W9-AUV-533

The Chambers Thesaurus
4th Edition

CHAMBERS
An imprint of Chambers Harrap Publishers Ltd
338 Euston Road, London, NWI 3BH

Chambers Harrap Publishers Ltd is an Hachette UK company

© Chambers Harrap Publishers Ltd 2012

Chambers® is a registered trademark of Chambers Harrap Publishers Ltd.

This fourth edition published by Chambers Harrap Publishers Ltd 2012.
First published 1996
Second edition published 2004
Third edition published 2009

Database right Chambers Harrap Publishers Ltd (makers)

A CIP catalogue record for this book is available from the British Library.

ISBN 978 0550 1024 85

10 9 8 7 6 5 4 3 2 1

We have made every effort to mark as such all words which we believe to be
trademarks. We should also like to make it clear that the presence of a word in
the thesaurus, whether marked or unmarked, in no way affects its legal status as a
trademark.

Every reasonable effort has been made by the author and the publishers to trace the
copyright holders of material quoted in this book. Any errors or omissions should be
notified in writing to the publishers, who will endeavour to rectify the situation for
any reprints and future editions.

www.chambers.co.uk

Designed by Chambers Harrap Publishers Ltd, Edinburgh
Typeset in Optima and Arial by Datapage (India) Pvt. Ltd.
Printed and bound in India

Contents

Contributors to this edition

Editorial Director
Sarah Cole

Commissioning Editor
Robert Williams

Editor
Mary O'Neill

Editorial Assistance
Laura Cremer

Production Controller
Georgina Cope

Preface

The English language moves at an astonishing rate. On its evolutionary journey it soaks up new words and creates extra meanings from around the world, adding to the rich history of English usage. This fourth edition of *The Chambers Thesaurus* aims to strike a balance between the established and the original and in doing so celebrate the brilliance and vibrancy of English. We revel in the quirky, the archaic, the beautiful and the practical. In browsing these pages you'll find thousands of alternative and opposite meanings for common words and phrases – old and new – to help you communicate with accuracy, precision and elegance.

This fourth edition contains hundreds of new and updated entries reflecting recent linguistic and social changes. Many of them hold up a mirror to contemporary trends. From the digital world comes the growth of 'citizen journalism', the menace of the 'cyberbully' and the tricky rules of 'netiquette'. The green agenda is explored through the evolution of recycling – 'precycle' and 'upcycle' – as well as the inclusion of 'organic' and 'e-waste'. From the economic recession comes 'agflation', 'NEET', 'cash-strapped' and the increasingly popular 'daycation'. As ever the worlds of fashion, politics and technology also contribute many new words to our language – think 'on-trend', 'wiggle room' and 'the cloud'.

At Chambers we enjoy browsing, discovering, collecting and using words and we know you do too. With this in mind we've created the *Word Lover's Gallimaufry*, an exquisite new supplement of fascinating collections of words and phrases. Offering practical advice for anyone wanting to write, present or speak creatively, it also celebrates all that's curious and enchanting in English. You'll uncover a range of intriguing and useful synonyms and expressions for our modern world. Learn the words to impress at an interview – 'soft skills' and 'proactive' - discover how to sound like a foodie or a fashionista - 'slow food' and 'fast fashion' - examine the rise of coffee culture - 'dead eye', 'flat white' and 'skinny' - and understand modern phobias – from 'affluenza' to 'password fatigue'.

As ever, *The Chambers Thesaurus* also includes hundreds of hyponym or 'types of' panels, many updated for this edition, giving extra depth in a range of fields from films and flowers to martial arts and marketing. There's also a host of intriguing quotations and proverbs to inspire and add context to your word search.

We know our love of language is shared by the users of the thesaurus and equally by those of *The Chambers Dictionary* – the ideal companion volume. As well as guiding you to the appropriate synonym or antonym, we hope you'll also be intrigued, inspired and delighted as you browse these pages. Chambers has long been an unrivalled treasure-trove of English and we are confident this new edition builds on that tradition of inquisitiveness and discovery.

Robert Williams
Commissioning Editor 2012

Features of the thesaurus

The following features are shown in context in the model of thesaurus layout on pages viii–ix. A discussion of how each can be put to use when writing creatively can be found on pages x–xiv.

Clear distinction of senses

Senses within an entry are distinguished by numbered sections and by either a key synonym in SMALL CAPITALS or an example in **bold italic**, eg

sad *adj*
  1 UNHAPPY, sorrowful…
  2 *sad news*
  upsetting, distressing…

Synonyms grouped by register

Synonyms are listed by range of context ('register') to show the appropriate styles within which words are used.

TECHNICAL
indicates a word that is restricted to a certain subject area such as music, philosophy, medicine or law, eg *codicil* (a supplement to a will) at **supplement**

OLD
indicates a word that is no longer in common use, be it obsolete, archaic or literary, eg *spoffish* at **fussy**

Shakesp and *Spenser* are extra labels used to annotate words featured in the works of Shakespeare and Spenser.

FORMAL
indicates a formal word, eg *discourse* and *colloquium* at **discussion**

COLLOQ.
indicates an informal word, eg *powwow* at **discussion**

SLANG
indicates a word used only very informally, eg *dough* and *dosh* at **money**

derog, *offensive* and *taboo* are extra labels used to annotate words considered particularly vulgar or which may give offence.

Countrywide and worldwide English

Terms from varieties of English from around Britain and around the world are included (eg North American *ornery* at **stubborn**), and labelled as

dialect	(usually indicates Northern English dialects)
Scot	(Scottish)
Welsh	
Irish	
N Am	(used mainly in the United States and, sometimes, Canada)
Can	(used mainly in Canada, rather than the United States)
Aust	(Australian)
NZ	(New Zealand)
S Afr	(South African)

Related adjectives

Where a headword has an adjective related to it, a note is included. For example, the entry **meaning** gives the related adjective *semantic*.

Proverbs and quotations

Many entries, eg **ambition** and **happiness**, feature proverbs and quotations that contain the entry word. These further eludicate the concept or provide extra inspiration for the writer.

Confusable words

Where a headword is sometimes confused with another word, eg **censor** or **censure**, **fatal** or **fateful**, concise explanatory notes are included to distinguish them.

Hyponym panels

Over 400 special panels show word families ('hyponyms'), and give lists of related words presenting

- different types of, eg **film**, **food** and **sport**
- parts of, eg the **brain**, a **flower** and a **motor vehicle**
- the terminology used in particular subject areas, eg **cookery**, **football** and **medicine**

Synonym nuances panels

Synonym nuances panels distinguish shades of meaning among synonyms in over 300 entries, identifying and exemplifying words that

- have particular associations or convey certain suggestions:
  unworldly suggests a vulnerability arising from lack of experience: *a schoolgirl who was unworldly in the extreme.*

- have a particular tone or convey an attitude on the part of the speaker:
  both **gullible** and **credulous** further imply a tendency to be duped, and are rather more contemptuous in tone: *he treated her as a credulous imbecile.*

- usually have a specific referent or context:
  Consort is a more formal term which tends to be reserved for a spouse: *the queen's consort.*

Abbreviations used in the thesaurus

adj	adjective		*N Am*	American English
adv	adverb		*NZ*	New Zealand English
Aust	Australian English		*prep*	preposition
Can	Canadian English		*pron*	pronoun
colloq.	colloquial		®	trademark
conj	conjunction		*S*	south, southern
derog	derogatory		*S Afr*	South African English
E	east, eastern		*Scot*	Scottish English
interj	interjection		*Shakesp*	found in Shakespeare's works
N	north, northern		*v*	verb
n	noun		*W*	west, western

Model of thesaurus layout

Headwords in bold type at the beginning of each entry

Synonyms or alternative words listed after the headword, and arranged according to shades of meaning

Proverbs and **quotations**

Register labels in bold small capitals

Antonyms, indicated by ⊟, in numbered sections corresponding to those of the synonyms

Parts of speech listed after the headword and treated in order within the entry

Geographical information in italic labels

Hyponym panels

---

absence *n*
1 *absence from school*
non-attendance, non-appearance, truancy; *N Am* playing hookey; absenteeism, non-existence
COLLOQ. skiving, bunking off
2 LACK, need, deficiency, scarcity, unavailability, default, omission, vacancy
FORMAL want, dearth, privation, paucity, vacuity
⊟ **1** presence, attendance, appearance **2** presence

> **PROVERBS**
> Absence makes the heart grow fonder

> **QUOTATIONS**
> Absence is to love what wind is to fire; / It extinguishes the small, it kindles the great
> COMTE DE BUSSY-RABUTIN, *Histoire Amoureuse des Gaules*

absent *adj, v*
♦ *adj*
1 *absent from the meeting*
missing, not present, not here, not there, not around, away, out, off, unavailable, gone, lacking, truant, AWOL
FORMAL *in absentia*
COLLOQ. when someone's back is turned
2 INATTENTIVE, daydreaming, dreamy, faraway, elsewhere, absent-minded, blank, preoccupied, unaware, oblivious, unheeding
FORMAL vacant, distracted
COLLOQ. miles away, in a world of your own
⊟ **1** present, here, there **2** attentive, alert, aware
■ **absent yourself**
take your leave, withdraw, retire, depart, exit, back out, retreat, slip away

absentee *n*
non-attender, no-show, truant

bag *v, n*
♦ *v*
1 CATCH, capture, trap, land, net, kill, shoot
2 OBTAIN, acquire, get, gain, come by, secure, net, corner, take, grab, appropriate, commandeer, reserve
♦ *n*
container, receptacle; *dialect* poke; *Scot* pock, pouch

Types of bag include:

attaché-case	flight bag	portfolio bag
backpack	Gladstone bag	record bag
baguette	grip	reticule
briefcase	handbag	rucksack
bumbag	haversack	sack
carpetbag	holdall	saddlebag
carrier bag	it bag	satchel
N Am carry-all	kitbag	shoulder bag
case	knapsack	sports bag
clutch bag	man bag	suitcase
ditty bag	messenger bag	tote bag
duffel bag	money bag	*Aust* tuckerbag
eco-bag	moneybelt	valise
N Am fanny pack	pack	vanity bag

branch *n, v*
♦ *n*
1 BOUGH, limb, sprig, shoot, stem, offshoot, arm, leg, lobe, loop, wing, prong, whip, withy; *Scot* cow, scrog
TECHNICAL ramus, axis, cladode, phylloclade
OLD braunch, rice
Related adjectives: ramal, rameal, rameous, ramous ⎯⎯⎯ **Related adjective** notes
2 *a different branch of the company*
department, office, local/regional office, agency, bureau, part, section, division, subsidiary, subsection, subdivision, affiliate, corps, wing, discipline
FORMAL succursal, ramification
3 *the branch of a river*
tributary, fork, division

■ **branch off**
divide, fork, diverge, deviate, separate
FORMAL bifurcate, furcate ⎯⎯⎯ **Idioms and phrasal verbs** highlighted separately at the end of entries
■ **branch out**
diversify, subdivide, vary, develop, expand, enlarge, spread out, extend, add to, broaden out, increase, multiply, proliferate
FORMAL ramify

brand *n, v*
♦ *n*
1 *different brands of soap* ⎯⎯⎯ **Different meanings** in numbered sections
make, brand-name, tradename, trademark, line, logo, symbol, sign, emblem, label, stamp, hallmark, marque
2 KIND, quality, class, kind, type, sort, line, variety, species ⎯⎯⎯ **Key synonyms** in small capitals
3 MARK, tag, identification, identifying mark
♦ *v*
1 *branded as a troublemaker*
mark, stamp, label, typecast, stigmatize, stain, taint, disgrace, discredit, denounce, censure
FORMAL besmirch
2 *brand cattle* ⎯⎯⎯ **Example phrases** in bold italics
mark, stamp, burn (in), sear

brandish *v*
wave, flourish, shake, raise, swing, wield, flash, flaunt, exhibit, display, parade
OLD wag, wampish; *(Spenser)* bless, hurtle ⎯⎯⎯ **Additional information** in bracketed italic labels

bravery *n*
courage, pluck, fearlessness, boldness, courageousness, daring, stalwartness, hardiness, fortitude, resolution, tenacity, stout-heartedness, valour, gallantry, chivalry, heroism, indomitability, mettle, spirit, dauntlessness, audacity, bravado, prowess
FORMAL intrepidity, valiance
COLLOQ. guts, grit, spunk
Ⓔ cowardice, fearfulness, faint-heartedness, timidity

🛈 **bravery** or **bravado**?
Bravery is courage: *soldiers decorated for bravery.*
Bravado is a boastful act of bravery intended to impress or intimidate or a boastful pretence of bravery aimed at concealing cowardice: *She felt her defiant bravado disintegrate like shattered glass.* ⎯⎯⎯ **Notes on words easily confused** indicated by 🛈

SYNONYM NUANCES

Courage is used in general contexts, whereas **pluck** has a very positive aspect of spiritedness, and is often used of facing up to difficulties rather than overt danger: *few people had the pluck to stand up to her.* **Fearlessness** suggests bravery that has more to do with an inability to experience fear than to confront it: *the fearlessness that only fanaticism confers.* **Indomitability** and **dauntlessness** are also suggestive of an inability to be conquered or frightened, whereas **mettle** and **spirit** more ⎯⎯⎯ **Synonym nuances** panels

Using the thesaurus to improve your style

This section explores the practical use of this thesaurus, showing how its different features can help you write the text you want. The subsections below examine each separate aspect of the thesaurus entries to show how you can make the best use of this book and apply its content to help you improve your writing.

Separating the meanings of entry words

Separate meanings of headwords are highlighted by numbers under the particular part-of-speech (word-class) marker.

Italic examples show you the typical usage of that word:

> **borrow** v
> **1** *borrow a friend's car*
> have the use of, take/have on loan, use temporarily, take out a loan, rent, hire, charter, lease; *dialect* scunge
> **TECHNICAL** lever
> **COLLOQ.** scrounge, cadge, sponge
> **2** *borrow words/ideas*
> adopt, take (over), draw, derive, obtain, use, acquire
> **FORMAL** appropriate

so using the example as a guide, you can select from all the options that are available to you in such a context. Instead of writing a sentence like:

> I am **borrowing** my friend's car.

you could write:

> I am **temporarily using** my friend's car.

You might use the second sentence, or one of similar construction, to emphasize the informality of the arrangement.

The SMALL CAPITAL synonym works in a similar way, showing you the key synonym in that block, and helping you pinpoint the exact meaning of the word that you want to use and the synonyms available for it:

> **present**^{2} v
> **1** AWARD, grant, give, donate, hand over, entrust, extend, hold out
> **FORMAL** confer, bestow
> **2** OFFER, tender, submit, put forward
> **FORMAL** proffer
> **3** SHOW, display, put on display, exhibit, demonstrate, organize, mount, stage, perform, put on, introduce, host, make known

so instead of writing:

> She was **presented** with a medal.

you could pick an alternative that conveys more accurately the situation you are describing:

> She was **awarded** a medal.

Using the synonyms

The synonyms listed within the entries are the heart of the thesaurus; these are the alternative words with similar meanings to the headword. It is often said that words have no exact synonyms, and this is true, but this central part of this thesaurus will nevertheless help you express yourself in the way you want.

Sometimes the words listed will be familiar to you and synonyms listed serve as a memory jogger. At other times the alternative words listed may be unfamiliar, and you may need to check their meaning and/or usage in another reference book before you include them in your document.

For example, you may have used the word *strong* in the usage *a strong case/argument* in a document you are writing. If you have to express the same idea again, you might very well want to use an alternative word to add variety to your style. Consulting the thesaurus takes you to **strong** sense 8:

> **8 *a strong case/argument***
> convincing, persuasive, powerful, potent, plausible, valid, sound, effective, telling, forceful, weighty, compelling, urgent
> **FORMAL** cogent, efficacious

Choosing, for example, ***convincing*** or ***persuasive*** as an alternative to *strong* could well work in the document you are writing and, as well as adding variety, it could add greater precision to what you are trying to convey:

a ***convincing*** *response/explanation*

persuasive *evidence/charm*

Understanding shades of meaning

Within each group of synonyms, the alternative words are arranged according to shades of meaning. This arrangement is intended to lend further assistance in making the correct choice of word.

> **context** *n*
> background, setting, surroundings, framework, frame of reference, state of affairs, situation, general situation, position, circumstances, factors, conditions, connection

Here, the alternatives begin with the aspect of meaning concerned with the facts that explain something (**background**) and then move on to the idea of 'context' as overall situation (**general situation**). However, note that because the shades do merge into each other, the listing has been kept in one sequence rather than separate senses because often you can use the same word in the different shades of meaning.

*Against a **background** of the strategic concerns outlined above, the government decided that it was not prepared to take the risk of rejection by the market.*

*The Education Act came into force, setting up a new **framework** for children with 'special educational needs', whether they attend ordinary or special schools.*

*The saying 'there is a time and a place for everything' means that there are certain **circumstances** when a particular action is appropriate.*

Applying level and style of usage

This thesaurus clearly distinguishes different levels of style. Those synonyms that are neutral are unmarked, while labels in capitals introduce groups of synonyms that are, for example, **FORMAL** or **COLLOQ.** (colloquial).

> **undertake** *v*
> **1** BEGIN, embark on, tackle, set about, try, attempt, endeavour, take on, accept, assume, deal with, shoulder, put/set your hand to, apply yourself to, turn your hand to, get down to, get to grips with
> **FORMAL** commence
> **COLLOQ.** grasp the nettle, get your teeth into, put your shoulder to the wheel, set your hand to the plough, take the bull by the horns
> **2** PLEDGE, promise, guarantee, agree, commit yourself, contract, covenant

Unmarked words may be used in general documents that are neither formal nor informal in style. **FORMAL** is used in official and serious writing, for example in business situations; **COLLOQ.** can be used in informal, everyday situations, for example conversations, conveying a more relaxed, friendly, and personal tone. Once you have settled on the tone of your piece, the labels can help you select vocabulary accordingly. Compare the following examples:

*Criminal prosecutions are **commenced** either in the Magistrates' Court if the matter is to be tried summarily or, following a committal before a Magistrates' Court, in the Crown Court if the matter is to be tried upon an indictment.*

*We've all had to **grasp the nettle** of global pollution.*

You can see here how using synonyms from different levels of language can set the tone of your text and has an effect on the overall impression of formality or informality it gives.

Other usage markers include **TECHNICAL** and **SLANG**, geographical markers such as *N Am* for usage in North America, and the time-marker **OLD** to indicate old-fashioned or archaic usages, which are sometimes further delineated by usage by a particular author.

> **drunk** *adj, n*
> ♦ *adj*
> under the influence, drunken, inebriated, intoxicated,
> incapable, tipsy, mellow, merry, foxed; *dialect* fairish; *Scot*
> capernoity, fou; *Scot & Irish* stotious; *N Am* jagged
> **OLD** overseen; (*Shakesp*) fap, paid
> **FORMAL** crapulent, ebriose
> **SLANG** stoned, tanked up, loaded, lit up, canned, paralytic,
> smashed, pissed, bombed, wasted, wrecked, trashed,
> mashed, trollied, stinko, whiffled, whistled, bonkers, bottled,
> Brahms and Liszt, juiced (up), in liquor, liquored,
> maggoty, mortal, up the pole, ripped; (*vulgar*) arseholed,
> rat-arsed, shitfaced; *Scot* blootered; *N Am* crocked, moon-
> eyed; *Aust* inky, inked; *Aust & NZ* shickered
> **F∃** sober, temperate, abstinent, teetotal

All these markers are intended to help you decide which words are and are not suitable in particular social and geographic contexts.

*Your Honour, I solemnly swear that on the night in question I was not **inebriated**.*

> **lake** *n*
> pond, pool, lagoon, sea, water, reservoir, dam, basin,
> mere, tarn, everglade, playa, salina, shott, nyanza; *Scot*
> loch; *Irish* lough; *N Am* bayou; *Can* saltchuck; *Aust* cowal

*Cameron had caught some fine trout in the beautiful **lochs** amongst the mountains of the Scottish Highlands.*

Consulting synonym nuance panels

This thesaurus lists nearly 400 special articles that elaborate on the subtle shades of meaning and contexts in which certain close synonyms can be used. These appear at the end of entries dealing with the synonyms.

For example, at **interesting**, the article includes *engaging*, *absorbing*, and *engrossing* as suggestive of completely capturing the attention:

*an **absorbing** book*

and *stimulating* and *thought-provoking* as appropriate for exciting intellectual interest:

*a **stimulating** public debate*

The synonym nuance panel at **interfere** comments on the tone, eg *intrude* is critical in that it suggests an uninvited or unwelcome encroachment.

The same panel at **interfere** also discusses *intervene*, describing it as more positive in that it suggests stepping in to assume a more controlling role:

*The government has **intervened** in environmental issues.*

Using these panels for guidance, you can select a more precise word that helps you focus the expression of your meaning more exactly. The panels are intended to help you feel confident about using the words you have found by showing that they correspond to the facts of the situation, <u>and the tone that you wish to convey</u>, as closely as you would wish.

Related adjectives

Related adjectives are listed at nouns that have a particular adjective associated with them, eg *annual* at **year**, and these give a further angle on finding an alternative word. For example, you are writing about birds and the adjective *avian* has momentarily slipped your mind. At the entry **bird** comes the related adjective *avian*.

A further example is at the entry **marriage**:

> *Related adjectives*: marital, matrimonial, conjugal,
> connubial

These related adjectives provide another means of expression:

*enjoy **marital** bliss*
*leave the **matrimonial** home*
*delight in **connubial** pleasures*

Using antonyms

Antonyms are shown at the end of some groups of synonyms. These are the opposites of the word, which can be used to give a further shade of meaning in your writing:

fortunate *adj*
ᴇ◄ unlucky, unfortunate, unhappy

*It was a far from **unfortunate** coincidence.* (ie it was actually a fortunate one)

significant *adj*
ᴇ◄ **1** insignificant, unimportant, trivial **2** meaningless

*The relationship between the two events is not **insignificant**.* (ie it may have some significance)

The literary term for this expression is *litotes*. This figure of speech means that you use a negative with the opposite of the original word. It achieves a subtle and ironic understatement, used for rhetorical effect. (For more information on devices used for rhetorical effect, see **21 words to make sense of rhetoric** in the *Word Lovers' Gallimaufry* in this book.)

3 *familiar with the procedure*
aware, acquainted, abreast, knowledgeable, versed, conversant, well up, au fait, *au courant*
ᴇ◄ **1** unfamiliar, strange **2** formal, reserved **3** unfamiliar, ignorant

After consulting the entry above, instead of saying:

*Jeff is **familiar** with Shakespeare's plays.*

you could use the negative word *not* with one of the antonyms:

*Jeff is **not unfamiliar** with Shakespeare's plays.*

*Jeff is **not ignorant** of Shakespeare's plays.*

These make the subtle suggestion that Jeff is not as familiar with Shakespeare's plays as he might be. However, you might use the antonym in a different way and so achieve a different effect:

*Jeff is **far from ignorant** of Shakespeare's plays.*

Here, a less subtle, more explicit statement results.

Consulting hyponym panels

A hyponym is a word that has a more specific meaning than a general term. This thesaurus contains over 400 panels that list hyponyms. For example at the word **signal**, over 80 different kinds of signal or warning are listed.

Kinds of signal and warning include:

alarm	car horn	gong	Lutine bell	semaphore signal	tattoo
alarm-bell	cue	green light	mayday	a shot across the	time signal (pips)
alarm clock	curfew bell	hand signal	Morse code	bows	tocsin
amber light	distress signal	heliograph	pager	shout	toot
beacon	drumbeat	honk	password	signal box	trafficator
Belisha beacon	final warning	hooter	personal alarm	signal letters	traffic lights
bell	fire	horn	police whistle	siren	Very light
bicycle bell	fire alarm	hurricane warning	red alert	smoke alarm	vigia
bleeper	flag	indicator	red card	smoke signal	warning light
bugle	flare	klaxon	red flag	SOS	whistle
buoy	flashing light	knell	red light	starter's gun	winker
burglar alarm	foghorn	larum	reveille	storm cone	written warning
buzzer	gale warning	larum-bell	rocket	storm signal	yellow card
car alarm	go-ahead	lighthouse beacon	security alarm	storm warning	yellow flag

As these panels of hyponyms give specific examples relating to the entry word, it follows that they are particularly helpful if you want to make your writing more specific.

Instead of simply writing *warning*, if you write **alarm**, **bleeper**, **gong**, **red alert** or **siren**, this adds creativity to your description and results in a more vivid mental image for your reader (for example by adding sound effects to the image):

*The **siren** went off and we knew an air raid was imminent.*

Although we use the term 'hyponym panels' for convenience, it is not always hyponyms that feature. The panels might contain 'parts of' (technically known as *meronyms*), for example at **castle**. Again, these words can help jog the memory or inspire the imagination, and help you create a distinct image.

*On top of the **battlements** a soldier on lookout called to him.*

Adding proverbs and quotations

Proverbs and quotations containing the headword are to be found at many entries throughout the book. As well as using them for general inspiration, you might choose to incorporate these in your text in some way.

References to proverbs – crystallized summaries of popular wisdom – can add liveliness to your composition:

> **PROVERBS**
> Nothing ventured, nothing gained

*As the proverb puts it, **nothing ventured, nothing gained** …*

> **PROVERBS**
> Never look a gift horse in the mouth
> You may take a horse to water but you can't make him drink

*We're all familiar with the saying **you may take a horse to water but you can't make him drink** …*

If, for example, you are preparing to give a speech, then a pithy quotation can be a useful device to engage the attention of your audience.

> **QUOTATIONS**
> Simply seek happiness, and you are not likely to find it. Seek to create and love without regard to your happiness, and you will likely be happy much of the time
> M SCOTT PECK, *The Different Drum*

> **QUOTATIONS**
> Pride goeth before destruction, and an haughty spirit before a fall
> *Bible, Proverbs*

The occasional humorous note can help relax and entertain your audience:

> **QUOTATIONS**
> Always do right. This will gratify some people, and astonish the rest
> MARK TWAIN

A

aback
■ **take aback**
surprise, astonish, astound, startle, stagger, stun, shock, disconcert, bewilder, dumbfound, dismay, upset
COLLOQ. knock out, flabbergast

abandon *v, n*
♦ *v*
1 *abandon a baby*
desert, leave (behind), maroon, strand, walk out on; *Scot* forhow
FORMAL forsake
COLLOQ. run out on, jilt, ditch, chuck, dump, leave in the lurch, leave for dead, give the elbow to, break (it) off with, leave high and dry
2 *abandon the boat*
vacate, evacuate, leave, depart from, withdraw from, go away from, bail out, escape, get out, break free from, break away, break loose, jump ship
COLLOQ. quit
3 *abandon an activity/your responsibilities*
give up, stop (doing), cease, let go, leave, abort, resign (from), jettison, surrender, waive, sacrifice
FORMAL renounce, part with, desist, discontinue, for(e)go, forswear, dispense with, relinquish, abdicate, yield, cede
COLLOQ. drop, scrap, ditch, leave it at that, quit, jack in, pack in, kick the habit
4 *abandon yourself to despair*
give way to, give yourself up to, yield to, lose yourself in, be overcome by
E∃ **1** support, maintain, stay (with), remain (with) **3** start, begin, continue
♦ *n*
carelessness, recklessness, unrestraint, uninhibitedness, wildness, impetuosity, impulsiveness, spontaneity, thoughtlessness
E∃ restraint, caution, inhibition(s), moderation, care, carefulness

> **SYNONYM NUANCES**
>
> *verb sense 1*
> To **desert** or **walk out on** someone or something implies abandonment of a duty or obligation: *deserting his regiment*; *walked out on his wife*. A quality that you are dependent on can also **desert** you: *his energy was deserting him*. **Maroon** and **strand** have the more specific meaning of abandoning someone or something in an isolated place with no means of leaving, or in a difficult situation with no help.
> Similarly, to **leave someone in the lurch** or **leave someone high and dry** is to leave them helpless in a difficult situation. **Leave behind** carries connotations of permanence and sometimes reluctance: *leaving behind my childhood*. Likewise, **forsake** is used of something that has been valued or enjoyed: *forced to forsake his country*; *forsook photography for film-making*.
> The colloquial terms **run out on**, **jilt**, **ditch**, **chuck**, **dump**, **give the elbow to**, or **break (it) off with** are usually used of a partner or lover. However, you can **ditch** any person or thing that is no longer useful: *ditched their manager*; *ditched plans*.

abandoned *adj*
1 *abandoned buildings*
deserted, unoccupied, unused, disused, empty, vacant, derelict, neglected, forlorn, desolate
FORMAL forsaken
2 *abandoned young people*
dissolute, wild, crazy, uninhibited, unrestrained, reckless, mad, wanton, wicked, debauched, immoral, corrupt
FORMAL reprobate, profligate
E∃ **1** (well-)kept, occupied **2** restrained, (self-) controlled

abandonment *n*
1 DESERTION, leaving (behind), neglect, marooning, stranding
FORMAL forsaking, decampment, dereliction
COLLOQ. running out on, jilting, ditching
2 *abandonment of an activity*
giving-up, stopping, resignation (from), surrender, waiving, sacrifice
FORMAL renunciation, relinquishment, cessation, discontinuation, discontinuance, abdication, cession
COLLOQ. dropping, scrapping, ditching

abase *v*
humble, humiliate, kowtow
FORMAL debase, demean, mortify, belittle, malign, disparage
COLLOQ. crawl, suck up to
E∃ elevate, honour, raise

abasement *n*
humbleness, humility, humiliation
FORMAL debasement, demeaning, mortification, disparagement
COLLOQ. crawling, sucking up to

abashed *adj*
ashamed, shamefaced, embarrassed, mortified, remorseful, humiliated, humbled, affronted, confused, taken aback, bewildered, nonplussed, confounded, dumbfounded, discomposed
FORMAL perturbed, disconcerted, discomfited, discountenanced
COLLOQ. floored
E∃ composed, at ease; *formal* audacious

abate *v*
1 *the storm abated*
decrease, subside, reduce, lessen, sink, dwindle, die down, ease, moderate, drop off, taper off, peter out, fall off, wane
FORMAL diminish, decline, attenuate
COLLOQ. let up
2 *abate anger/pain*
moderate, ease, relieve, lessen, decrease, reduce, alleviate, soothe, mitigate, pacify, quell, subside, weaken, wane, slacken, slow, fade
FORMAL remit
COLLOQ. let up
E∃ **1** increase, strengthen

abatement *n*
1 *the abatement of the storm; noise abatement*
reduction, lessening, subsidence, dying-down, dwindling, easing, lowering, dropping-off
FORMAL decline, diminution, attenuation

2 *abatement of anger*
moderation, easing, relief, lessening, decrease, alleviation, mitigation, weakening, wane, slackening
FORMAL remission, assuagement, palliation

abattoir *n*
slaughterhouse, butchery, shambles

abbey *n*
monastery, priory, friary, seminary, convent, nunnery, cloister, minster, cathedral

abbreviate *v*
shorten, cut (down), trim, clip, abridge, summarize, précis, abstract, digest, condense, compress, reduce, lessen, shrink, contract
FORMAL truncate, curtail, constrict
E3 extend, lengthen, expand, amplify

abbreviated *adj*
shortened, short, cut, abridged, contracted, reduced, condensed, clipped, truncated, summary, compact
E3 lengthened, long, extended

abbreviation *n*
shortening, short form, shortened form, contraction, acronym, initialism, clipping, curtailment, abridgement, summary, synopsis, résumé, précis, abstract, digest, compression, reduction
FORMAL truncated form, summarization, truncation
E3 long form, extension, expansion, amplification

> **QUOTATIONS**
> Abbreviations are the wheels of language, the wings of Mercury
> JOHN HORNE TOOKE, *The Diversions of Purley*

abdicate *v*
1 *the king abdicated*
resign, resign from the throne, stand down, step down, give up, give up the throne
FORMAL retire, relinquish/renounce the throne
COLLOQ. quit
2 *abdicate responsibility*
abandon, give up, reject, refuse to accept any longer, surrender, disown
FORMAL renounce, relinquish, cede, yield, forsake, for(e)go, abjure, abnegate, repudiate
COLLOQ. shirk, quit, turn your back on, wash your hands of

abdication *n*
1 *the abdication of the king*
resignation, retirement, standing-down, stepping-down, giving up of the throne
FORMAL renunciation/relinquishment of the throne
2 *abdication of responsibilities*
abandonment, rejection, refusal, surrender, giving-up, disowning
FORMAL renunciation, relinquishment, abjuration, abnegation, repudiation

abdomen *n*
belly, stomach, midriff, middle, maw
OLD ventricle, heart, little Mary
COLLOQ. guts, tummy, tum, insides, paunch, pot belly, corporation; *Aust* bingy
SLANG bread-basket
Related adjectives: coeliac, abdominal

abdominal *adj*
coeliac, ventral, intestinal, visceral, ventricular, gastric

abduct *v*
kidnap, seize, take (away) by force, capture, carry off, make off with, snatch, shanghai, take as hostage, hold to ransom, spirit away, lay hold of
FORMAL appropriate
COLLOQ. run away/off with

abduction *n*
kidnapping, kidnap, seizure, capture, snatching, taking as hostage, carrying off, ravishing, seduction, rape

aberrant *adj*
deviant, deviating, divergent, different, irregular, abnormal, anomalous, odd, peculiar, eccentric, rogue, defective, corrupt
FORMAL incongruous, atypical
COLLOQ. freakish, quirky
E3 regular, normal, typical

aberration *n*
1 *an aberration in behaviour*
deviation, straying, wandering, divergence, instability, irregularity, abnormality, nonconformity, oversight, anomaly, oddity, peculiarity, eccentricity, lapse, delusion
2 *scientific aberrations*
deviation, divergence, irregularity, abnormality, variation, anomaly, oddity, peculiarity, mistake
E3 1 conformity, regularity, normality

abet *v*
help, aid, assist, support, encourage, lend a hand, endorse, promote, sanction, spur, condone, collude with
FORMAL succour
COLLOQ. egg on
E3 prevent, hinder, discourage

abeyance
■ *in abeyance*
no longer in use, cancelled temporarily, postponed, not in operation, disused, suspended, in (a state of) suspension, pending
FORMAL dormant
COLLOQ. hanging fire, on ice, shelved
E3 in use, in operation, continued

abhor *v*
hate, detest, loathe, recoil from, spurn, despise, have an aversion to, cannot abide/bear, shudder at, shrink from
FORMAL abominate, execrate
COLLOQ. hate someone's guts, can't stand
E3 love, adore

abhorrence *n*
hate, hatred, aversion, loathing, horror, revulsion, disgust, distaste, contempt
FORMAL abomination, repugnance, execration, detestation, animosity, enmity, malice, odium
E3 love, adoration

abhorrent *adj*
repugnant, detestable, loathsome, abominable, obnoxious, hated, hateful, horrible, horrid, offensive, repellent, repulsive, revolting, nauseating, disgusting, distasteful
FORMAL execrable, heinous, odious, absonant
E3 delightful, attractive, lovable

abide *v*
1 BEAR, put up with, tolerate, accept, take, brook, endure; *Scot* thole
COLLOQ. stand, stomach, hack
2 REMAIN, last, endure, continue, survive, live on, persist
■ *abide by*
obey, observe, follow, go along with, carry out, discharge, stand by, hold to, keep to, agree to, comply with, adhere to, conform to, submit to, accept, respect, uphold, fulfil
COLLOQ. go by the book, stick to the rules, toe the line
E3 ignore, reject; *colloq.* flout

abiding *adj*
lasting, enduring, constant, continual, continuous, long-lasting, long-term, long-running, lifelong, persistent, persisting, unchanging, unchangeable, eternal, everlasting, immortal, unending, chronic, permanent, stable, standing, fixed, firm, durable
FORMAL immutable
E3 short-lived, short-term; *formal* ephemeral, transient

ability *n*
1 *the ability to teach*
capability, capacity, faculty, facility, power(s), means, resources
FORMAL potentiality, potential, propensity, wherewithal

2 *someone of great ability*
skill, competence, proficiency, qualification, talent, gift, calibre, endowment, expertise, savoir-faire, forte, strength, dexterity, aptitude, deftness, adeptness, adroitness, prowess, motivation
FORMAL competency
COLLOQ. knack, flair, touch, knowhow, genius, the hang, the knack, what it takes, savvy
F3 **1** inability **2** incompetence, weakness

> **! ability** or **capability**?
> *Ability* is the more general term, referring to the possession of particular skills, knowledge, powers, etc or the simple fact of something being possible: *his ability to write a catchy tune; our ability to work together. Capability* may refer to the possession of an aptitude, especially one that derives from a person's character: *my mother's organizational capabilities.*

ab initio *adv*
from the beginning, from the start, at first, at the beginning, at the start, to begin with, to start with, initially, primarily, originally, firstly

abject *adj*
1 *abject poverty*
miserable, wretched, forlorn, hopeless, woeful, awful, shameful, humiliating, pitiable, pitiful, pathetic, outcast, degraded
FORMAL execrable
2 *an abject coward*
contemptible, worthless, base, low, mean, dishonourable, deplorable, despicable, vile, sordid, debased, degenerate, submissive, servile, slavish, grovelling, ingratiating
FORMAL ignoble, ignominious
F3 **2** proud, exalted

abjure *v*
abandon, disown, deny, reject
FORMAL renounce, relinquish, retract, forswear, abdicate, dispense with, forsake, abnegate, disavow, disclaim, renege on
F3 agree, assent, support

ablaze *adj*
1 BURNING, alight, blazing, flaming, in flames, on fire, ignited, lighted, incandescent
OLD afire
FORMAL aflame
2 *a house ablaze with lights*
illuminated, luminous, glowing, aglow, alight, radiant, flashing, gleaming, sparkling, shimmering, brilliant, lit up
FORMAL incandescent
3 *eyes ablaze with passion*
impassioned, passionate, fervent, ardent, fiery, intense, enthusiastic, excited, exhilarated, stimulated, aroused, angry, furious, fuming, raging, incensed, frenzied

able *adj*
capable, competent, fit, fitted, dexterous, adroit, deft, adept, proficient, qualified, practised, experienced, skilled, accomplished, clever, intelligent, expert, masterly, skilful, ingenious, talented, gifted, strong, powerful, effective, efficient
COLLOQ. all there, on the ball, up to it, clued up, cut out for
F3 unable, incapable, incompetent, ineffective
■ **able to**
capable of, competent to, qualified to, fit to, prepared to, allowed to, free to

SYNONYM NUANCES

The words **capable**, **competent** and **proficient** are used of someone with sufficient ability or skill for a particular task, while **fit** and **fitted**, and the more colloquial **cut out for**, can be used to imply suitability in general.
　　While someone can be said to be **skilful** if they demonstrate skill in undertaking an action, **skilled** is more often used of someone who possesses specific skills and training. **Qualified** is used where someone has official recognition of having the necessary competency, while **practised**, **experienced** and **accomplished** are used of someone whose expertise has been honed by familiarity; **expert** and **masterly** can be used of someone who demonstrates complete mastery as a result. On the other hand, someone with a special innate skill or natural ability can be described by the words **talented** and **gifted**.
　　Clever, **intelligent** and **ingenious** suggest the use of highly developed mental ability, while **dexterous**, **adroit**, **deft** and **adept** may be used to suggest either physical or mental agility. **Strong**, **powerful** and **effective** can be used where stamina or technique are used to achieve a successful conclusion: *the most powerful lever for peace.* **Efficient**, however, suggests the ability to achieve satisfactory results with economy of effort.
　　Up to it suggests being able, although little more, and is usually used in the negative: *she wasn't up to it.*

able-bodied *adj*
fit, healthy, sound, in good health, strong, robust, hardy, tough, vigorous, powerful, hale, hearty, hale and hearty, fine, lusty, sturdy, rugged, strapping, stout, burly, stalwart, staunch
COLLOQ. as fit as a fiddle
F3 disabled, handicapped, infirm, delicate

ablution *n*
washing, cleaning, cleansing, bathing, showering, scrubbing, soaking, rinsing

abnegate *v*
give up, abstain, reject, refuse, abandon, surrender
FORMAL renounce, relinquish, forbear, abjure, forswear, disavow, repudiate, eschew

abnegation *n*
abstinence, self-denial, surrender, self-sacrifice, giving-up, temperance
FORMAL renunciation, relinquishment, forbearance, abjuration, repudiation, eschewal

abnormal *adj*
odd, strange, peculiar, curious, queer, weird, eccentric, idiosyncratic, paranormal, unnatural, uncanny, extraordinary, exceptional, unusual, uncommon, unexpected, irregular, erratic, wayward, deviant, divergent, different
FORMAL singular, anomalous, aberrant, atypical, outré, preternatural
COLLOQ. oddball
F3 normal, regular, typical

abnormality *n*
oddity, peculiarity, eccentricity, strangeness, bizarreness, unnaturalness, unusualness, uncommonness, irregularity, exception, anomaly, deformity, flaw, malformation, dysfunction, deviation, divergence, difference
FORMAL singularity, aberration, atypicality
F3 normality, regularity

aboard *adv, prep*
on, onto, in, into, on board, on board ship

abode *n*
home, lodgings, habitat
FORMAL dwelling, dwelling-place, residence, place of residence, domicile, habitation
COLLOQ. pad

abolish *v*
cancel, end, stop, do away with, quash, repeal, revoke, annul, invalidate, rescind, suppress, destroy, eliminate, put an end to, exterminate, annihilate, obliterate, sink, eradicate, overthrow, blot out, wipe out, get rid of, scrap, stamp out, subvert, overturn
FORMAL terminate, discontinue, nullify, vitiate, abrogate, expunge

COLLOQ. axe, chop, dump

E꜏ create, introduce, establish, institute, retain, authorize, continue

---

SYNONYM NUANCES

The fairly neutral term **cancel** is to abolish something not yet in place, but **end**, **stop** or **discontinue** are used of something currently happening. You can use **put an end to**, **scrap**, **get rid of** or **do away with** as general terms for removing something, although the latter two carry connotations of a welcome riddance.

Eliminate, **eradicate** and **stamp out** suggest complete and permanent removal, often as a result of strong measures. The words **destroy**, **exterminate**, **annihilate**, **obliterate**, **sink** and **wipe out** imply destruction with force. **Overthrow** is usually used for the toppling of regimes, but you can subvert or overturn a corrupt system or a decision.

You can also talk of someone in authority **quashing** a ruling or decision, while **repeal**, **revoke**, **annul**, **rescind** and **abrogate** are only used of legal or official measures; similarly **annul** and **terminate** describe the abolition of laws or contracts. **Axe**, **chop** and **dump** are very emotive informal terms to describe getting rid of someone or something; the first usually relates to jobs or services: *1220 jobs axed*. **Nullify** and **vitiate** are used where the results of an action are negated rather than abolished: *the costs would nullify any tax relief*.

To describe the removal of thoughts from the mind, you can use **expunge** or **blot out**: *to blot out the horror*.

---

abolition *n*
cancellation, annulment, ending, stopping, doing-away with, repeal, suppression, destruction, elimination, scrapping, annihilation, extinction, overthrow, blotting-out, quashing, withdrawal
FORMAL termination, invalidation, nullification, voiding, rescindment, revocation, vitiation, abrogation, rescission, obliteration, extermination, eradication, extirpation, dissolution, subversion
COLLOQ. axe, chop, chopping, dumping
E꜏ creation, introduction, retention, authorization, continuation

abominable *adj*
loathsome, detestable, hateful, horrid, horrible, abhorrent, offensive, repulsive, repellent, disgusting, revolting, repugnant, obnoxious, nauseating, foul, base, vile, atrocious, appalling, dreadful, terrible, contemptible, despicable, wretched, cursed, damnable
FORMAL execrable, odious, heinous, reprehensible
COLLOQ. god-awful
E꜏ delightful, pleasant, desirable

abominably *adv*
horribly, disgustingly, obnoxiously, appallingly, terribly, dreadfully
FORMAL odiously, reprehensibly, execrably

abominate *v*
abhor, hate, loathe, detest, despise, have an aversion to, condemn
FORMAL execrate
E꜏ love, adore

abomination *n*
1 *murder is an abomination*
outrage, offence, disgrace, horror, atrocity, evil, curse, plague, torment
FORMAL anathema
2 HATE, hatred, detestation, loathing, abhorrence, revulsion, disgust, distaste, aversion, hostility
FORMAL execration, repugnance, odium
E꜏ **2** adoration, delight

aboriginal *adj*
native, indigenous, original, earliest, initial, first, primal, primitive, ancient, local
FORMAL autochthonous, prim(a)eval

aborigine *n*
native, indigene, original inhabitant, earliest inhabitant, first inhabitant

abort *v*
1 *abort a pregnancy*
terminate, miscarry, have a miscarriage
2 *abort a plan*
end, bring/come to an end, stop, suspend, discontinue, halt, call off, cut short, check, frustrate, thwart, fail
FORMAL nullify
COLLOQ. axe, pull the plug on
E꜏ **2** continue, start, begin

abortion *n*
termination, miscarriage
FORMAL aborticide, foeticide

abortive *adj*
failed, unsuccessful, fruitless, unproductive, barren, sterile, vain, idle, futile, useless, ineffective, thwarted
OLD bootless
FORMAL unavailing, ineffectual, inefficacious
E꜏ successful, fruitful

abound *v*
be plentiful, flourish, swell, increase, swarm, teem, crowd, be full, be abundant, bristle, brim over, overflow
FORMAL proliferate, thrive, superabound, exuberate, luxuriate

about *prep, adv*
♦ *prep*
1 *write about a subject*
regarding, on, on the subject of, concerning, relating to, connected with, concerned with, as regards, referring to, with regard to, with respect to, with reference to, in the matter of, re, dealing with; *Scot* anent
FORMAL apropos of
2 *somewhere about the house*
close to, near, nearby, beside, adjacent to, in the vicinity of, around
3 *walk about the town*
round, around, surrounding, throughout, all over
FORMAL encircling, encompassing
♦ *adv*
1 *about twenty*
around, approximately, roughly, in the region of, in the neighbourhood of, more or less, almost, nearly, approaching, nearing
FORMAL circa
2 *run about*
to and fro, here and there, from place to place
OLD hither and thither
3 *Is there anyone about?*
near, nearby, close, close by, around, within reach
■ **about to**
going to, on the point of, on the verge of, all but, ready to, soon to, intending to, preparing to, all set to

about-turn *n*
about-face, volte-face, (complete) reversal, turnabout, turnaround
FORMAL enantiodromia
COLLOQ. U-turn

above *prep, adv, adj*
♦ *prep*
1 *above the clouds*
over, higher than, upon, on top of
FORMAL atop
2 *above the rank of sergeant*
superior to, senior to, higher than, over
3 *temperatures above the average*
in excess of, exceeding, beyond, higher than, greater than
FORMAL surpassing
4 *above suspicion*
beyond, not liable to, not open to, not exposed to, immune to, exempt from, superior to
E꜏ **1** below, under **2** below

♦ adv
1 *noise from above*
overhead, high up, higher
FORMAL aloft, on high
2 *as mentioned above*
earlier, before, previously
F3 **1** below, underneath **2** below
♦ adj
above-mentioned, previous, earlier, preceding
OLD prevenient
FORMAL above-stated, foregoing, prior, aforementioned,
aforesaid
■ **above all**
primarily, firstly, first of all, most importantly, chiefly, most
of all
■ **above yourself**
conceited, vain, proud, arrogant, haughty, boastful,
swollen-headed, immodest, egotistical, narcissistic, self-
important, full of yourself, puffed-up, supercilious, self-
satisfied, complacent, smug
FORMAL vainglorious
COLLOQ. cocky, bigheaded, stuck-up, toffee-nosed, too big
for your boots

above-board *adj*
honest, legitimate, straight, true, open, frank, candid,
straightforward, forthright, truthful, trustworthy,
honourable, reputable, upright
FORMAL guileless, veracious
COLLOQ. on the level, legit, kosher, fair and square, square
F3 dishonest, underhand, shady

abracadabra *n*
magic word, spell, open sesame, gibberish, hocus pocus
COLLOQ. mumbo-jumbo

abrade *v*
rub, graze, scratch, scrape, scrape away, scour, grate,
grind, chafe, erode, wear away/down

abrasion *n*
graze, scratch, cut, scrape, scratching, scraping, scouring,
grating, grinding, abrading, chafing, chafe, friction,
rubbing, erosion, wearing-away, wearing-down
FORMAL excoriation

abrasive *adj*
1 *abrasive material*
rough, scratching, scraping, grating, grinding, harsh,
chafing, corrosive
FORMAL erosive, frictional, attritional, erodent
2 *an abrasive person*
harsh, brusque, caustic, sharp, biting, grating, hurtful,
nasty, unpleasant, irritating, annoying
F3 **1** smooth **2** pleasant, kind

abreast *adj*
1 *walk abreast*
side by side, shoulder to shoulder, level, beside/alongside
each other, next to each other, cheek by jowl
2 *keep abreast of the news*
acquainted, informed, knowledgeable, *au courant*, up to
date, in touch, au fait, familiar, well up
FORMAL conversant
COLLOQ. in the picture, on the ball, with your finger on
the pulse
F3 **2** unaware, out of touch, unfamiliar

abridge *v*
shorten, cut (down), prune, curtail, abbreviate, cut short,
contract, reduce, decrease, lessen, summarize, précis,
abstract, digest, condense, compress, truncate, concentrate
FORMAL synopsize
COLLOQ. clip, lop
F3 expand, amplify; *colloq.* pad out

abridged *adj*
short, shorter, cut down, abbreviated, cut short,
contracted, reduced, digested, summarized
COLLOQ. clipped, potted

abridgement *n*
1 *the abridgement of the story*
shortening, cutting, reduction, decrease, diminishing,
concentration, contraction, restriction
FORMAL diminution, truncation
2 *an abridgement of a report*
summary, synopsis, résumé, short version, shortened
version, outline, précis, abstract, digest, epitome
FORMAL conspectus, abrégé
F3 **1** expansion; *colloq.* padding (out)

abroad *adv*
1 OVERSEAS, in/to a foreign country, in/to
foreign parts, out of the country, far and
wide, widely
2 *news spread abroad*
at large, widely, publicly, around, about, circulating,
extensively, far and wide, current
F3 **1** at home

> QUOTATIONS
> Abroad is bloody
> GEORGE VI

abrogate *v*
abolish, cancel, annul, end, stop, repeal, revoke,
do away with, invalidate, reverse
TECHNICAL disaffirm
FORMAL countermand, rescind, retract, dissolve,
repudiate, disenact, vitiate
COLLOQ. axe, scrap, chop, dump
F3 establish, institute, introduce

abrogation *n*
abolition, cancellation, annulment, repealing,
revocation, invalidation, reversal, overruling
TECHNICAL disaffirmation
FORMAL countermanding, rescinding, rescindment,
recision, dissolution, repudiation, vitiation
COLLOQ. axe, scrapping, chop, dumping

abrupt *adj*
1 *come to an abrupt end*
sudden, unexpected, unforeseen, unannounced,
unceremonious, surprising, startling, dramatic, quick,
rapid, swift, hasty, hurried, immediate, instant,
instantaneous
FORMAL precipitate
COLLOQ. snap
2 BRUSQUE, curt, terse, brisk, gruff, rough,
rude, offhand, dismissive, discourteous,
impolite, unfriendly, blunt, direct, uncivil
COLLOQ. short, off, snappy, snappish
3 *an abrupt slope*
sheer, steep, sharp, vertical
FORMAL precipitous, declivitous
F3 **1** gradual, slow, leisurely **2** friendly, expansive,
ceremonious, polite

abruptly *adv*
1 *the phone call ended abruptly*
suddenly, unexpectedly, unceremoniously,
quickly, rapidly, swiftly, hastily, hurriedly,
immediately, instantly, instantaneously
FORMAL precipitately
2 BRUSQUELY, curtly, tersely, briskly,
gruffly, roughly, rudely, offhand,
dismissively, discourteously, impolitely,
bluntly, directly
COLLOQ. shortly, snappily, snappishly
F3 **1** gradually, slowly **2** expansively, courteously,
politely

abscess *n*
swelling, ulcer, ulceration, boil, sore, infection,
inflammation, canker, noma
OLD impostume
COLLOQ. gathering

abscond *v*

run away, run off, make off, decamp, flee, fly, escape, disappear, vanish, bolt, take French leave
COLLOQ. quit, scram, skedaddle, vamoose, scarper, clear off/out, make a quick getaway, beat it, run for it, do one, do a runner, do a bunk, do a moonlight flit

absence *n*

1 *absence from school*
non-attendance, non-appearance, truancy; *N Am* playing hookey; absenteeism, non-existence
COLLOQ. skiving, bunking off
2 LACK, need, deficiency, scarcity, unavailability, default, omission, vacancy
FORMAL want, dearth, privation, paucity, vacuity
🖂 **1** presence, attendance, appearance **2** presence

> **PROVERBS**
> Absence makes the heart grow fonder

> **QUOTATIONS**
> Absence is to love what wind is to fire; / It extinguishes the small, it kindles the great
> COMTE DE BUSSY-RABUTIN, *Histoire Amoureuse des Gaules*

absent *adj, v*

♦ *adj*
1 *absent from the meeting*
missing, not present, not here, not there, not around, away, out, off, unavailable, gone, lacking, truant, AWOL
FORMAL in absentia
COLLOQ. when someone's back is turned
2 INATTENTIVE, daydreaming, dreamy, faraway, elsewhere, absent-minded, blank, preoccupied, unaware, oblivious, unheeding
FORMAL vacant, distracted
COLLOQ. miles away, in a world of your own
🖂 **1** present, here, there **2** attentive, alert, aware
■ **absent yourself**
take your leave, withdraw, retire, depart, exit, back out, retreat, slip away

absentee *n*

non-attender, no-show, truant

absently *adv*

absent-mindedly, inattentively, blankly, abstractedly
COLLOQ. in a world of your own, with your head in the clouds

absent-minded *adj*

forgetful, scatterbrained, having a bad memory, absent, withdrawn, faraway, distracted, preoccupied, absorbed, engrossed, musing, dreaming, dreamy, wool-gathering, inattentive, unaware, oblivious, unconscious, heedless, unheeding, unthinking, impractical, abstracted, pensive
FORMAL distrait(e)
COLLOQ. with a memory like a sieve, not all there, somewhere else, dead to the world, miles away, in a world of your own, scatty
🖂 attentive

absent-mindedly *adv*

absently, inattentively, blankly, abstractedly
COLLOQ. in a world of your own, with your head in the clouds

absolute *adj*

1 *in absolute confidence*
utter, total, complete, entire, full, thorough, exhaustive, supreme, definitive, conclusive, final, definite, unquestionable, indubitable, unambiguous, undivided, unlimited, categorical, decided, decisive, positive, sure, certain, genuine, pure, perfect, sheer, unmixed, unadulterated, unqualified, unconditional, unmitigated, unrestrained, unequivocal, unrestricted, downright, rank, out-and-out, outright
FORMAL consummate, peremptory

2 *absolute power*
totalitarian, unlimited, unrestricted, unrestrained, boundless
3 *an absolute ruler*
supreme, totalitarian, autocratic, tyrannical, despotic, dictatorial, sovereign, authoritarian, high-handed, almighty
FORMAL omnipotent, autarchic, autarchical
4 *absolute truth*
fixed, non-variable, unalterable, non-negotiable, set, established, settled, firm, rigid, universal

absolutely *adv*

1 *I agree with you absolutely*
utterly, totally, completely, entirely, fully, wholly, thoroughly, exhaustively, perfectly, supremely, unconditionally, finally, categorically, definitely, positively, in every way/respect, wholeheartedly, conclusively, unequivocally, unambiguously, unquestionably, decidedly, decisively, surely, certainly, infallibly, genuinely, truly, purely, exactly, precisely
COLLOQ. dead
2 *the despot ruled absolutely*
tyrannically, autocratically, despotically, dictatorially, high-handedly
3 *'He really ought to take more rest.' 'Absolutely.'*
certainly, of course, yes, surely, naturally, obviously, clearly, plainly, definitely, for sure, undoubtedly, without a doubt, no doubt, undeniably, unquestionably, by all means, doubtless, doubtlessly, assuredly, positively
COLLOQ. quite (so)

absolution *n*

forgiveness, pardon, pardoning, deliverance, freedom, liberation, release, mercy, redemption, acquittal, discharge, amnesty, emancipation
OLD shrift
FORMAL exoneration, remission, vindication, exculpation, purgation
COLLOQ. letting off

absolve *v*

excuse, clear, forgive, pardon, deliver, free, set free, discharge, liberate, release, loose, have mercy on, show mercy towards, emancipate
FORMAL exonerate, vindicate, justify, acquit, exculpate, remit
COLLOQ. let off

absorb *v*

1 *absorb liquid/heat*
take in, draw in, soak up, drink in, suck up, blot up, sponge up, assimilate, engulf
FORMAL ingest, imbibe, consume
COLLOQ. devour
2 *absorb facts*
take in, digest, assimilate, understand, receive, drink in, hold, retain
3 *absorb your attention*
engross, involve, fascinate, enthral, captivate, engage, hold, preoccupy, occupy, use up, fill (up), monopolize
COLLOQ. not be able to put down
4 *absorbed into a bigger company*
incorporate, integrate, assimilate
COLLOQ. swallow up
🖂 **1** give out; *formal* exude

absorbed *adj*

engrossed, involved, fascinated, interested, enthralled, captivated, preoccupied, occupied, taken up with, spellbound, riveted

absorbent *adj*

receptive, porous, permeable, pervious, spongy, soaking, blotting, retentive
TECHNICAL sorbefacient
FORMAL absorptive, assimilative, spongiform, resorbent
🖂 water-repellent, waterproof

absorbing *adj*

interesting, amusing, entertaining, enjoyable, diverting, engrossing, preoccupying, intriguing, fascinating,

captivating, enthralling, spellbinding, gripping, riveting, compelling, compulsive
COLLOQ. unputdownable
E3 boring, off-putting

absorption *n*
1 *the absorption of liquid/heat*
taking-in, drawing-in, soaking-up, assimilation
TECHNICAL osmosis
FORMAL ingestion, consumption
COLLOQ. devouring
2 *absorption of your attention*
engrossing, involvement, captivating, riveting, engagement, holding, preoccupation, occupation, immersion, raptness, attentiveness, concentration, intentness, monopoly

abstain *v*
1 *abstain from food*
refuse, reject, resist, shun, avoid, keep from, give up, do/go without, stop, stop short of, hold back
FORMAL refrain, decline, renounce, forbear, for(e)go, desist, deny yourself, eschew
COLLOQ. quit, cut out, jack in, think twice before doing something
2 *abstain in an election*
not vote, refuse to vote, be neutral
COLLOQ. sit on the fence
E3 **1** indulge

abstemious *adj*
temperate, moderate, abstinent, self-denying, self-disciplined, disciplined, sober, sparing, frugal, austere, ascetic, restrained
FORMAL self-abnegating
E3 intemperate, gluttonous, luxurious

abstention *n*
not voting, refusal to vote, declining to vote, neutrality
COLLOQ. sitting on the fence

abstinence *n*
1 *abstinence from sensual desires*
abstaining, self-denial, non-indulgence, avoidance, fasting, refusal, giving-up, going-without, restraint, self-restraint, self-control, self-discipline
FORMAL abstemiousness, continence, forbearance, refraining, declension, renunciation, desistance, eschewal, abjuration
2 TEETOTALISM, temperance, moderation, frugality, asceticism
FORMAL sobriety, nephalism
E3 **1** indulgence, self-indulgence

> **QUOTATIONS**
> For many, total abstinence is easier than perfect moderation
> ST AUGUSTINE, *On the Good of Marriage*

abstinent *adj*
abstaining, self-denying, non-indulgent, restrained, self-restrained, self-controlled, self-disciplined, temperate, moderate, frugal, ascetic, teetotal, sober
FORMAL abstemious, continent, forbearing
E3 self-indulgent

abstract *adj, n, v*
♦ *adj*
1 *abstract nouns*
non-concrete, conceptual, notional
2 *abstract reasoning*
theoretical, conceptual, notional, intellectual, hypothetical, unpractical, unrealistic, general, generalized, indefinite, philosophical, academic, complex, deep, profound, subtle
TECHNICAL metaphysical, ideational, ideative
FORMAL abstruse, arcane, recondite, suppositional, suppositive

3 *abstract paintings*
non-realistic, non-representational, symbolic, contrived
E3 **1** concrete **2** concrete, real, actual, practical **3** representational, realistic, figurative
♦ *n*
synopsis, outline, summary, recapitulation, résumé, précis, digest, abridgement, compression, compendium, syllabus
FORMAL epitome, conspectus
♦ *v*
1 *abstract a report*
summarize, outline, précis, digest, condense, compress, abridge, abbreviate, shorten, cut (down)
2 *abstract coal from the ground*
extract, remove, take away/out, withdraw, draw off, isolate, detach, tap, separate
FORMAL dissociate, prescind, subduce
E3 **1** expand, lengthen **2** insert, put in
■ **in the abstract**
theoretically, hypothetically, conceptually, notionally, generally, philosophically, *in abstracto*
COLLOQ. on paper

abstracted *adj*
preoccupied, absent-minded, distracted, forgetful, scatterbrained, absent, withdrawn, absorbed, engrossed, pensive, musing, dreaming, dreamy, bemused, wool-gathering, inattentive, unaware, oblivious, unconscious, heedless, unheeding, unthinking, impractical
COLLOQ. scatty, miles away
E3 attentive, alert; *colloq.* on the ball

abstractedly *adv*
absently, absent-mindedly, inattentively, blankly
COLLOQ. in a world of your own, with your head in the clouds

abstraction *n*
1 IDEA, notion, concept, thought, conception, theory, hypothesis, theorem, conjecture, formula, generalization, generality
2 INATTENTION, dream, dreaminess, absent-mindedness, preoccupation, remoteness, withdrawal
FORMAL distraction, pensiveness, absorption, bemusedness
3 EXTRACTION, withdrawal, removal, isolation, separation

abstruse *adj*
obscure, difficult to understand, deep, profound, complex, mysterious, cryptic, unfathomable, incomprehensible, high, long, Delphic, subtle, perplexing, puzzling
OLD exquisite
FORMAL arcane, esoteric, inscrutable, enigmatic, recherché, hermetic, recondite
E3 simple, obvious

absurd *adj*
ridiculous, ludicrous, preposterous, fantastic, illogical, paradoxical, unreasonable, irrational, nonsensical, meaningless, senseless, foolish, silly, stupid, idiotic, crazy, farcical, inane, comical, funny, humorous, harebrained, laughable, derisory, grotesque, priceless, unearthly
OLD Laputan
FORMAL incongruous, implausible, untenable, risible, asinine
COLLOQ. daft
SLANG *N Am* gonzo
E3 reasonable, logical, rational, sensible

absurdity *n*
ridiculousness, ludicrousness, preposterousness, illogicality, unreasonableness, meaninglessness, senselessness, foolishness, folly, silliness, fatuousness, idiocy, stupidity, craziness, inanity, paradox, humour, farce, charade, travesty, joke, caricature, nonsense, rubbish
FORMAL incongruity, irrationality, implausibility
COLLOQ. daftness, twaddle, gibberish, drivel, claptrap, balderdash, malarkey
E3 reasonableness, logicality, rationality, (good) sense

absurdly *adv*
ridiculously, ludicrously, preposterously, fantastically, paradoxically, unreasonably, irrationally, nonsensically,

meaninglessly, senselessly, foolishly, stupidly, idiotically, crazily, farcically, inanely, comically, funnily, humorously, laughably
FORMAL incongruously, implausibly, untenably
⊟ reasonably, logically, rationally, sensibly

abundance n
plenty, fullness, great supply, wealth, generosity, richness, riches, lavishness, overflow, land of milk and honey, glut, extravagance, excess, bonanza, fortune
FORMAL amplitude, bounty, plethora, copiousness, profusion, exuberance, luxuriance, munificence, plenitude, prodigality, opulence, affluence, plentifulness
COLLOQ. bags, heaps, masses, piles, loads, stacks, lashings, oodles, lots; N Am scads
⊟ shortage, scarcity; formal dearth, paucity

abundant adj
plentiful, in plenty, full, filled, ample, copious, profuse, bountiful, exuberant, more than enough, well-supplied, generous, rich, affluent, lavish, teeming, overflowing, galore
OLD plenteous, bounteous
FORMAL luxuriant, opulent
⊟ scarce, sparse, scant, insufficient

abundantly adv
1 *abundantly clear*
extremely, exceedingly, excessively, very, really, exceptionally, extraordinarily, intensely, thoroughly, remarkably, utterly, greatly, highly, unusually, unreasonably, immoderately, uncommonly, inordinately, acutely, severely, decidedly
OLD jolly
COLLOQ. awfully, terribly, dreadfully, frightfully, terrifically
2 *mushrooms found abundantly in early autumn*
in abundance, plentifully, copiously, profusely, in profusion, exuberantly, amply, extensively, prolifically

abuse n, v
♦ n
1 *the abuse of drugs/power*
misuse, exploitation, imposition, oppression, wrong
FORMAL misapplication, misemployment
2 *child abuse*
mistreatment, maltreatment, ill-treatment, cruelty, hurt, injury, interference, sexual assault, molestation, damage, harm, beating, torture
3 *shout abuse*
insult(s), swearing, swear-word, cursing, curse, offence, defamation, libel, slander, reproach, censure, scolding, billingsgate;
Scot snash
FORMAL affront, upbraiding, invective, castigation, malediction, vilification, vituperation, calumniation, calumny, contumely, denigration, derision, disparagement, tirade, diatribe, vitriol
COLLOQ. mud-slinging
SLANG jawing
⊟ **2** care, attention **3** compliment(s), praise
♦ v
1 *abuse authority*
misuse, exploit, take advantage of
FORMAL misapply, misemploy
2 *abuse children*
ill-treat, maltreat, mistreat, hurt, injure, damage, harm, beat, hit, batter, oppress, exploit, wrong, torture, molest, interfere with, rape, assault/harass sexually
3 INSULT, swear at, curse, hurl abuse at, call names, be rude to, defame, libel, slander, pick on, bully, smear, scold, rail, victimize, bullyrag
FORMAL malign, revile, slate, upbraid, calumniate, impugn, vituperate, castigate, denigrate, disparage, oppugn
COLLOQ. treat like dirt

SLANG slag off; Aust & NZ chuck off at
⊟ **2** cherish, care for, look after **3** compliment, praise

❗ abuse or **misuse?**
Abuse refers to the use of something for the wrong purposes: *substance abuse*, eg glue-sniffing. *Misuse* refers to the use of substances or objects in an incorrect way: *Bacteria may acquire resistance to a particular antibiotic by its overuse or misuse.*

abusive adj
insulting, offensive, rude, scathing, scornful, hurtful, harmful, injurious, cruel, brutal, destructive, defamatory, libellous, slanderous, derogatory, disparaging, pejorative, maligning, reviling, reproachful, scolding, scurrilous, blasphemous
OLD opprobrious
FORMAL vilifying, censorious, upbraiding, railing, vituperative, castigating, calumniating, contumelious, denigrating
COLLOQ. bitchy
⊟ complimentary, polite

abusively adv
insultingly, offensively, rudely, scathingly, scornfully, injuriously, cruelly, brutally, disparagingly, pejoratively, revilingly, reproachfully, scoldingly, scurrilously, blasphemously
OLD opprobriously
FORMAL censoriously, upbraidingly, vituperatively, calumniously, contumeliously, denigratingly
COLLOQ. bitchily
⊟ complimentarily, politely

abut v
border, be next to, verge on, join, touch, impinge
FORMAL adjoin, conjoin, be contiguous with

abysmal adj
dismal, shocking, disgraceful, dreadful, appalling, awful, terrible, frightful, complete, utter

abysmally adv
awfully, disgracefully, dreadfully, appallingly, terribly, frightfully

abyss n
fall into an abyss; the abyss of war
gulf, chasm, crevasse, fissure, gorge, canyon, ravine, crater, pit, bottomless pit, depth(s), void, swallow
OLD profound, Avernus Tartarus
FORMAL barathrum

academic adj, n
♦ adj
1 *academic qualifications*
educational, instructional, scholastic
FORMAL pedagogical
2 *she's very academic*
scholarly, intellectual, educated, well-educated, learned, well-read, studious, bookish, literary, highbrow, serious, donnish
FORMAL erudite
COLLOQ. brainy, smart
3 *an academic, not practical, approach*
theoretical, hypothetical, speculative, abstract, conceptual, impractical, irrelevant, ivory-tower
FORMAL conjectural, notional, suppositional
⊟ **3** practical, relevant, applied
♦ n
teacher, professor, don, master, fellow, lecturer, tutor, educator, instructor, trainer, student, scholar, man/woman of letters, pedant, bookworm
FORMAL pedagogue

academy n
college, school, university, institute, seminary, educational institution, training institute
OLD academe

accede v
1 *accede to a request*
accept, comply with, bow to, agree to, consent to,
admit, give in, back down
FORMAL assent to, acquiesce, concur
2 *accede to the throne*
come to, take over, inherit
FORMAL assume, attain, succeed (to)

accelerate v
1 *the car/driver accelerated*
quicken, speed, speed up, drive faster, go faster,
pick up/gather speed, gain momentum
COLLOQ. open up, put your foot down, step on it/the
gas/the juice, put on a spurt
2 *accelerate a process*
speed up, hurry, step up, stimulate, facilitate, advance,
further, promote, spur on, forward
TECHNICAL festinate
FORMAL hasten, expedite, precipitate
⊟ 1, 2 decelerate, slow down, delay

acceleration n
1 *the acceleration of a car*
speeding-up, rate of increase, gathering speed, momentum
2 *acceleration of a process*
speeding-up, stepping-up, stimulation, promotion,
forwarding, furtherance
FORMAL advancement, hastening, expedition
⊟ 1, 2 deceleration, slowing-down, delay

accent n
1 *speak with a strong Irish accent*
pronunciation, articulation, brogue, tone, pitch, intonation,
inflection, accentuation, stress, emphasis, intensity, force,
rhythm, beat, pulse
TECHNICAL cadence, timbre, modulation, enunciation
FORMAL diction, pulsation
COLLOQ. twang
2 *the accent comes on the second syllable*
stress, emphasis, accentuation, beat, force
TECHNICAL ictus
3 *the accent is on ease of use*
emphasis, prominence, importance, priority, stress,
underlining, highlighting
4 *with an acute accent*
diacritic, diacritical mark

accentuate v
accent, stress, emphasize, put the emphasis on, underline,
underscore, highlight, give prominence to, heighten,
intensify, strengthen, spotlight, deepen
COLLOQ. point up, drive the point home, make great play
of, show up
⊟ weaken; *colloq.* play down

accept v
1 *accept a job/an offer*
take, take up, receive, obtain, acquire, gain, welcome,
grasp, pocket, secure, get, come by, say yes to,
not say no to
FORMAL reply in the affirmative
COLLOQ. jump at
2 *accept advice*
take, welcome
FORMAL embrace
COLLOQ. take on board, take someone's point
3 *accept a decision*
acknowledge, recognize, admit, allow, approve, agree to,
consent to, take on, adopt, bow to, honour, comply with,
go along with, give in, back down
TECHNICAL *Scot* approbate
FORMAL abide by, accede to, acquiesce in, concur with
4 *accept responsibility/blame*
take on, undertake, bear, be responsible for, admit,
acknowledge, face up to
5 *accept an explanation*
believe (in), trust, credit, take, be certain of
COLLOQ. buy, swallow, fall for, wear

6 *accept into the family*
welcome, receive, receive warmly, embrace, integrate
7 *accept ill-treatment*
tolerate, stand, bear, abide, face up to, take, endure,
suffer, put up with, yield to, resign yourself to, be
resigned to, come to terms with, let go of
COLLOQ. stomach, swallow, make the best of
⊟ 1 refuse, turn down **2, 3, 4, 5, 6** reject

acceptable adj
1 *homework that is just acceptable*
satisfactory, tolerable, moderate, passable, adequate,
reasonable, all right, unexceptional
COLLOQ. OK, so-so
2 *acceptable not to smoke*
admissible, allowable, permissible, tolerable, agreeable,
appropriate, desirable
COLLOQ. the done thing
3 *a most acceptable present*
welcome, delightful, pleasant, pleasing, agreeable,
desirable, gratifying, appreciated
⊟ 1 unacceptable, unsatisfactory **2** unacceptable

acceptably adv
agreeably, desirably, appropriately, suitably, tolerably,
moderately, passably, adequately, satisfactorily, reasonably
⊟ 1 unacceptably

acceptance n
1 *acceptance of a job/an offer*
taking (-up), accepting, receipt, receiving, obtaining,
getting, acquiring, gaining, securing
FORMAL affirmative reply
2 *acceptance of advice*
taking, welcoming
FORMAL embracing
COLLOQ. taking on board, taking someone's point
3 *acceptance of the decision*
acknowledgement, admission, recognition, approval,
consent, affirmation, agreement, taking on, adoption,
going along with, compliance, giving-in, backing-down
FORMAL assent, accession, acquiescence, concurrence,
endorsement, ratification
COLLOQ. seal/stamp of approval, OK
4 *acceptance of responsibility/blame*
taking on, undertaking, assumption, admission,
acknowledgement
5 *the idea gained acceptance*
credence, belief, trust, faith
COLLOQ. buying, falling for
6 *acceptance into the family*
welcome, welcoming, receiving, recognition, integration
7 *acceptance of your situation*
tolerance, bearing, facing up to, endurance, resignation,
putting up with
COLLOQ. making the best of
⊟ 1 refusal **2, 3, 4, 5, 6** rejection

accepted adj
recognized, established, authorized, approved, ratified,
sanctioned, agreed, acknowledged, admitted, confirmed,
acceptable, correct, appropriate, conventional, orthodox,
traditional, customary, time-honoured, received, universal,
regular, standard, normal, usual, common
⊟ unconventional, unorthodox, controversial

access n, v
♦ n
1 *gain access to the building*
means of approach/entry, entry, entering, entrance,
gateway, door, way in, key, approach, passage, road,
path, drive, driveway, course
2 *deny access to the prisoner*
admission, admittance, right of entry, permission to
enter/see, accessibility, entrée
FORMAL ingress
⊟ 1 exit, outlet; *formal* egress
♦ v
locate, use, retrieve, read, gain access to

accessibility *n*
1 *easy accessibility to the site*
approachability, ease of access
OLD attainability
2 *the accessibility of affordable health care*
availability, convenience, obtainability, ease of access
3 *the programme's accessibility to ordinary people*
intelligibility, comprehensibility, approachability
F∃ 1 inaccessibility **2** unavailability **3** incomprehensibility

accessible *adj*
1 *accessible from the motorway*
reachable, attainable, approachable, open, achievable
OLD patent
COLLOQ. get-at-able
2 *financial help that is accessible to everyone*
obtainable, available, on hand, ready, handy, convenient, near, nearby
FORMAL procurable
3 *an accessible book/painting*
understandable, intelligible, comprehensible, easy to understand, easy to read, easy to follow
COLLOQ. user-friendly
F∃ 1 inaccessible, remote; *colloq.* out of the way, off the beaten track **3** incomprehensible, unintelligible

accession *n*
1 *accession to the throne*
taking over, inheritance
FORMAL assumption, attaining, succession
2 *accessions to the library*
addition, acquisition, increase, possession, gain, purchase, gift

accessorize *v*
add to, enhance, set off, contrast, complement, round off, supplement, augment, decorate, adorn, trim
OLD bedizen, bedaub

accessory *n, adj*
♦ *n*
1 *computer accessories*
extra, supplement, addition, attachment, extension, component, fitting
TECHNICAL peripheral, add-in, add-on
FORMAL appendage, adjunct
2 *accessories to match an outfit*
decoration, adornment, ornament, frill, trimming, supplement, complement, gloves, hat, belt, shoes, handbag, jewellery
FORMAL embellishment
3 *an accessory to a crime*
accomplice, partner, associate, colleague, confederate, assistant, helper, help, aid
TECHNICAL accessory before the fact, accessory after the fact, *particeps criminis*
FORMAL abettor, conniver
♦ *adj*
additional, extra, supplementary, subsidiary, contributory, incidental, secondary, ancillary, auxiliary, subordinate
FORMAL supplemental

accident *n*
1 *an accident with boiling water*
mishap, casualty, calamity, disaster, tragedy
FORMAL misfortune, mischance, misadventure
COLLOQ. blow
2 *a car accident*
collision, crash, fatality, RTA, road traffic accident
FORMAL contretemps
COLLOQ. pile-up, smash-up; *N Am* wreck
SLANG shunt, prang
3 *happen by accident*
chance, hazard, luck, good luck, fortune, good fortune, fate, freak, coincidence
OLD upcast
FORMAL fortuity, serendipity, contingency, hap, happenstance
COLLOQ. fluke

accidental *adj*
unintentional, unintended, inadvertent, unplanned, uncalculated, unpremeditated, unwitting, unexpected, unanticipated, unforeseen, unlooked-for, chance, uncertain, haphazard, random, casual, incidental
FORMAL fortuitous, adventitious, serendipitous, contingent, aleatory
COLLOQ. fluky
F∃ intentional, deliberate, calculated, premeditated

QUOTATIONS
Nothing is accidental in the universe – this is one of my Laws of Physics – except the entire universe itself, which is Pure Accident, pure divinity
JOYCE CAROL OATES, *Do What You Will*

SYNONYM NUANCES

The words **unintentional**, **unintended**, **unplanned** and **inadvertent** tend to be used of unwanted accidental events: *unintentional injuries*; *unplanned pregnancies*; *the leaks caused unplanned shutdowns*. Actions can also be described as **inadvertent**, **uncalculated** and **unpremeditated** if they have not been thought through, as can their generally negative results: *inadvertent use of an incorrect word*.

Unforeseen and **unanticipated** events also tend to come as an unpleasant surprise: *unanticipated allergic reactions*. **Unexpected**, **chance** and **unlooked-for** are more neutral, and are used to describe both pleasant and unpleasant events: *an unexpected windfall*. To say that something is **uncertain** is to suggest unreliability: *the uncertain economic climate*.

If you want to suggest that there is an element of human carelessness involved in accidental events, you might use **haphazard**, whereas **random** is a more neutral term to describe disordered events. To describe something as **casual** or **incidental** has the added implication that it is of relatively little importance: *a casual encounter*.

Fortuitous and **serendipitous** and the colloquial **fluky** express a good accidental outcome. **Adventitious** is now often used in scientific contexts; **aleatory** is only used in the context of music and poetry.

---

accidentally *adv*
unintentionally, inadvertently, unexpectedly, by chance, by accident, as luck would have it, by mistake, unwittingly, haphazardly, randomly, incidentally
FORMAL fortuitously, bechance, adventitiously, serendipitously
F∃ intentionally, deliberately

acclaim *v, n*
♦ *v*
praise, commend, extol, exalt, honour, hail, salute, welcome, applaud, clap, cheer, celebrate, fanfare, toast
FORMAL laud, eulogize
COLLOQ. rave about, give rave reviews to, give a good press to
F∃ condemn, criticize; *colloq.* give a bad press to
♦ *n*
praise, commendation, homage, tribute, exaltation, honour, welcome, approval, bouquets, applause, ovation, clapping, fanfare, cheers, cheering, shouting, celebration
FORMAL acclamation, approbation, eulogy, eulogium, extolment, laudation, plaudits
F∃ criticism, disapproval, condemnation; *formal* vituperation; *colloq.* brickbats, bad press

acclaimed *adj*
famous, famed, renowned, illustrious, celebrated, eminent, distinguished, admired, honoured, exalted, revered, great, noted, notable, prominent, outstanding, legendary
F∃ unknown, unsung, forgotten, obscure

acclamation n
praise, commendation, homage, tribute, exaltation, honour, welcome, approval, congratulations, applause, ovation, clapping, fanfare, cheering, bravos, shouting, celebration, enthusiasm
FORMAL approbation, eulogy, laudations, felicitations, paean, panegyric
E3 criticism, disapproval, condemnation

acclimatization n
adjustment, adaptation, accommodation, familiarization, orientation, naturalization; N Am acclimation
FORMAL habituation, acculturation

acclimatize v
adjust, adapt, accustom, get used to, find your way around, accommodate, familiarize, attune, conform, naturalize; N Am acclimate
FORMAL habituate, acculturate, inure
COLLOQ. find/get your bearings, find your feet

accolade n
award, honour, recognition, homage, tribute, testimonial, praise
COLLOQ. pat on the back

accommodate v
1 *accommodate someone in a hotel*
put up, take in, house, shelter, provide shelter for, cater for, lodge, board, billet, quarter
OLD bestow
FORMAL domicile
COLLOQ. put a roof over someone's head
2 *the hall accommodates 400*
take, hold, seat, have room/space for
3 *accommodate customers*
help, be helpful to, oblige, assist, aid, serve, provide, supply, comply, conform, fit in with
COLLOQ. give/lend a (helping) hand to
4 *accommodate yourself to new developments*
adapt, accustom, acclimatize, adjust, modify, fit, attune, harmonize, reconcile, settle, compose
FORMAL habituate

accommodating adj
obliging, indulgent, helpful, co-operative, agreeable, willing, compliant, kind, considerate, unselfish, sympathetic, friendly, hospitable
FORMAL complaisant
E3 disobliging, selfish

accommodation n
1 *find accommodation*
housing, shelter, board, rooms, quarter(s), lodging(s)
FORMAL dwelling, residence, abode
COLLOQ. a roof over someone's head, digs, pad, place
SLANG crashpad, gaff, crib
See panel below
2 *reach an accommodation*
agreement, compromise, understanding, negotiation(s), reconciliation, settlement, harmony, conformity

accompaniment n
1 *a musical accompaniment*
support, background, backing, backup
TECHNICAL obbligato, vamp

2 *wine as an accompaniment to food*
complement, accessory, supplement, addition
FORMAL concomitant, adjunct, coexistence

accompanist n
instrumentalist, accompanier, backing group
COLLOQ. comp

accompany v
1 *accompany someone on holiday*
escort, attend, go (along) with, travel with, walk with, associate with, come (along) with, tag along with, partner, chaperon(e), squire, usher, conduct, follow
FORMAL consort, convoy, wait upon
COLLOQ. hang around with
2 *a book accompanied by a study guide*
complement, supplement, belong to, go with, go together with, occur with
FORMAL coexist, coincide
3 *accompany someone on the guitar*
play with, back, support, provide backing/support for

SYNONYM NUANCES

sense 1
To **escort** or **squire** someone is to accompany them in a rather formal manner, the suggestion being that you are protecting or guarding them; **squire** is used where a man accompanies a woman, with the added suggestion of sexual relations. **Chaperon(e)** is only used where you accompany someone with the specific purpose of being responsible for them. **Attend** is archaic and rarely used, but always in the context of accompanying someone as an inferior with the intention of serving them, as is the more familiar **wait upon**.

To **partner**, **go (along) with** or **come (along) with** someone, however, is to join them on equal terms, but to **tag along with** them makes the implication that you are uninvited. To **associate with** someone suggests keeping more regular company, as does the colloquial **hang around with**. To **consort** with someone has negative connotations: *consort with the enemy*.

To **conduct** or **usher** someone would only be used of leading them or guiding them in a particular direction, with **usher** having the connotation of brusqueness, whereas **follow** specifically indicates that you are at the rear. **Convoy** is generally confined to military contexts, describing the accompanying of vehicles.

---

accomplice n
assistant, helper, abettor, mate, henchman, conspirator, collaborator, ally, confederate, partner, associate, colleague, aide, participator, accessory, right-hand man/woman
OLD complice, copesmate, fedarie, stale
COLLOQ. sidekick
SLANG swagsman; N Am shill
OLD SLANG button

accomplish v
achieve, attain, do, perform, carry out, manage, execute, fulfil, discharge, finish, complete, conclude, realize, bring about, bring off, engineer, produce, obtain, compass
OLD complish

Types of accommodation include:

apartment	billet	guest house	married quarters	rooms	villa
barracks	board	halls of residence	motel	self-catering	youth hostel
bed and board	boarding-house	hostel	pension	shelter	
bed and breakfast	digs	hotel	penthouse	squat	
bedsit	N Am dormitory	inn	N Am room and	studio	
bedsitter	flat	loft conversion	board	timeshare	

See also **house**; **room**.

FORMAL consummate, effect, carry into effect, effectuate
COLLOQ. hack it, pull it off, wangle, deliver the goods, bring home the bacon

accomplished *adj*
skilled, professional, practised, proficient, gifted, talented, skilful, experienced, adroit, adept, expert, masterly, polished, cultivated, learned, savant
OLD compleat
FORMAL consummate
COLLOQ. ace
SLANG wicked, shit-hot
⊟ unskilled, inexpert, incapable

accomplishment *n*
1 *no mean accomplishment*
feat, achievement, deed, act, performance, operation, triumph, exploit, stroke of genius
OLD qualification, virtue
COLLOQ. stroke, feather in your cap
2 SKILL, talent, ability, capability, proficiency, gift, quality, knack, forte, art
FORMAL aptitude, faculty
3 *the accomplishment of a task*
achievement, attainment, doing, performance, carrying-out, execution, discharge, fulfilment, finishing, completion, management, conclusion, perfection, realization, fruition, production
FORMAL consummation, effecting, futurition

accord *v, n*
♦ *v*
1 *not accord with the truth*
correspond, agree, square, harmonize, be in agreement/harmony, match, conform, suit
FORMAL concur
2 *accord someone recognition*
grant, give, tender, allow, endow, confer, present
FORMAL bestow, vouchsafe
⊟ **1** disagree **2** deny
♦ *n*
1 *sign an accord*
treaty, agreement, pact, settlement, convention, deal, contract
FORMAL compact, concordat
2 *to reach accord*
agreement, assent, unanimity, unity, correspondence, conformity, harmony, sympathy
FORMAL congruence, congruity, concurrence, consensus, accordance, concert
⊟ **2** conflict, discord, disharmony
■ **of your own accord**
voluntarily, of your own free will, freely, willingly, without being asked/forced, of your own volition
■ **with one accord**
unanimously, of one mind, in complete agreement

accordance
■ **in accordance with**
in agreement with, consistent with, in keeping with, obedient to, in conformity with, in line with, in proportion to, in relation to, after, in the light of, in the manner of
FORMAL commensurate with, in concert with, in consonance with

according
■ **according to**
1 *according to this book*
as said/claimed/stated by, on the report of
2 *play according to the rules*
in accordance with, in keeping with, obedient to, in conformity with, in line with, consistent with, after, in the light of, in the manner of, after the manner of, as per
3 *be paid according to experience*
in proportion to, in relation to, depending on, as per
FORMAL commensurate with

accordingly *adv*
1 *he was dishonest and was distrusted accordingly*
correspondingly, so, as a result, for that reason, consequently, in consequence, therefore
OLD hence
FORMAL thus, ergo
2 *act accordingly*
appropriately, properly, suitably, duly, fitly, consistently

accost *v*
approach, confront, address, waylay, stop, halt, detain, importune, solicit, attack, molest
COLLOQ. nobble, buttonhole

account *n, v*
♦ *n*
1 *an account of what happened*
story, tale, commentary, narrative, chronicle, history, memoir, record, statement, report, communiqué write-up, version, narration, portrayal, sketch, description, presentation, explanation, detail(s)
2 *pay an account*
bill, statement, invoice, tab, charges
3 *the accounts of a business*
ledger, books, journal, register, inventory
4 *a matter of no account*
importance, significance, consequence, regard
FORMAL distinction, esteem, import, moment
♦ *v*
consider, assess, believe, count, hold, reckon, look upon, regard as, view as, value, esteem
FORMAL adjudge, appraise, deem
■ **account for**
1 *account for the missing money*
explain, give reasons for, come up with an explanation, illuminate, clear up, rationalize, justify, answer for, say why
FORMAL elucidate, vindicate
2 *exports account for half our income*
make up, comprise, be responsible for, represent, supply, provide, give
FORMAL constitute
3 *account for an enemy*
defeat, destroy, kill, eliminate
■ **on account of**
because of, owing to, through, in view of, the reason is
■ **on no account**
under no circumstances, certainly not
COLLOQ. never, no way

accountability *n*
responsibility, answerability, liability, amenability, reporting, obligation

accountable *adj*
responsible, answerable, liable, amenable, obliged, bound, charged with, chargeable
FORMAL obligated

accoutrements *n*
paraphernalia, gear, equipment, decorations, fittings, fixtures, furnishings, appointments, kit, outfit, trimmings, adornments, things
FORMAL appurtenances, caparison
COLLOQ. stuff, clobber, bits and pieces, odds and ends

accredit *v*
endorse, recognize, authorize, approve, certify, license, commission, warrant
FORMAL depute, certificate

accredited *adj*
recognized, official, authorized, qualified, endorsed, appointed, approved, certified, licensed, commissioned
FORMAL certificated, deputed

accretion *n*
1 *the accretions of self-respect*
addition, growth, supplement, increment, add-on

2 *the accretion of fat*
collecting, accumulation, gathering, build-up, growth, increase
FORMAL cumulation, augmentation

accrue *v*
accumulate, increase, mount (up), be added, build up, collect, amass
FORMAL augment

accumulate *v*
gather, build up, assemble, collect, amass, accrue, grow, increase, multiply, pile up, hoard, stockpile, store, gain, acquire
FORMAL aggregate, augment, cumulate
COLLOQ. stash, tot up, snowball
Ea *formal* disseminate, diffuse

accumulation *n*
1 *small accumulations of mail*
hoard, mass, pile, stockpile, store, stack, stock, reserve, gain
2 *the gradual accumulation of blood*
gathering, build-up, building-up, collection, growth, gain, increase, multiplication, conglomeration, accrual, assembly, acquisition
FORMAL aggregate, augmentation, cumulation, accretion
Ea 2 *formal* dissemination

accumulative *adj*
increasing, growing, mounting, multiplying, enlarging
COLLOQ. snowballing

accuracy *n*
correctness, precision, exactness, authenticity, truth, truthfulness, closeness, faithfulness, carefulness, meticulousness
FORMAL veracity, fidelity, exactitude, scrupulosity, verity, veridicality
Ea inaccuracy

accurate *adj*
1 *an accurate report/translation*
faithful, true, factual, correct, exact, strict, literal, word-for-word, word-perfect, close, sound, truthful, valid, authentic, unerring, faultless, perfect, fair
FORMAL veracious, letter-perfect, veridical
2 *accurate calculations*
exact, correct, precise, right, valid, rigorous, meticulous
COLLOQ. spot-on, bang on
3 *an accurate gun/throw*
well-aimed, well-directed, precise, on target, on the mark
Ea 1, 3 inaccurate **2** inaccurate, imprecise, inexact

accurately *adv*
faithfully, truly, correctly, precisely, exactly, strictly, literally, closely, truthfully, unerringly, rigorously, meticulously, faultlessly, perfectly
FORMAL veraciously, veridically
Ea inaccurately, imprecisely, inexactly

accursed *adj*
damned, wretched, hateful, despicable, abominable, detestable, loathsome, condemned, doomed, bewitched
FORMAL execrable, anathematized, bedevilled
Ea blessed

accusation *n*
charge, allegation, denunciation, impeachment, recrimination, complaint, incrimination, blame, indictment, prosecution, information; *dialect* threap
OLD tax
FORMAL imputation, arraignment, inculpation, citation, crimination, gravamen, delation

accuse *v*
1 *accused of murder*
make accusations, bring/press charges, charge, lay to someone's charge, blame, prosecute, put on trial, allege, make allegations, denounce, impeach, confront, challenge, attribute, indict, incriminate, criminate, implicate, inform against

OLD attaint, detect; *(Shakesp & Spenser)* appeal; *(Shakesp)* peach, appeach
FORMAL impugn, impute, arraign, cite, criminate
OLD SLANG COLLOQ. frame, book
2 *accuse someone of cheating*
blame, hold responsible
FORMAL censure, recriminate
COLLOQ. point the finger at, throw the book at

accustom *v*
familiarize, adjust, adapt, accommodate, get used to, get familiar with, get acquainted with, conform
FORMAL habituate, inure, attune

accustomed *adj*
1 *accustomed to the dark*
used, in the habit of, given, acclimatized, acquainted
FORMAL habituated, inured, wont
COLLOQ. at home
2 *sitting in her accustomed chair*
normal, usual, ordinary, familiar, everyday, conventional, routine, regular, customary, habitual, traditional, established, fixed, prevailing, general
FORMAL wonted, consuetudinary
Ea 1 unaccustomed, unused

> **QUOTATIONS**
> He woke me from the torpor of the accustomed
> ROBERT PENN WARREN

ace *n, adj*
♦ *n*
champion, expert, genius, master, maestro, winner, virtuoso
COLLOQ. dab hand, hotshot, whizz
♦ *adj*
brilliant, excellent, first-class, superb, outstanding, great, very good, perfect
COLLOQ. top-notch, terrific, brill
SLANG cool, wicked

acerbic *adj*
sharp, harsh, biting, stinging, abrasive, sarcastic, caustic, acrimonious, spiky, rancorous
FORMAL astringent, vitriolic, mordant, trenchant
Ea mild, friendly, kind

ache *v, n*
♦ *v*
1 HURT, be sore, pain, be painful, suffer, be in agony, agonize, throb, pound, twinge, smart, sting
COLLOQ. play up, kill
2 *aching to tell her*
long, yearn, pine, hanker, desire, crave, hunger, thirst, itch
COLLOQ. yen
♦ *n*
1 PAIN, hurt, soreness, suffering, anguish, agony, throb, throbbing, pounding, pang, twinge, smarting, stinging
2 *an ache for the past*
longing, desire, hankering, yearning, craving, itch
COLLOQ. yen

achieve *v*
accomplish, attain, reach, get, obtain, acquire, gain, earn, win, succeed, manage, do, perform, carry out, execute, fulfil, finish, complete, bring about, realize, produce
FORMAL procure, consummate, effect, effectuate
COLLOQ. polish off, wrap up
Ea miss, fail

> **SYNONYM NUANCES**
> Whilst **do** is an unmarked neutral term, **accomplish**, **attain** and **reach** suggest achieving through effort. **Get**, **obtain** and **acquire** are again neutral terms with no connotations of effort, and are appropriate where possession of something has been achieved; **gain** is similar, but has the added suggestion that something has

been obtained to your advantage. Using the words **earn** and **win** suggest that labour or effort was involved, while **procure** has an undertone of disapproval, suggesting contrivance.

Succeed is quite positive in tone, with an undercurrent of admiration for someone's efforts — similarly **manage**, though less so. **Perform**, **carry out** and **execute**, as well as **finish** and **complete**, as well as **bring about**, **produce**, **effect** and **effectuate** are again all unmarked terms with few positive or negative implications. However, to hint at the sense of satisfaction in achieving, **fulfil** and **realize** could be used.

To emphasize the speed with which something has been achieved, you might use the colloquial term **polish off**, and if you want to stress completeness of an achievement, you could talk of **wrapping it up**. **Consummate** is nowadays usually associated with marriage.

achievement *n*

1 *the achievement of our aims*
accomplishment, attainment, performance, execution, fulfilment, completion, success, realization, fruition
OLD chevisance
FORMAL procurement, consummation, acquirement, fruition, effectuation
2 *great achievements*
accomplishment, act, action, activity, deed, performance, exploit, feat, stroke, stroke of genius, triumph, effort
COLLOQ. feather in your cap

achiever *n*

doer, performer, succeeder
COLLOQ. high-flyer, go-getter, live wire, success story, whizz kid

Achilles' heel *n*

weakness, weak point, weak spot, vulnerable point, fault, failing, imperfection
COLLOQ. chink in your armour

acid *adj*

1 *an acid taste*
acidic, sour, bitter, tart, vinegary, unsweetened, sharp, pungent, acerbic, caustic, corrosive
FORMAL acetic, acetous, acidulous
2 *an acid remark*
bitter, unkind, critical, sarcastic, stinging, biting, caustic, cutting, incisive, harsh, morose, hurtful
FORMAL acerbic, astringent, mordant, trenchant, vitriolic
COLLOQ. catty
E3 **1** alkaline **2** kind, complimentary

Types of acid include:

acetic (ethanoic)	fatty	pantothenic
acetylsalicylic	folic	pectic
acrylic	formic (methanoic)	phenol
amino	glutamic	phosphoric
aqua fortis	hydrochloric	propanoic
aqua regia	hydrocyanic	prussic
ascorbic	lactic	pteroic
aspartic	linoleic	pyruvic
benzoic	linolenic	RNA (ribonucleic)
boric	malic	salicylic
butanoic	nicotinic	spirits of salt
butyric	nitric	stearic
carbolic	nitrohydrochloric	sulphuric
chloric	nitrous	sulphurous
citric	nucleic	tannic
DNA (deoxyr-	oxalic	tartaric
ibonucleic)	palmitic	uric

See also **amino acid.**

acknowledge *v*

1 *acknowledge a fact/an error*
admit, recognize, accept, agree with, declare, affirm, grant, allow, confess, own up to, concede,
OLD agnize, avouch
FORMAL acquiesce, accede
2 *acknowledge him with a nod*
greet, wave to, signal to, address, notice, recognize
FORMAL salute, hail
3 *acknowledge a letter*
answer, write back to, reply to, respond to, react to, confirm
4 *acknowledge someone's help*
thank, say thank you, express/show your appreciation, be grateful, give thanks for, express your thanks/gratitude, honour, celebrate, mark, recognize
E3 **1** deny, disagree with **2** ignore

acknowledged *adj*

recognized, accepted, approved, declared, professed, confirmed
FORMAL accredited, attested, avowed

acknowledgement *n*

1 *an acknowledgement of defeat*
recognition, admission, confession, declaration, profession, acceptance, granting, appreciation
2 *a gesture of acknowledgement*
greeting, notice, recognition, welcome, nod, smile, wave
FORMAL salutation
3 *an acknowledgement of a letter*
answer, reply, response, reaction
COLLOQ. comeback
4 *an acknowledgement of assistance*
gratitude, appreciation, thanks, praise, expression of gratitude/appreciation/thanks, gratefulness, tribute, credit
COLLOQ. bouquets

acme *n*

high point, highest point, height, peak, pinnacle, apex, zenith, apogee, climax, culmination, crown, optimum, summit
E3 low point, nadir

acolyte *n*

follower, assistant, helper, attendant, adherent
COLLOQ. hanger-on, sidekick

acoustic *adj*

hearing, sound
FORMAL auditory, aural, audile

acquaint *v*

familiarize, let know, accustom, tell, notify, advise, inform, make aware of, brief, enlighten, divulge, disclose, reveal, announce
FORMAL make conversant, apprise
COLLOQ. put in the picture, give someone the lowdown, bring someone up to speed

acquaintance *n*

1 *friends and acquaintances*
associate, companion, colleague, friend, contact, connection
FORMAL confrère
2 *my acquaintance with them*
familiarity, association, relationship, intimacy, social contact, contact, fellowship, companionship
3 *some acquaintance with art*
familiarity, awareness, knowledge, understanding, experience
FORMAL cognizance, conversance

> **QUOTATIONS**
> If a man does not make a new acquaintance as he advances through life, he will soon find himself left alone
> SAMUEL JOHNSON

acquainted adj
 1 *acquainted with him*
 friendly, on friendly terms, on good terms
 2 *acquainted with that book*
 familiar, well-versed, knowledgeable, aware, abreast, au fait, *au courant*
 FORMAL conversant, cognizant, apprised
 COLLOQ. in the know, up to speed
 2 unfamiliar, unaware, ignorant

acquiesce v
 consent, submit, agree, accept, allow, permit, approve, defer
 FORMAL concur, accede
 COLLOQ. give in, give the go-ahead to, give the green light to, give the thumbs-up to, give the nod to
 disagree, object, resist

acquiescence n
 consent, agreement, acceptance, approval, compliance, submission, yielding, deference
 FORMAL concurrence, assent
 COLLOQ. go-ahead, green-light, thumbs-up, nod, say-so
 disagreement, resistance

acquiescent adj
 consenting, agreeable, agreeing, accepting, approving, amenable, obedient, compliant, submissive, yielding, deferential, servile
 FORMAL acceding, concurring, complaisant

acquire v
 buy, purchase, obtain, get, come by, receive, collect, gather, amass, accumulate, net, gain, secure, earn, take on, win, achieve, attain, realize
 FORMAL procure, appropriate
 COLLOQ. grab, pick up, snap up, splash out on
 SLANG bag, cop, collar
 relinquish, forfeit, sell

acquisition n
 1 *his latest acquisition*
 purchase, buy, gain, possession, accession, investment, takeover, property
 2 *the acquisition of a skill*
 securing, gaining, obtaining, achievement, attainment
 FORMAL procurement, appropriation

acquisitive adj
 greedy, covetous, hoarding, grasping
 FORMAL avaricious, avid, predatory, rapacious, voracious

acquisitiveness n
 greed, covetousness, cupidity, graspingness
 FORMAL avarice, avidity, predatoriness, rapacity, voracity

acquit v
 1 *acquitted of the crime*
 clear, reprieve, excuse, free, set free, liberate, deliver, relieve, release, dismiss, discharge, settle, satisfy, repay
 FORMAL absolve, exonerate, exculpate, vindicate
 COLLOQ. let off, let off the hook
 2 *acquit yourself well*
 perform, behave, act, do, conduct
 FORMAL comport, bear
 COLLOQ. make a good/bad job
 1 convict, condemn

acquittal n
 clearance, clearing, reprieve, excusing, freeing, liberation, deliverance, relief, release, dismissal, discharge
 FORMAL absolution, exoneration, exculpation, vindication, compurgation
 conviction, condemnation

acrid adj
 1 *an acrid smell*
 pungent, sharp, stinging, acid, sour, bitter, tart, harsh, burning, caustic, acerbic

 2 *an acrid comment*
 caustic, biting, cutting, incisive, sarcastic, sardonic, bitter, acrimonious, harsh, nasty, malicious, venomous
 FORMAL acerbic, astringent, mordant, trenchant, virulent, vitriolic

acrimonious adj
 bitter, biting, cutting, caustic, sharp, virulent, severe, spiteful, censorious, abusive, ill-tempered, waspish, venomous, rancorous, splenetic, petulant
 OLD atrabilious
 FORMAL acerbic, astringent, trenchant, vitriolic, irascible
 COLLOQ. crabbed, bitchy
 peaceable, kindly; *formal* irenic

acrimony n
 bitterness, resentment, spite, ill will, gall, ill temper, ill feeling, sarcasm, harshness, venom
 FORMAL causticity, rancour, petulance, irascibility, mordancy, trenchancy, vitriol, spleen, astringency, acerbity, asperity, acridity, virulence

acrobat n
 gymnast, tumbler, balancer, somersaulter, contortionist, trapeze artist, tightrope-walker, rope-walker, rope-dancer, stuntman, stuntwoman
 OLD *Scot* speel
 FORMAL funambulist, aerialist, equilibrist

acrobatics n
 gymnastics, balancing, somersaulting, tightrope-walking, rope-walking, wire-walking, stunts
 FORMAL funambulism, equilibrity

act v, n
 ♦ v
 1 *act fast*
 be, move, do, take action, take steps, take measures, be active, be busy, go about, react
 2 BEHAVE, perform, respond, react, function
 FORMAL conduct yourself, acquit yourself, exert yourself, comport yourself
 3 *the drug will act soon*
 take effect, have an effect, work, operate, function
 FORMAL be efficacious
 4 *the gear acts as a brake*
 work, function, serve, operate, do, do the job of
 5 *act upset*
 pretend, fake, put on, simulate
 FORMAL feign, affect, assume, dissemble, dissimulate
 COLLOQ. kid, sham
 6 *act in a play*
 perform, go on the stage, play, portray, represent, mime, characterize, enact, mimic, imitate, impersonate
 ♦ n
 1 *acts of bravery*
 deed, action, undertaking, enterprise, operation, manoeuvre, move, step, doing, execution, accomplishment, achievement, exploit, feat, stroke
 2 *the second act of the play*
 part, division, section, subsection, episode
 3 *put on an act*
 pretence, make-believe, counterfeit, fake
 FORMAL feigning, dissimulation, dissemblance, affectation
 COLLOQ. sham, show, put-up job, front
 4 *an act of parliament*
 law, statute, ordinance, canon, edict, decree, resolution, measure, ruling, bill
 5 *a juggler's act*
 turn, item, routine, sketch, performance, number
 COLLOQ. skit, gig
 ■ **act on**
 1 *act on orders*
 carry out, fulfil, comply with, conform to, obey, follow, heed, take

2 AFFECT, work on, influence, alter, modify, change, transform

■ **act up**
1 MISBEHAVE, behave badly, cause trouble, give bother
COLLOQ. play up, carry on, mess about, muck around
2 MALFUNCTION, break down, go wrong, fail, stop working
COLLOQ. play up, go kaput, pack up
SLANG conk out

acting *adj, n*
♦ *adj*
temporary, provisional, interim, stopgap, short-term, supply, stand-by, stand-in, standing in for, in place of, representing, covering, deputy, substitute, reserve, fill-in, relief, pro tem, surrogate
♦ *n*
theatre, drama, performing, performing arts, stagecraft, artistry, performance, play-acting, show business, melodrama, dramatics, theatricals, histrionics, footlights, portrayal, characterization, impersonation, imitating
FORMAL Thespianism
COLLOQ. showbiz
SLANG luvviedom

> **QUOTATIONS**
> Acting is a masochistic form of exhibitionism
> LAURENCE OLIVIER

action *n*
1 *his prompt action*
act, move, deed, exploit, step, measure, course of action, feat, accomplishment, achievement, performance, effort, endeavour, enterprise, undertaking, proceeding, process, activity
2 *put an idea into action*
operation, practice, effect, force, functioning, doing, performance, exercise, exertion, work, mechanism, movement, motion
3 *the action of a chemical on metal*
effect, operation, power, result, work, influence
4 *people of action*
vitality, liveliness, spirit, energy, vigour, power, force, forcefulness, activity
COLLOQ. get-up-and-go, pizzazz
5 *killed in action*
warfare, battle, conflict, combat, fight, fighting, fray, engagement, encounter, skirmish, clash, hostilities
FORMAL affray
6 *a legal action*
litigation, lawsuit, suit, case, prosecution, proceedings
7 *where the action is*
excitement, exhilaration, stimulation, activity, activities, events, happenings
COLLOQ. goings-on

> **PROVERBS**
> Actions speak louder than words

activate *v*
start, start working, set off, fire, switch/turn/put on, set in motion, mobilize, propel, move, stir, rouse, arouse, get going, set going, trigger (off), trip, stimulate, initiate, motivate, prompt, energize, excite, galvanize
OLD bestir
FORMAL actuate, animate, impel
COLLOQ. push/press the button, throw the switch, kick-start
🖪 deactivate, stop, arrest

active *adj*
1 *an active person*
busy, occupied, industrious, diligent, hard-working, forceful, spirited, vital, vibrant, forward, hyperactive, manic, frenetic; *Scot* birkie; *Irish* stirabout
FORMAL indefatigable, astir
COLLOQ. on the go
2 *active for his age*
agile, nimble, spry, sprightly, light-footed, quick, alert, animated, lively, energetic, mobile, vigorous; *Scot* yauld

OLD springe; (*Shakesp*) quiver; (*Spenser*) wimble
COLLOQ. zippy, bright-eyed and bushy-tailed
3 *active members*
devoted, engaged, involved, committed, contributing, militant, activist, enterprising, enthusiastic
4 *the system is active*
in operation, operational, functioning, working, operative, running, in force
OLD practive
FORMAL effectual
🖪 **1** passive **3** inactive

> **SYNONYM NUANCES**
>
> *sense 1*
> **Busy**, **occupied** and the more literary **astir** are fairly neutral in tone, and can be used of any active person or situation. The words **industrious**, **diligent**, **hard-working** and indefatigable suggest approbation of someone's untiring thoroughness: *a diligent search*.
> **Spirited**, **vital**, **vibrant** and the colloquial **on the go** are also positive terms to use, with the emphasis this time on animation and vigour: *a vibrant democracy*. **Forceful** and **forward** emphasize the energy and power something or someone has, but are not necessarily suggesting you are regarding it with favour.
> To describe an activity that is undesirably out of control, you might use the terms **manic** or **frenetic**: *a grin of manic glee*. **Hyperactive** is used in the field of medicine to describe abnormal activity: *hyperactive children*, but it can also be used figuratively without implying an opinion on the speaker's part: *hyperactive charm*.

activist *n*
militant, agitator, troublemaker, subversive, revolutionary, inciter, firebrand, incendiary, fomenter, henchman
COLLOQ. hacktivist, slacktivist, stirrer

activity *n*
1 *the office is full of activity*
business, liveliness, life, activeness, action, motion, movement, commotion, bustle, hustle and bustle, industry, labour, exertion, exercise
COLLOQ. hurly-burly, a hive of activity/industry, comings and goings, toing and froing
2 *holiday activities*
pursuit, hobby, pastime, interest, diversion, distraction, something to do, occupation, job, work, act, deed, project, scheme, task, venture, enterprise, endeavour, undertaking
FORMAL avocation
🖪 **1** inactivity, passivity

actor, actress *n*
play actor, film actor, movie actor, film star, movie star, comedian, tragedian, player, performer, stage performer, artist, dramatic artist, trouper, artiste, character actor, leading lady, leading man, understudy, extra, walk-on, impersonator, mime, mime artist, mummer
FORMAL Thespian, Roscius
COLLOQ. ham, luvvie, thesp

actual *adj*
real, existent, substantial, tangible, material, physical, concrete, positive, definite, absolute, certain, unquestionable, indisputable, confirmed, verified, factual, truthful, true, genuine, legitimate, bona fide, authentic, realistic
FORMAL de facto
COLLOQ. real live
🖪 theoretical, apparent, imaginary

actuality *n*
reality, fact, substance, existence, truth
TECHNICAL ens
FORMAL factuality, historicity, corporeality, materiality, substantiality

actually *adv*
1 *Did you actually see him fall?*
in fact, as a matter of fact, as it happens, in truth, in reality, really, truly, indeed, absolutely
OLD insooth, soothly
FORMAL de facto
2 *she took her degree eventually and actually got a first class*
even, though it may seem strange, surprisingly, believe it or not, as it happens

actuate *v*
move, stir, stimulate, activate, motivate, instigate, prompt, rouse, arouse, kindle, start, start working, set off, set going, trigger (off), switch/turn on, set in motion

acumen *n*
astuteness, shrewdness, sharpness, keenness, quickness, penetration, insight, intuition, discrimination, discernment, judgement, perception, sense, wit, wisdom, intelligence, cleverness, ingenuity
FORMAL judiciousness, percipience, perspicacity, perspicuity, sagacity, sapience
COLLOQ. smartness, gumption

acute *adj*
1 *an acute shortage*
severe, intense, extreme, violent, critical, dangerous, serious, grave, urgent, crucial, drastic, dire, vital, decisive, sharp, cutting, poignant, distressing, unbearable
2 *an acute mind*
sharp, sharp-witted, keen, incisive, penetrating, astute, shrewd, canny, judicious, discerning, clever, observant, perceptive, insightful, sensitive
FORMAL percipient, perspicacious, sapient
COLLOQ. smart
3 *an acute illness*
severe, serious, intense, dangerous, critical, grave
TECHNICAL peracute
Ea 1 mild, slight **3** mild, chronic, persistent

acutely *adv*
very, intensely, extremely, strongly, seriously, severely, gravely, sharply, keenly, markedly

adage *n*
maxim, saying, axiom, proverb, byword, precept, saw
FORMAL aphorism, apophthegm, gnome, paroemia

adamant *adj*
hard, resolute, determined, set, firm, insistent, rigid, stiff, inflexible, unbending, unrelenting, unyielding, stubborn, unwavering, uncompromising, tough, fixed, immovable, unshak(e)able
FORMAL intransigent, obdurate
Ea hesitant, flexible, yielding

adapt *v*
1 *adapt to a new environment*
adjust, acclimatize yourself, familiarize yourself, orientate yourself, accommodate yourself, get used/accustomed
FORMAL habituate yourself
2 *adapt a building*
alter, change, qualify, modify, adjust, convert, remodel, customize, fit, tailor, fashion, shape, harmonize, match, suit, conform, comply, prepare
OLD attemper, contemper

adaptable *adj*
flexible, compliant, amenable, easy-going, versatile, plastic, malleable, pliable, alterable, changeable, variable, modifiable, adjustable, convertible, open-ended, conformable
Ea inflexible; *formal* refractory

adaptation *n*
1 *adaptation to a different situation*
adjustment, acclimatization, familiarization, accommodation, getting used/accustomed
FORMAL habituation

2 *adaptation of a novel for TV*
alteration, change, modification, shift, transformation, revision, variation, adjustment, conversion, remodelling, customization, fitting, refitting, fashioning, refashioning, reworking, shaping, reshaping, harmonization, matching, conformity, preparation

add *v*
1 *add an introduction to the book*
put on, put in, include, complete, improve, attach, supplement, combine, build on
FORMAL adjoin, affix, append, annex, augment
COLLOQ. throw in
2 *add numbers*
count (up), total, work out/calculate the total
COLLOQ. tot up
3 *the rain added to her misery*
increase, raise, boost, intensify, deepen, heighten, extend
FORMAL augment
COLLOQ. hike up, aggravate
4 *'Thanks,' I added*
tack on, continue, go on, go on to say, carry on
Ea 1 take away, remove, reduce, decrease **2** subtract, take (away), deduct, remove

■ **add up**
1 *add up numbers*
add, sum up, add together, total, tally, count (up), reckon, calculate, compute, figure up
COLLOQ. tot up
2 *the total adds up to 100*
amount, make, come to, run to, include, spell
FORMAL constitute
3 *it doesn't add up*
be consistent, hang together, fit, be plausible, be reasonable, stand to reason, make sense, mean, signify, indicate, ring true
Ea 1 subtract

added *adj*
additional, supplementary, extra, more, another, fresh, further, new, spare
FORMAL adjunct

addendum *n*
appendix, addition, postscript, supplement; *N Am* annex
FORMAL codicil, adjunct, appendage, augmentation, attachment, endorsement, allonge

addict *n*
1 *a drug addict*
drug taker, drug user
COLLOQ. junkie, druggie, user, dope-fiend
SLANG freak, head, coke-head, crackhead, smackhead, tripper, mainliner, hop-head, hype, snowbird
2 *a chess addict*
enthusiast, fan, devotee, follower, adherent, fanatic, hound
COLLOQ. buff, fiend, freak

addicted *adj*
1 *addicted to drugs*
dependent, drug-dependent
COLLOQ. hooked, strung out
2 *addicted to TV*
obsessed, absorbed, devoted, dedicated, fond, inclined, fanatical
COLLOQ. hooked, wild, crazy, daft, nuts, potty

addiction *n*
1 *alcohol addiction*
dependence, dependency, compulsion, craving, habit
SLANG monkey
2 *addiction to chocolate*
craving, habit, obsession, compulsive behaviour, mania
COLLOQ. thing

> **QUOTATIONS**
> All sin tends to be addictive, and the terminal point of addiction is what is called damnation
>   W H AUDEN, *A Certain World*

addictive *adj*
habit-forming, compulsive, irresistible, uncontrollable, obsessive

addition *n*
1 *the index is a welcome addition*
supplement, attachment, extra, increment, additive, rider, afterthought, postscript, annexe, addendum, appendix, accessory
FORMAL adjunct, appendage, augmentation, appurtenance
2 *the addition of a separate phone line*
adding, extension, enlargement, increasing, increase, gain, inclusion
FORMAL annexation, accession, accretion
3 *addition of numbers*
summing-up, totalling, counting, reckoning, inclusion, computation
COLLOQ. totting-up
🖃 **2** removal, taking-away **3** subtraction, deduction
■ **in addition**
additionally, too, also, as well, besides, moreover, further, furthermore, over and above, not to mention; *Scot* forby
OLD to boot, withal
COLLOQ. into the bargain, for good measure

additional *adj*
added, extra, supplementary, spare, more, further, increased, other, new, fresh, another
FORMAL supplemental, adscititious, adventitious, supervenient, excrescent

additionally *adv*
in addition, too, also, as well, besides, moreover, further, furthermore, over and above; *Scot* forby
OLD to boot, withal
COLLOQ. into the bargain, for good measure

additive *n*
supplement, addition, extra, preservative

addle *v*
confuse, befuddle, bewilder, fluster, muddle, perplex, daze
COLLOQ. faze

addled *adj*
confused, befuddled, bewildered, lost, flustered, muddled, mixed-up, perplexed
COLLOQ. fazed
🖃 clear

address *n, v*
♦ *n*
1 *write down an address and phone number*
home, house, flat, apartment, lodging, directions, inscription, whereabouts, location, situation, place, poste restante, dwelling
FORMAL (place of) residence, abode
2 SPEECH, talk, lecture, sermon, oration, harangue, discourse, monologue, soliloquy, dissertation
FORMAL diatribe, philippic, apostrophe, allocution, disquisition
COLLOQ. spiel
3 *forms of address*
greeting, welcome
FORMAL salutation, invocation
♦ *v*
1 *address a letter*
direct, label, send, post, mail
FORMAL superscribe
2 *address an audience*
lecture, speak to, talk to, give a talk/speech to, make/deliver a speech, preach to, harangue
FORMAL sermonize, orate
3 *address a remark to someone*
communicate, direct, convey, send, intend for
FORMAL remit
4 *How should I address a duke?*
call, speak/write to, greet, designate

■ **address (yourself) to**
deal with, give your attention to, apply yourself to, devote yourself to, attend to, undertake, concentrate on, focus on, tackle, buckle down to, engage in, take care of

adduce *v*
cite, mention, allude to, refer to, name, quote, put forward, point out, present
FORMAL proffer, evidence

adept *adj, n*
♦ *adj*
skilled, accomplished, expert, masterly, experienced, versed, practised, polished, proficient, competent, capable, good, clever, able, adroit, deft, nimble
COLLOQ. ace, sharp, hot stuff, no flies on someone
SLANG wicked
🖃 bungling, incompetent, inept
♦ *n*
expert, genius, master, maestro, veteran
COLLOQ. dab hand, hot stuff, nobody's fool, wizard
🖃 bungler, incompetent

adequacy *n*
sufficiency, suitability, fitness, ability, competence, capability, serviceability, acceptability, satisfactoriness, reasonableness, passability, tolerability, tolerableness, fairness, indifference, mediocrity
FORMAL commensurateness, requisiteness
🖃 inadequacy, insufficiency

adequate *adj*
1 *adequate amounts of food*
enough, sufficient, suitable, appropriate
FORMAL commensurate, requisite
2 *adequate work*
acceptable, satisfactory, passable, reasonable, tolerable, unexceptional, indifferent, undistinguished, average, suitable, fit, able, competent, capable, serviceable
COLLOQ. all right, OK, will do, could be better/worse, no great shakes, patchy, fair to middling, ho-hum, run of the mill, nothing (much) to write home about, nothing (much) to shout about, not set the Thames on fire
🖃 **1** insufficient **2** inadequate

adequately *adv*
sufficiently, suitably, appropriately, satisfactorily, acceptably, passably, reasonably, tolerably
🖃 inadequately, insufficiently

adhere *v*
1 STICK, stick together, glue, paste, cement, grip, fix, fasten, attach, join, link, combine, coalesce, cohere, hold, hold fast, cling
FORMAL cleave to, accrete
2 *adhere to the agreement*
observe, follow, abide by, comply with, fulfil, obey, keep, heed, respect, stand by, go along with
COLLOQ. stick
3 *adhere to an opinion*
support, hold, defend, stand by, go along with, stick up for
FORMAL espouse

adherence *n*
support, advocacy, observance, compliance, fulfilment, respect, defence

adherent *n*
supporter, upholder, advocate, partisan, follower, disciple, satellite, henchman, devotee, admirer, fan, enthusiast
FORMAL votary, aficionado, sectary
COLLOQ. hanger-on, buff, freak, nut

adhesion *n*
adherence, adhesiveness, holding together, sticking (together), bond, attachment, grip, purchase, cohesion

adhesive *adj, n*
♦ *adj*
sticky, stick-on, tacky, self-adhesive, gummed, adhering, sticking, clinging, holding, attaching, cohesive

FORMAL adherent, glutinous, mucilaginous, emplastic
COLLOQ. gummy, gluey
♦ n
glue, gum, fixative, paste, cement, tape, sticky tape,
Sellotape®, passe-partout, Elastoplast®, Band-aid®, Cow
Gum®, Superglue®, Blu-tak®
FORMAL mucilage

ad hoc adj, adv
♦ adj
makeshift, improvised, extempore, ad-lib, unscripted,
unrehearsed, unprepared, spontaneous
COLLOQ. off-the-cuff
E⅃ rehearsed
♦ adv
without preparation, extempore, ad lib, spontaneously
COLLOQ. on the spur of the moment, off the top of your
head, off the cuff

adieu n, interj
♦ n
goodbye, farewell, leave-taking, au revoir
FORMAL valediction, valedictory
♦ interj
goodbye, farewell, au revoir, auf Wiedersehen, ciao,
adios, arrivederci
COLLOQ. cheerio, bye, bye-bye, cheers, see you (later), see
you around, be seeing you, all the best, mind how you
go, take care, have a nice day, ta-ta, so long

ad infinitum adv
for ever, evermore, perpetually, permanently, constantly,
at all times, continually, incessantly, endlessly, eternally,
until the end of time, till doomsday, till your dying day
OLD aye
COLLOQ. till the cows come home

adjacent adj
adjoining, touching, bordering, alongside, beside, next-
door, neighbouring, next, closest, nearest, close, near
FORMAL abutting, contiguous, juxtaposed, conterminant,
conterminate, conterminous, proximate, vicinal
E⅃ remote, distant

adjoin v
touch, meet, border, verge, neighbour, be next,
interconnect, link, connect, join, combine, unite, couple,
attach, add, annex
FORMAL abut, append, juxtapose

adjoining adj
adjacent, touching, bordering, near, neighbouring, next,
next door, verging, interconnecting, linking, connecting,
joining, combining, uniting
FORMAL contiguous, impinging, abutting, proximate,
juxtaposed, conjoining, vicinal

adjourn v
1 *adjourn a meeting*
stop temporarily, interrupt, suspend, break off, delay, stay,
defer, postpone, put off, pause
FORMAL discontinue, prorogue
COLLOQ. put on the back burner
2 *adjourn to the lounge*
withdraw, retreat
OLD betake yourself
FORMAL retire, repair
E⅃ 1 assemble, convene

adjournment n
interruption, suspension, break, pause, interval, recess,
intermission, delay, stay, postponement, putting-off
TECHNICAL moratorium
FORMAL discontinuation, deferment, deferral, dissolution,
prorogation
COLLOQ. let-up

adjudge v
decree, judge, consider, regard, deem, determine,
reckon

adjudicate v
judge, arbitrate, umpire, referee, settle, determine,
decide, pronounce, pass
FORMAL adjudge

adjudication n
judgement, arbitration, settlement, ruling, determination,
decree, decision, conclusion, pronouncement, verdict

adjudicator n
judge, arbitrator, umpire, referee, arbiter, mediator

adjunct n
addition, supplement, accompaniment, complement,
accessory
FORMAL appendage, concomitant

adjust v
1 *adjust to new circumstances*
become/grow accustomed, adapt, acclimatize yourself,
become acclimatized, orientate yourself, accommodate
yourself, reconcile yourself, harmonize, conform
FORMAL habituate yourself
COLLOQ. get used to
2 MODIFY, change, adapt, alter, convert, dispose, shape,
remodel, fit, accommodate, suit, measure, amend, revise,
make adjustments, rectify, regulate, balance, repair,
reshape, refashion, temper, tune, modulate, fix, set,
arrange, align, compose, settle, square
FORMAL coapt
COLLOQ. fine-tune, tweak
E⅃ 2 upset; *formal* disarrange

adjustable adj
adaptable, modifiable, convertible, flexible, alterable,
versatile, movable
E⅃ fixed, immovable

adjustment n
1 *minor adjustments to the engine*
modification, change, adaptation, alteration, conversion,
remodelling, shaping, fitting, accommodation,
amendment, revision, rectification, regulation, tuning,
fixing, setting, arranging, rearranging, arrangement,
rearrangement, ordering, settlement
COLLOQ. fine-tuning, tweaking
2 *adjustment to a new job*
orientation, adaptation, acclimatization, accommodation,
naturalization, reconciliation, harmonization, conforming,
settling down/in, getting used to
FORMAL habituation

ad-lib v, adj, adv
♦ v
improvise, make up, invent
FORMAL extemporize
COLLOQ. play it by ear, speak off the cuff/off the top of
your head, wing it
♦ adj
impromptu, improvised, unprepared, without preparation,
unpremeditated, unrehearsed, spontaneous, made-up
FORMAL extempore, extemporaneous, extemporized
COLLOQ. off-the-cuff, off the top of your head
E⅃ prepared
♦ adv
impromptu, spontaneously, impulsively
FORMAL extempore, extemporaneously
COLLOQ. off the cuff, off the top of your head

administer v
1 *administer a country/law/project*
organize, direct, conduct, manage, run, control, regulate,
superintend, supervise, oversee, govern, rule, lead, head,
guide, preside over, officiate
2 *administer a drug*
give, provide, supply, distribute, give out, measure out,
mete out, deliver, execute, impose, apply
FORMAL discharge, dispense, disburse, adhibit
COLLOQ. dole out

administration *n*

1 *reduce the cost of administration*
administering, management, running, paperwork, organization, direction, control, superintendence, supervision, overseeing, governing, ruling, command, leadership, execution
COLLOQ. red tape

2 *a country's administration*
government, governing body, regime, ministry, cabinet, leadership, directorship, management, parliament, council, senate, congress, executive, term of office
COLLOQ. powers that be, corridors of power

3 *the administration of a law/drug*
provision, supplying, execution, application, imposition
FORMAL dispensation, discharge

> **QUOTATIONS**
> An administration, like a machine, does not create. It carries on
> ANTOINE DE SAINT-EXUPÉRY, *Flight to Arras*

administrative *adj*
management, managerial, governmental, legislative, authoritative, executive, organizational, regulatory, supervisory
FORMAL directorial, gubernatorial

Administrative areas include:

area	enclave	state
borough	municipality	territory
city	parish	town
constituency	precinct	village
conurbation	province	ward
county	region	zone
district	sector	
division	shire	

---

administrator *n*
manager, organizer, director, controller, superintendent, supervisor, overseer, governor, ruler, leader, president, chairman, chief executive, executive, managing director, head, chief
FORMAL custodian, guardian, trustee
COLLOQ. boss, top dog, bigwig, big noise, big cheese

admirable *adj*
praiseworthy, commendable, creditable, deserving, worthy, respected, fine, excellent, magnificent, exceptional, superior, wonderful, exquisite, choice, rare, masterly, valuable
FORMAL estimable, laudable, meritorious
COLLOQ. cool, terrific, brill, out of this world, second to none
SLANG wicked, shit-hot
E3 contemptible, despicable, deplorable

admirably *adv*
commendably, deservingly, excellently, magnificently, exceptionally, wonderfully, eminently, supremely

admiration *n*
respect, (high) regard, (high) esteem, reverence, worship, idolism, adoration, affection, adulation, approval, praise, appreciation, kudos, pleasure, delight, wonder, astonishment, amazement, surprise, acclaim, commendation
FORMAL approbation, veneration, *fureur*
COLLOQ. yen
E3 contempt, disrespect, scorn

admire *v*

1 *admire his honesty*
respect, think highly of, have a high opinion of, hold in high regard, hold in high esteem, esteem (highly), look up to, like very much, revere, worship, idolize, adore, approve, praise, applaud
FORMAL venerate, laud, prize, iconize

COLLOQ. think the world of, hero-worship, put on a pedestal, take your hat off to
SLANG (*vulgar*) think the sun shines out of someone's arse

2 *admire a car*
appreciate, value, like, approve of
E3 1 despise, censure

> **SYNONYM NUANCES**
>
> *sense 1*
> **Respect** and **like very much** and **approve** are fairly restrained terms for admire; to suggest a higher level of admiration you might use **think highly of** or **have a high opinion of**, **hold in high esteem** or **regard**, **esteem** (**highly**), the rather colloquial **think the world of** or the more vulgar **think the sun shines out of someone's arse**. When you **prize** someone or something you also value them, but to use this term suggests you are doing so from a superior or possessive position.
> To say you **look up to** someone implies humility on the part of the speaker, and hints at emulation. This can be even more strongly conveyed with **hero-worship** or **put on a pedestal**. To express an extreme level of admiration, there are many other words you could use, for example **revere**, **worship**, **idolize**, **venerate**, **iconize** and **adore**. Although many of these terms are associated with admiration of deities, they can be used with a more light-hearted tone: *I adore cats; he worships his wife*.
> If you are talking of admiring someone for a particular achievement, you **take your hat off to** them; similarly **laud**, **praise** or **applaud** are usually used in the context of expressing your admiration: *I applaud your calmness in this situation*.

admirer *n*

1 *a great admirer of classical music*
follower, disciple, adherent, supporter, fan, enthusiast, devotee, worshipper, idolizer, idolater
FORMAL aficionado
COLLOQ. buff, fiend, freak

2 *a woman's admirers*
suitor, boyfriend, girlfriend, sweetheart, lover, beloved
FORMAL beau, wooer, gallant
E3 1 critic, opponent

admissible *adj*
acceptable, allowable, permissible, allowed, permitted, lawful, legitimate, justifiable, tolerable, tolerated, passable
FORMAL licit
COLLOQ. legit, OK
E3 inadmissible, illegitimate

admission *n*

1 *refuse admission*
permission, entrance, access, right of access, right of entry, entrée
FORMAL ingress

2 *admission is £5*
admission fee, entrance, entrance fee, entry charge

3 *an admission of guilt*
confession, granting, acknowledgement, recognition, acceptance, allowance, concession, affirmation, declaration, profession, disclosure, divulgence, revelation, exposé
FORMAL avowal, *mea culpa*, *peccavi*, asseveration
E3 1 exclusion, prohibition **3** denial, contradiction

> **!** **admission** or **admittance**?
> Each word means 'the act of entering' or 'permission to enter', but *admittance* is used in more formal styles: *Admission by ticket only; gain admittance to the palace of the President.*

admit *v*

1 CONFESS, own up, grant, acknowledge, recognize, accept, allow, concede, agree, declare, affirm, profess, own, yield, disclose, unburden yourself, divulge, reveal

COLLOQ. blurt out, eat your words, come clean
SLANG fess up
2 LET IN, allow to enter, allow entry, give access, give admission, accept, receive, take in, welcome, adopt, introduce, initiate
OLD adhibit
FORMAL intromit
Eᴣ 1 deny, hide **2** shut out, exclude, let out

SYNONYM NUANCES

sense 1

To **confess** or **own up** are widely used synonyms of admit, both used in the context of admitting some wrongdoing. **Grant**, **acknowledge** and **recognize** are also common synonyms, but used in the context of admitting that something is true or exists. **Accept** is a fairly straightforward term for simply complying or agreeing with something; but **allow** implies agreement with far less conviction: *he allowed that legislation could restrict liberty*. Similarly, if you **agree** with someone about something then you concur, and there is no implication of prior dissent; but to **concede**, **own** or **yield** suggests you admit something you previously opposed or denied.

To describe a public admission you could use **declare**, **affirm** or **profess**, with the latter having the added implication that the claims may be false: *they declared their opposition; she thrived on the publicity she professed to loathe*. **Disclose**, **divulge** and **reveal** would suggest publicly and willingly bringing secrets to light, while **unburden yourself** gives a strong sense of the relief felt on doing so. **Come clean** again suggests a deliberate act, with more emphasis on admitting all that you know. However, **blurt out** carries the distinct impression of an admission accidentally or unadvisedly made: *he blurted out his drugs secret*.

---

admittance *n*
admitting, admission, letting in, (right of) access, entrance, (right of) entry, entrée, acceptance, reception, introduction, initiation
FORMAL ingress
Eᴣ exclusion

> **Ⅰ admittance** or **admission**?
> *See panel at* **admission**.

admitted *adj*
confessed, acknowledged, recognized, accepted, declared, professed, confirmed, affirmed

admittedly *adv*
confessedly, allowedly, avowedly, granted, certainly

admixture *n*
mixture, compound, combination, blend, amalgamation, mix, fusion, amalgam, alloy
FORMAL commixture, intermixture, tincture

admonish *v*
scold, rebuke, reprimand, discipline, correct, reprove, warn, upbraid, chide, censure, exhort, counsel
FORMAL berate
COLLOQ. tell off, give someone a dressing-down, give someone an earful, tear a strip off, rap over the knuckles

admonition *n*
rebuke, reprimand, reproof, scolding, correction, warning, censure, exhortation, counsel
FORMAL berating, reprehension
COLLOQ. telling-off, ticking-off, dressing-down, earful, wigging

ad nauseam *adv*
endlessly, interminably, boringly, monotonously, perpetually, constantly, continually, continuously

ado *n*
fuss, bother, bustle, to-do, commotion
COLLOQ. hurly-burly, hassle, flap, tizzy, hoo-ha, song and dance

adolescence *n*
teens, teenage years, puberty, youth, young adulthood, minority, boyhood, girlhood, development, immaturity, youthfulness, boyishness, girlishness
FORMAL pubescence, juvenescence, juvenility
Related adjective: neanic

adolescent *adj, n*
◆ *adj*
1 *an adolescent son*
teenage, young, youthful, juvenile, boyish, girlish, growing, developing
FORMAL pubescent, juvenescent
2 *adolescent behaviour*
immature, puerile, childish, infantile
◆ *n*
teenager, youth, young person, young adult, juvenile, minor

adopt *v*
1 *adopt children*
take in, take as your own, foster
2 *adopt a policy*
take up, take on, accept, assume, follow, choose, select, support, maintain, back, endorse, ratify, approve
FORMAL appropriate, embrace, espouse, arrogate
3 *adopt a candidate*
select, choose, decide on, settle on, nominate, appoint, vote, elect
Eᴣ 1 disown **2** reject

adoption *n*
1 *the adoption of children*
taking as your own, taking-in, (long-term) fostering
2 *the adoption of a suggestion*
taking-on, acceptance, taking-up, choice, selection, support, backing, endorsement, ratification, approval
FORMAL appropriation, approbation, embracement, embracing, espousal
3 *adoption of a candidate*
selection, choice, vote, election, nomination, appointment

adorable *adj*
lovable, dear, darling, precious, appealing, sweet, winsome, charming, enchanting, captivating, winning, delightful, pleasing, attractive, wonderful, fetching, bewitching
Eᴣ hateful, abominable

adoration *n*
1 *adoration for someone*
love, admiration, devotion, cherishing, doting on, (high) regard, esteem
2 *adoration of God*
worship, praise, reverence, homage, idolization, exaltation, magnification, glorification, thanksgiving
FORMAL laudation, veneration
Eᴣ 1 abhorrence, detestation

adore *v*
1 *adore your parents*
love, cherish, be devoted to, dote on, hold dear, be fond of, admire, esteem (highly), honour, revere, worship
FORMAL venerate
COLLOQ. think the world of
2 *adore apricots*
love, like very much, enjoy greatly, be fond of, enjoy, savour, relish, be partial to
COLLOQ. have a weakness for, not be able to resist
Eᴣ 1, 2 hate, abhor

adorn *v*
decorate, deck, ornament, crown, trim, garnish, gild, enhance, embellish, enrich, grace
OLD bedeck, bedight, bedizen, begem, bejewel, bestick, bespangle, aguise, dight; (*Spenser*) attrap
FORMAL festoon, emblazon, furbish, adonize, apparel, array, attire, beautify, impearl, miniate
COLLOQ. do up, doll up, tart up

adornment n

1 *bodily adornment*
beautification, decorating, ornamentation, ornateness, enrichment, embellishment
OLD bedizenment
FORMAL garniture

2 *gold adornments*
accessory, ornament, decoration, jewellery, frill, trappings, trimmings, garnish, flounce, frippery
FORMAL falbala, fallal, fallalery, fandangle, figgery, furbelow, garnishry, gilding

adrift adj

1 *the boat had been cut adrift*
at sea, drifting, off course, unanchored, anchorless

2 *feel adrift and lonely*
aimless, rootless, directionless, disorientated, disoriented, having lost your bearings, goalless, insecure, lost, unsettled
Ε**1** anchored **2** stable, secure, settled

adroit adj
skilful, adept, able, clever, expert, resourceful, masterful, proficient, deft, dexterous
OLD habile
Ε clumsy, inept, maladroit

adroitly adv
skilfully, ably, cleverly, expertly, resourcefully, masterfully, proficiently, deftly, dexterously
Ε clumsily, ineptly

adroitness n
skill, skilfulness, adeptness, ability, cleverness, expertise, resourcefulness, mastery, facility, finesse, proficiency, competence, deftness, dexterity
Ε clumsiness, ineptitude

adulation n
flattery, idolization, personality cult, hero worship, admiration, praise, sycophancy, bootlicking, fawning
FORMAL blandishment
COLLOQ. pats on the back

adulatory adj
flattering, praising, complimentary, bootlicking, fawning, servile, sycophantic
FORMAL blandishing, fulsome, obsequious, unctuous
Ε unflattering

adult adj, n
♦ adj
1 *adult responsibilities*
grown-up, of age, full-grown, fully-grown, fully-fledged, developed, mature, ripe, ripened
2 *adult magazines*
sexually explicit, pornographic, obscene, indecent, hard-core
COLLOQ. blue, X-rated, raunchy, fruity, sleazy, near the knuckle/bone
Ε**1** immature
♦ n
grown person, grown-up, man, woman
Related adjective: ephebic

adulterate v
contaminate, pollute, taint, corrupt, defile, debase, degrade, dilute, water down, weaken, devalue, deteriorate, make impure
FORMAL attenuate, bastardize, vitiate
OLD (*Shakesp*) card
Ε purify, refine

adulteration n
contamination, pollution, corruption, defilement, debasement, dilution, weakening, deterioration
FORMAL vitiation

adulterer n
libertine, lecher, profligate, rake, roué, playboy, philanderer, womanizer, ladies' man, flirt, Casanova, Don Juan, deceiver, cad
OLD avouterer
COLLOQ. lady-killer, stud, wolf

adulterous adj
unfaithful, deceitful, false, disloyal, inconstant
COLLOQ. two-timing, cheating

adultery n
unfaithfulness, infidelity, affair, liaison, extramarital relations/relationship, extramarital sex, entanglement, flirtation, unchastity
OLD avoutry, fornication
COLLOQ. two-timing, cheating, a bit on the side
SLANG playing around, playing the field
Ε faithfulness, fidelity

advance v, n, adj
♦ v
1 PROCEED, go forward, move on, move forward, come forward, surge forward, go ahead
2 *advance the date of the wedding*
bring forward, move forward, make earlier
3 PROGRESS, make progress, make headway, forge ahead, develop, grow, improve, better, prosper, thrive, flourish
COLLOQ. make great strides, come on in leaps and bounds
4 FURTHER, promote, upgrade, foster, support, assist, help, benefit, facilitate, increase, grow
5 *advance an idea*
present, submit, put forward, suggest, allege, cite, bring forward, offer, provide, supply, furnish
FORMAL proffer, adduce
6 *advance a sum of money*
lend, loan, pay, pay beforehand, pay in advance, give
COLLOQ. sub
Ε**1** retreat **2** put back **4** impede, hinder
♦ n
1 *the army's advance*
progress, forward movement, onward movement, moving forward, going forward, marching forward
2 *recent advances in medicine*
breakthrough, step, step forward, development, furtherance, progression, headway, growth, increase, improvement
FORMAL advancement, betterment, amelioration
3 *an advance of £500*
deposit, down payment, prepayment, credit, loan, retainer
Ε**1** retreat, recession
♦ adj
1 *advance booking*
early, prior, forward, preliminary
2 *an advance party*
expeditionary, forward, leading, preliminary, vanguard
■ **in advance**
beforehand, previously, early, earlier, sooner, ahead of time, ahead, in front, in the lead, in the forefront
COLLOQ. up front
Ε later, behind

advanced adj
1 *an advanced design*
up-to-date, leading, foremost, ahead, forward, precocious, progressive, forward-looking, high-tech, state-of-the art, avant-garde, ultra-modern, ahead of the times, sophisticated, complex, higher, at the cutting/leading edge, at the bleeding edge
2 *an advanced course of studies*
high-level, complex
Ε**1** backward, retarded **2** elementary

SYNONYM NUANCES

sense 1
While something **up-to-date** has followed all the latest developments, the terms **leading** and **foremost**, and **at the cutting/leading edge** are reserved for something showing the way. To describe someone or something as **ahead**, **forward** or **higher** also places them in front of others: *forward thinking; a higher mind*. Someone who is **precocious** is strikingly advanced for their age or time, but this term often has the implication they are irksomely so: *a precocious young debater*.

    Progressive and **forward-looking** would appropriately describe something enlightened, having regard to the

future: *progressive moves towards full employment.*
High-tech and **state-of-the-art** are usually used to describe something advanced in a specialist field such as electronics. Technology with the most up-to-date devices could also be described as **sophisticated**, while **complex** things have evolved beyond the knowledge of many. **Ultra-modern**, although describing something entirely up-to-date, is ironically rather old-fashioned in tone.

Avant-garde is often used in the context of art and literature, and carries connotations of unconventionality and daring innovation; if you want to express an unconventionality that society may not be ready for you could use **ahead of the times**.

advancement *n*
1 *advancement in a career*
promotion, furtherance, betterment, upgrading, upward step
FORMAL preferment
COLLOQ. kick upstairs
2 *the advancement of science*
improvement, development, growth, evolution, rise, gain, advance, progress, headway
E∃ 1 demotion **2** retardation

advances *n*
overtures, addresses, approach(es), attentions, moves, proposition, offer, suggestion

advantage *n*
1 *the advantages of electric light*
asset, blessing, benefit, value, reward, good, good point, plus, plus point, virtue, pro, boon, fruit, welfare, interest, service, help, aid, assistance, use, convenience, helpfulness, usefulness, utility, profit, gain
OLD vantage, boot, obvention; *(Shakesp)* prize
FORMAL perquisite, avail
COLLOQ. beauty, pay-off
2 *an advantage over other candidates*
edge, lead, upper hand, head, superiority, precedence, dominance, pre-eminence, sway, leverage
COLLOQ. head start, whip hand; *Aust* box-seat; everything going for you, the odds in your favour
E∃ 1 disadvantage, drawback, hindrance

advantageous *adj*
beneficial, favourable, convenient, helpful, of assistance, of service, useful, worthwhile, valuable, profitable, gainful, remunerative, rewarding
FORMAL opportune, propitious, furthersome
E∃ disadvantageous, adverse, damaging

advent *n*
coming, appearance, approach, arrival, entrance, introduction, occurrence, emergence, looming, onset, dawn, birth, beginning
FORMAL accession, inception

adventitious *adj*
unplanned, unintended, accidental, uncalculated, unexpected, unforeseen
FORMAL fortuitous

adventure *n*
1 *exciting adventures*
exploit, venture, undertaking, enterprise, quest, escapade, risk, hazard, chance, speculation, experience, incident, happening, occurrence
OLD aunter
2 *a life of adventure*
excitement, enterprise, risk, danger, peril, romance, thrill
COLLOQ. kick(s)

SYNONYM NUANCES

sense 1
The words **occurrence**, **happening** and **experience** are generally neutral in tone: they can be used of any event that happens to someone without implying either

---

approval or disapproval, or that the person has any control over what happens: *his experiences in the Peruvian jungle; some occurrences in her younger life.* The word **incident** also implies that a person has no control over events, but can be more disapproving: *that unsavoury incident last Thursday.*

When you want to express approval, **exploit** is more appropriate: *heroic exploits.* On the other hand, **escapade** suggests something done with daring, but with comic or disreputable elements: *drunken escapades in Manchester.* The words **quest** and **undertaking** are only appropriate when there is something that a person deliberately sets out to achieve, **quest** having a more romantic tone: *a quest in search of lost civilizations.* When someone decides to do something requiring initiative or imagination, you can use **enterprise** or **venture**.

When you want to emphasize uncertainty about whether the person will be successful, you can use **speculation**, **hazard**, **risk** and **chance**. The words **undertaking**, **enterprise**, **venture** and **speculation** are often used in the context of business and finance.

---

adventurer *n*
opportunist, hero, heroine, traveller, venturer, voyager, wanderer, daredevil, pirate, filibuster, swashbuckler, *chevalier d'industrie*
OLD bandeirante, Odysseus, Ulysses, Argonaut

adventurous *adj*
1 *an adventurous person*
daring, intrepid, bold, headstrong, audacious, impetuous, reckless, rash, risky, venturesome, enterprising, daredevil
COLLOQ. spunky, gutsy
2 *an adventurous life*
exciting, enterprising, risky, dangerous, perilous, precarious, hazardous, romantic
E∃ 1, 2 unadventurous **1** cautious, chary, prudent

adversary *n*
enemy, opponent, antagonist, assailant, attacker, competitor, contestant, foe, opposer, rival
E∃ ally, supporter, friend

adverse *adj*
unfavourable, disadvantageous, hostile, antagonistic, opposing, opposite, counter, contrary, conflicting, counter-productive, negative, unfortunate, unlucky, detrimental, harmful, injurious, hurtful, unfriendly, uncongenial, inexpedient
OLD perverse
FORMAL inauspicious, inopportune, unpropitious, untoward
E∃ advantageous, favourable

❗ adverse or **averse**?
Adverse means 'unfavourable, hostile, harmful': *adverse criticism. Averse* means 'having a dislike, disinclined': *She's not averse to walking all over people to get what she wants.*

---

adversely *adv*
unfavourably, negatively, unfortunately, unluckily, harmfully, detrimentally
FORMAL inauspiciously, unpropitiously
E∃ favourably

adversity *n*
misfortune, ill fortune, bad luck, ill luck, reverse, hardship, hard times, misery, wretchedness, affliction, suffering, distress, sorrow, woe, trouble, trial, cross, calamity, disaster, catastrophe, traverse
FORMAL tribulation
COLLOQ. hell, living hell
SLANG the pits
E∃ prosperity

advertise v
1 *advertise a product*
publicize, promote, market, merchandize, sell, praise, talk up, tout
COLLOQ. push, plug, hype
2 *advertise the time of a performance*
announce, declare, proclaim, broadcast, publish, display, make known, make public, inform, notify
FORMAL promulgate

advertisement n
commercial, publicity, promotion, marketing, jingle, display, blurb, announcement, notice, poster, bill, placard, leaflet, handbill, circular, handout, propaganda, trailer, bulletin, banner, pop-up
COLLOQ. advert, ad, promo, plug, hype

advice n
1 *give someone advice*
warning, caution, dos and don'ts, injunction, instruction, counsel, counselling, help, guidance, direction, suggestion, recommendation, opinion, view, tip, wisdom, word, constructive criticism, encouragement
2 *a remittance advice*
notification, notice, memorandum, communication, information

> **QUOTATIONS**
> There is nothing which we receive with so much reluctance as advice
> JOSEPH ADDISON, *The Spectator*

> **SYNONYM NUANCES**
>
> *sense 1*
> The words **guidance** and **direction** can be used widely in situations where a person is looking to be told what they should do: *we give you guidance to make the right decision*. **Suggestion**, **recommendation** and **tip** are likely to be used where a specific course of action is being proposed: *the recommendation was made that Smith be appointed chairman*.
>   **Opinion**, **view** and **word**, on the other hand, are appropriate words to use when only a personal angle is called for, without the expectation that it will be acted upon.
>   However, with **dos and don'ts** and **instruction**, the tone is authoritative, and these terms carry the expectation that a proposed action is carried out. **Injunction** makes the most compelling demand for action, and is used mainly in legal contexts. A **warning** or a **caution** describes a type of advice that usually has not been sought, and suggests that there is danger in taking a particular course. It can also imply that the person giving it may take punitive action themselves.
>   Other words are more positive in tone: **wisdom** and **counsel** suggest advice given by someone with knowledge and experience, with the implication that it should be respected on those grounds. **Counselling** is typically used in the more specific sense of professional advice given to assist people with particular problems. Also conveying the idea of advice given to counter possible difficulties are **help**, **constructive criticism** and **encouragement**: *ask your solicitor for help in writing your will*.

advisability n
desirability, suitability, appropriateness, aptness, preferability, wisdom, judiciousness, prudence, soundness
FORMAL expediency
E3 inadvisability, folly

advisable adj
suggested, recommended, sensible, wise, wisest, prudent, expedient, judicious, sound, profitable, beneficial, best, desirable, preferable, suitable, appropriate, apt, fitting, fit, proper, correct

FORMAL politic
E3 inadvisable, foolish

advise v
1 COUNSEL, give counsel, guide, give guidance, warn, forewarn, caution, instruct, teach, tutor, suggest, give/offer/make suggestions, recommend, give/offer/make recommendations, commend, urge
FORMAL enjoin, forewarn
2 NOTIFY, inform, tell, acquaint, make known, report, give notice
FORMAL apprise
COLLOQ. fill in on, give the low-down

advisedly adv
cautiously, carefully, prudently, judiciously, after careful consideration

adviser n
counsellor, consultant, authority, guide, teacher, tutor, instructor, coach, mentor, helper, aide, right-hand man/woman, therapist, guru, confidant(e), counsel, lawyer

advisory adj
advising, consultative, consulting, counselling, helping, recommending
FORMAL consultatory

advocacy n
support, backing, adoption, campaigning, promotion, championing, defence, encouragement, patronage, proposal, recommendation, justification, upholding, propagation
FORMAL espousal, advancement, promulgation
COLLOQ. pushing

advocate v, n
♦ v
defend, champion, campaign for, press for, argue for, preach, plead for, justify, urge, encourage, advise, recommend, propose, prescribe, promote, endorse, back (up), support, uphold, patronize, adopt, subscribe to, favour, believe in, sympathize with, lobby
FORMAL espouse, countenance
COLLOQ. plug, push for, be behind, be pro, throw your weight behind
E3 *formal* impugn, disparage, deprecate
♦ n
1 *an advocate of an idea*
defender, supporter, upholder, champion, campaigner, pleader, vindicator, proponent, exponent, promoter, evangelist, speaker, spokesperson, spokesman, spokeswoman
2 *the advocate in a court of law*
lawyer, solicitor, barrister, counsel, attorney, paraclete; *Scot* peat
E3 1 opponent, critic

aegis n
support, backing, auspices, guardianship, patronage, sponsorship, wing, advocacy, championship, favour

aeon n
age, era, epoch, span, time, duration, generation, year(s)

aerate v
oxygenate, put air into, charge with air, charge with gas, gasify, refresh, ventilate, lighten

aerial adj, n
♦ adj
aerial combat
above the ground, in the air, midair, air-to-air
OLD aery
FORMAL aeolian
♦ n
antenna, booster, receiver, satellite dish
TECHNICAL dipole, duplex

aeroplane n
See panel at **aircraft**.

aesthetic *adj*
decorative, ornamental, adorning, embellishing, fine,
elegant, stylish, tasteful, artistic
FORMAL beautifying

afar *adv*
a long distance, a long way, far off, far away, distantly

affability *n*
friendliness, amiability, approachability, openness,
geniality, good humour, good nature, mildness,
benevolence, kindliness, graciousness, obligingness,
courtesy, amicability, congeniality, cordiality, warmth,
sociability, pleasantness
FORMAL benignity, conversableness
COLLOQ. chumminess, matiness, palliness
F3 unfriendliness, reserve, reticence, coolness

affable *adj*
friendly, amiable, approachable, open, expansive, genial,
good-humoured, good-natured, mild, benevolent, kindly,
gracious, obliging, courteous, amicable, congenial, cordial,
warm, sociable, pleasant, agreeable
OLD facile
COLLOQ. chummy, mat(e)y, pally
F3 unfriendly, reserved, reticent, cool

affair *n*
1 BUSINESS, transaction, operation, proceeding, undertaking,
activity, project, responsibility, interest, concern, matter,
question, issue, subject, topic, circumstance, happening,
occurrence, incident, episode, event, thing, ploy; *Scot*
effeir, hypothec
OLD gear
COLLOQ. show, pigeon, funeral, shebang
OLD COLLOQ. go
2 *have an affair*
relationship, liaison, intrigue, love affair, romance, *affaire,*
affaire d'amour, affaire de coeur, grande passion, amour
COLLOQ. fling, carry-on

affect *v*
1 *changes that affect the schedule*
have an effect/influence on, concern, regard, involve,
relate to, apply to, do to, bear upon, impinge upon, act
on, change, transform, alter, modify, influence, sway,
prevail over, impact
2 *deeply affected by the poverty*
move, touch, impress, interest, stir, upset, disturb, trouble,
overcome
FORMAL perturb
COLLOQ. faze, throw
3 *a disease affects the body*
attack, strike, take hold of
4 *affect an attitude*
adopt, simulate, imitate, fake, counterfeit, sham, pretend,
profess
FORMAL feign, assume
COLLOQ. put on

⚠ affect or **effect**?
Affect is usually a verb. Its most common meaning is
'to have an influence on; change the circumstances, etc
of': *The accident affected his eyesight. Effect* is used as
a noun or a verb: as a noun it means 'result or
consequence': *recover from the effects of his illness.* As
a verb it is used in formal styles to mean 'to cause or
bring about': *effect a reconciliation with his parents.*

SYNONYM NUANCES

sense 2
To say you are **moved** or **touched** suggests something
has aroused your sentiments, especially pity. The term
impress might be used instead to describe a profound
effect on the intellect rather than emotion, whereas to
interest is far less significant of any deep emotional
involvement.

To convey excitement, you could use **stir**: *a cause*
which stirred the electorate, but **upset** would only be
appropriate where a degree of distress has been caused.
Disturb, **trouble** and **perturb** are similar to upset,
though they have the added suggestion of agitation. To
express a more extreme effect, **overcome** suggests your
feelings have got the better of you: *overcome by grief.*
When something **fazes** you it worries, confuses or
unsettles you, and the similarly colloquial term **throw**
denotes much the same.

affectation *n*
airs, pretentiousness, mannerism, pose, act, show,
appearance, façade, pretence, charade, sham, false
display, simulation, imitation, artificiality, insincerity,
theatricism, airs and graces
F3 artlessness, ingenuousness

SYNONYM NUANCES

Many of these synonyms have a tone of disapproval; to
say someone has put on **airs** or **airs and graces** is to
accuse them of affecting superiority or refined behaviour;
pretentiousness goes further by suggesting someone
acting in a foolishly grandiose way. A **mannerism** is a
more neutral term to denote a marked peculiarity or a
trick of style or manner, whereas striking a **pose** is again
more marked by the suggestion of a false act and a
desire to impress.

Act and **show** also suggest a pretence, this time with
the aim to deceive: *I put on a show of contrition.* An
appearance similarly denotes an outward look or show,
and is not a particularly marked term; **façade**, too, can
be used to describe an outward display, but it is usually
showier and with little behind it: *the façade of*
respectability. **Pretence** also signifies an act put on
deliberately to mislead, while **false display** and **sham**
are even more strongly uncomplimentary terms
intimating an imposture or fraud.

Simulation and **imitation** can again be used as more
neutral terms to describe insincere acts, but **artificiality**
and **insincerity** again imply criticism, the latter carrying
a strong suggestion of hypocrisy. If you want to
emphasize the exaggerated nature of the affectation, you
might choose the word **theatricism**.

affected *adj*
pretentious, pompous, stiff, unnatural, insincere, twee,
simulated, artificial, fake, counterfeit, sham, contrived,
studied, precious, mannered
FORMAL assumed, feigned, literose, minikin
COLLOQ. put-on, la-di-da, hoity-toity, phoney
F3 genuine, natural

affecting *adj*
moving, touching, impressive, powerful, piteous, pitiable,
pitiful, poignant, heartbreaking, heart-rending, pathetic,
sad, stirring, troubling

affection *n*
fondness, attachment, devotion, love, tenderness, care,
caring, warmth, feeling, kindness, friendliness,
endearment, goodwill, favour, liking, partiality, inclination,
passion, desire
FORMAL amity, penchant, predilection, predisposition,
proclivity, propensity
F3 dislike, antipathy

affectionate *adj*
fond, attached, devoted, doting, loving, adoring, tender,
caring, warm, warm-hearted, kind, friendly, amiable,
cordial
F3 cold, undemonstrative

affectionately *adv*
fondly, lovingly, devotedly, adoringly, tenderly, kindly,
warmly, amiably, cordially
F3 coldly

affiliate v
join, associate, ally, amalgamate, unite, annex, combine, connect, incorporate, merge, team up, syndicate, band together
OLD filiate
FORMAL confederate, conjoin

affiliated adj
associated, allied, in partnership, in league, connected, related, incorporated, amalgamated, integrated
E3 independent

affiliation n
connection, relationship, link, tie, bond, alliance, union, amalgamation, association, coalition, combination, confederation, federation, incorporation, membership, joining, league, merger
OLD filiation

affinity n
1 RAPPORT, attraction, compatibility, empathy, sympathy, fondness, liking, good terms, bond, partiality
OLD affiance
FORMAL predisposition, propensity
COLLOQ. chemistry
2 RESEMBLANCE, similarity, likeness, relationship, correspondence, analogy, comparability, kin, kinship
FORMAL similitude
E3 **1** hatred **2** dissimilarity

affirm v
confirm, corroborate, endorse, ratify, uphold, support, certify, witness, testify, swear, maintain, state, assert, declare, pronounce
FORMAL asseverate, attest, aver, avouch, avow
E3 refute, deny

affirmation n
yes, assertion, statement, declaration, attestation, certification, confirmation, corroboration, endorsement, ratification, oath, pronouncement, protest, testimony, witness
FORMAL affirmance, asseveration, averment, deposition, avouchment, avowal

affirmative adj, n
♦ adj
agreeing, concurring, approving, assenting, consenting, positive, confirming, corroborative, emphatic
FORMAL assertory
E3 negative, dissenting
♦ n
yes, agreement, confirmation, acceptance, ratification
FORMAL concurrence, acquiescence
COLLOQ. OK
E3 negative

affix v
stick, glue, paste, adhere, pin on, tack, attach, add, annex, append, bind, connect, fasten, join, tag
FORMAL adjoin, subjoin
E3 detach

afflict v
strike, trouble, burden, oppress, distress, aggrieve, strain, stress, bother, bear hard upon, grieve, pain, hurt, ail, wound, harm, try, harass, plague, anguish, curse, gripe, torment, torture
OLD smite, visit; (Spenser) assay
FORMAL beset
E3 comfort; formal solace

> ⚠ **afflict** or **inflict**?
> Afflict means 'to cause pain or distress to': Pre-fight nerves afflict almost everyone. Inflict means 'to impose something unpleasant or unwanted': They inflicted heavy casualties on the enemy.

affliction n
distress, grief, sorrow, misery, depression, suffering, pain, torment, disease, illness, sickness, plague, curse, scourge, sore, night, cross, ordeal, trial, trouble, hardship, adversity, misfortune, calamity, disaster, woe, furnace, wretchedness
OLD languor, teen; (Spenser) tine; unweal, visitation
FORMAL tribulation
E3 comfort, blessing; formal consolation, solace

affluence n
wealthiness, wealth, riches, fortune, substance, property, prosperity, abundance, profusion, plenty
FORMAL opulence
COLLOQ. tidy sum, easy street
SLANG megabucks
E3 poverty

affluent adj
wealthy, rich, moneyed, well-off, prosperous, well-to-do, comfortable
FORMAL opulent
COLLOQ. well-heeled, flush, in the money, on easy street, rolling in it
SLANG loaded
E3 poor, impoverished

afford v
1 *afford school fees*
have enough for, pay for, have the money for, be able to pay, spare, allow, stretch to, manage, sustain, bear
2 *privileges afforded by the membership*
provide, supply, furnish, give, grant, offer, impart, present, produce, yield, generate

affordable adj
inexpensive, cheap, low-priced, low-cost, budget, economical, moderate, reasonable, manageable, sustainable

affray n
brawl, brush, contest, disturbance, fight, quarrel, riot, row, feud, fracas, fray, mêlée, scuffle, set-to, skirmish, squabble, tussle, wrangle
COLLOQ. punch-up, fisticuffs, scrap, free-for-all

affront v, n
♦ v
offend, insult, abuse, snub, slight, provoke, displease, irritate, annoy, anger, vex, incense, outrage, pique
E3 compliment, appease
♦ n
offence, insult, slur, rudeness, discourtesy, disrespect, indignity, snub, slight, wrong, injury, abuse, provocation, vexation, outrage
FORMAL aspersion
COLLOQ. facer, slap in the face, kick in the teeth
E3 compliment, pat on the back

affronted adj
injured, offended, insulted, slighted, displeased, irritated, annoyed, angry, vexed, incensed, outraged, piqued

aficionado n
devotee, fan, enthusiast, admirer, connoisseur, authority, expert, specialist
COLLOQ. buff, fiend, freak, nut

aflame adj
1 ALIGHT, burning, ablaze, on fire, ignited, lighted
2 AGLOW, lit up, illuminated, bright, radiant, shining

afloat adv
1 FLOATING, buoyant, unsinkable, swimming, drifting
COLLOQ. with your head above water
2 *keep business afloat*
solvent, viable, sound, out of debt
COLLOQ. in the black, with your head above water
E3 **1** sinking **2** colloq. in the red

afoot adv
about, around, circulating, current, going on, going about, in the air, in the wind, brewing
FORMAL abroad
COLLOQ. in the pipeline

aforementioned *adj*
already mentioned, previously mentioned
OLD aforesaid, aforenamed

afraid *adj*
1 FRIGHTENED, scared, alarmed, terrified, petrified, panic-stricken, fearful, timorous, daunted, intimidated, faint-hearted, cowardly, craven, reluctant, apprehensive, anxious, nervous, timid, distrustful, suspicious; *dialect* nesh; *Scot* rad
OLD affrayed, effraide, afear, adred; (*Spenser*) adrad
FORMAL tremulous, aghast
COLLOQ. scared out of your wits, scared to death, having kittens, in a cold sweat, in a blue funk, shaking in your shoes, shaking like a leaf, with your heart in your mouth
2 *I'm afraid she's badly hurt*
sorry, concerned, regretful, apologetic
E3 **1** unafraid, brave, bold, confident

SYNONYM NUANCES

sense 1
The words **frightened**, **scared** and **alarmed** are fairly straightforward synonyms of afraid; **terrified** and **petrified** might be used of more extreme fear, with the implication of being almost fixed in fear.
  Panic-stricken likewise indicates being struck by a panic or fear resulting in mental inaction. **Daunted** is a less extreme term, which more often nowadays suggests discouragement rather than fear. If you want to emphasize that something in particular is striking fear into someone and making them less able to act, you could say they are **intimidated**.
  To describe someone as **timid**, **faint-hearted**, **cowardly** or **craven** says they lack courage generally, often without good cause, and these terms are rather contemptuous; **craven** has a literary, old-fashioned tone. **Reluctant** is a fairly mild term suggesting only unwillingness.
  To convey an unwillingness or fear caused by the anticipation of something adverse, you could use **apprehensive**, **anxious** or **nervous**. **Tremulous** can be used to suggest a physical manifestation of fear or apprehensiveness. To describe someone as **aghast** would be appropriate where something in particular has struck them with horror, and they are showing signs of it: *they stood aghast at the news.*

---

afresh *adv*
anew, again, once again, once more, newly, over again

after *prep*
1 *life after death*
following, subsequent to
FORMAL posterior
2 *run after a thief*
in pursuit of, following, chasing
3 *be after the manager's job*
wanting, trying to get
4 *ask after someone*
about, regarding, with regard to, concerning
5 *named after his mother*
in honour of, given the same name as; *N Am* for
6 *after the way I've been treated*
because of, owing to, in consequence of, as a result of, on account of
E3 **1** before
■ **after all**
1 *it's only a game after all*
in spite of what was expected, despite what was expected
2 *you can't expect to learn English in a few days; after all it is a difficult language*
it must be remembered that, primarily, first of all, most importantly, most of all

after-effect *n*
result, consequence, repercussion, upshot, aftermath, spin-off

aftermath *n*
after-effects, effects, results, outcome, consequences, end, repercussions, upshot, wake

afterwards *adv*
next, later (on), subsequently, after that, then
OLD thereupon

again *adv*
once more, once again, yet again, one more time, another time, over again, afresh, anew, encore
■ **again and again**
repeatedly, continually, constantly, frequently, often, over and over again, time and time again, time and again

against *prep*
1 *against the wall*
adjacent to, close up to, touching, in contact with, on
FORMAL abutting
2 *against corporal punishment*
opposing, versus, opposed to, in opposition to, antagonistic to, hostile to, resisting, in defiance of, opposite to, facing, fronting, in the face of, confronting, in contrast to
COLLOQ. anti
3 *insure against fire*
in case of, as a protection from
4 *his youth is against him*
disadvantageous, unfavourable, harmful, detrimental, prejudicial
E3 **2** in favour of, for; *colloq.* pro

age *n, v*
♦ *n*
1 *the Ice Age*
era, epoch, day, days, generation, date, time, period, duration, span, years, aeon
2 *the experience of age*
old age, maturity, elderliness, seniority, dotage, senility, decline, advancing/declining years
FORMAL senescence, decrepitude
E3 **2** youth; *colloq.* salad days
♦ *v*
grow old/up, become old, come of age, mature, ripen, mellow, season, decline, deteriorate, degenerate, wither

---

QUOTATIONS
Old age is always wakeful
  HERMAN MELVILLE, *Moby Dick*

---

aged *adj*
old, elderly, advanced (in years), ag(e)ing, mature, senior, geriatric, grey, hoary, patriarchal, superannuated
FORMAL senescent
COLLOQ. getting on, past it, over the hill, have seen better days, no spring chicken, not as young as you were, not getting any younger, with one foot in the grave, ancient
E3 young, youthful

agency *n*
1 *a recruitment agency*
bureau, office, department, organization, business, firm, company, work
2 MEANS, medium, instrumentality, vehicle, power, force, influence, effect, intervention, action, activity, involvement, operation, mechanism, workings

agenda *n*
list, plan, programme, schedule, calendar, diary, timetable, to-do list, scheme, scheme of work, menu

agent *n*
1 *a travel agent*
representative, broker, middleman, go-between, liaison, intermediary, negotiator, substitute, deputy, delegate, envoy, emissary, minister, proxy, trustee, assignee, mover, doer, performer, operator, operative, functionary, worker, factor
COLLOQ. rep

2 *a secret agent*
spy, double agent, shadow, setter, emissary, sleeper, *mouchard*; *N Am* operative
OLD beagle, wait, spial, spie
COLLOQ. mole
SLANG nark, plant, spook
3 *water-purifying agents*
instrument, vehicle, channel, means, medium, agency, cause, force
4 *an agent of change*
instrument, vehicle, engine, medium, factor, channel, route, way, means, root, source, performer

age-old *adj*
ancient, old, very old, aged, time-worn, antique, long-lived
FORMAL prim(a)eval
E3 new

agglomeration *n*
accumulation, build-up, collection, gathering, mass, stockpile, increase, store, aggregate
FORMAL augmentation, aggregation
COLLOQ. stash

aggrandize *v*
make richer, make more powerful, advance, dignify, elevate, enhance, enlarge, ennoble, enrich, exaggerate, exalt, glamorize, glorify, inflate, amplify, magnify, promote, upgrade, widen
E3 belittle, debase

aggrandizement *n*
advancement, elevation, enlargement, enhancement, exaggeration, exaltation, promotion, magnification

aggravate *v*
1 *aggravate the problem*
worsen, make worse, compound, inflame, increase, intensify, heighten, magnify, exaggerate
FORMAL exacerbate
COLLOQ. add fuel to the fire/flames, add insult to injury, rub salt in the wound
2 ANNOY, irritate, vex, irk, exasperate, incense, provoke, tease, pester, harass
COLLOQ. wind up, get at, get on someone's nerves, get up someone's nose, get under someone's skin, rub up the wrong way, bug, needle
E3 1 improve, alleviate **2** soothe, appease, mollify

aggravation *n*
annoyance, exasperation, irritation, provocation, teasing, vexation, irksomeness
COLLOQ. aggro, hassle, thorn in the flesh

aggregate *n, adj*
♦ *n*
total, sum, sum total, grand total, amount, total/whole amount, whole, totality, entirety, generality, combination, collection, accumulation
♦ *adj*
total, entire, complete, whole, full, combined, gross, inclusive, comprehensive, accumulated

aggression *n*
1 ANTAGONISM, provocation, offence, injury, attack, offensive, assault, onslaught, raid, incursion, strike, encroachment, infringement, invasion, intrusion
2 AGGRESSIVENESS, militancy, belligerence, combativeness, hostility, forcefulness
FORMAL pugnacity, bellicosity
E3 1 peace, resistance **2** passivity, gentleness

aggressive *adj*
1 *an aggressive person*
argumentative, quarrelsome, contentious, belligerent, hostile, offensive, provocative, intrusive, invasive, ruthless, brutal, savage, ferocious, destructive
FORMAL pugnacious, bellicose
COLLOQ. cut-throat; *Can* chippy
SLANG *N Am* bad-ass

2 *an aggressive sales rep*
bold, assertive, pushy, go-ahead, competitive, forceful, vigorous, zealous
COLLOQ. feisty, full-on
SLANG in-your-face
E3 1 peaceable, friendly **2** submissive, unassertive, timid

aggressor *n*
invader, attacker, assailant, assaulter, intruder, offender, provoker, instigator
E3 victim

aggrieved *adj*
bitter, resentful, pained, distressed, saddened, unhappy, upset, angry, annoyed, wronged, offended, hurt, injured, insulted, maltreated, ill-used
COLLOQ. disgruntled, miffed, peeved
SLANG pissed off
E3 pleased, happy

aghast *adj*
shocked, appalled, horrified, horror-struck, thunderstruck, stunned, stupefied, amazed, astonished, astounded, startled, confounded, dismayed

agile *adj*
1 *an agile person*
active, lively, nimble, spry, sprightly, mobile, deft, dexterous, athletic, flexible, limber, lithe, fleet, quick, swift, brisk; *Scot* swank
COLLOQ. nifty
2 *an agile mind*
astute, sharp, acute, alert, quick-witted, clever
E3 1 clumsy, stiff **2** slow

agility *n*
1 *agility of movement*
activeness, liveliness, nimbleness, mobility, flexibility, deftness, quickness, swiftness, briskness
2 *agility of thought*
astuteness, sharpness, alertness, quick-wittedness
E3 1 clumsiness, stiffness **2** slowness

agitate *v*
1 *the news agitated them*
worry, trouble, upset, alarm, disturb, unsettle, disquiet, discompose, fluster, ruffle, flurry, unnerve, confuse, distract, disconcert, work up
OLD (*Shakesp*) betoss
FORMAL perturb
COLLOQ. faze, rattle
2 *agitate for reform*
campaign, argue, fight, battle, rouse, arouse, stir up, excite, stimulate, incite, inflame, ferment, work up
3 *agitate the mixture*
shake, rattle, convulse, rock, stir, beat, churn, toss, whisk, blend; *dialect* poss
OLD commove
E3 1 calm, tranquillize

agitated *adj*
worried, troubled, upset, disturbed, anxious, unsettled, flustered, ruffled, distraught, unnerved, disconcerted, nervous, wrought up
COLLOQ. in a lather, in a tizzy
E3 calm, composed

agitation *n*
1 ANXIETY, worry, concern, distress, trouble, alarm, disquiet, restlessness, tension
FORMAL perturbation
2 *periods of political agitation*
fighting, striving, struggle, battle, campaigning, crusade
3 *agitation of the particles*
shaking, moving, movement, stirring, whisking, beating, tossing, turning, blending
E3 1 calmness

agitator *n*
troublemaker, activist, subversive, rabble-rouser, revolutionary, *agent provocateur*, inciter, instigator, firebrand, fomenter
COLLOQ. stirrer

agnostic *n, adj*
♦ *n*
unbeliever, sceptic, doubter, questioner
COLLOQ. doubting Thomas
♦ *adj*
unbelieving, sceptical, doubting, questioning, disbelieving

ago *adv*
from that time, gone, past, in the past, before, since, previously, earlier

agog *adj*
eager, excited, curious, enthralled, enthusiastic, impatient, in suspense, keen, anxious, avid
COLLOQ. on the edge of your seat, on tenterhooks
E3 incurious

agonize *v*
worry, labour, strain, strive, struggle, fret, trouble, wrestle

agonizing *adj*
distressing, excruciating, harrowing, painful, tormenting, torturous, worrying, piercing, racking

agony *n*
anguish, torment, torture, pain, spasm, throes, suffering, affliction, distress, hurt, woe, misery, wretchedness
FORMAL tribulation

agrarian *adj*
agricultural, agronomic, farming, cultivated
OLD georgic
FORMAL bucolic, geoponic, praedial

agree *v*
1 *agree with someone*
concur, get on, settle, be of one mind, be of the same opinion, share the view, be at one, come to/reach an agreement, compromise, make concessions
OLD gree, fadge
FORMAL accord
COLLOQ. fall in with, see eye to eye, go along with, go with, meet halfway
2 *agree to your request*
consent, allow, permit, accept, grant, admit, concede, yield, comply, say yes to
OLD gree, underwrite
FORMAL assent, accede, acquiesce in
COLLOQ. give the go-ahead, give the green light, give the thumbs-up, rubber-stamp
3 *agree on a schedule*
decide, settle, make up your mind about, determine, reach an agreement on, strike a bargain
COLLOQ. clinch
4 *the reports do not agree*
match, suit, fit, tally, correspond, conform, be consistent, coincide, square, chime
OLD gree, congree, comport; (*Shakesp*) congrue, atone
FORMAL accord
E3 1 disagree **2** refuse **4** disagree, differ, conflict

SYNONYM NUANCES

sense 4
To say two things **match**, **tally**, **correspond** or **coincide** is simply to say they are exactly or nearly alike: *a manager with the credentials to match the club's aspirations*, but to say they **suit** or **fit** each other is to suggest that one has an effect on the outcome of the other: *the darkness suited his evil purpose*.
  However, **conform** would be used where an effort has to be made to make something agree. To **square** one thing with another suggests that you have to bring them into accord or reconcile them: *such optimism is hard to square with history*, but if they **chime** or **accord** then they already agree: *his poem chimes with our experience of loss*.

---

agreeable *adj*
1 *agreeable weather*
pleasant, enjoyable, delightful, fine, nice, acceptable
2 *an agreeable person*
pleasant, congenial, lik(e)able, nice, attractive, delightful, charming, friendly, good-natured, amicable, sympathetic
3 *agreeable to a suggestion*
willing, amenable, compliant
FORMAL complaisant
E3 1 disagreeable, nasty **2** unpleasant **3** unwilling, reluctant to accept

agreeably *adv*
acceptably, pleasantly, pleasingly, enjoyably, delightfully, attractively

agreement *n*
1 *a trade agreement*
settlement, covenant, treaty, pact, contract, deed, deal, bargain, arrangement, understanding
FORMAL concordat, compact, indenture
2 *be in agreement*
unanimity, union, harmony, sympathy, consensus, affinity
FORMAL assent, complaisance
3 *the agreement of the reports*
matching, fitting, tally, correspondence, consistency, conformity, compatibility, similarity
FORMAL concurrence, accord, concord, consonance
E3 2 disagreement **3** inconsistency

agricultural *adj*
agronomic, agrarian, farming, farmed, cultivated, rural, countryside, pastoral
OLD georgic
FORMAL bucolic, geoponic, praedial

agriculture *n*
farming, husbandry, cultivation, tilling, tillage
TECHNICAL agribusiness, agronomics, agronomy, agroscience, geoponics
Related adjective: geoponic

Types of agricultural implement and machinery include:

all-terrain vehicle (ATV)	fork	reaping hook
axe	fork-lift truck	reversible plough
baler	front end loader	rotary hoe
bale wrapper	harrow	Rotovator®
broadcaster	harvester	saw
chainsaw	hayfork	scarifier
clover fertilizer distributor	hayrake	scythe
combine harvester	hedgecutter	seed drill
combination seed-harrow	hoe	shovel
corn drill	irrigator	sickle
cultivator	mattock	slurry sprayer
disc harrow	milking machine	spade
drill	mower	tanker
fertilizer spreader	muckspreader	tedder
field sprinkler	pitchfork	tractor
flail mower	plough	trailer
	potato planter	wheelbarrow
	power lift	wheel plough
	rake	whetstone

---

aground *adj, adv*
ashore, beached, foundered, grounded, high and dry, marooned, stranded, stuck, wrecked, on the rocks
E3 afloat

ahead *adv*
1 *glance ahead*
forward(s), onward(s), leading, at the head, in front
2 *go on ahead*
in advance, in front, in the lead, in the vanguard
3 *ahead on points*
in the lead, leading, winning, at an advantage, advanced, superior, to the fore, in the forefront
4 *plan ahead*
in advance, before, earlier on
F3 1 behind

aid *v, n*
♦ *v*
1 *aid an invalid*
help, assist, rally round, relieve, support, subsidize, sustain, second, serve, favour, co-operate with
FORMAL succour, oblige, accommodate
2 *aid a process*
promote, boost, encourage, facilitate, speed up, ease
FORMAL expedite, hasten
F3 1 *colloq.* not lift a finger **2** hinder, impede, obstruct
♦ *n*
1 *aid for refugees*
relief, benefit, (financial) assistance, (financial) support, (financial) backing, subsidy, donation, gift, contribution, funding, grant, sponsorship, patronage, favour, encouragement, service
FORMAL subvention
2 *turn to someone for aid*
help, assistance, prop, support, backup, boost
FORMAL succour
COLLOQ. (helping) hand, a shot in the arm, a leg up
F3 2 hindrance, impediment, obstruction

aide *n*
adviser, assistant, right-hand man/woman, supporter, adjutant, advocate, aide-de-camp, attaché, confidant(e), disciple, follower

ail *v*
afflict, trouble, upset, bother, distress, fail, irritate, pain, sicken, weaken, worry
F3 comfort, flourish

ailing *adj*
1 UNWELL, ill, sick, poorly, suffering, languishing, sickly, diseased, invalid, infirm, unsound, unfit, frail, weak, feeble, failing, indisposed, debilitated
COLLOQ. out of sorts, under the weather, off-colour
2 *an ailing business*
failing, weak, foundering, insolvent, inadequate, poor, deficient
F3 1 healthy, fit **2** thriving, flourishing

ailment *n*
illness, sickness, complaint, malady, disease, infection, disorder, affliction, infirmity, disability, weakness
FORMAL indisposition
COLLOQ. *Aust* dog's disease

aim *v, n*
♦ *v*
1 POINT, direct, take aim, shoot at, level, line up, train, sight, target
COLLOQ. zero in on
2 *aim to achieve*
plan, aspire, want, wish, seek, resolve, purpose, intend, propose, mean, design, strive, try, attempt, endeavour, work towards, set your sights on
♦ *n*
purpose, motive, end, intention, object, objective, target, mark, goal, direction, course, plan, design, scheme, aspiration, mission, mission statement, ambition, hope, dream, desire, wish

aimless *adj*
pointless, purposeless, goalless, futile, unmotivated, irresolute, directionless, rambling, drifting, wandering,

undirected, unguided, unsettled, stray, chance, random, haphazard, erratic, unpredictable, wayward
F3 purposeful, positive, determined

air *n, v*
♦ *n*
1 *birds flying in the air*
atmosphere, oxygen, sky, heavens
FORMAL ether
Related adjective: aerial
2 *the air we breathe*
breath, fresh air, puff, waft, whiff, draught, breeze, wind, blast
FORMAL zephyr
Related adjective: pneumatic
3 APPEARANCE, look, aspect, aura, bearing, manner, mien, character, effect, impression, feeling, expression, carriage
FORMAL ambience, demeanour
♦ *v*
1 *air a room*
ventilate, aerate, freshen
2 *air an opinion*
utter, voice, express, give vent to, make known, communicate, tell, declare, state, reveal, disclose, divulge, expose, make public, broadcast, publish, ventilate, circulate, publicize
FORMAL disseminate
COLLOQ. speak your mind, have your say

airborne *adj*
flying, in the air, in flight, hovering, winging

aircraft

Types of aircraft include:

aeroplane	glider	spy plane
air-ambulance	ground-attack	stealth bomber
Airbus	aircraft	swing-wing
airship	hang-glider	taildragger
all-wing	helicopter	tanker
amphibian	hot-air balloon	trainer
aquaplane	intercepter	triplane
autogyro	jumbo	troop carrier
biplane	jump jet	turbojet
blimp	*colloq.* kite	turboprop
bomber	microlight	two-seater
slang chopper	monoplane	UAV (unmanned
Concorde	multiplane	aerial vehicle)
delta-wing	intercepter	VTOL (vertical
dirigible	plane	take-off and
dive-bomber	rocket plane	landing)
drone	seaplane	warplane
fighter	single-seater	zeppelin
fixed-wing	skiplane	
freighter	spitfire	

---

airily *adv*
casually, breezily, lightly, readily, flippantly, nonchalantly, light-heartedly, jauntily

airing *n*
1 *give clothes an airing*
ventilation, aeration, freshening, refreshing
2 *the airing of opinions*
expression, making known, communication, declaration, statement, revelation, disclosure, divulgence, exposure, uttering, voicing, venting, broadcast, publication, circulation
FORMAL dissemination

airless *adj*
unventilated, badly/poorly ventilated, stuffy, musty, stale, suffocating, stifling, sultry, muggy, close, heavy, oppressive
F3 airy, fresh

airs *n*
arrogance, artificiality, haughtiness, posing, pretensions, pretentiousness, superciliousness

FORMAL affectation, affectedness, hauteur, pomposity
COLLOQ. swank, snootiness

airtight adj
1 *an airtight container*
closed, sealed, impenetrable, impermeable, tight-fitting
2 *a simple airtight explanation*
indisputable, unquestionable, incontrovertible, indubitable,
irrefutable, incontestable, conclusive, beyond question,
beyond dispute, flawless

airy adj
1 *an airy room*
roomy, spacious, open, well-ventilated, draughty, fresh,
breezy, blowy, windy, gusty
2 ETHEREAL, unsubstantial, immaterial, intangible,
incorporeal, spirit-like, spiritual
3 CASUAL, cheerful, happy, light-hearted, high-spirited,
sprightly, lively, jaunty, nonchalant, breezy, flippant,
offhand
E3 1 airless, stuffy, close, heavy, oppressive

aisle n
gangway, corridor, passage, passageway, alleyway,
walkway, path, lane

ajar adj
open, unclosed, half open, slightly open, unfastened,
unbolted, unlocked, unlatched
E3 closed, shut, fastened, locked

akin adj
similar, like, close, related, near, corresponding,
equivalent, comparable

alacrity n
promptness, briskness, eagerness, keenness, readiness,
willingness, enthusiasm, fervour, ardour, impatience

alarm n, v
♦ n
1 FRIGHT, scare, fear, terror, panic, horror, shock,
consternation, dismay, distress, anxiety, nervousness,
apprehension, trepidation, uneasiness
OLD tirrit
FORMAL perturbation
2 *a burglar alarm*
danger signal, alert, warning, distress signal, siren, horn,
whistle, bell, alarm-bell
OLD larum
FORMAL tocsin
E3 1 calmness, composure
♦ v
frighten, scare, startle, terrify, panic, make afraid, unnerve,
daunt, dismay, distress, agitate
FORMAL perturb, affright
COLLOQ. put the wind up, rattle
E3 reassure, calm, soothe

alarming adj
frightening, startling, terrifying, unnerving, daunting,
ominous, worrying, threatening, dismaying, disturbing,
distressing, shocking, dreadful
FORMAL perturbing
COLLOQ. scary
E3 reassuring

alarmist n
scaremonger, pessimist, doomwatcher, doomsayer
COLLOQ. doom-merchant, prophet of doom
E3 optimist

alcohol n
drink, liquor, spirits, strong drink, intoxicant, grog, liqueur,
stimulus, slug; *Scot* skink, strunt
OLD fuddle; (*Shakesp*) tickle-brain
COLLOQ. hard stuff, the bottle, Dutch courage, firewater,
the creature, jar, tipple, tiddly, tinct, sauce
SLANG booze, jungle juice; *N Am* juice

alcoholic adj, n
♦ adj
intoxicating, inebriating, brewed, fermented, distilled,
strong, hard, ardent
♦ n
drunk, drunkard, inebriate, drinker, hard drinker, heavy
drinker, dipsomaniac, wine-bibber, Bacchus, bloat,
habitual; *N Am* souse
COLLOQ. tippler
SLANG boozer, wino, lush, alkie, dipso, soak, piss artist,
pisshead, toper, tosspot, sot, sponge

alcove n
niche, nook, recess, bay, corner, cubbyhole, opening,
compartment, cubicle, booth, carrel

alert adj, v, n
♦ adj
attentive, awake, wide-awake, watchful, vigilant, on the
lookout, sharp-eyed, observant, perceptive, sharp-witted,
active, lively, spirited, quick, brisk, agile, nimble, ready,
prepared, careful, heedful, circumspect, wary, on the
qui vive
COLLOQ. with your eyes open/peeled, on the ball, on your
toes
E3 slow, listless, unprepared
♦ v
warn, forewarn, notify, inform, tip off, signal, alarm
FORMAL apprise
♦ n
warning, notice, notification, alarm, caution, signal
COLLOQ. tip-off, wake-up call

alertness n
attentivenenss, watchfulness, vigilance, wariness,
observance, perceptiveness, sharp-wittedness

alias n, adv
♦ n
pseudonym, false name, assumed name, *nom de guerre*,
nom de plume, pen name, stage name, nickname
FORMAL so(u)briquet, allonym, anonym
SLANG monicker
♦ adv
also known as, also called, otherwise, otherwise known
as, under the name of, formerly, née
COLLOQ. aka

alibi n
defence, justification, story, explanation, vindication,
excuse, cover-up, pretext, reason

alien adj, n
♦ adj
1 *an alien culture*
foreign, exotic, extraterrestrial, extraneous, remote
OLD forinsec
2 *alien surroundings*
strange, unfamiliar, outlandish, odd, peculiar,
incongruous
3 *alien to her nature*
opposed, contrary, conflicting, unusual, antagonistic,
incompatible, repugnant
FORMAL inimical
♦ n
1 FOREIGNER, immigrant, newcomer, incomer, stranger,
outsider, non-native
2 EXTRATERRESTRIAL, ET, Martian
COLLOQ. LGM, little green man
E3 1 native, resident

alienate *v*
antagonize, set against, turn away, turn off, cut off, sever, make hostile, separate, divorce
FORMAL estrange, disaffect
E3 unite

alienation *n*
antagonization, turning away, indifference, remoteness, rupture, separation, detachment, isolation, severance, divorce, disunion, diversion
FORMAL estrangement, disaffection
E3 endearment

alight¹ *adj*
1 *set the rubbish alight*
lighted, lit, ignited, on fire, burning, blazing, ablaze, aflame, flaming, fiery
2 *eyes alight with excitement*
lit up, illuminated, bright, radiant, shining, gleaming, brilliant, lively, alive

alight² *v*
passengers alighting from buses
descend, get down, get off, land, touch down, come down, come to rest, settle, light, perch, pitch
OLD avale
FORMAL dismount, disembark, debark, detrain, disentrain
COLLOQ. pop
E3 ascend, board, get on, get on to, rise

align *v*
1 *align yourself with a political party*
ally, side, sympathize, associate, affiliate, join, co-operate, agree, join forces, combine, unite
2 *align two pieces of wood*
arrange, straighten, range, line up, make parallel, even (up), adjust, regulate, regularize, order, co-ordinate

alignment *n*
1 *alignment with a political party*
affiliation, association, alliance, co-operation, agreement, sympathy, siding
2 *alignment of the pieces*
arrangement, straightening, line, lining up, order, ranging

alike *adj, adv*
♦ *adj*
similar, resembling, comparable, akin, corresponding, equivalent, equal, the same, much the same, identical, indistinguishable, duplicate, parallel, even, uniform
FORMAL analogous, cognate
COLLOQ. like two peas in a pod
E3 different, dissimilar, unlike
♦ *adv*
similarly, in the same way, the same, analogously, correspondingly, equally, in common

alimony *n*
maintenance, support, upkeep, allowance, palimony, child support; *Scot* aliment

alive *adj*
1 LIVING, having life, live, animate, breathing, existent, in existence
OLD quick
FORMAL extant
COLLOQ. (still) going strong, in the land of the living, on the hoof
2 LIVELY, animated, spirited, awake, alert, active, brisk, energetic, full of life, vigorous, zestful, vivacious, vibrant, vital; *Scot* vive
COLLOQ. chirpy, bright-eyed and bushy-tailed
3 *keep a tradition alive*
active, surviving, carrying on, in existence, in force, in operation, functioning, running, working
FORMAL extant
4 *alive with tourists*
full of, teeming with, abounding in, overflowing with, thronged with
COLLOQ. crawling with, swarming with

5 *alive to the danger*
aware of, conscious of, heedful of, alert to, awake to, sensitive to
FORMAL cognizant of
E3 **1** dead, extinct **2** lifeless, apathetic **3** dead **5** unaware of, blind to, deaf to

all *adj, pron, adv*
♦ *adj*
1 *all people are equal*
each, every, each and every, every single, every one of, the whole of, every bit of, in its entirety, from start to finish
2 *run with all speed*
complete, entire, full, total, utter, outright, perfect, greatest
E3 **1** no, none
♦ *pron*
everything, everyone, everybody, sum, total, aggregate, total amount, whole amount, whole, entirety, utmost, comprehensiveness, universality
COLLOQ. the lot
E3 nothing, none
♦ *adv*
completely, entirely, wholly, fully, totally, utterly, without exception, altogether, wholesale

> **PROVERBS**
> All's well that ends well

allay *v*
alleviate, relieve, soothe, ease, smooth(e), calm, tranquillize, compose, quiet, quell, pacify, mollify, soften, blunt, lessen, reduce, decrease, diminish, check, moderate
OLD allege
E3 exacerbate, intensify

allegation *n*
accusation, charge, claim, profession, assertion, affirmation, declaration, statement, testimony, plea
FORMAL avowal, deposition, asseveration

allege *v*
assert, affirm, declare, state, maintain, insist, urge, hold, put forward, contend, claim, profess, plead
OLD obtend, trump
FORMAL attest, asseverate

alleged *adj*
supposed, reputed, inferred, so-called, professed, declared, stated, claimed, described, designated, doubtful, dubious, suspect
FORMAL ostensible, purported, putative

allegedly *adv*
supposedly, apparently, reportedly, by all accounts, doubtfully, dubiously
FORMAL ostensibly, purportedly, putatively

allegiance *n*
loyalty, fidelity, faithfulness, constancy, duty, obligation, obedience, devotion, support, adherence, solidarity, friendship
OLD (*Spenser*) foy
FORMAL fealty, liegedom
E3 disloyalty, enmity

allegorical *adj*
figurative, representative, symbolic, metaphorical, symbolizing, typical
FORMAL parabolic, emblematic, significative

allegory *n*
analogy, comparison, metaphor, symbol, parable, story, fable, myth, legend, tale, symbolism
FORMAL emblem, apologue

allergic *adj*
1 *allergic to shellfish*
sensitive, hypersensitive, susceptible, affected
2 *allergic to Mondays*
averse, disinclined, opposed, hostile, antagonistic
FORMAL dyspathetic

allergy *n*
1 *an allergy to dogs*
sensitivity, hypersensitivity, susceptibility
2 *an allergy to work*
opposition, hostility, antagonism, aversion,
disinclination
FORMAL antipathy, dyspathy

alleviate *v*
relieve, soothe, ease, mitigate, soften, cushion, dull,
deaden, allay, abate, lessen, assuage, reduce, diminish,
check, moderate, mollify, temper, take the edge off,
subdue
OLD allege
FORMAL palliate
COLLOQ. kill
ᴇᴁ aggravate

alleviation *n*
relief, soothing, easing, mitigation, dulling, deadening,
abatement, lessening, assuagement, reduction, moderation,
mollification
FORMAL palliation, diminution
ᴇᴁ aggravation

alley *n*
alleyway, back street, lane, street, road, mall, passage,
passageway, pathway, close, gate, walk; *dialect* ginnel;
Scot wynd, vennel

alliance *n*
partnership, confederation, federation, association,
affiliation, coalition, league, bloc, cartel, conglomerate,
consortium, syndicate, guild, union, marriage, agreement,
bond, pact, treaty, axis, combination, connection
FORMAL compact, concordat
ᴇᴁ separation, divorce, estrangement, enmity, hostility

allied *adj*
associated, connected, linked, bound, combined, in
league, joined, joint, kindred, related, affiliated,
amalgamated, federated, confederated, coupled, unified,
united, married, wed
COLLOQ. hand in glove, in cahoots
ᴇᴁ estranged

allocate *v*
assign, designate, budget, allow, earmark, set aside, issue,
task, allot, apportion, share out, distribute, deal out,
dispense, divide, parcel out, mete (out), ration
FORMAL admeasure
COLLOQ. dole out

allocation *n*
1 *the allocation of funds*
apportionment, distribution, giving-out, sharing-out,
allotment
2 *an allocation of tickets*
share, measure, lot, portion, stint, ration, quota, budget,
allowance, grant
COLLOQ. cut, whack, slice of the cake

allot *v*
divide, ration, apportion, share out, distribute, dispense,
mete (out), allocate, assign, designate, budget, allow,
grant, earmark, set aside
OLD stint; (*Shakesp*) rate, sort
FORMAL admeasure
COLLOQ. dole out

allotment *n*
1 *dig an allotment*
land, plot of land
2 *an allotment of funds*
division, partition, allocation, apportionment, distribution,
measure, percentage, lot, portion, share, stint, ration,
quota, allowance, grant
FORMAL apportionment
COLLOQ. cut, whack, slice of the cake

all-out *adj, adv*
♦ *adj*
complete, full, total, undivided, comprehensive,
exhaustive, thorough, intensive, thoroughgoing, wholesale,
vigorous, energetic, powerful, full-scale, maximum,
utmost, unlimited, unrestrained, unremitting, unstinted,
resolute, determined, forceful
COLLOQ. no-holds-barred
ᴇᴁ perfunctory, half-hearted
♦ *adv*
exhaustively, thoroughly, intensively, vigorously,
energetically, powerfully, unremittingly, resolutely,
determinedly, forcefully
ᴇᴁ half-heartedly

allow *v*
1 PERMIT, let, enable, authorize, sanction, warrant,
approve, say yes to, give your consent (to), consent (to),
agree to, give leave, tolerate, put up with, endure, suffer
COLLOQ. OK, okay, give the go-ahead to, green light, give
the green light to
2 ADMIT, confess, own, acknowledge, concede, grant,
agree
OLD (*Shakesp & Spenser*) beteem
3 *allow two hours for the journey*
allot, allocate, assign, earmark, apportion, afford, give,
provide, set aside, spare
ᴇᴁ **1** forbid, prevent **2** deny
■ **allow for**
take into account, make provision for, make allowances
for, provide for, foresee, plan for, arrange for, bear/keep in
mind, consider, include
ᴇᴁ discount

allowable *adj*
permissible, acceptable, admissible, justifiable, all right,
appropriate, approved, legal, legitimate, lawful
FORMAL licit, sanctionable
COLLOQ. legit
ᴇᴁ unacceptable

allowance *n*
1 PAYMENT, remittance, pocket money, grant, bursary,
income, maintenance, subsistence allowance, exhibition,
budget, capitation grant, table money, expenses, expense
allowance, contribution, benefit, child benefit, stipend,
pension, annuity, assistance, alimony, corrody, privy
purse; *Scot* aliment
COLLOQ. *N Am* baby bonus
2 REBATE, reduction, deduction, discount, concession,
subsidy, weighting
TECHNICAL cloff
3 ALLOCATION, lot, amount, portion, share, ration, quota,
feed
TECHNICAL tare
OLD diet, provand, livery, ratio, tret
■ **make allowances**
1 TAKE INTO ACCOUNT, take into consideration, bear/keep
in mind, consider, make concessions for
2 *make allowances for her inexperience*
excuse, bear with, pardon, forgive, overlook, condone

allowed *adj*
permitted, accepted, authorized, approved, tolerated
ᴇᴁ disallowed

alloy *n*
blend, compound, composite, amalgam, combination,
mixture, fusion, coalescence
FORMAL admixture, composite

all-powerful *adj*
almighty, supreme, pre-eminent, absolute, great,
totalitarian
FORMAL omnipotent
ᴇᴁ powerless

all-purpose *adj*
versatile, adaptable, flexible, all-round, multi-purpose,
general-purpose
ᴇᴁ inflexible

all right *adj, adv, interj*
♦ *adj*
1 SATISFACTORY, passable, unobjectionable, acceptable, reasonable, good enough, allowable, adequate, fair, average
COLLOQ. OK; *N Am* A-OK; *Aust* sweet
2 *Are you all right?*
well, healthy, unhurt, uninjured, unharmed, unimpaired, whole, sound, safe, secure
COLLOQ. OK, right as rain
E3 1 unacceptable, inadequate, unsatisfactory
♦ *adv*
1 SATISFACTORILY, well enough, passably, unobjectionably, acceptably, suitably, appropriately, adequately, reasonably
COLLOQ. OK
2 *it's true all right*
definitely, no doubt, certainly, absolutely, without question, indeed
E3 1 unsatisfactorily, unacceptably
♦ *interj*
OK, fine, right, agreed, okay, very well

allude *v*
mention, refer, remark, speak of, hint, imply, infer, insinuate, intimate, suggest, touch on/upon
FORMAL adumbrate

> **!** **allude** or **elude**?
> If you *allude* to something, you refer to it; if something *eludes* you, you cannot remember it or understand it.

allure *v, n*
♦ *v*
lure, entice, seduce, lead on, tempt, coax, cajole, persuade, win over, disarm, charm, enchant, attract, interest, fascinate, captivate, entrance, beguile, decoy, sirenize
OLD train, troll
COLLOQ. give the come-on, work on
E3 repel
♦ *n*
lure, enticement, seduction, temptation, appeal, attraction, magnetism, draw, pull, fascination, glamour, captivation, charm, enchantment

alluring *adj*
attractive, fascinating, intriguing, interesting, captivating, winning, enchanting, engaging, enticing, arousing, beguiling, bewitching, fetching, seductive, sensuous, sexy, desirable, tempting
COLLOQ. come-hither
E3 repellent, unattractive

allusion *n*
mention, reference, citation, quotation, remark, comment, observation, suggestion, hint, intimation, implication, insinuation

> **!** **allusion** or **illusion**?
> An *allusion* to something is an indirect reference to it; an *illusion* is a false belief or appearance.

ally *n, v*
♦ *n*
supporter, associate, consort, confederate, partner, colleague, co-worker, collaborator, helper, accomplice, accessory, friend
COLLOQ. sidekick
E3 enemy, antagonist
♦ *v*
associate, collaborate, join forces, band together, team up, go into partnership, fraternize, confederate, affiliate, league, side, join, connect, link, marry, unite, unify, amalgamate, combine
E3 estrange, separate

almanac *n*
yearbook, annual, calendar, register, ephemeris

almighty *adj*
1 *almighty God*
all-powerful, supreme, absolute, great, invincible
FORMAL omnipotent, plenipotent
2 ENORMOUS, severe, intense, very great, immense, huge, overwhelming, overpowering, terrible, awful, desperate
E3 1 impotent, weak

almost *adv*
nearly, practically, virtually, just about, as good as, all but, well-nigh, more or less, to all intents and purposes, close to/on, not far from, approaching, nearing, not quite, about, approximately
FORMAL quasi-
COLLOQ. pretty much/well

alms *n*
gifts, donations, handouts, contributions, charity, endowment, largesse

aloft *adv*
in the air, in the sky, off the ground, high, high up

alone
♦ *adv, adj adv*
1 *go for walks alone*
on your own, by yourself, singly, unaccompanied, unescorted, unattended, companionless
COLLOQ. on your tod
2 *left to cope alone*
by yourself, on your own, without help, unaided, unassisted, independently
COLLOQ. off your own bat
E3 1 together, accompanied, escorted
♦ *adj*
1 LONELY, isolated, lonesome, deserted, forsaken, forlorn, desolate, rejected, unhappy, miserable, sad
2 *you alone can put things right*
only, just, solely, exclusively, uniquely

> **SYNONYM NUANCES**
>
> *adjective sense 1*
> **Lonely** and **lonesome** carry a strong impression of sadness caused by being alone. The term **isolated** suggests a detached or secluded place, either physical or mental; **desolate** conveys this idea even more stongly, with a sense of insurmountable or frightening aloneness.
>   The terms **deserted**, **forsaken** and **forlorn** would be used where something or someone has been abandoned or left behind, and again have connotations of sadness and pity: *I looked back at his forlorn figure.*
>   **Rejected** would be used specifically where others have refused to accept you. However, to clearly and simply express sorrow as a result of being alone, you may choose to use the explicit terms **unhappy**, **miserable** or **sad**.

along *prep, adv*
♦ *prep*
1 *walk along a road*
down, up, in the same direction as
2 *trees growing along the river bank*
beside, at the side of, next to, alongside, adjacent to, close to, near
♦ *adv*
1 *driving along*
on, onwards, ahead, further
2 *bring a friend along*
with you, as a partner, as company
■ **along with**
together with, in addition to, including, over and above, not to mention, to say nothing of
■ **all along**
all the time, continually, constantly, always, for ever

aloof *adj*

distant, remote, offish, standoffish, haughty, supercilious, unapproachable, inaccessible, detached, forbidding, cool, chilly, cold, unsympathetic, unresponsive, indifferent, uninterested, reserved, unforthcoming, unfriendly, insular, unsociable, antisocial, formal, chill; *Scot* abeigh, skeigh
⊟ sociable, friendly, concerned

aloud *adv*

out loud, audibly, intelligibly, clearly, plainly, distinctly, for all to hear, loudly, resoundingly, sonorously, noisily, vociferously, *à haute voix*
⊟ silently

alphabet *n*

writing system, letters, ABC

> **QUOTATIONS**
> I struggled through the alphabet as if it had been a bramble-bush; getting considerably worried and scratched by every letter
>   CHARLES DICKENS, *Great Expectations*

Alphabets and writing systems include:

Arabic	Greek	Kufic
Braille	Gurmukhi	linear A
Byzantine	Hebrew	linear B
Chalcidian	hieroglyphs	logograph
alphabet	hiragana	nagari
cuneiform	ideograph	naskhi
Cyrillic	Initial Teaching	ogam
devanagari	Alphabet (ITA)	pictograph
estrangelo	International Pho-	romaji
finger-alphabet	netic Alphabet	Roman
futhark	(IPA)	runic
Georgian	kana	syllabary
Glagol	kanji	
Glossic	katakana	

---

already *adv*

1 *I've read the book already*
before now, beforehand, just now, previously
OLD heretofore, hitherto
2 *he can already count*
even now, even then, so soon (as this), so early by now, by that time, by then, by this time
FORMAL thus far

also *adv*

too, as well, and, plus, along with, including, as well as, additionally, in addition, besides, further, furthermore, moreover

alter *v*

change, vary, diversify, modify, qualify, shift, transpose, make different, adjust, adapt, convert, turn, transform, reform, reshape, rework, remodel, recast, revise, improve, amend, tweak
FORMAL emend, metamorphose, transmute
See Synonym nuances panel at **change**.
⊟ fix

alteration *n*

change, variation, variance, difference, diversification, shift, transposition, modification, adjustment, adaptation, conversion, transformation, transfiguration, reformation, reshaping, reworking, remodelling, revision, amendment, tweak
FORMAL emendation, metamorphosis, transmutation, vicissitude
⊟ fixity

altercation *n*

argument, dispute, clash, disagreement, difference, difficulty, bicker, breach, ruffle, discord, dissension, fracas, quarrel, row, squabble, wrangle, beef; *dialect* fratch, whid; *Scot* brattle, wap
OLD dependence, square

FORMAL logomachy
COLLOQ. set-to, dust-up, scrap, barney, breeze, broil, miff, bust-up, slanging match, punch-up; *Aust* yike

alternate *v, adj*

◆ *v*
interchange, reciprocate, rotate, take turns, take it in turns, follow one another, replace each other, substitute, change, alter, vary, oscillate, fluctuate, intersperse
COLLOQ. chop and change
◆ *adj*
1 *alternate weekends*
alternating, every other, every second
2 *alternate bouts of depression and happiness*
(repeated) one after the other, in turns, consecutive, interchanging, reciprocal, rotating

> **⚠** **alternate** or **alternative**?
> *Alternate* refers to something happening or coming every second day, week, etc or in turns: *He visits them on alternate Tuesdays; alternate bursts of hot and cold water*. *Alternative* refers to the choice of two possibilities: *If that doesn't work, we'll have to think of an alternative plan.*

alternative *n, adj*

◆ *n*
option, choice, selection, preference, other, recourse, substitute, back-up
◆ *adj*
1 *an alternative possibility*
substitute, second, another, other, different, surrogate
2 *alternative medicine*
unorthodox, unconventional, uncommon, unusual, fringe, nontraditional
COLLOQ. wacky, oddball
⊟ 2 conventional, traditional, orthodox, standard, regular

alternatively *adv*

otherwise, instead, on the other hand, as another option, as a substitute

although *conj*

though, even though, despite/in spite of the fact that, while, even if, even supposing, granted that
OLD howbeit
FORMAL albeit, whilst, notwithstanding

altitude *n*

height, elevation, loftiness, tallness, stature, depth

altogether *adv*

1 *altogether more efficient*
totally, completely, entirely, wholly, fully, utterly, absolutely, quite, perfectly, thoroughly
2 *the meal came to £60 altogether*
in total, in all, all told, *in toto*, all in all

altruism *n*

selflessness, unselfishness, disinterest, self-sacrifice, public-spiritedness, benevolence, generosity, considerateness
FORMAL magnanimity
⊟ selfishness

altruistic *adj*

selfless, unselfish, self-sacrificing, disinterested, public-spirited, philanthropic, charitable, humanitarian, benevolent, generous, considerate, humane
FORMAL magnanimous
⊟ selfish

always *adv*

1 *always be home by 6 o'clock*
every time, all the time, consistently, invariably, without exception, habitually, unfailingly, regularly, on every occasion, on each occasion, perpetually, *in perpetuum*, evermore

2 *always criticizing others*
again and again, continually, constantly, repeatedly, forever, endlessly, unceasingly, eternally
F3 1 never

amalgam *n*
mixture, blend, fusion, alloy, compound, merger, coalescence, synthesis, combination, union
TECHNICAL admixture, aggregate, commixture

amalgamate *v*
merge, blend, mingle, intermix, incorporate, alloy, integrate, compound, fuse, coalesce, synthesize, combine, unite, unify, ally
TECHNICAL commingle, homogenize
F3 separate

amalgamation *n*
merger, blend, incorporation, integration, joining, compound, fusion, coalescence, synthesis, combination, unity, union, unification, alliance
TECHNICAL admixture, commingling, homogenization
F3 separation

amass *v*
accumulate, accrue, assemble, collect, gather, heap (up), hoard, pile (up), store (up), gain, acquire
OLD foregather, garner
FORMAL agglomerate, agglutinate, aggregate

amateur *n*
non-professional, layman, lay person, dilettante, dabbler, enthusiast, fancier
COLLOQ. ham, buff
F3 professional, specialist

amateurish *adj*
non-professional, lay, unpaid, unqualified, untrained, unskilful, inexpert, unprofessional, clumsy, crude, incompetent, bungling, blundering, inept
F3 professional, expert, skilled

amatory *adj*
amorous, passionate, loving, affectionate, tender, fond, erotic, sexual, impassioned
COLLOQ. randy

amaze *v*
surprise, startle, astonish, astound, stun, stupefy, daze, stagger, dumbfound, shock, dismay, disconcert, confound, bewilder, flatten
OLD (*Spenser*) awhape
COLLOQ. floor, flabbergast, bowl over, gobsmack, wow, kill, blow your mind, knock for six, knock you down with a feather, strike dumb

amazed *adj*
surprised, startled, astonished, astounded, stunned, dazed, dumbfounded, bewildered, speechless
OLD (*Shakesp*) agazed
COLLOQ. floored, flabbergasted, gobsmacked, thunderstruck

amazement *n*
surprise, astonishment, shock, dismay, confusion, perplexity, bewilderment, admiration, wonder, marvel; *dialect* maze
FORMAL consternation, stupefaction, wonderment

amazing *adj*
surprising, astonishing, astounding, wonderful, magnificent, marvellous, impressive, dazzling, spectacular, formidable, awe-inspiring, exciting, thrilling, stunning, bewildering, overwhelming, staggering, disconcerting
COLLOQ. fabulous, incredible, jaw-dropping, eye-popping
SLANG far-out, unreal, awesome

ambassador *n*
1 *a country's ambassador*
envoy, diplomat, consul, nuncio, elchi
OLD ledger, leaguer
FORMAL emissary, legate, plenipotentiary

2 *an ambassador of peace*
representative, agent, deputy, delegate, minister, campaigner, advocate, supporter, backer

ambience *n*
atmosphere, air, aura, climate, milieu, mood, spirit, surroundings, environment, character, feel, feeling, flavour, impression, tenor, tone
COLLOQ. vibes, vibrations

ambiguity *n*
double meaning, double entendre, ambivalence, double-talk, double-speak, polysemy, equivocality, equivocation, confusion, obscurity, unclearness, vagueness, woolliness, imprecision, indeterminateness, dubiousness, doubt, doubtfulness, uncertainty, enigma, puzzle, paradox
FORMAL dubiety
F3 clarity

ambiguous *adj*
double-meaning, equivocal, multivocal, double-edged, two-edged, back-handed, cryptic, enigmatic, paradoxical, puzzling, confusing, obscure, unclear, vague, indefinite, imprecise, woolly, confused, dubious, doubtful, uncertain, inconclusive, indeterminate, louche
F3 clear, definite, unambiguous

SYNONYM NUANCES

If a statement is **double-meaning** then you might simply be saying that there is more than one way to interpret it; however, you might also use this term to suggest that the second meaning has a risqué element. If you say something is **equivocal** you mean it is capable of meaning two or more things, usually with the implication that this makes it vague and is a weakness. The more neutral **multivocal** can be used of a word or other item that can have many meanings.

However, when something is described as being **double-edged** or **two-edged** the suggestion is that it has two very different aspects, both positive and negative, and that it can be deceiving. **Back-handed** would usually be used of compliments, implying that the apparent meaning could have a different spin put on it: *her exclusion can be read as a back-handed compliment*.

If you say something is **cryptic** or **obscure**, you are emphasizing that it is mysterious or difficult to understand, whilst if you claim it is **enigmatic** you are suggesting it has a hidden meaning to be guessed at: *cryptic symbols*; *his reaction was enigmatic*. However, **paradoxical** is only appropriate when describing something of a self-contradictory nature. If you are perplexed by something ambiguous, you may describe it as **puzzling** or **confusing**.

Unclear, **vague**, **indefinite**, **imprecise**, and **woolly** are negative in tone, all emphasizing a lack of clarity, whilst **confused** suggests an undesirable lack of order. To stress the element of doubt you might use **dubious**, **doubtful** or **uncertain**: *doubtful authenticity*. Similarly **inconclusive** and **indeterminate** express an element of doubt; the former in the context of something that has not been settled, and the latter of something that remains unfixed or undefined.

---

ambit *n*
scope, extent, range, area, sphere, realm, sweep, breadth, compass, confines, bounds

ambition *n*
1 ASPIRATION, aim, goal, target, objective, intent, purpose, design, object, ideal, dream, holy grail, hope, wish, desire, yearning, longing, hankering, craving, hunger
2 *a woman of ambition*
enterprise, drive, determination, push, thrust, striving, eagerness, commitment, initiative, zeal

COLLOQ. get-up-and-go, fire in your belly, what it takes
2 apathy, diffidence

> **QUOTATIONS**
> All ambitions are lawful except those which climb
> upwards on the miseries or credulities of mankind
> JOSEPH CONRAD, *Some Reminiscences*

ambitious *adj*
1 ASPIRING, hopeful, desirous, intent, purposeful, bold,
assertive, pushy, go-ahead, enterprising, driving, energetic,
enthusiastic, eager, keen, striving, industrious, zealous,
determined
OLD (*Shakesp*) emulate
COLLOQ. power-hungry, full of go, go-getting, not
backward in coming forward
2 FORMIDABLE, hard, difficult, arduous, strenuous,
demanding, challenging, bold, exacting, impressive,
grandiose, elaborate
1 lazy, unassuming **2** modest, uninspiring

ambivalence *n*
contradiction, conflict, clash, opposition, inconsistency,
confusion, fluctuation, wavering, equivocation, hesitation,
irresoluteness, unsureness, uncertainty, doubt,
inconclusiveness
FORMAL vacillation
certainty

ambivalent *adj*
contradictory, conflicting, clashing, warring, opposed,
inconsistent, mixed, confused, fluctuating, wavering,
hesitant, irresolute, equivocal, undecided, unresolved,
unsettled, uncertain, unsure, doubtful, debatable,
inconclusive
FORMAL vacillating
unequivocal

amble *v*
walk, saunter, stroll, dawdle, wander, drift, meander,
ramble
FORMAL perambulate, promenade
COLLOQ. mosey along, toddle
stride, march

ambush *n, v*
♦ *n*
waylaying, surprise attack, trap, snare
OLD ambuscade, lurch; (*Spenser*) await
♦ *v*
lie in wait, waylay, lay a trap for, surprise, trap, entrap,
attack, ensnare; N Am bushwhack
OLD ambuscade, wait, lay wait, forelay, lie perdu(e)
COLLOQ. turn on, pounce on, jump

ameliorate *v*
alleviate, improve, better, make better, amend, benefit,
ease, elevate, enhance, mend, rectify, mitigate, promote,
relieve
exacerbate, worsen

amelioration *n*
alleviation, improvement, amendment, enhancement,
benefit, refinement, help, rectification, mitigation
exacerbation, worsening

amenable *adj*
accommodating, flexible, willing, open, agreeable,
biddable, persuadable, compliant, submissive, responsive,
susceptible, liable, responsible
FORMAL tractable, acquiescent, complaisant
unwilling, intractable

amend *v*
revise, correct, rectify, fix, repair, mend, remedy, heal,
redress, reform, change, alter, adjust, modify, qualify,
enhance, improve, better
FORMAL emend, emendate, ameliorate
impair, worsen

> **⚠ amend** or **emend**?
> If you *amend* a document, you alter or improve it; if
> you *emend* a text, you correct errors in it.

amendment *n*
revision, correction, remedy, reform, change,
alteration, adjustment, modification, improvement,
qualification, enhancement, clarification, addition,
attachment, adjunct
FORMAL corrigendum, rectification, emendation,
addendum
impairment, deterioration

amends *n*
atonement, expiation, requital, satisfaction, recompense,
compensation, indemnification, indemnity, reparation,
redress, restoration, restitution

amenity *n*
facility, advantage, convenience, opportunity,
arrangement, service, utility, resource

amiability *n*
friendliness, warmth, warm-heartedness, cheerfulness,
cordiality, kindness, lik(e)ability, pleasantness

amiable *adj*
affable, friendly, approachable, genial, warm, warm-
hearted, cordial, cheerful, good-tempered, good-natured,
kind, easy to get along/on with, gentle, obliging,
charming, engaging, lik(e)able, lov(e)able, sweet, pleasant,
agreeable, congenial, companionable, clubbable, sociable,
gemütlich
COLLOQ. mat(e)y, pally, chummy
unfriendly, curt, hostile

> **⚠ amiable** or **amicable**?
> *Amiable* is used to describe a person who is friendly,
> good-tempered and pleasant; *amicable* is used to
> describe relationships or agreements that are conducted
> in a friendly way without anger.

amicable *adj*
friendly, cordial, good-natured, civil, harmonious,
civilized, peaceful
hostile

amicably *adv*
cordially, good-naturedly, civilly, harmoniously, peaceably

amid *prep*
amidst, midst, in the midst of, in the thick of, among,
amongst, in the middle of, surrounded by

amino acid

Amino acids include:

alanine	glycine	proline
arginine	histidine	serine
asparagine	isoleucine	threonine
aspartic acid	leucine	trytophan
cysteine	lysine	tyrosine
glutamic acid	methionine	valine
glutamine	phenylalanine	

amiss *adj*
wrong, awry, defective, false, faulty, improper, out of
order, inaccurate, inappropriate, incorrect, unsuitable,
untoward, imperfect, out of kilter
COLLOQ. wonky
right, well

amity *n*
peace, peacefulness, understanding, accord, concord,
cordiality, fellowship, fraternity, brotherliness, friendliness,
friendship, goodwill, harmony, kindness, sympathy
FORMAL comity
discord, hostility

ammunition *n*
missiles, bullets, shells, rockets, projectiles, cartridges, explosives, slugs, grenades, bombs, shot, mine, gunpowder
COLLOQ. ammo
See panel at **weapon**.

amnesty *n*
pardon, forgiveness, absolution, mercy, lenience, indulgence, reprieve, remission, dispensation, immunity, release, discharge, freedom, liberty

amok *adv*
berserk, crazy, in a frenzy, frenzied, insanely, like a lunatic, madly, wildly, out of control, uncontrollably, violently, on the rampage

among *prep*
amongst, between, in the middle of, surrounded by, in the midst of, with, together with, in the company of, in the thick of
OLD amid, amidst, midst

amorous *adj*
passionate, loving, in love, affectionate, tender, fond, lovesick, gallant, erotic, sexual, impassioned, lustful
FORMAL amatory
COLLOQ. randy, kissy
☒ cold, indifferent

amorphous *adj*
formless, nebulous, shapeless, featureless, indeterminate, indistinct, irregular, undefined, unformed, unshapen, unstructured, vague
FORMAL inchoate
☒ definite, distinctive, shapely

amount *n, v*
quantity, number, sum, total, sum total, whole, entirety, lot, quota, supply, volume, mass, bulk, measure, magnitude, extent, expanse
TECHNICAL quantum
FORMAL aggregate
■ **amount to**
1 *amount to a total*
add up to, total, come to, make, equal, run into, run to
FORMAL aggregate
COLLOQ. tot up, tot up to
2 *giving presents to potential customers amounts to bribery*
mean, be tantamount to, be equivalent to, correspond to, come down to, boil down to

amphibian

Amphibians include:

axolotl	bullfrog	natterjack toad
eft	tree frog	newt
eel	toad	salamander
conger eel	horned toad	
frog	midwife toad	

---

ample *adj*
1 *ample opportunity/space*
(more than) enough, sufficient, adequate, considerable, substantial, plentiful, plenty, abundant, unrestricted, profuse, spacious, rich, good, handsome, great, copious
OLD plenteous
FORMAL commodious
2 *of ample proportions*
large, big, extensive, expansive, broad, wide, full, roomy, spacious, liberal, generous, substantial; *Scot* wally
FORMAL voluminous
☒ **1** insufficient, inadequate, meagre **2** small, thin, narrow

amplification *n*
1 *amplification of sound*
making louder, loudening, increase, boosting, intensification, strengthening, raising

2 *amplification of a statement*
enlargement, expansion, addition, supplement, development, elaboration
FORMAL augmentation

amplify *v*
1 *amplify sound*
make louder, louden, increase, heighten, enhance, boost, intensify, strengthen, deepen, raise
2 *amplify a statement*
enlarge on, expand, fill out, bulk out, add to, supplement, increase, extend, lengthen, widen, broaden, develop, elaborate on, go into details, flesh out
FORMAL augment, expatiate on
☒ **1** reduce, decrease, soften

amplitude *n*
expanse, vastness, volume, bulk, capacity, extent, size, fullness, greatness, largeness, magnitude, mass, profusion, spaciousness, width
FORMAL copiousness, plenitude, capaciousness

amputate *v*
cut off, remove, sever, dissever, separate, dock, chop off, hack off, lop off, curtail, truncate

amulet *n*
charm, talisman, mascot, fetish, juju, lucky charm, churinga, grisgris
OLD periapt
FORMAL braxas, pentacle, phylactery

amuse *v*
1 *the joke amused them*
make laugh, cheer (up), gladden, entertain, charm, delight, please, enthral
COLLOQ. tickle, crease, crack, tickle your funny bone
2 *amuse yourselves while I'm away*
occupy, entertain, divert, regale, engross, absorb, engage, interest, recreate, relax
FORMAL disport
☒ **1** displease **2** bore

amusement *n*
1 *a look of amusement at the joke*
fun, enjoyment, light-heartedness, pleasure, delight, hilarity, laughter
OLD merriment, mirth
2 *to the amusement of the onlookers*
entertainment, diversion, distraction, pleasure
3 PASTIME, game, sport, recreation, hobby, interest
COLLOQ. R & R

QUOTATIONS
All things considered, work is less boring than amusement
CHARLES BAUDELAIRE, *Mon coeur mis à nu*

amusing *adj*
funny, humorous, hilarious, comical, tickling, laughable, ludicrous, droll, drôle, quizzical, witty, facetious, jocular, jolly, waggish, enjoyable, pleasant, charming, light, delightful, entertaining, interesting
COLLOQ. zany, killing, a scream, a hoot
See Synonym nuances panel at **funny**.
☒ dull, boring

amusingly *adv*
humorously, hilariously, comically, wittily, enjoyably, pleasantly, delightfully, entertainingly, interestingly
☒ dully, boringly

anaemic *adj*
1 *a pale anaemic-looking girl*
bloodless, ashen, chalky, livid, pasty, pallid, sallow, whey-faced, pale, wan, colourless, insipid, weak, feeble, ineffectual, enervated, frail, infirm, sickly
TECHNICAL exsanguinous

2 *the most anaemic cup final for years*
weak, ineffective, feeble, insipid, poor, lame, unimaginative, uninspired, unoriginal, hackneyed, bland, stale, tame
▣ **1** ruddy, sanguine, full-blooded **2** strong, powerful

anaesthetic *n*
painkiller, sedative, analgesic, anodyne, narcotic, opiate, palliative, soporific, epidural, stupefacient, stupefactive, premedication, local/general anaesthetic

anaesthetize *v*
desensitize, numb, deaden, dull, drug, dope, stupefy

analogous *adj*
comparable, similar, like, resembling, matching, kindred, parallel, corresponding, equivalent, relative, correlative, agreeing
▣ disparate

analogy *n*
comparison, simile, metaphor, likeness, resemblance, similarity, parallel, correspondence, equivalence, relation, correlation, agreement
FORMAL similitude, semblance

analyse *v*
break down, separate, divide, take apart, dissect, reduce, resolve, construe, sift, investigate, inquire, study, examine, scrutinize, review, interpret, test, judge, evaluate, estimate, consider, process, critique, calendar
FORMAL anatomize, assay

analysis *n*
breakdown, separation, division, dissection, reduction, resolution, sifting, investigation, inquiry, study, examination, inspection, scrutiny, review, check, check-up, exposition, explication, explanation, interpretation, test, judgement, opinion, evaluation, estimation, reasoning, anatomy
FORMAL anatomization, assay

analyst *n*
analyser, dissector, inquirer, researcher, experimenter, experimentalist, tester, prober, chemist
FORMAL assayer

analytical *adj*
analytic, detailed, in-depth, searching, critical, questioning, inquiring, inquisitive, investigative, dissecting, diagnostic, systematic, methodical, logical, rational, interpretative, explanatory, expository, studious

anarchic *adj*
lawless, ungoverned, anarchistic, libertarian, nihilist, revolutionary, rebellious, mutinous, riotous, chaotic, disordered, confused, disorganized
▣ submissive, orderly

anarchism *n*
lawlessness, disorder, chaos, insurgency, insurrection, rebellion, revolution, sedition, mob-rule, racketeering
FORMAL ochlocracy
COLLOQ. mobocracy, rent-a-mob

anarchist *n*
revolutionary, rebel, insurgent, Bolshevik, libertarian, nihilist, terrorist

anarchy *n*
lawlessness, unrule, misrule, anarchism, revolution, rebellion, insurrection, mutiny, riot, pandemonium, chaos, disorder, confusion
▣ rule, control, order

anathema *n*
aversion, abhorrence, abomination, curse, object of loathing, bête noire, bugbear, bane, proscription, taboo

anatomy *n*
1 *the study of anatomy*
dissection, vivisection, zootomy
2 *an anatomy of contemporary life*
analysis, make-up, composition, constitution, construction, frame, framework, build, structure

Anatomical terms include:

aural	gastric	neural
cardiac	genital	ocular
cartilaginous	gingival	oesophagal
cerebral	hepatic	optical
cervical	intercostal	pectoral
cranial	jugular	pedal
crural	lachrymal	pulmonary
dental	laryngal	renal
diaphragmal (or	ligamental	spinal
diaphragmatic)	lumbar	tendinous
dorsal	mammary	umbilical
duodenal	membral	uterine
epidermal	muscular	uvular
epiglottal	nasal	

See also **bone**; **brain**; **ear**; **eye**; **gland**; **mouth**; **muscle**; **tooth**; **vein**.

ancestor *n*
forebear, forefather, progenitor, predecessor, forerunner, precursor, antecedent
FORMAL primogenitor
▣ descendant

ancestral *adj*
inherited, familial, parental, genealogical, hereditary, genetic
FORMAL lineal

ancestry *n*
ancestors, forebears, forefathers, progenitors, parentage, family, family tree, lineage, line, descent, blood, race, stock, stirps, roots, pedigree, genealogy, extraction, derivation, origin, heritage, heredity

anchor *n, v*
♦ *n*
1 HOOK, mooring
2 *trust in God as an anchor in life*
support, mainstay, bulwark, linchpin, backbone, foundation
COLLOQ. tower of strength
3 PRESENTER, anchorman/woman, announcer, newsreader, host, compère
♦ *v*
moor, berth, tie up, make fast, fasten, attach, affix, fix

Types of anchor include:

car	kedge	sea
double fluked	killick	stocked
drogue	mushroom	stockless
grapnel	navy	yachtsman

anchorite *n*
anchoress, recluse, ascetic, hermit, solitary, loner, monk, eremite, stylite, solitarian
OLD anchor

ancient *adj*
1 *ancient history*
early, earliest, first, antediluvian, prehistoric, fossilized, immemorial, old, aged, time-worn, age-old, antique
FORMAL pristine, prim(a)eval, primordial
COLLOQ. as old as the hills
2 OLD-FASHIONED, out-of-date, antiquated, archaic, outmoded, passé, démodé, obsolete, bygone, early, original
FORMAL superannuated, atavistic
COLLOQ. past its sell-by date
▣ **1** recent, contemporary **2** modern, up-to-date, original

ancillary adj

auxiliary, supporting, helping, accessory, contributory, extra, secondary, subordinate, additional, subsidiary, supplementary
FORMAL adjuvant, adminicular

and conj

also, too, together (with), besides, as well (as), with, along with, in addition (to), plus, including, furthermore, moreover, by the way, then
COLLOQ. what's more

androgynous adj

hermaphrodite, bisexual, male and female, polygamic
TECHNICAL androdioecious, gynodioecious, heterogamous, monoclinous, monoecious, protogynous

anecdotal adj

1 *anecdotal evidence*
informal, unofficial, everyday, unscientific
2 *anecdotal writing*
narrative, storytelling, reminiscing

anecdote n

story, tale, yarn, sketch, narrative, reminiscence

anew adv

afresh, again, once again, once more

angel n

1 *an angel of God*
divine messenger, messenger of God, heavenly messenger, heavenly being, principality, power
2 DARLING, treasure, saint, paragon, gem, ideal, nonpareil
1 devil, fiend

The nine orders of angels are:

angel	principality
archangel	seraph
cherub	throne
domination/dominion	virtue
power	

---

angelic adj

cherubic, seraphic, celestial, heavenly, divine, holy, pious, saintly, pure, innocent, unworldly, virtuous, lovely, beautiful, adorable
FORMAL beatific, ethereal, empyrean
devilish, fiendish

anger n, v

◆ n
annoyance, irritation, antagonism, displeasure, irritability, temper, pique, vexation, ire, rage, fury, wrath, exasperation, chagrin, outrage, indignation, gall, bitterness, rancour, resentment, fit of anger, boiling-point, bluster, pelt, blood, bad blood, paroxysm; *Scot* fuff, kippage
OLD mood, face, gram, teen
FORMAL choler, dudgeon
COLLOQ. huff, wax; *N Am* conniption
SLANG monkey, flake
forgiveness, forbearance
◆ v
annoy, irritate, irk, vex, rile, make angry, bother, ruffle, provoke, antagonize, offend, affront, gall, madden, enrage, incense, infuriate, inflame, exasperate, outrage
OLD emboil, move
COLLOQ. aggravate, wind up, get at, bug, drive mad, drive crazy, drive bananas, drive up the wall, drive round the bend/twist, miff, needle, nettle, make your blood boil, make someone see red, rattle someone's cage, ruffle someone's feathers, raise someone's dander, make someone's hackles rise, make sparks fly, get under someone's skin, get up someone's nose, get on someone's wick
SLANG nark, piss off

OLD SLANG get someone's shirt out
please, appease, calm

> **QUOTATIONS**
> Anger is never without an argument, but seldom with a good one
> GEORGE SAVILE, *Political Thoughts and Reflections*

> **SYNONYM NUANCES**
>
> *noun*
> **Annoyance**, **irritation** and **chagrin** suggest something which troubles you a little; **vexation** and **exasperation** are stronger terms, and suggest a greater degree of annoyance. **Displeasure**, however, would only be appropriate for very mild anger or annoyance. If you want to express a feeling of vexation arising from injured pride, you could use **pique**. **Indignation** is again used more specifically, for a feeling or display of justified anger, with the implication it is mingled with scorn.
>   **Antagonism** would be used where hostility is involved; **gall** and **bitterness** on the other hand could be used to put the emphasis on feelings of resentment. **Irritability** would be used more of the quality of being easily angered, while **temper** would appropriately describe a demonstration of uncontrolled anger. **Ire** is a fairly straightforward synonym of anger, but **rage**, **outrage**, **fury** and **wrath** are all indicative of overpowering, even violent, anger. The term **boiling-point** also suggests that you have reached the point at which you lose control of your anger. **Bluster** and **pelt** likewise imply loss of control, sharing the notion of a storm of rage. **Paroxysm** is similar, but is more suggestive of a fit of passion. **Blood** is generally used in the expression 'someone's blood being up': *Tabitha's blood was up*.

angle¹ n, v

◆ n
1 CORNER, intersection, projection, nook, bend, flexure, hook, crook, elbow, knee, crotch, edge, point, slant, gradient, inclination
2 ASPECT, outlook, facet, side, approach, direction, position, standpoint, viewpoint, point of view, slant, perspective
COLLOQ. spin, take
◆ v
face, point, turn, aim, direct, slant, tilt

angle²

■ **angle for**
seek, seek to obtain, aim, try to get, go for, shoot for, make a bid for
COLLOQ. fish for

angler n

fisherman, rod
OLD fisher, Waltonian
FORMAL piscator, piscatrix

angrily adv

crossly, irately, wrathfully, furiously, passionately, hotly, warmly, indignantly, bitterly, resentfully, rancorously
COLLOQ. stroppily
calmly

angry adj

annoyed, cross, in a temper, irritated, displeased, irate, enraged, incensed, livid, seething, infuriated, furious, raging, passionate, heated, hot, warm, riled, exasperated, outraged, high, beside yourself, black, evil, sullen, sultry, up in the air, wrathful, choleric, splenetic; *Scot* radge; indignant, bitter, resentful, rancorous, on the rampage
OLD moody; *(Shakesp)* moody-mad; foribund, wrath, stomachful; *(Spenser)* yond
COLLOQ. aggravated, ratty, uptight, mad, hopping mad, raving mad, seeing red, in a lather, disgruntled, up in arms, hot under the collar, stroppy, choked,

fit to be tied, on the warpath, in a paddy; *Aust* spewy, ropable; *Aust & NZ* crooked
SLANG pissed off, hairless; *N Am* ticked off, burned up, pissed
E3 content, happy, calm

Colloquial ways of expressing becoming angry and losing your temper include:

be fizzing	fly off the handle	have your monkey up
blow a fuse	foam at the mouth	
blow a gasket	freak out	hit the ceiling
blow up	get all steamed up	hit the roof
blow your cool	go ape	let off steam
blow your stack	go ballistic	lose your cool
blow your top	go berserk	lose your marbles
boil over	*Aust* go crook	lose your patience
burst a blood vessel	go mad	lose your rag
Aust & NZ do your block	go nuts	*Aust* perform
	go off the deep end	raise Cain
do your nut	*Aust* go to market	raise hell
explode	go up the wall	see red
flip your lid	have a fit	sizzle
fly into a rage	have kittens	throw a tantrum
		throw a wobbly

angst *n*
anxiety, worry, distress, apprehension, dread, anguish, foreboding, uneasiness, tension, stress
FORMAL disquietude, worriment

anguish *n*
agony, anxiety, desolation, distress, suffering, torment, torture, grief, heartache, heartbreak, misery, pain, pang, rack, sorrow, tribulation, woe, wretchedness, affliction
OLD dole, dolour
E3 happiness, solace

anguished *adj*
afflicted, tormented, stressed, distressed, harrowed, miserable, stricken, suffering, tortured, wretched
OLD dolorous

angular *adj*
bony, thin, gaunt, gawky, lank, lanky, lean, sharp-pointed, rawboned, scrawny, skinny, spare

animal *n, adj*
♦ *n*
1 *wild animals*
creature, mammal, beast
COLLOQ. furry friend; *N Am* critter
Related adjective: zoic
See panel below

2 *that man is an animal*
beast, brute, barbarian, savage, monster
COLLOQ. swine, pig
♦ *adj*
1 *animal fats*
TECHNICAL theriomorphic
FORMAL animalic, zoic
2 *animal instincts*
bestial, brutish, inhuman, savage, wild, instinctive, bodily, physical, carnal, fleshly, sensual

animate *adj, v*
♦ *adj*
alive, living, live, breathing, conscious
OLD quick
E3 inanimate
♦ *v*
activate, enliven, arouse, instigate, invigorate, galvanize, goad, spur, impel, stimulate, incite, energize, excite, fire, kindle, move, quicken, reactivate, revive, rouse, spark, stir, urge, vitalize, bring to life, encourage, inspire
FORMAL embolden, vivify, inspirit
COLLOQ. buck up
E3 dull, inhibit

animated *adj*
lively, spirited, buoyant, vibrant, ebullient, vivacious, alive, vital, quick, brisk, vigorous, energetic, active, passionate, impassioned, sparkling, vehement, ardent, fervent, glowing, radiant, excited, enthusiastic, eager, instinct
COLLOQ. peppy, chipper, chirpy, zappy, full of beans, bright and breezy, bright-eyed and bushy-tailed
E3 lethargic, sluggish, inert

animatedly *adv*
excitedly, enthusiastically, eagerly, vibrantly, vivaciously, briskly, vigorously, energetically, actively, passionately, vehemently, ardently, fervently, radiantly
E3 sluggishly, inertly

animation *n*
liveliness, spirit, action, activity, brio, ebullience, passion, elation, energy, enthusiasm, excitement, exhilaration, fervour, high spirits, life, radiance, sparkle, sprightliness, verve, vibrancy, vigour, vitality, zeal, zest
COLLOQ. pep, zing, go
E3 dullness, inertia

animosity *n*
ill feeling, ill will, acrimony, bitterness, rancour, resentment, spite, malice, malignity, malevolence, hate, hatred, loathing, abhorrence, antagonism, hostility, enmity, friction, feud
FORMAL odium, animus
E3 goodwill

Animals include:

aardvark	chimpanzee	gibbon	koala	panther	squirrel
antelope	cougar	giraffe	lemur	pig	tiger
ape	cow	gnu	leopard	platypus	wallaby
armadillo	deer	goat	lion	polar bear	walrus
baboon	dog	gorilla	llama	polecat	weasel
badger	dolphin	grizzly bear	mink	puma	whale
bear	eland	hamster	mole	rabbit	wolf
beaver	elephant	hare	mongoose	racoon	wolverine
bison	elk	hedgehog	monkey	rat	wombat
buffalo	ermine	hippopotamus	mouse	reindeer	zebra
bull	ferret	horse	moose	rhinoceros	
camel	fox	hyena	ocelot	seal	
caribou	gazelle	impala	orang-utan	sealion	
cat	gerbil	jaguar	otter	sheep	
cheetah	giant panda	kangaroo	panda	skunk	

See also **amphibian**; **bird**; **butterfly**; **cat**; **cattle**; **dog**; **fish**; **horse**; **insect**; **invertebrate**; **mammal**; **marsupial**; **mollusc**; **monkey**; **moth**; **reptile**; **rodent**.

See also **animal sounds** *at* **sound**[1].

See also **collective nouns**.

annals *n*
archives, chronicles, records, registers, history, journals, accounts, memoirs, reports

annex *v*
1 ADD, append, affix, attach, fasten, join, connect, unite, incorporate
FORMAL adjoin
2 SEIZE, appropriate, acquire, usurp, occupy, conquer, take over
FORMAL arrogate

> ❗ **annex** or **annexe**?
> *Annex*, stressed on the second syllable, is a verb meaning to add or acquire: *The USSR annexed Latvia in World War II*. The noun, stressed on the first syllable, may be spelt *annex* or *annexe*, but the form with -e is more common.

annexation *n*
seizure, appropriation, acquisition, usurping, occupation, conquest, takeover
FORMAL arrogation

annexe *n*
wing, extension, attachment, addition, supplement, expansion

> ❗ **annexe** or **annex**?
> *See panel at* **annex**.

annihilate *v*
eliminate, eradicate, obliterate, erase, wipe out, murder, assassinate, exterminate, extinguish, raze, destroy, abolish, conquer, defeat, rout
FORMAL extirpate
COLLOQ. liquidate, rub out, take out, thrash, trounce, bring to their knees

annihilation *n*
elimination, eradication, obliteration, erasure, murder, assassination, extermination, extinction, destruction, abolition, defeat
FORMAL extirpation
COLLOQ. liquidation

anniversary
See panels below

annotate *v*
note, add notes to, gloss, comment, explain, interpret, elucidate
FORMAL marginalize, explicate

annotation *n*
note, footnote, gloss, comment, commentary, exegesis, explanation, elucidation
FORMAL explication

announce *v*
declare, proclaim, report, state, make/issue a statement, reveal, disclose, divulge, make known/public, notify, intimate, give out, publish, broadcast, advertise, publicize
OLD blazon (abroad), betoken

FORMAL promulgate, propound, preconize
🔁 suppress

announcement *n*
1 *make an announcement*
statement, declaration, proclamation, release, report, communiqué, dispatch, bulletin, message, information, notification, intimation, revelation, disclosure, divulgence, publication, broadcast, advertisement, publicity
FORMAL pronunciamento, *ipse dixit*, promulgation
2 *the announcement of the news*
declaration, proclamation, reporting, revelation, disclosure, divulgence, making known/public, notification, intimation, giving-out, release, publication, publicizing

announcer *n*
broadcaster, newscaster, newsreader, commentator, compère, host, master of ceremonies, MC, presenter, anchor, anchorman, anchorwoman, town crier, herald, messenger

annoy *v*
irritate, rile, displease, anger, vex, irk, madden, exasperate, tease, provoke, ruffle, gall, trouble, nag, disturb, bother, pester, plague, harass, molest; *Scot* fash
COLLOQ. aggravate, bug, hassle, rub up the wrong way, wind up, get your blood up, make your blood boil, get on your nerves, get up your nose, get under your skin, get your goat, get on your wick, drive crazy/nuts/bananas, drive up the wall, drive round the bend/twist, get your back up, brass off, cheese off, make your hackles rise, make sparks fly, give you the hump, get your dander up; *N Am* tick/hack off
SLANG piss someone off
🔁 please, gratify, comfort

> **SYNONYM NUANCES**
>
> The terms **irritate** and **displease**, **vex**, **gall** and **irk** are fairly mild terms for annoy: *you sound a trifle irked; it galled him to have to sit in silence*. **Ruffle** would be used of slight annoyance, but to **rile** suggests making someone rather more angry (for which you could also use the very direct **anger**). **Madden** is similar, but more suggestive of constant mental derangement: *maddened with pain*; **exasperate** is the term to use if you want to convey feelings of frustration.
> **Provoke** indicates deliberate intent to annoy or anger. To use **tease** would imply annoying someone deliberately but in a playful, mischievous or unkind way. **Trouble**, **disturb** and **bother** suggest a more active annoyance: *stop bothering me with your questions*. To say something **nags** suggests it is continually worrying and upsetting. **Pester**, **plague** and **harass** also convey the idea of persistent annoyance, but again suggest more deliberate annoyance: *children often pester you to buy them things*. **Molest** is similar, but carries more connotation of evil intent.

Traditional names of wedding anniversary include:

1st paper	6th iron/sugar	10th tin/	14th ivory	35th coral	60th diamond
2nd cotton	7th copper/wool	aluminium	15th crystal	40th ruby	70th platinum
3rd leather	8th bronze/	11th steel	20th china	45th sapphire	
4th flowers/fruit	pottery	12th silk/linen	25th silver	50th gold	
5th wood	9th pottery/willow	13th lace	30th pearl	55th emerald	

Modern names of wedding anniversary include:

1st clocks	6th wood	10th diamond	13th textiles/fur	25th silver	50th gold
2nd china	7th desk sets	jewellery	14th gold	30th diamond	55th emerald
3rd crystal/glass	8th linen/lace	11th fashion	jewellery	35th jade	60th diamond
4th appliances	9th leather	jewellery	15th watches	40th ruby	70th platinum
5th silverware		12th pearl	20th platinum	45th sapphire	

annoyance *n*
1 NUISANCE, pest, disturbance, bother, trouble, bore, tease, provocation, irritant, bugbear, bête noire
COLLOQ. bind, drag, headache, thorn in the side, pain (in the neck)
SLANG bugger, pain in the backside/arse; *N Am* pain in the ass/butt
2 *express your annoyance*
irritation, displeasure, anger, vexation, exasperation, harassment; *Scot* sturt, fash
OLD
(*Shakesp & Spenser*) noyance
FORMAL chagrin
COLLOQ. aggravation
E3 2 pleasure, satisfaction, contentment

annoyed *adj*
irritated, cross, upset, displeased, angry, vexed, piqued, exasperated, provoked, indignant, harassed
OLD hipped
COLLOQ. peeved, miffed, narked, bugged, stroppy, shirty, hassled, driven crazy, driven nuts, cheesed off, brassed off, pig sick, got the hump, in a huff, in a paddy, hot under the collar; *N Am* ticked off
SLANG pissed off, chocker
E3 pleased

annoying *adj*
irritating, vexatious, irksome, troublesome, bothersome, tiresome, trying, maddening, infuriating, exasperating, galling, offensive, teasing, provoking, disturbing, intrusive, unwelcome, harassing
COLLOQ. aggravating, infernal, pesky
E3 pleasing, welcome

annual *n, adj*
♦ *n*
yearbook, almanac, calendar, register
♦ *adj*
yearly, every twelve months

annul *v*
nullify, invalidate, void, rescind, suspend, set aside, cancel, abolish, quash, repeal, revoke, countermand, negate, declare null and void, retract, recall, reverse, dissolve, disannul
OLD vacate, vacuate
FORMAL abrogate
E3 enact, restore

annulment *n*
invalidation, voiding, rescindment, abrogation, suspension, cancellation, abolition, quashing, repeal, countermand, negation, nullification, recall, reverse
FORMAL revocation, rescission
E3 enactment, restoration

anodyne *adj*
bland, inoffensive, neutral, dull, innocuous, deadening

anoint *v*
1 OIL, grease, lubricate, apply oil/lubrication to, rub, smear, daub
OLD anele
FORMAL embrocate
2 BLESS, consecrate, sanctify, set apart, hallow, dedicate, ordain

anomalous *adj*
abnormal, atypical, exceptional, irregular, inconsistent, incongruous, deviant, freakish, eccentric, peculiar, odd, unusual, singular, rare
COLLOQ. freak
E3 normal, regular, ordinary

anomaly *n*
abnormality, exception, irregularity, inconsistency, incongruity, aberration, deviation, divergence, departure, freak, misfit, eccentricity, peculiarity, oddity, rarity

anon *adv*
soon, quite soon, shortly, before long, in the near future, in a little while, by and by

anonymous *adj*
1 *an anonymous poem*
unnamed, nameless, unsigned, unacknowledged, unspecified, unidentified, unknown, unattributed, incognito
FORMAL unattested, innominate
2 *a row of anonymous-looking houses*
faceless, impersonal, nondescript, unremarkable, unexceptional
E3 1 named, signed, identifiable **2** distinctive

SYNONYM NUANCES

sense 1
The terms **unknown** and **unidentified** are fairly neutral; **unnamed** however implies that an identity is being kept secret deliberately: *the unnamed source of the story*. If something is **nameless** or **innominate**, then the implication is that it is not possible to be named: *nameless terrors*. **Unsigned** is used in fairly specific contexts where an author has not wished to make their identity known. To say something is **unacknowledged** suggests that it has gone unrecognized or unnoticed, whether the originator wanted it or not.
   To indicate that it is not known exactly what something is, **unspecified** is used: *some unspecified crime*. The unmarked term **unattributed** simply suggests that we do not know an origin or source: *unattributed stories*; while **unattested** only tells you that there have been no witnesses to it. **Incognito**, however, again would be used to refer to a deliberate attempt by someone to remain unidentified or even in disguise: *travelling incognito*.

---

another *adj*
1 ADDITIONAL, further, extra, more, added, spare, second
2 DIFFERENT, other, some other, alternative, not the same, variant

answer *n, v*
♦ *n*
1 REPLY, acknowledgement, response, reaction, rejoinder, retort, riposte, retaliation, rebuttal
FORMAL replication
COLLOQ. comeback
2 SOLUTION, explanation, result, key, resolution, unravelling
COLLOQ. quick fix
E3 1 question
♦ *v*
1 REPLY, acknowledge, respond, write back, react, refute, retaliate
COLLOQ. get/come back to
2 *answer a need*
fulfil, fill, meet, satisfy, match up to
3 *answer (to) a description*
fit, correspond to, match, correlate, conform, agree, suit, serve, pass
■ **answer back**
talk back, be cheeky to, retort, riposte, retaliate, contradict, disagree, argue, dispute, rebut
COLLOQ. *N Am* sass
■ **answer for**
1 *answer for her loyalty*
vouch for, be responsible for, be accountable for, be liable for, speak for
2 *answer for the crimes*
pay for, be punished for, suffer for
■ **answer to**
report to, be responsible to, be accountable to, work under

answerable *adj*
liable, responsible, accountable, chargeable, blameworthy, to blame

antagonism *n*
hostility, opposition, enmity, rivalry, antipathy, ill feeling/will, animosity, friction, discord, dissension, contention, conflict
OLD (*Shakesp*) oppugnancy
E∃ rapport, sympathy, agreement

antagonist *n*
opponent, adversary, enemy, foe, rival, competitor, contestant, contender
E∃ ally, supporter

antagonistic *adj*
conflicting, opposed, adverse, at variance, incompatible, hostile, belligerent, contentious, unfriendly, ill-disposed, averse
E∃ sympathetic, friendly

antagonize *v*
alienate, estrange, disaffect, repel, embitter, offend, insult, provoke, annoy, irritate, anger, rile, incense
FORMAL disaffect
COLLOQ. aggravate, wind up, get at, bug, drive mad, drive crazy, drive bananas, drive up the wall, drive round the bend/twist, miff, needle, nettle, make someone's blood boil, make someone see red, rattle someone's cage, ruffle someone's feathers, make sparks fly, get under someone's skin, get up someone's nose, get on someone's wick, make someone's hackles rise
E∃ disarm

antecedent *n*
1 *antecedents of the aeroplane*
precursor, forerunner, precedent
2 *with Welsh antecedents*
ancestors, forebears, forefathers, progenitors, blood, race, stock, stirps, roots, extraction, genealogy

antedate *v*
precede, come before, go before
FORMAL antecede, prevene

antediluvian *adj*
old, early, antiquated, archaic, outmoded, passé, bygone
COLLOQ. as old as the hills, old hat
E∃ modern, recent

anteroom *n*
antechamber, vestibule, foyer, hall, entrance hall, lobby, porch, waiting-room

anthem *n*
hymn, song, chorale, psalm, song of praise, canticle, chant
TECHNICAL motet
FORMAL paean

anthology *n*
selection, collection, compilation, compendium, digest, treasury, miscellany, omnibus
FORMAL spicilege, chrestomathy, florilegium

Antichrist *n*
the Beast, lawless one, man of sin, man of lawlessness

anticipate *v*
1 FORESTALL, pre-empt, intercept, prevent, second-guess
OLD prevene
FORMAL obviate, preclude
COLLOQ. second-guess, beat to it
2 EXPECT, foresee, predict, forecast, think likely, look for, await, look forward to, hope for, bank on, count on/upon, reckon on, prepare for; *N Am* figure on

anticipation *n*
1 *in anticipation of the shortage*
expectation, preparation, prediction, forecast
2 *eager anticipation*
excitement, expectancy, hope
COLLOQ. bated breath

anticlimax *n*
comedown, let-down, disappointment, fiasco
FORMAL bathos
COLLOQ. non-event, damp squib, not all that it was cracked up to be

antics *n*
foolery, tomfoolery, silliness, buffoonery, clowning, horseplay, frolics, capers, skylarking, playfulness, mischief, tricks, monkey-tricks, pranks, stunts, doings

antidote *n*
1 *an antidote to a sting*
cure, counter-agent, antitoxin, neutralizer, neutralizing agent, countermeasure, serum
TECHNICAL antivenin, mithridate, alexipharmic, alexipharmakon, naloxone
OLD treacle, Venice treacle, theriac
2 *an antidote to depression*
remedy, cure, corrective

antipathy *n*
aversion, dislike, hate, hatred, loathing, abhorrence, distaste, disgust, repulsion, antagonism, animosity, ill will, bad blood, enmity, hostility, opposition, incompatibility
FORMAL animus, odium
E∃ sympathy, affection, rapport

antiquated *adj*
obsolete, old-fashioned, outdated, outmoded, out-of-date, dated, bygone, anachronistic, ancient, antediluvian, archaic, démodé, fossilized, outworn, passé
COLLOQ. on the way out, old hat
E∃ forward-looking, modern

antique *adj, n*
♦ *adj*
antiquarian, ancient, old, veteran, vintage, quaint, antiquated, old-fashioned, outdated, archaic, obsolete
♦ *n*
antiquity, relic, bygone, period piece, heirloom, curio, museum piece, collector's item, curiosity, rarity, object of virtu

antiquity *n*
1 *the great civilizations of antiquity*
ancient times, time immemorial, distant past, olden days
OLD days of yore
2 *of great antiquity*
age, old age, oldness, ancientness, agedness
E∃ 1 modernity, novelty

antiseptic *adj, n*
♦ *adj*
disinfectant, medicated, aseptic, germ-free, clean, pure, unpolluted, uncontaminated, sterile, sterilized, sanitized, sanitary, hygienic
♦ *n*
disinfectant, germicide, bactericide, purifier, cleanser

antisocial *adj*
1 *an antisocial person*
unfriendly, unsociable, uncommunicative, reserved, retiring, withdrawn, alienated, unapproachable, unforthcoming, reclusive
2 *antisocial behaviour*
asocial, unacceptable, disruptive, disorderly, rebellious, lawless, belligerent, antagonistic, hostile, anarchic
E∃ 1 sociable, gregarious **2** acceptable, orderly

antithesis *n*
1 OPPOSITE, converse, reverse, opposite extreme
2 OPPOSITION, contrast, contradiction, reversal

antithetical *adj*
opposed, opposing, in opposition, contrary, conflicting, clashing, contradictory, incompatible, irreconcilable

anxiety *n*
worry, concern, care, distress, nervousness, apprehension, disquiet, dread, anguish, foreboding, misgiving,

uneasiness, restlessness, fretfulness, edginess, impatience, suspense, tension, stress, strain, rack
TECHNICAL dysthymia
OLD cark
FORMAL disquietude, solicitousness, solicitude, worriment
COLLOQ. tizzy, tiz, stew, hang-up, jitters, butterflies (in your stomach), collywobbles, heebie-jeebies, willies, fantods, fantigue
E3 calm, composure, serenity

SYNONYM NUANCES

Worry, **concern** and **care** are straightforward terms for troubled feeling: *inflation is causing worry*. **Distress** and **anguish**, on the other hand, are appropriate for extreme mental or emotional suffering. **Nervousness**, **apprehension**, **suspense** and **tension** all suggest uneasiness in anticipation of a future event. Similarly **dread** has a sense of something yet to happen, but suggests a great fear of it: *a dread of death*. Again looking to the future, **foreboding** can be used to describe an apprehension of coming evil. **Disquiet**, **misgiving** and **uneasiness** would appropriately describe a constant feeling that all is not well; **restlessness**, **fretfulness** and **impatience** all convey an image of a state of uneasy activity arising from such anxiety. **Stress**, **strain** and **rack** would all be used in the context of constant and often specific emotional or mental pressure, though the latter to a more extreme degree: *the rack of rejection*. The formal terms **disquietude**, **solicitousness**, **solicitude** and **worriment** all suggest a constant uneasiness of mind.

---

anxious *adj*
1 APPREHENSIVE, worried, concerned, nervous, afraid, fearful, upset, uneasy, restless, fretful, impatient, in suspense, on tenterhooks, tense, taut, distressed, dismayed, disturbed, troubled, tormented, overwrought, tortured
FORMAL solicitous
COLLOQ. uptight, jittery, het up, in a stew/tizzy, having butterflies in your stomach/tummy, tearing your hair out, climbing the walls, with your knickers in a twist, a bundle of nerves
SLANG *Aust* toey
2 EAGER, keen, longing, enthusiastic, yearning, desirous, expectant
COLLOQ. desperate
E3 1 calm, composed

anxiously *adv*
apprehensively, nervously, fearfully, uneasily, restlessly, fretfully, impatiently, tensely, tormentedly
FORMAL solicitously

any *adj, pron, adv*
♦ *adj*
some, a few, a bit of, whichever
♦ *pron*
one, a single one
♦ *adv*
to some extent, to any extent, at all, in the least, the least bit

anyhow *adv*
1 *it's too late to go and anyhow we've run out of petrol*
anyway, in any event, in any case, no matter what
2 *the books are arranged anyhow*
untidily, not in order, at random, haphazardly

apace *adv*
speedily, swiftly, double-quick, fast, hastily, quickly, rapidly, at full/top speed, without delay

apart *adv*
1 *stand apart from the others*
aside, to one side, away, afar, distant, aloof, excluded, isolated, cut off, separated, separate, distinct, piecemeal

2 *live apart*
separately, independently, separated, divorced, not together, not living together, individually, singly, alone, on your own, by yourself, privately
3 *tear apart*
to pieces, to bits, into parts, in pieces, in bits, piecemeal
OLD asunder
E3 2, 3 together
■ **apart from**
except (for), not counting, excepted, aside from, excluding, with the exception of, but for, save

apartment *n*
1 FLAT; *N Am* condominium, duplex apartment; *Scot* tenement; *Aust & NZ* home unit
OLD mansion, paradise
COLLOQ. pad; *N Am* condo
SLANG gaff
2 *the state apartments*
room, chamber, accommodation
OLD bower

apathetic *adj*
uninterested, uninvolved, indifferent, blasé, cool, unemotional, emotionless, impassive, unmoved, unconcerned, cold, unfeeling, numb, unresponsive, passive, listless, lethargic, unambitious, lukewarm, half-hearted
FORMAL insouciant
COLLOQ. ho-hum
E3 enthusiastic, involved, concerned, feeling, responsive

apathy *n*
uninterestedness, indifference, coolness, impassivity, unconcern, lack of interest, lack of concern/enthusiasm, coldness, insensibility, passivity, listlessness, lethargy, sluggishness, torpor, inertia
FORMAL languor, acedia, accidie
E3 enthusiasm, interest, concern

ape *v, n*
♦ *v*
copy, imitate, echo, mirror, parrot, mimic, caricature, parody, mock, counterfeit, affect
COLLOQ. take off, send up
♦ *n*
monkey, chimpanzee, gibbon, gorilla, baboon, orang-utan, magot
OLD jackanapes
Related adjective: simian

aperture *n*
gap, hole, opening, passage, perforation, breach, chink, cleft, crack, eye, fissure, rent, slit, slot, space, vent, mouth
TECHNICAL orifice, foramen, punctum
FORMAL interstice

apex *n*
top, high point, peak, pinnacle, point, summit, tip, climax, consummation, crest, crown, crowning point, culmination, height, acme, apogee, vertex, zenith
TECHNICAL fastigium
FORMAL apotheosis
E3 nadir

aphorism *n*
maxim, adage, axiom, dictum, precept, proverb, saw, saying, witticism
FORMAL apophthegm, epigram, gnome

aphrodisiac *n, adj*
♦ *n*
love potion, stimulant
♦ *adj*
stimulant, stimulative, erogenous, erotic
FORMAL amative, amatory, erotogenous, venerous

QUOTATIONS
Power is the ultimate aphrodisiac
HENRY KISSINGER

apiece adv
each, individually, per person, per head, per capita, respectively, separately, singly

aplomb n
poise, assurance, calmness, composure, confidence, coolness, equanimity, sangfroid, savoir-faire, self-assurance, self-confidence, self-possession
COLLOQ. unflappability
E3 discomposure

apocryphal adj
unauthenticated, unverified, unsubstantiated, unsupported, questionable, spurious, equivocal, doubtful, dubious, fabricated, concocted, fictitious, made-up, imaginary, legendary, mythical
E3 authentic, true

apologetic adj
sorry, repentant, penitent, contrite, remorseful, conscience-stricken, regretful, rueful
E3 unrepentant, impenitent, defiant

apologetically adv
penitently, repentantly, contritely, remorsefully, regretfully, ruefully
E3 unrepentantly, defiantly

apologia n
defence, vindication, explanation, argument
FORMAL explication

apologist n
defender, vindicator, supporter, advocate, backer, endorser, upholder

apologize v
say you are sorry, say sorry, regret, be apologetic, ask forgiveness, ask pardon, beg someone's pardon, acknowledge, confess, explain, justify, plead
COLLOQ. swallow your pride, eat your words, eat humble pie

apology n
1 *he accepted my apology*
saying sorry, acknowledgement, confession, excuse, regrets, explanation, justification, vindication, defence, plea
FORMAL palliation
2 *he has an apology for a brain*
mockery, travesty, caricature, corruption, distortion, excuse, poor substitute, poor specimen
E3 1 defiance

apoplectic adj
incensed, furious, very angry, annoyed, cross, in a temper, irritated, irate, enraged, livid, seething, infuriated, raging, passionate, exasperated, outraged, high, beside yourself, sullen, sultry, up in the air, wrathful, wroth, rancorous, choleric, splenetic; *Scot* radge; indignant, bitter, resentful, on the rampage
OLD moody, foribund, wrath
COLLOQ. ratty, uptight, mad, hopping mad, raving mad, seeing red, in a lather, disgruntled, up in arms, hot under the collar, stroppy, choked, fit to be tied, on the warpath, in a paddy; *N Am* ticked off; *Aust* spewy, ropable; *Aust & NZ* crooked
SLANG pissed off, hairless; *N Am* burned up

apostasy n
defection, desertion, disloyalty, faithlessness, falseness, treachery, unfaithfulness, heresy, rattery, ratting
FORMAL perfidy, recreance, recreancy, renegation, renunciation
E3 loyalty, orthodoxy

apostate n
renegade, defector, deserter, traitor, turncoat, heretic, runagate
OLD recreant
FORMAL recidivist, tergiversator
E3 follower

apostle n
1 *Jesus Christ's apostles*
disciple, messenger, preacher, evangelist, missionary, teacher, reformer, proselytizer
2 *apostles of a united Europe*
advocate, champion, supporter, crusader, pioneer, proponent
FORMAL apologist

apotheosis n
high point, peak, apex, pinnacle, point, summit, tip, climax, consummation, crest, crown, crowning point, culmination, height, acme, apogee, vertex, zenith
TECHNICAL fastigium

appal v
horrify, shock, outrage, disgust, dismay, disconcert, daunt, intimidate, unnerve, alarm, scare, frighten, terrify
E3 reassure, encourage

appalling adj
1 *work in appalling conditions*
horrifying, horrific, harrowing, shocking, outrageous, atrocious, disgusting, awful, dreadful, frightful, terrible, dire, grim, hideous, ghastly, horrible, horrid, loathsome, daunting, intimidating, unnerving, alarming, frightening, terrifying, nightmarish
2 *appalling handwriting*
terrible, awful, frightful, very bad, very disappointing, dreadful, poor, atrocious, inadequate, unsatisfactory, inferior, unacceptable, hopeless
COLLOQ. pathetic, lousy, rop(e)y
SLANG pants, the pits, naff
E3 1 reassuring, encouraging **2** excellent

appallingly adv
1 *an appallingly disfigured face*
horrifically, shockingly, frightfully, hideously, horribly
2 *behave appallingly*
awfully, terribly, frightfully, dreadfully, unsatisfactorily, unacceptably, hopelessly
COLLOQ. pathetically

apparatus n
1 *gym apparatus*
appliance, gadget, device, contraption, equipment, rig, gear, tackle, outfit, tools, implements, utensils, materials, machine, machinery
2 *the apparatus of government*
system, structure, network, set-up, mechanism, framework, means

apparel n
clothing, clothes, garments, dress, costume, garb, outfit, wardrobe
OLD raiment, habilments, vesture
FORMAL attire
COLLOQ. gear, clobber, togs, get-up, kit

apparent adj
1 *his distrust was all too apparent*
visible, evident, noticeable, perceptible, plain, clear, distinct, marked, unmistakable, conspicuous, be standing out, obvious, manifest, patent, open, declared
2 *their apparent calmness*
seeming, superficial, outward, visible, ostensible
E3 1 hidden, obscure

apparently adv
seemingly, ostensibly, outwardly, on the face of it, to all appearances, superficially, on the surface, reputedly, plainly, clearly, obviously, manifestly, patently, evidently

apparition n
ghost, spectre, phantom, phantasm, semblance, wraith, spirit, vision, manifestation, manifest, illusion, shape, materialization, presence, fetch, hobgoblin, doppelgänger, double; *dialect* gytrash; *Scot* taisch

FORMAL eidolon, chimera, visitant
COLLOQ. spook

appeal n, v
♦ n
1 REQUEST, application, claim, approach, petition,
suit, solicitation, plea, entreaty, supplication, prayer,
invocation
OLD conjuration
FORMAL imploration, adjuration, orison
2 ATTRACTION, allure, interest, fascination, enchantment,
charm, attractiveness, winsomeness, beauty, charisma,
magnetism
3 *an appeal in a lawcourt*
retrial, reconsideration, review, re-evaluation,
re-examination
TECHNICAL recusation
♦ v
1 *appeal for help*
ask (for), request, call, call on, apply, claim, address,
petition, solicit, plead, beg, beseech, implore, entreat,
pray, invoke, call upon
TECHNICAL *Scot* reclaim
OLD TECHNICAL avouch, provoke
OLD (*Spenser*) peal
FORMAL supplicate, sue
2 ATTRACT, draw, allure, lure, tempt, entice,
invite, interest, engage, fascinate, charm, please

appealing adj
pleasing, attractive, tempting, enticing,
inviting, alluring, interesting, fascinating, engaging,
winning, enchanting, charming, winsome, charismatic,
magnetic

appear v
1 ARRIVE, enter, turn up, attend, be present, materialize,
develop, show (up), come into sight/view, become visible,
come along, loom, rise, surface, arise, occur, crop up,
come to light, come out, emerge, issue, be published
COLLOQ. show up, roll up pop up
2 SEEM, look, give the impression of being, come across as,
show signs of, take the guise of, turn out
COLLOQ. **3** *appear in a show*
act, perform, play, take part, be a guest in, be on stage
4 *his book appeared in the shops*
be published, come out, become available
▣ **1** disappear, vanish

appearance n
1 APPEARING, arrival, advent, coming, coming into view,
rise, emergence, debut, introduction, attendance, presence
2 LOOK, expression, face, aspect, air, bearing, manner,
looks, figure, (outward) form, complexion, image
FORMAL mien, visage, demeanour
3 *keep up an appearance*
pretence, show, front, guise, illusion, impression, outward
impression, façade, image
OLD (*Shakesp*) ostent, outward
FORMAL semblance
▣ **1** disappearance

appease v
placate, pacify, reconcile, satisfy, mitigate,
make peace with, conciliate
FORMAL propitiate
▣ aggravate

appeasement n
reconciliation, conciliation, peacemaking, placation,
pacification, satisfaction

appellation n
epithet, name, nickname, title, designation,
description
FORMAL so(u)briquet, denomination
SLANG monicker

append v
add, affix, attach, fasten, join, tack on
FORMAL adjoin, annex, conjoin, subjoin

appendage n
addendum, appendix, addition, supplement,
adjunct, tailpiece

appendix n
addition, appendage, adjunct, addendum,
supplement, epilogue, codicil, postscript, rider

appertain v
pertain, relate, apply, be relevant, bear on,
have a bearing on, concern, refer, regard

appetite n
1 *a good appetite*
hunger, stomach, relish, zest, taste, desire, tooth
TECHNICAL malacia, orexis
COLLOQ. inner man, inner woman
SLANG twist
2 *appetite for sensation*
hunger, taste, thirst, inclination, liking, desire, longing,
urge, propensity, yearning, craving, lust, eagerness,
passion, zeal
OLD maw
COLLOQ. yen

appetizer n
starter, first course, canapé, *hors d'œuvre*, meze, apéritif,
cocktail, tapas, bhajee, whet, relish
OLD antepast

appetizing adj
mouthwatering, tempting, inviting, appealing, palatable,
tasty, delicious, succulent, piquant, savoury
COLLOQ. scrumptious, mor(e)ish, yummy
▣ disgusting, distasteful

applaud v
1 *the audience applauded*
clap, cheer, put your hands together for, give
an ovation/a standing ovation to, give a round of
applause, show your appreciation to
COLLOQ. give a big hand to
2 *applaud the government's efforts*
acclaim, compliment, congratulate, approve,
commend, praise
FORMAL laud, eulogize, extol

applause n
ovation, standing ovation, clapping, cheering, cheers,
bravos, acclaim, acclamation, accolade, congratulation,
approval, commendation, praise
FORMAL encomium
COLLOQ. a big hand
▣ criticism, censure

appliance n
1 *domestic appliance*
machine, device, contrivance, contraption,
gadget, tool, implement, instrument, apparatus,
mechanism, waldo
COLLOQ. gizmo
2 APPLICATION, use, value, relevance, function,
carrying-out
TECHNICAL praxis

applicable adj
relevant, apt, appropriate, fitting, suited, useful,
suitable, fit, proper, valid, legitimate
FORMAL pertinent, apposite
▣ inapplicable, inappropriate

applicant n
candidate, interviewee, claimant, contestant,
competitor, aspirant, suitor, petitioner, inquirer
TECHNICAL postulant

application n
1 REQUEST, appeal, petition, suit, claim,
inquiry, demand
2 RELEVANCE, function, purpose, use, value, bearing,
significance, aptness, germaneness
TECHNICAL praxis
FORMAL pertinence

3 DILIGENCE, hard work, industry, industriousness, effort, commitment, dedication, perseverance, keenness, attentiveness
FORMAL assiduity, sedulousness
4 *computer applications*
program, software
5 *the application of ointment*
putting on, smearing, spreading, rubbing, treatment, anointing

applied *adj*
practical, real, useful, functional, relevant, actual, hands-on
E3 pure, theoretical

apply *v*
1 REQUEST, ask for, requisition, put in for, put in an application for, fill in a form for, order, write away/off for, appeal, petition, solicit, sue, claim, inquire
2 *apply yourself to a task*
address, buckle down, settle down, commit, devote, dedicate, give, direct, concentrate, study, persevere, be diligent, be industrious, work hard, make an effort, commit/devote yourself
COLLOQ. knuckle down
3 USE, exercise, utilize, employ, bring into play, put into practice/operation, draw on, engage, harness, ply, wield, administer, execute, implement, assign, direct, bring to bear, exert, practise, resort to
4 REFER, relate, be relevant, be significant, fit, suit, affect, involve
FORMAL pertain, appertain
5 *apply ointment*
put on, spread on, lay on, cover with, paint, anoint, smear, rub, treat with
OLD appose
FORMAL adhibit

appoint *v*
1 NAME, nominate, be shortlisted, elect, install, choose, select, pick, engage, employ, take on, hire, recruit, commission, co-opt, delegate, assign, allot, designate, command, direct, charge, detail
2 DECIDE, determine, arrange, settle, fix, set, specify, assign, establish, ordain, decree, destine, designate, allot
E3 **1** reject, dismiss, discharge

appointed *adj*
determined, decided, scheduled, chosen, assigned, arranged, pre-arranged, settled, fixed, set, established, ordained, decreed, destined, preordained, designated, allotted

appointment *n*
1 ARRANGEMENT, engagement, date, meeting, arrangement to meet, interview, consultation, rendezvous
OLD tryst, assignation
2 JOB, position, situation, post, office, place
3 NAMING, nomination, election, choosing, choice, selection, commissioning, delegation

apportion *v*
assign, allocate, allot, distribute, divide, dispense, deal (out), hand out, grant, measure out, mete (out), ration (out), share (out), carve
OLD stint
FORMAL admeasure
COLLOQ. dole out

apportionment *n*
allocation, allotment, distribution, division, dispensation, assignment, dealing, grant, ration(ing), sharing, share
COLLOQ. handout

apposite *adj*
relevant, applicable, appropriate, apt, germane, suitable, suited, to the point, to the purpose
FORMAL pertinent, apropos, befitting
E3 inapposite

appraisal *n*
evaluation, assessment, survey, inspection, review, examination, estimate, estimation, judgement, reckoning, opinion, appreciation, valuation, rating
FORMAL assay
COLLOQ. once-over

appraise *v*
evaluate, assess, survey, inspect, review, examine, estimate, sum up, judge, value, rate; *N Am* valuate
FORMAL assay
COLLOQ. size up, once-over

> ⚠ **appraise** or **apprise**?
> If you *appraise* someone or something, you form an opinion about their quality, value, etc. If you are *apprised* of something, you are told about it.

appreciable *adj*
noticeable, significant, considerable, substantial, definite, perceptible, discernible, recognizable
E3 insignificant, imperceptible, negligible

appreciably *adv*
noticeably, significantly, considerably, substantially, definitely, markedly, perceptibly

appreciate *v*
1 ENJOY, relish, savour, prize, treasure, value, cherish, admire, respect, regard, like, welcome, take kindly to, think highly of, esteem
OLD apprize
2 UNDERSTAND, comprehend, perceive, realize, recognize, grasp, be aware of, be conscious of, be sensitive to, acknowledge, sympathize with, know, see, sense
3 *I appreciate your help*
be grateful for, express your gratitude/appreciation, thank, give thanks for, be appreciative, be indebted to
4 *appreciate in value*
grow, increase, rise, mount, go up, inflate, gain, strengthen, improve, enhance
E3 **1** despise, hate **2** overlook, ignore **4** depreciate, go down

---

SYNONYM NUANCES

sense 1
The word **enjoy** is a straightforward one to use for taking pleasure or delight in something. To express a deeper, more conscious appreciation and increased sensation, you could use **relish** and **savour**: *he savoured life to the full*; *she relished the experience*. The terms **prize**, **treasure** or **value** appropriately describe appreciation from the point of view of placing a high value on it, while **cherish** suggests doing the same but with more affection involved.
  Respect and **regard** are restrained terms, having more to do with treating with consideration, although **regard** in some contexts carries more implication of kindly feelings. To **think highly of** or **esteem** someone or something returns to the notion of highly respecting and appreciating their merits or qualities: *poets were highly esteemed*, whereas **like** is a far more mild, not particularly demonstrative term.
  To **take kindly to** is very similar, though its usage is generally in the negative: *she does not take kindly to criticism*. **Welcome** is used specifically of receiving something with pleasure: *Britain welcomes foreign investment*.

---

appreciation *n*
1 ENJOYMENT, relish, admiration, liking, respect, respecting, regard, high opinion, esteem, valuing
2 *send a present to show your appreciation*
gratitude, gratefulness, thankfulness, thanks, indebtedness, obligation

3 UNDERSTANDING, comprehension, perception, awareness, realization, recognition, grasp, acknowledgement, sympathy, sensitivity, responsiveness, valuation, assessment, estimation, judgement, knowledge
FORMAL cognizance
4 REVIEW, critique, evaluation, analysis, assessment, commentary, notice, praise
5 GROWTH, increase, rise, inflation, gain, improvement, escalation, enhancement
E3 **2** ingratitude **5** depreciation

appreciative *adj*
1 GRATEFUL, thankful, obliged, indebted, pleased
FORMAL beholden
2 ADMIRING, encouraging, enthusiastic, respectful, sensitive, responsive, supportive, perceptive, knowledgeable, conscious, mindful
E3 **1** ungrateful **2** ignorant, insensitive

apprehend *v*
1 CATCH, arrest, capture, detain, seize
COLLOQ. pick up, bust, nick, collar, grab, nab, run in, pull in
2 UNDERSTAND, comprehend, grasp, believe, conceive, perceive, realize, recognize, see
COLLOQ. twig

apprehension *n*
1 ANXIETY, dread, foreboding, misgiving, qualm, unease, uneasiness, worry, concern, disquiet, nervousness, alarm, fear, trepidation, doubt, suspicion, mistrust
FORMAL perturbation
COLLOQ. jitters, butterflies, butterflies in your stomach, collywobbles, heebie-jeebies, willies
2 ARREST, capture, detention, seizure, taking
3 UNDERSTANDING, comprehension, grasp, belief, conception, perception, discernment, realization, recognition, uptake
TECHNICAL noesis
FORMAL cognizance

apprehensive *adj*
nervous, anxious, worried, concerned, uneasy, doubtful, suspicious, mistrustful, distrustful, bothered, alarmed, afraid, fearful
COLLOQ. trepidatious, on tenterhooks, having the jitters, having butterflies in your stomach, having the collywobbles, having the willies, climbing the walls
SLANG *Aust* toey
E3 assured, confident

apprehensively *adv*
nervously, anxiously, uneasily, doubtfully, suspiciously, mistrustfully, distrustfully, fearfully
E3 assuredly, confidently

apprentice *n*
trainee, probationer, student, pupil, learner, novice, beginner, starter, recruit, newcomer, tyro, cadet, prentice, intern
OLD *Scot* servitor
COLLOQ. *N Am* rookie
E3 expert

apprenticeship *n*
training period, traineeship, studentship, trial period, probationary period, novitiate

apprise *v*
inform, notify, acquaint, advise, brief, communicate, enlighten, intimate, tell, warn
COLLOQ. tip off

> **❗ apprise** or **appraise**?
> See panel at **appraise**.

approach *v*, *n*
♦ *v*
1 GET CLOSER TO, come nearer/closer, advance towards, move towards, proceed towards, go near(er), draw near, near, gain on, catch up, reach, meet, arrive

2 SPEAK TO, talk to, address, make conversation with, greet, accost
3 TACKLE, deal with, begin, commence, set about, embark on, launch into, undertake, introduce, mention, treat
4 APPLY TO, appeal to, sound out, contact, get in touch with, get onto, invite, make advances, make overtures, broach
COLLOQ. buttonhole
5 *a speed approaching 200 km/h*
reach, come close to, border on, come near to, compare with, approximate
♦ *n*
1 *the approach of winter*
advance, coming, coming near/close, arrival
FORMAL advent
2 ATTITUDE, point of view, viewpoint, opinion, position, perspective, slant, standpoint, stance, angle
3 APPLICATION, appeal, overture(s), advances, suggestion(s), invitation, proposition, proposal, request, plea
4 METHOD, manner, style, technique, procedure, means, modus operandi, strategy, system, tactics, course of action
5 ACCESS, road, avenue, drive, driveway, way, passage, entrance, doorway, threshold

approachable *adj*
1 FRIENDLY, easy to get on/along with, sociable, congenial, warm, affable, agreeable, open, informal, pleasant, welcoming
2 ACCESSIBLE, attainable, reachable
COLLOQ. get-at-able
E3 **1** aloof, unapproachable **2** inaccessible, remote

approbation *n*
approval, good opinion, praise, respect, acceptance, favour, commendation, endorsement, encouragement, recognition, esteem
FORMAL laudation

appropriate *adj*, *v*
♦ *adj*
suitable, applicable, relevant, to the point, well-chosen, apt, fitting, fit, befitting, germane, seemly, becoming, proper, right, correct, accepted, well-timed, timely, seasonable, opportune
OLD meet
FORMAL pertinent, appurtenant, apropos, felicitous
COLLOQ. spot-on
E3 inappropriate, irrelevant, unsuitable
♦ *v*
1 SEIZE, take, take possession of, commandeer, requisition, confiscate, impound, assume, usurp
FORMAL expropriate, arrogate
2 STEAL, pocket, pilfer, embezzle, misappropriate, thieve, make off with
FORMAL purloin, peculate
COLLOQ. nick, pinch, swipe, nab, lift, filch, knock off

appropriately *adv*
suitably, fittingly, correctly, properly, relevantly
FORMAL felicitously

approval *n*
1 ADMIRATION, regard, respect, good opinion, esteem, liking, appreciation, acceptance, favour, recommendation, praise, commendation, acclaim, acclamation, honour, applause
OLD approof
FORMAL approbation
2 AGREEMENT, acceptance, assent, consent, permission, leave, sanction, authorization, licence, mandate, endorsement, blessing, certification, ratification, validation, confirmation, support
FORMAL approbation, concurrence, imprimatur
COLLOQ. go-ahead, green light, OK, rubber stamp, nod, wink, thumbs-up
E3 **1** disapproval, condemnation

sense 2
The general term **agreement** suggests approval given with accord, but **acceptance** does not carry the same implication of accord. **Assent** implies a degree of compliance whereas **consent** has more to do with accordance. Both **permission** and **leave** are general terms that might be used of any act of permitting or authorization. **Sanction** suggests more official approval, even more so **authorization**, which indicates being established by some form of authority: *authorization to carry a weapon.*

Meanwhile a **licence** can be used both of an official document and a more abstract permission: *licence to own a gun; his words gave me licence to act;* but a **mandate** again is an indication of legal authorization, usually to carry out an action. **Certification** is only used in the context of granting of a written declaration, and **ratification** also denotes approval that has been signed. **Validation** is especially appropriate where some checking has taken place before approval is granted.

If you talk of giving something your **endorsement** or the less formal **blessing** it implies that you are expressing personal agreement of it as well; **support** suggests an even more active backing: *his support for devolution.* **Approbation** can be used of a formal act of approval while **concurrence** leans more towards agreement and co-operation. An **imprimatur** refers specifically to permission to print: *now it has the imprimatur of the Pope, the Catechism will be sent for translation.*

approve v
1 ADMIRE, regard, like, think well/highly of, hold in high regard, be pleased with, appreciate, favour, recommend, praise, commend, acclaim, applaud, esteem
OLD countenance
2 *approve a proposal*
agree to, assent to, consent to, accede to, allow, permit, pass, sanction, authorize, mandate, bless, countenance, ratify, validate, endorse, support, hold with, uphold, second, back, accept, adopt, carry, confirm
FORMAL concur, homologate
COLLOQ. give the go-ahead to, give the green light to, OK, rubber-stamp, give the nod to, give the thumbs-up to, buy
OLD SLANG dig
E≥ 1 disapprove, condemn **2** reject

approved adj
accepted, authorized, orthodox, official, recommended, sanctioned, okayed, correct, favoured, permissible, permitted, preferred, proper, recognized
E≥ unauthorized, unorthodox

approving adj
admiring, appreciative, favourable, praising, respectful, supportive, commendatory
FORMAL laudatory

approvingly adj
admiringly, appreciatively, with pleasure, favourably

approximate adj, v
♦ *adj*
estimated, guessed, rough, inexact, imprecise loose, close, near, like, similar, relative
COLLOQ. ballpark
E≥ exact, precise
♦ *v*
approach, come close to, come near to, border on, verge on, be tantamount to, resemble, be similar to

approximately adv
roughly, around, about, some, something like, odd, circa, more or less, loosely, round about, or thereabouts, approaching, close to, nearly, just about, not far off, in the region/neighbourhood/vicinity of, somewhere in the region of, in round numbers, rounded up/down

COLLOQ. give or take
E≥ exactly

approximation n
1 ESTIMATE, rough calculation, rough idea, guess, estimation, conjecture
COLLOQ. guesstimate, ballpark figure
2 *an approximation to a dress*
likeness, resemblance, similarity, correspondence
FORMAL semblance

appurtenance n
accessories, equipment, belongings, trappings, paraphernalia, impedimenta

a priori adj
theoretical, deduced, hypothetical, inferred
FORMAL conjectural, suppositional

apron n
1 PINAFORE, bib, tablier, tabard, pinnie; N Am tier
OLD napron, barm-cloth, brat, placket
2 *the apron of the stage*
edge, fringe, periphery, skirt, rim, border
3 *aeroplanes on the apron*
standing, hard-standing, bay, loading bay, forecourt

apropos adj, prep
♦ *adj*
suitable, applicable, relevant, to the point, well-chosen, apt, fitting, befitting, becoming, proper, right, correct, accepted, timely, seasonable, opportune
OLD seemly
FORMAL pertinent, felicitous
E≥ inappropriate
♦ *prep*
with reference to, with regard to, with respect to, in relation to, in respect of, on the subject of, in connection with, re, regarding, respecting

apt adj
1 RELEVANT, applicable, appropriate, fitting, acceptable, suitable, fit, germane, seemly, proper, correct, accurate, timely, seasonable
FORMAL apposite
COLLOQ. spot-on
2 *apt to do something*
inclined, liable, prone, given, disposed, tending, likely, ready, subject
E≥ 1 inapt, unsuitable

aptitude n
ability, natural ability, capability, capacity, faculty, gift, talent, flair, facility, skill, proficiency, cleverness, intelligence, quickness, bent, inclination, leaning, disposition, tendency
E≥ inaptitude

aptly adv
suitably, appropriately, fittingly, fitly, relevantly, to thepoint
FORMAL appositely

aquatic adj
water, sea, river, marine, maritime, nautical, watery, fluid, liquid
FORMAL fluvial

arable adj
cultivable, ploughable, farmable, tillable, fertile, productive, fruitful
FORMAL fecund

Types of arable crop include:

N Am alfalfa	millet	soya bean
barley	mung bean	sugar beet
bean	oats	swede
cassava	oilseed rape	sweetcorn
corn	pea	sweet potato
fodder beet	popcorn	turnip
kale	potato	wheat
lucerne	rice	yam
linseed	rye	
mangel wurzel	sorghum	

arachnid
See panel at **insect**.

arbiter *n*
1 ADJUDICATOR, judge, referee, umpire
2 *an arbiter of style*
authority, expert, pundit, master, governor, judge, controller

arbitrarily *adv*
by chance, randomly, illogically, inconsistently, unreasonably, irrationally, subjectively

arbitrary *adj*
1 RANDOM, chance, capricious, whimsical, inconsistent, discretionary, subjective, personal, instinctive, unreasoned, illogical, irrational, unreasonable
2 DESPOTIC, tyrannical, dictatorial, autocratic, absolute, imperious, magisterial, domineering, overbearing, high-handed, dogmatic
E3 **1** reasoned, rational, circumspect

> **QUOTATIONS**
> To customs and beliefs, the very ones we hold sacred, sociology ruthlessly attaches the adjective 'arbitrary'
> RAYMOND CLAUDE FERDINAND ARON, *Politics and History*

arbitrate *v*
judge, adjudicate, pass judgement, sit in judgement, referee, umpire, mediate, settle, decide, determine

arbitration *n*
judgement, adjudication, intervention, mediation, negotiation, settlement, decision, determination
FORMAL arbitrament

arbitrator *n*
judge, adjudicator, arbiter, referee, umpire, moderator, mediator, negotiator, intermediary, go-between

arbour *n*
bower, shelter, alcove, grotto, bay, recess, retreat, sanctuary

arc *n, v*
♦ *n*
curve, curved line, bend, arch, bow, curvature, semicircle
♦ *v*
curve, bend, arch, bow, turn, round, spin, swerve

arcade *n*
gallery, cloister, colonnade, covered way, mall, piazza, portico, precinct, shopping mall, shopping precinct, plaza
TECHNICAL loggia, peristyle, stoa

arcane *adj*
secret, mysterious, concealed, obscure, hidden, abstruse, mystical, cryptic, enigmatic, esoteric, recondite, occult, profound

arch *n, v, adj*
♦ *n*
1 *the arches of a bridge*
archway, bridge, span, dome, vault, concave
2 ARC, bend, curve, curvature, bow, semicircle

♦ *v*
bend, curve, bow, arc, vault, camber
♦ *adj*
mischievous, playful, mysterious, cunning, sly

Types of arch include:

basket handle	keel	shouldered
convex	lancet	skew
corbel	Norman	stilted
equilateral	ogee	tented
four-centre	parabolic	trefoil
Gothic	round	Tudor
horseshoe	segmental	

archaeology
See panel below

archaic *adj*
antiquated, old-fashioned, outmoded, passé, outdated, out-of-date, obsolete, old, ancient, antique, quaint, bygone, primitive, medi(a)eval, antediluvian, obsolescent
COLLOQ. old hat, out of the ark
E3 modern, recent

archetypal *adj*
model, standard, typical, representative, characteristic, original, classic, ideal, stock
FORMAL exemplary, quintessential, paradigmatic

archetype *n*
pattern, model, standard, form, type, prototype, original, precursor, classic, paradigm, ideal, epitome, stereotype
FORMAL exemplar, quintessence, typification, entity

architect *n*
1 *the architect of the building*
designer, planner, master builder, draughtsman
2 *the architect of modern economics*
creator, author, inventor, engineer, maker, constructor, prime mover, originator, founder, instigator, shaper
COLLOQ. mastermind

architecture *n*
1 *study architecture*
designing, planning, building, construction
TECHNICAL architectonics
2 *Victorian architecture*
style, design, composition, structure, arrangement, make-up, framework
See panel on next page
3 *the architecture of a software program*
structure, framework, frame, construction, form, make-up, arrangement, organization, composition, constitution, system, set-up
FORMAL configuration, conformation

archives *n*
records, annals, chronicles, memorials, papers, documents, deeds, ledgers, registers, memorabilia, roll

arctic *adj*
1 *the Arctic Ocean*
polar, far northern
FORMAL boreal, hyperborean

Archaeological terms include:

agger	burin	flake	jar	mound	rock shelter
amphitheatre	cairn	flask	jug	mummy	sondage
amphora	cartouche	flint	kitchen-midden	neolith	spindle
artefact	cave art/rock art	handaxe	kurgan	obelisk	stele
barrow	cist	henge	ley lines	palmette	stone circle
beaker	cromlech	hieroglyph	loom weight	palstave	tell
blade	cup	hill fort	lynchet	papyrus	tumulus
bogman	dolmen	hoard	megalith	potassium-argon	urn
bowl	earthwork	hypocaust	microlith	dating	vallum
bracteate	eolith	incised decoration	mosaic	radiocarbon dating	whorl

Architectural and building terms include:

alcove	coving	elevation	frontispiece	pagoda	roughcast
annexe	dado	Elizabethan	gable	pantile	sacristy
architrave	decorated	façade	gargoyle	parapet	scroll
baluster	dogtooth	fanlight	gatehouse	pinnacle	soffit
barge-board	dome	fascia	Georgian	plinth	stucco
baroque	Doric	festoon	Gothic	Queen Anne	terrazzo
bas-relief	dormer	fillet	groin	rafters	Tudor
capstone	double glazing	finial	groundplan	Regency	Tuscan
casement window	drawbridge	flamboyant	half-timbered	reveal	wainscot
classical	dry-stone	Flemish bond	Ionic	ridge	weathering
coping stone	duplex	fletton	jamb	rococo	
Corinthian	Early English	fluting	lintel	Romanesque	
cornerstone	eaves	French window	mullion	roof	
cornice	Edwardian	frieze	Norman	rotunda	

See also **arch**; **roof**; **tower**; **wall**; **window**.

2 *arctic weather*
freezing, freezing cold, bitterly cold, frozen, frosty, Siberian, glacial, subzero
E3 **1** Antarctic **2** tropical

ardent *adj*
fervent, fiery, warm, passionate, impassioned, fierce, avid, vehement, intense, strong, spirited, enthusiastic, eager, keen, dedicated, devoted, zealous, evangelical, hot, burning, fervid, sanguine, mettled, mettlesome, spiritous
OLD perfervid
E3 apathetic, unenthusiastic

ardently *adv*
fervently, warmly, passionately, strongly, avidly, vehemently, intensely, hotly, enthusiastically, eagerly, devotedly, zealously
E3 unenthusiastically

ardour *n*
fervour, passion, fire, flame, heat, warmth, avidity, vehemence, intensity, spirit, enthusiasm, eagerness, animation, zest, keenness, dedication, devotion, zeal, lust, rage, *duende*
OLD covetise; (*Shakesp*) wrath
FORMAL empressement
E3 apathy, coolness, indifference

arduous *adj*
hard, difficult, tough, onerous, burdensome, heavy, rigorous, severe, harsh, formidable, strenuous, tiring, taxing, fatiguing, wearying, daunting, exhausting, backbreaking, punishing, gruelling, uphill, stiff, laborious
COLLOQ. be a slog, be murder
E3 easy

area *n*
1 *the Muslim areas of the city*
locality, neighbourhood, quarter, environment, environs, patch, terrain, district, region, parish, zone, sector, department, precinct, province, enclave, catchment area, reserve area
2 *an area of land*
expanse, width, breadth, stretch, extent, part, portion, section, tract
3 *an area of activity/knowledge*
field, sphere, domain, world, realm, territory, department, province, branch, sector, range, scope, compass, size, extent

arena *n*
1 STADIUM, field, ground, bowl, ring, area, amphitheatre, theatre, coliseum, hippodrome
2 *the political arena*
sphere, scene, domain, world, realm, department, province, battlefield, battleground, area of conflict

argot *n*
jargon, cant, slang, idiom, specialist language, parlance

arguable *adj*
debatable, open to question, questionable, disputable, open to doubt, contentious, uncertain, undecided, moot
FORMAL controvertible
E3 incontrovertible, indisputable, certain

arguably *adv*
probably, maybe, possibly, in all likelihood, most likely

argue *v*
1 QUARREL, squabble, bicker, row, have a row, wrangle, haggle, wrestle, remonstrate, take/join issue, fight, feud, fall out, disagree, dispute, quibble, rag, spar; *Scot* cangle
FORMAL altercate, moot
COLLOQ. be at each other's throats, be at loggerheads, hassle, have it out (with), have words, cross swords, have a bone to pick
2 REASON, assert, contend, hold, hold a brief, declare, maintain, claim, plead
FORMAL expostulate, logicize
3 *argue the point*
question, debate, discuss, reason
4 *argued them out of leaving*
persuade, dissuade, talk out of, convince
5 BE EVIDENCE FOR, exhibit, display, show, manifest, demonstrate, indicate, denote, prove, suggest, imply

argument *n*
1 QUARREL, squabble, row, wrangle, controversy, polemic, debate, discussion, dispute, disagreement, clash, difference of opinion, heated exchange, conflict, fight, feud, rumpus, ruckus, spat
OLD controverse
FORMAL altercation
COLLOQ. tiff, barney, argy-bargy, running battle, shouting-match, slanging-match, set-to, dust-up, ding-dong, bust-up; *Aust* yike
SLANG *Aust & NZ* blue
2 REASONING, reason, logic, rationale, assertion, declaration, contention, claim, demonstration, evidence, argumentation, debate, defence, case, justification
FORMAL expostulation
Related adjective: elenctic
3 *the argument of the book*
synopsis, summary, theme, topic, outline, plot, thesis

SYNONYM NUANCES

sense 1
Quarrel, **squabble** and **wrangle** are synonyms which suggest a personal argument with distinct viewpoints involved. **Row** is similar, but is often associated with domestic disagreements: *she had a row with her husband*. However, both **row** and **controversy** can suggest a more general argument, and one that is within the public domain: *political controversy*.

Debate and **discussion** are the terms to use when talking is the main expression of the dispute, especially where it has been deliberately organized; **dispute**, likewise, indicates a contest with words but with no formalization behind it.

The word **disagreement** is a general one with no strong associations, whereas **clash** implies noisy opposition or contradiction. Likewise, **difference of opinion** would describe a fairly tame argument on a matter on which two or more groups disagree, but **altercation** or **heated exchange** describe dialogue that has become angry. Both **conflict** and **fight** suggest a very passionate and intense struggle, often with a physical element implied, and **rumpus** puts the emphasis on noisiness or uproar: *a mighty rumpus*. **Feud** is used particularly of a persistent state of private enmity.

argumentation *n*
reasoning, debate, argument, rationale, logic, contention, claim, justification, evidence, case, defence
FORMAL expostulation

argumentative *adj*
quarrelsome, contentious, polemical, opinionated, belligerent, perverse, contrary, cantankerous
FORMAL captious, disputatious, litigious, dissentious, truculent
COLLOQ. stroppy; *Can* chippy
⊟ complaisant

arid *adj*
1 *an arid landscape*
dry, parched, waterless, moistureless, desiccated, torrid, dehydrated, baked, shrivelled up, barren, infertile, unproductive, desert, waste
FORMAL torrefied
2 DULL, uninteresting, boring, monotonous, tedious, dry, sterile, dreary, drab, flat, colourless, lifeless, spiritless, uninspired, vapid, jejune
⊟ **1** fertile **2** lively, exciting

aright *adv*
rightly, accurately, exactly, properly, correctly, truly, fitly, suitably, aptly
COLLOQ. OK

arise *v*
1 OCCUR, emerge, issue, appear, come to light, come up, present itself, happen, begin, start, commence, come into being/existence
COLLOQ. crop up
2 *points that arose from the report*
result, be a result of, be caused by, ensue, follow, derive, stem, come, spring, proceed, flow
3 RISE, get up, stand up, get to your feet, straighten up, rise up, go up, ascend, climb, mount, lift, soar, tower

aristocracy *n*
upper class, privileged class, gentry, aristocrats, lords, ladies, nobility, noblemen, noblewomen, peers, peerage, ruling class, gentility, high society, élite, rank
FORMAL patriciate, patricians, optimates, *haute monde*

COLLOQ. toffs, nobs, top drawer, upper crust
⊟ common people, lower classes, working class, proletariat, hoi polloi, riff-raff; *colloq.* plebs, proles

aristocrat *n*
noble, nobleman, noblewoman, peer, peeress, lord, lady, patrician, *grande dame*, *grand seigneur*
FORMAL grandee, eupatrid, optimate
COLLOQ. toff, nob
⊟ commoner

aristocratic *adj*
upper-class, highborn, well-born, noble, patrician, blue-blooded, titled, lordly, courtly, élite, dignified, elegant, refined, thoroughbred
COLLOQ. upper-crust, born with a silver spoon in your mouth
⊟ plebeian, vulgar

arm¹ *n*
1 *with folded arms*
limb, upper limb, appendage
TECHNICAL brachium
Related adjective: brachial
2 *the air arm of the fighting forces*
wing, section, division, detachment, department, branch, offshoot, extension, projection
3 *an arm of the sea*
inlet, estuary, bay, channel, firth, passage, cove, creek
4 *the arm of the law*
authority, power, force, strength
FORMAL might

arm² *v*
arm someone with weapons/information
provide, supply, issue, equip, rig, outfit, prime, prepare, forearm, rearm, gird, steel, brace, reinforce, strengthen, protect
FORMAL array, furnish, fortify, accoutre

armada *n*
fleet, flotilla, navy, naval force, squadron

armaments *n*
weapons, arms, artillery, guns, cannon, munitions, ammunition, ordnance, weaponry

armed services

Units in the armed services include:

garrison	battery	MARINES:
militia	brigade	commandos
task force	company	Royal Marines
AIR FORCE:	corps	
flight	patrol	NAVY:
squadron	platoon	convoy
wing	regiment	fleet
	squad	flotilla
ARMY:	troop	squadron
battalion		

See also **rank¹**.

Terms used in armour:

HEAD AND NECK:	nosepiece	hauberk	LEGS:	FOR HORSES:	lame
armet	sallet (or salade)	pectoral	cuisse	barding	palette
aventail	ventail		culet	chamfrain (or	plate armour
basinet (or	visor (or vizor)	SHOULDERS AND	greave	chamfron)	rondel
bascinet)		ARMS:	poleyn	crinet	splint armour
beaver	TORSO:	ailette	sabaton	pectoral	suit
casque	backpiece (or	brassard	shynbald	poitrel	surcoat
gorget	backplate)	couter	solleret		
grille	body armour	gauntlet	spur	MISCELLANEOUS:	
helmet	breastplate	pauldron (or	tasse	cap-à-pie	
mentonnière	corslet (or corselet)	pouldron)	tonlet	chain mail	
morion (or	cuirass	rerebrace	tuille	coat-armour	
morrion)	faulds	vambrace		gusset	

armistice *n*
ceasefire, truce, peace, peace treaty, pact, agreement to end/cease/suspend hostilities

armour *n*
protective covering, body armour, panoply, shield, mail, chain mail, iron-cladding, armature, garniture
See panel on previous page

armoured *adj*
armour-plated, steel-plated, iron-clad, toughened, reinforced, protected, bullet-proof, bomb-proof

armoury *n*
arsenal, ordnance depot, ammunition dump, magazine, (arms) depot, repository, stock, stockpile, garderobe

arms *n*
1 WEAPONS, weaponry, firearms, guns, cannon, missiles, projectiles, artillery, instruments of war, armaments, ordnance, munitions, ammunition
2 COAT-OF-ARMS, armorial bearings, shield, crest, insignia, emblem, heraldic device, escutcheon, heraldry, blazonry

army *n*
1 *a captain in the army*
armed force, military, militia, land forces, soldiers, soldiery, troops, infantry
Related adjective: military
2 *an army of workers*
legions, cohorts, multitude, throng, host, horde, pack, mob, crowd, swarm

> QUOTATIONS
> An army marches on its stomach
>   Napoleon I

aroma *n*
smell, odour, scent, perfume, fragrance, bouquet, savour, nose
FORMAL fumet(te), redolence

aromatic *adj*
perfumed, fragrant, sweet-smelling, sweet-scented, fresh, scented, balmy, savoury, spicy, pungent
FORMAL redolent, odoriferous
E3 acrid, foul-smelling

around *prep, adv*
♦ *prep*
1 SURROUNDING, round, encircling, encompassing, enclosing, on all sides of, on every side of, about, framed by
FORMAL circumambient, circumjacent
2 EVERYWHERE IN, to all parts of, about, all over
3 *around a dozen*
approximately, roughly, about, circa, more or less, close to, nearly
♦ *adv*
1 EVERYWHERE, all over, in all directions, on all sides, throughout, about, here and there, to and fro
2 CLOSE, close by, near, nearby, at hand, within reach

arousal *n*
1 SEXUAL STIMULATION, excitement, titillation
COLLOQ. getting going
2 *arousal to anger*
provocation, agitation, excitement, stirring, evocation, firing

arouse *v*
1 *arouse suspicion*
cause, instigate, induce, summon up, call forth, spark, kindle, inflame, whet, sharpen, quicken, animate, excite, prompt, provoke, stimulate, trigger, incur
2 *arouse someone to anger*
provoke, incite, agitate, stir up, excite, evoke, rouse, fire, startle, galvanize, goad, spur, whip up, get going
OLD upraise
FORMAL suscitate
3 *arouse from sleep*
wake up, waken, awaken, disentrance

OLD bestir
COLLOQ. knock up
4 *arouse sexually*
stimulate, excite, get going, titillate
COLLOQ. turn on
E3 2 calm, lull, quieten

arraign *v*
accuse, call to account, charge, impeach, indict, prosecute, impugn, incriminate, bring an action against

arraignment *n*
accusation, charge, trial, legal action, case, impeachment, incrimination, indictment, summons

arrange *v*
1 *arrange a meeting*
decide, settle on, agree, plan, organize, set up, make (an appointment)
COLLOQ. fix (up), pencil in, ink in
2 ORGANIZE, co-ordinate, prepare, fix, plan, project, design, devise, contrive, determine, settle
3 ORDER, put in order, tidy, range, marshal, dispose, distribute, position, set out, lay out, align, line up, group, class, classify, categorize, sort (out), sift, grade, list, file, systematize, catalogue, codify, methodize, regulate, adjust
FORMAL array
4 *arrange music*
adapt, set, score, orchestrate, instrument, harmonize
E3 3 untidy, disorganize, muddle

arrangement *n*
1 *make arrangements*
plan(s), preparation(s), detail(s), planning, preparing, groundwork
2 AGREEMENT, settlement, contract, terms, compromise, *modus vivendi*
3 ORDER, display, disposition, layout, line-up, positioning, grouping, classification, structure, system, method, set-up, organization, preparation, planning, plan, scheme, design, format, schedule
FORMAL array
4 ADAPTATION, version, interpretation, setting, score, orchestration, instrumentation, harmonization

arrant *adj*
absolute, complete, utter, downright, extreme, out-and-out, outright, rank, thorough, thoroughgoing, brazen, flagrant, gross, blatant, unmitigated, incorrigible, infamous, notorious, barefaced, vile
FORMAL egregious

array *n, v*
♦ *n*
arrangement, display, show, exhibition, exposition, assortment, collection, muster, order, formation, line-up, parade, disposition, marshalling
FORMAL assemblage
♦ *v*
1 ARRANGE, order, range, dispose, position, group, lay out, line up, align, draw up, marshal, assemble, muster, parade, display, show, exhibit
2 CLOTHE, dress, robe, deck, adorn, decorate
OLD bedizen, accoutre
FORMAL attire, apparel, habilitate

arrears *n*
debt(s), liabilities, outstanding payment/amount, sum of money owed, amount owed, money owing, balance, deficit
■ **in arrears**
owing, outstanding, behind(hand), in debt, overdue, late

arrest *v, n*
♦ *v*
1 *arrest a criminal*
capture, catch, seize, apprehend, detain, take into custody
COLLOQ. bust, nick, collar, grab, nab, book, run in, pick up, pull in, do, nail

2 STOP, stem, check, restrain, inhibit, halt,
interrupt, stall, delay, slow (down), retard, block,
obstruct, impede, hinder
COLLOQ. nip in the bud
3 *arrest your attention*
capture, attract, catch, grip, hold, engage,
absorb, engross, rivet, fascinate, intrigue
♦ *n*
capture, apprehension, detention, taking into custody,
seizure
■ **under arrest**
in custody, helping police with their inquiries, in captivity

arresting *adj*
striking, amazing, eyebrow-raising, surprising, stunning,
extraordinary, impressive, remarkable, engaging, notable,
noteworthy, conspicuous, noticeable, eye-catching,
outstanding, salient
ᕕ inconspicuous, unremarkable

arrival *n*
1 *the arrival of the president/fresh supplies*
appearance, entrance, entry, coming, approach,
emergence
FORMAL advent
2 *welcome new arrivals*
newcomer, incomer, comer, visitor, guest, entrant,
debutant(e), fresher; *N Am* freshman
FORMAL visitant
3 *the arrival of credit cards*
invention, appearance, coming, start, development,
emergence, occurrence, origin, birth, dawn
ᕕ **1** departure **2** leaver **3** death

arrive *v*
1 *arrive at the airport*
come, reach, get to, get there, get here, be present, reach
your destination, appear, put in an appearance, land,
touch down, dock, fetch, pull in, come in, check in, clock
in, materialize, enter, come on the scene, occur, happen
FORMAL accede
COLLOQ. show (up), turn up, rock up, make it, drop in,
blow in, swan in, roll up, pitch up, surface
2 APPEAR, become available, come on the market, be
produced
3 *arrive at a decision*
reach, come to, get, obtain, gain, achieve, accomplish,
attain, hammer out, thrash out
4 *he thinks he's really arrived*
succeed, be a success, become famous
COLLOQ. make it, get to the top
ᕕ **1** depart, leave

arrogance *n*
pride, conceit, boasting, haughtiness, vanity,
superciliousness, disdain, scorn, contempt, superiority,
egotism, condescension, lordliness, pomposity, high-
handedness, imperiousness, self-importance,
snobbishness, presumption, insolence
OLD surquedry; (*Shakesp*) opinion
FORMAL hauteur, hubris, contumely
COLLOQ. nerve
SLANG side
ᕕ humility, unassumingness, bashfulness

arrogant *adj*
proud, conceited, boastful, full of yourself, haughty,
supercilious, disdainful, scornful, contemptuous, superior,
egotistic, condescending, patronizing, imperious, lordly,
overbearing, overweening, high-handed, self-important,
snobbish, presumptuous, assuming, insolent, on the high
ropes; *dialect* cobby; *N Am* topping
OLD dangerous, stout, wanton
FORMAL hubristic
COLLOQ. bigheaded, stuck-up, high and mighty, uppity,
toffee-nosed, hoity-toity
ᕕ humble, unassuming, bashful

arrogantly *adv*
proudly, conceitedly, boastfully, haughtily,
superciliously, disdainfully, scornfully, contemptuously,
condescendingly, patronizingly, imperiously,
overbearingly, overweeningly, high-handedly,
self-importantly, snobbishly, presumptuously, insolently
FORMAL hubristically
ᕕ humbly, bashfully

arrogate *v*
seize, usurp, assume, presume, take over, commandeer,
misappropriate
FORMAL appropriate, possess yourself of

arrogation *n*
seizure, assumption, taking over, commandeering,
possession
FORMAL appropriation

arrow *n*
1 *shoot with an arrow*
shaft, bolt, dart, flight
OLD quarrel, quar'le; (*Shakesp*) butt-shaft
Related adjective: sagittal
2 *follow the arrows*
marker, indicator, pointer

arsenal *n*
armoury, ordnance depot, ammunition dump, weapons,
weaponry, magazine, (arms) depot, repository, stock,
stockpile, garderobe

arson *n*
fire-raising, incendiarism, pyromania, firebombing

arsonist *n*
fire-raiser, incendiary, pyromaniac, firebomber
COLLOQ. firebug
SLANG *N Am* torch

art *n*
1 FINE ART, painting, sculpture, drawing, artwork, design,
visual arts, craft, creative work, artistry, draughtsmanship,
craftsmanship
See panels on next page
2 SKILL, knack, technique, craft, method, aptitude, facility,
talent, flair, gift, dexterity, finesse, ingenuity, mastery,
expertise, virtuosity, adroitness, profession, trade
COLLOQ. knowhow
3 ARTFULNESS, cunning, craftiness, slyness, guile, deceit,
trickery, astuteness, shrewdness, wiliness, sleight, daubery

> QUOTATIONS
> There is no boundary line to art
> CHARLIE PARKER

artefact *n*
thing, something, object, item, tool, piece of jewellery

artery *n*
See panel at **vein**.

artful *adj*
cunning, crafty, sly, foxy, wily, tricky, scheming,
designing, deceitful, devious, subtle, sharp, shrewd, smart,
clever, masterly, ingenious, resourceful, skilful, dexterous
OLD (*Shakesp*) cautel
FORMAL vulpine
ᕕ artless, naive, ingenuous

artfully *adv*
cunningly, craftily, slyly, deceitfully, deviously,
shrewdly, cleverly, skilfully, ingeniously
ᕕ naively

article *n*
1 *articles in a magazine*
feature, report, story, account, piece, item, review,
commentary, write-up, composition, essay, paper,
monograph, offprint
2 ITEM, thing, something, object, commodity, unit,
artefact, part, constituent, piece, portion
COLLOQ. thingummy, thingummyjig, thingummybob,
what-d'you-call-it, whatsit

Arts and crafts include:

animation	collage	film	metalwork	photography	stained glass
animatronics	crochet	fresco	modelling	portraiture	tapestry
architecture	digital design	graphics	mosaic	pottery	video
batik	drawing	illustration	needlework	screenprinting	watercolour
calligraphy	embroidery	jewellery	oil painting	sculpture	weaving
caricature	enamelling	knitting	origami	silk-screen printing	woodcarving
ceramics	engraving	lithography	painting	sketching	woodcraft
cloisonne	etching	marquetry	patchwork	spinning	

See also **embroidery; painting; picture; sculpture**.

Schools of art include:

abstract	classicism	Gothic	Neoclassicism	Pre-Raphaelite	Stuckism
action painting	Conceptual Art	Hellenistic	Neoexpressionism	Brotherhood	Superrealism
Aestheticism	concrete art	Impressionism	Neohellenism	Primitivism	Suprematism
Art Brut	Constructivism	junk art	Neo-Impressionism	Purism	Surrealism
Art Deco	Cubism	Kinetic Art	Neo-Plasticism	quattrocento	Symbolism
Art Nouveau	Dadaism	magic realism	New Realism	Rayonism	tenebrism
Barbizon	Etruscan art	Mannerism	Op Art	Realism	Venetian
Baroque	Expressionism	medi(a)eval art	Orphism	renaissance	Vorticism
Bauhaus	Fauvism	Minimal Art	plastic art	Rococo	
Bohemian	Florentine	Modernism	Pointillism	Romanesque	
Brit art	folk art	the Nabis	Pop Art	Romanticism	
Byzantine	Futurism	Naturalism	Post-Impressionism	socialist realism	
classical revival	The Glasgow Boys	the Nazarenes	Post-Modernism	social realism	

---

3 *article 25 of the contract*
paragraph, section, subsection, clause, point

articulate *adj, v*

♦ *adj*
distinct, well-spoken, eloquent, clear, lucid, intelligible, comprehensible, understandable, communicative, coherent, fluent, vocal, expressive, meaningful
F3 inarticulate, incoherent

♦ *v*
say, utter, speak, talk, express, give expression to, voice, vocalize, verbalize, state, frame, pronounce, enunciate, enounce, breathe

> **SYNONYM NUANCES**
>
> *adjective*
> **Distinct** and **clear** are the most general and neutral terms to describe articulacy in expression, whereas to describe someone as **well-spoken** suggests approval of the grace and courtesy in their speech. **Eloquent** is also very admiring, this time of someone's expressive and fluent language. **Lucid** puts the focus on content and suggests that what you say is easily understood: *a beautifully lucid narrative*; likewise **intelligible**, **comprehensible** and **understandable** all simply suggest that something is capable of being understood, without any particular suggestion of approval.
> The terms **communicative** and **vocal** are properly used of a person's willingness to put their views across, although you would be more likely to use **vocal** if you did not particularly approve of it. **Coherent** and **fluent** tend to be interpreted as terms of praise; likewise **expressive** and **meaningful**, although these would put the emphasis again on the content of what is being said, rather than the delivery.

articulated *adj*
coupled, linked, hinged, interlocked, joined, attached, connected, fastened, segmented, fitted together, joint, jointed

articulately *adv*
distinctly, clearly, eloquently, lucidly, intelligibly, comprehensibly, coherently, fluently, expressively
F3 inarticulately, incoherently

articulation *n*

1 *a speaker with clear articulation*
saying, utterance, speaking, talking, expression, voicing, vocalization, verbalization, pronunciation, enunciation, diction, delivery
2 CONNECTION, junction, coupling
TECHNICAL arthrosis, diarthrosis, schindylesis, clavation

artifice *n*
1 TRICK, device, dodge, ruse, scheme, stratagem, strategy, subterfuge, tactic, wile, contrivance
COLLOQ. set-up, scam, con
2 DECEIT, trickery, artfulness, deception, deceit, deviousness, fraud, guile, craft, craftiness, cunning, slyness, subtlety, chicanery, cleverness

artificial *adj*
1 *artificial flowers*
synthetic, imitation, mock, faux, plastic, man-made, manufactured, simulated, non-natural, unnatural, processed
2 *an artificial smile*
false, fake, bogus, counterfeit, spurious, specious, sham, insincere, assumed, affected, mannered, studied, forced, contrived, made-up, feigned, pretended, simulated
COLLOQ. phoney, pseudo, pseud
F3 1 natural, real **2** genuine

> **SYNONYM NUANCES**
>
> *sense 1*
> All the synonyms for artificial can be negative in tone, depending on the context; **synthetic** and **simulated** are perhaps the least inherently marked: *a simulated coal fire*. **Imitation**, **mock** and **faux**, on the other hand, while they may be used without implication, can also be suggestive of cheap imitations of more luxurious fabrics, and so hint at bad taste. Similarly, if you describe something as **plastic**, it may well be made of plastic, or you may wish to imply that it is unattractively artificial. **Man-made** tends to be used widely and neutrally of materials that have been developed by man; whereas **manufactured** can also be used in various contexts to suggest undesirable artificiality: *manufactured pop bands and their manufactured songs*.
> Describing something as **non-natural** unavoidably conveys the powerful, negative suggestion that it is not

produced by or according to nature: *the non-natural use of land*; **unnatural** is even more marked in that it suggests being totally at odds with nature: *how unnatural our lifestyles have become*. The term **processed** is most commonly used of foodstuffs; while not particularly marked in itself, again the context may lend it a negative connotation.

artificiality *n*
1 UNNATURALNESS, simulation
2 FALSITY, spuriousness, insincerity, pretence, sham, speciousness

artificially *adv*
1 SYNTHETICALLY, unnaturally
2 FALSELY, spuriously, insincerely, speciously

artillery *n*
heavy guns, heavy weapons, guns, weapons, ordnance, cannons, munitions

artisan *n*
craftsperson, craftsman, craftswoman, artificer, journeyman, expert, skilled worker, mechanic, technician, operative
Related adjective: banausic

artist *n*
1 CREATOR, maker, inventor, designer, architect, founder, author, writer, poet, originator, composer, musician, actor, dancer, painter, sculptor
2 EXPERT, specialist, authority, professional, maestro; *N Am* maven, mavin
COLLOQ. dab hand, pro, ace

> **QUOTATIONS**
> The artist, like the idiot or clown, sits on the edge of the world, and a push may send him over it
> SIR OSBERT SITWELL, *The Scarlet Tree*

> **!** **artist** or **artiste**?
> An *artist* is someone who paints pictures or is skilled in one of the fine arts. An *artiste*, or *artist*, is a performer in a theatre or circus or on television; *artiste* is now regarded as old-fashioned or affected.

Types of artist include:

animator	draughtswoman	photographer
architect	engraver	portraitist
blacksmith	etcher	potter
caricaturist	goldsmith	printer
carpenter	graphic artist	screenprinter
cartoonist	graphic designer	sculptor
craftsman	illustrator	silversmith
craftswoman	lithographer	watercolourist
designer	master	weaver
digital artist	oil painter	
draughtsman	painter	

artiste *n*
performer, entertainer, variety artist, vaudevillian, comic, comedian, comedienne, player, trou
per, actor, actress, dancer, musician, singer

artistic *adj*
1 *an artistic person*
creative, sensitive, refined, cultured, original, expressive, gifted, cultivated, skilled, talented, imaginative
2 *an artistic design*
aesthetic, ornamental, decorative, beautiful, attractive, fine, exquisite, elegant, stylish, tasteful, graceful, harmonious
E3 **2** inelegant

artistry *n*
craftsmanship, workmanship, skill, craft, talent, flair, ability, brilliance, genius, finesse, style, mastery, expertise, proficiency, accomplishment, deftness, touch, sensitivity, creativity
E3 ineptitude

artless *adj*
simple, natural, unpretentious, genuine, guileless, honest, ingenuous, sincere, straightforward, open, plain, pure, childlike, innocent, naive, direct, frank, candid, true, trusting, unsophisticated, unwary, unworldly
E3 artful, cunning

artlessly *adv*
simply, naturally, unpretentiously, purely, innocently, naively, ingenuously, sincerely, straightforwardly, directly, frankly, openly, plainly, candidly, truly
E3 artfully, cunningly

as *conj, prep*
♦ *conj*
1 WHILE, when, just as, whilst, at the same time (that/as), simultaneously
2 SUCH AS, for example, for instance, like
3 IN THE SAME MANNER THAT, in the same way that, like
4 BECAUSE, since, seeing that, considering that, inasmuch as, being, the reason is ..., through, on account of, as a result of, owing to
OLD forasmuch
♦ *prep*
1 *work as a taxi-driver*
in the role of, with the part of, functioning as
2 *dressed as a man*
like, similar to, with the appearance of, in the guise of
■ **as for**
with reference to, as regards, with regard to, on the subject of, in connection with, in relation to, with relation to, concerning, respecting, with respect to, apropos
■ **as it were**
so to speak, in a manner of speaking, in a way, in some way, so to say, as it might be
■ **as yet**
so far, up to now, up to this point, up to the present moment, till now
OLD hitherto
FORMAL thus far

ascend *v*
rise, take off, lift off, go up, come up, move up, gain height, slope upwards, climb, scale, mount, tower, float up, fly up, soar, arise
E3 descend, go down

ascendancy *n*
dominance, domination, authority, command, control, power, dominion, superiority, lordship, mastery, supremacy, edge, predominance, pre-eminence, influence, prevalence, sway
FORMAL hegemony
COLLOQ. upper hand
E3 decline, subordination

ascendant *adj*
dominant, powerful, rising in power, superior, predominant, prevalent, growing, developing
COLLOQ. on the up and up

ascent *n*
1 ASCENDING, ascension, climb, climbing, scaling, escalation, rise, rising, mounting
2 SLOPE, gradient, incline, ramp, hill, elevation, rise
FORMAL acclivity
3 *their rapid ascent to power*
rise, advance, progress
FORMAL advancement
E3 **1** descent

ascertain *v*
find out, learn, discover, get to know, come to know, determine, fix, establish, settle, locate, detect, identify, verify, confirm, make certain
COLLOQ. suss out, twig, pin down

ascetic adj, n

♦ adj
self-denying, self-disciplined, austere, abstemious, abstinent, self-controlled, stern, strict, severe, rigorous, harsh, plain, puritanical, spartan
♦ n
hermit, recluse, solitary, anchorite, abstainer, celibate, monk, nun, puritan, stylite, pillarist, Nazarite, fakir, dervish, yogi, sadhu, sannyasi, Jainist, Montanist

asceticism n

self-denial, self-discipline, austerity, severity, harshness, self-control, abstinence, monasticism, ascesis

ascribe v

attribute, credit, give credit to, put down, assign, charge
FORMAL accredit, impute

ash n

embers, cinders, charcoal, residue
Related adjectives: cinereal, cinerary

ashamed adj

1 ashamed of your behaviour
sorry, apologetic, remorseful, contrite, guilty, conscience-stricken, sheepish, embarrassed, blushing, red-faced, mortified, humiliated, discomfited, abashed, humbled, crestfallen, distressed, discomposed, shamefaced, penitent
COLLOQ. not able to look someone in the face, having your tail between your legs, on a guilt trip
2 ashamed to admit his mistakes
reluctant, hesitant, unwilling, loath, self-conscious, bashful, modest
Ｆ **1** shameless, proud, defiant **2** proud

SYNONYM NUANCES

sense 1
The words **sorry** and **apologetic** imply an acknowledgement of guilt, and are used where regret is being expressed. **Guilty** suggests shame that is felt rather than expressed, as do the more intense terms **remorseful**, **penitent** and **conscience-stricken**, which are appropriate to describe a deep, burdensome guilt: *police found the remorseful robber desperate to give himself up.*

When you want to emphasize someone's embarrassment, you are more likely to use words such as **sheepish**, **embarrassed** or **abashed**; and **blushing** and **red-faced** could also be used of comparatively mild embarrassment. The stronger terms **shame-faced** and **crestfallen** again suggest physical displays of embarrassment, but with connotations of a deeper, moral ashamedness, while **mortified** and **humiliated** are stronger again, and can be used of a crippling embarrassment. **Humbled**, on the other hand, would be used in a context where you have been made to feel low by your shame, but can learn moral lessons from it: *he was humbled in the face of their selflessness.* If shame has led to a loss of composure, the words **discomfited** and **discomposed** could be used. **Distressed**, however, would be reserved to describe someone whose shame is causing mental pain.

---

ashen adj

pallid, pale, pale-faced, pasty, wan, white, anaemic, blanched, bleached, colourless, ghastly, grey, leaden, livid
Ｆ ruddy

ashore adv

onto the shore, onto the beach, onto the land, towards the shore

aside adv, n

♦ adv
1 move aside
to one side, on one side, alongside, apart, away, out of the way, separately, in isolation, alone, privately, secretly

2 his money aside
apart
FORMAL notwithstanding
♦ n
digression, parenthesis, incidental remark, cursory remark, departure, soliloquy, monologue, stage whisper, whisper
FORMAL apostrophe, *obiter dictum*

asinine adj

silly, stupid, foolish, senseless, nonsensical, idiotic, ludicrous, moronic, imbecilic, absurd, half-witted, fatuous, inane
COLLOQ. crazy, daft, potty, gormless
Ｆ intelligent, sensible

ask v

1 ask a question
inquire, enquire, query, question, put a question to, pose, put forward, propose, want to know the answer to, interrogate, suggest, cross-examine, cross-question, poll, canvass, interview, press; *Scot* speir
OLD yearn
FORMAL posit, postulate, propound
COLLOQ. grill, give a grilling to, fire off, give someone the third degree, pump, quiz, put on the spot
2 ask for advice
request, appeal, petition, sue, plead, beg, entreat, implore, clamour, pray, crave, demand, order, bid, require, seek, approach, solicit, invite, summon, requisition; *Aust* put the hard word on
OLD beseech, bespeak
FORMAL supplicate
3 ask them to dinner
invite, have round/over, entertain

SYNONYM NUANCES

sense 1
The word **inquire** is a fairly formal but neutral term to use in situations where someone is asking for, or seeking, information. **Question** can be used of someone asking questions but, like **query**, it can also imply that they are in some doubt about information they have already received: *he queried Miller's description.* You would use the terms **pose**, **put forward** or **propose** when someone has a specific question to ask or proposal to advance. If you use **suggest**, this also implies putting some proposition before people but with, perhaps, less assurance.

The term **press** has a tone of urgency, and suggests that you are urgently entreating someone for their response, before they are really willing to give it: *when pressed upon the issue he admitted the deal.* Generally **interrogate**, **cross-examine** and **cross-question** would be used in official contexts, but they may also be used more widely to suggest any thorough and intense questioning, particularly with an air of intimidation.

Interview, while still with an element of formality and used in official contexts, is less threatening in tone. **Poll** and **canvass** are generally confined to a process of questioning a group of people for their views: *an obvious and frequently canvassed solution.*

---

askance adv

suspiciously, disapprovingly, contemptuously, scornfully, disdainfully, distrustfully, doubtfully, dubiously, mistrustfully, sceptically, indirectly, sideways, obliquely
OLD asconce

askew adv, adj

crooked(ly), lopsided(ly), sideways, oblique(ly), at an oblique angle, off-centre, out of line, asymmetrical(ly), squint, tipsy; *Scot* agley
OLD *Scot* skivie
COLLOQ. skew, skew-whiff
Ｆ straight, level

asleep *adj*
sleeping, napping, snoozing, fast asleep, sound asleep, resting, inactive, inert, unconscious, numb, dozing
FORMAL dormant, reposing
COLLOQ. flaked out, nodded off, popped off, crashed out, conked out, comatose, dead to the world, out like a light, out for the count, having forty winks, in the land of Nod
SLANG sparked out

aspect *n*
1 *many aspects of life*
angle, direction, side, facet, feature, point, factor, dimension, position, standpoint, point of view, view, outlook, light
2 *take on a more promising aspect*
appearance, look, air, manner, bearing, face, expression, countenance
3 *a house with a northern aspect*
direction, position, standpoint, point of view, view, outlook

asperity *n*
sharpness, acerbity, harshness, roughness, severity, acrimony, astringency, abrasiveness, bitterness, churlishness, crabbedness, crossness, irascibility, irritability, peevishness, sourness
FORMAL causticity
E3 mildness

aspersion
■ **cast aspersions on**
make critical comments about, criticize, slate, censure, defame, reproach, run down, slander
FORMAL disparage, denigrate, deprecate, vilify, calumniate
COLLOQ. throw/sling mud at, slur, smear, knock, haul over the coals
E3 commend, compliment

asphyxiate *v*
suffocate, choke, smother, stifle, strangle, strangulate, throttle

asphyxiation *n*
suffocation, strangulation, choking, smothering, stifling

aspiration *n*
aim, intent, purpose, endeavour, object, objective, goal, ambition, hope, dream, ideal, wish, desire, yearning, longing, craving, hankering
COLLOQ. yen

aspire *v*
aim, intend, purpose, seek, pursue, hope, dream, wish, have as an ambition/aim/goal, desire, yearn, long, crave, hanker
COLLOQ. yen

aspiring *adj*
would-be, aspirant, striving, endeavouring, ambitious, enterprising, budding, keen, eager, intending, hopeful, optimistic, wishful, longing

ass *n*
1 *ride an ass*
donkey, mule, burro, hinny, jackass, pony, neddy; *Scot* cuddy
COLLOQ. moke
2 *call someone an ass*
fool, idiot, imbecile, halfwit, oaf, innocent, buffoon, clot, gull, lemming, neddy, jackass, muggins, soft, want-wit, mooncalf, Tom-noddy; *dialect* mumchance; *Scot* gowk, sumph, coof, dottle, numpty; *N Am* cluck, dumb-cluck, yap
OLD capocchia, cony, natural, nidget, fon, fondling, *Shakesp*)lack-brain, patch, snipe, sot, wigeon
COLLOQ. blockhead, nincompoop, ninny, nitwit, nit, mug, numskull, twerp, twit, dimwit, cretin, knuckle-head, lamebrain, proper Charlie, dope, gubbins, saphead; *Scot* bampot; *N Am* lunkhead; *Aust* dill
SLANG wally, dipstick, nerd, plonker, dork, geek, git, prat, goop, berk, nerk, dickhead, airhead, dweeb, joss, nana,

nig-nog, sawney, schlemiel, turkey, yo-yo; *Irish* omadhaun; *N Am* klutz, jughead, schmo, flathead; *Aust* galah, drongo; *Aust & NZ* nong
OLD SLANG cake
Related adjective: asinine

assail *v*
1 *assailed by the newspapers/foreign army*
attack, criticize, slate, lay into, set about, set upon, run down, malign, maltreat, strike, invade, bombard
COLLOQ. tear into, slam, rubbish, badmouth, slag off
2 *assailed by doubts*
beset, plague, worry, trouble, torment, disturb, bedevil, perplex

assailant *n*
attacker, invader, opponent, adversary, enemy, aggressor, assailer, assaulter, abuser, reviler
COLLOQ. mugger

assassin *n*
murderer, killer, slayer, cut-throat, executioner, gunman
COLLOQ. hatchet man, liquidator, contract man, hit-man

assassinate *v*
murder, kill, slay, slaughter, execute, dispatch, take someone's life
COLLOQ. eliminate, liquidate, hit, bump off, do in

assassination *n*
murder, killing, slaughter, execution, termination

assault *n, v*
♦ *n*
1 ATTACK, offensive, onslaught, blitz, strike, raid, invasion, incursion, storm, storming, charge, act of aggression
2 *charged with assault*
battery, violent act, grievous bodily harm, rape, abuse, molestation
COLLOQ. GBH, mugging
♦ *v*
attack, charge, invade, strike, hit, set upon, fall on, rape, molest, interfere with, abuse, bombard
OLD smite
COLLOQ. go for, lay into, beat up, do over, mug

assay *n*
test, evaluation, assessment, analysis, check, examination, inspection, judgement
FORMAL appraisal

assemblage *n*
accumulation, collection, gathering, group, mass, multitude, rally, crowd, flock, throng

assemble *v*
1 GATHER, congregate, muster, summon(s), rally, convene, meet, join up, flock, group, collect, accumulate, amass, bring/come together, get together, rendezvous, round up, marshal, mobilize, mass
OLD relide, troop
FORMAL convoke
2 CONSTRUCT, build, put together, piece together, fit together, compose, make, connect, join, fabricate, manufacture, set up, collate
E3 1 scatter, disperse **2** dismantle

assembly *n*
1 GATHERING, rally, meeting, convention, conference, congress, council, audience, chamber, court, plenum, group, body, body of people, company, congregation, flock, crowd, multitude, throng, collection
TECHNICAL synod, chapter, synagogue, synedrion, diet, Majlis, volksraad, gorsedd, indaba, kgotla
OLD agora, consistory, divan, ecclesia, moot, folkmoot, presence, frequence, gemot, thing
FORMAL convocation, panegyry, assemblage, concourse
See also **parliament**.
2 CONSTRUCTION, building, fabrication, manufacture, putting together, piecing together

assent *v, n*

♦ *v*

agree, approve, accept, comply, allow, consent, grant, permit, sanction, submit, subscribe, yield
FORMAL accede, acquiesce, concede, concur
COLLOQ. buy, give the thumbs-up, give the go-ahead, give the green light
Ⅎ disagree

♦ *n*

agreement, approval, acceptance, capitulation, concession, consent, permission, sanction, submission, compliance
FORMAL accord, acquiescence, concurrence, approbation
COLLOQ. thumbs-up, go-ahead, green light

SYNONYM NUANCES

verb

You can use **agree** as a general term to show that two parties share the same opinion; **concur** is a more formal word to express the same. The word **approve**, however, intimates that you are in a position of some power and your decision has an important part to play: *the acquisition of the stores was approved by the shareholders*. Similarly, **consent**, **permit** and **sanction** imply that others await your authorization before proceeding, with the latter used in more official contexts. **Accept** also indicates affirmation but with an element of reluctance suggested.

If you use **allow** you go further by giving the impression of surrender: *he allowed that legislation could restrict liberty*, whereas the term **grant** implies an element of equanimity in the decision. The word **submit** could be used to imply deference to the decision of another, while **yield** gives a stronger suggestion of defeat. On the other hand, **subscribe** suggests not only agreement but also support, although it is often used in the negative: *few engineers subscribe to this theory*.

Meanwhile, **accede**, **acquiesce**, **comply** and **concede** all return to the idea of reluctance to assent to something, or succumbing to the will of another.

assert *v*

1 *assert a fact*

declare, state, pronounce, profess, affirm, confirm, attest, argue, swear, testify to
FORMAL predicate

2 *assert your rights*

maintain, insist on, establish, stress, protest, defend, vindicate, uphold, claim, stand up for, contend, pose, lay down
OLD avouch
COLLOQ. crack the whip
Ⅎ 1 deny, refute

■ **assert yourself**

behave confidently, put yourself forward, make your presence felt, make your voice heard, make people sit up and take notice, make people sit up and listen

assertion *n*

affirmation, attestation, word, allegation, claim, contention, insistence, vindication, declaration, profession, statement, pronouncement; *Scot* threap
FORMAL averment, avowal, predication, constatation
Ⅎ denial

assertive *adj*

bold, confident, self-confident, self-assured, sure of yourself, positive, forward, insistent, emphatic, forceful, firm, decided, strong-willed, determined, dogmatic, opinionated, presumptuous, assuming, overbearing, domineering, dominant, aggressive, pushy
COLLOQ. not backward in coming forward; *N Am* feeling your oats
Ⅎ timid, diffident

SYNONYM NUANCES

Bold can be used to suggest assertiveness but is also imbued with a hint of risk-taking: *his bold, almost visionary, ideas*. **Confident**, however, along with **self-confident** and **self-assured**, is widely used to describe someone who is sure of their capabilities, as does **sure of yourself**, although this also hints at cockiness. The word **positive** can be generally used to describe someone who exhibits certainty, but if their certainty progresses to impudence, you could use the term **forward**.

Insistent, **emphatic** or **forceful** are more typically used to describe the way someone imparts their ideas and opinions, if they display no doubts that they are correct. The words **firm**, **decided**, **strong-willed** and **determined** are used slightly differently, usually to describe someone who is convinced of their opinions and will not be moved from them, rather than someone who wants to inflict them on others. **Dogmatic** and **opinionated** again imply certainty of opinion, but with the inference that there is an unreasonable element to their assertions. You would generally use the terms **presumptuous** and **assuming** when you wish to suggest that someone's certainty has to do with their expectations of others: *isn't it rather presumptuous to decide what he needs?*

On the other hand, to use the descriptions **overbearing**, **domineering** or **dominant** would suggest that someone uses the sheer force of their personality, to get the consensus they seek: *she was intimidated by his overbearing attitude*. **Aggressive**, meanwhile, although similar, goes further by implying that a more menacing approach could be deployed.

assertively *adv*

boldly, confidently, self-confidently, positively, insistently, firmly, forcefully, presumptuously, dominantly, aggressively
Ⅎ timidly

assess *v*

1 *assess a situation*

evaluate, gauge, estimate, appraise, review, judge, consider, weigh, size up, sum up
OLD cense
COLLOQ. check out

2 *assess the value of something*

compute, calculate, determine, estimate, fix, value, rate, tax, levy, impose, demand, teind; *Scot* stent
OLD assize, affeer

assessment *n*

1 *the assessment of a situation*

evaluation, estimation, appraisal, review, testing, judgement, consideration, opinion
COLLOQ. recce

2 *a tax assessment*

levy, computation, valuation, rate, toll, tariff, imposition, demand

assessor *n*

1 VALUER, estimator, measurer, gauger, valuator, appraiser

2 JUDGE, reviewer, examiner, inspector, arbitrator, arbiter, adjudicator, umpire, referee, estimator, recorder, expert, adviser, consultant, counsellor

asset *n*

1 *an asset to the school*

strength, strong point, resource, virtue, benefit, advantage, blessing, boon, help, aid, liability
COLLOQ. plus, plus point

2 *the assets of a company*

estate, property, possessions, goods, holdings, securities, money, wealth, capital, funds, reserves, savings, valuables, resources, means

asseverate v
declare, affirm, assert, claim, profess,
maintain, state, confirm
FORMAL aver, avow, attest

assiduity n
diligence, industry, industriousness,
meticulousness, hard work, conscientiousness, dedication,
devotion, constancy, perseverance, persistence,
indefatigability
FORMAL sedulity
ᴇᴈ laziness

assiduous adj
industrious, diligent, hard-working, careful, meticulous,
conscientious, constant, dedicated, devoted, attentive,
persevering, persistent, steady, studious, thorough,
unflagging, indefatigable, untiring
FORMAL sedulous
ᴇᴈ negligent

assign v
1 ALLOCATE, grant, give, dispense, distribute,
allot, hive off
OLD aret; (Shakesp) sort
FORMAL apportion
2 *a social worker is assigned to each family*
detail, delegate, name, nominate, designate, appoint,
choose, select, commission, install, determine, set, fix,
specify, stipulate, range, rank, station
FORMAL consign, adjudge
3 ATTRIBUTE, ascribe, put down
FORMAL accredit, impute, arrogate
COLLOQ. chalk up to
4 TRANSFER, grant, make over, hand over, consign,
transmit
TECHNICAL convey

assignation n
secret meeting, appointment, arrangement, date,
engagement, rendezvous
OLD tryst

assignment n
1 *written assignments*
task, project, job, position, post, duty, responsibility,
obligation, commission, errand, charge
2 *his assignment to the job*
appointment, delegation, designation, nomination,
selection, allocation, consignment, grant, distribution
3 TRANSFER, grant, consignment
TECHNICAL conveyance, disposition

assimilate v
1 *assimilate new ideas*
ABSORB, take in, pick up, incorporate, imbibe, internalize,
learn, grasp
2 INTEGRATE, absorb, blend, mix, mingle, unite, accustom,
adapt, adjust, acclimatize
FORMAL accommodate
ᴇᴈ 1, 2 reject

assimilation n
1 INTEGRATION, blending, mixing in, adaptation,
adjustment, acclimatization
FORMAL accommodation
2 ABSORPTION, learning, grasping, taking in, internalization,
incorporation
TECHNICAL osmosis, resorption

assist v
1 *assist with someone's work/expenses*
help, aid, give/lend a hand, lend a helping hand, abet,
rally round, co-operate, collaborate, back (up), second,
support, reinforce, sustain, relieve
FORMAL succour
COLLOQ. do your bit, give a leg up to, pitch in
2 *assist in the operation of a task*
facilitate, make easier, expedite, benefit, encourage, serve,
aid, enable, further, advance
ᴇᴈ 1 hinder 2 thwart

assistance n
help, aid, co-operation, collaboration,
backing, support, reinforcement, relief, benefit, service,
boost, furtherance
COLLOQ. a helping hand, a leg up
FORMAL succour
ᴇᴈ hindrance, resistance

assistant n
1 DEPUTY, subordinate, right-hand man, auxiliary,
ancillary, backer, second, second-in-command,
supporter, driving force
2 *a personal assistant*
helper, aide, accomplice, accessory, abettor,
collaborator, colleague, partner, ally, confederate,
associate, acolyte
TECHNICAL amanuensis, suffragan
3 *a shop assistant*
salesperson, salesman, saleswoman, checkout person;
N Am sales clerk

associate v, n
♦ v
1 CONNECT, link, think of together, couple,
pair, identify
OLD mell
FORMAL correlate, consociate
COLLOQ. speak of in the same breath,
go hand in hand
2 *associate with bad company*
socialize, mingle, mix, keep company, fraternize, haunt,
be involved
FORMAL consort
COLLOQ. hang around/about, pal, hobnob,
rub shoulders
3 AFFILIATE, confederate, ally, league, join, amalgamate,
combine, unite, link, connect, relate, couple,
attach, band together, syndicate, yoke
♦ n
partner, ally, confederate, affiliate, collaborator,
co-worker, mate, colleague, peer, compeer, fellow,
comrade, companion, friend, assistant, helper, follower,
confrère, yokefellow
COLLOQ. sidekick, pal, crony

associated adj
1 CONNECTED, linked, coupled, related,
corresponding, similar, alike
FORMAL correlated
2 AFFILIATED, allied, amalgamated, confederated,
combined, linked, in league, in partnership, related,
syndicated

association n
1 ORGANIZATION, corporation, company,
partnership, league, alliance, coalition, confederation,
confederacy, federation, affiliation, consortium, cartel,
syndicate, union, society, club, fraternity,
fellowship, guild, clique, group, band
FORMAL sodality
2 BOND, tie, connection, link,
correlation, relation, relationship, interrelation,
involvement, intimacy, friendship, companionship,
familiarity, identification

assorted adj
miscellaneous, mixed, varied, different,
differing, diverse, sundry, motley, various, several,
manifold, sortable
OLD divers, farraginous
FORMAL variegated, heterogeneous, multifarious

assortment n
miscellany, medley, potpourri, jumble, mix, mixture,
variety, diversity, collection, selection, choice,
arrangement, group(ing), lot, bunch, salmagundi, olla-
podrida, smörgåsbord, farrago
FORMAL array

assuage *v*
1 *assuage grief/pain*
relieve, ease, lessen, reduce, soften, allay, alleviate, calm, lighten, lower, lull, mitigate, moderate, soothe, mollify, pacify, palliate
2 *assuage your thirst*
alleviate, quench, satisfy, appease
FORMAL slake
E3 1 exacerbate, worsen

assume *v*
1 PRESUME, accept, take for granted, take as read, expect, understand, deduce, infer, posit, guess, suppose, presuppose, think, believe, imagine, fancy
FORMAL surmise, postulate
COLLOQ. take it ..., take someone's word for it
2 AFFECT, take on, feign, counterfeit, simulate, put on, pretend
3 *assume great importance*
take on, adopt, come to have, acquire
4 *assume command*
undertake, adopt, enter upon, take upon yourself, accept, bear, shoulder, embrace, seize, arrogate, commandeer, appropriate, usurp, pre-empt, take over

---

SYNONYM NUANCES

sense 1
You could use **presume** to imply that a supposition has been formed without any proof: *one man missing, presumed dead*. Similarly the terms **accept**, **take for granted**, **take as read** and **expect** all suggest an element of presumption but with a more passive or unconscious aspect: *she had always taken for granted that unemployment was an evil*.

However, if you use the terms **understand**, **deduce** and **infer** you are suggesting that any assumptions made have been reached by assessment of facts: *the occupational structure of the town can be deduced from the registers*. The opposite may be said of **guess** and **believe**, which imply conjecture or instinct rather than reason; similarly **imagine** and **fancy** eschew reason completely in favour of imagination: *sometimes he fancied a ghost in the room*.

When you use **suppose** you may suggest that something has been assumed provisionally, for argument's sake whilst **presuppose**, although similar in meaning, tends to be used in philosophical or theoretical contexts: *the principle of non-discrimination presupposed the existence of the concept of nationality*.

---

assumed *adj*
false, bogus, counterfeit, fake, sham, affected, feigned, simulated, pretended, made-up, fictitious, hypothetical
FORMAL supposititious, putative, pseudonymous
COLLOQ. phoney
E3 true, real, actual

assumption *n*
1 *make an assumption*
presumption, surmise, inference, conclusion, supposition, presupposition, guess, conjecture, theory, hypothesis, premise, postulate, idea, notion, axiom, belief, expectation, fancy
FORMAL postulation
2 *her assumption of power*
undertaking, adoption, taking upon yourself, embarkation, acceptance, shouldering, embrace, seizure, commandeering, takeover
FORMAL arrogation, appropriation, usurpation, pre-emption

assurance *n*
1 GUARANTEE, pledge, promise, security, vow, declaration, affirmation, assertion, word, certainty, undertaking, oath
OLD (*Shakesp*) surance
FORMAL positivism

2 CONFIDENCE, self-confidence, self-assurance, assuredness, aplomb, boldness, self-reliance, belief in yourself, audacity, courage, nerve, conviction, sureness, certainty, gall
COLLOQ. unflappability
E3 2 shyness, doubt, uncertainty

assure *v*
1 *assured me he would be safe*
convince, persuade, encourage, hearten, reassure, soothe, comfort, tell
OLD resolve
2 *success is assured*
guarantee, warrant, pledge, promise, seal, secure, ensure, confirm, affirm, vow, swear, certify; *Scot* hight
OLD avouch
FORMAL attest

assured *adj*
1 SURE, certain, indisputable, irrefutable, confirmed, promised, positive, definite, settled, fixed, ensured, guaranteed, secure
COLLOQ. cut and dried
2 SELF-ASSURED, confident, calm, self-confident, self-possessed, sure of yourself, bold, audacious, assertive
E3 1 uncertain **2** shy, bashful

assuredly *adv*
certainly, definitely, surely, indisputably, without doubt, without question, unquestionably
OLD (*Shakesp & Spenser*) perdie

astonish *v*
surprise, startle, amaze, astound, stun, stupefy, daze, stagger, dumbfound, take aback, take your breath away, shock, confound, bewilder
OLD stony
COLLOQ. floor, flabbergast, flummox, bowl over, gobsmack, blow your mind, knock for six, wow, make someone's hair stand on end, set back on your heels

astonished *adj*
surprised, startled, amazed, astounded, stunned, dazed, staggered, dumbfounded, taken aback, shocked, confounded, bewildered, open-eyed, wide-eyed
COLLOQ. lost for words, knocked for six, bowled over, flabbergasted, gobsmacked, thunderstruck

astonishing *adj*
surprising, startling, amazing, astounding, stunning, breathtaking, impressive, striking, staggering, shocking, bewildering
COLLOQ. mind-boggling

astonishment *n*
surprise, amazement, shock, disbelief, dismay, consternation, confusion, bewilderment, wonder
FORMAL stupefaction, wonderment

astound *v*
surprise, startle, amaze, astonish, stun, take your breath away, stupefy, overwhelm, shock, bewilder
COLLOQ. knock for six, floor, flummox, bowl over

astounding *adj*
surprising, startling, amazing, astonishing, stunning, breathtaking, stupefying, overwhelming, staggering, shocking, bewildering

astray *adv*
1 *lead someone astray*
into bad/foolish/wrong behaviour, off the straight and narrow
COLLOQ. off the rails
2 ADRIFT, off course, lost, missing, miss, amiss, wrong, awry, off the mark
OLD abroad, agate; (*Spenser*) miswandred

astringent *adj*
1 *an astringent liquid*
acerbic, acid, caustic
TECHNICAL styptic

2 *astringent criticism*
caustic, biting, trenchant, scathing, hard, harsh, critical, severe, stern
FORMAL mordant
F3 1, 2 bland

astronaut *n*
spaceman, spacewoman, space traveller, cosmonaut, taikonaut

astronomical *adj*
1 *the cost is astronomical*
enormous, huge, immense, vast, substantial, considerable, gigantic, massive, colossal, mammoth, tremendous, immeasurable, infinite
COLLOQ. whopping, thumping
2 *astronomical observations*
cosmological, cosmic, celestial, heavenly, stellar, interstellar, planetary

astute *adj*
shrewd, prudent, wise, canny, knowing, intelligent, sharp, sharp-witted, penetrating, keen, perceptive, discerning, subtle, clever, crafty, cunning, cute, sly, wily
FORMAL perspicacious, sagacious
SLANG wide
F3 stupid, slow

astutely *adv*
shrewdly, wisely, intelligently, keenly, sharp-wittedly, perceptively, craftily

asunder *adv*
in two, in pieces, to pieces, up

asylum *n*
1 *seek political asylum*
haven, sanctuary, refuge, shelter, retreat, place of safety
OLD frithsoken, grith
COLLOQ. port in a storm
2 *an asylum for the mentally ill*
mental hospital, psychiatric hospital, institution, Magdalen
OLD bedlam; (*Shakesp*) dark-house
SLANG funny farm, loony bin, bin, madhouse, nuthouse

asymmetrical *adj*
unsymmetrical, unbalanced, uneven, lopsided, crooked, awry, unequal, disproportionate, irregular, distorted, malformed
TECHNICAL anaxial
F3 symmetrical

asymmetry *n*
imbalance, unevenness, unsymmetry, crookedness, lopsidedness, inequality, disproportionateness, irregularity, distortion, malformation
F3 symmetry

atheism *n*
unbelief, non-belief, disbelief, scepticism, irreligion, ungodliness, godlessness, impiety, infidelity, paganism, heathenism, freethinking, rationalism
TECHNICAL nihilism

atheist *n*
unbeliever, non-believer, humanist, rationalist, disbeliever, sceptic, infidel, heretic, pagan, heathen, freethinker
TECHNICAL nihilist
FORMAL nullifidian

athlete *n*
sportsman, sportswoman, runner, gymnast, competitor, contestant, contender, player

athletic *adj*
1 *an athletic person*
fit, energetic, vigorous, active, sporty, muscular, muscly, sinewy, brawny, strapping, robust, sturdy, strong, powerful, well-knit, well-proportioned, wiry

2 *athletic events*
sports, sporting, gymnastic, games
F3 1 puny

Athletic events include:

TRACK EVENTS:	FIELD EVENTS:	race walking
sprint (100m, 200m and 400m)	high jump	COMBINED EVENTS:
middle-distance running (800m and 1500m)	long jump	biathlon
	triple jump	triathlon
	pole vault	pentathlon
long-distance running (3000m, 5000m and 10000m)	discus	heptathlon
	hammer	decathlon
	javelin	MISCELLANEOUS:
	shot put	cross-country running
hurdles	ROAD EVENTS:	
relay	half-marathon	
steeplechase	marathon	

athletics *n*
sports, games, matches, races, track events, field events, exercises, gymnastics
TECHNICAL aerobics, callisthenics

atmosphere *n*
1 AIR, sky, aerospace, heavens, ether
OLD firmament, empyrean, welkin
FORMAL vault of heaven
Related adjective: epedaphic
2 AMBIENCE, environment, surroundings, setting, milieu, background, air, aura, feel, feeling, mood, climate, spirit, tone, tenor, character, quality, flavour
COLLOQ. vibes

atom *n*
molecule, particle, bit, morsel, crumb, fragment, grain, spot, speck, mite, shred, scrap, hint, trace, scintilla, jot, iota, whit

Subatomic particles include:

anti-neutrino	kaon	pion
anti-neutron	lambda particle	positron
anti-proton	lepton	proton
baryon	meson (X particle)	psi particle
B-meson	muon	quark
boson	neutrino	sigma particle
electron	neutron	tau
gluon	omega particle	W particle
hadron	photon	Z particle

atone *v*
make amends, pay for, remedy, indemnify, reconcile, repent, compensate, recompense, make up for, make right, make good, make reparation, offset, redeem, redress, appease, satisfy, propitiate, expiate
OLD aby

atonement *n*
amends, reparation, repayment, reimbursement, ransom, redemption, requital, restitution, restoration, satisfaction, compensation, indemnity, payment, penance, recompense, redress, appeasement, propitiation, expiation
TECHNICAL acceptilation
COLLOQ. eye for an eye

atrocious *adj*
1 *atrocious behaviour*
shocking, appalling, abominable, dreadful, terrible, horrible, horrendous, hideous, ghastly, grievous, diabolical, savage, vicious, monstrous, fiendish, wicked, brutal, cruel, ruthless, merciless
FORMAL heinous, nefarious, flagitious
2 *atrocious weather*
dreadful, terrible, appalling, awful, frightful, disgusting
F3 1 admirable **2** fine

atrociously *adv*
shockingly, appallingly, abominably, dreadfully, terribly, horribly, monstrously, fiendishly, wickedly, brutally, cruelly, ruthlessly
FORMAL heinously

atrocity *n*
outrage, abomination, enormity, horror, monstrosity, savagery, barbarity, brutality, cruelty, viciousness, evil, villainy, wickedness, violation, vileness, hideousness, atrociousness
FORMAL heinousness, flagitiousness

atrophy *n, v*
♦ *n*
withering, shrivelling, wasting (away), emaciation, decay, decline, degeneration, deterioration, diminution, involution
TECHNICAL marasmus, tabefaction, amyotrophy
♦ *v*
wither, shrivel, waste (away), emaciate, decay, decline, degenerate, deteriorate, diminish, dwindle, fade, shrink
TECHNICAL tabefy

attach *v*
1 *attach a label*
affix, stick, adhere, fasten, fix, secure, tie, bind, pin, nail, weld, join, unite, connect, link, couple, add (on), annex, make secure, tack, harness
OLD adhibit
2 *attach yourself to a group*
join, affiliate with, associate with, combine with, align with, ally, unite
COLLOQ. latch onto
3 ASCRIBE, attribute, assign, put, place, lay, associate, relate to, belong
FORMAL impute
4 *a centre attached to the university*
link, affiliate, associate, connect, assign, allocate, detail, send, second
🔁 **1** detach, unfasten

attached *adj*
1 *very attached to her family*
affectionate, fond, loving, tender, liking, friendly, devoted
2 *Is she attached?*
married, engaged, spoken for, in a relationship, involved with someone
FORMAL affianced
COLLOQ. going steady
🔁 **1** unloving, indifferent **2** single, unattached, on your own

attachment *n*
1 ACCESSORY, fitting, fixture, fitment, extension, extra, supplement, supplementary part, addition, adjunct, codicil
FORMAL appendage, appurtenance, accoutrement
2 FONDNESS, affection, tenderness, love, liking, partiality, loyalty, devotion, friendship, affinity, attraction, bond, tie, link, closeness

attack *v, n*
♦ *v*
1 *attack a country/person*
raid, strike, storm, rush, charge, assail, assault, besiege, set about, set upon, fall on, lay into, go for, fly at, weight into, pounce on, ambush, sandbag
OLD aggress
COLLOQ. beat up, do over, mug, make a dead set at, jump, duff up, light into, get stuck into, leave for dead
SLANG knock into the middle of next week, have your guts for garters, take to the cleaners
2 CRITICIZE, find fault with, slate, censure, blame, denounce, revile, malign, abuse, run down, reprove, rebuke
FORMAL berate, impugn, fulminate against, vilify, inveigh, lampoon, oppugn, calumniate, decry
COLLOQ. slam, knock, blast, rubbish, clobber, pan, tear/pull to pieces, tear to shreds, pick holes in, pull apart, have a go at, bitch about

SLANG slag off; *Aust & NZ* chuck off at
3 *the disease attacks the nerves*
destroy, affect, infect, strike at
4 *attack a task*
tackle, deal with, address, attend to, focus on, begin, start, get started on, commence, set about, embark on, undertake, apply yourself to
🔁 **1** defend, protect
♦ *n*
1 OFFENSIVE, blitz, bombardment, air strike, invasion, incursion, foray, raid, strike, charge, storming, rush, onslaught, assault, sortie, push, sally, act of aggression, battery, *coup de main*, strafe
OLD (*Spenser*) bodrag
FORMAL irruption
2 *an attack on his reputation*
criticism, censure, abuse, broadside, snipe
FORMAL invective, impugnment, revilement, vilification
COLLOQ. slating, slamming, roasting, hatchet job, knocking, flak
3 SEIZURE, fit, convulsion, bout, paroxysm, spasm, stroke
TECHNICAL ictus
OLD *dialect* brash
FORMAL access

SYNONYM NUANCES

noun sense 1
The word **offensive** is generally used to talk about the course of action taken by an attacking party, whereas **blitz** has the more specific element of an attack or bombing from the air, although nowadays it may also be used of any overwhelming attack: *the book was launched with a marketing blitz*. Likewise the term **bombardment** has come to suggest any succession of blows: *the artillery bombardment*; *the constant press bombardment*.

Invasion, on the other hand, refers to an attack that makes inroads into another's territory; **incursion**, while similar, often suggests a degree of suddenness: *commercial groups are paying dearly for their rash incursion into property*. **Foray** and **raid** are similar manoeuvres implying a sudden swift inroad, generally undertaken for assault or seizure, whilst a **strike** is most commonly used of an attack by aircraft. The terms **charge**, **storming**, **rush**, and **onslaught** all suggest a swift, sometimes violent, impetuous forward movement, though onslaught is nowadays often used figuratively; *the storming of the Golden Temple*; *the cultural onslaught*. **Assault** similarly implies a sudden violent attack and it too has a spreading figurative usage: *Leeds are about to mount an assault on the European Cup*. **Sortie** and **sally** both suggest a sudden rush forward by a besieged party, whilst **push** is more generally connected with a concentrated, ongoing offensive: *the three main parties are prepared for a big push over the last weekend of the campaign*.

Generally you would use **act of aggression** to suggest an initial act of hostility, but **battery** would be more likely used (especially by legal practitioners) to describe a violent beating. **Strafe** was originally used of a machine-gun attack from the air, though nowadays the origin of the attack is less specific. If the attackers burst in they could be accused of **irruption**.

---

attacker *n*
assailant, aggressor, invader, raider, assaulter, striker, critic, detractor, reviler, abuser, persecutor
COLLOQ. mugger
🔁 defender, supporter

attain *v*
accomplish, achieve, fulfil, complete, effect, realize, earn, reach, touch, arrive at, hit, grasp, find, get, acquire, obtain, procure, secure, gain, win, net

attainable *adj*
achievable, feasible, viable, manageable, obtainable, possible, potential, practicable, probable, reachable, realistic, within reach, at hand, accessible, imaginable, conceivable
COLLOQ. doable
E∃ unattainable

attainment *n*
1 *artistic attainments*
accomplishment, achievement, feat, success, ability, capability, competence, proficiency, skill, art, talent, gift, aptitude, facility
2 *the attainment of his ambitions*
fulfilment, completion, consummation, realization, accomplishment, mastery
FORMAL procurement, acquirement

attempt *v, n*
♦ *v*
try, have a try, endeavour, aspire, set out, seek, strive, undertake, tackle, venture, aim, experiment, see if you can do, try your hand; *Scot* mint
OLD fand
FORMAL essay
COLLOQ. have a go/shot/crack/stab, give it a go/try/whirl, try your hand at, do your level best, bend over backwards, give it your best shot
♦ *n*
try, endeavour, go, push, effort, struggle, bid, undertaking, venture, trial, experiment, foray, shy, whack; *Scot* mint
FORMAL essay
COLLOQ. shot, stab, bash, crack; *Aust & NZ* burl

attend *v*
1 *attend a meeting*
be present at, take part in, be here, be there, go/come along, appear, put in/make an appearance at, go to, frequent, visit
COLLOQ. turn up, show (up)
2 PAY ATTENTION, concentrate, listen, hear, heed, mind, mark, watch, note, notice, take note/notice, follow, observe
3 ESCORT, chaperon(e), accompany, usher, follow, guard, squire
4 *attend the sick*
look after, take care of, care for, nurse, tend, minister to, help, serve, wait upon
■ **attend to**
deal with, see to, take care of, look after, cope with, manage, handle, process, direct, control, oversee, supervise, follow up (on), heed

attendance *n*
presence, appearance, appearing, audience, house, crowd, gate, turnout; *Aust* roll-up
COLLOQ. showing (up)

attendant *n, adj*
♦ *n*
assistant, aide, helper, auxiliary, steward, waiter, waitress, servant, page, retainer, guide, marshal, usher, escort, companion, follower, guard, custodian, chaperon(e)
♦ *adj*
accompanying, attached, associated, related, incidental, resultant, consequent, subsequent
FORMAL concomitant

attention *n*
1 *let your attention wander*
alertness, vigilance, concentration, heed, notice, observation, regard, mind, mindfulness, awareness, recognition, thought, focus of your thoughts, contemplation, consideration, preoccupation
FORMAL advertence, advertency
2 *attract great public attention*
notice, observation, regard, awareness, recognition, scrutiny, thought, contemplation, consideration, heed, concern
COLLOQ. limelight, high profile

3 *receive medical attention*
care, treatment, therapy, help, service
4 *flattered by his attentions*
respect, courtesy, politeness, civility, compliments, gallantry
E∃ 1 inattention, disregard, daydreaming **2** inattention, disregard **3** neglect
■ **pay attention to**
concentrate on, focus your mind/thoughts on, focus on, heed, devote your attention to, take notice, listen/watch carefully

> **QUOTATIONS**
> Let us fix our attention out of ourselves
> DAVID HUME, *A Treatise of Human Nature*

attentive *adj*
1 ALERT, awake, vigilant, aware, watchful, watching, observant, noticing, concentrating, heedful, mindful, careful, conscientious, on the qui vive, listening
OLD whist
FORMAL advertent
COLLOQ. all ears, on the ball
2 CONSIDERATE, thoughtful, kind, obliging, accommodating, civil, polite, courteous, devoted, gracious, conscientious, chivalrous, gallant, punctilious
E∃ 1 inattentive, heedless **2** inconsiderate

attentively *adv*
watchfully, observantly, mindfully, carefully, conscientiously
E∃ inattentively

attenuated *adj*
thin, narrow, slender, slim, fine, slight, skinny, bony, scraggy, scrawny
E∃ broad, fat

attest *v*
prove, confirm, corroborate, demonstrate, show, display, manifest, endorse, certify, affirm, assert, declare, vouch for, bear witness to, verify
FORMAL adjure, aver, asseverate, evince, evidence

attic *n*
loft, garret, mansard
OLD COLLOQ. sky parlour

attire *n*
dress, clothes, clothing, wear, garments, outfit, garb, costume, finery
OLD habiliments
FORMAL habit, apparel, accoutrements
COLLOQ. gear, togs, clobber, rig-out

attired *adj*
clothed, dressed, adorned, turned out
FORMAL arrayed, habilitated
COLLOQ. decked out, rigged out

attitude *n*
1 OPINION, feeling, disposition, sèntiment, mood, aspect, manner, position, point of view, view, viewpoint, approach, outlook, perspective, way of thinking, mentality, mindset, world-view, *Weltanschauung, Anschauung*
2 POSTURE, bearing, pose, stance, stand
FORMAL deportment, carriage

attorney *n*
lawyer, solicitor, barrister, advocate, counsel, QC, legal adviser, legal representative
COLLOQ. brief

attract *v*
pull, draw, lure, allure, entice, seduce, tempt, invite, induce, incline, appeal to, bring in, pull in, hook, rivet, magnetize, interest, engage, fascinate, enchant, charm, bewitch, captivate, excite
COLLOQ. tickle someone's fancy
E∃ repel, disgust

attraction n

1 *the attraction of an exotic lifestyle*
pull, draw, magnetism, lure, allure, bait, hook, enticement, inducement, seduction, temptation, invitation, appeal, affinity, interest, fascination, enchantment, charm, glamour, captivation

2 *tourist attractions*
sight, feature, building, activity, entertainment, diversion
E3 **1** repulsion

attractive adj

1 *an attractive person*
pretty, fair, fetching, good-looking, handsome, beautiful, gorgeous, striking, stunning, glamorous, elegant, lovely, pleasant, charismatic, picturesque, photogenic, personable, pleasing, cute, engaging, prepossessing, winsome, luscious, nubile, nymphic, desirable, sexy; *Scot* bonny
OLD comely, dashing
COLLOQ. all right, terrific, dishy, fanciable, hunky, hot stuff, knockout; *N Am* foxy
OLD COLLOQ. taky
SLANG beddable; *N Am* bad

2 *an attractive suggestion*
agreeable, appealing, winsome, winning, enticing, seductive, tempting, inviting, interesting, pleasant, toothsome, engaging, fascinating, charming, captivating, irresistible, catchy, magnetic

---

SYNONYM NUANCES

sense 1
The words **pretty** and **fair** are rather mild terms of praise generally used of women and girls, suggesting an element of daintiness. **Fetching** is more likely to be used of a garment or outfit, though it is possible for a person to look fetching: *a very fetching hat; she looked fetching in her uniform.*

Good-looking, **handsome** and **beautiful** are stronger adjectives, and all imply being blessed with regular facial features — **handsome** is generally used of men, although distinguished older women can also be described thus; similarly **beautiful**, although traditionally associated with women, may now sometimes be used to describe an attractive man.

Gorgeous, **striking** and **stunning** suggest attractiveness that is impossible to miss; **glamorous** has the added implication that the appeal is aided by clothes or artificial enhancements: *he seemed less glamorous out of uniform.* **Elegant**, on the other hand, conveys dignity combined with good taste.

The words **winsome**, **luscious**, **nubile** and **nymphic** are used specifically of sexually appealing females, but **desirable** and **sexy** are commonly used of either sex. The words **picturesque** and **photogenic** have more specific usages — the first to describe an exceedingly attractive place, the latter generally used of someone who is bound to photograph well: *the picturesque little French town; her photogenic face.*

Cute, on the other hand, is used of attractiveness that appeals to protective or nurturing instincts: *cute puppy dogs.* **Lovely, pleasant**, **personable**, **pleasing** and **engaging** are fairly restrained compliments, referring to attractive personal rather than physical qualities: *the chaplain was a pleasant gentleman.* The word **charismatic**, however, conjures up someone with a strong, indefinable quality that draws people: *a fiery, charismatic man.* The term **prepossessing**, however, is generally used in the negative, often implying a degree of distaste: *none of them were even slightly prepossessing.*

---

attribute v, n

♦ v
ascribe, credit, assign, put down, blame, charge, refer, apply
FORMAL accredit, impute

♦ n
property, quality, virtue, point, aspect, facet, feature, trait, characteristic, idiosyncrasy, peculiarity, quirk, note, mark, side, streak, sign, indicator, symbol

attrition n

1 FRICTION, abrasion, rubbing, scraping, chafing, erosion
FORMAL detrition

2 *a war of attrition*
wearing away, wearing down, weakening, grinding, harassment
FORMAL attenuation

attuned adj
acclimatized, assimilated, accustomed, familiarized, adapted, adjusted, regulated, co-ordinated, harmonized, set, tuned

atypical adj
uncharacteristic, unusual, exceptional, untypical, aberrant, abnormal, uncommon, anomalous, deviant, divergent, unconventional, eccentric, extraordinary, freakish
E3 typical

auburn adj
reddish-brown, dark-red, chestnut, tawny, russet, copper, rust, henna, Titian

audacious adj
adventurous, daring, enterprising, courageous, rash, reckless, risky, assuming, assured, unabashed, bold, brave, fearless, intrepid, dauntless, valiant, plucky, devil-may-care, disrespectful, impertinent, forward, presumptuous, impudent, insolent, cheeky, pert, brazen, rude, shameless
FORMAL venturesome
COLLOQ. fresh, lippy; *N Am* nervy
E3 cautious, reserved, timid

audacity n
adventurousness, daring, enterprise, courage, rashness, recklessness, risk, boldness, bravery, fearlessness, intrepidity, dauntlessness, valour, pluck, disrespectfulness, impertinence, forwardness, presumption, impudence, insolence, cheek, pertness, brazenness, effrontery, defiance, rudeness, shamelessness
COLLOQ. bottle, guts, grit
E3 caution, reserve, timidity

audible adj
clear, distinct, recognizable, perceptible, discernible, detectable, appreciable, hearable, heard
E3 inaudible, silent, unclear

audience n

1 *members of the audience*
spectators, onlookers, house, auditorium, listeners, viewers, crowd, turnout, gathering, assembly, congregation, fans, devotees, followers, regulars, following, patrons, public, ratings
COLLOQ. *Brit & Aust* bums on seats

2 MEETING, interview, hearing, consultation, discussion, reception, conference

audit n, v

♦ n
examination, inspection, check, verification, investigation, scrutiny, analysis, review, survey, statement, balancing

♦ v
examine, inspect, check, verify, investigate, scrutinize, analyse, review, go over, go through, work through, balance

auditorium n
concert hall, hall, chamber, conference hall, theatre, playhouse, opera house, assembly room

au fait adj
up to date, familiar, aware, abreast, in touch, knowledgeable, versed, conversant, *au courant*

augment *v*
add to, amplify, boost, enlarge, build up,
put on, expand, extend, grow, increase, make greater,
magnify, multiply, raise, inflate, enhance, heighten,
intensify, reinforce, strengthen, swell
OLD (*Shakesp*) eche
E₃ decrease

augmentation *n*
enlargement, increase, build-up, amplification,
expansion, extension, growth, strengthening,
magnification, intensification, boost
E₃ decrease

augur *v*
herald, prophesy, foretell, predict, promise,
be a sign of, signify; *Scot* spae
OLD betoken
FORMAL forebode, harbinger, bode, presage, portend

augury *n*
omen, herald, prophecy, prediction, foreboding,
prognostication, forerunner, forewarning, token, warning,
portent, promise, sign
TECHNICAL ornithoscopy
OLD sooth
FORMAL harbinger, haruspication, prodrome

august *adj*
dignified, exalted, distinguished, respected, solemn, noble,
impressive, imposing, glorious, grand, lofty, magnificent,
majestic, stately, awe-inspiring

aura *n*
air, ambience, atmosphere, mood, quality, emanation,
feel, feeling, hint, suggestion, vibrations
FORMAL nimbus
COLLOQ. vibes

auspices
■ **under the auspices of**
under the aegis of, under the authority of, with the
patronage/sponsorship of, with the backing/support/
approval of, under the supervision/control/influence/
guidance of, in the charge/care of

auspicious *adj*
favourable, encouraging, cheerful, bright, rosy, promising,
hopeful, optimistic, fortunate, lucky, opportune, timely,
happy, prosperous
FORMAL propitious, felicitous
E₃ unfavourable, inauspicious, ominous

austere *adj*
1 STARK, bleak, plain, simple, basic, functional, unadorned,
unornamented, grim, forbidding, sombre
2 SEVERE, stern, strict, cold, formal, distant, rigid, rigorous,
stringent, exacting, hard, harsh, spartan, grave, serious,
solemn, sober, abstemious, astringent, killjoy, unfeeling,
unbending, inflexible, self-denying, restrained, economical,
frugal, ascetic, self-disciplined, stoic, Dantean, puritanical,
Waldensian, chaste
OLD stoor
FORMAL self-abnegating
E₃ 1 ornate, elaborate **2** genial

austerity *n*
plainness, simplicity, severity, coldness, formality,
hardness, harshness, solemnity, abstemiousness,
abstinence, economy, asceticism, self-denial, self-
discipline, inflexibility, rigour, puritanism
E₃ elaborateness, extravagance, materialism

authentic *adj*
1 *an authentic signature*
genuine, real, actual, certain, attested,
undisputed, bona fide, lawful, legal, legitimate, valid,
sterling, *echt*
COLLOQ. the real thing, the genuine article, the real
McCoy
2 *an authentic description*
accurate, factual, true, true-to-life, historical, correct,
faithful, reliable, dependable, trustworthy, honest, credible

COLLOQ. kosher
E₃ 1 false, fake, counterfeit, spurious **2** inaccurate,
unfaithful

authentically *adv*
1 GENUINELY, really, actually, legitimately, lawfully
2 ACCURATELY, faithfully, reliably, historically, credibly
E₃ 1 falsely **2** inaccurately

authenticate *v*
verify, validate, certify, endorse, confirm, ratify,
corroborate, guarantee, warrant, vouch for, authorize,
prove, substantiate
FORMAL accredit, attest

authentication *n*
verification, validation, endorsement, confirmation,
authorization, ratification, corroboration, substantiation
FORMAL attestation, accreditation

authenticity *n*
genuineness, certainty, authoritativeness, validity, truth,
veracity, truthfulness, honesty, accuracy, correctness,
faithfulness, fidelity, reliability, dependability, credibility,
trustworthiness, legality, legitimacy
E₃ spuriousness, invalidity

author *n*
1 WRITER, novelist, man of letters, woman of letters,
biographer, dramatist, playwright, poet, essayist, composer,
contributor, screenwriter, librettist, lyricist, songwriter,
reporter, journalist, pen, penman, penwoman
Related adjective: auctorial
2 CREATOR, founder, originator, initiator, parent, prime
mover, mover, inventor, designer, architect, planner,
maker, producer

authoritarian *adj, n*
♦ *adj*
strict, disciplinarian, severe, harsh, rigid, tough, inflexible,
unyielding, dogmatic, doctrinaire, absolute, autocratic,
dictatorial, totalitarian, Orwellian, magisterial, despotic,
tyrannical, oppressive, domineering, imperious
E₃ liberal
♦ *n*
autocrat, absolutist, totalitarian, dictator, despot, tyrant

> **⚠ authoritarian** or **authoritative**?
> You describe a person or government as *authoritarian* if
> they try to control people instead of letting them have
> the freedom to make their own decisions. An
> *authoritative* account of something is one that is
> reliable; an *authoritative* person is one who inspires
> attention and obedience from others.

authoritarianism *n*
autocracy, despotism, totalitarianism, dictatorship,
absolutism, oppression, repression, Fascism, Nazism
E₃ democracy, liberalism

authoritative *adj*
1 *an authoritative study*
definitive, decisive, authentic, factual, true, truthful,
accurate, faithful, convincing, sound, reliable, dependable,
trustworthy, scholarly, learned, official, authorized,
legitimate, valid, approved, sanctioned, accepted
FORMAL cathedratic
2 *an authoritative person*
self-confident, confident, self-assured, self-possessed,
decisive, sure of yourself, bold, audacious, assertive,
imposing, commanding, magisterial, masterful
E₃ 1 unofficial, unreliable

> **⚠ authoritative** or **authoritarian**?
> *See panel at* **authoritarian**.

authoritatively *adv*
1 RELIABLY, dependably, definitively, decisively, factually,
authentically, accurately, faithfully, convincingly
2 SELF-CONFIDENTLY, confidently, boldly, audaciously,
assertively

authority *n*
1 GOVERNMENT, administration, establishment, management, officialdom, state, council, bureaucracy
COLLOQ. they, the powers that be
2 SOVEREIGNTY, supremacy, rule, sway, control, dominion, influence, command, power, force, jurisdiction
COLLOQ. clout, muscle
3 AUTHORIZATION, permission, sanction, permit, warrant, licence, credentials, right, power, prerogative, consent, leave, carte blanche
COLLOQ. go-ahead, green light, thumbs-up
4 *an authority on antiques*
expert, pundit, connoisseur, specialist, professional, master, scholar, sage, adept
COLLOQ. buff

authorization *n*
authority, permission, consent, sanction, approval, mandate, validation, ratification, confirmation, licence, entitlement, clearance, empowering, commission, warranty, permit, leave, credentials, passport, stamp, retainer
FORMAL accreditation
COLLOQ. OK, okay, go-ahead, green light, thumbs-up

authorize *v*
legalize, make legal, validate, ratify, confirm, license, entitle, empower, give authority to, enable, commission, warrant, permit, give permission to, allow, let, consent to, sanction, approve, mandate
FORMAL accredit
COLLOQ. OK, okay, give the go-ahead to, give the green light to, give the thumbs-up to

authorized *adj*
licensed, under licence, commissioned, permitted, warranted, official, approved, recognized, legal, lawful
FORMAL accredited

autobiography *n*
memoirs, life story, story of your life, diary, journal

> **QUOTATIONS**
> Only when one has lost all curiosity has one reached the age to write an autobiography
> EVELYN WAUGH, *A Little Learning*

autocracy *n*
absolutism, totalitarianism, dictatorship, despotism, tyranny, authoritarianism, fascism
🔁 democracy

autocrat *n*
absolutist, totalitarian, dictator, despot, tyrant, authoritarian, panjandrum
COLLOQ. (little) Hitler

autocratic *adj*
absolute, all-powerful, totalitarian, despotic, tyrannical, authoritarian, dictatorial, domineering, overbearing, imperious
FORMAL autarchic
🔁 democratic, liberal

autograph *n, v*
♦ *n*
signature, name, initials, countersignature, inscription, endorsement, mark
SLANG monicker
♦ *v*
sign, write your name, initial, countersign, endorse, put your mark

automatic *adj*
1 AUTOMATED, self-activating, mechanical, mechanized, programmed, self-regulating, computerized, push-button, robotic, self-propelling, unmanned
2 SPONTANEOUS, reflex, involuntary, mechanical, unwilled, unconscious, unthinking, natural, instinctive, routine,
necessary, certain, inevitable, unavoidable, inescapable, uncontrollable
COLLOQ. knee-jerk

automatically *adj*
1 MECHANICALLY, robotically
2 INVOLUNTARILY, spontaneously, mechanically, unconsciously, unthinkingly, naturally, instinctively, routinely, necessarily, certainly, inevitably, unavoidably, inescapably, uncontrollably

automobile *n*
car, motor car, motor vehicle, motor, vehicle
See panel at **car**.

autonomous *adj*
self-governing, self-directing, self-determining, independent, free, sovereign
🔁 dependent

autonomy *n*
self-government, self-rule, home rule, sovereignty, independence, self-determination, self-sufficiency, freedom, free will
FORMAL autarky
🔁 subjection, compulsion

autopsy *n*
post-mortem, dissection, necropsy

auxiliary *n, adj*
♦ *n*
ancillary, subordinate, helper, partner, supporter, right-hand man/woman, backer, second, second-in-command
♦ *adj*
ancillary, assistant, subsidiary, accessory, secondary, supporting, supportive, helping, assisting, aiding, extra, supplementary, additional, spare, reserve, back-up, emergency, substitute

avail *v*
make use of, use, utilize, exercise, accept, resort to, draw on, take advantage of
■ **to no avail**
without success, in vain, unsuccessfully, fruitlessly, vainly
FORMAL ineffectually

available *adj*
1 *have rooms available*
free, vacant, unoccupied, untaken, to hand, within reach, at hand, accessible, handy, convenient, on hand, at your disposal, disposable, ready, obtainable, usable, forthcoming
FORMAL procurable
COLLOQ. on tap, up your sleeve, up for grabs, yours for the asking/taking
2 *not available for comment*
free, not busy, contactable, at liberty
🔁 **1** unavailable, taken **2** unavailable

avalanche *n*
1 *an avalanche in the Alps*
landslide, landslip
2 *an avalanche of letters*
deluge, flood, cascade, torrent, inundation, wave, barrage

avant-garde *adj*
innovative, innovatory, pioneering, ground-breaking, experimental, unconventional, original, progressive, advanced, forward-looking, futuristic, enterprising, go-ahead, inventive, modern, contemporary
SLANG far-out, way-out
🔁 conservative

avarice *n*
covetousness, acquisitiveness, avidity, greed, greediness, meanness, miserliness, selfishness, materialism
OLD gourmandise; (*Shakesp*) misery
FORMAL pleonexia

SLANG *N Am* the gimmes
E3 generosity, liberality

avaricious *adj*
covetous, grasping, acquisitive, greedy,
griping, mercenary, mean, miserly, avid;
Scot gare, grippy
OLD gripple
FORMAL rapacious, pleonectic
E3 generous, liberal

avenge *v*
take revenge for, take vengeance for, punish, requite,
repay, pay back, retaliate
OLD wreak; (*Shakesp*) venge
COLLOQ. get even with, get back at, get your own back

avenue *n*
1 ROAD, street, drive, way, thoroughfare, boulevard,
broadway, passage
2 *an avenue for his missionary zeal*
way, method, line, approach, course of action, scheme,
modus operandi

aver *v*
state, declare, maintain, confirm, affirm, make known
FORMAL avow, attest

average *n, adj*
♦ *n*
mean, mid-point, median, norm, mode, standard, centre,
rule, par, medium, run
E3 extreme, exception
♦ *adj*
1 *the average age*
mean, medial, median, middle, intermediate, medium
2 *the average reader*
ordinary, everyday, common, usual, normal, regular,
standard, typical, routine, unexceptional
3 *an average performance*
mediocre, moderate, satisfactory, fair,
middling, fair to middling, indifferent,
passable, tolerable, undistinguished, unexceptional,
nothing special
COLLOQ. run-of-the-mill, so-so, common-or-garden, not up
to much, nothing much to write home about, not much
cop, no great shakes
E3 1 extreme **3** exceptional, remarkable
■ **on average**
normally, usually, generally, mainly, chiefly, mostly,
ordinarily, typically, routinely, as a rule, by and large, on
the whole, in the main

averse *adj*
reluctant, unwilling, loath, disinclined, ill-disposed, hostile,
opposed, antagonistic, unfavourable

FORMAL antipathetic
E3 willing, keen, sympathetic

> **!** **averse** or **adverse**?
> *See panel at* **adverse**.

aversion *n*
dislike, hate, hatred, loathing, abhorrence,
abomination, horror, phobia, reluctance, unwillingness,
disinclination, distaste, disgust, revulsion, repulsion,
hostility, opposition, antagonism
FORMAL detestation, repugnance
E3 liking, sympathy, desire

avert *v*
turn away, deflect, turn aside, parry,
head off, fend off, ward off, stave off, forestall,
frustrate, prevent, avoid, evade, stop
FORMAL obviate, preclude

aviation *n*
aeronautics, flying, flight, aircraft industry
See panel below

aviator *n*
pilot, flyer, airman, airwoman, aircraftsman,
aircraftswoman

avid *adj*
eager, earnest, keen, enthusiastic, fanatical, devoted,
dedicated, zealous, ardent, fervent, intense, great,
passionate, insatiable, ravenous, hungry, thirsty, athirst,
greedy, grasping, covetous
COLLOQ. crazy, mad
E3 indifferent

avidly *adv*
eagerly, earnestly, keenly, enthusiastically,
fanatically, devotedly, zealously, ardently, fervently,
intensely, passionately, insatiably, ravenously,
hungrily, thirstily, greedily, covetously
COLLOQ. madly
E3 indifferently

avoid *v*
evade, stay/keep away from, elude, sidestep,
escape, run away from, get out of, bypass, get round,
balk, decline, prevent, avert, shun, abstain
from, hold back from, shy away from, steer clear of,
make a detour, keep your distance from
OLD evite, evitate
FORMAL eschew, circumvent, refrain from, forbear
COLLOQ. hedge, duck, dodge, shirk, wriggle/worm your
way out of, give a miss, give a wide berth to

Aviation terms include:

aeronautics	altitude	flight crew	jet engine	parachute	taxi
aeroplane	automatic pilot	flight deck	jet propulsion	pilot	test flight
aerospace	biplane	flight recorder	jetstream	plane	test pilot
aileron	black box	fly-by	joystick	*slang* prang	thrust
aircraft	captain	fly-by-wire	jumbo jet	pressurized cabin	touchdown
airfield	*colloq.* chocks	fly-past	landing	propeller	undercarriage
airline	away	fuselage	landing gear	rotor blade	undershoot
air miss	cockpit	*slang* George	landing strip	rudder	vapour trail
N Am airplane	console	glider	lift-off	runway	vertical take-off
airport	control tower	ground control	loop-the-loop	solo flight	and landing
airship	crash dive	ground speed	Mach number	sonic boom	(VTOL)
airspace	crash-landing	hangar	maiden flight	sound barrier	windsock
air station	dive	helicopter	mid-air collision	spoiler	wingspan
air steward	drag	holding pattern	monoplane	subsonic	
airstrip	fixed-wing	hop	night-flying	supersonic	
air traffic control	flap	hot-air balloon	nose dive	swing-wing	
airway	flight	jet	overshoot	take-off	

See also **aircraft**.

Unlike the straightforward **stay** or **keep away from**, **evade** suggests an element of furtiveness: *I managed to evade detection*, and when something **eludes** someone it takes on an almost ethereal quality: *happiness has eluded him*. The word **sidestep** may be used to imply that someone has dodged something, either literally or figuratively: *he neatly sidestepped the questions*. Similarly **bypass** also suggests avoidance, through finding another route: *this leap of faith bypasses the truth*, whereas **escape** is suggestive of a more dramatic avoidance: *the thieves escaped detection*.

You can use the phrase **get out of** when talking about getting free of an unpleasant situation or responsibility, whilst **get round** implies that an alternative solution has been found: *the student got round the question in such an ingenious way*. **Balk** suggests a real aversion to doing something: *the banks have balked at new lending*, unlike **decline**, which describes a more restrained, less instinctive reaction.

Prevent, on the other hand, has more to do with stopping something from taking place, as does **avert**, although it is usually used of avoiding undesirable consequences: *the disaster was averted*. The word **shun** implies ignoring that which is to be avoided, whereas **abstain from** has more to do with not taking part. The phrases **shy away from** and **steer clear of** are similar in sense but differ in degree, the latter being used to emphasize a more determined avoidance.

avoidable *adj*
escapable, preventable, stoppable
OLD evitable
FORMAL avertible, eludible
≠ inevitable, inescapable

avow *v*
declare, admit, assert, maintain, state, profess, confess, acknowledge, swear, vow
OLD avouch
FORMAL attest, aver

avowed *adj*
sworn, declared, professed, self-proclaimed, self-confessed, confessed, admitted, acknowledged, open, overt
OLD (Shakesp) barefaced

await *v*
1 await his return
wait for, expect, hope for, anticipate, look forward to, look for
OLD bide, tarry
2 troubles that await us
be in store for, lie in wait for

awake *adj, v*
♦ *adj*
1 stay awake
wakeful, wide awake, stirring, aroused, alert, vigilant, watchful, observant, attentive, conscious
COLLOQ. tossing and turning, not sleeping a wink
2 awake to the possibilities
aware, sensitive, conscious, alive, appreciative, mindful
≠ **1** asleep, sleeping **2** unaware
♦ *v*
awaken, waken, wake, wake up, rouse, stir, arouse
OLD abraid

awaken *v*
1 awakened to the danger
cause to realize, generate, stir, rouse, stimulate, inspire, excite, engender
2 awakened by the alarm
awake, waken, wake, wake up, rouse, stir
OLD abraid

awakening *n*
awaking, wakening, waking, rousing, arousal, stimulation, animating, enlivening, activation, revival, birth
FORMAL vivification

award *n, v*
♦ *n*
1 an award for bravery
prize, trophy, decoration, medal, honours, reward, accolade, certificate, presentation, commendation, citation
COLLOQ. gong
See panel at **honour**.
2 an award for compensation
endowment, gift, grant, scholarship, bursary, allotment, allowance, settlement, payment, dispensation, bestowal, conferral, adjudication, judgement, decision, order
FORMAL subvention
♦ *v*
give, present, distribute, dispense, bestow, confer, decorate, accord, endow, gift, grant, allot, allocate, assign, allow, determine
OLD addeem; (Spenser) addoom; adward, aret
FORMAL apportion, adjudge

aware *adj*
1 aware of the problem
conscious, alive to, sensitive, acquainted, appreciative, mindful, heedful, attentive, observant, sharp, alert, vigilant
FORMAL sentient, sensible, recognizant
2 politically aware
familiar, conversant, acquainted, informed, enlightened, *au courant*, knowing, knowledgeable, shrewd
FORMAL cognizant, apprised
COLLOQ. clued up, in the know, on the ball, sussed
≠ **1** unaware, oblivious, insensitive

sense 1
Conscious may be used to show that something is continually present in your thoughts: *we were conscious of the insecurity of our situation*, whilst the term **alive to** is more suggestive of being actively receptive: *teachers need to be alive to cultural differences*. **Sensitive** again suggests being open but further implies a highly tuned awareness: *the profession must be sensitive to change*.

The term **acquainted**, however, suggests only a previous introduction to something: *pilgrimage acquainted men with the spiritual treasure in the world*; whereas **appreciative**, **mindful** and **heedful** imply that something is not only known of, but is also an active consideration: *mindful of the danger of tropical storms*. **Attentive** similarly suggests paying constant heed to something in particular, whilst **observant** implies a more inherent quality of watchfulness. If you describe someone as **sharp** or **alert** you again suggest that their lively minds would instantly pick up on something, whereas **vigilant** implies a degree of conscientious awareness of potential danger or wrongdoing: *the burglars were spotted by vigilant neighbours*.

awareness *n*
consciousness, appreciation, recognition, sensitivity, familiarity, knowledge, understanding, grasp, perception, acquaintance
FORMAL cognizance

awash *adj*
1 FLOODED, inundated, soaked, drenched, saturated, submerged
2 awash with reporters
crawling, teeming, swarming, alive, full, packed, inundated
FORMAL replete

away adv
1 *move away*
from here, from there, off, elsewhere, apart, aside
2 *I've been away in France*
not at home, not at work, absent, on holiday, on vacation, abroad
3 *live away from the city*
at a distance, far

awe n
wonder, reverence, respect, honour, admiration, amazement, astonishment, fear, terror, dread, apprehension
FORMAL wonderment, veneration, stupefaction
E3 contempt

awed adj
awe-struck, amazed, astonished, stunned, reverential, fearful
COLLOQ. lost for words

awe-inspiring adj
wonderful, sublime, magnificent, stupendous, overwhelming, breathtaking, striking, spectacular, stupefying, stunning, astonishing, amazing, impressive, dazzling, imposing, majestic, solemn, exalted, moving, awesome, formidable, daunting, intimidating, fearsome
FORMAL numinous
COLLOQ. mind-boggling
E3 contemptible, tame

awesome adj
impressive, formidable, extraordinary, overwhelming, breathtaking, spectacular, amazing, astonishing, stunning, daunting, intimidating
COLLOQ. mind-boggling, jaw-dropping

awestruck adj
amazed, astonished, impressed, awed, awe-struck
COLLOQ. lost for words

awful adj
1 *an awful accident*
horrific, terrible, dreadful, fearful, frightful, ghastly, unpleasant, nasty, horrible, horrid, gruesome, dire, atrocious, horrifying, shocking, appalling, alarming, disgusting, distressing
FORMAL heinous
2 *the film was awful*
unsatisfactory, very poor, abysmal, inferior, dreadful, inadequate, second-rate, third-rate
COLLOQ. terrible, lousy, pathetic, crummy, a load of rubbish
SLANG pants, naff, the pits;
(vulgar) shit, crap; *Aust* spewy
3 *I feel awful*
ill, unwell, sick, poorly, in pain, washed out
COLLOQ. terrible, rough, seedy, under the weather
E3 **1** wonderful **2** excellent **3** well

awfully adv
very, extremely, greatly, deeply, really, immensely, particularly, remarkably, absolutely, unbelievably
COLLOQ. terribly, dreadfully, tremendously

awhile adv
for a short time, for some time, for a moment

awkward adj
1 CLUMSY, gauche, inept, inexpert, unskilful, bungling, ham-fisted, handless, heavy-handed, left-handed, unco-ordinated, ungainly, graceless, ungraceful, gawky, inelegant, cumbersome, unwieldy, lubberly, chuckle-headed
FORMAL maladroit
COLLOQ. all thumbs, thumby, having two left feet

2 *feeling awkward in their presence*
uncomfortable, ill at ease, embarrassed, shy, bashful; *Scot* blate
3 *put me in an awkward position*
difficult, tricky, embarrassing, uncomfortable, delicate, troublesome, perplexing, problematic, annoying, inconvenient, fiddly
4 OBSTINATE, stubborn, unco-operative, obstructive, disobliging, troublesome, unaccommodating, irritable, touchy, prickly, oversensitive, rude, unpleasant, boorish, loutish, rustic, cubbish
COLLOQ. stroppy, bloody-minded
E3 **1** graceful, elegant, convenient, handy **2** comfortable, relaxed, at ease **3** straightforward, easy **4** amenable, pleasant

awkwardly adv
1 CLUMSILY, gracelessly, ungracefully, inelegantly, ineptly, inexpertly, unskilfully, ham-fistedly, heavy-handedly
FORMAL maladroitly
2 UNCOMFORTABLY, uneasily, shyly, bashfully
E3 **1** gracefully, elegantly **2** comfortably, confidently

awkwardness n
1 EMBARRASSMENT, self-consciousness, confusion, bashfulness, uneasiness
FORMAL discomfiture
2 CLUMSINESS, ungainliness, gracelessness, inelegance, gawkiness, heavy-handedness, lack of co-ordination
E3 **1** ease **2** grace, elegance

awning n
canopy, cover, covering, shade, shelter, sunshade

awry adv, adj
1 *clothing left awry*
askew, asymmetrical, cockeyed, crooked, misaligned, oblique, off-centre, skew-whiff, twisted, uneven; *Scot* agley
OLD skivie; (*Shakesp*) kam
COLLOQ. wonky
2 *plans gone awry*
wrong, amiss
E3 **1** straight, symmetrical

axe n, v
♦ n
hatchet, chopper, cleaver, tomahawk, battle-axe
♦ v
1 CUT DOWN, fell, hew, chop, cleave, split
2 CANCEL, terminate, discontinue, remove, withdraw, eliminate, get rid of, throw out, dismiss, discharge
COLLOQ. cut, sack, fire, give someone the sack, give someone their marching orders, give someone their cards
■ **get the axe**
be cancelled
COLLOQ. get the boot, get the chop

axiom n
principle, fundamental, truth, truism, precept, dictum, byword, maxim, adage, aphorism
TECHNICAL postulate

axiomatic adj
manifest, assumed, certain, given, granted, self-evident, understood, unquestioned, unquestionable, indubitable, presupposed, fundamental, accepted, proverbial
FORMAL aphoristic, apophthegmatic, gnomic

axis n
centre-line, vertical, horizontal, pivot, hinge

axle n
shaft, spindle, rod, pin, pivot
TECHNICAL mandrel

azure adj
sky-blue, light blue, pale blue, Cambridge blue, Saxe
OLD cerulean

B

babble *v, n*

♦ *v*
1 CHATTER, gabble, jabber, gibber, cackle, prate, mutter, mumble, murmur, prattle, twaddle, twattle
COLLOQ. rabbit on, waffle, gab, blabber, jaw, witter
2 *the stream babbled*
burble, gurgle, murmur
♦ *n*
chatter, gabble, prattle, clamour, hubbub, babel, gibberish, burble, murmur, twaddle, twattle, tongue-work
OLD bibble-babble
COLLOQ. waffle, gab, blabber, jawing, wittering

babe *n*
baby, child, infant, newborn, newborn baby, suckling, tot, tiny tot, babe in arms

babel *n*
babble, hubbub, clamour, bedlam, hullabaloo, chaos, commotion, confusion, din, disorder, pandemonium, tumult, turmoil, uproar

baby *n, adj*

♦ *n*
1 *she's expecting a baby*
babe, infant, newborn, newborn baby, suckling, child, tiny, toddler, tot, tiny tot;
Scot bairn
TECHNICAL neonate
COLLOQ. *Aust & NZ* bub, bubby
SLANG sprog
2 *take it easy, baby*
darling, sweetheart, love, dear, dearest
COLLOQ. sweetie, honey
♦ *adj*
miniature, small-scale, midget, small, little, tiny, minute, diminutive, dwarf; *Scot* wee
COLLOQ. mini, teeny, pint-size(d)

> **PROVERBS**
> Don't throw the baby out with the bathwater

> **QUOTATIONS**
> Every baby born into the world is a finer one than the last
> CHARLES DICKENS, *Nicholas Nickleby*

babyish *adj*
childish, juvenile, puerile, infantile, silly, foolish, baby, young, immature, naive
COLLOQ. soft, sissy
F∃ mature, precocious

back *n, v, adj, adv*

♦ *n*
1 *lie on your back*
backbone, spine
TECHNICAL dorsum, rachis, tergum
Related adjective: dorsal
2 *the back of an envelope*
rear, stern, end, rear end, tail, tail end, far end, hind part, hindquarters, posterior, backside, reverse, reverse side, other side
F∃ front, face

♦ *v*
1 GO BACKWARDS, move backwards, reverse, recede, backtrack, retreat, retire, withdraw, back away, recoil
FORMAL regress
2 SUPPORT, sustain, assist, help, aid, abet, side with, champion, advocate, encourage, promote, boost, favour, confirm, bolster, give countenance to, sanction, countenance, endorse, second, countersign, sponsor, finance, put up the money for, subsidize, underwrite
COLLOQ. throw your weight behind, get/be behind
3 BET, wager, gamble, speculate, risk, chance, venture, bid, stake
F∃ 1 advance, approach **2** discourage, weaken
♦ *adj*
1 *the back door*
rear, end, tail, posterior, hind, hindmost, reverse, other
2 *back copies*
past, previous, earlier, former, outdated, elapsed, bygone, out of date, obsolete
F∃ 1 front
♦ *adv*
1 BACKWARDS, to the rear, behind, off, away
2 *it happened several years back*
ago, past, previously, before, earlier
F∃ 1 forwards
■ **back away**
retreat, withdraw, draw back, fall back, move back, give ground, recoil, step back, recede
■ **back down**
abandon, yield, submit, surrender, concede, give in, retreat, withdraw, back-pedal, backtrack, climb down
■ **back out**
abandon, give up, withdraw, retreat, resign, recant, go back on, cancel
COLLOQ. pull out, get cold feet, chicken out
■ **back up**
support, confirm, corroborate, bear out, stand by, validate, substantiate, endorse, second, champion, reinforce, bolster, assist, aid
■ **behind your back**
secretly, without your knowledge, deceitfully, slyly, furtively, covertly, sneakily, surreptitiously
■ **turn your back on**
reject, exclude, ignore, repudiate, abandon, leave, throw out
COLLOQ. quit, wash your hands of, not touch with a bargepole

> **PROVERBS**
> It's the last straw that breaks the camel's back

> **SYNONYM NUANCES**
>
> *verb sense 2*
> The word **support** has positive connotations of actively and wholeheartedly backing, whereas **sustain** suggests merely keeping something going: *illegal trafficking is sustained by increasing demand*. **Assist**, **help** and **aid** all return to the positive aspect of active involvement; similarly **abet**, although it has a further implication of being associated with something illegal or undesirable: *politicians who have abetted our national decline*.

The term **side with** may be used of a dispute between rival parties, but **champion** supplies a dashing image of bringing a cause or ideology to people's attention: *he championed the cause of the poor*. **Advocate**, **promote**, **boost** and **bolster** similarly suggest an active role in the advancement of something: *the movement promoted single-issue politics*; whilst **encourage** has more to do with attracting people to it: *the children are encouraged to express themselves freely*. To **favour** something suggests having it as a preference over others, but to **confirm** it goes further by implying validation.

The words **sanction** and **countenance** also convey differing aspects; the first suggests a more positive commitment, the latter incorporates a degree of tolerance rather than committed backing: *this is widely sanctioned socially*; *such concessions could not be countenanced*. The terms **endorse**, **second**, and **countersign** all describe a public action whereby you are happy for your name to be linked with a cause, whilst **sponsor**, **finance**, **subsidize** and **underwrite** are used only when you are willing to put your money where your mouth is, and give financial backing.

backbiting *n, adj*
♦ *n*
criticism, slander, libel, defamation, abuse, insults, slurs, gossip, malice, scandalmongering, spite, spitefulness
FORMAL aspersion, calumny, disparagement, denigration, revilement, detraction, vilification, vituperation
COLLOQ. bitchiness, cattiness, slagging off, mud-slinging, rubbishing
F∃ praise
♦ *adj*
abusive, spiteful, malicious, slanderous, libellous, disparaging, scandalmongering
OLD (*Shakesp*) back-wounding
FORMAL vilifying
COLLOQ. bitchy, catty, cattish

backbone *n*
1 SPINE, spinal column, vertebrae, vertebral column
OLD chine
Related adjective: vertebrate, vertebrated
2 *the backbone of an organization*
mainstay, support, core, cornerstone, foundation, basis, nucleus
3 COURAGE, mettle, pluck, nerve, grit, determination, resolution, resolve, (strength of) character, firmness, tenacity, steadfastness, willpower, toughness, stamina, strength, power, vertebration
COLLOQ. bottle, guts
F∃ 3 spinelessness, weakness

backbreaking *adj*
arduous, exhausting, gruelling, strenuous, onerous, hard, heavy, crushing, laborious, punishing
COLLOQ. killing
F∃ easy

backchat *n*
impudence, impertinence, insolence, rudeness, cross-talk; *Scot* snash; *N Am* back talk
COLLOQ. cheek, nerve, sauciness, lip, face, mouth, brass neck

backer *n*
advocate, benefactor, promoter, second, seconder, sponsor, subscriber, supporter, underwriter, investor, subsidizer, funder, champion, patron, well-wisher, friend, bottle-holder
OLD stickler
COLLOQ. angel

backfire *v*
1 *the engine backfired*
misfire, explode, discharge, blow up, detonate

2 *the plans backfired*
recoil, rebound, ricochet, boomerang, strike back, miscarry, fail, defeat itself, be self-defeating, be counterproductive
COLLOQ. flop, come home to roost, score an own goal, blow up in your face

background *n*
1 SETTING, backdrop, backcloth, scene, surroundings, surround, environment, milieu, context, framework, circumstances, influences, factors
2 HISTORY, record, credentials, experience, qualifications, grounding, preparation, education, upbringing, family, (family) circumstances, breeding, social standing, status, origins, culture, tradition

back-handed *adj*
ambiguous, double-edged, two-edged, indirect, oblique, dubious, equivocal, ironic, sarcastic, sardonic
F∃ sincere, wholehearted

backing *n*
1 *financial backing*
support, accompaniment, aid, assistance, help, co-operation, helpers, championing, advocacy, encouragement, moral support, commendation, favour, approval, sanction, promotion, endorsement, seconding, patronage, sponsorship, finance, funds, grant, subsidy
2 *a plastic backing*
lining, padding, facing, interlining, stiffening, reinforcement
3 *musical backing*
accompaniment, support, backup
TECHNICAL obbligato, vamp

backlash *n*
reaction, response, repercussion, reprisal, retaliation, counteraction, recoil, kickback, backfire, boomerang

backlog *n*
accumulation, stock, supply, resources, reserve, reserves, heap, pile, excess, hoard
COLLOQ. mountain

back-pedal *v*
take back, retract, change your mind, about-face, about-turn, have second thoughts, abandon, yield, submit, surrender, concede, give in, retreat, withdraw, backtrack, go back on, climb down
FORMAL renege, tergiversate
COLLOQ. do a U-turn

backslide *v*
lapse, relapse, default, defect, turn away, turn your back, fall from grace, renege, desert, revert, go back, regress, sin, slip, stray, go astray
FORMAL apostatize, tergiversate
COLLOQ. leave the straight and narrow
F∃ persevere

backslider *n*
apostate, defaulter, defector, deserter, renegade, reneger, turncoat
OLD recreant
FORMAL recidivist, tergiversator

backsliding *n*
lapse, relapse, regression, apostasy, defection, desertion, defaulting
FORMAL tergiversation

backtrack *v*
back-pedal, climb down, go back on, withdraw, change your mind, have second thoughts
FORMAL renege, tergiversate
COLLOQ. do a U-turn

backup *n*
support, help, assistance, aid, encouragement, confirmation, endorsement, reinforcement, additional equipment/resources

backward adj

1 a backward step
rearward, reverse, to the back, retrograde,
retrogressive, regressive
2 a backward country/society
undeveloped, underdeveloped, unsophisticated
3 SHY, bashful, retiring, reticent, reluctant, unwilling,
hesitant, hesitating, shrinking, timid, wavering
4 a backward child
slow, immature, retarded, having learning difficulties,
subnormal
F₃ 1 forward **2** advanced, developed **3** bold, confident **4**
precocious

backwards adv
rearwards, to the back, retrogressively, regressively

backwash n

1 the backwash of a ship
wash, flow, swell, waves, wake, path
2 REPERCUSSIONS, aftermath, after effect(s), result(s),
consequence(s), reverberations

backwater n
isolated place, remote place
COLLOQ. Aust scrub, Woop Woop

backwoods n
isolated place, remote place, back of beyond, backwater,
bush, outback; Aust & NZ back-blocks; S Afr backveld
COLLOQ. middle of nowhere, the sticks; N Am the
boondocks, the boonies; Aust & NZ beyond the black
stump

bacteria n
germs, viruses, microbes, micro-organisms, parasites,
bacilli
COLLOQ. bugs

bad adj

1 UNPLEASANT, disagreeable, nasty, dreadful, appalling,
atrocious, undesirable, unfortunate, distressing, adverse,
detrimental, harmful, damaging, hurtful, dangerous,
injurious, unhealthy, unwholesome, destructive, ruinous
FORMAL deleterious
2 EVIL, wicked, sinful, criminal, corrupt, dishonest,
shameful, immoral, vile, offensive, degenerate, outrageous,
deplorable
FORMAL reprehensible, reprobate
3 bad workmanship; bad at speaking French
poor, inferior, inadequate, weak, mediocre, substandard,
shoddy, imperfect, faulty, defective, deficient,
unsatisfactory, unacceptable, second-rate, third-rate,
hopeless, incompetent, mismanaged, ineffective
FORMAL ineffectual
COLLOQ. awful, terrible, botched, lousy, crummy, pathetic,
ropy, useless; N Am hellacious; Aust onkus; a load of
rubbish, a load of garbage
SLANG the pits, pants, poxy, naff, crappy;
(vulgar) a load of crap/shit
4 feel bad today
unwell, sick, ill, poorly, diseased, painful, in pain, aching,
unhappy, despondent, gloomy
COLLOQ. under the weather
5 ROTTEN, mouldy, decayed, spoilt, putrid, rancid, sour,
off, tainted, contaminated, high
FORMAL putrefactive, putrescent
6 a bad child
naughty, mischievous, badly-behaved, ill-behaved,
disobedient, unruly, uncontrollable, wayward; Scot gallus
FORMAL refractory
COLLOQ. stroppy, bolshie
7 have a bad cold
serious, grave, severe, intense, critical, acute, harsh
8 a bad time to call
inconvenient, difficult, adverse, unfortunate, unfavourable,
unsuitable, inappropriate
FORMAL inauspicious
9 have a bad back
injured, hurt, diseased, wounded, weak, impaired

COLLOQ. gammy
10 in a bad mood
angry, bad-tempered, irritable, cross, snappy,
quick-tempered, grumpy, tetchy, testy, mean, foul, filthy,
black, gnarled, peppery, thin-skinned, prickly, fractious,
narky, petulant, impatient, choleric, bilious, splenetic,
dyspeptic; dialect stingy; Scot capernoity; Scot & Irish
carnaptious
FORMAL irascible, querulous, cantankerous
COLLOQ. stroppy, in a huff, in a sulk, having got out of
bed on the wrong side, having a short fuse, cross as a
bear with a sore head, crotchety, crabbed, crabby,
grouchy, shirty, ratty, edgy, feisty, humpy
11 feel bad about letting you down
guilty, sorry, ashamed, shamefaced, apologetic,
conscience-stricken, remorseful, contrite
12 bad language
rude, offensive, abusive, insulting, blasphemous, profane,
discourteous, impolite, crude, coarse, vulgar, indecent,
obscene, gross, dirty, smutty
COLLOQ. raunchy, blue, hot, juicy
F₃ 1 good, pleasant, mild **2** virtuous **3** skilled, skilful **4**
well, happy **5** fresh **6** well-behaved, obedient **8** good,
convenient, favourable; formal auspicious **10** good, good-
tempered, equable **12** polite
■ **not bad**
quite good, all right, tolerable, passable, acceptable, fair,
average, adequate, reasonable, satisfactory
COLLOQ. OK, so-so

SYNONYM NUANCES

sense 1
Unpleasant and **disagreeable** are both suggestive of bad
behaviour (towards someone), though they are less
intensive than **nasty**, which implies an inherent cruelty.
The terms **dreadful**, **appalling** and **atrocious** were
initially used to denote something truly horrific, but the
sense has weakened and can be used of many things:
that dreadful child; atrocious weather. **Undesirable** is
used more specifically, to describe something that falls
below accepted levels or standards: undesirable
practices.
    If something is described as **unfortunate** or
distressing you can infer that its failure to measure up
is a source of regret: her unfortunate gaffe. However the
terms **adverse**, **detrimental**, **harmful**, **damaging** and
hurtful are only used of something with definite negative
effects. **Dangerous**, **injurious**, **destructive** and **ruinous**
all suggest even more devastating effects, whilst
unhealthy and **unwholesome** are terms you can use
when your physical wellbeing or moral fibre is at risk:
an unhealthy obsession.

---

badge n

1 a school badge
identification, emblem, device, insignia, crest, shield,
escutcheon, rondel, sign, mark, token, stamp, brand,
trademark, logo, ensign
TECHNICAL episemon
2 a badge of power
sign, mark, token, symbol, indicator, indication

badger v
pester, plague, torment, harass, bait, bully, chivvy, go on
at, keep at, goad, harry, hound, nag, ride, bullyrag
FORMAL importune
COLLOQ. hassle

badinage n
banter, repartee, wordplay, jocularity, teasing,
waggery, chaff, drollery, give and take, humour,
mockery, raillery
OLD dicacity
FORMAL persiflage
COLLOQ. ribbing
SLANG Aust & NZ borak

badly adv

1 *a badly directed play*
poorly, inadequately, imperfectly, defectively, unsatisfactorily, unacceptably, uselessly, incompetently, wrongly, incorrectly, improperly, faultily, negligently, carelessly, ineptly
FORMAL ineffectually
COLLOQ. awfully, terribly, pathetically, appallingly
2 *badly hurt*
seriously, acutely, bitterly, painfully, desperately, severely, critically, dangerously, gravely, crucially
3 WICKEDLY, cruelly, criminally, immorally, shamefully, dishonestly, sinfully, evilly, offensively, unfairly
4 UNFAVOURABLY, adversely, critically, unfortunately, unsuccessfully, unhappily
5 *want something badly*
very much, greatly, exceedingly, enormously, tremendously, desperately, intensely, extremely, deeply
E3 1 well 2 slightly, mildly 3 well 4 favourably, fortunately

---

SYNONYM NUANCES

sense 1
Poorly can be used as a general term to suggest that something has failed to reach an acceptable standard, likewise if it is done **inadequately**. However, something done **imperfectly** implies that it has not been fully completed: *a new challenge, as yet imperfectly understood*. **Defectively** is rarely used and only in the context of an inherent fault, whilst **unsatisfactorily** and **unacceptably** both imply that the outcome of an action is fit only for rejection.
The word **uselessly** describes an ineffective action: *she peered uselessly into the dark corners*; whereas **incompetently** suggests one not done well. **Wrongly** and **incorrectly** are used of something done erroneously: *the paper incorrectly identified the former cricket player.* **Improperly** has to do with the manner of doing something and suggests that the correct procedures have not been followed. Another term rarely used is **faultily**, which suggests an inherent flaw.
If, however, you say that something has been done **negligently** or **carelessly**, it implies that it was not accorded the correct level of care or responsibility: *the fire had been started negligently*; whilst to use **ineptly** would suggest it was not done with the correct level of skill: *the game was ineptly refereed.*

---

badness n
wickedness, evil, dishonesty, corruption, depravity, vileness, immorality, sin, foulness, shamefulness, nastiness, unpleasantness, cruelty
E3 goodness

bad-tempered adj
irritable, cross, snappy, quick-tempered, grumpy, tetchy, testy, mean, black, gnarled, peppery, thin-skinned, prickly, fractious, in a (bad) mood, petulant, narky, impatient, choleric, bilious, splenetic, dyspeptic; *dialect* stingy; *Scot & Irish* carnaptious; *Scot* capernoity
FORMAL irascible, querulous, cantankerous
COLLOQ. stroppy, in a huff, in a sulk, having got out of bed on the wrong side, having a short fuse, cross as a bear with a sore head, crotchety, crabbed, crabby, grouchy, shirty, ratty, edgy, arsey, humpy, feisty
E3 good-tempered, genial, equable

baffle v
puzzle, perplex, nonplus, mystify, bemuse, bewilder, confuse, confound, dumbfound, daze, upset, fox, disconcert, foil, thwart, frustrate, hinder, block, bar, check, defeat; *Scot* bumbaze, fickle
OLD mate, bring to naught
COLLOQ. bamboozle, flummox, stump, throw, get, faze
E3 enlighten, help

baffling adj
puzzling, perplexing, mysterious, bewildering, cryptic, enigmatic, confusing, stupefying, disconcerting, surprising, amazing, astounding, bemusing, extraordinary, unfathomable
E3 enlightening, explanatory

bag v, n
♦ v
1 CATCH, capture, trap, land, net, kill, shoot
2 OBTAIN, acquire, get, gain, come by, secure, net, corner, take, grab, appropriate, commandeer, reserve
♦ n
container, receptacle; *dialect* poke; *Scot* pock, pouch

Types of bag include:

attaché-case	flight bag	portfolio bag
backpack	Gladstone bag	record bag
baguette	grip	reticule
briefcase	handbag	rucksack
bumbag	haversack	sack
carpetbag	holdall	saddlebag
carrier bag	it bag	satchel
N Am carry-all	kitbag	shoulder bag
case	knapsack	sports bag
clutch bag	man bag	suitcase
ditty bag	messenger bag	tote bag
duffel bag	money bag	*Aust* tuckerbag
eco-bag	moneybelt	valise
N Am fanny pack	pack	vanity bag

---

baggage n
luggage, suitcases, cases, bags, belongings, things, equipment, gear, paraphernalia, effects
FORMAL impedimenta, accoutrements
COLLOQ. clobber

baggy adj
loose, loose-fitting, slack, roomy, ill-fitting, billowing, bulging, ballooning, floppy, shapeless, sagging, droopy, oversize, extra large
E3 tight, firm

bail n, v
♦ n
security, surety, pledge, bond, guarantee, warranty, collateral
TECHNICAL *Scot* caution
OLD replevy
■ **bail out**
1 HELP, aid, assist, relieve, rescue, save, finance
2 WITHDRAW, retreat, quit, back out, escape, eject, get out, get clear

bait n, v
♦ n
lure, incentive, inducement, bribe, temptation, snare, enticement, decoy, allurement, incitement, attraction
E3 disincentive
♦ v
tease, provoke, goad, irritate, annoy, hound, taunt, irk, harass, persecute, torment, badger, plague, harry
COLLOQ. needle, hassle, give a hard time to

bake v
1 COOK, roast, oven-roast, pot-roast, spit-roast, brown
2 *clay baked in the sun*
dry, parch, harden, heat, fire, scorch, burn, wither, shrivel

balance v, n
♦ v
1 STEADY, poise, stabilize, level, square, equalize, even out, even up, equate, match
OLD (*Shakesp*) weigh; (*Shakesp & Spenser*) peise
2 *balance the cost against the benefits*
equalize, equate, match, correspond, agree, tally, counterbalance, counteract, counterweigh, neutralize, offset, set, adjust, juggle, compensate for

3 COMPARE, consider, weigh, weigh up, estimate, evaluate, appraise, review

◰ **1** unbalance, overbalance

♦ *n*

1 EQUILIBRIUM, steadiness, stability, evenness, symmetry, equality, parity, equity, equivalence, correspondence, uniformity

TECHNICAL stasis

FORMAL equipoise

2 COMPOSURE, calmness, self-possession, self-control, poise, assurance, aplomb, level-headedness, cool-headedness, equanimity

FORMAL sangfroid

COLLOQ. unflappability

3 REMAINDER, rest, residue, surplus, excess, difference

◰ **1** imbalance, instability

■ **in the balance**

uncertain, unsure, unknown, undetermined, indefinite, unpredictable;

COLLOQ. iffy, in the air, touch and go

■ **on balance**

in conclusion, all in all, overall, generally, taking everything into consideration

balanced *adj*

1 *a balanced report*

objective, fair, impartial, unbiased, unprejudiced, equitable

2 *a balanced diet*

well-rounded, healthy, sound, complete

3 *a balanced person*

calm, self-possessed, assured, level-headed, cool-headed, dispassionate, equitable, even-handed, sensible

◰ **1** prejudiced, biased

balcony *n*

terrace, veranda, portico, loggia, gallery, upper circle, gods

bald *adj*

1 BALD-HEADED, hairless, smooth, uncovered, tonsured, peeled, pollard

TECHNICAL glabrous, glabrate

FORMAL depilated

COLLOQ. bald as a coot

2 BARE, naked, unadorned, plain, simple, severe, stark, barren, exposed, treeless, unsheltered, bleak

3 *a bald statement*

forthright, direct, straight, blunt, outright, downright, straightforward, outspoken, simple, plain, unambiguous, unadorned

◰ **1** hairy, hirsute **2** adorned, covered **3** veiled, equivocal

balderdash *n*

rubbish, nonsense, drivel, gibberish, trash, tripe, twaddle, blague, doggerel; *dialect* faddle; havers; *Scot* blethers, clamjamphrie

OLD galimatias

COLLOQ. bunk, bunkum, claptrap, piffle, bilge, cock, poppycock, hot air, cobblers, rot, tommyrot, codswallop, baloney, blah, bosh, eyewash, hogwash, rhubarb, guff, hooey, malarkey, moonshine, stuff and nonsense; *Aust & NZ* bulldust; *Aust* bull's wool

SLANG bull;

(*vulgar*) balls, bollocks, crap, shit, bullshit; *N Am* jazz; *Aust & NZ* borak

balding *adj*

receding, losing your hair, thin on top, bald

baldness *n*

bald-headedness, bareness, hair loss, hairlessness, starkness

TECHNICAL calvities, calvousness, glabrousness, psilosis, madarosis

FORMAL alopecia

◰ hirsuteness

bale *n, v*

♦ *n*

bundle, truss, pack, package, parcel

■ **bale out**

WITHDRAW, retreat, quit, back out, escape, eject, get out, get clear

baleful *adj*

deadly, harmful, threatening, destructive, evil, hurtful, injurious, malevolent, malignant, menacing, mournful, noxious, ominous, pernicious, ruinous, sinister, venomous

◰ favourable

balefully *adv*

harmfully, hurtfully, destructively, menacingly, threateningly, dangerously, detrimentally

balk, baulk *v*

1 FLINCH, recoil, shrink, jib, boggle, hesitate, refuse, resist, dodge, evade, shirk

FORMAL eschew

2 THWART, frustrate, foil, forestall, disconcert, baffle, hinder, obstruct, check, stall, bar, prevent, impede, defeat, counteract

ball[1] *n*

a golf ball

sphere, globe, orb, globule, drop, conglomeration, projectile, pellet, pill, shot, bullet

COLLOQ. slug

■ **play ball**

co-operate, collaborate, go along, play along, show willing, respond, reciprocate

ball[2] *n*

an invitation to a ball

dance, dinner-dance, party, soirée, masquerade, carnival, assembly

ballad *n*

poem, song, folk-song, singsong, shanty, carol, ditty, calypso, cantilena, mento, romance, forebitter; *Scot* ballant

ballet *n*

ballet-dancing, dancing

SLANG leg-business

Terms used in ballet include:

à pointe	corps de ballet	leotard
arabesque	coryphée	pas de deux
attitude	dégagé	pas de seul
balancé	divertissement	pirouette
ballerina	écarté	plié
prima ballerina	échappé	ports de bras
ballon	élévation	premier danseur
barre	en l'air	première danseuse
battement	en pointe	prima ballerina
batterie	entrechat	assoluta
battu	figurant	principal male
bourrée	fish dive	dancer
brisé	five positions	régisseur
brisé volé	foudroyant	sur les pointes
cabriole	fouetté	sur place
capriole	fouetté en	répétiteur
chassé	tournant	ballet shoe
choreography	glissade	point shoe
ciseaux	jeté	splits
company	grande jeté	tutu

---

balloon *v*

1 *his cheeks ballooned*

bag, belly, billow, blow up, bulge, dilate, enlarge, expand, inflate, puff out, swell

FORMAL distend

2 *the deficit ballooned to 4 billion dollars*

soar, rocket, increase rapidly, snowball, grow rapidly, escalate, skyrocket

ballot *n*

poll, polling, vote, voting, election, referendum, plebiscite

ballyhoo *n*

fuss, hubbub, to-do, hullabaloo, clamour, commotion, excitement, disturbance, noise, racket, tumult, hue and cry, agitation, build-up, promotion, propaganda, publicity, advertising, hype

COLLOQ. kerfuffle

balm *n*
1 *soothing balm for the skin*
cream, lotion, salve, sedative, unguent, balsam, bromide, calmative, curative, embrocation, emollient, lenitive, ointment, palliative, restorative, anodyne, opobalsam
2 *balm for a troubled spirit*
comfort, consolation, relief
E3 1 irritant, vexation

balmy *adj*
warm, summery, gentle, mild, pleasant, soft, temperate, clement, soothing
E3 inclement

bamboozle *v*
confound, dumbfound, daze, upset, disconcert, trick, cheat, dupe, deceive, hoodwink, fool, swindle, puzzle, perplex, nonplus, mystify, bemuse, bewilder, confuse, mystify; *Scot* bumbaze
COLLOQ. con, gull, rook, diddle, lead up the garden path, pull a fast one on

ban *v, n*
♦ *v*
forbid, prohibit, disallow, bar, exclude, ostracize, outlaw, banish, suppress, veto, restrict, censor, disqualify
OLD (*Spenser*) band
FORMAL proscribe
E3 allow, permit, authorize
♦ *n*
prohibition, embargo, injunction, sanctions, veto, moratorium, boycott, stoppage, restriction, suppression, censorship, outlawry, bar, disqualification, banishment, condemnation, denunciation, curse, taboo
FORMAL interdiction, proscription
E3 permission, dispensation

SYNONYM NUANCES

noun
The word **prohibition** often has legal connotations: *the Sunday trading prohibition*; while **embargo** is usually used of government orders banning trade: *the US arms embargo*. **Sanctions** are more in use on the international stage, when penalties have been imposed: *China must open its markets or face sanctions.*
Injunction is used in the legal world, usually in the context of making someone refrain from certain actions. The term **veto**, although again often legal, can be used more widely to describe a ban on certain actions. Similarly **moratorium**, although it usually has a legal aspect, may also be used to talk about any enforced postponement: *a moratorium on commercial whaling*.
The term **boycott** usually suggests a pointed refusal to deal with someone; **stoppage** implies something organized, usually a cessation of labour. **Restriction** and **suppression** both suggest a ban that involves inhibiting development; the former through limiting it, the latter by more forceful means, quashing it completely.
Censorship is an appropriate word to refer to stifling expression such as writing or speech. The word **outlawry** is suggestive of a legal act of banning, but its use is rare nowadays, unlike the common **bar**, a more general term for the forbidding of something.
The word **curse** is a powerful term with supernatural overtones, implying an almost otherworldly preventative force; the unofficial but powerful restraining influence suggested by the word **taboo**, however, is more likely to be the conventions of this world: *the use of violence must remain a taboo in our society.*

---

banal *adj*
trite, commonplace, ordinary, everyday, mundane, humdrum, boring, dull, unimaginative, nondescript, bland, hackneyed, clichéed, stock, stereotyped, stale, overused, threadbare, tired, unoriginal, inane, wearing thin, empty, vapid

COLLOQ. corny, old hat
E3 original, fresh, imaginative

banality *n*
triteness, ordinariness, dullness, unimaginativeness, staleness, tiredness, unoriginality, inaneness, emptiness, vapidity, fatuity, cliché, commonplace, bromide, platitude, prosaicism, triviality, truism, old chestnut; *N Am* cornball, glittering generality
E3 originality

band[1] *n*
1 *a metal band*
strip, belt, ribbon, sash, girdle, tape, bandage, binding, tie, ligature, bond, strap, cord, chain, connection, link, shackle, manacle, fetter
2 STRIP, stripe, line, belt, bar, streak, swathe

band[2] *n, v*
♦ *n*
1 *bands of looters*
gang, crew, group, troop, herd, flock, party, body, gathering, crowd, throng, horde, contingent, association, company, society, club, clique
2 *the band played on*
group, music/musical group, pop group, orchestra, ensemble
♦ *v*
group, gather, join, unite, join forces, team up, close ranks, stand together, pull together, club together, ally, collaborate, consolidate, amalgamate, merge, affiliate, federate
COLLOQ. stick together
E3 disband, disperse

bandage *n, v*
♦ *n*
dressing, plaster, gauze, compress, lint, ligature, tourniquet, swathe, swaddle, Tubigrip®, Elastoplast®, Band-aid®
TECHNICAL capeline, spica
♦ *v*
bind (up), dress, wrap, cover, swathe, swaddle

bandit *n*
robber, thief, brigand, marauder, plunderer, outlaw, highwayman, pirate, buccaneer, hijacker, cowboy, gunman, desperado, gangster, crook, criminal, racketeer, raider
COLLOQ. mugger

bandy[1] *v*
bandy words about
exchange, swap, trade, barter, interchange, reciprocate, spread, pass, toss, throw, fling

bandy[2] *adj*
bandy-legged
bow-legged, curved, bowed, bent, misshapen, crooked

bane *n*
ruin, adversity, destruction, scourge, affliction, torment, trial, trouble, vexation, woe, annoyance, bête noire, blight, burden, calamity, curse, disaster, distress, downfall, evil, irritation, misery, misfortune, nuisance, ordeal, plague, pest, pestilence
COLLOQ. thorn in the flesh/side
E3 blessing

baneful *adj*
destructive, ruinous, troublesome, distressing, painful, harmful, noxious, annoying, disastrous, posionous, pernicious

bang *n, v, adv*
♦ *n*
1 *a loud bang*
explosion, detonation, pop, boom, crack, clap, peal, clang, clash, thud, thump, thwack, slam, noise, report, shot
FORMAL report

2 *a nasty bang on the head*
blow, hit, knock, bump, crash, collision, crack, smack, punch, thump, stroke, bash
COLLOQ. wallop, whack, sock
♦ v
1 STRIKE, hit, bump into, crash into, bash, knock, bump, rap, drum, hammer, pound, wham, thump, stamp
2 EXPLODE, burst, detonate, crack, blow up, boom, echo, resound, crash, slam, clatter, clang, peal, thunder
♦ adv
straight, directly, headlong, right, exactly, precisely, absolutely, slap, slap-bang, smack, hard, noisily, suddenly, abruptly
COLLOQ. dead

bangle n
bracelet, band, circlet, wristlet, anklet

banish v
1 *banish someone from their country*
expel, eject, evict, deport, transport, drive away, cast out, throw out, exile, outlaw, ban, bar, debar, exclude, shut out, ostracize, excommunicate, expatriate, repatriate, extradite
OLD (Spenser) band, forsay
FORMAL rusticate
2 *banish thoughts from your mind*
dismiss, oust, dislodge, remove, get rid of, drive away, send away, shut out, discard, dispel, eliminate, eradicate
FORMAL disimagine
Ⓔ **1** recall, welcome

SYNONYM NUANCES

sense 1
The words **expel**, **eject** and **evict** can all be used for the forcible removal of someone, though the first two imply greater force. **Deport** is used in the context of someone being removed from their land of residency: *many Madeirans were deported to the Azores*; while **transport** can be used when the destination is specified: *convicts transported to Australia*. The term **exile** could be used to intimate estrangement from one's native land or home. **Drive away** should be used if someone has been pressurized into choosing to leave a place, whereas the terms **cast out** and **throw out** return to the idea of a more physical enforcement.
The word **outlaw** has a narrower sense of being placed outside the law: *computer hacking should be outlawed*. The words **ban**, **bar** and **debar** are more generally used when admission has been refused.
Exclude and **shut out** similarly have to do with keeping someone out, and **ostracize** has the further suggestion of punishment or disapproval: *the new Federal Republic was internationally ostracized*. **Excommunicate** is only appropriate for exclusion from the church. The words **expatriate** and **repatriate** should also be used in specific contexts: the former of being forced from your native land, the latter of being sent back to it. **Extradite** similarly is used in the specific context of returning someone to a country, particularly for trial.

banishment n
expulsion, eviction, deportation, expatriation, transportation, exile, exclusion, ostracism, excommunication, extradition
FORMAL outlawry
Ⓔ return, recall, welcome

banisters n
railing, rail, handrail, balustrade

bank¹ n, v
♦ n
1 *a bank account*
financial institution, high-street bank, clearing bank, merchant bank, savings bank, building society, finance company/house

2 *a blood bank*
accumulation, fund, pool, reservoir, depository, repository, treasury, savings, reserve, store, stock, stockpile, hoard, cache
♦ v
deposit, save (up), keep, store, accumulate, stockpile, lay by, put aside
COLLOQ. stash away, save for a rainy day
Ⓔ spend
■ **bank on**
depend on, rely on, count on, bet on, trust, believe in
COLLOQ. bargain on, pin your hopes on

> **QUOTATIONS**
> A bank is a place that will lend you money if you can prove that you don't need it
> BOB HOPE

bank² n, v
♦ n
1 *the banks of a river*
side, embankment, slope, tilt, edge, shore, margin
Related adjective: riparian
2 *a bank of ground*
mound, earthwork, ridge, hillock, knoll, rampart, parapet, levee, parados, slope, rise, incline, terrace, heap, pile, mass
♦ v
1 SLOPE, incline, pitch, slant, tilt, tip
2 HEAP, heap up, pile, pile up, stack, stack up, mass, amass, accumulate, put together, mound, drift

bank³ n
a bank of switches
row, series, array, panel, bench, group, tier, rank, line, succession, sequence, train

banknote n
bill, note, paper money, treasury note; N Am greenback
SLANG flimsy

bankrupt adj, v, n
♦ adj
1 *the company went bankrupt*
insolvent, in liquidation, ruined, failed, folded, in administration, beggared, destitute, impoverished, spent
FORMAL penurious, impecunious
COLLOQ. bust, broke, broken, stony broke, hard up, gone to the wall, gone under, in the red, on the rocks, on your uppers; Aust bung
2 *bankrupt philosophies of life*
deficient, lacking, wanting, deprived, exhausted, depleted, without, bereft
Ⓔ **1** solvent, wealthy, flourishing, prospering, rich; colloq. in the black
♦ v
ruin, impoverish, break, bankrupt, cripple; Scot sequester
♦ n
insolvent, debtor, pauper, beggar, duck
OLD Scot dyvour

bankruptcy n
insolvency, (financial) ruin, liquidation, disaster, exhaustion, failure, indebtedness, lack, smash; Scot sequestration
OLD Scot dyvoury
FORMAL penury, beggary, ruination
COLLOQ. Carey Street
SLANG stumer
Ⓔ solvency, wealth

banner n
flag, standard, colours, ensign, pennant, jack, streamer, placard, sign, banderol, burgee, fanion, pennon, gonfalon, vexillum, oriflamme, labarum
OLD Scot gumphion

banquet n
feast, dinner, dinner party, meal, party, treat, spread

banter *n, v*
- *n*

joking, jesting, pleasantry, badinage, repartee, word play, chaff, chaffing, derision, mockery, ridicule, raillery, quiz
OLD dicacity
FORMAL persiflage
COLLOQ. kidding, ribbing
SLANG *Aust & NZ* borak
- *v*

joke, jest, chaff, deride, mock, ridicule, pun, make fun of
COLLOQ. kid, rib, rag, pull someone's leg
SLANG josh

baptism *n*
1 *the child's baptism*
christening, immersion, sprinkling, affusion, aspersion, purification, naming, dedication
TECHNICAL paedobaptism, parabaptism
OLD mersion
2 *a baptism of fire*
beginning, initiation, introduction, debut, launch, launching, inauguration

baptize *v*
christen, immerse, sprinkle, dip, purify, cleanse, name, call, term, style, title, introduce, initiate, admit, enrol, recruit

bar *n, v, prep*
- *n*

1 PUBLIC HOUSE, inn, tavern, saloon, taproom, lounge, lounge bar, cocktail bar, style bar, grill, brasserie, counter, table; *Scot* howf; *Can* beer-parlor, beverage room
COLLOQ. pub, hostelry, watering-hole
SLANG boozer
2 ROD, stick, shaft, pole, stake, stanchion, batten, lever, crosspiece, rail, railing, paling, barricade
3 SLAB, cake, block, lump, chunk, hunk, wedge, ingot, nugget
4 OBSTACLE, impediment, hindrance, obstruction, barrier, stop, check, deterrent, drawback
5 *called to the Bar*
barristers, lawyers, counsel, advocates, court, tribunal
- *v*

1 EXCLUDE, debar, ban, forbid, prohibit, prevent, hinder, obstruct, block, blockade, restrain, check, stop, disqualify, suspend, veto
FORMAL preclude
2 *bar the door*
barricade, lock, bolt, latch, fasten, secure, padlock
- *prep*

except (for), with the exception of, excepting, apart from, aside from, save, but for, excluding, omitting

barb *n*
1 *the barb on a fish hook*
arrow, point, spike, prong, needle, thorn, prickle, bristle, beard, tang
TECHNICAL harl, ramus, fluke, killick
2 *critical barbs at leaders*
gibe, insult, affront, sneer, rebuff, scorn
COLLOQ. dig, snark

barbarian *n, adj*
- *n*

savage, brute, wild person, ruffian, hooligan, vandal, lout, oaf, boor, philistine, ignoramus, illiterate
- *adj*

savage, brute, wild, rough, brutish, coarse, crude, uncivilized, uncouth, uncultivated, uncultured, unsophisticated, vulgar, loutish, hooligan
FORMAL tramontane
COLLOQ. Neanderthal

barbaric *adj*
barbarous, primitive, wild, savage, fierce, ferocious, vicious, cruel, inhuman, brutal, brutish, bestial, murderous, ruthless, uncivilized, uncouth, vulgar, coarse, crude, rude
E≡ humane, civilized, gracious

barbarism *n*
wildness, savagery, fierceness, ferocity, viciousness, cruelty, inhumanness, brutality, brutishness, bestiality, murderousness, ruthlessness, uncivilizedness, corruption, enormity, uncouthness, vulgarity, coarseness, crudeness, rudeness

barbarity *n*
barbarousness, wildness, savagery, ferocity, viciousness, cruelty, inhumanity, brutality, ruthlessness, brutishness, atrocity, outrage, enormity
E≡ civilization, humanity, civility

barbarous *adj*
1 *barbarous behaviour*
wild, savage, fierce, ferocious, vicious, cruel, inhuman, barbarian, barbaric, brutal, brutish, bestial, murderous, ruthless, heartless
2 *barbarous by modern standards*
primitive, ignorant, uncivilized, unrefined, unsophisticated, uncultured, unlettered, vulgar, rough, rude, crude
E≡ 2 civilized, cultured, educated

barbecue *n, v*
- *n*

N Am cookout; *S Afr* braaivleis
COLLOQ. BBQ; *Aust* barbie
- *v*

cook, grill, griddle, bake, brown, roast, spit-roast, stir-fry

barbed *adj*
1 PRICKLY, spiny, thorny, spiked, spiky, pronged, hooked, jagged, toothed, pointed; *Scot* jaggy
2 *a barbed remark*
sarcastic, cutting, caustic, acid, hurtful, unkind, wounding, nasty, snide, hostile, critical
COLLOQ. catty, bitchy

bare *adj, v*
- *adj*

1 NAKED, nude, in the nude, unclothed, undressed, with nothing on, stripped, denuded, uncovered, exposed
COLLOQ. in your birthday suit, in the raw, in the buff; *Scot* in the scud; *Irish* in the nip
2 *bare shelves/rooms*
empty, vacant, clear, unfurnished
3 *a bare tree/landscape*
barren, denuded, exposed, bleak, desolate, stark, unsheltered, treeless, unforested, unwooded, woodless
FORMAL defoliated
4 *the bare facts*
simple, plain, unadorned, barren, bald, stark, basic, essential, straightforward, cold, hard, sheer, absolute, mere
5 *the bare minimum*
mere, very least, very, sheer, no more than, utter, pure, absolute, complete
E≡ 1 clothed **2** full, decorated **3** wooded, sheltered, forested **4** detailed
- *v*

uncover, lay bare, unveil, strip, expose, unmask, peel, undress, unclothe, display, reveal

barefaced *adj*
brazen, shameless, blatant, bold, brash, flagrant, glaring, arrant, impudent, insolent, unabashed, undisguised, unconcealed, audacious, naked, manifest, open, palpable, patent, obvious, transparent, bald, bald-faced

barefooted *adj*
barefoot, shoeless, unshod
FORMAL discalced
E≡ shod

barely *adv*
hardly, scarcely, no sooner, only just, just, almost, none too, by a short head
OLD scrimp
COLLOQ. be a near/close thing, by the skin of your teeth, by a whisker

bargain n, v

♦ *n*

1 DEAL, transaction, contract, treaty, pact, pledge, promise, covenant, agreement, understanding, arrangement, negotiation

FORMAL concordat

2 DISCOUNT, reduction, special offer, good buy, cheap buy, value for money, *bon marché*; *Scot* wanworth

COLLOQ. snip, giveaway, steal

SLANG *N Am* whizz

♦ *v*

negotiate, haggle, beat down, deal, trade, traffic, broke; *N Am* broker; barter, buy, sell, transact, settle, clinch

OLD chaffer, indent

■ **bargain for**

expect, anticipate, plan for, be prepared for, include, reckon on, take into account, look for, foresee, imagine, contemplate, consider, figure on

■ **into the bargain**

as well, besides, additionally, also, furthermore

> QUOTATIONS
> A bargain is something you have to find a use for once you have bought it
> BENJAMIN FRANKLIN

bargaining n

negotiation, haggling, dealing(s), trade, trafficking, barter(ing), buying, selling, transaction, horsetrading, wheeling and dealing, wheeler-dealing

barge n, v

♦ *n*

canal-boat, flatboat, narrowboat, houseboat, lighter, wherry, pontoon, pram, scow, keel, keelboat, *barca*, budgerow, casco, piragua

OLD birlinn, Bucentaur, galley; *dialect* butty; *Scot* gabbart

♦ *v*

push (in), push your way, force your way, shove, rush, bump, hit, collide, press, jostle, elbow, smash, plough

■ **barge in**

interrupt, butt in, burst in, break in, cut in, gatecrash, intrude, interfere

bark[1] v, n

♦ *v*

1 *the dog barked*

yap, woof, yelp, snap, snarl, growl, bay, howl

2 *bark orders at someone*

yell, shout, cry, bawl, thunder, bellow, snap, snarl

♦ *n*

yap, woof, yelp, snap, snarl, growl, bay, howl

bark[2] n

the bark of a tree

covering, casing, crust, husk, rind, peel, skin, hide, shell

TECHNICAL cortex, integument

barmy adj

crazy, foolish, idiotic, insane, mad, odd, silly, stupid

COLLOQ. daft, batty, dippy, dotty, loony, loopy, nuts, crackers, nutty, off your head/rocker/nutter, need your head examining, round the bend/twist, off your trolley, out to lunch

ⓕ rational, sane, sensible, of sound mind

baron n

1 NOBLEMAN, peer, aristocrat, lord

2 *press barons*

magnate, tycoon, captain of industry, industrialist, mogul, entrepreneur, executive

COLLOQ. fat cat, bigwig, big shot

OLD SLANG big cheese

baroness n

noblewoman, peer, aristocrat, lady

baroque adj

elaborate, ornate, rococo, florid, flowery, flamboyant, embellished, exuberant, vigorous, bold, decorated, overelaborate, overdecorated, overwrought, extravagant, showy, fanciful, fantastic, whimsical, grotesque

TECHNICAL churrigueresque

FORMAL convoluted

ⓕ plain, simple, unadorned, austere

barrack v

heckle, jeer, taunt, hiss, boo, shout down, interrupt

barracking n

heckling, jeering, hissing, boos, interruption(s)

barracks n

garrison, camp, encampment, fort, guardhouse, quarters, billet, lodging, accommodation, casern, gendarmerie

SLANG glasshouse

barrage n

1 *a barrage of fire/criticism*

bombardment, shelling, gunfire, cannonade, battery, volley, salvo, burst, broadside, fusillade, assault, attack, onset, onslaught, deluge, torrent, flood, stream, storm, hail, rain, shower, mass, abundance, profusion

2 DAM, barrier, enbankment, wall, dyke, barricade, obstruction

barrel n

cask, keg, tun, butt, water-butt, firkin, hogshead, *pièce*, wood, tierce, rundlet

barren adj

1 *barren land/activity*

dry, arid, desert, desolate, waste, uncultivable, empty, addle

OLD effete, teemless; *Scot* hirstie

2 INFERTILE, sterile, childless, unprolific, unbearing; *Scot* yeld

FORMAL infecund

3 DULL, flat, vapid, uninteresting, uninspiring, uninformative, uninstructive, unrewarding, unbearing, unproductive, profitless, unfruitful, fruitless, pointless, useless, valueless, purposeless

ⓕ **1** fertile, productive **2** fertile **3** fruitful, useful

barrenness n

1 DRYNESS, aridity, emptiness, dullness, unfruitfulness, pointlessness, uselessness

2 INFERTILITY, sterility, unfruitfulness

TECHNICAL infecundity

barricade n, v

♦ *n*

blockade, obstruction, obstacle, barrier, bar, fence, stockade, bulwark, rampart, palisade, protection, defence

♦ *v*

block, obstruct, bar, blockade, close (up), shut (off), fortify, strengthen, defend, protect

barrier n

1 WALL, fence, railing, ha-ha, barricade, bar, gate, blockade, stockade, obstacle, roadblock, boom, cordon, rampart, fortification, ditch, frontier, boundary, check

2 *a barrier to success*

obstacle, hurdle, stumbling-block, impediment, obstruction, hindrance, handicap, limitation, restriction, drawback, check, restraint, difficulty

barring prep

except (for), except (in the event of), if, unless, bar

barrister n

lawyer, solicitor, advocate, counsel, QC; *N Am* attorney, counsellor

COLLOQ. brief

bartender n

barman, barmaid, barkeeper, publican, mixologist; *N Am* barkeep

barter v, n

♦ *v*

trade, exchange, bargain, swap, traffic, deal, truck, haggle, negotiate, sell, chop; *Scot* coup, niffer; *dialect* cope

♦ *n*
trade, trading, exchange, bargaining,
swapping, truck, trafficking, dealing, haggling,
negotiation; *N Am* dicker
OLD permutation

base¹ *n, v*
♦ *n*
1 *the base of the statue*
BOTTOM, foot, pedestal, plinth, stand, stay, rest, support,
prop, foundation, foundation stone, keystone, underneath,
substructure, understructure, bed, groundwork
TECHNICAL fundus
2 BASIS, foundation, fundamental, essential, component,
principal, key, heart, core, essence, backbone, bedrock,
root, origin, source
3 HEADQUARTERS, HQ, centre, post, station, camp,
settlement, depot, home, starting-point
4 *a biscuit base*
layer, thickness, bed, coating, covering
♦ *v*
1 *research based on fact*
found, establish, ground, build, construct, derive, have as
a basis, depend, rest, hinge
2 *based in Edinburgh*
locate, station, position, situate, site, install

base² *adj*
base behaviour
abject, contemptible, despicable, wicked, corrupt,
immoral, evil, vile, reprobate, vulgar, shameful, sordid,
depraved, unprincipled, disgraceful, disreputable,
wretched, worthless, ignominious, infamous, scandalous,
low, lowly, low-minded, mean, miserable, pitiful, poor,
valueless

baseless *adj*
groundless, unfounded, unsupported, unsubstantiated,
unauthenticated, unconfirmed, unjustified, uncalled-for,
unattested, untrue, fabricated, gratuitous
E3 justifiable, substantiated

basement *n*
cellar, crypt, vault
COLLOQ. *Scot* dunny

bash *v, n*
♦ *v*
hit, strike, knock, punch, belt, smash, smack, thump, slug,
break, crash
COLLOQ. wallop, whack, clobber, clock, biff, sock
♦ *n*
1 *a bash on the head*
knock, blow, bump, bang, box, thump, clip
2 *have a bash at something*
attempt, go, try
COLLOQ. crack, whirl, shot, stab
3 *throw a bash*
party, celebration
COLLOQ. thrash, blast, rave-up, rave

bashful *adj*
shy, coy, retiring, backward, reticent, reserved,
unforthcoming, hesitant, shrinking, nervous,
timid, timorous, diffident, modest, self-effacing, inhibited,
self-conscious, embarrassed, blushing, abashed,
shamefaced, sheepish; *Scot* laithfu', blate
E3 bold, confident, aggressive, assertive

bashfully *adv*
shyly, reticently, hesitantly, nervously, timidly, diffidently,
modestly, self-effacingly, self-consciously, sheepishly
E3 boldly, aggressively

bashfulness *n*
shyness, coyness, reticence, reserve, hesitancy,
nervousness, timidity, diffidence, modesty, self-effacement,
inhibition, self-consciousness, embarrassment, blushes,
shamefacedness, sheepishness
E3 boldness, confidence, assertiveness

basic *adj*
1 FUNDAMENTAL, elementary, primary, rudimentary, radical,
root, underlying, key, central, inherent, intrinsic, essential,
indispensable, vital, necessary, important, first, preparatory
2 *basic rate of pay*
standard, minimum, lowest level, starting
3 *basic accommodation*
primitive, elementary, plain, simple, minimal, staple,
unadorned, spartan, stark, austere, crude, unsophisticated
COLLOQ. *N Am* down-and-dirty
E3 **1** inessential, minor, peripheral **2** with commission,
premium **3** elaborate, sophisticated

basically *adv*
fundamentally, essentially, in essence, at bottom, at heart,
inherently, radically, intrinsically, principally, primarily,
substantially, mainly, in the main, when it comes
down to it

basics *n*
fundamentals, essentials, rudiments, (first) principles,
introduction, facts, necessaries, practicalities, ABC,
alphabet, realities, bedrock, rock bottom, core
COLLOQ. brass tacks, nitty-gritty, nuts and bolts

basin *n*
1 *a pudding basin*
bowl, dish, pot, pan, sink
TECHNICAL lavabo
2 *the basin of a river*
bed, crater, cavity, hollow, gully, valley, depression,
channel, dip
TECHNICAL playa

basis *n*
1 *research that forms the basis of the book*
foundation, support, base, bottom, footing, ground(s),
groundwork, cornerstone, bedrock, key, keynote, reason(s),
rationale, fundamental(s), fundamental point, starting-point,
premise, principle, first principles, main ingredient, alpha
and omega, essential(s), essence, heart, core, thrust
FORMAL quintessence, hypostasis
2 *on a particular basis*
arrangement, procedure, method, system, principle,
condition(s), terms, status, footing, way, approach

SYNONYM NUANCES

sense 1
Foundation, **support**, **base** and **footing** share wide
usage and imply the necessary first steps in establishing
any process: *basic research is an essential foundation for
applied research*; while **bottom** might also be used of
any fundamental aspect. **Groundwork** can also be used
of essential preparatory work: *the groundwork of the
veterinary art was medical science*. **Grounds**, however,
more appropriately describes a reason or excuse: *their
refusal was on religious grounds*.

The terms **cornerstone** and **bedrock**, although they
convey a physical image, are also widely used
figuratively, with connotations of strength and
immutability: *a cornerstone of government policy*; *the
bedrock of democracy*. **Key** and **keystone** may be used
of any factor considered crucial or central to a system or
policy, whereas **reason(s)** and **rationale** are appropriate
to describe a more intellectual explanation. Likewise
principle and **premise** tend to present a primary
assumption: *he starts with the premise that safety is
impossible*.

Essentials is a fairly unmarked term for necessary
things, but **essence**, **heart** or **core** have a more spiritual
tone, suggesting something's essential nature. **Thrust** is
rather different, in that it is suggestive of future direction:
economic reform will be the thrust of his plan.

---

bask *v*
1 *bask in the sun*
sunbathe, bathe, lie, lounge, relax, laze, loll, sprawl
OLD apricate

2 bask in someone's approval
revel, delight in, enjoy, take pleasure in, relish, savour, lap up, wallow
FORMAL luxuriate

basket n
hamper, container, bin, box, holder, receptacle, case, trolley, creel, pannier, punnet, bassinet, coop, skep, trug, scull, scuttle, van, chip, corbeil, crib, cabas, pottle, corf, frail, gabion, seedlip, petara; *dialect* cob, kipe, leap, maund, rip, willy, wisket; *Scot* murlain
OLD flasket

bass adj
deep, deep-pitched, deep-toned, low, low-pitched, low-toned, grave, full, full-toned, rich, resonant, sonorous

bastard n
illegitimate, illegitimate child, love child, natural child, misfortune, slink, by-blow, come-o'-will, come-by-chance, mamzer, *filius nullius*
OLD whoreson, sideslip
COLLOQ. basket, lucky-piece

bastardize v
adulterate, pervert, defile, contaminate, corrupt, debase, degrade, demean, depreciate, devalue, cheapen, distort
FORMAL vitiate

bastion n
stronghold, citadel, fortress, defence, bulwark, mainstay, support, prop, pillar, rock, protection
TECHNICAL lunette, moineau
FORMAL redoubt

batch n
lot, consignment, parcel, pack, bunch, set, assortment, collection, assemblage, cluster, accumulation, mass, group, conglomeration, contingent, amount, quantity, aggregate, crowd

bath n, v
♦ n
1 be in the bath
bathtub, tub, sauna, steam bath, hot tub, Jacuzzi®, whirlpool, bath, slipper bath, Turkish bath, steam room, spa, hamman, thermae
FORMAL balneary
Related adjective: balneal
2 have/take a bath
wash, scrub, soak, shower, douche, tub, dip
♦ v
bathe, have/take a bath, wash, clean, dip, soak, shower, freshen up

bathe v, n
♦ v
1 bathe in the sea
swim, bath, take a dip, surf, tub; *Scot* dook
2 bathe a wound
wet, moisten, immerse, wash, clean, cleanse, rinse, soak, steep, flood, cover
OLD embathe, lave, stew; (*Spenser*) beath, embay
3 bathed in light
suffuse, permeate, cover, saturate, steep
♦ n
swim, dip, paddle, wash, rinse, soak

bathos n
anticlimax, comedown, disappointment, let-down

baton n
stick, rod, staff, truncheon, cudgel
OLD warder

battalion n
1 an infantry battalion
army, force, garrison, brigade, regiment, squadron, company, platoon, division, detachment, section, contingent, legion, troops, unit
2 a battalion of people
crowd, mob, horde, multitude, throng, army, host, mass, herd

batten n, v
♦ n
strip, bar, bolt, board
♦ v
barricade, board up, clamp down, fasten, fix, nail down, secure, tighten

batter v
1 waves battering the pier
beat, pound, pummel, buffet, smash, dash, pelt, lash, bombard, damage, demolish, destroy, wear down, wear out, erode, mangle
2 battering his wife
abuse, maltreat, ill-treat, hit, strike, knock about, club, bash, beat, assault, hurt, injure, bruise, disfigure, maul
COLLOQ. lay into, wallop, thrash, whack, rough up
SLANG N Am lam
■ **batter down**
break down, smash, demolish, destroy, ruin, wreck

battered adj
1 a battered child
beaten, abused, hit, maltreated, ill-treated, injured, bruised
2 a battered old shed
weather-beaten, dilapidated, tumbledown, run-down, damaged, ramshackle, shabby, crumbling, crushed

battery n
1 a battery of tests
sequence, series, set, cycle, succession
2 a battery of cameras
set, row, bank, group
FORMAL array
3 assault and battery
attack, assault, beating, grievous bodily harm, force, striking, thrashing, violence
COLLOQ. mugging
4 the military battery
artillery, cannon, cannonry, emplacements, guns, ordnance

battle n, v
♦ n
war, warfare, hostilities, action, conflict, armed conflict, strife, combat, fight, engagement, final battle, Armageddon, field, encounter, attack, fray, skirmish, brawl, clash, struggle, free-for-all, contest, tournament, campaign, drive, race, competition, crusade, row, disagreement, confrontation, dispute, debate, controversy, stour; *Aust & NZ* stoush
FORMAL altercation
COLLOQ. scrap, set-to
♦ v
fight, combat, war, feud, contend, struggle, strive, campaign, crusade, agitate, clamour, contest, encounter, engage, argue, quarrel, disagree, dispute
OLD darraign

battle-axe n
1 POLEAXE, axe, bill
OLD gisarme, Jeddart staff, wifel
2 his battle-axe of a wife
dragon, disciplinarian, harridan, hag, shrew, fury, witch, martinet, Tartar, termagant, virago

battle-cry n
1 WAR CRY, war song, rallying cry/call, banzai
2 SLOGAN, motto, watchword, catchword, catchphrase

battlefield n
battleground, field of battle, field, front, front line, war/combat zone, theatre of operations, arena, Armageddon

batty adj
crazy, foolish, idiotic, insane, mad, demented, odd, eccentric, peculiar, silly, stupid
COLLOQ. daft, barmy, bats, bonkers, dippy, dotty, loony, loopy, nuts, crackers, nutty, off your head/rocker/nut, need your head examining, round the bend/twist, out to lunch
E3 rational, sane, sensible

bauble *n*
knick-knack, trinket, toy, plaything, trifle,
ornament, bagatelle, bibelot, gewgaw, gimcrack,
kickshaw, tinsel
OLD flamflew

baulk
see **balk, baulk**.

bawd *n*
brothel-keeper, madam, panderess, pimp, procuress,
procurer

bawdy *adj*
lewd, adult, pornographic, coarse, dirty, rude, vulgar,
erotic, obscene, X-rated, gross, improper, indecent,
indecorous, indelicate, lecherous, lascivious, licentious,
lustful, ribald, risqué, smutty, suggestive; *Scot* sculduddry
FORMAL libidinous, prurient, salacious
COLLOQ. blue, raunchy, near the knuckle
F3 chaste, clean

bawl *v*
1 *the baby bawled*
cry, weep, sob, blubber, wail, snivel, squall
2 *bawl loudly at someone*
yell, shout, cry (out), bellow, howl, roar, call (out),
scream, screech, yowl
OLD (*Shakesp*) gape
FORMAL vociferate
COLLOQ. holler
■ **bawl out**
scold, rebuke, reprimand, yell at
COLLOQ. tell off, give someone a telling-off, dress down,
give someone a dressing-down, give someone a piece of
your mind, tear someone off a strip, give someone an
earful

bay¹ *n*
moor the ship in a bay
gulf, bight, arm, sound, firth, inlet, indentation, fleet,
embayment, cove, lagoon, estuary; *Scot* loch, voe
OLD reach

bay² *n*
a bay in the lounge
recess, alcove, niche, nook, opening, compartment,
cubicle, cubbyhole, booth, stall, carrel
OLD classis

bay³ *v*
baying for blood
howl, clamour, roar, bellow, bell, bawl, cry, bark, yelp
COLLOQ. holler

bayonet *n, v*
♦ *n*
knife, blade, sword, pike, spear, dagger, poniard, white
arm
SLANG spike
♦ *v*
stab, impale, knife, pierce, spear, stick

bazaar *n*
1 MARKET, marketplace, mart, souk, alcaicería, alcázar,
exchange
2 *a school bazaar*
sale, fair, fête, bring-and-buy, jumble sale,
nearly-new sale

be *v*
1 EXIST, breathe, live, be alive, inhabit, be present, be
situated, be located, stand, lie, reside, dwell
2 STAY, remain, last, endure, persist, continue, survive,
stand, prevail, obtain
FORMAL abide
3 HAPPEN, occur, arise, come about, take place, come to
pass, develop, transpire
FORMAL befall
4 REPRESENT, constitute, make (up), form, amount to, add
up to, account for

beach *n, v*
♦ *n*
sand, sands, shingle, shore, seashore, seaside, water's
edge, coast, coastline, seaboard, machair, lido, plage
OLD strand
FORMAL littoral
Related adjective: littoral
♦ *v*
go ashore, run ashore, run aground, land, ground, strand,
be grounded, be stranded

beachcomber *n*
forager, loafer, loiterer, scavenger, wayfarer

beacon *n*
signal, fire, watch fire, bonfire, light, beam, lighthouse,
watchtower, flare, rocket, sign, warning light, danger
signal, needfire
OLD fanal
FORMAL pharos

bead *n*
1 *a string of beads*
ball, pearl, jewel, pellet, globule, spheroid, tear, bugle
TECHNICAL paternoster, knurl, ojime, spacer plate
OLD bede, gaud
2 *beads of sweat*
drop, droplet, drip, blob, dot, bubble
COLLOQ. glob

beak *n*
bill, mandibles, nib, neb, rostrum, nose, proboscis, snout,
rostellum
OLD becke

beaker *n*
glass, tumbler, jar, cup, mug, tankard

beam *n, v*
♦ *n*
1 *a beam of light*
ray, shaft, gleam, stream, flash, flare, glint, glimmer, glow,
streak, bar
2 PLANK, board, timber, rafter, joist, girder, spar, boom,
bar, support, stanchion, strut, transom, lintel, cantilever,
stringer, summer, lath, scantling
TECHNICAL purlin
3 SMILE, grin, laugh, smirk
♦ *v*
1 *beam a TV signal*
transmit, emit, broadcast, send, aim, direct, relay
2 *sunlight beaming through the window*
shine, emit, radiate, glare, gleam, glitter, glow, glimmer,
flash, sparkle
FORMAL effulge
3 SMILE, grin, laugh, smirk
■ **off beam**
wrong, mistaken, inaccurate, incorrect
COLLOQ. wide of the mark, off target

bean *n*
Related adjectives: fabaceous, leguminous
See panel on next page

bear *v*
1 CARRY, convey, transport, move, take, bring, fetch
COLLOQ. hump, tote
2 SUPPORT, hold (up), keep (up), carry, shoulder, uphold,
sustain
3 *bear children*
give birth to, breed, deliver, give up
OLD beget
FORMAL engender
4 TOLERATE, stand, put up with, endure, abide, suffer, like,
permit, allow, admit, endorse, accept, take, live with,
brook; *Scot* thole
OLD (*Shakesp*) abrooke
COLLOQ. stomach, hack, grin and bear it
5 *bear signs of a struggle*
carry, show, display, exhibit, have
6 *bear the cost*
pay, accept, support, carry, shoulder, sustain

Varieties of bean and pulse include:

ad(z)uki bean	cannellini bean (or	edamame bean	kidney bean	*N Am* navy bean	split pea
alfalfa	fasolia)	fava bean	legume	pea	string bean
bean sprout	carob (or locust)	flageolet bean	lentil	pinto bean	tonka bean
black bean	bean	French bean	*N Am* lima (or	puy lentil	wax bean
black-eye(d) bean	chickpea (or	gram	sugar) bean	red kidney bean	
(or cowpea)	garbanzo)	golden gram	mangetout (or	red lentil	
black gram	chilli bean	green bean	snow pea or	runner bean	
borlotti bean	d(h)al (or pigeon	green gram	sugar pea)	scarlet runner	
broad bean	pea)	green lentil	marrowfat pea	*N Am* snap bean	
butter bean	dwarf runner bean	haricot bean	mung bean	soy (or soya) bean	

See also **legumes and pulses** *at* **vegetable**.

---

7 *bear someone malice*
hold, have, maintain, entertain, harbour, foster, cherish
8 *bear fruit*
propagate, produce, generate, develop, yield, bring forth
FORMAL fructify
9 *bear yourself well*
carry, behave, act, conduct, acquit, move
OLD abear
FORMAL comport
10 *bear left at the junction*
veer, turn, move, go, drive, diverge, deviate, bend, curve, swerve

■ **bear down on**
advance on, approach, move in on, close in on, move threateningly towards, move menacingly towards

■ **bear in mind**
keep in, mind, remember, be mindful of, consider, note, take into account, make a mental note

■ **bear out**
confirm, endorse, support, back up, uphold, prove, demonstrate, corroborate, substantiate, validate, warrant, ratify, vindicate, justify, verify

■ **bear up**
persevere, cope, soldier on, carry on, suffer, endure, survive, withstand
COLLOQ. grin and bear it, keep your pecker up

■ **bear with**
tolerate, put up with, endure, suffer, forbear, be patient with, make allowances for

> **SYNONYM NUANCES**
>
> *sense 4*
> **Tolerate**, **stand** and **put up with** are fairly neutral terms in general use, while **endure** would imply a stronger test of one's stoicism: *she endured years of abuse*. The word **abide** is again more marked, and is invariably used in the negative to convey strong feeling: *I can't abide that man*. **Suffer** can also be used in the negative in a similar way: *he did not suffer fools gladly*. However, if it is not used in the negative, the suggestion is that great pain or distress is being borne. If you use **like**, however, the tone is positive.
> Unlike all the aforementioned words, **permit**, **allow**, **admit** and **accept** are not emotive, and they hint at an element of concession, whilst **endorse** implies collusion: *the plan endorses private ownership of land*. Both **take** and **live with** are again less intense terms referring to inaction and resignation, whilst **brook** is another generally found in negative usage and in more formal contexts: *he will brook no dissent*.

bearable *adj*
tolerable, endurable, sufferable, supportable, sustainable, passable, acceptable, admissible, manageable, liv(e)able
OLD (*Shakesp*) portable
E∃ unbearable, intolerable

beard *n, v*
♦ *n*
facial hair, stubble, bristle, goatee, imperial, vandyke, moustache, whiskers, five o'clock shadow, mutton chops, sideburns, sideboards, tuft, peak, Charlie, Newgate frill, kesh, pappus
SLANG beaver; *Aust* ziff
♦ *v*
brave, challenge, confront, dare, defy, face, oppose, stand up against

bearded *adj*
unshaven, bristly, stubbly, whiskered, bewhiskered, tufted, hairy, hirsute, shaggy, bushy
TECHNICAL pogoniate
E∃ beardless, clean-shaven, smooth

bearer *n*
1 *the bearer of bad news*
conveyor, courier, messenger, runner, agent
2 *the bearers of a coffin*
carrier, conveyor, porter, transporter
3 *the bearer of a document*
holder, possessor, owner, beneficiary, consignee, payee

bearing *n*
1 *have no bearing on the matter*
influence, relevance, significance, connection, relation, concern, reference
FORMAL pertinence
2 MANNER, air, aspect, attitude, behaviour, poise, carriage, gait, posture, stature
OLD
(*Shakesp & Spenser*) portance
FORMAL demeanour, comportment, deportment, mien
3 *find your bearings*
orientation, sense of direction, position, situation, location, whereabouts, course, track, way, direction, aim

beast *n*
1 *birds and beasts*
animal, creature, brute
2 *You selfish beast!*
brute, monster, savage, barbarian, pig, swine, devil, ogre, fiend
Related adjectives: bestial, theriomorphous

beastly *adj*
horrible, horrid, terrible, unpleasant, disagreeable, awful, nasty, rotten, foul, repulsive, mean, brutal, cruel, swinish

beat *v, n, adj*
♦ *v*
1 HIT, flog, lash, whip, flay, cane, birch, strap, thrash, lay into, punch, strike, swipe, knock, clout, bang, wham, club, bash, slap, smack, pound, hammer, batter, thump, drub, welt, thwack, buffet, pelt, bruise, box, cudgel, lambast, pummel
OLD contuse, knubble, knout, vapulate; (*Shakesp*) firk
COLLOQ. tan, wallop, whack, belt, clobber, knock about, biff, fill in
SLANG *N Am* lam
2 PULSATE, pulse, throb, thump, pound, race, palpitate, flutter, vibrate, quiver, tremble, shake, quake

3 *waves beating against the rocks*
pound, strike, dash, batter, lash

4 *beat a drum*
hit, strike, bang, tap, pound

5 *a bird's wings beating*
flap, flutter, shake, swing, quiver, thresh, thrash, vibrate

6 *beat the eggs*
stir, mix, whisk, blend, combine

7 *beat metal*
hammer, forge, knock, fashion, form, shape, mould, work, stamp
FORMAL malleate

8 CONQUER, overcome, overpower, best, get the better of, have the edge on, be more than a match for, outscore, outplay, outwit, outsmart, eclipse, excel, surpass, outmatch, subdue, overthrow, worst, repel, drub, trounce, overwhelm, rout, ruin, crush, quell, pulverize, bring someone to their knees, reject, throw out;
Scot granny
OLD put to the worse
FORMAL subjugate, vanquish, discomfit
COLLOQ. thrash, lick, hammer, thump, clobber, annihilate, smash, devastate, slaughter, make mincemeat (out) of, run rings round, wipe the floor with, paste, marmelize;
Scot gub
SLANG *N Am* lam
See Synonym nuances panel at **defeat**.

9 *beat the record*
surpass, excel, exceed, outdo, outstrip, outrun, transcend
♦ *n*

1 *the beat of a drum*
hit, stroke, strike, striking, bang, banging, blow, knocking, pounding

2 PULSATION, pulse, stroke, throb, pounding, thump, palpitation, vibration, flutter

3 RHYTHM, time, tempo, metre, measure, rhyme, pulse, stress, accent
FORMAL cadence

4 *a police officer's beat*
round, rounds, territory, circuit, course, journey, way, path, route, walk
♦ *adj*
exhausted, fatigued, tired, dog-tired, tired out, wearied, worn out,
COLLOQ. jiggered, dead-beat, all in, done in, whacked, knackered, bushed, clapped-out, zonked; *N Am* pooped (out), tuckered out

■ **beat off**
repel, drive back, repulse, fight off, hold off, ward off, force back, beat back, push back, keep at bay

■ **beat up**
attack, assault, knock about, knock around, batter
COLLOQ. do over, mug, rough up, clobber, knock someone's block off, beat the living daylights out of, knock into the middle of next week, *S Afr* donder

beaten *adj*

1 *beaten metal*
hammered, stamped, forged, wrought, worked, moulded, formed, shaped, fashioned

2 *beaten paths*
trampled, trodden, well-trodden, well-worn, well-used

3 WHISKED, whipped, mixed, blended, stirred, frothy, foamy

■ **off the beaten track**
remote, isolated, secluded, unfrequented, private, god-forsaken, outlying, out-of-the-way
COLLOQ. in the sticks

beatific *adj*
blissful, blessed, divine, exalted, sublime, glorious, heavenly, joyful, ecstatic, rapturous, angelic, seraphic

beatification *n*
canonization, sanctification, exaltation, glorification

beatify *v*
canonize, sanctify, bless, exalt, glorify
FORMAL macarize

beating *n*

1 CORPORAL PUNISHMENT, hitting, whipping, flogging, caning, the cane/birch/strap, thrashing, lashing, drubbing, punching, clubbing, slapping, smacking, battering, thumping, bruising, chastisement
COLLOQ. tanning, whacking, walloping, hiding, doing-over, belting, clobbering

2 DEFEAT, conquest, loss, rout, ruin, downfall, overthrow, trouncing, overwhelming, overpowering, annihilation, outwitting, outsmarting
FORMAL vanquishing
COLLOQ. hammering, slaughter, clobbering, thrashing

beatitude *n*
happiness, blessedness, ecstasy, rapture, contentedness, delight, elation

beau *n*

1 BOYFRIEND, admirer, suitor, sweetheart, lover, escort, fiancé
OLD spark
COLLOQ. guy

2 FOP, dandy, coxcomb, popinjay, Adonis
OLD muscadin

beautician *n*
beauty specialist, cosmetician, hairdresser, friseur
FORMAL visagiste

beautiful *adj*
attractive, fair, pretty, lovely, good-looking, handsome, gorgeous, radiant, ravishing, voluptuous, striking, stunning, pleasing, appealing, alluring, charming, delightful, fine, graceful, exquisite, becoming, magnificent;
Scot bonny
OLD comely, seemly
FORMAL pulchritudinous
COLLOQ. smashing, out of this world
SLANG drop-dead gorgeous
🖙 ugly, plain, hideous

SYNONYM NUANCES

Attractive and **lovely** can be used fairly generally to describe someone or something pleasing to look at, but **fair** and **pretty** are fairly mild terms usually reserved for females, though the latter may also be used of clothes and the like. **Good-looking** and **handsome**, on the other hand, are traditionally used of males, though both may also be applied to middle-aged women with distinguished features.

The term **voluptuous** is more usually reserved to conjure up the charms of more buxom women. You might use **radiant**, again usually of a woman, to suggest a more ethereal beauty that seems to shine from within, whilst **ravishing** carries a sense of being stunned by someone's or something's charms: *a ravishing smile*. Both **striking** and **stunning** may be used of both sexes, as well as scenery, and again suggest a breathtaking element. **Pleasing**, however, presents a much more restrained description.

You can use **appealing** to conjure up aspects of cuteness, whereas **alluring** suggests a more sensual aspect. **Charming** and **delightful** are now rather old-fashioned terms suggestive of a more quaint beauty: *a charming cottage*; whilst **fine**, along with **graceful** and **exquisite**, can be used to convey strongly an elegance of form or manner, the latter being generally used of things: *exquisite watercolours*. **Becoming** has an element of approval of something's suitability: *a few soft curls over each ear are very becoming*; whereas **magnificent** expresses extreme admiration of anything or anyone impressive.

beautifully *adv*
attractively, radiantly, strikingly, stunningly, pleasingly, pleasantly, charmingly, delightfully, gracefully

beautify *v*
embellish, smarten (up), enhance, improve, grace, gild, garnish, decorate, ornament, deck, adorn, array, glamorize, spruce up
OLD bedeck; (*Shakesp*) flourish
COLLOQ. titivate, tart up, doll up
E3 disfigure, spoil

beauty *n*
1 *the beauty of a woman/poem*
attractiveness, prettiness, loveliness, (good) looks, handsomeness, gorgeousness, radiance, appeal, allure, charm, delight, grace, gracefulness, exquisiteness, seemliness, excellence, harmony, symmetry
FORMAL pulchritude
Related adjective: pulchritudinous
2 *think her a real beauty*
belle, charmer, siren, Venus, *femme fatale*
COLLOQ. good-looker, smasher, corker, cracker, knockout, stunner, peach; *N Am* doozy, doozer
3 *the beauties of the plan*
attraction, advantage, benefit, good thing, plus point, good point, virtue, merit, glory, boon, blessing, strength, asset, bonus, dividend
E3 **1** ugliness, repulsiveness **2** frump **3** disadvantage

> **PROVERBS**
> Beauty is in the eye of the beholder
> Beauty is only skin-deep

> **QUOTATIONS**
> A thing of beauty is a joy for ever: / Its loveliness increases
> JOHN KEATS, *Endymion*

beaver
■ **beaver away**
work hard, work at, put a lot of effort in, persist, persevere
COLLOQ. slog, plug away, slave away

becalmed *adj*
at a standstill, at a halt, idle, motionless, still, stranded, marooned, stuck

because *conj*
as, for, for the reason that, since, owing to, due to, on account of, as a result of, the reason is ..., through, thanks to, in view of the fact that, in consideration of
FORMAL by reason of, by virtue of, forasmuch
COLLOQ. seeing as, 'cos

beckon *v*
1 *beckon to someone*
summon, motion, gesture, signal, nod, wave, waft, gesticulate
2 *fame beckons*
call, invite, attract, pull, draw, lure, allure, entice, tempt, induce, persuade, coax

become *v*
1 *become old-fashioned*
turn, grow (into), get, change into, be changed into, be transformed into, develop into, mature into, pass into, come to be, turn out to be, wax
2 SUIT, befit, flatter, look good on, enhance, grace, embellish, ornament, set off, harmonize
OLD (*Shakesp*) besort
■ **become of**
happen to, be the fate of
OLD befall

becoming *adj*
1 *a hat in a more becoming style*
attractive, charming, flattering, graceful, elegant, tasteful, fetching, pretty
OLD comely

2 *becoming behaviour*
appropriate, suitable, fit, fitting, befitting, consistent, congruous, compatible
E3 **1, 2** unbecoming

becomingly *adv*
attractively, charmingly, fetchingly, gracefully, elegantly, tastefully

bed *n, v*
♦ *n*
1 *get out of bed*
divan, couch, bunk, berth
SLANG sack, pit, hay, kip
2 LAYER, stratum, substratum, matrix, base, basis, bottom, floor, foundation, groundwork, watercourse, channel
3 *bed of flowers*
garden, border, patch, area, space, strip, row, plot
♦ *v*
base, embed, establish, fix, set, found, ground, implant, inlay, insert, bury, plant, settle
■ **bed down**
sleep, go to bed, settle down, call it a day, turn in
COLLOQ. doss down, hit the hay/sack, kip, kip down, get some kip
■ **go to bed with**
sleep with, have sex with, have sexual intercourse with, make love to
SLANG bed, have it off with, bonk; (*taboo*) fuck, screw, shag

Kinds of bed include:

adjustable bed	double bed	platform bed
bassinet	foldaway bed	Put-u-up®
bed settee	folding bed	put-you-up
berth	four-poster	queen-size(d)
box bed	futon	shakedown
bunk bed	hammock	single bed
camp-bed	high sleeper	sleigh bed
chaise longue	mid sleeper	sofa bed
cot	king-size(d)	trestle bed
couchette	lit bateau (or boat	truckle bed
cradle	bed)	trundle bed
crib	mattress	twin bed
day bed	pallet	water-bed
divan bed	palliasse	Z-bed

bedclothes *n*
bedding, bed-linen, covers

Kinds of bedclothes include:

bed canopy	coverlet	pillow sham
bedroll	*Aust* doona	pillowslip
bedspread	duvet	quilt
blanket	duvet cover	quilt cover
bolster	eiderdown	sheet
candlewick bed-	electric blanket	sleeping bag
spread	mattress cover	throwover
cellular blanket	patchwork quilt	valance
N Am comforter	pillow	valanced sheet
counterpane	pillowcase	

bedeck *v*
beautify, decorate, deck, adorn, embellish, festoon, garnish, ornament, array, trick out, trim; *N Am* trick up

bedevil *v*
afflict, torment, confound, frustrate, harass, irk, pester, plague, tease, annoy, besiege, torture, trouble, distress, vex, fret, worry, irritate
FORMAL beset

bedfellow *n*
associate, colleague, partner, ally, fellow, companion, friend

bedlam n

chaos, pandemonium, madhouse, commotion, confusion, furore, clamour, hubbub, hullabaloo, noise, tumult, turmoil, uproar, babel, anarchy
Ea calm

bedraggled adj

untidy, unkempt, dishevelled, disordered, scruffy, slovenly, messy, dirty, muddy, muddied, soiled, wet, soaked, soaking (wet), sodden, dripping, drenched
COLLOQ. like something the cat brought in
Ea neat, tidy, clean

bedridden adj

confined to bed, incapacitated, housebound;
N Am bedrid
COLLOQ. laid up, flat on your back

bedrock n

foundation, support, basis, base, bottom, footing, reason(s), rationale, fundamentals, basics, essentials, fundamental point, starting-point, premise, first principles, essence, heart, core

beef v

complain, criticize, grumble, moan, grouse, object, dispute, disagree, carp
COLLOQ. gripe
Ea approve
■ beef up
strengthen, consolidate, give new energy to, toughen (up), invigorate, build up, establish, reinforce, substantiate, flesh out
Ea weaken

beefy adj

brawny, muscular, bulky, burly, fat, fleshy, heavy, hefty, hulking, stalwart, stocky, robust, sturdy
FORMAL corpulent
COLLOQ. tubby
Ea slight

beer n

ale, brew, liquor
COLLOQ. *Aust & NZ* grog; *N Am* brewski; *Aust* amber liquid

Types of beer include:

abbey beer	green beer	milk stout
ale	gueuze	oatmeal stout
Altbier	Guinness®	old ale
amber ale	guest beer	pale ale
barley wine	harvest ale	Pils
Berliner Weisse	*Scot* heavy	Pilsener (or
bière de garde	Hefeweizen (or	Pilsner)
bitter	Hefe-Weissbier)	porter
black-and-tan	Helles	Rauchbier
black beer	honey beer	real ale
black lager	ice beer	red ale
bock	India Pale Ale	rice beer
bottled beer	(IPA)	sahti
brown ale	Irish ale	*Scot* seventy
cask-conditioned	keg beer	(shilling)
ale	Kölsch	shandy
Christmas ale	Kriek	*Scot* sixty (shilling)
cream ale	Kristall-Weizen	snakebite
draught	kvass	*N Am* steam beer
dry beer	lager	stone beer
Dunkel	lambic	sweet stout
Scot eighty	light ale	stout
(shilling)	low-alcohol	Trappist
Eisbock	*N Am* malt liquor	Vienna
export	March (or Märzen)	Weizenbier (or
Framboise (or	beer	Weissbier)
frambozen)	microbrew	wheat beer
fruit beer	mild	winter ale

See also **drink**.

beetle v

dash, hurry, nip, run, rush, scamper, scurry, bustle, tear, zip
COLLOQ. scoot

beetling adj

overhanging, protruding, poking out, projecting, jutting, leaning over, sticking out
FORMAL pendent

befall v

1 HAPPEN TO, come upon, overwhelm, strike, fall upon
2 TAKE PLACE, happen, occur, arrive, chance, result, ensue, fall, follow, materialize
OLD bechance
FORMAL betide, supervene

befit v

become, suit, sit, harmonize with, match, complement;
Scot set
OLD seem, befall, sort; *(Shakesp)* besort
FORMAL behove

befitting adj

appropriate, suitable, becoming, apt, correct, decent, fit, fitting, proper, right
OLD meet, seemly
Ea unbecoming

before prep, adv

♦ *prep*
1 *before breakfast*
earlier than, previous to, prior to, not later than, sooner than, in preparation for, in anticipation of, on the eve of
2 *perform before the king*
in front of, in the presence of, in the sight of
3 *all of his life before him*
in front of, ahead of
Ea 1 after **3** behind
♦ *adv*
1 *have been here before*
earlier, formerly, previously, already
2 *go on before*
ahead, in front, in advance
Ea 1 later **2** behind

beforehand adv

in advance, preliminarily, already, before, previously, earlier, sooner, ahead of time

befriend v

help, aid, assist, succour, back, support, protect, defend, look after, stand by, uphold, sustain, comfort, encourage, welcome, favour, benefit, take under your wing, keep an eye on, make friends with, make a friend of, get to know, fall in with, stick up for
FORMAL succour
Ea neglect, oppose

befuddle v

confuse, muddle, baffle, bewilder, daze, disorient, perplex, nonplus, puzzle, stupefy
COLLOQ. faze

beg v

1 *beg someone to do something*
ask for, request, require, desire, crave, plead, appeal, turn to, entreat, implore, pray, supplicate, petition, solicit, importune; *Scot* fleech
OLD beseech
2 *beg for money*
ask for money, cadge, stand pad, skelder;
Scot thig; *N Am* panhandle
OLD prog
COLLOQ. bum, scrounge, touch for money, sponge; *N Am* mooch (off)
SLANG *N Am* schnorr
OLD SLANG maund, maunder

sense 1
Ask for and **request** are in general use in situations where someone wishes to obtain something, whereas **require** implies an element of need. The word **desire**, on the other hand, expresses a wish for something, while **crave** and **plead** are appropriate words for making a more heartfelt request: *I must crave your indulgence.* If an approach is aimed directly at someone, often someone in a position of power, then **appeal** is used: *Amnesty appealed to the king to stop the torture;* whereas the term **turn to** hints at a request for help or advice. Both **entreat** and **implore**, however, are more urgent in tone, suggesting an earnest, even piteous, application to someone: *his friends entreated him not to go.*

To convey an element of humility in begging, you could use **pray** or the rarer **supplicate**: *I pray you forgive me!* **Solicit** is less marked in tone and can be used of applying for something of a more abstract nature: *solicited support; they solicited his intervention.* For official approaches, the terms **petition** and **importune** can be used; these also suggest repetition and persistence: *I bombarded the War Office and importuned the Red Cross to protest.*

beget *v*
1 CAUSE, bring about, create, breed, give rise to, lead to, occasion, result in, engender
FORMAL effect
2 *beget a child*
breed, father, generate, produce, propagate, sire, spawn
FORMAL procreate

beggar *n, v*
♦ *n*
mendicant, supplicant, pauper, down-and-out, tramp, vagrant, vagabond, craver, besognio, lazzarone, canter, whipjack; *dialect* randy; *Scot* beadsman, bedesman, gaberlunzie, hallan-shaker; *N Am* panhandler, down-and-outer
OLD blowze, palliard, ruffler; (*Shakesp*) bezonian
COLLOQ. cadger, scrounger, sponger, freeloader, bum; *N Am* moocher
SLANG bludger, blighter, toerag; *N Am* schnorrer
OLD SLANG maunder, mumper, upright-man, jarkman
Related adjective: mendicant
♦ *v*
defy, baffle, challenge, exceed, surpass, transcend

Beggars can't be choosers

beggarly *adj*
stingy, abject, meagre, mean, miserly, contemptible, despicable, inadequate, low, needy, niggardly, paltry, slight, insubstantial, modest, pathetic, pitiful, wretched
E3 affluent, generous

begin *v*
start, commence, set about, embark on, set in motion, get going, launch into, do first, activate, actuate, set off, originate, initiate, introduce, found, institute, open, instigate, arise, spring, emerge, appear, crop up
COLLOQ. kick off, get cracking, set the ball rolling, take the plunge
E3 end, stop, finish, cease, conclude

Start and **commence** are general terms to describe the initial action or operation of someone or something. **Set about** hints at preparation: *he set about ordering his life.* **Embark on** is used to imply that someone is at the beginning of a more lengthy undertaking: *He'd embarked on a thorough analysis of the historical data.* **Set in motion** could describe the actions of someone

with responsibility for the initial stages of a process: *the Home Secretary set in motion a review of the law.* If something or someone **gets going** a sense of moving into a phase of productive activity is conveyed: *the film was slow to start but when it got going it was outstanding.*

The term **launch into** can also be used to suggest great activity and enthusiasm, sometimes to the point of naivety, while **activate**, **actuate** and **set off** are also suggestive of moving something into action. On the other hand, **originate** and **initiate**, along with the terms **found** and **institute**, are more suggestive of creating something from scratch: *the alarm is activated when oxygen levels fall; psychological studies initiated by Freud.* **Instigate** is another word suggestive of providing the means for existence. **Introduce**, however, emphasizes bringing something to people's attention rather than creating it. **Open** may be used of abstracts, such as discussions, but equally of more tangible things: *they opened their first hotel.*

Arise and **spring** appropriately describe coming suddenly into being, and while **emerge** and **appear** are also used of something coming to light, it is at a more gradual pace. The informal term **crop up** would only be used to indicate something happening unexpectedly: *a problem had just cropped up.*

beginner *n*
novice, tiro, starter, learner, trainee, apprentice, student, probationer, initiate, freshman, fresher, pupil, recruit, raw recruit, cub, tenderfoot, fledgling, neophyte, Johnny-raw
OLD abecedarian
COLLOQ. greenhorn, rookie, newbie
SLANG noob, *Aust* new chum
E3 veteran, old hand, expert

A man ceases to be a beginner in any given science and becomes a master in that science when he has learned that … he is going to be a beginner all his life
R G COLLINGWOOD, *New Leviathan*

beginning *n*
start, commencement, onset, outset, first part, opening part, opening, preface, prelude, introduction, initiation, establishment, inauguration, institution, launch, inception, starting-point, birth, dawn, origin, source, fountainhead, root, seed, conception, genesis, emergence, rise, fresh start, new beginnings, pastures new; *N Am* get-go
FORMAL inchoation, incipience
COLLOQ. the word go, day one, square one, first base, kick-off, intro, new leaf
E3 end, finish, conclusion

begrudge *v*
resent, be resentful of, grudge, mind, object to, envy, covet, be jealous of, stint
E3 allow

beguile *v*
1 CHARM, enchant, bewitch, captivate, delight, attract, amuse, entertain, divert, distract, occupy, engross
2 DECEIVE, fool, hoodwink, dupe, trick, cheat, delude, mislead, seduce, cozen, wile
OLD blend; (*Spenser*) guile
COLLOQ. lead up the garden path, pull the wool over someone's eyes

beguiling *adj*
alluring, appealing, attractive, bewitching, captivating, charming, delightful, diverting, enchanting, entertaining, interesting, intriguing, enticing, seductive
E3 offensive, repulsive

behalf
■ **on behalf of**
for, representing, as a representative of, acting for, for the benefit/good of, for the sake of, in the name/authority of,

in the interests of, to the advantage/profit of, for account of, in support of

behave v

1 *behave aggressively*
act, conduct yourself, be, acquit yourself, respond, react, perform
FORMAL comport yourself

2 *tell the children to behave themselves*
be good, be well-behaved, act properly/politely, be on your best behaviour, mind your manners, stay out of trouble
COLLOQ. act your age, keep your nose clean, not mess about/muck about, stop fooling around, mind your p's and q's, not put a foot wrong

3 *electrons behave like this*
function, operate, work, act, perform, react
◼ **2** misbehave, get into trouble; *colloq.* act up, be up to no good

behaviour n

1 *the child's behaviour*
conduct, manner, manners, ways, habits, dealings, way of acting, response, reaction, attitudes
FORMAL demeanour, comportment, deportment

2 *the behaviour of chemical elements*
operation, performance, functioning, action, reaction

SYNONYM NUANCES

sense 1
Conduct is a general term used to describe the way a person acts, and **manner** may also be used in this way; **manners**, however, is used of behaviour in relation to expected social conventions: *he didn't have the manners to write*. **Ways**, on the other hand, would be used of the usual mannerisms peculiar to an individual: *he'd become set in his ways*; whilst **habits** may be used more narrowly to imply certain instilled traits. To talk of the way someone conducts their affairs, particularly in business, you might use the word **dealings**.
   The idea of **attitudes** returns us to the notion of generally held opinions within society, and their effect on behaviour: *puritanical attitudes in sexual matters*. **Response** and **reaction** are only appropriate where a person's actions are the result of something that has previously taken place.

---

behead v
decapitate, execute, kill, put to death, guillotine
OLD decollate, head

behest n
◼ **at the behest of**
with the authority of, at the bidding of, at the order/ command of, at the request of, on the instruction(s) of, on the wishes of
OLD at the hest of

behind prep, adv, n
◆ *prep*
1 *a shed behind the garage*
at the back of, at the rear of, on the other side of; *N Am* in back of
2 *walk behind the others*
after, following, at the back of, at the rear of, close on
3 *behind schedule*
late, later than, running late, overdue, slow, slower than usual
4 *we are behind you in your decision*
supporting, backing, endorsing, for, on the side of
5 *the reasons behind the change in policy*
responsible for, explaining, accounting for, instigating, causing, initiating, giving rise to, at the bottom of
◼ **1** in front of **2** ahead of **3** in advance of
◆ *adv*
1 *with a garden behind*
at the back/rear, in the rear

2 *with the stragglers following behind*
after, following, at the back, next, subsequently
3 *be behind with work/payments*
behindhand, late, delayed, overdue, in arrears, in debt
◆ *n*
bottom, buttocks, backside, rump
COLLOQ. bum, posterior; *N Am* ass, butt, heinie; *Scot* bahookie
SLANG
(*vulgar*) arse

behindhand adv
delayed, late, behind, behind schedule, remiss, slow, tardy, backward
FORMAL dilatory

behold v, interj
◆ *v*
consider, contemplate, descry, discern, espy, look at, see, watch, note, observe, mark, perceive, regard, scan, gaze at, survey, view, witness
◆ *interj*
look, mark, observe, see, watch, *voici, voila, ecce, la*
OLD lo

beholden adj
indebted, obligated, obliged, under (an) obligation, bound, grateful, owing, thankful, appreciative; *Scot* addebted

behove v
be proper, be to your advantage, benefit, profit, be advantageous, be necessary, be essential, be suitable for, be appropriate for
OLD be seemly
FORMAL befit

beige adj
buff, fawn, mushroom, camel, sandy, khaki, coffee, oatmeal, oyster, suede, tan, ecru, greige, taupe, neutral

being n
1 EXISTENCE, reality, life, living, animation, essence, substance, nature, soul, spirit
TECHNICAL haecceity, esse
FORMAL actuality
2 CREATURE, animal, beast, human being, human, man, woman, mortal, person, individual, thing, entity
3 *deep in my being*
soul, spirit, inner being, inner self, nature, psyche, heart, emotions, will, personality
COLLOQ. heart of hearts

belabour v
1 HIT, attack, beat, flog, thrash, strike, whip, belt, flay, pummel
OLD sauce, lay on load
2 *belabour the point*
harp on about, keep talking about, dwell on, reiterate
COLLOQ. go on and on about, flog to death

belated adj
late, tardy, overdue, delayed, behindhand, behind schedule, unpunctual
◼ punctual, on time, timely

belatedly adv
behind schedule, unpunctually, tardily
◼ punctually, on time

belch v, n
◆ *v*
1 *the baby belched*
burp, hiccup, bring up wind; *dialect* boke; *Scot* rift, yex, yesk
FORMAL eruct, eructate
2 *chimneys belching out smoke*
emit, give out, give off, discharge, issue, gush, vent, eject, disgorge, spew
◆ *n*
burp, hiccup
FORMAL eructation

beleaguered *adj*
1 *a beleaguered person*
harassed, pestered, troubled, tormented, badgered, bothered, worried, vexed, plagued, persecuted, beset
2 *a beleaguered city*
besieged, under siege, surrounded, blockaded

belie *v*
1 *the statistics belie the theory*
disprove, contradict, deny, refute, negate, run counter to
FORMAL gainsay, confute
2 *her looks belie her age*
conceal, disguise, misrepresent, falsify, mislead, deceive, cover up

belief *n*
1 OPINION, persuasion, feeling, intuition, impression, notion, theory, view, viewpoint, point of view, conviction, judgement
2 CONFIDENCE, reliance, trust, faith, credit, assurance, certainty, sureness, presumption, expectation
3 IDEOLOGY, faith, creed, doctrine, teaching, dogma, theory, ism, tenet, principle, ethic, ideal
E3 2 disbelief, doubt

believable *adj*
credible, imaginable, conceivable, acceptable, plausible, possible, likely, probable, authoritative, reliable, trustworthy, (well) within the bounds of possibility, not beyond the realms of possibility, with a ring of truth
E3 unbelievable, incredible, inconceivable, implausible, unconvincing

believe *v*
1 *I believe she's a professor*
think, be of the opinion that, accept, suppose, gather, reckon, assume, consider, hold, maintain, understand, speculate, conjecture, guess, imagine, judge; *N Am* figure
OLD ween, wis, wist
FORMAL deem, postulate, opine
2 *believe him/that he is telling the truth*
accept, trust, be convinced by, be persuaded by, have confidence in, be certain of, take someone's word for it
OLD trow
COLLOQ. take on board, swallow, fall for, buy, wear, fall for/swallow hook line and sinker
E3 2 disbelieve, doubt, question
■ **believe in**
1 *believe in God*
be sure of the existence/reality of, be convinced of
2 *believe in hard work*
approve of, favour, be in favour of, recommend, encourage, swear by, trust, be persuaded by, value highly, depend on, rely on, have confidence in, accept the importance of
FORMAL set great store by
COLLOQ. rate

> QUOTATIONS
> We can believe what we choose. We are answerable for what we choose to believe
> CARDINAL JOHN NEWMAN

believer *n*
convert, proselyte, disciple, follower, adherent, devotee, zealot, supporter, upholder
E3 unbeliever, sceptic

belittle *v*
demean, minimize, play down, trivialize, dismiss, underrate, understate, undervalue, underestimate, downgrade, deprecate, lessen, diminish, detract from, decry, slate, sell short, deride, scorn, ridicule
FORMAL disparage
COLLOQ. slam, knock, run down, rubbish, pick holes in, pull to pieces, tear to shreds, do a hatchet job on
SLANG slag (off); *N Am* dump on
E3 exaggerate, praise

bell *n*
gong, ring, chime, peal, knell, warning, signal, siren, horn, hooter, bleep, bleeper
OLD alarum

belle *n*
beauty, charmer, siren, Venus, *femme fatale*
COLLOQ. good-looker, smasher, corker, cracker, knockout, stunner, peach

bellicose *adj*
aggressive, militant, argumentative, quarrelsome, contentious, belligerent, combative, violent, bullying, antagonistic, warring, warlike
FORMAL pugnacious
E3 peaceable

belligerence *n*
aggression, militancy, argumentativeness, provocation, quarrelsomeness, unfriendliness, contentiousness, combativeness, violence, bullying, antagonism, war, warmongering, sabre-rattling
FORMAL pugnacity
E3 complaisance

belligerent *adj*
aggressive, militant, argumentative, provocative, hostile, quarrelsome, contentious, combative, violent, bullying, antagonistic, warring, warlike, warmongering, sabre-rattling
FORMAL pugnacious, disputatious, truculent
COLLOQ. scrappy; *Can* chippy
E3 peaceable

bellow *v, n*
♦ *v*
roar, yell, shout, bawl, cry, scream, shriek, howl, clamour, thunder, raise your voice, troat; *dialect* rout; *Scot* buller
COLLOQ. holler
♦ *n*
roar, yell, shout, bawl, cry, scream, shriek, howl, troat; *Scot* buller
COLLOQ. holler

belly *n*
stomach, abdomen, gut, guts, insides, intestines, paunch, pot-belly, beer belly; *dialect* wame
TECHNICAL venter
COLLOQ. tummy, corporation
SLANG bread basket
Related adjective: alvine

belong *v*
1 *this book belongs to me*
be owned by, be the possession of, be the property of, be under the ownership of, be yours
2 *belong to a rugby club*
be a member of, be affiliated to, be connected with, be associated with, be in, be an adherent of
3 *this lid belongs to that pan*
fit, go with, be part of, attach to, link up with, tie up with, be connected with, relate to
4 *Where do these toys belong?*
have as its place/home, go, be situated, be found, fit in, be sorted, be categorized, be classified, be included

belonging *n*
rapport, closeness, acceptance, affinity, association, attachment, compatibility, fellow-feeling, fellowship, affiliation, kinship, link(s), loyalty, relationship
E3 antipathy

belongings *n*
possessions, property, chattels, goods, (personal) paraphernalia
FORMAL effects, appurtenances, accoutrements
COLLOQ. gear, stuff, tackle, kit, clobber, things

beloved *adj, n*
- *adj*

loved, much loved, adored, cherished, endeared, treasured, prized, precious, pet, favourite, dearest, dear, darling, admired, revered, worshipped
OLD lief, alder-liefest; *(Shakesp)* tender
- *n*

sweetheart, darling, dear, dearest, love, loved one, true-love, fiancé, fiancée, betrothed, boyfriend, girlfriend, special friend, partner, spouse, husband, wife, favourite, lover, pet, precious, sweet, lady-love, joy; *Scot* jo
OLD *(Spenser)* belamoure; liking
FORMAL inamorata, inamorato
COLLOQ. angel, baby, sweetie, honey, bird, fella

below *adv, prep*
- *adv*

1 *the flat below mine*
beneath, under, underneath, down, lower, lower down
2 *see below for details*
later, at a later place, further on, underneath
🖃 **1, 2** above
- *prep*

1 UNDER, underneath, beneath, lower than
2 INFERIOR TO, lower (in rank) than, lesser than, subordinate to, subject to
🖃 **1, 2** above

belt *n, v*
- *n*

1 SASH, girdle, waistband, girth, strap, baldric, cingulum, bandoleer, zona
OLD cestus, mitre
FORMAL cummerbund, ceinture, cincture
2 *a conveyor belt*
strip, band, strap, cord, chain, loop
3 STRIP, area, region, district, sector, zone, swathe, stretch, tract, extent, layer
4 THUMP, hit, punch, strike, swipe, knock, clout, bang, blow, bashing, slap, smack, pelt, bruise, box
COLLOQ. tan, wallop, whack, biff, slosh
- *v*

1 HIT, strap, flog, lash, whip, flay, cane, birch, punch, strike, swipe, knock, clout, bang, slap, smack, thump, thwack, pelt, bruise, box
COLLOQ. bash, clobber, tan, wallop, whack, biff, give someone a good hiding
2 *belt along the road*
dash, tear, fly, rush, career, zip, charge, speed
■ **belt up**
shut up, be quiet
COLLOQ. pipe down, cut it out
SLANG put a sock in it, keep your trap shut, shut your mouth/face
■ **below the belt**
unfair, unjust, uncalled-for, unjustified, dishonest, underhand, unscrupulous, unethical
COLLOQ. dirty, out of order

bemoan *v*
lament, mourn, bewail, wail, deplore, grieve for, regret, rue, sigh for, sorrow over, weep for
🖃 gloat

bemuse *v*
confuse, bewilder, puzzle, baffle, perplex, daze, muddle, befuddle, stupefy
COLLOQ. bamboozle, throw, faze, floor
🖃 enlighten, illuminate

bemused *adj*
bewildered, confused, puzzled, perplexed, baffled, disconcerted, dazed, overwhelmed, muddled, befuddled, stupefied, astounded, astonished, mused; *N Am* pixilated
COLLOQ. bamboozled, fazed, floored
🖃 clear-headed, clear, lucid

bemusement *n*
confusion, puzzlement, bewilderment, perplexity, daze, bafflement, disorientation, stupefaction

bench *n*
1 SEAT, form, settle, pew, ledge
TECHNICAL thwart
OLD bink
2 *work at a bench*
counter, table, stall, board, workbench, worktable
3 COURT, courtroom, tribunal, judiciary, judicature, judge, magistrate, tribune, bank
TECHNICAL banc

benchmark *n*
criterion, example, level, model, norm, pattern, reference, reference-point, point of reference, guideline(s), standard, basis, gauge, scale, touchstone, yardstick

bend *v, n*
- *v*

1 *bend down to pick up a pin*
stoop, crouch, lean, incline, bow, kneel, squat
2 *bend the wire*
curve, make curved, turn, deflect, twist, contort, flex, crook, shape, mould, arch, bow, loop, buckle, warp
3 *the road bends*
curve, turn, deflect, veer, diverge, twist, wind, meander, zigzag, swerve, deviate
FORMAL incurve
4 *bend to their will*
mould, shape, persuade, influence, affect, sway, direct, manipulate, compel
🖃 **2** straighten
- *n*

curvature, curve, arc, bow, loop, hook, crook, elbow, angle, corner, hairpin bend, dog-leg, turn, twist, kink, zigzag, divergence, deflection
TECHNICAL flexure
FORMAL incurvation
■ **bend over backwards**
try very hard, exert yourself, go all out, do your best, put yourself out, trouble yourself
COLLOQ. leave no stone unturned, move heaven and earth, pull out all the stops

beneath *adv, prep*
- *adv*

below, under, underneath, lower, lower down
🖃 above
- *prep*

1 UNDER, underneath, below, lower than
2 UNWORTHY OF, unbefitting, unbecoming
🖃 **1** above

benediction *n*
blessing, prayer, thanksgiving, consecration, favour, grace, invocation
FORMAL benison
🖃 anathema, curse; *formal* execration

benefactor *n*
patron, sponsor, backer, supporter, promoter, donor, contributor, subscriber, provider, subsidizer, philanthropist, helper, friend, well-wisher, giver
COLLOQ. angel, fairy godmother
🖃 opponent, persecutor

beneficent *adj*
altruistic, liberal, benevolent, benign, bountiful, charitable, compassionate, generous, helpful, kind, unselfish, Grandisonian, benefic
FORMAL munificent
🖃 mean

beneficial *adj*
advantageous, favourable, useful, helpful, good, worthwhile, promising, profitable, serviceable, rewarding, valuable, improving, edifying, wholesome, salutary
FORMAL propitious
🖃 harmful, detrimental, useless

beneficiary *n*
payee, receiver, recipient, inheritor, legatee, heir, heiress, successor, the assured

benefit *n, v*

♦ *n*

1 *the benefits of exercise*
advantage, good, good point, gain, profit, asset, reward, merit, blessing, boon, interest, favour, bonus, benefaction, dividend, fringe benefit
OLD behoof
FORMAL perquisite
COLLOQ. pay-off, perk

2 *of benefit to children*
good, help, aid, assistance, service, use, sake, interest, behalf, welfare
OLD behoof
FORMAL avail

3 *child benefit; unemployment benefit*
income, allowance, pension, sick pay, payment, social security, credit, support, Job Seekers Allowance (JSA), unemployment benefit, income support; *Scot & Irish* buroo
COLLOQ. dole; *N Am* welfare
E3 1 disadvantage **2** harm, damage

♦ *v*
help, aid, assist, serve, be of service to, be advantageous to, be of advantage to, do good to, profit, gain, improve, enhance, better, further, advance, promote
FORMAL avail
E3 hinder, harm, undermine

benevolence *n*
philanthropy, humanitarianism, charitableness, generosity, liberality, magnanimity, altruism, humaneness, goodness, goodwill, kindness, kind-heartedness, friendliness, compassion, pity, mercy, grace, tolerance, care, considerateness
FORMAL munificence
E3 meanness

benevolent *adj*
philanthropic, humanitarian, charitable, generous, liberal, magnanimous, altruistic, benign, humane, kind, kind-hearted, soft-hearted, friendly, kindly, well-disposed, compassionate, merciful, gracious, tolerant, caring, considerate
FORMAL munificent
E3 mean, selfish, malevolent

benevolently *adv*
philanthropically, charitably, generously, liberally, magnanimously, altruistically, benignly, humanely, kindly, kind-heartedly, soft-heartedly, compassionately, mercifully, graciously, tolerantly, considerately
E3 selfishly, malevolently

benighted *adj*
ignorant, unenlightened, inexperienced, unknowing, uneducated, unschooled, uncultured, backward, illiterate, unlettered, unfortunate, nighted
OLD belated

benign *adj*

1 BENEVOLENT, charitable, good, gracious, gentle, kind, kindly, warm-hearted, obliging, friendly, amiable, affable, genial, avuncular, sweet, cordial, generous, liberal, sympathetic
OLD benefic

2 *benign conditions/climate*
favourable, advantageous, opportune, providential, beneficial, agreeable, temperate, mild, gentle, warm, refreshing, healthy, restorative, wholesome
OLD benedict
FORMAL auspicious, propitious, salubrious

3 *a benign tumour*
curable, harmless, non-malignant, treatable, innocent
E3 1 hostile **2** harmful, unpleasant **3** malignant, cancerous, dangerous

benignly *adv*
benevolently, charitably, graciously, generously, sympathetically, kindly, obligingly, genially, amiably, affably

bent *adj, n*

♦ *adj*

1 ANGLED, curved, bowed, arched, flexed, crooked, folded, doubled, twisted, hunched, stooped, sagged, warped, contorted

2 DISHONEST, illegal, criminal, corrupt, fraudulent, swindling, untrustworthy
COLLOQ. dodgy, crooked

3 HOMOSEXUAL, gay, lesbian
COLLOQ. camp, butch
SLANG
(*offensive*) queer, dykey
E3 1 straight, upright **2** honest, trustworthy

♦ *n*
tendency, inclination, disposition, leaning, preference, ability, capacity, faculty, aptitude, facility, gift, talent, fondness, knack, flair, forte
FORMAL predisposition, predilection, penchant, proclivity, propensity
COLLOQ. cup of tea

■ **bent on**
determined to, resolved to, set on, fixed on, insistent on, intent on, inclined to, disposed to

bequeath *v*

1 *bequeathed in her will*
leave, bestow, will, make over, give, endow, grant, consign, transfer, assign, entrust, commit
FORMAL demise, devise

2 *social problems bequeathed by past generations*
hand down, pass on, impart, transmit

bequest *n*
legacy, inheritance, heritage, trust, endowment, gift, donation, estate, settlement
FORMAL devisal, bestowal, bequeathal

berate *v*
scold, chide, reprimand, rebuke, tell off, reproach, reprove, censure, chastise, criticize, slate, rail at, revile, upbraid
FORMAL castigate, fulminate, vituperate
COLLOQ. blast, read the riot act to, dress down, tear a strip off, give a rocket to, rap over the knuckles, give hell, *N Am* chew out
E3 praise

bereaved *adj*
deprived, grieving, lost, dispossessed, divested, robbed, orphaned, widowed

bereavement *n*
loss, death, passing, passing-away, deprivation, dispossession, sadness, sorrow, grief
OLD orbity

bereft
■ **bereft of**
deprived of, robbed of, stripped of, destitute of, devoid of, lacking, wanting, parted from, cut off from, minus

berserk *adj*
mad, crazy, demented, insane, deranged, frantic, frenzied, crazed, wild, raging, furious, violent, rabid, manic, maniacal, raving, hysterical, uncontrollable, beside yourself
COLLOQ. barmy, batty, nuts, out of your mind, off your head, off the deep end
E3 sane, calm

berth *n, v*

♦ *n*

1 BED, bunk, hammock, billet

2 MOORING, anchorage, quay, wharf, dock, harbour, port

♦ *v*
anchor, dock, drop/cast anchor, land, moor, tie up
E3 weigh anchor, up anchor

■ **give a wide berth to**
avoid, evade, shun, steer clear of, keep your distance from, keep at arm's length

FORMAL eschew
COLLOQ. dodge, give a miss

beseech v
beg, call on, entreat, implore, ask, petition, plead, pray,
solicit, appeal to, supplicate, crave, desire
FORMAL adjure, importune, obsecrate,
sue, exhort

beset v
assail, attack, harass, entangle, worry,
pester, plague, press, torment, bedevil, hem in,
surround, besiege
OLD bego, belay; (Shakesp) lay; obsess
COLLOQ. hassle

besetting adj
compulsive, habitual, persistent, dominant,
inveterate, irresistible, uncontrollable, obsessive,
prevalent, constant, recurring, troublesome,
harassing

beside prep
next to, by, alongside, by the side of, abreast of, adjacent,
abutting, bordering, neighbouring, next door to, close to,
near, overlooking
■ **beside yourself**
berserk, insane, mad, crazy, crazed, delirious, demented,
deranged, overcome, out of your mind, frantic, frenetic,
frenzied, distraught, unbalanced, unhinged

besides adv, prep
♦ adv
also, as well, too, in addition, additionally, further,
furthermore, moreover
OLD forby, withal
COLLOQ. what's more
♦ prep
apart from, other than, aside from, in addition to, over and
above, as well as, excluding

besiege v
1 LAY SIEGE TO, blockade, surround, encircle, encompass,
confine, beleaguer
OLD (Spenser) assiege; belay, besit, obsess
2 besieged by reporters
surround, encircle, encompass, confine, shut in, hem in,
overwhelm
3 TROUBLE, worry, bother, oppress, torment, importune,
assail, beset, beleaguer, harass, pester, badger, nag, hound,
plague

besmirch v
defame, defile, dishonour, slander, smear,
soil, dirty, blacken, damage, stain, sully, tarnish,
besmear; dialect slur
OLD besmutch
🖃 enhance

besotted adj
infatuated, doting, obsessed, smitten, hypnotized,
spellbound, stupefied, bewitched, intoxicated,
bedazzled, sotted
COLLOQ. crazy, wild, mad, potty, bowled over,
swept off your feet
🖃 indifferent, disenchanted

bespatter v
spatter, splatter, splash, splodge, spray, sprinkle, shower,
scatter, dirty, soil, stain, smear

bespeak v
demonstrate, indicate, reveal, show, speak for, signify,
denote, display, exhibit, attest, proclaim, suggest, imply,
engage
FORMAL evince, evidence, betoken

best adj, adv, n, v
♦ adj
optimum, optimal, first, foremost, leading, top, ultimate,
prime, record-breaking, unequalled, unsurpassed,
unrivalled, unbeatable, matchless, peerless, incomparable,
supreme, pre-eminent, premium, of highest quality,

greatest, highest, largest, finest, worthiest, excellent,
outstanding, superlative, first-rate, first-class, ideal, perfect,
top-drawer
FORMAL nonpareil
COLLOQ. ace, star, number one, (the) tops, plum, second
to none, the pick of the bunch, one in a million, a cut
above the rest
🖃 worst
♦ adv
greatly, extremely, exceptionally, excellently,
outstandingly, superlatively, unsurpassedly, matchlessly,
incomparably, supremely, most, to the greatest/highest
degree
🖃 worst, least
♦ n
1 **students who are the best in their year**
finest, cream, prime, élite, top, first, pick, choice, flower,
jewel, favourite, star, highlight, crème de la crème, pièce
de résistance
COLLOQ. the pick of the bunch
2 **do your best**
hardest, utmost, greatest effort
COLLOQ. damnedest
🖃 **1** worst
♦ v
defeat, conquer, overcome, beat, get the better of,
overwhelm, overpower, subdue, rout, annihilate, outplay,
outwit, outsmart, worst, trounce, be more than a match
for, have the edge on
FORMAL vanquish
COLLOQ. hammer, slaughter, clobber, lick, thrash

> **QUOTATIONS**
> Grow old along with me! / The best is yet to be, / The
> last of life, for which the first was made
> ROBERT BROWNING, Dramatis Personae

SYNONYM NUANCES

adjective
Optimum and **optimal** are interchangeable and convey
the sense of something advantageous: the optimum
conditions for growth. On the other hand, **first**,
foremost, **leading** and **pre-eminent** are suitable terms to
describe the position held by someone or something in
relation to their peers: the foremost authority on the
subject; the pre-eminent players in the global market.
Top is similar, but possibly more suggestive of an
underlying hierarchy. **Worthiest** is applicable to
something outstanding in terms of merit: the worthiest of
causes.
  If you wish to emphasize thoroughly the outstanding
nature of something, you could use **unequalled**,
unsurpassed, **unrivalled**, **unbeatable**, **matchless**,
peerless, **incomparable** and **outstanding**, which
suggest that everyone or everything else is infinitely
inferior: a place of matchless beauty. The terms **ultimate**
or **supreme** go further by suggesting it cannot be
bettered: the ultimate weapon against crime; he was the
supreme all-rounder.
  Fine and **prime** are more restrained adjectives to use,
but can convey an impression of quality: one of the
finest poets; a prime tourist attraction. Similarly, you can
use **superlative** and **excellent** to suggest that something
is extraordinarily good, but **ideal** and **perfect** applied
literally suggest the aspirational rather than achievable,
though their everyday usage implies perfection is now
more easily reached: the perfect pint.

bestial adj
cruel, savage, brutal, animal, barbaric, barbarous, beastly,
inhuman, brutish, carnal, depraved, degraded, gross,
sensual, sordid, vile
FORMAL feral
🖃 civilized, humane

bestiality n
cruelty, savagery, animal behaviour, barbarism,
sordidness, inhumanity

bestir v
arouse, exert, awaken, stimulate,
energize, galvanize, incite, motivate, activate,
actuate, animate
Ⅎ calm, lull, quell

bestow v
award, present, grant, confer, endow, bequeath,
communicate, dispose, commit, entrust, impart,
transmit, allot, apportion, accord, give, donate, lavish,
wreak
OLD estate
Ⅎ withhold, deprive

bestride v
1 DOMINATE, command, overshadow
2 BESTRADDLE, cross, sit astride, stand
astride, straddle

bestseller n
blockbuster, hit, smash hit, success, triumph,
brand leader

bestselling adj
famous, popular, leading, top, unbeaten

bet v, n
♦ v
1 *bet money on a horse*
wager, gamble, punt, speculate, risk, hazard, chance,
venture, lay, stake, bid, pledge, back, put,
place, play for money
COLLOQ. have a flutter
2 *I bet she did it on purpose*
be certain, be sure, be convinced, expect,
not be surprised
♦ n
1 *place a bet*
wager, gamble, speculation, risk, venture, stake,
ante, bid, pledge, lottery, sweepstake, accumulator,
triple, perfecta; N Am superfecta; Aust trifecta
COLLOQ. flutter, punt
2 *my bet is that he'll stay*
opinion, feeling, intuition, impression, notion, theory,
view, viewpoint, point of view, conviction, judgement,
forecast, prediction
3 *your best bet*
choice, option, course of action, alternative

bête noire n
bugbear, bane, abomination, anathema, aversion,
curse, pet hate, pet aversion
COLLOQ. thorn in the flesh/side
Ⅎ favourite

betide v
chance, develop, ensue, happen, occur, take place,
overtake
OLD befall
FORMAL supervene

betoken v
signal, indicate, signify, suggest, token, bode,
forebode, presage, declare, denote, represent, manifest,
mark, promise
OLD bespeak
FORMAL augur, portend, evidence, prognosticate

betray v
1 *betray a friend*
inform on, double-cross, cross, desert, abandon,
turn traitor, be disloyal to, be unfaithful to, break faith
with, go back on, break your promise to, renege on,
abuse, let down, play false, deceive, delude,
mislead, dupe
OLD bewray
FORMAL forsake

COLLOQ. tell on, rat on, sell (out), sell down the river,
stab in the back, squeal on, blow the whistle on, shop,
walk out on, split on; Aust dob
SLANG grass, rumble, peach; N Am stool on
2 DISCLOSE, give away, tell, divulge, expose, reveal, show,
manifest, let slip, bring to light, unmask
Ⅎ 1 defend, protect, be loyal to 2 conceal, hide

SYNONYM NUANCES

sense 1
Most of the terms to describe the action of betraying
carry a tone of disapproval. **Inform on** is used generally
for the verbal identification of someone or their deeds,
whereas **double-cross** suggests a pretence of aiding
someone while actually working against them, and
carries a strong tone of disapprobation.
   Desert, **abandon** and **forsake** all share the idea of
leaving something or someone behind because it is no
longer of use: *politicians are willing to forsake their
principles*; whilst **go back on**, and **renege on** have
more to do with acting contrary to a promise: *the
country reneged on its pledge.* **Abuse** implies an
improper treatment of trust, and again carries a rather
strong note of criticism: *you abused your position as
police officer.*
   You might use **let down** to place more emphasis on
the disappointment felt by the betrayed person. **Deceive**
and **mislead** are the words to use when false
information has been given; likewise **dupe**, which
further implies trickery has been involved. **Delude** also
suggests a trick, but more likely one played on the mind:
ideas which delude people into thinking they are safe.

---

betrayal n
treachery, treason, sell-out, disloyalty,
unfaithfulness, double-dealing, double-crossing,
duplicity, backstabbing, deception, trickery, duping,
falseness, breaking faith
FORMAL perfidy
COLLOQ. stab in the back
Ⅎ loyalty, faithfulness, protection

betrayer n
traitor, Judas, informer, stool pigeon, double-crosser,
deceiver, conspirator, renegade, apostate
OLD traditor, treacher
COLLOQ. whistle-blower, backstabber
SLANG grass, supergrass; N Am stoolie
Ⅎ protector, supporter

betrothal n
engagement, proposal of marriage, promise,
vow(s), contract
OLD affiance, assurance, handfast, plighting of
your troth, troth
FORMAL espousal, fiançailles

betrothed adj
engaged, engaged to be married, contracted,
promised, pledged
OLD affianced, troth; (Shakesp) trothplight,
combinate
FORMAL espoused

better adj, v
♦ adj
1 SUPERIOR, bigger, larger, longer, greater, worthier,
of higher quality, finer, surpassing, preferable,
more acceptable, more fitting, more advantageous,
more valuable
COLLOQ. a cut above
2 IMPROVING, progressing, on the mend,
recovering, fitter, healthier, stronger, (fully)
recovered, restored, cured, healed, well
COLLOQ. on the mend
Ⅎ 1 inferior 2 worse

♦ *v*

1 IMPROVE, enhance, raise, make better, further, promote, forward, reform, mend, correct, rectify, enrich
FORMAL ameliorate
2 SURPASS, top, beat, outdo, exceed, improve on, outstrip, overtake, cap, go one better than
Ⅎ 1 worsen, deteriorate

betterment *n*
improvement, furtherance, advancement, edification, enhancement, enrichment
FORMAL amelioration, melioration
Ⅎ deterioration, impairment

between *prep*
in the middle (of), in the space between, among, halfway, mid, amid, amidst, amongst

bevel *n, v*
♦ *n*
oblique, slant, slope, tilt, angle, bias, splay, diagonal, mitre, basil, bezel, cant
TECHNICAL chamfer
♦ *v*
slant, slope, tilt, angle, mitre, bias, cant
TECHNICAL chamfer

beverage *n*
drink, draught, liquor, liquid, refreshment
OLD potation, potable

bevy *n*
gathering, group, band, gang, company, assembly, collection, troop, troupe, flock, gaggle, pack, bunch, crowd, throng

bewail *v*
grieve over, sorrow over, lament, bemoan, cry over, moan, mourn, regret, repent, rue, sigh over, beat your breast, deplore, keen
Ⅎ gloat, glory, vaunt

beware *v*
watch out, look out, mind (out), be careful, be cautious, be wary, take heed, steer clear of, avoid, shun, guard against, be on your guard, be on the lookout for
OLD ware
SLANG cave

bewilder *v*
confuse, muddle, mix up, disconcert, confound, baffle, puzzle, perplex, nonplus, mystify, daze, maze, stupefy, bemuse, disorient; *Scot* bumbaze, fickle
OLD wilder
COLLOQ. bamboozle, stump, flummox, faze, floor, wander, tie up in knots; *N Am* buffalo
SLANG take to town

bewildered *adj*
confused, muddled, uncertain, disoriented, distracted, baffled, puzzled, perplexed, mystified, taken aback, bemused, surprised, speechless, stunned, wandered, mixed up, muzzy, dizzy, fogged, pixy-led; *Scot* tavert, will, wull
OLD bemazed
COLLOQ. bamboozled, nonplussed, flummoxed, fazed, floored, jiggered; *N Am* pixilated; (all) at sea
Ⅎ unperturbed, collected

bewildering *adj*
puzzling, perplexing, baffling, confusing, mystifying, mysterious, surprising, amazing, astounding, dizzy, unfathomable, cryptic, enigmatic

bewilderment *n*
perplexity, confusion, uncertainty, daze, disconcertion, disorientation, mystification, puzzlement, stupefaction, surprise, awe, muddle, fog, mizmaze, *égarement*; *dialect* maze
OLD amaze
Ⅎ composure, confidence

bewitch *v*
charm, enchant, allure, beguile, spellbind, possess, enthral, captivate, enrapture, delight, obsess, fascinate, intrigue, tantalize, seduce, entrance, mesmerize, hypnotize, transfix, strike, take, witch, sirenize, overlook, hex, voodoo, hoodoo, obi; *dialect* wish; *Scot* forspeak
OLD ensorcell
Ⅎ disenchant, repel

beyond *prep*
1 *the fields beyond the house*
on the far side of, on the other side of, further than, away from, remote from, apart from
2 *beyond the age of 16*
after, past, later than, above, over, greater than, upwards of
3 *beyond me/my understanding*
out of reach of, out of range of, further than the limitations of

bias *n, v*
♦ *n*
1 *racial bias*
prejudice, partiality, favouritism, one-sidedness, unfairness, bigotry, intolerance, stereotyping, distortion, bent, leaning, inclination, tendency
FORMAL propensity, proclivity, predilection
2 *cut on the bias*
diagonal, angle, slant, oblique, cross
Ⅎ 1 impartiality, fairness
♦ *v*
prejudice, influence, sway, predispose, distort, colour, jaundice, twist, angle, load, slant, warp, weight
OLD earwig; (*Shakesp*) partialize
FORMAL prejudicate
COLLOQ. load the dice

biased *adj*
prejudiced, one-sided, unfair, bigoted, blinkered, jaundiced, influenced, swayed, partial, predisposed, discriminatory, interested, subjective, partisan, slanted, angled, skewed, distorted, warped, twisted, loaded, weighted
FORMAL prejudicate, tendentious
Ⅎ impartial, fair, objective

SYNONYM NUANCES

The word **prejudiced** is a fairly general term to describe a person with unfounded preconceived opinions, while **bigoted** is more emphatic, and can be used of someone displaying irrational dislike as a consequence of these opinions. **Discriminatory** also carries a negative aspect, implying unjustifiable exclusion: *discriminatory employment practices*.

One-sided is more likely to be used to suggest a lack of balance in an article or approach, especially in a narrative account: *one-sided reporting*; while **subjective** may be used to suggest the influence of personal taste or opinion. **Slanted**, **angled** and **skewed** all imply that a particular spin has been applied to present something in a particular way, and if you want to express that your distaste for this you might use **distorted**, **warped** or **twisted**, which imply deliberate misrepresentation. The terms **loaded** and **weighted** also imply being altered, but in order to achieve a specific outcome: *the arbitration must be independent, not loaded in their favour*.

Blinkered may be used if you wish to suggest a narrow viewpoint, unlike **jaundiced**, which implies a viewpoint adversely affected by experience: *a jaundiced view of the world*. Both these terms carry implicit criticism. **Influenced** can be used with more positive connotations, having more to do with being unduly in favour of something, and **swayed**, **partial** and **predisposed** echo this suggestion. **Partisan** is less likely to suggest approval of this favour: *his partisan commitment is foolish*.

Tendentious is used of a more intentional bias, one causing controversy: *the tendentious terms of their father's will*. To express disapproval of bias in any form, you might say it is **unfair**.

Bible *n*
1 *study the Christian Bible*
Scriptures, holy Scriptures, Holy Bible, holy writ, Old Testament, New Testament, Apocrypha, writings, canon, revelation, Pentateuch, law, prophets, Gospels, epistles, letters
COLLOQ. good book
2 *the gardener's bible; the cyclist's bible*
manual, handbook, authority, reference book, ABC, encyclopedia, dictionary, lexicon, guidebook, directory, companion, textbook, primer

bibliography *n*
book list, list of books, list of references, record, catalogue

bicker *v*
squabble, row, quarrel, wrangle, argue, spar, fight, clash, disagree, dispute, fall out
FORMAL altercate
COLLOQ. scrap, spat
F∃ agree, make up

bickering *adj*
squabbling, quarrelling, arguing, clashing, disagreeing, at odds, at one another's throats
COLLOQ. at loggerheads, scrapping, like cats and dogs

bicycle *n*
cycle, two-wheeler, pedal cycle
COLLOQ. bike, pushbike
See also panel below

Types of bicycle include:

all-terrain bike	mountain bike	sport utility
BMX (bicycle	penny farthing	bicycle
motocross)	racing bike (or	tandem
city bike	racer)	unicycle
cruiser	road bike	wetbike
hybrid bike	sit-up-and-beg	

---

bid *v, n*
♦ *v*
1 *bid for a painting*
offer, tender, submit, put up, put forward, advance, propose
FORMAL proffer

2 ASK, request, desire, instruct, direct, command, order, require, charge, call (for), demand, tell, summon, invite, solicit
FORMAL enjoin
3 *bid them farewell*
wish, greet, say, call, tell, wave
♦ *n*
1 OFFER, tender, sum, amount, price, advance, submission, proposal; *Scot* bode
OLD vie
2 ATTEMPT, effort, try, endeavour, venture
COLLOQ. go

biddable *adj*
amenable, submitting, obedient, subservient, tractable, malleable, easy-going, meek, compliant
COLLOQ. under someone's thumb

bidding *n*
request, desire, instruction, direction, command, order, charge, call, demand, summons, requirement, invitation, injunction
FORMAL behest

big *adj*
1 *a big house*
large, great, siz(e)able, considerable, substantial, huge, enormous, immense, vast, massive, colossal, gigantic, giant, mammoth, extensive, spacious, cavernous, extra large
FORMAL voluminous
COLLOQ. whopping, jumbo, bumper, ginormous, humungous
SLANG mega
2 *a big person*
well-built, large, burly, tall, huge, enormous, bulky, hulking, massive, beefy, brawny, muscular, fat, stout, obese
FORMAL corpulent
COLLOQ. hefty
3 *love your big brother*
older, elder, grown-up, adult, mature
4 *a big decision*
important, significant, momentous, major, serious, weighty, salient, critical, radical, fundamental
5 *a big name in the fashion world*
important, significant, well-known, famous, leading, main, principal, eminent, distinguished, prominent, influential, outstanding, noteworthy, valued, powerful
6 *that's big of you*
generous, gracious, kind-hearted, benevolent, unselfish
FORMAL magnanimous, munificent
F∃ **1, 2** small, little **3** younger, little **4** insignificant, unimportant **5** insignificant, unknown **6** mean, miserly, selfish

---

Parts of a bicycle include:

aero bars	chain guide	down tube	hanger	reflector	stabilizer
bar ends	chain guard	drive train	headset	rim brake	steering head
bell	chain link	drop handlebars	head tube	rim tape	steering tube
bottom bracket	chain ring	drum brake	hub	rod brake	stirrup guide
brake	chainset	dynamo	hub gear	roller chain	toe clip
brake block	chain stays	*N Am* fender	inner tube	saddle	tool bag
brake cable	chain wheel	fork	kickstand	Schrader® valve	top tube
brake caliper	clipless pedal	frame	lamp	seat pillar (or post)	tyre (or
brake lever	coaster brake	freewheel unit	lamp bracket	seat stays	*N Am* tire)
brake shoe	crank	gear	mudguard	seat tube	tyre valve
cable braking	crank lever	gear cable	pannier	shock absorber	wheel bearing
system	crankset	gear lever	pedal	side-pull brakes	wheel lock
carrier	crossbar	gear shifter	Presta® valve	speedometer	wheel nut
cassette	derailleur	gearwheel	prop stand	spokes	wheel rim
centre-pull brakes	diamond frame	handlebars	pulley	spoke nipples	wheel spindle
chain	disc brake	handlebar stem	pump	sprocket (wheel)	Woods® valve

sense 1

Large and **great** can be widely used to describe greatness of size, in relation to others: *a large population*; *a great portion of the foreground*. Similarly **sizable** can be used when something is above the average size, though perhaps less impressively so: *a sizable workforce*. Both **considerable** and **substantial** and **extensive** also suggest something worthy of attention, but you might tend to use them more of abstract ideas: *considerable success; a substantial increase.*

Immense and **vast** would tend to convey the extent of something: *vast plains*. **Huge**, **enormous**, **massive**, **colossal**, **gigantic**, **giant** and **mammoth** would be used to describe something of extraordinary size: *huge monuments; the colossal Ionic columns; a problem of mammoth proportions*. **Spacious** and **cavernous** are appropriate only when talking about space or capacity, with the latter having the association with darkness too: *cavernous tunnels.*

bigheaded *adj*
conceited, vain, arrogant, haughty, swollen-headed, self-important, full of yourself, self-satisfied, cocky; *N Am* swell-headed
FORMAL vainglorious
COLLOQ. stuck-up, too big for your boots

bigot *n*
sectarian, dogmatist, fanatic, zealot, partisan, chauvinist, racist, sexist, male chauvinist pig (MCP), religionist
E3 liberal, humanitarian

bigoted *adj*
prejudiced, biased, intolerant, one-sided, fanatical, illiberal, narrow-minded, narrow, blinkered, closed, dogmatic, hidebound, opinionated, obstinate, jaundiced, influenced, swayed, partial, warped, twisted
E3 tolerant, liberal, broad-minded, enlightened

bigotry *n*
prejudice, discrimination, bias, injustice, unfairness, intolerance, partiality, narrow-mindedness, dogmatism, fanaticism, chauvinism, jingoism, sectarianism, racism, racialism, sexism
E3 tolerance

bigwig *n*
celebrity, dignitary, personage, somebody, VIP, notable, mogul, panjandrum
COLLOQ. big gun, big noise, big shot, big cheese, heavyweight, nob; *N Am* honcho
E3 nobody, nonentity

bijou *adj*
small, little, tiny, minute, petite, diminutive, compact, pocket; *Scot* wee

bile *n*
anger, bitterness, bad temper, short temper, ill-humour, irascibility, irritability, testiness, peevishness, rancour, choler, gall, spleen

bilge *n*
rubbish, nonsense, drivel, gibberish, trash, tripe, twaddle; *dialect* faddle; *Scot* blethers, clamjamphrie
COLLOQ. claptrap, piffle, codswallop, poppycock, hot air, cobblers, rot, tommyrot, stuff and nonsense
SLANG
(*vulgar*) balls, bollocks, crap, shit, bullshit

bilious *adj*
1 IRRITABLE, bad-tempered, short-tempered, ill-tempered, ill-humoured, choleric, cross, grumpy, testy, peevish
COLLOQ. crotchety, grouchy, crabby, edgy
2 SICK, queasy, nauseated, sickly
COLLOQ. out of sorts

3 *bilious colours*
sickly, disgusting, nauseating, garish, lurid

bilk *v*
cheat, deceive, defraud, trick, fleece, swindle
COLLOQ. con, do, do out of, diddle, bamboozle, pull a fast one on
SLANG sting

bill[1] *n, v*
♦ *n*
1 INVOICE, statement, account, charges, reckoning, tally, score; *N Am* check
COLLOQ. *N Am* tab
2 CIRCULAR, leaflet, handout, bulletin, handbill, broadsheet, advertisement, notice, announcement, poster, flyer, placard, playbill, programme
COLLOQ. advert, ad
3 *parliamentary bill*
proposal, measure, (piece of) legislation, statute, act
♦ *v*
1 *bill you at the end of the month*
invoice, charge, debit, list costs, send a statement, send an account/invoice
2 *be billed to appear in a show*
advertise, announce, give notice, promote, post

bill[2] *n*
a bird's bill
beak, mandible, neb, nib, rostrum

billet *n, v*
♦ *n*
1 ACCOMMODATION, quarters, living quarters, rooms, barracks, lodging, housing, berth
OLD casern
2 EMPLOYMENT, post, job, position, situation, office, occupation
♦ *v*
accommodate, lodge, put up, quarter, station

billow *v, n*
♦ *v*
swell, expand, bulge, puff out, fill out, balloon, rise, heave, surge, roll, undulate; *dialect & N Am* roil
♦ *n*
cloud, mass, surge, rush, wave, flood, breaker

billowy *adj*
billowing, swelling, surging, heaving, rippling, rolling, tossing, swirling, undulating, waving

bin *n*
container, receptacle, box, holder, basket, chest

bind *v, n*
♦ *v*
1 FASTEN, tie (up), attach, fasten, secure, clamp, stick, join, lash, truss, rope, strap, fetter, tether, shackle, chain, bandage, cover, dress, wrap, tape, embale; *Scot* oup
OLD enfetter, wap
2 OBLIGE, force, compel, constrain, impel, require, necessitate, restrict, confine, restrain, hamper, yoke
OLD gage, objure, thirl
3 *bound together by a common grief*
unite, join, tie, unify, bond, stand together, knit together, pull together, close ranks
♦ *n*
1 BORE, difficulty, inconvenience, irritation, impasse, nuisance
COLLOQ. pain, pain in the neck
2 PREDICAMENT, dilemma, embarrassment, quandary
COLLOQ. hole, spot, tight spot

binding *adj, n*
♦ *adj*
obligatory, compulsory, mandatory, necessary, permanent, conclusive, irrevocable, unalterable, indissoluble, unbreakable, strict, stringent, rigorous, tight, valid
FORMAL requisite

♦ *n*

cover, covering, wrapping, border, edging, trimming, tape, bandage

binge *n*

spree, bout, fling, session, orgy, jag, guzzle
COLLOQ. do, beano, bender, blind, sesh
SLANG blow-out; *N Am* toot
E3 fast

biography *n*

life story, life, history, autobiography, memoir(s), journal(s), diary, diaries, letter(s), recollection(s), profile, curriculum vitae, CV, account, record, biopic, hagiography
FORMAL prosopography
COLLOQ. biog

biology *n*

See panels below

bird *n*

Related adjectives: avian, avine, volucrine, ornithoid
See panel on next page

> **PROVERBS**
> The early bird catches the worm
> A bird in the hand is worth two in the bush
> Birds of a feather flock together

birth *n*

1 CHILDBIRTH, labour, confinement, delivery, arrival, nativity
FORMAL parturition
COLLOQ. patter of tiny feet
Related adjective: natal
2 *of noble birth*
ancestry, family, parentage, origin(s), descent, line, lineage, genealogy, derivation, pedigree, blood, stock, race, strain, house, extraction, background, breeding
3 BEGINNING, rise, emergence, arrival, appearance, origin(s), start, starting-point, commencement, source, dawn, derivation, fountainhead, root, seed
FORMAL advent, genesis
E3 1 death 3 end, finish, conclusion
■ **give birth to**
cause to exist, bring into existence, give rise to, initiate, create, found, establish, inaugurate

> **QUOTATIONS**
> Our birth is but a sleep and a forgetting: / The soul that rises with us, our life's star
>   WILLIAM WORDSWORTH, 'Intimations of Immortality from Recollections of Early Childhood'

birthday *n*

anniversary, day of birth
Related adjectives: natalitial, genethliac

birthmark *n*

blemish, discoloration, mole, patch, naevus, strawberry mark
Related adjective: naevoid

birthplace *n*

place of origin, place of birth, native town, native country, fatherland, mother country, home, home town, root(s), provenance, source, fount, cradle

birthright *n*

privilege, prerogative, due, inheritance, legacy
OLD (*Shakesp*) birthdom

biscuit *n*

cake; *N Am* cookie; cracker, cracknel, pretzel, rusk, wafer, hardtack
COLLOQ. biccy

bisect *v*

halve, cut in half, divide, divide into two, cut in two, separate, split, intersect, cross, fork
FORMAL bifurcate

bisexual *adj*

androgynous, hermaphrodite
TECHNICAL gynandromorphic, gynandromorphous, monoclinous, epicene
COLLOQ. AC/DC, ambidextrous, bi, swinging both ways
E3 heterosexual, homosexual

bishop *n*

prelate, archbishop, primate, diocesan, metropolitan, patriarch, suffragan
OLD episcopant
Related adjective: episcopal

Biological terms include:

amino acid	conservation	evolution	germ	natural selection	respiration
anatomy	corpuscle	excretion	Golgi apparatus	nuclear membrane	reticulum
animal behaviour	cultivar	extinction	hereditary factor	nucleus	retrovirus
animal kingdom	cytoplasm	flora and fauna	homeostasis	nutrition	ribonucleic acid
bacillus	deoxyribonucleic	food chain	living world	order	(RNA)
bacteria	acid (DNA)	fossil	meiosis	organism	ribosome
biologist	diffusion	gene	membrane	osmosis	secretion
botanist	ecosystem	genetic engineer-	metabolism	parasitism	survival of the
cell	ectoplasm	ing	micro-organism	photosynthesis	fittest
chromosome	embryo	genetic fingerprint-	microbe	pollution	symbiosis
class	endoplasmic reti-	ing	mitosis	protein	virus
clone	culum (ER)	genetically mod-	molecule	protoplasm	
coccus	enzyme	ified (GM)	mutation	reproduction	

Fields of biology include:

aerobiology	bionomics	conservation biol-	enzymology	Mendelism	population genet-
agrobiology	biophysics	ogy	evolution	microbiology	ics
bacteriology	biopsychology	cryobiology	evolutionary biol-	molecular biology	radiobiology
biochemistry	biorhymics	cybernetics	ogy	morphology	sociobiology
biodynamics	bioscience	cytogenetics	genetics	natural history	stoichology
biogeochemisty	biosystematics	cytology	Haeckel's law	organography	systematics
biogeography	biotechnology	Darwinism	histology	palaeontology	taxonomy
bioinformatics	botany	developmental	human biology	parasitology	teratology
biomathematics	cellular biology	biology	hydrobiology	pathology	toxicology
biometeorology	chronobiology	neo-Darwinism	immunology	photobiology	virology
biometrics (or	computational	ecology	Lamarckism	phycology	zoology
biometry)	biology	embryology	macroecology	physiology	
bionics		endocrinology	marine biology		

Birds include:

bee-eater	robin	boatbill	knot	eagle	ptarmigan
blackbird	rook	chough	lapwing	falcon	quail
bluetit	sedge	coot	mallard	harrier	turkey
brambling	warbler	cormorant	moorhen	hawk	
bullfinch	shrike	crane	oyster-catcher	kestrel	**TROPICAL BIRDS:**
chaffinch	skylark	curlew	peewit	kite	ani
crow	sparrow	darter	pelican	osprey	barbet
cuckoo	starling	dipper	petrel	owl	bird of paradise
dove	swallow	duck	plover	sparrowhawk	budgerigar
dunnock	swift	dunlin	puffin	vulture	*colloq.* budgie
goldcrest	thrush	eider	rail		canary
greenfinch	tit	flamingo	roller	**FLIGHTLESS BIRDS:**	cockatiel
hedge sparrow	titlark	frigate	seagull	dodo	cockatoo
hoopoe	tree sparrow	bird	snipe	emu	kookaburra
jackdaw	wagtail	fulmar	stilt	kiwi	lovebird
jay	warbler	gallinule	stork	ostrich	macaw
lark	woodpecker	gannet	swan	peacock	mockingbird
linnet	wren	godwit	teal	penguin	myna bird
magpie	yellowhammer	golden eye	tern		parakeet
martin		goose	turnstone	**FOWL:**	parrot
nightingale	**WATER BIRDS:**	grebe	whimbrel	chicken	plume-bird
nutcracker	albatross	guillemot		francolin	toucan
pigeon	auk	heron	**BIRDS OF PREY:**	grouse	
pipit	avocet	ibis	buzzard	partridge	
raven	bittern	kingfisher	condor	pheasant	

bishopric *n*
diocese, episcopacy, see

bit *n*
fragment, part, segment, portion, piece, small piece, small portion, slice, crumb, grain, morsel, mouthful, drop, dash, chunk, lump, scrap, particle, atom, mite, whit, jot, iota, tittle, shred, flake, chip, sliver, speck, touch, tad, hint, trace, scintilla, soupçon, vestige
■ **a bit**
1 *a bit boring*
slightly, fairly, rather, a little, not much, not very
2 *wait a bit*
a while, a little while, a moment, a short time, minute, few minutes, few moments
COLLOQ. jiffy, tick
■ **bit by bit**
gradually, little by little, in stages, step by step, slowly, piecemeal
F∃ all at once, wholesale

bitch *n, v*
♦ *n*
1 *a bitch and her puppies*
female dog
2 *that woman's a bitch*
vixen, shrew, harpy, virago
COLLOQ. cat
SLANG (*offensive*) cow
3 ORDEAL, trial, torment, nightmare
COLLOQ. pig, swine
♦ *v*
complain, moan, grumble, criticize, find fault with, be spiteful about, talk about behind their back
COLLOQ. gripe, whinge, whine, badmouth

bitchiness *n*
nastiness, meanness, maliciousness, malice, cruelty, spite, venom
COLLOQ. cattiness
F∃ kindness

bitchy *adj*
snide, nasty, mean, spiteful, malicious, vindictive, cutting, backbiting, venomous, rancorous, shrewish, vixenish, cruel, vicious
COLLOQ. catty
F∃ kind, loving

bite *v, n*
♦ *v*
1 CHEW, eat, munch, gnaw, nibble, peck, chomp, champ, crunch, crush
OLD begnaw, pinch
FORMAL masticate
2 *the dog bit her hand*
nip, snap, pierce, wound, tear, rend, sink/get your teeth into
3 SMART, sting, tingle
4 *the rise in costs was beginning to bite*
grip, take effect, work, hold, seize, pinch
♦ *n*
1 NIP, snap, wound, sting, smarting, pinch, prick, puncture, lesion
Related adjective: morsal
2 *have a bite to eat*
snack, light meal, refreshment, mouthful, morsel, taste, piece, bit
3 POWER, force, effect, impact, impression, strength, influence
OLD (*Spenser*) remorse
4 PUNGENCY, piquancy, spiciness, spice, sharpness
COLLOQ. kick, punch

> **PROVERBS**
> Once bitten, twice shy

biting *adj*
1 COLD, freezing, sharp, bitter, harsh, severe, keen, penetrating, piercing, nipping, stinging
2 CUTTING, incisive, bitter, piercing, penetrating, acid, pointed, pungent, acrid, raw, stinging, sharp, tart, caustic, sarcastic, scathing, harsh, vicious, vitriolic, cynical, hurtful
OLD shrewd
FORMAL trenchant, mordant, mordacious, astringent
F∃ **1** mild **2** bland

bitter *adj*
1 ACID, tart, sharp, sour, vinegary, unsweetened, pungent, tangy; *Scot* wersh
FORMAL acrid, astringent, acerb, acerbic
2 RESENTFUL, embittered, begrudging, indignant, aggrieved, angry, disgruntled, sour, morose, jaundiced, cynical, sullen, hostile, acrimonious, rancorous, malevolent, spiteful, vindictive, venomous, scathing, caustic, sardonic, wry
FORMAL acerbic, vitriolic, vituperative, virulent

COLLOQ. with a chip on your shoulder
3 INTENSE, severe, harsh, fierce, cruel, savage, merciless, painful, sad, unhappy, disappointing, tragic, distressing, harrowing, heartbreaking, heart-rending, gut-wrenching
4 *bitter winds*
stinging, biting, sharp, freezing, freezing cold, arctic, raw, harsh, piercing, penetrating
COLLOQ. nippy, parky
E3 1 sweet **2** contented **3** mild, happy **4** warm, mild

bitterly *adv*
1 *bitterly cold*
bitingly, piercingly, penetratingly
2 *bitterly disappointed*
intensely, severely, cruelly, savagely, grievously, painfully
3 RESENTFULLY, embitteredly, grudgingly, begrudgingly, indignantly, angrily, sourly, morosely, cynically, sullenly, hostilely, spitefully, acrimoniously, rancorously, malevolently, vindictively, venomously, scathingly, caustically, sardonically, wryly
FORMAL acerbically, vituperatively, with vitriol

bitterness *n*
1 ACIDITY, tartness, sharpness, sourness, vinegar, pungency, tanginess
2 RESENTMENT, embitterment, grudge, indignation, anger, sourness, moroseness, jaundice, cynicism, sullenness, spleen, hostility, antagonism, acrimony, malevolence, rancour, enmity, spite, vindictiveness, venom
OLD gall, wormwood; (*Spenser*) fell
FORMAL acerbity, virulence
COLLOQ. chip on your shoulder
3 INTENSITY, severity, harshness, ferocity, cruelty, pain, painfulness, sadness, unhappiness, disappointment, tragedy, distress, heartbreaking, heart-rending
OLD marah
4 *the bitterness of the winter*
sharpness, coldness, iciness, chilliness, frostiness, rawness, harshness, penetration, bite

bitty *adj*
disconnected, disjointed, fragmented, broken, fitful, incoherent, scrappy, piecemeal

bizarre *adj*
strange, odd, queer, curious, weird, peculiar, funny, eccentric, outlandish, ludicrous, ridiculous, fantastic, surreal, comical, extravagant, grotesque, freakish, abnormal, deviant, unusual, uncommon, unconventional, extraordinary
COLLOQ. left-field, offbeat, oddball, wacky, Pythonesque
SLANG way-out; *N Am* gonzo, off the wall
E3 normal, ordinary, standard

bizarrely *adv*
strangely, oddly, curiously, weirdly, unusually, peculiarly, outlandishly, ludicrously, freakishly, abnormally, unconventionally, ridiculously, comically, extravagantly
E3 normally

blab *v*
blurt out, tell, reveal, disclose, divulge, let slip, gossip, tattle; *N Am* blat
COLLOQ. squeal, leak, give the game away, let the cat out of the bag, blow the gaff
E3 hide, hush up

blabber *v*
chat, chatter, prattle, gabble, twitter, twattle, gossip, jabber, babble, witter; *Scot* blether; *dialect* **AMP**, *N Am* blather

black *adj, v*
♦ *adj*
1 JET-BLACK, coal-black, pitch-black, jet, ebony, raven, sable, inky, sooty, dusky, swarthy
OLD (*Shakesp*) hell-black
FORMAL nigrescent
COLLOQ. black as coal
2 *black people*
dark-skinned, coloured;

(*offensive*) Negro, Negroid, nigger; swarthy
TECHNICAL melanistic
3 DARK, unlit, unilluminated, moonless, starless, overcast, dingy, dusky, dim, gloomy, sombre, funereal, pitch-black
FORMAL crepuscular, tenebrous, fuliginous, subfusc, Cimmerian, Stygian
4 FILTHY, dirty, soiled, stained, grimy, sooty, grubby, muddy, unclean
COLLOQ. grotty, gungy
5 *the future looks black*
bleak, gloomy, sad, depressing, distressing, melancholy, dismal, hopeless, sombre, mournful, funereal, awful, tragic
6 *in a black mood*
miserable, sad, unhappy, depressed, resentful, bitter, sullen, angry, threatening, menacing
FORMAL lugubrious
7 *black humour*
cruel, sick, cynical, tasteless, vulgar, gross, in bad taste
8 EVIL, wicked, bad, vile, cruel, malicious, malevolent, wrong, immoral, odious, devilish, satanic, demonic, diabolical
FORMAL nefarious, heinous
E3 1, 2 white **3** bright, light **4** clean, spotless **5** bright
♦ *v*
1 *black someone's eye*
bruise, blacken, punch, hit, injure
2 *they blacked the imported goods*
boycott, embargo, blacklist, ban, bar, taboo
■ **black out**
1 FAINT, pass out, lose consciousness, keel over, collapse
COLLOQ. flake out
2 DARKEN, eclipse, cover up
3 CENSOR, conceal, suppress, withhold, gag
■ **black and white**
1 *a black and white issue*
definite, clear-cut, well-defined, unambiguous, plain, distinct, unequivocal, categorical
2 *I've seen it in black and white*
printed, written, written down, on paper, on record
■ **in the black**
in credit, without debt, out of debt, solvent
COLLOQ. with your head above water

blackball *v*
vote against, ban, bar, blacklist, debar, ostracize, shut out, drum out, throw out, exclude, expel, oust, reject, repudiate, snub, veto, pill
COLLOQ. give the cold shoulder to

blacken *v*
1 DARKEN, black, nigrify, dirty, make dirty, soil, smudge, cloud, smoke
OLD besmut
2 DEFAME, malign, slander, libel, revile, detract, smear, besmirch, sully, stain, tarnish, taint, defile, denigrate, discredit, dishonour
FORMAL impugn, calumniate, vilify, decry
COLLOQ. run down
E3 2 praise, enhance

blackguard *n*
scoundrel, rascal, rogue, villain, devil, knave, miscreant, reprobate, wretch
COLLOQ. bleeder, blighter, bounder, rotter, stinker, crook, swine, scumbag
OLD SLANG sweep

blacklist *v*
debar, disallow, exclude, ban, outlaw, bar, boycott, expel, ostracize, reject, shut out, repudiate, snub, taboo, veto
FORMAL preclude, proscribe
E3 accept, allow

blackmail *n, v*
♦ *n*
extortion, intimidation, exaction, bribery, ransom, greenmail, chout
FORMAL chantage
COLLOQ. hush money

SLANG shakedown
OLD SLANG *N Am* strike
♦ *v*
extort, exact, hold to ransom, threaten, force, pressurize, compel, coerce, demand
COLLOQ. bleed, milk, squeeze, lean on, put the screws on
SLANG black

blackmailer *n*
bloodsucker, extortioner, extortionist, vampire, hijacker; *N Am* highbinder

blackout *n*
1 POWER FAILURE, power cut, electricity failure; *N Am* brownout
2 FAINT, coma, unconsciousness, passing out, loss of consciousness, swoon, oblivion
TECHNICAL syncope
COLLOQ. flaking-out
3 *a news blackout*
suppression, embargo, censorship, withholding, concealment, secrecy, silence
COLLOQ. cover-up

blade *n*
edge, cutting edge, knife, dagger, sword, scalpel, razor, vane

blame *v, n*
♦ *v*
hold responsible, say something is someone's fault, hold accountable, hold liable, accuse, charge, tax, reprimand, chide, reprove, upbraid, reprehend, admonish, rebuke, reproach, censure, attribute liability, thank, criticize, find fault with, fault, find guilty, disapprove, condemn, scapegoat
OLD wite
FORMAL berate, inculpate, discommend, dispraise
COLLOQ. tear into, point the finger at, lay at someone's door, pin it on, name names, name and shame
E3 exonerate, vindicate
♦ *n*
censure, criticism, reprimand, reproof, reproach, recrimination, condemnation, accusation, charge, incrimination, guilt, fault, responsibility, accountability, liability, onus; *dialect* wite; *Scot* dirdum
FORMAL culpability, berating, dispraise, odium
SLANG stick, rap

blameless *adj*
innocent, guiltless, clear, faultless, without fault, perfect, lily-white, unblemished, stainless, virtuous, sinless, upright, above reproach, irreproachable, irreprovable, unblamable, unimpeachable; *dialect* witeless
OLD
(*Shakesp & Spenser*) unreproved
FORMAL irreprehensible, inculpable
E3 guilty, blameworthy

blameworthy *adj*
at fault, guilty, discreditable, disreputable, shameful, unworthy, indefensible, inexcusable, reprehensible, responsible, reproachable
FORMAL culpable, flagitious
E3 blameless

blanch *v*
1 *blanch at the sight*
grow/become/turn pale, go/become/turn white, whiten, lighten, grow/become pallid, blench
TECHNICAL etiolate
2 *blanch vegetables*
boil, scald
E3 **1** colour, blush, redden

bland *adv*
1 *a bland person/statement*
boring, monotonous, humdrum, tedious, dull, uninspiring, uninteresting, unexciting, nondescript, characterless,

ordinary, mundane, inoffensive, flat, anodyne, smooth, suave, weak
COLLOQ. spammy
2 TASTELESS, insipid, flavourless, weak, mild
COLLOQ. vanilla
E3 **1** exciting, lively, stimulating **2** tasty, piquant, rich

blandishments *n*
flattery, compliments, enticements, fawning, inducements, ingratiation, blarney, cajolery, coaxing, persuasiveness, sycophancy, wheedling, treacle, lipsalve, *agréments*
OLD sooth
FORMAL inveiglement
COLLOQ. soft soap, flannel, spiel, sweet talk

blank *adj, n*
♦ *adj*
1 *a blank page*
empty, unfilled, void, clear, bare, unmarked, unwritten, plain, clean, white
2 EXPRESSIONLESS, deadpan, poker-faced, impassive, emotionless, without feeling, lifeless, apathetic, uninterested, indifferent, glazed, empty, vacant, vacuous, inscrutable, uncomprehending
♦ *n*
space, gap, break, void, emptiness, empty space, vacancy, vacuity, nothingness, vacuum

blanket *n, v, adj*
♦ *n*
1 *blankets on a bed*
cover, covering, bedcover, coverlet, bedspread, quilt, eiderdown, underblanket, manta; *dialect* whittle
OLD stroud
2 *a blanket of snow*
covering, coating, coat, layer, film, carpet, cloak, mantle, cover, sheet, envelope, overlay, wrapper, wrapping
♦ *v*
cover, coat, carpet, overlay, eclipse, hide, conceal, mask, cloak, surround, muffle, deaden, obscure, suppress, cloud
♦ *adj*
across-the-board, all-embracing, all-inclusive, comprehensive, inclusive, overall, global, total, wholesale, indiscriminate, sweeping, wide-ranging

blankly *adv*
expressionlessly, impassively, lifelessly, apathetically, uninterestedly, indifferently, vacantly, vacuously, emotionlessly, without feeling

blare *v, n*
♦ *v*
trumpet, clamour, roar, blast (out), boom (out), resound, sound loudly, thunder, ring, peal, clang, hoot, toot, honk
♦ *n*
clamour, roar, blast, boom, thunder, ring, peal, clang, hoot

blarney *n*
blandishments, cajolery, coaxing, flattery, persuasiveness, wheedling, soft sawder; *N Am* taffy
COLLOQ. soft soap, flannel, spiel, sweet talk

blasé *adj*
nonchalant, offhand, unimpressed, unmoved, unexcited, jaded, weary, bored, uninterested, uninspired, apathetic, indifferent, impassive, cool, lukewarm, unconcerned
FORMAL phlegmatic
E3 excited, enthusiastic, responsive

blaspheme *v*
swear, curse, profane, utter profanities, utter oaths, take the Lord's name in vain, desecrate, damn, revile, abuse
FORMAL execrate, imprecate, anathematize
OLD SLANG cuss

blasphemous *adj*
profane, impious, sacrilegious, godless, ungodly, irreligious, irreverent
OLD sulphurous
FORMAL imprecatory

blasphemously *adv*
profanely, sacrilegiously, irreverently, disrespectfully

blasphemy *n*
profanity, profaneness, curse, expletive, cursing, swearing, oaths, impiety, impiousness, ungodliness, irreverence, unholiness, sacrilege, desecration, violation, outrage
FORMAL execration, imprecation

blast *n, v*
♦ *n*
1 EXPLOSION, blow-up, detonation, shot, bang, crash, clap, crack, volley, burst, outburst, discharge
2 *a blast of cold air*
draught, gust, rush, gale, squall, storm, tempest, flurry, bluster, puff; *dialect* wuther; *Scot* waff, wap
TECHNICAL flatus
OLD sideration
3 SOUND, blow, blare, blaring, roar, roaring, boom, booming, thunder, clamour, bellow, peal, hoot, toot, honk, wail, scream, shriek, clang, tantara; *dialect* wuther
OLD trump
COLLOQ. parp
♦ *v*
1 EXPLODE, blow up, blow to pieces, burst, shatter, destroy, demolish, ruin, assail, attack, strike, bomb, shoot/gun down
2 SOUND, blare (out), boom (out), roar, thunder, peal, bellow, hoot, toot, honk, wail, scream, shriek, clang
COLLOQ. parp
3 CRITICIZE, slate, reprimand, rebuke, tell off, reprove, upbraid, scathe
OLD siderate
FORMAL berate
COLLOQ. slam, come down heavily on
■ **blast off**
take off, lift off, be launched

blasted *adj*
damned, cursed, confounded, infernal, flaming, annoying, unpleasant
COLLOQ. blooming, flipping, darned, ruddy, dratting
SLANG
(*taboo*) fucking

blatant *adj*
flagrant, brazen, barefaced, bald, blad-faced, shameless, unashamed, naked, arrant, open, overt, undisguised, ostentatious, glaring, conspicuous, manifest, patent, obtrusive, prominent, pronounced, hard-core, obvious, sheer, outright, unmitigated, out-and-out
COLLOQ. full-on

> ⚠ **blatant** or **flagrant**?
> *Blatant* means 'glaringly or shamelessly obvious': *a blatant lie/liar.* *Flagrant* implies a greater degree of condemnation and means 'scandalous, very obvious and wicked': *a flagrant misuse of his powers.*

blatantly *adv*
flagrantly, brazenly, unashamedly, shamelessly, openly, glaringly, conspicuously, obviously, patently, manifestly, out-and-out

blaze *n, v*
♦ *n*
1 FIRE, flames, inferno, bonfire, flare-up, explosion, blast; *Scot* lunt
FORMAL conflagration
2 *a blaze of colour*
radiance, brilliance, beam, glare, flash, gleam, glitter, glow, light, burst, outburst
♦ *v*
1 *the fire was blazing*
burn, flame, flare (up), be on fire, be alight, ignite, catch fire, burst into flames
2 *blazing with light*
shine, beam, glare, flash, flare, gleam, glitter, glow, light, burst, be radiant, be brilliant

3 *eyes blazing with anger*
blow up, explode, erupt, burst, burn, fire, flash, rage, boil, seethe
COLLOQ. see red
4 *guns blazing away*
shoot, fire, blast, discharge, let off, let fly, set off

blazon *v*
proclaim, publicize, announce, make known, broadcast, celebrate, flourish, trumpet, herald, flaunt, vaunt
⊟ deprecate, hush up

bleach *v*
whiten, make/turn white, blanch, decolour, decolorize, fade, pale, make/turn pale, lighten
TECHNICAL etiolate, peroxide

bleak *adj*
1 GLOOMY, sombre, leaden, grim, dreary, dismal, dark, drab, depressing, miserable, wretched, desperate, joyless, cheerless, comfortless, hopeless, discouraging, disheartening, unfavourable, unpromising
2 *a bleak landscape*
unsheltered, windy, windswept, exposed, open, barren, bare, empty, arid, soulless, spartan, desolate, chilly, cold
3 COLD, chilly, harsh, raw; *Scot* blae; weather-beaten, dreary, dull
⊟ 1 bright, cheerful **3** bright, fine, pleasant

bleakly *adv*
gloomily, sombrely, grimly, dismally, drearily, miserably, wretchedly, joylessly, cheerlessly, unfavourably, unpromisingly

bleary *adj*
bleary-eyed, blurred, blurry, cloudy, dim, tired, watery, rheumy, unfocused

bleat *v*
1 *sheep bleating*
baa, bray, maa, cry, call; *dialect* whicker; *N Am* blat
2 *bleating about price increases*
complain, grumble, moan, kvetch
COLLOQ. whine, whinge, beef, grouse, gripe

bleed *v*
1 HAEMORRHAGE, lose blood, shed blood, let blood, blood, gush, spurt, flow, flood, run, exude, weep, ooze, seep, trickle
TECHNICAL exsanguinate, phlebotomize, extravasate
2 DRAIN, suck dry, exhaust, squeeze, milk, sap, reduce, bleed white
FORMAL deplete
3 *bleed money*
extort, extract
COLLOQ. milk, squeeze
4 *the stain has bled into the wood*
run, merge, flow, glide, melt

blemish *n, v*
♦ *n*
1 *a blemish on her skin*
deformity, disfigurement, mark, speck, smudge, blotch, botch, blot, stain, discoloration
OLD mote
See panel on next page
2 *a blemish on his character*
flaw, imperfection, defect, fault, stain, taint, disgrace, dishonour
OLD want, mote
♦ *v*
tarnish, flaw, deface, disfigure, spoil, mar, damage, impair, spot, mark, blot, stain, sully, taint, compromise; *Scot* tash

blench *v*
falter, hesitate, recoil, flinch, shrink, pull back, draw back, shudder, cower, shy, start, wince, quail, quake, quiver

Kinds of blemish include:

acne	bump	corn	pockmark	strawberry mark
birthmark	bunion	freckle	pustule	verruca
blackhead	callus	mole	scab	wart
blister	carbuncle	naevus	scar	whitehead
boil	chilblain	pimple	spot	*slang* zit

blend v, n
♦ v
1 MERGE, combine, mix, mingle, amalgamate, coalesce, compound, synthesize, fuse, unite, homogenize, alloy, interweave, intertwine, stir, beat, whisk; *N Am* meld
FORMAL intermix, admix, commix, commingle, contemper
2 HARMONIZE, complement, fit, match, go (well) with, go together, suit, set off
F3 1 separate, divide **2** clash, jar
♦ n
compound, composite, alloy, amalgam, amalgamation, merging, synthesis, fusion, combination, union, uniting, mix, mixture, cross between two things, concoction
FORMAL admixture, commixture

bless v
1 ANOINT, sanctify, consecrate, hallow, dedicate, ordain, lay hands on
2 PRAISE, worship, extol, magnify, glorify, exalt, honour, thank
FORMAL laud
3 *the priest blessed the congregation*
ask God's favour for, ask God's protection for
4 *I bless the day I bought this washing machine*
give thanks for, be thankful for, be grateful for, favour
F3 1 curse **2** condemn

blessed adj
1 HOLY, sacred, hallowed, consecrated, sanctified, revered, adored, divine
2 HAPPY, contented, glad, joyful, joyous, lucky, fortunate, prosperous
3 *blessed with a good memory*
favoured, endowed, graced, provided
F3 1 cursed **2** unhappy, sad

blessing n
1 CONSECRATION, dedication, benediction, grace, thanksgiving, commendation
TECHNICAL darshan, kiddush
FORMAL invocation, benison
2 BENEFIT, advantage, favour, godsend, windfall, gift, gain, profit, help, service, bounty, boon, good thing, good fortune
3 *give a proposal your blessing*
approval, backing, support, agreement, authority, sanction, consent, permission, leave
FORMAL approbation, concurrence
COLLOQ. go-ahead, green light, OK, thumbs-up
F3 2 curse, blight **3** condemnation

QUOTATIONS
Life is the greatest of blessings, and death the worst of evils
HEINRICH HEINE, *Idéen, Das Buch le Grand*

blight n, v
♦ n
1 *affected by planning blight*
curse, misfortune, woe, trouble, calamity, bane, evil, scourge, blast, affliction, decay, pollution, contamination, corruption
OLD sideration
2 *potato blight*
disease, fungus, mildew, rot, infestation, cancer, canker
F3 1 blessing, boon
♦ v
spoil, mar, injure, undermine, ruin, wreck, crush, dash, shatter, destroy, damage, kill, annihilate, blast, wither, shrivel, frustrate, disappoint; *Scot* scouther
OLD strike
F3 bless

blind adj, v, n
♦ adj
1 SIGHTLESS, visually impaired, unsighted, unseeing, visionless, eyeless
See panel below
2 *blind to their needs*
unaware, ignorant, oblivious, unconscious, unobservant, imperceptive, slow, inattentive, neglectful, unmindful, indifferent, insensitive, thoughtless, inconsiderate
3 *love is blind*
unreasoning, uncritical, unthinking, irrational, injudicious, indiscriminate, heedless, mindless, impulsive, hasty, rash, impetuous, reckless, wild, mad, careless
4 CLOSED, obstructed, hidden, concealed, out of sight, obscured
F3 1 sighted **2** aware, sensitive **3** careful, cautious
♦ v
1 *blinded in the accident*
make blind, cause to lose your vision, deprive of sight, deprive of vision, put the eyes out of, gouge the eyes out of
2 *blinded by the car's headlights*
dazzle, block your vision, obscure your vision
3 *tolerance blinds you to faults*
cause to lose reason/sense, deceive, mislead, intimidate, trick, trap, confuse
♦ n
1 *a window blind*
screen, cover, curtain, (window) shade, shutter, roller blind, Austrian blind, Venetian blind, festoon blind
2 *operate as a blind for illegal activities*
cloak, mask, camouflage, masquerade, front, façade, distraction, screen, smokescreen, cover
COLLOQ. cover-up

PROVERBS
When the blind lead the blind, both shall fall into the ditch

blindly adv
1 *feel your way blindly*
without vision, without sight, sightlessly, unseeingly

Ways of describing sight impairment include:

amaurotic	colour-blind	hypermetropic	nyctalopic	short-sighted	visually handi-
astigmatic	far-sighted	long-sighted	partially-sighted	snow-blind	capped
colloq. blind as a	glaucomatous	myopic	presbyopic	stone-blind	visually impaired
bat	half-blind	near-sighted	purblind	trachomatous	
(having) cataracts	hemeralopic	night-blind	sand-blind		

2 UNCRITICALLY, unthinkingly, irrationally, indiscriminately, mindlessly, senselessly, thoughtlessly, impulsively, rashly, impetuously, recklessly, wildly, madly, carelessly, incautiously
2 critically, cautiously

blink v
1 *his eyes blinked*
wink, twinkle, twink, flicker, flutter
FORMAL nictate, nictitate
2 *the light blinked*
flash, flicker, twinkle, shine, gleam, glimmer, glitter, sparkle, scintillate

blip n
1 BLEEP, pip, buzz, squeal, screech
2 *a blip in the economy's recovery*
COLLOQ. glitch, hiccup, fly in the ointment, spanner in the works

bliss n
blissfulness, ecstasy, euphoria, rapture, joy, elation, happiness, gladness, blessedness, paradise, heaven, seventh heaven, utopia, nirvana
misery, hell, damnation

blissful adj
ecstatic, euphoric, elated, enraptured, idyllic, rapturous, delighted, enchanted, joyful, joyous, happy
miserable, wretched

blister n
sore, blain, swelling, cyst, boil, abscess, ulcer, pustule, pimple, canker, carbuncle
TECHNICAL bleb, bulla, furuncle, papilla, papula, phlyctaena, pompholyx, vesicle, vesicula, wen
OLD blab
Related adjective: vesicant

blistering adj
1 *blistering heat*
hot, scorching, withering, intense, extreme, fierce, ferocious
2 *blistering criticism*
cruel, vicious, savage, virulent, fierce, caustic, scathing, sarcastic

blithe adj
1 CASUAL, unthinking, thoughtless, careless, heedless, uncaring, unconcerned, carefree, untroubled
2 CHEERFUL, cheery, happy, light-hearted
1 serious **2** morose

blithely adv
casually, thoughtlessly, carelessly, unthinkingly

blitz n
1 *the blitz during the war*
bombardment, attack, offensive, raid, strike, campaign, onslaught, blitzkrieg
2 *have a blitz on the garden*
effort, all-out effort, attack, exertion, attempt, endeavour, campaign

blizzard n
snowstorm, squall, storm, tempest, buran

bloated adj
swollen, puffy, puffed out, puffed up, blown up, inflated, dilated, expanded, enlarged, full, stuffed
FORMAL distended
thin, shrunken, shrivelled

blob n
drop, droplet, globule, bead, pearl, bubble, dab, spot, splash, gob, lump, mass, ball, tear, pellet, pill
COLLOQ. glob

bloc n
alliance, group, league, coalition, federation, union, association, ring, syndicate, entente, axis, cabal, cartel, clique, faction

block n, v
♦ n
1 *a block of offices*
building, development, structure, complex
2 *a block of stone*
piece, lump, mass, slab, chunk, hunk, square, cube, wedge, cake, brick, bar
3 *a block of seats/tickets*
batch, cluster, quantity, group, series, section
4 OBSTACLE, barrier, bar, jam, blockage, stoppage, resistance, obstruction, impediment, hindrance, drawback, deterrent, stumbling-block, let, delay
♦ v
block a pipe/progress
choke, clog (up), plug, stop up, dam up, close, seal, bar, obstruct, be in the way, impede, hamper, hinder, stonewall, stop, check, arrest, halt, thwart, frustrate, scotch, deter
FORMAL occlude
COLLOQ. bung up
■ **block off**
shut off, seal, close (up), stop (up)
■ **block out**
1 *block out light*
hide, conceal, screen, blot out, obliterate, eclipse, obscure
2 *block out memories*
shut out, blank out, mask, screen, veil, suppress, repress

blockade n, v
♦ n
barrier, barricade, siege, obstruction, restriction, obstacle, block, stoppage, closure, encirclement
TECHNICAL investment
♦ v
keep from, prevent, hinder, stop, check, obstruct, prevent entering/reaching, prevent using, besiege, barricade, encircle, surround

blockage n
obstruction, blocking, stoppage, block, clot, jam, log jam, bottleneck, congestion, hindrance, impediment
FORMAL occlusion

blockhead n
fool, idiot, imbecile, dunce
COLLOQ. nincompoop, ninny, nitwit, numskull, twerp, dope, twit, dimwit; N Am bufflehead
SLANG wally, jerk, plonker, git, prat, dipstick, nerd, dork, geek
brain, genius

bloke n
man, boy, fellow, male, individual, character
COLLOQ. chap, guy

blond, blonde adj
fair, flaxen, golden, fair-haired, golden-haired, light, light-coloured, tow-coloured, bleached

blood n
1 *lose blood*
lifeblood, vital fluid, gore
Related adjectives: haemal, haemic, haematic, sanguineous
2 *of aristocratic blood*
extraction, birth, descent, lineage, family, kindred, relations, ancestry, descendants, kinship, relationship

PROVERBS
You can't get blood from a stone
Blood is thicker than water

bloodcurdling adj
horrifying, chilling, spine-chilling, hair-raising, terrifying, frightening, scary, dreadful, fearful, appalling, horrific, horrible, horrid, horrendous

bloodless adj
1 *a bloodless coup*
peaceful, non-violent, strife-free, unwarlike

2 *her bloodless face*
ashen, anaemic, colourless, pale, pallid, pasty, sallow, white, sickly, wan, chalky, cold, drained, feeble, insipid, languid, lifeless, listless, unfeeling, unemotional, passionless, spiritless, torpid
E3 1 bloody, violent **2** bloody, ruddy, vigorous

bloodshed *n*
killing, murder, slaughter, slaying, massacre, bloodbath, butchery, carnage, pogrom, gore, bloodletting, decimation

bloodsucker *n*
blackmailer, extortioner, extortionist
COLLOQ. leech, parasite, sponger

bloodthirsty *adj*
murderous, homicidal, warlike, savage, barbaric, barbarous, brutal, ferocious, vicious, cruel, inhuman, ruthless
FORMAL sanguinary

bloody *adj*
bleeding, bloodstained, gory, murderous, bloodthirsty, savage, brutal, ferocious, fierce, cruel
FORMAL sanguinary, sanguine, sanguineous, sanguinolent, ensanguinated

bloody-minded *adj*
awkward, difficult, obstinate, stubborn, unhelpful, unco-operative, obstructive, irritable, touchy
COLLOQ. stroppy

bloom *n, v*
♦ *n*
1 BLOSSOM, flower, bud
TECHNICAL efflorescence, florescence
2 PRIME, heyday, perfection, blush, flush, glow, rosiness, beauty, radiance, lustre, health, vigour, strength, freshness
♦ *v*
1 *the flowers were blooming*
bud, sprout, blossom, flower, open
2 *the children are blooming*
flourish, develop, mature, grow, blossom, prosper, thrive, glow
E3 1 fade, wither

blooming *adj*
blossoming, healthy, flowering, rosy, ruddy, bonny
TECHNICAL florescent
OLD (*Shakesp*) primy
E3 ailing

blossom *n, v*
♦ *n*
bloom, flower, bud
TECHNICAL efflorescence, florescence, pruina
OLD bloosme
♦ *v*
1 *the trees were blossoming*
bloom, flower
OLD bloosme
FORMAL burgeon
2 *blossom into a beautiful young woman*
develop, mature, grow, progress, bloom, flourish, thrive, prosper, succeed
FORMAL burgeon
E3 2 fade, wither

blot *n, v*
♦ *n*
1 *an ink blot*
spot, stain, smudge, blotch, smear, mark, dot, splodge, speck, blemish
2 *a blot on his reputation*
blemish, flaw, fault, defect, imperfection, taint, stain, disgrace, tarnishing, black mark
♦ *v*
1 *blot a surface*
spot, mark, stain, smudge, blur, dry (up), soak (up), absorb

2 *blotted his character*
sully, taint, tarnish, stain, blacken, spoil, mar, disfigure, disgrace
■ **blot out**
obliterate, cancel, delete, erase, darken, black out, obscure, hide, conceal, screen, shadow, eclipse
FORMAL efface, expunge

blotch *n*
patch, splodge, splotch, splash, smudge, blot, spot, mark, stain, blemish, monk

blotched *adj*
marked, spotted, spotty, stained, blemished, blotchy, scarred, pimply, freckly, scratched

blotchy *adj*
spotty, spotted, patchy, uneven, smeary, blemished, reddened, inflamed

blow^1 *v, n*
♦ *v*
1 *the wind was blowing*
gust, blast, flurry, puff
2 *blow leaves along the road*
waft, fan, flutter, float, flow, stream, drift, rush, whirl, whisk, sweep, carry, fling, buffet, drive, blast
3 BREATHE, breathe out, pant, puff (out)
TECHNICAL insufflate, exsufflate
FORMAL inhale, exhale
4 *blow a horn*
play, sound, pipe, trumpet, toot, blare, blast
5 *blow a lot of money*
fritter away, misspend, spend freely, squander
FORMAL dissipate
COLLOQ. spend like water, pour down the drain
6 *blow a chance/opportunity*
waste, spoil, ruin, wreck, bungle, make a mess of, miss out on
COLLOQ. botch, fluff, miss the boat; *N Am* flub
SLANG cock up, screw up
7 *the car blew a tyre*
blow out, burst, puncture, rupture, tear, split
8 *the fuse blew*
short-circuit, break, fuse, melt
■ **blow out**
1 EXTINGUISH, put out, smother, snuff out
2 BURST, puncture, rupture, tear, split
■ **blow over**
die down, subside, end, finish, cease, pass, vanish, disappear, be forgotten, settle down, fizzle out, peter out
FORMAL abate, dissipate
■ **blow up**
1 EXPLODE, go off, go up, detonate, burst, blast, bomb
2 INFLATE, pump up, swell, fill (out), puff up, balloon, bloat, dilate, expand, enlarge, magnify, exaggerate, overstate
FORMAL distend
3 LOSE YOUR TEMPER, become angry, get into a rage, take leave of your senses
COLLOQ. blow your top, hit the roof, fly off the handle, go mad, flip (your lid)
SLANG go ape, go ballistic
♦ *n*
puff, draught, flurry, gust, blast, wind, gale, storm, squall, tempest
OLD blore

blow^2 *n*
1 *a blow on the head*
hit, concussion, box, cuff, clip, swipe, bash, slap, smack, buffet, butt, bang, clap, clout, knock, rap, stroke, thump, punch, hook, uppercut, yank, souse, swat, thwack, wap, whang, whop, wuther, pelt, plug; *dialect* scat; *Scot* devvel, lounder, paik, skiff, spang, stot, waff, whample
TECHNICAL appel
OLD buff, dint, whirret; (*Spenser*) peise

COLLOQ. whack, wallop, belt
SLANG biff, sock, bop, conk
2 MISFORTUNE, affliction, reverse, setback, comedown, disappointment, upset, jolt, shock, surprise, bombshell, calamity, catastrophe, disaster
COLLOQ. shocker, bolt from the blue, rude awakening, whammy

blow-out n
1 PUNCTURE, flat tyre, burst tyre
COLLOQ. flat
2 PARTY, celebration, feast
COLLOQ. binge, bash, knees-up, rave, rave-up, beanfeast

blowy adj
breezy, windy, fresh, blustery, gusty, squally, stormy

blowzy adj
sloppy, slovenly, unkempt, untidy, bedraggled, dishevelled, ungroomed, tousled, messy, slipshod
E3 neat, smart

blubber v
cry, weep, blub, sob, snivel, sniffle, whimper

bludgeon v, n
♦ v
1 BEAT, strike, club, batter, hit, beat, cudgel
COLLOQ. clobber, cosh
2 FORCE, coerce, compel, intimidate, bulldoze, badger, hector, harass, browbeat, bully, dragoon, pressurize, terrorize
♦ n
club, baton, cosh, cudgel, truncheon

blue adj
1 AZURE, sky-blue, royal blue, ice-blue, sapphire, cornflower, cobalt, ultramarine, navy blue, navy, indigo, aquamarine, turquoise, cyan, cerulean, jacinth, dumortierite, haüyne
2 DEPRESSED, low, dejected, downcast, dispirited, downhearted, despondent, gloomy, glum, dismal, sad, unhappy, miserable, melancholy, morose
COLLOQ. fed up, down in the dumps
3 *a blue joke*
obscene, offensive indecent, improper, rude, coarse, vulgar, lewd, dirty, pornographic, X-rated, erotic, bawdy, fruity, saucy, smutty, racy, risqué, adult
COLLOQ. raunchy, steamy, near the knuckle/bone
E3 2 cheerful, happy **3** decent, clean

blueprint n
design, outline, draft, sketch, pilot, guide, plan, scheme, strategy, project, programme, archetype, prototype, representation, model, pattern

blues n
depression, despondency, unhappiness, sadness, gloom, gloominess, moodiness, glumness, melancholy, miseries, dejection, doldrums
COLLOQ. dumps
E3 euphoria

bluff[1] v, n
♦ v
was only bluffing
lie, pretend, feign, sham, fake, deceive, delude, mislead, hoodwink, blind, fool
COLLOQ. bamboozle
♦ n
lie, idle boast, bravado, humbug, pretence, show, sham, fake, fraud, trick, subterfuge, deceit, deception, feint
FORMAL braggadocio

bluff[2] adj, n
♦ adj
a bluff man
blunt, candid, direct, downright, open, outspoken, plain-spoken, straightforward, frank, genial, good-natured, hearty, affable
E3 diplomatic, refined

♦ n
cliff, crag, escarpment, peak, precipice, promontory, foreland, bank, brow, headland, height, ridge, scarp, escarp

blunder n, v
♦ n
mistake, error, inaccuracy, misjudgement, slip, indiscretion, gaffe, faux pas, oversight, fault, break, bevue, *bêtise*
FORMAL solecism
COLLOQ. howler, bloomer, clanger, boob, booboo, slip-up, bish, goof; N Am flub
SLANG cock-up, boner, floater; N Am pratfall
♦ v
make a mistake, stumble, flounder, bumble, err, miscalculate, misjudge, mess up, get wrong, go wrong, bungle, mismanage
COLLOQ. muck up, botch, slip up, fluff, drop a clanger; N Am flub
SLANG goof (up), cock up, screw up

blunt adj, v
♦ adj
1 UNSHARPENED, not sharp, dull, worn, pointless, edgeless, rounded, stubbed
2 FRANK, candid, direct, forthright, unceremonious, explicit, plain-spoken, honest, straightforward, downright, outspoken, tactless, insensitive, rude, impolite, uncivil, brusque, curt, stark, abrupt
COLLOQ. calling a spade a spade, speaking your mind, not beating about the bush, not mincing your words
E3 1 sharp, pointed **2** subtle, tactful
♦ v
dull, take the edge off, dampen, soften, deaden, numb, anaesthetize, alleviate, allay, weaken
FORMAL abate, hebetate
E3 sharpen, intensify

bluntly adv
frankly, candidly, directly, forthrightly, unceremoniously, explicitly, brusquely, rudely, impolitely, insensitively, tactlessly
E3 subtly, tactfully

blur v, n
♦ v
1 *the windscreen blurred*
smear, smudge, spot, blotch, stain, blear
2 *blurred memories/views*
obscure, make vague/indistinct, mask, conceal, mist, fog, befog, cloud, becloud, veil, dim, dull, darken, confuse, soften
COLLOQ. mudge
♦ n
1 *a blur on the picture*
smear, smudge, spot, blotch, stain, slur
TECHNICAL mackle
2 *my memories are a blur*
haze, mist, fog, cloudiness, fuzziness, indistinctness, obscurity, muddle, confusion, dimness

blurb n
advertisement, commendation, copy, puff
COLLOQ. hype, spiel

blurred adj
out of focus, fuzzy, unclear, indistinct, vague, ill-defined, lacking definition, faint, hazy, misty, foggy, cloudy, clouded, bleary, dim, obscure, confused
E3 clear, distinct

blurt v
■ **blurt out**
exclaim, cry (out), call out, come out with, gush, spout, utter, tell, reveal, disclose, divulge, let out, leak, let slip, plump; N Am blat
FORMAL ejaculate
COLLOQ. blab, let the cat out of the bag, give the game away, spill the beans
E3 bottle up, hush up

blush v, n

♦ v

flush, redden, go red, turn red, crimson, scarlet, colour (up), glow, rouge
OLD mantle

♦ n

flush, reddening, rosiness, ruddiness, colour, glow

blushing adj

flushed, red, rosy, glowing, apple-cheeked, confused, embarrassed, ashamed, modest
FORMAL erubescent
F3 pale, white, composed

bluster v, n

♦ v

boast, brag, crow, swagger, strut, vaunt, show off, rant, roar, storm, bully, harangue, hector, huff, roister
OLD ruffle
FORMAL rodomontade
COLLOQ. talk big

♦ n

boasting, crowing, bravado, bluff, swagger, domineering
OLD huff
FORMAL braggadocio, rodomontade

blustery adj

windy, gusty, squally, stormy, tempestuous, violent, wild, boisterous
F3 calm

board n, v

♦ n

1 *a wooden board*
sheet, panel, slab, plank, beam, timber, slat
2 COMMITTEE, council, panel, jury, commission, directorate, directors, trustees, governors, advisers, advisory group, working party, management, head office
3 MEALS, food, sustenance, provisions, rations
FORMAL victuals
SLANG grub, nosh

♦ v

get on, get in/into, embark, mount, step aboard, enter, catch
FORMAL embus, emplane, entrain

■ **board up**
close (up), cover (up), shut (up), seal

boast v, n

♦ v

1 *boasts about his qualifications*
brag, crow, claim, exaggerate, overstate, bluster, trumpet, vaunt, strut, swagger, prate, show off, sing your own praises; *dialect* crake
OLD yelp, gasconade, cry roast-meat
FORMAL rodomontade
COLLOQ. swank, talk big, loudmouth, blow your own trumpet; *N Am* blow your own horn; *Aust* big-note, skite
2 *boasts a new sauna*
exhibit, have, possess, enjoy, pride yourself on
F3 1 *formal* belittle, deprecate

♦ n

brag, crowing, blustering, self-praise, overstatement, claim, vaunt, pride, joy, gem, treasure
OLD gab
FORMAL fanfaronade, gasconade, gasconism, rodomontade, jactation
COLLOQ. hot air, swank

SYNONYM NUANCES

verb sense 1
Many of the synonyms are disapproving in tone; **brag** suggests arrogance in talking of one's achievements, whilst **crow** expresses a degree of gloating. **Claim**, however, hints that those achievements may not in fact be true, while **exaggerate** and **overstate** probably allow of their existence but imply they are less significant than projected: *I think you exaggerate your influence.*

Bluster could be used to describe voluble but perhaps unsubstantiated boasting; likewise **trumpet**. **Vaunt** has a narrower usage, generally of a public declaration of pride: *Canada's much vaunted multiculturalism*. **Prate** might be used of boastful speaking containing little of consequence; its usage is, surprisingly, rare. Both **strut** and **swagger** have connotations of a physical manner of carrying oneself, and can be used to emphasize this aspect: *he swaggered around in his new uniform*.

boastful adj

proud, conceited, vain, puffed up, bragging, crowing, cocky, swaggering, arrogant, self-flattering, egotistical, bigheaded, swollen-headed; *N Am* swell-headed
FORMAL vainglorious
COLLOQ. swanky
F3 modest, self-effacing, humble

boastfully adv

proudly, conceitedly, crowingly, cockily, arrogantly, egotistically
FORMAL vaingloriously
F3 modestly, self-effacingly, humbly

boat

See panel on next page

boatman n

ferryman, oarsman/woman, rower, sailor, yachtsman/woman, waterman, bargee, gondolier, voyageur

bob v

1 *a raft bobbing up and down*
bounce, float, move up and down shake, quiver, wobble, bobble, popple; *Scot* hod
FORMAL oscillate
2 *bobbed back into the house*
leap, spring, jump, jerk, jolt, twitch, nod, bow, curtsy, hop, skip
■ **bob up**
appear, emerge, arrive, materialize, rise, surface, pop up, spring up, crop up, arise
COLLOQ. show up

bode v

predict, foretell, prophesy, indicate, signify, intimate, herald, threaten, warn
OLD sign
FORMAL augur, adumbrate, forebode, foreshadow, foreshow, foretoken, forewarn, presage, betoken, portend, prognosticate, purport

bodge v

botch, bungle, mess (up), blunder, ruin, spoil
COLLOQ. muck up, foul up, fluff, make a hash of; *N Am* flub
SLANG goof (up), screw up, louse up

bodily adj, adv

♦ adj

physical, carnal, fleshly, real, actual, tangible, substantial, concrete, material
FORMAL corporeal
F3 spiritual

♦ adv

altogether, en masse, collectively, as a whole, as one, completely, fully, wholly, entirely, totally, in toto
F3 piecemeal

body n

1 *his whole body was aching*
physique, build, form, frame, figure, anatomy, skeleton, trunk, torso
Related adjective: corporal
2 CORPSE, cadaver, carcase, dead body
SLANG stiff
3 *sit in the body of the church*
main part, central part, largest part, bulk, heart, core, nub, kernel
4 ORGANIZATION, association, society, corporation, company, confederation, council, authority, bloc, cartel,

Types of boat or ship include:

airboat	corvette	frigate	lugger	schooner	trawler
aircraft-carrier	cruiser	galleon	man-of-war	scow	trimaran
barge	currach (or	gondola	minesweeper	skiff	trireme
battleship	curragh)	gulet	motor-boat	sloop	tug
brig	cutter	houseboat	motor-launch	smack	U-boat
cabin-cruiser	destroyer	hovercraft	narrow boat	speedboat	umiak
canal boat	dhow	hydrofoil	packet	square-rigger	vaporetto
canoe	dinghy	NZ jet boat	paddle steamer	steamer	warship
catamaran	dreadnought	junk	pedalo	submarine	whaler
clipper	dredger	kayak	proa	supertanker	wherry
coble (or cobble)	dugout	ketch	punt	swamp boat	windjammer
container-ship	ferry	lifeboat	rowing-boat	tall ship	yacht
coracle	freighter	liner	sampan	tanker	yawl

See also **sail**; **ship**.

---

syndicate, congress, collection, group, band, crowd, throng, multitude, mob, mass, phalanx
5 the body of a car
shell, framework, frame, chassis, structure, casing, skeleton
6 a body of water
expanse, area, range, stretch, extent
7 a body of information
quantity, amount, mass, lot, volume, weight, bulk
8 CONSISTENCY, density, solidity, firmness, bulk, mass, substance, essence, fullness, richness

> QUOTATIONS
> Our body is a machine for living
> LEO TOLSTOY, War and Peace

bodyguard n
guard, protector, defender, guardian
SLANG minder

boffin n
scientist, expert, engineer, designer, planner, inventor, mastermind, genius, brain, intellect, intellectual, thinker
COLLOQ. egghead, wizard, backroom-boy; N Am brainiac

bog n, v
♦ n
marsh, swamp, fen, mire, quagmire, quag, slough, morass, quicksands, marshland, swampland, wetlands; dialect sump; Can muskeg
■ **bog down**
encumber, hinder, overwhelm, deluge, sink, stick, trap, slow down, slow up, delay, halt, hold up, set back, stall
FORMAL impede, retard, mire

boggle v
astound, startle, amaze, surprise, wonder, marvel, overwhelm, stagger, alarm, confuse
COLLOQ. bowl over, flabbergast

boggy adj
marshy, miry, swampy, muddy, oozy, morassy, quaggy, soft, spongy, waterlogged, fenny
FORMAL paludal
arid

bogus adj
false, fake, counterfeit, forged, fraudulent, spurious, sham, make-believe, artificial, imitation, dummy
COLLOQ. spoof, phoney, pseudo, pseud
genuine, true, real, valid

bohemian adj, n
♦ adj
artistic, unconventional, unorthodox, nonconformist, alternative, original, avant-garde, eccentric, offbeat, bizarre, exotic
COLLOQ. boho, arty, oddball, off-the-wall
SLANG way-out
bourgeois, conventional, orthodox
♦ n
beatnik, hippie, drop-out, nonconformist

COLLOQ. boho
conformist

boil[1] v
1 boil water
simmer, stew, cook, heat, seethe, bring/come to the boil, brew, gurgle, bubble, fizz, effervesce, froth, foam, steam, parboil, decoct, wallop; dialect leep
2 boil with anger
erupt, explode, rage, rave, storm, fume, seethe
FORMAL fulminate
COLLOQ. blow your top, fly off the handle, fly into a rage, go off the deep end, blow a fuse, see red, hit the roof
■ **boil down**
amount, reduce, concentrate, distil, condense, digest, abstract, summarize, abridge

boil[2] n
a boil on the skin
pustule, abscess, gumboil, ulcer, sore, tumour, growth, ganglion, bunion, pimple, carbuncle, blister, inflammation, swelling, blain, furuncle
OLD botch
COLLOQ. gathering

boiling adj
1 boiling water
turbulent, gurgling, bubbling, steaming, scalding
2 HOT, baking, roasting, scorching, sweltering, blistering, torrid; N Am broiling
3 ANGRY, indignant, incensed, infuriated, enraged, furious, fuming, flaming

boisterous adj
exuberant, rollicking, romping, bouncy, active, hyperactive, lively, spirited, turbulent, energetic, animated, tumultuous, loud, noisy, clamorous, rowdy, rough, disorderly, riotous, wild, unrestrained, unruly, obstreperous, roisting; dialect randy; Scot goustrous
TECHNICAL strepitoso
OLD dithyrambic
COLLOQ. rumbustious, rambunctious
quiet, calm, restrained, docile

boisterously adv
exuberantly, actively, hyperactively, spiritedly, turbulently, energetically, animatedly, tumultuously, loudly, noisily, clamorously, rowdily, roughly, riotously, wildly, unrestrainedly, obstreperously
quietly, calmly, restrainedly

bold adj
1 BRAVE, dauntless, daring, audacious, fearless, undaunted, courageous, valiant, intrepid, heroic, gallant, adventurous, venturesome, enterprising, plucky, spirited, confident, outgoing
OLD haughty
FORMAL valorous
COLLOQ. bold as a lion
2 BRAZEN, brash, forward, shameless, unabashed, impudent, insolent, barefaced, bald-faced
COLLOQ. cheeky, saucy, brassy, pert, bold as brass

SLANG in-your-face
3 EYE-CATCHING, striking, conspicuous, prominent, strong, pronounced, distinct, definite, bright, vivid, colourful, loud, flashy, showy, flamboyant
4 *in bold print*
heavy, thick, pronounced
FE **1** cowardly, nervous, cautious, timid, shy **2** timid, modest, shy, diffident **3** faint, restrained **4** light

boldly *adv*
1 BRAVELY, daringly, courageously, confidently, fearlessly, audaciously, valiantly, intrepidly, heroically, adventurously, pluckily
2 VIVIDLY, strikingly, strongly, brightly, prominently, distinctly, definitely
FE **1** cowardly, cautiously, timidly **2** faintly

bolshie *adj*
awkward, obstinate, unhelpful, difficult, stubborn, unco-operative, irritable, touchy, prickly, oversensitive, rude, unpleasant, problem
COLLOQ. stroppy, bloody-minded
FE amenable, pleasant, co-operative, helpful

bolster *v, n*
♦ *v*
boost, aid, assist, help, maintain, prop, reinforce, strengthen, supplement, support, brace, buoy up, buttress, firm up, shore up, stay, stiffen, revitalize, invigorate
FORMAL augment
FE undermine
♦ *n*
pillow, support, cushion, Dutch wife

bolt *n, v*
♦ *n*
1 *a bolt on a door*
bar, rod, shaft, fastener, latch, catch, lock; *Scot* snib
2 *nuts and bolts*
screw, pin, peg, rivet
TECHNICAL pintle
3 *a bolt of lightning*
flash, shaft, burst, streak, ray, spark, blaze, flare
♦ *v*
1 FASTEN, secure, bar, latch, lock, rivet, pin, screw
OLD (*Spenser*) sperre
2 *bolt for the door*
escape, flee, fly, run (away), run off, sprint, rush, dash, dart, hurtle
FORMAL abscond
COLLOQ. scarper
3 *bolt your food down*
gulp, wolf (down), gobble, gorge, guzzle, devour, cram, stuff
COLLOQ. scoff

> **PROVERBS**
> It's no use shutting the stable door after the horse has bolted

bomb *n, v*
♦ *n*
bombshell, explosive, projectile, device
COLLOQ. pineapple
SLANG egg
See panel below
♦ *v*
bombard, shell, torpedo, attack, blow up, destroy

bombard *v*
1 *bombard the airport*
attack, assail, pelt, pound, strafe, blast, bomb, shell, torpedo, stone, blitz, raid, besiege
2 *bombard with criticism*
attack, hound, bother, harass, pester, flood, deluge, inundate, swamp

bombardment *n*
1 *aerial bombardment*
attack, assault, air raid, bombing, shelling, pounding, blitz, barrage, cannonade, fusillade, salvo, fire, flak, hail
SLANG stonk
2 *bombardment of questions*
attack, onslaught, besieging, hounding, bothering, harassing, pestering

bombast *n*
pomposity, pretentiousness, bluster, wordiness, heroics, rant, verbosity, turgidness; *N Am* sophomoric
OLD ampullosity, dithyramb
FORMAL grandiloquence, magniloquence, fustian, euphuism
COLLOQ. hot air

bombastic *adj*
pompous, pretentious, grandiose, verbose, wordy, turgid, ostentatious, affected, high-flown, inflated, bloated, windy
FORMAL grandiloquent, magniloquent, portentous, euphuistic, fustian
FE reserved, restrained

bona fide *adj*
genuine, real, valid, true, actual, authentic, lawful, legal, legitimate, kosher, honest
COLLOQ. the real McCoy
FE bogus

bonanza *n*
windfall, sudden wealth, godsend, stroke of luck, blessing, boon

bond *n, v*
♦ *n*
1 *bonds of friendship*
connection, relation, relationship, link, tie(s), binding, union, yoke, affiliation, attachment, rapport, friendship, affinity, chemistry
TECHNICAL nexus, ligament, valence
FORMAL vinculum
2 CONTRACT, covenant, agreement, pledge, promise, vow, pact, transaction, deal, treaty, word, obligation
3 FETTER, shackle, manacle, chain, cord, band, binding

Types of bomb include:

aerobomb	candle bomb	*colloq.* dumb	improvised explo-	neutron bomb	smoke bomb
anti-personnel	car bomb	bomb	sive device (IED)	nuclear bomb	stink bomb
bomb	cluster bomb	E-bomb	incendiary	parcel bomb	stun grenade
anti-tank bomb	cobalt bomb	firebomb	landmine	penetration bomb	thermobaric bomb
atom bomb	*colloq.* daisy-cutter	fission bomb	letter bomb	petrol bomb	thermonuclear
Bangalore torpedo	depth charge	flying bomb	mail bomb	pipe bomb	bomb
binary bomb	dime (dense inert	fragmentation	massive ordnance	plastic bomb	time bomb
blockbuster	metal explosive)	bomb	air burst (MOAB)	radium bomb	torpedo
bomblet	bomb	fusion bomb	megaton bomb	rifle grenade	vehicle-borne
booby-trap bomb	dirty bomb	general purpose	Mills bomb	roadside bomb	improvised
bouncing bomb	*old slang*	bomb	mine	rocket	explosive device
colloq. bunker	doodlebug	grenade	missile	sensor fuzed bomb	(VBIED)
buster	drogue bomb	hydrogen bomb	Molotov cocktail	shell	V-1
buzz bomb			nail bomb	smart bomb	V-2

♦ v
connect, fasten, bind, unite, fuse, join, stick, attach, glue, gum, paste, weld, seal

bondage *n*
imprisonment, captivity, confinement, restraint, slavery, enslavement, serfdom, servitude, subservience, subjection, subjugation, yoke
OLD thrall
FORMAL incarceration, thraldom, vassalage
Ƒ freedom, independence

bone *n*
Related adjectives: osseous, osteal

Human bones include:

carpal	malleus (hammer)	scapula (shoulder-
clavicle (col-	mandible (lower	blade)
larbone)	jawbone)	skull
coccyx	maxilla (upper	sternum (breast-
cranium	jawbone)	bone)
femur (thigh bone)	metacarpal	stapes (stirrup-
fibula	metatarsal	bone)
humerus (funny	patella (kneecap)	tarsal
bone)	pelvis	temporal
ilium	phalange	tibia
incus (anvil)	pubis	ulna
innominate bone	radius	vertebra
(hip bone)	rib	
ischium	sacrum	

bonhomie *n*
warm-heartedness, kind-heartedness, friendliness, conviviality, geniality, sympathy, tenderness, good nature, affability, amiability

bon mot *n*
witticism, quip, riposte, repartee, pleasantry, wisecrack
COLLOQ. one-liner

bonny *adj*
attractive, lovely, beautiful, pretty, fine, fair, blooming, handsome, bouncing, cheerful, cheery, joyful, merry
Ƒ ugly

bonus *n*
1 *pay a bonus*
commission, dividend, premium, prize, reward, honorarium, tip, gratuity, gift, fringe benefits, handout
FORMAL lagniappe
2 *the good weather is a bonus*
advantage, benefit, gain, extra
FORMAL perquisite
COLLOQ. plus, perk
Ƒ 2 disadvantage, disincentive

bony *adj*
thin, lean, angular, lanky, gawky, gangling, skinny, scrawny, scraggy, emaciated, skeletal, rawboned, gaunt, drawn
FORMAL osseous
Ƒ fat, plump

book *n, v*
♦ n
volume, tome, publication, work, booklet, tract
♦ v
1 *book a ticket*
arrange (in advance), reserve, make a reservation for, prearrange, engage, charter, procure, order, organize, schedule, programme
COLLOQ. bag
2 *booked for assault*
charge, accuse (of), blame
Ƒ 1 cancel
■ book in
register, enrol, check in, record your arrival

Types of book include:

album	guidebook	jotter
almanac	handbook	journal
annual	lexicon	ledger
anthology	libretto	notebook
atlas	manual	pad
A to Z	manuscript	scrapbook
autobiography	memoir	sketchbook
bestseller	novel	textbook
biography	omnibus	workbook
board book	penny dreadful	**CHURCH BOOKS:**
catalogue	phrase book	hymnal
children's book	picture book	hymn-book
coffee-table book	pocket companion	lectionary
comic book	primer	missal
compendium	reference book	prayer book
concordance	romantic novel	psalter
cookbook	story	
copybook	thesaurus	**FORMATS:**
crime	thriller	audio book
detective	treasury	blook
dictionary	yearbook	ebook
directory		enhanced ebook
encyclopedia	**WRITING BOOKS:**	hardback
fiction	album	Kindle®
foodoir	book of days	paperback
gazetteer	chapbook	softback
gradus	diary	vook
graphic novel	exercise book	
grimoire	Filofax®	

See also **literature**; **story**.

bookbinding
See panel on next page

booking *n*
reservation, arrangement, appointment, prior arrangement

bookish *adj*
studious, well-read, academic, scholarly, cultured, erudite, highbrow, intellectual, learned, literary, scholastic, lettered, donnish, bluestocking, pedantic
Ƒ lowbrow, unlettered

booklet *n*
leaflet, pamphlet, folder, circular, handout, notice

books *n*
accounts, ledgers, records, financial statement, balance sheet

boom *v, n*
♦ v
1 BANG, crash, roar, blare, thunder, roll, bellow, rumble, resound, reverberate, blast, explode, bombilate
2 FLOURISH, thrive, prosper, succeed, develop, grow, do well, increase, gain, progress, expand, swell, surge, leap, escalate, skyrocket, intensify, strengthen, go from strength to strength, mushroom, snowball, explode
FORMAL burgeon
Ƒ 2 fail, collapse, slump
♦ n
1 BANG, clap, crash, roar, thunder, rumble, reverberation, blast, blare, bellow, roll, resonance, explosion, burst, loud noise
2 INCREASE, growth, expansion, gain, upsurge, jump, surge, leap, spurt, boost, upturn, upswing, improvement, advance, progress, success, development, escalation, explosion
Ƒ 2 failure, collapse, slump, recession, depression

Terms used in bookbinding include:

adhesive binding	book block	fore edge	lining	rounding and	tail
all edges gilt (aeg)	buckram	front board	Linson®	backing	tailband
backboard	case	full bound	loose-leaf	saddle-stitch	thermal tape
backbone	casebound	gather	mechanical bind-	sewing	binding
back cornering	casing-in	half bound	ing	shoulder	thermoplastic
back lining	cloth-lined board	hardback	millboard	side-stitch	binding
N Am binder's	comb binding	head	morocco	signature	thread sewing
board	debossing	headband	notch binding	smashing	unsewn binding
binder's brass	doublure	headcap	open-flat	soft-cover	varnishing
binder's die	drawn-on	hinge	paperback	spine	velo binding
binding	drilling	hot foil stamping	pasteboard	spiral binding	whole bound
blind blocking	dust cover	jacket	perfect binding	square back	wire binding
blocking	embossing	laminating	quarter bound	stab-stitch	wire stitching
boards	endpaper	library binding	raised band	stamping	wiro binding
bolts	flyleaf	limp	ring binding	strawboard	yapp

boomerang v
rebound, bounce back, spring back, recoil, ricochet, reverse, backfire

boon[1] n
a great boon to the elderly
blessing, advantage, benefit, bonus, help, godsend, windfall, favour, kindness, gift, present, grant, gratuity
OLD bene
COLLOQ. plus
E3 disadvantage, blight

boon[2]
■ **boon companion**
close friend, dear friend, special friend, best friend, bosom friend, confidant(e)
OLD cupman, franion, Trojan

boor n
oaf, lout, barbarian, philistine, vulgarian, rustic, yahoo, hog, plebeian, clown, Grobian; *dialect* chuff; *Scot* keelie
OLD kern, Jack
COLLOQ. peasant, country bumpkin, clod, clodhopper, yokel, pleb, oik
SLANG yob, yobbo, slob

boorish adj
uncouth, oafish, loutish, ill-mannered, ill-bred, rude, coarse, rough, crude, vulgar, unrefined, uncivilized, gruff, impolite, rustic, uneducated, ignorant, crass, gross, lumpen, clodhopping; *Aust* ocker
OLD borrel, swain
E3 polite, refined, cultured, genteel

boost v, n
♦ v
1 *boost confidence*
bolster, lift, encourage, inspire, uplift, foster, support, stimulate; *Aust* rap
TECHNICAL potentiate
2 *boost sales*
increase, raise, put up, improve, enhance, develop, enlarge, expand, supplement, amplify, advance, help, aid, assist, maximize, promote, encourage, further, heighten
FORMAL augment
3 *boost a product*
advertise, promote, publicize, praise
COLLOQ. plug, hype, talk up
E3 **1** undermine **2** lower, deteriorate, hinder
♦ n
1 *a boost to morale*
lift, uplift, fillip, encouragement, inspiration, stimulus, spur, support; *Aust* rap
COLLOQ. shot in the arm, ego-trip
2 *a boost to sales*
increase, rise, improvement, enhancement, development, enlargement, expansion, increment, addition, supplement, amplification, advance, help, aid, assistance, furtherance
FORMAL augmentation

3 *a boost for a product*
advertisement, promotion, publicity, praise
COLLOQ. plug, hype
E3 **1** setback, blow **2** setback, deterioration

boot[1] v
kick, shove
■ **boot out**
dismiss, eject, expel, lay off, suspend, shed, give notice, make redundant
COLLOQ. kick out, fire, sack, give someone their cards, give the heave
See panel on next page

boot[2]
■ **to boot**
as well, in addition, besides, too
COLLOQ. into the bargain

booth n
cubicle, compartment, carrel, stall, stand, kiosk, hut, box; *Scot* bothan, crame, luckenbooth

bootleg adj
illegal, unlawful, illicit, criminal, wrong, forbidden, prohibited, banned, outlawed, barred, unauthorized, under-the-counter, black-market
FORMAL proscribed, interdicted
E3 legal

bootless adj
fruitless, futile, vain, ineffective, useless, pointless, profitless, sterile, unavailing, unsuccessful, worthless, unproductive, barren
E3 profitable, useful

booty n
loot, plunder, pillage, spoil(s), haul, gains, takings, pickings, prize, profits, winnings; *Scot* creagh
OLD purchase
SLANG swag

booze n, v
♦ n
alcohol, drink, liquor, spirits, strong drink, intoxicant, grog, liqueur, stimulus, slug; *Scot* skink, strunt
OLD fuddle
COLLOQ. hard stuff, the bottle, Dutch courage, firewater, the creature; *Scot & Irish* the cratur; jar, tipple, tiddly, tinct
SLANG jungle juice; N Am juice
♦ v
drink, indulge, have a drink, be a hard drinker, be a heavy drinker
COLLOQ. tipple, hit the bottle, drink like a fish
SLANG get pissed

boozer n
1 PUB, bar, saloon, public house, tavern, inn, lounge, lounge bar; *Scot* howf
COLLOQ. local, hostelry, watering-hole
2 DRINKER, alcoholic, drunk, drunkard, inebriate, hard drinker, heavy drinker, dipsomaniac, wine-bibber, Bacchus, bloat, habitual; *N Am* souse

---

Types of boot include:

ankle boot	climbing-boot	gambado	lace-boot	rugby boot	walking-boot
balmoral	clodhopper	gumboot	larrigan	*colloq.* scarpetto	wellington
biker boot	*old* crow boot	half-boot	moon boot	shoeboot	*colloq.* welly
bootee	derby	Hessian boot	muckluck	skating boot	
bottine	Doc Marten®	high shoe	overshoe	snowboot	
old buskin	finnesko	jemima	platform boot	top-boot	
Chelsea boot	football boot	kamik	riding boot	Ugg® boot	
chukka boot	galosh	kid	rock boot	wader	

COLLOQ. tippler
SLANG wino, lush, alkie, dipso, soak, piss artist, pisshead, toper, tosspot, sot, sponge

bop *n, v*
♦ *n*
dance, hop, twist, jive, stomp
COLLOQ. boogie
♦ *v*
dance, leap, jump, move to music, rock, spin, sway, gyrate, twirl, pirouette, whirl, trip the light fantastic
COLLOQ. hoof it, hop, jig, shake a leg

border *n, v*
♦ *n*
1 BOUNDARY, frontier, line, state line, marchlands, marches
2 *herbaceous borders*
bed, edge, rim, brim, verge, margin, fringe, periphery, surround, perimeter, circumference, bound, bounds, confine, confines, limit, demarcation, borderline, brink
3 HEM, frill, valance, skirt, trimming, frieze, selvage, list, rand, welt
TECHNICAL limb, mat, bordure, orle, cartouche, dado, guilloche, furbelow, purfle
OLD swage
♦ *v*
1 *Sweden borders Norway*
lie/be next to, be adjacent to, join, touch, connect, trench
FORMAL adjoin, abut, impinge, be contiguous with
2 *streets bordered with trees*
edge, bound, skirt, flank, fringe, rim, surround, enclose, trim, selvage, hem
OLD emborder, engrail
FORMAL circumscribe
■ **border on**
verge on, be almost, be nearly, resemble, approximate to, be tantamount to, approach

borderline *n, adj*
♦ *n*
demarcation line, boundary, differentiation, line, dividing-line, divide, division, limit
♦ *adj*
marginal, problematic, indefinite, doubtful, uncertain, indecisive, indeterminate, ambivalent
COLLOQ. iffy
E3 certain, definite, clear-cut

bore[1] *v, n*
♦ *v*
the speech bored them
tire, make tired, weary, wear out, fatigue, exhaust, pall on, be tedious to, jade, trouble, bother, worry, irritate, annoy, vex, irk
COLLOQ. turn off, send to sleep, bore the pants off
E3 interest, excite
♦ *n*
nuisance, bother
COLLOQ. bind, drag, turn-off, headache, pain, pain in the neck
E3 pleasure, delight

bore[2] *v*
bore a hole
drill, mine, pierce, perforate, penetrate, puncture, sink, dig (out), burrow, hollow (out), tap, tunnel, undermine, sap

bored *adj*
uninterested, unexcited, tired, wearied, exhausted
FORMAL ennuied, ennuyé
COLLOQ. bored to tears, bored stiff, bored out of your mind, cheesed off, fed up, turned off, sick and tired, in a rut, brassed off, browned off
E3 interested, excited

boredom *n*
tedium, tediousness, monotony, humdrum, dullness, sameness, flatness, apathy, listlessness, weariness, world-weariness, frustration
FORMAL ennui, malaise, acedia
E3 interest, excitement

> **QUOTATIONS**
> The effect of boredom on a large scale in history is underestimated. It is a main cause of all revolutions
> WILLIAM INGE, *The End of an Age*

boring *adj*
tedious, dull, monotonous, routine, repetitious, uninteresting, unexciting, uneventful, mundane, dreary, drab, humdrum, tiring, tiresome, unvaried, commonplace, trite, unimaginative, uninspired, uninspiring, dry, stale, flat, insipid, stodgy, prosaic, long-winded
OLD stultifying, jejune
COLLOQ. samey, dull as ditchwater, soul-destroying, with the novelty worn off, ho-hum
E3 interesting, exciting, stimulating, original

> **SYNONYM NUANCES**
>
> **Tedious** may be used to imply the cause of boredom could well be excessive length: *reasons too tedious to relate*. The words **monotonous**, **routine** and **repetitious**, point to the same thing happening over and over: *her life is a monotonous routine*. **Dull**, **uninteresting**, **unexciting**, **uneventful** and **unvaried**, on the other hand, express a lack of anything new or stimulating. **Dreary** and **humdrum** are similar, suggesting a lack of variety, but with more emotional effect: *she was sick of her humdrum existence*. **Tiring** can be used to suggest something so boring that is physically or mentally draining: *a tiring journey*; whilst **tiresome** suggests it is irritating: *a truly tiresome and boring movie*.
>
> **Commonplace**, **unimaginative** and **uninspired** can be used of boring speech or writing to indicate there it contains nothing of distinction. Both **flat** and **insipid** also point to a lack of inspiration, while **prosaic** similarly is lacking in imagination: *news reports are commonly prosaic and patronising*. The word **dry**, while also generally used of the written or spoken word, appropriately describes a heaviness of style with little in the way of light relief; whereas **stale** has more of a suggestion that it has already been experienced many times before: *stale jokes*.
>
> **Long-winded**, however, is appropriate when many more words have been used than are actually required. **Trite** tends to be used more narrowly of over-used words or phrases: *trite accolades*.

boringly *adv*
tediously, dully, monotonously, repetitiously, uninterestingly, unexcitingly, uneventfully, drearily,

tiresomely, tritely, unimaginatively, flatly, insipidly, prosaically, long-windedly
OLD stultifyingly
⊞ interestingly, excitingly

borough n
town, district, area, community, constituency, parish; Scot burgh

borrow v
1 *borrow a friend's car*
have the use of, take/have on loan, use temporarily, take out a loan, rent, hire, charter, lease; dialect scunge
TECHNICAL lever
COLLOQ. scrounge, cadge, sponge
2 *borrow words/ideas*
adopt, take (over), draw, derive, obtain, use, acquire
FORMAL appropriate
⊞ **1** lend

borrowing n
1 *borrowing of money*
use, temporary use, loan, rental, hire, charter, leasing
2 *English borrowings in German*
loan, loan-translation, loan-word, adoption, takeover, derivation, use, acquisition
TECHNICAL calque
⊞ **1** lending

bosom n, adj
♦ n
1 BUST, breasts, chest, breast; dialect pap, diddy
COLLOQ. boob, booby
SLANG bristol, knocker, tit, titty; Aust nork
2 *in the bosom of the family*
heart, core, centre, midst, protection, shelter, sanctuary
♦ adj
close, intimate, dear, devoted, loving, faithful, confidential, boon

boss n, v
♦ n
employer, master, owner, captain, head, chief, leader, top man, top woman, supremo, administrator, executive, director, chairman, chairperson, chairwoman, manager, superior, foreman, superintendent, overseer, governor, supervisor; S Afr oubaas
COLLOQ. gaffer, gov, guv, bigwig, big cheese, top dog, top banana; N Am honcho
♦ v
order around, order about, domineer, tyrannize, bully, bulldoze, browbeat, give orders to, dominate
COLLOQ. push around, throw your weight about, lay down the law

bossiness n
authoritarianism, high-handedness, imperiousness, assertiveness, autocracy, tyranny, despotism
⊞ unassertiveness

bossy adj
authoritarian, autocratic, tyrannical, despotic, dictatorial, domineering, overbearing, oppressive, lordly, high-handed, dominating, imperious, insistent, assertive, demanding, exacting
⊞ unassertive

botch v, n
♦ v
bungle, mess (up), make a mess of, blunder, mar, mismanage, ruin, spoil, patch; N Am mux
COLLOQ. foul up, fluff, muck up, muff, make a hash of, make a bad job of, bodge; N Am flub
SLANG goof (up), louse up, screw up, cock up, balls up; (taboo) fuck up
⊞ accomplish, succeed
♦ n
blunder, bungle, failure, muddle, mess, miscarriage
COLLOQ. flop, farce, shambles, hash
SLANG cock-up, balls-up
⊞ success

both adj
the two, each, the pair, the one and the other

bother v, n
♦ v
1 *not bother to reply*
concern yourself, trouble, make the/an effort, think necessary
2 *the heat bothered us*
worry, upset, trouble, concern, annoy, dismay, alarm, distress, vex; Scot fash, deave
COLLOQ. bug
3 *don't bother her*
disturb, inconvenience, put out, trouble, pester, plague, harass, nag, annoy, irritate, molest
FORMAL incommode
COLLOQ. hassle
♦ n
1 *not worth the bother*
trouble, inconvenience, effort, problem, difficulty, fuss, exertion, pains, bustle, flurry
COLLOQ. hassle
SLANG shtook
2 *office paperwork is a real bother*
nuisance, annoyance, irritation, problem, difficulty, vexation, worry, strain
COLLOQ. aggravation, pest, pain in the neck
3 *a spot of bother in the pub*
trouble, fighting, disturbance, disorder, unrest, rumpus
COLLOQ. aggro
SLANG bovver

bothersome adj
troublesome, annoying, irksome, irritating, infuriating, vexatious, vexing, inconvenient, distressing, exasperating, laborious, boring, tedious, tiresome, wearisome; Scot fashious
OLD brickle
COLLOQ. aggravating, pesky

bottle n, v
♦ n
1 container
See panel on next page
2 COURAGE, bravery, boldness, daring, valour, intrepidity
COLLOQ. guts, nerve, spunk, grit
■ **bottle up**
hide, conceal, restrain, curb, keep back, hold back, keep in check, suppress, repress, inhibit, restrict, shut in, enclose, contain, disguise
⊞ unbosom, unburden

bottleneck n
hold-up, traffic jam, snarl-up, congestion, gridlock, clogging, blockage, obstruction, block, obstacle, restriction, constriction, narrowing

bottom n, adj
♦ n
1 UNDERSIDE, underneath, sole, base, foot, plinth, pedestal, support, foundation, substructure, basis, underpinning, ground, nadir
2 *at the bottom of the sea*
floor, bed, depths
3 *at the bottom of the garden*
end, far end, furthest end, farthest end
4 *children at the bottom of the class*
lowest level, least important position
5 *sitting on his bottom*
rear, behind, buttocks, seat, rump
COLLOQ. posterior, backside, tail, bum; N Am butt, heinie, booty; Scot bahookie
SLANG
(vulgar) arse; N Am ass, tush; Aust coit, quoit
⊞ **1** top **2** surface **4** top
♦ adj
lowest, lower, underside, undermost

Types of bottle include:

ampulla	carboy	feeding bottle	hot-water bottle	poison bottle	torpedo bottle
apothecary bottle	codd bottle	flacon	jack	scent bottle	vial
beer bottle	cruet	flagon	lagena	screwtop	vinegar bottle
calabash	decanter	flask	milk bottle	snuff bottle	wine bottle
canteen	demijohn	gourd	phial	*Aust* stubby	
carafe	dumpy	hip flask	pitcher	Thermos® flask	

See also **wine bottle sizes**.

bottomless *adj*
a bottomless pit/supply of funds
deep, profound, fathomless, unfathomed, unplumbed, unbottomed, immeasurable, unfathomable, measureless, infinite, boundless, limitless, unlimited, inexhaustible
TECHNICAL subjacent
OLD unfounded
FORMAL abysmal, abyssal
E3 shallow, limited

bough *n*
branch, limb

boulder *n*
rock, stone, niggerhead; *Aust* gibber
OLD bowlder

boulevard *n*
avenue, mall, parade, promenade, drive, road, street, prospect, thoroughfare

bounce *v, n*
♦ *v*
1 *bounce a ball*
rebound, spring back, bob, ricochet, recoil, throw, dap; *Scot* stoit, stot
2 *children bouncing about*
spring, jump, leap, bound
♦ *n*
1 *allowed one bounce of the ball*
rebound, bound, spring, jump, leap; *Scot* stot
2 SPRING, springiness, elasticity, give, resilience, rebound, recoil
3 EBULLIENCE, exuberance, vitality, vivacity, energy, vigour, animation, dynamism, spiritedness, liveliness
COLLOQ. go, get-up-and-go, zip
■ **bounce back**
recover, get better, get back to normal, improve, make a comeback

bouncing *adj*
healthy, lively, robust, strong, vigorous, thriving, blooming, bonny

bouncy *adj*
1 SPRINGY, resilient, flexible, elastic, stretchy, rubbery, spongy
2 LIVELY, active, energetic, alive, spirited, dynamic, vivacious, vigorous, sprightly
COLLOQ. full of beans

bound[1] *adj*
1 *bound to go wrong*
sure, certain, definite, fated, destined, doomed
2 LIABLE, committed, duty-bound, pledged, obliged, required, forced, compelled, constrained
FORMAL beholden
3 FASTENED, secured, fixed, tied (up), chained, roped, fettered, tethered, held, attached, clamped, lashed, trussed, strapped, shackled, restricted, bandaged
■ **bound up with**
tied up with, connected with, linked with, related to, associated with, dependent on
COLLOQ. (going) hand in hand with

bound[2] *adj*
be bound for Norway
heading, headed, off (to), on your way to, travelling, going, coming, proceeding

bound[3] *v, n*
♦ *v*
she bounded down the stairs
jump, leap, vault, hurdle, spring, bounce, bob, hop, skip, dance, frisk, gambol, frolic, caper, prance, cavort, lollop, galumph; *Scot* scoup, skelp, spang, stend
♦ *n*
jump, leap, vault, spring, bounce, bob, hop, skip, gambol, frolic, caper, dance, prance; *Scot* spang, stend
TECHNICAL gambado

bound[4] *n, v*
♦ *n*
1 BORDER, line, limit(s), borderline, demarcation, confine(s), margin, verge, brink, edge, perimeter, circumference, extremity, termination
2 LIMITATION, limit, restriction, check, curb, restraint
♦ *v*
1 BORDER, outline, limit, enclose, edge, skirt, flank, fringe, surround; *dialect* mere
2 RESTRICT, regulate, control, limit, moderate, restrain, contain
FORMAL circumscribe

boundary *n*
border, frontier, barrier, line, borderline, demarcation, bounds, confine(s), limit(s), margin, fringe, verge, brink, edge, perimeter, extremity, termination, point of no return, Rubicon, score; *dialect* mere; *Scot* meith
OLD bourn, limes, list, mark
Related adjectives: perimetric, peripheral

bounded *adj*
enclosed, surrounded, bordered, edged, encircled, encompassed, limited, restrained, restricted, confined, walled in, hemmed in, controlled, defined, demarcated
FORMAL circumscribed, delimited

bounder *n*
cad, cheat, blackguard, rogue, miscreant, cur, dastard, knave
COLLOQ. blighter, rotter, pig, swine, rat, dirty dog

boundless *adj*
unbounded, limitless, unlimited, illimitable, unconfined, countless, incalculable, numberless, innumerable, untold, vast, immense, measureless, immeasurable, infinite, endless, unending, never-ending, interminable, everlasting, inexhaustible, unflagging, indefatigable
E3 limited, restricted

bounds *n*
restrictions, confines, limits, borders, marches, demarcations, margins, fringes, boundaries, periphery, circumference, perimeter, edges, extremities, parameters, scope
■ **out of bounds**
off limits, prohibited, forbidden, not allowed

bountiful *adj*
abundant, plentiful, exuberant, profuse, ample, prolific, overflowing, ungrudging, unstinting, boundless, copious, generous, lavish, liberal, open-handed, princely
FORMAL magnanimous, munificent, bounteous, plenteous, luxuriant
E3 meagre, mean, sparse

bounty *n*
1 REWARD, recompense, premium, bonus, gratuity, tip, gift, present, donation, grant, allowance
2 GENEROSITY, liberality, largesse, almsgiving, charity, philanthropy, kindness
FORMAL munificence, beneficence, magnanimity

bouquet *n*
1 *a bouquet of flowers*
bunch, posy, nosegay, spray, corsage, buttonhole, boutonnière, wreath, garland
2 AROMA, smell, odour, scent, perfume, fragrance, nose
FORMAL redolence, odoriferousness
3 COMPLIMENT, favour, approval, honour, congratulations, praise, commendation, accolade, tribute
FORMAL eulogy, felicitation
COLLOQ. pat on the back

bourgeois *adj*
middle-class, materialistic, money-orientated, conservative, traditional, conformist, conventional, hidebound, unadventurous, ordinary, dull, humdrum, banal, commonplace, trite, pedestrian, uninspired, unoriginal, uncreative, unimaginative, *Biedermeier*, uncultured
Ⓔ bohemian, unconventional, original

bout *n*
1 PERIOD, spell, time, stint, turn, term, stretch, run, course, session, spree, jag
COLLOQ. go, binge, splurge, sesh
2 *a bout of illness*
attack, fit, spasm, touch
3 FIGHT, battle, engagement, encounter, struggle, wrestle, set-to, match, contest, competition, round, heat

bovine *adj*
1 *bovine animals*
cattlelike, cowlike
2 *his bovine response*
stupid, slow, dull, slow-witted
COLLOQ. dense, dumb, thick, doltish, dim-witted
Ⓔ 2 quick

bow¹ *v, n*
♦ *v*
1 *bow your head*
incline, bend, nod, bob, curtsy, kowtow, salaam, stoop, curve, arch, crook, crouch; *Scot* jouk
FORMAL genuflect, make obeisance
2 YIELD, give in, give way to, consent, surrender, capitulate, submit, succumb, concede, accept, comply, defer
FORMAL accede, acquiesce
3 SUBDUE, overpower, conquer, crush, humble, humiliate
FORMAL subjugate, vanquish
♦ *n*
inclination, bending, nod, bob, curtsy, arc, kowtow, salaam, salutation, acknowledgement; *Scot* beck, jouk
FORMAL genuflexion, obeisance, prostration
■ **bow out**
withdraw, pull out, desert, abandon, defect, back out, retire, resign, leave, stand down, step down, give up
COLLOQ. chicken out, quit

bow² *n*
the bow of a ship
front, beak, head, prow, stem, forepart, rostrum
Ⓔ stern

bow³ *n*
tie a bow
loop, ring, circle, knot, lavallière

bowdlerize *v*
censor, cut, edit, excise, expunge, expurgate, purge, clean up, purify, modify, blue-pencil

bowels *n*
1 INTESTINES, entrails, guts, colon
TECHNICAL viscera
COLLOQ. insides, innards

2 *in the bowels of the earth*
depths, interior, inside, middle, centre, core, heart, belly, cavity

bower *n*
arbour, shelter, alcove, grotto, bay, recess, retreat, sanctuary

bowl¹ *n*
a washing-up bowl
receptacle, container, vessel, dish, basin, sink, pan, piggin, tazza, pottinger, porringer; *Scot* coggie
OLD monteith

bowl² *v*
1 *bowl a ball*
throw, hurl, fling, pitch, propel, roll, spin, whirl, rotate, revolve
2 *bowl along in a car*
move steadily, motor, speed, race, career, rush, hurry
■ **bowl over**
1 *bowled over by the news*
overwhelm, affect deeply, impress greatly, surprise, amaze, astound, astonish, shock, startle, stagger, stun, dumbfound
COLLOQ. flabbergast, floor, wow
2 *bowl over a person*
knock down, fell, topple, unbalance, push into

box¹ *n, v*
♦ *n*
boxes of books
container, receptacle, case, carton, packet, present, bijou, casket, pyxis, pyx, chest, coffret
♦ *v*
package, pack, wrap, parcel, case, encase
■ **box in**
enclose, surround, block in, cordon off, hem in, shut in, fence in, corner, trap, confine, restrain, coop up, restrict, imprison, cage, contain
FORMAL circumscribe

Types of box include:

ballot-box	dispatch box	sewing box
bin	hatbox	shoebox
black box	jewellery box	snuffbox
box-file	knife box	strongbox
caddy	locker	suggestion box
canister	matchbox	tea chest
cardboard box	pack	tin
cartridge	package	toolbox
casket	pencilbox	trinket box
cigarette box	pillar box	trunk
coffer	pillbox	*Aust* tuckerbox
coffin	postbox	vesta
collection-box	punnet	writing-slope
coolbox	safe	
crate	sarcophagus	

---

box² *v, n*
♦ *v*
1 *learn to box*
fight, spar, engage in fisticuffs
2 *box someone's ears*
punch, hit, strike, slap, batter, thump, buffet, clout, cuff, rap
COLLOQ. wallop, whack, slug
SLANG sock
♦ *n*
punch, hit, strike, slap, batter, thump, buffet, clout, cuff
COLLOQ. wallop, whack, slug
SLANG sock

boxer *n*
fighter, prizefighter, sparring partner
FORMAL pugilist
COLLOQ. ham

boxing n
prizefighting, fighting, fisticuffs, sparring
FORMAL pugilism
Related adjective: pugilistic

Weight divisions in professional boxing:

heavyweight	junior-lightweight/super-
cruiserweight/junior-heavy-	featherweight
weight	featherweight
light-heavyweight	super-bantamweight/junior-
super-middleweight	featherweight
middleweight	bantamweight
light-middleweight/junior-	super-flyweight/junior-ban-
middleweight	tamweight
welterweight	flyweight
light-welterweight/junior-wel-	light-flyweight/junior-fly-
terweight	weight
lightweight	mini-flyweight/straw-weight/
	minimum weight

boy n
son, lad, youngster, stripling, youth, junior, schoolboy, fellow, child, adolescent, teenager, young man, male, garçon, groom, hokra; *Scot* gilpy, loon, chield, knave-bairn, nickum; *Irish* gossoon, spalpeen; *N Am* bub
OLD dandiprat, galopin, kinchin-cove; (*Shakesp*) Jack-a-Lent
COLLOQ. kid, nipper, whippersnapper, guttersnipe, sprog, shaver; *Irish* bucko
SLANG boyo

boycott v, n
♦ *v*
refuse, reject, embargo, black, ban, prohibit, disallow, bar, exclude, blacklist, outlaw, ostracize, ignore, avoid, spurn, snub
FORMAL eschew, proscribe
COLLOQ. cold-shoulder, send to Coventry
E∃ encourage, support, advocate, defend, champion, patronize
♦ *n*
refusal, rejection, embargo, ban, prohibition, spurning, snub, exclusion, ostracism
FORMAL proscription

boyfriend n
young man, man, admirer, sweetheart, lover, suitor, best boy, fiancé, beau, date, steady, partner, cohabitee, live-in lover, common-law spouse
COLLOQ. fellow, fella, guy, bloke, toyboy, significant other, squeeze

boyish adj
youthful, childlike, adolescent, childish, immature, innocent, juvenile, puerile, tomboy, unfeminine, unmaidenly, young
COLLOQ. green

brace¹ n, v
♦ *n*
fit braces to strengthen a wall
support, stay, strap, prop, clamp, fastener, vice, beam, strut, reinforcement, truss, buttress, shoring
FORMAL stanchion
♦ *v*
1 STRENGTHEN, reinforce, bolster, buttress, prop (up), shore (up), support, hold up, steady, secure, tighten, fasten, tie, strap, bind, bandage
FORMAL fortify
2 brace yourself for bad news
prepare, get ready, compose, nerve, steel
FORMAL fortify
COLLOQ. gear up, psych up

brace² n
a brace of pheasant
pair, couple, twosome, duo

bracelet n
bangle, band, circlet, wristlet
OLD armilla
Related adjective: armillary

bracing adj
fresh, crisp, refreshing, reviving, strengthening, fortifying, tonic, rousing, stimulating, exhilarating, invigorating, enlivening, energizing, brisk, energetic, vigorous
E∃ weakening, draining, debilitating; *formal* enervating

bracket n
1 SUPPORT, stay, prop, frame, rest, holder
2 CLASSIFICATION, group, grouping, class, category, batch, lot, cohort

brackish adj
bitter, briny, saline, salt, saltish, salty; *S Afr* brak
FORMAL salsuginous
E∃ fresh, clean, clear

brag v
bluster, boast, show off, swagger, vaunt, vapour
OLD gab, cry roast-meat
FORMAL hyperbolize
COLLOQ. blow your own trumpet; *N Am* blow your own horn; crow, talk big, lay it on thick/with a trowel; *Aust* big-note
SLANG bull
E∃ be modest

braggart n
boaster, bluffer, blusterer, show-off, braggadocio, fanfaron, gascon, rodomontader, swaggerer, swashbuckler
OLD puckfist; (*Shakesp*) swasher
COLLOQ. big mouth, windbag, loud-mouth

bragging n
showing-off, bluster, boastfulness, boasting, bravado, exaggeration
FORMAL vauntery
COLLOQ. hot air
E∃ modesty, unobtrusiveness

braid n, v
♦ *n*
cord, thread, yarn, twine, plait; *dialect* pleat; tress, caddis, sennit, soutache, passement
♦ *v*
plait, interweave, interlace, intertwine, weave, lace, twine, entwine, ravel, twist, wind
OLD embraid
E∃ undo, unravel

brain n
1 damage to the brain
cerebrum
TECHNICAL encephalon, sensorium
OLD (*Shakesp*) pia mater
SLANG upper storey
Related adjectives: cerebral, encephalic
See panel on next page
2 MIND, head, intellect, intelligence, wit, reason, sense, common sense, shrewdness, understanding
FORMAL acumen, sagacity
COLLOQ. grey matter, brains, nous, savvy
3 the real brain in the family
mastermind, intellectual, scholar, expert, pundit, highbrow, genius, prodigy
COLLOQ. egghead, boffin, brainbox, cleverclogs; *N Am* brainiac
E∃ simpleton, idiot

brainless adj
silly, stupid, crazy, daft, foolish, incompetent, half-witted, simple-minded, idiotic, inept, mindless, thoughtless, senseless
E∃ sensible, shrewd, wise

Parts of the brain include:

brainstem	cerebral hemi-	corpus callosum	medulla oblongata	optic thalamus	spinal cord
Broca's area	sphere	forebrain	meninges	parietal lobe	temporal lobe
cerebellum	cerebrum	frontal lobe	mesencephalon	pineal body	thalamus
cerebral cortex	cinerea (grey	hindbrain	midbrain	pituitary gland	Wernicke's area
	matter)	hypothalamus	occipital lobe	pons	

brainteaser *n*
riddle, puzzle, problem, conundrum, mind-bender, poser; *N Am* brain-twister

brainwashing *n*
indoctrination, conditioning, pressurizing, re-education, grilling, intellectual suicide, mind-bending, persuasion
FORMAL menticide

brainy *adj*
intellectual, intelligent, clever, gifted, smart, bright, brilliant, wise
FORMAL sapient
E3 dull, stupid

brake *n, v*
♦ *n*
check, curb, rein, restraint, control, restriction, constraint, drag
FORMAL retardment
♦ *v*
slow (down), decelerate, reduce speed, retard, drag, slacken, moderate, check, halt, stop, pull up
FORMAL retard
E3 accelerate

branch *n, v*
♦ *n*
1 BOUGH, limb, sprig, shoot, stem, offshoot, arm, leg, lobe, loop, wing, prong, whip, withy; *Scot* cow, scrog
TECHNICAL ramus, axis, cladode, phylloclade
OLD braunch, rice
Related adjectives: ramal, rameal, rameous, ramous
2 *a different branch of the company*
department, office, local/regional office, agency, bureau, part, section, division, subsidiary, subsection, subdivision, affiliate, corps, wing, discipline
FORMAL succursal, ramification
3 *the branch of a river*
tributary, fork, division
■ **branch off**
divide, fork, diverge, deviate, separate
FORMAL bifurcate, furcate
■ **branch out**
diversify, subdivide, vary, develop, expand, enlarge, spread out, extend, add to, broaden out, increase, multiply, proliferate
FORMAL ramify

brand *n, v*
♦ *n*
1 *different brands of soap*
make, brand-name, tradename, trademark, line, logo, symbol, sign, emblem, label, stamp, hallmark, marque
2 KIND, quality, class, kind, type, sort, line, variety, species
3 MARK, tag, identification, identifying mark
♦ *v*
1 *branded as a troublemaker*
mark, stamp, label, typecast, stigmatize, stain, taint, disgrace, discredit, denounce, censure
FORMAL besmirch
2 *brand cattle*
mark, stamp, burn (in), sear

brandish *v*
wave, flourish, shake, raise, swing, wield, flash, flaunt, exhibit, display, parade
OLD wag, wampish; *(Spenser)* bless, hurtle

brash *adj*
1 BRAZEN, forward, impertinent, impudent, insolent, rude, cocky, self-confident, assertive, assured, bold, audacious
COLLOQ. pushy
2 RECKLESS, rash, impetuous, impulsive, hasty, foolhardy, incautious, indiscreet
FORMAL precipitate
E3 **1** reserved, unassuming, modest, unobtrusive **2** cautious, wary, prudent

brashly *adv*
1 BRAZENLY, forwardly, impertinently, impudently, insolently, rudely, cockily, self-confidently, assertively, assuredly, boldly, audaciously
COLLOQ. pushily
2 RECKLESSLY, rashly, impetuously, impulsively, hastily, foolhardily, incautiously, indiscreetly
FORMAL precipitately
E3 **1** reserved, unassuming, modest, unobtrusive **2** cautious, wary, prudent

brashness *n*
1 BRAZENNESS, impertinence, impudence, insolence, rudeness, self-confidence, assertiveness, boldness, audacity
COLLOQ. pushiness
2 RECKLESSNESS, rashness, hastiness, foolhardiness, incaution
E3 **1** modesty **2** caution

brass *n*
brazenness, impertinence, impudence, insolence, gall, rudeness, presumption, audacity
FORMAL effrontery, temerity
COLLOQ. cheek, nerve, chutzpah, brass neck, brass nerve; *N Am* sass
E3 timidity; *formal* circumspection

brassy *adj*
1 *brassy music*
noisy, loud, blaring, dissonant, grating, hard, harsh, jangling, jarring, piercing, raucous, strident
2 *a brassy blonde*
shameless, forward, brash, insolent, cocky, bold, loud, brazen
COLLOQ. pushy, loud-mouthed, saucy; *N Am* sassy

brat *n*
kid, youngster, rascal, brach; *Scot* get, gyte
OLD bantling
COLLOQ. nipper, guttersnipe, jackanapes, puppy, whippersnapper

bravado *n*
swagger, boasting, bragging, bluster, talk, boast, showing-off, parade, show, pretence
FORMAL vaunting, bombast, braggadocio, fanfaronade, rodomontade
E3 modesty, restraint

brave *adj, v*
♦ *adj*
courageous, plucky, unafraid, fearless, undaunted, unflinching, bold, daring, intrepid, stalwart, hardy, stoical, resolute, stout-hearted, lion-hearted, valiant, gallant, heroic, indomitable, manly, yeomanly
FORMAL dauntless, audacious, valorous, doughty
COLLOQ. gutsy, spunky, gritty, feisty
E3 cowardly, afraid, timid, craven, faint-hearted; *colloq.* yellow, spineless, wimpish, chicken
♦ *v*
face, confront, defy, challenge, dare, stand up to, put up with, face up to, suffer, endure, bear, withstand

COLLOQ. face the music, keep a stiff upper lip, put a bold/brave face on it, not turn a hair, keep your chin up
E3 yield, capitulate, give in; *colloq.* get cold feet, chicken out

bravely *adv*
courageously, pluckily, fearlessly, undauntedly, unflinchingly, boldly, daringly, intrepidly, stalwartly, hardily, stoically, resolutely, stout-heartedly, valiantly, gallantly, heroically, indomitably
FORMAL dauntlessly, audaciously, valorously, doughtily

bravery *n*
courage, pluck, fearlessness, boldness, courageousness, daring, stalwartness, hardiness, fortitude, resolution, tenacity, stout-heartedness, valour, gallantry, chivalry, heroism, indomitability, mettle, spirit, dauntlessness, audacity, bravado, prowess
FORMAL intrepidity, valiance
COLLOQ. guts, grit, spunk
E3 cowardice, fearfulness, faint-heartedness, timidity

> **!** **bravery** or **bravado**?
> *Bravery* is courage: *soldiers decorated for bravery.*
> *Bravado* is a boastful act of bravery intended to impress or intimidate or a boastful pretence of bravery aimed at concealing cowardice: *She felt her defiant bravado disintegrate like shattered glass.*

SYNONYM NUANCES

Courage is used in general contexts, whereas **pluck** has a very positive aspect of spiritedness, and is often used of facing up to difficulties rather than overt danger: *few people had the pluck to stand up to her.* **Fearlessness** suggests bravery that has more to do with an inability to experience fear than to confront it: *the fearlessness that only fanaticism confers.* **Indomitability** and **dauntlessness** are also suggestive of an inability to be conquered or frightened, whereas **mettle** and **spirit** more appropriately describe an inborn intrepid nature: *these crises will test his mettle.*

The terms **boldness**, **daring**, **audacity** and **bravado** strongly suggest the idea of taking risks and perhaps even showing off: *the audacity of criminals*; in contrast to the uncommon **stalwartness**, which suggests a more down-to-earth dependability in the face of difficulty. **Hardiness**, **fortitude** and **stout-heartedness** also imply innate strength of spirit and an ability to persevere, whereas **resolution** and **tenacity** emphasize more intellectual determination: *a tenacity of purpose.*

Heroism is a word generally reserved for those responsible for acts that endanger themselves whilst safeguarding others: *the heroism of the firefighters.* **Valour** is usually used in the context of the battlefield: *he received a medal for valour.* **Gallantry** and **chivalry** are more romantic in tone, and suggest the qualities associated with dashing warriors from the past, though still recognized today: *his gallantry in action.*

---

bravura *n*
spirit, dash, sparkle, brilliance, magnificence, élan

brawl *n, v*
♦ *n*
fight, scuffle, mêlée, free-for-all, fray, affray, broil, skirmish, fracas, rumpus, disorder, row, argument, quarrel, squabble, dispute, clash, fisticuffs, Donnybrook, *bagarre*; *dialect* fratch; *Aust & NZ* stoush
OLD brangle; (*Shakesp*) brabble; *Scot* tuilyie
FORMAL altercation
COLLOQ. punch-up, bust-up, dust-up, scrap, ruckus
♦ *v*
fight, scuffle, wrestle, tussle, argue, quarrel, squabble, wrangle, dispute; *Scot* flyte; *Aust & NZ* stoush
FORMAL altercate

OLD brabble
COLLOQ. scrap, row

brawn *n*
strength, might, muscle, muscles, bulk, bulkiness, muscularity, power, robustness, sinews; *N Am* headcheese
COLLOQ. beef, beefiness

brawny *adj*
muscular, sinewy, meaty, athletic, well-built, burly, hefty, solid, bulky, hulking, massive, strapping, strong, powerful, vigorous, sturdy, robust, hardy, stalwart
COLLOQ. beefy, husky, hunky
E3 slight, frail, skinny, weak, weedy

bray *v*
neigh, whinny, heehaw, blare, hoot, roar, screech, trumpet, bell, bellow

brazen *adj, v*
♦ *adj*
bold, forward, barefaced, bald-faced, impudent, insolent, defiant, shameless, unashamed, unabashed, immodest, blatant, flagrant, brash, pert
FORMAL audacious
COLLOQ. pushy, brassy, saucy, hard-boiled
SLANG in-your-face
E3 shy, shamefaced, modest, cautious
■ **brazen it out**
be unashamed, defy, be defiant, be impenitent
COLLOQ. put a brave/bold face on it

brazenly *adv*
boldly, impudently, insolently, defiantly, shamelessly, unashamedly, immodestly, blatantly, flagrantly
FORMAL audaciously
E3 modestly, cautiously

breach *n, v*
♦ *n*
1 *a breach of the rules*
breaking, violation, contravention, infringement, trespass, disobedience, offence, lapse, disruption
FORMAL infraction, transgression
2 *a breach in international relations*
quarrel, disagreement, dissension, difference, variance, schism, rift, rupture, split, division, gulf, chasm, separation, parting, severance, alienation, dissociation
FORMAL disaffection, estrangement
3 *a breach in the defences*
break, crack, rift, rupture, split, fissure, cleft, crevice, opening, aperture, gap, space, hole, gulf, chasm
♦ *v*
1 *breach an agreement*
violate, break, contravene, infringe
2 *breach the sea wall*
rupture, break (open), open up, break through, burst through, split

---

SYNONYM NUANCES

noun sense 1
Breaking, **violation**, **infringement** and **contravention** are widely used in instances where official specifications have not been adhered to: *a clear violation of international law; his persistent infringement of school laws; each side made repeated raids in contravention of treaty terms.* You would probably use the word **trespass** primarily of illegal entry, and **disobedience** to describe orchestrated action, taken usually to get a certain change in the law: *civil disobedience by peace protesters.* **Disruption** is more usually associated with creating conditions to make it difficult for a rule or law to function.

Other terms are less forceful in tone. **Offence** is often qualified to convey a degree of severity: *a minor offence*; while **transgression** nowadays is perhaps more appropriate for an act at odds with social mores. The word **lapse** also suggests a failure to follow social or personal rules: *I gave up smoking, then had a lapse.*

bread *n*

1 *bread and jam*
crusts, roll, loaf, bap, plait, cob, sandwich
Related adjective: panary
2 *our daily bread*
food, provisions, diet, fare, nourishment, necessities
FORMAL nutriment, sustenance, subsistence, victuals
3 CASH, money, funds
COLLOQ. the necessary
SLANG dough, dosh, lolly, spondulicks

Kinds of bread include:

bagel	focaccia	puri
baguette	fougasse	roti
bara brith	French stick	rye bread
barmbrack	Granary®	soda bread
brioche	matzo	sourdough
challah	milk bread	spelt bread
chapati	multigrain	stottie
ciabatta	naan	tortilla
croissant	paratha	wholemeal
damper	pitta	wholewheat
farl	pretzel	
flatbread	pumpernickel	

---

breadth *n*

1 *the breadth of the garden*
width, broadness, wideness, latitude, thickness, size, magnitude, measure
2 *a great breadth of interests*
range, scale, reach, scope, compass, span, sweep, extent, expanse, spread, comprehensiveness, extensiveness, vastness
FORMAL amplitude

break *v, n*

♦ *v*
1 *break a plate*
fracture, crack, snap, split, sever, separate, divide, rend, smash, disintegrate, splinter, shiver, shatter, ruin, destroy, demolish
2 *break the law*
violate, contravene, infringe, breach, disobey, flout, dishonour
3 *the television has broken*
stop working, fail
FORMAL malfunction
COLLOQ. go on the blink, pack up, conk out, go kaput, go phut, crash, cut out
4 *break for lunch*
pause, halt, stop, interrupt, suspend, rest
FORMAL discontinue
5 *break a silence*
interrupt, suspend, disturb, interfere with, bring to an end
FORMAL discontinue
COLLOQ. cut off
6 *the news broke his spirit*
destroy, crush, overcome, subdue, tame, weaken, enfeeble, impair, undermine, demoralize
7 *the injury broke her skin*
pierce, perforate, puncture, open (up)
8 *break the news*
tell, inform, impart, divulge, disclose, reveal, announce
9 *break a record*
exceed, beat, better, excel, surpass, outdo, outstrip
10 *the weather broke*
change (for the better/worse), vary, improve, worsen
11 *the branches broke his fall*
weaken, soften, lessen, reduce, cushion, diminish
12 *break a habit*
give up, stop, abandon
FORMAL discontinue, relinquish
COLLOQ. quit, kick, shake off
13 *as day broke*
dawn, lighten, begin, appear, emerge, rise, be born

14 *waves breaking against the raised bank*
dash, pound, smash, strike, lash, beat, crash
15 *his voice broke*
falter, stammer, stutter, stumble
16 *break a code*
crack, decipher, decode, decrypt, unravel, solve, work/figure out
E3 **1** mend, put together **2** keep, obey, observe, abide by **3** mend, fix **4** start again, resume **6** encourage, strengthen **12** start, take up **13** end

♦ *n*
1 *a break in the defences/diplomatic relations*
fracture, crack, split, rift, rupture, schism, separation, tear, gash, fissure, cleft, crevice, opening, gap, hole, breach
FORMAL estrangement
2 *have a break for coffee*
interval, intermission, interlude, interruption, stop, pause, halt, lull, respite, rest; *Aust* smoke-ho
COLLOQ. let-up, breather, time-out
3 *go away for a short break*
time off, holiday; *N Am* vacation
COLLOQ. vac
4 *a lucky break*
opportunity, chance, advantage, fortune, (stroke of) luck, opening

■ **break away**
separate, split (off), part company, detach, secede, leave, depart, quit, run away, escape, flee, fly
COLLOQ. make a run for it

■ **break down**
1 *the van broke down*
fail, stop, stop working, give way, collapse
COLLOQ. pack up, conk out, go phut, seize up
2 *negotiations broke down*
fail, collapse, come to nothing, founder
COLLOQ. fall through
3 *break down in tears*
lose control, be overcome, collapse
COLLOQ. go to pieces, crack up
4 *break down a door*
knock down, smash, demolish, destroy
5 *break down the figures*
analyse, dissect, separate, itemize, categorize, detail

■ **break in**
1 *break in with unhelpful remarks*
interrupt, butt in, cut in, interject, intervene, intrude, encroach, impinge
FORMAL interpose
2 *break in and steal the money*
burgle, rob, raid, enter illegally
3 *break in a horse/pair of walking boots*
train, condition, wear, accustom, prime, get used to

■ **break off**
1 DETACH, separate, part, divide, disconnect, sever
FORMAL dissever
COLLOQ. snap off
2 *break off as the phone rang; break off a relationship*
pause, interrupt, suspend, halt, stop, cease, end, finish, bring to an end
FORMAL discontinue, terminate

■ **break out**
1 *war broke out in 1939*
begin (suddenly), start, arise, emerge, happen, occur, erupt
FORMAL commence
COLLOQ. blow up, flare up, burst out
2 *break out of prison*
escape, bolt, flee
FORMAL abscond
3 *'Just a minute,' she broke out*
exclaim, shout, interject
COLLOQ. burst out
4 *break out into a rash*
erupt, come out in, flare up

■ **break through**
emerge, gain ground, leap forward, make headway, pass, penetrate, progress, succeed, overcome

■ break up
1 *break up a monopoly*
dismantle, take apart, demolish, destroy, disintegrate, splinter, sever, divide, split (up), part, separate
2 *the couple broke up*
separate, part, part company, divorce, finish
COLLOQ. split up
3 *the meeting broke up*
disband, disperse, dissolve, adjourn, suspend, stop, finish, bring/come to an end
FORMAL discontinue, terminate
■ break with
finish with, part with, reject, separate from
FORMAL renounce, repudiate
COLLOQ. drop, jilt, ditch

breakable *adj*
brittle, fragile, delicate, flimsy, insubstantial, frail, easily broken
FORMAL friable, frangible
COLLOQ. jerry-built
E3 unbreakable, durable, sturdy, long-lasting, shatterproof

breakaway *adj*
rebel, dissenting, separatist, renegade, heretical
FORMAL apostate, schismatic, seceding, secessionist

breakdown *n*
1 *the breakdown of the talks/car*
failure, collapse, disintegration, interruption, stoppage
FORMAL malfunction
2 *a nervous breakdown*
collapse
COLLOQ. going to pieces, cracking-up
3 ANALYSIS, dissection, itemization, classification, categorization

breaker *n*
wave, roller, billow, white horses

break-in *n*
burglary, house-breaking, robbery, raid, invasion, intrusion, trespass, larceny

breakneck *adj*
very fast, very quick, rapid, swift, speedy, express, headlong
FORMAL precipitate
COLLOQ. like lightning

breakthrough *n*
discovery, find, finding, invention, innovation, advance, progress, headway, step, gain, leap, step/leap forward, quantum leap (forward), development, improvement, milestone

break-up *n*
divorce, separation, parting, split, rift, finish, end, dispersal, disintegration, crumbling, dissolution, debacle, upbreak
FORMAL termination
COLLOQ. splitting-up

breakwater *n*
groyne, mole, bulwark, sea wall, jetty, pier, quay, spur, wharf, dock

breast *n*
1 *beat your breast in sorrow*
bosom, bust, chest, front, heart, thorax
2 *a woman's breasts*
bust, nipple, teat; *dialect* diddy
TECHNICAL mamma
COLLOQ. boob, booby
SLANG banger, bristol, knocker, tit, titty; *Aust* nork
Related adjective: mammary

breath *n*
1 *take deep breaths to relax*
air, breathing, respiration, sigh, gasp, pant, gulp
FORMAL flatus, inhalation, inspiration, exhalation
Related adjectives: respiratory, aspiratory

2 *a breath of fresh air*
breeze, puff, waft, gust
FORMAL pneuma
3 *a breath of autumn in the air*
aroma, smell, odour, whiff
4 *a breath of scandal*
hint, suggestion, suspicion, undertone, whisper, murmur

breathe *v*
1 *breathe deeply*
sigh, gasp, pant, puff, snore
OLD embreathe, suspire
FORMAL inhale, inbreathe, exhale, respire, expire, insufflate
2 *not breathe a word to anyone*
express, voice, murmur, whisper, tell, articulate, utter, impart
3 *breathe new life into a project*
instil, imbue, infuse, inject, inspire
FORMAL transfuse

breather *n*
break, rest, constitutional, pause, halt, recess, relaxation, walk
FORMAL respite
COLLOQ. breathing space

breathless *adj*
1 *breathless from climbing*
short-winded, out of breath, panting, puffing, puffed (out), exhausted, winded, gasping, wheezing, choking
COLLOQ. N Am pooped (out), tuckered out
2 *breathless anticipation*
expectant, impatient, in suspense, eager, agog, excited, open-mouthed, feverish, anxious

breathtaking *adj*
awe-inspiring, impressive, magnificent, spectacular, overwhelming, amazing, astonishing, stunning, stupendous, exciting, thrilling, stirring, moving
COLLOQ. drop-dead, eye-popping

breathtakingly *adv*
overwhelmingly, amazingly, astonishingly, stunningly, spectacularly, stupendously, excitingly, thrillingly, stirringly, awe-inspiringly, impressively

breed *v, n*
♦ *v*
1 *breed dogs*
reproduce, procreate, multiply, hatch, bear, give birth to, rear, raise, bring up, bring forth
FORMAL propagate, pullulate
2 *breed suspicion*
produce, create, originate, arouse, cause, occasion, bring about, give rise to, generate, make, foster, nurture, nourish, cultivate, develop
FORMAL engender
♦ *n*
1 *breeds of cattle*
species, strain, variety, family, stamp, stock, race, line, lineage, pedigree, hybrid
FORMAL progeny
2 *the new breed of leader*
kind, type, sort, variety, calibre, class

breeding *n*
1 *the breeding of cattle*
reproduction, nurture, development, rearing, raising, upbringing, ancestry, lineage, stock, genetic engineering
FORMAL procreation
2 *have breeding*
(good) manners, politeness, gentility, refinement, cultivation, culture, polish, education, training
FORMAL civility, urbanity
E3 **2** vulgarity, bad manners

breeding-ground *n*
nest, nursery, school, training ground, cradle, hothouse
COLLOQ. hotbed

breeze *n, v*

♦ *n*

wind, gust, flurry, waft, puff, breath, draught, air, snift, cat's paw
OLD zephyr

♦ *v*

glide, sail, hurry, sweep, trip, wander, saunter
COLLOQ. flit, sally

breezy *adj*

1 WINDY, blowing, blowy, fresh, airy, gusty, brisk, blustery, squally
2 LIVELY, confident, animated, jaunty, buoyant, debonair, carefree, cheerful, casual, informal, relaxed, easy-going, light-hearted, light, bright, exhilarating, vivacious
OLD blithe
E3 1 still, calm, windless **2** staid, serious, quiet, sad

brevity *n*

1 *the brevity of the speech*
briefness, shortness, conciseness, compactness, succinctness, pithiness, economy, economy of language, crispness, incisiveness, abruptness, curtness
FORMAL terseness, concision, laconism
2 *the brevity of life*
briefness, shortness
FORMAL impermanence, ephemerality, transience, transitoriness
E3 1 long-windedness, wordiness; *formal* verbosity, prolixity **2** permanence; *formal* longevity

QUOTATIONS
Brevity is the soul of wit
   WILLIAM SHAKESPEARE, *Hamlet*

brew *v, n*

♦ *v*

1 *brew tea*
stew, boil, prepare, soak, steep, cook, make
FORMAL infuse, seethe, ferment, prepare
2 *the tea is still brewing*
infuse, be in preparation, mash
3 *brew beer*
ferment, make
4 *trouble/a storm is brewing*
build up, gather, develop, loom, be in the offing, be on its way
5 *brew a scheme*
plot, scheme, plan, project, devise, contrive, concoct, hatch, excite, foment

♦ *n*

1 *boil up a hot brew*
drink, liquor, potion
FORMAL beverage, infusion
2 *a powerful brew of sex and violence*
mixture, blend, compound, combination, preparation, fermentation, distillation
FORMAL concoction

bribe *n, v*

♦ *n*

incentive, inducement, allurement, enticement, bonus, dash, kickback, douceur, palm-grease, palm-oil, pension
OLD gift, gratification, vail
COLLOQ. carrot, back-hander, refresher, sweetener, hush money, pay-off, slush fund, protection money; *N Am* payola, boodle
SLANG bung, the drink

♦ *v*

corrupt, reward, suborn, square, hamper
COLLOQ. buy/pay off, grease, grease someone's palm, fix, take care of, keep sweet
SLANG nobble, bung

bribery *n*

corruption, inducement, protection, malversation, subornation, embracery
COLLOQ. palm-greasing, graft

bric-à-brac *n*

knick-knacks, ornaments, curios, antiques, trinkets, baubles, trumpery, gewgaws, bibelots, gimcracks, bits and pieces, odds and ends

brick *n*

1 *bricks and mortar*
breeze block, adobe, firebrick, block, briquette, header, klinker, stretcher, rock, stone
2 *a huge brick of fresh butter*
block, piece, lump, mass, slab, wedge, bar
3 *be a real brick for helping*
mate, pal, real friend, chum; *N Am* buddy

PROVERBS
You can't make bricks without straw

bridal *adj*

wedding, nuptial, marriage, marital
FORMAL conjugal, matrimonial, connubial

bride *n*

honeymooner, newly-wed, wife, wife-to-be, bride-to-be, spouse, marriage partner, war bride, GI bride

bridegroom *n*

honeymooner, newly-wed, husband, husband-to-be, spouse, marriage partner, groom

bridge *n, v*

♦ *n*

1 *a bridge over the river*
arch, span, causeway, link
2 *act as a bridge between the different factions*
link, connection, bond, tie

♦ *v*

span, cross, go over, reach across, fill, link, connect, couple, join, unite, bind
FORMAL traverse

PROVERBS
Don't cross your bridges until you come to them

QUOTATIONS
What is great in man is that he is a bridge and not a goal
   FRIEDRICH NIETZSCHE, *Thus Spake Zarathustra*

Types of bridge include:

aqueduct	cantilever bridge	railway bridge
arch bridge	drawbridge	rope bridge
Bailey bridge	flying bridge	suspension bridge
bascule bridge	flyover	swing bridge
beam bridge (or	footbridge	toll bridge
girder bridge)	humpback bridge	viaduct
box girder bridge	overbridge	
cable-stayed	overpass	
bridge	pontoon bridge	

bridle *v, n*

♦ *v*

1 *bridle your temper*
check, curb, restrain, control, govern, master, subdue, moderate, repress, hold back, contain
2 *bridle at someone's anger*
bristle, become indignant, be offended by

♦ *n*

check, halter, control, curb, restraint, hackamore; *Scot* branks

brief *adj, n, v*

♦ *adj*

1 *a brief report*
short, terse, succinct, concise, pithy, crisp, compressed, condensed, abridged, thumbnail
FORMAL aphoristic

2 *a brief manner*
abrupt, sharp, short, brusque, blunt, curt, surly
FORMAL laconic
3 *a brief visit; this brief life*
short-lived, momentary, transient, fleeting, passing,
transitory, temporary, limited, cursory, hasty, quick, swift
FORMAL fugacious, ephemeral, evanescent
F3 **1** lengthy, long-winded, extensive, verbose, protracted
♦ *n*
1 *with a brief to reduce crime*
responsibility, orders, instructions, directions, remit,
mandate, directive, advice, briefing, data, information
2 *a brief of the day's events*
outline, summary, précis, abstract, abridgement, digest
3 *a legal brief*
dossier, case, defence, argument, evidence, data
TECHNICAL breviate
♦ *v*
instruct, direct, explain, guide, advise, prepare, prime,
inform, tell, bring up to date
COLLOQ. fill in, gen up, give someone the run-down/low-
down, put someone in the picture

SYNONYM NUANCES

adjective sense 1
Short is a neutral term to describe something that is
limited in length or duration, whereas **terse** is more
usually applied to speech or text with no extraneous
material, with the added suggestion of an unwelcome
abruptness: *an economical, even terse, style.* **Succinct**
and **concise**, however, are more expressive of favour,
suggesting that a lack of unnecessary material leads to a
more satisfactory outcome: *our goal is a set of succinct
definitions.* To use **pithy** likewise would suggest that you
approve of this economy with words: *pithy, punchy
posters*; while **crisp** is another positive term to speak
about words, with overtones of clarity and neatness.
   Condensed and **compressed** are not necessarily
positive, both terms suggestive of squeezing an
abundance into less or limited space: *patterns stored in
the memory are compressed.* **Abridged** is a neutral term
describing something has been cut in order to fit.
Thumbnail is usually reserved for shortened
representations: *a thumbnail sketch of the scene.*

---

briefing *n*
meeting, conference, preparation, priming, information,
advice, guidance, directions, instructions, orders
FORMAL intimation
COLLOQ. filling-in, gen, run-down, low-down

briefly *adv*
1 *speak briefly*
concisely, succinctly, cursorily, precisely, quickly,
summarily, tersely, to the point
2 *briefly, the answer is no*
in brief, in a word, in a few words
COLLOQ. in a nutshell
F3 **1** at length, fully

brigade *n*
group, band, body, company, unit, corps, crew, force,
party, squad, team, troop, contingent

brigand *n*
bandit, robber, desperado, gangster, outlaw, marauder,
plunderer, ruffian, highwayman, freebooter, haiduk
OLD cateran, trailbaston

bright *adj*
1 *bright lights/colours*
brilliant, luminous, illuminated, light, radiant, shining,
beaming, flashing, gleaming, glistening, glittering,
sparkling, twinkling, shimmering, glowing, glorious,
splendid, dazzling, blinding, glaring, blazing, intense, vivid
FORMAL resplendent, effulgent, refulgent, lustrous,
incandescent
2 HAPPY, cheerful, glad, joyful, merry, jolly, lively, genial

FORMAL vivacious
3 *the future looks bright*
promising, favourable, rosy, optimistic, hopeful,
encouraging
FORMAL propitious, auspicious
4 CLEVER, smart, intelligent, quick-witted, quick, sharp,
acute, alert, keen, astute, perceptive
COLLOQ. brainy, bright as a button
5 *a bright day*
fine, sunny, cloudless, unclouded, pleasant
F3 **1** dull, drab, colourless, pale, dim, soft **2** sad, gloomy,
depressed; *colloq.* down **3** depressing, gloomy; *formal*
inauspicious **4** stupid; *colloq.* thick **5** dark, overcast,
cloudy

brighten *v*
1 *brighten up a room*
light up, illuminate, lighten, make bright, smarten up,
enhance, refurbish
FORMAL irradiate
2 *brighten up the silver*
polish, burnish, rub (up), shine, gleam, glow
3 *brighten at the prospect*
cheer up, gladden, hearten, encourage, liven up, buoy up
FORMAL enliven
COLLOQ. buck up, perk up, pep up
F3 **1** darken, shadow **2** dull, tarnish

brightly *adv*
1 *a light shining brightly*
brilliantly, radiantly, intensely, splendidly, glowingly,
dazzlingly, blindingly, glaringly, ablaze
2 *smile brightly*
happily, cheerfully, gladly, joyfully
FORMAL vivaciously

brilliance *n*
1 *brilliance at the piano*
talent, virtuosity, genius, greatness, distinction, excellence,
aptitude, cleverness, prowess, bravura
2 *the brilliance of the sun*
radiance, brightness, sparkle, dazzle, intensity, vividness,
gloss, lustre, sheen, tone, glamour, glory, magnificence,
splendour
FORMAL resplendence, effulgence, refulgence, fulgency,
coruscation

brilliant *adj*
1 *a brilliant flautist*
gifted, talented, accomplished, expert, skilful, masterly,
exceptional, outstanding, superb, illustrious, famous,
celebrated
2 *a brilliant light/show*
sparkling, glittering, scintillating, dazzling, glaring, blazing,
intense, vivid, bright, shining, glossy, showy, glorious,
magnificent, splendid
OLD splendent
FORMAL resplendent, effulgent, refulgent, fulgent, lambent
3 *a brilliant mind*
clever, bright, intelligent, quick, astute
FORMAL erudite
COLLOQ. brainy
4 *a brilliant performance*
clever, skilful, masterly, remarkable, magnificent, superb,
resourceful, enterprising
5 *What a brilliant game!*
great, excellent, fantastic, superb, wonderful, magnificent
COLLOQ. brill, cool, top-notch, smashing, terrific, neat, ace,
out of this world, second to none
SLANG mega, wicked, radical, crucial
F3 **1** undistinguished, untalented **2** dull, dim **3** stupid,
slow **4** ordinary; *colloq.* run-of-the-mill **5** awful, bad

brilliantly *adv*
1 *a brilliantly acted play*
superbly, magnificently, wonderfully, masterfully, skilfully,
cleverly

2 *brilliantly coloured*
dazzlingly, intensely, vividly, brightly, gloriously, magnificently, splendidly
FORMAL resplendently

brim *n, v*
♦ *n*
rim, perimeter, circumference, lip, edge, margin, border, brink, verge, top, limit
♦ *v*
be full with, be (packed) full with, be filled with, overflow with, be overflowing with

brimful *adj*
full, filled, filled to capacity, abrim, overflowing, bulging, crammed, stuffed, jammed
COLLOQ. chock-a-block, packed out

brindled *adj*
dappled, streaked, speckled, mottled, stippled, dotted, flecked, variegated, piebald, pied

bring *v*
1 *bring a drink; bring you home later*
take, carry, transport, fetch, deliver, escort, accompany, usher, guide, conduct, lead, convey
FORMAL bear
2 *bring misery*
cause, produce, result in, create, make happen, prompt, provoke, force
FORMAL engender
3 *bring a charge*
present, put forward, initiate, lay, submit
■ **bring about**
cause, occasion, create, produce, generate, accomplish, achieve, fulfil, realize, manage
FORMAL effect
■ **bring back**
suggest, call up, evoke, remind, take you back to, make you think of
■ **bring down**
1 *bring down the government*
overthrow, unseat, depose, oust, defeat, destroy
FORMAL vanquish
COLLOQ. topple, knock down, shoot down
2 REDUCE, decrease, lower, cause to fall/drop
■ **bring forward**
1 ADVANCE, put forward, make earlier
2 PROPOSE, suggest, present, raise, put forward
F∃ **1** postpone, put back
■ **bring in**
1 *bring in new laws*
introduce, initiate, originate, pioneer, set up, launch, usher in
FORMAL inaugurate
2 *bring in £30,000*
earn, net, gross, produce, make, fetch, return, yield
FORMAL accrue, realize
■ **bring off**
succeed in, achieve, fulfil, perform, accomplish, discharge
FORMAL execute, consummate
COLLOQ. pull off
■ **bring on**
1 *bring on a headache*
cause, lead to, give rise to, generate, inspire, prompt, make happen, provoke
FORMAL occasion, induce, precipitate
2 *bring on the plant's growth*
advance, accelerate, foster, nurture, improve
FORMAL expedite, precipitate
■ **bring out**
1 *bring out a point in a story*
emphasize, stress, highlight, enhance, draw out, accentuate, make someone aware of
2 *bring out a book*
publish, print, issue, launch, introduce, produce
■ **bring round**
1 REVIVE, resuscitate, bring to, rouse, wake up, awaken

2 *bring someone round to your way of thinking*
persuade, convince, win over, convert, coax, cajole
■ **bring up**
1 *bring up children*
care for, raise, rear, foster, nurture, educate, teach, train, form
2 *bring up a matter for discussion*
raise, introduce, broach, mention, touch on, submit, propose
3 *bring up food*
vomit, regurgitate
COLLOQ. throw up, puke

brink *n*
verge, threshold, edge, margin, fringe, border, boundary, limit, extremity, lip, rim, brim, bank
OLD marge

brio *n*
vigour, energy, liveliness, spirit, verve, gusto, animation, force, dash, dynamism
FORMAL vivacity
COLLOQ. zip, oomph, pep

brisk *adj*
1 *go for a brisk walk*
energetic, vigorous, quick, rapid, snappy, lively, spirited, active, busy, bustling, agile, nimble, alert
2 *a brisk manner*
lively, quick, businesslike, no-nonsense
3 *brisk business*
busy, active, lively, bustling, rapid, good
4 *brisk weather*
invigorating, exhilarating, stimulating, bracing, refreshing, cold, fresh, crisp
F∃ **1** unenergetic, slow **2** slow, lethargic **3** slow, sluggish

briskly *adv*
1 *walk briskly*
quickly, rapidly, energetically, vigorously, nimbly
TECHNICAL con moto
2 *products selling briskly*
rapidly, quickly, well, busily
3 *work briskly*
quickly, decisively, sharply, abruptly, brusquely

bristle *n, v*
♦ *n*
1 *shave off bristles*
hair, whisker, stubble
2 *bristles on an animal's back*
spine, prickle, barb, quill, thorn, awn; *Scot* birse
TECHNICAL seta, setule, striga, vibrissa
♦ *v*
1 *the hairs on the back of my head bristled*
stand on end, rise
2 *bristling with anger*
seethe (with), draw yourself up, bridle at, be incensed at, bridle, make someone's hackles rise
TECHNICAL horripilate
3 *bristling with police*
teem with, swarm with
FORMAL abound in
COLLOQ. be thick with, hum with

bristly *adj*
hairy, whiskered, bearded, unshaven, stubbly, rough, spiny, prickly, spiky, thorny
TECHNICAL hispid, barbellate, echinate
FORMAL hirsute
F∃ clean-shaven, smooth

brittle *adj*
1 BREAKABLE, easily broken, fragile, delicate, frail, hard, crisp, crackly, crumbly, crumbling, shattery, spall; *dialect* frowy; *Scot* birsy, bruckle, frush; *N Am* brash
FORMAL friable, frangible
2 *a brittle situation*
unstable, fragile, delicate
3 *a brittle manner*
tense, curt, irritable, harsh, nervous

COLLOQ. edgy, nervy
4 *a brittle laugh*
short hard, sharp, harsh, grating
E3 1 durable, resilient, sturdy **2** stable, secure,
constant

broach *v*
1 INTRODUCE, raise, mention, propose, suggest, bring up,
allude to, refer to, hint at
2 *broach a cask*
tap, pierce, open
OLD (*Shakesp*) strike

broad *adj*
1 *broad avenues/valleys*
wide, large, vast, roomy, spacious, ample, extensive,
widespread
FORMAL capacious, latitudinous
2 *a broad education*
wide-ranging, far-reaching, encyclopedic, extensive, all-
embracing, inclusive, comprehensive, general, sweeping,
universal, unlimited
FORMAL catholic, eclectic, compendious
3 *the broad meaning of the term*
general, vague, not detailed
4 *broad support*
widespread, extensive, general
5 *a broad hint*
obvious, clear, plain, direct, undisguised,
unconcealed
6 *a broad accent*
strong, marked, noticeable, obvious, evident
E3 1 narrow **2** limited, restricted **3** narrow, detailed,
specific, precise **4** limited **5** veiled, disguised **6** slight

> **⚠ broad** or **wide**?
> *Broad* refers to the extent across something and often
> has the connotation of spaciousness or ampleness,
> whereas *wide* refers to the distance separating, or the
> gap between, sides or edges: *a person's broad back;
> broad shoulders; wide sleeves; a wide doorway.*

broadcast *v, n*
♦ *v*
1 *broadcast TV programmes*
transmit, air, show, beam, relay, televise,
cable, radiate
2 *broadcast the decision widely*
make known, report, announce, publicize, advertise,
publish, circulate, spread, scatter
FORMAL promulgate, disseminate
♦ *n*
transmission, programme, show, access broadcast,
community broadcast, simulcast, simultaneous
transmission, television première, teletext, satellite
programme, telebridge, webcast

broaden *v*
widen, spread, enlarge, expand, extend, stretch, increase,
develop, open up, branch out, diversify
FORMAL augment
E3 narrow, reduce, restrict

broadly *adv*
1 GENERALLY, usually, normally, mostly, in most cases,
commonly, mainly, largely, as a rule, more or less, by and
large, on the whole, for the most part
2 EXTENSIVELY, widely, generally, thoroughly, fully,
comprehensively

broad-minded *adj*
liberal, tolerant, permissive, forbearing, enlightened, free-
thinking, progressive, indulgent, impartial, open-minded,
receptive, unbiased, unprejudiced, dispassionate
E3 narrow-minded, intolerant, biased, prejudiced

broadside *n*
1 *fire a broadside at a ship*
attack, assault, volley, salvo, battering, cannonade, blast,
bombardment, counterblast, tire

2 *verbal broadsides*
criticism, denunciation, censure
FORMAL philippic, diatribe, fulmination, harangue,
invective
COLLOQ. brickbat, stick

brochure *n*
leaflet, booklet, pamphlet, prospectus, broadsheet,
handbill, circular, handout, folder, flyer;
N Am throwaway

broil *v*
grill, cook, fry, toast, barbecue, roast

broiling *adj*
sweltering, boiling, hot, baking, roasting, scorching,
blistering

broke *adj*
penniless, bankrupt, ruined, poor, impoverished, poverty-
stricken, destitute
FORMAL insolvent, impecunious, penurious, indigent
COLLOQ. bust, skint, stony-broke, strapped (for cash),
cleaned out, on your uppers, on your beam ends, not
having two pennies to rub together
E3 rich, affluent, solvent

broken *adj*
1 *a broken pipe*
fractured, burst, ruptured, severed, separated, shattered,
smashed, damaged, destroyed, demolished
COLLOQ. broken to smithereens
2 *broken machinery*
faulty, damaged, defective, out of order/action, not
working, gone wrong
FORMAL malfunctioning, inoperative
COLLOQ. bust, kaput, duff, on the blink, wonky;
N Am on the fritz
3 *broken sleep*
disjointed, disconnected, fragmentary, interrupted,
disturbed, fitful, intermittent, spasmodic, erratic
FORMAL discontinuous
4 *a broken marriage*
failed, ended, divorced
5 *speak broken German*
hesitating, stammering, halting, faltering, imperfect,
disjointed
6 *a broken man*
beaten, defeated, crushed, demoralized, dispirited, weak,
feeble, exhausted, tamed, subdued, oppressed
FORMAL vanquished
COLLOQ. down, knackered
E3 1 mended, intact, whole **2** mended, in order/action,
working **3** continuous, uninterrupted **5** fluent, perfect

broken-down *adj*
1 *a broken-down machine*
faulty, damaged, defective, broken, out of order
FORMAL inoperative
COLLOQ. on the blink, bust, kaput, duff;
N Am on the fritz
2 *a broken-down old house*
dilapidated, in disrepair, decrepit, ramshackle, rickety,
ruined, decayed, collapsed

broken-hearted *adj*
heartbroken, inconsolable, devastated, grief-stricken,
desolate, despairing, miserable, wretched, mournful,
sorrowful, sad, unhappy, dejected, despondent, crestfallen,
disappointed
FORMAL dolorous, forlorn, disconsolate, prostrated
COLLOQ. down, down in the dumps

broker *n, v*
♦ *n*
agent, middleman, dealer, factor, handler, intermediary,
negotiator, go-between, stockbroker, jobber, stockjobber
TECHNICAL arbitrageur
♦ *v*
negotiate, deal, mediate, arbitrate, bargain, arrange, settle,
organize, complete, agree, job

FORMAL conclude, execute
COLLOQ. clinch

bromide *n*
1 PLATITUDE, banality, cliché, commonplace, stereotype, truism
FORMAL anodyne
2 TRANQUILLIZER, sedative, calmative, sleeping pill, opiate, narcotic, barbiturate
COLLOQ. downer

bronze *adj*
copper, copper-coloured, auburn, chestnut, reddish-brown, rust, tan, Titian
OLD brass

bronzed *adj*
bronze, tanned, suntanned, brown, browned, sunburnt

brooch *n*
badge, pin, clip, clasp, breastpin, lapel pin, tiepin, fibula
OLD broch, ouch
SLANG prop

brood *v, n*
♦ *v*
1 *brood over lost opportunities*
ponder, meditate, muse, mull over, go over, dwell on, worry about, fret about, sulk, agonize
FORMAL , rehearse, ruminate
COLLOQ. fret, mope
2 *hens brood*
incubate, sit, cover; *Scot* clock; hatch
♦ *n*
1 *a brood of birds*
clutch, chicks, hatch, litter, young, offspring, issue, progeny, nest, nid, spawn; *Scot* cleck
OLD kindle, sperm, team
2 *a brood of children*
children, family, household, clan; *Scot* bairn-team, bairn-time
COLLOQ. tribe

brook[1] *n*
a brook running by the cottage
stream, rivulet, beck, watercourse, channel, inlet, gill, runnel, fleet, rill; *Scot* burn; *N Am* branch, kill; *N Am, Aust & NZ* creek
OLD purl

brook[2] *v*
will brook no interference
tolerate, allow, accept, permit, bear, endure, stand, put up with, support, withstand
OLD abrooke
FORMAL countenance
COLLOQ. stomach

brothel *n*
bordello, bawdy-house, house of ill fame, house of ill repute, whorehouse, bagnio, disorderly house; *Irish* kip; *N Am* sporting house
OLD bordel, flash-house, stew, vaulting-house, Corinth; (*Shakesp*) hothouse, leaping-house
COLLOQ. red light
SLANG knocking-shop, crib; *N Am* cathouse

brother *n*
1 *brothers and sisters*
sibling, blood-brother, full brother, twin-brother, half-brother, relation, relative, sib; *N Am* brer
OLD german, brother-german
COLLOQ. bro
Related adjective: fraternal
2 *brothers in the struggle against injustice*
comrade, friend, mate, partner, colleague, associate, fellow, companion
COLLOQ. chum, pal, buddy
3 *brothers in a monastery*
monk, friar, *fra*

brotherhood *n*
1 *feelings of brotherhood*
fellowship, comradeship, friendship, friendliness, fraternalism, camaraderie
2 *a brotherhood of monks*
fraternity, association, society, league, confederation, confederacy, alliance, union, guild, fellowship, confraternity, confrère, community, clique

brotherly *adj*
fraternal, loyal, affectionate, amicable, caring, sympathetic, friendly, kind, loving, benevolent, philanthropic
F3 callous, unbrotherly

brow *n*
1 *sweat on your brow*
forehead, temples
2 *the brow of the hill*
summit, ridge, top, tip, peak, verge, brink, cliff

browbeat *v*
bully, coerce, force, intimidate, threaten, tyrannize, hector, hound, dragoon, domineer, overbear, oppress
COLLOQ. bulldoze
F3 coax, flatter; *colloq.* sweet-talk

brown *adj, v*
♦ *adj*
1 *brown in colour*
mahogany, chocolate, coffee, *café au lait*, Mocha, hazel, bay, chestnut, auburn, umber, burnt umber, raw umber, sepia, ginger, beige, fawn, tan, tawny, honey, biscuit, bistre, cinnamon, earth-tone, nut-brown, walnut, oatmeal, pine, teak, vandyke brown, fuscous, infuscate, russet, rust, rusty, brunette, dark, dusky
OLD burnet, orange-tawny
2 *brown from lying in the sun*
sunburnt, tanned, bronze, bronzed, browned
♦ *v*
cook, seal, fry, grill, toast, singe, embrown

browned off *adj*
bored, fed up, discontented, discouraged, disheartened, annoyed, irritated, exasperated, weary
COLLOQ. bored stiff, brassed off, cheesed off, hacked off, disgruntled
SLANG pissed off
F3 fascinated, interested, intrigued

browse *v, n*
♦ *v*
1 *browse through a book*
survey, scan, leaf through, flick through, dip into, skim
FORMAL peruse
2 *sheep browsing in the fields*
graze, pasture, feed, eat, nibble
♦ *n*
scan, skim, quick read, look, flick-through

bruise *v, n*
♦ *v*
1 *bruise your leg*
discolour, blacken, mark, blemish, injure, wound, pound, stun
OLD beat, surbate, to-bruise; (*Shakesp*) frush
FORMAL contuse
2 *bruise someone's feelings*
hurt, injure, insult, offend, grieve, upset, crush
3 *bruise fruit*
damage, mark, spoil, blemish, crush, discolour, break
♦ *n*
discoloration, mark, blemish, injury, lesion; *Scot* clour
TECHNICAL ecchymosis
OLD intuse
FORMAL contusion

COLLOQ. black eye, shiner
SLANG rainbow

bruiser *n*
ruffian, thug, tough, rough, roughneck, hoodlum,
bully, bully boy
COLLOQ. bovver boy

brunt *n*
burden, thrust, (main) force, impact, impetus,
pressure, (full) weight, shock, strain

brush[1] *n, v*
♦ *n*
1 *sweep the room with a brush*
broom, sweeper, besom, whisk
2 *give the room a good brush*
sweep, clean, clear, dust, wipe
♦ *v*
1 *brush the room*
clean, sweep, flick, burnish, polish, shine
2 *brush against the table*
touch, contact, graze, kiss, stroke, caress, rub,
scrape, scuff
■ **brush aside**
dismiss, ignore, flout, disregard, override
FORMAL belittle
COLLOQ. pooh-pooh
■ **brush off**
disregard, ignore, slight, snub, rebuff, dismiss,
spurn, reject, repulse, disown
FORMAL repudiate
COLLOQ. cold-shoulder
■ **brush up**
1 *brush up your Spanish*
revise, relearn, improve, polish up, study, go over,
read up
COLLOQ. swot, bone up on, cram
2 *go and brush up*
refresh (yourself), freshen up, clean (yourself up), tidy (up)

brush[2] *n*
a ball lost in the brush
bush, scrub, thicket, bushes, shrubs, brushwood,
undergrowth, underwood, ground cover, frith

brush[3] *n*
a brush with the police
confrontation, encounter, disagreement, argument, clash,
conflict, fight, skirmish, tussle, fracas
COLLOQ. dust-up, set-to, scrap

brush-off *n*
discouragement, dismissal, rebuff, refusal, rejection,
repudiation, repulse, slight, snub
FORMAL repudiation
COLLOQ. cold shoulder
SLANG N Am kiss-off
☒ encouragement

brusque *adj*
abrupt, sharp, short, terse, curt, blunt, downright, gruff,
surly, discourteous, impolite, uncivil, tactless, undiplomatic
☒ courteous, polite, tactful

brutal *adj*
1 *a brutal murder/attacker*
savage, bloodthirsty, vicious, ferocious, cruel, inhumane,
animal, inhuman, beastly, barbarous, boarish, doggish,
Rottweiler, ruffian, brutish, remorseless, pitiless, merciless,
ruthless, callous
FORMAL bestial
2 *brutal frankness*
harsh, insensitive, unfeeling, heartless, iron-hearted,
unsparing, plain, straightforward, frank, severe, tough
☒ **1** kindly, humane, civilized **2** kind, gentle, sensitive

brutality *n*
savagery, bloodthirstiness, viciousness, ferocity, cruelty,
inhumanity, violence, atrocity, ruthlessness, callousness,
roughness, coarseness, barbarism, barbarity, brutishness

FORMAL callosity
☒ gentleness, kindness

brutalize *v*
1 HARDEN, deaden, desensitize, inure, dehumanize
2 ATTACK, assault, beat, pound, batter, thrash, hit, flog

brutally *adv*
1 *brutally honest*
harshly, insensitively, unfeelingly, heartlessly,
straightforwardly, frankly, severely
2 SAVAGELY, viciously, ferociously, cruelly, inhumanely,
barbarously, brutishly, pitilessly, mercilessly, ruthlessly,
callously
☒ **1** gently, sensitively **2** humanely, kindly

brute *n, adj*
♦ *n*
animal, beast, swine, creature, monster, ogre, devil, fiend,
savage, sadist, bully, lout, yahoo, ruffian, *bête*, Rottweiler,
Caliban
♦ *adj*
physical, senseless, unthinking, bodily, carnal, coarse,
depraved, fleshly, gross, instinctive, mindless, sensual

brutish *adj*
brutal, uncivilized, barbarian, barbaric, barbarous, animal,
coarse, crass, crude, cruel, gross, loutish, savage, stupid,
uncouth, vulgar
FORMAL bestial, feral, ferine
☒ refined, civilized, polite

bubble *n, v*
♦ *n*
1 *soap bubbles*
ball (of air), air-bell, drop, droplet, bead, blister, fizz,
foam, froth, head, lather, suds, effervescence, globule,
spume, bleb, bell, air-lock
OLD (*Spenser*) rowndell
FORMAL vesicle
2 *a bubble in glass*
dimple, depression, blister, blowhole, seed
3 *the bubble of all their dreams burst*
delusion, fantasy, fraud, illusion, trifle, vanity
♦ *v*
1 SPARKLE, froth, foam, seethe, boil, burble, gurgle,
effervesce, gloop; *Scot* wallop
OLD mantle
COLLOQ. fizz
2 *bubble with enthusiasm*
be filled, be excited, sparkle, be elated
COLLOQ. bounce

bubbly *adj*
1 SPARKLING, carbonated, frothy, foaming, sudsy,
effervescent
COLLOQ. fizzy
2 LIVELY, happy, merry, elated, excited, exuberant,
vivacious
FORMAL animated, ebullient
COLLOQ. bouncy
☒ **1** flat, still **2** lethargic

buccaneer *n*
pirate, corsair, filibuster, freebooter, privateer, sea robber,
sea rover, sea wolf

buck *v*
1 *buck the trend*
resist, ignore, oppose, break the rules, contradict
2 *feel very bucked*
encourage, cheer, hearten, reassure, buoy up
■ **buck up**
1 *buck someone up*
cheer (up), encourage, improve, rally, stimulate, take
heart, hearten, enliven
FORMAL inspirit
COLLOQ. perk up
2 *Buck up or we'll be late!*
hurry (up)
FORMAL hasten

COLLOQ. get a move on, get your skates on, step on it
E∃ 1 discourage **2** slow down

bucket *n, v*
♦ *n*
pail, can, bail, scuttle, pitcher, vessel, tub, ladle, dip, kibble
OLD situla, stoup, stoop
■ **bucket down**
pour (down), rain heavily, pelt down
COLLOQ. rain cats and dogs, come down in buckets/stair rods/torrents

buckle *n, v*
♦ *n*
1 *a buckle on a belt*
clasp, clip, catch, fastener, hasp
2 *a buckle in metal*
bulge, warp, distortion, twist, kink
FORMAL contortion
♦ *v*
1 FASTEN, clasp, catch, hook, hitch, connect, close, secure
2 *the metal buckled*
bend, warp, twist, distort, bulge, fold, wrinkle, crumple, collapse
COLLOQ. cave in
■ **buckle down**
knuckle down, start to work hard, get down to it
COLLOQ. pull your finger out, go all out, pull out all the stops

bucolic *adj*
pastoral, rural, agrarian, agricultural, country
FORMAL rustic
COLLOQ. countrified
E∃ industrial, urban

bud *n, v*
♦ *n*
shoot, sprout, sprig, germ, embryo, button, knot
TECHNICAL bulbil, gemma, knosp, turion
OLD knop
FORMAL plumule
♦ *v*
shoot, sprout, develop, grow
FORMAL burgeon, pullulate
E∃ wither, waste away

budding *adj*
potential, promising, embryonic, developing, growing, up-and-coming, flowering, fledgling
FORMAL incipient, nascent, burgeoning
E∃ experienced, mature

buddy *n*
friend, good friend, companion, comrade
COLLOQ. buddy-buddy, pal, mate, chum, crony

budge *v*
1 *the door won't budge*
move, stir, shift, remove, dislodge, push, roll, slide; *Scot* jee
OLD bouge, bodge
2 *not budge from your position*
change, bend, yield, give (way), give in, change your mind, not compromise, sway, influence, persuade, convince

budget *n, v*
♦ *n*
finances, funds, resources, economics, means, allowance, allotment, quota, allocation, (financial) plan, (financial) estimate, what you can afford
OLD bouget, bowget
♦ *v*
plan, estimate, schedule, allow, allot, allocate, set aside, ration, afford
FORMAL apportion

buff¹ *adj, v*
♦ *adj*
buff-coloured envelopes
yellowish-brown, yellowish, straw, sandy, fawn, khaki, beige, natural, nankeen, tan
♦ *v*
polish, burnish, shine, smooth, rub (up), brush
■ **in the buff**
naked, nude, bare, with nothing on, undressed, unclothed, uncovered, stripped, stark-naked
COLLOQ. in the altogether, in the raw, starkers, not a stitch on

buff² *n*
a computer buff
expert, connoisseur, enthusiast, fan, fanatic, admirer, devotee, addict; *N Am* maven
FORMAL aficionado
COLLOQ. freak, fiend

buffer *n, v*
♦ *n*
shock absorber, bumper, fender, pad, cushion, pillow, intermediary, screen, shield, bulwark
♦ *v*
cushion, soften, deaden, absorb, suppress, lessen, reduce, diminish, mitigate, protect

buffet¹ *n*
1 *a railway buffet*
snackbar, counter, café, cafeteria
2 *a buffet supper*
self-service, cold meal, smorgasbord, cold table
COLLOQ. help yourself

buffet² *v, n*
♦ *v*
1 *buffeted by the storm*
batter, hit, strike, knock, bang, bump, push, pound, pummel, beat, shove, thump, box, cuff, clout, slap
2 *a government buffeted by corruption*
trouble, afflict, disturb, weigh (down), burden, distress, harm, oppress, tax, blight
♦ *n*
blow, knock, bang, bump, jar, jolt, push, thump, box, cuff, clout, slap, smack, shove
OLD buff

buffoon *n*
clown, comedian, comic, fool, harlequin, jester, joker, wag, droll, tomfool, zany, *farceur*, mime, mountebank
OLD antic, Jack-pudding, merry-andrew, mome, Punchinello, Scoggin, Scaramouch, Vice, Iniquity

buffoonery *n*
clowning, jesting, pantomime, tomfoolery, waggishness, drollery, nonsense, silliness, farce, pantaloonery, Pantagruelism

bug *n, v*
♦ *n*
1 INSECT, flea, mite
COLLOQ. creepy-crawly
2 *a stomach bug*
virus, bacterium, germ, microbe, micro-organism, infection, illness, disease
COLLOQ. *Aust* wog
SLANG *N Am* cootie
3 *a bug in a computer program*
fault, defect, flaw, blemish, imperfection, failing, error
COLLOQ. gremlin
4 *bitten by the decorating bug*
craze, fad, obsession, mania
COLLOQ. thing
5 *put a bug in a room*
hidden microphone, listening device
COLLOQ. wire-tap, phone-tap
♦ *v*
1 *their attitude bugs me*
annoy, irritate, vex, irk, bother, disturb, harass
COLLOQ. aggravate, needle, wind up

2 bug an office
tap, listen in (on/to), monitor
FORMAL eavesdrop (on)
COLLOQ. wiretap, phone-tap

bugbear n
anathema, bane, bête noire, pet hate, dread,
fiend, horror, nightmare, bogle, bogy, poker, rawhead
OLD bug

build v, n
♦ v
1 build a new hotel
construct, put up, erect, raise, fabricate, make, form,
constitute, assemble, put together, knock together, shape,
fashion, rear, mason, substruct, throw out, overbuild,
upbuild; Scot big
OLD edify
2 build a fairer society
inaugurate, initiate, institute, begin, start, develop, enlarge,
extend, increase, escalate, intensify
FORMAL augment
E∃ **1** destroy, demolish; colloq. knock down **2** lessen
♦ n
physique, figure, body, form, shape, size, frame,
structure; dialect set
■ **build up**
1 build up a navy
assemble, put together, piece together, extend, enlarge, set
up, establish
2 build up your strength
reinforce, extend, expand, develop, grow, amplify,
increase, escalate, intensify, heighten, strengthen, boost,
improve, enhance
FORMAL fortify
3 build a person up as important
publicize, advertise, promote
COLLOQ. plug, hype
4 ACCUMULATE, increase, mount (up), add, gather, collect,
amass, snowball
FORMAL augment

SYNONYM NUANCES

verb sense 1
Construct may be used generally to talk about creating
something, whereas **erect** and **raise** would be used
starting from the lowest level and elevating into position:
barriers erected to prevent trespassing. **Put up** can cover
both nuances: they put up very inferior dwellings; they
put up statues of him.
　Fabricate and, especially, **make** are widely used to
mean creating something, while **form**, **shape** and
fashion convey an idea of giving something shape: the
attic, formed by the steep-sided pitched roof; the
scoured branches, fashioned by the weather.
　Constitute is used of the parts making up the whole: a
trolley of books constituted the hospital library; whereas
assemble and **put together** is used of making
something from those parts: sculptures assembled from
pieces of scrap iron. While the preceding terms are
neutral in tone, the terms **knock together** and **throw out**
may be taken as pejorative in that they carry the
suggestion of carelessness.
　Rear revisits the idea of elevating, and its tone tends to
the poetic, and so is fairly uncommon.
　Usually **mason** has the narrower application of
building stonework, whilst **substruct**, with its sole
application to foundation work, is rarely used.

---

builder n
construction worker, labourer, manual worker, mason,
craftsman, craftsperson, craftswoman, skilled worker

building n
construction, development, fabrication, structure, erection,
architecture
FORMAL edifice, dwelling

Related adjective: tectonic
See panels on next page

build-up n
1 a build-up of fat
enlargement, expansion, development, increase, gain,
growth, accumulation, escalation
FORMAL accretion
2 build-up of nuclear weapons
accumulation, mass, load, heap, stack, drift, store,
stockpile
3 build-up to the competition
publicity, promotion, advertising, marketing
COLLOQ. plug, hype, puff
E∃ **1** reduction, decrease, contraction

built-in adj
1 built-in wardrobes
fitted, integral, in-built, fixed, included
2 built-in safeguards
inherent, included, incorporated, implicit, in-built,
inseparable, integral, intrinsic, essential, fundamental,
necessary

bulbous adj
rounded, swollen, swelling, bulging, convex, bloated,
puffed (out)
TECHNICAL pulvinate(d), tuberous
FORMAL distended

bulge n, v
♦ n
1 a bulge on the wall
swelling, bump, lump, hump, bias, blister, shoulder,
pouch
FORMAL projection, protuberance, distension
2 a bulge in the production figures
rise, increase, surge, upsurge, intensification
♦ v
swell, hump, expand, enlarge, bulb, project, protrude,
bag, belly, billow; dialect strout
OLD strut
FORMAL dilate, distend
COLLOQ. puff out, sag; N Am bug

bulk n, v
♦ n
1 the vast bulk of the ship
size, magnitude, dimensions, extent, bigness, largeness,
immensity, volume, mass, weight, substance, body,
quantity; Scot bouk
OLD great
FORMAL amplitude
2 MAJORITY, most, nearly all, preponderance, weight, gross;
Scot feck
COLLOQ. lion's share
■ **bulk out/up**
expand, extend, make bigger, increase, pad out, fill out,
fill (up)

bulky adj
substantial, big, large, huge, enormous, immense, ample,
volumed, gross, lusty, mammoth, massive, colossal,
hulking, hefty, heavy, weighty, unmanageable, unwieldy,
awkward, cumbersome, lofty
FORMAL voluminous
E∃ insubstantial, small, handy

bulldoze v
1 bulldoze buildings
clear, flatten, demolish, level, raze
COLLOQ. knock down
**2 bulldoze someone into buying; bulldoze plans through
a committee**
force, push (through), intimidate, browbeat
FORMAL coerce
COLLOQ. bully, steamroller

bullet n
shot, pellet, ball, missile, propellant, cartridge, cartouche,
dumdum

Types of building include:

abbey	chapel	garage	mausoleum	pier	*N Am* sliver
N Am apartment	chateau	gazebo	mews	power station	building
building (or	church	gurdwara	mill	prison	sports hall
apartment house)	cinema	gymnasium	monastery	*colloq.* pub	stable
arena	college	high-rise	monument	public house	store
barn	*N Am*	hospital	mosque	restaurant	summerhouse
barracks	condominium	hotel	multiplex	school	synagogue
beach hut	cottage	house	museum	shed	temple
block of flats	dovecote	inn	oast house	shop	theatre
boathouse	exhibition centre	library	observatory	showroom	tower block
bungalow	factory	lighthouse	office block	silo	university
cabin	farmhouse	low-rise	outhouse	*Aust* skillion (or	villa
café	farmscraper	maisonette	pagoda	skilling)	warehouse
castle	fort	mandir	palace	skyscraper	windmill
cathedral	fortress	mansion	pavilion		

See also **house**; **restaurant**; **shop**.

Types of building material include:

aggregate	cladding	granite	marble	reinforced con-	steel beam
aluminium	clapboard	gravel	mastic	crete	stone
asbestos	clay	grout	matchboard	roofing felt	tarmac
ashlar	concrete	gypsum	medium density	roof tile	thatch
asphalt	decking	hardboard	fibreboard (MDF)	sand	tile
bitumen	*N Am* drywall	hard core	mortar	sandstone	timber
breeze block	fixings	insulation	paving stone	*Scot & NZ* sarking	wall tile
brick	flagstone	foam insulation	pavior	shingle	wattle and daub
building block	floor tile	loose fill insulation	plaster	*N Am* siding	wood
cast iron	girder	lagging	plasterboard	slate	
cement	glass	lintel	plastic	stainless steel	
chipboard	glass fibre	*N Am* lumber	plywood	steel	

OLD Biscayan
FORMAL projectile
COLLOQ. slug
OLD SLANG lead towel

bulletin *n*
1 *televison news bulletins*
report, newsflash, dispatch, communiqué, statement, announcement, notification, communication, message, update, release
2 *an office bulletin*
news sheet, newspaper, newsletter, leaflet, update

bullish *adj*
optimistic, confident, hopeful, positive, cheerful, buoyant
FORMAL sanguine
COLLOQ. upbeat

bully *n, v*
♦ *n*
persecutor, tormentor, browbeater, intimidator, cyberbully, tyrant, bully-boy, ruffian, thug, bouncer, hoodlum, swashbuckler, bucko
OLD brave, cuttle, huff, killcow, Drawcansir
COLLOQ. heavy, tough
♦ *v*
persecute, torment, terrorize, bulldoze, coerce, browbeat, bullyrag, intimidate, cow, tyrannize, prey, bluster, hector, haze, pick on, victimize, domineer, overbear, oppress
COLLOQ. push around
E∃ coax, persuade, encourage

bulwark *n*
bastion, buttress, defence, wall, guard, safeguard, security, protection, support, mainstay, outwork, buffer, embankment, fortification, partition, rampart
TECHNICAL redoubt

bum¹ *n*
sitting on his bum
bottom, buttocks, behind, rear, seat, rump
COLLOQ. backside, tail; *N Am* butt, booty; *Scot* bahookie
SLANG arse; *N Am* ass

bum² *n, v, adj*
♦ *n*
end up as a drunken bum
tramp, vagrant, hobo, vagabond; *Scot* gangrel
SLANG dosser
♦ *v*
cadge, scrounge, beg, borrow
COLLOQ. sponge
♦ *adj*
poor, bad, worthless, low, useless, unpleasant, disagreeable, adverse, inadequate, imperfect, unsatisfactory, unacceptable
COLLOQ. awful, terrible, rubbish, duff, crummy
SLANG naff, crappy

bumble *v*
blunder, stumble, falter, stagger, lurch, totter, teeter

bumbling *adj*
bungling, awkward, inept, blundering, botching, clumsy, inefficient, incompetent, lumbering, muddled, stumbling
FORMAL maladroit
E∃ competent, efficient

bump *v, n*
♦ *v*
1 *bump into the wall/against the table*
hit, strike, knock, bang, crash, collide (with), barge; *dialect* jowl; *Scot* dunch
COLLOQ. slam, prang
2 *bump along a track*
jolt, jerk, jar, jostle, rattle, shake, bounce, jounce
♦ *n*
1 *hear a bump*
blow, hit, knock, bang, thump, thud, smash, crash, collision, impact, jolt, jar, shock, whop
2 *a bump on your head*
lump, swelling, bulge, injury, hump, irregularity
TECHNICAL papilla, knur, nodule
FORMAL protrusion, protuberance, tumescence

3 *a bump on a road*
lump, bulge, hump, protuberance, speed bump,
sleeping policeman
■ **bump into**
come across, meet (unexpectedly), meet by chance,
encounter
FORMAL chance upon, happen upon, light upon
COLLOQ. run into
■ **bump off**
kill, murder, assassinate, remove
COLLOQ. eliminate, liquidate, do in, rub out,
blow away, top

bumper *adj*
plentiful, abundant, rich, large, great, enormous,
massive, excellent, exceptional
COLLOQ. whopping, jumbo, ginormous
E3 small, tiny

bumpkin *n*
country bumpkin, country yokel, boor, lout, clodhopper,
clodpoll, rustic, oaf, peasant, provincial, hawbuck;
N Am yap; *N Am & Aust* bushwhacker
OLD putt
COLLOQ. hillbilly, hick, hayseed
SLANG *N Am* rube

bumptious *adj*
self-important, pompous, officious, overbearing, pushy,
assertive, over-confident, presumptuous, forward, full of
yourself, impudent, arrogant, cocky, brash, conceited,
swaggering, boastful, egotistic
COLLOQ. too big for your boots
E3 humble, modest, unassertive

bumpy *adj*
1 *a bumpy road*
rough, lumpy, pot-holed, knobbly, knobby, uneven,
irregular
2 *a bumpy ride*
rough, uneven, jerky, jolting, bouncy, choppy
E3 1 smooth, level **2** smooth, even, uncomfortable

bunch *n, v*
♦ *n*
1 *a bunch of grapes*
bundle, sheaf, tuft, club, clump, cluster, string,
racemation; *dialect* bob
2 *a bunch of keys/papers*
batch, lot, wad, heap, pile, stack, mass, number,
quantity, collection, assortment
FORMAL agglomeration, fascicle, fascicule
3 *a bunch of flowers*
bouquet, posy, spray, nosegay, corsage,
tussie mussie
OLD boughpot
4 *a bunch of people*
gang, band, troop, crew, team, party, gathering,
flock, swarm, crowd, mob, multitude
♦ *v*
group, bundle, cluster, collect, gather, flock,
herd, crowd, mass, pack, huddle
FORMAL assemble, congregate
E3 disperse, scatter, spread out

bundle *n, v*
♦ *n*
1 *a bundle of hay/sticks*
bunch, sheaf, shook, roll, bale, truss, faggot, wad, wisp,
woolpack, bavin, bottle; *dialect* knitch, wap, yelm; *Scot*
dorlach
OLD fasces
FORMAL fascicle, fascine, fascicule
2 *carry bundles of clothes*
pack, batch, parcel, package, packet, carton, box, bag;
Aust swag, bluey, drum
OLD *Aust* shiralee
FORMAL consignment

3 *a bundle of books/paper*
group, set, collection, assortment, quantity, mass,
accumulation, pile, stack, heap, skein
OLD trousseau
♦ *v*
1 *bundle papers together*
pack, wrap, bale, truss, cluster, gather, parcel,
bind, tie, fasten, huddle
2 *bundle someone into a van*
rush, hurry, push roughly, shove, tumble

bung *n*
stopper, plug, cork, seal, spigot

bungle *v*
mismanage, make a mess of, botch, ruin,
spoil, mar, fudge, blunder, mishandle, muddle, fluff,
bumble, duff, mangle, mull; *Scot* bauchle, blunk,
misguggle; *N Am* bobble
COLLOQ. foul up, mess up, louse up, bodge,
boob, muck up, foozle, muff; *N Am* flub
SLANG goof (up), cock up, screw up

bungler *n*
incompetent, blunderer, bumbler, tinker; *Scot* blunk
COLLOQ. botcher, butterfingers,
duffer, muff
SLANG schlemiel

bungling *adj*
awkward, clumsy, incompetent, inept,
unskilful, messy, amateurish
FORMAL maladroit
COLLOQ. blundering, botching, cack-handed,
ham-fisted, ham-handed

bunkum *n*
nonsense, rubbish
COLLOQ. balderdash, baloney, bilge, bosh,
bunk, blah, garbage, cobblers, hooey, piffle, malarkey,
codswallop, poppycock, rot, stuff and nonsense,
tommyrot, trash, tripe, twaddle; *N Am* hogwash,
horsefeathers, BS; *Aust & NZ* bulldust
SLANG bull;
(*vulgar*) balls, bollocks, bullshit

buoy *n, v*
♦ *n*
float, marker, signal, beacon, mooring, dan, dolphin
■ **buoy up**
support, sustain, raise, lift, boost, encourage,
cheer (up), hearten
E3 depress, discourage

buoyancy *n*
1 LIGHTNESS, floatability
2 CHEERFULNESS, happiness, gladness, joy,
light-heartedness, enthusiasm, geniality, jolliness,
brightness, confidence, optimism, good spirits
COLLOQ. bounce, pep
3 *the buoyancy of the economy*
strength, vigour, toughness, resilience, growth,
development

buoyant *adj*
1 *a buoyant mood*
light-hearted, carefree, bright, cheerful,
optimistic, happy, joyful, lively, blithe, bullish,
debonair, animated, vivacious, youthful
COLLOQ. bouncy, peppy
2 *a buoyant raft*
floatable, floating, afloat, light, weightless
3 *a buoyant economy*
strong, tough, resilient, hardy, adaptable, growing,
developing, thriving
E3 1 depressed, despairing **2** heavy

burble *v*
babble, gurgle, lap, murmur, purl

burden *n, v*

♦ *n*

1 *put down a heavy burden*
cargo, load, weight, dead-weight
OLD burthen; (*Shakesp*) carriage

2 *the burdens of office*
obligation, responsibility, duty, onus, imposition, millstone,
pressure, strain, stress, worry, anxiety, weight, care,
trouble, trial, affliction, cross, grievance, sorrow,
overburden, yoke
FORMAL encumbrance, cumbrance
SLANG monkey

♦ *v*

burdened with a heavy load/worldly cares
weigh down, lade, handicap, bother, worry, tax, strain,
charge, land with, lumber, saddle, overload, overburden,
overstress, overextend, lie heavy/hard on, oppress,
overwhelm, crush, task
OLD cark; (*Shakesp*) overbulk
FORMAL encumber
Ｅｄ unburden, relieve

burdensome *adj*
onerous, crushing, difficult, weighty, exacting, heavy,
irksome, oppressive, taxing, troublesome, trying,
wearisome, grievous
OLD chargeable, importune
Ｅｄ easy, light

bureau *n*

1 *the Federal Bureau of Investigation*
office, service, agency, branch, department, division,
counter

2 *sit at a bureau*
desk, writing-desk

bureaucracy *n*

1 *a bureaucracy of thousands of civil servants*
administration, government, ministry, civil service, the
authorities, the system; *N Am* city hall

2 *try to reduce bureaucracy*
administration, rules and regulations, paperwork,
officialdom, officiousness, beadledom
COLLOQ. red tape

bureaucrat *n*
officer, official, office-holder, administrator, civil servant,
functionary, (government) minister, committee member,
mandarin, apparatchik, Eurocrat, chinovnik
SLANG suit

> **QUOTATIONS**
> There is something about a bureaucrat that does not like
> a poem
> GORE VIDAL, *Sex, Death and Money*

bureaucratic *adj*
official, administrative, governmental, ministerial,
complicated, procedural, inflexible, rigid

burgeon *v*
grow, develop, increase, expand, extend, enlarge, swell,
escalate, proliferate, snowball

burglar *n*
housebreaker, robber, thief, pilferer, trespasser, cat-burglar,
cracksman; *N Am* yegg

burglary *n*
housebreaking, break-in, robbery, theft, stealing, trespass,
pilferage, larceny
COLLOQ. heist

burgle *v*
break into, rob, steal from, burst into, force your way into;
N Am burglarize

burial *n*
burying, funeral, committal
FORMAL interment, entombment, obsequies, exequies,
inhumation, sepulchre

burial place *n*
graveyard, cemetery, churchyard, God's acre, vault, crypt,
catacomb, mausoleum, necropolis, tumulus
OLD charnel, kurgan

burlesque *n, adj*

♦ *n*
caricature, mock, mockery, parody, ridicule, satire,
travesty, Pantagruelism
COLLOQ. take-off, send-up, spoof, mickey-taking

♦ *adj*
comic, derisive, farcical, mocking, parodying, satirical,
heroi-comic
FORMAL caricatural, hudibrastic
Ｅｄ serious

burly *adj*
well-built, thickset, hulking, hefty, heavy, stocky, big,
sturdy, brawny, beefy, muscular, athletic, strapping, strong,
powerful; *Scot* buirdly
Ｅｄ small, puny, thin, slim

burn *v*

1 *the fire's burning*
be on/catch fire, be in flames, burst into flames,
blaze, be/catch ablaze, go up in smoke, flame, inflame,
flare (up), flash, glow, flicker, smoulder, smoke
OLD bren, brenne

2 *burn rubbish*
ignite, light, set fire to, put a match to, set alight, kindle,
incinerate, cremate, consume, corrode, burn down,
destroy, go up in flames, gut, put to the torch, combust,
chark
TECHNICAL cense
OLD increate, conflagrate
FORMAL deflagrate

3 *burn your hand on the oven; burn a hole in a cardigan*
scald, scorch, parch, shrivel, singe, char, toast, fry, grill,
brand, sear, inure; *dialect* plot, sweal; *Scot* scouther
FORMAL cauterize

4 *make your throat burn*
smart, sting, bite, hurt, tingle

5 *burn with anger*
fume, simmer, seethe
OLD emboil

6 *burn to be with someone*
long, desire, yearn, itch, be eager, be consumed by

burning *adj*

1 *a burning building*
ablaze, aflame, afire, fiery, flaming, blazing, flashing,
gleaming, glowing, smouldering, alight, lit, illuminated,
quick
OLD conflagrant, flagrant, swealing

2 *a burning forehead; a burning hot day*
hot, scalding, scorching
OLD swealing

3 *a burning sensation*
searing, piercing, acute, smarting, stinging, prickling,
tingling, biting, caustic, pungent, urent
FORMAL acrid

4 *burning desire*
passionate, ardent, fervent, eager, earnest, intense, fiery,
vehement, impassioned, frantic, frenzied, consuming
OLD inburning
FORMAL fervid

5 *a burning issue*
urgent, pressing, important, significant, crucial, essential,
vital, live
Ｅｄ **2** cold **4** apathetic **5** unimportant

burnish *v*
polish (up), brighten, buff, glaze, shine

burp *v, n*

♦ *v*
belch, bring up wind
FORMAL eructate

♦ *n*
belch
FORMAL eructation

burrow *n, v*
♦ *n*
warren, hole, earth, set, den, lair, retreat,
shelter, tunnel; *dialect* bury
♦ *v*
1 TUNNEL, dig, delve, excavate, mine, undermine,
gopher; *Scot* howk
2 *burrow for the keys*
rummage, delve, search, root

bursar *n*
treasurer, cashier, purser

bursary *n*
scholarship, grant, award, endowment, fellowship,
exhibition

burst *v, n*
♦ *v*
1 *the tyre burst*
puncture, rupture, tear, split (open), blow, crack, break
(open), fragment, shatter, shiver, disintegrate, spring,
disrupt, part, pull apart
OLD (*Spenser*) distrain
2 *the dam burst*
gush, spout, rush, erupt
3 *burst into a room*
rush, run, hurry, race, dart, fly, bounce, plump,
break in on
COLLOQ. barge, push your way
4 *the bomb burst*
explode, blow up, go off
COLLOQ. go pop, go bang
♦ *n*
1 *have a burst on the motorway*
puncture
COLLOQ. blow-out
2 *a burst of gunfire; a sudden burst of activity*
discharge, volley, salvo, gush, spurt, surge,
rush, spate, torrent, outpouring, outburst, outbreak,
fit, bang, clap, flash, blaze, blitz, start, gust
FORMAL fusillade
■ **burst out**
1 *burst out crying*
begin, start
FORMAL commence
2 EXCLAIM, cry (out), call out, utter
COLLOQ. blurt out

bury *v*
1 *bury the dead*
lay to rest, shroud; *Scot* yird
OLD earth, grave; (*Shakesp*) inhearse
FORMAL inter, entomb, tomb, sepulchre, inhume, inearth
COLLOQ. put six feet under
SLANG plant
2 *bury your face in your hands; bury a memory*
sink, submerge, plant, implant, embed, conceal, hide,
cover, engulf, immerse, enclose
FORMAL enshroud
3 *buried yourself in work*
immerse, engross, occupy, engage, absorb
E3 1 *formal* disinter, exhume **2** uncover,
discover, expose

bush *n*
1 *a rose bush*
shrub, hedge, plant, thicket; *dialect* scrog
OLD tod, todde; (*Spenser*) busket
2 *go camping in the bush*
scrub, brush, scrubland, backwoods, wilds, outback
■ **not beat about the bush**
speak plainly/openly, come to the point,
commit yourself
COLLOQ. call a spade a spade

bushy *adj*
shaggy, thick, bristling, bristly, fluffy, fuzzy, luxuriant,
woody, spreading, stiff, unruly, rough, wiry
TECHNICAL dasyphyllous, dumose, dumous
E3 thin, neat, tidy, trim, well-kept

busily *adv*
actively, diligently, assiduously, earnestly, energetically,
hard, industriously, purposefully, briskly, speedily,
strenuously

business *n*
1 *do business*
trade, commerce, industry, manufacturing, dealings,
transactions, bargaining, trading, buying, selling,
merchandizing
2 *set up a new business*
company, firm, industry, corporation,
establishment, organization, concern, operation, franchise,
enterprise, private enterprise, flagship, venture,
management buyout, consortium, syndicate, holding
company, parent/subsidiary company, conglomerate,
multinational
3 *a line of business*
job, occupation, work, employment, trade, profession,
line, calling, career, vocation, duty, task, responsibility,
métier
4 *none of your business*
affair, concern, matter, issue, subject, topic, question,
problem, point
COLLOQ. baby, pigeon
5 *the business of the meeting*
topic, subject, issue, question, matter

businesslike *adj*
professional, efficient, thorough, systematic,
methodical, organized, orderly, well-ordered, slick,
painstaking, practical, pragmatic, matter-of-fact, precise,
correct, formal, impersonal
E3 inefficient, wasteful, disorganized; *colloq.* sloppy

businessman, businesswoman *n*
executive, entrepreneur, industrialist, trader, merchant,
tycoon, magnate, capitalist, financier, employer,
manufacturer, Babbitt
COLLOQ. city gent

busker *n*
street-entertainer, street-musician

bust[1] *n*
1 *a bust of the President*
sculpture, head, torso, statue
TECHNICAL herm, term, terminus
2 *a woman's bust*
bosom, breasts, chest, breast
COLLOQ. boobs
SLANG bristols, knockers, tits

bust[2] *v, adj*
♦ *v*
someone's bust the television
break, damage, shatter, crack, smash, destroy
♦ *adj*
broken, faulty, defective, out of order/action
COLLOQ. on the blink, wonky, phut, kaput, duff;
N Am on the fritz
■ **go bust**
become bankrupt, become insolvent, fail, collapse,
founder, crash, close down
COLLOQ. fold, flop, go to the wall, *Aust* go bung

bustle *v, n*
♦ *v*
hurry, dash, rush, scamper, scurry, rush to and fro,
scramble, fuss, bumble, fluster, trot; *dialect* whew
FORMAL hasten, bestir
COLLOQ. tear, belt, to and fro
SLANG buzz

♦ *n*

activity, stir, commotion, to-do, tumult,
agitation, excitement, fuss, scramble, flurry, hurry, hurly-
burly, hustle and bustle, rush hour, the rush, hurry-scurry;
Irish stirabout; *N Am* rustle
OLD (*Shakesp*) ruffle
FORMAL haste, pother, ado
COLLOQ. a hive of activity, comings
and goings

bustling *adj*

lively, active, energetic, busy,
hectic, buzzing, rushing, crowded,
eventful, full, humming, restless, stirring, swarming,
teeming
FORMAL astir, abustle, thronged
COLLOQ. on the trot
F3 quiet, sleepy, restful

busy *adj, v*

♦ *adj*

1 *be busy at the moment*
occupied, engaged, otherwise engaged,
employed, unavailable, working, having a previous
engagement/prior appointment
FORMAL in conference
COLLOQ. tied up, hard at it, on the job, in the
thick of it, busy as a bee
2 *a very busy day*
active, lively, energetic, strenuous, tiring,
full, crowded, swarming, vibrant, teeming,
bustling, hectic, frantic, eventful
3 *busy preparing for the meeting*
occupied, involved, engrossed, working
4 *a busy person*
active, having a lot to do, time-poor, energetic, lively,
diligent, industrious, assiduous, restless, tireless; *Scot*
eident; *Irish* stirabout
FORMAL sedulous
COLLOQ. on the go, having a lot on, having
your hands full, fully stretched, rushed off
your feet, under pressure, snowed under,
up to your eyes in something, on the trot
F3 1 free, available **2** quiet, leisured, empty, slack **3**
unoccupied **4** lazy, idle; *colloq.* at a loose end

♦ *v*

occupy, involve, engage, employ, engross,
absorb, immerse, interest, concern, go about,
bustle
OLD embusy

SYNONYM NUANCES

adjective sense 2
The words **active**, **lively**, **energetic** and **vibrant** are
positive in tone, with the suggestion that the activity is
enjoyable: *an active campaign*; *lively discussion*; *vibrant
Rhodes*. However, **strenuous** and **tiring** put a negative
slant on any activity: *strenuous manual work*.
  Full and **eventful** would usually be applied to a time
characterized by numerous incidents, and are fairly
neutral in tone, although **eventful** is sometimes used
facetiously when a day has been too packed with
incident for your liking: *the car broke down and the
toaster blew up — you could call it an eventful day*.
Crowded carries the negative implication that too much
has been packed into a time or place, whilst **swarming**
and **teeming** have the restricted use of describing too
many animate things in a confined area, although
swarming has a far more pejorative feel than **teeming**:
the beach was swarming with people; *hillsides teeming
with deer*.
  The term **bustling** may be applied to crowded places
as well as busy people, but implies a favourable view of
the underlying excitement: *bustling waiters*. Both **hectic**
and **frantic**, on the other hand, would appropriately
describe stressful activity.

---

busybody *n*

meddler, interferer, intruder, pry, gossip,
eavesdropper, snoop, snooper, troublemaker,
mischief-maker, scandalmonger
OLD pragmatic
FORMAL pantopragmatic, quidnunc
COLLOQ. Nosey Parker

but *conj, prep, adv*

♦ *conj*

however, nevertheless, nonetheless, anyway,
even so, all/just the same, for all that
FORMAL notwithstanding

♦ *prep*

except, excepting, apart from, other than, with the
exception of, aside from, save, omitting, leaving out,
excluding, besides, bar, barring

♦ *adv*

only, just, at most, merely, simply, purely, no more than

butch *adj*

masculine, male, manlike, mannish, virile
COLLOQ. macho

butcher *n, v*

♦ *n*

1 *buy meat from the butcher's*
meat counter, meat retailer, meat trader, supermarket; *Scot*
flesher
2 SLAUGHTERER, destroyer, killer, (mass) murderer, slayer

♦ *v*

slaughter, massacre, assassinate, exterminate, kill,
liquidate, mutilate, slay, destroy

butchery *n*

1 SLAUGHTER, massacre, (mass) murder, carnage, killing,
mass destruction, blood-letting, bloodshed
2 MEAT-SELLING, meat trade, meat retailing, butcher's

butt[1] *n*

1 *the butt of a gun/tool*
end, butt end, base, foot, shaft, stock, handle, haft
2 *the butt of a cigarette*
stub, tip, end, tail end
COLLOQ. fag end, dog-end; *Scot* dout, nip; *Aust* bumper
SLANG *N Am* snipe, roach
3 *sit on your butt*
bottom, buttocks
COLLOQ. bum, posterior
SLANG
(*vulgar*) arse

butt[2] *n*

the butt of jokes
target, mark, object, subject, victim, laughing-stock,
dupe, scapegoat
OLD stooge, jesting-stock, table-sport

butt[3] *v*

butt someone with its horns
hit, bump, knock, buffet, push, ram, thrust,
shove, punch, jab, prod, poke, bunt, horn; *Scot* box,
dunch, dunsh
SLANG nut
■ **butt in**
interrupt, cut in, break in, intrude, meddle, interfere
FORMAL interpose, interject
COLLOQ. stick your nose in, put your oar in

butt[4] *n*

a water-butt
cask, barrel, keg, tun, tierce, rundlet, firkin,
hogshead

butter
■ **butter up**
flatter, praise, blarney, cajole, coax, pander to, wheedle,
kowtow to
FORMAL be obsequious to
COLLOQ. suck up to, soft-soap

Types of butterfly include:

apollo	Cleopatra	Glanville fritillary	Lulworth skipper	purple hairstreak	silver-washed
black hairstreak	clouded yellow	grayling	map	Queen of Spain	fritillary
brimstone	comma	green hairstreak	marbled white	fritillary	small copper
brown argus	common blue	green-veined white	marsh fritillary	red admiral	swallowtail
brown hairstreak	dingy skipper	grizzled skipper	meadow brown	ringlet	tortoiseshell
cabbage white	Duke of Burgundy	hairstreak	monarch	Scotch argus	wall
Camberwell	fritillary	heath fritillary	orange-tip	silver-spotted skip-	white admiral
beauty	Essex skipper	hermit	painted lady	per	white letter
chalkhill blue	fritillary	holly blue	peacock	silver-studded blue	hairstreak
chequered skipper	gatekeeper	large copper	purple emperor		wood white

See also **moth**.

---

butterfly n
Related adjectives: papilionaceous, rhopaloceral, rhopalocerous
See panel above

buttocks n
bottom, rump, hindquarters, rear, behind, seat, breech, haunches, *derrière*; *Scot* doup, fud, hinderlings, hurdies
TECHNICAL gluteus, nates
OLD crouper
COLLOQ. backside, bum, posterior, fundament, tail; *N Am* butt, heinie, booty
SLANG duff, prat;
(*vulgar*) arse; *N Am* ass, can, fanny, keister, tush; *Aust* coit, quoit
Related adjective: gluteal

button n
1 *buttons on a shirt*
fastener, fastening, catch, clasp, link, stud, frog, olivet
2 *press the button*
knob, disc, switch, lever

buttonhole v
accost, waylay, catch, take aside, detain
FORMAL importune
COLLOQ. grab, nab, corner, collar

buttress n, v
♦ n
support, prop, shore, stay, brace, pier, strut, mainstay, reinforcement
TECHNICAL counterfort, tambour
FORMAL abutment, stanchion
♦ v
support, prop up, shore up, hold up, back up, brace, underpin, strengthen, reinforce, bolster up, sustain
Ⅰ undermine, weaken

buxom adj
plump, ample, large-breasted, full-breasted, bosomy, busty, chesty, well-endowed, well-rounded, full-figured, Junoesque, Rubenesque, zaftig; *Scot* sonse
OLD bucksom
FORMAL voluptuous, comely
COLLOQ. busty
SLANG well-stacked, pneumatic
Ⅰ petite, slim, small

buy v, n
♦ v
1 *buy a car*
pay for, acquire, obtain, get, go shopping, do the shopping, shop around, shop for, stock up on, invest in, speculate, take, hedge, job, market, trade, merchandize, underbuy, overbuy, panic-buy, redeem, subsidize; *Scot* coff
TECHNICAL engross
OLD chop
FORMAL purchase, procure
COLLOQ. snap up, pick up, splash out on; *N Am* scalp
2 *buy the tax man*
bribe, buy off, suborn
COLLOQ. fix, grease someone's palm

SLANG nobble
Ⅰ **1** sell
♦ n
purchase, acquisition, bargain, deal
FORMAL emption
Ⅰ selling

buyer n
purchaser, shopper, consumer, customer, client, patron, broker, dealer
FORMAL vendee, emptor
Ⅰ seller; *formal* vendor

buzz v, n
♦ v
1 *bees buzzing round*
hum, whirr, drone, murmur
FORMAL bombilate, bombinate, susurrate
2 *the clock buzzed*
ring, purr, reverberate, resound, resonate
3 *buzz with excitement*
hum, throb, pulse, bustle, race
♦ n
1 *the buzz of bees*
hum, whirr, buzzing, drone, murmur, purr, thrum
TECHNICAL tinnitus
FORMAL bombilation, bombination, susurration, susurrus
2 *give someone a buzz*
ring, (phone) call
3 *the latest buzz*
rumour, gossip, scandal, latest, hearsay
COLLOQ. word on the street
4 THRILL, excitement, stimulation
COLLOQ. kick(s), high

by prep, adv
♦ prep
1 *a low table by the chair*
near, next to, close to, beside, alongside
2 *enter by the window*
along, over, through, via
3 *earn money by working hard*
by means of, through the agency of, through, using
FORMAL under the aegis of
4 *get home by noon*
before, no later than, at
5 *by any standard*
according to, in relation to
♦ adv
near, close (by), handy, at hand, past, beyond, away, aside
OLD forby

bygone adj
past, ancient, departed, forgotten, former, previous, lost, olden, one-time, antiquated, antique, dinosauric
OLD forepast
FORMAL erstwhile,
Ⅰ modern, recent, future, forthcoming

bypass *v, n*
♦ *v*
avoid, find a way round, sidestep, ignore, neglect, evade, steer clear of, omit, sidetrack, shunt
FORMAL circumvent
COLLOQ. dodge, skirt
♦ *n*
ring road, slip road, alternative route, detour, diversion

by-product *n*
1 *cattle feed is a by-product of whisky*
derivative, spin-off
2 *by-products of modern life*
consequence, result, side effect, repercussion, after-effect, spin-off, knock-on effect
FORMAL concomitant, entailment, epiphenomenon
COLLOQ. fallout

bystander *n*
spectator, onlooker, looker-on, watcher, observer, witness, eyewitness, passer-by
COLLOQ. rubberneck
E3 participant

byword *n*
1 *a byword for efficiency*
model, example, standard, ideal, paragon, perfect example, embodiment
FORMAL exemplar, epitome
2 SLOGAN, catchword, watchword, dictum, maxim, proverb, motto, saw, saying, precept, adage, aphorism
OLD nayword; (*Shakesp*) ayword
FORMAL apophthegm

C

cab *n*
1 *hire a cab*
taxi, taxicab, minicab, hackney carriage, four-wheeler,
droshky, vettura
OLD fiacre, hansom, two-wheeler
OLD SLANG growler
2 *the cab in a lorry*
compartment, driver's compartment,
cabin, quarters

cabal *n*
clique, faction, party, plotters, coalition, league, set,
coterie, conclave junta, junto, camarilla

cabaret *n*
1 ENTERTAINMENT, show, performance, dancing, singing,
comedy, acts, turns, variety
2 NIGHT CLUB, club, restaurant

cabin *n*
1 *a log cabin*
HUT, shack, shanty, lodge, chalet, cottage, shed, shelter;
Scot bothy; refuge; *N Am* cabana
2 BERTH, quarters, sleeping quarters, compartment, room,
stateroom, saloon, coach, cuddy, roundhouse

cabinet *n*
1 *a medicine cabinet*
cupboard, closet, dresser, case, store, chest, locker,
console, secretaire, shrine, almirah, bahut, chiffonier,
encoignure, vargueño
2 *Cabinet ministers*
government, ministers, leadership, senate, administration,
executive, Privy Council

cable *n, v*
♦ *n*
1 *tie with cable*
line, rope, cord, chain, guy, stay, hawser
2 *electric cable*
wire, flex, lead, coaxial, co-ax
3 *send a message by cable*
telegram, telegraph, Telemessage®, wire, fax, facsimile,
email
♦ *v*
send a telegram/telemessage/wire, send by telegraph,
telegraph, wire, transmit, radio, fax, email

cache *n*
store, accumulation, collection, fund, hoard, reserve,
stock, stockpile, storehouse, supply, garner, treasure-store,
hidden treasure
FORMAL repository
COLLOQ. stash

cachet *n*
estimation, prestige, reputation, approval, favour, esteem,
distinction, eminence, status
COLLOQ. street cred

cack-handed *adj*
clumsy, awkward, unco-ordinated, ham-fisted, heavy-
handed, unskilful, inept, bungling, blundering, ungraceful
COLLOQ. gawky, all thumbs

cackle *v, n*
♦ *v*
laugh loudly, laugh unpleasantly, chortle, chuckle, clack,
gabble, gaggle, crow, giggle, snigger, titter; *Scot* keckle

♦ *n*
loud laugh, unpleasant laugh, chortle, chuckle, clack,
gabble, crow, giggle, snigger, titter

cacophonous *adj*
raucous, loud, strident, grating, harsh, discordant,
dissonant, inharmonious, jarring
FORMAL horrisonant
⊟ harmonious, pleasant

cacophony *n*
raucousness, stridency, harshness, racket, din, discord,
dissonance, disharmony, jarring, caterwauling, charivari
FORMAL horrisonance
⊟ harmony

cad *n*
blackguard, scoundrel, rascal, rogue, villain, devil, knave,
deceiver, miscreant, reprobate, wretch
COLLOQ. bleeder, blighter, bounder, rotter, stinker, rat, oik,
swine, scumbag

cadaver *n*
dead body, body, corpse, remains, carcase
SLANG stiff

cadaverous *adj*
corpse-like, death-like, pale, ashen, wan, ghostly, gaunt,
haggard, thin, emaciated, skeletal
COLLOQ. like death warmed up

cadence *n*
intonation, lilt, modulation, inflection, accent, rhythm,
beat, stress, tempo, measure, metre, pattern, swing, pulse,
throb, rate, fall, close

cadge *v*
scrounge, beg
COLLOQ. sponge, bum, mooch; *Aust* bot

cadre *n*
team, small group, squad, crew, corps,
gang, band, set

café *n*
coffee shop, tea shop, tea room, coffee bar, cybercafé,
cafeteria, snackbar, buffet, bistro, wine bar, brasserie,
restaurant
SLANG caff, greasy spoon

cafeteria *n*
self-service café, self-service restaurant, self-service
canteen, café, canteen, restaurant, buffet
SLANG caff

cage *n*
aviary, coop, hutch, enclosure, pen,
pound, lock-up, corral, grate, corf, tumbler, mew; *Scot*
cavie, keavie

caged *adj*
encaged, cooped up, shut up, confined, restrained, fenced
in, imprisoned, impounded, locked up, mewed
OLD encaged
FORMAL incarcerated
⊟ released, let out, free

cagey *adj*
careful, chary, cautious, discreet, guarded, non-committal,
secretive, shrewd, wary, wily
FORMAL circumspect

COLLOQ. playing your cards close to your chest
☒ frank, indiscreet, open

cahoots
■ **in cahoots**
colluding, in collusion, in league, in alliance, collaborating, conspiring
COLLOQ. hand in glove

cajole v
coax, persuade, get round, wheedle, flatter, blandish, blarney, tempt, lure, seduce, entice, beguile, mislead, dupe, wile, soothe, humbug, diddle; *Scot* cuittle, whilly, whillywha
OLD beflum
FORMAL inveigle
COLLOQ. sweet-talk, butter up, soft-soap, work yourself, chat up
SLANG moody
☒ bully, force, compel

cajolery n
cajolement, coaxing, persuasion, wheedling, flattery, blarney, enticement, inducement(s), beguilement, misleading, duping, wiles; *Scot* whillywha
FORMAL blandishments, inveiglement, inveigling
COLLOQ. sweet talk, soft soap
☒ bullying, force, compulsion

cake n, v
♦ n
1 *tea and cakes*
gateau, fancy, pastry, bun, pie, tart, flan
2 LUMP, mass, bar, slab, block, tablet, cube, chunk, loaf
♦ v
coat, cover, encrust, plaster, dry, harden, solidify, consolidate, coagulate, congeal, thicken

PROVERBS
You can't have your cake and eat it

Kinds of cake and pastry include:

angel food cake	custard slice	plum-cake
apple pie	Danish pastry	pound cake
Bakewell tart	date and walnut	profiterole
baklava	cake	queen cake
banana cake	death by	rock cake
banana-nut cake	chocolate cake	roulade
Banbury cake	doughnut	Sachertorte
bannock	drop scone	saffron cake
banoffee pie	Dundee cake	Sally Lunn
Battenburg cake	Eccles cake	sandwich cake
birthday cake	éclair	savarin
black bun	fairy cake	scone
Black Forest	flan	*N Am* shoofly pie
gateau	fruitcake	simnel cake
brownie	gateau	sponge cake
N Am bundt cake	Genoa cake	stollen
cannoli	gingerbread	strawberry short-
carrot cake	hot cross bun	cake
cheesecake	lady's finger	strudel
Chelsea bun	*Aust* lamington	sultana cake
cherry pie	lardy cake	Swiss roll
chocolate cake	lemon drizzle	tarte tatin
Christmas cake	cake	teacake
churro	Madeira cake	tipsy cake
coffee cake	madeleine	turnover
cream cake	marble cake	upside-down cake
cream horn	meringue	Victoria sponge
cream puff	mince pie	waffle
crêpe	muffin	wedding cake
crumpet	pancake	yeast cake
cup cake	panettone	Yule log

See also **dessert**.

calamitous adj
disastrous, catastrophic, ruinous, devastating, deadly, fatal, cataclysmic, dire, ghastly, dreadful, wretched, tragic, woeful, grievous
☒ good, fortunate, happy

calamity n
disaster, catastrophe, mishap, misadventure, mischance, misfortune, blow, adversity, scourge, reverse, trial, tribulation, affliction, distress, tragedy, ruin, downfall, trouble, woes, sword of Damocles
OLD ruth
☒ blessing, godsend

calculate v
1 WORK OUT, compute, count, enumerate, reckon (up), figure, determine, make, derive, measure, weigh, assess, rate, value, estimate, gauge; *N Am* work
OLD cast, cipher
2 *a plan calculated to make him jealous*
judge, consider, plan, intend, aim, design

SYNONYM NUANCES
sense 1
Work out is a general, widely used term to suggest going through something systematically to reach a solution: *how is holiday pay worked out?*; whereas **compute**, **count** and **enumerate** would all be used for the involvement of figures: *the index is computed from actual prices*. **Reckon** is more generally used to imply an addition based on estimates: *he reckoned he had spent £30,000*; while the less common **reckon up** suggests a more accurate totalling. The words **figure** and **make** also suggest a less exact calculation and that there might be an element of inaccuracy in the conclusions: *I make it ten pounds; what do you make it?*
Determine and **derive**, however, appropriately describe a more methodical approach and conclusions reached from what is already known: *interest rates are to be politically determined*; *he derived that this must indeed be the murder weapon*. **Rate**, **value**, **estimate**, **assess** and **gauge** share the idea of a calculation involving prediction and guesswork: *the significance of the market can be gauged from these tables*.

calculated adj
considered, deliberate, intended, intentional, planned, measured, well-judged, tactical, purposeful, wilful, premeditated
FORMAL purposed
☒ unintended, unplanned

calculating adj
crafty, cunning, sly, devious, scheming, designing, contriving, manipulative, sharp, shrewd, wily, Machiavellian
☒ artless, naive

calculation n
sum, computation, working-out, answer, result, arithmetic, figurework, reckoning, figuring, estimate, estimation, forecast, assessment, judgement, planning, deliberation
TECHNICAL mensuration, alligation, evolution, logistic

calibre n
1 DIAMETER, bore, gauge, size, measure
2 *candidates of the right calibre*
talent, gifts, strength, worth, merit, quality, character, ability, capacity, faculty, league, excellence, competence, endowments, stature, distinction

call v, n
♦ v
1 NAME, christen, baptize, title, entitle, dub, style, term, label, brand, describe as, designate, rename
FORMAL denominate
2 SHOUT, yell, exclaim, cry (out), scream, shriek, bellow, roar, bawl

3 TELEPHONE, phone (up), ring (up), contact,
give someone a ring
COLLOQ. buzz, give someone a buzz,
give someone a tinkle
4 *call a doctor*
ask to come in/round, ask for, send for, contact, order
FORMAL summon
5 *call to collect the money*
call in/round, drop in, pay a visit, stop by, come by
COLLOQ. pop in
6 *call a meeting*
invite, bid, assemble
FORMAL convene, summon
♦ *n*
1 CRY, exclamation, shout, yell, scream, shriek
2 VISIT, ring, summons, invitation
3 *a telephone call*
ring
COLLOQ. buzz, tinkle, bell
4 *calls for his resignation*
APPEAL, request, plea, order, command, claim,
announcement, signal
5 *there's no call for it*
demand, market, need, occasion, cause, excuse,
justification, reason, grounds, right, run
■ **call for**
1 FETCH, collect, pick up, go for
2 DEMAND, require, need, make necessary,
necessitate, justify, involve, occasion, suggest,
press for, push for
FORMAL entail, warrant
■ **call off**
cancel, drop, abandon, discontinue, break off,
withdraw
FORMAL rescind, revoke
COLLOQ. scrub, shelve
■ **call on**
1 *call on a friend*
pay someone a (short) visit, visit, look in on,
go and see
2 *call on the government to resign*
appeal, appeal to, ask, bid, demand, urge, request, plead,
press for
FORMAL summon, supplicate, entreat
■ **call up**
1 TELEPHONE, phone (up), ring (up), contact,
give someone a ring
COLLOQ. buzz, give someone a buzz,
give someone a tinkle
2 ENLIST, sign up, recruit, conscript, take on
3 CHOOSE, select, pick, settle on, invite
■ **on call**
ready, on standby, standing by, on duty

call girl *n*
prostitute, whore, harlot, loose woman, woman of the
streets, street-walker, lady of the night
COLLOQ. hooker, hustler
SLANG tart

calling *n*
mission, vocation, career, profession,
occupation, job, trade, business, line, line of
business/work, work, employment, field, province,
pursuit, métier

callous *adj*
heartless, hard-hearted, cold, cold-hearted,
cold-blooded, harsh, tough, indifferent, uncaring,
unsympathetic, unfeeling, insensitive,
hardened, case-hardened, hard-bitten, hard as nails,
stony, stony-hearted, iron-headed, thick-skinned, horny,
seared
FORMAL obdurate, indurate, insensate, insensible
COLLOQ. hard-boiled
See Synonym nuances panel at **cold**.
⊟ kind, caring, sympathetic, sensitive

callously *adv*
heartlessly, hard-heartedly, coldly, cold-bloodedly, harshly,
unsympathetically, unfeelingly, insensitively
⊟ sympathetically, sensitively
callow *adj*
inexperienced, immature, naive, innocent, guileless,
juvenile, puerile, raw, fledgling, uninitiated,
unsophisticated, unfledged, untried
FORMAL jejune
COLLOQ. green, rookie
⊟ experienced
calm *adj, v, n*
♦ *adj*
1 COMPOSED, self-possessed, self-controlled, collected,
quiet, serene, cool, cool-headed, dispassionate,
unemotional, impassive, unmoved, placid, sedate, centred,
poised, imperturbable, nerveless, phlegmatic, unexcitable,
unpassionate, relaxed, unexcited, unruffled, unflustered,
unperturbed, undisturbed, untroubled, unapprehensive,
steady, even, on an even keel
FORMAL reposed
COLLOQ. laid-back, unflappable, cool as a cucumber; *N
Am* supercool
2 *calm waters/weather*
smooth, still, waveless, windless, unclouded, mild,
tranquil, serene, peaceful, quiet, undisturbed, restful,
unclouded; *Scot* lown
⊟ **1** excitable, worried, anxious, upset **2** rough, wild,
windy, stormy
♦ *v*
compose, soothe, relax, sedate, tranquillize,
de-stress, hush, lull, quieten, still, settle (down), allay,
pacify, ease
FORMAL mollify, placate, appease, assuage, smooth,
becalm, sleek
COLLOQ. cool down, simmer down, keep your head,
lighten up, pour oil on troubled waters
⊟ excite, worry, upset
♦ *n*
calmness, stillness, tranquillity, restfulness, composure,
contentment, serenity, equanimity, peacefulness, peace,
quiet, hush, lull, impassiveness, impassivity, presence of
mind
FORMAL quietude, repose, placidity, sangfroid,
ataraxia
COLLOQ. unflappability, cool
⊟ storminess, restlessness, trouble, excitement

> **QUOTATIONS**
> We are as calm in our delight / As is the crescent moon
> so bright / Among the scattered stars
> WILLIAM WORDSWORTH, 'Peter Bell'

> **SYNONYM NUANCES**
>
> *adjective sense 1*
> **Composed** and **collected** may be used quite widely of
> someone who is in control of their emotions, while
> **quiet** and, especially, **serene** and **sedate** go further by
> suggesting an inner peace. **Cool, unemotional,
> impassive** and **unmoved**, on the other hand, more
> accurately describe someone completely unaffected by
> emotion in a given circumstance, perhaps with the
> implication that it is an unnatural reaction;
> **dispassionate** further suggests a consequent lack of
> prejudice: *his admirable dispassionate analysis of the
> issues.*
> **Unexcitable, unpassionate, imperturbable** and
> **nerveless**, however, are stronger terms to use,
> suggesting that someone is never likely to be upset or
> anxious. The term **phlegmatic** may be used
> appropriately of resignation or a lack of reaction: *he is
> phlegmatic enough to accept his lot.* **Steady** and **even**
> have the positive connotation of a calmness that is
> constant and dependable: *his steady honesty.*

calmly *adv*
steadily, on an even keel,
unemotionally, phlegmatically, dispassionately,
impassively

calumny *n*
slander, abuse, attack, backbiting, defamation,
insult, libel, lying, misrepresentation, mud pie
FORMAL aspersion, denigration, obloquy, revilement,
derogation, detraction,
disparagement, vilification, vituperation, smear
SLANG slagging-off

camaraderie *n*
brotherhood, brotherliness, companionship,
comradeship, *esprit de corps*, fellowship, friendship,
fraternization, good fellowship, sociability, closeness,
affinity, intimacy, togetherness

camera

Types of camera include:

advanced photo	film	single-lens reflex
system (APS)	folding reflex	(SLR)
antishake	half-plate	sliding box
automatic	Instamatic®	sound
bellows	large-format	Steadicam®
binocular	LCD monitor	still
box Brownie®	miniature	stereo
camcorder	subminiature	Super 8®
camera obscura	panoramic	surveillance
cine	pinhole	twin-lens reflex
cinematographic	plate	(TLR)
compact	quarter-plate	TV
daguerreotype	point-and-press	video
digicam	Polaroid®	view
digital	press	Webcam
disc	reflex	wet-plate
disposable	security	
dry-plate	self timer	

See also **photographic**.

Parts of a camera include:

accessory shoe	focus control/	pentaprism
AF lenses	setting	program card
aperture	focusing hood	program reset
aperture setting	focusing ring	button
control	frame counter	rangefinder win-
autofocus (AF)	function adjust-	dow
autofocus sensor	ment button	reflex viewer
automatic focusing	function selector	registration pin
system	key	release button
battery chamber	hot shoe	rewind handle/
blind	iris diaphragm	crank
cable release	LCD panel	self timer
card door	leaf shutter	sensor
card on/off key	LED indicator	shutter
card window	lens	shutter release
compact lens	lens cap	shutter speed
compound lens	lens release	control
data panel/display	light control	shutter/film speed
diaphragm	long-focus lens	indicator
docking port	magazine	spool
exposure meter	medium focal-	spool knob
exposure mode	length lens	take-up reel/spool
button	memory	telephoto lens
film advance/	menu button	USB port
transport	meter cell	viewfinder
film gate	microphone	viewfinder eye-
film holder	mirror	piece
fisheye lens	mirror lens	viewing lens
flash contact	mirror shutter	wide-angle lens
flash setting	mode dial/switch	zoom lens
focal plane shutter	object lens	

camouflage *n, v*
♦ *n*
disguise, guise, masquerade, mask, cloak, screen, blind,
front, cover, cover-up, protective colouring, concealment,
deception, façade, maskirovka
♦ *v*
disguise, mask, cloak, veil, screen, cover, cover up,
conceal, hide, obscure
E3 uncover, reveal

camp[1] *n, v*
♦ *n*
1 *a Scout camp*
campsite, camping-site, camping-ground, encampment,
tents, bivouac
OLD leaguer
2 *the union camp*
side, faction, group, party, section, set, crowd, caucus,
clique
♦ *v*
pitch tents, pitch camp, set up camp, sleep outdoors,
bivouac, tent
OLD gypsy, outlie
FORMAL encamp
COLLOQ. rough it
E3 break camp, strike camp, decamp, rise

camp[2] *adj*
camp behaviour
affected, artificial, campy, exaggerated, mannered,
ostentatious, posturing, theatrical, effeminate,
homosexual
COLLOQ. over the top, poncy
SLANG (*offensive*) queer, queeny

campaign *n, v*
♦ *n*
crusade, movement, promotion, drive, push, course of
action, strategy, offensive, attack, battle, expedition,
operation, war
OLD journey
COLLOQ. blitz
♦ *v*
crusade, promote, push, drive, advocate, lobby, canvass,
work, fight, strive, struggle, battle, attack

campaigner *n*
crusader, advocate, champion, promoter, activist,
enthusiast, reformer, zealot, fighter

camp-follower *n*
hanger-on, henchman, lackey, toady

can *n*
tin, container, receptacle, canister, jar, jerrycan, pail

canal *n*
1 *the Grand Union canal*
waterway, watercourse, navigation, channel, ditch, trench,
moat, foss, zanja
2 *the alimentary canal*
tube, channel, passage, duct

cancel *v*
1 *cancel a concert*
call off, abort, abandon, drop, postpone
COLLOQ. scrap, scrub, shelve, axe, wash out,
wipe, kill
2 *cancel a reservation/debt*
abolish, annul, quash, stop, break off, repeal,
delete, erase, obliterate, undo, write off, cross
out, red-line, eliminate, dissolve, override, strike out,
withdraw, declare off
TECHNICAL adeem
FORMAL discontinue, countermand, rescind, revoke, nullify,
invalidate, retract, abrogate, vitiate
SLANG nix
■ **cancel out**
offset, compensate, make up for, redeem, counterbalance,
balance, neutralize, counteract, nullify

cancellation *n*
calling-off, abandoning, abandonment, abolition, dropping, stopping, deletion, elimination, neutralization, quashing, repeal
FORMAL annulment, revocation, invalidation, nullifying
COLLOQ. shelving, scrubbing

cancer *n*
1 TUMOUR, growth, malignancy, malignant growth
TECHNICAL carcinoma
COLLOQ. Big C
2 EVIL, blight, canker, pestilence, sickness, disease, plague, scourge, corruption, rot

candelabrum *n*
candlestick, menorah, lampadary

candid *adj*
frank, open, truthful, honest, sincere, forthright, straightforward, ingenuous, guileless, simple, plain, plain-spoken, clear, unequivocal, blunt, outspoken, round, liberal, heart-to-heart
Ⅎ guarded, evasive, devious

QUOTATIONS
Laugh where we must, be candid when we can
ALEXANDER POPE, *An Essay on Man*

candidate *n*
1 *candidates for a job*
applicant, aspirant, contender, contestant, competitor, seeker, runner, possibility, nominee
2 *candidates for an exam*
entrant

candidly *adv*
frankly, openly, truthfully, honestly, sincerely, forthrightly, straightforwardly, ingenuously, guilelessly, simply, plainly, clearly, unequivocally, bluntly, outspokenly, roundly, liberally
Ⅎ guardedly, evasively

candle *n*
taper, tallow candle, cerge, wax light, torch, dip, amandine, bougie, votive candle, shammes, tealight

candour *n*
frankness, openness, truthfulness, honesty, plain-dealing, sincerity, forthrightness, straightforwardness, directness, brusqueness, ingenuousness, guilelessness, naivety, artlessness, simplicity, plainness, unequivocalness, bluntness, outspokenness, liberality, *franchise*
Ⅎ guardedness, evasiveness, deviousness

candy *n*
sweets, confectionery, chocolates, toffees

cane *n*
stick, staff, crook, rod, walking-stick, switch, swish, tickler, alpenstock, rattan, supplejack, whangee, swagger-stick
OLD jambee

canker *n*
1 EVIL, blight, cancer, pestilence, sickness, disease, plague, scourge, bane, corrosion, corruption, rot
2 *canker in an animal's ear*
sore, ulcer, boil, infection, lesion

cannabis *n*
marijuana, hemp, hashish, bhang
COLLOQ. dope, ganja, grass, hash, pot, spliff, bifter, puff, tea, kef, wacky baccy
SLANG blow, weed, skunk, punk, leaf

cannibal *n*
people-eater, man-eater
TECHNICAL anthropophagite
OLD (*Shakesp*) anthropophaginian

cannibalism *n*
man-eating, people-eating
TECHNICAL anthropophagy, endophagy, exophagy

cannibalistic *adj*
man-eating, people-eating, Thyestean
TECHNICAL anthropophagous, endophagous, exophagous

cannily *adv*
shrewdly, acutely, sharply, astutely, cleverly, knowingly, skilfully, subtly

cannon *n*
gun, mortar, field gun, howitzer, artillery, battery, ordnance, falcon
OLD basilisk, bombard, carronade, chamber, culverin, demi-culverin, monkey, murderer, Quaker, saker, serpentine, stern-chaser, zumbooruk
COLLOQ. big gun
OLD SLANG barker

❗ cannon or **canon**?
A *cannon* is a large gun. A *canon* is a Christian priest who helps to run the work of a cathedral, and also a general rule or belief: *the canons of literary taste*.

cannonade *n*
barrage, bombardment, shelling, volley, broadside, pounding, salvo

canny *adj*
shrewd, acute, sharp, astute, careful, cautious, prudent, clever, knowing, skilful, sly, subtle, wise, worldly-wise, artful; *Scot* pawky, wice
FORMAL circumspect, perspicacious, judicious, sagacious
COLLOQ. no flies on someone
Ⅎ foolish, imprudent

canoe *n*
dugout, kayak, monoxylon, montaria, piragua, woodskin

canon *n*
1 *a cathedral canon*
prebendary, clergyman, vicar, priest, minister, reverend, residentiary, vice-dean
2 *the canons of literary taste*
principle, rule, regulation, statute, criterion, standard, law, precept, dictate, yardstick, line, brocard
OLD square, squire

❗ canon or **cannon**?
See panel at **cannon**.

canonical *adj*
authorized, recognized, accepted, sanctioned, approved, authoritative, orthodox, regular

canonize *v*
beatify, saint, declare to be a saint, sanctify, bless
OLD besaint

canopy *n*
awning, cover, covering, shade, shelter, sunshade, umbrella, tester, tilt, baldachin, tabernacle, dais, chuppah, cloth of state, marquise
OLD estate, state, pavilion, hearse

cant *n*
1 *insincere cant*
insincerity, hypocrisy, pretentiousness, sanctimoniousness, snivel, snuffle
2 *underworld cant*
argot, jargon, lingo, slang, vernacular, rogues'/thieves' Latin

cantankerous *adj*
irritable, irascible, grumpy, crusty, testy, bad-tempered, quick-tempered, ill-humoured, cross, peevish, difficult, perverse, contrary, quarrelsome; *Scot & Irish* carnaptious; *N Am* ornery
COLLOQ. crabbed, crabby, crotchety, grouchy
Ⅎ good-natured, pleasant, easy-going

canteen *n*
cafeteria, restaurant, snackbar, café, buffet, refectory, commissary

canter *n, v*
♦ *n*
amble, trot, jog, jogtrot, lope, gallop, run, tittup; *S Afr* tripple
OLD false gallop

♦ v
amble, trot, jog, jogtrot, lope, gallop, run;
S Afr tripple

canvass v
1 ELECTIONEER, agitate, campaign, solicit votes,
ask for votes, seek votes, poll, drum up
support
2 EXAMINE, inspect, find out, scrutinize, study, scan,
investigate, explore, survey, examine, inquire into, analyse,
sift, evaluate, poll, discuss, debate

canyon n
gorge, ravine, gully, valley, chasm, abyss;
N Am cañada

cap n, v
♦ n
1 HAT, bonnet; Scot bunnet
See panel at **hat**.
2 LID, top, cover, stopper, plug, bung, ferrule
♦ v
1 cap someone's story
exceed, excel, surpass, transcend, better, beat, outdo,
outstrip, outshine, eclipse, go one better than
2 mountains capped with snow
crown, top, cover, coat
3 cap council spending
limit, restrict, curb, restrain, control

> **PROVERBS**
> If the cap fits, wear it

capability n
ability, capacity, faculty, power, potential, means, facility,
competence, qualification, skill, skilfulness,
accomplishment, proficiency, talent, aptitude, efficiency
E3 inability, incompetence

> 🛇 **capability** or **ability**?
> See panel at **ability**.

capable adj
1 a capable person
able, competent, efficient, qualified, experienced,
accomplished, skilful, adept, proficient, gifted, talented,
masterly, clever, intelligent, smart, businesslike
See Synonym nuances panel at **able**.
2 capable of winning
fitted, suited, apt to, liable to, disposed to, inclined to,
tending to, having the inclination/tendency to, allowing,
needing
E3 1 incompetent, useless **2** incapable

capably adv
competently, ably, efficiently, skilfully, proficiently,
cleverly, intelligently, adeptly
E3 incompetently

capacious adj
ample, big, vast, wide, broad, huge, large, roomy, sizable,
spacious, comfortable, comprehensive, expansive,
extensive, generous, liberal, substantial, elephantine
OLD (Shakesp) womby
FORMAL commodious, voluminous
E3 cramped, small

capacity n
1 CAPABILITY, ability, faculty, power, potential, competence,
proficiency, efficiency, skill, gift, talent, genius, cleverness,
intelligence, aptitude, resources, readiness
2 VOLUME, space, room, size, dimensions, proportions,
magnitude, extent, largeness, compass, range, scope
3 in her capacity as president
role, function, position, office, post, appointment, job

cape¹ n
wear a cape
cloak, shawl, wrap, mantle, robe, poncho, pelisse,
pelerine, coat

cape² n
the Cape of Good Hope
headland, head, promontory, point, ness, neck, tongue,
peninsula

caper v, n
♦ v
cavort, frisk, frolic, gambol, bounce, bound, dance, hop,
jump, leap, romp, skip, spring
♦ n
antic, escapade, high jinks, jest, lark, mischief, prank,
stunt, jape, affair, business
COLLOQ. N Am dido

capital n, adj
♦ n
1 need capital to expand the business
funds, finance, principal, money, cash, savings,
investment(s), wealth, means, wherewithal, resources,
assets, liquid assets, property, stock, reserves
2 the capital of France
main city, most important city, administrative centre, seat
of government
3 write in capitals
block letter, block capital, capital letter,
upper-case letter
FORMAL majuscule, uncial
♦ adj
1 PRINCIPAL, important, leading, primary, prime, main,
major, cardinal, central, chief, first, foremost
2 a capital offence
serious, punishable by death
E3 1 minor, unimportant **2** minor

capitalism n
private enterprise, free enterprise, private ownership,
laissez-faire

> **QUOTATIONS**
> Capitalism was doomed ethically before it was doomed
> economically, a long time ago
> ALEKSANDR SOLZHENITSYN, Cancer Ward

capitalist n
banker, financier, investor, moneyman, tycoon, magnate,
mogul, person of means, plutocrat
OLD moneyer
COLLOQ. moneybags, money-spinner
SLANG fat cat

capitalize
■ capitalize on
take advantage of, profit from, make the most of, exploit
COLLOQ. cash in on

capitulate v
surrender, yield, give in, give up, relent, back down,
submit, succumb
COLLOQ. throw in the towel/sponge

capitulation n
surrender, yielding, giving-in, giving-up, relenting, backing-
down, submission, succumbing

caprice n
whim, fad, fancy, impulse, whimsy, fantasy, notion, quirk,
vagary, vapour, fickleness, fitfulness, inconstancy, humour,
freak
OLD megrim, spleen

capricious adj
changeable, inconstant, mercurial, erratic, arbitrary,
wayward, fickle, uncertain, unpredictable, variable, fitful,
petulant, perverse, fanciful, fantastic, whimsical, freakish,
impulsive, odd, queer, quirky; Scot capernoity, kittle
OLD humorous, wanton
E3 sensible, steady

capsize v
overturn, turn over, turn turtle, invert, keel over, tip over,
roll over, upset, purl; dialect whemmle

capsule n
1 *a capsule of medicine*
pill, tablet, caplet, lozenge, receptacle, container
2 *a seed capsule*
shell, sheath, pod
3 *a space capsule*
craft, module, probe

captain n, v
♦ *n*
officer, commander, master, skipper, pilot, head, chief, leader, commodore, shipmaster, master-mariner, patron, patroon, old man, cid
OLD (*Spenser*) capitayn; ritt-master, protospatharius
COLLOQ. boss
SLANG owner
♦ *v*
lead, command, skipper, control, direct, manage, supervise, be in charge of

caption n
heading, note, title, legend, wording, inscription, underline

captious adj
carping, critical, quibbling, nit-picking, hypercritical, niggling, hair-splitting, peevish

captivate v
charm, enchant, bewitch, beguile, fascinate, delight, enthral, hypnotize, mesmerize, lure, allure, seduce, win, get, attract, enamour, infatuate, enrapture, take by storm, dazzle
☒ repel, disgust, appal

captivating adj
attractive, charming, fascinating, beautiful, enchanting, bewitching, beguiling, delightful, catching, taking, enthralling, alluring, seductive, winsome, dazzling
☒ ugly, unattractive

captive n, adj
♦ *n*
prisoner, hostage, slave, detainee, internee, convict, jailbird
♦ *adj*
imprisoned, caged, confined, restricted, secure, locked up/away, shut up, interned, detained, held in custody, restrained, enchained, enslaved, ensnared, in bondage, subject
OLD (*Spenser*) caitive
FORMAL incarcerated
☒ free, liberated

captivity n
custody, detention, imprisonment, internment, confinement, restraint, constraint, bondage, duress, slavery, enslavement, exile
OLD endurance
FORMAL incarceration, servitude
☒ freedom, liberation

captor n
guard, custodian, warder, keeper, jailor, incarcerator

capture v, n
♦ *v*
1 *capture a prisoner*
catch, trap, entrap, hunt down, snare, ensnare, net, land, occupy, take, take possession of, seize, arrest, apprehend, imprison, take prisoner, recapture, pick up, carry, run down, rush, secure, win, mop up
COLLOQ. nab, collar, nick, cop
SLANG snaffle, snabble
2 *capture a mood*
encapsulate, represent, record, express, reproduce, embrace
♦ *n*
catching, trapping, taking, taking captive, taking prisoner, seizure, arrest, imprisonment
COLLOQ. nabbing, collaring, nicking

SYNONYM NUANCES

verb sense 1
Trap and **entrap** contain a suggestion that a plan or even trickery has been involved in capture; **snare** and **ensnare** are similar, but with the added notion of getting caught up in something restrictive: *they were snared in a police sting*; *they became ensnared in the rush-hour traffic*. The word **net** has literal associations: *netted fish*; along with **land**, it is also often used in the context of a total taken, or getting something worthwhile despite competition: *the raid netted him £500 million*; *he landed a part in the musical*.

The terms **occupy**, **take** and **seize** are appropriate when an element of force has been used; **rush** would suggest greater force and speed.

The term **pick up** has an element of casualness about it: *the railways picked up some custom from the bus strike*. **Hunt down** and **run down**, however, would be used when capture has involved a lengthy pursuit or an exhaustive chase.

The term **secure** implies that possession is assured: *the team secured victory early in the game*, whereas **win** is usually used to suggest that something has been gained against the odds or in competition: *human rights can be won*.

---

car n
automobile, motor car, motor vehicle, motor, vehicle
OLD horseless carriage

Types of car include:

all-roader	gas-sipper	panda car
banger	hatchback	patrol car
Beetle®	high-occupancy	Range Rover®
bubble-car	vehicle (HOV)	saloon
buggy	hybrid	*N Am & Aust*
cab	jalopy	sedan
cabriolet	jeep	shooting brake
convertible	Land Rover®	sports car
coupé	*colloq.* limo	sports-utility vehi-
crossover-utility	limousine	cle (SUV)
vehicle (CUV)	Mini®	*N Am, Aust & NZ*
electric car	minivan	station wagon
estate	multi-purpose	supercar
fastback	vehicle (or MPV	taxi
four-wheel drive	or people carrier)	veteran car
gas-guzzler	off-roader	vintage car

See also **motor vehicle**.

---

carafe n
bottle, decanter, flagon, flask, jug, pitcher

caravan n
1 MOBILE HOME, van, camper van, Dormobile®; *N Am* trailer, motor home, recreational vehicle, RV, Winnebago®
2 *a caravan of traders crossing the desert*
convoy, line, group, train, cafila

carbuncle n
boil, inflammation, bunion, lump, bump, pimple, sore, blister, anthrax

carcase n
1 *the carcase of an animal*
body, dead body, corpse, cadaver, remains
2 *the carcase of a building*
shell, structure, framework, hulk, skeleton

card
■ **on the cards**
likely, probable, possible, being a strong possibility, looking like, looking as if
COLLOQ. the chances are

cardinal *adj*
chief, main, principal, fundamental, basic, greatest, highest, important, key, leading, paramount, pre-eminent, primary, prime, central, essential, first, foremost, capital

care *n, v*
♦ *n*
1 *handle with care*
carefulness, caution, prudence, forethought, watchfulness, vigilance, pains, meticulousness, accuracy, consideration
OLD attendance
FORMAL circumspection
2 *children need care*
looking-after, concern, attention, tending, minding, protection, watching-over, heed, regard, consideration, interest
3 *in their care*
keeping, safekeeping, custody, guardianship, protection, ward, charge, responsibility, control, supervision, tutelage
4 WORRY, anxiety, stress, strain, pressure, responsibility, burden, concern, trouble, distress, affliction, fear, disquiet
FORMAL tribulation, vexation
COLLOQ. hang-up
E∃ **1** carelessness, recklessness **2** carelessness, thoughtlessness, inattention, neglect
♦ *v*
worry, mind, bother, be concerned, be interested
COLLOQ. give a damn
E∃ neglect, ignore, be indifferent; *slang* not give a hoot/hang/damn/toss, not give a monkey's, not give a tinker's cuss/brass farthing
■ **care for**
1 LOOK AFTER, take care of, nurse, tend, mind, watch over, protect, provide for, minister to, attend, maintain
2 BE FOND OF, feel affection for, love, be in love with, be keen on, be close to, enjoy, delight in, cherish
3 *Would you care for a cup of tea?*
like, want, desire

career *n, v*
♦ *n*
vocation, calling, life-work, life, occupation, pursuit, profession, trade, job, employment, métier, livelihood
♦ *v*
rush, dash, tear, hurtle, race, run, gallop, speed, shoot, bolt, whang

carefree *adj*
unworried, untroubled, unconcerned, easy-going, blithe, breezy, happy-go-lucky, cheery, light-hearted, cheerful, happy, halcyon, rollicking, fancy-free, thoughtless, irresponsible, debonair
FORMAL insouciant, nonchalant
COLLOQ. laid-back
E∃ worried, anxious, troubled, distressed, despondent

careful *adj*
1 CAUTIOUS, aware, wary, chary, vigilant, watchful, alert, attentive, mindful, heedful, prudent, discreet, tactful, guarded, softly-softly
OLD (*Spenser*) heedy
FORMAL circumspect, judicious
2 METICULOUS, painstaking, conscientious, diligent, assiduous, scrupulous, fastidious, rigorous, thorough, detailed, showing great attention to detail, close, deliberate, methodical, systematic, particular, accurate, precise, thoughtful; *dialect* eyeful
FORMAL punctilious, solicitous
3 *careful with money*
prudent, thrifty, economical, sensible, wise, penny-wise, frugal, sparing, mean, miserly, niggardly, close-fisted, close-handed, fast-handed
FORMAL parsimonious
COLLOQ. tight, tight-fisted, hard-fisted, stingy, penny-pinching
E∃ **1** careless, inattentive, thoughtless, reckless **2** careless **3** extravagant, wasteful

---

SYNONYM NUANCES

sense 2
Many of the synonyms are approving in tone.
Meticulous is a fairly positive term to describe an extreme attention to detail; **painstaking** is similar in meaning but perhaps a little more neutral in tone: *painstaking precision*. The terms **conscientious**, **diligent**, **assiduous** and **scrupulous** all describe thoroughness, often where it arises from a sense of duty, and again would suggest a favourable view: *assiduous planning brings results*. **Fastidious**, **rigorous** and **thorough** also describe an exacting application, but more neutrally: *you must fold it with fastidious care*.

  Detailed and **close** have the emphasis on taking note of minutiae: *detailed analysis of the facts*. To emphasize that something is carried out in a rational sequence you might prefer to use **deliberate**, **methodical** and **systematic**: *you should record the findings on a more methodical basis*. **Particular** has connotations of fussiness, but **precise** and **accurate** are more suggestive of a desirable level of correctness: *precise in detail*.

  To use **thoughtful** would shift the emphasis back to attentiveness in practice, rather than the accuracy of the results: *a clear, thoughtful exploration of the theory*.

carefully *adv*
1 METICULOUSLY, painstakingly, conscientiously, diligently, assiduously, scrupulously, fastidiously, rigorously, thoroughly, with great attention to detail, closely, deliberately, methodically, systematically, accurately, precisely, thoughtfully
FORMAL punctilious, solicitous
2 CAUTIOUSLY, warily, charily, vigilantly, watchfully, attentively, mindfully, heedfully, prudently, discreetly, tactfully, guardedly
FORMAL circumspectly, judiciously
E∃ **1** carelessly **2** carelessly, thoughtlessly, recklessly

careless *adj*
1 UNTHINKING, thoughtless, inattentive, inconsiderate, uncaring, unconcerned, heedless, incautious, unmindful, forgetful, remiss, negligent, absent-minded, irresponsible, reckless, indiscreet, tactless, unguarded, regardless; *Scot* untenty
OLD secure
COLLOQ. asleep at the wheel
2 *careless work*
inaccurate, messy, untidy, disorganized, disorderly, neglectful, slack, lax, slipshod, slapdash, hasty, perfunctory, cursory, superficial, offhand, casual, shoddy
COLLOQ. sloppy
3 *careless charm*
casual, easy-going, carefree, unworried, untroubled, simple, artless, breezy, light-hearted, cheerful, happy-go-lucky
FORMAL insouciant, nonchalant
COLLOQ. laid-back, happy as a sandboy; *N Am* happy as a clam
E∃ **1** thoughtful, careful **2** careful, accurate, meticulous

QUOTATIONS
To lose one parent, Mr Worthing, may be regarded as a misfortune; to lose both looks like carelessness
  OSCAR WILDE, *The Importance of Being Earnest*

SYNONYM NUANCES

sense 2
Inaccurate describes the introduction of error through carelessness, although it is not strongly critical; on the other hand, **messy** and **untidy**, along with **disorganized** and **disorderly**, are marked by disapproval. Other inherently critical terms are **slack**, **lax** and **slipshod**, which strongly suggest a lack of care and precision: *he was becoming slipshod in his editing*; whilst both

slapdash and **hasty** could be used of something that has been done too quickly: *the book is full of slapdash theories.* Less marked terms to use include **perfunctory** or **cursory**, which suggest that something has been completed with the minimum effort. **Superficial** similarly implies lack of depth or exertion, while **offhand** and **casual** also suggest something undertaken without due consideration: *an offhand reply.* More critical, however, is **shoddy**, which is very strongly marked by disapproval of something badly done: *we will not tolerate shoddy service.*

carelessly *adv*
1 *a carelessly planned project*
hastily, perfunctorily, cursorily, superficially, offhandedly, casually, shoddily
COLLOQ. sloppily
2 *he spoke carelessly*
unthinkingly, thoughtlessly, inattentively, inconsiderately, uncaringly, unconcernedly, heedlessly, incautiously, unmindfully, forgetfully, remissly, negligently, absent-mindedly, irresponsibly, recklessly, indiscreetly, tactlessly, unguardedly
F3 **1** careful, accurately, meticulously **2** thoughtfully, carefully

caress *v, n*
♦ *v*
stroke, pet, fondle, cuddle, hug, embrace, kiss, touch, rub, nuzzle, bill
COLLOQ. canoodle, grope; *N Am* lallygag
SLANG feel up, touch up
♦ *n*
stroke, touch, pat, fondle, cuddle, hug, embrace, kiss, petting, butterfly kiss, endearment
COLLOQ. slap and tickle

caretaker *n, adj*
♦ *n*
janitor, porter, watchman, keeper, custodian, curator, warden, superintendent, concierge, steward, ostiary, doorkeeper, verger, sexton, dvornik, shammes
♦ *adj*
acting, temporary, provisional, substitute, short-term, fill-in, stand-in, pro tem
F3 permanent

careworn *adj*
tired, weary, worn, worn-out, exhausted, fatigued, gaunt, haggard, anxious, worried
F3 lively, sprightly

cargo *n*
freight, load, payload, haul, lading, tonnage, shipment, consignment, contents, goods, merchandise, baggage

caricature *n, v*
♦ *n*
cartoon, parody, lampoon, burlesque, satire, mimicry, imitation, representation, distortion, travesty
COLLOQ. send-up, take-off
♦ *v*
parody, mock, ridicule, satirize, mimic, distort, exaggerate
COLLOQ. send up, take off

caring *adj*
kind, kind-hearted, good-natured, helpful, thoughtful, compassionate, sympathetic, warm, tender-hearted, tender, benevolent, friendly, loving, affectionate, devoted, fond, philanthropic, altruistic
F3 uncaring, inconsiderate

carnage *n*
bloodshed, bloodbath, butchery, slaughter, killing, murder, mass murder, massacre, genocide, ethnic cleansing, holocaust

carnal *adj*
sensual, sexual, erotic, fleshly, physical, human, natural, animal, bodily, impure, lascivious, lecherous, lewd, licentious, lustful
TECHNICAL belly
FORMAL corporeal, libidinous
F3 chaste, pure, spiritual

carnival *n*
festival, fiesta, gala, jamboree, fête, fair, holiday, jubilee, celebration, merrymaking, revelry, *Mardi Gras, Fasching*
SLANG *N Am* carny

carnivorous *adj*
meat-eating
TECHNICAL creophagous, zoophagous

carol *n*
Christmas song, noel, song, hymn, strain, wassail, chorus
OLD carrel

carouse *v*
make merry, revel, drink, drink freely, party, celebrate, quaff, roister, wassail, spree; *dialect* birl
FORMAL imbibe
SLANG booze

carousing *n*
celebrating, drinking, merrymaking, partying, compotation
OLD mallemaroking

carp *v*
complain, criticize, censure, reproach, find faults, nag, quibble, go on at; *Aust* have a shot at
OLD yerk, pinch
FORMAL ultracrepidate
COLLOQ. knock, nit-pick
F3 praise, compliment

carpenter *n*
woodworker, joiner, cabinet-maker; *Scot* wright
SLANG chips, chippy

carpet *n, v*
♦ *n*
1 *fit a new carpet*
floor-covering, covering, mat, rug, matting, Axminster, Aubusson, Wilton, Kidderminster, kali, kilim, Persian carpet, moquette, Bessarabian, Kirman, Brussels
2 *a carpet of leaves*
layer, blanket, covering, bed
♦ *v*
cover, spread, blanket, dress, clothe, coat, wrap, overlay, encase, cake

carping *n*
complaining, criticizing, fault-finding, nagging, quibbling
COLLOQ. nit-picking

carriage *n*
1 COACH, wagon, cab, car, vehicle, turnout, equipage, trap, buggy, hackney, stagecoach; *Scot* hurly-hacket, clatch; *vettura, voiture*
OLD diligent, dilly, job
2 POSTURE, bearing, air, manner, attitude, stance, presence, guise, behaviour, conduct, poise, set, tenue
OLD (*Shakesp & Spenser*) portance
FORMAL deportment, demeanour, mien, port
3 CARRYING, conveyance, transport, transportation, delivery, freight, truckage, postage, porterage

---

Types of carriage include:

barouche	chaise	ekka
berlin	chariot	four-in hand
britzka	clarence	gig
brougham	coupé	hansom
cabriolet	désobligeante	herdic
calash	dogcart	jump-seat
cariole	drag	landau
caroche	dray	phaeton
carryall	droshky	pillbox

post chaise	stanhope	victoria
ricksha	sulky	vis-à-vis
rockaway	surrey	wagonette
sociable	T-cart	
spider phaeton	tilbury	

carrier *n*
bearer, conveyor, delivery-person, roundsperson,
messenger, porter, runner, transmitter, transporter, vehicle,
vector; *dialect* tranter

carry *v*
1 BRING, convey, transport, haul, move,
transfer, relay, release, take, drive, fetch,
shift, conduct, pipe, deliver, hand over
COLLOQ. lug, cart, hump, tote
2 BEAR, shoulder, support, underpin, maintain,
hold (up), uphold, sustain, suffer, stand, take
someone's weight
3 *carry a disease*
transmit, pass on, be infected with
4 *the proposal was carried*
pass, vote for, vote in favour, accept, approve, adopt,
authorize, ratify, sanction
5 *she carries herself well*
bear, behave, hold, acquit, act
FORMAL comport
6 *drug-smuggling carries a risk*
bear, involve, have (as a consequence),
lead to, mean
FORMAL entail
7 *the newspaper carried the story*
cover, contain, display, show, present, communicate,
print, publish, release, broadcast
FORMAL disseminate
8 *carry several brands*
stock, keep in stock, sell, retail, have, have for sale
9 *the crime carries a year's imprisonment*
have, lead to, result in, present, show
10 *her voice carried far*
be heard, be audible, reach, travel
■ **carry off**
1 *carry a project off*
achieve, complete, succeed in
COLLOQ. crack
2 *carry off a prize*
win, gain, secure, pick up
COLLOQ. come away with, land, net
■ **carry on**
1 CONTINUE, proceed, last, endure, maintain, go on, keep
(on), keep up, persist, persevere, progress, return to,
resume, restart
2 *carry on a business*
operate, run, manage, conduct, engage in,
administer
3 *children carrying on*
misbehave, behave foolishly
COLLOQ. mess around, play up
4 *carrying on with a colleague at work*
have an affair, be involved
COLLOQ. play around
[≡] **1** stop, finish **3** behave (well)
■ **carry out**
do, perform, undertake, discharge, conduct,
execute, implement, fulfil, accomplish,
achieve, realize, bring off, put into
effect/operation/practice
FORMAL effect
COLLOQ. deliver (the goods)
■ **get carried away**
become excited, become overexcited,
lose your self-control
COLLOQ. lose it

carry-on *n*
fuss, bother, trouble, commotion, stir
COLLOQ. hassle, to-do, hoo-ha, flap, kerfuffle

cart *n, v*
♦ *n*
barrow, handcart, wheelbarrow, wagon, truck,
dray, float, cariole, gill, jill, hackery, pram, tumbrel;
dialect shandry; *Welsh* gambo; *N Am* gurney;
Aust furby
OLD car; *N Am* democrat
♦ *v*
move, convey, transport, haul, bear, carry,
transfer, shift; *dialect* jag, lead
COLLOQ. lug, hump, tote

carton *n*
box, packet, pack, case, container, package,
parcel, tub

cartoon *n*
1 *newspaper cartoons*
sketch, drawing, picture, bubble, balloon, caricature, strip
cartoon, parody, lampoon, burlesque
COLLOQ. send-up, take-off
2 *watch cartoons on TV*
comic strip, animation, animated film, *fumetto*

cartridge *n*
cassette, canister, cylinder, tube, container, case, capsule,
shell, torpedo, magazine, round, charge

carve *v*
1 *carve meat*
cut (up), slice, chop, hack, unlace, truncheon
OLD dismember, kerve
2 *carve stone*
sculpt, sculpture, shape, form, fashion, mould, hew, cut,
whittle, chisel, chip
OLD entail
3 *carve a design*
etch, engrave, write, incise, notch, indent
OLD sculp, insculp
■ **carve up**
divide, share (out), separate, partition, parcel out,
distribute, split (up)

carving *n*
bust, incision, sculpture, statue, statuette, model, cut,
knotwork
TECHNICAL dendroglyph, lithoglyph, petroglyph, mezzo-
relievo, tondo
Related adjective: glyptic

cascade *n, v*
♦ *n*
rush, gush, outpouring, flood, deluge, torrent, avalanche,
cataract, waterfall, fall, falls, fountain, chute, shower,
trickle
♦ *v*
rush, gush, surge, flood, overflow, spill, tumble, fall,
descend, shower, pour, plunge, pitch

case[1] *n*
1 OCCURRENCE, circumstances, context, state, condition,
position, situation, occasion, event, specimen, example,
instance, illustration, point
FORMAL contingency
2 LAWSUIT, suit, trial, proceedings, action, process, cause,
argument, dispute
3 *a doctor's case*
patient, invalid, victim, client
4 *a murder case*
crime, investigation, inquiry, incident, affair
5 *argue the case against the death penalty*
evidence, reasoning, argument, grounds, defence

case[2] *n*
1 CONTAINER, receptacle, holder, trunk, crate, box, carton,
casket, chest, cabinet, showcase, casing, canister,
cartridge, shell, capsule, sheath, cover, jacket, wrapper
2 SUITCASE, briefcase, vanity-case, bag, holdall,
portmanteau, valise, overnight bag, flight bag, hand
luggage, travel bag, attaché case, portfolio, trunk

cash *n, v*

♦ *n*

1 *pay by cash*

money, hard money, ready money, banknotes, notes, coins, change, legal tender, currency, hard currency, bullion

2 *have no cash for a holiday*

funds, resources, capital, finance, wherewithal

SLANG loot, readies, ready, megabucks, dough, dosh, bread, lolly, spondulicks, brass, gravy, greens, shekels, moolah, greenies, scratch, smash, stumpy; *Aust & NZ* Oscar

OLD SLANG blunt, rhino

See Synonym nuances panel at **money**.

♦ *v*

exchange, realize, liquidate, change, turn into cash, encash

cashier[1] *n*

a bank cashier

clerk, bank clerk, teller, treasurer, bursar, purser, banker, accountant, financial controller, checker

cashier[2] *v*

be cashiered from the army

discharge, dismiss, drum out, expel, break, discard, throw out, get rid of

COLLOQ. sack, give someone the boot, unfrock

casing *n*

cover, covering, wrapping, jacket, envelope, shell, sheath, sheathing, trunking, protection, housing, core

TECHNICAL cowling, binnacle

cask *n*

barrel, tun, keg, firkin, vat, tub, butt, casket, barrico, octave, pin, pipe, tierce, wood

OLD hogshead, kilderkin, leaguer, puncheon

casket *n*

1 *keep jewels in a casket*

box, case, chest, coffer, jewel-box, kist, pyxis, cassette

2 COFFIN, box, sarcophagus, shell; *Scot* kist

OLD larnax

SLANG *N Am* pine overcoat, wooden overcoat, wooden kimono

cast *v, n*

♦ *v*

1 THROW, hurl, lob, pitch, fling, toss, sling, heave, shy, launch, impel, drive

2 *cast light*

direct, project, shed, emit, give out, give off, radiate, diffuse, spread, scatter

3 *cast your eyes/a glance*

look (at), glimpse, glance, see, view, catch sight, turn, throw

4 *cast doubt/suspicion*

place, put, throw, put in jeopardy

COLLOQ. put a question mark over

5 *cast your vote*

vote, register, record, mark with a cross

6 MOULD, shape, form, model, fashion, found

♦ *n*

1 COMPANY, troupe, actors, players, performers, entertainers, characters, dramatis personae

2 CASTING, mould, shape, form, die, model, covering

■ **cast aside**

reject, discard, turn down, say no to

FORMAL dispense with

COLLOQ. get rid of

■ **cast down**

depress, discourage, dishearten, deject, sadden, crush, desolate

🔄 cheer up, encourage

caste *n*

class, social class, social standing, order, group, position, rank, station, status, grade, lineage, background, degree, estate, stratum, race

castigate *v*

criticize, reprimand, chasten, chastise, rebuke, scold, discipline, punish, correct, censure, chide, reprove, upbraid, berate

FORMAL admonish

COLLOQ. dress down, haul over the coals, rap on the knuckles, tear a strip off, give someone hell

castle *n*

stronghold, fort, fortress, fastness, citadel, keep, tower, château, palace, mansion, stately home, country house, *schloss*, villa

> **QUOTATIONS**
> A man's house is his castle
> SIR EDWARD COKE, *The Third Part of the Institutes of the Laws of England*

Parts of a castle include:

approach	curtain wall	outer bailey
arrow-slit	ditch	parados
bailey	donjon	parapet
barbican	drawbridge	portcullis
bartizan	dungeon	postern
bastion	embrasure	rampart
battlements	enclosure wall	scarp
berm	fosse	stockade
brattice	gatehouse	tower
buttress	inner wall	lookout tower
chapel	keep	turret
corbel	loophole	wall walk
courtyard	merlon	ward
crenel	moat	watchtower
crenellation	motte	
crosslet	mound	

---

castrate *v*

emasculate, geld, neuter, unman, unsex, cut, knacker, swig

OLD alter; (*Shakesp*) glib

FORMAL evirate

COLLOQ. doctor

casual *adj*

1 UNCONCERNED, nonchalant, blasé, lackadaisical, lukewarm, negligent, apathetic, indifferent, informal, offhand, relaxed, easy-going

FORMAL insouciant

COLLOQ. couldn't-care-less, laid-back, happy-go-lucky, free-and-easy

2 *casual clothes*

informal, comfortable, relaxed, leisure

3 *casual work*

temporary, irregular, intermittent, occasional, part-time, short-term, provisional

4 *a casual meeting*

chance, accidental, spontaneous, unintentional, unpremeditated, unexpected, unforeseen, irregular, random, occasional, incidental, superficial, cursory

FORMAL fortuitous, serendipitous

🔄 **1** worried, concerned **2** formal **3** permanent, regular, full-time **4** deliberate, planned

casually *adv*

1 *'I'm sorry,' I added casually*

spontaneously, parenthetically, on the spur of the moment

COLLOQ. off the cuff, off the top of your head

2 *dress casually*

informally, comfortably, sportily

🔄 **2** formally, smartly

casualty *n*

injury, loss, death, fatality, victim, sufferer, injured, injured person, wounded, dead person, missing

casuistry *n*

chicanery, sophism, sophistry, speciousness, equivocation

cat *n*
tabby, kitten, mouser, tomcat
OLD grimalkin
COLLOQ. puss, pussy, pussy cat, mog, moggy
Related adjective: feline

> **PROVERBS**
> When the cat's away, the mice will play

> **QUOTATIONS**
> Macavity, Macavity, there's no one like Macavity, /
> There never was a Cat of such deceitfulness and suavity
> TS ELIOT, 'Macavity: the Mystery Cat'
>
> What is the victory of a cat on a hot tin roof? – I wish I
> knew ... Just staying on it, I guess, for as long as she can
> TENNESSEE WILLIAMS, *Cat on a Hot Tin Roof*

Breeds of cat include:

Abyssinian	domestic tabby	Persian
American short-	Egyptian Mau	rag-doll
hair	Exotic shorthair	rex
Balinese	Foreign Blue	Russian Blue
Birman	Foreign spotted	Scottish Fold
Bombay	shorthair	Siamese
British longhair	Foreign White	silver tabby
British shorthair	Havana	Singapura
Burmese	Himalayan	Somali
Carthusian	Japanese Bobtail	Tiffany
chinchilla	Korat	Tonkinese
Cornish rex	Maine Coon	tortoiseshell
Cymric	Manx	Turkish Angora
Devon rex	Norwegian Forest	Turkish Van

---

cataclysm *n*
disaster, calamity, catastrophe, debacle, devastation,
upheaval, blow, collapse, convulsion

cataclysmic *adj*
catastrophe, disastrous, tragic, fatal, calamitous,
devastating, terrible, dreadful, awful

catacomb *n*
underground passages, underground rooms, underground
tunnels, underground cemetery, burial-vault, vault, tomb,
crypt, mausoleum
FORMAL ossuary

catalogue *n, v*
♦ *n*
list, inventory, roll, register, roster, schedule, checklist,
record, table, classification, index, directory, gazetteer,
brochure, guide, prospectus, manifest, calendar, bulletin,
specialogue, litany
TECHNICAL iconography, notitia
OLD catelog, ragman
COLLOQ. magalog
♦ *v*
list, compile/make a list, register, record, index, classify,
alphabetize, file, categorize

catapult *n, v*
♦ *n*
sling; *N Am* slingshot; *Aust & NZ* shanghai
OLD bricole
♦ *v*
propel, hurl, fling, throw, pitch, toss, sling, hurtle, launch,
shoot, fire

cataract *n*
waterfall, falls, rapids, force, cascade, overfall, downpour,
torrent, deluge

catastrophe *n*
disaster, calamity, debacle, fiasco, failure, ruin,
devastation, tragedy, blow, reverse, mischance, misfortune,
adversity, trouble, doom, upheaval
FORMAL cataclysm, affliction

catastrophic *adj*
disastrous, tragic, fatal, calamitous, devastating, terrible,
dreadful, awful, of the first magnitude
FORMAL cataclysmic

catcall *n*
jeer, boo, gibe, hiss, whistle, barracking;
N Am Bronx cheer
COLLOQ. raspberry

catch *v, n*
♦ *v*
1 *catch a ball*
hold, grab, take, seize, grasp, snatch, grip,
clutch, field
2 *catch an animal/a prisoner*
capture, trap, entrap, hunt down, snare, ensnare, hook,
net, seize, lay hold of, arrest, apprehend, corner, round
up, recapture
COLLOQ. nab, collar, nick
3 *catch a train*
get, get on, make, board, be in time for
4 *catch what someone says*
hear, make out, perceive, recognize, understand, follow,
take in, fathom, grasp
FORMAL comprehend
COLLOQ. get the hang of, twig, get it
5 *catch someone doing something wrong*
surprise, catch red-handed/in the act, expose, unmask,
startle, find (out), discover, detect, discern
OLD (*Shakesp*) watch
6 *catch a cold*
get, develop, go down with, pick up, become infected
with, become ill with
FORMAL contract, succumb to
7 *catch someone's attention*
attract, draw, grasp, hold, capture, engage
E₃ 1 drop **2** release, free **3, 4** miss
♦ *n*
1 FASTENER, clip, hook, clasp, hasp, latch, lock, bolt;
dialect sneck
2 *herring catches*
haul, net, bag
3 DISADVANTAGE, drawback, snag, hitch, obstacle, problem,
difficulty
COLLOQ. fly in the ointment
■ **catch on**
1 *the new style is catching on quickly*
become popular, become fashionable
COLLOQ. become all the rage
2 *catch on to what she said*
understand, follow, take in, fathom, grasp, comprehend
■ **catch up**
draw level, gain on, overtake

catching *adj*
infectious, contagious, communicable, transmittable,
transmissible

catchphrase *n*
saying, slogan, motto, jingle, watchword, byword,
catchword, formula, password, parrot-cry
SLANG wheeze

catchy *adj*
memorable, unforgettable, haunting, popular,
melodic, tuneful, ear-catching, attractive, captivating,
appealing
E₃ dull, boring, instantly forgettable

catechize *v*
instruct, interrogate, question, cross-examine, examine,
test, drill
COLLOQ. grill, give the third degree

categorical *adj*
absolute, total, utter, unqualified, unreserved,
unconditional, downright, positive, definite, emphatic,
unequivocal, clear, conclusive, explicit, express, direct
E₃ tentative, qualified, vague

categorically *adv*
absolutely, utterly, unconditionally, emphatically, unequivocally, unreservedly, definitely, clearly, directly, positively, explicitly, expressly

categorization *n*
classification, grouping, sorting, ranking, ordering, arrangement, listing

categorize *v*
class, classify, group, sort, grade, rank, order, arrange, list, tabulate, stereotype, pigeonhole

category *n*
class, classification, group, grouping, kind, sort, type, variety, genre, section, division, department, chapter, head, heading, title, rubric, grade, rank, order, list, listing, bracket
TECHNICAL superclass, superorder, superphylum, taxon, stirps

cater *v*
1 cater for people's needs/interests
provide, supply, furnish, serve
FORMAL provision, victual
2 cater to someone's desires
indulge, pander, satisfy

caterwaul *v*
wail, scream, cry, screech, shriek, bawl, howl, miaow, squall, yowl
OLD (*Spenser*) wrawl

catharsis *n*
cleansing, purging, purification, purifying, release
TECHNICAL abreaction, abstersion, epuration, lustration

cathartic *adj*
cleansing, purging, purgative, purifying, release
TECHNICAL abreactive, abstersive, lustral, eccoprotic

cathedral *n*
minster, duomo, procathedral
OLD dome

catholic *adj*
broad, broad-based, diverse, wide, wide-ranging, widespread, varied, universal, global, general, comprehensive, inclusive, all-inclusive, all-embracing, all-encompassing, liberal, tolerant, open-minded, broad-minded
FORMAL eclectic
F3 narrow, limited, narrow-minded, bigoted

cattle *n*
cows, bulls, oxen, livestock, stock, beasts
Related adjective: bovine

Breeds of cattle include:

Aberdeen Angus	Chillingham	Longhorn
Africander	Devon	Luing
Alderney	dexter	Red Poll
Ankole	Durham	Romagnola
Ayrshire	Friesian	Santa Gertrudis
Belgian Blue	Galloway	Shetland
Blonde d'Aqui-	Guernsey	Shorthorn
taine	Hereford	Simmenthaler
Brahman	Highland	South Devon
Brown Swiss	Holstein	Teeswater
cattabu	Jersey	Ukrainian
cattalo	Latvian	Welsh Black
Charolais	Limousin	(British) White

---

catty *adj*
bitchy, malicious, spiteful, venomous, vicious, mean, ill-natured, malevolent, rancorous, backbiting
F3 kind, pleasant

caucus *n*
assembly, meeting, session, convention, gathering, conclave, get-together, parley, set, clique

causative *adj*
causing, root
TECHNICAL factitive, factive

cause *n, v*
♦ *n*
1 SOURCE, origin, beginning, root, basis, factor, spring, mainspring, originator, creator, producer, maker, author, mover, prime mover, agent, agency
2 REASON, motive, grounds, justification, explanation, basis, motivation, stimulus, incentive, inducement, impulse
3 *a worthy cause*
object, purpose, end, aim, ideal, principle, belief, conviction, movement, undertaking, enterprise
F3 **1** effect, result, consequence
♦ *v*
begin, give rise to, be the cause of, be at the root of, lead to, result in, occasion, bring about, make, make happen, produce, generate, originate, create, breed, precipitate, trigger (off), motivate, stimulate, provoke, incite, induce, prompt, force, compel
FORMAL effect, render
F3 stop, prevent

SYNONYM NUANCES

verb
Begin, **give rise to**, **lead to** and **result in** are fairly general and neutral terms: *his pioneering work began a new era; the delay gave rise to suspicion.* **Bring about** and **make happen** are similar, but suggest a more active involvement: *his speech brought about a change of heart.* **Breed** and **occasion** often have the narrower use of providing the correct conditions, though the former is often used of negative consequences: *oppression breeds violence,* and the latter is rather more formal sounding: *the marches occasioned violent encounters with the police.* **Precipitate** should be used of causing something to happen quickly: *the surge of nationalism which precipitated the end of the colonial era.* **Trigger** (**off**) could be used of sudden, unavoidable consequences, very often negative: *the economic downturn has triggered a rash of redundancies.* **Motivate**, **stimulate** and **prompt** might be used to convey positive aspects of encouraging, but **provoke** and **incite** tend to be used of actions with less favourable developments: *the violence, incited by propaganda.* The words **force** and **compel** are confined to circumstances in which no other outcome would be allowed, or even possible.

---

caustic *adj*
1 caustic chemicals
corrosive, acid, destructive, burning, stinging, erodent, escharotic
2 a caustic remark
biting, cutting, stinging, keen, pungent, bitter, acid, sarcastic, scathing, virulent, severe, acrimonious, vitriolic, snide
FORMAL astringent, mordant, trenchant
F3 **1** soothing **2** mild, kind

caustically *adv*
bitterly, scathingly, sarcastically, severely, acrimoniously, vitriolically, virulently
FORMAL trenchantly

cauterize *v*
burn, sterilize, disinfect, scorch, sear, singe, carbonize
TECHNICAL fire

caution *n, v*
♦ *n*
1 CARE, carefulness, watchfulness, vigilance, alertness, guard, mindfulness, heed, heedfulness, discretion, prudence, forethought, deliberation, wariness
FORMAL circumspection
OLD cautel
2 WARNING, injunction, reprimand, advice, counsel
FORMAL admonition, caveat

COLLOQ. tip-off
E 1 carelessness, recklessness
♦ v
warn, advise, counsel, urge, alert, deter
FORMAL admonish
COLLOQ. tip off

cautious adj
careful, watchful, vigilant, alert, heedful, shrewd, prudent, discreet, tactful, defensive, chary, wary, guarded, safe, tentative, conservative, deliberate, Fabian, unadventurous
OLD cautelous
FORMAL circumspect, judicious
COLLOQ. cagey, softly-softly, gingerly
E reckless, rash, foolhardy

cautiously adv
carefully, prudently, discreetly, tactfully, defensively, tentatively, deliberately, conservatively
FORMAL circumspectly, judiciously
COLLOQ. gingerly
E recklessly, rashly

cavalcade n
procession, parade, march-past, troop, array, retinue, cortège, train, sowarry, motorcade

cavalier n, adj
♦ n
1 HORSEMAN, equestrian, horse soldier, cavalryman, knight, chevalier, Bashi-Bazouk, chasseur, Ironside, spahi
2 GENTLEMAN, gallant, escort, partner
♦ adj
supercilious, patronizing, condescending, lordly, haughty, lofty, arrogant, swaggering, insolent, scornful, disdainful, curt, offhand, casual, free-and-easy

cavalry n
horsemen, equestrians, horse soldiers, cavalrymen, horse, light-horse, mounted troops, troopers, dragoons, hussars, lancers, sabreurs, chasseurs, risaldars, the heavies
OLD reiters, ritt-masters

cave n, v
♦ n
cavern, grotto, hole, pothole, tunnel, dugout, underground chamber, hollow, cavity
OLD antre, delve; (Shakesp) antar
Related adjective: speleological
■ **cave in**
collapse, subside, give way, yield, fall (in), slip

caveat n
caution, warning, proviso, alarm
FORMAL admonition

cavern n
cave, cavity, den, grotto, hollow, pothole, vault, vaultage, tunnel, dugout, underground chamber, cove, Erebus

cavernous adj
hollow, concave, gaping, yawning, echoing, resonant, deep, unfathomable, bottomless, large, huge, immense, vast, spacious, dark, gloomy, sunken, depressed

cavil v
complain, carp, criticize, censure, reproach, quarrel, find faults, nag, quibble, haggle
COLLOQ. nit-pick
E praise, compliment

cavity n
hole, gap, dent, hollow, excavation, crater, pit, well, bore, chamber, pocket, vein, tear, sinus, womb; dialect vug; N Am & Aust thunder-egg
TECHNICAL antrum, atrium, cell, orifice, ventricle, aperture, lacuna, camera, sac, vesicle, acetabulum, blastocoel, cochlea, concha, eardrum, coelom, vestibule, splanchnocele, cotyle, crypt, druse, geode, haematocele, lumen, mediastinum, neuroblastoma, pelvis, rhynchocoel, vacuole, vitta
OLD TECHNICAL conceptacle, purse
OLD mine

cavort v
caper, frolic, gambol, prance, skip, dance, frisk, sport, romp

cease v
stop, refrain, halt, call a halt, come/bring to a halt, break off, leave (off), finish, end, come/bring to an end, conclude, terminate, suspend, let up, peter out, fail, die; Scot devall
OLD surcease, unbe; (Spenser) cesse, blin, lin
FORMAL abate, discontinue, desist
COLLOQ. fizzle out, pack in, quit; N Am poop (out)
E begin, start, commence

ceaseless adj
endless, unending, never-ending, eternal, everlasting, continuous, non-stop, incessant, unceasing, interminable, constant, perpetual, continual, persistent, untiring, uninterrupted, unremitting
E occasional, irregular

ceaselessly adv
endlessly, unendingly, eternally, everlastingly, for ever, for ever and ever, uninterruptedly, continuously, incessantly, unremittingly, constantly, unceasingly, interminably, day in day out
COLLOQ. till the cows come home

cede v
surrender, give up, resign, abandon, yield, relinquish, convey, transfer, hand over, turn over, grant, deliver, allow, concede
FORMAL abdicate, renounce

ceiling n
1 *a decorated ceiling*
vault, plafond, roof, overhead, overhead covering, rafters, beams, awning, canopy
TECHNICAL laquearia
OLD seeling, soffit; (Spenser) loft
2 LIMIT, upper limit, maximum, most, cut-off point

celebrate v
1 *celebrate a birthday*
commemorate, remember, observe, keep, mark, hold, record, honour, do something in someone's honour, have/throw a party, rejoice, enjoy yourself, have fun, go out, toast, drink to, extol, revel, sonnet, sound, trumpet, sing, hymn, carol, chant
OLD besing, emblaze, maffick
FORMAL laud, tune, emblazon, renown, repeat, procession
COLLOQ. rave, binge, have a ball, live it up, whoop it up, go out on the town, go on the razzle, paint the town red, kill the fatted calf, put the flags out, push the boat out
SLANG wet
2 *the priest celebrated Communion*
bless, perform, observe, solemnize, concelebrate

celebrated adj
famous, well-known, famed, renowned, illustrious, glorious, eminent, distinguished, great, notable, noted, prominent, outstanding, legendary, popular, acclaimed, admired, exalted, revered
COLLOQ. with your name in lights
E unknown, obscure, forgotten

celebration n
observance, merrymaking, jollification, revelry, orgy, festivity, feast, festival, occasion
COLLOQ. rave, rave-up, binge, spree, do, shindig; Irish hooley
SLANG S Afr jol

Celebrations include:

anniversary	centenary	festival
banquet	christening	fête
baptism	coming-of-age	First Communion
bar mitzvah	commemoration	gala
bat mitzvah	confirmation	graduation
birthday	feast	harvest festival

harvest-home	marriage	retirement
homecoming	May Day	reunion
Independence	name-day	saint's day
Day	party	thanksgiving
jubilee	reception	tribute
Labour Day	remembrance	wedding

See also **anniversary**; **party**.

See also **church services** at **church**; **religious festivals** at **religious**.

---

celebrity n
1 STAR, personality, name, famous person, A-lister, superstar, megastar, legend, legend in their own lifetime, living legend, household name, dignitary
FORMAL personage, notable, luminary, worthy
COLLOQ. celeb, VIP, big name, bigwig, big shot
SLANG sleb
2 FAME, renown, stardom, distinction, prominence, eminence, esteem, greatness, notability, note, reputation, illustriousness
F3 1 nobody, unknown, nonentity

celerity n
rapidity, fastness, quickness, speed, swiftness, velocity, dispatch, expedition, fleetness, haste, promptness
F3 slowness

celestial adj
heavenly, divine, godlike, spiritual, angelic, seraphic, elysian, empyrean, ethereal, paradisaic, eternal, immortal, sublime, supernatural, transcendental, astral, starry
F3 earthly, mundane

celestially adv
divinely, spiritually, angelically, eternally, immortally, sublimely, supernaturally, transcendentally
F3 mundanely

celibacy n
singleness, bachelorhood, spinsterhood, maidenhood, virginity, chastity, purity, self-denial, self-restraint, abstinence, continence
FORMAL abnegation

> **QUOTATIONS**
> Marriage may often be a stormy lake, but celibacy is almost always a muddy horsepond
> THOMAS LOVE PEACOCK, *Melincourt*

celibate adj
chaste, pure, abstinent, virgin, single, unmarried, unwed, bachelor, spinster

cell n
1 *a prison cell*
prison, jail, dungeon, lock-up, room, cubicle, chamber, compartment, enclosure
2 *living cells*
unit, organism
TECHNICAL protoplasm, cytoplasm, protoplast, gamete, zygote, spore, nucleus, matrix
Related adjective: cytoid
3 *a political cell*
faction, nucleus, group, party, unit, section, set, crowd, caucus, clique

cellar n
basement, crypt, vault, storeroom, wine cellar;
Scot dunny

cement n, v
 ♦ n
plaster, mortar, concrete, screed, compo, putty, pointing, grout, grouting, gunite, lute, mastic, fixative, matrix, bonding, adhesive, glue, paste
TECHNICAL ciment fondu
OLD maltha

 ♦ v
stick, bond, weld, solder, join, fasten, fix, cohere, unite, combine, bind, affix, attach, glue, gum, solution; *dialect* lime

cemetery n
burial ground, burial place, burial site, graveyard, churchyard, necropolis, charnel house, God's acre, graves, tombs, urnfield, *campo santo*
SLANG boneyard

censor v, n
 ♦ v
cut, make cuts, ban, edit, delete, blue-pencil, bowdlerize, expurgate
 ♦ n
inspector, examiner, editor, bowdlerizer, expurgater

> **❗ censor** or **censure**?
> To *censor* books, films, etc is to examine them, deleting parts of them or forbidding publication: *His letters home were censored.* To *censure* someone is to criticize them severely: *The President was severely censured for abusing his powers.*

censorious adj
condemnatory, disapproving, disparaging, fault-finding, carping, cavilling, critical, hypercritical, overcritical, severe
FORMAL captious
F3 complimentary, approving

censoriously adv
disapprovingly, disparagingly, critically, hypercritically, overcritically, severely
FORMAL captiously
F3 approvingly

censure v, n
 ♦ v
condemn, denounce, blame, criticize, disapprove of, reprehend, reprove, reproach, rebuke, reprimand, scold
FORMAL castigate, admonish, remonstrate, upbraid
COLLOQ. tell off, haul over the coals, come down heavy on, pull to pieces
F3 praise, compliment, approve
 ♦ n
condemnation, blame, disapproval, criticism, denunciation, reprehension, reproof, reproach, rebuke, reprimand, scolding
FORMAL admonition, admonishment, castigation, upbraiding, remonstrance, obloquy, vituperation
COLLOQ. telling-off
F3 praise, compliments, approval

> **❗ censure** or **censor**?
> See panel at **censor**.

central adj
1 MIDDLE, centre, mid, inner, interior, medial, median
2 PRINCIPAL, main, major, most important, chief, key, primary, fundamental, foremost, dominant, vital, crucial, significant, focal, pivotal, basic, essential, core, prime
F3 1 peripheral **2** minor, secondary

centralization n
concentration, convergence, consolidation, incorporation, rationalization, amalgamation, unification, focusing, streamlining

centralize v
concentrate, converge, bring/gather together, consolidate, incorporate, rationalize, focus, streamline, amalgamate, compact, condense, unify
F3 decentralize

centre n, v
 ♦ n
middle, midpoint, heart, core, nucleus, kernel, pivot, hub, focus, focal point, crux, linchpin, arena
COLLOQ. bull's-eye
F3 edge, periphery, outskirts
 ♦ v
focus, concentrate, converge, gravitate, revolve, pivot, hinge

centrepiece n
most significant feature, focus of attention, highlight, high point, high spot, most interesting part, best, peak, climax, cream

ceramics n
pottery, earthenware, ware, bisque, faience, ironstone, porcelain, raku
See panel at **pottery**.

cereal n
1 *cereal crops*
barley, grain, corn, wheat, maize, millet, oats, rye, sorghum, rice, amarant
2 *breakfast cereal*
cornflakes, muesli, porridge, oatmeal; *N Am* granola
Related adjective: farinaceous

ceremonial adj, n
♦ *adj*
formal, official, stately, state, solemn, dignified, ritual, ritualistic
F∃ informal, casual
♦ *n*
ceremony, formality, protocol, custom, solemnity, ritual, rite

> **!** **ceremonial** or **ceremonious**?
> *Ceremonial* means 'relating to or appropriate for a ceremony': *ceremonial dress; a ceremonial occasion.* *Ceremonious* means 'very formal or polite': *He ushered her through with a ceremonious bow.*

ceremonially adv
formally, officially, solemnly, ritually
F∃ informally, casually

ceremonious adj
stately, dignified, grand, imposing, solemn, ritual, civil, official, majestic, polite, courteous, deferential, courtly, formal, stiff, starchy, exact, precise, scrupulous
FORMAL punctilious
F∃ unceremonious, informal, relaxed

> **!** **ceremonious** or **ceremonial**?
> See panel at **ceremonial**.

ceremoniously adv
grandly, solemnly, ritualistically, civilly, officially, politely, courteously, deferentially, formally, stiffly, starchily, exactly, precisely, scrupulously
FORMAL punctiliously
F∃ unceremoniously, informally

ceremony n
1 *wedding ceremony*
service, rite, sacrament, ordinance, liturgy, commemoration, occasion, observance, festival, celebration, formality, solemnity, function, custom, tradition, parade, anniversary, inauguration, dedication, induction, initiation, graduation, coronation, investiture, unveiling; *N Am* exercise, commencement
2 ETIQUETTE, formality, protocol, form, order, circumstance, niceties, ceremonial, ritual, pomp, pageantry, show, gaud
FORMAL decorum, propriety, punctilio
COLLOQ. spit and polish

Ceremonies include:

amrit	christening	marriage
baptism	chuppah	matrimony
bar mitzvah	committal	matsuri
bat mitzvah	confirmation	maundy
bris milah (or brit	doseh	nipter
milah)	fire-walking	nuptials
colloq. capping	First Communion	tangi
chanoyu	graduation	wedding

---

certain adj
1 *I'm certain he's telling the truth*
sure, positive, assured, confident, convinced, persuaded

2 *it's certain that she left yesterday*
indisputable, unquestionable, undeniable, undoubted, indubitable, incontrovertible, irrefutable, evident, obvious, clear, plain, sure, conclusive, absolute, convincing, true
COLLOQ. no two ways about it, no ifs and buts, sure as eggs is eggs; *Aust* dead set
3 *success is certain*
inevitable, unavoidable, inescapable, bound, bound to happen, meant to happen, assured, destined, fated, doomed
FORMAL inexorable, ineluctable
COLLOQ. cut and dried, open-and-shut, home and dry, in the bag
4 *below a certain income*
specific, special, particular, individual, precise, express, fixed, established, settled, decided, definite, determined
5 *to a certain extent*
some, partial, small, limited
F∃ 1 uncertain, unsure, hesitant, doubtful **3** unlikely

certainly adv
surely, of course, naturally, obviously, clearly, plainly, definitely, for sure, undoubtedly, without a doubt, no doubt, undeniably, unquestionably, beyond question, absolutely, by all means, doubtlessly, assuredly, positively

certainty n
1 *identify someone with certainty*
sureness, positiveness, assurance, confidence, conviction, faith, trust, assuredness
2 *it's a certainty that she'll get the job*
inevitability, foregone conclusion, matter of course, truth, validity, fact, reality
COLLOQ. sure thing, safe bet, dead cert
SLANG *Aust* moral
F∃ 1 uncertainty, doubt, hesitation

certificate n
document, award, diploma, qualification, credentials, testimonial, guarantee, endorsement, proof, warrant, licence, authorization, register, pass, voucher
TECHNICAL lines, marriage-lines, patent, aegrotat, testamur, bill of health, clearance, navicert, cocket, docket, debenture, scrip, securities, title; *N Am* land-scrip
OLD TECHNICAL smart-ticket, Tyburn-ticket
FORMAL certificatory
SLANG ticket

certify v
declare, assure, guarantee, endorse, confirm, pronounce, vouch, testify, witness, bear witness to, substantiate, verify, authenticate, validate, warrant, ratify, authorize, recognize, license
FORMAL attest, aver, corroborate, accredit

certitude n
(full) assurance, assuredness, certainty, confidence, conviction, sureness, positiveness
FORMAL plerophoria, plerophory
F∃ doubt

cessation n
halt, halting, ceasing, discontinuation, discontinuing, end, ending, remission, respite, rest, standstill, stay, stoppage, stopping, conclusion, suspension, termination, pause, recess, break, let-up, interruption, intermission, interval
FORMAL abeyance, desistance, discontinuance, hiatus
F∃ beginning, start, commencement

chafe v
1 *chafe someone's skin*
rub, grate, irritate, rasp, scrape, fret, bind, inflame, scratch, wear (away), wear down
OLD chauf, chauff
FORMAL abrade, excoriate
2 *chafing at the rules*
anger, annoy, enrage, exasperate, incense, provoke, inflame, vex, be angry
COLLOQ. peeve, get on someone's nerves, get on someone's wick

chaff *n, v*

♦ *n*

1 HUSKS, shells, pods, cases
Related adjective: paleaceous
2 BANTER, teasing, joking, jesting, badinage, repartee
COLLOQ. kidding, ribbing, have-on

♦ *v*

tease, joke, jest, banter, mock, make fun of
COLLOQ. kid, rib, rag, pull someone's leg, chip
SLANG josh, rot

chagrin *n, v*

♦ *n*

annoyance, exasperation, indignation, disappointment, displeasure, irritation, vexation, disquiet, dissatisfaction, discomposure, embarrassment, mortification, humiliation, shame, fretfulness
FORMAL discomfiture
F3 delight, pleasure

♦ *v*

annoy, exasperate, disappoint, displease, irritate, vex, irk, disquiet, dissatisfy, embarrass, humiliate, mortify
COLLOQ. peeve

chain *n, v*

♦ *n*

1 FETTER, manacle, restraint, bond, shackle, trammel, link, coupling, union
Related adjective: catenary
2 *a hotel chain*
group, company, firm
3 *a chain of islands*
string, line, row, range, train, set
FORMAL concatenation
4 *a chain of events*
series, sequence, succession, progression, string

♦ *v*

fasten, secure, bind, tie, hitch, restrain, tether, confine, fetter, shackle, manacle, handcuff, enslave
F3 free, release, liberate

chair *n, v*

♦ *n*

1 SEAT, armchair, recliner, swivel-chair, stool, bench, form
2 *Sally is the new chair*
chairperson, chairman, chairwoman, president, convenor, organizer, director, master of ceremonies, MC, toastmaster, speaker

♦ *v*

lead, act as chairperson/chairman/chairwoman, convene, direct, supervise, preside over, moderate

Chairs include:

armchair	estate	office chair
Barcelona chair	fauteuil	pouffe
beanbag	fiddle-back	prie-dieu
bench	form	recliner
bergère	guérite	rocker
carver	high chair	rocking chair
commode	jampan	sedan
Cromwellian	kitchen chair	stool
dining chair	ladder-back	swivel-chair
easy chair	lounger	throne

See also **stool**.

chairman, chairwoman *n*

chairperson, president, convenor, organizer, director, spokesman, spokeswoman, spokesperson, master of ceremonies, MC

chalk
■ **chalk up**
1 ACHIEVE, attain, gain, log, score, tally, register, record, accumulate
2 ASCRIBE, attribute, charge, credit, put down

chalky *adj*

1 ASHEN, pale, pallid, white, wan, colourless
2 POWDERY, dusty, ground, crushed, granulated
FORMAL calcareous, cretaceous

challenge *v, n*

♦ *v*

1 DARE, defy, confront, brave, summon, invite, accost, tackle; *Scot* hen
OLD provoke, champion, darraign, defy; (*Shakesp*) assay
COLLOQ. throw down the gauntlet, throw your hat into the ring
2 *challenged his authority*
question, dispute, query, protest, disagree with, object to, take exception to, call in(to) question
FORMAL demur
3 *challenged my ability*
test, tax, try, stretch, strain

♦ *n*

1 *the new job is a real challenge*
test, trial, hurdle, obstacle, problem, risk, hazard, opportunity
COLLOQ. big ask
2 *take up the challenge to fight*
dare, defiance, confrontation, provocation, call, summons, bidding
OLD vie
3 *a challenge to their powers*
dispute, protest, opposition, defiance, disagreement, objection, calling into question, questioning, interrogation, stand, confrontation, ultimatum

challenging *adj*

exciting, exacting, demanding, testing, taxing, stretching
F3 undemanding

chamber *n*

1 HALL, assembly room, auditorium, meeting-place, moot-hall
2 ROOM, apartment, compartment, bedroom, boudoir
3 *the chambers of the heart*
cavity, ventricle, compartment, hollow
4 *the upper chamber of parliament*
assembly, legislature, parliament, council, house

champion *n, v*

♦ *n*

1 *the school chess champion*
winner, victor, conqueror, title-holder, hero, ace, expert
OLD kemp, kemper
COLLOQ. champ; *Aust & NZ* gun
2 *a champion of animal rights*
guardian, protector, defender, vindicator, patron, backer, supporter, upholder, advocate, tribune, protagonist, messiah, saviour, asserter, deliverer, apostle
TECHNICAL promachos
FORMAL proponent
COLLOQ. angel

♦ *v*

defend, stand up for, stand for, back, support, protect, maintain, uphold, advocate, promote, hold a brief for
FORMAL espouse

chance *n, v, adj*

♦ *n*

1 *meet someone by chance*
accident, coincidence, luck, fortune, providence, fate, destiny, risk, gamble, speculation
FORMAL fortuity, serendipity
COLLOQ. fluke
2 *there's a chance that I'll be late*
possibility, prospect, probability, likelihood, odds
3 *a second chance*
opportunity, opening, occasion, time; *N Am, Aust & NZ* show
COLLOQ. break, golden opportunity, chance of a lifetime, your best shot
F3 1 certainty

♦ *v*

1 RISK, hazard, take a chance, gamble, wager, stake, try, speculate, venture
FORMAL essay
COLLOQ. chance your luck, push your luck, play a hunch, bet your boots/life, bet your bottom dollar
2 HAPPEN, occur, come about, take place, arise, crop up, develop, result, follow

♦ *adj*

casual, accidental, inadvertent, unintentional, unintended, unforeseen, unexpected, unanticipated, unlooked-for, random, arbitrary, haphazard, incidental
FORMAL fortuitous, serendipitous
COLLOQ. flukey
E3 deliberate, intentional, foreseen, certain

■ **chance on/upon**
meet, meet unexpectedly, find by chance, discover, come across, run across, stumble on
COLLOQ. run into, bump into

■ **by chance**
accidentally, unintentionally, inadvertently, unexpectedly, by accident, as luck would have it, by mistake, unwittingly, haphazardly, randomly, incidentally
OLD bechance
FORMAL fortuitously, adventitiously, serendipitously

> **QUOTATIONS**
> Revolving in his altered soul / The various turns of chance below
> JOHN DRYDEN, *Alexander's Feast*

> **SYNONYM NUANCES**
> *noun sense 1*
> **Accident** is widely used to suggest any unplanned incident, whereas a **coincidence** more specifically refers to the unlikely occurrence of two related events. **Luck** refers to circumstances over which you have no control, as does **fortune**, although when used without any qualification the implication is usually of something beneficial: *an adventitious stroke of fortune*. **Providence** connotes a benevolent divine contribution, and **fate** and **destiny** an element of preordination: *his heroic struggle against his destiny*.
> The terms **risk** and **gamble** are suggestive of possible unhappy consequences: *a risk of thundery showers*; whilst **speculation** would be an appropriate term for chance based on theories or unfounded conclusions.

chancy *adj*
risky, speculative, tricky, uncertain, unpredictable, fraught, hazardous, dangerous, problematical
COLLOQ. dicey, dodgy
E3 safe, secure

change *v, n*
♦ *v*

1 *water changes into ice; prices keep changing*
make/become different, alter, vary, convert, turn, go, become, develop, modify, reorganize, reform, restructure, remodel, revise, renew, amend, adapt, customize, adjust, transform, evolve, transfer, move, shift, fluctuate, vacillate, be in a state of flux
TECHNICAL mutate, transmutate, metamorphose, transfigure
COLLOQ. do a U-turn
2 *change one thing for another*
substitute, replace, alternate, interchange, rotate, transpose, exchange, swap, trade, switch, barter
COLLOQ. chop and change
3 *change buses*
transfer, connect, make a connection
♦ *n*
1 *a change in the weather*
difference, alteration, variation, conversion, modification, reorganization, shake-up, transition, trend, movement, diversion, novelty, innovation, variety, revolution,

upheaval, development, reform, restructuring, remodelling, reconstruction, revision, renewal, amendment, adaptation, customization, adjustment, transformation, evolution, transfer, move, shift, fluctuation, vacillation, state of flux, reversal, about-turn, about-face, volte-face, turnabout, ebb and flow
TECHNICAL mutation, transmutation, metamorphosis, transfiguration
FORMAL vicissitude
COLLOQ. U-turn
2 *a change of government*
exchange, transposition, interchange, substitution, substitute, replacement, alternation, rotation, swap, trade, switch, barter
3 *Have you got any change?*
coins, cash, silver, coppers

> **PROVERBS**
> A change is as good as a rest

> **SYNONYM NUANCES**
> *noun sense 1*
> **Conversion** is suggestive of a complete change, or can be used of being turned to a different purpose, while **modification**, **amendment**, **adaptation**, **customization** and **adjustment** all suggest more minor interference to make something better suited for its purpose.
> **Shake-up**, **revolution** and **upheaval**, on the other hand, are appropriate words to use where there has been a dramatic process of change: *a radical shake-up of commercial TV*. **Transition**, **movement**, **development**, **evolution**, **move** and **shift** all suggest something more gradual. The term **trend** is usually used in the context of changing fashions or current influences: *the trend towards early retirement*.
> Both **novelty** and **innovation** suggest the introduction of something new and unlike anything else, whilst **reform**, **revision** and **renewal** all have to do with new approaches to something current.
> **Transformation** returns to the idea of something being turned into something else, often with the implication that it is a postive change: *aim for self-improvement and personal transformation*. **Fluctuation** and **vacillation** appropriately describe constant moving between states, whereas **reversal** and **turnabout** are often used of a single, dramatic change in thought or action: *a rapid turnabout in attitudes*.

changeable *adj*
variable, varying, fluctuating, fluid, kaleidoscopic, versatile, shifting, mobile, movable, unsettled, unstable, uncertain, unpredictable, unreliable, changeful, erratic, irregular, inconstant, inconsistent, fickle, flighty, whimsy, capricious, volatile, skittish, windy, unsteady, wavering, vacillating, mercurial, labile, chameleonic, chamelion-like, Protean; *dialect* wankle
OLD various, voluble
FORMAL mutable, vicissitudinous
See Synonym nuances panel at **variable**.
E3 constant, settled, reliable

changeless *adj*
unchangeable, unalterable, unchanging, invariable, static, permanent, fixed, final, eternal, timeless
FORMAL immutable

channel *n, v*
♦ *n*
1 *a channel for rainwater; irrigation channels*
passage, duct, conduit, main, groove, furrow, trough, bed, way, ditch, gutter, gully, trench, canal, flume, course, trunk, culvert, watercourse, waterway, strait, narrows, cut-off, offtake, hollow, siphon, aqueduct, chamfer, gut, grough, artery, drain, sewer, sluice, overflow, spill-stream, fairway, feed, lead, level, tube, gate, lane, neck, sound; *dialect* ea, eau, gullet; *Scot*

sheuch, stank; *N Am* kill, snye; *Aust* wash-away; *S Afr* sluit, sloot
TECHNICAL chime, glyph, race, headrace, millrace, tailrace, limbers
OLD lake, falaj
2 *channels of communication*
route, course, path, avenue, way, means, medium, use, approach, passage, agent, agency
♦ *v*
direct, guide, conduct, convey, send, transmit, force, concentrate, focus, major

chant *n, v*
♦ *n*
1 *the football supporters' chants*
shout, cry, slogan, warcry
2 *a religious chant*
plainsong, psalm, song, melody, chorus, refrain, ditty, incantation, recitation, intonation, mantra
♦ *v*
sing, chorus, recite
FORMAL intone, incant

chaos *n*
disorder, confusion, disorganization, disarray, anarchy, lawlessness, tumult, upheaval, disruption, pandemonium, uproar, riot, bedlam, madhouse, mess
FORMAL tohu bohu
COLLOQ. pig's breakfast, dog's dinner, shambles
SLANG *N Am* snafu
E3 order

chaotic *adj*
disordered, confused, disorganized, topsy-turvy, disorderly, deranged, anarchic, lawless, orderless, riotous, tumultuous, unruly, uncontrolled, disrupted
COLLOQ. shambolic, at sixes and sevens, all over the place/shop, higgledy-piggledy
SLANG *N Am* snafu
E3 ordered, organized

chap *n*
fellow, man, boy, male person, individual, character, sort, type, codger; *dialect* cod
COLLOQ. bloke, guy, shaver; *Irish* bucko; *Aust* cove
SLANG sod, bastard, cat, Johnny, boyo, oik

chaperon, chaperone *n, v*
♦ *n*
companion, escort, duenna
♦ *v*
escort, accompany, attend, guard, protect, safeguard, shepherd, take care of, look after, mind, watch over

chapped *adj*
sore, chafed, cracked, raw, sprayed

chapter *n*
1 *read chapter 3*
section, division, part, clause, portion, topic
2 *a new chapter in my life*
episode, period, phase, stage, time
3 *the local chapter of a club*
branch, division, section, department

char *v*
burn, cauterize, scorch, sear, singe, carbonize, blacken, brown, coal

character *n*
1 *the cruel side of his character; the character of the countryside*
nature, essential quality, essence, ethos, personality, disposition, temperament, temper, constitution, make-up, individuality, identity, peculiarity, feature, attributes, characteristics, quality, property, type, stamp, calibre, reputation, psyche, status, position, trait, image
FORMAL persona
COLLOQ. what makes someone tick
2 *he has character; this house has character*
strength, strength of purpose, backbone, determination, courage, honesty, integrity, uprightness, honour, moral

fibre, charm, appeal, attractiveness, attractive features, distinctive features, arresting qualities, specialness, style, interest
3 ECCENTRIC, eccentric person, original, oddity
COLLOQ. oddball, case
4 *the characters in a play*
individual, person, human being, role, part, sort, type
5 LETTER, figure, symbol, sign, mark, type, device, logo, emblem, cipher, rune, hieroglyph, ideograph

---

SYNONYM NUANCES

sense 1
Nature and **essence** are both used of the innate qualities that contribute to identity, while **ethos** is more likely to be used of the beliefs or credo that distinguishes a particular group: *the public ethos of the health service.* The word **psyche** is generally used of mental character: *Scotland's footballing psyche.*
  Personality is associated more with the way people project their character, while **disposition**, **temperament** and **temper** emphasize their dominant emotions and the way they are affected by them. Terms such as **constitution** and **make-up**, which convey a picture of various elements making up the whole, and **feature**, **attributes**, **characteristics**, **quality**, **property** and **trait** are all neutral terms to use when describing any aspect of character: *physical attributes; personality traits.*
  The terms **individuality**, **identity** and **peculiarity** are more suggestive of something unique: *litigation was a peculiarity of modern America.* Both **stamp** and **calibre** may be used positively to suggest quality: *mathematicians of the finest calibre*; whereas **reputation**, **status**, **position** and **image** would more appropriately be used in contexts describing how the character of something is perceived or ranked.

---

characteristic *n, adj*
♦ *n*
feature, trait, attribute, property, quality, essential quality, mark, hallmark, factor, peculiarity, idiosyncrasy, mannerism, symptom
♦ *adj*
distinctive, distinguishing, individual, idiosyncratic, peculiar, specific, special, typical, representative, symbolic, symptomatic
E3 uncharacteristic, untypical

characteristically *adv*
typically, distinctively, individually, peculiarly, idiosyncratically

characterization *n*
description, representation, presentation, depiction, portrayal

characterize *v*
1 *materialism that characterizes life*
typify, mark, stamp, brand, identify, distinguish, indicate, specify, designate
2 DESCRIBE, represent, portray, present, depict

charade *n*
farce, mockery, parody, pretence, fake, travesty, sham, pantomime

charge *v, n*
♦ *v*
1 *charge a high price*
ask, ask for, ask someone to pay, demand, demand in payment, set/fix a price, levy, exact, debit, bill, put down to
2 ACCUSE, indict, impeach, incriminate, blame
FORMAL arraign, impute
3 ATTACK, assail, assault, storm, rush (forward), tear
4 FILL, pervade, affect, imbue, infuse, suffuse, burden, saturate, overwhelm

◆ *n*

1 PRICE, cost, fee, rate, amount, expense, expenditure, outlay, payment, premium, rent, rental, dues, toll, levy, tax, tariff, tithe

2 ACCUSATION, indictment, allegation, impeachment, blame, incrimination
FORMAL arraignment, imputation

3 ATTACK, assault, onslaught, sortie, incursion, offensive, storming, rush onrush

4 *in your charge*
custody, keeping, care, safekeeping, guardianship, ward, protection, trust, responsibility, duty, burden, obligation

■ **in charge of**
responsible for, managing, leading, controlling, directing, supervising, overseeing, heading up, looking after, taking care of

charisma *n*
charm, appeal, lure, allure, attraction, magnetism, drawing-power, draw, pull

charismatic *adj*
charming, magnetic, attractive, glamorous, appealing, fascinating, captivating, irresistible

charitable *adj*
philanthropic, humanitarian, benevolent, benign, kind, compassionate, sympathetic, understanding, considerate, generous, open-handed, liberal, tolerant, broad-minded, kindly, lenient, forgiving, indulgent, gracious
FORMAL magnanimous, beneficent, bounteous, eleemosynary
Fა uncharitable, inconsiderate, unforgiving

charitably *adv*
kindly, compassionately, sympathetically, considerately, generously, tolerantly, open-mindedly, liberally, graciously
FORMAL bounteously

charity *n*

1 fund, trust, foundation, caritas, voluntary organization, non-profit-making organization, not-for-profit organization, mission, institution, confraternity
OLD hospital

2 *live on charity*
gift, donation, handout, aid, relief, contribution, funding, (financial) assistance, alms

3 GENEROSITY, goodwill, bountifulness, almsgiving, philanthropy, unselfishness, altruism, benevolence, benignness, kindness, goodness, humanity, compassion, considerateness, thoughtfulness, tender-heartedness, love, affection, tolerance, clemency, indulgence
FORMAL beneficence, munificence

4 *show some charity*
compassion, kindness, sympathy, kind-heartedness, graciousness, consideration, concern, tolerance, leniency
Fა **3** selfishness, malice

PROVERBS
Charity begins at home

charlatan *n*
impostor, cheat, fake, fraud, confidence trickster, pretender, bogus caller/official, quack, sham, swindler, mountebank, deceiver
COLLOQ. phoney, con man

charm *n, v*

◆ *n*

1 ATTRACTION, allure, allurement, magnetism, appeal, delightfulness, attractiveness, desirability, fascination, enchantment, captivation, glamour, prestige, aroma; *dialect* comether
COLLOQ. it, what it takes

2 *a lucky charm*
trinket, ornament, talisman, medicine, phylactery, mascot, amulet, fetish, idol, grisgris, ju-ju, obi, periapt, *porte-bonheur*, hand of glory
SLANG *N Am* mojo

3 *the magician's charm*
spell, sorcery, magic, abracadabra, abraxas
OLD *Scot* weird

◆ *v*
please, delight, enrapture, captivate, fascinate, beguile, enchant, bewitch, mesmerize, attract, draw, take, allure, intrigue, cajole, win, enamour, seduce
OLD becharm, encharm
Fა repel, disgust

charming *adj*
pleasing, delightful, pleasant, lovely, captivating, enchanting, attractive, fetching, appealing, tasteful, sweet, cute, winsome, alluring, engaging, tempting, glamorous, seductive, winning, irresistible
FORMAL delectable
Fა ugly, unattractive, repulsive

QUOTATIONS
All charming people have something to conceal, usually their total dependence on the appreciation of others
CYRIL CONNOLLY, *Enemies of Promise*

charmingly *adv*
pleasingly, delightfully, pleasantly, attractively, enchantingly, sweetly, winsomely, alluringly, glamorously, irresistibly
FORMAL delectably
Fა unattractively, repulsively

chart *n, v*

◆ *n*

1 *a chart showing the patient's temperature*
diagram, table, graph, map, plan, blueprint, bar chart, flow chart, pie chart, histogram, worm, flow sheet, Mind Map®
TECHNICAL nomogram, nomograph

2 *number one in the charts*
hit parade, top twenty, list, league

◆ *v*

1 *chart an area*
map, map out, sketch, draw, draft, outline, delineate, mark, plot, place

2 MONITOR, document, record, keep a record of, put on record, note, register, observe, follow

charter *n, v*

◆ *n*
right, privilege, prerogative, authority, authorization, permit, licence, franchise, concession, contract, covenant, indenture, deed, bond, warrant, sanction, document
TECHNICAL *Scot* novodamus
OLD charta, carta
FORMAL accreditation

◆ *v*
hire, rent, lease, commission, engage, employ, authorize, sanction, license

chary *adj*
careful, prudent, cautious, wary, shy, tender, guarded, heedful, uneasy, unwilling, reluctant, slow, suspicious, leery
FORMAL circumspect
COLLOQ. cagey
Fა heedless, unwary

chase *v, n*

◆ *v*
pursue, follow, hunt, run after, give chase, track, drive, trail, tail, shadow, hound, expel, send away, rush, hurry, course, chivvy, sick
OLD prosecute, scorse
COLLOQ. be hot on someone's heels

◆ *n*
pursuit, trail, running after, hunt, hunting, coursing, rush
OLD chivvy

chasm *n*

1 *a chasm in the rocks*
crack, rift, split, cleft, fissure, crevasse, canyon, gorge, ravine, gap, gape, opening, gulf, abyss, void, hollow, cavity, crater, breach, yawn
2 *a chasm between two people*
rift, split, gulf, gap, opening, breach, divorce, separation, estrangement, alienation, disagreement, quarrel

chassis *n*
framework, bodywork, frame, fuselage, skeleton, structure, substructure, undercarriage

chaste *adj*

1 *a chaste person*
pure, virginal, unsullied, undefiled, immaculate, abstinent, continent, celibate, unmarried, single, virtuous, moral, innocent, demure, vestal
OLD graced, honest
2 *a chaste style*
modest, decent, plain, simple, restrained, classic, bare, austere, unadorned, unembellished
F3 **1** promiscuous, immoral, corrupt **2** unrestrained, decorated

chasten *v*
humble, humiliate, tame, subdue, repress, curb, restrain, moderate, soften, discipline, punish, correct, reprove
FORMAL chastise, castigate

chastise *v*
punish, discipline, reprimand, correct, reprove, scold, censure, beat, flog, whip, lash, scourge, smack, spank, strap, cane
OLD disple, swinge; (*Spenser*) reform
FORMAL admonish, castigate, upbraid, berate
COLLOQ. haul over the coals, dress down, take to task, wallop
SLANG fix
F3 praise, encourage

chastisement *n*
punishment, discipline, correction, censure, scolding, beating, flogging, whipping, smacking, spanking
FORMAL admonition, castigation
COLLOQ. dressing-down, walloping

chastity *n*
purity, virginity, maidenhood, modesty, abstinence, temperateness, continence, continency, celibacy, unmarried state, singleness, virtue, honour, innocence, immaculateness
OLD (*Shakesp*) honesty
F3 promiscuity, immorality

chat *v, n*
♦ *v*
talk, gossip, chatter, tittle-tattle, chitchat, coze, babble, jabber; *dialect* cosher; *Scot* blether; *Scot & N Am* crack; *Aust* yabber
FORMAL converse
COLLOQ. natter, rabbit (on), gas, waffle, prattle, chinwag, jaw, chew the rag/fat, shoot the breeze; *Aust* wongi
SLANG schmooze
♦ *n*
talk, conversation, gossip, tête-à-tête, heart-to-heart, cosy chat, small talk, tittle-tattle, causerie, coze; *Scot* blether; *Aust* yabber
COLLOQ. natter, confab, chinwag, rap; *N Am* visit; *Aust* wongi
SLANG schmooze

■ **chat up**
flirt with, try to get off with, make a pass at, make advances to, ogle, leer at, eye
COLLOQ. come on to

chatter *v, n*
♦ *v*
chat, chitchat, gossip, tattle, tittle-tattle, gabble, babble, jabber, rattle (on), cackle, clack,

clatter, jargon, palaver; *dialect* chitter, mag; *Scot* blether
COLLOQ. pass the time of day, natter, witter, rabbit (on), gab, gas, waffle, prattle, chinwag, earbash, jaw, talk the hind legs off a donkey, chunter
♦ *n*
talk, conversation, gossip, tête-à-tête, chitchat, natter, jabber, witter, prattle, babble, tittle-tattle, jaw, tattle, twattle, patter, jargon, clitter-clatter, gibble-gabble, talkee-talkee, tongue-work; *dialect* mag; *Scot* blether, clash, yatter, gabnash, nashgab
COLLOQ. confab, chinwag, yap
SLANG gammon

chatterbox *n*
chatterer, babbler, gossipper, gossip, talker, conversationalist, jabberer, tittle-tattler, tattler
COLLOQ. natterer, windbag, gasbag, gasser, gabber, big mouth, blabbermouth, loudmouth

chatty *adj*

1 *a chatty person*
talkative, gossipy, conversational, communicative, garrulous, gushing, effusive, verbose, long-winded, glib
FORMAL loquacious
COLLOQ. gabby, mouthy
2 *a chatty letter*
newsy, friendly, informal, casual, colloquial, conversational, gossipy, familiar
F3 quiet, taciturn

chauvinism *n*
jingoism, nationalism, bias, prejudice, partisanship, flag-waving, sexism, male chauvinism

chauvinist *adj, n*
♦ *adj*
jingoist, nationalist, biased, prejudiced, flag-waving, sexist, male chauvinist
♦ *n*
jingoist, nationalist, male chauvinist
COLLOQ. MCP, male chauvinist pig

chauvinistic *adj*
biased, prejudiced, sexist, jingoistic, nationalistic

cheap *adj*

1 INEXPENSIVE, reasonable, low-price, low-cost, affordable, bargain, reduced, cut-price, knock-down, marked-down, discounted, slashed, rock-bottom, giveaway, throwaway, budget, economy, sale, economical, no-frills, cheap-rate, reduced-rate, concessional-rate, on special offer, value-for-money, a good buy, bargain-basement, à *bon marché*
OLD good-cheap
COLLOQ. bargainous, a snip, a steal, going for a song, dirt-cheap, dog-cheap, ten a penny, on a shoestring
2 SHODDY, cheap and nasty, tatty, tawdry, inferior, second-rate, worthless, vulgar, tasteless, common, chintz, gingerbread, sixpenny, improvised, ramshackle, poor, cheapjack, paltry
COLLOQ. cheapo, tacky; *N Am* two-bit, a dime a dozen, jitney
3 *cheap comments*
mean, contemptible, despicable, low, vulgar, sordid
F3 **1** expensive, costly, dear **2** superior, good quality **3** noble, admirable

---

SYNONYM NUANCES

sense 1
Reasonable and **affordable** are both positive-sounding terms, suggesting simply that something is not overpriced: *Stilton is an affordable substitute for Roquefort.* **Bargain** is similarly positive, in that it suggests you getting a good deal for your money, as is **giveaway**, which is usually applied to price to create the impression of a virtual gift. Other terms with much the same meaning have different connotations, however;

throwaway, for instance, connotes something of little value rather than a desirably low price.
   Budget and **economy**, although they can be used straightforwardly to describe something cheap because it is the lower end of a scale, may also have associations of poor quality or discomfort: *economy air travel.*
Economical is different again, however, having as it does the positive implication of long-term savings for the buyer: *the development of a more economical car.*

cheapen *v*
devalue, degrade, lower, demean, depreciate, belittle, discredit, downgrade
FORMAL disparage, denigrate, derogate

cheaply *adv*
inexpensively, affordably, economically, reasonably, at low cost, at an affordable price, on special offer, at a cheap rate, at a reduced/discounted rate, at rock-bottom prices, with no frills, à *bon marché*
F∃ expensively

cheat *v, n*
♦ *v*
1 *cheat someone*
defraud, swindle, diddle, short-change, double-cross, mislead, deceive, dupe, fool, trick, hoodwink, gull, beguile, cozen, fiddle, fleece, fake, bluff, welsh, cajole, rogue, skelder, hocus, chouse, cog, smouch, fudge, jink; (*offensive*) jew; *Scot* begunk
OLD baffle, colt, cully, fob, mump, slur; (*Shakesp*) cony-catch
COLLOQ. do, do one over on, do the dirty on, con, take, pull the wool over someone's eyes, two-time, bilk, fix, rig, bamboozle, bam, clip, fox; *Aust & NZ* duckshove
SLANG take for a ride, screw, sting, touch, trim, chisel, chizz, swiz, gum, queer, rip off, stiff, take to the cleaners, do a flanker; *N Am* hornswoggle
2 *cheated out of their inheritance*
prevent, deprive, deny, thwart, frustrate, check
OLD (*Shakesp*) bob
COLLOQ. do, have
♦ *n*
cheater, dodger, crook, fraud, swindler, extortioner, double-crosser, impostor, charlatan, deceiver, trickster, confidence trickster, rogue, cozener, sharper, chouse, picaroon
OLD biter; (*Shakesp*) cony-catcher, gull-catcher
COLLOQ. con man, shark
SLANG chiseller, chizz, intake; *N Am* gyp; *Aust* dingo
OLD SLANG snap

SYNONYM NUANCES

verb sense 1
Predictably, many of the synonyms for cheat have strong implications of disapproval. The terms **defraud**, **swindle**, and **diddle** generally suggest cheating someone out of money, as can the word **fiddle**, which can also be used of tampering with something with the aim of deceiving: *he fiddled the statistics in his thesis.*
Short-change, although used literally of money, can be used in wider contexts: *the victim's family felt short-changed by the sentence.*
   Double-cross carries an emotive suggestion of betrayal, and **welsh** is similarly marked, but used in the context of dereliction of an obligation or financial debt. The terms **mislead**, **deceive**, **dupe**, **fool**, **trick**, **hoodwink** and the less common **gull** would usually be used in the context of convincing someone of a falsehood: *don't be hoodwinked into thinking money brings happiness.*

Beguile has strong associations of cheating someone through charm, and **cajole**, through persuasion: *she could not be cajoled into agreeing.* If, however, you imply that something has been made less clear in order to obscure the truth, you could use **fudge**: *the media fudged the events.*

check *v, n*
♦ *v*
1 EXAMINE, inspect, scrutinize, look at (closely), go through, scan, investigate, probe, inquire into, test, monitor, police, study, research, analyse, compare, cross-check, screen, take stock, make sure, confirm, verify
FORMAL corroborate, substantiate, validate
COLLOQ. give the once-over
2 *check an impulse*
curb, bridle, restrain, control, limit, contain, rein in, repress, inhibit, damp, thwart, hinder, impede, obstruct, bar, delay, slow (down), stop, staunch, stem, arrest, halt, bring to a standstill
FORMAL retard
♦ *n*
1 EXAMINATION, inspection, scrutiny, check-up, investigation, inquiry, audit, test, research, monitoring, analysis, probe, confirmation, verification
COLLOQ. once-over
2 BILL, invoice, statement, account, charges, reckoning, tally; *N Am* tab
■ **check in**
register, book in, enrol, record your arrival, report your arrival
■ **check out**
1 *check out of a hotel*
leave, pay the bill, settle up
2 *check out the procedure*
examine, investigate, test, study, look into
COLLOQ. recce
■ **check up**
investigate, inspect, evaluate, assess, analyse, probe, inquire into, ascertain, make sure, confirm, verify
■ **hold/keep in check**
restrain, hold back, keep back, suppress, repress, curb, bridle, rein in, stop, arrest, prevent, hinder, obstruct, impede

check-up *n*
examination, inspection, work-up, scrutiny, investigation, inquiry, audit, test, research, monitoring, analysis, evaluation, appraisal, probe, confirmation, verification

cheek *n*
1 *his cheeks went red*
jowl, jaw, chop, chap, dimple; *Scot* chafts
TECHNICAL gena
OLD wang
Related adjectives: buccal, malar
2 IMPERTINENCE, impudence, insolence, disrespect, brazenness, audacity, gall
FORMAL effrontery, temerity
COLLOQ. nerve, sauce, lip, mouth, attitude, neck, brass neck, chutzpah
SLANG *Aust* arse

cheekily *adv*
impertinently, impudently, insolently, disrespectfully, pertly
F∃ respectfully, politely

cheeky *adj*
impertinent, impudent, insolent, disrespectful, impolite, forward, brazen, pert, audacious, overfamiliar
COLLOQ. fresh, saucy, lippy, mouthy; *N Am* sassy
SLANG gobby
F∃ respectful, polite

cheep *v, n*
chirp, chirrup, tweet, peep, trill, sing, twitter, warble, pipe, whistle

cheer v, n

♦ v

1 ACCLAIM, hail, clap, applaud, salute, welcome, celebrate, fanfare, shout, support; *Aust & NZ* barrack for
COLLOQ. root for
2 COMFORT, console, brighten, gladden, warm, uplift, raise/lift the spirits of, elate, exhilarate, encourage, hearten, enliven, buoy up
FORMAL solace, inspirit
COLLOQ. buck up, perk up
🔁 **1** boo, jeer **2** dishearten, discourage

♦ n

1 *the cheers of the crowd*
acclamation, hurrah, bravo, applause, clapping, ovation
FORMAL plaudits
2 CHEERFULNESS, gladness, happiness, hopefulness, joyfulness, high spirits, light-heartedness, merriment, merrymaking, revelry
🔁 criticism

■ **cheer up**
comfort, console, encourage, brighten (up), hearten, liven (up), take heart, rally
COLLOQ. buck up, perk up

> QUOTATIONS
> Cheer up – the worst is yet to come
> PHILANDER CHASE JOHNSON

cheerful adj
1 *a cheerful person*
happy, glad, contented, joyful, joyous, blithe, carefree, light-hearted, cheery, good-humoured, sunny, optimistic, enthusiastic, hearty, genial, jovial, jolly, gay, merry, lively, animated, exuberant, bright, smiling, laughing, spirited, in good spirits, chirpy, breezy, jaunty, buoyant, sparkling, upbeat
2 *painted in a cheerful yellow*
attractive, pleasing, pleasant, agreeable, delightful, warm, sunny, bright, comforting, encouraging, heartening, inspiring, stirring
🔁 **1** sad, dejected, depressed **2** depressing, disheartening

cheerily adv
happily, gladly, light-heartedly, cheerfully, enthusiastically, jovially, brightly
🔁 sadly, unhappily

cheerio interj
goodbye, farewell, adieu, *au revoir*
COLLOQ. cheers, so long, bye, bye-bye, see you, see you later, ta-ta; *Aust* hooray

cheerless adj
gloomy, dismal, dreary, dull, depressing, dejected, despondent, austere, barren, desolate, forlorn, grim, bleak, cold, sad, unhappy, sombre, sorrowful, comfortless, joyless, lonely, melancholy, miserable, mournful, dank, dark, dingy, drab, sullen, sunless, wintery, uninviting

FORMAL disconsolate, dolorous
🔁 bright, cheerful

cheers interj
1 *say cheers as a toast*
bottoms up, here's to you, your good health, here's looking to you, here's mud in your eye, here's to ..., to absent friends, down the hatch, happy landings, all the best, chin-chin, *prosit, skol, slàinte*
2 THANK YOU, thank you very much, bless you, much obliged
COLLOQ. many thanks, thanks a lot, ta
3 GOODBYE, farewell, adieu, *au revoir*
COLLOQ. so long, bye, bye-bye, see you, see you later, ta-ta

cheery adj
happy, glad, contented, joyful, carefree, light-hearted, cheerful, optimistic, enthusiastic, hearty, genial, jovial, jolly, gay, merry, lively, animated, exuberant, bright, smiling, laughing, spirited, in good spirits, chirpy, breezy, jaunty, buoyant, sparkling
🔁 downcast, sad

cheese n
Related adjective: caseous
See panel below

cheesed off adj
fed up, disappointed, bored, depressed, discontented, disgruntled, dissatisfied, annoyed, disgusted
COLLOQ. brassed off, browned off, hacked off, sick and tired
SLANG pissed off; *N Am* pissed
🔁 contented, happy

chemistry

Terms used in chemistry include:

acid	chlorination	gas
alkali	combustion	halogen
analysis	compound	hydrolysis
atom	corrosion	immiscible
atomic number	covalent bond	indicator
atomic structure	crystal	inert gas
subatomic parti-	cycle	ion
cles	decomposition	ionic bond
base	diffusion	isomer
bond	dissociation	isotope
buffer	distillation	lipid
catalysis	electrochemical	liquid
catalyst	cell	litmus paper
chain reaction	electrode	litmus test
chemical bond	electrolysis	mass
chemical com-	electron	matter
pound	emulsion	metallic bond
chemical element	fermentation	mixture
chemical equation	fixation	mole
chemical reaction	formula	molecule
chemist	free radical	neutron

Varieties of cheese include:

Amsterdam	Cheshire	Dunlop	Jarlsberg®	Parmesan	Saint-Paulin
Asiago	chevreton	Edam	Killarney	pecorino	scamorza
Bel Paese	Churnton	Emmental	Lancashire	Petit Suisse	smoked cheese
Bleu d'Auvergne	Comté	Emmentaler	Leerdammer	Pont-l'Évêque	Stilton
Blue Cheshire	cottage cheese	ewe-cheese	Leicester	Port Salut	stinking bishop
Blue Vinny	cream cheese	Feta	Limburg(er)	processed cheese	stracchino
Boursin	crottin	Fontina	Lymeswold	provolone	Vacherin
Brie	Crowdie	fromage frais	manchego	quark	vegetarian cheese
Caboc	curd cheese	Gloucester	mascarpone	reblochon	Wensleydale
Caerphilly	Danish blue	Gorgonzola	Monterey Jack	Red Leicester	
Camembert	Derby	Gouda	mouse-trap	Red Windsor	
Cantal	Dolcelatte	Grana Padano	mozzarella	ricotta	
Carré	Dorset Blue	Gruyère	Neufchâtel	Roquefort	
Cheddar	Double Gloucester	Huntsman	Orkney	sage Derby	

noble gas	radioactivity	solvent
nucleus	reaction	substance
oxidation	reduction	suspension
periodic table	respiration	symbol
pH	salt	synthesis
polymer	solids	valency
proton	solution	zwitterion

See also **acid**; **gas**; **mineral**.

chequered *adj*
1 *a chequered tablecloth*
checked, multicoloured, variegated, particoloured, striped, diced
TECHNICAL checky, chequy
2 VARIED, mixed, diverse, with good and bad parts, with ups and downs, with sad and happy downs, with its fair share of rough and tumble

cherish *v*
1 *cherish someone*
care for, look after, love, take (good) care of, hold dear, have at heart, encourage, make much of, treasure, adore, hug, support, foster, nurture, nourish, nurse, sustain
OLD refocillate, tender
2 *cherish a tradition/privilege*
foster, nurture, sustain, hold dear, value, prize, treasure, enshrine
3 *cherish hopes/memories*
harbour, shelter, entertain, hold dear, value, prize, treasure, nourish, brood on

cherub *n*
angel, seraph

cherubic *adj*
adorable, appealing, cute, sweet, innocent, lov(e)able, lovely, heavenly, angelic, seraphic

chest *n*
1 *a man with a hairy chest*
breast
TECHNICAL sternum, thorax
Related adjective: pectoral, thoracic
2 *a treasure chest*
trunk, crate, box, case, casket, coffer, strongbox, bunker, hutch, ark, chiffonier, commode, tallboy, bahut, *cassone*, cub, slop-chest; *Scot* kist, corn-kist, girnel, meal-ark; *N Am* bureau, dresser
OLD cap-case, larnax, scrine, shrine

chew *v*
bite, gnaw, munch, champ, chomp, crunch, grind, eat, ruminate; *dialect* chaw, chumble
FORMAL masticate, manducate

■ **chew over**
consider, meditate on, mull over, ponder, weigh up, muse on, deliberate upon
FORMAL ruminate on
COLLOQ. put on your thinking cap

chic *adj*
elegant, fashionable, sophisticated, modish, smart, stylish, dapper, à la mode
COLLOQ. snazzy, trendy, with it
≝ outmoded, unfashionable

chicanery *n*
trickery, deception, fraud, deceitfulness, dishonesty, deviousness, cheating, double-dealing, guile, hoodwinking, duplicity, artifice, intrigue, sharp practice, underhandedness, sophistry, subterfuge, wiles
COLLOQ. dodge, jiggery-pokery

chide *v*
scold, tell off, blame, criticize, censure, lecture, rebuke, chastise, reprehend, reprimand, reproach, reprove, row, dress, rate; *Scot* quarrel
OLD shend
FORMAL admonish, berate, upbraid, objurgate
≝ praise

chief *adj, n*
♦ *adj*
leading, foremost, uppermost, highest, supreme, grand, arch, head, premier, principal, main, key, central, prime, prevailing, predominant, dominant, pre-eminent, outstanding, vital, most important, essential, primary, major, controlling, directing, supervising
≝ minor, unimportant
♦ *n*
ruler, chieftain, lord, overlord, master, supremo, head, principal, leader, commander, captain, governor, boss, director, manager, premier, prime minister, president, suzerain, chair, chairperson, chairman, chairwoman, chief executive, managing director, superintendent, superior, ringleader
COLLOQ. gaffer, top dog, top banana, big cheese, big noise, big gun
SLANG *Scot* head bummer; *N Am* honcho

chiefly *adv*
mainly, mostly, for the most part, in the main, predominantly, principally, primarily, essentially, especially, generally, on the whole, usually

child *n*
youngster, young person, little one, little 'un, young one, young 'un, baby, infant, toddler, minor, juvenile, boy, little boy, girl, little girl, son, daughter, grandchild, stepchild, schoolchild, adolescent, teenager, youth, young adult, descendant, godchild, orphanmite, changeling, innocent, suckling, weanling, tiny, trot, littling, pledge, *enfant*, papoose; (*offensive*) pickaninny; preschooler, underfive, preteen, weeny-bopper, prodigy, wunderkind, ragamuffin, imp, waif, brat, jackanapes, bambino, cherub, elf, chick, chit, guttersnipe, Benjamin, olive branch; *Scot* bairn, wean, tyke, knave-bairn, gyte, smout; *N Am* subteen
OLD bantling, dilling, wanton, wench; (*Shakesp*) eyas-musket; *Scot* gangrel
FORMAL offspring, issue, progeny
COLLOQ. tot, tiny tot, kid, nipper, sprog; *N Am* hellion; *Scot* get
SLANG kinchin, ankle-biter; *N Am* rug rat
OLD SLANG butter-print

childbirth *n*
labour, delivery, confinement, child-bearing, lying-in, pregnancy, maternity
TECHNICAL parturition
FORMAL travail, accouchement, puerperal

childhood *n*
babyhood, infancy, boyhood, girlhood, schooldays, early days, early years, youth, adolescence, minority, immaturity

> **QUOTATIONS**
> Childhood is the kingdom where nobody dies. / Nobody that matters, that is
> EDNA ST VINCENT MILLAY, *Wine From These Grapes*

childish *adj*
babyish, boyish, girlish, infantile, puerile, juvenile, immature, irresponsible, silly, foolish, frivolous
≝ mature, sensible

> **!** **childish** or **childlike**?
> You describe someone as *childish* if you think they are behaving in a silly immature way: *Stop being so childish! Childlike* is a neutral term: *childlike innocence.*

childishly *adv*
immaturely, irresponsibly, foolishly

childlike *adj*
innocent, naive, ingenuous, artless, guileless, credulous, trusting, trustful, simple, natural, unaffected

> **!** **childlike** or **childish**?
> *See panel at* **childish**.

chill *n, v, adj*

♦ *n*

1 *a wintry chill in the air*
coolness, cold, coldness, rawness, bite, nip, crispness, iciness

2 *catch a chill*
cold, fever, flu, influenza, virus

3 *a chill ran down my spine*
shiver, fear, anxiety, apprehension, dread

E₃ 1 warmth

♦ *v*

1 COOL, cool down, refrigerate, make/become cold(er), freeze, ice

2 FRIGHTEN, terrify, dismay, scare, dishearten, petrify, discourage, depress, dampen

E₃ 1 warm, heat

♦ *adj*
cold, cool, raw, sharp, biting, icy, freezing, wintry, chilly, frigid, depressing, bleak

COLLOQ. nippy, parky

E₃ warm, hot

■ **chill out**
calm down, relax, have a rest, unwind

COLLOQ. take it easy

chilly *adj*

1 *chilly weather*
cold, fresh, brisk, crisp, cool, raw, sharp, biting, icy, freezing, frigid, wintry

COLLOQ. nippy, parky

2 *a chilly response*
cool, frigid, unsympathetic, unwelcoming, aloof, stony, distant, unresponsive, unfriendly, unenthusiastic, hostile

E₃ 1 warm **2** friendly

chime *v, n*

♦ *v*
sound, strike, toll, ring, peal, clang, ding, dong, jingle, tinkle, reverberate, boom, resound

FORMAL tintinnabulate

♦ *n*
toll, ring, peal, clang, ding, dong, tinkle, boom, reverberation

■ **chime in**

1 *chime in when someone is talking*
interrupt

FORMAL interject, interpose

COLLOQ. chip in, butt in, cut in

2 *his analysis chimed in with mine*
fit in, harmonize, correspond, blend, agree, be consistent, be similar

chimera *n*
illusion, fantasy, delusion, dream, fancy, idle fancy, figment of the imagination, hallucination, will-o'-the-wisp, spectre

chimney *n*
shaft, stack, chimney stalk, vent, flue, funnel, cleft, crevice, lum, femerall

china *n*

1 *a vase made of china*
porcelain, ceramic, pottery, earthenware, terracotta

2 *serve the best china*
crockery, plates, dishes, cups and saucers, tableware, dinner service

Chinese calendar

The animals representing the years in which people are born:

rat	dragon	monkey
buffalo	snake	rooster
tiger	horse	dog
rabbit (or hare)	goat (or sheep)	pig

chink *n*
crack, rift, cleft, fissure, crevice, cut, split, slit, slot, cavity, opening, aperture, gap, space

chip *n, v*

♦ *n*

1 *fish and chips*
fried potato, (French) fry

2 NOTCH, nick, crack, scratch, dent, flaw

3 FRAGMENT, bit, piece, scrap, wafer, splinter, sliver, flake, shred, shard, shaving, paring

4 *gambling chips*
counter, disc, token

♦ *v*
chisel, whittle, nick, crack, fragment, break (off), crumble, notch, gash, snick, damage

■ **chip in**

1 CONTRIBUTE, make a donation, donate, club together, have a collection, pay, subscribe

COLLOQ. have a whip-round

2 *chip in when someone is talking*
interrupt

FORMAL interject, interpose

COLLOQ. chime in, butt in, cut in

chirp *v, n*
chirrup, tweet, cheep, peep, trill, twitter, warble, sing, pipe, whistle

chirpy *adj*
cheerful, cheery, bright, happy, glad, jolly, merry, gay, jaunty, blithe

COLLOQ. perky

E₃ downcast, sad

chit-chat *n*
chat, chatter, talk, conversation, gossip, idle gossip, tête-à-tête, heart-to-heart, cosy chat, small talk, tittle-tattle

COLLOQ. natter, confab, chinwag

chivalrous *adj*
gentlemanly, polite, courteous, well-mannered, gallant, heroic, valiant, brave, courageous, bold, gracious, noble, honourable, knightly

E₃ ungallant, cowardly

chivalry *n*
gentlemanliness, politeness, courtesy, graciousness, good manners, courtliness, gallantry, bravery, courage, boldness, honour, truthfulness, integrity, bushido

chivvy *v*
badger, harass, annoy, hound, goad, nag, urge, pester, plague, pressure, hurry (up), prod, torment

FORMAL importune

COLLOQ. bug, hassle

chock-a-block *adj*
packed, crammed, full, overfull, jammed, crowded, congested, brimful

COLLOQ. jam-packed, packed like sardines, full to bursting

SLANG chocker

E₃ empty

choice *n, adj*

♦ *n*

1 *a choice of several dishes; make a choice between two things*
selection, variety, range, choosing, opting, picking, preference, decision, election, discrimination

2 *have no choice but to go*
option, alternative, answer, solution

♦ *adj*
select, best, superior, prime, plum, excellent, first-class, first-rate, fine, finest, exquisite, exclusive, hand-picked, special, prize, valuable, precious

E₃ inferior, poor

> **QUOTATIONS**
> You pays your money and you takes your choice
> *Punch*

choke v

1 STRANGLE, throttle, asphyxiate, suffocate, stifle, smother, suppress, overpower, overwhelm
OLD worry
2 OBSTRUCT, constrict, congest, clog, block, dam (up), bar, close, stop, plug, glut, silt (up)
OLD (*Spenser*) accloy; stap
FORMAL occlude
3 COUGH, gag, retch
■ **choke back**
suppress, restrain, contain, control, check, curb, repress, inhibit, fight back

choleric adj
fiery, hot-tempered, angry, bad-tempered, ill-tempered, quick-tempered, testy, touchy, irascible, irritable, petulant
COLLOQ. crabbed, crabby, crotchety
E3 calm, placid

choose v

1 *choose a new dress*
pick (out), select, single out, take, go for, opt for, vote for, decide on, settle on, fix on, designate, adopt, take up, appoint, elect, predestine
FORMAL espouse
COLLOQ. plump for
2 *choose to do something*
decide, prefer, wish, desire, make up your mind, want, favour, see fit

---

SYNONYM NUANCES

sense 1
Pick (out), **decide on**, **settle on** and **fix on** are terms that could be used to refer to choosing after some thought. **Select** is similar, but with more implication of discrimination in your choice: *he was selected for the England squad*. **Take**, **opt for** or **go for** sometimes imply instinct rather than careful discrimination: *I opted for the quickest route home*.
 Single out might be used where there is an element of drawing special attention to something: *the over-40s are being singled out as potential customers*. To refer to purposefully marking something out for specific recognition, you may wish to use **designate**: *nursing staff designated specifically for the care of the elderly*. Both **adopt** and **take up** suggest a degree of support or activity is involved: *they took up the theme of citizenship*; whilst **appoint** and **elect** are generally used in the context of deciding on suitable candidates for office, though the latter may also be suggestive of deciding a course of action: *they elected to live together*.
 The term **predestine** lends itself to a narrower range of uses and specifically suggests a preordained decision: *he was predestined to be black sheep of the family*.

---

choosy adj
selective, discriminating, fussy, particular, finicky, fastidious, exacting, faddy
COLLOQ. picky, pernickety; *N Am* persnickety
E3 undemanding

chop v
cut (up), hack, fell, hew, lop, saw, sever, truncate, slice, carve, cleave, divide, dissect, split, slash, axe
■ **chop up**
cut (up), cut into pieces, slice (up), divide, cube, dice, shred, mince, grind, grate

choppy adj
rough, turbulent, tempestuous, stormy, squally, blustery, ruffled, wavy, uneven, broken
E3 calm, still, peaceful

chore n
task, job, errand, routine, duty, burden, piece of work

chortle v
cackle, chuckle, guffaw, laugh, crow, snigger, snort

chorus n
1 REFRAIN, response, burden, strain, call, shout
2 CHOIR, choristers, singers, vocalists, ensemble, choral group

Christ n
Messiah, Saviour, Son of God, Son of Man, deliverer, Redeemer, I am, Immanuel, Lord, Lord of lords, King of kings, Word of God, Lamb of God, Good Shepherd

christen v
1 *christen a baby*
baptize, name, give a name to, sprinkle, immerse
2 *christened it 'the emerald forest'*
name, call, dub, title, style, term, designate
3 *christen the wine glasses*
inaugurate, use for the first time, begin using

Christmas n
Xmas, Noel, Christmas-tide, Christmas-time, Nativity, Yule, Yuletide
COLLOQ. Chrissie, Crimbo

chronic adj
1 *a chronic illness*
persistent, deep-seated, recurring, incessant, constant, continual, long-lasting, long-standing, long-term, ingrained, deep-rooted
2 *a chronic worrier*
inveterate, confirmed, habitual, hardened, incorrigible
3 *the film was chronic*
awful, terrible, dreadful, appalling, atrocious, frightful, abysmal
COLLOQ. ropy, a load of rubbish
SLANG naff, crappy, the pits, pants
E3 1 temporary **3** excellent

chronically adv
1 *chronically sick*
persistently, recurrently, incessantly, constantly, continually, long-term, deep-rootedly
2 *chronically disorganized*
inveterately, habitually, incorrigibly

chronicle n, v
♦ n
account, record, register, annals, archives, diary, calendar, history, journal, narrative, story, saga, epic
♦ v
recount, narrate, relate, report, tell, write down, set down, record, put on record, register, enter, list

chronicler n
historian, archivist, annalist, diarist, narrator, recorder, reporter, scribe, historiographer, chronographer, chronologer

chronological adj
consecutive, sequential, in sequence, progressive, ordered, in order, serial, historical

chubby adj
plump, fat, podgy, fleshy, flabby, stout, portly, round, full, tubby, paunchy, roly-poly
FORMAL rotund
E3 slim, skinny

chuck v
1 THROW, cast, toss, fling, heave, hurl, jettison, pitch, put, shy, sling
2 *chuck a habit/your boyfriend*
give up, abandon, reject, discard, get rid of, jilt
FORMAL forsake
COLLOQ. quit, dump, pack in, give the brush-off, give the elbow

chuckle v
laugh, laugh quietly, giggle, titter, snigger, chortle, snort, cackle, crow

chum n
friend, companion, comrade
COLLOQ. mate, pal, crony, buddy
E3 enemy

chummy *adj*
friendly, affectionate, close, intimate, sociable
COLLOQ. mat(e)y, pally, thick

chunk *n*
lump, hunk, mass, wedge, block, slab, piece, dollop, portion
COLLOQ. wodge

chunky *adj*
1 *a chunky man*
heavy, broad, well-built, stocky, solid, thickset, dumpy
2 *a chunky bag*
large, thick, bulky, substantial, weighty, heavy, unwieldy, awkward, cumbersome
F3 1 tall, skinny **2** small, light

church *n*
1 *go to church*
place of worship, chapel, house of God, Lord's house, house of prayer, house of worship, cathedral, minster, abbey, tabernacle, meeting-house, bethel, chantry, shrine, basilica, Bethesda, preaching-house, procathedral, temple; *Scot* kirk
2 *the Methodist Church*
denomination, tradition, grouping, sect, cult
3 CONGREGATION, assembly, fellowship, community, people of God, body of Christ, bride of Christ, flock, fold
TECHNICAL ecclesia
Related adjective: ecclesiastical
See panels below

churchyard *n*
graveyard, cemetery, God's acre, burial ground, burial place, burial site, necropolis, charnel, house; *Scot* kirkyard, kirkyaird
SLANG boneyard

churlish *adj*
bad-tempered, ill-tempered, harsh, impolite, morose, rough, brusque, rude, sullen, surly, uncivil, unmannerly, ill-mannered, ill-bred, discourteous, unneighbourly, unsociable, loutish, boorish, oafish
COLLOQ. crabbed
F3 polite, urbane

churn *v*
1 *my stomach is churning*
heave, turn, vomit, be sick, retch
COLLOQ. throw up, puke
2 *churn up mud*
move about violently, agitate, beat, stir, disturb, swirl, toss, writhe, convulse, boil, foam, froth, seethe
■ **churn out**
turn out, produce in great quantities, pump out, throw together, knock up

chute *n*
channel, incline, slide, slope, ramp, runway, shaft, funnel, gutter, trough

chutzpah *n*
cheek, impertinence, impudence, gall, insolence, disrespect, brazenness, audacity
COLLOQ. nerve, sauce, lip, mouth, brass neck

cigarette *n*
cigar, menthol, filter-tip, king-size, high-tar, low-tar, roll-up, roll-your-own, smoke, whiff
OLD paper-cigar
COLLOQ. cig, ciggy, fag, tab, fag end, dog end, gasper, joint, spliff, weed, burn, reefer, tailor-made; *N Am* roach
SLANG cancer-stick, coffin-nail, snout
See also panel at **tobacco**.

cinch *n*
COLLOQ. child's play, doddle, piece of cake, snip, scoosh, no-brainer, stroll, walkover, pushover; *N Am* cakewalk

cinders *n*
embers, ashes, clinker, charcoal, coke, slag

cinema *n*
1 FILMS, pictures, movies, motion pictures
OLD flicks; *N Am* nickelodeon
COLLOQ. big screen, silver screen
2 PICTURE-HOUSE; *N Am & Aust* theatre; *S Afr* bioscope; film theatre, movie theatre, movies, entertainment centre, multiplex, picture-palace
COLLOQ. fleapit; *S Afr* scope

cipher *n*
1 CODE, secret writing, secret system, coded message, cryptogram, cryptograph
2 NONENTITY, nobody, yes-man

Parts of a church or cathedral include:

adytum	bell tower	deambulatory	parclose	rood	stall
aisle	chancel	diaconicon	parvis	rood screen	stasidion
almonry	chapel	fenestella	pew	sacellum	stations of the
altar	chapterhouse	font	pinnacle	sacrarium	cross
ambulatory	chevet	frithstool	piscina	sacristy	steeple
antechoir	choir	frontal	porch	sanctuary	stoup
apse	clerestory	gallery	portal	schola cantorum	tambour
arcade	cloister	keystone	predella	sedile	tomb
arch	confessional	lectern	presbytery	sepulchre	tower
atrium	corona	lucarne	pulpit	shrine	transept
baptistery	credence	misericord	reredos	slype	triforium
belfry	crossing	narthex	retrochoir	spire	vault
bell screen	crypt	nave	ringing chamber	squint	

See also **places of worship** *at* **worship**.

Names of church services include:

Advent	Christmas	evening service	Lord's Supper	Mothering Sunday	Requiem Mass
Ascension Day	communion	evensong	marriage	Nones	Vigil Mass
Ash Wednesday	confirmation	funeral	Mass	nuptial Mass	
baptism	dedication	Good Friday	Midnight Mass	Palm Sunday	
benediction	Easter	High Mass	memorial service	Pentecost	
christening	Epiphany	Holy Communion	morning prayers	Remembrance	
Christingle	Eucharist	Holy Matrimony	morning service	Sunday	

See also **celebration**.

circa *adv*
about, approximately, roughly, around, some, something like, odd, more or less, loosely, round about, or thereabouts, approaching, close to, nearly, just about, not far off, in the region/neighbourhood/vicinity of, somewhere in the region of
E‑ exactly

circle *n, v*
◆ *n*
1 RING, hoop, round, annulus, epicycle, disc, discus, ball, sphere, orb, globe, circumference, perimeter, circuit, lap, compass, cordon, girdle, band, belt, orbit, loop, revolution, cycle, rotation, gyration, spiral, coil, curl, halo, circlet, coronet, crown, plate, saucer, turn, tyre, wheel, wreath
Related adjective: circular
2 *circle of friends*
group, band, company, crowd, set, clique, coterie, gang, ring, club, society, assembly, fellowship, fraternity
◆ *v*
1 RING, loop, encircle, surround, belt, gird, encompass, enclose, envelop, hem in, hedge in
FORMAL circumscribe, circumnavigate
2 ROTATE, revolve, move round, pivot, gyrate, circulate, whirl, turn, swivel, wheel, coil, wind

circuit *n*
1 *a racing circuit; run a circuit*
race track, track, running-track, lap, orbit, revolution, course, route, round, beat
FORMAL perambulation
2 *the circuit of the gardens*
circumference, boundary, bounds, limit, range, compass, ambit
3 *a judge's circuit*
tour, district, area, region

circuitous *adj*
roundabout, indirect, oblique, devious, tortuous, winding, meandering, rambling
FORMAL periphrastic, labyrinthine
E‑ direct, straight

circular *adj, n*
◆ *adj*
round, annular, ring-shaped, hoop-shaped, disc-shaped, spherical
◆ *n*
handbill, leaflet, pamphlet, notice, announcement, advertisement, letter, flyer

circulate *v*
1 *circulate information*
spread (around), spread about, diffuse, broadcast, transmit, publicize, publish, issue, give out, propagate, pass round, distribute, go/get around, utter
FORMAL disseminate, promulgate
2 GO ROUND, rotate, revolve, gyrate, whirl, swirl, flow

circulation *n*
1 BLOOD-FLOW, flow, motion, movement, rotation, circling, cycle
TECHNICAL cyclosis
2 SPREAD, transmission, currency, issuing, publication, readership, distribution, publicity, propagation
FORMAL dissemination
■ **in circulation**
in use, available, around, published, issued, printed, current, distributed, spread about/around, afloat

circumference *n*
circuit, circle, perimeter, rim, edge, girth, round, outline, boundary, border, bounds, limits, confines, compass, extremity, margin, arc, verge, fringe, periphery

circumlocution *n*
diffuseness, discursiveness, tautology, indirectness, euphemism, redundancy, roundaboutness, wordiness, verbosity

FORMAL convolution, periphrasis, pleonasm, prolixity
COLLOQ. beating about the bush

circumlocutory *adj*
diffuse, discursive, tautological, indirect, euphemistic, redundant, roundabout, wordy, verbose
FORMAL convoluted, periphrastic, pleonastic, prolix

circumscribe *v*
bound, limit, restrain, restrict, confine, curtail, trim, define, delimit, delineate, demarcate, surround, encircle, enclose, encompass, hem in, pen in

circumspect *adj*
careful, cautious, prudent, attentive, deliberate, discreet, guarded, observant, wary, canny, watchful, vigilant, discriminating, wise
FORMAL sagacious, judicious, politic
E‑ unguarded, unwary, reckless

circumspection *n*
care, carefulness, caution, deliberation, discretion, prudence, guardedness, canniness, chariness, wariness, vigilance
E‑ recklessness

circumstance *n*
1 *died in mysterious circumstances*
condition, fact, factor, situation, position, state, state of affairs, background, environment, arrangement, detail, particular, item, thing, element, event, occurrence, happening, respect, lie of the land, how the land lies
2 *in impoverished circumstances*
situation, means, resources, status, (financial) position, case, lifestyle, plight
3 *a victim of circumstance*
fate, fortune, lot

circumstantial *adj*
conjectural, presumed, deduced, contingent, hearsay, incidental, indirect, provisional, inferred
FORMAL evidential, presumptive, inferential

circumvent *v*
avoid, get round, get out of, get past, evade, bypass, sidestep, steer clear of, dodge, thwart, outwit

circumvention *n*
avoidance, evasion, bypassing, sidestepping, steering clear, thwarting, dodging

cissy
see **sissy, cissy**.

cistern *n*
tank, reservoir, sink, basin, vat

citadel *n*
fortress, stronghold, bastion, castle, keep, tower, fort, fortification, acropolis

citation *n*
1 AWARD, commendation, honour
2 QUOTATION, quote, cutting, excerpt, illustration, mention, passage, reference, source, allusion

cite *v*
quote, mention, refer to, name, specify, state, allude to, exemplify, give an example, enumerate, advance, bring up
FORMAL adduce, evidence

citizen *n*
city-dweller, townsman, townswoman, inhabitant, denizen, resident, householder, voter, taxpayer, freeman, burgher, national, subject, urbanite, local
FORMAL oppidan

city *n*
metropolis, town, urban district, conurbation, megalopolis, metropolitan area, inner city, city centre, downtown, concrete jungle, urban sprawl, precinct, micropolis, cosmopolis, municipality, pentapolis; *N Am* metroplex
COLLOQ. big smoke
Related adjectives: civic, urban

civic *adj*
city, metropolitan, urban, town, municipal, borough, local, public, communal, community

civil *adj*
1 *civil affairs*
domestic, home, national, internal, interior, state, municipal, civic, public, communal, local, community, secular, civilian
2 POLITE, courteous, well-mannered, mannerly, well-bred, cultivated, courtly, refined, civilized, polished, urbane, affable, respectful, complaisant, obliging, accommodating
⟺ 1 international, military, religious **2** uncivil, discourteous, rude

civility *n*
politeness, courteousness, courtesy, breeding, refinement, (good) manners, respect, urbanity, tact, graciousness, affability, pleasantness, amenity
FORMAL comity
⟺ discourtesy, rudeness, uncouthness

civilization *n*
1 *ancient civilizations*
society, human society, culture, customs, community, people
2 *modern western civilization*
progress, advancement, development, education, enlightenment, cultivation, refinement, sophistication, urbanity
⟺ 2 barbarity, primitiveness

civilize *v*
educate, enlighten, instruct, cultivate, refine, edify, polish, sophisticate, socialize, improve, perfect, tame, humanize

civilized *adj*
1 *a civilized society*
advanced, developed, educated, enlightened, cultured, refined, sophisticated, cultivated, urbane, polite, sociable
2 *a polite, civilized manner*
reasonable, sensible, polite, courteous, refined, well-mannered, urbane, cultured, cultivated
⟺ 1 uncivilized, barbarous, primitive **2** harsh, coarse, unreasonable, unsophisticated

civilly *adv*
politely, courteously, urbanely, respectfully, mannerly, courtly, obligingly
⟺ uncivilly, discourteously, rudely

clad *adj*
clothed, wearing, covered, dressed
FORMAL attired

claim *v, n*
◆ *v*
1 MAINTAIN, allege, profess, state, affirm, declare, assert, maintain, contend, hold, insist, pretend
FORMAL avow, aver, postulate, purport, assume
2 *claim a refund*
ask, request, put in for, require, need, demand, exact, take, collect, lay claim to, have a right to, be entitled to, deserve
FORMAL requisition
3 *claimed the lives of three people*
take, cause, kill
◆ *n*
1 ALLEGATION, pretension, affirmation, assertion, contention, declaration, profession, insistence
FORMAL avowal, averment, asseveration

2 APPLICATION, petition, request, requirement, demand, call, right, privilege, entitlement

claimant *n*
applicant, candidate, petitioner, suppliant, supplicant, litigant, pretendant, pretender

clairvoyance *n*
psychic powers, ESP, extrasensory perception, telepathy, second sight, fortune-telling
TECHNICAL cryptaesthesia, hyperaesthesia

clairvoyant *adj, n*
◆ *adj*
psychic, prophetic, visionary, telepathic, extrasensory
◆ *n*
psychic, fortune-teller, prophet, prophetess, visionary, seer, soothsayer, augur, oracle, diviner, telepath

clamber *v*
scramble, claw, climb, scrabble, shin, scale, mount, ascend; *N Am* shinny

clammy *adj*
damp, moist, sweaty, sweating, sticky, slimy, dank, muggy, heavy, close

clamorous *adj*
noisy, blaring, vociferous, vocal, loud, deafening, lusty, riotous, tumultuous, uproarious, vehement, insistent
⟺ quiet, silent

clamour *v, n*
◆ *v*
demand, ask for noisily, call for, press for, claim, insist, urge, bark
OLD brabble
◆ *n*
noise, uproar, commotion, shouting, din, racket, blare, agitation, hubbub, cry, outcry, hue and cry, complaints, brouhaha, rout, rumour; *Scot* stramash, reird; *N Am* katzenjammer
OLD (*Spenser*) outrage; (*Shakesp*) utis
FORMAL vociferance, vociferation
⟺ quietness, silence

clamp *n, v*
◆ *n*
vice, grip, press, brace, clasp, bracket, fastener, hand-screw, pinchcock, immobilizer
◆ *v*
fasten, secure, fix, clinch, clench, squeeze, press, grip, hold, brace, immobilize
■ **clamp down on**
control, limit, crack down on, come down hard on, restrict, confine, restrain, suppress, stop, put a stop to, prevent

clampdown *n*
control, limit, restriction, restraint, suppression, prevention, stop, crackdown, blitz

clan *n*
1 *the Macleod clan*
tribe, family, house, race, name, kindred, line, sept
OLD gens
2 GROUP, circle, society, brotherhood, fraternity, confraternity, sect, faction, band, set, clique, coterie, horde

clandestine *adj*
secret, surreptitious, undercover, underhand, concealed, hidden, covert, fraudulent, sly, sneaky, stealthy, underground, closet, furtive, private
COLLOQ. backroom, behind-door, cloak-and-dagger, under-the-counter
⟺ open

clandestinely *adv*
secretly, surreptitiously, covertly, fraudulently, slyly, stealthily, sneakily, privately, furtively
COLLOQ. under the counter
⟺ openly

clang v, n
- v

clash, jangle, clank, clink, clunk, clatter, peal, bong, chime, resound, reverberate, ring, toll
- n

clash, jangle, clank, clink, clunk, clatter, peal, bong, chime, resound, reverberation, ring, toll

clanger n

mistake, error, blunder, inaccuracy, misjudgement, slip, indiscretion, gaffe, faux pas, oversight, fault
FORMAL solecism
COLLOQ. howler, bloomer, boob, booboo, slip-up; N Am flub
SLANG boner, goof, cock-up

clank v, n
- v

clang, clash, jangle, clink, clunk, clatter, resound, reverberate, ring, toll
- n

clang, clash, jangle, clink, clunk, clatter, resounding, reverberation, ring, toll

clannish adj

cliquey, cliquish, unfriendly, select, exclusive, insular, narrow, parochial, sectarian
E3 friendly, open

clap v, n
- v

1 APPLAUD, acclaim, cheer, put your hands together for
2 SLAP, smack, strike, pat, hit, bang
OLD chop
COLLOQ. wallop, whack
- n

1 APPLAUSE, round of applause, acclaim, handclap, ovation, standing ovation
2 *a clap of thunder*
bolt, crack, flash, shaft, burst, streak, ray, spark, blaze, flare

claptrap n

rubbish, nonsense, drivel, gibberish, trash, tripe, twaddle, blarney; *dialect* faddle; *Scot* blethers
COLLOQ. bunk, bunkum, claptrap, piffle, bilge, baloney, blah, bosh, eyewash, hogwash, rhubarb, guff, poppycock, hot air, cobblers, codswallop, rot, tommyrot
SLANG bull; (*vulgar*) balls, bollocks, shit, bullshit

clarification n

explanation, simplification, interpretation, exposition, definition, gloss, illumination
FORMAL elucidation
E3 *formal* obfuscation

clarify v

1 EXPLAIN, make clear, throw light on, shed light on, simplify, resolve, spell out, clear up, make plain, define, illuminate, gloss
FORMAL elucidate
2 REFINE, purify, filter, clear
E3 1 obscure, confuse **2** cloud

clarity n

1 *clarity of thought*
lucidity, simplicity, intelligibility, comprehensibility, plainness, explicitness, unambiguousness, obviousness
2 *clarity of the water/her diction*
clearness, transparency, precision, sharpness, definition, visibility
E3 1 vagueness, woolliness **2** cloudiness, obscurity, imprecision

clash v, n
- v

1 CRASH, bang, strike, collide, fall foul (of), clank, clang, jangle, clatter, rattle, jar, swash
OLD hurtle
2 CONFLICT, disagree, quarrel, wrangle, grapple, fight, contend, feud, war

3 *two events clash*
happen at the same time, coincide
FORMAL co-occur
4 *the styles clash*
not match, not go with, not go together, look unpleasant, be incompatible, be discordant, jar
COLLOQ. scream
E3 4 match, be compatible, harmonize, go well together
- n

1 CRASH, striking, bang, clank, jangle, clatter, noise, snap
2 *a clash with the police*
confrontation, showdown, conflict, disagreement, argument, fight, brush, collision, warring, fighting, feud, quarrel, wrangle
FORMAL altercation
3 *a clash of colours*
mismatch, jarring, discordance, incompatibility, misalliance, irregularity

clasp n, v
- n

1 FASTENER, buckle, clip, pin, hasp, hook, fastening, catch, hair slide, slide, brooch, safety pin
TECHNICAL agraffe
OLD tach, spang; (*Shakesp*) tassel
2 HOLD, grip, grasp, embrace, hug, cuddle, bosom
- v

1 HOLD, grip, grasp, clutch, embrace, enfold, hug, squeeze, press, cling to, embosom, enclasp
2 FASTEN, connect, attach, grapple, hook, clip, pin, interlock, unite
TECHNICAL infibulate

class n, v
- n

1 *a French class*
lesson, period, lecture, seminar, tutorial, workshop, teach-in, course, year, form, study group, set, stream; N Am grade
2 *a social class*
social order, social status, status, (social) standing, standing in society, social division, rank, level, (social) background, caste
COLLOQ. pecking order
3 CATEGORY, classification, group, set, section, division, department, sphere, grouping, order, league, rank, status, caste, quality, grade, type, genre, sort, kind, species, genus, style
TECHNICAL phylum
FORMAL denomination
4 *he has class*
taste, style, stylishness, elegance, sophistication, chic, distinction
- v

categorize, classify, group, sort, rank, arrange, order, grade, rate, pigeonhole, designate, brand

---

Social classes/groups include:

aristocracy	upper class	bourgeoisie
nobility	*colloq.* Sloane	proletariat
gentry	Ranger	hoi polloi
landed gentry	ruling class	commoners
gentlefolk	jet set	serfs
élite	*colloq.* glitterati	plebeians
colloq. nobs	middle class	*colloq.* plebs
high society	lower class	
top drawer	working class	

See also **nobility**.

---

classic adj, n
- adj

1 *a classic film*
first-class, first-rate, outstanding, brilliant, ideal, best, finest, definitive, masterly, authoritative, excellent
FORMAL consummate

2 TYPICAL, prime, representative, characteristic, archetypal, standard, regular, usual, true
FORMAL paradigmatic, quintessential
3 *classic style*
traditional, time-honoured, established, archetypal, model, exemplary, ageless, timeless, immortal, undying, lasting, enduring, abiding, simple, understated, undecorated, unsophisticated, elegant
E3 1 second-rate **2** unrepresentative
♦ *n*
standard, model, prototype, masterwork, masterpiece, established work, great, *pièce de résistance*
FORMAL exemplar

classical *adj*
1 *classical style/form*
traditional, elegant, refined, excellent, plain, pure, simple, restrained, well-proportioned, symmetrical, harmonious
2 *classical music*
serious, traditional, concert, symphonic
3 *classical studies/languages*
ancient Greek, Grecian, Hellenic, ancient Roman, Latin, Attic
E3 1 modern

classically *adv*
1 *a classically trained musician*
traditionally, historically, originally, purely
2 *a classically beautiful profile*
simply, elegantly, traditionally, plainly, purely, symmetrically, harmoniously
3 *classically the term should only be applied in technical contexts*
typically, usually, normally, ordinarily, characteristically, customarily, as a rule
FORMAL quintessentially

classification *n*
categorization, sorting, classing, grading, grouping, arrangement, systematization, codification, tabulation, cataloguing
TECHNICAL taxonomy

classify *v*
categorize, class, group, pigeonhole, sort, grade, rank, arrange, order, type, distribute, systematize, codify, tabulate, file, catalogue
FORMAL dispose

classy *adj*
stylish, elegant, sophisticated, up-market, expensive, exclusive, exquisite, fine, grand, high-class, select, superior, gorgeous
COLLOQ. posh, ritzy, swanky
E3 dowdy, plain, unstylish

clatter *n, v*
bang, strike, clank, clunk, clang, jangle, crash, rattle, jar

clause *n*
article, item, part, section, subsection, particle, paragraph, heading, chapter, passage, phrase, condition, proviso, provision, rider, specification, point, loophole
TECHNICAL adjunct, clausula, novodamus, reddendum, salvo, tenendum

claw *n, v*
♦ *n*
talon, nail, pincer, nipper, gripper, pounce; *Scot* claut
TECHNICAL chela, unguis
OLD clutch, fang, griff, sere
♦ *v*
scratch, scrabble, scrape, graze, tear, rip, lacerate, maul, mangle, crab; *Scot* claut
OLD clapperclaw; (*Shakesp*) cloye

clay *n*
earth, loam, ground, soil, kaolin, lute, marl, brick, pottery, ceramics, slip, bole, clunch, gley, pisé, pug; *dialect* cloam; *Scot* cam, caum, calm, till
TECHNICAL illuvium, argil, cimolite, fango, laterite, plastilina, wax

clean *adj, adv*
♦ *adj*
1 WASHED, laundered, sterile, aseptic, antiseptic, hygienic, sanitary, sterilized, cleansed, decontaminated, purified, pure, unadulterated, fresh, unpolluted, uncontaminated, immaculate, spotless, unspotted, unstained, unsoiled, unsullied, perfect, speckless, spick and span, faultless, flawless, unblemished
COLLOQ. clean as a new pin
2 *a clean life*
innocent, guiltless, virtuous, pure, good, upright, moral, honest, honourable, righteous, reputable, upstanding, respectable, decent, chaste
COLLOQ. squeaky-clean
3 *a clean sheet of paper*
blank, new, fresh, unmarked, unused, empty
4 *a clean joke*
decent, wholesome, proper, modest, appropriate, ethical
5 *a clean game*
fair, just, honest, according to the rules, even-handed, proper
COLLOQ. above board
6 *clean lines*
simple, well-defined, clean-cut, graceful, elegant, smooth, regular, straight, neat, tidy
7 *made a clean break with his past life*
complete, whole, total, utter, perfect, decisive, conclusive, final
E3 1 dirty, polluted **2** dishonourable, indecent **4** dirty; *colloq.* blue **5** dirty, rough **6** ragged
♦ *adv*
completely, straight, directly, entirely, fully, totally, quite

> **PROVERBS**
> A new broom sweeps clean

> **SYNONYM NUANCES**
>
> *adj sense 1*
> **Sterile**, **aseptic**, **antiseptic** and **sterilized** suggest freedom from germs rather than a less defined cleanliness, and so lend a rather clinical tone, especially if they are not used in specifically clinical contexts. **Hygienic** and **sanitary** are similar, though not quite so stark: *the hygienic handling of chemicals*.
> The terms **cleansed**, **purified** and **decontaminated** imply that something harmful has now been removed, the first having the most scientific association: *the instruments are decontaminated after use*. **Pure**, **unadulterated**, **unpolluted** and **uncontaminated** suggest always having been free from anything harmful: *unadulterated essential oils for aromatherapy*; of these, **pure** is the most widely applied and the most suggestive of favour.
> The words **immaculate**, **spotless**, **unspotted**, **unstained** and the less common **speckless** might all be used with regard to appearance; of these, **immaculate** and **spotless** are more approving in tone: *the woodwork was an immaculate white*. **Unsullied** tends to have a narrower implication of having avoiding contact with anything odious or undesirable: *the unsullied emotions of childhood*; whereas **perfect**, **flawless** and **unblemished** could be used to convey admiration of cleanliness, literal or figurative, that is exemplary: *a flawless complexion*; *an unblemished career*.

Ways to clean include:

bath	clear	dry-clean
bathe	comb	dust
bleach	decontaminate	filter
brush	deodorize	floss
buff	disinfect	flush
cleanse	distil	freshen

freshen up	rinse	spring-clean
fumigate	rub	spruce
groom	sandblast	spruce up
Hoover®	sanitize	steep
launder	scour	sterilize
mop	scrape	swab
muck out	scrub	sweep
pasteurize	shampoo	swill
pick	shine	tidy
polish	shower	vacuum
purge	soak	valet
purify	soap	wash
refine	sponge	wipe

clean-cut *adj*
neat, tidy, orderly, smart, fresh, spruce, trim
COLLOQ. natty

cleaner *n*
char, charlady, charwoman, daily, Mrs Mop(p), wiper,
orderly

cleanliness *n*
cleanness, purity, freshness, spotlessness, perfection
🖃 dirtiness

> QUOTATIONS
> Cleanliness is next to Godliness
>   CHARLES DICKENS, *Great Expectations*

cleanse *v*
1 *cleanse a wound*
disinfect, sterilize, clean, bathe, wash, rinse
FORMAL deterge
2 *cleansed from sin/cleanse your soul*
absolve, purify, purge, make free from, clear
FORMAL lustrate
🖃 **1** dirty **2** defile

cleanser *n*
soap, soap powder, detergent, cleaner, solvent, scourer,
scouring powder, purifier, disinfectant

clear *adj, v*
♦ *adj*
1 PLAIN, distinct, comprehensible, understandable,
intelligible, coherent, lucid, explicit, precise, unambiguous,
well-defined, apparent, evident, patent, obvious, manifest,
conspicuous, unmistakable, unquestionable, sure,
unequivocal, incontrovertible, beyond question, crystal-
clear, beyond doubt, certain, positive, definite, convinced
2 *clear thinking*
sharp, keen, perceptive, penetrating, quick, sensible,
reasonable, logical
3 *clear water*
transparent, limpid, crystalline, glassy, translucent, see-
through, clean, unclouded, colourless
FORMAL pellucid, diaphonous
4 *a clear day*
cloudless, unclouded, fine, fair, bright, sunny, light,
luminous, undimmed
5 UNOBSTRUCTED, unblocked, open, free, empty,
unhindered, unimpeded
6 *a clear conscience*
guiltless, innocent, blameless, untroubled, having no
qualms, in the clear
FORMAL having/feeling no compunction
7 AUDIBLE, perceptible, pronounced, distinct, recognizable
COLLOQ. clear as a bell
🖃 **1** unclear, vague, ambiguous, confusing, unsure **2**
muddled, woolly **3** opaque, cloudy **4** dull, cloudy, rainy,
misty **5** blocked, jammed **6** guilty, troubled **7** inaudible,
indistinct, faint
♦ *v*
1 *clear the dishes/room*
remove, take away, empty, unload, vacate, evacuate,
void, move, shift, get rid of, rid, free, clean, fine, filter,
tidy, wipe, erase, cleanse, refine

2 UNBLOCK, unclog, unstop, decongest, free, rid, extricate,
disentangle, loosen
3 *clear a fence*
jump (over), vault, leap over, go over
4 *the fog cleared*
disappear, vanish, go, evaporate, melt away
FORMAL evanesce
5 ACQUIT, exonerate, absolve, pardon, vindicate, find not
guilty, excuse, justify, free, liberate, release, let go
FORMAL exculpate
6 *cleared for publication*
permit, give permission, allow, authorize, approve, pass,
sanction
COLLOQ. give the green light, give the go-ahead
7 *clear £1000*
earn, take home, net, make a profit, make, gain, land,
bring (in), pocket
🖃 **1** dirty, mess up **2** block, jam **5** condemn, find guilty **6**
prohibit, veto
■ **clear off**
go away, run along
COLLOQ. buzz off, get out, push off, shove off
■ **clear out**
1 *been told to clear out*
get out, leave, go away, depart, withdraw
COLLOQ. get lost, beat it, clear off, push off, shove off, hop
it
SLANG piss off
2 *clear out a cupboard*
tidy (up), empty, sort (out), throw out
■ **clear up**
1 EXPLAIN, clarify, elucidate, unravel, solve, resolve,
answer, straighten (out), sort out, iron out
COLLOQ. crack
2 TIDY, order, sort, rearrange, put in order, straighten (up),
remove
3 *the weather cleared up*
clear, become fine, become sunny, stop raining, brighten
(up), improve

clearance *n*
1 *clearance of old buildings*
demolition, removal, taking-away, emptying, unloading,
vacating, evacuation, clearing, moving, shifting, freeing,
cleansing
2 AUTHORIZATION, sanction, endorsement, permission,
consent, leave
COLLOQ. OK, go-ahead, green light, say-so
3 SPACE, gap, room, headroom, margin, allowance

clear-cut *adj*
definite, explicit, well-defined, clear, precise, specific,
straightforward, unambiguous, unequivocal, distinct,
trenchant, plain
COLLOQ. cut and dried, black and white
🖃 ambiguous, vague

clear-headed *adj*
sensible, rational, intelligent, wise, sober, realistic,
practical

clearing *n*
space, gap, opening, glade, dell

clearly *adv*
1 *speak clearly*
plainly, distinctly, comprehensibly, intelligibly, coherently,
lucidly, explicitly, conspicuously, patently
2 OBVIOUSLY, without doubt, undoubtedly, undeniably,
evidently, incontestably, incontrovertibly, indisputably,
unmistakably, manifestly, plainly, patently, distinctly,
openly, markedly

cleave[1] *v*
cleave the tree in two
split (open), divide, separate, sever, cut, slice, chop, crack
(open), disunite, halve, hew, open, part, pierce, rend
FORMAL dissever, sunder
🖃 join, unite

cleave² v

cleave to your marriage partner
adhere, cling, cohere, hold, stick, remain, attach, unite

cleft n

fissure, opening, gap, fracture, breach, break, chasm, chink, crack, cranny, crevice, crevasse, rent, split, rift; *Scot* cloff, riva, slack
TECHNICAL pharynx, jag, chimney
FORMAL scissure

clemency n

mercy, mercifulness, pity, compassion, forbearance, forgiveness, generosity, humanity, indulgence, kindness, sympathy, leniency, mildness, moderation, soft-heartedness, tenderness
FORMAL magnanimity
E3 harshness, ruthlessness

clench v

grip, hold, clasp, close (tightly), squeeze, press (together), seal, fasten, shut, clutch, double, grasp, grit

clergy n

clergymen, clergywomen, churchmen, churchwomen, clerics, the church, the cloth, ministry, priesthood, holy orders
OLD spirituality
Related adjectives: clerical, ecclesiastical

clergyman, clergywoman n

churchman, churchwoman, cleric, ecclesiastic, divine, man of God, woman of God, man of the cloth, woman of the cloth, minister, priest, reverend, bishop, preacher, vicar, pastor, padre, parson, rector, canon, dean, prebendary, father, mother, deacon, deaconess, chaplain, curate, presbyter, prelate, secular, spintext, squarson, arch-priest, rural dean, diocese, superintendent, clerk, Nonjuror, vartabed; *N Am* dominie; rabbi, imam, muezzin, mullah
SLANG Levite, sky pilot; *Aust* josser

clerical adj

1 ADMINISTRATIVE, office, secretarial, white-collar, official, filing, typing, keyboarding
COLLOQ. pen-pushing
2 ECCLESIASTICAL, pastoral, ministerial, priestly, episcopal, canonical, sacerdotal
See panel below

clerk n

account-keeper, record-keeper, book-keeper, assistant, official, administrative officer, administrator, notary, receptionist, secretary, typist, stenographer, shop-assistant, writer, copyist, protocolist
COLLOQ. pen-pusher

clever adj

1 *a clever student*
intelligent, bright, brilliant, smart, witty, gifted, talented, expert, knowledgeable, adroit, apt, able, capable, deft, quick, quick-witted, sharp, sharp-witted, keen, shrewd, knowing, perceptive, discerning, cute, cunning; *Scot* gleg, souple
OLD apprehensive, artful, conceited, notable
FORMAL sapient, sagacious
COLLOQ. brainy
2 *a clever plan*
inventive, resourceful, sensible, rational, ingenious, cunning, shrewd, pretty
COLLOQ. natty
E3 1 foolish, stupid, senseless, ignorant **2** foolish, irrational

---

SYNONYM NUANCES

sense 1
Intelligent, **bright**, and **smart** are fairly broad and straightforward synonyms, whereas **brilliant** would suggest clever to a more extreme degree: *the most brilliant poet of her generation*. **Witty** would more appropriately be used of sharp humour and expression. **Gifted** and **talented**, meanwhile, imply a particularly outstanding aptitude, but one which is instinctive rather than learned: *a gifted painter*. **Expert** and **knowledgeable**, on the other hand, would be appropriate to convey a high degree of learning.
    Adroit, **deft**, **quick**, **sharp** and **keen** are also approving terms, highly suggestive of speed and directness of thought: *adroit manipulation of language; a keen analytical mind*. The terms **shrewd** and **knowing** describe innate practical judgement, although an element of potential underhandedness may be suggested.
    Perceptive is a more positive term, appropriately describing someone with an ability to identify all aspects of a situation, with **discerning** further implying an element of good taste: *readers were becoming more discerning*. To use **cute** and **cunning**, however, implies an underhand element to someone's smartness, and so often sounds unfavourable: *the Minister was cute enough to cultivate the backbenchers*.

---

cleverly adj

1 INTELLIGENTLY, expertly, knowledgeably, ably, capably, discerningly, quick-wittedly
2 INGENIOUSLY, skilfully, astutely, craftily, shrewdly, artfully
E3 1 foolishly, stupidly **2** foolishly, artlessly

cliché n

platitude, hackneyed phrase/expression, commonplace, banality, truism, bromide, (old) chestnut, stereotype; *N Am* glittering generality

click v, n

♦ *v*
1 *the machine clicked*
clack, clink, snap, snick, snip, tick, beat
2 *it suddenly clicked*
(begin to) understand, make sense, become clear, fall into place
COLLOQ. twig, cotton on
3 *they clicked and became close friends*
hit it off, get on, get on well, get along, relate well to each other
COLLOQ. get on like a house on fire
♦ *n*
beat, clack, clink, snap, snick, snip, tick

client n

customer, patron, regular, buyer, purchaser, shopper, consumer, user, patient, applicant
COLLOQ. punter

clientèle n

business, clients, customers, following, market, patronage, patrons, regulars, trade, buyers, purchasers, shoppers, consumers, users

cliff n

precipice, overhang, bluff, face, rock-face, scar, scarp, escarpment, crag, tor, promontory

---

Types of clerical vestment include:

alb	clerical collar	ephod	maniple	scapular	tallith
amice	cope	frock	mantle	scarf	tippet
biretta	cotta	Geneva bands	mitre	skullcap	tunicle
cassock	cowl	Geneva gown	mozzetta	soutane	wimple
chasuble	dalmatic	habit	pallium	stole	yarmulka
chimere	*colloq.* dog-collar	hood	rochet	surplice	

climactic *adj*
decisive, critical, final, crucial, exciting, paramount
Ⅎ trivial

climate *n*
1 *a cold climate*
weather, weather conditions, temperature
2 *a hostile political climate*
atmosphere, feeling, mood, temper, disposition, setting, milieu, environment, spirit, ambience, tendency, trend

climax *n*
culmination, height, high point, highlight, acme, zenith, peak, pinnacle, summit, apex, apogee, top, head
Ⅎ low point, nadir

climb *v, n*
♦ *v*
1 *climb the stairs*
go up, ascend, scale, shin up, clamber, scramble, mount, ramp, surmount; *Scot* speel, sclim
TECHNICAL herringbone, jumar, prusik
OLD scan, sty
2 *climb into the car*
move, stir, shift, clamber, scramble
3 *unemployment is climbing*
increase, go up, rise, soar, shoot up, top
♦ *n*
ascent, going up, clamber, scramble, uphill struggle, upward slope; *Scot* speel
TECHNICAL jumar
Ⅎ descent
■ **climb down**
retract, back down, admit that you are wrong, concede, retreat, surrender, yield
COLLOQ. eat your words

SYNONYM NUANCES

verb sense 1
Go up is a term that can be widely used for any movement that takes you in an upward direction, similarly **ascend**, although it is more formal sounding and perhaps suggestive of a more dignified or gradual movement.
Scale, on the other hand, would be used for the physical act of climbing, and is particularly suggestive of height: *the crew scaled the masts barefoot*. **Shin up** is more descriptive of the physical way progress is made: *the animal shinned up his leg*. **Clamber** and **scramble** are equally descriptive, but suggestive of a rather ungainly and desperate manner: *I scrambled up the embankment*.
Mount could be used of reaching the top after a climb, or often in the more specific context of getting on to a horse or bike. **Surmount** is more often used figuratively to imply overcoming an obstacle: *the challenge could not be surmounted*.

---

climb-down *n*
withdrawal, retraction, retreat, concession, surrender, yielding

clinch *v*
settle, secure, seal, close, conclude, decide, determine, confirm, verify
COLLOQ. land

cling *v*
1 *cling to a branch*
clasp, clutch, grasp, grip, hold on to, stick, adhere, cleave, fasten, embrace, hug
2 *cling to old ideas*
adhere, stick, support, hold, defend, stand by, be faithful, stay true

clinic *n*
medical centre, health centre, hospital, infirmary, sanatorium, doctor's, outpatients' department

clinical *adj*
1 *clinical trials of the drug*
medical, hospital, patient
2 *a clinical design*
simple, plain, austere, stark, basic, unadorned
3 *a clinical attitude*
impersonal, analytic, businesslike, cold, emotionless, unemotional, unfeeling, detached, disinterested, dispassionate, uninvolved, impassive, objective, scientific
Ⅎ **2** decorated, ornamented **3** warm, biased, subjective

clinically *adv*
clinically proven remedies
medically, scientifically

clip *n, v*
♦ *n*
1 *a paper clip*
fastener, staple, pin
2 *a clip from a newspaper*
cutting, snippet, quotation, citation, passage, section, excerpt, extract
3 *a clip round the ear*
punch, slap, smack, cuff, box, clout, thump
COLLOQ. wallop, whack
♦ *v*
1 *clipped the pen to her pocket*
pin, staple, fasten, attach, fix, hold
2 *clip a bush*
trim, snip, cut, cut short, prune, pare, shear, crop, dock, poll, pollard, truncate, curtail, shorten, abbreviate
3 HIT, strike, graze, tough, collide with, crash into, run into

clipping *n*
cutting, snippet, quotation, citation, passage, section, excerpt, extract, clip

clique *n*
circle, set, coterie, group, bunch, band, pack, gang, crowd, in-crowd, society, fraternity, faction, clan

cloak *n, v*
♦ *n*
1 *wear a cloak*
cape, mantle, robe, wrap, shawl, coat, cover
2 *a cloak of secrecy*
coat, cover, shield, mask, front, screen, blind, veil, pall, mantle, shroud, pretext
♦ *v*
cover, veil, mask, screen, hide, conceal, obscure, shroud, disguise, shield, camouflage
OLD palliate

Types of cloak include:

abolla	gaberdine	*old* pelisse
amice	gallabea(h)	pilch
buffalo-robe	grego	poncho
capa	himation	rail
capote	manta	*Scot* rokelay
Capuchin	manteel	roquelaure
cardinal	mantilla	sagum
chlamys	mousquetaire	sarafan
cope	paenula	talma
djellaba	pall	visite
domino	paludament	

See also **clothes**; **coat**.

---

clobber[1] *n*
clothing, equipment, things, garments, belongings, possessions, baggage, tackle, kit, paraphernalia
COLLOQ. gear, togs, stuff, bits and pieces, bits and bobs

clobber[2] *v*
1 HIT, strike, bash, knock, clout, slap, thrash, punch, thump
COLLOQ. wallop, whack, belt, sock, zap
2 DEFEAT, overwhelm, beat, conquer, crush, rout, ruin
COLLOQ. thrash, wallop, lick, hammer, trounce

clock

■ **clock up**
reach, record, register, achieve, log, attain, chalk up, notch up

■ **round the clock**
day and night, all day and all night, continuously, ceaselessly, without stopping, constantly
COLLOQ. twenty-four seven, 24-7

> **QUOTATIONS**
> Stands the Church clock at ten to three? / And is there honey still for tea?
> *Rupert Brooke*, 'The Old Vicarage, Grantchester'

Types of clock or watch include:

CLOCKS:	digital clock	travelling clock
alarm clock	grandfather clock	
analogue clock	grandmother clock	WATCHES:
atomic clock	longcase clock	fob-watch
bracket clock	mantel clock	pendant watch
carriage clock	quartz clock	repeating watch
chronograph	speaking clock	ring-watch
chronometer	sundial	stopwatch
cuckoo-clock	*colloq.* Tim	wristwatch

---

clod *n*
lump, clump, chunk, hunk, mass, block, slab, wedge
OLD glebe

clog *v*
block, choke, stop up, bung up, dam (up), congest, jam, obstruct, impede, hinder, hamper, encumber, burden
FORMAL occlude
⊟ unblock, free, clear

cloister *n*
walkway, pavement, corridor, aisle, arcade, portico, ambulatory

cloistered *adj*
sheltered, secluded, confined, restricted, enclosed, shielded, withdrawn, insulated, protected, isolated
FORMAL reclusive, sequestered, cloistral, hermitic
⊟ open

close[1] *v, n*
♦ *v*
1 SHUT, shut up, fasten, secure, lock (up), bar, bolt, padlock
2 *close a road/bottle*
obstruct, block (off/up), shut, clog, plug, cork, stop up, fill, seal
FORMAL occlude
3 END, bring to an end, draw to an end, finish, complete, conclude, terminate, adjourn, wind up, round off, stop, cease
FORMAL discontinue
4 *the shop closes at 6 o'clock*
shut, close for the night
5 *the factory closed in March*
close down, close permanently, cease operating, cease operations, shut down, go bankrupt, fail
COLLOQ. fold, flop, go bust, go to the wall
6 *pursuers closing on you*
catch up with, get closer to, come closer, approach, near, gain on
7 *close a gap*
join, unite, fuse, seal, narrow, lessen
8 *close a deal*
settle, secure, seal, clinch, conclude, decide, determine, establish, confirm, verify
⊟ **1** open, separate **3** start, begin **4** open, open for business **7** widen

♦ *n*
end, finish, completion, conclusion, culmination, ending, finale, dénouement, termination, adjournment, winding-up, stop, pause
FORMAL cessation
⊟ start, beginning

■ **close in**
come nearer, draw near, approach, surround, encircle

close[2] *n*
live in a close
courtyard, enclosure, quadrangle, square, place, court, road, street, row, terrace, lane, mews, cul-de-sac

close[3] *adj*
1 NEAR, close by, nearby, at hand, not far, neighbouring, adjacent, adjoining, in the vicinity, in close proximity, impending, imminent
COLLOQ. on your doorstep, in your own backyard, a stone's throw
2 INTIMATE, dear, familiar, attached, inseparable, devoted, loving, close-knit, tight, best, good, bosom
3 *close relations*
immediate, direct
4 *a close resemblance*
strong, near, distinct, marked, similar, like, comparable, corresponding
5 *a close game*
evenly matched, well-matched, hard-fought
COLLOQ. neck and neck
6 *close to tears*
near, on the verge of, on the brink of, approaching
7 HUMID, heavy, stuffy, fuggy, muggy, oppressive, sultry, sweltering, airless, stifling, suffocating, unventilated, sticky
8 MISERLY, mean, stingy, niggardly, penny-pinching
FORMAL parsimonious
COLLOQ. tight
9 SECRETIVE, uncommunicative, unforthcoming, quiet, taciturn, reticent, private, secret, confidential
10 *a close translation*
exact, precise, accurate, strict, literal, faithful, true
11 *pay close attention*
fixed, concentrated, thorough, rigorous, painstaking, detailed, methodical, careful, intense, keen, searching
12 DENSE, compact, condensed, solid, tight, packed, crowded, cramped
⊟ **1** far, distant **2** cool, unfriendly, distant **3** distant **7** fresh, cool **8** generous, liberal **9** open **10** rough, loose

> **SYNONYM NUANCES**
>
> *sense 1*
> **Near**, **nearby** and **close by** are synonyms with a wide range of applications for things that are close in space, or time: *the near future*. **At hand** tends to have a less physical aspect, and is often used of abstracts: *help was at hand*; *success was at hand*. The words **neighbouring**, **adjacent** and **adjoining** are limited to where two things are side by side: *neighbouring countries*; *adjacent streets*; *the park adjoining the palace*.
> The term **in the vicinity** is rather vague as to distance: *there are three villages in the vicinity*; whereas **in close proximity** is more explicit and puts great emphasis on the physical nearness of something: *The UFO was seen at close proximity*.
> If you want to say that some event is very near in time, you might prefer to use **impending** or **imminent**: *impending motherhood*; *a flu epidemic was imminent*.

closet *n, adj, v*
♦ *n*
cupboard, wardrobe, storage room, recess, press, cabinet
♦ *adj*
secret, private, unrevealed, hidden, covert, furtive, underground, surreptitious, undercover
⊟ open, having come out

♦ v

cloister, shut away, confine, seclude, isolate

closure n

1 *the closure of the factory*
closing-down, permanent closing, shutdown, failure,
bankruptcy, winding-up
FORMAL cessation of operations
COLLOQ. folding
2 *the closure of the road*
obstruction, block, blocking, shutting, stopping-up

clot n, v

♦ n

1 *a blood clot*
lump, mass, glob, clump, thrombus, thrombosis, clotting,
obstruction, coagulation; *dialect* lopper; *Scot* lapper; *Scot
& N Am* splatch
TECHNICAL embolus, cruor, grume, crassamentum
OLD gobbet
2 FOOL, idiot, imbecile
COLLOQ. nit, mug, blockhead, nincompoop, twit, twerp,
dope; *N Am* bufflehead
SLANG wally, nerd, plonker, dork, git, prat

♦ v

coalesce, curdle, coagulate, congeal, thicken, solidify, set,
gel

cloth n

1 FABRIC, material, stuff, textile, upholstery
See panel at **fabric**.
2 RAG, facecloth, flannel, dishcloth, floorcloth, duster,
towel; *S Afr* lap, lappie
3 THE CLERGY, the church, clergymen,
clergywomen, churchmen, churchwomen,
the ministry, holy orders

clothe v

1 DRESS, put on, robe, deck, outfit, fit out,
rig, vest, drape, cover
FORMAL attire, apparel, accoutre, habit, invest,
bedizen, caparison
2 *mountains clothed in verdure*
cover, overlay, envelop, blanket, drape, carpet
E3 **1** undress, strip, disrobe

clothes n

clothing, garments, wear, garb, outfit, dress, costume,
uniform, wardrobe, vestments
OLD weed
FORMAL attire, apparel, raiment, habiliments, vesture
COLLOQ. gear, clobber, togs, get-up, hand-me-downs,
cast-offs
SLANG threads
Related adjectives: sartorial, habilatory
See panel on next page
See also panel at **hat**.

> **PROVERBS**
> Clothes make the man

cloud n, v

♦ v

mist, fog, blur, dull, dim, darken, shade, shadow,
overshadow, eclipse, cover, veil, shroud, mantle, obscure,
muddle, confuse
FORMAL obfuscate
E3 clear
Related adjective: nubiform

> **PROVERBS**
> Every cloud has a silver lining

> **QUOTATIONS**
> I wandered lonely as a cloud / That floats on high o'er
> vales and hills
>   WILLIAM WORDSWORTH, 'I Wandered Lonely as a
> Cloud'

Types of cloud include:

altocumulus	cumulonimbus	nimbostratus
altostratus	cumulus	stratocumulus
cirrocumulus	fractocumulus	stratus
cirrostratus	fractostratus	
cirrus	mammatus	

cloudless adj

unclouded, fine, bright, clear, sunny, fair, dry,
pleasant
E3 cloudy, overcast

cloudy adj

1 *a cloudy sky*
overcast, dull, dark, murky, gloomy, sombre,
grey, leaden, heavy, lowering, dim, sunless,
hazy, misty, foggy
2 *a cloudy liquid*
opaque, milky, muddy, murky
3 *cloudy issues*
indistinct, obscure, nebulous, hazy, misty, foggy, blurred,
blurry, vague, confused, muddled
E3 **1** bright, sunny, cloudless **2** clear **3** clear,
distinct, plain

clout v, n

♦ v

punch, strike, smack, hit, slap, cuff, box
COLLOQ. thump, wallop, whack
SLANG sock, slug

♦ n

1 *gave him a clout*
punch, strike, smack, hit, slap, cuff, box
COLLOQ. thump, wallop, whack
SLANG sock, slug
2 *political clout*
influence, weight, authority, power,
standing, prestige
COLLOQ. pull, muscle

cloven adj

divided, split, bisected, cleft
E3 solid

clown n, v

♦ n

1 *clowns at a circus*
buffoon, comic, comedian, joker, jester, fool, harlequin,
Joey, rustic, bumpkin, merry-andrew, gracioso, Pierrot,
august
OLD zany, antic, pickle-herring, Owl-glass
OLD SLANG joskin
2 *some clown has parked in front of the gates*
fool, idiot, blockhead, imbecile
COLLOQ. nincompoop, ninny, nitwit, numskull,
twerp, twit, dimwit
SLANG wally, jerk, dipstick, nerd, dork, geek

♦ v

fool around, act foolishly, act/play the fool, jest, joke
COLLOQ. mess around, muck about
SLANG N Am goof around

cloying adj

disgusting, nauseating, sickening, sickly, excessive,
choking, oversweet, fulsome
E3 pleasing, pleasant

club n, v

♦ n

1 ASSOCIATION, society, organization, group, league, guild,
order, union, auxiliary, fraternity, federation, company,
brotherhood, sisterhood, set, circle, clique, social club,
chapter, fasciol, free-and-easy; *N Am* glee club, sorosis
OLD hetairia
2 NIGHTCLUB, discotheque, bar, cabaret
COLLOQ. disco

Clothes include:

DRESSES:	jumper	jazz pants	**WOMEN'S UNDER-**	**MEN'S UNDERWEAR:**	**ACCESSORIES:**
caftan	polo neck	jeans	**WEAR:**	boxer-shorts (or	belt
dinner-gown	polo shirt	jeggings	basque	boxers)	bow tie
evening dress	pullover	jodhpurs	body stocking	singlet	braces
frock	shirt	leggings	bra	string vest	cravat
kimono	smock	Levis®	brassière	underpants	cummerbund
maxidress	sweater	palazzo pants	briefs	vest	earmuffs
sari	sweatshirt	pedal-pushers	camiknickers	Y-fronts	fascinator
sheath dress	tabard	peg trousers	camisole		gloves
shift dress	tank top	plus-fours	corset	**SPORTSWEAR:**	leg warmers
shirtwaister	tee-shirt	shorts	French knickers	bathing costume	mittens
sweater dress	T-shirt	slacks	garter	bikini	muffler
	tunic		girdle	cycling shorts	necktie
SKIRTS:	turtleneck	**SUITS:**	g-string	jockstrap	pashmina
culottes	twinset	boiler suit	hold-ups	leotard	scarf
dirndl	waistcoat	catsuit	hosiery	monokini	shahtoosh
divided skirt		*N Am* coveralls	knickers	salopette	shawl
kilt	**TROUSERS:**	double-breasted	liberty bodice	swimming cos-	shrug
mini skirt	bell-bottoms	dress suit	lingerie	tume	snood
pencil skirt	Bermuda shorts	jogging suit	panties	swimming trunks	socks
pinafore skirt	breeches	jumpsuit	pantihose	swimsuit	sporran
rah-rah skirt	Capri pants	leisure suit	pants		stole
sarong	cargo pants	lounge suit	petticoat	**NIGHTWEAR:**	tie
tulip skirt	combat trousers	morning suit	shift	bed-jacket	
	cords	overall	slip	bedsocks	**MISCELLANEOUS:**
TOPS:	denims	playsuit	stockings	dressing-gown	burka
blouse	drainpipes	power suit	suspender belt	housecoat	veil
cardigan	dungarees	shell suit	suspenders	*colloq.* jimjams	yashmak
crop top	501s®	single-breasted	teddy	negligee	
dress shirt	flannels	three-piece suit	thong	nightdress	
fleece	harem pants	tracksuit	tights	*colloq.* nightie	
guernsey	hipsters	trouser suit	*colloq.* tit tape	nightshirt	
hoodie	hot pants	wet suit		*colloq.* PJs	
jersey				pyjamas	

See also **clerical**; **coat**; **fabric**; **footwear**; **hat**.

3 STICK, staff, bat, bludgeon, truncheon, cudgel, mace, life-preserver, knobkerrie; *N Am* blackjack, billy, billystick; *Aust* waddy, nulla-nulla
TECHNICAL bandy, priest, shinty-stick, caman, hurley
OLD bourdon, trunnion, polt
COLLOQ. cosh
See panel at **golf club**.
♦ *v*
hit, strike, beat (up), bash, clout, bludgeon, batter, pummel
COLLOQ. clobber, cosh
■ **club together**
give money, share the cost, join forces, contribute, chip in
COLLOQ. have a whip-round

clue *n*
hint, tip, suggestion, idea, notion, lead, tip-off, pointer, sign, indication, evidence, trace, suspicion, inkling, intimation

clueless *adj*
ignorant, inexperienced, unschooled, unlearned, uninitiated, uninformed
COLLOQ. dense, thick, not all there; (*offensive*) dumb

clump *n, v*
♦ *n*
cluster, bundle, bunch, tuft, thicket, mass, accumulation, collection, lot, group
FORMAL agglomeration, agglutination
♦ *v*
1 *clump around*
tramp, clomp, stamp, stomp, stumble, plod, trudge, lumber, thump, thud
2 *clump together*
group, accumulate, amass, cluster, bunch, bundle

clumsy *adj*
1 *a clumsy person*
awkward, unco-ordinated, ham-fisted, ham, accident-prone, unhandy, heavy-handed, unskilful, inept, bungling, blundering, lumbering, gauche, ungainly, ungraceful, wooden, cack-handed, oafish, squab, banana-fingered, two-fisted, thumby, chuckle, chuckle-headed, hippopotamian, looby
OLD unhandsome
FORMAL maladroit
COLLOQ. gawky, all thumbs, having two left feet
SLANG (*offensive*) spastic
2 *clumsy objects*
awkward, unwieldy, ungainly, heavy, bulky, hulking, unmanageable, cumbersome, ill-made, shapeless, Dutch-built
COLLOQ. clumping, clunky
3 *a clumsy attempt to comfort her*
insensitive, rude, tactless, awkward, uncouth, rough, crude
E3 1 co-ordinated, skilful, careful, graceful, natural **2** elegant, dainty **3** sensitive, tactful

---

SYNONYM NUANCES

sense 1
Both **awkward** and **unco-ordinated** are fairly mild terms to describe a clumsy manner or movement: *his arms moved in the most unco-ordinated way*; whilst **ham-fisted** is a more disparaging term, with an added implication of incompetence: *the ham-fisted police hunt allowed the criminals to escape detection*. **Heavy-handed**, **unskilful**, **inept** and the less common **unhandy** also suggest a lack of the required precision, and are again rather pejorative in tone; the terms **bungling**, **blundering** and **lumbering** are highly pejorative, and

imply that a clumsy approach may prove a distinct liability: *bungling bureaucratic incompetence.*

Gauche appropriately describes a clumsiness born of being ill at ease and lacking in sophistication: *this imposing woman made her feel gauche;* whereas **ungainly**, **ungraceful** and **wooden** are fairly straightforward descriptions physical movement: *an ungainly walk.* **Oafish**, on the other hand, is strongly suggestive of an inherent ignorance, and is therefore highly derogatory: *her oafish, idiot son.*

cluster *n, v*

♦ *n*

bunch, clump, batch, group, knot, band, mass, crowd, gathering, huddle, collection, assembly, assortment
TECHNICAL inflorescence, raceme, panicle, truss
FORMAL assemblage, agglomeration

♦ *v*

bunch, group (together), gather, collect, assemble, congregate, come together, flock

clustered *adj*

bunched, gathered, grouped, assembled, massed
FORMAL glomerate

clutch *v, n*

♦ *v*

hold, get/take hold of, clasp, grip, hang on to, grasp, cling to, clench, seize, snatch, grab, catch, grapple, embrace

♦ *n*

1 *in someone's clutches*
control, grasp, grip, power, sway, dominion, possession, hands, keeping, custody, embrace, mercy, claws, jaws
2 *a clutch of eggs*
set, setting, group, hatching, incubation

clutter *n, v*

♦ *n*

litter, mess, jumble, untidiness, disorder, disarray, muddle, chaos, confusion

♦ *v*

litter, encumber, fill (untidily), mess (up), make a mess, make untidy, cover, strew, scatter

coach *n, v*

♦ *n*

1 *travel by coach*
express coach, bus, minibus; *N Am* Greyhound
OLD charabanc, motor-bus, motor-coach
2 *a train of twelve coaches*
carriage, car, wagon
3 *a football coach*
trainer, instructor, tutor, teacher, educator, mentor
4 *a coach and horses*
carriage, wagon, cab, trap, hackney, hansom, gig, landau, brougham, barouche, cabriolet, droshky

♦ *v*

train, drill, instruct, teach, tutor, prime, cram, prepare

coagulate *v*

congeal, thicken, solidify, gel, melt, clot, cake, curdle

coagulation *n*

congealing, thickening, solidifying, clotting

coalesce *v*

amalgamate, join (together), blend, mix, unite, combine, consolidate, cohere, fuse, incorporate, integrate, merge, affiliate
FORMAL commingle, commix

coalescence *n*

amalgamation, blending, mixture, combination, consolidation, fusion, incorporation, integration, merger, affiliation
OLD immixture

coalition *n*

alliance, merger, amalgamation, combination, integration, fusion, joining, league, bloc, compact, federation, confederation, confederacy, association, partnership, affiliation, union
FORMAL conjunction, compact

coarse *adj*

1 ROUGH, unpolished, unfinished, uneven, lumpy, unpurified, unrefined, unprocessed, rugged, hairy, bristly, scaly, prickly
2 *coarse humour*
bawdy, ribald, earthy, obscene, smutty, vulgar, crude, offensive, foul-mouthed, boorish, loutish, rude, impolite, ill-mannered, crass, rough, gross, rank, indelicate, improper, indecent, immodest, off-colour
COLLOQ. blue, raunchy
F3 1 smooth, fine **2** refined, sophisticated, polite, clean

---

SYNONYM NUANCES

sense 2

Bawdy, **ribald** and **earthy** may be used of something with sexually explicit content, suggesting a lack of refinement: *bawdy limericks;* they are fairly neutral in tone and do not suggest disapproval. **Smutty**, on the other hand, implies a degree of disfavour on the speaker's part.

Obscene, **offensive**, and the more informal **off-colour** put the emphasis on audience sensibilities, clearly implying that they will be upset: *the Obscene Publications Act.* The words **indelicate**, **improper**, and **immodest** suggest a lack of decorum and propriety, and are understated, and even rather euphemistic terms: *improper sexual conduct;* **indecent** could be used to be more direct.

The terms **vulgar**, **crude**, **gross** and **rank** also describe a lack of delicacy, but are very pejorative in tone: *his crude jokes were not funny.* Similarly, **impolite** and **ill-mannered** are fairly mild terms; to suggest unacceptably coarse behaviour you could use **foul-mouthed**, **loutish** or **rude**.

---

coarsely *adv*

1 ROUGHLY, unevenly, ruggedly, irregularly
2 BAWDILY, obscenely, crudely, vulgarly, rudely, impolitely, offensively, roughly, immodestly, indecently, improperly, boorishly, loutishly
F3 1 smoothly **2** politely

coarsen *v*

roughen, thicken, blunt, deaden, desensitize, dull, harden
FORMAL indurate
F3 sensitize

coarseness *n*

1 OBSCENITY, bawdiness, ribaldry, smut, smuttiness, vulgarity, crassitude, crudity, earthiness, indelicacy, offensiveness, indecency, immodesty
2 ROUGHNESS, unevenness, ruggedness, irregularity, hairiness, prickliness
F3 1 delicacy, politeness, sophistication **2** smoothness

coast *n, v*

♦ *n*

coastline, seaboard, shore, seashore, beach, seaside, strand, foreshore
FORMAL littoral
Related adjectives: littoral, orarian

♦ *v*

freewheel, glide, slide, sail, cruise, taxi, drift

coat *n, v*

♦ *n*

1 FUR, hair, fleece, wool, pelt, hide, skin
2 LAYER, coating, covering, cover, overlay, film, blanket, sheet, mantle, glaze, varnish, finish, veneer, laminate, lamination, cladding
TECHNICAL integument, pellicle

♦ v

cover, paint, spread, layer, smear, daub, apply, put on/over, overlay, plaster, pave, cake, encrust

PROVERBS
Cut your coat according to your cloth

Types of coat include:

Afghan	Eton jacket	raincoat
anorak	frock-coat	redingote
blanket	fur coat	reefer
blazer	greatcoat	safari jacket
blouson	hacking-jacket	tail coat
body-warmer	jacket	shooting-jacket
bomber jacket	jerkin	snorkel
Burberry®	mackintosh	N Am, Aust & NZ
cagoul(e)	colloq. mac	sports coat
cape	matinee jacket	sports jacket
car-coat	overcoat	trench coat
cloak	parka	tuxedo
dinner jacket	pea-jacket	windcheater
donkey jacket	poncho	
duffel coat	puffa jacket	

coating n
covering, layer, dusting, wash, coat, blanket, sheet, membrane, film, skin, finish, overlay, veneer, glaze, varnish, enamel, lamination, crust
FORMAL patina

coax v
persuade, cajole, wheedle, blandish, draw, get round, talk into, win over/round, flatter, beguile, allure, induce, entice, tempt, prevail upon, wile; dialect carny; Scot cuittle, fleech, whillywha
OLD collogue
FORMAL inveigle
COLLOQ. sweet-talk, soft-soap

cobble
■ **cobble together**
make/prepare/produce roughly, make/prepare/produce quickly, improvise, knock up, put together
COLLOQ. throw together

cock n, v
♦ n
rooster, capon, cockerel, chicken, chanticleer
♦ v
lift, raise, point, slant, incline, bend, tip, tilt

cockeyed adj
1 CROOKED, lopsided, askew, asymmetrical, awry, skew-whiff
2 SENSELESS, absurd, crazy, ludicrous, nonsensical, preposterous
COLLOQ. daft, barmy, half-baked
🔁 2 sensible, sober

cockily adv
cheekily, impertinently, impudently, insolently, disrespectfully
🔁 respectfully, politely

cocksure adj
cocky, arrogant, self-important, conceited, vain, swollen-headed, swell-headed, egotistical, swaggering, brash, self-assured, self-confident, overconfident
🔁 humble, modest, shy

cocktail n
mixture, mixed drink, blend, concoction

QUOTATIONS
When evening quickens in the street, comes a pause in the day's occupation that is known as the cocktail hour
BERNARD DE VOTO, The Hour

Cocktails include:

Acapulco	Harvey Wall-	rattlesnake
American beauty	banger	rickey
bellini	horse's neck	Rob Roy
between the	kir	rusty nail
sheets	kir royale	salty dog
black Russian	Long Island iced	satan's whiskers
black velvet	tea	Sazerac®
bloody Mary	long vodka	screwdriver
blue lagoon	mai tai	sea breeze
brandy Alexander	Manhattan	sex on the beach
Bronx	margarita	Shirley Temple
brown cow	Martini®	sidecar
buck's fizz	mimosa	Singapore sling
caipirinha	mint julep	snowball
champagne	mocktail	St Clements
cocktail	mojito	stinger
cosmopolitan	Molotov cocktail	tequila slammer
daiquiri	Moscow mule	tequila sunrise
eggnog	negroni	Tom and Jerry
G&T	old-fashioned	Tom Collins
gimlet	piña colada	Virgin Mary
gin-and-tonic	pink gin	whisky mac
gloom raiser	pink lady	whisky sour
grasshopper	planter's punch	white lady
	prairie oyster	white Russian

cocky adj
arrogant, self-important, conceited, vain, swollen-headed, egotistical, swaggering, brash, cocksure, self-assured, self-confident, overconfident, bumptious
FORMAL hubristic
🔁 humble, modest, shy

cocoon v
protect, overprotect, isolate, preserve, defend, envelop, cushion, insulate, wrap, cover, swathe, cloister

coddle v
pamper, pet, spoil, protect, overprotect, mollycoddle, cosset, humour, indulge, baby

code n
1 ETHICS, rules, regulations, laws, principles, morals, morality, system, custom, convention, etiquette, manners, practice, conduct
2 *written in code*
cipher, secret language, secret writing, secret message, cryptograph, cryptogram, Morse code
3 *a book's code number*
numbers, letters, signs, symbols, bar code, QR code®, postcode, postal code, zip code, dialling code, local code, national code, international code, machine code

codify v
order, systematize, organize, classify, group, sort out, marshal, catalogue

coerce v
force, use force, drive, compel, constrain, pressurize, pressure, bully, intimidate, browbeat, bludgeon, dragoon, pressgang
COLLOQ. put the screws on, bulldoze, strongarm, twist someone's arm, lean on

coercion n
force, duress, compulsion, constraint, pressure, bullying, intimidation, threats, direct action, browbeating, arm-twisting, strongarm tactics
COLLOQ. heat

coffee n
COLLOQ. N Am joe

Types of coffee include:

COFFEE DRINKS:	caffè con	flat white	mocha	BEANS AND	half-caf
(caffè) Americano	panna	frappé	mochaccino	PREPARATIONS:	(or half-and-half)
black coffee	Canadiano	Frappuccino®	quad	Arabica	instant
black eye	cappuccino	granita	red eye	dark roast	intense roast
breve	corretto	iced coffee	ristretto	decaffeinated	light roast
café au lait	cortado	Irish coffee	skinny latte	colloq. decaf	medium roast
café bonbon	dead eye (or green	latte	soy coffee	drip	percolated
café crème	eye)	lazy eye	soy latte	filter	colloq. perked
café filtre	espresso	lungo	Turkish coffee	freshly ground	rich roast
café noir	espresso	macchiato	white coffee	ground	Robusta
café noisette	Romano	misto			

See also **tea**.

Terms used in coffee preparation include:

barista	crema	drip brewer	grind	percolator	tall
bean-to-cup	demitasse	dry	grinder	pod	tamp
brew	doppio	foam	harmless	pull	tamper
cafetière (or	dose	froth	ibrik	shot	to go (or with legs)
French press or	doser	frother	moka pot	skinny	venti
plunger pot)	double	grande	no fun	solo	wet

coffer n
1 *jewels hidden in a coffer*
casket, case, box, chest, trunk, ark, safe, strongbox, treasury, moneybox, repository
2 *the coffers of an organization*
funds, finance, resources, assets, capital, backing, money, cash, wealth, means

coffin n
sarcophagus, shell; *Scot* kist; *N Am* casket
OLD larnax
SLANG *N Am* wooden kimono, wooden overcoat, pine overcoat

cogency n
power, strength, force, potency, forcefulness, influence, weight, plausibility, effectiveness, urgency

cogent adj
convincing, compelling, conclusive, potent, powerful, strong, forceful, forcible, influential, weighty, irresistible, persuasive, unanswerable, effective, urgent
Fꓱ weak, ineffective, unsound

cogently adv
convincingly, compellingly, conclusively, potently, powerfully, strongly, forcefully, forcibly, persuasively, effectively, urgently
Fꓱ weakly, ineffectively

cogitate v
think deeply, consider, contemplate, deliberate, meditate, muse, ponder, reflect, mull over
FORMAL ruminate, cerebrate

cognate adj
related, affiliated, associated, connected, kindred, akin, alike, allied, analogous, corresponding, similar
TECHNICAL agnate, consanguine, congeneric
Fꓱ unrelated, unconnected

cognition n
perception, awareness, consciousness, knowledge, apprehension, learning, discernment, insight, comprehension, understanding, thinking, intelligence, enlightenment, reason, reasoning, rationality

cognizance n
■ **take cognizance of**
acknowledge, regard, recognize, take notice of, become aware of, accept

cognizant adj
aware, conscious, conversant, familiar, informed, knowledgeable, acquainted, versed, witting

FORMAL apprised
Fꓱ unaware

cohabit v
live together, live together as man and wife, live with, sleep together
OLD live in sin, occupy, company
COLLOQ. bed
SLANG shack up
OLD SLANG live tally

cohere v
1 STICK, adhere, cling, fuse, unite, bind, combine, coalesce, consolidate
2 *the argument does not cohere*
agree, square, correspond, harmonize, hold, hang together, make sense, be consistent, add up
Fꓱ separate

coherence n
agreement, harmony, consistency, correspondence, connection, sense, logicality, union, unity
FORMAL congruity, consonance, concordance
Fꓱ incoherence

coherent adj
articulate, intelligible, comprehensible, easy to understand, meaningful, lucid, clear, consistent, logical, reasoned, rational, sensible, orderly, systematic, organized, well-structured, well-planned
Fꓱ incoherent, unintelligible, meaningless

cohesion n
union, unity, whole, agreement, harmony, consistency, correspondence, solidarity, connection, sense
COLLOQ. togetherness

cohesive adj
coherent, close, united, joined, joined-up, continuous, connected, interrelated
COLLOQ. together

cohort n
1 *Roman cohorts*
troop, division, legion, regiment, squadron, band, brigade, squad, body, column, company, contingent, unit
2 GROUP, unit, set, body, lot, batch, combination, class, classification, bracket, category, categorization
3 COMPANION, partner, accomplice, assistant, supporter, associate, follower, myrmidon
COLLOQ. mate, buddy, sidekick

coil v, n
♦ v
wind, spiral, curl, loop, turn, twist, writhe, snake, fake, twirl, wreathe, twine, entwine

OLD wring
FORMAL convolute
♦ *n*
roll, curl, loop, turn, ring, spiral, spire, corkscrew, helix, twist, twine, whorl, wreathe, skein, hank, rouleau, bight, fake; *Scot* fank
OLD (*Spenser*) bought
FORMAL convolution, volution

coin *n, v*
♦ *n*
piece, bit, money, cash, change, small change, loose change, silver, copper
FORMAL specie
Related adjectives: numismatic, nummulary, nummary
♦ *v*
1 *coin a new word*
invent, make up, think up, conceive, dream up, devise, formulate, originate, create, fabricate, produce, neologize
2 *coin money*
produce, mint, stamp, cast, strike, forge

Types of coin include:

angel	half-crown	rap
bezant	half guinea	real
colloq. bob	halfpenny	sesterce
copper	half sovereign	shilling
crown	ha'penny	sixpence
dandiprat	krugerrand	solidus
denarius	louis d'or	sou
dime	moidore	sovereign
doubloon	napoleon	spade guinea
ducat	nickel	stater
farthing	noble	*colloq.* tanner
florin	obol	thaler
groat	penny	threepenny bit
guilder	pound	
guinea	*colloq.* quid	

coincide *v*
1 *the two events coincided*
happen at the same time, happen together, clash, take place simultaneously, coexist, synchronize
FORMAL concur
2 *our opinions coincide*
be the same, agree, correspond, square, tally, harmonize, be consistent with, match
FORMAL concur, accord

coincidence *n*
1 CHANCE, accident, luck, eventuality, synchronicity
FORMAL fortuity, serendipity
COLLOQ. fluke
2 COEXISTENCE, correspondence, happening at the same time, happening together, clash, clashing, taking place simultaneously, synchronization
FORMAL concurrence, conjunction, correlation

coincident *adj*
1 SIMULTANEOUS, contemporaneous, coinciding, coexisting
FORMAL concurrent
2 SIMILAR, the same, like, alike, close, related, corresponding, equivalent, comparable, consistent, in agreement, in harmony
FORMAL concurrent

coincidental *adj*
accidental, chance, casual, unintentional, unplanned, lucky
FORMAL fortuitous, serendipitous
COLLOQ. flukey
E3 deliberate, planned, arranged

coincidentally *adv*
accidentally, by chance, unintentionally, luckily

coitus *n*
sexual intercourse, sex, union, intimacy, copulation, coupling, lovemaking, marriage-bed, bed, sleeping with someone, going to bed with someone, mating, relations
OLD commixtion, embraces
FORMAL carnal knowledge, congress, consummation, coition
COLLOQ. how's your father, it, the other; *Aust & NZ* naughty
SLANG lay, bang, bonk, leg-over, wham bam thank you ma'am, greens, jig-a-jig, knee-trembler, quickie, nooky, pussy, rumpy-pumpy, tail; *N Am* jazz, poontang; (*taboo*) fuck, fucking, screw, screwing, shag, shagging

cold *adj, n*
♦ *adj*
1 UNHEATED, cool, chilled, ice-cold, chilly, chill, shivery, raw, biting, cutting, bitter, fresh, wintry, bleak, frigid, frosty, icy, rimy, glacial, arctic, Siberian, polar, freezing, frozen, numbed, keen, Decemberish; *Scot* cauld
OLD frore
FORMAL gelid, brumal, brumous
2
COLLOQ. nippy, parky
3 *feel cold*
shivery, chilly, freezing, frozen, numb, agued
4 UNFEELING, unmoved, unsympathetic, unemotional, frigid, icy, impersonal, unfriendly, distant, remote, aloof, standoffish, reserved, chilly, clinical, undemonstrative, unresponsive, passionless, unexcitable, indifferent, lukewarm, stony, callous, insensitive, heartless, biting, dead, uncaring, antagonistic, hostile, repulsive; *Scot* fremd
FORMAL phlegmatic
E3 1 hot, warm **2** hot **3** friendly, responsive, warm
♦ *n*
coldness, chill, chilliness, coolness, frigidity, iciness, rawness, winter, frost, snow, ice; *Scot* cauld, jeel
E3 warmth, heat

> **QUOTATIONS**
> Cold – cold as truth, cold as life. No, nothing can be as cold as life
> JEAN RHYS, *Voyage in the Dark*

> **SYNONYM NUANCES**
> *adj sense 1*
> **Cool** is a fairly positive synonym, suggesting a level of coldness that may be desirable: *the evening was pleasantly cool; cool drinks*. **Fresh** may be used in a similar way, to imply an invigorating aspect: *fresh, bracing breezes*. **Chilled**, **chilly** and **chill**, however, may be used to suggest a stronger, although not severe coldness, with the strong connotation of a potential effect on the body: *the chilly station foyer*. **Chilled** is often used specifically of foodstuffs and other objects that have been deliberately cooled.
>   **Ice-cold** suggests a severely low temperature, again with a connotation of physical sensation: *he fell into the ice-cold lake*. The terms **keen**, **raw**, **biting**, **cutting** and **bitter** are the most strongly suggestive of physical effects, and are appropriately used of the natural elements: *the biting cold penetrated our clothes; bitter frosty nights*.
>   **Freezing** and **frozen** could be used literally or figuratively to convey severe coldness; however, **glacial**, **arctic**, **Siberian** and **polar** would only be used in the context of extremes of low temperature: *arctic conditions hampered the expedition*. **Wintry** and **bleak** can be used evoke the desolation that cold weather may bestow: *many resorts can be bleak and damp in winter*.

cold-blooded *adj*
cruel, inhuman, brutal, savage, barbaric, barbarous, merciless, ruthless, pitiless, callous, unfeeling, heartless, iron-headed
E3 compassionate, merciful

cold-hearted adj
unfeeling, unkind, uncaring, insensitive, unsympathetic, uncompassionate, callous, stony-hearted, cold, heartless, indifferent, detached, flinty, inhuman, iron-headed
➡ warm-hearted

coldly adv
unfeelingly, unsympathetically, unemotionally, undemonstratively, callously, insensitively, heartlessly, antagonistically
➡ warmly, responsively

collaborate v
1 WORK TOGETHER, co-operate, join, join forces, work jointly, work as partners, combine forces, team up, associate with, unite, participate
2 *collaborate with the enemy*
conspire, collude, fraternize, betray, turn traitor

collaboration n
1 *in collaboration with local industry*
association, alliance, partnership, teamwork, co-operation, participation, union, combined/joint/collective effort
2 *collaboration with the enemy*
conspiring, collusion, fraternizing

collaborator n
1 *collaborators in the research*
co-worker, associate, partner, teammate, fellow worker, colleague, assistant
2 *traitors and collaborators*
conspirator, accomplice, traitor, turncoat, betrayer, colluder, fraternizer, quisling, renegade

collapse v, n
♦ v
1 *the bridge collapsed*
fall down, fall in, fall to pieces, come apart, fall apart, sink, founder, disintegrate, crumble, subside, give way, cave in
2 *the business collapsed*
fail, founder, break down, fall through, finish, disintegrate, come to an end, come to nothing, slump, go to the wall
COLLOQ. fold, flop, tank; *Aust* go bung
3 *collapse with exhaustion*
faint, pass out, lose consciousness, black out, keel over, swoon, crumple
4 *collapse in tears*
break down, lose control, fall apart, go to pieces, have a (nervous) breakdown
COLLOQ. crack up
♦ n
1 *the collapse of the roof*
falling-down, falling-in, falling to pieces, coming apart, sinking, foundering, disintegration, subsidence, giving way, cave-in
2 *the collapse of the talks*
failure, foundering, breakdown, falling-through, disintegration, downfall, ruin, debacle
COLLOQ. flop

3 *his collapse in the street*
fainting, passing-out, loss of consciousness, blackout, keeling-over, swoon
4 BREAKDOWN, nervous breakdown, loss of control, attack

collar n, v
♦ n
neckband, band, ring, dog-collar, choker, gorget, ruff, bertha, ruche, vandyke, rollcollar, turn-down, ox-bow, jampot
TECHNICAL collet, chevesaile, holderbat
OLD carcanet, mousquetaire, partlet, piccadilly, rebato, whisk, rabatine
♦ v
stop, grab, capture, catch, seize, arrest, apprehend
COLLOQ. nab, nick, bust, haul in

collate v
gather, collect, sort, arrange, order, put in order, organize, compare, compose, compile, edit, put together

collateral n
security, guarantee, pledge, surety, assurance, deposit, funds

collation n
gathering, arrangement, ordering, organization, composition, compilation, editing, putting together

colleague n
workmate, co-worker, teammate, partner, collaborator, ally, associate, confederate, confrère, comrade, fellow worker, companion, aide, helper, assistant, auxiliary

collect v
1 *collect firewood*
gather, accumulate, amass, heap, hoard, pile up, stockpile
FORMAL aggregate
2 *a crowd collected*
gather, form, come together, amass, mass, converge, congregate, assemble, convene, muster, rally
3 *collect them from the station*
fetch, pick up, meet, get, call for, come for, go and get, go and take, go and bring; *Scot & NZ* uplift
4 *collect for a charity*
raise money, ask for money, ask people to give, solicit, acquire
5 *collect stamps*
acquire, save, amass, have as a hobby, be interested in
6 *collect your thoughts*
compose, gather (together), assemble, recover, prepare;
COLLOQ. *N Am* recombobulate
➡ **2** disperse, scatter **3** drop off, leave

collected adj
composed, controlled, self-controlled, self-possessed, placid, serene, calm, unruffled, unshaken, unperturbed, imperturbable, poised, cool
COLLOQ. unflappable, unfazed
➡ anxious, worried, agitated

Collective nouns (by animal) include:

shrewdness of *apes*	pack of *dogs*	tribe of *goats*	swarm of *locusts*	nye of *pheasants*	murmuration of *starlings*
cete of *badgers*	school of *dolphins*	husk of *hares*	tittering of *magpies*	litter of *pigs*	ambush of *tigers*
sloth of *bears*	dole of *doves*	cast of *hawks*	troop of *monkeys*	school of *porpoises*	rafter of *turkeys*
swarm of *bees*	team of *ducks*	brood of *hens*	watch of *nightingales*	bury of *rabbits*	turn of *turtles*
obstinacy of *buffalos*	parade of *elephants*	bloat of *hippopotami*	family of *otters*	colony of *rats*	descent of *woodpeckers*
clowder of *cats*	busyness of *ferrets*	string of *horses*	parliament of *owls*	unkindness of *ravens*	gam of *whales*
drove of *cattle*	charm of *finches*	pack of *hounds*	pandemonium of *parrots*	crash of *rhinoceros*	rout of *wolves*
brood of *chickens*	shoal of *fish*	troop of *kangaroos*	covey of *partridges*	building of *rooks*	zeal of *zebras*
bask of *crocodiles*	skulk of *foxes*	kindle of *kittens*	muster of *peacocks*	pod of *seals*	
murder of *crows*	army of *frogs*	exaltation of *larks*	muster of *penguins*	flock of *sheep*	
herd of *deer*	gaggle/skein of *geese*	leap of *leopards*			
		pride of *lions*			

Names of collectors and enthusiasts include:

zoophile (*animals*)
antiquary (*antiques*)
tegestologist (*beer mats*)
campanologist (*bell-ringing*)
ornithologist (*birds*)
bibliophile (*books*)
audiophile (*broadcast sound*)
lepidopterist (*butterflies*)
cartophilist (*cigarette cards*)
numismatist (*coins/medals*)
gamer (*computer games*)

conservationist (*countryside*)
cruciverbalist (*crosswords*)
planganologist (*dolls*)
environmentalist (*the environment*)
vexillologist (*flags*)
xenophile (*foreigners*)
gourmet (*good food*)
gastronome (*good food and wine*)
discophile (*gramophone records*)
chirographist (*handwriting*)
hippophile (*horses*)

entomologist (*insects*)
phillumenist (*matches/matchboxes*)
monarchist (*the monarchy*)
deltiologist (*postcards*)
arachnologist (*spiders/arachnids*)
philatelist (*stamps*)
arctophile (*teddy bears*)
oenophile (*wine*)
etymologist (*words*)

collection *n*
1 *an art collection; the collection of information*
group, cluster, accumulation, gathering, assembly, conglomeration, mass, heap, pile, hoard, stockpile, store, assortment, job-lot
FORMAL assemblage
2 *a collection of poems*
set, anthology, compilation, collected works, selection, series
3 *a collection for charity*
donation(s), gift(s), contribution(s), subscription, offering, offertory
COLLOQ. whip-round

collective *adj, n*
♦ *adj*
united, combined, concerted, co-operative, collaborative, joint, common, shared, corporate, democratic, composite, aggregate, unanimous, cumulative
F∃ individual
♦ *n*
commune, co-operative, community, kibbutz, kolkhoz, moshav

collective nouns
See panel on previous page

collector
See panel above

college *n*
educational institution, educational establishment, university, institute, college of further education, technical college, adult education centre, academy, school, seminary
OLD polytechnic, poly
Related adjective: collegiate

collide *v*
1 *the cars collided*
crash (into), meet head on, smash (into), bump (into), run into, go into, plough into, hit
COLLOQ. prang
2 *their opinions collided*
clash, conflict, be in conflict, disagree, quarrel, wrangle, grapple, fight, contend, feud, war

collision *n*
1 *in collision with a lorry*
crash, impact, bump, smash, accident, pile-up, wreck, disaster
COLLOQ. prang
2 *a collision of interests*
clash, conflict, confrontation, opposition, showdown, disagreement, fight, brush, collision, warring, fighting, feud, quarrel, wrangle

colloquial *adj*
conversational, informal, familiar, everyday, vernacular, casual, idiomatic, chatty, popular
FORMAL demotic
F∃ formal

colloquially *adv*
informally, familiarly, popularly, conversationally
F∃ formally

collude *v*
conspire, plot, connive, collaborate, scheme, intrigue
FORMAL machinate
COLLOQ. be in cahoots

collusion *n*
complicity, deceit, conspiracy, plot, connivance, collaboration, league, scheme, scheming, intrigue, artifice
FORMAL machination
COLLOQ. cahoots

colonist *n*
colonial, settler, colonizer, immigrant, emigrant, pioneer

colonize *v*
settle, occupy, people, pioneer, found, populate

colonnade *n*
arcade, cloisters, portico, covered walk, stoa
FORMAL columniation, peristyle

colony *n*
1 *Britain's former colonies*
settlement, outpost, dependency, dominion, protectorate, possession, satellite, satellite state, territory, province
OLD plantation
2 *a colony of birds*
group, association, community, settlement
TECHNICAL hive, swarm, apery, coenobium, formicarium, polyzoarium

colossal *adj*
huge, enormous, immense, vast, massive, great, gigantic, mammoth, monstrous, monumental, herculean, gargantuan
FORMAL Brobdingnagian
COLLOQ. whopping, jumbo
F∃ tiny, minute

colossus *n*
giant, titan, Goliath, Hercules, monster, ogre, Cyclops

colour *n, v*
♦ *n*
1 HUE, shade, tinge, tone, tincture, tint, dye, paint, wash, pigment, pigmentation, colorant, coloration, complexion
2 *the colour of her cheeks*
rosiness, redness, ruddiness, pinkness, glow
3 *regardless of colour or creed*
skin colour, pigmentation, race, racial group, ethnic group, nationality
4 VIVIDNESS, liveliness, life, richness, brilliance, animation
COLLOQ. kick, oomph, pizzazz
5 *a nation's colours*
flag, standard, banner, emblem, ensign, insignia, badge
6 *a team's colours*
strip, kit, tackle, clothing
COLLOQ. get-up
♦ *v*
1 PAINT, crayon, dye, tint, stain, tinge, wash, highlight
2 BLUSH, flush, redden, go/turn red
3 *colour your judgement*
affect, bias, prejudice, influence, sway, distort, slant, pervert, exaggerate, overstate, misrepresent, falsify, taint
Related adjective: chromatic

The range of colours includes:

red	coral	chocolate	chartreuse	blue	rose
crimson	salmon	tan	green	sapphire	magnolia
scarlet	peach	sepia	eau de nil	gentian	cream
vermilion	amber	taupe	emerald	indigo	ecru
cherry	brown	beige	jade	anil	milky
cerise	chestnut	fawn	bottle green	navy	white
magenta	mahogany	yellow	avocado	violet	grey
maroon	bronze	lemon	olive	purple	silver
burgundy	auburn	canary	sage	mauve	charcoal
ruby	rust	ochre	khaki	plum	ebony
orange	umber	saffron	turquoise	lavender	jet
tangerine	copper	topaz	aquamarine	lilac	black
apricot	cinnamon	gold	cobalt	pink	

QUOTATIONS
Color possesses me. I don't have to pursue it. It will possess me always ... Color and I are one
PAUL KLEE, *The Diaries of Paul Klee*

colourful *adj*
1 MULTICOLOURED, kaleidoscopic, variegated, many-coloured, parti-coloured, polychrome, vivid, bright, brilliant, rich, deep, intense, vibrant, gaudy, garish
2 *a colourful description*
vivid, graphic, picturesque, animated, lively, stimulating, exciting, interesting, rich, vibrant
F3 **1** colourless, drab

colourfully *adv*
brightly, brilliantly, vibrantly, intensely, kaleidoscopically

colourless *adj*
1 TRANSPARENT, neutral, uncoloured, monochrome, white, in black and white, bleached, washed out, faded, pale, ashen, sickly, anaemic, wan
2 INSIPID, lacklustre, dull, dreary, drab, plain, characterless, unmemorable, boring, uninteresting, tame
F3 **1** colourful, polychrome **2** bright, exciting

column *n*
1 PILLAR, post, shaft, pole, upright, support, pier, obelisk
TECHNICAL asta, caryatid, telamon, Atlas, pilaster, newel
2 *a column of people*
line, row, rank, file, procession, queue, string, parade, list
3 *a column in a newspaper*
article, item, piece, feature, story
Related adjectives: columnal, columnar

columnist *n*
journalist, reporter, reviewer, writer, correspondent, contributor, critic, editor

coma *n*
unconsciousness, hypnosis, insensibility, lethargy, oblivion, stupor, torpor, trance, drowsiness
TECHNICAL PVS, persistent vegetative state, catalepsy, sopor
FORMAL somnolence

comatose *adj*
unconscious, out, out cold, in a coma, insensible, lethargic, drowsy, sleepy, sluggish, stupefied, stunned, dazed, torpid
TECHNICAL cataleptic, soporose
FORMAL somnolent
F3 conscious

comb *v*
1 *comb your hair*
groom, neaten, tidy, arrange, dress, untangle, disentangle
2 SEARCH, hunt, scour, sweep, explore, sift, screen, rake, rummage, ransack, go through
COLLOQ. go over with a fine-tooth comb, turn upside down

combat *n*, *v*
♦ *n*
war, warfare, hostilities, action, battle, fight, fighting, skirmittle, do battle, war, wage war, take up arms, strive, struggle, contend, contest, oppose, resist, withstand, defy

combatant *n*
fighter, warrior, soldier, serviceman, servicewoman, enemy, opponent, adversary, antagonist, belligerent, contender

combative *adj*
aggressive, antagonistic, belligerent, warring, argumentative, contentious, militant, quarrelsome, warlike, hawkish
FORMAL bellicose, pugnacious, truculent
F3 pacific, peaceful

combination *n*
1 *in combination with other subjects*
association, co-operation, conjunction, co-ordination, union, amalgamation, coalition, unification, alliance, federation, confederation, confederacy, combine, consortium, syndicate, merger, integration, synergy
2 BLEND, mix, mixture, composite, cross, amalgam, amalgamation, merger, union, fusion, conflation, coalescence, collection, connection, group, synthesis, compound, solution

combine *v*
merge, amalgamate, bring together, put together, club together, unify, blend, stir, mix, mingle, integrate, incorporate, synthesize, compound, alloy, fuse, bond, bind, conflate, weld, join, join forces, connect, link, marry, unite, pool, ally, associate, team up, co-operate
FORMAL admix, homogenize
F3 divide, separate, detach

combustible *adj*
1 *combustible gas*
explosive, flammable, incendiary, ignitable, inflammable
2 *a combustible temper*
excitable, sensitive, explosive, stormy, tense, volatile, charged
F3 incombustible, non-flammable, flameproof

combustion *n*
burning, igniting, ignition, firing

come *v*
1 *they came to me*
advance, move towards, travel towards, move forward, approach, move nearer, near, draw near
2 *come to the river/party*
reach, attain, arrive, enter, get here, get there, appear, put in an appearance, attend, materialize
COLLOQ. turn up, show up, surface, burst in, barge in
3 *come to power*
reach, attain, achieve, gain, secure, pass into
4 *the time for action has come*
arrive, occur, take place, happen, come about, present itself, come to pass, transpire

5 *she comes from Belgium*
originate, be, be a native of, be ... by birth, have as your home, hail from, have as its source/origin
6 *his arrogance comes from his insecurity*
result from, be caused by, follow, issue, develop, arise, stem, evolve
7 *it may come to war*
pass into, become, turn, evolve into, develop into, enter, go as far as
8 *the idea came to me*
think of, remember, strike, occur to, come to the mind of, dawn on
9 *this wallpaper comes in blue or green*
be available, be produced, be on the market, be on offer
10 REACH AN ORGASM, have an orgasm, climax
⊟ **1** go, retreat **2** depart, leave **3** fall from, lose **8** forget

■ **come about**
happen, occur, come to pass, take place, result, arise, transpire
FORMAL befall

■ **come across**
1 FIND (BY CHANCE), discover, meet by chance, stumble across, encounter, notice
FORMAL chance upon, happen upon
COLLOQ. run into, bump into
2 *his speech came across well*
come over, seem, appear, communicate, give the impression of being

■ **come along**
1 PROGRESS, make progress, develop, get better, improve, show an improvement, make headway, advance, rally, mend, recover, recuperate
2 HURRY UP
COLLOQ. get a move on, get cracking, shake a leg, get your skates on, pull your finger out

■ **come apart**
collapse, disintegrate, fall to bits/pieces, break (up), separate, split, tear, crumble

■ **come back**
1 RETURN, reappear, come home, go back, get back
2 BE REMEMBERED, remind, be recalled, be recollected, be suggested

■ **come between**
separate, part, divide, split up, disunite, alienate, cause a rift between
FORMAL estrange

■ **come by**
acquire, get, get hold of, obtain, secure, come into someone's possession, fall into someone's hands
FORMAL procure

■ **come clean**
acknowledge, admit, confess, own up, reveal, tell all
COLLOQ. make a clean breast of something, spill the beans
SLANG fess up

■ **come down**
decrease, fall, drop, reduce, descend, decline, deteriorate, worsen, degenerate

■ **come down on**
blame, criticize, rebuke, reprimand, find fault with, chide, reprove, upbraid, reprehend, admonish
FORMAL berate
COLLOQ. slate, knock, tear into

■ **come down to**
mean, be tantamount to, be equivalent to, correspond to, amount to, add up to, boil down to

■ **come down with**
catch, become/fall ill with, get, develop, go down with, pick up, become infected with, become ill with
FORMAL contract, succumb to

■ **come forward**
offer (yourself), offer your services, volunteer, step forward

■ **come in**
enter, appear, arrive, finish receive
COLLOQ. show up
⊟ go out

■ **come in for**
receive, get, suffer, endure, bear, undergo, experience, be subjected to, sustain

■ **come into**
inherit, be left, have bequeathed to you, be heir to, acquire, receive

■ **come off**
succeed, be successful, be effective, go well, work (out), happen, occur, take place, end up
COLLOQ. pay off

■ **come on**
begin, appear, advance, proceed, progress, make progress, develop, improve, show an improvement, get better, thrive, succeed, rally, mend, recover, recuperate

■ **come out**
1 *it came out that she never liked him*
become known, emerge, leak out, come to light, appear, be revealed, be made public
2 *the magazine comes out monthly*
be published, appear, be produced, be released, become available
3 *everything came out all right in the end*
result, end (up), finish, conclude, terminate
4 *gay people coming out*
come out of the closet, declare yourself to be, declare openly, admit

■ **come out with**
say, state, affirm, declare, utter, exclaim, disclose, divulge, blurt out

■ **come round**
1 *come around from the anaesthetic*
come to, recover, recover/regain consciousness, wake, awake
2 YIELD, change your mind, agree, be converted to, be persuaded, be won over, relent, concede, allow, grant, accede
3 *spring comes round again*
occur, happen, take place, recur, reappear
⊟ **1** pass out

■ **come through**
endure, withstand, survive, ride out, pull through, prevail, triumph, succeed, accomplish, achieve

■ **come to**
1 *come to after the operation*
come round, recover, recover/regain consciousness, wake, awake
2 *come to a total*
add up to, total, aggregate, amount to, make, equal, run to

■ **come up**
rise, arise, happen, occur, present itself, crop up, turn up

■ **come up to**
reach, meet, match up to, measure up to, live up to, make the grade, compare with, approach, bear comparison with

■ **come up with**
suggest, put forward, propose, offer, present, think of, dream up, conceive, devise, advance, produce, submit

comeback *n*
return, reappearance, resurgence, revival, recovery, rally

comedian *n*
comic, clown, humorist, funny man, funny woman, comedienne, entertainer, wit, joker, gagman
COLLOQ. wag, gagster

comedown *n*
anticlimax, let-down, disappointment, deflation, blow, reverse, reversal, decline, descent, demotion, humiliation, degradation
TECHNICAL bathos

comedy *n*
1 *comedy on TV*
farce, entertainment, humour, pantomime, burlesque, vaudeville, slapstick, satire, situation comedy, sitcom, tragicomedy, commedia dell'arte

2 *the comedy of the situation*
humour, hilarity, funniness, fun, drollery, clowning, wit, joking, jesting, facetiousness
E3 1 tragedy

comely *adj*
attractive, beautiful, pretty, lovely, good-looking, blooming, buxom, fair, graceful, pleasing, winsome; *Scot* bonny
FORMAL pulchritudinous

come-on *n*
encouragement, inducement, enticement, lure, allurement, temptation, attraction

comeuppance *n*
deserts, just deserts, what you deserve, dues, merit, punishment, rebuke, chastening, recompense, requital, retribution

comfort *n, v*
♦ *n*
1 EASE, relaxation, luxury, plenty, snugness, cosiness, wellbeing, satisfaction, contentment, enjoyment, freedom from pain, freedom from worry/unhappiness, freedom from difficulties
FORMAL repose, opulence
COLLOQ. easy street
2 CONSOLATION, compensation, cheer, reassurance, encouragement, condolence, alleviation, relief, help, aid, support
FORMAL solace, succour
E3 1 discomfort **2** distress
♦ *v*
ease, soothe, relieve, alleviate, assuage, console, cheer, gladden, reassure, hearten, encourage, help, support, sympathize, empathize, invigorate, strengthen, enliven, refresh
OLD encheer, stay, speak to the heart, recomfort
FORMAL solace, bring solace to, succour

QUOTATIONS
I beg cold comfort
WILLIAM SHAKESPEARE, *King John*

comfortable *adj*
1 SNUG, cosy, relaxing, restful, easy, convenient, pleasant, agreeable, enjoyable, delightful, warm, homelike, kindly, well, *gemütlich*; *Scot* couthie, bein, tosh
OLD commodious
COLLOQ. comfy
2 *comfortable clothes*
well-fitting, loose-fitting, loose, roomy
3 AFFLUENT, well-off, well-to-do, without financial problems, pleasant, prosperous, luxurious; *Scot* bein
FORMAL opulent
COLLOQ. cushy
4 UNHURRIED, leisurely, slow, relaxed, easy, gentle, carefree, lazy, armchair
COLLOQ. laid-back
5 *feel comfortable talking about it*
relaxed, at ease, unembarrassed, confident, happy, contented, safe, secure
E3 1 uncomfortable, unpleasant **2** uncomfortable, tight **3** poor, hard-up **5** uneasy, awkward, nervous, offended, embarrassed, threatened

SYNONYM NUANCES
sense 1
Snug and **cosy** and are highly suggestive of security and shelter: *they're snug in their beds*; *a cosy place by the fire.* **Homelike** would be used to describe a similar place which prompts a feeling of familiarity. **Relaxing** and **restful** suggest the removal of tension, either physical or mental, while **easy** has the added connotation of absence of any discomfort: *he has had an easy life.*
The word **convenient** perhaps conveys the least feeling, merely suggesting suitability: *convenient working*

hours. **Pleasant** and **agreeable** are suggestive of mild pleasure gained from comfort: *an agreeable spot on the beach*; whilst **enjoyable** and **delightful** are similar but more effusive.

comforting *adj*
soothing, reassuring, encouraging, heartening, heartwarming, helpful, cheering, consolatory, consoling
FORMAL inspiriting
E3 worrying

comic *adj, n*
♦ *adj*
funny, hilarious, side-splitting, comical, droll, humorous, witty, amusing, entertaining, diverting, joking, facetious, jocular, light, farcical, ridiculous, ludicrous, absurd, laughable, zany, buffo
COLLOQ. priceless, rich, knee-slapping
E3 tragic, serious, straight
♦ *n*
comedian, clown, humorist, funny man, funny woman, entertainer, wit, joker, gagman, buffoon, buffo
COLLOQ. wag, gagster

comical *adj*
funny, hilarious, droll, humorous, witty, amusing, entertaining, diverting, laughable, farcical, absurd, ridiculous, ludicrous
E3 sad, unamusing

comically *adv*
funnily, hilariously, humorously, wittily, amusingly, absurdly, ridiculously, ludicrously, farcically
E3 sadly

coming *adj, n*
♦ *adj*
1 *in the coming months*
next, forthcoming, upcoming, impending, imminent, due, approaching, advancing, near, nearing, future
2 *the coming man*
aspiring, promising, rising, up-and-coming
♦ *n*
advent, approach, arrival, nearing, birth, dawn, accession

command *v, n*
♦ *v*
1 ORDER, bid, give orders to, charge, enjoin, direct, instruct, require, demand, compel
FORMAL adjure
2 LEAD, head, rule, reign, govern, control, be in charge/control of, direct, dominate, manage, superintend, supervise, preside over
3 *command respect*
be given, gain, receive, get, obtain, secure
♦ *n*
1 COMMANDMENT, decree, edict, precept, mandate, order, bidding, charge, injunction, dictate, directive, direction, instruction, requirement
OLD (*Shakesp*) impose; (*Spenser*) hest
FORMAL behest
2 *be in command*
power, authority, leadership, control, charge, domination, dominion, mastery, rule, sway, government, ascendancy, management, supervision, superintendence

commandeer *v*
seize, take possession of, take, confiscate, impound, hijack, usurp
FORMAL appropriate, requisition, expropriate, arrogate, sequester, sequestrate

commander *n*
leader, head, chief, director, commander-in-chief, general, admiral, captain, commanding officer, officer, chieftain, governor, master, superintendent
COLLOQ. boss
SLANG bloke

Types of commander include:

aga	meer	*old* taxiarch
old chiliarch	*old* polemarch	*old* tetrarch
encomendero	*old* phylarch	*old* trierarch
old hipparch	*old* prefect	*old* turcopolier
imperator	privateer	warlord
mir	risaldar	

commanding *adj*
1 *in a commanding lead*
powerful, strong, superior, advantageous, dominant, dominating, controlling, directing
2 *a commanding personality*
authoritative, forceful, powerful, assertive, confident, autocratic
FORMAL peremptory
3 *the castle's commanding position*
dominating, imposing, impressive, lofty

commemorate *v*
celebrate, solemnize, remember, mark, honour, pay tribute to, salute, immortalize, observe, keep, recognize
FORMAL memorialize

commemoration *n*
celebration, observance, remembrance, memory, tribute, honour, honouring, ceremony, salute, recognition, dedication

commemorative *adj*
memorial, celebratory, remembering, marking, honouring, saluting, dedicatory, in memory of, in memoriam, in remembrance of, in honour of, as a tribute to, in recognition of

commence *v*
begin, make a beginning, start, make a start, embark on, originate, initiate, inaugurate, open, launch, go ahead
E3 finish, end, cease

commencement *n*
beginning, start, initiation, origin, opening, launch, outset, onset
COLLOQ. kick-off
E3 finish, end, conclusion

commend *v*
1 PRAISE, compliment, acclaim, extol, applaud, speak highly of
FORMAL laud, eulogize
2 *commend this book*
recommend, suggest, approve, propose, advocate, put in a good word for
3 COMMIT, entrust, trust, confide, consign, hand over, give, deliver, yield
E3 1 criticize, censure

commendable *adj*
admirable, excellent, noble, praiseworthy, worthy, creditable, exemplary, deserving, estimable
FORMAL laudable, meritorious
E3 blameworthy, poor

commendation *n*
praise, acclaim, acclamation, accolade, applause, congratulation, high/good opinion, good word, approval, credit, recognition, encouragement, recommendation, seal/stamp of approval, special mention
FORMAL approbation, encomium, panegyric
COLLOQ. brownie points
E3 blame, criticism

commensurate *adj*
proportionate, equivalent, equal, corresponding, comparable, in proportion to, according to, corresponding to, consistent with, appropriate to, compatible with, acceptable, adequate, sufficient, due, fitting

comment *v, n*
♦ *v*
remark, give an opinion, observe, note, mention, say, point out, explain, interpret, gloss, speak to
OLD descant, gloze
FORMAL interpose, interject, elucidate, opine
♦ *n*
opinion, statement, remark, observation, view, note, annotation, footnote, marginal note, sidenote, explanation, illustration, exposition, commentary, criticism
FORMAL elucidation, scholion, scholium

commentary *n*
1 *a commentary on a football match*
narration, voice-over, analysis, description, report, account, review
2 *a Bible commentary*
explanation, interpretation, analysis, notes, annotation, treatise, critique
FORMAL elucidation, exegesis, exposition, postil

commentator *n*
1 *a sports commentator*
broadcaster, reporter, correspondent, sportscaster, newscaster, narrator, commenter
2 *a commentator on the text*
annotator, interpreter, critic
FORMAL expositor, exegete

commerce *n*
trade, business, industry, private enterprise, buying and selling, dealings, relations, dealing, traffic, trafficking, exchange, marketing, merchandizing

> **QUOTATIONS**
> The commerce of the world is conducted by the strong, and usually it operates against the weak
>   HENRY WARD BEECHER, *Proverbs from the Plymouth Pulpit*

commercial *adj, n*
♦ *adj*
1 *buildings for commercial use*
trade, trading, business, industrial
2 *a commercial success*
profitable, profit-making, lucrative, moneymaking, money-spinning, sellable, saleable, popular, monetary, financial, entrepreneurial, profit-orientated, materialistic, mercenary, venal
♦ *n*
advertisement, publicity, promotion, marketing, jingle, display, blurb, announcement, notice, poster, bill, placard, leaflet, handbill, circular, handout, propaganda
COLLOQ. advert, ad, plug, hype

commiserate *v*
express/offer sympathy, send/offer condolences, sympathize, comfort, feel for, feel sorry for, understand, console, show consideration

commiseration *n*
pity, sympathy, compassion, consolation, comfort, consideration, understanding, condolence(s)
FORMAL solace

commission *n, v*
♦ *n*
1 ASSIGNMENT, mission, errand, task, job, duty, function, appointment, employment, mandate, work, piece of work, warrant, authority, charge, trust, responsibility
2 COMMITTEE, board, delegation, council, advisory group/body, deputation, representative
3 *commission on a sale*
percentage, share, royalty, allowance, fee, brokerage, compensation
COLLOQ. cut, rake-off
♦ *v*
nominate, select, appoint, arrange, contract, engage, employ, assign, authorize, empower, delegate, depute,

send, order, place/put in an order for, request, ask for, mandate

commit v
1 *commit a crime*
do, carry out, get up to, indulge in, perform, execute, enact
FORMAL effect, perpetrate
2 ENTRUST, trust, confide, commend, consign, deliver, hand over, give, assign, deposit
3 *commit yourself to do something*
promise, pledge, bind, engage, decide, dedicate, covenant, cross the Rubicon
FORMAL obligate
4 *committed to a mental hospital*
admit, send, assign, confine
COLLOQ. put away

commitment n
1 DEDICATION, involvement, adherence, devotion, allegiance, loyalty, hard work, effort
2 DUTY, responsibility, undertaking, obligation, engagement, liability, tie
3 *make a commitment*
undertaking, guarantee, assurance, promise, word, covenant, pledge, vow
E3 1 vacillation, wavering

committal n
admission, confinement, consignment, sending

committed adj
active, dedicated, devoted, loyal, involved, enthusiastic, zealous, fervent, red-hot, evangelical, hardworking, diligent, industrious, studious
FORMAL engagé
COLLOQ. card-carrying, paid up, sold out (on)
E3 apathetic, uncommitted

SYNONYM NUANCES

Active and **involved** are neutral terms suggesting participation: *an active campaigner*. **Dedicated** and **devoted** would imply centring your life on someone or something, and any inference is likely to be favourable: *a dedicated priest*; *a devoted husband*. The term **loyal** is similar, this time with the focus on fidelity: *a loyal customer base*.

Enthusiastic implies an intense and lively interest, and there is a note of approval in this term; both **zealous**, **fervent** and **red-hot** are similar, but usually refer to an extreme degree of enthusiasm, and not necessarily with favour: *a zealous evangelist*. The term **evangelical** implies the wish to convert people to the same way of thinking, and again a slightly disapprobatory feeling is likely to come across: *her evangelical attitude to breastfeeding*.

The more approbatory terms **hardworking**, **diligent** and **industrious** appropriately describe a committed application to work, and **studious** could be used to refer to a similar application to learning.

---

committee

Types of committee include:

advisory group/ body	discussion group	steering group
assembly	focus group	sub-committee
board	group	synod
caucus	jury	task force
commission	legation	team
congress	mission	*colloq.* think tank
council	panel	user group
delegation	quango	working group
deputation	quorum	working party
	steering committee	workshop

commodious adj
roomy, spacious, large, ample, comfortable, expansive, extensive
FORMAL capacious
E3 cramped

commodity n
product, thing, article, item, goods, merchandise, material, output, produce, stock, wares

common adj
1 *a common response*
frequent, familiar, customary, habitual, usual, daily, everyday, routine, ordinary, normal, regular
COLLOQ. two/ten a penny, dime a dozen
2 *share a common belief*
mutual, shared, joint, collective
3 *common land*
communal, community, public
4 *common knowledge*
widespread, prevalent, general, universal, conventional, accepted, popular, commonplace
5 *a common soldier*
ordinary, standard, average, plain, simple, workaday, run-of-the-mill, undistinguished, unexceptional
COLLOQ. bog standard
6 VULGAR, coarse, unrefined, crude, inferior, low, ill-bred, uncouth, loutish, plebeian
COLLOQ. common as muck
SLANG chavvy
E3 1 uncommon, unusual, rare, noteworthy **5** different, special **6** tasteful, refined

commonly adv
generally, normally, usually, often, frequently, regularly, typically, routinely, as a rule, for the most part
E3 rarely

commonplace adj
ordinary, unexceptional, everyday, common, routine, humdrum, dull, pedestrian, banal, trite, widespread, frequent, hackneyed, stock, stale, obvious, worn out, boring, uninteresting, threadbare, mundane, prosaic
E3 memorable, exceptional

common sense n
good sense, sense, sensibleness, level-headedness, sanity, soundness, reason, pragmatism, hard-headedness, realism, experience, discernment, wisdom, shrewdness, astuteness, judgement, native intelligence, prudence, practicality
FORMAL judiciousness
COLLOQ. gumption, nous, savvy
E3 folly, stupidity

common-sense adj
commonsensical, matter-of-fact, sensible, level-headed, sane, sound, reasonable, practical, down-to-earth, pragmatic, hard-headed, realistic, experienced, wise, discerning, prudent, shrewd, astute
FORMAL judicious
E3 foolish, unreasonable, unrealistic

commotion n
agitation, hurly-burly, turmoil, tumult, excitement, ferment, fuss, bustle, ado, uproar, furore, racket, hubbub, rumpus, row, clamour, fracas, upheaval, disturbance, confusion, disorder, disquiet, riot, stir; *Irish* stirabout
COLLOQ. ballyhoo, hullabaloo, to-do, brouhaha, bust-up

communal adj
public, community, shared, joint, collective, general, common
E3 private, personal

communally adv
collectively, jointly, generally, commonly, community
E3 personally, privately

commune n, v
♦ *n*
collective, co-operative, kibbutz, community, fellowship, colony, settlement

♦ v

converse, discourse, communicate, make contact, feel/get close to, feel/get in touch, relate spiritually

communicable adj

infectious, contagious, transmittable, transmissible, transferable, conveyable, catching, spreadable
FORMAL infective

communicate v

1 ANNOUNCE, impart, inform, acquaint, intimate, notify, publish, broadcast, relay, spread, diffuse, pass on, transmit, convey, declare, proclaim, make known, report, reveal, disclose, divulge, unfold, express, get across, get over, put across, put over, deliver, reach, mediate
FORMAL disseminate

2 TALK, speak, converse, commune, correspond, write, phone, telephone, contact, get/be in touch, liaise, keep the lines open

communication n

information, intelligence, intimation, disclosure, contact, connection, transmission, message
FORMAL dissemination
See panel below

communicative adj

talkative, voluble, expansive, informative, chatty, sociable, friendly, forthcoming, outgoing, extrovert, unreserved, free, open, frank, candid
F3 quiet, reserved, reticent, secretive

communion n

1 *communion with nature*
sharing thoughts, sharing feelings, communing, closeness, sympathy, empathy, togetherness, unity, harmony, fellowship, participation, rapport, affinity, community
FORMAL accord, concord, intercourse

2 *Holy Communion*
Lord's Supper, Eucharist, Mass, Sacrament
TECHNICAL agape
OLD Scot occasion

communiqué n

announcement, bulletin, (official) communication, press release, dispatch, message, report, statement, newsflash

communism n

collectivism, sovietism, revisionism, socialism, totalitarianism, Bolshevism, Leninism, Marxism, Stalinism, Trotskyism, Maoism, Titoism

communist n

collectivist, socialist, leftist, soviet, revisionist, Bolshevist, Leninist, Marxist, Stalinist, Trotskyist, Trotskyite, Maoist, Spartakist
COLLOQ. red, tanky; (derog) commie, comrade;
Aust commo

community n

1 *the local community*
district, region, locality, locale, neighbourhood, population, people, populace, public, residents

2 *the Bangladeshi community*
population, people, populace, public, residents, nation, state, section, group, body, colony, fellowship, brotherhood, fraternity

3 *a religious community*
commune, kibbutz, society, association, fellowship, brotherhood, sisterhood, fraternity
Related adjectives: communal, civil

commute v

1 *commute by train*
travel to work, travel to and from work, journey, shuttle

2 *commute the death sentence*
reduce, decrease, shorten, curtail, lighten, soften, lessen, mitigate, remit, adjust, modify

commuter n

traveller, passenger
COLLOQ. strap-hanger, suburbanite

compact[1] adj, v

♦ adj

a compact book
small, neat, short, brief, terse, succinct, concise, pithy, condensed, pocket, little, compressed, pressed together, close, close-packed, close-pressed, dense, impenetrable, solid, firm
F3 large, rambling, diffuse

♦ v

to compact collected refuse
compress, press down, press together, condense, consolidate, pack down, cram, flatten, ram, squeeze, tamp

compact[2] n

the compact between the nations
agreement, alliance, pact, treaty, arrangement, transaction, deal, settlement, bargain, understanding, accord, bond, indenture, concordat, contract, covenant, entente

companion n

fellow, comrade, friend, intimate, confidant(e), ally, confederate, colleague, associate, partner, consort, escort, chaperon(e), attendant, aide, assistant, accomplice, follower, workmate, compeer, lad, playmate, *bon vivant(e)*, inseparable, shadow, barnacle, compadre, *compagnon de voyage*, compotation, pew-fellow; *dialect* marrow
OLD book-mate, convive, copes-mate, copemate, Trojan, Ephesian, fere, pheere, franion, skaines mate; (Shakesp) co-mate; (Spenser) beau-pere
COLLOQ. mate, pal, buddy, crony, sidekick, cohort

Forms of communication include:

advertising	computer	journal	newspaper	sign language	subscription TV
aerogram	conversation	junk mail	note	SMS (short	pay TV
announcement	correspondence	leaflet	notice	message service)	pay-per-view
answering	data communica-	letter	pager	speech	telex
machine	tion	loud-hailer	pamphlet	statement	text message
bleeper	dialogue	magazine	PDA (Personal	tannoy	typewriter
blog (or weblog)	dictaphone	mailshot	Digital Assistant)	telecommunica-	wireless
Braille	dispatch	mass media	podcast	tions	video
broadband	email	media	post	telegram	video-conferencing
broadcasting	facsimile	megaphone	postcard	Telemessage®	video-on-demand
brochure	fax	memo	poster	telephone	voice mail
bulletin	gossip	message	press	teleprinter	walkie-talkie
cable	grapevine	MMS (multimedia	press release	teletext	webcast
call-conferencing	information tech-	messaging ser-	publicity	television (or TV)	website
catalogue	nology (IT)	vice)	radar	access TV	wire
chain letter	intercom	Morse code	radio	cable TV	word
circular	the Internet (or the	news	report	digital TV	word processor
communiqué	Net)	newsflash	semaphore	satellite TV	World Wide Web

See also **telephone**.

companionable *adj*
friendly, affable, sympathetic, familiar, genial, amiable, congenial, convivial, sociable, extrovert, outgoing, approachable, gregarious, cordial, informal, neighbourly
🔁 unfriendly

companionship *n*
fellowship, comradeship, camaraderie, *esprit de corps*, support, friendship, company, togetherness, closeness, conviviality, association, social intercourse, intimacy, sympathy, rapport
Related adjective: contubernal

company *n*
1 *a manufacturing company*
firm, business, business organization, concern, association, corporation, establishment, house, partnership, syndicate, cartel, trust, consortium, conglomerate, multinational, holding company, subsidiary, public limited company (PLC or plc), private limited company, limited company, limited liability company
2 TROUPE, group, band, ensemble, cast, set, circle, crowd, throng, body, troop, crew, party, assembly, gathering, community, society, team
OLD (*Shakesp*) heap
3 GUESTS, visitors, callers
4 *be glad of company*
friendship, companionship, support, togetherness, closeness, fellowship, comradeship, conviviality, attendance, contact, presence

comparable *adj*
similar, like, alike, related, close, near, akin, corresponding, analogous, equivalent, tantamount, proportional, proportionate, commensurate, parallel, equal
FORMAL cognate
🔁 dissimilar, unlike, unequal

> ❗ **comparable** or **comparative**?
> *Comparable* means 'of the same kind, to the same degree, etc': *cheaper than any comparable hotel*.
> *Comparative* means 'judged by comparing with something else': *After they had stopped playing so noisily there was a period of comparative silence*.

comparably *adv*
similarly, correspondingly, analogously, proportionally, proportionately, equally

comparative *adj*
relative, by/in comparison

> ❗ **comparative** or **comparable**?
> See panel at **comparable**.

comparatively *adv*
relatively, by/in comparison

compare *v*
1 *compare the new edition with the old one*
contrast, juxtapose, balance, weigh, measure, set against, set side by side, note the differences between, correlate
OLD confer, confront, paragon
2 *compare her to an angel*
liken, equate, link, correlate, regard as the same, show the similarities between, draw analogies with, draw a parallel between; *dialect* even
OLD resemble; (*Shakesp*) like
FORMAL analogize
3 *not compare with his predecessor*
resemble, match, equal, parallel, bear comparison, be comparable to, be as good as, touch
COLLOQ. hold a candle to
■ **beyond compare**
without equal, without parallel, matchless, unmatched, incomparable, unequalled, unrivalled, unsurpassed, brilliant, superb, supreme, superlative, nonpareil, peerless

comparison *n*
juxtaposition, analogy, parallel, correlation, relationship, likeness, resemblance, similarity, comparability, contrast, differences, differentiation, distinction

compartment *n*
section, division, subdivision, part, category, pigeonhole, cubbyhole, niche, alcove, bay, area, stall, booth, cubicle, locker, partition, carrel, cell, chamber, berth, carriage

compartmentalize *v*
categorize, classify, group, sort, file, tag, slot, catalogue, pigeonhole, alphabetize, sectionalize

compass *n*
limit(s), range, scope, stretch, space, extent, sphere, area, reach, field, realm(s), boundary, bounds, circle, circuit, circumference, enclosure, round, scale, zone

compassion *n*
kindness, gentleness, tenderness, tender-heartedness, heart, fellow-feeling, humanity, mercy, pity, leniency, sympathy, commiseration, condolence, sorrow, benevolence, consideration, concern, care, understanding; *S Afr* ubuntu
OLD bowels; (*Spenser*) remorse
🔁 cruelty, indifference

> **QUOTATIONS**
> I see compassion may become a justice, though it be a weakness, I confess, and nearer a vice than a virtue
> BEN JONSON, *Bartholomew Fair*

compassionate *adj*
kind-hearted, kindly, tender-hearted, tender, gentle, caring, warm-hearted, benign, benevolent, charitable, humanitarian, humane, merciful, clement, lenient, pitying, forgiving, forbearing, feeling, sympathetic, understanding, supportive
OLD bleeding, piteous, remorseful; (*Shakesp*) passionate
See Synonym nuances panel at **kind**.
🔁 cruel, indifferent

compatibility *n*
suitability, harmony, consistency, match, adaptability, sympathy, rapport, like-mindedness

compatible *adj*
harmonious, in harmony, consistent, matching, suitable, suited, reconcilable, adaptable, conformable, sympathetic, having rapport, like-minded, well-matched, well-suited, similar
FORMAL congruous, congruent, accordant, consonant
🔁 incompatible, antagonistic, contradictory

compatriot *n*
fellow citizen, fellow national, countryman, fellow countryman, countrywoman, fellow countrywoman

compel *v*
force, make, constrain, oblige, necessitate, drive, urge, enforce, impel, insist on, coerce, pressure, pressurize, hustle, browbeat, bully, intimidate, press-gang, dragoon; *Scot* gar
OLD coact, compulse, efforce
COLLOQ. bulldoze, strongarm, twist someone's arm, lean on, put the screws on

compelling *adj*
1 *a compelling story*
fascinating, gripping, riveting, enthralling, spellbinding, absorbing, mesmeric, irresistible, compulsive
COLLOQ. unputdownable
2 *compelling reasons*
forceful, imperative, urgent, pressing, overriding, powerful, cogent, persuasive, convincing, weighty, conclusive, incontrovertible, irrefutable
🔁 **1** boring **2** weak, unconvincing

compendious *adj*
brief, short, concise, succinct, compact, terse, condensed, to the point, crisp, summary, comprehensive, complete, all-embracing

compendium *n*
companion, handbook, manual, collection, anthology, compilation, digest, summary, synopsis, vade-mecum

compensate *v*
1 *compensate you for any loss*
repay, refund, reimburse, indemnify, recompense, reward, remunerate
2 *compensate for doing wrong*
make amends, make reparation, make good, make up for, restore, requite, atone, redeem, redress, satisfy
3 COUNTERACT, balance (out), counterbalance, cancel, neutralize, nullify, offset
FORMAL countervail, counterpoise

compensation *n*
1 *pay compensation*
recompense, reward, payment, remuneration, requital, repayment, refund, reimbursement, indemnification, indemnity, damages, reparation, return
TECHNICAL demurrage, solatium
OLD boot, reprisal
SLANG *Aust* compo
2 *make compensation for wrongdoing*
amends, redress, satisfaction, restoration, restitution, atonement, consolation, comfort, correction

compère *n*
host, link person, presenter, master of ceremonies, MC, announcer, anchor, anchorman, anchorwoman
COLLOQ. emcee

compete *v*
1 *compete against/with other firms*
vie, contest, contend, fight, battle, struggle, strive, oppose, challenge, pit yourself, rival, jostle
2 *compete in a contest*
contend, participate, enter, run, race, take part, go in for

competence *n*
1 ABILITY, proficiency, capability, aptitude, capacity, skill, technique, experience, expertise, facility, fitness
2 *challenge the competence of the court*
power, authority, jurisdiction, legal capacity
⊟ 1 incompetence

competent *adj*
1 *competent to deal with them*
capable, able, adept, efficient, trained, qualified, well-qualified, skilled, skilful, accomplished, experienced, proficient, expert, masterly, equal
2 *competent work*
satisfactory, acceptable, reasonable, passable, respectable, adequate, sufficient, fit, suitable, appropriate
⊟ 1 incompetent, incapable, unable, inefficient **2** excellent, outstanding

competition *n*
1 CONTEST, championship, tournament, cup, event, race, match, game, quiz, bout, meet, encounter
2 RIVALRY, opposition, challenge, contest, contention, conflict, struggle, strife, vying, competitiveness, combativeness
3 COMPETITORS, rivals, opponents, opposition, challengers, field

competitive *adj*
1 AMBITIOUS, combative, contentious, antagonistic, aggressive, pushy, keen
COLLOQ. cut-throat, dog-eat-dog
2 *competitive prices*
moderate, reasonable, modest, just, fair, average, inexpensive, low, cut-rate
COLLOQ. bargain-basement

competitively *adv*
competitively priced
moderately, reasonably, modestly, fairly, inexpensively, low

competitiveness *n*
combativeness, contentiousness, antagonism, assertiveness, challenge, aggression, aggressiveness, rivalry, ambition, ambitiousness, keenness
FORMAL pugnacity

COLLOQ. pushiness, rat race, survival of the fittest
⊟ backwardness, sluggishness

competitor *n*
contestant, contender, entrant, candidate, participant, challenger, player, opponent, adversary, antagonist, rival, emulator, competition, opposition

compilation *n*
composition, collection, accumulation, collation, anthology, selection, organization, arrangement, thesaurus, treasury, album, compendium, miscellany, omnibus, potpourri, corpus, opus, work, segue
FORMAL assemblage, amassment, collectanea, florilegium, chrestomathy

compile *v*
compose, put together, collect, gather, garner, cull, accumulate, amass, assemble, collate, marshal, organize, arrange

complacency *n*
smugness, self-satisfaction, gloating, triumph, pleasure, pride, self-righteousness, serenity, self-assurance, gratification, contentment, satisfaction, self-content
⊟ diffidence, discontent

complacent *adj*
smug, self-satisfied, gloating, triumphant, proud, self-righteous, serenity, unconcerned, serene, self-assured, pleased, gratified, contented, self-contented, satisfied
⊟ diffident, concerned, discontented

> **!** **complacent** or **complaisant**?
> *Complacent* means 'smugly pleased with yourself or your own abilities': *One of the dangers of success is that you can become complacent. Complaisant* means 'being cheerfully willing to do what others want': *Franca's complaisant kindness was too much for him.*

complain *v*
1 *complain to the manager; always complaining*
criticize, find fault, file/lodge a complaint, take something up with someone, kick up a fuss, object, protest, air your grievances, grumble, carp, fuss, lament, bemoan, bewail, moan, nag, whine, carry on, groan, growl, kvetch; *dialect* girn; *Scot* mump, mean
OLD plain; *(Spenser)* grutch
FORMAL remonstrate, expostulate, repine
COLLOQ. beef, bellyache, moan and groan, grouse, gripe, grump, bleat, whinge, squawk, squeal, raise a stink, have a bone to pick
SLANG bitch
OLD SLANG bind
2 *complain of an illness*
suffer from, endure, be in pain, feel pain, hurt, ache

> **SYNONYM NUANCES**
>
> *sense 1*
> **Criticize** and **find fault** emphasize the element of dissatisfaction in a complaint, whereas **file/lodge a complaint** or **take up something with someone** are fairly mild, neutral terms for conveying dissatisfaction to someone. **Object**, **protest** and **air your grievances** are appropriate terms for more vehement claims: *the former employees protested at their treatment by the company.* **Kick up a fuss** also suggests less inhibited complaining, creating a disturbance as you do so.
> While these terms do not convey any particular view of the complaining, to use **grumble**, which suggests a less distinct mode of expression, would imply that you think it unconstructive or unnecessary: *he grumbled to himself about the way he was treated.* **Carp**, **kvetch** and **fuss** are similar, and can be used to suggest bothering about trivialities, or even pettiness: *his carping and negative attitude; I can't stand people who fuss about their health.* When someone complains in a sorrowful or pained way, you can use the words **groan**, **lament**, **bemoan** and **bewail**: *she bewailed her ill-fortune;* **moan**

and **whine** are similar, but more strongly imply a self-pitying aspect.

To refer to constant, repetitive complaining, you could use **nag**, but this term will also convey disapproval of this behaviour: *I am ashamed to say I nagged my mother until she gave in.*

complainer *n*
grumbler, moaner, niggler, fault-finder
COLLOQ. bellyacher, grouser, fusspot, nit-picker, whiner, whinger; *N Am* fussbudget

complaint *n*
1 PROTEST, objection, grumble, moan, grievance, dissatisfaction, annoyance, fault-finding, criticism, carping, censure, accusation, charge, representation
OLD querimony; *(Shakesp)* plaining
COLLOQ. beefing, bellyaching, grouse, gripe, bleating, whingeing
2 *a chest complaint*
ailment, illness, sickness, disease, disorder, infection, trouble, upset, condition
FORMAL indisposition, affliction, malady, malaise

complaisant *adj*
agreeable, amenable, amiable, accommodating, willing, obliging, solicitous, biddable, compliant, deferential, conciliatory, docile, obedient, conformable
FORMAL tractable
F3 obstinate, perverse

> **!** complaisant or complacent?
> *See panel at* **complacent.**

complement *n, v*
♦ *n*
1 *wine as a complement to the dinner*
companion, counterpart, addition, accessory, accompaniment, completion
FORMAL consummation
2 *the ship's complement*
allowance, quota, total, totality, aggregate, sum, amount, capacity, entirety
♦ *v*
go well with, go well together, combine well with, accompany, match, set off, contrast, round off, complete, crown

> **!** complement, compliment or supplement?
> One thing is a *complement* to another when it makes a pleasant contrast or makes the combination of the two things pleasantly balanced: *Yoghurt can be used as a complement to spicy dishes.* You pay someone a *compliment* when you praise them. A *supplement* is something added to something else that is already complete or to make up for a deficiency: *a magazine supplement; take vitamin supplements.*

complementary *adj*
finishing, completing, perfecting, reciprocal, interdependent, correlative, interrelated, corresponding, matching, twin, fellow, companion, compatible, harmonious, supporting
F3 contradictory, incompatible

> **!** complementary, complimentary or supplementary?
> Two things are *complementary* if they complement each other: *use complementary colours in all the furnishings.* You say something *complimentary* to someone as an expression of admiration or praise to them; a *complimentary* ticket is one given free of charge. You use *supplementary* to describe something that is added: *ask a supplementary question.*

complete *adj, v*
♦ *adj*
1 ENTIRE, integral, whole, entire, full, unbroken, undivided, total, intact, plenary, unabbreviated, unabridged,

unshortened, unedited, unexpurgated, detailed, comprehensive, exhaustive
2 FINISHED, ended, completed, concluded, over, done, accomplished, finalized, settled, achieved
FORMAL terminated
3 UTTER, total, absolute, outright, downright, out-and-out, thorough, unqualified, unmitigated, unconditional, perfect, consummate
F3 1 abridged **2** incomplete **3** partial
♦ *v*
1 *complete the work*
finish, end, close, conclude, finalize, settle, perform, discharge, execute, fulfil, realize, accomplish, achieve, make up, crown, cap, round off, wind up, perfect
FORMAL terminate, consummate
COLLOQ. polish off, clinch
2 *complete a form*
fill in, fill out, answer

> **SYNONYM NUANCES**
>
> *verb sense 1*
> **Conclude**, **finalize** and **settle** have a strong element of finality about them and are suggestive of tying up all the relevant loose ends to reach the final state: *the Cabinet finalized the budget for the fiscal year.* **Perform** and **discharge** could be used if you want to put more emphasis on the manner in which tasks have been completed: *she discharged her duties with detached severity.* **Execute** is similar, with strong connotations of efficiency: *brilliantly executed colour illustrations.*
>
> The terms **fulfil** is appropriate in the context of completing duties or aims: *he fulfilled his obligations,* and **realize** in the context of carrying plans through to completion. The positive terms **accomplish** and **achieve** could be used if you want to convey the idea of completing something successfully.
>
> **Crown**, **cap** and **perfect** are also positive terms to use and again suggest an impressive achievement, surpassing what has gone before: *the striker capped his team's rousing display with his audacious goal; the ancient art of batik has been perfected over the centuries.* **Make up**, on the other hand, has a more restrained tone and merely suggests the provision of something previously lacking: *I was just there to make up the numbers.*

completely *adv*
totally, utterly, wholly, fully, in full, absolutely, perfectly, quite, thoroughly, through and through, altogether, entirely, solidly
COLLOQ. in every respect, lock stock and barrel, from first to last, root and branch, every inch, heart and soul, hook line and sinker

completion *n*
finish, end, close, conclusion, finalization, settlement, discharge, execution, fulfilment, realization, accomplishment, achievement, attainment, fruition, culmination, perfection
FORMAL termination, consummation

complex *adj, n*
♦ *adj*
complicated, intricate, elaborate, involved, difficult, circuitous, tortuous, devious, mixed, varied, diverse, multiple, composite, compound, ramified
FORMAL convoluted, Byzantine
F3 simple, easy
♦ *n*
1 NETWORK, structure, system, scheme, composite, organization, establishment, institute, development
FORMAL aggregation
2 FIXATION, obsession, preoccupation, phobia, disorder, neurosis
COLLOQ. hang-up, thing

SYNONYM NUANCES

SYNONYM NUANCES

adjective
Intricate, **elaborate** and **involved** convey fairly straightforwardly the idea of something multi-faceted: *a long and elaborate trial*. **Complicated** is similar, but can be used with the added implication of being difficult to follow or understand. To use **difficult**, however, would make a clear comment that something is too complex to understand or use easily.

Circuitous and **devious** are more likely to be used in the context of an indirect route, or an indirect approach to dealing with a matter, but again have the negative implication that it is unnecessarily or tiresomely complex. **Tortuous** similarly describes a far from straightforward method or route, but is even more suggestive of associated frustration: *six years of tortuous legal battles*.

The terms **mixed**, **varied** and **diverse** are neutral terms conveying the idea of variety of elements, while **multiple**, **composite** and **compound** are similarly neutral, but suggest several components: *a composite remedy of five different flowers*. **Ramified** could be used of situations with a variety of possible or actual consequences: *he was involved in a bitter and ramified dispute*.

complexion *n*
1 SKIN, colour, colouring, tone, texture, pigmentation
2 LOOK, appearance, aspect, attitude, guise, light, character, perspective, nature, cast, type, stamp, kind, sort

complexity *n*
complication, complicatedness, intricacy, elaboration, involvement, circuitousness, tortuousness, deviousness, multifariousness, multiplicity, variety, diverseness, compositeness, entanglement, ramification, repercussion
FORMAL convolution
E3 simplicity

compliance *n*
obedience, submissiveness, submission, agreement, accordance, assent, conformability, deference, passivity, yielding
FORMAL acquiescence, complaisance, concurrence
E3 defiance, disobedience

QUOTATIONS
All I wanted was compliance with my wishes after reasonable discussion
SIR WINSTON CHURCHILL

compliant *adj*
obedient, submissive, subservient, pliable, accommodating, agreeable, biddable, conformable, amenable, deferential, passive, docile, yielding, indulgent
FORMAL acquiescent, complaisant, tractable
E3 disobedient, intractable

complicate *v*
compound, elaborate, make difficult, involve, make involved, muddle, mix up, confuse, jumble, tangle, entangle
E3 simplify

complicated *adj*
complex, intricate, elaborate, involved, tortuous, difficult, puzzling, perplexing, problematic, cryptic, labyrinthine, Byzantine
FORMAL convoluted
COLLOQ. fiddly
E3 simple, easy

complication *n*
difficulty, problem, drawback, snag, obstacle, ramification, repercussion, complexity, intricacy, elaboration, convolution, tangle, web, confusion, mixture

complicity *n*
collusion, collaboration, connivance, involvement, agreement, approval, knowledge
FORMAL concurrence, abetment
COLLOQ. being in cahoots
E3 ignorance, innocence

compliment *n, v*
♦ *n*
1 *pay someone a compliment*
flattery, flattering remark, admiration, favour, approval, congratulations, tribute, honour, accolade, commendation, praise, sugarplum
OLD douceur
FORMAL eulogy, homage, felicitation, encomium, laudation
COLLOQ. bouquet
2 *sends his compliments*
greetings, regards, best wishes, good wishes, congratulations, remembrances, respects
FORMAL salutation, devoirs
E3 **1** insult, criticism
♦ *v*
flatter, admire, commend, speak highly/well of, praise, extol, congratulate, applaud, salute
FORMAL felicitate, laud, eulogize
COLLOQ. pat on the back
E3 insult, condemn

❗ **compliment**, **complement** or **supplement**?
See panel at **complement**.

complimentary *adj*
1 FLATTERING, admiring, favourable, approving, appreciative, congratulatory, commendatory
FORMAL eulogistic, panegyrical
2 *complimentary ticket*
free, gratis, for nothing, honorary, courtesy
COLLOQ. on the house
E3 **1** insulting, unflattering, critical

❗ **complimentary**, **complementary** or **supplementary**?
See panel at **complementary**.

comply *v*
agree, consent, assent, yield, submit, defer, respect, observe, obey, abide by, all in, conform, follow, perform, discharge, fulfil, satisfy, meet, oblige, accommodate
FORMAL acquiesce, accord, accede
E3 defy, disobey

component *n, adj*
♦ *n*
part, constituent, constituent part, integral part, ingredient, element, factor, item, unit, piece, section, module, bit, spare part
♦ *adj*
constituent, integral, essential, basic, intrinsic, inherent

comport *v*
acquit, conduct, carry, bear, act, behave, perform
FORMAL demean, deport

compose *v*
1 *the board is composed of four directors*
make up, constitute, form, comprise
2 CREATE, write, arrange, produce, make (up), think of/up, devise, form, fashion, build, construct, frame, invent, concoct, put together, assemble
3 CALM, calm down, soothe, quiet, collect, still, settle, steady, tranquillize, quell, assuage, pacify, control

composed *adj*
calm, calmed down, tranquil, quiet, quietened down, serene, relaxed, unworried, unruffled, level-headed, cool, collected, cool and collected, self-possessed, controlled, self-controlled, confident, imperturbable, placid, sedate, centred, at ease
COLLOQ. unflappable, cool as a cucumber
E3 agitated, worried, troubled

composer *n*
musician, arranger, songwriter, songsmith, tunesmith, melodist, author, writer, creator, maker, master, originator, producer, poet, bard

composite *adj, n*
♦ *adj*
compound, conglomerate, complex, blended, combined, fused, mixed, patchwork, synthesized
FORMAL heterogeneous, agglutinate
E3 homogeneous, uniform
♦ *n*
compound, conglomerate, blend, combination, alloy, amalgam, amalgamation, fusion, conflation, mixture, synthesis, pastiche, patchwork
FORMAL agglutination

composition *n*
1 CONSTITUTION, make-up, combination, mixture, form, structure, configuration, layout, arrangement, organization, character, harmony, consonance, balance, symmetry
FORMAL conformation
2 *a musical composition*
creation, work, work of art, opus, piece, arrangement, adaptation, accompaniment, symphony, opera, study, exercise, poem, picture, painting, drawing, story, novel
3 MAKING, production, formation, creation, invention, arranging, devising, putting together, concoction, design, formulation, writing, compilation, proportion
4 ESSAY, paper, article, piece, text, assignment, task, review, dissertation, thesis

compost *n*
fertilizer, humus, mulch, manure, peat, dressing, leaf-mould, leaf-soil, grow-bag, growing-bag

composure *n*
calm, tranquillity, serenity, ease, coolness, self-possession, self-control, level-headedness, confidence, assurance, self-assurance, poise, dignity, imperturbability, placidity, equanimity, dispassion, impassivity
FORMAL aplomb
E3 agitation, nervousness, discomposure

SYNONYM NUANCES

Calm, **tranquillity** and **serenity**, along with **equanimity** and **placidity**, are suggestive of a naturally peaceful, undisturbed state of mind: *the monk exuded serenity*. If you want to place the emphasis on an ability to keep emotions in check, you might use the terms **coolness**, **self-possession** or **self-control**: *he displays remarkable coolness, in view of his inexperience.*
Level-headedness suggests composure with common sense at its core. The terms **confidence**, **assurance** and **self-assurance** imply being imbued with a sense of self-belief: *he went about his illegal business with a brazen assurance*; **poise** and **dignity** have positive connotations of a stately demeanour. **Dispassion** or **impassivity** could be used for composure stemming from lack of emotion: *they viewed the scene with worldly dispassion; her face was a white mask of impassivity.*

---

compound¹ *n, adj, v*
♦ *n*
a chemical compound
blend, mixture, medley, hybrid, composite, amalgam, alloy, synthesis, fusion, composition, amalgamation, combination, conglomerate
TECHNICAL admixture
♦ *adj*
composite, blended, combined, fused, mixed, synthesized, multiple, complex, complicated, intricate, conglomerate
♦ *v*
1 COMBINE, put together, amalgamate, unite, fuse, coalesce, synthesize, alloy, blend, mix, mingle, intermingle
2 WORSEN, exacerbate, aggravate, make matters worse, complicate, intensify, heighten, magnify, add to, increase

FORMAL augment
COLLOQ. add insult to injury, add fuel to the fire/flames, rub salt in the wound

compound² *n*
a prison compound
enclosure, yard, pen, fold, pound, paddock, stockade, corral, court

comprehend *v*
1 UNDERSTAND, conceive, see, grasp, sense, make sense of, make out, fathom, penetrate, realize, appreciate, know, catch, apprehend, perceive, discern, take in, assimilate, compass, put your finger on; *Aust & NZ* get the strength of
COLLOQ. tumble to, twig, get it
2 INCLUDE, comprise, take in, encompass, involve, contain, embrace, cover, generalize
E3 **1** misunderstand, misapprehend

comprehensible *adj*
understandable, easy to understand, intelligible, graspable, discernible, conceivable, coherent, explicit, clear, lucid, plain, simple, accessible, straightforward
E3 incomprehensible, obscure

comprehension *n*
understanding, conception, grasp, realization, appreciation, knowledge, apprehension, perception, discernment, judgement, sense, insight, intelligence
COLLOQ. ken
E3 incomprehension, unawareness

comprehensive *adj*
thorough, exhaustive, full, complete, detailed, encyclopedic, compendious, broad, wide, widespread, extensive, sweeping, general, blanket, inclusive, overall, all-inclusive, all-embracing, across-the-board
E3 partial, incomplete, selective

comprehensively *adv*
thoroughly, exhaustively, fully, completely, broadly, widely, widespread, extensively
E3 partially, selectively

compress *v*
1 *compress petrol and air*
press, squeeze, crush, squash, flatten, jam, wedge, cram, tamp, stuff, pack, pinch, pump, compact, condense, constrict, strangulate, strain, consolidate, impact, pressurize, concentrate, crowd, lace, screw, shoehorn
TECHNICAL astringe
OLD astrict
2 *compress an article*
abridge, condense, contract, telescope, shorten, abbreviate, reduce, summarize, synopsize
FORMAL coarctate
E3 **2** expand, diffuse

compression *n*
constriction, consolidation, concentration, condensing, pressing, squashing, stuffing, packing, pinching, pumping

comprise *v*
1 *the flat comprises three rooms*
consist of, be composed of, include, contain, take in, incorporate, embody, involve, encompass, cover
FORMAL comprehend, embrace
2 *the countries that comprise Great Britain*
make up, constitute, compose, form

compromise *v, n*
♦ *v*
1 NEGOTIATE, bargain, arbitrate, settle (for), agree, concede, make concessions, meet halfway, come to/reach an understanding, give and take, adapt, adjust
2 *compromise your principles*
weaken, undermine, expose, endanger, imperil, jeopardize, risk, prejudice
3 DISHONOUR, discredit, shame, bring shame to, bring into disrepute, damage, embarrass, involve, implicate
♦ *n*
settlement, agreement, concession, negotiation, mediation, understanding, bargain, deal, co-operation,

accommodation, adjustment, trade-off, middle way, give-and-take, balance, composition, *modus vivendi*
OLD temperament
⊟ disagreement, intransigence

compulsion *n*
1 *use compulsion to obtain something*
force, coercion, duress, constraint, obligation, pressure, demand, insistence
2 *feel a compulsion to do something*
urge, drive, impulse, desire, longing, need, necessity, temptation, obsession, preoccupation

compulsive *adj*
1 IRRESISTIBLE, overwhelming, overpowering, uncontrollable, obsessive, compelling, driving, besetting, urgent
2 *a compulsive gambler*
obsessive, habitual, addicted, dependent, hardened, inveterate, chronic, incorrigible, irredeemable, incurable, hopeless
COLLOQ. pathological, hooked
3 *compulsive viewing*
compelling, fascinating, gripping, riveting, enthralling, spellbinding, absorbing, mesmeric, irresistible, unavoidable

compulsively *adv*
1 OBSESSIVELY, habitually, chronically, incorrigibly, incurably
COLLOQ. pathologically
2 IRRESISTIBLY, unavoidably, involuntarily, inevitably

compulsory *adj*
obligatory, mandatory, imperative, forced, set, stipulated, binding, contractual, essential, necessary, required
FORMAL requisite, *de rigueur*
⊟ optional, voluntary, discretionary

compunction *n*
remorse, regret, repentance, penitence, shame, contrition, sorrow, qualm(s), misgiving(s), guilt, reluctance, hesitation, unease, uneasiness
⊟ callousness, defiance

computation *n*
calculation, sum, answer, result, figuring, working-out, reckoning, estimation, forecast, forecasting

compute *v*
calculate, count (up), work out, sum, tally, add up, total, enumerate, reckon, estimate, assess, evaluate, figure, measure, rate

computer *n*

> **QUOTATIONS**
> The computer is a fast idiot, it has no imagination; it cannot originate action. It is, and will remain, only a tool to man
> AMERICAN LIBRARY ASSOCIATION

Types of computer include:

Apple® Mac	MacBook®	personal computer
slang big iron	Macintosh® (or	(PC)
biocomputer	Mac®)	quantum compu-
client	mainframe	ter
desktop	microcomputer	server
e-reader (or e-	minicomputer	supercomputer
book reader)	nanocomputer	super-
handheld	netbook	minicomputer
iMac®	notebook	tablet
iPad®	palmtop	terminal
laptop		workstation

comrade *n*
fellow, companion, friend, intimate, confidant(e), ally, confederate, colleague, associate, partner, consort, escort, chaperon(e), attendant, aide, assistant, accomplice, follower, *bon camarade*, frater, tovarish, Achates; *dialect* butty; *Scot* billy

OLD bully-rook
COLLOQ. mate, pal, buddy, crony, sidekick

comradeship *n*
camaraderie, companionship, fellowship, friendship, sociability, closeness, togetherness, affinity, brotherhood, brotherliness, sisterhood, sisterliness, *esprit de corps*

con *v, n*
♦ *v*
trick, cheat, hoax, dupe, deceive, mislead, hoodwink, double-cross, swindle, fleece, defraud, rook
FORMAL inveigle
COLLOQ. do, bamboozle
SLANG rip off
♦ *n*
confidence trick, trick, bluff, deception, swindle, cheating, fraud, racket
COLLOQ. fiddle, scam

concatenation *n*
sequence, series, course, progress, progression, succession, string, chain, connection, interlinking, interlocking, linking, nexus, thread, trail, procession, train

concave *adj*
hollow, hollowed, curved in, bending inwards, cupped, scooped, excavated, sunken, indented, depressed
FORMAL incurvate, incurved
⊟ convex

conceal *v*
1 *conceal a body*
hide, obscure, disguise, camouflage, mask, screen, veil, cloak, shroud, cover, bury, submerge, keep hidden, keep out of sight, tuck away
FORMAL secrete
COLLOQ. stash
2 *conceal a secret*
hide, keep dark, keep secret, keep quiet, suppress
FORMAL dissemble
COLLOQ. cover up, hush up, sweep under the carpet, put the lid on, whitewash
⊟ **1** uncover **2** reveal, disclose

concealed *adj*
hidden, covered, screened, unseen, covert, disguised, inconspicuous, latent, tucked away
⊟ clear, plain, visible

concealment *n*
1 *concealment of guns*
hideaway, hideout, hiding, disguise, camouflage, mask, protection, screen, veil, shroud, cloak, cover, secrecy, shelter
FORMAL secretion
2 *concealment of information*
hiding, suppression, keeping dark, keeping secret, secrecy
COLLOQ. cover-up, whitewash, smokescreen
⊟ **1** uncovering, exposing **2** openness, revelation

concede *v*
1 ADMIT, confess, acknowledge, recognize, own (up), grant, allow, accept
FORMAL accede
2 YIELD, give up, surrender, relinquish, forfeit, sacrifice, hand over
FORMAL cede
⊟ **1** deny

conceit *n*
1 VANITY, conceitedness, pride, arrogance, haughtiness, immodesty, boastfulness, swagger, egotism, self-love, narcissism, self-importance, self-admiration, superciliousness, cockiness, self-satisfaction, complacency
FORMAL vainglory
COLLOQ. bigheadedness
2 *literary conceits*
image, comparison, simile, metaphor, figurative expression, figure of speech
OLD device
⊟ **1** modesty, diffidence

conceited *adj*
vain, proud, arrogant, haughty, boastful, swollen-headed, swell-headed, immodest, egotistic, egotistical, narcissistic, self-important, full of yourself, puffed up, supercilious, self-satisfied, complacent, smug, overweening, above yourself, cocky, cat-witted, windy; *Scot* upsetting
OLD flory
FORMAL vainglorious
COLLOQ. bigheaded, stuck-up, toffee-nosed, snotty, too big for your boots; *Aust* having tickets on yourself
E3 modest, self-effacing, diffident, humble

conceivable *adj*
imaginable, credible, believable, thinkable, tenable, possible, likely, probable, plausible
E3 inconceivable, unimaginable

conceivably *adv*
possibly, probably, imaginably, plausibly
E3 inconceivably

conceive *v*
1 IMAGINE, envisage, visualize, see, picture, grasp, understand, perceive, apprehend, comprehend, realize, appreciate, believe, think, fancy, suppose, guess, get into your head
OLD conceit, contrive, fantasy; (*Shakesp*) brain
FORMAL gestate
2 INVENT, design, devise, formulate, think of/up, come up with, create, originate, form, take, contrive, produce, develop
3 *conceive a baby*
become pregnant, get pregnant, become fertilized, be fertile, become impregnated, become inseminated, reproduce, give birth to, start
OLD enwomb

concentrate *v, n*
♦ *v*
1 FOCUS, converge, centre, direct, centralize, rivet, consolidate, cluster, crowd, congregate, gather, collect, accumulate, amass
2 APPLY YOURSELF, think, give your (undivided) attention, pay/devote attention, attend, put/keep your mind, consider, mind
3 CONDENSE, evaporate, boil down, reduce, compress, distil, thicken, intensify
E3 **1** disperse **3** dilute
♦ *n*
essence, extract, distillation, juice
TECHNICAL apozem, decoction, decocture
FORMAL quintessence, elixir

concentrated *adj*
1 *concentrated liquid*
condensed, evaporated, reduced, distilled, thickened, compressed, dense, rich, strong, undiluted
2 INTENSE, intensive, all-out, concerted, vigorous, strenuous, hard, deep
E3 **1** diluted **2** half-hearted

concentration *n*
1 ATTENTION, deep/close thought, heed, absorption, application, mind, devotion, single-mindedness, engrossment, intensity
2 CONVERGENCE, centralization, focusing, cluster, mass, crowd, grouping, collection, congregation, accumulation, consolidation, conglomeration
FORMAL agglomeration
3 COMPRESSION, evaporation, boiling-down, distillation, reduction, consolidation, denseness, thickness
E3 **1** distraction **2** dispersal **3** dilution

concept *n*
idea, notion, plan, theory, hypothesis, thought, abstraction, conception, conceptualization, visualization, image, view, picture, impression

conception *n*
1 CONCEPT, idea, notion, thought, plan, abstraction, theory, hypothesis, image, view, vision, picture, impression, intention
2 KNOWLEDGE, understanding, comprehension, appreciation, perception, visualization, image, picture, vision, impression, idea, inkling, clue
3 INVENTION, design, birth, beginning, origin, origination, outset, initiation, inauguration, formation, launching
OLD inception, genesis
4 *from conception to birth*
impregnation, insemination, fertilization, conceiving, pregnancy, reproduction
FORMAL fecundation

conceptual *adj*
notional, abstract, theoretical, hypothetical, speculative, thematic, classificatory

concern *v, n*
♦ *v*
1 WORRY, distress, trouble, disturb, bother, upset, alarm, make worried, make anxious, prey on your mind
OLD reck
FORMAL perturb
2 *concern yourself with their problems*
give your attention to, involve, interest, busy, devote, affect, touch, reckon
OLD meddle, cern
3 BE ABOUT, relate to, refer to, regard, deal with, be connected with, have to do with, involve, cover, apply to, bear on
FORMAL appertain to, pertain to
♦ *n*
1 *a cause for concern*
anxiety, worry, unease, disquiet, care, sorrow, distress, apprehension, disturbance, strain, pressure, anguish
OLD concernment
FORMAL perturbation
2 REGARD, consideration, attention, attentiveness, care, heed, thought
OLD (*Shakesp*) tender
FORMAL solicitude
3 *it's not my concern*
duty, responsibility, charge, job, task, field, business, affair, matter, lookout, problem, interest, part, involvement
OLD concernment
COLLOQ. baby, pidgin, pidgeon, pigeon
4 ISSUE, matter, affair, problem, point, subject, topic, question, debate, argument
OLD concernment
COLLOQ. *S Afr* indaba
5 COMPANY, firm, business, corporation, association, establishment, enterprise, organization, partnership, syndicate
E3 **1** joy **2** indifference

concerned *adj*
1 ANXIOUS, worried, uneasy, apprehensive, upset, unhappy, distressed, troubled, disturbed, bothered
FORMAL perturbed
2 *concerned teachers*
attentive, caring, considerate, kind, thoughtful, helpful, charitable, unselfish, altruistic, gracious, sensitive
3 CONNECTED, related, involved, implicated, interested, affected
E3 **1** unconcerned, indifferent, apathetic **2** inconsiderate, thoughtless, selfish

concerning *prep*
about, regarding, with regard to, as regards, respecting, with respect to, with reference to, referring to, relating to, relevant to, in the matter of, on the subject of, re
FORMAL apropos

concert n

1 *a musical concert*
performance, entertainment, presentation, production, show, recital, appearance, engagement, rendering, rendition, gig, jam session, prom, soirée
COLLOQ. *N Am* hootenanny
2 *work in concert with others*
agreement, harmony, unanimity, union, unison, collaboration, co-operation, partnership
OLD quill
FORMAL accord, concord, concordance, consonance
⊟ 2 disunity, disharmony, conflict, opposition

concerted adj

combined, united, joint, collective, shared, co-operative, collaborative, co-ordinated, interactive, organized, concentrated, prearranged, planned
⊟ separate, unco-ordinated, disorganized

concession n

1 YIELDING, giving-up, surrender, relinquishment, forfeit, sacrifice, handover, admission, acknowledgement, recognition, grant, allowance, compromise, adjustment, acceptance
FORMAL ceding
COLLOQ. sop
2 *tax concessions*
reduction, decrease, cut, discount, (special) right, (special) privilege, favour, grant, allowance, exception, bending of the rules

conciliate v

reconcile, pacify, placate, appease, restore harmony to, satisfy, soften, soothe, disarm, disembitter, mollify, propitiate
⊟ antagonize

conciliation n

reconciliation, peacemaking, pacification, placation, appeasement, mollification, propitiation
⊟ alienation, antagonization

conciliator n

reconciler, mediator, negotiator, peacemaker, intermediary, broker, middleman, go-between, intercessor, dove
⊟ troublemaker, hawk

conciliatory adj

reconciliatory, peacemaking, peaceable, appeasing, disarming, mollifying, pacific, assuaging
FORMAL irenic, pacificatory, placatory, propitiative, propitiatory
⊟ antagonistic

concise adj

short, brief, terse, curt, succinct, pithy, crisp, compendious, elliptic, compact, compressed, condensed, abridged, abbreviated, summary, to the point, thumbnail, tight, laconic
FORMAL synoptic, epigrammatic, aphoristic
⊟ diffuse, verbose, wordy

concisely adv

briefly, tersely, succinctly, curtly, pithily, crisply, laconically, to the point, in brief, in short, in a word
⊟ diffusely, verbosely

conclave n

assembly, (secret) meeting, council, conference, session, gathering, cabinet, cabal
FORMAL confabulation
COLLOQ. powwow, parley

conclude v

1 END, bring/come/draw to an end, cease, close, finish, discontinue, complete, culminate
FORMAL consummate, terminate
COLLOQ. wind up, polish off, top off
2 INFER, deduce, come to the conclusion, assume, reason, gather, suppose, reckon, judge, decide
FORMAL conjecture, surmise
COLLOQ. put two and two together

3 SETTLE, resolve, close, decide, establish, determine, negotiate, accomplish, agree, arrange, work out
FORMAL effect
COLLOQ. wrap up, bring off, pull off, clinch
⊟ 1 begin, start, commence

conclusion n

1 INFERENCE, deduction, assumption, opinion, conviction, judgement, verdict, decision, resolution, settlement, result, consequence, outcome, upshot, issue, answer, solution
OLD consectary
FORMAL illation
2 END, ending, close, finish, completion, culmination, point, finale, epilogue, *finis*, punchline; *Scot* pirlicue
TECHNICAL coda
OLD fine, explicit
FORMAL consummation, cessation, termination, discontinuance, omega, peroration
COLLOQ. come-off
3 SETTLING, resolution, decision, establishment, determination, negotiation, brokering, accomplishment, agreement, arrangement, working-out
FORMAL effecting
COLLOQ. pulling-off, clinching
■ in conclusion
finally, to conclude, in closing, to sum up
OLD in fine

conclusive adj

final, ultimate, definitive, decisive, clear, convincing, definite, undeniable, irrefutable, indisputable, incontrovertible, unarguable, unanswerable
⊟ inconclusive, questionable

conclusively adv

definitively, decisively, clearly, convincingly, definitely, undeniably, irrefutably, indisputably, incontrovertibly, unarguably, finally, ultimately
⊟ inconclusively

concoct v

1 *concoct a meal*
put together, mix, prepare, make, develop, blend, cook (up), brew
COLLOQ. fix, rustle up
2 *concoct a story*
fabricate, invent, make up, think up, devise, contrive, formulate, plan, plot, hatch, dream up
FORMAL decoct
COLLOQ. cook up

concoction n

1 MIXTURE, brew, potion, preparation, blend, combination, compound, creation
2 FABRICATION, fiction, fable, story, myth, untruth
COLLOQ. cock-and-bull story, fairy story

concomitant adj, n

◆ *adj*
complementary, accompanying, associative, attendant, co-existent, coincidental, incidental, simultaneous, synchronous, contributing
FORMAL concurrent, contemporaneous, conterminous, syndromic
⊟ accidental, unrelated
◆ *n*
accompaniment, by-product, incidental, secondary, symptom, side effect
FORMAL epiphenomenon

concord n

harmony, accord, agreement, friendship, entente, consensus, unanimity, unison, union, amicability, peace, compact, treaty, rapport
FORMAL amity, consonance
⊟ discord

concourse n

1 *the station concourse*
hall, entrance, foyer, lobby, lounge, piazza, plaza

2 *a concourse of people*
gathering, multitude, crowd, swarm, throng, assembly, collection, meeting, crush, press

concrete *adj*
1 *concrete objects*
real, actual, solid, physical, material, substantial, tangible, touchable, perceptible, visible
2 *concrete evidence*
firm, definite, positive, specific, explicit, genuine, factual, solid
⊟ 1 abstract, immaterial **2** weak, vague

concubine *n*
mistress, kept woman, paramour, lover, courtesan, leman, lorette, apple-squire, sultana
OLD madam; (*Shakesp*) guinea-hen

concupiscence *n*
appetite, desire, libido, lasciviousness, lechery, lewdness, lust, lustfulness, sexual desire
OLD concupy
FORMAL libidinousness, lubricity
COLLOQ. randiness, horniness

concupiscent *adj*
lascivious, lecherous, lewd, lustful
FORMAL libidinous, lubricious
COLLOQ. randy, horny

concur *v*
agree, approve, comply, consent, co-operate, harmonize, be in harmony
FORMAL accede, assent, accord, acquiesce
⊟ disagree

concurrence *n*
1 *concurrence on the decision*
agreement, association, convergence, common ground, acceptance, approval
FORMAL assent, acquiescence
2 *the concurrence of the two events*
coincidence, coexistence, synchrony
FORMAL contemporaneity, juxtaposition, simultaneity
⊟ 1 difference, disagreement

concurrent *adj*
simultaneous, synchronous, contemporaneous, coinciding, coincident, coexisting, coexistent
FORMAL concomitant

concussion *n*
unconsciousness, head injury, brain injury, water hammer

condemn *v*
1 *condemn his actions*
disapprove, criticize, reproach, blame, revile, deplore, denounce, censure
FORMAL reprehend, reprove, deprecate, berate, upbraid, castigate, disparage, decry, slate, run down
COLLOQ. slam, knock
2 *condemn a prisoner*
sentence, give/pass a sentence, punish, find guilty, convict, judge, damn, accurse
3 *condemned to a life of poverty*
doom, compel, coerce, force, consign, ordain, destine
4 *condemn a building*
declare unsafe, declare unfit, demolish, destroy, bar, ban
⊟ 1 praise, approve **2** acquit, pardon

condemnation *n*
disapproval, criticism, reproof, reproach, blame, censure, denunciation, damnation, conviction, sentence, judgement
FORMAL castigation, deprecation, disparagement
COLLOQ. thumbs-down
⊟ praise, approval

condemnatory *adj*
critical, judgemental, disapproving, discouraging, incriminating, unfavourable, accusatory, accusing, damnatory

FORMAL censorious, denunciatory, deprecatory, proscriptive, reprobative, reprobatory
⊟ approving, complimentary, indulgent; *formal* laudatory

condensation *n*
1 *condensation of liquid*
distillation, liquefaction, precipitation, concentration, moisture, steam, evaporation, reduction, boiling-down, consolidation
TECHNICAL deliquescence
2 ABRIDGEMENT, précis, synopsis, digest, summary, contraction, compression, curtailment

condense *v*
1 *condense a book*
shorten, cut (down), curtail, abbreviate, abridge, précis, summarize, encapsulate, contract, compress, compact, capsulize
FORMAL epitomize
2 DISTIL, precipitate, concentrate, evaporate, reduce, thicken, solidify, coagulate, compress, boil down, intensify
TECHNICAL condensate, deliquesce, inspissate
⊟ 1 expand **2** dilute

condensed *adj*
1 *a condensed book*
shortened, cut (down), curtailed, abridged abbreviated, summarized, abstracted, reduced, contracted, compact, concise
2 *condensed liquid*
concentrated, evaporated, reduced, thickened, compressed, clotted, coagulated, dense, rich, strong, undiluted
⊟ 1 expanded **2** diluted

condescend *v*
1 *condescend to do something*
deign, see fit, stoop, bend, lower yourself, demean yourself, humble yourself, descend
OLD vouchsafe
FORMAL decline
2 *condescend to people*
patronize, talk down to, treat condescendingly, be snobbish to

condescending *adj*
patronizing, disdainful, supercilious, snooty, snobbish, haughty, lofty, superior, lordly, imperious
COLLOQ. stuck-up, toffee-nosed
⊟ gracious, humble

condescendingly *adv*
patronizingly, superciliously, imperiously, disdainfully, snobbishly

condescension *n*
disdain, haughtiness, superciliousness, superiority, loftiness, snobbishness, lordliness, airs
⊟ humility

condition *n, v*
♦ *n*
1 STATE, circumstances, factor(s), case, position, situation, predicament, plight, quandary
2 *the conditions in which people work*
surroundings, environment, milieu, setting, atmosphere, climate, background, context, circumstances, factors, way of life, situation, state, set-up
3 REQUIREMENT, obligation, prerequisite, terms, stipulation, demand, necessity, essential, precondition, provision, proviso, qualification, limit, limitation, restriction, rule
4 *out of condition*
fitness, health, state, state of health, shape, form, order, working order, fettle, kilter
COLLOQ. nick
5 *a heart condition*
disorder, defect, weakness, infirmity, problem, complaint, disease, illness, ailment
FORMAL malady

♦ *v*

1 *a shampoo that conditions*
tone, make healthy, restore, revive, treat, improve, nourish, groom

2 *conditioned by experience*
influence, mould, shape, transform, educate, train, teach, groom, equip, prepare, prime, accustom, familiarize, season, temper, adapt, adjust, tune, indoctrinate, brainwash

conditional *adj*
provisional, qualified, limited, restricted, tied, relative, subject, based, dependent, contingent
E3 unconditional, absolute

conditionally *adv*
provisionally, qualifiedly, with qualification, limitedly, relatively
E3 unconditionally, absolutely

conditioning *n*
moulding, shaping, transforming, preparation, adaptation, adjustment, influence

condolence *n*
sympathy, commiseration, compassion, pity, comfort, consolation, support
E3 congratulation

condom *n*
sheath, contraceptive, female condom, Femidom®; *N Am* prophylactic, protective
SLANG French letter, johnnie, rubber; *N Am* scumbag, safe

condone *v*
forgive, pardon, excuse, overlook, ignore, disregard, tolerate, brook, let pass, allow, accept
COLLOQ. turn a blind eye to
E3 condemn, censure

conducive *adj*
leading, tending, contributing, contributory, productive, promoting, advantageous, beneficial, favourable, helpful, useful, instrumental, encouraging
E3 detrimental, adverse, unfavourable

conduct *v*, *n*
♦ *v*
1 CARRY OUT, perform, do, administer, manage, run, organize, direct, orchestrate, chair, control, be in charge of, handle, regulate
2 ACCOMPANY, show, take, bring, escort, usher, lead, guide, direct, pilot, steer
3 *conduct heat*
convey, carry, bear, transmit
4 *conduct yourself*
behave, acquit, act
FORMAL comport
♦ *n*
1 *good conduct*
behaviour, actions, ways, manners, bearing, practice, attitude
FORMAL comportment, demeanour, deportment
2 ADMINISTRATION, management, direction, running, organization, operation, control, supervision, leadership, guidance

conduit *n*
channel, pipe, tunnel, passage, passageway, duct, tube, drain, gutter, culvert, ditch, flume, chute, watercourse, waterway, canal, main, trough, trunk, wireway

confectionery *n*
sweets, sweetmeats, chocolates, candy, toffees, bonbons
OLD junkets
COLLOQ. sweeties, goodies

confederacy *n*
union, federation, alliance, coalition, confederation, league, partnership
FORMAL compact

confederate *n*, *adj*
♦ *n*
accomplice, ally, assistant, associate, colleague, friend, partner, supporter, collaborator, abettor, accessory, conspirator
♦ *adj*
federate, federal, allied, associated, combined, united

confederation *n*
union, federation, alliance, association, coalition, amalgamation, confederacy, league, partnership
FORMAL compact

confer *v*
1 DISCUSS, debate, deliberate, consult, talk, converse, exchange views
2 BESTOW, award, present, give (out), grant, accord, impart, lend

conference *n*
meeting, convention, congress, summit, symposium, forum, discussion, debate, consultation, dialogue, colloquium, seminar, council of war, diet, palaver, parley, powwow, pourparler; *S Afr* indaba
FORMAL convocation, imparlance
COLLOQ. get-together, huddle

confess *v*
admit, confide, own (up), accept blame, accept responsibility, grant, concede, acknowledge, recognize, affirm, assert, profess, declare, disclose, reveal, make known, divulge, expose, unbosom, unburden
TECHNICAL shrive
OLD agnize
FORMAL avow
COLLOQ. come clean, make a clean breast of, get off your chest, come out with it, spill the beans, spill your guts, tell all
SLANG cough, fess up
E3 deny, conceal

confession *n*
admission, acknowledgement, owning-up, affirmation, assertion, profession, declaration, disclosure, making known, divulgence, exposure, revelation, unbosoming, unburdening, short shrift
OLD (*Shakesp*) submission
FORMAL avowal, *amende honorable*
E3 denial, concealment

> **QUOTATIONS**
> 'I know of no joy,' she airily began, 'greater than a cool white dress after the sweetness of confession'
> RONALD FIRBANK, *Valmouth*

confidant, confidante *n*
friend, close friend, bosom friend, best friend, intimate, companion
COLLOQ. crony, pal, mate, chum, buddy, bosom buddy

confide *v*
confess, admit, tell a secret, reveal, disclose, divulge, whisper, breathe, tell, impart, intimate, unburden, unbosom, pour out your heart to
COLLOQ. get off your chest
E3 hide, suppress, conceal

confidence *n*
1 *have confidence in someone*
trust, faith, reliance, dependence, credence, belief, conviction, certainty
2 SELF-ASSURANCE, assurance, composure, calmness, self-possession, self-confidence, self-reliance, self-assurance, belief in yourself, poise, boldness, courage
FORMAL aplomb
3 SECRET, confidential matter, private matter, intimacy
E3 **1** distrust **2** diffidence
■ *in confidence*
privately, in privacy, in private, confidentially, in secret, personally, between ourselves, *entre nous*, behind closed doors, within these four walls

COLLOQ. between you and me, between you me and the gatepost/bedpost

🖃 openly

confident *adj*

1 *confident that it will happen*
sure, certain, positive, convinced, definite, unhesitating, comfortable

2 *a confident person*
assured, sure of yourself, sure-footed, composed, self-possessed, calm, cool, self-confident, self-reliant, self-assured, unselfconscious, bold, courageous, fearless, secure, hardy, positive, happy, optimistic, sanguine, dauntless, unabashed; *Scot* crouse

COLLOQ. upbeat, cocksure

🖃 **1** doubtful, unsure **2** diffident, insecure

SYNONYM NUANCES

sense 2

Assured suggests a strong element of self-belief, as do **self-possessed**, **self-confident** and **self-assured**: *a self-possessed manner touching on the arrogant*. **Composed**, **cool** and **calm** are more passive in tone, suggesting an absence of disturbance or doubt. **Self-reliant** would appropriately describe a confident and independent nature, whilst **unselfconscious** places the emphasis on lack of embarrassment.

The term **bold** suggests a degree of daring: *a bold programme of reforms*, as do **courageous** and **fearless**. The words **dauntless** and **unabashed** would suggest no impediment will be permitted to someone's view: *Dauntless, he set off the climb the mountain*. You could use **positive**, **optimistic** or **sanguine** to describe a hopeful outlook where the best outcome is expected.

---

confidential *adj*

secret, top secret, classified, restricted, off-the-record, private, personal, intimate, bosom, sensitive, man-to-man, woman-to-woman, tête-à-tête; *Scot* pack

TECHNICAL a latere

OLD privy, inward

COLLOQ. hush-hush

confidentially *adv*

privately, in privacy, in private, in confidence, in secret, personally, between ourselves, *entre nous*, behind closed doors, on the quiet, within these four walls

OLD privily

FORMAL in camera

COLLOQ. between you and me, between you me and the gatepost/bedpost

🖃 openly

confidently *adv*

assuredly, composedly, calmly, coolly, unselfconsciously, unhesitatingly, comfortably, boldly, courageously, fearlessly, positively, optimistically

configuration *n*

arrangement, composition, figure, form, outline, shape, contour, cast

FORMAL conformation, disposition

confine *v, n*

♦ *v*

1 *confine a disease; confine yourself to something*
restrict, limit, keep within limits, bound, bind, constrain, control, fix, regulate, delimit

FORMAL circumscribe

2 *confine in prison*
imprison, cage, enclose, shut (up), hold prisoner, hold captive, hold in custody, intern, impound, keep in, lock up/away, coop up, bind, shackle, trammel, restrain, repress, inhibit

FORMAL incarcerate, immure

🖃 **1** derestrict **2** free, release

♦ *n*

limit, limitation, restriction, scope, parameter, bound, boundary, frontier, border, circumference, perimeter, edge

confined *adj*

restricted, limited, narrow, constrained, constricted, cramped, controlled, enclosed, housebound, impounded

FORMAL circumscribed

🖃 free, unrestricted

confinement *n*

1 IMPRISONMENT, internment, custody, detention, captivity, house arrest

FORMAL incarceration

2 CHILDBIRTH, birth, labour, delivery

TECHNICAL parturition

🖃 **1** freedom, liberty

confirm *v*

1 PROVE, corroborate, substantiate, verify, check, validate, authenticate, give credence to, evidence, demonstrate, endorse, back, support

2 ESTABLISH, fix, settle, ratify, sanction, approve, authorize, warrant, endorse, validate

COLLOQ. clinch

3 *confirm that he will go*
affirm, assert, assure, pledge, promise, guarantee

FORMAL asseverate, aver

4 *confirmed me in my decision*
strengthen, reinforce, harden, support, uphold

FORMAL fortify

🖃 **1** refute, deny

confirmation *n*

affirmation, validation, authentication, corroboration, substantiation, verification, proof, evidence, testimony, ratification, sanction, approval, assent, acceptance, agreement, endorsement, backing, support

FORMAL accreditation

🖃 denial

confirmed *adj*

inveterate, entrenched, dyed-in-the-wool, rooted, firm, fixed, set, established, long-established, long-standing, habitual, chronic, through and through, seasoned, hardened, incorrigible, incurable

FORMAL inured

confiscate *v*

seize, remove, take away, take possession of, impound, commandeer

TECHNICAL escheat, sequester

OLD forfeit

FORMAL appropriate, expropriate, arrogate

🖃 return, restore

confiscation *n*

seizure, removal, takeover, impounding, commandeering

FORMAL appropriation, distrainment, distraint, escheat, expropriation, sequestration, forfeiture

🖃 restoration

conflagration *n*

blaze, fire, flames, inferno, holocaust

FORMAL deflagration

conflate *v*

combine, amalgamate, merge, bring/put together, blend, integrate, incorporate, compound, synthesize

conflict *n, v*

♦ *n*

1 DISAGREEMENT, quarrel, dissension, dispute, opposition, antagonism, hostility, friction, collision, strife, unrest, confrontation, feud, discord, contention, ill-will, difference of opinion, variance, clash, clashing, incompatibility, row, jar

TECHNICAL antinomy, dissonance

FORMAL antipathy

COLLOQ. bust-up, dust-up

2 BATTLE, war, warfare, combat, fight, contest, struggle, front line, engagement, skirmish, fracas, brawl, quarrel, feud, encounter, row, clash, mêlée

OLD agony, agon, camp, muss; *(Shakesp)* close

COLLOQ. set-to, bust-up, scrap, scrape

🖃 **1** agreement, harmony, concord

♦ *v*

differ, clash, collide, disagree, be at variance, be at loggerheads, be at odds, be inconsistent with, contradict, oppose, be in opposition, contest, go against, fight, combat, battle, war, strive, struggle, contend, thwart
FORMAL be incongruous
F3 agree, harmonize

> **QUOTATIONS**
> Never in the field of human conflict has so much been owed by so many, to so few
> Sir Winston Churchill

SYNONYM NUANCES

noun sense 1
Disagreement, **dissension** and **variance** may be used of any difference of opinion between two parties, however mild. **Quarrel** and **dispute** are similar, but imply a more heated exchange, and the more informal **row** and **clash** could refer to being violently at odds. Similarly, the term **opposition** can be used to express varying degrees, whereas **antagonism** and **hostility** suggest something more keenly felt and expressed: *French antagonism towards England was still very much alive.*
   Friction could be used of annoyance between two parties: *the incompatible demands of the various departments resulted in friction*; while the terms **strife** and **unrest** could be used in the context of dissatisfaction within a group, especially where knock-on effects are possible: *internecine strife*; *industrial unrest.*
   To refer to a long-term conflict and enmity between two parties, you could use **feud**; for the existence of more general bad feelings towards someone you might use the term **discord**, the more formal term **antipathy**, or, to be more explicit, **ill-will.**

---

conflicting *adj*
contradictory, contrary, opposing, clashing, inconsistent, incompatible, at variance, at odds
FORMAL incongruous, antithetical
F3 consistent

confluence *n*
convergence, junction, meeting, meeting-point, concurrence, union, watersmeet
FORMAL conflux

conform *v*
1 *conform to a law*
obey, follow, comply (with), fall in with, observe, abide by, adapt, adjust, accommodate
2 *conform in your behaviour*
follow, be conventional, be uniform, do the same thing
COLLOQ. follow the crowd, go with the flow/stream, toe the line
3 *conform to a pattern*
agree, harmonize, match, suit, fit, correspond, tally, square
FORMAL accord
F3 1 disobey 2 rebel 3 differ, conflict

conformist *n*
conventionalist, traditionalist
COLLOQ. yes-man, stick-in-the-mud, rubber-stamp
F3 bohemian, nonconformist

conformity *n*
1 *in conformity with the law*
compliance, observance, obedience, allegiance adaptation, adjustment, accommodation, affinity, agreement, harmony, correspondence, likeness, similarity, resemblance
FORMAL consonance, congruity
2 *conformity in behaviour*
conventionality, orthodoxy, traditionalism, uniformity
F3 1 disobedience, non-compliance 2 nonconformity, rebellion

confound *v*
1 CONFUSE, bewilder, baffle, perplex, mystify, puzzle, nonplus, surprise, startle, amaze, astonish, astound, dumbfound, stun, stupefy
FORMAL discomfit
COLLOQ. bamboozle, flabbergast, flummox, throw, floor, faze, stump
2 *confound their plans*
thwart, frustrate, upset, beat, defeat, overwhelm, overthrow, destroy, demolish, ruin

confront *v*
1 *confront a problem*
face, face up to, brave, tackle, address, deal with, cope with, contend with, reckon with, come to terms with
COLLOQ. come to grips with, meet head on, face the music
2 *confront the enemy*
face, face up to, meet, encounter, stand up to, challenge, oppose, brave, defy, resist, withstand, attack, assault, accost
3 *confront him with the facts*
challenge, present, face, show

confrontation *n*
encounter, clash, conflict, collision, showdown, disagreement, fight, battle, quarrel, engagement, contest, brush
COLLOQ. set-to

confuse *v*
1 BEWILDER, baffle, perplex, mystify, confound, dizzy, maze, dither, puzzle, bemuse, disorient, disorientate, disconcert, fluster, discompose, distract, dumbfound, jumble, flurry, surprise, upset, embarrass, mortify; *dialect* moider; *Scot* bumbaze, fickle
OLD embrangle
COLLOQ. throw, flummox, faze, stump, floor, tie in knots, blind with science
2 MUDDLE, mix up, mistake, jumble, disarrange, disorder, tangle, entangle, involve, mingle, fog, fuddle, mudge, mizzle; *Scot* burble
OLD bemuddle, bemud
3 COMPLICATE, make more difficult, compound, elaborate, make difficult, involve, make involved
F3 1 enlighten, orient 3 simplify, clarify

confused *adj*
1 BEWILDERED, baffled, perplexed, mystified, confounded, puzzled, bemused, nonplussed, disconcerted, flustered, disorientated, dazed, unbalanced
COLLOQ. flummoxed, floored, not knowing whether you are coming or going, up a gumtree, in a flat spin, in a flap, all at sea, like a headless chicken
2 MUDDLED, jumbled, disarranged, disordered, untidy, messy, disorderly, chaotic, disorganized, mixed-up, out of order
COLLOQ. higgledy-piggledy, at sixes and sevens, having your wires crossed
SLANG with your knickers in a twist
F3 2 orderly

confusing *adj*
puzzling, baffling, bewildering, muddling, perplexing, unclear, difficult, ambiguous, complicated, involved, contradictory, inconclusive, inconsistent, misleading, cryptic, tortuous
F3 clear, definite

confusion *n*
1 DISORDER, disarray, untidiness, mess, clutter, jumble, muddle, mix-up, disorganization, disarrangement, chaos, turmoil, commotion, upheaval
COLLOQ. shambles
2 MISUNDERSTANDING, puzzlement, perplexity, mystification, bewilderment, bafflement, muddle
F3 1 order, organization 2 clarity, enlightenment

confute *v*
disprove, refute, contradict, prove false, rebut, discredit
FORMAL negate, controvert

COLLOQ. debunk
⊟ confirm, prove

congeal v
clot, curdle, coalesce, coagulate, thicken, stiffen, harden, concentrate, fuse, solidify, set, cake, gel, freeze
⊟ dissolve, melt, liquefy

congenial adj
agreeable, pleasant, pleasing, relaxing, delightful, favourable, friendly, companionable, genial, sympathetic, homely, compatible, complaisant, cosy, like-minded, suitable, well-suited
⊟ disagreeable, unpleasant

congenital adj
1 a congenital disease
hereditary, inborn, inbred, inherited, innate, inherent, constitutional, natural
TECHNICAL connate
2 a congenital liar
inveterate, entrenched, habitual, compulsive, chronic, seasoned, hardened, incorrigible, incurable, complete, thorough, utter
FORMAL inured

congested adj
1 congested roads
blocked, clogged, jammed, packed, stuffed, crammed, full, crowded, overcrowded, overflowing, teeming
2 a congested nose
blocked, clogged, choked, engorged
⊟ **1, 2** clear

congestion n
1 congestion on the roads
clogging, blockage, crowding, overcrowding, jam, traffic jam, snarl-up, gridlock, bottleneck, pinchpoint
2 nasal congestion
clogging, blockage, blocking, choking

conglomerate n
corporation, multinational, merger, cartel, trust, consortium, combine, group, company, firm, business, business organization, concern, association, partnership, establishment

conglomeration n
mass, agglomeration, aggregation, accumulation, collection, assemblage, composite, assortment, medley, hotchpotch

congratulate v
praise, compliment, say well done to, wish well, wish happiness to, send/offer good wishes to, send/offer best wishes to
OLD gratulate, greet
FORMAL felicitate
COLLOQ. take your hat off to, pat on the back
⊟ commiserate
■ **congratulate yourself**
pride, preen, plume
COLLOQ. give yourself a pat on the back, delight in

congratulations n
compliments, good wishes, best wishes, greetings
FORMAL felicitations
COLLOQ. pat on the back, bouquet(s)
⊟ commiserations, condolences

congregate v
gather, assemble, collect, muster, rally, rendezvous, meet, come together, convene, converge, flock, swarm, crowd, throng, form, mass, accumulate, cluster, clump
⊟ disperse

congregation n
assembly, crowd, group, throng, mass, multitude, host, meeting, flock, fold, parishioners, parish, laity, fellowship

congress n
assembly, conference, convention, council, legislature, meeting, gathering, forum, parliament, synod, diet
FORMAL conclave, convocation

congruence n
correspondence, consistency, agreement, conformity, coincidence, harmony, compatibility, similarity, resemblance, identity, match, parallelism
FORMAL concinnity, concurrence, consonance
⊟ incongruity

congruent adj
consistent, compatible, harmonious, similar, parallel, corresponding
FORMAL concurrent, consonant

conical adj
cone-shaped, pyramidal, pyramid-shaped, funnel-shaped, tapering, tapered, pointed
FORMAL infundibular, infundibulate, turbinate

conjectural adj
hypothetical, assumed, surmised, tentative, theoretical, speculative, supposed, academic, suppositional
FORMAL posited, postulated
⊟ factual, real

conjecture v, n
♦ v
speculate, theorize, hypothesize, guess, estimate, reckon, fancy, suppose, presuppose, surmise, assume, presume, infer, imagine, suspect
♦ n
speculation, theory, hypothesis, fancy, notion, guesswork, guess, estimate, supposition, presupposition, surmise, suspicion, assumption, presumption, conclusion, inference, extrapolation, projection
COLLOQ. guesstimate

conjoin v
combine, amalgamate, unite, unify, join (together), link, connect, match, synthesize
FORMAL concur

conjugal adv
marital, nuptial, married, wedded, bridal
FORMAL matrimonial, connubial, epithalamic, spousal, hymeneal

conjunction n
coincidence, co-occurrence, coexistence, combination, amalgamation, association, union, unification
FORMAL concurrence, juxtaposition
■ **in conjunction with**
together with, with, along with, alongside, combined with, in partnership with, in collaboration with, in association with, in company with

conjure v
1 conjuring at the children's party
do tricks, perform tricks, do magic, perform magic
2 conjure handkerchiefs from a hat
summon, invoke, call up, evoke, make appear, materialize, rouse, raise, bewitch, charm, fascinate, compel
■ **conjure up**
evoke, create, produce, excite, awaken, recollect, recall, call/bring to mind, summon up

conjurer n
magician, illusionist, miracle-worker, sorcerer, wizard
FORMAL prestidigitator, prestigiator, thaumaturge

conk v
■ **conk out**
break down, collapse, fail
COLLOQ. pack up, go bust, go on the blink, go haywire, go phut, go kaput

con man n
con artist, confidence trickster, cheat, liar, deceiver, swindler, overcharger, usurer, extortionist
COLLOQ. rip-off artist, crook, hustler; N Am bunco, bunco artist, grifter
SLANG blagger; Aust illy whacker

connect v
1 *connect two objects*
join, link, unite, couple, bridge, combine, fasten, secure, affix, tie, clamp, fuse, attach
FORMAL concatenate
2 *connected with the murder*
relate (to), correlate, associate, bracket, identify, link, couple, equate, ally
1 disconnect, cut off, detach

connected adj
joined, linked, united, coupled, tied, combined, fastened, secured, related, akin, associated, affiliated, allied
disconnected, unconnected

connection n
1 *a connection between pipes; a connection between smoking and cancer*
junction, coupling, joint, fastening, attachment, clasp, bond, tie, link, association, alliance, relation, relationship, interrelation, contact, communication, parallel, correlation, analogy, correspondence, relevance, reference
2 *use your connections to get a job*
friend, acquaintance, relation, relative, contact, sponsor, person of influence, person of importance
1 disconnection
■ **in connection with**
with regard to, in regard to, as regards, regarding, concerning, with reference to, with respect to, in relation to, re, about, as to, on the subject of
FORMAL apropos

connivance n
collusion, complicity, condoning, consent, abetment, abetting, conspiracy

connive v
1 *connive with someone to commit an offence*
collude, conspire, intrigue, plot, scheme, collaborate
FORMAL complot, cabal, coact
2 *connive at wrongdoing*
overlook, ignore, disregard, condone, tolerate, brook, let go, let pass, pass over, gloss over, allow, wink at
COLLOQ. turn a blind eye to

conniving adj
scheming, colluding, conspiring, plotting, nasty, immoral, unscrupulous, corrupt, manipulative

connoisseur n
authority, specialist, expert, judge, arbiter, pundit, devotee, cognoscente, gourmet, gastronome, epicure, virtuoso, aesthete
FORMAL aficionado
COLLOQ. buff

connotation n
implication, suggestion, intimation, intent, hint, nuance, allusion, undertone, overtone, insinuation, colouring, association, undercurrent
TECHNICAL comprehension

connote v
imply, suggest, intimate, hint at, allude to, insinuate, signify, indicate, associate
OLD betoken
FORMAL import, purport, connotate

conquer v
1 *conquer an enemy/your fears*
defeat, beat, overthrow, overpower, rout, crush, subdue, quell, overrun, best, get the better of, worst, overcome, surmount, master, suppress, humble
OLD debel
FORMAL vanquish, subjugate
COLLOQ. trounce
See Synonym nuances panel at **defeat**.
2 SEIZE, take, annex, occupy, possess, take possession of, acquire, obtain, win, control
FORMAL appropriate
1 surrender, yield, give in

conqueror n
victor, winner, champion, hero, master, lord
FORMAL vanquisher, subjugator, conquistador
COLLOQ. champ

conquest n
1 *the conquest of the country*
victory, triumph, win, success, defeat, beating, overthrow, overpowering, coup, rout, crushing, mastery, subjection, invasion, overrunning, possession, occupation, capture, seizing, annexation, acquisition
FORMAL appropriation, subjugation, vanquishment
COLLOQ. trouncing
2 *his latest conquest*
captive, lover, catch, acquisition

conscience n
principles, standards, morals, ethics, sense of right, sense of right and wrong, moral sense, moral code, still small voice, voice within, scruples, qualms
TECHNICAL syneidesis, synteresis
OLD inwit

> **QUOTATIONS**
> The one thing that doesn't abide by majority rule is a person's conscience
> HARPER LEE, *To Kill a Mockingbird*

conscience-stricken adj
ashamed, sorry, contrite, guilt-ridden, guilty, penitent, regretful, remorseful, repentant, disturbed, troubled
FORMAL compunctious
COLLOQ. on a guilt trip
unashamed, unrepentant

conscientious adj
diligent, hard-working, scrupulous, painstaking, methodical, thorough, meticulous, punctilious, industrious, dedicated, assiduous, particular, careful, attentive, responsible, upright, honest, faithful, dutiful
careless, irresponsible, unreliable

conscious adj
1 AWAKE, alive, responsive, sensible, rational, reasoning, alert
TECHNICAL conscient
FORMAL sentient
2 AWARE, self-conscious, heedful, mindful, alert
FORMAL cognizant, recognizant, percipient, sensible
3 *a conscious effort to be polite*
deliberate, intentional, on purpose, calculated, premeditated, studied, knowing, wilful, voluntary, witting
FORMAL volitional
1 unconscious **2** unaware **3** involuntary, unintentional

consciously adv
deliberately, intentionally, knowingly, wilfully, voluntarily, on purpose
unintentionally

consciousness n
1 *enter his consciousness*
awareness, mind, knowledge, intuition, perception, apprehension, realization, recognition, psyche
TECHNICAL coenaesthesis
FORMAL cognizance, sentience, sensibility
2 *lose consciousness*
being awake, wakefulness, awareness, alertness
2 unconsciousness

conscript v, n
♦ *v*
recruit, enlist, draft, call up, take on, round up, muster
volunteer
♦ *n*
recruit, enlistee, draftee
volunteer

consecrate v
sanctify, bless, anoint, hallow, make holy, dedicate, devote, vow, ordain, venerate, revere, exalt

consecutive *adj*
successive, sequential, serial, continuous, unbroken, uninterrupted, following, succeeding, running, one after the other, in turn, straight, in a row
FORMAL seriate
COLLOQ. on the trot, back to back
Ea discontinuous

consecutively *adv*
successively, sequentially, continuously, uninterruptedly, one after the other, in turn, in a row
COLLOQ. on the trot, back to back

consensus *n*
agreement, consent, harmony, majority view, unanimity, unity
FORMAL concord, concurrence, consentience, consension
Ea disagreement

consent *v, n*
◆ *v*
agree, accept, approve, permit, allow, authorize, grant, admit, concede, yield, submit, go along with, comply
OLD afford, condescend
FORMAL concur, assent, accede, acquiesce, homologate
COLLOQ. give the go-ahead, give the green light, give the thumbs-up
Ea refuse, decline, oppose
◆ *n*
agreement, acceptance, approval, authorization, permission, clearance, sanction, concession, compliance
FORMAL concurrence, assent, acquiescence
COLLOQ. go-ahead, green light
Ea disagreement, refusal, opposition
Related adjective: consensual

consequence *n*
1 RESULT, outcome, issue, end, upshot, effect, side effect, eventuality, implication, repercussion, reverberation
2 *of no consequence*
importance, significance, concern, value, weight, substance, note, eminence, prominence, distinction
FORMAL import, moment
Ea 1 cause **2** unimportance, insignificance

consequent *adj*
resultant, resulting, ensuing, subsequent, following, successive, sequential

consequential *adj*
1 RESULTANT, resulting, ensuing, subsequent, following, successive, sequential
2 IMPORTANT, significant, momentous, noteworthy, material, relevant, crucial, weighty, valuable, serious, far-reaching, substantial, vital, key, prominent
Ea 2 unimportant, insignificant

consequently *adv*
as a result, therefore, with the result that, so that, accordingly, consequentially, necessarily, subsequently, then
FORMAL inferentially, ergo, hence, thus

conservation *n*
keeping, safe-keeping, custody, saving, care, economy, husbandry, maintenance, upkeep, preservation, protection, safeguarding, ecology, environmentalism
Ea destruction

conservatism *n*
conservativeness, conventionalism, orthodoxy, traditionalism
Ea radicalism

conservative *adj, n*
◆ *adj*
1 *conservative politicians*
Tory, right-wing, hidebound, diehard, reactionary, establishmentarian
2 *conservative opinions/estimates*
unprogressive, conventional, traditional, traditionalist, orthodox, inflexible, set in your ways; *N Am* old-line;

hidebound, moderate, middle-of-the-road, careful, cautious, guarded, sober
COLLOQ. *N Am* buttoned-down, square
Ea 1 left-wing, radical **2** innovative, progressive
◆ *n*
Tory, right-winger, diehard, stick-in-the-mud, reactionary, traditionalist, moderate; *N Am* old-liner
Ea left-winger, radical

conservatory *n*
1 *grow plants in the conservatory*
greenhouse, glasshouse, hothouse
2 *study music at the conservatory*
conservatoire, school, college, academy, institute, music school, drama college

conserve *v*
keep, keep back, keep in reserve, save, store up, hoard, maintain, preserve, protect, take care of, guard, safeguard
Ea use, waste, squander

consider *v*
1 PONDER, deliberate, reflect, contemplate, meditate, muse, mull over, examine, study, weigh (up), debate, respect, remember, note, make a mental note of, give thought to, bear/keep in mind, take into account/consideration
FORMAL cogitate, ruminate
COLLOQ. chew over, toy with
2 *consider it an honour*
regard as, think, believe, judge, rate, count, hold, feel
FORMAL deem

considerable *adj*
great, large, big, siz(e)able, substantial, ample, plentiful, abundant, lavish, generous, marked, noticeable, perceptible, appreciable, reasonable, tolerable, respectable, important, significant, noteworthy, distinguished, influential, serious
COLLOQ. tidy
Ea small, slight, insignificant, unremarkable

considerably *adv*
significantly, substantially, greatly, markedly, much, noticeably, remarkably, appreciably, abundantly
Ea slightly

considerate *adj*
kind, thoughtful, caring, attentive, obliging, helpful, charitable, unselfish, concerned, selfless, altruistic, gracious, sympathetic, compassionate, generous, sensitive, tactful, discreet, solicitous
Ea inconsiderate, thoughtless, selfish

consideration *n*
1 THOUGHT, deliberation, reflection, contemplation, meditation, examination, analysis, scrutiny, review, inspection, attention, notice, heed, regard, reckoning, account
FORMAL cogitation, rumination
2 KINDNESS, thoughtfulness, care, attention, regard, respect, helpfulness, unselfishness, concern, selflessness, altruism, graciousness, sympathy, compassion, generosity, sensitivity, tact, discretion
3 *the cost is a major consideration*
fact, circumstance, factor, issue, point, concern
Ea 1 disregard, dismissal **2** thoughtlessness, lack of concern
■ **take into consideration**
take into account, consider, plan for, allow for, make allowances for, bear in mind, keep in mind, give thought to

considering *prep*
1 *considering her age*
taking into account/consideration, bearing in mind, making allowances for, in view of, in the light of
2 *he's very well, considering*
all things considered, all in all

consign v

entrust, assign, commend, commit, devote, hand over, give over, transfer, transmit, deliver, send, convey, ship, banish, relegate
OLD recommend

consignment n

cargo, shipment, load, batch, delivery, goods

consist v

1 *a jury consists of twelve people*
comprise, be composed, be made up, contain, include, incorporate, embody, be formed, embrace, involve, amount to
2 *the poem's beauty consists in its simplicity*
inhere, lie, reside, exist, be contained, have as its main feature
FORMAL subsist

consistency n

1 *the consistency of the porridge*
thickness, density, firmness, cohesion, smoothness
TECHNICAL viscosity
2 STEADINESS, regularity, evenness, uniformity, continuity, sameness, identity, constancy, steadfastness, stability, persistence, dependability, reliability, unchangeableness, lack of change
3 AGREEMENT, accordance, correspondence, compatibility, harmony
FORMAL congruity, consonance
F3 3 inconsistency

consistent adj

1 STEADY, stable, regular, uniform, straight, unchanging, undeviating, constant, same, persistent, unfailing, dependable, predictable
2 *not consistent with his colleague's version*
agreeing, compatible, corresponding, coinciding, matching, harmonious, conforming, logical, coherent, hanging together
FORMAL accordant, consonant, congruous, consentaneous
F3 1 irregular, erratic 2 inconsistent

consistently adv

regularly, constantly, persistently, unfailingly, uniformly, dependably, predictably

consolation n

comfort, cheer, encouragement, help, support, reassurance, aid, sympathy, commiseration, relief, ease, soothing, alleviation
OLD (*Shakesp*) recomforture
FORMAL solace, succour, assuagement
F3 discouragement

console¹ v

console the bereaved
comfort, cheer, hearten, encourage, help, support, reassure, sympathize with, commiserate with, relieve, soothe, calm
FORMAL solace, succour
F3 upset, agitate

console² n

an instrument console
panel, control panel, board, dashboard, keyboard, instruments, controls, switches, knobs, dials, buttons, levers

consolidate v

1 *consolidate power/support*
reinforce, strengthen, make strong(er), secure, make (more) secure, stabilize, make (more) stable, cement
FORMAL fortify
2 *consolidate businesses*
unite, join, combine, amalgamate, merge, unify, fuse

consolidation n

1 *consolidation of power*
reinforcement, strengthening, securing, stabilization, cementing
FORMAL fortification

2 *consolidation of businesses*
uniting, joining, combination, amalgamation, merger, unification, affiliation, alliance, association, confederation, federation, fusion

consonance n

compatibility, agreement, consistency, conformity, correspondence, harmony, suitability
FORMAL accordance, congruity, concord
F3 dissonance

consonant adj

compatible, consistent, correspondent, conforming, harmonious, in harmony, agreeing, in agreement, suitable, in accordance, according
FORMAL accordant, congruous
F3 dissonant

consort n, v

♦ *n*
partner, companion, associate, escort, plus-one, spouse, husband, wife
♦ *v*
associate, spend time, keep company, fraternize, mingle, mix

consortium n

partnership, confederation, federation, association, affiliation, coalition, league, corporation, company, bloc, cartel, conglomerate, alliance, organization, syndicate, guild, union, marriage, agreement, compact, bond, pact, treaty, combination

conspicuous adj

apparent, visible, noticeable, easily seen/noticed, marked, clear, obvious, evident, recognizable, observable, discernible, perceptible, patent, manifest, prominent, eminent, remarkable, shining, striking, blatant, flagrant, glaring, ostentatious, showy, flashy, garish; *dialect* kenspeckle
COLLOQ. standing out a mile
F3 inconspicuous, concealed, hidden

conspicuously adv

noticeably, visibly, markedly, clearly, obviously, evidently, recognizably, observably, discernibly, perceptibly, patently, manifestly, prominently, remarkably, strikingly, blatantly, flagrantly, glaringly, ostentatiously, showilyy, flashily, garishly
F3 inconspicuously

conspiracy n

plot, scheme, intrigue, stratagem, league, cabal, collusion, collaboration, connivance, treason, confederacy
OLD complot, consult, covin
FORMAL machination
COLLOQ. fix, frame-up, set-up

conspirator n

conspirer, plotter, schemer, intriguer, colluder, collaborator, traitor; *N Am* highbinder
OLD practisant

conspire v

1 *conspire to oust the president*
plot, hatch a plot, scheme, intrigue, manoeuvre, plan, connive, collude, collaborate
FORMAL machinate
2 *events conspiring for their harm*
combine, join, join forces, work/act together, connect, link, unite, ally, associate, co-operate

constancy n

1 STABILITY, steadiness, permanence, consistency, unchangeability, firmness, regularity, uniformity
2 LOYALTY, faithfulness, fidelity, devotion, steadfastness, dependability, trustworthiness, firmness, steadiness, persistence, resolution, perseverance, tenacity
F3 1 change, irregularity 2 fickleness

constant adj

1 *a constant barrage of questions*
continual, unbroken, never-ending, non-stop, endless, ceaseless, interminable, incessant, eternal, everlasting, perpetual, persistent, chronic, continuous, unremitting, uninterrupted, without respite, relentless, unflagging, unwavering

2 *his temperature is constant*
stable, steady, unchanging, unvarying, changeless, invariable, unalterable, consistent, permanent, firm, even, regular, uniform
FORMAL immutable

3 *a constant friend*
loyal, faithful, staunch, steadfast, dependable, trustworthy, true, devoted, firm, steady, persistent, resolute, persevering
E3 **1** fitful, occasional **2** variable, irregular **3** disloyal, fickle

constantly adv
always, continually, all the time, for ever, permanently, continuously, endlessly, non-stop, ceaselessly, everlastingly, incessantly, interminably, invariably, perpetually, perennially, daily, relentlessly, ad nauseam, on and on, day in day out; *dialect* aye
OLD still
COLLOQ. twenty-four seven, 24-7
E3 occasionally

constellation n
See panel below

consternation n
alarm, dismay, anxiety, fear, distress, dread, horror, fright, shock, terror, panic, awe, bewilderment
FORMAL disquietude, perturbation, trepidation
E3 composure

constituency n
area, region, district, borough, zone, division, ward, parish, community, shire, electorate; *Scot* burgh; *N Am* precinct

constituent n, adj
♦ n
1 *voting by constituents*
elector, voter
2 *the constituents of the mixture*
ingredient, element, factor, principle, component, component part, part, content, bit, section, unit
E3 **2** whole, total
♦ adj
component, integral, essential, basic, intrinsic, inherent

constitute v
1 *six counties constitute the province*
comprise, make up, form, compose
2 *his remarks constitute a challenge to the leadership*
be, represent, mean, form, make, be equivalent to, amount to, add up to, be tantamount to, be regarded as
3 *constitute a committee*
form, create, establish, set up, found, inaugurate, initiate, institute, appoint, authorize, commission, charter, empower

constitution n
1 *a country's constitution*
laws, rules, statutes, basic principles, code, social code, state, charter, codified law, bill of rights, *fuero*
OLD policy
FORMAL polity
2 COMPOSITION, make-up, structure, organization, formation, nature
FORMAL configuration
3 HEALTH, condition, physique, physical condition, make-up, disposition, temperament, temper, temperature, character, nature, habit, idiosyncrasy, upmake

> QUOTATIONS
> Some men look at Constitutions with sanctimonious reverence and deem them like the Ark of the Covenant – too sacred to be touched
> THOMAS JEFFERSON

constitutional adj, n
♦ adj
statutory, by law, according to the law, legal, legitimate, lawful, legislative, governmental, authorized, vested, codified, ratified
♦ n
walk, stroll, saunter, amble, promenade, turn, airing

constrain v
1 FORCE, compel, coerce, oblige, necessitate, drive, put, impel, pressurize, pressure, urge
OLD strain
2 LIMIT, confine, constrict, restrain, check, curb, bind, restrict, hinder, hold back
OLD perstringe

constrained adj
uneasy, embarrassed, inhibited, reticent, reserved, guarded, stiff, forced, unnatural, awkward
E3 relaxed, free

The constellations (with common English names) are:

Andromeda	Capricornus (Sea Goat)	Crux (Southern Cross)	Indus (Indian)	Pavo (Peacock)	Taurus (Bull)
Antlia (Air Pump)			Lacerta (Lizard)	Pegasus (Winged Horse)	Telescopium (Tele-scope)
Apus (Bird of Paradise)	Carina (Keel)	Cygnus (Swan)	Leo (Lion)	Perseus	Triangulum (Trian-gle)
	Cassiopeia	Delphinus (Dol-phin)	Leo Minor (Little Lion)	Phoenix	
Aquarius (Water Bearer)	Centaurus (Cen-taur)	Dorado (Swordfish)	Lepus (Hare)	Pictor (Easel)	Triangulum Aus-trale (Southern Triangle)
Aquila (Eagle)	Cepheus	Draco (Dragon)	Libra (Scales)	Pisces (Fishes)	
Ara (Altar)	Cetus (Whale)	Equuleus (Little Horse)	Lupus (Wolf)	Piscis Austrinus (Southern Fish)	
Aries (Ram)	Chamaeleon (Cha-meleon)	Eridanus (River Eridanus)	Lynx	Puppis (Ship's Stern)	Tucana (Toucan)
Auriga (Charioteer)			Lyra (Harp)		Ursa Major (Great Bear)
Boötes (Herdsman)	Circinus (Com-passes)	Fornax (Furnace)	Mensa (Table)	Pyxis (Mariner's Compass)	Ursa Minor (Little Bear)
Caelum (Chisel)		Gemini (Twins)	Microscopium (Microscope)		
Camelopardalis (Giraffe)	Columba (Dove)	Grus (Crane)	Monoceros (Uni-corn)	Reticulum (Net)	Vela (Sails)
Cancer (Crab)	Coma Berenices (Berenice's Hair)	Hercules		Sagitta (Arrow)	Virgo (Virgin)
Canes Venatici (Hunting Dogs)	Corona Australis (Southern Crown)	Horologium (Clock)	Musca (Fly)	Sagittarius (Archer)	Volans (Flying Fish)
Canis Major (Great Dog)	Corona Borealis (Northern Crown)	Hydra (Sea Serpent)	Norma (Level)	Scorpius (Scorpion)	Vulpecula (Fox)
			Octans (Octant)	Sculptor	
Canis Minor (Little Dog)	Corvus (Crow)	Hydrus (Water Snake)	Ophiuchus (Ser-pent Bearer)	Scutum (Shield)	
	Crater (Cup)		Orion	Serpens (Serpent)	
				Sextans (Sextant)	

See also **star**.

constraint n
1 FORCE, duress, compulsion, coercion, pressure, necessity, obligation, demand, insistence, forcedness
2 RESTRICTION, limitation, hindrance, restraint, check, curb, damper, shackle, impediment
3 INHIBITION, restraint, self-control, reticence, guardedness, stiffness, unnaturalness, awkwardness

constrict v
1 *constrict an air passage*
squeeze, compress, pinch, cramp, narrow, make narrow, tighten, contract, close, shrink, choke, strangle, strangulate
2 *constricted by lower budgets*
limit, restrict, confine, constrain, check, curb, bind, hinder, impede, hold back, obstruct, hamper, inhibit
E3 1 expand, widen, open

constriction n
1 *feel a constriction in the chest*
squeezing, narrowing, pressure, tightness, tightening, compression, cramp, blockage
TECHNICAL stricture, stenosis
FORMAL constringency
2 *constrictions in the budget*
restriction, constraint, limitation, reduction, check, curb, hindrance, impediment
E3 1 expansion, widening

construct v
1 *construct a building*
build, erect, raise, elevate, make, manufacture, fabricate, assemble, structure, establish, put up, put together, set up, carpenter, craft, patch, weave
OLD fabric
COLLOQ. throw up, throw together, knock up, knock together
2 *construct a theory*
compose, form, put together, shape, fashion, fabricate, model, devise, design, engineer, create, found, establish, formulate
E3 1 demolish, destroy

construction n
1 *houses under construction*
building, erection, fabrication, assembly, elevation, making, manufacture, establishment
2 *the cathedral is a magnificent construction*
structure, building, edifice, assembly, fabric, form, shape, framework, figure, model
3 *the construction put on his remarks*
interpretation, meaning, inference, deduction, reading
4 *the art of sentence construction*
structure, formation, arrangement, order, organization, composition, make-up
FORMAL configuration, disposition
E3 1 demolition, destruction

constructive adj
practical, productive, positive, helpful, useful, valuable, beneficial, advantageous
E3 destructive, negative, unhelpful

constructively adv
productively, positively, practically, helpfully, usefully, beneficially, advantageously
E3 destructively, negatively, unhelpfully

construe v
interpret, explain, understand, see as, regard as, read, render, take to mean, deduce, infer, analyse
FORMAL expound

consul n
ambassador, envoy, diplomat, representative, agent, delegate, minister, nuncio, elchi
OLD ledger, leaguer
FORMAL emissary, legate, plenipotentiary

consult v
1 *consult an expert*
ask/seek advice, ask/seek information, ask someone's opinion, question, interrogate, turn to, see
COLLOQ. pick someone's brains
2 *consult with business partners*
confer, discuss, debate, talk, deliberate
3 *consult a map*
look up, refer to, turn to

consultant n
adviser, expert, authority, specialist, associate

consultation n
discussion, deliberation, talk, dialogue, conference, meeting, hearing, interview, examination, appointment, forum, session

consultative adj
advisory, advising, consulting, counselling, helping, recommending
FORMAL consultatory

consume v
1 EAT, eat up, drink (up), swallow, devour, dispose of, gobble, take
OLD bezzle
FORMAL ingest
COLLOQ. tuck in, guzzle, scoff, snarf, polish off, touch, shift, discuss, get stuck into, murder, kill, punish
SLANG mainline
2 USE UP, use, absorb, spend, get through, go through, expend, drain, exhaust, squander, waste, fritter away
FORMAL deplete, dissipate, utilize
3 DESTROY, demolish, annihilate, devastate, burn, gut, ravage, lay waste, waste, wear (down), damage
OLD pine
4 *consumed with jealousy*
devour, dominate, absorb, engross, preoccupy, grip, obsess, monopolize, overwhelm, torment
COLLOQ. eat up

consumer n
user, end-user, customer, buyer, purchaser, shopper, patron, client, mouth

consuming adj
dominating, compelling, absorbing, preoccupying, devouring, engrossing, gripping, obsessive, immoderate, monopolizing, overwhelming, tormenting

consummate adj, v
♦ adj
absolute, complete, total, utter, perfect, supreme, superior, ultimate, superb, transcendent, unqualified, skilled, accomplished, finished, gifted, practised, exact, proficient, distinguished, matchless, exemplary, polished
OLD replenished; (*Shakesp*) made up
E3 imperfect
♦ v
perfect, accomplish, fulfil, realize, complete, perform, achieve, crown, cap, end, finish, conclude
FORMAL terminate, execute, effectuate

consummation n
perfection, accomplishment, achievement, fulfilment, realization, completion, performance, culmination, crowning, capping, end, finish, conclusion
FORMAL termination, execution, actualization, effectuation

consumption n
1 EATING, drinking, swallowing, devouring
FORMAL ingestion
COLLOQ. tucking-in, guzzling, scoffing
2 USING-UP, absorption, spending, getting-through, going-through, draining, exhaustion, squandering, waste
FORMAL depletion, expending, expenditure, utilization

contact n, v

♦ n

1 *in contact with an object*
touching, touch, impact, meeting, junction, union, proximity
FORMAL juxtaposition, contiguity
2 *in contact with old friends*
touch, communication, connection, association
3 *use your contacts to get a job*
friend, acquaintance, relation, relative, connection, sponsor, person of influence, person of importance, network of contacts

♦ v

approach, get onto, apply to, reach, get hold of, get in touch with, get through to, communicate with, notify, write to, speak to, telephone, phone, ring, call, fax, email, message, text

contagion n
infection, contamination, pollution, defilement, tainting, poison, corruption

contagious adj
1 *a contagious disease*
infectious, catching, communicable, transmissible, transmittable, spreading, epidemic, pandemic
2 *contagious laughter*
infectious, compelling, irresistible, catching, spreading

contain v
1 INCLUDE, take in, comprise, incorporate, embody, involve, embrace, enclose, have inside, hold, carry, take, accommodate, seat
2 *contain your feelings*
repress, suppress, stifle, restrain, control, keep under, keep back, hold in, check, keep in check, curb, limit, stop, rein in, prevent from spreading
E3 1 exclude

container n
receptacle, vessel, holder
FORMAL repository
See panel below

containment n
control, restraint, limitation, check, curb, suppression, repression, stifling

contaminate v
infect, pollute, decay, adulterate, taint, soil, sully, defile, corrupt, harm, foul, spoil, make impure, deprave, debase, stain, tarnish
FORMAL vitiate
COLLOQ. spike
E3 purify, decontaminate

contamination n
infection, pollution, decay, adulteration, taint, soiling, sullying, defilement, desecration, corruption, harm, foulness, rottenness, spoiling, filth, impurity, debasement, stain, tarnish
FORMAL vitiation
E3 purification, decontamination

contemplate v
1 *contemplate leaving; contemplate the meaning of life*
consider, think about, deliberate, reflect on, ponder, meditate, muse, mull over, give thought to, dwell on, examine, study, weigh (up), turn over in your mind, have in mind/view, expect, foresee, envisage, plan, design, propose, intend
FORMAL cogitate, ruminate
2 *contemplate the view*
look at, regard, view, observe, scrutinize, survey, examine, inspect

contemplation n
1 *religious contemplation*
consideration, thought, deliberation, reflection, recollection, pondering, meditation, musing, mulling-over, dwell, examination, study, weighing (up)
FORMAL cogitation, rumination, cerebration
2 *contemplation of the view*
gazing, regard, regarding, view, viewing, observation, scrutiny, survey, examination, inspection
OLD beholding

contemplative adj
thoughtful, reflective, meditative, introspective, musing, pensive, rapt, intent, deep in thought
FORMAL cerebral, ruminative
E3 impulsive, thoughtless

contemporaneous adj
simultaneous, coexistent, synchronous
FORMAL concurrent, coetaneous, coeval

contemporary adj, n

♦ adj

1 MODERN, current, present, present-day, present-time, today's, topical, recent, latest, up-to-date, fashionable, on-trend, fashion-forward, up-to-the-minute, ultra-modern, avant-garde, futuristic
OLD contemporanean
COLLOQ. trendy, new-fangled, with it, now
2 CONTEMPORANEOUS, coexistent, parallel, synchronous, simultaneous
OLD contemporanean
FORMAL concurrent, coetaneous, coeval
E3 1 out-of-date, old-fashioned

♦ n

fellow, partner, associate, peer, equal, colleague, co-worker, confrère, counterpart, collateral
OLD contemporanean
FORMAL coeval

contempt n
scorn, disdain, condescension, derision, ridicule, mockery, disrespect, dishonour, disregard, neglect, dislike, loathing, hatred
FORMAL detestation, contumely
E3 respect, admiration, regard

contemptible adj
despicable, shameful, low, mean, vile, base, detestable, lamentable, loathsome, abject, wretched, hateful, degenerate, unworthy, pitiful, paltry, worthless

---

Types of container include:

bag	can	crock	kettle	purse	tube
barrel	canister	cup	locker	sack	tumbler
basin	carton	cylinder	mug	suitcase	tureen
basket	case	dish	pack	tank	urn
bath	cask	drum	packet	tea caddy	vase
beaker	casket	dustbin	pail	tea chest	vat
bin	cauldron	glass	pan	teapot	waste bin
bottle	chest	hamper	pannier	tin	wastepaper basket
bowl	churn	jar	pitcher	trough	water-butt
box	cistern	jug	pot	trunk	well
bucket	crate	keg	punnet	tub	

See also **box**[1].

OLD (*Shakesp*) pelting
FORMAL ignominious
F3 admirable, honourable

contemptuous *adj*
scornful, disdainful, sneering, supercilious, condescending, arrogant, haughty, high and mighty, tossy, cynical, derisive, derisory, insulting, mocking, jeering, disrespectful, insolent, withering
OLD dispiteous
FORMAL contumelious
F3 respectful, polite, humble

contend *v*
1 *contend with a problem*
deal, cope, grapple, face, face up to, brave, tackle, address, reckon, come to terms
COLLOQ. come to grips, meet head on
2 MAINTAIN, state, hold, argue, allege, assert, declare, affirm, profess, claim
FORMAL aver, asseverate
3 COMPETE, vie, contest, dispute, clash, wrestle, grapple, struggle, strive, tussle, oppose, challenge, fight, battle, combat, war

content[1] *n*
1 *the contents of the package*
constituents, parts, elements, ingredients, components, component parts, load, items, what is contained, things inside
2 *the contents of the book*
chapter, division, section, subject, subject matter, topic, theme
3 SUBSTANCE, matter, material, essence, gist, meaning, significance, text, theme, subject matter, ideas, contents, load, burden
4 AMOUNT, proportion, capacity, volume, size, measure

content[2] *adj, n, v*
♦ *adj*
content with the arrangements
satisfied, fulfilled, contented, comfortable, unworried, untroubled, pleased, happy, glad, cheerful, willing, at ease
F3 dissatisfied, troubled
♦ *n*
comfort, contentment, satisfaction, fulfilment, delight, pleasure, happiness, gladness, cheerfulness, peace, peacefulness, ease, serenity, gratification, equanimity
F3 discontent
♦ *v*
satisfy, humour, indulge, gratify, please, be happy, be pleased, be glad, delight, appease, pacify, placate, soothe
F3 displease

contented *adj*
happy, glad, pleased, cheerful, comfortable, relaxed, content, satisfied, fulfilled, unworried, untroubled
OLD perfect
F3 discontented, troubled, unhappy, annoyed

contention *n*
1 *it is my contention that ...*
belief, contention, opinion, persuasion, feeling, intuition, impression, notion, theory, view, viewpoint, point of view, thesis, conviction, claim, judgement, plea, stand, position, assertion, argument
2 *a matter of contention*
disagreement, argument, controversy, dispute, debate, discord, dissension, enmity, feuding, hostility, strife, struggle, rivalry, wrangling

contentious *adj*
1 *a contentious issue*
controversial, polemical, disputed, doubtful, questionable, debatable, disputable
FORMAL tendentious
2 *a contentious person*
argumentative, antagonistic, quarrelsome, hostile, perverse, querulous, bickering, captious

FORMAL pugnacious
F3 **1** uncontroversial, straightforward **2** co-operative, peaceable

contentment *n*
contentedness, happiness, gladness, cheerfulness, pleasure, gratification, comfort, ease, complacency, peace, peacefulness, serenity, equanimity, content, satisfaction, fulfilment
F3 unhappiness, discontent, dissatisfaction

contest *n, v*
♦ *n*
competition, game, match, race, championship, tournament, event, encounter, fight, battle, combat, conflict, struggle, skirmish, dispute, vying, debate, controversy, challenge, bout, *concours*
COLLOQ. set-to
♦ *v*
1 DISPUTE, debate, question, call into question, doubt, challenge, oppose, argue against, object to, deny, refute
TECHNICAL litigate
2 COMPETE, be in competition with, vie, contend, strive, struggle, fight, battle, try to beat, tussle
F3 **1** accept

contestant *n*
competitor, contender, player, participant, entrant, candidate, aspirant, rival, opponent, adversary, prizer, disputant

context *n*
background, setting, surroundings, framework, frame of reference, state of affairs, situation, general situation, position, circumstances, factors, conditions, connection

contiguous *adj*
adjacent, adjoining, touching, beside, bordering, near, close, neighbouring, next, tangential
TECHNICAL vicinal
FORMAL abutting, conjoining, conterminous, juxtaposed, juxtapositional

continent *n*
mainland, terra firma

contingency *n*
eventuality, possibility, accident, randomness, arbitrariness, chance, chance event, emergency, event, happening, incident, uncertainty
FORMAL fortuity, juncture

contingent *n, adj*
♦ *n*
body, company, deputation, delegation, mission, representatives, detachment, section, division, group, band, set, batch, quota, party, complement
♦ *adj*
dependent, conditional, subject, based, relative

continual *adj*
constant, perpetual, incessant, interminable, eternal, everlasting, regular, frequent, recurrent, repeated, repetitive, persistent
F3 occasional, intermittent, temporary

⚠ continual or **continuous**?
Continual means 'very frequent, happening again and again': *I've had continual interruptions all morning.*
Continuous means 'without a pause or break': *continuous rain.*

---

continually *adv*
constantly, perpetually, incessantly, interminably, ceaselessly, ever, forever, eternally, everlastingly, always, endlessly, on and on, non-stop, regularly, frequently, recurrently, repeatedly, persistently, habitually, all the time
F3 occasionally, intermittently

continuance *n*
continuation, duration, endurance, period, term, permanence, persistence
FORMAL protraction

continuation *n*

1 *continuation after a pause*
resumption, recommencement, starting again, carrying-on, renewal, maintenance, development, furtherance, addition, supplement, sequel

2 *the continuation of the road*
prolongation, lengthening, extension
FORMAL protraction
E₃ 1 *formal* cessation, termination

continue *v*

1 *continue doing something*
go on, carry on, not stop, keep, keep on (with), proceed, pursue, stay, persist in, persevere in, progress, press on
COLLOQ. stick at, soldier on

2 *the course continues next term*
resume, recommence, renew, proceed (again), start again, begin again, take up again, carry on, go on
COLLOQ. pick up the threads, pick up where you have left off

3 *if the storm continues; continue your training*
last, endure, remain, abide, survive, hold (out), stay, rest, pursue, sustain, maintain, keep up, lengthen, prolong, extend, persist, keep on, project
OLD dure
FORMAL subsist

4 *'I'm not sure,' she continued*
start talking again, resume, go on

5 *continue on your way*
keep going, keep travelling, keep walking, keep moving, move on, keep on, carry on, proceed, press ahead
E₃ 1, 2, 3, 4 stop

continuity *n*
flow, progression, succession, sequence, linkage, interrelationship, connection, cohesion, continuousness, uninterruptedness, unchangeableness
E₃ discontinuity

continuous *adj*
unbroken, uninterrupted, consecutive, non-stop, not stopping, without a break, endless, seamless, unending, never-ending, solid, unceasing, ceaseless, interminable, persistent, relentless, constant, unremitting, prolonged, extended, continued, lasting
COLLOQ. with no let-up
E₃ discontinuous, broken, sporadic

> **!** **continuous** or **continual**?
> See panel at **continual**.

> **SYNONYM NUANCES**
>
> **Unbroken**, **uninterrupted**, **solid** and **non-stop** are used quite neutrally of something carrying on without interruption: *the remedy for irritability is uninterrupted sleep; three months of non-stop rain*.
> **Unending**, **unceasing**, **unremitting** and **endless** go further by suggesting the feeling that something will carry on forever, and are often used in figurative contexts, either negatively or positively: *endless summer evenings; an unremitting battle against prejudice*. **Interminable** again suggests the feeling that it will never end, with a clear implication of monotony: *bogged down in interminable discussions*. **Prolonged** also hints at something gruelling, but is used in the context of unexpected additional time: *prolonged talks on the economy*.

> **Seamless** may be used similarly to suggest the apparent flow of one thing into another, and is often used as a term of approbation: *a professional and seamless show*. You can use **persistent** or **relentless**, however, to describe repeated action and imply a perhaps unwelcome tenacity: *the persistent questions of a newspaper reporter*. **Lasting** would be used with the positive implication that something will endure: *a deep and lasting friendship*.

continuously *adv*
uninterruptedly, consecutively, endlessly, ceaselessly, interminably, persistently, relentlessly, constantly, unremittingly
COLLOQ. twenty-four seven, 24-7
E₃ sporadically

contort *v*
twist, distort, warp, wrench, disfigure, deform, misshape, bend out of shape, screw up, gnarl, knot, writhe, squirm, wriggle
FORMAL convolute

contortionist *n*
acrobat, gymnast, tumbler, balancer, somersaulter, trapeze artist, rope-walker, rope-dancer, stuntman, stuntwoman
FORMAL funambulist, aerialist, equilibrist

contour *n*
outline, silhouette, shape, form, figure, curve, lines, relief, profile, character, aspect
TECHNICAL isobase, isobath
FORMAL contorno, tournure

contraband *n*
banned/black-market goods, smuggling, forbidden/illegal traffic, bootlegging, prohibited/unlawful goods
FORMAL proscribed goods
COLLOQ. hot goods

contraceptive
See panel below

contract *v, n*
♦ *v*

1 SHRINK, lessen, diminish, reduce, decrease, shorten, make/become shorter, make/become smaller, curtail, abbreviate, abridge, condense, compress, constrict, narrow, tighten, tense, draw in, shrivel, wrinkle

2 *contract pneumonia*
catch, get, go/come down with, develop, pick up, become infected with, become ill with, be taken ill with
FORMAL succumb to

3 PLEDGE, promise, undertake, engage, agree, stipulate, covenant, arrange, agree terms, settle, negotiate, bargain
E₃ 1 expand, enlarge, lengthen
♦ *n*
agreement, bond, commitment, engagement, covenant, treaty, convention, pact, transaction, deal, bargain, settlement, arrangement, understanding
FORMAL compact, concordat

■ contract out
1 SUBCONTRACT, pass/give to others, delegate, farm out, outsource
2 WITHDRAW, get out, drop out

> **QUOTATIONS**
> A verbal contract isn't worth the paper it's written on
> SAM GOLDWYN

Contraceptives and other forms of birth control include:

barrier contraceptive	condom	female condom	intrauterine device (IUD)	oral contraceptive	sheath
barrier method	contraceptive ring	Femidom®	*slang* johnnie	pill	spermicide
cervical cap	contraceptive sponge	*slang* French letter	loop	*N Am* prophylactic	vaginal ring
coil	diaphragm	injectable contraceptive	minipill	protective	withdrawal method
coitus interruptus	Dutch cap		morning-after pill	rhythm method	
				slang rubber	

contraction n
1 *'Don't' is a contraction of 'do not'*
abbreviation, shortening, shortened form, abridgement
2 *the contraction of muscles*
constriction, compression, narrowing, tightening, tensing, drawing-in, shrivelling, shrinkage, lessening, reduction, curtailment
TECHNICAL astringency
F3 2 relaxation, expansion, growth

contradict v
1 *contradict someone*
deny, challenge, oppose, dispute, rebut, counter, go against, argue with; *dialect* threap
TECHNICAL sublate, traverse
OLD nay, outface
FORMAL disaffirm, confute, refute, impugn, gainsay, contrary
2 *one statement contradicts another*
disagree with, clash with, conflict with, contrast with, go against, be at variance with, be at odds with, be in conflict with, be inconsistent with
FORMAL negate, belie
COLLOQ. fly in the face of
F3 1 agree **2** agree with, confirm; *formal* corroborate

contradiction n
1 *the contradiction between theory and practice*
clash, variance, odds, conflict, inconsistency, disagreement, paradox
FORMAL incongruity, negation, antithesis
2 *contradiction of an earlier report*
denial, challenge, opposition, dispute, rebuttal, counter-argument
FORMAL disaffirmance, disaffirmation, confutation, refutation
F3 1, 2 agreement

contradictory adj
contrary, opposite, opposing, paradoxical, conflicting, clashing, inconsistent, incompatible, antagonistic, irreconcilable, opposed
FORMAL discrepant, dissentient, repugnant, incongruous, antithetical
F3 consistent

SYNONYM NUANCES

The word **contrary** suggests going against something established: *contrary to popular belief*. **Opposite** and **opposing** imply being at the furthest extremities of anything: *the stark polarization of these opposing views*. The term **paradoxical** is appropriately used only to describe a contradiction with apparent absurdity: *the paradoxical view of ugliness as a special kind of beauty*.
You might use **incompatible** if two or more things are simply unable to co-exist, or **irreconcilable** where inherent differences mean no area of agreement can be found: *the irreconcilable differences between landowners and conservationists*. **Antagonistic** would be most appropriately used to suggest a more violent disagreement, and to convey this notion further, you could use **conflicting** or **clashing**.

---

contraption n
contrivance, device, gadget, waldo, apparatus, rig, machine, mechanism, invention
COLLOQ. gizmo, widget, doodah; *N Am* doodad; thingamy, thingamybob, thingamyjig, what's-its-name
SLANG doofer

contrary adj, n
♦ adj
1 OPPOSITE, counter, reverse, conflicting, clashing, inconsistent, incompatible, irreconcilable, antagonistic, opposed, opposing, adverse, hostile
2 PERVERSE, awkward, disobliging, difficult, unco-operative, wayward, obstinate, stubborn, headstrong, intractable, cantankerous

FORMAL refractory
COLLOQ. stroppy
F3 1 like **2** obliging
♦ n
opposite, converse, reverse
FORMAL antithesis
■ **on the contrary**
conversely, quite/just the reverse, quite/just the opposite, *per contra, au contraire, tout au contraire*
■ **contrary to**
in opposition to, at variance with, at odds with, in conflict with, inconsistent with

contrast n, v
♦ n
difference, dissimilarity, divergence, distinction, differentiation, comparison, foil, set-off, opposite, opposition, relief
TECHNICAL chiasmus, contraposition, counterchange
FORMAL disparity, dissimilitude, antithesis
F3 similarity, resemblance
♦ v
1 *contrast two people*
compare, differentiate, distinguish, discriminate
2 *her expression contrasted sharply with her dress*
disagree, contradict, clash, conflict, differ, oppose, go against, be at variance, be at odds, be in conflict, be inconsistent with
■ **in contrast to**
as distinguished from, opposed to, in opposition to, rather than, as against

contravene v
infringe, violate, break, breach, disobey, defy, flout
FORMAL transgress
F3 uphold, observe, obey

contravention n
infringement, violation, breaking, breach
FORMAL transgression, dereliction
F3 observance, compliance

contretemps n
argument, disagreement, squabble, clash, brush, tiff, difficulty, accident, misadventure, misfortune, mishap, hitch, predicament

contribute v
1 *contribute money to charity*
give, donate, give a donation, subscribe, grant, present, endow, provide, supply, furnish
FORMAL bestow
COLLOQ. chip in; *Aust* chuck in
2 *poor design contributed to the disaster*
cause, play a part in, give rise to, lead to, result in, occasion, bring about, make, make happen, produce, generate, originate, create, promote, help, add to, be a factor in, be instrumental in
FORMAL conduce
3 *contribute an article for a magazine*
write, compose, create, compile, prepare, edit, submit, supply, provide

contribution n
1 *a contribution of £1000*
donation, subscription, gift, gratuity, handout, grant, levy, tax, mite, present, endowment, superannuation, offering, input, addition, proportion, shot, Peter's pence
FORMAL bestowal
2 *a contribution to a magazine*
article, story, feature, item, piece, column, report, review, paper, feuilleton

contributor n
1 DONOR, subscriber, giver, patron, benefactor, sponsor, backer, supporter
2 WRITER, author, journalist, reporter, compiler, correspondent, reviewer, critic, columnist, freelance

contrite adj
sorry, regretful, remorseful, repentant, penitent, penitential, guilt-ridden, conscience-stricken, chastened, humble, ashamed, red-faced

contrition n
remorse, sorrow, regret, shame, humiliation, penitence, repentance, sackcloth and ashes, self-reproach
FORMAL compunction

contrivance n
1 INVENTION, device, contraption, gadget, implement, appliance, machine, mechanism, tool, apparatus, equipment, gear
COLLOQ. gizmo, widget, doodah; N Am doodad; thingamy, thingamybob, thingamyjig, what's-its-name
SLANG doofer
2 STRATAGEM, ploy, trick, dodge, ruse, expedient, tactic, plan, design, project, scheme, plot, intrigue
FORMAL machination, artifice

contrive v
1 *somehow contrived to blame me*
manage, succeed, arrange, bring about, create, design, devise, find a way
2 *contrive a meeting between them*
engineer, manoeuvre, orchestrate, stage-manage, plan, plot, scheme, fabricate, create, devise, invent, concoct, construct
COLLOQ. set up, wangle

contrived adj
unnatural, artificial, false, forced, strained, laboured, mannered, elaborate, overdone
COLLOQ. set-up
F3 natural, genuine, spontaneous

control n, v
♦ n
1 POWER, charge, authority, command, mastery, dominance, sway, supremacy, government, rule, reign, direction, management, oversight, supervision, superintendence, discipline, guidance, influence
FORMAL jurisdiction
2 RESTRAINT, self-restraint, self-control, self-discipline, constraint, check, curb, repression
3 *price controls*
restriction, constraint, limitation, regulation, limit, reduction, brake, check, curb, hindrance, impediment
4 INSTRUMENT, dial, switch, button, knob, lever
♦ v
1 LEAD, be in charge of, have authority over, govern, rule, command, direct, manage, run, head, oversee, preside over, dominate, supervise, superintend
COLLOQ. be the boss, be in the driving seat, be in the saddle, pull the strings, rule the roost, run the show, call the tune/shots, wear the trousers
2 *control a machine/the temperature*
run, operate, work, make go, regulate, modulate, adjust, monitor, verify
3 *control wages*
restrict, limit, regulate, constrain, constrict, reduce, check, curb
OLD perstringe
COLLOQ. keep a tight rein on, put the brakes on
4 *control your temper*
restrain, check, curb, subdue, repress, hold back, keep, keep in check, contain
See Synonym nuances panel at **restrain**.

controversial adj
contentious, polemical, disputed, doubtful, questionable, debatable, disputable, at issue, moot
FORMAL tendentious, eristic

controversy n
debate, discussion, war of words, difference of opinion, dispute, disagreement, argument, quarrel, squabble, wrangle, strife, contention, discord, friction, dissension, *cause célèbre*
OLD debatement

FORMAL polemic, altercation
F3 accord, agreement
Related adjective: eristic

contusion n
bruise, bump, discoloration, mark, blemish, injury, knock, lump, swelling
TECHNICAL ecchymosis

conundrum n
puzzle, problem, enigma, difficulty, quandary, poser, riddle, word game, anagram
COLLOQ. brainteaser, brain-twister

conurbation n
city, metropolitan area, metropolis, megalopolis, inner city, city centre, downtown, concrete jungle, urban sprawl, precinct, ghetto, suburbia, micropolis, cosmopolis, pentapolis, municipality, town, urban area, urban district; N Am metroplex
COLLOQ. big smoke

convalesce v
recuperate, recover, get better, get well, get stronger, regain your strength, improve, pick up, rally, revive
COLLOQ. pull through

convalescence n
recuperation, getting better, improvement, recovery, rehabilitation, restoration

> QUOTATIONS
> I enjoy convalescence. It is the part that makes illness worth while
> GEORGE BERNARD SHAW, *Back to Methuselah*

convene v
1 *convene a meeting*
call/bring (together), rally, summon
2 *the court convened*
assemble, meet, gather, collect, congregate, muster, come together
FORMAL convoke

convenience n
1 ACCESSIBILITY, availability, handiness, usefulness, use, ease of use, usability, utility, serviceability, service, benefit, advantage, advantageousness, help, suitability, fitness, appropriateness, opportuneness
FORMAL expediency, propitiousness, propinquity
2 *all modern conveniences*
facility, amenity, appliance, device, labour-saving device, gadget, service, resource
F3 **1** inconvenience

convenient adj
nearby, at hand, near/close at hand, within reach, within walking/driving distance, accessible, available, at your disposal, handy, useful, beneficial, helpful, labour-saving, easy, adapted, fitted, suited, suitable, fitting, appropriate, opportune, timely, well-timed, expedient; *dialect* gain
OLD advantageable, commodious, handsome, hend
COLLOQ. just/only round the corner, at your fingertips
F3 inconvenient, awkward

conveniently adv
accessibly, helpfully, usefully, suitably, appropriately, nearby, at hand, near/close at hand, within reach, within walking/driving distance
COLLOQ. just/only round the corner, at your fingertips
F3 inconveniently

convent n
nunnery, priory, cloister, abbey

convention n
1 CUSTOM, tradition, practice, use, usage, fashion, ceremony, protocol, etiquette, formality, matter of form, code, ethos, mores
FORMAL propriety, punctilio
2 ASSEMBLY, congress, conference, meeting, gathering, council, delegates, representatives, synod
FORMAL convocation, conclave

3 *the Geneva convention*
agreement, bond, commitment, engagement, covenant, treaty, pact, contract, transaction, deal, bargain, settlement, arrangement, understanding
FORMAL accord, compact, concordat

conventional *adj*
1 *a conventional person*
traditional, conservative, proper, correct, formal, conformist, hidebound
2 *a conventional approach*
unoriginal, routine, usual, customary, regular, standard, normal, ordinary, mainstream, straight, stereotyped, trite, pedestrian, commonplace, common, traditional, orthodox, formal, prevalent, prevailing, accepted, received, expected, ritual
COLLOQ. common-or-garden, run-of-the-mill
⊟ **1** unconventional, nonconformist **2** unusual, original, exotic, alternative

---

SYNONYM NUANCES

sense 1
Traditional suggests adherence to, or a liking for, long-established customs, and is often used with a tone of approval: *traditional pubs, lovingly restored*; whereas **conservative** tends more to suggest a reluctance to change, and is not particularly marked by favour or disfavour: *police society's conservative outlook*. The term **formal** suggests an adherence to etiquette, as do **proper** and **correct**, which also imply some agreement with this view.
Conformist has more to do with adherence to social norms, and, like **conservative**, is likely to take its tone from its context: *scientists tend to be more conformist than artists*. **Hidebound**, however, is more suggestive of being restricted by out-of-date practices, and so is inherently critical in tone: *hidebound attitudes of bureaucracy*.

---

conventionally *adv*
traditionally, formally, routinely, usually, commonly, regularly, normally, ordinarily
⊟ unconventionally, unusually

converge *v*
1 *crowds converged on the car*
approach, move towards, gather, close in, form, mass, focus, concentrate
2 *the roads converge at the bridge*
meet, join, combine, merge, coincide, unite, come together, intersect
⊟ **1** disperse **2** diverge

convergence *n*
concentration, approach, merging, combination, blending, meeting, coincidence, junction, intersection, union
FORMAL confluence
⊟ divergence, separation

conversant
■ **conversant with**
familiar with, acquainted with, experienced in, informed about, knowledgeable about, practised in, proficient in, skilled in, versed in, au fait with
FORMAL apprised of
⊟ ignorant of

conversation *n*
talk, chat, gossip, chitchat, discussion, discourse, dialogue, exchange, communication, tête-à-tête, heart-to-heart, cosy chat, table talk, small talk, pillow talk; *Aust* yabber
OLD parlance; *(Shakesp)* question; *(Spenser)* board
FORMAL colloquy, interlocution
COLLOQ. chinwag, natter, confab; *Aust* wongi

conversational *adj*
informal, chatty, colloquial, communicative, talkative, relaxed, casual

converse[1] *v*
converse with people
talk, speak, discuss, confer, communicate, chat, chitchat, gossip, chatter
OLD *(Shakesp)* propose, question, reason, relate
FORMAL commune, discourse
COLLOQ. natter

converse[2] *n, adj*
♦ *n*
the converse is true
opposite, reverse, contrary, obverse
FORMAL antithesis
COLLOQ. other way round, other side of the coin
♦ *adj*
opposite, opposing, reverse, counter, contrary, reversed, transposed, obverse
FORMAL antithetical

conversely *adv*
on the other hand, on the contrary, contrarily, contrariwise, obversely
FORMAL antithetically

conversion *n*
1 *a loft conversion*
alteration, change, transformation, turning, adaptation, modification, remodelling, reshaping, reconstruction, reorganization, customization, adjustment
TECHNICAL metamorphosis, transfiguration, mutation, transmutation
2 *conversion of pounds into francs*
change, exchange, substitution, switch
3 *conversion to Judaism*
persuasion, conviction, reformation, regeneration, rebirth, evangelization, proselytization, preaching

convert *v, n*
♦ *v*
1 *convert the building*
alter, change, turn, transform, make, adapt, customize, adjust, modify, go over to, transfer, switch, reform, restructure, remodel, reshape, refashion, restyle, revise, reorganize, rebuild, reconstruct
TECHNICAL metamorphose, transfigure, mutate, transmute
2 *convert inches into centimetres*
change, exchange, substitute, turn into, switch from
3 WIN OVER, convince, persuade, cause to change beliefs/religion, reform, evangelize, proselytize
4 CHANGE RELIGION, change beliefs, reform, move over, turn
COLLOQ. *Scot* jump/loup the dyke
♦ *n*
disciple, believer, new person, changed person, proselyte, neophyte, adherent

convertible *adj*
adaptable, adjustable, changeable, exchangeable, modifiable, interchangeable
FORMAL permutable

convex *adj*
rounded, curved out, bending outwards, bulging, swelling, protuberant, bow-fronted, gibbous
TECHNICAL nowy
⊟ concave, hollow

convey *v*
1 *convey feelings*
communicate, express, tell, relate, reveal, disclose, announce, make known, transmit, hand on, pass on
FORMAL impart
2 TRANSPORT, carry, bear, bring, fetch, move, transport, drive, shift, send, forward, deliver, transfer, conduct, guide, channel, pipe

conveyance *n*
1 VEHICLE, car, taxi, cab, bus, coach, bicycle, motorcycle, lorry, truck, van, wagon, carriage

2 *the conveyance of bicycles*
transport, transportation, movement, carriage, transfer, transference

3 *the conveyance of property*
transfer, transference, granting, transmission, consignment, delivery, bequeathal, ceding

convict *v, n*
♦ *v*
condemn, find guilty, sentence, judge, imprison
TECHNICAL crime
OLD reprove, attaint; (*Shakesp*) approve
♦ *n*
criminal, lawbreaker, felon, culprit, villain, offender, wrongdoer, prisoner, inmate, old hand, *forçat*
OLD emancipist
COLLOQ. crook, jailbird; *N Am* yardbird
SLANG lag, con; *Aust* canary

conviction *n*
1 BELIEF, view, opinion, faith, creed, tenet, principle
2 *speak with conviction*
assurance, confidence, fervour, wholeheartedness, earnestness, certainty, firmness, persuasion
FORMAL certitude
3 *previous convictions*
condemnation, pronouncement of guilt, sentence, judgement, imprisonment

convince *v*
assure, persuade, prove to, sway, talk into, talk over, win over, bring round, bring home, sell, induce, influence, prompt, satisfy
OLD resolve
FORMAL prevail upon

convincing *adj*
persuasive, powerful, telling, impressive, credible, plausible, likely, probable, conclusive, compelling, forceful, incontrovertible
FORMAL cogent
E3 unconvincing, improbable

SYNONYM NUANCES

Persuasive implies having the power to influence the mind or passions in a subtle way: *persuasive tax advantages*, whilst **compelling**, **forceful** and **powerful** could be used of a stronger, more immediately apparent case: *there is a compelling case for routine cancer screening; a powerful argument.*

The term **telling** may be used if you also want to suggest an action or idea has some significance: *the speech is short but very telling.* **Impressive** is the word to use to convey the additional sense of something producing a profound and positive effect: *he has impressive credentials.*

Both **credible** and **plausible** would suggest that some notion is highly believable or possible; to put more emphasis on the idea of it actually being true, you might choose **likely** or **probable.** **Conclusive** and **incontrovertible**, on the other hand, would be reserved for an unquestionable finality: *conclusive evidence; the facts were hard and incontrovertible.*

---

convincingly *adv*
persuasively, powerfully, tellingly, impressively, credibly, plausibly, conclusively, compellingly, forcefully
FORMAL cogently
E3 unconvincingly

convivial *adj*
friendly, sociable, genial, cheerful, cordial, festive, affable, hearty, jolly, jovial, lively, merry, fun-loving
E3 taciturn

conviviality *n*
friendliness, geniality, cheer, cordiality, sociability, gaiety, jollity, joviality, good feeling, bonhomie, liveliness, mirth, festivity, merrymaking, fun

convocation *n*
congress, convention, forum, council, assembly, conference, congregation, meeting, diet, synod
FORMAL conclave, forgathering, assemblage

convoluted *adj*
convoluted carvings/ideas
twisting, winding, meandering, tortuous, involved, complicated, complex
E3 straight, straightforward

convolution *n*
1 *convolutions in the design*
coil, twist, whorl, turn, spiral, helix, loop, coiling, winding, sinuousness, sinuosity
TECHNICAL gyrus
FORMAL curlicue
2 *convolutions in relationships*
complexity, intricacy, complication, entanglement, involvement, tortuousness

convoy *n*
fleet, line, escort, guard, protection, attendance, train, group, company

convulse *v*
suffer a fit/seizure, shake uncontrollably/violently, jerk, shudder, seize, unsettle, disturb

convulsion *n*
1 FIT, seizure, attack, paroxysm, spasm, cramp, contraction, tic, tremor
TECHNICAL ictus
2 *major political convulsions*
eruption, outburst, furore, disturbance, unrest, disorder, commotion, tumult, turmoil, agitation, turbulence, upheaval

convulsive *adj*
jerky, spasmodic, fitful, sporadic, uncontrolled, violent

cook *v*
prepare, heat, warm, put on, put together, make, improvise, undercook, underdo, overcook, overdo, burn
COLLOQ. rustle up, scare up, throw together
■ **cook up**
concoct, prepare, brew, invent, make up, falsify, fabricate, contrive, devise, plan, plot, scheme

---

PROVERBS
Too many cooks spoil the broth

Terms used in cookery include:

à la crème	caramelize	farci
à la Grècque	carve	fillet
à la mode	casserole	flambé
a la plancha	chargrill	flash fry
al dente	chasseur	Florentine
au gratin	chill	fold in
au naturel	chop	freeze
au poivre	chop suey	fricassee
bake	coddle	fry
bake blind	cordon bleu	fusion
balti	core	fu yung
barbecue	cream	glaze
bargar	crumble	grate
baste	cure	griddle
bhuna (or bhoona)	curry	grill
bind	deep-fry	grind
blanch	defrost	haute cuisine
blend	deglaze	ice
boil	devil	jalfrezi
bone	dopiaza	joint
bonne femme	drizzle	jug
braise	dum	jus
broil	dust	knead
brown	en cocotte	knock back
brûlé	en croûte	korma
cacciatore	en papillote	liquidize

Lyonnaise	poach	sieve
madras	pot-roast	sift
Marengo	potted	simmer
Marie Rose	*colloq.* prep	skim
marinate	preserve	smoke
masala	prove	souse
mash	Provençale	sous vide
microwave	purée	spit-roast
mince	reduce	steam
mix	re-heat	stew
mornay	rest	stir
mull	rise	stir-fry
Niçoise	roast	strain
nouvelle cuisine	rogan josh	stuff
oven-roast	roulade	sweat
parboil	roux	sweet-and-sour
peel	rub in	thicken
peppered	sauté	toast
pickle	scramble	truss
plate (up)	sear	whisk

See also **kitchen utensils**.

cool *adj, v, n*

♦ *adj*
1 CHILLY, fresh, breezy, nippy, cold, bracing, crisp, draughty
COLLOQ. parky
2 *a cool drink*
cold, chilled, iced, ice-cold, refreshing
3 CALM, unruffled, unexcited, composed, self-possessed, level-headed, collected, unemotional, dispassionate, quiet, relaxed, impassive, unmoved, placid, sedate, poised, imperturbable, unexcitable, unflustered, unperturbed, undisturbed, untroubled, unapprehensive
COLLOQ. laid-back, unflappable, cool as a cucumber
4 *a cool reception*
unfriendly, unwelcoming, cold, frigid, frosty, lukewarm, tepid, half-hearted, unenthusiastic, apathetic, uninterested, unresponsive, uncommunicative, undemonstrative, reserved, distant, aloof, standoffish
5 *look cool in that outfit*
sophisticated, fashionable, elegant, smart, stylish, chic
COLLOQ. trendy, streetwise
6 *a really cool party*
great, wonderful, excellent, fantastic, marvellous
COLLOQ. smashing, terrific, neat, ace, brill, out of this world, second to none
SLANG mega, wicked
E3 **1, 2** warm, hot **3** excited, angry **4** friendly, welcoming

♦ *v*
1 CHILL, refrigerate, ice, freeze, make/become cold, make/become colder, get/turn cold, get/turn colder, fan, air-condition
2 MODERATE, lessen, temper, dampen, diminish, subside, reduce, quiet, calm, allay
FORMAL abate, assuage
E3 **1** warm, heat **2** excite

♦ *n*
1 *keep/lose your cool*
composure, coolness, calmness, collectedness, poise, self-possession, self-discipline, self-control, control, temper
2 *the cool of the early morning*
chill, freshness, breeze, nippiness, cold, coldness, chilliness, crispness, draught
TECHNICAL defervescence, defervescency

cooling *n, adj*

♦ *n*
chilling, refrigeration, air-conditioning, ventilation
TECHNICAL defervescence, defervescency
E3 heating, warming

♦ *adj*
freezing, refrigerant, refrigerative, refrigeratory
E3 warming

coolly *adv*

1 CALMLY, unexcitedly, composedly, level-headedly, collectedly, unemotionally, dispassionately, quietly, impassively, placidly, sedately, imperturbably, unexcitably
2 *coolly received ideas*
half-heartedly, unenthusiastically, apathetically, uninterestedly, unresponsively, reservedly, distantly, standoffishly, coldly, frostily

coop *n, v*

♦ *n*
cage, box, enclosure, pen, hutch, pound, run
■ **coop up**
imprison, cage, enclose, shut (up), confine, impound, shut in, keep in, close in, lock up/away, pen
FORMAL incarcerate, immure

co-operate *v*

collaborate, work together, pull together, band together, team up, help, assist, aid, contribute, participate, combine, unite, join forces, play along, work side by side, share, pool, pool your resources, put your heads together, pull your weight, conspire
COLLOQ. play ball

co-operation *n*

helpfulness, help, helping hand, assistance, aid, contribution, participation, collaboration, teamwork, working together, unity, co-ordination, joint action, concerted action/effort, give-and-take, team spirit, *esprit de corps*
E3 opposition, rivalry, competition

co-operative *adj*

1 COLLECTIVE, joint, shared, combined, united, concerted, co-ordinated, collaborative, working together
2 HELPFUL, helping, assisting, supportive, responsive, obliging, accommodating, willing, compliant
FORMAL coactive
E3 **2** unco-operative, rebellious

co-ordinate *v*

1 ORGANIZE, arrange, systematize, order, work together, co-operate, collaborate, tabulate, integrate, mesh, synchronize, correlate, regulate
FORMAL ordinate
COLLOQ. join up
2 *co-ordinate colours*
harmonize, match, complement, blend (in), adapt, go, go together, go well, be/make compatible
COLLOQ. mix 'n' match

co-ordination *n*

1 ORGANIZATION, ordering, arrangement, co-operation, collaboration, integration
2 COMPATIBILITY, harmony, matching, complementation, blending

cop *n, v*

♦ *n*
police officer, officer, policeman, policewoman, constable, PC
COLLOQ. copper, bobby, rozzer
SLANG pig, nark, bizzy, flatfoot, bluebottle, bull
■ **cop out**
avoid, evade, stay/keep away from, elude, sidestep, escape, run away from, get out of, bypass, get round, balk, prevent, avert, shun, abstain from, hold back from, shy away from, steer clear of, make a detour, keep your distance from
COLLOQ. hedge, duck, dodge, shirk, wriggle/worm your way out of, give a miss, give a wide berth to

cope *v*

manage, carry on, survive, get by, get through, make do, succeed, take in your stride
FORMAL subsist

■ **cope with**
deal with, encounter, contend with, struggle with, grapple with, wrestle with, handle, manage, treat, weather, endure, face
🔁 *colloq.* not hack it

copious *adj*
abundant, plentiful, inexhaustible, overflowing, profuse, rich, lavish, bountiful, liberal, full, ample, generous, extensive, numerous, great, huge
FORMAL plenteous, bounteous, luxuriant
COLLOQ. bags of
🔁 scarce, meagre

cop-out *n*
excuse, dodge, evasion, fraud, pretence, pretext, alibi
COLLOQ. get-out, shirking, passing the buck

copse *n*
coppice, wood, thicket, grove, bush, brush

copulate *v*
mate, make love, have sex, have sexual intercourse, go to bed with, enjoy, horse, line
OLD gender, mell
COLLOQ. fool around, get off with, go all the way
SLANG get your leg over, have, lay, make it with, have it off with, bed, bonk, bang; (taboo) screw, hump, shag, stuff, fuck

copulation *n*
sexual intercourse, sex, union, intimacy, coupling, love-making, marriage-bed, bed, sleeping with someone, going to bed with someone, mating, relations
OLD commixtion, embraces
FORMAL consummation, coitus, coition, carnal knowledge, congress
COLLOQ. how's your father, it; *Aust & NZ* naughty
SLANG lay, bang, bonk, leg-over, wham bam thank you ma'am, greens, jig-a-jig, knee-trembler, quickie; *N Am* jazz, poontang, nooky, pussy, rumpy-pumpy, tail; (taboo) fuck, fucking, screw, screwing, shag, shagging

copy *n, v*
♦ *n*
1 *copies of the letter*
duplicate, facsimile, fax, carbon copy, photocopy, Photostat®, Xerox®, reproduction, print, tracing, transcript, transcription, replica, model, pattern, archetype, representation, image, likeness, counterfeit, forgery, fake, imitation, borrowing, plagiarism, crib
COLLOQ. knock-off
2 *buy a copy of the magazine*
issue, sample, example, specimen
🔁 1 original
♦ *v*
duplicate, photocopy, Photostat®, Xerox®, reproduce, print, trace, transcribe, fax, scan, forge, counterfeit, pirate, simulate, imitate, impersonate, mimic, ape, parrot, repeat, echo, mirror, follow, emulate, borrow, plagiarize, crib
FORMAL replicate

SYNONYM NUANCES

verb
Duplicate can be used to suggest creating something identical, but may occasionally further imply wastefulness: *efforts to eliminate duplicating research and expenditure.* **Scan** has the specific usage of using photographic technology for copying purposes.
  Pirate, like **forge** and **counterfeit**, is only used in the context of illegal activity; **plagiarize** and **crib** also imply dishonest copying, this time stealing another's ideas. To convey the idea of copying a person's style, you could use **imitate** or **mirror**, especially where there is an element of trying to be like someone admired: *his style imitated that of Keats*; this is even more strongly suggested by **follow** and **emulate**.
  However, if you want to convey the idea of assuming another's character for humour or ridicule, you could use **impersonate** or **mimic**: *I mimicked his slow accent.*

Ape similarly suggests imitation but further implies that it is not completely successful: *the bourgeoisie, who aped aristocratic style.*
  The terms **repeat** and **echo** have more to do with copying sounds and speech, though the latter may also be used figuratively; *he echoed the thoughts of many.*
Parrot is similar in sense but tends to be rather derogatory in tone: *all he does is parrot what his boss says.*

---

coquettish *adj*
flirtatious, seductive, amorous, provocative, dallying, flighty, flirty, inviting, teasing
COLLOQ. come-hither, vampish

cord *n*
string, twine, thread, ribbon, lace, rope, line, cable, flex, connection, link, bond, tie
Related adjective: funicular

cordial *adj*
friendly, amicable, affable, affectionate, agreeable, cheerful, genial, sociable, pleasant, heartfelt, warm, warm-hearted, welcoming, wholehearted, earnest, hearty, stimulating, invigorating
🔁 hostile, aloof, cool

cordiality *n*
friendliness, affability, affection, agreeableness, cheerfulness, geniality, sociability, heartiness, warmth, welcome, wholeheartedness, earnest, sincerity
🔁 coolness, hostility

cordially *adv*
amicably, affably, cheerfully, genially, sociably, pleasantly, warmly, warm-heartedly, wholeheartedly

cordon *n, v*
♦ *n*
line, ring, barrier, chain, fence, column
■ **cordon off**
close off, fence off, seal off, isolate, separate, encircle, enclose, surround

core *n, adj*
♦ *n*
kernel, nucleus, heart, centre, middle, interior, nub, crux, essence, substance, gist
FORMAL quintessence
COLLOQ. nitty-gritty
🔁 surface, exterior
♦ *adj*
essential, fundamental, basic, intrinsic, inherent, innate, underlying, principal, main, key, central, crucial, vital, characteristic, definitive, typical, constituent
🔁 incidental

cork *n*
stopper, plug, bung, seal, stop, cover, lid

corn *n*
arable crop, cereal crop, cereal, wheat, barley, oats, rye, maize, grain
Related adjective: frumentarious

corner *n, v*
♦ *n*
1 *round the corner*
angle, joint, crook, bend, curve, turning, fork, junction, intersection
2 NOOK, cranny, niche, recess, crevice, cavity, hole, hideout, hideaway, retreat
3 *in a tight corner*
predicament, plight, situation, hardship, straits
COLLOQ. tight spot, nowhere to turn, hole, jam, fix, scrape, pickle
♦ *v*
1 *corner an animal*
force into a place, trap, hunt down, catch, cut off, block off, run to earth, confine

2 *corner the market*
monopolize, control, dominate, have sole rights in
COLLOQ. hog
■ **round/around the corner**
1 IMMINENT, impending, approaching, coming, near, close, looming, in the air, about to happen
2 NEAR, nearby, close, close by, within reach, within range, at hand, accessible, convenient, local, neighbouring
COLLOQ. a stone's throw (away)

cornerstone *n*
basis, support, base, groundwork, bedrock, mainstay, key, keystone, keyhole, fundamental(s), fundamental point, starting-point, (basic) principle, first principles, main ingredient, alpha and omega, essential(s), essence, heart, core, thrust

corny *adj*
banal, commonplace, hackneyed, stale, overused, stereotyped, trite, clichéd, sentimental, dull, feeble, maudlin, mawkish, old-fashioned, platitudinous
Ea new, original

corollary *n*
consequence, conclusion, result, upshot, deduction, induction, inference
FORMAL illation
TECHNICAL function

coronation *n*
enthronement, crowning, accession to the throne

coronet *n*
crown, diadem, tiara, circlet, wreath, garland

corporal *adj*
anatomical, bodily, fleshly, carnal, material, substantial, concrete, actual, physical, tangible, corporeal
FORMAL somatic
Ea spiritual

corporate *adj*
combined, collective, concerted, joint, common, communal, merged, pooled, shared, united, allied, amalgamated, collaborative

corporation *n*
1 *a business corporation*
firm, company, business, concern, association, organization, establishment, house, partnership, syndicate, cartel, trust, consortium, conglomerate, multinational, industry, holding company
2 *the Corporation of London*
council, authority, authorities, governing body
3 PAUNCH, belly, pot-belly, beer belly

corporeal *adj*
actual, material, physical, substantial, concrete, tangible, bodily, fleshly, human, mortal, carnal, corporal
Ea spiritual

corps *n*
band, body, detachment, unit, squad, team, division, brigade, company, contingent, crew, regiment, squadron

corpse *n*
body, dead body, carcase/carcass, cadaver, skeleton, remains, mummy, zombie; *Scot* like
OLD relics, corse
COLLOQ. deader
SLANG stiff, flatliner

corpulent *adj*
fat, fattish, large, obese, overweight, plump, stout, beefy, bulky, burly, fleshy, portly, pot-bellied, podgy, roly-poly, tubby, well-padded
FORMAL rotund, adipose
Ea thin

corpus *n*
collection, compilation, body, entirety, whole
FORMAL aggregation

corral *n*
enclosure, fold, pound, stall, coop, sty, kraal

correct *adj, v*
♦ *adj*
1 *the correct answer*
right, accurate, precise, exact, strict, true, truthful, actual, real, faithful, word-perfect, faultless, flawless, unerring
COLLOQ. spot-on, bang on
2 PROPER, acceptable, accepted, standard, regular, right, just, appropriate, suitable, fitting, conventional
OLD seemly
COLLOQ. OK
Ea **1** incorrect, wrong, inaccurate
♦ *v*
1 *correct an error*
rectify, put right, right, set right, sort (out), put straight, fix, remedy, cure, debug, redress, adjust, regulate, revise, improve, amend, tweak
FORMAL emend, ameliorate, disabuse
COLLOQ. put the record straight
2 PUNISH, discipline, reprimand, reprove, scold, rebuke, reform, rehabilitate
FORMAL admonish

correction *n*
1 *corrections to the text*
rectification, remedying, adjustment, alteration, modification, amendment, improvement, tweak
FORMAL emendation, amelioration
2 PUNISHMENT, discipline, reprimand, chastisement, reproof, scolding, rebuke, reform, reformation, rehabilitation
FORMAL admonition

corrective *adj*
1 *corrective measures*
remedial, curative, medicinal, palliative, restorative, therapeutic
FORMAL emendatory
2 DISCIPLINARY, disciplinary, penal, punitive, reformatory, rehabilitative

correctly *adv*
1 ACCURATELY, rightly, right, exactly, precisely, actually, faultlessly, flawlessly, unerringly
2 PROPERLY, acceptably, appropriately, suitably, fittingly, conventionally
Ea **1** incorrectly, wrongly, inaccurately

correlate *v*
associate, compare, connect, show a connection/relationship, co-ordinate, correspond, agree, equate, tally, interact, link, parallel, relate, tie in

correlation *n*
association, connection, relationship, correspondence, equivalence, interaction, interchange, interdependence, interrelationship, link, reciprocity, fit

correspond *v*
1 MATCH, match up, fit (together), answer, conform, tally, square, agree, be in agreement, be consistent, coincide, harmonize, sympathize, balance, dovetail, complement, be similar, be equivalent, represent
TECHNICAL assonate
FORMAL concur, correlate, accord, be analogous
2 COMMUNICATE, write, pen, exchange letters, keep in touch

correspondence *n*
1 COMMUNICATION, writing, letters, post, mail, email
2 CONFORMITY, agreement, coincidence, relation, analogy, comparison, comparability, similarity, resemblance, equivalence, harmony, match, fit
FORMAL concurrence, correlation, congruity, consonance
Ea **2** divergence, incongruity

correspondent *n*
journalist, reporter, contributor, columnist, writer, letter-writer, pen friend, pen pal

corresponding *adj*
matching, complementary, reciprocal, interrelated, comparable, relative, equivalent, similar, like, agreeing, congruent, parallel, identical
FORMAL commensurate, analogous

corridor *n*
aisle, passageway, passage, gangway, hallway, hall, lobby

corroborate *v*
confirm, prove, bear out, verify, support, back up, endorse, ratify, certify, substantiate, validate, authenticate, document, underpin, uphold, sustain
FORMAL evidence, attest
F3 contradict

corroboration *n*
confirmation, verification, endorsement, ratification, substantiation, authentication, validation
FORMAL attestation
F3 contradiction

corroborative *adj*
confirming, confirmatory, supporting, supportive, verifying, endorsing, substantiating, validating
FORMAL confirmative, evidential, evidentiary, verificatory

corrode *v*
erode, wear away, eat away, etch, consume, destroy, waste, burn, fret, rust, oxidize, tarnish, impair, deteriorate, rot, crumble, disintegrate
FORMAL abrade

corrosion *n*
erosion, wasting, burning, rusting, tarnishing, deterioration, rot, rotting, disintegration
FORMAL abrasion

corrosive *adj*
corroding, acid, caustic, cutting, abrasive, wearing, consuming, destructive, wasting
TECHNICAL erosive

corrugated *adj*
ridged, fluted, grooved, channelled, furrowed, wrinkled, folded, crinkled, rumpled, creased
TECHNICAL striate

corrupt *adj, v*
♦ *adj*
rotten, unscrupulous, unprincipled, unethical, immoral, evil, wicked, fraudulent, dishonest, untrustworthy, bribable, venal, depraved, degenerate, debauched, obscene, abusive, barbarous, dissolute, tainted, contaminated, impure
COLLOQ. shady, bent, crooked
F3 ethical, virtuous, upright, honest, fair, trustworthy
♦ *v*
1 CONTAMINATE, spoil, pollute, decay, canker, poison, putrefy, rot, adulterate, taint, infect, mar, blight, defile, debase, debauch, pervert, deprave, demoralize, subvert, barbarize, bastardize, warp, be a bad influence, lead astray, lure, seduce, bribe, suborn
OLD empoison, inquinate
COLLOQ. buy (off), grease someone's palm
2 *corrupt a piece of text*
tamper with, adulterate, contaminate, falsify, defile, debase, doctor
FORMAL vitiate
F3 1 purify

corruption *n*
1 IMMORALITY, unscrupulousness, impurity, depravity, degeneration, degradation, perversion, debauchery, abuse, distortion, dishonesty, fraud, bribery, subornation, extortion, sharp practice, vice, wickedness, iniquity, evil, criminality, villainy, contamination, pollution, rottenness; N Am graft
COLLOQ. wheeling and dealing, crookedness, shadiness, sleaze
2 *a corruption of a Maori word*
alteration, adaptation, modification
F3 1 honesty, virtue, fairness, trustworthiness

SYNONYM NUANCES

sense 1
Immorality can be widely used to suggest behaviour that is inconsistent with accepted moral standards. **Impurity** implies being tainted in some way, and can be used both of physical and moral corruption: *there was a lethal impurity in the drug*. **Contamination** and **pollution** echo this idea, while **rottenness** suggests the ultimate state of decay or badness, and implies a very unfavourable judgement.

Depravity is a powerful term suggesting a state of complete wickedness, while **degeneration** is only slightly less condemnatory, and suggests heading down that route: *unrivalled degeneration among the young*. **Degradation** is another emotive word, but has elements of disgrace or humiliation: *the degradation of women through pornography*. **Debauchery** is more suggestive of a lewd lifestyle and is strongly censorious in tone. You can use **vice**, **wickedness**, **iniquity** and **evil** to suggest the varying degrees of extreme moral corruption, but all of these make a clear judgement.

The term **sharp practice** describes acts that perhaps just manage to stay just within the law, while **criminality** is specifically used of illegal activity: *the dividing line between sharp practice and criminality is becoming increasingly thin*. **Villainy** is similar but rather old-fashioned or literary in tone.

---

corset *n*
girdle, panty girdle, shaper, belt, bodice, corselet, foundation garment, stays, busk, roll-on, waspie

cortège *n*
procession, retinue, suite, train, column, entourage, cavalcade, parade

cosily *adv*
snugly, comfortably, warmly, safely, securely, initmately

cosmetic *adj*
1 *a cosmetic substance*
make-up, beauty, beautifying
2 *cosmetic changes*
superficial, surface, external, shallow, skin-deep, peripheral, minor, slight, trivial
F3 2 basic, essential

cosmetics

Types of cosmetics include:

blusher	face powder	mascara
bronzer	false eyelashes	moisturizer
cleanser	foundation	nail polish
concealer	greasepaint	nail varnish
eyebrow pencil	highlighter	pancake make-up
eyelash dye	kohl pencil	panstick
eyeliner	lip gloss	pressed powder
eye shadow	lip liner	rouge
face cream	lipstick	toner
face mask	loose powder	
face pack	maquillage	

---

cosmic *adj*
1 *cosmic forces*
worldwide, universal, in/from space, infinite, limitless, measureless
2 *changes of cosmic proportion*
immense, vast, huge, enormous, colossal, massive, grandiose, infinite, limitless, immeasurable, measureless
SLANG mega, seismic

cosmonaut *n*
astronaut, spaceman, spacewoman, space traveller, taikonaut

cosmopolitan *adj*
1 *a very cosmopolitan city*
international, universal, multiracial, multicultural
2 *a very cosmopolitan outlook*
worldly, worldly-wise, well-travelled, broad-minded,
sophisticated, cultured, urbane
⊟ 2 insular, parochial

cosmos *n*
universe, creation, galaxy, system, worlds

cosset *v*
coddle, mollycoddle, baby, pamper, indulge, overindulge,
spoil, pet, fondle, cuddle, cherish

cost *n, v*
♦ *n*
1 EXPENSE, outlay, payment, expenditure, charge, price,
selling price, asking price, rate, fee, tariff, levy, toll,
quotation, amount, figure, value, valuation, worth
FORMAL disbursement
COLLOQ. damage
2 *cover costs*
budget, expenses, expenditure, spending, outgoings,
outlay, overheads
FORMAL disbursements
3 *the cost to her health of smoking*
harm, injury, hurt, loss, suffering, deprivation, detriment,
sacrifice, penalty, price
♦ *v*
1 *it costs £500*
pay, charge, be priced at, ask for, sell for, retail at, buy
for, be valued at, be worth, fetch, go for, come to, amount
to
COLLOQ. set back, knock back
2 *cost a job*
price, estimate, cost out, quote, value, calculate, work out
3 *cost him his life*
cause the loss/sacrifice of, cause harm/injury, destroy,
deprive, take, harm, injure, hurt, be a high price to pay

costly *adj*
1 EXPENSIVE, dear, exorbitant, extortionate, excessive, lavish,
rich, splendid, valuable, precious, high-cost, high-priced,
overpriced, priceless
OLD chargeful
COLLOQ. steep, pricey, posh, sky-high, costing an arm and
a leg, costing the earth, costing a bomb, daylight robbery;
N Am big-ticket
OLD SLANG salt
2 HARMFUL, damaging, destructive, detrimental, disastrous,
ruinous, catastrophic, loss-making
FORMAL deleterious
⊟ 1 cheap, inexpensive

costume *n*
outfit, uniform, livery, ensemble, robes, vestments, suit,
dress, style of dress, fashion, clothes, clothing, garments,
garb, habit, fancy dress
FORMAL apparel, attire
COLLOQ. get-up, clobber, rig-out
SLANG threads

cosy *adj*
snug, comfortable, warm, sheltered, secure, safe, homely,
congenial, intimate
COLLOQ. comfy
⊟ uncomfortable, cold

coterie *n*
set, circle, clique, group, club, association, community,
faction, camp, caucus, cabal, gang

cottage *n*
lodge, chalet, bungalow, villa, hut, cabin, shack,
shanty

couch *n, v*
♦ *n*
sofa, settee, chesterfield, chaise-longue, ottoman, divan,
bed, day bed, sofa bed

♦ *v*
express, frame, phrase, word, set, bear, support,
utter, cradle

cough *v, n*
♦ *v*
clear your throat, bark, hack, hawk, hem
♦ *n*
bark, hack, rasp, croak, hawking, hem, clearing your
throat
TECHNICAL tussis
OLD (*Shakesp*) tisick
COLLOQ. frog in your throat
■ **cough up**
pay up, pay, pay out, hand over, give;
N Am ante up
COLLOQ. fork out, shell out, stump up

council *n*
1 *the town council*
local authority, corporation, cabinet, ministry, chamber,
parliament, government, governing body, senate,
administration, executive
2 *the Arts Council*
advisory body, advisory group, committee, panel, jury,
commission, directorate, directors, trustees, governors,
advisers, board, working party, focus group, management
3 *a ministerial council*
congress, assembly, convention, conference, forum,
gathering, rally, meeting, convocation, group, body, body
of people, company, congregation, flock, crowd,
multitude, throng
FORMAL convocation
Related adjective: conciliar

> **❗ council** or **counsel**?
> A *council* is 'a body of people who organize, control,
> advise or take decisions': *a county council. Counsel* is
> a rather formal word for 'advice': *give wise counsel.*

counsel *n, v*
♦ *n*
1 ADVICE, suggestion, recommendation, guidance,
direction, information, consultation, conferring,
conference, deliberation, consideration, forethought,
opinion, viewpoint, moralism
OLD (*Spenser*) read
FORMAL exhortation, admonition
2 *counsel for the defence*
lawyer, advocate, solicitor, attorney, barrister, *avocat*
consultant
♦ *v*
advise, warn, caution, suggest, recommend, advocate,
urge, exhort, guide, give guidance, direct, teach, instruct,
give your opinion
OLD aread, rede
FORMAL admonish

counsellor *n*
consultant, authority, guide, teacher, tutor,
instructor, coach, mentor, therapist, guru,
confidant(e)

count *v, n*
♦ *v*
1 NUMBER, enumerate, list, include, reckon, calculate,
compute, tell, check, add (up), total, score, tally
COLLOQ. tot up
2 MATTER, be important, signify, qualify, carry weight,
make a difference, make an impression, mean something
COLLOQ. cut some ice
3 *count yourself lucky*
consider, regard, judge, think, reckon, look upon, hold,
feel
FORMAL esteem, deem
4 *if you count children*
include, take account of, take into account, take into
consideration, consider, allow for

♦ *n*
numbering, enumeration, poll, reckoning, calculation,
computation, sum, total, tally, number, whole, full amount
COLLOQ. totting-up

■ **count in**
include, involve, let in on, put in, introduce, allow for,
allow to take part in
COLLOQ. rope in

■ **count on**
depend on, rely on, bank on, lean on, reckon on, swear
by, expect, believe, trust

■ **count out**
exclude, eliminate, ignore, leave out, omit, pass over,
disregard, include out
E3 include, consider

> **PROVERBS**
> Don't count your chickens before they are hatched

countenance *n, v*
♦ *n*
face, expression, appearance, features, look
FORMAL mien, physiognomy, visage
♦ *v*
tolerate, agree, allow, permit, approve, brook,
stand for, put up with, back, condone, endorse, endure,
sanction

counter[1] *n*
1 *serve at the counter*
worktop, surface, work surface, table, stand, bar
2 *a counter in a game*
disc, token, chip, piece, coin, marker

counter[2] *v, adv, adj*
♦ *v*
counter someone's argument
parry, resist, oppose, combat, dispute, offset, answer,
respond, retaliate, retort, hit back at, return, meet
♦ *adv*
against, in opposition, contrary, conversely
♦ *adj*
contrary, opposite, opposing, conflicting, contradictory,
contrasting, opposed, against, adverse

counteract *v*
neutralize, counterbalance, offset, act against, oppose,
resist, hinder, check, thwart, frustrate, prevent, foil, defeat,
undo, annul, invalidate
FORMAL negate, countervail
E3 support, assist

counterbalance *v*
balance, compensate for, make up for, equalize,
neutralize, offset, undo
FORMAL counterpoise, countervail

counterfeit *adj, n, v*
♦ *adj*
fake, faked, false, forged, copied, pirate, fraudulent, bogus,
sham, spurious, imitation, artificial, simulated, pretended,
borrowed, queer, base, snide, postiche
FORMAL feigned, simular
COLLOQ. phoney, pseud, pseudo, brummagem
E3 genuine, authentic, real
♦ *n*
fake, forgery, copy, reproduction, imitation, fraud, sham,
dummy
COLLOQ. dud
♦ *v*
fake, forge, fabricate, copy, imitate, disguise, phantasm,
reproduce, pirate, impersonate, falsify, pretend, simulate,
sham, camouflage
FORMAL feign
COLLOQ. phoney

countermand *v*
cancel, reverse, annul, override, overturn, quash, repeal
FORMAL abrogate, rescind, revoke

counterpart *n*
equivalent, opposite number, equal, complement,
supplement, parallel, match, fellow, mate, peer, twin,
duplicate, copy, obverse

counterpoint *n, v*
♦ *n*
contrast, foil, differentiation, set-off, opposite, relief,
complement
♦ *v*
contrast, differentiate, set off, foil, enhance, heighten,
intensify, throw into relief

countless *adj*
innumerable, myriad, numberless, unnumbered, untold,
incalculable, infinite, endless, without end, legion,
immeasurable, measureless, inexhaustible, limitless,
boundless
COLLOQ. umpteen
E3 finite, limited

countrified *adj*
rural, rustic, pastoral, provincial, idyllic, agricultural,
agrarian, outback
FORMAL bucolic
COLLOQ. hick
E3 urban; *formal* oppidan

country *n, adj*
♦ *n*
1 STATE, nation, kingdom, realm, republic, power,
community, principality, inhabitants, people, population,
populace, public, residents, citizens, voters, electors
2 COUNTRYSIDE, green belt, farmland, moorland, rural area,
outback, bush
COLLOQ. provinces, backwater, backwoods, wilds, sticks,
back of beyond, middle of nowhere; *Aust & NZ* beyond
the black stump
Related adjective: rural
3 TERRAIN, land, territory, region, area, district,
neighbourhood, locality
E3 2 town, city
♦ *adj*
rural, rustic, pastoral, landed, provincial, idyllic,
agricultural, agrarian
FORMAL bucolic
E3 urban

> **QUOTATIONS**
> I vow to thee, my country – all earthly things above – /
> Entire and whole and perfect, the service of my love
>   SIR CECIL SPRING-RICE, *I Vow To Thee, My Country*
>
> My country is the world, and my religion is to do good
>   THOMAS PAINE, *The Rights of Man*
>
> The city has a face, the country a soul
>   JACQUES DE LACRETELLE, *Idées dans un chapeau*

countryman, countrywoman *n*
1 *fellow countrywomen*
compatriot, fellow citizen, fellow national
2 *local countrymen's skills*
farmer, yokel, boor, clodhopper, rustic, peasant,
provincial, backwoodsman, bushwhacker; *Scot* hind
COLLOQ. bumpkin, hillbilly, hick, hayseed

countryside *n*
landscape, scenery, country, green belt, farmland,
moorland, rural area, outdoors

county *n*
shire, province, region, area, state, territory, district,
department
Related adjective: comital

coup *n*
1 *a military coup*
coup d'état, overthrow, revolution, (military) takeover,
uprising, insurrection, palace revolution, putsch, rebellion,
revolt

2 *a big coup for the company*
feat, success, triumph, masterstroke, stroke, accomplishment, deed, exploit, stunt, action, manoeuvre, tour de force

coup de grâce *n*
death blow, finishing blow
FORMAL quietus
COLLOQ. clincher, kiss of death, kibosh, kill

coup d'état *n*
coup, overthrow, revolution, (military) takeover, uprising, insurrection, palace revolution, putsch, rebellion, revolt

couple *n, v*
♦ *n*
pair, husband and wife, newlyweds, partners, lovers, brace, twosome, duo
♦ *v*
pair, match, marry, wed, unite, join, link, connect, combine, integrate, ally, associate, attach, fasten, hitch, clasp, bind, buckle, yoke
FORMAL conjoin

coupon *n*
voucher, token, slip, check, stub, counterfoil, docket, ticket, certificate, form

courage *n*
bravery, pluck, fearlessness, dauntlessness, heroism, gallantry, valour, boldness, audacity, intrepidity, daring, determination, resolution, spirit, mettle, backbone, heart, gumption
FORMAL fortitude
COLLOQ. nerve, guts, bottle, spunk, grit, stomach
SLANG balls; *N Am* cojones, moxie
See Synonym nuances panel at **bravery**.
◄ cowardice, fear

courageous *adj*
brave, plucky, fearless, dauntless, indomitable, heroic, gallant, valiant, lion-hearted, stout-hearted, full-hearted, high-hearted, hardy, bold, audacious, daring, intrepid, adventurous, determined, resolute
FORMAL valorous
COLLOQ. gutsy, spunky, feisty
◄ cowardly, afraid

courageously *adv*
bravely, boldly, fearlessly, audaciously, intrepidly, dauntlessly, indomitably, heroically, gallantly, valiantly, resolutely, adventurously
◄ fearfully, timidly

courier *n*
1 *the courier delivered the parcels*
messenger, carrier, dispatch rider, runner, bearer, emissary, envoy, representative, herald, legate, nuncio, estafette, pursuivant
2 *a guided tour by the courier*
guide, travel guide, tour guide, escort, company representative
COLLOQ. rep

course *n, v*
♦ *n*
1 CURRICULUM, syllabus, programme, schedule, classes, lessons, lectures, studies
2 FLOW, movement, advance, march, rise, progress, development, unfolding, furtherance, order, sequence, series, succession, progression
3 DURATION, time, period, lapse, term, spell, span, passing, passage
4 ROUTE, direction, way, passage, path, track, tack, road, lane, run, channel, trail, line, circuit, orbit, ambit, trajectory, flight path
5 *course of action*
plan, schedule, programme, policy, procedure, system, process, manner, method, way, approach, tack
FORMAL mode
6 *the last hole on the course*
golf course, racecourse, racetrack, track, ground, circuit

7 *chicken for main course*
dish, part, stage, remove, starter, *hors d'œuvre*, appetizer, entrée, main course, dessert, sweet, pudding, entremets
8 *a course of medical treatment*
sequence, series, programme, schedule, regimen
♦ *v*
1 *tears coursing down her cheeks*
flow, run, move, pour, gush, stream, surge, race, dash
2 *coursing hares*
chase, hunt, pursue, run after, follow, track, race
■ **in due course**
in time, in due time, sooner or later, in the fullness of time, in the course of time, finally, eventually
■ **of course**
naturally, certainly, surely, by all means, definitely, without a doubt, no doubt, undoubtedly, doubtlessly, needless to say, to be sure
FORMAL indubitably
SLANG natch

court *n, v*
♦ *n*
1 LAWCOURT, bench, bar, judiciary, tribunal, trial, session, assizes, see
2 *tennis courts*
playing area, game area, enclosure, track, ground, arena, ring, alley, green
3 COURTYARD, yard, quadrangle, square, patio, cloister, forecourt, enclosure, plaza, esplanade, piazza
COLLOQ. quad
4 *at the king's court*
palace, castle, royal residence
5 ENTOURAGE, attendants, household, retinue, suite, train, cortège
♦ *v*
1 *court a young lady*
woo, pursue, chase, go out with, go around/round with, go with, date, go steady
2 *court support/publicity*
cultivate, try to win, solicit, flatter, pander to, curry favour with, ingratiate yourself with, attract, prompt, provoke, incite, seek, invite, risk
COLLOQ. *N Am* cozy up with

Types of court include:

Admiralty Division	court of justice	International Court
assizes	Court of	of Justice
Central Criminal	Protection	juvenile court
Court	Court of Session	Lord Chancellor's
Chancery Division	criminal court	Court
children's court	crown court	magistrates' court
circuit court	district court	municipal court
civil court	divorce court	Old Bailey
coroner's court	European Court of	police court
county court	Justice	Privy Council
court-martial	family court	sheriff court
court of appeals	federal court	small claims court
court of claims	High Court	Supreme Court
Court of Common	High Court of	
Pleas	Justiciary	
Court of	House of Lords	
Exchequer	Industrial tribunals	

---

courteous *adj*
polite, civil, respectful, well-mannered, well-bred, deferential, ladylike, gentlemanly, mannerly, gracious, obliging, considerate, kind, diplomatic, tactful, attentive, gallant, chivalrous, courtly, urbane, debonair, refined, polished
◄ discourteous, impolite, rude

courteously *adv*
politely, civilly, respectfully, deferentially, graciously, obligingly, considerately, kindly, diplomatically, tactfully, attentively, gallantly, chivalrously, urbanely, refinedly
◄ discourteously, impolitely, rudely

courtesy n

politeness, civility, respect, etiquette, (good) manners, (good) breeding, deference, graciousness, consideration, kindness, favour, generosity, tact, attention, gallantry, chivalry, refinement, urbanity, gentility, devoir
OLD gentilesse; (Shakesp) gentry
FORMAL comity
E3 discourtesy, incivility, rudeness

courtier n

noble, nobleman, lord, lady, lady-in-waiting, steward, page, attendant, cup-bearer, train-bearer, subject, liegeman, follower, flatterer, sycophant, toady

courtly adj

gracious, dignified, polite, refined, obliging, polished, elegant, stately, aristocratic, high-bred, lordly, ceremonious, gallant, chivalrous, civil, formal, decorous, flattering
E3 inelegant, provincial, rough

courtship n

wooing, pursuit, suit, courting, chasing, going-out, dating, going steady, romance, affair
OLD (Shakesp) love-suit

courtyard n

yard, quadrangle, area, enclosure, court, square, cloister, forecourt, plaza, patio, esplanade, atrium, cortile, garth, marae
COLLOQ. quad

cove n

bay, bight, inlet, estuary, firth, fiord, creek

covenant n, v

♦ n
arrangement, promise, contract, bond, commitment, deed, engagement, pact, pledge, treaty, trust, convention, stipulation, undertaking
OLD warranty
FORMAL testament, indenture, compact, concordat
Related adjective: federal
♦ v
agree, contract, promise, stipulate, undertake, engage, pledge, vow

cover v, n

♦ v
1 HIDE, put/place over, conceal, bury, obscure, shroud, veil, wreathe, screen, mask, disguise, camouflage
2 covered with mud
be over, coat, spread, overspread, daub, plaster, cake, encase, wrap, envelop, blanket, carpet, swaddle, clothe, dress, overlay
FORMAL attire, accoutre
3 SHELTER, put/place over, protect, shield, guard, safeguard, defend
4 cover a topic
deal with, treat, consider, examine, investigate, give details of, review, survey, report, describe, encompass, embrace, incorporate, embody, involve, include, contain, comprise, take in
5 cover 25 miles
travel (over), cross, go, go across, journey, do
FORMAL traverse
6 cover for a colleague
stand in for, fill in for, deputize, relieve, replace, take over from, be a replacement/substitute for
COLLOQ. N Am pinch-hit for
7 the estate covers some 500 acres
extend over, stretch, continue, measure
8 £50 to cover expenses
pay for, be enough for, recompense, make up for, compensate for, counterbalance, balance out
9 the insurance will cover it
protect, insure, underwrite, provide for
FORMAL indemnify

10 journalists covering an event
report, describe, give details of, tell, talk/write about, give an account of, narrate, present, investigate, analyse
E3 1 uncover 2 strip 3 expose 4 exclude
♦ n
1 SHELTER, refuge, protection, shield, guard, defence, concealment, hiding-place, sanctuary, disguise, camouflage
2 COVERING, coating, top, lid, cup, jacket, wrapper, sleeve, binding, case, envelope, package, coat, layer, film, skin, carpet, mantle, clothing, dress, bedclothes, bedding, blankets, duvet, bedspread, throw, canopy
3 as a cover for illegal activity
cover-up, concealment, screen, smokescreen, veil, mask, front, façade, pretence, conspiracy, complicity
COLLOQ. whitewash
4 insurance cover
protection, insurance, security, compensation, assurance
FORMAL indemnity, indemnification

■ cover up

conceal, hide, suppress, keep secret, keep dark, repress, gloss over
FORMAL dissemble
COLLOQ. whitewash, hush up
E3 disclose, reveal

coverage n

reporting, report(s), description, account, investigation, analysis, item, story, reportage

covering n, adj

♦ n
layer, coat, coating, blanket, carpet, film, veneer, skin, crust, case, shell, casing, housing, wrapping, clothing, protection, shelter, mask, overlay, cover, top, roof, roofing, awning, tarpaulin
♦ adj
accompanying, explanatory, descriptive, introductory

covert adj

hidden, secret, private, clandestine, concealed, disguised, veiled, sneaky, stealthy, furtive, sidelong, surreptitious, unsuspected, ulterior, underhand
FORMAL dissembled, subreptitious
COLLOQ. under the table
E3 open, overt

covertly adv

secretly, privately, furtively, surreptitiously
E3 openly, overtly

cover-up n

concealment, screen, smokescreen, front, faõcade, pretence, deception, conspiracy, complicity
COLLOQ. whitewash

covet v

desire, crave, long for, yearn for, hanker for, want, hunger/thirst for, lust after, envy, begrudge
COLLOQ. fancy

covetous adj

yearning, craving, wanting, longing, hankering, hungering, thirsting, acquisitive, grasping, greedy, insatiable, jealous, envious
FORMAL desirous, avaricious, rapacious
E3 generous, temperate

covey n

cluster, flight, flock, group, brood, hatch, party, set, band, company, bevy, nid, skein

cow v

intimidate, domineer, browbeat, bully, terrorize, frighten, scare, overawe, subdue, unnerve, daunt, dishearten, discourage, chasten, dismay
COLLOQ. rattle
E3 encourage

coward n

craven, faint-heart, weakling, poltroon, renegade, deserter
OLD cowheard, cowherd, recreant, dastard, nithing, hilding, viliaco, viliago

COLLOQ. chicken, scaredy-cat, yellow-belly, sissy, crybaby, wimp; *Aust* sook
SLANG wuss; *Aust* cat, dingo
🔁 hero

> **QUOTATIONS**
> The sea hates a coward!
> EUGENE O'NEILL, *Mourning Becomes Electra*

cowardice *n*
cowardliness, faint-heartedness, weak-spiritedness, fearfulness, spiritlessness, timidity, timorousness, spinelessness
FORMAL pusillanimity
🔁 courage, bravery, valour

cowardly *adj*
faint-hearted, craven, fearful, timid, coward, dastardly, timorous, scared, unheroic, unmanly, chicken-hearted, chicken-livered, white-livered, lily-livered, spiritless, spineless, weak, weak-spirited, weak-kneed, soft, jittery; *dialect* mangy, nesh
OLD faint, nithing; (*Shakesp*) cowish, milk-livered, meacock
FORMAL pusillanimous
COLLOQ. chicken, gutless, wimpish, yellow-bellied, yellow, showing the white feather
🔁 brave, courageous, bold

> **SYNONYM NUANCES**
> **Faint-hearted**, **fearful**, **timid** and **timorous** simply suggest a lack of spirit or mettle: *the mountain pass is a sore trial for a timid car driver*. **Craven** makes a strong statement by further implying total temerity: *craven abdication of his duty*. **Dastardly** is similar but literary in tone, and suggests an underhand element: *a dastardly plan was hatched*.
> **Unheroic** and **unmanly** suggest a lack of certain expected qualities and are in themselves rather negative, although in particular contexts the tone may not necessarily be unfavourable: *a modest leader with an unheroic attitude to war*; *American officers consider community policing as 'unmanly'*.
> The terms **chicken-hearted**, **chicken-livered** and **white-livered** are insulting ways to suggest that someone lacks courage; **spiritless**, **spineless** and **soft**, as well as **weak**, **weak-spirited**, **weak-kneed** all suggest a lack of fortitude or resolution, but are similarly derogatory: *the authorities are being spineless*.

cowboy *n*
1 *cowboys to look after cattle*
drover, cattleman, cowhand, herdsman, cattleherder, herder, stockman, rancher, ranchero, waddy; *N Am* bronco-buster, buckaroo, cowpoke, cowpuncher, gaucho, vaquero, wrangler
2 *a plumbing firm full of cowboys*
bungler, incompetent, rascal, rogue, cheat, fraudster, scoundrel, swindler
🔁 **2** professional

cower *v*
crouch, grovel, skulk, shrink, flinch, draw back, recoil, wince, cringe, quail, tremble, quake, shake, shiver

co-worker *n*
colleague, workmate, teammate, partner, collaborator, ally, associate, confederate, confrère, comrade, fellow worker, companion, aide, helper, assistant, auxiliary

coy *adj*
modest, demure, prudish, prim, diffident, shy, bashful, timid, shrinking, backward, retiring, self-effacing, withdrawn, reserved, reticence, evasive, arch, flirtatious, coquettish, skittish, kittenish
🔁 bold, forward

coyly *adv*
modestly, bashfully, demurely, primly, prudishly, diffidently, timidly, self-effacingly, evasively, flirtatiously, coquettishly
🔁 boldly, forwardly

crabbed, crabby *adj*
bad-tempered, cross, ill-tempered, irritable, fractious, morose, snappish, cantankerous, petulant, perverse, acrid, acrimonious, awkward, difficult, harsh, tough, sour, captious, churlish, fretful, snappy, surly, tart, testy, prickly, splenetic
FORMAL iracund, iracundulous, irascible, misanthropic
COLLOQ. crotchety, grouchy
🔁 calm, placid

crack *v, n, adj*
♦ *v*
1 SPLIT, burst, fracture, break, snap, shatter, splinter, fragment, chip
2 EXPLODE, go bang, bang, detonate, boom, burst, pop, crackle, snap, crash, bash, hit, beat, strike, clap, clout, slap, bump
COLLOQ. whack, wallop
3 *crack under pressure*
lose control, collapse, break down, go to pieces, cave in
4 *crack a code*
decipher, docode, decrypt, work out, solve, resolve, unravel, figure out, find the answer to
COLLOQ. *N Am* dope (out)
♦ *n*
1 BREAK, fracture, flaw, chip, split, rift, breach, rupture, gap, crevice, fissure, cleft, cavity, chink, line, cranny
2 EXPLOSION, bang, boom, detonation, burst, pop, snap, crash, clap, clout, blow, smack, slap, hit, bump
FORMAL report
COLLOQ. whack
3 *have a crack at something*
attempt, go, try, effort
COLLOQ. bash, shot, stab, whirl
4 JOKE, quip, witticism, one-liner, wisecrack, gibe, repartee
COLLOQ. gag, dig
♦ *adj*
first-class, first-rate, excellent, outstanding, brilliant, superior, choice, hand-picked, expert, skilled, skilful
COLLOQ. top-notch
■ **crack down on**
clamp down on, end, stop, put a stop to, crush, suppress, check, control, limit, restrict, confine, repress, act against
COLLOQ. get tough on
■ **crack up**
1 BREAK DOWN, lose control, go to pieces, fall apart, have a nervous breakdown, collapse, go mad, go crazy
SLANG go ballisitic
2 LAUGH UNCONTROLLABLY, dissolve into laughter
COLLOQ. be rolling in the aisles, fall about, split your sides

crackdown *n*
clampdown, crushing, end, check, blitz, stop, repression, suppression

cracked *adj*
1 *a cracked glass*
broken, chipped, damaged, defective, flawed, imperfect, faulty, fissured, rimose, split, torn
2 *they're cracked*
crazy, insane, deranged, crazed, foolish, idiotic
COLLOQ. daft, barmy, batty, crackbrained, crackpot, nuts, nutty, round the bend; *Aust & NZ* dingbats
SLANG loony, off your rocker, out of your tree
🔁 **1** flawless, perfect **2** sane, of sound mind

crackers *adj*
cracked, crazy, mad, foolish, idiotic
COLLOQ. daft, batty, crackbrained, crackpot, nuts, nutty, round the bend
SLANG loony
🔁 sane, sound

crackle v, n

♦ v
snap, crack, sizzle, rustle
FORMAL crepitate, decrepitate
♦ n
snap, crack, sizzle, rustle
FORMAL crepitation, crepitus, decrepitation

crackpot n
idiot, fool
COLLOQ. freak, weirdo, oddball, nutter, nutcase
SLANG loony, basket case

cradle n, v

♦ n
1 COT, carry-cot, Moses basket, travel-cot, crib, bassinet, bed, berceau
FORMAL cunabula
2 SOURCE, origin, spring, wellspring, fount, fountain-head, birthplace, starting-point, beginning
FORMAL incunabula
3 *put the telephone receiver back on its cradle*
rocker, holder, rest, prop, stand, base, support, mount, mounting, frame, framework
♦ v
hold, support, rock, lull, nestle, nurse, shelter, nurture, tend

craft n
1 SKILL, expertise, mastery, talent, knack, flair, ability, skilfulness, expertness, aptitude, dexterity, cleverness, artistry, art, handicraft, handiwork, workmanship, technique
2 TRADE, business, calling, vocation, job, occupation, work, employment, line, activity, pursuit
3 VESSEL, boat, ship, aircraft, spacecraft, spaceship, landing craft
4 CUNNING, cunningness, craftiness, slyness, art, artfulness, trickery, deviousness, subtlety, deceit, deceitfulness, guile, wiles, sharpness, shrewdness, astuteness, ingenuity, cleverness, imaginativeness, sleight, inventiveness, resourcefulness, deftness, finesse, adroitness, fiendishness, Machiavellianism
OLD (Shakesp) foxship

craftily adv
slyly, cunningly, artfully, deviously, deceitfully, guilefully, fraudulently, shrewdly, astutely
F3 naively

craftsman, craftswoman n
artist, artisan, technician, mechanic, expert, master, maker, tradesman, tradeswoman, tradesperson, craftsperson, skilled worker, wright, smith

craftsmanship n
artistry, workmanship, skill, skilfulness, technique, dexterity, expertise, mastery

crafty adj
sly, cunning, artful, wily, foxy, devious, subtle, scheming, calculating, conniving, designing, deceitful, guileful, fraudulent, sharp, shrewd, astute, canny, tricksy, knackish, knacky, Machiavellian, versute, slim, subdolous; Scot loopy
FORMAL duplicitous, disingenuous
COLLOQ. crooked
F3 artless, naive, guileless

crag n
bluff, cliff, escarpment, scarp, ridge, peak, pinnacle, rock, tor

craggy adj
1 *a craggy cliff*
precipitous, rocky, rough, rough-hewn, rugged, cragged, stony, jagged, uneven
2 *a craggy face*
rough, rugged, jagged, uneven, weather-beaten, marked
F3 2 smooth

cram v
1 *cram sweets into your mouth*
stuff, jam, ram, force, press, squeeze, crush, compress, pack, crowd, overcrowd, fill (up), overfill, glut, gorge
FORMAL compact
2 *cram for an exam*
revise, study hard
COLLOQ. swot, mug up, bone up on, grind

cramp n, v

♦ n
pain, ache, twinge, pang, contraction, convulsion, spasm, muscular contraction, crick, stitch, pins and needles, stiffness
♦ v
hinder, hamper, obstruct, impede, inhibit, handicap, thwart, frustrate, check, restrict, limit, bridle, rein, hamstring, arrest, constrain, restrain, confine, stymie, shackle, tie

cramped adj
narrow, tight, small, uncomfortable, poky, restricted, confined, crowded, packed, squashed, squeezed, closed in, hemmed in, overcrowded, full, overfull, jam-packed, congested
COLLOQ. no room to swing a cat
F3 spacious

crane n
derrick, hoist, tackle, winch, block and tackle, davit

crank n, v

♦ n
eccentric, character, madman, idiot
COLLOQ. freak, weirdo, oddball, nutter, kook, crackpot
SLANG loony

■ **crank up**
increase, intensify, step up, build up, add to, further, strengthen
COLLOQ. hike up

cranky adj
1 ECCENTRIC, odd, peculiar, unconventional, strange, bizarre, freakish, fey, queer, idiosyncratic
COLLOQ. wacky, dotty, screwy
2 BAD-TEMPERED, cross, ill-tempered, irritable, cantankerous, awkward, difficult, harsh, snappy, surly, tart, testy, prickly
COLLOQ. crabby, crotchety, grouchy
F3 1 normal, sensible 2 calm, placid

cranny n
chink, cleft, crack, crevice, fissure, rent, gap, hole, slit, nook, opening, cleavage
FORMAL interstice

crash n, v, adj

♦ n
1 *a car crash*
accident, collision, bump, pile-up, wreck; Scot frush
OLD rack
COLLOQ. smash, smash-up, prang; Aust bingle
2 BANG, clash, clatter, clang, clank, thud, thump, boom, explosion, thunder, thunderclap, clap, smash, racket, din
OLD fragor
3 *stock market crash*
collapse, failure, ruin, downfall, fall, bankruptcy, depression, meltdown, black Monday
♦ v
1 COLLIDE, hit, knock, bump, bang, run into, go into, drive into, smash into, plough into, ditch
COLLOQ. bash, prang, shunt, wham
2 BREAK, fracture, smash, batter, dash, pound, shatter, splinter, shiver, fragment, disintegrate
3 FALL, topple, pitch, plunge, collapse, fail, fold (up), founder, go under, go into liquidation
COLLOQ. go bust, go to the wall
4 *the computer crashed*
cut out, break down, stop working, fail
FORMAL malfunction
COLLOQ. pack up, go on the blink, go phut, go kaput

♦ *adj*
intensive, rapid, accelerated, concentrated, telescoped, emergency, immediate, round-the-clock, urgent

crass *adj*
stupid, indelicate, tasteless, insensitive, tactless, unrefined, unsophisticated, blundering, rude, crude, coarse, dense, oafish, clumsy, unsubtle, witless
FORMAL obtuse
E3 refined, sensitive

crassly *adv*
stupidly, clumsily, indelicately, insensitively, tactlessly, rudely, crudely, coarsely, tastelessly
E3 sensitively

crate *n*
container, box, case, chest, tea chest, packing-box, packing-case; *dialect & Scot* kist

crater *n*
hollow, depression, hole, basin, bowl, dip, pit, cavity, chasm, abyss

crave *v*
hunger for, thirst for, long for, yearn for, pine for, sigh for, hanker after, pant for, lust after, desire, covet, want, dream of, wish, need, require
COLLOQ. be dying for, fancy
E3 dislike

craven *adj*
cowardly, faint-hearted, fearful, timorous, timid, scared, afraid, unheroic, chicken-hearted, white-livered, chicken-livered, lily-livered, mean-spirited, spineless, spiritless, weak, weak-spirited, weak-kneed, soft
OLD recreant, poltroon
FORMAL pusillanimous
COLLOQ. chicken, gutless, yellow
E3 brave, courageous, bold

craving *n*
appetite, hunger, thirst, longing, yearning, pining, sighing, hankering, panting, lust, desire, wish, need, urge
E3 dislike, distaste

crawl *v*
1 CREEP, go on all fours, move on your hands and knees, inch, edge, slither, wriggle, squirm, writhe, drag, move/advance slowly
2 GROVEL, cringe, toady, fawn, flatter, bow and scrape, curry favour
FORMAL be obsequious to
COLLOQ. be all over, suck up, creep, kowtow
3 *the city centre crawling with police*
teem, swarm, seethe, bristle, be full of

craze *n*
fad, novelty, fashion, vogue, mode, trend, obsession, preoccupation, mania, frenzy, passion, infatuation, whim, enthusiasm
COLLOQ. rage, the latest, thing

crazed *adj*
mad, insane, lunatic, unbalanced, deranged, demented, crazy, wild, berserk, unhinged, out of your mind
COLLOQ. nuts, round the bend, round the twist
SLANG loony, off your rocker

crazily *adv*
madly, insanely, wildly, franctically, frenetically, manically

crazy *adj*
1 MAD, insane, lunatic, unbalanced, disturbed, deranged, demented, crazed, wild, berserk, frantic, unhinged, distracted, distraught, frenetic, maniac, out of your mind, infuriate; *Scot* gyte
OLD frantic-mad, lymphatic, bestraught
COLLOQ. nuts, nutty, nutty as a fruitcake, wacky, mad as a hatter, barmy, bonkers, batty, cracked, crackers, dippy, daffy, dotty, loopy, potty, off your nut, off your head, wrong in the head, out of your head, off the wall, out to lunch, round the bend, round the twist, bats, having bats in the belfry, cuckoo, off the rails, screwy, screwball, up the wall, haywire, raving, not all there; *N Am* buggy, flaky, fruity; *Aust & NZ* dingbats
SLANG loony, mental, bananas, barking, wacko, doolally, off your rocker, off your chump, off your trolley, out of your tree, needing your head examined, having lost your marbles, having a screw loose, having a tile loose, having several cards short of a full deck, with one sandwich short of a picnic, meshuga; *N Am* gonzo, loco, wiggy
2 *What a crazy idea!*
silly, foolish, idiotic, stupid, senseless, unwise, imprudent, nonsensical, absurd, odd, peculiar, ludicrous, ridiculous, preposterous, outrageous, impracticable, unrealistic, foolhardy, irresponsible, wild; *Aust* strange
COLLOQ. daft, barmy, batty, potty, half-baked, hare-brained, crackbrained, crackpot
3 *crazy about golf*
enthusiastic, fanatical, zealous, devoted, fond, keen, avid, ardent, passionate, infatuated, enamoured, smitten, mad, wild
COLLOQ. daft, nuts, potty
E3 **1** sane **2** sensible **3** indifferent

SYNONYM NUANCES

sense 1
Mad can be widely used to suggest any incomprehensible behaviour or deviation from mental norms, whilst **insane** and **lunatic** may be used to suggest extreme irrationality: *a policy of lunatic aggression*. Both **distracted**, which is a fairly mild term, and **distraught**, which is rather stronger, could be used where someone's whole attention is taken up by something, usually upsetting: *distraught at the separation from her husband.*
    Unbalanced and **disturbed** suggest being out of kilter, possibly mildly, while **unhinged**, **deranged** and **demented** imply situations where the mind has undergone more deeply troubling changes, and someone's mental ability has degenerated: *demented by grief*. **Wild** and **berserk** are appropriately used of outrageous behaviour; **frenetic** and **maniac** of a highly excited manner: *a frenetic flurry of activity*. The term **frantic** is similar, but hints at a strong element of anxiety: *frantic signalling*.

---

creak *v*
squeak, groan, grate, scrape, rasp, scratch, grind, squeal, screech

creaky *adj*
squeaky, squeaking, groaning, grating, scraping, rasping, scratching, grinding, squealing, screeching, rusty, unoiled

cream *n, adj*
♦ *n*
1 PASTE, emulsion, oil, lotion, ointment, preparation, application, salve, cosmetic
TECHNICAL emollient, liniment, unguent
2 BEST, pick, élite, flower, choice/select part, prime, finest, pick of the bunch, crème de la crème
♦ *adj*
yellowish-white, whitish-yellow, off-white, ivory, pale, pasty, milky

creamy *adj*
1 CREAM-COLOURED, off-white, ivory, yellowish-white, whitish-yellow, pale, pasty, milky
2 MILKY, buttery, oily, smooth, velvety, rich, thick

crease *v, n*
♦ *v*
fold, pleat, wrinkle, pucker, crumple, rumple, crinkle, crimp, tuck, corrugate, groove, furrow, ridge
♦ *n*
fold, line, pleat, tuck, wrinkle, pucker, ruck, crinkle, corrugation, furrow, ridge, groove

■ **crease up**
make laugh, amuse
COLLOQ. make someone fall about, make someone split their sides, have rolling in the aisles

create v
invent, coin, formulate, compose, design, devise, concoct, hatch, originate, initiate, found, establish, set up, institute, cause, cause to happen, bring about, occasion, give rise to, produce, bring into being, bring into existence, generate, engender, make, form, shape, mould, develop, build, construct, erect, frame, fabricate, appoint, install, invest, inaugurate, ordain, lead to, result in
ℱℲ destroy

creation n
1 MAKING, formation, constitution, invention, concoction, origination, foundation, establishment, institution, production, generation, origin, conception, initiation, birth, development, design, construction, fabrication
TECHNICAL biopoiesis
FORMAL procreation, genesis
2 *God's creation*
world, universe, cosmos, nature, life, everything
3 INVENTION, innovation, brainchild, concept, product, production, achievement, work, work of art, handiwork, masterpiece, composition, design, *pièce de résistance*, *chef d'oeuvre*
ℱℲ **1** destruction

creative adj
artistic, inventive, original, imaginative, inspired, visionary, full of ideas, innovative, talented, gifted, clever, ingenious, resourceful, fertile, productive, intuitive
ℱℲ unimaginative

creativity n
artistry, inventiveness, originality, imagination, imaginativeness, inspiration, vision, talent, gift, cleverness, ingenuity, resourcefulness, fertility, productiveness
ℱℲ unimaginativeness

creator n
maker, inventor, designer, architect, author, originator, producer, initiator, builder, composer, founder, father, mother, prime mover, first cause

creature n
animal, beast, bird, fish, insect, organism, being, living thing, mortal, individual, person, human being, human, man, woman, body, soul, mortal; *Scot & Irish* cratur
COLLOQ. *N Am* critter

credence n
belief, confidence, trust, faith, dependence, reliance, acceptance, support, credibility, credit
ℱℲ distrust

credentials n
diploma, certificate, reference, testimonial, recommendation, authorization, warrant, licence, permit, passport, identity card, proof of identity, papers, documents, deed, title
FORMAL accreditation

credibility n
integrity, reliability, trustworthiness, plausibility, probability, likelihood, reasonableness
ℱℲ implausibility

credible adj
believable, imaginable, convincing, conceivable, thinkable, tenable, plausible, likely, probable, possible, reasonable, persuasive, sincere, honest, trustworthy, reliable, dependable
OLD credent
COLLOQ. with a ring of truth
ℱℲ incredible, unbelievable, implausible, unreliable

⬛ **credible, creditable** or **credulous**?
Credible means 'believable, even if untrue': *a credible theory*. *Creditable* means 'worthy of praise or respect': *a very creditable performance*. *Credulous* means 'too easily convinced; easily fooled': *Only the most credulous of voters would believe all the party's election promises.*

SYNONYM NUANCES

Believable, **imaginable**, **conceivable**, **thinkable**, **plausible** and **tenable** may be widely used, simply to say that something is very possible: *it was conceivable that a foreign investor might be tempted; it appeared to them a tenable meaning to the words*. **Likely** and **probable**, on the other hand, further suggest there is a good chance of something happening: *the probable effects of higher taxation*.
    Convincing suggests there may be strong evidence of verity, while the term **reasonable** suggests that judgement grants something may be the case: *a reasonable supposition*, and **persuasive** implies outside forces have been brought to bear on this perception: *influenced by his persuasive argument*.
    Sincere and **honest** might be used of people as well as more abstract notions and carry the positive suggestion of inherent believability, similarly **trustworthy**, **reliable** and **dependable**, which are all approbatory and appropriately describe something inspiring justifiable confidence: *any information system should be reliable*.

credibly adv
believably, imaginably, convincingly, conceivably, thinkably, plausibly, possibly, reasonably, persuasively, sincerely, honestly, trustworthy, reliably, dependably

credit n, v
♦ n
1 *get the credit for his success*
acknowledgement, recognition, thanks, approval, commendation, praise, acclaim, tribute, plaudits
FORMAL laudation
2 *your loyalty does you credit*
glory, fame, prestige, distinction, honour, reputation, asset, boast, pride, esteem, estimation
COLLOQ. feather in your cap, pride and joy
3 *give someone credit for their ability*
belief, trust, faith, credence, confidence
ℱℲ **1** blame, discredit, shame
♦ v
1 *credited with the invention*
attribute, ascribe, put down, assign, charge
FORMAL accredit, impute
2 *the reports are difficult to credit*
believe, accept, subscribe to, trust, have faith, rely on
COLLOQ. swallow, buy
ℱℲ **2** disbelieve
■ **in credit**
have money in your bank account, solvent
COLLOQ. in the black
■ **on credit**
on account, by instalments, by deferred payment, on hire purchase
COLLOQ. on tick, on the slate, on the tab, on the never-never

creditable adj
honourable, reputable, respectable, estimable, admirable, commendable, praiseworthy, good, excellent, exemplary, worthy, deserving
FORMAL laudable, meritorious
ℱℲ shameful, blameworthy

⬛ **creditable, credible** or **credulous**?
See panel at **credible**.

creditably *adv*
well, excellently, honourably, respectably, admirably, commendably
F3 shamefully

creditor *n*
person/business you owe money to, lender, moneylender
FORMAL debtee
COLLOQ. loan shark
F3 debtor

credulity *n*
naivety, gullibility, credulousness, dupability, silliness, simplicity, stupidity, uncriticalness
F3 scepticism

credulous *adj*
naive, gullible, wide-eyed, trusting, overtrusting, dupable, unsuspecting, uncritical
F3 sceptical, suspicious

> **!** **credulous, credible** or **creditable**?
> *See panel at* **credible**.

creed *n*
belief, faith, persuasion, credo, catechism, doctrine, teaching, principles, tenets, articles, canon, dogma, ideology

creek *n*
inlet, estuary, cove, bay, bight, firth, fiord, fjord

creep *v, n*
♦ *v*
crawl, inch, edge, tiptoe, steal, sneak, slink, move unnoticed, slither, worm, wriggle, squirm, grovel, writhe, snake
♦ *n*
1 *You little creep!*
sneak, fawner, sycophant, toady
COLLOQ. yes-man, bootlicker
SLANG geek
2 *gave me the creeps*
fear, horror, revulsion, terror, alarm, unease, disquiet

creeper *n*
climber, climbing plant, trailer, trailing plant, plant, rambler, runner, trailing, vine, liana

creepy *adj*
eerie, sinister, threatening, frightening, terrifying, hair-raising, bloodcurdling, spine-chilling, nightmarish, macabre, gruesome, horrible, horrifying, horrific, unpleasant, menacing, ominous, disturbing, weird
COLLOQ. scary, spooky

crescent-shaped *adj*
bow-shaped, sickle-shaped
FORMAL falcate, falcated, falciform, lunate, lunated, lunular

crest *n*
1 *the crest of the hill*
ridge, crown, top, peak, summit, pinnacle, apex, head, edge, chine, comb, cornice
2 TUFT, tassel, plume, comb, cockscomb, mane, aigrette, caruncle, panache
TECHNICAL crista
OLD copple
3 INSIGNIA, regalia, device, symbol, emblem, badge, coat of arms

crestfallen *adj*
disappointed, downhearted, dejected, sad, depressed, despondent, discouraged, disheartened, dispirited, downcast
FORMAL disconsolate
COLLOQ. cheesed off, in the doldrums, down in the dumps
F3 elated

cretin *n*
fool, blockhead, moron, fathead, dolt, dunce, dimwit, simpleton, halfwit, idiot, imbecile, ignoramus
COLLOQ. nincompoop, ass, chump, ninny, clot, dope, twit, nitwit, nit, sucker, mug, twerp, birdbrain; *N Am* bufflehead
SLANG wally, jerk, dumbo, pillock, prat, dork, geek, plonker, prick; *N Am* schmuck, jughead, schmo

crevasse *n*
abyss, chasm, cleft, crack, fissure, gap, bergschrund

crevice *n*
crack, fissure, split, rift, cleft, slit, chink, cranny, gap, hole, opening, break
FORMAL interstice

crew *n*
team, party, squad, troop, corps, company, complement, force, gang, band, pack, group, unit, bunch, crowd, mob, set, lot

crib *n, v*
♦ *n*
carry-cot, cot, crib, travel-cot, Moses basket, bassinet, bed
♦ *v*
copy, cheat, steal, reproduce, pirate, plagiarize
FORMAL purloin
COLLOQ. lift, pinch

crick *n*
pain, spasm, stiffness, convulsion, cramp, rick, twinge

cricket
See panel below

crier *n*
announcer, proclaimer, messenger, bearer of tidings, herald, town crier

crime *n*
lawbreaking, lawlessness, delinquency, illegal act, unlawful act, offence, felony, misdemeanour, misdeed,

---

Terms used in cricket include:

all-rounder	county champion-	googly	long leg	point	stump
the Ashes	ship	gully	long off	pull	stumped
bail	cover	half-volley	long on	run	sweep
ball	crease	hat-trick	maiden	run out	sweeper
bat	cut	hook	mid off	scorer	swing bowler
batsman	drive	howzat?	mid on	seam bowler	test match
block	duck	ICC (International	mid-wicket	short leg	thigh pad
bouncer	Duckworth-Lewis	Cricket Council)	nightwatchman	short	third man
boundary	method	infield	no ball	sightscreen	twelfth man
bowled	extra cover	innings	off spinner	silly point	umpire
bowler	extras	lbw (leg before	one-day match	single	whites
box	fast bowler	wicket)	outfield	six	wicket
bye	fielder	leg bye	over	slip	wicketkeeper
caught	fine leg	leg spinner	pace bowler	spin bowler	wide
century	four	limited-overs	pad	square	wrong 'un
chinaman	full toss	match	pavilion	square cut	yorker
	glance	long hop	pitch	square leg	

wrongdoing, misconduct, violation, sin, iniquity, vice, villainy, wickedness, atrocity, outrage

OLD (Shakesp) malefaction

FORMAL malfeasance, transgression

Crimes include:

abduction	embezzlement	money laundering
actual bodily	extortion	mugging
harm	false imprisonment	murder
arson	forgery	netcrime
assassination	fraud	perjury
assault	colloq. GBH	pilfering
battery	grievous bodily	piracy
blackmail	harm	poaching
breach of the	grooming	possession
peace	handling stolen	racketeering
breaking and	goods	rape
entering	hate crime	receiving stolen
bribery	hijack	goods
burglary	homicide	rioting
computer hacking	hooliganism	robbery
corruption	housebreaking	sabotage
counterfeiting	identity theft	sedition
cybercrime	incitement	shoplifting
dangerous driving	insider dealing/	stalking
disorder	trading	terrorism
domestic violence	joy-riding	theft
drink-driving	kidnapping	treason
drug dealing	larceny	trespassing
drug-driving	looting	vandalism
drug smuggling	manslaughter	
drunk and	mobile phone	
disorderly	driving	

criminal n, adj

♦ n

lawbreaker, felon, delinquent, offender, wrongdoer, miscreant, culprit, villain, convict, prisoner, perpetrator

FORMAL malefactor

COLLOQ. crim, fence, N Am perp

♦ adj

1 a criminal offence

illegal, unlawful, illicit, lawless, lawbreaking, wrong, indictable, dishonest, villainous, corrupt, wicked, evil, iniquitous

FORMAL culpable, felonious, nefarious

COLLOQ. crooked, bent

2 a criminal waste

scandalous, deplorable, disgraceful, outrageous, preposterous, infamous, disgusting, shameful, reprehensible

COLLOQ. obscene

⊟ 1 legal, lawful, honest, upright

crimp v

flute, pleat, fold, gather, furrow, ridge, corrugate, groove, wrinkle, pucker, crease, crumple, rumple, crinkle, tuck

cringe v

1 the sight made me cringe

shrink, recoil, shy, start, flinch, draw back, wince, blench, quail, tremble, quiver, cower, crouch, bend, bow, stoop

2 GROVEL, toady, fawn, flatter, bow and scrape, tug the forelock, curry favour

COLLOQ. crawl, creep, kowtow, be all over, suck up

crinkle n, v

♦ n

fold, line, pleat, crease, tuck, ruffle, rumple, twist, wave, wrinkle, pucker, ruck, crinkle, corrugation, furrow, ridge, groove

♦ v

fold, pleat, crease, wrinkle, pucker, curl, twist, crumple, rumple, crinkle, crimp, tuck, corrugate, groove, furrow, ridge

crinkly adj

fluted, pleated, folded, gathered, furrowed, ridged, corrugated, grooved, wrinkled, wrinkly, puckered, curly, frizzy, kinky, creased, crimped, crumpled, rumpled, crinkled, tucked

⊟ smooth, straight

cripple v

crippled by the accident/the tax increase

paralyse, disable, handicap, injure, maim, lame, immobilize, mutilate, damage, impair, spoil, ruin, destroy, sabotage, weaken, debilitate, hamstring, hamper, impede

FORMAL incapacitate, vitiate

crippled adj

lame, paralysed, disabled, handicapped, deformed

FORMAL incapacitated

crisis n

emergency, extremity, catastrophe, disaster, calamity, critical situation, crossroads, dilemma, quandary, predicament, difficulty, trouble, problem, turn, turning-point, brunt, crise

TECHNICAL solution

OLD acme, fit

FORMAL exigency

COLLOQ. crunch, mess, scrape, pickle, jam, fix, hole, stew, hot water

crisp adj

1 a crisp biscuit

crispy, crunchy, brittle, crumbly, breakable, firm, hard

FORMAL friable

2 BRACING, invigorating, refreshing, fresh, brisk, chilly, cool

3 BRIEF, pithy, terse, brief, short, succinct, concise, clear, incisive

COLLOQ. snappy

⊟ 1 soggy, limp, flabby 2 muggy, humid 3 wordy, vague

Types of criminal include:

abductor	car-thief	forger	killer	racketeer	strangler
armed robber	cat burglar	gangster	slang lag	ram-raider	swindler
arsonist	counterfeiter	gunman	larcenist	rapist	terrorist
assassin	cracksman	hacker	looter	receiver	thief
bandit	crook	highwayman	N Am mobster	rioter	thug
batterer	dope pusher	hijacker	mugger	robber	trespasser
bigamist	drink-driver	slang hood	murderer	rustler	vandal
blackmailer	drug dealer	hoodlum	paedophile	saboteur	war criminal
bogus caller	drug-driver	housebreaker	pederast	safecracker	
bootlegger	drug smuggler	colloq. jailbird	perjurer	sexual abuser	
brigand	embezzler	joyrider	pickpocket	shoplifter	
buccaneer	extortionist	kerb-crawler	pirate	smuggler	
burglar	fire-raiser	kidnapper	poacher	stalker	

criterion n
standard, norm, touchstone, benchmark, yardstick, basis, measure, gauge, rule, scale, law, principle, model, canon, test, shibboleth
OLD square
FORMAL exemplar

critic n
1 *a music critic*
reviewer, commentator, analyst, pundit, authority, monitor, observer, expert, judge
2 *a critic of the government*
judge, censor, censurer, carper, fault-finder, attacker
OLD find-fault
COLLOQ. backbiter, nit-picker, knocker

> **QUOTATIONS**
> Critics are like eunuchs in a harem. They're in there every night, they see how it should be done every night, but they can't do it themselves
> BRENDAN BEHAN

critical adj
1 *at the critical moment*
crucial, vital, essential, important, all-important, significant, momentous, major, deciding, decisive, historic, fateful, pivotal, urgent, serious, compelling, pressing
FORMAL exigent, climacteric
2 *in a critical condition*
dangerous, serious, grave, precarious
FORMAL perilous
3 UNCOMPLIMENTARY, derogatory, disparaging, condemnatory, judgemental, disapproving, disapprobative, censorious, scathing, carping, fault-finding, captious, niggling, quibbling, hypercritical, venomous, vitriolic
FORMAL vituperative
COLLOQ. cavilling, nit-picking
4 ANALYTICAL, diagnostic, penetrating, probing, discerning, evaluative, explanatory, interpretative, perceptive
FORMAL expository
E3 **1** unimportant, insignificant **3** complimentary, appreciative

critically adv
1 *critically important*
significantly, vitally, crucially, seriously, decisively, urgently
2 *critically ill*
dangerously, seriously, gravely, acutely
FORMAL perilously
3 *look critically*
disparagingly, disapprovingly, captiously, hypercritically
4 *evaluate critically*
analytically, diagnostically
E3 **3** appreciatively

criticism n
1 CONDEMNATION, disapproval, fault-finding, censure, reproof, blame
FORMAL animadversion, disparagement
COLLOQ. brickbat, flak, slating, slamming, nit-picking, niggle, knocking, stick
2 REVIEW, critique, assessment, evaluation, appraisal, judgement, analysis, commentary, write-up, appreciation, explanation, interpretation
FORMAL exposition, explication
COLLOQ. bad press
E3 **1** praise, commendation

criticize v
1 CONDEMN, carp, disapprove of, find fault with, pass judgement on, denounce, speak ill of, run down, attack, slate, censure, blame, canvass, niggle, peck at, scarify, slash, snipe at, tilt at; N Am score
FORMAL disparage, cast aspersions on, animadvert, excoriate, decry, denigrate, vituperate, castigate, impugn
COLLOQ. nag, slam, hammer, knock, come down on, give someone some stick, go to town on, haul over the coals, pick holes in, pan, take apart, pull/tear apart, pull to

pieces, tear to shreds, tear a strip off, nit-pick, do a hatchet job on, badmouth, rubbish, trash, put the boot in, cut up, roast, have a go at, wade into; N Am & Aust bag; Aust have a shot at
SLANG slag (off), take to the cleaners; N Am rip into, zing
2 REVIEW, assess, evaluate, appraise, judge, analyse, explain, interpret
E3 **1** praise, commend

> **SYNONYM NUANCES**
>
> *sense 1*
> **Condemn** and **censure** may be used to convey speaking out vehemently against, as can the term **attack**: *the Prime Minister attacked the doom-mongers*; **denounce** has a narrower suggestion of public accusation: *they denounced him as a traitor*. **Disparage** has a strong element of humiliation or belittling: *there are many students who feel disparaged by teachers*.
>   **Carp**, **niggle** and **peck at** could be used of continuous and implicitly irritating fault-finding, whereas **scarify**, though rarely used, suggests the fault-finding is much more severe: *a columnist who scarified our leading politicians*. **Snipe at** and **tilt at** are likely to be used of a fairly mild, possibly veiled verbal assault: *the critic tilted at the art world's honours system*. **Wade into**, on the other hand, could be used of a much more blatant onslaught: *he waded into his father with anger*.

critique n
review, essay, assessment, evaluation, appraisal, judgement, analysis, commentary, write-up, appreciation, explanation, interpretation
FORMAL exposition, explication

croak v, n
♦ n
rasp, squawk, caw, crow, croup, wheeze, speak harshly, gasp, grunt; *dialect* crake
♦ n
rasp, squawk, caw, wheeze, gasp, grunt

crock n
jar, pot, urn, vessel

crockery n
dishes, tableware, china, porcelain, earthenware, stoneware, pottery

---

Items of crockery include:

basin	dinner plate	salad bowl
beaker	dinner service	saucer
bowl	dish	side plate
butter dish	gravy boat	soup bowl
cafétière	jug	sugar bowl
cakestand	meat dish	tea cup
cereal bowl	milk jug	teapot
coffee cup	mug	tea set
coffee pot	percolator	tureen
cruet	plate	
cup	pot	

---

croft n
farm, plot, smallholding, farmland

crony n
friend, companion, familiar, intimate, confidant(e), associate, colleague, accomplice, ally, comrade, follower, sidekick
COLLOQ. mate, pal, chum, buddy

crook n, v
♦ n
1 CRIMINAL, thief, robber, offender, lawbreaker, swindler, operator, cheat, rogue, fraud, villain
COLLOQ. shark, con man
2 BEND, twist, slant, angle, hook, curve, bow, kink, distortion

♦ *v*
bend, twist, tilt, slant, angle, hook, curve, flex, bow, distort, warp, deform

crooked *adj*
1 ASKEW, awry, lopsided, asymmetric, irregular, uneven, off-centre, tilted, slanting, bent, angled, hooked, curved, bowed, warped, distorted, misshapen, deformed, contorted, twisted, buckled, tortuous, sinuous, winding, zigzag; *Scot* camsho, thrawn
OLD wrong
FORMAL anfractuous
COLLOQ. skew-whiff
2 CRIMINAL, illegal, unlawful, illicit, criminal, dishonest, deceitful, corrupt, fraudulent, shifty, underhand, treacherous, unscrupulous, unprincipled, unethical
FORMAL nefarious
COLLOQ. bent, shady
E3 1 straight **2** honest

crookedly *adv*
lopsidedly, askew, awry, asymmetrically, unevenly, off-centre

croon *v*
sing, hum, warble, lilt, vocalize

crop *n, v*
♦ *n*
1 *grow crops*
growth, yield, produce, fruits, harvest, vintage, gathering, reaping, gleaning
See also panel **arable crop** *at* **arable**.
2 *this year's crop of graduates*
batch, group, lot, set, collection
♦ *v*
cut, snip, clip, shear, trim, pare, prune, mow, lop, shorten, reduce, curtail
■ **crop up**
arise, emerge, appear, arrive, occur, happen, come up, turn up, present itself, come to pass, take place

cross *n, v, adj*
♦ *n*
1 CRUX, transverse
Related adjective: crucial
2 BURDEN, load, misfortune, trouble, adversity, worry, disaster, catastrophe, trial, grief, misery, pain, suffering, woe
FORMAL affliction, tribulation
3 CROSSBREED, hybrid, mongrel, blend, mix, mixture, mixed breed, amalgam, combination
♦ *v*
1 *cross the river*
go across, travel across, pass over, ford, bridge, arch, span
FORMAL traverse
2 INTERSECT, meet, join, converge, criss-cross, lace, interweave, intertwine
3 CROSSBREED, interbreed, mongrelize, hybridize, cross-fertilize, cross-pollinate, blend, mix
4 THWART, frustrate, foil, hinder, hamper, impede, obstruct, block, check, defy, resist, oppose
♦ *adj*
1 IRRITABLE, annoyed, angry, vexed, bad-tempered, ill-tempered, grumpy, put out, splenetic, irate, short, snappy, snappish, surly, sullen, fractious, cantankerous, awkward, difficult, prickly, harsh, fretful, disagreeable, impatient
FORMAL irascible
COLLOQ. peeved, shirty, crotchety, grouchy, crabby
2 TRANSVERSE, crosswise, oblique, diagonal, intersecting, opposite, reciprocal
E3 1 placid, pleasant
■ **cross out**
delete, remove, cancel, rub out, strike out, obliterate, edit out, cut out, blue-pencil

Types of cross include:

ankh	fleury	quadrate
Avelian	fylfot	rood
botoné	Geneva	Russian
Calvary	Greek	saltire
capital	Jerusalem	St Andrew's
cardinal	Latin	St Anthony's
Celtic	Lorraine	St George's
Constantinian	Maltese	St Peter's
Cornish	moline	swastika
crosslet	papal	tau
crucifix	patriarchal	Y-cross
encolpion	potent	

cross-examination *n*
interrogation, questioning, cross-questioning, examination, quiz, quizzing
COLLOQ. grilling, the third degree

cross-examine *v*
interrogate, question, cross-question, quiz, examine
COLLOQ. grill, pump, give someone the third degree

crossing *n*
1 *meet at the crossing*
junction, intersection, crossroads
2 *a pedestrian crossing*
pedestrian crossing, zebra crossing, pelican crossing, Toucan crossing; *N Am* crosswalk
3 *a sea crossing*
journey, trip, passage, voyage

crosswise *adv*
diagonally, crossways, crisscross, across, over, sideways, transversely, aslant, obliquely, athwart, awry
FORMAL catercorner, catercornered

crotch *n*
crutch, groin, genitals

crotchety *adj*
grumpy, awkward, bad-tempered, ill-tempered, cross, irritable, difficult, disagreeable, obstreperous, peevish, prickly, surly, testy, petulant, fractious, cantankerous, contrary, crusty
FORMAL irascible, iracund, iracundulous
COLLOQ. crabby, crabbed, grouchy
E3 calm, placid, pleasant

crouch *v*
squat, kneel, stoop, bend, bow, hunch, duck, cower, ruck, cringe
OLD dare

crow *v*
bluster, boast, brag, show off, gloat, rejoice, triumph, exult, flourish, vaunt
OLD cry roast-meat
COLLOQ. blow your own trumpet, talk big; *N Am* blow your own horn

crowd *n, v*
♦ *n*
1 THRONG, multitude, army, host, mob, masses, populace, people, public, riff-raff, rabble, horde, swarm, flock, herd, drove, huddle, pack, press, crush, squash, assembly, collection, company; *dialect* mong; *Scot* meinie
OLD (*Shakesp*) varletry
2 *all the college crowd*
group, bunch, lot, set, circle, band, clique, fraternity
3 SPECTATORS, viewers, watchers, listeners, gate, attendance, audience, house, turnout; *Aust* roll-up
♦ *v*
1 *crowd around the pop star*
cluster, gather, congregate, muster, converge, huddle, hustle, mass, mob, throng, swarm, flock, surge, stream

2 *crowd into a van*
push, shove, elbow, jostle, thrust, press, surge, squeeze, bundle, pile, pack, cram, jam, stuff, compress, congest, overflow

crowded *adj*
full, filled, packed, jammed, congested, crammed, cramped, crushed, overfull, overcrowded, overpopulated, busy, teeming, swarming, overflowing
COLLOQ. full to bursting, jam-packed, packed like sardines, chock-a-block, thick on the ground
SLANG chocker
F3 empty, deserted

crown *n, v*
♦ *n*
1 CORONET, diadem, tiara, circlet, wreath, corona, taj
TECHNICAL aureola
OLD pschent, garland
Related adjective: coronal
2 PRIZE, trophy, reward, honour, award, title, distinction, glory, kudos, garland, laurels, bays
3 SOVEREIGN, monarch, king, queen, emperor, empress, ruler, sovereignty, monarchy, royalty, empire
4 MONARCHY, sovereignty, royalty, empire
TECHNICAL ultimus haeres
5 TOP, tip, crest, summit, pinnacle, peak, acme, apex, climax, height, culmination; *S Afr* krantz
TECHNICAL corona
6 *the crown of the head*
pate; *Scot* cantle
TECHNICAL vertex
OLD sconce, foretop, noll
♦ *v*
1 *crown the king*
enthrone, invest, induct, install, anoint, adorn, festoon, honour, dignify, reward, laureate
2 TOP, cap, complete, perfect, fulfil, finalize, round off, be the culmination of
FORMAL consummate

crowning *adj, n*
♦ *adj*
culminating, final, perfect, supreme, top, ultimate, unmatched, unsurpassed, paramount, sovereign
FORMAL climactic, consummate
♦ *n*
coronation, enthronement, installation, investiture, inauguration
FORMAL incoronation

crucial *adj*
urgent, pressing, vital, essential, key, pivotal, central, important, momentous, major, deciding, decisive, critical, trying, testing, compelling, searching, historic
F3 unimportant, trivial

crucially *adv*
critically, vitally, essentially, centrally, momentously, importantly, decisively
F3 unimportantly, trivially

crucify *v*
1 *Christ was crucified*
kill on the cross, execute, put to death
2 *crucified by the critics*
criticize, run down, slate, mock, ridicule, persecute, torment, punish, torture, rack
FORMAL excoriate, denigrate
COLLOQ. slam, rubbish, knock, tear to pieces, tear to shreds, pull to pieces

crude *adj*
1 RAW, unprocessed, unrefined, untreated, rough, coarse, unfinished, unpolished
2 *a crude cabin*
rough, natural, primitive, makeshift, unfinished, undeveloped, simple, basic, rudimentary
FORMAL rude
COLLOQ. *N Am* down-and-dirty

3 *a crude remark*
vulgar, coarse, rude, indecent, obscene, uncouth, risqué, offensive, gross, dirty, lewd, earthy, bawdy, smutty
COLLOQ. raunchy, blue, hot, juicy
F3 1 refined, finished **3** polite, decent, tasteful

crudely *adv*
1 *a crudely-painted building*
roughly, simply, basically, primitively
2 RUDELY, coarsely, offensively, indecently, obscenely

cruel *adj*
fierce, ferocious, vicious, savage, barbarous, barbaric, bloodthirsty, murderous, cold-blooded, bloody, butcherly, sadistic, raw, brutal, inhuman, inhumane, unkind, heathenish, nasty, mean, evil, wicked, malevolent, fiendish, spiteful, malicious, callous, heartless, unfeeling, merciless, pitiless, flinty, hard-hearted, stony-hearted, iron-headed, implacable, ruthless, remorseless, blistering, unrelenting, inexorable, grim, hellish, diabolic, Neronian, atrocious, bitter, severe, cutting, painful, excruciating, fell, wanton
OLD felon, immane, marble-breasted, marble-hearted, truculent
FORMAL vengeful, indurate
F3 kind, compassionate, merciful

> **SYNONYM NUANCES**
>
> **Fierce**, **ferocious** and **vicious** all imply an unrestrained element, whilst **savage**, **barbarous** and **barbaric** more strongly suggest cruelty with an uncivilized aspect; **raw**, **brutal**, **inhuman** and **inhumane** also convey this idea: *his brutal reign of terror; the inhuman system of slavery.*
>   The terms **cold-blooded**, **callous**, **heartless**, **unfeeling**, **merciless**, **pitiless**, **ruthless** and **wanton** could all be used to emphasize the idea of absent feeling, while **flinty**, **hard-hearted** and **stony-hearted** continue this suggestion.
>   **Bloodthirsty** and **sadistic**, however, put the emphasis on relish and enjoyment of cruelty. The terms **nasty**, **mean**, **spiteful** and **malicious** all conjure up a somewhat underhand malevolence: *spiteful taunts.* **Implacable**, however, should be used specifically of an inability to be appeased even by cruelty: *the implacable tyranny of time;* **remorseless**, **unrelenting** and **inexorable** of a cruelty that is constant: *the war was a bitter and remorseless struggle.*

cruelly *adv*
fiercely, ferociously, viciously, savagely, cold-bloodedly, brutally, inhumanly, inhumanely, unkindly, spitefully, maliciously, callously, heartlessly, pitilessly, mercilessly, hard-heartedly, implacably, painfully, ruthlessly, remorselessly
OLD immanely, truculently
F3 kindly, compassionately, mercifully

cruelty *n*
ferocity, viciousness, savagery, barbarity, bloodthirstiness, murderousness, violence, sadism, abuse, bullying, brutality, bestiality, inhumanity, spite, malice, venom, callousness, heartlessness, hard-heartedness, mercilessness, ruthlessness, tyranny, unkindness, meanness, harshness, severity
F3 kindness, compassion, mercy

> **QUOTATIONS**
> Cruelty is the law pervading all nature and society; and we can't get out of it if we would!
>   THOMAS HARDY, *Jude the Obscure*

cruise *n, v*
♦ *n*
holiday, voyage, sail, journey, trip
♦ *v*
1 *cruising round the Mediterranean*
sail, travel, journey, voyage

2 *cruising along comfortably*
sail, coast, drift, freewheel, glide, slide, taxi

crumb *n*
piece, scrap, morsel, bit, titbit, particle, grain, atom, fragment, flake, speck, iota, jot, mite, shred, sliver, snippet, soupçon

crumble *v*
1 *the plaster is crumbling*
fragment, break up, come away, decompose, disintegrate, decay, degenerate, deteriorate, collapse, crush, pound, grind, powder, pulverize
2 *the organization began to crumble*
collapse, fail, fall to pieces, fall apart, disintegrate, decay, degenerate, deteriorate, break down, rot

crumbly *adj*
brittle, powdery, short
FORMAL friable, pulverulent

crummy *adj*
inferior, miserable, poor, rotten, shoddy, trashy, cheap, useless, weak, worthless, contemptible, substandard, second-rate, third-rate
COLLOQ. grotty, pathetic, rubbishy, half-baked
SLANG crappy
E3 excellent

crumple *v*
crush, wrinkle, pucker, crinkle, rumple, crease, fold, collapse, fall

crunch *v, n*
♦ *v*
1 *crunch a biscuit*
munch, chomp, champ, chew, bite, grind, crush
FORMAL masticate
2 *snow crunching*
grind, crush, scrunch, smash
♦ *n*
crisis, crux, critical point/situation, emergency, test, moment of truth
COLLOQ. pinch

crusade *n, v*
♦ *n*
1 *the Crusades*
holy war, jihad
2 *the crusade against nuclear power*
campaign, drive, struggle, push, movement, cause, undertaking, expedition, strategy, war, battle, offensive
♦ *v*
campaign, promote, push, drive, advocate, work, fight, strive, struggle, battle, attack

crusader *n*
advocate, campaigner, champion, promoter, enthusiast, reformer, zealot, activist, fighter, battler, missionary

crush *v, n*
♦ *v*
1 SQUASH, compress, squeeze, squelch, pinch, stamp, tread, trample, mash, press, pulp, break (up), smash, mill, pound, pulverize, bruise, mangle, shatter, screw up, grind, crunch, scrunch, champ, crumble, crumple, rumple, crease, crinkle, wrinkle, telescope; *dialect* thrutch
TECHNICAL contuse
OLD oppress; (*Shakesp*) pash
FORMAL comminute, triturate
2 *the rebels were crushed*
conquer, demolish, devastate, defeat, overpower, overwhelm, overcome, quash, quell, suppress, squelch, subdue, step on, put down
FORMAL vanquish
COLLOQ. squabash
3 *crushed by the criticism*
upset, devastate, annihilate, mortify, humiliate, shame, abash; *dialect* mush
COLLOQ. put down

♦ *n*
1 *injured in the crush*
crowd, pack, press, squash, throng, horde, jam
2 *a crush on the French teacher*
infatuation, passion, obsession, love, liking
COLLOQ. pash

crust *n*
surface, exterior, outside, covering, topping, coat, coating, layer, film, casing, mantle, skin, rind, shell, husk, scab, caking
TECHNICAL incrustation, concretion

crusty *adj*
1 *crusty bread*
crispy, crunchy, brittle, crumbly, breakable, firm, hard, well-done, baked, well-baked
FORMAL friable
2 *a crusty old man*
grumpy, awkward, bad-tempered, short-tempered, brusque, gruff, cross, irritable, difficult, disagreeable, obstreperous, peevish, prickly, surly, testy, touchy, petulant, fractious, splenetic, cantankerous, contrary
FORMAL irascible
COLLOQ. crabby, crabbed, grouchy
E3 1 soft, soggy **2** calm, placid, pleasant

crux *n*
nub, heart, core, essence, centre, kernel, nucleus
COLLOQ. the bottom line

cry *v, n*
♦ *v*
1 WEEP, sob, be in/shed tears, wail, howl, bawl, whimper, whine, snivel; *Scot* greet
COLLOQ. blub, blubber, burst into tears, cry your eyes out, turn on the waterworks; *Scot* bubble
2 SHOUT, call (out), exclaim, roar, bellow, yell, scream, howl, bawl, shriek, screech
♦ *n*
1 WEEP, sob, tears, wail, howl, bawl, whimper, whine, snivel; *Scot* greet
COLLOQ. blubber; *Scot* bubble
2 SHOUT, call, plea, exclamation, roar, bellow, yell, scream, howl, bawl, shriek, screech
■ **cry off**
cancel, withdraw, excuse yourself, back out, decide against, change your mind
■ **cry out for**
need, call for, demand, want, require, necessitate

SYNONYM NUANCES

verb sense 1
Weep can be widely used, without any suggestion of disapproval, to refer to the shedding of tears, generally as an expression of grief; **sob** suggests a more dramatic act with a convulsive catching of the breath: *she sobbed, gasping for air*. **Blubber** also suggests the effusive shedding of tears, but carries a further implication of impatience from those witnessing it: *he was blubbering like a child*.
   Wail, **howl** and **bawl**, however, would be appropriate to use of a usually prolonged, loud sound: *the cat wailed to be let out*; *he bawled loudly when getting his hair washed*. For a quieter, almost muffled, low crying sound, you could use **whimper**: *the children whimpered piteously*; **whine**, although similar, often has a further accusation of peevishness: *the babies were whining and fractious*. If you use **snivel**, you are implying contempt for the person doing it: *oh, do stop snivelling!*

---

crypt *n*
tomb, vault, burial chamber, catacomb, mausoleum, undercroft
Related adjective: cryptal

cryptic *adj*
enigmatic, ambiguous, equivocal, puzzling, perplexing, mysterious, strange, bizarre, secret, hidden, veiled, obscure, dark, occult
FORMAL abstruse, esoteric
EXT straightforward, clear, obvious

cryptically *adv*
enigmatically, ambiguously, mysteriously, strangely, secretly, bizarrely, obscurely
EXT clearly, obviously

crystallize *v*
1 *the substance crystallized*
solidify, harden, materialize, form
2 *the idea crystallized*
make/become clear, make/become definite, clarify, appear, emerge, form

cub *n*
1 *fox cubs*
offspring, pup, puppy, whelp, baby, young
2 *a cub reporter*
beginner, novice, tiro, starter, learner, trainee, apprentice, student, probationer, initiate, freshman, fresher, recruit, raw recruit, tenderfoot, fledgling, neophyte, youngster, youth
COLLOQ. greenhorn, rookie, newbie

cubbyhole *n*
compartment, niche, pigeonhole, slot, recess, booth, cubicle, den, hideaway, hole, tiny room

cube *n*
dice, die, solid, block, cuboid, hexahedron

cuddle *v, n*
♦ *v*
hug, embrace, clasp, hold, enfold, nurse, nestle, snuggle, pet, fondle, caress
COLLOQ. snog, canoodle, neck, smooch
♦ *n*
hug, embrace, clasp, hold, snuggle
COLLOQ. snog, canoodle, neck, smooch

cuddly *adj*
cuddlesome, lov(e)able, huggable, plump, soft, warm, cosy

cudgel *n, v*
♦ *n*
club, stick, mace, bludgeon, bat, truncheon; *Irish* shillelagh, alpeen; bastinado
COLLOQ. cosh
♦ *v*
hit, strike, beat, club, bash, clout, thwack, pound, bludgeon, batter
COLLOQ. clobber, cosh

cue *n*
signal, sign, nod, hint, suggestion, intimation, indication, reminder, prompt, incentive, stimulus

cuff *v*
hit, thump, box, clip, knock, buffet, slap, smack, strike, clout, beat
COLLOQ. biff, clobber, belt, whack
■ **off the cuff**
impromptu, extempore, without preparation, ad lib, spontaneously, improvised, unprepared, unrehearsed, unscripted
COLLOQ. off the top of your head, on the spur of the moment

cuisine *n*
cooking, cookery, haute cuisine, cordon bleu, nouvelle cuisine

cul-de-sac *n*
no through road, dead end, blind alley

cull *v*
1 *cull information*
collect, gather, choose, pick (out), select, sift, glean, pluck, amass

2 *cull wild animals*
kill, destroy, slaughter, thin (out)

culminate *v*
climax, come to a climax, come to a head, end (up), terminate, close, conclude, finish, peak
FORMAL consummate
COLLOQ. wind up
EXT start, begin

culmination *n*
climax, height, high point, peak, apex, acme, zenith, pinnacle, summit, top, crown, perfection, finale, conclusion, completion
FORMAL consummation
EXT start, beginning

culpability *n*
responsibility, accountability, liability, answerability, blame, guilt, fault

culpable *adj*
to blame, wrong, in the wrong, at fault, responsible, guilty, liable, offending, answerable, blam(e)able, blameworthy, censurable, reprehensible, sinful
FORMAL peccant
EXT blameless, innocent

culprit *n*
guilty party, offender, wrongdoer, miscreant, lawbreaker, criminal, felon, delinquent, convict, villain

cult *n*
1 SECT, denomination, religion, faith, belief, affiliation, school, movement, party, faction
2 CRAZE, fad, fashion, vogue, obsession, mania, fixation, trend
COLLOQ. in-thing

cultivate *v*
1 FARM, till, work, plough, dig, prepare, grow, sow, plant, tend, raise, bring on, fertilize, produce, harvest, garden; *dialect* labour
OLD husband, manure
FORMAL culture
2 FOSTER, nurture, cherish, help, aid, assist, support, back, encourage, promote, further, forward, advance, enhance, work on, pursue, court, woo, develop, train, prepare, polish, refine, improve, enrich, enlighten
EXT 2 neglect

cultivated *adj*
refined, cultured, civilized, sophisticated, polished, genteel, urbane, advanced, enlightened, educated, well-read, well-informed, scholarly, highbrow, discerning, discriminating

cultivation *n*
1 FARMING, agriculture, growing, sowing, planting, tilling, working, preparation, harvesting
2 FOSTERING, encouragement, nurture, nurturing, cherishing, assistance, support, backing, furthering, forwarding, advancing, development, improvement, refinement

cultural *adj*
1 *cultural events*
artistic, aesthetic, liberal, civilizing, humanizing, enlightening, educational, educative, edifying, improving, broadening, developmental, enriching, elevating
2 *cultural heritage*
communal, national, ethnic, folk, tribal, traditional
TECHNICAL anthropological
FORMAL societal

culture *n*
1 *popular culture*
the arts, humanities, painting, philosophy, music, literature, history, learning
2 CIVILIZATION, society, lifestyle, way of life, customs, traditions, heritage, habits, behaviour
FORMAL mores

3 *cell culture*
growth, production, crop, tendering, nurturing

cultured *adj*
cultivated, civilized, advanced, enlightened, educated, well-educated, well-read, well-informed, learned, scholarly, highbrow, intellectual, erudite, artistic, well-bred, refined, polite, polished, sophisticated, genteel, tasteful, urbane
COLLOQ. arty; *(derog)* arty-farty
E3 uncultured, uneducated, ignorant

culvert *n*
channel, conduit, drain, duct, gutter, sewer, watercourse

cumbersome *adj*
1 *a cumbersome machine*
awkward, inconvenient, bulky, unwieldy, unmanageable, burdensome, onerous, heavy, weighty
FORMAL incommodious, cumbrous
2 *a cumbersome process*
complicated, complex, involved, difficult, inefficient, badly organized, wasteful, slow
E3 1 convenient, manageable **2** simple, efficient

cumulative *adj*
increasing, growing, mounting, multiplying, enlarging, progressive, collective
COLLOQ. snowballing

cunning *adj, n*
   ♦ *adj*
1 *a cunning person*
crafty, sly, artful, wily, tricky, devious, subtle, deceitful, arch, sneaky, guileful, manipulative, sharp, shrewd, astute, canny, knowing, deep, insidious, varmint, vulpine, knackish, leery, *rusé*; *dialect* carny; *Scot* sleekit
OLD quaint
COLLOQ. shifty, cunning as a fox
2 *a cunning plan*
clever, imaginative, ingenious, skilful, inventive, resourceful, deft, dexterous, fiendish
E3 1 naive, ingenuous, gullible
   ♦ *n*
cunningness, craftiness, slyness, artfulness, trickery, deviousness, subtlety, deceit, deceitfulness, guile, wiles, sharpness, shrewdness, astuteness, ingenuity, cleverness, imaginativeness, skill, art, craft, policy, sleight, inventiveness, resourcefulness, deftness, finesse, adroitness, fiendishness, Machiavellianism
OLD *(Shakesp)* cautel; *(Spenser)* practic

cup *n*
1 *drink from a cup*
mug, tankard, beaker, goblet, chalice
2 *win a cup*
trophy, award, medal, prize, reward
3 *claret cup*
punch, wine

cupboard *n*
cabinet, locker, closet, wardrobe, pantry, sideboard, tallboy, dresser, Welsh dresser, chest

cupidity *n*
acquisitiveness, greed, greediness, avarice, avariciousness, graspingness, covetousness, eagerness, hunger, hankering, itching, longing, yearning
FORMAL avidity, rapaciousness, rapacity, voracity

curable *adj*
remediable, treatable, operable, medicable, reparable, rectifiable, reformable
E3 incurable

curative *adj*
healing, healthful, health-giving, therapeutic, tonic, medicinal, remedial, restorative, corrective, salutary
TECHNICAL febrifugal
FORMAL alleviative, vulnerary

curator *n*
keeper, attendant, conservator, custodian, caretaker, steward, warden, warder, guardian

curb *v, n*
   ♦ *v*
restrain, constrain, restrict, contain, control, keep under control, check, keep in check, rein, moderate, reduce, bridle, muzzle, keep back, hold back, suppress, subdue, repress, inhibit, hinder, impede, hamper
FORMAL retard
E3 encourage, foster
   ♦ *n*
limitation, restriction, check, control, constraint, restraint, brake, rein, bridle, deterrent, damper, holding-back, suppression, repression, hindrance, hamper, impediment
FORMAL retardant

curdle *v*
coagulate, congeal, clot, solidify, thicken, turn, sour, turn sour, ferment
OLD *(Shakesp)* posset; *(Spenser)* cruddle

cure *v, n*
   ♦ *v*
1 HEAL, remedy, correct, restore, treat, repair, fix, rectify, mend, relieve, ease, alleviate, help, make better, make well
2 PRESERVE, dry, smoke, salt, pickle, kipper
   ♦ *n*
remedy, antidote, panacea, cure-all, solution, medicine, corrective, restorative, healing, treatment, therapy, alleviation, recovery
TECHNICAL specific
FORMAL elixir

cure-all *n*
panacea, universal remedy, nostrum
FORMAL elixir, catholicon, diacatholicon, panpharmacon

curio *n*
antique, bygone, curiosity, knick-knack, trinket, bibelot, *objet d'art*, object of virtu, *objet de vertu*

curiosity *n*
1 INQUISITIVENESS, interest, questioning, querying, search, inquiry, prying, snooping, interference
COLLOQ. nosiness
2 CURIO, *objet d'art*, antique, bygone, novelty, trinket, knick-knack
3 ODDITY, rarity, peculiarity, freak, phenomenon, spectacle, wonder, marvel, exotica

PROVERBS
Curiosity killed the cat

curious *adj*
1 INQUISITIVE, questioning, querying, searching, inquiring, interested, intrigued, fascinated, keen to know, wanting to learn, prying, meddling, snooping, agog, meddlesome, interfering
COLLOQ. nos(e)y
2 *a curious sight*
odd, queer, funny, strange, peculiar, bizarre, mysterious, puzzling, extraordinary, out of the ordinary, unusual, remarkable, rare, unique, novel, exotic, unconventional, weird, freakish, unorthodox, quaint
E3 1 uninterested, indifferent **2** ordinary, usual, normal

curiously *adv*
1 INQUISITIVELY, questioningly, inquiringly, meddlesomely, interferingly
2 ODDLY, strangely, peculiarly, mysteriously, unusually, remarkably, unconventionally, quaintly, bizarrely, out of the ordinary
E3 2 usually, normally

curl *v, n*

♦ *v*

crimp, crimple, frizz, frizzle, wave, roll, crinkle, ripple, kink, bend, curve, meander, loop, turn, twist, wind, wreathe, twirl, twine, coil, spiral, snake, corkscrew, scroll, tong, purl, becurl

OLD frounce

ᴇᴈ uncurl

♦ *n*

wave, kink, swirl, twist, roll, ring, ringlet, coil, crimp, crinkle, frizz, frizzle, curlicue, helix, spiral, whorl, dildo, heartbreaker, kiss-curl, wreath

OLD frounce, earlock, favourite, lovelock, pinch

curly *adj*

curled, crimped, permed, frizzy, fuzzy, wavy, kinky, curling, looping, turning, twisting, winding, wreathing, twirling, coiling, spiralled, spiralling, corkscrew

ᴇᴈ straight

currency *n*

1 MONEY, legal tender, coinage, coins, notes, cash, bills
2 ACCEPTANCE, publicity, popularity, vogue, circulation, prevalence, exposure

FORMAL dissemination

current *adj, n*

♦ *adj*

1 *current events*

present, ongoing, existing, contemporary, present-day, present-time, modern, fashionable, in fashion, up-to-date, up-to-the-minute, in vogue, popular, topical

FORMAL extant

COLLOQ. trendy, in, now

2 *still current in the 1800s*

(generally) accepted, widespread, prevalent, common, popular, general, prevailing, reigning, in circulation, valid

COLLOQ. going around

ᴇᴈ 1 obsolete, old-fashioned

♦ *n*

draught, stream, mainstream, jet, flow, swirl, movement, drift, ebb, tide, course, progress, trend, direction, tendency, undercurrent, tenor, mood, feeling

currently *adv*

now, at present, at the present time, right now, just now, at the moment, for the time being, at this time, today, these days; *N Am* presently

curriculum *n*

syllabus, core curriculum, national curriculum, subjects, course of studies, discipline, course, course of study, module, educational programme, timetable

curse *v, n*

♦ *v*

1 SWEAR, use bad language, blaspheme, damn

FORMAL imprecate

COLLOQ. damn and blast, blind, eff and blind

SLANG cuss

2 CONDEMN, damn, denounce, blast

OLD ban, shrew; (*Shakesp*) beshrew

FORMAL accurse, execrate, imprecate, anathematize, fulminate

COLLOQ. put a jinx on

3 BLIGHT, plague, scourge, afflict, harm, ruin, trouble, beset, torment

ᴇᴈ 2 bless

♦ *n*

1 SWEAR-WORD, oath, expletive, blasphemy, obscenity, profanity, bad language; *N Am* curse-word

FORMAL imprecation

COLLOQ. four-letter word

SLANG cuss; *N Am* cussword

2 JINX, spell, anathema, Indian sign, bane, evil, plague, scourge, blight, affliction, trouble, torment, ordeal, calamity, misfortune, disaster; *Scot* winze

OLD pox, woe, maugre, vengeance, ban, malison

FORMAL execration, malediction, tribulation

COLLOQ. *Aust* moz

ᴇᴈ 2 blessing, advantage

cursed *adj*

damned, detestable, abominable, hateful, loathsome, odious, vile, fiendish, annoying, unpleasant, pernicious, infamous

FORMAL execrable

COLLOQ. blasted, blooming, blinking, flipping, flaming, darned, dashed, confounded, infernal, dratting

SLANG bloody, cussed; (*taboo*) fucking, frigging

cursory *adj*

brief, slight, summary, superficial, desultory, quick, rapid, fleeting, hasty, hurried, offhand, dismissive, passing, perfunctory, careless, casual, slapdash

ᴇᴈ painstaking, thorough

curt *adj*

abrupt, blunt, rude, sharp, brusque, gruff, laconic, offhand, short, short-spoken, tart, terse, snappish, unceremonious, uncivil, ungracious, brief, pithy, concise, succinct, summary

ᴇᴈ voluble

curtail *v*

reduce, limit, restrict, shorten, truncate, cut, cut down, cut short, cut back (on), trim, shrink, abridge, abbreviate, lessen, decrease, pare, pare down/back, prune, slim, guillotine

ᴇᴈ lengthen, extend, increase

curtailment *n*

reduction, limitation, restriction, shortening, truncation, cut, cutback, trimming, shrinkage, abridgement, abbreviation, contraction, lessening, decrease, paring, docking, pruning, slimming, guillotine

FORMAL retrenchment

ᴇᴈ extension, lengthening, increase

curtain *n*

blind, screen, cover, shutter, net curtain, hanging, window hanging, backdrop, portière, drapery, tapestry; *N Am* drape

curtly *adv*

abruptly, bluntly, rudely, sharply, brusquely, laconically, gruffly, tersely, unceremoniously, uncivilly, ungraciously, briefly, pithily, concisely, succinctly

curtsy *v*

bob, bow, kowtow, salaam

FORMAL genuflect

curvaceous *adj*

shapely, well-proportioned, well-rounded, buxom, comely, curvy, bosomy, voluptuous

SLANG well-stacked

ᴇᴈ skinny

curve *v, n*

♦ *v*

bend, arch, arc, bow, bulge, swell, hook, crook, turn, wind, twist, round, swerve, loop, spiral, coil

FORMAL incurve

♦ *n*

bend, turn, bow, loop, arc, arch, circle, crescent, trajectory, helix, spiral, winding, meandering, camber, kink, curvature, flexure

curved *adj*

bent, arched, bowed, rounded, humped, bulging, swelling, convex, concave, bending, cupped, scooped, crooked, twisted, warped, sweeping, sinuous, tortuous, serpentine

TECHNICAL arcuate, curviform

ᴇᴈ straight

cushion *n, v*

♦ *n*

pillow, bolster, headrest, squab, beanbag, hassock, kneeler, pad, padding, mat, bum roll, pillion, buffer, protection, shock absorber; *Scot* cod
TECHNICAL pulvinus
Related adjectives: pulvillar, pulvinar

♦ *v*

soften, deaden, dampen, absorb, muffle, stifle, suppress, lessen, reduce, diminish, mitigate, protect, bolster, buttress, buffer, prop up, support

cushy *adj*

comfortable, easy, undemanding
COLLOQ. jammy, soft, plum
Fᴣ demanding, tough, taxing

custodian *n*

caretaker, conservator, curator, guard, guardian, warden, warder, keeper, overseer, superintendent, watchdog, watchman, protector, castellan

custody *n*

1 KEEPING, possession, charge, care, safekeeping, protection, preservation, custodianship, trusteeship, guardianship, wardship, guidance, supervision, responsibility
2 DETENTION, confinement, imprisonment, captivity, arrest
FORMAL incarceration

custom *n*

1 *national customs*
tradition, usage, use, habit, routine, procedure, practice, policy, way, manner, style, form, fashion, way of behaving, convention, etiquette, ethos, mores, formality, observance, ritual, rite, institution
2 *take my custom elsewhere*
business, trade
FORMAL patronage

> **QUOTATIONS**
> Often, the less there is to justify a traditional custom, the harder it is to get rid of it
>   Mᴀʀᴋ Tᴡᴀɪɴ, *The Adventures of Tom Sawyer*

SYNONYM NUANCES

sense 1
The word **tradition** appropriately describes something that has been passed down through the generations and has positive associations, whereas **usage** and **use** are more neutral, suggesting only the constant use of something until it becomes established. Both **habit** and **routine** can be used of custom that has been established by repetition: *get into the habit of separating recyclable material from the rest of the household rubbish.*

The terms **procedure** and **practice** are the words to use to convey an established way of going about something: *police procedure; accepted hospital practice;* **policy** is appropriate where an official declaration of this has been made: *it's not company policy to allow extra days off.* **Form** also conveys this notion of what is or is not accepted, but might be used with a more social slant: *it's not good form to turn up drunk to a party.*

Convention and **etiquette** also relate to custom conforming to an established set of rules, although convention can have the widest application: *the conventions of the detective story.* **Fashion** is similar, but would most appropriately be used of customs conforming to current trends.

The term **ethos** has connotations of an intrinsic and usually positive distinguishing character: *the American ethos of freedom and liberty.* **Observance**, **rite** and **ritual** are more appropriate where ceremony is involved:

the observance of Remembrance Day. **Institution**, meanwhile, is again quite positive in tone, referring to something that forms the bedrock of everyday life: *the pub is a great British institution.*

customarily *adv*

traditionally, conventionally, habitually, routinely, regularly, as a rule, usually, normally, ordinarily, commonly, generally, popularly, fashionably
Fᴣ unusually, occasionally, rarely

customary *adj*

traditional, conventional, obligatory, accepted, established, set, habitual, routine, regular, usual, normal, ordinary, everyday, familiar, common, general, popular, fashionable, prevailing
Fᴣ unusual, rare

customer *n*

client, patron, regular, consumer, shopper, buyer, purchaser, prospect
COLLOQ. punter

customize *v*

adapt, convert, modify, tailor, alter, adjust, tweak, suit, fit, transform, personalize
COLLOQ. fine-tune

customs *n*

taxes, duties, dues, tariffs, levies, exise
FORMAL impost

cut *v, n*

♦ *v*

1 *cut the paper/your finger; cut a hole*
slit, pierce, slice, sever, chop, hack, hew, carve, split, dock, lop, prune, excise
2 *cut meat*
dissect, divide, carve, slice, chop (up), dice, mince, shred, grate
FORMAL cleave
3 *cut hair/grass/a plant*
shorten, trim, clip, crop, snip, shear, mow, shave, pare, prune, poll, dock
4 *cut glass*
engrave, incise, chisel, score
5 *cut someone's throat*
stab, wound, nick, slash, lacerate, gash, slit
6 *cut costs*
reduce, decrease, lower, diminish, lessen, curtail, curb, prune
COLLOQ. slash, axe
7 *cut a story/broadcast*
shorten, make shorter, curtail, abbreviate, abridge, condense, précis, summarize, edit, delete, omit
FORMAL excise, expurgate
8 *cut a supply*
stop, end, bring to an end, halt, suspend, disconnect, break off, block, obstruct, intercept
FORMAL discontinue
9 *cut a recording*
record, make, tape, tape-record, videotape, burn
10 *cut someone dead*
ignore, spurn, avoid, pretend not to see/notice, shun, snub, slight, rebuff, insult, scorn
COLLOQ. cut dead, cold-shoulder, look right through, blank, send to Coventry, not give someone the time of day

♦ *n*

1 INCISION, wound, nick, gash, slit, slash, rip, laceration, notch, score
2 *go for a cut at the barber's*
trim, clip, crop, shave
3 *spending cuts*
reduction, decrease, lowering, cutback, saving, economy, lessening
FORMAL retrenchment
4 *a cut of meat*
joint, section, slice, piece, bit, part

5 *a power cut*
failure, fault, breakdown, breaking-down, cutting-out
FORMAL malfunctioning
6 *a cut of the profits*
share, allocation, proportion, portion, quota, ration
COLLOQ. slice, slice of the cake, rake-off, whack
7 *the cut of a garment*
shape, style, fashion, form, profile, design

■ **cut across**
transcend, surmount, go beyond, rise above, leave behind

■ **cut back**
check, crop, curb, curtail, decrease, economize, lessen, lop, lower, prune, reduce, trim, scale down
FORMAL retrench
COLLOQ. slash, downsize, pull/tighten the purse strings

■ **cut down**
1 *cut down a tree*
fell, chop down, hew, saw, lop, level, raze
2 REDUCE, decrease, lower, lessen, diminish, curtail, curb, prune

■ **cut in**
interrupt, break in, butt in, intervene, intrude
FORMAL interpose, interject
COLLOQ. barge in

■ **cut off**
1 *cut off his head*
remove, sever, detach, amputate, chop off, take off, break off, tear off
2 *feel cut off from friends*
separate, isolate, keep apart, detach, seclude, sever, insulate, shelter
3 *cut off a supply*
stop, end, bring to an end, halt, suspend, disconnect, break off, block, obstruct, intercept
FORMAL discontinue
4 *get cut off on the phone*
disconnect, break off, unhook, separate, detach, intercept, interrupt

■ **cut out**
1 *cut out a coupon*
extract, remove, separate, take out, tear out
FORMAL excise
2 OMIT, cut, exclude, leave out, drop, delete, edit
FORMAL excise
3 stop, refrain, cease
FORMAL desist, discontinue
COLLOQ. quit, leave off, lay off, knock off, pack in
4 *the engine cut out*
stop working, fail, break down, go wrong
FORMAL malfunction
COLLOQ. pack up, go on the blink, go phut, go kaput
SLANG conk out

■ **cut up**
carve, slice(up), chop (up), dice, mince, dissect, dismember, divide, slash

■ **cut out for**
suitable, suited, right, appropriate, qualified, made, good

■ **cut and dried**
clear, definite, certain, settled, decided, fixed, organized, prearranged, automatic, predetermined
COLLOQ. sewn up

■ **cut up**
upset, unhappy, hurt, annoyed, distressed, bothered, saddened, troubled
COLLOQ. put out, het up, worked up

cutback *n*
cut, saving, economy, reduction, decrease, curtailment, lowering, lessening
FORMAL retrenchment
COLLOQ. slashing

cute *adj*
sweet, endearing, lov(e)able, charming, appealing, attractive, pretty, lovely, delightful, adorable
🔁 unpleasant, unattractive, nasty

cutlery

Items of cutlery include:

apostle spoon	corn holders	salt spoon
bread knife	dessertspoon	soupspoon
butter knife	fish fork	spoon
caddy spoon	fish knife	spork
cake server	fish slice	steak knife
canteen of cutlery	fork	sugar tongs
carving fork	knife	tablespoon
carving knife	ladle	teaspoon
cheese knife	pickle fork	vegetable knife
chopsticks	salad servers	

See also **kitchen utensils**.

cut-price *adj*
reduced, sale, discount, bargain, cheap, low-priced, cut-rate, marked-down

cutter

Types of cutter include:

adze	jigsaw	scissors
axe	knife	scythe
billhook	lawnmower	secateurs
blade	lopper	shears
chainsaw	machete	shredder
chisel	mower	sickle
chopper	penknife	spokeshave
clippers	pinking shears	Stanley knife®
flick knife	plane	Strimmer®
fretsaw	pocket knife	Swiss army knife
guillotine	razor	sword
hacksaw	saw	
hedgetrimmer	scalpel	

See also **cutlery**; **saw¹**; **weapon**.

cut-throat *adj*
ruthless, pitiless, merciless, relentless, fierce, highly/fiercely competitive, keen, keenly contested, cruel, brutal
COLLOQ. dog-eat-dog

cutting *adj, n*
♦ *adj*
1 *a cutting wind*
bitter, raw, chill, sharp, keen, penetrating
2 *a cutting comment*
pointed, incisive, bitter, penetrating, piercing, wounding, hurtful, stinging, biting, caustic, acid, scathing, sarcastic, snide, malicious
FORMAL mordant, trenchant
COLLOQ. bitchy
♦ *n*
clipping, clip, extract, excerpt, piece

cycle *n*
circle, round, rotation, oscillation, rhythm, biorhythm, body clock, revolution, rota, series, sequence, order, pattern, succession, phase, period, era, age, epoch, aeon

cyclical *adj*
cyclic, recurring, recurrent, repeated, repetitive, regular

cyclone *n*
hurricane, monsoon, tempest, tropical storm, storm, tornado, typhoon, whirlwind; *Aust* willy-willy

cylinder *n*
column, barrel, drum, reel, bobbin, spool, spindle

cynic *n*
sceptic, doubter, pessimist, killjoy, scoffer
FORMAL misanthrope
COLLOQ. knocker, spoilsport

cynical *adj*
sceptical, doubtful, doubting, distrustful, disillusioned, disenchanted, pessimistic, negative, critical, scornful, derisive, suspicious, contemptuous, sneering, unsentimental, surly, scoffing, mocking, sarcastic, sardonic, ironic, bitter, embittered, worldly-wise, streetwise
FORMAL Diogenic, Mephistophelean
COLLOQ. hard-boiled, hardnosed

cynically *adv*
sceptically, distrustfully, pessimistically, critically, scornfully, derisively, suspiciously, contemptuously, mockingly, bitterly, negatively

cynicism *n*
scepticism, doubt, disbelief, distrust, disillusionment, disenchantment, pessimism, scorn, suspicion, contempt, sneering, scoffing, mocking, sarcasm, irony
FORMAL misanthropy

SYNONYM NUANCES

Scepticism may be used of a general lack of trust, similar to **distrust** and **suspicion**, though perhaps with a more world-weary view: *rising scepticism over politicians' promises*. **Doubt** suggests hesitancy in accepting something, whilst **disbelief** goes further and would only be appropriate to describe a complete lack of faith.

Both **disillusionment** and **disenchantment**, however, emphasize the idea of being let down by something you did previously believe in: *his growing disenchantment with communism*; while the term **pessimism** is suggestive of a generally bleak outlook, anticipating the worst.

Contempt and **sneering** could be used of an actively expressed cynicism born of a complete lack of regard: *their total contempt for democracy*. **Scorn**, **scoffing** and **mocking** might be used of vociferous cynicism involving jeering derision. **Sarcasm** is only appropriate where there is an element of cutting verbal expression: *social commentaries, loaded with sarcasm*.

---

cyst *n*
growth, sac, vesicle, blister, wen, abscess, bladder, bleb

TECHNICAL atheroma, utricle, ranula, steatoma, chalazion, dermoid, hydatid

D

dab *v, n*

♦ *v*
pat, daub, swab, wipe, touch, press, blot, mop, tap
♦ *n*
1 BIT, drop, dash, speck, spot, trace, trickle, splash, sprinkle, tinge, smear, smudge, fleck
COLLOQ. dollop, tad, smidgen
2 TOUCH, pat, stroke, tap, mop, wipe, press
■ **dab hand**
expert, pastmaster, wizard, ace, adept

dabble *v*
1 TRIFLE, play, tinker, toy, dally, dip, flirt, fiddle, potter; *N Am* putter
2 PADDLE, moisten, wet, dampen, sprinkle, dip, immerse, splash, splatter

dabbler *n*
amateur, lay person, dilettante, trifler, dallier, tinkerer
E3 professional, expert

daemon *n*
spirit, good spirit, genius, *genius loci*, force, animus, deva, geist, evil spirit, devil, demon, cacodemon

daft *adj*
1 *a daft idea*
foolish, crazy, silly, stupid, absurd, ridiculous, ludicrous, preposterous, farcical, laughable, outrageous, nonsensical, senseless, unwise, imprudent, odd, peculiar, impracticable, unrealistic, foolhardy, irrational, irresponsible, wild, idiotic, fatuous, inane
COLLOQ. dotty; *(offensive)* dumb; barmy, batty, potty, half-baked, hare-brained, addle-brained, crackbrained, crackpot, wacky; *Aust & NZ* dingbats
2 *a daft boy*
simple, simple-minded, stupid, dim, dull, dense, slow, slow-witted
COLLOQ. thick, thick as a plank/two short planks, dim-witted, dopey, gormless, dumb
3 INSANE, mad, lunatic, crazy, unbalanced, disturbed, deranged, demented, crazed, wild, berserk, touched, unhinged, out of your mind
COLLOQ. loopy, bonkers, nuts, nutty, nutty as a fruitcake, round the bend, round the twist
SLANG mental, loony, off your rocker, needing your head examining
4 INFATUATED, passionate, enamoured, smitten, obsessed, mad, wild, enthusiastic, fanatical, zealous, devoted, fond, keen, avid, ardent
COLLOQ. crazy, nuts, potty, sweet
E3 1 sensible **2** sane **3** indifferent

dagger *n*
knife, blade, poniard
OLD baselard, bodkin, dudgeon, puncheon

Daggers include:

bayonet	kukri	stiletto
dirk	misericord	whinger
handjar	push dagger	whinyard
jambiya	sai	yatagan
kirpan	skene	
kris	skene-dhu	

---

daily *adj, adv*

♦ *adj*
1 REGULAR, routine, everyday, customary, common, commonplace, ordinary, habitual
2 EVERYDAY
OLD *(Shakesp)* journal; *(Spenser)* adays
FORMAL diurnal, quotidian, circadian
♦ *adv*
every day, day after day, day by day

dainty *adj, n*

♦ *adj*
1 DELICATE, elegant, pretty, exquisite, petite, little, small, refined, fine, graceful, neat, trim, charming
2 *a dainty morsel*
tasty, delicious, delightful, enjoyable, appetizing, choice, palatable mouth-watering, luscious, succulent, juicy, savoury
FORMAL delectable
3 FASTIDIOUS, fussy, particular, discriminating, hard to please, finicky, scrupulous
COLLOQ. choosy, faddy
E3 1 gross, clumsy, unwieldy **2** unpalatable
♦ *n*
delicacy, fancy, titbit, sweetmeat, bonbon, bonne-bouche

dais *n*
platform, stage, rostrum, podium, stand, staging

dale *n*
valley, vale, glen, dell, coomb, cwm; *dialect* griff, grike; *Scot* heuch, strath; *N Am* gulch; dean, den, dene, ria, slade, dingle, gill

dalliance *n*
1 PLAYING, sporting, toying, flirting, trifling
2 DELAY, dawdling, pottering, tarrying, loitering

dally *v*
1 DAWDLE, linger, loiter, delay, take your time
FORMAL procrastinate, tarry
2 *dally with an idea*
toy, play, flirt, trifle, frivol, carry on
E3 1 hasten, hurry

dam *n, v*

♦ *n*
barrier, barrage, embankment, weir, wall, blockage, barricade, obstruction, hindrance
♦ *v*
block, confine, restrict, check, barricade, staunch, stem, obstruct

damage *v, n*

♦ *v*
harm, injure, hurt, spoil, ruin, destroy, break, impair, mar, abuse, wreck, deface, scar, vandalize, sabotage, desecrate, mutilate, weaken, tamper with, play/wreak havoc with, incapacitate
FORMAL vitiate
E3 mend, repair, fix
♦ *n*
1 *extensive damage after the fire*
harm, injury, hurt, destruction, ruin, devastation, havoc, loss, abuse, suffering, mischief, mutilation, impairment, detriment, defacement, vandalism, desecration, vandalization, defilement

2 pay damages
compensation, fine, indemnity, indemnification, reimbursement, recompense, reparation, restitution, satisfaction
3 What's the damage?
cost, expense, charge, price
☰ 1 repair

SYNONYM NUANCES

verb
Harm is in general use to suggest physical, emotional or moral damage: *motherhood harmed her career*; **hurt** and **injure** may be used in the same way: *the scandal hurt the campaign*. The terms **spoil**, **ruin** and **mar** could be used of the irreparable damaging of a variety of things: *low cloud spoiled our view*; *the mud ruined my shoes*; *the text was marred by careless errors*. **Destroy** and **wreck** are fairly emotive terms conveying the notion of causing the end of something: *his cruelty had wrecked her love for him*; if something or someone has simply been put out of action, you might use **incapacitate**.
 Impair and **weaken**, however, is more vague in the level of damage it suggests: *pollution is impairing our health*. **Abuse** could be used of various forms of maltreatment, but **deface** and **vandalize** suggest deliberate and wanton acts of physical damage: *textbooks defaced by doodles*. **Sabotage**, too, could be used of deliberate action, but usually to foil an end purpose: *the massacre sabotaged the resumption of negotiations*. **Tamper with** also suggests ill-intentioned interference: *someone has tampered with the brakes*.
 The term **desecrate** is usually reserved to talk about damage to something sacred, while **mutilate** is usually used to refer to bodily maiming, but you may also use it to convey strong distaste for other forms of damage: *I managed to mutilate my life by making these choices*. The phrases **play/wreak havoc on** are very strong terms for creating problems: *the floods wrought havoc on the roads*.

---

damaging *adj*
harmful, hurtful, injurious, unfavourable, bad, detrimental, disadvantageous, pernicious, prejudicial, ruinous, destructive
FORMAL deleterious
COLLOQ. toxic
☰ favourable, helpful

dame *n*
1 Dame Edith Evans
lady, noblewoman, baroness, dowager, peeress, aristocrat
2 WOMAN, female; (*offensive*) broad

damn *v, n*
♦ *v*
1 CURSE, swear, blast, doom, blaspheme, use bad language, sink
FORMAL accurse, imprecate, execrate, maledict, anathematize, fulminate
2 CONDEMN, revile, denounce, criticize, slate, run down, censure, attack, denunciate
FORMAL berate, castigate, inveigh, excoriate, decry, denigrate
COLLOQ. slam, pan, knock, come down on, pick holes in, pull to pieces, tear to shreds
SLANG slag (off)
☰ 1 bless **2** praise, commend
♦ *n*
iota, jot
COLLOQ. dang, darn, dash
SLANG toss, monkey's, brass farthing, hoot, two hoots, tinker's cuss

damnable *adj*
abominable, atrocious, horrible, unpleasant, disagreeable, objectionable, offensive, despicable, detestable, iniquitous, cursed, infernal, damned, hellish, diabolical, wicked

FORMAL execrable
☰ admirable, praiseworthy

damnation *n*
condemnation, doom, denunciation, hell, hell-fire, perdition, excommunication, anathema
FORMAL proscription

damned *adj*
1 the damned in hell
condemned, doomed, lost, cursed, accursed, reprobate, anathematized
FORMAL execrated
2 a damned disgrace
cursed, detestable, despicable, abominable, confounded, infernal, hateful, loathsome, odious, vile, fiendish, annoying, unpleasant, pernicious
FORMAL execrable
COLLOQ. blasted, blooming, flipping, darned, dashed, dratting, flaming, blinking
SLANG bloody, effing; (*taboo*) fucking, frigging
☰ 1 blessed

damning *adj*
incriminating, condemning, implicating
FORMAL accusatorial, condemnatory, damnatory, implicative, inculpatory

damp *adj, n, v*
♦ *adj*
moist, moistened, wet, wettish, clammy, dank, humid, dewy, muggy, rainy, drizzly, misty, soggy, vaporous, rheumy
OLD moisty
☰ dry, arid
♦ *n*
dampness, moisture, clamminess, dankness, humidity, wet, wetness, dew, rain, drizzle, fog, mist, vapour
☰ dryness
■ **damp down**
calm, dull, deaden, restrain, check, reduce, lessen, moderate, decrease, diminish

dampen *v*
1 MOISTEN, wet, spray, damp
2 DISCOURAGE, dishearten, damp down, deter, dash, dull, deaden, restrain, check, depress, dismay, reduce, lessen, moderate, decrease, diminish, put a damper on, muffle, inhibit, stifle, smother
☰ 1 dry **2** encourage

damper
■ **put a damper on**
discourage, dishearten, damp down, deter, dash, dull, deaden, restrain, check, depress, dismay, reduce, lessen, moderate, decrease, diminish, muffle, inhibit, stifle, smother
☰ encourage

dampness *n*
damp, moisture, clamminess, dankness, humidity, wet, wetness, dew, rain, drizzle, fog, mist, vapour

damsel *n*
maiden, girl, lass, young woman, young lady; *Scot* lassie

dance *v, n*
♦ *v*
1 learn to dance
move to music, rock, spin, sway, gyrate, twirl, pirouette, whirl, trip the light fantastic
COLLOQ. bop, hoof it, hop, jig, shake a leg
2 dance for joy
skip, leap, jump, bounce, frisk, caper, cavort, frolic, gambol, juke, kantikoy, prance, spin, stomp, sway, swing, tread a measure, whirl
3 lights dancing on the water
leap, sway, flicker, twinkle, flash, shimmer, sparkle, waver, play, ripple, move lightly

♦ *n*
ball, social
COLLOQ. bop, hop, knees-up, shindig
Related adjectives: orchestic, terpsichorean

> **QUOTATIONS**
> To dance is to discover and to recreate, above all when the dance is the dance of love
> LÉOPOLD SÉDAR SENGHOR

Dances include:

allemande	gigue	paso doble
beguine	habanera	Paul Jones
belly dance	Highland fling	polka
black bottom	hoedown	polonaise
bogle	hokey-cokey	quadrille
bolero	hora	quickstep
bop	jig	reel
bossanova	jitterbug	rock 'n' roll
bourrée	jive	rondeau
can-can	kazachoc	rumba
ceroc	krump	salsa
cha-cha	lambada	samba
Charleston	Lambeth Walk	sarabande
Circassian circle	Lancers	schottische
clog dance	limbo	square dance
conga	line dance	stomp
courante	macarena	Strip the Willow
Dashing White	mambo	tango
Sergeant	mashed potato	tarantella
fandango	mazurka	turkey trot
flamenco	merengue	twist
foxtrot	military two-step	valeta
galliard	minuet	vogue
gavotte	morris dance	waltz
Gay Gordons	one-step	

Types of dancing include:

ballet	flamenco	line-dancing
ballroom	folk	morris dancing
bogling	Highland	old-time
break-dancing	hip-hop	pole dancing
clog-dancing	Irish	robotics
country	Latin-American	street dancing
disco	limbo-dancing	tap

See also **ballet**.

Dance functions include:

ball	disco	*N Am* prom
barn dance	fancy dress ball	rave
ceilidh	*colloq.* hop	shindig
charity ball	hunt ball	social
dance	knees-up	tea dance

dancer *n*
danseur, danseuse, ballerina, ballet dancer, baladin, coryphee, figurant, comprimario, tap-dancer, morisco, belly-dancer, showgirl
COLLOQ. bopper, hoofer

dandle *v*
jiggle, bounce, dance, toss, cradle, fondle, pet, cuddle; *Scot* doodle

dandy *n, adj*
♦ *n*
fop, coxcomb, beau, man about town, Adonis, blade, dapperling, dude, exquisite, peacock, popinjay, swell, toff
OLD (*Shakesp*) princox
SLANG *Aust* lair
♦ *adj*
fine, capital, excellent, first-rate, great, splendid

danger *n*
1 *in danger of falling*
insecurity, jeopardy, precariousness, perilousness, liability, vulnerability
FORMAL endangerment, imperilment
2 *the dangers of smoking*
risk, threat, peril, hazard, menace, pitfall
F3 1 safety, security **2** safety

dangerous *adj*
unsafe, insecure, risky, high-risk, fraught with danger, threatening, breakneck, hazardous, chancy, perilous, precarious, reckless, treacherous, vulnerable, defenceless, menacing, ominous, exposed, susceptible, alarming, critical, severe, serious, grave, daring, nasty
FORMAL minacious
COLLOQ. dicey, hairy, dodgy
F3 safe, secure, harmless

> **SYNONYM NUANCES**
>
> **Unsafe** and **insecure** can be widely used to suggest an inherent lack of safety, physical or otherwise: *his job was very insecure*. To describe a situation or condition that has likely pitfalls you could use **perilous** or **precarious**, the latter giving a strong impression of potential failure: *in some areas farming is a precarious business*. Both **risky** and **high-risk**, as well as **chancy**, suggest an element of actively gambling on something. The term **daring**, meanwhile, would be appropriately used of a bold but dangerous exploit. **Hazardous** can be similarly used to suggest taking a chance: *setting up as an artist is a hazardous undertaking*, although it can also be used of more unavoidable dangers: *hazardous driving conditions*. **Breakneck** is specifically used of high speed, while **reckless** could be used to describe an approach that gives no regard to safety. **Treacherous** implies hidden dangers: *prematurely aged by the treacherous sun*.
> The terms **vulnerable**, **defenceless** and **exposed** could be used of a dangerous situation offering no protection; **susceptible** is similar but is even more suggestive of actually being prone to an attack. **Menacing**, on the other hand, emphasizes the intimidating aspect of danger, whereas **ominous** is strongly suggestive of foreboding evil or harm: *the ominous escalation of tension*.

dangerously *adv*
perilously, precariously, menacingly, threateningly, seriously, critically, gravely, severely, acutely, alarmingly

dangle *v*
1 HANG, droop, swing, sway, sag, wave, flap, trail
2 TEMPT, entice, flaunt, flourish, offer, seduce, lure, hold out, tantalize

dank *adj*
damp, moist, wet, clammy, sticky, dewy, musty, chilly, slimy, soggy
F3 dry

dapper *adj*
trim, well-dressed, well-turned-out, well-groomed, debonair, chic, dainty, neat, tidy, smart, spruce, stylish, nimble, active, brisk, spry
COLLOQ. natty
F3 dishevelled, dowdy, scruffy, shabby, sloppy

dappled *adj*
speckled, mottled, spotted, blotched, blotchy, streaked, stippled, dotted, flecked, freckled, variegated, bespeckled, piebald, pied, chequered

dare *v, n*
♦ *v*
1 RISK, venture, brave, be brave/bold enough, have the courage, hazard, adventure, endanger, stake, gamble, go so far as
COLLOQ. go out on a limb

2 CHALLENGE, goad, provoke, taunt, defy, invite, throw down the gauntlet
COLLOQ.
3 DEFY, face, brave, confront, resist, flout, stand up to
♦ *n*
challenge, venture, risk, provocation, taunt, goad, ultimatum, gauntlet

daredevil *n, adj*
♦ *n*
adventurer, desperado, madcap, hothead, swashbuckler, stuntman
E3 coward
♦ *adj*
adventurous, daring, bold, fearless, dauntless, intrepid, brave, plucky, audacious, hasty, reckless, rash, impetuous, impulsive, valiant, madcap, hotheaded

daring *adj, n*
♦ *adj*
bold, adventurous, intrepid, courageous, fearless, brave, plucky, audacious, valiant, venturesome, dauntless, undaunted, reckless, wild, rash, impulsive, foolhardy
E3 cautious, timid, afraid
♦ *n*
boldness, fearlessness, courage, bravery, adventurousness, audacity, intrepidity, valour, defiance, pluck, nerve, spirit, gall, prowess, wildness, recklessness, rashness, foolhardiness
COLLOQ. guts, grit, bottle, spunk
E3 caution, timidity, cowardice

daringly *adv*
boldly, adventurously, courageously, fearlessly, bravely, audaciously

dark *adj, n*
♦ *adj*
1 *a dark room/day*
unlit, badly/poorly/dimly lit, overcast, black, dim, unilluminated, shady, shadowy, sunless, cloudy, murky, misty, foggy, dusky, gloomy, dingy
FORMAL tenebrous, crepuscular
2 *dark hair*
black, brown, auburn, tawny, chestnut, dark-haired, brunette
3 *dark skin*
dark-skinned, swarthy, Black, dusky, tanned, suntanned, bronzed, olive
4 *a dark manner*
gloomy, grim, sad, cheerless, joyless, drab, dismal, bleak, forbidding, sombre, sinister, dejected, mournful, morose, moody, ominous, menacing
5 *the dark days of war*
unpleasant, tragic, disastrous, awful, worrying, sad, gloomy, distressing, hopeless, frightening, bleak, dismal, black
6 *dark secrets*
hidden, mysterious, obscure, secret, concealed, veiled, inscrutable, unintelligible, puzzling, enigmatic, intricate, cryptic
FORMAL abstruse, arcane, recondite, esoteric
7 *dark deeds*
evil, wicked, bad, wrong, horrible, iniquitous, immoral, base, vile, despicable, foul
COLLOQ. dirty, crooked
E3 **1** light, bright, clear **2** fair, blond(e) **3** light, pale **4** bright, cheerful **5** happy, joyful **6** comprehensible **7** good
♦ *n*
1 DARKNESS, dimness, night, night-time, nightfall, evening, blackness, gloom, gloominess, dusk, twilight, half-light, shadows, shade, shadiness, murkiness, sunlessness, cloudiness, mist, fog
FORMAL tenebrity, tenebrosity
2 IGNORANCE, secrecy, privacy, concealment, obscurity, mystery
E3 **1** light, brightness, daylight, lightness **2** enlightenment, openness

---

adjective sense 1
Unlit or **unilluminated** simply describe any situation where no light has been introduced, whereas **cloudy** and **overcast** specifically mean clouds are blocking the sun's light, which in itself can create an ominous or gloomy impression: *the sky was growing overcast and threatening.* **Black**, although literally describing the colour, can again sound vaguely threatening when describing something very dark: *black pools of water; the black woods.* **Dim**, however, simply suggests lacking brightness: *dim streetlamps.*
   The term **shady** implies pleasant protection from light and heat: *a shady patio*; the less positive **shadowy** suggests a more hostile or threatening darkness: *the empty shadowy corridors.* **Misty** and **foggy** again describe atmospheric conditions: *the misty valley; foggy autumn days.* **Murky**, on the other hand, suggests an unpleasant lack of clarity, possibly exacerbated by the presence of dirt: *the murky waters.* The term **dusky** tends to be more narrowly used to suggest the idea of muted evening light, and the connotations may be quite pleasant. However, to use **gloomy** and **dingy** of a lack of light results in a somewhat depressing impression: *a dingy bedsit.*

darken *v*
1 DIM, become/grow darker, obscure, blacken, cloud (over), fog, shadow, overshadow, shade, fade, eclipse
OLD obnubilate
2 DEPRESS, sadden, deject, make gloomy, cast down, weigh down, grow/become angry, look angry, frown
E3 **1** lighten **2** brighten

darkly *adv*
1 DIMLY, obscurely, blackly, at/by night, in the shadows
2 GLOOMILY, dismally, glumly, sullenly
3 MYSTERIOUSLY, enigmatically, cryptically, inscrutably
E3 **1** lightly **2** happily

darling *n, adj*
♦ *n*
1 *come here, darling*
beloved, dear, dearest, favourite, sweetheart, love, pet, poppet, treasure, precious; *Irish* mavourneen, acushla, asthore
COLLOQ. angel, honey, sweetie, sugar
2 *the darling of the fashion world*
favourite, pet, celebrity, idol, hero, apple of your eye
COLLOQ. blue-eyed boy, teacher's pet; *N Am* fair-haired boy
♦ *adj*
dear, dearest, beloved, loved, adored, cherished, prized, precious, treasured

darn *v*
mend, repair, stitch, sew (up), patch, cobble

dart *v, n*
♦ *v*
1 DASH, bound, sprint, flit, flash, fly, rush, run, race, spring, leap, tear, bolt, scurry, start, pounce, skit; *Scot* cook, wheech
OLD endart
COLLOQ. scoot
2 THROW, cast, hurl, fling, shoot, toss, sling, strike, launch, project, propel, send, flash, glance
OLD lance
♦ *n*
bolt, arrow, barb, feather, flight, shaft, fléchette, harpoon, banderilla

dash *v, n*
♦ *v*
1 RUSH, fly, hurry, tear, dart, scuttle, dive, race, sprint, run, speed, bolt, bound, hurtle;
Scot wheech
COLLOQ. nip, pop

2 *waves dashing against rocks*
smash, strike, lash, pound, beat, break, throw, crash, toss, slam, hurl, fling
OLD (*Shakesp*) pash
3 *dash your hopes*
crush, smash, shatter, disappoint, discourage, dishearten, let down, depress, sadden, dampen, confound, blight, ruin, destroy, spoil, frustrate, thwart, devastate, wreck
♦ *n*
1 DROP, pinch, grain, touch, flavour, soupçon, spot, speck, trace, suggestion, hint, tinge, bit, little
COLLOQ. tad, smidgen
2 SPRINT, dart, bolt, rush, spurt, race, run
3 *everything she did showed dash and determination*
verve, vitality, vivacity, animation, energy, élan, liveliness, sparkle, vigour, passion, fervour, enthusiasm, gusto, life, relish, spirit, force, brio
COLLOQ. pizzazz, zip
■ **dash off**
scribble, jot down, scrawl

dashing *adj*
1 LIVELY, vigorous, spirited, energetic, animated, gallant, daring, bold, plucky, exuberant
2 SMART, stylish, fashionable, elegant, debonair, showy, flamboyant, attractive, dapper, rakish, raffish
F3 **1** lethargic **2** dowdy

dastardly *adj*
wicked, iniquitous, evil, fiendish, diabolical, low, mean, base, contemptible, underhand, vile, cowardly, craven, despicable, faint-hearted, lily-livered
F3 heroic, noble

data *n*
information, documents, facts, input, statistics, figures, details, material, research, particulars, features

date *n, v*
♦ *n*
1 TIME, age, period, era, stage, epoch, day, week, month, year, decade, century, millennium
2 APPOINTMENT, engagement, meeting, rendezvous
OLD tryst
FORMAL assignation
3 FRIEND, boyfriend, girlfriend, young man, young lady, man friend, woman friend, lady friend, partner, escort
COLLOQ. steady
♦ *v*
1 *date back to the 18th century*
originate, go back, come/exist from, belong
2 *buy styles that won't date*
become old-fashioned/obsolete, go out, go out of use, show its age
FORMAL obsolesce
3 *date someone*
go out with, take out, go with, be involved with, be together, go steady with, court
■ **out of date**
old-fashioned, unfashionable, outdated, obsolete, dated, outmoded, antiquated, archaic, passé
F3 fashionable, modern
■ **to date**
so far, until now, as yet, yet, until the present time, up to now, up to the present
■ **up to date**
fashionable, modern, current, contemporary, up-to-the-minute, latest, recent, present-day
COLLOQ. trendy, now, in, cool, with it, hip, all the rage, state-of-the-art
F3 old-fashioned, dated

dated *adj*
old-fashioned, obsolete, outdated, outmoded, out-of-date, passé, superseded, unfashionable, unstylish, obsolescent, antiquated, archaic
COLLOQ. old hat, square
F3 fashionable, up-to-the-minute

daub *v, n*
♦ *v*
smear, plaster, coat, paint, cover, smirch, bedaub, splash, dab, beplaster, smudge, spatter, bespatter, splatter, stain, sully
♦ *n*
smear, splash, splodge, splotch, spot, stain, blot, blotch

daughter *n*
girl, child, lass, lassie, offspring, descendant, inhabitant, disciple

daunt *v*
intimidate, unnerve, alarm, scare, dismay, frighten, disconcert, cow, overawe, take aback, discourage, dishearten, demoralize, disillusion, put off, dispirit, abash, shake, ruffle, deter
COLLOQ. faze, rattle
F3 encourage, hearten

daunting *adj*
intimidating, unnerving, alarming, frightening, disconcerting, discouraging, disheartening, demoralizing, dispiriting
COLLOQ. scary
F3 encouraging, heartening

dauntingly *adv*
intimidatingly, unnervingly, alarmingly, frighteningly, disconcertingly, discouragingly, dishearteningly, demoralizingly, dispiritingly
COLLOQ. scarily
F3 encouragingly

dauntless *adj*
fearless, undaunted, resolute, brave, courageous, bold, determined, indomitable, intrepid, daring, plucky, valiant, doughty
F3 discouraged, disheartened

dawdle *v*
delay, loiter, lag, go slowly, go at a snail's pace, hang about, linger, dally, take your time, take too long, trail, potter; *N Am* putter
FORMAL tarry
COLLOQ. dilly-dally, drag your feet, faff about
F3 hurry

dawn *n, v*
♦ *n*
1 SUNRISE, daybreak, break of day, morning, daylight, first light, crack of dawn, cock-crow, sunrise, sun-up, Aurora
Related adjectives: auroral, aurorean
2 BEGINNING, start, emergence, onset, origin, birth, arrival, rise
FORMAL commencement, advent, inception, genesis
F3 **1** dusk **2** end
♦ *v*
1 BREAK, brighten, lighten, become/grow light, gleam, glimmer
2 BEGIN, appear, emerge, open, break, arrive, develop, originate, be born, come into being, rise
FORMAL commence
■ **dawn on**
realize, strike, occur to, sink in, register with, come into your mind
COLLOQ. hit, click

day *n*
1 DAYTIME, daylight, daylight hours
2 AGE, period, time, date, era, generation, epoch
3 *he must have been good-looking in his day*
heyday, peak, prime, flush, bloom, golden age
F3 **1** night
■ **day after day**
regularly, repeatedly, again and again, time and (time) again, continually, endlessly, persistently, monotonously, perpetually, relentlessly
■ **day by day**
gradually, progressively, slowly but surely, steadily

■ **day in, day out**
every day, regularly, repeatedly, again and again, time and (time) again, continually, endlessly, persistently, monotonously

■ **have had its day**
be no longer fashionable/popular, be no longer useful/successful, be out of date
COLLOQ. be past it
Related adjective: diurnal

PROVERBS
Absence makes the heart grow fonder

QUOTATIONS
What are days for? / Days are where we live. / They come, they wake us / Time and time over. / They are to be happy in: / Where can we live but days?
PHILIP LARKIN, 'Days'

---

daybreak n
sunrise, dawn, break of day, morning, daylight, first light, crack of dawn, cock-crow, sun-up, Aurora
E≡ sunset, sundown

daydream n, v
◆ n
fantasy, imagining, reverie, castles in the air, pipe dream, vision, musing, wish, dream, inattention, figment, trance, woolgathering
◆ v
fantasize, imagine, muse, fancy, dream, be lost in space, not pay attention, let your thoughts wander, stare into space, be in a brown study, build castles in the air
COLLOQ. switch off
SLANG zone out

daydreamer n
fantasizer, fantasist, dreamer, romantic, idealist, escapist, visionary, Walter Mitty, Don Quixote

daylight n
1 *during daylight hours*
light, natural light, day, daytime, sunlight
2 SUNRISE, dawn, daybreak, break of day, morning, first light, crack of dawn, cock-crow, sun-up
E≡ **1** night, dark

daze v, n
◆ v
1 STUN, stupefy, shock, numb, paralyse, knock out, knock unconscious
2 DAZZLE, bewilder, blind, confuse, baffle, dumbfound, amaze, surprise, shock, stun, startle, perplex, astonish, astound, stagger, take aback
COLLOQ. flabbergast, bowl over, blow away, knock for six
◆ n
bewilderment, confusion, stupor, numbness, trance, shock, distraction, spin, whirl

dazed adj
1 STUNNED, stupefied, shocked, numbed, paralysed, unconscious
COLLOQ. out
2 DAZZLED, bewildered, confused, baffled, dumbfounded, speechless, amazed, surprised, shocked, stunned, startled, perplexed, astonished, astounded, staggered, taken aback
COLLOQ. flabbergasted, bowled over, blown away

dazzle v, n
◆ v
1 DAZE, blind, confuse, blur
2 SPARKLE, fascinate, impress, strike, overwhelm, awe, overawe, overpower, scintillate, bedazzle, amaze, astonish, bewitch, hypnotize, dumbfound, stupefy
COLLOQ. bowl over, knock out, wow
◆ n
1 *the dazzle of the headlights*
glare, brightness, blaze, flare, gleam, flash, brilliance

2 *the glamour and dazzle of the theatre*
sparkle, brilliance, brightness, magnificence, splendour, scintillation, glitter
COLLOQ. razzmatazz

dazzling adj
1 *a dazzling light*
bright, glaring, shining, brilliant, blinding
2 *a dazzling performance*
brilliant, splendid, impressive, stunning, awe-inspiring, breathtaking, spectacular, glaring, glittering, shining, sparkling, glorious, radiant, ravishing, scintillating, sensational, grand, superb

dazzlingly adv
1 *dazzlingly coloured*
brightly, glaringly, brilliantly, blindingly
2 *dazzlingly talented*
brilliantly, impressively, breathtakingly, spectacularly, gloriously, radiantly, sensationally, superbly

deactivate v
disable, immobilize, paralyse, stop, put out of action
FORMAL render inoperative

dead adj, adv
◆ adj
1 LIFELESS, inanimate, defunct, departed, passed on, passed away, perished, extinct, late, gone, no more, asleep
FORMAL deceased, expired
COLLOQ. dead as a dodo, dead as a doornail, pushing up the daisies, six feet under; *Aust* bung
2 *dead leaves*
inanimate, lifeless, barren, inert
FORMAL insentient, insensate, exanimate
3 *a dead language*
obsolete, extinct, discontinued, disused, defunct, no longer spoken
4 *that issue is dead*
dated, out of date, passé, no longer of interest
COLLOQ. old hat, dead as a dodo
5 *this town is dead*
boring, dull, humdrum, tedious, uninteresting, unexciting, with nothing happening, quiet, flat, sleepy
6 *my fingers have gone dead*
numb, unfeeling, not feeling anything, gone to sleep, paralysed, benumbed
FORMAL insensate
7 UNRESPONSIVE, apathetic, dull, indifferent, insensitive, numb, cold, emotionless, unemotional, unfeeling, frigid, lukewarm, unsympathetic, torpid
8 *dead centre*
exact, absolute, perfect, unqualified, utter, outright, complete, entire, total, downright, thorough
9 EXHAUSTED, tired, tired out, worn out
COLLOQ. knackered, dead beat, ready to drop
10 *the telephone line is dead*
out of order, not working, broken, broken-down, defunct, ineffective
COLLOQ. kaput, on the blink, conked out, bust; *N Am* on the fritz
E≡ **1** alive **3** living **7** lively **9** refreshed **10** working
◆ adv
1 *the post office is dead opposite the library*
directly, straight, exactly, immediately
COLLOQ. bang, smack
2 *it's dead easy*
very, absolutely, completely, extremely, exceptionally, really, terribly, awfully
3 *the train stopped dead*
completely, absolutely, quite, utterly

SYNONYM NUANCES

adjective sense 1
Lifeless can be used of any lack of movement or any other sign of life: *his lifeless body*. **Inanimate** would only be used when life was never present: *inanimate objects*. **Defunct**, on the other hand, describes something that

was formerly functioning: *the now defunct air-conditioning*.

The terms **departed**, **passed on** and **passed away** are rather euphemistic ways of referring gently to the death of any living creature, especially man: *my dear departed grandmother*. **Gone** and **no more** are also indirect ways of describing a person or animal that has died, as is the even more euphemistic **asleep**.

Perished, though also used of previously living things, is more suggestive of having met an unnatural end: *they perished when their boats capsized*. **Extinct** would be used specifically of an entire group or species ceasing to exist: *the red squirrel is virtually extinct in parts of the country*. **Late** is a more formalized way of referring to someone who has expired: *it was her late grandfather's house*.

deaden v
1 *deaden pain*
reduce, blunt, muffle, dull, lessen, quieten, suppress, weaken, numb, diminish, stifle, mitigate, alleviate, soothe, moderate, take the edge off, anaesthetize, desensitize, smother, check, allay, assuage, subdue, dampen, hush, mute, paralyse
FORMAL abate
2 *deaden imagination*
numb, benumb, desensitize, make insensitive, harden
F₃ **1** heighten

deadline n
time limit, target date, time, time up, term

deadlock n
standstill, stalemate, checkmate, impasse, dead end, halt, stoppage, log jam; *N Am* stand-off

deadly adj, adv
♦ adj
1 *deadly poison*
lethal, fatal, dangerous, venomous, toxic, destructive, life-threatening, death-dealing, pernicious, noxious, malignant, murderous, mortal
2 *deadly enemies*
implacable, irreconcilable, mortal, murderous, hated, grim, fierce, savage, bitter
3 *in deadly earnest*
great, serious, marked, intense, extreme
4 *a deadly lecture*
dull, boring, uninteresting, unexciting, tedious, monotonous, humdrum
5 *deadly aim*
unerring, unfailing, precise, accurate, perfect, flawless, sure, effective, true
F₃ **1** harmless **4** exciting
♦ adv
utterly, thoroughly, dreadfully, absolutely, completely, entirely, perfectly, quite, totally

deadpan adj
blank, empty, expressionless, unexpressive, impassive, inexpressive, inscrutable, poker-faced, straight-faced, dispassionate
F₃ expressive

deaf adj
1 HARD OF HEARING, stone-deaf, with impaired hearing
COLLOQ. deaf as a post
2 UNCONCERNED, indifferent, impervious, unmoved, unaffected, untouched, oblivious, heedless, unmindful
F₃ **2** aware, conscious

PROVERBS
There's none so deaf as those that will not hear

deafening adj
piercing, very loud, very noisy, ear-splitting, ear-piercing, booming, resounding, thundering, thunderous, ringing, reverberating, roaring, overwhelming
F₃ quiet

deal v, n
♦ v
1 DISTRIBUTE, give out, share, dole out, divide, allot, dispense, assign, mete out
FORMAL apportion, bestow
2 TRADE, do business, buy and sell, negotiate, traffic, export, bargain, transact, handle, treat, operate, market, stock
OLD (*Shakesp*) mart
FORMAL vend
COLLOQ. flog, push
3 *deal a blow*
deliver, administer, direct, mete, inflict, dispense
♦ n
1 QUANTITY, lot, load, amount, extent, degree, portion, share
2 AGREEMENT, contract, understanding, pact, transaction, bargain, buy, arrangement, covenant
3 ROUND, hand, distribution
■ **deal with**
1 *deal with a situation*
attend to, concern yourself with, see to, manage, handle, tackle, cope with, get to grips with, take care of, look after, sort out, process
2 *her novel deals with the future*
treat, consider, be about, concern, cover, tackle, have to do with

dealer n
trader, seller, salesman, saleswoman, salesperson, merchant, retailer, wholesaler, supplier, distributor, marketer, merchandizer, vendor, trafficker, agent, broker, brinjarry, hawker, pedlar, chapman, coper, monger; *Scot* couper
COLLOQ. pusher, tout

dealing n
1 *drug dealing*
trading, business, trade, commerce, transaction, operation, traffic, trafficking, marketing
2 *my dealings with you*
relations, association, connections, communication
FORMAL intercourse
COLLOQ. truck

dean n
1 *the dean of the Faculty of Law*
head of faculty, head of department, head, principal, director, doyen
2 *dean of the cathedral*
chapter head, rural dean, cardinal-bishop, vicar-forane

dear adj, n
♦ adj
1 LOVED, beloved, treasured, valued, cherished, adored, favoured, esteemed, precious, favourite, intimate, respected, close, darling, familiar, endearing
2 EXPENSIVE, high-priced, costly, high-cost, overpriced, excessive, exorbitant, not cheap, extortionate
OLD chargeful
COLLOQ. steep, pricey, posh, sky-high, costing an arm and a leg, costing the earth, costing a bomb, daylight robbery; *N Am* big-ticket
OLD SLANG salt
F₃ **1** disliked, hated **2** cheap, inexpensive
♦ n
beloved, loved one, precious, darling, pet, sweetheart, treasure
COLLOQ. angel, honey, sweetie, sugar

dearly adv
1 *he loves her dearly*
fondly, affectionately, with affection, lovingly, devotedly, adoringly, tenderly, intimately, with favour/respect
2 *I wish it dearly*
greatly, extremely, very much, deeply, profoundly, a great deal

3 *pay dearly for something*
at a great cost, at a high price, with great loss,
with much suffering

dearth *n*
scarcity, shortage, deficiency, insufficiency, inadequacy,
lack, absence, scantiness, sparsity, need, poverty, famine,
meagreness
FORMAL paucity, want, exiguousness
F3 excess, abundance

death *n*
1 *people in danger of death*
loss, departure, loss of life, fatality, passing, passing away,
passing on, perishing, end, finish, the grave
OLD (*Shakesp & Spenser*) funeral; (*Shakesp*) defunction
FORMAL expiration, decease, demise, quietus
COLLOQ. last farewell, curtains
Related adjective: mortal
2 *the death of the welfare state*
ruin, destruction, end, finish, undoing, annihilation,
downfall, extermination, dissolution, extinction
FORMAL demise, obliteration, eradication, extirpation,
termination, cessation
F3 1 life, birth
■ **put to death**
execute, kill, hang, electrocute, shoot, guillotine, behead,
decapitate, gas, send to the electric chair, exterminate,
martyr
COLLOQ. do in, take out
SLANG bump off, knock off, rub out, waste, blow away

> **QUOTATIONS**
> Yea, though I walk through the valley of the shadow of
> death, I will fear no evil: for thou art with me
> *Bible, Psalms*
>
> Death is not an event in life: we do not live to
> experience death
> LUDWIG WITTGENSTEIN, *Tractatus Logico-
> Philosophicus*

deathless *adj*
immortal, imperishable, eternal, everlasting, undying,
never-ending, timeless, incorruptible, inextinguishable,
memorable, unforgettable

deathly *adj*
1 ASHEN, grim, haggard, pale, pallid, ghastly, wan, white,
colourless, cadaverous, ghostly, ghost-like
2 FATAL, deadly, mortal, intense, extreme, terrible, harmful,
utmost

debacle *n*
fiasco, catastrophe, failure, collapse, defeat, devastation,
disaster, downfall, havoc, cataclysm, overthrow, reversal,
rout, turmoil, disintegration, ruin, ruination, stampede,
farce
COLLOQ. hash, foul-up, washout
SLANG cock-up, balls-up, screw-up

debar *v*
ban, bar, forbid, prohibit, eject, exclude, shut out, keep
out, expel, stop, hamper, hinder, obstruct, prevent,
segregate, restrain, deny, blackball
FORMAL preclude, proscribe
F3 admit, allow

debase *v*
degrade, demean, devalue, disgrace, dishonour, discredit,
shame, humble, humiliate, cheapen, lower, reduce, abase,
defile, contaminate, pollute, corrupt, adulterate, bastardize,
embase, alloy, dilute, taint
FORMAL vitiate
F3 elevate, enhance, purify

debased *adj*
degraded, devalued, disgraced, dishonoured, discredited,
shamed, humbled, humiliated, cheapened, abased,
defiled, contaminated, impure, polluted, perverted,

corrupt, debauched, immoral, sinful, fallen, low,
degenerate, adulterated, tainted, base, sordid, vile
F3 elevated, pure, honourable

debasement *n*
degradation, devaluation, disgrace, dishonour, shame,
humiliation, cheapening, depravation, abasement,
defilement, contamination, pollution, perversion,
corruption, degeneration, adulteration
F3 elevation, purification

debatable *adj*
questionable, arguable, uncertain, unsure, unclear,
disputable, contestable, controversial, open to question,
doubtful, contentious, undecided, unsettled, problematical,
dubious, moot
F3 unquestionable, certain, indisputable, incontrovertible

debate *n, v*
♦ *n*
discussion, argument, controversy, deliberation,
consideration, forum, exchange of views, contention,
dispute, reflection, polemic; *Scot* flyte
FORMAL disputation, altercation
COLLOQ. powwow
♦ *v*
1 DISPUTE, argue, reason, discuss, talk about/over/through,
contend, contest, wrangle, thrash out
FORMAL altercate
COLLOQ. kick about/around, knock about/around
2 CONSIDER, think over, deliberate, ponder, reflect,
meditate on, mull over, weigh
FORMAL cogitate

debauch *v*
corrupt, lead astray, deprave, over-indulge, pervert,
pollute, subvert, ravish, ruin, seduce, violate, whore
FORMAL vitiate
F3 cleanse, purge, purify

debauched *adj*
depraved, abandoned, immoral, corrupt, corrupted,
debased, perverted, degenerate, degraded, intemperate,
overindulgent, dissipated, dissolute, excessive, decadent,
promiscuous, wanton, lewd, carousing, riotous
FORMAL licentious
F3 decent, pure, virtuous, chaste

debauchery *n*
depravity, immorality, corruption, degeneracy,
degradation, intemperance, overindulgence, rakishness,
dissoluteness, excess, decadence, wantonness, lewdness,
carousal, orgy, revel, lust, riot
FORMAL dissipation, licentiousness, libertinism
F3 restraint, temperance, morality

debilitate *v*
weaken, undermine, sap, incapacitate, wear out, exhaust,
drain, tire, fatigue, impair, cripple
FORMAL enervate, enfeeble, devitalize
F3 strengthen, invigorate, energize

debilitating *adj*
weakening, undermining, incapacitating, wearing out,
fatiguing, tiring, exhausting, impairing, crippling
FORMAL enervating, enervative, enfeebling
F3 invigorating, strengthening

debility *n*
weakness, infirmity, tiredness, fatigue, weariness,
exhaustion, faintness, feebleness, frailty, incapacity,
lack of energy/vitality
TECHNICAL asthenia, atonicity, atony, myasthenia
FORMAL decrepitude, enervation, enfeeblement, languor,
malaise
F3 strength, vigour

debonair *adj*
suave, refined, urbane, well-bred, sophisticated, cultured,
dignified, stylish, smooth, dashing, elegant, affable, breezy,
buoyant, charming, courteous, cheerful, jaunty, light-
hearted

debrief v
interview, question, examine, interrogate, cross-examine, cross-question
COLLOQ. grill, give the third degree

debris n
remains, ruins, rubbish, refuse, waste, wreck, wreckage, litter, fragments, rubble, trash, pieces, bits, sweepings, scrap, dross, drift
TECHNICAL eluvium, tephra, pyroclastics
FORMAL detritus

debt n
1 *their debts amounted to £10,000*
overdraft, money owing/due, due, amount owing/due, arrears, liability, debit, duty, bill, account, hock, claim, score
2 *he owed them a debt of gratitude*
indebtedness, obligation, commitment, liability
1 credit, asset
■ **in debt**
insolvent, in arrears, in overdraft, owing money
COLLOQ. gone to the wall, gone under, in the red, in Queer Street
■ **in someone's debt**
indebted, obliged, honour-bound, thankful, appreciative
FORMAL beholden

debtor n
borrower, bankrupt, insolvent, defaulter, mortgagor
COLLOQ. N Am deadbeat
creditor

debunk v
expose, deflate, puncture, show up, ridicule, mock, explode, disprove, lampoon
COLLOQ. cut down to size, quash, shoot down in flames

debut n
first appearance, first performance, first night, first recording, first time, introduction, launch, launching, beginning, entrance, presentation, inauguration, première, coming-out, initiation

decadence n
corruption, debasement, debauchery, depravity, dissolution, immorality, degeneracy, degenerateness, degeneration, deterioration, self-indulgence, decay, decline, fall, perversion
FORMAL dissipation, licentiousness, retrogression
flourishing, rise

decadent adj
1 CORRUPT, debased, debauched, depraved, dissolute, dissipated, immoral, degenerate, degraded, self-indulgent, unprincipled
FORMAL licentious
2 DECAYING, declining, degenerating, deteriorating, debased
1 moral **2** resurgent

decamp v
make off, run away, take off, run off, abscond, bolt, desert, escape, flee, flit, fly
COLLOQ. scarper, skedaddle, vamoose, scrap, split, make tracks, do a runner, do a bunk, do a moonlight flit, hightail it, absquatulate
SLANG N Am lam it, take in on the lam

decant v
pour out, draw off, siphon off, transfer, drain, tap

decapitate v
behead, execute, guillotine, unhead

decay v, n
♦ v
1 ROT, go bad, go off, decompose, spoil, fester, perish, rust, corrode
FORMAL putrefy
2 DECLINE, deteriorate, disintegrate, corrode, crumble, waste away, degenerate, atrophy, wear away, weaken, dwindle, fail, shrivel, wither, sink

COLLOQ. go downhill, go the the dogs, go to pot
2 flourish, grow
♦ n
1 ROT, rotting, going bad, decomposition, perishing, mould, fungus, mildew
FORMAL putrefaction, putrescence, putridity
2 DECLINE, deterioration, disintegration, degeneration, collapse, crumbling, decadence, debasement, weakening, wasting, failing, atrophy, withering, fading

decayed adj
rotten, rotting, bad, off, stale, sour, rank, addled, carious, decomposed, spoiled, mouldy, mildewed, perished, corroded, carrion, wasted, withered
FORMAL putrefied, putrid, putrescent

decease n
death, dying, demise, departure, end, passing, passing away, passing on, dissolution, rest
FORMAL expiration, demise

deceased adj, n
♦ adj
dead, departed, former, late, lost, defunct, gone, no more, asleep, finished, extinct
FORMAL expired
COLLOQ. dead as a doornail, pushing up the daisies, six feet under
♦ n
dead, departed

deceit n
deception, pretence, cheating, misrepresentation, fraud, trickery, fraudulence, double-dealing, underhandedness, chicanery, fake, guile, subterfuge, swindle, treachery, hypocrisy, artifice, ruse, cunning, slyness, craftiness, wiliness, stratagem, wile, imposition, feint, abuse
OLD barrat, glozing, cozenage; (*Spenser*) malengine; *Aust & NZ* slenter
FORMAL duplicity
COLLOQ. sham, con, game, monkey business, dodge; *N Am* gold brick; *Aust & NZ* slinter
honesty, openness, frankness

deceitful adj
dishonest, untruthful, lying, deceptive, deceiving, false, insincere, untrustworthy, double-dealing, double, fraudulent, treacherous, guileful, underhand, sneaky, counterfeit, crafty, sly, cunning, hypocritical, designing, illusory, knavish
FORMAL mendacious, duplicitous, dissembling, perfidious
COLLOQ. crooked, two-faced, tricky, foxy, sharp
honest, open

deceitfully adv
dishonestly, untruthfully, deceptively, deceivingly, falsely, insincerely, fraudulently, treacherously, underhandedly, sneakily, craftily, slyly, cunningly, hypocritically
FORMAL mendaciously, duplicitously, perfidiously
honestly, openly

deceive v
mislead, delude, cheat (on), betray, fool, trick, hoax, defraud, bluff, dupe, swindle, outsmart, outwit, impose upon, lead on, misguide, hoodwink, beguile, set a trap for, entrap, ensnare, camouflage, abuse, seduce, gull; *Aust* slip up
OLD (*Shakesp*) misuse
FORMAL dissemble
COLLOQ. con, kid, bamboozle, have on, do, string along, double-cross, two-time, pull someone's leg, pull a fast one on, pull the wool over someone's eyes, put up a smokescreen, lead up the garden path, put one over on; *N Am* pull/yank someone's chain
SLANG take for a ride

QUOTATIONS
Oh what a tangled web we weave, / When first we practise to deceive!
SIR WALTER SCOTT, *Marmion*

deceiver n

liar, deluder, cheat, betrayer, fake, fraud, hypocrite, trickster, hoaxer, swindler, impostor, charlatan, abuser, seducer, mountebank
OLD guiler, guyler, treacher, tregetour; (Spenser) treachetour, falser
FORMAL dissembler, inveigler
COLLOQ. con man, diddler, crook, double-dealer

decelerate v

slow down, slow, go more slowly, brake, put the brakes on, reduce speed

decency n

respectability, uprightness, integrity, civility, correctness, fitness, good taste, etiquette, courtesy, politeness, modesty, helpfulness
OLD seemliness
FORMAL propriety, decorum
E3 impropriety, discourtesy

decent adj

1 *decent behaviour*
respectable, upright, worthy, proper, fitting, dignified, correct, tasteful, chaste, virtuous, ethical, suitable, modest, appropriate, presentable, pure, fit, becoming, befitting, nice
OLD seemly
FORMAL decorous
2 *a decent person*
kind, obliging, courteous, helpful, accommodating, generous, thoughtful, honest, dependable, trustworthy, civil, polite, gracious
3 ADEQUATE, acceptable, satisfactory, reasonable, sufficient, tolerable, fair, competent
COLLOQ. OK
E3 **1** indecent **2** disobliging **3** unsatisfactory

SYNONYM NUANCES

sense 1
Respectable and **upright** are fairly restrained terms to describe someone (or the behaviour of someone) who merits the esteem of others, as is **worthy**, although this may be used with a slightly sneering or facetious implication: *the classics teacher was a worthy pedant.* The terms **proper**, **fitting** and **correct**, as well as **fit** and **befitting**, may all be used to approve of something appropriate to the situation: *his fitting tribute*; *a welcome befitting their status*; **suitable** and **appropriate** are similar, but more neutral in tone.
   Dignified puts the emphasis on a degree of stateliness and decorum, while **tasteful** could be used to suggest an element of discernment: *a tasteful joke.* **Chaste**, **pure** and **virtuous** strongly imply approval of moral or sexual decency, and **modest** implies decency born of a sense of propriety. **Ethical** has more to do with adhering to a moral code: *the City's ethical standards seem to have disappeared.*
   Presentable, meanwhile, might be used of a decent appearance, although it may be used to suggest being little more than passable: *give me time to make myself look presentable.*

---

decently adv

1 *act decently*
respectably, properly, correctly, ethically, honestly, suitably, appropriately, presentably, becomingly, nicely, obligingly, courteously, politely, graciously, helpfully, generously, thoughtfully
FORMAL decorously
2 *a decently sized share*
adequately, acceptably, satisfactorily, reasonably, sufficiently, tolerably, fairly

decentralize n

devolve, regionalize, localize, delegate, deconcentrate, spread downwards/outwards
E3 centralize

deception n

deceit, pretence, deceptiveness, insincerity, treachery, hypocrisy, cheating, misrepresentation, trickery, fraudulence, double-dealing, underhandedness, chicanery, trick, cheat, imposture, lie, hoax, fraud, bluff, ruse, snare, guile, sham, subterfuge, artifice, swindle, stratagem, illusion, smoke and mirrors, wile, craftiness, cunning
FORMAL dissembling, duplicity
COLLOQ. con, set-up, scam, put-up job, leg-pull, flim-flam
E3 openness, honesty

deceptive adj

misleading, dishonest, false, fraudulent, cheating, cunning, sly, crafty, underhand, unreliable, illusive, fake, illusory, spurious, specious, mock, bogus, sham, ambiguous
FORMAL fallacious, dissembling, duplicitous
COLLOQ. crooked, foxy, sharp
E3 genuine, artless, open

deceptively adv

misleadingly, illusively, ambiguously, spuriously, speciously, dishonestly, falsely, fraudulently

decide v

1 *decide to do something*
make up your mind, come to/arrive at a decision, reach/make a decision, come to/reach a conclusion, determine, resolve, commit yourself, opt in
2 *decide an issue/a case*
settle, resolve, determine, work out, conclude, fix, establish, adjudicate, arbitrate, judge, rule, give a judgement/ruling
COLLOQ. clinch, wrap up
3 *decide on a new car*
choose, pick, select, opt for, settle
COLLOQ. go for, plump for

decided adj

1 DEFINITE, clear, certain, marked, obvious, undeniable, indisputable, unequivocal, absolute, clear-cut, pronounced, undisputed, unmistakable, unquestionable, positive, unambiguous, categorical, express, distinct, emphatic
2 RESOLUTE, decisive, determined, purposeful, firm, unhesitating, unswerving, unwavering, deliberate, forthright
E3 **1** inconclusive **2** irresolute

decidedly adv

very, absolutely, certainly, downright, positively, quite, unquestionably, unequivocally, unmistakably, clearly, definitely, distinctly, markedly, noticeably, obviously, decisively

decider n

clincher, *coup de grâce*, determiner

deciding adj

decisive, determining, conclusive, critical, crucial, significant, final, chief, influential, prime, principal, key, supreme
COLLOQ. crunch
E3 insignificant

decimate v

destroy, devastate, obliterate, flatten, annihilate, eliminate, eradicate

decipher v

decode, unscramble, unravel, interpret, translate, make out, work out, solve, make sense of, understand, transliterate
FORMAL construe
COLLOQ. crack, figure out, suss out; N Am dope (out)
E3 encode

decision n

1 CONCLUSION, result, outcome, verdict, finding, settlement, resolution, recommendation, judgement, arbitration, adjudication, ruling, decree, pronouncement, opinion

2 DETERMINATION, decisiveness, firmness, resolve, forcefulness, purpose, strong-mindedness, single-mindedness

---

SYNONYM NUANCES

sense 1

Conclusion is used to refer to a decision arrived at through consideration, although it is often based on inference: *don't jump to the wrong conclusion.* **Result** and **outcome** put less emphasis on the human element, and more on how something turns out: *press reports influenced the outcome of the trial.*

Judgement may also be used to suggest that everything has been duly considered before coming to a decision, as does **verdict**, which has strong associations with legal judgements and has connotations of finality. Although **finding** is more suggestive of action based on what has been elicited, this word too is often used in a courtroom context: *the tribunal's finding of unfair dismissal.* The terms **settlement** and **resolution** might be used of the agreed end of a dispute, and you may choose the terms **arbitration** or **adjudication** where there has been external mediation: *independent adjudication found in favour of the company.*

Recommendation would be used specifically where a decision is accompanied by strong advice, often official: *the recommendation of the Law Commission.* The terms **ruling** and **decree** can be used of a decision with the weight of law behind them, but a **pronouncement**, however authoritative, is really just a declaration: *an official pronouncement on terrorism.*

---

decisive *adj*
1 CONCLUSIVE, deciding, definite, definitive, determining, absolute, final, critical, crucial, key, influential, significant, momentous, prime, principal, fateful
2 *a decisive person*
determined, resolute, decided, positive, firm, forceful, forthright, purposeful, strong, strong-minded, single-minded, unwavering, unswerving
E₃ 1 inconclusive, insignificant **2** indecisive

decisively *adv*
1 CONCLUSIVELY, definitively, absolutely, critically, crucially, influentially, significantly, momentously, fatefully
2 *act decisively*
determinedly, resolutely, positively, firmly, forcefully, forthrightly, purposefully, strongly, single-mindedly, unwaveringly, unswervingly
E₃ 1 inconclusively **2** indecisively

deck *v*
decorate, ornament, adorn, beautify, embellish, trim, garnish, garland, festoon, grace, enrich, prettify, trick out; *N Am* trick up
FORMAL array, bedeck
COLLOQ. tart up
■ **deck out**
dress, decorate, dress up, clothe, robe, garb
FORMAL array
COLLOQ. do up, rig, tog, tart up, get up, doll up

declaim *v*
speak boldly/dramatically, proclaim, hold forth, pronounce, lecture, harangue, rant, sermonize
OLD bespout
FORMAL orate, perorate, expostulate
COLLOQ. spiel, spout, sound off

declamation *n*
speech, address, lecture, oration, sermon, recitation, harangue, tirade, rant, speechifying

declamatory *adj*
bold, dramatic, rhetorical, bombastic, discursive, grandiloquent, grandiose, high-flown, inflated, oratorical, overblown, pompous, stagy, theatrical, stilted
TECHNICAL parlando
FORMAL magniloquent, orotund, fustian

declaration *n*
1 ANNOUNCEMENT, notification, communication, pronouncement, statement, proclamation, edict, decree, manifesto, broadcast
FORMAL promulgation
2 AFFIRMATION, acknowledgement, assertion, statement, confession, testimony, confirmation, disclosure, profession, revelation
FORMAL attestation, avowal, affidavit, asseveration, averment

declare *v*
1 ANNOUNCE, proclaim, make known, reveal, express, communicate, pronounce, decree, publish, broadcast
FORMAL promulgate
2 AFFIRM, assert, claim, profess, maintain, state, certify, pronounce, confess, confirm, disclose, make known, reveal, show, swear, testify, witness, validate
FORMAL aver, avow, attest, asseverate

decline *v, n*
♦ *v*
1 DIMINISH, become/get less, go/come down, decrease, de-escalate, dwindle, lessen, fade, fall, sink, subside, reduce, slide, drop, wane, weaken, wither, ebb, flag, plummet, plunge, slump, tail off, peter out
FORMAL abate
2 REFUSE, turn down, say no to, reject, deny, repudiate, for(e)go, avoid, balk
COLLOQ. give the thumbs-down to, give the red light to
3 DECAY, deteriorate, worsen, degenerate, sink, rot, slip, fall off, lapse
FORMAL regress
COLLOQ. go to pot, go to pieces, go downhill
4 DESCEND, sink, slope, dip, slant
E₃ 1 grow, increase **2** accept **3** improve **4** rise
♦ *n*
1 DECREASE, reduction, lessening, lowering, dwindling, drop, downturn, downswing, slump
2 DETERIORATION, dwindling, lessening, decrease, reduction, de-escalation, decay, degeneration, weakening, worsening, failing, failure, downturn, waning, fall, falling-off, recession, slump
FORMAL diminution, abatement
3 DESCENT, dip, declination, hill, slope, incline, divergence, deviation
FORMAL declivity
E₃ 1 increase **2** improvement **3** rise

decode *v*
decipher, decrypt, interpret, unscramble, unravel, translate, make out, work out, understand, transliterate, uncipher
FORMAL construe
COLLOQ. crack, figure out; *N Am* dope (out)
E₃ encode

decomposable *adj*
biodegradable, degradable, destructible, decompoundable

decompose *v*
disintegrate, rot, decay, go bad, go off, break down, break up, crumble, fragment, spoil, dissolve, separate, fester
FORMAL putrefy

decomposition *n*
rot, rotting, going bad, going off, decay, perishing, corruption, disintegration, dissolution
FORMAL putrefaction, putrescence, putridity
E₃ combination, unification

decontaminate *v*
disinfect, sterilize, fumigate, sanitize, cleanse, purify, purge, clean
E₃ contaminate

décor *n*
decoration, ornamentation, furnishings, colour scheme, scenery

decorate v
1 ORNAMENT, adorn, beautify, embellish, trim, garnish, deck, garland, festoon, grace, enrich, prettify, trick out; N Am trick up
OLD bedizen, bedaub
FORMAL array
COLLOQ. tart up
2 RENOVATE, paint, paper, wallpaper, colour, smarten, refurbish, furbish
COLLOQ. do up, spruce up, tart up
3 HONOUR, crown, cite, reward, give a medal/honour to, give an award to, garland, bemedal

decoration n
1 ORNAMENT, adornment, ornamentation, trimming, embellishment, beautification, enhancement, décor, furnishings, mural, colour scheme, garnish, flourish, enrichment, elaboration, bunting, frill, scroll, trinket, bauble, knick-knack
2 AWARD, medal, order, badge, garland, crown, colours, ribbon, cross, laurel, wreath, star, emblem, insignia, honour, title

decorative adj
ornamental, fancy, adorning, beautifying, embellishing, non-functional, pretty, prettifying, ornate, elaborate, enhancing, rococo
COLLOQ. flashy
E3 plain

decorous adj
polite, refined, correct, courtly, decent, dignified, proper, well-behaved, appropriate, suitable, becoming, befitting, comely, comme il faut, fit, mannerly, modest, sedate, staid
OLD seemly
E3 indecorous

decorum n
good manners, good form, etiquette, respectability, conformity, protocol, behaviour, decency, dignity, restraint, politeness, courtesy, modesty, grace, breeding
OLD seemliness
FORMAL propriety, deportment
E3 bad manners; formal impropriety

decoy n, v
♦ n
lure, trap, snare, enticement, inducement, ensnarement, allurement, pretence, attraction, temptation, bait, diversion, pitfall, stall, dummy
OLD roper, trepan; (Shakesp) tame cheater
COLLOQ. red herring
SLANG shill
OLD SLANG button
♦ v
bait, lure, entrap, entice, ensnare, allure, tempt, deceive, attract, seduce, lead, draw; N Am tole
FORMAL inveigle

decrease v, n
♦ v
lessen, make/become less, go/come down, lower, diminish, dwindle, decline, de-escalate, fall (off), reduce, subside, slide, plummet, plunge, cut back/down, contract, drop, ease, shrink, taper (off), wane, slim (down), let up, slacken, peter out, curtail, scale down, trim
FORMAL abate
E3 increase
♦ n
lessening, reduction, decline, de-escalation, lowering, drop, fall, falling-off, dwindling, loss, cutback, contraction, downturn, ebb, shrinkage, subsidence, step-down
FORMAL diminution, abatement
E3 increase

SYNONYM NUANCES

verb
Lessen, **lower** and **reduce** are neutral terms with very little inherent association: *his comments lessened their fears*; *the price rise lowered demand*. While these terms are often used transitively and suggest an outside influence, both **diminish** and **dwindle** are usually intransitive and suggest a gradual becoming less, often with the implication of negative effects: *football attendances are dwindling and revenue is down*. **Decline**, similarly, implies a gradual deterioration, and can be negative in its implication: *declining standards of behaviour*. **Drop** and the rather more informal **fall off**, however, could be used to suggest a speedier decrease.
   The term **subside** appropriately describes weakened intensity, and can be used in positive contexts: *the panic has subsided*, whereas **slide** suggests a relentless and undesirable drop: *the country was sliding into anarchy*. Both **plummet** and **plunge** further convey the idea of a rapid and uncontrollable descent.
   Cut back/down are again used transitively, often of decreasing motivated by economy or discipline: *many companies are cutting back on training; he cut down on alcohol*. The term **scale down** also suggests a deliberate, practical decrease: *the police have scaled down their search*; **slim** (**down**) and **trim** have the added association of removing excess: *the new team managed to trim the business costs*. **Contract** and **shrink**, on the other hand, are often intransitive, and you might use them to move the emphasis away from active influences: *the contracting labour force*.
   Ease is suggestive of a slow but usually comforting process: *the pressure to do well has eased*; **taper** (**off**), **wane** and **peter out** are slightly more negative in tone: *interest in traditional games has sadly waned*. **Let up** and **slacken**, however, would be the terms to use of a slowing down of something previously brisk: *I slackened my pace; business in the shop has slackened since Christmas*.

decree n, v
♦ n
order, command, law, ordinance, regulation, ruling, judgement, directive, rule, statute, act, enactment, edict, fiat, proclamation, mandate, manifesto, precept
FORMAL interlocution, indiction, promulgation, ukase, firman, rescript, psephism
Related adjective: decretal
♦ v
order, command, rule, lay down, dictate, direct, decide, determine, ordain, prescribe, proclaim, pronounce, enact
FORMAL enjoin

decrepit adj
1 *a decrepit building*
dilapidated, run-down, ramshackle, rickety, broken-down, battered, worn-out, old, in bad condition/shape, tumbledown, crumbling, falling apart/to bits/to pieces
COLLOQ. clapped-out; Aust warby
2 *a decrepit person*
weak, aged, feeble, enfeebled, frail, worn-out, infirm, elderly, doddering, tottering
FORMAL senescent
COLLOQ. getting on, past it, over the hill

decrepitude n
ruin, dilapidation, decay, degeneration, deterioration, ricketiness, disability, debility, weakness, feebleness, infirmity, incapacity, incapacitation, dotage, old age, senility
FORMAL senescence
E3 good repair, fitness

decriminalize v
legalize, legitimize, license, permit, sanction, allow, authorize, warrant, validate, approve, ratify

decry v
criticize, condemn, carp, snipe, disapprove of, find fault with, denounce, attack, slate, tear to shreds, belittle, run down, come down on, blame, crab, preach down, depreciate, devalue, underrate, undervalue

FORMAL censure, disparage, declaim against, animadvert, excoriate, derogate, inveigh against, denigrate, traduce
COLLOQ. knock, slam, pan, pull to pieces, tear a strip off, nit-pick, do a hatchet job on
E3 praise, value

dedicate v
1 DEVOTE, commit, assign, bind, give, give over to, pledge, present, offer, sacrifice, surrender
2 *dedicate a book*
inscribe, address, name
3 CONSECRATE, bless, sanctify, set apart, hallow, make holy

dedicated *adj*
1 *a dedicated teacher*
devoted, committed, enthusiastic, single-minded, wholehearted, single-hearted, zealous, staunch, dyed-in-the-wool, given over to, purposeful, hard working, industrious, diligent
COLLOQ. card-carrying, sold out (on)
2 CUSTOMIZED, custom-built, bespoke
E3 **1** uncommitted, apathetic
See Synonym nuances panel at **committed**.

dedication *n*
1 COMMITMENT, devotion, single-mindedness, wholeheartedness, allegiance, attachment, adherence, faithfulness, loyalty, enthusiasm, zeal, self-sacrifice
2 INSCRIPTION, address
3 CONSECRATION, hallowing, blessing, benediction, sanctification, presentation, wake
E3 **1** apathy

deduce v
derive, infer, gather, conclude, come to the conclusion, work out, reason, surmise, understand, draw, glean
COLLOQ. figure out, suss; *N Am* dope (out)

deduct v
subtract, take away/off/from, remove, reduce by, decrease by, withdraw
COLLOQ. knock off, dock
E3 add

deduction *n*
1 SUBTRACTION, reduction, decrease, taking away/off, withdrawal, removal, discount, allowance, off-reckoning
OLD reprise
FORMAL diminution, abatement
COLLOQ. dock
2 INFERENCE, reasoning, finding, conclusion, consequence, corollary, surmising, assumption, presumption, result
OLD consectary
FORMAL hypothesis
E3 **1** addition, increase

deed *n*
1 ACTION, act, activity, achievement, performance, accomplishment, undertaking, exploit, feat, attainment, endeavour, fact, truth, reality
FORMAL actuality
2 DOCUMENT, contract, agreement, record, title, transaction
FORMAL mortgage, indenture, enfeoffment

deem v
judge, believe, suppose, think, conceive, consider, estimate, hold, imagine, account, esteem, reckon, regard
FORMAL adjudge

deep *adj, adv, n*
♦ *adj*
1 *a deep river/pit*
profound, bottomless, unplumbed, fathomless, unfathomed, immeasurable, yawning, cavernous, gaping, uncrossable
2 *a deep sleep/crisis/feeling*
intense, serious, earnest, extreme, profound, very great, severe, heart-felt, passionate, impassioned, wholehearted, fervent, ardent, strong, vigorous, grave

3 *a deep person*
perceptive, discerning, profound, wise, learned, knowledgeable, astute, clever, serious, intellectual, quiet, reserved
FORMAL sagacious, perspicacious
COLLOQ. deep as a well
4 *deep in thought*
preoccupied, absorbed, engrossed, immersed, intent, rapt, lost, faraway
5 LOW, low-pitched, bass, resonant, sonorous, resounding, booming, rich, full, full-toned, strong, powerful
6 *a deep colour*
strong, intense, rich, vivid, brilliant, warm, glowing, dark
7 OBSCURE, mysterious, difficult
FORMAL abstruse, esoteric, recondite, arcane
E3 **1** shallow, open **2** light **3** superficial, shallow, frivolous **5** high, high-pitched **6** light, pale **7** clear, plain, open
♦ *adv*
far, a long way, a great distance
♦ *n*
sea, high seas, ocean, main
COLLOQ. briny, the drink

deepen v
1 INTENSIFY, grow, increase, strengthen, reinforce, heighten, extend, magnify, build up, step up, mushroom, deteriorate, worsen, get worse
COLLOQ. hike up, bump up
2 EXCAVATE, hollow, dig out, scrape out, scoop out

deeply *adv*
intensely, seriously, earnestly, extremely, completely, thoroughly, profoundly, very much, greatly, severely, passionately, fervently, ardently, movingly, strongly, vigorously, keenly, sharply, acutely, distressingly, feelingly, gravely, mournfully, sadly, to the quick
COLLOQ. from the bottom of your heart
E3 slightly

deep-seated *adj*
ingrained, entrenched, deep-rooted, fixed, confirmed, deep, profound, fundamental, settled
E3 superficial, eradicable, temporary

deer *n*
buck, doe, hart, reindeer, roe, stag
Related adjective: cervine

deface v
damage, spoil, disfigure, blemish, impair, mutilate, mar, sully, tarnish, vandalize, deform, obliterate, ruin, injure, destroy
E3 repair

de facto *adv, adj*
♦ *adv*
actually, in effect, really, in practice
E3 de jure
♦ *adj*
actual, existing, real
E3 de jure

defamation *n*
slander, libel, slur, smear, smear campaign, innuendo, scandal, character assassination, backbiting
FORMAL vilification, disparagement, aspersion, calumny, traducement, denigration, derogation, obloquy, opprobrium, malediction
COLLOQ. mud-slinging, slamming, slagging-off, badmouthing
E3 commendation, praise

defamatory *adj*
slanderous, libellous, disparaging, pejorative, insulting, injurious, derogatory
FORMAL vilifying, denigrating, contumelious, calumnious, maledictory
COLLOQ. mud-slinging
E3 complimentary, appreciative

defame v

slander, libel, discredit, disgrace, dishonour, malign, blacken, smear, blemish, cloud, speak evil of, run down, stigmatize
OLD disparage, infame, bespatter, besmirch, deface, detract, scandal
FORMAL cast aspersions, denigrate, asperse, calumniate, traduce, vilify, vituperate
COLLOQ. slam, badmouth, drag through the mud, sling/throw mud at
SLANG slag (off)
E∃ compliment, praise

default v, n

♦ v
fail, evade, defraud, neglect, dodge, swindle, backslide
♦ n
failure, absence, neglect, negligence, non-payment, omission, deficiency, lapse, fault, lack, defect
FORMAL want, dereliction

defaulter n

non-payer, offender, absentee, non-appearer

defeat v, n

♦ v
1 CONQUER, beat, overcome, overpower, best, get the better of, have the edge on, pip at the post, inch out, be more than a match for, outscore, outplay, outwit, outsmart, eclipse, excel, surpass, outmatch, subdue, overthrow, worst, repel, drub, trounce, overwhelm, rout, ruin, crush, quell, pulverize, bring someone to their knees, reject, throw out; *Scot* granny
OLD put to the worse
FORMAL subjugate, vanquish, discomfit
COLLOQ. thrash, lick, hammer, thump, clobber, annihilate, smash, devastate, slaughter, make mincemeat (out) of, run rings round, wipe the floor with, paste, marmelize; *Scot* gub
SLANG pwn; *N Am* lam
2 FRUSTRATE, confound, balk, get the better of, disappoint, foil, thwart, baffle, puzzle, perplex, checkmate, block, obstruct
♦ n
1 CONQUEST, beating, overthrow, overcoming, rout, repulsion, ruin, crushing, rejection, loss, debacle
OLD defeasance
FORMAL subjugation, vanquishment
COLLOQ. trouncing, thrashing, pasting
2 FRUSTRATION, failure, setback, reverse, breakdown, downfall, disappointment, thwarting, checkmate

QUOTATIONS
In defeat: defiance. In victory: magnanimity
  SIR WINSTON CHURCHILL, *The Second World War*

SYNONYM NUANCES

verb sense 1
Overcome suggests a hard-fought achievement, as does **conquer**, which has an added suggestion of gaining control over someone or something and has a vaguely triumphant tone: *as one disease is conquered, another appears*. **Overpower** and **overwhelm** could be used to emphasize superior strength. **Overthrow**, likewise, suggests using strength, but usually against those in authority: *a conspiracy to overthrow the government*.
  Eclipse implies a very definite defeat, and complete overshadowing: *young tennis players who have eclipsed their more renowned contemporaries*. **Excel** and **surpass** similarly suggest outstanding superiority. The less forceful term **repel** is appropriate for referring to foiling invaders.
  Where defeat has put a total end to opposition, you could use the words **subdue**, **crush** or **quell**, or **rout** or **pulverize**, which are even more strongly suggestive of damage: *the party's left wing was routed; their spokesman was pulverized by her expertise*. **Ruin**,

although similar, perhaps does not convey the same sense of relish. In the narrower context of defeating proposals, you might use **reject** or **throw out**: *the appeals court threw out the previous verdict.*

defeatist n, adj

♦ n
pessimist, quitter, yielder, doomwatcher, doomsayer, prophet of doom
E∃ optimist
♦ adj
pessimistic, resigned, fatalistic, despondent, helpless, hopeless, despairing, gloomy, negative
E∃ optimistic

defecate v

empty/move your bowels, evacuate, excrete, pass a motion, relieve yourself, void excrement, poop; *dialect* mute
OLD scumber, ease yourself, cover the feet
FORMAL egest
COLLOQ. do your business, do number two
SLANG poo, poop, plop; *(vulgar)* shit, crap

defect n, v

♦ n
imperfection, fault, flaw, deficiency, failing, mistake, error, inadequacy, blemish, taint, deformity, shortcoming, shortfall, weakness, frailty, lack, spot, weak spot, snag, absence, omission
FORMAL want
COLLOQ. bug
♦ v
desert, abandon, break faith, change sides, rebel, revolt, turn traitor, abscond
FORMAL renege, apostatize, tergiversate
COLLOQ. *Scot* jump/loup the dyke

SYNONYM NUANCES

noun
Imperfection is a fairly mild term for some minor element that makes the whole fall short of perfection: *Nature is full of imperfections*, but both **fault** and **flaw** more decidedly suggest something that is wrong: *there is a fault on the line; there is a basic flaw in that argument*. **Deficiency** or **shortcoming** might be used where something is lacking: *deficiencies common to many secondary schools; a moral shortcoming*, while to refer to a more general falling short of what is required you might use **inadequacy**. **Failing** and **weak spot** usually apply to an area of human vulnerability or relate to a man-made defect: *his old failing — impetuosity*.
  Both **mistake** and **error** make a clear suggestion that something has been done wrongly to create a defect. The term **blemish** is suggestive of something that spoils the whole, while the more marked **taint** has undercurrents of contamination: *the taint of corruption*. You may use **deformity** to state clearly that something is physically shaped other than it should be, but it is a word that should be used sensitively of living creatures.
  Shortfall should be used specifically of something missing, usually money or items: *a shortfall of several thousand*. **Snag** is usually reserved for a defect in a material.

defection n

desertion, abandonment, disloyalty, backsliding, rebellion, revolt, mutiny, betrayal, absconding, treason
FORMAL renegation, apostasy, defalcation, dereliction, perfidy, tergiversation

defective adj

faulty, imperfect, out of order, flawed, deficient, broken, in disrepair, abnormal
FORMAL malfunctioning
COLLOQ. bust, duff, on the blink, kaput; *N Am* on the fritz
E∃ in order, working; *formal* operative

> **!** **defective** or **deficient**?
> *Defective* means 'having a fault or flaw': *The crash was caused by defective wiring in the signalling system.* *Deficient* means 'inadequate, lacking in what is needed': *a diet deficient in essential vitamins and minerals.*

defector *n*
deserter, traitor, turncoat, betrayer, rebel, Judas, quisling, mutineer, backslider
OLD recreant
FORMAL renegade, apostate, tergiversator
COLLOQ. rat

defence *n*
1 PROTECTION, resistance, security, fortification, cover, safeguard, shelter, guard, shield, screen, deterrence, deterrent, barricade, bastion, keep, fortress, outpost, stronghold, garrison, immunity, bulwark, rampart, buttress
OLD (Shakesp) propugnation
2 *a country's defences*
military resources, armed forces, army, navy, air force, troops, soldiers, military, weapons, weaponry, armaments
3 JUSTIFICATION, explanation, excuse, argument, plea, vindication, pleading, testimony, alibi, case
OLD propugnation
FORMAL apologia, apologetic, explication, extenuation, exoneration
Eâ **1** attack, assault **3** accusation, attack

defenceless *adj*
unprotected, undefended, unarmed, unguarded, vulnerable, exposed, susceptible, open to attack, weak, helpless, powerless, impotent
Eâ protected, guarded

defend *v*
1 PROTECT, guard, safeguard, watch over, shelter, secure, preserve, shield, screen, cover, resist, withstand, oppose, hold, keep from harm, contest, deter, barricade, garrison, buttress, bulwark
OLD bestride, enguard, fend, warrant
FORMAL fortify
2 SUPPORT, stand up for, stand by, back, uphold, endorse, vindicate, champion, bolster, argue for, speak up for, make a case for, maintain, explain, justify, plead, assert, fight/stand your corner
FORMAL exonerate
COLLOQ. stick up for
Eâ **1** attack **2** accuse, attack

> **SYNONYM NUANCES**
>
> *sense 1*
> The term **safeguard** is slightly more emotive in tone than **guard**, and suggests keen efforts to look after someone or something that it is worth defending: *regulations designed to safeguard the health of the workforce.* **Watch over** is likely to suggest a more personal involvement: *she watched over us as if we were her children.* The term **shelter** might be used of taking someone or something in to a place of safety, whilst **secure** may be used to describe defending a place by making it safe: *secured with a giant lock.*
> You would use the word **preserve** of taking action to maintain the existence of someone or something: *peace must be preserved.* **Shield**, **screen** and **cover**, however, all suggest providing some form of barrier against danger, whilst **resist**, **withstand** and **oppose** all convey the idea of encountering dangerous forces by standing firm against them. Similarly, **hold** suggests taking a stand, but in order to keep control of something: *they held the city for fifteen weeks.*
> **Contest** continues the idea of defence through offering resistance, whilst **deter** would only be appropriate of discouraging any possible threat: *an alarm system to deter burglars.*

defendant *n*
accused, offender, prisoner
TECHNICAL litigant, appellant, respondent

defender *n*
1 PROTECTOR, guard, bodyguard, keeper
2 SUPPORTER, guardian, advocate, vindicator, backer, endorser, upholder, preserver, champion, patron, sponsor, counsel, apologist
Eâ **1** attacker **2** accuser, detractor

defensible *adj*
justifiable, tenable, arguable, permissible, plausible, valid, maintainable, safe, secure, unassailable, impregnable, pardonable, vindicable
Eâ indefensible, insecure

defensive *adj*
1 PROTECTIVE, defending, safeguarding, protecting, wary, opposing, cautious, watchful
2 SELF-JUSTIFYING, apologetic, self-defensive, oversensitive

defer¹ *v*
defer a meeting
delay, postpone, put off, adjourn, hold over, put back, shelve, suspend, waive
FORMAL procrastinate, prorogue, protract
COLLOQ. put on ice, put on the back burner, take a raincheck on
Eâ bring forward

defer² *v*
defer to an expert opinion
yield, give way, comply, submit, surrender, give in, capitulate, respect, bow
FORMAL accede, acquiesce

deference *n*
1 RESPECT, respectfulness, regard, esteem, honour, reverence, courtesy, civility, politeness, attentiveness, consideration, thoughtfulness
2 SUBMISSION, submissiveness, servility, obedience, compliance, yielding
FORMAL acquiescence
Eâ **1** contempt **2** resistance

deferential *adj*
respectful, reverent, reverential, courteous, civil, dutiful, humble, polite, attentive, ingratiating
FORMAL morigerous, regardful, complaisant, obeisant, obsequious
Eâ arrogant, immodest

deferment *n*
delay, postponement, deferral, putting-off, adjournment, holding-over, shelving, suspension, stay, moratorium, waiving
FORMAL procrastination, prorogation

defiance *n*
opposition, confrontation, resistance, challenge, disobedience, rebelliousness, contempt, insubordination, disregard, insolence
FORMAL recalcitrance, truculence, contumacy
Eâ compliance, acquiescence, submissiveness

defiant *adj*
challenging, resistant, antagonistic, aggressive, rebellious, insubordinate, disobedient, intransigent, bold, insolent, contemptuous, scornful, obstinate, unco-operative, militant, provocative
OLD roisting
FORMAL recalcitrant, refractory, truculent, contumacious
Eâ compliant, acquiescent, submissive

defiantly *adv*
rebelliously, insubordinately, disobediently, intransigently, obstinately, unco-operatively, militantly, boldly, insolently, contemptuously, scornfully, provocatively, antagonistically, aggressively
FORMAL recalcitrantly, truculently, contumaciously
Eâ compliantly, submissively

deficiency n

1 SHORTAGE, lack, inadequacy, scarcity, insufficiency, dearth, want, scantiness, poverty, absence, deficit
2 IMPERFECTION, shortcoming, weakness, fault, defect, flaw, failing, frailty
⊟ 1 excess, surfeit **2** perfection

deficient adj

inadequate, insufficient, scarce, short, low, poor, lacking, meagre, scant, scanty, skimpy, incomplete, unsatisfactory, imperfect, inferior, weak, bankrupt
FORMAL wanting, exiguous, defectible
COLLOQ. minus
⊟ excessive

> ⚠ **deficient** or **defective**?
> See panel at **defective**.

deficit n

shortage, shortfall, deficiency, loss, arrears, lack, default
⊟ excess

defile v, n

♦ v
pollute, violate, contaminate, degrade, dishonour, desecrate, defame, debase, soil, dirty, infect, stain, spoil, sully, tarnish, taint, make impure/unclean, profane, treat sacrilegiously, corrupt, blacken, disgrace
OLD inquinate, defoul, file, moil; (Shakesp) enseam, ray
FORMAL denigrate, vitiate, maculate
⊟ clean, cleanse, purify
♦ n
pass, gorge, valley, gully, passage, ravine, gate; dialect halse
TECHNICAL col

defilement n

contamination, degradation, pollution, impurity, violation, desecration, defamation, debasement, staining, sullying, tarnishing, tainting, profanity
OLD conspurcation
FORMAL denigration
⊟ cleansing, purification

definable adj

ascertainable, definite, identifiable, describable, determinable, perceptible, fixed, specific, exact, precise
FORMAL explicable
⊟ indefinable

define v

1 define the meaning
explain, characterize, describe, interpret, determine, designate, specify, spell out, detail, clarify
FORMAL expound, elucidate
2 define the boundaries
bound, limit, delimit, establish, determine, demarcate, mark out, fix
FORMAL circumscribe, delineate

> QUOTATIONS
> He who defines himself can't know who he really is
> LAO-TZU, Tao Te Ching

definite adj

1 CLEAR, clear-cut, exact, precise, specific, explicit, particular, firm, obvious, marked, noticeable, unmistakable
2 CERTAIN, settled, sure, positive, fixed, decided, determined, assured, guaranteed
⊟ 1 vague, unclear **2** indefinite, provisional

> ⚠ **definite** or **definitive**?
> Definite means 'clear' or 'certain': I'll give you a definite answer later. Definitive means 'final, settling things once and for all': a definitive study of Ben Jonson.

definitely adv

positively, surely, unquestionably, without question, absolutely, certainly, categorically, undeniably, clearly, undoubtedly, doubtless, without doubt, no denying, unmistak(e)ably, for sure, plainly, obviously, indeed, easily
FORMAL indubitably

definition n

1 EXPLANATION, meaning, significance, sense, description, interpretation, clarification, determination
TECHNICAL denotation
FORMAL exposition, elucidation
2 DISTINCTNESS, clarity, precision, clearness, focus, sharpness, visibility, contrast

definitive adj

decisive, conclusive, final, authoritative, standard, correct, ultimate, reliable, exhaustive, perfect, classic, exact, absolute, complete, categorical
⊟ interim

> ⚠ **definitive** or **definite**?
> See panel at **definite**.

definitively adv

decisively, conclusively, finally, authoritatively, absolutely, completely, categorically

deflate v

1 FLATTEN, puncture, collapse, let down, exhaust, squash, empty, contract, void, shrink, squeeze
2 deflate his opinion of himself
humiliate, debunk, dash, disappoint, dispirit, subdue, humble, mortify, chasten, disconcert
COLLOQ. put down, burst someone's bubble, rain on someone's parade
3 DEPRECIATE, devalue, reduce, lessen, lower, diminish, decrease, depress, slow (down)
⊟ 1 inflate **2** boost **3** inflate, increase

deflect v

deviate, diverge, turn (aside), swerve, veer, change course, sidetrack, drift, twist, avert, head off, wind, glance (off), bend, ricochet, snick
TECHNICAL refract
OLD withdraw

deflection n

deviation, divergence, turning, turning aside, diversion, swerve, veer, changing course, sidetracking, drift, twisting, glancing-off, bend, ricochet
TECHNICAL refraction
FORMAL aberration

deflower v

violate, assault, defile, rape, seduce, spoil, desecrate, force, harm, mar, molest, ruin
FORMAL ravish, despoil

deform v

distort, contort, disfigure, deface, malform, misshape, warp, mar, pervert, ruin, spoil, damage, maim, mutilate, twist, buckle

deformation n

bend, curve, distortion, contortion, disfiguration, defacement, malformation, misshapenness, mutilation, twist, twisting, warp, buckle
TECHNICAL diastrophism

deformed adj

distorted, misshapen, malformed, contorted, disfigured, crippled, crooked, gnarled, bent, twisted, warped, buckled, defaced, mangled, maimed, marred, ruined, mutilated, perverted, corrupted

deformity n

distortion, misshapenness, malformation, disfigurement, defacement, abnormality, irregularity, imperfection, misproportion, defect, ugliness, crookedness, vileness, grossness, monstrosity, corruption, perversion

defraud v

cheat, swindle, dupe, rob, trick, fleece, rook, wrong, deceive, delude, mislead, fool, hoodwink, outwit, embezzle, beguile, nick
OLD lurch

FORMAL cozen
COLLOQ. fiddle, rush, do, diddle, con
SLANG screw, sting, rip off, swiz, take to the cleaners

defray v
reimburse, refund, repay, recompense, discharge, meet, pay, cover, square, settle
E∃ incur

deft adj
adept, handy, dexterous, nimble, skilful, adroit, agile, expert, nifty, proficient, able, neat, clever
E∃ clumsy, awkward

deftly adv
skilfully, adeptly, nimbly, expertly, ably, cleverly, neatly, proficiently
E∃ awkwardly

defunct adj
1 DEAD, deceased, departed, gone, expired, extinct
2 OBSOLETE, disused, unused, invalid, expired, passé, outmoded, bygone
FORMAL inoperative
E∃ **1** alive, live **2** functioning; formal operative

defuse v
1 *defuse a tense situation*
calm (down), quieten, relieve, alleviate
COLLOQ. cool (down), clear the air, pour oil on troubled waters
2 *defuse a bomb*
deactivate, disarm, disable, immobilize
FORMAL render inoperative
E∃ **1** intensify, make worse **2** activate

defy v
1 *defy the authorities*
challenge, confront, resist, dare, outdare, brave, face, repel, spurn, beard, flout, slight, withstand, stand up to, disobey, rebel against, disrespect, disregard, ignore, scorn, mock, despise, defeat, provoke, frustrate, thwart, fly in the face of
2 *her writings defy categorization*
elude, avoid, frustrate, baffle, foil
E∃ **1** obey, comply **2** permit, allow

degeneracy n
dissoluteness, debauchery, depravation, degradation, debasement, decadence, corruption, fallenness, immorality, vileness, wickedness, sinfulness, degeneration, perversion, deterioration
FORMAL effeteness
E∃ morality, uprightness

degenerate adj, v, n
♦ adj
dissolute, debauched, depraved, degraded, debased, base, low, abandoned, decadent, corrupt, fallen, immoral, mean, ignoble, vile, wicked, sinful, degenerated, perverted, deteriorated
OLD (Shakesp) derogate
FORMAL effete, profligate
COLLOQ. off the rails
E∃ moral, upright
♦ v
decline, deteriorate, sink, decay, rot, fail, slip, worsen, fall off, lapse, decrease, bastardize
OLD degender; (Shakesp) recoil
FORMAL regress
COLLOQ. go downhill, go to pot, go down the tubes
E∃ improve
♦ n
reprobate, miscreant, rake, roué, wrongdoer, criminal, evildoer, sinner, rogue, rascal, scoundrel, scamp, scallywag, villain, vagabond, wretch, mischief-maker, ne'er-do-well, knave, dastard, troublemaker
FORMAL profligate

degeneration n
decline, deterioration, debasement, decay, rot, failure, slip, worsening, falling-off, sinking, drop, slide, lapse, atrophy, decrease

FORMAL regression
E∃ improvement

degradation n
1 ABASEMENT, humiliation, mortification, dishonour, disgrace, shame, ignominy, decadence, degeneracy, dissoluteness, debauchery, depravation, debasement, corruption, fallenness, immorality, vileness, wickedness, sinfulness, degeneration, perversion
2 DETERIORATION, degeneration, decline, downgrading, demotion
E∃ **1** virtue **2** enhancement

degrade v
1 DISHONOUR, disgrace, debase, abase, shame, humiliate, humble, put down, discredit, mortify, demean, belittle, diminish, lower, sink, devalue, weaken, impair, deteriorate, cheapen, adulterate, pervert, sully, defile, corrupt, prostitute, brutalize, embase
2 DEMOTE, depose, downgrade, deprive, cashier, reduce/lower in rank, relegate, unseat, declass, disennoble
COLLOQ. drum out, take down a peg or two
E∃ **1** exalt, elevate **2** promote

degrading adj
humiliating, dishonourable, disgraceful, debasing, base, shameful, contemptible, discrediting, mortifying, demeaning, belittling, cheapening, ignoble, undignified, unworthy
E∃ enhancing

degree n
1 *to a great degree*
extent, measure, range, stage, step, level, amount, point, intensity, strength, standard
2 GRADE, class, rank, rung, order, position, standing, status, stage, level, limit, unit, point, mark

dehydrate v
dry, dry up, dry out, evaporate, lose water, drain, parch
FORMAL desiccate, exsiccate, effloresce

dehydration n
drying, evaporation, parching, dehumidifying
FORMAL desiccation

deification n
exaltation, elevation, worship, glorification, idolization, extolling, revering, reverence, immortalization, ennoblement, idealization
FORMAL veneration, apotheosis, divinification, divinization

deify v
exalt, elevate, worship, glorify, idolize, extol, revere, immortalize, ennoble, idealize
FORMAL aggrandize, venerate

deign v
condescend, stoop, lower yourself, consent, demean yourself

deity n
god, goddess, divinity, divine being, supreme being, godhead, idol, demigod, spirit, power, eternal, immortal

dejected adj
downcast, despondent, depressed, downhearted, discouraged, disheartened, down, low, melancholy, sad, miserable, cast down, gloomy, glum, crestfallen, crushed, demoralized, dismal, wretched, doleful, morose, spiritless, dispirited
FORMAL disconsolate
COLLOQ. blue, down in the dumps
SLANG US bummed
E∃ cheerful, high-spirited, happy

dejectedly adv
despondently, sadly, miserably, glumly, gloomily, dismally, wretchedly, morosely
FORMAL disconsolately
E∃ cheerfully, happily

dejection n
despondency, depression, downheartedness, discouragement, low spirits, despair, melancholy, sadness,

sorrow, unhappiness, misery, gloom, gloominess,
wretchedness, dolefulness, moroseness, dispiritedness
FORMAL disconsolateness, disconsolation
COLLOQ. blues, dumps
E3 happiness, high spirits

de jure *adv, adj*
legally, rightfully, legal, rightful
E3 de facto

delay *v, n*
♦ *v*
1 OBSTRUCT, hinder, impede, hamper, hold up, check,
hold back, set back, slow, stay, stop, halt, detain,
stonewall, filibuster, keep, restrain, retard, stave
2 POSTPONE, put off, put back, defer, suspend,
shelve, hold over, detain, reprieve, adjourn, stall
OLD (*Shakesp & Spenser*) forslow
FORMAL procrastinate
COLLOQ. sit on, put on ice, put on the back burner
3 DAWDLE, hang on, linger, hesitate, lag (behind), loiter,
dither, hold back
FORMAL tarry
COLLOQ. dilly-dally, faff about
E3 **1** accelerate **2** bring forward **3** hurry, keep up
♦ *n*
1 OBSTRUCTION, hindrance, impediment, hold-up, check,
setback, stay, stoppage, halt, retardation, interruption, lull,
interval, wait
OLD let
2 POSTPONEMENT, deferment, putting-off, adjournment,
holding-over, shelving, suspension, detaining, detention,
stay, respite, moratorium, waiving, reprieve
TECHNICAL demurrage, mora
OLD frist
FORMAL procrastination, cunctation
3 DAWDLING, lingering, loitering, stalling,
hesitance, lag
FORMAL tarrying
COLLOQ. dilly-dallying
E3 **1** hastening, continuation **3** hurry

SYNONYM NUANCES

verb sense 1
Both **obstruct** and **impede** may be used to refer to
placing something in the way, perhaps deliberately: *UN
officials accused the government of obstructing relief
operations*. The terms **check**, **stay**, **hold back** and **set
back** again suggest preventing progress, although they
are perhaps less strong terms: *a tax credit checked the
slump*. **Hinder**, **hamper**, and **hold up** are similar, though
perhaps more suggestive of action that slows something
down rather than stops it temporarily: *failing eyesight
which hampered his work*; **detain** could be used where
a person has been kept somewhere and so delayed:
unforeseen business detained him.
  The words **keep** and **restrain** could also be used
especially where there is a deliberate effort to keep
something in check: *efforts to restrain the lava flows
from the volcano*. To refer to delaying development, you
might choose **retard**: *the monetary squeeze is already
retarding recovery*. **Stave**, however, is more suggestive
of delaying something by warding it off: *employers
skilfully staved off demands for big wage increases*. Both
stonewall and **filibuster** are used specifically of delaying
tactics used within government.

---

delectable *adj*
1 DELICIOUS, appetizing, palatable, tasty, dainty,
luscious, mouthwatering, succulent, flavoursome,
savoury
COLLOQ. scrumptious, yummy
2 ATTRACTIVE, pleasant, delightful, adorable, charming,
beautiful, lovely, enchanting, engaging, exciting, pleasing,
agreeable
E3 **1** unpalatable **2** unpleasant

delectation *n*
enjoyment, delight, happiness, pleasure, comfort,
contentment, gratification, refreshment, relish, satisfaction,
amusement, diversion, entertainment
E3 distaste

delegate *n, v*
♦ *n*
representative, agent, envoy, messenger, deputy, second,
secondary, substitute, ambassador, spokesperson,
spokesman, spokeswoman, legate, emissary, proxy,
commissioner
TECHNICAL vicar
OLD TECHNICAL syndic
♦ *v*
authorize, appoint, depute, charge, commission, commit,
give, pass on/over, assign, empower, entrust, devolve,
consign, leave, designate, ordain, nominate, name, hand
over

delegation *n*
1 DEPUTATION, representatives, commission, legation,
mission, contingent, embassy
2 *delegation of responsibility*
committal, transference, assignment, consignment,
entrusting, passing on/over, devolution, empowerment

delete *v*
erase, remove, cross out, cancel, rub out, strike (out), take
out, obliterate, edit (out), cut (out), blot out, blue-pencil
FORMAL excise, efface, expunge
E3 add, insert

deleterious *adj*
destructive, detrimental, harmful, hurtful, injurious, bad,
damaging, ruinous, pernicious, prejudicial
FORMAL noxious
E3 enhancing, helpful

deliberate *adj, v*
♦ *adj*
1 INTENTIONAL, planned, calculated, prearranged, set,
premeditated, preplanned, preconceived, willed, wilful,
conscious, witting, designed, considered, advised, *voulu*
TECHNICAL volitive
OLD propense
2 CAREFUL, unhurried, thoughtful, methodical, cautious,
studied, studious, prudent, slow, ponderous, steady,
leisurely, measured, heedful, resolute, unhesitating,
unwavering
FORMAL circumspect
E3 **1** unintentional, accidental **2** hasty, casual
♦ *v*
consider, ponder, reflect, think (over), think about,
meditate, mull over, muse, debate, discuss, evaluate,
weigh (up), consult
OLD advise
FORMAL cogitate, ruminate, excogitate

deliberately *adv*
1 INTENTIONALLY, on purpose, consciously, pointedly,
calculatingly, by design, in cold blood, coldbloodedly,
knowingly, wittingly, wilfully, with malice aforethought
2 CAREFULLY, unhurriedly, thoughtfully, methodically,
cautiously, prudently, slowly, ponderously, steadily,
studiously
FORMAL circumspectly
E3 **1** unintentionally, by accident, accidentally, by mistake
2 hastily, casually

deliberation *n*
1 CONSIDERATION, reflection, thought, calculation,
forethought, meditation, pondering, musing, mulling,
brooding, study, evaluation, weighing-up
FORMAL cogitation, rumination, excogitate
2 *secret deliberations*
debate, discussion, consultation, conferring
3 CARE, carefulness, caution, thoughtfulness, unhurriedness,
slowness, steadiness, prudence
FORMAL circumspection

delicacy *n*
1 DAINTINESS, fineness, elegance, exquisiteness, lightness, fragility, precision
2 SENSITIVITY, tact, diplomacy, discretion, care, consideration, subtlety, finesse, discrimination, niceness
3 TITBIT, dainty, taste, treat, luxury, sweetmeat, savoury, relish, speciality, bonne-bouche
OLD delice
E3 1 coarseness, roughness **2** tactlessness, insensitivity

delicate *adj*
1 FINE, dainty, exquisite, elegant, slight, graceful, ethereal
OLD (*Shakesp*) incony
2 FRAIL, sickly, weak, ailing, infirm, unwell, in poor health, faint, debilitated; *dialect* nesh
3 *delicate china*
fragile, breakable, easily damaged/broken, frail, flimsy, brittle, insubstantial, light
4 *a delicate situation*
sensitive, tricky, difficult, problematic, critical, awkward, touchy, controversial
5 *needs delicate handling*
tactful, sensitive, diplomatic, careful, considerate, discreet
COLLOQ. softly-softly, kid-glove
6 SUBTLE, muted, pastel, pale, subdued, soft, faint, mild, bland
7 *a delicate instrument*
precision, sensitive, precise, exact, accurate
E3 1 coarse, clumsy **2** healthy, strong **3** strong, tough **4** easy, straightforward **6** strong, bold

delicately *adv*
1 DAINTILY, finely, exquisitely, elegantly, gracefully
2 SUBTLY, softly, faintly, mildly, blandly, palely
3 SENSITIVELY, critically, carefully, finely, tactfully, gently, diplomatically

delicious *adj*
1 TASTY, palatable, appetizing, mouth-watering, juicy, succulent, toothsome, savoury, good, choice, tempting, melting in the mouth
FORMAL delectable, nectareous, ambrosial
COLLOQ. delish, mor(e)ish, scrumptious, yummy, scrummy, lip-smacking
SLANG goluptious
2 ENJOYABLE, pleasant, agreeable, delightful, charming, enchanting, captivating, pleasurable, pleasing, gratifying, entertaining, fascinating, exquisite
E3 1 unpalatable, tasteless **2** unpleasant

SYNONYM NUANCES

sense 1
Tasty is a very widely used and approbatory term to describe something that really appeals to our sense of taste; **toothsome** is similar, though much less common: *toothsome vegetable-based dishes*. **Palatable**, however, is less effusive and simply describes something pleasing, or even merely tolerable: *safe, palatable drinking water*. The terms **appetizing** and **tempting** could be used of something that prompts our desire to eat, whilst **mouth-watering** goes even further by suggesting an ability to provoke salivation: *mouth-watering desserts on offer*.
    The words **juicy** and **succulent** return to the idea of how things taste, as opposed to the response they provoke, and, as both suggest lushness, would be used of more moist foods. **Melting in the mouth** also has more to do with the texture of the food, this time describing something tender. **Savoury** was originally used to suggest having full flavour, but tends nowadays to be used simply as the converse of sweet: *a savoury smell*; *savoury snacks*.

---

delight *n, v*
♦ *n*
happiness, joy, pleasure, contentment, enjoyment, gladness, glee, rapture, transport, bliss, exultation, euphoria, ecstasy, elation, gratification, jubilation, amusement, entertainment
OLD delice, mirth
FORMAL delectation, felicity
E3 disgust, displeasure
♦ *v*
1 *the prospect of being parents delighted them*
please, charm, gratify, cheer, gladden, excite, enchant, captivate, enrapture, entrance, tickle, thrill, ravish, give enjoyment to, amuse, entertain
OLD rape
COLLOQ. bowl over, tickle pink, take your breath away
2 *delight in something*
enjoy, relish, like, love, appreciate, revel in, feast, take pleasure in, take pride in, glory in, boast of, wallow in, savour
OLD (*Spenser*) fain
E3 1 disappoint, displease, dismay **2** dislike, hate

delighted *adj*
happy, pleased, glad, enchanted, captivated, enraptured, entranced, elated, euphoric, ecstatic, thrilled, excited, joyful, overjoyed, gleeful, jubilant, gratified, charmed
FORMAL joyous
COLLOQ. over the moon, tickled pink, happy as Larry/a sandboy, pleased as Punch
E3 disappointed, dismayed

delightful *adj*
charming, enchanting, captivating, enjoyable, pleasant, thrilling, exciting, agreeable, pleasurable, engaging, attractive, beautiful, pleasing, gratifying, appealing, fascinating, amusing, diverting, entertaining
FORMAL delectable
COLLOQ. out of this world, great, magic, ace, divine, the tops
E3 nasty, unpleasant

delimit *v*
bound, demarcate, determine, establish, fix, set, mark, define

delineate *v*
describe, depict, portray, set forth, outline, draw, sketch, trace, design, chart, render, represent, define, mark, bound, determine, establish, fix

delineation *n*
description, depiction, portrayal, tracing, rendering, representation

delinquency *n*
crime, offence, misdeed, wrongdoing, misbehaviour, misconduct, lawbreaking, misdemeanour, criminality
FORMAL transgression

delinquent *n, adj*
♦ *n*
offender, criminal, wrongdoer, lawbreaker, hooligan, young offender, culprit, ruffian, vandal, *Halbstarker*
FORMAL miscreant, malefactor
♦ *adj*
criminal, offending, lawbreaking, lawless, guilty, negligent
FORMAL remiss, culpable
E3 blameless, careful

delirious *adj*
1 *delirious because of fever*
demented, raving, incoherent, beside yourself, irrational, deranged, frenzied, light-headed, wild, mad, frantic, frenetic, insane, crazy, unhinged, babbling, rambling, wandering, out of your mind
COLLOQ. gone, spaced out
2 *delirious with excitement*
ecstatic, euphoric, overjoyed, elated, jubilant, rapturous, hysterical, beside yourself, carried away
COLLOQ. over the moon
E3 1 sane

deliriously *adv*
ecstatically, jubilantly, rapturously, hysterically

delirium *n*
1 *feverish delirium*
derangement, raving, incoherence, irrationality, fever, frenzy, passion, wildness, madness, insanity, lunacy, dementia, craziness, hallucination, hysteria
COLLOQ. jimjams
2 *the delirium of first love*
ecstasy, euphoria, joy, elation, rapture, excitement, jubilation, wildness, passion
F∃ 1 sanity

deliver *v*
1 *deliver a parcel*
convey, bring, take, send, give, carry, supply, distribute, give out
FORMAL dispatch
2 SURRENDER, hand over, turn over, render, relinquish, yield, transfer, grant, entrust, commit
FORMAL cede
3 *deliver a speech*
utter, make, speak, give, proclaim, declare, announce, pronounce, express, voice, give voice to
FORMAL enunciate
4 ADMINISTER, deal, give, inflict, launch, direct, aim, strike
5 *deliver the promised benefits*
fulfil, provide, supply, do, carry out, implement, live up to
6 *deliver a baby*
help give birth to, assist in/at the delivery of, bring into the world
7 SET FREE, liberate, save, rescue, release
FORMAL emancipate, ransom, redeem, manumit

deliverance *n*
rescue, liberation, salvation, freedom, release, escape, extrication
FORMAL emancipation, ransom, redemption

delivery *n*
1 CONVEYANCE, supply, distribution, transport, transportation, carriage, consignment, transmission, transfer, shipment
FORMAL dispatch
2 CONSIGNMENT, batch, load, shipment
3 ARTICULATION, pronunciation, speech, utterance, intonation, elocution
FORMAL enunciation
4 CHILDBIRTH, birth, labour, confinement
FORMAL parturition, travail

dell *n*
valley, vale, dale, hollow, dean, dingle, slade

delude *v*
deceive, mislead, beguile, dupe, fool, take in, lead on, trick, hoodwink, hoax, cheat, cajole, misguide, misinform
OLD blend, put the change on
COLLOQ. bamboozle, have on, kid, take for a ride, double-cross, two-time, pull someone's leg, pull a fast one on, pull the wool over someone's eyes

deluge *n, v*
♦ *n*
1 *a deluge of rain*
flood, inundation, downpour, overflowing, torrent
2 *a deluge of letters*
flood, torrent, avalanche, spate, barrage, rush, wave
♦ *v*
1 *deluged by rain*
flood, inundate, drench, drown, soak, engulf, submerge
2 *deluged by queries*
overwhelm, inundate, swamp, flood, snow under

delusion *n*
illusion, hallucination, fancy, misconception, misapprehension, false belief/impression, deception, misbelief, fallacy, misinformation, tricking

> **! delusion** or **illusion**?
> A *delusion* is a false belief arising in your own mind, whereas an *illusion* is a false impression coming into your mind from the world outside it.

de luxe, deluxe *adj*
luxury, luxurious, select, choice, quality, expensive, costly, special, exclusive, grand, lavish, fine, elegant, palatial, rich, splendid, sumptuous, superior
FORMAL opulent
COLLOQ. plush, swish

delve *v*
burrow, rummage, search, dig into, hunt in/through, poke, scrabble, ransack, root, probe, examine, explore, investigate, go/look into, research

demagogue *n*
agitator, orator, speaker, public speaker, firebrand, haranguer, rabble-rouser, tub-thumper

demand *v, n*
♦ *v*
1 ASK (FOR), request, tell, call for, insist on, urge, press for, hold out for, order, dictate, stipulate, solicit, claim, clamour, petition, exact, inquire, question, interrogate
2 REQUIRE, need, necessitate, take, call for, involve, cry out for
♦ *n*
1 REQUEST, question, claim, petition, call, plea, order, inquiry, desire, pressure, insistence, clamour, interrogation
2 NEED, necessity, call, requirement, want
FORMAL exigency
3 *there's no demand for it*
call, market, need, desire, run
■ **in demand**
popular, fashionable, asked for, requested, desired, sought after
COLLOQ. big, trendy, in, of the moment

demanding *adj*
hard, difficult, challenging, exacting, taxing, tough, exhausting, wearing, back-breaking, insistent, nagging, harassing, pressing, testing, urgent, trying
FORMAL exigent
COLLOQ. high-maintenance, a tall order
F∃ easy, undemanding

demarcate *v*
determine, establish, fix, mark (out), mark off, divide, separate, delimit, define, bound

demarcation *n*
boundary, bound, differentiation, distinction, division, separation, enclosure, limit, line, margin, determination, establishment, fixing, marking off/out, delimitation, definition

demean *v*
lower, humble, degrade, belittle, deprecate, humiliate, debase, abase, descend, demote, stoop, condescend
F∃ exalt, enhance

demeaning *adj*
degrading, humiliating, dishonourable, disgraceful, debasing, base, shameful, contemptible, discrediting, mortifying, belittling, cheapening, ignoble, undignified, unworthy
F∃ enhancing

demeanour *n*
manner, conduct, behaviour, air, carriage
FORMAL bearing, deportment, mien, comportment

demented *adj*
mad, insane, lunatic, unbalanced, disturbed, deranged, crazy, crazed, wild, berserk, frantic, unhinged, distracted, distraught, frenetic, maniac, out of your mind, infuriate; *Scot* gyte
OLD frantic-mad, lymphatic, bestraught
COLLOQ. demented, nuts, nutty, nutty as a fruitcake, wacky, mad as a hatter, barmy, bonkers, batty, cracked, crackers, dippy, daffy, dotty, loopy, potty, off your nut, off your head, wrong in the head, out of your head, off the wall, out to lunch, round the bend, round the twist, bats, having bats in the belfry, cuckoo, off the rails, screwy, up the wall, raving, not all there; *N Am* buggy, flaky, fruity; *Aust & NZ* dingbats

SLANG loony, mental, bananas, barking, wacko, doolally, off your rocker, off your chump, off your trolley, out of your tree, needing your head examined, having lost your marbles, having a screw loose, having a tile loose, having several cards short of a full deck, with one sandwich short of a picnic, meshuga, ape, apeshit; *N Am* gonzo, loco, wiggy; *Aust* out of your tree
E3 sane

demise *n*
1 DEATH, decease, end, dying, passing, departure
FORMAL termination, expiration, cessation
2 DOWNFALL, fall, end, collapse, failure, ruin, disintegration

demobilize *v*
disperse, disband, break up, dismiss
COLLOQ. demob
E3 assemble, conscript

democracy *n*
self-government, commonwealth, autonomy, republic

> QUOTATIONS
> It has been said that democracy is the worst form of Government except all those other forms that have been tried from time to time
> SIR WINSTON CHURCHILL

democratic *adj*
self-governing, representative, elected, egalitarian, autonomous, popular, populist, republican

demolish *v*
1 DESTROY, dismantle, knock down, pull down, take down, ruin, flatten, bulldoze, raze, tear down, break up, pulverize, level, unbuild
OLD abate, ruinate
2 *demolish the opponents*
beat, overcome, overpower, get the better of, conquer, excel, surpass, subdue, overthrow, repel, overwhelm, rout, ruin, crush, quell, break down, bring someone to their knees
FORMAL subjugate, vanquish
COLLOQ. thrash, lick, hammer, annihilate, devastate, massacre, slaughter
3 *demolish an argument*
destroy, ruin, wreck, overturn, undo, tear down
COLLOQ. drive a coach and horses through
E3 **1** build up, erect, construct

demolition *n*
1 DESTRUCTION, dismantling, knocking-down, pulling-down, flattening, razing, tearing-down, breaking-up, levelling
2 *demolition of the opposing team*
beating, overpowering, surpassing, overthrow, overwhelming, rout
COLLOQ. thrashing, clobbering, licking, hammering, annihilation, massacre, slaughter

demon *n*
1 DEVIL, fiend, evil spirit, fallen angel, imp, ghoul, warlock, familiar, daemon, satyr, cacodemon, afrit, rakshas, incubus, succubus, *duende*
2 VILLAIN, devil, rogue, monster, fiend, beast, ogre, savage, brute
3 *a demon at chess*
addict, fanatic, fiend, buff, wizard
COLLOQ. ace, freak, dab hand

demonic *adj*
fiendish, devilish, diabolical, hellish, infernal, satanic, possessed, mad, maniacal, manic, crazed, frantic, frenetic, frenzied, furious

demonstrable *adj*
verifiable, provable, arguable, attestable, self-evident, obvious, evident, certain, clear, positive
FORMAL evincible
E3 unverifiable

demonstrate *v*
1 PROVE, determine, show, establish, verify, indicate
FORMAL validate, substantiate
2 SHOW, display, exhibit, express, indicate, register, betray
OLD remonstrate
FORMAL manifest, testify to, bear witness to, evince, betoken, bespeak
3 EXPLAIN, illustrate, describe, show, teach, communicate, make clear
FORMAL expound
4 PROTEST, march, parade, rally, picket, sit in

demonstration *n*
1 DISPLAY, expression, indication, exhibition, proof, confirmation, evidence, testimony, verification, affirmation
FORMAL manifestation, evincement, substantiation, validation
2 EXPLANATION, illustration, description, presentation, communication, test, trial
FORMAL exposition, elucidation
3 PROTEST, march, rally, mass rally, picket, sit-in, parade, civil disobedience
COLLOQ. demo

demonstrative *adj*
affectionate, expressive, extrovert, unreserved, effusive, gushing, expansive, emotional, open, loving, warm
E3 reserved, introvert, cold, restrained

demonstratively *adv*
expressively, openly, emotionally, warmly, affectionately, lovingly
E3 coldly

demoralize *v*
1 DISCOURAGE, dishearten, dispirit, depress, deject, cast down, crush, disconcert, make despondent, daunt, lower, undermine, weaken
2 CORRUPT, deprave, debase, pervert, contaminate, defile
E3 **1** encourage, inspire confidence **2** improve

demoralizing *adj*
discouraging, disheartening, depressing, disconcerting, daunting, weakening, dispiriting
E3 encouraging

demote *v*
downgrade, reduce in rank, degrade, relegate, humble, cashier
E3 promote, upgrade

demotic *adj*
popular, vernacular, colloquial, vulgar
FORMAL enchorial, enchoric

demotion *n*
downgrading, relegation, degrading
E3 promotion

demur *v, n*
♦ *v*
disagree, dissent, object, take exception, refuse, protest, dispute, balk, cavil, scruple, doubt, express doubts, hesitate, be unwilling
♦ *n*
disagreement, dissent, hesitation, objection, protest, misgiving, qualm, reservation, doubt, scruple
FORMAL compunction, demurral

demure *adj*
modest, reserved, unassuming, reticent, coy, shy, timid, quiet, serious, retiring, prissy, grave, prudish, sober, strait-laced, prim, staid
E3 wanton, forward

demurely *adv*
modestly, unassumingly, reticently, quietly, seriously, coyly, shyly, timidily, primly, staidly

den *n*
1 *a wolf's den*
lair, hideout, hole, hollow

2 *a den of forgers*
haunt, meeting-place, patch, pitch, hotbed
COLLOQ. dive, joint
3 *study in his den*
retreat, study, studio, hideaway, shelter, sanctuary

denial *n*
1 CONTRADICTION, opposition, disagreement, dissent,
disclaimer, dismissal, renunciation
OLD denay, denegation
FORMAL negation, disavowal, disaffirmation, abjuration,
refutation, rebuttal, repudiation
2 REFUSAL, rebuff, rejection, dismissal, prohibition, veto
3 *denial of your parents*
disowning, renunciation, repudiation, forsaking
FORMAL disavowal

denigrate *v*
run down, slander, belittle, abuse, assail, criticize,
deprecate, cheapen
FORMAL disparage, cast aspersions on, revile, defame,
malign, vilify, decry, besmirch, impugn, calumniate,
vilipend
COLLOQ. fling/sling/throw mud, pick holes in
☒ praise, acclaim

denigration *n*
slander, belittling, abuse, deprecation, degradation
FORMAL disparagement, vilification, calumny
☒ praise

denizen *n*
citizen, dweller, inhabitant, occupant, resident, townsman,
townswoman, habitant, habitué

denomination *n*
1 RELIGION, persuasion, Church, sect, religious body/group,
belief, faith, creed, communion, cult, school, order,
constituency, tradition
2 *the denomination of a banknote*
value, face value, worth, unit, grade, class, kind, sort,
designation

denote *v*
indicate, be a sign of, stand for, signify, represent,
symbolize, mean, refer to, express, designate, typify, mark,
show, imply, suggest
OLD betoken

dénouement *n*
climax, culmination, conclusion, outcome, upshot, finale,
resolution, clarification, unravelling, finish, last act,
solution, close
COLLOQ. pay-off

denounce *v*
condemn, censure, denunciate, accuse, attack, run down,
criticize, inform against, betray, indict, pronounce
FORMAL deplore, revile, decry, castigate, impugn, vilify,
arraign, declaim, fulminate, inculpate, execrate, proscribe
COLLOQ. slate, knock, pick holes in, pull/tear to pieces,
rubbish, badmouth, put the boot in
SLANG slag (off)
☒ acclaim, praise

dense *adj*
1 *a dense crowd/forest*
solid, packed, crammed, jammed together, close-packed,
tightly packed, crowded, thick, compact, compressed,
condensed, close, close-knit, heavy; *dialect* rank
2 *dense smoke*
thick, opaque, impenetrable, concentrated
3 STUPID, dim, dull, slow, slow-witted
FORMAL obtuse
COLLOQ. thick, thick as two short planks, dim-witted,
dopey, dumb, gormless
☒ **1** thin, sparse **3** quick-witted, clever

densely *adv*
solidly, closely, thickly, heavily, firmly, tightly, compactly
☒ sparsely

density *n*
body, mass, bulk, closeness, compactness, consistency,
denseness, solidity, solidness, thickness, tightness,
impenetrability
☒ sparseness

dent *n, v*
♦ *n*
1 HOLLOW, depression, dip, concavity, indentation, crater,
dimple, dint, pit
2 REDUCTION, lessening, deduction, cut, drop, fall
♦ *v*
1 DEPRESS, gouge, push in, indent
2 REDUCE, lessen, diminish, damage, weaken

denude *v*
strip, divest, expose, uncover, bare, clear, deforest,
defoliate
☒ cover, clothe

denunciation *n*
condemnation, denouncement, censure, accusation,
incrimination, attack, criticism
FORMAL invective, decrial, castigation, obloquy,
fulmination
☒ acclaim, praise

deny *v*
1 *deny the allegations*
contradict, oppose, disagree with, disprove, repudiate,
rebut, nay
TECHNICAL sublate, traverse
OLD denay, renay
FORMAL refute, disaffirm, negate, abnegate, nullify, abjure,
gainsay, forswear, renege
2 *deny him access to his children*
refuse, turn down, forbid, prohibit, reject, withhold,
dismiss, rebuff, veto
FORMAL decline, disallow
3 *deny your parents*
disown, disclaim, repudiate, turn your back on, unget
FORMAL renounce, disavow, recant
☒ **1** admit **2** allow

deodorant *n*
anti-perspirant, deodorizer, scent, air-freshener,
disinfectant, fumigant, fumigator

deodorize *v*
freshen, purify, refresh, sweeten, disinfect, fumigate,
aerate, ventilate

depart *v*
1 GO, go away, go off, leave, withdraw, exit, make off,
part, decamp, take your leave, absent yourself, set off, set
out, start out, pull out, get going, remove, retreat, migrate,
escape, disappear, retire, vanish, take wing
OLD avaunt
COLLOQ. push along/off, make tracks, quit, scat, scoot,
scram, take off, take to your heels, make yourself scarce,
shove off, bunk off, clear off, split, scarper, skedaddle,
vamoose, skive, do a runner, do a bunk, do a moonlight
flit, hit the road/trail, make a bolt/break for it, up sticks,
hightail it, sling your hook
SLANG N Am lam it, take it on the lam
2 DEVIATE, digress, differ, diverge, fork, branch off, swerve,
turn aside, veer, vary
☒ **1** arrive, return **2** keep to

SYNONYM NUANCES

sense 1
The terms **withdraw** and **exit** are suggestive of moving
out of a specific place: *we exited the aircraft*. You may
use **make off** to imply haste, with, perhaps, an element
of guilt attached: *two men had made off as the police
arrived*. You would use **part** to place emphasis on the
idea of moving from a place or person. **Remove** could
be used to refer to permanent departure to another
place, and **decamp**, although it has the literal use of
breaking up camp, is more widely used, sometimes

facetiously or with a suggestion of secretiveness, of moving away from one place to another: *fashionable society decamped from London to Bath*.

The phrases **absent yourself** and **take your leave** are suggestive of a somewhat formal departure, the latter sometimes including farewells: *he bowed and took his leave*. If you want to talk about embarking on a journey, you could use **set off**, **set out**, **start out** or **get going**, whereas to use **retreat** would imply an element of running away from something, and **escape**, though similar, would further suggest departing previous restrictions and therefore relief.

Migrate is used of movement from one country to another, whilst **retire** tends towards the idea of taking yourself away to a much closer location: *she retired to her room*. Both **vanish** and **disappear** can be used fairly informally to suggest going away at speed: *his brother had vanished upstairs*, whilst **take wing** similarly suggests speed of departure.

departed *adj*
dead, gone, late, lost, passed away
FORMAL deceased, expired

department *n*
1 DIVISION, branch, subdivision, section, sector, wing, office, bureau, agency, organization, station, unit, region, district
2 SPHERE, realm, province, domain, field, area, concern, responsibility, interest, function, speciality, line

departure *n*
1 EXIT, going, going away/off, leaving, leave-taking, removal, withdrawal, retirement, retreat, escape, exodus, setting-off, setting-out
2 DEVIATION, digression, divergence, variation, innovation, branching (out), forking, difference, change, shift, veering
1 arrival, return

depend *v*
1 *the cost depends on the quantity*
hinge on, be dependent on, rest on, revolve around, be subject to, hang on, be decided by, be determined by, be based on, ride on
FORMAL turn on, be contingent on
2 *depend on her for support*
rely on, count on, calculate on, reckon on, build upon, trust in, have confidence in, lean on, need, not manage without, cling to, expect; *Scot* lippen
COLLOQ. bank on

dependable *adj*
reliable, trustworthy, steady, trusty, responsible, faithful, unfailing, sure, honest, conscientious, steadfast, certain, stable, rock-solid
COLLOQ. tried and tested, a safe pair of hands
unreliable, fickle

dependant *n*
child, minor, relative, charge, protégé, ward, client, hanger-on, henchman, minion, subordinate, parasite

dependence *n*
1 RELIANCE, confidence, faith, trust, need, expectation
2 ADDICTION, attachment, dependency, subservience, abuse, helplessness, subordination
1 independence

dependency *n*
1 COLONY, province, protectorate, dominion, satellite
2 RELIANCE, helplessness, weakness, immaturity, support, subordination
3 ADDICTION, attachment, habit, subservience, abuse

dependent *adj*
1 RELIANT, helpless, weak, immature, subject, sustained, leaning, supported, supporting, vulnerable
2 *the profit is dependent on the quantity bought*
conditional, decided, determined, controlled, dictated, based, influenced, relative, subject, subordinate

FORMAL contingent
1, 2 independent

depict *v*
1 *depicted in a painting*
portray, illustrate, sketch, outline, draw, picture, paint, trace, show, represent, describe
2 *novels depicting Victorian life*
portray, describe, recount, characterize, detail, illustrate, outline, trace, show, represent, render, reproduce, record
FORMAL delineate

depiction *n*
portrayal, description, characterization, detailing, drawing, illustration, image, likeness, picture, caricature, sketch, outline, representation, rendering
FORMAL delineation

deplete *v*
empty, drain, exhaust, impoverish, bankrupt, weaken, evacuate, use up, consume, spend, expend, run down, reduce, lessen, decrease, diminish, eat into, erode, whittle away
FORMAL attenuate
increase; *formal* augment

depletion *n*
exhaustion, impoverishment, weakening, evacuation, consumption, using-up, expenditure, reduction, lessening, decrease, deficiency, dwindling, lowering, shrinkage
FORMAL attenuation, diminution
increase, supply; *formal* augmentation

deplorable *adj*
disgraceful, reprehensible, scandalous, outrageous, shameful, dishonourable, disreputable, blameworthy, abominable, despicable, lamentable, pitiable, grievous, regrettable, unfortunate, wretched, distressing, sad, miserable, heartbreaking, melancholy, disastrous, dire, appalling, chronic
excellent, commendable

deplorably *adv*
disgracefully, scandalously, unfortunately, miserably, appallingly, outrageously, shamefully, despicably, abominably, lamentably
commendably

deplore *v*
1 DISAPPROVE OF, condemn, criticize, reproach, blame, revile, denounce
FORMAL reprehend, reprove, deprecate, berate, upbraid, castigate, disparage, censure, slate
COLLOQ. slam
2 GRIEVE FOR, lament, mourn, regret, bemoan, bewail, pine, rue, weep, cry, shed tears
1 extol

deploy *v*
arrange, position, station, spread out, scatter, use, make use of, utilize, distribute
FORMAL dispose

depopulate *v*
empty, dispeople, unpeople

deport[1] *v*
deported from a country
expel, banish, exile, extradite, repatriate, transport, oust, ostracize

deport[2] *v*
deport yourself well
conduct, bear, behave, carry, hold, manage, act, perform
FORMAL acquit, comport

deportation *n*
expulsion, banishment, exile, extradition, repatriation, transportation, ousting, ostracism

deportment *n*
manner, air, appearance, aspect, bearing, behaviour, carriage, conduct, pose, posture, gait, stance, etiquette
FORMAL comportment, demeanour, mien

depose v

oust, overthrow, dismiss, fire, remove, unseat, topple, disestablish, displace, demote, dethrone, discharge, downgrade
COLLOQ. sack

deposit v, n

♦ v

1 LAY, drop, plant, place, put (down), set (down), settle, park, sit, locate, land, ware
TECHNICAL precipitate, depone, sediment, sublime, oviposit
FORMAL reposit
COLLOQ. dump, bung
2 SAVE, store, hoard, bank, amass, consign, entrust, lodge, file, stow, put away, put by, pay in

♦ n

1 SECURITY, stake, down payment, pledge, retainer, instalment, part payment, margin; *S Afr* lay-by
OLD gage
FORMAL earnest
2 SEDIMENT, accumulation, dregs, lees, silt, bed, dew, soot, warp
TECHNICAL alluvium, fall-out, precipitate
FORMAL deposition

Types of deposit include:

amyloid	globigerina ooze	salamander
arcus	hypostasis	Saturn's tree
bergmehl	infiltration	shell-marl
black earth	loess	sinter
bone-bed	moorlog	tar-sand
cave-earth	placer	tartar
coral reef	precipitation sub-	terramara
crag	limate	tophus
delta	pteropod ooze	tree of silver
Diana's tree	radiolarian ooze	Zechstein
diatom ooze	red clay	
diluvium	saburra	

deposition n

1 *the deposition of the ruler*
ousting, overthrow, dismissal, removal, unseating, toppling, displacement, dethronement
2 *the witness's deposition*
affidavit, declaration, statement, testimony, evidence, information
FORMAL attestation

depository n

storehouse, store, warehouse, bonded warehouse, depot, repository, arsenal, cache

depot n

1 *military depot*
storehouse, store, warehouse, depository, repository, cache, arsenal
2 *bus depot*
station, garage, terminal, terminus

deprave v

corrupt, debauch, debase, degrade, pervert, subvert, warp, infect, demoralize, lead astray, seduce, pollute, defile, contaminate
E3 improve, reform

depraved adj

corrupt, debauched, degenerate, perverted, debased, warped, reprobate, dissolute, immoral, obscene, base, shameless, wicked, sinful, vile, evil, iniquitous, criminal
FORMAL licentious
E3 moral, upright

depravity n

corruption, debauchery, degeneracy, perversion, debasement, reprobacy, dissoluteness, immorality, baseness, wickedness, sinfulness, vileness, evil, iniquity, vice
FORMAL turpitude
E3 uprightness

deprecate v

condemn, disapprove of, censure, criticize, object to, protest at, reject, reproach, reprove, berate, upbraid, blame, revile, run down, slate, denounce
FORMAL deplore, reprehend, deprecate, castigate, disparage
COLLOQ. slam, knock, rubbish
E3 approve, commend

> ! **deprecate** or **depreciate**?
> *Deprecate* is a formal word meaning 'to disapprove of': *The government deprecated the soldiers' actions.* *Depreciate* most commonly means 'to fall or cause to fall in value': *Property shares have depreciated rapidly.* A rarer meaning of *depreciate* is 'to speak of as having little value or importance': *to depreciate your achievements*.

deprecatory adj

disapproving, censorious, condemnatory, reproachful, dismissive, protesting, apologetic, regretful
E3 encouraging; *formal* commendatory

depreciate v

1 DEVALUE, deflate, downgrade, decrease/fall/go down in value, reduce, lower, drop, fall, lessen, decline, slump
2 BELITTLE, undervalue, underestimate, underrate, slight, run down, make light of
FORMAL disparage, denigrate, revile, defame, malign
E3 1 appreciate **2** overrate

> ! **depreciate** or **deprecate**?
> See panel at **deprecate**.

depreciation n

1 DEVALUATION, deflation, depression, slump, fall, reduction in price/value, mark-down, cheapening
2 BELITTLEMENT, underestimation
FORMAL disparagement, denigration

depredation n

desolation, destruction, devastation, laying waste, ravaging, marauding, pillage, looting, plunder, plundering, raiding, ransacking, harrying, robbery, theft
FORMAL despoiling, denudation

depress v

1 DEJECT, sadden, make sad, dishearten, discourage, cast down, bring down, weigh down, oppress, upset, daunt, burden, overburden
COLLOQ. get down, break someone's heart
2 WEAKEN, undermine, debilitate, sap, tire, drain, exhaust, weary, impair, reduce, lessen, press, lower, level
FORMAL enervate
3 DEVALUE, bring down, reduce, lower, cut, depreciate, cheapen
COLLOQ. slash
4 *depress a lever*
push, push down, press, press down, lower, hold down
E3 1 cheer **2** vitalize, energize; *formal* fortify **3** increase, raise

depressant n

sedative, tranquillizer, downer, relaxant, calmant, calmative
COLLOQ. downer
E3 stimulant

depressed adj

1 DEJECTED, low-spirited, melancholy, dispirited, sad, unhappy, low, low in spirits, out of spirits, down, downcast, disheartened, miserable, moody, cast down, discouraged, gloomy, glum, downhearted, moping, broken-hearted, heartsick, cowed, dumpish, distressed, despondent, morose, crestfallen, pessimistic, exanimate, *accablé*
OLD jaw-fallen
COLLOQ. fed up, blue, doomy, a peg too low, down in the dumps; *N Am* in a funk
2 POOR, disadvantaged, deprived, needy, run-down, destitute, poverty-stricken, under hatches
3 SUNKEN, recessed, low, concave, hollow, indented, dented, pushed in

TECHNICAL emarginate
F3 **1** cheerful **2** thriving, affluent **3** convex, protuberant

depressing adj
dejecting, dismal, bleak, gloomy, saddening, cheerless, dreary, disheartening, unhappy, sad, melancholy, sombre, grey, black, daunting, discouraging, dispiriting, heartbreaking, distressing, upsetting, hopeless, grave
F3 cheerful, happy, encouraging

depressingly adv
dishearteningly, dauntingly, discouragingly, dispiritingly, heartbreakingly, distressingly, unhappily, sadly, bleakly, gloomily, cheerlessly, drearily
F3 encouragingly, happily

depression n
1 DEJECTION, despair, despondency, melancholy, low spirits, unhappiness, sadness, gloom, gloominess, doldrums, glumness, downheartedness, broken-heartedness, pessimism, hopelessness, desolation, discouragement
TECHNICAL melancholia
COLLOQ. blues, dumps, black dog
2 RECESSION, slump, stagnation, crash, hard times, decline, inactivity, slowdown, standstill
3 INDENTATION, hollow, hole, dip, trough, concavity, dent, dimple, valley, pit, sink, dint, bowl, cavity, basin, impression, dish, excavation
F3 **1** cheerfulness, happiness, euphoria **2** prosperity, boom **3** convexity; *formal* protuberance

> **QUOTATIONS**
> It's a recession when your neighbour loses his job; it's a depression when you lose yours
> HARRY S TRUMAN

deprivation n
1 *deprivation of sleep*
denial, withdrawal, withholding, removal, lack, dispossession
2 *deprivation in inner cities*
hardship, poverty, impoverishment, want, need, disadvantage
FORMAL destitution, privation, penury

deprive v
take away, dispossess, strip, divest, rob, confiscate, bereave, deny, withhold, refuse
FORMAL denude, expropriate
F3 endow, provide

> **SYNONYM NUANCES**
> **Take away** may be broadly used of removing something from someone's possession, while **dispossess** tends more usually to relate to having land or property removed: *the dispossessed peasantry of old Ireland*. Both **strip** and **divest** suggest removal of clothing, sometimes the formal trappings of office and often a title or station, and so these terms can carry connotations of indignity: *divested of her robes*.
>   If you use **rob** the implication is that something is being removed illegally or at least unfairly, but **confiscate** suggests having the force of law behind it: *the government confiscated all the TV footage*. The terms **deny**, **withhold** and **refuse** are all fairly unmarked terms for having something within your power or possession that you deliberately refuse to pass on to someone else: *he was denied permission to appeal*; *she was withholding evidence*; *he was refused the right to call witnesses*.
>   **Bereave**, meanwhile, is more appropriately used of depriving by death: *she was bereaved of two daughters*.

deprived adj
poor, needy, in need, underprivileged, disadvantaged, impoverished, destitute, lacking, bereft
F3 prosperous, privileged

depth n
1 DEEPNESS, profoundness, extent, measure, drop
FORMAL profundity
2 *depth of feeling*
intensity, strength, thoroughness, seriousness, severity, gravity, earnestness, passion, vigour, fervour
3 *a person of great depth*
wisdom, insight, discernment, perception, penetration, awareness, intuition, astuteness, cleverness, shrewdness, acumen
FORMAL profundity
4 *the depths of their knowledge*
extent, extensiveness, scope, range, amount
FORMAL profundity
5 *depth of colour*
intensity, strength, richness, vividness, brilliance, warmth, glow, darkness
6 *the depths of the sea*
remotest area, bed, floor, bottom, abyss, deep, gulf, middle, midst
F3 **1** shallowness **6** surface
■ **in depth**
comprehensively, thoroughly, exhaustively, extensively, in detail
F3 superficially, broadly

deputation n
commission, delegation, embassy, mission, representatives, legation, committee

depute v
appoint, authorize, charge, commission, second, designate, nominate, empower, entrust, mandate, delegate, consign, hand over
FORMAL accredit

deputize n
represent, stand in for, fill in for, take over, substitute, replace, act for, understudy, take the place of, double, relieve, cover
COLLOQ. sub for; N Am pinch-hit for

deputy n, adj
♦ *n*
representative, agent, delegate, proxy, substitute, stand-in, second-in-command, second, ambassador, envoy, commissioner, lieutenant, legate, surrogate, alternate, subordinate, assistant, locum, locum tenens, spokesperson, vice-president, vice-chairperson, vice-regent, commissary, commis, official
COLLOQ. sidekick, mate
♦ *adj*
assistant, representative, substitute, stand-in, surrogate, subordinate, vice-; *Scot* -depute

derail v
derail peace talks; the train was derailed
hold back, obstruct, prevent, impede, upset, displace, disturb, throw off course, disrupt

deranged adj
disordered, demented, crazy, mad, lunatic, insane, of unsound mind, *non compos mentis*, unbalanced, unstable, unhinged, fey, unsettled, distracted, disturbed, irrational, confused, frantic, frenzied, frenetic, wild, manic, maniac, maniacal, crazed, delirious, distraught, berserk, out of your mind, out of your senses, psychotic
OLD frantic-mad, lymphatic, bestraught
COLLOQ. nuts, nutty, nutty as a fruitcake, wacky, mad as a hatter, barmy, bonkers, batty, cracked, crackers, dippy, daffy, dotty, loopy, potty, off your nut, off your head, wrong in the head, out of your head, off the wall, out to lunch, round the bend, round the twist, bats, having bats in the belfry, cuckoo, off the rails, screwy, up the wall, raving, not all there; N Am buggy, flaky, fruity; Aust & NZ dingbats
SLANG loony, mental, bananas, barking, wacko, doolally, off your rocker, off your chump, off your trolley, out of your tree, needing your head examined, having lost your marbles, having a screw loose, having a tile loose, having

several cards short of a full deck, with one sandwich short of a picnic, meshuga, ape, apeshit; *N Am* gonzo, loco, wiggy; *Aust* out of your tree
☒ sane, calm

derangement *n*
aberration, agitation, confusion, delirium, dementia, disorder, distraction, disturbance, frenzy, hallucination, mania, insanity, lunacy, madness
☒ order, sanity

derelict *adj, n*
♦ *adj*
abandoned, neglected, deserted, forsaken, desolate, discarded, dilapidated, falling to pieces, ramshackle, tumbledown, run-down, ruined, in disrepair
♦ *n*
tramp, vagrant, dosser, beggar, wretch, vagabond, down-and-out, drifter, hobo, outcast, no-good, good-for-nothing, no-hoper, ne'er-do-well; *N Am* down-and-outer
COLLOQ. *Scots* jakey

dereliction *n*
1 DILAPIDATION, abandonment, neglect, desertion, forsaking, desolation, ruin(s), disrepair
2 *dereliction of duty*
neglect, negligence, abdication, abandonment, desertion, evasion, failure, faithlessness, forsaking, betrayal, relinquishment, remissness
FORMAL apostasy, renegation, renunciation
☒ **2** devotion, faithfulness, fulfilment

deride *v*
ridicule, laugh at, mock, scoff at, scorn, jeer at, sneer at, make fun of, satirize, gibe, insult, belittle, disdain, taunt, tease, rag
FORMAL disparage
COLLOQ. knock, pooh-pooh; *Aust* chiack
☒ respect, praise

de rigueur *adj*
conventional, fashionable, fitting, necessary, correct, decent, done, proper, expected, required, compulsory, right
FORMAL decorous
COLLOQ. the done thing

derision *n*
ridicule, mockery, scorn, contempt, scoffing, hissing, satire, sneering, taunting, disrespect, insult, teasing, ragging, disdain
FORMAL disparagement
☒ respect, praise

derisive *adj*
mocking, scornful, contemptuous, scoffing, disrespectful, insulting, irreverent, jeering, disdainful, taunting
☒ respectful, flattering

> ⚠ **derisive** or **derisory**?
> *Derisive* means 'mocking; showing derision': *derisive laughter*. *Derisory* means 'ridiculous; deserving mockery or derision': *The management offered a derisory pay increase.*

derisively *adv*
scornfully, contemptuously, disrespectfully, irreverently, disdainfully
☒ respectfully

derisory *adj*
laughable, ludicrous, absurd, ridiculous, contemptible, insulting, outrageous, preposterous, small, tiny, inadequate, insufficient, paltry
FORMAL risible

> ⚠ **derisory** or **derisive**?
> See panel at **derisive**.

derivation *n*
source, origin, root, beginning, etymology, extraction, foundation, genealogy, ancestry, basis, descent, deduction, inference

derivative *adj, n*
♦ *adj*
unoriginal, acquired, copied, borrowed, derived, imitative, obtained, second-hand, secondary, plagiarized, hackneyed, trite
COLLOQ. cribbed, rehashed
☒ original, inventive, innovative
♦ *n*
derivation, offshoot, by-product, development, branch, outgrowth, spin-off, product, descendant

derive *v*
1 *derive pleasure from something*
gain, obtain, get, take, draw, extract, receive, reap, acquire, borrow
FORMAL procure
2 ORIGINATE, arise, spring, flow, have as the source, have its origin/roots in, descend, stem, issue, follow, develop, evolve
FORMAL emanate, proceed

derogatory *adj*
disparaging, insulting, pejorative, belittling, offensive, critical, disapproving, unfavourable, slighting, uncomplimentary, injurious
FORMAL depreciative, defamatory, vilifying, denigratory
☒ flattering, favourable, complimentary

descend *v*
1 GO DOWN, come down, move down, drop, fall, dive, plummet, plunge, tumble, swoop, pitch, parachute, pancake, sink, arrive, alight, dismount, dip, slope, incline, subside, *dégringoler*
2 CONDESCEND, deign, sink, stoop, lower yourself
3 DEGENERATE, deteriorate, decline
COLLOQ. go downhill, go to the dogs, go to pot
4 ORIGINATE, issue, spring, stem, derive
FORMAL proceed, emanate
5 *family descended on us*
invade, arrive suddenly, storm, swoop, take over
☒ **1** ascend, rise

descendants *n*
offspring, children, issue, progeny, successors, heirs, lineage, line, scions, posterity
FORMAL seed
☒ ancestors

descent *n*
1 FALL, going-down, drop, plunge, sinking, subsiding, dip, decline, incline, slope, slant, gradient
FORMAL declivity
2 COMEDOWN, debasement, degradation, deterioration, decline, degeneration, degeneracy, decadence
3 ANCESTRY, parentage, heredity, family tree, genealogy, lineage, line, stock, extraction, origin
☒ **1** ascent, rise

describe *v*
1 *describe a situation*
portray, depict, illustrate, characterize, specify, draw, define, detail, give details of, explain, express, tell, talk, write, narrate, outline, relate, recount, present, represent, report
FORMAL delineate, elucidate
2 *describe someone as clever*
call, portray, consider, think, style, label, designate, brand, hail
3 *skaters describing circles on the ice*
mark out, draw, sketch, trace, outline
FORMAL delineate

description *n*
1 PORTRAYAL, representation, characterization, account, depiction, sketch, portrait, presentation, report, statement, outline, explanation, narration, commentary, chronicle, profile
FORMAL delineation, exposition, elucidation
2 SORT, type, kind, variety, specification, order, class, designation, category, style, breed, brand, make

---

SYNONYM NUANCES

sense 1

Portrayal and **presentation** suggest the use of words, drawings or even performance to show what someone is like: *the portrayal of women in the media; one textbook distorted its presentation of the data;* whereas **representation** and **depiction** suggest something more definite, perhaps less subjective: *the representation of movement in drawings; the depiction of country life.* **Characterization** is usually limited to suggesting the nature of a particular person or thing.

Both **sketch** and **portrait** are used in a literal way of drawings, but they may sometimes be used of pictures drawn from words, though **sketch** is usually less clearly defined: *a sketch of the proceedings.* **Outline** and **profile** also suggest a general overview minus details. To describe a continuous vocal description of something that has happened or is happening, the terms **narration** or **commentary** may be used: *narration of past events; a running commentary on the match.* **Chronicle** could also be used of the idea of a continuous record, although usually written.

---

descriptive *adj*
illustrative, explanatory, expressive, detailed, graphic, colourful, pictorial, striking, vivid
FORMAL elucidatory

descry *v*
discern, catch sight of, mark, notice, observe, perceive, recognize, discover, distinguish, glimpse, see, spot, detect
OLD espy

desecrate *v*
defile, violate, pervert, pollute, profane, contaminate, debase, dishallow, dishonour, insult, abuse, blaspheme, vandalize

desecration *n*
defilement, violation, blasphemy, debasement, dishonouring, pollution, profanation, sacrilege, impiety, insult

desegregate *v*
integrate, assimilate, merge, blend, join, incorporate, intermix, harmonize

desert¹ *n, adj*
♦ *n*
the Sahara desert
wasteland, wilderness, wilds, barrenness, void, dust bowl
Related adjective: eremic
♦ *adj*
bare, barren, waste, wild, uninhabited, empty, uncultivated, dry, dried up, arid, parched, moistureless, infertile, unproductive, desolate, sterile, lonely, solitary

desert² *v*
1 *desert his family*
abandon, leave, maroon, strand, give up, walk out on
FORMAL renounce, forsake, relinquish, cast off, abscond; *Scot* forhow
COLLOQ. jilt, quit, throw over, run out on, leave in the lurch, leave high and dry, rat on, chicken out; *N Am* bug out
2 *the soldier deserted*
decamp, defect, run away, fly, flee, go AWOL
FORMAL abscond, tergiversate
3 *desert a political party*
abandon, give up, turn your back on, deny, betray, defect, change sides
FORMAL forsake, relinquish, renounce, recant, apostasize, tergiversate
F∃ **1** stand by, support **3** support

desert³ *n*
1 DUE, right, reward, deserts, what you deserve, return, retribution, payment, recompense, remuneration
COLLOQ. comeuppance

2 WORTH, merit, virtue
OLD demerit

deserted *adj*
abandoned, empty, derelict, desolate, god-forsaken, forsaken, neglected, underpopulated, stranded, isolated, bereft, left, vacant, betrayed, lonely, solitary, uninhabited, unoccupied
F∃ populous

deserter *n*
runaway, absconder, escapee, truant, renegade, defector, traitor, turncoat, fugitive, betrayer, backslider, delinquent
FORMAL apostate
COLLOQ. rat; *N Am* bug-out

desertion *n*
1 *desertion of his family*
abandonment, leaving, give up
FORMAL forsaking, relinquishment, absconding, casting-off, renunciation
COLLOQ. jilting, quitting; *N Am* bug-out
2 *desertions from the armed forces*
defection, decamping, running-away, flight, going AWOL, truancy
FORMAL absconding, dereliction
3 *desertion of a political party*
abandonment, giving-up, denial, betrayal
FORMAL renunciation, forsaking, relinquishment, apostasy, renegation, tergiversation
F∃ **3** support

deserve *v*
earn, be worthy of, merit, be entitled to, warrant, justify, have a right to, win, rate, incur
COLLOQ. have it coming (to you)

deserved *adj*
due, earned, merited, justifiable, justified, warranted, right, rightful, well-earned, suitable, proper, fitting, fair, just, appropriate, apt, legitimate
FORMAL meet, apposite, condign
F∃ gratuitous, undeserved

deservedly *adv*
justifiably, duly, rightly, rightfully, by rights, justly, fairly, suitably, properly, fittingly, appropriately

deserving *adj*
worthy, estimable, exemplary, praiseworthy, admirable, commendable, upright, righteous, virtuous
FORMAL laudable, meritorious
F∃ undeserving, unworthy

desiccated *adj*
dehydrated, drained, dried, dried up, dry, arid, dead, lifeless, parched, powdered, sterile
FORMAL exsiccated

desiccation *n*
dehydration, dryness, aridity, parching, sterility
FORMAL exsiccation, xeransis

desideratum *n*
requirement, requisite, prerequisite, need, want, necessity, essential, sine qua non
COLLOQ. must

design *v, n*
♦ *v*
1 DRAW, plan, sketch, draw up, draft, outline, plot
FORMAL delineate
2 INVENT, originate, conceive, create, think up, develop, construct, fashion, form, model, fabricate, hatch, make
3 INTEND, plot, plan, devise, purpose, contrive, aim, scheme, shape, project, propose, tailor, mean, gear
♦ *n*
1 BLUEPRINT, draft, pattern, plan, prototype, sketch, drawing, outline, map, diagram, scheme, model, guide
FORMAL delineation
2 MOTIF, style, pattern, logo, shape, form, figure, device, emblem, monogram, cipher, format, structure,

organization, arrangement, composition, make-up, construction
3 AIM, intention, goal, purpose, plan, end, object, objective, scheme, plot, project, meaning, target, point, wish, desire, hope, dream, enterprise, undertaking
■ **by design**
intentionally, deliberately, on purpose, consciously, pointedly, calculatingly, knowingly, wittingly, wilfully

designate v
1 *designated as a listed building*
call, name, title, entitle, term, dub, style, describe, class, classify, christen
2 *designated to be chairman*
choose, appoint, nominate, select, elect, assign, specify, define, stipulate, earmark, set aside, show, denote, indicate

designation n
1 NAME, title, term, label, epithet, nickname, description, style, sobriquet
FORMAL appellation, denomination
COLLOQ. tag
2 SPECIFICATION, description, definition, denoting, marking, classification, category, stipulation, indication
3 NOMINATION, appointment, selection, election

designer n
deviser, originator, maker, stylist, inventor, creator, contriver, producer, fashioner, planner, architect, author

designing adj
artful, crafty, scheming, conspiring, calculating, devious, intriguing, plotting, tricky, wily, sly, deceitful, cunning, guileful, underhand, sharp, shrewd
F3 artless, naive

desirability n
1 *the desirability of qualifications*
advantage, profit, advisability, benefit, preference, usefulness, merit, worth, excellence, popularity
2 *the desirability of the woman*
attractiveness, attraction, allure, seductiveness, appeal
COLLOQ. sexiness
F3 **1** disadvantage, inadvisability, undesirability

desirable adj
1 *a desirable qualification*
advantageous, sought-after, profitable, worthwhile, advisable, appropriate, expedient, beneficial, preferable, sensible, eligible, good, pleasing, pleasant, agreeable, popular, in demand
2 *a desirable woman*
attractive, alluring, seductive, fetching, tempting, tantalizing
COLLOQ. sexy
SLANG beddable, hot
F3 **1** undesirable **2** unattractive

desire v, n
♦ v
1 WANT, wish for, covet, long for, like, need, crave, hunger for, gasp for, yearn for, set your heart on, fancy, feel like, hanker after, envy
OLD (Spenser) fain
FORMAL desiderate
COLLOQ. be dying for, have your eyes on, have designs on, give the world for
2 *desire a man*
lust after, burn for, take to
COLLOQ. fancy, be crazy about, have a crush on, take a shine to
SLANG have the hots for
♦ n
1 WANT, longing, wish, need, fancy, yearning, craving, hankering, lust, appetite, greed, preference, aspiration, demand, *besoin*
OLD covetise; (Shakesp) bosom
FORMAL predilection, predisposition, proclivity, cacoëthes
COLLOQ. itch, yen

2 LUST, passion, sexual attraction, sexuality, sex drive, ardour, libido, sensuality, lasciviousness
TECHNICAL ephebophilia
FORMAL concupiscence
Related adjective: epithymetic

desired adj
required, proper, accurate, appropriate, correct, exact, expected, fitting, necessary, particular, right
F3 undesired, unintentional

desirous adj
ready, willing, ambitious, aspiring, avid, burning, craving, itching, eager, enthusiastic, fervent, fervid, hopeful, hoping, keen, longing, anxious, wishing, yearning
FORMAL cupidinous
F3 reluctant, unenthusiastic

desist v
stop, leave off, end, break off, give up, halt, suspend, pause, peter out, cease
FORMAL abstain, refrain, discontinue, remit, forbear
F3 continue, resume

desk n
table, bureau, lectern, reading-desk, davenport, écritoire, secretaire, writing-table, ambo

desolate adj, v
♦ adj
1 DESERTED, uninhabited, unoccupied, abandoned, unfrequented, barren, bare, arid, desert, bleak, gloomy, dismal, dreary, lonely, solitary, isolated, god-forsaken, forsaken, waste, wild, depressing; *Scot* gousty
2 MISERABLE, forlorn, bereft, depressed, dejected, forsaken, despondent, distressed, melancholy, gloomy, unhappy, sad, disheartened, dismal, downcast, broken-hearted, heartbroken, wretched, drearisome
F3 **1** populous **2** cheerful
♦ v
devastate, upset, disconcert, overwhelm, take aback, confound, nonplus, get down
FORMAL discomfit
COLLOQ. shatter, floor

desolation n
1 DESTRUCTION, ruin, devastation, ravages, laying waste
2 BARRENNESS, bleakness, emptiness, forlornness, loneliness, isolation, solitude, remoteness, wildness, wilderness
3 DEJECTION, despair, despondency, gloom, misery, sadness, melancholy, sorrow, unhappiness, broken-heartedness, anguish, depression, grief, distress, wretchedness

despair v, n
♦ v
lose heart, lose hope, give up, give in, be despondent, be discouraged, collapse, surrender
COLLOQ. hit rock bottom, throw in the towel
F3 hope
♦ n
despondency, gloom, hopelessness, desperation, dejection, anguish, distress, inconsolableness, melancholy, misery, depression, pessimism, wretchedness
TECHNICAL dysthymia
OLD wanhope
F3 cheerfulness, resilience

> **QUOTATIONS**
> Vaunting aloud, but racked with deep despair
>   JOHN MILTON, *Paradise Lost*

despairing adj
despondent, distraught, inconsolable, desolate, desperate, heartbroken, suicidal, grief-stricken, hopeless, depressed, discouraged, disheartened, dejected, miserable, anguished, wretched, sorrowful, pessimistic, dismayed, downcast, *au désespoir*
FORMAL disconsolate
F3 cheerful, hopeful

despatch
see **dispatch, despatch**.

desperado *n*
bandit, criminal, brigand, terrorist, gangster, gunman, outlaw, ruffian, thug, cut-throat, lawbreaker; *N Am* badman
COLLOQ. hoodlum, mugger

desperate *adj*
1 HOPELESS, inconsolable, wretched, despondent, abandoned, distraught, desolate, heartbroken, suicidal, grief-stricken, depressed, discouraged, disheartened, dejected, miserable, anguished, sorrowful, pessimistic, dismayed, downcast
FORMAL disconsolate
COLLOQ. at rock-bottom
2 RECKLESS, rash, impetuous, bold, audacious, daring, dangerous, do-or-die, foolhardy, risky, hazardous, hasty, wild, violent, lawless, frantic, frenzied, incautious, determined
FORMAL precipitate
3 CRITICAL, dire, acute, crucial, serious, grave, severe, extreme, urgent, compelling, pressing, great, dangerous
4 *desperate to leave school*
wanting very much, needing very much, crying out for, in great need
COLLOQ. dying
E3 1 hopeful, optimistic **2** cautious, considered

desperately *adv*
dangerously, critically, gravely, acutely, hopelessly, seriously, severely, badly, urgently, greatly, extremely, dreadfully, fearfully, frightfully

desperation *n*
despair, despondency, anguish, hopelessness, gloom, misery, agony, distress, pain, wretchedness, sorrow, trouble, worry, anxiety, depression

despicable *adj*
contemptible, vile, worthless, detestable, disgusting, mean, low, degrading, base, wretched, disgraceful, disreputable, shameful, abominable, loathsome, reprobate
OLD dastardly, caitiff
FORMAL reprehensible
COLLOQ. lowdown
E3 admirable, noble

despise *v*
scorn, hold in contempt, look down on, disdain, condemn, spurn, undervalue, slight, dislike, hate, detest, loathe, abhor, shun, mock, sneer
OLD contemn, forhow, set at naught/nought
FORMAL revile, deplore, deride, vilipend
E3 admire

despite *prep*
in spite of, regardless of, in the face of, undeterred by, against, defying
FORMAL notwithstanding

despoil *v*
destroy, devastate, loot, maraud, pillage, plunder, ransack, ravage, deprive, dispossess, divest, rifle, rob, strip, vandalize, wreck
FORMAL denude, depredate, spoliate
E3 adorn, enrich

despondency *n*
broken-heartedness, dejection, depression, despair, desperation, discouragement, dispiritedness, downheartedness, gloom, glumness, hopelessness, inconsolability, melancholia, melancholy, distress, misery, sadness, sorrow, grief, wretchedness
FORMAL disconsolateness
COLLOQ. blues, heartache
E3 cheerfulness, hopefulness

despondent *adj*
depressed, dejected, disheartened, downcast, down, low, gloomy, glum, discouraged, distressed, miserable, melancholy, sad, sorrowful, doleful, despairing, heartbroken, heartsick, inconsolable, mournful, wretched
COLLOQ. down in the dumps, blue
E3 cheerful, heartened, hopeful

despot *n*
autocrat, tyrant, dictator, oppressor, absolute ruler, absolutist, boss, sultan, tsar

despotic *adj*
autocratic, tyrannical, imperious, oppressive, dictatorial, authoritarian, domineering, high-handed, absolute, overbearing, arbitrary, arrogant
E3 democratic, egalitarian, liberal, tolerant

despotism *n*
autocracy, totalitarianism, tyranny, dictatorship, absolutism, oppression, repression
E3 democracy, egalitarianism, liberalism, tolerance

dessert *n*
sweet, sweet dish, sweet course, pudding
COLLOQ. afters, pud
See panel below

destination *n*
1 GOAL, aim, objective, object, purpose, target, end, intention, aspiration, design, ambition
2 JOURNEY'S END, terminus, station, stop, final port of call, end of the line, landing place

destined *adj*
1 FATED, doomed, inevitable, certain, meant, unavoidable, inescapable, fatal, born, marked, intended, designed, appointed, predetermined, ordained, preordained, set apart
FORMAL foreordained
2 *passengers destined for Glasgow*
bound, directed, routed, en route, headed, heading, scheduled, assigned, intended, booked

destiny *n*
fate, future, doom, fortune, lot, luck, karma, kismet, Moira
FORMAL portion, predestination, predestiny

Desserts and puddings include:

baked Alaska	cheesecake	Eton mess	millefeuilles	rice pudding	tiramisu
baklava	Christmas pudding	Eve's pudding	mousse	roly-poly pudding	trifle
banana split	clafoutis	frangipane	mud pie	sorbet	vacherin
banoffee pie	*Scot* clootie	fruit cocktail (or	*N Am* pandowdy	soufflé	verrine
bavarois	dumpling	salad)	panna cotta	spotted dick	yogurt
blancmange	cobbler	fruit crumble	parfait	sticky toffee	zabaglione
bombe	compote	ice cream	pavlova	pudding	
bread-and-butter	cranachan	jelly	peach Melba	summer pudding	
pudding	crème brûlée	knickerbocker	plum-duff	sundae	
N Am Brown	crème caramel	glory	plum pudding	syllabub	
Betty	crêpe suzette	kulfi	profiteroles	tapioca	
charlotte russe	egg custard	milk pudding	queen of puddings	tartufo	

See also **cake**.

destitute *adj*
1 POOR, hard up, badly off, penniless, poverty-stricken, impoverished, distressed, bankrupt
FORMAL impecunious, indigent, penurious
COLLOQ. broke, stony-broke, down-and-out, on the breadline, cleaned out, strapped for cash, with your back to the wall, on your beam-ends, dirt-poor
SLANG skint, rooked
2 LACKING, needy, wanting, innocent of, deprived, deficient, depleted
FORMAL devoid of, bereft
E3 1 prosperous, rich

destitution *n*
poverty, pennilessness, impoverishment, distress, bankruptcy, beggary, starvation, straits
FORMAL impecuniousness, indigence, penury, pauperdom
E3 prosperity, wealth

destroy *v*
1 DEMOLISH, ruin, shatter, wreck, devastate, smash, break, crush, subdue, overthrow, sabotage, undo, stamp out, dismantle, knock down, pull down, tear down, flatten, obliterate, thwart, undermine, waste, lay waste, gut, level, spoil, ravage, raze, ransack, torpedo, unshape
OLD (*Shakesp*) ruinate
FORMAL extirpate
2 KILL, kill off, annihilate, eliminate, extinguish, eradicate, dispatch, slaughter, put down, put to sleep, put out of its misery
FORMAL slay, nullify, vitiate
COLLOQ. decimate
E3 1 build up **2** create

SYNONYM NUANCES

sense 1
Demolish can be used to suggest knocking down, literally or figuratively: *he demolished the class barrier*, while both **level** and **raze** would be used with the literal sense of reducing to the ground. **Ruin**, **shatter** and **wreck** are descriptive terms all suggestive of action causing irredeemable damage. The even stronger term **devastate** similarly suggests destruction on a huge scale, and **obliterate** further suggests the removal of any trace: *the park was completely obliterated beneath the snow*.

    Smash, **crush** and **break**, however, all have implications of deliberate harm, with the first two possibly implying an element of zeal. **Undo** has gentler associations, more suggestive of reversing what has already been done, while **dismantle** is also less forceful, suggesting a taking apart piece by piece: *after the British and French dismantled their empires*. The term **stamp out** can be used of putting an end to something perceived as undesirable, and again there is an underlying sense of eagerness: *a need to stamp out violence*.

    If you want to convey the destruction of more abstract notions such as plans, systems or feelings, then you might use **thwart** or **undermine**, the latter appropriately describing a severe weakening rather than outright destruction: *aggressive actions can undermine international stability*.

    Lay waste is best used of rendering land desolate, while **gut** may be used of buildings, especially the interior: *the church was gutted by fire*. **Ravage** also conveys images of desolation, and has additional connotations of plunder, as indeed has **ransack**. **Torpedo**, with its image of a rapid and violent attack, has connotations of complete and irreversible destruction: *the outbreak of fighting torpedoed the peace talks*.

---

destroyer *n*
wrecker, annihilator, demolisher, desolater, despoiler, ransacker, ravager, vandal, locust, kiss of death
E3 creator

destruction *n*
1 RUIN, devastation, shattering, smashing, crushing, wreckage, demolition, knocking-down, pulling-down, tearing-down, vandalism, defeat, downfall, overthrow, ruination, desolation, obliteration, undoing, wastage, razing, levelling, dismantling, havoc, ravagement
FORMAL depredation
2 ANNIHILATION, killing, killing-off, extermination, eradication, elimination, extinction, slaughter, murder, massacre, end, liquidation
FORMAL nullification
E3 2 creation

destructive *adj*
1 *destructive storms*
devastating, damaging, catastrophic, disastrous, deadly, harmful, fatal, disruptive, lethal, ruinous, injurious, detrimental, hurtful, malignant, pernicious, mischievous
FORMAL noxious, nullifying, deleterious, baneful, slaughterous
2 *destructive criticism*
adverse, hostile, antagonistic, negative, discouraging, unfavourable, unfriendly, disparaging, contrary, derogatory, undermining, subversive, vicious
FORMAL denigrating
E3 1 creative **2** constructive, favourable

destructively *adv*
disastrously, catastrophically, harmfully, hurtfully, detrimentally, lethally
E3 creatively

desultorily *adv*
casually, aimlessly, erratically, half-heartedly, loosely, fitfully
E3 methodically

desultory *adj*
random, erratic, aimless, casual, disorderly, chaotic, haphazard, irregular, half-hearted, spasmodic, inconsistent, undirected, unco-ordinated, unsystematic, unmethodical, fitful, disconnected, rambling, loose
FORMAL capricious
E3 systematic, methodical

detach *v*
1 *detach the reply slip*
separate, take/tear off, disconnect, unfasten, disjoin, cut off, disengage, remove, undo, uncouple, unhitch, sever, dissociate, isolate, loosen, free, unfix, segregate, divide, disentangle
2 *detach yourself from something*
separate, sever, split, cut off, dissociate, isolate, loosen, free, segregate, divorce
FORMAL estrange
E3 1 attach **2** involve

detachable *adj*
remov(e)able, mov(e)able, separable, eradicable, transferable

detached *adj*
1 SEPARATE, disconnected, unfastened, dissociated, severed, free, loose, divided, discrete
2 ALOOF, remote, dispassionate, impersonal, neutral, impartial, independent, indifferent, unconcerned, disinterested, cold, clinical, unemotional, objective
E3 1 connected **2** involved

detachment *n*
1 ALOOFNESS, remoteness, coolness, reserve, unconcern, indifference, impassivity, disinterestedness, neutrality, dispassion, dispassionateness, lack of emotion, impartiality, objectivity, lack of bias, fairness
2 SEPARATION, disconnection, unfastening, uncoupling, disengagement, removal, withdrawal, undoing, severance, isolation, loosening, disentangling
FORMAL disunion
3 SQUAD, unit, force, corps, brigade, patrol, task force, detail
E3 1 concern, bias, prejudice

detail *n, v*
♦ *n*
1 *personal details*
particular, item, factor, element, aspect, characteristic, component, feature, point, fact, circumstance, respect, specific, specification, ingredient, attribute, technicality, complication, intricacy
2 *attention to detail*
minutiae, triviality, nicety, thoroughness, elaboration, meticulousness, precision, complexity, refinement
COLLOQ. ins and outs, nitty-gritty, nuts and bolts
3 SQUAD, unit, force, corps, brigade, patrol, task force
♦ *v*
1 LIST, set out, enumerate, itemize, specify, catalogue, spell out, tabulate, describe, present, portray, depict, point out, recount, relate
FORMAL delineate, rehearse
2 ASSIGN, appoint, choose, allocate, charge, delegate, commission
■ **in detail**
point by point, carefully, thoroughly, comprehensively, exhaustively, fully, item by item, at length, in depth

detailed *adj*
comprehensive, exhaustive, complete, full, itemized, thorough, minute, in-depth, exact, precise, specific, particular, intricate, elaborate, complex, complicated, meticulous, descriptive
FORMAL convoluted
COLLOQ. blow-by-blow
F3 cursory, general

detain *v*
1 DELAY, hold (up), make late, hold back, keep (back), inhibit, hinder, impede, check, slow, stay, stop
FORMAL retard
2 CONFINE, arrest, intern, hold, restrain, keep, keep/hold in custody, take into custody, lock up, put in prison, imprison
FORMAL incarcerate
F3 2 release

detect *v*
1 NOTICE, ascertain, sense, note, observe, perceive, become aware of, make out, recognize, discern, distinguish, identify, sight, catch, spot, spy
2 UNCOVER, catch, discover, disclose, expose, find (out), turn up, track down, uncover, unearth, unmask, reveal, bring to light

detectable *adj*
noticeable, discoverable, perceivable, discernible, perceptible, recognizable, identifiable, visible, apparent, clear, distinct, before your eyes

detection *n*
1 NOTICING, ascertaining, note, observation, perception, recognition, discernment, distinguishing, identification, sighting
2 UNCOVERING, discovery, disclosure, exposé, exposure, tracking-down, smelling-out, sniffing-out, unearthing, unmasking, revelation

> **QUOTATIONS**
> Detection is, or ought to be, an exact science, and should be treated in the same cold and unemotional manner
> SIR ARTHUR CONAN DOYLE, *The Sign of Four*

detective *n*
police officer, (private) investigator, thief-catcher, thief-taker, plain-clothes officer, sherlock, plant, Pinkerton, shadow; *N Am* operative
COLLOQ. 'tec, private eye, sleuth, sleuth-hound, bloodhound, gumshoe, shamus, dick, tail, busy, jack, prodnose

detention *n*
1 DETAINMENT, custody, confinement, imprisonment, captivity, restraint, constraint, internment, quarantine, punishment
FORMAL incarceration
2 DELAY, hindrance, holding-back, slowing-up
F3 1 release

deter *v*
discourage, disincline, put off, talk out of, inhibit, frighten, intimidate, scare off, daunt, check, caution, warn, restrain, hinder, prevent, prohibit, stop
FORMAL dissuade
COLLOQ. turn off
F3 encourage

detergent *n*
cleaner, cleanser, soap, washing powder, washing-up liquid
TECHNICAL abstergent

deteriorate *v*
1 WORSEN, get/become/grow worse, decline, degenerate, depreciate, drop, fail, fall off, lapse, go from bad to worse, slide, relapse, slip, wane, ebb, tail off/away
FORMAL retrograde, retrogress
COLLOQ. go downhill, go down, go to pot, go down the tube, go/run to seed
2 DECAY, disintegrate, decompose, spoil, degrade, degenerate, go bad, break up, fall apart, fall to pieces, weaken, fade
OLD starve
F3 1 improve, get better

> **SYNONYM NUANCES**
>
> *sense 1*
> **Decline** is suggestive of becoming less rather than simply getting worse: *his health rapidly declined.* **Degenerate** suggests becoming something inferior, and has an element of judgement: *the loan scheme has degenerated into a farce.* The term **depreciate** can be used to convey a straightforward lessening in value: *your car has depreciated since you bought it.* **Drop** and **fall off** similarly suggest a decrease in level or value, but perhaps a sharper one: *audience figures fell off during the second series.*
> **Fail** has inherently negative connotations, and is appropriate to use where there are unhappy effects: *my eyesight is failing,* whilst **lapse**, **slide** and **slip** simply suggest a quiet or gradual descent into a worse state: *he lapsed into a coma.* **Relapse** would only be used of a return to a worse state. The terms **wane** and **ebb** can both be used of deteriorating very gradually, with the implication that it will happen until nothing remains: *her confidence ebbed away; prosperity waned.*

deterioration *n*
worsening, decline, degeneration, drop, failure, falling-off, downturn, lapse, slide, relapse, slipping, waning, ebb, decay, atrophy, corrosion, debasement, degradation, disintegration
FORMAL retrogression, exacerbation, pejoration
F3 improvement

determinate *adj*
fixed, absolute, certain, clear-cut, distinct, explicit, express, conclusive, decided, decisive, defined, settled, specific, specified, definite, definitive, established, positive, precise, quantified
F3 indeterminate

determination *n*
1 RESOLUTENESS, tenacity, firmness, willpower, perseverance, persistence, purpose, resolution, resolve, backbone, steadfastness, single-mindedness, will, insistence, conviction, dedication, push, drive, thrust, stamina, strength of character, firmness of purpose
FORMAL fortitude
COLLOQ. guts, grit

2 DECISION, judgement, sentence, settlement, conclusion, ruling, decree, verdict, opinion
TECHNICAL arbitrament, assay, value
FORMAL resolution
F∃ **1** irresolution, indetermination

Colloquial expressions showing determination include:

be hell-bent	go the whole hog	pull out all the
dig your heels in	hang on like grim	stops
do your utmost	death	put your heart and
get stuck into	hold your ground	soul into
give your all	leave no stone	stay the course
go all out	unturned	stick to your guns
go for it	mean business	stop at nothing
go to extremes	move heaven and	strain every nerve
go to great lengths	earth	

determine v
1 AFFECT, influence, govern, control, condition, dictate, direct, guide, prompt, impel, regulate, ordain
2 DISCOVER, establish, find out, learn, ascertain, identify, check, detect, verify
3 DECIDE, settle, set, make up your mind, choose, conclude, agree on, establish, fix (on), resolve, elect, finish
FORMAL purpose
COLLOQ. clinch

determined adj
resolute, firm, purposeful, strong-willed, single-minded, persevering, persistent, strong, strong-minded, steadfast, tenacious, dogged, insistent, intent, set, resolved, fixed, bent, dedicated, convinced, decided, unflinching, unwavering, uncompromising, stubborn, obstinate, dour
COLLOQ. hell-bent, dead set, out
F∃ irresolute, wavering

> **SYNONYM NUANCES**
>
> **Resolute** describes someone who has made up their mind and will not be swayed from it, and it is a term with favourable connotations of strength of mind or character. **Fixed**, although similar, is associated more with the negative quality of narrow-mindedness than the positive one of conviction: *try not to have too many fixed ideas about the job.*
>
> **Purposeful** would suggest someone has a specific aim, whilst **strong-willed** and **single-minded** could be used of those who neither need nor want advice. These three terms can be used without implying any judgement. The term **persevering** may be used of someone who will endure in their pursuit, which may be perceived as admirable: *their persevering efforts to remove oppression*, whereas to describe someone as **persistent** suggests they may be more likely to annoy: *persistent telephone salespeople.* **Strong** and **strong-minded**, however, are again more approving in tone in that they return to the idea of strength of character, and the ability to see things through; **steadfast** is similarly positive in its connotation of constancy. **Dedicated**, **unflinching** and **unwavering** further suggest positive elements of devotion and strength of purpose.
>
> **Uncompromising** implies a reluctance to yield in any respect, and might be used with a hint of admiration of this determination: *he is a tough, uncompromising boxer*, while **stubborn**, although similar in meaning, strongly hints at obstinacy rather than conviction and is more disapproving in tone.

determinedly adv
resolutely, firmly, strongly, purposefully, single-mindedly, strong-mindedly, persistently, steadfastly, tenaciously, insistently, decidedly, stubbornly, uncompromisingly, unflinchingly
F∃ irresolutely

deterrence n
prevention, hindrance, avoidance, heading-off, warding-off, elimination
FORMAL dissuasion, obviation
F∃ encouragement

deterrent n
hindrance, impediment, obstacle, repellent, check, bar, barrier, block, discouragement, disincentive, obstruction, curb, restraint, difficulty
F∃ incentive, encouragement

detest v
hate, loathe, abhor, dislike, recoil from, deplore, despise
FORMAL abominate, execrate
COLLOQ. can't stand
F∃ adore, love

detestable adj
hateful, loathsome, abhorrent, repellent, obnoxious, despicable, abominable, odious, contemptible, revolting, repulsive, repugnant, offensive, vile, disgusting, distasteful, shocking, sordid
FORMAL execrable, accursed, reprehensible, heinous
F∃ adorable, admirable

detestation n
hate, hatred, loathing, abhorrence, dislike, anathema, animosity, hostility, antipathy, aversion, repugnance, revulsion
FORMAL abomination, execration, odium
F∃ adoration, approval, love

dethrone v
depose, oust, topple, unseat, unthrone, uncrown
F∃ crown, enthrone

detonate v
blow up, discharge, blast, explode, ignite, kindle, set off, let off, go off, spark off, shoot, knock
FORMAL fulminate

detonation n
bang, blast, explosion, blow-up, blowing-up, boom, burst, discharge, igniting, ignition
FORMAL fulmination, report

detour n
deviation, diversion, indirect route, circuitous route, roundabout route, scenic route, digression, byroad, byway, bypath, bypass

detract v
diminish, subtract from, take away from, spoil, mar, reduce, lessen, lower, devaluate, depreciate, belittle
FORMAL disparage
F∃ add to, enhance, praise

detractor n
backbiter, belittler, defamer, slanderer, critic, muck-raker, reviler, scandalmonger, enemy
FORMAL denigrator, disparager, traducer, vilifier
F∃ flatterer, supporter, defender

detriment n
damage, harm, hurt, disadvantage, loss, ill, injury, impairment, disservice, wrong, evil, mischief, prejudice
F∃ advantage, benefit

detrimental adj
damaging, harmful, hurtful, adverse, disadvantageous, prejudicial, mischievous, pernicious, destructive
FORMAL deleterious, injurious, inimical
F∃ advantageous, favourable, beneficial

detritus n
remains, rubbish, debris, rubble, fragments, garbage, junk, litter, scum, waste, wreckage

devalue v
1 *devalue someone's work*
make light of, demean, play down, run down, slate, minimize, dismiss, underrate, undervalue
FORMAL disparage
COLLOQ. knock, slam, pull/tear to pieces
SLANG slag (off)

2 *devalue a currency*
deflate, devaluate, lower, reduce, decrease
FORMAL devalorize

devastate v
1 DESTROY, desolate, lay waste, demolish, spoil, despoil, wreck, ruin, ravage, waste, ransack, plunder, level, flatten, raze, pillage, sack
2 DISCONCERT, overwhelm, overcome, shock, take aback, confound, nonplus, discompose, traumatize
FORMAL perturb, discomfit
COLLOQ. shatter, floor

devastated adj
shocked, overwhelmed, crushed, heartbroken, overcome, taken aback, upset, distressed, desolate, appalled, traumatized, stunned, horrified, in anguish
COLLOQ. gutted, in bits, knocked for six

devastating adj
1 *devastating storms*
destructive, disastrous, ruinous, damaging, harmful, catastrophic
2 *a devastating blow to his pride*
effective, incisive, overwhelming, crushing, shocking, traumatizing, stunning
COLLOQ. shattering
3 *in devastating form*
stunning, brilliant, striking, impressive, spectacular, extraordinary, remarkable, wonderful, lovely, gorgeous, dazzling, magnificent, marvellous, great, staggering
COLLOQ. smashing, fabulous

devastation n
destruction, desolation, waste, havoc, ruin(s), damage, wreckage, ravages, demolition, annihilation, pillage, plunder, spoliation

develop v
1 ADVANCE, grow, evolve, expand, enlarge, progress, foster, nurture, flourish, mature, prosper, improve, branch out, spread
2 ELABORATE, amplify, argument, enhance, unfold, work out, expand on, enlarge
FORMAL dilate on
3 ACQUIRE, begin, start, generate, create, invent, produce, originate, establish, set about/off, set in motion, initiate, bring about, effect, found, institute, pioneer
FORMAL contract, commence
4 RESULT, come about, grow, ensue, arise, follow, happen
5 *develop an illness*
catch, get, go down with, pick up, become infected with, become/fall ill with
FORMAL contract, succumb to

development n
1 GROWTH, evolution, advance, blossoming, elaboration, furtherance, progress, progression, unfolding, expansion, enlargement, extension, spread, increase, improvement, maturing, maturity, flourishing, prosperity, promotion, refinement, issue
2 OCCURRENCE, happening, event, turn of events, incident, circumstance, change, outcome, situation, result, phenomenon
3 *a housing development*
complex, centre, block, estate, land, area

SYNONYM NUANCES

sense 1
Growth tends to suggest increasing in size, whereas **evolution** suggests changing to a more advanced state: *linguistic evolution*. **Advance** can be used of a positive move forward: *recent advances in technology*; **progress** and **progression** are both similar but suggest a continual move. **Blossoming** could be used of a coming to fruition, with a hint at its inevitability: *the blossoming of your career*.
   Elaboration, on the other hand, has more to do with working out the details: *there is no elaboration of the reasoning behind the diagnosis*, whereas **furtherance**

---

implies moving forward with some help: *his personal sacrifices for the furtherance of his son's career*.
Unfolding could be used a gradual disclosure of events: *the unfolding of the plot*. You could use **improvement** to emphasize that something has become better than it was, while **refinement** would be the word to use of development by attending to fine details.
   Maturing and **maturity** imply that any benefits have come through age, and again would be used positively: *intellectual maturity*. Both **flourishing** and **prosperity** are very positive terms suggestive of success, usually financial in the latter instance, but **promotion** might simply be used in the context of something being made known or widespread.

---

deviance n
divergence, aberration, anomaly, abnormality, irregularity, variance, eccentricity, perversion
FORMAL disparity
Ⓔ normality

deviant adj, n
♦ adj
divergent, aberrant, anomalous, abnormal, irregular, variant, bizarre, eccentric, quirky, freakish, perverse, perverted, twisted, wayward, bent
FORMAL disparate
COLLOQ. kinky, oddball, with a screw loose, with bats in the belfry
Ⓔ normal, straight
♦ n
freak, oddity, eccentric, nonconformist, misfit, dropout, odd sort, pervert
COLLOQ. oddball, kook, crank, weirdo
SLANG geek, goof
Ⓔ COLLOQ. straight

deviate v
diverge, veer, turn (aside), digress, sheer, swerve, deflect, incline, change, vary, differ, depart, stray, oblique, yaw, wander, err, go astray, drift, part, decline
TECHNICAL sport
OLD prevaricate
FORMAL aberrate
COLLOQ. go off the rails

deviation n
divergence, aberration, departure, abnormality, irregularity, difference, variance, variation, digression, eccentricity, anomaly, deflection, turning-aside, alteration, discrepancy, detour, fluctuation, inconsistency, change, drift, quirk, shift, freak
OLD prevarication
FORMAL disparity
Ⓔ conformity, regularity

device n
1 TOOL, implement, appliance, gadget, waldo, contrivance, contraption, apparatus, utensil, instrument, machine, mechanism
COLLOQ. gizmo
2 SCHEME, ruse, strategy, stratagem, plan, plot, ploy, tactic, gambit, manoeuvre, wile, trick, artifice, stunt
FORMAL machination
COLLOQ. dodge; Aust & NZ slinter
3 EMBLEM, symbol, motif, logo, colophon, design, insignia, crest, badge, shield, seal, token, coat of arms

---

SYNONYM NUANCES

sense 1
Tool is widely used of something created to be of help in accomplishing a manual task, whereas **implement** is more vague, and often used when its actual identity is unknown: *an implement may have been used in the attack*. **Appliance** suggests domestic devices, often electrical: *kitchen appliances such as toasters*, whereas **gadget** generally implies something small but ingenious: *a gadget to remove bobbles from knitwear*.

Both **contrivance** and **contraption** are less approving, and suggestive of something rather complicated. **Apparatus** is most appropriately used in technical applications, of a variety of things set up as required, or sometimes even one thing with a specific function: *the laboratory apparatus for this experiment*; *the stinging apparatus of the wasp*. **Utensil**, on the other hand, tends now to be associated with cooking.

The term **instrument** suggests something usually used for precise work: *dental instruments*, whilst **machine** might be used of something larger, which is capable of completing a task: *a sewing machine*. A **mechanism**, on the other hand, is usually a component necessary for such a thing to work, and would generally describe part of a larger device.

devil *n*

1 SATAN, arch-fiend, Lucifer, Evil One, the wicked one, Prince of Darkness, Adversary, Beelzebub, Mephistopheles, Apollyon, Belial, the Tempter, arch-traitor, bogy, man of sin, ragman, deuce, dickens, sorrow; *Scot* the deil, Hornie, Clootie, Cloots, Mahoun, worricow
OLD (*Shakesp*) goodyear, yoke-devil; Ragamuffin
COLLOQ. Old Nick, Old Harry, Old One, Old Poker, Old Scratch, Davy Jones, mischief, goodman
Related adjective: diabolic
2 DEMON, fiend, evil spirit, imp, incubus, succubus, daemon, cacodemon; *Scot* fient
OLD Ragamuffin
3 BRUTE, rogue, monster, ogre, savage, beast, demon, terror, imp, rascal, wretch

> **PROVERBS**
> Needs must when the devil drives
> The devil finds work for idle hands to do
> The devil looks after his own
> Better the devil you know than the devil you don't

> **QUOTATIONS**
> If the devil doesn't exist, but man has created him, he has created him in his own image and likeness
> FYODOR DOSTOEVSKY, *The Brothers Karamazov*

devilish *adj, adv*

♦ *adj*
1 DIABOLICAL, diabolic, fiendish, satanic, demonic, hellish, damnable, evil, infernal, wicked, cruel, vile, atrocious, dreadful, outrageous, shocking, disastrous, excruciating, accursed
FORMAL execrable, nefarious
2 *a devilish problem*
tricky, difficult, awkward, problematic, complicated, knotty, thorny, sensitive, delicate, ticklish
♦ *adv*
extremely, exceedingly, excessively, very, really, exceptionally, extraordinarily, intensely, thoroughly, remarkably, greatly, highly, unusually, unreasonably, immoderately, uncommonly, severely
OLD jolly
COLLOQ. awfully, terribly, dreadfully, frightfully

devil-may-care *adj*

careless, reckless, rash, casual, cavalier, easy-going, flippant, frivolous, happy-go-lucky, heedless, nonchalant, unconcerned, unworried, swaggering, swashbuckling
FORMAL insouciant

devilry *n*

wickedness, evil, depravity, vileness, atrocity, abomination, corruption, corruptness, foulness, fiendishness, immorality, shamefulness, sin, sinfulness, impiety, unrighteousness, enormity, amorality
FORMAL dissoluteness, heinousness, iniquity, reprobacy
E3 uprightness

devious *adj*

1 UNDERHAND, deceitful, dishonest, double-dealing, unscrupulous, scheming, insidious, insincere, designing, calculating, crafty, cunning, evasive, wily, sly, artful, surreptitious, treacherous, misleading
FORMAL disingenuous
COLLOQ. tricky, slippery, crooked
2 INDIRECT, circuitous, rambling, roundabout, wandering, winding, deviating, tortuous, erratic
E3 **1** straightforward **2** direct

devise *v*

invent, contrive, plan, plot, design, conceive, come up with, work out, think up, dream up, put together, arrange, formulate, imagine, scheme, construct, originate, create, concoct, forge, fabricate, hatch, frame, project, shape, form, compose
COLLOQ. cook up

> **SYNONYM NUANCES**
>
> **Contrive**, though similar, suggests a degree of complexity or difficulty rather than creativity: *they contrived an ingenious scheme of tunnels*. **Plot** and **scheme** can have rather sinister, clandestine undertones: *they plotted his downfall*; *he schemed to retain power*, whilst **hatch** also generally implies malign intentions: *they hatched a plot to subvert the constitution*.
>
> While **plan**, **design** and **work out** convey the idea of lengthy or careful deliberation, **conceive** and **come up with** suggest a more spontaneous idea: *they came up with an ideal slogan*. **Think up**, **dream up** and **imagine** are similar, but suggest that the idea may not be particularly practical: *he dreamed up some harebrained plan*. **Put together**, **construct** and **compose** are appropriate to describe drawing together separate components: *we've put together a basic guide*; **formulate**, **shape** and **form** emphasizes giving a clear form to: *he formulated their education policy*; and **frame** similarly suggests deciding what form something should take: *his question was framed to elicit a yes or no reply*.
>
> **Originate** and **create** have an implication of innovation; **concoct** and **fabricate**, on the other hand, suggest an element of effort or even untruth: *some concocted yarn*; *officers fabricated evidence*. **Forge** implies a successful beginning, or an element of constancy or unity: *a tradition forged over two hundred years ago*.

devoid *adj*

lacking, wanting, without, free, bereft, destitute, deprived, bare, barren, empty, vacant, void
FORMAL deficient
E3 endowed

devolution *n*

decentralization, delegation of power, distribution, transference of power, dispersal
E3 centralization

devolve *v*

hand down, pass down, delegate, transfer, consign, convey, deliver, depute, entrust, commission, fall to, rest with

devote *v*

dedicate, consecrate, commit, give yourself, set apart, set aside, reserve, consign, apply, allocate, allot, sacrifice, enshrine, assign, appropriate, surrender, offer, give, put in, pledge

> **SYNONYM NUANCES**
>
> **Commit** suggests a deep involvement: *a government committed to free enterprise*, while **dedicate** can be used with the positive implication of being really giving of time and effort: *dedicated musicians*. To use the terms **give yourself** and **surrender** make a clear statement of complete devotion: *he gave himself to God*; **sacrifice** is appropriate to refer to devotion at a personal cost.

The terms **set aside** and **reserve** straightforwardly refer to retaining for a specific purpose: *time set aside for training*, as do **allocate**, **allot**, and **assign**. **Put in** is similar, but more generally implies effort: *he put in a strenuous two hours at the gym.*

Pledge would be best used of giving a solemn promise: *candidates pledged to unilateral disarmament*, whilst **consecrate** most strongly suggests devoting to some religious purpose: *the day, consecrated by the Romans to the sun.*

You may use **consign** to suggest entrusting to an appropriate place, though this usually implies a reduction in status: *consigning to a museum; consigned to obscurity.*

devoted *adj*
dedicated, ardent, committed, loyal, faithful, devout, loving, staunch, steadfast, true, constant, fond, unswerving, tireless, concerned, attentive, caring
E3 indifferent, disloyal

SYNONYM NUANCES

Dedicated suggests being completely given over to a cause, whilst **ardent** is more suggestive of strong passion: *an ardent fan of opera.* **Committed** also suggests deep involvement, whilst **loyal**, **faithful** and **steadfast**, along with **unswerving** and **tireless**, are positive terms describing continuing support and implying approval of this constancy: *faithful customers; his steadfast character.* **Staunch** is similar in meaning, but is less approbatory (although not necessarily negative) in tone. **True** and **constant** also suggest unwavering and genuine support: *he was a true democrat.*

Devout generally suggests strict religious observance, but can be more widely applied to convey depth of feeling: *a devout capitalist.* **Loving**, however, would be appropriate to describe being enamoured, while the term **fond** is less strong, and simply suggestive of a partiality. You may use **concerned** to emphasize the element of care or worry: *we crept about like concerned parents around a sleeping child*, whilst **attentive** and **caring** will similarly emphasize involvement with another's needs: *attentive service.*

devotedly *adv*
committedly, dedicatedly, ardently, loyally, faithfully, devoutly, staunchly, steadfastly, unswervingly, tirelessly, attentively, caringly, fondly, lovingly
E3 indifferently

devotee *n*
enthusiast, fan, fanatic, lover, addict, follower, supporter, zealot, adherent, admirer, disciple, hound; *Irish* voteen
FORMAL aficionado
COLLOQ. buff, freak, merchant, fiend

devotion *n*
1 DEDICATION, commitment, consecration, ardour, loyalty, faithfulness, allegiance, adherence, trueness, staunchness, constancy, solidarity, zeal, support, love, passion, fervour, fondness, attachment, admiration, warmness, closeness, adoration, affection, reverence, steadfastness, regard, earnestness
FORMAL fidelity
2 DEVOUTNESS, piety, godliness, faith, holiness, spirituality, sanctity, religiousness
3 PRAYER, worship, observance
E3 1 inconstancy **2** irreverence

devotional *adj*
devout, holy, pietistic, religious, reverential, sacred, solemn, spiritual, dutiful, pious

devour *v*
1 EAT, eat up, consume, finish off, guzzle, gulp, gorge, gobble, bolt, swallow, stuff, cram, gormandize, feast on, relish, revel in; *Scot* worry
OLD (*Spenser*) engorge; raven
COLLOQ. wolf down, polish off, tuck into, scoff, put away, knock back, snarf; *N Am* scarf, chow down
2 DESTROY, devastate, lay waste, consume, absorb, engulf, envelop, ravage, dispatch, deprecate
3 *devour a book*
be engrossed in, take in, drink in, appreciate, enjoy, relish, feast on

devout *adj*
1 PIOUS, godly, religious, reverent, prayerful, saintly, holy, orthodox, church-going, committed, practising
2 SINCERE, earnest, devoted, fervent, genuine, staunch, steadfast, ardent, passionate, serious, wholehearted, dedicated, committed, constant, faithful, intense, vehement, heartfelt, zealous, unswerving, deep, profound
E3 1 irreligious **2** insincere

devoutly *adv*
1 *devoutly religious*
piously, religiously, reverently, prayerfully
2 SINCERELY, deeply, earnestly, fervently, staunchly, steadfastly, ardently, passionately, wholeheartedly, faithfully, zealously

dewy *adj*
1 *dewy grass*
bedewed, roral, rorid, roric
OLD roscid
2 BLOOMING, innocent, starry-eyed, youthful

dexterity *n*
deftness, adeptness, address, adroitness, agility, handiness, nimbleness, proficiency, mastery, readiness, skilfulness, ability, skill, expertise, aptitude, art, artistry, expertness, facility, knack, finesse, legerdemain, sleight, ingenuity, effortlessness
E3 clumsiness, awkwardness, ineptitude

dexterous *adj*
deft, adept, adroit, agile, able, nimble, proficient, skilful, clever, expert, accomplished, nippy, handy, facile, nimble-fingered, neat-handed
COLLOQ. nifty
E3 clumsy, inept, awkward

diabolical *adj*
devilish, fiendish, demonic, hellish, damnable, evil, infernal, satanic, wicked, vile, sinful, dreadful, outrageous, shocking, appalling, disastrous, monstrous, excruciating, atrocious, nasty
FORMAL execrable

diadem *n*
circlet, coronet, crown, tiara, headband, mitre, round

diagnose *v*
identify, determine, recognize, pinpoint, distinguish, analyse, explain, isolate, detect, interpret, investigate

diagnosis *n*
identification, verdict, explanation, conclusion, answer, interpretation, judgement, analysis, opinion, investigation, recognition, detection, examination, scrutiny

diagnostic *adj*
analytical, indicative, interpretative, interpretive, recognizable, symptomatic, demonstrative, distinguishing

diagonal *adj*
oblique, slanting, cross, crossing, crosswise, sloping, crooked, angled, cornerways, catercorner

diagonally *adv*
obliquely, crossways, crosswise, at an angle, cornerwise, on the cross, on the slant, slantwise, aslant, on the bias

diagram *n*
plan, sketch; *N Am* plat; chart, bar chart, pie chart, flow chart, Mind Map®, run chart, drawing, figure, representation, schema, illustration, outline, draft, graph,

picture, exploded view, cutaway, layout, table, floor plan, indicator, key, scheme, tree, family tree
FORMAL delineation

diagrammatic *adj*
diagrammatical, schematic, graphic, illustrative, representational, tabular
ᴇ∃ imaginative, impressionistic

dial *n, v*
♦ *n*
circle, disc, face, clock, control
♦ *v*
phone, telephone, ring, call (up)
COLLOQ. give a buzz/a bell

dialect *n*
idiom, language, regionalism, localism, patois, provincialism, vernacular, variety, argot, jargon, accent, speech, diction
COLLOQ. lingo

dialectic *adj, n*
♦ *adj*
dialectical, logical, rational, argumentative, analytical, rationalistic, logistic, polemical, inductive, deductive
FORMAL disputatious
♦ *n*
dialectics, logic, reasoning, rationale, analysis, debate, argumentation, contention, discussion, polemics, deduction
FORMAL disputation, induction, ratiocination

dialogue *n*
1 CONVERSATION, communication, talk, chat, tête-à-tête, gossip, exchange, discussion, discourse, conference
FORMAL interchange, converse, debate, colloquy, interlocution
2 LINES, script

diametrically *adv*
directly, completely, absolutely, utterly
FORMAL antithetically

diaphanous *adj*
cobwebby, delicate, filmy, fine, gauzy, gossamer, gossamery, chiffony, light, see-through, sheer, thin, translucent, transparent, veily
FORMAL pellucid
ᴇ∃ heavy, opaque, thick

diarrhoea *n*
looseness of the bowels, gippy tummy, holiday tummy, dysentery
COLLOQ. the runs, the trots, Spanish tummy, Delhi belly, Montezuma's revenge
SLANG (*vulgar*) the shits
ᴇ∃ constipation

diary *n*
journal, day-book, logbook, chronicle, memoir, year-book, appointment book, engagement book, Filofax®

diatribe *n*
tirade, abuse, harangue, attack, onslaught, denunciation, criticism, insult, reviling, upbraiding, reproof, reprimand, rebuke
FORMAL invective, vituperation, philippic
COLLOQ. knocking, slating, slamming, running-down
ᴇ∃ praise, eulogy

dicey *adj*
risky, chancy, unpredictable, uncertain, tricky, problematic, dangerous, difficult, dubious
COLLOQ. iffy, hairy, dodgy
ᴇ∃ certain

dichotomy *n*
difference, dissimilarity, discrepancy, divergence, variation, variance, conflict, division, opposition, deviation, differentiation
FORMAL disparity

dicky *adj*
unsound, unsteady, weak, ailing, frail, infirm, shaky
ᴇ∃ healthy, robust

dictate *v, n*
♦ *v*
1 SAY, read, read aloud, read out, speak, utter, announce, pronounce, transmit
OLD dite, indite
2 COMMAND, lay down, set down, impose, demand, insist, order, give orders to, direct, decree, instruct, rule
OLD dite, indite
FORMAL prescribe, promulgate
♦ *n*
command, decree, precept, principle, rule, direction, charge, injunction, edict, order, ruling, statute, requirement, law, bidding, mandate, ultimatum, word
FORMAL ordinance, behest, promulgation

dictator *n*
despot, absolute ruler, autocrat, tyrant, oppressor, Caesar, Führer, Hitler
FORMAL autarchist
COLLOQ. supremo, Big Brother, little Hitler

dictatorial *adj*
tyrannical, despotic, totalitarian, all powerful, authoritarian, autocratic, oppressive, imperious, domineering, absolute, unlimited, unrestricted, repressive, overbearing, arbitrary, dogmatic
FORMAL omnipotent, peremptory, autarchic
COLLOQ. bossy
ᴇ∃ democratic, egalitarian, liberal

dictatorship *n*
tyranny, despotism, totalitarianism, authoritarianism, autocracy, absolute rule, fascism, police state, reign of terror, Hitlerism
ᴇ∃ democracy, egalitarianism

diction *n*
speech, articulation, language, elocution, intonation, pronunciation, inflection, fluency, delivery, expression, phrasing
FORMAL enunciation, locution

dictionary *n*
lexicon, glossary, thesaurus, vocabulary, wordbook, encyclopedia, concordance

dictum *n*
1 RULING, pronouncement, direction, proclamation, decree, dictate, edict, precept, command, order
FORMAL fiat
2 SAYING, maxim, axiom, utterance, proverb, aphorism

didactic *adj*
instructive, educational, informative, prescriptive, pedantic, moralizing, moral
FORMAL educative, pedagogic

die *v*
1 *he died in terrible pain*
pass away, pass on, pass, depart, depart this life, breathe your last, draw your last breath, lose your life, perish, fail, go, drown, starve, go west, succumb, close your eyes, go over to the majority
OLD exit, famish, be gathered to your fathers, give up the ghost, go the way of all flesh, go the way of the earth, pip out, sterve, swelt; (*Shakesp*) go off; (*Spenser*) quell
FORMAL expire, decease
COLLOQ. peg out, bite the dust, pop off, have had it, meet your maker, push up daisies, shuffle off this mortal coil; *Aust* go bung; slip the cable, turn up your toes
SLANG snuff it, cash in your chips, cash/pass in your checks, kick the bucket, kick off, kiss off, spark out, choke, croak, flatline, hop the twig, pop your clogs; *N Am* buy the farm, go belly up; *Aust* cark
2 DWINDLE, fade, pass, ebb, sink, wane, peter out, wilt, wither, decline, decay, decrease, finish, lapse, end, come to an end, disappear, vanish, subside, dissolve, melt away

3 *the machine died*
stop, break down, fail, lose power, cut out
SLANG conk out
4 LONG FOR, pine for, yearn, desire, be desperate
COLLOQ. be crazy, be mad, be nuts, be wild, be raring
■ **die away**
fade, fall, become weak, become faint, disappear
OLD evanish
■ **die down**
decrease, subside, decline, quieten, drop, quench, slake,
stop, blow over
FORMAL abate
■ **die out**
become rarer/less common, disappear, vanish, extinguish,
peter out
Ｆ３

> **QUOTATIONS**
> What passing-bells for these who die as cattle?
> WILFRED OWEN, 'Anthem for Doomed Youth'

diehard *n, adj*
♦ *n*
reactionary, hardline, ultra-conservative, rightist, fanatic,
zealot
COLLOQ. blimp, old fogey, stick-in-the-mud
♦ *adj*
hardline, reactionary, ultra-conservative, rightist, fanatical,
traditionalist, conservative, dyed-in-the-wool
FORMAL intransigent
COLLOQ. stick-in-the-mud
Ｆ３ progressive

diet *n, v*
♦ *n*
1 FOOD, nutrition, rations, foodstuffs, fare, subsistence
OLD provisions
FORMAL sustenance, victuals, comestibles, viands
2 FAST, abstinence, regimen, regime
♦ *v*
lose weight, slim, fast, reduce, cut down, abstain
COLLOQ. weight-watch

differ *v*
1 VARY, diverge, deviate (from), depart from, be a
departure from, contradict, contrast, be unlike, be
dissimilar
2 DISAGREE, argue, conflict, oppose, dispute, be at odds
with, be at variance, clash, quarrel, fall out, debate,
contend, not see eye to eye, take issue
FORMAL dissent, altercate
Ｆ３ **1** conform **2** agree

difference *n*
1 DISSIMILARITY, unlikeness, discrepancy, divergence,
diversity, variation, variance, variety, distinctness,
distinction, deviation, differentiation, contrast, singularity,
exception
FORMAL dissimilitude, antithesis, incongruity, dichotomy,
disparity
2 DISAGREEMENT, clash, dispute, conflict, argument,
misunderstanding, quarrel, row, set-to, contention
FORMAL controversy, disputation, altercation
COLLOQ. spat, tiff
3 REMAINDER, rest, balance, residue
Ｆ３ **1** conformity **2** agreement

> **SYNONYM NUANCES**
>
> *sense 1*
> **Dissimilarity** and the less commonly used **unlikeness**
> may be used generally of a difference between things; to
> suggest more strongly the idea of things being opposites
> you can use **contrast**. **Discrepancy**, however, usually
> suggests that one of two things amounts to less, and can
> be negative in that it hints at potential problems: *the
> discrepancy between the actual and the expected rates
> of inflation*. The term **divergence**, though, has to do
> with separation out from a single standard: *the*

> *divergence of opinion*, while **deviation** has more to do
> with turning away from an accepted form: *this deviation
> from the general trend*.
> The terms **diversity** and **variety** would refer to the
> existence of many types, which, especially in the case of
> **variety**, could be viewed as a positive thing: *cultural
> diversity*; *a variety of entertainments*. **Variation**
> straightforwardly suggests a slightly different form of
> something: *there is appetising variation in the diet*,
> whereas **variance** can often be suggestive of a negative
> element of dispute: *ideas at variance with prevailing
> medical views*.
> **Singularity** is more positively suggestive of uniqueness:
> *the singularity of a work of art*, like the rarely used
> **distinctness**, which is unlike, surprisingly, **distinction**,
> which is more likely to refer simply to the main area
> where two things differ: *the distinction between
> punishment and rehabilitation*.

different *adj*
1 DISSIMILAR, unlike, contrasting, divergent,
inconsistent, deviating, at odds, at variance,
clashing, opposed
COLLOQ. a far cry, poles/worlds apart, different
as chalk and cheese
2 VARIED, various, varying, separate, diverse,
miscellaneous, assorted, many, numerous, several, sundry,
other, another
FORMAL disparate, discrete
COLLOQ. mixed bag
3 UNUSUAL, unconventional, unique, distinct, distinctive,
extraordinary, individual, original, special, strange,
remarkable, odd, peculiar, rare, bizarre, anomalous, out of
the ordinary
4 INCONVENIENT, awkward, unsuitable, unfavourable,
unmanageable, ill-timed, untimely, inopportune
Ｆ３ **1** similar, identical **2** same **3** conventional, ordinary **4**
convenient

differential *n, adj*
♦ *n*
difference, variance, divergence, discrepancy, contrast, gap
FORMAL disparity
♦ *adj*
different, distinctive, separate, divergent, contrasting
FORMAL disparate

differentiate *v*
distinguish, tell apart, discriminate, contrast, separate, mark
off, individualize, particularize

differentiation *n*
distinction, distinguishing, discrimination, contrast,
separation, demarcation, individualization,
particularization, modification
Ｆ３ assimilation, association, confusion, connection

differently *adv*
diversely, dissimilarly, contrastingly, inconsistently,
incompatibly, at odds, at variance
COLLOQ. a far cry, poles/worlds apart, different
as chalk and cheese

difficult *adj*
1 HARD, laborious, demanding, arduous, strenuous,
tough, gruelling, tiring, wearisome, exhausting,
back-breaking, uphill, formidable, exacting,
burdensome, onerous
2 COMPLEX, complicated, intricate, hard, involved, obscure,
dark, knotty, thorny, problematical, puzzling, perplexing,
abstract, baffling, tricky
FORMAL abstruse, intractable, recondite, arcane, esoteric
3 UNMANAGEABLE, awkward, perverse, troublesome, trying,
demanding, hard to please, unco-operative, tiresome,
stubborn, obstinate
FORMAL intractable, recalcitrant, refractory
Ｆ３ **1** easy **2** straightforward, simple, intelligible **3**
manageable, helpful

sense 1
The simple synonym **hard** is widely used of something that will take much effort or thought, whilst **laborious** is more suggestive of something being much work, with a further implication that it will take up a lot of time and is possibly unnecessary: *the laborious old-style methods of wheat-grinding.* **Demanding** and **exacting**, however, could be used of an activity that requires much attention or precision, and often a particular skill: *intellectually demanding projects; an exacting regimen of exercises.*

The terms **arduous** and **tough** can be used of any activity that can be a problem to accomplish: *a tough assignment,* whereas **strenuous** and the stronger **back-breaking** suggest physical exertion. **Gruelling**, **tiring**, **wearisome** and **exhausting** all have strong associations with using up energy reserves and consequent fatigue: *a gruelling four-month tour.* **Uphill** and **formidable** are fairly gentle terms to use of something that will actually require strength and commitment, but they do also have the implication of something rather daunting: *an uphill struggle; a formidable rival.*

To suggest very oppressive difficulty you might use **burdensome** or **onerous**, which have the added implication of being almost too much to bear: *for many elderly people the effort of daily living becomes burdensome.*

difficulty *n*
1 HARDSHIP, trouble, labour, strain, arduousness, strenuousness, painfulness, trial, struggle, struggling, awkwardness
FORMAL tribulation, exigency
2 PROBLEM, predicament, complication, snag, dilemma, quandary, perplexity, embarrassment, plight, distress, hang-up, obstacle, hindrance, hurdle, impediment, objection, opposition, block, barrier, obstruction, pitfall, stumbling-block, cleft stick
COLLOQ. fix, mess, jam, spot, hiccup, hole, stew, dire straits, pickle, tall order, hot/deep water, fly in the ointment, Catch-22, how-d'you-do, devil, tight spot, pretty pass
SLANG bitch, bugger, pain in the arse
F3 1 ease
■ **in difficulties**
having problems, in trouble
COLLOQ. up against it, stumped, at the end of your tether, out of your depth, not knowing which way to turn, in the soup, in a fix/mess/jam/hole, in dire straits, in a scrape, in hot/deep water, in a stew, in a tight spot
SLANG up shit creek (without a paddle)

diffidence *n*
unassertiveness, modesty, shyness, self-consciousness, self-effacement, timidity, insecurity, reserve, bashfulness, humility, inhibition, meekness, self-distrust, self-doubt, hesitancy, reluctance, backwardness
F3 confidence

diffident *adj*
unassertive, modest, shy, timid, self-conscious, self-effacing, insecure, nervous, bashful, abashed, meek, reserved, withdrawn, tentative, shrinking, inhibited, hesitant, reluctant, unsure, shamefaced, sheepish
F3 assertive, confident

diffuse *v, adj*
♦ *v*
spread, scatter, disperse, distribute, propagate, send out, dispense, permeate, circulate
FORMAL disseminate, dissipate, promulgate
F3 concentrate
♦ *adj*
1 *diffuse outbreaks of rain*
scattered, unconcentrated, diffused, dispersed, disconnected

2 *a diffuse prose style*
verbose, imprecise, wordy, rambling, long-winded, profuse, vague, discursive
FORMAL prolix, loquacious, periphrastic, circumlocutory
COLLOQ. waffling
F3 1 concentrated 2 succinct

diffusion *n*
spreading, scattering, dispersal, distribution, propagation, permeation, circulation
FORMAL dissemination, dissipation, promulgation

dig *v, n*
♦ *v*
1 EXCAVATE, penetrate, burrow, make a hole, mine, quarry, scoop, scratch, spade, fork, hollow, channel, tunnel, till, turn over, work, break up, spit, spud, cultivate, harrow, plough, gouge, delve, pierce, grub (up/out), ditch, trench, entrench, disinter, unearth, undermine; *dialect* graft; *Scot* cast, howk; *Aust* fossick
OLD grave
2 POKE, prod, jab, punch
3 INVESTIGATE, probe, go into, research, search, delve
4 UNDERSTAND, grasp, take in, follow, figure out, realize, appreciate
COLLOQ. get, click, twig, get the hang of
♦ *n*
1 *a dig in the ribs*
poke, prod, jab, punch
2 GIBE, jeer, sneer, taunt, crack, insinuation, insult, wisecrack,
OLD gird
COLLOQ. snark
■ **dig up**
discover, unearth, uncover, root out, bring to light, disinter, expose, extricate, find, retrieve, track down
FORMAL exhume
F3 bury, obscure

digest *v, n*
♦ *v*
1 ABSORB, assimilate, incorporate, process, dissolve, break down
FORMAL macerate
2 TAKE IN, absorb, understand, comprehend, assimilate, grasp, study, consider, contemplate, meditate, mull over, ponder
3 SHORTEN, summarize, condense, compress, reduce, abridge
FORMAL comprehend
♦ *n*
summary, abridgement, abstract, précis, synopsis, résumé, reduction, abbreviation, compression, compendium

digestion *n*
absorption, assimilation, breaking-down, transformation
FORMAL ingestion, eupepsia, maceration

digit *n*
1 FINGER, thumb
2 NUMBER, numeral, figure, integer

dignified *adj*
stately, solemn, imposing, grand, majestic, noble, august, lordly, courtly, ceremonious, lofty, exalted, formal, distinguished, grave, impressive, reserved, honourable
FORMAL decorous
F3 undignified, lowly

dignify *v*
honour, distinguish, grace, exalt, enhance, adorn, glorify, advance, elevate, ennoble, promote, raise
FORMAL aggrandize, apotheosize
F3 degrade, demean

dignitary *n*
worthy, notable, high-up, personage, grandee, somebody, name
FORMAL luminary
COLLOQ. VIP, bigwig, big name, big gun, big shot, top brass

dignity _n_

stateliness, solemnity, nobleness, courtliness, self-possession, grandeur, loftiness, majesty, honour, eminence, importance, excellence, honourability, nobility, self-respect, self-esteem, self-importance, standing, poise, respectability, greatness, elevation, status, pride
FORMAL propriety, decorum

> **QUOTATIONS**
> Official dignity tends to increase in inverse ratio to the importance of the country in which the office is held
> ALDOUS HUXLEY, _Beyond the Mexique Bay_

> **SYNONYM NUANCES**
> Many of these synonyms are approbatory in tone. **Stateliness** may be used to suggest an elegance of carriage and conduct, while **solemnity** is more suggestive of an observance of ritual, often with a degree of pomposity: _he was laid to rest with great solemnity in Poets' Corner._ Both **nobleness** and **courtliness** have echoes of aristocracy, and consequently imply refinement. **Grandeur** and **majesty** are highly connotative terms, suggesting an elegant and imposing air: _the house has all the grandeur of a small manor._ **Loftiness** has the implication of haughtiness, whilst **self-possession** and **poise** can be used fairly neutrally of dignity through personal composure.
> The terms **respectability**, the stronger **honour** and **honourability**, and the more common **nobility** have more to do with a moral code and suggest a fineness of character. Both **self-respect** and **self-esteem** have the positive implication of valuing yourself, whilst **self-importance** makes the negative suggestion of over-valuing yourself unduly.
> The words **standing** and **status** can be used of dignity acquired from a perceived place within a group: _he held the office with standing for many years_, whilst **greatness** and **elevation** are similar but less reserved. **Pride**, meanwhile, can be suggestive either of a desirable sense of self-worth, or a rather less admirable conceit.

digress _v_

diverge, deviate, stray, wander, go off at a tangent, go off the subject, drift, depart, ramble, turn aside, be sidetracked

digression _n_

divergence, deviation, straying, wandering, aside, departure, diversion, footnote, parenthesis
FORMAL apostrophe, divagation, _obiter dictum_, excursus

digs _n_

lodgings, accommodation, quarters, billet, boarding-house, rooms, place
COLLOQ. pad, a roof over your head

dilapidated _adj_

ramshackle, shabby, broken-down, neglected, tumbledown, uncared-for, rickety, shaky, decrepit, crumbling, run-down, worn-out, beat-up, ruined, in ruins, decayed, decaying, falling apart, in a state of disrepair

dilapidation _n_

decay, ruin, disrepair, collapse, demolition, destruction, deterioration, disintegration, waste

dilate _v_

enlarge, expand, spread (out), broaden, widen, increase, extend, stretch, swell, bloat, inflate
FORMAL distend
E₃ contract, constrict, shorten

dilatory _adj_

delaying, slow, sluggish, lingering, dawdling, lazy, lackadaisical, slack, snail-like, time-wasting, postponing, stalling
FORMAL procrastinating, tardy, tarrying
E₃ prompt

dilemma _n_

quandary, conflict, predicament, problem, vicious circle, difficulty, puzzle, embarrassment, mess, perplexity, plight, cleft stick, _crise de conscience_
TECHNICAL double bind
OLD why-not
COLLOQ. Catch-22, spot, fix, no-win situation, tight corner, the devil and the deep (blue) sea, a rock and a hard place

dilettante _n_

dabbler, amateur, non-professional, trifler, potterer
FORMAL aesthete, sciolist
E₃ professional

diligence _n_

assiduity, assiduousness, industry, conscientiousness, attention, care, thoroughness, dedication, attentiveness, application, constancy, earnestness, intentness, laboriousness, perseverance
FORMAL pertinacity, sedulousness
E₃ laziness

diligent _adj_

assiduous, industrious, hard-working, conscientious, painstaking, busy, attentive, tireless, careful, thorough, dedicated, meticulous, persevering, persistent, studious, earnest, constant
FORMAL sedulous
E₃ negligent, lazy

dilly-dally _v_

dally, dawdle, delay, falter, hesitate, hover, linger, loiter, dither, potter, vacillate, waver, take your time, waste time
FORMAL procrastinate, tarry
COLLOQ. shilly-shally, faff about

dilute _v_

adulterate, water down, thin (out), make thinner, weaken, make weaker, diffuse, diminish, decrease, lessen, reduce, temper, moderate, tone down
FORMAL attenuate, mitigate
E₃ concentrate

diluted _adj_

watered down, watery, weak, thinned (out)
E₃ concentrated

dim _adj, v_

♦ _adj_
1 DARK, dull, dusky, cloudy, clouding, overcast, grey, shadowy, gloomy, leaden, sombre, dingy, unlit, lacklustre, feeble
OLD caliginous
FORMAL crepuscular, tenebrous
2 INDISTINCT, blurred, hazy, ill-defined, obscure, misty, unclear, foggy, fuzzy, vague, faint, weak, feeble, pale, confused, imperfect
FORMAL obfuscated
3 STUPID, simple, simple-minded, dense, dull, obtuse, slow, slow-witted, doltish
COLLOQ. thick, dumb, dopey, gormless, dim-witted
4 **dim prospects**
unpromising, unfavourable, gloomy, discouraging, adverse
FORMAL inauspicious
E₃ 1 bright 2 distinct 3 bright, intelligent 4 hopeful, promising
♦ _v_
darken, dull, obscure, cloud, blur, make/become blurred, fade, make/become faint, pale, tarnish, shade, dusk, blear
OLD bedim, appal, becloud
E₃ brighten, illuminate

dimension _n_

1 _the dimensions of the room_
extent, measurement, measure, size, length, width, breadth, height, depth, area, proportions, scope, magnitude, largeness, volume, capacity, mass
2 _the dimensions of a problem_
extent, size, scale, range, bulk, importance, magnitude, greatness

3 *add a new dimension to the matter*
aspect, facet, side, factor, element, feature

diminish *v*
1 DECREASE, lessen, become/grow less, reduce, lower, detract, drop, deactivate, contract, decline, dwindle, shrink, recede, wane, weaken, become/grow weaker, impair, pare (down), fade, peter out, sink, subside, deflate, ebb, slacken, taper off, wear down, whittle (down/away), die away, die out, cut, take the edge off, mince, minify
TECHNICAL damp, rebate
OLD bate, minish
FORMAL abate, retrench
2 BELITTLE, devalue, defame
FORMAL disparage, deprecate, denigrate, derogate, vilify
F3 1 increase, grow **2** exaggerate

diminution *n*
reduction, lessening, contraction, decline, ebb, decrease, cut, cutback, curtailment, deduction, decay, subsidence, weakening, shortening, shrinkage
FORMAL abatement, retrenchment
F3 enlargement, increase, growth

diminutive *adj*
small-scale, tiny, little, undersized, small, miniature, minute, microscopic, infinitesimal, elfin, petite, midget, compact, Lilliputian, pocket(-sized), pygmy, dwarfish; *dialect & Scot* tottie; *Scot* wee
FORMAL homuncular
COLLOQ. mini, teeny, teeny-weeny, dinky, pint-size(d)
F3 big, large, oversized

dimly *adv*
1 DARKLY, dully, sombrely, gloomily, dingily, feebly
2 FAINTLY, weakly, unclearly, indistinctly, obscurely, hazily, mistily
F3 1 brightly **2** clearly, distinctly

dimness *n*
darkness, dullness, dusk, cloudiness, mist, greyness, twilight, half-light, dinginess
TECHNICAL caligo
OLD caliginosity
FORMAL crepuscule

dimple *n*
concavity, depression, dint, hollow, indentation
TECHNICAL fovea, umbilicus

dimwit *n*
idiot, fool, blockhead, nitwit, dunce, dullard, dunderhead, ignoramus, halfwit, clot
COLLOQ. bonehead, numskull, twit, dope, knuckle-head
SLANG plonker, dork, geek, dweeb, berk, git, prat, dickhead

din *n*
noise, loud noise, row, racket, clash, clatter, clamour, clangour, pandemonium, uproar, tumult, commotion, crash, hubbub, brouhaha, outcry, shout, shouting, yelling, babble
COLLOQ. hullabaloo
F3 quiet, calm

dine *v*
eat, have dinner, feast, sup, lunch, banquet, feed

dingy *adj*
dark, drab, grimy, murky, faded, dull, dim, shabby, soiled, discoloured, dirty, dreary, gloomy, dismal, cheerless, seedy, sombre, obscure, run-down, colourless, dusky, worn
F3 bright, clean

dinky *adj*
dainty, fine, small, little, petite, neat, trim, miniature
COLLOQ. natty, mini

dinner *n*
meal, main meal, evening meal, supper, tea, banquet, feast, spread

FORMAL repast, refection
COLLOQ. blow-out
Related adjective: prandial

dinosaur

Dinosaurs include:

Allosaurus	Corythosaurus	Pachycephalo-
Ankylosaurus	Deinonychus	saurus
Apatosaurus	Diplodocus	Parasaurolophus
Barosaurus	Heterodontosaurus	Plateosaurus
Brachiosaurus	Iguanodon	Saurischia
Brontosaurus	microraptor	Stegosaurus
Camptosaurus	Ophiacodon	Styracosaurus
Coelophysis	Ornithischia	Triceratops
Compsognathus	Ornithomimus	Tyrannosaurus

dint *n*
dent, indentation, impression, hollow, depression, blow, concavity, stroke
■ *by dint of*
by means of, by the agency of, through the medium of, with the assistance of
FORMAL by virtue of

dip *v, n*
♦ *v*
1 PLUNGE, immerse, submerge, duck, dunk, dap, dib, dive, nod, lower, bathe, soak, douse, souse, sink, baptize; *dialect* plot
TECHNICAL dibble
OLD dop, immerge, merge
2 DECREASE, go down, decline, drop, fall, descend, subside, slump, sink, lower
3 *the track dips*
slope, descend, go down, decline, drop, fall, sink, delve
♦ *n*
1 HOLLOW, basin, decline, hole, drop, concavity, incline, descent, indentation, dent, depression, fall, slope
2 DECREASE, slump, lowering, lessening, fall, decline, reduction
3 SWIM, bathe, immersion, plunge, soaking, ducking, swim, drenching, dive
FORMAL infusion
4 *an avocado dip*
sauce, cream, dressing, relish
■ *dip into*
1 *dip into a book*
look at, leaf through, look through, run through, flick through, thumb through, skim, browse
2 *dip into your savings*
spend, draw on, use

diplomacy *n*
1 TACT, tactfulness, finesse, sensitivity, delicacy, discretion, prudence, savoir-faire, cleverness, subtlety, skill, craft
FORMAL judiciousness
2 STATECRAFT, statesmanship, international relations, politics, negotiation(s), manoeuvring

diplomat *n*
go-between, mediator, negotiator, ambassador, envoy, emissary, legate, attaché, consul, plenipotentiary, *chargé d'affaires*, conciliator, peacemaker, arbitrator, moderator, politician, statesman

diplomatic *adj*
1 *diplomatic relations*
consular, ambassadorial
2 TACTFUL, prudent, discreet, subtle, sensitive, clever, skilful
FORMAL politic, judicious
F3 tactless

diplomatically *adv*
1 POLITICALLY, by negotiation, conciliatorily, with diplomacy
2 TACTFULLY, discreetly, sensitively, skilfully, prudently
FORMAL judiciously
F3 2 tactlessly

dipsomaniac *n*
alcoholic, drunk, drunkard, inebriate, drinker, hard
drinker, heavy drinker, wine-bibber, Bacchus, bloat,
habitual; *N Am* souse
COLLOQ. tippler
SLANG boozer, wino, lush, alkie, dipso, soak, toper,
tosspot, sot, sponge, piss artist, pisshead

dire *adj*
1 DISASTROUS, dreadful, terrible, frightful, awful, appalling,
calamitous, catastrophic, horrible, atrocious, shocking,
alarming, distressing
2 DESPERATE, urgent, grave, drastic, crucial, extreme, vital,
pressing, ominous

direct *adj, v, adv*
◆ *adj*
1 STRAIGHT, undeviating, unswerving, through,
uninterrupted, non-stop, unbroken
2 STRAIGHTFORWARD, outspoken, blunt, bluff, frank, straight,
forthright, plainspoken, unequivocal, sincere, candid,
honest, explicit, unambiguous
COLLOQ. up-front
3 IMMEDIATE, first-hand, face-to-face, personal
F3 **1** indirect, circuitous **2** equivocal **3** indirect
◆ *v*
1 CONTROL, be in control of, manage, run, administer, be
in charge of, organize, lead, govern, regulate, superintend,
preside over, oversee, supervise, handle, mastermind
COLLOQ. call the shots, be the boss of
2 INSTRUCT, command, order, tell, give orders, issue
instructions, charge
FORMAL adjure
3 GUIDE, lead, conduct, point, show, steer, show/point the
way, escort, usher
4 AIM, point, focus, turn, intend, mean, level, target,
market
◆ *adv*
directly, straight, right, uninterruptedly, non-stop

direction *n*
1 CONTROL, administration, management, government,
running, handling, supervision, guidance, leadership,
superintendency, overseeing, regulation
2 ROUTE, way, line, road, course, path, track, bearing,
orientation
3 *change the direction of your career*
course, trend, tendency, inclination, drift, tenor, current
aim, orientation
4 *give someone directions*
instructions, guidelines, orders, brief, briefing, information,
guidance, recommendations, indication, plan, rules,
regulations

directive *n*
command, instruction, order, direction, regulation, ruling,
imperative, dictate, decree, charge, bidding, mandate,
injunction, ordinance, edict, notice
FORMAL fiat

directly *adv*
1 IMMEDIATELY, instantly, at once, promptly, right away,
speedily, forthwith, instantaneously, quickly, soon,
presently, straightaway, without delay, as soon as possible,
straight, right, exactly
COLLOQ. pronto
2 FRANKLY, bluntly, candidly, honestly, straightforwardly,
unequivocally, sincerely, clearly, plainly, explicitly,
unambiguously
3 SQUARELY, straight, unswervingly, right, dead, just,
exactly, precisely
COLLOQ. bang, smack, plumb

directness *n*
1 IMMEDIACY, immediateness, uninterruptedness
2 CANDIDNESS, straightforwardness, outspokenness,
bluntness, frankness, forthrightness, plainspokenness,
honesty

director *n*
manager, managing director, board of directors, head,
boss, chief, controller, executive, chief executive,
principal, governor, leader, president, superintendent,
organizer, supervisor, overseer, administrator, producer,
chairman, chairwoman, chairperson, chair, conductor,
régisseur
COLLOQ. top dog, top banana

directory *n*
catalogue, index, list, listing, inventory, guide

dirge *n*
elegy, lament, funeral song, requiem, dead-march,
coronach, threnody, monody

dirt *n*
1 EARTH, soil, clay, dust, mud, loam
2 FILTH, grime, soot, pollution, muck, mire, bilge,
excrement, stain, smudge, sludge, slime, tarnish; *dialect*
clart; *Aust & NZ* scunge
COLLOQ. gunge, yuck, grot
SLANG crud, gunk, grunge, crap
3 INDECENCY, impurity, obscenity, pornography, lewdness,
sordidness, salaciousness
COLLOQ. smut, sleaze

dirty *adj, v*
◆ *adj*
1 FILTHY, grimy, grubby, mucky, soiled, greasy, unclean,
unwashed, unhygienic, foul, messy, muddy, dusty, sooty,
polluted, slimy, squalid, insanitary, miry, scruffy, shabby,
sullied, stained, defiled, tarnished, clouded, cloudy, black,
dark, dull, grungy; *dialect* clart, grufted; *Aust & NZ* scungy
COLLOQ. grotty, yucky, flea-bitten, cruddy, manky, skanky;
Aust & NZ chatty
2 UNPLEASANT, dishonest, unfair, immoral, deceitful,
unscrupulous, bad, foul, nasty, contemptible, despicable,
undesirable
SLANG cruddy, poxy
3 INDECENT, improper, obscene, coarse, filthy, smutty,
sordid, salacious, suggestive, risqué, vulgar, pornographic,
X-rated, contaminated, corrupt, lewd, bawdy, ribald
COLLOQ. blue, raunchy, sleazy
F3 **1** clean **2** honest **3** decent
◆ *v*
pollute, soil, stain, foul, mess up, defile, contaminate,
adulterate, smear, smirch, spoil, smudge, splash, sully,
tarnish, mud, muddy, blacken, discolour, draggle, mess,
muck up; *dialect* clart, soss
OLD assoil, bedaggle; *(Shakesp)* ray
FORMAL besmirch, begrime
F3 clean, cleanse

SYNONYM NUANCES

adjective sense 1
Whilst **grimy** and **soiled** appropriately describe
something superficially unclean, **filthy** and **foul** are more
emotive and would generally suggest being disgustingly
dirty. **Grubby**, **shabby** and **mucky** possibly fall midway,
but can imply disgust at a moral aspect: *his was a
grubby little life*. **Messy** is more suggestive of untidiness.
Greasy, **muddy**, **dusty** and **sooty** are all fairly literal
and mild terms, although **greasy** has a tactile element to
it; **slimy** again is tactile in its suggestion but has a far
more repulsive element: *horrible, slimy worms*.
   Unhygienic and **insanitary** are used only in contexts
of carrying germs or dirt posing a threat to health, like
polluted, which could be used of poisonous dirt caused
by a variety of things, often by-products of industry:
polluted by radiation; polluted rivers. **Squalid** is more
suggestive of neglect, and often poverty, but again has
highly negative connotations of unhealthiness: *the
squalid housing estates*.
   Scruffy returns to the idea of a more superficial
untidiness, whereas **sullied** and **stained**, **defiled** and
tarnished suggest deeper and irreversible marks, and
often suggest being tainted in a moral sense.

disability *n*
handicap, disablement, disorder, inability, incapability, incapacity, infirmity, defect, unfitness, disqualification, illness, ailment, complaint, weakness
FORMAL impairment, affliction, malady

disable *v*
1 *disable a person*
cripple, lame, damage, handicap, hamstring, make unfit, disqualify, weaken, debilitate, immobilize, invalidate, paralyse, prostrate
FORMAL incapacitate, impair, enfeeble
2 *disable a machine*
immobilize, paralyse, stop, deactivate, defuse, put out of action
FORMAL render inoperative

disabled *adj*
handicapped, infirm, unfit, crippled, lame, immobilized, debilitated, maimed, weak, weakened, out of action, paralysed, bed-ridden, wrecked
FORMAL incapacitated, impaired, indisposed, enfeebled
E3 able, able-bodied

disabuse *v*
disillusion, disenchant, disappoint, enlighten

disadvantage *n*
1 DRAWBACK, snag, hindrance, liability, handicap, impediment, limitation, inconvenience, disamenity, flaw, defect, nuisance, weakness, weak point, trouble, penalty, catch; *N Am* out
OLD disinterest
FORMAL disbenefit, disutility
COLLOQ. downside, minus, hang-up, spanner in the works, fly in the ointment, weak link in the chain, chink in your armour, Achilles heel, own goal
2 HARM, damage, detriment, hurt, injury, loss, prejudice, hardship, lack, disservice
FORMAL privation
E3 1 advantage, benefit, asset

disadvantaged *adj*
deprived, underprivileged, poor, poverty-stricken, handicapped, impoverished, struggling, in need, in distress, in want
E3 privileged

disadvantageous *adj*
unfavourable, harmful, detrimental, inopportune, prejudicial, adverse, unfortunate, unlucky, damaging, hurtful, injurious, inconvenient, ill-timed, inexpedient
FORMAL hapless, deleterious
E3 advantageous, favourable; *formal* auspicious

disaffected *adj*
disloyal, hostile, alienated, antagonistic, rebellious, mutinous, dissatisfied, disgruntled, discontented, unfriendly, seditious
FORMAL estranged
E3 loyal, friendly, satisfied

disaffection *n*
disloyalty, hostility, alienation, discontentment, resentment, ill-will, dissatisfaction, disgruntlement, animosity, coolness, unfriendliness, antagonism, disharmony, discord, disagreement, aversion, dislike
FORMAL estrangement
E3 loyalty, contentment

disagree *v*
1 *disagree with someone; the two sides disagree*
conflict, clash, contradict, diverge, differ, beg to differ, agree to differ, vary, not see eye to eye with, be at odds with, be at loggerheads with, quarrel, argue, bicker, wrangle, fight, squabble, contend, dispute, contest, take issue
FORMAL dissent, discord
COLLOQ. fall out
2 *disagree with an idea*
disapprove of, think wrong, oppose, object, contradict, take issue with, argue against, be against

FORMAL dissent
3 *food disagreeing with you*
upset, make unwell, cause illness, sicken, nauseate
E3 1 agree **2** approve, accept **3** agree

SYNONYM NUANCES

sense 1
Conflict may be used to suggest being in marked or vociferous opposition: *these proposals conflicted with official policy*; whilst **contradict** and **be at odds with** can be used of asserting the opposite in a more restrained way: *his version was contradicted by eyewitness accounts*. **Diverge** suggests that elements, often formerly unified, are going their separate ways: *we diverged from the original strategy*.

Clash would suggest only very forceful opposition or highly marked or significant disagreement: *MPs clashed openly in a chaotic parliament*. **Quarrel** can be used to refer to any verbal expression of disagreement or discord, as can **argue**, **bicker**, **wrangle** and **squabble**, although **quarrel** is perhaps a more vociferous expression. **Fight** is similar in that it suggests forceful opposition as well as disagreement. **Contend** is slightly less forceful, although it suggests rigorously maintaining something to be the case, in disagreement with others: *the president contended the elections were free*. To refer to questioning the validity of a claim, the terms **dispute** and **contest** are appropriate: *officials disputed the need for nuclear weapons*.

---

disagreeable *adj*
1 *disagreeable old man*
bad-tempered, ill-humoured, impolite, difficult, unfriendly, ill-natured, awkward, unhelpful, peevish, rude, surly, churlish, irritable, nasty, disobliging, contrary, cross, brusque
COLLOQ. grouchy
2 *a disagreeable taste*
disgusting, unpleasant, offensive, repulsive, repellent, repugnant, obnoxious, unsavoury, horrible, dreadful, abominable, objectionable, nasty
E3 1 amiable, pleasant **2** agreeable, pleasant

disagreeably *adv*
unpleasantly, horribly, dreadfully, nastily, objectionably, obnoxiously, offensively, repulsively, disgustingly
E3 pleasantly

disagreement *n*
1 DISPUTE, argument, difference/variance of opinion, friction, fight, disharmony, disunion, conflict, quarrel, row, clash, dissent, dissension, contention, strife, misunderstanding, squabble, wrangle
FORMAL altercation, discord, disputation, dissidence, dissonance
COLLOQ. falling-out, tiff, bust-up, flak
2 DIFFERENCE, variance, unlikeness, discrepancy, deviation, conformity, dissimilarity, incompatibility, inconsistency, divergence, diversity
FORMAL disparity, incongruity, dissimilitude
E3 1 agreement, harmony **2** similarity, conformity

disallow *v*
ban, cancel, forbid, prohibit, refuse, reject, debar, dismiss, embargo, disown, rebuff, repudiate, veto, say no to, exclude
FORMAL abjure, disaffirm, disavow, disclaim, proscribe, interdict
E3 allow, permit

disappear *v*
1 VANISH, wane, recede, fade, evaporate, melt away, drop away, die away, peter out, dissolve, ebb, go out of sight, pass from sight, get lost, go missing, dematerialize, ghost
FORMAL dissipate, evanesce
COLLOQ. make tracks, walk
2 GO, depart, withdraw, retire, exit, flee, fly, escape, hide, take flight

COLLOQ. scarper, vamoose, slope
3 END, perish, pass, cease, die out, die away, become extinct, go cold
FORMAL expire
E **1** appear **3** emerge, start, begin

disappearance *n*
1 VANISHING, fading, passing from sight, evaporation, melting away, departure, withdrawal, exit, loss, going, passing, desertion, flight
2 END, passing, dying-out, expiry, extinction
FORMAL evanescence
E **1** appearance, manifestation **2** start, beginning

disappoint *v*
let down, fail, dissatisfy, disillusion, dismay, discourage, depress, dispirit, disenchant, sadden, thwart, vex, baffle, frustrate, foil, dishearten, disgruntle, disconcert, hamper, hinder, deceive, betray, mock, make a fool of, break someone's heart, defeat, delude, dash someone's hopes; *dialect* misslippen; *Scot* mistryst; *Aust* slip up
OLD deceive
COLLOQ. devastate
E satisfy, please, delight

disappointed *adj*
let-down, frustrated, thwarted, disenchanted, deflated, disillusioned, dissatisfied, upset, vexed, discouraged, disgruntled, disheartened, distressed, downhearted, saddened, cast down, despondent, depressed, betrayed
COLLOQ. miffed, devastated, gutted, bummed
E pleased, satisfied

disappointing *adj*
unsatisfactory, inferior, inadequate, insufficient, unworthy, pathetic, sad, sorry, unhappy, discouraging, disconcerting, depressing, disagreeable, anticlimactic
COLLOQ. not all it's cracked up to be, underwhelming
E encouraging, pleasant, satisfactory

disappointment *n*
1 FRUSTRATION, dissatisfaction, failure, disenchantment, disillusionment, displeasure, discouragement, discontent, distress, regret, chagrin, sadness, despondency, dispiritedness
COLLOQ. cold comfort
2 FAILURE, let-down, anticlimax, setback, comedown, non-event, blow, misfortune, fiasco, disaster, calamity
COLLOQ. washout, wipeout, damp squib, swiz, swizzle, bummer, bitter pill (to swallow)
E **1** pleasure, satisfaction, delight **2** success

disapprobation *n*
blame, censure, condemnation, criticism, denunciation, disapproval, disfavour, dissatisfaction, dislike, displeasure, objection, exception, reproach, reproof
FORMAL remonstration, disparagement
E approval; *formal* approbation

disapproval *n*
censure, condemnation, criticism, blame, displeasure, reproach, exception, objection, dissatisfaction, denunciation, dislike, rejection, veto, rebuke, reproof
OLD disallowance, misliking
FORMAL disapprobation, remonstration, disparagement
COLLOQ. the thumbs-down
E approval; *formal* approbation

disapprove *v*
censure, condemn, blame, take exception to, be against, object to, find unacceptable, deplore, denounce, dislike, reject, veto, spurn, look down on, think little of, hold in contempt, frown on, take a dim view of, think badly of, have a low opinion of, not hold with, harrumph, reprobate
OLD disallow, disprove; (*Spenser*) disproove; mislike
FORMAL disparage, deprecate, discountenance, disfavour, disesteem, animadvert
COLLOQ. look down your nose at, give the thumbs-down
E approve, agree, have a high opinion of

SYNONYM NUANCES

Both **censure** and **condemn** involve speaking out strongly against: *a judicial inquiry severely censured police behaviour*; whereas **blame** involves holding someone or something responsible, whether voiced or not. **Deplore** suggests strength of feeling and being appalled by, whilst **denounce** returns to the idea of strongly and publicly vilifying, and the milder **disparage** can be used for talking slightingly about: *the art critical establishment is still sniffily disparaging about his work*.
Where disapproval is expressed in a refusal to accept, you could use the terms **reject** and **spurn**, and, in official contexts, **veto**: *their diplomatic overtures were spurned by the French government*.
Meanwhile, the phrases **look down on** and **hold in contempt** suggest a feeling of superiority behind any disapproval; **think little of**, **frown on**, **take a dim view of**, **think badly of** and **have a low opinion of** can be used to refer to varying degrees of disapprobation, from the mild to the severe, and which may be keenly felt but not expressed. **Take exception to** and **not hold with** are also fairly restrained but imply active objection.

disapproving *adj*
censorious, condemnatory, critical, reproachful, reproving, derogatory, pejorative
FORMAL deprecatory, disparaging, disapprobative, disapprobatory, improbative, improbatory

disarm *v*
1 DISABLE, unarm, demilitarize, demobilize, deactivate, disband, immobilize, lay down arms/weapons, make powerless, put out of action
FORMAL render inoperative
2 APPEASE, conciliate, win over, mollify, placate, persuade, charm
E **1** arm

disarmament *n*
demilitarization, demobilization, deactivation, laying-down of arms/weapons, arms control/limitation/reduction

disarming *adj*
charming, winning, persuasive, conciliatory, irresistible, likeable, mollifying

disarmingly *adv*
charmingly, pleasantly, persuasively, irresistibly

disarrange *v*
untidy, disorganize, disorder, confuse, disturb, jumble, mess, dislocate, shuffle, unsettle, put out of place
FORMAL derange
E arrange, tidy

disarray *n*
disorder, confusion, chaos, mess, muddle, disorganization, clutter, untidiness, dishevelment, unruliness, unsettledness, jumble, indiscipline, tangle, upset
COLLOQ. shambles
E order

disassemble *v*
dismantle, take apart, pull apart, separate, pull/take to pieces
E assemble, put together

disassociate *v*
dissociate, separate, cut off, remove, withdraw, break

disaster *n*
calamity, catastrophe, misfortune, reverse, reversal, adversity, tragedy, blow, accident, act of God, cataclysm, debacle, mishap, misadventure, setback, failure, fiasco, ruin, stroke, trouble, mischance, ruination, mucker, sticky end; *N Am* providence
OLD shipwreck
COLLOQ. flop, washout, wipeout, holocaust, horror story
SLANG screw-up
E success, triumph

disastrous *adj*
calamitous, catastrophic, cataclysmic, devastating,
ravaging, ruinous, tragic, unlucky, unfortunate, adverse,
dreadful, dire, terrible, appalling, shocking, destructive,
harmful, injurious, ill-fated, ill-starred, fatal, miserable
⊟ successful; *formal* auspicious

disavow *v*
repudiate, deny, disown, contradict, reject
FORMAL renounce, disaffirm, abjure
COLLOQ. wash your hands of

disavowal *n*
repudiation, denial, contradiction, rejection, dissent
FORMAL renunciation, disaffirmation, abjuration

disband *v*
disperse, break up, scatter, dismiss, demobilize, part
company, separate, dissolve, go separate ways
COLLOQ. demob
⊟ assemble, gather, muster

disbelief *n*
unbelief, incredulity, doubt, scepticism, questioning,
suspicion, distrust, mistrust, discredit, rejection
FORMAL dubiety
⊟ belief, conviction

disbelieve *v*
discount, discredit, repudiate, reject, distrust, mistrust,
suspect, question, doubt, be unconvinced
COLLOQ. take something with a pinch of salt
⊟ believe, trust, give credence to, accept

disbeliever *n*
doubter, agnostic, atheist, unbeliever, non-believer,
questioner, sceptic, scoffer, doubting Thomas
FORMAL nullifidian
⊟ believer

disbelieving *adj*
incredulous, unbelieving, unconvinced, sceptical, cynical,
suspicious, uncertain, doubtful, doubting, distrustful

disburse *v*
pay out, spend, lay out
FORMAL expend
COLLOQ. fork out, shell out, dish out, cough up

disbursement *n*
payment, outlay, spending, expenditure
FORMAL disbursal, disposal

disc *n*
1 CIRCLE, face, plate, ring, round, saucer, counter, discus
2 RECORD, album, LP, CD, vinyl, gramophone record
3 DISK, diskette, hard disk, floppy disk, compact disk, CD-
ROM, microfloppy

discard *v*
reject, abandon, dispose of, get rid of, throw away, throw
out, jettison, dispense with, cast aside, toss out, drop,
scrap, shed, remove, relinquish, repudiate
FORMAL forsake
COLLOQ. ditch, dump, chuck away/out
⊟ retain, adopt

discern *v*
perceive, make out, observe, detect, recognize, see, get,
tell (from), pick out, ascertain, notice, determine, discover,
spot, distinguish, differentiate, judge, discriminate
OLD scerne, wit
FORMAL descry

discernible *adj*
perceptible, noticeable, detectable, appreciable, distinct,
distinguishable, observable, recognizable, visible,

apparent, manifest, clear, obvious, plain, conspicuous,
patent, discoverable
⊟ imperceptible

discerning *adj*
discriminating, perceptive, astute, prudent, clear-sighted,
sensitive, shrewd, wise, ingenious, intelligent, clever,
quick, sharp, subtle, penetrating, acute, piercing, critical,
selective, tasteful, eagle-eyed, sound
FORMAL sagacious, judicious, perspicacious, percipient,
sapient
⊟ dull, obtuse

discernment *n*
judgement, discrimination, perception, perceptiveness,
acuteness, clear-sightedness, shrewdness, wisdom,
sharpness, ingenuity, insight, intelligence, cleverness,
understanding, awareness, acumen, keenness, (good) taste,
penetration
FORMAL ascertainment, percipience, perspicacity, sagacity

discharge *v, n*
♦ *v*
1 LIBERATE, free, set free, let go, pardon, release, clear,
absolve, acquit, relieve, dismiss
FORMAL exonerate, exculpate
2 *discharge from employment*
remove, dismiss, expel, get rid of, discard, oust, eject
COLLOQ. sack, fire, turf out, boot out, give the boot to,
give the elbow, give someone their marching orders, give
someone their cards/jotters, give someone the heave-ho,
axe
3 FULFIL, carry out, perform, do
FORMAL dispense
4 FIRE, shoot, let off, detonate, explode, set off
5 *discharge fumes*
emit, let off/out, give off, send out, pour, release, exude,
ooze, leak, disgorge, gush
FORMAL excrete, disembogue
6 *discharge a debt*
settle, pay, clear, honour, satisfy, meet
⊟ 1 detain **2** appoint, hire **3** neglect
♦ *n*
1 LIBERATION, release, acquittal, clearance, absolution
FORMAL exoneration, exculpation
2 *discharge from employment*
dismissal, removal, expulsion, ousting, cashiering
COLLOQ. sacking, the sack, firing, the boot, the elbow, the
heave-ho
3 EMISSION, secretion, ejection, flow, leak, exuding, release,
pus
FORMAL excretion, suppuration
4 FULFILMENT, accomplishment, performance, carrying-out,
doing, execution, achievement
5 *discharge of a debt*
settling, payment, repayment, clearance, honouring
⊟ 1 confinement, detention **2** hiring, appointment **3**
absorption **4** neglect

disciple *n*
follower, convert, proselyte, adherent, believer, devotee,
supporter, upholder, learner, pupil, student, votary

disciplinarian *n*
authoritarian, (hard) taskmaster, autocrat, stickler, despot,
tyrant, martinet

discipline *n, v*
♦ *n*
1 TRAINING, direction, control, regulation, exercise, drill,
practice, routine, regimen
2 PUNISHMENT, correction
FORMAL chastisement, castigation
3 STRICTNESS, control, self-control, self-discipline, restraint,
self-restraint, regulation, orderliness
4 SUBJECT, area of study, field of study, course of study,
branch, speciality
⊟ 3 indiscipline

♦ v

1 TRAIN, instruct, drill, teach, educate, exercise, break in, ground
FORMAL inculcate, inure
2 CHECK, keep in check, control, keep under control, curb, correct, restrain, govern, regulate, limit, restrict
3 PUNISH, chasten, rebuke, reprove, penalize, correct, reprimand, make an example of, teach someone a lesson
OLD disple
FORMAL chastise, castigate

disclaim v
deny, disown, repudiate, abandon, reject, decline, refuse
FORMAL renounce, abjure, disavow
COLLOQ. wash your hands of
🖃 accept, confess

disclaimer n
denial, repudiation, rejection, contradiction
FORMAL renunciation, abjuration, abnegation, disavowal, disaffirmation, disownment, retraction

disclose v
make known, reveal, tell, confess, let slip, let drop, blurt out, relate, publish, broadcast, communicate, make public, expose, divulge, impart, betray, tell a tale, show, exhibit, uncover, unfold, lay bare, unveil, bring to light, develop, discover, evolve, open out, unlock, unrip
OLD propale; (Spenser) unhele, unheal
COLLOQ. let on, leak, blab, squeal, let the cat out of the bag, spill the beans, blow the gaff, blow the whistle, give the game away, take the wraps off
🖃 conceal

disclosure n
revelation, exposure, exposé, uncovering, publication, discovery, admission, confession, acknowledgement, announcement, broadcast, declaration, bringing to light, laying bare
FORMAL divulgence
COLLOQ. leak

discoloration n
blemish, stain, spot, streak, mark, patch, blot, blotch, splotch
TECHNICAL dyschroa, ecchymosis

discolour v
disfigure, fade, stain, soil, mark, mar, rust, streak, tarnish, tinge, weather

discomfit v
embarrass, disconcert, discompose, unsettle, demoralize, abash, confound, baffle, confuse, perplex, fluster, ruffle, frustrate, thwart, outwit
FORMAL perturb
COLLOQ. faze, rattle

discomfiture n
unease, uneasiness, embarrassment, confusion, abashment, discomposure, demoralization, frustration, disappointment, humiliation, chagrin

discomfort n
1 ACHE, pain, soreness, tenderness, hurt, twinge, pang, jet lag
TECHNICAL irritation, cardialgia
2 UNEASE, uneasiness, embarrassment, trouble, distress, disquiet, hardship, vexation, irritation, annoyance, misery, worry, apprehension, restlessness
FORMAL malaise
COLLOQ. hell, purgatory
3 INCONVENIENCE, difficulty, trouble, disadvantage, drawback, worry, nuisance, bother, irritation, annoyance
COLLOQ. hassle
🖃 **2** comfort, ease

discomposure n
unease, uneasiness, upset, agitation, restlessness, fluster, disturbance, anxiety, irritation, annoyance
FORMAL disquietude, inquietude, perturbation
🖃 formal composure

disconcert v
unsettle, disturb, confuse, upset, unnerve, put off/out, shake, alarm, startle, take aback, throw off balance, surprise, fluster, ruffle, bewilder, nonplus, embarrass, baffle, perplex, dismay
FORMAL perturb
COLLOQ. faze, rattle, throw, put someone's nose out of joint
SLANG N Am discombobulate

disconcerting adj
disturbing, confusing, upsetting, unnerving, unsettling, daunting, alarming, bewildering, distracting, embarrassing, awkward, baffling, perplexing, dismaying, bothersome
FORMAL perturbing
COLLOQ. off-putting

disconnect v
cut off, disengage, uncouple, sever, separate, detach, de-energize, unplug, undo, unhook, unhitch, part, divide, split
🖃 attach, connect, join, unite

disconnected adj
confused, incoherent, garbled, rambling, unco-ordinated, unintelligible, loose, wandering, irrational, disjointed, illogical, jumbled, mixed-up, abrupt, staccato
🖃 coherent, connected

disconnection n
separation, division, detachment, disengagement, uncoupling, severance, unplugging, undoing
🖃 connection, linking

disconsolate adj
desolate, dejected, dispirited, sad, melancholy, depressed, unhappy, wretched, miserable, despondent, gloomy, downcast, forlorn, inconsolable, low, low-spirited, down, crushed, heavy-hearted, hopeless, heartbroken, grief-stricken
COLLOQ. down in the dumps
🖃 cheerful, joyful

disconsolately adv
sadly, unhappily, miserably, wretchedly, desolately, dejectedly, despondently, inconsolably, heavy-heartedly
🖃 happily, cheerfully

discontent n
uneasiness, dissatisfaction, disquiet, disaffection, restlessness, fretfulness, unrest, impatience, vexation, regret, displeasure, misery, unhappiness, wretchedness
COLLOQ. fed-upness
🖃 content, satisfaction, happiness

> **QUOTATIONS**
> Now is the winter of our discontent / Made glorious summer by this son of York
>   WILLIAM SHAKESPEARE, Richard III

discontented adj
dissatisfied, disgruntled, unhappy, restless, inpatient, disaffected, miserable, wretched, exasperated, displeased, complaining
COLLOQ. fed up, browned off, cheesed off
SLANG pissed off
🖃 contented, satisfied, happy

discontinue v
stop, come to a stop, end, come to an end, cease, finish, break off, refrain, do away with, halt, drop, suspend, abolish, abandon, cancel, interrupt
FORMAL terminate
COLLOQ. quit, scrap
🖃 begin, continue, produce

discontinuity n
disjointedness, disconnectedness, incoherence, interruption, breach, break, disconnection, disruption, disunion, rupture
🖃 continuity, coherence

discontinuous *adj*
intermittent, broken, disconnected, fitful, interrupted,
irregular, sporadic, spasmodic, periodic, punctuated
E3 continuous

discord *n*
1 CONFLICT, disagreement, clashing, disunity,
incompatibility, difference, difference of opinion, dispute,
contention, friction, division, opposition, strife, split,
wrangling, argument, row, dissent
FORMAL dissension, discordance
2 DISCORD OF SOUNDS, disharmony, jangle, jangling,
jarring, harshness
TECHNICAL suspension
FORMAL dissonance, cacophony, inharmonicity
E3 1 concord, agreement **2** harmony

discordant *adj*
1 DISAGREEING, conflicting, at odds, at variance, opposing,
clashing, hostile, contradictory, differing, dissenting,
incompatible, inconsistent
FORMAL incongruous
2 DISSONANT, grating, jangling, jarring, harsh, strident,
sharp, flat
TECHNICAL atonal
FORMAL cacophonous, inharmonious
E3 1 agreeing **2** harmonious

discount *n, v*
♦ *n*
reduction, rebate, allowance, cut price, cut, concession,
deduction, mark-down
♦ *v*
1 DISREGARD, ignore, overlook, dismiss, disbelieve, pass
over, gloss over
COLLOQ. pooh-pooh
2 REDUCE, deduct, mark down, take off
COLLOQ. knock off, slash
E3 1 pay attention to, take notice of **2** increase

discourage *v*
1 DISHEARTEN, dampen, damp, dispirit, depress,
demoralize, dismay, unnerve, put off, daunt, deject,
disappoint, cast down, chill, put a damper on
FORMAL discountenance
COLLOQ. pour/throw cold water on
2 DETER, dissuade, hinder, put off, restrain, prevent, hold
back, talk out of, advise against, choke off
E3 1 encourage, hearten **2** encourage, persuade

discouraged *adj*
disheartened, let down, deflated, dispirited, depressed,
demoralized, dejected, dismayed, downcast, glum,
pessimistic, daunted, dashed, crestfallen
COLLOQ. down in the dumps
E3 encouraged, heartened

discouragement *n*
1 DOWNHEARTEDNESS, despondency, pessimism, dismay,
depression, dejection, despair, disappointment,
hopelessness, gloom
2 DETERRENT, damper, setback, impediment, obstacle, curb,
barrier, disincentive, opposition, hindrance, restraint, rebuff
E3 1 encouragement **2** incentive

discouraging *adj*
disheartening, dispiriting, depressing, disappointing,
demoralizing, off-putting, unfavourable, dampening,
daunting
FORMAL dehortatory, dissuasive, dissuasory, inauspicious,
unpropitious
E3 encouraging, heartening

discourse *n, v*
♦ *n*
1 CONVERSATION, dialogue, chat, communication, talk,
discussion
FORMAL converse, colloquy, confabulation
COLLOQ. chit-chat

2 SPEECH, address, lecture, sermon, essay, treatise,
dissertation, homily
FORMAL oration, disquisition
♦ *v*
converse, talk, speak, discuss, debate, confer, lecture,
preach, hold forth

discourteous *adj*
rude, bad-mannered, ill-mannered, impolite, boorish,
uncouth, disrespectful, unpleasant, offensive, ill-bred,
uncivil, unmannerly, ungracious, unceremonious,
impertinent, impudent, insolent, offhand, curt, brusque,
abrupt, short, gruff
E3 courteous, polite

discourteously *adv*
rudely, impolitely, disrespectfully, uncivilly, unpleasantly,
offensively, ungraciously, unceremoniously, impertinently,
impudently, insolently, offhandedly, curtly, brusquely,
abruptly, gruffly
E3 courteously, politely

discourtesy *n*
rudeness, bad manners, impoliteness, disrespectfulness, ill-
breeding, unmannerliness, ungraciousness, incivility,
impertinence, insolence, curtness, brusqueness, rebuff,
slight, snub, insult, affront
FORMAL indecorousness, indecorum
E3 courtesy, politeness

discover *v*
1 FIND OUT ABOUT, determine, realize, notice, make out,
recognize, perceive, see, spot, trace, discern, establish,
learn, detect, unmask, spy, come to know, fathom (out),
sound out, analyse
OLD espy
FORMAL ascertain, descry, excogitate
COLLOQ. twig, suss out, get wise to, rumble, get onto, get
wind of, hit on, smoke out
2 FIND, come across, uncover, unearth, dig up, disclose,
reveal, stumble across/on, turn up, come to light, ferret
out, light on, locate
3 ORIGINATE, invent, pioneer, devise, create, work out,
compose
E3 1 conceal, cover (up) **2** miss

discoverer *n*
explorer, finder, founder, pioneer, initiator, inventor,
originator, author, deviser, creator

discovery *n*
1 FINDING, determination, realization, recognition,
discernment, learning, disclosure, detection, revelation,
location
2 BREAKTHROUGH, find, finding(s), origination, introduction,
innovation, research, invention, devising, exploration,
pioneering

discredit *v, n*
♦ *v*
1 *discredit someone*
dishonour, degrade, defame, damage, disgrace, bring into
disrepute, give someone a bad name, run down, belittle,
slate, slander, slur, smear, tarnish, reproach, reflect (badly)
on, put in a bad light
FORMAL disparage, vilify, cast aspersions on
COLLOQ. rubbish, badmouth
SLANG slag (off)
2 *discredit a theory*
disprove, disbelieve, distrust, doubt, question, mistrust,
challenge, invalidate, deny, discard, reject, explode,
debunk, shake your faith in
FORMAL refute
E3 1 honour **2** believe
♦ *n*
dishonour, disrepute, censure, disgrace, blame, shame,
reproach, slur, stigma, smear, scandal, infamy, humiliation
FORMAL aspersion, opprobrium, ignominy
E3 honour, respect

discreditable *adj*
improper, dishonourable, disreputable, disgraceful, scandalous, blameworthy, shameful, infamous, degrading
FORMAL reprehensible
Ⓔ creditable

discreet *adj*
tactful, careful, diplomatic, cautious, prudent, delicate, reserved, guarded, wary, sensible, wise, considerate
FORMAL politic, judicious, circumspect
Ⓔ tactless, indiscreet

> **❗ discreet** or **discrete**?
> *Discreet* means 'prudent, cautious, not saying or doing anything that might cause trouble': *My secretary won't ask awkward questions; she's very discreet. Discrete* means 'separate, not attached to others': *a suspension of discrete particles in a liquid.*

discreetly *adv*
tactfully, carefully, diplomatically, cautiously, delicately, prudently, sensibly, wisely, considerately
FORMAL judiciously, circumspectly
Ⓔ tactlessly, indiscreetly

discrepancy *n*
inconsistency, difference, variance, variation, dissimilarity, deviation, divergence, disagreement, conflict, contradiction, inequality
FORMAL disparity, discordance, incongruity

discrete *adj*
separate, distinct, detached, disconnected, unattached, individual, discontinuous, disjoined
FORMAL disjunct

> **❗ discrete** or **discreet**?
> *See panel at* **discreet**.

discretion *n*
1 TACT, diplomacy, caution, wisdom, discernment, judgement, good sense, care, carefulness, prudence, reserve, consideration, wariness, guardedness
FORMAL judiciousness, circumspection volition, predilection
2 CHOICE, freedom, preference, will, wish, desire, inclination
Ⓔ 1 indiscretion

> **PROVERBS**
> Discretion is the better part of valour

discretionary *adj*
optional, voluntary, elective, open
Ⓔ fixed, mandatory, compulsory, automatic

discriminate *v*
1 DISTINGUISH, differentiate, discern, tell apart, tell/recognize the differences, draw/make a distinction, segregate, separate
2 BE PREJUDICED, show prejudice, be biased, victimize, treat differently, treat unfairly, be intolerant
Ⓔ 1 confuse, confound **2** favour

discriminating *adj*
discerning, fastidious, selective, critical, perceptive, particular, tasteful, keen, astute, shrewd, sensitive, cultivated

discrimination *n*
1 BIAS, prejudice, intolerance, unfairness, bigotry, favouritism, narrow-mindedness, inequity, segregation, racism, colour bar, sexism, male chauvinism, ageism, homophobia, heterosexism, classism, lookism, siz(e)ism
SLANG *N Am* Jim Crow
2 DISCERNMENT, judgement, acumen, perception, acuteness, insight, shrewdness, astuteness, penetration, subtlety, keenness, sensitivity, refinement, distinction, taste
OLD skill
FORMAL perspicacity
Ⓔ 1 equal opportunities

discriminatory *adj*
biased, prejudiced, favouring, inequitable, prejudicial, unfair, unjust, discriminative, partial, partisan, preferential, loaded, weighted, one-sided
Ⓔ fair, impartial, unbiased

discursive *adj*
rambling, digressing, wandering, wordy, long-winded, meandering, wide-ranging, circuitous, diffuse, verbose
FORMAL prolix
Ⓔ terse

discuss *v*
debate, talk about/over, confer, argue, consider, go into, weigh up, deliberate, converse, consult, exchange views on, canvass, examine, study, review, analyse, reason, handle, treat, critique, go into detail, deal with, thrash out, speak to, take up, agitate
TECHNICAL interplead
OLD parley; *(Shakesp)* question
FORMAL discourse, confabulate, expostulate, pro and con
COLLOQ. kick about/around, knock about/around, put your heads together

> **SYNONYM NUANCES**
>
> **Debate** may be used of a more formal or official method of discussing various aspects, whilst **talk about/over** would be appropriately used of a more informal chat. **Confer** and **consult** might be used of seeking the opinions of others: *she had conferred with her lawyers,* unlike **argue**, which implies pushing personal opinions: *he argued for an increase in hospital funding.*
> The terms **consider**, **go into**, **weigh up** and **deliberate**, and the more explicit terms **examine**, **study** and **analyse** might be used where there is a thorough discussion and examination of all the facts. The word **review**, however, is reserved for looking again at a previous decision or practice: *the party will review its industrial relations policy,* while **reason** is best applied to discussion applying logic. Discussing with the aim of finding a solution or answering questions is suggested by the terms **handle**, **treat** and **deal with**: *training strategies should be handled at a local level; other civilizations will be treated in separate studies.* The more informal **thrash out** which also gives the impression of an exhaustive exchange.
> **Critique** and **agitate**, on the other hand, are suggestive of critical questioning with the purpose of raising problematic issues rather than solving them: *they had long been agitating for land reform.*

discussion *n*
debate, conference, argument, conversation, talk, talks, dialogue, exchange, consultation, forum, negotiations, deliberation, consideration, analysis, review, examination, study, scrutiny, seminar, symposium; *NZ* korero
OLD parley; *(Shakesp)* question
FORMAL discourse, colloquium
COLLOQ. powwow

disdain *n, v*
♦ *n*
scorn, contempt, arrogance, haughtiness, derision, sneering, dislike, snobbishness
FORMAL disparagement, deprecation, contumely
Ⓔ admiration, respect
♦ *v*
scorn, look down on, despise, slight, disregard, snub, ignore, reject, spurn, rebuff, turn down, belittle, sneer at, undervalue
FORMAL contemn, deride, disavow
COLLOQ. pooh-pooh, cold shoulder
Ⓔ admire, respect

disdainful *adj*
scornful, contemptuous, derisive, haughty, aloof, arrogant, supercilious, sneering, slighting, pompous, superior, proud, insolent

Diseases and disorders include:

Addison's disease	bubonic plague	encephalitis	Legionnaires' dis-	Paget's disease	severe acute
AIDS	bulimia	endometriosis	ease	Parkinson's disease	respiratory syn-
alopecia	cancer	enteritis	leprosy	peritonitis	drome (SARS)
Alzheimer's dis-	cerebral palsy	farmer's lung	leukaemia	pneumonia	shingles
ease	chickenpox	*colloq.* flu	lockjaw	poliomyelitis	silicosis
anaemia	cholera	foot-and-mouth	Lyme disease	psittacosis	smallpox
angina	cirrhosis	disease	malaria	psoriasis	swine flu
anorexia nervosa	coeliac disease	gangrene	mastoiditis	pyorrhoea	syphilis
anthrax	common cold	German measles	measles	rabies	tapeworm
arthritis	consumption	gingivitis	meningitis	rheumatic fever	tetanus
asbestosis	Creutzfeldt-Jakob	glandular fever	Ménière's disease	rheumatoid arthri-	thrombosis
asthma	disease (CJD)	glaucoma	motor neuron	tis	thrush
athlete's foot	Crohn's disease	gonorrhoea	disease	rickets	tinnitus
avian flu	croup	haemophilia	multiple sclerosis	ringworm	tuberculosis (TB)
autism	cystic fibrosis	hepatitis	(MS)	rubella	typhoid
Bell's Palsy	deep-vein throm-	herpes	mumps	scabies	typhus
beriberi	bosis (DVT)	Hodgkin's disease	muscular dystro-	scarlet fever	vertigo
bird flu	diabetes	Huntington's	phy	schistosomiasis	West Nile virus
Black Death	diphtheria	chorea	myalgic encepha-	schizophrenia	whooping cough
botulism	dropsy	hydrophobia	lomyelitis (ME)	scurvy	yellow fever
Bright's disease	dysentery	impetigo	nephritis	septicaemia	
bronchitis	eclampsia	influenza	osteomyelitis		
brucellosis	emphysema	Lassa fever	osteoporosis		

FORMAL disparaging
E∃ respectful

disease *n*
  illness, sickness, ill-health, infirmity, complaint, disorder,
  ailment, condition, disability, infection, contagion, epidemic
  FORMAL indisposition, malady, affliction
  COLLOQ. bug, virus
  E∃ health
  See panel above

diseased *adj*
  sick, ill, unhealthy, unwell, infirm, ailing, unsound,
  contaminated, infected, blighted
  E∃ healthy, well

disembark *v*
  land, arrive, dismount, leave, get off, step off
  FORMAL alight, debark, detrain, deplane
  E∃ embark

disembarkation *n*
  landing, arrival
  FORMAL alighting
  E∃ embarkation

disembodied *adj*
  bodiless, ghostly, phantom, spiritual, immaterial, intangible
  FORMAL incorporeal, discarnate, spectral

disembowel *v*
  disbowel, draw, embowel, gut, gralloch, paunch
  FORMAL eviscerate, exenterate

disenchanted *adj*
  disillusioned, disappointed, let down, discouraged,
  dissatisfied, jaundiced, cynical, soured, blasé, indifferent
  COLLOQ. fed up

disenchantment *n*
  disillusionment, disillusion, disappointment, dissatisfaction,
  cynicism, revulsion
  COLLOQ. fed-upness

disengage *v*
  disconnect, disunite, detach, loosen, free, extricate,
  withdraw, undo, unfasten, untie, uncouple, unhitch,
  unhook, remove, release, liberate, separate, disentangle
  E∃ connect, engage, unite

disengaged *adj*
  detached, liberated, loose, released, free(d), disentangled,
  separate(d), unattached, unconnected, unhitched
  E∃ connected, joined, united

disengagement *n*
  withdrawal, removal, taking away, detachment,
  disconnection, loosening, release, disentanglement, retreat,
  retirement

disentangle *v*
  1 LOOSE, release, free, extricate, disconnect, untangle,
  unwind, unfasten, disengage, detach, unravel, ravel out,
  unsnarl, untwist, undo, unknot, separate, unfold, straighten
  (out); *Scot* redd
  OLD debarrass
  FORMAL disinvolve
  2 RESOLVE, clarify, simplify, distinguish, separate,
  distance
  E∃ 1 entangle

disfavour *n*
  1 *fall into disfavour*
  unpopularity, discredit, disrepute
  FORMAL ignominy, opprobrium
  2 *look with disfavour at someone*
  dislike, disapproval, displeasure, distaste, dissatisfaction,
  disregard, low opinion
  FORMAL disapprobation, disesteem
  E∃ 1, 2 favour

disfigure *v*
  deface, blemish, mutilate, maim, scar,
  mar, deform, distort, damage, injure, ruin,
  spoil, flaw, make ugly
  E∃ adorn, embellish

disfigurement *n*
  blemish, defacement, defect, deformity, mutilation, scar,
  spot, blotch, stain, disgrace, impairment, injury, distortion,
  uglification
  OLD (*Shakesp*) defeature
  E∃ adornment

disgorge *v*
  discharge, empty, eject, expel, vomit, spew, spout, pour
  out, belch, regurgitate
  FORMAL effuse
  COLLOQ. throw up

disgrace *n, v*
  ♦ *n*
  shame, disrepute, disrespect, dishonour, contempt,
  discredit, disfavour, humiliation, loss of face, defamation,
  degradation, infamy, indignity, scandal, reproach, reproof,
  blot, slur, smear, stain, stigma, black mark

TECHNICAL atimy
OLD TECHNICAL disworship, villainy
FORMAL ignominy, debasement, disapprobation, opprobrium, obloquy, attainder
COLLOQ. skeleton in the cupboard
E3 honour, esteem
♦ v
shame, bring shame on, put to shame, dishonour, abase, defame, humiliate, cause to lose face, put someone's nose out of joint, blot someone's copybook, disfavour, degrade, debase, belittle, discredit, reproach, blame, slur, sully, taint, stain, stigmatize
OLD attaint, baffle, indignify, scandal, shend
FORMAL disparage, denigrate
COLLOQ. drag through the mud
E3 honour, respect

disgraced adj
discredited, shamed, dishonoured, humiliated, degraded, branded, stigmatized, under a cloud
COLLOQ. in the doghouse, in someone's black books
E3 honoured, respected

disgraceful adj
shameful, dishonourable, disreputable, scandalous, outrageous, despicable, contemptible, blameworthy, infamous, shocking, unworthy, dreadful, terrible, awful, appalling
FORMAL ignominious, culpable, reprehensible
E3 honourable, respectable

disgracefully adv
shamefully, dishonourably, disreputably, scandalously, outrageously, despicably, contemptibly, shockingly, dreadfully, terribly, awfully, appallingly
FORMAL ignominiously, reprehensibly
E3 honourably, respectably

disgruntled adj
discontented, dissatisfied, displeased, annoyed, exasperated, grumpy, irritated, peeved, peevish, resentful, sulky, sullen, testy, vexed, put out, petulant
FORMAL malcontent
COLLOQ. fed up, hacked off, cheesed off, browned off, brassed off
E3 pleased, satisfied

disguise n, v
♦ n
concealment, camouflage, cloak, cover, costume, mask, front, façade, face, masquerade, deception, misrepresentation, false picture, pretence, travesty, screen, veil, shroud
OLD visor
FORMAL coverture
♦ v
1 CONCEAL, cover, cover up, be under cover, camouflage, mask, hide, dress up, impersonate, cloak, screen, veil, shroud, colour, mantle, veneer, suppress, repress
OLD palliate, vizard; (Shakesp) immask
FORMAL dissemble, dissimulate
COLLOQ. put on a brave face
2 FALSIFY, deceive, pretend, misrepresent, gloss over, fake, fudge
FORMAL dissemble, feign
COLLOQ. cook the books, whitewash, put up a smokescreen, ring
E3 1 reveal, expose

QUOTATIONS
No mask like open truth to cover lies, / As to go naked is the best disguise
WILLIAM CONGREVE, The Double Dealer

disguised adj
camouflaged, cloaked, veiled, hidden, made up, masked, incognito, under cover, unrecognizable, fake, false
FORMAL covert, feigned

disgust v, n
♦ v
offend, displease, nauseate, revolt, sicken, repel, shock, outrage, put off, make your gorge rise
COLLOQ. turn off, turn your stomach
E3 delight, please
♦ n
revulsion, repulsion, repugnance, detestation, distaste, aversion, nausea, loathing, abhorrence, hatred, disapproval, displeasure

SYNONYM NUANCES
verb
Offend is a fairly mild term for hurting someone's sensibilities, whereas **displease** makes the even more restrained suggestion of doing something with which they are unhappy. The terms **nauseate**, **revolt** and **sicken**, however, are highly marked terms, suggestive of feelings of utmost abhorrence: *the whole country was revolted by the bombing*. **Repel**, while similar in the reaction it conveys, is slightly less emotive: *some were repelled by his reactionary views*. Both **shock** and **outrage** again are strong terms suggestive of profound feelings, this time suggesting disgust at the breaking of moral codes: *outraged by the scale of corruption*.
Put off is a much milder term to use and suggests being discouraged, often in a physical way: *they were put off the food by the smell of garlic*; whereas **make your gorge rise** returns to the idea of filling with loathing, and is strongly connotative of physical manifestations of disgust.

disgusted adj
repelled, repulsed, revolted, sickened, offended, appalled, outraged, put off
COLLOQ. up in arms
E3 attracted, delighted

disgusting adj
repellent, repulsive, revolting, repugnant, offensive, sickening, nauseating, nauseous, off-putting, odious, foul, unappetizing, unpalatable, distasteful, unpleasant, bad, vile, obscene, abominable, detestable, disgraceful, appalling, objectionable, nasty, shocking, outrageous
OLD ugsome
FORMAL rebarbative
COLLOQ. yucky, gross
E3 delightful, pleasant, acceptable

dish n, v
♦ n
plate, bowl, platter, food, fare, recipe, speciality, delicacy, course
■ **dish out**
distribute, give out, share out, hand out, hand round, pass round, dispense, dole out, allocate, mete out, inflict
■ **dish up**
serve, present, ladle, spoon, scoop, dispense, offer

disharmony n
conflict, clash, discord, friction, strife, incompatibility
FORMAL disaccord, discordance, dissonance
E3 harmony

dishearten v
discourage, dispirit, dampen, cast down, demoralize, depress, make depressed, dismay, dash, disappoint, deject, weigh down, daunt, crush, deter, put a damper on
E3 encourage, hearten

disheartened adj
discouraged, dispirited, downcast, depressed, disappointed, dismayed, downhearted, dejected, demoralized, daunted, crestfallen, crushed
E3 encouraged, heartened

dishevelled adj
tousled, unkempt, uncombed, untidy, bedraggled, messy, in a mess, ruffled, rumpled, slovenly, scruffy, disordered

FORMAL disarranged
COLLOQ. *Aust & NZ* daggy
◪ neat, tidy

dishonest adj
untruthful, fraudulent, deceitful, false, lying, deceptive, double-dealing, cheating, treacherous, untrustworthy, unscrupulous, unprincipled, swindling, corrupt, disreputable, dishonourable, crafty, cunning, sly, devious, irregular
FORMAL perfidious, mendacious, duplicitous
COLLOQ. crooked, shady, bent, shifty, fishy, iffy
◪ honest, trustworthy, scrupulous

SYNONYM NUANCES

Although many of these synonyms are marked by disapproval, **untruthful** is perhaps the least implicitly judgemental. **Fraudulent** carries strong implications of illegal activity, often with regard to money: *fraudulent benefit claims.* **False**, **deceptive**, and the more explicit **deceitful**, invariably suggest something deliberately misleading: *false news accounts of the war*; *the board ruled that the advertisement was deceptive.* The term **lying** makes an explicit accusation to this effect. **Double-dealing** suggests an element of treachery: *double-dealing spies*, whilst **cheating** and **treacherous** are explicit in their suggestion of a breach of trust.

Swindling is a disapprobatory term used in the context of tricking someone out of money, while **corrupt**, although similarly disapproving, can be used in wider contexts such as being amenable to questionable dealings, often for financial gain: *corrupt city officials allowed the supermarket to be built.* The term **disreputable** is rather milder, appropriately used of something known for unreliability: *a disreputable opportunist*, whilst **dishonourable** is more marked, and implies shameful behaviour: *the government is backing the cause for dishonourable reasons.*

Crafty, **cunning**, **sly** and **devious** would all hint at dishonesty, with an element of a sneaky cleverness which is by no means admirable: *a cunning ploy*; *devious schemes*, whereas **irregular** is an almost euphemistic term to describe something of questionable legitimacy: *this accounting practice is highly irregular and we will be consulting our lawyers.*

---

dishonestly adv
fraudulently, deceitfully, falsely, deceptively, treacherously, unscrupulously, corruptly, disreputably, dishonourably, deviously
FORMAL perfidiously
◪ honestly, scrupulously

dishonesty n
deceit, falsehood, falsity, fraudulence, fraud, criminality, insincerity, untruthfulness, treachery, cheating, double-dealing, corruption, unscrupulousness, trickery, chicanery, sharp practice, irregularity
FORMAL duplicity, improbity, perfidy
COLLOQ. crookedness, shadiness, dirty trick
◪ honesty, truthfulness

dishonour v, n
♦ v
1 *dishonour the family's name*
disgrace, shame, humiliate, debase, defile, wrong, degrade, defame, discredit, stain, sully, abuse, insult, offend, affront, demean, debauch
2 *dishonour an agreement/a cheque*
refuse, reject, turn down
◪ **1** honour **2** honour, accept
♦ n
disgrace, abasement, humiliation, shame, degradation, disrepute, infamy, indignity, reproach, slight, slur, scandal, stigma, insult, offence, outrage, abuse, discourtesy
OLD disworship

FORMAL discredit, ignominy, disfavour, aspersion, debasement, opprobrium
◪ honour

dishonourable adj
disreputable, unprincipled, unscrupulous, untrustworthy, unethical, unworthy, corrupt, discreditable, treacherous, scandalous, shameful, shameless, disgraceful, contemptible, despicable, infamous, ignoble
FORMAL ignominious, perfidious
COLLOQ. shady
◪ honourable

dishy adj
good-looking, attractive, charming, handsome
COLLOQ. gorgeous, hunky, sexy
◪ ugly

disillusion v, n
♦ v
disenchant, disappoint, undeceive
FORMAL disabuse
♦ n
disillusionment, disenchantment, disappointment

disillusioned adj
disenchanted, undeceived, disappointed, let-down
FORMAL disabused

disincentive n
deterrent, barrier, constraint, damper, determent, discouragement, dissuasion, hindrance, impediment, obstacle, repellent, restriction, turn-off
◪ encouragement, incentive

disinclination n
reluctance, unwillingness, hesitation, dislike, loathness, objection, opposition, resistance, alienation, averseness, aversion, repugnance
FORMAL antipathy
◪ inclination, enthusiasm

disinclined adj
reluctant, unwilling, resistant, indisposed, unenthusiastic, loath, opposed, hesitant
FORMAL averse
◪ inclined, willing, enthusiastic

disinfect v
sterilize, fumigate, sanitize, decontaminate, clean, cleanse, purify, purge
◪ contaminate, infect

disinfectant n
antiseptic, sterilizer, sanitizer, fumigant, decontaminant, bactericide, germicide

disingenuous adj
insincere, deceitful, dishonest, devious, designing, guileful, wily, sly, crafty, artful, cunning, two-faced, shifty, insidious, uncandid
FORMAL duplicitous, feigned
◪ artless, frank, ingenuous, naive

disingenuously adv
insincerely, deceitfully, dishonestly, deviously, slyly, cunningly, artfully, insidiously
◪ ingenuously, frankly, naively

disinherit v
cut off, reject, abandon, dispossess, impoverish, repudiate, cut someone out of your will
FORMAL renounce
COLLOQ. cut off without a penny, turn your back on

disintegrate v
break up, decompose, fall apart, break apart, crumble, rot, decay, moulder, separate, shatter, smash, splinter, fall to pieces

disintegration n
breakup, falling-apart, crumbling, decaying, separation, shattering, decomposition

disinter v
dig up, unearth, exhume, excavate, disentomb, unbury, uncover, expose, reveal, bring to light
FORMAL disinhume
⊟ bury

disinterest n
disinterestedness, impartiality, neutrality, detachment, unbiasedness, dispassionateness, fairness

disinterested adj
unbiased, neutral, impartial, objective, unprejudiced, dispassionate, detached, uninvolved, open-minded, fair, equitable, just, even-handed, unselfish
⊟ biased, prejudiced, concerned

> ⚠ **disinterested** or **uninterested**?
> *Disinterested* means 'not biased, not influenced by private feelings or selfish motives': *I think we need the opinions of a few disinterested observers*. *Uninterested* means 'not interested, not showing any interest': *uninterested in politics*.

disjointed adj
1 INCOHERENT, aimless, directionless, confused, disordered, loose, unconnected, bitty, wandering, rambling, spasmodic
2 DISCONNECTED, dislocated, divided, separated, disunited, displaced, broken, fitful, split, disarticulated
COLLOQ. bitty
⊟ **1** coherent

dislike n, v
♦ n
aversion, hatred, hostility, distaste, disapproval, disinclination, displeasure, resentment, animosity, antagonism, enmity, detestation, repugnance, disgust, loathing, down
OLD mislike
FORMAL disapprobation, disrelish, dyspathy, disfavour, disesteem, antipathy, animus
COLLOQ. allergy, thing, needle
SLANG *Aust* derry
⊟ liking; *formal* predilection
♦ v
hate, detest, object to, loathe, abhor, abominate, disapprove, regard with distaste, shun, despise, scorn, lump, take against; *Scot* take a scunner to
OLD defy, distaste, mind, mislike
FORMAL execrate, disfavour, disrelish, disesteem
COLLOQ. hate someone's guts, not stand the sight of, not be someone's cup of tea, be sick to the back teeth of, be no love lost between
SLANG *Aust* have a derry on
⊟ like, favour

> **SYNONYM NUANCES**
>
> *noun*
> The word **disapproval** is quite restrained and suggests an intellectual or moral dislike, while **distaste** implies a more instinctive element of recoiling: *a distaste for all that is foreign*. The term **aversion** suggests a much stronger disinclination, and **hatred**, **detestation**, **disgust** and **loathing** leave no room for doubt about its intensity: *an abiding loathing of racism*.
> **Displeasure** has an element of being annoyed at something, and while **resentment** also implies irritable feelings, these have more to do with a perceived injury or affront: *the promotions caused resentment among those who were passed over*.
> The terms **hostility**, **animosity**, **antagonism** and **enmity** all suggest an active expression of strong feelings against someone or something disliked: *public antagonism to the institution runs high*. The more informal **down**, on the other hand, is much less extreme, implying only unkind feelings: *the boy had a down on his school*.

dislocate v
1 *dislocate a bone*
disjoint, put out of joint/place, displace, misplace, twist, strain, sprain, pull, disengage, put out, disorder, shift, disconnect, disunite
TECHNICAL luxate
COLLOQ. do in
2 *dislocate plans*
disrupt, disturb, disorganize, confuse, throw into confusion

dislocation n
disruption, disturbance, disarray, disorder, disorganization
⊟ order

dislodge v
displace, eject, remove, oust, extricate, force out, shift, move, uproot

disloyal adj
treacherous, faithless, false, traitorous, deceitful, double-dealing, two-faced, unfaithful, untrue, unpatriotic
FORMAL apostate, perfidious
⊟ loyal, faithful, trustworthy, constant

disloyalty n
treachery, unfaithfulness, falseness, falsity, breach of trust, betrayal, treason, double-dealing, deceit, infidelity, adultery
FORMAL apostasy, inconstancy, perfidiousness, perfidy, sedition
⊟ loyalty, faithfulness

dismal adj
1 DREARY, gloomy, depressing, bleak, cheerless, dull, dark, dingy, drab, low-spirited, melancholy, desolate, sad, sombre, forlorn, despondent, miserable, sorrowful, hopeless, discouraging, glum
FORMAL lugubrious
COLLOQ. long-faced
2 *a dismal failure*
awful, terrible, bad, poor, frightful, dreadful, unsuccessful
COLLOQ. ropy, lousy, crummy, useless
SLANG naff, crappy
⊟ **1** cheerful, bright **2** good, successful

dismally adv
1 DREARILY, gloomily, sadly, despondently, miserably, darkly, drably
2 TERRIBLY, badly, frightfully, dreadfully, unsuccessfully
⊟ **1** happily, cheerfully **2** successfully, well

dismantle v
demolish, take apart, disassemble, strip (down), pull apart, separate, take to pieces
⊟ assemble, put together

dismay n, v
♦ n
alarm, distress, agitation, dread, fear, fright, horror, terror, discouragement, disappointment
FORMAL consternation, apprehension, trepidation
⊟ boldness, encouragement
♦ v
alarm, daunt, frighten, unnerve, unsettle, upset, shake, scare, put off, dispirit, cast down, distress, disconcert, disturb, shock, take aback, dishearten, discourage, disillusion, depress, horrify, appal, dread, worry, bother, concern, disappoint
OLD amate, heart-strike
FORMAL perturb, consternate
⊟ encourage, hearten

dismember v
disjoint, amputate, dissect, dislocate, mutilate, sever, divide, separate, break up, pull apart
⊟ assemble, join, unify

dismemberment n
dissection, mutilation, division, separation, breakup, amputation
⊟ assembly

dismiss *v*
1 *the class was dismissed*
discharge, free, let go, release, send away/off, remove, dissolve, drop, discord, banish
SLANG chassé
2 *dismiss employees*
make redundant, give notice, suspend, give someone their papers, lay off, discharge, relegate, expel, remove, cashier
COLLOQ. send packing, boot out, sack, fire, give someone their cards, give someone the sack/push/boot/elbow/bird/bum's rush/heave-ho, show someone the door
3 *dismiss it from your mind*
discount, disregard, banish, reject, repudiate, set aside, put away, put out of your mind, shelve, spurn, pour cold water on, brush aside/off
F3 1 retain, gather **2** appoint, hire **3** accept, think about

dismissal *n*
notice, redundancy, laying-off, discharge, removal, expulsion, marching-orders
COLLOQ. papers, sacking, firing, sack, push, boot, elbow, bird, bum's rush, heave-ho
F3 appointment, hiring

dismissive *adj*
contemptuous, disdainful, scornful, sneering, off-hand
FORMAL dismissory
F3 concerned, interested

dismissively *adv*
contemptuously, disdainfully, scornfully, sneeringly, off-handedly
F3 concernedly, interestedly

dismount *v*
descend, get down, get off
FORMAL alight, disembark, light, unmount
F3 mount

disobedience *n*
unruliness, waywardness, defiance, rebellion, wilfulness, contrariness, indiscipline, mutiny, revolt
OLD contumacity, contumacy
FORMAL infraction, insubordination, recalcitrance
F3 obedience

disobedient *adj*
unruly, wayward, defiant, rebellious, wilful, contrary, disorderly, obstreperous, naughty, mischievous
OLD contumacious
FORMAL froward, insubordinate, intractable, refractory, recalcitrant, recusant
F3 obedient

SYNONYM NUANCES

Unruly may be used to describe something unmanageable: *a drunk, unruly audience*, whilst **wayward** is perhaps less disapproving in tone in that it is more suggestive of being unpredictable or having lost your way: *he saw boarding school as a last chance for his wayward daughter*. **Defiant** would appropriately describe a person or actions resisting authority, while **rebellious** suggests openly flouting it, but both of these terms might be used with a hint at admiration: *a defiant sense of moral righteousness*. **Wilful**, on the other hand, may be used to suggest a less than admirable stubbornness: *her wilful refusal to go to school*, while **contrary** is similar in tone when describing something deliberately and troublesomely contradictory.

The term **disorderly** returns to the idea of being out of control: *disorderly conduct*, whilst **obstreperous** further suggests a noisy, rowdy element, but without the same tone of disapprobation. The word **naughty** is fairly mild and generally reserved for disobedient children, while **mischievous**, which further suggests an element of playfulness, may be applied to people of all ages with a hint that it is actually endearing: *he takes mischievous delight in baiting them*.

---

disobey *v*
infringe, go against someone's wishes, overstep, step out of line, flout, disregard, defy, ignore, resist, rebel
FORMAL contravene, violate, transgress
F3 obey, comply with

disobliging *adj*
unhelpful, unwilling, unco-operative, unaccommodating, awkward, disagreeable, discourteous, rude, uncivil, bloody-minded
F3 obliging, helpful

disorder *n*
1 CONFUSION, chaos, muddle, disarray, mess, untidiness, clutter, disorganization, disorderliness, jumble
COLLOQ. shambles
2 DISTURBANCE, unrest, tumult, riot, breach of the peace, confusion, disruption, commotion, uproar, fracas, brawl, fight, rumpus, rout, clamour, quarrel, brouhaha, mêlée
3 ILLNESS, complaint, disease, sickness, disability, ailment, condition
FORMAL affliction, malady
See panel at **disease**.
F3 1 neatness, order **2** law and order, peace

disordered *adj*
1 UNTIDY, messy, unkempt, confused, muddled, disorganized, jumbled, cluttered, upside-down
2 DISTURBED, deranged, confused, troubled, upset, maladjusted, unbalanced
F3 1 organized, tidy

disorderly *adj*
1 DISORGANIZED, confused, chaotic, irregular, messy, untidy, jumbled, cluttered, in disarray
COLLOQ. at sixes and sevens
SLANG fubar
2 UNRULY, undisciplined, unmanageable, uncontrollable, obstreperous, rowdy, rough, boisterous, tumultuous, turbulent, rebellious, wild, lawless, disobedient
FORMAL refractory
F3 1 neat, tidy **2** well-behaved

disorganization *n*
disarray, chaos, confusion, disorder, disruption, dislocation, untidiness, muddle
COLLOQ. shambles
F3 order, tidiness

disorganize *v*
disorder, disrupt, disturb, disarrange, muddle, upset, confuse, discompose, jumble, play havoc with, play hell with, dislocate, unstring, unsettle, break up, mess up, mix up, destroy
OLD unmechanize
F3 organize

disorganized *adj*
1 CONFUSED, disordered, haphazard, jumbled, muddled, chaotic, unsorted, unsystematized, topsy-turvy
COLLOQ. shambolic
2 UNMETHODICAL, unorganized, unstructured, undisciplined, unsystematic, careless, muddled
COLLOQ. untogether
F3 1 organized, tidy **2** organized, methodical

disorientate *v*
confuse, disorient, mislead, perplex, puzzle, upset, muddle
COLLOQ. faze

disorientated *adj*
disoriented, confused, bewildered, mixed up, muddled, perplexed, puzzled, unsettled, unbalanced, lost, adrift, astray, (all) at sea, upset

disorientation *n*
lostness, confusion, bewilderment, muddle, perplexity, puzzlement

disown *v*
repudiate, disclaim, deny, cast off, disallow, reject, turn your back on, abandon, unget
OLD reprobate

FORMAL renounce, forsake, disavow, abnegate, disacknowledge

▪ accept, acknowledge

disparage v
belittle, criticize, defame, slander, decry, slate, run down, degrade, detract from, disdain, discredit, dishonour, malign, ridicule, scorn, cry down, lessen, sell short, minimize, dismiss, underestimate, underrate, undervalue, depreciate, mock, slur, impeach
OLD disvalue; (Shakesp) disable
FORMAL denigrate, deprecate, deride, cast aspersions on, vilify, traduce, vilipend, derogate, calumniate
COLLOQ. knock, slam, rubbish
SLANG slag (off)
▪ praise

disparagement n
belittlement, condemnation, criticism, slander, contempt, denunciation, discredit, disdain, ridicule, scorn, debasement, degradation, detraction, underestimation
FORMAL derision, deprecation, aspersion, derogation, decrial, decrying, contumely, vilification
▪ praise

disparaging adj
derisive, derogatory, mocking, scornful, critical, insulting, dismissive
FORMAL deprecating, deprecatory, derisive
COLLOQ. snide, knocking
▪ flattering, praising

disparate adj
contrasting, different, dissimilar, unequal, unlike, contrary, diverse, distinct
FORMAL discrepant
▪ equal, similar

disparity n
difference, contrast, discrepancy, gap, gulf, dissimilarity, distinction, imbalance, inequality, inconsistency, unevenness, unlikeness, disproportion, bias, unfairness
FORMAL dissimilitude, incongruity, inequity
▪ equality, similarity, parity

dispassionate adj
detached, objective, impartial, neutral, disinterested, unbiased, unprejudiced, equitable, impersonal, fair, cool, calm, calm and collected, composed, unemotional, unexcited, self-possessed, self-controlled
▪ biased, emotional, involved

dispassionately adv
objectively, impartially, disinterestedly, fairly, equitably, impersonally, coolly, unemotionally, unexcitedly
▪ emotionally

dispatch, despatch v, n
♦ v
1 SEND, mail, post, courier, express, transmit, forward, consign, expedite, convey, remit, accelerate,
2 DISPOSE OF, finish, perform, discharge, conclude, settle, deal with
3 KILL, murder, execute, put to death, assassinate, slaughter
COLLOQ. bump off, knock off, do in
▪ 1 receive
♦ n
1 SENDING, mailing, posting, consignment, transmittal, forwarding
2 COMMUNICATION, message, report, bulletin, communiqué, news, letter, article, account, item, piece
3 PROMPTNESS, speed, expedition, celerity, haste, rapidity, swiftness
FORMAL alacrity, promptitude
▪ 3 slowness

dispel v
banish, drive away, chase away, get rid of, rid, dismiss, disperse, allay, eliminate, expel, rout, scatter, melt away
FORMAL dissipate, disseminate

dispensable adj
unnecessary, disposable, expendable, inessential, non-essential, replaceable, superfluous, needless, gratuitous, useless
▪ indispensable, essential

dispensation n
1 PERMISSION, exemption, exception, release, remission, relief, reprieve, immunity, licence
2 ISSUE, distribution, allocation, allotment, provision, handing out, sharing out
FORMAL apportionment, endowment, bestowal
3 SYSTEM, order, arrangement, plan, scheme, direction, administration, organization, authority, discharge, application
FORMAL economy

dispense v
1 DISTRIBUTE, pass round, give out, deal out, hand out, dole out, share out, apportion, allot, allocate, assign, share, divide out, mete out, bestow
FORMAL confer
2 ADMINISTER, carry out, apply, implement, issue, deliver, enforce, discharge, execute, operate
FORMAL effectuate

■ dispense with
dispose of, get rid of, abolish, do away with, do without, not need, discard, omit, disregard, give up, cancel, for(e)go, ignore, waive, relinquish
FORMAL rescind, revoke, renounce

dispersal n
scattering, breakup, breaking-up, dismissal, disbanding, separation, distribution
▪ gathering

disperse v
scatter, dispel, spread, distribute, diffuse, dissolve, break up, split up, melt away, thin out, dismiss, disband, separate, go their separate ways
FORMAL dissipate, disseminate
▪ gather

dispersion n
spreading, scattering, distribution, circulation, dispersal, diffusion, broadcast
TECHNICAL diaspora
FORMAL dissemination, dissipation

dispirit v
dishearten, discourage, deject, depress, dash, demoralize, dampen, damp, sadden, put a damper on, deter
▪ encourage, hearten

dispirited adj
disheartened, discouraged, dejected, depressed, demoralized, despondent, sad, downcast, cast down, crestfallen, gloomy, glum, morose, low
OLD (Shakesp) pale-hearted
COLLOQ. fed up, cheesed off, down, down in the dumps, brassed off, browned off
▪ encouraged

displace v
1 DISLODGE, move, shift, misplace, disturb, dislocate, relocate
2 DEPOSE, oust, remove, force out, dislodge, replace, dismiss, discharge, supplant, eject, expel, evict, succeed, supersede
COLLOQ. turf out, boot out

displacement n
disarrangement, dislodging, dislocation, shifting, moving, disturbance, misplacement
TECHNICAL ectopia, ectopy, heterotaxis, heterotopia
▪ order, arrangement

display v, n
♦ v
1 EXHIBIT, present, demonstrate, show, put on show, unveil, advertise, promote, publicize
2 BETRAY, disclose, reveal, show, expose
FORMAL evince, manifest

3 SHOW OFF, flourish, parade, flaunt, boast, blazon
F3 **1** conceal **2** disguise
♦ *n*
show, exhibition, exhibit, demonstration, presentation, parade, spectacle, pageant, array, revelation, evidence, disclosure
FORMAL manifestation, evincement

displease *v*
offend, annoy, irritate, anger, upset, dissatisfy, infuriate, provoke, exasperate, incense, irk, vex, disturb, discompose
OLD dislike, mislike, misplease, displeasure
FORMAL perturb
COLLOQ. put out, aggravate, bug
F3 please, satisfy

displeased *n*
annoyed, angry, exasperated, furious, infuriated, irritated, offended, upset, disgruntled, peeved, piqued
COLLOQ. aggravated, put out
F3 pleased

displeasure *n*
offence, annoyance, disapproval, irritation, resentment, discontentment, disfavour, dissatisfaction, disgruntlement, distaste, disgust, anger, exasperation, indignation, chagrin, ire, pique, wrath
FORMAL disapprobation, perturbation
F3 pleasure

disport *v*
divert, amuse, entertain, cheer, delight, play, revel, romp, frisk, frolic, cavort, gambol, sport

disposable *adj*
throwaway, expendable, replaceable, non-returnable, biodegradable

disposal *n*
1 ARRANGEMENT, grouping, ordering, order, positioning
2 CONTROL, direction, command
3 REMOVAL, riddance, getting rid of, throwing-away, clearance, discarding, jettisoning, scrapping
■ **at someone's disposal**
available, obtainable, at/to hand, ready
COLLOQ. on tap

dispose *v*
1 *dispose of a problem*
deal with, decide, settle, determine, finish, attend to, see to, handle, tackle, look after, take care of, sort out, dismiss, dispatch, make short work of
COLLOQ. polish off, sew up, wrap up
2 *dispose of old books*
get rid of, discard, throw away/out, clear away/out, shed, scrap, destroy, jettison, clear out
COLLOQ. dump, get shot of, chuck out
3 *dispose troops*
arrange, align, group, place, position, plot, put, set, situate, order, organize, line up
OLD battle, dispone
4 *dispose of a person*
kill, murder, destroy, do away with, put to death
COLLOQ. do in, bump off
F3 **2** keep

disposed *adj*
liable, inclined, bent, prone, likely, apt, minded, subject, ready, prepared, willing, eager
FORMAL predisposed
F3 disinclined

disposition *n*
1 *a friendly disposition; a disposition to obey*
character, nature, temperament, inclination, make-up, bent, leaning, constitution, habit, mood, temper, spirit, humour, tendency, proneness
FORMAL predisposition, propensity, predilection, proclivity
COLLOQ. what makes someone tick
2 *the disposition of troops*
arrangement, alignment, placing, positioning, order, line-up, pattern, grouping, sequence, system

3 *the disposition of property*
distribution, giving-over, allocation, disposal, transfer, conveyance

dispossess *v*
deprive, take away, divest, strip, rob, eject, evict, expel, oust, dislodge
F3 give, provide

disproportion *n*
inequality, unevenness, imbalance, lopsidedness, discrepancy, inadequacy, insufficiency
FORMAL asymmetry, disparity, incommensurateness
F3 balance, equality

disproportionate *adj*
unequal, uneven, unbalanced, excessive, inordinate, unreasonable, out of proportion, undue
FORMAL incommensurate
F3 balanced; *formal* commensurate

disproportionately *adv*
unevenly, excessively, unreasonably, inordinately
FORMAL incommensurately

disprove *v*
rebut, discredit, invalidate, contradict, prove false, deny, expose, give the lie to
OLD refel, reprove
FORMAL refute, negate, controvert, confute
COLLOQ. debunk
F3 confirm, prove

disputable *adj*
arguable, debatable, questionable, controversial, doubtful, dubious, uncertain, moot
FORMAL litigious
F3 indisputable, unquestionable

disputation *n*
debate, argument, discussion, argumentation, controversy, dispute, deliberation, polemics
TECHNICAL quodlibet
FORMAL dissension

disputatious *adj*
argumentative, contentious, polemical, quarrelsome, cantankerous, captious
FORMAL litigious, pugnacious

dispute *v, n*
♦ *v*
argue, debate, question, call into question, contend, challenge, contest, discuss, doubt, contradict, deny, quarrel, clash, wrangle, bicker, squabble, wrestle, have words, moot, differ, cross swords, spar; *Scot* threap
TECHNICAL litigate, plea
OLD discept
FORMAL altercate, controvert, gainsay, traverse
F3 agree
♦ *n*
argument, debate, disagreement, controversy, conflict, contention, contest, quarrel, row, wrangle, feud, turf war, spat, strife, squabble, variance, odds, tilt, tug-of-love; *Scot* cangle
TECHNICAL litigation
OLD controverse, disceptation
FORMAL altercation
F3 agreement, settlement

disqualification *n*
ban, bar, prohibition, veto, elimination, disentitlement, ineligibility
FORMAL preclusion

disqualified *adj*
banned, eliminated, ineligible, struck off
FORMAL debarred, precluded, disentitled
F3 accepted, eligible, qualified

disqualify *v*
1 *disqualified from the competition*
ban, bar, rule out, declare ineligible, eliminate, prohibit, suspend, strike off

FORMAL preclude, disentitle, debar
2 INCAPACITATE, disable, invalidate, immobilize, handicap, debilitate
FORMAL impair
⊟ 1 qualify, accept

disquiet *n, v*
♦ *n*
anxiety, worry, concern, unease, nervousness, uneasiness, restlessness, alarm, distress, agitation, fretfulness, fear, foreboding, anguish, dread, disturbance, upset, trouble
FORMAL disquietude, inquietude, perturbation
⊟ calm, reassurance
♦ *v*
worry, make anxious, unsettle, make uneasy, unnerve, discompose, distress, agitate, annoy, bother, trouble, upset, concern, disturb, fret, shake, ruffle, harass, pester, plague, vex
FORMAL incommode, perturb
COLLOQ. hassle
⊟ calm, reassure

disquieting *adj*
worrying, distressing, upsetting, disturbing, anxious, unsettling, unnerving, trying, troublesome
FORMAL perturbing
COLLOQ. nail-biting
⊟ reassuring

disquisition *n*
explanation, dissertation, paper, essay, thesis, treatise, monograph, sermon
FORMAL discourse, exposition

disregard *v, n*
♦ *v*
1 IGNORE, overlook, discount, neglect, take no notice of, pass over, gloss over, disobey, flout, make light of, set aside, brush aside, put/rule out of court, oversee, close your eyes to, set at naught
OLD omit, waive
FORMAL dispense with
COLLOQ. turn a blind eye to, laugh off, smile at, bend
2 SLIGHT, affront, offend, snub, shun, insult, despise, disdain
FORMAL disparage, denigrate, disoblige
COLLOQ. cold-shoulder, give the go-by to, walk all over
⊟ 1 heed, pay attention to, listen to **2** respect
♦ *n*
neglect, negligence, carelessness, inattention, oversight, indifference, disrespect, contempt, disdain, sacrilege, desperation
OLD (*Shakesp*) non-regardance
FORMAL denigration, disesteem
COLLOQ. brush-off, cold shoulder
⊟ attention, heed, notice

disrepair *n*
dilapidation, deterioration, decay, collapse, ruin, rack and ruin, shabbiness
⊟ good repair

disreputable *adj*
1 DISGRACEFUL, discreditable, dubious, suspicious, dishonourable, unprincipled, unrespectable, notorious, infamous, scandalous, outrageous, shameful, unworthy, base, contemptible, corrupt, low, mean, shocking, louche
FORMAL ignominious, opprobrious
COLLOQ. shady, shifty, dodgy
2 SCRUFFY, shabby, seedy, unkempt, slovenly, untidy, dishevelled
⊟ 1 honourable, respectable **2** smart

disrepute *n*
disgrace, dishonour, shame, disfavour, discredit, disreputation, infamy
FORMAL disesteem, ignominy, obloquy
⊟ honour, esteem

disrespect *n*
impoliteness, disregard, discourtesy, incivility, irreverence, rudeness, dishonour, contempt, scorn, insolence, impertinence, impudence, cheek
FORMAL misesteem
⊟ respect, politeness, civility, consideration

disrespectful *adj*
rude, discourteous, inconsiderate, impertinent, impolite, impudent, insolent, uncivil, unmannerly, cheeky, insulting, irreverent, contemptuous
COLLOQ. N Am sassy
⊟ polite, respectful, civil, considerate

disrespectfully *adv*
rudely, discourteously, impertinently, impolitely, impudently, insolently, uncivilly, cheekily, insultingly, irreverently, contemptuously
⊟ politely, respectfully

disrobe *v*
undress, unclothe, take off, divest, bare, uncover, strip, remove, shed, denude
FORMAL disapparel
⊟ cover, dress

disrupt *v*
disturb, disorganize, confuse, cause confusion in, interfere with, interrupt, butt in, break up, unsettle, intrude, upset, throw into confusion/disorder/disarray, disarrange, dislocate, hamper, impede, sabotage
COLLOQ. throw a spanner in the works, put a spoke in someone's wheel
SLANG screw up

disruption *n*
disorder, disordering, confusion, disorganization, turmoil, disarray, disorderliness, disturbance, interference, interruption, stoppage, upheaval, upset

disruptive *adj*
troublesome, unruly, undisciplined, obstreperous, troublemaking, disorderly, boisterous, noisy, turbulent, distracting, disturbing, unsettling, upsetting
⊟ well-behaved, manageable

dissatisfaction *n*
discontent, displeasure, dislike, discomfort, disappointment, disapproval, frustration, restlessness, anger, annoyance, irritation, exasperation, unhappiness, regret, resentment, vexation, chagrin
FORMAL disapprobation, disaffection, malcontentedness
COLLOQ. fed-upness
⊟ satisfaction

dissatisfied *adj*
discontented, displeased, disgruntled, disappointed, disillusioned, disenchanted, frustrated, angry, annoyed, irritated, exasperated, unfulfilled, unhappy, unsatisfied
FORMAL disaffected, malcontent, malcontented
COLLOQ. fed up, cheesed off, brassed off, browned off
SLANG pissed off
⊟ fulfilled, satisfied

dissatisfy *v*
displease, disappoint, let down, discontent, disgruntle, anger, annoy, irritate, exasperate, frustrate, put out, vex

dissect *v*
1 DISMEMBER, cut up, vivisect
FORMAL anatomize
2 ANALYSE, break down, investigate, scrutinize, examine, inspect, study, probe, explore, pore over

dissection *n*
1 dismemberment, cutting up, vivisection
TECHNICAL autopsy, necropsy
2 analysis, breakdown, investigation, scrutiny, examination, inspection, study, probe, exploration
Related adjective: prosectorial

dissemble v
feign, pretend, hide, conceal, disguise, simulate, camouflage, cloak, mask, counterfeit, fake, falsify, sham, play possum
FORMAL affect, dissimulate
COLLOQ. cover up
E3 admit

dissembler n
pretender, deceiver, liar, hypocrite, impostor, trickster, charlatan, fake, feigner, fraud, whited sepulchre
FORMAL dissimulator
COLLOQ. con man

disseminate v
circulate, distribute, spread, broadcast, scatter, sow, diffuse, disperse, publish, publicize, propagate, proclaim
FORMAL promulgate

dissemination n
circulation, distribution, spread, spreading, broadcasting, publishing, publication, diffusion, dispersion, propagation
FORMAL promulgation

dissension n
disagreement, discord, dissent, dispute, contention, argument, conflict, strife, friction, quarrel, variance, difference of opinion
E3 agreement

dissent v, n
♦ v
disagree, differ, protest, object, dispute, refuse, quibble
OLD disconsent
FORMAL demur
E3 assent
♦ n
disagreement, difference, dissension, discord, disharmony, friction, dispute, difference of opinion, controversy, resistance, opposition, objection, protest
E3 agreement, conformity

dissenter n
dissident, objector, protestant, protester, demonstrator, nonconformist, disputant, rebel, recusant, heretic, revolutionary, sectary, schismatic
FORMAL dissentient

dissentient adj
disagreeing, dissenting, dissident, opposing, nonconformist, protesting, conflicting, differing, rebellious, heretical, revolutionary, recusant
E3 arguing

dissertation n
thesis, treatise, critique, essay, monograph, paper
TECHNICAL prolegomena, propaedeutic
FORMAL discourse, disquisition, exposition

disservice n
disfavour, injury, wrong, bad turn, harm, hurt, unkindness, injustice, sharp practice
COLLOQ. dirty trick, con trick, kick in the teeth
E3 favour

dissidence n
disagreement, discordance, dispute, dissent, feud, recusancy, rupture, schism, variance
E3 agreement, peace

dissident adj, n
♦ adj
disagreeing, differing, discordant, nonconformist, opposing, protesting, conflicting, rebellious, heretical, revolutionary
FORMAL dissenting, heterodox
E3 acquiescent, orthodox
♦ n
dissenter, protester, objector, nonconformist, rebel, agitator, revolutionary, heretic, schismatic, recusant
E3 assenter

dissimilar adj
unlike, unalike, different, divergent, deviating, unrelated, contrasting, incompatible, mismatched, distinct, diverse, varying, various
TECHNICAL bifacial, hemimorphic
FORMAL disparate, heterogeneous
COLLOQ. like chalk and cheese
E3 similar, like, alike

dissimilarity n
unlikeness, difference, discrepancy, divergence, distinction, unrelatedness, contrast, incomparability, diversity, variety, incompatibility
FORMAL disparity, dissimilitude, heterogeneity
E3 compatibility, similarity

dissimulate v
pretend, hide, lie, fake, conceal, mask, cloak, disguise, camouflage
FORMAL feign, dissemble, affect
COLLOQ. cover up

dissipate v
1 *he dissipated his inheritance*
spend, waste, exhaust, squander, use up, expend, consume, lavish, drain, deplete, fritter away, burn up, run/get through
COLLOQ. blow, splurge, spend (money) like there was no tomorrow
2 *the clouds dissipated*
disperse, drive away, scatter, break up, vanish, disappear, dispel, diffuse, evaporate, dissolve, melt away
E3 1 accumulate **2** appear, gather

dissipated adj
dissolute, debauched, abandoned, self-indulgent, rakish, wasted, corrupt, wild, depraved, degenerate
FORMAL intemperate, profligate, licentious
E3 conserved, virtuous, upright

dissipation n
1 *the dissipation of all fears*
dispersal, diffusion, evaporation, disappearance, squandering, expenditure, consumption, depletion
2 DEBAUCHERY, extravagance, licence, immorality, abandonment, self-indulgence, excess, prodigality, corruption, depravity
FORMAL intemperance, licentiousness
E3 1 conservation **2** virtue

dissociate v
1 *dissociate one thing from another*
separate, detach, break off/up, disunite, disassociate, disengage, disconnect, cut off, sever, disband, set apart, divorce, disrupt, isolate, segregate
2 *dissociate yourself from something*
distance, disconnect, cut off, break off, withdraw, disassociate, separate
FORMAL secede
COLLOQ. quit
E3 associate, join

dissociation n
separation, detachment, break, division, divorce, disconnection, disengagement, dissevering, distancing, disassociation, segregation, isolation, setting apart, cutting-off, severance, severing, split
FORMAL disunion
E3 association, union

dissolute adj
dissipated, debauched, degenerate, depraved, wanton, self-indulgent, abandoned, corrupt, immoral, lewd, rakish, unrestrained, wild
FORMAL intemperate, profligate, licentious
E3 restrained, virtuous

dissolution n
1 *the dissolution of an organization/a marriage*
ending, breakup, conclusion, suspension, divorce, annulment
FORMAL termination, discontinuation

2 *the dissolution of the monarchy*
break-up, destruction, overthrow
FORMAL cessation
3 *dissolution of family life*
break-up, disintegration, collapse, decomposition,
separation, division, disposal, evaporation, disappearance

dissolve v
1 *sugar dissolves in water*
liquefy, melt, go into solution, digest
TECHNICAL deliquesce, solvate
OLD TECHNICAL discandy
2 *the marriage/partnership dissolved*
end, bring to an end, finish, break up, divorce, unmarry,
annul, disintegrate, wind up, dismiss, disband, separate,
disperse, solve
FORMAL terminate, discontinue, rescind, revoke, nullify,
invalidate
3 *my fears gradually dissolved*
disappear, vanish, evaporate, disperse, dwindle, melt
away, crumble
FORMAL dissipate, evanesce
4 *dissolve into tears*
collapse, be overcome with, lose control, break, burst,
begin, start

dissonance n
discord, clash, disagreement, dissension, difference,
incompatibility, inconsistency, variance, disharmony,
discordance, discrepancy, harshness, jangle, stridency,
grating, jarring, cacophony
FORMAL inharmoniousness, disparity, incongruity
E3 harmony, agreement

dissonant adj
discordant, clashing, jarring, disagreeing, jangling, grating,
differing, harsh, incompatible, irregular, inconsistent,
irreconcilable, raucous, strident, cacophonous, unmusical,
tuneless, unmelodious
FORMAL inharmonious, anomalous, incongruous
E3 compatible, harmonious

dissuade v
deter, discourage, put off, stop, persuade not to, talk out
of, prevent, disincline
OLD discounsel
FORMAL dehort
COLLOQ. nobble
E3 persuade

dissuasion n
discouragement, deterrence, deterring, caution
FORMAL expostulation, remonstrance, remonstration,
dehortation
E3 persuasion

distance n, v
♦ *n*
1 SPACE, interval, gap, separation, extent, stretch, range,
reach, span, length, width, breadth, depth, height
2 REMOTENESS, farness, inaccessibility
3 ALOOFNESS, reserve, coolness, coldness, remoteness,
formality, unfriendliness, detachment, stiffness
E3 **1** closeness **2** accessibility **3** approachability, closeness,
warmth
♦ *v*
separate, cut off, dissociate, disassociate, remove,
withdraw, break, detach
FORMAL secede

> **QUOTATIONS**
> The distance does not matter; it is only the first step that
> counts
> MARQUISE DU DEFFAND

distant adj
1 FAR, faraway, far-flung, far-off, out-of-the-way, remote,
outlying, isolated, abroad, dispersed
COLLOQ. back of beyond

2 *a distant relative*
not close, slight, remote, indirect
3 ALOOF, cool, reserved, formal, cold, unfriendly,
restrained, detached, stiff, unapproachable,
uncommunicative, unresponsive, antisocial, withdrawn
COLLOQ. stand-offish
4 *a distant expression in her eyes*
detached, distracted, absent-minded, blank, preoccupied,
faraway, dreamy, daydreaming
FORMAL vacant
E3 **1** close, nearby **2** close **3** approachable, warm

distantly adv
1 FAR AWAY, a long way, great/some distance
COLLOQ. miles
2 VAGUELY, slightly, imprecisely, faintly, dimly
3 UNEMOTIONALLY, coolly, formally, coldly, stiffly,
unresponsively, vacantly
4 *distantly related*
remotely, not closely
E3 **1** near **2** distinctly **3** emotionally **4** closely

distaste n
dislike, aversion, disgust, revulsion, repugnance, horror,
loathing, abhorrence, disfavour, displeasure
FORMAL antipathy
E3 liking

distasteful adj
disagreeable, offensive, displeasing, unpleasant, disgusting,
revolting, objectionable, repellent, repulsive, repugnant,
obnoxious, undesirable, uninviting, unsavoury,
unpalatable, detestable, loathsome, abhorrent
E3 pleasing

distend v
bloat, swell, dilate, enlarge, expand, fill out, inflate, bulge,
balloon, puff, stretch, widen
TECHNICAL intumesce
E3 deflate, contract, shrink

distended adj
bloated, swollen, dilated, enlarged, expanded, inflated,
puffed-out, puffy, stretched, astrut
TECHNICAL emphysematous, tumescent, varicose
E3 deflated, shrunken

distension n
swelling, bloating, enlargement, expansion, extension,
spread, dilation
TECHNICAL emphysema, intumescence, tumescence

distil v
vaporize, evaporate, condense, extract, press out, draw out,
derive, express, drip, trickle, leak, flow, purify, refine, still
TECHNICAL rectify, sublimate

distillation n
extract, extraction, evaporation, condensation, purification,
essence, spirit

distinct adj
1 CLEAR, plain, evident, obvious, clear-cut, apparent,
manifest, marked, defined, well-defined, sharp, definite,
noticeable, recognizable, unambiguous, unmistakable
2 SEPARATE, different, detached, individual, dissimilar,
unconnected, unassociated
FORMAL discrete, disparate
E3 **1** indistinct, vague

> **!** **distinct** or **distinctive**?
> *Distinct* means 'definite', 'clearly or easily seen, heard,
> smelt, etc': *a distinct smell of alcohol; a distinct*
> *Scottishness in her pronunciation*. *Distinctive* means
> 'characteristic', 'distinguishing one person or thing from
> others': *She has a very distinctive walk; the distinctive*
> *call of a barn owl.*

distinction n
1 DIFFERENTIATION, discrimination, discernment, separation,
difference, dissimilarity, division, contrast
FORMAL contradistinction, dissimilitude

2 EXCELLENCE, renown, fame, celebrity, prominence, eminence, importance, significance, reputation, greatness, honour, prestige, repute, superiority, worth, merit, credit, quality
FORMAL consequence
3 CHARACTERISTIC, peculiarity, individuality, feature, quality, mark
E3 2 unimportance, obscurity

distinctive adj
characteristic, distinguishing, individual, peculiar, different, typical, unique, particular, special, original, noteworthy, extraordinary, idiosyncratic
FORMAL singular
E3 ordinary, common

! distinctive or **distinct**?
See panel at **distinct**.

distinctiveness n
individuality, peculiarity, uniqueness, originality, noteworthiness, extraordinariness, idiosyncrasy
FORMAL singularity

distinctly adv
clearly, plainly, obviously, evidently, definitely, markedly, decidedly, noticeably, unmistak(e)ably, manifestly, unambiguously

distinguish v
1 DIFFERENTIATE, tell apart, tell from, set apart, discriminate, determine, tell the difference between, single out, mark off, divide, characterize, particularize, typify, mark, stamp, categorize, classify, signalize
FORMAL contradistinguish, secern
2 DISCERN, perceive, identify, ascertain, make out, recognize, see, detect, notice, pick out, discriminate, judge
FORMAL descry
3 *distinguish yourself academically*
excel, do well, acquit yourself well, bring fame to, bring honour to, bring acclaim to, glorify, dignify, ennoble

distinguishable adj
recognizable, discernible, clear, plain, plainly seen, evident, noticeable, conspicuous, obvious, manifest, perceptible, appreciable, observable
E3 indistinguishable

distinguished adj
famous, eminent, celebrated, well-known, famed, acclaimed, illustrious, prominent, notable, noted, renowned, honoured, esteemed, outstanding, striking, marked, extraordinary, noble, aristocratic, refined, conspicuous
E3 insignificant, obscure, unimpressive
See Synonym nuances panel at **eminent**.

distinguishing adj
differentiating, different, distinctive, individual, individualistic, marked, peculiar, typical, characteristic, unique, discriminative, discriminatory
FORMAL singular, diacritical

distort v
1 DEFORM, contort, bend, misshape, disfigure, pull about, rack, twist, jumble, screw up, warp, buckle, hamper, torment, torture, wrench, wrest, wring; *Scot* thraw
OLD detort, writhe
2 FALSIFY, misrepresent, pervert, slant, twist, bias, colour, garble, mangle, tamper with, fudge, skew
COLLOQ. cook the books

distorted adj
1 DEFORMED, bent, misshapen, out of shape, disfigured, twisted, warped, awry, skew, skewed, wry; *Scot* thrawn
2 FALSE, falsified, biased, perverted, misrepresented
E3 1 straight **2** accurate

distortion n
1 DEFORMITY, twist, bend, buckle, contortion, crookedness, skew, slant, warp
2 MISREPRESENTATION, falsification, perversion, bias, twisting, colouring, garbling

distract v
1 DIVERT, sidetrack, deflect, draw away, turn aside/away, put off
2 AMUSE, occupy, divert, entertain, engross
3 CONFUSE, disconcert, bewilder, confound, disturb, perplex, puzzle, fluster, discompose

distracted adj
1 DISTRAUGHT, agitated, anxious, overwrought, upset, distressed, grief-stricken, beside yourself, worked up, frantic, hysterical, raving, mad, wild, crazy
2 *their attention was distracted*
abstracted, wandering, absent-minded, preoccupied, inattentive, dreaming
COLLOQ. miles away, not with it
E3 1 calm, untroubled **2** attentive

distracting adj
disturbing, disconcerting, confusing, bewildering, unsettling, annoying, irritating
FORMAL perturbing
COLLOQ. off-putting

distraction n
1 DISTURBANCE, interrupted, diversion, interference, confusion
FORMAL derangement
2 DIVERSION, amusement, entertainment, game, sport, hobby, pastime, recreation, divertissement
■ **drive to distraction**
upset, annoy, anger, madden, exasperate
COLLOQ. drive crazy, get someone's blood up, make your blood boil

distraught adj
agitated, anxious, overwrought, upset, worried, distressed, distracted, beside yourself, worked up, frantic, hysterical, raving, mad, wild, crazy
COLLOQ. in a state, het up
E3 calm, untroubled

distress n, v
♦ n
1 ANGUISH, grief, misery, sorrow, heartache, suffering, discomfort, torment, wretchedness, sadness, worry, anxiety, unease, desolation, pain, agony, torture
FORMAL woe, tribulation, affliction, perturbation
2 ADVERSITY, hardship, poverty, need, danger, destitution, calamity, misfortune, trouble, difficulties, trial
FORMAL peril, privation, indigence, penury
E3 1 content **2** comfort, ease
♦ v
upset, cause suffering to, grieve, disturb, trouble, sadden, make miserable, worry, make anxious, pain, vex, torment, harass, harrow, hurt, agonize, break someone's heart
FORMAL afflict, perturb
COLLOQ. cut up
E3 comfort

distressed adj
upset, hurt, troubled, worried, disturbed, dismayed, unsettled, discomposed, put out, bothered, aggrieved
FORMAL perturbed
COLLOQ. in a state, uptight, worked up
E3 calm

distressing adj
upsetting, worrying, alarming, disturbing, unsettling, off-putting, disconcerting, frightening, startling
FORMAL perturbing
E3 comforting

distribute v
1 DISPENSE, allocate, give out, hand out, pass out/round, dole out, dish out, ladle (out), part, serve out, share, deal (out), divide, measure out, mete out, carve, allot, issue, assort, dispose, digest; *N Am* prorate
FORMAL apportion
2 DELIVER, supply, hand out, spread, issue, circulate, pass round, transmit
TECHNICAL reticulate

3 SCATTER, diffuse, disperse, discharge
FORMAL disseminate
F3 2 collect

distribution *n*
1 DELIVERY, supply, transport, transportation, dealing, handling, conveyance
2 ALLOCATION, giving-out, handing-out, division, sharing; *N Am* proration
FORMAL apportionment
3 CIRCULATION, spreading, scattering, dispersal
FORMAL dissemination
4 ARRANGEMENT, grouping, classification, organization, placement, position
F3 1 collection

district *n*
region, area, quarter, neighbourhood, locality, sector, precinct, zone, block, parish, place, locale, community, vicinity, ward, constituency, domain, territory, shire, county, province, municipality, suburb, belt, bounds, circumscription, patch, pale, hunt, walk, *faubourg, quartierbarrio; N Am* section
TECHNICAL circuit

distrust *v, n*
♦ *v*
mistrust, doubt, have doubts about, disbelieve, suspect, be suspicious of, question, be sceptical about, discredit, be wary of
F3 trust
♦ *n*
mistrust, doubt, doubtfulness, disbelief, suspicion, misgiving, wariness, scepticism, question, questioning, qualm, chariness, discredit
F3 trust, confidence, faith

> **QUOTATIONS**
> We have to distrust each other. It's our only defence against betrayal
> TENNESSEE WILLIAMS, *Camino Real*

distrustful *adj*
mistrustful, distrusting, doubtful, doubting, dubious, disbelieving, suspicious, wary, sceptical, untrustful, untrusting, chary, uneasy, cynical
F3 trustful, unsuspecting

disturb *v*
1 DISRUPT, interrupt, put off, distract, bother, butt in on, break someone's train of thought, pester
2 AGITATE, trouble, unsettle, upset, distress, worry, make anxious, shake, fluster, annoy, bother, concern, discompose, disquiet, fret, disconcert, dismay, stir, vex, infest, racket, ruffle, touch; *Scot* mismake, sturt
OLD affray, commove, rouse, distrouble, inquiet, tumult
FORMAL discomfit, perturb, concuss
COLLOQ. beat up, turn up, hassle
3 DISARRANGE, disorder, confuse, upset, disorganize, dislocate, muddle, unsettle, throw into confusion; *Scot* jee
F3 2 reassure **3** order

disturbance *n*
1 DISRUPTION, agitation, interference, interruption, distraction, intrusion, upheaval, upset, confusion, disorder, muddle, annoyance, bother, trouble, hindrance
FORMAL inquietude
COLLOQ. hassle
2 DISORDER, uproar, commotion, tumult, turmoil, fracas, fray, brawl, riot, row, rumpus, hullabaloo, racket; *Scot* sturt
3 *emotional disturbance*
illness, sickness, disorder, complaint, neurosis
F3 1 peace **2** order

disturbed *adj*
1 *disturbed by the news*
anxious, apprehensive, bothered, concerned, troubled, worried, upset, confused, discomposed, uneasy, flustered
OLD inquiet

2 *emotionally disturbed*
troubled, maladjusted, neurotic, unbalanced, unstable, dysfunctional, psychotic, mentally ill, paranoid, upset
COLLOQ. screwed-up, hung-up
F3 1 calm

disturbing *adj*
alarming, distressing, troubling, unsettling, upsetting, worrying, disconcerting, bewildering, confusing, dismaying, disquieting, discouraging, agitating, frightening, startling, threatening
FORMAL disturbant, disturbative, perturbing
F3 reassuring, comforting

disunited *adj*
divided, split, separated, disrupted, alienated
FORMAL estranged
F3 unify

disunity *n*
disagreement, conflict, discord, division, dissension, dissent, rupture, schism, split, strife, party spirit, alienation, breach
FORMAL estrangement, discordance
F3 unity

disuse *n*
neglect, abandonment, decay
FORMAL desuetude, discontinuance
F3 use

disused *adj*
unused, neglected, idle, abandoned, decayed, obsolete
FORMAL discontinued
F3 used

ditch *n, v*
♦ *n*
trench, dyke, channel, canal, gully, gutter, furrow, moat, drain, level, watercourse, trough
♦ *v*
abandon, get rid of, throw away/out, discard, dispose of, drop, jettison, scrap
COLLOQ. dump, chuck

dither *v, n*
♦ *v*
hesitate, waver, vacillate, hang back, delay, falter, take your time
COLLOQ. be in two minds, shilly-shally, dilly-dally, faff about
♦ *n*
panic, indecision, bother, flutter, fluster
COLLOQ. flap, pother, stew, tizzy
F3 decision

divan *n*
couch, settee, sofa, sofa bed, chaise-longue, day bed, lounge, lounger, ottoman, chesterfield

dive *v, n*
♦ *v*
1 *dive into water*
plunge, jump, plummet, dip, submerge, leap, nose-dive, fall, drop, swoop, descend, go down/under, pitch, duck, sound
2 *dive for cover*
move quickly, leap, dash, rush, hurry, fly, tear, bolt
♦ *n*
1 PLUNGE, lunge, header, jump, leap, plummet, nose-dive, swoop, dash, spring, fall, drop, jackknife, tailspin
COLLOQ. belly-flop
2 *make a dive for the door*
leap, dash, rush, dart, bolt, spring
3 BAR, club, pub, saloon, nightclub
COLLOQ. dump, joint, hole

diverge *v*
1 DIVIDE, branch (off), fork, part, separate, spread (out), split, subdivide, radiate
TECHNICAL divaricate
FORMAL bifurcate

2 DIFFER, vary, disagree, dissent, conflict, clash, contradict, be at variance
3 DEVIATE, digress, stray, wander, depart, drift
FORMAL divagate
E3 **1** converge **2** agree

divergence n
difference, disagreement, variation, clash, conflict, deviation, separation, parting, deflection, departure, digression, branching-out
TECHNICAL divarication
FORMAL disparity
E3 agreement

divergent adj
different, differing, disagreeing, conflicting, dissimilar, variant, varying, separate, diverging, diverse, deviating, tangential
TECHNICAL divaricate
E3 similar

divers adj
varying, varied, various, different, many, numerous, several, some, miscellaneous, sundry
FORMAL manifold, multifarious

diverse adj
various, varied, varying, sundry, all means of, different, differing, assorted, mixed, unlike, dissimilar, contrasting, miscellaneous, separate, several, distinct
FORMAL manifold, discrete, heterogeneous
E3 similar, identical

diversification n
modification, alteration, extension, variation, branching-out, spreading-out
FORMAL variegation

diversify v
vary, change, expand, extend, branch out, bring variety to, spread out, modify, alter, mix, assort
FORMAL variegate

diversion n
1 DEVIATION, detour, alternative route, redirection, rerouteing, switching
2 AMUSEMENT, entertainment, distraction, hobby, pastime, recreation, relaxation, play, game, sport, fun, divertissement
3 ALTERATION, change, redirection, deviation

diversionary adj
distracting, deflecting, divertive

diversity n
variety, dissimilarity, difference, diversification, variance, assortment, miscellany, multifariousness, embroidery, range, mixture, medley
TECHNICAL biodiversity
FORMAL variegation, dissimilitude, pluralism, heterogeneity
E3 similarity, likeness

divert v
1 DEFLECT, redirect, reroute, switch, sidetrack, avert, distract, deflect, draw/turn away
2 AMUSE, entertain, occupy, distract, delight, interest, absorb, engross, intrigue

diverting adj
enjoyable, entertaining, amusing, fun, pleasant, pleasurable, funny, humorous, witty
E3 irritating

divest v
deprive, strip, remove, dispossess, undress, unclothe, disrobe
OLD doff
FORMAL denude, despoil
E3 clothe

divide v, n
♦ v
1 SPLIT, separate, sever, part, cut (up), break up/down, detach, bisect, disconnect, segregate, diverge, branch, fork
OLD cleave

2 DISTRIBUTE, share (out), allocate, deal out, allot, dispense, hand out, dole out, measure out
FORMAL apportion
3 DISUNITE, separate, alienate, segregate, split (up), break up, drive apart, come between, set someone against another, polarize
FORMAL estrange
4 CLASSIFY, group, sort (out), grade, arrange, order, rank, categorize, segregate
E3 **1** join **2** collect **3** unite
♦ n
division, gulf, gap, opening, separation, rift, split, breach, divergence

■ **divide up**
share (out), allocate, allot, dole out, measure out, parcel out
FORMAL apportion

dividend n
1 *shareholders' dividends*
share, bonus, portion, surplus, gain, percentage
COLLOQ. cut, divvy, whack
2 BENEFIT, bonus, extra, gain, advantage, plus
FORMAL perquisite
COLLOQ. perk

divination n
clairvoyance, divining, foretelling, prophecy, prediction, fortune-telling, dukkeripen, second sight, crystal-gazing, soothsaying, augury, -mancy, presage; *Scot* taghairm
FORMAL hariolation, prognostication, rhabdomancy
Related adjective: mantic

divine adj, n, v
♦ adj
1 GODLIKE, godly, superhuman, supernatural, mystical, celestial, heavenly, angelic, seraphic, saintly, spiritual
2 HOLY, sacred, sanctified, consecrated, hallowed, spiritual, transcendent, exalted, glorious, religious, supreme
3 DELIGHTFUL, beautiful, charming, lovely, wonderful, excellent, glorious, heavenly
E3 **1** human **2** mundane
♦ n
churchman, churchwoman, clergyman, clergywoman, minister, priest, pastor, parson, reverend, cleric, ecclesiastic, prelate, theologian
♦ v
guess, deduce, suppose, infer, surmise, suspect, understand, foretell, apprehend, perceive
FORMAL conjecture, intuit, prognosticate

divinely adv
1 *divinely inspired poetry*
heavenly, supernaturally, mystically, celestially, angelically, spiritually
2 *a divinely beautiful girl*
delightfully, charmingly, wonderfully, excellently, gloriously
E3 **1** humanly

diviner n
clairvoyant, astrologer, augur, oracle, prophet, seer, visionary, crystal-gazer, soothsayer, haruspex, sibyl, water-finder, dowser
OLD divinator

divinity n
1 *worship a divinity; claims to divinity*
god, goddess, deity, divineness, godliness, holiness, sanctity, godhead, spirit
2 THEOLOGY, religious studies, religious education, religious knowledge, religion

division n
1 SEPARATION, dividing (up), detaching, parting, cutting (up), disunion, severance
2 BREACH, rupture, split, schism, rift, disunion, disunity, disagreement, feud, discord, conflict, alienation, difference of opinion
FORMAL estrangement
3 DISTRIBUTION, sharing (out), allotment, allocation

FORMAL apportionment
4 SECTION, group, sector, segment, part, department, category, class, subsection, compartment, branch, arm
5 BOUNDARY, divide, dividing-line, frontier, border, partition, demarcation line
E3 **1** union **2** unity **3** collection **4** whole

divisive adj
alienating, damaging, injurious, disruptive, troublesome, troublemaking, inharmonious, schismatic
FORMAL discordant, estranging
E3 harmonious, unifying

divorce n, v
♦ n
dissolution, annulment, break-up, split-up, split, rupture, separation, breach, division, partition, disunion, severance
TECHNICAL talaq
OLD divorcement
♦ v
separate, part, annul, break up, split up, sever, dissolve, divide, detach, dissociate, disconnect, disunite, isolate
OLD repudiate
COLLOQ. bust up, put away
E3 marry, unite

divulge v
reveal, disclose, make known, tell, communicate, broadcast, publish, proclaim, confess, declare, let slip, betray, expose, uncover
FORMAL impart, promulgate
COLLOQ. leak, break the news, let the cat out of the bag, spill the beans, blow the gaff, put your cards on the table

dizziness n
giddiness, faintness, light-headedness
FORMAL vertiginousness
COLLOQ. wooziness

dizzy adj
1 GIDDY, faint, light-headed, wobbly, shaky, reeling, off-balance, weak at the knees, with your head swimming
FORMAL vertiginous
COLLOQ. woozy
2 CONFUSED, bewildered, dazed, muddled; dialect mazy
3 a dizzy blonde
silly, irresponsible, foolish, feather-brained, scatterbrained
COLLOQ. rattle-brained, airheaded, addle-headed; N Am ditsy

do v, n
♦ v
1 PERFORM, carry out, execute, accomplish, achieve, fulfil, implement, complete, discharge, undertake, work, put on, present, produce, end, finish, put into practice
FORMAL conclude, effectuate
2 BEHAVE, act, conduct yourself, acquit yourself
FORMAL comport yourself
3 do the tea
prepare, get ready, fix, organize, arrange, deal with, look after, take care of, manage, be in charge of, be responsible for, produce, make, create, cause, proceed
4 Will this do?
be enough, be adequate, be sufficient, be satisfactory, fit the bill, satisfy, serve
FORMAL suffice
5 What do you do?
have as a job, work as, be employed as, earn a living as
6 do something about a problem
try to solve, deal with, work out, find the answer to, sort out, resolve, figure out, tackle
COLLOQ. crack, get to the bottom of; N Am dope (out)
7 do French at school
study, learn, master, read, work at/on, take, major in
8 do deliveries for you
provide, supply, furnish, offer
9 do 150 kph
travel at, go at, reach, achieve

10 do well/badly; How are you doing?
get on, get along, come on, come along, fare, progress, develop, manage, make a good/bad job of
11 do the crossword
solve, work out, figure out, resolve, puzzle out
COLLOQ. N Am dope (out)
12 do the sitting room
clean (up), decorate, tidy (up)
COLLOQ. do up, tart up
13 do your hair
arrange, style, adjust, wash, comb, brush
COLLOQ. fix
14 do Paris
visit, tour, go round, sightsee, explore, travel round
15 CHEAT, defraud, swindle, trick, deceive, dupe, fleece, hoodwink
COLLOQ. con, have
SLANG rip off, take for a ride
♦ n
function, affair, event, gathering, party, reception, celebration, soirée, occasion
COLLOQ. bash, knees-up, rave-up
■ **do away with**
1 GET RID OF, discard, dispose of, abolish, annul, remove, eliminate
FORMAL discontinue, nullify
2 KILL, murder, put to death, finish off, slaughter, slay, exterminate, assassinate
COLLOQ. do in, knock off, bump off
■ **do down**
critcize, condemn, blame, censure, belittle, find fault with
FORMAL disparage
COLLOQ. slam, rubbish, badmouth
SLANG slag (off)
■ **do in**
kill, murder, put to death, slaughter, slay, exterminate, assassinate
COLLOQ. knock off, bump off
■ **do out of**
prevent from having, deprive of, cheat out of, trick out of, swindle out of, fleece
COLLOQ. con out of, diddle out of
■ **do up**
1 FASTEN, tie (up), lace, button, zip up, pack
2 RENOVATE, redecorate, decorate, restore, modernize, repair, refurbish, recondition
■ **do without**
go without, manage without, give up, dispense with, deny yourself, refrain
FORMAL for(e)go, eschew, abstain from, relinquish
■ **dos and don'ts**
rules, regulations, code, instructions, standards, customs, etiquette

---

SYNONYM NUANCES

verb sense 1
Perform, **carry out** and **execute** are fairly straightforward synonyms for seeing something through; **discharge** too could be used of successfully meeting objectives, often in an official capacity: he discharged his duties well.
    Accomplish suggests a successful completion, with an element of satisfaction involved. **Achieve** likewise implies reaching a successful and satisfying outcome, while **fulfil**, although similar, is more suggestive of meeting all the original goals: he fulfilled his campaign promise. **Implement** and **put into practice**, on the other hand, have more to do with putting something into effect: the Act is due to be implemented fully by April. The terms **put on** and **undertake** put the focus on setting about a task rather than its completion, and **undertake** suggests a commitment to seeing it through: we undertook to restore the cathedral. **Work** would be used where some kind of labour is involved: she worked in accountancy.

You might choose to use **present** or **produce** if what is being done involves causing or creating: *the proposals presented difficulties*; *we have produced the relevant data*.

docile *adj*
tractable, co-operative, manageable, submissive, obedient, compliant, amenable, willing, controllable, controlled, obliging, yielding, dutiful
E3 truculent, unco-operative

docilely *adv*
amenably, willingly, obediently, compliantly, obligingly, co-operatively, dutifully
E3 unco-operatively

docility *n*
amenability, tractability, manageability, submissiveness, obedience, compliance, biddableness, meekness, pliability, pliancy
FORMAL complaisance, ductility
E3 truculence, unco-operativeness

dock¹ *n, v*
♦ *n*
the ship is in dock
harbour, wharf, quay, boat yard, pier, waterfront, jetty, marina
♦ *v*
anchor, moor, drop anchor, land, berth, put in, tie up

dock² *v*
1 *dock an animal's tail*
crop, clip, cut, shorten, curtail, truncate
2 *dock someone's pay*
deduct, reduce, lessen, withhold, decrease, subtract, remove, diminish

docket *n, v*
♦ *n*
certificate, ticket, label, receipt, tab, tag, bill, chit, chitty, counterfoil, coupon, voucher, tally, document, documentation, paperwork
♦ *v*
label, mark, tab, tag, ticket, register, record, document, catalogue, file, index

doctor *n, v*
♦ *n*
physician, medical officer, consultant, clinician
OLD (*Shakesp*) medicine
COLLOQ. doc, medic
SLANG bones, sawbones, quack
♦ *v*
1 ALTER, tamper with, interfere with, falsify, misrepresent, pervert, adulterate, change, disguise, dilute, massage, manipulate
COLLOQ. fiddle, cook
2 CONTAMINATE, drug, weaken, lace, add drugs/poison to, adulterate
COLLOQ. spike
3 STERILIZE, castrate, spay, neuter

QUOTATIONS
Who shall decide when doctors disagree?
ALEXANDER POPE, *Moral Essays*

Types of medical doctor include:

consultant	hospital doctor	registrar
dentist	houseman	resident
family doctor	intern	veterinary surgeon
family practitioner	locum	*colloq.* vet
general practi- tioner (GP)	medical officer (MO)	

See also **medical specialists**; **surgeon**.

doctrinaire *adj*
dogmatic, inflexible, rigid, insistent, opinionated, pedantic, biased, fanatical
E3 flexible

doctrine *n*
dogma, creed, belief, tenet, principle, teaching, precept, conviction, opinion, canon, credo

document *n, v*
♦ *n*
paper, certificate, deed, record, proof, evidence, report, form, charter, writ
TECHNICAL affidavit
FORMAL instrument
♦ *v*
1 RECORD, put on record, keep on record, commit to film/paper, write down, report, write up, chronicle, list, detail, register, cite, chart
2 SUPPORT, back up, prove, verify, give weight to
FORMAL corroborate, substantiate, validate

documentary *adj*
documented, recorded, chronicled, detailed, charted, written, factual

documentation *n*
paperwork, papers, record, authority, verification, evidence, qualifications

doddering *adj*
decrepit, weak, aged, feeble, frail, infirm, elderly, tottering

doddery *adj*
unsteady, shaky, weak, faltering, doddering, tottering, tottery, staggering, feeble, infirm, aged
E3 hale, youthful

dodge *v, n*
♦ *v*
1 AVOID, elude, evade, swerve, jump away, bypass, get out of, get round, side-step, shirk, shun, shift, steer clear of, fend off, veer
COLLOQ. duck
2 MOVE SUDDENLY, duck, dive, dart, dash, rush, bolt
♦ *n*
trick, ruse, ploy, wile, scheme, stratagem, manoeuvre, device, contrivance, subterfuge, deception, sharp practice
FORMAL machination
COLLOQ. *Aust & NZ* slinter
SLANG *Aust* lurk

dodger *n*
evader, avoider, shirker, trickster, slacker, layabout, dreamer
COLLOQ. lead-swinger, skiver, slyboots, lazybones
SLANG *N Am* goldbricker, goof-off

dodgy *adj*
1 SUSPECT, doubtful, dubious, unreliable, disreputable
COLLOQ. fishy, iffy; *Aust & NZ* crook
2 CHANCY, risky, dangerous, unsafe, unreliable, uncertain, fraught, problematical
COLLOQ. dicey
E3 1 honest **2** reliable

doer *n*
achiever, activist, organizer, worker, accomplisher, executor, bustler, dynamo
COLLOQ. go-getter, live wire, powerhouse, mover and shaker
E3 thinker, contemplatist

doff *v*
take off, discard, remove, shed, throw off, lift, raise, tip, touch
E3 don

dog *n, v*
♦ *n*
1 *cats and dogs*
hound, cur, mongrel; *NZ* kuri; canine, puppy, pup, bitch
COLLOQ. mutt, pooch
SLANG *Aust* tripehound

Related adjective: canine
See panel below
2 VILLAIN, scoundrel, rascal, rogue, wretch
♦ *v*
pursue, follow, trail, track, tail, hound, shadow, stalk, plague, harry, haunt, trouble, worry

> **PROVERBS**
> Give a dog a bad name and hang him
> You can't teach an old dog new tricks
> Let sleeping dogs lie
> Barking dogs seldom bite

> **QUOTATIONS**
> There will always be a lost dog somewhere that will prevent me being happy
> JEAN ANOUILH, *La Sauvage*
>
> Let Hercules himself do what he may, / The cat will mew, and dog will have his day
> WILLIAM SHAKESPEARE, *Hamlet*

dogged *adj*
determined, resolute, persistent, persevering, intent, tenacious, firm, steadfast, staunch, single-minded, tireless, indefatigable, steady, unshak(e)able, stubborn, obstinate, relentless, unyielding, unflagging, unfaltering
FORMAL indomitable, obdurate, pertinacious
🖃 irresolute, apathetic

doggedly *adv*
resolutely, persistently, tenaciously, firmly, steadfastly, staunchly, single-mindedly, tirelessly, indefatigably, unshak(e)ably, stubbornly, obstinately, relentlessly
🖃 apathetically

doggedness *n*
determination, resolution, persistence, perseverance, tenaciousness, tenacity, firmness, steadfastness, steadiness, single-mindedness, stubbornness, obstinacy, relentlessness, endurance
FORMAL indomitability, pertinacity

dogma *n*
doctrine, creed, belief, precept, principle, code (of belief), article (of faith), credo, tenet, conviction, teaching, opinion, maxim

dogmatic *adj*
opinionated, assertive, affirmative, authoritative, canonical, positive, doctrinaire, domineering, dictatorial, doctrinal, categorical, emphatic, overbearing, arbitrary, insistent, arrogant, imperious, intolerant, authoritarian, ex cathedra, unquestionable, unchallengeable, pontifical
FORMAL peremptory

dogmatically *adv*
assertively, authoritatively, domineeringly, dictatorially, categorically, emphatically, insistently, arrogantly, intolerantly, imperiously

dogmatism *n*
opinionatedness, assertiveness, imperiousness, dictatorialness, bigotry, presumption, arbitrariness, positiveness
FORMAL peremptoriness

dogsbody *n*
gofer, drudge, slave, lackey, doormat, galley-slave, menial, factotum, maid-of-all-work, man-of-all-work
COLLOQ. skivvy
SLANG bitch

doings *n*
activities, actions, acts, exploits, feats, achievements, enterprises, deeds, events, goings-on, happenings, dealings, affairs, concerns, adventures, handiwork, proceedings, transactions

doldrums *n*
depression, dejection, downheartedness, gloom, melancholy, listlessness, low-spiritedness, apathy, boredom, tedium, dullness, inertia, stagnation, sluggishness, torpor
FORMAL ennui, lassitude, malaise, acedia
COLLOQ. blues, dumps

dole *n, v*
♦ *n*
benefit, Job Seekers Allowance (JSA), unemployment benefit, state benefit, social security, allowance, payment, income, credit, support
■ **dole out**
distribute, allocate, give out, hand out, dish out, apportion, allot, mete out, share (out), divide (up), deal (out), issue, ration, dispense, administer, assign
FORMAL apportion

doleful *adj*
cheerless, depressing, distressing, dismal, dreary, forlorn, gloomy, melancholy, miserable, wretched, sad, sorrowful, mournful, sombre, rueful, painful, pathetic, pitiful, woeful
FORMAL dolorous, lugubrious, woebegone, disconsolate
COLLOQ. blue, down in the dumps
🖃 cheerful

dolefully *adv*
gloomily, mournfully, unhappily, dismally, forlornly, miserably, wretchedly, sadly, pathetically
FORMAL disconsolately

doll *n, v*
♦ *n*
figure, puppet, marionette, plaything, toy, figurine, moppet, dolly, Barbie®, Sindy®
■ **doll up**
dress up, preen, primp, deck out, trick out, titivate
COLLOQ. tart up; *N Am* trick up

dollop *n*
lump, blob, clump, bunch, ball, glob, gob, gobbet

dolorous *adj*
anguished, distressing, melancholy, miserable, wretched, sad, sorrowful, doleful, grievous, harrowing, heart-rending, painful, mournful, rueful, sombre, woeful

---

Breeds of dog include:

Afghan hound	cairn terrier	fox terrier	komondor	poodle	shih tzu
Airedale	chihuahua	German Shepherd	Labradoodle	pug	springer spaniel
alsatian	chow	golden retriever	Labrador	Rottweiler	Staffordshire terrier
Australian terrier	cocker spaniel	Great Dane	lhasa apso	saluki	St Bernard
basset-hound	collie	greyhound	lurcher	*colloq.* Samoyed	terrier
beagle	corgi	husky	Maltese	sausage-dog	water spaniel
Border collie	dachshund	Irish (or red) setter	Norfolk terrier	schnauzer	West Highland
borzoi	Dalmatian	Irish wolfhound	Old English	*colloq.* Scottie	terrier
boxer	Doberman pin-	Jack Russell	sheepdog	Scottish terrier	*colloq.* Westie
bulldog	scher	Kerry Blue (terrier)	Pekingese	Sealyham	whippet
bull-mastiff	English terrier	King Charles	pit bull terrier	setter	wolfhound
bull terrier	foxhound	spaniel	pointer	sheltie	Yorkshire terrier

FORMAL lugubrious, woebegone
E∃ happy

dolour *n*
anguish, distress, grief, misery, sadness, sorrow, heartache, heartbreak, mourning, suffering, lamentation

dolt *n*
fool, idiot, imbecile, simpleton
COLLOQ. ass, blockhead, nincompoop, ninny, nitwit, numskull, twerp, dope, chump, clot, nutcase, twit, dimwit
SLANG wally, dipstick, nerd, plonker, dork, geek, git

domain *n*
1 DOMINION, kingdom, realm, territory, region, empire, estate, lands, province
2 FIELD, area, speciality, concern, section, arena, department, region, province, realm, sphere, world, discipline, jurisdiction

dome *n*
cupola, vault, rotunda, tholus, mound, hemisphere
TECHNICAL astrodome, brachydome, macrodome, tope

domestic *adj, n*
♦ *adj*
1 HOME, family, household, home-loving, stay-at-home, homely, domesticated, house-trained, tame, pet, private, personal
FORMAL domiciliary
2 INTERNAL, indigenous, native, national, home, local
3 DOMESTICATED, tame, tamed, pet, house-trained, broken (in)
E∃ 2 foreign, international, export 3 wild
♦ *n*
servant, maid, charwoman, char, help, daily help, domestic help, daily, au pair

domestically *adv*
internally, locally, at/near home, nationally, in private

domestic appliances
See panel below

domesticate *v*
tame, house-train, break, break in, train, accustom, familiarize, acclimatize, naturalize, assimilate
FORMAL habituate

domesticated *adj*
1 TAME, tamed, pet, house-trained, broken (in), domestic, naturalized
2 HOME-LOVING, homely, house-proud, housewifely, naturalized
E∃ feral, wild

domestication *n*
taming, house-training, breaking-in, training, naturalization, assimilation
FORMAL habituation

domesticity *n*
homemaking, housecraft, homecraft, housekeeping, home economics, domestic science, domestication

domicile *n, v*
♦ *n*
home, house, residence, lodging(s), residency, mansion, quarters, settlement
FORMAL abode, dwelling, habitation
♦ *v*
make your home, live, settle, establish, take up residence, put down roots

dominance *n*
supremacy, authority, power, command, pre-eminence, superiority, control, rule, domination, sway, leadership, mastery, government
FORMAL ascendancy, hegemony, paramountcy

dominant *adj*
1 AUTHORITATIVE, controlling, governing, ruling, presiding, powerful, all-powerful, strong, assertive, influential
2 PRINCIPAL, main, outstanding, chief, major, key, central, important, most important, predominant, overriding, primary, paramount, prime, prominent, leading, pre-eminent, supreme, prevailing, prevalent, commanding, besetting
E∃ 1 submissive 2 subordinate

SYNONYM NUANCES

sense 2
Principal and **main**, **chief** and **major** are fairly neutral terms, whilst **outstanding** and **paramount** imply superiority: *areas of outstanding beauty*. To convey the idea of something being necessary, you could use **key** and **central**: *the banks' participation was central to this bill*.
    Predominant implies enjoying a high position or great number: *the predominant life forms on the planet*. Similarly, **pre-eminent** and **supreme** imply that something has high status and is the most influential: *the world's pre-eminent expert on asbestos*. **Overriding**, however, is stronger in that it suggests having power over other elements or possibilities: *the overriding sentiment was for peace*. The term **commanding** is similar in its suggestion of a dominance that lends power or requires respect: *this win gives him a commanding lead*. **Primary** and **prime** might be used to convey the idea of coming first: *the primary cause of war; the prime suspect*.
    Prominent is a fairly restrained term to describe something that stands out in some way, but **leading** suggests being at the forefront and showing the way. To describe a dominant force whose influence may not be permanent, you might use **prevailing** or **prevalent**; the latter also suggests being widespread: *the prevailing arbiters of taste; nationalism is less prevalent now*.

Domestic appliances include:

FOR CLOTHES:		FOR PREPARING FOOD:	
clothes airer	cylinder cleaner	electric cooker	slow cooker
iron	floor polisher	electric grill	spit
steam iron	Hoover®	fan oven	stove
steam press	upright cleaner	gas stove	toaster
trouser press	vacuum cleaner	griddle	waffle iron
tumble-drier	wet-and-dry clea-	grill	
washer	ner	hob	
washing machine	FOR COOKING:	hotplate	
washer/drier	Aga®	kitchen range	
carpet shampooer	barbecue	microwave oven	
FOR FLOORS:	cooker	oven	
carpet sweeper	deep fryer	rotisserie	
	Dutch oven	sandwich maker	

FOR PREPARING FOOD:
blender
coffee mill
electric knife
electric tin opener
ice-cream maker
juicer
juice extractor
food processor
food slicer
kettle
knife sharpener
liquidizer
mixer
percolator
tea/coffee maker
timer
water filter
FOR COOLING:
deep-freeze
icebox
freezer
colloq. fridge
fridge/freezer
refrigerator
MISCELLANEOUS:
dishwasher
fire extinguisher
hostess-trolley
humidifier
ionizer

See also **kitchen utensils**.

dominate v

1 CONTROL, domineer, govern, preside, rule, direct, command, monopolize, predominate, master, lead, overrule, prevail, overbear, intimidate, tyrannize
FORMAL have ascendancy over
COLLOQ. have the upper/whip hand over, have under your thumb, have over a barrel, throw your weight around, wear the trousers, have on toast
SLANG rule OK
2 OVERSHADOW, eclipse, dwarf, overlook, tower over

dominating adj

commanding, powerful, strong, superior, advantageous, dominant, controlling, directing, authoritative, assertive, confident

domination n

command, control, authority, influence, power, leadership, rule, government, sway, mastery, supremacy, superiority, despotism, dictatorship, oppression, subjection, subordination, suppression, repression, tyranny, pre-eminence, predominance
FORMAL ascendancy

domineering adj

overbearing, authoritarian, imperious, autocratic, dictatorial, despotic, masterful, high-handed, iron-handed, forceful, coercive, oppressive, tyrannical, arrogant, haughty, aggressive, pushy
FORMAL peremptory
COLLOQ. bossy
E3 meek, servile

dominion n

1 POWER, authority, domination, command, control, rule, direction, sway, jurisdiction, government, lordship, mastery, supremacy, sovereignty
FORMAL ascendancy
2 DOMAIN, country, territory, province, colony, dependency, protectorate, realm, kingdom, empire

don v, n

♦ v
put on, get into, dress in, slip into, clothe yourself in
E3 doff
♦ n
lecturer, teacher, tutor, academic, scholar, professor, fellow, reader

donate v

give, give away, contribute, present, make a gift, make a donation, pledge, bequeath, subscribe
FORMAL bestow, confer
COLLOQ. cough up, fork out, chip in, club together, shell out
E3 receive

donation n

gift, present, offering, grant, gratuity, largess(e), contribution, presentation, subscription, alms, charity, bequest
FORMAL benefaction

done adj, interj

♦ adj
1 FINISHED, over, accomplished, complete, completed, ended, settled, realized, fulfilled, executed, acheived
FORMAL concluded, terminated, consummated
2 CONVENTIONAL, acceptable, proper, right, correct, suitable, appropriate, fitting
OLD seemly
FORMAL decorous
3 COOKED, well-done, tender, ready, prepared, finished, baked, boiled, browned, fried, crisp, roasted, stewed
♦ interj
settled, agreed, accepted, arranged, decided, right, absolutely
COLLOQ. OK

■ **done for**

ruined, destroyed, finished, lost, wrecked, undone, doomed, beaten, broken, dashed, defeated, foiled

FORMAL vanquished
COLLOQ. for the high jump

■ **done in**

exhausted, tired out, worn out, weary, fatigued
COLLOQ. all in, fit to drop, bushed, dead, dead beat, dog-tired, fagged out, whacked, knackered, zonked, on your last legs, flaked out, shattered, worn to a frazzle; N Am tuckered out

■ **have done with**

finished with, over with, thrash with, no longer involved/associated with
COLLOQ. over and done with

donkey n

ass, mule, burro, hinny, jackass, jenny, jennet, neddy, Jerusalem pony; Scot cuddy
OLD cardophagus
COLLOQ. moke
Related adjective: asinine

donnish adj

academic, serious, intellectual, bookish, erudite, learned, pedantic, studious, scholarly, scholastic, formalistic, pedagogic

donor n

giver, donator, benefactor, backer, supporter, contributor, philanthropist, provider
COLLOQ. fairy godmother, angel
E3 beneficiary

doom n, v

♦ n
1 FATE, fortune, destiny, portion, lot
2 DESTRUCTION, catastrophe, downfall, disaster, ruin, ruination, death, death-knell, rack and ruin
3 CONDEMNATION, judgement, sentence, verdict, pronouncement
OLD dome
♦ v
condemn, damn, consign, judge, sentence, decree, pronounce, predestine, fate, destine; Scot weird
OLD devote

doomed adj

condemned, damned, fated, ill-fated, star-crossed, ill-omened, cursed, destined, ruined, hopeless, unlucky, luckless, ill-starred, bedevilled; Scot fey

door n

1 the door of the house
opening, entrance, entry, exit, doorway, portal, hatch
2 OPPORTUNITY, open door, entrance, opening, way in, access, route, way, gateway, road

doorkeeper n

commissionaire, doorman, gatekeeper, usher, caretaker, janitor, porter, concierge, ostiary

dope n, v

♦ n
1 NARCOTIC, drugs, marijuana, cannabis, heroin, opiate, hallucinogen, barbiturate, amphetamine, crack, acid, LSD, Ecstasy
COLLOQ. grass, weed, hash, pot, speed, coke
SLANG E
2 FOOL, dolt, idiot, dunce, simpleton, buffoon, halfwit, oaf, clot
COLLOQ. half-wit, dimwit, clot, blockhead, nincompoop, ninny, nitwit, twerp, twit
SLANG plonker, dork, geek, git, prat, berk, dickhead
3 INFORMATION, facts, inside information, details, specifics, particulars
COLLOQ. low-down, info, gen
♦ v
drug, sedate, anaesthetize, stupefy, medicate, narcotize, inject, knock out, doctor
COLLOQ. spike, lace

dopey adj

1 SLEEPY, dozy, groggy, drowsy, nodding, lethargic, confused, muddled

FORMAL somnolent, torpid
2 STUPID, foolish, silly, daft, simple
COLLOQ. dozy, addle-brained
F∃ 1 awake, alert **2** clever, bright

dormancy n
inactivity, inertness, sleep, rest, slumber, hibernation, latency
F∃ activity

dormant adj
1 INACTIVE, asleep, sleeping, inert, resting, slumbering, sluggish, hibernating, latent, fallow
TECHNICAL comatose
FORMAL torpid, quiescent
2 LATENT, unrealized, potential, undeveloped, undisclosed
F∃ 1 active, awake **2** realized, developed

dosage n
dose, measure, amount, portion, quantity

dose n, v
 ♦ n
measure, dosage, amount, portion, quantity, draught, potion, prescription, shot
 ♦ v
medicate, administer, prescribe, dispense, treat

dossier n
file, folder, papers, portfolio, report, case, documents, data, information, notes

dot n, v
 ♦ n
point, spot, speck, mark, fleck, dab, circle, pin-point, atom, particle, decimal point, full stop, iota, jot
 ♦ v
spot, speckle, mark, scatter, pepper, sprinkle, stud, dab, stipple, punctuate
■ **on the dot**
punctually, promptly, precisely, exactly, on time, sharp

dotage n
old age, senility, agedness, elderliness, second childhood, infirmity, weakness, feebleness, imbecility, evening/autumn of life
FORMAL decrepitude

dote
■ **dote on**
adore, idolize, worship, treasure, admire, love, hold dear, indulge, pamper, spoil

doting adj
adoring, devoted, fond, loving, affectionate, tender, soft, indulgent

dotty adj
crazy, eccentric, feeble-minded, peculiar, touched, weird
OLD frantic-mad, lymphatic, bestraught
COLLOQ. demented, nuts, nutty, nutty as a fruitcake, wacky, mad as a hatter, barmy, bonkers, batty, cracked, crackers, dippy, daffy, dotty, loopy, potty, off your nut, off your head, wrong in the head, out of your head, off the wall, out to lunch, round the bend, round the twist, bats, having bats in the belfry, cuckoo, off the rails, screwy, up the wall, raving, not all there; N Am buggy, flaky, fruity; Aust & NZ dingbats
SLANG loony, mental, bananas, barking, wacko, doolally, off your rocker, off your chump, off your trolley, out of your tree, needing your head examined, having lost your marbles, having a screw loose, having a tile loose, having several cards short of a full deck, with one sandwich short of a picnic, meshuga, ape, apeshit; N Am gonzo, loco, wiggy; Aust out of your tree
F∃ sensible

double adj, v, n
 ♦ adj
1 *double doors; a double yellow line*
dual, twofold, twice, duplicate, twin, paired, doubled, duplex, two-ply, coupled
FORMAL bifarious, binate

2 AMBIGUOUS, double-meaning, double-edged, two-edged, ambivalent, equivocal, paradoxical
F∃ 1 single, half **2** unambiguous
 ♦ v
1 *double your income*
duplicate, enlarge, increase twofold, repeat, multiply by two, fold, magnify
2 *double as someone/something*
have a second job/purpose, have a dual/second role, do/function also
3 *double for someone*
substitute, stand in, fill in, understudy, be an understudy
 ♦ n
twin, duplicate, copy, clone, replica, doppelgänger, lookalike, match, image, facsimile, counterpart, impersonator
COLLOQ. spitting image, ringer
■ **double back**
return, reverse, backtrack, circle, dodge, evade, loop, go back the way you came, retrace your steps
■ **at the double**
immediately, at once, without delay, right away, straight away, quickly, at full speed, as fast as your legs can carry you

double-cross v
cheat, swindle, defraud, trick, hoodwink, betray, mislead
COLLOQ. con, two-time, pull a fast one on
SLANG take for a ride

double-dealing n
cheating, swindling, betrayal, treachery, defrauding, tricking, hoodwinking, misleading, two-facedness, two-timing
FORMAL dissembling, duplicity, perfidy, mendacity
COLLOQ. two-timing, crookedness

double entendre n
double meaning, innuendo, suggestiveness, ambiguity, play on words, wordplay, pun

doubly adv
twice, twofold, again, especially, extra
FORMAL bis

doubt n, v
 ♦ n
1 DISTRUST, suspicion, mistrust, scepticism, reservation, misgiving, qualm, mixed feeling, incredulity, apprehension, hesitation, uneasiness
TECHNICAL scepsis
2 UNCERTAINTY, difficulty, confusion, ambiguity, problem, query, question, scruple, indecision, hesitation, hesitancy, wavering, perplexity, dilemma, quandary
TECHNICAL aporia
F∃ 1 trust, confidence, faith **2** certainty, belief
 ♦ v
1 DISTRUST, mistrust, query, question, call in question, suspect, be suspicious, have misgivings/qualms about, fear, wonder
OLD misdoubt, scruple, impeach
FORMAL disbelieve
COLLOQ. take with a pinch of salt
2 BE UNCERTAIN, be dubious, hesitate, vacillate, waver, be undecided
OLD dubitate, mammer
FORMAL demur
F∃ 1 believe, trust, have confidence in **2** be certain, decide
■ **in doubt**
uncertain, undecided, doubtful, unresolved, unreliable, ambiguous, in question, open to question, questionable, open to debate, debatable, moot
COLLOQ. up in the air
■ **no doubt**
doubtless, without doubt, without a shadow of a doubt, undoubtedly, definitely, unquestionably, certainly, surely, of course, no denying, probably, most likely, presumably, in anyone's book

doubter *n*
questioner, sceptic, disbeliever, unbeliever, non-believer, agnostic, doubting Thomas, cynic, scoffer
E∃ believer

doubtful *adj*
1 *it is doubtful that he will win*
unlikely, improbable, uncertain, in doubt, open to question, debatable
COLLOQ. touch and go
2 *doubtful about his future*
uncertain, unsure, undecided, suspicious, distrustful, uneasy, apprehensive, having reservations/misgivings, irresolute, wavering, hesitant, vacillating, tentative, sceptical
COLLOQ. in two minds
3 *writing of doubtful origin*
dubious, questionable, suspect, unclear, inconclusive, ambiguous, vague, obscure, debatable
COLLOQ. fishy, shady, iffy; *Aust & NZ* crook
E∃ 1 certain **2** certain, decided, confident **3** definite, settled, trustworthy

doubtfully *adv*
hesitantly, uncertainly, uneasily, apprehensively, irresolutely, sceptically

doubtless *adv*
certainly, without doubt, without a shadow of a doubt, undoubtedly, unquestionably, indisputably, no doubt, clearly, surely, of course, truly, precisely, probably, presumably, most likely, assuredly, seemingly, supposedly, in anyone's book
FORMAL indubitably
COLLOQ. bang to rights

doughty *adj*
fearless, bold, brave, confident, courageous, daring, intrepid, valiant, heroic, gallant, plucky, dauntless, unafraid, unapprehensive, unabashed, undaunted, unflinching, lion-hearted, unblenching, unblinking
FORMAL indomitable, valorous
COLLOQ. gutsy, spunky, gritty
E∃ afraid, timid

dour *adj*
1 GLOOMY, dismal, forbidding, grim, morose, unfriendly, unsmiling, charmless, dreary, austere, sour, sullen, churlish, gruff
2 HARD, harsh, inflexible, unyielding, rigid, severe, stern, rigorous, strict, obstinate
E∃ 1 cheerful, bright **2** easy-going

douse, dowse *v*
1 SOAK, pour water over, saturate, flood, deluge, steep, submerge, immerse, immerge, wet, dip, souse, duck, drench, dunk, plunge, splash
2 EXTINGUISH, put out, blow out, smother, quench, snuff

dovetail *v*
fit together, correspond, match, coincide, conform, agree, tally, harmonize, join, interlock, link
FORMAL accord

dowdy *adj*
unfashionable, ill-dressed, frumpish, drab, shabby, frowsy, dingy, old-fashioned, slovenly
COLLOQ. tatty, tacky
E∃ fashionable, smart

down[1] *prep, adv, adj, v*
♦ *prep, adv*
down the road
to a lower level/position, to the ground, to the floor, to the bottom
E∃ up

♦ *adj*
1 SAD, depressed, unhappy, melancholy, miserable, downhearted, dejected, downcast, dispirited, wretched, low
COLLOQ. blue, down in the dumps
2 *the computer is down*
out of order, out of action, not working, crashed
FORMAL inoperative, malfunctioning
COLLOQ. bust, kaput, on the blink, wonky; *N Am* on the fritz
SLANG conked out
E∃ 1 happy **2** working, operational
♦ *v*
1 KNOCK DOWN, fell, floor, bring down, prostrate, throw, topple
2 SWALLOW, consume, drink, gulp (down)
COLLOQ. swig, put away, knock back, toss off, swill
■ **down with**
get rid of, away with

down[2] *n*
quilts made of down
soft feathers, fine hair, wool, pile, shag, nap, fluff, floss, fuzz, floccus, flue, bloom
TECHNICAL pappus
Related adjectives: pappose, pappous

down-and-out *adj, n*
♦ *adj*
derelict, destitute, impoverished, on your uppers, homeless, penniless, ruined
♦ *n*
tramp, vagrant, vagabond, piker, *clochard*, floater, straggle, stroller; *dialect* walker; *Scot* caird, gangrel, hallan-shaker, landloper, rinthereout, (*derog*) tinkler; *N Am* hobo, down-and-outer; *Aust* sundowner
OLD cursitor, rogue, scatterling, truant, vagrom
COLLOQ. loser, knight of the road, Weary Willie; *Scot* jakey
SLANG dosser, bum, toerag; (*offensive*) gook; *N Am* dingbat

down-at-heel *adj*
1 ILL-DRESSED, frayed, tattered, ragged, drab, frowsy, dowdy, shabby, poor, slovenly
2 *the pub looked down-at-heel*
dingy, run-down, dilapidated, ramshackle, in disrepair, neglected, tumbledown, uncared for
COLLOQ. tatty, tacky, seedy

downbeat *adj*
1 RELAXED, easy-going, calm, low, downcast, informal, casual, nonchalant, unhurried, unworried
FORMAL insouciant
COLLOQ. laid-back
2 GLOOMY, pessimistic, fearing the worst, negative, depressed, low, downcast, despondent, cheerless, cynical
E∃ 1 upbeat **2** happy

downcast *adj*
dejected, depressed, despondent, sad, unhappy, wretched, miserable, down, low, low-spirited, disheartened, downhearted, dispirited, discouraged, disappointed, crestfallen, daunted, dismayed, glum, gloomy, dull, hanging
OLD downlooked
FORMAL disconsolate
COLLOQ. blue, fed up
E∃ cheerful, happy, elated

downfall *n*
fall, ruin, failure, collapse, destruction, disgrace, debasement, degradation, debacle, undoing, overthrow
E∃ rise

downgrade *v*
1 DEGRADE, demote, lower, humble, reduce/lower in rank, relegate, depose, deflate
FORMAL disparage, denigrate
COLLOQ. take down a peg or two, take the wind out of someone's sails

2 BELITTLE, run down, decry, minimize, defame,
make light of
FORMAL disparage
COLLOQ. do down, sell short
F∃ 1 upgrade, improve **2** praise

downhearted adj
depressed, dejected, despondent, sad, downcast,
disappointed, discouraged, disheartened, dispirited, low-
spirited, daunted, unhappy, gloomy, glum, dismayed
FORMAL disconsolate
F∃ cheerful, enthusiastic

down-market adj
cheap, inexpensive, low-price, low-cost, affordable,
bargain, reduced, cut-price, knock-down, marked-down,
discounted, rock-bottom, giveaway, throwaway, budget,
economy, sale, economical, no-frills, cheap-rate, bargain-
basement, shoddy, cheap and cheerful, tatty, tawdry,
inferior, second-rate, worthless, common, ramshackle,
poor, cheapjack
COLLOQ. cheapo, tacky
F∃ up-market

downpour n
cloudburst, deluge, rainstorm, flood, inundation, torrent

downright adv, adj
♦ adv
absolutely, plainly, utterly, clearly, completely, totally,
thoroughly, positively, simply, categorically
♦ adj
outright, complete, total, out-and-out, absolute, plain,
utter, clear, sheer, thorough, wholesale, categorical,
unqualified, unequivocal

downside n
disadvantage, drawback, snag, liability, impediment,
limitation, inconvenience, flaw, defect, nuisance,
weakness, weak point, trouble, penalty
COLLOQ. minus, spanner in the works, fly in the ointment,
weak link in the chain, chink in your armour, Achilles
heel
F∃ advantage, benefit, asset

downsize v
reduce, make smaller, contract, shrink, slim, minimize,
moderate, diminish
F∃ increase

down-to-earth adj
commonsense, commonsensical, hard-headed, matter-of-
fact, mundane, no-nonsense, plain-spoken, practical,
realistic, sane, sensible, unsentimental
F∃ fantastic, impractical, idealistic

downtrodden adj
oppressed, subservient, exploited, trampled on, weighed-
down, burdened, overwhelmed, abused, tyrannized,
bullied, victimized, helpless, powerless
FORMAL subjugated

downward adj
descending, declining, going/moving down, downhill,
sliding, slipping
F∃ upward

downy adj
soft, feathery, fine, smooth, velvety, woolly, fluffy, fleecy,
fuzzy
FORMAL pappose, pappous

dowry n
1 MARRIAGE SETTLEMENT, marriage portion, inheritance,
legacy, portion, provision, share, wedding-dower, dot,
endowment; Scot tocher
2 FACULTY, gift, talent

doxology n
hymn/song of praise, praise, hymn, psalm, song, chant,
anthem, response, chorale, recessional, gloria, glorification

doze v, n
♦ v
sleep, nap, catnap, take a nap, drift off, go off, drop off

COLLOQ. snooze, kip, nod off
SLANG zizz
♦ n
nap, catnap, siesta
COLLOQ. snooze, forty winks, kip, shut-eye
SLANG zizz
■ **doze off**
fall asleep, drift off, catnap
COLLOQ. nod off, snooze, have forty winks

dozy adj
1 DROWSY, sleepy, tired, weary, nodding, dreamy,
yawning, half-asleep, dopey
FORMAL somnolent, torpid
2 STUPID, foolish, silly, daft, simple
COLLOQ. dopey
F∃ 1 awake, alert **2** clever, bright

drab adj
dull, dingy, dreary, dismal, gloomy, flat, grey, colourless,
lacklustre, cheerless, lifeless, sombre, shabby, featureless,
tedious, boring, uninteresting
F∃ bright, cheerful, lively

drabness n
dullness, dinginess, dreariness, gloom, sombreness,
greyness, shabbiness, colourlessness, cheerlessness,
lifelessness
F∃ cheerfulness

Draconian adj
harsh, severe, cruel, strict, iron-handed, iron-fisted,
abrasive, stern, grim, savage, brutal, unsympathetic,
unfeeling, hard, inhuman, pitiless, ruthless, merciless

draft n, v
♦ n
1 OUTLINE, sketch, rough sketch, plan, abstract, rough,
preliminary version, drawing, blueprint
FORMAL delineation, protocol
2 a bank draft
bill of exchange, cheque, money order, letter of credit,
postal order
♦ v
draw (up), outline, sketch, plan, design, formulate,
compose
FORMAL delineate

drag v, n
♦ v
1 DRAW, pull, haul, lug, tug, trail, tow, yank
2 GO SLOWLY, creep, crawl, lag, become boring/tedious,
wear on, go on and on, go on for ever
♦ n
bore, annoyance, nuisance, bother, pest, trouble
COLLOQ. pain, pain in the neck, bind, headache
■ **drag on**
go on, run on, continue, persist, be lengthy, be long-
drawn-out
■ **drag out**
spin out, prolong, draw out, extend, hang on, lengthen,
persist
FORMAL protract
■ **drag up**
rake up, remind, bring up, raise, mention, introduce,
revive

dragoon v
coerce, compel, constrain, drive, force, pressure,
pressurize, harass, impel, intimidate, browbeat, bully
COLLOQ. strongarm

drain v, n
♦ v
1 EMPTY, remove, evacuate, draw off, pump off, extract,
withdraw, strain, dry, milk, bleed, tap, sap, sponge, tile,
ladle, leach, leech, sluice, buzz, dewater, ditch, quaff,
underdrain; dialect sew; Scot pour
TECHNICAL exsanguinate, pot, unwater
OLD emulge
FORMAL void

2 *waste draining into the stream*
trickle, flow out, discharge, seep out, leak, ooze
FORMAL exude, effuse
3 EXHAUST, consume, sap, use up, drink up, suck, swallow,
strain, tax, bleed, bleed dry, bleed white
FORMAL deplete
⊞ 1 fill
◆ *n*
1 CHANNEL, conduit, culvert, duct, outlet,
trench, ditch, pipe, sink, gutter, sluice, sewer,
gully, delf, fleet, grip, nulla, sough; *Scot* cundy,
sheuch, stank, syver
TECHNICAL cunette, piscina
OLD common-shore
2 *a drain on resources*
exhaustion, consumption, sap, strain, tax
OLD lickpenny
FORMAL depletion

drama *n*
1 PLAY, acting, theatre, show, piece, spectacle, stagecraft,
scene, comedy, melodrama, tragedy, dramatics,
dramaturgy
2 EXCITEMENT, thrill, sensation, crisis, dilemma, tension,
turmoil, histrionics

dramatic *adj*
1 *a dramatic change*
striking, sudden, marked, significant, substantial,
considerable, abrupt, noticeable, distinct
2 EXCITING, striking, stirring, thrilling, tense, spectacular,
vivid, graphic, sensational, expressive, effective,
impressive, unexpected
3 HISTRIONIC, theatrical, exaggerated, melodramatic,
flamboyant, artificial
4 *dramatic art*
theatrical, stage, Thespian

dramatically *adv*
1 SUDDENLY, abruptly, significantly, substantially,
considerably, noticeably
2 SPECTACULARLY, vividly, impressively, expressively,
strikingly

dramatist *n*
playwright, writer, scriptwriter, play-writer, screen writer,
comedian, dramaturge, dramaturgist, tragedian

dramatization *n*
staging, adaptation, presentation, arrangement

dramatize *v*
1 STAGE, put on, adapt, present as a play/film, arrange for
2 EXAGGERATE, play-act, act, overdo, overstate
COLLOQ. ham (up), lay it on thick, blow up out of all
proportion, make a big thing of

drape *v*
hang, cover, wrap, envelop, overlay, shroud, cloak, veil,
arrange, decorate, adorn, fold, drop, droop, suspend

drapery *n*
cloth, covering(s), curtain(s), hanging(s), blind(s), arras,
backdrop, tapestry, valance

drastic *adj*
extreme, radical, strong, serious, forceful,
severe, harsh, rigorous, far-reaching, desperate, dire,
Draconian
⊞ moderate, cautious

drastically *adv*
greatly, severely, seriously, rigorously, extremely, strongly,
radically, forcefully
⊞ moderately

draught *n*
1 PUFF, breath, current, flow, rush, movement
FORMAL influx
2 DRINK, gulp, swallow, swig, quantity, cup, potion
3 PULLING, dragging, drawing, traction

draw *v, n*
◆ *v*
1 *draw a picture*
sketch, portray, trace, pencil, paint, represent, map out,
depict, design, chart, scribble, doodle
FORMAL delineate
2 *the procession drew nearer*
move, go, proceed, progress, travel, walk, drive, come,
approach, advance
3 PULL, drag, haul, tow, tug, lug, trail
4 *draw a knife*
take out, pull out, bring out, produce, extract, remove,
withdraw
5 *draw water from a well*
extract, drain, remove, withdraw, pump, suck, siphon, tap,
milk
6 *draw a breath*
breathe in
FORMAL inhale, respire, inspire
7 *draw money from a bank*
take, get, receive, obtain
FORMAL procure
8 *draw attention to something*
attract, allure, lure, entice, bring in, influence, persuade,
elicit, prompt
9 *draw a conclusion*
conclude, deduce, infer, gather, come to, reason
10 *draw lots*
pick, choose, select, decide on, go for
COLLOQ. plump for
11 TIE, be equal, be even
COLLOQ. be all square
⊞ 3 push **8** repel
◆ *n*
1 ATTRACTION, enticement, lure, allure, appeal, bait,
interest, magnetism
2 RAFFLE, lottery, sweepstake, sweep, tombola
3 TIE, stalemate, dead heat
■ **draw back**
recoil, wince, flinch, shrink, start back, withdraw, retract,
retreat
■ **draw on**
make use of, use, put to use, call on, exploit, apply,
employ, quarry, rely on, have recourse to
FORMAL utilize
■ **draw out**
1 *the train drew out of the station*
pull out, move out, set out, depart, leave, start
2 EXTEND, prolong, lengthen, spin out, drag out, elongate,
stretch
FORMAL protract
3 *draw someone out*
encourage to talk, induce to talk/speak, put at ease, make
feel less nervous, make
⊞ 2 shorten
■ **draw up**
1 DRAFT, compose, formulate, prepare, frame, write out,
put in writing
2 PULL UP, stop, halt, run in

drawback *n*
disadvantage, snag, hitch, obstacle, hurdle, barrier,
impediment, hindrance, difficulty, problem, flaw, fault,
catch, stumbling-block, nuisance, trouble, defect, weak
spot, handicap, deficiency, liability, limitation,
imperfection, damper, discouragement
COLLOQ. fly in the ointment
⊞ advantage, benefit

drawing *n*
sketch, picture, outline, representation, portrayal,
illustration, cartoon, graphic, portrait, composition,
depiction, diagram, study
FORMAL delineation

drawl *v*
speak/say slowly, draw out your vowels, drone, haw-haw,
protract, twang

drawn *adj*
tired, fatigued, worn, haggard, gaunt, pinched, strained, stressed, taut, tense, fraught, harassed, sapped, washed out
COLLOQ. hassled

dread *v, n, adj*
♦ *v*
fear, shrink from, quail, cringe at, flinch, shy, shudder, tremble, be afraid of, be scared of, be terrified by, be frightened (to death) by, be anxious/worried about
COLLOQ. get cold feet about
⊟ look forward to
♦ *n*
fear, apprehension, misgiving, dismay, alarm, horror, terror, fright, fit of terror, blind panic, cold sweat, hair standing on end, disquiet, worry, qualm
FORMAL trepidation, perturbation
COLLOQ. (blue) funk
⊟ confidence, security
♦ *adj*
dreaded, feared, frightening, frightful, terrifying, terrible, dreadful, awful, awe-inspiring, alarming, ghastly, grisly, gruesome, horrible, dire

dreadful *adj*
awful, terrible, frightful, horrible, appalling, dire, shocking, outrageous, frightening, terrifying, alarming, ghastly, horrendous, horrific, grim, tragic, grievous, hideous, unpleasant, nasty
FORMAL heinous
⊟ wonderful, comforting

dreadfully *adv*
1 *I'm dreadfully sorry*
awfully, terribly, frightfully, very, extremely, exceedingly
2 *suffer dreadfully*
appallingly, shockingly, horrendously, awfully, terribly, atrociously

dream *n, v, adj*
♦ *n*
1 VISION, illusion, reverie, trance, fantasy, daydream, nightmare, hallucination, delusion, imagination, phantasmagoria, phantom
OLD sweven; *Irish* aisling
Related adjectives: oneiric, somnial
2 ASPIRATION, ambition, wish, hope, desire, yearning, ideal, goal, design, aim, plan, speculation, expectation, castles in the air
3 DAYDREAM, fantasy, reverie, pipe dream, inattention; *Scot* dwam
4 *their new house is a dream*
ideal, beauty, perfection, joy, delight, marvel
♦ *v*
1 *dream during sleep*
imagine, envisage, fantasize, fancy, hallucinate
FORMAL somniate
2 DAYDREAM, fantasize, imagine, muse, fancy, be lost in space, not pay attention, let your thoughts wander, stare into space
COLLOQ. switch off
3 *dream of becoming a doctor*
want very much, long, desire, yearn, crave
♦ *adj*
perfect, ideal, model, supreme, superb, excellent, wonderful
■ **dream up**
invent, devise, conceive, think up, conjure up, imagine, concoct, hatch, create, fabricate, spin, contrive
■ **not dream of**
not think, not imagine, not consider, not conceive

QUOTATIONS
They are not long, the days of wine and roses: / Out of a misty dream / Our path emerges for a while, then closes / Within a dream
ERNEST DOWSON, 'Vitae Summa Brevis'

SYNONYM NUANCES

noun sense 1
Vision may be used where things are envisaged in the future: *the government's vision for the inner cities*, whilst **illusion** suggests a deceptive conception or appearance, with the implication that it can never become real: *the illusion of success*. To state this idea explictly, you might choose the term **delusion**: *to think you can beat him is a dangerous delusion*.
   The term **reverie**, however, is more appropriate for succumbing to an undirected train of thoughts, and the connotations are pleasant ones: *he drifted into a momentary reverie*. **Trance**, although similar, has more to do with absence of thought and is used of a hypnotic state that has been induced.
   The term **fantasy** could be used negatively to suggest either a misguided belief: *it is fantasy to believe this bill can be implemented*, or, more positively, of an idyllic mental projection: *we all enjoy an escapist fantasy*; whilst **daydream** likewise implies conjuring up an ideal scenario, and has pleasant connotations.
   Nightmare, conversely, can only refer to something really unpleasant, dreamed while asleep or dreaded when awake: *meeting her was his worst nightmare*. The terms **hallucination**, **delusion** and **phantom** also have unpleasant associations and again suggest something deceptive which your mind may unconsciously produce, sometimes through illness or drugs: *the ghastly phantoms of his delirious brain*, whereas **imagination** is more positive in its suggestion of conscious creativity.
Phantasmagoria is restricted to an incredible series of unreal images or real forms: *it was a phantasmagoria of horror and mystery combined*.

dreamer *n*
idealist, visionary, fantasist, fantasizer, romancer, daydreamer, stargazer, theorizer, romantic, Utopian
⊟ realist, pragmatist

dreamily *adv*
gently, softly, peacefully, pleasantly, romantically

dreamlike *adj*
surreal, illusory, unreal, trance-like, hallucinatory, insubstantial, unsubstantial, visionary, chimerical, fantastic, phantom, phantasmagoric, phantasmagorical, Alice-in-Wonderland
FORMAL ethereal

dreamy *adj*
1 FANTASTIC, unreal, imaginary, shadowy, unclear, indistinct, vague, misty, hazy, faint, ethereal, dim
2 DAYDREAMING, fanciful, fantasizing, romantic, idealistic, impractical, visionary, faraway, absent, musing, pensive, thoughtful, absent-minded, preoccupied, abstracted
COLLOQ. with your head in the clouds
3 *dreamy music*
relaxing, soothing, lulling, calming, gentle, soft, romantic
⊟ **1** real, clear **2** practical, down-to-earth

drearily *adv*
depressingly, dismally, boringly, tediously, routinely, monstrously

dreary *adj*
gloomy, depressing, drab, dismal, bleak, sombre, cheerless, sad, mournful, overcast, dark, boring, tedious, uninteresting, uneventful, dull, humdrum, routine, monotonous, unvaried, wearisome, commonplace, colourless, lifeless, featureless, run-of-the-mill
⊟ cheerful, interesting

dredge
■ **dredge up**
dig up, discover, uncover, unearth, raise, drag up, draw up, fish up, rake up, scoop up

dregs *n*

1 SEDIMENT, deposit, residue, lees, grounds, scourings, scum, dross, trash, waste, tailings, excrement, faeces
TECHNICAL precipitate, sublimate, bottoms, draff, dunder, fecula, greaves, mother, taplash
OLD lags
FORMAL residuum, detritus
COLLOQ. ullage
2 OUTCASTS, rabble, riff-raff, scum, down-and-outs, tramps, vagrants, *faex populi*
OLD legge
SLANG dossers

drench *v*

soak, soak to the skin, saturate, steep, wet, douse, souse, immerse, inundate, duck, flood, swamp, imbue, drown, permeate

dress *n, v*

♦ *n*
1 FROCK, gown, robe
2 CLOTHES, clothing, garment(s), outfit, costume, ensemble, garb
FORMAL attire, apparel, habiliment
COLLOQ. clobber, get-up, gear, togs
Related adjective: sartorial
♦ *v*
1 CLOTHE, put on, get into, slip into, garb, rig, robe, wear, don, decorate, deck (out), garnish, trim, adorn, turn out, fit (out), drape
FORMAL attire, array, accoutre
COLLOQ. throw on
2 *dress your hair*
arrange, adjust, dispose, prepare, groom, style, straighten, tidy, comb, do, primp, preen
3 BANDAGE, bind up, put a plaster on, clean, cover, tend, treat, swathe
4 *dress meat*
clean, prepare, get ready
🔁 **1** strip, undress

■ **dress down**
1 DRESS CASUALLY, dress informally
2 REBUKE, reprimand, reprove, scold, chide
FORMAL berate, castigate, upbraid
COLLOQ. carpet, haul over the coals, tear off a strip, tell off, give someone an earful

■ **dress up**
1 DRESS SMARTLY, dress formally
COLLOQ. doll up
2 BEAUTIFY, improve, adorn, decorate, ornament, embellish, deck, gild, disguise
COLLOQ. tart up, jazz up

SYNONYM NUANCES

verb sense 1
The phrase **slip into** suggests easy, unobtrusive movements: *he slipped into his dressing gown*. The terms **garb** and **rig** put the emphasis on the garments you are dressing in, with the suggestion they are formal or in some way untypical: *garbed in funereal black; a cavalry regiment rigged in green and gold*. **Robe** is similar, but is most appropriately used of official vestments: *the fully robed civic dignitaries*. **Drape** also puts the emphasis on the clothing, but would be used of garments which hang loosely: *draped in a loose shawl*.
To use **don** puts the emphasis back on the actual act of dressing, and suggests a very conscious act of putting on particular garments: *we donned our rain gear*. You may use **decorate** and **adorn** if you want to suggest the addition of something fancy: *a beautiful ring adorned her finger*, whilst you could use **deck (out)** to imply a slightly ludicrous effect: *decked out in a cowboy hat*.
Both **garnish** and **trim** return to the idea of adding something decorative but perhaps with the suggestion it is unnecessary. The term **turn out** may be used to emphasize the manner in which you present yourself and the impression it will give: *ensure that you're well*

---

turned out for the inspection, whilst **fit out**, which also has connotations of formal or elegant dress, emphasizes the way someone organizes your attire: *he had been fitted out in a very handsome silk suit*.

---

dressing *n*

1 *a salad dressing*
sauce, condiment, relish, jus, coulis
2 BANDAGE, plaster, Elastoplast®, Band-aid®, gauze, lint, compress, poultice, tourniquet, pad, spica, ligature

dressmaker *n*

tailor, tailoress, couturier, modiste, needlewoman, garment-maker, seamstress, sewing woman, midinette

dressy *adj*

elegant, formal, smart, stylish, elaborate, ornate
COLLOQ. classy, natty, ritzy, swish
🔁 dowdy, scruffy

dribble *v, n*

♦ *v*
1 TRICKLE, drip, leak, run, seep, drop, ooze
FORMAL exude
2 DROOL, slaver, slobber, drivel, foam, froth
♦ *n*
1 DRIP, trickle, droplet, leak, seepage, sprinkling
2 SALIVA, drool, spit, drivel, slaver, slobber, foam, froth

dried *adj*

arid, dehydrated, desiccated, drained, parched, wilted, withered, wizened, shrivelled, mummified
FORMAL exsiccated

drift *v, n*

♦ *v*
1 WANDER, waft, stray, float, freewheel, coast, go with the stream, be carried along, roam, rove, crab, sag, wisp
OLD hull, rack
2 GATHER, accumulate, pile up, heap up, bank, drive, amass
♦ *n*
1 ACCUMULATION, mound, pile, bank, mass, heap, wreath
2 SHIFT, movement, trend, tendency, course, direction, flow, stream, current, variation, digression, rush, sweep
3 MEANING, intention, implication, gist, vein, tenor, thrust, course, direction, trend, tendency, significance, essence, core, substance, aim, point, design, scope
FORMAL import, purport

drifter *n*

wanderer, traveller, nomad, vagrant, itinerant, rover, tramp, vagabond, rolling stone, swagman, beachcomber; *N Am* hobo

drill *n, v*

♦ *n*
1 BORER, awl, bit, gimlet
2 INSTRUCTION, training, practice, coaching, grounding, exercise, repetition, tuition, preparation, discipline, indoctrination, procedure, routine
FORMAL inculcation
♦ *v*
1 TEACH, train, instruct, coach, practise, school, rehearse, exercise, discipline, ground, put someone through their paces
FORMAL inculcate
2 BORE, pierce, make a hole in, penetrate, puncture, perforate, prick, punch

drink *v, n*

♦ *v*
1 IMBIBE, swallow, have, sip, drain, down, gulp, sup, quaff, absorb, guzzle, swill
FORMAL partake of
COLLOQ. swig, knock back, throw back
2 GET DRUNK, have one too many, have (a drop) too much, overdrink, indulge, carouse, revel, be a hard drinker, be a heavy drinker, have a drink problem

COLLOQ. tipple, tank up, have one over the eight, drink like a fish; *Aust* grog on; hit the bottle, knock back a few, polish off
SLANG booze, lush, get pissed; *Aust* go on the shout
3 drink someone's health
drink to, toast, propose a toast to, salute, wish someone success
◆ *n*
1 BEVERAGE, liquid, brew, infusion, soft drink, cold drink, hot drink, thirst-quencher, refreshment, draught, sip, swallow, gulp
COLLOQ. swig; *Scot* swally
See panel below
2 ALCOHOL, strong drink, spirits, liquor
OLD (*Shakesp*) tickle-brain
COLLOQ. tipple, the bottle, stiffener, hard stuff, hoo(t)ch, Dutch courage, firewater, the creature, jar, tiddly, tinct, sauce; *Aust & NZ* grog
SLANG booze, jungle juice, gnat's piss, rotgut; *N Am* juice; *Aust & NZ* shicker
See panel below
■ **drink in**
absorb, take in, digest, realize, appreciate, grasp

SYNONYM NUANCES

verb sense 1
Imbibe is generally used to imply that alcohol has been consumed: *flushed with the Scotch he'd imbibed*.
Swallow emphasizes the act of moving food or drink down the throat, and like **down**, **gulp**, **knock back** and **throw back** it suggests drinking hastily and possibly greedily: *he downed half his wine in one gulp*. **Sip** is, by contrast, descriptive of drinking in small delicate mouthfuls, whilst **drain** suggests a more deliberate movement, trying to get the most out of your last mouthful: *she drained the last of her coffee*.
   The less common **sup** and **quaff** are old-fashioned terms which are quite literary in tone, and which may also be used to describe the manner of drinking, with **sup** having connotations of relish and enjoyment, and **quaff** suggesting a faster, zealous action: *he quaffed pint after pint*. Both **guzzle** and **swill** return to the idea of greedily consuming copious amounts of drink: *champagne was guzzled like lemonade; they swilled gin in the afternoon*.

---

drinkable *adj*
clean, safe, fit to drink, potable

drinker *n*
hard/serious drinker, heavy drinker, drunk, drunkard, inebriate, dipsomaniac, imbiber
COLLOQ. tippler
SLANG boozer, wino, lush, alkie, dipso, soak, piss artist, toper, tosspot, sot, sponge
E3 abstainer, teetotaller

drip *v, n*
◆ *v*
drop, dribble, trickle, leak, ooze, plop, drizzle, splash, sprinkle, weep, filter, percolate
◆ *n*
1 DROP, trickle, dribble, leak, splash, plop, bead, tear
2 WEAKLING, bore
COLLOQ. wimp, softy, wet, weed, pansy, sissy, ninny

drive *v, n*
◆ *v*
1 STEER, ride, travel (by car), go/come (by car), motor, be behind/at the wheel, be at the controls, pilot, operate
2 TRANSPORT, take, convey, carry, move, send, run, chauffeur, give a lift to
3 PROPEL, impel, direct, power, control, manage, operate, run, handle, hurl, press, thrust
4 FORCE, compel, impel, coerce, constrain, press, move, push, urge, spur, prod, herd, round up, dragoon, goad, guide, oblige, leave someone with no choice/option
5 MOTIVATE, force, compel, pressure, pressurize, impel, lead, prompt, actuate, incite, provoke, persuade, move, spur
6 STRIKE, hammer, screw, knock, thump, dash, dig, sink, ram, thrust, plunge
7 OVERBURDEN, overwork, tax, overtax, work too hard, overdo it, exert yourself too much, burden
COLLOQ. kill yourself
◆ *n*
1 EXCURSION, outing, journey, ride, run, trip, jaunt
COLLOQ. spin, turn
2 AVENUE, driveway, road, roadway, approach
3 ENERGY, enterprise, ambition, initiative, vigour, verve, motivation, determination, will, resolve, push, spirit, effort, action

---

Non-alcoholic drinks include:

beef tea	Ovaltine®	*colloq.* Coke®	limeade	squash	**WATER:**
coffee	milk	cordial	Lucozade®		mineral water
tea	milk shake	cream soda	orangeade	**MIXERS:**	Perrier®
tisane	smoothie	energy drink	Pepsi®	bitter lemon	seltzer
		fizzy drink	*colloq.* pop	Canada Dry®	sparkling water
MILKY DRINKS:	**SOFT DRINKS:**	fruit juice	relaxation drink	ginger ale	still water
cocoa	Aqua Libra®	ginger beer	Ribena®	soda (water)	Vichy water
float	barley water	Irn-Bru®	root beer	tonic	
Horlicks®	cherryade	lemonade	sarsaparilla	(water)	
hot chocolate	Coca Cola®				

See also **coffee**; **tea**.

Alcoholic drinks include:

BEER AND LAGER:	Armagnac	hot toddy	Scotch and soda	*colloq.* plonk	Wincarnis®
ale	bourbon	Irish coffee	sloe gin	port	
beer	brandy	ouzo	tequila	red wine	**MISCELLANEOUS:**
black-and-tan	Calvados	peach schnapps	vermouth	retsina	alcopop
Guinness®	Campari	Pimm's®	vodka	rosé wine	cider
lager	Cognac	pink gin	whisky	sangria	*N Am* malternative
porter	eggnog	poteen		sherry	mead
shandy	G&T	rum	**WINE:**	vin blanc	perry
snakebite	gin	rye	*colloq.* bubbly	*colloq.* vino	
stout	gin-and-tonic	sake	champagne	vin rosé	
	grappa	schnapps	ginger wine	vin rouge	
SPIRITS:	grog	Scotch	hock	white wine	
aquavit			Marsala		

See also **beer**; **cocktail**; **liqueur**; **wine**.

FORMAL tenacity
COLLOQ. get-up-and-go, pizazz, vim, zip
4 CAMPAIGN, crusade, appeal, effort, action, movement, fight, struggle, battle
COLLOQ. push
5 POWER, thrust, surge, pressure, propulsion, transmission, propeller shaft
6 URGE, instinct, impulse, pressure, need, desire, appetite

■ **drive at**
imply, allude to, intimate, mean, suggest, hint, have in mind, intend, refer to, signify, insinuate, indicate, aim at
COLLOQ. get at

drivel *n*
nonsense, rubbish, gibberish, gobbledygook, garbage
OLD balderdash
COLLOQ. bunkum, mumbo-jumbo, waffle, rot, baloney, blah, eyewash, hogwash, rhubarb, guff, hooey, malarkey, poppycock, tripe, claptrap, twaddle
SLANG bull; (*vulgar*) crap, bullshit, balls, bollocks

driver *n*
motorist, motorcyclist, rider, chauffeur, cabbie, trucker

driving *adj*
compelling, forceful, vigorous, dynamic, energetic, forthright, heavy, violent, sweeping

drizzle *n, v*
♦ *n*
mist, mizzle, (light/fine) rain, spray, shower, mizzle; *dialect* skiffle; *Scot* smur
♦ *v*
1 *it's drizzling*
spit, spray, sprinkle, rain (lightly/finely), spot, shower, mizzle; *Scot* scouther, smur
2 TRICKLE, dribble, pour, sprinkle, drip, drop

droll *adj*
bizarre, odd, queer, eccentric, peculiar, comical, amusing, humorous, ridiculous, laughable, ludicrous, funny, clownish, zany, farcical, waggish, whimsical, witty, comic, diverting, entertaining, jocular
FORMAL risible

drone *v, n*
♦ *v*
1 HUM, buzz, purr, thrum, vibrate, whirr, drawl, chant, bombilate, bombinate
2 *the lecturer droned on and on*
go on and on, speak interminably, talk monotonously, intone
♦ *n*
1 HUM, buzz, purr, thrum, vibration, whirr, whirring, murmuring, chant
2 LAZY PERSON, idler, loafer, slacker, dreamer, layabout, parasite, leech, hanger-on
COLLOQ. lazybones, sponger, scrounger
SLANG *N Am* goldbricker, goof-off

drool *v*
1 DRIBBLE, slobber, salivate, drivel, slaver, water at the mouth
2 *drool over the new baby*
dote, enthuse, gloat, gush, slobber over

droop *v*
1 HANG DOWN, dangle, sag, bend, wilt, weep, stoop, bow, nod, fall down, sink, drop, slump, slouch
TECHNICAL nutate
OLD slink; (*Shakesp*) lob
2 LANGUISH, decline, flag, falter, slump, lose heart, wilt, wither, drop, faint, fall down, fade, slouch, peak
E3 **1** straighten **2** flourish, rise

droopy *adj*
drooping, limp, floppy, falling, dropping, sagging, saggy, slack, loose, lax, weak, feeble

drop *v, n*
♦ *v*
1 FALL, sink, decline, plunge, plummet, tumble, dive, descend, droop

2 LET FALL, let go (of), lower
3 DRIP, trickle, leak, dribble, plop
4 LOWER, decrease, lessen, weaken, diminish, decline, dwindle, slacken off, plummet, plunge, sink
5 ABANDON, give up, desert, reject, finish (with), jilt, disown, walk out on
FORMAL forsake, relinquish, repudiate, renounce
COLLOQ. chuck, ditch, run out on, throw over
6 END, stop, cease, finish, leave out, miss out, omit, exclude, eliminate
FORMAL dispense with, discontinue, terminate, for(e)go, relinquish, repudiate, renounce
COLLOQ. quit
7 *drop me at the corner*
take, bring, deliver, carry, put off, transport
8 DISMISS, discharge, make redundant
COLLOQ. sack, fire, turf out, boot out
SLANG *N Am* can
E3 **1** rise
♦ *n*
1 DROPLET, bead, tear, drip, bubble, blob, globule, trickle
FORMAL goutte, globulet, spheroid, gutta
2 LITTLE, mouthful, sprinkle, bit, pinch, sip, nip, tot, trace, dab, splash; *N Am* tad
FORMAL modicum
COLLOQ. dash, spot, smidgen
3 DESCENT, fall, precipice, cliff, slope, chasm, abyss, plunge
FORMAL declivity
4 DECLINE, falling-off, fall-off, lowering, downturn, decrease, reduction, cutback, slump, plunge, depreciation, devaluation, deterioration
5 *chocolate drops*
sweet, bonbon, candy, pastille, lozenge
COLLOQ. sweetie

■ **drop back**
fall behind, lag (behind), fall back
FORMAL retreat

■ **drop in**
call (round), call by, come over, come round, visit, come by
COLLOQ. pop in

■ **drop off**
1 FALL ASLEEP, drift off, doze (off), go off, catnap
COLLOQ. nod off, snooze, have forty winks
2 DECLINE, fall off, decrease, dwindle, lessen, diminish, slacken off, plummet, plunge, sink
3 DELIVER, set down, deposit, unload, hand in
E3 **1** wake up **2** increase

■ **drop out**
withdraw, leave, give up, abandon
FORMAL renounce, forsake
COLLOQ. back out, cry off, quit

■ **drop out of**
back out of, withdraw from, leave, opt out, pull out, abandon
FORMAL renounce, renege
COLLOQ. cry off from, quit

dropout *n*
nonconformist, rebel, Bohemian, dissenter, hippie, beatnik, loner, deviant
FORMAL dissentient, malcontent, renegade

droppings *n*
excrement, dung, manure, ordure, spraint
TECHNICAL excreta, stools
FORMAL egesta, faeces

dross *n*
rubbish, remains, refuse, trash, waste, scum, debris, dregs, impurity, lees, slag, slack, junk
TECHNICAL scoria
FORMAL recrement

drought *n*
dryness, aridity, parchedness, dehydration, shortage, want, drouth
FORMAL desiccation

drove n
herd, horde, gathering, crowd, multitude, swarm, throng, flock, pack, host, company, mob, press, crush

drown v
1 *she drowned in the canal*
go under, suffocate in water, die, perish, go, founder, lose your life
OLD drench
COLLOQ. go to Davy Jones's locker
2 SUBMERGE, immerse, inundate, flood, sink, deluge, engulf, drench
3 *the end of her speech was drowned by applause*
drown out, silence, overwhelm, overpower, overcome, swamp, wipe out, howl out
OLD outvoice

> QUOTATIONS
> I was much too far out all my life / And not waving but drowning
>   Stevie Smith, 'Not Waving but Drowning'

drowsily adv
sleepily, wearily, lethargically, sluggishly, dopily, dozily

drowsiness n
sleepiness, tiredness, weariness, lethargy, sluggishness, dopiness, doziness
FORMAL oscitancy, somnolence, torpor
COLLOQ. grogginess

drowsy adj
sleepy, tired, weary, lethargic, nodding, dreamy, dozing, dozy, dopey, yawning, half-asleep, hardly able to keep your eyes open
FORMAL somnolent, torpid
F3 alert, awake

drubbing n
defeat, beating, flogging, pounding, pummelling, trouncing, walloping, whipping, hammering
COLLOQ. clobbering, licking, thrashing

drudge n, v
♦ n
toiler, menial, hack, labourer, servant, slave, factotum, worker, galley-slave, lackey
COLLOQ. dogsbody, skivvy
♦ v
plod, toil, work, slave, labour

COLLOQ. plug away, grind, beaver, slog away, keep your nose to the grindstone, work your fingers to the bone
F3 idle, laze

> QUOTATIONS
> Lexicographer. A writer of dictionaries, a harmless drudge
>   SAMUEL JOHNSON, *A Dictionary of the English Language*

drudgery n
labour, menial work, hackwork, slavery, sweat, sweated labour, toil, skivvying, chore
COLLOQ. donkey-work, grunt work, slog, grind

drug n, v
♦ n
medication, medicine, remedy, potion, cure
See panels below
♦ v
medicate, sedate, tranquillize, anaesthetize, make unconscious, dose, stupefy, deaden, numb, shanghai
COLLOQ. dope, knock out

drug addict n
COLLOQ. junkie, druggie, user, dope-fiend
SLANG freak, head, coke-head, tripper, mainliner, hop-head, hype, snowbird

drugged adj
stupefied
TECHNICAL comatose
COLLOQ. knocked out, high, spaced out, turned on, doped, zonked, on a trip
SLANG stoned, ripped, wasted

drum v
beat, pulsate, tap, throb, thrum, tattoo, reverberate, rap, knock
■ **drum into**
din into, drive home, hammer, harp on, instil, reiterate, inculcate
■ **drum out**
expel, discharge, dismiss
COLLOQ. throw out
■ **drum up**
obtain, round up, collect, gather, summon, solicit, canvass, petition, attract, get

---

Drugs include:

slang acid	chloroform	*colloq.* dope	laudanum	propranolol	tamoxifen
allopurinol	chloroquin(e)	*colloq.* ecstasy	LSD	Prozac®	temazepam
amoxicillin	cocaine	(or E)	marijuana	quinine	tetracycline
amphetamine	co-codamol	heparin	methadon(e)	ranitidine	Valium®
amyl nitrate	codeine	heroin	morphine	Ritalin®	Viagra®
aspirin	cortisone	hydrocortisone	neomycin	Rohypnol	warfarin
cannabis	*slang* crack	ibuprofen	opium	salbutamol	
chlorambucil	diazepam	insulin	paracetamol	*slang* smack	
chloramphenicol	digitalis	ipecacuanha	penicillin	*slang* speed	

Types of drug include:

ACE-inhibitor	anticoagulant	beta-blocker	diuretic	inhibitor	statin
agonist	anticonvulsant	biologic (or	*slang* downer	interferon	steroid
alpha-blocker	antidepressant	biological)	excitant	laxative	stimulant
anaesthetic	antiemetic	biopharmaceutical	expectorant	narcotic	stupefacient
analeptic	antifungal	broncho-con-	hallucinogenic	NSAID (non-	sulphonamide
analgesic	antihistamine	strictor	hepatic	steroidal anti-	tranquillizer
antacid	anti-inflammatory	bronchodilator	hypnotic	inflammatory	*slang* upper
antagonist	antiretroviral	corticosteroid	immunomodulator	drug)	vasoconstrictor
antibacterial	antiviral	decongestant	immuno-sup-	opiate	vasodilator
antibiotic	barbiturate	depressant	pressant	sedative	

See also **medicine**.

drunk *adj, n*

♦ *adj*

under the influence, drunken, inebriated, intoxicated, incapable, tipsy, mellow, merry, foxed; *dialect* fairish; *Scot* capernoity, fou; *Scot & Irish* stotious; *N Am* jagged
OLD overseen; (*Shakesp*) fap, paid
FORMAL crapulent, ebriose
COLLOQ. a sheet in the wind, three sheets in/to the wind, tight, tiddly, tiddled, well-oiled, blotto, drunk as a lord/ newt, drunk as a piper, drunk as a skunk, sloshed, stewed, blind drunk, roaring drunk, the worse for drink, soused, squiffy, happy, legless, hammered, plastered, sozzled, pickled, bibulous, woozy, one over the eight, under the table, bevvied, having had a few, tired and emotional, high, footless, full, half-cut, obfuscated, pie-eyed, sow-drunk, under the weather, the worse for wear
OLD COLLOQ. corked, moppy, overshot
SLANG stoned, tanked up, loaded, lit up, canned, paralytic, smashed, pissed, bombed, wasted, wrecked, trashed, mashed, trolleyed, stinko, whiffled, whistled, bonkers, bottled, Brahms and Liszt, juiced (up), in liquor, liquored, maggoty, mortal, up the pole, ripped; (*vulgar*) arseholed, rat-arsed, shitfaced; *Scot* blootered; *N Am* crocked, moon-eyed; *Aust* inky, inked; *Aust & NZ* shickered
E3 sober, temperate, abstinent, teetotal

♦ *n*

drunkard, alcoholic, inebriate, drinker, hard drinker, heavy drinker, dipsomaniac
COLLOQ. tippler
SLANG boozer, wino, lush, alkie, dipso, soak, piss artist, pisshead, toper, sot, tosspot, sponge; *Aust & NZ* shicker

---

SYNONYM NUANCES

adjective
The term **under the influence** has legal connotations, but could also be used facetiously: *he claimed he was in no way 'under the influence'*. **Drunken**, however, implies a propensity to overindulge in alcohol generally: *his violent drunken father*, whereas **incapable**, although slightly euphemistic, would be used if someone is drunk to such an extent that they are rendered helpless on a particular occasion: *he was in this incapable state most afternoons*.

Terms such as **mellow** and **merry**, on the other hand, are less judgemental, even positive, terms for someone in a relaxed or happy state induced by alcohol, though they too can often be used jocularly: *you seem particularly mellow tonight!* **Tipsy** similarly carries no tone of disapproval, and is reserved for mild drunkenness, sometimes with connotations of mischievousness: *mum is a bit tipsy and talking too much*. The term **foxed** is not often used nowadays, superseded by the abundance of colloquialisms coined, but conveys the impression of drunken confusion.

---

drunkard *n*

drunk, alcoholic, inebriate, drinker, hard drinker, heavy drinker, dipsomaniac, wine-bibber, bloater, fuddler, habitual; *N Am* souse
COLLOQ. tippler
SLANG boozer, wino, lush, alkie, dipso, soak, piss artist, pisshead, toper, sot, tosspot, sponge; *Aust & NZ* shicker

drunken *adj*

1 DRUNK
FORMAL inebriate, intoxicated, crapulent
COLLOQ. merry, tight, tipsy, tiddly, sloshed, happy
SLANG boozy, stoned, loaded, lit up, pissed, bombed
2 *a drunken party*
debauched, dissipated, riotous, intemperate, baccanalian
FORMAL crapulent
E3 1 sober

drunkenness *n*

intemperance, alcoholism, hard/serious drinking, debauchery, dipsomania

---

TECHNICAL methysis
FORMAL inebriation, inebriety, insobriety, intoxication, crapulence, ebriety, ebriosity, temulence
COLLOQ. bibulousness, tipsiness
E3 sobriety

dry *adj, v*

♦ *adj*

1 ARID, parched, baked, scorched, thirsty, dehydrated, barren, unwatered, waterless, rainless, moistureless, torrid, shrivelled, withered, wilted
TECHNICAL xeric
FORMAL desiccated
COLLOQ. dry as a bone
2 THIRSTY, dehydrated
COLLOQ. parched, gasping
3 TEETOTAL, abstinent, prohibitionist, temperate, alcohol-free, abstemious
COLLOQ. on the wagon
4 BORING, dull, dreary, tedious, monotonous, uninteresting, unexciting, wearisome, flat
COLLOQ. dry as dust
5 *dry humour*
witty, ironic, subtle, cynical, droll, clever, deadpan, sarcastic, cutting, low-key, laconic
E3 1 wet, damp **4** interesting, imaginative

♦ *v*

make/become dry, dehydrate, parch, scorch, drain, wipe, shrivel, wither, wilt
FORMAL desiccate
E3 soak, wet

■ **dry up**
1 FAIL, stop being productive, come to an end, disappear, stop, dwindle, wane, fade, die out
2 STOP TALKING, forget your lines, shut up, someone's mind goes blank

dryness *n*

aridity, aridness, drought, barrenness, dehydration, thirst, thirstiness
E3 wetness

dual *adj*

double, twofold, duplicate, duplex, binary, combined, paired, coupled, twin, two-piece, matched

duality *n*

doubleness, duplication, duplicity, combination, polarization, opposition, separation

dub *v*

name, call, entitle, confer, designate, label, nickname, style, tag, term, christen
FORMAL bestow

dubiety *n*

doubt, doubtfulness, indecision, uncertainty, misgiving, scepticism, suspicion, mistrust, qualm, hesitation
FORMAL incertitude
E3 certainty

dubious *adj*

1 DOUBTFUL, uncertain, undecided, unsure, wavering, vacillating, unsettled, suspicious, sceptical, hesitant, irresolute
2 QUESTIONABLE, debatable, unreliable, untrustworthy, ambiguous, suspect, suspicious, obscure
COLLOQ. fishy, shady, iffy, shifty; *Aust & NZ* crook
E3 1 certain **2** trustworthy

dubiously *adv*

1 *dubiously legal*
questionably, debatably, ambiguously, suspiciously
2 *she eyed the caller dubiously*
uncertainly, undecidedly, suspiciously, hesitantly

duck *v*

1 CROUCH, stoop, bob, bend, bow down, drop, squat
2 AVOID, evade, shirk, shun, sidestep, steer clear of, elude, dodge
COLLOQ. wriggle out of, worm your way out of, skive

3 DIP, immerse, plunge, dunk, dive, submerge, douse, souse, wet, lower

duct *n*

pipe, tube, channel, conduit, passage, vessel, canal, funnel, wireway
TECHNICAL deferent, diffuser, emunctory, excretory, ureter, vas, Venturi
FORMAL fistula

ductile *adj*

amenable, biddable, flexible, plastic, malleable, manageable, pliable, pliant, tractable, manipulable, yielding
FORMAL compliant
E∃ intractable; *formal* refractory

dud *n, adj*

♦ *n*
failure, flop, disappointment, let-down
COLLOQ. washout
♦ *adj*
broken, faulty, failed, valueless, worthless
FORMAL inoperative, nugatory
COLLOQ. bust, duff, kaput
SLANG conked out
E∃ working

due *adj, adv, n*

♦ *adj*
1 OWED, owing, payable, unpaid, outstanding, in arrears
2 RIGHTFUL, right, fitting, appropriate, proper, earned, merited, deserved, justified, suitable, correct
3 ADEQUATE, enough, sufficient, ample, plenty of
FORMAL requisite
4 EXPECTED, scheduled, anticipated, awaited, long-awaited, required
E∃ 1 paid **3** inadequate
♦ *adv*
exactly, direct(ly), precisely, straight
COLLOQ. dead
♦ *n*
1 *give him his due*
rights, (just) deserts, merits, prerogative, privilege, birthright
COLLOQ. comeuppance
2 *pay dues*
charge(s), contribution, fee, membership fee, levy, subscription

■ **due to**

owing to, as a result of, caused by, because of

duel *n*

affair of honour, *affaire d'honneur*, combat, contest, fight, clash, struggle, battle, competition, rivalry, engagement, encounter, tilt
OLD dependence, duello
FORMAL monomachy

duff *adj*

bad, poor-quality, poor, inferior, inadequate, weak, mediocre, substandard, imperfect, faulty, defective, deficient, unsatisfactory, unacceptable, second-rate, third-rate, hopeless, incompetent, mismanaged, ineffective
COLLOQ. awful, terrible, botched, lousy, crummy, pathetic, ropy, useless, a load of rubbish, a load of garbage
SLANG the pits, pants, poxy, naff, crappy

duffer *n*

bungler, blunderer, fool, idiot, ignoramus, oaf
COLLOQ. bonehead, clod, clot, dolt, dimwit, halfwit
SLANG plonker, dork, geek, git, prat

dulcet *adj*

sweet, sweet-sounding, gentle, pleasant, melodious, harmonious, mellow, soothing, soft, agreeable
FORMAL mellifluous

dull *adj, v*

♦ *adj*
1 BORING, uninteresting, unexciting, flat, dreary, monotonous, stereotyped, tedious, tiresome, wearisome, stultifying, uneventful, humdrum, unimaginative,

pedestrian, dismal, lifeless, plain, bland, insipid, heavy, ponderous
COLLOQ. dull as ditchwater
2 DARK, sombre, gloomy, drab, dreary, murky, indistinct, grey, dark, cloudy, lacklustre, matt, opaque, dim, overcast
3 UNINTELLIGENT, dense, dim, stupid, slow
COLLOQ. dimwitted, thick, dumb, birdbrained, dopey, dozy, slow on the uptake
4 *dull weather*
overcast, grey, cloudy, dim, dark, leaden, dreary, sombre, gloomy
5 *feel dull*
sluggish, slow, inactive, inert, idle, heavy, lethargic, slack
FORMAL torpid
6 *a dull pain*
weak, faint, mild, troublesome, uncomfortable, distressing
7 *a dull sound/thud*
muted, indistinct, weak, soft, quiet, feeble, muffled
8 BLUNT, unsharpened, edgeless
E∃ 1 interesting, exciting, lively **2** bright **3** intelligent, clever **4** fine, sunny **5** lively, energetic **6** sharp, intense, acute **7** sharp, loud **8** sharp
♦ *v*
1 BLUNT, alleviate, moderate, lessen, reduce, decrease, diminish, relieve, soften, allay, assuage, tone down
FORMAL mitigate
2 DEADEN, numb, paralyse, stupefy, drug, tranquillize, desensitize
OLD (*Shakesp*) mull
3 DISCOURAGE, dampen, subdue, lower, sadden, dishearten, depress, deject
4 DIM, obscure, darken, blacken, fade, wash out

dullard *n*

idiot, imbecile, ignoramus, moron, oaf, simpleton, dunce
COLLOQ. blockhead, bonehead, chump, clod, clot, dumbo, dimwit, dolt, dope, dunderhead, nitwit, numskull; *N Am* bufflehead
SLANG plonker, dork, git, prat
E∃ brain

dullness *n*

dreariness, emptiness, flatness, dryness, plainness, monotony, slowness, tedium, sluggishness
FORMAL torpor, vacuity, vapidity
E∃ excitement, interest, sharpness, brightness, clarity

duly *adv*

accordingly, appropriately, correctly, fitly, fittingly, properly, rightfully, suitably, sure enough, deservedly
FORMAL befittingly, decorously

dumb *adj*

1 *deaf and dumb*
silent, mute, soundless, speechless, tongue-tied, inarticulate, without speech, at a loss for words, lost for words
COLLOQ. mum
SLANG shtoom
2 STUPID, unintelligent, foolish, dense
COLLOQ. dim-witted, thick, brainless, gormless, dopey, dozy, as thick as two short planks

dumbfound *v*

astonish, surprise, startle, amaze, astound, stun, stupefy, daze, stagger, take aback, take your breath away, shock, confound, bewilder
COLLOQ. floor, flabbergast, flummox, bowl over, gobsmack, blow your mind, knock for six, wow

dumbfounded *adj*

astonished, amazed, astounded, overwhelmed, speechless, taken aback, startled, stunned, overcome, confounded, lost for words, staggered, confused, baffled, bewildered, dumb, nonplussed, paralysed
COLLOQ. thrown, flabbergasted, bowled over, floored, gobsmacked, knocked for six

dumbly *adv*

silently, mutely, soundlessly, speechlessly, inarticulately

dumbstruck adj
speechless, dumbfounded, thunderstruck, amazed, astounded, shocked, aghast, tongue-tied, inarticulate, mute, dumb, silent, mum
FORMAL obmutescent
🖃 talkative

dummy n, adj
♦ n
1 COPY, duplicate, imitation, mock-up, counterfeit, substitute, representation, reproduction, sample
2 MODEL, lay-figure, mannequin, figure, form
3 TEAT, pacifier
4 IDIOT, imbecile, fool, oaf
COLLOQ. blockhead, chump, clot, dimwit, numskull, nitwit; N Am bufflehead
SLANG plonker, dork, git, prat
♦ adj
1 ARTIFICIAL, fake, imitation, false, bogus, mock, sham
FORMAL feigned
COLLOQ. phoney
2 a dummy run
simulated, practice, trial

dump v, n
♦ v
1 DEPOSIT, put down, set down, lay down, place, drop, offload, throw down, let fall, fling down, unload, empty out, tip out, discharge, pour out, park
COLLOQ. plonk, bung
2 GET RID OF, discard, scrap, throw away, throw out, dispose of, ditch, tip, jettison
COLLOQ. chuck away
3 he dumped his girlfriend
leave, abandon, walk out on, desert, jilt
FORMAL forsake
COLLOQ. ditch, chuck, give the elbow/heave-ho to
♦ n
1 RUBBISH TIP, junkyard, rubbish heap, tip, scrapyard; Scot midden
2 HOVEL, slum, shack, shanty, mess
COLLOQ. hole, joint, tip, pigsty; N Am pigpen
■ down in the dumps
sad, depressed, unhappy, melancholy, miserable, downhearted, dejected, downcast, dispirited, low
COLLOQ. blue

dumpy adj
short, plump, stout, chubby, chunky, podgy, pudgy, squab, squat, stubby, tubby
🖃 tall

dun adj
greyish-brown, dull, dingy, mud-coloured, mouse-coloured

dunce n
fool, idiot, imbecile, dullard, loggerhead
COLLOQ. blockhead, bonehead, nincompoop, ninny, nitwit, numskull, twerp, twit, dimwit; N Am bufflehead
SLANG wally, dipstick, nerd, plonker, dork, git, prat
🖃 brain, intellectual

dung n
excrement, animal waste, droppings, manure, ordure, spraint, dirt, muck, mulch, soil, turd, album Graecum, argol, chip, buffalo chips, buttons, cock, guano, scumber, spraints; dialect tath; Scot sharn
OLD fumets, fewmets; (Shakesp) shard, siege
FORMAL faeces
COLLOQ. cack, doo-doo
SLANG dreck

dungeon n
cell, prison, jail, gaol, cage, lock-up, keep, oubliette, vault

dupe v, n
♦ v
deceive, delude, fool, trick, outwit, cheat, hoax, swindle, take in, hoodwink, defraud

COLLOQ. con, bamboozle, diddle, lead up the garden path, pull the wool over someone's eyes
SLANG rip off, take to the cleaners; N Am goldbrick
♦ n
victim, fool, gull, pawn, puppet, instrument, simpleton
COLLOQ. sucker, mug, pushover, fall guy, stooge

duplicate v, adj, n
♦ v
copy, reproduce, repeat, do again, photocopy, Xerox®, Photostat®, fax, facsimile, double, clone, echo
FORMAL replicate
♦ adj
identical, matching, twin, twofold, corresponding, paired, matched
♦ n
copy, replica, reproduction, model, photocopy, Xerox®, Photostat®, carbon (copy), match, mate, facsimile, fax, double, twin, clone, imitation, forgery
COLLOQ. lookalike, (dead) ringer, spitting image

duplication n
repetition, copy(ing), photocopy(ing), reproduction, doubling, clone, cloning
FORMAL dittography, gemination, replication
Related adjectives: phonocampticl

duplicity n
deceit, deceitfulness, deception, dishonesty, falsehood, fraud, guile, hypocrisy, double-dealing, treachery, betrayal, artifice, chicanery
FORMAL dissimulation, mendacity, perfidy

durability n
permanence, imperishability, persistence, stability, strength, endurance, constancy, lastingness
FORMAL durableness, longevity
🖃 fragility, impermanence, weakness

durable adj
lasting, enduring, long-lasting, abiding, hard-wearing, heavy-duty, reinforced, strong, solid, sturdy, tough, robust, unchanging, unfading, substantial, sound, reliable, dependable, stable, resistant, persistent, persisting, constant, permanent, firm, fixed, fast
🖃 changeable, perishable, weak, fragile

duration n
time, time span, time scale, extent, continuation, continuance, perpetuation, prolongation, fullness, length, length of time, period, span, spell, stretch, term
🖃 shortening

duress n
constraint, coercion, compulsion, pressure, restraint, threat, force, enforcement, exaction
COLLOQ. arm-twisting

during conj
at/in the time of, for the time of, in, throughout, in the course of, all the while

dusk n
twilight, sunset, nightfall, evening, sundown, darkness, dark, gloom, shadows, shade
OLD gloaming, owl-light
FORMAL crepuscule
🖃 dawn, brightness

dusky adj
1 SHADOWY, dark, dim, gloomy, murky, cloudy, foggy, misty, hazy, twilit
FORMAL crepuscular, tenebrous, fuliginous, subfusc
2 DARK-SKINNED, dark-coloured, dark-complexioned, swarthy, tawny, black, brown
🖃 1 bright 2 white

dust *n, v*

♦ *n*

powder, particles, dirt, earth, soil, ground, clay, grit, grime, soot, ashes, smut, smoke, smother, coom, culm, fallout, fuzz, mote, pother; *Scot* stour; *Aust* bulldust

TECHNICAL cryoconite, haemoconia, lemel, limail, bort, meteor streams, micro-meteorite, stardust, pozzolana

♦ *v*

1 CLEAN, wipe, brush, mop, burnish, polish, spray
2 SPRINKLE, powder, scatter, cover, spread, seed
OLD bedust

dust-up *n*

conflict, disagreement, quarrel, argument, disturbance, encounter, fight, fracas, brawl, brush, commotion, scuffle, skirmish, tussle

COLLOQ. argy-bargy, punch-up, bust-up, scrap, set-to, barney

dusty *adj*

1 DIRTY, grubby, grimy, filthy, dust-covered, sooty
2 POWDERY, granular, crumbly, chalky, sandy
FORMAL friable
E3 1 clean **2** solid, hard

dutiful *adj*

obedient, respectful, conscientious, devoted, filial, reverential, deferential, compliant, submissive, thoughtful, considerate

duty *n*

1 OBLIGATION, responsibility, burden, onus, assignment, calling, charge, part, role, task, job, chore, business, function, work, office, service, commission, mission, requirement
2 OBEDIENCE, respect, loyalty, allegiance, faithfulness
FORMAL fidelity
3 TAX, toll, tariff, levy, customs, excise, dues

■ **off duty**

not working, on holiday, off, off work, free, resting, inactive

■ **on duty**

at work, working, on call, engaged, busy, occupied, active
COLLOQ. tied up

QUOTATIONS

Your duty, your reward, your destiny are here and now
DAG HJALMAR AGNE CARL HAMMARSKJÖLD,
Vägmarken

SYNONYM NUANCES

sense 1

Obligation is often used of something legally or morally binding: *journalists have an obligation to protect their sources*, whilst **responsibility** and **charge** have the added implication of being accountable for something: *the manager has responsibility for the computer system; he handed the project over to their charge.* **Burden**, however, would only be appropriate of a duty that is cumbersome, as would **onus**.

For a particular, allocated duty the terms **task** or **job**, or the more specific **assignment** or **commission**, could be used: *his commission was to review teaching methods.* The term **mission** likewise suggests being assigned a specific, and highly important, purpose: *the unit's mission was to prevent any nation from mounting an attack.* **Chore** further implies a set duty that is unpleasant or tedious: *my daily household chores tire me out.*

Both **business** and **work** emphasize the aspect of labour and refer to a more continuous duty, similarly **function**, which suggests a specific purpose that is peculiar to an office or job: *the proper function of government is to manage things well.*

---

dwarf *n, adj, v*

♦ *n*

1 PERSON OF RESTRICTED GROWTH, midget, pygmy, Tom Thumb, Lilliputian
2 GNOME, goblin

♦ *adj*

miniature, little, small, tiny, pocket, diminutive, minute, petite, Lilliputian, baby, pygmy, stunted, undersized
COLLOQ. mini
E3 large

♦ *v*

1 STUNT, retard, check, arrest, atrophy
2 OVERSHADOW, tower over, dominate
COLLOQ. stand head and shoulders above

dwell *v*

live, inhabit, stay, settle, populate, people, lodge, rest
OLD (*Shakesp*) remain
FORMAL reside, abide, be domiciled
COLLOQ. hang out

■ **dwell on**

brood on, think about, meditate on, turn over in your mind, reflect on, mull over, harp on, linger over, elaborate, emphasize
FORMAL expatiate, ruminate on
E3 pass over

dweller *n*

inhabitant, occupant, occupier, resident
FORMAL denizen

dwelling *n*

home, house, establishment, residence, place, quarters, flat, apartment, tenement, penthouse, *pied-à-terre*; *Scot* single-end, weem; *S Afr* pondok; dwelling-house, lodge, lodging, cottage, hut, shanty, bothy, tent, roof, hovel, doghole, dug
TECHNICAL messuage
OLD bower, cot, won; (*Spenser*) grange
FORMAL abode, domicile, habitation

dwindle *v*

diminish, decrease, decline, reduce, become/grow less, lessen, subside, ebb, fade, weaken, taper off, tail off, shrink, fall, wane, peter out, waste away, die out, wither, shrivel, vanish, disappear
E3 increase, grow

dye *n, v*

♦ *n*

colour, colouring, agent, stain, wash, pigment, tint, shade, hue, tinge

♦ *v*

colour, tint, stain, shade, pigment, tinge, imbue
Related adjective: tinctorial

dyed-in-the-wool *adj*

entrenched, inveterate, deep-rooted, diehard, established, long-standing, settled, fixed, hard-core, hardened, inflexible, unchangeable, uncompromising, unshak(e)able, through and through, thorough, confirmed, complete, card-carrying
E3 superficial

dying *adj*

1 *a dying woman*
close/near to death, not long for this world, at death's door, on your deathbed, passing, going, mortal, perishing, failing, fading, vanishing, ebbing
FORMAL moribund
COLLOQ. with one foot in the grave, on your last legs
2 *the dying moments of the match*
last, final, closing, concluding, finishing
E3 1 reviving

dynamic *adj*

forceful, powerful, active, strong, energetic, full of energy, vigorous, high-powered, driving, go-ahead, effective, self-starting, spirited, vital, lively, potent
COLLOQ. go-getting
E3 inactive, apathetic

dynamically *adv*
forcefully, powerfully, actively, strongly, energetically, vigorously, effectively, vitally
◨ inactively

dynamism *n*
energy, forcefulness, drive, initiative, liveliness, vigour, spirit, enterprise
COLLOQ. get-up-and-go, go, pep, pizzazz, push, vim, zap, zip
◨ apathy, inactivity, slowness

dynasty *n*
house, line, lineage, succession, dominion, regime, government, authority, rule, jurisdiction, empire, sovereignty

dyspepsia *n*
dyspepsy, heartburn, cardialgia, acidity, pyrosis, water-brash

dyspeptic *adj*
bad-tempered, irritable, gloomy, indigested, peevish, short-tempered, snappish, testy, touchy

COLLOQ. stroppy, in a huff, in a sulk, having got out of bed on the wrong side, having a short fuse, cross as a bear with a sore head, crotchety, crabbed, crabby, grouchy, shirty, ratty, edgy, feisty, humpy

each *adj, pron, adv*
♦ *adj*
every, every single, every individual
♦ *pron*
each one, each in their own way, each and
every one
♦ *adv*
apiece, individually, per capita, per head,
per person, respectively, separately, singly

eager *adj*
1 ENTHUSIASTIC, keen, fervent, intent, earnest,
wholehearted, zealous, impatient, avid,
ardent, diligent; *Scot* frack;
N Am gung-ho
OLD fain, rath; (*Shakesp*) prone
SLANG up for it
2 LONGING, yearning, anxious, impatient,
keen, intent, wishing, greedy,
thirsty, hungry
COLLOQ. desperate, dying
F3 1 unenthusiastic, indifferent, reluctant

eagerly *adv*
keenly, enthusiastically, fervently, intently,
earnestly, wholeheartedly, impatiently, ardently,
avidly, zealously, greedily
F3 apathetically, listlessly

eagerness *n*
keenness, enthusiasm, fervency, fervour,
intentness, earnestness, wholeheartedness,
impatience, ardour, avidity, impetuosity, zeal,
longing, yearning, greediness, hunger, thirst
FORMAL fervidity
COLLOQ. yen
F3 apathy, disinterest

ear *n*
1 *deaf in his right ear*
earhole; *dialect* souse
TECHNICAL auricle
COLLOQ. lug
SLANG shell-like, lughole
Related adjectives: aural, auricular, otic
2 ATTENTION, heed, notice, regard, attentiveness
3 *an ear for language*
perception, sensitivity, discrimination,
appreciation, hearing, skill,
ability, taste
■ *play it by ear*
ad-lib, extemporize, improvise
COLLOQ. wing it, take things as they come,
think on your feet

Parts of the ear include:

anvil (incus)	eustachian tube	round window
auditory canal	hammer (malleus)	semicircular canal
auditory nerve	helix	stirrup (stapes)
auricle	labyrinth	tragus
cochlea	lobe	tympanum
concha	oval window	vestibular nerve
eardrum	pinna	vestibule

early *adj, adv*
♦ *adj*
1 *early symptoms/stages*
forward, advanced, advance, premature, untimely,
undeveloped, precocious, first, initial, opening
2 *early theatre*
primitive, ancient
TECHNICAL autochthonous
FORMAL prim(a)eval, primordial
F3 1 late **2** modern, contemporary
♦ *adv*
1 *early in the day*
in the (early) morning, at dawn, at daybreak
2 AHEAD OF TIME, ahead of schedule, in good time,
beforehand, before the usual/arranged/expected time,
with time to spare, in advance, too soon, prematurely
F3 1 late

earmark *v*
set aside, put aside, lay aside, designate, allocate, keep
back, reserve, label, mark out, tag

earn *v*
1 *earn a good salary*
receive, be/get paid, obtain, make, get, draw, clear, gain,
realize, gross, net, collect, pocket, take home, reap
COLLOQ. bring in, pull in, rake in
2 *earn your reputation*
deserve, merit, be owed, be someone's by right, warrant,
win, rate, obtain, secure, attain, achieve
F3 1 spend, lose

earnest¹ *adj*
1 SERIOUS, sincere, solemn, grave, heartfelt, intense,
dedicated, committed, thoughtful, zealous, devout
OLD sad, dear
FORMAL assiduous
2 RESOLUTE, devoted, ardent, conscientious, diligent, intent,
keen, fervent, firm, fixed, eager, enthusiastic, steady,
persistent, urgent
OLD forward, wistful
F3 1 frivolous, flippant **2** apathetic
■ *in earnest*
1 SERIOUSLY, resolutely, ardently, conscientiously, intently,
steadily, wholeheartedly, passionately, purposefully,
zealously
2 SINCERE, genuine, serious, not joking
F3 2 in jest, as a joke

earnest² *n*
the earnest of heavenly gifts
deposit, down payment, guarantee, pledge, token,
security, assurance, determination, promise, resolution,
seriousness, sincerity, truth
OLD arles, earnest-penny, press-money

earnestly *adv*
seriously, sincerely, intently, resolutely, firmly, keenly,
eagerly, fervently, warmly, zealously
F3 flippantly, listlessly

earnestness *n*
seriousness, sincerity, gravity, purposefulness, resolution,
intentness, determination, ardour, devotion, eagerness,
enthusiasm, fervency, fervour, zeal, keenness, passion,
vehemence, warmth
F3 apathy, flippancy

earnings n
pay, income, salary, wages, profits, take home pay, net pay, gross pay, gain, proceeds, reward, receipts, return, revenue, fee, remuneration, honorarium, stipend
FORMAL emolument
E3 expenditure, outgoings

earth n
1 WORLD, planet, globe, sphere, orb
Related adjectives: terrestrial, telluric
2 LAND, ground, soil, topsoil, turf, clay, loam, sod, humus, dirt

earthenware n
pottery, ceramics, crockery, stoneware, pots

earthly adj
1 *our earthly life*
material, physical, human, worldly, mortal, mundane, fleshly, secular, sensual, materialistic, profane, temporal
FORMAL terrestrial, tellurian, telluric
2 *no earthly explanation*
possible, likely, imaginable, conceivable, slightest, feasible
E3 1 spiritual, heavenly

SYNONYM NUANCES

sense 1
Material suggests having a physical substance, and is often used as the opposite of spiritual: *our material needs*; **physical** has more to do with matters of the body: *physical pain*. **Human** is suggestive of mankind, and tends to be used in speaking of its limitations: *human nature*. **Worldly**, on the other hand, while it can be used literally of being of this world: *this is a worldly paradise*, can also be used to imply a preoccupation with material aspects: *a worldly, go-ahead, businessman*.
The term **mortal**, with its suggestion of eventual and inevitable death, is again suggestive of limitations: *no mortal man could have travelled this far*. The word **temporal** may also be used to suggest the finite nature of things: *the king rules over the Church as well as his temporal kingdom*. **Mundane** returns to the idea of being of this world: *mundane and this-worldly considerations*; however, it is more often suggestive of ordinariness: *the mundane aspects of working life*. The term **fleshly** again puts the emphasis firmly on the body and the idea of being corporeal.
You may use **secular** without any implication if you are referring to something that is not concerned with religion; **profane**, though similar in meaning, further suggests irreverence or blasphemy: *the deep gulf between sacred and profane*. **Sensual**, meanwhile, emphasizes the senses as distinct from the mind: *I take sensual pleasure in the natural world*. **Materialistic**, which is a fairly disapproving term, describes being overly concerned with material goods.

---

earthquake n
earth-tremor, tremor, quake, seism, shake, upheaval, convulsion, shock, aftershock
Related adjectives: seismic, seismal, terremotive

earthy adj
1 *an earthy smell*
soillike, earthlike, claylike, dirtlike
2 DOWN TO EARTH, natural, simple, direct, unsophisticated, unrefined, uninhibited
3 *earthy humour*
crude, coarse, rude, vulgar, bawdy, rough, ribald
FORMAL indecorous
COLLOQ. raunchy, blue
E3 2 inhibited **3** proper, modest

ease n, v
♦ *n*
1 EFFORTLESSNESS, facility, skilfulness, deftness, adroitness, dexterity, naturalness, cleverness

2 COMFORT, contentment, enjoyment, peace, peacefulness, affluence, prosperity, wealth, leisure, relaxation, rest, quiet, happiness, lap of luxury
FORMAL repose, opulence
COLLOQ. bed of roses, easy street, life of Riley
E3 1 difficulty **2** discomfort
♦ *v*
1 *ease the pain*
alleviate, moderate, grow/become less, lessen, reduce, diminish, lighten, relieve, relent, allay, assuage, relax, comfort, calm, soothe, facilitate, smooth, quieten, salve
FORMAL mitigate, abate, ameliorate, palliate
2 *ease it into position*
inch, steer, edge, slide, manoeuvre, guide
E3 1 aggravate, intensify, worsen
■ **ease off**
decrease, become less, die away, die down, diminish, moderate, relent, slacken, subside, wane
FORMAL abate
E3 increase
■ **at ease**
relaxed, natural, composed, calm, secure, at home, comfortable

easily adv
1 EFFORTLESSLY, comfortably, readily, simply, fluently, straightforwardly
2 *easily the best*
by far, undoubtedly, without doubt, indisputably, definitely, certainly, doubtlessly, clearly, far and away, undeniably, simply, surely, probably, well
COLLOQ. by a country mile
E3 1 laboriously

easy adj
1 SIMPLE, effortless, uncomplicated, undemanding, straightforward, foolproof, manageable, painless, natural
COLLOQ. cushy, a cinch, a doddle, a piece of cake, a pushover, a cakewalk, a walk in the park, easy as ABC, easy-peasy, easy as pie, child's play, like falling off a log, not rocket science
SLANG (*vulgar*) a piece of piss
2 RELAXED, carefree, easy-going, comfortable, informal, calm, natural, leisurely, casual, unforced
COLLOQ. laid-back
E3 1 difficult, hard, demanding, exacting **2** tense, uneasy

---

SYNONYM NUANCES

sense 1
Simple a fairly positive word that can be used, as it often is in advertising, to play down potential difficulty: *a simple task; simple to use; a simple mistake*. **Effortless** makes the appealing suggestion of requiring little exertion, while **painless** also has to do with causing minimum upset: *a painless solution to council overspending*.
Natural could be used of something that is easy because it is instinctive, so implying that it requires little or no thought: *French life proceeds at its natural, inviting pace*. The terms **uncomplicated** and **straightforward** again convey the positive idea of something that may be easily followed, without any troublesome complexity: *an uncomplicated skincare routine; straightforward logic*.
The term **undemanding** can have a slightly negative aspect as it may suggest lacking a challenge: *undemanding and tedious work*. The implication of **foolproof** is that anyone could succeed with it, so it is infallible. **Manageable**, however, is not such an emphatic term, which you could use of something one is able to deal with rather than do easily: *a relatively manageable task on the computer*.

---

easy-going adj
relaxed, tolerant, lenient, amenable, undemanding, carefree, nonchalant, calm, equable, even-tempered, serene, placid

FORMAL insouciant, imperturbable
COLLOQ. laid-back, happy-go-lucky
☒ strict, intolerant, critical

eat v
1 CONSUME, feed, swallow, devour, chew, munch, pick, have a snack, have a bite, breakfast, lunch, dine, gulp down, bolt down, gobble, cram, chop, binge
OLD mess
FORMAL ingest, partake of, gormandize, manducate
COLLOQ. scoff, snarf, put away, wolf down, tuck in(to), polish off, graze, knock back, peck, guts; N Am chow down
SLANG grub, nosh, pig, pig out; N Am scarf
2 CORRODE, erode, wear away, bite into, decay, rot, crumble, dissolve, undermine, fret
OLD begnaw

SYNONYM NUANCES

sense 1
The word **consume** is a relatively unmarked term, but can sometimes carry the added suggestion of using or taking up completely, whether literally or figuratively: *vast quantities of food were consumed; she was consumed with envy.* **Feed** is often used of animals, and to use the term of humans can suggest, perhaps even with a hint a disgust, an instinctive or greedy action of taking in as nourishment: *we fed hungrily on the leftovers.*

Swallow suggests the act of moving food or drink down the throat, and like **gulp down**, **bolt down** and **gobble**, it suggests eating quickly and greedily. The term **devour** also suggests doing this with great gusto. **Gormandize** is a less common word for eating with what might seem an unappealing voraciousness. **Cram**, likewise, suggests packing in as much food as possible in the shortest time, and suggests an unpleasantly greedy action. The term **chew** is suggestive of a slower, more deliberate action, as is **munch**, which often also implies an element of enthusiasm and is used in positive contexts: *she munched on a cake and felt better.*

The verb **pick**, on the other hand, could be used more negatively to imply a lack of interest in eating: *she seemed lifeless and picked at her meal.* The terms **breakfast**, **lunch** and **dine** tell you very little about the manner of eating, but are neutral terms which put the emphasis on the formal situation of taking a meal.

---

eatable adj
edible, palatable, good, wholesome, digestible
FORMAL comestible
☒ inedible, unpalatable

❗ eatable or edible?
If something is *edible*, it is by nature safe or good to eat, whereas if it is *eatable*, it is in a condition that makes it possible to eat it (whether or not it is safe to do so). Poisonous mushrooms are *eatable* but they are not *edible*, while a bag of flour is perfectly *edible* but would scarcely be *eatable*.

---

eavesdrop v
listen in, spy, overhear, monitor
COLLOQ. snoop, tap, bug

eavesdropper n
listener, monitor, spy
COLLOQ. snoop, snooper

ebb v, n
♦ v
1 *the tide ebbed*
fall, fall back, flow back, go out, recede
FORMAL retrocede
2 *his confidence ebbed away*
decline, decrease, diminish, drop, dwindle, flag, weaken, deteriorate, decay, degenerate, fade away, shrink, sink, slacken, subside, recede, lessen, wane, peter out

FORMAL abate
☒ **1** rise **2** increase, rise
♦ n
1 *at ebb tide*
low tide, low water, fall, going-out, flowing-back, receding, retreat
2 *her health is at a low ebb*
decline, decrease, drop, decay, lagging, lessening, deterioration, degeneration, slackening, weakening, subsiding, subsidence, wane, waning, dwindling
FORMAL abatement
☒ **1** rise, flow **2** increase

ebony adj
black, dark, jet, jet-black, jetty, inky, sable, sooty

ebullience n
exhilaration, effusiveness, enthusiasm, excitement, exuberance, brightness, buoyancy, elation, vivacity, high spirits, breeziness, zest
COLLOQ. chirpiness, bubbliness
☒ apathy, dullness, lifelessness

ebullient adj
exhilarated, effusive, enthusiastic, excited, exuberant, bright, buoyant, elated, gushing, vivacious, effervescent, breezy, irrepressible, zestful
COLLOQ. chirpy, bubbly
☒ apathetic, dull, lifeless

eccentric adj, n
♦ adj
odd, peculiar, abnormal, unconventional, strange, quirky, weird, off, queer, outlandish, idiosyncratic, bizarre, freakish, erratic, singular, fey
FORMAL aberrant
COLLOQ. way-out, wacky, dotty, off-beat, off the wall, nutty, loopy, kinky, screwy, kooky; N Am flaky, ditsy
SLANG loony, spacy; N Am loony tunes
☒ conventional, orthodox, normal
♦ n
nonconformist, oddity, crank
COLLOQ. oddball, freak, character, case, card, nut, nutter, nutjob, nutcase, weirdo, wacko, crackpot, kook, odd fish, square peg in a round hole, fish out of water; N Am flake, ditz, screwball
SLANG loony, loon, geek; N Am dingbat, wack, cupcake; Aust dag

eccentricity n
unconventionality, strangeness, unorthodoxy, peculiarity, nonconformity, abnormality, oddity, bizarreness, weirdness, idiosyncrasy, singularity, quirk, quirkiness, freakishness, anomaly
FORMAL aberration, capriciousness
☒ conventionality, ordinariness

ecclesiastic n
churchman/woman, cleric, clergyman/woman, man/woman of God, man/woman of the cloth, minister, priest, reverend, father, vicar, pastor, padre, parson, rector, canon, dean, deacon, deaconess, chaplain, curate, presbyter, preacher

ecclesiastical adj
church, churchly, religious, clerical, priestly, holy, divine, spiritual, pastoral, ministerial
FORMAL sacerdotal
☒ secular, temporal

echelon n
level, rank, grade, rung, tier, degree, position, place, status

echo n, v
♦ n
1 REVERBERATION, ringing, resounding, reiteration, repetition, reflection
OLD (Shakesp) replication
2 IMITATION, copy, reproduction, reflection, mirror image, image, parallel, repeat, clone, duplicate

3 REMINDER, memory, remembrance, allusion, hint, trace, remains, vestige
FORMAL evocation
Related adjective: phonocamptic
♦ *v*
1 REVERBERATE, resound, resonate, repeat, reflect, reiterate, ring
2 IMITATE, copy, reproduce, mirror, reflect, resemble, mimic, repeat, parallel, parrot

éclat *n*
glory, brilliance, lustre, style, stylishness, ostentation, flamboyance, show, distinction, display, success, splendour, acclaim, renown, acclamation, applause, approval, effect, fame, celebrity
FORMAL plaudits
🖙 disapproval, dullness

eclectic *adj*
diverse, wide-ranging, wide, many-sided, catholic, broad, comprehensive, diversified, general, all-embracing, liberal, varied, selective
FORMAL heterogeneous, multifarious
🖙 narrow, one-sided, exclusive

eclipse *v, n*
♦ *v*
1 BLOT OUT, obscure, cloud, cover, block, conceal, veil, shroud, darken, dim, cast a shadow over
2 OUTDO, overshadow, outshine, surpass, exceed, transcend, excel, dwarf, put into the shade, leave someone standing
COLLOQ. run rings around
♦ *n*
1 OVERSHADOWING, blotting-out, darkening, concealing, covering, veiling, shading, dimming
FORMAL obscuration
2 DECLINE, failure, fall, loss, decay, ebb, weakening

economic *adj*
1 COMMERCIAL, business, industrial, trade
2 FINANCIAL, budgetary, fiscal, monetary
FORMAL pecuniary
3 PROFITABLE, profit-making, moneymaking, productive, cost-effective, viable, rewarding, remunerative

> **QUOTATIONS**
> The most basic law of economics ... that one cannot get something for nothing
> SIR ROY HARROD, *Towards a Dynamic Economics*

> **!** **economic** or **economical**?
> *Economic* means 'relating to economics or the economy of a country': *economic history; the country's economic future*. It also means 'giving an adequate profit or fair return', as in *We must charge an economic rent/price*. *Economical* means 'thrifty', 'not wasteful, expensive, or extravagant': *This car is very economical on petrol; the economical use of limited supplies*.

economical *adj*
1 THRIFTY, careful, prudent, saving, sparing, frugal, provident, scrimping, skimping
FORMAL parsimonious
2 CHEAP, inexpensive, low-price, low-priced, low-cost, low-budget, bargain-basement, reasonable, cost-effective, budget, modest, efficient
🖙 **1** wasteful **2** expensive, uneconomical

economics
See panels on next page

economize *v*
save, cut back, budget, cut expenditure, use less, buy cheaply, keep down costs, live on the cheap, cut costs, be economical, scrimp and save
FORMAL retrench
COLLOQ. tighten your belt, pull/tighten the purse strings, cut corners, cut your coat according to your cloth
🖙 waste, squander

economy *n*
1 *the country's economy*
system of wealth, wealth, financial state, financial resources, financial system, financial organization, business resources
2 THRIFT, saving, restraint, carefulness, care, frugality, parsimony, providence, prudence, husbandry, scrimping, skimping
🖙 **2** extravagance

ecstasy *n*
delight, rapture, bliss, elation, joy, jubilation, euphoria, frenzy, exultation, fervour, transports of delight, pleasure
🖙 misery, torment

> **QUOTATIONS**
> This is the very ecstasy of love, / Whose violent property fordoes itself / And leads the will to desperate undertakings
> WILLIAM SHAKESPEARE, *Hamlet*

ecstatic *adj*
elated, blissful, joyful, jubilant, rapturous, enraptured, in raptures, overjoyed, euphoric, delirious, frenzied, fervent
FORMAL rhapsodic
COLLOQ. jumping for joy, on cloud nine, in seventh heaven, over the moon, tickled pink, high as a kite; *Aust & NZ* rapt
🖙 downcast

ecumenical *adj*
interdenominational, nondenominational, nonsectarian, broad-based, all-embracing, universal, catholic

eddy *n, v*
♦ *n*
whirlpool, swirl, swirling, vortex, twist, maelstrom
♦ *v*
swirl, whirl, spin, turn, twist, twirl, reel, roll, swish

edge *n, v*
♦ *n*
1 BORDER, rim, boundary, frontier, limit, brim, threshold, brink, fringe, margin, outline, outer limit, side, verge, line, extremity, perimeter, periphery, lip
2 ADVANTAGE, superiority, force, dominance, head, lead
FORMAL ascendancy
COLLOQ. upper hand, whip hand
3 SHARPNESS, acuteness, keenness, incisiveness, severity, zest, bite, sting
FORMAL pungency, acerbity, causticity, trenchancy
♦ *v*
creep, crawl, inch, ease, steal, sidle, elbow, worm, pick your way
■ **on edge**
nervous, tense, anxious, apprehensive, ill at ease, highly-strung, keyed-up, touchy, irritable
COLLOQ. uptight, nervy, edgy
🖙 calm, at ease

edgy *adj*
on edge, nervous, tense, anxious, highly-strung, ill at ease, keyed-up, touchy, irritable
COLLOQ. uptight, nervy
🖙 calm, at ease

edible *adj*
eatable, fit to eat, safe to eat, palatable, digestible, wholesome, good, harmless
FORMAL comestible
🖙 inedible

> **!** **edible** or **eatable**?
> *See panel at* **eatable**.

edict *n*
command, order, proclamation, law, decree, regulation, pronouncement, rule, ruling, act, mandate, statute, fiat, injunction, manifesto, pronunciamento, ukase

Economics terms include:

acquisition
alternative asset
annuity
asset
autarky
bad bank
bailout
balance of trade
bear market
black economy
boiler room
boom
budget
budget deficit
bull market
business cycle
buy-back
capital
capital expenditure
capitalism
cartel
cash flow
cash ratio
CAT standard
Central Bank
Chancellor of the
  Exchequer
(the) City
clearing-house
club deal
command econ-
  omy
commercial bank
commodity
common market
consumer
consumer good

corporation tax
cost-benefit
  analysis
credit
colloq. credit
  crunch
credit easing
credit rating
credit squeeze
dead cat bounce
debt
deficit
deflation
deleverage
depression
devaluation
discount
discount rate
disequilibrium
dividend
double dip
Dow-Jones aver-
  age or index
econometrics
economic deter-
  minism
economic rent
economic sanc-
  tions
economy of scale
e-economy
embargo
enterprise culture
equity finance
European Mone-
  tary Union
  (EMU)

excise duty or tax
financial year
fiscal drag
fiscal stimulus
fiscal year
fixed capital
flash crash
foreign exchange
free-market econ-
  omy
free-trade area
FTSE
funds
futures
General Agree-
  ment on Tariffs
  and Trade
  (GATT)
gilt-edged security
gold reserve
gold standard
green fund
grey economy
gross domestic
  product (GDP)
gross national
  product (GNP)
gross profit
  margin
Group of 7 (G7)
Group of 8 (G8)
hidden economy
human capital
income tax
input-output analy-
  sis
interest

International
  Monetary Fund
  (IMF)
law of supply and
  demand
leverage
liability
liquid asset
liquidity
liquidization
listed company
marginal cost or
  revenue
market economy
mature
merchant bank
mixed economy
monetary
money supply
monopoly
mortgage
NASDAQ®
new economy
offshoring
old economy
oligopoly
open economy
Organization for
  Economic Co-
  operation and
  Development
  (OECD)
overheating
overleveraging
personal equity
  plan (PEP)
Phillips curve

planned economy
political economy
Ponzi scheme
price control
(retail) price index
private enterprise
private sector
producer
product
productivity
profits warning
protectionism
public sector
quantitative easing
rationalization
recession
reflation
reserve bank
reserve currency
savings
Sedol number
share
siege economy
single currency
slump
socio-economic
(the) Square Mile
stagflation
stakeholder
stakeholder econ-
  omy
stamp duty
sterling overnight
  interbank average
  rate (SONIA)
stock
stock exchange

stock market
stop-go policy
structured invest-
  ment vehicle
  (SIV)
tariff
taxation
tax avoidance
tax evasion
tax haven
tiger economy
toxic asset
toxic bank
toxic debt
trade cycle
trade gap/deficit
trademark
trader
trade union
transaction
Troubled Assets
  Relief Program
  (TARP)
trust
unit trust
Wall Street
working capital
World Trade
  Organization
  (WTO)
yield
zombie bank

Economic theories or schools include:

Austrian school
Chicago school
Classical school

Game theory
Keynesian
Marxian

Mercantilism
Neo-classical
Neo-Keynesian

Neo-Ricardian
New classical
  economics

Physiocracy
Post-Keynesian

Types of economics include:

agronomics
cliometrics
econometrics

macroeconomics
microeconomics

edification *n*
  instruction, improvement, enlightenment, guidance,
  education, teaching, coaching, tuition, upbuilding,
  elevation, uplifting

edifice *n*
  building, construction, structure, erection

edify *v*
  instruct, build up, improve, enlighten, inform,
  guide, educate, tutor, nurture, teach, school, coach,
  elevate, uplift

edit *v*
  1 *edit a text*
  correct, revise, rewrite, rephrase, reorder, rearrange, adapt,
  modify, check, compile, subedit, copy-edit, proofread,
  select, polish, annotate, blue-pencil
  FORMAL emend, redact
  2 *edit a newspaper*
  be in charge of, direct, head (up), be responsible for
  3 *edit an anthology*
  compile, choose, select, put together, arrange, assemble,
  collect, gather, organize

edition *n*
  copy, volume, impression, printing, publication, issue,
  version, number

editor *n*
  1 *a newspaper editor*
  publisher, director, journalist, writer, reporter,
  correspondent, reviewer, newspaperman/woman,
  newsman/woman, newscaster
  2 *a freelance editor*
  reviser, checker, amender, corrector, rewriter, subeditor,
  copy editor, proofreader

educable *adj*
  instructible, teachable, trainable
  E3 ineducable

educate *v*
  teach, train, instruct, tutor, coach, school, inform,
  cultivate, edify, enlighten, drill, improve, prepare, prime,
  discipline, indoctrinate, develop, bring up, nurture,
  nourish, take in hand
  OLD institute, uptrain
  FORMAL inculcate

educated *adj*
learned, taught, schooled, literate, trained, knowledgeable, enlightened, informed, instructed, lettered, well-read, cultured, civilized, cultivated, wise, tutored, refined, well-bred
FORMAL erudite, sagacious
COLLOQ. brainy, all there, clever-clever
E∃ uneducated, uncultured

education *n*
teaching, training, schooling, tuition, tutoring, coaching, guidance, instruction, informing, drilling, cultivation, culture, letters, scholarship, improvement, enlightenment, edification, knowledge, nurture, preparation, fostering, upbringing, development, indoctrination
FORMAL inculcation
See panels below

> QUOTATIONS
> The most fundamental value of a liberal education is that it makes life more interesting
> KINGMAN BREWSTER, JR

educational *adj*
academic, learning, teaching, cultural, edifying, enlightening, educative, improving, informative, instructive, minds-on
FORMAL didactic, scholastic, pedagogic, pedagogical
E∃ uninformative

educative *adj*
instructive, improving, informative, edifying, educational, enlightening
FORMAL catechetic, catechismal, catechistic(al), didactic
E∃ uninformative

educator *n*
instructor, teacher, tutor, schoolteacher, schoolmaster, master, schoolmistress, mistress, educationalist, lecturer, professor, academic, trainer, coach
FORMAL pedagogue

eerie *adj*
weird, strange, unnatural, unearthly, mysterious, sinister, uncanny, ghostly, frightening, scaring, scary, bloodcurdling
COLLOQ. spooky, creepy, spine-chilling

eerily *adv*
weirdly, strangely, unnaturally, mysteriously, uncannily

efface *v*
remove, destroy, delete, rub out, wipe out, cancel, eliminate, eradicate, obliterate, erase, blank out, blot out, cross out
FORMAL excise, expunge, extirpate

effect *n, v*
◆ *n*
1 OUTCOME, result, conclusion, consequence, upshot, fruit, impact, aftermath, issue
2 POWER, force, impact, action, impression, strength, influence
FORMAL efficacy
3 MEANING, significance, sense, drift, tenor, thread
FORMAL import, purport
4 *personal effects*
belongings, possessions, property, goods, mov(e)ables, paraphernalia, baggage, luggage, things, trappings
FORMAL chattels, accoutrements
COLLOQ. gear, stuff, clobber
◆ *v*
cause, execute, bring about, carry out, create, achieve, accomplish, perform, produce, make, initiate, give rise to, fulfil, complete
FORMAL generate, effectuate
■ **in effect**
in fact, actually, in actual fact, really, in reality, in truth, to all intents and purposes, in practice, for all practical purposes, essentially, effectively, virtually
■ **take effect**
be effective, become operative, come into force, come into operation, come into service, be implemented,

---

Educational establishments include:

academy	college	convent school	*Aust* kinder	preparatory school	sixth-form college
adult-education centre	college of further education	faith school	kindergarten	primary school	summer-school
beacon school	college of	finishing school	*Aust & NZ* kindy	private school	Sunday school
boarding school	technology	foundation school	middle school	public school	technical college
business school	combined school	grammar school	non-denomina-	secondary modern	university
city academy	community school	grant-maintained	tional	secondary school	upper school
city technical	comprehensive	school	nursery school	secretarial college	voluntary school
college (CTC)	school	high school	*old colloq.* poly	seminary	
		infant school	*old* polytechnic	single faith school	

Educational terms include:

Advanced Higher	discipline	higher education	National Literacy	playtime	student
A-level	double-first	Higher Grade	Strategy	prefect	student grant
assisted places scheme	educational pro-	homework	National Numer-	primary education	student loan
(international)	gramme	IGCSE (Interna-	acy Strategy	proctor	study
baccalaureate	eleven-plus	tional General	NQT (Newly	professor	subject
board of governors	enrolment	Certificate of	Qualified	pupil	syllabus
break time	examination	Secondary	Teacher)	quadrangle	teacher
bursar	exercise book	Education)	NVQ (National	qualification	teacher training
campus	final exam	intake	Vocational	refresher course	teaching assistant
catchment area	finals	invigilator	Qualification)	register	test paper
certificate	further education	lecture	numeracy	report	textbook
classroom	GCSE (General	literacy	Ofsted (Office for	SATs (Standard	thesis
classroom assistant	Certificate of	literacy hour	Standards in	Assessment Tasks)	timetable
coeducation	Secondary	matriculation	Education)	scholarship	top-up fees
common entrance	Education)	matron	O-level	school term	truancy
course	governor	mixed-ability	opting out	secondary educa-	university entrance
course of studies	graduation	teaching	parent governor	tion	work experience
curriculum	half-term	modular course	PTA (parent-	special education	YTS (Youth
degree	head boy	module	teacher associa-	Standard Grade	Training Scheme)
diploma	head girl	national curricu-	tion)	statemented	
	head teacher	lum	playground	streaming	

become law, become valid, begin, work, take, produce results, function
COLLOQ. kick in, talk

> **❗ effect** or **affect**?
> *See panel at* **affect**.

effective *adj*
1 EFFICIENT, productive, adequate, sufficient, capable, useful, helpful, fruitful, practical, successful, worthwhile
FORMAL efficacious
2 OPERATIVE, in force, in effect, in operation, functioning, legal, valid, current, active
FORMAL implemental
3 STRIKING, impressive, forceful, powerful, exciting, attractive, persuasive, convincing, compelling, potent, telling, prevailing
FORMAL cogent
COLLOQ. devastating
4 ACTUAL, practical, virtual, essential
E₃ 1 ineffective, powerless **4** theoretical

> **❗ effective** or **effectual**?
> *Effective* has a number of meanings: 'producing, or likely to produce, the intended result': *Aspirin is effective against many types of pain* ; 'impressive', 'powerful': *He's a very effective speaker* ; 'in operation, in force': *The new regulations become effective at midnight* ; 'in reality, even if not in theory': *Although not the king, he was the effective ruler of the country for twenty years.* *Effectual* puts more emphasis on the actual achievement of the desired result than *effective* does. If the police take *effective* measures to combat the rising crime rate, these measures have the desired effect, or are expected to, whereas if the police take *effectual measures*, there is no doubt that these measures are succeeding in reducing the crime rate.

effectively *adv*
1 IN EFFECT, in fact, actually, in actual fact, really, in reality, in truth, to all intents and purposes, in practice, for all practical purposes, essentially, virtually
2 SUCCESSFULLY, efficiently, productively, fruitfully

effectiveness *n*
success, strength, force, influence, productiveness, fruitfulness, usefulness, use, power, ability, capability, efficiency, validity, vigour, weight
FORMAL cogency, efficacy, potency
COLLOQ. clout
E₃ ineffectiveness, uselessness

effectual *adj*
1 *an effectual plan*
successful, effective, useful, capable, influential, serviceable, operative, sound, powerful, productive, forcible
FORMAL perficient
2 *effectual contracts*
binding, authoritative, lawful, legal, valid, authentic, proper
E₃ 1 ineffective, useless

> **❗ effectual** or **effective**?
> *See panel at* **effective**.

effeminate *adj*
unmanly, womanly, womanish, feminine, delicate
OLD (*Shakesp*) meacock
COLLOQ. sissy, wimpish
E₃ manly

effervesce *v*
1 *mineral water effervescing*
sparkle, bubble, fizz, boil, foam, froth, ferment
2 *effervescing with conversation*
be lively, be vivacious, be animated, be exhilarated, sparkle
FORMAL be ebullient

effervescence *n*
1 SPARKLE, bubbles, bubbling, fizz, fizziness, gas, gassiness, foam, foaming, froth, frothing, ferment, fermentation

2 LIVELINESS, vivacity, vitality, sparkle, animation, buoyancy, enthusiasm, high spirits, excitedness, excitement, exhilaration, exuberance
FORMAL ebullience
COLLOQ. vim, zing, zip

effervescent *adj*
1 BUBBLY, bubbling, sparkling, fizzy, fizzing, gassy, aerated, frothy, carbonated, foaming, fermenting
2 LIVELY, vivacious, animated, buoyant, exhilarated, enthusiastic, exuberant, sparkling, excited, vital, irrepressible
FORMAL ebullient
E₃ 1 flat **2** dull

effete *adj*
weak, feeble, enfeebled, debilitated, exhausted, drained, fruitless, unfruitful, unproductive, played out, spent, sterile, tired out, worn out, spoiled, used up, unprolific, wasted, decayed, barren, corrupt, debased, decrepit, degenerate, decadent
FORMAL enervated, ineffectual, infecund
E₃ vigorous

efficacious *adj*
effective, productive, capable, useful, successful, competent, powerful, potent, strong, adequate, sufficient, active, effectual, operative
E₃ ineffective, useless

efficacy *n*
effectiveness, effect, usefulness, use, success, successfulness, power, energy, force, influence, potency, strength, capability, ability, competence, virtue
E₃ ineffectiveness, uselessness

efficiency *n*
effectiveness, competence, proficiency, skill, expertise, skilfulness, capability, ability, productivity, order, orderliness, organization
E₃ inefficiency, incompetence

efficient *adj*
effective, competent, proficient, skilful, capable, able, productive, organized, well-organized, well-ordered, streamlined, rationalized, methodical, systematic, businesslike, workmanlike, smart, practical, strong, powerful, well-run, well-conducted, expert
E₃ inefficient, incompetent

effigy *n*
figure, statue, carving, representation, likeness, picture, portrait, image, icon, idol, dummy, guy, Jack-straw
OLD sign

effluent *n*
waste, liquid waste, discharge, sewage, emission, outflow, pollutant, pollution
FORMAL effluence, effluvium, efflux, emanation, exhalation

effort *n*
1 EXERTION, strain, application, struggle, sweat, trouble, energy, hard work, power, force, stress, toil, striving, pains, labour, muscle power
FORMAL travail
COLLOQ. elbow-grease, sweat of your brow, beef, muscles
2 ATTEMPT, try, endeavour
COLLOQ. go, shot, stab, crack, bash, whirl
3 ACHIEVEMENT, accomplishment, feat, attainment, exploit, production, creation, deed, product, result, work, opus

effortless *adj*
easy, simple, undemanding, facile, painless, uncomplicated, unexacting, straightforward, smooth
E₃ difficult, complicated, exacting, demanding

effrontery *n*
audacity, impertinence, insolence, impudence, temerity, boldness, brazenness, cheekiness, cheek, gall, nerve, presumption, disrespect, arrogance, brashness
COLLOQ. face, brass, brass neck, lip, chutzpah; *N Am* sass
E₃ respect, timidity

effulgent *adj*
brilliant, radiant, shining, glowing, splendid, glorious
FORMAL resplendent, refulgent, incandescent

effusion *n*
outpouring, outburst, outflow, gush, discharge, emission, stream, shedding
FORMAL effluence, efflux, voidance

effusive *adj*
fulsome, gushing, gushy, unrestrained, unreserved, expansive, demonstrative, profuse, overflowing, enthusiastic, exuberant, extravagant, lavish, talkative, voluble, lyrical
FORMAL ebullient, rhapsodic
COLLOQ. gabby, gassy, over the top, OTT, all mouth, big-mouthed
E3 reserved, restrained

egalitarian *adj*
democratic, fair, just, equitable, sharing

egg *n, v*
♦ *n*
ovum, ovule
TECHNICAL oocyte, oosphere
■ **egg on**
encourage, incite, push, urge, drive, excite, stimulate, spur, prompt, coax, talk into, goad, prod, prick
FORMAL exhort
E3 discourage

PROVERBS
You can't make an omelette without breaking eggs

egghead *n*
boffin, brain, intellect, intellectual, academic, thinker, scholar, bookworm, genius, Einstein
COLLOQ. know-all, know-it-all, brainbox; *N Am* brainiac

ego *n*
self, (sense of) identity, self-esteem, self-importance, self-confidence, self-image, self-worth

egocentric *adj*
self-centred, selfish, self-seeking, self-serving, self-interested, egotistic(al), narcissistic, self-absorbed, thinking only of yourself, wrapped up in yourself
E3 altruistic

egoism *n*
self-interest, self-centredness, self-importance, self-absorption, self-love, self-regard, self-seeking, selfishness, narcissism, egocentricity, egomania, egotism, amour-propre
E3 altruism

egoist *n*
self-seeker, narcissist, egotist, egomaniac

egoistic *adj*
self-absorbed, self-important, self-involved, self-centred, self-pleasing, self-seeking, narcissistic, egocentric, egoistical, egotistic, egotistical, egomaniacal
E3 altruistic

egotism *n*
egoism, egomania, self-centredness, no thought for others, self-importance, egocentricity, selfishness, superiority, conceitedness, self-regard, self-love, self-conceit, narcissism, self-admiration, pride, boastfulness, vanity, snobbery
FORMAL braggadocio
COLLOQ. bigheadedness, swank, blowing your own trumpet; *N Am* blowing your own horn
E3 humility

egotist *n*
boaster, bluffer, show-off, self-admirer, braggart, egoist, egomaniac, swaggerer, braggadocio
COLLOQ. bighead, big mouth, smart alec, clever clogs, clever dick

egotistic *adj*
egoistic, egocentric, self-centred, selfish, self-important, self-admiring, narcissistic, conceited, swollen-headed, swell-headed, superior, vain, proud, boasting, bragging
COLLOQ. bigheaded
E3 humble

egregious *adj*
grievous, outrageous, scandalous, shocking, gross, rank, infamous, notorious, insufferable, intolerable, appalling, monstrous, flagrant, glaring, arrant
FORMAL heinous
E3 slight

egress *n*
exit, way out, outlet, vent, issue, exodus, emergence, leaving, departure, escape, escape route

ejaculate *v*
1 DISCHARGE, eject, spurt, emit, release, expel
COLLOQ. come
2 EXCLAIM, call (out), blurt (out), cry (out), shout (out), yell, utter, scream

ejaculation *n*
1 *ejaculation of semen*
discharge, ejection, emission, spurt, release, expulsion, orgasm, climax
COLLOQ. coming
2 EXCLAMATION, call, cry, scream, shout, yell, utterance, interjection

eject *v*
1 EMIT, expel, discharge, release, ejaculate, spout, spew, spit, splutter, disgorge, evacuate, vomit, excrete, belch, expectorate
TECHNICAL degas
FORMAL exude, excrete
2 OUST, evict, get rid of, throw out, drive out, turn out, expel, remove, banish, deport, dismiss, discharge, exclude, exile, bounce
OLD expulse
COLLOQ. fire, sack, boot out, kick out, turf out, chuck out, give someone the boot, give someone their cards, give someone the bum's rush, show someone the door
See Synonym nuances panel at **banish**.
3 BAIL OUT, propel, thrust out, throw out, get out

ejection *n*
eviction, expulsion, removal, banishment, dismissal, discharge, exile, deportation, ousting
COLLOQ. firing, sacking, the boot, the sack

eke
■ **eke out**
1 *eke out supplies*
make something stretch, stretch, spin out, fill out, husband, economize on, be economical with, add to, increase, supplement
COLLOQ. go easy with
2 *eke out a living*
scrimp and save, scrape, scratch, get by, survive
COLLOQ. live from hand to mouth, feel the pinch

elaborate *adj, v*
♦ *adj*
1 *elaborate plans*
detailed, complicated, complex, intricate, careful, thorough, exact, extensive, painstaking, precise, perfected, minute, laboured, studied
2 *elaborate designs*
intricate, complex, complicated, involved, ornamental, ornate, fancy, decorated, extravagant, ostentatious, showy, fussy, rococo, overwrought, highwrought, historiated, storiated
OLD quaint
E3 **2** simple, plain
♦ *v*
amplify, develop, enlarge on, expand on, work out, flesh out, polish, improve, refine, enhance, devise, explain

FORMAL expatiate
🖅 précis, simplify

élan *n*
panache, liveliness, flair, flourish, style, stylishness, spirit, verve, vigour, vivacity, animation, confidence, zest, dash, esprit
COLLOQ. brio, oomph, pizzazz
🖅 apathy, lifelessness

elapse *v*
pass, lapse, go by, go on, go past, slip away, slip by

elastic *adj*
1 PLIABLE, flexible, stretchable, stretchy, supple, resilient, yielding, springy, rubbery, pliant, elasticated, plastic, bouncy, buoyant
2 ADAPTABLE, accommodating, flexible, tolerant, adjustable, fluid, compliant
COLLOQ. easy
🖅 **1** rigid **2** inflexible

elasticity *n*
1 PLIABILITY, flexibility, resilience, stretch, stretchiness, springiness, suppleness, plasticity, bounce, buoyancy
COLLOQ. give, play
2 ADAPTABILITY, flexibility, tolerance, adjustability
🖅 **1** rigidity **2** inflexibility

elated *adj*
exhilarated, excited, delighted, euphoric, ecstatic, thrilled, rapturous, exultant, jubilant, overjoyed, joyful, happy, blissful
FORMAL joyous, rhapsodic
COLLOQ. over the moon, on cloud nine
🖅 despondent, downcast

elation *n*
exhilaration, delight, transports of delight, euphoria, ecstasy, thrill, rapture, bliss, exultation, glee, high spirits, happiness, joy, joyfulness, jubilation
FORMAL joyousness
🖅 depression, despondency

elbow *v*
jostle, nudge, push, force, bump, knock, crowd, shoulder
COLLOQ. shove, barge

elbow-grease *n*
effort, hard work, energy, strength, exertion, muscle power
COLLOQ. sweat of your brow, beef, muscles

elbow-room *n*
space, room, breathing space, play, scope, leeway, freedom, latitude, *Lebensraum*
COLLOQ. wiggle room

elder *adj, n*
♦ *adj*
older, senior, first-born, ancient
🖅 younger
♦ *n*
1 *no respect for their elders*
senior, older person, old person
COLLOQ. oldie
2 *a church elder*
leader, deacon, father

elderly *adj, n*
♦ *adj*
aging, aged, old, grey-haired, hoary, senile, mature, badgerly
FORMAL senescent
COLLOQ. silver, not as young as you were, not getting any younger, over the hill, long in the tooth, past it, not long for this world
🖅 young, youthful
♦ *n*
old people, older generation, older adults, senior citizens, retired people, pensioners, old-age pensioners, OAPs; *N Am* golden agers
COLLOQ. oldies, wrinklies, has-beens
SLANG fossils

eldest *adj*
first, first-born, oldest
🖅 youngest

elect *v, adj, n*
♦ *v*
choose, pick, opt for, select, vote for, cast a vote, go to the polls, decide on, prefer, adopt, designate, appoint, determine, co-opt, return
OLD voice
COLLOQ. plump for
♦ *adj*
chosen, designate, -to-be, future, picked, prospective, selected, preferred, hand-picked
TECHNICAL nominate
♦ *n*
chosen, élite, select
COLLOQ. chosen few

election *n*
choice, selection, vote, voting, ballot, poll, hustings, referendum, appointment, determination, decision, preference, choosing, picking

electioneering *n*
campaigning, promotion, lobbying, canvassing, crusading, championing, fighting, struggling; *Can* mainstreeting

elector *n*
voter, selector, constituent, electorate

electric *adj*
1 *an electric light*
electric-powered, mains-operated, battery-operated, rechargeable, cordless, powered, live
2 *the atmosphere was electric*
electrifying, exciting, stimulating, thrilling, startling, charged, dynamic, stirring, tense, rousing
🖅 **2** unexciting, flat

electrical components

Types of electrical components and devices include:

adaptor	earthed plug	multimeter
ammeter	electrical	neon lamp
armature	screwdriver	socket
battery	electricity meter	test lamp
bayonet fitting	extension lead	three-core cable
cable	fluorescent tube	three-pin plug
ceiling rose	fuse	transducer
circuit breaker	fusebox	transformer
conduit	fuse carrier	two-pin plug
continuity tester	high voltage tester	universal test
copper conductor	insulating tape	meter
dimmer switch	lampholder	voltage doubler
dry-cell battery	light bulb	wire strippers

electricity and electronics

Electricity and electronic terms include:

alternating current	conductivity	galvanic
(AC)	coulomb	galvanometer
alternator	digital signal	generator
amp	diode	grid system
ampere	direct current	henry
amplifier	(DC)	impedance
analogue signal	Dolby® (system)	induced current
anode	dynamo	inductance
band-pass filter	eddy current	integrated circuit
battery	electrode	isoelectric
bioelectricity	electrolyte	isoelectronic
capacitance	electromagnet	logic gate
capacitor	electron tube	loudspeaker
cathode	farad	microchip
cathode-ray tube	Faraday cage	mutual induction
cell	Foucault current	NICAM®
commutator	frequency	ohm
condenser	modulation	optoelectronics

oscillator	solenoid	triode
oscilloscope	solid state circuit	truth table
piezoelectricity	static electricity	turboalternator
polarity	step-down	tweeter
power station	transformer	valve
reactance	superconductivity	volt
resistance	switch	voltage amplifier
resistor	thermionics	voltaic
rheostat	thermistor	watt
semiconductor	thyristor	Wheatstone bridge
siemens	transformer	woofer
silicon chip	transistor	

electrify v

thrill, excite, shock, charge, invigorate, animate, stimulate, stir, rouse, fire, jolt, galvanize, amaze, astonish, astound, stagger

E3 bore

elegance n

style, chic, fashionableness, stylishness, sophistication, smartness, refinement, polish, beauty, dignity, distinction, grace, gracefulness, discernment, taste, gentility, politeness, tastefulness, poise, exquisiteness, grandeur, luxury, sumptuousness

FORMAL propriety, concinnity

E3 inelegance

> QUOTATIONS
>
> Elegance is good taste plus a dash of daring
> CARMEL SNOW, *The World of Carmel Snow*
>
> Fashion anticipates, and elegance is a state of mind
> OLEG LOLEWSKI CASSINI, *In My Own Fashion*

elegant adj

stylish, chic, fashionable, modish, smart, refined, polished, cultivated, genteel, classy, charming, sophisticated, debonair, urbane, smooth, tasteful, lovely, fine, exquisite, beautiful, cultured, graceful, gracious, handsome, delicate, neat, artistic, bijou, humane; *Scot* jimp

OLD (*Spenser*) dainty

FORMAL concinnous

COLLOQ. ritzy, snazzy, swanky, la-di-da

E3 inelegant, unrefined, unfashionable

elegiac adj

lamenting, funereal, mournful, doleful, melancholic, sad, plaintive, valedictory, keening

FORMAL threnetic, threnetical, threnodial, threnodic

E3 happy

elegy n

dirge, lament, requiem, funeral poem, funeral song, burial hymn, plaint

FORMAL threnody, threnode

Related adjectives: epicedial, epicedian

element n

1 *the elements of our discussion*

factor, component, constituent, ingredient, member, part, piece, fragment, feature, strand

2 *the elements of a subject*

basics, foundations, fundamentals, principles, first principles, rudiments, essentials

3 *an element of truth*

small amount, grain, trace, touch, hint, suspicion, soupçon

4 *the criminal element in society*

individual(s), group, faction, set, party, clique

5 *exposed to the elements*

weather, wind and rain, storms, climate, atmospheric conditions, meteorological conditions, atmospheric forces

6 *in his element*

natural environment, habitat, territory, niche, haunt

E3 1 whole

elemental adj

basic, fundamental, primary, principal, natural, rudimentary, primitive, radical, immense, powerful, forceful, uncontrolled

elementary adj

basic, fundamental, rudimentary, principal, primary, clear, easy, introductory, straightforward, uncomplicated, simple

E3 advanced, complicated

elephantine adj

large, vast, immense, huge, enormous, massive, great, bulky, hulking, heavy, weighty, awkward, clumsy, lumbering

elevate v

1 LIFT, raise, hoist, uplift, heighten, intensify, magnify, exalt

COLLOQ. hike up

2 PROMOTE, advance, exalt, aggrandize, refine, ennoble, upgrade

COLLOQ. move up the ladder, put on a pedestal, kick upstairs

3 UPLIFT, rouse, boost, buoy up, brighten, cheer, gladden, give a lift to

E3 1 lower **2** downgrade **3** depress

elevated adj

1 IMPORTANT, great, lofty, exalted, grand, noble, dignified

2 *elevated thoughts*

advanced, lofty, exalted, grand, high, noble, dignified, moral

FORMAL sublime

3 *elevated ground*

raised, lifted (up), rising, high, hoisted, uplifted

elevation n

1 RISE, promotion, advancement, preferment, upgrading, aggrandizement

COLLOQ. step up the ladder, leg-up, go-getting

2 EXALTATION, loftiness, grandeur, eminence, nobility, dignity

FORMAL sublimity

3 HEIGHT, altitude, tallness, hill, rise, mound, mount

4 *the east elevation*

face, façade, aspect, front, back, side

E3 1 demotion **3** dip

elf n

fairy, sprite, imp, pixie, goblin, hobgoblin, gnome, brownie, leprechaun, troll, banshee, puck, pygmy

OLD urchin

Related adjectives: elfish, elfin, elvan, elvish

elfin adj

small, petite, delicate, dainty, charming, elfish, elflike, frolicsome, sprightly, playful, impish, mischievous, puckish

elicit v

evoke, draw out, bring out, derive, extract, obtain, exact, extort, cause, wrest

FORMAL call forth, educe

COLLOQ. worm out

eligibility n

qualification, condition, suitability, entitlement, allowance, acceptability, desirability

eligible adj

qualified, fit, fitting, appropriate, suitable, acceptable, entitled, worthy, proper, desirable

E3 ineligible

eliminate v

1 GET RID OF, remove, cut out, take out, exclude, delete, dispense with, abolish, put an end/a stop to, rub out, omit, reject, disregard, dispose of, drop, do away with, eradicate, expel, extinguish, stamp out

2 DEFEAT, conquer, beat, overwhelm

COLLOQ. knock out, thrash, lick, hammer, annihilate

3 KILL, murder, do away with, exterminate

COLLOQ. wipe out, liquidate, rub out, bump off, do in; *N Am* whack, ice

E3 1 include, accept

elimination n

removal, exclusion, abolition, omission, rejection, deletion, eradication, expulsion, disposal

élite *n, adj*
♦ *n*
best, pick, cream, elect, aristocracy, upper classes, nobility, gentry, crème de la crème, establishment, high society
COLLOQ. pick of the bunch, jet set
♦ *adj*
choice, best, exclusive, selected, first-class, aristocratic, noble, upper-class

elixir *n*
cure-all, panacea, remedy, solution, mixture, concentrate, essence, extract, pith, potion, principle, quintessence, syrup, tincture, nostrum

elliptical *adj*
1 OVAL, egg-shaped, oviform, ovoid(al)
2 OBLIQUE, cryptic, obscure, ambiguous, incomprehensible, unfathomable, concise, concentrated, condensed, laconic, terse, succinct
FORMAL abstruse, recondite
2 clear, direct, verbose

elocution *n*
delivery, articulation, diction, pronunciation, voice production, rhetoric, speech, utterance, phrasing
FORMAL enunciation, oratory

elongate *v*
lengthen, extend, draw out, prolong, make longer, stretch (out)
FORMAL protract

elongated *adj*
lengthened, extended, prolonged, protracted, stretched, long

elope *v*
run off, run away, decamp, bolt, make off, abscond, flee, escape, slip away, steal away, leave, disappear
COLLOQ. do a bunk, scarper, skedaddle, vamoose, do a runner, do a moonlight flit, hit the road/trail, make a bolt/break for it, hightail it

eloquence *n*
expressiveness, fluency, flow of words, expression, persuasiveness, articulateness, diction, facility, forcefulness, oratory, rhetoric
FORMAL facundity
COLLOQ. gift of the gab, blarney, gassiness
inarticulateness

eloquent *adj*
articulate, fluent, well-expressed, well-spoken, glib, expressive, vocal, voluble, persuasive, moving, honey-tongued, silver-tongued, forceful, graceful, plausible, stirring, effective, vivid, Demosthenic, Mercurial
inarticulate, tongue-tied

elsewhere *adv*
somewhere else, in/to another place, not here, absent, removed, abroad
here, present

elucidate *v*
explain, clarify, make clear, clear up, interpret, spell out, simplify, state simply, illustrate, illuminate, unfold, throw/shed light on, fill in, exemplify, give an example
FORMAL explicate, expound
confuse

elucidation *n*
explanation, clarification, comment, commentary, illumination, illustration, interpretation, footnote, gloss, annotation, marginalia
FORMAL explication, exposition

elude *v*
1 AVOID, escape, evade, shirk, shake off, flee, bilk, get away from, give someone the slip, throw someone off the scent; *Scot* jink
FORMAL circumvent
COLLOQ. dodge, duck, slip through someone's fingers

2 PUZZLE, frustrate, baffle, confound, thwart, stump, evade, foil
OLD delude

elusive *adj*
1 INDEFINABLE, difficult to describe, intangible, unanalysable, subtle, puzzling, baffling, deceptive, misleading, transient, transitory
2 EVASIVE, difficult to find, hard to catch, slippery, tricky
COLLOQ. shifty, dodgy

elusiveness *n*
indefinability, intangibility, subtlety, puzzle, evasiveness, transience, transitoriness

emaciated *adj*
thin, gaunt, lean, haggard, drawn, wasted, bony, anorexic, scrawny, skinny, skeletal, pinched, meagre
FORMAL attenuated, cadaverous
COLLOQ. thin as a rake, all skin and bone
plump, well-fed

emaciation *n*
thinness, gauntness, leanness, haggardness, boniness, scrawniness, atrophy
plumpness

emanate *v*
1 RADIATE, send out, emit, give out, give off, exude, discharge
FORMAL exhale
2 ORIGINATE, proceed, arise, derive, issue, spring, stem, flow, come, emerge

emanation *n*
discharge, emission, flow, effluent, effluence, radiation
FORMAL effluvium, efflux, effluxion, effusion

emancipate *v*
free, liberate, release, set free, enfranchise, deliver, discharge, loose, set loose, unchain, untie, unshackle, unfetter, unyoke
FORMAL manumit
enslave

emancipation *n*
liberation, freedom, setting free, freeing, release, deliverance, liberty, discharge, enfranchisement, unbinding, unfettering, unchaining
FORMAL manumission
enslavement

emasculate *v*
1 CASTRATE, geld, neuter, spay
2 WEAKEN, impoverish, cripple, debilitate, soften
FORMAL enervate
2 boost, vitalize

emasculation *n*
weakening, impoverishment, debilitation, reduction, diminishment, moderation, lessening
FORMAL abatement

embalm *v*
preserve, mummify, store, lay out, enshrine, cherish, consecrate, conserve, treasure

embankment *n*
causeway, dam, rampart, mound, bank, levee, earthwork; *NZ* stopbank

embargo *n, v*
♦ *n*
restriction, ban, prohibition, restraint, bar, barrier, impediment, check, hindrance, obstruction, blockage, stoppage, seizure
FORMAL proscription, interdiction
♦ *v*
restrict, ban, bar, prohibit, restrain, block, check, impede, obstruct, seize, stop
FORMAL interdict, proscribe
allow

embark *v*
board (ship), go aboard, take ship

OLD (*Shakesp*) inship
◨ disembark
■ **embark on**
begin, start, commence, set about, launch into, undertake, venture into, enter (on), initiate, engage
◨ complete, finish

embarkation *n*
boarding, mounting, entrance, getting-on, embussing, emplaning, entrainment

embarrass *v*
make awkward/ashamed, disconcert, mortify, show up, discompose, fluster, humiliate, shame, distress, upset, confuse
FORMAL discomfit, discountenance

embarrassed *adj*
awkward, uncomfortable, ill at ease, uneasy, self-conscious, upset, confused, distressed, disconcerted, unnatural, constrained, ashamed, shamed, guilty, shown up, humiliated, mortified, abashed
FORMAL discomfited
COLLOQ. sheepish, hot under the collar
◨ unembarrassed

SYNONYM NUANCES

Awkward and **uncomfortable** can be used, perhaps with qualifying adverbs, of various degrees of embarrassed feelings: *there was a slightly awkward silence*. Both **ill at ease** and **uneasy** are similar, but may further imply a degree of apprehension: *she felt intimidated and uneasy*. You could use the term **self-conscious** of an embarrassed feeling characterized by a preoccupation with how you are perceived.

The terms **upset** and **distressed** would be appropriate only where embarrassment has caused mental pain or suffering. **Disconcerted**, although similar, further suggests a loss of self-possession: *she appeared disconcerted, even flustered, at his remarks*.

The terms **guilty** and **ashamed** suggest deep embarrassment at one's own actions or possibly, in the case of **ashamed**, those of a close associate; **humiliated** and **mortified** are even stronger terms which could refer to embarrassment at oneself, but are often reserved for deep feelings of injured self-respect. **Shamed**, on the other hand, suggests a more public embarrassment caused by exposition by others: *shamed Cabinet minister resigns*. **Shown up** also conveys the idea of being publicly humbled: *the team were shown up by their performance*. To refer to suddenly being struck by feelings of shame or embarrassment, you might use the word **abashed**: *abashed at being caught snooping*.

---

embarrassing *adj*
awkward, uncomfortable, disconcerting, distressing, upsetting, sensitive, mortifying, humiliating, shameful, shaming, tricky, compromising, painful
FORMAL discomfiting, indelicate, discountenancing
COLLOQ. touchy, cringeworthy

embarrassment *n*
1 DISCOMPOSURE, self-consciousness, mortification, humiliation, shame, guilt, awkwardness, unease, uneasiness, confusion, distress, bashfulness
FORMAL chagrin, discomfiture
COLLOQ. sheepishness
2 DIFFICULTY, constraint, predicament, distress, dilemma, mess, plight
COLLOQ. fix, scrape, jam, pickle
3 *an embarrassment of riches*
abundance, surplus, excess, superabundance, overabundance
FORMAL profusion

embassy *n*
consulate, legation, ministry, delegation, deputation, mission

embed *v*
implant, plant, fix, insert, root, set, sink, hammer, drive

embellish *v*
1 *embellish a design*
adorn, ornament, decorate, deck, dress up, beautify, gild, garnish, trim, festoon
OLD bedeck, bespangle
2 *embellish a story*
elaborate, embroider, enrich, exaggerate, enhance, grace
COLLOQ. sex up
◨ **1** simplify; *formal* denude

embellishment *n*
adornment, ornament, ornamentation, decoration, elaboration, garnish, trimming, gilding, enrichment, enhancement, embroidery

embers *n*
live coals, ashes, cinders, charcoal, residue, clinker

embezzle *v*
steal, swindle, pilfer, rob
FORMAL appropriate, misappropriate, purloin, defalcate, peculate
COLLOQ. filch, pinch, nab, nick, have your fingers/hand in the till
SLANG rip off

embezzlement *n*
pilfering, fraud, stealing, theft
FORMAL appropriation, misappropriation, defalcation
COLLOQ. filching, nabbing, nicking

embezzler *n*
cheat, fraud, thief, robber
FORMAL defalcator, peculator
COLLOQ. crook, diddler, con man

embittered *adj*
bitter, resentful, disaffected, sour, rancorous, disillusioned, disenchanted, discouraged, disheartened, angry, exasperated, piqued, rankled

emblazon *v*
1 DECORATE, adorn, ornament, blazon, embellish, depict, display, colour, illuminate, paint
2 PROCLAIM, publicize, publish, extol, praise, glorify, trumpet
FORMAL laud

emblem *n*
symbol, sign, token, representation, logo, insignia, device, crest, mark, badge, figure, image

emblematic *adj*
representative, representing, symbolic, symbolical, figurative, allegorical, emblematical

embodiment *n*
personification, incarnation, exemplification, expression, epitome, example, type, model, incorporation, realization, representation, concentration
FORMAL manifestation

embody *v*
1 PERSONIFY, exemplify, represent, stand for, typify, symbolize, incorporate, express
FORMAL manifest
2 INCLUDE, contain, integrate, incorporate, assimilate, collect, combine, bring together, take in

embolden *v*
encourage, inspire, make brave/bold, give courage to, invigorate, reassure, rouse, stimulate, stir, strengthen, vitalize, animate, fire, cheer, hearten, inflame, nerve
◨ dishearten

embrace *v, n*
♦ *v*
1 HUG, clasp, cuddle, hold, grasp, put/throw your arms around, take into your arms, squeeze, enfold, fold, enlace, inarm, lock, strain; *Scot* halse; clip

OLD coll, inclip, wrap, complect, compress
COLLOQ. neck, canoodle, smooch, tangle with
SLANG snog
2 INCLUDE, encompass, incorporate, contain, cover, involve, take in, span
OLD (*Spenser*) brace; complect
FORMAL comprise
3 ACCEPT, take up, welcome, receive eagerly, receive wholeheartedly
FORMAL espouse
COLLOQ. take on board
♦ *n*
hug, cuddle, hold, clasp, squeeze, bosom, abrazo
OLD colling, accolade, embrasure
COLLOQ. clinch, necking, slap and tickle, smooch

embrocation *n*
cream, lotion, ointment, salve
FORMAL epithem

embroider *v*
1 DECORATE, sew, stitch
2 EMBELLISH, enrich, exaggerate, colour, enhance, elaborate, dress up, garnish

embroidery *n*
fancywork, needlework, sewing, tapestry, tatting, needlepoint

---

Types of embroidery stitch include:

backstitch	French knot	Romanian
blanket	half-cross	couching
bullion	herringbone	running
chain	lazy-daisy	satin
chevron	longstitch	stem
cross	long-and-short	straight
feather	moss	Swiss darning
fishbone	Oriental couching	tent

---

embroil *v*
involve, implicate, entangle, enmesh, mix up, catch up in, draw into, incriminate

embryo *n*
1 UNBORN CHILD, foetus
2 *the embryo of the plan*
nucleus, germ, seed, beginning, root, rudiments, basics

embryonic *adj*
undeveloped, rudimentary, immature, beginning, emerging, fledgling, unformed, early, germinal, elementary, primary
FORMAL incipient, inchoate
🔁 developed

emend *v*
correct, rectify, edit, revise, rewrite, polish, refine, improve, alter, amend, fix, repair
FORMAL redact

> ❗ **emend** or **amend**?
> *See panel at* **amend**.

emendation *n*
correction, editing, revision, rewriting, refinement, improvement, alteration, amendment
FORMAL corrigendum, rectification, redaction

emerge *v*
1 *emerge from the office*
come out, come forth, come into view, emanate, issue, proceed, arise, rise, surface, appear, develop, turn up, materialize
2 *the facts emerged*
become known, come out, come to light, be revealed, become apparent, appear, transpire, turn out
COLLOQ. crop up
🔁 **1** disappear

emergence *n*
appearance, rise, coming, dawn, development, arrival, springing-up, unfolding, disclosure, issue
FORMAL advent
🔁 disappearance

emergency *n, adj*
♦ *n*
crisis, danger, accident, catastrophe, disaster, extremity, calamity, difficulty, predicament, plight, pinch, strait, dilemma, quandary
FORMAL exigency
COLLOQ. scrape, mess, pickle, fix, hot water
♦ *adj*
1 *an emergency meeting*
urgent, crisis, immediate, top-priority, extraordinary
2 *emergency supplies*
alternative, back-up, reserve, spare, substitute, extra, fall-back

emergent *adj*
budding, coming (out), fledgling, developing, emerging, embryonic, rising, independent
FORMAL burgeoning
🔁 declining, disappearing

emetic *adj, n*
♦ *adj*
emetical, vomitive, vomitory
♦ *n*
vomit, vomitary, vomitive

emigrate *v*
migrate, move abroad, relocate, move, depart, leave your home/native country, resettle

emigration *n*
moving abroad, migration, removal, departure, exodus, journey, relocation, expatriation

eminence *n*
distinction, fame, pre-eminence, prominence, renown, reputation, illustriousness, greatness, importance, esteem, celebrity, notability, note, prestige, dignity, rank

> **QUOTATIONS**
> Eminence engenders enemies
>   C L R JAMES, *The Black Jacobins*

eminent *adj*
distinguished, famous, prominent, illustrious, outstanding, notable, pre-eminent, prestigious, celebrated, renowned, noted, noteworthy, conspicuous, esteemed, important, well-known, elevated, respected, great, high-ranking, high, first, superlative, grand, superior
🔁 unknown, obscure, unimportant

> **SYNONYM NUANCES**
>
> **Distinguished** is a mild term for having a distinction that sets someone apart from their peers: *a distinguished philosopher*, while **prominent** would emphasize being known for this distinction: *he was among the most prominent political leaders*. You can also use **outstanding** or **pre-eminent** to appropriately describe someone who is more important or influential than most or all others.
>
> The terms **celebrated**, **renowned**, **respected** and **esteemed** similarly echo the idea of being widely known and having high status, as do the stronger **illustrious**, **prestigious** and the particularly unequivocal **great**: *Sherlock Holmes, the world's greatest detective*. **Famous**, **well-known** and **noted**, while still positive, are perhaps less admiring in tone, in that they put the emphasis on wide recognition rather than status: *Dr Jones is a noted specialist in her field*; **conspicuous** is the least inherently approving term, given its frequent application to negative qualities. **Notable** and **noteworthy** are more approbatory, however, in their implication that something is worthy of regard.

Elevated, along with **high-ranking**, **high** and **first** simply suggest being rated among the foremost, and do not suggest any particular attitude; **superior** and **superlative** are more marked terms to use in that they further imply supremacy: *the superlative grandeur of Verdi's music*.

eminently *adv*
highly, well, very, greatly, most, exceedingly, exceptionally, extremely, outstandingly, prominently, remarkably, notably, signally, strikingly, conspicuously, surpassingly, par excellence

emissary *n*
ambassador, agent, envoy, messenger, delegate, herald, courier, representative, diplomat, scout, deputy, intermediary, go-between, spy

emission *n*
discharge, issue, ejection, emanation, giving-out, giving-off, diffusion, transmission, exhalation, outpouring, radiation, release, production, exudation, vent

emit *v*
1 *emit fumes*
discharge, issue, eject, emanate, exude, pour out, give out, throw out, give off, send out, send forth, diffuse, radiate, release, shed, vent, ooze, leak, spew, produce, let out, express
FORMAL excrete
2 *emit a long low laugh*
produce, utter, speak, say, voice, vocalize, verbalize, express, sound
E3 1 absorb

emollient *adj, n*
♦ *adj*
1 SOOTHING, assuaging, mollifying, moisturizing, palliative, softening
FORMAL assuasive, balsamic, demulcent, lenitive, mitigative
2 CONCILIATORY, placatory, appeasing, calming
FORMAL propitiatory
♦ *n*
cream, lotion, moisturizer, oil, ointment, balm, poultice, salve
FORMAL lenitive, liniment, unguent

emolument *n*
pay, salary, wages, payment, remuneration, return, reward, allowance, benefit, earnings, fee, gain, charge, profit(s), hire, honorarium, stipend, compensation, recompense

emotion *n*
feeling, passion, sensation, sense, affection, movement, sensibility, transport, sentiment, ardour, fervour, spirit, warmth, reaction, vehemence, excitement, thrill, joy, happiness, ecstasy, sadness, sorrow, grief, reverence, sublimity, surprise, fear, despair, dread, hate, anger, pang, spasm, shock, turn, whirl, upsurge
TECHNICAL affect, anoesis
OLD motion

emotional *adj*
1 FEELING, passionate, sensitive, responsive, loving, ardent, tender, warm, roused, demonstrative, excitable, enthusiastic, fervent, fervid, glowing, radiant, swelling, impassioned, moved, sentimental, zealous, hot-blooded, red-hot, white-hot, heated, tempestuous, overcharged, temperamental, fiery, psychological, soulful, susceptible
2 EMOTIVE, moving, poignant, thrilling, touching, stirring, heartwarming, soul-stirring, tearful, exciting, effusive, gushing, full-hearted, sentimental, pathetic
COLLOQ. tear-jerking, soppy, schmaltzy
E3 1 unemotional, cold, detached, calm

emotionally *adv*
1 *emotionally involved*
passionately, lovingly, ardently, fervently, tenderly, warmly, demonstratively, with all your heart, enthusiastically, zealously, temperamentally, poignantly, touchingly, heartwarmingly, sentimentally, psychologically

2 *emotionally charged negotiations*
awkwardly, controversially, delicately, sensitively, tensely, nervously, under pressure

emotionless *adj*
cold, cold-blooded, cool, distant, undemonstrative, unaffected, unemotional, unfeeling, unmoved, unblinking, impassive, detached, clinical, indifferent, insensible, remote, blank, toneless, frigid, glacial, cold-fish
OLD impassible
FORMAL imperturbable, phlegmatic
E3 emotional

emotive *adj*
controversial, delicate, inflammatory, sensitive, awkward, touchy

empathize *v*
share, identify with, feel for, comfort, support, understand, have a rapport, be sensitive towards
COLLOQ. be on the same wavelength, put yourself in someone's shoes

emperor *n*
ruler, sovereign, king, queen, imperial, imperator, kaiser, mikado, shogun, tsar, czar
Related adjective: imperial

emphasis *n*
1 IMPORTANCE, stress, weight, significance, priority, focus, underscoring, accent, accentuation, force, power, prominence, pre-eminence, attention, intensity, strength, urgency, positiveness, insistence, mark, moment
2 *the emphasis is on the second syllable*
stress, accent, weight, force

emphasize *v*
1 *emphasize the differences*
stress, accentuate, underline, highlight, call/draw attention to, accent, feature, dwell on, weight, point up, spotlight, play up, insist on, press home, intensify, heighten, strengthen, punctuate, bring to the fore
COLLOQ. drive the point home
2 *emphasize a syllable*
put stress on, accent, stress, accentuate
E3 1 play down, understate

emphatic *adj*
1 *an emphatic gesture*
forceful, positive, insistent, certain, definite, decided, unequivocal, absolute, categorical, earnest, marked, pronounced, significant, unmistak(e)able, distinctive, strong, striking, vigorous, distinct, energetic, forcible, vehement, firm, important, impressive, momentous, powerful, punctuated, telling, vivid, direct
2 *an emphatic win*
decisive, marked, distinctive, conclusive, momentous, unmistak(e)able
E3 1 tentative, hesitant, understated

emphatically *adv*
1 *reply emphatically*
forcefully, insistently, unequivocally, strongly, firmly, distinctively, vigorously, vehemently
2 *this is emphatically not a lie*
certainly, definitely, absolutely, categorically
E3 1 hesitantly

empire *n*
1 DOMAIN, dominion, kingdom, realm, province, commonwealth, territory
Related adjective: imperial
2 SUPREMACY, sovereignty, rule, authority, dominion, command, government, jurisdiction, control, power, sway
3 *a cosmetics empire*
corporation, organization, multinational, conglomerate, consortium, business, firm, company

empirical *adj*
practical, pragmatic, experimental, observed
FORMAL experiential
E3 theoretical, conjectural, speculative

empirically adv
experimentally, practically, pragmatically
FORMAL experientially
⊞ theoretically

employ v
1 ENGAGE, hire, appoint, take on, recruit, sign up, enlist, commission, put on the payroll, retain, fill, occupy, take up, apprentice
2 USE, utilize, make use of, put to use, apply, draw on, exploit, take advantage of, bring to bear, bring into play, ply, exercise, exert

employed adj
working, in work, in employment, with a job, earning, hired, occupied, engaged, active, preoccupied, busy
⊞ unemployed, jobless

employee n
worker, working man/woman, working person, blue-collar worker, white-collar worker, member of staff, job-holder, hand, wage-earner, assistant, labourer, operative, casual, help, man, woman
OLD waterclerk
SLANG rainmaker; N Am gofer, munchkin

employer n
proprietor, owner, manager, head, management, director, executive, company, firm, business, establishment, organization, entrepreneur, governor, master, mistress, workmaster, workmistress, taskmaster, taskmistress
COLLOQ. boss, skipper, gaffer, guv

employment n
1 JOB, work, position, post, occupation, situation, business, calling, profession, vocation, trade, service, métier, pursuit, craft
COLLOQ. line
2 ENLISTMENT, employ, engagement, hire, hiring, taking-on, recruitment, apprenticeship, signing-up
⊞ 1 unemployment

emporium n
shop, store, establishment, bazaar, market, boutique, market-place, mart, fair

empower v
1 AUTHORIZE, warrant, enable, license, certify, sanction, permit, entitle, commission, delegate, qualify
FORMAL accredit
2 EQUIP, enable, set free, give power/means to

empress n
ruler, sovereign, queen, imperator, imperial, kaiserin, tsarina, czarina

emptiness n
1 VACUUM, vacantness, void, voidness, hollowness, hunger, bareness, barrenness, desolation
FORMAL hiatus
2 FUTILITY, meaninglessness, uselessness, worthlessness, aimlessness, purposelessness, senselessness, ineffectiveness, insubstantiality, hollowness, unreality
⊞ 1 fullness

empty adj, v
♦ adj
1 VACANT, with nothing in it, containing nothing, void, unoccupied, free, available, uninhabited, unfilled, deserted, barren, bare, hollow, desolate, blank, clear
2 an empty gesture
futile, aimless, meaningless, senseless, trivial, vain, idle, worthless, useless, fruitless, unreal, insubstantial, ineffective, insincere
FORMAL ineffectual
3 an empty period of life
aimless, meaningless, senseless, purposeless, futile, pointless, vain, hollow, worthless, useless
4 VACUOUS, inane, expressionless, blank, vacant, deadpan
⊞ 1 full **2** meaningful **3** interesting, eventful

♦ v
drain, exhaust, discharge, issue, clear, turn out, evacuate, vacate, leave, go out, pour out, flow out, use up, unload, unpack, void, gut
⊞ fill

SYNONYM NUANCES

adjective sense 1
Vacant, **unoccupied** and **unfilled** tend to be used of an empty place or unfilled position, and **void**, although similar, has connotations of a more wasteful emptiness: *the cathedral has vast arches and void spaces*. **Free** and **available**, on the other hand, have more positive associations of potential which is yet to be fulfilled: *is this seat free?*; *there are still places available for this trip*. **Uninhabited** is specifically used to refer to a lack of resident people, while **deserted** more evocatively suggests abandonment by people: *the streets were deserted while the big match was on television*.
 Barren is more suggestive of a lack of vegetation, but again has connotations of waste. **Bare**, however, may be widely used of a lack of any form of covering, although any associations tend to be negative: *the room was bare and filthy*. You might use the word **desolate** to convey a bleak, forsaken appearance: *the dark and desolate moorlands*.
 Blank has more to do with being unmarked or, more specifically, not written on, and is not particularly connotative: *blank pages*; *a blank screen*; but **clear** has a more positive association of being free of any unwanted contents: *a clear, sunny sky*; *a clear conscience*.

---

empty-headed adj
inane, silly, stupid, foolish, unintelligent, frivolous
COLLOQ. scatter-brained, scatty, feather-brained, rattle-brained, daft, dopey, batty, dotty, dippy; N Am ditsy
⊞ intelligent

emulate v
match, copy, mimic, follow, imitate, model yourself on, echo, reproduce, compete with, contend with, rival, vie with
COLLOQ. take a leaf out of someone's book

emulation n
copying, mimicry, following, imitation, echoing, matching, challenge, competition, contention, contest, rivalry, strife

enable v
1 AUTHORIZE, equip, qualify, entitle, empower, sanction, warrant, allow, permit, prepare, fit, license, commission, endue
FORMAL accredit, validate
2 FACILITATE, make possible, make easier, let, allow, permit, help, further, clear/pave the way for
⊞ prevent, inhibit, forbid

enact v
1 DECREE, ordain, order, authorize, command, legislate, rule, sanction, approve, ratify, pass, make law, establish
2 ACT OUT, perform, play, portray, represent, depict, appear as
⊞ 1 repeal, rescind

enactment n
1 PASSING, authorization, approval, sanction, ratification, legislation, rule, bill, act, statute, law, order, decree, edict, command, commandment, ordinance, regulation
2 PERFORMANCE, play, playing, performing, acting, portrayal, representation, staging
⊞ 1 repeal

enamoured adj
charmed, infatuated, in love with, enchanted, captivated, entranced, bewitched, enthralled, smitten, besotted, keen, wild, mad, taken, fascinated, fond

en bloc adv
en masse, all at once, all together, as a group, as a whole, as one, ensemble, in a body, wholesale

encampment n
camp, camping-ground, campsite, base, bivouac, barracks, quarters, tents

encapsulate v
sum up, summarize, typify, exemplify, epitomize, capture, include, contain, take in, represent, condense, digest, abridge, compress, précis

encapsulation n
summary, representation, digest, précis, exemplification, expression

encase v
cover, surround, enclose, bound, envelop, confine, frame, wrap

enchant v
1 CAPTIVATE, charm, fascinate, enrapture, enamour, attract, allure, appeal, delight, thrill, sirenize
OLD becharm
2 ENTRANCE, enthral, bewitch, beguile, spellbind, spell, hypnotize, mesmerize
E∃ 1 repel

enchanter n
conjurer, magician, magus, mesmerist, necromancer, reim-kennar, sorcerer, spellbinder, warlock, witch, wizard, archimage

enchanting adj
charming, delightful, attractive, fascinating, appealing, lovely, pleasant, wonderful, alluring, bewitching, captivating, endearing, entrancing, irresistible, mesmerizing, ravishing, winsome
E∃ boring, repellent

enchantment n
1 DELIGHT, fascination, charm, appeal, attractiveness, allure, allurement, glamour, bliss, rapture, ecstasy
2 SPELL, magic, witchcraft, witching, wizardry, hypnotism, sorcery, incantation, charm, mesmerism
OLD gramary, malefice
FORMAL conjuration, necromancy
E∃ 1 disenchantment

enchantress n
1 SORCERESS, magician, spellbinder, witch, conjurer, fairy, Circe, lamia
FORMAL necromancer
2 SEDUCTRESS, charmer, siren, vamp, femme fatale

encircle v
surround, encompass, compass, ring, circle, orbit, girdle, enclose, enfold, envelop, crowd, close in, hem in
FORMAL circumscribe, gird

enclose v
1 SURROUND, encircle, encompass, ring, circle, fence, hedge, hem in, bound, encase, embrace, envelop, confine, frame, cage, cocoon, hold, shut in, close in, wrap, pen, cover, corral
OLD (Shakesp) inhoop, womb
FORMAL circumscribe
2 INCLUDE, insert, contain, put in, send with
FORMAL comprehend

enclosure n
1 herded into the enclosure
pen, pound, compound, paddock, fold, stockade, sty, run, arena, area, corral, kraal, court, yard, ring, fencing, close, cloister; Irish bawn; S Afr camp
2 INSERTION, inclusion, addition

encode v
encrypt, encipher, cipher, put into code, scramble, ravel, garble, obscure, disguise, make mysterious
E∃ decode

encompass v
1 ENCIRCLE, circle, ring, surround, envelop, close in, shut in, hem in, confine, enclose, hold
FORMAL gird, circumscribe
2 INCLUDE, cover, embrace, contain, take in, admit, incorporate, involve, embody, span
FORMAL comprise, comprehend

encore n
repeat, repetition, replay, additional/extra performance

encounter v, n
♦ v
1 encounter difficulties
confront, face, be faced with, experience, be/come up against, deal with, cope with, tackle
2 MEET, come across, run across, stumble across
FORMAL happen on, chance upon
COLLOQ. run into, bump into
3 FIGHT, clash with, combat, engage, grapple with, struggle, strive, contend, tussle, do battle with, come into conflict with, compete with, match
COLLOQ. cross swords with
♦ n
1 MEETING, contact, rendezvous, brush, confrontation, rencounter
2 CLASH, fight, combat, conflict, struggle, contest, battle, dispute, engagement, action, skirmish, brush, run-in, collision, joust, tilt, passage of arms
OLD ruffle; (Shakesp) close
COLLOQ. set-to

encourage v
1 HEARTEN, stimulate, motivate, spur, reassure, rally, give moral support to, be supportive to, animate, stir, inspire, incite, buoy up, cheer, urge, rouse, comfort, embolden, console; Aust & NZ barrack for
FORMAL exhort
COLLOQ. pep up, buck up
2 encourage someone to do something
persuade, influence, sway, win over, coax, convince, prompt, talk into
FORMAL exhort
COLLOQ. egg on
3 PROMOTE, advance, aid, boost, forward, further, foster, back, support, help, assist, advocate, favour, strengthen
E∃ 1 discourage, depress **2** discourage, dissuade **3** discourage

encouragement n
1 REASSURANCE, inspiration, motivation, cheer, cheering, heartening, incitement, urging, coaxing, persuasion, stimulation, consolation
FORMAL exhortation, succour
COLLOQ. pep talk
2 PROMOTION, help, aid, assistance, boost, incentive, support, backing, endorsement, stimulus, furtherance
COLLOQ. shot in the arm
E∃ 1 discouragement, disapproval

encouraging adj
heartening, promising, hopeful, reassuring, stimulating, inspiring, uplifting, cheering, comforting, supportive, bright, rosy, cheerful, satisfactory
FORMAL auspicious
E∃ discouraging

encroach v
intrude, invade, impinge, trespass, infringe, usurp, overstep, overrun, infiltrate, make inroads
COLLOQ. muscle in on, tread on someone's toes

encroachment n
intrusion, invasion, trespass, trespassing, infringement, overstepping, infiltration
FORMAL incursion

encrypt v
encode, encipher, cipher, put into code, scramble, ravel, garble, obscure, disguise, make mysterious
E∃ decode

encumber v
1 BURDEN, overload, load, weigh down, saddle, strain, stress, oppress, handicap, hamper, hinder, impede,

restrain, slow down, obstruct, constrain, inconvenience,
prevent, check, cramp
FORMAL retard
2 BLOCK, congest, jam, pack, stuff, cram

encumbrance n
burden, load, weight, cross, millstone, albatross, difficulty,
restraint, constraint, handicap, impediment, obstruction,
obstacle, inconvenience, strain, stress, hindrance, liability,
obligation, responsibility
FORMAL cumbrance

encyclopedic adj
complete, exhaustive, comprehensive, thorough,
thoroughgoing, in-depth, wide-ranging, vast, all-inclusive,
broad, all-embracing, all-encompassing, universal,
compendious
E3 incomplete, narrow

end n, v
♦ n
1 FINISH, conclusion, close, ending,
completion, culmination, epilogue, finale,
dénouement
FORMAL termination, cessation
2 EXTREMITY, boundary, border, edge, limit, margin, tip,
butt, stub
3 REMAINDER, tip, butt, remnant, stub, scrap, vestige,
fragment, leftovers
4 AIM, object, objective, purpose, intention, goal, target,
point, reason, motive, design
FORMAL intent
5 RESULT, outcome, consequence, issue, upshot
6 DEATH, dying, destruction, extermination, downfall,
doom, ruin, extinction, dissolution
FORMAL demise
7 PART, aspect, side, area, field, section,
department, branch
E3 **1** beginning, start **6** birth
♦ v
1 FINISH, come/bring to an end, close, stop,
cease, be over, expire, complete, round off,
culminate, break off, die out, fade away, run out
OLD (Shakesp) fine, period
FORMAL conclude, terminate, discontinue
COLLOQ. wind up
See Synonym nuances panel at **stop**.
2 DESTROY, annihilate, exterminate, extinguish, ruin,
abolish, dissolve
E3 **1** begin, start; formal commence
■ **the end**
intolerable, unbearable, unendurable,
too much, enough, beyond endurance, insufferable,
the worst
COLLOQ. the limit, the last straw, the final blow

endanger v
hazard, risk, put at risk, jeopardize, put in jeopardy,
expose, threaten, put in danger, compromise
FORMAL imperil
E3 protect

endearing adj
lov(e)able, charming, appealing, attractive, winsome,
engaging, delightful, sweet, adorable, cute, captivating,
enchanting

endearment n
1 AFFECTION, love, fondness, attachment
2 *whispered endearments*
sweet nothing, sweet talk, term of affection, diminutive,
pet-name
FORMAL hypocorism

endeavour v, n
♦ v
attempt, try, strive, struggle, aim, aspire, undertake,
venture, try your hand at, labour, take pains,
do your best
FORMAL seek

♦ n
attempt, effort, try, undertaking, enterprise, aim, venture,
striving
COLLOQ. go, shot, stab, bash, crack

ending n
end, close, finish, completion, conclusion, culmination,
climax, resolution, dénouement, finale, epilogue
FORMAL termination, consummation, cessation
E3 beginning, start

endless adj
1 INFINITE, without end, unending, boundless, limitless,
unlimited, measureless
2 EVERLASTING, perpetual, ceaseless, constant, continual,
continuous, undying, eternal, interminable, boring,
monotonous
OLD (Shakesp) fineless
3 UNBROKEN, continuous, constant, uninterrupted,
entire, whole
E3 **1** finite, limited **2** temporary

endlessly adv
infinitely, without end, without stopping, ceaselessly,
unendingly, limitlessly, perpetually, constantly,
continually, continuously, eternally, interminably,
uninterruptedly, day in day out, day after day, through
thick and thin
COLLOQ. till the cows come home

endorse v
1 APPROVE, sanction, authorize, support, back, be/get
behind, favour, ratify, confirm, affirm, vouch for,
advocate, uphold, warrant, recommend, subscribe to,
sustain, adopt
COLLOQ. throw your weight behind
2 SIGN, countersign, sign on the back of, initial

endorsement n
1 APPROVAL, sanction, authorization, support, backing,
ratification, confirmation, affirmation, advocacy, warrant,
recommendation, commendation, seal of approval,
testimonial, subscription
FORMAL approbation
COLLOQ. OK, green light, thumbs-up
2 SIGNATURE, countersignature, initialling

endow v
1 FINANCE, give, donate, pay for, grant,
boast, present, award, fund, support, make over,
leave, will
FORMAL bestow, bequeath, confer
2 HAVE, possess, give, provide, furnish,
supply, present, enjoy, boast, be endued with,
be blessed with

endowment n
1 FINANCE, award, grant, fund, funding, gift, present,
provision, settlement, donation, dowry, legacy, income,
revenue
FORMAL bequest, bestowal, benefaction
2 TALENT, attribute, faculty, gift, aptitude, capability, ability,
quality, flair, power, capacity, genius, qualification,
character

endurable adj
bearable, tolerable, supportable, manageable,
withstandable, sustainable, sufferable
E3 intolerable, unbearable

endurance n
patience, staying power, stamina, resignation, stoicism,
sufferance, tenacity, perseverance, resolution, stability,
durability, backbone, persistence, strength, tolerance,
toleration
FORMAL fortitude
COLLOQ. guts, spunk, bottle, stickability

endure v
1 *endure hardship*
bear, stand, put up with, tolerate, abide, weather, brave,
cope with, face, go through, encounter, meet, experience,
submit to, suffer, sustain, swallow, undergo, withstand,

take, have, hold, stick, allow, permit, support, brook;
dialect abear; *Scot* dree, thole
OLD bide, abrooke, outstand
COLLOQ. stomach, stick it, sweat it out, tough it out
2 *a peace that will endure for ever*
last, remain, live, survive, stay, persist, continue, hold,
hold out, keep, wear, prevail
OLD aby, dure, perdure
FORMAL abide

enduring *adj*
lasting, long-lasting, durable, permanent, perpetual,
abiding, remaining, continuing, long-standing, stable,
steady, firm, steadfast, persistent, persisting, chronic,
prevailing, surviving, unfaltering, unwavering, eternal,
immortal, imperishable
OLD (*Spenser*) dureful
E3 changeable, fleeting

enemy *n*
adversary, opponent, rival, antagonist, the
opposition, competitor, the competition,
opposer, other side
FORMAL foe
E3 friend, ally

QUOTATIONS
Ye have heard that it hath been said, Thou shalt love thy
neighbour, and hate thine enemy. But I say unto you,
Love your enemies, bless them that curse you, do good
to them that hate you, and pray for them which
despitefully use you, and persecute you
Bible, St Matthew

SYNONYM NUANCES

Adversary may be used to refer to someone who
hostilely opposes you, and sounds vaguely literary: *the
compelling menace of his adversary*. Other gentler terms
include **opponent** which, although similar, is often used
in the context of arranged competition, and does not
necessarily have the same connotations of aggression.
The opposition and **the other side** might also be used
of a body of people who simply object to your views or
actions.
  Rival and **competitor**, along with **the competition**, are
also used specifically of people who are not necessarily
enemies, but who are pursuing the same objective: *he
began his campaign for the presidency with more
support than his rivals*. The word **antagonist**, however,
suggests someone involved in contention or a struggle,
and has a more marked note of enmity: *the USA and
USSR were dangerous antagonists in the Cold War*.

energetic *adj*
lively, vigorous, active, animated, dynamic, spirited,
tireless, boisterous, zestful, brisk, strong, forceful, potent,
powerful, strenuous, high-powered, indefatigable; *dialect*
wick
COLLOQ. bursting with energy, full of beans, go-getting,
zippy, punchy
E3 lethargic, sluggish, inactive, idle

energize *v*
stimulate, arouse, stir, motivate, enliven, invigorate, liven,
quicken, animate, vitalize, vivify, activate, electrify,
galvanize
COLLOQ. pep up, fire up
E3 daunt

energy *n*
1 FUEL, propellant, motive power
TECHNICAL kinetic energy, potential energy, renewable
energy, alternative energy
See also **fuel**.
2 LIVELINESS, vigour, activity, animation, drive, dynamism,
enthusiasm, life, spirit, verve, vivacity, vitality, sparkle,
effervescence, zest, zeal, ardour, fire, efficiency, force,

forcefulness, effectiveness, strength, power, potency,
intensity, exertion, stamina
FORMAL might
COLLOQ. get-up-and-go, zip, push, pep, brio, pizzazz
See Synonym nuances panel at **vigour**.
E3 **2** lethargy, inertia, weakness, anergy

enervated *adj*
tired, weak, exhausted, feeble, fatigued, worn out,
weakened, incapacitated, debilitated, paralysed,
undermined, unmanned, unnerved, sapped, devitalized,
limp, spent
FORMAL effete, enfeebled
COLLOQ. done in, run-down, washed-out; *N Am* pooped
(out), tuckered out; *Aust & NZ* beaten
E3 active, energetic

enervating *adj*
tiring, wearying, wearisome, fatiguing, exhausting,
draining, demanding, hard, tough, difficult, exacting,
taxing, arduous, strenuous, laborious

enfeeble *v*
weaken, exhaust, fatigue, reduce, diminish, wear out, sap,
geld, undermine, debilitate, unhinge, unnerve, deplete,
devitalize
FORMAL enervate
E3 strengthen

enfold *v*
1 ENCLOSE, envelop, shroud, swathe, encircle, encompass,
fold, enwrap, wrap (up)
2 EMBRACE, clasp, hug, hold, clutch

enforce *v*
1 IMPOSE, administer, implement, carry out, apply, execute,
discharge, fulfil
2 COMPEL, insist on, oblige, urge, constrain, require,
necessitate, force, pressure, pressurize, coerce, exact,
prosecute, reinforce
COLLOQ. lean on, put the screws on

enforced *adj*
compulsory, binding, necessary, required, unavoidable,
imposed, involuntary, forced, obliged, obligatory,
mandatory, compelled, constrained, dictated, ordained,
prescribed

enforcement *n*
imposition, administration, implementation, application,
execution, discharge, fulfilment, insistence, coercion,
obligation, compulsion, constraint, pressure, prosecution,
requirement
FORMAL coaction

enfranchise *v*
give the right to vote to, give the vote to, free, liberate,
release
FORMAL emancipate, manumit, give suffrage to
E3 disenfranchise

enfranchisement *n*
giving the right to vote, voting rights, freedom, freeing,
liberating, liberation, release
FORMAL emancipation, manumission, suffrage
E3 disenfranchisement

engage *v*
1 PARTICIPATE, take part, embark on, take up, practise, do,
enter into, undertake, join, involve, share, become
involved in/with
FORMAL partake of
2 ATTRACT, allure, draw, win, gain, captivate, capture,
charm, catch
3 OCCUPY, engross, absorb, employ, fill, hold, preoccupy,
busy, tie up, grip
4 EMPLOY, hire, appoint, take on, sign up/on, enlist, enrol,
commission, recruit, contract, enter into an agreement, put
on the payroll
5 INTERLOCK, mesh, enmesh, interconnect, join, fit together,
interact, attach

6 FIGHT, battle with, attack, take on, encounter, assail, clash with, combat, join in battle with, wage war with
2 repel **4** dismiss, discharge **5** disengage

engaged adj
1 *engaged in his work*
occupied, busy, engrossed, immersed, absorbed, preoccupied, involved, active, employed
COLLOQ. tied up
2 *engaged to be married*
promised, pledged, committed
FORMAL betrothed, affianced, plighted, espoused
COLLOQ. spoken for
3 *the phone is engaged*
busy, unavailable, occupied, in use, taken
COLLOQ. tied up

engagement n
1 APPOINTMENT, meeting, interview, date, arrangement, commitment, assignation, booking, reservation, fixture, rendezvous
COLLOQ. gig, snap
2 PROMISE, pledge, commitment, obligation, agreement, contract, bond, assurance, vow
OLD plight; *Irish* hand-promise
FORMAL betrothal, betrothment, espousal, troth
3 INVOLVEMENT, participation, taking part, undertaking, sharing
FORMAL partaking
4 FIGHT, battle, combat, conflict, attack, clash, war, assault, strife, struggle, offensive, action, encounter, confrontation, contest

engaging adj
charming, attractive, appealing, captivating, pleasing, delightful, winsome, winning, lov(e)able, adorable, sweet, lik(e)able, pleasant, fetching, fascinating, enchanting, agreeable
repulsive, repellent

engender v
cause, produce, occasion, bring about, give rise to, instigate, lead to, incite, induce, create, inspire, generate, arouse, excite, encourage, nurture, kindle, breed, propagate, provoke
OLD beget
FORMAL effect

engine n
1 *a car engine*
motor, machine, machinery, mechanism, appliance, contraption, apparatus, device, instrument, tool, implement, locomotive, generator, dynamo
2 *a major engine of economic growth*
cause, instrument, vehicle, agent, medium, factor, channel, way, means, source

---

Types of engine include:

compression-ignition	gas	reciprocating
diesel	internal-combustion	rocket
external-combustion	jet	steam
fuel-injection	oil	turbine
	petrol	V-engine
		water

Parts of an automotive engine and its ancillaries include:

air filter	crankshaft pulley	fuel and ignition ECU (electronic control unit)
alternator	cylinder block	
camshaft	cylinder head	
camshaft cover	drive belt	fuel injector
carburettor		gasket
choke	exhaust manifold	ignition coil
connecting rod	exhaust valve	ignition distributor
colloq. con-rod		inlet manifold
cooling fan	fan belt	inlet valve
crankshaft	flywheel	oil filter

oil pump	push-rod	sump
oil seal	radiator	tappet
petrol pump	rocker arm	thermostat
piston	rocker cover	timing belt
piston ring	rotor arm	timing pulley
power-steering	spark plug	turbocharger
pump	starter motor	

---

engineer n, v
♦ n
1 MECHANIC, technician, operator, machinist, driver, engine driver, controller, handler
2 DESIGNER, originator, planner, builder, inventor, deviser, mastermind, architect, civil engineer, electrical engineer, mechanical engineer, chemical engineer, sound engineer
♦ v
plan, contrive, devise, manoeuvre, cause, manipulate, control, direct, bring about, mastermind, originate, arrange, orchestrate, plot, scheme, stage-manage, manage, create, rig
FORMAL effect

engorged adj
full, overfull, swollen, puffy, inflated, enlarged, expanded

engrave v
1 INSCRIBE, cut, carve, chisel, etch, mark, print, imprint, impress, incise, chase
2 *engraved on her mind*
imprint, impress, fix, stamp, lodge, set, embed, engrain, brand

engraving n
print, impression, imprint, inscription, carving, etching, cutting, cut, woodcut, plate, block, chiselling, mark
TECHNICAL dry-point, intaglio

> QUOTATIONS
> Engraving then, is, in brief terms, the Art of Scratch
> JOHN RUSKIN, *Ariadne Florentina*

engross v
absorb, occupy, engage, interest, grip, hold, preoccupy, rivet, fascinate, captivate, enthral, arrest, involve, intrigue
bore

engrossed adj
absorbed, occupied, taken up, preoccupied, gripped, engaged, caught up, enthralled, fascinated, captivated, immersed, intent, intrigued, rapt, riveted, mesmerized, wrapped, lost, fixated
bored, disinterested

engrossing adj
absorbing, fascinating, enthralling, captivating, intriguing, gripping, interesting, compelling, riveting, suspenseful
COLLOQ. unputdownable
boring

engulf v
overwhelm, swamp, flood, deluge, drown, inundate, plunge, immerse, submerge, overrun, overtake, swallow up, devour, consume, bury, absorb, engross, envelop

enhance v
heighten, intensify, increase, improve, upgrade, elevate, add to, enrich, magnify, swell, exalt, raise, lift, boost, strengthen, emphasize, stress, reinforce, embellish
FORMAL augment
COLLOQ. sex up
reduce, minimize

enhancement n
heightening, increase, improvement, elevation, enrichment, magnification, intensification, boost, emphasis, stress, reinforcement
FORMAL augmentation

enigma n

mystery, riddle, puzzle, paradox, conundrum, problem, dilemma, quandary, brain-teaser; N Am brain-twister
COLLOQ. poser

enigmatic adj

mysterious, mystifying, puzzling, cryptic, obscure, strange, baffling, perplexing, paradoxical, incomprehensible, inexplicable, unfathomable
FORMAL arcane, esoteric, recondite
⊟ simple, straightforward

enjoin v

1 ORDER, command, demand, urge, direct, instruct, decree, ordain, advise, encourage, require, charge
2 PROHIBIT, forbid, ban, bar
FORMAL disallow, interdict, proscribe

enjoy v

1 *enjoy dancing*
take pleasure in, delight in, appreciate, like, relish, revel in, love, be fond of, rejoice in, savour
OLD joy, taste
COLLOQ. fancy, go for, go a bundle on, get a buzz out of, get a kick out of
See Synonym nuances panel at **appreciate**.
2 *enjoy an advantage*
have, have the use of, possess, be blessed with, be endowed with, be favoured with, benefit from
OLD wield, undergo
FORMAL partake of
COLLOQ. have something going for
⊟ **1** dislike, hate

■ **enjoy yourself**
have a good time, have fun, make merry, sport
COLLOQ. have a whale of a time, live it up, party, let your hair down, paint the town red, have a ball, have a blast, get your jollies, get your kicks, have it large, large it
SLANG N Am ball; S Afr jol

enjoyable adj

pleasant, agreeable, delightful, pleasing, entertaining, amusing, fun, pleasurable, delicious, fine, lovely, good, nice, satisfying
FORMAL gratifying, delectable
COLLOQ. smashing, cool, ace, wizard, brilliant, brill, super, fantastic, fab, fabulous; N Am neat; S Afr lekker
SLANG radical, wicked, bad, mega
⊟ disagreeable

enjoyment n

1 PLEASURE, delight, amusement, entertainment, relish, joy, fun, gladness, happiness, diversion, recreation, indulgence, zest, satisfaction
FORMAL gratification, delectation
2 POSSESSION, use, advantage, benefit, privilege, favour, blessing
⊟ **1** displeasure

enlarge v

1 *enlarge the garden; glands enlarging*
make/become larger, make/become bigger, increase, expand, extend, magnify, add to, supplement, inflate, swell, stretch, multiply, develop, amplify, widen, broaden, lengthen, heighten
TECHNICAL distend, dilate, intumesce
FORMAL augment, elongate
2 *enlarge a photograph*
make bigger, blow up, expand, magnify
3 *enlarge on something*
expand on, go into details, elaborate on
FORMAL expatiate on, dilate on
⊟ **1** diminish, shrink

enlargement n

1 *enlargement of the building/a gland*
increase, expansion, growth, extension, magnification, inflation, swelling, stretching, multiplication, development, amplification
TECHNICAL distension, dilation, intumescence, oedema
FORMAL augmentation

2 *a photographic enlargement*
blow-up, magnification
⊟ **2** contraction, decrease, reduction

enlighten v

instruct, edify, cultivate, educate, inform, illuminate, teach, tutor, counsel, apprise, advise, notify, make aware, open your eyes
⊟ confuse

enlightened adj

informed, aware, knowledgeable, educated, civilized, cultivated, refined, cultured, sophisticated, conversant, wise, learned, intellectual, reasonable, liberal, broad-minded, open-minded, literate
FORMAL erudite
⊟ ignorant, confused

enlightenment n

awareness, knowledge, teaching, understanding, illumination, light, education, instruction, wisdom, information, insight, comprehension, civilization, cultivation, refinement, learning, literacy, edification, sophistication, broad-mindedness, open-mindedness, eye-opener, *Aufklärung*
TECHNICAL satori
FORMAL erudition, sapience
⊟ confusion, ignorance

enlist v

1 *enlist in the army*
engage, enrol, register, sign up, recruit, conscript, hire, take on, employ, volunteer, join (up), gather, muster
2 *enlist someone's help*
secure, obtain, enter, win, engage, get
FORMAL procure

enliven v

excite, exhilarate, brighten (up), cheer (up), gladden, hearten, invigorate, rouse, wake up, liven (up), stimulate, revitalize, inspire, animate, buoy up, fire, kindle, quicken, spark
FORMAL vivify
COLLOQ. pep up, perk up, give a lift to
⊟ subdue

en masse adv

all at once, all together, as a group, as a whole, as one, ensemble, in a body, together, en bloc, wholesale

enmeshed adj

involved, associated, concerned, caught up, entangled, mixed up

enmity n

animosity, hostility, antagonism, discord, strife, feud, antipathy, bitterness, acrimony, malevolence, hate, hatred, aversion, ill-will, bad blood, rancour, malice, venom
⊟ friendship, reconciliation

ennoble v

dignify, uplift, elevate, raise, exalt, enhance, glorify, honour, magnify
FORMAL aggrandize, nobilitate

ennui n

boredom, tiredness, dissatisfaction, tedium, lassitude, listlessness, languor, malaise
FORMAL accidie, acedia
COLLOQ. the doldrums

enormity n

atrocity, outrage, iniquity, horror, evil, crime, abomination, violation, monstrosity, outrageousness, wickedness, vileness, depravity, evilness, atrociousness, viciousness

> ❗ **enormity** or **enormousness**?
> Of these two nouns, only *enormousness* should be used when referring to size: *the enormousness of his ambitions*. *Enormity* means 'great wickedness, seriousness (of a crime, etc)': *the enormity of his assault on the little girl*.

enormous *adj*
huge, immense, vast, gigantic, massive, colossal, large-scale, gross, gargantuan, astronomic, monstrous, mammoth, considerable, tremendous, stupendous, prodigious, giant, Titanic
COLLOQ. jumbo, great big, whopping, walloping, whacking, whaling, plonking, hulking great, ginormous, humongous, monster, God-almighty
SLANG mega
F∃ small, tiny

enormously *adv*
very, extremely, to a vast/huge/immense extent, hugely, exceptionally, extraordinarily, exceedingly, especially, massively, tremendously, immensely
OLD jolly
COLLOQ. terribly, devilish, well, dead

enormousness *n*
hugeness, immensity, immenseness, vastness, massiveness, largeness, greatness, magnitude, expanse, extensiveness

⚠ enormousness or enormity?
See panel at **enormity**.

enough *adj, n, adv*
♦ *adj*
sufficient, adequate, ample, plenty, abundant
F∃ insufficient, inadequate
♦ *n*
sufficiency, adequacy, plenty, abundance, ample supply
FORMAL amplitude
♦ *adv*
sufficiently, adequately, reasonably, tolerably, passably, moderately, fairly, satisfactorily, amply

en passant *adv*
in passing, by the way, while on the subject, incidentally, cursorily
FORMAL parenthetically

enquire, enquirer, enquiring, enquiringly, enquiry
see **inquire, inquirer, inquiring, inquiringly, inquiry**.

enrage *v*
incense, infuriate, anger, make angry, annoy, madden, provoke, incite, inflame, agitate, exasperate, irritate, rile, irk, vex
COLLOQ. needle, bug, wind up, hack off, drive someone up the wall, drive someone round the bend, make someone's blood boil, make someone's hackles rise, put/get someone's back up, push too far
SLANG piss off
F∃ calm, placate

enraged *adj*
incensed, infuriated, angry, angered, furious, livid, raging, seething, storming, inflamed, annoyed, irritated, irate, exasperated, fuming
COLLOQ. aggravated, mad, wild
SLANG pissed off; *N Am* pissed
F∃ calm

enrapture *v*
enchant, fascinate, charm, thrill, delight, please greatly, captivate, bewitch, beguile, enthral, entrance, spellbind, transport, ravish

enrich *v*
1 ENDOW, enhance, improve, refine, develop, cultivate, add to, supplement
FORMAL augment, aggrandize, ameliorate
2 ADORN, ornament, beautify, embellish, decorate, garnish, grace, gild
F∃ 1 impoverish

enrol *v*
1 REGISTER, enlist, sign on, sign up, join up, recruit, go in for, enter, put your name down, engage, admit
2 RECORD, list, note, enter, put down
FORMAL inscribe

enrolment *n*
registration, recruitment, enlistment, enlisting, signing on/up, joining up, admission, acceptance

en route *adv*
in transit, on the move, on the way, on the road, on/during the journey

ensconce *v*
install, settle, establish, entrench, nestle, put, place, lodge, protect, shelter, shield, screen, locate

ensemble *n*
1 WHOLE, total, entirety, entity, unit, sum, set, group, collection, accumulation
FORMAL aggregate
COLLOQ. whole caboodle, whole (bang) shoot
2 OUTFIT, costume, suit, co-ordinates
COLLOQ. get-up, rig-out
3 GROUP, band, orchestra, company, troupe, circle, chorus, cast

enshrine *v*
preserve, set down, lay down, protect, guard, shield, treasure, cherish, immortalize, consecrate, dedicate, exalt, hallow, revere, sanctify, idolize, embalm
FORMAL apotheosize

enshroud *v*
cloak, cloud, shroud, veil, pall, wrap, conceal, hide, cover, enclose, enfold, envelop, enwrap, obscure

ensign *n*
banner, standard, flag, colours, pennant, jack, badge, crest, shield, coat of arms, sign, pennon, gonfalon
OLD pavilion

enslave *v*
subject, dominate, bind, enchain, yoke, trap
FORMAL subjugate, disenfranchise
F∃ free, emancipate

enslavement *n*
slavery, subjection, servitude, bondage, captivity, oppression, repression, serfdom, vassalage
FORMAL dulosis, enthralment, subjugation, thraldom, disenfranchisement
F∃ emancipation

ensnare *v*
trap, catch, capture, net, snare, embroil, enmesh, entangle, entrap

ensue *v*
follow, issue, proceed, succeed, result, arise, happen, occur, transpire, turn out, flow, derive, develop, stem, come next
FORMAL befall
F∃ precede

ensure *v*
1 MAKE CERTAIN, make sure, guarantee, warrant, secure, certify
FORMAL effect
2 PROTECT, make safe, guard, safeguard, secure

entail *v*
involve, necessitate, occasion, need, require, call for, demand, cause, produce, bring about, give rise to, lead to, result in

entangle *v*
1 *entangled in the net*
tangle, twist, knot, ravel, intertwine, enmesh, ensnare, snare, mix up
2 EMBROIL, involve, implicate, complicate, confuse, jumble, muddle
F∃ 1, 2 disentangle

entanglement *n*
1 TANGLE, knot, mesh, tie, trap, jumble, ensnarement, entrapment, snare
2 INVOLVEMENT, complication, embarrassment, confusion, muddle, snarl-up, difficulty, mess, mix-up, predicament, liaison, relationship, affair
F∃ 1 , 2 disentanglement

entente *n*
agreement, arrangement, friendship, deal, pact, treaty, understanding, entente cordiale
FORMAL compact

enter *v*
1 COME IN TO, go in (to), get in (to), arrive, gain access to, cross the threshold, burst in, sneak in, break in, worm your way in, insert, introduce, board, infiltrate, penetrate, pierce, occupy
COLLOQ. pop in
2 JOIN, become a member of, enlist, set about, sign up, put your name down for, take up, participate, take part, go in for, undertake, embark upon, enrol, start, begin, engage in, get involved in
FORMAL commence
3 RECORD, log, note, list, register, put down, take down, write down, set down, inscribe, lodge, put on record, submit, go in for, input
4 *the country entered a new period of reform*
begin, start, embark on, launch into, introduce
F3 **1** depart **3** delete

enterprise *n*
1 UNDERTAKING, venture, project, plan, effort, operation, campaign, programme, endeavour, task, scheme
OLD design, expedience, emprise; *(Shakesp)* designment
COLLOQ. show
2 INITIATIVE, resourcefulness, drive, adventurousness, adventure, courage, boldness, imagination, ambition, energy, enthusiasm, strong feeling, spirit, vitality, gumption
COLLOQ. get-up-and-go, push, oomph
3 BUSINESS, company, firm, establishment, operation, concern, industry
F3 **2** apathy

> **QUOTATIONS**
> If Enterprise is afoot, Wealth accumulates whatever may be happening to Thrift; and if Enterprise is asleep, Wealth decays, whatever Thrift may be doing
> JOHN MAYNARD KEYNES, *A Treatise on Money*

enterprising *adj*
venturesome, adventurous, bold, daring, imaginative, resourceful, entrepreneurial, self-reliant, self-motivated, enthusiastic, energetic, keen, eager, zealous, ambitious, aspiring, pushy, go-ahead, spirited, vigorous, active, ingenious, undertaking
COLLOQ. goey
F3 unenterprising, lethargic

entertain *v*
1 AMUSE, divert, please, delight, cheer, interest, occupy, engage, engross, charm, captivate, distract
2 RECEIVE, have guests, ask over/round, have round, invite over/round, accommodate, play host to, provide hospitality, put up, treat, host, regale, junket, harbour
3 HARBOUR, contemplate, consider, think about, imagine, have, conceive, foster, nurture, cherish
FORMAL countenance
COLLOQ. flirt with
F3 **1** bore **3** reject

entertainer

Entertainers include:

acrobat	disc jockey	magician
actor	*colloq.* DJ	mime artist
actress	escapologist	mimic
artiste	fire-eater	mind-reader
busker	game-show host	minstrel
chat-show host	hypnotist	musician
clown	ice-skater	performer
comedian	impressionist	player
comic	jester	pole dancer
conjuror	juggler	presenter
dancer	lap dancer	singer
song-and-dance act	stripper	trapeze artist
stand-up comic	striptease artist	turntablist
	tightrope walker	ventriloquist

See also **musician, singer**.

entertaining *adj*
amusing, diverting, fun, recreational, enjoyable, delightful, interesting, pleasant, pleasing, pleasurable, humorous, funny, comical, witty
F3 boring

entertainment *n*
1 AMUSEMENT, diversion, recreation, enjoyment, play, hobby, pastime, fun, sport, leisure activity, distraction, pleasure
2 SHOW, spectacle, performance, play, presentation, extravaganza

Forms of entertainment include:

airshow	fête	radio
barbecue	firework party	reality television
cabaret	fleadh	recital
carnival	game show	revue
cartoon show	gymkhana	rodeo
casino	infotainment	*colloq.* show biz
chat show	karaoke	show business
cinema	laser-light show	sitcom
circus	magic show	soap opera
computer game	makeover show	television
concert	musical	theatre
dance	music hall	variety show
disco	nightclub	video
discothèque	opera	video game
documentary	pageant	waxworks
docusoap	pantomime	zoo
DVD	Punch-and-Judy	
edutainment	show	
festival	puppet show	

See also **performance**; **theatrical**.

enthral *v*
captivate, entrance, enchant, fascinate, charm, beguile, bewitch, thrill, enrapture, delight, intrigue, spellbind, hypnotize, mesmerize, engross, grip, rivet, absorb
F3 **1** bore

enthralling *adj*
captivating, entrancing, enchanting, fascinating, intriguing, beguiling, charming, thrilling, riveting, gripping, compulsive, compelling, spellbinding, hypnotizing, mesmerizing, mesmeric
F3 boring

enthuse *v*
praise, rave, wax lyrical, gush, drool, excite, inspire, motivate, fire, bubble over, effervesce, go into raptures

enthusiasm *n*
1 ZEAL, ardour, fervour, passion, keenness, eagerness, vehemence, warmth, zest, frenzy, fire, excitement, acclamation, furore, furor, earnestness, relish, spirit, brio, wholeheartedness, commitment, devotion, fanaticism, ecstasy, delirium
OLD verve
FORMAL ebullience, schwärmerei, *entraînement*, *estro*
COLLOQ. buzz, hype, oomph
2 INTEREST, hobby, pastime, passion, preoccupation, craze, mania, rage
COLLOQ. thing
F3 **1** apathy

enthusiast *n*
devotee, zealot, admirer, fan, supporter, follower, fanatic, lover
OLD zeal

FORMAL aficionado
COLLOQ. buff, freak, fiend, nut

enthusiastic adj
keen, ardent, eager, fervent, vehement, intense, passionate, warm, wholehearted, zealous, vigorous, spirited, earnest, devoted, avid, committed, self-motivated, excited, fanatical, gung-ho, exuberant
FORMAL ebullient
COLLOQ. crazy, mad, wild, daft, nuts, potty, up for it; N Am rootin'-tootin'
See Synonym nuances panel at **intense**.
F3 unenthusiastic, apathetic

entice v
tempt, lure, allure, attract, seduce, lead on, draw, coax, persuade, induce, beguile, cajole
FORMAL inveigle
COLLOQ. sweet-talk

enticement n
inducement, lure, allure, attraction, seduction, bait, persuasion, coaxing, temptation, decoy, allurement, beguilement, cajolery
FORMAL blandishments, inveiglement
COLLOQ. come-on, sweet-talk

enticing adj
attractive, tempting, alluring, appealing, enticing, seductive, inviting, charming, captivating, irresistible

entire adj
1 the entire factory
complete, whole, total, full
2 entire agreement
absolute, utter, complete, total, whole, full, unqualified, unmitigated, outright
F3 **1** incomplete, partial

entirely adv
completely, wholly, totally, fully, utterly, unreservedly, absolutely, in toto, thoroughly, altogether, perfectly, only, solely, exclusively, in every respect, in every way, every inch
F3 partially

entirety n
totality, total, fullness, completeness, wholeness, whole, sum

entitle v
1 AUTHORIZE, give someone the right, qualify, empower, enable, make eligible, allow, permit, license, warrant, sanction
FORMAL accredit
2 NAME, call, term, title, give the title, know as, style, christen, dub, label, designate

entitlement n
right, claim, due, authority, privilege, prerogative, title, warrant, opportunity

entity n
being, existence, thing, body, creature, individual, organism, substance, object

entomb v
bury, lay to rest, shroud
FORMAL inter, tomb, sepulchre, inhume, inearth
COLLOQ. put six feet under
SLANG plant

entombment n
burial, laying to rest
FORMAL interment, inhumation, sepulture

entourage n
retinue, attendants, company, companions, followers, following, escort, staff, suite, court, train, retainers, associates, cortège, coterie
COLLOQ. hangers-on, gang, posse

entrails n
intestines, offal, viscera, bowels, internal organs, vital organs, giblets, umbles
COLLOQ. guts, innards, insides

entrance[1] n
1 OPENING, way in, entry, access, door, doorway, gate, gateway, approach, threshold, drive, driveway, passageway, lobby, porch, hall, vestibule, foyer, anteroom
2 ARRIVAL, appearance, debut, initiation, introduction, start
3 ACCESS, admission, admittance, entry, right of entry, entrée
FORMAL ingress
F3 **1** exit **2** departure

entrance[2] v
entranced by her beauty
charm, enchant, enrapture, captivate, enthral, bewitch, beguile, spellbind, fascinate, delight, ravish, transport, hypnotize, mesmerize
F3 repel

entrancing adj
enchanting, charming, delightful, attractive, fascinating, appealing, lovely, pleasant, wonderful, alluring, bewitching, captivating, endearing, irresistible, mesmerizing, ravishing, winsome
F3 boring, repellent

entrant n
1 NOVICE, beginner, starter, newcomer, new arrival, initiate, convert, probationer, apprentice, fresher, freshman, learner, student, pupil, trainee
2 COMPETITOR, candidate, contestant, contender, entry, applicant, participant, player, rival, opponent

entrap v
1 CATCH, trap, capture, snare, ensnare, entangle, enmesh, embroil, ambush, net
2 TRICK, deceive, delude, entice, seduce, tempt, implicate, beguile, allure, lure
FORMAL inveigle

entreat v
beg, implore, plead with, crave, pray, ask, petition, solicit, request, appeal to
FORMAL beseech, supplicate, invoke, importune

entreaty n
appeal, plea, prayer, petition, suit, cry, solicitation, request
FORMAL supplication, invocation

entrée n
1 MAIN COURSE, main dish
2 STARTER, appetizer, first course
3 ACCESS, admission, admittance, entry, right of entry
FORMAL ingress

entrench v
establish, fix, embed, dig in, ensconce, install, lodge, root, ingrain, settle, seat, plant, anchor, set, stop a gap, take up position
F3 dislodge

entrenched adj
deep-rooted, deep-seated, rooted, established, well-established, firm, fixed, implanted, ingrained, inbred, set, inflexible, diehard, unshak(e)able, dyed-in-the-wool, indelible, ineradicable
FORMAL intransigent
COLLOQ. stick-in-the-mud

entrepreneur n
business executive, businessman, businesswoman, financier, industrialist, middleman, promoter, agent, dealer, broker, contractor, magnate, tycoon, speculator, moneymaker, manager, undertaker, enterpriser, impresario

entrepreneurial adj
business, commercial, industrial, trade, contractual, managerial, financial, monetary, economic, budgetary, professional

entrust v
trust, commit, make someone responsible for, put in charge, confide, consign, authorize, charge, assign, turn over, hand over, commend, depute, invest, endow, delegate, deliver

entry *n*

1 APPEARANCE, entrance, admittance, admission, arrival, access, entrée, introduction
2 ACCESS, admission, admittance, entry, right of entry, entrée
FORMAL ingress
3 RECORD, item, minute, note, memorandum, description, statement, account, listing
4 ENTRANT, competitor, contestant, contender, candidate, applicant, participant, player, rival, opponent
5 OPENING, entrance, door, doorway, access, threshold, way in, passage, gate, gateway, approach, lobby, porch, hall, vestibule, foyer, anteroom
₣ **5** exit

entwine *v*

wind, twist, intertwine, interlace, interlink, interweave, intwine, coil, braid, knit, plait, twine, weave, wreathe, knot, ravel, entangle, embroil
₣ unravel

enumerate *v*

list, name, itemize, cite, detail, specify, catalogue, count, number, relate, recount, spell out, tell, mention, calculate, quote, recite, reckon, compute

enunciate *v*

1 ARTICULATE, pronounce, vocalize, voice, express, say, speak, utter, sound
2 STATE, declare, express, utter, proclaim, affirm, announce, put forward
FORMAL propound, promulgate

enunciation *n*

1 ARTICULATION, pronunciation, vocalization, expression, speech, sound, sounding, utterance
2 STATEMENT, declaration, expression, proclamation, affirmation, announcement
FORMAL promulgation

envelop *v*

wrap, enfold, enwrap, encase, cover, swathe, shroud, engulf, enclose, encircle, encompass, surround, cloak, veil, blanket, conceal, obscure, hide

envelope *n*

wrapper, wrapping, wrap, cover, case, casing, sleeve, sheath, covering, shell, skin, holder, jacket, coating

enviable *adj*

desirable, privileged, favoured, blessed, fortunate, lucky, attractive, advantageous, sought-after, invidious, excellent, fine
₣ unenviable

envious *adj*

covetous, jealous, resentful, green (with envy), dissatisfied, grudging, begrudging, jaundiced, spiteful
COLLOQ. green-eyed

enviously *adv*

with envy, jealously, resentfully, grudgingly, desirously, covetously, begrudgingly

environment *n*

1 *a restful environment*
surroundings, conditions, climate, circumstances, milieu, atmosphere, habitat, situation, element, medium, background, ambience, scene, setting, locale, context, mood, influences, territory, domain
COLLOQ. the lie of the land, which way the wind is blowing
2 *respect the environment*
nature, creation, mother earth/nature, earth, Gaia, natural world/surroundings

---

SYNONYM NUANCES

sense 1
Surroundings may be used generally of the concrete things around you: *situated in beautiful surroundings*; whereas **conditions** has more to do with the state in which things exist: *children growing up in appalling*

---

living conditions. **Habitat** returns to the more concrete referent of a place that is lived in.

You can use **element** to refer to the substances necessary to life, or more figuratively, the state best suited to a particular person: *the hypothetical is their element*; whilst **medium** tends to refer more narrowly to a place with the necessary attributes for supporting life: *the plant has some exacting demands as to its medium.* The term **climate** may be used of weather patterns, but can be extended to refer to the current trend in a particular area: *education has suffered in the climate of recent cuts.*

Milieu has to do with the centre of a particular place or way of thinking: *the exotic milieu of Montparnasse; the limitations of the milieu in which she was born.* **Atmosphere** is more suggestive of pervading feeling: *an atmosphere of trust.* The terms **ambience** and **mood** similarly conjure up an idea of surrounding influences or prevailing feelings: *an ambience of unashamed luxury.*

Both **scene** and **setting** would be used to refer to where something takes place, and **locale**, likewise, may be used of a place in respect of an event: *they see the countryside as a locale for recreation.* **Context** similarly links the nature of something with its position: *literature should be read in its cultural context.*

environmentalist *n*

conservationist, ecologist, preservationist, Friends of the Earth
COLLOQ. ecofreak, econut, green; *Aust* greenie

environs *n*

neighbourhood, surroundings, surrounding area, vicinity, outskirts, suburbs, district, locality, precincts, purlieus
FORMAL circumjacencies, vicinage

envisage *v*

visualize, imagine, picture, see coming, envision, conceive of, preconceive, predict, anticipate, foresee, image, see, think of, contemplate

envision *v*

imagine, visualize, envisage, picture, see coming, see, think of, contemplate

envoy *n*

agent, representative, ambassador, diplomat, messenger, legate, consul, attaché, emissary, minister, delegate, deputy, courier, mediator, intermediary, go-between

envy *n, v*

♦ *n*
covetousness, desire, jealousy, resentfulness, resentment, dissatisfaction, grudge, ill-will, malice, spite
♦ *v*
covet, resent, begrudge, grudge, crave

ephemeral *adj*

transient, short-lived, fleeting, brief, momentary, passing, short, temporary, transitory, impermanent, flitting
FORMAL evanescent, fugacious, fungous
₣ enduring, lasting, perpetual

epic *adj, n*

♦ *adj*
heroic, grand, majestic, elevated, exalted, lofty, imposing, impressive, vast, ambitious, long, large, large-scale, great, colossal, huge
FORMAL grandiloquent, sublime
₣ ordinary
♦ *n*
long story/poem, narrative, history, legend, saga, myth, romance

epicure *n*

gourmet, connoisseur, *bon vivant*, *bon viveur*, gastronome, epicurean, gourmand, glutton, hedonist, sensualist, Sybarite, voluptuary

epicurean adj
gourmet, gastronomic, gormandizing, sensual, sensualist, voluptuous, luxurious, self-indulgent, gluttonous, luscious, lush, unrestrained, hedonistic, Sybaritic, libertine

epidemic adj, n
♦ adj
widespread, prevalent, extensive, rife, rampant, sweeping, wide-ranging, pervasive, prevailing, endemic
FORMAL pandemic
♦ n
1 PLAGUE, outbreak, scourge, pest
FORMAL pandemia
2 *the epidemic of fatherless families*
spread, rash, spate, upsurge, growth, increase, rise, wave

epigram n
witticism, quip, *bon mot*, saying, proverb, maxim, pun, play on words, aphorism, gnome
TECHNICAL apophthegm
COLLOQ. old chestnut

epigrammatic adj
concise, succinct, brief, short, terse, laconic, pithy, aphoristic, incisive, piquant, pointed, sharp, pungent, witty, ironic

epilogue n
afterword, postscript, PS, appendix, coda, conclusion, swan song
E3 foreword, prologue, preface

episode n
1 INCIDENT, event, occurrence, happening, occasion, circumstance, experience, adventure, affair, matter, business
2 INSTALMENT, part, chapter, passage, section, scene
3 *an episode of an illness*
attack, spell, bout, period, fit, spasm
Related adjective: episodic

episodic adj
periodic, intermittent, irregular, occasional, spasmodic, sporadic, disconnected, disjointed, digressive, anecdotal
FORMAL picaresque

epistle n
letter, communication, message, missive, correspondence, bulletin, note, line, encyclical

epitaph n
commemoration, elegy, inscription, rest in peace, RIP, obituary, funeral oration
TECHNICAL lapidary expression

epithet n
description, descriptive adjective, descriptive phrase/ expression, designation, name, nickname, tag, title, sobriquet, by-name, to-name
FORMAL appellation, denomination

epitome n
1 PERSONIFICATION, embodiment, representation, model, example, archetype, type, prototype, essence
FORMAL quintessence, exemplar
2 SUMMARY, abstract, abridgement, digest, synopsis, outline, précis, résumé

epitomize v
1 PERSONIFY, embody, represent, exemplify, incorporate, encapsulate, illustrate, typify, symbolize, sum up
FORMAL incarnate
2 ABRIDGE, shorten, summarize, abbreviate, abstract, précis, reduce, compress, condense, contract, curtail, cut
E3 2 elaborate, expand

epoch n
age, era, period, time, span, date

equable adj
1 *an equable person*
even-tempered, placid, calm, cool and collected, serene, unexcitable, tranquil, composed, level-headed, easy-going
FORMAL imperturbable
COLLOQ. unflappable, unfazed, laid-back

2 *an equable climate*
uniform, even, consistent, constant, regular, moderate, temperate, unchanging, unvarying, steady, stable, smooth
E3 1 excitable 2 variable, extreme

> **! equable** or **equitable**?
> *Equable* means 'even-tempered': *That child would infuriate the most equable parent* ; 'not extreme and without great variation': *an equable climate*. *Equitable* means 'fair, just': *a more equitable distribution of profits*.

equably adv
calmly, placidly, serenely, unexcitably, tranquilly, level-headedly

equal adj, n, v
♦ adj
1 IDENTICAL, the same, alike, like, equivalent, corresponding, commensurate, comparable
2 EVEN, uniform, regular, constant, level, unchanging, symmetrical, unvarying, balanced, well balanced, matched, evenly matched, on an equal footing
COLLOQ. fifty-fifty, neck and neck, even-steven(s)
3 IMPARTIAL, fair, just, unbiased, neutral, non-partisan
4 *equal to a task*
competent, able, adequate, sufficient, fit, strong, capable, suitable, suited
E3 1 different 2 unequal 3 biased 4 unsuitable
♦ n
peer, counterpart, equivalent, coequal, match, parallel, twin, fellow, mate, compeer
♦ v
1 *equal a number*
match, correspond to, be the same as, add up to, amount to, balance, parallel, square with, tally with, coincide with, be equivalent to, equalize, equate with, make, total
2 *equal someone's score*
match, rival, emulate, reach, be level with, be on a par with, come up to
3 *no other dancer equals her for passion*
be as good as, compare with, match, be a match for, match up to, measure up to, rival, contend, view, keep up with

> **QUOTATIONS**
> All animals are equal but some animals are more equal than others
> GEORGE ORWELL, *Animal Farm*

equality n
1 UNIFORMITY, evenness, equivalence, correspondence, comparability, parallelism, balance, parity, par, symmetry, proportion, identity, sameness, likeness, similarity
2 IMPARTIALITY, fairness, justice, neutrality, partisanship, equal rights, equal opportunities, egalitarianism
E3 2 inequality

equalization n
standardization, compensation, levelling, matching, balancing, evening-out

equalize v
level, even up, make even, even out, match, equal, equate, draw level, keep pace, balance, redress the balance, square, standardize, regularize, compensate, smooth

equally adv
1 *treat people equally*
fairly, justly, evenly, uniformly, proportionally, proportionately, on equal terms
2 *equally important*
just as, similarly, as, as important, correspondingly, likewise, in the same way, in like manner, by the same token

equanimity n
composure, calm, calmness, tranquillity, serenity, ease, coolness, self-possession, self-control, level-headedness,

confidence, assurance, self-assurance, aplomb, poise, dignity, placidity, impassivity
FORMAL imperturbability, sangfroid
COLLOQ. unflappability
⊟ alarm, anxiety, discomposure

equate v
1 *equate wealth with happiness*
compare (to/with), liken to, match with, identify with, connect with, link with, pair with, juxtapose with, regard as the same, bracket together
2 *costs equate to a quarter of the income*
correspond to, correspond with, balance, parallel, equalize, be equal, offset, square with, agree with, tally with

equation n
1 *a differential equation*
mathematical expression, mathematical statement, calculation
2 *the equation between cheap food and the plight of farmers*
equality, correspondence, equivalence, balancing, agreement, parallel, pairing, comparison, match, matching, likeness, identity, identification, similarity
FORMAL juxtaposition

equestrian n, adj
♦ n
horseman, horsewoman, rider, courier, cavalryman, knight, cavalier, hussar, trooper, cowboy, cowgirl, rancher, herder, jockey
♦ adj
mounted, riding, horse-riding
FORMAL equine

equilibrium n
1 BALANCE, poise, symmetry, evenness, stability, steadiness
TECHNICAL stasis
FORMAL equipoise, counterpoise
2 EQUANIMITY, self-possession, composure, calmness, coolness, serenity, tranquillity, self-control, level-headedness, confidence, assurance, self-assurance, aplomb, poise, dignity
FORMAL imperturbability, sangfroid
COLLOQ. unflappability
⊟ **1** imbalance, instability **2** anxiety

equip v
provide, fit out, supply, furnish, prepare, arm, issue, fit up, outfit, kit out, stock, endow, rig, dress, clothe, deck out
OLD equipage, accomplish, accoutre; (*Spenser*) aguise; apparel, appoint, bedight, dight

equipment n
apparatus, gear, supplies, tackle, kit, tools, material, furnishings, luggage, baggage, outfit, paraphernalia, accessories, appliances, articles, furniture, hardware
FORMAL accoutrements, apparelment
COLLOQ. stuff, things, rig-out

equipoise n
equilibrium, balance, evenness, stability, steadiness, symmetry, poise, ballast, counterbalance, counter-weight
FORMAL counterpoise, equibalance, equiponderance
⊟ imbalance

equitable adj
even-handed, fair, proper, reasonable, right, rightful, due, fair-and-square, square, honest, ethical, impartial, just, unbiased, unprejudiced, legitimate, disinterested, dispassionate, objective
⊟ inequitable, unfair

> **!** **equitable** or **equable**?
> *See panel at* **equable**.

equitably adv
fairly, justly, impartially, even-handedly, reasonably, rightfully, honestly, ethically, disinterestedly, dispassionately
⊟ unfairly, inequitably

equity n
even-handedness, equitableness, fairness, fair play, fair-mindedness, reasonableness, righteousness, uprightness, honesty, integrity, justice, justness, objectivity, impartiality, disinterestedness
FORMAL rectitude
⊟ inequity

equivalence n
identity, identicalness, correspondence, agreement, likeness, sameness, equality, interchangeability, comparability, similarity, substitutability, correlation, parallel, conformity
FORMAL parity
⊟ unlikeness, dissimilarity

equivalent adj, n
♦ adj
equal, same, similar, identical, substitutable, parallel, corresponding, alike, like, comparable, interchangeable, even, twin
TECHNICAL homologous
FORMAL tantamount, commensurate
⊟ unlike, different
♦ n
counterpart, opposite number, equal, parallel, match, fellow, double, twin, peer, alternative, correspondent
TECHNICAL homologue
FORMAL correlative

equivocal adj
ambiguous, uncertain, ambivalent, obscure, vague, indefinite, evasive, oblique, misleading, dubious, questionable, suspicious, confusing
⊟ unequivocal, clear, definite

equivocate v
prevaricate, evade, dodge, fence, hedge, mislead, change your mind
FORMAL tergiversate, vacillate
COLLOQ. shilly-shally, pussyfoot, waffle, chop and change, change your tune, beat about the bush, hedge your bets, run with the hare and hunt with the hounds

equivocation n
prevarication, evasion, dodging the issue, hedging, double talk, quibbling, shifting, shuffling
FORMAL tergiversation
COLLOQ. flannel, waffle, weasel words, pussyfooting
⊟ directness

era n
age, epoch, period, date, day, days, time, times, generation, aeon, season, cycle, stage, century

eradicate v
eliminate, annihilate, get rid of, remove, do away with, root out, uproot, suppress, destroy, exterminate, extinguish, weed out, stamp out, wipe out, crack down on, abolish, erase, obliterate
FORMAL efface, expunge, extirpate

eradication n
elimination, annihilation, removal, riddance, obliteration, abolition, suppression, destruction, extermination, extinction
FORMAL effacement, extirpation, deracination, expunction

erasable adj
removable, washable, eradicable
FORMAL effaceable
⊟ permanent, ineradicable

erase v
obliterate, rub out, delete, blot out, wipe out, cancel, get rid of, remove, eradicate, put out of your mind
FORMAL expunge, efface, excise

erasure n
obliteration, deletion, elimination, eradication, rubbing-out, blotting-out, wiping-out, removal, cancellation, cleansing
FORMAL erasement, effacement, expunction

erect *v, adj*

♦ *v*

1 BUILD, construct, put up, put together, establish, set up, elevate, assemble, raise, rear, lift, mount, pitch, create
2 *erect a system*
found, form, institute, initiate, set up, put up, create, organize, establish

♦ *adj*

1 UPRIGHT, straight, vertical, upstanding, standing, raised
2 RIGID, hard, firm, stiff
TECHNICAL tumescent

erection *n*

1 BUILDING, construction, edifice, structure, assembly, establishment, manufacture, fabrication, creation, elevation, raising
COLLOQ. pile
2 RIGIDITY, stiffness
TECHNICAL tumescence, priapism
COLLOQ. hard
SLANG hard on, horn, stiffy, boner

ergo *adv*

therefore, consequently, accordingly, for this reason, in consequence, so, then, this being the case
FORMAL hence, thus

erode *v*

wear away, eat away, eat into, wear down, corrode, consume, grind down, destroy, disintegrate, deteriorate, fragment, deplete, spoil, undermine
FORMAL abrade, excoriate

erosion *n*

wear, wearing away, corrosion, disintegration, deterioration, destruction, undermining
FORMAL abrasion, attrition, denudation, excoriation

erotic *adj*

aphrodisiac, seductive, sensual, titillating, adult, pornographic, lascivious, stimulating, suggestive, erogenous, sexually arousing, amorous, venereal, carnal, lustful, voluptuous, Lesbian, Anacreontic
FORMAL amatory
COLLOQ. sexy, blue, raunchy, steamy, hot, dirty
SLANG horny

erotically *adv*

suggestively, sensually, seductively, pornographically, explicitly, anacreontically
COLLOQ. raunchily, steamily

err *v*

1 MAKE A MISTAKE, be wrong, be incorrect, miscalculate, mistake, misjudge, make a slip, slip up, blunder, misunderstand, misconstrue
COLLOQ. boob, make a booboo, mess up, duff it, bark up the wrong tree, get hold of the wrong end of the stick, put your foot in it, drop a clanger, come a cropper; *N Am* flub
SLANG goof (up), louse up, balls up, cock up, screw up
2 DO WRONG, sin, misbehave, go astray, offend, deviate, fall from grace
FORMAL transgress

QUOTATIONS
To err is human; to forgive, divine
ALEXANDER POPE, *An Essay on Criticism*

SYNONYM NUANCES

sense 1
Make a mistake is an unmarked term for committing a single error: *he made a mistake when he pumped too much money into the economy*, whilst **be wrong** and **be incorrect** are equally unmarked but would refer to a continuous state of being in error: *the country was wrong in its aggressions of the 1930s*.
   The term **make a slip** returns to a single act of doing something wrong, though the term itself is understated and suggests something minor, whereas the term

---

blunder suggests a gross mistake and implies an unfavourable judgement: *the government has blundered in its treatment of eastern affairs*. Returning to more neutral terms, **miscalculate** and **misjudge** are appropriate where previously-made conclusions or judgements are proved wrong, and **mistake** and **misunderstand** could be used convey the idea of error in comprehension: *they mistook the poisonous toadstools for wild mushrooms*. To refer to interpreting something wrongly, you could use **misconstrue**: *the referee had misconstrued the rules and allowed the goal to stand*.

errand *n*

task, job, duty, chore, commission, charge, mission, undertaking, assignment, message

errant *adj*

1 WAYWARD, wrong, erring, stray, straying, deviant, offending, criminal, lawless, disobedient, sinful, sinning, loose
FORMAL aberrant, peccant
2 ROAMING, rambling, roving, itinerant, journeying, wandering, nomadic
FORMAL peripatetic

erratic *adj*

changeable, variable, fitful, fluctuating, inconsistent, intermittent, sporadic, irregular, unsteady, unstable, shifting, varying, inconstant, unpredictable, volatile, unsettled, unreliable, abnormal, eccentric, wandering, meandering, vagrant
FORMAL aberrant, capricious, desultory
F3 steady, consistent, stable

erratically *adv*

changeably, unpredictably, variably, fitfully, inconsistently, unreliably, intermittently, irregularly, inconstantly, sporadically
F3 steadily, consistently

erring *adj*

wayward, wrong, errant, stray, straying, deviant, offending, criminal, lawless, disobedient, guilty, sinful, sinning, loose
FORMAL culpable, peccant

erroneous *adj*

incorrect, wrong, mistaken, false, untrue, spurious, specious, inaccurate, inexact, invalid, illogical, unfounded, faulty, flawed, misguided, misplaced
FORMAL fallacious
F3 correct, right

error *n*

mistake, inaccuracy, slip, blunder, gaffe, faux pas, lapse, slip of the tongue, mix-up, miscalculation, misunderstanding, misinterpretation, misjudgement, misconception, misapprehension, misprint, literal, spelling mistake, oversight, omission, fallacy, flaw, fault, wrong
OLD (Spenser) mesprize
FORMAL solecism, aberration
COLLOQ. slip-up, howler, clanger, blooper, boob, booboo, foul-up, own goal, cardinal sin, glitch, typo; *N Am* flub
SLANG goof, cock-up, balls-up

■ **in error**
mistakenly, wrongly, by mistake, erroneously, incorrectly, falsely, inaccurately, inappropriately, misguidedly, unfairly, unjustly
FORMAL fallaciously

ersatz *adj*

fake, substitute, imitation, artificial, synthetic, man-made, simulated, counterfeit, sham, bogus
COLLOQ. phoney

erstwhile *adj*

one-time, former, sometime, ex, late, old, once, past, previous, bygone

erudite *adj*
learned, scholarly, well-educated, knowledgeable, lettered, educated, well-read, literate, academic, cultured, intellectual, wise, highbrow, profound
COLLOQ. brainy
⊟ illiterate, ignorant

erudition *n*
learning, scholarship, education, knowledge, facts, knowledgeableness, learnedness, scholarliness, wisdom, culture, letters
FORMAL profundity, reconditeness

erupt *v*
1 *the volcano erupted*
burst open, explode, emit lava, discharge lava, pour forth lava
2 *lava erupting from the volcano*
belch, pour forth, discharge, burst, gush, spew, spout, eject, vent, expel, emit
3 *violence erupted*
break out, flare up, explode, blow up
4 *her skin erupted in boils*
break out, flare up

eruption *n*
1 OUTBURST, discharge, ejection, emission, venting, outbreak, explosion, flare-up, blow-up
2 RASH, outbreak, inflammation

escalate *v*
increase, intensify, grow, accelerate, rise, step up, heighten, raise, spiral, magnify, mushroom, enlarge, expand, extend, develop, mount, ascend, climb, soar, shoot up, amplify
COLLOQ. rocket, go through the roof, hit the roof
⊟ decrease, diminish

escalation *n*
increase, intensification, growth, acceleration, rise, heightening, magnification, expansion, extension, development, soaring, mushrooming
⊟ decrease

escalator *n*
lift, elevator, moving staircase, moving walkway, travolator

escapable *adj*
avoidable, evadable, avertible, eludible
⊟ inevitable

escapade *n*
adventure, exploit, fling, prank, frolic, caper, romp, spree, antic, stunt, trick
COLLOQ. lark, skylarking
SLANG *N Am* monkey shine

escape *v, n*
♦ *v*
1 GET AWAY, break free, run away, make your escape, make your getaway, bolt, abscond, flee, elope, fly, decamp, break loose, break out, flit, slip away, shake off, slip, bail out, cut and run; *dialect* overrun
COLLOQ. scoot, scram, scat, scarper, do a runner, do a bunk, run for it, do a moonlight flit, make a bolt/break for it, take to your heels, run for your life, slip through someone's fingers, have it away, take to the boats
SLANG leg it, *N Am* lam it, take it on the lam
2 AVOID, evade, elude, skip, shun, steer clear of, sidestep
FORMAL circumvent
COLLOQ. dodge, duck, ditch
3 LEAK, seep, flow, drain, spurt, gush, issue, discharge, ooze, trickle, pour out/forth, pass
4 *his name escapes me*
forget, not place, not be remembered/recalled, not know
COLLOQ. be on the tip of your tongue, not be able to put your finger on
♦ *n*
1 GETAWAY, flight, bolt, flit, breakout, absconding, decampment, jailbreak
OLD scape

COLLOQ. bunk
SLANG *N Am* lam
2 AVOIDANCE, evasion, go-by
FORMAL circumvention
COLLOQ. dodging, ducking
3 LEAK, seepage, leakage, outflow, gush, drain, hole, loophole, out, vent, discharge, issue, emission, spurt, outpour, emanation
TECHNICAL blower, efflux, extravasation
4 ESCAPISM, diversion, distraction, dreaming, fantasy, fantasizing, wishful thinking, recreation, relaxation, pastime, safety-valve

escapee *n*
absconder, escaper, jailbreaker, defector, deserter, fugitive, runaway, truant, refugee

escapism *n*
diversion, distraction, dreaming, fantasy, fantasizing, wishful thinking, recreation, relaxation, pastime, safety-valve
COLLOQ. pie in the sky, castles in the air
⊟ realism

escapist *n*
dreamer, daydreamer, fantasizer, wishful thinker, non-realist, Don Quixote, Walter Mitty
COLLOQ. ostrich
⊟ realist

eschew *v*
avoid, give up, abandon, keep clear of, repudiate, shun, spurn, disdain
FORMAL abjure, abstain from, refrain from, for(e)go, forswear, renounce
⊟ embrace

escort *n, v*
♦ *n*
1 COMPANION, chaperon(e), partner, attendant, aide, squire, guide, bodyguard, guard, protector, defender, beau
COLLOQ. date
2 ENTOURAGE, company, retinue, suite, train, guard, convoy, cortège, attendants
♦ *v*
accompany, partner, chaperon(e), bring, come (along) with, take, take out, attend on, guide, lead, usher, conduct, guard, protect, defend, shepherd, walk

esoteric *adj*
obscure, cryptic, inscrutable, mysterious, mystic, mystical, occult, hidden, secret, confidential, private, inside
FORMAL recondite, abstruse, arcane
⊟ well-known, familiar

especial *adj*
particular, special, marked, specific, striking, pre-eminent, notable, noteworthy, exceptional, outstanding, express, unique, exclusive, extraordinary, peculiar, singular, signal, uncommon, unusual, distinctive, remarkable

especially *adv*
1 PARTICULARLY, specially, markedly, notably, exceptionally, outstandingly, expressly, supremely, uniquely, exclusively, unusually, extraordinarily, uncommonly, remarkably, strikingly, very
2 CHIEFLY, mainly, principally, primarily, pre-eminently, mostly, above all, most of all

espionage *n*
counter-intelligence, infiltration, intelligence, investigation, probing, penetration, reconnaissance, spying, cloak-and-dagger operations/activities/tactics, surveillance, intercepting, secret service, industrial espionage, counter-espionage, undercover operations/work, fifth column, tradecraft
OLD scout
COLLOQ. snooping, bugging, wiretapping

> **QUOTATIONS**
> There is no place where espionage is not possible
> SUN TZU, *Art of War*

espousal n

adoption, embracing, support, advocacy, backing, promotion, choice, defence, taking-up, championing, championship, maintenance

espouse v

take up, adopt, embrace, support, advocate, back, choose, stand up for, defend, champion, patronize, maintain, opt for

esprit de corps n

group loyalty, team spirit, camaraderie, public spirit, friendly relations, mutual feeling, mutal respect

espy v

notice, see, catch sight of, glimpse, observe, detect, discern, perceive, make out, sight, spot, spy, discover, distinguish, behold

essay n, v

♦ n

1 *an essay on 'Hamlet'*
composition, dissertation, paper, article, study, assignment, thesis, theme, piece, commentary, critique, treatise, review, leader, tract, sketch
FORMAL discourse, disquisition, causerie, prolusion
2 ATTEMPT, try, endeavour, push, go, venture
COLLOQ. bash, crack, stab, shot
♦ v
try, attempt, endeavour, test, go for, take on, strain, strive, struggle, tackle, undertake
OLD assay
COLLOQ. have a bash, have a crack, have a go, have a stab

essence n

1 NATURE, character, essential character, being, substance, reality, actuality, soul, spirit, core, centre, heart, meaning, point, quality, significance, life, entity, crux, kernel, marrow, pith, characteristics, attributes, principle
FORMAL quintessence
2 CONCENTRATE, extract, concentration, distillation, spirits
FORMAL distillate

■ **in essence**
basically, fundamentally, essentially, substantially, at bottom, to all intents and purposes

■ **of the essence**
crucial, indispensable, necessary, essential, vital, required, needed, important
FORMAL requisite

essential adj, n

♦ adj

1 FUNDAMENTAL, basic, intrinsic, inherent, innate, underlying, principal, main, key, central, integral, characteristic, definitive, typical, constituent
2 CRUCIAL, indispensable, necessary, vital, required, needed, important, key
FORMAL requisite
1 incidental **2** dispensable, inessential
♦ n
necessity, prerequisite, requisite, requirement, basic, fundamental, rudiment, necessary, principle, gist, main point(s), key point(s)
FORMAL sine qua non
COLLOQ. must

essentially adv

fundamentally, basically, in essence, at heart, deep down, inherently, intrinsically, primarily

establish v

1 SET UP, found, start, form, institute, bring into being, open, create, begin, organize, inaugurate, introduce, install, plant, settle, secure, lodge, base
2 PROVE, demonstrate, show, authenticate, ratify, verify, certify, confirm, affirm, attest
FORMAL substantiate, validate, corroborate
1 uproot **2** refute

established adj

respected, experienced, traditional, conventional, accepted, secure, settled, entrenched, ensconced, fixed, steadfast, proved, proven, tried and tested
impermanent, unreliable

establishment n

1 FORMATION, setting up, founding, forming, creation, foundation, installation, institution, organization, inauguration
FORMAL inception
2 BUSINESS, company, firm, institute, organization, concern, institution, corporation, enterprise, shop, store
3 RULING CLASS, the system, the authorities, the powers that be, the government
COLLOQ. them

estate n

1 POSSESSIONS, effects, assets, belongings, havings, holdings, property, goods, grounds, land(s), landholding, real estate, manor, domain, park, pen, princedom, hacienda, latifundia; *Scot* udal; *N Am* realty, plantation
TECHNICAL trust, personalty, demesne, allodium, entail, executry, conditional fee, patrimony, taluk
2 AREA, development, centre, site, land, region, tract
3 STATUS, standing, situation, position, class, place, condition, state, rank

estate agent n

property agent; *N Am* realtor, real-estate agent

esteem n, v

♦ n

respect, regard, good opinion, appreciation, estimation, judgement, admiration, honour, consideration, reverence, credit, reckoning, count, account, love
FORMAL veneration, approbation
♦ v
respect, admire, honour, regard highly, revere, reverence, value, cherish, reckon, rate, regard, think, view, consider, treasure, count, judge, hold, believe, account
FORMAL adjudge, deem, venerate

esteemed adj

admired, respected, well-respected, well-thought-of, worthy, highly-regarded, honoured, revered, treasured, valued, honourable, admirable, reputable, respectable, distinguished, excellent, prized
FORMAL venerated

estimable adj

esteemed, respected, worthy, creditable, admirable, commendable, distinguished, reputable, respectable, honourable, excellent, good, notable, noteworthy, praiseworthy, valuable, valued
FORMAL laudable, meritorious
despicable, insignificant

estimate v, n

♦ v

assess, reckon, evaluate, calculate roughly, work out approximately, gauge, guess, value
FORMAL conjecture
♦ n
1 ROUGH CALCULATION, approximate cost/price/value/quantity, quotation, reckoning, valuation, judgement, (rough) guess, approximation, assessment, estimation, evaluation, computation
COLLOQ. guesstimate, ballpark figure
2 JUDGEMENT, consideration, opinion, belief, view, thinking, conclusion, evaluation, assessment, reckoning

estimation n

1 JUDGEMENT, opinion, belief, consideration, estimate, view, (way of) thinking, feeling, evaluation, assessment, reckoning, conception, calculation, computation, conclusion
2 RESPECT, regard, appreciation, esteem, credit
3 ROUGH CALCULATION, approximate cost/price/value/quantity, valuation, (rough) guess, assessment, estimate, evaluation

estrange v
alienate, disaffect, antagonize, disunite, divide, divorce, split up, break up, separate, sever, drive apart, part, set at variance, set against, withhold, withdraw
COLLOQ. drive a wedge between, put a barrier between
⊟ attract, bind, unite

estranged adj
divided, separate, separated, divorced, alienated, disaffected, antagonized
⊟ reconciled, united

estrangement n
alienation, disaffection, antagonism, disunity, division, dissociation, parting, separation, severance, split, breach, break-up, hostility, unfriendliness, antipathy, withdrawal, withholding

estuary n
inlet, mouth, firth, fjord, creek, cove, bay, arm, sea-loch

et cetera adv
and so on, and so forth, and the like, and the rest, &c, and suchlike, et al
COLLOQ. and what have you, and/or whatever

etch v
cut, carve, engrave, burn, furrow, dig, eat in, groove, impress, imprint, incise, ingrain, inscribe, bite, corrode, stamp

etching n
carving, cut, engraving, inscription, impression, imprint, print, sketch
TECHNICAL aqua fortis, aquatint

eternal adj
1 *eternal bliss*
unending, endless, ceaseless, everlasting, never-ending, infinite, limitless, immortal, deathless, undying, imperishable, indestructible
2 *eternal truths*
unchanging, timeless, enduring, lasting, perennial, abiding
3 *eternal quarrelling*
constant, continuous, perpetual, persistent, incessant, interminable, endless, never-ending, non-stop, relentless, remorseless
FORMAL unremitting
⊟ 1 temporary; *formal* ephemeral **2** changeable

SYNONYM NUANCES

sense 1
The words **unending**, **endless** and **everlasting** can be positive or negative depending on the context: *an unending supply of money*; *his endless questions annoyed me*; *his everlasting complaints*; *everlasting glory*. **Ceaseless**, though similar, may have further implications of mundanity: *her life was a ceaseless round of hard work*; **never-ending** also tends to be used rather derogatively, again implying tediousness: *the never-ending management-union battle*.
The terms **infinite** and **limitless**, however, can be used of something not just without end in time but also without any other fixed boundaries, and they often have positive associations: *my father had infinite patience*; *an athlete with limitless energy*.
Immortal, meanwhile, is generally reserved for deities, whilst **undying**, and the uncommon **deathless**, are used in a positive way of more earthly notions: *undying love*. **Imperishable**, however, shifts the focus to not being subject to decay or deterioration: *the imperishable soul*, and **indestructible** emphasizes the inability to be destroyed: *CDs are not indestructible as once claimed*.

---

eternally adv
1 EVERLASTINGLY, endlessly, ceaselessly, indestructibly, for ever, permanently
2 INTERMINABLY, constantly, continually, lastingly, always, for ever, perpetually, incessantly

COLLOQ. 24-7
⊟ briefly, temporarily

eternity n
1 EVERLASTINGNESS, endlessness, forever, everlasting, imperishability, infinity, timelessness, perpetuity, immutability, after-life, hereafter, immortality, deathlessness, everlasting life, heaven, paradise, next world, world to come, world without end
2 AGE, ages, long time, ages and ages
COLLOQ. donkey's years, yonks

ethereal adj
1 DELICATE, immaterial, dainty, exquisite, fine, light, gossamer, subtle, tenuous, insubstantial, intangible, airy-fairy, impalpable
FORMAL diaphanous
2 HEAVENLY, spiritual, celestial, refined, rarefied, unearthly, unworldly, elemental
FORMAL empyreal, empyrean
⊟ 2 earthly, solid

ethical adj
moral, principled, just, right, proper, virtuous, honourable, fair, upright, decent, above reproach, righteous, honest, good, correct, high-minded, responsible, commendable, fitting, noble
OLD seemly
FORMAL decorous
⊟ unethical

ethically adv
morally, rightly, justly, honestly, moralistically, virtuously, honourably, respectfully, responsibly, high-mindedly, reputably, nobly, ideologically

ethics n
moral values, values, morality, morals, principles, moral principles, standards, moral standards, code, moral code, moral philosophy, rules, beliefs, conscience, equity, principles of behaviour, principles of right and wrong
TECHNICAL deontology, descriptivism
FORMAL propriety

ethnic adj
racial, native, indigenous, traditional, tribal, folk, cultural, national, aboriginal
TECHNICAL ethnological, anthropological
FORMAL societal, autochthonous

ethnically adv
racially, culturally, socially, humanistically, tribally, traditionally
TECHNICAL anthropologically
FORMAL societally

ethos n
attitude, beliefs, standards, manners, ethics, morality, code, principles, spirit, tenor, flavour, atmosphere, rationale, character, disposition

etiquette n
code, code of behaviour, formalities, standards, correctness, conventions, customs, code of practice, code of conduct, rules, manners, good manners, form, good form, politeness, courtesy, ceremony, decency, unwritten law
COLLOQ. netiquette
FORMAL protocol, civility, decorum, propriety

etymology n
word history, word origins, word-lore, linguistics, origin, derivation, source, philology, semantics, lexicology

eulogize v
praise, acclaim, sing/sound the praises of, wax lyrical, applaud, approve, celebrate, exalt, extol, glorify, honour, magnify, commend, compliment, congratulate
FORMAL laud, panegyrize
COLLOQ. rave about, hype, plug
⊟ condemn

eulogy *n*
praise, tribute, acclaim, acclamation, accolade,
commendation, exaltation, glorification, compliment,
applause, plaudit
FORMAL encomium, laud, laudation, laudatory, paean,
panegyric
Ⅎ condemnation

euphemism *n*
evasion, polite term, indirect expression, substitution,
substitute, softening, genteelism, politeness,
understatement, mild alternative
Ⅎ dysphemism

euphemistic *adj*
polite, neutral, vague, indirect, substitute, evasive, soft-
toned, genteel, understated, mild

euphonious *adj*
harmonious, melodious, melodic, musical, silvery, soft,
sweet, dulcet, mellow, pleasant, sweet-sounding, sweet-
toned, tuneful, clear
FORMAL canorous, consonant, dulcifluous, dulciloquent,
euphonic, mellifluous, symphonious
Ⅎ cacophonous

euphoria *n*
elation, ecstasy, bliss, rapture, high spirits, buoyancy,
wellbeing, exhilaration, exultation, joy, intoxication,
jubilation, transport, glee, exaltation, enthusiasm,
happiness, cheerfulness
COLLOQ. high
Ⅎ depression, despondency

euphoric *adj*
elated, ecstatic, blissful, rapturous, exhilarated, enraptured,
enthusiastic, buoyant, intoxicated, exultant, exulted, joyful,
gleeful, happy, cheerful, jubilant
FORMAL joyous
COLLOQ. high
Ⅎ depressed, despondent

euthanasia *n*
mercy killing, assisted suicide, release, happy/merciful
release, quietus

evacuate *v*
1 LEAVE, go away from, depart, withdraw, remove, move
out of, retreat, retire from, abandon, desert, vacate,
decamp, relinquish
FORMAL forsake
COLLOQ. quit, clear (out), pull out of
2 EMPTY, make empty, eject, void, clear, remove, expel,
discharge, eliminate, purge, ease, relieve
TECHNICAL getter
OLD stool, vacuate
FORMAL defecate, excrete, stercorate
SLANG *(vulgar)* shit

evacuation *n*
1 DEPARTURE, leaving, withdrawal, retreat, exodus, flight,
removal, desertion, abandonment, clearance,
relinquishment, retirement, vacating
FORMAL forsaking
COLLOQ. quitting
2 EMPTYING, expulsion, ejection, discharge, clearance,
removal, elimination, purging, urination
OLD vacuation
FORMAL defecation

evade *v*
1 *evade your duties*
elude, avoid, escape, shirk, steer clear of, shun, sidestep,
get round, wriggle, balk, fend off, back out of, sheer
OLD blink, shift, waive
FORMAL circumvent
COLLOQ. dodge, duck, skive, chicken out, cop out, weasel
out; *Aust & NZ* duckshove
SLANG skrimshank; *N Am* gold brick; *Aust & NZ* bludge
2 *evade a question*
prevaricate, equivocate, fence, fudge, avoid, parry,
quibble, bypass, shuffle

COLLOQ. hedge, dodge, duck, beat about the bush
Ⅎ **1** confront, face

evaluate *v*
value, assess, estimate, reckon, calculate, gauge, measure,
get/take/have the measure of, judge, determine, rate, size
up, weigh, compute, rank
FORMAL appraise

evaluation *n*
valuation, assessment, estimation, estimate, appraisal,
judgement, reckoning, calculation, opinion, determination,
computation

evanescent *adj*
fading, fleeting, brief, short-lived, transient, transitory,
impermanent, momentary, temporary, unstable,
disappearing, vanishing, passing, evaporating,
insubstantial, perishable
FORMAL ephemeral
Ⅎ permanent

evangelical *adj*
1 *evangelical Christianity*
biblical, Bible-believing, scriptural, orthodox,
fundamentalist, missionary, converting, crusading
COLLOQ. Bible-bashing, Bible-thumping, Bible-punching
2 ENTHUSIASTIC, zealous, campaigning, crusading,
evangelistic, missionary, propagandizing, propagandist,
proselytizing

evangelist *n*
preacher, missionary, missioner, revivalist, (hot) gospeller,
televangelist, proselytizer, crusader, campaigner

evangelize *v*
preach, campaign, spread the word, crusade, convert,
proselytize, baptize, gospelize, missionarize, missionize,
propagandize

evaporate *v*
1 DISAPPEAR, dematerialize, vanish, end, melt (away),
dissolve, disperse, dispel, fade
FORMAL dissipate, evanesce
2 VAPORIZE, dry, dehydrate, boil away, distil, exhale
TECHNICAL vapour, volatilize
FORMAL desiccate

evaporation *n*
vaporization, drying, dehydration, condensation,
distillation, dematerialization, dissolution, fading, melting,
vanishing
FORMAL desiccation

evasion *n*
1 AVOIDANCE, equivocation, prevarication,
escape, shirking, trickery, subterfuge, fencing, steering
clear of, shunning
FORMAL circumvention, tergiversation
COLLOQ. hedging, ducking, cop-out, dodge, skiving
SLANG skrimshank
2 *evasions rather than straight answers*
excuse, quibble, quibbling, deception, deceit, trickery,
fudging, prevarication, equivocation, shuffling
COLLOQ. ducking, hedging, dodge, dodging
Ⅎ **1** frankness, directness

evasive *adj*
equivocating, indirect, vague, prevaricating, devious,
unforthcoming, misleading, deceitful, deceptive, fudging,
quibbling, oblique, secretive, tricky, cunning
COLLOQ. shifty, slippery, cagey, waffling
Ⅎ direct, frank

evasiveness *n*
equivocation, indirectness, vagueness, prevarication,
deceit, deceptiveness, fudging, quibbling, secrecy,
cunning
COLLOQ. caginess

eve *n*
day before, time before, period before, verge, brink,
edge, threshold

even adj, adv, v

◆ adj

1 LEVEL, flat, smooth, horizontal, flush, parallel, uniform, true, plane

2 STEADY, unvarying, unchanging, stable, constant, regular, uniform, consistent, unwavering

3 EQUAL, balanced, matching, same, identical, similar, like, alike, evenly matched, on an equal footing, symmetrical, level, drawn, side by side

COLLOQ. fifty-fifty, neck and neck, quits, even-steven(s)

4 EVEN-TEMPERED, calm, placid, serene, tranquil, composed, cool, equable, unruffled, unexcitable

FORMAL unperturbable

COLLOQ. unflappable

5 EVEN-HANDED, balanced, equitable, stable, fair, impartial, just, neutral, non-partisan

E3 1 uneven **3** unequal

◆ adv

1 *even worse*

all the more, still, yet, more, to a greater extent/degree

2 *even a child could do that*

surprisingly, unexpectedly, unusually, oddly, as well, also, too, still more, likewise

3 *sad, even depressed*

more exactly, more precisely, actually, indeed

4 *not even write his own name*

hardly, scarcely, at all, so much as

◆ v

smooth, flatten, level, plane, match, regularize, balance (out), equalize, make equal, make uniform, align, square, stabilize, steady, straighten

COLLOQ. strike a balance

■ **even so**

however, but, all the same, despite that, in spite of that, however that may be, nevertheless, nonetheless, still, yet

FORMAL notwithstanding that

■ **get even**

pay back, take/have your revenge, revenge/avenge yourself, reciprocate, requite

COLLOQ. give as good as you get, get your own back, settle a score

even-handed adj

fair, just, impartial, balanced, disinterested, dispassionate, equitable, neutral, unbiased, unprejudiced, reasonable, non-discriminatory, square, fair and square, without fear or favour

E3 inequitable, discriminatory

evening n

night, nightfall, dusk, close of day, eve, eventide, twilight, sunset, sundown

evenly adv

1 STEADILY, stably, constantly, regularly, uniformly, consistently

2 EQUALLY, similarly, symmetrically, evenly matched, on an equal footing

3 *she replied evenly*

calmly, placidly, serenely, tranquilly

event n

1 HAPPENING, occurrence, incident, occasion, proceeding, affair, circumstance, episode, experience, matter, case, adventure, business, fact, possibility, milestone

FORMAL eventuality

2 GAME, match, fixture, competition, contest, round, race, tournament, engagement, meeting, meet, item

3 CONSEQUENCE, result, outcome, conclusion, end, aftermath, upshot, effect, issue

FORMAL termination

■ **in any event**

anyway, anyhow, in any case, no matter what, whatever happens

---

SYNONYM NUANCES

sense 1

Happening is a very general synonym, whilst occurrence implies an event that it is unplanned or unforced: *machine failure is a common occurrence*. **Incident**, while also suggestive of an unanticipated (and often unpleasant) event, would be appropriately used of a more specific one: *she reported the incident to the police*. **Circumstance** also conveys the idea of something unplanned taking place, but as one element in a causal chain: *what to do in the circumstance of a fire*, while you might use **episode** of a distinct event taking place within a finite period of time: *the sinking of the cruiser was a highly suspicious episode*. **Case** shares this notion of a particular instance, but you would use it of an event that is being given as an example of something significant: *a case of unwitting collusion*.

Occasion, on the other hand, tends to suggest something that has been planned, usually a grand or happy event: *on the occasion of your silver wedding*, while **affair** insinuates business that has been ongoing and is of some consequence: *extremists had set the whole affair in motion; the contemporary art show was a very significant affair*. The term **proceeding** suggests a deliberate event that involves advancement, but it is fairly formal-sounding, and has legal and political connotations. **Matter** also has connotations of seriousness, and suggests something that may cause concern or must be dealt with: *they had deeply-held views on the matter of the stolen money*. You may use **experience** to emphasize the aspect of personal engagement: *the whole experience had been a lot of fun*, while **adventure** suggests an event with an element of excitement. This is unlike **business**, which has a more pedestrian association, often further implying something complex or awkward: *the family makes rather a fuss over the whole business of baptism*.

The term **milestone** is reserved for an event that marks an important stage: *the milestone of buying your first home*.

---

even-tempered adj

calm, level-headed, equable, placid, stable, tranquil, serene, composed, cool, cool and collected, steady, peaceful, peaceable

FORMAL imperturbable

COLLOQ. unflappable, unfazed, laid-back

E3 excitable, erratic

eventful adj

busy, exciting, lively, active, full, interesting, remarkable, important, significant, memorable, momentous, historic, crucial, critical, notable, noteworthy, unforgettable

COLLOQ. action-packed

SLANG ripsnorting

E3 dull, ordinary

eventual adj

final, ultimate, last, resulting, closing, concluding, ensuing, future, later, subsequent, prospective, projected, planned, impending

eventuality n

possibility, probability, likelihood, chance, contingency, event, incidence, occurrence, happening, circumstance, case, outcome, crisis, emergency, mishap

FORMAL happenstance

eventually adv

finally, ultimately, at last, in the end, at length, subsequently, after all, sooner or later, in the long run, in due course, in the fullness of time

COLLOQ. at the end of the day, when all is said and done, in the final analysis

ever adv

1 ALWAYS, evermore, for ever, perpetually, permanently, constantly, at all times, continually, incessantly, endlessly,

eternally, until the end of time, till doomsday, till your dying day
COLLOQ. till the cows come home, till hell freezes over
2 AT ANY TIME, in any case, in/under any circumstances, at all, on any account, on any occasion
▣ **1** never
■ **ever so**
very, very much, really, extremely, exceptionally, immensely, exceedingly
OLD jolly
COLLOQ. tremendously, frightfully, terribly, awfully

everlasting adj
1 ETERNAL, undying, never-ending, unending, endless, immortal, infinite, imperishable, constant, permanent, perpetual, indestructible, deathless, timeless
OLD perdurable, sempiternal
2 *everlasting noise*
constant, continual, perpetual, persistent, incessant, interminable, continuous, endless, never-ending, non-stop, relentless, remorseless
FORMAL unremitting
▣ temporary, transient

> **QUOTATIONS**
> From everlasting to everlasting, thou art God
>   *Bible, Psalms*

evermore adv
always, for ever, eternally, ever, ever after, for ever and a day, for ever and ever, unceasingly, to the end of time, till doomsday
FORMAL henceforth, hereafter, in perpetuum
COLLOQ. till the cows come home, till hell freezes over

every adj
1 EACH, every single, every individual
2 *make every effort*
all possible, as much as possible
3 *have every confidence*
all, complete, total, full, entire

everybody n
everyone, one and all, each one, each person, every person, all and sundry, the whole world
COLLOQ. all the world and his wife, every Tom Dick and Harry, every man Jack, every mother's son, Uncle Tom Cobleigh and all

everyday adj
ordinary, common, commonplace, day-to-day, familiar, run-of-the-mill, regular, standard, basic, plain, routine, usual, workaday, normal, average, customary, stock, accustomed, conventional, daily, habitual, monotonous, unimaginative, frequent, simple, informal
COLLOQ. common-or-garden
▣ unusual, exceptional, special

everyone n
everybody, one and all, each one, each person, every person, all and sundry, the whole world
COLLOQ. all the world and his wife, every Tom Dick and Harry, every man Jack, every mother's son, Uncle Tom Cobleigh and all

everything n
all, all things, each thing, the lot, the whole lot, the entirety, the sum, the total, lock, stock and barrel
FORMAL the aggregate
COLLOQ. the whole caboodle, the whole kit and caboodle, the whole shooting-match, the whole shebang, the whole bag of tricks, the works, everything but the kitchen sink

everywhere adv
all around, in/to all places, in/to each place, the world over, all over, throughout, far and near, near and far, far and wide, high and low, ubiquitous
COLLOQ. left, right and centre, here there and everywhere; *N Am* every place

evict v
expel, eject, dispossess, put out, turn out, throw out, force out, force to leave, remove, cast out, oust, dislodge
FORMAL expropriate
COLLOQ. turf out, kick out, chuck out, show someone the door, throw out on the streets, turn out of house and home

eviction n
expulsion, ejection, dispossession, removal, clearance, dislodgement
FORMAL defenestration, expropriation
COLLOQ. the bum's rush, the boot, the push, the elbow

evidence n, v
♦ n
1 PROOF, verification, confirmation, affirmation, grounds, support, documentation, data, test, token, credentials, warranty, guarantee, exhibit
TECHNICAL title
OLD argument, document; (*Shakesp*) avouch, instance
FORMAL substantiation, corroboration
COLLOQ. smoking gun
2 TESTIMONY, declaration, deed
TECHNICAL affidavit, adminicle, precognition, surrebut
OLD compurgation
FORMAL attestation
3 INDICATION, suggestion, sign, trace, mark, hint, demonstration, token, symptom, stamp
FORMAL manifestation
♦ v
show, indicate, reveal, demonstrate, display, exhibit, prove, witness, signify, confirm, affirm, establish, betray
OLD assert, bespeak
FORMAL attest, denote, evince, manifest, vouch
■ **in evidence**
clear, obvious, apparent, plain, patent, visible, conspicuous, noticeable, clear-cut, unmistakable

evident adj
clear, obvious, apparent, plain, patent, visible, conspicuous, noticeable, clear-cut, unmistakable, perceptible, distinct, discernible, tangible, manifest, undoubted, incontestable, indisputable, incontrovertible

evidently adv
1 CLEARLY, apparently, plainly, patently, obviously, manifestly, undoubtedly, doubtless(ly), indisputably
2 SEEMINGLY, apparently, outwardly, as it would seem/appear, so it seems/appears, to all appearances, on the face of it
FORMAL ostensibly

evil adj, n
♦ adj
1 WICKED, wrong, sinful, bad, immoral, vicious, vile, cruel, base, corrupt, malicious, malignant, malevolent, devilish, demonic, diabolic, depraved, mischievous, sinister, black
FORMAL iniquitous, reprehensible, nefarious, heinous
2 HARMFUL, pernicious, destructive, injurious, deadly, detrimental, hurtful, bad, poisonous
FORMAL deleterious
3 DISASTROUS, ruinous, calamitous, catastrophic, adverse, dire, unfortunate, unlucky, unfavourable
FORMAL inauspicious, unpropitious
4 OFFENSIVE, noxious, foul, nasty, vile, stinking
FORMAL noisome
▣ **1** good **3** fortunate
♦ n
1 WICKEDNESS, wrongdoing, wrong, immorality, misconduct, badness, sin, sinfulness, vice, viciousness, vileness, depravity, baseness, corruption, devilishness, mischief
FORMAL iniquity, malignity, heinousness
2 ADVERSITY, calamity, disaster, misfortune, suffering, sorrow, ruin, catastrophe, blow, curse, distress, hurt, harm, ill, pain, injury, misery, woe
FORMAL affliction

SYNONYM NUANCES
adjective sense 1
Obviously, many of these synonyms are highly marked
with disapprobation. **Wicked** is a strongly judgemental
and disapproving term describing the worst extremity of
badness, whilst **wrong** is comparatively tame in its
suggestion of being at odds with accepted moral codes.
Sinful and **immoral** are similar in meaning but stronger
in tone, with **sinful** having strong religious associations.
The word **corrupt** and the rather stronger term **depraved**
also have connotations of immoral behaviour: *corrupt
pleasure.*
  You could use **base** or **vile** to imply that you find
something loathsome or disgusting: *vile exploitation of
poor workers.* **Vicious** and **cruel**, on the other hand,
along with **malicious** and **malignant**, are appropriate
terms for evil expressed through spite and ferocity
towards others. **Devilish**, **demonic** and **diabolic** all
convey images of the supreme spirit of evil, and so are
highly judgemental: *the Nazis' demonic crimes.* The
terms **sinister** and **black** have more to do with the
threat of evil or potential harm: *sinister undertones, the
black arts of propaganda.* Compared to all these terms,
mischievous is fairly mild in its suggestion of a malign
playfulness.

evildoer *n*
wrongdoer, bad person, criminal, delinquent,
offender, miscreant, reprobate, sinner, scoundrel,
rogue, villain
FORMAL transgressor

evildoing *n*
badness, wickedness, corruption, depravity, vileness,
immorality, sin, sinfulness, iniquity, nastiness, cruelty

evince *v*
show, reveal, indicate, display, exhibit, make clear,
express, signify, demonstrate, confess, declare, betray,
establish
FORMAL attest, bespeak, betoken, evidence, manifest
⊟ conceal, suppress

eviscerate *v*
disembowel, gut, draw, gralloch
FORMAL exenterate

evocation *n*
summoning-up, calling, elicitation, invocation, inducing,
arousal, stirring, stimulation, suggestion, activation,
excitation, kindling, recall, echo

evocative *adj*
suggestive, expressive, indicative, reminiscent, vivid,
graphic, memorable
FORMAL redolent

evoke *v*
summon (up), call, elicit, invoke, induce, arouse, stir,
bring/call to mind, raise, kindle, stimulate, bring about,
cause, call forth, call up, conjure up, awaken, provoke,
excite, recall, bring back memories of, make someone
think of
⊟ suppress

evolution *n*
development, growth, progression, progress, expansion,
increase, ripening, derivation, descent, unrolling,
unfolding, unravelling, working-out, opening-out
TECHNICAL natural selection, survival of the fittest

evolve *v*
develop, grow, increase, mature, progress, advance,
unravel, unroll, unfold, work out, open out, expand,
enlarge, emerge, descend, derive, result, elaborate

exacerbate *v*
aggravate, worsen, make worse, make things/matters
worse, compound the problem, heighten, increase,
provoke, sharpen, intensify, exaggerate, inflame,
exasperate, deepen, embitter, enrage, infuriate, irritate, vex
COLLOQ. add fuel to the fire/flames, fan the flames, add
insult to injury, rub salt in the wound
⊟ soothe

exacerbation *n*
worsening, aggravation, intensification, exaggeration,
exasperation, irritation
⊟ soothing

exact *adj, v*
♦ *adj*
1 PRECISE, accurate, correct, faithful, literal, flawless,
faultless, right, true, definite, explicit, detailed, specific,
strict, unerring, close, just, factual, identical, express,
word-perfect
FORMAL veracious
COLLOQ. blow-by-blow, on the nail, spot on, bang on, on
the button
2 CAREFUL, scrupulous, particular, rigorous, precise,
methodical, meticulous, orderly, exacting, painstaking,
thorough
FORMAL punctilious
⊟ **1** inexact, imprecise **2** careless
♦ *v*
extort, extract, claim, insist on, wrest, wring, compel,
demand, command, call for, force, impose, insist, require,
squeeze
COLLOQ. milk, bleed

exacting *adj*
demanding, challenging, difficult, hard, laborious, arduous,
onerous, stringent, tiring, rigorous, taxing, tough, harsh,
firm, painstaking, severe, strict, stern, unsparing, unyielding
⊟ easy

exactitude *n*
accuracy, precision, exactness, correctness, faultlessness,
carefulness, care, meticulousness, orderliness, rigorousness,
rigour, scrupulousness, thoroughness, conscientiousness,
painstakingness, perfectionism, strictness, detail
⊟ inaccuracy, carelessness, imprecision

exactly *adv, interj*
♦ *adv*
1 PRECISELY, accurately, literally, faithfully, correctly,
specifically, rigorously, scrupulously, verbatim, carefully,
faultlessly, without error, unerringly, strictly, religiously, to
the letter, particularly, methodically, explicitly, expressly
OLD (Shakesp) jump
FORMAL veraciously
COLLOQ. dead
2 ABSOLUTELY, definitely, precisely, indeed, certainly, truly,
quite, just, unequivocally
COLLOQ. bang on, spot on, on the dot, on the button, on
the nail, to a T, smash, plumb
⊟ **1** inaccurately, roughly, vaguely
♦ *interj*
precisely, yes, quite, of course, just so, indeed, absolutely,
agreed, certainly, right, that's right, true
COLLOQ. you got it

exactness *n*
accuracy, precision, exactitude, correctness, faultlessness,
carefulness, care, meticulousness, orderliness, rigorousness,
rigour, scrupulousness, thoroughness, strictness
⊟ inaccuracy, carelessness, imprecision

exaggerate *v*
overstate, overdo, magnify, overemphasize, emphasize,
stress, make too much of, overdo (it/things), dramatize,
overdramatize, embellish, embroider, colour, stretch (the
truth), enlarge, amplify, enhance, oversell, overplay,
goliathize, bounce
FORMAL aggrandize, distend
COLLOQ. sex up, lay/pile it on, lay/pile in on thick, lay/pile
it on with a trowel, over-egg the pudding, make a

mountain out of a molehill, blow something up out of all proportion, shoot a line, make a drama out of a crisis
E∃ understate, play down

exaggerated adj
overstated, overdone, overestimated, overcharged, excessive, extravagant, pretentious, embellished, amplified, bombastic, inflated, overblown, caricatured, burlesqued, exalted
TECHNICAL euphuistic
FORMAL hyperbolic
COLLOQ. tall, camp
E∃ understated, played down

exaggeration n
overstatement, overemphasis, emphasis, magnification, overestimation, excess, extravagance, embellishment, enlargement, pretentiousness, amplification, burlesque, caricature, parody
FORMAL hyperbole
E∃ meiosis, understatement

exalt v
1 PRAISE, extol, glorify, magnify, acclaim, applaud, bless, honour, adore, revere, worship, reverence, eulogize
FORMAL laud, venerate
2 DELIGHT, elate, overjoy, transport, uplift, enliven, excite, exhilarate
3 RAISE, advance, promote, prefer, elevate, upgrade
FORMAL aggrandize

exaltation n
1 ELATION, ecstasy, rapture, bliss, joy, jubilation, excitement, exhilaration, high spirits
2 PRAISE, glorification, acclaim, honour, glory, reverence, worship, adoration, eulogy
FORMAL veneration
3 ELEVATION, raising, promotion, advancement
FORMAL aggrandizement

exalted adj
1 LOFTY, high, elevated, grand, regal, lordly, eminent, stately, noble, idealistic, virtuous, moral
2 ELATED, ecstatic, blissful, exultant, joyful, happy, jubilant, rapturous, in high spirits
COLLOQ. in seventh heaven

exam n
test, examination, exercises, questions, multiple-choice questions, practical, quiz, paper, viva, oral, final

examination n
1 INSPECTION, inquiry, scrutiny, study, survey, search, analysis, assessment, exploration, investigation, probe, observation, research, review, scan, perusal, check, check-up, audit, critique, post-mortem
FORMAL appraisal
COLLOQ. once-over
2 TEST, exam, quiz, questioning, cross-examination, cross-questioning, trial, inquisition, interrogation, viva, oral

---

SYNONYM NUANCES

sense 1
Inspection suggests a very close look, often in an official capacity, whilst **inquiry**, although also often official, has more to do with asking relevant questions to reach the truth. **Scrutiny**, however, implies highly detailed consideration: *parliamentary scrutiny of public sector contracts*, whilst **study**, although still suggesting attentiveness, is unlikely to delve as deeply.
  Survey, on the other hand, is more appropriate a term for a general overview: *a chronological survey of art*, or sometimes, more officially, a critical look at effectiveness: *a transport survey*. **Review** is similar, but retrospective: *a review of existing legislation*. **Critique**, however, generally concentrates on the negative aspects: *a critique of society*.
  If you use **search** and **research**, the implication is that you expect to uncover something, unlike **analysis**, which is suggestive of looking in detail to ascertain or

---

resolve, whilst **assessment** has more to do with evaluation. The words **exploration**, **investigation** and **probe** suggest delving deeply into, **exploration** usually to discover something new, the other two to expose something: *a probe into the cause of the air crash*. A **post-mortem** can now refer to any thorough examination that takes place after an unfortunate event to establish what went wrong.
  To refer to a more detached act of watching and noting you may choose to use the term **observation**. **Scan** suggests a quicker action, fleetingly looking over written material, while **perusal** would be the term to convey the idea of reading attentively. **Check-up** is usually used solely of a medical examination.

examine v
1 INSPECT, investigate, scrutinize, study, look at, look into, look over, view, observe, survey, analyse, dissect, go into, search, explore, inquire, discuss, reason, eye, consider, probe, research, review, scan, check (out), check over, ponder, pore over, sift, vet, weigh up, overhaul, assess, audit, peruse, collate, process, revise, test, try, canvass
TECHNICAL assay, cognosce
OLD quote, seek, speculate, depose; (*Spenser*) appose; overhaile
FORMAL appraise
COLLOQ. go over with a fine-tooth comb
SLANG case
2 TEST, quiz, question, cross-examine, cross-question, interrogate
OLD appose
FORMAL catechize
COLLOQ. grill, pump, give the third degree to, give someone a roasting, go to town on, put the screws on

examinee n
entrant, candidate, competitor, contestant, applicant, interviewee

examiner n
adjudicator, assessor, tester, inspector, interviewer, judge, marker, questioner, reviewer, reader, analyst, censor, critic, auditor, arbiter, scrutineer, scrutinizer
TECHNICAL assayer
FORMAL examinant, interlocutor, scrutator

example n
1 SAMPLE, specimen, prototype
FORMAL exemplar, archetype
2 INSTANCE, case, case in point, illustration, exemplification, representation/typical case, epitome
3 MODEL, role model, guide, lead, pattern, ideal, standard, criterion, type
FORMAL precedent, paradigm
4 LESSON, warning, caution, punishment
FORMAL admonition
■ **for example**
eg, for instance, like, such as, as an example/instance, say, to illustrate, by way of illustration, to give as an illustration

exasperate v
infuriate, annoy, anger, incense, irritate, madden, provoke, enrage, irk, rile, rankle, rouse, goad, vex, gall
COLLOQ. get on someone's nerves, get to, needle, bug, aggravate, wind up, drive up the wall, make someone's blood boil, put someone's back up, get someone's dander, get on someone's wick, put someone's nose out of joint
E∃ appease, pacify

exasperated adj
infuriated, annoyed, angry, indignant, angered, incensed, irritated, maddened, provoked, riled, vexed, piqued, irked, galled, goaded
COLLOQ. aggravated, at the end of your tether, bugged, fed up, needled, nettled, peeved
E∃ calm, satisfied

exasperating adj
infuriating, annoying, bothersome, maddening, provoking, troublesome, disagreeable, irksome, irritating, vexing, galling, pernicious, vexatious
COLLOQ. aggravating, confounded, infernal

exasperation n
annoyance, irritation, anger, rage, fury, chagrin, indignation, discontent, disgruntlement
COLLOQ. aggravation, stroppiness

excavate v
dig (out), dig up, hollow (out), burrow, tunnel, delve, unearth, mine, quarry, disinter, cut, gouge, scoop, reveal, uncover
FORMAL exhume

excavation n
1 HOLE, hollow, pit, quarry, mine, colliery, dugout, dig, diggings, burrow, cavity, crater, trench, trough, shaft, ditch, cutting
2 DIGGING (OUT), hollowing (out), burrowing, tunnelling, unearthing, mining
FORMAL exhumation

exceed v
surpass, go beyond, be greater/larger than, be more than, outnumber, outdo, outstrip, beat, better, be superior to, pass, overtake, top, outshine, eclipse, outreach, outrun, outrace, outweigh, transcend, cap, overdo, overstep, go over

exceedingly adv
very, very much, extremely, greatly, highly, unusually, exceptionally, especially, enormously, excessively, hugely, immensely, vastly, inordinately, unprecedentedly, superlatively, surpassingly, amazingly, astonishingly, extraordinarily

excel v
1 BE EXCELLENT, succeed, shine, stand out, be outstanding, be skilful, be pre-eminent, predominate
2 SURPASS, outdo, beat, be superior to, outclass, outperform, outrank, outrival, eclipse, better, be better than
OLD (Shakesp) outpeer

excellence n
superiority, pre-eminence, distinction, merit, supremacy, high quality, quality, worth, value, fineness, skill, eminence, goodness, greatness, virtue, perfection, purity, transcendence

excellent adj
wonderful, brilliant, marvellous, fantastic, superior, first-class, first-rate, high-quality, very good, prime, superlative, unequalled, unparalleled, matchless, rare, exceptional, outstanding, surpassing, remarkable, distinguished, great, eminent, flawless, faultless, perfect, above reproach, good, best, exemplary, select, superb, admirable, magnificent, shining, sterling, commendable, splendid, pre-eminent, praiseworthy, noteworthy, notable, noted, top-drawer, fine, A1, high, noble, worthy, inspired, Utopian, brave; Scot wally
OLD eximious, pure
COLLOQ. top-notch, smashing, stunning, terrific, cool, neat, ace, brill, boffo, out of this world, second to none, divine, heavenly, fabulous, sensational, not half bad, boss, bully, classic, crack, dilly, famous, jammy, knockout, the bee's knees; N Am hunky, jim-dandy; Aust bonzer, grouse; Aust & NZ trimmer
OLD COLLOQ. capital, champion, spiffing
SLANG mega, mean, wicked, sick, fierce, nang, stonking, radical, rad, crucial, way-out, shit-hot, groovy, clinking, def, fab, peachy, elegant, ripping, stellar, tipping, triff, triffic; (vulgar) the dog's bollocks; N Am copacetic, dicty, righteous, socko; Aust beaut, castor
OLD SLANG lummy, topping
E≡ inferior, second-rate

excellently adv
wonderfully, brilliantly, marvellously, well, fantastically, superlatively, exceptionally, remarkably, eminently, perfectly, superbly, admirably, commendably, splendidly
COLLOQ. terrifically, divinely, sensationally
E≡ poorly

except prep, v
♦ prep
excepting, but, but for, apart from, other than, with the exception of, aside from, save, omitting, not counting, leaving out, excluding, except for, besides, bar, barring, minus, less, short of
♦ v
leave out, omit, bar, exclude, reject, rule out, pass over

exception n
oddity, deviation, departure, abnormality, irregularity, peculiarity, inconsistency, rarity, special case, freak, quirk
FORMAL anomaly
■ **take exception**
object, protest, oppose, disapprove, refuse, complain, rebut, repudiate, withstand, resist, argue, challenge, beg to differ, take issue, take a stand against
FORMAL demur, expostulate, remonstrate
■ **with the exception of**
excepting, but, apart from, other than, save, omitting, not counting, leaving out, excluding, except for, besides, bar, barring, minus, less

PROVERBS
the exception proves the rule

exceptionable adj
objectionable, unpleasant, disagreeable, offensive, unacceptable, disgusting, deplorable, abhorrent, repugnant
E≡ acceptable, agreeable

exceptional adj
1 OUTSTANDING, remarkable, marvellous, excellent, extraordinary, brilliant, phenomenal, notable, noteworthy, superior, unequalled
FORMAL prodigious
COLLOQ. one in a thousand, one in a million
2 ABNORMAL, unusual, strange, odd, irregular, extraordinary, out of the ordinary, peculiar, special, rare, atypical, uncommon
FORMAL anomalous, aberrant, singular
E≡ **1** mediocre **2** normal

exceptionally adv
1 EXTREMELY, extraordinarily, notably, outstandingly, especially, amazingly, remarkably, wonderfully
2 UNUSUALLY, uncommonly, irregularly, abnormally, rarely

excerpt n
extract, passage, portion, section, selection, quote, quotation, part, piece, cutting, clip, clipping, citation, scrap, fragment
TECHNICAL pericope

excess n, adj
♦ n
1 SURFEIT, too much, more than enough, overabundance, oversupply, glut, superabundance, surplus, backlog, overflow, overkill, remainder, rest, residue, leftovers
FORMAL plethora, superfluity
COLLOQ. bellyful; Aust & NZ gutful
2 OVERINDULGENCE, dissoluteness, immoderateness, immoderation, extravagance, unrestraint, debauchery
FORMAL dissipation, intemperance, prodigality
E≡ **1** deficiency **2** restraint
♦ adj
extra, surplus, too much, spare, redundant, remaining, residual, left-over, additional, superfluous
FORMAL supernumerary
E≡ inadequate
■ **in excess of**
more than, over, above

excessive adj

immoderate, inordinate, extreme, too much, undue, uncalled-for, disproportionate, overdone, unnecessary, unneeded, needless, unwarranted, superfluous, overabundant, superabundant, unreasonable, lavish, exorbitant, extravagant
COLLOQ. steep, over the top, OTT, eye-watering
Ⅎ insufficient

excessively adv

immoderately, inordinately, extremely, too much, to a fault, unduly, unreasonably, overly, overmuch, disproportionately, unnecessarily, needlessly, superfluously, exorbitantly, exaggeratedly, extravagantly, intemperately
Ⅎ insufficiently, inadequately

exchange v, n

♦ v
barter, change, trade, swap, switch, replace, interchange, convert, commute, transpose, substitute, stand in for, reciprocate, bargain, bandy
♦ n
1 INTERCHANGE, swap, switch, replacement, substitution
FORMAL reciprocity
COLLOQ. give and take
2 TRADE, commerce, dealing, market, traffic, barter, bargain, trade-off
3 CONVERSATION, discussion, chat, argument, dialogue
Related adjective: catallactic

excise[1] n

excise duty
duty, tax, VAT, customs, levy, surcharge, tariff, toll
FORMAL impost

> **QUOTATIONS**
> Excise. A hateful tax levied upon commodities
> SAMUEL JOHNSON, *A Dictionary of the English Language*

excise[2] v

excise sensitive material
cut, cut out, remove, extract, destroy, eradicate, erase, delete, exterminate
FORMAL expunge, expurgate, extirpate, rescind

excision n

removal, deletion, eradication, destruction, expunction
FORMAL expurgation, extermination, extirpation

excitable adj

temperamental, volatile, mercurial, passionate, emotional, highly-strung, fiery, hot-headed, hasty, nervous, hot-tempered, irascible, quick-tempered, sensitive, susceptible
FORMAL choleric, mercurial
COLLOQ. edgy
Ⅎ calm, stable

excite v

1 excite a feeling
stir up, thrill, impress, touch, move, agitate, disturb, upset, arouse, rouse, animate, awaken, evoke, stir, enliven, irritate, tickle, engender, inspire, kindle, enkindle, ferment, fire, inflame, ignite, intoxicate, flush, wake, work up, wind up, whet, waken, warm, yerk
OLD commove, upraise; (*Shakesp*) accite; (*Spenser*) emmove
COLLOQ. turn on
2 excite an action
provoke, motivate, stimulate, bring about, instigate, impel, urge, incite, induce, galvanize, generate, sway, electrify, work up, suscitate
3 excite sexually
arouse, stimulate, awaken, titillate, provoke
COLLOQ. turn on
Ⅎ 1 calm

excited adj

aroused, roused, stimulated, stirred, exhilarated, thrilled, elated, in high spirits, enthusiastic, eager, moved, beside yourself, animated, worked up, wrought-up, overwrought, agitated, restless, frantic, frenzied, wild
COLLOQ. high, on the edge of your seat, on tenterhooks, thrilled to bits, turned on, uptight, hyper, fired up, hyped up, amped, pumped
Ⅎ calm, apathetic

> **SYNONYM NUANCES**
>
> Both **aroused** and **roused** suggest a response has been elicited by something: *their secretiveness aroused considerable suspicion*, while **stimulated** could be used where interest rather than excitement has been prompted. **Stirred** and **moved** are suggestive of having the emotions activated: *stirred by thoughts of heroic deeds*, whereas **exhilarated** and **thrilled** have more to do with being thoroughly enlivened: *I was exhilarated by the run and wasn't tired*.
>
> Both **in high spirits** and the even more emphatic **elated** suggest excitement with a strong element of enjoyment or happiness. **Enthusiastic** focuses on an element of zealous anticipation, as does **eager**.
>
> To convey the sense of lively behaviour brought on by excitement you could use the term **animated**, whereas **worked up**, the fairly uncommon **wrought-up** and **overwrought** imply expending the same energy but in agitation or anxiety rather than pleasure. **Agitated**, likewise, has to do with being emotionally perturbed, whilst **restless** is similarly negative in its connotation of unease. The terms **frantic**, **frenzied** and **wild** would be appropriate only for a manic, uncontrolled excitedness: *frantic efforts to get home; a frenzied rage*.

excitement n

1 the excitement of winning
thrill, passion, adventure, emotion, sensation, exhilaration, pleasure, animation, elation, enthusiasm, restlessness, ferment, fever, eagerness, stimulation, agitation, discomposure
FORMAL perturbation
COLLOQ. kick(s)
2 UNREST, ado, action, activity, commotion, stir, fuss, tumult, flurry, furore
Ⅎ 1 apathy **2** calm

exciting adj

stimulating, stirring, intoxicating, exhilarating, thrilling, dramatic, rousing, moving, enthralling, electrifying, striking, breathtaking, sensational, provocative, inspiring, interesting
COLLOQ. nail-biting, cliff-hanging, action-packed, sexy
Ⅎ dull, unexciting

exclaim v

cry (out), declare, come out with, blurt (out), call, yell, shout, roar, shriek, bellow, proclaim, utter
FORMAL vociferate, ejaculate

exclamation n

cry, call, yell, shout, expletive, interjection, outcry, utterance, roar, shriek, bellow
FORMAL ejaculation

exclude v

1 BAN, bar, prohibit, refuse, disallow, veto, forbid, debar, blacklist
FORMAL interdict
2 OMIT, leave out, miss out, delete, keep out, refuse, reject, ignore, shut out, rule out, ostracize, eliminate, except
FORMAL preclude
COLLOQ. drop, skip, count out, include out
3 EXPEL, eject, evict, throw out, remove, excommunicate, ostracize, boycott, freeze out, ice out, lock out
COLLOQ. boot out, turf out, kick out, send to Coventry
Ⅎ 1 admit **2** include, consider

excluding prep

except, except for, with the exception of, excepting, exclusive of, not including, not counting, omitting, leaving out, ruling out, barring, debarring

exclusion n

1 OMISSION, rejection, elimination, ruling out, refusal, repudiation
FORMAL preclusion
2 BAN, bar, prohibition, embargo, veto, boycott
FORMAL interdict, proscription
3 EJECTION, expulsion, eviction, removal, boycott, exception
E3 1 inclusion 2 allowance 3 admittance

exclusive adj, n

♦ adj
1 SOLE, single, individual, unique, only, undivided, unshared, complete, whole, total, peculiar
2 RESTRICTED, limited, closed, private, narrow, restrictive, choice, select, discriminative, cliquey, chic, elegant, fashionable, up-market, high-class, upper-crust, snobbish
COLLOQ. classy, posh, snazzy, ritzy, plush, swish
♦ n
scoop, coup, inside story, revelation, exposé, sensation

■ **exclusive of**
except, except for, with the exception of, excepting, excluding, not including, not counting, omitting, leaving out, ruling out, barring, debarring
E3 inclusive of

SYNONYM NUANCES

adjective sense 2
Restricted and **limited** have a vaguely negative tone in that they describe something not available to everyone: *restricted access; limited edition;* **closed** explicitly describes something that is only for a particular group: *a closed military court.* **Private** puts less emphasis on limitation and so suggests a more desirable exclusivity: *a private party for a few guests.*
 Both **narrow** and **restrictive** again have less positive connotations, by emphasizing the lack of scope: *restrictive social conventions,* unlike **choice** and **select** which suggest an element of suitability or desirability: *select schools.* **Discriminative**, on the other hand, puts the emphasis on the observance of distinctions and so can be negative in its implication, whilst **cliquey** is clearly derogatory in tone, and implicitly critical of the exclusivity of a group.
 Chic and **elegant** are admiring in tone and can be used to refer to the exclusivity of something stylish: *the chic cuisine of today,* while **up-market**, **high-class** and **upper-crust**, although less suggestive of admiration, have resonances with the fine living associated with the wealthier classes. **Snobbish**, however, is a markedly disapproving term, with suggestions of affectation and condescension behind the exclusivity.

---

excommunicate v

ban, banish, eject, denounce, exclude, expel, remove, bar, blacklist, debar, outlaw, repudiate, disfellowship, unchurch
FORMAL anathematize, proscribe, execrate

excommunication n

expulsion, exclusion, disfellowship, unchurching, banning, banishment, ejection, denunciation, barring, outlawing

excoriate v

condemn, carp, snipe, disapprove of, find fault with, run down, slate, denounce, attack, censure, blame
FORMAL animadvert, disparage, decry, denigrate, vituperate
COLLOQ. nag, slam, knock, come down on, give someone some stick, nit-pick

excrement n

waste matter, biosolids, excretion, dung, ordure, droppings, turd, mess
TECHNICAL egesta, frass, scats, guano
OLD sir-reverence

FORMAL faeces, stool, rejectamenta
COLLOQ. flux, jobbie, doo-doo
SLANG poop, crud; (*vulgar*) crap, shit
Related adjective: excrementitious

excrescence n

1 GROWTH, swelling, bump, lump, knob, appendage, outgrowth, projection, prominence, tumour, wart, boil, cancer
FORMAL intumescence, protuberance
2 MONSTROSITY, blot, disfigurement, eyesore

excrete v

void, pass, eject, discharge, expel, evacuate, exude, secrete
FORMAL defecate, urinate
SLANG (*vulgar*) crap, shit

excretion n

discharge, excrement, droppings, dung, evacuation, ordure, perspiration
FORMAL defecation, excreta, urination, faeces, stool
SLANG (*vulgar*) crap, shit

excruciating adj

agonizing, painful, severe, tormenting, unbearable, insufferable, acute, intolerable, intense, sharp, piercing, extreme, atrocious, racking, harrowing, savage, burning, bitter

excruciatingly adv

unbearably, intolerably, painfully, severely, acutely, intensely, extremely, atrociously

exculpate v

clear, discharge, excuse, free, justify, let off, pardon, release, vindicate, forgive, deliver, absolve, acquit
FORMAL exonerate
E3 blame, condemn

excursion n

1 OUTING, trip, day trip, jaunt, expedition, journey, tour, airing, breather, ride, drive, walk, ramble
COLLOQ. daycation, junket
2 DIGRESSION, departure, straying, wandering, detour, diversion

excusable adj

understandable, minor, slight, allowable, permissible, defensible, explainable, forgivable, pardonable, justifiable
E3 blameworthy

excuse v, n

♦ v
1 FORGIVE, pardon, overlook, absolve, acquit, tolerate, make allowances for, ignore, indulge
FORMAL exonerate, exculpate
2 RELEASE, free, discharge, liberate, let off, relieve, spare, exempt
3 CONDONE, explain, justify, vindicate, defend, apologize for
FORMAL mitigate
E3 1 criticize 2 punish
♦ n
justification, explanation, grounds, defence, plea, alibi, reason, vindication, apology, pretext, pretence, evasion, shift, substitute
FORMAL exoneration, mitigation, mitigating circumstances
COLLOQ. cop-out, front, cover-up, get-out

execrable adj

deplorable, abhorrent, abominable, disgusting, foul, dreadful, awful, appalling, atrocious, despicable, detestable, offensive, shocking, repulsive, revolting, horrible, loathsome, vile, nauseous, obnoxious, odious, damnable, accursed, hateful
FORMAL heinous
E3 admirable, estimable

execrate v

deplore, hate, abhor, loathe, abominate, condemn, denounce, denunciate, despise, detest, revile, curse, damn, imprecate

FORMAL excoriate, fulminate, inveigh against, vilify, anathematize
COLLOQ. blast
F3 commend, praise

execute v
1 PUT TO DEATH, kill, hang, electrocute, shoot, guillotine, behead, crucify
FORMAL decapitate
COLLOQ. liquidate
2 CARRY OUT, perform, do, accomplish, achieve, fulfil, complete, bring off, discharge, put into effect, put into practice, enact, deliver, enforce, finish, implement, administer, engineer, realize, dispatch, validate, serve, render, stage
FORMAL effect, consummate, expedite

execution n
1 DEATH PENALTY, death sentence, capital punishment, putting to death, killing
2 ACCOMPLISHMENT, operation, performance, completion, achievement, administration, effect, carrying-out, enactment, implementation, realization, fulfilment, discharge, dispatch, enforcement
FORMAL consummation, effecting
3 STYLE, technique, rendition, rendering, delivery, performance, staging, manner, mode, presentation

---

Means of execution include:

beheading	electrocution	lynching
burning	firing squad	shooting
Colombian neck-	garrotting	stoning
tie	gassing	*colloq.* stringing
crucifixion	guillotining	up
decapitation	hanging	
electric chair	lethal injection	

---

executioner n
hangman, firing squad, headsman, Jack Ketch, axeman, killer, murderer, exterminator, assassin, slayer
OLD (*Shakesp*) deathsman
COLLOQ. hit man, liquidator

executive n, adj
◆ n
1 ADMINISTRATOR, manager, organizer, leader, controller, director, governor, official, chairman, chairwoman, chairperson, superior, superintendent
2 ADMINISTRATION, management, government, leadership, hierarchy
COLLOQ. top brass, big guns, big shots
◆ adj
administrative, managerial, controlling, supervisory, regulating, decision-making, governing, lawmaking, organizing, directing, directorial, organizational, leading, guiding

> **QUOTATIONS**
> It is unfortunate we can't buy many business executives for what they are worth and sell them for what they think they are worth
> MALCOLM STEVENSON FORBES, JR

exegesis n
explanation, interpretation, clarification, opening-up
FORMAL exposition, expounding, explication

exemplar n
example, standard, model, pattern, type, ideal, prototype, paragon, copy, criterion, yardstick, epitome, illustration, instance, specimen
FORMAL archetype, embodiment, exemplification, paradigm

exemplary adj
1 MODEL, ideal, perfect, admirable, excellent, faultless, flawless, correct, good, commendable, praiseworthy, worthy, honourable
FORMAL laudable, estimable, meritorious

2 CAUTIONARY, warning
FORMAL admonitory
F3 1 imperfect, unworthy

exemplify v
illustrate, be an example of, demonstrate, show, instance, cite, represent, typify, characterize, embody, personify, epitomize, exhibit, depict, display
FORMAL manifest

exempt v, adj
◆ v
excuse, release, relieve, let off, free, grant immunity to, absolve, discharge, dismiss, liberate, spare, exclude, waive, make an exception
FORMAL exonerate
◆ adj
excused, not liable, not subject, immune, released, spared, absolved, discharged, excluded, free, liberated, dismissed, clear
F3 liable

exemption n
exception, exclusion, immunity, privilege, indulgence, release, freedom, indemnity, discharge
FORMAL absolution, dispensation, exoneration
F3 liability

exercise v, n
◆ v
1 USE, utilize, employ, make use of, apply, exert, practise, implement, bring to bear, bring into play, wield, try, discharge, exploit
2 TRAIN, work out, do exercises, drill, practise, keep fit, exert yourself, warm up, warm down
COLLOQ. pump iron
3 WORRY, disturb, trouble, upset, burden, distress, concern, vex, annoy, agitate, afflict, preoccupy
FORMAL perturb
◆ n
1 TRAINING, drill, movement, practice, effort, exertion, activity, keep-fit, sports, gymnastics, PE, physical education, PT, physical training, warm-up, warm-down, jogging, running, cardio, labour
COLLOQ. physical jerks, workout
2 USE, utilization, employment, application, implementation, practice, operation, discharge, assignment, fulfilment, accomplishment, exertion
3 TASK, assignment, lesson, work, discipline, problem, project, piece of work

---

Exercise systems include:

aerobics	eurhythmics	t'ai chi
Bikram yoga	falun gong	yoga
boxercise	isometrics	Yogalates®
Callanetics	Pilates	Zumba®
callisthenics	qigong	
dancercise	Tae-Bo®	

---

exert v
use, utilize, employ, apply, exercise, bring to bear, bring into play, wield, spend, expend
■ **exert yourself**
strive, struggle, try hard, strain, make every effort, take pains, do your best/utmost, toil, labour, work, endeavour, apply yourself, give your all
COLLOQ. sweat, go all out, pull out all the stops, slog away, give it your best shot, keep your nose to the grindstone, work your socks off

exertion n
1 EFFORT, industry, labour, toil, work, exercise, struggle, diligence, assiduousness, perseverance, pains, endeavour, attempt, strain, stress, trial
FORMAL travail
COLLOQ. (hard) graft

2 USE, utilization, employment, application, exercise, operation, action
Ƨ 1 idleness, rest

exhalation n
breathing-out, respiration, evaporation, discharge, emission, expulsion
FORMAL expiration

exhale v
breathe (out), give off, blow (out), discharge, emit, expel, issue, respire, steam, evaporate
FORMAL emanate, expire
Ƨ inhale

exhaust v, n
♦ v
1 TIRE (OUT), weary, fatigue, tax, sap, drain, strain, weaken, overwork, overtax, overtire, wear out
FORMAL enervate
COLLOQ. do in, fag out, knock out, whack, knacker, take it out of, nearly/almost kill; *N Am* tucker out
2 CONSUME, empty, drain, sap, spend, expend, run through, waste, squander, impoverish, use up, finish, dry, bankrupt
FORMAL deplete, dissipate
Ƨ 1 refresh **2** renew
♦ n
emission, exhalation, discharge, fumes, smoke, steam, vapour
FORMAL emanation

exhausted adj
1 TIRED OUT, dead tired, worn out, fatigued, weak, washed-out, drained, jaded; *Scot* wabbit
FORMAL enfeebled, enervated
COLLOQ. dead-beat, all in, done (in), whacked, fagged out, knackered, bushed, burnt out, dog-tired, ready to drop, zonked, jiggered, shagged out; *N Am* pooped (out), tuckered out; *Aust & NZ* beaten
SLANG *Aust & NZ* euchred out
2 EMPTY, finished, consumed, spent, used up, drained, dry, worn out, void
FORMAL depleted
Ƨ 1 vigorous **2** fresh

exhausting adj
tiring, strenuous, taxing, wearying, wearing, gruelling, arduous, hard, laborious, backbreaking, draining, debilitating, severe, testing, punishing, formidable
FORMAL enervating
Ƨ refreshing, invigorating

exhaustion n
fatigue, tiredness, weariness, weakness, feebleness, lethargy, jet-lag
FORMAL enervation
Ƨ freshness, liveliness

exhaustive adj
comprehensive, all-embracing, all-inclusive, far-reaching, complete, total, extensive, encyclopedic, full-scale, thorough, full, in-depth, intensive, detailed, definitive, all-out, sweeping
Ƨ incomplete, restricted

exhaustively adv
comprehensively, all-inclusively, completely, totally, extensively, encyclopedically, thoroughly, fully, intensively, definitively
Ƨ incompletely

exhibit v, n
♦ v
display, put on display, show, present, demonstrate, expose, unveil, parade, reveal, express, make clear, make plain, disclose, indicate, air, flaunt, offer, set out, set forth
FORMAL manifest, array
Ƨ conceal, hide

♦ n
display, exhibition, show, showing, demonstration, illustration, model, presentation

exhibition n
display, show, demonstration, exhibit, presentation, diorama, pavilion, spectacle, showing, fair, performance, airing, representation, showcase, preview, retrospective, Salon, indication, expression, revelation, disclosure
TECHNICAL panopticon
FORMAL manifestation, exposition
COLLOQ. expo

exhibitionism n
showing-off, boastfulness, flaunting, self-display, flamboyance, histrionics, dramatics, overacting, staginess

exhibitionist n
show-off, extrovert, poseur, poser, self-advertiser

exhilarate v
thrill, excite, make excited, elate, make happy, cheer up, delight, gladden, animate, enliven, invigorate, vitalize, revitalize, raise/lift the spirits of, intoxicate, stimulate, brighten, lift
COLLOQ. perk up
Ƨ bore, discourage

exhilarating adj
thrilling, exciting, delightful, cheerful, gladdening, cheering, enlivening, stimulating, revitalizing, invigorating, heady, breathtaking, intoxicating
COLLOQ. mind-blowing
Ƨ boring, discouraging

exhilaration n
excitement, thrill, happiness, cheerfulness, gladness, delight, euphoria, elation, joy, joyfulness, exaltation, glee, high spirits, liveliness, vivacity, zeal, enthusiasm, animation, ardour, invigoration, revitalization, stimulation, gusto, dash, gaiety, mirth, hilarity
FORMAL élan
Ƨ boredom, discouragement

exhort v
urge, persuade, encourage, implore, goad, incite, inflame, inspire, instigate, spur, warn, bid, call on/upon, press, advise, counsel, caution, prompt
FORMAL admonish, beseech, enjoin, entreat

exhortation n
urging, persuasion, encouragement, call, appeal, goading, incitement, advice, caution, warning, counsel, bidding, lecture, sermon
FORMAL admonition, beseeching, enjoinder, entreaty, paraenesis, protreptic

exhumation n
disinterment, disentombment, excavation, unearthing

exhume v
disinter, dig up, disentomb, excavate, unbury, unearth, resurrect
FORMAL disinhume
Ƨ bury

exigency n
1 DEMAND, requirement, need, necessity
2 EMERGENCY, urgency, crisis, criticalness, difficulty, distress, imperativeness, pressure, plight, quandary, predicament, stress

exigent adj
urgent, demanding, insistent, necessary, pressing, stringent, exacting, critical, crucial

exiguous adj
meagre, insufficient, inadequate, scant, scanty, negligible, sparse, slight, slim, bare

exile n, v
♦ n
1 BANISHMENT, deportation, expatriation, expulsion, uprooting, ostracism, separating, separation, transportation, Babylon
TECHNICAL Galut

2 EXPATRIATE, refugee, émigré, expat, deportee, fugitive, displaced person, Diaspora, outcast, outlaw, pariah
OLD (*Spenser*) exul; wretch
♦ *v*
banish, expel, deport, extradite, expatriate, repatriate, drive out, cast out, uproot, separate, ostracize, oust, excommunicate, eject, outlaw, ban, bar

exist *v*
1 BE, live, have life, be alive, abide, continue, endure, have being, have existence, breathe, have breath
2 SUBSIST, survive, live, eke out a living, eke out an existence
3 BE PRESENT, occur, happen, be available, be found, remain, last, continue, prevail

existence *n*
1 BEING, life, living, reality, actuality, fact, continuance, continuation, endurance, survival, breath, subsistence
2 WAY OF LIFE, way of living, life, lifestyle
FORMAL mode of living
3 ENTITY, creature, being, thing
4 CREATION, the world
F3 **1** death, non-existence

existent *adj*
existing, in existence, actual, real, current, present, living, alive, enduring, remaining, surviving, standing, abiding, prevailing
FORMAL obtaining, extant
COLLOQ. around
F3 non-existent

exit *n, v*
♦ *n*
1 DEPARTURE, going, leaving, retreat, withdrawal, leave-taking, retirement, farewell, exodus, flight
2 DOOR, way out, doorway, gate, vent, outlet; *Scot & dialect* outgate
FORMAL egress
F3 **1** entrance, arrival **2** entrance
♦ *v*
depart, leave, go (out), retire, withdraw, take your leave, retreat, issue
F3 arrive, enter

exodus *n*
departure, evacuation, mass departure, mass evacuation, flight, fleeing, escape, leaving, migration, retirement, long march, retreat, withdrawal, exit, hegira

exonerate *v*
1 ABSOLVE, acquit, clear, excuse, vindicate, justify, pardon, declare innocent, discharge
FORMAL exculpate
2 EXEMPT, excuse, spare, let off, free, liberate, discharge, release, relieve
F3 **1** incriminate

exoneration *n*
1 ACQUITTAL, clearing, excusing, vindication, justification, pardon, discharge, amnesty, absolution, dismissal
FORMAL exculpation
2 EXEMPTION, excusing, discharge, liberation, freeing, release, relief, immunity, indemnity
F3 **1** incrimination

exorbitant *adj*
excessive, unreasonable, unwarranted, undue, inordinate, immoderate, extravagant, extortionate, enormous, preposterous, monstrous
COLLOQ. eye-watering, daylight robbery, a rip-off
F3 reasonable, moderate, fair

exorbitantly *adv*
excessively, unreasonably, unduly, inordinately, immoderately, extravagantly, extortionately
F3 reasonably, moderately

exorcism *n*
casting out, deliverance, freeing, expulsion, purification
TECHNICAL exsufflation, insufflation
FORMAL adjuration

exorcize *v*
cast out, drive out, free, expel, purify
TECHNICAL exsufflate, insufflate
FORMAL adjure

exotic *adj*
1 FOREIGN, alien, imported, introduced, tropical, external, non-native
2 UNUSUAL, striking, different, remarkable, unfamiliar, extraordinary, bizarre, curious, strange, impressive, fascinating, colourful, glamorous, peculiar, outlandish, extravagant, outrageous, sensational
F3 **1** native **2** ordinary, common

exotically *adv*
unusually, strikingly, remarkably, extraordinarily, curiously, strangely, impressively, sensationally, outlandishly, tropically

expand *v*
increase, grow, become/make larger/bigger, extend, enlarge, develop, amplify, spread, stretch, swell, widen, lengthen, thicken, intensify, escalate, magnify, multiply, inflate, broaden, blow up, open out, fill out, put out, fatten, puff out, unfold, unfurl, pad, branch out, diversify, mushroom, work up
OLD intend
FORMAL distend, dilate, dispread, intumesce
F3 contract

■ **expand on**
enlarge on, elaborate on, embroider, flesh out, go into details
FORMAL expatiate on, dilate on

expanse *n*
extent, space, area, breadth, range, stretch, region, sweep, field, plain, tract, vastness, extensiveness
OLD main

expansion *n*
growth, increase, extension, development, amplification, spread, expanse, swelling, enlargement, lengthening, thickening, broadening, magnification, multiplication, inflation, unfolding, unfurling, diversification
FORMAL augmentation, diffusion, dilation, distension, dilatation
F3 contraction

expansive *adj*
1 EXTENSIVE, broad, comprehensive, wide, sweeping, wide-ranging, widespread, all-embracing, thorough
2 COMMUNICATIVE, friendly, genial, outgoing, open, affable, sociable, talkative, warm, forthcoming, effusive, uninhibited
FORMAL loquacious
3 EXPANDING, growing, increasing, enlarging, developing, diversifying, magnifying, multiplying
F3 **1** restricted, narrow **2** reserved, cold **3** contracting

expatiate *v*
expand, enlarge, amplify, elaborate, embellish, develop, expound, dwell on, hold forth on
FORMAL dilate

expatriate *n, v, adj*
♦ *n*
emigrant, émigré, exile, refugee, displaced person, outcast, expat
♦ *v*
banish, exile, deport, extradite, drive out, uproot, expel, oust, repatriate, ostracize
FORMAL proscribe
♦ *adj*
banished, exiled, deported, expelled, uprooted, emigrant, émigré

expect *v*
1 *expect you're right*
suppose, assume, believe, think, presume, imagine, reckon, trust
OLD ween

FORMAL surmise, conjecture
COLLOQ. guess
2 *expect the money soon*
anticipate, await, look forward to, hope for, trust, look for, watch for, bank on, bargain for, envisage, predict, forecast, contemplate, project, foresee; *Scot* lippen
3 *expect you to comply*
require, want, wish, insist on, demand, call for, ask for, look for, hope for, rely on, count on, figure on

---

SYNONYM NUANCES

sense 2
Anticipate would be appropriate for something likely, as would **look forward to**, though with the further implication of it being something pleasant: *she was looking forward to the holidays*. **Await** suggests a greater degree of certainty about something in the future: *I await your response to my complaint.*

Hope for has a strong element of desire, while **trust** can be used as a more tentative, polite term to suggest assumption: *I trust you find everything satisfactory*. The term **look for** similarly implies confidence in the expectation at a superficial level, but might actually be used with an element of hope: *I'll be looking for your support*. **Bank on** is similar, but would be used to hint at dependency: *I am banking on you to perform well so we win the match*. **Bargain for** is different in that it would be used negatively to refer to not expecting something: *they hadn't bargained for a dramatic change in the weather.*

For expressing what you think could happen, you might use **envisage** if it is within the realms of your imaginings: *I could envisage a long-drawn-out court case*. If you have applied what you know to your expectation for the future you might use the terms **predict**, **forecast**, **project** or **foresee**: *the fog has cleared, so I do not foresee any travel problems.*

---

expectancy *n*
anticipation, eagerness, expectation, hope, suspense, waiting, curiosity
FORMAL conjecture

expectant *adj*
1 AWAITING, anticipating, looking forward, hopeful, in suspense, ready, apprehensive, anxious, watchful, eager, excited, on tenterhooks, with bated breath, curious
2 PREGNANT, going to have a baby, carrying, big-bellied
TECHNICAL gravid
OLD with child, great, quick, in an interesting condition/state/situation
FORMAL enceinte
COLLOQ. expecting, in the family way, in the club, in a certain condition, in trouble
SLANG preggers, with a bun in the oven, in the pudding club, up the duff, up the spout

expectantly *adv*
in anticipation, eagerly, expectingly, hopefully, in suspense, apprehensively, optimistically

expectation *n*
hope, belief, anticipation, assumption, presumption, surmise, supposition, calculation, forecast, projection, prediction, eagerness, requirement, demand, insistence, promise, want, wish, reliance, trust, prospect, confidence, assurance, suspense, optimism, possibility, probability, outlook
FORMAL conjecture

expecting *adj*
pregnant, going to have a baby, expectant, carrying, big-bellied
TECHNICAL gravid
OLD with child, great, quick, in an interesting condition/state/situation

FORMAL enceinte
COLLOQ. in the family way, in the club, in a certain condition, in trouble
SLANG preggers, with a bun in the oven, in the pudding club, up the duff, up the spout

expedience *n*
convenience, suitability, appropriateness, fitness, aptness, advantageousness, effectiveness, desirability, helpfulness, properness, profitableness, usefulness, practicality, pragmatism, prudence, advisability, benefit, advantage, profitability, expediency, utility, utilitarianism
FORMAL judiciousness, propriety

expedient *adj, n*
♦ *adj*
convenient, suitable, appropriate, fitting, opportune, politic, in your own interest, profitable, prudent, useful, beneficial, advantageous, advisable, sensible, practical, pragmatic, tactical
🖅 inexpedient
♦ *n*
stratagem, scheme, means, method, measure, tactic, ploy, manoeuvre, plan, trick, shift, contrivance, device, stopgap
COLLOQ. dodge

expedite *v*
speed up, accelerate, step up, quicken, hasten, hurry, further, facilitate, assist, promote, press, dispatch, discharge, hurry through
FORMAL precipitate
🖅 delay

expedition *n*
1 JOURNEY, excursion, trip, voyage, tour, outing, exploration, field trip, trek, safari, hike, sail, ramble, raid, quest, pilgrimage, adventure, undertaking, enterprise, project, campaign, mission, crusade, warpath
OLD hosting
2 TEAM, group, party, crew, company
3 PROMPTNESS, speed, swiftness, haste
FORMAL alacrity, celerity

expeditious *adj*
quick, efficient, rapid, speedy, swift, fast, hasty, immediate, instant, diligent, prompt, active, alert, brisk, ready
COLLOQ. meteoric
🖅 slow

expel *v*
1 DRIVE OUT, eject, evict, banish, throw out, cast out, ban, bar, oust, dismiss, sideline, reject, exile, outlaw, expatriate
FORMAL proscribe
COLLOQ. boot out, chuck out, kick out
2 DISCHARGE, let out, eject, belch, evacuate, void, cast out, spew out
🖅 **1** welcome

expend *v*
1 SPEND, pay (out), buy, afford, overspend, waste, fritter, squander
FORMAL purchase, disburse, procure
COLLOQ. fork out, lay out, shell out, blow, splash out
2 CONSUME, use (up), get through, go through, exhaust, empty, drain, sap, employ, utilize
FORMAL dissipate, deplete
🖅 **1** save **2** conserve

expendable *adj*
dispensable, disposable, replaceable, unimportant, unnecessary, inessential, non-essential, throwaway
🖅 indispensable, necessary

expenditure *n*
1 *huge amounts of public expenditure*
spending, expense, expenses, costs, outlay, outgoings, payment, output, waste, squandering
FORMAL disbursement

2 *the expenditure of effort*
use, application, consumption, draining, sapping,
employment, utilization
FORMAL dissipation
⊟ income

expense *n*
1 *underestimate the expense of moving house*
spending, expenditure, outlay, payment, paying-out, loss,
cost, price, charge, fee, rate
FORMAL disbursement
2 *expenses will be reimbursed*
costs, outgoings, incidentals, outlay, overheads, incidental
expenses, out-of-pocket expenses, miscellaneous expenses,
spending
Related adjective: sumptuary
3 *at the expense of his life*
cost, sacrifice, loss, harm, disadvantage, detriment

expensive *adj*
dear, high-priced, high-cost, costly, costing a lot,
exorbitant, extortionate, overpriced, excessive, extravagant,
lavish, splendid, executive
OLD chargeful
COLLOQ. steep, pricey, posh, sky-high, costing an arm and
a leg, costing the earth, costing a bomb, daylight robbery;
N Am big-ticket
OLD SLANG salt
⊟ cheap, inexpensive

experience *n, v*
♦ *n*
1 KNOWLEDGE, familiarity, contact, skill, involvement,
exposure, participation, practice, training, understanding,
learning, observation
COLLOQ. knowhow
2 INCIDENT, event, episode, happening, encounter,
occurrence, circumstance, adventure, affair, case, ordeal
COLLOQ. *Aust & NZ* spin
⊟ **1** inexperience
♦ *v*
undergo, go through, live through, suffer, feel, endure,
encounter, face, meet, know, try, perceive, sustain,
become familiar with, participate in

> QUOTATIONS
> Experience is the child of Thought, and Thought is the
> child of Action
> BENJAMIN DISRAELI, *Vivian Grey*

experienced *adj*
1 PRACTISED, knowledgeable, familiar, capable, competent,
proficient, adept, well-versed, expert, accomplished,
qualified, skilful, skilled, tried, trained, professional, au fait,
au courant
2 MATURE, seasoned, wise, veteran, sophisticated,
worldly wise, suave
COLLOQ. have been around, streetwise
⊟ **1** inexperienced, unskilled **2** inexperienced,
unsophisticated

experiment *n, v*
♦ *n*
trial, test, testing, investigation, experimentation, research,
inquiry, demonstration, examination, observation, analysis,
trial run, venture, try-out, trial and error, attempt,
procedure, proof, pilot study, piloting, dummy run,
dry run
♦ *v*
try (out), test, investigate, examine, research, trial, sample,
verify, observe, explore, carry out tests, conduct an
experiment

experimental *adj*
trial, test, exploratory, tentative, provisional, investigative,
scientific, observational, speculative, pilot, preliminary,
trial-and-error, at the trial/exploratory stage
TECHNICAL empirical
FORMAL peirastic

experimentally *adv*
tentatively, provisionally, speculatively, innovatively,
scientifically, investigatively, by trial and error,
by rule of thumb
TECHNICAL empirically

experimentation *n*
investigation, exploration, research, research and
development, R & D, verification, rule of thumb,
pragmatism, inventiveness
TECHNICAL empiricism

expert *n, adj*
♦ *n*
specialist, connoisseur, authority, pundit, master, past
master, old master, old hand, practitioner, professional,
maestro, virtuoso, crack, proficient, cognoscente, nark;
Aust & NZ don
COLLOQ. pro, dab hand, ace, buff, egghead, boffin,
hotshot, whizz, wise guy; *N Am* mavin, maven;
Aust & NZ gun; *S Afr* fundi
♦ *adj*
proficient, adept, skilled, skilful, knowledgeable,
experienced, able, practised, professional, accomplished,
masterly, excellent, brilliant, specialist, qualified, virtuoso,
dexterous
OLD sly
COLLOQ. top-notch, up on, well up on, crack, ace; *Aust &
NZ* gun
⊟ amateurish, novice

expertise *n*
expertness, proficiency, ability, skill, skilfulness, deftness,
knowledge, understanding, professionalism, mastery,
command, dexterity, facility, cleverness, virtuosity,
savoir-faire
OLD skill
COLLOQ. knowhow, knack
⊟ inexperience, inexpertness

expertly *adv*
skilfully, proficiently, competently, ably, capably,
professionally, excellently, efficiently, masterly

expiate *v*
atone for, make amends for, purge, do penance for, make
up for, pay for, redress

expiation *n*
atonement, redemption, ransom, reparation, redress,
penance, amends, recompense, shrift

expire *v*
1 END, come to an end, cease, finish, stop, close, run out,
be no longer valid, lapse
FORMAL terminate, conclude, discontinue
2 DIE, depart, perish, pass away, pass on, depart this life,
breathe your last, lose your life
FORMAL decease
COLLOQ. peg out, bite the dust, pop off, give up the ghost,
have had it, meet your maker
SLANG snuff it, cash in your chips, kick the bucket
⊟ **1** begin, be valid **2** live, be born

expiry *n*
end, finish, close, expiration, lapse
FORMAL cessation, conclusion, termination, discontinuation
⊟ beginning, continuation

explain *v*
1 INTERPRET, clarify, describe, define, make clear,
throw/shed light on, open up, simplify, resolve, solve, spell
out, translate, elaborate, unfold, unravel, untangle,
decipher, decode, illustrate, demonstrate, disclose, teach,
set out
FORMAL elucidate, expound, delineate,
explicate
2 JUSTIFY, excuse, account for, rationalize,
vindicate, defend, give a reason for, explain away,
lie behind
⊟ **1** obscure, confound

explanation *n*
1 INTERPRETATION, clarification, definition, illustration, demonstration, simplification, account, description, report, note, comment, commentary, gloss, footnote, annotation, unfolding, deciphering, decoding
FORMAL elucidation, exegesis, expounding, delineation, explication
2 JUSTIFICATION, excuse, reason, account, motive, meaning, answer, warrant, rationalization, vindication, defence, alibi
FORMAL apologia

explanatory *adj*
descriptive, demonstrative, illustrative, justifying
FORMAL interpretative, interpretive, explicative, expository, exegetical, elucidatory

expletive *n*
swear-word, oath, curse, blasphemy, obscenity, profanity, bad language
FORMAL anathema, imprecation, execration
COLLOQ. four-letter word
SLANG cuss; *N Am* cussword

explicable *adj*
explainable, accountable, definable, determinable, intelligible, justifiable, resolvable, understandable, solvable
FORMAL interpretable, exponible

explicate *v*
explain, interpret, clarify, describe, define, make clear, illustrate, demonstrate, spell out, set forth, unfold, unravel, untangle, work out
FORMAL elucidate, expound
E3 confuse, obscure

explication *n*
explanation, interpretation, clarification, description, illustration
FORMAL elucidation, exposition

explicit *adj*
1 CLEAR, distinct, clearly expressed, exact, categorical, absolute, direct, certain, positive, precise, specific, unequivocal, unambiguous, express, definite, declared, detailed, stated, straightforward
2 OPEN, direct, frank, candid, outspoken, straightforward, forthright, unreserved, unrestrained, uninhibited, plain, plain-spoken
3 *explicit sex scenes*
uncensored, offensive, shocking, obscene, pornographic, dirty, filthy, smutty, X-rated, adult

COLLOQ. near the knuckle/bone
E3 **1** implicit, unspoken, vague **2** reserved, restrained, cagey

explicitly *adv*
clearly, overtly, directly, specifically, unequivocally, unambiguously, plainly, definitely, straightforwardly
E3 implicitly, vaguely

explode *v*
1 BLOW UP, burst, go off, go up, set off, detonate, discharge, blast, spring
OLD displode
FORMAL erupt
COLLOQ. go bang
2 *explode with rage*
lose your temper, blow up, erupt, flare up, burst out
FORMAL fulminate
COLLOQ. blow a fuse, blow your cool, blow your top, boil over, burst a blood vessel, do your nut, fly into a rage, fly off the handle, go off the deep end, go up the wall, hit the ceiling, hit the roof, lose your cool, lose your rag, see red
3 DISCREDIT, disprove, give the lie to, debunk, invalidate, rebut, repudiate
FORMAL refute
4 GROW RAPIDLY, increase suddenly, escalate, accelerate, boom, leap, surge, mushroom, rocket
E3 **3** prove, confirm

exploit *n, v*
♦ *n*
deed, feat, adventure, achievement, accomplishment, attainment, activity, action, act, stunt
♦ *v*
1 USE, apply, employ, draw on, put to good use, make use of, utilize, capitalize on, use to good advantage, profit by, turn to account, take advantage of, make capital out of, tap
COLLOQ. cash in on, milk
2 MISUSE, abuse, take advantage of, take liberties, profiteer, oppress, ill-treat, impose on, fleece, manipulate
COLLOQ. milk, bleed, put something across someone, pull a fast one on, walk all over, play off against
SLANG rip off, take for a ride

exploitation *n*
1 *the exploitation of children*
taking (unfair) advantage, misuse, abuse, oppression, manipulation
COLLOQ. fleecing, milking, bleeding
SLANG rip-off, taking for a ride
2 *the exploitation of fossil fuels*
use, utilization, employment, application, putting to good use, making use of
COLLOQ. cashing in on, milking

exploration *n*
1 INVESTIGATION, examination, inquiry, research, scrutiny, study, inspection, observation, analysis, probe
2 EXPEDITION, survey, reconnaissance, search, trip, tour, voyage, travel, safari

exploratory *adj*
investigative, fact-finding, experimental, pilot, probing, searching, analytic, tentative, trial

explore *v*
1 INVESTIGATE, examine, look into, study, inspect, research, scrutinize, probe, analyse, consider, survey, inquire into, review
2 TRAVEL, tour, search, reconnoitre, prospect, scout, survey
FORMAL traverse
COLLOQ. see the world, do

explorer n
traveller, discoverer, navigator, tourer, prospector, scout, surveyor, reconnoitrer

explosion n
1 DETONATION, blast, blow-up, burst, outburst, discharge, eruption, bang, boom, outbreak, clap, crack, thunder, rumble, roll, fit; *Scot* pluff
OLD displosion
FORMAL report
2 *population explosion*
boom, surge, leap, sudden increase, dramatic growth
3 *explosion of anger*
outburst, eruption, fit, flare-up, rage, tantrum, paroxysm

explosive n, adj
♦ n
dynamite, gelignite, gunpowder, jelly, nitroglycerine, TNT, cordite, Semtex®
♦ adj
1 *an explosive device*
charged, hazardous, dangerous, unstable, volatile
FORMAL perilous
2 *an explosive situation*
tense, sensitive, fraught, charged, critical, powerful, nerve-racking, unstable, volatile, volcanic
3 FIERY, angry, unstable, volatile, overwrought, worked-up, violent, stormy, unrestrained, wild, raging, sensitive, touchy
4 *explosive growth*
sudden, dramatic, rapid, unexpected, mushrooming, rocketing, exponential, burgeoning, abrupt
COLLOQ. meteoric
1, 2 stable, calm **3** composed

explosively adv
1 *explosively combustible*
dangerously, hazardously, unstably, destructively
2 *grow explosively*
suddenly, rapidly, dramatically, unexpectedly, exponentially
3 *reply explosively*
fierily, angrily, violently, wildly
4 *the play opens explosively*
tensely, critically, powerfully, volcanically, like a bolt from the blue
3 calmly

exponent n
1 ADVOCATE, promoter, supporter, upholder, defender, backer, adherent, spokesman, spokeswoman, spokesperson, champion
FORMAL proponent
2 PRACTITIONER, adept, expert, master, specialist, player, performer

export v, n
♦ v
trade, deal with, sell abroad/overseas, traffic in, transport, re-export
♦ n
exported product/commodity/goods, re-export, transfer, trade, foreign trade, international trade

expose v
1 REVEAL, show, exhibit, display, disclose, uncover, bring to light, bring out into the open, make known, present, detect, divulge, betray, unveil, unmask, unearth, lay bare, denounce
FORMAL manifest
COLLOQ. blow the whistle, take the lid off
2 ENDANGER, jeopardize, imperil, risk, hazard, put at risk, put in jeopardy, make vulnerable
3 *expose the public to art*
familiarize with, bring into contact with, acquaint with, introduce to, present with, lay open to, subject to
4 *expose yourself*
show your genitals, commit indecent exposure
COLLOQ. flash
1 conceal, cover up **2** protect

exposé n
disclosure, divulgence, exposure, revelation, uncovering, account, article

exposed adj
bare, open, in the open, revealed, laid bare, unprotected, without protection, open to the elements, vulnerable, exhibited, on display, on show, on view, shown, susceptible
covered, sheltered

exposition n
1 EXPLANATION, description, analysis, unfolding, clarification, illumination, commentary, interpretation, account, illustration, critique, presentation, paper, study, thesis, monograph
FORMAL discourse, elucidation, exegesis, explication
2 EXHIBITION, show, fair, display, demonstration
COLLOQ. expo

expository adj
explanatory, descriptive, illustrative, interpretative
TECHNICAL exegetic, hermeneutic
FORMAL declaratory, elucidative, explicatory, interpretive

expostulate v
protest, argue, plead, reason, dissuade, disagree
FORMAL remonstrate

exposure n
1 REVELATION, uncovering, disclosure, exposé, showing, unmasking, unveiling, display, airing, exhibition, presentation, publicity, discovery, detection, divulgence, denunciation
FORMAL manifestation
2 FAMILIARITY, experience, knowledge, contact, acquaintance, awareness
3 JEOPARDY, danger, hazard, risk, vulnerability, susceptibility
4 PUBLICITY, public attention, advertising, promotion
COLLOQ. plug, hype

expound v
explain, analyse, dissect, unfold, unravel, untangle, clarify, illuminate, describe, illustrate, interpret, comment on, set forth, set out, spell out, open (up), preach, sermonize
FORMAL elucidate, explicate

express v, adj
♦ v
1 ARTICULATE, verbalize, put into words, utter, voice, give voice to, say, speak, state, communicate, put/get over, pronounce, word, tell, announce, report, assert, declare, put across, formulate, point out, intimate, testify, convey, vent, ventilate, air
FORMAL enunciate
2 SHOW, demonstrate, exhibit, disclose, divulge, reveal, indicate, denote, depict, embody, couch
FORMAL manifest
3 SYMBOLIZE, stand for, represent, signify, designate
♦ adj
1 SPECIFIC, explicit, exact, definite, clear, categorical, precise, distinct, well-defined, clear-cut, certain, plain, particular, stated, unambiguous, unequivocal, special, sole
FORMAL manifest
2 FAST, speedy, rapid, quick, swift, high-speed, brisk, non-stop
FORMAL expeditious
1 vague

expression n
1 LOOK, air, aspect, appearance, scowl, grimace, gesture
FORMAL countenance, mien
2 REPRESENTATION, demonstration, indication, intimation, exhibition, communication, illustration, embodiment, show, sign, symbol, style
FORMAL manifestation
3 UTTERANCE, verbalization, voicing, communication, articulation, vocalization, statement, assertion, proclamation, announcement, declaration, pronouncement, speech, wording, intimation

4 PHRASE, word, wording, term, turn of phrase, saying, maxim, adage, proverb, aphorism, axiom, set phrase, phrasing, idiom, language
5 TONE, intonation, delivery, style, idiom, diction, enunciation, modulation, phrasing
FORMAL locution
6 FEELING, emotion, passion, depth, force, power, vigour, vividness, intensity, imagination, artistry, creativity, style

expressionless adj
dull, blank, deadpan, impassive, emotionless, straight-faced, inscrutable, empty, vacuous, glassy, glazed
COLLOQ. poker-faced
E3 expressive

expressive adj
1 ELOQUENT, articulate, meaningful, forceful, telling, revealing, informative, communicative, demonstrative, emphatic, moving, evocative, poignant, lively, striking, animated, suggestive, significant, thoughtful, vivid, sympathetic
2 INDICATIVE, showing, demonstrating, revealing, suggesting

expressively adv
meaningfully, informatively, eloquently, demonstratively, emphatically, suggestively, evocatively, vividly
TECHNICAL espressivo

expressiveness n
articulateness, articulacy, demonstrativeness, meaningfulness, communicativeness, evocativeness, poignancy, vividness

expressly adv
specifically, explicitly, exactly, definitely, clearly, categorically, absolutely, precisely, distinctly, plainly, particularly, unambiguously, unequivocally, specially, solely, especially, decidedly, intentionally, on purpose, purposely, pointedly
FORMAL manifestly

expropriate v
take, take away, seize, take possession of, commandeer, confiscate, impound, usurp, assume, dispossess, annex, unhouse
TECHNICAL sequester, disseise
FORMAL appropriate, arrogate, requisition

expropriation n
taking-away, seizure, confiscation, impounding, dispossession
TECHNICAL sequestration
FORMAL appropriation, arrogation

expulsion n
1 EJECTION, eviction, exile, banishment, removal, discharge, exclusion, dismissal, throwing out, rejection
COLLOQ. sacking, the sack, the boot
2 DISCHARGE, ejection, belching, evacuation, voiding, excretion

expunge v
erase, remove, wipe out, cancel, obliterate, eradicate, destroy, exterminate, extinguish, raze, get rid of, abolish, annihilate, annul, blot out, delete, cross out, rub out
FORMAL efface, extirpate

expurgate v
censor, cut, emend, clean up, blue-pencil, bowdlerize, purge, purify, sanitize

exquisite adj
1 BEAUTIFUL, attractive, dainty, delicate, fine, charming, elegant, delightful, lovely, pretty, pleasing, fragile
2 PERFECT, flawless, fine, excellent, choice, precious, rare, outstanding
3 REFINED, discriminating, meticulous, sensitive, discerning, cultivated, cultured, impeccable
4 INTENSE, keen, sharp, acute, piercing, poignant
E3 **1** ugly **2** flawed **3** unrefined

exquisitely adv
beautifully, attractively, daintily, delicately, finely, charmingly, elegantly, delightfully, pleasingly

extant adj
surviving, remaining, existent, existing, still existing, in existence, alive, living, subsistent, subsisting
E3 extinct, non-existent, dead

extempore adv, adj
♦ adv
impromptu, ad lib, on the spur of the moment, spontaneously
COLLOQ. off the cuff, off the top of your head
♦ adj
impromptu, improvised, ad-lib, unscripted, spontaneous, unplanned, unrehearsed, unprepared, extemporaneous
COLLOQ. off-the-cuff, off the top of your head
E3 planned

extemporize v
ad-lib, improvise, play it by ear, think on your feet, make up
COLLOQ. wing it, speak off the cuff, do something off the top of your head

extend v
1 SPREAD, stretch, reach, continue, carry on, run, last, come (up/down) to, go as far as, go down/up to
2 ENLARGE, increase, expand, develop, amplify, intensify, step up, lengthen, widen, broaden, draw out, stretch, prolong, spin out, drag out, unwind
FORMAL elongate, protract, augment
3 OFFER, give, grant, hold out, put out, reach out, impart, present
FORMAL bestow, confer, proffer
4 *the job extends to doing the cleaning*
include, take in, span, involve
FORMAL embrace, comprehend
E3 **2** contract, shorten **3** withhold

extendable adj
enlargeable, expandable, stretchy, stretchable, elastic, magnifiable, extensive
FORMAL dilatable

extended adj
lengthy, long, lengthened, prolonged, increased, enlarged, expanded, developed, amplified

extension n
1 ENLARGEMENT, increase, stretching, broadening, widening, lengthening, expansion, development, enhancement, continuation, prolongation, proliferation
FORMAL elongation, protraction, diffusion
2 ADDITION, supplement, appendix, annexe, wing, add-on, adjunct
FORMAL addendum
3 DELAY, postponement, deferral, more/additional time

extensive adj
1 COMPREHENSIVE, far-reaching, large-scale, thorough, wide, wide-ranging, broad, widespread, universal, complete, extended, all-inclusive, unlimited, boundless, general, pervasive, prevalent
2 LARGE, huge, roomy, spacious, vast, long, lengthy, wide, substantial, fair-sized, sizeable, spread out, outspread
FORMAL capacious, commodious, voluminous
E3 **1** restricted, narrow **2** small

extensively adv
1 *deal with a subject extensively*
comprehensively, thoroughly, completely, generally, boundlessly
2 *used extensively in industry*
greatly, widely, largely, generally, substantially

extent n
1 DIMENSION(S), amount, magnitude, expanse, size, area, bulk, degree, level, breadth, quantity, spread, coverage,

stretch, volume, width, measure, length,
duration, term, time
2 LIMIT, bounds, lengths, range, reach, scope, compass,
stretch, sphere, play, sweep

extenuate v
diminish, excuse, lessen, minimize, make allowances for,
modify, qualify, soften
FORMAL mitigate

extenuating adj
moderating, qualifying, justifying, palliative, diminishing,
excusing, lessening, minimizing, modifying, softening
FORMAL mitigating, exculpatory, extenuative, extenuatory

exterior n, adj
♦ n
outside, surface, outer surface, covering, coating, face,
façade, shell, skin, finish, externals, external surface,
appearance
▣ inside, interior
♦ adj
outer, outside, outermost, surface, external, superficial,
surrounding, outward, peripheral, extrinsic
▣ inside, interior

exterminate v
annihilate, kill, eradicate, destroy, eliminate, massacre,
slaughter, abolish, wipe out
FORMAL extirpate
COLLOQ. do in, do away with, bump off, knock off

extermination n
annihilation, killing, eradication, elimination,
destruction, massacre, genocide
FORMAL extirpation

external adj
1 OUTER, surface, outside, exterior, superficial,
outward, outermost, apparent, visible, extraneous,
peripheral, extrinsic
2 *external students*
extramural, independent, visiting, non-resident, outside
▣ 1 internal **2** resident

externally adv
outwardly, visibly, superficially, apparently,
extraneously, peripherally
▣ internally

extinct adj
1 DEFUNCT, dead, died out, non-existent,
gone, obsolete, ended, exterminated, terminated,
vanished, lost, wiped out, abolished
2 EXTINGUISHED, quenched, inactive, out,
burnt out
3 OBSOLETE, invalid, expired, old, passé,
outmoded, former, bygone, antiquated
FORMAL terminated
▣ 1 living, existing, existent **2** active, erupting

extinction n
annihilation, extermination, death, dying-out, vanishing,
disappearance, eradication, obliteration, destruction,
abolition, excision
FORMAL termination

extinguish v
1 PUT OUT, blow out, snuff out, stifle,
smother, choke, douse, quench, dampen
down, stub out
2 ANNIHILATE, exterminate, eliminate, destroy, kill,
eradicate, erase, abolish, remove, end, suppress
FORMAL expunge, extirpate
COLLOQ. rub out

extirpate v
destroy, annihilate, eliminate, wipe out,
eradicate, cut out, remove, weed out, root out, uproot,
abolish, exterminate, extinguish, erase
FORMAL deracinate, expunge

extol v
praise, acclaim, exalt, magnify, glorify, sing the praises of,
applaud, celebrate, commend, wax lyrical
FORMAL laud, eulogize, rhapsodize
▣ blame; *formal* denigrate

extort v
extract, wring, exact, coerce, force, get out of, wrest,
blackmail, squeeze, bully
COLLOQ. milk, bleed
SLANG screw

extortion n
force, coercion, blackmail, oppression, demand,
exaction, racketeering
FORMAL malversation
COLLOQ. milking

extortionate adj
exorbitant, excessive, outrageous, grasping, exacting,
immoderate, unreasonable, inordinate, preposterous,
oppressive, severe, hard, harsh
FORMAL rapacious

extortionist n
extortioner, profiteer, racketeer, exploiter, blackmailer,
exactor, yakuza

extra adj, n, adv
♦ adj
1 ADDITIONAL, added, auxiliary, supplementary, new,
another, more, further, ancillary, fresh, other,
subsidiary
2 EXCESS, excessive, spare, superfluous, surplus,
unused, unneeded, unnecessary, left-over, reserve,
redundant
FORMAL supernumerary
▣ 1 integral **2** essential
♦ n
1 ADDITION, supplement, extension, accessory, appendage,
bonus, complement, additive, adjunct, attachment
FORMAL addendum
2 *employ extras in the film*
bit player, supernumerary, spear-carrier, walk-on, walk-on
part, minor role
♦ adv
1 ESPECIALLY, exceptionally, extraordinarily,
particularly, unusually, remarkably, uncommonly,
extremely
2 IN ADDITION, also, as well, together with, along with,
besides, too, additionally, and so on, not to mention, not
forgetting, let alone, above and beyond
COLLOQ. into the bargain

extract v, n
♦ v
1 REMOVE, take out, draw out, cut out, get out, pull (out),
exact, uproot, prise, pluck, wrench, withdraw, suck, gut,
quarry, recover, grog
TECHNICAL enucleate, decoct, render
OLD educe
FORMAL deracinate
2 DERIVE, draw, distil, boil down, obtain, get, gather, glean,
wrest, wring, elicit, worm
3 CHOOSE, pick, select, cull, abstract, excerpt, copy, cite,
quote, reproduce
▣ 1 insert
♦ n
1 DISTILLATION, essence, concentrate, spirits, juice
TECHNICAL decoction, euonymin, logwood
FORMAL distillate
2 EXCERPT, passage, selection, clip, clipping, cutting,
quotation, abstract, citation, gobbet
TECHNICAL estreat, pericope

SYNONYM NUANCES

verb sense 1
Cut out and **pull out** emphasize the manner of
extracting; **draw out** is similar but suggests a slower,
more deliberate movement, whereas **get out** may

sometimes imply a degree of difficulty: *he finally got the device out of its wrapper.* **Exact** is also suggestive of difficulty but further suggests the use of strongly persuasive methods or even force: *the allies exacted a heavy price for their help.*

The term **uproot** would be used literally of extracting plants from the soil, but when used more figuratively, for instance of people moving from their place of origin, the implication is of a painful action, undertaken with reluctance or regret: *many were uprooted by drought or flood.* **Prise**, similarly, suggests a slow action made with effort, in this instance often physical: *he prised her fingers from the handle;* likewise **wrench**, which has further connotations of force. **Pluck**, meanwhile, would describe a much quicker, snatching movement.

Withdraw can be used of the act of extracting when it is not forceful or physical: *the bank withdrew its sponsorship.* The term **suck** is often used figuratively to suggest a slow draining, and the connotations are rarely positive: *the darkness sucked all the courage from his body,* whereas **gut** is more suggestive of violently extracting the contents from something and emphasizes the completeness of the result: *the whole house has been gutted, carpets pulled up and curtains torn down.*

extraction *n*
1 REMOVAL, taking-out, uprooting, drawing, drawing-out, pulling, withdrawal, separation, obtaining, derivation
2 ORIGIN, descent, ancestry, birth, blood, lineage, derivation, family, stock, parentage, pedigree, race
F3 1 insertion

extradite *v*
send back, send home, deport, repatriate, hand over, banish, expel, exile

extradition *n*
sending back, deportation, banishment, expulsion, handover, repatriation, exile

extraneous *adj*
superfluous, supplementary, redundant, irrelevant, immaterial, inapplicable, inappropriate, inessential, inapt, incidental, tangential, needless, unnecessary, unneeded, non-essential, unessential, unrelated, unconnected, extra, additional, peripheral, exterior, external, extrinsic, alien, strange, foreign
FORMAL inapposite
F3 integral, essential

extraordinarily *adv*
remarkably, unusually, uncommonly, exceptionally, notably, uniquely, specially, significantly, particularly, unexpectedly, strangely, oddly, bizarrely, curiously, amazingly, astoundingly
F3 ordinarily

extraordinary *adj*
remarkable, unusual, exceptional, notable, noteworthy, outstanding, unique, special, unexpected, strange, peculiar, odd, bizarre, curious, unconventional, rare, uncommon, surprising, amazing, astounding, wonderful, unprecedented, marvellous, fantastic, significant, particular, emergency
FORMAL singular
COLLOQ. out of this world
F3 commonplace, ordinary

extrapolate *v*
project, plan, estimate, approximate, reckon, calculate, sample, gauge, expect

extravagance *n*
1 OVERSPENDING, squandering, waste, wastefulness, thriftlessness, recklessness, imprudence
FORMAL profligacy, prodigality, improvidence
2 EXCESS, excessiveness, exaggeration, immoderation, recklessness, profusion, outrageousness, folly, wildness,

ornateness, ostentation, vanity, pretentiousness, lavishness, dissipation, splurge
OLD riotise
3 LUXURY, extra, treat
F3 1 thrift **2** moderation, restraint

extravagant *adj*
1 WASTEFUL, spendthrift, squandering, thriftless, reckless, imprudent
FORMAL prodigal, profligate, improvident
2 IMMODERATE, exaggerated, excessive, flamboyant, preposterous, outrageous, ostentatious, pretentious, lavish, ornate, fanciful, fantastic, wild, unrestrained, bizarre, outré
TECHNICAL baroque, rococo, churrigueresque
COLLOQ. flashy, over the top, OTT
3 OVERPRICED, exorbitant, expensive, excessive, extortionate, costly, dear
COLLOQ. steep, pricey, spendy, sky-high, costing an arm and a leg, costing the earth, costing a bomb, daylight robbery
F3 1 thrifty **2** moderate, restrained **3** reasonable

extravaganza *n*
spectacular, pageant, display, show, spectacle

extreme *adj, n*
♦ *adj*
1 INTENSE, great, immoderate, inordinate, utmost, uttermost, out-and-out, maximum, acute, downright, extraordinary, exceptional, greatest, highest, supreme, ultimate, unreasonable, remarkable
2 FARTHEST, far-off, faraway, distant, endmost, outermost, outlying, remotest, most remote, uttermost, final, last, terminal, ultimate
3 RADICAL, zealous, extremist, fanatical, hardline, immoderate, excessive, unreasonable
4 DRASTIC, dire, uncompromising, unrelenting, unyielding, stern, strict, rigid, severe, harsh, desperate, serious, stringent, iron-fisted, iron-handed, Draconian
F3 1 mild **3** moderate
♦ *n*
extremity, limit, maximum, ultimate, utmost, excess, top, mark, line, pinnacle, peak, height, acme, apex, zenith, end, climax, depth, edge, pole
FORMAL termination

■ **in the extreme**
exceedingly, excessively, very, exceptionally, extraordinarily, intensely, remarkably, utterly, greatly, highly, immoderately, uncommonly, inordinately
COLLOQ. awfully, terribly, dreadfully, frightfully, terrifically

extremely *adv*
exceedingly, excessively, very, really, exceptionally, extraordinarily, intensely, thoroughly, remarkably, utterly, greatly, highly, unusually, unreasonably, immoderately, uncommonly, inordinately, tremendously, acutely, severely, decidedly; *N Am* mighty
OLD jolly
COLLOQ. seriously, awfully, terribly, dreadfully, frightfully, terrifically
SLANG majorly

SYNONYM NUANCES

Very and **really** have a very general use to add emphasis. **Greatly**, **highly** and the more emphatic **exceedingly** make a stronger suggestion of great degree, whilst **excessively** is negative in tone, and clearly implies too great a degree. **Intensely**, however, is appropriate for something that is concentrated to an extreme level: *the most intensely populated region.* You can use the term **exceptionally** to imply that something is outside of the average, whereas **remarkably**, **unusually**, **uncommonly** and **extraordinarily** go further by suggesting something is beyond the norm: *an extraordinarily gifted performer.*

More disapproving terms include **unreasonably**, which describes levels that exceed the bounds of reason, and **immoderately**, which suggests extravagance that crosses the boundaries of taste. **Inordinately** similarly suggests that something is unrestrained or unwarranted: *inordinately proud of her son*. The tone of both **acutely** and **severely** is not judgemental but negative in a different way, emphasizing something felt very keenly or deeply and connotative of difficulty: *the stuntman was acutely aware of what could go wrong; I am severely disappointed at your attitude*. Meanwhile **decidedly** hints at the truth of conclusions based on the degree to which something is happening: *nationalism is decidedly on the wane; that shelf is decidedly crooked*.

extremism *n*
fanaticism, radicalism, zeal, excessiveness, unreasonableness, terrorism
FORMAL zealotry
E∃ moderation

extremist *n*
fanatic, hardliner, fundamentalist, militant, radical, zealot, diehard, ultra, terrorist
E∃ moderate

extremity *n*
1 EXTREME, limit, boundary, brink, verge, periphery, bound, border, frontier, height, tip, top, edge, excess, end, ending, termination, peak, pinnacle, apex, acme, zenith, apogee, margin, terminal, terminus, ultimate, pole, maximum, minimum, depth
2 *extremities of the body*
limb, arm, hand, finger, foot, leg, toe, tail
3 CRISIS, danger, emergency, plight, hardship, adversity, misfortune, trouble, outrance
OLD utterance, exigent
FORMAL indigence, exigency
COLLOQ. fix, mess, jam, spot, tight spot, pickle, hole, dire straits

extricate *v*
disentangle, extract, clear, disengage, detach, let loose, free, deliver, liberate, release, rescue, relieve, remove, get out, withdraw
E∃ involve

extrinsic *adj*
external, extraneous, exterior, outside, alien, exotic, foreign, imported
E∃ intrinsic

extrovert *n*
mixer, socializer, mingler, outgoing person, sociable person, conversationalist, joiner, life and soul of the party

extroverted *adj*
outgoing, friendly, sociable, amicable, amiable, exuberant, hearty, demonstrative, outward-looking
COLLOQ. hail-fellow-well-met
E∃ introverted

extrude *v*
force out, squeeze out, press out, thrust out, mould

exuberance *n*
1 LIVELINESS, vitality, high spirits, zest, effervescence, enthusiasm, eagerness, excitement, animation, elation, buoyancy, exhilaration, effusiveness, cheerfulness, fulsomeness, life, vigour, energy
FORMAL ebullience, vivacity
COLLOQ. pizzazz
2 ABUNDANCE, copiousness, lushness, richness, superabundance, lavishness, luxuriance, rankness, exaggeration, excessiveness
FORMAL plenitude, prodigality, profusion
E∃ 1 apathy, lifelessness **2** scantiness

exuberant *adj*
1 LIVELY, vivacious, spirited, zestful, high-spirited, effervescent, enthusiastic, sparkling, excited, animated, elated, buoyant, exhilarated, effusive, cheerful, full of life, vigorous, energetic, unrestrained, fulsome, irrepressible, exaggerated
FORMAL ebullient
2 PLENTIFUL, lavish, overflowing, luxurious, lush, rich, profuse, abundant, thriving, rank
FORMAL plenteous
E∃ 1 apathetic **2** scarce

exude *v*
1 *exude confidence*
radiate, ooze, display, show, emanate, emit, exhibit
FORMAL manifest
2 DISCHARGE, issue, flow out, bleed, excrete, leak, secrete, give off/out, seep, perspire, sweat, trickle, weep, well

exult *v*
rejoice, revel, delight, be joyful, be delighted, glory, celebrate, relish, crow, gloat, triumph
COLLOQ. be over the moon

exultant *adj*
delighted, rejoicing, revelling, elated, thrilled, exulting, gleeful, joyful, overjoyed, jubilant, transporting, enraptured, triumphant
FORMAL joyous
COLLOQ. cock-a-hoop, over the moon, on cloud nine, in seventh heaven
E∃ depressed

exultation *n*
rejoicing, joy, delight, elation, glee, revelling, glory, glorying, joyfulness, jubilation, merriness, transport, triumph, celebration, crowing, gloating
FORMAL joyousness, paean, eulogy
E∃ depression

eye *n, v*
♦ *n*
1 *blind in one eye*
Scot & dialect keeker
TECHNICAL ocellus, ommateum
OLD light; *dialect* pigsney
COLLOQ. ocular, optic, water pump; *dialect & N Am* winker
SLANG peeper, peep, goggler, blinker, glim, lamp
Related adjectives: ocular, ophthalmic, optical
2 VISION, sight, eyesight, power of seeing, faculty of sight, observation
3 APPRECIATION, discrimination, discernment, perception, awareness, recognition, judgement, sensitivity, taste
4 VIEWPOINT, opinion, view, point of view, way of thinking, judgement, mind, estimation, belief
5 WATCH, observation, lookout, view, notice, watchfulness, vigilance, surveillance
♦ *v*
look at, see, watch, regard, observe, stare at, gaze at, glance at, view, scrutinize, scan, examine, peruse, study, survey, inspect, contemplate, look up and down, assess
■ **keep an eye on**
watch closely, mind, attend to, take responsibility for, look after, take care of, monitor, keep tabs on
■ **see eye to eye**
agree, be of one mind, be at one, reach an agreement
FORMAL concur
COLLOQ. go along with, go with, speak the same language, be on the same wavelength
■ **set eyes on**
see, notice, observe, come across, come upon, lay eyes on, clap eyes on, meet, encounter
FORMAL behold

■ **up to your eyes**
busy, occupied, involved, engrossed, overwhelmed, inundated
COLLOQ. snowed under, fully stretched, overstretched, having your hands full, tied up
E₃ free, idle

QUOTATIONS
Take a pair of sparkling eyes
Sɪʀ W S Gɪʟʙᴇʀᴛ, *The Gondoliers*

Parts of the eye include:

anterior chamber	fovea	pupil
aqueous humour	iris	retina
blind spot	lacrimal duct	rod
choroid	lens	sclera
ciliary body	lower eyelid	suspension
cone	ocular muscle	ligament
conjunctiva	optic nerve	upper eyelid
cornea	papilla	vitreous humour
eyelash	posterior chamber	

eye-catching *adj*
striking, arresting, attractive, spectacular, captivating, beautiful, stunning, gorgeous, imposing, impressive, showy, conspicuous, noticeable, prominent
E₃ plain, unattractive

eye-opener *n*
revelation, disclosure, surprising thing/fact, wonder, quite something, something incredible

eyesight *n*
vision, sight, perception, observation, power of seeing, faculty of sight, view
Related adjectives: optical, ocular, visual

eyesore *n*
ugliness, blemish, scar, monstrosity, blot, blot on the landscape, disfigurement, defacement, horror, blight, disgrace, atrocity, mess, carbuncle

eyewitness *n*
witness, observer, spectator, looker-on, onlooker, bystander, viewer, passer-by, watcher

fable *n*
Aesop's fables; fact or fable?
allegory, parable, story, tale, moral tale, yarn, myth,
legend, epic, saga, fiction, fabrication, invention, lie,
untruth, falsehood, *Märchen*
COLLOQ. tall story, old wives' tale
FORMAL apologue

fabled *adj*
legendary, renowned, celebrated, famous, famed,
remarkable
Ea unknown

fabric *n*
1 CLOTH, material, textile, stuff, web, texture
2 STRUCTURE, framework, construction, make-up,
constitution, organization, infrastructure, frame,
foundations

Fabrics include:

alpaca	flannelette	paisley
angora	fleece	pashmina
astrakhan	gaberdine	piqué
barathea	georgette	polycotton
bouclé	gingham	polyester
brocade	Gore-Tex®	poplin
Brussels lace	gossamer	rayon
buckram	grosgrain	sateen
calico	Harris tweed®	satin
cambric	hessian	seersucker
candlewick	horsehair	serge
canvas	huckaback	shahtoosh
cashmere	jean	shantung
chambray	jersey	sharkskin
chamois	kid	sheepskin
Chantilly	lace	Shetland wool
cheesecloth	lamé	silk
chenille	lawn	suede
chiffon	leather	taffeta
chino	leather-cloth	terry towelling
chintz	linen	Terylene®
cord	lisle	ticking
corduroy	Lurex®	tulle
cotton	Lycra®	tweed
crêpe	madras	velour
crêpe de Chine	mohair	velvet
Crimplene®	moire	vicuña
crocodile skin	moleskin	Viyella®
damask	muslin	voile
denim	needlecord	webbing
drill	net	winceyette
duffel	nylon	wool
felt	organdie	worsted
flannel	organza	

---

fabricate *v*
1 FAKE, falsify, forge, counterfeit, invent, make up, trump
up, concoct, hatch, spin
COLLOQ. cook up
2 MANUFACTURE, make, construct, assemble, build, erect,
put together, produce, form, shape, fashion, create, frame,
devise
Ea 2 demolish, destroy

fabrication *n*
1 FAKE, falsehood, forgery, invention, concoction, fable,
fiction, figment, story, myth, untruth
COLLOQ. cock-and-bull story, fairy story
2 MANUFACTURE, assembly, building, construction,
erection, production
FORMAL assemblage
Ea 1 truth

fabulous *adj*
1 WONDERFUL, marvellous, fantastic, tremendous,
remarkable, great, superb, breathtaking, spectacular,
phenomenal, amazing, astounding, astonishing,
unbelievable, incredible, inconceivable, unimaginable
COLLOQ. out of this world, top-notch, super, cool, magic,
divine, heavenly, sensational, not half bad
SLANG way-out, def, fab, triff, mega, wicked, stonking,
radical, rad, crucial, mean
2 *a fabulous beast*
mythological, mythical, legendary, fabled,
fantastic, fictitious, fictional, invented, made-up,
imaginary, unreal
Ea 2 real

façade *n*
1 FRONT, exterior, frontage, face
2 SHOW, semblance, appearance, front, cover, cloak, veil,
guise, mask, disguise, pretence, veneer

face *n, v*
♦ *n*
1 *she has a lovely face*
features, façade, profile
FORMAL countenance, visage, physiognomy
COLLOQ. mug, kisser, phiz, pan, clock, dial
SLANG puss
Related adjectives: facial
2 EXPRESSION, look, appearance, air, aspect
FORMAL mien, demeanour
3 *pull a face*
grimace, frown, scowl, pout, moue
4 EXTERIOR, outside, surface, cover, front, frontage, façade,
aspect, side, flank
5 *changing the face of the city*
appearance, nature, look(s), aspect, form
6 *save/lose face*
reputation, prestige, name, standing, respect, honour,
esteem, admiration
Related adjective: facial
♦ *v*
1 BE OPPOSITE, give on to, front, overlook, look onto, look
towards, look out on
2 CONFRONT, face up to, deal with, come up against, cope
with, tackle, defy, oppose, brave, resist, withstand, have to
reckon with, encounter, meet, experience
3 COVER, line, coat, dress, clad, overlay, smooth, polish,
veneer
■ **face up to**
accept, come to terms with, resign yourself to, reconcile
yourself to, acknowledge, recognize, cope with, deal with,
confront, meet head-on, stand up to
■ **face to face**
opposite, facing, eye to eye, confronting,
in confrontation
COLLOQ. eyeball to eyeball

■ **fly in the face of**
contradict, oppose, disagree, clash, conflict, contrast, go against, be at variance, be at odds, be in conflict, be inconsistent with

■ **on the face of it**
apparently, seemingly, ostensibly, outwardly, to all appearances, superficially, on the surface, reputedly, plainly, clearly, obviously, manifestly, patently

■ **pull a face**
frown, grimace, lour, pout, scowl, sulk, glower, knit your brows

> **QUOTATIONS**
> Was this the face that launched a thousand ships, / And burnt the topless towers of Ilium
> CHRISTOPHER MARLOWE, *Doctor Faustus*

facelift *n*
1 COSMETIC SURGERY, plastic surgery
TECHNICAL rhytidectomy
2 REDECORATION, renovation, restoration, refurbishment, refit, makeover, transformation

facet *n*
surface, plane, slant, side, face, aspect, element, angle, point, feature, characteristic, factor

facetious *adj*
flippant, frivolous, playful, jocular, jocose, jesting, glib, joking, tongue-in-cheek, light-hearted, funny, amusing, humorous, comic, comical, droll, witty
🖃 serious

facile *adj*
shallow, superficial, easy, simple, simplistic, uncomplicated, ready, quick, hasty, glib, fluent, smooth, slick, plausible
🖃 complicated, profound

facilitate *v*
ease, make easier, help, assist, encourage, further, smooth, smooth the way, lubricate, promote, advance, forward, accelerate, speed up
FORMAL expedite

facilitation *n*
assistance, furthering, helping, encouragement, promotion, acceleration, forwarding
FORMAL expediting

facility *n*
1 *a facility for learning languages*
effortlessness, ease, readiness, quickness, fluency, eloquence, articulateness, aptitude, proficiency, skill, skilfulness, talent, gift, knack, ability, dexterity
2 *sports facilities*
amenity, service, utility, convenience, resource, provision, appliance, equipment, means, feature, prerequisite, opportunity, advantage, aid
COLLOQ. mod con

facing *n*
coating, covering, lining, cladding, dressing, reinforcement, façade, overlay, surface, trimming, veneer, false front
TECHNICAL revetment

facsimile *n*
copy, imitation, reproduction, repro, replica, carbon copy, carbon, duplicate, image, fax, photocopy, Photostat®, Xerox®, mimeograph, transcript, print

fact *n*
1 *facts and figures*
information, datum, detail, particular, specific, point, item, feature, factor, circumstance, component, element, event, incident, occurrence, happening, act, deed, fait accompli
COLLOQ. gen, info, low-down, score, ins and outs; *N Am* poop
2 REALITY, factuality, certainty, truth
FORMAL actuality
🖃 2 fiction

■ **in fact**
actually, in actual fact, in point of fact, as a matter of fact, in practice, in reality, really, indeed, truly, in truth
COLLOQ. come to that

faction *n*
1 SPLINTER GROUP, ginger group, minority, division, section, contingent, party, band, side, group, camp, set, sector, ring, caucus, clique, coterie, cabal, junta, lobby, pressure group
2 DISAGREEMENT, conflict, argument, friction, quarrels, discord, disharmony, division, trouble, contention, infighting, strife, dissension

factious *adj*
conflicting, clashing, divisive, divided, split, partisan, sectarian, quarrelsome, discordant, quarrelling, at odds, at loggerheads, warring, troublemaking, turbulent, tumultuous, dissident, rival, contentious, mutinous, seditious, insurrectionary, rebellious
FORMAL disputatious, refractory
🖃 calm, co-operative

factitious *adj*
unnatural, artificial, bogus, sham, counterfeit, imitation, pretended, false, fabricated, contrived
🖃 genuine

factor *n*
cause, influence, circumstance, contingency, consideration, element, ingredient, component, constituent, part, point, aspect, facet, fact, item, detail, characteristic, feature
FORMAL determinant

factory *n*
works, plant, mill, shop floor, assembly line, assembly shop, yard, workshop, foundry, manufactory

factotum *n*
do-all, handyman, jack-of-all-trades, maid-of-all-work, Man (or Girl) Friday, odd-jobman

factual *adj*
true, historical, actual, real, genuine, authentic, true-to-life, correct, accurate, truthful, precise, exact, literal, faithful, close, strict, detailed, realistic, unbiased, unprejudiced, objective
🖃 false, fictitious, imaginary, fictional

factually *adv*
in reality, really, actually, truly, truthfully, historically, genuinely

faculties *n*
wits, senses, intelligence, reason, powers, capabilities

faculty *n*
1 ABILITY, capability, capacity, power, facility, proficiency, knack, flair, gift, talent, skill, aptitude, bent
2 *Faculty of Medicine*
department, organization, division, section, school

fad *n*
craze, mania, (passing) fashion, mode, vogue, trend, enthusiasm, whim, fancy
FORMAL affectation
COLLOQ. trendlet, rage

faddy *adj*
fussy, particular, fastidious, finicky, hard-to-please, exact
COLLOQ. pernickety, choosy, picky, nit-picking; *N Am* persnickety

fade *v*
1 DISCOLOUR, lose colour, bleach, blanch, blench, pale, become paler, become/grow pale, tone down, whiten, dim, dull, wash out
TECHNICAL etiolate
COLLOQ. go as white as a sheet
2 DECLINE, fall, diminish, dwindle, ebb (away), wane, fail, waste away, disappear, vanish, recede, melt (away), dissolve, pale, flag, weaken, become weaker, droop, wilt, wither, shrivel, perish, die (away), peter out, die out
FORMAL evanesce

COLLOQ. fizzle out
⊟ brighten

faeces *n*
waste matter, body waste, biosolids, excrement, droppings, dung, ordure, turd
TECHNICAL egesta, frass, scats, guano
OLD sir-reverence
FORMAL stool, excreta, rejectamenta
COLLOQ. flux, jobbie, doo-doo
SLANG poo, poop, crud; (*vulgar*) crap, shit
Related adjectives: stercoraceous, stercoral

fag *n*
1 CIGARETTE, filter-tip, king-size, high-tar, low-tar, roll-up, roll-your-own, smoke, whiff
COLLOQ. cig, ciggy, fag end, dog end, gasper, joint
SLANG cancer-stick, coffin-nail
2 NUISANCE, inconvenience, irritation, bind, bore, slog, grind, bother, chore, pest
COLLOQ. drag

fagged *adj*
exhausted, fatigued, weary, worn out, jaded, wasted
COLLOQ. all in, beat, knackered, on your last legs, deadbeat, done (in), whacked, bushed, burnt out, dog-tired, ready to drop, zonked, jiggered; *N Am* pooped (out), tuckered out; *Aust & NZ* beaten, euchred (out)
⊟ refreshed

fail *v*
1 GO WRONG, be unsuccessful, break down, collapse, miscarry, abort, fall through, fall down, founder, come to grief, come to nothing, get nowhere, underachieve
COLLOQ. flop, fold, flunk, not come off, not make it, not come up to scratch, fall flat, bottle it, blow it, blow your chances, bite the dust, crash and burn, come a cropper, come unstuck, come unglued, come undone, not come up with the goods, fizzle out, score an own goal; *N Am* bomb; *Aust & NZ* come a gutser
2 *fail to pay the bill*
omit, neglect, forget, not do something
3 LET DOWN, disappoint, leave, desert, neglect, abandon
FORMAL forsake
4 *the engine failed*
break down, go wrong, stop, not work, cut out, not start
FORMAL malfunction
COLLOQ. pack up, crash, play up, go on the blink, go kaput, go phut; *N Am* go on the fritz; *Aust* go bung
SLANG conk out
5 *the business failed*
collapse, founder, go bankrupt, go under, become insolvent, sink
COLLOQ. fold, flop, tank, crash, go bust, go broke, go to the wall, go into the red; *N Am* go belly-up
6 *his health failed*
weaken, fade, wane, ebb, sink, collapse, flag, decline, dwindle, diminish, decay, deteriorate, droop
⊟ **1** succeed **4** work **5** prosper
■ **without fail**
without exception, unfailingly, constantly, regularly, dependably, conscientiously, reliably, faithfully, predictably, punctually, religiously
COLLOQ. like clockwork
⊟ unpredictably, unreliably

> **QUOTATIONS**
> I think I fail a bit less than everyone else
> JACK NICKLAUS

SYNONYM NUANCES

sense 1
Go wrong and **be unsuccessful** can be used to describe a wide variety of things that do not go as intended: *servicemen died when an invasion exercise went wrong*, whereas **break down** suggests that something has ceased functioning: *the negotiations broke*

down. You could use **fall through** of plans which have come to little or no result, whilst **miscarry** has more to do with not achieving the intended end: *the plot miscarried and we were caught*.

Collapse suggests a more dramatic or sudden failure: *war was declared when peace talks collapsed*. **Abort**, on the other hand, implies bringing to an end prematurely and usually deliberately. **Fall down** might be used of a less deliberate failure and could be used where a cause is being identified: *where the theory fell down was in its assessment of the prospects of revolution*. The terms **founder** and **come to grief** similarly suggest failing through encountering a major setback or disaster: *many geniuses have foundered due to their lack of direction; the scheme came to grief because of entrenched opposition*.

Come to nothing and **get nowhere** are more suggestive of never actually getting underway, and hint at the frustration involved: *despite his plans, his attempts to write the novel came to nothing*.

failing *n*, *prep*
♦ *n*
weakness, foible, fault, defect, imperfection, flaw, blemish, drawback, deficiency, shortcoming, failure, lapse, error, weak spot
⊟ strength, advantage
♦ *prep*
in the absence of, lacking, without, in default of, wanting

failure *n*
1 *our efforts ended in failure*
lack of success, defeat, collapse, breakdown, meltdown, downfall, miscarriage, abortion, frustration, coming to nothing
COLLOQ. flop, washout, let-down, mess
2 *the plan was a failure*
disappointment, misfortune, disaster, calamity, miss, fiasco, debacle
COLLOQ. flop, hash, botch, washout, shambles, slip-up, no go, wipeout
SLANG cock-up, balls-up, screw-up
3 *his failure to return home*
omission, neglect, negligence, disregard, oversight, forgetfulness, default
FORMAL dereliction, remissness
4 *feel that you are a failure*
loser, born loser, misfit, reject, victim
COLLOQ. dropout, non-starter, washout, write-off, no-hoper, also-ran, flop, has-been, dead loss, waste of space
5 *the failure of the machine*
breakdown, cutting-out, shutdown, stopping, stalling
FORMAL malfunction, malfunctioning
COLLOQ. crash, packing-up
SLANG conking-out
6 *the failure of the business*
collapse, bankruptcy, ruin, insolvency, foundering
COLLOQ. crash, folding, flop, going under, going to the wall
7 *the failure of his health*
weakening, fading, decline, sinking, flagging, waning, ebbing, collapse, breakdown, deterioration
⊟ **1, 2** success **3** observance **4** success **6** prosperity

faint *adj*, *v*, *n*
♦ *adj*
1 SLIGHT, weak, feeble, soft, low, hushed, quiet, muffled, subdued, muted, faded, bleached, mild, light, pale, dull, dim, hazy, indistinct, unclear, obscure, blurred, vague
2 *I feel faint*
dizzy, giddy, unsteady, lightheaded, weak, feeble, exhausted
COLLOQ. woozy
3 *a faint smile*
slight, feeble, weak, unenthusiastic, half-hearted
⊟ **1** strong, clear

♦ *v*
black out, lose consciousness, pass out, collapse, drop
OLD swoon; *Scot* swelt
COLLOQ. flake out, keel over
♦ *n*
blackout, loss of consciousness, collapse, unconsciousness
TECHNICAL syncope
OLD swoon

faint-hearted *adj*
timid, timorous, weak, lily-livered, spiritless,
diffident, half-hearted, irresolute, cowardly, craven, fearful,
scared, white-livered, spineless, weak-spirited,
weak-kneed, soft, jittery
FORMAL pusillanimous
COLLOQ. yellow, chicken, chicken-hearted,
chicken-livered, gutless, wimpish, wussy, yellow-bellied,
showing the white feather
F3 courageous, confident

faintly *adv*
slightly, vaguely, a little, a bit, somewhat,
weakly, feebly, softly

fair[1] *adj*
1 JUST, equitable, square, even-handed,
dispassionate, impartial, objective, disinterested, unbiased,
unprejudiced, detached, right, proper,
above board, lawful, legitimate, honest, trustworthy,
upright, honourable
COLLOQ. on the level, straight up, legit, kosher, going/
done/played by the book
2 *a fair number; a fair chance of success*
reasonable, moderate, respectable, satisfactory, modest,
decent, sporting
3 FAIR-HAIRED, fair-headed, blond(e), yellow, light, light-
haired, golden, flaxen
4 *fair skin*
pale, cream, light, white, ivory
5 ADEQUATE, sufficient, middling, not bad, all right,
satisfactory, acceptable, tolerable, reasonable, passable,
mediocre
COLLOQ. OK, so-so
6 *fair weather*
fine, dry, sunny, bright, clear, warm, cloudless, unclouded
F3 1 unfair, unjust **3** dark, brunette **5** excellent, poor **6**
inclement, cloudy

SYNONYM NUANCES

sense 1
Just is a fairly general synonym of fair, while **equitable**
has more to do with natural or moral laws and the idea
of treating everyone the same way: *equitable social and
economic policies*. **Even-handed** and **impartial** describe
a lack of favouritism: *the reports are politically impartial*,
and the terms **dispassionate**, **detached**, **objective**,
disinterested, **unbiased** and **unprejudiced** may likewise
be appropriately used of being unaffected by personal
feelings: *dispassionate, professional judgement; the
detached scientific observer is a myth.*
   The terms **right** and **proper** return to the idea of moral
correctness and imply approval of this: *it is only right
that we should be sent a bill for the damage we caused.*
The terms **above board**, **lawful** and **legitimate** are all
suggestive of fairness with an official element of legality,
whilst **honest** and **trustworthy** are more general terms
which have more to do with being morally
irreproachable. Similarly, **upright** and **honourable** are
approving terms, which can be used to describe
something or someone principled: *upright Victorians
with a strong sense of family.*

---

fair[2] *n*
1 *a county fair*
market, craft fair, bazaar, exchange, fete, festival,
carnival, gala
Related adjective: nundinal

2 *a trade fair*
exhibition, show, exposition, trade fair
COLLOQ. expo

fairly *adv*
1 QUITE, rather, somewhat, reasonably, tolerably, passably,
moderately, adequately, pretty
2 POSITIVELY, absolutely, impartially, really, fully, veritably
3 JUSTLY, equitably, honestly, objectively, unbiasedly,
impartially, neutrally, properly, legally, lawfully
F3 3 unfairly

fair-minded *adj*
fair, just, equitable, square, even-handed, dispassionate,
impartial, objective, disinterested, unbiased, unprejudiced,
detached, right, proper, honest, trustworthy, upright,
honourable
COLLOQ. on the level, straight up

fairness *n*
justice, equitableness, equity, even-handedness,
unbiasedness, impartiality, legitimacy, rightfulness,
rightness, uprightness, disinterestedness, decency,
legitimateness
F3 unfairness

fairy *n*
elf, pixie, imp, brownie, sandman, leprechaun, sprite,
Robin Goodfellow, Puck, hob, hobgoblin, nymph, rusalka,
peri, *fée*, Mab
OLD faerie, fay

fairy tale *n*
1 FAIRY STORY, folk-tale, myth, romance, fiction, fantasy
2 LIE, untruth, invention, fabrication
COLLOQ. fib, cock-and-bull story, tall story

faith *n*
1 BELIEF, trust, reliance, dependence, conviction,
confidence, assurance
FORMAL credit, credence
2 RELIGION, denomination, persuasion, church, belief,
creed, teaching, doctrine, dogma, sect
3 FAITHFULNESS, fidelity, loyalty, obedience, commitment,
devotion, dedication, honour, sincerity, honesty,
truthfulness
OLD allegiance, fealty
F3 1 mistrust, uncertainty **3** unfaithfulness, treachery,
betrayal

QUOTATIONS
And his disciples came to him, and awoke him, saying,
Lord, save us: we perish. And he saith unto them, Why
are ye fearful, O ye of little faith?
   Bible, St Matthew

Back of every creation, supporting it like an arch, is faith
   HENRY MILLER, *The Air-Conditioned Nightmare*

---

faithful *adj, n*
♦ *adj*
1 LOYAL, devoted, committed, dedicated, staunch,
steadfast, constant, trusty, trustworthy, reliable,
dependable, unwavering, unflagging, unswerving,
obedient, true
2 *a faithful description*
accurate, precise, exact, strict, close, true, truthful
F3 1 disloyal, treacherous **2** inaccurate, vague
♦ *n*
adherents, followers, supporters, believers, congregation,
communicants, brethren

faithfully *adv*
1 LOYALLY, devotedly, staunchly, firmly, steadfastly,
constantly, reliably, dependably
2 ACCURATELY, precisely, exactly, strictly, closely, truly
F3 1 disloyally **2** inaccurately

faithfulness *n*
1 LOYALTY, fidelity, devotion, dedication, commitment,
allegiance, steadfastness, constancy, trustworthiness,
reliability, dependability, staunchness

OLD fealty
2 ACCURACY, closeness, exactness, strictness, scrupulousness
E∃ 1 disloyalty, treachery **2** inaccuracy

faithless *adj*
1 DISLOYAL, unfaithful, inconstant, fickle, false, false-hearted, unreliable, untrue, untrustworthy, untruthful, traitorous, treacherous, adulterous
FORMAL perfidious
2 UNBELIEVING, doubting, disbelieving, agnostic, atheistic
FORMAL nullifidian
E∃ 1 faithful **2** believing

faithlessness *n*
unfaithfulness, disloyalty, deceit, infidelity, fickleness, inconstancy, treachery, betrayal, adultery, apostasy
FORMAL perfidy
E∃ 1 faithfulness

fake *adj, v, n*
♦ *adj*
forged, counterfeit, false, spurious, pseudo, bogus, fraudulent, assumed, sham, artificial, simulated, mock, faux, imitation, reproduction, ersatz
FORMAL affected
COLLOQ. phoney, pseud, pretend
E∃ genuine
♦ *v*
forge, fabricate, counterfeit, copy, pirate, imitate, simulate, feign, sham, pretend, put on, assume, fudge
FORMAL affect
COLLOQ. phoney
♦ *n*
forgery, copy, reproduction, replica, imitation, mountebank, simulation, sham, counterfeit, hoax, fraud, impostor, charlatan; *Aust & NZ* bodgie
COLLOQ. phoney, quack

fall *v, n*
♦ *v*
1 TUMBLE, stumble, trip, fall down, slip, topple (over), keel over, collapse, slump, crash, slide, pitch (forward)
COLLOQ. *Aust & NZ* come a gutser
2 DESCEND, go down, come down, drop, slope, incline, slant, slide, sink, dive, plunge, plummet, nose-dive, pitch
OLD (*Shakesp*) precipitate
3 DECREASE, lessen, decline, go down, diminish, dwindle, fall off, subside, recede, ebb, slump, plummet, plunge, dive, nose-dive
4 *fall ill*
become, get, grow (into), turn, come to be
5 *fall in battle*
be killed, die, perish, lose your life, be lost
FORMAL be slain
6 *the town fell in the battle*
lose control, be defeated, be conquered, be taken, surrender, yield, capitulate, submit, give in, pass into enemy hands
FORMAL be vanquished
7 *my birthday falls on a Tuesday this year*
happen, occur, take place, come about
E∃ 2 rise **3** increase
♦ *n*
1 TUMBLE, stumble, trip, topple, keeling-over, collapse, slip, slide, crash
COLLOQ. *Aust & NZ* gutzer
2 DROP, fall-off, decrease, decline, cut, reduction, lessening, dwindling, slump, descent, depreciation, crash, plunge, plummeting, nose-dive
3 DEFEAT, capture, conquest, overthrow, loss of control, downfall, collapse, ruin, failure, destruction, surrender, capitulation, submission, yielding, giving-in, resignation
FORMAL demise
4 *the fall of humanity*
sin, original sin, disobedience, wrongdoing, offence
FORMAL transgression
5 WATERFALL, falls, cascade, chute, cataract, torrent

■ **fall apart**
1 *the old clothes fell apart*
break, break into pieces, fall to bits/pieces, come/go to pieces, go to bits, break up, come away, shatter, disintegrate, collapse, dissolve, crumble, decompose, decay, rot
2 CRACK UP, break down, lose control, go to pieces, have a nervous breakdown
■ **fall asleep**
pass into sleep, drift off, drop off, doze (off)
COLLOQ. nod off, flake out, go out like a light
■ **fall away**
1 SLOPE DOWN, slope away, go down, drop (away)
2 DECLINE, dwindle, drop off
■ **fall back**
retreat, withdraw, recoil, draw back, pull back, back off, disengage, depart
■ **fall back on**
resort to, make use of, have recourse to, use, employ, turn to, look to, call on, call into play
■ **fall behind**
lag (behind), trail, straggle, drop back, not keep up
E∃ keep up, make progress, keep pace
■ **fall down**
fail, break down, be unsuccessful, collapse, founder, come to nothing
COLLOQ. flop, not come up to scratch, come a cropper, come unstuck, come unglued
■ **fall for**
1 FALL IN LOVE WITH, be attached to, become infatuated with, become besotted with, desire, take to
COLLOQ. fancy, be crazy about, have a crush on, fall head over heels in love with
2 ACCEPT, be taken in by, be fooled by, be deceived by
COLLOQ. swallow, buy
■ **fall in**
1 CAVE IN, come down, collapse, crash, give way, subside, sink
2 LINE UP, get in(to) formation, stand in line
FORMAL array
■ **fall in with**
1 AGREE WITH, go along with, accept, comply with, co-operate with, support
FORMAL assent to
2 BECOME FRIENDS WITH, get involved with, go around with
COLLOQ. hang with, hang about/around/out with
■ **fall off**
decrease, lessen, drop (off), slump, decline, deteriorate, worsen, slow, slacken
COLLOQ. crash
■ **fall on**
attack, descend on, set upon, lay into, pounce on, snatch, assail, assault
■ **fall out**
quarrel, argue, squabble, bicker, fight, clash, disagree, differ
E∃ agree
■ **fall through**
come to nothing, go wrong, fail, miscarry, abort, founder, collapse, come to grief
E∃ come off, succeed
■ **fall to**
1 *the responsibility fell to her*
be the duty of, be the responsibility of, be an opportunity for, be the task of
2 APPLY YOURSELF, begin, get stuck in, set about, set to, start
FORMAL commence

fallacious *adj*
false, wrong, untrue, incorrect, mistaken, deceptive, erroneous, inaccurate, inexact, illogical, misleading, spurious, delusive, delusory, illusory, fictitious
FORMAL casuistical, sophistic, sophistical
E∃ correct, true

fallacy *n*

misconception, misapprehension, miscalculation, misjudgement, delusion, mistake, mistaken belief, error, flaw, inconsistency, falsehood, false idea, illusion, myth
formal casuistry, sophism, sophistry
TECHNICAL equivocation, idolum, ignoratio elenchi, illicit process of the major/minor, undistributed middle
OLD idolism
⊟ truth

fallen *adj*

1 *fallen in battle*
killed, murdered, died, dead, lost, perished, slaughtered
FORMAL slain
2 *fallen women*
immoral, loose, promiscuous, degenerate, shamed, disgraced
⊟ 2 chaste

fallibility *n*

imperfection, failing, weakness, mortality, inaccuracy, unreliability
⊟ infallibility, inerrancy

fallible *adj*

imperfect, errant, erring, frail, weak, flawed, human, mortal, ignorant, uncertain, unreliable
⊟ infallible

fallow *adj*

uncultivated, unploughed, unplanted, unsown, undeveloped, unused, idle, inactive, unproductive, dormant, resting, barren, lea

false *adj*

1 WRONG, incorrect, mistaken, untrue, erroneous, inaccurate, inexact, misleading, faulty, invalid, illusory
FORMAL fallacious
2 ARTIFICIAL, synthetic, imitation, simulated, mock, fake, faux, counterfeit, fraudulent, forged, fabricated, invented, feigned, pretended, sham, bogus, assumed, fictitious
COLLOQ. phoney, pretend, trumped-up
3 *false friends*
disloyal, unfaithful, faithless, lying, unreliable, deceitful, dishonest, insincere, untrustworthy, hypocritical, two-faced, double-dealing, treacherous, traitorous
FORMAL duplicitous, perfidious
⊟ 1 true, right **2** real, genuine **3** faithful, reliable, genuine

---

SYNONYM NUANCES

sense 1
The terms **incorrect**, **inaccurate** and **faulty** are suggestive of error, especially where information or conclusion is concerned: *your theory about what happened is incorrect*; *you gave me inaccurate information*. This idea is continued with **mistaken** and **erroneous**, which are further suggestive of something being misconstrued or misapprehended: *erroneous assumptions*. **Untrue**, on the other hand, could be used of something that is not genuine, but not necessarily through error: *an untrue depiction of life in that era*.

Inexact is perhaps a less marked term to use, since it suggests a lack of precision rather than complete falseness: *an inexact calculation of the costs*. You may use **misleading** of something that prompts a wrong conclusion, giving the term an inherently negative tone: *the misleading use of figures by politicians*. **Invalid**, on the other hand, has more to do with a lack of legitimacy given accepted facts: *an invalid argument*; *the test results were invalid*, whereas **illusory** would be used to convey a deceptive element: *access to information remains an illusory right*.

---

falsehood *n*

untruth, lie, story, fairy story, fiction, fabrication, invention, untruthfulness, deceit, deception, dishonesty, insincerity, hypocrisy, two-facedness, double dealing, treachery
TECHNICAL perjury
FORMAL duplicity, perfidy

COLLOQ. fib, porky, tall story
SLANG (*vulgar*) bullshit
⊟ truth, truthfulness

falsely *adv*

1 WRONGLY, wrongfully, incorrectly, mistakenly, by mistake, erroneously, in error
FORMAL fallaciously
2 INSINCERELY, hypocritically, dishonestly, deceitfully, deviously, treacherously, artificially, fraudulently
⊟ 1 truly, correctly **2** sincerely, genuinely

falsetto *n*

high voice, high pitch, high note, shrillness

falsification *n*

alteration, tampering, distortion, perversion, misrepresentation, change, adulteration, deceit, forgery
FORMAL dissimulation

falsify *v*

alter, tamper with, doctor, distort, adulterate, twist, pervert, misrepresent, misstate, forge, counterfeit, fake, rig, fiddle, manipulate, massage
COLLOQ. cook

falter *v*

1 TOTTER, stumble, be unsteady, be shaky
2 *falter while talking*
stammer, stutter, stumble
COLLOQ. fluff your lines
3 HESITATE, waver, vacillate, delay, flinch, quail, shake, tremble, flag, fail
COLLOQ. shilly-shally, dilly-dally, be in two minds, sit on the fence, drag your feet, take your time

faltering *adj*

uncertain, hesitant, unsteady, weak, tentative, irresolute, stammering, stumbling, timid, broken, failing, flagging
⊟ firm, strong

fame *n*

renown, celebrity, stardom, prominence, distinction, eminence, notability, note, illustriousness, glory, honour, greatness, importance, reputation, repute, name, kudos, esteem

famed *adj*

renowned, well-known, widely-known, famous, recognized, noted, prominent, celebrated, acclaimed, esteemed
⊟ unknown

familiar *adj*

1 EVERYDAY, usual, routine, repeated, conventional, household, common, commonplace, ordinary, accustomed, customary, frequent, habitual, run-of-the-mill, well-known, known, recognized, recognizable, unmistakable
2 INTIMATE, close, near, dear, confidential, friendly, informal, free, free-and-easy, easy, relaxed, casual, comfortable, sociable, open, natural, unceremonious, unreserved
COLLOQ. pally, chummy
3 *familiar with the procedure*
aware, acquainted, abreast, knowledgeable, versed, conversant, well up, au fait, *au courant*
COLLOQ. clued up, genned up, up to speed
4 FORWARD, over-familiar, over-friendly, presumptuous, impertinent, bold, disrespectful
COLLOQ. smarmy
⊟ 1 unfamiliar, strange **2** formal, reserved **3** unfamiliar, ignorant

familiarity *n*

1 INTIMACY, liberty, closeness, nearness, friendliness, ease, casualness, sociability, openness, naturalness, informality, unceremoniousness
COLLOQ. palliness, chumminess
2 AWARENESS, acquaintance, experience, skill, knowledge, understanding, comprehension, grasp, mastery

3 FORWARDNESS, over-familiarity, over-friendliness, presumption, liberty, liberties, impertinence, boldness, disrespect, impudence, intrusiveness
COLLOQ. pushiness

> **PROVERBS**
> Familiarity breeds contempt

> **QUOTATIONS**
> Familiarity breeds contempt – and children
> MARK TWAIN

familiarize v
accustom, acclimatize, make familiar, make aware, make acquainted, acquaint, teach, school, train, coach, instruct, indoctrinate, prime, brief
FORMAL habituate
COLLOQ. clue up, gen up, get/keep up to speed

family n
1 RELATIVES, relations, household, nuclear family, extended family, one-parent family, single-parent family, next of kin, kin, kindred, kinsmen, people, parents, your own flesh and blood, you and yours, ancestors, forebears, children, offspring, issue, progeny, descendants, scions
COLLOQ. folk, little ones, kids, kiddies, patter of tiny feet
2 CLAN, tribe, race, dynasty, house, pedigree, ancestry, parentage, descent, line, lineage, extraction, blood, stock, strain, birth
3 CLASS, group, order, species, genus, type, subclass, kind, classification
TECHNICAL stirps
■ **family tree**
ancestry, pedigree, genealogy, line, lineage, descent, extraction, background

> **QUOTATIONS**
> The family – that dear octopus from whose tentacles we never quite escape
> DODIE SMITH, *Dear Octopus*

Members of a family include:

ancestor	grandchild	old man
aunt	grand-daughter	parent
brother	grandfather	sibling
cousin	grandmother	sister
colloq. dad	*colloq.* granny	son
colloq. daddy	grandparent	spouse
daughter	grandson	stepbrother
descendant	half-brother	stepchild
father	half-sister	*colloq.* stepdad
forebear	heir	stepfather
forefather	husband	stepmother
foster-child	*N Am colloq.*	*colloq.* stepmum
foster-parent	mom	step-parent
godchild	mother	stepsister
god-daughter	*colloq.* mum	twin-brother
godfather	*colloq.* mummy	twin-sister
godmother	nanny	uncle
godson	nephew	wife
colloq. gran	niece	
colloq. grandad	offspring	

---

famine n
starvation, hunger, malnutrition, lack, deprivation, scarcity, shortage of food, dearth, death
FORMAL destitution, want, exiguousness
E3 plenty

famished adj
starved, starving, famishing, ravenous, hungry, undernourished, voracious
E3 sated

famous adj
well-known, famed, renowned, celebrated, acclaimed, world-famous, noted, great, distinguished, illustrious, eminent, honoured, respected, esteemed, glorious, legendary, legend, remarkable, notable, popular, A-list, prominent, signal, venerable, having (made) a name for yourself, your name on everyone's lips, notorious, infamous
E3 unheard-of, unknown, obscure, Z-list

> **QUOTATIONS**
> In the future, everybody will be famous for fifteen minutes
> ANDY WARHOL

> **SYNONYM NUANCES**
>
> **Famed** is an appropriate word to use when suggesting a specific cause of someone's or something's renown: *a city famed for its hospitality*. This idea continues with **acclaimed**, which carries the further notion of enthusiastic approval: *the acclaimed production of Madam Butterfly*. **Popular** also implies being much liked, if more unofficially: *the most popular singer of his day*. **Eminent** is a more formal, restrained term to use: *eminent scientists of the day*.
>
> **Honoured** is suggestive of something that has attracted plaudits, while **venerable** emphasizes that something is worthy of reverence. **Glorious**, although it again implies distinction, is more emotive and highly marked with approval: *the country's glorious history*. Both **notorious** and **infamous**, however, carry a disapproving tone, and suggest being widely known for your misdeeds rather than good works. The terms **legendary** and **legend** could be used of someone or something long-established, and have connotations of an exaggerated fame: *the legendary blues singer*. **Remarkable** has more to do with being singular in one's achievements and is fairly approbatory in tone: *a remarkable phase in the nation's history*.
>
> **Signal** is not particularly marked in tone, and returns to the idea of being singularly conspicuous and significant: *his expulsion from All Souls was the signal point of his academic career*.

famously adv
1 NOTABLY, eminently, prominently, conspicuously, popularly, notoriously, infamously
2 *get on famously*
well, greatly, happily, wonderfully, superbly, brilliantly, splendidly
COLLOQ. swimmingly

fan[1] n
football fans
enthusiast, admirer, supporter, backer, follower, adherent, devotee, addict, lover
FORMAL aficionado
COLLOQ. buff, fiend, freak, nut
SLANG groupie

fan[2] v, n
♦ v
1 COOL, ventilate, air, air-condition, air-cool, aerate, blow, freshen, refresh, winnow
2 INCREASE, provoke, intensify, stimulate, incite, instigate, rouse, arouse, excite, agitate, ignite, kindle, stir up, work up, whip up
♦ n
extractor, extractor fan, ventilator, air-conditioner, blower, cooler, air cooler, propeller, vane, wing, winnow, punka, Colmar
TECHNICAL flabellum, rhipidion
■ **fan out**
spread (out), move out, open (out), unfold, unfurl

fanatic n

zealot, devotee, enthusiast, addict, maniac, visionary, radical, bigot, extremist, militant, activist, fundamentalist
COLLOQ. fiend, freak

fanatical adj

overenthusiastic, extreme, passionate, zealous, fervent, burning, mad, wild, frenzied, rabid, obsessive, fundamentalist, activist, militant, immoderate, extremist, radical, single-minded, bigoted, narrow-minded, dogmatic
E3 moderate, unenthusiastic

fanaticism n

extremism, monomania, single-mindedness, fundamentalism, activism, militancy, obsessiveness, madness, wildness, frenzy, infatuation, bigotry, narrow-mindedness, zeal, zealotry, fervour, dogmatism, enthusiasm, dedication
E3 moderation

fancier n

breeder, keeper, enthusiast, fan, devotee, follower
COLLOQ. fiend, freak

fanciful adj

1 IMAGINARY, mythical, flighty, fabulous, fantastic, legendary, visionary, romantic, unrealistic, unreal, make-believe, illusory, fairytale, airy-fairy, vaporous, whimsical, wild
2 ELABORATE, ornate, decorated, extravagant, exotic, wild, creative, imaginative, fantastic, curious
E3 1 real, ordinary, realistic 2 simple, plain

fancy v, n, adj

◆ v

1 LIKE, want, feel like, wish (for), prefer, favour, desire, take a liking to, take to, go for, have in mind, not mind, not say no to, long for, yearn for, covet
2 BE ATTRACTED TO, find attractive, desire, take to, go for, have a soft spot for, think the world of, be interested in, lust after
COLLOQ. have a crush on, have eyes for, be mad about, be wild about, be crazy about, want
SLANG have the hots for
3 THINK, conceive, imagine, dream of, picture, believe, suppose, reckon, guess
FORMAL conjecture, surmise
E3 1 dislike

◆ n

1 DESIRE, whim, caprice, craving, urge, want, wish, liking, fondness, longing, yearning, inclination, impulse, preference
FORMAL penchant, predilection
COLLOQ. itch, yen
2 NOTION, thought, idea, opinion, impression, imagination, creativity, dream, fantasy, vision, illusion, delusion
E3 1 dislike, aversion 2 fact, reality

◆ adj

elaborate, ornate, decorated, adorned, ornamented, embellished, rococo, baroque, elegant, extravagant, ostentatious, showy, lavish, fantastic, fanciful, far-fetched
E3 plain, ordinary, simple

■ **fancy yourself**

have a high opinion of yourself, flatter yourself
COLLOQ. think that you are the cat's whiskers/pyjamas, think that you are God's gift to someone

fanfare n

1 *a fanfare of trumpets*
flourish, trumpet call, trump, fanfarade
OLD tucket
2 *he arrived with little fanfare*
show, display, ostentation, publicity, flamboyance, pageantry, parade, fuss

fang n

tooth, prong, tusk, tang, venom-tooth

fantasize v

imagine, daydream, dream, hallucinate, invent, romance
COLLOQ. build castles in Spain/the air, live in a dream

fantastic adj

1 WONDERFUL, marvellous, sensational, superb, excellent, first-rate, tremendous, impressive, terrific, great, brilliant, incredible, unbelievable, amazing, remarkable, phenomenal, overwhelming, enormous, extreme
COLLOQ. top-notch, super, cool, magic, brill, smashing, ace, out of this world, neat
SLANG mega, wicked, radical
2 STRANGE, weird, odd, eccentric, bizarre, exotic, outlandish, extravagant, wild, absurd, fanciful, fabulous, imaginary, illusory, unreal, imaginative, visionary, romantic
E3 1 ordinary 2 real

fantastically adv

extremely, tremendously, terrifically, incredibly, unbelievably, amazingly, phenomenally

fantasy n

1 DREAM, daydream, reverie, pipe dream, nightmare, vision, hallucination, illusion, mirage, apparition, figment of the imagination, invention, fancy, flight of fancy, myth, story, speculation, delusion, misconception, creativity, imagination, originality, unreality, moonshine
COLLOQ. cloud-cuckoo-land, pie in the sky
2 IMAGINATION, imaginativeness, creativity, inventiveness, fancifulness, speculation, originality, inspiration, resourcefulness
E3 1 reality

far adv, adj

◆ adv
a long way, a good way, great distance, some distance, distantly, nowhere near, much, very much, greatly, considerably, extremely, markedly, decidedly, significantly, incomparably, immeasurably
COLLOQ. miles
E3 near, close

◆ adj
distant, far-off, faraway, far-flung, outlying, remote, inaccessible, secluded, out-of-the-way, godforsaken, removed, far-removed, further, opposite, other
COLLOQ. N Am in the boondocks/boonies; Aust (beyond) the black stump, back o' Bourke
E3 nearby, close, accessible

■ **far and wide**
extensively, far and near, widely, everywhere, in/from all places, all about, broadly, worldwide

■ **far out**
extreme, strange, exotic, radical, bizarre, unusual, unconventional, unorthodox, weird, outlandish
COLLOQ. way out
E3 orthodox, conventional

■ **go far**
succeed, be successful, achieve success, get on
COLLOQ. get on in the world, make your mark, make a name for yourself, arrive, go places

■ **so far**
1 UP TO NOW, up to this point, up to the present moment, till now, to date
FORMAL thus far, hitherto
2 TO A CERTAIN EXTENT, to a limited extent, to some extent, within limits

faraway adj

1 DISTANT, remote, outlying, far-flung, far-off, far
2 DREAMY, absent-minded, absent, abstracted, preoccupied, lost
E3 1 nearby 2 alert

farce n

1 COMEDY, slapstick, buffoonery, satire, parody, burlesque, burletta, exode, *lazzo*, mime, *opera bouffe*
OLD jig
2 TRAVESTY, sham, parody, joke, mockery, ridiculousness, absurdity, nonsense, pantomime
COLLOQ. shambles

farcical *adj*
ridiculous, absurd, ludicrous, preposterous, nonsensical, stupid, laughable, comic, silly, derisory, diverting
E3 sensible

fare *n, v*
♦ *n*
1 *pay your fare*
charge, cost, price, fee, ticket, passage
2 FOOD, eatables, nourishment, nutriment, rations, meals, diet, menu, board, table
OLD provisions
FORMAL sustenance, victuals, viands
3
COLLOQ. nosh, eats
♦ *v*
be, do, get along, get on, go, go on, happen, make out, manage, proceed, progress, prosper, succeed, turn out

farewell *n, interj*
♦ *n*
goodbye, adieu, leave-taking, *au revoir*
FORMAL valediction, valedictory
♦ *interj*
goodbye, adieu, *au revoir, auf Wiedersehen, ciao, adios, arrivederci, sayonara*
COLLOQ. cheerio, bye, bye-bye, cheers, see you (later), see you around, be seeing you, all the best, mind how you go, take care, have a nice day, ta-ta, so long; N Am later

far-fetched *adj*
implausible, unrealistic, improbable, unlikely, dubious, incredible, unbelievable, unconvincing, fantastic, fanciful, preposterous, crazy
E3 plausible

farm *n, v*
♦ *n*
ranch, farmstead, grange, croft, homestead, station, co-operative, land, farmland, holding, acreage, acres
♦ *v*
cultivate, till, plough, work the land, plant, operate
■ **farm out**
subcontract, pass/give to others, delegate, contract out, outsource

---

Types of farm include:

arable farm	free-range farm	sheep station
biodynamic farm	hill farm	skyscraper farm
cattle ranch	mixed farm	smallholding
croft	organic farm	stud farm
dairy farm	ostrich farm	turkey farm
deer farm	pig farm	vertical farm
estate	plantation	wave farm
fish farm	server farm	wind farm

---

farmer *n*
agriculturist, crofter, smallholder, husbandman, rancher, grazier, yeoman, stock-farmer, mailer, *métayer, campesino, estanciero*; Scot store farmer; N Am sodbuster, sharecropper; *Aust & NZ* cockatoo, cocky
TECHNICAL agronomist

farming *n*
agriculture, cultivation, husbandry, tilling, crofting
TECHNICAL agribusiness, agronomy, agroscience, geoponics

far-off *adj*
faraway, far, distant, remote, outlying, far-flung
E3 near

farrago *n*
hotchpotch, hodgepodge, jumble, medley, miscellany, mixture, mélange, pot-pourri, hash, mishmash, gallimaufry, salmagundi
COLLOQ. dog's breakfast

far-reaching *adj*
broad, extensive, widespread, sweeping, important, wide-ranging, wide, comprehensive, thorough, global, significant, momentous
E3 limited, restricted, insignificant

far-sighted *adj*
wise, forward-looking, far-seeing, shrewd, discerning, cautious, acute, canny, provident, prudent
FORMAL circumspect, judicious, politic, prescient
E3 imprudent, unwise

farther *adj, adv*
♦ *adj*
further, more distant, remoter, more extreme
♦ *adv*
to a greater distance, to a more distant/remote/onward/advanced point

farthest *adj*
furthest, most distant, remotest, most extreme

fascia *n*
1 SIGN, panel, board, front
2 CONSOLE, panel, dashboard, instrument panel

fascinate *v*
absorb, engross, intrigue, delight, charm, allure, lure, draw, attract, entice, captivate, enchant, beguile, bewitch, spellbind, enthral, enrapture, rivet, transfix, hypnotize, mesmerize
E3 bore, repel

fascinated *adj*
absorbed, engrossed, curious, intrigued, delighted, charmed, enticed, spellbound, enthralled, entranced, captivated, bewitched, beguiled, hypnotized, mesmerized, infatuated, smitten
COLLOQ. hooked
E3 bored, uninterested

fascinating *adj*
intriguing, gripping, exciting, interesting, engaging, engrossing, irresistible, compelling, alluring, bewitching, captivating, enchanting, riveting, enticing, seductive, tempting, charming, absorbing, stimulating, delightful, mesmerizing
E3 boring, uninteresting

fascination *n*
interest, attraction, delight, appeal, lure, allure, compulsion, magnetism, pull, draw, charm, preoccupation, captivation, enchantment, spell, sorcery, magic
E3 boredom, repulsion

fascism *n*
autocracy, dictatorship, absolutism, authoritarianism, totalitarianism, Hitlerism, Falangism, Sinarchism

fascist *adj, n*
♦ *adj*
autocratic, absolutist, authoritarian, totalitarian, Hitlerist, Hitlerite, sinarchist
♦ *n*
autocrat, absolutist, authoritarian, totalitarian, Blackshirt, Hitlerite, Hitlerist, Brownshirt, Falangist, sinarchist

fashion *n, v*
♦ *n*
1 MANNER, way, method, mode, approach, style, system, shape, form, make, design, pattern, line, cut, look, appearance, type, sort, kind
2 VOGUE, trend, mode, style, fad, craze, custom, tendency, practice, convention
COLLOQ. rage, latest, in thing
3 COUTURE, clothes, clothes industry, haute couture, fashion business, high fashion, designer label
COLLOQ. rag trade

♦ *v*

create, form, shape, mould, model, build,
construct, manufacture, design, fit, tailor, alter, adjust,
adapt, suit

■ **after a fashion**

not very well, to some extent, to a certain extent, in a
manner of speaking

■ **in fashion**

fashionable, on-trend, chic, smart, elegant, stylish,
designer, modish, à la mode, in vogue, in, popular,
prevailing, current, latest, up-to-the-minute, up-to-date,
contemporary, modern
COLLOQ. trendy, all the rage, hot, natty, glitzy, ritzy,
snazzy, swanky, funky, hip, with it, swinging, cool,
dressed to the nines

■ **out of fashion**

unfashionable, outmoded, dated, out of date,
out, passé, old-fashioned, *démodé*, antiquated,
obsolete, unpopular
COLLOQ. old hat, square
E3 fashionable

QUOTATIONS

Fashion is only the attempt to realize Art in living forms
and social intercourse
OLIVER WENDELL HOLMES, *The Professor at the
Breakfast Table*

Every generation laughs at the old fashions, but follows
religiously the new
HENRY THOREAU, *Walden, or Life in the Woods*

SYNONYM NUANCES

noun sense 2
The term **vogue** is suggestive of what people are
preferring to do or wear at a certain time: *the vogue for
dressing down*, while **trend** similarly refers to an
inclination at a particular time, but suggests
something that is gradually increasing in
popularity: *the trend towards earlier retirement*. The term
tendency is similar, but might be used of a less
significant or marked fashion: *the growing tendency
towards eating out*.

   Mode, however, would be more appropriate to refer to
a particular way that something is done: *the dominant
literary mode in New York*, while **style** could refer to
the form something takes, but perhaps without the same
connotations of transitoriness: *the plain façade belies the
style and elegance of the interior*.

   Both **fad** and **craze** strongly suggest being currently
prevalent, with the further implication of being short-
lived: *the latest fad in clubland*. **Custom** and **practice**
suggest an accepted and possibly long-established
manner of doing things. **Convention**, likewise, is
suggestive of an established method or set of rules: *she
has made a virtue of flying in the face of business
convention*.

---

fashionable *adj*

chic, smart, elegant, stylish, designer,
modish, à la mode, in vogue, in, popular, prevailing,
current, on-trend, latest, up-to-the-minute, up-to-date,
contemporary, modern
COLLOQ. trendy, all the rage, hot, natty, glitzy, ritzy,
snazzy, swanky, funky, hip, with it, swinging, cool,
dressed to the nines
E3 unfashionable

fast¹ *adj, adv*

  ♦ *adj*

1 QUICK, swift, rapid, brisk, accelerated, speedy,
express, high-speed, hasty, hurried, flying
OLD fleet
COLLOQ. nippy
See Synonym nuances panel at **quick**.

2 *the fast life*

exciting, exhilarating, thrilling, wild, turbulent,
boisterous, riotous, shameless, self-indulgent, immoral,
dissipated
COLLOQ. action-packed
SLANG ripsnorting
E3 1 slow, unhurried **2** quiet, dull

  ♦ *adv*

quickly, swiftly, rapidly, speedily, hastily, hurriedly, in a
hurry, apace, presto
COLLOQ. like a flash, like a shot, as fast as your legs will
carry you, before you can say Jack Robinson, at a rate of
knots, hell for leather, like lightning, like greased lightning,
like the wind, like crazy, like mad, like the clappers, like
a bat out of hell, lickety-spit, pdq
E3 slowly, gradually

fast² *adj, adv*

  ♦ *adj*

1 FASTENED, shut, closed, secure, fixed, immovable,
immobile, firm, tight
2 *fast colours*
indelible, permanent, fixed
E3 1 loose **2** non-fast

  ♦ *adv*

1 FIRMLY, securely, tightly, immovably, fixedly, resolutely,
doggedly, stubbornly
2 *fast asleep*
sound, deeply, fully

fast³ *v, n*

  ♦ *v*

fast for religious reasons
go hungry, diet, slim, deny yourself, starve, refrain
FORMAL abstain

  ♦ *n*

fasting, diet, starvation, abstinence, hunger strike
E3 gluttony, self-indulgence

fasten *v*

1 FIX, affix, attach, clamp, grip, anchor, rivet, nail, pin,
clip, tack, seal, close, latch, shut, lock, bolt, secure, tie,
tether, hitch, bind, chain, link, interlock, connect, join,
unite, do up, button, zip up, lace, buckle
2 *fasten your attention*
focus, direct, concentrate, fix, rivet, point, aim, zero in
E3 1 unfasten, untie, undo

fastener

Types of fastener include:

alligator clip	hinge	rivet
bond	holder	screw
bulldog clip	hook	shoelace
button	hook-and-eye	split pin
catch	knot	staple
clasp	lace	stitch
clip	latch	stud
collar stud	link	tie
cotter	lock	toggle
crocodile clip	loop	treasury tag
cufflink	nail	Velcro®
eyelet	padlock	zip
frog	paperclip	*N Am* zipper
hasp	press stud	

---

fastidious *adj*

fussy, particular, finicky, hard-to-please, scrupulous, faddy,
discriminating, hypercritical, meticulous, precise,
punctilious, overnice, squeamish, difficult, dainty
COLLOQ. choosy, pernickety, picky; *N Am* persnickety
E3 undemanding

fat *adj, n*

  ♦ *adj*

1 PLUMP, overweight, obese, tubby, dumpy, stout, portly,
round, paunchy, well-endowed, pot-bellied, large, heavy,

solid, chubby, podgy, fleshy, fleshed, buxom, tubbish, squab, pursy; *Scot* sonsy, fozy
TECHNICAL steatopygous
OLD (*Shakesp*) gor-bellied
FORMAL rotund, corpulent
COLLOQ. beefy, flabby, gross, fat as a pig, porky, well-upholstered
2 FATTY, oily, greasy, rich
TECHNICAL lipoid, pinguid
FORMAL oleaginous, adipose, sebaceous
3 *a fat book*
thick, wide, broad, big, heavy, solid, substantial
4 *fat profits*
large, handsome, considerable, generous, siz(e)able
E3 1 thin, slim **2** low-fat **3** narrow, slim, thin **4** slim, meagre, miserable, poor
♦ *n*
1 FATNESS, obesity, plumpness, stoutness, solidness, bulk, chubbiness, overweight, paunch, pot (belly), blubber
TECHNICAL lipomatosis
FORMAL corpulence
COLLOQ. flab, spare tyre
2 *fats such as cream*
butter, margarine, cream, cheese, lard, suet, shortening, animal fat, vegetable fat, saturated fat, polyunsaturated fat, tallow, blubber, grease, oil, wax, dripping, lanolin; *Scot* creesh
TECHNICAL chylomicron, degras, deutoplasm, palmitin
OLD keech, kitchen-fee

SYNONYM NUANCES

adjective sense 1
Plump may be used to suggest roundness and softness in appearance, and has positive connotations; the term **chubby** is also suggestive of being round and soft: *she was pretty in a chubby sort of way.* **Podgy**, although similarly used of an endearing kind of plumpness, typical of young children, might also be used to suggest a slightly less appealing appearance: *the little one was podgy with puppy fat and had a front tooth missing.*
    The term **overweight** is more technical in tone, although it can be used in a euphemistic way, referring to weighing more than is recommended for your age and height. **Obese** shares this more clinical tone, but goes further by suggesting abnormal fatness: *being obese, it was not easy for them to climb stairs.*
    Tubby, on the other hand, conveys the idea of being round, almost barrel-like, while **dumpy** suggests shortness of stature as well as width. You could use **stout** and **solid** to hint at strength behind the large size, and the word **heavy** usually suggests solidity with weight (although it also might be used euphemistically). **Portly** too gives an impression of substantial but solid girth, and is unlikely to be used of the young. The term **round** suggests being as wide as your height, unlike **paunchy**, which is generally used to imply a large stomach, as is **pot-bellied**, although it tends to conjure up a more concentrated mass and sounds insulting if used of people.
    Well-endowed, however, while usually reserved to describe a man with large genitals or a woman with large breasts, might be used in a facetious way with regard to fatness. **Large** may be widely used to suggest general bigness, and again could be used as a vaguely euphemistic, polite term: *clothes for larger ladies*. Both **fleshy** and **fleshed** suggest fatness but often with a sensual implication: *fleshy thighs*, whilst **buxom** suggests the comeliness of women.

---

fatal *adj*
deadly, lethal, mortal, killing, incurable, malignant, terminal, final, destructive, calamitous, catastrophic, disastrous
E3 harmless

! **fatal** or **fateful**?
Fatal means 'causing death or disaster': *a fatal accident; She made the fatal mistake of telling him what she really thought. Fateful* means 'of great importance, having important consequences, etc', as in: *At last the fateful day arrived, the day she was to be married.*

---

fatalism *n*
resignation, stoicism, acceptance, passivity, endurance

fatalistic *adj*
resigned, reconciled, philosophical, stoical, patient, long-suffering, passive, submissive, yielding, defeatist
FORMAL acquiescent

fatality *n*
death, mortality, loss, casualty, dead, deadliness, lethality, disaster, catastrophe

fate *n*
destiny, providence, God's will, kismet, karma, chance, future, luck, fortune, horoscope, stars, lot, doom, end, issue, outcome, ruin, disaster, destruction, catastrophe, defeat, death
FORMAL predestiny

QUOTATIONS
I could never begin a poem: 'When I am dead' / In case it tempted Fate, and Fate gave way
ROGER McGOUGH, 'When I am dead'

---

fated *adj*
doomed, destined, predestined, preordained, unavoidable, inevitable, inescapable, certain, sure
FORMAL ineluctable, foreordained
E3 avoidable

fateful *adj*
crucial, critical, decisive, important, momentous, significant, pivotal
E3 unimportant

! **fateful** or **fatal**?
See panel at **fatal**.

---

fatefully *adv*
momentously, crucially, critically, decisively, importantly, significantly

father *n, v*
♦ *n*
1 PARENT, birth father, patriarch, ancestor
FORMAL begetter, procreator, progenitor, sire, paterfamilias, pater
COLLOQ. dad, daddy, da, pop, pa, papa, old man
Related adjective: paternal
2 ANCESTOR, patriarch, elder, forefather, forebear, predecessor, progenitor
3 FOUNDER, creator, originator, inventor, initiator, maker, architect, author, patron, leader, prime mover, guiding light
4 PRIEST, padre, pastor, parson, clergyman, minister, abbé, curé
♦ *v*
produce, engender, give life to
OLD beget, sire
FORMAL procreate

fatherland *n*
native land, home, homeland, land of your birth, mother-country, motherland, old country

fatherly *adj*
paternal, kind, kindly, affectionate, protective, supportive, benevolent, benign, tender, forbearing, indulgent, patriarchal
FORMAL avuncular
E3 cold, harsh, unkind

fathom *v*
1 MEASURE, gauge, plumb, sound, probe, estimate

2 UNDERSTAND, comprehend, grasp, see, perceive, work out, search out, interpret, penetrate, get to the bottom of
COLLOQ. get, twig, get the hang of, latch onto, rumble, suss out, get your head round

fathomless *adj*
deep, impenetrable, immeasurable, infinite, bottomless, endless, mysterious, enigmatic, complex, complicated, intricate

fatigue *n, v*
♦ *n*
tiredness, weariness, exhaustion, lethargy, listlessness, lassitude, weakness
FORMAL debility, enervation
F3 energy
♦ *v*
tire, wear out, weary, exhaust, drain, sap, tax, weaken, overwork
FORMAL debilitate, enervate
COLLOQ. take it out of
F3 invigorate, refresh

fatigued *adj*
exhausted, jaded, jiggered, overtired, tired, tired out, wasted, weary
COLLOQ. all in, beat, bushed, dead-beat, fagged (out), knackered, whacked, zonked, done in; *N Am* pooped (out), tuckered out; *Aust & NZ* beaten, euchred (out)
F3 refreshed

fatness *n*
plumpness, overweight, obesity, bulk, bulkiness, heaviness, largeness, tubbiness, stoutness, portliness, podginess, grossness, grease
TECHNICAL pinguidity, pinguitude
FORMAL corpulence, rotundity
COLLOQ. flab

fatten *v*
feed, feed up, nourish, nurture, build up, overfeed, flesh, lard, soil, cram, stuff, bloat, swell, fill out, spread, expand, widen, broaden, thicken
TECHNICAL pinguefy, saginate
OLD batten, battle, frank; (*Shakesp*) engross

fatty *adj*
fat, greasy, oily, creamy, buttery, fleshy, waxy
TECHNICAL pinguid, adipose, sebaceous, lipoid
FORMAL oleaginous, oleic, unctuous

fatuous *adj*
idiotic, foolish, silly, stupid, ludicrous, ridiculous, absurd, daft, inane, mindless, vacuous, moronic, puerile, brainless, lunatic, dense, asinine, weak-minded, witless
F3 sensible

fault *n, v*
♦ *n*
1 DEFECT, flaw, blemish, imperfection, deficiency, shortcoming, weak point, weakness, failing, foible, default, demerit, vice, beam
COLLOQ. bug, glitch, hitch
See Synonym nuances panel at **defect**.
2 ERROR, mistake, blunder, slip, lapse, negligence, omission, oversight
COLLOQ. slip-up, boob, booboo, fluff; *N Am* flub
SLANG goof
3 MISDEED, offence, wrong, wrongdoing, sin, delinquency, *culpa levis*, lapse, indiscretion, peccadillo
FORMAL misdemeanour
4 *it's your fault*
responsibility, accountability, liability, answerability, blameworthiness
FORMAL culpability
♦ *v*
find fault with, criticize, slate, censure, blame, call to account, judge, nag, carp, impeach, nibble, quarrel, reprehend, scold
OLD pinch
FORMAL impugn, inculpate

COLLOQ. pick holes in, knock, slam, pull to pieces
F3 praise, approve
■ **at fault**
(in the) wrong, blameworthy, to blame, responsible, accountable, guilty, at a loss, out
FORMAL culpable
■ **to a fault**
excessively, extremely, too much, inordinately, unduly, unnecessarily, disproportionately, in the extreme, to extremes, immoderately, out of all proportion
COLLOQ. over the top

fault-finding *n, adj*
♦ *n*
criticism, grumbling, complaining, complaint, carping, quibbling, cavilling, nagging, niggling, hypercriticism
FORMAL ultracrepidation
COLLOQ. finger-pointing, hair-splitting, nit-picking
F3 praise
♦ *adj*
critical, grumbling, nagging, captious, carping, cavilling, censorious, hypercritical
OLD pettifogging
FORMAL querulous, ultracrepidarian
COLLOQ. nit-picking
F3 complimentary

faultless *adj*
perfect, flawless, unblemished, without blemish, spotless, immaculate, unimpeachable, impeccable, unsullied, pure, blameless, exemplary, model, correct, accurate
F3 faulty, imperfect, flawed

faulty *adj*
1 NOT WORKING, defective, imperfect, damaged, out of order, out of action, broken
FORMAL malfunctioning, inoperative
COLLOQ. on the blink, bust, kaput, duff, wonky, playing up
SLANG conked out
2 FLAWED, defective, inaccurate, incorrect, wrong, erroneous, illogical, invalid, weak
FORMAL fallacious, casuistic
F3 1 working **2** sound

faux pas *n*
blunder, gaffe, indiscretion, mistake
FORMAL impropriety, solecism
COLLOQ. boob, booboo, clanger, slip-up, howler
SLANG goof

favour *n, v*
♦ *n*
1 APPROVAL, esteem, support, backing, commendation, sympathy, kindness, friendliness, goodwill, patronage, assistance, aid, favouritism, preference, partiality
FORMAL approbation
2 *he did me a favour*
kindness, act of kindness, service, good turn, good deed, courtesy, benefit
F3 1 disapproval
♦ *v*
1 PREFER, choose, select, opt for, like, pick, approve, support, back, recommend, endorse, advocate, champion, sanction, take kindly to
COLLOQ. go for, plump for
2 HELP, assist, aid, benefit, promote, encourage, pamper, spoil, indulge
FORMAL succour
F3 1 dislike **2** mistreat
■ **in favour of**
for, all for, pro, supporting, on the side of, backing, behind
F3 against

favourable *adj*
1 *a favourable reaction*
positive, sympathetic, agreeable, well-disposed, approving, complimentary, enthusiastic, friendly, amicable, kind, understanding, encouraging, reassuring, heartening

2 *a favourable impression*
positive, good, agreeable, pleasing, effective, promising
3 *favourable conditions*
good, advantageous, beneficial, promising, fair,
encouraging, convenient, suitable, appropriate, opportune
FORMAL auspicious, propitious
⊟ **1, 2** negative **3** unhelpful

favourably *adv*
well, positively, sympathetically, agreeably, approvingly,
enthusiastically, helpfully, advantageously, fortunately,
conveniently, opportunely, profitably
FORMAL auspiciously, propitiously
⊟ unfavourably

favoured *adj*
preferred, chosen, selected, recommended, favourite,
privileged, advantaged, blessed, élite
FORMAL predilected

favourite *adj, n*
♦ *adj*
preferred, favoured, pet, best-loved, most-liked, dearest,
beloved, treasured, chosen, great, esteemed, special
⊟ hated
♦ *n*
1 PREFERENCE, choice, first choice, number one, pick, pet,
beloved, darling, idol, minion, white boy, nostrum
OLD gracioso, peat
COLLOQ. blue-eyed boy, teacher's pet, the apple of your
eye, particular, best boy/girl, boyfriend, girlfriend, flavour
of the week/month; *N Am* fair-haired boy
SLANG fave, winger
2 CERTAINTY, odds-on favourite, nap, likely winner, form
horse
⊟ **1** bête noire, pet hate

favouritism *n*
nepotism, preferential treatment, preference, partiality,
prejudice, inequality, inequity, one-sidedness, partisanship,
bias, unfairness, injustice
⊟ impartiality, equality

fawn[1] *adj*
a fawn coat
beige, buff, yellowish-brown, pale brown, sand-coloured,
sandy, khaki

fawn[2] *v*
fawning over someone famous
flatter, grovel, bow and scrape, court, curry favour, dance
attendance, kowtow, pay court, ingratiate yourself, toady
FORMAL be obsequious to
COLLOQ. bootlick, crawl, creep, cringe, smarm, lick
someone's boots, suck up to, butter up, soft-soap, cosy up
(to); *N Am* cozy up (with)

fawning *adj*
servile, sycophantic, deferential, flattering, grovelling,
ingratiating, bowing and scraping, abject, toadying,
toadyish
OLD (*Shakesp*) knee-crooking
FORMAL obsequious, unctuous
COLLOQ. bootlicking, crawling, cringing
SLANG (*vulgar*) arse-licking
⊟ cold, proud

faze *v*
surprise, shock, startle, stun, shake, unnerve, unsettle,
dumbfound, dismay, disconcert, fluster, disturb, put off/
out, take aback, puzzle
FORMAL perturb
COLLOQ. rattle

fear *n, v*
♦ *n*
1 TERROR, dread, alarm, fright, panic, fearfulness, agitation,
apprehension, foreboding, dismay, distress, trembling,
shaking, quivering, phobia, aversion, horror, nightmare,
bête noire
OLD (*Spenser*) affray
FORMAL trepidation, consternation

2 ANXIETY, worry, concern, unease, uneasiness, qualms,
misgivings, disquiet, suspicion, doubt
FORMAL solicitude
3 AWE, reverence, respect, wonder, honour, fear of God,
terror, dread
FORMAL veneration
4 *no fear of being misunderstood*
chance, risk, likelihood, likeliness, possibility, probability,
prospect, expectation, scope
⊟ **1** courage, bravery, confidence **3** contempt
♦ *v*
1 BE AFRAID OF, be scared of, dread, shudder at, shrink
from, tremble at, lose your nerve, take fright at, have a
horror of, have a phobia about, panic
COLLOQ. have your heart in your mouth, your heart melts,
your stomach turns, get the wind up, be in a cold sweat,
be in a blue funk, freak out, lose your bottle
2 WORRY, be anxious about, be uneasy about, be
concerned about, have misgivings/qualms about,
tremble for
3 *fear God*
stand in awe of, revere, hold in reverence, reverence,
wonder at
FORMAL venerate
4 *I fear I can't help you*
be afraid, regret, suspect, expect, foresee, anticipate
COLLOQ. have a sneaking suspicion

> **QUOTATIONS**
> Let me assert my belief that the only thing that we have
> to fear is fear itself – nameless, unreasoning, unjustified
> terror that paralyses needed efforts to convert retreat into
> advance
> FRANKLIN D ROOSEVELT, US president, inaugural
> address 4 March 1933
>
> Doubt is a necessary precondition to meaningful action.
> Fear is the great mover in the end
> DONALD BARTHELME, *Sadness*, 'The Rise of
> Capitalism'

> **SYNONYM NUANCES**
>
> *noun sense 1*
> **Terror** may be used to refer to an extreme state of fear,
> whilst **dread** would be used of being scared of what
> might or will happen in future: *a dread of old age*.
> **Alarm**, on the other hand, is more suggestive of being
> alerted to danger, whereas **fright** implies a sudden
> reaction, and **panic** suggests a chaotic loss of control: *if
> there was a fire there could be panic and havoc*.
> **Fearfulness** may be used of a continuous state of being
> afraid, whilst **agitation** is more suggestive of being
> perturbed through fear.
> Both **apprehension** and **foreboding** contain the idea
> of anxiety about future events, though the latter suggests
> a greater intensity: *a foreboding of imminent danger*.
> You can use **dismay** to emphasize elements of upset
> and concern: *I watched with dismay as the boat sank*,
> but **distress** has greater implications of severe mental
> suffering: *the threats caused me great distress*.
> **Phobia**, which is usually reserved for a deep
> psychological fear of some particular thing, can also
> imply irrationality. **Aversion** is similar, but suggests a
> less obsessive feeling, and implies an overwhelming
> dislike, whilst **horror** goes further by suggesting an
> intense repugnance: *she had a horror of moths*. The
> terms **trembling**, **shaking**, and **quivering** all put the
> emphasis on the physical effects of being frightened, and
> so imply an intense fear.

fearful *adj*
1 FRIGHTENED, afraid, scared, alarmed, in dread, nervous,
anxious, tense, uneasy, apprehensive, agitated, trembling,

shaking, quivering, petrified, hesitant, nervy, panicky, faint-hearted, timid
OLD affrayed, effraide, adred, afear
FORMAL tremulous, aghast
COLLOQ. scared out of your wits, scared to death, having kittens, in a cold sweat, in a blue funk, shaking in your shoes, shaking like a leaf, with your heart in your mouth, spineless, yellow
2 TERRIBLE, dreadful, awful, frightful, atrocious, shocking, dire, harrowing, distressing, appalling, horrific, monstrous, gruesome, hideous, ghastly, horrible, grim;
Scot ferly
FORMAL fearsome
E3 1 brave, courageous, fearless **2** wonderful, delightful

fearfully adv
1 APPREHENSIVELY, anxiously, nervously, uneasily, hesitantly, timidly, in fear and trembling
2 *fearfully insecure*
extremely, highly, intensely, unusually, exceedingly, exceptionally, very, most, incredibly, unbelievably
COLLOQ. awfully, terribly, frightfully, dreadfully, well, jolly, terrifically

fearless adj
bold, brave, confident, courageous, daring, intrepid, valiant, heroic, gallant, plucky, dauntless, aweless, unafraid, unapprehensive, unabashed, undaunted, unflinching, lion-hearted, unblenching, unblinking
OLD impavid
FORMAL doughty, indomitable, valorous
COLLOQ. game, gutsy, feisty, spunky, gritty
SLANG ballsy
E3 afraid, timid

fearsome adj
formidable, awe-inspiring, awesome, awful, daunting, terrifying, frightening, frightful, hair-raising, horrendous, horrible, horrific, horrifying, menacing, terrible, unnerving, alarming, appalling, dismaying
E3 delightful

feasibility n
practicability, achievability, workability, practicality, reasonableness, possibility, viability, expedience

feasible adj
practicable, practical, workable, doable, achievable, attainable, realizable, accomplishable, viable, expedient, reasonable, possible, likely, realistic
E3 impossible

feast n, v
♦ n
1 BANQUET, dinner, spread, junket, treat, carousal, luau;
NZ kaikai
TECHNICAL love-feast, agape
FORMAL repast, epulation
OLD regale
COLLOQ. blow-out, binge, beano, slap-up meal, do
SLANG pig
2 *a feast for the eyes*
wealth, abundance, profusion
FORMAL cornucopia
3 FESTIVAL, holiday, gala, fete, celebration, carnival, saint's day, *jour de fête*, feast day, religious festival, holy day, revels, festivities, gaudy, junketing;
N Am potlatch
OLD ale
Related adjective: festal
♦ v
gorge, eat your fill, wine and dine, indulge in, treat, entertain, regale, revel, banquet, junket
OLD convive
FORMAL partake of
COLLOQ. pig out

feat n
exploit, deed, act, action, accomplishment, achievement, attainment, performance, undertaking

feather n
plume, quill, down, tuft, crest
TECHNICAL penna, plumule, plumula, aigrette, egret, pinion
Related adjectives: pennaceous, plumose, plumous

feathery adj
1 *feathery birds*
feathered, featherlike, fleecy, fluffy, wispy, downy
TECHNICAL pennaceous, penniform, plumate, plumed, plumose, plumous, plumy
2 *feathery clouds*
soft, light, delicate, fluffy, wispy, flimsy

feature n, v
♦ n
1 ASPECT, facet, point, factor, attribute, quality, property, side, trait, characteristic, peculiarity, mark, hallmark, speciality, highlight, attraction, focal point
2 *a person's facial features*
face, looks
FORMAL countenance, lineaments, physiognomy, visage
SLANG mug, phiz, phizog, kisser, pan, clock, dial
3 *a magazine feature*
column, article, report, story, piece, item, comment
4 *a water feature*
highlight, centrepiece, focus, focus of attention, most interesting/exciting part
♦ v
1 EMPHASIZE, highlight, spotlight, play up, call/draw attention to, accentuate, promote, show, present
2 APPEAR, figure, participate, act, perform, star

featureless adj
nondescript, indeterminate, undistinctive, undistinguished, indistinguishable, unexceptional, ordinary, commonplace, plain, dull, vague, bland, anaemic, insipid, uninspiring, uninteresting, unattractive, unremarkable, unclassified
COLLOQ. run of the mill, common or garden, vanilla;
N Am cookie cutter
E3 distinctive, remarkable

febrile adj
feverish, delirious, fevered, flushed, fiery, hot, inflamed, burning
FORMAL pyretic

feckless adj
incompetent, weak, feeble, useless, worthless, aimless, futile, hopeless, irresponsible
FORMAL ineffectual
COLLOQ. wimpish, no-good, wet
E3 efficient, sensible

fecund adj
fertile, productive, fruitful, prolific, teeming
FORMAL feracious, fructiferous, fructuous
E3 infertile

fecundity n
fertility, productiveness, fruitfulness
FORMAL feracity, fructiferousness
E3 infertility

federal adj
confederated, amalgamated, allied, integrated, united, unified, in league, combined, associated

federate v
confederate, amalgamate, integrate, join together, ally, league, syndicate, unify, unite, combine, associate
E3 disunite, separate

federation n
confederation, confederacy, alliance, league, amalgamation, association, coalition, combination, syndicate, union, copartnership, federacy

fed up adj
depressed, bored, discontented, annoyed, dismal, dissatisfied, gloomy, glum, tired, weary, have had enough

COLLOQ. blue, brassed off, browned off, cheesed off, down, sick and tired, pig sick, hacked off, have had it up to here, at the end of your tether
SLANG pissed off
E3 contented

fee *n*
charge, terms, bill, account, pay, remuneration, payment, cost, price, subscription, reward, recompense, hire, rent, retainer, wage, salary, honorarium, toll, appearance money
FORMAL emolument

feeble *adj*
1 WEAK, faint, exhausted, frail, slight, delicate, puny, sickly, infirm, ailing, failing, powerless, helpless, decrepit, rickety, wastrel, washy, wishy-washy, debile, spiritless, dispirited, graspless, namby-pamby; *dialect* wearish; *Scot* sober, wersh, daidling, foisonless, fushionless, fizzenless
OLD impuissant, sackless, silly; (*Spenser*) lustless
FORMAL effete, debilitated, enervated
2 *a feeble excuse*
inadequate, lame, poor, weak, futile, thin, flimsy, unconvincing, tame, ineffective, unsuccessful
FORMAL ineffectual
3 *a feeble person*
ineffective, weak, incompetent, indecisive, feckless
FORMAL ineffectual
COLLOQ. pathetic, wimpish, wet
SLANG wussy
E3 1 strong, powerful

feeble-minded *adj*
slow-witted, half-witted, stupid, moronic, simple, silly, weak-minded, retarded, deficient, idiotic, imbecile, imbecilic
COLLOQ. dim-witted, dumb, slow on the uptake, soft in the head, two bricks short of a load, running on three wheels, not the sharpest knife in the box, not all there, mouth breathing; *Aust* not the full quid
E3 bright, intelligent

feebly *adv*
1 WEAKLY, faintly, slightly, powerlessly, helplessly, dispiritedly
2 *he apologized feebly*
ineffectively, weakly, indecisively, lamely
COLLOQ. pathetically

feed *v, n*
♦ *v*
1 *feed the baby*
give food to, nurture, nourish, cater for, provide for, suckle
2 *what does he feed on?*
eat, dine (on), consume, take in
FORMAL partake of
3 *animals feeding*
graze, pasture, browse, crop
FORMAL ruminate
4 *feed your sense of self-worth*
strengthen, gratify, fuel, foster, nurture, encourage, support
FORMAL fortify
5 *feed data into a computer*
put, insert, give, introduce, provide, supply, deliver, slide, slip
♦ *n*
food, fodder, foodstuff, forage, pasture, silage, provender

feedback *n*
response, answer, reply
OLD respondence
COLLOQ. comeback

feel *v, n*
♦ *v*
1 EXPERIENCE, be, go through, live through, undergo, suffer, bear, endure, be overcome by, give way to, harbour, nurse, know, enjoy
2 TOUCH, finger, handle, manipulate, hold, contact, stroke, massage, rub, caress, fondle, paw, maul, poke, fumble, grope, clutch, grasp

3 *feel soft*
seem, appear, look
4 THINK, believe, consider, reckon, judge, hold
FORMAL deem
5 SENSE, perceive, notice, observe, know, understand, realize, detect, discern, be aware of, feel in your bones
♦ *n*
1 *the feel of the material*
texture, surface, finish, touch, consistency
2 *have a feel for computer programming*
touch, knack, ability, skill, aptitude, gift, talent, faculty, flair, bent
3 *the feel of a place*
atmosphere, impression, feeling, quality, mood, air, aura, ambience
COLLOQ. vibes
■ **feel for**
pity, sympathize (with), empathize with, commiserate (with), be sorry for, be moved by, grieve for, weep for
■ **feel like**
want, desire, wish, would like, fancy

feeler *n*
1 ANTENNA, horn, tentacle, sense organ
TECHNICAL palp, palpus
2 *put out feelers*
advance, approach, overture(s), probe, trial balloon, ballon d'essai

feeling *n*
1 EMOTION, passion, intensity, warmth, compassion, love, sympathy, understanding, pity, concern, care, affection, fondness, spirit, ardour, sentiment, sentimentality, susceptibility, sensibility, sensitivity, appreciation, fervour
FORMAL sentience
2 SENSE, perception, sensation, instinct, intuition, hunch, theory, suspicion, inkling, impression, idea, belief, thought, notion, opinion, view, point of view, way of thinking
COLLOQ. sneaking suspicion, feeling in your bones
3 *hurt someone's feelings*
emotions, passions, self-esteem, sensitivities, sensibilities, susceptibilities, ego
FORMAL affections
4 AIR, aura, atmosphere, mood, quality, feel, impression
COLLOQ. vibes
5 *have a feeling for finance*
natural ability, ability, knack, aptitude, skill, gift, talent, flair, bent

feign *v*
simulate, assume, fabricate, fake, forge, imitate, pretend, put on, put it on, sham, make a show of, make believe, invent, counterfeit, act, fable
OLD dissemble, false, falsify, fayne, gammon, misfeign; (*Shakesp*) take upon yourself
FORMAL affect, dissimulate

feint *n*
play, pretence, ruse, artifice, distraction, expedient, gambit, manoeuvre, stratagem, subterfuge, blind, bluff, deception, sham, make-believe, mock-assault, wile
OLD dissemblance
COLLOQ. dodge

feisty *adj*
tough, courageous, brave, bold, plucky, spirited, lively, determined
COLLOQ. spunky, gutsy, gritty

felicitous *adj*
1 APPOSITE, appropriate, apt, fitting, suitable, well-chosen, opportune, timely, well-timed, well-turned, fortunate
FORMAL apropos
2 DELIGHTFUL, happy, inspired, fortunate, advantageous
FORMAL propitious
E3 inappropriate

felicity *n*
1 BLISS, joy, delight, euphoria, rapture, ecstasy, happiness
FORMAL delectation

2 APPROPRIATENESS, applicability, aptness, eloquence, suitability, suitableness
FORMAL propriety
E₃ **1** sadness **2** inappropriateness

feline *adj, n*
♦ *adj*
catlike, graceful, sleek, slinky, smooth, stealthy, seductive, sensual, sinuous, leonine
♦ *n*
cat, kitten, tomcat, tom, tabby, queen, mouser, wildcat, alleycat, grimalkin, Tibert, eyra, jaguarundi, manul, ocelot, ounce, quoll, rumpy, sealpoint, serval; *dialect* malkin; *Scot* baudrons
TECHNICAL felid
COLLOQ. puss, pussy, moggy

fell¹ *v*
fell trees
cut down, hew, knock down, chop down, strike down, floor, level, flatten, raze, raze to the ground, demolish, overthrow

fell²
■ **at one fell swoop**
all at once, at one time, in one go, by a single action

fellow *n, adj*
♦ *n*
1 MAN, male, boy, individual, person, character
COLLOQ. chap, bloke, guy, lad; *Aust* cove
2 PEER, compeer, equal, partner, associate, colleague, co-worker, confrère, contemporary, compatriot, companion, comrade, friend, counterpart, match, mate, twin, double
COLLOQ. crony, pal, chum, buddy
♦ *adj*
co-, associate, associated, related, like, similar

fellow feeling *n*
empathy, commiseration, compassion, care, feeling, sympathy, understanding

fellowship *n*
1 COMPANIONSHIP, camaraderie, comradeship, communion, familiarity, friendship, amiability, sociability, compatibility, affability, intimacy
COLLOQ. chumminess, matiness, palliness
2 ASSOCIATION, league, guild, society, club, union, affiliation, fraternity, brotherhood, sisterhood, order

female *adj*
feminine, she-, girlish, womanly, ladylike
E₃ male

feminine *adj*
1 FEMALE, womanly, ladylike, pretty, graceful, gentle, tender, delicate
2 EFFEMINATE, unmanly, womanish, girlish, girly, weak
COLLOQ. cissy, wimpish
E₃ **1** masculine **2** manly

SYNONYM NUANCES

sense 1
Female can be used to refer to a person's or animal's gender and has no connotations beyond specifyng sex: *most of the applicants were female.* **Womanly** has to do with the natural attributes associated with women, and is often associated with the more positive ones: *her eyes had a gentle, womanly strength.* **Ladylike**, is a rather old-fashioned sounding term to modern ears, with connotations of propriety: *she spoke with ladylike reserve.* **Pretty** implies an attractive appearance with archetypally feminine features: *his girlfriend was very pretty with a flawless complexion.*
   Other terms widely associated with femininity focus on features that are considered desirable in women; the term **graceful**, for instance, may be used to suggest an elegance of carriage or manner, **gentle** and **tender** are suggestive of being soft-hearted and **delicate** can imply a physical fragility: *her delicate white skin.*

---

femininity *n*
feminineness, womanhood, womanishness, womanliness, girlishness, effeminacy, prettiness, gracefulness, gentleness, tenderness, delicacy
COLLOQ. sissiness
E₃ masculinity

feminism *n*
women's movement, women's lib(eration), female emancipation, women's rights

femme fatale *n*
charmer, seductress, enchantress, temptress, siren, vamp, Circe, Lorelei, Mata Hari, Sirens, Delilah

fen *n*
bog, marsh, morass, moss, quag, quagmire, slough, swamp

fence *n, v*
♦ *n*
1 BARRIER, railing, rail, paling, wall, hedge, windbreak, guard, defence, barricade, stockade, enclosure, rampart, palisade
TECHNICAL sepiment
2 RECEIVER OF STOLEN GOODS/PROPERTY, trafficker
COLLOQ. pusher
♦ *v*
1 SURROUND, encircle, bound, hedge, wall, enclose, shut in, pen, coop, confine, restrict, separate, protect, secure, guard, defend
FORMAL fortify, circumscribe
2 PARRY, evade, hedge, equivocate, quibble, stonewall, prevaricate
FORMAL vacillate, tergiversate
COLLOQ. dodge, pussyfoot, shilly-shally, beat about the bush
■ **sit on the fence**
be irresolute, be uncommitted, be undecided, be unsure, be uncertain, vacillate, dither
COLLOQ. shilly-shally, blow hot and cold

---

fencing

Fencing terms include:

appel	foil	reprise
attack	forte	riposte
balestra	hit	counter-riposte
barrage	lunge	sabre
coquille	on guard	tac-au-tac
disengage	parry	thrust
en garde	counter-parry	touch
épée	pink	touché
feint	piste	volt
flèche	plastron	
foible	remise	

---

fend *v*
1 *fend for yourself*
look after, take care of, support, maintain, sustain, provide
2 *fend off an attack*
ward off, beat off, head off, parry, deflect, divert, avert, resist, repel, repulse, hold at bay, keep off, stave off, shut out, turn aside

feral *adj*
wild, ferocious, fierce, savage, vicious, brutal, brutish, bestial, undomesticated, unbroken, untamed
E₃ tame, domesticated

ferment *v, n*
♦ *v*
1 BUBBLE, effervesce, froth, foam, boil, seethe, smoulder, fester, work, brew, rise, yeast; *dialect* fret
2 ROUSE, arouse, stir up, excite, work up, agitate, foment, incite, provoke, inflame, cause, heat, yeast

♦ *n*

1 UNREST, agitation, turbulence, stir, excitement, turmoil, disruption, commotion, confusion, fuss, tumult, hubbub, stew, uproar, furore, brouhaha, frenzy, fever

2 *the action of a ferment*
leaven, zyme, enzyme, mould, bacteria
TECHNICAL ptyalin
E3 1 calm

ferocious *adj*

1 VICIOUS, savage, fierce, wild, untamed, barbarous, barbaric, brutal, inhuman, cruel, sadistic, murderous, bloodthirsty, violent, merciless, pitiless, bitter, ruthless
FORMAL feral
2 INTENSE, wild, vigorous, strong, extreme, severe, deep
E3 1 tame 2 gentle, mild

ferocity *n*

savagery, fierceness, violence, bloodthirstiness, ruthlessness, cruelty, inhumanity, brutality, viciousness, sadism, barbarity, wildness, intensity, severity, extremity
E3 gentleness, mildness

ferret *v*

search, rummage, hunt, go through, scour, forage, rifle

■ **ferret out**
discover, search out, find, hunt down, track down, trace, elicit, determine, extract, unearth, dig up, nose out, root out, worm out, run to earth
COLLOQ. suss out

ferry *n, v*

♦ *n*
ferry-boat, car ferry, ship, boat, vessel, packet, packet boat, shuttle

♦ *v*
transport, ship, convey, carry, take, shuttle, taxi, drive, run, move, shift, ply

fertile *adj*

1 *fertile soil*
fruitful, productive, rich, abundant; *dialect* battle
OLD pregnant
FORMAL fecund, luxuriant

2 *a fertile imagination*
creative, resourceful, inventive, prolific, productive, ingenious, imaginative, inspired, visionary

3 *fertile animals*
generative, prolific, able to have children, potent, reproductive, virile
OLD broody
FORMAL fecund
E3 1 unfruitful, unproductive 2 barren 3 sterile, infertile, barren

fertility *n*

1 FRUITFULNESS, productiveness, abundance, richness
FORMAL luxuriance, fecundity

2 *fertility tests*
generativeness, prolificness, potency, reproductiveness, virility
E3 1 aridity 2 barrenness, sterility

fertilization *n*

impregnation, implantation, insemination, conception, pollination, propagation
FORMAL fecundation, procreation

fertilize *v*

1 IMPREGNATE, inseminate, pollinate, make pregnant, make fruitful
FORMAL procreate, fecundate, fructify

2 *fertilize land*
enrich, feed, dress, compost, manure, dung, mulch, top-dress

fertilizer *n*

dressing, compost, manure, dung, top-dressing, plant food, mulch, bone meal, humus

fervent *adj*

ardent, earnest, eager, sincere, enthusiastic, wholehearted, excited, energetic, vigorous, fiery, spirited, intense, vehement, passionate, full-blooded, zealous, devout, impassioned, heartfelt, emotional, warm
E3 cool, indifferent, apathetic

fervently *adv*

ardently, earnestly, eagerly, sincerely, enthusiastically, wholeheartedly, intensely, passionately, emotionally, excitedly, energetically, vigorously
E3 indifferently, apathetically

fervour *n*

ardour, eagerness, earnestness, sincerity, enthusiasm, excitement, animation, energy, vigour, spirit, verve, intensity, wholeheartedness, fire, vehemence, passion, emotion, zeal, warmth; *Welsh* hwyl
E3 apathy, indifference

fester *v*

1 *the wound was festering*
infect, ulcerate, gather, suppurate, discharge
TECHNICAL maturate

2 *cheese festered on the filthy counter*
rot, decay, go bad, decompose, moulder, perish
FORMAL putrefy

3 *hatred was festering*
rankle, irk, chafe, anger, annoy, gall, smoulder, brew

festival *n*

celebration, commemoration, anniversary, jubilee, holiday, feast, gala, gala day, fair, fete, carnival, fiesta, party, merrymaking, entertainment, festivities

festive *adj*

celebratory, holiday, gala, carnival, festal, happy, joyful, merry, hearty, cheerful, cheery, light-hearted, jolly, jovial, cordial, jubilant, convivial
FORMAL joyous
E3 gloomy, sombre, sober

festivity *n*

celebration, jubilation, feasting, banqueting, fun, enjoyment, pleasure, entertainment, festival, party, fun and games, carousal, junketing, sport, amusement, cheerfulness, cheeriness, merriment, merrymaking, revelry, revel, jollity, joviality, conviviality

festoon *v, n*

♦ *v*
adorn, deck, garland, wreathe, drape, hang, swathe, decorate, ornament, garnish
OLD bedeck, bedizen
FORMAL array

♦ *n*
garland, wreath, swathe, chaplet, swag

fetch *v*

1 *fetch a bucket*
get, go and get, collect, bring, carry, transport, deliver, escort, convey, conduct

2 SELL FOR, go for, bring in, yield, realize, make, earn

■ **fetch up**
end up, finish up, arrive, materialize, turn up
COLLOQ. wind up, show up

fetching *adj*

attractive, pretty, sweet, cute, charming, enchanting, appealing, fascinating, captivating, alluring, winsome, adorable
E3 repellent

fete, fête *n, v*

♦ *n*
fair, bazaar, sale of work, garden party, gala, carnival, festival

♦ *v*
entertain, treat, regale, welcome, honour, lionize

fetid, foetid *adj*

stinking, disgusting, foul, filthy, sickly, nauseating, smelly, odorous, offensive, rancid, rank, reeking
FORMAL malodorous, noisome, noxious, mephitic
COLLOQ. pongy, whiffy, humming
E3 fragrant

fetish *n*
1 FIXATION, obsession, mania, *idée fixe*
COLLOQ. thing
2 CHARM, amulet, talisman, idol, image, cult object, ju-ju, totem, obi

fetter *v*
hamper, restrain, hinder, obstruct, restrict, impede, constrain, bind, chain, confine, encumber, curb, shackle, tie (up), hamstring, manacle, truss, entrammel
E3 free

fetters *n*
1 CONSTRAINTS, obstructions, restraints, restrictions, hindrances, checks, curbs, inhibitions, captivity, bondage
2 CHAINS, bonds, bracelets, handcuffs, irons, shackles, manacles

fettle
■ **in fine fettle**
in (good) shape, fit, healthy, in good health, sound, strong, trim, in good condition, on form, in fine form, shipshape, hale and hearty
COLLOQ. in good nick

feud *n, v*
♦ *n*
vendetta, quarrel, row, argument, disagreement, dispute, bickering, conflict, strife, discord, animosity, ill will, bitterness, enmity, hostility, antagonism, rivalry, bad blood
E3 agreement, peace
♦ *v*
quarrel, argue, row, squabble, bicker, clash, contend, dispute, duel, fight, brawl, war, wrangle, be at odds
FORMAL altercate
E3 agree

fever *n*
1 FEVERISHNESS, (high) temperature, delirium, ague
TECHNICAL pyrexia
OLD calenture
Related adjective: febrile
2 EXCITEMENT, agitation, turmoil, unrest, restlessness, heat, passion, ecstasy, frenzy, ferment

fevered *adj*
1 EXCITED, impatient, restless, nervous, worked up, passionate, frenzied, frantic
2 FEVERISH, with a temperature, hot, burning, flushed, red
FORMAL febrile

feverish *adj*
1 DELIRIOUS, with a temperature, hot, burning, flushed, red
FORMAL febrile
2 EXCITED, impatient, agitated, restless, nervous, overwrought, worked up, passionate, frenzied, frantic, hectic, rushed, hasty, hurried, flustered, troubled, bothered
COLLOQ. hot and bothered, in a kerfuffle, in a tizzy, in a tizz, in a dither
E3 1 cool **2** calm

few *adj, pron*
♦ *adj*
scarce, rare, uncommon, sporadic, infrequent, sparse, thin, scant, scanty, meagre, negligible, inconsiderable, inadequate, insufficient, in short supply
COLLOQ. thin on the ground
E3 many
♦ *pron*
not many, hardly any, scarcely any, one or two, a couple, a small number of, scattering, sprinkling, handful, some, a minority
E3 many

fey *adj*
whimsical, fanciful, quirky, playful, mischievous, impulsive, childish, unpredictable, eccentric, funny, droll, curious, shy, unusual, weird, odd, peculiar, quaint
FORMAL capricious
COLLOQ. dotty

fiancé, fiancée *n*
betrothed, intended, husband-to-be, bridegroom-to-be, future/prospective husband, wife-to-be, bride-to-be, future/prospective wife

fiasco *n*
failure, catastrophe, calamity, collapse, debacle, disaster, ruin, rout, mess
COLLOQ. cropper, damp squib, flop, washout; *N Am* bomb
E3 success

fiat *n*
order, command, directive, edict, decree, injunction, mandate, sanction, warrant, authorization, ordinance, permission, dictate, precept, dictum, proclamation, diktat
COLLOQ. OK

fib *n, v*
♦ *n*
lie, untruth, white lie, falsehood, story, tale, yarn, fable, concoction, fantasy, fiction, invention, misrepresentation, evasion, prevarication
COLLOQ. whopper, porky
♦ *v*
evade, fabricate, falsify, fantasize, invent, lie, prevaricate, sidestep
FORMAL dissemble

fibre *n*
1 FILAMENT, strand, thread, tendril, fibril, nerve, sinew, pile, texture, material, cloth, substance, stuff
2 *moral fibre*
character, nature, make-up, disposition, temperament, calibre, backbone, strength, stamina, toughness, courage, resolution, resoluteness, resolve, determination, willpower, strength of character, firmness (of purpose)

fickle *adj*
inconstant, disloyal, unfaithful, faithless, treacherous, unreliable, unpredictable, variable, changeable, irresolute, vacillating, volatile, unstable, unsteady, inconsistent, flighty, wind-changing, mutable, volage; *Scot* kittle
OLD choiceful
FORMAL capricious, mercurial, labile
E3 constant, steady, stable

fickleness *n*
inconstancy, disloyalty, unfaithfulness, faithlessness, treachery, unreliability, unpredictability, changeability, changeableness, volatility, unsteadiness, instability, fitfulness, flightiness, mutability
FORMAL capriciousness
E3 constancy

fiction *n*
1 *read fiction*
novels, fantasy, romance, story, stories, tale, yarn, fable, parable, legend, myth, storytelling, creative writing
2 PRETENCE, lie, falsehood, untruth, fabrication, invention, concoction
COLLOQ. fib, tall story, cock-and-bull story
E3 1 non-fiction **2** fact, truth

fictional *adj*
literary, invented, made-up, imaginary, make-believe, legendary, mythical, mythological, fabulous, non-existent, unreal
E3 factual, real

fictitious *adj*
false, untrue, invented, made-up, fabricated, fake, fictive, apocryphal, imaginary, non-existent, bogus, counterfeit, sham, spurious, assumed, supposed, concocted, improvised
E3 true, genuine

fiddle *v, n*
♦ *v*
1 *fiddling with her necklace*
play, tinker, toy, trifle, tamper, mess around, fool around, meddle, interfere, fidget, fuss

2 CHEAT, falsify, fraud, swindle, juggle, manoeuvre, racketeer
COLLOQ. cook the books, diddle, fix, graft
♦ *n*
swindle, fraud, racket, sharp practice
COLLOQ. con, graft, fix
SLANG rip-off; *N Am* gold brick

fiddling *adj*
trifling, petty, trivial, insignificant, negligible, paltry
F3 important, significant

fidelity *n*
1 FAITHFULNESS, loyalty, allegiance, devotion, devotedness, constancy, reliability, dependability, trustworthiness
2 ACCURACY, exactness, precision, closeness, adherence, strictness, faithfulness, authenticity
F3 1 disloyalty, unfaithfulness, infidelity, inconstancy, treachery **2** inaccuracy

fidget *v*
squirm, wriggle, writhe, toss and turn, shuffle, twitch, niggle, jerk, jump, jiggle, twiddle, fret, fuss, bustle, fiddle, mess about, play around, tinker, toy, trifle, tamper; *Scot* footer, fike, hirsle, hotch

fidgety *adj*
restless, impatient, uneasy, nervous, agitated, excited, jumpy, twitchy, on edge
FORMAL restive
COLLOQ. jittery, uptight, afraid of your shadow, like a cat on hot bricks
F3 still

field *n, v*
♦ *n*
1 GRASSLAND, meadow, pasture, paddock, playing-field, ground, pitch, green, lawn
OLD lea, mead, sward, glebe
Related adjectives: agrestic, campestral
2 RANGE, scope, bounds, limits, confines, territory, area, province, domain, sphere, environment, department, discipline, speciality, line, forte, regime, scene
3 PARTICIPANTS, entrants, contestants, competitors, contenders, runners, candidates, applicants, opponents, opposition, competition, possibles
♦ *v*
1 CATCH, retrieve, stop, pick up, return
2 ANSWER, cope with, deal with, handle, parry, deflect
3 *field a team*
play, choose to play, select, put up, present, send out

fiend *n*
1 EVIL SPIRIT, demon, devil, monster, savage, beast, brute, ogre, ghoul; *Scot* fient
2 *a health fiend*
enthusiast, fanatic, fan, addict, devotee
FORMAL aficionado
COLLOQ. freak, nut, buff

fiendish *adj*
1 *a fiendish person/plot*
devilish, diabolical, infernal, wicked, malevolent, cunning, cruel, inhuman, savage, brutal, aggressive, vicious, ferocious, ruthless, bloodthirsty, barbaric, monstrous, unspeakable
2 *a fiendish problem/plan*
difficult, intricate, involved, complex, complicated, obscure, horrendous, infernal, devilish, diabolical, challenging, cunning, clever, imaginative, ingenious, resourceful

fierce *adj*
1 FEROCIOUS, vicious, savage, cruel, brutal, wild, merciless, ruthless, aggressive, dangerous, fell, bloodthirsty, murderous, frightening, menacing, threatening, stern, grim, terrible, relentless
OLD stout, truculent; *(Shakesp)* walleyed
2 INTENSE, strong, powerful, passionate, wild, raging, rampant, angry, violent, furious, tempestuous, severe, grave, keen, cut-throat, hot, uncontrolled, relentless

OLD felon, wood; *(Spenser)* breme
F3 1 gentle, kind **2** calm

fiercely *adv*
ferociously, viciously, savagely, cruelly, brutally, wildly, mercilessly, murderously, ruthlessly, aggressively, dangerously, menacingly, threateningly, sternly, terribly, intensely, implacably, fanatically, bitterly, strongly, powerfully, passionately, relentlessly, violently, furiously, tempestuously, severely, keenly
COLLOQ. tooth and nail
F3 gently, kindly

fiery *adj*
1 BURNING, afire, flaming, aflame, blazing, ablaze, red-hot, glowing, aglow, flushed, hot, torrid, sultry
2 PASSIONATE, inflamed, ardent, fervent, impassioned, impatient, excitable, impetuous, impulsive, hot-headed, fierce, violent, heated
3 SPICY, spiced, seasoned, hot, pungent, piquant, sharp
F3 1 cold **2** impassive

fiesta *n*
party, festival, celebration, jubilee, holiday, feast, gala, carnival, merrymaking

fight *v, n*
♦ *v*
1 WRESTLE, box, fence, joust, brawl, punch, hit, set about, take on, scuffle, tussle, skirmish, combat, battle, do battle, war, wage war, make war, be at war, clash, conflict, cross swords, duel, militate, spar, engage, attack, grapple, struggle, contend, come to blows; *Aust & NZ* stoush
OLD debate, camp, strike, digladiate, measure swords, snickersnee; *(Shakesp)* meddle
COLLOQ. scrap, lay into, weigh into; *N Am* duke it out
2 QUARREL, argue, have a row, row, bandy words, dispute, squabble, bicker, wrangle, feud, be at odds
OLD debate
FORMAL altercate
COLLOQ. fall out, be at each other's throats
3 OPPOSE, contest, campaign against, champion, combat, work against, resist, withstand, defy, hold out against, stand up to, dispute, object to, take issue with, strive, struggle against, do battle against
OLD repugn
4 RESIST, restrain, repress, suppress, curb, thwart, hold back, keep back, force back, stem, stifle, smother
COLLOQ. bottle up
♦ *n*
1 BOUT, contest, duel, combat, action, battle, war, warfare, bloodshed, hostilities, attack, brawl, scuffle, tussle, struggle, brush, skirmish, exchange, clash, engagement, encounter, confrontation, conflict, spar, fray, row, disturbance, free-for-all, fracas, rout, ruckus, ruction, riot, mêlée, ruffle, shindy, Donnybrook, fisticuffs, cockfight, dogfight, gunfight, pell-mell, monomachy; *Scot* wap, rammy; *N Am* mix-in; *Aust & NZ* stoush
OLD graplement, medley; *Scot* tuilyie
COLLOQ. aggro, bovver, scrap, set-to, scrape, punch-up, pasting, bashing
SLANG ruck, rumble, bundle
2 QUARREL, row, disagreement, difference of opinion, argument, dispute; *Aust* yike
OLD debate
FORMAL dissension, discord, altercation
COLLOQ. dust-up, ding-dong
SLANG *Aust & NZ* blue
3 *the fight for freedom*
campaign, crusade, movement, drive, struggle, battle
4 *lose all his fight*
determination, willpower, tenacity, firmness, resolve, resoluteness, drive, spirit, aggression, will to live, pluck
COLLOQ. bottle, grit, guts, spunk

■ **fight back**
1 RETALIATE, defend yourself, resist, put up a fight, counter-attack, hold out against, retort, reply

2 *fight back tears*
hold back, force back, restrain, curb, control, repress, contain, suppress, check
COLLOQ. bottle up
■ **fight off**
hold off, keep/hold at bay, ward off, stave off, resist, repel, rebuff, beat off, rout, put to flight

> **QUOTATIONS**
> We shall fight on the beaches, we shall fight on the landing grounds, we shall fight in the fields and in the streets, we shall fight in the hills. We shall never surrender
> Sɪʀ Wɪɴsᴛᴏɴ Cʜᴜʀᴄʜɪʟʟ

> **SYNONYM NUANCES**
>
> *noun sense 1*
> **Bout** and **spar** are specifically used of an organized match in boxing or wrestling, but could be used figuratively, whilst **contest** is similar but not so restricted to sports: *the election will be a close contest*. **Duel**, on the other hand, has the more narrow referent of a prearranged fight between two people, although it may now be used to suggest a decisive struggle between two people: *the race soon developed into its final desperate duel*.
> The terms **combat** and **action** are more suggestive of fighting in ongoing, official war, whilst **battle** has associations of one particular engagement of two opposing sides, while **attack** would be reserved for making the first aggressive move. You can use **hostilities** or **engagement** of a continuous state of antagonism, especially war, although the tone is rather formal, even euphemistic: *the commencement of hostilities is expected later this week*. **Bloodshed**, on the other hand, is an emotive and inherently disapproving term which evokes the outcome of large-scale fighting.
> **Encounter** is a very mild term, and one which can be more widely used to imply any meeting of opposing parties: *an encounter with his rival in the semi-final*, whilst **confrontation** has more hostile implications. **Conflict** and **clash** clearly imply a more violent struggle. The terms **brawl**, **scuffle**, **tussle**, **brush** and **skirmish** are all suggestive of and appropriate for minor or limited physical disturbances: *a pub brawl*, while **struggle** implies a more protracted effort: *the struggle for human rights*.
> The term **row** is usually used to suggest a verbal disagreement, whilst **disturbance** suggests a noisy outburst and smaller-scale actions: *a disturbance in the street kept me awake*. **Fracas** and **ruckus** suggest greater uproar: *she had never heard such a ruckus*, whilst **riot** implies a large-scale display which can extend into lawlessness. **Mêlée**, however, is more suggestive of confusion and disorder, as is **fray**, which is appropriate to use figuratively of bustling, active contests as well as burgeoning warfare: *other countries have been drawn into the fray over the border; key ministers have joined the election fray*.

fighter *n*
combatant, contestant, contender, rival, opponent, adversary, antagonist, attacker, disputant, boxer, wrestler, prizefighter, sparring partner, soldier, trouper, mercenary, warrior, man-at-arms, swordsman, gladiator
FORMAL pugilist

figment
■ **figment of your imagination**
invention, fabrication, falsehood, fancy, fiction, illusion, delusion, improvisation, fable, deception, concoction

figurative *adj*
metaphorical, symbolic, emblematic, representative, allegorical, parabolic, descriptive, pictorial, naturalistic
Ⓔ literal

figure *n, v*
♦ *n*
1 NUMBER, numeral, digit, integer, sum, amount, total
2 *good at figures*
arithmetics, mental arithmetic, calculations, mathematics, maths, statistics
COLLOQ. sums
3 SHAPE, form, outline, silhouette
4 BODY, frame, build, physique, torso
5 *public figure*
dignitary, celebrity, leader, personality, character, person, personage, notable, worthy, authority
6 DIAGRAM, illustration, picture, drawing, sketch, image, representation, symbol, sign, emblem, design, pattern
♦ *v*
1 RECKON, guess, estimate, judge, think, suppose, believe, consider, conclude
2 FEATURE, appear, crop up, be mentioned in, be included in
■ **figure on**
bargain for, expect, plan for, be prepared for, depend on, reckon on, take into account
■ **figure out**
work out, calculate, make, compute, reckon, count, estimate, puzzle out, resolve, fathom, reason, understand, see, make out, decipher
COLLOQ. twig, tumble to, latch onto, get the picture; *N Am* dope (out)
■ **figure of speech**
figure, image, imagery, rhetorical device, turn of phrase
See panel at **rhetorical**.

figurehead *n*
1 *the president is merely a figurehead*
front man, name, mouthpiece, dummy, puppet, image, man of straw, nominal head, titular head, token
2 *a figurehead on a ship's prow*
figure, bust, carving

filament *n*
fibre, strand, thread, hair, whisker, wire, tendril, string, cord, cable, pile

filch *v*
steal, take, pilfer, thieve, rob, embezzle, palm, crib
FORMAL misappropriate, peculate, purloin
COLLOQ. lift, nab, nobble, nick, pinch, knock off, snaffle, snitch, swipe
SLANG rip off

file¹ *n, v*
♦ *n*
1 FOLDER, dossier, papers, portfolio, binder, case, box, box file, lever arch file, record, document, data, information, particulars, details
2 *a computer file*
document, text, data set, program, format
3 LINE, queue, column, row, procession, cortège, crocodile, train, string, stream, trail, rake
♦ *v*
1 *file papers*
record, register, note, enter, process, store, classify, categorize, pigeonhole, organize, catalogue, put in place
2 *file a complaint/file for divorce*
make, put in, submit, apply, ask
3 *file out of the building*
walk in line, trail, process, stream, march, parade, troop

file² *v*
file a rough surface
rub (down), sand, abrade, scour, scrape, grate, rasp, hone, whet, shave, plane, smooth, polish, shape; *Scot* risp

filial *adj*
dutiful, loyal, respectful, devoted, affectionate, loving, fond, daughterly
Ⓔ disloyal, unfilial

filibuster *n, v*

♦ *n*
delay, delaying tactics, impediment, obstruction, postponement, hindrance
FORMAL procrastination, speechifying, peroration
♦ *v*
delay, obstruct, impede, put off, prevent, hinder, stall, waste time
FORMAL procrastinate, speechify, perorate
E3 expedite

filigree *n*
fretwork, lacework, lattice, latticework, interlace, lace, scrollwork, tracery, wirework

fill *v, n*

♦ *v*
1 *fill a bucket with water*
make full, stock, supply, furnish, satisfy, provide, pack, crowd, occupy, cram, stuff, congest, block, clog, plug, bung, cork, stop (up), close, seal
FORMAL replenish
2 PERVADE, imbue, permeate, soak, impregnate, saturate, charge, spread throughout, riddle
FORMAL suffuse
3 *fill a post*
take up, hold, occupy, fulfil, complete, perform
E3 1 empty, drain
♦ *n*
enough, abundance, ample, plenty, sufficiency, sufficient, all you want, more than enough, all you can take

■ **fill in**
1 *fill in a form*
complete, fill out, answer
2 STAND IN, deputize, understudy, substitute, replace, represent, act for
COLLOQ. *N Am* pinch-hit for
3 INFORM, brief, advise, acquaint, bring up to date

■ **fill out**
1 *fill out a form*
complete, fill in, answer
2 *the child filled out*
become/grow fatter, put on/gain weight, become plumper/chubbier

filling *n, adj*

♦ *n*
contents, inside, stuffing, padding, wadding, filler, substance

♦ *adj*
satisfying, nutritious, rich, square, solid, stodgy, substantial, heavy, large, big, generous, ample, hearty
E3 insubstantial

fillip *n*
boost, incentive, stimulus, inducement, stimulant, stimulation, encouragement, motivation, goad, impetus, spur, prod, push
COLLOQ. shove
E3 damper

film *n, v*

♦ *n*
1 MOTION PICTURE, picture, video, cassette, video cassette, cartridge, reel, spool, feature film, short, documentary, screenplay, footage
COLLOQ. movie, flick
Related adjective: cinematic
See panel below
2 LAYER, covering, cover, dusting, coat, coating, glaze, patina, skin, membrane, tissue, sheet, veil, blanket, screen, cloud, mist, haze
♦ *v*
photograph, shoot, record on film, televise, video, videotape

■ **film over**
cloud over, mist over, glaze, become blurred, blur, fog, dull

filmy *adj*
cobwebby, delicate, fragile, fine, gauzy, gossamer, gossamery, light, chiffony, see-through, sheer, shimmering, thin, translucent, transparent, insubstantial, flimsy, floaty
FORMAL diaphanous
E3 opaque

filter *v, n*

♦ *v*
strain, sieve, sift, riddle, screen, refine, purify, clarify, percolate, ooze, seep, leak, trickle, dribble, drain, leach
FORMAL filtrate
♦ *n*
strainer, sieve, sifter, colander, mesh, netting, gauze, riddle, membrane

filth *n*
1 DIRT, grime, muck, dross, dung, manure, excrement, sewage, refuse, rubbish, garbage, trash, slime, sludge, soil, effluent, pollution, contamination, corruption, defilement, impurity, uncleanness, foulness, sordidness, squalor, bilge, sullage, wallow; *dialect* addle

---

Kinds of film include:

action	CGI (computer-	disaster	horse opera	realist	social problem
actioneer	generated ima-	Disney	James Bond	remake	space-age
adult	gery)	documentary	kitchen sink	rites of passage	space exploration
adventure	chapter-play	drama	love story	road movie	space opera
animated	Charlie Chaplin	dramedy	low-budget	robbery	spaghetti western
anime	*colloq.* chick flick	Ealing comedy	machinima	romantic	spoof
auteur	*slang* chopsocky	epic	martial arts	romantic comedy	spy
avant-garde	cinéma-vérité	erotic	medi(a)eval	romantic tragedy	surrealist
biopic	classic	escapist	melodrama	*colloq.* rom-com	swashbuckler
black comedy	claymation	ethnographic	multiple-story	satirical	tear-jerker
blaxploitation	cliffhanger	expressionist	murder	*slang* schlock	thriller
blockbuster	comedy	family	murder mystery	horror	tragedy
colloq. blue	comedy thriller	fantasy	musical	science-fiction	tragicomedy
B-movie	comic-book hero	farce	newsreel	*colloq.* sci-fi	travelogue
Bollywood	computer-ani-	*slang* fem-jep	new wave	screenplay	underground
colloq. Bond film	mated	film à clef	nouvelle vague	screwball comedy	Victorian
bonkbuster	costume drama	film noir	passion	serial	adaptation
buddy	cowboy and	flashback	period drama	sexual fantasy	vogue
burlesque	Indian	gangster	police	short	war
campus	crime	gay-lesbian	police thriller	silent	war hero
classic	cult	historical romance	political	*slang* skin flick	*colloq.* weepie
Carry-on	*colloq.* date movie	Hitchcock	pornographic	*slang* slasher	western
cartoon	detective	Hollywood	psychological	*slang* snuff movie	whodunnit
	director's cut	horror	thriller	social comedy	

TECHNICAL colluvies
OLD gore
FORMAL faeces, putrefaction, putrescence
COLLOQ. gunge, yuck, grot
SLANG crud, gunk, grunge, crap, dreck
2 OBSCENITY, pornography, indecency, vulgarity,
coarseness, dirty books
COLLOQ. smut, sleaze, porn, hard porn, blue films,
sexploitation, raunchiness
E3 1 cleanness, cleanliness, purity

filthy adj
1 DIRTY, soiled, unwashed, grimy, grubby, black, mucky,
muddy, slimy, sooty, unclean, contaminated, polluted,
decaying, rotten, impure, foul, gross, sordid, squalid,
swinish, Augean
FORMAL faecal, putrid, putrefying
COLLOQ. yucky
SLANG crappy, cruddy, manky
2 OBSCENE, dirty, foul, pornographic, smutty, bawdy, adult,
suggestive, indecent, explicit, offensive, foul-mouthed,
vulgar, coarse, lewd, corrupt, depraved
COLLOQ. blue, raunchy, X-rated
3 DESPICABLE, contemptible, worthless, wretched, nasty,
vile, low, base, mean
4 filthy weather
foul, nasty, bad, disagreeable, wet, rainy, stormy, dirty,
rough, wild
5 in a filthy mood
angry, bad, bad-tempered, irritable, cross, mean
COLLOQ. stroppy, ratty, crabby, shirty
E3 1 clean, pure **2** decent **4** fine, fair **5** good

final adj
1 LAST, latest, closing, concluding, finishing, end, ultimate,
terminal, dying, last-minute, eventual
FORMAL terminating
2 CONCLUSIVE, definitive, decisive, definite, settled,
incontrovertible, indisputable, irrevocable, unalterable,
irrefutable
FORMAL determinate
E3 1 first, initial **2** provisional

finale n
climax, dénouement, culmination, crowning glory, end,
ending, conclusion, close, final act, curtain, epilogue

finality n
conclusiveness, conviction, decidedness, decisiveness,
definiteness, certitude, firmness, resolution, inevitability,
inevitableness, unavoidability, incontrovertibility,
irreversibility, irrevocability
FORMAL ultimacy

finalize v
conclude, finish, complete, round off, work out,
resolve, settle, agree, decide, close
COLLOQ. clinch, sew up, wrap up, put the icing on the
cake, put the finishing touches to

finally adv
lastly, in conclusion, to conclude, ultimately, eventually,
at last, at length, in the end, conclusively, once and for
all, for ever, for good, permanently, irreversibly,
irrevocably, decisively, definitely, in fine
COLLOQ. when all is said and done

finance n, v
♦ n
1 corporate finance
economics, money management, accounting, banking,
investment, stock market, business, commerce, trade,
money, funding, sponsorship, subsidy
2 the company's finances
accounts, affairs, budget, bank account, income,
revenue, liquidity, resources, funding, assets,
means, capital, wealth, money, cash, funds,
wherewithal, savings

♦ v
pay for, fund, sponsor, back, support,
underwrite, guarantee, subsidize, capitalize,
float, set up

financial adj
monetary, money, economic, fiscal, budgetary,
commercial, entrepreneurial
FORMAL pecuniary

financier n
financialist, banker, stockbroker, moneymaker,
industrialist, investor, speculator, trader

find v, n
♦ v
1 DISCOVER, locate, track down, trace, spot, retrieve,
recover, regain, get back, unearth, uncover, dig out, turn
up, expose, reveal, bring to light, come across, come by,
stumble across/on, meet, encounter, detect, recognize,
notice, observe, perceive, realize, learn
FORMAL happen upon, chance upon
2 ATTAIN, achieve, win, reach, gain, earn, acquire,
secure, obtain, get
FORMAL procure
3 find it difficult
consider, think, judge, rate, gauge, declare,
believe
FORMAL deem
4 vitamin A is found in carrots
be, exist, be present, occur
5 the judge found him guilty
judge, adjudicate, arbitrate, try, sit in judgement,
deliver/pronounce a verdict, referee, umpire, decree,
mediate, examine, sentence, pass sentence, give a
sentence, review, rule
FORMAL adjudge
E3 1 lose
♦ n
acquisition, asset, catch, coup, discovery, boon,
godsend, bargain, good buy
■ **find out**
1 LEARN, ascertain, establish, identify, understand, pinpoint,
discover, detect, note, observe, perceive, see, gather,
realize
COLLOQ. get wind of, suss out, twig, cotton on to
2 UNMASK, expose, show up, uncover, reveal,
disclose, get at, detect, bring to light, lay bare, catch
COLLOQ. tumble to
SLANG rumble

finding n
1 DISCOVERY, find, breakthrough, innovation
2 DECISION, conclusion, judgement, verdict,
order, pronouncement, decree, recommendation,
award

fine¹ adj, adv, interj
♦ adj
1 EXCELLENT, outstanding, exceptional, first-class, first-rate,
great, superior, exquisite, splendid, magnificent, admirable,
brilliant, beautiful, handsome, attractive, lovely, nice,
good, select, choice
2 HEALTHY, in good health, well, fit, strong, flourishing,
vigorous, all right, in (good) shape, sound, in good
condition, on form, shipshape, hale and hearty
3 SATISFACTORY, acceptable, all right,
agreeable, good
COLLOQ. OK, up to scratch; N Am A-OK
4 fine weather
bright, sunny, clear, cloudless, dry, fair, clement,
temperate
5 THIN, slender, slim, slight, sheer, gauzy, diaphanous,
powdery, flimsy, light, lightweight, fragile, delicate, dainty,
narrow, sharp
6 POWDERY, ground, crushed, fine-grained, gossamer
7 EXPENSIVE, elegant, smart, fashionable, stylish, discerning
8 a fine distinction
exact, precise, accurate, nice, critical, subtle, minute

COLLOQ. hair-splitting
☒ **1** mediocre, poor **4** cloudy, dull, inclement, stormy **5** thick, heavy, coarse
♦ *adv*
well, acceptably, all right, satisfactorily, properly, correctly, successfully
COLLOQ. OK
♦ *interj*
all right, very well, very good, good, excellent, agreed, right, yes
COLLOQ. OK

fine² *n, v*

♦ *n*
a speeding fine
penalty, punishment, forfeit, forfeiture, damages
FORMAL amercement, mulct
♦ *v*
penalize, punish
FORMAL amerce, mulct
COLLOQ. sting

finely *adv*

1 EXCELLENTLY, admirably, brilliantly, attractively, magnificently, splendidly
2 THINLY, delicately, lightly, sharply
3 SUBTLY, critically, precisely, exactly, nicely, minutely
☒ **1** badly, poorly **2** thickly, coarsely **3** generally, widely

finery *n*

decorations, frippery, regalia, best clothes, Sunday best, jewellery, ornaments, showiness, splendour, gaudery, trappings
FORMAL bedizenment
COLLOQ. glad rags, best bib and tucker

finesse *n, v*

♦ *n*
skill, flair, expertise, deftness, adeptness, adroitness, cleverness, delicacy, diplomacy, tact, tactfulness, discretion, subtlety, savoir-faire, elegance, gracefulness, polish, neatness, refinement, sophistication, quickness
COLLOQ. knowhow
♦ *v*
bluff, evade, manipulate, manoeuvre, trick

finger *v*

touch, handle, manipulate, feel, stroke, caress, fondle, paw, fiddle with, toy with, play about with, meddle with
■ **put your finger on**
pinpoint, indicate, isolate, pin down, hit upon, identify, discover, find out, remember, place, locate, recall
COLLOQ. hit the nail on the head

finicky *adj*

1 PARTICULAR, finickety, fussy, fastidious, meticulous, scrupulous, critical, hypercritical, selective, discriminating, faddy
COLLOQ. pernickety, choosy, nit-picking, picky; N Am persnickety
2 FIDDLY, intricate, tricky, difficult, delicate
☒ **1** easy-going **2** easy

finish *v, n*

♦ *v*
1 END, bring/come to an end, stop, cease, be over, complete, accomplish, attain, achieve, fulfil, carry out, get through, discharge, deal with, do, close, settle, round off, culminate, perfect
OLD absolve, outwork
FORMAL conclude, terminate, discontinue, consummate
COLLOQ. wind up, polish off, pack in, wrap up, sew up, be done with, get shot of, be through, call it a day, put paid to
2 USE UP, use, consume, devour, eat, drink, exhaust, drain, empty, run out of
FORMAL deplete, expend
COLLOQ. down, guzzle, scoff, polish off
3 DESTROY, ruin, exterminate, get rid of, do away with, annihilate, defeat, overcome, overwhelm, overpower,

conquer, rout, overthrow, crush, topple, bring down, get the better of
COLLOQ. wipe out
4 VENEER, apply, lacquer, varnish, coat, polish, gloss, glaze
☒ **1** begin, start; *formal* commence
♦ *n*
1 END, completion, conclusion, close, ending, finale, culmination, accomplishment, achievement, perfection, fulfilment, discharge, ruin, destruction
FORMAL termination, cessation
COLLOQ. winding-up, wind-up, curtains
2 SURFACE, appearance, texture, grain, polish, shine, gloss, glaze, coating, veneer, lacquer, lustre, lamination, smoothness
☒ **1** beginning, start; *formal* commencement

finished *adj*

1 COMPLETED, complete, concluded, dealt with, over, at an end
FORMAL consummated
COLLOQ. over and done with, through, wrapped up, sewn up
2 USELESS, defeated, ruined, doomed, lost, drained, exhausted, empty, spent, undone, unwanted, unpopular
COLLOQ. done for, played out, zonked
3 *a finished performance*
accomplished, proficient, professional, expert, polished, impeccable, faultless, flawless, perfect, masterly, consummate, refined, sophisticated, urbane, virtuoso
☒ **1** unfinished, incomplete **2** useful, productive **3** incompetent; *colloq.* hopeless

finite *adj*

limited, restricted, bounded, demarcated, terminable, definable, fixed, measurable, calculable, countable, numbered
☒ infinite

fire *n, v*

♦ *n*
1 FLAMES, blaze, bonfire, inferno, burning, combustion, holocaust
FORMAL conflagration
Related adjective: igneous
2 GUNFIRE, attack, firing, bombing, shelling, sniping, bombardment, barrage, cannonade, fusillade, salvo, flak
3 HEATER, radiator, convector, fan
4 PASSION, feeling, ardour, excitement, dynamism, eagerness, enthusiasm, spirit, energy, liveliness, life, vigour, animation, vivacity, verve, fervour, intensity, heat, radiance, inventiveness, creativity, sparkle
5 CRITICISM, condemnation, disapproval, fault-finding, censure, reproof, blame
FORMAL disparagement
COLLOQ. brickbat, flak, slating, slamming, knocking, stick
♦ *v*
1 IGNITE, light, put a match to, kindle, set fire to, set on fire, set alight, set ablaze
COLLOQ. torch
2 *fire a missile*
shoot, launch, set off, let off, detonate, discharge, explode, trigger, hurl
3 DISMISS, discharge, eject, get rid of
COLLOQ. sack, axe, boot out, kick out, show someone the door, give someone their cards, give someone the sack/push/boot/elbow
4 EXCITE, whet, enliven, galvanize, electrify, stir (up), arouse, rouse, motivate, stimulate, inspire, animate, inflame, incite, spark off, trigger off
■ **on fire**
1 IN FLAMES, burning, alight, ignited, flaming, aflame, blazing, ablaze
2 ENTHUSIASTIC, passionate, excited, eager, ardent, fiery, energetic, creative, inventive, sparkling, inspired

firearm n
gun, weapon, automatic, handgun, pistol, revolver, rifle, shotgun, musket
See panel at **weapon**.

firebrand n
revolutionary, radical, fanatic, militant, extremist, agitator, troublemaker, rabble-rouser, incendiary, rebel, insurrectionist, insurgent

fireplace

Types of fireplace include:

backboiler	forge	kiln
boiler	furnace	open fire
bonfire	gas fire	oven
brazier	grate	stove
campfire	hearth	paraffin stove
electric fire	incinerator	wood burning
firebox	ingle	stove

fireproof adj
non-flammable, incombustible, non-inflammable, flameproof, fire-resistant, flame-resistant
EƷ flammable, inflammable, combustible

fireworks n
1 PYROTECHNICS, explosions, illuminations, feux d'artifice
2 UPROAR, trouble, outburst, frenzy, fit, rage, rows, storm, temper, sparks, hysterics

Types of firework include:

banger	flare	rocket
cake	fountain	roman candle
Catherine wheel	golden rain	shell
Chinese cracker	indoor firework	sky-rocket
cracker	jumping-jack	sparkler
firecracker	mine	squib
firewriting	pinwheel	waterfall

firm[1] adj
1 firm ground
dense, compressed, compact, close-grained, concentrated, set, solid, solidified, substantive, hard, hardened, unyielding, stiff, rigid, inflexible, inelastic
2 FIXED, embedded, established, fast, tight, secure, secured, fastened, anchored, riveted, immovable, motionless, unshak(e)able, stationary, steady, stable, set, sturdy, strong
3 a firm handshake
strong, vigorous, forceful, solid, substantial
4 a firm decision
definite, settled, fixed, decided, established, unchangeable, unalterable
5 ADAMANT, unshak(e)able, resolute, resolved, decided, determined, dogged, unwavering, unfaltering, unswerving, unflinching, strict, hard, inflexible, stubborn, obstinate, constant, steadfast, staunch, tenacious
FORMAL obdurate
6 firm friends
close, dependable, true, sure, committed, unchanging, constant, long-standing, long-lasting, good, boon, steady, stable, steadfast, staunch
EƷ 1 soft, flabby **2** unsteady, shaky **3** limp, weak **4** vague, changeable **5** hesitant, non-committal

firm[2] n
a firm of accountants
company, corporation, business, enterprise, concern, house, establishment, institution, organization, association, partnership, syndicate, conglomerate

firmament n
sky, skies, heaven(s), atmosphere, space, expanse, the blue, ether
OLD empyrean, welkin

firmly adv
securely, tightly, steadily, stably, sturdily, strongly, robustly, unshakably, unwaveringly, strictly, immovably, unalterably, unchangeably, unflinchingly, resolutely, inflexibly, decisively, definitely, determinedly, doggedly, enduringly, staunchly, steadfastly
EƷ loosely, vaguely, hesitantly, uncertainly

firmness n
1 STIFFNESS, hardness, rigidity, solidity, density, compactness, inflexibility, inelasticity, tautness, tension, fixity, immovability, tightness
2 STRENGTH, strength of will, determination, resolution, resolve, dependability, reliability, staunchness, steadfastness, steadiness, willpower, constancy, conviction, changelessness, stability, strictness, resistance, sureness, doggedness
FORMAL indomitability, obduracy
EƷ 1 softness **2** uncertainty

first adj, adv, n
♦ adj
1 INITIAL, opening, introductory, preliminary, beginning, inaugural, elementary, primary, basic, fundamental, rudimentary
2 ORIGINAL, earliest, earlier, prior, primitive, initial, oldest, eldest, senior
FORMAL prim(a)eval, primordial
3 CHIEF, main, key, cardinal, principal, head, leading, foremost, ruling, sovereign, highest, greatest, uppermost, paramount, best, prime, supreme, predominant, pre-eminent
EƷ 1 last, final
♦ adv
initially, to begin with, at first, first of all, firstly, in the first place, to start with, first and foremost, at the beginning, at the outset, beforehand, before anything else, originally, in preference, rather, sooner
♦ n
beginning, start, opening, introduction, outset, origin(s), original, prototype, unveiling, première
FORMAL commencement, inception
COLLOQ. the word go, square one

first-born adj
elder, eldest, older, oldest, senior
OLD eigne, primogenit
FORMAL aîné(e), primogenital, primogenitary, primogenitive

first-class adj
first-rate, second-to-none, matchless, peerless, top, top-flight, leading, supreme, superior, prime, excellent, outstanding, superlative, premier, exceptional, splendid, superb, fine, admirable
COLLOQ. super, cool, fabulous, top-notch, A1, ace, crack, out of this world
SLANG way-out, radical, mega, mean, wicked, crucial

firsthand adj, adv
direct(ly), immediate(ly), personal(ly), in service, on the job
COLLOQ. straight from the horse's mouth, hands-on
EƷ indirect(ly)

firstly adv
in the first place, initially, to begin with, at first, first of all, to start with, first and foremost, at the outset

first name n
forename, Christian name, given name, baptismal name

first-rate *adj*
first-class, second-to-none, matchless, peerless,
top, top-flight, leading, supreme, superior, prime,
excellent, outstanding, superlative, premier,
exceptional, splendid, superb, fine, admirable
COLLOQ. super, fabulous, top-notch, A1, ace, crack,
out of this world
SLANG way-out, cool, radical, mega, mean, wicked, crucial
F3 inferior

fiscal *adj*
financial, tax, monetary, money, economic, budgetary,
treasury, capital
FORMAL pecuniary

fiscally *adv*
financially, economically
FORMAL pecuniarily
COLLOQ. moneywise

fish *n, v*
Related adjectives: piscine, ichthyic, ichthyoid
♦ *v*
1 GO FISHING, angle, trawl
2 *she fished in her bag for a pen*
delve, hunt, search, grope
3 *fish for information*
try to get, try to obtain, angle, look, ask
FORMAL seek
■ **fish out**
produce, take out, extract, find, retrieve, haul out, pull out,
come up with, dredge up

> **PROVERBS**
> There are as good fish in the sea as ever came out of it

Types of fish, shellfish and crustacean include:

bass	goldfish	rainbow trout
bloater	guppy	roach
Bombay duck	haddock	roughy
bream	hake	salmon
brill	halibut	sardine
brisling	herring	scallop
candiru	hoki	shark
carp	king prawn	shrimp
catfish	kipper	skate
chub	lantern fish	snapper
clam	ling	sole
cockle	lobster	sprat
cod	mackerel	squid
coley	marlin	stickleback
conger eel	minnow	stingray
crab	monkfish	sturgeon
crayfish (or *N Am*	mullet	swordfish
crawfish)	mussel	tench
cuttlefish	octopus	trout
dab	oyster	tuna
dace	perch	turbot
dogfish	pike	whelk
dory	pilchard	whitebait
Dover sole	piranha	whiting
eel	plaice	*Aust* yabbie
flounder	pollock	
fugu	prawn	

See also **shark**.

fisherman *n*
angler, fisher, rod, rodfisher, rodman, rodsman, rodster
FORMAL piscator, piscatorian

fishing *n*
catching fish, angling, trawling
Related adjectives: piscatorial, piscatory, halieutic

fishy *adj*
1 *a fishy taste*
fish-like

FORMAL piscatorial, piscatory, piscine
2 ODD, suspicious, questionable, shady, suspect,
doubtful, dubious, implausible, improbable, funny,
irregular, queer
F3 honest, legitimate

fission *n*
splitting, breaking, division, rupture,
parting, rending, schism, severance, scission,
cleavage, cleaving

fissure *n*
crack, opening, cleft, fracture, breach,
break, cranny, crevasse, crevice, rent, rift,
rupture, chasm, hole, gap, gape, gash, slit,
split, chink, fault, vein, shake
TECHNICAL grike, foramen, sulcus, porta, zygon
OLD rime
FORMAL cleavage, interstice, scissure

fist *n*
palm, hand, clenched hand, knuckles
COLLOQ. paw
SLANG mitt, bunch of fives

fit[1] *adj, v, n*
♦ *adj*
1 HEALTHY, well, in good health, able-bodied, in good
form, in good shape, in shape, in good condition, in trim,
sound, sturdy, strong, hardy, robust, vigorous, flourishing,
hale and hearty
2 SUITABLE, appropriate, apt, fitting, correct, right, good
enough, proper, due, convenient, ready, prepared, able,
capable, competent, qualified, equipped, trained, eligible,
worthy
OLD seemly
FORMAL decorous, pertinent
F3 1 unfit, out of condition **2** unsuitable, unworthy
♦ *v*
1 *Do the shoes fit you?*
get into, be the right size for, be the right shape for, be a
good fit
COLLOQ. fit like a glove
2 MATCH, correspond, conform, follow, agree, tally, suit,
be suitable, be appropriate, harmonize, go, be right, be
consistent, belong, dovetail, interlock, connect, join, put
together, meet, accommodate
FORMAL concur, be consonant
3 *fit a washing machine*
install, insert, put in, position, place, put in position/place,
attach, arrange, fix
4 ALTER, modify, change, adjust, adapt, regulate, tailor,
shape, fashion, accommodate
5 EQUIP, qualify, train, make suitable, prepare, provide,
make ready, prime, condition, arm, coach, groom, tailor
♦ *n*
correlation, relationship, correspondence, equivalence,
conformity, agreement
FORMAL concurrence
■ **fit in**
match, correspond, conform, agree, square, belong, slot,
squeeze
FORMAL accord, concur
■ **fit out/up**
equip, rig out, kit out, outfit, provide, supply, furnish,
prepare, arm
FORMAL accoutre

fit[2] *n*
1 SEIZURE, convulsion, spasm, paroxysm, attack
TECHNICAL ictus
2 OUTBREAK, bout, spell, burst, surge, outburst, eruption,
explosion, tantrum
■ **in fits and starts**
sporadically, fitfully, spasmodically, intermittently,
occasionally, irregularly, unevenly, brokenly, erratically,
off and on
F3 regularly, steadily

fitful *adj*
sporadic, intermittent, occasional, spasmodic, erratic, irregular, disconnected, haphazard, uneven, broken, disturbed, patchy
E3 steady, regular, continuous

fitfully *adv*
in/by fits and starts, spasmodically, sporadically, intermittently, occasionally, unevenly, erratically, irregularly, haphazardly
E3 steadily, regularly, continuously

fitness *n*
1 SUITABILITY, qualifications, readiness, preparedness, eligibility, capability, appropriateness, aptness, competence, adequacy, applicability, condition
OLD opportunity, property
FORMAL pertinence
2 HEALTH, healthiness, strength, vigour, condition, shape, trim, good health, robustness, haleness
E3 1 unsuitability **2** unfitness

fitted *adj*
1 *fitted wardrobe*
built-in, permanent, integral, integrated, fixed
2 EQUIPPED, rigged out, provided, furnished, appointed, prepared, armed, tailored, shaped
3 SUITED, right, suitable, fit, qualified, cut out

fitting *adj, n*
♦ *adj*
apt, appropriate, suitable, fit, correct, right, proper, desirable, deserved
OLD seemly, meet
FORMAL decorous
E3 unsuitable, improper
♦ *n*
1 *light fittings*
attachment, accessory, connection, part, component, piece, unit, fitment, fixture
2 *the price includes fittings*
equipment, furnishings, furniture, fixtures, installations, fitments, accessories, extras
FORMAL accoutrements, appointments

fix *v, n*
♦ *v*
1 FASTEN, secure, tie, bind, attach, join, connect, link, couple, anchor, affix, clamp, pin, nail, screw, rivet, stick, glue, cement, set, harden, solidify, stiffen, stabilize, plant, root, implant, embed, establish, install, station, lodge, locate, situate, position
2 *fix a date/price*
arrange, set, specify, define, agree on, decide, determine, name, settle, resolve, finalize, arrive at, sort
TECHNICAL valorize
3 MEND, repair, patch up, correct, rectify, adjust, restore, remedy, see to, put right
4 *fix your eyes/attention*
direct, aim, focus, concentrate, turn, point, level, hold, attract, draw
5 *fix your hair*
arrange, tidy, groom, adjust, dress, prepare, put in order, order, do, neaten, straighten, comb
6 *fix a race*
rig, set up, falsify, fake, manoeuvre, tamper with, manipulate
COLLOQ. fiddle
7 *fix some food for you*
prepare, make, get ready, put together, cook
COLLOQ. knock up, throw together
E3 1 move, shift **3** damage **5** untidy
♦ *n*
1 DILEMMA, quandary, predicament, plight, difficulty, corner, mess, muddle
COLLOQ. hole, (tight) spot, bind, pickle, scrape, jam, the soup
2 *there's no quick fix to the problem*
solution, answer, remedy, resolution, way out

3 INJECTION, dose, shot, hit
COLLOQ. score, slug, bang
4 RIGGING, manipulation, scam
COLLOQ. fiddle
SLANG set-up
■ **fix up**
arrange, organize, settle, agree on, plan, lay on, provide, supply, furnish, equip, sort out, produce, bring about

fixated *adj*
obsessed, preoccupied, infatuated, compulsive, pathological, dominated, gripped, phobic, neurotic
COLLOQ. hung up on

fixation *n*
preoccupation, obsession, mania, fetish, infatuation, compulsion, complex, *idée fixe*, phobia, neurosis
COLLOQ. thing, hang-up

fixed *adj*
1 *fixed times/opinions*
decided, settled, established, constant, definite, arranged, planned, set, firm, rigid, inflexible, entrenched, immobile, steady, secure, fast, rooted, permanent
COLLOQ. cast/set in stone
2 *a fixed smile*
fake, insincere, false, pretended
COLLOQ. pretend, phoney
E3 1 variable, varying, flexible, mobile

fixedly *adv*
intently, attentively, hard, watchfully, closely, steadily, searchingly, staringly

fixity *n*
permanence, persistence, constancy, stability, steadiness, fixedness
FORMAL immutability

fixture *n*
1 *fixtures and fittings*
equipment, furnishings, furniture, installations
2 *a sports fixture*
event, match, game, competition, contest, race, round, meeting

fizz *v, n*
♦ *v*
effervesce, sparkle, bubble, froth, foam, fizzle, hiss
♦ *n*
1 EFFERVESCENCE, bubbles, bubbling, fizz, fizziness, gas, gassiness, sparkle, foam, foaming, froth, frothing, ferment, fermentation
2 LIVELINESS, sparkle, vivacity, vitality, animation, buoyancy, enthusiasm, high spirits, excitedness, excitement, exhilaration, exuberance
COLLOQ. vim, zing, zip

fizzle
■ **fizzle out**
collapse, come to nothing, die away, die down, fall through, fail, come to grief, stop, subside, disappear, evaporate, taper off, peter out
FORMAL dissipate
COLLOQ. fold, flop

fizzy *adj*
effervescent, sparkling, aerated, carbonated, gassy, bubbly, bubbling, frothy, foaming

flab *n*
fat, fatness, obesity, plumpness, stoutness, solidness, bulk, chubbiness, overweight, paunch, pot (belly), blubber
FORMAL corpulence
COLLOQ. spare tyre

flabbergasted adj
amazed, confounded, astonished, astounded, staggered, dumbfounded, speechless, stunned, dazed, nonplussed, overcome, overwhelmed
COLLOQ. bowled over, blown away, knocked for six, gobsmacked

flabby adj
1 FLESHY, soft, yielding, flaccid, limp, floppy, drooping, hanging, sagging, slack, loose, lax, fat, overweight, plump
2 flabby business corporations
wasteful, uneconomical, disorganized, inefficient, sloppy, slack, lax
E3 1 firm, strong, lean, toned **2** lean

flaccid adj
limp, drooping, droopy, flabby, floppy, lax, loose, sagging, slack, soft, toneless, weak, nerveless, relaxed, clammy
E3 firm, hard

flag[1] n, v
♦ n
Related adjective: vexillary
♦ v
1 SIGNAL, wave, salute, motion, hail, wave down, signal to stop
2 MARK, indicate, label, tag, note

Types of flag include:

banderol	ensign	signal flag
banner	gonfalon	standard
bunting	jack	streamer
burgee	oriflamme	swallow tail
colours	pennant	vexillum
cornet	pilot flag	

Names of flags include:

Blue Ensign	Red Crescent	Star-spangled Banner
Blue Peter	Red Cross	ner
Crescent	Red Ensign	Tricolour
Hammer and	Rising Sun	Union Jack
Sickle	Saltire	White Ensign
Jolly Roger	Skull and	Yellow Jack
Old Glory	Crossbones	
Olympic Flag	Stars and Stripes	

flag[2] v
spirits were beginning to flag
lessen, diminish, decline, fall (off), subside, wane, ebb, sink, slump, dwindle, peter out, taper off, fade, fail, weaken, slow, falter, tire, grow tired, weary, wilt, droop, hang down, sag, flop, faint, die
FORMAL abate
E3 revive

flagellation n
beating, whipping, flogging, lashing, scourging, thrashing, flaying, whaling
OLD verberation
FORMAL castigation, chastisement, vapulation

flagging adj
lessening, diminishing, declining, subsiding, sinking, dwindling, ebbing, waning, decreasing, fading, failing, weakening, slowing, faltering, sagging, tiring, drooping, wilting
FORMAL abating
E3 returning, reviving

flagon n
bottle, decanter, carafe, jug, pitcher, flask, ewer, vessel, container

flagrant adj
scandalous, outrageous, glaring, disgraceful, dreadful, shameless, open, blatant, atrocious, enormous, infamous, notorious, bold, brazen, audacious, ostentatious, barefaced, naked, conspicuous, unashamed, undisguised, overt, rank, gross, arrant
FORMAL egregious, heinous
E3 covert, secret

> **flagrant** or **blatant**?
> *See panel at* **blatant**.

flail v
wave uncontrolledly, swing wildly, thresh, thrash, batter, beat, whip, strike

flair n
1 SKILL, ability, natural ability, aptitude, faculty, gift, talent, bent, facility, knack, mastery, genius, feel
2 STYLE, taste, discernment, acumen, elegance, stylishness, panache
E3 1 inability, ineptitude

flak n
criticism, blame, censure, complaints, disapproval, fault-finding, hostility, opposition, abuse, condemnation
FORMAL animadversions, aspersions, disapprobation, disparagement, invective
COLLOQ. bad press, brickbats, stick, knocking, panning

flake n, v
♦ n
scale, peeling, paring, shaving, scurf, sliver, shiver, wafer, chip, splinter, bit, particle, fragment, smut, spangle, flaught
TECHNICAL squama, flocculus, desquamation, exfoliation, furfur
OLD (Shakesp) flaw
♦ v
scale, peel, chip, splinter, blister
TECHNICAL desquamate, exfoliate
■ **flake out**
collapse, pass out, faint, keel over, drop, fall asleep, relax completely

flaky adj
dry, scaly, scurfy, laminar, layered
TECHNICAL squamate, squamose, squamous, flocculent, desquamative, desquamatory, exfoliative, furfuraceous, scabrous

flamboyance n
showiness, ostentation, colour, brilliance, glamour, extravagance, style, dash, élan, panache, theatricality
COLLOQ. pizzazz
E3 diffidence, restraint

flamboyant adj
showy, ostentatious, flashy, gaudy, bright, colourful, brilliant, exciting, dazzling, striking, dashing, extravagant, rich, glamorous, elaborate, ornate, florid, baroque, rococo, theatrical
E3 modest, restrained

flame v, n
♦ v
1 BURN, catch fire, flare, blaze, burst into flames
2 GLOW, glare, flash, beam, shine, sparkle, gleam, radiate, flush, go/become/turn red, redden
♦ n
1 FIRE, blaze, light, brightness, gleam, glow, heat, warmth
FORMAL conflagration
2 PASSION, ardour, fervour, warmth, fervency, excitement, enthusiasm, eagerness, keenness, zeal, intensity, radiance, fire
3 an old flame
lover, partner, boyfriend, girlfriend, sweetheart
■ **in flames**
on fire, burning, alight, ignited, flaming, aflame, blazing, ablaze

flameproof adj
fireproof, non-flammable, incombustible, non-inflammable, fire-resistant, flame-resistant
E3 flammable, inflammable, combustible

flaming *adj*

1 *a flaming torch*
burning, alight, aflame, blazing, on fire, in flames, fiery, brilliant, scintillating, red-hot, glowing, raging, smouldering

2 *a flaming red*
intense, vivid, bright, brilliant, blazing

3 *a flaming row/temper*
furious, angry, enraged, raging, infuriated, incensed, mad, violent

4 CURSED, damned, wretched, detestable, abominable, hateful, loathsome, odious, vile, fiendish, annoying, unpleasant, pernicious, infamous
FORMAL execrable
COLLOQ. blasted, blooming, blinking, flipping, darned, dashed, confounded, infernal, dratting
SLANG bloody; (*vulgar*) frigging; (*taboo*) fucking

flammable *adj*
inflammable, ignitable, combustible, burnable
⊟ non-flammable, incombustible, flameproof, fire-resistant, flame-resistant

flank *n, v*
♦ *n*

1 *the animal's flank*
side, quarter, wing, loin, haunch, hip, thigh

2 *the enemy's flank*
side, edge, wing
♦ *v*
edge, fringe, skirt, line, border, bound, confine, wall, screen

flannel *n*
nonsense, rubbish, flattery, blarney, smooth talk
FORMAL blandishments
COLLOQ. waffle, rot, sweet talk, soft soap, spiel

flap *v, n*
♦ *v*
flutter, vibrate, wave, agitate, shake, wag, waggle, flag, flip, slat, swing, sway, swish, thrash, thresh, beat, move up and down, move from side to side; *dialect* flacker, waff, wap; *Scot* flaff, wallop
OLD winnow
♦ *n*

1 FOLD, fly, lapel, overhang, overlap, covering, fall, tongue, tab, lug, tag, tail, skirt, apron, lap, lappet
TECHNICAL aileron, elevon, visor, epiglottis, loma, great omentum, epiploon, tuner, barn-door
OLD aventail

2 FLUTTER, fluttering, wave, shake, wag, waggle, beat, swing, sway, swish; *Scot* flaff, wap

3 PANIC, fuss, commotion, fluster, agitation, flutter, dither
COLLOQ. state, tiswas, tizwas, tizzy, stew

flare *v, n*
♦ *v*

1 FLAME, burn, blaze, glare, glow, gleam, glitter, sparkle, flash, flicker, burst, explode, erupt

2 BROADEN, widen, flare out, spread out, splay
♦ *n*

1 FLAME, blaze, glare, flash, flicker, burst, glimmer, gleam, dazzle

2 SIGNAL, distress signal, warning signal, beacon, light, rocket, beam

3 BROADENING, widening, spread, splay

■ **flare up**
erupt, break out, blaze, burst out, lose your temper, lose control
COLLOQ. explode, blow up, boil over, lose your cool, blow a fuse, blow your top, burst a blood vessel, do your nut, flip your lid, fly into a rage, fly off the handle, foam at the mouth, freak out, go ape, go ballistic, go berserk, go mad, go off the deep end, go up the wall, hit the roof, lose your rag, throw a wobbly; *Aust* go to market; *Aust & NZ* do your block

flare-up *n*
eruption, outburst, discharge, ejection, emission, venting, outbreak, explosion, rash, inflammation

flash *v, n, adj*
♦ *v*

1 BEAM, shine, light up, lighten, flare, blaze, glare, glance, gleam, glimmer, glisten, glint, flicker, twinkle, sparkle, blink, glitter, shimmer, scintillate, dance
FORMAL coruscate, fulgurate, fulminate

2 *the train flashed past*
streak, fly, shoot, speed, dart, race, dash, tear, zoom, rush, bolt, career, bound

3 *flashed her engagement ring*
flourish, brandish, flaunt, show off, display

4 EXPOSE YOURSELF, show your genitals, commit indecent exposure
♦ *n*

1 *flash of lightning*
beam, ray, shaft, spark, blaze, flare, burst, streak, lightning, bolt, fork, glare, glimmer, glitter, gleam, glint, flicker, twinkle, sparkle, shimmer, scintillation, flaught, *bluette*
OLD fire-flag, fire-flaught; (*Spenser*) flake; *Scot* glaiks
FORMAL coruscation, fulguration

2 *a flash of inspiration*
burst, outburst, outbreak, sudden appearance, show, display, exhibition, concetto
♦ *adj*
showy, ostentatious, smart, fashionable, expensive, glamorous, gaudy, kitsch, pretentious

■ **in a flash**
in an instant, instantly, in a moment, in a split second, in a twinkling, in the twinkling of an eye, in no time (at all), in less than no time, in a trice
COLLOQ. pdq, pronto, in a jiffy, in two shakes of a lamb's tail, before you can say Jack Robinson

---

SYNONYM NUANCES

verb sense 1
Beam suggests directing a shaft of light, whilst **shine** conveys an image of constant, reflecting light: *the spotlight shone on the models*. The term **light up**, may be used to suggest infusing with light. **Flare** and **blaze** suggest a quick explosion of light or flame.
  You can use **glare** to suggest a constant, dazzling effect: *the glare of headlights*. The terms **glance** and **glint** suggest a momentary catching of the light causing a flash: *a light that glinted on the glancing raindrops*. **Gleam** and **glimmer** imply a more muted light, and **glisten** is suggestive of a wet or oily appearance: *the rain glistened on his skin*. To convey the idea of constant subtle movement of light you could use **flicker** or **scintillate**: *the waters of the river were broken and scintillating*, or **twinkle**, which is usually associated with an attractive sight such as the stars: *the stars twinkled in the black sky*.
  A sense of movement and prettiness is also conveyed in the verbs **sparkle** and **glitter**. **Blink** implies a broken ray but does not have the same appealing connotations, while **dance** implies a much more erratic but attractive movement: *the light danced on the water*, and **shimmer** conjures up images of waves of light: *a heat haze shimmered above the fields*.

---

flashy *adj*
showy, ostentatious, flamboyant, glamorous, bold, loud, garish, gaudy, jazzy, flash, pretentious, tawdry, cheap, vulgar, tasteless, kitsch, showing poor taste
COLLOQ. tacky, glitzy; *Aust* lairy
SLANG bling, blingy
⊟ plain, tasteful

flask *n*
bottle, carafe, flagon, decanter, vessel, container, matrass; *dialect* flacket; *Can* mick
OLD lekythos

flat *n, adj, adv*

♦ *n*

apartment, penthouse, maisonette, tenement, flatlet, rooms, suite, bedsit(ter); *Aust & NZ* home unit

COLLOQ. pad

♦ *adj*

1 LEVEL, plane, even, smooth, uniform, unbroken, levelled, horizontal, outstretched, prostrate, prone, recumbent, reclining, low, spread-eagled

TECHNICAL homaloidal

FORMAL supine

COLLOQ. flat as a pancake

2 SHALLOW, not deep, not thick, not tall

3 *a flat tyre*

punctured, burst, deflated, collapsed, ruptured

COLLOQ. blown-out

4 *a flat battery*

dead, used up, finished

COLLOQ. bust, kaput, duff

5 DULL, boring, monotonous, tedious, uninteresting, unexciting, stale, lifeless, toneless, dead, spiritless, lacklustre, drab, vapid, insipid, bland, weak, watery, empty, pointless

6 *a flat refusal*

absolute, utter, total, unequivocal, categorical, positive, unconditional, unqualified, outright, out-and-out, downright, point-blank, direct, straight, explicit, plain, final, definite, complete

7 *feel flat*

depressed, low, discouraged, dejected, downcast, despondent, miserable, inactive, sluggish, slack, slow

COLLOQ. down

8 *charge a flat price*

set, fixed, standard, definite, stock, regular, firm, rigid, planned, arranged

9 *the market was flat*

sluggish, slow, inactive, quiet, slack, sleepy, stagnant, dull, dead, lifeless

10 STILL, dead, no longer fizzy

E **1** bumpy, vertical, upright **2** deep, thick, tall **4** charged **5** exciting, full **6** equivocal **7** happy, cheerful, lively **8** variable, negotiable **9** active, busy **10** fizzy, effervescent, sparkling

♦ *adv*

directly, outright, categorically, absolutely, straight, point-blank, completely, totally, utterly, entirely, exactly, plainly, precisely

■ **flat out**

at top speed, at full speed, all out, as fast as possible, hard, as hard as possible, for all you are worth

flatly *adv*

categorically, point-blank, positively, absolutely, completely, uncompromisingly, unconditionally, unhesitatingly

FORMAL peremptorily

flatness *n*

1 EVENNESS, levelness, smoothness, horizontality, uniformity

2 DULLNESS, monotony, tedium, boredom, staleness, emptiness, tastelessness, insipidity, vapidity

FORMAL languor

flatten *v*

1 SMOOTH, iron, press, roll, crush, squash, compress, plane, level, make flat, make even, even out

2 KNOCK DOWN, knock to the ground, prostrate, floor, fell, demolish, raze, tear down, defeat, overwhelm, subdue

flatter *v*

1 PRAISE, compliment, adulate, fawn, cringe, sing the praises of, wheedle, toady, kowtow, humour, play up to, court, pay court to, curry favour with, palaver, sawder, soft-sawder, tickle the ear of, soap, soothe, adulate; *Scot* fleech, phrase; *Irish* soothe; *N Am* stroke

OLD claw, collogue, gloze, smooth it, bear in hand, beslobber, beslaver; (*Shakesp*) make fair weather, word

FORMAL sycophantize, eulogize, inveigle, blandish

COLLOQ. flannel, sweet-talk, butter up, creep, suck up to, make up to, soft-soap, massage someone's ego, lay it on; *N Am* cozy up (with)

2 *that dress flatters you*

show off, make someone look attractive, look good on, become, suit, enhance, embellish, grace, show to advantage, befit

E **1** criticize

flatterer *n*

adulator, sycophant, fawner, groveller, lackey, toady, bootlicker, lickspittle

FORMAL encomiast, eulogizer

COLLOQ. back-scratcher, creep, creeper, crawler, yes-man

E critic, opponent

flattering *adj*

complimentary, kind, favourable, enhancing, gratifying, becoming, adulatory, ingratiating, fawning, fulsome, effusive, servile, smooth-spoken, smooth-tongued, honeyed, honey-tongued, sugared, sugary

OLD gnathonic

FORMAL laudatory, obsequious, sycophantic, unctuous

COLLOQ. sweet-talking, soft-soaping

E candid, uncompromising, unflattering

flattery *n*

adulation, praise, blarney, fulsomeness, compliments, cajolery, cajolement, fawning, toadyism, ingratiation, servility, butter, flapdoodle, soft sawder; *dialect* carny; *Scot* fleeching, fleechment; *N Am* taffy

OLD glozing, fair words, court holy water

FORMAL eulogy, sycophancy, blandishments, laudation

COLLOQ. sweet talk, soft soap, flannel, back scratching

SLANG sugar

OLD SLANG soap

E criticism

QUOTATIONS

Imitation is the sincerest form of flattery
CHARLES CALEB COLTON, *Lacon*

---

flatulence *n*

wind, windiness, gas, gassiness

FORMAL eructation, flatus, borborygmus, ventosity

COLLOQ. farting

flatulent *v*

windy, gassy

FORMAL ventose

flaunt *v*

show off, display, parade, flourish, brandish, exhibit, boast, air, sport, vaunt, wield, dangle, flash; *dialect* strout; *Scot* skyre

OLD disport, strut

⚠ flaunt or flout?

To *flaunt* something is 'to show it off or display it ostentatiously': *She was flaunting her new fur coat in front of her colleagues.* Flout means 'to treat with contempt, to refuse to obey or comply with': *He constantly flouts authority/the law.*

---

flavour *n, v*

♦ *n*

1 TASTE, tang, smack, savour, relish, piquancy, zest, aroma, odour

COLLOQ. zing

2 QUALITY, property, character, style, aspect, feeling, feel, atmosphere, tone, spirit, essence, nature, soul

3 HINT, indication, impression, suggestion, touch, tinge, tone

♦ *v*

season, spice (up), ginger up, infuse, imbue, lace

flavouring *n*

seasoning, flavour, spice, zest, tang, relish, piquancy, essence, extract, additive

COLLOQ. zing

flaw *n*
defect, imperfection, fault, weakness, weak spot, Achilles' heel, foible, shortcoming, failing, fallacy, lapse, slip, error, mistake, blemish, spot, mark, speck, crack, crevice, fissure, cleft, rent, split, tear, rift, chip, break, fracture, craze
TECHNICAL brack, thief, windshake, hamartia
OLD gall
COLLOQ. fly in the ointment

flawed *adj*
imperfect, defective, faulty, blemished, marked, damaged, spoilt, marred, cracked, chipped, broken, unsound, fallacious, erroneous
F3 flawless, perfect

flawless *adj*
perfect, faultless, unblemished, without blemish, spotless, immaculate, impeccable, stainless, sound, intact, whole, unbroken, undamaged, unimpaired
F3 flawed, imperfect, blemished

flay *v*
1 SKIN, skin alive, upbraid, revile, scourge, flog, flench
OLD uncase
FORMAL excoriate, castigate, execrate, lambast
2 CRITICIZE, condemn, find fault with, attack, denounce, run down, slate
COLLOQ. slam, knock, pan, pull/tear apart, pull to pieces, tear a strip off

fleck *v, n*
♦ *v*
dot, spot, mark, speckle, dapple, mottle, stipple, freckle, streak, sprinkle, dust, spatter
♦ *n*
dot, point, spot, mark, stain, speck, speckle, freckle, streak

fledgling *n, adj*
♦ *n*
beginner, newcomer, novice, apprentice, learner, recruit, trainee, tiro, neophyte, novitiate, tenderfoot
COLLOQ. greenhorn, rookie
♦ *adj*
emergent, budding, coming (out), developing, emerging, embryonic, rising, independent
FORMAL burgeoning, nascent

flee *v*
run away, bolt, fly, take flight, take off, make off, cut and run, escape, get away, rush, decamp, abscond, leave, depart, withdraw, retreat, vanish, disappear, make yourself scarce
COLLOQ. get out, push along/off, make tracks, quit, scat, scoot, scram, take to your heels, make yourself scarce, shove off, bunk off, clear off, split, scarper, skedaddle, vamoose, skive, do a runner, do a bunk, do a moonlight flit, hit the road/trail, make a bolt/break for it, up sticks, hightail it, sling your hook
F3 stay

fleece *n, v*
♦ *n*
down, coat, wool
♦ *v*
swindle, rob, steal, cheat, defraud, overcharge, plunder, mulct, bilk
COLLOQ. do, bleed, con, diddle, squeeze, fiddle, gull, have someone on, string along, pull a fast one, put one over on
SLANG rip off, sting, take for a ride, take to the cleaners

fleecy *adj*
downy, woolly, soft, velvety, shaggy, nappy, fluffy, hairy
TECHNICAL floccose, flocculate, lanuginose, pilose, eriophorous
F3 bald, smooth

fleet *n, adj*
♦ *n*
flotilla, armada, navy, task force, naval force, squadron
♦ *adj*
swift, fast, quick, rapid, nimble, flying, speedy, agile, light-footed, winged, mercurial, meteoric

FORMAL expeditious
F3 slow

fleeting *adj*
short, brief, flying, short-lived, quick, sudden, rushed, momentary, transient, transitory, passing, temporary
FORMAL evanescent, fugacious, ephemeral
COLLOQ. here today and gone tomorrow
F3 lasting, permanent

fleetingly *adv*
briefly, for a moment, for an instant, for a second, quickly, momentarily, casually

flesh *n, v*
♦ *n*
1 *an animal's flesh*
body, tissue, fat, muscle, brawn, skin, meat, pulp
2 SUBSTANCE, matter, physicality, pith, stuff, solidity, significance, weight
3 *pleasures of the flesh*
human nature, body, physical nature, sinful nature, carnal nature, physicality, sensuality, sexuality
FORMAL carnality, corporeality
Related adjectives: carnal, carneous, carnose
■ **flesh out**
add/give details, elaborate on, expand on, make complete, make more substantial
■ **flesh and blood**
family, relative, relations, kin, kindred
COLLOQ. folks
■ **in the flesh**
in person, in real life, in actual life, before your own eyes

fleshly *adj*
worldly, earthy, physical, earthly, bodily, human, animal, sensual, sexual, bestial, carnal, lustful, erotic, material, brutish
FORMAL corporal, corporeal
F3 spiritual

fleshy *adj*
fat, ample, beefy, chubby, chunky, brawny, hefty, meaty, obese, plump, podgy, portly, tubby, stout, paunchy, overweight, well-padded
FORMAL corpulent, rotund
COLLOQ. flabby
F3 thin, slim

flex *n, v*
♦ *n*
cable, wire, lead, cord
♦ *v*
bend, bow, curve, angle, crook, ply, double up, stretch, tighten, contract
F3 straighten, extend

flexibility *n*
1 BENDABILITY, pliability, pliancy, elasticity, resilience, spring, springiness, suppleness, give, flexion
FORMAL tensility
2 ADAPTABILITY, agreeability, adjustability, amenability
FORMAL complaisance
F3 1, 2 inflexibility

flexible *adj*
1 BENDABLE, pliable, pliant, plastic, malleable, mouldable, elastic, stretchy, springy, yielding, supple, lithe, limber, double-jointed, agile, lissome, mobile, withy
COLLOQ. bendy
2 ADAPTABLE, adjustable, changeable, amenable, accommodating, variable, open, open-ended, yielding, manageable, complying, pliable, pliant, tractable
F3 1 inflexible, rigid 2 fixed, inflexible, rigid

flick *v, n*
♦ *v*
hit, strike, rap, tap, touch, dab, flip, swish, snap, click, jerk, whip, lash, fillip, flirt
♦ *n*
rap, tap, touch, dab, flip, jerk, click, lick, snap, swish

■ flick through
flip through, browse through, thumb through, leaf through, run through, glance at, glance over, skip, skim, scan

flicker v, n
♦ v
flash, blink, wink, twinkle, sparkle, glimmer, glitter, flare, glint, shimmer, gutter, flutter, vibrate, bat, jump, lick, play, quiver, waver, flaught
♦ n
flash, gleam, glint, twinkle, glimmer, glitter, sparkle, spark, trace, drop, iota, atom, indication
FORMAL lambency

flier n
handout, leaflet, circular, bulletin, statement, press release, brochure, pamphlet, literature

flight¹ n
1 FLYING, aviation, aeronautics, air transport, air travel
2 JOURNEY, trip, voyage, shuttle, globetrotting
3 *a flight of steps*
staircase, set, stairway, stairs, steps

flight² n, v
♦ n
his flight from the police
fleeing, escape, running away/off, getaway, breakaway, rush, absconding, exit, departure, exodus, retreat, withdrawal
■ take flight
run, run away, bolt, flee, fly, take off, make off, cut and run, escape, get away, rush, decamp, abscond, leave, depart, withdraw, retreat, vanish, disappear
COLLOQ. push along/off, make tracks, quit, scat, scoot, scram, take to your heels, make yourself scarce, shove off, bunk off, clear off, split, scarper, skedaddle, vamoose, skive, do a runner, do a bunk, do a moonlight flit, hit the road/trail, make a bolt/break for it, up sticks, hightail it, sling your hook
SLANG leg it; *N Am* lam it, take it on the lam

flighty adj
inconstant, scatterbrained, impetuous, impulsive, changeable, irresponsible, silly, skittish, thoughtless, fickle, frivolous, lightheaded, rattle-brained, rattle-headed, erratic, unstable, unsteady, volatile, unbalanced, wild, mercurial, giddy, butterfly, skipping, unballasted, volage, whisky-frisky, bubble-headed; *Scot* loup-the-dyke, weather-headed, hellicat
FORMAL capricious
COLLOQ. birdbrained, hare-brained
E3 steady, responsible, sensible

flimsy adj
1 *flimsy clothing/structures*
thin, fine, light, slight, insubstantial, ethereal, lightweight, fragile, delicate, filmy, sheer, shaky, rickety, ramshackle, jerry-built, makeshift
2 *a flimsy excuse*
weak, feeble, meagre, inadequate, shallow, superficial, trivial, poor, thin, trifling, unconvincing, implausible
E3 1 sturdy, strong 2 convincing, plausible

flinch v
wince, start, cringe, cower, crouch, quail, tremble, shake, quake, shudder, shiver, shrink, shrink back, blench, recoil, falter, draw back, pull back, balk, shy away, avoid, shirk, withdraw, retreat, flee
COLLOQ. duck, dodge, funk

fling v, n
♦ v
throw, hurl, pitch, lob, toss, cast, sling, catapult, launch, propel, send, send flying, let fly, heave, jerk
COLLOQ. chuck
♦ n
1 THROW, hurl, pitch, lob, toss, cast, shot, heave
2 SPREE, venture, indulgence, good time, gamble, binge, whirl, go, trial, try, turn, attempt
COLLOQ. crack

3 AFFAIR, relationship, liaison, intrigue, love affair, romance, affaire, affaire d'amour, grande passion, amour
COLLOQ. carry-on

flinty adj
stony, hard, emotionless, blank, expressionless, deadpan, poker-faced, cold, frigid, icy, frosty, chilly, indifferent, unfeeling, heartless, adamant, steely, unresponsive, callous, merciless, pitiless, severe, stern, unforgiving, inexorable, hostile
E3 warm, soft-hearted, friendly

flip v, n
♦ v
flick, spin, twirl, twist, turn, toss, throw, cast, pitch, jerk, flap, click, snap
♦ n
flick, spin, twirl, twist, turn, toss, jerk, flap, click, snap
■ flip through
flick through, browse through, thumb through, leaf through, glance at, glance over, skip, skim, scan

flippancy n
facetiousness, light-heartedness, frivolity, superficiality, shallowness, thoughtlessness, disrespect, disrespectfulness, glibness, pertness, impertinence, irreverence, levity
FORMAL persiflage
COLLOQ. cheek, cheekiness, sauciness
E3 earnestness, seriousness

flippant adj
facetious, light-hearted, frivolous, superficial, shallow, thoughtless, offhand, flip, glib, pert, impudent, impertinent, rude, disrespectful, irreverent, irresponsible
FORMAL insouciant
COLLOQ. saucy, cheeky
E3 serious, respectful

flippantly adv
facetiously, light-heartedly, frivolously, superficially, thoughtlessly, glibly, impertinently, rudely, disrespectfully, irreverently, irresponsibly
E3 seriously, respectfully

flipping adj
wretched, cursed, damned, fiendish, annoying, unpleasant
COLLOQ. blasted, blooming, blinking, darned, dashed, confounded, infernal, dratting

flirt v, n
♦ v
chat up, make eyes at, ogle, eye up, make a pass at, make up to, lead on, philander, dally
COLLOQ. carry on
OLD SLANG mash
♦ n
tease, vamp, trifler, heart-breaker, philanderer, wanton, hussy, coquet(te), gillet
OLD gillflirt
SLANG chippy
OLD SLANG masher
■ flirt with
consider, entertain, toy with, play with, trifle with, dabble in, try

flirtation n
affair, chatting up, dalliance, dallying, philandering, coquetry, intrigue, teasing, toying, trifling, sport
FORMAL amour
COLLOQ. come-on

flirtatious adj
provocative, coquettish, flirty, loose, promiscuous, teasing, sportive, amorous, wanton
OLD flirtish
COLLOQ. come-hither, come-on

flit v
dart, speed, dash, rush, flash, fly, wing, flutter, flitter, whisk, skim, skip, slip, pass, bob, dance

float v
1 GLIDE, stay afloat, sail, swim, bob, be buoyant, slide, drift, waft, hover, wander, hang, suspend
2 LAUNCH, initiate, set up, establish, promote, get going, get off the ground, be in at the beginning of, get the show on the road
3 *float an idea with you*
suggest, recommend, put forward, submit, present, propose, come up with, table
E3 **1** sink

floating adj
1 AFLOAT, buoyant, unsinkable, sailing, swimming, bobbing, drifting, wafting, hovering
2 VARIABLE, fluctuating, movable, migratory, transitory, wandering, unsettled, unattached, free, uncommitted, indecisive
COLLOQ. sitting on the fence
E3 **1** sinking, submerged **2** fixed, settled, committed

flock v, n
◆ v
herd, swarm, troop, converge, mass, bunch, cluster, huddle, mill, crowd, throng, group, assemble, come together, gather, collect, congregate
◆ n
herd, pack, crowd, throng, drove, fold, host, multitude, mass, bunch, cluster, group, gathering, collection, assembly, congregation; *Aust & NZ* mob

flog v
1 BEAT, whip, lash, scourge, birch, cane, strap, flay, drub, thrash, belt, chastise, punish, horsewhip, swish, tat, breech, knout; *S Afr* sjambok
OLD taw
FORMAL flagellate, vapulate
COLLOQ. whack, wallop, hide, larrup
2 SELL, deal in, handle, trade, peddle, hawk, offer for sale, put up for sale

flogging n
beating, whipping, lashing, scourging, birching, caning, flaying, strapping, belting, thrashing, horsewhipping
FORMAL flagellation, vapulation
COLLOQ. whacking, walloping, hiding

flood v, n
◆ v
1 DELUGE, inundate, soak, drench, saturate, fill, overflow, surge, swell, brim over, immerse, submerge, drown, engulf, swamp, overwhelm, smother
FORMAL transgress
2 FLOW, pour, stream, rush, surge, gush, saturate, swamp, inundate
◆ n
1 DELUGE, inundation, downpour, torrent, flash flood, flow, tide, stream, rush, spate, outpouring, overflow, cataclysm, bore, eagre, freshet
TECHNICAL debacle
OLD (*Shakesp*) rage
FORMAL alluvion, diluvium
2 EXCESS, torrent, series, succession, abundance, profusion, glut, tide, spring tide
FORMAL superfluity, plethora
E3 **1** drought, trickle **2** trickle, dearth, lack

floor n, v
◆ n
1 FLOORING, ground, base, basis
2 *on the third floor*
storey, level, stage, landing, deck, tier
◆ v
1 BAFFLE, defeat, overwhelm, beat, frustrate, confound, perplex, nonplus, dumbfound, puzzle, bewilder, disconcert, throw
FORMAL discomfit
COLLOQ. stump, flummox
2 KNOCK DOWN, strike down, fell, level, prostrate

flop v, n
◆ v
1 COLLAPSE, slump, tumble, droop, hang, dangle, sag, drop, fall, topple, plump, whop
OLD swap
COLLOQ. flump
2 FAIL, be unsuccessful, collapse, misfire, fall flat, founder, sink
COLLOQ. fold, tank, pack up, crash, go bust, go broke, go to the wall, come a cropper, go into the red; *N Am* bomb, lay an egg
◆ n
failure, fiasco, debacle, disaster
COLLOQ. washout, non-starter, shambles, slip-up, no-hoper, also-ran, has-been; *N Am* bomb

floppy adj
droopy, hanging, dangling, sagging, limp, loose, baggy, soft, flabby, flaccid
E3 firm

flora n
botany, plant life, plants, vegetable kingdom, vegetation, herbage, plantage

florid adj
1 FLOWERY, ornate, elaborate, fussy, overelaborate, extravagant, embellished, verbose, pompous, high-flown, high-sounding, bombastic, baroque, rococo, flamboyant
TECHNICAL melismatic
FORMAL grandiloquent
2 *a florid complexion*
ruddy, red, red-faced, reddish, blushing, flushed, purple, sanguine
FORMAL rubicund
E3 **1** plain, simple **2** pale

flotsam n
jetsam, wreckage, floating wreckage, debris, rubbish, junk, oddments, odds and ends
FORMAL detritus
COLLOQ. dreck

flounce[1] v
flounce out of the room
bounce, spring, stamp, storm, toss, jerk, twist, throw, fling, bob

flounce[2] n
a flounce of flannel petticoat
frill, fringe, ruffle, trimming, valance, falbala
OLD furbelow

flounder v
wallow, thresh about, flail about, struggle, grope, fumble, blunder, stagger, stumble, falter, dither, be confused, be in difficulties, go under, be out of your depth, not know which way to turn

flourish v, n
◆ v
1 THRIVE, grow, wax, increase, flower, blossom, bloom, bear fruit, be strong, develop, progress, get on, do well, prosper, succeed, boom
FORMAL burgeon
2 BRANDISH, wave, shake, twirl, swing, swish, wag, display, wield, flaunt, show off, parade, exhibit, vaunt
E3 **1** decline, languish, fail
◆ n
1 DISPLAY, parade, show, gesture, wave, sweep, fanfare, ornament, decoration, panache, élan
COLLOQ. pizzazz
2 *a flourish on the lettering*
swirl, curlicue, serif, twist

flourishing adj
thriving, blooming, blossoming, prosperous, successful, booming
FORMAL burgeoning

flout v

defy, disobey, break, disregard, go against, spurn, treat with contempt, show contempt for, disdain, reject, scorn, jeer at, scoff at, sneer at, mock, laugh at, ridicule
FORMAL violate
E3 obey, respect, regard

> **!** **flout** or **flaunt**?
> See panel at **flaunt**.

flow v, n

♦ v
1 CIRCULATE, move, go, run, proceed, course, ooze, seep, trickle, ripple, bubble, well, spout, spew, spurt, squirt, gush, jet, leak, drip, spill, pour, cascade, rush, stream, teem, flood, overflow, surge, sweep, drift, slip, slide, babble, gurgle, glide, roll, swirl, whirl
2 ORIGINATE, derive, arise, spring, emerge, issue, result, stem, proceed
FORMAL emanate
♦ n
course, flux, tide, current, drift, movement, passage, stream, deluge, cascade, spurt, gush, outpouring, flood, spate, abundance, plenty
OLD (Shakesp) recourse
FORMAL effusion, plethora

flower n, v

♦ n
1 BLOOM, blossom, bud, floret, floweret
TECHNICAL efflorescence, florescence, inflorescence
Related adjective: floral
2 BEST, cream, pick, finest, choice, select, élite, crème de la crème
3 PRIME, height, peak, pinnacle, acme, zenith, heyday, blossom, bloom, culmination, best part, maturity, perfection
♦ v
bud, bloom, blossom, open, sprout, come out, develop, grow, mature, prosper, thrive, flourish, succeed
FORMAL burgeon

Garden flowers include:

African violet	foxglove (digitalis)	petunia
alyssum	freesia	phlox
amaryllis	fritillary	pink (dianthus)
anemone	fuchsia	poinsettia
aster	gardenia	polyanthus
aubrietia	geranium	poppy
azalea	gladioli	primrose
begonia	grape hyacinth	primula
bluebell	hollyhock	rose
busy lizzie	hyacinth	salvia
(impatiens)	iris (flag)	scilla
calendula	jonquil	snapdragon
candytuft	lily	(antirrhinum)
carnation	lily-of-the-valley	snowdrop
chrysanthemum	lobelia	stock
coneflower	lupin	sunflower
cornflower	marigold	sweet pea
cowslip	montbretia	sweet william
crocus	narcissus	tulip
crown imperial	nasturtium	verbena
cyclamen	nemesia	viola
daffodil	nicotiana	violet
dahlia	night-scented	wallflower
daisy	stock	zinnia
delphinium	orchid	
forget-me-not	pansy	

See also **plant**; **shrub**; **wild flower**.

Parts of a flower include:

anther	nectary	spadix
calyx	ovary	spike
capitulum	ovule	stalk
carpel	panicle	stamen
corolla	pedicel	stigma
corymb	petal	style
dichasium	pistil	thalamus
filament	raceme	torus
gynoecium	receptacle	umbel
monochasium	sepal	

flowery adj

florid, ornate, elaborate, fancy, chintzy, bloomy, blossomy, baroque, rhetorical, high-flown, verbose, pompous, bombastic
TECHNICAL euphuistic
FORMAL grandiloquent
E3 plain, simple

flowing adj

1 *flowing rivers/traffic*
moving, oozing, seeping, bubbling, welling, gushing, pouring, rushing, cascading, streaming, surging, sweeping, overflowing
2 FLUENT, effortless, easy, natural, smooth, continuous, uninterrupted, unbroken
3 *flowing hair*
hanging, hanging loose, loose, floppy, hanging freely, falling, rolling, flaccid

fluctuate v

vary, change, alter, differ, shift, rise and fall, seesaw, go up and down, come and go, ebb and flow, alternate, swing, sway, undulate, vacillate, waver, hesitate, range, balance, trim, yo-yo
TECHNICAL float
FORMAL oscillate
COLLOQ. chop and change
E3 be steady

fluctuation n

variation, change, shift, swing, alternation, variability, range, instability, unsteadiness, wavering, irresolution, inconstancy, ambivalence, fickleness
TECHNICAL floating, nutation, seiche
FORMAL oscillation, capriciousness, vacillation

flue n

shaft, pipe, duct, vent, channel, passage, tunnel, chimney, uptake
TECHNICAL fluework
OLD tewel

fluency n

ease, eloquence, smoothness, articulateness, assurance, command, control, facility, readiness, outpouring, glibness, slickness
FORMAL facundity, volubility
E3 incoherence

fluent adj

flowing, smooth, easy, effortless, free-flowing, fluid, natural, graceful, elegant, articulate, eloquent, silver-tongued, slick, glib, ready
FORMAL voluble, mellifluous
COLLOQ. facile
E3 broken, inarticulate, tongue-tied

fluently adv

smoothly, easily, effortlessly, naturally, gracefully, elegantly, articulately, eloquently, glibly, pat

fluff n, v

♦ n
down, nap, pile, fuzz, floss, lint, dust
♦ v
botch, do badly, make a bad job of, mismanage, bungle, mess up, make a mess of, muck up, muddle, fumble, muff, spoil

COLLOQ. blot your copybook, boob, put your foot in it, foul up, blow
SLANG balls up, cock up, screw up
➤ bring off

fluffy *adj*
furry, fuzzy, downy, feathery, fleecy, woolly, hairy, shaggy, velvety, silky, soft

fluid *n, adj*
♦ *n*
liquid, solution, liquor, juice, gas, vapour
♦ *adj*
1 LIQUID, liquefied, aqueous, watery, flowing, running, runny, melted, molten
2 *a fluid situation*
variable, changeable, unstable, inconstant, shifting, mobile, adjustable, adaptable, flexible, open, unsettled, fluctuating, unsteady
FORMAL protean
3 *fluid movements*
flowing, free-flowing, smooth, effortless, easy, graceful, elegant, natural
➤ **1** solid, rigid **2** inflexible, fixed

fluke *n*
stroke, stroke of luck, lucky break, accident, quirk, blessing, windfall, break, chance, coincidence
FORMAL fortuity, serendipity
COLLOQ. freak

fluky *adj*
accidental, lucky, chance, fortunate, coincidental, uncertain, incalculable
FORMAL fortuitous, serendipitous
COLLOQ. jammy, freakish

flummox *v*
confuse, confound, baffle, bewilder, mystify, perplex, puzzle, nonplus, fox, defeat, stymie
COLLOQ. bamboozle, stump, floor, faze

flummoxed *adj*
baffled, confounded, bewildered, confused, perplexed, puzzled, mystified, nonplussed, foxed, stymied, at a loss, at sea
COLLOQ. bamboozled, stumped, floored, fazed

flunk *v*
be unsuccessful, founder, come to grief
COLLOQ. flop, fold, flunk, not come off, not make it, not come up to scratch, fall flat, blow it, blow your chances, bite the dust, come a cropper, come unstuck, come unglued, come undone, not come up with the goods; *N Am* bomb

flunkey *n*
lackey, assistant, servant, steward, menial, minion, slave, manservant, valet, underling, drudge, footman, hanger-on, cringer, toady, bootlicker, yes-man

flurried *adj*
upset, disturbed, flustered, unsettled, unnerved
FORMAL perturbed
COLLOQ. fazed, rattled, in a flap, in a tizzy, in a tizz, having kittens, all of a lather

flurry *n, v*
♦ *n*
1 BURST, outbreak, spell, shower, bout, spurt, gust, blast, squall, scurry, swirl, whirl
2 BUSTLE, hurry, hubbub, fluster, fuss, commotion, tumult, whirl, disturbance, agitation, excitement, stir; *Scot* swither
FORMAL perturbation
COLLOQ. to-do, flap
♦ *v*
fluster, hurry, hustle, agitate, bewilder, bother, bustle, flutter, fuss, unsettle, upset, confuse, ruffle, disconcert, disturb
FORMAL discountenance, perturb
COLLOQ. hassle, rattle

flush[1] *v, n, adj*
♦ *v*
1 BLUSH, go/turn red, redden, crimson, colour (up), burn, glow, flame
OLD gild
FORMAL suffuse
2 CLEANSE, wash, rinse, hose, swab, clear, scour, sluice, empty, eject, evacuate, expel
♦ *n*
bloom, freshness, vigour, glow, blush, reddening, colour, redness, rosiness, ruddiness, heyday
OLD rud
♦ *adj*
1 ABUNDANT, lavish, generous, full, overflowing, rich, wealthy, moneyed, prosperous, well-off, well-heeled, well-to-do
FORMAL replete
2 LEVEL, even, smooth, flat, plane, square, true

flush[2] *v*
flush the enemy out of the forest
force out, drive out, run to earth, discover, uncover, expel, eject, start, rouse, disturb

flushed *adj*
1 RED, rosy, ruddy, blushing, burning, crimson, scarlet, florid, aflame, ablaze, glowing, aglow, hot, embarrassed, blowzy
OLD hectic; (*Shakesp*) rosed
FORMAL rubicund
2 ELATED, thrilled, enthused, excited, exhilarated, exultant, animated, aroused, inspired, intoxicated, sanguine
➤ **1** pale

fluster *v, n*
♦ *v*
bother, upset, embarrass, disturb, agitate, ruffle, flap, discompose, confuse, confound, unsettle, unnerve, make nervous, disconcert, put off, distract, pother
OLD flustrate
FORMAL perturb
COLLOQ. rattle, faze
➤ calm
♦ *n*
flurry, bustle, commotion, disturbance, confusion, agitation, upset, turmoil, panic, embarrassment
OLD flustration
FORMAL perturbation
COLLOQ. state, flap, dither, tizzy, tizz
➤ calm

fluted *adj*
grooved, furrowed, channelled, corrugated, ribbed, ridged

flutter *v, n*
♦ *v*
flap, wave, beat, bat, flicker, vibrate, palpitate, agitate, shake, tremble, quiver, shiver, ruffle, flitter, ripple, twitch, pulsate, toss, waver, fluctuate, dance, hover
♦ *n*
1 FLAPPING, wave, beat, flicker, vibration, agitation, palpitation, tremble, tremor, quiver, shiver, shudder, twitch, ripple, ruffle
2 BET, gamble, wager, speculation, risk
COLLOQ. punt

flux *n*
fluctuation, instability, unrest, change, changeability, alteration, modification, fluidity, flow, movement, motion, transition, development, mutation
➤ stability, rest

QUOTATIONS
All is flux, nothing is stationary
HERACLITUS

fly[1] v

1 TAKE OFF, travel/go by air, rise, ascend, mount, soar, glide, float, hover, flit, flutter, wing
2 *fly an aeroplane*
control, operate, pilot, guide, manoeuvre, steer
3 *fly a flag*
show, wave, display, exhibit, present, reveal
4 RACE, sprint, dash, tear, rush, go/pass quickly, slip by, hurry, speed, zoom, shoot, bolt, dart, career, jet
FORMAL hasten
5 FLEE, run away, bolt, take flight, take off, make off, cut and run, escape, get away, rush, decamp, abscond, leave, depart, withdraw, retreat, vanish, disappear
COLLOQ. get out, push along/off, make tracks, quit, scat, scoot, scram, take to your heels, make yourself scarce, shove off, clear off, split, scarper, skedaddle, vamoose, skive, do a runner, do a bunk, do a moonlight flit, hit the road/trail, make a bolt/break for it
E3 stay

■ **fly at**
attack, assault, go for, fall upon, hit, strike, lay into, charge, lash out at, let someone have it, let fly
COLLOQ. bite someone's head off, have a go at, jump down someone's throat

fly[2] adj
he's a fly fellow
alert, artful, sharp, shrewd, astute, canny, careful, prudent, cunning
FORMAL sagacious
COLLOQ. nobody's fool, on the ball, smart

fly-by-night adj
disreputable, discreditable, questionable, shady, unreliable, untrustworthy, undependable, irresponsible, dubious, short-lived
FORMAL ephemeral
COLLOQ. cowboy, here today gone tomorrow
E3 reliable

flying adj
1 *flying insects*
gliding, floating, hovering, flapping, fluttering, airborne, winged, winging, wind-borne, soaring, mobile
2 *a flying visit*
brief, hurried, fleeting, rapid, fast, hasty, rushed, speedy
COLLOQ. whistle-stop

foam n, v
♦ n
froth, lather, suds, head, bubbles, fizz, spume, effervescence, mousse, surf, scum
OLD (*Shakesp*) yeast
♦ v
froth, lather, bubble, effervesce, fizz, boil, seethe, spume
OLD befoam; (*Spenser*) fry

foamy adj
frothy, lathery, bubbly, foaming, spumy, sudsy
FORMAL spumescent

fob
■ **fob off**
foist, pass off, get rid of, dump, unload, inflict, impose, deceive, put off
COLLOQ. palm off

focus n, v
♦ n
1 *the focus of concern*
focal point, target, centre, heart, core, nucleus, kernel, crux, hub, axis, linchpin, pivot, hinge
2 *the focus is on competition*
attention, priority, emphasis, importance, stress, weight, significance, concentration, underscoring, accent, accentuation, prominence, pre-eminence
♦ v
concentrate, aim, direct, turn, fix, spotlight, pinpoint, home in, zoom in, converge, meet, join, centre, bring into focus
COLLOQ. zero in

■ **in focus**
clear, sharp, distinct, crisp, well-defined
■ **out of focus**
blurred, ill-defined, indistinct, hazy, fuzzy, blurry, muzzy

fodder n
feed, food, foodstuff, forage, eatage, nourishment, rations, silage, soilage, provender, lucerne, browsing, provand, proviant, pabulum; *dialect* fother
OLD stover

foe n
enemy, adversary, antagonist, opponent, combatant, rival, ill-wisher
E3 friend

foetus n
unborn child, unborn baby, embryo
Related adjective: foetal

fog n, v
♦ n
1 MIST, haze, mistiness, haziness, cloud, gloom, murkiness, smog, smoke, pea-souper, pease-soup, pea-soup
FORMAL brume
2 PERPLEXITY, puzzlement, confusion, bewilderment, bafflement, disorientation, daze, trance, stupor, vagueness, obscurity, blur, haze
♦ v
1 MIST, steam up, cloud, dull, dim, darken, obscure
OLD befog
2 CONFUSE, blur, muddle, bewilder, baffle, perplex
FORMAL obfuscate

foggy adj
1 MISTY, hazy, smoggy, cloudy, clouded, overcast, murky, damp, dark, grey, shadowy, gloomy, dim
FORMAL brumous
2 *foggy recollections*
indistinct, vague, obscure, unclear, muddled
E3 1, 2 clear

foible n
quirk, weakness, weak point, idiosyncrasy, imperfection, eccentricity, oddity, failing, fault, defect, oddness, peculiarity, shortcoming, strangeness, habit

foil[1] v
foil someone's plans
defeat, outwit, frustrate, thwart, prevent, baffle, stump, counter, nullify, stop, check, balk, obstruct, block, elude, hinder, hamper
OLD foyle
FORMAL circumvent
COLLOQ. scuttle, scupper, pip
E3 abet

foil[2] n
a foil to her dark hair
contrast, complement, balance, setting, set-off, background, relief, beauty spot
OLD foyle
FORMAL antithesis

foist v
force, impose, introduce, thrust, unload, saddle, pass off, get rid of, fob off, wish on
COLLOQ. palm off

fold[1] v, n
♦ v
1 BEND, ply, double, overlap, tuck, pleat, crease, gather, turn under, turn down, turn over, crumple, crimp, crinkle
2 ENFOLD, embrace, hug, clasp, squeeze, envelop, wrap (up), enclose, entwine, intertwine
3 *the business folded*
fail, shut down, close, collapse, crash, go bankrupt, go out of business
COLLOQ. flop, pack up, go to the wall, go broke, go bust
♦ n
bend, turn, layer, ply, overlap, tuck, pleat, gather, crease, knife-edge, line, wrinkle, crinkle, pucker, ruffle, furrow, corrugation

fold² n

1 ENCLOSURE, pen, pound, compound, paddock, stockade, court, yard, ring, kraal
2 CONGREGATION, church, assembly, flock, community, gathering, company, parishioners, fellowship

folder n

file, binder, folio, portfolio, envelope, holder, wallet, pocket

foliage n

leaves, greenery, leafage, vegetation, foliation
TECHNICAL frondescence, foliature, vernation
FORMAL verdure

folk n, adj

♦ n
1 PEOPLE, society, nation, persons, humans, public, population, race, tribe, clan, ethnic group
2 RELATIONS, family, parents, relatives, kin, kindred, kinsfolk
♦ adj
ethnic, national, traditional, popular, native, indigenous, tribal, ancestral

folklore n

fables, folktales, legends, myths, mythology, lore, stories, tales, customs, beliefs, tradition, superstitions

folksy adj

1 *a folksy country table*
traditional, time-honoured, rustic, plain, simple, natural, crude, basic, unsophisticated, ordinary
2 AMIABLE, affable, genial, convivial, cordial, kind, kindly, warm, neighbourly, helpful, sympathetic, fond, affectionate, familiar, intimate, inseparable, close, companionable, sociable, outgoing, approachable, receptive, hospitable, comradely, amicable, good-natured
COLLOQ. mat(e)y, pally, chummy, thick, tight

follow v

1 *night follows day*
come after, succeed, come next, replace, supersede, supplant, take the place of, step into the shoes of
2 CHASE, pursue, go after, run after, hunt, track, trail, shadow, tail, stalk, dog, give chase, hound, catch, be at someone's heels
3 ACCOMPANY, go (along) with, escort, attend, trail, go behind, come behind, walk behind, tread behind, tag along
4 RESULT, ensue, develop, emanate, arise, issue, spring, flow, proceed
5 OBEY, adhere to, heed, mind, observe, note, accept, yield to, comply with, conform to, carry out, stick to, practise, take your cue from
FORMAL comply with
6 UNDERSTAND, grasp, comprehend, fathom, take in, appreciate
COLLOQ. twig, latch onto, suss (out)
7 *follow someone's example*
copy, imitate, repeat, emulate, mimic, ape
8 *she followed her father into medicine*
succeed, replace, take the place of, supplant
9 KEEP UP WITH, support, be interested in, be devoted to, be a fan of, be a supporter of, keep up to date with
E3 **1** precede **3** abandon, desert **5** disobey
■ **follow through**
continue, pursue, see through, finish, complete, conclude, fulfil, implement, bring to completion
■ **follow up**
investigate, check out, look into, research, continue, pursue, reinforce, consolidate

follower n

backer, supporter, admirer, enthusiast, fan, devotee; *Irish* voteen; disciple, apostle, acolyte, pupil, imitator, emulator, adherent, hanger-on, believer, convert, attendant, retainer, helper, companion, escort
COLLOQ. sidekick, freak, buff

following adj, n

♦ adj
subsequent, next, succeeding, successive, resulting, ensuing, consequent, later
E3 previous
♦ n
followers, suite, retinue, entourage, circle, fans, fanbase, admirers, adherents, supporters, support, body of support, backing, backers, patrons, patronage, clientèle, audience, public, coterie

folly n

1 FOOLISHNESS, stupidity, senselessness, rashness, recklessness, imprudence, irresponsibility, indiscretion, craziness, inanity, madness, lunacy, insanity, idiocy, imbecility, silliness, ludicrousness, ridiculousness, absurdity, nonsense, illogicality, foolhardiness, vanity, foolery, foppery, *folie*
OLD idiotcy
FORMAL fatuousness, moria
2 MONUMENT, tower, whim, belvedere, gazebo
E3 **1** wisdom, prudence, sanity

foment v

incite, instigate, excite, stir up, agitate, arouse, rouse, encourage, kindle, promote, prompt, provoke, raise, activate, stimulate, spur, quicken, goad, whip up, work up, foster, brew
E3 quell

fond adj

1 *fond of someone/something*
liking, partial to, attached to, keen on, having a soft spot for, addicted to, thinking the world of
FORMAL enamoured of
COLLOQ. hooked on, crazy about, mad about, daft about, dotty about, hot, nuts about/on
2 AFFECTIONATE, warm, tender, caring, loving, adoring, devoted, doting, indulgent, amorous, amatory, spoony
3 *fond expectations*
foolish, naive, deluded, credulous, absurd, impractical, over-optimistic, vain

fondle v

caress, stroke, pat, pet, hug, cuddle, smuggle, cosset, dandle, cocker
COLLOQ. grope, touch up

fondly adv

affectionately, warmly, tenderly, lovingly, amorously

fondness n

affection, devotion, kindness, tenderness, love, liking, fancy, attachment, enthusiasm, inclination, leaning, partiality, preference, weakness, soft spot, taste, susceptibility, *tendre*, tendresse
OLD well-liking
FORMAL penchant, predilection
E3 aversion, hate

food n

FOODSTUFFS, comestibles, provisions, meals, stores, rations, refreshments, sustenance, nourishment, nutrition, nutriment, subsistence, feed, fodder, diet, fare, dish, speciality, delicacy, cooking, cuisine, menu, board, table; *NZ* kai, kaikai
OLD aliment, pabulum; (*Spenser*) pasture; (*Shakesp*) repasture
FORMAL viands, victuals
COLLOQ. eatables, eats, scran, tuck
SLANG grub, nosh, chow, scoff; *Aust & NZ* tucker
See panel on next page
See also panels at **meat**.
■ **food for thought**
mental stimulation, something to be seriously considered, something to think about

fool n, v

♦ n
blockhead, fat-head, dunce, dimwit, simpleton, halfwit, idiot, cretin, imbecile, ignoramus, moron, dupe, stooge, butt, laughing-stock, clown, comic, buffoon, jester,

Kinds of food include:

SOUPS AND STEWS:
borsch
bouillabaisse
broth
chowder
cockaleekie
consommé
cullen skink
gazpacho
gumbo
minestrone
pho
succotash
vichyssoise

POTATO DISHES:
boxty
bubble and squeak
champ
chips
colcannon
dauphinoise potatoes
duchesse potatoes
French fries
gnocchi
gratin
mash
rösti
Scot stovies

SEAFOOD:
calamari
caviar
ceviche
crab stick
fish and chips
fishcake
fisherman's pie
fish-finger
gefilte fish

kedgeree
kipper
pickled herring
prawn cocktail
scampi

SALADS:
caesar salad
coleslaw
Greek salad
green salad
mesclun
potato salad
Russian salad
salade niçoise
tabbouleh
Waldorf salad
winter salad

VEGETABLE DISHES:
cauliflower cheese
macaroni cheese
nut cutlet
pease pudding
Quorn®
ratatouille
stuffed mushroom
tofu

MEAT AND GAME:
bacon
boeuf bourguignon
casserole
cassoulet
cottage pie
faggot
goulash
hotpot
Irish stew

roast beef and
  Yorkshire
  pudding
salami
sausage
Scotch woodcock
shepherd's pie
stroganoff
toad-in-the-hole
turducken

EGG DISHES:
eggs Benedict
frittata
omelette
quiche

FAST FOOD:
Big Mac®
N Am corn dog
hamburger
hot dog
KFC®
McDonald's®
Wimpy®

INTERNATIONAL AND REGIONAL:
baba ganoush
balti
bhajee (or bhaji)
biriyani
burrito
chillada
chilli con carne
chop suey
chorizo
couscous
curry
dal (or dhal)
dolma

empanada
enchilada
fajita
falafel
feijoada
fondue
frankfurter
fritter
gado-gado
gyoza
haggis
imam bayildi
kebab
kofta
laksa
latke
macédoine
moussaka
paella
pakora
peperonata
pilau
pissaladière
pizza
polenta
ragout
raita
risotto
samosa
sauerkraut
smorgasbord
sushi
taco
tagine
tortilla
Wiener schnitzel

SNACKS AND NIBBLES:
antipasto

canapé
gyro
panini
panzerotto
sandwich
smushi
vol-au-vent
welsh rarebit
wrap

BISCUITS:
amaretti
Anzac
biscotto
bourbon
brandy snap
cookie
cracker
cream cracker
crispbread
digestive
flapjack
Florentine
Garibaldi
ginger nut
ginger snap
langue de chat
macaroon
oatcake
parkin
petit four
ratafia
shortbread
N Am soda
  cracker
wafer
water biscuit
zwieback

DIPS:
guacamole

hummus
salsa
tahina
taramasalata
tzatziki

SAUCES AND DRESSINGS:
apple
balsamic vinegar
barbecue
bechamel
caponata
cranberry
fish
French dressing
harissa
hoisin
hollandaise
mint
nam pla
olive oil
pesto
ponzu
red wine sauce
salad cream
tartare
Thousand Island
  dressing
tomato ketchup
vinaigrette
white sauce
white wine sauce
Worcestershire

CONDIMENTS:
chutney
horseradish
mayonnaise
mustard
Tabasco®

See also **bread**; **cake**; **cheese**; **cook**; **dessert**; **fish**; **fruit**; **kitchen utensils**; **meat**; **nut**; **pasta**; **pastry**; **sugar**; **sweet**; **vegetable**.

---

muggins, gull, Jack-fool, jackass, lemming, mooncalf, soft, softy, Tom-noddy, tomfool, punk; *dialect* gowk, mumchance, barmpot, gump, haverel; *Scot* coof, dottle; *Scot & Irish* eejit; *Irish* omadhaun; *N Am* cluck, dumb-cluck, yap

OLD cony, fon, fondling, want-wit, patch, sot, wigeon; (*Shakesp*) lack-brain, bauble, capocchia, snipe

COLLOQ. nincompoop, ass, chump, ninny, neddy, clot, dope, twit, nitwit, nit, sucker, mug, twerp, birdbrain, lamebrain, knuckle-head, muttonhead, silly-billy, berk, (proper) Charlie, gubbins, sap, saphead, wazzock, dum-dum, coot, goat, head-banger; *Scot* bampot; *N Am* lunkhead, chowderhead, putz, doofus; *Aust* dill, boofhead

SLANG wally, jerk, dumbo, muppet, pillock, prat, dork, geek, plonker, git, nerd, nerk, nelly, goop, josser, nig-nog, sawney, schlemiel, turkey, cloth head, dipstick, goof, kook, tosspot; *N Am* jughead, schmo, dingbat, dweeb; (*taboo*) prick, fuckwit, knobhead, dickhead; *Aust* galah, nana; *Aust & NZ* nong

OLD SLANG cake

♦ *v*

1 DECEIVE, take in, delude, mislead, beguile, make a fool of, dupe, gull, hoodwink, put one over on, trick, hoax, cheat, swindle, bluff, tease, joke, jest, play tricks, pretend, feign, sham

OLD fon

COLLOQ. con, diddle, string along, have on, kid, pull someone's leg, bamboozle

2 *stop fooling about*
lark about, play about, monkey about/around; *N Am* futz around

COLLOQ. horse around, mess about/around

SLANG fart about/around, ponce about/around, piss about/around

3 *fooling about with my wife*
philander, flirt, play around, have an affair, womanize

COLLOQ. carry on, sleep around, mess about/around

■ **play the fool**
fool around, fool about, mess about, mess around, muck about, muck around, clown around, monkey around, play the giddy goat

OLD fon

COLLOQ. act the fool, horse around

> **PROVERBS**
> A fool and his money are soon parted
> There's no fool like an old fool

> **QUOTATIONS**
> For fools rush in where angels fear to tread
> ALEXANDER POPE, *An Essay on Criticism*

foolery *n*
silliness, folly, fooling, nonsense, tomfoolery, antics, buffoonery, drollery, waggery, zanyism, capers, carry-on, clowning, farce, childishness, horseplay, larks, high jinks,

mischief, practical jokes, pranks, monkey tricks, shenanigans

foolhardiness *n*
recklessness, rashness, imprudence, irresponsibility, impulsiveness, boldness
E3 caution, prudence

foolhardy *adj*
rash, reckless, ill-advised, irresponsible, imprudent, incautious, impulsive, bold, daring, daredevil
FORMAL temerarious
E3 cautious, prudent

foolish *adj*
stupid, senseless, silly, absurd, ridiculous, ludicrous, imbecile, nonsensical, unwise, ill-advised, ill-considered, vacuous, short-sighted, half-baked, crazy, mad, insane, idiotic, moronic, hare-brained, half-witted, simple-minded, simple, ignorant, unintelligent, inept, inane, pointless, unreasonable, *étourdi*; *Scot* doilt, dottle, fool, glaik; *Welsh* twp; *N Am* fool
OLD fond, gudgeon, peevish
FORMAL fatuous, risible, injudicious
COLLOQ. daft, crack-brained, rattle-brained, gormless, dumb, dotty, wacky, potty, batty, barmy, nutty, not in your right mind, out of your mind, with a screw missing, needing to have your head examined; *Aust* dilly
SLANG goofy
E3 wise, prudent; *formal* judicious

foolishly *adv*
stupidly, senselessly, absurdly, ridiculously, unwisely, imprudently, ill-advisedly, idiotically, incautiously, indiscreetly, mistakenly, ineptly, short-sightedly
OLD fonly
FORMAL fatuously, injudiciously
COLLOQ. daftly, crazily, madly, wackily
E3 wisely

foolishness *n*
folly, stupidity, silliness, senselessness, absurdity, irresponsibility, weakness, craziness, madness, lunacy, nonsense, rubbish, foolery, inanity, ineptitude, indiscretion, imprudence
FORMAL incaution, unreason, unwisdom
COLLOQ. bunkum, claptrap, baloney, daftness, hogwash, rot, piffle, poppycock, bunk, bilge, cobblers
SLANG (*vulgar*) crap, balls, bullshit
E3 wisdom, prudence

foolproof *adj*
idiot-proof, infallible, unfailing, safe, fail-safe, sure, certain, dependable, trustworthy, guaranteed
COLLOQ. sure-fire
E3 unreliable

foot *n*
1 *an animal's feet*
paw, hoof, pad, trotter, leg, toe, sole, heel
TECHNICAL pes
COLLOQ. tootsie, tootsy-wootsy
Related adjectives: pedal, pedate
2 *at the foot of the hill*
bottom, end, far end, limit, extremity, border, base, foundation
E3 2 head, top, summit

football
See panel on next page

footing *n*
1 BASIS, base, foundation, ground, relations, relationship, terms, conditions, state, standing, status, grade, rank, position
2 FOOTHOLD, balance, support, position, grip

footling *adj*
paltry, trifling, minor, trivial, insignificant, petty, irrelevant
COLLOQ. piffling
E3 major, significant

footloose *adj*
uncommitted, unattached, uninvolved, available, free, fancy-free
E3 committed; *colloq.* tied down

footnote *n*
annotation, note, marginal note, gloss, comment, commentary, marginalia
FORMAL scholium

footprint *n*
footmark, track, trail, trace, step, tread, spoor
FORMAL vestige

footstep *n*
footmark, track, step, tread, footfall, plod, tramp, trudge

footwear

Types of footwear include:

ballet shoe	galosh	running shoe
slang beetle-crusher	gladiator sandal	sabot
	gumboot	sandal
boat shoe	hiking-boot	shoe
boot	Hush Puppies®	shoeboot
bootee	jelly	slingback
bowling shoe	kitten heel	slip-on
brogue	lace-up	slipper
colloq. brothel creeper	loafer	sneaker
	moccasin	snowshoe
casual	mule	stiletto heel
Chelsea boot	overshoe	*S Afr slang* tacky
climbing-boot	Oxford	tennis shoe
clog	pantofle	thong
combat boot	*old* patten	trainer
court shoe	platform heel	wader
deck shoe	plimsoll	walking-boot
Doc Martens®	pump	wedge heel
espadrille	riding boot	wellington boot
flatform heel	rock boot	*colloq.* welly
flip-flop	rock shoe	
football boot	rugby boot	

See also **boot**.

---

fop *n*
dandy, coxcomb, beau, popinjay, dude, exquisite, peacock, swell, toff, Jack-a-dandy, *petit maître*
OLD muscadin, fantastic, skipjack; (*Shakesp*) barber-monger

foppish *adj*
dapper, dressy, spruce, overdressed, preening, vain, dandyish, dandified, affected, dainty, finical, coxcombic, apish
OLD fallal, fantastic; (*Shakesp*) fangled, fashionmongering
COLLOQ. la-di-da, natty, swellish
E3 unkempt

forage *n, v*
♦ *n*
fodder, pasturage, feed, food, foodstuffs, provender
♦ *v*
rummage, search, seek, cast about, scour, scratch, hunt, scavenge, ransack, plunder, assault, ravage, loot, raid, invade

foray *n*
raid, offensive, attack, assault, ravage, sortie, sally, swoop, invasion, inroad, incursion, reconnaissance

forbear *v*
avoid, decline, hesitate, hold, hold back, keep from, stop, cease, withhold, stay, restrain yourself, omit, pause
FORMAL refrain, abstain, desist, eschew

forbearance *n*
self-control, patience, moderation, endurance, leniency, mildness, restraint, temperance, tolerance, toleration,

Terms used in football include:

AMERICAN FOOTBALL:		ASSOCIATION FOOTBALL:			GAELIC FOOTBALL:
American Football Conference (AFC)	National Football League (NFL)	banana kick	nutmeg	bouncing	All-Ireland Championships
audible	neutral zone	bicycle kick	offside	boundary umpire	charge
backfield	nickelback	Bundesliga	overhead kick	Brownlow Medal	corner-back
blitz	nose tackle	Champions League	own goal	bump	corner-forward
block	offensive line	chip	pass	centre bounce	Croke Park
centre	offside	corner (kick)	pass back	centre circle	crossbar
complete	out of bounds	cross	penalty	centre square	divot
cornerback	overtime	defender	penalty shoot-out	charge	fist
defensive end	pass interference	dugout	Premiership	checking	45m free kick
defensive tackle	pass rush	dummy	promotion	drop punt	foul
down	pocket	European Championships	red card	field umpire	free kick
draw	point after	extra time	referee	50m penalty	full-forward
endzone	punt	FA Cup	relegation	flank	Gaelic Athletic Association (GAA)
face mask	punter	FIFA (Fédération Internationale de Football Association)	Serie A	footpass	goal (3 points)
fair catch	quarterback		silver goal	free kick	handpass
field goal	red zone		skipper	goal (6 points)	kick-out
flag	running back	First Division	stoppage time	goal line	one-handed pass
flanker	rush	formation	striker	goal square	overcarry
fullback	sack	foul	*colloq.* sub	goal umpire	overhold
fumble	safety	fourth official	substitute	guernsey	parallelogram
guard	scrimmage	free kick	sweeper	handball	penalty kick
hail Mary	scrimmage line	full back	tackle	interchange	point
halfback	secondary	goal	technical area	mark	Sam Maguire Cup
holding	shotgun	*colloq.* goalie	throw-in	Melbourne Cricket Ground (MCG)	side-line kick
huddle	snap	goalkeeper	UEFA (Union of European Football Associations)	nineteenth man	solo
incomplete	split end	golden goal		out of bounds	square ball
interception	Super Bowl®	half-time	wing back	pockets	throw-in
kicker	tackle	handball	winger	quarter	tipping
kickoff	tailback	header	World Cup	rover	toe-tap
lateral	tee	injury time	yellow card	ruck	toss
linebacker	tight end	kickabout		ruck-rover	two-handed pass
lineman	touchback	kick-off	AUSTRALIAN RULES:	runner	
National Football Conference (NFC)	touchdown	marking	advantage	shepherding	
	turnover	midfielder	Australian Football League (AFL)	siren	
	two-point conversion		ball-up	*colloq.* torp	
	wide receiver		behind (1 point)	torpedo punt	

---

avoidance, self-denial, clemency, long-suffering, resignation, refraining, sufferance
FORMAL abstinence
⊟ intolerance

forbearing *adj*
long-suffering, patient, moderate, lenient, self-controlled, restrained, tolerant, merciful, mild, easy, forgiving, indulgent, clement
⊟ intolerant, merciless

forbid *v*
prohibit, disallow, not allow, not let, ban, veto, refuse, deny, outlaw, debar, blacklist, exclude, rule out, prevent, block, hinder, inhibit
FORMAL proscribe, interdict, preclude
COLLOQ. give the thumbs-down to; give the red light to
⊟ allow, permit, let, approve

> **SYNONYM NUANCES**
>
> The verbs **prohibit** and **ban** are appropriate for forbidding in official contexts: *tourist coaches are to be banned from the town centre*, whilst **veto** similarly implies using official power to stop something: *the scheme was vetoed by the Treasury*, and **outlaw** is specifically used of making something illegal: *secondary picketing has been outlawed*.
>   **Debar** and **exclude** are best used of forbidding entry: *lack of education debars half the population from employment*, whereas **blacklist** is more specific about who is forbidden in that it has to do with compiling a list of undesirables. The term **rule out** best describes forbidding something by discounting it as a possibility:

lack of funds rules out any more building work, while **prevent** and **block** convey the idea of taking action to stop something from occurring: *MPs blocked moves to hold more talks with the French*.
  Hinder and **inhibit** would appropriately describe actions more likely to restrict or impede than to halt completely: *the conservatism that has hindered development in the past; his depression inhibited his writing*.

forbidden *adj*
prohibited, banned, excluded, taboo, vetoed, debarred, illicit, outlawed, out of bounds
TECHNICAL haram
OLD (*Shakesp*) restrained
FORMAL proscribed
COLLOQ. not on

forbidding *adj*
stern, formidable, awesome, severe, harsh, grim, hostile, unfriendly, daunting, off-putting, uninviting, menacing, threatening, ominous, sinister, foreboding, frightening
⊟ approachable, friendly, congenial

force *v, n*
♦ *v*
1 COMPEL, make, oblige, urge, coerce, constrain, press, pressure, pressurize, put pressure on, pressgang, bulldoze, bully, railroad, drive, propel, impel, push, thrust, impose, inflict
COLLOQ. lean on, put the screws on, twist someone's arm, breathe down someone's neck

2 PRISE, force open, break open, crack, blast, wrench, wrest, extort, exact, wring, extract

♦ *n*

1 COMPULSION, impulse, necessity, influence, coercion, constraint, pressure, duress, enforcement, violence, aggression
COLLOQ. arm-twisting, strongarm tactics, the screws, the third degree
2 POWER, might, strength, intensity, effort, energy, vigour, exertion, stamina, muscle, momentum, impetus, drive, dynamo, dynamism, vitality, passion, vehemence, determination, stress, emphasis, influence, power, significance, persuasiveness, effectiveness
FORMAL cogency
3 MEANING, sense, substance, significance, gist, essence, thrust
4 ARMY, troop, body, corps, regiment, squad, platoon, squadron, battalion, division, unit, group, detachment, patrol
2 weakness

■ **in force**

1 IN OPERATION, functioning, valid, binding, working, effective, current, on the statute book
FORMAL operative
2 IN STRENGTH, in crowds, in large/great numbers, in flocks, in droves

---

SYNONYM NUANCES

verb sense 1
Compel and **make** may be used to suggest that your actions are determined by certain external pressures: *he was compelled to resign because he'd been embezzling the funds*. **Oblige**, on the other hand, has more to do with feeling that something is morally binding: *I feel obliged to leave a tip even when the service is not good*.

The terms **urge** and **press** imply a powerful attempt to persuade: *he urged them to reform before it was too late*, while **coerce** suggests being made to do something against your will. Both **pressure** and **pressurize** suggest applying stronger methods to get your way, and **pressgang** has suggestions of being physically forced against your will. **Bulldoze** is a negative term echoing this use of strong tactics, or even physical strength: *the new tax was to be bulldozed through parliament*, and **bully** also suggests the use of menacing behaviour.

You can use **railroad** to further imply undue haste: *she refused to be railroaded into a decision*, whereas **drive** and **propel** have more to do with motivating factors: *driven by a need to maximize profit*. **Impel** also implies a cause for action, this time coming from within: *because he disagreed so strongly, he was impelled to speak out*. **Push** can be used to imply a determined bid to force something to be done: *they pushed the bill through parliament*, but **thrust**, although similar, can often be used to suggest a physical action: *the actor was thrust into the public eye; she thrust a leaflet in my hand*.

The forcing of unwelcome demands or measures can be conveyed in the terms **impose** and **inflict**: *the new laws were imposed without public consultation*.

---

forced *adj*

1 UNNATURAL, stiff, wooden, stilted, laboured, strained, false, artificial, contrived, feigned, insincere, overdone
FORMAL affected
2 COMPULSORY, obligatory, binding, involuntary, enforced, compelled
FORMAL mandatory
1 spontaneous, natural, sincere

forceful *adj*

strong, mighty, powerful, potent, effective, compelling, convincing, impressive, persuasive, telling, valid, weighty, urgent, emphatic, vehement, forcible, dynamic, high-powered, assertive, energetic, vigorous

FORMAL cogent
COLLOQ. *N Am* gutsy
weak, feeble

forcefully *adv*

strongly, powerfully, effectively, emphatically, convincingly, persuasively, vehemently, assertively, energetically, vigorously
weakly, feebly

forcible *adj*

1 VIOLENT, aggressive, coercive, forced, by/using force
2 POWERFUL, strong, compelling, compulsory, effective, impressive, telling, weighty, cogent, energetic, forceful, vehement, mighty, potent
1, 2 feeble, weak

forcibly *adv*

violently, by force, using force, against your will, compulsorily, obligatorily, under compulsion, under duress, vigorously, vehemently, emphatically, willy-nilly

ford *n*

causeway, crossing, crossing place; *S Afr* drift

forebear *n*

ancestor, forefather, father, predecessor, forerunner, antecedent
FORMAL progenitor, primogenitor
descendant

foreboding *n*

misgiving, anxiety, worry, apprehension, apprehensiveness, suspicion, dread, fear, omen, sign, token, premonition, warning, prediction, intuition, feeling, sixth sense, hoodoo
OLD abodement
FORMAL presentiment, prognostication, presage

forecast *v, n*

♦ *v*

predict, prophesy, foretell, foresee, forewarn, anticipate, expect, tip off, estimate, calculate, extrapolate, project
FORMAL conjecture, prognosticate, portend, divine, augur, presage
COLLOQ. second-guess

♦ *n*

prediction, prophecy, expectation, forewarning, outlook, projection, extrapolation, calculation, permutation, guess, tip, speculation
TECHNICAL metcast
FORMAL prognosis, conjecture, prognostication, augury
COLLOQ. guesstimate

forefather *n*

ancestor, forebear, father, predecessor, forerunner, antecedent
FORMAL progenitor, primogenitor
descendant

forefront *n*

front, front line, firing line, van, vanguard, spearhead, lead, head, fore, leading/foremost position, avant-garde
OLD (*Shakesp*) vaward
rear

forego, forgo *v*

give up, yield, surrender, sacrifice, forfeit, waive, abandon, resign, pass up, do without, go without
FORMAL refrain from, relinquish, renounce, abstain from, eschew, abjure

foregoing *adj*

preceding, above, previous, earlier, former, prior
FORMAL antecedent, precedent, aforementioned, aforesaid
following

foregone

■ **foregone conclusion**
inevitability, certainty, fact
COLLOQ. sure thing

foreground *n*

fore, forefront, front, prominence, leading/foremost position, centre, limelight
background

forehead *n*
brow, temple(s), front
TECHNICAL metope
Related adjectives: metopic, frontal

foreign *adj*
1 *foreign policy*
international, overseas, external, alien, immigrant,
imported, outside, exotic, ethnic, migrant, faraway, distant
2 *the technique was foreign to her*
unfamiliar, unknown, strange, outlandish, peculiar, odd,
uncharacteristic, unconnected, extraneous, borrowed
E3 1 home, domestic **2** familiar, known

foreigner *n*
alien, immigrant, incomer, stranger, outsider, newcomer,
visitor, tramontane, outlander, *étranger*, *Ausländer*, *gaijin*
OLD *S Afr* uitlander; barbarian
E3 native

foreknowledge *n*
foresight, premonition, forewarning, clairvoyance, second
sight
TECHNICAL precognition, prescience
FORMAL prevision, prognostication

foreman *n*
supervisor, superintendent, manager, leader, overseer,
steward, ganger, overman, charge hand
COLLOQ. boss, gaffer; *N Am* honcho

foremost *adj*
first, leading, most important, front, chief, main, prime,
principal, primary, top, cardinal, paramount, central,
highest, advanced, uppermost, supreme, premier, pre-
eminent

foreordained *adj*
fated, destined, predestined, predetermined, appointed,
preordained, prearranged
FORMAL foredoomed

forerunner *n*
precursor, predecessor, ancestor, antecedent, forefather,
herald, envoy, sign, token
OLD (*Shakesp*) precurrer
FORMAL harbinger
E3 successor, follower

foresee *v*
envisage, anticipate, expect, forecast, predict, prophesy,
foretell, foreknow, forebode
OLD previse
FORMAL prognosticate, divine

foreshadow *v*
predict, prophesy, signal, indicate, signify, mean, suggest,
promise
FORMAL bode, prefigure, presage, augur, portend,
prognosticate

foresight *n*
anticipation, planning, forward planning, forethought, far-
sightedness, vision, caution, discernment, discrimination,
care, prudence, readiness, preparedness, provision,
precaution
FORMAL circumspection, perspicacity, judiciousness,
prevision
E3 improvidence

forest *n*
wood, woodland, woods, trees, greenwood, monte,
plantation, urman; *Aust* brush

Types of forest and wood include:

ancient forest	equatorial ever-	littoral
boreal	green rainforest	lowland
chaparral	evergreen	mangrove
cloud forest	gallery forest	maquis
coastal	garrigue	moist evergreen
coastal temperate	greenwood	moist forest
coniferous	heath forest	monsoon rain-
deciduous	igapò	forest
montane rainforest	secondary rain-	temperate decid-
peat forest	forest	uous
primary rainforest	selva	temperate rain-
rainforest	taiga	forest
savanna forest	temperate broad-	tropical rainforest
seasonal rainforest	leaf	vàrzea forest
		wetland

See also **tree**; **wood**.

---

forestall *v*
pre-empt, anticipate, stop, avert, head off, ward off, stave
off, parry, balk, frustrate, thwart, obstruct, hinder, prevent,
impede, intercept, get ahead of
FORMAL preclude, obviate
COLLOQ. second-guess

forested *adj*
wooded, reafforested

forestry *n*
forestation, woodcraft, woodmanship, forest management
TECHNICAL afforestation, arboriculture, dendrology,
silviculture

foretaste *n*
forewarning, foretoken, preview, trailer, sample, taster,
appetizer, specimen, example, whiff, indication,
anticipation, pre-echo, warning, premonition, *avant-goût*
OLD antepast
FORMAL pregustation, prelibation

foretell *v*
prophesy, forecast, predict, foresee, signify, foreshadow,
indicate, forewarn
FORMAL prognosticate, augur, presage, divine

forethought *n*
preparation, planning, forward planning, provision,
precaution, anticipation, foresight, far-sightedness,
prudence, caution, discernment
FORMAL circumspection, perspicacity, judiciousness
E3 improvidence, carelessness

forever *adv*
1 ETERNALLY, always, ever, evermore, for all time,
permanently, till the end of time
COLLOQ. till kingdom come, till the cows come home, for
good, until hell freezes over
2 CONTINUALLY, constantly, always, persistently,
incessantly, perpetually, endlessly
FORMAL interminably
COLLOQ. all the time

forewarn *v*
alert, advise, caution, tip off, give notice, warn, give
advance warning to
FORMAL apprise, admonish, dissuade, previse

> PROVERBS
> Forewarned is forearmed

forewarning *n*
advance warning, advance notice, early warning
COLLOQ. tip-off

foreword *n*
preface, introduction, preliminary matter, prelims,
frontmatter, prologue
FORMAL prolegomenon
E3 appendix, postscript, epilogue

forfeit *v*, *n*
♦ *v*
lose, give up, hand over, surrender, sacrifice, for(e)go,
abandon
FORMAL relinquish, renounce
COLLOQ. pass up
♦ *n*
penalty, loss, surrender, confiscation, fine, damages,
relinquishment, sconce; *dialect* rue-bargain

TECHNICAL sequestration, amercement
OLD cheat

forfeiture n
giving up, surrender, confiscation, loss, relinquishment, sacrifice, for(e)going
TECHNICAL escheat, attainder, sequestration
FORMAL déchéance

forge¹ v
1 MAKE, mould, cast, shape, form, fashion, found, beat out, hammer out, beat into shape, work, create, build, construct, invent, frame, devise, put together
2 *forge a document*
fake, counterfeit, falsify, copy, imitate, simulate, feign

forge²
■ **forge ahead**
progress, make progress, move steadily, advance, go/move forward, make headway, push forward

forged adj
counterfeit, fake, faked, false, copied, pirate, fraudulent, bogus, sham, spurious, imitation, artificial, simulated, pretended, borrowed
FORMAL feigned, simular
COLLOQ. phoney, pseud, pseudo
E3 genuine, authentic, real

forger n
counterfeiter, contriver, faker, falsifier, framer, coiner, fabricator

forgery n
fake, counterfeit, copy, replica, reproduction, imitation, sham, fraud, faking, falsification, counterfeiting
COLLOQ. dud, phoney
E3 original

forget v
omit, fail, fail to remember, have no recollection of, neglect, let slip, overlook, disregard, ignore, lose sight of, dismiss, stop thinking about, think no more of, unlearn, not place, slip your mind, put out of your mind, put behind you, put aside; *dialect* disremember; *Scot* misremember
COLLOQ. go in one ear and out the other, have a memory like a sieve, dry up, wipe
SLANG corpse
E3 remember, recall, recollect
■ **forget yourself**
misbehave, behave badly, be naughty, be guilty of misconduct

forgetful adj
absent-minded, scatterbrained, preoccupied, distracted, abstracted, dreamy, inattentive, oblivious, negligent, neglectful, remiss, lax, careless, heedless, unheeding
COLLOQ. with a head/memory like a sieve, not all there; *N Am* ditsy
E3 attentive, mindful, heedful

forgetfulness n
absent-mindedness, inattention, obliviousness, oblivion, dreaminess, heedlessness, carelessness, neglect, woolgathering, abstraction, amnesia, lapse, laxness
FORMAL obliviscence
E3 attentiveness, heedfulness

forgivable adj
excusable, pardonable, condonable, minor, petty, slight, trifling, innocent, venial
E3 unforgivable

forgive v
pardon, absolve, excuse, acquit, remit, let off, let it go, clear, spare, overlook, condone, forgive and forget, let bygones be bygones
FORMAL exonerate, exculpate
COLLOQ. shake hands, shake on it, think no more of, bury the hatchet
E3 punish, censure

SYNONYM NUANCES

Pardon may be used generally to suggest a willingness to put aside someone's wrongdoings, and in official contexts, specifically of allowing them to go unpunished: *the president pardoned thirty-five prisoners in an amnesty*. The term **spare** is reserved for relieving someone of their punishment.

Absolve and **clear** go somewhat further by implying a complete discharge from blame: *the King was formally absolved from complicity in Becket's murder*. **Excuse** may be widely used to suggest making allowances for someone's behaviour, whereas **acquit** has more to do with rejecting accusations against someone and is usually reserved for legal contexts: *they were acquitted of illegally importing arms*. The term **remit**, although formerly used to suggest giving pardon, tends now to imply refraining from exacting: *parliament remitted all obligation on the king to repay*.

Similarly, **let off** and **overlook** are suggestive of allowing someone to get away with something they have done wrong, whilst **let it go** implies a degree of reluctance about ignoring it: *I'll let it go this time, but be careful in future*. **Condone** would suggest acceptance or approval as well as forgiveness, although it is often used in the negative: *I cannot condone the behaviour of these children*.

---

forgiveness n
pardon, absolution, acquittal, remission, amnesty, mercy, leniency
FORMAL clemency, exoneration
E3 punishment, censure, blame

forgiving adj
merciful, pitying, lenient, tolerant, forbearing, indulgent, kind, humane, compassionate, soft-hearted, mild
FORMAL magnanimous, clement, placable
E3 merciless, censorious, harsh

forgo
see **forego, forgo.**

forgotten adj
unremembered, unrecalled, blotted out, disregarded, ignored, neglected, obliterated, overlooked, omitted, out of mind, past recollection, past recall, gone, left behind, buried, bygone, past, lost, irrecoverable, irretrievable, unretrieved, in the shade, in the wilderness
OLD oblivious
E3 remembered

fork v, n
♦ *v*
split, divide, part, separate, diverge, branch (off), go separate ways
TECHNICAL divaricate
FORMAL bifurcate
♦ *n*
branching, divergence, separation, split, division, junction, intersection
TECHNICAL divarication, furcation
FORMAL bifurcation
■ **fork out**
pay (up), give
COLLOQ. cough up, shell out, stump up

forked adj
branched, branching, divided, split, separated, Y-shaped, pronged
TECHNICAL divaricated, forficate, furcate, furcal, furcular
FORMAL tined, bifurcate

forlorn adj
1 *a forlorn place*
deserted, abandoned, forsaken, forgotten, neglected, bereft, friendless, lonely, lost, homeless, uncared-for, destitute, desolate

2 *a forlorn person*
unhappy, miserable, sad, desperate, despairing, hopeless, cheerless, wretched, helpless, pathetic, pitiable
FORMAL disconsolate
E3 1, 2 cheerful

forlornly *adv*
unhappily, miserably, sadly, desperately, despondently, hopelessly, pointlessly, unsuccessfully, in vain, to no avail
E3 happily, successfully

form *n, v*
♦ *n*
1 APPEARANCE, shape, mould, cast, cut, guise, outline, silhouette, figure, build, construction, frame, framework, structure, format, formation, model, pattern, design, arrangement, planning, order, organization, system
FORMAL configuration, disposition, manifestation
2 *a form of punishment*
type, kind, sort, order, species, genus, variety, genre, style, manner, nature, character, description
3 CLASS, year, grade, stream, set
4 *on top form*
health, fitness, shape, trim, fettle, condition, spirits
5 ETIQUETTE, protocol, custom, usage, correct practice, convention, ritual, behaviour, polite behaviour, manners
COLLOQ. the done thing
6 QUESTIONNAIRE, document, application (form), paper, sheet
♦ *v*
1 SHAPE, mould, model, fashion, forge, make, manufacture, produce, create, found, establish, build, construct, assemble, put together, set up, devise, formulate, conceive, draw up, arrange, organize, order, line up, develop, acquire
2 COMPRISE, constitute, make (up), compose, serve as, be a part of
3 APPEAR, take shape, materialize, crystallize, come into existence, show up, grow, develop, become visible

formal *adj*
1 OFFICIAL, ceremonial, ritual, ritualistic, stately, solemn, conventional, customary, traditional, established, orthodox, correct, prescribed, approved, proper, fixed, set, standard, regular, ordered, organized, methodical
2 PRIM, starchy, stiff, strait-laced, strict, rigid, inflexible, unbending, precise, exact, punctilious, ceremonious, stilted, remote, reserved, aloof
3 *a formal garden*
symmetrical, ordered, orderly, controlled, arranged, regular, conventional
E3 1 informal **2** informal, casual

formality *n*
custom, convention, ceremony, ceremoniousness, ritual, procedure, rule, form, matter of form, bureaucracy, red tape, protocol, etiquette, correctness, politeness
FORMAL decorum, propriety, punctilio
E3 informality

formalization *n*
structuring, arrangement(s), arranging, standardization, organization, ordering, systematization, confirmation

formalize *v*
make formal, make official, structure, arrange, affirm, confirm, ordain, ratify, standardize, regularize, order, systematize, organize, fix, set, stylize, ritualize

formally *adv*
1 OFFICIALLY, conventionally, correctly, properly, methodically, ceremonially, ritually, solemnly
2 PRIMLY, rigidily, inflexibly, precisely, exactly, punctiliously
E3 1, 2 informally

format *n*
appearance, form, order, presentation, design, layout, pattern, plan, shape, structure, style, arrangement, make-up, look, type, construction, dimensions
FORMAL configuration

formation *n*
1 STRUCTURE, construction, composition, constitution, format, order, organization, arrangement, layout, make-up, grouping, pattern, design, figure
FORMAL configuration, disposition, phalanx
2 CREATION, generation, production, construction, building, making, shaping, manufacture, emergence, appearance, development, starting, founding, institution, establishment, inauguration

formative *adj*
determining, controlling, influential, dominant, shaping, growing, guiding, moulding, developmental, impressionable, teachable, malleable, mouldable, plastic, pliant, susceptible, sensitive
FORMAL determinative, creant
E3 destructive

former *adj*
past, ex-, one-time, sometime, late, departed, old, old-time, ancient, bygone, historical, earlier, prior, previous, preceding, long ago, long-gone, first, first-mentioned, antecedent, foregoing, above
FORMAL erstwhile, quondam, of yore
E3 current, present, future, following

formerly *adv*
once, in the past, previously, historically, earlier, at an earlier time, before, at one time
FORMAL heretofore, hitherto, erst, erstwhile
E3 currently, now, later

formidable *adj*
daunting, challenging, redoubtable, intimidating, threatening, menacing, frightening, terrifying, horrifying, alarming, terrific, frightful, horrific, fearful, great, huge, colossal, mammoth, tremendous, impressive, powerful, awesome, dreadful, overwhelming, staggering, onerous
FORMAL prodigious
COLLOQ. scary, mind-blowing, spooky

formidably *adv*
menacingly, frightfully, fearfully, shockingly, horrifically, tremendously, dreadfully, awfully, overwhelmingly

formless *adj*
amorphous, shapeless, confused, chaotic, disorganized, indefinite, indeterminate, incoherent, nebulous, vague, unshaped, unformed
FORMAL inchoate, indigest
E3 definite, orderly

formula *n*
recipe, prescription, proposal, blueprint, code, fixed/set expression, wording, rubric, rule, principle, form, precept, procedure, technique, convention, method, way

formulate *v*
devise, create, compose, prepare, conceive, think up, invent, originate, found, form, give form to, work out, plan, design, map out, draw up, frame, cast, propose, define, express, articulate, state, set down, put down, lay down, specify, detail, itemize, symbolize, develop, evolve
OLD formate

formulation *n*
1 *an experimental formulation*
production, preparation, composition, formula, product
2 *the formulation of a strategy*
devising, creating, composition, preparation, conception, framing, definition, expression, specification, development

fornication *n*
extramarital relations/relationship, extramarital sex, adultery, unfaithfulness, infidelity, affair, liaison, entanglement, flirtation, unchastity
OLD avoutry
COLLOQ. two-timing, cheating, a bit on the side
SLANG playing around, playing the field
E3 faithfulness, fidelity

forsake _v_
desert, abandon, throw over, discard, jettison, cast off, reject, repudiate, set aside, disown, leave, give up, surrender, for(e)go
OLD destitute, forlese, waive
FORMAL relinquish, renounce
COLLOQ. jilt, quit, ditch, chuck, leave in the lurch, have done with, turn your back on

forsaken _adj_
abandoned, deserted, neglected, godforsaken, remote, isolated, desolate, forlorn, lonely, marooned, solitary, derelict, dreary, destitute, cast off, discarded, disowned, rejected, shunned, outcast, ignored, friendless
COLLOQ. jilted, left in the lurch

forswear _v_
abandon, give up, for(e)go, repudiate, drop, disown, disclaim, reject, deny, do without, renege, lie, perjure yourself
FORMAL forsake, renounce, recant, disavow, abjure, retract
COLLOQ. cut out, pack in, jack in
E3 revert to

fort _n_
fortress, castle, tower, watchtower, citadel, keep, stronghold, fortification, turret, battlements, parapet, garrison, station, camp, donjon, redoubt

forte _n_
strong point, strength, skill, speciality, gift, talent, aptitude, bent, métier
E3 weak point, inadequacy

forth _adv_
out, away, off, outside, on, onwards, forwards, into existence, into view

forthcoming _adj_
1 _their forthcoming wedding_
impending, imminent, approaching, coming, future, upcoming, prospective, in the offing, projected, expected
2 AVAILABLE, accessible, obtainable, ready, at your disposal
COLLOQ. on tap, up for grabs, yours for the asking/taking
3 COMMUNICATIVE, talkative, chatty, conversational, sociable, friendly, informative, expansive, open, frank, direct
FORMAL loquacious, voluble
E3 3 reticent, reserved

forthright _adj_
direct, straightforward, blunt, frank, candid, plain, plain-spoken, open, honest, bold, outspoken, four-square, trenchant
COLLOQ. up-front
E3 devious, secretive

forthwith _adv_
immediately, as soon as possible, at once, directly, instantly, straightaway, right away, without delay, quickly
COLLOQ. pronto, asap

fortification _n_
defence, strengthening, reinforcement, protection, castle, citadel, fort, fortress, keep, stronghold, earthwork, rampart, bulwark, bastion, battlements, parapet, barricade, palisade, buttressing, bawn, embattlement, entrenchment, munition, outwork, redoubt, stockade
TECHNICAL contravallation

fortify _v_
1 STRENGTHEN, reinforce, brace, shore up, buttress, fence, fort, mound, rampart, wall, garrison, defend, guard, protect, secure, cover, embattle, entrench
OLD munite
FORMAL munify
2 INVIGORATE, sustain, support, boost, revive, energize, brace, encourage, hearten, cheer, reassure, strengthen, buoy up
E3 1 weaken

fortitude _n_
courage, bravery, valour, pluck, nerve, resolution, determination, tenacity, perseverance, patience, firmness, strength of mind, backbone, mettle, willpower, hardihood, endurance, stoicism
FORMAL forbearance
COLLOQ. guts, grit, spine
E3 cowardice, fear

fortress _n_
stronghold, castle, fort, citadel, fortification, fastness, tower, keep, garrison, battlements

fortuitous _adj_
accidental, chance, random, arbitrary, casual, haphazard, incidental, unforeseen, unexpected, unplanned, unintentional, lucky, fortunate, providential
COLLOQ. fluky
E3 intentional, planned, anticipated

fortuitously _adv_
accidentally, by chance, randomly, at random, arbitrarily, casually, haphazardly, incidentally, inadvertently, unexpectedly, unintentionally, fortunately, luckily
E3 intentionally

fortunate _adj_
lucky, providential, happy, prosperous, flourishing, successful, well-off, well, rich, timely, well-timed, opportune, convenient, advantageous, favourable, encouraging, promising, profitable, blessed, favoured; _Scot_ canny
OLD seely
FORMAL felicitous, propitious, auspicious, providential
E3 unlucky, unfortunate, unhappy

SYNONYM NUANCES

While **lucky** is a very general synonym, **providential** is more suggestive of divine intervention having brought something about: _their progress was aided by a providential wind._ **Happy** could describe a stroke of fortune that causes something to turn out very well: _I met my wife due to a happy coincidence._ The terms **prosperous**, **well-off** and **rich** have more to do with being in a fortunate financial state, though **rich** may occasionally be used of less material possessions: _rich rewards._

Flourishing, **successful** and **profitable** could also be used of something that is thriving and generating wealth. The terms **timely**, **well-timed** and **opportune** describe something happening at the most appropriate time, whilst **convenient** is a rather more restrained term which has wider suggestions of general suitability: _the switch of dates was convenient for my plans._ You could also use **advantageous** or **favourable** of something having a beneficial element, whereas **encouraging** and **promising** put the emphasis on offering hope of future good fortune: _there have been encouraging results in trials of the new drug._

The terms **blessed** and **favoured** suggest being the recipient of a fortuitous gift, and again there is a divine aspect: _I considered myself blessed to be given another chance._

fortunately _adv_
luckily, happily, thankfully, conveniently, encouragingly
FORMAL providentially
E3 unfortunately

fortune _n_
1 WEALTH, riches, treasure, income, means, substance, assets, estate, property, possessions, affluence, prosperity, success
FORMAL opulence
COLLOQ. mint, pile, packet, bundle, bomb
SLANG megabucks, big bucks
2 LUCK, chance, coincidence, accident, providence, fate, destiny, doom, lot, portion, cup, life, history, future
FORMAL serendipity

3 *the fortunes of the company*
experience, circumstances, position, condition, situation,
state of affairs

> **QUOTATIONS**
> Fortune favours the brave
>   TERENCE, 'Phormio'
> Fortune, that favours fools
>   BEN JONSON, *The Alchemist*

fortune-teller *n*
prophet, prophetess, visionary, soothsayer, clairvoyant,
seer, augur, diviner, oracle, sibyl, psychic, telepath

forum *n*
meeting, meeting-place, arena, rostrum, stage, assembly,
gathering, conference, discussion, debate, symposium

forward *adj, adv, v*
♦ *adj*
1 FIRST, head, front, fore, foremost, leading, advance,
onward, advancing, progressing, progressive, prospective,
future, forward-looking, go-ahead, enterprising
FORMAL frontal
2 CONFIDENT, over-confident, assertive, over-assertive, bold,
audacious, brazen, brash, barefaced, impudent,
impertinent, cheeky, cocky, familiar, overfamiliar,
presumptuous, presuming, aggressive, thrusting, pushy
COLLOQ. fresh
3 EARLY, advance, precocious, premature, advanced, well-
advanced, well-developed
4 *forward planning*
long-range, medium-range, long-term, medium-term,
future
E3 1 backward, retrograde **2** shy, modest **3** late, retarded
♦ *adv*
forwards, ahead, on, onward, onwards, out, forth, into
view, into the open
♦ *v*
1 ADVANCE, promote, further, foster, encourage, support,
back, favour, help, assist, aid, facilitate, accelerate, speed
(up), step up, hurry, hasten, dispatch
FORMAL expedite
2 SEND (ON), pass on, redirect, readdress, post, mail,
transport, deliver, ship
E3 1 impede, obstruct, hinder, slow

forward-looking *adj*
far-sighted, enterprising, progressive, reforming, modern,
innovative, dynamic, enlightened, avant-garde, liberal
COLLOQ. go-getting, goey, go-ahead
E3 conservative, retrograde

forwardness *n*
confidence, over-confidence, boldness, audacity,
brashness, brazenness, pertness, presumption,
presumptuousness, impertinence, impudence,
aggressiveness
OLD *N Am* forth-putting
COLLOQ. cheek, cheekiness, neck, brass neck, pushiness
E3 reserve, retiring

forwards *adv*
forward, ahead, on, onwards, out, forth

fossil *n*
remains, remnant, petrified remains/impression, ammonite,
relic, reliquiae
TECHNICAL graptolite, coprolite, trilobite

fossilized *adj*
1 HARDENED, stony
FORMAL petrified, ossified
2 OUT OF DATE, archaic, obsolete, old-fashioned, passé,
outmoded, prehistoric, antediluvian, anachronistic,
antiquated, extinct, dead
E3 2 up-to-date

foster *v*
1 *foster a child*
raise, rear, bring up, nurse, care for, take care of, look
after, nurture, nourish, feed, sustain
2 *foster an activity*
help, assist, aid, back, support, uphold, promote, advance,
encourage, stimulate, further, boost, cultivate, nurture,
hold, cherish, make much of, entertain, harbour, nurse,
foment
OLD nuzzle
E3 2 neglect, discourage

foul *adj, v*
♦ *adj*
1 DISGUSTING, offensive, repulsive, revolting, repellent,
dirty, soiled, filthy, mucky, unclean, tainted, infected,
impure, defiled, polluted, contaminated, rank, f(o)etid,
stinking, smelly, foul-smelling, mephitic, putrid, decayed,
rotting, rotten, sickening, nauseating, abominable,
loathsome, odious, squalid
OLD (*Shakesp*) reeky
FORMAL putrescent, putrefactive
2 *foul language*
obscene, lewd, smutty, dirty, filthy, indecent, coarse,
colourful, off-colour, ribald, indelicate, vulgar, gross, low,
blasphemous, profane, offensive, abusive
COLLOQ. blue
3 NASTY, disagreeable, wicked, vicious, vile, base, mean,
low, loathsome, despicable, offensive, revolting, repulsive,
disgusting, abhorrent, detestable, horrible, disgraceful,
shameful, contemptible
FORMAL iniquitous, heinous, execrable, nefarious
4 *foul weather*
bad, nasty, unpleasant, disagreeable, rainy, wet, stormy,
squally, blustery, rough, dirty, wild
FORMAL inclement
5 *in a foul temper*
bad, angry, bad-tempered, irritable, cross, mean, snappy,
quick-tempered, grumpy, tetchy, testy, black, gnarled,
peppery, prickly, fractious, narky, impatient, choleric,
bilious, splenetic, dyspeptic; *dialect* stingy; *Scot*
capernoity; *Scot & Irish* carnaptious
COLLOQ. stroppy, ratty, shirty, crotchety, crabbed, crabby,
grouchy, edgy, feisty, humpy
E3 1, 2 clean **4** fine **5** good
♦ *v*
1 DIRTY, soil, stain, sully, muddy, blacken, defile, taint,
pollute, contaminate
2 ENTANGLE, catch, snarl, twist, ensnare, tangle
3 BLOCK, obstruct, clog, choke, jam, foul up
E3 1 clean **2** disentangle **3** clear
■ *foul play*
criminal violence/activity, crime, unfair/dishonest
behaviour, breach of the rules, deception, dirty work,
double-dealing
COLLOQ. funny business, sharp practice
E3 fair play, justice

foul-mouthed *adj*
coarse, obscene, offensive, profane, abusive, blasphemous
FORMAL foul-spoken

found *v*
1 ESTABLISH, originate, create, bring into being, organize,
initiate, institute, inaugurate, set up, constitute, develop,
start, endow
2 BASE, ground, bottom, root, rest, set, settle, fix, plant,
locate, position, raise, build, erect, construct

foundation *n*
1 *the foundations of a building*
base, foot, bottom, ground, bedrock, substance, basis,
footing, underpinning, understructure, substructure,
substratum
2 *the foundation of a belief*
basis, support, base, groundwork, bedrock, key, keynote,
reason(s), rationale, fundamental(s), fundamental point,
starting-point, premise, principle, first principles, main

ingredient, alpha and omega, essential(s), essence, heart, core, thrust
FORMAL quintessence, hypostasis
3 *the foundation of the college in 1900*
setting-up, establishment, founding, institution, inauguration, initiation, creation, constitution, endowment, organization, groundwork
4 *a charitable foundation*
organization, institution, charity, endowment, fund
5 *the story is without foundation*
grounds, justification, base, basis, excuse, vindication, reason, motive, inducement, cause, occasion, call, score, account, argument, principle

founder[1] *n*
the founder of the university
originator, initiator, father, mother, benefactor, creator, author, architect, designer, inventor, prime mover, maker, builder, constructor, organizer, institutor, establisher, developer, discoverer

founder[2] *v*
1 *the ship foundered*
sink, go down, go to the bottom, submerge, capsize
2 *the plan foundered*
subside, collapse, break down, fall, be unsuccessful, come to grief, fail, misfire, miscarry, abort, fall through, come to nothing, go wrong
🗲 **2** succeed

foundling *n*
stray, orphan, waif, abandoned infant, outcast, urchin, *enfant trouvé*

fount *n*
source, origin, rise, well, cause, birth, beginning, mainspring, fountainhead, wellhead
FORMAL commencement, inception

fountain *n*
1 SPRAY, jet, *jet d'eau*, spout, spring, spurt, fount, well, wellspring, source, reservoir; *dialect* pant
OLD waterworks, conduit, gerbe, laver, scuttlebutt, scuttle cask
2 SOURCE, origin, fount, rise, well, cause, birth, beginning, mainspring, fountainhead, wellhead
OLD font
FORMAL commencement, inception

four-square *adv*
firmly, squarely, resolutely, solidly, frankly, honestly

fowl *n*
bird, duck, chicken, cock, hen, bantam, goose, turkey, pheasant, wildfowl, poultry
Related adjective: gallinaceous

foxy *adj*
crafty, canny, devious, cunning, artful, astute, sharp, shrewd, sly, tricky, wily, fly, knowing, guileful
🗲 naive, open

foyer *n*
entrance hall, hall, hallway, reception, lobby, vestibule, antechamber, anteroom

fracas *n*
brawl, disturbance, fight, free-for-all, quarrel, riot, trouble, uproar, row, rumpus, scuffle, barney, affray, ruckus, ruction, rout, ruffle, shindy, mêlée , Donnybrook
COLLOQ. aggro, bust-up, scrap, spat, set-to

fraction *n*
proportion, amount, ratio, subdivision, part, bit

fractional *adj*
slight, small, little, minute, partial, insignificant, negligible, insubstantial, imperceptible, subtle

fractious *adj*
awkward, quarrelsome, cross, irritable, grumpy, touchy, bad-tempered, petulant, testy, unruly, choleric, captious, fretful, peevish
FORMAL querulous, recalcitrant, refractory

COLLOQ. crabby, crotchety, grouchy
🗲 complaisant, placid

fracture *n, v*
♦ *n*
break, breakage, crack, fissure, cleft, rupture, split, splitting, rift, rent, schism, breach, gap, opening, aperture, slit
TECHNICAL fault
♦ *v*
break, crack, rupture, split, splinter, chip, snap
🗲 join

fragile *adj*
1 BRITTLE, breakable, frail, delicate, tender, flimsy, dainty, fine, slight, insubstantial, unstable
FORMAL frangible
2 *feel fragile after an illness*
weak, feeble, delicate, infirm
🗲 **1** robust, tough, durable, sturdy **2** strong

fragility *n*
brittleness, breakableness, delicacy, frailty, weakness, feebleness, infirmity
FORMAL frangibility
🗲 durability, robustness, strength

fragment *n, v*
♦ *n*
piece, bit, part, portion, fraction, particle, crumb, morsel, scrap, end, remainder, remains, remnant, shred, snip, snippet, chip, splinter, shatter, shiver, sliver, chink, shard, smithereen(s), patch, morceau, mite, snatch, cantlet, flitter, potsherd; *dialect* ort; *Scot* blaud, blad
TECHNICAL sequestrum, sheave, spar, xenolith
OLD quantity, flinder, fritter, frust, rift; (*Shakesp*) flaw
♦ *v*
break, shatter, splinter, shiver, crumble, disintegrate, come to pieces, come apart, break up, divide, split (up), disunite, smash to pieces/smithereens
🗲 hold together, join

fragmentary *adj*
bitty, piecemeal, scrappy, broken, disjointed, disconnected, separate, scattered, sketchy, partial, incomplete, uneven, discontinuous, incoherent
🗲 whole, complete

fragmentation *n*
break-up, shattering, crumbling, disintegration, decomposition, division, separation, splitting, splitting-up

fragmented *adj*
broken, divided, separate, disintegrated, disjointed, disunited, departmentalized, compartmentalized, in pieces, in bits, incomplete
🗲 complete, whole

fragrance *n*
perfume, scent, smell, sweet smell, odour, aroma, bouquet, balm, attar, otto
FORMAL redolence

fragrant *adj*
perfumed, scented, sweet-smelling, sweet-scented, sweet, balmy, aromatic, odorous
FORMAL redolent, odoriferous
🗲 unscented

frail *adj*
delicate, brittle, breakable, easily broken, fragile, flimsy, insubstantial, slight, puny, weak, feeble, infirm, unwell, unsound, vulnerable, susceptible
FORMAL frangible
🗲 robust, tough, strong

frailty *n*
weakness, weak point, foible, failing, deficiency, shortcoming, fault, defect, flaw, blemish, imperfection, infirmity, fallibility, susceptibility, vulnerability, brittleness, fragility, delicacy
🗲 strength, robustness, toughness

frame *n, v*

♦ *n*

1 STRUCTURE, fabric, framework, skeleton, carcase, shell, casing, chassis, substructure, foundation, construction, support, bodywork, body, build, form, physique, figure, size, shape

2 MOUNT, mounting, setting, surround, border, edge

♦ *v*

1 COMPOSE, formulate, conceive, establish, create, devise, contrive, concoct, plan, map out, plot, sketch, draw up, draft, shape, form, model, fashion, mould, forge, assemble, put together, build, set up, erect, construct, fabricate, make, manufacture
COLLOQ. cook up

2 SURROUND, enclose, box in, case, encase, mount

3 *I've been framed*
trap, incriminate, plant
COLLOQ. set up, fit up, stitch up, pin on, cook up a charge

■ **frame of mind**
state (of mind), mood, condition, humour, temper, disposition, spirit, outlook, attitude

frame-up *n*

fabrication, trap, plot, conspiracy
COLLOQ. fit-up, fix, put-up job, trumped-up charge

framework *n*

structure, fabric, bare bones, skeleton, shell, frame, casing, outline, plan, foundation, groundwork, substructure, trestle, trestlework, lattice, rack, scheme, constraints, parameters

franchise *n*

concession, licence, charter, warrant, authorization, permission, consent, privilege, right, prerogative, liberty, freedom, immunity, exemption
FORMAL suffrage, enfranchisement

frank *adj, v*

♦ *adj*

honest, truthful, sincere, genuine, candid, blunt, open, free, plain, plain-spoken, direct, forthright, straight, straightforward, downright, hard-hitting, outspoken, explicit, bluff
COLLOQ. straight from the shoulder, up-front
⊟ insincere, evasive

♦ *v*

stamp, mark, postmark, cancel

SYNONYM NUANCES

adjective
Honest is a positive term in that it implies an absence of deception in all areas of life, whilst **truthful** is more neutral and more narrow, referring only to always telling what is true. Both **sincere** and **genuine** are also approbatory terms, describing those who have belief in what they say or do. **Candid** is more neutral, having more to do with being unreservedly open: *the book's candid discussion of sexual matters*. **Blunt** is rather more disapproving, implying a lack of tact; **bluff** is similar, but also has connotations of heartiness: *he expressed himself in a macho, bluff way*.

The terms **plain** and **straight** suggest a lack of adornment: *the plain facts*, with **plain-spoken**, **straightforward**, **direct** and **forthright** suggesting a similar absence of evasion in speech, with their use being unmarked by approval or disapproval. On the other hand, **downright**, although similar in meaning, usually suggests less admirable attributes: *downright rudeness*.

Both **hard-hitting** and **outspoken** imply that the frankness may provoke a reaction: *an outspoken campaigner for democracy*, while **explicit** emphasizes that something is unambiguous: *art critics are not always explicit in their evaluations of works*.

---

frankly *adv*

to be frank, to be honest, to be blunt, in truth, to tell you the truth, honestly, candidly, bluntly, truthfully, openly,

freely, plainly, directly, straight, explicitly, without reserve, straight from the shoulder, eye to eye, eyeball to eyeball
COLLOQ. straight out, laying it on the line, not beating about the bush, not mincing your words
⊟ insincerely, evasively

frankness *n*

bluntness, candour, forthrightness, plain speaking, openness, directness, sincerity, outspokenness, truthfulness
FORMAL ingenuousness
⊟ reserve

frantic *adj*

agitated, overwrought, fraught, desperate, beside yourself, furious, raging, mad, wild, raving, frenzied, berserk, frenetic, distressed, distracted, distraught, delirious, out of control, panic-stricken, hectic
COLLOQ. at your wits' end
⊟ calm, composed

frantically *adv*

desperately, furiously, madly, wildly, hysterically, out of control, beside yourself
COLLOQ. at your wits' end, tearing your hair out

fraternity *n*

comradeship, brotherhood, kinship, camaraderie, companionship, set, society, association, circle, club, company, guild, order, league, union, fellowship, clan

fraternize *v*

mix, mingle, socialize, associate, keep company, move, go around, affiliate, unite, sympathize, cordialize
FORMAL consort, forgather
COLLOQ. hang about, hobnob, pal up with, gang up with, rub shoulders
⊟ shun, ignore

fraud *n*

1 DECEIT, deception, guile, fraudulence, cheating, swindle, swindling, double-dealing, sharp practice, embezzlement, fake, counterfeit, forgery, sham, hoax, trick, trickery, racket, roguery, humbug, imposture, supercherie
TECHNICAL stellionate, *fraus pia*
FORMAL duplicity, chicanery
COLLOQ. con, riddle, scam, fix, diddle, swiz, take-in
SLANG rip-off; *N Am* gold brick
2 CHARLATAN, impostor, pretender, sham, fake, bluffer, hoaxer, cheat, swindler, fraudster, embezzler, double-dealer, trickster, quack, mountebank
COLLOQ. phoney, con man

fraudulent *adj*

dishonest, criminal, deceitful, deceptive, false, bogus, sham, counterfeit, swindling, cheating, double-dealing, unscrupulous, exploitative, shameless, surreptitious
FORMAL duplicitous
COLLOQ. crooked, shady, phoney; *Aust* cronk
⊟ honest, genuine

fraudulently *adv*

dishonestly, deceitfully, falsely, unscrupulously, shamelessly, corruptly, illegally
⊟ honestly

fraught *adj*

1 FULL, filled, charged, abounding, accompanied, attended, bristling
FORMAL laden, replete
2 ANXIOUS, tense, agitated, worried, under stress, distressed, distraught, overwrought
COLLOQ. uptight, stressed out
⊟ calm, untroublesome

fray *v, n*

♦ *v*

1 *the rope is fraying*
become ragged, become threadbare, wear (out), frazzle, rag, unravel, wear thin
OLD fridge

2 *tempers were fraying*
irritate, vex, strain, stress, tax, overtax, make tense, make nervous, push too far, put on edge

♦ *n*

brawl, scuffle, free-for-all, set-to, clash, conflict, fight, combat, battle, quarrel, row, rumpus, disturbance, riot, affray, excitement, challenge
OLD wigs on the green
COLLOQ. dust-up, aggro, bovver, scrap, scrape, punch-up, pasting, bashing

frayed *adj*

ragged, tattered, worn, threadbare, unravelled, thin, worn thin

freak *n, adj, v*

♦ *n*

1 MONSTER, mutant, mutation, freak of nature, monstrosity, deformity, irregularity
TECHNICAL *lusus naturae*
FORMAL malformation
2 ANOMALY, abnormality, aberration, oddity, curiosity, quirk, whim, vagary, twist, turn
FORMAL caprice
COLLOQ. oddball, weirdo
SLANG *N Am* geek
3 ENTHUSIAST, fanatic, addict, devotee, fan
FORMAL aficionado
COLLOQ. buff, fiend, nut
♦ *adj*
abnormal, atypical, unusual, exceptional, odd, queer, bizarre, erratic, unpredictable, unexpected, surprise, chance
FORMAL aberrant, capricious, fortuitous
COLLOQ. fluky
E3 normal, common
■ **freak out**
go crazy, go wild, go berserk, go out of your mind, lose control, lose your self-control
COLLOQ. throw a wobbly, explode, go off the deep end, go bananas
SLANG *N Am* wig out

freakish *adj*

unusual, odd, abnormal, strange, peculiar, unconventional, unpredictable, weird, outlandish, freaky, whimsical, fanciful, fantastic, grotesque, monstrous, malformed, arbitrary, fitful, changeable, erratic
FORMAL aberrant, capricious
E3 ordinary, normal

free *adj, v, adv*

♦ *adj*

1 *free tickets*
gratis, without charge, free of charge, for nothing, at no cost, at no extra cost, complimentary, with compliments
COLLOQ. on the house
SLANG buckshee
2 *free to move*
at liberty, at large, loose, on the loose, unattached, unrestrained, unconfined, out
COLLOQ. free as a bird
3 *a free country*
liberated, emancipated, sovereign, independent, democratic, self-governing, self-ruling, autonomous
FORMAL autarchic
4 *free of dirt*
lacking, without, unaffected by, immune to, exempt from, safe from, clear of
FORMAL devoid of
5 *free time; a free seat*
spare, available, idle, unemployed, unoccupied, off duty, with time on your hands, untaken, vacant, empty
6 CLEAR, unobstructed, unimpeded, open, unblocked, unhampered, unrestricted
7 GENEROUS, liberal, open-handed, lavish, charitable, giving, hospitable, unstinting
FORMAL munificent
8 *with his free hand*
unattached, unfastened, loose, unsecured

9 *a free translation*
loose, rough, general, broad, vague, inexact, imprecise
10 *his free manner; free movement*
easy, relaxed, easy-going, smooth, natural, uninhibited, casual, spontaneous, fluid
COLLOQ. laid-back, doing your own thing, doing as you please
E3 2 imprisoned, bound, tied, fettered, confined, restricted **4** liable to, affected by **5** busy, occupied, at work, reserved, engaged; *colloq.* tied up **6** blocked, obstructed **7** mean, stingy **8** attached **9** literal, rigorous, exact, precise **10** inhibited, formal, tense
♦ *v*
1 *free a prisoner*
release, discharge, let go, let out, loose, turn loose, set loose, set free, untie, unbind, unchain, unleash, liberate, emancipate
2 *free someone trapped*
rescue, deliver, save, ransom, disentangle, disengage, extricate
3 *free someone from debt*
clear, make available, rid, relieve, unburden, exempt, excuse, except, absolve, acquit
E3 1 imprison, confine
♦ *adv*
1 FOR NOTHING, for free, without charge, gratis, freely, for love
2 GENEROUSLY, liberally, lavishly, extravagantly, abundantly, copiously
E3 2 meanly
■ **free and easy**
casual, informal, easy-going, relaxed, happy-go-lucky, carefree, spontaneous, tolerant
COLLOQ. laid-back
E3 inhibited, formal
■ **free hand**
authority, freedom, latitude, liberty, licence, free rein, carte blanche, permission, power, scope, discretion

freedom *n*

1 LIBERTY, emancipation, deliverance, release, exemption, immunity, impunity
2 INDEPENDENCE, autonomy, self-government, sovereignty, democracy, emancipation, home rule
FORMAL autarchy
3 RANGE, scope, play, leeway, flexibility, margin, latitude, licence, opportunity, privilege, right, power, prerogative, free rein, free hand; *Aust & NZ* open slather
E3 1 captivity, confinement **3** restriction

> **QUOTATIONS**
> Freedom is only the distance / between the hunter and his prey
> ZHENKAI ZHAO, 'Answer'

free-for-all *n*

brawl, fight, scrap, scuffle, mêlée, fray, affray, broil, skirmish, fracas, rumpus, ruckus, disorder, row, argument, quarrel, squabble, dispute, clash, fisticuffs, Donnybrook, bagarre; *dialect* fratch; *Aust & NZ* stoush
OLD brabble, brangle; *Scot* tuilyie
FORMAL altercation
COLLOQ. punch-up, bust-up, dust-up

freely *adv*

1 READILY, willingly, voluntarily, of your own volition, of your own free will, spontaneously, easily
2 *give freely*
generously, liberally, lavishly, extravagantly, amply, abundantly
3 *speak freely*
frankly, candidly, bluntly, unreservedly, openly, plainly, spontaneously, ad-lib
4 *move freely*
easily, smoothly, naturally, loosely, frictionlessly, without jerking, without resistance, in all directions
E3 2 grudgingly **3** evasively, cautiously

freethinker n
rationalist, sceptic, agnostic, doubter, nonconformist, libertine, independent, deist, unbeliever, infidel

freethinking adj
rationalist, sceptical, agnostic, nonconformist, broad-minded, open-minded, liberal, independent, unconventional

free will n
freedom, liberty, independence, self-determination, self-sufficiency, spontaneity
TECHNICAL autarky
FORMAL volition, autonomy
■ **of your own free will**
voluntarily, willingly, freely, intentionally, consciously, deliberately, purposely, spontaneously, by choice, on your own initiative, of your own accord
F3 involuntarily, unwillingly

freeze v, n
♦ v
1 ICE OVER, ice up, congeal, solidify, set, harden, stiffen
TECHNICAL glaciate
2 DEEP-FREEZE, ice, refrigerate, chill, cool, preserve, freeze-dry, enfreeze
3 GET COLD, shiver, quiver, catch a chill, turn blue with cold, your teeth be chattering
4 STOP, suspend, fix, immobilize, halt, stand still, stop dead in your tracks, become paralysed, hold
5 FIX, hold, suspend, peg
♦ n
1 FROST, freeze-up, cold snap
2 STOPPAGE, halt, standstill, shutdown, suspension, interruption, postponement, stay, embargo, fixing, moratorium
■ **freeze out**
expel, eject, evict, throw out, remove, excommunicate, ostracize, boycott, ignore, snub, cut, ice out, lock out
COLLOQ. boot out, turf out, kick out, brush off, give the cold shoulder to, send to Coventry

freezing adj
icy, frosty, glacial, arctic, polar, Siberian, wintry, raw, bitter, bitterly cold, biting, cutting, piercing, penetrating, numbing, stinging, numb, cold, chilly
COLLOQ. baltic
SLANG brass monkeys
F3 hot, warm

freight n
1 CARGO, load, lading, payload, contents, goods, merchandise, consignment, shipment
OLD fraught
2 TRANSPORTATION, conveyance, carriage, haulage, freightage, portage

frenetic adj
frantic, wild, frenzied, hectic, overwrought, demented, distraught, excited, unbalanced, mad, insane, berserk, hysterical, manic, maniacal, obsessive, hyperactive
F3 calm, placid

frenetically adv
frantically, hectically, wildly, excitedly, intensely, madly, hysterically, manically
F3 calmly, placidly

frenzied adj
frantic, frenetic, hectic, feverish, desperate, furious, overwrought, distraught, distracted, crazed, wild, uncontrolled, mad, berserk, amok, raving, demented, hysterical, manic, panic-stricken, out of control, beside yourself, obsessive, at your wits' end
F3 calm, composed

frenzy n
1 TURMOIL, agitation, wildness, distraction, madness, lunacy, insanity, mania, hysteria, delirium, fever
TECHNICAL must, musth, phrenesis
OLD derangement
COLLOQ. tailspin

2 BURST, fit, bout, spasm, paroxysm, convulsion, seizure, outburst, transport, passion, rage, fury
TECHNICAL nympholepsy, oestrus
F3 1 calm, composure

frequency n
frequentness, incidence, prevalence, recurrence, rate of occurrence, repetition, commonness, constancy
OLD oftenness
FORMAL periodicity
F3 infrequency

frequent adj, v
♦ adj
common, commonplace, happening often, normal, everyday, familiar, usual, customary, accustomed, habitual, prevailing, prevalent, predominant, numerous, countless, incessant, constant, continual, persistent, repeated, recurring, recurrent, regular, hourly, daily, weekly, thick
OLD often
F3 infrequent
♦ v
visit, visit often, go to frequently, go to regularly, patronize, attend, haunt, associate with, lobby
OLD habituate, practise
COLLOQ. hang out at, hang about at

frequenter n
regular, regular visitor, customer, client, patron, haunter, habitué

frequently adv
often, commonly, many times, much, many a time, over and over, repeatedly, persistently, continually, habitually, customarily, regularly, hourly, daily, weekly, thick; N Am oftentimes
COLLOQ. half the time, nine times out of ten, more times than you've had hot dinners
F3 infrequently, seldom

fresh adj
1 ADDITIONAL, supplementary, extra, more, further, other
2 NEW, novel, innovative, original, different, brand-new, unconventional, revolutionary, modern, up-to-date, recent, latest, exciting, unusual
COLLOQ. new-fangled
3 REFRESHING, bracing, invigorating, brisk, crisp, keen, cool, chilly, windy, fair, bright, clean, clear, pure, unfaded, unpolluted
4 *fresh fruit*
raw, natural, unprocessed, crude, firm, crisp, unpreserved, uncured, undried
5 REFRESHED, revived, restored, renewed, rested, invigorated, stimulated, energetic, vigorous, lively, vibrant, enthusiastic, alert, vital, bouncing
COLLOQ. raring to go, ready for more, yourself again, a new person, fresh as a daisy, bright-eyed and bushy-tailed
6 *a fresh complexion*
healthy, healthy-looking, glowing, bright, clear, blooming, fair, pink, rosy
7 *fresh from university*
straight, just, right, direct
8 PERT, disrespectful, impudent, insolent, impertinent, cheeky, cocky, bold, brazen, forward, familiar, overfamiliar, presumptuous
COLLOQ. saucy; N Am sassy
F3 2 old, hackneyed **3** stale **4** preserved, tinned, processed **5** tired

freshen v
1 AIR, ventilate, purify, clean, clear, deodorize
2 REFRESH, restore, revitalize, revive, reinvigorate, liven (up), enliven, stimulate, rouse
COLLOQ. tart up
F3 2 tire
■ **freshen up**
tidy yourself up, have a wash, wash yourself, get washed, spruce yourself up, get spruced up

freshly *adv*

recently, lately, of late, newly, barely, just, in the last few days, in the past few days/weeks, not long ago, a short time ago, a little while back

▰ long ago

freshman *n*

first-year, fresher, first-year student, underclassman, newcomer

COLLOQ. *N Am* frosh

freshness *n*

brightness, cleanness, clearness, newness, originality, novelty, bloom, shine, glow, sparkle, vigour, wholesomeness

▰ staleness, tiredness

fret *v*

1 WORRY, be anxious, be upset, agonize, anguish, be distressed, brood, pine, mope, concern yourself, make a fuss

2 VEX, irritate, nettle, bother, trouble, concern, anger, annoy, exasperate, infuriate, rile, torment

fretful *adj*

worried, anxious, unhappy, upset, distressed, disturbed, uneasy, fearful, tense, restless, troubled

COLLOQ. edgy, uptight

▰ calm

fretfully *adv*

anxiously, worriedly, uneasily, fearfully, tensely, restlessly

COLLOQ. edgily

▰ calmly

friable *adj*

brittle, crumbly, crisp, powdery

FORMAL pulverizable

▰ solid

friar *n*

monk, religioner, mendicant, religious, prior, abbot, brother

friction *n*

1 DISAGREEMENT, dispute, disharmony, disunity, clashing, conflict, strife, quarrelling, arguing, antagonism, hostility, opposition, rivalry, animosity, bad/ill feeling, bad blood, resentment

FORMAL dissension, discord, disputation

2 RUBBING, chafing, irritation, scraping, grating, rasping, erosion, gnawing, wearing away, resistance, traction

FORMAL abrasion, abrading, attrition, excoriation

▰ **1** agreement, unity

friend *n*

1 COMPANION, good friend, close friend, best friend, intimate, confidant(e), bosom friend, soul mate, comrade, ally, partner, associate, familiar, playmate, pen friend, acquaintance, well-wisher, boyfriend, girlfriend, best boy/ girl, better half, schoolfriend, compadre, sparring partner, alter ego, *ami(e), belle amie, bon ami, amigo, paisano, fidus Achates*

OLD gossip, gossib, ingle, mucker, paranymph, privado; *(Shakesp)* inward, lover, cater-cousin, co-mate; *(Spenser)* belamy

COLLOQ. mate, pal, gal pal, chum, buddy, buddy-buddy, crony, sidekick, bestie, BFF; *N Am* homeboy, homey

2 SUPPORTER, backer, patron, well-wisher, sponsor, benefactor, subscriber, back-friend

▰ **1** enemy **2** opponent

> **PROVERBS**
> A friend in need is a friend indeed

> **SYNONYM NUANCES**
> *sense 1*
> **Companion** can be used of anyone who frequently keeps company with another, but an **intimate** is someone who is very close to another: *christened Richard, but called Dick by his intimates*. **Confidant(e)**

similarly implies closeness but further involves the sharing of private secrets, whilst **soul mate** or **alter ego** would be reserved for someone with whom you feel a unique affinity.

> **Comrade** is more suggestive of someone with a shared, often military, experience which generates closeness: *his comrade in crime*, whereas **ally** has more to do with providing support. The term **partner** implies an equal relationship, either social or professional, but **associate** is generally reserved for varying depths of business relationships: *a close political associate and friend of Nelson Mandela*. **Compadre** also suggests an equal relationship, and might be used quite humorously of a male companion, whilst the equally light-hearted **sparring partner** suggests someone with whom you are comfortable enough to enjoy arguing.

> You can use **acquaintance** to suggest anyone of whom you have slight knowledge, while a **well-wisher** could be someone you do not necessarily know particularly well, but who, like a friend, is generally concerned for your welfare.

> The terms **boyfriend** and **girlfriend** can be used of a platonic friend of the specified sex, but usually refer to a person with whom you are having a sexual or romantic relationship. The old fashioned terms **best boy** and **best girl** are similar but would probably be used facetiously. The formal expression **fidus Achates** carries strong connotations of faithfulness and reliability.

friendless *adj*

alone, companionless, unpopular, unloved, unbefriended, solitary, shunned, ostracized, lonely, isolated, forlorn, abandoned, lonesome, lonely-heart, deserted, forsaken, unattached, unbeloved, by yourself, with no one to turn to

COLLOQ. cold-shouldered

friendliness *n*

affability, amiability, companionability, congeniality, conviviality, approachability, kindness, kindliness, warmth, neighbourliness, sociability, geniality, *Gemütlichkeit*

COLLOQ. matiness, palliness, chumminess

▰ coldness, unsociableness

friendly *adj*

1 AMIABLE, affable, genial, convivial, cordial, kind, kindly, warm, neighbourly, helpful, fond, affectionate, familiar, intimate, inseparable, close, companionable, sociable, outgoing, approachable, receptive, hospitable, comradely, amicable, peaceable, well-disposed, favourable, agreeable, good-natured, sympathetic

COLLOQ. mat(e)y, pally, chummy, thick, tight, folksy

2 *a friendly atmosphere*

convivial, congenial, cordial, welcoming, warm, pleasant, close, amicable, familiar

▰ **1** hostile, unsociable, unfriendly **2** cold, unwelcoming, hostile

friendship *n*

companionship, closeness, intimacy, familiarity, amiability, affinity, rapport, attachment, affection, fondness, warmth, love, harmony, concord, understanding, goodwill, friendliness, kindliness, friendly relationship, alliance, fellowship, comradeship, camaraderie

FORMAL amity

▰ enmity, animosity

> **QUOTATIONS**
> To like and dislike the same things, that is indeed true friendship
> SALLUST, *Bellum Catilinae*

fright *n*

shock, scare, alarm, dismay, dread, apprehension, fear, fearfulness, terror, horror, panic, disquiet; *Scot* fleg, gliff; *S Afr* skrik

OLD affright, affrightment, tirrit

FORMAL trepidation, consternation, perturbation
COLLOQ. blind panic, cold sweat, hair standing on end, blood running cold, knocking knees, shivers, jitters, creeps, willies, heebie-jeebies, funk, blue funk, bombshell, bolt from the blue

frighten v
alarm, daunt, unnerve, unman, dismay, intimidate, terrorize, scare, startle, scare stiff, give someone a fright, terrify, petrify, horrify, appal, shock, panic; *Scot* fleg
OLD affright, affrighten; (*Spenser*) afear; (*Shakesp*) gallow, gast, ghast
COLLOQ. rattle, spook, boggle, scare out of your wits, make your blood run cold, scare the living daylights out of, scare silly, make your hair stand on end, make you jump out of your skin, put the frighteners on, put the wind up
SLANG scare the hell/shit out of
E3 reassure, calm

SYNONYM NUANCES

Alarm would describe the action of causing apprehension at the prospect of danger: *the public have been alarmed by warnings of terrorist attacks*, whilst **daunt** and **dismay** are less dramatic, suggesting discouragement: *voluntary organizations are often daunted by local bureaucracy*.

Unnerve and **unman**, however, are more suggestive of being disconcerted and losing courage. **Intimidate** has more to do with the restriction of someone's actions through perceived or deliberate and real threats: *she was intimidated by his aggressive manner*. You might use the word **terrorize** of deliberately causing a more extreme fear: *elderly people terrorized by young thugs*. **Scare** implies a lesser degree of fear, although the extended term, **scare stiff**, is stronger in its image of making someone unable to move.

Terrify can be used of causing great fear, and **petrify** returns to the image of being rendered immobile by it: *he was sitting petrified but unhurt in the wreckage*. Both **horrify** and **appal** suggest an element of outrage or disgust in the fear caused, whilst **shock**, may be more appropriately used when someone's sensibilities are offended rather than feeling fear. **Panic** has more to do with causing a frantic, often irrational, reaction: *I was panicked into leaving town when they made their empty threats*.

---

frightened adj
afraid, dismayed, scared, terrified, unnerved, terrorized, terror-stricken, alarmed, cowed, frozen, petrified, scared stiff, startled, trembly, quivery, panicky, panic-stricken; *dialect* frit; *Scot* feart
COLLOQ. scared out of your wits, scared to death, having kittens, in a blue funk, shaking like a leaf, with your heart in your mouth
See Synonym nuances panel at **afraid**.
E3 calm, courageous

frightening adj
alarming, daunting, formidable, grim, fearsome, forbidding, terrifying, hair-raising, creepy, bloodcurdling, spine-chilling, petrifying, traumatic
COLLOQ. scary, hairy, spooky, white-knuckle

frightful adj
1 UNPLEASANT, disagreeable, awful, nasty, dreadful, fearful, terrible, alarming, appalling, shocking, horrendous, harrowing, unspeakable, dire, grim, ghastly, hideous, horrible, horrid, horrific, grisly, macabre, gruesome, revolting, repulsive, abhorrent, odious, loathsome, unbearable, fearsome, frightsome, *schrecklich*
OLD affrightful, ugly
COLLOQ. like nothing on earth
2 *get into a frightful mess*
awful, dreadful, very bad, terrible, appalling, horrendous
E3 **1** pleasant, agreeable

frightfully adv
very, much, greatly, extremely, exceedingly, thoroughly, desperately, decidedly
COLLOQ. terribly, awfully
E3 slightly

frigid adj
1 FROZEN, bitter, freezing, icy, frosty, glacial, arctic, cold, very cold, chill, chilly, wintry, polar, Siberian
2 UNFEELING, unresponsive, unemotional, passionless, unloving, unmoved, unsympathetic, cool, chilly, icy, distant, remote, reserved, formal, clinical, impersonal, aloof, standoffish, passive, unexcitable, indifferent, stiff, dry, lifeless, stony
E3 **1** hot, temperate **2** responsive, enthusiastic, approachable

---

SYNONYM NUANCES

sense 2
The terms **unfeeling** and **unemotional** appropriately describe a complete and general lack of emotion, while **unmoved**, **unsympathetic** and **unresponsive** are suggestive of an inability to identify with another's specific problems. All these terms have an inherent if not highly marked note of criticism.

Rather more deliberately disapproving in tone are **chilly** and **icy**, which are fairly emotive terms to describe an unwelcoming manner.

Impersonal and **clinical**, on the other hand, are not necessarily such marked terms, in that they are often more suggestive of formality and a disinterested but necessary detachment: *a clinical account of the incident*. The terms **reserved**, **distant** and **remote** all imply an inability or reluctance to relate with another: *she felt remote from her companion*; **aloof** and **standoffish** would be used of a more deliberate choice not to interact, and are therefore rather critical in tone.

Unexcitable and **indifferent** can be used fairly neutrally of a lack of any strong feeling or response, while **passionless** carries a more critical connotation of incapacity for deeply felt emotion. **Stony**, **stiff**, **dry** and **lifeless**, however, create images of a complete lack of potential for feeling, and are even more derogatory in tone: *Evelyn tried a smile, but it was met with stony indifference*.

---

frigidity n
unresponsiveness, unapproachability, frostiness, iciness, impassivity, lifelessness, passivity, stiffness, cold-heartedness, coldness, aloofness, chill, chilliness
E3 responsiveness, warmth

frill n
1 *a blouse with frills*
flounce, gathering, ruff, ruffle, trimming, tuck, valance, fold, fringe, furbelow, ruche, ruching, purfle, orphrey
2 *the basic model without the frills*
trimmings, addition, extra, ornamentation, decoration, embellishment, fanciness, accessory, ostentation, superfluity, finery, frilliness, fandangle, frippery

frilly adj
ruffled, crimped, gathered, frilled, flounced, trimmed, lacy, fancy, ornate
E3 plain

fringe n, adj, v
♦ n
1 MARGIN, periphery, outskirts, edge, perimeter, limit, rim, border, verge, borderline
2 BORDER, edging, edge, trimming, tassel, frill, valance, pelmet, fall, bullion, macramé, thrum, bangs, *frisette*
TECHNICAL fimbria, loma, peristome
♦ adj
unconventional, unorthodox, unofficial, alternative, avant-garde, experimental, off-beat
COLLOQ. left-field
E3 conventional, mainstream

◆ v
border, edge, trim, skirt, hem, surround, enclose, purl
TECHNICAL fimbria

fringed adj
bordered, edged, fringy, trimmed, hemmed, tasselled,
tassely
TECHNICAL fimbriated

frippery n
finery, adornments, decorations, ornaments, ostentation,
pretentiousness, showiness, gaudiness, fanciness,
flashiness, frilliness, fussiness, tawdriness, triviality,
baubles, fandangles, trinkets, knickknacks, gewgaws,
trifles, trivia, frills, froth, nonsense, glad rags, foppery
FORMAL meretriciousness
▱ plainness, simplicity

frisk v
1 JUMP, leap, skip, hop, bounce, prance, caper, dance,
gambol, frolic, romp, cavort, play, sport, trip
2 BODY-SEARCH, search, inspect, check; N Am shake down

friskily adv
actively, spiritedly, exuberantly, playfully
▱ quietly

frisky adj
lively, active, spirited, high-spirited, in high spirits,
exuberant, dashing, frolicsome, playful, romping,
rollicking, bouncy
COLLOQ. high, alive and kicking, full of beans, hyper
▱ quiet, subdued

fritter v
waste, squander, go through, get through, idle, misuse,
misspend, overspend
FORMAL dissipate
COLLOQ. spend like water
SLANG blow

frivolity n
fun, gaiety, flippancy, facetiousness, jest, light-heartedness,
levity, triviality, superficiality, inanity, silliness, folly,
foolishness, pettiness, nonsense, senselessness
COLLOQ. froth
▱ seriousness

frivolous adj
1 *a frivolous person*
shallow, superficial, flippant, jocular, light, light-hearted,
juvenile, puerile, facetious, foolish, silly, skittish, empty-
headed, featherbrained, giddy-headed, bubble-headed,
airheaded
2 *frivolous activities*
futile, vain, pointless, senseless, unimportant, petty,
irresponsible, trivial, trifling, shallow, superficial, inane,
puerile, juvenile, foolish, silly, idle
▱ 1 serious, sensible 2 useful, sensible

frivolously adv
irresponsibly, foolishly, idly, vainly, pointlessly, senselessly,
jocularly, light-heartedly, whimsically
▱ sensibly, seriously

frizzle[1] v
frizzled her hair
curl, crimp, crimple, frizz, wave, roll, crinkle, kink, bend,
curve, loop, turn, twist, wind, wreathe, twirl, twine, coil,
spiral, scroll, tong, purl, becurl

frizzle[2] v
frizzled on the fire
fry, scorch, sizzle, hiss, crackle, spit, sputter

frizzy adj
curled, curly, crimped, crisp, frizzed, wiry, corrugated
▱ straight

frock n
dress, gown, robe

frolic v, n
◆ v
gambol, caper, romp, play, lark around, rollick, make
merry, frisk, prance, cavort, dance, leap, skip, hop,
bounce, sport; dialect gammock
◆ n
fun, fun and games, amusement, sport, game, gaiety,
jollity, merriment, mirth, revel, romp, prank, lark, caper,
spree, high jinks, antics, escapade; dialect gammock
COLLOQ. razzle, razzle-dazzle

frolicsome adj
playful, ludic, frisky, lively, merry, gay, sprightly, sportive,
rollicking, coltish, skittish
▱ quiet, serious, solemn

front n, adj, v
◆ n
1 *the front of the building*
face, aspect, frontage, façade, outside, exterior, facing,
cover, obverse, top, head, lead, vanguard, van, forefront,
front line, firing line, foreground, forepart, bow
2 PRETENCE, show, air, appearance, look, expression,
manner, exterior, façade, cover, mask, disguise, pretext,
cover-up, blind
FORMAL countenance
3 *fighting at the front*
front line, vanguard, firing line, battle zone
▱ 1 back, rear
◆ adj
leading, foremost, head, first, fore
▱ back, rear, last
◆ v
face, confront, look over, look out on, meet, oppose,
overlook
■ **in front**
leading, ahead, first, in advance, to the fore, before,
preceding
▱ behind
■ **in front of**
1 AHEAD OF, in advance of, before, facing
2 *in front of the children*
in the presence of, under the nose of, before

frontier n
border, boundary, borderline, limit, edge, perimeter,
confines, marches, bounds, verge, partition

front-runner n
favourite, odds-on favourite, certainty, nap, likely winner,
finalist, top seed, form horse
▱ underdog, also-ran

frost n
freeze, freeze-up, ice, Jack Frost, hoar-frost, rime, coldness

frostily adv
coldly, coolly, stiffly, in an unfriendly manner
▱ warmly, responsively, enthusiastically

frosty adj
1 ICY, frozen, freezing, frigid, wintry, cold, bitterly cold,
chilly, rimy, glacial, arctic, Siberian, polar
COLLOQ. nippy, parky
2 UNFRIENDLY, unwelcoming, cool, cold, icy, aloof,
standoffish, stiff, discouraging, hostile
▱ 1 warm, hot 2 warm, friendly, responsive, welcoming,
enthusiastic

froth n, v
◆ n
1 BUBBLES, effervescence, fizz, foam, lather, suds, head,
scum, spume
2 TRIVIA, trifles, trivialities, irrelevancies
COLLOQ. pap
◆ v
foam, lather, ferment, fizz, effervesce, bubble, spume
Related adjectives: spumous, spumy

frothy adj
1 BUBBLING, bubbly, foaming, foamy, yeasty, sudsy
FORMAL spumescent, spumous, spumy

COLLOQ. fizzy
2 INSUBSTANTIAL, empty, trivial, frivolous, trifling, slight, light, lightweight, vain
Ƒ 1 flat, still **2** substantial, significant

frown v, n
♦ v
scowl, glower, lour, glare, grimace, mow, pout
COLLOQ. give someone a dirty look, look daggers at
Ƒ approve of, go along with
♦ n
scowl, glower, glare, grimace, moue, raised eyebrow
COLLOQ. dirty look
■ **frown on**
disapprove of, object to, dislike, discourage, take a dim view of, not take kindly to, think badly of, have a low opinion of, raise your eyebrows

frowsty adj
fusty, stuffy, airless, unventilated, fuggy, musty
Ƒ airy

frowsy adj
untidy, dishevelled, scruffy, unwashed, unkempt, ungroomed, dirty, messy, frumpish, frumpy, slatternly, sloppy, slovenly, sluttish
Ƒ well-groomed

frozen adj
iced, chilled, icy, frosty, icebound, ice-covered, arctic, ice-cold, bitterly cold, raw, polar, Siberian, frigid, freezing, numb, hard, frosted, solidified, stiff, frozen-stiff, rigid, fixed
Ƒ warm

frugal adj
thrifty, penny-wise, niggardly, penny-pinching, miserly, stingy, careful, prudent, provident, saving, scrimping and saving, economical, sparing, meagre, paltry, scanty, inadequate
FORMAL parsimonious
Ƒ wasteful, extravagant

frugality n
thrift, economy, husbandry, saving, scrimping and saving, conservation, prudence, carefulness
FORMAL parsimony
Ƒ extravagance, waste

frugally adv
thriftily, carefully, prudently, economically, meagrely, scantily, inadequately
FORMAL parsimoniously
Ƒ wastefully, extravagantly

fruit n
1 CROP, harvest, produce, fruitage
2 BENEFIT, consequence, advantage, effect, outcome, reward, return, result, yield, product, profit

---

Varieties of fruit include:

APPLES:	lime	colloq. goosegog
Braeburn	mandarin	loganberry
Bramley	mineola	pineberry
Cox's Orange	nectarine	raspberry
Pippin	orange	redcurrant
crab apple	pink grapefruit	strawberry
Golden Delicious	satsuma	whitecurrant
Granny Smith	Seville orange	
Pink Lady	tangerine	PLUMS:
Royal Gala	Ugli®	damson
		greengage
PEARS:	BERRIES:	
Asian pear	bilberry	MELONS:
Conference	blackberry	cantaloupe
William	blackcurrant	casaba
	blueberry	Galia
CITRUS FRUIT:	boysenberry	honeydew
blood orange	cranberry	watermelon
clementine	elderberry	
grapefruit	goji berry	TROPICAL FRUIT:
Jaffa orange	gooseberry	açaí
lemon		date

dragon fruit (or pitahaya)	star fruit (or carambola)	olive
fig		peach
guava	OTHER:	persimmon (or sharon fruit)
kiwi fruit	apricot	pomegranate
mango	avocado	rhubarb
papaya (or pawpaw)	cherry	sloe
passion fruit	grape	tomato
pineapple	kumquat	
	lychee	

---

fruitful adj
1 FERTILE, rich, teeming, plentiful, abundant, prolific, productive, fruit-bearing
OLD plenteous, pregnant; (Shakesp) conceptious, increaseful
FORMAL fecund, feracious, fructive
2 REWARDING, profitable, advantageous, beneficial, effective, worthwhile, well-spent, useful, successful, productive, fat
OLD increaseful
FORMAL effectual, efficacious
Ƒ 1 barren, unproductive **2** fruitless, vain

fruitfully adv
successfully, profitably, advantageously, beneficially, effectively, usefully, productively
Ƒ fruitlessly, unsuccessfully

fruitfulness n
productiveness, profitability, fertility, usefulness
FORMAL fecundity, fecundation, feracity
Ƒ fruitlessness

fruition n
realization, fulfilment, attainment, achievement, completion, maturity, ripeness, perfection, success, enjoyment
FORMAL consummation, actualization

fruitless adj
unsuccessful, abortive, useless, futile, pointless, vain, idle, hopeless, worthless, unproductive, barren, sterile
OLD infructuous
FORMAL ineffectual
Ƒ fruitful, successful, profitable, productive

fruitlessly adv
in vain, vainly, unproductively, unsuccessfully, uselessly, pointlessly, hopelessly
Ƒ fruitfully, successfully

fruity adj
1 a fruity voice
rich, mellow, resonant, deep, low, full
2 INDECENT, bawdy, indelicate, juicy, suggestive, naughty, saucy, risqué, titillating, vulgar, salacious, spicy, sexy, smutty, racy
COLLOQ. blue
Ƒ 2 decent

frumpy adj
dowdy, dreary, drab, badly-dressed, frumpish, dingy, ill-dressed, dated, out of date
Ƒ chic, well-groomed

frustrate v
1 DISAPPOINT, discourage, dishearten, dissatisfy, embitter, depress, anger, annoy, irritate, exasperate, rile, infuriate
COLLOQ. aggravate, wind up, needle, get at, bug, miff, drive mad, drive crazy, get under someone's skin
SLANG nark, piss off
2 THWART, foil, balk, baffle, block, check, stop, defeat, hinder, obstruct, hamper, impede, forestall, counter, nullify, neutralize, inhibit
COLLOQ. stymie, scupper, spike, nobble
Ƒ 1 encourage **2** further, promote

frustrated adj
disappointed, discontented, discouraged, dissatisfied, disheartened, embittered, resentful, angry, annoyed, thwarted, dashed, blighted, repressed

COLLOQ. dished
⊟ fulfilled, satisfied

frustrating *adj*
disappointing, discouraging, disheartening, annoying, irritating, exasperating, maddening, infuriating
⊟ fulfilling

frustration *n*
1 DISAPPOINTMENT, discouragement, dissatisfaction, resentment, annoyance, anger, vexation, irritation, exasperation
2 THWARTING, foiling, balking, blocking, defeat, curbing, failure, non-fulfilment, obstruction, contravention
FORMAL circumvention
⊟ **1** fulfilment, contentment **2** furthering, promoting

fuddled *adj*
hazy, confused, muddled, stupefied, muzzy, bemused, addled, drunk, groggy, woozy, inebriated, intoxicated, sozzled, tipsy
⊟ clear, sober

fuddy-duddy *n, adj*
♦ *n*
conservative, traditionalist, conformist, museum piece, fossil, stick-in-the-mud
COLLOQ. old fogey, square, back number, stuffed shirt
♦ *adj*
old-fashioned, old-fogeyish, stick-in-the-mud, stuffy, carping, censorious, prim
COLLOQ. *N Am* buttoned-down
⊟ up-to-date

fudge *v*
avoid, dodge, equivocate, evade, hedge, stall, shuffle, misrepresent, fake, falsify
COLLOQ. cook, fiddle, fix

fuel *n, v*
♦ *n*
1 COMBUSTIBLE, propellant, motive power
2 PROVOCATION, incitement, encouragement, ammunition, goading, incentive, stimulus, material
♦ *v*
incite, inflame, fire, encourage, fan, boost, stimulate, feed, nourish, sustain, stoke up
⊟ discourage, damp down

Fuels include:

acetylene	coke	methane
alternative fuel	derv	methylated spirit
anthracite	diesel	nuclear power
biodiesel	electricity	oil
bioenergy	flex-fuel	paraffin
bioethanol	fossil fuel	peat
biofuel	gas	petrol
butane	gasoline	propane
calor gas®	hydroelectricity	red diesel
charcoal	kerosine	wood
coal	logs	

---

fug *n*
stuffiness, staleness, reek, stink, frowstiness, fustiness, f(o)etidness
⊟ airiness

fuggy *adj*
stuffy, airless, close, stale, suffocating, unventilated, foul, f(o)etid, frowsty, fusty
FORMAL noisome, noxious
⊟ airy

fugitive *n, adj*
♦ *n*
escapee, runaway, runner, hideaway, deserter, refugee, maroon, runagate
♦ *adj*
1 RUNAWAY, refugee, deserter, AWOL

2 FLEETING, transient, transitory, passing, short, short-lived, momentary, brief, flying, temporary, elusive
FORMAL ephemeral, evanescent, fugacious
⊟ **2** permanent

fulfil *v*
complete, finish, perfect, realize, achieve, accomplish, perform, execute, discharge, implement, carry out, live out, comply with, observe, keep, obey, conform to, satisfy, fill, meet, answer, qualify, stand up to, act up to, come up to scratch; *N Am* fill
FORMAL conclude, consummate, effect
⊟ fail, break

fulfilled *adj*
satisfied, gratified, pleased, happy, content
⊟ dissatisfied, discontented, unhappy

fulfilling *adj*
satisfying, gratifying, pleasing, comforting, satisfactory
⊟ unfulfilling

fulfilment *n*
completion, perfection, realization, achievement, accomplishment, success, performance, execution, discharge, implementation, observance, satisfaction
FORMAL consummation
⊟ failure

full *adj, adv*
♦ *adj*
1 FILLED, loaded, laden, packed, crowded, crammed, stuffed, overflowing, bulging, well-stocked, flush, jammed, filled to capacity, full to the brim
COLLOQ. chock-a-block, chock-full, chocker, packed out, bursting at the seams, packed like sardines
2 ENTIRE, whole, intact, total, complete, unabridged, unexpurgated
3 THOROUGH, comprehensive, exhaustive, all-inclusive, broad, vast, extensive, detailed, ample, filled, generous, abundant, plentiful, copious, profuse, sufficient
4 *feel full*
satisfied, well fed, gorged, sated, stuffed
FORMAL satiated, replete
COLLOQ. bursting
5 *a full sound*
rich, resonant, loud, deep, clear, strong, distinct, fruity, sonorous
6 *at full speed*
maximum, top, highest, greatest, utmost
7 *lead a full life*
busy, active, lively, eventful, exciting, tiring, hectic, frantic
8 *a full flavour*
strong, rich, deep, intense, full-bodied, fruity, warm, vibrant
9 *a full figure*
rounded, well-rounded, plump, chubby, stout, fat, overweight, large, round, shapely, buxom, obese
FORMAL corpulent, rotund
10 *a full skirt*
wide, baggy, loose, loose-fitting
FORMAL voluminous
⊟ **1** empty, bare **2** partial, incomplete **3** superficial, cursory **4** hungry, peckish **6** minimum, lowest **7** empty, boring
♦ *adv*
directly, squarely, straight, right, exactly
COLLOQ. bang, smack
■ *in full*
fully, completely, wholly, in detail, with all the details, in its entirety, in total, uncut, with nothing missed out
■ *to the full*
fully, to the greatest possible extent, to the utmost, completely, entirely, thoroughly, utterly

full-blooded *adj*
committed, dedicated, devoted, enthusiastic, wholehearted, thorough, out-and-out, vigorous, hearty
⊟ half-hearted

full-blown *adj*
full, full-scale, all-out, out-and-out, complete, intense, major, total, thorough, full-fledged

full-bodied *adj*
full, strong, rich, deep, intense, fruity

full-frontal *adj*
1 *full-frontal nudity*
complete, unexpurgated, total, absolute
2 *a full-frontal attack*
complete, out-and-out, thorough, forceful, strong, direct

full-grown *adj*
adult, grown-up, fully-grown, of age, mature, ripe, developed, fully-developed, fully-fledged, full-blown, full-scale
F3 young, undeveloped

fullness *n*
1 THOROUGHNESS, comprehensiveness, vastness, extensiveness, abundance, plenty, profusion, ampleness, completeness, totality, wholeness
2 INTENSITY, strength, depth, greatness, power, force, loudness, richness, resonance
3 SATISFACTION, glut, fill, satedness
FORMAL satiation, satiety, repletion
4 BREADTH, width, largeness, shapeliness, plumpness, curvaceousness, voluptuousness
5 SWELLING, enlargement, inflammation, growth
TECHNICAL tumescence
FORMAL dilation
F3 1 incompleteness **3** emptiness
■ **in the fullness of time**
eventually, in due course, in time, finally, ultimately, in the end
COLLOQ. when all is said and done, in the final analysis

full-scale *adj*
exhaustive, extensive, complete, sweeping, thorough, thoroughgoing, wide-ranging, comprehensive, all-out, in-depth, all-encompassing, intensive, major
F3 partial

fully *adv*
completely, totally, utterly, wholly, entirely, in all respects, thoroughly, altogether, quite, positively, without reserve, unreservedly, perfectly, satisfactorily, sufficiently
F3 partly

fully-fledged *adj*
professional, qualified, trained, senior, graduate, mature, proficient, experienced, fully-developed, full-blown
F3 inexperienced

fulminate *v*
criticize, condemn, curse, denounce, slate, protest, rage, rail, fume, thunder
FORMAL animadvert, inveigh, vituperate, declaim, decry
COLLOQ. slam
F3 praise

fulmination *n*
condemnation, criticism, denunciation, thundering, tirade, detonation
FORMAL diatribe, invective, obloquy, philippic, decrial
COLLOQ. brickbat, slating
F3 praise

fulsome *adj*
extravagant, excessive, immoderate, overdone, gross, inordinate, insincere, adulatory, enthusiastic, effusive, fawning, ingratiating, sycophantic, sickening, nauseating, cloying, nauseous, offensive, saccharine, fat, luscious
FORMAL obsequious, unctuous
COLLOQ. smarmy, slimy, buttery, over the top, OTT
F3 sincere

fulsomely *adv*
extravagantly, excessively, immoderately, inordinately, insincerely, effusively, sickeningly, nauseatingly
COLLOQ. over the top

fumble *v*
grope, feel (about), scrabble, blunder, bungle, botch, mishandle, mismanage, flounder, spoil, bobble
COLLOQ. faff (about)

fume *v*
1 SMOKE, smoulder, boil, steam
2 RAGE, be furious, storm, rant, rave, seethe, boil, be livid
COLLOQ. explode, blow up, blow your top, boil over, fly into a rage, fly off the handle, go mad, go off the deep end, lose your rag, rant and rave, blow/lose your cool, burst a blood vessel, hit the roof

fumes *n*
exhaust, smoke, gas(es), vapour(s), haze, fog, smog, pollution, stink, smell, stench, reek
FORMAL exhalation

fumigate *v*
deodorize, disinfect, sterilize, purify, cleanse, sanitize

fumigation *n*
disinfecting, sterilization, cleansing, sanitization, purifying, purification

fuming *adj*
angry, enraged, furious, livid, incensed, raging, seething, boiling
COLLOQ. ranting and raving, steamed up, uptight, mad, hopping mad, raving mad, seeing red, in a lather, disgruntled, up in arms, hot under the collar; *N Am* ticked off
F3 calm

fun *n, adj*
♦ *n*
enjoyment, pleasure, amusement, entertainment, relaxation, diversion, distraction, recreation, play, sport, game, foolery, tomfoolery, buffoonery, horseplay, skylarking, romp, merrymaking, celebration, laughter, laughs, mirth, cheerfulness, gladness, jollity, jocularity, hilarity, joy, joking, joke, jest, jesting; *dialect* gammock, gig; *Irish* craic, crack; *N Am* music
OLD bourd
♦ *adj*
entertaining, amusing, diverting, recreational, delightful, pleasurable, enjoyable; *S Afr* lekker; lively, witty
■ **for fun**
for a laugh, for enjoyment, for no particular reason
COLLOQ. for kicks, for the hell of it
■ **in fun**
as a joke, jokingly, for a laugh, to tease, in jest, playful(ly), mischievous(ly), teasingly, tongue in cheek
■ **make fun of**
ridicule, mock, laugh at, jeer at, scoff at, sneer at, tease, taunt, humiliate, poke fun at, banter, joke, jolly
FORMAL deride
COLLOQ. rib, send up, pull someone's leg, take the mickey, get at; *Aust* have a shot at
SLANG take the piss, cod, guy; *N Am* goof; *Aust & NZ* poke borak at

function *n, v*
♦ *n*
1 ROLE, part, office, duty, charge, responsibility, concern, capacity, job, post, chore, task, occupation, situation, employment, business, activity, purpose, mission, use
2 RECEPTION, party, gathering, affair, social event, dinner, luncheon
COLLOQ. do
3 COROLLARY, concomitant, consequence, conclusion, result, upshot, deduction, induction, inference

◆ *v*

work, be in working order, operate, run, go, serve, act, perform, behave, play the part of, have the job of

▣ break down; *formal* malfunction; *slang* conk out

functional *adj*

working, operational, operative, running, practical, useful, utilitarian, utility, plain, hard-wearing, serviceable

▣ useless, decorative

functionally *adv*

operationally, practically, usefully, efficiently

functionary *n*

bureaucrat, employee, officer, official, office-bearer, office-holder, dignitary

fund *n, v*

◆ *n*

1 *contribute to the restoration fund*

pool, kitty, reserve, treasury, collection, grant, endowment, foundation, investment

2 *raise funds for the repairs*

money, finance, backing, capital, resources, savings, wealth, cash, means, assets

COLLOQ. the necessary, readies

SLANG megabucks, dough, dosh, bread, lolly, spondulicks, brass, loot, gravy, greens, shekels, moolah, gelt

OLD SLANG rhino

3 *a fund of funny stories*

reserve, repository, storehouse, store, stock, collection, accumulation, hoard, cache, stack, mine, well, source, supply, reservoir

◆ *v*

finance, provide finance for, capitalize, endow, subsidize, pay for, underwrite, sponsor, back, support, promote, float

fundamental *adj*

basic, primary, first, elementary, underlying, foundational, integral, central, principal, cardinal, prime, main, chief, key, essential, indispensable, vital, necessary, crucial, important, initial, original, profound

FORMAL rudimentary, basal, elemental

fundamentalist *adj*

rigorous, rigid, uncompromising, strict, orthodox

fundamentally *adv*

1 *fundamentally, this is a criminal, not civil, matter*

basically, essentially, in essence, at bottom, at heart, deep down, inherently, intrinsically, primarily, substantially

2 *differ fundamentally*

profoundly, deeply, inherently, intrinsically, critically, crucially, radically, acutely

fundamentals *n*

basics, essentials, first principles, laws, rules, rudiments, facts, necessaries, practicalities

COLLOQ. brass tacks, nitty-gritty, nuts and bolts

funeral *n*

burial, cremation, wake

FORMAL interment, entombment, inhumation, exequies, obsequies

funereal *adj*

solemn, serious, grave, mournful, sad, sombre, depressing, dismal, dreary, gloomy, lamenting, woeful, sepulchral, dark, deathlike

FORMAL exequial, funeral, funebrial, lugubrious

▣ happy, lively

fungus *n*

FORMAL thallophyte

Related adjective: fungous

Types of fungus include:

black spot	grey mould	saprophyte
blight	mushroom	scab
botritis	orange-peel	smut
brewer's yeast	fungus	sooty mould
brown rot	penicillium	toadstool
candida	potato blight	yeast
downy mildew	powdery mildew	
ergot	rust	

See also **mushrooms and toadstools**.

funk *v, n*

◆ *v*

balk at, flinch from, recoil from, blench, duck out of, shirk from, dodge

COLLOQ. chicken out of, cop out

◆ *n*

panic, alarm, fright, fear, terror, frenzy, fuss, commotion, fluster, agitation, dither

COLLOQ. flap, cold sweat, state, tiswas, tizwas, tizzy, stew, blue funk

funnel *v, n*

◆ *v*

channel, direct, convey, guide, move, transfer, pass, go, pour, siphon, filter

◆ *n*

chimney, smokestack, stack, vent, flue, shaft, tube, pipe, channel

TECHNICAL drogue, infundibulum, swallow hole, sink hole, windsail

OLD tun-dish

funnily *adv*

surprisingly, amazingly, astonishingly, incredibly, remarkably

funny *adj*

1 HUMOROUS, amusing, entertaining, diverting, comic, comical, hilarious, witty, facetious, droll, farcical, laughable, ridiculous, absurd, silly, hysterical, side-splitting, uproarious, riotous, rich

FORMAL risible

COLLOQ. killing, corny, rum, a scream, a hoot, knee-slapping

2 ODD, strange, peculiar, curious, queer, weird, bizarre, unusual, remarkable, puzzling, perplexing, mysterious, suspicious, dubious

COLLOQ. shady, oddball, way-out, off-beat, wacky

▣ **1** serious, solemn, sad **2** normal, ordinary, usual

SYNONYM NUANCES

sense 1

Humorous can be used of anything that causes a laugh or a smile, whilst **amusing** similarly suggests a cheery diversion. **Entertaining** implies having a wider appeal than just comedy, and **diverting** similarly suggests being engaging in a pleasurable way: *his inimitable way of telling diverting anecdotes*. Both **comic** and **comical** return to the idea of simply prompting laughter, whereas **hilarious**, **hysterical** and **side-splitting** would be reserved for something causing uncontrollable mirth.

Witty, on the other hand, suggests a more subtle effect, and implies a sharp intelligence behind the funniness, while **facetious** goes a bit further by suggesting a degree of deprecation: *a facetious sketch on contemporary politicians*, and something **droll** would have an element of wryness about it: *his droll observations on hospital food*.

The term **farcical** conjures up a sense of the ludicrous, whilst **laughable** and **ridiculous** also imply something unworthy of serious consideration, and all of these terms are often used of things that are not actually funny: *a laughable attempt to look cool*. Likewise, **absurd** suggests something that would prompt a degree of scorn: *trouserless men look absurd in socks*, and **silly** is similar, but with a lesser degree of scorn.

Both **riotous** and **uproarious** suggest causing a commotion, and so appropriately describe more extreme, boisterous humour and its effects. **Rich**, on the other hand, suggests having comedic potential: *that's rich, coming from you!*

fur *n*

coat, hair, hide, down, fleece, pelt, fell, skin, wool, mane, pelage

furbish *v*

renovate, restore, renew, recondition, repair, overhaul, modernize, refurbish, refit, redecorate, remodel, reform, rehabilitate, revamp, improve
COLLOQ. do up, give a facelift to

furious *adj*

1 ANGRY, livid, indignant, irate, enraged, infuriated, incensed, inflamed, incandescent, raging, fuming, boiling, seething, frenzied, purple with rage
COLLOQ. mad, hopping mad, sizzling, up in arms, in a stew, in a paddy, in a lather, in a huff, gone off the deep end, hot under the collar, foaming at the mouth
2 VIOLENT, wild, fierce, intense, vigorous, frantic, boisterous, stormy, tempestuous, vehement
E∃ 1 calm, pleased **2** restrained

furiously *adv*

1 ANGRILY, in anger, indignantly, irately, crossly, passionately, infuriatingly
COLLOQ. madly, seeing red, up in arms, hot under the collar, in a paddy
2 VIOLENTLY, wildly, fiercely, intensely, vigorously, vehemently, stormily, tempestuously
E∃ 1, 2 calmly, gently

furnish *v*

equip, fit out, kit out, decorate, rig, appoint, stock, provide, supply, afford, grant, give, offer, present, endue
FORMAL bestow
E∃ divest

furniture *n*

equipment, appliances, furnishings, fittings, appointments, fitments, household goods, movables, possessions, effects, things

Types of furniture include:

TABLES:	sofa	china cabinet
bedside table	stool	dumb waiter
card table	studio couch	sideboard
coffee table	suite	Welsh dresser
dining table	swivel-chair	
gateleg table		FIREPLACE:
kitchen table	BEDS:	fender
lowboy	bed-settee	firescreen
occasional table	bunk	overmantel
refectory table	camp-bed	
side table	chaise-longue	BEDROOM FURNI-
	cot	TURE:
CHAIRS:	cradle	armoire
armchair	daybed	blanket box
beanbag	divan	chest
carver	four-poster	chest of drawers
chesterfield	water bed	chiffonier
couch		coffer
dining chair	STUDY FURNITURE:	commode
easy chair	bookcase	dressing table
footstool	bureau	ottoman
highchair	computer desk	tallboy
kitchen chair	secretaire	vanity unit
pouffe		wardrobe
recliner	DINING-ROOM FUR-	washstand
rocking chair	NITURE:	
settee	buffet	MISCELLANEOUS:
	cabinet	coatstand

hallstand — mirror
magazine rack — umbrella stand

See also **bed**; **chair**; **stool**.

Styles of furniture include:

Adam	Cromwellian	Louis-Quinze
Anglo-Colonial	Dutch Colonial	provincial
Anglo-Indian	Dutch Neoclassi-	Queen Anne
Art Deco	cal	Regency
Art Nouveau	Edwardian	Restoration
Arts and Crafts	Empire	rococo
Baroque	French Provincial	Shaker
Biedermeier	French Second	Sheraton
boulle	Empire	Shibayama
buhl	Gainsborough	Transitional
Charles II	Georgian	Vernis Martin
Chippendale	Gothic	Victorian
Colonial	Hepplewhite	William and Mary
Continental	Louis Philippe	William IV
Empire	Louis-Quatorze	Windsor

furore *n*

uproar, disturbance, outcry, commotion, fuss, frenzy, fury, hullabaloo, outburst, rage, stir, to-do, tumult, storm, excitement
COLLOQ. flap
E∃ calm

furrow *n, v*

♦ *n*
1 GROOVE, channel, trench, hollow, trough, rut, track, stria, gutter, chamfer, list; *Scot* feerin, fur
TECHNICAL sulcus, canaliculus, vallecula, rill
2 WRINKLE, line, crease, crinkle, trench, crow's foot
♦ *v*
crease, wrinkle, draw together, knit, seam, flute, channel, corrugate, gouge, plough, groove, engroove, rut, mill
Related adjective: sulcal

furry *adj*

hairy, woolly, fleecy, fuzzy, downy, soft, fluffy

further *adj, v, adv*

♦ *adj*
1 MORE, additional, supplementary, extra, fresh, new, other
2 FARTHER, more distant, remoter, more extreme
E∃ 2 nearer
♦ *v*
advance, forward, promote, champion, encourage, foster, help, aid, assist, ease, facilitate, develop, speed (up), hasten, accelerate
FORMAL expedite
COLLOQ. push
E∃ stop, frustrate
♦ *adv*
moreover, furthermore, besides, in addition, additionally, also, as well, too
COLLOQ. what's more

furtherance *n*

advancement, promotion, advancing, backing, boosting, encouragement, help, facilitation, carrying-out, championing, promoting, advocacy, pursuit, speeding
FORMAL preferment

furthermore *adv*

moreover, in addition, further, besides, also, too, as well, additionally
COLLOQ. what's more, into the bargain

furthermost *adj*

furthest, farthest, remotest, outermost, outmost, extreme, ultimate, utmost, uttermost
E∃ nearest

furthest *adj*

farthest, furthermost, remotest, outermost, outmost, extreme, ultimate, utmost, uttermost
E∃ nearest

furtive *adj*
surreptitious, sly, stealthy, secretive, underhand, hidden, cloaked, veiled, covert, secret, sneaky
FORMAL clandestine
🖃 open

furtively *adv*
surreptitiously, slyly, secretively, secretly, covertly
🖃 openly

fury *n*
anger, rage, wrath, ire, frenzy, madness, passion, vehemence, fierceness, ferocity, violence, wildness, intensity, severity, force, turbulence, power
🖃 calm, peacefulness

fuse *v*
combine, integrate, unite, join, amalgamate, blend, conflate, put together, coalesce, meld, melt, solder, weld, flux, smelt, merge, run, synthesize, intermix, mingle, interfuse
OLD colliquate
FORMAL agglutinate, commingle, intermingle

fusillade *n*
barrage, volley, discharge, burst, fire, hail, outburst, salvo, broadside

fusion *n*
melting, smelting, welding, union, synthesis, blend, blending, coalescence, amalgamation, integration, conflation, running, merger, federation
OLD colliquation

fuss *n, v*
♦ *n*
bother, trouble, palaver, furore, ado, squabble, row, commotion, stir, fluster, confusion, upset, worry, agitation, excitement, bustle, flurry, brouhaha, chichi, hurry, racket, pother, piece of work; *Scot* fikery, paraffle, stooshie
OLD coil, do
COLLOQ. hassle, to-do, hoo-ha, flap, carry-on, kerfuffle, ballyhoo, tizzy, a song and dance, storm in a teacup, pantomime
🖃 calm
♦ *v*
complain, grumble, fret, worry, panic, take pains, bother, bustle, fidget
COLLOQ. flap, stir, make a song and dance, be in a tizzy, create, be all over, make a thing

fussiness *n*
choosiness, finicality, finicalness, pernicketiness, perfectionism, meticulousness, niceness, niggling, particularity, busyness
🖃 unfastidiousness

fusspot *n*
worrier, perfectionist, hyper-critic, stickler, fidget; *N Am* fussbudget
COLLOQ. nit-picker, old maid, old woman, fantod

fussy *adj*
1 PARTICULAR, fastidious, scrupulous, finicky, finical, difficult, hard to please, grandmotherly, discriminating, faddy, fiddle-faddle, demanding, quibbling, niggling, pettifogging, pedantic, selective, prissy, chichi

OLD spoffish
COLLOQ. pernickety, choosy, picky, nit-picking, old-maidish; *N Am* persnickety
2 FANCY, elaborate, ornate, overdecorated, cluttered, busy, baroque, rococo
🖃 1 casual, uncritical 2 plain, simple

fusty *adj*
1 OLD-FASHIONED, antiquated, archaic, outdated, out-of-date, passé
COLLOQ. old-fogeyish
2 STALE, damp, dank, airless, stuffy, unventilated, fuggy, ill-smelling, musty, mouldy, mouldering, frowsty, rank
FORMAL malodorous
🖃 1 up-to-date 2 airy

futile *adj*
pointless, useless, worthless, vain, in vain, idle, wasted, fruitless, meaningless, profitless, unavailing, to no avail, unsuccessful, abortive, unprofitable, unproductive, ineffective, barren, empty, hollow, forlorn, feckless, sleeveless
FORMAL ineffectual, nugatory, otiose
COLLOQ. no go
🖃 fruitful, profitable

futility *n*
pointlessness, uselessness, fruitlessness, meaninglessness, worthlessness, ineffectiveness, waste, unproductiveness, vanity, emptiness, hollowness, barrenness, aimlessness
FORMAL nugatoriness
🖃 use, purpose, success

future *n, adj*
♦ *n*
hereafter, tomorrow, time to come, coming times, outlook, prospects, expectations
🖃 past
♦ *adj*
prospective, next, designate, to be, to come, forthcoming, in the offing, imminent, impending, coming, approaching, expected, planned, unborn, later, subsequent, eventual, fated, destined
🖃 past
■ **in future**
from now on, from this time on, from this day on, after this
FORMAL henceforth, henceforward, hereafter, hereinafter, hence

fuzz *n*
down, floss, fluff, fug, hair, lint, nap, pile, fibre, flock

fuzzy *adj*
1 FRIZZY, fluffy, furry, woolly, fleecy, downy, linty, velvety, napped
2 BLURRED, unfocused, ill-defined, indefinite, unclear, indistinct, vague, faint, hazy, foggy, shadowy, woolly, muffled, distorted, fuddled, confused
COLLOQ. muzzy
🖃 2 clear, distinct, focused

G

gab *v, n*

♦ *v*

chatter, talk, drivel, gossip, jaw, prattle, tattle, babble, blabber, jabber, buzz; *dialect & N Am* blather; *Scot* blether

COLLOQ. yak

♦ *n*

chat, chatter, chitchat, conversation, prattle, prattling gossip, blab, blarney; *Scot* blethering; small talk, tittle-tattle, tongue-wagging

FORMAL loquacity

COLLOQ. yackety-yak, yak

gabble *v, n*

♦ *v*

babble, chatter, jabber, prattle, spout, splutter, cackle, sputter, gaggle, gibber, rattle, blab, blabber; *Scot* blether; rabble, patter

♦ *n*

babble, chatter, blabber, cackling prattle, jabber, twaddle; *Scot* blethering; waffle, nonsense, drivel, gibberish, gibble-gabble, ribble-rabble

gad

■ **gad about**

gallivant, run around, travel, roam, wander, range, rove, flit about, ramble, stray, traipse, jaunt, dot about

gadabout *n*

gallivanter, rambler, rover, runabout, wanderer, pleasure-seeker; *Scot* stravaiger

gadget *n*

tool, implement, appliance, device, instrument, apparatus, mechanism, contrivance, invention, contraption, thing novelty, gimmick, toy, widget, waldo

COLLOQ. thingamy, thingummy, thingamybob, thingummyjig gismo, whatsit, whatnot, doodah, gubbins, jigamaree, jiggumbob, jimjam; *N Am* hickey

gaffe *n*

blunder, mistake, slip, error, indiscretion, faux pas, gaucherie

FORMAL solecism

COLLOQ. bloomer, boob, boo-boo, brick, clanger, howler, slip-up; *N Am* flub

SLANG goof

gaffer *n*

foreman, manager, overseer, superintendent, supervisor, overman, ganger

COLLOQ. boss, gov, guv, bigwig big cheese; *N Am* honcho

gag¹ *v*

1 SILENCE, muffle, muzzle, quiet, stifle, smother, block, plug clog put a gag on, throttle, strangle, suppress, restrain, curb, check, still

2 RETCH, choke, heave, nearly vomit

gag² *n*

a comedian telling gags

joke, jest, quip, wisecrack, one-liner, pun, witticism

COLLOQ. crack, funny

gaga *adj*

crazy, insane, mad, unbalanced, disturbed, deranged, demented, unhinged, distracted

COLLOQ. dotty, batty, loopy, barmy, nuts, potty, off the rails, cuckoo, mad as a hatter, raving wrong in the head, not all there

SLANG loony, doolally, off your rocker

gaiety *n*

happiness, glee, cheerfulness, joy, pleasure, delight, joie de vivre, jollity, merriment, mirth, gladness, blitheness, hilarity, fun, merrymaking revelry, festivity, celebration, frolics, joviality, good humour, high spirits, light-heartedness, liveliness, exuberance, buoyancy, brightness, brilliance, sparkle, glitter, colour, colourfulness, show, showiness

FORMAL vivacity

▣ sadness, drabness, gloom

gaily *adv*

happily, joyfully, merrily, cheerfully, blithely, light-heartedly, brightly, brilliantly, colourfully, flamboyantly

▣ sadly, dully

gain *v, n*

♦ *v*

1 OBTAIN, achieve, capture, secure, get, acquire, bring in, gather, win

FORMAL procure

COLLOQ. collar, nab

2 EARN, make, produce, realize, gross, net, clear, profit, yield, bring in, reap, harvest

COLLOQ. rake in

3 REACH, arrive at, come to, get to, attain, achieve, realize

4 *gain speed*

increase, pick up, gather, collect, add, put on, advance, progress, improve

▣ **1, 2, 4** lose

♦ *n*

earnings, proceeds, income, revenue, winnings, pickings, takings, profit, return, reward, yield, interest, dividend, growth, addition, increase, increment, rise, advance, progress, headway, improvement, advantage, benefit, attainment, achievement, acquisition

FORMAL emolument, advancement, augmentation, accretion

▣ loss

■ **gain on**

close with, close in on, narrow the gap, approach, get nearer/closer to, catch up on/with, level with, overtake, outdistance

▣ leave behind

■ **gain time**

delay, stall, play for time, temporize

FORMAL procrastinate

COLLOQ. drag your feet, dilly-dally

SYNONYM NUANCES

verb sense 1

Obtain, **get** and **acquire** refer to something coming into your possession, with no suggestion as to how it was done: *he recently acquired an honours degree.* **Achieve**, although similar, implies an element of effort was involved. The term **capture** suggests taking something usually with effort or even by force, whilst **secure** might be used of having taken the necessary steps to gain something desirable: *his skilful play secured a place in* *the finals.* **Win** is similar, but emphasizes a competitive element: *although the bidding was competitive, our company won the lucrative contract.*

The term **bring in** suggests a productive effect: *her literary work brings in the bulk of her income*, and **reap** and **harvest** similarly suggest yielding profitable returns from an initial effort or outlay, either literally or figuratively: *the prestige reaped from the royal visit was incalculable.* **Gather**, however, would be best used where bringing together or collecting is involved: *information, gathered from a variety of sources.*

gainful *adj*
profitable, beneficial, advantageous, fruitful, lucrative, remunerative, moneymaking paying productive, rewarding financially rewarding useful, worthwhile
FORMAL fructuous
F3 useless

gainfully *adv*
profitably, productively, usefully, beneficially, advantageously, lucratively
F3 uselessly

gainsay *v*
deny, contradict, disagree with, dispute, oppose, challenge
FORMAL contravene, controvert, disaffirm
F3 agree

gait *n*
walk, pace, step, stride, tread, bearing carriage, manner
OLD going
FORMAL deportment

gala *n*
festivity, celebration, party, festival, carnival, jubilee, jamboree, fete, fair, pageant, procession·

galaxy *n*
1 STARS, star system, solar system, the Milky Way, constellation, cluster, nebula
Related adjective: galactic
2 ARRAY, host, collection, gathering group assembly, mass, multitude

gale *n*
1 WIND, squall, storm, hurricane, tornado, typhoon, cyclone
2 BURST, outburst, outbreak, fit, eruption, explosion, blast

gall[1] *n*
1 IMPERTINENCE, impudence, brazenness, insolence, presumption, presumptuousness, chutzpah
FORMAL effrontery
COLLOQ. nerve, neck, cheek, sauciness, brass, brass neck
2 BITTERNESS, rancour, sourness, spite, animosity, hostility, enmity, antipathy, malice, venom, virulence, malevolence
FORMAL acrimony, animus
F3 **1** modesty, reserve **2** friendliness

gall[2] *v*
it galls me to have to ask his permission
annoy, irritate, irk, exasperate, vex, bother, get to, nettle, peeve, pester, provoke, plague, rile, rankle, ruffle, harass, nag
COLLOQ. aggravate, get up your nose, get/put your back up, get on your wick
F3 please

gallant *adj, n*
♦ *adj*
chivalrous, gentlemanly, courteous, polite, gracious, attentive, thoughtful, considerate, courtly, noble, honourable, dashing manly, heroic, valiant, brave, courageous, fearless, dauntless, intrepid, audacious, bold, daring plucky
OLD chivalric
F3 ungentlemanly, cowardly
♦ *n*
cavalier, chevalier, dandy, fop, beau, *cavaliere servente*, cicisbeo
OLD chamberer, gay

gallantly *adv*
chivalrously, courteously, politely, graciously, thoughtfully, considerately, nobly, honourably, heroically, valiantly, bravely, courageously, fearlessly, dauntlessly, intrepidly, audaciously

gallantry *n*
chivalry, gentlemanliness, courtesy, courteousness, politeness, graciousness, attentiveness, thoughtfulness, consideration, courtliness, nobility, honour, manliness, heroism, valour, bravery, courage, courageousness, spirit, fearlessness, dauntlessness, boldness, intrepidity, audacity, pluck, daring
FORMAL valiance
F3 cowardice, ungentlemanliness

QUOTATIONS
What men call gallantry, and gods adultery, / Is much more common where the climate's sultry
LORD BYRON, *Don Juan*

gallery *n*
art gallery, showroom, exhibition area, display room, museum, arcade, passage, walk, balcony, veranda, circle, spectators
COLLOQ. gods

galling *adj*
annoying irritating irksome, exasperating humiliating infuriating vexing provoking nettling plaguing rankling vexatious, bitter, embittering bothersome, harassing
COLLOQ. aggravating
F3 pleasing

gallivant *v*
gad about, run around, travel, roam, wander, ramble, range, rove, stray, traipse, flit about, dot about; *Scot* stravaig

gallop *v*
bolt, canter, run, sprint, race, career, fly, dash, tear, speed, zoom, scurry, shoot, dart, rush, hurry
FORMAL hasten
F3 amble

gallows *n*
scaffold, gibbet, the rope, Tyburn-tree
Related adjective: patibulary

galore *adv*
in abundance, in profusion, lots of, plenty, in numbers, to spare, everywhere
OLD aplenty
COLLOQ. heaps of, tons of, stacks of, millions of
F3 scarce

galvanize *v*
electrify, shock, jolt, prod, spur, urge, provoke, stimulate, stir, startle, move, arouse, rouse, awaken, quicken, excite, fire, inspire, enliven, animate, invigorate, vitalize, energize

gambit *n*
device, manoeuvre, move, ploy, tactic(s), ruse, play, stratagem, trick, wile, artifice
FORMAL machination

gamble *v, n*
♦ *v*
bet, wager, try your luck, put money on, back, punt, play, play for money, play the horses, game, stake, chance, chance it, take a chance, risk, take a risk, hazard, venture, speculate, invest
COLLOQ. have a flutter
♦ *n*
bet, wager, punt, lottery, sweepstake, chance, risk, hazard, venture, speculation, pot luck
COLLOQ. flutter, leap in the dark, spec, toss-up

gambler *n*
better, punter, risk-taker, gamester, plunger, throwster; *N Am* tinhorn; tipster, bookmaker, turf accountant, desperado, daredevil

gambling *n*
betting speculation, gaming risk-taking playing for money, playing the market

gambol *v*
caper, frolic, frisk, cavort, dance, skip, leap, romp, jump, bound, spring hop, bounce, prance, kick up your heels
OLD disport

game[1] *n*
1 RECREATION, play, sport, pastime, diversion, distraction, entertainment, amusement, merriment, fun, frolic, romp, joke, practical joke, jest, prank, trick
See panels below
2 COMPETITION, contest, match, round, tournament, event, meeting meet, bout
3 GAME BIRDS, animals, wild animals, meat, flesh, wild fowl, prey, quarry, bag spoils
See panel below

> **QUOTATIONS**
> 'The game,' said he, 'is never lost till won.'
>   GEORGE CRABBE, *Tales of the Hall*, 'Gretna Green'

Types of video game include:

action adventure game	god game	game (MMPORPG)
action game	hack and slash	platform game
adventure game	Japanese role-playing game (JRPG)	puzzle
alternative reality game (ARG)	life simulation	racing game (or racer)
arcade game	light-gun shooter	real-time strategy (RTS)
arcade racer	massively multi-player online first person shooter (MMOFPS)	rhythm action
beat 'em up		role-playing game (RPG)
driving game		
fighting game	massively multi-player online role-playing	shoot 'em up (or shmup)
first person shooter (FPS)		simulation (SIM)
flight simulation		

sports simulation	tactical shooter	tower defence game
stealth game		
strategy game	third person shooter	vehicle simulation
survival horror		

game[2] *adj*
1 *game for anything*
willing inclined, interested, ready, prepared, eager, enthusiastic
FORMAL desirous
COLLOQ. up for
2 BOLD, daring intrepid, brave, courageous, fearless, resolute, spirited, unflinching gallant, plucky, valiant, lion-hearted
F3 1 unwilling 2 cowardly, afraid, fearful

gamekeeper *n*
keeper, warden
OLD venerer

gamely *adv*
resolutely, boldly, intrepidly, bravely, courageously, fearlessly, unflinchingly, valiantly

gamut *n*
scale, series, range, sweep, scope, compass, spectrum, sequence, field, area, variety

gang *n, v*
♦ *n*
group, band, ring pack, herd, mob, crowd, gathering horde, circle, clique, coterie, set, lot, club, team, crew, squad, shift, party, troupe, company, core, coffle, coven; *Aust* push
OLD ging; (*Shakesp*) tribulation
COLLOQ. outfit
SLANG posse
■ **gang up on/against**
join forces against, unite against, team up against, band together against, conspire against

---

Types of indoor game include:

BOARD GAMES:	Scrabble®	*colloq.* crib	picquet	craps	table football
backgammon	snakes and ladders	cribbage	poker	dice	table tennis
bagatelle	Trivial Pursuit®	draw poker	pontoon	dominoes	Yahtzee®
N Am checkers		faro	rummy	Dungeons & Dragons®	
chess	**CARD GAMES:**	gin rummy	snap		**FLOOR GAMES:**
Cluedo®	baccarat	happy families	solitaire	foosball	bowling
draughts	beggar-my-neighbour	hearts	solo whist	Jenga®	bowls
halma		nap	stud poker	mah-jong	ten-pin bowling
ludo	bezique	napoleon	twenty-one	pinball	
Monopoly®	blackjack	newmarket	vingt-et-un	ping pong	**TARGET GAMES:**
Mouse Trap®	brag	old maid	whist	pool	darts
nine men's morris	bridge	partner whist		roulette	
Pictionary®	canasta	patience	**TABLE GAMES:**	shove ha'penny	
Risk®	chemin de fer	Pelmanism	billiards	snooker	

Types of children's game include:

battleships	fivestones	jacks	noughts and crosses	pin the tail on the donkey	spillikins
blindman's buff	forfeits	jackstraws	pass the parcel	postman's knock	spin the bottle
charades	hangman	Kim's game	piggy-in-the-middle	sardines	tiddlywinks
Chinese whispers	hide-and-seek	kiss chase		Simon says	tug-of-war
conkers	hopscotch	musical chairs		sleeping lions	
consequences	I-spy				

Types of game (killed for sport) include:

antelope	buffalo	elk	hazel grouse	quail	stag
badger	capercailzie	fallow deer	lion	rabbit	tiger
bear	caribou	fox	moose	red deer	waterfowl
bison	deer	goose	mountain lion	roe deer	wild boar
blackcock	duck	grouse	partridge	snipe	woodcock
boar	elephant	hare	pheasant	squirrel	woodgrouse

gangling *adj*
lanky, gawky, gangly, skinny, spindly, bony, angular, raw-boned, loose-jointed, awkward, tall, ungainly, rangy, gauche

gangster *n*
mobster, desperado, hoodlum, ruffian, rough, tough, thug terrorist, racketeer, bandit, brigand, robber, criminal; *N Am* wise guy; yakuza
OLD tumbler
COLLOQ. Al, crook; *N Am* goodfella
SLANG enforcer, greaser, heavy, steamer, Yardie; *N Am* gangsta, goombah, hood

gangway *n*
aisle, corridor, passage, passageway, walkway

gaol
see **jail, gaol.**

gaoler
see **jailer, gaoler.**

gap *n*
1 SPACE, blank, void, hole, cavity, aperture, opening crack, chink, crevice, cleft, cranny, breach, rift, fracture, rent, divide, gulf, divergence, difference
TECHNICAL interstice
FORMAL orifice, lacuna, vacuity, discontinuity, disparity
2 INTERRUPTION, break, recess, pause, lull, interlude, intermission, interval
FORMAL hiatus

gape *v*
1 STARE, gaze, wonder, goggle
COLLOQ. gawp, gawk
SLANG *N Am* rubberneck
2 OPEN, yawn, part, split, crack

gaping *adj*
open, yawning broad, wide, vast, cavernous
[E3] tiny

garage *n*
lock-up, car port, petrol station, service station; *N Am* gas station

garb *n, v*
♦ *n*
1 CLOTHES, clothing garment, costume, dress, outfit, wear, robes, uniform, vestments, habiliment
FORMAL apparel, array, attire, raiment
COLLOQ. gear, get-up, rig-out, togs
SLANG clobber
2 APPEARANCE, guise, aspect, look, form, fashion, style
♦ *v*
clothe, cover, dress, robe
FORMAL apparel, array, attire, habilitate
COLLOQ. rig out

garbage *n*
1 WASTE, rubbish, refuse, remains, leftovers, scourings, scraps, slops, swill, filth, muck, debris, dross, junk, litter, bits and pieces, odds and ends, sweepings; *N Am* trash
FORMAL detritus
2 NONSENSE, rubbish, gibberish, trash, tripe, twaddle, drivel
COLLOQ. bunk, bunkum, claptrap, piffle, bilge, cock, poppycock, hot air, cobblers, rot, tommyrot, stuff and nonsense, codswallop, baloney, blah, bosh, eyewash, hogwash, rhubarb, guff, hooey, malarkey, moonshine
SLANG bull; (*vulgar*) balls, bollocks, crap, bullshit, shit; *dialect* shite

garble *v*
confuse, muddle, jumble, scramble, mix up, twist, distort, corrupt, pervert, warp, slant, doctor, misrepresent, misinterpret, falsify, tamper with, mutilate, edit
[E3] decipher

garbled *adj*
jumbled, confused, muddled, scrambled, mixed-up, unintelligible, undecipherable

garden *n*
yard, backyard, lawn, plot; *S Afr* erf; park

Types of garden include:

allotment	herb garden	rose arbour
alpine garden	hop garden	rose bed
arboretum	indoor garden	rose garden
arbour	Japanese garden	shrubbery
beer garden	kitchen garden	sink garden
border	knot garden	sunken garden
botanical garden	lawn	tea garden
bottle garden	market garden	terrarium
cottage garden	orchard	vegetable plot
curtilage	ornamental garden	vertical garden
fruit garden	raised bed	walled garden
garden of rest	rockery	water garden
hanging garden	rock garden	window box
herbaceous border	roof garden	winter garden

---

gargantuan *adj*
colossal, huge, enormous, giant, gigantic, massive, immense, vast, tremendous, towering mammoth, large, big monumental, titanic, monstrous, elephantine
FORMAL leviathan, prodigious, Brobdingnagian
COLLOQ. ginormous, humongous
[E3] small, tiny, minute

garish *adj*
gaudy, lurid, loud, glaring flashy, showy, flaunting tawdry, vulgar, tasteless, cheap, glittering tinselly, raffish, jazzy, criant; *Scot* roary
FORMAL meretricious
COLLOQ. glitzy, flash
[E3] quiet, tasteful

garishly *adv*
gaudily, luridly, loudly, glaringly, jazzily, tastelessly
COLLOQ. glitzily
[E3] tastefully

garland *n, v*
♦ *n*
wreath, festoon, decoration, flowers, laurels, honours, crown, coronet, coronal, headband, lei, bays, chaplet, toran
OLD crants, girlond
FORMAL stemma
♦ *v*
wreathe, festoon, decorate, deck, adorn, crown, engarland

garments *n*
clothes, clothing wear, outfit, dress, costume, uniform
FORMAL attire, apparel
COLLOQ. gear, togs, get-up, garb

garner *v*
gather, collect, accumulate, amass, assemble, heap, pile up, stack up, hoard, lay up, put by, reserve, save, stockpile, cull, store, stow away, deposit, treasure, husband
[E3] dissipate

garnish *v, n*
♦ *v*
decorate, adorn, ornament, trim, deck (out), festoon, embellish, enhance, grace, set off, beautify
[E3] divest
♦ *n*
decoration, ornament, ornamentation, adornment, trimming embellishment, enhancement, relish

garret *n*
attic, loft, mansard, roof space

garrison *n, v*
♦ *n*
1 ARMED FORCE, detachment, troops, unit, command
2 FORT, fortress, fortification, stronghold, station, post, base, barracks, camp, encampment, casern, zareba
Related adjective: presidiary

◆ *v*
1 PROTECT, defend, guard, engarrison
OLD stuff
2 OCCUPY, position, place, mount, station, assign, furnish, man, post

garrulous *adj*
talkative, chatty, windy, long-winded, verbose, wordy, voluble, gassy, glib; *Aust* yabbering; gossiping gushing chattering babbling effusive, prattling prating
OLD wordish
FORMAL loquacious, prolix, voluble
COLLOQ. mouthy, gabby
◄ taciturn, terse

garrulousness *n*
talkativeness, long-windedness, verboseness, verbosity
OLD wordishness
FORMAL loquaciousness, loquacity, prolixity, volubility
COLLOQ. mouthiness

gas *n*
Related adjective: pneumatic

> **QUOTATIONS**
> All is gas and gaiters
> CHARLES DICKENS, *Nicholas Nickleby*

Types of gas include:

acetylene	ethylene	neon
ammonia	firedamp	nerve gas
black damp	helium	nitrogen
butane	hydrogen sulphide	nitrous oxide
carbon dioxide	ketene	ozone
carbon monoxide	krypton	propane
chloroform	laughing gas	radon
chokedamp	marsh gas	sarin gas
CS gas	methane	tear gas
cyanogen	mustard gas	town gas
ether	natural gas	xenon

gash *v, n*
◆ *v*
cut, wound, slash, slit, incise, lacerate, tear, rend, split, score, gouge, nick
◆ *n*
cut, wound, slash, slit, incision, laceration, tear, rent, split, score, gouge, nick

gasp *v, n*
◆ *v*
pant, puff, blow, breathe, catch your breath, wheeze, heave, choke, gulp; *dialect* chink, kink
◆ *n*
pant, puff, blow, breath, choke, gulp, exclamation; *dialect* chink, kink

gassy *adj*
effervescent, sparkling aerated, carbonated, bubbly, bubbling frothy, foaming

gastric *adj*
stomach, intestinal, abdominal, coeliac, stomachic, enteric

gate *n*
barrier, door, wicket, doorway, gateway, opening entrance, exit, access, passage
FORMAL portal

gather *v*
1 CONGREGATE, convene, muster, rally, round up, assemble, summon, marshal, collect, come/bring together, meet, group, crowd, cluster, attract, draw, pull (in), amass, mass, accumulate, converge, hoard, stockpile, heap, pile up, hoard up, build, rake in, garner
COLLOQ. stash away
2 INFER, deduce, conclude, surmise, assume, understand, learn, hear, believe

3 *gather flowers*
pick, pluck, cull, select, reap, harvest, crop, collect, glean, garner
4 *gather speed*
gain, increase, grow, pick up, build up, add, advance, progress, improve, develop
5 FOLD, pleat, tuck, pucker, ruffle, shirr
◄ **1** scatter, dissipate

> **SYNONYM NUANCES**
>
> *sense 1*
> **Congregate** creates an image of a group of people coming together in one place: *the beggars congregated at tube-station entrances*, while **converge** conveys the idea of people reaching the same place simultaneously. The term **convene** suggests a more formal arrangement: *a hastily convened committee meeting*. **Round up** has connotations of gathering animals together, and so is generally suggestive of getting everyone together in the same location physically, and not always voluntarily: *police have been rounding up school truants*; the word **assemble** has a more voluntary aspect to it.
> **Summon** would imply ordering people to gather, whilst **marshal** is more suggestive of bringing together in an orderly fashion: *she marshalled her thoughts*. The word **muster**, on the other hand, can be used specifically of military personnel or, more generally, of getting people or things to join together for a cause: *he mustered support for his scheme*; **rally** likewise suggests gathering in support of a specific cause: *the government tried to rally people behind their manifesto*.
> The terms **group** and **crowd** tend to suggest larger numbers, while **cluster** puts the emphasis on formation, conveying an image of small tight units. The terms **amass**, **mass** and **accumulate** are appropriate for a gradual adding to what is initially present, as is **garner**, which tends to be used transitively and which you might use of gathering information or other more abstract concepts.
> Both **heap** and **pile up** again tend to be intransitive, though these suggest a more physical image and one which is often negative: *my work is piling up*. **Build** is similar in sense, although it has more constructive connotations: *I built a fine collection of miniature paintings*. **Stockpile** refers to saving up reserves for the future, and so suggests a more considered action, but without the grasping implications of **hoard** and **hoard up**. **Rake in** suggests more rapid acquisition, but also has connotations of greed: *syndicates raking in huge profits from sales of drugs*.

gathering *n*
assembly, convention, meeting round-up, rally; *Irish* feis; get-together, jamboree, party, bevy, group, band, company, congregation, mass, crowd, flock, throng mob, horde, turnout
FORMAL convocation, conclave, assemblage
COLLOQ. *NZ* hui

gauche *adj*
awkward, clumsy, shy, ungainly, inelegant, ungraceful, unpolished, gawky, graceless, uncultured, unsophisticated, ignorant, ill-bred, ill-mannered, insensitive, inept, farouche, tactless
FORMAL maladroit
◄ graceful, elegant, urbane

gaudiness *n*
brightness, brilliance, garishness, loudness, harshness, showiness, tawdriness, tastelessness, raffishness
COLLOQ. flashiness
◄ plainness, simplicity

gaudy *adj*
bright, too bright, brilliant, colourful, multicoloured, glaring garish, loud, shrieking harsh, stark, flashy, showy,

kitsch, flaunting ostentatious, tinselly, tawdry, vulgar, tasteless, raffish
FORMAL meretricious
COLLOQ. glitzy, flash, snazzy
Ⴋ drab, plain, simple

gauge *v, n*
♦ *v*
estimate, guess, judge, assess, evaluate, value, rate, reckon, figure, calculate, compute, count, measure, weigh, determine, check
FORMAL apprise, ascertain
COLLOQ. guesstimate
♦ *n*
1 SCALE, meter, measure
See panel at **measuring instruments**.
2 STANDARD, basic, guide, norm, criterion, benchmark, yardstick, touchstone, rule, guideline, indicator, measure, meter, test, sample, example, model, pattern
FORMAL exemplar
3 SIZE, magnitude, measure, capacity, bore, calibre, thickness, width, span, extent, area, scope, height, depth, degree

gaunt *adj*
1 HAGGARD, hollow-eyed, angular, bony, thin, lean, lank, skinny, skin and bones, scraggy, scrawny, spindly, skeletal, emaciated, wasted
FORMAL cadaverous
2 BLEAK, stark, bare, barren, desolate, forlorn, dismal, dreary, forbidding grim, harsh
Ⴋ 1 plump

gauzy *adj*
filmy, flimsy, delicate, sheer, thin, transparent, light, see-through, gossamer, insubstantial, unsubstantial
FORMAL diaphanous
Ⴋ heavy, thick

gawk *v*
gape, gawp, goggle, stare, gaze, look, ogle

gawky *adj*
awkward, clumsy, gauche, inept, loutish, oafish, ungainly, gangling lanky, unco-ordinated, graceless, lumbering
FORMAL maladroit
Ⴋ graceful

gawp *v*
gawk, gape, goggle, stare, gaze, look, ogle

gay *adj, n*
♦ *adj*
1 HOMOSEXUAL, lesbian, bisexual
FORMAL sapphic
COLLOQ. pink, camp, butch
SLANG (*offensive*) queer, bent, dykey, homo, poofy, limp-wristed
2 HAPPY, joyful, jolly, merry, cheerful, bright, blithe, sunny, carefree, debonair, fun-loving pleasure-seeking vivacious, lively, animated, exuberant, sprightly, playful, light-hearted, in good/high spirits
3 *gay colours*
vivid, rich, bright, brilliant, sparkling festive, colourful, gaudy, garish, flashy, showy, flamboyant
Ⴋ 1 heterosexual; *slang* straight **2** sad, gloomy
♦ *n*
homosexual, lesbian
TECHNICAL invert
OLD bardash, homophile, urning
SLANG (*offensive*) queer, poof, dyke, faggot, fag fairy, bent, pansy, queen, homo, nancy, woofter, butch, closet queen, fruit, Mary, powder puff, puff, punk, quiff, shirtlifter; *Aust* tonk
Ⴋ heterosexual; *colloq.* straight

gaze *v, n*
♦ *v*
stare, stare fixedly/intently, contemplate, regard, watch, view, look, look vacantly, gape, wonder, goggle, eye, muse, outstare, pore

OLD aftereye, wait upon
COLLOQ. gawk, moon around/about
♦ *n*
stare, look, fixed look, gape
OLD gazement

SYNONYM NUANCES

verb
Stare is a fairly general synonym of gaze, with little suggestion of motivation or manner inherent in the word, unlike **contemplate**, which suggests quiet consideration of what is being looked at: *he dropped anchor and contemplated the horizon*. **Regard** is similar, although you might wish to use an adverb to elaborate on the manner: *they regarded each other silently*, while **watch** can be used generally to suggest prolonged and deliberate observation.

Look vacantly suggests not actually registering what your eyes see. You can use **gape** in the same way or, as **goggle**, to imply being open-mouthed in awe or amazement: *he gaped at the damage to his new car*; **wonder** likewise suggests marvelling at something but usually in a more positive fashion.

The word **eye** returns to the idea of concentrated observation to ascertain something: *he eyed me up and down*, whilst **pore** also suggests close and steady attention, generally of written matter: *they pored over the contracts*. The term **muse** is also suggestive of deeper scrutiny, but of a more internalized nature. **Outstare** would specifically be used of keeping your eyes fixed on someone until they are forced to look away.

---

gazebo *n*
belvedere, summerhouse, shelter, pavilion, hut

gazette *n*
newspaper, journal, magazine, news-sheet, broadsheet, tabloid, periodical, paper, organ, dispatch, notice

gear *n, v*
♦ *n*
1 EQUIPMENT, kit, outfit, tackle, apparatus, tools, implements, instruments, appliances, accessories, supplies, utensils, contrivances
FORMAL accoutrements
COLLOQ. stuff, things
2 GEARWHEEL, cogwheel, tooth-wheel, toothed wheel, ratchet, cog gearing mechanism, machinery, works
FORMAL engrenage
3 BELONGINGS, possessions, personal possessions, things, baggage, luggage, paraphernalia, kit
FORMAL effects
COLLOQ. stuff
4 CLOTHES, clothing garments, dress
FORMAL attire, apparel
COLLOQ. garb, togs, get-up
SLANG threads, clobber
♦ *v*
adapt, fit, design, tailor, devise, prepare, organize

gel, jell *v*
set, congeal, coagulate, crystallize, harden, thicken, solidify, stiffen, materialize, come together, finalize, form, take shape

gelatinous *adj*
jelly-like, jellied, congealed, rubbery, glutinous, gummy, gluey, sticky, viscous, viscid
FORMAL mucilaginous
COLLOQ. gooey

geld *v*
emasculate, castrate, neuter, cut, unman, unsex

gem *n*
1 GEMSTONE, precious stone, stone, jewel

2 TREASURE, prize, masterpiece, *pièce de résistance*, crème de la crème
COLLOQ. pride and joy, the bee's knees

Gems and gemstones include:

agate	fire opal	rhinestone
amber	garnet	rose quartz
amethyst	jade	ruby
aquamarine	jasper	sapphire
beryl	jet	spessartite
bloodstone	lapis lazuli	spinel ruby
chrysoprase	marcasite	tiger's eye
citrine	moonstone	topaz
coral	morganite	tourmaline
cornelian	mother-of-pearl	turquoise
cubic zirconia	onyx	uvarovite
demantoid	opal	white sapphire
diamond	pearl	zircon
emerald	peridot	

---

gen *n, v*

♦ *n*
information, facts, details, data, knowledge, background
COLLOQ. info, low-down, dope

■ **gen up on**
find out about, be well-informed about, research, read up on, study
COLLOQ. swot up on, bone up on, brush up on

genealogy *n*
family tree, family history, pedigree, lineage, ancestry, descent, derivation, extraction, family, dynasty, line, birth, parentage, breeding

general *adj*
1 *a general statement*
broad, sweeping blanket, all-inclusive, comprehensive, universal, global, total, across-the-board, widespread, wide-ranging prevailing prevalent, extensive, overall, accepted, popular, common, panoramic
2 VAGUE, broad, ill-defined, indefinite, imprecise, inexact, approximate, loose, rough, unspecific
3 USUAL, regular, normal, typical, ordinary, standard, everyday, customary, conventional, common, habitual, public
4 *a general store*
mixed, varied, assorted, diverse, miscellaneous
FORMAL heterogeneous, variegated
F∃ 1 particular, limited **2** specific, detailed, precise **3** rare

---

SYNONYM NUANCES

sense 1
Broad and **wide-ranging** can be used neutrally of something covering a wide area or range: *a wide-ranging speech*, and **blanket**, **total**, **universal** and **global** can describe covering everything: *a blanket ban on tobacco advertising*. **Sweeping** has further implications of being indiscriminate: *sweeping cuts in the public sector*. The terms **all-inclusive** and **comprehensive** can be used where everything has been taken into account: *a comprehensive study of classroom practice*. **Across-the-board** is best used in narrower contexts to do with, for instance, pay increases.

Both **prevailing** and **prevalent** are more suggestive of being widely practised or accepted, though they carry a further suggestion of being current: *the prevailing conditions of censorship*, while **accepted** and **popular** would state these ideas more explicitly. The terms **extensive** and **widespread** could be used of something widely but more accidentally occurring although the latter might suggest more negative concepts: *a widespread financial need*. The term **panoramic** is generally reserved for a wide or complete view: *panoramic views of the coastline*.

---

generality *n*
1 GENERALIZATION, generality, sweeping statement, general statement, impreciseness, indefiniteness, inexactness, looseness, approximateness, vagueness
2 COMMONNESS, extensiveness, popularity, prevalence, universality, comprehensiveness, breadth, catholicity, ecumenicity, miscellaneity
3 MAJORITY, bulk, (the) many, most, greater/larger part, more than half, nearly all
F∃ 1 detail, exactness, particular **2** uncommonness **3** minority

generalization *n*
sweeping statement, general statement, impreciseness, indefiniteness, inexactness, looseness, approximateness, vagueness

generalize *v*
theorize, assume, deduce, infer, conclude, deal in generalities, make a sweeping statement, standardize

generally *adv*
usually, normally, in general, ordinarily, commonly, habitually, customarily, as a rule, by and large, overall, for the most part, on the whole, more or less, mostly, in most cases, predominantly, mainly, chiefly, broadly, largely, at large, universally

generate *v*
produce, engender, whip up, arouse, cause, bring about, bring into being give rise to, create, originate, initiate, occasion, make, form, breed, propagate
F∃ prevent

generation *n*
1 AGE GROUP, age, days, era, epoch, period, time
2 PRODUCTION, creation, origination, formation, engendering reproduction, propagation, breeding
FORMAL genesis, procreation

generic *adj*
1 GENERAL, common, comprehensive, inclusive, universal, sweeping wide, all-inclusive, all-encompassing blanket, collective
2 *generic drugs*
unbranded, non-trademarked, untrademarked, non-registered, non-proprietary
F∃ 1 particular, specific **2** branded, trademarked, registered, proprietary

generically *adv*
generally, commonly, comprehensively, inclusively, universally, all-inclusively

generosity *n*
liberality, open-handedness, bounty, charity, philanthropy, kindness, big-heartedness, benevolence, goodness, lavishness, unselfishness, selflessness
FORMAL magnanimity, munificence
F∃ meanness, selfishness

generous *adj*
1 LIBERAL, free, bountiful, open-handed, free-handed, unstinting unsparing lavish
2 CHARITABLE, philanthropic, public-spirited, unselfish, selfless, altruistic, kind, big-hearted, benevolent, good, high-minded, noble, lofty
FORMAL magnanimous, beneficent, munificent
COLLOQ. big
3 AMPLE, lavish, full, plentiful, abundant, rich, copious, overflowing
F∃ 1 mean, miserly **2** selfish **3** meagre

generously *adv*
1 LIBERALLY, freely, bountifully, lavishly, open-handedly
2 CHARITABLY, unselfishly, selflessly, philanthropically, nobly
FORMAL magnanimously
3 AMPLY, lavishly, fully, plentifully, richly, abundantly, copiously
F∃ 1 meanly **2** selfishly **3** meagrely

genesis *n*
origin, beginning birth, outset, root, source, start, foundation, founding generation, initiation, engendering formation, propagation, creation, dawn
FORMAL commencement, inception
F3 end, finish

genetic *adj*
hereditary, inherited, chromosomal, biological
TECHNICAL genomic

genial *adj*
affable, amiable, friendly, amicable, convivial, cordial, kindly, kind, sociable, warm-hearted, warm, hearty, jovial, jolly, cheerful, happy, good-natured, good-humoured, easy-going agreeable, pleasant
COLLOQ. mat(e)y, pally, chummy
F3 cold, unfriendly

geniality *n*
affability, amiability, friendliness, conviviality, congenialness, cordiality, kindliness, kindness, warm-heartedness, warmth, joviality, jollity, cheerfulness, happiness, gladness, cheeriness, good nature, agreeableness, pleasantness, bonhomie
F3 coldness, unfriendliness

genially *adv*
affably, amiably, amicably, cordially, warmly, warm-heartedly, heartily, cheerfully, pleasantly
F3 coldly

genie *n*
spirit, fairy, demon, jinni, jinnee, jann

genitals *n*
sexual organs, reproductive organs, private parts, clitoris, labia majora/minora, vagina, womb, uterus, penis, scrotum, testicles
TECHNICAL pudenda, pudendum, fourchette, vulva
FORMAL genitalia
COLLOQ. groin, privates, naughty bits, willy
SLANG (*taboo*) fanny, pussy, muff, punani, cunt, cock, prick, dick, balls

genius *n*
1 VIRTUOSO, maestro, prodigy, master, past master, expert, adept, intellectual, mastermind, brain, intellect, wizard, sage
COLLOQ. egghead, brains, boffin; *N Am* brainiac
2 INTELLIGENCE, brightness, brilliance, cleverness, fine mind, intellect, wisdom, ability, aptitude, gift, talent, flair, knack, bent, inclination, capacity, faculty
FORMAL propensity
COLLOQ. brains, nous, grey matter, little grey cells

> **QUOTATIONS**
> Genius is one percent inspiration, ninety-nine percent perspiration
> THOMAS EDISON, *Life*

genocide *n*
extermination, massacre, slaughter, ethnocide, ethnic cleansing

genre *n*
type, form, style, class, fashion, brand, group, kind, sort, variety, category, character, school, strain
TECHNICAL genus

genteel *adj*
respectable, refined, cultivated, polished, elegant, polite, stylish, fashionable, cultured, aristocratic, formal, civil, gentlemanly, graceful, mannerly, well-mannered, well-bred, courteous, courtly, ladylike, urbane
F3 crude, rough, unpolished, vulgar

gentility *n*
1 NOBILITY, aristocracy, high birth, gentle birth, good family, upper class, nobles, rank, breeding élite, gentry, blue blood

2 COURTESY, respectability, formality, elegance, politeness, etiquette, civility, courtliness, manners, mannerliness, refinement, culture, urbanity
FORMAL decorum, propriety
COLLOQ. poshness
F3 crudeness, discourteousness, roughness

gentle *adj*
1 KIND, kindly, amiable, tender, tender-hearted, soft-hearted, compassionate, sympathetic, lenient, humane, merciful, charitable, benign, mild, placid, calm, tranquil, serene, soft, meek, sweet, maidenly, tame, milky
OLD mansuete
2 *a gentle slope*
gradual, slow, easy, smooth, moderate, slight, light, imperceptible, delicate, low-pitched
3 SOOTHING, peaceful, serene, quiet, soft, smooth
4 *gentle winds*
mild, light, moderate, calm, pleasant, balmy
FORMAL clement
F3 1 unkind, rough, harsh, wild **2** steep, severe **4** strong violent

gentlemanly *adj*
courteous, polite, refined, polished, urbane, well-bred, well-mannered, cultivated, civilized, civil, honourable, mannerly, gentlemanlike, noble, gallant, chivalrous, genteel, reputable, suave, obliging
OLD gent
F3 impolite, rough

gentleness *n*
kindness, warmth, tenderness, compassion, sympathy, humaneness, mildness, calmness, softness, meekness, sweetness, mercy
F3 unkindness, harshness

gently *adv*
1 *smile gently*
sympathetically, warmly, compassionately, tenderly, charitably, mildly, calmly, serenely, tranquilly
2 *gently sloping hills*
gradually, slowly, slightly, moderately
3 *blowing gently in the wind*
lightly, moderately, calmly, pleasantly
F3 1 unkindly, harshly **2** steeply **3** strongly, violently

gentry *n*
nobility, nobles, upper class, privileged classes, aristocracy, élite, gentility
COLLOQ. top drawer, upper crust

genuflect *v*
bow, bend the knee, kneel, pay your respects, humble yourself
FORMAL prostrate yourself, make/pay obeisance

genuine *adj*
1 REAL, actual, natural, pure, original, authentic, factual, veritable, true, sound, bona fide, legitimate, legal, lawful, unadulterated, pukka
COLLOQ. real McCoy, kosher; *Aust & NZ* dinkum; *Aust* ridgy-didge
See Synonym nuances panel at **real**.
2 SINCERE, honest, frank, candid, earnest, with integrity, truthful, open, natural
F3 1 artificial, false, fake, counterfeit **2** insincere, deceitful

> **SYNONYM NUANCES**
> *sense 1*
> **Real** and **actual** are used of something that definitely exists. **Natural** suggests not being artificial or man-made, and has positive overtones: *made with natural ingredients*. **Pure** has further and again positive connotations of being untainted with anything else: *pure dairy butter*, whilst **unadulterated**, although it would convey this idea clearly, is more clinical in tone.
>   You can use **original** to imply that something has remained as it has always been; **authentic** likewise makes the positive suggestion that something has not

been modified or tampered with: *authentic flamenco dancing*. **Factual** has to do with truthful details or real events: *a factual account of the war*, and while **veritable** is used of something which is undeniable, the term is often used and taken in a rather tongue-in-cheek way: *she became a veritable bag of nerves*.

   Sound refers to something that is genuine in that it is well-founded: *sound arguments*. **Bona fide** would appropriately describe something which is truly what it appears: *a bona fide charity*. To emphasize that something genuine can be justified as such, you might describe it as **legitimate**: *legitimate industrial action*, while **legal** and **lawful** would be reserved for something that is actually backed by the law.

genuinely *adv*
sincerely, really, honestly, earnestly, actually

genus *n*
species, race, breed, genre, order, sort, set, type, division, subdivision, kind, group, category, class
TECHNICAL taxon

germ *n*
1 MICRO-ORGANISM, microbe, bacterium, bacillus, virus
COLLOQ. bug
2 BEGINNING, start, origin, source, fountain, cause, spark, rudiment, nucleus, root, seed, embryo, bud, sprout
FORMAL commencement, inception

germane *adj*
relevant, appropriate, suitable, apt, applicable, fitting material, proper, related, connected, akin, allied
FORMAL pertinent, apposite, apropos
F₃ irrelevant

germinal *adj*
generative, developing embryonic, seminal, preliminary, rudimentary, undeveloped

germinate *v*
bud, sprout, shoot, develop, originate, grow, swell, spring up, take root
FORMAL burgeon

gestation *n*
development, incubation, pregnancy, conception, evolution, ripening planning drafting
FORMAL maturation

gesticulate *v*
wave, signal, gesture, motion, indicate, sign, make a sign

gesticulation *n*
wave, signal, gesture, motion, movement, indication, sign, body language
FORMAL chironomy

gesture *n, v*
♦ *n*
movement, motion, indication, sign, signal, wave, gesticulation, act, action
♦ *v*
indicate, sign, motion, beckon, point, signal, wave, gesticulate
OLD gest

get *v*
1 OBTAIN, acquire, come by, receive, be given, earn, gain, have, buy, bring in, clear, make, win, secure, achieve, realize
FORMAL procure, purchase
2 *it's getting dark*
become, turn, go, grow, come to be
OLD wax
3 *get him to help*
persuade, coax, induce, talk into, urge, influence, sway, win over, convince
FORMAL prevail upon
4 MOVE, go, come, travel, reach, arrive
5 FETCH, collect, go for, pick up, bring take, catch, capture, seize, grab

6 *get a disease*
catch, pick up, develop, come/go down with, become infected with, be afflicted by
FORMAL contract, succumb to
7 *get to see the exhibition*
succeed, manage, have the opportunity, organize, arrange, find a way
COLLOQ. work it, wangle
8 *get breakfast*
prepare, get ready, cook, put together; *N Am* fix
COLLOQ. rustle up
9 *get a joke*
understand, comprehend, see, follow, take in, work out, grasp, fathom
COLLOQ. figure out, twig get the hang of, get the point, get it, suss (out)
10 *get a thief/an animal*
catch, capture, trap, hunt down, snare, lay hold of, arrest, hit, kill
FORMAL apprehend
COLLOQ. nab, collar, nick, bust, pick up
11 *not get what she said*
hear, make out, catch, recognize, understand, follow, take in, grasp
12 *his snoring really gets me*
annoy, irritate, infuriate, exasperate, vex, provoke, rile, bother
COLLOQ. aggravate, wind up, bug get on someone's nerves, rub someone up the wrong way, drive crazy, get on someone's wick, get up someone's nose
F₃ 1 lose **4** leave

■ **get about**
move about, move around, go/travel (widely)

■ **get across**
communicate, transmit, convey, express, impart, put across, put over, get over, make clear, bring home to

■ **get ahead**
advance, progress, get on, thrive, flourish, prosper, do well, succeed, make good, make it
COLLOQ. go places, get there, get somewhere, go great guns, make the big time, make your mark, go up in the world
F₃ fall behind, fail

■ **get along**
1 COPE, manage, get by, survive, fare, progress, develop
COLLOQ. make out
2 AGREE, be on friendly terms, harmonize, get on, relate, be on the same wavelength
COLLOQ. hit it off

■ **get at**
1 REACH, attain, gain access to, find, discover, obtain
2 BRIBE, suborn, corrupt, influence
COLLOQ. nobble
3 MEAN, intend, imply, insinuate, hint, suggest
4 CRITICIZE, find fault with, slate, pick on, attack, make fun of
COLLOQ. knock, slam, pick holes in

■ **get away**
escape, get out, break out, break away, break free, run away, flee, depart, leave
COLLOQ. scoot, scram, scat, scarper, do a runner/bunk, run for it, do a moonlight flit, make a bolt/break for it, take to your heels, run for your life
SLANG sling your hook

■ **get back**
1 RETURN, go/come back, go/come home
2 RECOVER, regain, recoup, repossess, retrieve
3 PAY BACK, retaliate, get even with, take revenge on, take vengeance on, avenge yourself on

■ **get by**
cope, get along manage, survive, exist, fare
FORMAL subsist
COLLOQ. make ends meet, scrape through, hang on, keep your head above water, keep the wolf from the door, weather the storm, see it through

■ **get down**
1 DEPRESS, sadden, make sad, dishearten, dispirit
2 DESCEND, dismount, disembark, alight, get off
F∃ 1 encourage **2** board
■ **get in**
enter, penetrate, infiltrate, arrive, come, land, embark
■ **get off**
1 *get off a train*
alight from, leave, get out (of), dismount, climb off, descend
FORMAL disembark
2 REMOVE, detach, separate, shed, get down
F∃ 1 get on, board **2** put on
■ **get on**
1 BOARD, climb on, get in, get into, embark, mount, ascend
2 COPE, manage, fare, get along prosper, succeed
COLLOQ. make out
3 CONTINUE, proceed, press on, advance, progress
4 AGREE, be on friendly terms, harmonize, relate, be on the same wavelength
COLLOQ. hit it off
F∃ 1 get off
■ **get out**
1 ESCAPE, flee, break out, extricate yourself, free yourself, leave, depart, withdraw, vacate, evacuate, clear out
COLLOQ. scoot, scram, scat, scarper, do a runner/bunk, run for it, do a moonlight flit, make a bolt/break for it, take to your heels, run for your life
2 *she got out a pen*
take out, produce
3 *the news got out*
become public, become known, come out, leak out, be leaked, spread, circulate
■ **get out of**
avoid, escape, evade, shirk, dodge
COLLOQ. skive
SLANG N Am gold-brick, goof off
■ **get over**
1 RECOVER FROM, shake off, recuperate from, pull through, get well/better, respond to treatment, be restored, survive
2 SURMOUNT, overcome, master, get round, defeat, deal with, complete
3 COMMUNICATE, get across, convey, put over, impart, explain, make clear
■ **get ready**
prepare, arrange, fix up, ready, rehearse, set out
■ **get rid of**
do away with, dispense with, dispose of, throw away, rid yourself of, shake off, remove, unload, dump, eject, eliminate, expel, jettison
COLLOQ. get shot of, ditch
F∃ accumulate, acquire
■ **get round**
1 BYPASS, evade, avoid
FORMAL circumvent
2 PERSUADE, win over, talk round, coax, cajole, induce, sway
FORMAL prevail upon
■ **get there**
advance, arrive, prosper, succeed, make good
COLLOQ. go places, make it
■ **get together**
meet, assemble, collect, gather, congregate, rally, join, unite, collaborate, organize
■ **get up**
stand (up), arise, rise, stir, get out of bed, ascend, climb, mount, scale

getaway *n*
escape, breakout, flight, start, absconding decampment, break

get-together *n*
party, reception, meeting reunion, function, gathering rally, assembly, social, soirée
COLLOQ. do, bash

get-up *n*
set, outfit, clothes, clothing garments, kit
COLLOQ. rig-out, gear, togs
SLANG clobber, threads

ghastliness *n*
awfulness, dreadfulness, frightfulness, grimness, gruesomeness, hideousness, nastiness

ghastly *adj*
1 AWFUL, dreadful, frightful, frightening terrifying terrible, grim, gruesome, hideous, horrible, horrid, horrendous, loathsome, nasty, repellent, shocking appalling lurid, macabre; *Scot* gash
OLD greisly, griesly
2 *look/feel ghastly*
ill, sick, unwell, poorly, rotten, dreadful, awful, terrible
COLLOQ. lousy, rop(e)y, off colour, under the weather
3 *a ghastly mistake*
serious, bad, grave, critical, dangerous, awful, terrible, dreadful, frightful, shocking appalling unrepeatable
F∃ 1 delightful, attractive **2** well, healthy

SYNONYM NUANCES

sense 1
Awful, **dreadful** and **frightful** are now fairly restrained terms to describe anything thoroughly unpleasant: *a dreadful row took place between them*, while **terrible**, although still widely applied, suggests a stronger response: *I had such a terrible day at work I wanted to resign*. **Frightening** has more to do with arousing fear, as does **terrifying**, though to a greater extent, while **grim** is more suggestive of being harsh and unappealing: *a grim picture of life in the prison*. **Gruesome** suggests provoking a shudder and has overtones of disgust, as does **hideous**, although it can also be used in inoffensive contexts: *hideous injuries; a young man in a hideous jacket*. **Horrible**, although similar, again implies a strong emotional response: *I think the new building is horrible*.
   The term **horrid** nowadays tends to be suggestive merely of something highly disagreeable: *a horrid little boy*. By contrast, **horrendous** implies greater horror on a larger scale: *a horrendous loss of life*.
   You can use **loathsome** to convey an element of contempt, while **repellent** would suggest complete aversion, and **shocking** or the even stronger **appalling** implies startling as well as offending the senses. For unsavoury descriptions or images, especially those deliberately created, you could use the term **lurid**. **Macabre** would appropriately describe something with elements of strangeness or death: *a macabre memento of a hangman's noose*.

---

ghost *n*
1 SPECTRE, phantom, apparition, visitant, spirit, wraith, soul, shadow, presence, spook, fetch, manifest, poltergeist, revenant, duppy, jumby, lemur, umbra, *duende*; *dialect* gytrash; *Scot* waff; *N Am* haunt
TECHNICAL astral body
OLD shade, larva
COLLOQ. spook
2 TRACE, suggestion, hint, shadow, impression, semblance

SYNONYM NUANCES

sense 1
Spectre can be used to suggest a being not of this world, however it now more commonly implies any haunting fear of something unpleasant: *the spectre of war*, whilst **phantom** can be used generally of anything illusory. **Apparition** is suggestive of the unexpected appearance of something with an unreal quality: *he was startled by the apparition of a strange man with a black dog*, while **manifest** suggests the form taken by such an apparition or ghost.

Visitant would be used of a supernatural visitor, perhaps with a specific purpose, and the more rare **revenant** could be used to refer to someone who has returned from the dead. The term **spirit** may be widely used to refer to any incorporeal body, whereas **wraith** and **fetch** would have the more narrow referent of a vision of someone living although not present.

Soul has less frightening connotations, suggesting merely the essence of a living creature that is believed to survive death, whilst **shadow** and **presence** are more appropriate for the influence cast by someone who has died, rather than a vision of them: *his father's shadow hung over him.* The word **spook** can be used to suggest someone otherworldly, but is now generally and relatively light-heartedly used to suggest creepiness: *his friends are real spooks.* **Poltergeist** specifically refers to a mysterious invisible force that is blamed for throwing or rearranging things.

ghostly *adj*
eerie, creepy, weird, supernatural, unearthly, ghostlike, spectral, wraith-like, phantom, illusory, shadowy
COLLOQ. spooky

ghoulish *adj*
grisly, gruesome, macabre, morbid, unhealthy, unwholesome, revolting sick

giant *n, adj*
♦ *n*
monster, titan, colossus, behemoth, ogre, Briarean, Patagonian
OLD eten, rounceval
See panel below
♦ *adj*
gigantic, colossal, titanic, mammoth, king-size, huge, enormous, massive, immense, vast, tremendous, monumental, gargantuan, cyclopean, large
FORMAL prodigious, Brobdingnagian, leviathan
COLLOQ. jumbo, great big whopping ginormous, humongous
E3 tiny, miniature

gibber *v*
babble, blab, blabber; *dialect & N Am* blather; gabble, jabber, prattle, chatter, cackle, cant

gibberish *n*
nonsense, rubbish, drivel, jargon, twaddle, balderdash, prattle, yammer, ravings
OLD (*Shakesp*) linsey
COLLOQ. gobbledygook, mumbo-jumbo, poppycock, tommyrot, cobblers, bunkum, baloney, blah, bosh, eyewash, hogwash, stuff and nonsense, codswallop, rhubarb, guff, hooey, malarkey, moonshine
E3 sense

gibe, jibe *n, v*
♦ *n*
jeer, sneer, mockery, ridicule, teasing taunt, derision, scoff, poke, quip
COLLOQ. dig crack
♦ *v*
jeer, sneer, mock, ridicule, taunt, tease, scoff, make fun of
FORMAL deride
SLANG *N Am* goof

giddily *adv*
1 DIZZILY, unsteadily, lightheadedly
COLLOQ. woozily

2 EXCITEDLY, dizzily, wildly, restlessly, frantically, enthusiastically, euphorically

giddiness *n*
1 DIZZINESS, faintness, lightheadedness, wooziness, wobbliness, nausea, vertigo
2 EXCITEMENT, dizziness, frenzy, exhilaration, thrill, animation

giddy *adj*
1 DIZZY, faint, lightheaded, unsteady, reeling
FORMAL vertiginous
COLLOQ. woozy
2 EXCITED, wild, dizzy, exhilarated, stirred, stimulated, thrilled, elated, frenzied, silly, flighty
COLLOQ. high

gift *n, v*
♦ *n*
1 PRESENT, offering donation, contribution, bounty, largesse, gratuity, tip, bonus, inheritance, legacy, bequest, endowment
COLLOQ. freebie
2 TALENT, genius, flair, skill, aptitude, aptness, bent, knack, facility, endowment, proficiency, power, faculty, attribute, ability, capability, capacity, turn
♦ *v*
give, present, offer, contribute, donate
FORMAL bestow, confer

> **QUOTATIONS**
> The only gift is a portion of thyself
> RALPH WALDO EMERSON, *Essays: Second Series*, 'Gifts'

gifted *adj*
talented, endowed, adept, skilful, expert, masterly, skilled, accomplished, able, capable, proficient, clever, intelligent, bright, brilliant, sharp
COLLOQ. smart

gigantic *adj*
huge, enormous, immense, vast, giant, massive, colossal, king-size, monumental, titanic, mammoth, gargantuan, Herculean, Patagonian
OLD rounceval
FORMAL Brobdingnagian
COLLOQ. jumbo, great big whopping ginormous, humongous
SLANG mega
E3 tiny, Lilliputian

giggle *v, n*
titter, snigger, chuckle, chortle, laugh, snicker

gild *v*
enhance, ornament, elaborate, deck, enrich, adorn, grace, beautify, embellish, embroider, festoon, garnish, brighten, dress up, paint, coat, trim
FORMAL array, bedeck

gilded *adj*
gilt, gold, golden, gold-plated, gold-layered

gimcrack *adj*
cheap, shoddy, jerry-built, tawdry, trashy, rubbishy, trumpery
COLLOQ. tacky
E3 solid, well-made

gimmick *n*
attraction, publicity, novelty, ploy, stratagem, ruse, scheme, trick, stunt, dodge, device, contrivance, gadget

---

Famous and mythological giants include:

Albion	Briareus	Galligantus	Jotun	Polyphemus
Antaeus	Cyclops	Gargantua	Magog	Titans
Ashuras	Enceladus	Gog	Orion	Tityus
Atlas	Fionn MacCumhail	Goliath	Pantagruel	Ymir
Balor	Fomorians	Hagrid	Paul Bunyan	Ysbaddaden

gimmickry n
novelty, modernity, innovation

gingerly adv
tentatively, hesitantly, warily, watchfully, cautiously, with
caution, prudently, carefully, charily, attentively, delicately
FORMAL judiciously
E⅃ boldly, carelessly

Gipsy
see **Gypsy, Gipsy**.

gird v
1 PREPARE, ready, get ready, brace, steel
FORMAL fortify
2 FASTEN, belt, bind, girdle, hem in, pen, surround,
encircle, enclose, ring encompass, enfold

girdle n, v
♦ n
belt, sash, band, waistband, corset
FORMAL cummerbund, ceinture, cestus, cincture, cingulum
♦ v
surround, encircle, circle, enclose, encompass, go round,
gird, bind, bound, hem, ring

girl n
lass, youngster, young woman, young lady, female,
madam, miss, schoolgirl, girlfriend, sweetheart, maiden,
daughter, child, teenager, adolescent, au pair, tomboy,
hussy, *fille, jeune fille*, shiksa, geisha, mousmee, gill,
belle, cutie, dolly, dolly bird, baby, beauty queen,
Cinderella, cub, fizgig flirt, gamine, minx, moppet,
princess, puss, nymphet, romp; *dialect* gal, mauther; *Scot*
lassie, cummer, kimmer, cutty, gilpy, quean, randy,
tawpie; *Irish* colleen; *N Am* bachelorette
OLD damsel, wench, gerle, jill, grisette, peat, pigeon,
popsy, backfisch, blowze, blushet, gig giglet; (*Shakesp*)
maid-child
COLLOQ. kid, nipper, hen, babe, teeny-bopper; *Aust* sheila
OLD COLLOQ. filly, bobby-dazzler, bobbysoxer
SLANG chick, peach, bit, number, chit, jail-bait; (*offensive*)
bit of stuff/fluff, tart, tit, tottie; *Aust* tabby
OLD SLANG Judy, dell, flapper, kinchin-mort

girlfriend n
young lady, girl, lady, lass, partner, date, sweetheart, lover,
fiancée, woman, mistress, old flame, cohabitee, live-in
lover, common-law spouse, best girl
COLLOQ. steady, babe/baby, significant other, squeeze
SLANG bird, chick, bint

girlish adj
youthful, childlike, adolescent, childish, immature,
innocent, unmasculine

girth n
circumference, perimeter, measure, size, bulk, strap, band

gist n
pith, essence, marrow, substance, matter, meaning
significance, sense, idea, drift, direction, point, crux,
nucleus, nub, core, keynote
FORMAL import, quintessence

give v, n
♦ v
1 PRESENT, award, let someone have, slip, offer, lend,
donate, contribute, provide, supply, distribute, administer,
furnish, grant, endow, gift, make over, hand over, turn
over, deliver, entrust, bequeath, leave, will, commit,
devote
FORMAL confer, bestow, accord, proffer
2 *give news*
communicate, transmit, transfer, convey, tell, utter,
announce, declare, pronounce, publish, show, set forth
FORMAL impart
3 CONCEDE, allow, admit, yield, give way, give up,
surrender
FORMAL cede
4 *give trouble*
cause, occasion, make, create, produce, do, perform

5 *give an impression*
show, indicate, display, present, exhibit, reveal, set forth,
cause to have
FORMAL manifest
6 *give a speech*
make, perform, carry out, do
7 *give attention to something*
concentrate, direct, aim, focus, turn
8 *give someone a fright*
cause to experience/undergo, make, do, perform,
occasion, create, give rise to
9 *give something a value*
allow, offer, estimate, grant
10 SINK, yield, bend, buckle, give way, break (down),
collapse, fall, fall apart
11 *give a party*
organize, arrange, put on, be responsible for, have, take
charge of, lay on
COLLOQ. throw
12 *be given to understand something*
lead, make, cause, move, dispose, incline, prompt, induce
E⅃ 1 take, withhold 10 withstand
♦ n
yielding slack, elasticity, springiness, stretch, stretchiness
COLLOQ. play
■ **give away**
betray, inform on, expose, uncover, divulge, let slip,
disclose, reveal, leak, let out, concede
E⅃ keep
■ **give in**
surrender, capitulate, submit, yield, give way, concede,
admit/concede defeat, give up, succumb
COLLOQ. quit, throw in the towel/sponge, chuck it in, pack
it in, jack in, call it a day, show the white flag
E⅃ hold out
■ **give off/out**
emit, discharge, release, give out, send out, throw out,
pour out, exhale, vent, exude, produce
■ **give on to**
lead to, open on to, overlook
■ **give out**
1 DISTRIBUTE, disperse, hand out, pass around, share out,
dole out, mete out, allot, deal
COLLOQ. dish out
2 ANNOUNCE, declare, broadcast, publish, make known,
circulate, disseminate, communicate, transmit, impart,
notify, advertise
3 STOP WORKING, break down
COLLOQ. pack up
SLANG conk out
4 RUN OUT, come to an end, be (all) mixed up, be
exhausted
FORMAL be depleted
■ **give up**
1 STOP, cease, resign, abandon, waive, leave off, sacrifice
FORMAL relinquish, discontinue, forswear, renounce, forgo
COLLOQ. quit, cut out
2 SURRENDER, capitulate, give in, admit defeat, concede,
concede defeat
COLLOQ. quit, throw in the towel, turn in
SLANG *Aust* drop your bundle
E⅃ 1 start 2 hold out

SYNONYM NUANCES

verb sense 1
Present can be used to suggest giving something to
someone in a formal way, and **award**, while still
suggesting formality, also implies that the recipient has
been selected on merit. **Slip**, on the other hand, has
connotations of shadiness and subterfuge: *she slipped
me a fiver while his back was turned*, unlike **offer** which
would only be used where someone is being given a
choice.
    Contribute and **donate** are more suggestive of giving
to a worthy cause, although **contribute** also implies that

you are not the only donor, whilst **provide** and **supply** are appropriate where something essential is being made available: *the agency provides practical care in the home*, and **distribute** suggests there are a number of recipients. The term **administer** is best used of dispensing in a professional context: *the courts administered justice*; *he administered first aid*, whereas **furnish** is more suggestive of equipping and can be used of the giving of information: *the Inspector was furnished with all the documentary evidence*.

   Grant, however, is often used in official contexts and implies a degree of concession in the giving: *delays in granting exit visas*, unlike **endow** or **gift** which have more voluntary implications, and suggest the giving of something valuable: *they bought the play area and gifted it to the town*. The terms **entrust** and **commit** are suggestive of passing over for safekeeping: *the courts can commit children into care*, and **devote** can be used to imply it is to the exclusion of everything else: *I've devoted my time and energy to my work*. **Bequeath**, **leave** and **will** are generally used of the transfer of your belongings after death.

give-and-take *n*
adaptability, compromise, negotiation, flexibility, co-operation, goodwill, willingness, compliance

given *adj, prep*
♦ *adj*
1 *a given number*
specified, particular, definite, specific, stated, individual, distinct
2 INCLINED, disposed, likely, liable, prone
♦ *prep*
considering taking into account/consideration, bearing in mind, making allowances for, in view of, in the light of, assuming

giver *n*
benefactor, patron, sponsor, backer, supporter, promoter, donor, contributor, subscriber, provider, subsidizer, philanthropist, helper, friend, well-wisher
COLLOQ. angel, fairy godmother
E3 opponent, persecutor

glacial *adj*
1 FREEZING, frozen, biting bitter, chill, chilly, cold, frosty, raw, wintry, stiff, frigid, icy, piercing polar, arctic, Siberian
FORMAL brumous, gelid
2 UNFRIENDLY, antagonistic, cold, icy, frosty, hostile
FORMAL inimical
E3 **1** hot **2** warm

glad *adj*
1 PLEASED, delighted, gratified, contented, satisfied, happy, joyful, overjoyed, thrilled, elated, merry, cheerful, cheery, gleeful, welcome, bright
OLD gladsome, fain
COLLOQ. over the moon, chuffed, tickled pink
2 WILLING, eager, keen, ready, prepared, inclined, happy, pleased
FORMAL disposed
E3 **1** sad, unhappy **2** unwilling reluctant

gladden *v*
brighten, cheer, encourage, delight, please, hearten, gratify, rejoice, elate, enliven, exhilarate, raise the spirits of
COLLOQ. buck up
E3 sadden

glade *n*
clearing dell, space, gap, opening

gladly *adv*
happily, cheerfully, freely, willingly, readily, with good grace, with pleasure
OLD gladsomely, fain, fainly
E3 sadly, unwillingly, reluctantly

gladness *n*
happiness, joy, cheerfulness, delight, pleasure, brightness, high spirits, jollity, glee, hilarity, mirth, gaiety
FORMAL felicity, joyousness
E3 sadness

glamorous *adj*
smart, elegant, well-dressed, attractive, beautiful, lovely, gorgeous, enchanting captivating alluring charming appealing fascinating exciting thrilling dazzling glittering glossy, colourful
COLLOQ. glam, glitzy, flashy, ritzy, glammy
E3 plain, drab, boring

glamour *n*
attraction, attractiveness, allure, appeal, fascination, excitement, thrill, captivation, enchantment, charm, magic, beauty, elegance, glitter, prestige

> **QUOTATIONS**
> Glamour is what makes a man ask for your telephone number. But it also is what makes a woman ask for the name of your dressmaker
>   LILLY DACHÉ, 'Lilly Daché's Secrets of Lifelong Glamour Book'

glance *v, n*
♦ *v*
peep, peek, glimpse, catch a glimpse of, view, look, look quickly/briefly at, scan, skim, leaf, flip, flick, thumb, dip, browse
♦ *n*
peep, peek, glimpse, look, quick/brief look
COLLOQ. butcher's, dekko, gander; *Aust & NZ* squiz
■ **glance off**
bounce off, deflect, rebound, ricochet, spring back
■ **at first glance**
apparently, at first sight, seemingly, ostensibly, outwardly, on the face of it, to all appearances, superficially, on the surface
FORMAL *prima facie*

gland *n*
Related adjectives: adenoid, glandular

Types of gland include:

adrenal	lymph	parotid
apocrine	lymph node	pineal
cortex	mammary	pituitary
eccrine	medulla	prostate
endocrine	merocrine	sebaceous
exocrine	ovary	testicle
holocrine	pancreas	thymus
lachrymal	parathyroid	thyroid

glare *v, n*
♦ *v*
1 GLOWER, look frown, scowl, stare, frown
COLLOQ. daggers, give someone a dirty look
2 DAZZLE, blaze, flame, flare, shine, beam, reflect
♦ *n*
1 *his fiery glare*
glower, frown, scowl, stare, look
COLLOQ. dirty look, black look
2 BRIGHTNESS, brilliance, glow, blaze, flame, flare, dazzle, spotlight

glaring *adj*
blatant, flagrant, open, conspicuous, patent, obvious, manifest, overt, outrageous, gross, lurid, plain as a pikestaff
E3 hidden, concealed, minor

glaringly *adv*
blatantly, flagrantly, obviously, manifestly, openly, conspicuously, patently, overtly

glass *n*
1 BEAKER, tumbler, goblet
2 CRYSTAL, glassware, vitrics
Related adjectives: vitreous, hyaline
3 SPECTACLES, eyewear, lens, contact lenses, lorgnette, eyeglasses, opera-glasses, pince-nez, monocle
COLLOQ. specs
See also **spectacles**.

glassy *adj*
1 GLASSLIKE, smooth, polished, slippery, icy, shiny, glossy, transparent, clear, crystal clear, mirrorlike
2 *a glassy stare*
expressionless, blank, empty, vacant, dazed, unmoving fixed, deadpan, glazed, vacuous, cold, lifeless, dull

glaze *v, n*
♦ *v*
coat, cover, enamel, gloss, varnish, lacquer, polish, burnish, flambé
♦ *n*
coat, coating finish, enamel, varnish, lacquer, polish, shine, lustre, gloss

gleam *n, v*
♦ *n*
glint, flash, beam, ray, shaft, flare, flicker, glimmer, shimmer, sparkle, glitter, gloss, glow, lustre, brightness
♦ *v*
glint, flash, glance, flare, shine, radiate, beam, glisten, glimmer, glitter, sparkle, scintillate, shimmer, glow

glean *v*
gather, collect, find out, learn, pick (up), select, accumulate, amass, harvest, garner, reap, cull

glee *n*
delight, cheerfulness, pleasure, fun, joy, joyfulness, merriment, mirth, gladness, liveliness, exhilaration, exuberance, exultation, elation, hilarity, jocularity, jollity, joviality, gaiety, gratification, triumph, verve
FORMAL joyousness

gleeful *adj*
delighted, cheerful, pleased, happy, beside yourself, joyful, overjoyed, elated, exuberant, exultant, merry, mirthful, jubilant, jovial, gratified, triumphant
FORMAL joyous
COLLOQ. over the moon, cock-a-hoop
F3 sad

gleefully *adv*
cheerfully, happily, joyfully, exuberantly, merrily, jubilantly, triumphantly
FORMAL joyously

glib *adj*
fluent, easy, facile, quick, ready, talkative, plausible, insincere, smooth, slick, suave, smooth-tongued, smooth-talking silver-tongued
FORMAL loquacious, voluble
COLLOQ. with the gift of the gab, gabby, gassy
F3 tongue-tied, implausible

glibly *adv*
fluently, easily, quickly, insincerely, slickly, smoothly

glide *v*
slide, move smoothly/effortlessly, slip, skate, skim, fly, float, drift, sail, coast, roll, run, flow, pass

glimmer *v, n*
♦ *v*
glow, shimmer, glisten, glitter, sparkle, twinkle, wink, blink, flash, flicker, gleam, shine
OLD glimpse
♦ *n*
1 GLOW, shimmer, shine, sparkle, twinkle, flicker, glint, gleam, ray, flash; *Scot* styme
2 TRACE, hint, suggestion, inkling grain, flicker, ray

glimmering *n*
inkling suspicion, idea, notion, clue, hint, intimation, insinuation, innuendo, suggestion, allusion, indication, sign, pointer
COLLOQ. faintest, foggiest, whisper

glimpse *n, v*
♦ *n*
peep, peek, squint, glance, look, quick/brief look, sight, sighting view, blink, aperçu; *dialect* whiff; *Scot* gledge, gliff, glim, glisk, styme, waff
♦ *v*
spy, spot, catch sight of, sight, view
FORMAL espy

glint *v, n*
♦ *v*
flash, gleam, shine, reflect, glitter, sparkle, glisten, twinkle, glimmer, shimmer, scintillate
♦ *n*
flash, gleam, shine, reflection, glitter, sparkle, glistening twinkle, glimmer, shimmer

glisten *v*
shine, gleam, glint, glitter, flash, sparkle, twinkle, flicker, glimmer, shimmer
FORMAL coruscate

glitch *n*
snag delay, hold-up, trouble, problem, difficulty, mishap, setback, hiccup, drawback, catch, impediment, hindrance, obstacle, block, check, barrier, obstruction

glitter *v, n*
♦ *v*
sparkle, spangle, scintillate, twinkle, shimmer, glimmer, flicker, glisten, glint, gleam, flash, shine, dazzle, flare
OLD glister
FORMAL coruscate
♦ *n*
1 SPARKLE, scintillation, twinkle, shimmer, glimmer, flicker, glint, gleam, flash, shine, lustre, sheen, brightness, radiance, brilliance, splendour
FORMAL coruscation
2 SHOWINESS, glamour, tinsel, flashiness, gilt
COLLOQ. glitz, razzle-dazzle, razzmatazz

glitz *n*
showiness, flamboyance, pretentiousness, glitter, ostentation, razzle-dazzle, attractiveness, tastelessness, gaudiness
COLLOQ. flashiness, pizzazz, razzmatazz, swank
F3 restraint

glitzy *adj*
showy, flashy, flamboyant, ostentatious, gaudy, garish, glittering brilliant, vivid, loud, tawdry, fancy, ornate, pretentious, cheap, tasteless, pompous
COLLOQ. swanky, flash, posh, ritzy
F3 quiet, restrained

gloat *v*
triumph, glory, exult, rejoice, revel in, delight in, relish, crow, boast, vaunt
COLLOQ. rub it in

global *adj*
1 WORLDWIDE, universal, international
2 GENERAL, all-encompassing total, thorough, exhaustive, comprehensive, all-inclusive, encyclopedic, wide-ranging universal
F3 1 parochial **2** limited

globally *adv*
universally, throughout the world, worldwide, everywhere, in every place, in every country/land, internationally, generally, under the sun

globe *n*
world, earth, planet, sphere, ball, orb, round

globular *adj*
ball-shaped, round, globate, spherical
FORMAL orbicular, spheroid

globule *n*
bead, ball, bubble, drop, droplet, globulet, pearl, pellet, particle
TECHNICAL vesicle, vesicula

gloom *n*
1 DARK, darkness, blackness, shade, shadow, dusk, twilight, dimness, obscurity, cloud, cloudiness, dullness, murkiness
2 DEPRESSION, low spirits, despondency, dejection, sadness, unhappiness, glumness, melancholy, grief, sorrow, woe, misery, hopelessness, pessimism, desolation, despair, discouragement, damp, mood, shadow
COLLOQ. the blues
≠ 1 brightness **2** cheerfulness, happiness

gloomily *adv*
despondently, downheartedly, sadly, miserably, glumly, pessimistically, depressingly, morosely, drearily, cheerlessly, dismally
≠ cheerfully, happily

gloomy *adj*
1 DARK, sombre, shadowy, dim, obscure, overcast, dull, dreary, dismal, dire, dingy, unlit
FORMAL tenebrous, crepuscular
2 DEPRESSED, down, low, despondent, dejected, downcast, dispirited, downhearted, sad, miserable, glum, morose, dreary, drear, pessimistic, cheerless, melancholy, downbeat, sorrowful, dismal, depressing desolate, in low spirits
FORMAL disconsolate
COLLOQ. down in the dumps
≠ 1 bright **2** happy, cheerful

glorification *n*
1 PRAISE, worship, adoration, honouring thanking gratitude, reverence, extolling
FORMAL lauding veneration
2 *glorification of war*
celebration, praise, magnification, lionization, idolization, romanticization

glorify *v*
1 *glorify God*
praise, worship, exalt, adore, honour, thank, bless, magnify, revere, extol, sanctify
FORMAL laud, venerate
2 *glorify violence/war*
celebrate, praise, magnify, hail, lionize, idolize, elevate, enshrine, immortalize, romanticize, panegyrize
FORMAL eulogize
≠ 1 denounce; *formal* vilify

glorious *adj*
1 ILLUSTRIOUS, eminent, distinguished, famous, renowned, honoured, noted, great, noble, celebrated, famed, splendid, magnificent, grand, majestic, supreme, excellent, victorious, triumphant
2 MARVELLOUS, splendid, beautiful, gorgeous, superb, perfect, excellent, wonderful, delightful, dazzling heavenly
COLLOQ. super, terrific, great
3 *glorious weather*
fine, bright, radiant, shining brilliant
≠ 1 unknown

glory *n, v*
♦ *n*
1 FAME, renown, celebrity, illustriousness, greatness, eminence, distinction, honour, recognition, acclaim, prestige, accolade, kudos, triumph, *gloire*
2 PRAISE, homage, tribute, worship, veneration, adoration, exaltation, blessing thanksgiving gratitude
TECHNICAL doxology, gloria, preface

3 BRIGHTNESS, radiance, brilliance, beauty, splendour, halo, sun, resplendence, magnificence, pomp, grandeur, majesty, dignity, impressiveness, crown, diadem
TECHNICAL aureola, gloriole
OLD (*Shakesp & Spenser*) garland
♦ *v*
revel, delight, exult, pride yourself, rejoice, take great pleasure, triumph, relish, boast, crow, gloat
OLD strut, triumph

> **QUOTATIONS**
> How quickly the glory of the world passes
> ST THOMAS À KEMPIS, *The Imitation of Christ*

gloss¹ *n, v*
♦ *n*
1 SHEEN, polish, varnish, lustre, shine, brightness, gleam, shimmer, sparkle, brilliance
2 SHOW, appearance, semblance, surface, front, façade, veneer, camouflage, mask, disguise, veil, window-dressing
■ **gloss over**
conceal, hide, veil, draw a veil over, mask, disguise, camouflage, cover up, whitewash, explain away, evade, avoid, ignore, smooth over, deal with quickly

gloss² *n, v*
♦ *n*
glosses to the text
annotation, note, footnote, explanation, interpretation, translation, definition, comment, commentary
FORMAL elucidation, explication, scholion
♦ *v*
annotate, add glosses to, define, explain, interpret, construe, translate, comment
FORMAL elucidate

glossary *n*
word list, wordbook, index, dictionary, lexicon, concordance, thesaurus

glossy *adj*
shiny, sheeny, lustrous, sleek, silky, smooth, glassy, polished, burnished, glazed, gleaming enamelled, bright, shining shimmering sparkling brilliant
≠ matt

glove *n*
mitten, mitt, gauntlet, gage, mousquetaire glove, oven glove

glow *n, v*
♦ *n*
1 LIGHT, gleam, glimmer, radiance, glory, brightness, vividness, richness, brilliance, splendour, afterglow, sunglow, outflush
TECHNICAL phosphorescence, gegenschein
OLD leam
FORMAL luminosity, incandescence
2 ARDOUR, fervour, intensity, warmth, passion, enthusiasm, excitement, happiness, satisfaction
3 FLUSH, blush, rosiness, rose, redness, reddening pinkness, burning bloom
♦ *v*
1 SHINE, radiate, gleam, glimmer, burn, smoulder
2 *their faces glowed*
flush, blush, colour, redden, burn, grow/look pink

glower *v, n*
♦ *v*
glare, frown, scowl, stare
COLLOQ. look daggers, give someone a dirty look
♦ *n*
glare, frown, scowl, stare, look
COLLOQ. black look, dirty look

glowing *adj*
1 BRIGHT, luminous, vivid, vibrant, rich, warm, flushed, red, ruddy, flaming smouldering
TECHNICAL phosphorescent
FORMAL incandescent

2 *a glowing review*
complimentary, enthusiastic, favourable, ecstatic, rhapsodic
FORMAL laudatory, eulogistic, panegyrical
COLLOQ. rave
E3 1 dull, colourless **2** restrained

glue *n, v*
♦ *n*
adhesive, gum, paste, size, cement, fixative, mortar
♦ *v*
1 STICK, affix, gum, paste, seal, bond, cement, fix
FORMAL agglutinate
2 *glued to the radio*
grip, rivet, engross, absorb, engage, compel, hypnotize, mesmerize

gluey *adj*
adhesive, gummy, sticky, viscid, viscous
FORMAL glutinous

glum *adj*
gloomy, unhappy, forlorn, sad, miserable, depressed, despondent, moody, dejected, morose, pessimistic, doleful, crestfallen, sour, sulky, sullen, surly, grumpy, gruff, ill-humoured, churlish
COLLOQ. crabbed, down, low, down in the dumps
E3 ecstatic, happy

glumly *adv*
gloomily, unhappily, forlornly, sadly, miserably, despondently, dejectedly, morosely, sourly, sullenly, grumpily, gruffily
E3 ecstatically, happily

glut *n, v*
♦ *n*
surplus, excess, superfluity, surfeit, overabundance, superabundance, saturation, overflow
E3 scarcity, lack
♦ *v*
saturate, oversupply, overload, inundate, flood, deluge, overfeed, sate, satiate, stuff, gorge, fill, cram, choke, clog

glutinous *adj*
adhesive, sticky, cohesive, gluey, gummy, mucous, viscous
FORMAL mucilaginous, viscid

glutton *n*
gourmand, gormandizer, gobbler, belly-god, free-liver, cormorant; *Aust & NZ* gutzer
OLD lurcher
COLLOQ. guzzler, greedy guts, gorger, pig
E3 ascetic

gluttonous *adj*
greedy, gluttonish, voracious, ravenous, insatiable, gormandizing
OLD gluttonish
FORMAL edacious, esurient, omnivorous, rapacious
COLLOQ. hoggish, piggish
E3 abstemious, ascetic

gluttony *n*
gourmandism, greed, greediness, voracity, insatiability, surfeit
OLD gulosity
FORMAL edacity, esurience
COLLOQ. piggishness
E3 abstinence, asceticism

gnarled *adj*
gnarly, knotted, knotty, bumpy, lumpy, twisted, contorted, distorted, rough, wrinkled, rugged, weather-beaten, leathery

gnash *v*
grind, grate, grit, scrape

gnaw *v*
1 BITE, nibble, munch, chew, crunch, eat, devour, consume, erode, wear, haunt
FORMAL masticate

2 WORRY, nag niggle, fret, trouble, plague, prey, torment, harass, harry

go *v, n*
♦ *v*
1 MOVE, pass, advance, progress, proceed, make for, head, drive, travel, journey, walk, start, begin, go away, depart, leave, take your leave, set off, set out, retreat, withdraw, disappear, vanish, melt away
FORMAL repair
COLLOQ. clear off, quit, scat, scoot, scram, make tracks, beat it; *Aust* shoot through
2 OPERATE, function, work, run, act, perform, be in working order
3 EXTEND, spread, stretch, reach, lead, span, continue, carry on, unfold
4 *time goes quickly*
pass, pass by, elapse, lapse, proceed, roll on, go by, slip away, slip by, tick away
5 *go mad*
become, turn, get, grow, come to be, be changed into
6 *the machine goes 'beep'*
emit, sound, make a sound, give off, send out, release
7 *the books go here*
belong have as its usual place, fit in, be found, be kept, be located, be situated
8 *the interview went well*
turn out, work out, progress, proceed, manage, fare, occur, result, end up, develop
FORMAL eventuate
COLLOQ. pan out
9 *Where does all the money go?*
be used up, be spent, be finished, be exhausted, be consumed
10 *100 jobs will go*
get rid of, be discarded, be thrown away, be dismissed, be made redundant
COLLOQ. be axed, be given the sack, be sacked, be fired, be given the push, be given your cards, be shown the door, be given your marching orders; *N Am* be given the pink slip; be given your P45
11 *most of the income goes on rent*
be spent on, be given to, be allotted to, be assigned to, be awarded to
12 *the proceeds will go to charity*
be given, be donated, be presented, be pledged
13 *the hat goes well with the dress*
match, harmonize, co-ordinate, blend, go together, complement, suit, fit, correspond, go with each other
FORMAL accord
14 DIE, pass away, pass on, pass, depart, depart this life, breathe your last, draw your last breath, lose your life, perish, fail, drown, starve, close your eyes
FORMAL expire, decease
COLLOQ. peg out, bite the dust, pop off, give up the ghost, push up daisies, pop your clogs
SLANG snuff it, cash in your chips, kick the bucket, croak; *Aust* cark or kark (it)
E3 1 stop **2** break down, fail **13** clash
♦ *n*
1 *have a go*
attempt, try, bid, turn, endeavour, effort
COLLOQ. shot, bash, stab, crack, whirl
2 ENERGY, vitality, life, force, spirit, dynamism, vigour, animation
COLLOQ. get-up-and-go, push, pizzazz, oomph, zip, zing

■ **go about**
approach, begin, set about, embark on, address, tackle, attend to, undertake, do, engage in, perform

■ **go ahead**
begin, proceed, carry on, continue, advance, progress, make progress, move

■ **go along with**
accept, agree with, obey, follow, fall in with, support, abide by
FORMAL comply with, concur with

■ **go around/round**
circulate, be spread around, be passed round, be talked about, go about

■ **go at**
set about, tackle, attack, blame, criticize, argue

■ **go away**
depart, leave, abscond, withdraw, retreat, disappear, vanish
COLLOQ. scoot, scram, do a runner/bunk, run for it, make a bolt/break for it, take to your heels, run for your life

■ **go back**
return, revert, backslide, retreat

■ **go back on**
renege on, default on, deny, break, break your promise

■ **go by**
1 PASS, elapse, lapse, flow
2 *go by the rules*
observe, follow, obey, heed
FORMAL comply with

■ **go down**
1 DESCEND, sink, be submerged, set, fall (down), drop, decrease, be reduced, decline, deteriorate, degenerate, fail, founder, go under, collapse
COLLOQ. fold
2 LOSE, be beaten, be defeated, suffer defeat, fail
COLLOQ. come a cropper
3 *the joke went down badly*
be received, have as a response, be reacted to, be met with, sustain
4 *go down in history*
be remembered, be recorded, be honoured, be recognized

■ **go down with**
catch, pick up, develop, come down with, become infected with, be afflicted by
FORMAL contract, succumb to

■ **go for**
1 CHOOSE, select, prefer, favour, aim for, like, admire, enjoy
2 ATTACK, assail, assault, rush at, set about, lunge at

■ **go in for**
enter, take part in, participate in, engage in, go into, take up, embrace, adopt, undertake, practise, pursue, follow
FORMAL espouse

■ **go into**
discuss, consider, review, examine, study, research, look into, scrutinize, investigate, inquire into, check out, probe, delve into, analyse, dissect

■ **go off**
1 DEPART, leave, set out, abscond, vanish, disappear
COLLOQ. quit
2 EXPLODE, blow up, blast, burst, detonate, be fired, be discharged
COLLOQ. go bang
3 *the milk has gone off*
deteriorate, turn, sour, go bad, rot, go stale

■ **go on**
1 CONTINUE, carry on, proceed, persist, stay, endure, last, remain
2 CHATTER, ramble on
COLLOQ. rabbit, witter, natter, gab, gas, talk the hind legs off a donkey
3 HAPPEN, occur, take place

■ **go out**
1 EXIT, depart, leave, withdraw
2 *the light went out*
be switched off, be turned off, be extinguished
3 *go out with a boy*
go with, go around/round, court, see each other, date, go steady

■ **go over**
examine, peruse, study, revise, scan, read, look over, inspect, discuss, think about, check, review, repeat, rehearse, list

■ **go round**
SPIN, turn (round), revolve, rotate, circle, twist, gyrate, twirl, swivel, pirouette, wheel, whirl, whirr, swirl, reel
See **go around** *above*

■ **go through**
1 SUFFER, undergo, experience, bear, tolerate, endure, face, withstand, stand, be subjected to
2 INVESTIGATE, check, examine, look through, search, hunt, explore
3 USE UP, consume, exhaust, spend, squander, get through
4 *the proposal has gone through*
be approved, be passed, be authorized, be accepted, be confirmed, be adopted, be carried, be signed

■ **go together**
match, harmonize, fit, suit, blend, co-ordinate, complement
FORMAL accord

■ **go under**
1 CLOSE DOWN, collapse, default, die, fail, go out of business, founder, go bankrupt
COLLOQ. fold, flop, go to the wall, go bust
2 SINK, go down, founder, submerge, succumb, drown

■ **go with**
1 MATCH, harmonize, co-ordinate, blend, complement, suit, fit, correspond
2 ACCOMPANY, escort, take, usher
◧ 1 clash

■ **go without**
abstain, deny yourself, for(e)go, do without, manage without, lack, want

goad v
prod, prick, spur, impel, push, drive, jolt, provoke, incite, induce, instigate, arouse, stimulate, inspire, motivate, pressurize, prompt, urge, nag hound, harass, taunt, annoy, irritate, vex

go-ahead n, adj
◆ n
permission, authorization, clearance, sanction, approval, assent, consent, warranty, agreement, confirmation
COLLOQ. green light, OK, thumbs-up
◧ ban, veto, embargo
◆ adj
enterprising pioneering progressive, resourceful, ambitious, forward, forward-looking opportunist, up-and-coming dynamic, vigorous, energetic, aggressive, pushy
COLLOQ. go-getting
◧ unenterprising sluggish

goal n
target, mark, objective, aim, intention, object, purpose, end, design, ambition, ideal, aspiration

gobble v
bolt, guzzle, gorge, eat quickly, cram, stuff, devour, consume, swallow, gulp, slabber
COLLOQ. put away, wolf, scoff, snarf; N Am chow down

gobbledygook n
gibberish, jargon, officialese, journalese, computerese, psychobabble, buzz words, nonsense, rubbish, drivel, twaddle, balderdash, prattle

go-between n
intermediary, mediator, liaison, contact, middleman, broker, dealer, agent, factor, messenger, medium
OLD (Shakesp) ring-carrier

goblet n
glass, cup, chalice, beaker, tumbler

goblin n
imp, brownie, fiend, hobgoblin, gnome, elf, sprite, spirit, gremlin, nixie, bogey, leprechaun, kelpie, kobold, demon, troll, puck, bogle, lubber fiend, barghest, *duende, esprit*

follet, nis; *dialect* knocker; *Scot* bodach, redcap, red-cowl, shellycoat; *Irish* pooka
OLD gobbeline, pug

gobsmacked *adj*
stunned, dumbfounded, astonished, amazed, astounded, overwhelmed, speechless, taken aback, startled, overcome, confounded, lost for words, staggered, confused, baffled, bewildered, dumb, nonplussed, paralysed
COLLOQ. thrown, flabbergasted, bowled over, floored, knocked for six

God *n*
Deity, Supreme Being Divine Being Godhead, prime mover, Creator, Maker, Providence, Lord, King Almighty, Holy One, Jehovah, Yahweh, Father, Allah, Brahma, Zeus, Judge, Saviour, Eternal, Everlasting
Related adjective: divine

god, goddess *n*
deity, divine being divinity, spirit, power, icon, idol, graven image
Related adjective: divine
See panel on next page

god-forsaken *adj*
remote, isolated, lonely, bleak, desolate, abandoned, deserted, forlorn, dismal, dreary, gloomy, miserable, wretched, depressing

godless *adj*
ungodly, atheistic, heathen, pagan, irreligious, agnostic, faithless, unholy, unrighteous, impious, sacrilegious, profane, irreverent, bad, evil, sinful, wicked
OLD atheous
FORMAL nullifidian
E∃ godly, pious

godlessness *n*
ungodliness, irreligion, faithlessness, unfaithfulness, impiety, irreverence, wickedness, atheism, agnosticism, paganism
E∃ godliness

godlike *adj*
divine, celestial, heavenly, exalted, saintly, holy, sacred, perfect, sublime, transcendent, superhuman
FORMAL deiform, theomorphic

godliness *n*
holiness, piety, devoutness, belief, religion, righteousness, morality, purity
E∃ godlessness

godly *adj*
religious, holy, pious, devout, God-fearing believing righteous, good, moral, virtuous, saintly, pure, innocent
E∃ godless, impious

godsend *n*
blessing boon, stroke of luck, bonanza, windfall, benediction, miracle
E∃ blow, setback

goggle *v*
stare, gaze, wonder
COLLOQ. gawp, gawk

going-over *n*
1 EXAMINATION, inspection, investigation, study, survey, analysis, check, check-up, work-up, review, scrutiny
2 BEATING, attack, criticism, reprimand, scolding, rebuke, pasting, chiding, thrashing, whipping, row
FORMAL castigation, chastisement
COLLOQ. dressing-down, trouncing

goings-on *n*
events, activities, occurrences, happenings, affairs, scenes, business, misbehaviour, mischief
COLLOQ. funny business

gold *n*
bullion, nugget, bar, ingot, precious metal
Related adjectives: auric

golden *adj*
1 GOLD, gilded, gilt, gold-coloured, goldish, yellow, blond(e), hyacinthine, red, fair, flaxen, bright, shining gleaming brilliant, dazzling lustrous
OLD gilden, inaurate
FORMAL resplendent, aureate, aurelian
2 PROSPEROUS, successful, glorious, excellent, treasured, precious, happy, joyful, delightful, rosy, favourable, promising flourishing bright, rewarding millennial, Saturnian
FORMAL auspicious, propitious

golf club

Types of golf club include:

baffy	mashie	putter
brassy	mashie iron	putting-cleek
bulger	mashie niblick	sand wedge
cleek	midiron	spade mashie
driver	midmashie	spoon
driving iron	niblick	wedge
iron	pitching niblick	wood
jigger	pitching wedge	

gone *adj*
departed, absent, away, astray, defunct, disappeared, vanished, lost, missing, finished, done, over, elapsed, past, used, spent, dead, extinct
COLLOQ. over and done with

goo *n*
matter, ooze, slime, stickiness, slush, sludge, mud, scum, mire, muck, grease, grime
COLLOQ. gunge, yuck, grot, gloop
SLANG crud, gunk, grunge

good *adj, n, interj*
♦ *adj*
1 *have a good day; do good work*
enjoyable, cheerful, pleasing pleasurable, satisfying commendable, excellent, first-class, first-rate, superior, fine, wonderful, marvellous, fantastic, terrific, superb, exceptional, acceptable, satisfactory, pleasant, agreeable, nice, adequate, passable, reasonable, tolerable, desirable
COLLOQ. great, super, brill, fabulous, smashing cracking top
SLANG fab, mega, wicked, awesome, cushty
2 *good at her job*
competent, proficient, skilled, expert, accomplished, professional, skilful, clever, talented, gifted, fit, brilliant, able, capable, dependable, reliable, efficient, adept, dexterous
3 KIND, considerate, thoughtful, gracious, friendly, sympathetic, benevolent, charitable, altruistic, philanthropic, kind-hearted, well-disposed
4 VIRTUOUS, exemplary, moral, upright, honest, trustworthy, worthy, honourable, noble, admirable, righteous, ethical
COLLOQ. salt of the earth
5 ADVANTAGEOUS, beneficial, favourable, helpful, useful, worthwhile, profitable, convenient, appropriate, suitable, fitting lucky, fortunate
FORMAL auspicious, propitious
6 WELL-BEHAVED, obedient, compliant, well-mannered, polite, respectful, under control
COLLOQ. good as gold
7 *in good health*
fine, healthy, strong vigorous, sound, hale and hearty
COLLOQ. in the pink, the picture of health, fit as a fiddle
8 *a good reason*
sound, sensible, valid, right, genuine, persuasive, convincing
9 *be good friends*
close, dear, intimate, best, loving bosom, true, reliable, faithful

Gods and goddesses include:

GREEK GODS:
Adonis (vegetation and rebirth)
Aeolus (winds)
Apollo (prophecy, music, youth, archery, healing)
Ares (war)
Asclepius (healing)
Atlas (Titan who bears Earth)
Attis (vegetation)
Boreas (north wind)
Cronus (father of Zeus)
Dionysus (wine, vegetation, ecstasy)
Eros (love)
Ganymede (rain)
Hades (underworld)
Helios (sun)
Hephaestus (fire)
Hermes (messenger of the Gods)
Hypnos (sleep)
Morpheus (dreams)
Nereus (sea)
Oceanus (river Oceanus)
Pan (male sexuality, woods, shepherds)
Poseidon (sea)
Thanatos (death)
Zeus (sky, king of the gods)

GREEK GODDESSES:
Alphito (barley, goddess of Argos)
Aphrodite (love, beauty)
Arethusa (springs and fountains)
Artemis (fertility, chastity, hunting)
Athene (prudence and wisdom, protectress of Athens)
Cybele (earth)
Demeter (harvest)
the Fates (destiny)
the Furies (or Erinyes) (vengeance)
Gaia (Earth)
the Graces (charm and beauty)
Hebe (youth)
Hecate (moon)
Hera (marriage and childbirth, queen of the gods)
Hestia (hearth)
the Horae (seasons)
Iris (rainbow)
the Muses (the liberal arts)
Nemesis (destiny, vengeance)
Nike (victory)
Persephone (underworld, corn)
Rhea (mother of Zeus)
Selene (moon)

ROMAN GODS:
Apollo (sun)
Bacchus (wine and ecstasy)
Cupid (love)
Faunus (crops and herbs)
Fides (honesty)
Genius (protector of individuals and the state)

Janus (entrances, travel, dawn)
Jupiter (sky, sun, moon, thunder etc)
Lares (house)
Liber Pater (human and agricultural fertility)
Mars (war)
Mercury (messenger of the gods, god of merchants)
Mithra (sun, regeneration)
Neptune (sea)
Orcus (death)
the Penates (food and drink)
Picus (woods)
Pluto (underworld)
Portunus (husbands)
Saturn (fertility, agriculture)
Silvanus (trees and forests)
Tellus (mother earth)
Vertumnus (fertility)
Vulcan (fire)

ROMAN GODDESSES:
Bellona (war)
Ceres (corn, agriculture)
Diana (fertility, hunting)
Egreria (fountains, childbirth)
Fauna (fertility)
Flora (fruitfulness, flowers)
Fortuna (chance)
Juno (marriage, childbirth, light)
Luna (moon)
Maia (fertility)
Minerva (war, craftsmen, education, arts)
Ops (harvest)
Pales (protectress of flocks)
Pomona (fruits)
Proserpina (underworld)
Rumina (nursing mothers)
Venus (spring, gardens, love)
Vesta (hearth)
Victoria (victory)

EGYPTIAN GODS:
Amun-Ra (universal god)
Anubis (funerals)
Apis (fertility)
Atum (ancestor of the human race)
Geb (the earth)
Horus (sun)
Osiris (vegetation, death)
Ptah (creation, protector of artists and artisans)
Seth (evil)
Thoth (moon, learning, scribe)

EGYPTIAN GODDESSES:
Hathor (love, fertility)
Isis (magic, fertility, mother-goddess)
Maat (order, law, justice)
Nepthys (funerals)
Nut (sky)

NORSE GODS:
Aegir (sea)
the Aesir (race of warlike gods)
Balder (son of Odin, god of light)
Bragi (poetry)

Frey (fertility, sunshine, growth)
Heimdall (sentinel-god of the dawn)
Loki (mischief)
Njord (ships, the sea)
Odin (or Woden or Wotan) (father-god, war, magic, law, poetic inspiration)
Thor (thunder, war)
Tyr (battle, sky)
the Vanir (race of benevolent gods)

NORSE GODDESSES:
Freyja (libido)
Frigg (fertility, wife of Odin)
Hel (underworld)
Nerthus (earth)
the Valkyrie (warrior-women, helpers of gods of war)

HINDU GODS:
Agni (fire)
Brahma (creator, father of gods and men)
Krishna
Ganesh (wisdom, success)
Hanuman (monkey god)
Indra (life, light, fertility, rain)
Rama
Ravana
Savitri (order)
Shiva (destruction, reproduction)
Vishnu (fertility)

HINDU GODDESSES:
Devi
Durga
Kali (death, destruction)
Lakshmi (happiness, beauty, prosperity)
Parvati
Sarasvati (knowledge, education)
Uma

AZTEC GODS:
Huitzilopochtil (war, sun)
Quetzalcoatl (creator, god of wind)
Tezcatlipoca (trickster-god of sun)
Tlaloc (rain, mountains, springs)
Xiuhtecuhtli (fire, light)
Xochipilli (flowers, love, song and dance)

AZTEC GODDESSES:
Chalchiuhtlicue (water)
Coatlicue (earth goddess)
Xochiquetzal (flowers, love, childbirth)

MAYAN GODS:
the Bacabs (wind gods)
Hunab Ku (supreme god and creator)
Itzamna (founder of Mayan culture, god of maize, fertility, moon)
Kukulkan (god of 4 elements, creator)

MAYAN GODDESSES:
Aknah (birth)

Ixazaluoh (water, inventor of weaving)
Ixchel (storm-goddess)

INCA GODS:
Apu Punchau (sun)
Catequil (thunder and lightning)
Inti (sun-god, father of Viracocha)
Manco Capac (sun-god, father of Incans)
Pachacamac (earth-god, creator)
Viracocha (supreme creator)

INCA GODDESSES:
Chasca (Venus, protectress of virgins)
Mama Oella (inventor of spinning)
Mama Quilla (moon-goddess)
Pachamama (earth-goddess)

CELTIC GODS:
Aengus Mac Og (youth, love, beauty)
Balor (death)
Bran the Blessed (prophecy, arts, war)
Cernunnos (fertility, underworld, animals)
the Dagda (earth-god, fertility, prosperity)
Goibniu (smithcraft)
Gwydion (enchantment, illusion)
Gwynn ap Nudd (underworld)
Lir/Llyr (sea, water)
Lug (sun-god, arts, healing, father of Cuchulainn)
Manannan Mac Lir/Manawydan ap Llyr (sea-god, regeneration)
Nuada/Nuadu (harpers, healing, learning, warfare)
Ogma (eloquency, physical strength)
Pryderi (underworld)
Pwyll
Tuatha Dé Danann (magical race)

CELTIC GODDESSES:
Aine (love, fertility)
Badhb (battle, enlightenment)
Boann (water, fertility)
Branwen (love, beauty)
Brigit/Brigid (agriculture, smithcraft, inspiration)
Cliodhna (beauty)
Danu/Don (mother of the gods, rivers, wisdom, magic)
Epona (horses, prosperity)
Eriu
Macha (warrior-goddess, death, cunning)
Morrigan (war-goddess, lust, revenge, magic)
Rhiannon (divine queen, wit)

10 THOROUGH, complete, whole, substantial, considerable, siz(e)able, large

🖃 1 bad, poor **2** incompetent **3** unkind, inconsiderate **4** wicked, immoral **5** inconvenient, useless **6** naughty, disobedient **7** poor **8** bad

◆ *n*

1 VIRTUE, morality, goodness, integrity, honesty, honour, uprightness, righteousness, right, ethics, morals
FORMAL rectitude
2 USE, purpose, avail, advantage, profit, gain, worth, merit, usefulness, service
3 *for your own good*
benefit, welfare, wellbeing interest, sake, behalf, convenience

◆ *interj*

fine, perfect, all right, very well, right, agreed, indeed, just so
COLLOQ. OK

■ **for good**
for ever, always, ever, evermore, for all time, permanently, till the end of time, eternally
COLLOQ. till kingdom come, till the cows come home, until hell freezes over

■ **make good**
1 PUT RIGHT, make amends for, make recompense for, compensate for, make restitution for, repair
2 SUCCEED, get ahead, go far, progress, be successful, get on in the world
COLLOQ. arrive, make it
3 *make good a threat/promise*
fulfil, carry out, do, live up to, put into action
FORMAL effect

> **QUOTATIONS**
> Do all the good you can / By all the means you can /
> In all the ways you can / In all the places you can / To
> all the people you can / As long as ever you can
>   JOHN WESLEY, 'Rules of Conduct'

goodbye *interj, n*

◆ *interj*

farewell, adieu, *au revoir, auf Wiedersehen, ciao, arrivederci, adiós, sayonara*
COLLOQ. cheerio, bye, bye-bye, cheers, see you (later), see you around, be seeing you, all the best, mind how you go, take care, have a nice day, ta-ta, so long; *N Am* later; *Aust* hooray

◆ *n*

farewell, adieu, *au revoir*, leave-taking parting
swan song
FORMAL valediction, valedictory

good-for-nothing *adj, n*

◆ *adj*

lazy, useless, worthless, idle, irresponsible, reprobate, no-good
FORMAL profligate, indolent, feckless
🖃 conscientious, successful

◆ *n*

layabout, ne'er-do-well, reprobate, idler, waster, wastrel, slacker
FORMAL profligate
COLLOQ. black sheep, lazybones, loafer, skiver
SLANG bum; *Aust & NZ* bludger
🖃 achiever, success, winner

good-humoured *adj*

cheerful, happy, jovial, genial, affable, amiable, friendly, congenial, pleasant, good-tempered, approachable
🖃 ill-humoured

good-looking *adj*

attractive, handsome, beautiful, fair, pretty, lovely, personable, presentable
OLD comely
See Synonym nuances panel at **attractive**.
🖃 ugly, plain

goodly *adj*

substantial, siz(e)able, considerable, ample, large, good, significant, sufficient
COLLOQ. tidy
🖃 inadequate

good-natured *adj*

kind, kindly, kind-hearted, sympathetic, benevolent, generous, helpful, neighbourly, gentle, good-tempered, warm-hearted, approachable, friendly, tolerant, patient
🖃 ill-natured

goodness *n*

virtue, uprightness, integrity, righteousness, honesty, kindness, compassion, graciousness, mercy, goodwill, excellence, benefit, benevolence, unselfishness, generosity, altruism, friendliness, helpfulness, wholesomeness
FORMAL rectitude, probity, beneficence
🖃 badness, wickedness, selfishness

goods *n*

1 PROPERTY, chattels, effects, possessions, belongings, paraphernalia, things
COLLOQ. gear, stuff
FORMAL accoutrements, appurtenances
2 MERCHANDISE, wares, commodities, products, things, lines, stock, freight

good-tempered *adj*

kind, kindly, kind-hearted, sympathetic, benevolent, generous, helpful, neighbourly, gentle, good-natured, warm-hearted, approachable, friendly, tolerant, patient

goodwill *n*

benevolence, kindness, compassion, generosity, favour, friendliness, friendship, zeal, well-wishing
OLD (*Spenser*) gree
FORMAL amity
🖃 ill-will

goody-goody *adj*

self-righteous, sanctimonious, pious, priggish
FORMAL unctuous, ultra-virtuous

gooey *adj*

1 STICKY, soft, gluey, glutinous, viscous, tacky, thick, syrupy
FORMAL mucilaginous, viscid
COLLOQ. gungy
2 SENTIMENTAL, slushy, sloppy, syrupy, nauseating maudlin, mawkish, sickly, cloying

gore *v, n*

◆ *v*

pierce, penetrate, stab, spear, stick, impale, wound, horn
OLD (*Spenser*) cloy, engore

◆ *n*

blood, bloodiness, bloodshed, slaughter, butchery, carnage
TECHNICAL cruor, grume

gorge *n, v*

◆ *n*

canyon, ravine, gully, defile, chasm, abyss, crevice, cleft, fissure, rift, gap, pass; *N Am* barranca

◆ *v*

feed, guzzle, gobble, devour, bolt, gulp, swallow, cram, stuff, fill, sate, surfeit, glut, overeat, stodge
COLLOQ. wolf
🖃 fast

gorgeous *adj*

1 MAGNIFICENT, splendid, grand, glorious, superb, fine, impressive, rich, sumptuous, luxurious, brilliant, dazzling marvellous, wonderful, delightful, pleasing lovely, enjoyable, good, showy, glamorous
FORMAL resplendent, opulent
2 ATTRACTIVE, beautiful, pretty, fine, sweet, glamorous, handsome, good-looking lovely
FORMAL pulchritudinous
COLLOQ. sexy, stunning ravishing
🖃 dull, plain

gorgeously *adv*
magnificently, splendidly, gloriously, brilliantly, impressively, superbly, richly, sumptuously, luxuriously, marvellously, wonderfully, delightfully
F3 opulently, resplendently

gory *adj*
bloody, bloodstained, blood-soaked, grisly, brutal, savage, violent, murderous
FORMAL sanguinary

gospel *n*
1 LIFE OF CHRIST, teaching of Christ, message of Christ, good news, New Testament
2 TEACHING, doctrine, creed, credo, certainty, truth, fact
TECHNICAL kerygma
FORMAL evangel, verity

gossamer *adj*
thin, light, delicate, flimsy, fine, cobwebby, insubstantial, sheer, shimmering silky, airy, transparent, see-through, translucent, gauzy
FORMAL diaphanous
F3 heavy, opaque, thick

gossip *n, v*
♦ *n*
1 IDLE TALK, prattle, chitchat, tittle-tattle, tattle, rumour, hearsay, report, whisper, scandal, causerie, bush telegraph, reportage, *chronique scandaleuse*; *Scot* clatters, claver, clash, clish-clash, clishmaclaver, clash-ma-clavers; *Irish* crack
COLLOQ. goss, mud-slinging smear campaign, buzz, dirt
SLANG gup; *N Am* scuttlebutt
2 GOSSIP-MONGER, scandalmonger, whisperer, prattler, babbler, chatterbox, busybody, talebearer, tell-tale, tattler; *Scot* blether, cummer, sweetie-wife; *N Am* tattletale, yenta
OLD aunt
COLLOQ. Nosey Parker
♦ *v*
talk, chat, natter, chatter, schmooze, jabber, gabble, prattle, babble, tattle, tittle, spread gossip, tell tales, whisper, rumour, spread/circulate a rumour, chitchat; *Scot* blether, clash; *dialect & N Am* blather; *Scot & N Am* crack
COLLOQ. rabbit (on), gas, waffle, chinwag jaw, chew the rag/fat

gouge *v*
chisel, cut, hack, incise, score, groove, scratch, claw, gash, slash, dig scoop, hollow, extract

gourmand *n*
glutton, gormandizer
FORMAL omnivore
COLLOQ. gorger, guzzler, hog pig
F3 ascetic

> **!** **gourmand** or **gourmet**?
> A *gourmand* is a glutton; a person who enjoys eating large quantities of food. A *gourmet* is a person who has an expert knowledge of, and a passion for, good food and wine.

gourmet *n*
gastronome, epicure, epicurean, connoisseur, *bon vivant*
COLLOQ. foodie

govern *v*
1 RULE, reign, be in power, hold office, direct, manage, administer, be responsible for, superintend, supervise, oversee, preside, lead, head, be in charge of, command, order, control, influence, guide, conduct, steer, pilot
2 *govern your temper*
dominate, master, control, regulate, curb, check, keep in check, hold/keep back, restrain, contain, quell, constrain, bridle, rein in, subdue, tame, discipline

governess *n*
teacher, guide, instructress, tutoress, tutress, mentor, companion, duenna
OLD gouvernante

governing *adj*
ruling controlling regulatory, commanding reigning guiding leading supreme, uppermost, dominant, overriding predominant, prevailing transcendent
FORMAL dominative

government *n*
1 *blame the government*
administration, executive, ministry, Establishment, authorities, state, régime, congress, parliament, council, cabinet, leadership
COLLOQ. powers that be
2 RULE, sovereignty, sway, direction, management, superintendence, supervision, surveillance, command, charge, authority, power, guidance, conduct, domination, dominion, control, regulation, restraint

> **QUOTATIONS**
> All Governments like to interfere; it elevates their position to make out that they can cure the evils of mankind
> WALTER BAGEHOT, *Economic Studies*

Government systems include:

absolutism	empire	plutocracy
autocracy	federation	puppet govern-
commonwealth	hierocracy	ment
communism	junta	republic
democracy	kingdom	theocracy
despotism	kleptocracy	triumvirate
dictatorship	monarchy	

governor *n*
ruler, commissioner, administrator, executive, chief executive, director, manager, leader, head, chief, president, viceroy, commander, superintendent, supervisor, master, regulator, guide, warden, overseer, controller, corrector, alderman, lieutenant-governor
OLD governess, grieve, gubernator, rector, rectrix, intendant, legate; *(Shakesp)* dominator
COLLOQ. boss
Related adjective: gubernatorial
See panel on next page

gown *n*
robe, dress, frock, dressing-gown, garment, habit, costume, shift
COLLOQ. garb
See panel at **clothes**.

grab *v, n*
♦ *v*
seize, snatch, take, pluck, snap up, catch/take/lay hold of, grasp, clutch, grip, catch, capture, commandeer, usurp, annex
FORMAL appropriate
COLLOQ. nab, bag collar, nail, swipe
♦ *n*
grasp, grip, clutch, snatch, catch, capture
■ **up for grabs**
available, obtainable, at hand
COLLOQ. for the asking to be had

grace *n, v*
♦ *n*
1 GRACEFULNESS, poise, beauty, attractiveness, loveliness, shapeliness, smoothness, elegance, ease, fluency, finesse, tastefulness, good taste, refinement, polish, breeding cultivation, manners, etiquette, decorum, decency, consideration, courtesy, charm
OLD comeliness
FORMAL propriety

Types of governor include:

adelantado (*of a Spanish province*)
alcaide (*of a Spanish fortress*)
castellan (*of a castle*)
eparch (*of a modern Greek province*)
ethnarch (*of an ethnic group*)
hakim (*in Pakistan*)

mudir (*in Turkey and Egypt*)
naik (*in India*)
nomarch (*of a province in modern Greece*)
pentarch (*in a government of five rulers*)
stadtholder (*of a Dutch province*)
tuchun (*Chinese military governor*)

vali (*of a Turkish province*)
HISTORICAL TERMS:
Ban (*of a district on the boundaries of the Hungarian kingdom*)
beglerbeg (*of a Turkish province*)
bey (*Turkish governor*)

burgrave (*of a German town or castle*)
catapan (*of Calabria and Apulia*)
dey (*of Algiers*)
exarch (*Byzantine provincial governor*)
harmost (*Spartan governor of a subject province*)

hospodar (*of Moldavia or Wallachia*)
khan (*in Ancient Persia*)
legate (*of a Papal province*)
nomarch (*of a province in Ancient Egypt*)
podestà (*in Italy*)
proconsul (*in the Roman Empire*)

proveditor (*in the republic of Venice*)
satrap (*in Ancient Persia*)
subahdar (*in the Mogul empire*)
voivode (*in central and eastern Europe*)

---

2 KINDNESS, kindliness, compassion, consideration, goodness, virtue, generosity, charity, benevolence, goodwill, favour, forgiveness, indulgence, mercy, mercifulness, leniency, pardon, reprieve, quarter
FORMAL beneficence, clemency
3 *say grace*
blessing benediction, thanksgiving prayer, prayer of thanks
E3 2 cruelty, harshness
♦ *v*
favour, honour, dignify, distinguish, embellish, enhance, enrich, set off, trim, garnish, decorate, ornament, adorn
E3 spoil, detract from

graceful *adj*
1 FLOWING, easy, fluid, smooth, supple, agile, deft, nimble, natural, slender, fine, tasteful, elegant, beautiful, attractive, appealing charming cultured, refined, polished, cultivated, suave
2 POLITE, kind, courteous, pleasant, agreeable, cheerful, generous, respectful, gracious, tactful, diplomatic
E3 1 graceless, awkward, clumsy, ungainly **2** rude, unpleasant

gracefully *adv*
1 SMOOTHLY, deftly, nimbly, naturally, elegantly, beautifully, attractively, tastefully
2 *with good grace*
politely, courteously, pleasantly, agreeably, cheerfully, generously, respectfully, graciously, tactfully, diplomatically
E3 1 awkwardly **2** rudely, unpleasantly

graceless *adj*
clumsy, awkward, unattractive, forced, gauche, gawky, ungainly, ungraceful, inelegant, rough, rude, vulgar, coarse, crude, uncouth, unsophisticated, impolite, improper, unmannerly, ill-mannered, barbarous, shameless; *Scot* menseless
FORMAL indecorous
E3 graceful, refined

gracelessly *adv*
clumsily, awkwardly, ungracefully, inelegantly, roughly, impolitely, rudely
E3 gracefully

gracious *adj*
1 POLITE, courteous, well-mannered, refined, considerate, sweet, obliging accommodating kind, compassionate, kind-hearted, kindly, friendly, pleasant, benevolent, generous, charitable, hospitable, forgiving indulgent, lenient, mild, clement, merciful, benign;
Scot menseful
OLD hend, handsome
FORMAL beneficent, magnanimous
2 ELEGANT, luxurious, comfortable, tasteful, sumptuous
E3 1 ungracious

graciously *adv*
politely, courteously, civilly, kindly, pleasantly, respectfully, tactfully, diplomatically

gradation *n*
change, progression, degree, grading sorting ordering progress, succession, arrangement, sequence, series, stage, step, level, mark, shading rank
FORMAL array

grade *n, v*
♦ *n*
rank, status, standing station, place, position, level, stage, degree, step, rating rung notch, mark, brand, quality, standard, condition, size, order, group, type, class, category, classification
FORMAL echelon
♦ *v*
sort, arrange, categorize, order, group, class, rate, size, rank, range, classify, evaluate, assess, value, mark, brand, label, pigeonhole, type
■ **make the grade**
succeed, pass, come/win through, reach the expected standard
COLLOQ. come up to scratch

gradient *n*
slope, incline, hill, bank, rise, grade
FORMAL acclivity, declivity

gradual *adj*
slow, leisurely, unhurried, easy, gentle, moderate, regular, even, measured, steady, continuous, progressive, step-by-step
E3 sudden, steep, precipitate

gradually *adv*
little by little, bit by bit, imperceptibly, inch by inch, step by step, successively, continuously, progressively, by degrees, piecemeal, slowly, gently, cautiously, gingerly, moderately, regularly, evenly, steadily, unhurriedly

graduate *v, n*
♦ *v*
1 *graduate from medical school*
pass, qualify, complete studies
2 CALIBRATE, mark off, measure out, proportion, grade, arrange, range, order, rank, sort, group, classify, categorize
3 PROGRESS, move up, move forward, advance, be promoted, make headway, go/forge ahead
♦ *n*
qualified/skilled person, expert, specialist, consultant, professional, bachelor, doctor, master, fellow, member, graduand, alumna, alumnus, valedictorian
COLLOQ. whizz kid

graft¹ *v, n*
♦ *v*
grafted onto a tree
engraft, implant, insert, transplant, join, splice, bud, inoculate

TECHNICAL autograft
OLD graff, imp, inarch
FORMAL affix

♦ *n*

implant, implantation, transplant, growth, splice, bud,
sprout, shoot, scion, take
TECHNICAL allograft, autograft, heterograft, homograft,
xenograft
OLD graff, imp

graft² *n*

1 EFFORT, hard word, toil, labour, exertion
COLLOQ. sweat of your brow, slog
2 BRIBERY, corruption, dishonesty, extortion
COLLOQ. con tricks, shady business, dirty
tricks/dealings, wheeling and dealing sharp
practices, sleaze
SLANG scam, rip-off, sting

grain *n*

1 BIT, piece, fragment, scrap, morsel, crumb,
granule, particle, molecule, atom, jot, iota,
mite, speck, modicum, trace, hint, suggestion, soupçon,
scintilla
2 SEED, kernel, corn, cereals, wheat, rye, barley, oats,
maize
3 TEXTURE, fabric, fibre, weave, pattern,
marking surface, nap

grammar *n*

grammatical rules, linguistic rules, correct English, good
English, style, usage
TECHNICAL syntax, syntactic structure

grammatical *adj*

structural, linguistic, correct, acceptable, well-formed,
well-structured, appropriate
TECHNICAL syntactic, syntactical

grand *adj*

1 MAJESTIC, regal, stately, palatial, splendid, magnificent,
glorious, superb, sublime, exalting fine, excellent,
outstanding first-rate, impressive, imposing striking
monumental, large, luxurious, lavish, sumptuous, noble,
lordly, lofty, pompous, pretentious, grandiose, showy,
ostentatious, ambitious
FORMAL opulent
2 SUPREME, pre-eminent, leading head, chief, main,
principal, arch, highest, senior, great, illustrious
3 *have a grand day out*
excellent, wonderful, splendid, marvellous,
fantastic, superb, enjoyable, delightful, outstanding
first-rate
COLLOQ. great, cool, super, terrific, smashing pretty,
precious
SLANG fab, mega, wicked
4 *a grand total*
complete, final, comprehensive, inclusive,
all-inclusive, in full
E3 1 humble, plain, simple common, poor

SYNONYM NUANCES

sense 1
Majestic, **regal** and **stately** are all suggestive of a
dignified manner or appearance. **Palatial** is generally
used of buildings to suggest being not only luxurious,
but on a grand scale, whereas **splendid** can be used of
anything that merits admiration. The terms **magnificent**,
glorious and **superb** are extremely admiring terms for
something grand, whilst **sublime** would be reserved for
something supreme.
   Exalting is suggestive of lifting your spirits: *this road is*
one of the most exalting in the Pyrenees, while the more
restrained **fine** suggests a high quality, and **excellent**
goes further by suggesting it cannot be improved on.
Likewise, **outstanding** and **first-rate** are
highly approving terms which imply superiority.
Impressive, **imposing** and **striking** all suggest a

commanding appearance: *its striking black and white*
plumage.
   While **large** is a neutral and restrained term
describing size, **monumental** suggests being on a
massive scale. **Luxurious**, **lavish** and
sumptuous are all highly expressive of opulence and
comfort.
   The terms **noble**, **lofty** and **lordly**, on the other hand,
suggest an aristocratic demeanour, although **lofty** and
lordly can have a rather negative connotation of
aloofness. The term **pompous** is more markedly
disapproving and suggests self-importance, whilst
pretentious goes further by suggesting affectation, and
grandiose is generally used nowadays to imply that
something is overblown: *small countries dreaming of a*
grandiose role for themselves. Both **showy** and
ostentatious can also imply an excessive, even gaudy,
display, whilst **ambitious** is more neutral, emphasizing
an aspiration to grandeur.

grandeur *n*

majesty, stateliness, pomp, state, dignity, splendour,
magnificence, impressiveness, luxuriousness, lavishness,
nobility, greatness, illustriousness, importance, fame,
renown, eminence, prominence
FORMAL opulence
E3 humbleness, lowliness, simplicity

QUOTATIONS
From the war of nature, from famine and death, the
most exalted object which we are capable of conceiving
namely, the production of the higher animals, directly
follows. There is grandeur in this view of life
   CHARLES DARWIN, *The Origin of Species by Means of*
   Natural Selection

grandfather *n*

grandparent; *Scot* luckie-dad; *dialect* granfer; *S Afr* oupa
OLD grandsire; *Scot* goodsire, gudesire, gutcher
COLLOQ. grandpa, grandpapa, papa, grand(d)ad,
grand(d)addy; *N Am* gramps

grandiloquent *adj*

exaggerated, pretentious, high-flown, high-sounding
inflated, pompous, bombastic, flowery, rhetorical, fustian,
euphuistic, swollen, turgid
FORMAL grandiloquous, magniloquent, orotund
E3 plain, restrained, simple

grandiose *adj*

pompous, pretentious, high-flown, high-sounding
bombastic, lofty, ambitious, extravagant, ostentatious,
showy, flamboyant, grand, majestic, splendid, striking
stately, magnificent, impressive, imposing monumental
OLD mausolean
FORMAL magniloquent
COLLOQ. over-the-top
E3 unpretentious

grandly *adv*

impressively, magnificently, gloriously, excellently,
strikingly, majestically, regally, pompously, pretentiously

grandmother *n*

grandparent, babushka; *S Afr* ouma
OLD beldam, grandam, grannam; *Scot* good-dame, gude-
dame
COLLOQ. grandma, granny, gran, nanny, nan, nana,
grandmama, grandmamma

PROVERBS
Don't teach your grandmother to suck eggs

grant *v, n*

♦ *v*

1 GIVE, donate, present, award, impart, transmit, dispense,
assign, allot, allocate, provide, supply, contribute
FORMAL confer, bestow, apportion, furnish

2 ADMIT, acknowledge, concede, allow, permit, let, consent to, accept, agree to
FORMAL accede to, vouchsafe
F3 1 withhold **2** deny
♦ *n*
allowance, subsidy, concession, award, bursary, scholarship, gift, donation, endowment, bequest, annuity, pension, honorarium, contribution

granular *adj*
grainy, granulated, gritty, sandy, lumpy, rough, crumbly, friable

granule *n*
piece, particle, grain, scrap, crumb, bead, speck, fragment, iota, jot, atom, molecule, pellet, seed, pearl
TECHNICAL microsome, bioblast, chondrule, plastid

graph *n*
diagram, chart, table, grid, plot, curve, worm, bar graph, bar chart, pie chart, scatter diagram
TECHNICAL nomogram, nomograph

graphic *adj*
1 VIVID, descriptive, expressive, striking telling lively, realistic, explicit, effective, clear, lucid, specific, detailed, well-defined, blow-by-blow
FORMAL cogent
2 VISUAL, pictorial, diagrammatic, symbolic, drawn, illustrative, representational
FORMAL delineative
F3 vague, impressionistic

graphically *adv*
vividly, descriptively, expressively, strikingly, clearly, realistically, explicitly

grapple *v*
1 GRASP, seize, snatch, grab, grip, tackle, clutch, clasp, hold, lay hold of, wrestle, tussle, struggle, contend, battle, fight, combat, clash, engage, close, clinch
OLD craple
2 *grapple with a problem*
face, confront, encounter, tackle, address, deal with, cope with, get to grips with, wrestle, struggle
COLLOQ. take the bull by the horns
F3 1 release **2** avoid, evade

grasp *v, n*
♦ *v*
1 HOLD, clasp, clutch, grip, grapple, seize, snatch, grab, catch, lay hold of, clench
2 *grasp a concept*
understand, follow, comprehend, see, perceive, master, realize, take in, catch on, latch onto
FORMAL apprehend
COLLOQ. get
♦ *n*
1 GRIP, clasp, hold, embrace, clutches, possession, control, power, command, rule, dominion, mastery
2 UNDERSTANDING, comprehension, apprehension, mastery, familiarity, knowledge, awareness, perception

grasping *adj*
greedy, acquisitive, covetous, griping mercenary, mean, selfish, miserly, close-fisted, niggardly, gripple
OLD (*Shakesp*) large-handed
FORMAL avaricious, rapacious, parsimonious
COLLOQ. money-grubbing tight-fisted, stingy; *N Am* grabby
F3 generous

grass *n, v*
♦ *n*
turf, lawn, green, grassland, common, field, meadow, pasture, downs, prairie, pampas, savanna, steppe, veld, veldt
OLD lea, mead, sward
Related adjective: graminaceous
♦ *v*
inform, betray, incriminate, denounce, blab

COLLOQ. tell on, squeal, rat, blow the whistle on, sell down the river, split, snitch, stitch up
SLANG shop; *N Am* stool on; *Aust & NZ* dob in

> **PROVERBS**
> The grass is always greener on the other side of the fence

Types of grass include:

bamboo	Kentucky blue-	rattan
barley	grass	reed
beard grass	knot grass	rice
bent	maize	rye
brome	marijuana	ryegrass
buckwheat	marram grass	sorghum
cane	meadow foxtail	squirrel-tail grass
cocksfoot	meadow grass	sugar cane
corn	melick	switch grass
dog's-tail	millet	timothy grass (or
English ryegrass	moor grass	cat's-tail)
esparto	oats	twitch grass
fescue	paddy	vernal grass
Italian ryegrass	pampas grass	wheat
kangaroo grass	papyrus	wild oat
	quaking grass	

grate *v*
1 GRIND, shred, mince, pulverize, rub, rasp, scrape, scratch
OLD gride
FORMAL triturate
2 SCRATCH, squeak, screech, rasp, creak, grit, bray
3 JAR, set your teeth on edge, annoy, irritate, vex, irk, exasperate, gall, rankle
COLLOQ. aggravate, peeve, get on your nerves, get under your skin, get someone's goat

grateful *adj*
thankful, appreciative, pleased, indebted, obliged, obligated
FORMAL beholden
F3 ungrateful

gratefully *adv*
thankfully, appreciatively, with gratitude, expressing your appreciation

gratification *n*
pleasure, satisfaction, contentment, delight, elation, enjoyment, joy, thrill, relish, indulgence, glee
COLLOQ. kicks
F3 frustration, disappointment

gratify *v*
1 PLEASE, cheer, charm, gladden, delight, thrill, make happy
2 SATISFY, fulfil, indulge, pander to, humour, favour, pamper, spoil, cosset, placate
F3 1 frustrate **2** thwart

grating[1] *adj*
a grating noise
harsh, rasping scraping grinding scratching creaking gritting braying squeaky, screeching strident, discordant, raucous, jarring annoying irritating galling unpleasant, disagreeable, offensive, exasperating irksome
F3 harmonious, pleasing

grating[2] *n*
a grating over a window
grate, grille, grid, lattice, trellis, frame, fire-grate
TECHNICAL graticule, cancelli

gratis *adv*
free, without charge, free of charge, for nothing at no cost, complimentary
COLLOQ. on the house
SLANG buckshee

gratitude *n*
gratefulness, thankfulness, thanks, appreciation, acknowledgement, recognition, indebtedness, obligation
⊟ ingratitude, ungratefulness

gratuitous *adj*
1 WANTON, unnecessary, needless, superfluous, unwarranted, unjustified, groundless, unfounded, undeserved, unprovoked, uncalled-for, unasked-for, unmerited, unsolicited, without reason
2 VOLUNTARY, free, free of charge, gratis, for nothing complimentary, unrewarded, unpaid
⊟ 1 justified, provoked

gratuitously *adv*
needlessly, unnecessarily, unjustifiably, undeservedly
⊟ justifiably

gratuity *n*
tip, bonus, gift, present, donation, reward, recompense, bounty, boon, largesse, baksheesh, pourboire, donative, drink-money, lagniappe; *Scot* mags; dash, cumshaw; *S Afr* bonsella
OLD glove-money, primage; (*Shakesp*) gratillity
FORMAL perquisite
COLLOQ. perk, beer-money

grave¹ *n*
1 *buried in a grave*
burial place, tomb, vault, crypt, last resting-place, sepulchre, mausoleum, pit, burial mound, burial site, barrow, tumulus, cairn, dust, long home, moulds; *Scot* mouls
OLD graff
2 DEATH, loss of life, loss, departure, fatality, passing passing away
FORMAL expiration, decease, demise
COLLOQ. last farewell, curtains

grave² *adj*
1 SOLEMN, dignified, sober, sedate, serious, earnest, sombre, severe, thoughtful, pensive, grim, gloomy, austere, long-faced, quiet, reserved, subdued, restrained, staid, saturnine, heavy, matronal, high
OLD sad
2 *a grave mistake*
important, significant, weighty, momentous, serious, critical, vital, crucial, urgent, pressing acute, severe, menacing threatening dangerous, hazardous
FORMAL exigent, perilous
⊟ 1 cheerful, smiling **2** trivial, light, slight

gravel *n*
shingle, grit, pebbles, stones, chesil, hogging
OLD grail

gravelly *adj*
1 GRAINY, granular, pebbly, shingly, gritty
OLD glareous
FORMAL sabulose, sabulous
2 *a gravelly voice*
harsh, rough, thick, hoarse, guttural, throaty, grating gruff
⊟ 2 clear, fine

gravely *adv*
1 *he shook his head gravely*
solemnly, seriously, earnestly, thoughtfully, pensively, quietly, gloomily
2 *gravely ill*
critically, importantly, significantly, seriously, crucially, dangerously, urgently, acutely, severely

gravestone *n*
tombstone, headstone, stone, memorial

graveyard *n*
cemetery, burial ground, burial place, burial site, churchyard, necropolis, charnel house, God's acre

gravitas *n*
seriousness, gravity, solemnity, earnestness
⊟ light-heartedness

gravitate *v*
fall, descend, drop, head for, move, precipitate, sink, incline, lean, tend, drift, be attached to, be drawn to, settle

gravity *n*
1 IMPORTANCE, significance, seriousness, weightiness, momentousness, consequence, urgency, acuteness, severity, danger, hazard
OLD state
FORMAL exigency, peril
2 SOLEMNITY, dignity, seriousness, earnestness, severity, thoughtfulness, sombreness, grimness, gloominess, reserve, restraint
FORMAL sobriety
3 GRAVITATION, attraction, pull, weight, heaviness
⊟ 1 triviality **2** levity

graze¹ *v*
the cattle are grazing
crop, feed, fodder, pasture, browse
OLD gride
FORMAL ruminate

graze² *v, n*
♦ *v*
1 SCRATCH, scrape, skin, bruise, rub, chafe
FORMAL abrade
2 BRUSH, skim, touch, kiss, shave, glance off
♦ *n*
scratch, scrape, abrasion

grease *n*
oil, lubrication, fat, lard, dripping tallow; *Scot* creesh
OLD (*Shakesp*) seam

greasy *adj*
oily, fatty, lardy, buttery, smeary, slimy, slippery, smooth, waxy
FORMAL oleaginous, oleic, adipose, sebaceous, unctuous

great *adj*
1 LARGE, big siz(e)able, huge, enormous, massive, colossal, gigantic, mammoth, immense, vast, extensive, boundless, spacious, impressive
COLLOQ. great big whopping jumbo, ginormous, humongous
SLANG mega
2 *with great care*
considerable, pronounced, substantial, extreme, excessive, inordinate
3 FAMOUS, renowned, celebrated, famed, illustrious, eminent, distinguished, prominent, successful, noteworthy, notable, noted, remarkable, outstanding
FORMAL august
4 FINE, grand, glorious, impressive, imposing magnificent, splendid
5 IMPORTANT, significant, serious, major, crucial, critical, principal, primary, main, chief, leading powerful, essential, momentous, vital, paramount, salient
6 EXCELLENT, first-rate, superb, wonderful, marvellous, admirable, splendid, tremendous, fantastic, fabulous
COLLOQ. super, terrific, smashing ace, top-notch, brilliant, brill, cracking
SLANG cool, mega, wicked, awesome, cushty
7 *feel great*
healthy, well, fit, energetic, lively, enthusiastic, eager
8 EXPERT, proficient, adept, skilled, skilful, knowledgeable, experienced, able, practised, professional, accomplished, masterly, excellent, brilliant, specialist, qualified, virtuoso, dexterous
COLLOQ. top-notch, up on, well up on, crack, ace
⊟ 1 small, limited **2** slight **3** unknown **5** unimportant, insignificant **6** poor, mediocre, second-rate; *colloq.* rubbish **7** ill **8** amateurish, novice

PROVERBS
Great oaks from little acorns grow

greatly adv
much, very much, considerably, enormously, highly, extremely, immensely, vastly, noticeably, significantly, remarkably, impressively, notably, substantially, markedly, mightily, tremendously, hugely, powerfully, exceedingly, abundantly, sorely
SLANG majorly

greatness n
fame, renown, illustriousness, eminence, heroism, distinction, note, significance, importance, weight, momentousness, seriousness, power, success, successfulness, magnitude, intensity, excellence, glory, genius, grandeur
E3 insignificance, pettiness, smallness

greed n
1 HUNGER, ravenousness, gluttony, gourmandism, insatiability
OLD (*Spenser*) gourmandise
FORMAL voracity, edacity, esurience
COLLOQ. piggishness, hoggishness, bingeing stuffing yourself
2 ACQUISITIVENESS, covetousness, desire, craving longing eagerness, impatience, selfishness, itching palm
FORMAL avidity, avarice, rapacity, cupidity, pleonexia
E3 1 abstemiousness, self-restraint

> **QUOTATIONS**
> Greed begins where poverty ends
> HONORÉ DE BALZAC, *Illusions perdues*, 'Les deux poètes'
> The world has enough for everyone's need, but not enough for everyone's greed
> MAHATMA GANDHI

greedily adv
ravenously, eagerly, impatiently, selfishly
FORMAL avidly, avariciously, rapaciously, esuriently

greedy adj
1 HUNGRY, starving ravenous, gluttonous, gormandizing insatiable, open-mouthed
FORMAL voracious, edacious, esurient, omnivorous
COLLOQ. hoggish, piggish
2 ACQUISITIVE, covetous, desirous, craving grabbing eager, impatient, grasping selfish, having gripple; *Scot* gare
FORMAL avid, avaricious, rapacious, cupidinous, pleonectic
COLLOQ. on the make, money-grubbing; *N Am* grabby
E3 1 abstemious **2** generous, benevolent

green adj, n
♦ adj
1 EMERALD, jade, pine, vert, olive, avocado, sage, pea-green, apple-green, lime, chartreuse, eau de nil, aquamarine, sea-green
OLD virent
FORMAL virid, virescent, viridescent, glaucous
2 GRASSY, leafy, unripe, lush, unseasoned, tender, raw, fresh, budding blooming flourishing healthy, vigorous
OLD virent
FORMAL verdant, virescent, verdurous
3 ECOLOGICAL, environmental, conservationist, eco-friendly, environmentally aware, environmentally safe, environmentally friendly, organic, sustainable, renewable, biodegradable, preservationist
4 IMMATURE, naive, simple, unsophisticated, ignorant, unqualified, inexperienced, untrained, inexpert, unversed, raw, new, recent, young
COLLOQ. wet behind the ears
5 *green with envy*
envious, covetous, jealous, grudging resentful
E3 4 mature, experienced, qualified, expert
♦ n
common, lawn, grass, turf, field, grassland, meadow, pasture
OLD sward, lea

greenery n
foliage, vegetation, greenness
FORMAL verdure, verdancy, viridity, viridescence, virescence

greenhorn n
novice, apprentice, beginner, learner, initiate, recruit, neophyte, tenderfoot, tiro, newcomer, newbie, fledgling
COLLOQ. rookie
E3 veteran; *colloq.* old hand

greenhouse n
glasshouse, hothouse, conservatory, pavilion, vinery, orangery

greet v
salute, acknowledge, hail, address, say hello to, shake hands with, kiss, wave to, nod to, accost, meet, receive, welcome, bow, doff/tip your hat, pay your compliments, shake hands, pass the time of day, remember, bid; *dialect* pass the seel of the day; *S Afr* wish
OLD congreet, halse; (*Shakesp*) regreet
COLLOQ. give someone five
E3 ignore

greeting n
salutation, acknowledgement, wave, hallo, nod, handshake, the time of day, seasonal greeting address, reception, welcome, kiss, accost, hail; *N Am* glad hand
COLLOQ. *N Am* high five

greetings n
regards, kind/warm regards, respects, compliments, best wishes, good wishes, congratulations, love, salutations, remembrances, salaams, salve
OLD (*Shakesp*) regreet(s)

gregarious adj
sociable, outgoing extrovert, friendly, affable, social, companionable, convivial, cordial, warm, hospitable
E3 unsociable

grey adj
1 *a grey colour*
neutral, colourless, pale, pallid, ashen, wan, leaden
2 *a grey morning*
dull, cloudy, overcast, dim, dark, dismal, dreary, bleak, cheerless, foggy, misty, murky
3 GLOOMY, dismal, cheerless, depressing dreary, bleak, dull, uninteresting colourless
4 *a grey area*
unclear, uncertain, doubtful, ambiguous, debatable, open to question

grid n
grating frame, grille, grill, gridiron, lattice, trellis
TECHNICAL graticule

grief n
sorrow, sadness, unhappiness, depression, dejection, desolation, despondency, despair, distress, misery, woe, heartbreak, mourning, bereavement, heartache, anguish, agony, pain, suffering, dolour, trouble, regret, remorse
OLD bemoaning, dolorousness
FORMAL affliction, lamentation, tribulation
E3 happiness, delight
■ **come to grief**
go wrong, be unsuccessful, break down, collapse, fall through, fall down, founder, come to nothing
COLLOQ. flop, fold, not come off, fall flat, bite the dust, crash and burn, come a cropper, come unstuck, come unglued; *N Am* bomb

grief-stricken adj
sorrowful, sad, unhappy, sorrowing grieving mourning depressed, dejected, desolate, despondent, distressed, despairing broken, broken-hearted, heartbroken, inconsolable, overcome, overwhelmed, devastated, crushed, anguished, troubled, wretched
FORMAL disconsolate, woebegone, afflicted
E3 overjoyed, delighted

grievance *n*
complaint, resentment, objection, protest, charge, wrong injustice, unfairness, offence, injury, damage, trouble, hardship, trial
FORMAL affliction, tribulation
COLLOQ. moan, grumble, grouse, gripe, bone to pick

grieve *v*
1 SORROW, lament, mourn, wail, cry, weep, sob, mope, brood, pine away, ache, suffer, condole; *dialect* hone
OLD rue, vex, bemoan; (*Spenser*) engrieve, wayment
2 SADDEN, upset, dismay, distress, afflict, pain, hurt, wound, crush, horrify, offend, shock, break someone's heart
E3 **1** rejoice **2** please, gladden

grievous *adj*
1 SEVERE, grave, tragic, appalling distressing dreadful, atrocious, burdensome, calamitous, devastating damaging shameful, harmful, outrageous, overwhelming shocking deplorable, intolerable, unbearable, monstrous, flagrant, glaring
OLD doloriferous, dolorific
FORMAL sorrowful
2 WOUNDING, injurious, hurtful, painful, damaging sore
OLD dolorous
FORMAL afflicting

grievously *adv*
severely, tragically, dreadfully, appallingly, outrageously, shockingly, unbearably, intolerably
OLD dolorously

grill *n, v*
♦ *n*
grille, gridiron, grid, grating barbecue, lattice, frame
OLD wicket
♦ *v*
cook, heat, roast, flame-grill, toast; *N Am* broil

grim *adj*
1 STERN, severe, harsh, dour, forbidding formidable, fierce, menacing threatening surly, sullen, morose, gloomy, depressing unattractive
2 UNPLEASANT, horrible, horrid, horrendous, dire, ghastly, gruesome, grisly, sinister, dreadful, awful, frightening fearsome, terrible, shocking appalling harrowing unspeakable
3 RESOLUTE, determined, dogged, tenacious, persistent, stubborn, inexorable, unyielding unshak(e)able
FORMAL obdurate
E3 **1** attractive **2** pleasant

grimace *n, v*
♦ *n*
frown, scowl, moue, pout, smirk, sneer, face
♦ *v*
pull a face, make a face, frown, scowl, mow, pout, smirk, mouth, sneer

grime *n*
dirt, muck, filth, soot, dust, mud
COLLOQ. gunge, yuck, grot
SLANG crud, grunge

grimly *adv*
sternly, harshly, fiercely, sullenly, morosely, gloomily

grimy *adj*
dirty, mucky, grubby, soiled, stained, filthy, sooty, smutty, dusty, muddy, smudgy
FORMAL besmirched
E3 clean

grin *v, n*
smile, beam, smirk, leer, sneer, laugh, chuckle, giggle, snigger, titter

grind *v, n*
♦ *v*
1 CRUSH, pound, pulverize, crumble, powder, chew, crunch, grit, mill, granulate, grate, scrape, gnash, bray, meal, pug slime, stamp

TECHNICAL kibble, levigate, comminute, triturate
FORMAL masticate
COLLOQ. graunch
2 SHARPEN, whet, smooth, polish, sand, file, rub, abrade
TECHNICAL chamfer
3 GRATE, scrape, rub, rasp, grit
♦ *n*
drudgery, chore, toil, labour, round, routine, exertion, task, slavery, sweat

■ **grind down**
wear down, oppress, crush, trouble, persecute, plague, torment, harass, harry, hound, tyrannize
FORMAL afflict

grip *n, v*
♦ *n*
1 HOLD, grasp, clasp, clutch, embrace, clench, hug
2 CONTROL, power, command, influence, mastery, domination, clutches
3 BAG, case, holdall, kitbag shoulder bag valise, suitcase, overnight bag travelling bag
♦ *v*
1 HOLD, grasp, clasp, get/catch/grab hold of, clutch, clench, latch onto, cling seize, grab, catch
2 FASCINATE, thrill, enthral, spellbind, mesmerize, hypnotize, entrance, rivet, engross, absorb, involve, engage, compel

■ **come/get to grips with**
deal with, tackle, cope with, take care of, look after, encounter, confront, handle, face up to, take on, grasp

gripe *v, n*
♦ *v*
complain, grumble, protest, moan, nag groan
COLLOQ. beef, bellyache, carp, grouch, grouse, whine, whinge, have a bone to pick
SLANG bitch
♦ *n*
complaint, groan, grumble, moan, objection, protest, grievance
COLLOQ. beef, grouch, grouse, griping whinge
SLANG bitch

gripping *adj*
fascinating thrilling enthralling compelling enchanting compulsive, exciting suspenseful, spellbinding entrancing riveting engrossing absorbing
COLLOQ. unputdownable

grisly *adj*
gruesome, gory, grim, macabre, horrid, horrible, horrifying ghastly, awful, frightful, terrible, dreadful, repulsive, revolting disgusting hideous, loathsome, abhorrent, abominable, appalling shocking
E3 delightful

gristly *adj*
hard, tough, rubbery, leathery, sinewy, stringy, fibrous
FORMAL cartilaginous

grit *n, v*
♦ *n*
1 GRAVEL, pebbles, shingle, sand, dust, swarf
Related adjectives: sabulous, sabulose
2 DETERMINATION, courage, bravery, strength, resolve, resolution, hardness, toughness, mettle, endurance, perseverance, doggedness, steadfastness, tenacity
COLLOQ. backbone, guts
♦ *v*
clench, gnash, grate, rasp, scrape, grind

gritty *adj*
1 GRAINY, dusty, gravelly, sandy, shingly, pebbly, powdery, granular, rough, abrasive
FORMAL sabulous, sabulose
2 DETERMINED, courageous, brave, resolute, hardy, tough, mettlesome, dogged, tenacious, steadfast, spirited, plucky
COLLOQ. spunky, feisty, gutsy
E3 **1** fine, smooth **2** cowardly; *colloq.* spineless

grizzle v
cry, whimper, whine, whinge, sniffle, snivel, snuffle, fret, moan, complain, grumble

grizzled adj
grey, grey-haired, grey-headed, greying hoary, hoar, pepper-and-salt
TECHNICAL griseous
FORMAL canescent

groan n, v
♦ n
1 MOAN, sigh, cry, whine, whimper, wail, lament
2 COMPLAINT, grumble, objection, protest, outcry, grievance, moan
COLLOQ. beef, grouch, grouse, griping
♦ v
1 MOAN, sigh, cry, whine, whimper, wail, lament
2 COMPLAIN, grumble, object, protest
COLLOQ. whine, whinge, beef, bellyache, grouse

grocer n
dealer, storekeeper, supplier, supermarket, greengrocer
FORMAL purveyor, victualler

groggy adj
weak, dopey, unsteady, wobbly, shaky, staggering stunned, dazed, confused, befuddled, bewildered, stupefied, punch-drunk, dizzy, faint, reeling
COLLOQ. muzzy, woozy
E∃ healthy, strong lucid

groin n
crotch, crutch, genitals; dialect lisk
Related adjective: inguinal

groom v, n
♦ v
1 SMARTEN, neaten, tidy (up), spruce up, prepare, put in order, arrange, adjust, fix, do, smooth
2 CLEAN, brush, comb, curry, preen, dress
3 groomed for her new post
prepare, make ready, train, school, teach, educate, instruct, tutor, drill, coach, prime
♦ n
1 BRIDEGROOM, honeymooner, newly-wed, husband, husband-to-be, spouse, marriage partner
2 STABLEBOY, stableman, stable lad/lass, stable hand

groove n
furrow, rut, track, slot, channel, canal, chamfer, gutter, trough, ditch, trench, hollow, gouge, indentation, cut, score, ridge, fissure, slide, throat, chase, race, riffle, rigol; Scot raggle
TECHNICAL rabbet, rebate, sulcus, cannelure, croze, cullis, diglyph, flute, quirk, fossula, kerf, key-seat, mark, oche, pod, scrobe, sipe, vallecula
Related adjective: sulcal

grooved adj
channelled, fluted, furrowed, rutted, scored, chamfered
TECHNICAL rabbeted, scrobiculate
FORMAL sulcal, sulcate, exarate
E∃ ridged

grope v
1 FUMBLE, feel, scrabble, flounder, pick
2 SEARCH, hunt, scrabble, fish, probe, cast about
3 FONDLE, touch, molest, abuse, abuse sexually, interfere with
COLLOQ. touch up, feel up

gross adj, v
♦ adj
1 gross misconduct
serious, grievous, blatant, flagrant, glaring obvious, manifest, plain, sheer, utter, outright, shameful, shocking outrageous
FORMAL egregious
2 OBSCENE, lewd, improper, dirty, filthy, risqué, pornographic, indecent, offensive, rude, coarse, crude, vulgar, ribald, bawdy, smutty, salacious, earthy, tasteless
COLLOQ. blue

3 FAT, obese, overweight, big large, huge, colossal, immense, massive, hulking bulky, heavy
FORMAL corpulent
4 gross earnings
inclusive, all-inclusive, total, entire, complete, comprehensive, whole, before deductions, before tax
FORMAL aggregate
5 TASTELESS, vulgar, unpleasant, uncultured, unsophisticated, unrefined, insensitive, coarse, boorish
6 DISGUSTING, repulsive, revolting repugnant, offensive, sickening nauseating nauseous, off-putting odious, foul, unappetizing unpalatable, distasteful, unpleasant, disgraceful, nasty
COLLOQ. yucky
E∃ 2 polite **3** slight **4** net **5** tasteful **6** delightful
♦ v
earn, make, take, bring in, accumulate, total
FORMAL aggregate
COLLOQ. pull in, rake in

grossly adv
extremely, exceedingly, excessively, very, really, exceptionally, extraordinarily, intensely, thoroughly, remarkably, utterly, greatly, highly, unusually, unreasonably, immoderately, uncommonly, inordinately, acutely, severely, decidedly
COLLOQ. awfully, terribly, dreadfully, frightfully, terrifically

grotesque adj
bizarre, odd, weird, strange, peculiar, unnatural, freakish, monstrous, hideous, ugly, unsightly, misshapen, deformed, malformed, distorted, twisted, fantastic, fanciful, whimsical, extravagant, ridiculous, ludicrous, absurd, outlandish, surreal, macabre
E∃ normal, graceful

grotesquely adv
bizarrely, strangely, unnaturally, hideously, unpleasantly, outlandishly

grotto n
cave, cavern, chamber, catacomb, underground chamber, subterrane

grotty adj
1 a grotty little flat
seedy, shabby, dirty, untidy, scruffy, tatty, mangy, squalid, run-down, dilapidated, decaying
COLLOQ. crummy, sleazy
2 feel grotty
ill, sick, poorly, unwell, ailing off-colour
COLLOQ. groggy, rough, under the weather, out of sorts
E∃ 2 well

grouch n
1 COMPLAINER, grumbler, moaner, fault-finder, murmurer, mutterer, grouser, kvetch, kvetcher
FORMAL malcontent
COLLOQ. grump, bellyacher, crosspatch, whiner, whinger, sourpuss, griper
2 COMPLAINT, grievance, grumble, objection, moan
COLLOQ. gripe, grouse, whinge

grouchy adj
bad-tempered, irritable, cross, dissatisfied, discontented, grumpy, sulky, surly, complaining grumbling testy, ill-tempered, irascible, captious, churlish, peevish, petulant
FORMAL cantankerous, querulous, truculent
COLLOQ. crotchety
E∃ contented

ground n, v
♦ n
1 EARTH, soil, clay, loam, dirt, dust, dry land, terra firma, land, terrain, bottom, foundation, surface
2 a football ground
field, pitch, stadium, arena, park
3 the palace grounds
estate, property, territory, domain, gardens, lawns, park, campus, surroundings, fields, acres, land, terrain, holding plot

4 *no grounds for such harsh treatment*
base, foundation, justification, excuse, vindication, reason, motive, inducement, cause, occasion, call, score, account, argument, principle, basis
5 *coffee grounds*
dregs, sediment, deposit, residue, lees, scourings
TECHNICAL precipitate
♦ *v*
1 BASE, found, establish, set, fix, settle
2 PREPARE, introduce, initiate, familiarize with, acquaint with, inform, instruct, teach, educate, train, drill, coach, tutor

groundless *adj*
baseless, unfounded, unsubstantiated, unsupported, empty, imaginary, false, illusory, unjustified, unwarranted, unprovoked, uncalled-for, without reason
₣₃ well-founded, reasonable, justified

groundwork *n*
basis, base, essentials, foundation, fundamentals, preparation, preliminaries, research, homework, cornerstone, footing spadework, underpinnings

group *n, v*
♦ *n*
band, gang pack, team, crew, troop, squad, detachment, unit, party, faction, set, circle, clique, sect, coterie, cohort, contingent, club, society, association, guild, league, organization, company, gathering congregation, body, assembly, trio, sextet, nonet, crowd, flock, collection, bunch, clump, cluster, knot, batch, lot, combination, element, bracket, formation, grouping class, category, classification, genus, species, family, school
FORMAL conglomeration
♦ *v*
1 GATHER, collect, assemble, congregate, unite, mass, cluster, clump, bunch, huddle
2 *group them according to size*
sort, range, arrange, marshal, line up, organize, order, rank, grade, class, classify, categorize, band, bracket, link, associate

---

SYNONYM NUANCES

noun

The terms **band**, **gang** and **pack** suggest an informal group and can have connotations of lawless intent: *a band of outlaws*. **Team** and **crew** are associated more with official or organized groups with a specific role or task: *the crew manning the ship*. **Team** in particular would be used for a competing group, and can have connotations of co-operation and camaraderie: *for this game, divide into two teams*. **Squad**, **detachment** and **unit** are similar, but tend to be associated more with the armed services, and the term **contingent**, while formerly applied to armed forces, now tends to be used more loosely where a group is taken to represent something: *the British contingent at this year's Games*.

Party is appropriate to refer to a group who have gathered to take part in a particular activity: *a tour party; the shooting party*, and, of course, an organized political group. **Faction** would also be used in a political context, but to refer specifically to a group within a larger party, particularly a group which is potentially troublesome or divisive.

The words **set** and **circle** are appropriate to refer to a social group that is not official but widely recognized, and **set** in particular can have connotations of glamour or fashionability: *the modern art set*. **Cohort**, **clique** and **coterie** are similar in meaning but suggest a much smaller group, and while **clique** has negative overtones of insularity, **coterie** has further, and again negative, connotations of pandering to someone: *the president had a coterie of aides and sycophants*.

Club, **society**, **association**, **guild** and **league** would refer to an organized group of individuals who have come together voluntarily to practise or promote something; **body**, **organization** and **company** are

similar, but more likely to be used in a business or administrative context. On the other hand, **gathering**, **congregation**, and **assembly** suggest a group of people who have gathered for a particular purpose on a specific occasion: *she addressed a gathering of civil servants*, while **crowd** or **flock**, although suggesting large numbers, move the emphasis away from the idea of a group as individuals: *the crowd was thickening and filling the square*.

A smaller group of people or things that are so close together that the identities or natures of the individuals are unimportant or indistinguishable, could be referred to as a **bunch**, **clump**, **cluster** or **knot**: *a clump of spectators; there was a knot of people around the prostrate body*. The term **collection**, on the other hand, reinforces the idea of individual items making up the whole: *a motley collection of characters*.

---

grouse *v, n*
♦ *v*
complain, grumble, moan, find fault
COLLOQ. beef, bellyache, carp, grouch, gripe, whine, whinge
SLANG bitch
₣₃ acquiesce
♦ *n*
complaint, groan, grumble, moan, objection, protest, grievance
COLLOQ. bellyache, gripe, grouch, whine, whinge

grove *n*
wood, woodland, thicket, spinney, coppice, copse, plantation, covert, arbour, avenue
Related adjective: nemoral

grovel *v*
1 INGRATIATE YOURSELF, crawl, creep, toady, flatter, fawn, cringe, cower, kowtow, defer, demean yourself
COLLOQ. butter someone up, suck up, bow and scrape, lick someone's boots, eat humble pie, kiss up to
SLANG cheese; (*vulgar*) kiss someone's arse
2 CRAWL, creep, kneel, crouch, stoop, lie low, prostrate yourself, lie down, bow down, cower, fall on your knees

grow *v*
1 BECOME LARGER, become/get taller, become/get bigger, increase in size/height, extend, develop, expand, enlarge, lengthen, elongate, widen, broaden, thicken, deepen, swell, fill out
2 GERMINATE, shoot, sprout, spring bud, flower, mature, develop
FORMAL burgeon
3 INCREASE, rise, expand, enlarge, swell, spread, extend, stretch, develop, multiply, escalate, mushroom, wax
FORMAL proliferate
4 *grow cold*
become, get, go, turn, come to be, change, develop
5 PROGRESS, thrive, flourish, prosper, succeed, improve, advance, make headway
6 ORIGINATE, arise, issue, stem, spring
7 CULTIVATE, farm, produce, propagate, breed, raise, sow, plant, harvest
₣₃ **1** shrink **3** decrease **5** fail

growl *v*
snarl, snap, yap, bark, howl, yelp, grumble, rumble, roar, gnar; *Scot* gurl
OLD groin; (*Spenser*) royne

grown-up *adj, n*
♦ *adj*
adult, mature, of age, full-grown, fully-grown, fully-developed, fully-fledged
₣₃ young immature
♦ *n*
adult, man, woman
₣₃ child

growth *n*
1 INCREASE, rise, extension, enlargement, expansion, spread, multiplication, magnification, amplification, deepening development, evolution, progress, advance, improvement, success, headway, prosperity
FORMAL proliferation, augmentation, aggrandizement
2 GERMINATION, shooting sprouting springing budding flowering development
FORMAL maturation, burgeoning
3 TUMOUR, lump, swelling protuberance, outgrowth
TECHNICAL intumescence, excrescence
1 decrease, decline, failure

> **QUOTATIONS**
> All growth is a leap in the dark, a spontaneous unpremeditated act without benefit of experience
> HENRY MILLER, *The Wisdom of the Heart,* 'The Absolute Collection'

grub *v, n*
♦ *v*
dig burrow, delve, excavate, probe, root, rummage, forage, ferret, hunt, search, scour, unearth, uncover, explore
♦ *n*
1 LARVA, maggot, worm, pupa, caterpillar, chrysalis
2 FOOD, provision, meals, refreshment(s), sustenance, nutrition
COLLOQ. eats, tuck
SLANG nosh; *Aust & NZ* tucker

grubby *adj*
dirty, soiled, unwashed, mucky, grimy, filthy, squalid, seedy, messy, scruffy, shabby
3 clean

grudge *n, v*
♦ *n*
resentment, bitterness, envy, jealousy, pique, spite, malice, enmity, antagonism, hate, hatred, venom, dislike, animosity, antipathy, aversion, ill-will, hard feelings, grievance
FORMAL malevolence, rancour, animus
3 favour
♦ *v*
begrudge, resent, envy, covet, be jealous of, dislike, take exception to, object to, mind, feel aggrieved about

grudging *adj*
reluctant, unwilling hesitant, half-hearted, unenthusiastic, resentful, envious, jealous

gruelling *adj*
hard, difficult, taxing demanding tiring exhausting laborious, arduous, strenuous, trying backbreaking draining crushing grinding harsh, severe, tough, punishing
3 easy

gruesome *adj*
horrible, disgusting repellent, repugnant, repulsive, revolting sickening hideous, grisly, macabre, grim, ghastly, awful, terrible, horrific, horrid, frightful, dreadful, appalling shocking monstrous, abhorrent, abominable, loathsome
3 pleasant

gruesomely *adv*
horribly, repulsively, hideously, grimly, terribly, frightfully, dreadfully, monstrously
3 pleasantly

gruff *adj*
1 CURT, brusque, abrupt, blunt, rude, surly, sour, sullen, grumpy, bad-tempered, churlish, testy, tetchy, impolite, unfriendly, discourteous
COLLOQ. crotchety, crabbed
2 *a gruff voice*
rough, harsh, rasping guttural, throaty, husky, hoarse, croaking thick
3 1 friendly, courteous, polite

gruffly *adv*
1 BRUSQUELY, rudely, impolitely, curtly, abruptly, discourteously
2 ROUGHLY, harshly, hoarsely, huskily, gutturally

grumble *v, n*
♦ *v*
1 COMPLAIN, moan, object, protest, bleat, find fault
OLD groin
COLLOQ. bellyache, beef, grouch, gripe, whine, whinge, carp
2 RUMBLE, murmur, gurgle, growl
♦ *n*
1 COMPLAINT, moan, grievance, objection, protest
COLLOQ. beef, gripe, grouch, grouse, whinge, bleat
SLANG bitch
2 RUMBLE, murmur, muttering gurgle, growl, roar

grumbler *n*
complainer, moaner, niggler, fault-finder
COLLOQ. bellyacher, grouser, fusspot, nit-picker, whiner, whinger; *N Am* fussbudget

grumpily *adv*
churlishly, crossly, sullenly, sulkily
COLLOQ. grouchily, in a huff, in a sulk, having got out of bed on the wrong side

grumpy *adj*
bad-tempered, ill-tempered, churlish, cross, irritable, surly, sullen, sulky, tetchy, snappy, petulant, discontented, grumpish
FORMAL cantankerous
COLLOQ. crotchety, crabbed, grouchy, ratty, in a huff, in a sulk, having got out of bed on the wrong side; *dialect* mardy
3 contented

grunt *v*
snort, croak, snore, cough, grate, rasp
OLD groin

guarantee *n, v*
♦ *n*
warranty, warrant, guaranty, insurance, assurance, promise, word of honour, pledge, oath, bond, covenant, contract, security, collateral, surety, endorsement, testimonial, token
TECHNICAL *appellation contrôlée*
OLD *Scot* warrandice
FORMAL earnest
♦ *v*
assure, give an assurance, promise, pledge, swear, vouch for, answer for, warrant, certify, underwrite, provide security/collateral/surety for, endorse, support, back, sponsor, secure, protect, insure, ensure, make sure, make certain
OLD vouchsafe, avouch, gage, stipulate

guarantor *n*
underwriter, guarantee, sponsor, supporter, backer, surety, warrantor, referee, voucher, bondsman, bailsman, covenantor
COLLOQ. angel

guard *v, n*
♦ *v*
protect, safeguard, save, preserve, shield, secure, screen, shelter, cover, defend, patrol, police, escort, supervise, oversee, watch, keep, keep watch, be alert, look out, take care, mind, beware, sentinel, fence, hedge, preserve; *Scot* wear, weir
OLD ward, warden; (*Shakesp*) enguard, fortress; (*Spenser*) savegard
See Synonym nuances panel at **defend.**
♦ *n*
1 PROTECTOR, defender, custodian, warder, wardress, escort, bodyguard, keeper, captor, conductor, watch, scout, watchman, lookout, sentry, sentinel, picket, patrol, security, guardian, garda

OLD bostangi
SLANG minder
2 PROTECTION, safeguard, defence, wall, barrier, fence, screen, shield, bumper, fender, buffer, pad, cushion, rail, splasher
3 SURVEILLANCE, watch, lookout, observation, inspection, superintendence, supervision, vigilance, stewardship, guardianship, monitoring scrutiny, check, care, charge, control, direction, regulation

■ **off your guard**
careless, unprepared, unaware(s), unready, unwary, inattentive, napping unsuspecting surprised, with your defences down
COLLOQ. red-handed, with your pants down

■ **on your guard**
alert, watchful, vigilant, cautious, careful, ready, prepared, attentive, on the lookout, wary, wide awake, on the alert
FORMAL circumspect, excubant

guarded adj
cautious, wary, chary, careful, watchful, discreet, non-committal, reluctant, reticent, reserved, restrained, secretive
FORMAL circumspect
COLLOQ. cagey
Ⓔ communicative, frank

guardedly adv
cautiously, warily, carefully, charily, non-committally, reluctantly, secretively
FORMAL circumspectly

guardian n
trustee, curator, custodian, steward, caretaker, keeper, warden, protector, preserver, defender, champion, guard, warder, escort, attendant

guardianship n
trust, care, guidance, trusteeship, curatorship, custodianship, custody, tutelage, stewardship, patronage, attendance, guard, hands, keeping wardenship, wardship, preservation, protection, safekeeping defence
FORMAL aegis

guerrilla n
freedom fighter, terrorist, irregular, resistance fighter, partisan, sniper, guerrillero, franc-tireur, haiduk, bushwhacker
OLD SLANG (offensive) gook

guess v, n
♦ v
speculate, make a guess, predict, estimate, judge, reckon, hypothesize, work out, put something at, suppose, assume, think, believe, consider, imagine, fancy, feel, suspect
FORMAL conjecture, surmise, postulate
COLLOQ. guesstimate
♦ n
prediction, estimate, speculation, assumption, belief, judgement, reckoning fancy, idea, notion, theory, hypothesis, guesswork, opinion, feeling suspicion, intuition, hunch
FORMAL conjecture, supposition, surmise
COLLOQ. guesstimate, ballpark figure, shot in the dark

guesstimate n
rough calculation, approximate cost/price/value/quantity, quotation, reckoning valuation, judgement, (rough) guess, approximation, assessment, estimation, evaluation, computation
COLLOQ. ballpark figure

guesswork n
speculation, estimation, reckoning prediction, assumption, intuition, theory, hypothesis
FORMAL conjecture, supposition, surmise
COLLOQ. guesstimate

guest n
visitor, caller, boarder, lodger, resident, patron, regular, invitee, umbra

TECHNICAL synoecete
FORMAL visitant

guesthouse n
boarding-house, hostel, hostelry, inn, hotel, pension, rooming-house, taverna, B & B
FORMAL xenodochium

guff n
rubbish, nonsense, drivel, gibberish, trash, tripe, twaddle, stuff and nonsense
COLLOQ. bunk, bunkum, claptrap, piffle, bilge, cock, poppycock, hot air, cobblers, rot, tommyrot, codswallop, baloney, blah, bosh, eyewash, hogwash, rhubarb, hooey, malarkey, moonshine
SLANG bull; (vulgar) balls, bollocks, crap, shit, bullshit

guffaw v, n
♦ v
laugh loudly, roar, bellow, hoot, cackle, shriek, whoop
♦ n
loud laugh, roar, bellow, hoot, cackle, shriek, whoop

guidance n
leadership, direction, management, rule, charge, control, teaching instruction, advice, counsel, counselling help, assistance, information, instructions, directions, guidelines, indication(s), pointer(s), hint(s), tip(s), recommendation(s), suggestion(s)

guide v, n
♦ v
1 LEAD, conduct, direct, navigate, point, steer, pilot, manoeuvre, usher, escort, show, show the way, accompany, attend
COLLOQ. hold someone's hand
2 CONTROL, govern, manage, direct, be in charge of, rule, preside over, oversee, supervise, superintend, command
3 ADVISE, counsel, give directions/recommendations to, influence, educate, teach, instruct, train
♦ n
1 MANUAL, handbook, guidebook, catalogue, directory, key, ABC
2 LEADER, courier, navigator, pilot, helmsman, steersman, conductor, director, ranger, usher, escort, chaperon(e), attendant, companion
3 ADVISER, counsellor, mentor, guru, teacher, instructor, tutor
4 GUIDELINE, example, model, pattern, norm, gauge, standard, criterion, measure, benchmark, yardstick, tombstone, indication, pointer, signpost, sign, signal, key, marker, mark, beacon
FORMAL exemplar, archetype

guidebook n
guide, handbook, manual, instruction book, book of directions, ABC, companion, prospectus, Baedeker, A to Z®

guideline n
instruction, recommendation, suggestion, direction, advice, information, indication, rule, regulation, standard, criterion, measure, benchmark, yardstick, touchstone, framework, parameter, constraint, procedure, principle, terms

guild n
organization, association, alliance, federation, society, club, union, fellowship, league, order, company, chapel, brotherhood, lodge, fraternity, sorority, corporation, incorporation

guile n
deceit, deception, cunning treachery, double-dealing fraud, trickery, trickiness, wiliness, cleverness, slyness, craft, craftiness, deviousness, artfulness, artifice, ruse, gamesmanship, knavery
FORMAL duplicity
Ⓔ artlessness, guilelessness

guileless adj
artless, direct, straight, straightforward, genuine, honest, frank, sincere, trusting truthful, innocent, naive, candid,

natural, open, simple, transparent, unreserved, unsophisticated, unworldly
FORMAL ingenuous
E3 artful, cunning

guilt n
1 *he confessed his guilt*
responsibility, blame, blameworthiness, disgrace, dishonour, wrong wrongdoing criminality, misconduct, unlawfulness
TECHNICAL blood-guilt
FORMAL culpability
2 *a feeling of guilt*
guilty conscience, conscience, disgrace, dishonour, shame, self-condemnation, self-reproach, self-accusation, regret, remorse, contrition, repentance, penitence
FORMAL compunction
COLLOQ. guilt trip
E3 1 innocence, righteousness **2** shamelessness

guiltily adv
wrongly, illegally, unlawfully, illicitly, responsibly, unforgivably, reprehensibly, to blame, at fault, without excuse, shamefully, contritely, regretfully, penitentially, remorsefully, with sorrow, in sackcloth and ashes, caught in the act, caught red-handed

guiltless adj
blameless, innocent, clear, clean, pure, irreproachable, above reproach, sinless, spotless, faultless, stainless, immaculate, impeccable, unblamable, unimpeachable, undefiled, unspotted, unsullied, untainted, untarnished
FORMAL inculpable
E3 guilty, tainted

guilty adj
1 *guilty of a crime*
responsible, blamable, blameworthy, to blame, at fault, offending wrong illegal, unlawful, delinquent, criminal, convicted, illicit, sinful, wicked, damned, evil
FORMAL culpable
2 CONSCIENCE-STRICKEN, ashamed, guilt-ridden, bad, with a bad conscience, on your conscience, shamefaced, sheepish, sorry, regretful, remorseful, contrite, penitent, repentant
FORMAL compunctious
E3 1 innocent, guiltless, blameless **2** shameless

guise n
appearance, form, shape, features, likeness, manner, disguise, mask, pretence, show, façade, front, behaviour, custom, air, aspect, face, semblance
FORMAL demeanour

gulf n
1 BAY, bight, cove, inlet, basin
2 GAP, opening separation, division, divide, rift, split, breach, cleft, fissure, crevice, chasm, gorge, hole, ravine, abyss, void, hollow, canyon, maw
OLD vorago

gullet n
throat, craw, crop, maw
TECHNICAL oesophagus
OLD weasand
Related adjective: oesophageal

gullibility n
credulity, innocence, simplicity, naivety, trustfulness, foolishness
E3 astuteness

gullible adj
credulous, suggestible, impressionable, trusting trustful, overtrusting ingenuous, unsuspecting easily deceived, foolish, naive, green, inexperienced, unsophisticated, innocent
COLLOQ. wet behind the ears
E3 astute

gully n
channel, ravine, gorge, valley, canyon, watercourse, gutter, ditch, couloir, grough; *Scot* geo; *N Am* gulch
TECHNICAL donga

gulp v, n
♦ v
swallow, swig swill, quaff, bolt, gobble, guzzle, devour, stuff, gollop; *dialect* gulch
COLLOQ. knock back, wolf, tuck into
OLD SLANG swipe
E3 sip, nibble
♦ n
swallow, swig draught, mouthful; *N Am* slug

gum n, v
♦ n
adhesive, glue, paste, cement, fixative, resin
Related adjective: mucilaginous
♦ v
stick, glue, paste, fix, cement, seal, clog
FORMAL affix
■ **gum up**
obstruct, hinder, impede, choke, clog

gummy adj
sticky, adhesive, gluey, gooey, tacky, viscous
FORMAL viscid

gumption n
common sense, initiative, resourcefulness, cleverness, astuteness, nous, enterprise, shrewdness, wit, discernment, acumen, ability, acuteness
FORMAL sagacity
COLLOQ. savvy
E3 foolishness

gun n
firearm, weapon
COLLOQ. piece, shooter, shooting iron
See panel at **weapon**.

gunfire n
shooting firing gunshots, bombardment, shelling pounding cannonade, salvo, flak

gunman n
assassin, terrorist, thug killer, sniper, shootist, murderer, bandit, armed robber, gangster, mobster, bravo, desperado, gunslinger
COLLOQ. hatchet man, hit man

gurgle v, n
♦ v
BABBLE, bubble, burble, murmur, ripple, lap, splash, plash
♦ n
BABBLE, bubbling murmur, ripple, crow, burble

guru n
expert, authority, instructor, master, teacher, tutor, leader, mentor, luminary, guiding light, pundit, maharishi, Svengali, swami, sage

gush v, n
♦ v
1 FLOW, run, pour, stream, surge, cascade, flood, rush, burst, spurt, spout, jet, well, issue, fountain, regurgitate, regorge; *dialect* boke
OLD rail
2 ENTHUSE, effervesce, bubble over, effuse, chatter, babble, fuss, jabber; *dialect & N Am* blather; drivel
COLLOQ. go on, rave
♦ n
flow, outflow, stream, surge, torrent, cascade, flood, tide, rush, burst, outburst, spurt, spout, outpouring spate, jet

gushing adj
effusive, over-enthusiastic, excessive, cloying emotional, saccharine, sentimental, sickly, fulsome, mawkish
COLLOQ. gushy
E3 restrained, sincere

gust *n, v*

♦ *n*

1 *a gust of wind*
blast, burst, rush, flurry, blow, puff, breeze, wind, gale, storm, squall, surge

2 *gusts of temper*
outburst, outbreak, fit, eruption, surge

♦ *v*

blast, blow, puff, squall, bluster, breeze, rush, surge, burst out, erupt

gustily *adv*
stormily, windily, breezily, tempestuously, wildly
E3 calmly

gusto *n*
zest, relish, appreciation, enjoyment, pleasure, delight, enthusiasm, exhilaration, exuberance, energy, fervour, élan, verve, zeal
E3 distaste, apathy

gusty *adj*
stormy, blowy, squally, windy, blustering blustery, breezy, tempestuous
E3 calm

gut *n, v, adj*

♦ *n*

1 INTESTINES, belly, stomach, bowels, viscera, entrails, vital organs, insides, internal organs
COLLOQ. innards
Related adjectives: enteral, enteric, splanchnic

2 *have the guts to own up*
courage, bravery, pluck, boldness, audacity, tenacity, nerve, mettle
FORMAL fortitude
COLLOQ. grit, backbone, bottle, spunk
SLANG balls

♦ *v*

1 *gut fish*
disembowel, draw, clean (out)
FORMAL eviscerate, exenterate

2 STRIP, clear, empty, rifle, ransack, plunder, loot, sack, rob, destroy, devastate, ravage, clear out

♦ *adj*

instinctive, intuitive, emotional, unthinking basic, deep-seated, heartfelt, innate, involuntary, natural, spontaneous, strong

gutless *adj*
weak, cowardly, feeble, irresolute, timid, faint-hearted, lily-livered, craven, abject
COLLOQ. chicken, chicken-hearted, chicken-livered, spineless
E3 courageous

gutsily *adv*
bravely, boldly, courageously, resolutely, indomitably, passionately, staunchily
COLLOQ. spunkily

gutsy *adj*
bold, brave, courageous, determined, resolute, plucky, indomitable, mettlesome, passionate, spirited, staunch, gallant, game
COLLOQ. spunky
SLANG ballsy
E3 quiet, timid

gutter *n*
drain, sluice, sewer, ditch, trench, trough, channel, gully, duct, conduit, culvert, passage, pipe, tube, grip, kennel, rigol; *Scot* strand
TECHNICAL cullis

> **QUOTATIONS**
> We are all in the gutter, but some of us are looking at the stars
> OSCAR WILDE, *Lady Windermere's Fan*

guttersnipe *n*
urchin, waif, ragamuffin, gamin, mudlark, tatterdemalion

guttural *adj*
rasping throaty, croaking hoarse, harsh, gruff, rough, grating gravelly, husky, deep, low, thick
E3 dulcet

guy *n*
fellow, man, boy, youth, lad, person, individual, character
COLLOQ. bloke, chap, fella; *Irish* bucko;
Aust cove
SLANG sod; *N Am* dude; boyo, geezer

guzzle *v*
bolt, devour, gobble, gormandize, stuff, cram, gulp, swallow, swill, quaff, swig
COLLOQ. wolf, scoff, polish off, put away, tuck into, knock back

Gypsy, Gipsy *n*
Romany, Romani, Roma, traveller, rom, rye, wanderer, roamer, rover, rambler, hawker, huckster, nomad, tzigany, *Zigeuner, Zincalo, Zingaro,* Bohemian, tinker, diddicoy, faw, *gitano; Scot* caird, (*derog*) tinkler; *Scot & Irish* (*derog*) tinker
OLD Egyptian, gipsen
SLANG (*offensive*) gippo

gyrate *v*
turn, revolve, rotate, twirl, pirouette, spin, whirl, wheel, swirl, swivel, circle, spiral

gyration *n*
turn, revolution, rotation, twirl, pirouette, spin, spinning whirl, whirling swirl, swivel, wheeling circle, spiral
FORMAL convolution

H

habit *n*
1 CUSTOM, usage, practice, routine, rule, procedure, matter of course, second nature, way(s), manner, mannerism, mode, policy, wont, inclination, tendency, leaning bent, quirk, ethos
FORMAL propensity, proclivity
2 ADDICTION, dependence, fixation, obsession, weakness
3 GARMENT, costume, dress, clothing outfit, uniform, robe, vestment
COLLOQ. get-up, gear, togs

> **PROVERBS**
> Old habits die hard

habitable *adj*
fit to live in, suitable to live in, good enough to live in, inhabitable

habitat *n*
home, domain, element, environment, natural environment, surroundings, dwelling locality, territory, terrain, station
TECHNICAL metropolis, niche
FORMAL abode

habitation *n*
1 OCCUPANCY, occupation, quarters, residence, tenancy, housing lodging inhabitance, inhabitancy, inhabitation
2 HOME, house, cottage, accommodation, flat, apartment, hut, quarters, living quarters, lodging mansion
FORMAL abode, domicile, dwelling dwelling-place, residence, residency
COLLOQ. digs, pad, joint, roof over your head
SLANG gaff

habitual *adj*
1 CUSTOMARY, traditional, accustomed, routine, usual, ordinary, common, natural, normal, set, standard, regular, recurrent, fixed, established, systematic, familiar
FORMAL wonted
2 *habitual drinker*
confirmed, inveterate, chronic, hardened, addicted, dependent, constant, great, intemperate, pathological, persistent, obsessive
E3 1 occasional, infrequent

habitually *adv*
usually, normally, generally, as a rule, ordinarily, typically, traditionally, regularly, routinely, commonly, by and large, on the whole, mainly, chiefly, mostly, for the most part, on average, in the main
COLLOQ. nine times out of ten
E3 exceptionally

habituate *v*
acclimatize, accustom, make used, adapt, familiarize, make familiar with, break in, condition, train, school, discipline, tame, harden, inure, season

habitué *n*
regular, regular customer, frequenter, frequent visitor, patron, denizen

hack¹ *v*
hacked them to death
cut, chop, hew, fell, saw, clear, notch, gash, slash, lacerate, mutilate, mangle

■ **hack it**
cope, manage, carry on, get on/along get by, get through, muddle through
COLLOQ. make out

hack² *n*
write as a hack
scribbler, writer, journalist, reporter, drudge, slave

hackle
■ **make someone's hackles rise**
anger, annoy, irritate, irk, vex, rile, make angry, needle, nettle, bother, ruffle, provoke, antagonize, offend, affront, gall, madden, enrage, incense, infuriate, exasperate, outrage
COLLOQ. aggravate, get at, wind up, miff, make someone's blood boil, bug hassle, rub up the wrong way, get someone's blood up, get on someone's nerves, rattle someone's cage, ruffle someone's feathers, raise someone's dander, make sparks fly, get under someone's skin, get up someone's nose, get on someone's wick
SLANG nark, piss off

hackneyed *adj*
stale, old, overworked, overused, tired, worn-out, time-worn, threadbare, wearing thin, unoriginal, cliché-ridden, clichéed, stereotyped, stock, banal, trite, commonplace, common, pedestrian, uninspired, unimaginative
FORMAL platitudinous
COLLOQ. corny, run-of-the-mill, yawn-making
E3 original, new, fresh

haft *n*
handle, grip, handgrip, knob, stock, shaft, hilt

hag *n*
crone, witch, shrew, gorgon, termagant, vixen, virago, harridan, fury, harpy
COLLOQ. battle-axe

haggard *adj*
drawn, gaunt, careworn, thin, wasted, drained, shrunken, pinched, hollow-cheeked, emaciated, pale, pallid, wan, ghastly
E3 hale

haggle *v*
bargain, negotiate, barter, beat down, chaffer, higgle, wrangle, squabble, bicker, quarrel, dispute; N Am dicker

hail¹ *v*
1 GREET, address, acknowledge, salute, say hello to, nod to, wave to, communicate, speak; S Afr hail
2 SIGNAL TO, flag down, wave down, wave to, call out to
3 ACCLAIM, applaud, honour, welcome, praise, cheer, exalt
FORMAL laud
4 *hail from Malawi*
come, originate, have your home/roots in, be born in

hail² *n, v*
♦ *n*
1 *a hail storm*
frozen rain, frozen ice, sleet, hailstones, hail-storm
TECHNICAL precipitation
2 *a hail of arrows*
barrage, bombardment, volley, torrent, shower, storm
♦ *v*
pelt, bombard, shower, rain, beat, batter, attack, assail

hail-fellow-well-met *adj*
convivial, friendly, sociable, genial, cheerful, cordial, festive, affable, hearty, jolly, jovial, lively, merry, fun-loving

hair *n*
locks, tresses, shock, mop, mane, fleece, wool, coat, fur, pelt, hide
COLLOQ. barnet
Related adjectives: pilose, pileous, crinal, capillaceous, trichoid

■ **let your hair down**
relax, let yourself go, have a good time, throw off your inhibitions
COLLOQ. hang loose, loosen up
SLANG let it all hang out, chill out

■ **make someone's hair stand on end**
shock, frighten, terrify, disgust, revolt, repel, appal, outrage, scandalize, horrify, startle, astound, stagger, amaze, stun, daze, stupefy, numb, paralyse, traumatize, jolt, jar, shake, agitate, unsettle, upset, distress, disquiet, unnerve, bewilder, take aback, confound, dumbfound, dismay
FORMAL perturb
E∃ delight, please, gratify, reassure

■ **not turn a hair**
remain calm, remain composed
COLLOQ. see it coming not bat an eyelid, keep your cool, stay cool

■ **split hairs**
find fault, quibble, cavil, pettifog argue over unimportant details
COLLOQ. nit-pick

> **QUOTATIONS**
> Only God, my dear, / Could love you for yourself alone / And not your yellow hair
> W B YEATS, 'For Anne Gregory'

haircut, hairdo *n*
hairstyle, coiffure, cut, style, set

hairdresser *n*
hairstylist, stylist, barber, coiffeur, coiffeuse

hairless *adj*
bald, bald-headed, shorn, tonsured, shaven, clean-shaven, beardless
E∃ hairy, hirsute

hairpiece *n*
wig toupee, postiche, scratch-wig spencer, bobwig Brutus, buzz-wig tie-wig; *Scot* gizz, jiz
OLD periwig peruke, transformation, bagwig caxon, major, Ramilie
OLD COLLOQ. jasey
SLANG rug

hair-raising *adj*
frightening scary, terrifying horrifying shocking bloodcurdling spine-chilling petrifying eerie, alarming startling thrilling exciting
COLLOQ. creepy

hair's-breadth *n*
fraction, hair, inch, jot
COLLOQ. whisker
E∃ mile

hairstyle *n*
style, coiffure, cut, haircut, set
COLLOQ. hairdo, barnet
See panel below

hairy *adj*
1 HIRSUTE, bearded, shaggy, bushy, fuzzy, furry, woolly, fleecy, unshaven
FORMAL pilose, crinose, crinigerous, crinite
2 DANGEROUS, unsafe, insecure, risky, high-risk, fraught with danger, threatening breakneck, hazardous, chancy, perilous, precarious, reckless, treacherous, vulnerable, menacing ominous, exposed, susceptible, alarming critical, severe, serious, grave, daring nasty
COLLOQ. dicey, dodgy
E∃ 1 bald, clean-shaven **2** safe, secure

halcyon *adj*
peaceful, happy, flourishing prosperous, carefree, calm, balmy, mild, gentle, golden, pacific, placid, quiet, serene, still, tranquil, undisturbed
E∃ stormy

hale *adj*
healthy, fit, well, youthful, strong sound, vigorous, robust, flourishing athletic, hearty, able-bodied, blooming
COLLOQ. in the pink, in fine fettle
E∃ ill

half *n, adj, adv*
♦ *n*
fifty per cent, equal part/share, bisection, hemisphere, semicircle, section, segment, portion, share, fraction
♦ *adj*
semi-, halved, divided, divided in two, bisected, hemispherical, fractional, part, partial, incomplete, moderate, limited, slight
E∃ whole
♦ *adv*
partly, partially, incompletely, inadequately, insufficiently, moderately, slightly, barely
E∃ completely

■ **by half**
very, considerably, excessively, too

■ **by halves**
incompletely, imperfectly, inadequately, insufficiently
E∃ thoroughly

■ **not half**
1 *not half as clever*
not at all, not nearly
2 *not half get into trouble*
very, very much, really, indeed

■ **too ... by half**
unduly, too, over, excessively, immoderately, inordinately, disproportionately, out of all proportions, unreasonably, unjustifiably, unnecessarily

---

Hairstyles include:

Afro	chignon	*slang* duck's arse	marcel wave	pouffe	tonsure
backcombed	combover	(or DA)	mohican	quiff	topknot
bangs	corn rows	Eton crop	mullet	ringlets	undercut
beehive	cowlick	fishtail braid	number 1,2,3 etc	shed	updo
bob	crewcut	flat-top	pageboy	shingle	weave
bouffant	crimped	fohawk	perm	short back and	
braid	crop	French pleat	pigtail	sides	
bun	curled	fringe	plait	sideboards	
bunches	dreadlocks	frizette	pompadour	sideburns	
buzzcut		hair extension	ponytail	skinhead	

half-baked *adj*
impractical, stupid, ill-conceived, unplanned, undeveloped, ill-judged, short-sighted, silly, crazy, foolish, senseless
COLLOQ. harebrained, crackpot
🔁 sensible, thought out

half-caste *n*
Creole, griff(e), mestee, mestiza, mestizo, metif, Métis, Métisse, miscegen, miscegene, miscegine, mongrel, mulatta, mulatto, mulattress, quadroon, quarteroon, quarter-blood, quintroon, sambo

half-hearted *adj*
lukewarm, tepid, cool, weak, feeble, passive, apathetic, lacklustre, listless, uninterested, unenthusiastic, indifferent, unconcerned, neutral, Laodicean
🔁 wholehearted, enthusiastic

half-heartedly *adv*
unenthusiastically, feebly, apathetically, listlessly, neutrally
🔁 wholeheartedly, enthusiastically

halfway *adv, adj*
◆ *adv*
midway, in/to the middle, centrally
◆ *adj*
middle, central, equidistant, mid, midway, intermediate, mean, median
■ **meet someone halfway**
compromise, reach a compromise, negotiate, make concessions, come to/reach an understanding give and take, steer a middle course, find a happy medium, make a deal
COLLOQ. go fifty-fifty with, split the difference

halfwit *n*
fool, blockhead, fat-head, dunce, dimwit, simpleton, idiot, cretin, imbecile, ignoramus, moron, dupe, stooge, butt, laughing-stock, clown, comic, buffoon, jester
COLLOQ. nincompoop, ass, chump, ninny, airhead, clot, dope, twit, nitwit, nit, sucker, mug twerp, birdbrain; *Scot & Irish* eejit; *Scot* numpty; *N Am* doofus; *Aust & NZ* dill
SLANG wally, dumbo, pillock, prat, dork, geek, git, berk, nerk, plonker, prick; *Aust & NZ* nong; *Aust* galah
🔁 brain

half-witted *adj*
simple-minded, feeble-minded, silly, foolish, idiotic, stupid, crazy, dull, moronic, simple
COLLOQ. dim-witted, crack-brained, crackpot, dumb, dotty, potty, batty, barmy, nutty, wacky, two bricks short of a load, two sandwiches short of a picnic; *Aust* not the full quid
🔁 clever

hall *n*
1 HALLWAY, corridor, passage, passageway, entrance-hall, foyer, vestibule, lobby
2 CONCERT HALL, auditorium, chamber, assembly hall, assembly room, conference hall

hallmark *n*
1 *a hallmark on gold*
official mark/stamp, mark/stamp of authenticity
2 *the hallmark of her music*
typical quality, distinctive feature, stamp, mark, trademark, brand-name, sign, indication, indicator, symbol, emblem, device, badge

hallo *interj*
hello, hullo, good morning good afternoon, good evening greetings, welcome, holloa; *Can* chimo
OLD hillo
COLLOQ. hi; *Aust* g'day

hallowed *adj*
honoured, revered, sacred, sacrosanct, blessed, sanctified, consecrated, holy, dedicated, established, inviolable, age-old

hallucinate *v*
dream, imagine, imagine things, see things, see visions, daydream, fantasize
SLANG freak out, trip

hallucination *n*
illusion, mirage, vision, apparition, dream, daydream, fantasy, figment, figment of the imagination, delusion, delirium, phantasmagoria
TECHNICAL autoscopy
SLANG freak-out, trip

halo *n*
circle of light, crown, ring corona, glory, nimbus, radiance, aura, aureole, aureola, gloria, gloriole, halation

halt *v, n*
◆ *v*
stop, cease, come/bring to a stop, draw up, pull up, pause, wait, rest, come to (a) rest, break off, finish, bring/draw to a close, end, put an end to, check, stem, curb, obstruct, block, arrest, crush, hold back, impede
FORMAL discontinue, desist, terminate
COLLOQ. quit, call it a day
🔁 start, continue
◆ *n*
stop, stoppage, arrest, interruption, break, interval, pause, rest, respite, breathing space, standstill, end, close, deadlock, stalemate
FORMAL termination, cessation, discontinuance, discontinuation, desistance
🔁 start, continuation

halting *adj*
hesitant, stuttering stammering faltering stumbling fumbling for words, uncertain, broken, imperfect, laboured, awkward, unsteady
🔁 fluent, certain

halve *v*
bisect, cut in half, split in two, divide, divide equally, split, sever, share, cut down, reduce, lessen
FORMAL dichotomize

halved *adj*
divided, split, cut, shared, bisected
FORMAL dimidiate

ham-fisted *adj*
clumsy, awkward, unco-ordinated, ham, accident-prone, unhandy, heavy-handed, unskilful, inept, bungling blundering lumbering cack-handed, two-fisted, thumby
FORMAL maladroit
COLLOQ. gawky, all thumbs
🔁 co-ordinated, skilful

hammer *v, n*
◆ *v*
1 HIT, strike, beat, drum, bang bash, hit, slap, pound, batter, knock, drive, shape, form, make, mould, fashion, forge, dolly
TECHNICAL malleate, rivet
OLD (*Spenser*) martel
2 CRITICIZE, condemn, slate, attack, blame, censure, run down
FORMAL decry, denigrate
COLLOQ. slam, knock, tear a strip off, haul over the coals
3 *hammer the opposition*
beat, trounce, defeat, overcome, overwhelm, rout, annihilate, outplay
COLLOQ. clobber, slaughter, lick, thrash, run rings round, wipe the floor with, walk all over, make mincemeat of
SLANG take to the cleaners, pwn
4 *hammer an idea into someone*
force, drum, din, drive home, instil, reiterate
5 *hammer away at his essay*
persevere, pound, persist, keep on, labour, work away, plug grind, drudge, slog
◆ *n*
mallet, gavel, beetle, claw hammer, sledgehammer, steam hammer, stone hammer, tack hammer, tilt-hammer, trip hammer, water hammer, pick, about-sledge, madge, maul, monkey; *Scot* knapping-hammer
TECHNICAL axe, bully, percussor, plexor
OLD mall

■ hammer out
settle, sort out, negotiate, thrash out, achieve eventually, produce, bring about, work out, carry through, accomplish, complete, finish, resolve

hamper v, n
◆ v
hinder, impede, obstruct, slow down, hold up, stop, inhibit, frustrate, thwart, baulk, prevent, handicap, hamstring shackle, cramp, restrict, curb, restrain, block, clog check, bridle, encumber, fetter, foil
FORMAL retard
COLLOQ. stymie
F3 aid, facilitate
◆ n
basket, box, container, creel, pannier

hamstring v
hinder, impede, hold up, stop, frustrate, baulk, thwart, cramp, restrict, restrain, block, check, encumber, foil, cripple, disable, handicap, incapacitate, paralyse
COLLOQ. stymie

hand n, v
◆ n
1 FIST, palm
TECHNICAL manus
COLLOQ. paw
SLANG mitt, fin
Related adjective: manual
2 give me a hand
help, helping hand, aid, assistance, support, participation, part, influence
FORMAL succour
3 in someone's hands
responsibility, care, custody, possession, charge, authority, command, control, power, management, supervision, clutches
4 give someone a hand
applause, round of applause, clapping handclap, cheering acclaim, ovation
5 INDICATOR, pointer, needle, arrow, marker
6 HANDWRITING, writing script, penmanship, calligraphy
COLLOQ. fist
7 WORKER, manual worker, employee, operative, workman, workwoman, labourer, farm-hand, hireling
◆ v
give, pass, offer, submit, present, yield, deliver, hand over, transmit, conduct, convey

■ hand down
bequeath, will, pass on, pass down, transfer, give, grant, leave

■ hand on
pass on, transfer, give, supply, let someone have, surrender

■ hand out
distribute, deal out, pass out, give out, share out, mete out
FORMAL dispense, disseminate
COLLOQ. dish out

■ hand over
yield, relinquish, surrender, turn over, deliver, consign, release, give up, give, donate, present, pass, transfer
F3 keep, retain

■ at hand
near, close, to hand, handy, accessible, available, at someone's disposal, ready, readily available, imminent, about to happen

■ by hand
manually, using your hands, with your hands

■ from hand to mouth
precariously, dangerously, insecurely, uncertainly, in poverty, from day to day
COLLOQ. on the breadline

■ hand in glove
very closely, in close collaboration/co-operation, in close association
COLLOQ. in cahoots

■ hand in hand
1 HOLDING HANDS, with hands joined/clasped/held
2 CLOSELY RELATED, closely together, in close association

■ in hand
1 BEING DEALT WITH, under way, considered, attended to, under control
2 SPARE, in reserve, put by, ready, available

■ to hand
near, close, at hand, nearby, handy, accessible, available, at someone's disposal, ready, imminent, about to happen

■ try your hand
attempt, try, seek, strive, see if you can do
COLLOQ. have a go, have a shot/crack/stab

■ win hands down
win easily/effortlessly, win without effort

> **PROVERBS**
> Many hands make light work

handbag n
clutch bag flight bag grip, handgrip, holdall, vanity bag shoulder bag; *N Am* purse

handbill n
circular, leaflet, pamphlet, flier, notice, announcement, advertisement, letter

handbook n
manual, instruction book, book of directions, ABC, guide, guidebook, companion, prospectus

handcuff v
fetter, shackle, manacle, fasten, secure, tie
SLANG cuff

handcuffs n
manacles, fetters, shackles, wristlets, snippers, cuffs
COLLOQ. cuffs, darbies, mittens, nippers, bracelets
OLD SLANG snitchers

handful n
1 SMALL NUMBER, few, little, small amount, sprinkling scattering smattering
2 NUISANCE, bother, pest
COLLOQ. pain in the neck, thorn in the flesh, pain
F3 1 a lot, many

handgun n
pistol, gun, revolver, sidearm, six-shooter; *N Am* derringer
SLANG piece, rod, iron; *N Am* gat
See also panel at **weapon**.

handicap n, v
◆ n
obstacle, obstruction, check, block, barrier, impediment, stumbling-block, hindrance, encumbrance, constraint, drawback, disadvantage, restriction, limitation, penalty, disability, impairment, abnormality, defect, shortcoming
F3 assistance, advantage
◆ v
impede, hinder, disadvantage, put at a disadvantage, put on the back foot, hold back, hamper, impair, obstruct, block, check, bridle, curb, burden, encumber, restrict, limit, disable
FORMAL retard
F3 help, assist

handicapped adj
disabled, differently abled, disadvantaged, incapacitated, having special needs, challenged

handicraft n
craft, art, craftwork, craftsmanship, skill, handwork, handiwork, workmanship

handily adv
1 CONVENIENTLY, practically, usefully, helpfully
2 SKILFULLY, cleverly, practically, adeptly, adroitly
3 ACCESSIBLY, within reach, readily, nearly, to hand, at hand
F3 1 inconveniently **2** clumsily **3** inaccessibly

handiwork *n*
work, doing responsibility, achievement, action, product, result, design, invention, creation, production, skill, workmanship, craftsmanship, artisanship, handicraft, craft, art, craftwork

handkerchief *n*
tissue, Kleenex®, rag romal, foulard, kerchief, blind, bandana, monteith; *Scot* napkin
OLD muckender, orarium
COLLOQ. hankie
SLANG fogle, nose-rag
OLD SLANG wipe

handle *n, v*
♦ *n*
grip, handgrip, knob, stock, shaft, hilt, haft
Related adjective: manubrial
♦ *v*
1 TOUCH, finger, feel, fondle, pick up, hold, grasp, grip
COLLOQ. paw
2 *handle a situation*
tackle, treat, deal with, manage, cope with, control, supervise, be in charge of, take care of
3 *handle a car*
operate, control, drive, steer, work
4 TRADE IN, do business in, deal in, market, stock, traffic, operate

---

SYNONYM NUANCES

verb sense 1
Touch refers to coming into physical contact with, but may suggest that contact is brief, whilst **hold** is suggestive of prolonged retention. The verb **finger** is indicative of movement: *she fingered the flowers to see if they were real*. Similarly, **fondle** would be used of a caressing movement, particularly an affectionate or appreciative one, but it also has sexual connotations. The terms **grasp** and **grip** imply forceful holding: *he grasped my hand fiercely*.

---

handling *n*
management, conduct, approach, operation, running treatment, direction, administration, discussion, transaction, manipulation

handout *n*
1 CHARITY, alms, gifts, dole, largesse, share, issue, free sample
COLLOQ. freebie
2 LEAFLET, circular, bulletin, statement, press release, brochure, pamphlet, literature

handover *n*
transfer, change, changeover, transposition, move, shift, removal, relocation, displacement, transmission, assignment, transference
TECHNICAL conveyance

hand-picked *adj*
choice, select, selected, chosen, elect, élite, picked, screened, recherché

handsome *adj*
1 GOOD-LOOKING, attractive, fair, personable, dashing elegant, fine, dignified, stately
OLD brave, comely, seemly, featous, featurely; (*Shakesp*) goodfaced
COLLOQ. gorgeous, dishy, hunky
2 GENEROUS, liberal, large, considerable, ample, lavish, plentiful, abundant, bountiful, siz(e)able, magnanimous, unsparing unstinting
F₃ 1 ugly, unattractive **2** mean

handsomely *adv*
generously, lavishly, plentifully, richly, amply, abundantly, bountifully, liberally, magnanimously, unsparingly, unstintingly
FORMAL munificently
F₃ stingily

handwriting *n*
writing script, hand, penmanship, calligraphy, autograph
COLLOQ. fist, scrawl, scribble

handy *adj*
1 CONVENIENT, practical, useful, helpful, functional, practicable
2 AVAILABLE, to hand, ready, at hand, near, nearly, accessible, within reach
COLLOQ. at your fingertips
3 SKILFUL, proficient, expert, skilled, clever, practical, dexterous, adroit, adept, nimble
F₃ 1 inconvenient **3** clumsy

handyman *n*
DIYer, odd-jobman, odd-jobber, Jack-of-all-trades, factotum

hang *v*
1 SUSPEND, be suspended, hang down, put up, dangle, swing drape, drop, flop, droop, sag trail, lean, bend
2 FASTEN, attach, fix, stick, glue, paste, cement
FORMAL affix, append
3 *hang in the air*
float, drift, hover, flit, flutter, linger, remain, cling
4 *the prisoners were hanged*
execute, lynch, put to death, send to the gallows/scaffold/gibbet, kill
COLLOQ. string up
■ **hang about**
1 LOITER, hang around, linger, dawdle, waste time
SLANG mike
2 ASSOCIATE WITH, keep company with, frequent, haunt
COLLOQ. hang out
■ **hang back**
hold back, be reluctant, hesitate, shy away, shrink back, recoil, stay behind
FORMAL demur
■ **hang fire**
hold back, hang back, delay, hold on, stall, stick, stop, wait
FORMAL procrastinate, vacillate
F₃ press on
■ **hang on**
1 WAIT, hold on, remain, hold out, endure, continue, carry on, persevere, persist
2 GRIP, grasp, cling clutch, hold fast
3 DEPEND ON, hinge on, turn on, rest on, be conditional on, be determined by
FORMAL be contingent on
F₃ 1 give up
■ **hang over**
impend, loom, menace, threaten, approach, be imminent
■ **get the hang of**
understand, grasp, comprehend, learn, master, fathom, get the knack of
COLLOQ. twig

QUOTATIONS
Depend upon it, Sir, when a man knows he is to be hanged in a fortnight, it concentrates his mind wonderfully
  SAMUEL JOHNSON

---

hangdog *adj*
abject, browbeaten, defeated, guilty, shamefaced, cowed, cringing downcast, miserable, wretched, sneaking furtive
F₃ bold

hanger-on *n*
follower, minion, henchman, lackey, toady, sycophant, parasite, appendage, freeloader, dependant, client, courtling flunkey
COLLOQ. sponger, sponge

hanging adj, n

♦ adj
suspended, dangling swinging draping drooping flopping floppy, flapping loose, unattached, unsupported
FORMAL pendent, pendulous, pensile
♦ n
curtain, drape, drapery, drop, frontal, drop-scene, dossal, dossel

hang-out n

haunt, den, meeting-place, home, patch, local, stamping-ground
COLLOQ. dive, joint, watering-hole

hangover n

after-effects, katzenjammer, morning after, the morning after the night before
FORMAL crapulence

hang-up n

inhibition, difficulty, problem, obsession, preoccupation, fixation, phobia, *idée fixe*, block, mental block, neurosis
COLLOQ. thing

hank n

skein, coil, loop, length, roll, piece, twist; *Scot* fank

hanker

■ **hanker after/for**
crave, hunger for, thirst for, want, wish for, desire, covet, yearn for, long for, pine for, itch for, set your heart on
COLLOQ. be dying for

hankering n

craving hunger, thirst, wish, desire, yearning longing pining itch, urge

hanky-panky n

mischief, trickery, tricks, deception, dishonesty, jiggery-pokery, nonsense, chicanery, subterfuge, devilry, affair, adultery
FORMAL machinations
COLLOQ. cheating funny business, monkey business, shenanigans, carry-on, fooling around, bit on the side, slap and tickle, fling
SLANG nookie
F3 openness

haphazard adj

random, chance, casual, arbitrary, hit-or-miss, hitty-missy, wild, indiscriminate, irregular, aimless, orderless, unsystematic, disorganized, disorderly, careless, slapdash, slipshod, unmethodical, unplanned, promiscuous, rough-and-tumble
OLD tumultuary
F3 methodical, orderly

haphazardly adv

randomly, by chance, arbitrarily, carelessly, wildly, indiscriminately, irregularly, unmethodically, unsystematically, willy-nilly
COLLOQ. higgledy-piggledy

hapless adj

unlucky, unhappy, unfortunate, wretched, miserable, ill-fated, ill-starred, cursed, luckless, jinxed, star-crossed
F3 lucky

happen v

1 OCCUR, take place, fall, arise, crop up, develop, present itself, turn up, go on, come about, come true, result, ensue, follow, turn out, appear, come into being
FORMAL transpire, supervene, eventuate
COLLOQ. materialize
2 *happen to do something*
have the good/bad luck to, have the good/bad fortune to
3 *happen on something*
find, discover, hit on, light on, stumble on, come/run across, chance on
COLLOQ. bump into
4 *I wonder what happened to my schoolfriend*
become of, be the fate of
OLD befall

happening n

occurrence, phenomenon, event, incident, episode, occasion, adventure, experience, accident, chance, proceedings, circumstance, case, affair, thing action, scene, business
FORMAL eventuality

happily adv

1 GLADLY, joyfully, merrily, cheerfully, gleefully, heartily, delightedly, contentedly, agreeably, enthusiastically, willingly
FORMAL joyously
2 FORTUNATELY, luckily, providentially, by chance, fittingly, as luck would have it
FORMAL auspiciously, opportunely, propitiously
F3 **1, 2** unhappily

happiness n

joy, joyfulness, gladness, cheerfulness, cheeriness, contentment, pleasure, delight, enjoyment, gaiety, glee, life, merriment, merriness, light-heartedness, exuberance, high spirits, good spirits, elation, bliss, ecstasy, euphoria
FORMAL blitheness, felicity
F3 unhappiness, sadness

> **QUOTATIONS**
> Simply seek happiness, and you are not likely to find it. Seek to create and love without regard to your happiness, and you will likely be happy much of the time
> M SCOTT PECK, *The Different Drum*

> **SYNONYM NUANCES**
> The terms **joy** and **joyfulness** would be reserved for an intense feeling of happiness, whilst **gladness** has connotations of gratitude or relief: *she was full of gladness at her deliverance*. **Cheerfulness** and **cheeriness** suggest a happy disposition that is projected to others, whereas **contentment** has more to do with a more internalized satisfaction at a current state of affairs.
>   The words **pleasure** and **delight** are appropriate for the gratification to be derived from something in particular: *his delight in music*, with **enjoyment** similarly suggesting happiness while undertaking an agreeable occupation. You can use **gaiety**, **merriment** and **merriness** to refer to a bright and lively state, particularly one that has been deliberately engendered: *the day is celebrated with traditional feasting and merriment*, whilst **glee** is connotative of a degree of mischievousness, if not maliciousness: *their rivals' defeat was greeted with glee*.
>   **Life**, like **exuberance**, could be used of vivacity and a zest for living: *she was full of life and energy; the sheer exuberance of youth*; and **high spirits** is also connotative of a degree of friskiness and playfulness: *the exploits were undertaken with schoolboy high spirits*. **Light-heartedness**, which has similar associations with being carefree, would be appropriate for a less boisterously expressed emotion. **Elation** is more suggestive of exhilaration, whereas **bliss** and **ecstasy** imply an unworldly, exalted state of rapture: *sexual ecstasy*. **Euphoria** is also fairly extreme, but implies a highly exaggerated sense of happiness that is usually short-lived: *a year after the revolution the euphoria has faded*.

happy adj

1 JOYFUL, jolly, merry, cheerful, glad, pleased, delighted, thrilled, elated, ecstatic, rapturous, overjoyed, exuberant, gleeful, euphoric, satisfied, gratified, in good/high spirits, in a good mood, content, contented, gay, carefree, light-hearted, jovial, radiant, smiling untroubled, unconcerned, unworried
FORMAL joyous, blithe
COLLOQ. chuffed, cock-a-hoop, on top of the world, happy as Larry/a sandboy, over the moon, on cloud nine, in

seventh heaven, walking/floating on air, tickled pink;
N Am happy as a clam
2 *a happy coincidence*
lucky, fortunate, favourable, advantageous, convenient,
helpful, beneficial, appropriate, apt, fitting proper,
opportune
OLD seely
FORMAL felicitous, auspicious, propitious, apposite
F₃ **1** unhappy, sad, discontented **2** unfortunate,
inappropriate

happy-go-lucky *adj*
carefree, casual, nonchalant, easy-going cheerful,
devil-may-care, light-hearted, unconcerned,
untroubled, unworried, reckless, irresponsible, heedless,
improvident
FORMAL blithe, insouciant
F₃ anxious, wary

harangue *n, v*
♦ *n*
diatribe, tirade, lecture, speech, address
FORMAL peroration, exhortation
♦ *v*
lecture, preach, hold forth, spout, address
FORMAL declaim

harass *v*
pester, badger, harry, plague, torment, hound, afflict, bait,
chivvy, distract, distress, grind, harrow, pinch, dragoon,
persecute, pursue, exasperate, vex, annoy, nag provoke,
antagonize, irritate, fret, bother, disturb, trouble, worry,
stress, tire, wear out, exhaust, fatigue, weary, overdo,
press, trash, infest; *Scot* pingle
OLD cark, dun, trounce, turmoil
FORMAL importune
COLLOQ. hassle, have it in for, put the wind up, put the
frighteners on, drive round the bend/twist, breathe down
someone's neck, give someone grief

> **SYNONYM NUANCES**
>
> **Pester** can be used especially of one person persistently
> annoying another, while **badger**, although similar, is
> generally used to achieve a specific objective: *he
> badgered her into going*. **Harry**, on the other hand, is
> more suggestive of being troubled or beset by numerous
> problems: *the harried executive forgot the meeting*.
> **Afflict**, **plague** and **torment** would be used where
> something is a constant source of extreme worry or
> distress.
> **Hound** and **pursue** are suggestive of being constantly
> chased: *the young star was hounded by the press*.
> **Chivvy** also suggests chasing after someone to make
> them do something: *busy young mothers chivvied and
> scolded their children*. **Dragoon** is appropriate where
> someone is being forced into something: *she was
> dragooned into helping with the housework*. The word
> **bait** can be used to imply more deliberate, spiteful
> harassing especially when verbal; similarly **persecute**
> has to do with persistent bullying but suggests a more
> extreme action.
> The term **nag** tends to suggest making continual
> reprimands, while **vex**, **annoy** and the stronger
> **exasperate** put more emphasis on the victim's reaction,
> in this case anger or frustration. **Worry** and **stress** are
> appropriate for putting under mental pressure and again
> put emphasis on the feelings of the victim. The terms
> **tire**, **wear out**, **exhaust** and **fatigue** could be used if
> harassment has worn down the victim's energy.

harassed *adj*
distraught, pressurized, pressured, stressed,
under pressure, under stress, strained, distressed, troubled,
worried, careworn, hounded, pestered, plagued,
tormented, harried, vexed
COLLOQ. hassled, stressed-out, uptight
F₃ carefree

harassment *n*
annoyance, nuisance, pestering trouble, molest,
molestation, persecution, pressuring torment, bother,
distress, aggravation, badgering bedevilment, irritation,
vexation
COLLOQ. hassle, grief
F₃ assistance

harbinger *n*
herald, forerunner, precursor, messenger, omen, portent,
warning sign, indication, *avant-courier*
FORMAL foretoken

harbour *n, v*
♦ *n*
port, dock, quay, wharf, marina, mooring anchorage,
haven, shelter, refuge, lodging
♦ *v*
1 HIDE, conceal, protect, shield, shelter, house, take in
OLD herd; *Scot* reset
2 *harbour a feeling*
hold, retain, cling to, entertain, maintain, foster, nurse,
bear, nurture, cherish, receive, believe, imagine

hard *adj, adv*
♦ *adj*
1 SOLID, firm, unyielding tough, strong dense, condensed,
compressed, compact, compacted, impenetrable, resistant,
stiff, rigid, inflexible, unpliable
COLLOQ. hard as stone/iron/rock
2 *a hard question/problem*
complicated, difficult, complex, involved, intricate, knotty,
baffling puzzling perplexing bewildering
3 *building a wall is hard work*
strenuous, difficult, arduous, onerous, laborious, tough,
tiring toilsome, exhausting backbreaking heavy, exacting
rigorous
4 HARSH, severe, strict, callous, unfeeling unsympathetic,
cruel, cold-hearted, hard-hearted, stern, tyrannical,
oppressive, pitiless, merciless, ruthless, implacable,
unsparing unyielding unrelenting distressing painful,
unpleasant, grim
FORMAL obdurate
COLLOQ. hard as flint, standing no nonsense, ruling with a
rod of iron
5 *hard times*
tough, unpleasant, difficult, harsh, grim, severe, painful,
distressing uncomfortable, disagreeable, austere
6 *a hard worker*
hard-working industrious, diligent, assiduous,
conscientious, zealous, enthusiastic, keen, busy, energetic
FORMAL sedulous
7 *a hard push*
forceful, powerful, strong intense, heavy, sharp, violent
8 *a hard winter*
cold, severe, harsh, raw, bitter, freezing
9 *hard evidence*
true, reliable, indisputable, undeniable, unquestionable,
definite, actual, certain, real, verified
10 *hard drugs*
addictive, harmful, habit-forming narcotic, heavy, strong
potent
F₃ **1** soft, yielding **2** easy, simple **4** kind, pleasant,
compassionate, gentle **5** easy, comfortable **6** lazy, idle **8**
mild **9** uncertain, unreliable
♦ *adv*
1 FORCEFULLY, powerfully, energetically, intensely, strongly,
heavily, sharply, forcibly, violently, vigorously
FORMAL with all your might
2 *work hard*
diligently, industriously, assiduously, conscientiously,
energetically, intensely, busily, enthusiastically, eagerly,
keenly
3 *look/think hard*
carefully, attentively, closely, intently, sharply, keenly
4 *a hard-won victory*
with difficulty, arduously, strenuously, laboriously, after a
struggle, vigorously

5 *the recession hit them hard*
severely, acutely, critically, badly, intensely, deeply, harshly
6 *snowing hard*
intensely, severely, strongly, heavily, steadily
E3 **3** carelessly **4** effortlessly **5, 6** lightly
■ **hard and fast**
binding fixed, definite, immutable, incontrovertible, inflexible, invariable, rigid, set, strict, stringent, unalterable, unchangeable, unchanging uncompromising
E3 flexible
■ **hard up**
penniless, impoverished, in the red, bankrupt, short, lacking
FORMAL impecunious
COLLOQ. broke, bust, stony broke, skint, cleaned out, strapped (for cash), on your uppers, on your beam ends, not having two pennies to rub together, dirt-poor
E3 rich

hard-bitten *adj*
callous, case-hardened, cynical, down-to-earth, hard-boiled, hard-headed, hard-nosed, toughened, inured, matter-of-fact, practical, realistic, ruthless, shrewd, tough, unsentimental
E3 callow

hard-boiled *adj*
tough, cynical, hard-headed, down-to-earth, unsentimental

hard-core *adj*
steadfast, dedicated, blatant, obstinate, rigid, staunch, explicit, extreme, intransigent, dyed-in-the-wool, diehard
E3 moderate

harden *v*
solidify, set, freeze, congeal, bake, cake, stiffen, petrify, strengthen, reinforce, concrete, buttress, brace, steel, gird, nerve, toughen, temper, deaden, season, accustom, train, inure, indurate, flesh
TECHNICAL anneal, vulcanize, calcify, case-harden, work-harden, chill, sclerose
OLD bronze; (*Spenser*) endure
FORMAL fortify, habituate, indurate
E3 soften, weaken

hardened *adj*
incorrigible, inveterate, irredeemable, seasoned, set, shameless, toughened, inured, reprobate, habitual, accustomed, habituated, chronic, unfeeling callous
FORMAL obdurate
E3 soft, callow

hard-headed *adj*
shrewd, astute, businesslike, sharp, level-headed, clear-thinking cool-headed, sensible, realistic, rational, pragmatic, practical, hard-bitten, hard-boiled, tough, unsentimental, down-to-earth
COLLOQ. hard-nosed
E3 unrealistic, sentimental, idealistic, impractical

hard-hearted *adj*
callous, unfeeling uncaring unconcerned, unkind, cold, hard, stony, stony-hearted, heartless, unsympathetic, cruel, inhuman, pitiless, merciless
OLD (*Shakesp*) flint-heart
E3 kind, merciful, compassionate, concerned

hard-hitting *adj*
bold, direct, blunt, forthright, frank, straight, vigorous, forceful, tough, uncompromising condemnatory, critical, unsparing
COLLOQ. no-holds-barred, pulling no punches
E3 mild

hardihood *n*
boldness, audacity, adventurousness, daring enterprise, courage, rashness, recklessness, risk, bravery, fearlessness, intrepidity, dauntlessness, valour, pluck
COLLOQ. bottle, guts, grit
E3 caution, reserve, timidity

hardiness *n*
robustness, toughness, resilience, resolution, boldness, courage, valour, ruggedness, sturdiness, intrepidity
FORMAL fortitude
E3 timidity

hardline *adj*
strict, tough, extreme, immoderate, inflexible, militant, uncompromising unyielding undeviating
FORMAL intransigent
E3 moderate, flexible

hardly *adv*
barely, scarcely, just, only just, not quite, not at all, almost not, by no means, none too, with difficulty; *Scot* jimp, jimply
OLD uneath

hardness *n*
toughness, severity, harshness, sternness, firmness, rigidity, difficulty, laboriousness, insensitivity, pitilessness, inhumanity, coldness
E3 ease, mildness, softness

hard-nosed *adj*
hard-boiled, hard-headed, hard-bitten, tough, ruthless, realistic, practical, unsentimental
COLLOQ. no-nonsense

hard-pressed *adj*
hard-pushed, hard put, harassed, harried, pushed, under pressure, under stress, overburdened, overtaxed
COLLOQ. up against it, in a corner, in a tight spot, between a rock and a hard place, with your back to the wall
E3 untroubled

hardship *n*
misfortune, adversity, trouble, difficulty, affliction, pain, distress, suffering burdens, trial, want, need, austerity, poverty, destitution, deprivation, misery
FORMAL tribulation, privation
E3 ease, comfort, prosperity

hardware *n*
apparatus, equipment, gear, supplies, tackle, kit, tools, outfit, paraphernalia, accessories, appliances, articles, furniture
FORMAL accoutrements, apparelment
COLLOQ. rig-out, stuff, things

hard-wearing *adj*
durable, lasting well-made, made/built to last, strong tough, sturdy, stout, rugged, resilient
E3 delicate

hard-working *adj*
industrious, diligent, assiduous, conscientious, enthusiastic, keen, zealous, busy, energetic
FORMAL sedulous
COLLOQ. with your nose to the grindstone
E3 idle, lazy

hardy *adj*
1 STRONG, tough, sturdy, durable, heavy-duty, robust, vigorous, fit, sound, healthy, indurate, indurated, iron-sided
2 BRAVE, courageous, plucky, fearless, undaunted, bold, daring intrepid, stalwart, stoical, stout, stout-hearted, heroic, indomitable, trusty
E3 **1** weak, tender **2** cowardly, unfaithful, fickle

hare-brained *adj*
foolish, stupid, silly, wild, daft, ill-conceived, careless, rash, reckless, inane, giddy
COLLOQ. half-baked, crackpot, scatty, scatterbrained
E3 sensible

hark *v*
listen, hear, give ear, mark, note, notice, pay attention, pay heed
OLD hearken
■ **hark back**
remember, recall, recollect, go back, turn back, revert
FORMAL regress

harlequin *n*
fool, jester, clown, comic, buffoon, zany, joker

harlot *n*
prostitute, callgirl, whore, trollop
OLD hussy, strumpet, wagtail
COLLOQ. pro, streetwalker, tramp, hooker, working girl
OLD COLLOQ. fallen woman, loose woman
SLANG scrubber, tart, slapper, slag, skank

harm *n, v*
♦ *n*
damage, loss, injury, hurt, pain, detriment, ill, misfortune, adversity, suffering ruin, destruction, wrong abuse, impairment, disservice
F3 benefit, service
♦ *v*
damage, impair, work against, blemish, spoil, mar, ruin, hurt, destroy, injure, wound, ill-treat, maltreat, abuse, molest, misuse, be detrimental to
F3 benefit, improve

harmful *adj*
damaging detrimental, bad, pernicious, unhealthy, unwholesome, injurious, wounding dangerous, hazardous, poisonous, toxic, destructive
FORMAL noxious, deleterious
F3 harmless

harmless *adj*
safe, innocuous, non-toxic, inoffensive, gentle, mild, blameless, innocent, -friendly
F3 harmful, dangerous, destructive

harmonious *adj*
1 MELODIOUS, tuneful, musical, sweet-sounding harmonizing rhythmic, symphonious, euphonious, dulcet, pleasant, mellow
FORMAL mellifluous, consonous, symphonious
2 MATCHING, co-ordinated, balanced, compatible, consistent
OLD according
FORMAL congruous, consonant
COLLOQ. in sync
3 a harmonious relationship
agreeable, cordial, amiable, amicable, friendly, sympathetic, like-minded, peaceful, peaceable, compatible, Apollonian
FORMAL concordant, concordial, concinnous
F3 1 discordant

harmoniously *adv*
1 racial groups in the population that exist together harmoniously
amicably, cordially, agreeably, sympathetically, peacefully, compatibly, in a balanced way
2 colours that blend harmoniously
in a balanced way, symmetrically, consistently, compatibly
FORMAL congruously

harmonization *n*
co-ordination, matching balancing correspondence, reconciliation, agreement, accommodation, adaptation, arrangement

harmonize *v*
match, co-ordinate, balance, mix, blend, fit in, suit, tone, correspond, go together, get on with, agree, reconcile, coincide, accommodate, adapt, arrange, attune, compose
FORMAL be congruous, be congruent, accord
F3 clash, conflict

harmony *n*
1 TUNEFULNESS, tune, melody, melodiousness, euphony, chiming
OLD concent
FORMAL mellifluousness
2 live in harmony
agreement, unison, unanimity, oneness, unity, compatibility, like-mindedness, peace, goodwill, rapport, sympathy, understanding amicability, tune, friendliness, co-operation
FORMAL accord, concord, amity, assent, concurrence
3 CO-ORDINATION, balance, blending symmetry, correspondence, conformity, consistency, keeping
FORMAL concord, consonance, concinnity
F3 1 discord 2 conflict

harness *n, v*
♦ *n*
tackle, gear, equipment, straps, tack
FORMAL accoutrements
See panel at **tack**.
♦ *v*
control, channel, use, utilize, exploit, make use of, employ, mobilize, apply
■ **in harness**
1 CO-OPERATING, in co-operation, collaborating together
2 back in harness
at work, working busy, active, employed

harp
■ **harp on**
go/keep on about, keep talking about, dwell on, labour, belabour the point, press, reiterate, renew, repeat, nag
COLLOQ. go on and on about, flog to death

harpoon *n*
arrow, barb, dart, spear, trident, grains

harridan *n*
virago, vixen, witch, dragon, harpy, nag scold, shrew, tartar, fury, gorgon, termagant, Xanthippe, hell-cat
COLLOQ. battle-axe

harried *adj*
worried, anxious, agitated, troubled, bothered, distressed, harassed, hard-pressed, pressured, pressurized, plagued, tormented, ravaged, beset
COLLOQ. hassled
F3 untroubled

harrowing *adj*
distressing upsetting heart-rending disturbing alarming daunting tormenting frightening terrifying nerve-racking traumatic, agonizing excruciating
FORMAL perturbing
F3 encouraging heartening

harry *v*
badger, pester, nag chivvy, harass, oppress, plague, hound, torment, persecute, annoy, vex, worry, trouble, bother, pressurize, disturb, assail, molest
COLLOQ. hassle

harsh *adj*
1 SEVERE, austere, barren, stark, bitter, bleak, grim, comfortless, desolate, wild, inhospitable, spartan
2 CRUEL, strict, abrasive, severe, stern, grim, savage, brutal, unsympathetic, unfeeling unkind, hard, inhuman, pitiless, ruthless, merciless, Draconian
FORMAL acerbic
3 a harsh sound
rasping rough, coarse, croaking guttural, hoarse, gruff, grinding grating jarring jangling discordant, strident, ear-piercing raucous, sharp, shrill, unpleasant, dissonant, metallic
4 BRIGHT, dazzling glaring showy, flashy, gaudy, lurid, garish, bold
F3 1 mild, comfortable 2 compassionate, feeling lenient 3 harmonious, soft, gentle 4 gentle

---

SYNONYM NUANCES

sense 1
Severe can be widely applied as a synonym of harsh, while **austere** and **spartan** have implications of lacking embellishments: *prisons should be austere but decent.*
Barren goes even further by suggesting being totally bare: *a barren rolling landscape*, whilst **stark** returns to the idea of being completely unadorned. You could use **bitter** to suggest physical or mental pain: *we were*

buffeted by bitter winds, or if you want to imply acrimony: *a bitter argument*.

  Bleak is more suggestive of physical emptiness or psychological pessimism: *a bleak forecast for the economy*. **Grim** strongly suggests a lack of respite or hope, while **comfortless** would more explicitly convey a lack of physical or mental ease: *a comfortless bed; comfortless days*. **Desolate** has echoes of loneliness or forlornness: *a desolate wasteland of charred tree-stumps*, whereas **wild** would be applied to a landscape or conditions that are untamed and hostile.

harshly *adv*
1 *harshly treated*
cruelly, brutally, unkindly, severely, sternly, grimly, ruthlessly, pitilessly, mercilessly, unsympathetically
2 *sounds that grate harshly*
roughly, hoarsely, gruffly, discordantly, stridently, sharply, unpleasantly
F3 1 compassionately, comfortably, leniently **2** harmoniously, softly, gently

harshness *n*
bitterness, acrimony, coarseness, roughness, severity, ill-temper, rigour, starkness, sternness, strictness, hardness, sourness, abrasiveness, brutality
FORMAL acerbity, asperity
F3 mildness, softness, gentleness

harum-scarum *adj*
reckless, hasty, rash, impetuous, irresponsible, ill-considered, imprudent, wild, careless, haphazard, erratic
FORMAL precipitate
COLLOQ. hare-brained, scatterbrained, scatty
F3 sensible

harvest *n, v*
  ♦ *n*
1 HARVEST-TIME, autumn, ingathering reaping harvesting harvest-home, collection, store, supply, stock, accumulation, horde, rabi, *Spätlese*, vendange; *dialect* hockey; *Scot* hairst, kirn, tattie-lifting tattie-howking
2 CROP, yield, return, produce, product, fruits, result, consequence, effect, returns
  ♦ *v*
reap, mow, pick, glean, pluck, garner, gather (in), ingather, in, silage, collect, accumulate, amass, horde, gain, obtain, acquire, secure

hash *n*
1 MESS, botch, muddle, bungle, mix-up, jumble, confusion, mismanagement, hotchpotch, mishmash
2 GOULASH, stew, hotpot, lobscouse, lob's course

hashish *n*
hash, hemp, marijuana, bhang cannabis
COLLOQ. dope, ganja, grass, pot, weed

hassle *n, v*
  ♦ *n*
bother, inconvenience, nuisance, difficulty, trouble, problem, struggle, argument, disagreement, quarrel, squabble, trial, upset, fight, dispute, bickering wrangle
FORMAL altercation
COLLOQ. aggro
F3 agreement, peace
  ♦ *v*
bother, pester, trouble, annoy, worry, badger, harass, hound, harry, chivvy
COLLOQ. bug breathe down someone's neck, give someone grief
F3 assist, calm

hassled *adj*
harassed, distraught, pressurized, pressured, stressed, under pressure, under stress, strained, distressed, troubled, worried, careworn, hounded, pestered, plagued, tormented, harried, vexed
COLLOQ. stressed-out, uptight

haste *n*
hurry, rush, hustle, bustle, speed, velocity, rapidity, swiftness, quickness, briskness, fastness, urgency, rashness, recklessness, carelessness, foolhardiness, impulsiveness, impetuosity
FORMAL alacrity, celerity, expeditiousness
■ in haste
fast, quickly, rapidly, speedily, promptly, straightaway, apace
F3 slowness

hasten *v*
hurry (up), be quick, go fast/quickly, rush, run, sprint, dash, tear, race, fly, bolt, scamper, accelerate, speed (up), quicken, dispatch, urge, assist, help, aid, boost, press, advance, forward, step up, push forward
OLD make haste
FORMAL expedite, precipitate
COLLOQ. get a move on, step on it/the gas, hotfoot it, put your foot down
F3 dawdle, delay

hastily *adv*
1 RASHLY, recklessly, hurriedly, impetuously, heedlessly, impulsively
FORMAL precipitately
2 FAST, quickly, rapidly, hurriedly, speedily, promptly, straightaway, apace
COLLOQ. double-quick, chop-chop
F3 1 carefully, deliberately **2** slowly

hasty *adj*
1 *a hasty decision*
hurried, rushed, rash, reckless, heedless, thoughtless, careless, impetuous, impulsive, impatient, headlong hotheaded
FORMAL precipitate
2 *a hasty look at the newspaper*
fast, quick, rapid, swift, speedy, rushed, hurried, brisk, prompt, short, brief, cursory, fleeting transitory, perfunctory
FORMAL expeditious
F3 1 careful, deliberate **2** slow

hat
See panel on next page

hatch *v*
1 INCUBATE, brood, sit on, breed
2 CONCOCT, formulate, originate, think up, dream up, invent, conceive, devise, contrive, plot, scheme, design, plan, project

hatchet *n*
axe, chopper, cleaver, tomahawk, battle-axe, mattock, pickaxe, machete

hate *v, n*
  ♦ *v*
1 DISLIKE, despise, detest, loathe, abhor, not stand, recoil from, have an aversion to, feel revulsion at, spite
FORMAL abominate, execrate
COLLOQ. hate someone's guts
2 *I hate to disturb you*
regret, apologize, be sorry, be reluctant, be unwilling be loath
F3 1 like, love
  ♦ *n*
hatred, aversion, dislike, loathing abhorrence, animosity, ill-will, grudge, bitterness, resentment, antagonism, hostility, enmity, spite
FORMAL abomination, rancour
F3 liking love

Hats include:

Balaclava	busby	flat cap	mitre	*N Am*	sunhat
balmoral	bycoket	forage cap	mitre-wort	poke-bonnet	taj
baseball cap	cahperon	glengarry	mob cap	pork-pie hat	tammy
beanie	chapka	helmet	montero	sailor hat	Tam o' Shanter
bearskin	cheesecutter	Homburg	mortarboard	school cap	ten-gallon hat
beret	cloche	hood	muffin-cap	shako	top hat
bicorn	*Scot* cockernony	*Scot* hummle	*Scot* mutch	ski mask	toque
biggin	cock's-comb	bonnet	nightcap	skullcap	toy
biretta	college cap	hunting-cap	panama	snood	trapper
boater	deerstalker	jockey cap	peaked	sombrero	trencher cap
bobble hat	*N Am* derby	kalpak	cap	sou'wester	trilby
bonnet	*S Afr* doek	kepi	picture hat	Stetson®	tuque
bowler	fedora	Kilmarnock	pileus	stovepipe hat	turban
Bronx hat	fez	Kilmarnock cowl	pillbox	straw hat	yarmulka

■ **pet hate**
bugbear, anathema, bane, bête noire, dread, fiend, horror, nightmare, bogle, bogey, poker, rawhead

> **QUOTATIONS**
> A time to love, and a time to hate; a time of war, and a time of peace
>   *Bible, Ecclesiastes*

> **SYNONYM NUANCES**
>
> *verb sense 1*
> **Dislike** is a fairly mild term for something simply being displeasing whilst **despise** is far stronger and implies an element of contempt. Both **detest** and **loathe** would similarly refer to something deeply felt, suggesting extreme hatred, while **not stand** is also suggestive of an inability to bear: *she could not stand the sight of him, so she left the room*. **Recoil from** and **have an aversion to** put the emphasis on being more instinctively repulsed: *we recoil from the prospect of people suffering*, while **feel revulsion at** is even more strongly suggestive of complete abhorrence and disgust: *we feel some revulsion at these discriminatory policies*.

hateful *adj*
horrid, horrible, loathsome, detestable, abominable, offensive, disgusting repellent, repugnant, obnoxious, odious, revolting repulsive, nasty, unpleasant, disagreeable, despicable, vile, contemptible, foul, evil
FORMAL abhorrent, execrable, heinous
Ea pleasing

hatred *n*
hate, aversion, dislike, abhorrence, loathing disgust, revulsion, animosity, ill-will, grudge, bitterness, resentment, antagonism, hostility, enmity, spite
FORMAL detestation, repugnance, abomination, execration, rancour, antipathy, animus
Ea liking love

haughtily *adv*
arrogantly, proudly, imperiously, superciliously, disdainfully, contemptuously, scornfully, cavalierly
COLLOQ. snootily
Ea humbly

haughtiness *n*
arrogance, pride, conceit, contempt, contemptuousness, disdain, aloofness, loftiness, snobbishness, superciliousness, airs, hauteur, insolence, pomposity
FORMAL hubris
COLLOQ. snootiness
Ea friendliness, humility

haughty *adj*
arrogant, proud, conceited, vain, swollen-headed, lofty, imperious, high, lordly, stiff-necked, supercilious, cavalier, cavalierish, contemptuous, disdainful, scornful, superior,

self-important, egotistical, overbearing condescending patronizing snobbish, aloof, assuming; *Scot* paughty
OLD fastuous, haught, superb, orgulous, stomachful, stomachous, stomachy; (*Shakesp*) surly
COLLOQ. snooty, stuck-up, high and mighty, hoity-toity, with your nose in the air, toploftical, on your high horse
Ea humble, modest

haul *v, n*
♦ *v*
pull, heave, tug draw, tow, drag trail, move, transport, convey, ship, convoy, carry, cart, lug push
COLLOQ. hump
♦ *n*
loot, booty, plunder, spoils, takings, gain, yield, find
SLANG swag

haunches *n*
thighs, hips, buttocks, rear end, rump, nates, huckles, hucks, hunkers

haunt *v, n*
♦ *v*
1 *a ghost haunts the house*
walk, visit, appear often in, materialize, spook, possess, curse
OLD (*Shakesp*) spright
COLLOQ. show up
2 FREQUENT, patronize, spend time in, visit (regularly)
COLLOQ. hang about/around in
3 *memories haunted her*
plague, torment, trouble, disturb, worry, burden, recur, prey on, beset, harry, oppress, obsess, possess
♦ *n*
resort, stamping-ground, den, local, meeting-place, rendezvous, favourite spot; *Scot* howf
COLLOQ. hangout

haunted *adj*
1 POSSESSED, cursed, eerie, ghostly, jinxed, hag-ridden
COLLOQ. spooky
2 TROUBLED, worried, plagued, tormented, obsessed, preoccupied

haunting *adj*
memorable, unforgettable, persistent, recurrent, evocative, nostalgic, atmospheric, poignant
Ea unmemorable

hauteur *n*
arrogance, pride, conceit, contempt, contemptuousness, disdain, aloofness, loftiness, snobbishness, superciliousness, airs, insolence, pomposity
FORMAL hubris
COLLOQ. snootiness

have *v*
1 OWN, possess, get, obtain, gain, be given, acquire, secure, take, receive, accept, keep, hold, use
FORMAL procure

2 FEEL, experience, enjoy, suffer, undergo, submit to, be subjected to, endure, tolerate, put up with, go through, find, meet, encounter
3 CONTAIN, include, take in, embody, incorporate, consist of
FORMAL comprise, embrace, comprehend
4 *have a party*
hold, arrange, organize, take part in, participate in
5 *have to go now*
must, be forced, be compelled, be obliged, be required, ought, should
6 *have someone do something*
cause to, make, arrange, get, oblige, require, persuade, talk into, ask, tell, request, order, command, bid, force, compel, coerce
FORMAL enjoin, prevail upon
7 *I've had measles*
suffer from, get, develop, become infected with
FORMAL contract, succumb to
8 *have an invitation to the party*
receive, get, obtain, be given, gain, acquire
9 *have pity on someone*
show, demonstrate, display, exhibit, express, feel
FORMAL manifest
10 *have food/drink*
eat, swallow, consume, take, drink, devour, down, gulp, guzzle
FORMAL partake of
COLLOQ. put away, tuck into, knock back, wolf down
11 *have a baby*
give birth to, bear, bring into the world, be delivered of
OLD beget, bring forth
12 *I won't have such behaviour*
tolerate, put up with, take, accept, allow, permit, endure, abide, brook
COLLOQ. stand
13 *you've been had*
deceive, dupe, fool, trick, cheat, swindle, take in
COLLOQ. con, diddle
E3 **1** lack
■ **have done with**
finish with, give up, stop, cease, be through with
FORMAL desist
COLLOQ. throw over, wash your hands of
■ **have had it**
be in trouble, have no hope, be defeated, be exhausted, be lost, have no chance of success
COLLOQ. bite the dust, come to a sticky end
■ **have on**
1 WEAR, be dressed in, be clothed in
2 *What have you got on this week?*
have an engagement, have an appointment, have arranged, have planned
3 TEASE, trick, play a joke on
COLLOQ. kid, rag pull someone's leg lead up the garden path, wind someone up
SLANG take for a ride

haven *n*
harbour, port, dock, bay, anchorage, shelter, refuge, sanctuary, asylum, retreat, oasis

haversack *n*
backpack, rucksack, knapsack, kitbag

havoc *n*
chaos, confusion, disorder, disruption, mayhem, damage, destruction, ruin, ruination, wreck, wreckage, rack and ruin, devastation, waste, ravaging desolation
FORMAL despoliation
COLLOQ. shambles

hawk[1] *n*
hawks and other birds of prey
buzzard, kite, harrier, sparrowhawk, falcon, haggard, goshawk, tercel
Related adjective: accipitrine

hawk[2] *v*
hawking goods at people's houses
sell, offer for sale, peddle, market, offer, cry, tout, vend, bark

hawker *n*
seller, trader, dealer, pedlar, vendor, door-to-door salesman, crier, huckster, colporteur, barrow-boy, chapman, costermonger, coster

haywire *adj*
wrong out of control, crazy, mad, wild, chaotic, confused, disordered, disorganized, tangled, topsy-turvy

hazard *n, v*
♦ *n*
risk, danger, jeopardy, menace, threat, deathtrap, pitfall, accident, chance, luck; *N Am* crapshoot
OLD venture, wager, risque; (*Shakesp*) jump; (*Spenser*) hazardize
FORMAL peril, endangerment
E3 safety
♦ *v*
1 RISK, endanger, jeopardize, expose to danger, put at risk, put in jeopardy
OLD wage
2 CHANCE, gamble, stake, venture, suggest, put forward, submit, offer, speculate
OLD wage

hazardous *adj*
risky, dangerous, unsafe, precarious, menacing threatening insecure, chancy, uncertain, unpredictable, difficult, tricky
OLD jeopardous
FORMAL perilous
COLLOQ. hairy
E3 safe, secure

hazardously *adv*
dangerously, riskily, precariously, insecurely, uncertainly, unpredictably
OLD jeopardously
FORMAL perilously
E3 safely, securely

haze *n*
1 MIST, fog smog cloud, steam, vapour, film, mistiness, fogginess, cloudiness, smokiness, dimness, obscurity
2 BLUR, confusion, muddle, bewilderment, daze, uncertainty, indistinctness, vagueness

hazy *adj*
misty, foggy, smoky, clouded, cloudy, overcast, milky, fuzzy, blurred, muzzy, ill-defined, veiled, obscure, dim, faint, unclear, indistinct, vague, indefinite, uncertain
E3 clear, bright, definite

head *n, adj, v*
♦ *n*
1 SKULL, cranium
TECHNICAL caput
OLD (*Shakesp*) mazard, pash
COLLOQ. noddle, nut, conk, bonce
Related adjectives: capital, cephalic
2 MIND, brain, mentality, mental abilities, intellect, intelligence, wit(s), sense, understanding wisdom, thought, reasoning common sense
COLLOQ. brains, loaf, noddle, little grey cells, grey matter, upper storey
3 TOP, peak, summit, crown, crest, tip, apex, vertex, height, climax
4 FRONT, fore, forefront, vanguard, van, lead
5 LEADER, chief, captain, commander, director, manager, managing director, superintendent, supervisor, principal, head teacher, headmaster, headmistress, ruler, controller, administrator, president, governor, chair, chairman, chairwoman, chairperson
COLLOQ. boss, big cheese, bigwig top banana
6 COMMAND, control(s), leadership, directorship, management, supervision, charge

7 *have a head for figures*
gift, talent, genius, flair, skill, aptitude, aptness, bent, knack, facility, endowment, proficiency, power, faculty, attribute, ability, capability, capacity
8 *come to a head*
crisis, critical point, climax, emergency, catastrophe, calamity, dilemma
COLLOQ. crunch
9 *the head of a river*
source, origin, fount, spring rise, wellspring wellhead
10 *no head on the beer*
froth, foam, bubbles, fizz, suds, lather
🗲 **1** foot, tail **3** base, foot **4** back **5** subordinate
♦ *adj*
leading front, foremost, first, chief, main, prime, principal, top, topmost, highest, supreme, premier, dominant, pre-eminent
♦ *v*
1 *head the queue*
be at the front of, be first in, go first, lead
2 LEAD, rule, govern, command, direct, be in charge of, be in control of, manage, run, superintend, oversee, supervise, administer, control, guide, steer
■ **head for**
make for, go/move/travel towards, direct towards, go in the direction of, aim for, point to, turn for, steer for
■ **head off**
forestall, intercept, intervene, deflect, divert, turn aside, cut off, fend off, ward off, avert, prevent, stop
FORMAL interpose
■ **head over heels**
completely, utterly, uncontrollably, wholeheartedly, recklessly, thoroughly, intensely, wildly
■ **head up**
lead, direct, manage, be in charge of, take charge of, be responsible for
■ **go to your head**
1 MAKE DRUNK, intoxicate, inebriate, make dizzy, befuddle
COLLOQ. make woozy
2 *success has gone to his head*
make arrogant, make conceited, make proud, make someone full of themselves
COLLOQ. puff up
■ **keep your head**
keep calm, stay calm and collected, keep control of yourself, keep/maintain your composure
COLLOQ. keep your cool
■ **lose your head**
panic, lose control of yourself, lose your composure
COLLOQ. lose your cool, flap, freak out, go round like a headless chicken

headache *n*
1 *suffer from headaches*
migraine, neuralgia
TECHNICAL cephalalgia, hemicrania
COLLOQ. splitter
2 BOTHER, nuisance, trouble, inconvenience, problem, worry, pest, vexation, bane
COLLOQ. hassle, pain in the neck

heading *n*
title, name, headline, rubric, caption, section, division, classification, subject, category, class, head

headland *n*
promontory, cape, head, point, ness, foreland

headlong *adj, adv*
♦ *adj*
hasty, impetuous, impulsive, rash, reckless, careless, dangerous, breakneck, head-first
FORMAL precipitate
♦ *adv*
head first, hurriedly, hastily, prematurely, rashly, recklessly, carelessly, heedlessly, impetuously, impulsively, thoughtlessly, without thinking wildly
FORMAL precipitately

headman *n*
chief, leader, captain, ruler, chieftain, muqaddam, sachem

head-on *adj*
a head-on crash/confrontation
direct, full-frontal, straight-on, straight
COLLOQ. eyeball-to-eyeball

headquarters *n*
HQ, base (camp), head office, main office, centre of operations, nerve centre

headstone *n*
gravestone, tombstone, memorial, plaque

headstrong *adj*
stubborn, obstinate, intractable, wayward, pigheaded, wilful, self-willed, not listening to reason, perverse, contrary, unruly, ungovernable
FORMAL obdurate, refractory, recalcitrant, intransigent
🗲 tractable, docile

headway *n*
advance, progress, ground, way, improvement, movement, development

heady *adj*
intoxicating strong stimulating overpowering exhilarating invigorating thrilling exciting potent, ecstatic, euphoric, rousing

heal *v*
cure, make better, make well, remedy, mend, restore, improve, treat, soothe, comfort, salve, settle, reconcile, make good, patch up, put/set right
FORMAL assuage, palliate

health *n*
fitness, constitution, form, shape, trim, fettle, condition, tone, state, healthiness, good condition, wellbeing welfare, good shape, soundness, robustness, strength, vigour
OLD sanity
🗲 illness, infirmity

> QUOTATIONS
> Health is worth more than learning
> THOMAS JEFFERSON

healthily *adv*
well, soundly, robustly, strongly, vigorously, in condition, in good shape, in fine fettle

healthy *adj*
1 WELL, fit, good, fine, in condition, in good shape, in fine fettle, sound, sturdy, robust, strong
vigorous, hale, hale and hearty, blooming
flourishing thriving able-bodied,
healthsome, jolly
OLD lustick, well-disposed
COLLOQ. hardy, fit as a fiddle, right as rain, in the pink, a picture of health
2 *healthy food*
wholesome, nutritious, nourishing bracing good, beneficial, invigorating healthful
OLD (*Spenser*) hartie-hale
3 *healthy fresh air*
bracing invigorating refreshing stimulating
FORMAL salubrious
4 *a healthy economy*
successful, strong sound, robust, vigorous
5 *a healthy respect for authority*
wise, sensible, prudent, sound
FORMAL judicious
🗲 **1** ill, sick, infirm **2** colloq. junk **4** ailing

> SYNONYM NUANCES
> *sense 1*
> **Well**, **good** and **fine** are suggestive of being in satisfactory rather then remarkable health, and tend to be used in answer to inquiries: *he was a bit poorly at the weekend, but now he's fine*. **Sound** has the narrower suggestion of being unimpaired, but has added

implications of constant good health: *you are overweight but otherwise sound.*

The terms **robust** and **strong** could be used of someone or something with a healthy, working constitution, whilst **sturdy** is more suggestive of a strong physical build. **Fit** is generally used to suggest being in good condition and able to take on physical challenges, or you could use **vigorous** to emphasize the energy afforded by someone's good health.

The terms **blooming**, **flourishing** and **thriving** could be applied to anyone or anything progressing in a successful manner: *the flourishing tourist industry.* You would use **able-bodied** specifically to describe a person without any disability or physical impediments.

heap *n, v*

♦ *n*
1 MOUND, pile, stack, mountain, lot, mass, bundle, accumulation, collection, hoard, stockpile, supply, store, bulk, cumulus, cairn, drift, rick, ruck, clamp, pit, congeries, imbroglio; *dialect* bing tass; *Scot* rickle, toorie
OLD acervation, quarry, raff
FORMAL assemblage, agglomeration
2 A LOT, great deal, plenty, abundance, quantities, lots, mass, lashings; *N Am* raft
COLLOQ. load(s), stack(s), tons, oodles, pot(s), millions, scores

♦ *v*
1 PILE, stack, mound, bank, build, amass, accumulate, cumulate, collect, gather, assemble, hoard, stockpile, store (up), load, burden, lumber, mow, ruck, congest, uphoard
TECHNICAL coacervate
2 *heap criticism/praise on someone*
shower, lavish
FORMAL confer, bestow

hear *v*
1 LISTEN, catch, pick up, make out, get, perceive, be in touch with, overhear, eavesdrop, heed, pay attention, take in
COLLOQ. latch onto
2 LEARN, find out, discover, pick up, understand, gather, be informed, be told
FORMAL ascertain
3 JUDGE, pass judgement, try, examine, investigate, consider, inquire, adjudicate

hearing *n*
1 EARSHOT, sound, range, hearing distance, reach, ear, perception
2 *gave him a fair hearing*
opportunity to speak, opportunity to express yourself, chance to speak
3 TRIAL, inquiry, investigation, examination, review, case, judgement, inquest, inquisition, adjudication, audition, interview, audience

hearsay *n*
rumour, word of mouth, talk, common talk, common knowledge, gossip, tittle-tattle, report, say-so, *on-dit*
COLLOQ. buzz

heart *n*
1 SOUL, mind, character, disposition, nature, temperament
2 FEELING, emotion, sentiment, love, affection, passion, tenderness, kindness, compassion, concern, sympathy, pity, responsiveness, warmth
3 *lose heart*
courage, bravery, boldness, heroism, fearlessness, intrepidity, pluck, stout-heartedness, spirit, resolution, determination, enthusiasm, eagerness, keenness
FORMAL fortitude
COLLOQ. guts, bottle, spunk
4 CENTRE, middle, core, substance, kernel, nucleus, hub, nub, crux, essence, essential part, pith, marrow

FORMAL quintessence
3 cowardice **4** periphery
Related adjective: cardiac

■ **at heart**
basically, really, fundamentally, essentially, in essence, at bottom
■ **by heart**
by rote, parrot-fashion, pat, off pat, from memory, word for word, verbatim
■ **change of heart**
change of mind, rethink, second thoughts
■ **from the bottom of your heart**
deeply, sincerely, passionately, fervently, earnestly, profoundly, devoutly
■ **heart and soul**
eagerly, enthusiastically, completely, unreservedly, wholeheartedly, devotedly, gladly, heartily, absolutely, entirely
■ **set your heart on**
wish for, long for, desire, yearn, crave
■ **take heart**
be encouraged, brighten up, cheer up, rally, revive
COLLOQ. buck up, perk up
■ **take to heart**
be affected by, be moved by, be upset by, be disturbed by

> **QUOTATIONS**
> Only with the heart can a person see rightly; what is essential is invisible to the eye
> ANTOINE DE SAINT-EXUPÉRY, *Le Petit Prince*

Parts of the heart include:

aortic valve	left pulmonary	right atrium
ascending aorta	artery	right pulmonary
bicuspid valve	left pulmonary	artery
carotid artery	veins	right pulmonary
descending	left ventricle	veins
thoracic aorta	mitral valve	right ventricle
epicardium	myocardium	superior vena cava
inferior vena cava	papillary muscle	tricuspid valve
left atrium	pericardium	ventricular septum
	pulmonary valve	

heartache *n*
sorrow, anxiety, worry, grief, despair, anguish, agony, heartbreak, pain, suffering despondency, dejection, bitterness, distress, remorse, torment, torture
FORMAL affliction

heartbreak *n*
distress, sadness, suffering sorrow, dejection, despair, pain, grief, misery, agony, anguish, desolation
elation, joy, relief

heartbreaking *adj*
distressing sad, tragic, harsh, harrowing heart-rending pitiful, agonizing painful, excruciating grievous, bitter, cruel, disappointing poignant
heartwarming heartening

heartbroken *adj*
broken-hearted, desolate, sad, miserable, sorrowful, in low spirits, dejected, despondent, downcast, suffering, crestfallen, disappointed, disheartened, dispirited, grieved, crushed, anguished
COLLOQ. in bits
delighted, elated

heartburn *n*
indigestion, cardialgia, dyspepsia, brash
TECHNICAL peptic/reflux oesophagitis

hearten *v*
comfort, console, reassure, cheer (up), encourage, boost, inspire, invigorate, stimulate, energize, revitalize, animate, rouse, raise the spirits of

COLLOQ. buck up, pep up
E3 dishearten, depress, dismay

heartening *adj*
cheering heartwarming encouraging uplifting gladdening touching moving affecting pleasing gratifying rewarding satisfying

heartfelt *adj*
deep, profound, sincere, honest, genuine, unfeigned, devout, earnest, ardent, fervent, wholehearted, warm, compassionate
E3 insincere, false

heartily *adv*
1 ENTHUSIASTICALLY, eagerly, earnestly, deeply, profoundly, warmly, warm-heartedly, gladly, cordially, feelingly, sincerely, resolutely, unfeignedly, zealously, staunchly, vigorously, genuinely
2 ABSOLUTELY, completely, very, totally, entirely, extremely, thoroughly

heartless *adj*
unfeeling uncaring cold, hard, hard-hearted, cold-hearted, cold-blooded, callous, unkind, cruel, inhuman, harsh, brutal, ruthless, pitiless, merciless, unsympathetic, unmoved, inconsiderate
E3 kind, considerate, sympathetic, merciful

heartlessly *adv*
coldly, cold-heartedly, hard-heartedly, unsympathetically, callously, cruelly, harshly, brutally, pitilessly, mercilessly
E3 sympathetically, kindly

heart-rending *adj*
harrowing heartbreaking agonizing pitiful, piteous, pathetic, tragic, sad, distressing moving affecting poignant

heartsick *adj*
sad, heavy-hearted, despondent, dejected, disappointed, depressed, downcast, melancholy, glum

heart-throb *n*
pin-up, star, idol
COLLOQ. hunk
OLD COLLOQ. dreamboat

heart-to-heart *n*
cosy chat, private conversation, tête-à-tête, friendly talk, honest talk, personal conversation

heartwarming *adj*
cheering heartening encouraging uplifting gladdening touching moving affecting pleasing gratifying rewarding satisfying
E3 heartbreaking

hearty *adj*
1 ENTHUSIASTIC, eager, wholehearted, unreserved, heartfelt, sincere, genuine, unfeigned, warm, warm-hearted, affable, friendly, cordial, jovial, cheerful, ebullient, effusive, exuberant, bluff, bouncing staunch, stalwart
COLLOQ. mat(e)y, blokeish
2 *a hearty breakfast*
large, siz(e)able, substantial, filling solid, nourishing nutritious, ample, abundant, generous
3 STRONG, energetic, vigorous, boisterous, robust, healthy, sound, hardy
E3 **1** inhibited, reserved, cold, half-hearted **3** weak, feeble

heat *n, v*
♦ *n*
1 HOTNESS, warmth, sultriness, torridness, swelter, closeness, heaviness, high temperature, fever, feverishness
TECHNICAL calefaction
Related adjectives: calorific, thermal
2 ARDOUR, fervour, fervency, fieriness, passion, warmth, intensity, vehemence, fury, anger, excitement, impetuosity, earnestness, eagerness, enthusiasm, zeal
E3 **1** cold(ness) **2** coolness
♦ *v*
1 WARM, boil, toast, cook, microwave, bake, roast, reheat, warm up
TECHNICAL calefy

2 INFLAME, excite, animate, stir, rouse, arouse, stimulate, enrage, annoy, flush, glow
E3 **1** cool (down), chill

heated *adj*
angry, furious, raging passionate, impassioned, fiery, stormy, tempestuous, bitter, fierce, intense, vehement, violent, frenzied, enraged, inflamed, excited, animated, stirred, fired, roused, stimulated
COLLOQ. worked-up
E3 calm

heatedly *adv*
angrily, furiously, passionately, excitedly, intensely, vehemently, violently, bitterly, fiercely
E3 calmly

heater *n*
fire, radiator, boiler, central heating immersion heater, gas heater, electric heater, fan heater, convector, storage heater, solar heater

heath *n*
moor, moorland, fell, upland

heathen *n, adj*
♦ *n*
pagan, unbeliever, infidel, philistine, nations, idolater, idolatress, barbarian, savage
TECHNICAL Gentile
OLD paynim, proselyte of the gate
FORMAL nullifidian
E3 believer
♦ *adj*
pagan, unbelieving infidel, philistine, uncivilized, unenlightened, idolatrous, godless, irreligious, savage, barbaric
FORMAL nullifidian
E3 godly, believing

heave *v*
1 PULL, haul, drag tug raise, lift, hitch, hoist, lever, rise, surge
2 THROW, fling hurl, cast, toss, send, pitch, let fly
COLLOQ. chuck, sling
3 RETCH, vomit, be sick, spew, bring up, cough up, gag cat, disgorge; *dialect* boke
OLD egurgitate, parbreak
COLLOQ. throw up, sick up, chuck up, puke
SLANG fetch up, honk, barf; *N Am* upchuck; *Aust* chunder
4 *heave a sigh*
give, utter, express, let out, breathe

heaven *n*
1 PARADISE, home of God, glory, on high, bliss, next world, hereafter, life to come, afterlife, utopia, Elysium, elysian fields, happy hunting-ground, New Jerusalem, promised land, Zion, nirvana, Valhalla, Swarga, Land o' the Leal, Asgard, Olympus
OLD firmament, empyrean, welkin
FORMAL abode of God, vault of heaven
COLLOQ. up there
2 SKY, firmament, skies, the blue, ether
3 ECSTASY, rapture, bliss, happiness, complete happiness, joy, delight, transports of delight
COLLOQ. seventh heaven
E3 **1** hell

> **QUOTATIONS**
> The mind is its own place, and in itself / Can make a heav'n of hell, a hell of heav'n
> JOHN MILTON, *Paradise Lost*

heavenly *adj*
1 CELESTIAL, unearthly, supernatural, extraterrestrial, cosmic, other-worldly, spiritual, divine, ethereal, godlike, angelic, seraphic, cherubic, immortal, holy, sublime, blessed, beatific
FORMAL empyreal, empyrean

2 BLISSFUL, wonderful, glorious, marvellous, rapturous, beautiful, lovely, exquisite, perfect, enchanting delightful, enjoyable
COLLOQ. out of this world, divine
E3 1 infernal, mundane **2** hellish

heaven-sent *adj*
unexpectedly welcome, favourable, fortunate, happy, bright, timely, opportune
FORMAL auspicious
E3 *formal* inauspicious

heavily *adv*
1 PONDEROUSLY, slowly, clumsily, awkwardly, laboriously, with difficulty, painfully, hard, sluggishly, weightily, woodenly
2 COMPACTLY, closely, densely, solidly, thick, thickly
3 COMPLETELY, utterly, decisively, thoroughly, roundly, soundly
4 EXCESSIVELY, to excess, too much, abundantly, immoderately, copiously
E3 1 lightly **2** loosely

heaviness *n*
1 WEIGHT, weightiness, ponderousness, heftiness, bulk, density, solidity, thickness
2 *a heaviness in the air*
dejection, depression, despondency, melancholy, sadness, seriousness, oppression, oppressiveness, burdensomeness, onerousness, drowsiness, sleepiness, sluggishness, deadness, gloom, gloominess
FORMAL languor, lassitude, somnolence
3 INTENSITY, seriousness, severity, depth, greatness
E3 2 lightness, liveliness

heavy *adj*
1 WEIGHTY, hefty, ponderous, burdensome, cumbersome, awkward, massive, substantial, large, bulky, hulking solid, dense, thick
COLLOQ. weighing a ton, heavy as lead
2 *heavy work*
hard, difficult, tough, arduous, laborious, strenuous, troublesome, demanding taxing exacting harsh, severe
3 SERIOUS, intense, grave, sombre, deep, profound, dull, tedious, dry, uninteresting
4 *heavy fighting; a heavy shower*
severe, intense, extreme, excessive, considerable, strong great
5 *a heavy blow on the head*
forceful, hard, powerful, strong intense, sharp, violent
6 *heavy responsibilities*
burdensome, onerous, unbearable, intolerable, crushing difficult, weighty, exacting irksome, oppressive, taxing troublesome, trying wearisome
7 *with a heavy heart*
sad, miserable, despondent, depressed, discouraged, downcast, gloomy, sorrowful, crushed
8 *a heavy meal*
filling substantial, solid, big large, stodgy, rich, hearty, indigestible, starchy
9 *tables heavy with food*
laden, loaded, full, burdened, weighed down, encumbered, groaning
10 *the weather is heavy*
sultry, humid, oppressive, muggy, close, steamy, sticky, clammy
11 *a heavy sky*
dark, cloudy, overcast, dull, grey, gloomy, leaden
12 *a heavy drinker*
excessive, immoderate, intemperate, inordinate, overindulgent
E3 1 light **2** easy **3** light **4, 5** gentle **6, 8** light **10** cool, fresh **11** bright

SYNONYM NUANCES

sense 1
Weighty puts the emphasis quite simply on weighing a lot, whilst **hefty** implies being of a substantial size as well as weight. **Ponderous** goes further with its implication of being massive, and this rather negative aspect is developed in **burdensome** and **cumbersome**, which suggest something is unmanageable or troublesome: *computers were meant to do away with cumbersome paper files.* **Awkward** similarly suggests being unwieldy as much as heavy.
The terms **bulky** and **hulking** suggest something is difficult to manipulate due to size and weight: *his big hulking frame loomed over me.* To use a term such as **massive**, on the other hand, puts the emphasis firmly on enormous size, and the terms **solid**, **substantial** and **dense** can be used to suggest hardness and compactness in addition to weight and size.

heavy-duty *adj*
durable, lasting enduring long-lasting abiding hard-wearing reinforced, strong solid, sturdy, tough, robust, substantial, sound, resistant
E3 weak, perishable

heavy-handed *adj*
clumsy, awkward, blundering bungling unsubtle, tactless, insensitive, thoughtless, inept, oppressive, forceful, severe, harsh, stern, overbearing domineering autocratic, despotic
FORMAL maladroit
COLLOQ. ham-fisted, cack-handed, all fingers and thumbs, like a bull in a china shop
E3 skilful

heavy-hearted *adj*
sorrowful, sad, depressed, discouraged, disappointed, disheartened, downcast, downhearted, despondent, gloomy, miserable, morose, mournful, melancholy, glum, forlorn, crushed, heartsick
E3 light-hearted

heckle *v*
barrack, shout down, interrupt, disrupt, jeer, taunt, pester, gibe, catcall, bait, needle

hectic *adj*
busy, frantic, frenetic, chaotic, fast, feverish, excited, bustling heated, furious, frenzied, tumultuous, turbulent, wild
E3 leisurely

hector *v*
bully, intimidate, badger, chivvy, harass, menace, threaten, nag provoke, worry, browbeat, bluster, bullyrag huff
COLLOQ. bulldoze

hedge *n, v*
♦ *n*
1 FENCE, hedgerow, screen, windbreak, barrier, protection, dyke, boundary, raddle, sepiment
OLD haw, hay, mound, ox-fence
2 SAFEGUARD, protection, shield, cover, guard
♦ *v*
1 SURROUND, enclose, encircle, edge, hem in, confine, restrict, limit, guard, shield, protect, safeguard, cover, insure
FORMAL fortify
2 STALL, equivocate, sidestep, evade, quibble, prevaricate, dodge
FORMAL temporize
COLLOQ. duck, sit on the fence, waffle

hedonism *n*
gratification, luxuriousness, self-indulgence, sensualism, sensuality, voluptuousness, pleasure-seeking Epicureanism, epicurism, *dolce vita*, sybaritism
E3 asceticism

hedonist *n*
pleasure-seeker, sensualist, voluptuary, epicure, epicurean, *bon vivant, bon viveur,* sybarite
E3 ascetic

hedonistic *adj*
luxurious, pleasure-seeking self-indulgent, voluptuous, epicurean, sybaritic
E3 ascetic, austere

heed *v, n*
◆ *v*
listen, pay attention to, mind, mark, attend to, take note/notice of, take into account, take into consideration, bear in mind, consider, note, regard, observe, follow, obey
E3 ignore, disregard
◆ *n*
attention, regard, note, notice, consideration, mind, thought, watchfulness, care, caution, heedfulness, respect, ear
OLD (*Shakesp*) observance
FORMAL animadversion
E3 inattention, indifference, unconcern

heedful *adj*
attentive, watchful, mindful, observant, careful, prudent, cautious, vigilant, chary, wary
FORMAL circumspect, regardful
E3 heedless, unthinking

heedless *adj*
oblivious, unthinking careless, remiss, negligent, rash, reckless, irresponsible, foolhardy, inattentive, unobservant, unwary, incautious, unguarded, indiscreet, tactless, thoughtless, inconsiderate, unaware, regardless, uncaring unconcerned, unmindful, absent-minded, forgetful
FORMAL precipitate
E3 heedful, mindful, attentive, watchful, vigilant

SYNONYM NUANCES

Many of these synonyms are inherently disapproving in tone, for example **unthinking, thoughtless** and **inattentive**: *the storyline has twists to challenge inattentive viewers*. **Inconsiderate** clearly implies selfishness on the part of the person or actions you are describing while **uncaring** and **unconcerned** are disapproving of someone's lack of emotional involvement. To simply suggest a lack of care or regard for the consequences, you can use **incautious, regardless, heedless** or **unmindful**: *warriors, heedless of the dangers*. **Incautious** further implies a lack of care, possibly even a degree of recklessness: *the wine made her incautious*.

Both **forgetful** and **absent-minded** might be used of a slightly endearing vagueness, whereas **remiss** and **negligent** are more negative, implying the less forgivable aspect of neglect: *the Home Office has been remiss about security*. The terms **irresponsible** and **reckless** are again strongly marked by disapproval, and might be used of casualness verging on danger. **Tactless**, another critical term, has the narrower use of a tendency to hurt people's feelings. **Indiscreet** and **unguarded** both would be used more in the context of divulging secrets: *unguarded gossip*.

---

heedlessly *adv*
carelessly, unthinkingly, thoughtlessly, negligently, inattentively, rashly, recklessly
E3 attentively, watchfully, vigilantly

heel *v*
list, lean over, tilt, bank, tip, slope, slant, angle, sway
TECHNICAL seel

hefty *adj*
1 LARGE, big huge, strapping burly, hulking beefy, muscular, brawny, strong powerful, vigorous, robust, massive, stout

2 *a hefty blow*
forceful, hard, heavy, weighty, powerful, vigorous, solid, substantial, massive, immense, colossal, bulky, awkward, unwieldy
3 *a hefty sum of money*
substantial, considerable, generous, ample, siz(e)able
E3 1 small, slight **2** weak **3** small

height *n*
1 HIGHNESS, altitude, elevation, tallness, loftiness, stature
2 TOP, summit, peak, pinnacle, mountain top, hill top, apex, vertex, zenith, apogee, crest, crown, culmination, climax, perfection, extremity, maximum, limit, ultimate, uttermost, ceiling
E3 1 depth

heighten *v*
raise, elevate, lift, increase, add to, build up, magnify, intensify, strengthen, sharpen, improve, boost, amplify, enhance, exalt
FORMAL augment
E3 lower, decrease, diminish

heinous *adj*
evil, monstrous, atrocious, abominable, detestable, loathsome, abhorrent, contemptible, despicable, iniquitous, outrageous, shocking flagrant, vicious, wicked, awful, hideous, villainous, revolting hateful, odious, infamous, unspeakable, grave
FORMAL execrable, facinorous, nefarious

heir, heiress *n*
beneficiary, co-heir, fellow-heir, inheritor, inheritress, inheritrix, successor, next in line, scion
TECHNICAL parcener, legatee, substitute
OLD tanist

helix *n*
spiral, twist, coil, curl, whorl, loop, wreathe, screw, corkscrew
TECHNICAL curlicue, volute

hell *n*
1 *heaven and hell*
underworld, inferno, infernal regions, lower regions, abyss, fire, fire and brimstone, bottomless pit, pit, netherworld, Hades, Sheol, Acheron, Gehenna, Tophet, Abaddon, Tartarus, Malebolge, Erebus
FORMAL perdition, abode of the devil
COLLOQ. below, down there, other place
2 TORTURE, suffering anguish, agony, torment, ordeal, nightmare, misery, wretchedness
FORMAL tribulation
3 *What the hell are you doing here?*
on earth
COLLOQ. the blazes, the heck
OLD COLLOQ. the deuce, the dickens
E3 1 heaven
■ **give someone hell**
1 TROUBLE, annoy, torment, pester, vex, harass, punish, scold, beat, flog
2 CHASTISE, criticize
COLLOQ. tell off, haul over the coals, tear off a strip, give someone an earful
■ **hell for leather**
very fast/quickly, as fast/quickly as possible, hurriedly, quickly, rapidly, swiftly, recklessly, rashly, wildly, post-haste
FORMAL precipitately
COLLOQ. like crazy, like the clappers
■ **raise hell**
1 OBJECT NOISILY, protest loudly, be very angry, be furious
COLLOQ. hit the roof
2 MAKE TROUBLE, run riot, cause a commotion

PROVERBS
The road to hell is paved with good intentions

hell-bent *adj*
determined, bent, intent, fixed, resolved, set, settled,
tenacious, dogged, inflexible, unhesitating unwavering
FORMAL intransigent, obdurate

hellish *adj, adv*
♦ *adj*
infernal, devilish, satanic, diabolical, demonic, fiendish,
accursed, damnable, monstrous, savage, barbaric, wicked,
cruel, abominable, atrocious, dreadful, nasty, disagreeable,
unpleasant
FORMAL nefarious, execrable
E3 heavenly
♦ *adv*
dreadfully, awfully, very, extremely, exceptionally,
intensely, immensely, unpleasantly

hello *interj*
hallo, hullo, good morning good afternoon, good evening
greetings, welcome, holloa, *bonjour*, *buon giorno*
OLD hillo
COLLOQ. hi; *Aust* g'day; *N Am* howdy, yo

helm *n*
tiller, rudder, wheel
■ **at the helm**
in control, in command, in charge, leading
directing in the driving seat, holding the reins,
in the saddle

help *v, n*
♦ *v*
1 AID, assist, be of assistance, lend a hand, do something
for, do someone a good turn, serve, be of use, guide,
collaborate, co-operate, stand by, rally round, support,
back, encourage, oblige, contribute to, promote, nurse,
give a boost to
COLLOQ. do your bit
2 IMPROVE, relieve, soothe, assuage, cure, heal, remedy,
ease, facilitate, further
FORMAL ameliorate, alleviate, mitigate
E3 1 hinder 2 worsen
♦ *n*
1 AID, assistance, helping hand, collaboration, co-
operation, encouragement, boost, backup, support,
backing advice, guidance, service, charity, relief, use,
utility, avail, benefit, advantage
FORMAL succour
COLLOQ. shot in the arm, tower of strength
2 REMEDY, relief, cure, healing improvement, restorative,
moderator, balm, salve
FORMAL alleviation, amelioration, mitigation
COLLOQ. oil on troubled waters
3 *a daily help*
helper, home help, cleaner, worker, employee,
charwoman
COLLOQ. Mrs Mop
E3 1 hindrance
■ **cannot help**
be unable to stop, be unable to control, be unable to
prevent yourself
FORMAL be unable to refrain/abstain

SYNONYM NUANCES

verb sense 1
Aid can be widely used of supplying help, while **assist**
suggests a more active involvement: *parent volunteers
assisted in running the school library*. The phrase **lend a
hand** is suggestive of contributing to the efforts of others,
unlike **do something for** which implies undertaking
something on someone else's behalf. **Do someone a
good turn** and **oblige** have implications of a favour for
which they may owe a debt. **Serve** suggests being
subordinate, whereas **guide** has more to do with taking
a controlling advisory role.
   The word **co-operate** has connotations of togetherness
and joint effort, although it may not always refer to a
willing action: *unions were asked to co-operate with*

management *to improve production levels*. **Collaborate**
would only be used where there is mutual, usually
voluntary, involvement: *three prestigious galleries have
collaborated in an exhibition of his works*.
   You can use **support** and **stand by** to suggest
remaining true to someone in troubled times when help
is required, while **rally round** would be used of a
number of people coming together for someone in need:
*the neighbours rallied round when she became
housebound*. **Support** and **aid** can also be used like
back, of providing practical or financial help or
endorsement, whilst **encourage** has more to do with
providing motivation. **Promote** and **give a boost to** can
also be used of helping something's progress: *the new
laws promote good relations in the workplace*.

helper *n*
assistant, deputy, auxiliary, subsidiary, attendant, aid, aide,
adjutant, right-hand man/woman, PA, mate, helpmate,
partner, associate, colleague, collaborator, accomplice,
worker, co-worker, subordinate, ally, supporter, second,
second-in-command, employee, man/girl Friday, maid,
servant
FORMAL paraclete

helpful *adj*
1 USEFUL, of use, practical, of service, constructive,
worthwhile, valuable, beneficial, profitable, advantageous,
instrumental
OLD furthersome, second
2 *a helpful person*
co-operative, obliging accommodating neighbourly,
friendly, caring considerate, kind, benevolent, charitable,
sympathetic, supportive
E3 1 useless, futile 2 unfriendly, cruel

helpfully *adv*
kindly, obligingly, sympathetically, considerately,
reassuringly, usefully, conveniently

helping *n*
serving portion, share, ration, amount, plateful, bowlful,
spoonful, piece
COLLOQ. dollop

helpless *adj*
weak, feeble, powerless, dependent, vulnerable, exposed,
unprotected, defenceless, abandoned, friendless, destitute,
forlorn, desolate, incapable, incompetent, infirm, disabled,
impotent, paralysed
FORMAL debilitated
COLLOQ. helpless as a newborn babe
E3 strong independent, competent

helplessly *adv*
powerlessly, defencelessly, desolately, impotently, weakly,
feebly, vulnerably

helpmate *n*
partner, support, assistant, associate, companion,
consort, helper, helpmeet, better half, other half,
spouse, husband, wife

helter-skelter *adv, adj*
♦ *adv*
carelessly, confusedly, recklessly, wildly, hastily, hurriedly,
pell-mell, rashly, impulsively, headlong
♦ *adj*
confused, disordered, disorganized, jumbled,
muddled, random, unsystematic, hit-or-miss, haphazard,
topsy-turvy
COLLOQ. higgledy-piggledy

hem *n, v*
♦ *n*
edge, edging border, margin, fringe, trim, trimming frill,
valance, flounce
TECHNICAL fimbria
♦ *v*
fringe, edge, trim, bind, border, skirt, fold
TECHNICAL fimbriate

■ **hem in**
surround, enclose, box in, close in, shut in, confine, restrict, limit, hedge in, pen in, trap, constrain

hence *adv*
therefore, thus, for this reason, accordingly, consequently, as a consequence
FORMAL ergo

henceforth *adv*
from now on, from this time on, in the future, henceforward, hereafter, hereinafter, hence

henchman *n*
aide, associate, subordinate, supporter, attendant, follower, right-hand man/woman, minion, bodyguard, lackey, underling
COLLOQ. heavy, hit man, hatchet man, crony, minder, sidekick

henpecked *adj*
dominated, subjugated, browbeaten, bullied, intimidated, criticized, harassed, pestered, badgered, tormented, meek, timid
OLD (*Shakesp*) woman-tired
COLLOQ. under someone's thumb, tied to someone's apron strings, like a puppet on a string
E∃ dominant

herald *n, v*
♦ *n*
messenger, courier, announcer, crier, forerunner, precursor, blazoner, usher, omen, token, signal, sign, indication
FORMAL harbinger, portent, augury
♦ *v*
1 ANNOUNCE, proclaim, broadcast, advertise, publicize, make known, make public, trumpet, fanfare
FORMAL promulgate
2 PRECEDE, usher in, show, indicate, signal, promise, foreshadow
FORMAL harbinger, augur, portend, presage
COLLOQ. pave the way

heraldry

Heraldic terms include:

addorsed	emblazonry	quarter
annulet	emblem	quatrefoil
arms	ensign	rampant
badge	escutcheon	regalia
bezant	field	roundel
blazon	fleur-de-lis	salient
bordure	gardant	saltire
caboched	griffin	sejant
camelopard	gyronny	semé
canton	hatchment	shield
centre	helmet	sinister
charge	impale	statant
chevron	insignia	supporters
cinquefoil	lozenge	tierced
coat of arms	mantling	trefoil
cockatrice	martlet	undee
compartment	motto	unicorn
couchant	mullet	urdé
crest	orle	urinant
dexter	pile	volant
displayed	pall	wivern
dormant	passant	
dragon	phoenix	

---

herbs and spices
See panel on next page

herculean *adj*
arduous, laborious, onerous, toilsome, demanding strong tough, exacting difficult, enormous, powerful, exhausting strenuous, tremendous, colossal, large, gigantic, massive, great, huge, mammoth, formidable, daunting gruelling heavy, hard

herd *n, v*
♦ *n*
1 *a herd of cattle*
drove, flock, swarm, pack; *Aust & NZ* mob
2 *follow the herd*
press, crush, mass, horde, throng multitude, crowd, mob, host, the masses, rabble
COLLOQ. riff-raff, plebs, proles
♦ *v*
1 FLOCK, congregate, gather, collect, get together, assemble, rally, huddle, muster
2 LEAD, guide, shepherd, look after, take care of, round up, urge, drive, goad, force

herdsman *n*
shepherd, cowherd, cowman, drover, stockman, grazier, wrangler; *N Am* vaquero

here *adv*
1 *come here*
in/to/at this place, present, around, in
2 *I must finish here*
at this point, at this time, now, at this stage
E∃ 1 there, away, absent, missing **2** then

hereabouts *adv*
here, near here, around here, in these parts, in this place

hereafter *adv, n*
♦ *adv*
from now on, from this time forward/onwards, hence, henceforth, henceforward, in the future, later, eventually
♦ *n*
afterlife, heaven, paradise, life after death, life to come, next world, elysian fields, happy hunting-ground

here and there *adv*
in different places, in various places, hither and thither, to and fro, sporadically
COLLOQ. from pillar to post

hereditary *adj*
1 *a hereditary title*
inherited, bequeathed, handed down, family, ancestral, left, willed, transferred
2 *hereditary diseases*
inborn, inbred, innate, inherent, inherited, natural, congenital, genetic, transmissible

heredity *n*
genetics, hereditary character, gene(s), genetic make-up, DNA, chromosomes, inheritance

heresy *n*
heterodoxy, unorthodoxy, nonconformity, free-thinking apostasy, dissidence, dissent, dissension, unbelief, atheism, agnosticism, scepticism, schism, error, sectarianism, separatism, revisionism, blasphemy
OLD recusance
E∃ orthodoxy

heretic *n*
free-thinker, nonconformist, apostate, dissident, dissenter, unbeliever, atheist, agnostic, sceptic, revisionist, separatist, schismatic, sectarian, renegade, miscreant
OLD recusant, zendik
E∃ conformist

heretical *adj*
heterodox, unorthodox, free-thinking dissident, dissenting revisionist, separatist, sectarian, renegade, unbelieving atheistic, agnostic, sceptical, rationalistic, schismatic, impious, irreverent, iconoclastic, blasphemous
OLD recusant
E∃ orthodox, conventional, conformist

heritage *n*
1 INHERITANCE, legacy, bequest, endowment, lot, portion, share, estate, birthright, due
2 HISTORY, past, tradition, culture, cultural, traditions, background, ancestry, descent, lineage, family, extraction, dynasty

Herbs and spices include:

allspice	cardamon	comfrey	hyssop	nutmeg	St John's wort (or
angelica	catmint	coriander	lavender	paprika	hypericum)
anise	cayenne	cumin	lemon balm	parsley	tarragon
basil	pepper	curry	lovage	pepper	thyme
bay	chervil	dill	mace	rosemary	turmeric
bergamot	chilli	fennel	marjoram	saffron	vanilla
borage	chives	gaillardia	mint	sage	
camomile	cinnamon	garlic	mustard	savory	
caraway seeds	cloves	ginger	oregano	sorrel	

hermaphrodite *adj*
androgynous, bisexual, male and female, polygamic
TECHNICAL androdioecious, gynodioecious, heterogamous, monoclinous, monoecious, protogynous

hermetic *adj*
airtight, sealed, watertight, shut, hermetical

hermit *n*
recluse, solitary, loner, monk, ascetic, anchorite, anchoress, ancress, eremite, stylite, pillarist, pillar-saint

hermitage *n*
retreat, refuge, haven, sanctuary, cloister, shelter, asylum, hideaway, hideout, hiding-place

hero *n*
1 *the hero of a play*
protagonist, leading male role/part, leading actor, lead actor, male lead, lead
2 *heroes in battle*
conqueror, victor, champion, brave person, person of courage, cavalier, lion, celebrity
COLLOQ. good guy
See panel below
3 IDOL, star, superstar, pin-up, ideal, paragon, celebrity, god
COLLOQ. heart-throb
Ea 1 villain

> **QUOTATIONS**
> Being a hero is about the shortest-lived profession on earth
> WILL ROGERS

heroic *adj*
brave, courageous, fearless, dauntless, undaunted, lion-hearted, stout-hearted, valiant, bold, daring intrepid, adventurous, gallant, chivalrous, noble, determined, selfless, epic, Homeric
FORMAL valorous, doughty
Ea cowardly, timid

heroically *adv*
bravely, courageously, boldly, valiantly, nobly, selflessly, fearlessly, dauntlessly
Ea timidly

heroine *n*
1 *the heroine of a play*
protagonist, leading female role/part, leading actress/lady, female lead, lead actor, lead, diva, prima donna, prima ballerina
2 *heroines in battle*
conqueror, victor, champion, brave woman, woman of courage, celebrity, Amazon
See panel below
3 IDOL, star, superstar, pin-up, ideal, paragon, celebrity, goddess
Ea 1 villain

heroism *n*
bravery, courage, courageousness, valour, fearlessness, dauntlessness, boldness, daring intrepidity, gallantry, chivalry, prowess, selflessness, determination, stout-heartedness, lion-heartedness
FORMAL fortitude, doughtiness
Ea cowardice, timidity; *formal* pusillanimity

hero-worship *n*
admiration, idolization, adoration, worship, exaltation, glorification, adulation, idealization, deification
FORMAL veneration
COLLOQ. putting on a pedestal

hesitancy *n*
reluctance, misgiving qualm, scruples, unwillingness, disinclination, doubt, doubtfulness, reservation, uncertainty, indecision, wavering
FORMAL demur, irresolution
Ea willingness, certainty

hesitant *adj*
hesitating reluctant, unwilling disinclined, half-hearted, uncertain, unsure, doubtful, sceptical, dubious, indecisive,

Legendary, historical and fictional heroes and heroines include:

GREEK MYTH:	Telemachus	Lancelot	**SUMERIAN:**	**UNITED STATES:**	Tarzan
Achilles	Theseus	Percival (Parsifal)	Gilgamesh	Daniel Boone	William Tell
Agamemnon				Paul Bunyan	
Ajax	**CELTIC MYTH:**	**HINDU:**	**JAPANESE:**	Davy Crockett	**SUPERHEROES:**
Argonauts	Bran	Rama	Raiko	Molly Pitcher	Batman
Atalanta	Cúchulainn		Yamato Take	Paul Revere	Daredevil
Bellerophon	Fionn MacCumhail	**PERSIAN:**	Yorimasa		Elektra
Cadmus	Pwyll	Rustam	Yoshitsune		Fantastic Four
Diomedes				**LITERATURE AND**	Iron Man
Hector	**GERMANIC AND**	**RUSSIAN:**	**SCOTTISH:**	**ROMANCE:**	Spiderman
Hercules	**NORSE MYTH:**	Ivan Tsarevich	Rob Roy	Beowulf	Superman
Jason	Brunhilde	Mikula	William	Gawain	Wonder Woman
Odysseus	Siegfried (Sigurd)		Wallace	Ivanhoe	X-Men
Perseus		**SPANISH:**		Ogier the Dane	
Seven against	**ARTHURIAN LEGEND:**	El Cid	**BRITISH:**	Robinson Crusoe	
Thebes	Galahad		Boudicca	Roland	
	Gawain	**CHINESE:**	Robin Hood	Tam o'Shanter	
		Yu the Great			

See also **God**.

irresolute, vacillating delaying stalling wavering tentative, wary, shy, timid, halting stammering stuttering

FORMAL demurring

E∃ decisive, resolute, confident, fluent

hesitate v

1 PAUSE, delay, wait, think twice, doubt, hold back, hang back, hang fire, falter, stumble, halt, stammer, stutter; *Scot* swither

OLD dubitate, demur; *(Shakesp)* mammer

COLLOQ. shilly-shally, dilly-dally, hum and haw

2 BE RELUCTANT, be unwilling be disinclined, shrink from, scruple, boggle, vacillate, waver, balance, stall, be uncertain, dither; *Scot* tarrow; *N Am* dicker

FORMAL demur

COLLOQ. shilly-shally, dilly-dally

E∃ **2** decide

PROVERBS
He who hesitates is lost

SYNONYM NUANCES

sense 1
You could use the word **pause** to suggest a very short cessation: *he paused to think before answering*, whereas **delay** and the more informal **hang fire** would suggest putting off for a longer time: *he delayed his decision until he had more information*. You could use the term **think twice** specifically of stopping to reconsider one's actions: *think twice before doing anything rash*.
    Doubt would convey uncertainty about a course of action; **hold back** suggests restraint: *she started forward to hug him, then held back*; **hang back** implies reluctance to perform some action: *I hung back when volunteers were called for*. **Falter** and **stumble** are both suggestive of wavering in your intent: *their resolution failed, they faltered and then fled*. **Stammer** and **stutter** are specifically used with regard to speech, suggesting involuntary breaks or hesitation: *she started to argue, stammered, and went quiet*.

---

hesitation n

pause, delay, holding-back, hanging-back, waiting reluctance, unwillingness, disinclination, hesitance, scruple(s), qualm(s), misgivings, doubt, doubtfulness, scepticism, second thoughts, vacillation, wavering uncertainty, unsureness, indecision, stalling faltering stumbling stammering stuttering

FORMAL irresolution, demure, cunctation

COLLOQ. dilly-dallying shilly-shallying

E∃ eagerness, assurance

heterodox adj

unorthodox, unsound, dissident, dissenting free-thinking heretical, heretical, schismatic, iconoclastic, revisionist

E∃ orthodox

heterogeneous adj

diverse, varied, miscellaneous, assorted, different, mixed, motley, diversified, divergent, catholic, opposed, unlike, unrelated, dissimilar, contrary, contrasted, discrepant, piebald

TECHNICAL polymorphic

FORMAL multiform, disparate, incongruous

E∃ homogeneous

heterogeneously adv

diversely, differently, divergently, dissimilarly, contrarily

FORMAL disparately, incongruously

E∃ homogeneously

heterosexual adj, n

COLLOQ. straight

SLANG hetero, breeder

E∃ homosexual, gay

het up adj

worked up, angry, indignant, offended, resentful, upset, in a rage, beside yourself, tense, stressed, anxious, worried, agitated

COLLOQ. wound up, uptight, stressed-out

SLANG pissed off

hew v

1 CHOP cut, fell, saw, axe, lop, hack, sever, prune, trim, split

2 FORM, carve, sculpt, sculpture, cut, chip, whittle, chisel, hammer, fashion, model, shape, make

heyday n

peak, pinnacle, prime, flush, bloom, flowering culmination, golden age, boom time

hiatus n

break, gap, breach, opening rift, space, void, chasm, blank, discontinuity, pause, rest, lull, interruption, interval, lapse, suspension

FORMAL aperture, discontinuance, lacuna

hiccup n

snag delay, hold-up, hitch, trouble, problem, difficulty, mishap, setback, drawback, catch, impediment, hindrance, obstacle, block, check, barrier, obstruction

COLLOQ. glitch

hidden adj

1 *a hidden door*
concealed, covered, shrouded, veiled, masked, disguised, camouflaged, unseen, secret, out of sight

2 OBSCURE, dark, occult, secret, covert, close, cryptic, indistinct, mysterious, abstruse, mystical, latent, ulterior

FORMAL arcane, recondite

COLLOQ. under wraps

E∃ **1** showing apparent, revealed, visible, on view **2** obvious, clear, distinct

hide[1] v

1 CONCEAL, cover, cloak, shroud, veil, draw a veil over, put out of sight, screen, mask, disguise, camouflage, obscure, shadow, eclipse, darken, cloud, obstruct, bury, store, stow, secrete, withhold, keep dark, keep secret, suppress

FORMAL dissemble

COLLOQ. stash away, bottle up, keep under your hat, sweep under the carpet, keep under wraps

2 TAKE COVER, shelter, conceal yourself, lie low, go to ground, go into hiding keep out of sight, cover your tracks, lurk

COLLOQ. hole up, disappear into thin air, keep a low profile, lie doggo, lay a false scent

E∃ **1** reveal, show, display

SYNONYM NUANCES

sense 1
Conceal suggests keeping something out of view, whilst **cover**, **cloak** and **shroud** are more specific, in the sense of placing something over an object or person: *the moon was shrouded in mist*. **Veil** is similar, but implies disguising something unpleasant or undesirable: *a thinly veiled threat*, and **draw a veil over** also implies discouraging further talk on the subject: *let's draw a veil over last night's debacle*. **Screen**, likewise, has censorial aspects: *unpleasant facts screened by fawning officials*, although it can also be used more literally: *the hedge screened the washing area*. **Mask**, **disguise** and **camouflage** suggest that something has being altered so as not to stand out or be recognized for what it is, so these terms might also be used of hiding unpleasant things: *nosiness disguised as concern*.
    If something is coming between the viewer and their view, the terms **obscure** and **obstruct** are appropriate: *the safety notices were obscured by plants*, and both **shadow** and **eclipse** could be used where something has obstructed the light: *the square was eclipsed by tall buildings*. The term **bury** suggests putting something beneath many layers: *plants buried beneath a carpet of dead leaves*.
    The terms **store**, **stow** and **secrete** can all be used of deliberately hiding something to keep for your own use: *she stowed the money in her jeans pocket when his*

back was turned, whereas **withhold** and **suppress** are more appropriate for the deliberate hiding of information or facts, by preventing others from getting them: *he was withholding vital information from the public.*

hide² *n*
the hide of an animal
skin, pelt, fell, fur, coat, fleece, leather

hideaway *n*
retreat, hiding-place, hideout, refuge, sanctuary, shelter, cloister, hermitage, haven, nest, den, lair, hole

hidebound *adj*
set, rigid, fixed, entrenched, narrow, narrow-minded, intolerant, strait-laced, conventional, ultra-conservative, bigoted, uncompromising reactionary
FORMAL intractable
E3 liberal, progressive

hideous *adj*
ugly, repulsive, repellent, grotesque, monstrous, unsightly, horrid, ghastly, awful, dreadful, frightful, terrible, grim, gruesome, macabre, abominable, terrifying shocking outrageous, appalling horrifying disgusting revolting horrible, horrendous; *Scot* gash
OLD deform, loathly, ugsome
E3 beautiful, attractive

hideously *adv*
repulsively, grotesquely, horridly, dreadfully, frightfully, terribly, gruesomely, abominably, terrifyingly, shockingly, outrageously, disgustingly, horribly, horrendously
E3 beautifully, attractively

hideout *n*
retreat, hiding-place, hideaway, refuge, sanctuary, shelter, cloister, hermitage, haven, nest, den, lair, hole

hiding¹ *n*
go into hiding
concealment, cover, veiling screening disguise, shroud, veil, mask, camouflage

hiding² *n*
give someone a good hiding
beating flogging whipping caning spanking thrashing drubbing battering
COLLOQ. walloping tanning whacking belting licking

hiding-place *n*
hideaway, hideout, lair, den, hole, hide, nest, cache, cover, shelter, refuge, haven, sanctuary, retreat, cloister

hierarchy *n*
pecking order, ranking grading scale, series, ladder, echelons, strata, system, structure

hieroglyphics *n*
1 *decipher Egyptian hieroglyphics*
signs, symbols, secret symbols, picture writing pictograms, runes, code, cipher
2 *cannot understand his hieroglyphics*
scribble, squiggle, bad/illegible handwriting bad/illegible writing scratch, scrabble
FORMAL cacography

higgledy-piggledy *adv, adj*
♦ *adv*
any old how, anyhow, indiscriminately, untidily, confusedly, haphazardly, pell-mell, topsy-turvy
♦ *adj*
confused, disorderly, disorganized, untidy, jumbled, muddled, haphazard, indiscriminate, topsy-turvy

high *adj, n*
♦ *adj*
1 TALL, lofty, elevated, soaring towering
2 GREAT, strong powerful, forceful, vigorous, violent, intense, extreme

3 IMPORTANT, influential, powerful, eminent, distinguished, notable, prominent, chief, top, principal, leading senior, high-ranking high-level, elevated, exalted
4 *a higher form of life*
advanced, complex, elaborate, progressive, ultra-modern, high-tech
5 *a high standard*
good, excellent, fine, outstanding great, perfect, exemplary, commendable, noteworthy, first-class, first-rate, superior, superlative, surpassing unequalled, unparalleled, select, choice, quality, de luxe, gilt-edged, tiptop, top-class, blue-chip
COLLOQ. classy
6 *have a high opinion of someone*
favourable, good, positive, well-disposed, approving complimentary, admiring agreeable, appreciative
7 *high moral principles*
noble, moral, ethical, lofty, virtuous, upright, admirable, honourable, worthy
8 *a high price*
expensive, dear, costly, exorbitant, excessive, inflated, unreasonable, extortionate
COLLOQ. steep
9 *high winds*
strong intense, severe, extreme, forceful, violent, stormy, gusty, blustery, squally
10 HIGH-PITCHED, high-frequency, soprano, treble, falsetto, sharp, shrill, tinny, piping piercing penetrating acute
11 *high on drugs*
intoxicated, inebriated, hallucinating
COLLOQ. turned on, having your mind blown, doped, on a trip, stoned, freaked out, spaced out, wasted, zonked; *N Am* wired
SLANG bombed, loaded, blitzed, blasted, out of it
12 *meat going high*
bad, off, rotting smelling smelly, gamy, decayed, putrid, rancid
E3 1 low, short **2** low, slight **3** unimportant, lowly **4** low **5** low, poor, inferior **6** low, poor, bad **7** low **8** cheap **9** light, gentle **10** deep, low
♦ *n*
1 *feeling on a high*
intoxication, inebriation, hallucination
COLLOQ. trip, turn-on, freak-out
2 RECORD, height, summit, peak, top, zenith
E3 1, 2 low

■ **high and dry**
abandoned, marooned, stranded, helpless, bereft, destitute
COLLOQ. ditched, dumped

■ **high and low**
everywhere, all around, in all places, in each/every place, all over, throughout, far and near
COLLOQ. left right and centre, here there and everywhere; *N Am* every place

■ **high and mighty**
arrogant, conceited, haughty, overbearing self-important, snobbish, superior, proud, egotistic, condescending patronizing disdainful, cavalier, imperious, overweening
OLD hogen-mogen
COLLOQ. stuck-up, swanky, toploftical, toplofty

high-born *adj*
noble, aristocratic, blue-blooded, thoroughbred, well-born, patrician
E3 low-born

highbrow *n, adj*
♦ *n*
intellectual, scholar, genius, mastermind, academic
COLLOQ. egghead, brains, brainbox, know-it-all, clever clogs, boffin
♦ *adj*
intellectual, sophisticated, cultured, cultivated, academic, scholarly, bookish, deep, profound, serious, classical

COLLOQ. brainy
⊞ lowbrow

high-class *adj*
upper-class, top-class, top-flight, high-quality, quality, de luxe, luxurious, élite, elegant, superior, excellent, first-rate, choice, select, exclusive
COLLOQ. posh, classy, super
⊞ ordinary, mediocre

highfalutin, highfaluting *adj*
pretentious, pompous, supercilious, bombastic, grandiose, high-flown, high-sounding lofty
FORMAL affected, magniloquent
COLLOQ. la-di-da, swanky

high-flown *adj*
florid, extravagant, exaggerated, elaborate, flamboyant, ornate, ostentatious, pretentious, grand-sounding high-sounding grandiose, pompous, bombastic, turgid, artificial, stilted, affected, lofty, highfalutin, supercilious
FORMAL grandiloquent
COLLOQ. la-di-da

high-handed *adj*
overbearing domineering arrogant, haughty, imperious, dictatorial, autocratic, despotic, tyrannical, oppressive, arbitrary
FORMAL peremptory
COLLOQ. bossy

high-handedness *n*
arrogance, imperiousness, arbitrariness, inflexibility
FORMAL peremptoriness
COLLOQ. bossiness

high jinks *n*
horseplay, clowning buffoonery, foolery, fooling fooling around, tomfoolery, skylarking pranks, capers, antics, practical jokes, fun and games, rough-and-tumble
COLLOQ. monkey business

highland *n*
mountain, hill, upland, elevation, rise, mound, mount, height, ridge, plateau

> **QUOTATIONS**
> My heart's in the Highlands, my heart is not here, / My heart's in the Highlands a chasing the deer; / Chasing the wild deer, and following the roe; / My heart's in the Highlands, wherever I go
>   ROBERT BURNS, 'My Heart's in the Highlands'

highlight *n, v*
♦ *n*
high point, high spot, most interesting/exciting part, most significant feature, main feature, focus, peak, climax, best, cream
♦ *v*
underline, emphasize, put emphasis on, focus on, feature, call attention to, stress, accentuate, accent, play up, point up, spotlight, illuminate, show up, set off

highly *adv*
1 VERY, very much, greatly, most, thoroughly, really, considerably, decidedly, extremely, certainly, immensely, vastly, hugely, tremendously, exceptionally, extraordinarily
2 *think highly of someone*
favourably, approvingly, enthusiastically, warmly, well, appreciatively

highly-strung *adj*
sensitive, neurotic, nervous, easily upset, nervy, jumpy, on edge, temperamental, excitable, restless, overwrought, tense, stressed
COLLOQ. wound up, uptight, edgy
⊞ calm

high-minded *adj*
lofty, noble, pure, moral, ethical, principled, high-principled, idealistic, elevated, virtuous, upright, righteous, honourable, fair, good, worthy
⊞ immoral, unscrupulous

high-pitched *adj*
soprano, treble, falsetto, sharp, shrill, tinny, piping piercing penetrating acute
⊞ deep, low

high-powered *adj*
forceful, strong mighty, powerful, potent, effective, compelling convincing impressive, persuasive, telling valid, weighty, urgent, emphatic, vehement, forcible, dynamic, assertive, pushy, energetic, vigorous, go-ahead
⊞ weak, feeble

high-priced *adj*
expensive, dear, costly, exorbitant, excessive, extortionate, high, pricey, unreasonable
COLLOQ. steep, stiff
⊞ cheap

high-sounding *adj*
grandiose, flamboyant, ostentatious, overblown, pompous, florid, artificial, bombastic, extravagant, high-flown, ponderous, pretentious, stilted, strained
FORMAL affected, grandiloquent, magniloquent, orotund

high-speed *adj*
quick, swift, rapid, brisk, accelerated, speedy, express, hasty, hurried, flying
OLD fleet
⊞ slow

high-spirited *adj*
boisterous, bouncy, exuberant, effervescent, frolicsome, ebullient, sparkling animated, vigorous, vibrant, vivacious, lively, active, dynamic, energetic, spirited, dashing bold, daring
COLLOQ. full of beans
⊞ quiet, sedate, placid

high spirits *n*
boisterousness, exhilaration, exuberance, ebullience, animation, energy, spirit, boldness, liveliness, sparkle, good cheer, vivacity, capers, hilarity, buoyancy, joie de vivre
COLLOQ. bounce

highway *n*
road, roadway, route, thoroughfare, avenue, boulevard, broadway, grove, high street, main road, motorway, primary route, trunk road, bypass, ring road, arterial road, carriageway, clearway, dual carriageway, flyover, toll road; *N Am* expressway, freeway, turnpike

highwayman *n*
bandit, robber, land-pirate, rank-rider, knight of the road, footpad

hijack *v*
commandeer, skyjack, seize, take over
FORMAL expropriate

hike *v, n*
♦ *v*
1 RAMBLE, walk, trek, wander, march, tramp, trudge, plod
2 RAISE, increase, put up, lift, pull up
COLLOQ. jack up, push up
3 *hike up your clothing*
pull, tug jerk, hoist, jack, hitch, raise, lift
COLLOQ. yank
♦ *n*
ramble, walk, trek, wander, tramp, trudge, march

hilarious *adj*
funny, amusing comical, humorous, side-splitting farcical, laughable, riotous, uproarious, noisy, boisterous, rollicking merry, entertaining jolly, jovial
FORMAL risible

COLLOQ. hysterical, killing a scream
E3 serious, grave

hilariously adv
comically, humorously, farcically, laughably, uproariously, boisterously
COLLOQ. hysterically

hilarity n
mirth, laughter, fun, amusement, comedy, levity, frivolity, merriment, jollity, conviviality, high spirits, boisterousness, exuberance, exhilaration
E3 seriousness, gravity

hill n
1 HILLOCK, knoll, mound, hummock, prominence, eminence, elevation, rise, rising ground, hilltop, foothill, down, fell, tor, mountain, mount, height, saddleback, sugarloaf, dun, dune, pike, pimple, holt, mamelon, monadnock, morro, jebel, tell; dialect how, knot, pap, toot; Scot dod, kip, law; N Am butte, coast, cuesta, loma, mesa; S Afr berg kop, koppie
TECHNICAL cone, monticule
OLD barrow, low
2 a steep hill
slope, incline, gradient, ramp, rise, ascent, drop, descent, declivity
FORMAL acclivity
■ **over the hill**
old, getting on, past your prime
COLLOQ. past it, to be no spring chicken

hillbilly n
bumpkin, country bumpkin, country yokel, boor, lout, clodhopper, clodpoll, rustic, oaf, peasant, provincial, hawbuck; N Am & Aust bushwhacker
COLLOQ. hick, hayseed

hillock n
mound, hummock, knoll, dune, barrow, knap, knob, monticle, monticulus, tump; Scot knowe

hilt n
handle, grip, handgrip, shaft, haft, heft, helve
■ **to the hilt**
completely, fully, as fully as possible, wholly, entirely, utterly, to the full, to the end, to the maximum extent, in every respect
COLLOQ. all the way, from first to last, from beginning to end

hind adj
rear, back, hinder, tail, after, posterior, caudal
E3 fore

hinder v
hamper, obstruct, block, impede, encumber, keep off, handicap, hamstring hold up, delay, slow down, hold back, check, curb, halt, stop, forestall, arrest, prevent, bar, debar, deter, trammel, stunt, dwarf, cumber, foil, frustrate, thwart, balk, oppose, inhibit, interfere with, interrupt, overslaugh; Scot taigle
TECHNICAL estop
OLD embar, let
FORMAL retard, preclude
COLLOQ. stymie, put a spoke in someone's wheel
E3 help, aid, assist

SYNONYM NUANCES

Hamper can be used to suggest interrupting the progress of something perhaps temporarily, while **obstruct** and **block** suggest a more permanent situation. **Impede** suggests getting in the way of; **inhibit**, **encumber** and the rarer **cumber** have more to do with holding something's progress back: the country was encumbered by a poorly developed industrial sector. The terms **check** and **curb** suggest putting restraints on something and **handicap** and **hamstring** are equally suggestive of restrictions: as a doctor, I can't be hamstrung by sentiment.

Both **foil** and **frustrate** are appropriate of spoiling a plan, while **thwart** more definitely implies putting an end to it. The terms **arrest** and **prevent** clearly indicate that something has been stopped. **Stunt** and **dwarf** would be used of hindering or stopping the growth of something.
Forestall has more to do with taking anticipatory action: she tried to sidestep him but he forestalled her movement. You can use **bar** and **debar** where something is hindered by exclusion or prevention, whereas **deter** implies active discouragement, and the less common **trammel** suggests an element of confinement: the tightness of her skirt trammelled her steps.

hindmost adj
last, farthest behind, furthest back, rearmost, tail, endmost, furthest, final, remotest, trailing ultimate, concluding terminal
E3 foremost

hindrance n
obstruction, impediment, handicap, encumbrance, obstacle, stumbling-block, block, barrier, bar, check, curb, restraint, restriction, thwarting interference, interruption, stoppage, hold-up, delay, limitation, difficulty, drag snag hitch, drawback, disadvantage, inconvenience, deterrent, foil
OLD let
E3 help, aid, assistance

hindsight n
retrospect, afterthought, thinking back, reflection, re-examination, review, survey, recollection, remembrance
E3 prospect

hinge v
centre, turn, revolve, pivot, hang depend, rest
FORMAL be contingent

hint n, v
♦ n
1 TIP, advice, suggestion, help, clue, inkling suspicion, tip-off, cue, reminder, indication, sign, pointer, mention, allusion, intimation, whisper, insinuation, implication, innuendo
COLLOQ. wrinkle
2 a hint of garlic
touch, trace, overtone, tinge, taste, dash, soupçon, sprinkling speck, whiff, suspicion, suggestion, nuance
♦ v
suggest, prompt, indicate, signal, imply, insinuate, intimate, allude, mention
COLLOQ. tip off, tip someone the wink

hinterland n
interior, hinderland, back-country, backveld, back-blocks

hip¹ n
she broke her hip
haunch, loin, thigh, pelvis, hindquarters, posterior, buttocks, rump, croup, huck, huckle

hip² adj
parents trying to be hip
trendy, fashionable, modish, stylish, up to the minute, voguish
COLLOQ. all the rage, cool, funky, in, happening with it
OLD COLLOQ. groovy
E3 unfashionable

hippie n
beatnik, flower child, rebel, loner, bohemian
COLLOQ. dropout

hire v, n
♦ v
1 RENT, let, lease, charter, commission, book, reserve

2 EMPLOY, take on, sign up, sign on, engage, appoint, enlist, retain

Eǝ 2 dismiss; *colloq.* fire

♦ *n*

rental, rent, lease, fee, charge, pay, cost, price, salary, wage

hire-purchase *n*

instalment plan, easy terms, HP, deferred payments

COLLOQ. never-never

hirsute *adj*

hairy, bearded, unshaven, bristly, bewhiskered, shaggy

TECHNICAL hispid

FORMAL crinal, crinate, crinigerous, crinose, crinite

Eǝ bald, hairless

hiss *v, n*

♦ *v*

1 WHISTLE, shrill, whiss, whizz, sizzle, fizzle, effervesce, siffle

TECHNICAL assibilate

FORMAL sibilate

2 JEER, mock, scoff at, scorn, ridicule, taunt, boo, hoot, shout down, catcall

OLD (*Shakesp*) hizz

FORMAL deride

COLLOQ. blow raspberries, give someone the bird, goose

♦ *n*

1 WHISTLE, hissing buzz

FORMAL sibilance, sibilation

2 JEER, mockery, scoffing scorn, taunting contempt, hoot, boo, catcall

FORMAL derision

COLLOQ. raspberry, the bird

historian *n*

chronicler, archivist, annalist, diarist, narrator, recorder, historiographer, chronologer

historic *adj*

famous, famed, renowned, celebrated, momentous, important, significant, epoch-making notable, memorable, remarkable, outstanding extraordinary

FORMAL consequential

COLLOQ. red-letter

Eǝ unimportant, insignificant, unknown

⚠ **historic** or **historical**?

Historic means 'famous or important in history': *a historic battle*. *Historical* means 'of or about history': *books on military and historical topics* ; or 'having actually happened or lived, in contrast to existing only in legend or fiction': *Is Macbeth a historical person?*

---

historical *adj*

1 *of historical interest*

past, old, former, prior, ancient, bygone

FORMAL of yore

2 REAL, actual, authentic, factual, documented, recorded, chronicled, confirmed, verified, verifiable

FORMAL attested

Eǝ 2 legendary, fictional

historically *adv*

in the past, formerly, in former times, once, long ago, some time ago, in years gone by, originally, from past experience, yesterday, in the good old days

history *n*

1 THE PAST, bygone/olden days, former times, days of old, the (good) old days, antiquity, yesterday

FORMAL yesteryear, days of yore

2 CHRONICLE, record(s), annals, archives, chronology, account, study, report(s), narrative, story, tale, saga, biography, life, autobiography, memoirs

3 BACKGROUND, experience, record, credentials, qualifications, education, family, circumstances

---

QUOTATIONS

History, at least in its ideal state of perfection, is a compound of poetry and philosophy
THOMAS BABINGTON MACAULAY, 'Hallam's *Constitutional History'*

If men could learn from history, what lessons it might teach us
SAMUEL TAYLOR COLERIDGE, *Table Talk*

---

histrionic *adj*

dramatic, exaggerated, theatrical, melodramatic, insincere, sensational, unnatural, forced, artificial, bogus, ham

FORMAL affected

histrionics *n*

overacting theatricality, dramatics, performance, melodrama, artificiality, insincerity, unnaturalness, sensationalism, staginess, tantrums, scene

FORMAL affectation

COLLOQ. ranting and raving

hit *v, n*

♦ *v*

1 STRIKE, knock, tap, smack, slap, thrash, bash, slam, bat, thump, punch, beat, pound, batter, buffet, clout, cuff, box

COLLOQ. whack, belt, wallop, biff, sock, clock, clobber

SLANG twat

2 BUMP, collide with, bang, clip, crash into, smash into, run into, meet head-on, plough into, damage, harm

COLLOQ. prang

3 AFFECT, have an effect on, upset, disturb, trouble, devastate, overwhelm, move, touch

FORMAL perturb

COLLOQ. knock for six

4 *the thought hit me*

come to mind, come to, strike, be remembered, be thought of, occur to, dawn on, enter your mind

♦ *n*

1 STROKE, shot, blow, knock, tap, slap, smack, buffet, thrashing, beating, punch, cuff, box, clout, bash, bump, collision, impact, crash, smash

COLLOQ. whack, belt, wallop, clobbering, sock, prang

2 SUCCESS, triumph, winner, blockbuster

COLLOQ. knockout, wow

Eǝ 2 failure

■ **hit back**

retaliate, reciprocate, counter-attack, respond, strike back, criticize in return

■ **hit it off**

get along with, get on (well) with, be/become friendly with, become friends, warm to, grow to like, relate well to each other, get on good terms with

COLLOQ. click, get on like a house on fire, become thick as thieves

■ **hit on**

realize, arrive at, guess, think of, chance on, stumble on, light on, uncover, discover, invent

■ **hit out**

lash out, assail, attack, rail, strike out, denounce, condemn, criticize

FORMAL inveigh, vilify

hitch *v, n*

♦ *v*

1 FASTEN, attach, tie, harness, tether, bind, yoke, couple, connect, join, unite

2 PULL, heave, tug jerk, hoist

COLLOQ. yank, hike (up)

Eǝ 1 unhitch, unfasten

♦ *n*

snag delay, hold-up, trouble, problem, difficulty, mishap, setback, drawback, catch, impediment, hindrance, obstacle, block, check, barrier, obstruction

COLLOQ. glitch, hiccup

hitherto adv

until now, up to now, till now, so far, previously, formerly, beforehand, thus far
FORMAL heretofore

hit-or-miss adj

disorganized, haphazard, indiscriminate, undirected, unplanned, careless, offhand, casual, aimless, random, trial-and-error, perfunctory, lackadaisical, apathetic, cursory, uneven
▸ directed, planned, organized

hoard n, v

♦ n
collection, accumulation, mass, heap, pile, fund, reservoir, supply, reserve, store, stockpile, cache, treasure-trove; Scot pose
FORMAL aggregation, conglomeration
COLLOQ. stash
SLANG plant
♦ v
collect, gather, amass, accumulate, heap (up), stack up, buy up, save, set aside, put by, put away, lay in, lay up, store, stock up, stockpile, coffer, salt away, squirrel away, pile up, keep, treasure, uplay, uphoard
OLD hutch, mucker, spare
COLLOQ. stash away
▸ use, spend, squander

> **! hoard** or **horde**?
> A *hoard* is a store or hidden stock of something: *He had a hoard of chocolate bars under the bed.* A *horde* is a crowd or large number of people, etc: *Hordes of tourists come here every year.*

hoarder n

collector, saver, gatherer, miser, niggard, magpie, squirrel

hoarse adj

husky, croaky, croaking throaty, guttural, gravelly, gruff, growling rough, harsh, rasping raspy, grating raucous, discordant
▸ clear, smooth

hoarsely adv

roughly, harshly, raucously, croakily, huskily, gutturally, gruffly
▸ clearly, smoothly

hoary adj

1 WHITE-HAIRED, white, grey, grey-haired, silvery, grizzled, venerable, old, aged, ancient, antique, antiquated
FORMAL canescent, senescent
2 *that hoary old joke*
old, familiar, clichéd, trite, banal, overfamiliar, predictable, ancient, archaic
COLLOQ. old-hat

hoax n, v

♦ n
trick, prank, practical joke, put-on, joke, jest, ruse, fake, fraud, canard, deception, bluff, humbug cheat, swindle
COLLOQ. leg-pull, con, put-up job, frame-up, fast one, scam, spoof
SLANG N Am gold brick
♦ v
trick, deceive, play a practical joke on, take in, fool, dupe, gull, delude, swindle, cheat, hoodwink, bluff
COLLOQ. con, bamboozle, have on, pull someone's leg lead up the garden path, pull the wool over someone's eyes, pull a fast one on, double-cross, two-time
SLANG take for a ride

hoaxer n

joker, practical joker, jokester, prankster, trickster, hoodwinker, mystifier, humbug
COLLOQ. bamboozler, spoofer

hobble v

limp, walk with a limp, stumble, falter, stagger, totter, reel, dodder, shuffle, walk awkwardly, walk lamely

hobby n

pastime, interest, diversion, recreation, relaxation, pursuit, leisure activity/pursuit, sideline, game, sport, entertainment, amusement, divertissement, fad, avocation

hobgoblin n

goblin, imp, elf, dwarf, gnome, spectre, spirit, evil spirit, mischievous fairy, sprite, apparition, bugbear, bogey, bugaboo; *dialect* buggan, bull-beggar; *Scot* worricow

hobnob v

associate, fraternize, keep company, mingle, mix, go around, socialize
FORMAL consort
COLLOQ. hang about, pal around

hocus-pocus n

trickery, swindle, deception, delusion, chicanery, gibberish, humbug imposture, nonsense, mumbo-jumbo, spell, magic words, rigmarole, sleight of hand, legerdemain, trompe-l'oeil, artifice, cant, jargon, gobbledygook, abracadabra, cheat, hoax, deceit, conjuring
FORMAL prestidigitation

hodgepodge n

hotchpotch, mishmash, medley, miscellany, collection, mix, mixture, melange, jumble, confusion, mess

hog n, v

♦ n
pig boar, wild boar, porker, grunter, swine
♦ v
monopolize, control, dominate, corner, take over, keep to yourself

hogwash n

rubbish, nonsense, drivel, gibberish, trash, tripe, twaddle
COLLOQ. bunk, bunkum, claptrap, piffle, bilge, poppycock, hot air, cobblers, baloney, blah, bosh, guff, hooey, malarkey, moonshine, eyewash, tosh, balderdash, rot, tommyrot
SLANG (*vulgar*) balls, bollocks, crap, shit, bullshit

hoi polloi n

the common people, the ordinary people, the masses, the proletariat, the third estate, the peasants, the rabble, the herd, the great unwashed
OLD (*Shakesp*) varletry
FORMAL the populace
COLLOQ. riff-raff, the plebs, the proles
▸ aristocracy, élite, nobility

hoist v, n

♦ v
lift, elevate, raise, erect, jack up, winch up, heave, rear, uplift
♦ n
jack, winch, crane, tackle, pulley, capstan, lift, elevator

hoity-toity adj

arrogant, proud, overweening conceited, haughty, scornful, snobbish, supercilious, lofty, disdainful, pompous
COLLOQ. stuck-up, high and mighty, toffee-nosed, snooty, uppity

hold v, n

♦ v
1 GRIP, have in your hand(s), grasp, clutch, clasp, seize, cling to, embrace, enfold, hug have, own, possess, keep, retain
2 *hold a meeting*
run, organize, conduct, carry on, continue, call, summon, convene, assemble, preside over
3 *hold someone's attention*
keep (up), engage, occupy, maintain, catch, arrest, absorb, engross, fascinate, enthral, captivate, rivet, fill, monopolize
4 CONSIDER, regard, esteem, judge, reckon, suppose, view, treat, think, believe, maintain, assume, presume

FORMAL deem, adjudge

5 BEAR, support, hold up, keep up, sustain, carry, take, buttress, prop up, brace

6 DETAIN, imprison, confine, impound, hold in custody, lock up, stop, arrest, check, curb, restrain

FORMAL incarcerate

7 CLING, stick, adhere, stay, remain

8 *the bus holds 53 passengers*

contain, accommodate, take, have space/room for, have a capacity of

FORMAL compromise

9 *hold office as prime minister*

occupy, fill, take up, continue, fulfil, have, hold down

10 *the fine weather will hold*

continue, carry on, last, remain, stay, go on, keep up

11 *the invitation/theory still holds*

stay, apply, remain, remain in force, remain valid/true, be in force/operation, hold up

☐ 1 drop **5** collapse, fall, break **6** release, free, liberate

♦ *n*

1 GRIP, grasp, clasp, embrace, hug

TECHNICAL purchase

2 INFLUENCE, power, sway, mastery, dominance, dominion, authority, control, grip, leverage

COLLOQ. clout

■ **hold back**

1 CONTROL, keep back, curb, check, bar, restrain, impede, stop, delay, prevent, obstruct, suppress, stifle, retain, withhold, repress, contain, inhibit

FORMAL retard

2 HESITATE, delay, pause, shrink, refuse

FORMAL desist, refrain, forbear

☐ 1 release, disclose

■ **hold down**

1 *hold down a job*

keep, have, occupy, continue in

2 *hold someone down*

keep down, oppress, dominate, tyrannize, suppress

■ **hold forth**

speak, talk, speak/talk at length, lecture, discourse, preach, harangue

FORMAL orate, declaim

COLLOQ. spout

■ **hold off**

1 FEND OFF, fight off, ward off, stave off, keep off, keep at bay, repel, resist, rebuff

2 DELAY, postpone, put off, defer, avoid, wait

■ **hold on**

1 GRASP, grip, clutch, clasp, seize, cling to

2 CONTINUE, endure, remain, persevere, wait, carry on, keep going survive

COLLOQ. hang on

■ **hold out**

1 OFFER, give, present, extend

FORMAL proffer

2 LAST, last out, continue, carry on, persist, endure, persevere, stand fast, stand firm, resist, withstand

COLLOQ. hang on

☐ 2 give in, yield

■ **hold over**

defer, postpone, put off, put back, delay, adjourn, suspend, shelve

■ **hold up**

1 SHOW, display, present, exhibit, hold high

2 SUPPORT, bear, carry, hold, sustain, brace, shore up, prop up, lift, raise

3 DELAY, detain, slow, hinder, impede, obstruct, set/put back

FORMAL retard

4 ROB, steal from, burgle, knock over, break into; *N Am* burglarize

COLLOQ. mug stick up, knock off, nobble

5 APPLY, stay, remain, remain in force, remain valid/true, be in force/operation

■ **hold water**

bear scrutiny/examination, convince, be convincing make sense, ring true, work, stand up, pass the test

COLLOQ. wash

■ **hold with**

agree with, go along with, approve of, support, subscribe to, accept

FORMAL countenance

■ **hold your own**

resist, withstand, survive, stand fast, stand firm, stand your ground

COLLOQ. keep your head above water

☐ be defeated, lose ground

■ **get hold of**

1 OBTAIN, get, acquire, get your hands on

2 CONTACT, reach, get in touch with, speak to, communicate with, get through to

■ **put on hold**

delay, postpone, put off, hold off, defer

COLLOQ. put on the back burner

holder *n*

1 *holders of tickets*

bearer, owner, possessor, proprietor, keeper, purchaser, custodian, occupant

FORMAL incumbent

2 CONTAINER, receptacle, case, housing casing cover, sheath, rest, stand

holdings *n*

investments, shares, stocks, securities, bonds, assets, resources, land, real estate, possessions, property, estate, tenure

hold-up *n*

1 DELAY, wait, hitch, setback, snag difficulty, problem, trouble, obstruction, stoppage, (traffic) jam, bottleneck

2 ROBBERY, burglary, theft, break-in, raid

COLLOQ. mugging

SLANG heist, stick-up, stick-up job

hole *n, v*

♦ *n*

1 *dig a hole*

dent, dimple, depression, excavation, crater, mine, shaft, pothole, scoop, hollow, cavity, pit, chasm, cave, cavern, chamber, pocket, recess

2 *a hole in the roof*

aperture, opening space, break, gap, pore, puncture, perforation, eyelet, tear, split, crack, fissure, breach, rift, vent, notch, slit, gash, rent, outlet, shaft, slot

FORMAL orifice

3 *an animal's hole*

burrow, nest, lair, den, covert, set

4 *a hole in a theory*

flaw, fault, mistake, error, defect, loophole, inconsistency, discrepancy, weakness

5 HOVEL, slum, shack

COLLOQ. dump, tip, pigsty; *N Am* pigpen

6 *in a hole*

predicament, difficulty, quandary, snag plight

COLLOQ. fix, mess, jam, spot, corner, bind, pickle, hot/deep water, pretty pass

♦ *v*

puncture, perforate, pierce, breach, break, crack, stab, spike, slit, gash, rent

■ **hole up**

hide, conceal yourself, take cover, lie low, go to ground, go into hiding

■ **pick holes in**

criticize, find fault with, slate, run down

COLLOQ. pull to pieces, nit-pick

SLANG slag (off)

hole-and-corner *adj*

secretive, secret, underhand, clandestine, covert, furtive, stealthy, surreptitious

COLLOQ. back-door, backstairs, hush-hush, sneaky, under-the-counter

☐ open, public

holiday *n*
1 *go on holiday*
vacation, trip, recess, leave, leave of absence, time off, day off, break, awayday, rest, half-term, furlough
2 *a national holiday*
public holiday, bank holiday, legal holiday, feast day, festival, celebration, anniversary, saint's day, holy day
Related adjectives: ferial, festal

> **QUOTATIONS**
> One can always tell when one is getting old and serious by the way that holidays seem to interfere with one's work
> BOB EDWARDS, *Eye Opener*

holier-than-thou *adj*
self-righteous, sanctimonious, self-satisfied, complacent, self-approving smug priggish, pietistic, pious, religiose
FORMAL unctuous
COLLOQ. goody-goody
E3 humble, modest, meek

holiness *n*
sacredness, sanctity, spirituality, divinity, piety, devoutness, godliness, consecration, dedication, saintliness, blessedness, religiousness, goodness, virtuousness, righteousness, purity, perfection, sinlessness
OLD halidom, sanctimony
E3 impiety

holler *n, v*
yell, shout, bawl, bellow, roar, call, cheer, shriek, clamour, cry, howl, yelp, yowl, whoop

hollow *adj, n, v*
♦ *adj*
1 CONCAVE, indented, depressed, caved-in, sunken, deep-set, deep, cavernous, empty, vacant, void, unfilled
FORMAL incurvate
2 FALSE, artificial, deceptive, insincere, hypocritical, pretended, deceitful, sham, meaningless, empty, vain, futile, fruitless, useless, pointless, profitless, worthless, valueless, unavailing of no avail, Pyrrhic
3 *a hollow sound*
dull, flat, low, muffled, deep, rumbling echoing reverberant
E3 **1** solid **2** real
♦ *n*
1 HOLE, pit, well, cavity, crater, excavation, cavern, cave, depression, basin, pan, bowl, cup, dimple, dent, dip, niche, recess, nook, cranny, indentation, groove, channel, trough
FORMAL concavity
2 VALLEY, gorge, ravine, dell, glen, vale, dale, cirque
♦ *v*
dig excavate, burrow, tunnel, scoop, gouge, channel, groove, furrow, pit, dent, indent
■ **beat someone hollow**
defeat soundly/convincingly, rout, overwhelm
COLLOQ. thrash, lick, hammer, trounce, annihilate, devastate, slaughter, clobber, wipe the floor with

holocaust *n*
conflagration, flames, inferno, destruction, disaster, cataclysm, catastrophe, devastation, annihilation, extermination, extinction, massacre, carnage, mass murder, genocide, ethnic cleansing sacrifice, slaughter, pogrom, hecatomb
FORMAL immolation

holy *adj*
1 *holy ground*
sacred, hallowed, consecrated, sanctified, sacrosanct, dedicated, blessed, venerated, revered, religious, spiritual, divine
2 PIOUS, religious, devout, godly, God-fearing pietistic, saintly, virtuous, good, righteous, moral, faithful, pure, perfect, sinless
E3 **1** unsanctified **2** impious, irreligious

holy of holies *n*
most holy place, shrine, altar
FORMAL sanctum, inner sanctum, sanctum sanctorum

homage *n*
recognition, acknowledgement, tribute, honour, praise, adulation, admiration, regard, respect, esteem, deference, reverence, adoration, awe, worship, devotion
FORMAL veneration

home *n, adj, v*
♦ *n*
1 *invite someone to your home*
house, flat, apartment, bungalow, cottage, address
FORMAL residence, abode, domicile, dwelling dwelling-place, habitation
COLLOQ. pad, digs, semi-, roof over your head, somewhere to live
Related adjective: domestic
2 BIRTHPLACE, roots, home town, native town, homeland, native country, country of origin, mother country, motherland, fatherland
3 INSTITUTION, residential home, nursing home, retirement home, old people's home, sheltered housing children's home, Dr Barnardo's home, refuge, hostel, centre, retreat, asylum, safe place
4 *the home of jazz*
place of origin, birthplace, source, fount, cradle, habitat, natural environment, element
♦ *adj*
domestic, household, family, internal, local, national, native, inland, interior
E3 foreign, international, overseas
■ **home in on**
pinpoint, aim, direct, focus, concentrate, zero in on, zoom in on
■ **at home**
1 COMFORTABLE, relaxed, at ease
2 FAMILIAR, knowledgeable, experienced, confident, skilled, conversant, competent
COLLOQ. well up
■ **bring home**
make someone understand, make someone aware, make someone realize, impress, emphasize, instil, inculcate
■ **nothing to write home about**
not interesting not exciting dull, drab, boring ordinary, mediocre, inferior, predictable
COLLOQ. OK, not enough to set the Thames on fire, no great shakes, nothing earthshattering

> **PROVERBS**
> There's no place like home

homecoming *n*
return (home), arrival (at home), coming-back, return of the prodigal

homeland *n*
native land, country of origin, native country, home, fatherland, motherland, mother country

homeless *adj, n*
♦ *adj*
itinerant, travelling nomadic, wandering vagrant, rootless, unsettled, displaced, dispossessed, evicted, exiled, outcast, abandoned, forsaken, destitute, without a roof over your head
FORMAL of no fixed abode
COLLOQ. down-and-out, sleeping rough, on the streets
SLANG dossing
♦ *n*
travellers, vagabonds, vagrants, tramps, squatters
FORMAL derelicts
COLLOQ. down-and-outs
SLANG dossers

homelessness *n*
vagrancy, rootlessness, displacement, abandonment, destitution, not having a roof over your head

FORMAL no fixed abode
COLLOQ. sleeping rough
SLANG dossing

homely adj
1 *a homely room*
homelike, homey, comfortable, cosy, snug relaxed, informal, friendly, welcoming cheerful, hospitable, intimate, familiar
2 SIMPLE, plain, everyday, ordinary, domestic, natural, modest, unassuming unpretentious, unsophisticated, folksy, homespun
3 *a homely person*
plain, unattractive, unlovely, ugly, unprepossessing
COLLOQ. not much to look at
■ **1** grand, formal **3** attractive, lovely, good-looking

homespun adj
plain, simple, uncomplicated, unpolished, unrefined, unsophisticated, rough, rude, crude, rustic, homely, home-made, inelegant, amateurish, coarse, artless, folksy
■ sophisticated

homework n
prep, preparation, groundwork, spadework

homey adj
homelike, comfortable, cosy, snug relaxed, informal, friendly, welcoming cheerful, hospitable, intimate, familiar

homicidal adj
deadly, lethal, murderous, violent, bloodthirsty, mortal, death-dealing maniacal
FORMAL sanguinary

homicide n
murder, manslaughter, assassination, killing bloodshed, slaughter, slaying

homily n
sermon, lecture, talk, speech, address, harangue, preaching
OLD prone
FORMAL discourse, postil, oration
COLLOQ. spiel

homogeneity n
uniformity, consistency, identicalness, similarity, sameness, resemblance, likeness, oneness, correspondence, agreement, analogousness, comparability
FORMAL consonancy, similitude
■ difference, disagreement

homogeneous adj
uniform, consistent, unvarying unvaried, identical, similar, alike, (all) the same, of the same kind, all of a piece, akin, kindred, analogous, corresponding comparable, harmonious, compatible
FORMAL cognate, correlative
■ heterogeneous, different

homogeneously adv
uniformly, consistently, (all) the same, of the same kind, all of a piece, similarly, identically, correspondingly
■ heterogeneously

homogenize v
blend, merge, combine, amalgamate, make similar/uniform, coalesce, fuse, unite

homologous adj
related, matching similar, parallel, comparable, analogous, equivalent, like, correspondent, corresponding
■ different, dissimilar

homosexual n, adj
♦ n
gay, lesbian, bisexual
SLANG (*offensive*) queer, poof, dyke, faggot, fag fairy, bent, queen, homo, nancy, pansy, woofter, butch, closet queen, fruit, powder puff, puff, punk, quiff, shirtlifter; *Aust* tonk
■ heterosexual; *colloq.* straight
♦ adj
gay, lesbian, bisexual
COLLOQ. pink; (*offensive*) camp, butch

SLANG (*offensive*) queer, bent, dykey, homo
■ heterosexual; *colloq.* straight

hone v
sharpen, whet, point, edge, grind, file, polish, develop

honest adj
1 LAW-ABIDING, virtuous, upright, upstanding ethical, moral, principled, high-minded, right-minded, scrupulous, honourable, dependable, reputable, respectable, reliable, trustworthy, trusty, incorruptible, true, genuine, real, right, round, white, yeomanly; *dialect* even-down; *Scot* aefald
OLD soothful
COLLOQ. clean; *N Am* jake; *Aust & NZ* dinkum, dinky-di
SLANG *N Am* righteous
2 TRUTHFUL, true, sincere, frank, candid, blunt, outspoken, direct, straight, outright, forthright, straightforward, plain, simple, open, plain-speaking plain-hearted
OLD single
COLLOQ. up-front, four-square
3 FAIR, just, impartial, objective, equitable, above-board, legitimate, legal, lawful, square, bona fide
COLLOQ. on the level, fair and square, honest as the day is long straight as a die, on the up and up
■ **1** dishonourable **2** dishonest **3** unjust

SYNONYM NUANCES

sense 1
The term **law-abiding** creates a picture of someone who is honest in an everyday sense rather than especially so, and who is unlikely to cause problems: *law-abiding citizens should not have to put up with this kind of behaviour*, while **virtuous** has more to do with inherent goodness, although it can sound rather old-fashioned and hint at pomposity. **Upright**, however, is suggestive of moral rectitude, and **upstanding** suggests a basic decency.

The terms **ethical** and **moral** can be applied to someone or something that follows the accepted codes of conduct: *ethical practices in accounting*, while **principled**, although similar, would tend to be used of a more personal or voluntary quality: *a principled commitment to better housing*. **High-minded**, although suggestive of lofty principles, also has connotations of arrogance or conceit, unlike **right-minded**, which is straightforwardly descriptive of being naturally drawn to what is correct. **Scrupulous**, although guided by moral considerations, also has associations with thoroughness in these considerations: *he was scrupulous about his business affairs*, while the term **incorruptible** has more to do with unflinching rectitude even in the face of temptations.

The terms **dependable** and **reliable**, **trustworthy** and **trusty** are approving ones which would put the emphasis on the confidence merited by someone's honesty, while **reputable** and **respectable** emphasize their worthiness of esteem: *we are a reputable law firm*.

---

honestly adv
1 REALLY, truly, truthfully, sincerely, frankly, to be honest
COLLOQ. straight up, not to put too fine a point on it, no messing
2 LEGITIMATELY, legally, lawfully, morally, ethically, fairly, justly, objectively, honourably, in good faith
COLLOQ. on the level
3 TRUTHFULLY, truly, sincerely, frankly, directly, direct, straightforwardly, plainly, simply
COLLOQ. up-front
4 FAIRLY, justly, impartially, objectively, equitably, legitimately, legally, lawfully, above board
COLLOQ. fair and square
■ **2** dishonestly, dishonourably **3** dishonestly **4** unfairly

honesty n
1 VIRTUE, uprightness, honour, integrity, morality, morals, ethics, principles, righteousness, incorruptibility, scrupulousness, trustworthiness, genuineness, veracity

FORMAL probity, rectitude
2 TRUTHFULNESS, sincerity, frankness, candour, bluntness, outspokenness, forthrightness, straightforwardness, plain-speaking explicitness, openness
3 FAIRNESS, legitimacy, legality, equity, justness, objectivity, impartiality, balance, even-handedness
2 dishonesty **3** bias, prejudice, partiality

honeyed adj
sweet, pleasant, delightful, pleasing lovely, attractive, beautiful, pretty, winning cute, engaging appealing charming agreeable, affectionate, tender, kind, precious, dear, flattering
FORMAL mellifluous, unctuous

honorarium n
fee, pay, payment, salary, remuneration, recompense, reward
FORMAL emolument

honorary adj
unpaid, unofficial, titular, nominal, in name only, honorific, ex officio, formal
paid

honour n, v
♦ n
1 REPUTATION, good name, repute, renown, fame, glory, distinction, regard, respect, esteem, credit, dignity, self-respect, pride, integrity, uprightness, honesty, morals, ethics, principles, virtue, goodness, morality, decency, righteousness, trustworthiness, truthfulness
FORMAL rectitude, probity
2 AWARD, accolade, decoration, prize, reward, trophy, crown, title, distinction, laurel, commendation, acknowledgement, compliment, recognition, tribute, favour, privilege
See panel on next page
3 PRAISE, acclaim, acclamation, applause, homage, admiration, reverence, worship, adoration
4 CHASTITY, purity, virginity, maidenhood, modesty, abstinence, temperateness, continence, continency, celibacy, unmarried state, singleness, virtue, innocence, immaculateness
1 dishonour, disgrace
♦ v
1 PRAISE, acclaim, applaud, commend, have a high regard for, compliment, exalt, glorify, pay homage to, pay tribute to, acknowledge, recognize, decorate, crown, celebrate, commemorate, remember, admire, respect, esteem, revere, worship, prize, value
FORMAL venerate
2 *honour a promise*
keep, observe, respect, fulfil, carry out, discharge, execute, perform, be true to
3 *honour a cheque/bill*
pay, accept, clear, take
1 dishonour, disgrace

honourable adj
great, eminent, distinguished, renowned, famous, notable, noted, illustrious, respected, worthy, prestigious, trusty, reputable, respectable, admirable, virtuous, upright, upstanding straight, honest, trustworthy, truthful, true, sincere, dependable, reliable, noble, high-minded, principled, high-principled, moral, ethical, fair, just, right, righteous, good, decent
dishonourable, unworthy, dishonest

honourably adv
nobly, reputably, respectably, worthily, virtuously, honestly, truly, sincerely, well, decently, morally, ethically
dishonourably

hood n
cowl, scarf, capuche, capeline, domino

hoodlum n
1 HOOLIGAN, ruffian, rowdy, vandal, mobster, thug tough, lout, brute
COLLOQ. mugger
SLANG bovver boy, yob
2 CRIMINAL, lawbreaker, felon, offender, gangster, armed robber, gunman
COLLOQ. N Am mobster, hood

hoodoo n
voodoo, witchcraft, sorcery, magic, wizardry, occultism, the occult, the black art, black magic, enchantment, spell, incantation, divination, jinx
FORMAL necromancy, conjuration

hoodwink v
deceive, dupe, fool, take in, delude, mislead, outwit, hoax, trick, cheat, rook, gull, defraud, swindle, get the better of
COLLOQ. bamboozle, have on, con, lead up the garden path, pull a fast one on, pull the wool over someone's eyes
SLANG take for a ride

hoof n
foot, trotter, cloven hoof, cloot
TECHNICAL ungula

hoofed adj
cloven-footed, cloven-hoofed
TECHNICAL ungulate, unguligrade

Honours and awards include:

DENMARK:	NETHERLANDS:	CBE (Commander of the British Empire)	George Cross (GC)

DENMARK:
Order of Dannebrog
Order of the Elephant

FRANCE:
Croix de Guerre
Légion d'Honneur

GERMANY:
Iron Cross
Order of Merit

ITALY:
Ordine al Merito della
  Repubblica Italiana

NETHERLANDS:
Militaire Willemsorde
  Orde van Oranje Nassau
Nederlandsche Leeuw

UNITED KINGDOM:
The Most Excellent Order of
  the British Empire – GBE
  (Knight or Dame Grand
  Cross)
KBE/DBE (Knight or Dame
  Commander of the British
  Empire)

CBE (Commander of the
  British Empire)
OBE (Officer of the British
  Empire)
MBE (Member of the British
  Empire)
The Most Noble Order of the
  Garter (KG)
The Most Distinguished
  Order of St Michael and St
  George
The Distinguished Service
  Order

George Cross (GC)
Victoria Cross (VC)
Victoria Medal

UNITED STATES:
Bronze Star
Congressional Medal of
  Honour
Distinguished Service Cross
Legion of Merit
Medal for Merit
Purple Heart
Silver Star

---

hook *n, v*

♦ *n*

1 *a hook on a door/dress*
catch, peg barb, fastener, clasp, hasp, clip, hinge, tenter, tenterhook, goose-neck; *dialect* snig crome; *Scot* cleek
TECHNICAL becket, dog cantdog chape, crummock, gaff, tenaculum
OLD angle, crotchet, grappling-iron, gripple
FORMAL uncus, hamulus
2 SICKLE, scythe
3 BEND, curve, crook, angle, loop, elbow, bow, arc
4 BLOW, hit, stroke, box, thump, punch, cuff, clout, clip, knock, rap
COLLOQ. wallop

♦ *v*

1 BEND, crook, curve, curl
2 CATCH, capture, bag grab, trap, entrap, snare, ensnare, enmesh, entangle, strike; *Scot* cleek
TECHNICAL gaff
3 FASTEN, clasp, hitch, fix, attach, secure

■ **by hook or by crook**
by any means, by some means, somehow, one way or another, come what may
COLLOQ. by fair means or foul, come hell or high water

■ **hook, line and sinker**
completely, totally, utterly, wholly, fully, in full, absolutely, perfectly, quite, thoroughly, through and through, altogether, entirely, solidly
COLLOQ. in every respect, lock stock and barrel, from first to last, root and branch, every inch, heart and soul

■ **off the hook**
cleared, acquitted, in the clear
FORMAL exonerated, vindicated
COLLOQ. scot free

hooked *adj*
1 CURVED, bent, curled, beaked, barbed, beaky, aquiline, sickle-shaped
FORMAL falcate, hamate, hamose, hamous, hamular, hamulate, uncate, unciform, uncinate, adunc
2 ADDICTED, dependent, devoted, obsessed, enamoured

hooligan *n*
ruffian, rowdy, hoodlum, mobster, thug tough, rough, lout, vandal, tearaway, delinquent
COLLOQ. mugger; *Aust & NZ* hoon
SLANG bovver boy, yob; *Scot* ned

hoop *n*
ring circle, round, loop, wheel, band, girdle, circlet, stirrup, tire, basket, bail, hula-hoop, trundle; *Scot* gird, girr
TECHNICAL laggen-gird
OLD trochus

hoot *v, n*

♦ *v*

1 *an owl hooting*
call, cry, whoop, screech, tu-whit tu-whoo
FORMAL ululate
2 *the car hooted*
toot, beep, blare, whistle

3 *the audience hooted*
shout, shriek, cry, yell, whoop, howl, sneer, ridicule, taunt, mock, jeer, boo, hiss, howl down

♦ *n*

1 *the hoot of an owl*
call, cry, whoop, screech, tu-whit tu-whoo
2 *the hoot of a car*
toot, beep, whistle
3 *the hoots of the audience*
shout, shriek, cry, yell, whoop, howl, sneer, ridicule, taunt, mock, jeer, boo, hiss
4 *he's a real hoot*
amusing person/situation, joker, comic, wit
COLLOQ. character, scream, laugh, riot

■ **not give a hoot**
not care in the slightest, not be bothered
COLLOQ. not give a damn, not give a monkey's, not care a toss, not give a tinker's cuss/damn

hop *v, n*

♦ *v*

1 JUMP, leap, spring bound, vault, skip, dance, prance, frisk, limp, hobble
2 *hop over to Paris*
pop, nip, fly quickly

♦ *n*

1 JUMP, leap, spring bound, vault, bounce, step, skip, dance
2 *a quick hop by plane*
(quick) flight, trip, journey, excursion, jaunt
3 DANCE, disco, social, party
COLLOQ. knees-up, shindig

■ **caught on the hop**
caught unprepared/unawares, caught in the act, unready, ill-equipped
COLLOQ. caught with your trousers down

hope *n, v*

♦ *n*
hopefulness, optimism, ambition, aspiration, wish, desire, longing yearning craving dream, pipe dream, expectance, expectancy, expectation, anticipation, prospect, promise, belief, confidence, assurance, conviction, assumption, faith, trust
OLD (*Shakesp*) esperance
ЕЗ pessimism, despair

♦ *v*
aspire, wish, desire, long yearn, crave, dream, expect, be hopeful, await, look forward to, anticipate, aim, seek, be ambitious, contemplate, foresee, believe, trust, have confidence, pray, rely, reckon on, assume
COLLOQ. keep your fingers crossed, pin your hopes on, hope against hope
ЕЗ despair

> **QUOTATIONS**
> Hope springs eternal in the human breast: / Man never
> Is, but always To be blest
> ALEXANDER POPE, *An Essay on Man*

hopeful *adj*
1 OPTIMISTIC, confident, assured, expectant, sanguine, cheerful, buoyant, aspiring aspirant, positive
COLLOQ. bullish
2 *a hopeful sign*
promising encouraging heartening gladdening reassuring optimistic, pleasant, favourable, positive, rosy, bright, cheerful
FORMAL propitious, auspicious
E3 1 pessimistic, despairing **2** discouraging

hopefully *adv*
1 *hopefully the weather will improve*
I hope, if all goes well, with luck, all being well, probably, conceivably, it is to be hoped that
2 EXPECTANTLY, with hope, with anticipation, confidently, eagerly, optimistically, expectedly
FORMAL sanguinely
COLLOQ. bullishly

hopefulness *n*
optimism, ambition, aspiration, wish, desire, longing yearning craving expectation, anticipation, prospect, belief, confidence, assurance, conviction, assumption, faith, trust

hopeless *adj*
1 PESSIMISTIC, defeatist, negative, despairing desperate, gloomy, demoralized, downhearted, dejected, downcast, despondent, forlorn, wretched
2 UNATTAINABLE, unachievable, impracticable, impossible, vain, grave, foolish, futile, useless, pointless, worthless, poor, helpless, lost, past praying for, irreversible, irremediable, beyond remedy, irreparable, beyond repair, incurable
COLLOQ. all up (with), no-hope, not having a hope in hell
3 *hopeless at speaking French*
useless, incompetent, bad, weak
COLLOQ. lousy, pathetic, awful
E3 1 hopeful, optimistic **2** curable **3** skilled, expert

hopelessly *adv*
1 UNHAPPILY, pessimistically, negatively, despairingly, gloomily, desperately, despondently, dejectedly
2 INCOMPETENTLY, badly, weakly, uselessly, inefficiently
COLLOQ. pathetically, awfully

hopelessness *n*
despondency, pessimism, discouragement, despair, misery, gloom, gloominess, dejection, wretchedness, forlorn hope
OLD wanhope
COLLOQ. blues, dumps

horde *n*
band, gang pack, troop, crew, herd, drove, flock, swarm, crowd, mob, throng mass, multitude, host, army

> **!** **horde** or **hoard**?
> See panel at **hoard**.

horizon *n*
1 SKYLINE, vista, prospect, range, range of vision
2 *widen your horizons*
experience, scope, perspective, compass, outlook, perception
■ on the horizon
imminent, impending forthcoming in the offing approaching fast approaching coming on the way, near, close, looming menacing threatening brewing in the air, at hand, about to happen, almost upon you

horizontal *adj*
level, flat, plane, smooth, levelled, on its side
FORMAL supine

horny *adj*
1 *a horny shell*
hard, corny, callous
TECHNICAL ceratoid
FORMAL corneous
2 LUSTFUL, ardent, sexy, aroused, lascivious, lecherous, ruttish

FORMAL concupiscent, libidinous
COLLOQ. randy
E3 2 cold, frigid

horrendous *adj*
horrible, horrific, shocking appalling horrifying terrifying frightening terrible, dreadful, frightful

horrible *adj*
1 *horrible scenes of murder*
horrific, shocking appalling horrifying terrifying frightening harrowing bloodcurdling hair-raising terrible, black, horrendous, dreadful, frightful, repulsive, revolting abominable, grim, hideous, gruesome, monstrous, ghastly, awful, grisly, grisy
OLD ugly
COLLOQ. scary
See Synonym nuances panel at **ghastly**.
2 *that fish smells horrible*
unpleasant, disagreeable, nasty, unkind, obnoxious, horrid, disgusting revolting loathsome, repulsive, detestable, abominable, offensive, ghastly, awful, terrible, dreadful, frightful, horrendous
E3 1 attractive **2** pleasant, agreeable, lovely

horribly *adv*
1 HORRIFICALLY, appallingly, terribly, dreadfully, frightfully, repulsively, grimly, hideously, gruesomely
2 UNPLEASANTLY, disagreeably, awfully, terribly, dreadfully, frightfully

horrid *adj*
1 HORRIFIC, shocking appalling horrifying terrifying frightening harrowing bloodcurdling hair-raising terrible, dreadful, frightful, repulsive, revolting abominable, grim, hideous, gruesome, ghastly, awful
2 UNKIND, mean, nasty, awful, cruel, dreadful, obnoxious, hateful
COLLOQ. beastly
E3 1, 2 lovely, pleasant

horrific *adj*
horrifying shocking appalling awful, terrible, frightful, dreadful, ghastly, gruesome, terrifying frightening harrowing bloodcurdling
COLLOQ. scary

horrifically *adv*
shockingly, appallingly, terribly, dreadfully, frightfully, repulsively, disagreeably, awfully

horrify *v*
shock, appal, offend, outrage, scandalize, disgust, repel, revolt, sicken, nauseate, dismay, alarm, startle, scare, panic, frighten, terrify, terrorize, intimidate
OLD abhor
COLLOQ. spook, make your blood run cold, make your hair stand on end, make your flesh creep, give you the shivers, give you the heebie-jeebies, put the wind up, put the frighteners on, scare out of your wits, scare the living daylights out of, scare to death
E3 please, delight

horror *n*
1 *recoil in horror*
shock, outrage, disgust, distaste, revulsion, repugnance, abhorrence, loathing abomination, hate, dismay, alarm, fright, fear, terror, panic, dread, apprehension
FORMAL consternation, trepidation, detestation
2 GHASTLINESS, awfulness, frightfulness, hideousness, unpleasantness
E3 1 approval, delight

horror-struck *adj*
appalled, shocked, frightened, horrified, terrified, horror-stricken, aghast, stunned, petrified, scared stiff
E3 delighted, pleased

Breeds of horse include:

Akhal-Teké	British Warmblood	Frederiksborg	Karabair	Murgese	Salerno
Alter-Réal	Brumby	Freiberger	Karabakh	Mustang	Sardinian
American Quarter	Budyonny	French Saddle	Kladruber	New Kirgiz	Shagya Arab
Horse	Calabrese	Horse	Knabstrup	Nonius	Shire
American Saddle	Charollais	French Trotter	Kustanair	North Swedish	Suffolk Punch
Horse	Halfbred	Friesian	Latvian Harness	Oldenburg	Swedish Halfbred
American Trotter	Cleveland Bay	Furioso	Horse	Orlov Trotter	Tchenaran
Andalusian	Clydesdale	Gelderland	Limousin Halfbred	Palomino	Tennessee
Anglo-Arab	Comtois	German Trotter	Lipizzaner	Paso Fino	Walking Horse
Anglo-Norman	Criollo	Groningen	Lithuanian Heavy	Percheron	Tersky
Appaloosa	Danubian	Hanoverian	Draught	Peruvian Stepping	Thoroughbred
Arab	Døle	Hispano	Lokai	Horse	Toric
Ardennias	Gudbrandsdal	Holstein	Lusitano	Pinto	Trait du Nord
Auxois	Døle Trotter	Iomud	Mangalarga	Pinzgauer Noriker	Trakehner
Barb	Don	Irish Draught	Maremmana	Plateau Persian	Vladimir Heavy
Bavarian	Dutch Draught	Irish Hunter	Masuren	Poitevin	Draught
Warmblood	East Bulgarian	Italian Heavy	Mecklenburg	Rhineland Heavy	Waler
Boulonnais	East Friesian	Draught	Metis Trotter	Draught	Welsh Cob
Brabançon	Einsiedler	Jutland	Morgan	Russian Heavy	Württemberg
Breton	Finnish	Kabardin	Muraköz	Draught	

The points of a horse are:

back	elbow	gaskin	loins	nostril	tail
breast	eye	haunch	lower jaw	pastern	throat
cannon	face	head	lower (or under)	root	upper lip
chestnut	fetlock	hind leg	lip	(or dock) of	withers
crest of the neck	forearm	hip	mane	the tail	
croup (or rump)	forefoot	hock	mouth	shoulder	
crupper	forehead	hoof	neck	spur vein	
ear	forelock	knee	nose	stifle (joint)	

Breeds of pony include:

Connemara	Exmoor	Hackney	Przewalski's	Welsh Mountain
Dales	Falabella	Highland	Horse	Pony
Dartmoor	Fell	New Forest	Shetland	Welsh Pony

horse n
steed, mount, stallion, nag mustang mare, colt, filly, bay, sorrel, roan, hack, bronc(h)o, charger, cob, dobbin, hackney, centaur; *Welsh* keffel; *Scot* yaud; *Aust* brumby, yarraman
SLANG *Aust & NZ* moke; *Aust* neddy
Related adjectives: equine, caballine, hippic
See panels above

> **PROVERBS**
> Never look a gift horse in the mouth
> You may take a horse to water but you can't make him drink

horseman, horsewoman n
equestrian, rider, jockey, cavalryman, horse soldier, hussar, dragoon, knight

horseplay n
clowning buffoonery, foolery, fooling fooling around, tomfoolery, skylarking pranks, capers, antics, high jinks, practical jokes, fun and games, rough-and-tumble
COLLOQ. monkey business

hortatory adj
encouraging edifying heartening inspiriting instructive, practical, stimulating homiletic
FORMAL didactic, exhortative, exhortatory, hortative, preceptive
COLLOQ. pep

horticulture n
gardening cultivation, agriculture
TECHNICAL arboriculture, floriculture

hosanna n
praise, worship, alleluia, save us
FORMAL laudation

hose n
pipe, tube, tubing piping channel, conduit, duct

hosiery n
socks, stockings, tights, hold-ups, stay-ups, leggings, leg-coverings, hose

hospitable adj
friendly, sociable, welcoming neighbourly, receptive, cordial, amicable, congenial, convivial, genial, warm, helpful, kind, kind-hearted, gracious, generous, open-handed, liberal, bountiful
F3 inhospitable, unfriendly, hostile

hospital n
medical centre, health centre, clinic, infirmary, institute, sanatorium, hospice
Related adjective: nosocomial

hospitality n
friendliness, sociability, welcome, neighbourliness, accommodation, entertainment, congeniality, conviviality, warmth, cheer, generosity, kindness, liberality, helpfulness, open-handedness, open house
FORMAL philoxenia
COLLOQ. tea and sympathy
F3 unfriendliness, hostility
Related adjective: xenial

host[1] n, v
♦ n
1 COMPÈRE, master of ceremonies, MC, presenter, announcer, anchor, anchorman, anchorwoman, linkman, media personality, entertainer, party-giver
COLLOQ. emcee
2 PUBLICAN, innkeeper, landlord, landlady, proprietor, proprietress

♦ *v*
present, introduce, give, compère

host² *n*
a host of letters
multitude, myriad, array, army, horde, crowd, throng
mass, swarm, pack, troop, herd, mob, crush, band

hostage *n*
prisoner, captive, detainee, pawn, surety,
security, pledge

hostel *n*
youth hostel, bed and breakfast, B & B, YMCA, YWCA,
boarding-house, guesthouse, hotel, inn, motel, pension,
hospice; *N Am* dormitory
OLD hospital, entry
FORMAL residence
SLANG dosshouse; *N Am* flophouse

hostelry *n*
public house, inn, tavern, bar, hotel,
boarding-house, guesthouse, pension, motel;
S Afr canteen
COLLOQ. pub

hostile *adj*
1 BELLIGERENT, antagonistic, aggressive, warlike,
ill-disposed, unsympathetic, unfriendly, inhospitable,
inimical, opposed, malevolent
FORMAL bellicose
2 ADVERSE, unfavourable, contrary, opposite
FORMAL inauspicious
3 *hostile to trade unions*
disapproving averse, opposed, antagonistic, unfavourable,
disinclined, ill-disposed
FORMAL antipathic
E3 **1** receptive, friendly, welcoming **2** favourable

hostilities *n*
war, warfare, battle, fighting conflict, strife, action,
bloodshed

hostility *n*
opposition, aggression, belligerence, militancy, war,
enmity, antagonism, animosity, unfriendliness, cruelty,
ill-will, malice, resentment, hard feelings, anger, bitterness,
abhorrence, hate, hatred, malevolence, dislike, aversion,
prejudice, unpleasantness, disfavour
OLD envy
FORMAL estrangement, bellicosity, antipathy, animus
E3 friendliness, friendship

hot *adj*
1 WARM, heated, fiery, burning scalding scorching
blistering red hot, roasting baking boiling piping steaming
sizzling sweltering parching summery, balmy, searing
sultry, torrid, tropical
2 SPICY, spiced, peppery, piquant, sharp, pungent,
strong fiery
3 FEVERISH, delirious, burning flushed, red, with a
temperature
4 *his hot temper*
fiery, furious, angry, indignant, raging boiling
seething fuming livid, violent, heated, inflamed, incensed,
enraged
5 *hot competition*
fierce, intense, strong furious, keen, cut-throat
COLLOQ. dog-eat-dog
6 *not very hot on the idea*
keen, enthusiastic, eager, warm, earnest, zealous,
diligent, devoted
7 *hot news*
recent, new, fresh, latest, up-to-date, exciting
8 *hot goods*
illegally obtained/imported, contraband, stolen, illicit,
pilfered, ill-gotten
9 FASHIONABLE, chic, stylish, in vogue, in, popular,
prevailing current, latest, up-to-the-minute, up-to-date,
contemporary, modern

COLLOQ. trendy, all the rage, glitzy, ritzy, snazzy, swanky,
funky, hip, with it, cool
OLD COLLOQ. swinging
E3 **1** cold, cool, chilly **2** mild, bland **4** calm **7** old, stale
■ **blow hot and cold**
vacillate, waver, hesitate, fluctuate, sway,
oscillate, keep changing your mind, haver,
temporize
COLLOQ. dilly-dally, shilly-shally, hum and ha(w)
■ **hot air**
nonsense, empty talk, emptiness,
mere words, bluster, bombast, vapours, foam, froth;
Scot blethers
FORMAL verbiage
COLLOQ. balderdash, bosh, bunk, bunkum,
claptrap, gas, cobblers, piffle, bilge, codswallop,
baloney, eyewash, stuff and nonsense
SLANG (*vulgar*) bullshit, crap, shit
E3 wisdom

SYNONYM NUANCES

sense 1
Warm can be used of anything that is even mildly hot,
whilst **heated** is similar, but more suggestive of having
heat applied: *a heated swimming pool*, though, if used
of conversation, it is a little more marked in its
suggestion of a confrontational element: *a heated
discussion*. **Fiery**, however, is often used of being hot to
taste, or is more suggestive of being somewhat
tempestuous: *theirs was a fiery relationship*.

The terms **burning** and **scalding**, along with
scorching and **blistering**, suggest that damage could be
sustained and thus imply dangerously high temperatures,
while *red hot* offers its own warning. The terms
roasting, **baking** and **steaming**, and **piping** and
sizzling, make reference to how heat may have been
applied or is manifesting.

Sweltering, on the other hand, is usually reserved for
very hot climatic conditions, as are **sultry** and **tropical**,
and while **summery** and **balmy** also suggest weather of
a seasonal nature, they are associated with milder, more
comfortable temperatures. **Parching**, however, puts the
emphasis on the dryness effected by extreme heat: *a
parching desert dust storm*, and **searing** suggests great
intensity: *it was impossible to walk in the searing heat of
the outback*.

---

hotbed *n*
breeding-ground, den, hive, nest, seedbed, cradle, nursery,
school, forcing-house

hot-blooded *adj*
passionate, temperamental, excitable, spirited, wild, rash,
impulsive, impetuous, high-spirited, heated, fervent, fiery,
bold, eager, ardent, lustful, sensual, lusty
FORMAL perfervid, precipitate
E3 cool, dispassionate

hotchpotch *n*
mishmash, medley, miscellany, collection, mix, mixture,
melange, jumble, confusion, mess; *N Am* hodgepodge

hotel *n*
boarding-house, guesthouse, pension, motel, inn, bed and
breakfast, B & B, public house, tavern, hostel, hostelry,
aparthotel

hotfoot *adv*
speedily, at top speed, quickly, rapidly, swiftly, without
delay, hurriedly, in haste, hastily, posthaste, helter-skelter,
pell-mell
COLLOQ. at the double, at a rate of knots, flat out, hell for
leather, like the clappers, like greased lightning; *N Am*
lickety-split
E3 slowly; *formal* dilatorily
■ **hotfoot it**
hurry, rush, speed, race, tear, zoom, career, bowl along
sprint, gallop, dash, accelerate, quicken

COLLOQ. belt, hurtle, pelt, put your foot down, step on it
Ⓕ slow, delay

hothead n
tearaway, terror, madcap, madman, daredevil, desperado, hotspur

hotheaded adj
headstrong impetuous, impulsive, hasty, rash, foolhardy, reckless, wild, fiery, excitable, volatile, explosive, volcanic, hot-tempered, quick-tempered, short-tempered, irascible
Ⓕ cool, calm

hothouse n
greenhouse, glasshouse, conservatory, orangery, vinery

hotly adv
1 *a hotly debated issue*
passionately, forcefully, vehemently, strongly, vigorously, keenly, fiercely, ardently, fervently, intensely
2 *hotly pursued*
closely, at close quarters, at close range, narrowly, near, nearly, tightly
FORMAL nigh

hot-tempered adj
fiery, choleric, explosive, quick-tempered, short-tempered, violent, volcanic, testy, hasty, irascible, irritable, petulant
COLLOQ. ratty, stroppy; *Scot & Irish* crabbit
Ⓕ calm, cool; *formal* imperturbable

hound v
chase, pursue, follow, hunt (down), track, stalk, trail, drive, force, goad, prod, urge, chivvy, nag pester, disturb, bully, badger, harry, harass, provoke, persecute

house n, v
♦ n
1 BUILDING, home
FORMAL dwelling residence, domicile, habitation; *NZ* whare
SLANG gaff, pad, crib
2 HOUSEHOLD, family, family circle, home, ménage
Related adjectives: domestic, domal
3 *a publishing/design house*
firm, company, establishment, business, enterprise, corporation, organization
4 ASSEMBLY, legislative assembly, body, chamber, legislature, parliament, congress
5 *a full house at the theatre*
audience, auditorium, gathering assembly, turnout, crowd, spectators, onlookers, listeners, viewers
6 DYNASTY, family, clan, tribe, line, lineage, ancestry, blood, strain, race, kindred
♦ v
1 LODGE, quarter, billet, board, accommodate, put up, take in, have room/space for, shelter, harbour
2 HOLD, contain, protect, cover, guard, shelter, sheathe, place, keep, store
■ on the house
free, free of charge, without charge/cost/payment, for nothing at no (extra) cost, gratis

> **QUOTATIONS**
> A man's house is his castle
> SIR EDWARD COKE, *The Third Part of the Institutes of the Laws of England*

Types of house include:

apartment	dacha	hall
bedsit	detached	homestead
bungalow,	*N Am* duplex	hut
Scot but and ben	eco-lodge	igloo
chalet	farmhouse	lodge
chalet bungalow	flat	log cabin
condominium	ger	maisonette
cottage	grange	manor
council house	granny flat	manse
croft	hacienda	mansion
mia-mia	*colloq.* semi	town house
parsonage	semi-detached	treehouse
penthouse	shack	vicarage
pied-à-terre	shanty	villa
S Afr pondok	*Scot* single-end	*Aust* villa home
prefab	*NZ* state house	(or unit)
ranch house	studio	*Scot* weem
rectory	terraced	*Aust* wurley
riad	thatched cottage	yurt

See also **building**.

household n, adj
♦ n
family, family circle, house, home, ménage, establishment, set-up
♦ adj
1 DOMESTIC, home, family, ordinary, plain
2 *a household name*
everyday, common, familiar, well-known, famous, established

householder n
resident, tenant, occupier, occupant, owner, landlady, freeholder, leaseholder, proprietor, landlord, home-owner, head of the household

housekeeping n
home economics, domestic science, household management, running a home, domestic work/matters, homemaking housewifery

houseman n
1 DOCTOR, junior doctor, house-physician, house-surgeon, intern(e), resident
2 MANSERVANT, servant, butler, valet, retainer, gentleman's gentleman

house-trained adj
domesticated, tame, tamed, well-mannered, house-broken
Ⓕ unsocial

housing n
1 ACCOMMODATION, houses, homes, shelter
FORMAL dwellings, habitation
2 CASING, case, container, holder, covering guard, cover, sheath, jacket, protection

hovel n
shack, shanty, cabin, hut, shed, slum
COLLOQ. dump, hole

hover v
1 HANG, be suspended, poise, float, drift, fly, flutter, flap
2 *he hovered by the door*
pause, linger, hang about, loiter, hesitate, waver, fluctuate, alternate, seesaw
FORMAL vacillate, oscillate

however adv
nevertheless, nonetheless, still, yet, even so, regardless, though, anyhow, just the same, in any case, as it comes, at the same time, actually, howsoever, leastaways; *dialect* but, howsomever, howsomdever; *N Am* leastwise
OLD howbeit
FORMAL notwithstanding

howl v, n
♦ v
wail, cry, shriek, scream, bawl, shout, yell, roar, bellow, bay, yelp, yowl, hoot, moan, groan, wow, yawl; *dialect* gowl
♦ n
wail, cry, shriek, scream, bawl, shout, yell, roar, bellow, bay, yelp, yowl, hoot, moan, groan, wow, yawl

howler n
error, mistake, blunder, gaffe, malapropism
FORMAL solecism
COLLOQ. bloomer, clanger, boob; *N Am* flub
SLANG goof

hub n
centre, middle, focus, focal point, axis, pivot, linchpin, nerve centre, core, heart

hubbub n
noise, racket, din, clamour, commotion, disturbance, riot, uproar, hullabaloo, rumpus, confusion, disorder, tumult, hurly-burly, chaos, pandemonium
Ea peace, quiet

hubris n
arrogance, pride, conceit, boasting haughtiness, vanity, superciliousness, disdain, scorn, contempt, superiority, egotism, condescension, lordiness, pomposity, high-handedness, imperiousness, self-importance, snobbishness, presumption, insolence
FORMAL hauteur, contumely
COLLOQ. nerve
Ea humility, unassumingness, bashfulness

huckster n
hawker, dealer, trader, salesperson, barker, tinker, vendor, haggler, packman, pedlar, pitcher

huddle v, n
♦ v
cluster, gravitate, converge, meet, gather, congregate, crowd, flock, cram, pack, herd, throng press, squeeze, cuddle, snuggle, nestle, curl up, crouch, hunch
Ea disperse
♦ n
1 CLUSTER, clump, knot, mass, crowd, heap, muddle, jumble
2 MEETING, conclave, conference, discussion, consultation
COLLOQ. powwow

hue n
colour, shade, tint, dye, tinge, nuance, tone, complexion, aspect, light

hue and cry n
furore, fuss, hullabaloo, outcry, commotion, rumpus, uproar, brouhaha, clamour, ado, chase
COLLOQ. ruction, to-do, hoo-ha, carry-on, kerfuffle, ballyhoo, tizzy, a song and dance

huff n
pique, sulks, mood, bad mood, anger, rage, passion
COLLOQ. paddy, stew

huffily adv
crossly, angrily, resentfully, snappily, irritably, morosely, peevishly, in a huff, in a temper
COLLOQ. hot under the collar, in a paddy, in a strop

huffy adj
cross, angry, resentful, snappy, disgruntled, grumpy, irritable, offended, sulky, surly, testy, touchy, moping morose, moody, crusty, short, peevish, petulant, waspish
FORMAL querulous
COLLOQ. crabbed, crotchety, miffed, shirty, stroppy
Ea cheery, happy

hug v, n
♦ v
1 EMBRACE, cuddle, squeeze, enfold, hold, hold close, press, clasp, clutch, grip, cling to, enclose
2 *the path hugs the wall for a mile*
stay close to, follow closely, stay near, keep close to
♦ n
embrace, cuddle, squeeze, clasp, hold, clinch

huge adj
immense, vast, enormous, massive, colossal, titanic, giant, gigantic, mammoth, monumental, tremendous, stupendous, great, big, large, extensive, cavernous, monstrous, Herculean, gargantuan, bulky, heavy, unwieldy
OLD hideous, immane
FORMAL prodigious
COLLOQ. XXL, jumbo, frightful, ginormous, humongous

SLANG whopping, mega
Ea tiny, minute

hugely adv
enormously, immensely, vastly, massively, extremely, very, very much, really, thoroughly, greatly, highly, extraordinarily, tremendously, largely
COLLOQ. frightfully, terribly, awfully, terrifically

hugger-mugger adj
1 CONFUSED, muddled, jumbled, disarranged, disordered, untidy, disorderly, chaotic, disorganized, mixed-up, out of order
COLLOQ. higgledy-piggledy, at sixes and sevens
2 SECRET, clandestine, surreptitious, undercover, underhand, concealed, hidden, covert, fraudulent, sly, sneaky, stealthy, underground, closet, furtive, private
COLLOQ. backroom, behind-door, cloak-and-dagger, under-the-counter
Ea 1 orderly

hulk n
1 WRECK, shipwreck, remains, derelict, frame, hull, shell
2 LOUT, lump, lubber, oaf
COLLOQ. clod, clodhopper

hulking adj
massive, heavy, weighty, unwieldy, cumbersome, bulky, big large, awkward, clumsy, lumbering ungainly
Ea small, delicate

hull¹ n
the hull of a ship
body, frame, framework, skeleton, structure, casing covering

hull² n, v
♦ n
the hull of a fruit
husk, pod, capsule, legume, skin, rind, peel, shell; *N Am* shuck
TECHNICAL epicarp
♦ v
husk, pare, peel, shell, strip, skin, trim; *N Am* shuck

hullabaloo n
fuss, palaver, outcry, furore, hue and cry, noise, din, racket, brouhaha, uproar, pandemonium, rumpus, disturbance, commotion, hubbub, turmoil, tumult
COLLOQ. ruction, to-do, hoo-ha, carry-on, kerfuffle, ballyhoo, tizzy, a song and dance
Ea calm, peace

hum v, n
♦ v
1 BUZZ, whirr, purr, drone, thrum, throb, croon, sing
2 MURMUR, mumble
3 *humming with activity*
throb, be busy, pulse, vibrate, buzz
♦ n
buzz, buzzing whirr, whirring purring thrum, drone, murmur, mumble, throb, throbbing pulsation, vibration
■ **hum and haw**
be indecisive, dither, vacillate, waver, hesitate, fluctuate, sway, oscillate, keep changing your mind
COLLOQ. dilly-dally, shilly-shally, blow hot and cold

human adj, n
♦ adj
1 MORTAL, physical, fleshly, fallible, flesh and blood, weak, susceptible, vulnerable, reasonable, rational
FORMAL anthropoid
2 KIND, considerate, understanding humane, compassionate, sympathetic, tolerant
Ea 2 inhuman
♦ n
human being mortal, man, woman, child, person, individual, body, soul
TECHNICAL Homo sapiens

humane *adj*
kind, compassionate, sympathetic, understanding
thoughtful, kind-hearted, good-natured, considerate, gentle,
tender, loving mild, lenient, merciful, forgiving forbearing
kindly, generous, benevolent, charitable, humanitarian,
good, benign
E3 inhumane, cruel

humanely *adv*
compassionately, sympathetically, thoughtfully, kindly,
kind-heartedly, gently, lovingly, tenderly, generously,
mildly, mercifully
E3 inhumanely, cruelly

humanitarian *adj, n*
♦ *adj*
benevolent, charitable, philanthropic, public-spirited,
welfare, compassionate, humane, kind, sympathetic,
understanding considerate, generous, altruistic, unselfish
E3 selfish, self-seeking
♦ *n*
philanthropist, benefactor, good Samaritan, do-gooder,
altruist
E3 egoist, self-seeker

humanitarianism *n*
benevolence, charitableness, charity, goodwill,
philanthropy, humanism, compassionateness, generosity,
loving-kindness
FORMAL beneficence
E3 egoism, self-seeking

humanities *n*
arts, liberal arts, literature, classics, classical studies,
philosophy

humanity *n*
1 HUMAN RACE, humankind, mankind, womankind,
mortals, mortality, people, man
TECHNICAL Homo sapiens
2 HUMANENESS, kindness, compassion, fellow-feeling
brotherly love, understanding tenderness, sympathy,
gentleness, thoughtfulness, benevolence, tolerance,
generosity, goodwill, kind-heartedness, goodness, pity,
mercy; *S Afr* ubuntu
E3 2 inhumanity, cruelty

humanize *v*
improve, better, polish, refine, domesticate, tame, civilize,
cultivate, educate, enlighten, edify

humankind *n*
humanity, human race, mankind, womankind, mortals,
mortality, people, man
TECHNICAL Homo sapiens

humanness *n*
human nature, humanity, kindness, compassion,
understanding tenderness, sympathy, gentleness,
thoughtfulness, benevolence, tolerance, generosity,
goodwill, kind-heartedness, goodness

humble *adj, v*
♦ *adj*
1 MEEK, submissive, unassertive, modest, unassuming self-
effacing polite, respectful, deferential, servile, subservient,
sycophantic, prideless, supplicatory
OLD (*Spenser*) afflicted; demiss, demissive
FORMAL obsequious
2 LOWLY, low, mean, insignificant, unimportant, common,
commonplace, ordinary, poor, small, inferior, low-ranking
plain, simple, modest, unassuming unpretentious,
unostentatious, undistinguished, unrefined, yeomanly
OLD base, silly
E3 1 proud, assertive **2** important, pretentious
♦ *v*
bring down, lower, bring low, abase, demean, sink,
discredit, belittle, disgrace, shame, put to shame,
humiliate, mortify, chasten, crush, depress, deflate, subdue
OLD afflict, pluck
FORMAL disparage

COLLOQ. put someone in their place, bring/take someone
down a peg or two, cut down to size
E3 exalt

humbleness *n*
humility, modesty, unassertiveness, unassumingness, self-
effacement, diffidence, meekness, submissiveness,
deference, self-abasement, servility, lowliness,
unpretentiousness
E3 pride, arrogance, assertiveness

humbly *adv*
modestly, unassumingly, meekly, respectfully, simply,
submissively, unpretentiously, deferentially, diffidently,
docilely, subserviently, servilely
FORMAL obsequiously
COLLOQ. sheepishly, cap in hand
E3 confidently, defiantly

humbug *n*
1 DECEPTION, pretence, sham, fraud, swindle, trick, hoax,
deceit, trickery, cheating hypocrisy
COLLOQ. con
SLANG *N Am* gold brick
2 NONSENSE, rubbish, bluff, cant, hypocrisy
COLLOQ. bunkum, claptrap, eyewash, balderdash,
poppycock, cobblers, rot
SLANG baloney; (*vulgar*) balls, shit
3 CHARLATAN, fraud, cheat, bluffer, actor, swindler,
impostor, fake, sham, trickster, rogue
COLLOQ. con man, poser

humdrum *adj*
boring tedious, monotonous, routine, dull, repetitious,
tiresome, dreary, uninteresting uneventful, unvaried,
ordinary, mundane, everyday, commonplace, run-of-the-
mill, banal
E3 varied, lively, unusual, exceptional

humid *adj*
damp, moist, dank, wet, clammy, sticky, close, heavy,
oppressive, muggy, sultry, steamy
E3 dry

humidity *n*
humidness, damp, dampness, moisture, moistness,
dankness, wetness, stickiness, closeness, heaviness,
clamminess, mugginess, sultriness, steaminess, sogginess,
vaporousness, dew, mist
FORMAL vaporosity
E3 dryness

humiliate *v*
mortify, embarrass, confound, crush, break, deflate,
chasten, shame, bring shame on, disgrace, abash,
discredit, degrade, demean, humble, bring low, abase
FORMAL discomfit
COLLOQ. put down, put someone in their place, make
someone lose face, bring/take someone down a peg or
two, cut someone down to size, take the wind out of
someone's sails
E3 dignify, exalt

humiliating *adj*
humbling mortifying shaming crushing chastening deflating
degrading embarrassing disgraceful, ignominious,
inglorious, disgracing snubbing
FORMAL discomfiting humiliant, humiliative, humiliatory
E3 gratifying triumphant

humiliation *n*
mortification, embarrassment, shame, disgrace, chastening
crushing confounding dishonour, discredit, debasement,
indignity, ignominy, abasement, humbling degradation,
deflation, snub, rebuff, affront
FORMAL discomfiture
COLLOQ. put-down, loss of face, humble pie
E3 gratification, triumph

humility *n*
modesty, unassertiveness, unassumingness, self-effacement,
diffidence, meekness, submissiveness, deference, self-

abasement, servility, humbleness, lowliness,
unpretentiousness
E3 pride, arrogance, assertiveness

> **QUOTATIONS**
> The only wisdom we can hope to acquire / Is the
> wisdom of humility: humility is endless
> T S ELIOT, *Four Quartets*, 'East Coker'

hummock *n*
hillock, hump, knoll, mound, barrow, elevation,
prominence

humorist *n*
wit, satirist, caricaturist, cartoonist, comedian, comic,
joker, wag jester, clown, gagman

humorous *adj*
funny, amusing comic, entertaining witty, satirical,
facetious, playful, waggish, droll, whimsical, comical,
farcical, ludicrous, absurd, ridiculous, laughable, hilarious,
humoristic, side-splitting Falstaffian, Gilbertian,
Rabelaisian; *Scot* pawky
OLD (*Shakesp*) capricious
FORMAL jocular, risible
COLLOQ. zany, knee-slapping
E3 serious, humourless

humour *n, v*
♦ *n*
1 WIT, wittiness, gags, drollery, jokes, jesting badinage,
repartee, facetiousness, absurdity, ridiculousness, hilarity,
comedy, fun, amusement
FORMAL jocularity
COLLOQ. wisecracks
See Synonym nuances panel at **wit**.
2 *in a bad humour*
mood, temper, frame/state of mind, spirits, disposition,
temperament, vein, kidney
♦ *v*
go along with, comply with, accommodate, satisfy, gratify,
indulge, pamper, spoil, cosset, favour, permit, please,
mollify, flatter, pander to, tolerate, coax, jolly
OLD (*Shakesp*) observe
FORMAL acquiesce in

Types of humour include:

barrack-room	farcical	satirical
black	gallows	scatological
colloq. blue	*N Am colloq.*	sick
Chaplinesque	gross-out	slapstick
dark	ironic	whimsical
dry	Pythonesque	wry

---

humourless *adj*
boring tedious, dull, dry, solemn, serious, grave, earnest,
sombre, glum, morose, unsmiling unlaughing grim, long-
faced, dour
COLLOQ. po-faced
E3 humorous, witty

hump *n, v*
♦ *n*
hunch, lump, knob, bump, projection, protuberance,
outgrowth, bulge, swelling mound, ramp, mass,
prominence, protrusion; *Scot* humph
TECHNICAL sleeping policeman
OLD bunch
FORMAL excrescence, intumescence
♦ *v*
1 ARCH, curve, crook, bend, hunch
2 CARRY, lug haul, lift, heave, hoist, shoulder
■ *get the hump*
sulk, mope, be annoyed, be irritated,
be exasperated
COLLOQ. be rubbed up the wrong way,
get the pip

■ *give someone the hump*
annoy, irritate, rile, anger, vex, irk, madden, exasperate,
tease, provoke, ruffle, gall, trouble, nag disturb, bother,
pester, plague, harass
COLLOQ. aggravate, bug hassle, rub up the wrong way,
wind up, get someone's blood up, get on someone's
nerves, get up someone's nose, get under someone's skin,
get someone's goat, get on someone's wick, drive up the
wall, drive round the bend/twist, get someone's back up,
brass off, cheese off, make someone's hackles rise, make
sparks fly, get someone's dander up; *N Am* tick/hack off
■ *over the hump*
past the crisis, past the difficulty, over the worst

hump-backed *adj*
crookbacked, hunchbacked, hunched, crooked, stooped,
humped, deformed, misshapen, gibbous
TECHNICAL kyphotic
OLD (*Shakesp*) bunch-backed
E3 straight, upright

humped *adj*
arched, bent, curved, crooked, hunched, gibbous
E3 flat, straight

hunch *n, v*
♦ *n*
1 HUMP, lump, knob, bump, projection, protuberance,
outgrowth, bulge, swelling mound, ramp, mass,
prominence, protrusion
2 SUSPICION, premonition, intuition, feeling impression,
idea, inkling guess, sixth sense
FORMAL presentiment
♦ *v*
hump, bend, curve, arch, stoop, crouch, squat, huddle,
draw in, curl up

hunger *n, v*
♦ *n*
1 HUNGRINESS, emptiness, starvation, malnutrition, famine,
famishment, appetite, ravenousness, greed, greediness
TECHNICAL bulimia
FORMAL voracity, esurience, esuriency
2 *hunger for power*
desire, craving longing yearning pining hankering want,
need, yen, itch, thirst, appetite
♦ *v*
starve, want, wish, desire, need, crave, have a craving for,
hanker, long have a longing for, yearn, pine, ache, itch,
thirst, raven

> **PROVERBS**
> Hunger is the best sauce

> **SYNONYM NUANCES**
> *noun sense 1*
> The word **emptiness** places the emphasis on the
> physical sensations caused by needing food, but does
> not necessarily suggest an extreme condition. **Starvation**,
> however, goes much further, by suggesting a debilitated
> physical state caused by lack of food, and **malnutrition**
> also suggests consequent bad health, either through a
> lack of food or an absence of nourishing food: *many
> elderly find it difficult to cook, and suffer from
> malnutrition*. The term **famine** would be reserved for a
> widespread scarcity of food, usually with extreme results:
> *the famine left up to a million dead*, while the rarer
> **famishment** again suggests the effects of such a scarcity.
>   **Appetite**, on the other hand, suggests an everyday
> hunger caused by a natural desire for food: *they lost
> weight by taking appetite suppressors*, whereas
> **ravenousness** would be appropriate for immense
> hunger, although it can be used in a more light-hearted
> tone. Both **greed** and **greediness** are disapproving in
> that they have to do with craving much larger quantities
> than you actually require.

hungrily *adv*
ravenously, greedily, covetously, insatiably, eagerly, longingly, avidly

hungry *adj*
1 STARVING, underfed, undernourished, malnourished, empty, hollow, famished, ravenous, greedy, insatiable, having a wolf in the stomach, hungerful; *Scot* yaup
OLD ahungered; (*Shakesp*) hungerly, sharp
FORMAL voracious
COLLOQ. peckish, could eat a horse
2 *hungry for knowledge*
desirous, craving longing aching yearning pining hankering itching thirsty, eager, avid, needing covetous
E3 1 satisfied, full

hunk *n*
1 CHUNK, lump, piece, block, slab, wedge, mass, dollop, clod, gobbet
2 STRONG MAN, macho man, he-man
COLLOQ. dish, beefcake, stud
OLD COLLOQ. dreamboat

hunt *v, n*
♦ *v*
1 CHASE, pursue, follow, shadow, hound, run, dog stalk, track, trail, run to ground, persecute, prey on, tire down, chivvy, course, scare up, halloo, beagle, cub, ride to hounds, ferret, hawk, rabbit, seal, mouse, rat, slug turtle
2 SEEK, look for, search, try to find, scour, rummage, fish, ferret, forage, investigate; *N Am* still-hunt
COLLOQ. scrounge
♦ *n*
chase, pursuit, search, stalking tracking scouring rummaging quest, investigation, battue
OLD chivvy, venation

hunter *n*
huntsman, chaser, chasseur, woodman, woodsman, jäger, montero, hound, beagler, hawker, rabbiter, ratter, turtler, wolfer, lion-hunter, Nimrod, seal-fisher, shikar; *N Am* still-hunter
OLD venator, venerer

hunting *n*
field sports, chase, coursing trapping stalking beagling cubbing falconry, lamping wolfing wolving ratting turtling birding shikar
OLD venation, venery
Related adjectives: cynegetic, venatic, venatical

hurdle *n*
jump, fence, wall, hedge, railing bar, barrier, barricade, obstacle, obstruction, stumbling-block, hindrance, impediment, handicap, problem, snag difficulty, complication

hurl *v*
throw, toss, fling sling pitch, cast, heave, catapult, project, propel, fire, launch, send, let fly
COLLOQ. chuck

hurly-burly *n*
bustle, hustle, commotion, confusion, trouble, disorder, disruption, unrest, pandemonium, uproar, chaos, furore, upheaval, tumult, turbulence, turmoil, frenzy, distraction, agitation, hubbub, brouhaha, bedlam
COLLOQ. hassle

hurricane *n*
gale, tornado, typhoon, cyclone, whirlwind, squall, storm, tempest

hurried *adj*
rushed, hectic, hasty, speedy, fast, quick, breakneck, swift, rapid, passing fleeting transient, transitory, brief, short, cursory, superficial, offhand, perfunctory, shallow, careless, slapdash
FORMAL precipitate
COLLOQ. rush job
E3 leisurely, unhurried

hurriedly *adv*
speedily, at top speed, quickly, rapidly, swiftly, without delay, in haste, hastily, posthaste, helter-skelter, pell-mell, hotfoot
COLLOQ. at the double, at a rate of knots, flat out, hell for leather, like the clappers, like greased lightning; *N Am* lickety-split
E3 slowly; *formal* dilatorily

hurry *v, n*
♦ *v*
rush, dash, run, fly, hasten, make haste, press on, quicken, speed (up), accelerate, chase, drive, scurry, beetle, hustle, push
OLD hie, festinate
FORMAL expedite
COLLOQ. mosey, vamoose, bettle off, run like hell, cut and run, go all out, belt, hightail it
E3 slow down, delay
♦ *n*
rush, haste, quickness, swiftness, fastness, rapidity, speed, urgency, hustle, bustle, flurry, commotion, hubbub, confusion
OLD dispatch
FORMAL expedition, celerity, precipitation
E3 leisureliness, calm

hurt *v, n, adj*
♦ *v*
1 *my leg hurts*
ache, be painful, be sore, pain, throb, sting smart, burn, tingle
2 INJURE, wound, maltreat, ill-treat, bruise, cut, scratch, lacerate, damage, burn, torture, maim, impair, disable
FORMAL debilitate
3 DAMAGE, impair, harm, mar, spoil, blemish, blight
4 UPSET, sadden, cause sadness, grieve, distress, wound, pain, offend, annoy
FORMAL afflict
♦ *n*
pain, soreness, aching throbbing burning tingling smarting discomfort, suffering injury, wound, cut, bruise, scratch, damage, harm, distress, sadness, upset, sorrow, grief, misery
FORMAL affliction
♦ *adj*
1 INJURED, wounded, bruised, grazed, cut, scarred, lacerated, maimed, painful, sore, aching throbbing burning tingling smarting
2 UPSET, sad, saddened, sorrowful, grief-stricken, miserable, in anguish, distressed, aggrieved, annoyed, offended, affronted

hurtful *adj*
1 UPSETTING, wounding vicious, cruel, mean, unkind, nasty, malicious, spiteful, catty, derogatory, offensive, distressing scathing cutting
FORMAL injurious, malefactory
2 HARMFUL, damaging detrimental, pernicious, destructive, ruinous
FORMAL injurious, deleterious
E3 1 helpful, kind, innocuous **2** advantageous

hurtle *v*
dash, tear, race, fly, shoot, speed, rush, career, charge, plunge, dive, crash, rattle
COLLOQ. belt, pelt, put your foot down, step on it/the gas/the juice

husband *n, v*
♦ *n*
spouse, partner, mate, groom, man, married man, consort, *mari complaisant*; *dialect* master
OLD goodman, hoddy-doddy; *N Am* gander-mooner
COLLOQ. hubby, better half, other half, old boy
Related adjective: marital

♦ *v*
conserve, economize, eke out, use sparingly, use carefully, manage, preserve, reserve, put aside, put by, budget, save, save up, store, ration, hoard
F3 squander, waste

husbandry *n*
1 FARMING, agriculture, cultivation, tillage, land management, farm management, conservation
TECHNICAL agribusiness, agronomics, agronomy
2 MANAGEMENT, saving thrift, thriftiness, frugality, economy, good housekeeping
F3 2 wastefulness, squandering

hush *v, n, interj*
♦ *v*
quieten, silence, shush, still, settle, compose, calm, soothe, mollify, subdue
COLLOQ. pipe down, shut up, cut the cackle, dry up
F3 disturb, rouse
♦ *n*
quietness, quiet, silence, peace, peacefulness, stillness, calm, calmness, tranquillity, serenity
FORMAL repose
F3 noise, clamour
♦ *interj*
quiet, be quiet, hold your tongue, shut up, not another word
COLLOQ. belt up, button it, cut the cackle, dry up, enough said, give it a rest, give over, hold your peace, pack it in, pipe down, put a sock in it, say no more, shut your face, shut your mouth, wrap up
■ **hush up**
keep dark, keep secret, suppress, conceal, cover up, stifle, smother, gag
F3 publicize

hush-hush *adj*
secret, confidential, classified, restricted, top-secret
COLLOQ. under wraps
F3 open, public

husk *n*
covering case, shell, pod, capsule, legume, hull, rind, peel, skin, bran, chaff; *N Am* shuck
TECHNICAL epicarp
OLD (*Shakesp*) shale

huskily *adv*
deeply, hoarsely, croakily, gutturally, gruffly, gravelly, harshly

husky *adj*
1 HOARSE, croaky, croaking low, deep, throaty, guttural, gruff, gravelly, rasping rough, thick, coarse, harsh
2 BRAWNY, muscular, burly, hefty, strong strapping well-built
COLLOQ. beefy

hussy *n*
loose woman, minx, temptress; *dialect* huzzy, limmer
COLLOQ. floozie, vamp
SLANG slut, tart, scrubber, tramp, slag, skank

hustle *v, n*
♦ *v*
rush, hurry, dash, fly, bustle, hasten, force, pressurize, push, shove, manhandle, thrust, bundle, elbow, nudge, jostle, crowd
♦ *n*
bustle, activity, stir, commotion, tumult, agitation, fuss, hurry, rush, hurly-burly

hut *n*
cabin, shack, shanty, booth, shed, lean-to, shelter, den; *S Afr* pondok

hybrid *n, adj*
♦ *n*
cross, crossbreed, half-breed, half-blood, mongrel, composite, combination, mixture, amalgam, compound
FORMAL conglomeration

♦ *adj*
crossbred, mongrel, composite, combined, mixed, heterogeneous, compound
F3 pure-bred

hybridize *v*
crossbreed, cross, interbreed, bastardize, reproduce together

hygiene *n*
sanitariness, sanitation, sterility, disinfection, cleanliness, purity, wholesomeness
F3 insanitariness

hygienic *adj*
sanitary, sterile, sterilized, aseptic, germ-free, disinfected, clean, pure, healthy, wholesome
FORMAL salubrious
F3 unhygienic, insanitary, contaminated, polluted

hymn *n*
song of praise, song chorus, spiritual, psalm, anthem, air, carol, chant, cantata, canticle, motet, doxology, introit, choral(e), offertory, paean, paraphrase, hymeneal, procession, recessional, dirge, mantra
TECHNICAL cathisma, sticheron, trisagion, troparion, dies irae, Stabat Mater, Tantum ergo, Te Deum, sequence

hype *n, v*
♦ *n*
publicity, advertisement, advertising promotion, puff, puffery, ballyhoo, build-up, racket, fuss
COLLOQ. plugging razzmatazz
♦ *v*
promote, publicize, advertise, build up
COLLOQ. plug talk up

hyped up *adj*
excited, anxious, overwrought, stimulated, stirred, exhilarated, thrilled, elated, in high spirits, enthusiastic, eager, moved, beside yourself, animated, worked up, wrought-up, agitated, restless, frantic, frenzied, wild
COLLOQ. high, on the edge of your seat, on tenterhooks, thrilled to bits, uptight, hyper, fired up
F3 calm

hyperbole *n*
overstatement, exaggeration, excess, magnification, extravagance, overkill
F3 understatement; *technical* meiosis

hypercritical *adj*
fault-finding over-particular, pedantic, finicky, fussy, quibbling hair-splitting niggling captious, carping strict, cavilling censorious
FORMAL ultracrepidarian
COLLOQ. nit-picking pernickety, choosy, picky; *N Am* persnickety
F3 tolerant, uncritical

hypnotic *adj*
mesmerizing soporific, sleep-inducing sedative, numbing spellbinding fascinating compelling irresistible, magnetic
FORMAL somniferous, stupefactive

hypnotism *n*
hypnosis, mesmerism, suggestion, auto-suggestion

hypnotize *v*
mesmerize, put into a state of unconsciousness, put to sleep, spellbind, bewitch, enchant, entrance, fascinate, captivate, beguile, magnetize

hypochondria *n*
neurosis, hypochondrianism, hypochondriasis
FORMAL valetudinarianism

hypochondriac *n, adj*
♦ *n*
hypochondriast
FORMAL valetudinarian
♦ *adj*
hypochondriacal, neurotic
FORMAL valetudinarian

hypocrisy n
insincerity, double-talk, double-dealing two-facedness, dishonesty, falsity, deceit, deceitfulness, deception, pretence, pretended goodness, sanctimoniousness, lip service, wearing a mask, cant, pharisaism
FORMAL dissimulation, dissembling duplicity
COLLOQ. phoneyness
🞐 sincerity

QUOTATIONS
Hypocrisy is the most difficult and nerve-racking vice that any man can pursue; it needs an unceasing vigilance and a rare detachment of spirit. It cannot, like adultery or gluttony, be practised at spare moments; it is a whole-time job
W SOMERSET MAUGHAM, *Cakes and Ale*

hypocrite n
deceiver, fraud, impostor, pretender, mountebank, Pharisee, canter, charlatan, whited sepulchre, Holy Willie, Pecksniff, Tartuffe, Janus
FORMAL dissembler
COLLOQ. phoney, pseud, pseudo

hypocritical adj
insincere, two-faced, self-righteous, sanctimonious, double, double-dealing false, specious, hollow, deceptive, fraudulent, spurious, deceitful, dishonest, lying histrionic, self-pious, pharisaical, Pecksniffian, Tartuffian, Janian-faced, Janus-faced
OLD (*Shakesp*) false-faced
FORMAL dissembling perfidious, duplicitous
COLLOQ. phoney
🞐 sincere, genuine, truthful

hypothesis n
theory, thesis, theorem, axiom, proposition, notion, supposition, presumption, assumption, speculation
FORMAL premise, postulate, conjecture

hypothetical adj
theoretical, imaginary, imagined, supposed, assumed, presumed, proposed, speculative
FORMAL conjectural
🞐 real, actual

hypothetically adv
in theory, theoretically, supposedly, speculatively, ideally
FORMAL conjecturally

hysteria n
agitation, frenzy, panic, hysterics, neurosis, mania, delirium, madness
COLLOQ. (screaming) habdabs
🞐 calm, composure, control

hysterical adj
1 FRANTIC, frenzied, berserk, out of control, uncontrollable, mad, raving crazed, beside yourself, delirious, demented, overwrought, neurotic, in a panic
2 HILARIOUS, extremely funny, uproarious, farcical, ridiculous, ludicrous, side-splitting
COLLOQ. priceless, rich
🞐 1 calm, composed, self-possessed

hysterically adv
1 FRANTICALLY, uncontrollably, neurotically, madly, beside yourself, in a panic, out of control, out of your mind
2 HILARIOUSLY, uproariously, ridiculously, farcically, ludicrously, absurdly
COLLOQ. screamingly

hysterics n
agitation, frenzy, panic, hysteria, neurosis, mania, delirium, madness
COLLOQ. (screaming) habdabs

I

ice *n, v*

♦ *n*

1 FROZEN WATER, hail, sleet, frost, rime, icicle, glacier, floe, brash, black ice, dry ice, ground ice, anchor-ice, frazil, drift-ice, pack-ice, sea ice, shelf ice, shell ice, snow-ice, stream-ice, hummock, verglas, tickly-benders; *Scot* grue, grew; *N Am* slob ice
TECHNICAL crust, virga
2 ICINESS, frostiness, coldness, chill, coolness, unresponsiveness, distance

♦ *v*

freeze (over), refrigerate, chill, cool, frost, glaze, harden, enfreeze

■ **put on ice**
shelve, delay, postpone, put off, defer
FORMAL hold/leave in abeyance
COLLOQ. put on the back burner

iceberg *n*
berg calf, growler

ice-cold *adj*
frozen, iced, chilled, icy, frosty, icebound, arctic, bitterly cold, raw, polar, glacial, Siberian, frigid, freezing numb, hard, frosted, solidified, stiff, frozen-stiff, chilled to the bone, rigid, fixed
TECHNICAL algid
FORMAL gelid
COLLOQ. baltic
E₃ warm, hot

icily *adv*
coldly, coolly, stiffly, formally, rudely, morosely, forbiddingly
E₃ warmly, responsively

icon *n*
idol, portrait, image, likeness, figure, representation, symbol, portrayal

iconoclast *n*
critic, denouncer, dissenter, denunciator, dissident, radical, sceptic, rebel, opponent, questioner, heretic, unbeliever, image-breaker
E₃ devotee, believer

iconoclastic *adj*
critical, dissident, irreverent, innovative, questioning radical, rebellious, sceptical, subversive, heretical, impious
FORMAL denunciatory, dissentient
E₃ uncritical, unquestioning trustful

icy *adj*
1 ICE-COLD, glacial, freezing frozen, frosty, raw, bitter, biting cold, chill, chilly, frigid, arctic, polar, Siberian
FORMAL gelid
2 *icy roads*
frosty, slippery, glassy, frozen, icebound, frostbound, rimy, slippy
3 HOSTILE, cold, stony, cool, frigid, frosty, indifferent, unfriendly, aloof, stiff, reserved, restrained, distant, formal, rude, morose, forbidding
E₃ 1 hot **3** friendly, warm, welcoming responsive

idea *n*
1 THOUGHT, concept, notion, theory, hypothesis, guess, belief, opinion, feeling, view, viewpoint, judgement, conception, conceptualization, vision, image, motif,
impression, perception, interpretation, understanding, inkling, suspicion, fancy, clue
FORMAL conjecture, abstraction
2 *a good idea*
brainwave, suggestion, proposal, proposition, recommendation, plan, scheme, design
COLLOQ. lightbulb moment
3 AIM, intention, purpose, reason, point, end, goal, target, object, objective

ideal *n, adj*

♦ *n*

1 PERFECTION, epitome, acme, paragon, example, model, pattern, prototype, type, image, criterion, standard, yardstick, benchmark
FORMAL exemplar, archetype, nonpareil
2 PRINCIPLE, morals, ethics, moral standards/values, ethical standards/values

♦ *adj*

1 PERFECT, dream, utopian, best, optimum, optimal, supreme, highest, complete, absolute, model
FORMAL archetypal, quintessential, consummate
2 UNREAL, imaginary, conceptual, philosophical, theoretical, hypothetical, abstract, unattainable, impractical, visionary, romantic, fanciful, idealistic, utopian

> **QUOTATIONS**
> Good friends, good books and a sleepy conscience: this is the ideal life
> MARK TWAIN, *Notebook*

idealism *n*
impracticality, perfectionism, romanticism, utopianism
E₃ pragmatism, realism

idealist *n*
perfectionist, visionary, dreamer, optimist, romantic, romanticist
E₃ realist, pragmatist

idealistic *adj*
perfectionist, utopian, visionary, romantic, quixotic, starry-eyed, optimistic, unrealistic, impractical, impracticable
E₃ realistic, pragmatic, practical

idealization *n*
romanticization, romanticizing glamorization, glorification, worship, exaltation, idolization, ennoblement
FORMAL apotheosis

idealize *v*
utopianize, romanticize, glamorize, glorify, exalt, worship, idolize
E₃ caricature

ideally *adv*
perfectly, in a perfect world, in an ideal world, at best, in theory, theoretically, hypothetically

idée fixe *n*
fixation, obsession, complex, hang-up, leitmotiv, fixed idea
FORMAL monomania

identical *adj*
same, self-same, one and the same, indistinguishable, interchangeable, twin, duplicate, like, alike, similar,

corresponding matching equal, equivalent, consistent, right, precise
TECHNICAL cloned, congruent, identic, syngeneic
OLD self, numeric
FORMAL analogous, coincident
COLLOQ. as like as two peas in a pod, a dead ringer, spitting image
≠ different

identically *adv*
interchangeably, indistinguishably, alike, in the same way, just the same, similarly, equally, equivalently, correspondingly, consistently
FORMAL congruently, analogously
≠ differently

identifiable *adj*
recognizable, discernible, noticeable, known, perceptible, detectable, distinguishable, unmistakable
FORMAL ascertainable
≠ unidentifiable, indefinable, unfamiliar, unknown

identification *n*
1 RECOGNITION, detection, spotting pointing-out, diagnosis, naming labelling classification
2 EMPATHY, association, involvement, connection, rapport, relationship, sympathy, fellow feeling
3 IDENTITY CARD, documents, ID, papers, credentials, badge, driving licence, birth certificate, passport; *S Afr* passbook
4 ASSOCIATION, bond, tie, connection, link, correlation, relation, relationship, interrelation, involvement

identify *v*
1 RECOGNIZE, know, pick out, single out, point out, distinguish, perceive, make out, discern, discover, find out, establish, notice, detect, diagnose, name, label, tag specify, pinpoint, spot, place, catalogue, classify
FORMAL ascertain
2 ASSOCIATE, connect, relate, involve, place, think of together, couple
3 *identify with other sufferers*
empathize with, relate to, associate with, respond to, sympathize with, feel for

identity *n*
1 INDIVIDUALITY, particularity, distinctiveness, uniqueness, self, selfhood, personhood, name, ego, personality, character, existence, background, roots
FORMAL singularity
2 SAMENESS, likeness, selfsameness, closeness, similarity, resemblance, indistinguishability, oneness, unity, interchangeability, correspondence, equality, equivalence
3 *a company's corporate identity*
impression, image, profile, face, appearance, public persona, public face, public recognition

ideologist *n*
thinker, theorist, visionary, philosopher, teacher, doctrinaire, ideologue

ideology *n*
philosophy, world-view, ideas, principles, teaching theory, tenets, doctrine(s), convictions, belief(s), opinion(s), faith, dogma, thesis
FORMAL creed, credo

idiocy *n*
folly, stupidity, silliness, senselessness, lunacy, craziness, absurdity, foolhardiness, insanity, inanity
FORMAL fatuousness
COLLOQ. daftness
≠ wisdom, sanity

idiom *n*
phrase, expression, colloquialism, language, turn of phrase, phraseology, style, usage, jargon, speech, talk, vernacular
FORMAL locution

idiomatic *adj*
colloquial, everyday, natural, vernacular, native, grammatical, correct, dialectal, dialectical, idiolectal
≠ unidiomatic

idiosyncrasy *n*
peculiarity, individuality, speciality, oddity, eccentricity, freak, quirk, habit, mannerism, trait, feature, characteristic, quality
FORMAL singularity

idiosyncratic *adj*
personal, individual, characteristic, distinctive, peculiar, odd, eccentric, quirky
FORMAL singular
≠ general, common

idiot *n*
fool, imbecile, fat-head, dunce, dimwit, simpleton, halfwit, cretin, clown, ignoramus, oaf, innocent, moron
OLD natural, nidget; (*Shakesp*) malt-horse
COLLOQ. thickhead, numskull, nincompoop, airhead, ass, chump, ninny, clot, dope, twit, nitwit, nit, sucker, mug, twerp, birdbrain, pea-brain, berk, dum-dum, knuckle-head, blockhead, lamebrain, mouth-breather, wazzock; *dialect* barmpot; *Scot* bampot, bammer, numpty; *Scot & Irish* eejit; *N Am* putz, chowderhead, bufflehead, doofus; *Aust & NZ* dill; *Aust* boofhead
SLANG jerk, nerd, wally, dumbo, divvy, pillock, prat, muppet, dork, dipstick, geek, schlub, plonker, cloth head, butthead, nana, nerk, nelly; (*taboo*) dickhead, knobhead, prick, fuckwit; *N Am* flathead, jughead, klutz, schmuck, schmo, dumb-ass; *Aust & NZ* nong; *Aust* galah; *Irish* (*vulgar*) gobshite

idiotic *adj*
foolish, stupid, senseless, silly, absurd, ridiculous, ludicrous, nonsensical, unwise, ill-advised, ill-considered, short-sighted, half-baked, crazy, mad, insane, moronic, oafish, hare-brained, half-witted, simple-minded, simple, ignorant, unintelligent, inept, inane, pointless, unreasonable, gormless; *Welsh* twp
FORMAL fatuous, risible, injudicious
COLLOQ. thick-headed, daft, crack-brained, dumb, dotty, potty, batty, barmy, nutty, wacky, knuckle-headed, dozy, dim-witted
SLANG dorky, goofy; *N Am* dumb-ass
≠ sensible, sane

idle *adj, v*
♦ *adj*
1 INACTIVE, not working inoperative, unused, dormant, dead, mothballed, unoccupied, unemployed, jobless, redundant
COLLOQ. on the dole
*See Synonym nuances panel at **inactive**.*
2 LAZY, work-shy, lethargic, sluggish, lackadaisical, do-nothing loafish, bone-idle
FORMAL indolent, slothful
3 *idle threats*
empty, futile, vain, pointless, useless, worthless, fruitless, unsuccessful, ineffective, unproductive
FORMAL ineffectual
4 *idle gossip*
casual, trivial, petty, foolish, shallow, light, unimportant, insignificant
≠ **1** active, hardworking **2** busy **4** important, deep
♦ *v*
1 DO NOTHING, laze, lounge, while, take it easy, sit back, relax, kill time, while away, potter, loiter, dawdle, dally, fritter, waste, loaf, slack, shirk, fiddle about/around, lollop, pootle, twiddle your thumbs, wanton, whip the cat; *Scot* daidle; *N Am* putter
COLLOQ. skive, horse around, fester; *N Am* lallygag
SLANG sod about, bum around, fart about, arse around, mike, lig; *Irish* doss; *N Am* gold-brick, goof off; *Aust & NZ* bludge

2 *the engine is idling*
tick over, be operational, be ready to work/run, move
F3 1 work, be busy

idleness *n*
laziness, lazing sluggishness, torpor, inaction, inactivity, inertia, vegetating shiftlessness, leisure, loafing pottering ease, unemployment
FORMAL indolence, sloth, slothfulness
COLLOQ. skiving
F3 activity, employment, occupation

idler *n*
loafer, dawdler, slacker, lounger, malingerer, shirker, good-for-nothing laggard, sluggard, waster, wastrel, layabout, do-nothing do-naught, drone, clock-watcher, bumble, fine gentleman/lady; *dialect* donnot
OLD Lollard, truant
FORMAL sloth
COLLOQ. dodger, lazybones, skiver, spiv, couch potato
SLANG *Irish* dosser; *N Am* gold brick, goof-off; *Aust & NZ* bludger

idol *n*
1 HERO, heroine, favourite, darling star, superstar, pet, beloved
COLLOQ. blue-eyed boy, pin-up
2 *worship idols*
effigy, icon, image, graven image, likeness, god, deity, fetish, mammet

idolater *n*
admirer, worshipper, adorer, devotee, idol-worshipper, idolatress, idolist, iconolater, votary

idolatrous *adj*
adoring worshipping glorifying lionizing adulatory, idolizing idol-worshipping reverential, uncritical, pagan, heretical

idolatry *n*
worshipping admiration, reverence, adoration, adulation, deification, exaltation, glorification, hero-worship, idolizing idolism, iconolatry, icon worship, paganism, heathenism, fetishism
F3 vilification

idolize *v*
hero-worship, lionize, exalt, glorify, worship, deify, revere, admire, adore, adulate, reverence, love, dote on
FORMAL venerate
COLLOQ. put on a pedestal
F3 despise

idyllic *adj*
perfect, idealized, heavenly, blissful, delightful, wonderful, charming picturesque, pastoral, rustic, unspoiled, peaceful, romantic, happy
F3 unpleasant, spoiled, noisy

if *conj*
in the event of, in case of, on condition that, as/so long as, provided, providing assuming (that), supposing (that)

iffy *adj*
1 *my German is a bit iffy*
unsatisfactory, substandard, disappointing imperfect, defective, low-grade, second-rate
COLLOQ. dodgy, not up to scratch
2 UNCERTAIN, doubtful, dubious, tentative, undecided, unsettled

ignite *v*
set fire to, set alight, light, catch fire, flare up, burn, burst into flames, conflagrate, fire, inflame, kindle, touch off, put a match to, spark off, torch
F3 quench

ignoble *adj*
low, mean, petty, base, vulgar, wretched, contemptible, despicable, shameful, vile, infamous, disgraceful, dishonourable
FORMAL heinous
F3 noble, worthy, honourable

ignobly *adv*
meanly, pettily, wretchedly, contemptibly, despicably, shamefully, disgracefully, dishonourably, without honour, vilely, infamously
F3 nobly

ignominious *adj*
humiliating mortifying degrading undignified, shameful, dishonourable, discreditable, sorry, disreputable, disgraceful, despicable, infamous, abject, base, contemptible, scandalous, embarrassing
F3 triumphant, honourable, glorious

ignominiously *adv*
shamefully, disgracefully, dishonourably, disreputably, despicably, scandalously

ignominy *n*
humiliation, mortification, degradation, shame, dishonour, discredit, disgrace, disrepute, reproach, scandal, contempt, indignity, infamy, stigma
FORMAL obloquy, odium, opprobrium
F3 credit, honour, dignity

ignoramus *n*
dunce, dimwit, halfwit, imbecile, simpleton, fool, illiterate, know-nothing blockhead, dullard
OLD ignaro, ignorant
COLLOQ. numskull, bonehead, ass, duffer, dolt
F3 scholar, intellectual, highbrow

ignorance *n*
unintelligence, illiteracy, unawareness, unconsciousness, obliviousness, oblivion, unfamiliarity, inexperience, innocence, naivety, stupidity
COLLOQ. greenness, thickness
F3 knowledge, wisdom, education, intelligence

PROVERBS
Where ignorance is bliss, 'tis folly to be wise

ignorant *adj*
uneducated, illiterate, innumerate, backward, unknowing unread, untaught, untrained, inexperienced, unschooled, unlearned, stupid, uninitiated, unenlightened, in the dark, uninformed, ill-informed, unwitting unaware, unfamiliar, unacquainted, unconscious, oblivious, having no idea, know-nothing blind, innocent, naive;
N Am redneck
OLD benighted, ingram, inscient, lack-Latin, lewd; (*Shakesp*) unconfirmed
FORMAL nescient
COLLOQ. clueless, dense, thick, thick as two short planks, dumb, in the dark
SLANG not knowing one's arse from one's elbow
OLD SLANG not knowing a B from a battledore, not knowing a B from a broomstick, not knowing a B from a bull's foot
F3 educated, knowledgeable, learned, clever, wise; *formal* conversant

ignore *v*
disregard, take no notice of, not take any notice of, overlook, take for granted, pay no attention to, be oblivious to, pass over, pass by, bypass, neglect, omit, brush aside, shrug off, reject, snub, spurn, disown, slight, cut (dead), tune out, balk, discount, high-hat
OLD blink
COLLOQ. close/shut your eyes to, turn a blind eye to, look the other way, turn a deaf ear to, not listen to, cold-shoulder, turn your back on, keep in the dark, bury your head in the sand, run away from, leave out in the cold
SLANG scrub round
F3 notice, observe, pay attention to

ilk *n*
kind, sort, type, make, style, variety, brand, breed, class, stamp, character, description

ill *adj, n, adv*

♦ *adj*

1 SICK, poorly, unwell, laid up, ailing off-colour, out of sorts, seedy, queasy, diseased, unhealthy, infirm, frail, weak, feeble, bedridden
FORMAL afflicted, indisposed, valetudinarian
COLLOQ. in a bad way, dicky, crummy, under the weather, run down, rough, groggy, like death warmed up, green about the gills; *Aust* cronk; *Aust & NZ* crook

2 *an ill omen*
bad, evil, damaging harmful, unpleasant, injurious, destructive, ruinous, detrimental, adverse, unfavourable, unpromising sinister, ominous, threatening unlucky, unfortunate, difficult, harsh, severe
FORMAL inauspicious, unpropitious, infelicitous, deleterious

3 *ill feelings*
unkind, unfriendly, antagonistic, hostile, resentful, belligerent
F₃ 1 well, healthy **2** good, favourable, fortunate **3** kind, friendly

♦ *n*

1 TROUBLE, problem, trial(s), pain, misfortune, suffering disaster, unpleasantness
2 HARM, evil, hurt, cruelty, destruction, injury, sorrow
FORMAL tribulation, affliction
F₃ 1 benefit **2** good

♦ *adv*

1 BADLY, unfavourably, unkindly, disapprovingly, adversely, unfortunately, unsuccessfully, unluckily, wrongfully
FORMAL inauspiciously
2 SCARCELY, hardly, barely, by no means, insufficiently, inadequately, poorly, scantily, amiss
F₃ 1 well

■ **ill at ease**
uncomfortable, awkward, fidgety, hesitant, embarrassed, self-conscious, strange, unsure, nervous, on edge, restless, tense, unrelaxed, unsettled, uneasy, worried, anxious, disquieted, disturbed
COLLOQ. edgy, like a cat on hot bricks, on tenterhooks
F₃ at ease

■ **speak ill of**
criticize, condemn, carp, disapprove of, find fault with, pass judgement on, denounce, attack, slate, censure, blame, niggle, peck at, scarify, slash, snipe at, tilt at, run down; *N Am* score
FORMAL animadvert, excoriate, decry, denigrate, disparage, vituperate, castigate, impugn, cast aspersions on
COLLOQ. nag slam, hammer, knock, come down on, give someone some stick, go to town on, haul over the coals, pick holes in, pan, take apart, pull/tear apart, pull to pieces, tear to shreds, tear a strip off, nit-pick, do a hatchet job on, badmouth, rubbish, trash, put the boot in, wade into, cut up, roast, have a go at
SLANG slag (off)

SYNONYM NUANCES

adjective sense 1
Sick and the less common **ailing** can be widely applied as a synonym of ill, whilst **poorly** and **unwell**, while implying a fairly mild condition, suggest being in constant poor health: *she was poorly throughout most of her childhood.* The term **laid up** would be reserved for having to take to your bed, whereas **bedridden** suggests a similar, but a far more serious and permanent state.
    Off-colour is a fairly vague term which would suggest simply not feeling as well as one should, while both **seedy** and **queasy** would be appropriate for feeling mild nausea: *she felt seedy throughout the long bus journey.* **Diseased** is a more highly marked term, appropriate only for being affected by a distinctive illness: *diseased heart valves,* whereas **unhealthy** is less specific, implying continuing poor health as much as illness: *an unhealthy pallor.*

   Infirm and **frail** suggest being in a continuous debilitated or delicate state, and are often associated with ageing: *he became very infirm in his last years.* Both **weak** and **feeble**, likewise, put the emphasis on lacking strength and vigour as a consequence of illness: *he was too feeble to get out of bed.*

ill-advised *adj*
unwise, foolish, ill-considered, thoughtless, careless, hasty, rash, imprudent, reckless, short-sighted, misguided, inappropriate
FORMAL injudicious
F₃ wise, sensible, well-advised, cautious; *formal* politic, circumspect

ill-assorted *adj*
incompatible, inharmonious, discordant, unsuited, mismatched, uncongenial, misallied
FORMAL incongruous
F₃ harmonious, well-matched

ill-bred *adj*
bad-mannered, ill-mannered, discourteous, impolite, rude, loutish, boorish, coarse, crude, vulgar, crass, uncouth, indelicate, uncivil, uncivilized
FORMAL unseemly
F₃ well-bred, polite, gentlemanly, ladylike

ill-considered *adj*
ill-advised, ill-judged, careless, foolish, hasty, heedless, rash, imprudent, unwise, overhasty
FORMAL improvident, injudicious, precipitate
F₃ sensible, wise

ill-defined *adj*
indistinct, unclear, vague, nebulous, imprecise, indefinite, blurred, fuzzy, hazy, woolly, blurry, dim, shadowy
F₃ clear

ill-disposed *adj*
unfriendly, unsympathetic, hostile, antagonistic, opposed, unco-operative, unwelcoming against
FORMAL averse, inimical
COLLOQ. anti
F₃ well-disposed

illegal *adj*
unlawful, illicit, criminal, wrong forbidden, prohibited, illegitimate, fraudulent, banned, outlawed, barred, unauthorized, under-the-counter, black-market, unconstitutional, bootleg wrongful, criminalized
OLD wrongous
FORMAL felonious, proscribed, interdicted
COLLOQ. crooked
F₃ legal, lawful, permitted, allowed

illegality *n*
wrong wrongfulness, wrongness, crime, criminality, illegitimacy, illicitness, lawlessness, unconstitutionality, unlawfulness
TECHNICAL felony, malfeasance
F₃ legality

illegally *adv*
unlawfully, illicitly, wrongly, against the law, contrary to the law, without authority, illegitimately, disobediently, guiltily, wrongfully, criminally
F₃ legally, lawfully

illegible *adj*
unreadable, indecipherable, hard to read, scrawled, obscure, faint, indistinct, unintelligible, hieroglyphic
F₃ legible, clear

illegitimacy *n*
illegitimateness, bastardism, bastardy, fatherlessness, birth out of wedlock
TECHNICAL baton-sinister, bend-sinister

illegitimate *adj*

1 *an illegitimate child*
natural, love, bastard, fatherless, misbegotten, adulterine, unfathered, spurious

OLD base, base-born; (*Shakesp*) misbegot
FORMAL born out of wedlock
COLLOQ. born on the wrong side of the blanket
2 ILLEGAL, unlawful, illicit, lawless, unauthorized, unwarranted, unlicensed, improper
3 ILLOGICAL, incorrect, inadmissible, spurious, invalid, unsound
≢ 1 legitimate **2** legal **3** well-reasoned

ill-equipped *adj*
unprovided (for), unsupplied, ill-supplied, exposed, unprotected, underresourced, underfinanced, underfunded, undercapitalized, understaffed, under strength, undermanned

ill-fated *adj*
doomed, ill-starred, ill-omened, blighted, unfortunate, unlucky, luckless, unhappy
FORMAL hapless
≢ lucky

ill-favoured *adj*
hideous, plain, repulsive, ugly, unattractive, unlovely, unprepossessing unsightly; *N Am* homely
≢ beautiful, attractive

ill-feeling *n*
ill-will, bad blood, bitterness, grudge, hard feelings, resentment, sourness, spite, malice, hostility, enmity, animosity, antagonism, dissatisfaction, frustration, offence, anger, indignation, wrath, disgruntlement, dudgeon
FORMAL animus, odium, rancour
≢ friendship, goodwill

ill-founded *adj*
baseless, groundless, without foundation, unjustified, unsupported, unconfirmed
≢ substantiated, verified

ill-gotten *adj*
obtained dishonestly, obtained illegally, stolen, pilfered, taken, swiped
FORMAL purloined
COLLOQ. nicked, nobbled, knocked off, ripped off, dodgy
SLANG hot, bent

ill-humoured *adj*
bad-tempered, acrimonious, cross, impatient, irascible, quick-tempered, irritable, sharp, snappy, snappish, disagreeable, cantankerous, grumpy, sulky, sullen, petulant, huffy, moody, morose, peevish, tart, testy, waspish
COLLOQ. stroppy, shirty, ratty, crabbed, crabby, crotchety, grouchy
≢ amiable

illiberal *adj*
mean, narrow-minded, intolerant, petty, prejudiced, reactionary, small-minded, bigoted, hidebound, ungenerous, uncharitable, stingy, miserly, niggardly, close-fisted
FORMAL parsimonious
COLLOQ. tight-fisted, tight
≢ broad-minded, liberal

illicit *adj*
illegal, unlawful, criminal, wrong illegitimate, improper, forbidden, prohibited, banned, barred, unauthorized, unlicensed, black-market, bootleg contraband, ill-gotten, under-the-table, under-the-counter, furtive, clandestine, secretive, surreptitious, stealthy, black; *Aust* sly
SLANG *Aust* shonky
≢ legal, permissible

illicitly *adv*
unlawfully, illegally, wrongly, against the law, contrary to the law, without authority, illegitimately, disobediently, guiltily, wrongfully, criminally
≢ legally, lawfully

illiteracy *n*
inability to read, inability to read and/or write, ignorance, lack of education, lack of schooling
≢ literacy

illiterate *adj*
ignorant, uneducated, unschooled, unlearned, untaught, unlettered, untutored, uncultured
TECHNICAL analphabetic
OLD benighted
≢ literate

ill-judged *adj*
ill-advised, ill-considered, short-sighted, unwise, foolish, foolhardy, misguided, hasty, overhasty, rash, reckless, imprudent, incautious, indiscreet, wrong-headed
FORMAL impolitic, injudicious
COLLOQ. daft
≢ sensible

ill-mannered *adj*
rude, impolite, badly-behaved, bad-mannered, insolent, discourteous, ill-bred, ill-behaved, unmannerly, uncivil, loutish, uncouth, boorish, churlish, coarse, crude, insensitive
≢ polite, well-mannered

ill-natured *adj*
spiteful, vindictive, nasty, perverse, mean, surly, sulky, sullen, unfriendly, unkind, unpleasant, vicious, bad-tempered, cross, disagreeable, malicious, malevolent, malignant, churlish, petulant
COLLOQ. crabbed
≢ good-natured

illness *n*
disease, disorder, complaint, condition, ailment, sickness, ill/poor health, infirmity, disability, attack, bout, touch
FORMAL indisposition, malady, affliction
See panel at **disease**.

SYNONYM NUANCES

Disease would only be used of specific, and usually serious, illness characterized by a distinctive set of symptoms, while **disorder** can be used of varying degrees of illness, but particularly where some part of the body is malfunctioning: *suffering from a kidney disorder*. Similarly, **complaint** and **ailment** can be widely used of any, even minor, health problem that troubles you, while **condition** has connotations of a more permanent state, especially one that is a particular cause for concern: *an incurable heart condition*.
  Sickness can be fairly widely applied to the state of being ill, although it also has associations with vomiting. **Indisposition**, on the other hand, is more suggestive of a fairly mild illness resulting in the temporary inability to perform your usual functions, unlike **infirmity**, which implies a continuous state of poor health and physical inability, often arising from age. **Disability**, however, might be used more narrowly where illness involves a particular physical or mental handicap.
  Attack and **bout** are different in that they suggest a sudden and severe but temporary affliction: *an attack of gout; a bout of flu*, while **touch** clearly suggests a very minor case: *a touch of food poisoning*.

---

illogical *adj*
irrational, unreasonable, unscientific, untenable, invalid, unsound, faulty, specious, spurious, inconsistent, (*offensive*) Irish, ; fallible, senseless, meaningless, absurd, incorrect, wrong
FORMAL fallacious, sophistical, casuistic
≢ logical, rational, reasonable

illogicality *n*
irrationality, unreasonableness, unreason, unsoundness, absurdity, senselessness, speciousness, fallacy, inconsistency, invalidity

FORMAL fallaciousness
logicality

ill-starred *adj*
doomed, ill-fated, unfortunate, unhappy, unlucky, star-crossed, blighted
FORMAL inauspicious, hapless
fortunate

ill-tempered *adj*
bad-tempered, acrimonious, cross, ill-natured, ill-humoured, impatient, irritable, irascible, spiteful, vicious, curt, grumpy, cantankerous, testy, tetchy, touchy, choleric, sharp
COLLOQ. stroppy, shirty, ratty, crabbed, crabby, crotchety, grouchy
good-tempered

ill-timed *adj*
inopportune, inconvenient, inappropriate, unseasonable, untimely, wrong-timed, mistimed, unwelcome, unfortunate, awkward, tactless, inept, crass
well-timed

ill-treat *v*
mistreat, abuse, maltreat, injure, harm, damage, neglect, mishandle, misuse, wrong oppress

ill-treatment *n*
abuse, mistreatment, maltreatment, damage, harm, injury, ill-use, manhandling mishandling misuse, neglect
care

illuminate *v*
1 LIGHT, light up, lighten, shine on, throw light on, floodlight, brighten, twilight
OLD illumine; (*Shakesp*) overshine
2 CLARIFY, clear up, elucidate, illustrate, explain, edify, instruct, enlighten, limelight
3 DECORATE, ornament, adorn, embellish, illustrate
OLD limn, miniate
1 darken **2** mystify

illuminating *adj*
informative, instructive, helpful, edifying enlightening revealing
FORMAL explanatory, revelatory
unhelpful

illumination *n*
1 LIGHT, lights, lighting beam, ray, irradiation, brightness, radiance, flash, candlelight
2 ENLIGHTENMENT, awareness, insight, light, understanding instruction, perception, learning education, revelation
3 DECORATION, ornamentation, adornment, embellishment, illustration
1 darkness

illusion *n*
apparition, mirage, spectre, phantom, will-o'-the-wisp, hallucination, figment of the imagination, déjà vu, fantasy, fancy, delusion, misapprehension, misconception, misjudgement, error, false impression, deception, phantasm
TECHNICAL maya
OLD prestige
FORMAL chimera, fallacy
reality, truth

> **!** illusion or allusion?
> See panel at **allusion**.

> **!** illusion or delusion?
> See panel at **delusion**.

illusory *adj*
illusive, illusionary, deceptive, misleading apparent, seeming deluding delusive, unreal, delusory, fancied, imagined, specious, unsubstantial, sham, false, untrue, mistaken, erroneous
FORMAL chimerical, fallacious
real, actual

illustrate *v*
1 DEMONSTRATE, exemplify, instance, explain, interpret, clarify, draw, sketch, depict, picture, show, exhibit
FORMAL elucidate
2 ILLUMINATE, decorate, ornament, adorn, embellish
FORMAL miniate

illustrated *adj*
decorated, embellished, illuminated, pictorial, with drawings/pictures
FORMAL miniated

illustration *n*
1 PICTURE, plate, half-tone, photograph, drawing sketch, figure, diagram, chart, artwork, design, representation, graphic, blow-up, frontispiece, vignette, decoration, ornamentation, adornment, embellishment
TECHNICAL bleed, hors texte
2 EXAMPLE, specimen, instance, case, case in point, sample, analogy, demonstration, exemplification, explanation, interpretation, clarification, quotation, quote, comment, remark, observation, note, gloss, sidelight
FORMAL exemplar, elucidation, exponent

illustrative *adj*
explanatory, descriptive, representative, typical, exemplifying sample, specimen, diagrammatic, graphic, pictorial, interpretative
FORMAL explicatory, expository, delineative, illustrational, illustratory

illustrious *adj*
great, noble, eminent, distinguished, celebrated, acclaimed, honoured, esteemed, famous, famed, renowned, well-known, noted, prominent, outstanding pre-eminent, remarkable, notable, brilliant, excellent, splendid, magnificent, glorious, exalted
ignoble, inglorious

ill-will *n*
hostility, antagonism, bad blood, enmity, unfriendliness, malevolence, malice, spite, animosity, ill-feeling resentment, hard feelings, grudge, dislike, aversion, hatred, antipathy, anger, indignation, wrath
FORMAL animus, rancour, odium
goodwill, friendship

image *n*
1 IDEA, notion, concept, conception, thought, fancy, impression, perception, vision
2 REPRESENTATION, likeness, resemblance, portrayal, depiction, picture, portrait, icon, graven image, effigy, figure, figurine, statue, statuette, bust, idol, replica, doll
3 REPRODUCTION, reflection, photograph, picture, copy, facsimile
4 *improve the company's image*
impression, identity, corporate identity, profile, face, appearance, public persona, public face, public recognition
5 *the image of his father*
likeness, representation, double, twin, duplicate, copy, clone, replica, doppelgänger, lookalike, match
COLLOQ. spitting image, (dead) ringer
6 *images in a poem*
figure of speech, figurative expression, turn of phrase, rhetorical device, imagery, simile, metaphor

imaginable *adj*
conceivable, thinkable, believable, credible, supposable, feasible, plausible, likely, possible, probable
unimaginable, inconceivable

imaginary *adj*
imagined, fanciful, fancied, illusory, hallucinatory, visionary, pretend, make-believe, dreamy, shadowy, ghostly, spectral, insubstantial, unreal, non-existent, fictive, fictional, fantastic, fabulous, legendary, mythological, mythical, made-up, invented, fictitious, assumed, supposed, hypothetical, notional
FORMAL chimerical
real

imagination n
1 CREATIVITY, imaginativeness, inventiveness, fancifulness, originality, inspiration, insight, ingenuity, ingeniousness, resourcefulness, enterprise, wit, vision
2 *see them in my imagination*
mind's eye, fancy, flight of fancy, fantasy, phantasy, mental view, contemplation, illusion, vision, dream, conceptualization, imagery, schema, dreamland
OLD wit, project
FORMAL chimera
E3 1 unimaginativeness **2** reality

imaginative adj
creative, inventive, innovative, full of ideas, original, inspired, visionary, ingenious, clever, resourceful, enterprising fanciful, whimsical, fantastic, vivid
E3 unimaginative

imagine v
1 PICTURE, form a picture of, visualize, see, see in your mind's eye, envisage, conceive, fancy, fantasize, daydream, dream, pretend, make believe, conjure up, dream up, think up, invent, devise, create, scheme, plan, opine, project, vision
OLD image; (Shakesp) ween
FORMAL ideate
2 *I imagine so*
think, believe, judge, suppose, guess, reckon, assume, presume, gather, fancy, figure
OLD conceit; (Shakesp) propose
FORMAL conjecture, deem, surmise
COLLOQ. take it

imbalance n
unevenness, inequality, variance, disparity, disproportion, unfairness, partiality, bias
FORMAL inequity
E3 balance, parity

imbecile n, adj
♦ n
idiot, halfwit, simpleton, moron, cretin, fool, blockhead, bungler, dunce, dimwit
COLLOQ. thickhead, numskull, nincompoop, ass, chump, ninny, clot, dope, twit, nitwit, nit, sucker, mug, twerp, birdbrain, berk, dum-dum, knuckle-head, lamebrain, mouth-breather, wazzock; *Scot* bampot, bammer, numpty; *Scot & Irish* eejit; *N Am* putz, chowderhead, doofus
SLANG jerk, nerd, wally, dumbo, pillock, prat, dork, geek, plonker, cloth head, nana, nerk; *N Am* flathead, jughead, klutz; *Aust & NZ* nong
♦ adj
stupid, silly, foolish, idiotic, inane, ludicrous, absurd, crazy, moronic, witless, asinine
FORMAL fatuous
COLLOQ. thick-headed, daft, crack-brained, dumb, dotty, potty, batty, barmy, nutty, wacky, knuckle-headed
SLANG dorky, goofy
E3 intelligent, sensible

imbecility n
foolishness, idiocy, inanity, stupidity, incompetence, cretinism, asininity, childishness
TECHNICAL amentia
FORMAL fatuity
COLLOQ. daftness, craziness
E3 intelligence, sense

imbibe v
1 DRINK, consume, swallow, gulp, sip, quaff
FORMAL ingest
COLLOQ. knock back, swig
2 ABSORB, take in, assimilate, drink in, receive, soak up, acquire, gain, gather
COLLOQ. lap up

imbroglio n
entanglement, tangle, involvement, confusion, difficulty, dilemma, complication, muddle, mess, quandary, embroilment
COLLOQ. scrape

imbue v
permeate, impregnate, pervade, suffuse, fill, saturate, inject, ingrain, inspire, charge, steep, inculcate, instil, tinge, tint

imitate v
1 COPY, take as a model, follow, follow suit, do likewise, ape, mimic, impersonate, do an impression of, caricature, parody, mock, act, hit, parrot, repeat, echo, mirror
FORMAL emulate
COLLOQ. take off, send up, spoof, take a leaf out of someone's book
2 REPRODUCE, duplicate, simulate, copy, fake, counterfeit, forge
FORMAL replicate

SYNONYM NUANCES

sense 1
Copy is a very general synonym, whilst **follow** implies imitating a person or adopting a style because it is believed to be better, and has vague implications of slavishness: *we would be better off following their system.* **Echo** would be used of displaying similarities to someone or something rather than copying them: *their buildings echoed those of Imperial Paris.*
  Both **ape** and **mimic** are suggestive of copying someone to rather ludicrous effect: *their lifestyle aped that of the royal household*, while **impersonate** would be reserved for pretending to be them. The terms **caricature** and **parody** are appropriate for presenting an exaggerated, often grotesque, representation, again for comic effect: *he parodied her accent*, and **mock** suggests a similarly disrespectful action. Both **parrot** and **repeat** might be used of saying something previously said by someone else, without any changes or embellishments: *he simply repeated my speech, word for word.*

---

imitation n, adj
♦ n
1 MIMICRY, impersonation, aping apery, impression, caricature, parody, mocking mockery, travesty
COLLOQ. take-off, send-up, spoof
2 COPY, duplicate, reproduction, replica, simulation, counterfeit, fake, forgery, sham, likeness, resemblance, reflection, dummy
FORMAL emulation
COLLOQ. knock-off
♦ adj
artificial, synthetic, man-made, ersatz, fake, mock, reproduction, simulated, sham, dummy
COLLOQ. phoney, pseudo
E3 genuine

QUOTATIONS
Imitation is the sincerest form of flattery
CHARLES CALEB COLTON, *Lacon*

---

imitative adj
copying mimicking parrot-like, unoriginal, derivative, plagiarized, second-hand, simulated, mock
FORMAL emulating mimetic
COLLOQ. me-too
E3 original

imitator n
mimic, impersonator, impressionist, parrot, ape, echo, parodist, plagiarist, copier, copyist, follower, epigone
FORMAL emulator
COLLOQ. copycat

immaculate adj
perfect, unblemished, flawless, faultless, impeccable, spotless, unsoiled, clean, spick and span, pure, unsullied, undefiled, incorrupt, untainted, stainless, blameless, guiltless, sinless, innocent
COLLOQ. squeaky clean
E3 blemished, stained, contaminated

immaculately *adv*
spotlessly, perfectly, to perfection, flawlessly, faultlessly, impeccably, purely, incorruptly, blamelessly, without blame, innocently, guiltlessly, without guilt, sinlessly, without sin

immanent *adj*
inherent, intrinsic, innate, ingrained, permeating all-pervading
FORMAL ubiquitous, omnipresent

> ⚠ **immanent** or **imminent**?
> *Immanent* means 'dwelling within', 'inherent': *divinity is immanent in many forms*. *Imminent* means 'approaching': *an imminent storm*.

immaterial *adj*
irrelevant, insignificant, unimportant, minor, trivial, petty, trifling inconsequential, of no account
⮕ relevant, important

immature *adj*
young under-age, adolescent, juvenile, childish, puerile, infantile, babyish, raw, crude, callow, jejune, inexperienced, naive, unripe, undeveloped, unmellowed, incomplete, budding fledgling embryonic, unformed, unsiz(e)able, untimely, vealy, unready, unprepared, half-baked, unbaked
FORMAL ingenuous
COLLOQ. wet behind the ears, innocent as a newborn babe, green
⮕ mature, fully-developed, grown-up

immaturity *n*
youth, adolescence, juvenility, childishness, puerility, babyishness, rawness, crudeness, crudity, callowness, inexperience, immatureness, unpreparedness, imperfection, unripeness, greenness
⮕ maturity, mellowness

immeasurable *adj*
vast, immense, infinite, limitless, unlimited, illimitable, boundless, fathomless, unfathomable, unbounded, endless, never ending interminable, bottomless, inexhaustible, incalculable, inestimable
⮕ limited

immeasurably *adv*
infinitely, limitlessly, boundlessly, illimitably, beyond measure, endlessly, interminably, inexhaustibly, incalculably, inestimably, vastly, immensely

immediacy *n*
urgency, importance, criticalness, instancy, spontaneity, instantaneity, promptness, swiftness, simultaneity, directness, imminence
⮕ remoteness, distance

immediate *adj*
1 INSTANT, instantaneous, direct, sudden, without delay, prompt, swift, speedy
2 URGENT, pressing important, vital, crucial, critical, current, present, existing
COLLOQ. top-priority, high-priority
3 NEAREST, closest, next, adjacent, next-door, near, close, recent
FORMAL adjoining abutting
4 the immediate cause of death
direct, primary, basic, fundamental, chief, main, principal
⮕ 1 delayed 3 distant 4 indirect

immediately *adv*
now, then, straight away, right away, right now, at once, next, there and then, instantly, instantaneously, directly, speedily, quickly, without delay, no sooner ... than, as soon as, promptly, unhesitatingly, without hesitation, without question, this minute/instant, on the instant, on the spot, at a glance, in the wake of, without further/more ado, straightforth, *statim*; *Scot & N Am* presently
TECHNICAL subito
OLD thereupon, straightway, therewithal, anon, incessantly, incontinent, incontinently, on the morrow

FORMAL forthwith
COLLOQ. pronto, yesterday, before you know it, before you can say Jack Robinson, in two shakes of a lamb's tail, like a shot, ASAP; *N Am* lickety-split
⮕ eventually, never

immemorial *adj*
age-old, timeless, ancient, archaic, long-standing fixed, time-honoured, hoary, traditional, ancestral
FORMAL of yore
⮕ recent

immense *adj*
vast, great, extremely large, huge, enormous, massive, giant, gigantic, colossal, extensive, cosmic, limitless, myriad, tremendous, fabulous, monumental, mammoth, herculean, elephantine, titanic, Brobdingnagian, cyclopean
COLLOQ. whopping bumper, jumbo, ginormous, humungous, mega
⮕ tiny, minute, Lilliputian

immensely *adv*
enormously, extremely, exceedingly, excessively, very, really, exceptionally, extraordinarily, intensely, remarkably, utterly, greatly, highly, massively, unusually, unreasonably, immoderately, uncommonly, inordinately, acutely, severely, decidedly
OLD jolly
COLLOQ. awfully, terribly, dreadfully, frightfully, terrifically

immensity *n*
magnitude, bulk, expanse, vastness, greatness, hugeness, enormousness, massiveness, giganticness, extensiveness, limitlessness
⮕ minuteness

immerse *v*
1 PLUNGE, submerge, submerse, sink, duck, dip, dunk, douse, souse, saturate, drench, wallow, soak, bathe, baptize
TECHNICAL blanch
OLD demerge, demerse, embathe, immerge
2 ENGROSS, preoccupy, occupy, absorb, bury, wrap up in, engage, involve, engulf

immersed *adj*
absorbed, engrossed, involved, occupied, preoccupied, consumed, buried, busy, deep, taken up, wrapped up, rapt, sunk

immersion *n*
1 SUBMERSION, plunging sinking ducking dip, dipping dunking dousing saturation, drenching soaking baptism, bathe
2 PREOCCUPATION, absorption, engrossing engagement, involvement, concentration

immigrant *n*
incomer, settler, migrant, economic migrant, newcomer, new arrival, outsider, foreigner, alien
⮕ native

immigrate *v*
come in, move in, migrate, settle, resettle, remove
⮕ emigrate

imminence *n*
approach, nearness, closeness, immediacy, instancy, menace, threat
FORMAL propinquity
⮕ remoteness

imminent *adj*
impending forthcoming upcoming in the offing approaching fast approaching coming on the way, near, close, looming menacing threatening brewing in the air, at hand, about to happen, almost upon you, on the horizon
COLLOQ. round the corner
⮕ remote, far-off

> ⚠ **imminent** or **immanent**?
> *See panel at* **immanent**.

immobile *adj*
motionless, stationary, unmoving immobilized, at rest, still, stock-still, static, immovable, rooted, fixed, frozen, rigid, stiff, riveted
E3 mobile, moving

immobility *n*
motionlessness, immovability, steadiness, stillness, firmness, fixedness, fixity, stability, inertness, disability
E3 mobility

immobilize *v*
stop, halt, inactivate, freeze, transfix, paralyse, cripple, disable, deactivate, put out of action/operation
E3 mobilize

immoderate *adj*
excessive, unreasonable, unjustified, unwarranted, undue, exaggerated, fulsome, enormous, exorbitant, lavish, extravagant, extreme, wanton, inordinate, uncalled-for, uncontrolled, unrestrained, outrageous, unlimited, unrestricted, unbridled, uncurbed, intemperate, self-indulgent, distemperate, overweening
FORMAL unconscionable, profligate, hubristic, egregious
COLLOQ. over the top, OTT, steep
E3 moderate

immoderately *adv*
excessively, exorbitantly, extravagantly, extremely, inordinately, exaggeratedly, unduly, unjustifiably, unrestrainedly, without measure, unreasonably, wantonly
E3 moderately

immoderation *n*
excess, excessiveness, exorbitance, extravagance, lavishness, immoderateness, intemperance, inordinacy, overindulgence, unreason, unrestraint
FORMAL prodigality, dissipation
E3 moderation

immodest *adj*
improper, indecent, revealing shameless, forward, bold, boastful, impudent, cheeky, cocky, brazen, immoral, obscene, lewd, coarse, risqué
FORMAL indecorous
COLLOQ. fresh, saucy
E3 modest

immodesty *n*
audacity, boldness, forwardness, gall, impudence, shamelessness, temerity, bawdiness, coarseness, impurity, lewdness, obscenity, indelicacy
FORMAL indecorousness, indecorum
COLLOQ. brass
E3 modesty

immolate *v*
sacrifice, kill, offer (up), burn

immoral *adj*
unethical, wrong bad, sinful, evil, wicked, unscrupulous, unprincipled, dishonest, vile, vicious, corrupt, depraved, base, degenerate, debauched, reprobate, dissolute, loose, lewd, indecent, pornographic, obscene, licentious, impure, questionable, against nature, wanton
OLD naught, unhonest
FORMAL iniquitous, nefarious
COLLOQ. blue, raunchy, juicy
E3 moral, right, good

SYNONYM NUANCES

Unethical is a straightforward synonym for going against the accepted code of conduct, while **unscrupulous** and **unprincipled** are more suggestive of a disregard for basic rules of morality. The words **wrong** and **bad** can be applied more widely, but imply a stronger judgement on the part of the speaker: *it was wrong of you to lie to your mother*. **Sinful** is similarly judgemental, but has added implications of offending religious tenets: *you must confess your sinful thoughts*, while **evil** and **wicked** make an extreme judgement.

You can use **vile** to suggest that something is loathsome, while **vicious** has more to do with a penchant for inflicting hurt. Both **corrupt** and **depraved** have connotations of perversion of accepted morals, while the terms **degenerate** and **debauched** suggest a decline into a low moral state which is demonstrated by a person's behaviour: *a debauched lifestyle*. **Reprobate** similarly suggests being steeped in shame: *I have no excuse for my reprobate behaviour*. **Dissolute**, **licentious**, **loose** and **wanton** are more suggestive of a lack of discipline or restraint in one's behaviour: *gambling and other dissolute pursuits; he was accused of wanton conduct*.

Lewd and **indecent**, and the stronger terms **pornographic** and **obscene** would only be applied to something of a sexual nature that is offensive. **Impure** suggests being tainted by immorality: *this impure world*, while **questionable** is a milder term in that it simply implies being of a morally dubious nature: *these are questionable legal practices*.

---

immorality *n*
wrong wrongdoing badness, sin, sinfulness, evil, wickedness, dishonesty, vileness, corruption, vice, depravity, dissoluteness, debauchery, impurity, lewdness, indecency, pornography, obscenity, licentiousness
OLD indiscretion
FORMAL iniquity, profligacy, turpitude
E3 morality

immortal *adj, n*
♦ *adj*
1 UNDYING, deathless, imperishable, indestructible, unfading eternal, everlasting perpetual, endless, ceaseless, lasting enduring abiding constant, perennial, timeless, ageless, fadeless, ambrosial
OLD amarantin; (*Shakesp*) ever-living
FORMAL sempiternal
2 *recall those immortal words*
memorable, unforgettable, well-known, celebrated, famous, honoured, distinguished
E3 1 mortal
♦ *n*
deity, god, goddess, divinity, divine being great, hero, genius, Olympian

QUOTATIONS
Each human spirit is immortal – for time cannot destroy whatever element within us reverences the glory of a dawn in the mountains
DERVLA MURPHY, *In Ethiopia with a Mule*

immortality *n*
1 ETERNAL LIFE, everlasting life, eternity, endlessness, deathlessness, incorruptibility, imperishability, indestructibility, timelessness, perpetuity
2 FAME, glorification, gloriousness, glory, greatness, renown, celebrity, honour, distinction
E3 1 mortality

immortalize *v*
celebrate, commemorate, memorialize, perpetuate, glorify, enshrine, eternalize
FORMAL laud

immovable *adj*
1 FIXED, rooted, immobile, stuck, fast, secure, stable, moored, riveted, anchored, jammed, constant, firm, set
2 STEADFAST, determined, resolute, adamant, unshak(e)able, stubborn, obstinate, uncompromising unyielding set, firm, constant, inflexible, dogged, unwavering unswerving
FORMAL intransigent
E3 1 movable **2** flexible

immune *adj*
invulnerable, unsusceptible, resistant, proof, protected, safe, exempt, free, clear, secure, spared, excused, released, relieved, absolved
F∃ susceptible, liable, subject, exposed, open

The immune system's components and responses include:

COMPONENTS:	adaptive immune system
antibody	allergy
antigen (or antibody	artificially acquired
generator)	immunity (immunization)
B-lymphocytes	autoimmune response
commensals	cell-mediated immunity
complement system	cellular response
cytotoxic cells	humoral immunity/response
helper T-cells	immunosurveillance
histamine	inflammatory response
immunoglobulins	innate immune system
interferon	naturally acquired immunity
killer T-cells	non-specific immune
leucocyte	response
lymphocyte	passive immunity
lysosome	phagocyte action
lysozyme	(adherence/ingestion/
memory T-cells	digestion)
phagocyte	phagocytosis
plasma cells	primary response
receptor (binding) site	secondary response
T-cells	sneeze reflex
T-lymphocytes	specific immune
RESPONSES:	response
acquired immunity	tissue rejection

---

immunity *n*
resistance, protection, immunization, vaccination, inoculation, safety, exemption, indemnity, exception, impunity, freedom, liberty, release, licence, franchise, privilege, right, permission
TECHNICAL mithridatism
FORMAL exoneration
F∃ susceptibility

immunization *n*
vaccination, inoculation, injection, protection, jab

immunize *v*
vaccinate, inoculate, inject, protect, safeguard, shield

immure *v*
enclose, confine, wall in, shut up, cage, imprison, incarcerate, jail, put behind bars, cloister, enwall
F∃ free

immutability *n*
changelessness, immutableness, invariability, unalterableness, unchangeableness, permanence, constancy, durability, fixedness, stability
F∃ mutability

immutable *adj*
changeless, inflexible, invariable, unalterable, unchangeable, perpetual, permanent, abiding constant, enduring fixed, lasting stable, steadfast, sacrosanct
F∃ mutable, changeable

imp *n*
1 SPRITE, demon, devil, goblin, hobgoblin, gnome, elf, puck
2 MISCHIEVOUS CHILD, rascal, rogue, scamp, brat, minx, troublemaker, mischief-maker, trickster, prankster, flibbertigibbet, gamin, urchin, limb

impact *n, v*
♦ *n*
1 *the impact of the reforms*
effect, consequences, results, repercussions, reverberations, impression, power, influence, significance, meaning

2 COLLISION, crash, smash, bang bump, blow, knock, contact, clash, jolt, force, shock, brunt
♦ *v*
1 COLLIDE, crash, hit, clash, crush, fix, strike, press together
2 AFFECT, have an effect on, influence, act, work, apply to, impinge

impair *v*
damage, harm, injure, hinder, mar, spoil, cripple, disable, worsen, deteriorate, undermine, weaken, reduce, decrease, lessen, diminish, blunt
FORMAL debilitate, enervate, vitiate, enfeeble
F∃ improve, enhance

impaired *adj*
defective, faulty, flawed, poor, weak, disabled, handicapped, imperfect, damaged, spoilt, unsound
FORMAL vitiated
F∃ enhanced

impairment *n*
disability, handicap, disablement, injury, weakness, damage, deterioration, reduction, harm, hurt, fault, flaw, ruin
FORMAL dysfunction, vitiation
F∃ enhancement

impale *v*
pierce, puncture, perforate, run through, spear, lance, spike, skewer, spit, stick, stab, prick, transfix, disembowel

impalpable *adj*
imperceptible, inapprehensible, insubstantial, unsubstantial, elusive, indistinct, intangible, indefinable, shadowy, tenuous, thin, fine, delicate, airy
FORMAL incorporeal
F∃ palpable

impart *v*
1 CONVEY, tell, relate, communicate, make known, transmit, disclose, divulge, reveal, report, pass on
2 GIVE, grant, offer, contribute, lend, assign
FORMAL confer, bestow, accord
F∃ 1, 2 withhold

impartial *adj*
objective, dispassionate, detached, disinterested, neutral, non-partisan, unbiased, unprejudiced, uncommitted, open-minded, fair, fair-minded, just, equitable, judicial, even-handed, equal, candid, crossbench
COLLOQ. not having an axe to grind
F∃ biased, prejudiced

impartiality *n*
neutrality, non-partisanship, objectivity, unbiasedness, fairness, justice, even-handedness, open-mindedness, detachment, disinterest, disinterestedness, dispassion, equality, equity
F∃ bias, prejudice, favouritism, discrimination

impassable *adj*
blocked, closed, obstructed, unnavigable, unpassable, untraversable, pathless, trackless, impenetrable, insurmountable, insuperable, unassailable, invincible
F∃ passable

impasse *n*
deadlock, stalemate, checkmate, dead end, cul-de-sac, blind alley, halt, standstill, log jam

impassioned *adj*
fervent, ardent, passionate, intense, inspired, stirring heartfelt, spirited, rousing emotional, enthusiastic, eager, excited, fervid, vigorous, forceful, violent, furious, fiery, vehement, animated, glowing inflamed, heated, blazing
F∃ apathetic, mild

impassive *adj*
expressionless, stone-faced, emotionless, calm, composed, unruffled, unconcerned, apathetic, cool, unfeeling unemotional, unmoved, unexcitable, stoical, indifferent, dispassionate
FORMAL imperturbable, phlegmatic

COLLOQ. unflappable, laid-back
E3 responsive, moved

impassively *adv*
calmly, emotionlessly, unemotionally, unfeelingly,
dispassionately, apathetically, coolly, with a straight face
FORMAL imperturbably, phlegmatically

impatience *n*
1 IRRITABILITY, intolerance, shortness, brusqueness,
abruptness, curtness, tenseness, nervousness, edginess,
agitation, uneasiness
OLD indignance
FORMAL dysphoria
2 EAGERNESS, keenness, excitability, restlessness, anxiety,
haste, rashness, impetuosity
E3 **1** contentment **2** reluctance, unwillingness

impatient *adj*
1 IRRITABLE, jittery, snappy, testy, hot-tempered, quick-
tempered, angry, intolerant, brusque, abrupt, short, curt,
tense, nervous, fidgety
FORMAL querulous
COLLOQ. ratty, narky, edgy
2 EAGER, keen, excitable, restless, anxious, impetuous,
hasty, on tenterhooks
COLLOQ. champing at the bit, straining/panting at the
leash, biting on the bridle, with ants in your pants
E3 **1** pleased, happy, contented **2** reluctant, unwilling

impeach *v*
accuse, charge, denounce, criticize, revile, attack, censure,
blame
TECHNICAL indict, arraign
FORMAL impugn, disparage

impeachment *n*
accusation, charge
TECHNICAL arraignment, indictment
FORMAL disparagement

impeccable *adj*
perfect, faultless, precise, exact, correct, exemplary,
flawless, unblemished, stainless, immaculate, pure,
upright, irreproachable, blameless, innocent
E3 faulty, flawed, corrupt

impecunious *adj*
poor, poverty-stricken, insolvent, destitute, impoverished,
penniless, needy
FORMAL indigent, penurious
COLLOQ. broke, stony-broke, skint, dirt-poor, cleaned out,
strapped, on your uppers
E3 rich

impede *v*
hinder, hamper, obstruct, block, handicap, clog slow
(down), hold up, hold back, delay, check, curb, restrain,
thwart, disrupt, stop, bar
FORMAL retard
E3 aid, promote, further

impediment *n*
1 HINDRANCE, obstacle, obstruction, barrier, bar, block,
setback, stumbling-block, snag difficulty, handicap,
burden, encumbrance, check, curb, restraint, restriction
2 *a speech impediment*
defect, handicap, stutter, stammer
E3 **1** aid

impedimenta *n*
baggage, luggage, equipment, gear, belongings,
paraphernalia
FORMAL effects, accoutrements
COLLOQ. things, stuff, bits and pieces

impel *v*
urge, force, oblige, compel, constrain, drive, propel, move,
get going push, put, press, pressure, pressurize, spur, prod,
goad, prompt, incite, stimulate, excite, instigate, strike,
motivate, inspire
E3 deter, dissuade

impending *adj*
imminent, forthcoming in the offing approaching coming
upcoming close, near, at hand, on the way, looming
menacing threatening brewing in the air, about to happen,
on the horizon
E3 remote, far-off

impenetrable *adj*
1 *impenetrable jungle*
impassable, solid, thick, dense, overgrown
2 UNINTELLIGIBLE, incomprehensible, unfathomable,
indiscernible, puzzling baffling mysterious, cryptic,
enigmatic, obscure, dark, inscrutable
FORMAL abstruse, recondite
E3 **1** accessible **2** understandable

impenitence *n*
impenitency, stubbornness, defiance, hard-heartedness,
incorrigibility
FORMAL obduracy
E3 penitence, remorse

impenitent *adj*
unrepentant, unremorseful, uncontrite, unashamed, defiant,
hardened, incorrigible, remorseless, without remorse,
without regret, unabashed, unreformed, unregenerate
FORMAL obdurate
E3 penitent, contrite

imperative *adj*
vital, essential, crucial, pressing urgent, compulsory,
critical, necessary, obligatory, indispensable
E3 optional, unimportant

imperceptible *adj*
inappreciable, indiscernible, unapparent, indistinguishable,
undetectable, unnoticeable, inaudible, faint, slight,
muffled, negligible, impalpable, infinitesimal, microscopic,
minute, tiny, minuscule, small, fine, subtle, gradual,
unclear, obscure, vague, indistinct, indefinite
E3 perceptible, noticeable, clear

imperceptibly *adv*
inappreciably, indiscernibly, unnoticeably, unobtrusively,
unseen, slowly, subtly, gradually, bit by bit, little by little
FORMAL insensibly
E3 perceptibly

imperfect *adj*
faulty, flawed, defective, damaged, broken, blemished,
impaired, chipped, deficient, inadequate, insufficient,
unsound, incomplete, embryonic, sketchy
OLD unperfect
E3 perfect, whole

imperfection *n*
fault, flaw, defect, blemish, deformity, crack, dent, break,
tear, cut, scratch, blot, blotch, stain, taint, spot, deficiency,
impairment, shortcoming foible, weakness, failing
inadequacy, insufficiency
TECHNICAL malconformation
E3 perfection

imperial *adj*
sovereign, supreme, absolute, royal, regal, monarchical,
kingly, queenly, majestic, grand, magnificent, glorious,
splendid, great, noble, lofty, stately

> **!** **imperial** or **imperious**?
> *Imperial* means 'of an empire or emperor': *the imperial
> crown*. *Imperious* means 'proud and overbearing',
> 'behaving as if expecting to be, or in the habit of being
> obeyed': *She disliked his imperious manner.*

imperialism *n*
empire-building colonialism, expansionism,
acquisitiveness, adventurism
COLLOQ. flag-waving flag-wagging

imperil *v*
endanger, put in danger, jeopardize, put in jeopardy, risk,
expose to risk, hazard, take a chance, expose, harm,
injure, compromise, threaten

imperious *adj*
overbearing domineering autocratic, despotic, tyrannical, dictatorial, high-handed, lordly, masterful, commanding assertive, arrogant, haughty
FORMAL peremptory, overweening
Ⓕ humble

> ⚠ **imperious** or **imperial**?
> *See panel at* **imperial**.

imperishable *adj*
enduring permanent, incorruptible, indestructible, inextinguishable, undying unfading unforgettable, abiding perpetual, perennial, eternal, everlasting immortal, deathless
Ⓕ perishable

impermanence *n*
transience, transiency, temporariness, inconstancy, transitoriness, briefness, elusiveness
FORMAL ephemerality
Ⓕ permanence

impermanent *adj*
transient, temporary, passing short-lived, momentary, transitory, inconstant, brief, elusive, fleeting flying unfixed, unsettled, unstable, mortal, perishable, fugitive
FORMAL ephemeral, evanescent, fugacious
COLLOQ. fly-by-night
Ⓕ permanent

impermeable *adj*
impervious, impenetrable, impassable, sealed, watertight, hermetic, non-porous, damp-proof, waterproof, proof, water-resistant, resistant, water-repellent
Ⓕ permeable, porous

impersonal *adj*
1 COLD, cool, frigid, formal, official, aloof, remote, distant, clinical, stiff, stuffy, businesslike, detached, unemotional, unfeeling
2 OBJECTIVE, neutral, dispassionate, detached, unbiased, unprejudiced
Ⓕ **1** friendly, informal **2** biased

impersonally *adv*
objectively, neutrally, dispassionately, fairly, equitably, justly, without bias/prejudice, without favouritism, open-mindedly, with an open mind
COLLOQ. not having an axe to grind

impersonate *v*
imitate, mimic, parody, caricature, mock, ape, masquerade as, pose as, pass off as, act, portray
COLLOQ. take off, send up

impersonation *n*
imitation, impression, mimicry, parody, caricature, aping apery, burlesque
COLLOQ. take-off, send-up, spoof

impertinence *n*
rudeness, impoliteness, disrespect, discourtesy, insolence, impudence, effrontery, audacity, boldness, brazenness, forwardness, presumption, shamelessness, gall, chutzpah
COLLOQ. cheek, brass, brass neck, nerve, sauce, lip, attitude, face, mouth; *Scot* snash; *N Am* sass
Ⓕ politeness, respect, civility

impertinent *adj*
rude, impolite, ill-mannered, unmannerly, discourteous, disrespectful, insolent, impudent, pert, bold, audacious, brash, brazen, forward, presumptuous, shameless
COLLOQ. cheeky, saucy, fresh; *N Am* sassy
SLANG smartarse
Ⓕ polite, respectful

imperturbability *n*
calmness, composure, coolness, complacency, self-possession, equanimity, tranquillity
Ⓕ jitteriness, touchiness

imperturbable *adj*
unexcitable, calm, tranquil, composed, collected, even-tempered, self-possessed, cool, impassive, unmoved, unruffled, untroubled, complacent
COLLOQ. unflappable, unfazed, laid-back, calm and collected
Ⓕ excitable, ruffled

impervious *adj*
1 IMPERMEABLE, waterproof, damp-proof, proof, non-porous, watertight, hermetic, closed, sealed, resistant, impenetrable
2 *impervious to criticism*
immune, invulnerable, untouched, unaffected, unmoved, closed, resistant
Ⓕ **1** porous, pervious **2** responsive, vulnerable

impetuosity *n*
impetuousness, impulsiveness, rashness, haste, hastiness, spontaneity, foolhardiness, recklessness, thoughtlessness, impatience, dash, élan, vehemence
FORMAL precipitateness
Ⓕ caution, wariness; *formal* circumspection

impetuous *adj*
impulsive, spontaneous, unplanned, unthinking unpremeditated, spur-of-the-moment, hasty, impatient, headlong uncontrolled, bull-headed, hot-headed, fiery, tearaway, violent, foolhardy, rash, reckless, thoughtless, ill-conceived, unreasoned; *N Am* brash
OLD sturdy
FORMAL precipitate
Ⓕ cautious, wary; *formal* circumspect

impetuously *adv*
rashly, impulsively, unthinkingly, recklessly, spontaneously, passionately, vehemently
FORMAL precipitately
Ⓕ cautiously

impetus *n*
stimulus, incentive, motivation, influence, encouragement, inspiration, actuation, impulse, momentum, force, energy, power, drive, urging boost, push, goad, spur

impiety *n*
irreverence, irreligion, profaneness, profanity, sinfulness, ungodliness, unholiness, unrighteousness, wickedness, godlessness, blasphemy, sacrilege, sacrilegiousness
FORMAL iniquity, hubris
Ⓕ piety, reverence

impinge *v*
encroach, infringe, affect, influence, hit, touch (on), intrude, trespass, invade

impious *adj*
irreverent, irreligious, profane, sinful, ungodly, godless, unholy, unrighteous, wicked, blasphemous, sacrilegious
FORMAL iniquitous, hubristic
Ⓕ pious, reverent

impish *adj*
mischievous, naughty, roguish, rascally, sportive, devilish, elfin, gamin, tricksome, frolicsome, tricksy, pranksome, waggish

implacability *n*
implacableness, inexorability, relentlessness, remorselessness, mercilessness, pitilessness, ruthlessness, rancorousness, unforgivingness, vengefulness, irreconcilability, inflexibility
FORMAL intransigence, intractability
Ⓕ placability

implacable *adj*
inexorable, relentless, unrelenting remorseless, merciless, pitiless, unappeasable, irreconcilable, vengeful, cruel, heartless, deadly, mortal, unforgiving ruthless, rancorous, inflexible, adamant, uncompromising unyielding
OLD impacable
FORMAL intransigent, intractable
Ⓕ compassionate, forgiving

implant v
1 *implant ideas in someone's mind*
sow, plant, fix, root, instil, inculcate, introduce
2 *implant a new heart/new skin tissue*
insert, place, put, engraft, graft, transplant
3 EMBED, fix, sow, plant, place, root

implausible adj
improbable, unlikely, hard to believe, unbelievable,
inconceivable, incredible, far-fetched, dubious, doubtful,
questionable, suspect, unconvincing weak, flimsy, thin,
transparent
E∃ plausible, probable, likely, reasonable

implausibly adv
improbably, unbelievably, incredibly, inconceivably,
doubtfully, questionably
E∃ probably, plausibly, reasonably

implement n, v
♦ n
tool, instrument, utensil, gadget, device, apparatus,
appliance, contrivance
See panel at **tool**.
♦ v
enforce, bring about, carry out, perform, do, apply,
execute, discharge, fulfil, complete, accomplish, realize,
put into effect, put into action/operation
FORMAL effect

implementation n
carrying-out, performance, performing fulfilling fulfilment,
application, execution, discharge, accomplishment,
completion, operation, action, enforcement, realization
FORMAL effecting

implicate v
involve, embroil, entangle, incriminate, compromise,
include, concern, connect, associate, be a part of, be (a)
party to
FORMAL inculpate
E∃ absolve; *formal* exonerate

implicated adj
involved, embroiled, entangled, incriminated,
compromised, included, concerned, connected,
associated, responsible, party to, suspected
FORMAL inculpated
E∃ exonerated

implication n
1 INFERENCE, deduction, insinuation, suggestion, meaning
significance, overtone, undertone, ramification,
repercussion, effect, consequence, conclusion
2 INVOLVEMENT, entanglement, embroilment, incrimination,
connection, association
FORMAL inculpation

implicit adj
1 IMPLIED, inferred, deducible, insinuated, suggested,
hinted, indirect, unsaid, unspoken, unexpressed, unstated,
tacit, understood, inherent, hidden, latent
2 *implicit belief*
unquestioning unhesitating utter, total, full, entire,
complete, absolute, perfect, sheer, positive, unqualified,
unreserved, unconditional, steadfast, wholehearted
E∃ 1 explicit **2** half-hearted

implicitly adv
absolutely, totally, utterly, completely, unconditionally,
unhesitatingly, unquestioningly, unreservedly, steadfastly,
wholeheartedly, firmly
E∃ explicitly

implied adj
implicit, tacit, indirect, insinuated, suggested, hinted,
assumed, understood, unspoken, unexpressed, unstated,
undeclared, inherent
E∃ stated

implore v
beg entreat, ask, appeal, request, press, crave, plead, pray
FORMAL importune, solicit, supplicate, beseech

imply v
suggest, insinuate, hint, intimate, infer, say indirectly, give
someone to understand/believe, mean, signify, point to,
indicate, signal, involve, require, entail, state
FORMAL denote

⚠ imply or infer?
Imply means 'to suggest or hint at (something) without
actually stating it': *Are you implying that I'm a liar?*
Infer means 'to form an opinion by reasoning from
what you know': *I inferred from your silence that you
were angry.*

impolite adj
rude, discourteous, bad-mannered, unmannerly, ill-
mannered, ill-bred, uncivil, unrefined, ungentlemanly,
unladylike, ungracious, inconsiderate, disrespectful,
impertinent, insolent, rough, loutish, boorish, coarse,
crude, vulgar, abrupt
FORMAL indecorous
COLLOQ. cheeky
E∃ polite, courteous

impolitely adv
rudely, discourteously, uncivilly, ungraciously,
inconsiderately, disrespectfully, impertinently, insolently,
crudely
FORMAL indecorously
E∃ politely, courteously

impoliteness n
rudeness, discourtesy, bad manners, unmannerliness,
disrespect, insolence, impertinence, incivility,
inconsiderateness, boorishness, churlishness, crassness,
indelicacy, roughness, coarseness, abruptness, gaucherie
FORMAL indecorousness, indecorum
E∃ politeness, courtesy

impolitic adj
unwise, ill-advised, inexpedient, imprudent, ill-judged,
misguided, ill-considered, short-sighted, undiplomatic,
indiscreet, rash, foolish
FORMAL injudicious, maladroit
COLLOQ. daft
E∃ wise, prudent; *formal* politic

import n, v
♦ n
1 *exports and imports*
imported product/commodity/goods,
foreign product/commodity/goods, reimport,
foreign trade
2 IMPORTANCE, consequence, significance, weight,
substance, seriousness
OLD state
FORMAL moment
3 CONTENT, sense, substance, nub, meaning implication,
intention, thrust, message, drift, essence, gist
FORMAL purport
♦ v
bring in, buy in, buy from abroad, ship in, reimport,
introduce

importance n
1 MOMENTOUSNESS, significance, urgency, criticalness,
graveness, substance, matter, concern, interest, usefulness,
value, worth, weight
OLD state
FORMAL consequence, import
2 *people of importance in society*
influence, power, mark, prominence, eminence,
distinction, noteworthiness, prestige, status, standing
esteem
E∃ 1, 2 unimportance, insignificance

important adj
1 MOMENTOUS, noteworthy, significant, meaningful,
relevant, material, salient, urgent, critical, paramount,
crucial, vital, essential, key, central, primary, principal,
major, main, chief, priority, substantial, valuable, valued,

weighty, mighty, ultimate, serious, grave, far-reaching
pivotal, historic, fateful, epoch-making world-shaking
world-shattering
FORMAL seminal
SLANG heavy
2 the most important person in the school
leading foremost, high-level, high-ranking top, influential,
chief, main, powerful, pre-eminent, prestigious, prominent,
outstanding eminent, notable, distinguished, valued,
esteemed, noted
F3 1 unimportant, insignificant, trivial 2 powerless

SYNONYM NUANCES

sense 1

Momentous can be used to suggest that something is
worthy of remembrance, or you can use **historic** to
suggest that something merits a place in history. **Fateful**
echoes the idea of having great consequence in history:
Titanic's fateful maiden voyage. **Noteworthy** is much
more restrained in its suggestion that something is
worthy of attention. **Significant** and **material** have
implications of being of consequence: *a significant
proportion of the population are opposed to this tax; the
merger involved material changes to the hierarchy*, while
pivotal suggests that everything else hinges on it: *our
pivotal problem is getting people to see the sense in this
plan.*

You could use **paramount, primary** or **principal** to
suggest something is supreme or foremost: *his primary
concern was the safety of his family*, while **salient**
would be used of something prominent among other
things: *we will deal with the salient points of the case
first of all.* **Priority, urgent** or **critical** can be used in
cases where immediate action is essential.

The terms **serious** and **grave**, on the other hand,
suggest a cause for intense concern: *the resurgence of
hostage-taking has grave implications*, whereas **weighty**
is most appropriate for people or things that can exert
power or influence: *the weighty issues of the day.*

---

importunate *adj*
insistent, persistent, troublesome, impatient, tenacious,
dogged, pressing urgent
FORMAL pertinacious

importune *v*
pester, badger, harass, hound, cajole, plague, appeal, beg
request, press, urge, plead with, solicit, beset
FORMAL supplicate

importunity *n*
insistence, persistence, pressing pestering harassing
hounding urgency, urging solicitation, harassment,
cajolery, entreaties

impose *v*
1 ENFORCE, exact, levy, apply, charge, set, fix, put (on),
place (on), lay (on), introduce, institute, establish, decree,
inflict, burden, encumber, saddle, force, thrust, foist
2 FOIST, force yourself, thrust yourself, intrude, butt in,
break in, encroach, trespass, obtrude, presume, exploit,
put upon, abuse, mislead, take liberties, take advantage of

imposing *adj*
impressive, striking grand, stately, majestic, splendid,
dignified, lofty, august
F3 unimposing modest

imposition *n*
1 ENFORCEMENT, introduction, infliction, exaction, levying
application, setting fixing establishment, decree, institution
2 CHARGE, tax, tariff, levy, toll, burden, constraint, load,
encumbrance, duty, task, punishment
3 INTRUSION, encroachment, trespassing burden, pressure
COLLOQ. hassle

impossibility *n*
hopelessness, impracticability, unattainableness,
unobtainableness, unacceptability, untenability, unviability,

inability, inconceivability, preposterousness, absurdity,
ludicrousness, ridiculousness
COLLOQ. no-no, non-starter, squaring the circle
F3 possibility

impossible *adj*
hopeless, impracticable, unworkable, unattainable,
unachievable, unobtainable, insoluble, unreasonable,
unacceptable, beyond you, inconceivable, unimaginable,
unthinkable, out of the question, preposterous, incredible,
unbelievable, absurd, ludicrous, ridiculous, outlandish,
intolerable, unbearable, prohibitive
COLLOQ. out, not by any stretch of the imagination, and
pigs might fly, like flogging a dead horse, anybody's guess
F3 possible

impostor *n*
fraud, fake, quack, charlatan, sham, mountebank,
impersonator, pretender, deceiver, deluder, hoodwinker,
swindler, cheat, trickster, defrauder, rogue, bunyip
OLD faitor, faitour, idol, phantasm
COLLOQ. phoney, con man
SLANG *N Am* ringer

imposture *n*
deception, fraud, pretence, misrepresentation,
impersonation, quackery, swindle, trick, counterfeit, cheat,
hoax, artifice
COLLOQ. con, con trick

impotence *n*
powerlessness, helplessness, uselessness, inability,
inadequacy, incapacity, incompetence, ineffectiveness,
weakness, feebleness, frailty, disability, infirmity, paralysis
FORMAL enervation, inefficacy, impuissance
F3 strength

impotent *adj*
powerless, helpless, useless, worthless, futile, unable,
incapable, ineffective, incompetent, inadequate, weak,
feeble, frail, worn out, exhausted, infirm, disabled,
incapacitated, paralysed, crippled
FORMAL debilitated, enervated, impuissant
F3 potent, strong

impound *v*
1 CONFISCATE, seize, remove, take away, take possession
of, commandeer
FORMAL appropriate, expropriate
2 CONFINE, shut up, cage, keep in, lock up, coop up, hem
in, pen in
FORMAL incarcerate, immure

impoverish *v*
bankrupt, break, ruin, beggar, make poor, weaken,
reduce, deplete, exhaust, drain, diminish, denude
FORMAL pauperize
F3 enrich

impoverished *adj*
1 POOR, needy, poverty-stricken, destitute, down-and-out,
bankrupt, penniless, ruined
FORMAL impecunious, penurious, indigent
COLLOQ. bust, skint, broke, stony-broke, without a bean,
cleaned out, on your uppers, on your beam ends, not
having two pennies to rub together, dirt-poor
2 WEAKENED, drained, exhausted, desolate, empty, waste,
dead, barren, bare
F3 1 rich

impracticability *n*
unworkability, infeasibility, unsuitableness, unviability,
uselessness, impossibility, futility, hopelessness
F3 practicability

impracticable *adj*
unworkable, unfeasible, unattainable, unachievable,
impossible, out of the question, unviable, non-viable,
unrealistic, visionary, wild, useless, unserviceable,
inoperable
OLD unpracticable
F3 practicable, feasible

> ⚠ **impracticable** or **impractical**?
> *Impracticable* means 'cannot be carried out or put into practice': *The whole project has become completely impracticable.* When referring to suggestions, plans, etc, *impractical* means 'possible to carry out but not sensible or convenient': *In a modern economy barter is totally impractical* ; when referring to a person, *impractical* means 'not able to do or make things in a sensible and efficient way': *He was impractical and dreamy, with a head full of foolish notions.*

impractical *adj*
unrealistic, idealistic, romantic, starry-eyed, visionary, theoretical abstract, academic, ivory-tower, impracticable, unworkable, impossible, awkward, crazy, inconvenient, unserviceable
F3 practical, realistic, sensible

impracticality *n*
idealism, romanticism, unworkability, unworkableness, impossibility, hopelessness, infeasibility
F3 practicality

imprecation *n*
curse, blasphemy, denunciation, abuse, anathema
FORMAL execration, malediction, profanity, vituperation, vilification

imprecise *adj*
inexact, inaccurate, approximate, estimated, rough, loose, indefinite, vague, woolly, blurred, hazy, ill-defined, sloppy, inexplicit, ambiguous, equivocal
F3 precise, exact

imprecision *n*
inexactitude, inexactness, inaccuracy, approximation, estimate, vagueness, ambiguity, haze, sloppiness
F3 precision, exactness

impregnable *adj*
impenetrable, unconquerable, invincible, unbeatable, unassailable, indestructible, inviolable, fortified, strong solid, secure, safe, invulnerable, unquestionable, irrefutable
F3 vulnerable

impregnate *v*
1 SOAK, steep, saturate, drench, fill, permeate, pervade, suffuse, imbue, infuse, penetrate
2 INSEMINATE, fertilize, make pregnant
FORMAL fecundate

impregnation *n*
fertilization, fertilizing insemination, saturation, imbuing
FORMAL fructification, fructifying fecundation

impresario *n*
manager, organizer, director, producer, promoter, exhibitor

impress *v*
1 *I'm not impressed*
strike, move, touch, sway, affect, influence, stir, inspire, rouse, excite, overwhelm, possess, prepossess, bear in upon
COLLOQ. grab, bowl over, knock for six, knock out, wow, slay, go over big (with)
SLANG N Am gas
2 EMPHASIZE, stress, highlight, underline, bring home, hammer home, press, drum, enforce, engrave, print, indent, instil, inculcate, fix deeply
3 STAMP, imprint, print, engrave, strike, emboss, deboss, incuse, mark

impressed *adj*
moved, excited, affected, struck, influenced, marked, taken, touched, stamped, stirred, overawed
COLLOQ. grabbed, bowled over, knocked out, knocked for six, wowed
F3 unimpressed

impression *n*
1 FEELING, awareness, consciousness, sense, sensation, illusion, idea, notion, opinion, belief, thought, conviction, suspicion, fancy, hunch, memory, recollection
COLLOQ. funny feeling gut feeling vibes
2 *make a good impression*
effect, impact, influence, power, control, sway
3 STAMP, mark, print, dent, indentation, imprint, pressure, outline
4 IMPERSONATION, imitation, parody, mimicry, caricature, burlesque
COLLOQ. take-off, send-up, spoof

impressionability *n*
naivety, gullibility, susceptibility, vulnerability, sensitivity, receptiveness, receptivity, suggestibility, greenness
FORMAL ingenuousness

impressionable *adj*
naive, gullible, easily influenced, persuadable, susceptible, vulnerable, sensitive, pliable, mouldable, responsive, open, receptive
FORMAL ingenuous

impressive *adj*
striking, imposing, grand, breathtaking, spectacular, superb, magnificent, commanding, dramatic, powerful, effective, dazzling, awe-inspiring, awesome, scintillating, stirring, inspiring, exciting, rousing, moving, affecting, touching, emphatic, epic, monumental, noble, stately
FORMAL portentous
COLLOQ. whizzy
SLANG shit-hot, stonking
F3 unimpressive, uninspiring

impressively *adv*
strikingly, grandly, spectacularly, magnificently, powerfully, effectively, emphatically, awesomely

imprint *n, v*
♦ *n*
1 PRINT, mark, stamp, impression, indentation, sign, logo, emblem, badge, colophon
2 EFFECT, consequences, results, repercussions, reverberations, impression, power, influence, significance, meaning
♦ *v*
stamp, print, mark, brand, impress, fix, establish, engrave, emboss, etch

imprison *v*
put in prison, send to prison, jail, intern, detain, lock up, cage, pen, confine, shut in
OLD lumber
FORMAL incarcerate, immure
COLLOQ. send down, put away
SLANG bang up, lag shop, quod
F3 release, free

imprisoned *adj*
jailed, locked up, behind bars, confined, caged, captive
FORMAL incarcerated, immured
COLLOQ. inside, put away, sent down, doing time
SLANG doing bird, doing porridge, banged up
F3 free

imprisonment *n*
internment, detention, custody, captivity, confinement
FORMAL incarceration
SLANG porridge, bird
F3 freedom, liberty

improbability *n*
uncertainty, doubt, doubtfulness, dubiousness, unlikelihood, unlikeliness, far-fetchedness, preposterousness, ridiculousness, implausibility
FORMAL dubiety
F3 probability

improbable *adj*
uncertain, questionable, doubtful, unlikely, dubious, implausible, unconvincing far-fetched, preposterous, ridiculous, unbelievable, incredible
E3 probable, likely, convincing

impromptu *adj, adv*
♦ *adj*
improvised, extempore, ad-lib, unscripted, unrehearsed, unprepared, spontaneous
COLLOQ. off-the-cuff
E3 rehearsed
♦ *adv*
without preparation, extempore, ad lib, spontaneously
COLLOQ. on the spur of the moment, off the top of your head, off the cuff

improper *adj*
1 INDECENT, rude, vulgar, shocking risqué, indelicate, immodest, indiscreet, immoral
FORMAL unseemly, indecorous, unbecoming
2 WRONG, incorrect, irregular, false, erroneous, unlawful
3 UNSUITABLE, inappropriate, unfitting inopportune, inadequate, out of place
FORMAL incongruous
E3 1 decent **2** correct, lawful **3** suitable, appropriate

improperly *adv*
1 INDECENTLY, rudely, immodestly, indiscreetly, immorally
FORMAL indecorously
2 WRONGLY, incorrectly, irregularly, falsely, unlawfully, erroneously
3 UNSUITABLY, inappropriately, unfittingly
FORMAL incongruously
E3 1 decently **2** correctly, lawfully **3** suitably, appropriately

impropriety *n*
mistake, lapse, slip, blunder, faux pas, gaffe, bad taste, vulgarity, gaucherie, immodesty, indecency, unsuitability
FORMAL incongruity, indecorousness, indecorum, solecism, unseemliness
E3 *formal* propriety

improve *v*
better, make better, enhance, enrich, perfect, polish, touch up, mend, rectify, put right, set right, correct, amend, revise, reform, help, upgrade, modernize, streamline, revamp, work on/upon, increase, rise, pick up, develop, look up, advance, grow, progress, make headway, get better, recover, convalesce, recuperate, rally, rehabilitate, gain strength
FORMAL ameliorate, meliorate
COLLOQ. be on the up and up, get your act together, turn over a new leaf, mend your ways, perk up, give a facelift to, do for, do up, fix up
E3 worsen, deteriorate, decline

SYNONYM NUANCES

Better can be used to suggest surpassing a previous state, while **enhance** would suggest adding to it: *oak furniture enhances the light feel of the room*. You might use **enrich** to suggest increasing the worth: *our lives are enriched by literature*. **Perfect** implies doing something continually until it cannot be improved upon. **Polish**, on the other hand, is more suggestive of bringing something up to a higher standard: *a slick and polished dance routine*. **Touch up** implies covering flaws.
   Both **revise** and **reform** likewise imply changes for the better, while the terms **upgrade**, **modernize** and **revamp** would be appropriate for making newer, and better, substitutions or alterations, and **streamline** has implications of doing away with anything unnecessary. You can use **pick up** to suggest that something previously disappointing has begun to get better: *trade*

---

picked up towards the end of the year, whilst **develop** is more suggestive of steady progression.
   Look up, however, is more suggestive that things are about to improve: *Smith's fortunes in track events are looking up*. The terms **advance**, **progress** and **make headway** suggest a move forwards to a more satisfactory state or improved position: *science is making particular headway in this field*.
   The terms **get better** and **recover** are suggestive of prior failure or weakness, while **convalesce** and **recuperate** would be specifically used of getting better after a period of illness. **Rally** can also be used of getting into a better condition than previously, usually through one's own efforts: *the players rallied well but too late to save themselves from defeat*.

improvement *n*
betterment, enhancement, rectification, rectifying correction, amendment, revision, emendation, reform, reformation, rehabilitation, upgrading modernizing increase, rise, upswing gain, development, advance, growth, progress, headway, furtherance, recovery, rally, pick-up
FORMAL amelioration
E3 deterioration, decline, worsening

improvident *adj*
thriftless, unthrifty, spendthrift, extravagant, shiftless, uneconomical, wasteful, imprudent, careless, reckless, heedless, inattentive, thoughtless, negligent, unprepared, underprepared, Micawberish
FORMAL prodigal, profligate
E3 thrifty, economical

improvisation *n*
ad-lib, ad-libbing extemporizing extemporization, impromptu, invention, spontaneity, makeshift, expedient, vamp
FORMAL autoschediasm

QUOTATIONS
There's nothing that makes you so aware of the improvisation of human existence as a song unfinished. Or an old address book
  CARSON MCCULLERS, *The Ballad of the Sad Café*, 'The Sojourner'

---

improvise *v*
1 CONTRIVE, devise, concoct, invent, put together quickly, make do
COLLOQ. throw together, cobble together, knock up, rig up, run up
2 EXTEMPORIZE, ad-lib, compose/perform without preparation, vamp
COLLOQ. say whatever comes into your head/mind, speak off the cuff, speak off the top of your head, play by ear, wing it, have a brainwave

improvised *adj*
extempore, ad-lib, spontaneous, extemporaneous, extemporized, makeshift, unrehearsed, unprepared, unscripted
COLLOQ. off-the-cuff
E3 rehearsed

imprudence *n*
folly, foolhardiness, short-sightedness, rashness, recklessness, haste, irresponsibility, carelessness, heedlessness, thoughtlessness
E3 wisdom, caution, prudence

imprudent *adj*
unwise, ill-advised, ill-considered, ill-judged, foolish, foolhardy, short-sighted, rash, reckless, hasty, irresponsible, unthinking careless, heedless, thoughtless, indiscreet
FORMAL impolitic, injudicious, improvident
E3 wise, cautious, wary, prudent

impudence n

impertinence, boldness, brazenness, pertness, insolence, rudeness, presumption, chutzpah; *Scot* snash
FORMAL effrontery
COLLOQ. cheek, nerve, sauciness, attitude, lip, face, mouth, brass neck; *N Am* sass
F3 politeness

impudent adj

impertinent, bold, forward, shameless, immodest, cocky, brazen, insolent, rude, impolite, cheeky, disrespectful, presumptuous, audacious, pert
COLLOQ. saucy, fresh; *N Am* sassy
SLANG smartarse
F3 polite

impugn v

challenge, attack, assail, question, call in(to) question, criticize, oppose, resist, dispute
FORMAL berate, censure, revile, vilify, vituperate, traduce, vilipend
F3 praise, compliment

impulse n

1 URGE, wish, desire, inclination, whim, notion, caprice, instinct, feeling passion, drive, pulse, signal, thought-wave
TECHNICAL premotion, conatus, nisus
2 IMPETUS, momentum, force, pressure, drive, impact, thrust, motion, movement, propulsion, impulsion, surge, push, incitement, incentive, inducement, stimulation, stimulus, motive, motivation
■ **on impulse**
impulsively, impetuously, rashly, recklessly, impatiently, irresponsibly, hastily, suddenly, spontaneously, automatically, instinctively, intuitively, thoughtlessly, without thinking

impulsive adj

impetuous, rash, reckless, foolhardy, thoughtless, unthinking impatient, madcap, headstrong hasty, quick, sudden, ill-judged, ill-considered, spontaneous, automatic, instinctive, emotional, passionate, intuitive
FORMAL precipitate
F3 cautious, premeditated

impulsively adv

impetuously, rashly, recklessly, impatiently, irresponsibly, hastily, suddenly, spontaneously, automatically, instinctively, intuitively, thoughtlessly, without thinking on impulse
F3 cautiously

impulsiveness n

impetuosity, impetuousness, rashness, recklessness, foolhardiness, thoughtlessness, impatience, haste, hastiness, quickness, suddenness, spontaneity, instinct, emotion, passion, intuitiveness
FORMAL precipitateness, precipitation
F3 caution

impunity n

exemption, freedom, immunity, liberty, licence, dispensation, permission, security, amnesty, excusal
F3 liability
■ **with impunity**
safely, in safety, freely, without being punished, without risk

impure adj

1 UNREFINED, adulterated, alloyed, mixed, blended, combined, diluted, drossy, contaminated, polluted, tainted, infected, corrupt, defiled, debased, sullied, unclean, dirty, foul, filthy
OLD TECHNICAL vicious
2 OBSCENE, indecent, dirty, crude, coarse, vulgar, offensive, immoral, shameless, improper, promiscuous, depraved, unchaste, sexy, immodest, lustful, lewd, lecherous, licentious, risqué, suggestive, pornographic, erotic, smutty, bawdy, ribald
F3 **1** pure **2** chaste, decent

impurity n

1 *impurities in the petrol*
adulteration, mixture, blend, dilution, contamination, pollution, taint, infection, corruption, debasement, dirtiness, contaminant, pollutant, dirt, filth, grime, foulness, dross, foreign body, mark, spot
2 OBSCENITY, indecency, crudity, coarseness, vulgarity, offensiveness, immorality, shamelessness, impropriety, promiscuity, unchastity, looseness, immodesty, lustfulness, lewdness, licentiousness, pornography, eroticism, smut
F3 **2** purity

impute v

ascribe, assign, attribute, put down to, charge, credit, refer
FORMAL accredit

in prep, adj
♦ prep
1 *in the box*
within, inside, enclosed by, surrounded by
2 *in the autumn*
during during the time/course of, throughout, through
3 *one in ten people*
per, each, every
♦ adj
fashionable, in vogue, popular, current, smart, stylish, modish
COLLOQ. all the rage, trendy, cool, hip, funky
■ **in for**
due to receive, about to experience, going to suffer
■ **in on**
involved in, aware of, knowledgeable about, acquainted with
COLLOQ. clued up on
■ **in with**
friendly with, on good terms with, on friendly terms with, liked by

inability n

incapability, incapacity, powerlessness, impotence, inadequacy, incompetence, ineffectiveness, weakness, ineptitude, handicap, disability, uselessness
F3 ability

inaccessibility n

remoteness, isolation, distance, separation, unapproachableness, unattainability
F3 accessibility

inaccessible adj

isolated, remote, out of the way, god-forsaken, unfrequented, unapproachable, unreachable, out of reach, beyond reach, unattainable, impenetrable, unavailable
COLLOQ. unget-at-able
F3 accessible

inaccuracy n

mistake, error, miscalculation, slip, blunder, gaffe, fault, defect, imprecision, inexactness, unreliability, erroneousness, mistakenness
FORMAL corrigendum, erratum, fallaciousness
COLLOQ. boo-boo, slip-up, howler; *N Am* flub
SLANG goof
F3 accuracy, precision

> **QUOTATIONS**
> A little inaccuracy sometimes saves tons of explanation
> SAKI, *The Square Egg*, 'Clovis on the Alleged Romance of Business'

inaccurate adj

incorrect, wrong erroneous, mistaken, false, faulty, flawed, imperfect, defective, imprecise, inexact, out, loose, unreliable, unfaithful, untrue, unsound
FORMAL fallacious
COLLOQ. adrift
F3 accurate, correct, true, right, sound

inaccurately *adv*
incorrectly, wrongly, erroneously, falsely, imperfectly, defectively, imprecisely, inexactly, unreliably, unfaithfully, loosely, wildly, carelessly, clumsily
E3 accurately, correctly

inaction *n*
inactivity, immobility, motionlessness, inertia, rest, idleness, passivity, slowness, lifelessness, sluggishness, lethargy, stagnation
FORMAL torpor
E3 action

inactivate *v*
disable, immobilize, paralyse, stop, deactivate, cripple, mothball, stabilize
COLLOQ. knock the bottom out of, scupper
E3 activate

inactive *adj*
immobile, motionless, stationary, still, unactive, inert, idle, unused, unemployed, dormant, dead, passive, sedentary, lazy, slow, lifeless, lethargic, sluggish, vegetating stagnant, sleepy, hibernating shadow, slothful
FORMAL inoperative, indolent, torpid, quiescent
E3 active, working busy, functioning in use

SYNONYM NUANCES

Both **immobile** and **motionless** can be used where there is a total absence of movement. **Stationary** has more to do with staying in the same spot. **Still** suggests being completely at rest and has connotations of calmness: *we relaxed by the still waters*. The rare **unactive** and more common **inert**, when not used in scientific contexts, have associations with disinclination and sluggishness: *she was too inert to refuse this ridiculous request*. **Idle**, likewise, would strongly suggest disinclination to do anything: *idle days in front of the television*, but may also have connotations of wasted potential: *factories lying idle*.
  Dormant returns to the idea of not currently being in action: *dormant volcano*. **Dead** would be appropriate where there is no potential for activity. **Passive** has more to do with a lack of participation: *you don't want a pantomime audience to be passive*. **Sedentary** would be specifically applied to being seated: *office work and sedentary occupations*.
  Lazy and **slothful** are disapproving terms to describe disinclination to do anything. You can use **lifeless** if you want to suggest a lack of vitality: *lifeless little villages*, whereas **lethargic** and **sluggish** have suggestions of torpor: *the sluggish global economy*, and **vegetating** goes further by implying an absence of mental activity. **Stagnant** implies not moving at all, with further connotations of being unhealthy: *stagnant and badly circulating air encourages disease to settle*.

---

inactivity *n*
immobility, inaction, inertia, inertness, idleness, unemployment, dormancy, passivity, laziness, sluggishness, lifelessness, lethargy, sloth, vegetation, stagnation, hibernation, languor, dullness, heaviness
TECHNICAL stasis
FORMAL indolence, lassitude, quiescence, dilatoriness, torpor, abeyance
E3 activeness

inadequacy *n*
1 INSUFFICIENCY, lack, shortage, deficit, dearth, deficiency, scarcity, scantiness, meagreness
FORMAL want, paucity
2 DEFECTIVENESS, ineffectiveness, inability, incapability, incompetence
FORMAL inefficacy
3 *the inadequacies of the system*
fault, defect, imperfection, weakness, foible, failing shortcoming flaw
E3 1 adequacy 3 strong point

inadequate *adj*
1 INSUFFICIENT, short, wanting deficient, too little/few, scanty, scant, scarce, skimpy, sparse, meagre, niggardly
FORMAL incommensurate
COLLOQ. thin on the ground
2 INCOMPETENT, bad, incapable, inexpert, unproficient, careless, not good enough, unequal, unqualified, ineffective, faulty, defective, imperfect, unsatisfactory, poor, unfit, substandard, disappointing sketchy, leaving a lot to be desired
OLD unequal
FORMAL ineffectual, inefficacious
COLLOQ. pathetic, not up to scratch
E3 1 adequate, enough 2 satisfactory

inadequately *adv*
insufficiently, poorly, meagrely, scantily, sketchily, skimpily, sparsely, thinly, imperfectly, badly, carelessly
E3 adequately

inadmissible *adj*
unacceptable, irrelevant, immaterial, inappropriate, unallowable, disallowed, prohibited, improper
FORMAL precluded, inapposite
E3 admissible, allowable

inadvertent *adj*
accidental, chance, unintentional, unintended, unplanned, unguarded, unpremeditated, uncalculated, careless, negligent, thoughtless, unwitting unconscious, involuntary
OLD (*Spenser*) unadvised
E3 deliberate, conscious, careful

inadvertently *adv*
accidentally, by accident, by mistake, by chance, unintentionally, unthinkingly, unwittingly, unconsciously, involuntarily, carelessly, heedlessly, negligently, mistakenly, remissly, thoughtlessly
E3 deliberately

inadvisable *adj*
unwise, foolish, silly, ill-advised, ill-judged, ill-considered, imprudent, inexpedient, misguided, indiscreet
FORMAL injudicious
E3 advisable, wise

inalienable *adj*
inherent, inviolable, unassailable, non-negotiable, non-transferable, untransferable, unremovable, permanent, sacrosanct, absolute
E3 impermanent

inane *adj*
senseless, foolish, stupid, unintelligent, silly, idiotic, absurd, ridiculous, ludicrous, frivolous, trifling puerile, mindless, nonsensical, vapid, empty, vacuous, vain, worthless, futile
FORMAL fatuous
E3 sensible

inanely *adv*
foolishly, stupidly, idiotically, absurdly, ridiculously, ludicrously, nonsensically, vacuously, futilely
FORMAL fatuously
E3 sensibly

inanimate *adj*
lifeless, dead, defunct, extinct, unconscious, inactive, lazy, inert, dormant, immobile, stagnant, spiritless, dull, apathetic, lethargic, wooden
TECHNICAL insentient, insensate
FORMAL torpid
E3 animate, living alive

inanity *n*
senselessness, folly, foolishness, stupidity, silliness, absurdity, ridiculousness, ludicrousness, frivolity, puerility, imbecility, vapidity, vacuity, asininity, emptiness
FORMAL fatuity
COLLOQ. daftness, waffle
E3 sense

inapplicable *adj*
irrelevant, immaterial, inapt, inappropriate, unsuitable, unsuited, unrelated, unconnected
FORMAL inapposite, inconsequent
F3 applicable; *formal* germane, pertinent

inapposite *adj*
unsuitable, inappropriate, irrelevant, immaterial, out of place

inappreciable *adj*
indiscernible, imperceptible, unapparent, indistinguishable, undetectable, unnoticeable, inaudible, faint, slight, muffled, negligible, impalpable, infinitesimal, microscopic, minute, tiny, minuscule, small, fine, subtle, gradual, unclear, obscure, vague, indistinct, indefinite
F3 perceptible, noticeable, clear

inappropriate *adj*
unsuitable, unappropriate, inapt, ill-suited, ill-fitted, irrelevant, out of place, untimely, ill-timed, inopportune, tactless, improper, unbecoming undue, unfitting tasteless, facetious
OLD unseemly
FORMAL inapposite, incongruous, indecorous, infelicitous, malapropos
F3 appropriate, suitable

inappropriately *adv*
unsuitably, out of place, irrelevantly, without relevance, off/beside the point, inopportunely, tactlessly, tastelessly
FORMAL incongruously, infelicitously

inapt *adj*
inappropriate, unsuitable, unsuited, ill-suited, ill-fitted, irrelevant, out of place, ill-timed, inopportune, unfortunate
FORMAL inapposite, infelicitous
F3 apt

inarticulacy *n*
inarticulateness, incoherence, unintelligibility, incomprehensibility, mumbling indistinctness, hesitancy, stumbling stammering stuttering speechlessness, tongue-tiedness
F3 articulacy

inarticulate *adj*
incoherent, unintelligible, incomprehensible, unclear, indistinct, mumbled, blurred, muffled, hesitant, hesitating stumbling stammering stuttering trembling shaking quavery, faltering gibbering disjointed, halting tongue-tied, speechless, voiceless, dumb, mute, soundless
F3 articulate

inattention *n*
carelessness, negligence, disregard, heedlessness, thoughtlessness, unmindfulness, inattentiveness, absent-mindedness, forgetfulness, daydreaming dreaminess, preoccupation, distraction
F3 attention, care

inattentive *adj*
distracted, dreamy, daydreaming, preoccupied, absent-minded, wool-gathering, unmindful, heedless, regardless, disregarding, careless, thoughtless, negligent, forgetful, remiss
FORMAL distrait
COLLOQ. miles away, in a world of your own, somewhere else, asleep at the wheel
F3 attentive

inaudible *adj*
silent, noiseless, imperceptible, faint, indistinct, muffled, stifled, muted, soft, dull, low, mumbled, muttered, murmured, whispered
F3 audible, loud

inaugural *adj*
opening introductory, first, initial, launching original, maiden
FORMAL exordial
F3 closing final

inaugurate *v*
1 *inaugurate a scheme*
institute, originate, begin, start, set up, open, launch, introduce, usher in, initiate, set in motion, put into operation, get going
OLD auspicate, handsel
FORMAL commence
COLLOQ. set/start the ball rolling
2 *inaugurate the president*
induct, invest, install, ordain, instate, enthrone, admit to office, swear in
3 *inaugurate a new building*
dedicate, consecrate, open officially, commission

inauguration *n*
1 INSTITUTION, setting up, starting opening launch, launching initiation
FORMAL commencement
2 INDUCTION, ordination, investiture, consecration, enthronement, installation, installing swearing-in

inauspicious *adj*
unfavourable, bad, unlucky, unfortunate, unpromising untimely, ill-fated, ill-starred, discouraging threatening ominous, black
FORMAL infelicitous, unpropitious
F3 promising; *formal* auspicious

inborn *adj*
innate, inherent, natural, native, congenital, inbred, hereditary, inherited, in the family, ingrained, instinctive, intuitive
FORMAL connate
F3 learned

inbred *adj*
innate, inherent, natural, native, ingrained, incrossed, constitutional
TECHNICAL sib
FORMAL connate, ingenerate
F3 learned

inbuilt *adj*
built-in, integral, constituent, inherent, basic, fundamental, essential, elemental

incalculable *adj*
countless, innumerable, numberless, without number, untold, inestimable, immeasurable, measureless, limitless, boundless, unlimited, endless, infinite, immense, vast, enormous
F3 limited, restricted

incandescence *n*
glow, brilliance, brightness, gleam, glimmer, radiance, glory, vividness, richness, splendour, afterglow, sunglow, outflush
TECHNICAL phosphorescence
OLD leam
FORMAL luminosity

incandescent *adj*
1 GLOWING, aglow, shining dazzling gleaming brilliant, bright, white-hot
2 FURIOUS, angry, livid, indignant, irate, enraged, infuriated, incensed, inflamed, raging fuming boiling seething frenzied, purple with rage
COLLOQ. mad, hopping mad, sizzling up in arms, in a lather, hot under the collar, foaming at the mouth

incantation *n*
chant, charm, spell, abracadabra, formula, magic formula, invocation, mantra, mantram, rune, hex
FORMAL conjuration

incapable *adj*
unable, powerless, impotent, helpless, useless, weak, feeble, unfit, unsuited, unqualified, unfitted, incompetent, inept, inadequate, ineffective
FORMAL ineffectual
COLLOQ. not up to scratch, not hacking it, out of your league
F3 capable, experienced

incapacitate v
disable, cripple, paralyse, immobilize, disqualify, put out of action, lay up
FORMAL debilitate
COLLOQ. scupper

incapacitated adj
disabled, crippled, paralysed, immobilized, disqualified, out of action, unfit, unwell, hamstrung prostrate, drunk
FORMAL indisposed
COLLOQ. laid up, scuppered, tipsy
E■ operative

incapacity n
incapability, inability, disability, unfitness, disqualification, powerlessness, impotence, ineffectiveness, ineptitude, weakness, feebleness, inadequacy, incompetence, incompetency, uselessness
FORMAL ineffectuality
E■ capability

incarcerate v
imprison, put in prison, jail, gaol, put in jail, lock up, intern, confine, impound, commit, detain, put away, restrain, restrict, cage, encage, coop up, wall in
FORMAL immure
COLLOQ. send down, put inside
SLANG bang up
E■ free, release

incarceration n
imprisonment, internment, jail, custody, detention, confinement, bondage, captivity, restraint, restriction
E■ freedom, liberation

incarnate adj
human, in human form, embodied, made flesh, in the flesh, fleshly, personified, typified
OLD impersonate, incardinate
FORMAL corporeal

incarnation n
human form, appearance in the flesh, personification, embodiment, manifestation, impersonation
TECHNICAL avatar

incautious adj
careless, imprudent, ill-judged, ill-advised, ill-considered, unthinking thoughtless, inconsiderate, inattentive, unwary, unwatchful, unobservant, foolish, foolhardy, rash, reckless, hasty, impulsive
FORMAL injudicious, uncircumspect, precipitate
E■ cautious, careful, vigilant

incendiary adj, n
♦ adj
1 an incendiary bomb
fire-raising flammable, combustible, pyromaniac
2 INCITING, inflammatory, provocative, stirring seditious, subversive, dissentious, rabble-rousing
FORMAL proceleusmatic
E■ **2** calming
♦ n
1 AGITATOR, insurgent, revolutionary, demagogue, rabble-rouser, firebrand
2 FIRE-RAISER, pyromaniac, arsonist, firebug pétroleur, pétroleuse
3 FIREBOMB, bomb, explosive, charge, grenade, mine, petrol bomb

incense¹ n
smell the incense
perfume, scent, aroma, balm, bouquet, fragrance, joss-stick, pastille, myrrh, frankincense, benzoin, stacte

incense² v
incense his teacher
anger, enrage, infuriate, madden, exasperate, inflame, agitate, irritate, irk, vex, nettle, rile, provoke, excite
COLLOQ. aggravate, hassle, get someone's blood up, make someone's blood boil, get under someone's skin, drive up the wall, get someone's dander up
E■ calm

incensed adj
enraged, angry, fuming furious, exasperated, mad, maddened, steamed up, indignant, infuriated, irate, ireful, wrathful
FORMAL furibund
COLLOQ. aggravated, cross, ratty, uptight, hopping mad, raving mad, seeing red, in a lather, disgruntled, up in arms, hot under the collar, stroppy, in a strop, choked, fit to be tied, on the warpath, in a paddy; N Am ticked off; Aust spewy, ropable; Aust & NZ crooked
SLANG pissed off, hairless; N Am burned up
E■ calm

incentive n
bait, lure, enticement, reward, encouragement, fillip, inducement, incitement, reason, motive, impetus, spur, stimulus, goad, stimulant, bribe, motivation
COLLOQ. carrot, sweetener
E■ disincentive, discouragement, deterrent

inception n
inauguration, initiation, opening installation, establishment, beginning start, birth, origin, dawn, outset, rise
FORMAL commencement
COLLOQ. kick-off
E■ end

incessant adj
ceaseless, unceasing endless, never-ending unending continual, persistent, constant, perpetual, eternal, everlasting continuous, unbroken, uninterrupted, recurrent, unremitting non-stop
FORMAL interminable
E■ intermittent, sporadic, periodic, temporary

incessantly adv
ceaselessly, endlessly, unendingly, eternally, everlastingly, for ever, for ever and ever, uninterruptedly, continuously, unremittingly, constantly, unceasingly, interminably
COLLOQ. till the cows come home; N Am twenty-four seven

incidence n
frequency, commonness, prevalence, extent, range, amount, degree, rate, occurrence

incident n
1 EVENT, occurrence, happening episode, adventure, experience, proceeding affair, matter, occasion, instance, circumstance, passage, scene, subject, period, affaire, page
2 CONFRONTATION, clash, conflict, fight, skirmish, commotion, disturbance, scene, row, fracas, brush, upset, mishap

incidental adj
accidental, chance, by chance, random, minor, non-essential, petty, trivial, small, secondary, subordinate, background, subsidiary, ancillary, peripheral, supplementary, accompanying attendant, related, contributory
FORMAL fortuitous, concomitant
E■ important, essential

incidentally adv
1 BY THE WAY, in passing secondarily, parenthetically, as a digression, as an aside, episodically, en passant
FORMAL apropos
COLLOQ. by the by
2 ACCIDENTALLY, by accident, coincidentally, unexpectedly, by chance, casually, digressively
FORMAL fortuitously

incinerate v
burn, cremate, reduce to ashes, carbonize

incineration n
burning cremation, carbonization, turning/reduction to ashes

incipient adj
beginning originating starting inaugural, developing rudimentary, embryonic, newborn, impending

FORMAL commencing inceptive, inchoate, nascent
🔁 developed

incise v
cut, cut into, carve, chisel, engrave, sculpt, sculpture, etch, gash, slit, slash, nick, notch

incision n
cut, opening slit, gash, notch, slash, nick

incisive adj
cutting keen, sharp, acute, piercing penetrating surgical, biting stinging pungent, caustic, acid, astute, perceptive, shrewd, sarcastic
FORMAL trenchant, mordant, perspicacious

incisively adv
keenly, sharply, acutely, penetratingly, piercingly, astutely, pungently, sarcastically, tartly, caustically
FORMAL trenchantly, mordantly

incisiveness n
keenness, sharpness, acuteness, penetration, astuteness, acidity, pungency, sarcasm, tartness
FORMAL perspicacity, astucity, trenchancy

incite v
prompt, instigate, rouse, arouse, inflame, foment, stir up, whip up, work up, agitate, excite, animate, provoke, stimulate, spur, goad, prod, induce, impel, drive, urge, encourage
COLLOQ. egg on
🔁 restrain

incitement n
prompting instigation, rousing agitation, provocation, spur, goad, prod, impetus, stimulus, stimulation, animation, urging drive, motivation, encouragement, inducement, incentive
🔁 discouragement

inciting adj
incendiary, rabble-rousing inflammatory, provocative, stirring seditious, subversive
FORMAL proceleusmatic
🔁 calming

incivility n
impoliteness, discourtesy, discourteousness, rudeness, disrespect, unmannerliness, bad manners, ill-breeding inurbanity, boorishness, coarseness, roughness, vulgarity
🔁 civility

inclemency n
harshness, bitterness, rawness, severity, storminess, tempestuousness, roughness, foulness
🔁 clemency

inclement adj
intemperate, harsh, bitter, cold, raw, severe, wet, stormy, tempestuous, rough, foul, nasty, blustery, squally
🔁 fine, clement

inclination n
1 LIKING, fondness, affection, attraction, affinity, taste, preference, partiality, bias, tendency, trend, disposition, leaning
FORMAL propensity, proclivity, predisposition, predilection, penchant
2 *an inclination of 45 degrees*
angle, slope, gradient, incline, ascent, steepness, bank, ramp, lift, pitch, slant, tilt, bend, bow, nod
FORMAL acclivity, declivity
🔁 1 disinclination, dislike

incline v, n
♦ v
1 DISPOSE, influence, persuade, affect, sway, bend, bias, prejudice, tend, prefer
2 LEAN, slope, slant, bank, tilt, tip, bend, curve, list, bow, nod, stoop, veer, deviate, swing
♦ n
slope, gradient, ramp, hill, rise, ascent, dip, descent
FORMAL acclivity, declivity

inclined adj
liable, likely, tending given, apt, disposed, of a mind, willing
FORMAL predisposed, wont

include v
comprise, incorporate, embody, contain, enclose, hold, encompass, cover, take in, span, admit, insert, introduce, add, enter, put in, allow for, add in, count in, take into account, involve, let in on, reckon, carry
FORMAL comprehend, embrace, subsume, connote
COLLOQ. rope in, throw in
🔁 exclude, omit, eliminate

including prep
counting inclusive of, with, together with, as well as, included
🔁 excluding

inclusion n
incorporation, involvement, embodiment, encompassing addition, insertion
FORMAL comprehension, subsumption
🔁 exclusion

inclusive adj
comprehensive, full, all-in, all-inclusive, all-embracing across-the-board, general, catch-all, overall, sweeping
COLLOQ. blanket
🔁 exclusive, narrow

incognito adj
in disguise, disguised, masked, veiled, camouflaged, unmarked, unidentified, unrecognizable, unidentifiable, keeping your identity secret, unknown, under an assumed/a false name, nameless
🔁 undisguised

incognizant adj
unaware, unconscious, unacquainted, uninformed, unenlightened, ignorant, unknowing unobservant, inattentive
🔁 aware; *formal* apprised

incoherence n
unintelligibility, incomprehensibility, inarticulateness, stammer, stutter, mumble, mutter, brokenness, garbledness, muddle, mix-up, jumble, confusion, wildness, disconnectedness, disjointedness, illogicality, inconsistency
🔁 coherence

incoherent adj
unintelligible, incomprehensible, inarticulate, wandering rambling stammering stuttering mumbled, muttered, unconnected, disconnected, broken, garbled, scrambled, confused, muddled, mixed-up, jumbled, disjointed, disordered, loose, illogical, inconsistent, unclear, rigmarole, unjointed
OLD skimble-skamble
🔁 coherent, intelligible

incombustible adj
fireproof, flameproof, fire-resistant, flame-resistant, flame-retardant, non-flammable, non-inflammable, unburnable
🔁 combustible

income n
revenue, returns, proceeds, gains, profits, interest, takings, receipts, earnings, pay, salary, wages, means, remuneration, allowance, independency, penny-rent, rent roll, rente
OLD benefice
🔁 expenditure, expenses, outgoings

> **QUOTATIONS**
> Annual income twenty pounds, annual expenditure nineteen nineteen six, result happiness. Annual income twenty pounds, annual expenditure twenty pounds ought and six, result misery
> CHARLES DICKENS, *David Copperfield*

incoming adj
arriving entering approaching coming homeward,
returning ensuing succeeding next, new
☷ outgoing

incommensurate adj
disproportionate, insufficient, inadequate, unequal,
excessive, extravagant, extreme
FORMAL incommensurable, inequitable, inordinate
☷ appropriate

incommunicable adj
indescribable, inexpressible, unspeakable, unutterable,
unimpartable
FORMAL ineffable
☷ expressible, communicable

incomparable adj
matchless, unmatched, beyond compare, unequalled,
without equal, unparalleled, without parallel, second to
none, unrivalled, unsurpassed, peerless, inimitable,
nonpareil, paramount, supreme, superlative, superb,
brilliant
☷ ordinary, run-of-the-mill, poor

incomparably adv
by far, far and away, beyond compare, immeasurably,
infinitely, easily, supremely, superbly, superlatively,
eminently, brilliantly
COLLOQ. by a country mile
☷ poorly, slightly

incompatibility n
irreconcilability, contradiction, clash, conflict, variance,
inconsistency, difference, disagreement, discrepancy,
antagonism, mismatch, uncongeniality
FORMAL disparateness, disparity, incongruity
☷ compatibility

incompatible adj
irreconcilable, contradictory, conflicting in conflict,
exclusive, at odds, alien, at variance, inconsistent, clashing
antagonistic, disagreeing discordant, ill-matched,
mismatched, ill-assorted, unsuited, uncongenial, wrong
repugnant
TECHNICAL dissonant
OLD insociable
FORMAL incongruous, disparate
COLLOQ. like a fish out of water, like a square peg in a
round hole, like chalk and cheese
☷ compatible, complementary, going well together

incompetence n
incapability, inability, unfitness, unsuitability, stupidity,
uselessness, ineptitude, ineptness, ineffectiveness,
inefficiency, inadequacy, insufficiency, bungling
FORMAL ineffectuality, ineffectualness
☷ competence

incompetent adj
incapable, unable, unfit, unqualified, unsuitable,
inefficient, inexpert, amateurish, unskilful, bungling
awkward, clumsy, fumbling stupid, useless, botched,
ineffective, inadequate, insufficient, deficient
COLLOQ. awful, terrible, lousy, crummy, pathetic, rop(e)y,
a load of rubbish, a load of garbage
SLANG the pits, pants, poxy, naff, crappy, not able to
organize a piss-up in a brewery; (vulgar) a load of crap, a
load of shit
☷ competent, able

incomplete adj
deficient, lacking short, unfinished, unaccomplished,
undeveloped, embryonic, rudimentary, abridged,
shortened, partial, part, half, sketchy, fragmentary, broken,
scrappy, piecemeal, imperfect, defective
TECHNICAL catalectic
FORMAL wanting
☷ complete, accomplished, exhaustive, total

incomprehensible adj
unintelligible, unreadable, impenetrable, unfathomable,
unfamiliar, unaware, complex, complicated, involved,
above/over your head, puzzling perplexing baffling deep,
profound, enigmatic, mysterious, inscrutable, obscure,
opaque
FORMAL abstruse, recondite
COLLOQ. double Dutch, all Greek to you
☷ comprehensible, intelligible

incomprehension n
unintelligibility, lack of understanding ignorance,
unperceptiveness, incognizance, unawareness,
unfamiliarity, impenetrability, complexity, mysteriousness,
inscrutability, obscurity, profundity
☷ comprehension, intelligibility

inconceivable adj
unthinkable, unimaginable, staggering unheard-of,
impossible, unbelievable, incredible, implausible,
ridiculous, ludicrous, absurd, outrageous, shocking
COLLOQ. mind-boggling
☷ conceivable, imaginable, not on

inconclusive adj
unsettled, undecided, indefinite, open, open to question,
uncertain, indecisive, ambiguous, vague, unconvincing
unsatisfying
FORMAL indeterminate
COLLOQ. up in the air, left hanging
☷ conclusive; colloq. open-and-shut

incongruity n
inappropriateness, unsuitability, inconsistency,
incompatibility, conflict, clash, irreconcilability,
contradiction, discrepancy, inharmoniousness, inaptness
FORMAL disparity, dissociability, dissociableness
☷ consistency, harmoniousness

incongruous adj
inappropriate, unsuitable, out of place, out of keeping
inconsistent, conflicting clashing jarring incompatible,
irreconcilable, contradictory, contrary, at odds, odd,
absurd, strange
☷ consistent, compatible

incongruously adv
unsuitably, inappropriately, out of place, irrelevantly,
without relevance, off/beside the point, inopportunely
FORMAL infelicitously

inconsequential adj
minor, trivial, trifling petty, unimportant, of no importance,
insignificant, neither here nor there, negligible, immaterial,
inappreciable
☷ important, significant

inconsiderable adj
small, slight, negligible, trivial, petty, trifling minor,
unimportant, insignificant
☷ considerable, large

inconsiderate adj
unkind, uncaring unconcerned, uncharitable, selfish, self-
centred, egotistic, intolerant, insensitive, tactless, rude,
thoughtless, unthinking careless, heedless, undiscerning
☷ considerate, thoughtful, gracious, kind

inconsiderateness n
unkindness, unconcern, selfishness, self-centredness,
intolerance, insensitivity, tactlessness, rudeness,
thoughtlessness, carelessness
☷ considerateness, thoughtfulness, kindness

inconsistency n
1 CONTRADICTION, irreconcilability, incompatibility,
discrepancy, disagreement, divergence, paradox, conflict,
variance, odds, gallimaufry
FORMAL contrariety, disparity, incongruity
2 CHANGEABLENESS, unpredictability, instability,
unsteadiness, unreliability, fickleness, inconstancy
☷ 1 consistency 2 consistency, constancy

inconsistent adj
1 CONFLICTING, at variance, at odds, out of place/keeping
in opposition, incompatible, contradictory, contrary,

differing discordant, irreconcilable, dissimilar, alien, jarring unagreeable, repugnant, self-repugnant
TECHNICAL disconformable
FORMAL incongruous
2 CHANGEABLE, variable, irregular, erratic, unpredictable, varying unstable, unsteady, inconstant, fickle, capricious, mercurial, playing fast and loose
COLLOQ. in and out, blowing hot and cold
F3 **1** consistent **2** consistent, constant

inconsolable adj
heartbroken, broken-hearted, devastated, desolate, despairing wretched, miserable, grief-stricken
FORMAL disconsolate

inconspicuous adj
unobtrusive, plain, ordinary, indistinct, unremarkable, undistinguished, discreet, low-key, hidden, concealed, camouflaged, modest, unassuming quiet, retiring insignificant, in the background
F3 conspicuous, noticeable, obtrusive

inconspicuously adv
unobtrusively, unassumingly, quietly, modestly, faintly, insignificantly, in the background
F3 conspicuously, obtrusively

inconstancy n
variableness, unsteadiness, fluctuation, variation, change, shift, swing alternation, variability, range, instability, wavering irresolution, ambivalence, fickleness
FORMAL oscillation, vacillation

inconstant adj
changeable, variable, varying changeful, erratic, mutable, unsteady, fluctuating inconsistent, unsettled, unstable, volatile, wavering uncertain, undependable, unreliable, unfaithful, irresolute, capricious, mercurial, wayward, fickle
OLD (Shakesp) giglet
FORMAL vacillating
F3 constant

incontestable adj
incontrovertible, indisputable, undeniable, indubitable, irrefutable, unquestionable, certain, obvious, clear, evident, self-evident, sure
F3 uncertain

incontinent adj
uncontrollable, uncontrolled, ungovernable, ungoverned, unrestrained, unbridled, unchecked, loose, promiscuous, unchaste, dissipated, dissolute, debauched, lewd, licentious, lascivious, lecherous, lustful, wanton
F3 continent

incontrovertible adj
indisputable, unquestionable, beyond question, undeniable, irrefutable, indubitable, beyond doubt, certain, clear, self-evident
F3 questionable, uncertain

incontrovertibly adv
indisputably, unquestionably, beyond question, beyond doubt, undeniably, irrefutably, indubitably, certainly, clearly

inconvenience n, v
♦ n
1 cause inconvenience
awkwardness, difficulty, annoyance, vexation, nuisance, bother, trouble, fuss, discomfort, disruption
FORMAL incommodity, incommodiousness
COLLOQ. hassle
2 a minor inconvenience
difficulty, problem, annoyance, worry, nuisance, hindrance, drawback, bother, trouble, fuss, upset, disturbance, disadvantage, burden, burr
COLLOQ. drag pain, bore, bind, headache, turn-off
F3 **1, 2** convenience
♦ v
bother, disturb, disrupt, put out, trouble, upset, irk, annoy, worry, fuss, burden, impose upon
FORMAL discommode

COLLOQ. hassle
F3 convenience

inconvenient adj
awkward, ill-timed, untimely, unseasonable, unsuitable, inappropriate, inexpedient, difficult, embarrassing annoying troublesome, bothersome, untoward, unwieldy, unmanageable, cumbersome
OLD unhandsome
FORMAL inopportune, incommodious
F3 convenient, suitable, handy

incorporate v
include, embody, contain, take in, build in, absorb, assimilate, integrate, combine, amalgamate, unite, unify, merge, blend, mix, fuse, coalesce, consolidate
OLD incorpse, piece up
FORMAL subsume, embrace
F3 separate

incorporation n
inclusion, absorption, embodiment, assimilation, integration, combination, amalgamation, unification, unifying blend, fusion, coalescence, association, company, merger, society, federation
FORMAL subsuming
F3 separation, splitting off

incorporeal adj
bodiless, unfleshy, spiritual, unreal, illusory, intangible, ethereal, spectral, phantasmal, phantasmic, ghostly
F3 real, fleshy

incorrect adj
wrong not right, mistaken, erroneous, inaccurate, imprecise, inexact, false, untrue, bad, ill, faulty, ungrammatical, improper, illegitimate, inappropriate, unsuitable
FORMAL fallacious
COLLOQ. (way) off beam
F3 correct, accurate

incorrectly adv
wrongly, mistakenly, by mistake, in error, erroneously, falsely, inaccurately, inappropriately, misguidedly, unfairly, unjustly
FORMAL fallaciously

incorrectness n
wrongness, mistakenness, erroneousness, error, inaccuracy, imprecision, inexactitude, falseness, faultiness, impreciseness, inexactness, speciousness, unsoundness, unsuitability
FORMAL fallacy
F3 correctness, accuracy

incorrigible adj
irredeemable, incurable, inveterate, hardened, hopeless, beyond hope, beyond redemption, dyed-in-the-wool
F3 redeemable

incorruptibility n
honesty, honour, integrity, uprightness, virtue, morality, trustworthiness, justness, nobility
FORMAL probity
F3 corruptibility

incorruptible adj
honest, straight, upright, virtuous, moral, ethical, honourable, high-principled, trustworthy, unbribable, just
F3 corruptible, dishonest

increase v, n
♦ v
1 the number of tourists has increased
become greater, go up, be on the increase, climb, rise; N Am tick up; mount, soar, maximize, improve, advance, progress, grow, develop, build up, intensify, strengthen, heighten, appreciate, extend, expand, spread, swell, multiply, proliferate, escalate, mushroom, snowball, rocket, skyrocket, spiral
COLLOQ. go through the roof

2 increase the public's awareness
raise, boost, add to, improve, enhance, advance, further,
step up, intensify, strengthen, heighten, develop, build up,
accumulate, enlarge, magnify, broaden, widen, deepen,
extend, prolong expand, spread, breed, propagate,
scale up
FORMAL augment
COLLOQ. hike up, bump up, bring to a head,
bring to the boil
F3 1 decrease, reduce, decline, fall 2 decrease, reduce
♦ n
rise, growth, surge, upsurge, upturn, gain, boost, addition,
increment, uptick, advance, step-up, build-up,
intensification, heightening development, enlargement,
extension, expansion, spread, proliferation, escalation,
mushrooming snowballing rocketing
FORMAL augmentation
COLLOQ. hike, bounce
F3 decrease, reduction, decline

SYNONYM NUANCES

verb sense 1
Climb and **rise** are suggestive of increasing by a large
amount; **mount** may be found in wider contexts
suggesting a steep ascent: *mounting criticism.* **Soar**
implies a huge rise, but is usually applied to figures:
crime rates have soared in the past year. **Improve** would
be used where there is a growth in price or value with a
positive effect: *improved trading figures give a healthier
look to the economy.*
While **grow** suggests a natural increase, **develop** and
build up can be used of a natural or a planned
expansion: *we have built up our clientele over the years.*
Intensify is suggestive of becoming concentrated:
yesterday's increase intensified fears for the economy.
The terms **extend**, **expand** and **spread** are all
suggestive of horizontal growth, either physical or more
figurative: *we are extending the garden by two metres;
my waistline is expanding.*
Swell suggests a more marked, inflated outcome: *the
number of tourists has swelled,* and **multiply** would be
used of an increase in numbers, as could **proliferate**,
especially if you wish to suggest a resulting abundance.
The terms **escalate**, **mushroom** and **snowball** use
differing images to suggest the unstoppable speed with
which an increase comes about. **Spiral**, **rocket** and
skyrocket imply a fast and uncontrolled increase,
especially where the outcome is negative: *spiralling
debts have left many companies in trouble.*

increasingly *adv*
more and more, all the more, more so, to an increasing
degree/extent, on the increase, progressively, cumulatively
TECHNICAL exponentially

incredible *adj*
1 give some incredible excuse
unbelievable, improbable, implausible, far-fetched,
preposterous, absurd, impossible, inconceivable,
beyond/past belief, unthinkable, unimaginable
2 walk an incredible distance
extraordinary, amazing surprising astonishing astounding
fantastic, remarkable, magnificent, formidable, exceptional,
marvellous, wonderful, great
COLLOQ. tremendous, terrific, smashing out of this world,
mind-boggling jaw-dropping
F3 1 credible, believable

incredible or **incredulous**?
Incredible means 'unbelievable'; *incredulous* means
'not believing showing disbelief'. If you are told an
incredible story, you may be *incredulous.*

incredibly *adv*
unimaginably, unbelievably, inconceivably, impossibly,
very, extremely, greatly, highly, extraordinarily,

inexpressibly, unspeakably, amazingly, surprisingly,
fantastically, remarkably, exceptionally, wonderfully,
marvellously
COLLOQ. terrifically, tremendously

incredulity *n*
unbelief, disbelief, scepticism, cynicism, suspicion, doubt,
distrust, mistrust
F3 credulity

incredulous *adj*
unbelieving disbelieving unconvinced, sceptical, cynical,
suspicious, doubting distrusting distrustful, dubious,
doubtful, uncertain
F3 credulous

incredulous or **incredible**?
See panel at **incredible**.

increment *n*
increase, gain, addition, step-up, advancement, extension,
supplement, growth, enlargement, expansion, growth ring
FORMAL accretion, accrual, accrument, addendum,
augmentation
F3 decrease

incriminate *v*
implicate, involve, accuse, charge, impeach, blame, put
the blame on
TECHNICAL indict, arraign
FORMAL inculpate
COLLOQ. point the finger at
F3 exonerate

inculcate *v*
instil, drum into, hammer into, din into, drill into, implant,
fix, imprint, engrain, impress, infuse, teach, indoctrinate

inculpate *v*
blame, put the blame on, censure, accuse, charge,
impeach, incriminate, involve, implicate, recriminate
TECHNICAL indict, arraign
F3 exonerate

incumbent *adj, n*
♦ adj
binding necessary, obligatory, compulsory,
prescribed, up to
FORMAL mandatory
♦ n
office-holder, office-bearer, bearer, holder, official, officer,
functionary, member

incur *v*
sustain, suffer, provoke, arouse, bring upon yourself, lay
yourself open to, expose yourself to, risk, run, experience,
meet with, run up, gain, earn, contract

incurable *adj*
1 an incurable disease
terminal, fatal, untreatable, unhealable, inoperable,
hopeless
2 INCORRIGIBLE, inveterate, hardened, hopeless, beyond
hope, beyond redemption, dyed-in-the-wool
F3 1 curable

incurably *adv*
1 TERMINALLY, fatally, inoperably, hopelessly
2 INCORRIGIBLY, inveterately, hopelessly, beyond hope

incursion *n*
raid, attack, assault, invasion, onslaught, foray, sortie, sally,
infiltration, inroads, penetration
FORMAL irruption

indebted *adj*
obliged, grateful, thankful, appreciative
FORMAL beholden

indebtedness *n*
obligation, debt of gratitude, gratitude, appreciation

indecency *n*
immodesty, impurity, indecent behaviour, obscenity,
pornography, lewdness, licentiousness, vulgarity,
coarseness, crudity, foulness, grossness, offensiveness

FORMAL indecorum
▣ decency, modesty

indecent adj
1 IMPURE, immodest, improper, indelicate, suggestive, offensive, free, obscene, pornographic, lewd, immoral, corrupt, perverted, depraved, degenerate, licentious, vulgar, coarse, crude, dirty, filthy, smutty, foul, gross, bawdy, ribald, risqué, outrageous, shocking off colour
COLLOQ. blue, raunchy, sleazy, fruity, close to/near the bone, near the knuckle
2 *indecent haste*
improper, unbecoming unsuitable, inappropriate
OLD uncomely, unseemly
FORMAL indecorous
▣ **1** decent, modest

indecipherable adj
indistinguishable, unreadable, illegible, unintelligible, indistinct, unclear, tiny, crabbed, cramped
▣ readable

indecision n
indecisiveness, irresolution, wavering fluctuation, hesitation, hesitancy, dithering ambivalence, uncertainty, tentativeness, suspense, doubt
FORMAL vacillation
COLLOQ. shilly-shallying
▣ decisiveness, resolution

> **QUOTATIONS**
> My Indecision is Final
> JAKE EBERTS, *My Indecision is Final*

indecisive adj
1 UNDECIDED, undecisive, irresolute, undetermined, fluctuating wavering ambivalent, hesitating hesitant, faltering tentative, uncertain, unsure, indefinite, doubtful
FORMAL vacillating
COLLOQ. in two minds, weak-willed, pussyfooting shilly-shallying wishy-washy, blowing hot and cold, humming and hawing chopping and changing sitting on the fence, giving someone the runaround
2 INCONCLUSIVE, indefinite, unclear, open, undecided, unsettled
FORMAL indeterminate
COLLOQ. up in the air, hanging in the balance
▣ **1** decisive **2** decisive; *colloq.* open-and-shut

indecorous adj
undignified, improper, immodest, indecent, rough, impolite, rude, vulgar, in bad taste, tasteless, uncouth, unsuitable, inappropriate, coarse, crude, uncivil, unmannerly, ungentlemanly, unladylike, ill-mannered, ill-bred, boorish, churlish
FORMAL unseemly, untoward
▣ decorous

indecorum n
immodesty, indecency, roughness, rudeness, impoliteness, uncivility, tastelessness, bad taste, coarseness, crudity, vulgarity
FORMAL impropriety, unseemliness

indeed adv
really, actually, in fact, in point of fact, in truth, certainly, absolutely, positively, yes, truly, undeniably, without doubt, undoubtedly, doubtlessly, for sure, to be sure, even, definitely, for that matter, rather, in anyone's book, aye, la; *Scot* atweel, deed
OLD sooth, forsooth, insooth; (*Spenser*) soothly; yea, faith, marry, quotha, in good time
FORMAL nay
COLLOQ. just, quite

indefatigable adj
untiring tireless, untireable, unflagging unfailing unwearied, unwearying unweariable, unresting relentless, unremitting dogged, inexhaustible, diligent, patient, persevering indomitable, undying
▣ flagging slothful

indefatigably adv
tirelessly, unflaggingly, unfailingly, relentlessly, unremittingly, unrestingly, doggedly, diligently, patiently, indomitably

indefensible adj
1 UNJUSTIFIABLE, inexcusable, unforgivable, unpardonable, insupportable, untenable, wrong faulty, flawed, specious
2 *an indefensible place*
vulnerable, exposed, defenceless, unshielded, unarmed, disarmed, unprotected, unguarded, undefendable, ill-equipped
FORMAL unfortified
▣ **1** defensible, excusable **2** defensible, protected, guarded

indefinable adj
indescribable, inexpressible, indistinct, unrealized, nameless, obscure, unclear, vague, subtle, dim, hazy, impalpable
▣ definable

indefinite adj
unknown, uncertain, unsettled, unresolved, inconclusive, undecided, undetermined, unfixed, undefined, unspecified, unlimited, ill-defined, vague, indistinct, unclear, blurred, confused, hazy, fuzzy, obscure, ambivalent, equivocal, ambiguous, doubtful, imprecise, inexact, loose, general, nondescript
FORMAL indeterminate
COLLOQ. the jury is still out
▣ definite, limited, clear

indefinitely adv
for ever, eternally, endlessly, always, permanently, without limit, continually, ad infinitum
COLLOQ. till the cows come home

indelible adj
lasting enduring permanent, fast, unfading ineffaceable, ineradicable, ingrained, imperishable, indestructible
▣ erasable

indelibly adv
enduringly, permanently, ineradicably, indestructibly

indelicacy n
immodesty, indecency, obscenity, rudeness, vulgarity, offensiveness, suggestiveness, tastelessness, bad taste, coarseness, crudity, grossness, smuttiness
FORMAL impropriety
▣ delicacy

indelicate adj
rude, embarrassing suggestive, immodest, improper, indecent, offensive, tasteless, in bad taste, unbecoming vulgar, coarse, crude, gross, low, obscene, risqué
FORMAL indecorous, unseemly, untoward
COLLOQ. blue, off-colour
▣ delicate

indemnify v
protect, secure, underwrite, guarantee, insure, endorse, exempt, free, reimburse, compensate, repair, repay, requite, satisfy, pay, remunerate

indemnity n
compensation, reimbursement, remuneration, repayment, restitution, requital, redress, reparation, insurance, assurance, guarantee, security, protection, safeguard, immunity, exemption, amnesty

indent v
1 CUT, mark, nick, notch, dent, dint, pink, serrate, scallop
2 ORDER, ask for, apply for, request, demand
FORMAL requisition

indentation n
notch, nick, cut, serration, dent, groove, furrow, depression, dip, hollow, pit, dimple

indenture n
contract, agreement, certificate, deed, bond, covenant, commitment, deal, settlement

independence n

independency, autonomy, self-government, self-determination, self-rule, home rule, sovereignty, freedom, liberty, individualism, separation, self-sufficiency, self-reliance, decolonization, nationalism
TECHNICAL autarky
⊟ dependence

independent adj

1 AUTONOMOUS, self-governing self-determining self-ruling self-legislating sovereign, absolute, non-aligned
TECHNICAL autarkic
FORMAL autarchic
2 FREE, free-thinking liberated, unconstrained, unrestrained, freelance, individualistic, individualist, unconventional, self-sufficient, self-supporting self-reliant, unaided
COLLOQ. standing on your own two feet, doing your own thing with a mind of your own, going your own way, doing something off your own bat, paddling your own canoe
3 SEPARATE, self-contained, individual, unconnected, unattached, unrelated, free-standing distinct
FORMAL discrete
4 FAIR, just, unprejudiced, neutral, impartial, unbiased, dispassionate, objective, disinterested
⊟ 1 dependent 4 biased

independently adv

alone, by yourself, on your own, individually, separately, solo, unaided, autonomously
COLLOQ. under your own steam, on your tod
⊟ together

indescribable adj

inexpressible, indefinable, undefinable, unutterable, unspeakable, incredible, extraordinary, exceptional, amazing
FORMAL ineffable
⊟ describable

indescribably adv

inexpressibly, unutterably, unspeakably, incredibly, extraordinarily, exceptionally, amazingly, extremely, very, highly, greatly

indestructible adj

unbreakable, durable, tough, strong lasting enduring abiding permanent, eternal, everlasting immortal, endless, undecaying inextinguishable, imperishable
FORMAL infrangible
⊟ breakable, mortal

indeterminate adj

indefinite, unspecified, unstated, undefined, unknown, unfixed, imprecise, inexact, unclear, vague, hazy, ill-defined, open-ended, undecided, undetermined, unpredictable, uncertain, ambiguous, equivocal, ambivalent
⊟ known, specified, fixed

index n

1 *an index of names*
table, key, list, catalogue, directory, guide, concordance
2 INDICATOR, pointer, needle, dial, hand, sign, token, mark, indication, hint, clue, symptom
TECHNICAL alidad
OLD gnomon
3 RATIO, proportion, rate, number, average, formula, scale, indicator, correspondence, difference, percentage, fraction
TECHNICAL exponent, power

indicate v

1 *shrugging shoulders indicates a lack of care*
show, reveal, display, mark, signify, mean, express, tell, make known, suggest, imply, represent, be symptomatic of
FORMAL manifest, evince, denote
2 *indicate the way to someone*
point out, show, point to, designate, specify
3 *he indicated that he would not oppose the plan*
say, declare, state, tell, announce, report, communicate, assert, affirm, specify, present, express, put, set out, make known, formulate, articulate, voice, utter, reveal, divulge, disclose
4 *the gauge indicates temperature*
show, register, record, read

indicated adj

needed, required, suggested, desirable, necessary, called-for, advisable, recommended

indication n

sign, mark, evidence, symptom, signal, record, register, warning omen, intimation, expression, suggestion, hint, clue, note, explanation
FORMAL manifestation, augury, portent

indicative adj

symptomatic, suggestive, demonstrative, characteristic, typical, telltale, significant, symbolic
FORMAL denotative, exhibitive, indicatory, indicant

indicatively adv

symptomatically, characteristically, significantly, typically, symbolically, as a sign, as a symbol, as evidence, as an expression

indicator n

pointer, needle, marker, hand, index, sign, symbol, token, signal, display, dial, gauge, meter, guide, flasher, bezel, barometer, litmus test, mark, signpost; *N Am* turn signal
OLD gnomon

indict v

charge, accuse, impeach, summon, summons, prosecute, put on trial, incriminate
TECHNICAL arraign
FORMAL inculpate
⊟ absolve; *formal* exonerate

indictment n

charge, accusation, impeachment, allegation, recrimination, summons, prosecution, incrimination
TECHNICAL arraignment
FORMAL inculpation
⊟ exoneration

indifference n

apathy, unconcern, lack of concern, lack of interest, lack of feeling coldness, coolness, inattention, disregard, heedlessness, negligence, impassivity, nonchalance, neutrality, disinterestedness
⊟ interest, concern

indifferent adj

1 UNINTERESTED, unenthusiastic, unexcited, apathetic, unconcerned, unmoved, unresponsive, unfeeling unemotional, uncaring unsympathetic, blasé, callous, cold, cool, distant, aloof, detached, lukewarm, dispassionate, uninvolved, impassive, neutral, nonchalant, disinterested, careless, heedless
COLLOQ. easy, all the same to you
2 MEDIOCRE, average, middling passable, moderate, fair, adequate, undistinguished, ordinary, medium, bad, not good
COLLOQ. OK, so-so, could be better/worse, run of the mill, nothing to write home about
⊟ 1 interested, caring 2 excellent

SYNONYM NUANCES

sense 1
The word **apathetic** is fairly disapproving in tone and can be used to show that someone cannot be bothered: *young people are notoriously apathetic about voting.* **Blasé**, on the other hand, is less marked in that it suggests indifference arising from overfamiliarity. **Nonchalant** is appropriate of a very casual and perhaps studied display of indifference, while **careless** and **heedless** suggest an irresponsible lack of concern: *rushing onwards with heedless bravery.*

Other more neutral terms are **unconcerned**, **unmoved**, **unemotional**, **unsympathetic** and **uninvolved**, which are simply concerned with the absence of a particular emotion, but **unresponsive**,

unfeeling and **uncaring** have a more disapprobatory feel, suggesting an unnatural lack of fellow feeling. **Callous** is even more strongly suggestive of a hardened attitude to the suffering of others.

Both **cold** and **cool**, however, have connotations of varying degrees of unfriendliness, and **distant** and **detached** suggest a simple lack of emotional involvement, whereas **impassive** would be appropriate for not showing it. **Aloof** has further, more disapproving implications of standoffishness. **Neutral** and **disinterested** have more to do with impartiality and not taking sides in a dispute.

indigence *n*
poverty, distress, destitution, deprivation, necessity, need, want
FORMAL penury, privation
E∃ affluence

indigenous *adj*
native, aboriginal, original, local, home-grown
FORMAL autochthonous
E∃ foreign

indigent *adj*
poverty-stricken, impoverished, poor, destitute, needy, penniless, in dire straits, in want, in need
FORMAL penurious, impecunious, necessitous
COLLOQ. down and out, bust, skint, broke, stony-broke, cleaned out, on your uppers, on your beam ends, up against it, not having two pennies to rub together, dirt-poor
E∃ affluent

indigestion *n*
dyspepsia, dyspepsy, heartburn, cardialgia, acidity, pyrosis, water-brash, grass/stomach staggers
OLD apepsia

indignant *adj*
annoyed, angry, cross, irate, heated, fuming livid, furious, incensed, infuriated, enraged, exasperated, outraged, riled, aggrieved, disgruntled, wrathful, acrimonious, bitter, resentful
COLLOQ. hot under the collar, steamed up, mad, up in arms, peeved, miffed, narked, got the hump, in a huff, in a strop
E∃ pleased, delighted

indignantly *adv*
angrily, crossly, irately, furiously, reproachfully, acrimoniously, resentfully, bitterly
COLLOQ. hot under the collar, steamed up, up in arms, in a huff

indignation *n*
annoyance, anger, ire, wrath, rage, fury, exasperation, outrage, pique, scorn, contempt, resentment
E∃ pleasure, delight

indignity *n*
humiliation, abuse, insult, slight, snub, affront, shame, contempt, mistreatment, offence, disgrace, outrage, reproach, dishonour, disrespect, incivility, injury
FORMAL contumely, obloquy, opprobrium
COLLOQ. slap in the face, kick in the teeth, cold shoulder, putdown
E∃ honour

indirect *adj*
1 ROUNDABOUT, circuitous, divergent, devious, remote, oblique, wandering rambling curving winding meandering zigzag tortuous, discursive, allusive, back-handed, squint
FORMAL periphrastic, circumlocutory
2 *an indirect effect*
secondary, incidental, unintended, subordinate, subsidiary, ancillary, bye, mediate
E∃ **1** direct **2** primary

indirectly *adv*
roundaboutly, obliquely, second-hand, deviously, in a roundabout way, hintingly, incidentally, allusively

FORMAL periphrastically, circumlocutorily
E∃ directly

indiscernible *adj*
imperceptible, minuscule, minute, microscopic, tiny, undiscernible, undetectable, unapparent, unclear, indistinct, obscure, indistinguishable, unnoticeable, invisible, hidden, impalpable
E∃ clear, apparent

indiscreet *adj*
tactless, undiplomatic, insensitive, unwise, imprudent, ill-advised, ill-judged, ill-considered, foolish, foolhardy, rash, reckless, hasty, careless, heedless, unthinking unwary, immodest, indelicate, shameless
FORMAL impolitic, injudicious
E∃ discreet, cautious

indiscreetly *adv*
tactlessly, undiplomatically, unwisely, foolishly, rashly, recklessly, carelessly, heedlessly, immodestly, indelicately, insensitively, shamelessly
E∃ discreetly, cautiously

indiscretion *n*
mistake, error, slip, faux pas, gaffe, blunder, lapse, tactlessness, rashness, recklessness, imprudence, foolishness, folly, carelessness, immodesty, indelicacy, shamelessness
COLLOQ. boob, slip-up; *N Am* flub
E∃ caution, diplomacy, etiquette

indiscriminate *adj*
general, sweeping wholesale, random, haphazard, hit or miss, hit and miss, aimless, careless, confused, chaotic, unsystematic, unmethodical, unselective, undifferentiating undiscriminating mixed, varied, diverse, motley, miscellaneous
E∃ selective, specific, precise

indiscriminately *adv*
generally, wholesale, haphazardly, randomly, unselectively, aimlessly, carelessly, unsystematically, unmethodically, without fear or favour, in the mass
E∃ deliberately, selectively

indispensable *adj*
vital, essential, basic, fundamental, important, key, crucial, imperative, required, needed, necessary, needful
FORMAL requisite
E∃ dispensable, unnecessary

indisposed *adj*
1 ILL, sick, unwell, poorly, ailing confined to bed, laid up
FORMAL incapacitated
COLLOQ. groggy, under the weather, out of sorts, like death warmed up
2 RELUCTANT, unwilling not willing not of a mind (to), disinclined, averse, loath
E∃ **1** well **2** inclined

indisposition *n*
1 ILLNESS, ailment, disease, complaint, disorder, sickness, ill health, bad health
FORMAL malady
2 RELUCTANCE, unwillingness, hesitancy, disinclination, aversion, dislike, distaste
E∃ **1** health **2** inclination

indisputable *adj*
incontrovertible, unquestionable, undeniable, indubitable, irrefutable, incontestable, absolute, undisputed, inarguable, unarguable, definite, positive, certain, sure, beyond question
SLANG *Aust* dead set
E∃ doubtful, uncertain

indissoluble *adj*
indestructible, permanent, inseparable, imperishable, incorruptible, enduring lasting eternal, fixed, inviolable, abiding binding solid, unbreakable
FORMAL sempiternal
E∃ impermanent, short-lived

indistinct *adj*
unclear, ill-defined, out of focus, blurred, fuzzy, misty, hazy, shadowy, obscure, dim, pale, faded, faint, low, muted, muffled, muttered, confused, unintelligible, indistinguishable, indecipherable, vague, woolly, ambiguous, indefinite, undefined
≠ distinct, clear, in focus

indistinctly *adv*
unclearly, vaguely, fuzzily, hazily, obscurely, dimly, unintelligibly, indistinguishably, out of focus
≠ clearly, distinctly

indistinguishable *adj*
identical, interchangeable, same, twin, alike, hard to make out the difference, cloned, tantamount
COLLOQ. as like as two peas in a pod
≠ distinguishable, unalike, different, dissimilar

individual *n, adj*
♦ *n*
person, being human being creature, party, body, soul, mortal, type, sort, character, fellow
COLLOQ. singleton
♦ *adj*
distinctive, characteristic, typical, idiosyncratic, peculiar, unique, exclusive, original, special, personal, own, lone, solitary, isolated, proper, respective, several, separate, distinct, specific, personalized, particular, single, sole, private
FORMAL singular
≠ collective, shared, general

QUOTATIONS
The masses are wrong; individuals are always right
BORIS VIAN, *L'Écume des jours*

individualism *n*
independence, originality, self-direction, self-interest, self-reliance, freethinking freethought, eccentricity, egocentricity, egoism, anarchism, libertarianism
≠ conventionality

individualist *n*
independent, freethinker, free spirit, egoist, egocentric, nonconformist, original, bohemian, eccentric, maverick, loner, lone wolf, libertarian, anarchist
≠ conventionalist

individualistic *adj*
independent, individual, nonconformist, unorthodox, eccentric, bohemian, original, self-reliant, unconventional, egocentric, egoistic, idiosyncratic, special, typical, unique, particular, libertarian, anarchistic
≠ conventional

individuality *n*
character, personality, distinctiveness, identity, peculiarity, uniqueness, originality, separateness, distinction
OLD property; (*Shakesp*) propriety
FORMAL singularity
≠ sameness, anonymity

individually *adv*
separately, singly, one by one, one at a time, independently, particularly, personally
FORMAL severally, in several
≠ together

indivisible *adj*
inseparable, undividable, indissoluble, impartible
FORMAL indiscerptible
≠ divisible

indoctrinate *v*
brainwash, propagandize, teach, instruct, school, ground, train, drill, impress, inculcate, instil

indoctrination *n*
brainwashing instruction, schooling training teaching grounding inculcation, drilling instilling
FORMAL catechesis, catechetics

indolence *n*
idleness, laziness, inactivity, inertia, inertness, lethargy, heaviness, listlessness, do-nothingism, apathy, slacking sloth, sluggishness
FORMAL languidness, languor, torpidity, torpidness, torpitude, torpor
COLLOQ. shirking
≠ activeness, enthusiasm, industriousness

indolent *adj*
idle, bone-idle, lazy, inactive, inert, lethargic, listless, do-nothing shiftless, apathetic, slack, slow, sluggish, slothful, sluggard, lackadaisical, lumpish
FORMAL fainéant, languid, torpid
≠ active, enthusiastic, industrious

indomitable *adj*
invincible, unconquerable, unbeatable, undefeatable, impregnable, unassailable, brave, courageous, fearless, valiant, bold, intrepid, stalwart, lion-hearted, resolute, staunch, firm, intransigent, determined, steadfast, undaunted, unflinching unyielding
≠ compliant, timid, submissive

indubitable *adj*
indisputable, beyond dispute, unanswerable, undeniable, beyond doubt, undoubted, undoubtable, unquestionable, unarguable, incontestable, incontrovertible, irrefutable, sure, absolute, certain, obvious, evident
FORMAL irrebuttable, irrefragable
≠ arguable

indubitably *adv*
doubtless, certainly, without doubt, undoubtedly, unquestionably, indisputably, no doubt, clearly, surely, of course, truly, precisely, probably, presumably, most likely, assuredly

induce *v*
1 CAUSE, bring about, occasion, give rise to, lead to, bring on, get, set in motion, incite, instigate, originate, prompt, provoke, produce, generate
FORMAL effect
2 COAX, prevail upon, encourage, press, persuade, talk into, move, influence, draw, tempt, inspire, motivate, urge, actuate, impel, force, seduce
OLD entreat, procure
≠ 2 discourage, deter

inducement *n*
lure, bait, attraction, enticement, encouragement, incentive, impetus, incitement, influence, reward, spur, goad, stimulus, motive, reason
COLLOQ. carrot, sweetener
≠ disincentive

induct *v*
inaugurate, initiate, install, invest, ordain, introduce, consecrate, enthrone, swear in, admit

induction *n*
1 INAUGURATION, initiation, installation, institution, investiture, ordination, introduction, enthronement, consecration
2 INFERENCE, conclusion, deduction, generalization

indulge *v*
1 GRATIFY, satisfy, humour, pander to, go along with, give in to, yield to, give way to, cater to, favour, pet, cosset, mollycoddle, pamper, spoil, treat, regale
2 *indulge in something*
give way to, give free rein to, give yourself up to, revel in, wallow in, luxuriate in

indulgence *n*
1 EXTRAVAGANCE, luxury, treat, excess, gratification, self-gratification, mollycoddling pampering spoiling satisfaction, fulfilment, immoderation, intemperance, dissipation, dissoluteness
2 FAVOUR, tolerance, generosity, lenience, forbearance, pardon, remission
≠ 1 restraint

indulgent *adj*
tolerant, lenient, permissive, generous, forgiving merciful,
compassionate, sympathetic, humane, liberal, easy-going
kind, fond, tender, understanding patient, pampering
humouring spoiling cosseting mollycoddling
FORMAL forbearing
E3 strict, harsh

indulgently *adv*
tolerantly, leniently, generously, liberally, compassionately,
mercifully, sympathetically, humanely, kindly, fondly,
tenderly, patiently, with compassion, with mercy, with
sympathy
E3 strictly, harshly

industrial *adj*
manufacturing commercial, business, trade

industrialist *n*
manufacturer, producer, magnate, tycoon, baron, captain
of industry, capitalist, financier

industrious *adj*
busy, productive, hard-working hard, diligent, assiduous,
conscientious, laborious, steady, dedicated, studious,
workful, zealous, active, energetic, tireless, indefatigable,
persistent, persevering determined, dogged, vigorous;
dialect deedy
OLD notable
FORMAL sedulous
COLLOQ. busy as a bee, on the go, slogging your guts out
E3 lazy, idle

industriously *adv*
diligently, conscientiously, assiduously, steadily, hard,
perseveringly, doggedly, sedulously
COLLOQ. with your nose to the grindstone
E3 lazily

industry *n*
1 *the steel industry*
business, trade, commerce, manufacturing production,
service, enterprise, line, field
2 INDUSTRIOUSNESS, diligence, conscientiousness,
assiduousness, assiduity, application, intentness,
concentration, effort, labour, laboriousness, toil,
persistence, hard work, zeal, energy, vigour, activity,
perseverance, steadiness, determination, productiveness,
tirelessness
FORMAL sedulity, sedulousness
COLLOQ. stickability
E3 2 laziness, indolence

inebriated *adj*
under the influence, drunk, drunken
FORMAL intoxicated, crapulent
COLLOQ. merry, tight, tipsy, tiddly, tiddled, well-oiled,
blotto, drunk as a lord/newt, drunk as a piper, sloshed,
stewed, blind drunk, roaring drunk, the worse for drink,
soused, squiffy, happy, legless, plastered, sozzled, pickled,
bibulous, woozy, one over the eight, under the table,
bevvied, having had a few, tired and emotional, high,
footless, full, half-cut, obfuscated, pie-eyed, sow-drunk,
under the weather, the worse for wear, steaming; *Irish*
jarred; *Scot & Irish* stocious
SLANG stoned, tanked up, loaded, lit up, canned, paralytic,
smashed, pissed; *Scot* pished; ossified, off your face,
bladdered, hammered, bombed, ripped, wasted, wrecked,
trolleyed, stinko, whiffled, whistled, bonkers, bottled,
Brahms and Liszt, juiced (up), in liquor, liquored,
maggoty, mortal, up the pole; (*vulgar*) arseholed, rat-
arsed; *N Am* crocked, moon-eyed; *Aust* inky, inked,
rotten; *Aust & NZ* shickered
OLD SLANG corked, moppy
E3 sober, temperate, abstinent, teetotal

inedible *adj*
uneatable, unpalatable, stale, indigestible, not fit to eat,
unconsumable, rotten, off, bad, rancid, harmful, noxious,
poisonous, deadly
E3 edible, wholesome

ineducable *adj*
unteachable, incorrigible, indocile
E3 educable

ineffable *adj*
indescribable, inexpressible, unspeakable, unutterable,
beyond words, remarkable, fearful, incommunicable,
unimpartible
E3 describable

ineffably *adv*
inexpressibly, indescribably, unspeakably, unutterably,
absolutely, remarkably, fearfully, beyond words

ineffective *adj*
1 *an ineffective attempt*
useless, worthless, vain, idle, futile, unavailing to no avail,
abortive, profitless, fruitless, unproductive, unsuccessful
FORMAL ineffectual
2 POWERLESS, impotent, inadequate, weak, feeble, inept,
idle, lame, incompetent
E3 1, 2 effective

ineffectiveness *n*
uselessness, worthlessness, fruitlessness, unproductiveness,
inadequacy, weakness, feebleness, futility
E3 effectiveness

ineffectual *adj*
1 *ineffectual methods*
useless, vain, futile, worthless, fruitless, unproductive,
unavailing abortive
FORMAL inefficacious
2 *an ineffectual person*
weak, feeble, powerless, inadequate, incompetent,
impotent, inept, lame
COLLOQ. wimpy
E3 1, 2 effectual

ineffectually *adv*
weakly, feebly, lamely, uselessly, unsuccessfully,
fruitlessly, unproductively, in vain, to no purpose, to no
avail
E3 effectually

inefficacy *n*
ineffectiveness, unproductiveness, uselessness, futility,
inadequacy
FORMAL ineffectuality, ineffectualness
E3 efficacy

inefficiency *n*
waste, wastefulness, disorganization, carelessness,
negligence, slackness, laxity, ineptitude, sloppiness,
incompetence, muddle
E3 efficiency

inefficient *adj*
uneconomic, wasteful, money-wasting time-wasting
ineffective, incompetent, inexpert, unworkmanlike,
slipshod, sloppy, maladroit, slack, lax, inept, careless,
disorganized, unorganized, negligent
E3 efficient

inelegant *adj*
graceless, ungraceful, clumsy, awkward, ham-fisted,
gauche, ungainly, laboured, ugly, unrefined, ill-bred,
crude, vulgar, unpolished, rough, homespun,
unsophisticated, uncultured, uncultivated, unfinished,
uncouth
OLD unpolite
E3 elegant

ineligible *adj*
disqualified, ruled out, unacceptable, undesirable,
unworthy, unsuitable, unfit, unfitted, unqualified,
unequipped
TECHNICAL incompetent
E3 eligible

ineluctable *adj*
inescapable, inevitable, unavoidable, destined, fated,
certain, sure, assured, irrevocable, unalterable, inexorable
OLD ineludible

inept adj

awkward, clumsy, bungling heavy-handed, incompetent, incapable, inadequate, unskilful, inexpert, unsuccessful, foolish, stupid, useless, appalling
FORMAL maladroit
COLLOQ. pathetic, cack-handed, lousy, ham-fisted
F3 competent, skilful

ineptitude n

ineptness, awkwardness, clumsiness, bungling unhandiness, gaucheness, gaucherie, incompetence, incapability, unskilfulness, inexpertness, stupidity, unfitness, uselessness, crassness
FORMAL fatuity, incapacity
F3 aptitude, skill

inequality n

unequalness, imbalance, difference, discrepancy, contrast, variation, diversity, dissimilarity, nonconformity, unevenness, roughness, irregularity, disproportion, bias, prejudice, discrimination
FORMAL disparity
F3 equality, balance

inequitable adj

unfair, unjust, unequal, wrongful, one-sided, biased, prejudiced, discriminatory, bigoted, intolerant, partisan, partial, preferential
F3 equitable

inequity n

unfairness, unjustness, injustice, maltreatment, mistreatment, abuse, inequality, wrongfulness, one-sidedness, prejudice, bias, discrimination, partiality
F3 equity

inert adj

1 IMMOBILE, motionless, unmoving still, stock-still, inactive, static, stationary, inanimate, lifeless, dead, passive, cold, unresponsive
FORMAL comatose
2 SLUGGISH, lethargic, lazy, inactive, slack, listless, dull, apathetic, idle, dormant, stagnant, torpid, sleepy
FORMAL indolent
F3 1 moving 2 lively, animated

inertia n

inertness, immobility, motionlessness, stillness, stagnation, inactivity, inaction, passivity, unresponsiveness, apathy, idleness, laziness, sloth, slothfulness, lethargy, listlessness
FORMAL indolence, languor, torpor
F3 activity, liveliness

inescapable adj

inevitable, unavoidable, destined, fated, certain, sure, assured, irrevocable, unalterable, inexorable
OLD ineludible
FORMAL ineluctable
F3 escapable, preventable

inescapably adv

inevitably, unavoidably, inescapably, irrevocably, inexorably, necessarily, definitely, certainly, surely, automatically, assuredly
F3 avoidably

inessential adj, n

♦ adj
unnecessary, irrelevant, superfluous, surplus, redundant, non-essential, needless, unasked-for, uncalled-for, unimportant, secondary, spare, accidental, unessential, dispensable, expendable, extraneous, optional, extrinsic
F3 essential, necessary
♦ n
non-essential, extra, extravagance, luxury, superfluity, accessory, trimming appendage
F3 essential

inestimable adj

incalculable, measureless, infinite, immeasurable, invaluable, precious, priceless, unlimited, uncountable, unfathomable, incomputable, immense, vast, untold
FORMAL prodigious

COLLOQ. mind-boggling worth a fortune
F3 insignificant

inevitability n

certainty, absolute certainty, foregone conclusion, matter of course, truth, validity, fact, reality
COLLOQ. sure thing safe bet, dead cert

inevitable adj

unavoidable, inescapable, necessary, definite, certain, sure, decreed, ordained, destined, predestined, fated, fateful, automatic, infallible, assured, fixed, settled, unalterable, irrevocable, inexorable, unpreventable
OLD unshunned; (Shakesp) unavoided
FORMAL ineluctable
F3 avoidable, uncertain, alterable

inevitably adv

unavoidably, inescapably, irrevocably, inexorably, necessarily, infallibly, definitely, certainly, surely, automatically, assuredly, fatefully
F3 avoidably

inexact adj

imprecise, approximate, inaccurate, incorrect, erroneous, indefinite, indistinct, fuzzy, loose, woolly, lax, muddled
FORMAL indeterminate, fallacious
F3 exact, accurate

inexactitude n

inexactness, impreciseness, imprecision, inaccuracy, incorrectness, indefiniteness, approximation, miscalculation, woolliness, looseness, mistake, blunder, error
F3 exactitude, accuracy

inexcusable adj

indefensible, unforgivable, unpardonable, unjustifiable, intolerable, unacceptable, outrageous, shameful, blameworthy
FORMAL reprehensible
F3 excusable, justifiable

inexcusably adv

indefensibly, unjustifiably, unacceptably, outrageously, shamefully
FORMAL reprehensibly
F3 justfiably

inexhaustible adj

1 an inexhaustible supply
unlimited, limitless, boundless, unbounded, unrestricted, measureless, infinite, endless, never-ending abundant, unfailing
FORMAL illimitable
2 INDEFATIGABLE, tireless, untiring unflagging unfailing unwearied, unwearying weariless
F3 1 limited

inexorable adj

relentless, unrelenting remorseless, unalterable, inevitable, unpreventable, unavertable, irresistible, irrevocable, inescapable, immovable, implacable, intransigent, unyielding unceasing incessant, unstoppable, unfaltering ordained, destined, fated, definite, certain, sure
FORMAL ineluctable
F3 avoidable, preventable

inexorably adv

relentlessly, remorselessly, inescapably, irresistibly, inevitably, irrevocably, definitely, certainly, surely, resistlessly, implacably, pitilessly, mercilessly
FORMAL ineluctably

inexpedient adj

unwise, unsuitable, inappropriate, disadvantageous, misguided, detrimental, unadvisable, unfavourable, indiscreet, foolish, senseless, wrong imprudent, ill-advised, inadvisable, ill-chosen, ill-judged, inconvenient, impractical, undesirable, undiplomatic
FORMAL impolitic, injudicious
F3 expedient

inexpensive *adj*
cheap, low-priced, low-price, reasonable, modest, bargain, budget, low-cost, cut-rate, economical, reduced, discounted
COLLOQ. a snip, a steal, going for a song dirt-cheap, dog-cheap, ten a penny, on a shoestring
≢ expensive, dear

inexperience *n*
inexpertness, ignorance, unfamiliarity, strangeness, newness, freshness, rawness, immaturity, naiveness, innocence
≢ experience

inexperienced *adj*
inexpert, untrained, unqualified, untutored, new to the job, unskilled, amateur, probationary, apprentice, unacquainted, uninformed, ignorant, unfamiliar, unaccustomed, unseasoned, new, fresh, raw, callow, young immature, naive, unsophisticated, innocent, fledgling unfledged
OLD unseen; (*Shakesp*) puny, unexperient
COLLOQ. rookie, green, wet behind the ears, out of your depth, wide-eyed
≢ experienced, mature

> **SYNONYM NUANCES**
>
> **Untrained**, **unqualified** and **unskilled** are straightforward synonyms, suggesting a lack of requisite knowledge. **Inexpert** and **amateur**, however, can have rather negative connotations of being unprofessional in one's practices and of the effects of this on one's work: *an enthusiastic, if amateur, cameraman*. **Unacquainted** and **uninformed**, as well as **unfamiliar** and **unaccustomed**, return to the idea of simply not having had the requisite information or introduction: *he was unacquainted with the new practices*, but **ignorant** can imply not just a lack of knowledge, but also intelligence.
> The terms **unseasoned**, **raw** and **fresh** suggest having newly come to something: *raw recruits*, while **fledgling** and **unfledged**, along with **callow**, **young** and **immature**, which also have connotations of vulnerability, continue the idea of being in the early stages: *callow undergraduates; a fledgling democracy*. **Naive**, **unsophisticated** and **innocent** put further emphasis on ingenuousness as a consequence of inexperience.

inexpert *adj*
unskilled, unskilful, untaught, untrained, unpractised, unworkmanlike, unprofessional, untutored, unqualified, amateur, amateurish, awkward, clumsy, unhandy, incompetent, inept, bungling blundering
FORMAL maladroit
COLLOQ. cack-handed, ham, ham-fisted
≢ expert

inexplicable *adj*
incomprehensible, unexplainable, unintelligible, unaccountable, strange, mystifying puzzling perplexing baffling bewildering mysterious, insoluble, enigmatic, weird, unfathomable, incredible, unbelievable, miraculous
FORMAL abstruse
≢ explicable

inexplicably *adv*
incomprehensibly, unexplainably, incredibly, unaccountably, strangely, mysteriously, mystifyingly, bafflingly, puzzlingly, miraculously
≢ explicably

inexpressible *adj*
indescribable, undescribable, unspeakable, unutterable, incommunicable, indefinable, nameless, unsayable, untellable
OLD (*Shakesp*) termless
FORMAL ineffable

inexpressibly *adv*
indescribably, unspeakably, unutterably, beyond words
FORMAL ineffably

inexpressive *adj*
unexpressive, expressionless, deadpan, poker-faced, inscrutable, blank, vacant, empty, lifeless, dead, cold, emotionless, impassive
≢ expressive

inextinguishable *adj*
unquenchable, indestructible, imperishable, irrepressible, unconquerable, unquellable, unsuppressible, deathless, enduring lasting eternal, everlasting undying immortal
≢ impermanent, perishable

inextricable *adj*
inseparable, indissoluble, indivisible, indistinguishable, intricate, irretrievable, inescapable, irreversible

inextricably *adv*
inseparably, indissolubly, indivisibly, indistinguishably, intricately, irresolubly, irretrievably, inescapably, irreversibly

infallibility *n*
accuracy, unerringness, faultlessness, inerrancy, perfection, dependability, reliability, safety, supremacy, sureness, trustworthiness, impeccability, irreproachability, inerrability
FORMAL irrefutability, omniscience
≢ fallibility

infallible *adj*
accurate, unerring unfailing foolproof, fail-safe, certain, sure, reliable, dependable, trustworthy, sound, perfect, flawless, faultless, impeccable, inerrable
COLLOQ. sure-fire
≢ fallible

infamous *adj*
notorious, ill-famed, disreputable, disgraceful, discreditable, dishonourable, shameful, shocking outrageous, abominable, detestable, scandalous, evil, bad, base, vile, wicked, hateful
OLD dastardly
FORMAL iniquitous, ignominious, egregious, nefarious
≢ illustrious, glorious

infamy *n*
notoriety, disrepute, disgrace, discredit, shame, dishonour, wickedness, evil, baseness, vileness, depravity, villainy
FORMAL ignominy, turpitude
≢ glory

infancy *n*
1 BABYHOOD, childhood, youth
2 BEGINNING, start, outset, birth, dawn, cradle, seeds, roots, genesis, emergence, rise, origin(s), early stages
FORMAL commencement, inception
≢ 1 adulthood

infant *n, adj*
♦ *n*
baby, toddler, child, little one, nurseling; *Scot* bairn
FORMAL babe, babe in arms
COLLOQ. tot, sprog
≢ adult
♦ *adj*
newborn, baby, young youthful, juvenile, immature, beginning growing developing dawning emergent, rudimentary, early, initial, new, fledgling
FORMAL nascent, burgeoning
≢ adult, mature

infantile *adj*
babyish, childish, puerile, juvenile, young youthful, adolescent, immature
≢ adult, mature

infatuated *adj*
besotted, obsessed, enamoured, in love, spellbound, bewitched, mesmerized, captivated, fascinated, enraptured, ravished, carried away
OLD assott, assotted
FORMAL *entêté(e)*
COLLOQ. crazy/mad/daft/nuts/potty about, sweet on, wild about/for, sold on, far gone, having a crush, bowled over, swept off your feet, having a thing smitten, head over heels in love
⊟ indifferent, disenchanted

infatuation *n*
besottedness, obsession, craze, fixation, mania, passion, love, fondness, fascination
FORMAL engouement
COLLOQ. crush, thing pash, shine, rave
OLD COLLOQ. mash
⊟ indifference, disenchantment

infect *v*
contaminate, pollute, defile, taint, blight, mar, spoil, ulcerate, poison, corrupt, pervert, spread to, pass on, influence, affect, excite, stimulate, animate, move, touch, inspire

infection *n*
illness, disease, complaint, condition, virus, bacteria, germ, epidemic, contagion, pestilence, contamination, pollution, defilement, taint, tainting spoiling fouling blight, poison, corruption, influence
TECHNICAL sepsis
COLLOQ. bug

infectious *adj*
1 *an infectious disease*
contagious, communicable, transmissible, transmittable, infective, catching spreading epidemic, virulent, deadly, toxic, contaminating polluting defiling corrupting
TECHNICAL septic
FORMAL noxious
2 *infectious laughter*
contagious, compelling irresistible, catching spreading

infelicitous *adj*
1 INAPPROPRIATE, unfitting unsuitable, unfortunate, inopportune, untimely, disadvantageous
FORMAL incongruous
2 UNHAPPY, unfortunate, sad, miserable, sorrowful, unlucky, despairing wretched
⊟ **1** appropriate, apt **2** happy

infer *v*
deduce, derive, extrapolate, conclude, come to a conclusion, reason, assume, presume, surmise, gather, understand, allude
FORMAL conjecture
COLLOQ. figure out

❗ **infer** or **imply**?
See panel at **imply**.

inference *n*
deduction, conclusion, consequence, assumption, presumption, construction, interpretation, reasoning reading
FORMAL extrapolation, corollary, conjecture, surmise

inferior *adj, n*
♦ *adj*
1 LOWER, lesser, minor, secondary, junior, subordinate, ancillary, subsidiary, second-class, low, lowly, humble, menial, subservient
COLLOQ. not in the same league, low-rent
2 *inferior work*
substandard, second-rate, low-quality, mediocre, weak, inadequate, poor, bad, awful, unsatisfactory, unacceptable, imperfect, faulty, defective, deficient, incompetent, slipshod, shoddy, cheap, useless, hopeless
COLLOQ. crummy, rop(e)y, low-rent, grotty, rubbish, pathetic

SLANG naff
⊟ **1** superior **2** excellent
♦ *n*
subordinate, junior, underling minion, vassal, menial
⊟ superior

SYNONYM NUANCES

sense 2
Poor, **weak** and **inadequate** may all be used to show that something is not up to achieving its purpose: *inadequate protection*, while **ineffective** would usually be applied to an action that has failed to make a difference: *ineffective aid schemes*. Similarly **second-rate**, **mediocre** and **substandard** all suggest that something fails to reach the accepted standard.
  Imperfect, however, implies a specific fault or faults rather than overall shoddiness. Similarly **faulty** and **defective** are used of something with particular, identifiable flaws: *a faulty valve*. **Deficient**, on the other hand, is more likely to point to a lack: *deficient in imagination*.
  Slipshod and **shoddy** make the critical implication that insufficient care has been taken with something: *he was becoming slipshod in his editing*. The terms **useless** and **hopeless** would be reserved for people or things so far below standard that they have no practical application: *hopeless public transport*, while **incompetent** is another inherently critical term used mainly of people or the results of their efforts: *incompetent scientists*.

---

inferiority *n*
1 SUBORDINATION, subservience, humbleness, lowliness, meanness, insignificance
2 MEDIOCRITY, imperfection, inadequacy, faultiness, defectiveness, low/poor/bad quality, unsatisfactoriness, slovenliness, shoddiness, incompetence
COLLOQ. crumminess, ropiness, grottiness
⊟ **1** superiority **2** excellence, perfection

infernal *adj*
1 HELLISH, satanic, devilish, diabolical, demonic, fiendish, accursed, damned, Hadean
2 WICKED, evil, malevolent, vile, atrocious
FORMAL execrable
3 *What an infernal mess!*
damned, wretched, cursed, confounded, fiendish
COLLOQ. blasted, flipping blooming blinking flaming darned, dashed
SLANG *Irish* fecking; (*taboo*) fucking
⊟ **1** heavenly

infertile *adj*
barren, sterile, childless, unproductive, non-productive, unfruitful, arid, parched, dried-up
FORMAL effete, unfructuous, infecund
⊟ fertile, fruitful, productive, prolific

infertility *n*
barrenness, sterility, unfruitfulness, unproductiveness, aridity, aridness
FORMAL effeteness, infecundity
⊟ fertility

infest *v*
swarm, teem, crawl, bristle, throng flood, overrun, overspread, spread through, plague, take over, beset, invade, infiltrate, penetrate, permeate, pervade, ravage

infestation *n*
affliction, pestilence, scourge, plague, blight, pest, visitation, overrunning infiltration, pervasion, verminousness

infested *adj*
swarming teeming crawling bristling beset, alive, pervaded, plagued, ravaged, ridden, overrun, overspread, infiltrated, permeated, vermined

infidel *n*

pagan, heathen, disbeliever, unbeliever, heretic, sceptic, atheist, freethinker, irreligionist
FORMAL nullifidian
Ea believer

infidelity *n*

1 ADULTERY, unfaithfulness, falseness, affair, relationship, liaison, intrigue, romance, armour
COLLOQ. fooling around, playing around, cheating
2 DISLOYALTY, faithlessness, treachery, betrayal
FORMAL duplicity, perfidy
Ea 1 fidelity **2** faithfulness

infiltrate *v*

penetrate, enter, creep into, insinuate, intrude, invade, slip, pervade, permeate, filter, percolate, seep, soak

infiltration *n*

penetration, entr(y)ism, insinuation, intrusion, pervasion, invasion, permeation, percolation
FORMAL interpenetration

infiltrator *n*

penetrator, insinuator, intruder, spy, subversive, subverter, seditionary, entr(y)ist

infinite *adj*

limitless, unlimited, boundless, unbounded, endless, never-ending interminable, inexhaustible, bottomless, fathomless, innumerable, numberless, without number, uncountable, countless, untold, incalculable, inestimable, immeasurable, unfathomable, illimitable, vast, extensive, immense, enormous, huge, absolute, total, unconditioned
FORMAL indeterminable
Ea finite, limited

> **!** **infinite** or **infinitesimal**?
> *Infinite* means 'without limits', or, loosely, 'extremely large or great': *If we follow that course of action, the dangers are infinite*; *infinitesimal* means 'infinitely small' or, loosely, 'extremely small': *Personally, I consider the dangers infinitesimal.*

infinitely *adv*

endlessly, limitlessly, boundlessly, interminably, inexhaustibly, absolutely, inestimably, enormously, immensely, without limit, without end, ad infinitum

infinitesimal *adj*

tiny, minute, microscopic, minuscule, inconsiderable, insignificant, trifling negligible, inappreciable, imperceptible; *Scot* wee
COLLOQ. teeny
Ea great, large, enormous

> **!** **infinitesimal** or **infinite**?
> *See panel at* **infinite**.

infinitesimally *adv*

minutely, microscopically, tinily, insignificantly, negligibly, inappreciably, imperceptibly
Ea greatly

infinity *n*

eternity, perpetuity, limitlessness, boundlessness, allness, endlessness, inexhaustibility, countlessness, immeasurableness, extensiveness, vastness, immensity, enormousness
Ea finiteness, limitation

> **QUOTATIONS**
> To see a world in a grain of sand, / And heaven in a wild flower, / Hold infinity in the palm of your hand, / And Eternity in an hour
> WILLIAM BLAKE, *Auguries of Innocence*

infirm *adj*

weak, feeble, frail, ailing ill, unwell, poorly, sickly, decrepit, failing faltering unsteady, shaky, wobbly, doddery, old, lame, disabled

FORMAL debilitated
Ea healthy, strong

infirmity *n*

weakness, feebleness, frailty, ailment, illness, ill health, disease, complaint, sickness, sickliness, disorder, failing decrepitude, vulnerability, instability, dodderiness
FORMAL debility, malady
Ea health, strength

inflame *v*

anger, enrage, infuriate, incense, exasperate, madden, rile, incite, provoke, stimulate, work up, stir, excite, rouse, arouse, agitate, stir (up), whip up, foment, impassion, kindle, ignite, fire, heat, fan, fuel, increase, intensify, worsen, make worse, aggravate
FORMAL exacerbate
Ea cool, quench

inflamed *adj*

sore, swollen, septic, infected, festered, poisoned, red, hot, heated, fevered, angry, feverish, flushed, reddened, glowing

inflammable *adj*

flammable, combustible, burnable, ignitable
Ea non-flammable, incombustible, flameproof, fire-resistant, flame-resistant

inflammation *n*

soreness, painfulness, tenderness, swelling abscess, festering infection, redness, heat, hotness, rash, sore, irritation, eruption
TECHNICAL empyema, erythema, sepsis, septicity

inflammatory *adj*

1 PROVOCATIVE, incendiary, explosive, fiery, rabble-rousing rabid, riotous, seditious, insurgent, intemperate, inciting incitative, inflaming instigative, anarchic, demagogic
2 SORE, painful, tender, swollen, allergic, festering septic, infected
Ea 1 calming pacific

inflate *v*

1 *inflate a life jacket*
blow up, pump up, fill with air, bloat, expand, dilate, enlarge, aerate, swell, puff up, puff out, balloon; *dialect* blast
OLD sufflate
FORMAL distend
2 *inflate prices*
increase, raise, boost, step up, escalate, amplify, extend, intensify
FORMAL augment
COLLOQ. hike up, push up
3 *inflate the importance of something*
exaggerate, overstate, overrate, overestimate, boost, magnify
FORMAL aggrandize, bombast
Ea 1 deflate **2** decrease, lower **3** understate, play down

inflated *adj*

1 BLOWN UP, swollen, puffed out, dilated, bloated, ballooned
FORMAL distended, tumefied, tumid
2 INCREASED, raised, escalated, extended, intensified
3 EXAGGERATED, overblown, ostentatious, pompous
FORMAL bombastic, grandiloquent, magniloquent, euphuistic
Ea deflated

inflation *n*

expansion, increase, rise, escalation, hyperinflation, agflation
Ea deflation

inflection *n*

change of tone/intonation, pitch, modulation, stress, emphasis, rhythm
TECHNICAL cadence

inflexibility *n*
rigidity, hardness, stiffness, fixity, immovability, immutability, immutableness, inelasticity, obstinacy, stubbornness, stringency, unsuppleness
FORMAL intractability, intransigence, obduracy
ᴇ꒱ flexibility

inflexible *adj*
1 *an inflexible mass*
stiff, firm, hard, rigid, solid, set, fixed, unelastic, unsupple, unbending taut, iron, ramrod
FORMAL calcified
2 *inflexible rules/people*
fast, immovable, immutable, unchangeable, unvarying uniform, standard, standardized, firm, rigorous, taut, strict, stern, stringent, unbending unbendable, unyielding adamant, resolute, relentless, pitiless, merciless, implacable, intolerant, uncompromising unaccommodating stubborn, obstinate, steely, entrenched, dyed-in-the-wool, tramlined
FORMAL intransigent, obdurate, intractable, calcified
COLLOQ. hard and fast
ᴇ꒱ **1** flexible, soft, elastic, supple **2** flexible, adaptable

inflict *v*
impose, enforce, perpetrate, wreak, administer, apply, deliver, deal (out), mete out, lay, burden, exact, levy

> ⚠ **inflict** or **afflict**?
> *See panel at* **afflict**.

infliction *n*
imposition, enforcement, perpetration, wreaking administration, application, delivery, affliction, exaction, burden, punishment, trouble, worry, penalty
FORMAL retribution, castigation, chastisement

influence *n, v*
♦ *n*
power, sway, rule, authority, domination, dominance, supremacy, mastery, hold, control, direction, guidance, bias, prejudice, pull, pressure, effect, impact, weight, importance, prestige, standing mark, toll
COLLOQ. clout, pull
SLANG *N Am* drag
♦ *v*
dominate, control, manipulate, direct, guide, determine, manoeuvre, change, alter, modify, transform, affect, have an effect on, impress, move, mould, shape, stir, arouse, rouse, sway, persuade, impact on, induce, incite, instigate, prompt, impel, motivate, dispose, incline, colour, condition, bias, prejudice
COLLOQ. have clout, carry weight, pull strings, pull wires, have under your thumb, hold over a barrel, wheel and deal

influential *adj*
dominant, controlling leading authoritative, charismatic, persuasive, meaningful, convincing compelling inspiring moving powerful, potent, effective, telling strong far-reaching prestigious, weighty, momentous, important, significant, considerable, instrumental, guiding
ᴇ꒱ ineffective, unimportant

influx *n*
inflow, inrush, invasion, arrival, intrusion, stream, flow, rush, flood, inundation
FORMAL ingress, incursion

inform *v*
1 TELL, advise, notify, let know, communicate, announce, relate, impart, leak, tip off, acquaint, brief, instruct, enlighten, illuminate, give notice, certify, possess
OLD advertise, resolve; (*Shakesp*) recommend; (*Spenser*) partake; *N Am* avail
FORMAL apprise
COLLOQ. fill in, put in the picture, clue up, clue in, put wise, wise up, keep posted, cue in
2 *inform on your friends*
betray, incriminate, denounce, blab

COLLOQ. tell on, squeal, rat, blow, blow the whistle on, sell down the river, split, snitch; *N Am* sing (like a canary); *Aust* put someone's pot on; *Aust & NZ* dob in
SLANG grass, shop, rumble, peach, fink, nark, blow the gaff; *N Am* stool on
3 CHARACTERIZE, typify, mark, stamp, brand, identify, distinguish, permeate

informal *adj*
unofficial, unceremonious, casual, everyday, relaxed, easy, easy-going free, natural, simple, unpretentious, familiar, colloquial, vernacular
ᴇ꒱ formal, solemn, serious, official

informality *n*
unceremoniousness, casualness, congeniality, ease, freedom, familiarity, naturalness, relaxation, simplicity, unpretentiousness, approachability, homeliness, cosiness
ᴇ꒱ formality, ceremony

informally *adj*
unofficially, unceremoniously, casually, easily, familiarly, simply, colloquially, freely, confidentially, privately, on the quiet
ᴇ꒱ formally

information *n*
facts, details, particulars, data, input, intelligence, news, report, bulletin, communiqué, propaganda, message, word, advice, counsel, notice, briefing instruction, knowledge, enlightenment, file, record, dossier, database, databank, clues, evidence
FORMAL tidings
COLLOQ. gen, info, low-down, dope, SP, score; *N Am* poop

informative *adj*
educational, instructive, edifying enlightening illuminating revealing forthcoming communicative, chatty, gossipy, newsy, helpful, useful, constructive
ᴇ꒱ uninformative

informed *adj*
1 *we'll keep you informed*
familiar, conversant, acquainted, enlightened, aware, briefed, primed, posted, up to date, abreast, au fait
COLLOQ. in the know, in the loop, clued-up, up to speed
2 *an informed opinion*
well-informed, authoritative, expert, versed, well-versed, well-read, well-briefed, erudite, learned, knowledgeable, well-researched
ᴇ꒱ **1** ignorant, unaware

informer *n*
informant, betrayer, traitor, Judas, tell-tale, sneak, spy, squeaker, whisperer
OLD approver, discoverer, promoter, sycophant
COLLOQ. mole, rat, finger, squealer, whistle-blower, snitch, snitcher, canary, fink, nose
SLANG grass, supergrass, stool pigeon, peacher, nark, snout; *N Am* stoolie; *Aust* fizgig
OLD SLANG stag

infraction *n*
breaking breach, violation, infringement, contravention, encroachment
FORMAL transgression
ᴇ꒱ observance, compliance

infrequent *adj*
exceptional, intermittent, occasional, rare, scanty, sparse, spasmodic, sporadic, uncommon, unusual
COLLOQ. few and far between, like gold dust
ᴇ꒱ frequent

infringe *v*
1 BREAK, violate, contravene, overstep, disobey, defy, flout, ignore
FORMAL transgress
2 INTRUDE, encroach, impinge, trespass, invade

infringement n
1 *infringement of the rules*
breach, breaking disobedience, violation, defiance, contravention, evasion, non-compliance, non-observance
FORMAL infraction, transgression
2 INTRUSION, encroachment, trespass, invasion

infuriate v
anger, vex, enrage, incense, exasperate, madden, inflame, provoke, rouse, annoy, irritate, rile, antagonize
COLLOQ. aggravate, wind up, get at, bug drive mad, drive crazy, drive bananas, drive up the wall, drive round the bend/twist, miff, needle, nettle, make someone's blood boil, make someone see red, rattle someone's cage, ruffle someone's feathers, raise someone's dander, make someone's hackles rise, make sparks fly, get under someone's skin, get up someone's nose, get on someone's wick, put someone's back up
SLANG nark, piss off
OLD SLANG get someone's shirt out
F∃ calm, pacify

infuriated adj
angry, exasperated, enraged, agitated, provoked, roused, vexed, furious, incensed, irate, irritated, violent, wild, heated, beside yourself
COLLOQ. flaming maddened, peeved, miffed, narked, aggravated, cross, ratty, uptight, mad, hopping mad, raving mad, seeing red, in a lather, disgruntled, up in arms, hot under the collar, stroppy, choked, fit to be tied, on the warpath, in a paddy; *Scot* radge; *N Am* ticked off; *Aust* spewy, ropable; *Aust & NZ* crooked
SLANG pissed off, hairless; *N Am* burned up
F∃ calm, gratified, pleased

infuriating adj
annoying exasperating irritating unbearable, intolerable, frustrating galling provoking thwarting
FORMAL vexatious
COLLOQ. maddening aggravating; *N Am* pesky
F∃ agreeable, pleasing

infuse v
fill, breathe into, imbue, impart to, introduce, implant, inculcate, inspire, instil, inject, steep, soak, saturate, pervade, brew, draw

infusion n
implantation, inculcation, infusing instillation, steeping soaking brew

ingenious adj
clever, shrewd, astute, adept, adroit, cunning crafty, wily, sly, sharp, smart, skilful, masterly, bright, brilliant, neat, pretty, imaginative, creative, inventive, resourceful, talented, gifted, original, innovative
OLD artificial, quaint, witty
COLLOQ. natty, nifty, slick, patent
F∃ unimaginative

> **!** **ingenious** or **ingenuous**?
> *Ingenious* means 'clever, skilful' or 'cleverly made or thought out': *an ingenious plan. Ingenuous* means 'frank, trusting not cunning or deceitful': *It was rather ingenuous of you to believe a compulsive liar like him.*

ingeniously adv
cleverly, cunningly, skilfully, brilliantly, imaginatively, originally
COLLOQ. niftily

ingenuity n
ingeniousness, cleverness, shrewdness, astuteness, sharpness, skill, skilfulness, creativeness, adroitness, cunning slyness, innovativeness, invention, inventiveness, deftness, originality, resourcefulness, genius, gift, faculty, flair, knack
COLLOQ. nattiness, niftiness, slickness
F∃ clumsiness, dullness

ingenuous adj
artless, guileless, innocent, honest, sincere, genuine, frank, candid, open, direct, forthright, plain, simple, unsophisticated, naive, trusting trustful
FORMAL undissembling
F∃ cunning deceitful, artful, sly

> **!** **ingenuous** or **ingenious**?
> *See panel at* **ingenious**.

ingenuously adv
artlessly, guilelessly, without guile, innocently, honestly, sincerely, genuinely, openly, directly, plainly, simply, naively, trustingly
F∃ deceitfully, artfully

ingenuousness n
artlessness, guilelessness, innocence, genuineness, honesty, openness, naivety, trustfulness, candour, frankness, forthrightness, directness, unsophisticatedness, unreserve
F∃ deceit, cunning slyness, artfulness, subterfuge

inglorious adj
shameful, disgraceful, discreditable, dishonourable, disreputable, humiliating blameworthy, ignoble, infamous, mortifying unsuccessful, unhonoured, unheroic, unknown, obscure, unsung
FORMAL ignominious
F∃ glorious

ingrain v
fix, root, entrench, engrain, embed, establish, build in, impress, imprint, imbue, implant, infix, instil, dye

ingrained adj
fixed, implanted, rooted, deep-rooted, deep-seated, entrenched, embedded, established, immovable, ineradicable, permanent, inbuilt, built-in, inborn, inbred, inherent

ingratiate v
curry favour, flatter, creep, crawl, grovel, fawn, get in with, toady, play up to
COLLOQ. suck up to, lick someone's boots, bow and scrape, get on the right side of, get into someone's good books, soft-soap, butter someone up; *Scot & dialect* sook; *N Am* cozy up (with)
SLANG (*vulgar*) kiss/lick someone's arse, brown-nose; *N Am* (*vulgar*) kiss ass

ingratiating adj
flattering servile, crawling fawning toadying sycophantic, smooth-tongued, suave, time-serving
FORMAL obsequious, unctuous
COLLOQ. bootlicking

ingratitude n
ungratefulness, thanklessness, unappreciativeness, unthankfulness, ungraciousness
F∃ gratitude, thankfulness, appreciation

ingredient n
constituent, element, factor, unit, component, item, feature, part

ingress n
access, means of approach/entry, entrance, entry, admission, admittance, right of entry, permission to enter

inhabit v
live in, occupy, possess, colonize, settle, make your home in, people, populate, stay in
FORMAL dwell in, reside in

inhabitable adj
fit to live in, suitable to live in, good enough to live in, habitable

inhabitant n
resident, citizen, native, settler, occupier, occupant, inmate, tenant, lodger
FORMAL dweller, habitant, denizen

inhabited *adj*
lived-in, occupied, peopled, populated, settled, possessed, colonized, held, developed, tenanted
E3 uninhabited

inhalation *n*
breathing breath, inhaling inspiration, suction
TECHNICAL respiration, spiration

inhale *v*
breathe in, draw in, draw, suck in, inspire, whiff
TECHNICAL respire
FORMAL inbreathe

inharmonious *adj*
1 UNMELODIOUS, unharmonious, tuneless, grating harsh, strident, clashing jangling jarring discordant, raucous, cacophonous, untuneful, unmusical, atonal
2 INCOMPATIBLE, conflicting out of place, contradictory, clashing irreconcilable, unfriendly, unsympathetic, quarrelsome, perverse
FORMAL dissonant, antipathetic, inconsonant
E3 1, 2 harmonious

inherent *adj*
inborn, inbred, innate, inherited, hereditary, in the blood, native, natural, inbuilt, built-in, intrinsic, ingrained, essential, fundamental, basic

---
SYNONYM NUANCES

Inborn and **innate** can be used of something that is within from birth: *many mammals have an inborn fear of poisonous snakes*, whereas **inbred**, **inherited** and **hereditary**, although similar, would describe a characteristic that has been passed down directly by your forebears: *intelligence is an inherited characteristic; hereditary diseases*. **Native**, on the other hand, has more to do with being pertinent to your origins: *her native language*, whereas **natural** is positive in tone, suggesting something which has not been affected or tampered with since birth: *she has natural beauty; a natural ability*.

You can use **inbuilt** and **built-in** to convey the idea of structure, and suggest that something is part of your genetic make-up, while **intrinsic** and **essential**, **fundamental** and **basic**, are appropriate to describe a crucial or prominent inherent element of that structure: *the stubbornness that is fundamental to his character*. **Ingrained**, however, is suggestive of being deeply instilled rather than inborn: *ingrained prejudices*.

---

inherently *adv*
intrinsically, basically, fundamentally, centrally, essentially, inwardly, constituently, integrally, constitutionally

inherit *v*
succeed to, assume, take over, come into, be left, be heir to, receive, be bequeathed; *dialect* heir
OLD (*Shakesp*) succeed
FORMAL accede to

inheritance *n*
legacy, bequest, heritage, endowment, birthright, heredity, descent, succession
TECHNICAL patrimony, primogeniture, secundogeniture
OLD fee
FORMAL accession

inheritor *n*
heir, heiress, inheritress, inheritrix, successor, beneficiary, recipient, reversionary, co-heir, next in line, scion, fellow-heir
TECHNICAL devisee, legatee, legatary, substitute
OLD tanist
FORMAL heritor, heritress, heritrix

inhibit *v*
discourage, repress, hold back, suppress, curb, rein in, check, bridle, restrain, constrain, hinder, impede, obstruct,

restrict, interfere with, frustrate, thwart, hamper, balk, prevent, stop, stanch, stem, slow down
E3 encourage, assist

inhibited *adj*
repressed, self-conscious, shy, embarrassed, reticent, withdrawn, introverted, self-restrained, reserved, guarded, subdued, restrained, constrained, frustrated
COLLOQ. uptight
E3 uninhibited, open, relaxed

inhibition *n*
1 *lose all our inhibitions*
repression, self-consciousness, shyness, reticence, coyness, embarrassment, reserve
COLLOQ. hang-up
2 RESTRAINT, curb, check, hindrance, impediment, obstruction, restriction, interference, hampering frustration, thwarting bar
E3 1 openness **2** freedom

inhospitable *adj*
1 *an inhospitable place*
uninhabitable, forbidding bare, barren, bleak, desolate, empty, lonely, uncongenial, unfavourable, uninviting hostile
FORMAL inimical
2 *an inhospitable person*
unwelcoming unfriendly, unreceptive, unsociable, antisocial, ungenerous, unkind, unneighbourly, uncivil, cold, cool, aloof, xenophobic
E3 favourable, hospitable

inhuman *adj*
1 BARBARIC, barbarous, animal, bestial, vicious, savage, sadistic, cold-blooded, brutal, cruel, harsh, merciless, ruthless, diabolical, fiendish
2 NON-HUMAN, strange, odd, animal
E3 1, 2 human

! **inhuman** or **inhumane**?
When referring to cruel conditions, treatment, behaviour, etc, *inhuman* is stronger than *inhumane*. *Inhumane* means 'unkind, cruel, showing lack of compassion', whereas *inhuman* means 'showing cruelty and lack of compassion to a degree almost unbelievable in a human being'.

---

inhumane *adj*
unkind, insensitive, inconsiderate, callous, unfeeling uncaring unsympathetic, heartless, cold-hearted, hard-hearted, pitiless, cruel, harsh, brutal, dehumanized
E3 humane, kind, compassionate

inhumanity *n*
atrocity, barbarism, barbarity, savageness, brutality, brutishness, cruelty, cold-bloodedness, viciousness, pitilessness, ruthlessness, sadism, callousness, unkindness, cold-heartedness, hard-heartedness, heartlessness
E3 humanity

inimical *adj*
hostile, adverse, antagonistic, destructive, opposed, harmful, injurious, hurtful, pernicious, intolerant, unfavourable, unfriendly, unwelcoming inhospitable, ill-disposed, disaffected, antipathetic, contrary, repugnant
FORMAL noxious
E3 favourable, friendly, sympathetic

inimitable *adj*
unique, incomparable, matchless, unmatched, unparalleled, unrivalled, unsurpassable, unsurpassed, unequalled, peerless, consummate, sublime, superlative, supreme, distinctive, exceptional, nonpareil, unexampled

iniquitous *adj*
evil, wicked, unrighteous, immoral, unjust, sinful, accursed, atrocious, base, vicious, awful, dreadful, criminal, abominable, infamous, reprobate
OLD facinorous
FORMAL nefarious, reprehensible, heinous, flagitious
E3 virtuous

iniquity n

wickedness, injustice, offence, misdeed, wrong
wrongdoing evil, evil-doing sin, sinfulness, enormity,
baseness, vice, viciousness, infamy, abomination, crime,
lawlessness, unrighteousness, ungodliness
FORMAL heinousness, transgression
E3 virtue

initial adj, v

♦ adj

first, beginning opening starting introductory, inaugural,
original, primary, prime, early, basic, elementary,
foundational, formative
FORMAL commencing inceptive, inchoate,
incipient
E3 final, last

♦ v

write your initials on, sign, autograph, endorse,
countersign

initially adv

at first, at the beginning at the start, to begin with, to start
with, originally, first, firstly, first of all, in the first instance,
at the outset
COLLOQ. first off
E3 finally, in the end

initiate v, n

♦ v

1 BEGIN, start, start up, originate, pioneer, institute, set up,
establish, bring about, introduce, launch, open, inaugurate,
instigate, activate, trigger, prompt, stimulate, cause,
induce, sow the seeds of
OLD auspicate
FORMAL commence
COLLOQ. kick off, set the ball rolling set the wheels in
motion, get off the ground, get under way, set in motion,
get things moving
2 TEACH, instruct, train, drill, crash, tutor, inculcate,
instil
3 *initiated into the organization*
accept, admit, let in, introduce, receive,
welcome, enter, enrol, sign up, induct, install, invest,
ordain

♦ n

new member, recruit, entrant, learner, newcomer, novice,
beginner, convert, catechumen, novitiate, neophyte,
probationer, proselyte, tenderfoot, tiro
COLLOQ. greenhorn, rookie
E3 authority, expert, connoisseur, sage

initiation n

1 BEGINNING, start, origination, setting-up, launching
opening inauguration
FORMAL inception
2 ADMISSION, reception, entrance, entry, debut,
introduction, admittance, enrolment, enlistment, induction,
investiture, installation, ordination, inauguration, baptism,
rite of passage

initiative n

1 ENTERPRISE, resourcefulness, inventiveness, originality,
innovativeness, creativity, energy, drive, dynamism,
gumption, ambition, lead, lead-off
COLLOQ. get-up-and-go, go, push
2 SUGGESTION, recommendation, scheme,
proposal, plan, action, first move, opening move, first step,
démarche

inject v

1 *inject drugs*
inoculate, immunize, vaccinate, syringe
COLLOQ. jab
SLANG shoot (up), mainline, hype (up)
2 INTRODUCE, insert, add, bring (in), infuse, instil

injection n

1 INOCULATION, immunization, vaccination, dose
COLLOQ. jab, shot
SLANG fix
2 INTRODUCTION, insertion, addition, infusion, instilling

injudicious adj

ill-advised, ill-judged, imprudent, inexpedient, ill-timed,
unwise, inadvisable, incautious, inconsiderate, foolish,
stupid, hasty, rash, misguided, unthinking indiscreet,
wrong-headed
FORMAL impolitic
E3 wise, cautious, prudent; *formal* judicious

injunction n

command, order, directive, ruling mandate, direction,
instruction, precept, dictum, dictate
FORMAL admonition

injure v

1 HURT, harm, damage, impair, spoil, mar, ruin, disfigure,
deface, blemish, blight, weaken, undermine, mutilate,
mangle, deform, wound, cut, break, fracture, maim,
disable, cripple, lame
2 OFFEND, ill-treat, maltreat, abuse, wrong upset,
put out

injured adj

1 HURT, harmed, damaged, wounded, bruised, sore,
tender, lame, disabled, crippled, weakened
2 OFFENDED, upset, hurt, ill-treated, maltreated, misused,
pained, put out, wronged, unhappy, aggrieved, maligned,
abused, defamed, insulted, grieved, bruised, sore,
displeased, disgruntled, vulnerable, cut to the quick

injurious adj

damaging detrimental, harmful, hurtful, disadvantageous,
destructive, prejudicial, unconducive, pernicious, adverse,
corrupting baneful, ruinous, unhealthy, unjust, bad,
wrongful, insulting libellous, slanderous
FORMAL calumnious, deleterious, iniquitous, noxious
E3 beneficial, favourable

injury n

1 WOUND, cut, bruise, sore, lesion, fracture,
gash, abrasion, laceration, trauma, hurt, mischief,
ill, harm, damage, impairment, ruin, disfigurement,
mutilation
TECHNICAL contusion
FORMAL affliction
2 WRONG, ill-treatment, abuse, insult, grievance, offence,
injustice

injustice n

unfairness, unjustness, wrong injury, abuse, ill-treatment,
offence, inequality, discrimination, oppression, bias,
prejudice, one-sidedness, partisanship, partiality,
favouritism
OLD unreason
FORMAL disparity, iniquity, inequity
E3 justice, fairness

> **QUOTATIONS**
> The love of justice in most men is simply the fear of
> suffering injustice
>   FRANÇOIS DE LA ROCHEFOUCAULD, *Réflexions, ou*
>   *sentences et maximes morales*

inkling n

suspicion, idea, notion, glimmering clue, hint, intimation,
insinuation, innuendo, suggestion, allusion, indication,
sign, pointer
COLLOQ. faintest, foggiest, whisper

inky adj

black, jet-black, coal-black, pitch-black, jet, sooty,
dark-blue

inlaid adj

set, inset, enamelled, mosaic, tiled, lined, studded,
enchased, damascened
FORMAL tessellated, empaestic

inland adj

interior, inner, internal, central, domestic, up-country,
landward, midland, upland
OLD within land

inlay *n*
setting inset, enamel, mosaic, tiling lining studding damascene
FORMAL tessellation, emblema

inlet *n*
bay, cove, bight, creek, fiord, firth, opening entrance, passage, sound

inmate *n*
patient, prisoner, convict, detainee, case, client

inmost *adj*
deepest, deep, central, innermost, intimate, personal, dearest, private, secret, confidential, closest, essential, hidden, buried, basic
FORMAL esoteric

inn *n*
public house, tavern, hostelry, hotel, bar, halfway house, house, posthouse, roadhouse, *auberge*, imaret, serai, khan, ryokan, *albergo*, *posada*; *Scot* change-house, howff
OLD caravanserai, watering-house
COLLOQ. pub, local

innards *n*
1 *the innards of an animal*
insides, guts, internal organs, interior, intestines, entrails, entera, organs, umbles, viscera, vitals
2 *the innards of a machine*
works, mechanism, inner workings

innate *adj*
inborn, inbred, congenital, inherited, hereditary, inherent, intrinsic, native, indigenous, natural, instinctive, intuitive
FORMAL connate
🔄 acquired, learnt

innately *adv*
intrinsically, inherently, basically, fundamentally, centrally, essentially, inwardly, constituently, integrally, constitutionally

inner *adj*
internal, interior, inside, inward, innermost, central, middle, concealed, obscure, hidden, secret, private, personal, intimate, deep, profound, restricted, mental, psychological, spiritual, emotional
FORMAL esoteric
🔄 outer, outward, revealed

innermost *adj*
deepest, deep, central, inmost, intimate, personal, dearest, private, secret, confidential, closest, essential, hidden, buried, basic
FORMAL esoteric

innkeeper *n*
landlord, landlady, hotel-keeper, hotelier, proprietor, manager, publican, host, hostess, mine host, barkeeper, restaurateur, innholder, padrone

innocence *n*
1 GUILTLESSNESS, blamelessness, irreproachability, unimpeachability, honesty, integrity, virtue, righteousness, sinlessness, faultlessness, impeccability, immaculateness, stainlessness, spotlessness, purity, chastity, virginity, incorruptibility
FORMAL inculpability
2 ARTLESSNESS, guilelessness, ingenuousness, naiveness, naivety, inexperience, ignorance, naturalness, simplicity, openness, frankness, unsophistication, unworldliness, childlikeness, credulity, gullibility, trustfulness
3 HARMLESSNESS, innocuousness, inoffensiveness, safety, playfulness
🔄 **1** guilt **2** experience **3** harmfulness

innocent *adj, n*
♦ *adj*
1 *innocent of the crime*
guiltless, blameless, clear, irreproachable, above suspicion, unblameworthy, unimpeachable, honest, upright, virtuous, righteous, sinless, faultless, impeccable, stainless, spotless,

immaculate, unsullied, unblemished, untainted, uncontaminated, pure, chaste, virginal, white, uncorrupted, incorrupt, crimeless
OLD offenceless, sackless
FORMAL inculpable
2 ARTLESS, guileless, ingenuous, naive, inexperienced, fresh, natural, simple, open, frank, unsophisticated, unworldly, childlike, angelic, credulous, gullible, trusting trustful, dewy-eyed, unsuspecting Arcadian
OLD (*Spenser*) seely
COLLOQ. green, wet behind the ears, innocent as a newborn babe
3 HARMLESS, inoffensive, innocuous, safe, playful, unsuspicious, dovelike, lamblike, gentle, bland, anodyne
🔄 **1** guilty, to blame **2** experienced, sophisticated **3** harmful, offensive
♦ *n*
beginner, infant, novice, child, tenderfoot, babe, babe in arms, neophyte, ingénue, greenhorn
🔄 connoisseur, expert

SYNONYM NUANCES

sense 1
Clear, **guiltless** and **blameless** can be used in specific cases where someone is not responsible for a wrongful action, but they can also be used to suggest not having done anything wrong generally, as can **impeccable** and **irreproachable**: *his private life was irreproachable*. The more uncommon **unblameworthy**, along with **unimpeachable**, similarly suggest being free from fault, whereas **honest** is more suggestive of being generally trustworthy.
Likewise **upright**, **virtuous** and **righteous** all convey very positive images of integrity, while **sinless** and **faultless** would emphasize instead the lack of moral defects. **Stainless** and **spotless** imply never having been tainted by dishonest actions: *who can claim to have led a spotless life?* **Immaculate** has almost religious overtones of being free from sin, while the terms **unsullied**, **unblemished**, **untainted** and **uncontaminated** return to the idea of never having been tarnished in any way.
You can use **pure** of being free from defilement, and **chaste**, **virginal**, and **white** share similar associations, usually of sexual innocence. Both **uncorrupted** and **incorrupt**, meanwhile, are appropriate for having resisted bad influences: *he remained incorrupt while in office, never accepting the bribes offered to him*.

---

innocently *adv*
naively, artlessly, blamelessly, harmlessly, innocuously, inoffensively, unoffendingly, trustfully, trustingly, simply, ingenuously, credulously, unsuspiciously
COLLOQ. like a lamb to the slaughter

innocuous *adj*
harmless, safe, inoffensive, unobjectionable, innocent, playful, mild, bland, unobtrusive, anodyne
🔄 harmful, dangerous, toxic

innovation *n*
new product, new method, newness, novelty, neologism, introduction, modernization, progress, reform, change, alteration, variation, departure
OLD novelism, novity
FORMAL novation

innovative *adj*
new, fresh, original, creative, imaginative, inventive, resourceful, enterprising go-ahead, progressive, reforming bold, daring adventurous, groundbreaking trail-blazing avant-garde, Promethean
🔄 conservative, unimaginative

innovator *n*
originator, fresh thinker, progressive, creator, pioneer, source, deviser, developer, trailblazer, reformer, modernizer

innuendo n
insinuation, slur, whisper, hint, intimation, suggestion, implication, allusion, overtone
FORMAL aspersion

innumerable adj
countless, uncountable, numerous, numberless, unnumbered, untold, incalculable, infinite, many
COLLOQ. umpteen, oodles, tons, loads, masses, heaps, piles, stacks, dozens, hundreds, thousands, millions, gazillions

inoculate v
immunize, vaccinate, inject, protect, safeguard
COLLOQ. give a jab/shot to

inoculation n
vaccination, immunization, protection, injection
COLLOQ. shot, jab

inoffensive adj
harmless, innocuous, safe, innocent, unobjectionable, unexceptionable, peaceable, mild, bland, anodyne, unobtrusive, unassertive, quiet, retiring
Ⓔ offensive, harmful, provocative

inoperable adj
incurable, untreatable, unhealable, unremovable, irremovable, terminal, fatal, deadly, hopeless
FORMAL intractable
Ⓔ operable

inoperative adj
not working not operative, out of order, out of action, out of service, out of commission, defective, broken, broken-down, non-functioning unserviceable, unused, unworkable, useless, invalid, idle, ineffective, inadequate, inefficient, futile, worthless
FORMAL ineffectual, inefficacious, nugatory
COLLOQ. kaput, on the blink, bust, duff; N Am on the fritz
Ⓔ working operative

inopportune adj
untimely, inconvenient, unsuitable, inappropriate, tactless, ill-timed, ill-chosen, mistimed, wrong-timed, unfortunate, unseasonable, clumsy
FORMAL inauspicious, unpropitious, infelicitous
Ⓔ opportune

inordinate adj
excessive, immoderate, extreme, exorbitant, unwarranted, unrestricted, unrestrained, undue, unreasonable, outrageous, preposterous, disproportionate, great
COLLOQ. over the top, OTT
Ⓔ moderate, reasonable

inorganic adj
inanimate, lifeless, dead, mineral, non-natural, artificial
Ⓔ organic

input v, n
♦ v
feed in, insert, key in, put in, enter, load, code, capture, process, store
♦ n
information, data, facts, figures, statistics, material, details, particulars, resources
Ⓔ output

inquest n
inquiry, investigation, examination, hearing post-mortem, inspection

inquietude n
uneasiness, restlessness, worry, anxiety, nervousness, agitation, unease, apprehension, discomposure, disquiet, jumpiness
FORMAL disquietude, perturbation, solicitude
Ⓔ composure

inquire, enquire v
ask, question, quiz, query, investigate, look into, see, research, study, probe, examine, inspect, scrutinize, scan, search, explore, interrogate; Scot speir
OLD (Spenser) inquere
COLLOQ. snoop

inquirer, enquirer n
questioner, student, seeker, researcher, searcher, explorer, interrogator, investigator

inquiring enquiring adj
inquisitive, interested, questioning searching curious, analytical, eager, investigative, investigatory, interrogatory, outward-looking probing prying wondering doubtful, sceptical
FORMAL zetetic
COLLOQ. nos(e)y
Ⓔ incurious, unquestioning

inquiringly, enquiringly adv
inquisitively, curiously, eagerly, keenly, wonderingly, questioningly, analytically

inquiry, enquiry n
question, query, investigation, inquest, hearing inquisition, interrogation, examination, inspection, scrutiny, study, demand, survey, poll, search, probe, exploration, sounding reconnaissance, quest, interrogatory, star chamber
TECHNICAL aetiology
OLD inquire
FORMAL perquisition

inquisition n
interrogation, cross-examination, cross-questioning examination, investigation, questioning quizzing inquiry, inquest
COLLOQ. grilling the third degree, witch hunt

inquisitive adj
curious, inquiring questioning probing searching scrutinizing prying peeping peering snooping spying interfering meddlesome, intrusive
COLLOQ. nos(e)y, snoopy

inquisitively adv
curiously, eagerly, keenly, inquiringly, searchingly, questioningly, interferingly, meddlesomely

inroad n
advance, progress, encroachment, foray, impingement, incursion, intrusion, trespassing invasion, irruption, onslaught, attack, assault, offensive, charge, raid, sally, sortie, trespass

insane adj
1 MAD, lunatic, unbalanced, psychotic, disturbed, deranged, maniacal, out of your mind, out of your senses, of unsound mind, unhinged, crazed, unstable, non compos mentis, frenzied, wild, berserk, manic, maniac, distracted, distraught, fey, frenetic, frantic, stone-crazy, queer; Scot gyte, red-mad
OLD frantic-mad, horn-mad, lymphatic, bestraught; (Shakesp) wood; (Spenser) yond
COLLOQ. crazy, demented, nuts, nutty, nutty as a fruitcake, wacky, mad as a hatter, barmy, bonkers, batty, cracked, crackers, dippy, daffy, dotty, loopy, potty, off your nut, off your head, wrong in the head, out of your head, off the wall, out to lunch, round the bend, round the twist, bats, having bats in the belfry, cuckoo, off the rails, screwy, up the wall, raving not all there; N Am buggy, flaky, fruity; Aust & NZ dingbats
SLANG loony, mental, bananas, barking wacko, doolally, off your rocker, off your chump, off your trolley, out of your tree, needing your head examined, having lost your marbles, having a screw loose, having a tile loose, having several cards short of a full deck, with one sandwich short of a picnic, meshuga, ape, apeshit; N Am gonzo, loco, wiggy
2 FOOLISH, stupid, senseless, mad, crazy, impractical, idiotic, nonsensical, absurd, ridiculous

COLLOQ. daft, potty, barmy, half-baked, hare-brained, crackbrained, crackpot
⊟ 1 sane **2** sensible

> **QUOTATIONS**
> Man is quite insane. He wouldn't know how to make a maggot, and he makes Gods by the dozen
> MICHEL EYQUEM DE MONTAIGNE, *Essais*

insanely *adv*
madly, ridiculously, absurdly, ludicrously, senselessly, foolishly, outrageously

insanitary *adj*
unhygienic, unsanitary, unclean, impure, unhealthy, unsanitized, dirty, dirtied, contaminated, polluted, infected, disease-ridden, filthy, foul, infested
FORMAL unhealthful, noisome, noxious, insalubrious, feculent
⊟ sanitary, clean

insanity *n*
1 *suffer from insanity*
insaneness, madness, craziness, lunacy, mental illness, neurosis, mania, dementia, delirium, frenzy, derangement, *folie,* craze
TECHNICAL psychosis, psychopathy, hebephrenia
2 FOLLY, madness, craziness, lunacy, foolishness, stupidity, senselessness, absurdity, ridiculousness, irresponsibility, *folie*
COLLOQ. daftness
⊟ 1 sanity **2** sensibleness

> **SYNONYM NUANCES**
>
> *sense 1*
> **Madness** suggests a mental disorder which manifests itself in irrational behaviour, while **craziness** and **lunacy** are more informal terms suggesting any generally outlandish behaviour, not necessarily caused by a mental disorder. **Neurosis**, on the other hand, is a more clinical term which emphasizes internal effects, and has narrower implications of a specific set of disorders: *anxiety neurosis; obsessional neurosis.*
> The term **mania** tends to be suggestive of euphoria, and informal usage has also leant it implications of wild behaviour. The more straightforwardly medical term **dementia** is used of mental deterioration. **Delirium** suggests a fevered mental state with physical manifestations: *she thrashed and mumbled in delirium.* **Frenzy** has more to do with a state of violent excitement: *in a frenzy of wrath.* The term **derangement** is less suggestive of behaviour and returns to the general idea of mental disturbance causing disordered thought.

insatiable *adj*
voracious, unquenchable, unsatisfiable, unappeasable, ravenous, hungry, greedy, gluttonous, craving avid, immoderate, inordinate
FORMAL rapacious

inscribe *v*
1 ENGRAVE, etch, carve, cut, incise, imprint, impress, stamp, brand, mark, print
2 WRITE, sign, enrol, enlist, register, record, address, autograph, dedicate

inscription *n*
engraving etching epitaph, caption, legend, lettering wording words, writing signature, autograph, message, dedication

inscrutable *adj*
incomprehensible, unfathomable, impenetrable, deep, unintelligible, inexplicable, unexplainable, unreadable, baffling puzzling mysterious, enigmatic, cryptic, hidden
FORMAL arcane
⊟ comprehensible, expressive

insect

Insects include:

aphid	glowworm	midge
bee	gnat	mosquito
beetle	grasshopper	moth
blackfly	hornet	nit
bumblebee	horsefly	onion fly
butterfly	flea	*N Am* roach
cicada	froghopper	stick insect
cockroach	greenfly	termite
cranefly	lacewing	tsetse-fly
cricket	ladybird	wasp
colloq. daddy	*N Am* ladybug	water boatman
longlegs	leatherjacket	weevil
dragonfly	locust	whitefly
earwig	louse	woodlouse
fly	mayfly	woodworm

See also **butterfly**; **moth**.

Arachnids include:

harvester (or harvestman)	spider
mite	tick
scorpion	

Parts of an insect include:

abdomen	head	ocellus
antenna	hindwing	ovipositor
cercus	legs	segment
compound eye	mandible	spiracle
forewing	mouthpart	thorax

insecure *adj*
1 ANXIOUS, worried, nervous, uncertain, unsure, unassured, lacking confidence, afraid, apprehensive, fearful, hesitant, doubtful
2 UNSAFE, dangerous, hazardous, perilous, precarious, unsteady, unstable, shaky, loose, weak, frail, flimsy, unprotected, unguarded, defenceless, exposed, vulnerable, open to attack
OLD (*Shakesp & Spenser*) tickle
⊟ 1 confident, self-assured **2** secure, safe, protected

insecurity *n*
1 ANXIETY, worry, nervousness, uncertainty, unsureness, apprehension, fear, uneasiness, lack of confidence
2 UNSAFETY, unsafeness, danger, hazard, peril, precariousness, unsteadiness, shakiness, instability, weakness, frailness, flimsiness, defencelessness, vulnerability
⊟ 1 confidence, self-assurance **2** safety, security

insensate *adj*
insensible, unfeeling unconscious, unaware, anaesthetized, numb, senseless, unresponsive, oblivious, unmindful, ignorant, blind, deaf
FORMAL insentient, comatose

insensible *adj*
1 UNCONSCIOUS, anaesthetized, numb, senseless, unresponsive
FORMAL insentient, comatose
COLLOQ. out, zonked, knocked out, out for the count, dead to the world
2 UNAWARE, unconscious, oblivious, unmindful, ignorant, blind, deaf
3 CALLOUS, insensitive, unfeeling emotionless, detached, untouched, unmoved, unaffected, cold, hard-hearted, hard, aloof, distant
4 IMPERCEPTIBLE, indiscernible, indistinguishable, undetectable, unapparent, faint, slight
⊟ 1 conscious **2** aware, knowing **3** sensitive

insensitive *adj*
hardened, tough, resistant, impenetrable, impervious, immune, unsusceptible, thick-skinned, case-hardened, unfeeling impassive, oblivious, indifferent, unaffected, unresponsive, unmoved, untouched, unsympathetic, uncaring unconcerned, dead, hard, hard-hearted, iron, callous, heartless, thoughtless, tactless, crass, obtuse
TECHNICAL hypalgesic, anomalous
FORMAL pachydermatous
E3 sensitive, responsive, affected

insensitivity *n*
hardness, toughness, resistance, impenetrability, imperviousness, immunity, unresponsiveness, hard-heartedness, hard-headedness, unconcern, bluntness, callousness, indifference, tactlessness, crassness, obtuseness
TECHNICAL hypalgesia, hypalgia
E3 sensitivity, responsiveness

inseparable *adj*
indivisible, indissoluble, undividable, inextricable, close, intimate, bosom, constant, devoted
E3 separable

inseparably *adv*
inextricably, intimately, closely, firmly, hand in hand, arm in arm, indivisibly, indissolubly, together, as one

insert *v, n*
♦ *v*
put, place, press, put in, enclose, stick in, push in, thrust in, slide in, slip in, introduce, enter, implant, embed, engraft, infix, inlay, set, inset, let in, interleave, interject
FORMAL interpose, interpolate, intercalate
♦ *n*
insertion, enclosure, inset, notice, advertisement, circular, supplement, addition, inlay

insertion *n*
addition, entry, inclusion, insert, inset, introduction, implant, supplement, intrusion
FORMAL intercalation, interpolation, intromission

inside *n, adv, adj*
♦ *n*
interior, content, contents, middle, centre, heart, core
COLLOQ. guts, belly
E3 outside
♦ *adv*
within, indoors, internally, inwardly, secretly, privately
E3 outside
♦ *adj*
1 INTERIOR, internal, inner, implicit, inherent, intrinsic, innermost, inward
2 SECRET, classified, confidential, internal, private, restricted, reserved
COLLOQ. hush-hush

insider *n*
member, participant, staff member, co-worker
COLLOQ. one of us, one of the in-crowd

insides *n*
internal organs, entrails, guts, intestines, bowels, organs, viscera, belly, stomach, abdomen
COLLOQ. innards, tummy

insidious *adj*
subtle, sly, crafty, cunning wily, artful, deceptive, deceitful, dishonest, devious, stealthy, surreptitious, furtive, sneaking sneaky, tricky, treacherous, insincere, Machiavellian
FORMAL duplicitous, perfidious
E3 direct, straightforward

insidiously *adv*
subtly, slyly, cunningly

insight *n*
awareness, knowledge, comprehension, understanding realization, grasp, apprehension, perception, intuition, sensitivity, discernment, judgement, acumen, penetration,

sharpness, shrewdness, observation, vision, wisdom, intelligence, aperçu, epiphany
OLD sight
FORMAL perspicacity

insightful *adj*
perceptive, astute, sharp, shrewd, observant, penetrating understanding acute, discerning seeing intelligent, knowledgeable, wise, prudent
OLD inscient
FORMAL perspicacious, sagacious, percipient
E3 superficial

insignia *n*
emblem, badge, regalia, crest, sign(s), ensign, medallion, ribbon, decoration, mark, hallmark(s), symbol, trademark, brand, logo

insignificance *n*
unimportance, irrelevance, meaninglessness, immateriality, inconsequence, inconsequentiality, negligibility, smallness, pettiness, paltriness, tininess, insubstantiality, triviality, meanness, worthlessness
FORMAL nugatoriness
E3 significance

insignificant *adj*
unimportant, irrelevant, meaningless, immaterial, inconsequential, minor, trivial, trifling petty, paltry, meagre, scanty, slight, small, tiny, insubstantial, inconsiderable, negligible, non-essential, peripheral, not worth mentioning marginal, minimal, fractional, insect, nebbich, scrub
FORMAL nugatory
OLD petit, puisne
COLLOQ. piddling cutting no ice, no great shakes, small-time; *N Am* dinky, jerkwater, no-account
SLANG Mickey Mouse, C-list
E3 significant, important

insincere *adj*
hypocritical, two-faced, double-dealing lying untruthful, dishonest, deceitful, underhand, devious, unfaithful, faithless, disloyal, untrue, treacherous, false, feigned, pretended, hollow, pretentious
FORMAL mendacious, disingenuous, dissembling duplicitous, perfidious
COLLOQ. phoney
E3 sincere, genuine

insincerely *adv*
hypocritically, dishonestly, deceitfully, untruthfully, deviously, unfaithfully, disloyally, treacherously, falsely, pretentiously
FORMAL duplicitously, perfidiously

insincerity *n*
hypocrisy, untruthfulness, dishonesty, deceitfulness, deviousness, pretence, hollowness, pretentiousness, falseness, falsity, faithlessness, artificiality, cant, evasiveness
FORMAL disingenuousness, dissembling dissimulation, duplicity, mendacity, perfidy
COLLOQ. phoniness, humbug lip service
E3 sincerity

insinuate *v*
imply, suggest, allude, hint, mention, intimate, indicate
COLLOQ. get at, whisper
■ **insinuate yourself**
curry favour, ingratiate, sidle, work, worm, wriggle
COLLOQ. get in with

insinuation *n*
suggestion, implication, allusion, hint, intimation, inference, introduction, slant, slur, innuendo
FORMAL aspersion
COLLOQ. insinuendo

insipid *adj*
1 TASTELESS, flavourless, unsavoury, unappetizing watery, weak, thin, bland
COLLOQ. wishy-washy

2 UNINTERESTING, dull, monotonous, boring tedious, wearisome, tame, flat, lifeless, inanimate, spiritless, vapid, characterless, trite, banal, unimaginative, dry, anaemic, colourless, drab
COLLOQ. wishy-washy
E3 1 tasty, spicy, piquant, appetizing **2** interesting exciting lively

insist v
demand, require, urge, entreat, stress, emphasize, repeat, reiterate, dwell on, harp on, assert, declare, stipulate, state firmly, ask for firmly, maintain, claim, contend, hold, press, vow, swear, persist, stand firm, stand on, stand your ground, refuse to accept an alternative, stick out for, hang out for, stick to your guns; *dialect* threap
OLD (*Shakesp*) strain
FORMAL aver
COLLOQ. put your foot down, not take no for an answer

insistence n
demand, requirement, entreaty, urging stress, emphasis, repetition, reiteration, maintenance, assertion, declaration, claim, contention, persistence, determination, resolution, firmness, assertiveness
FORMAL exhortation

insistent adj
demanding importunate, emphatic, resolute, determined, adamant, forceful, pressing urgent, dogged, tenacious, persistent, persevering assertive, constant, repeated, relentless, unrelenting unremitting unyielding inexorable, incessant
FORMAL exigent

insobriety n
drunkenness, hard drinking intemperance, inebriation, inebriety, intoxication
FORMAL crapulence
COLLOQ. tipsiness
E3 sobriety

insolence n
rudeness, abuse, insults, impudence, impertinence, gall, arrogance, audacity, boldness, forwardness, pertness, presumption, presumptuousness, disrespect, contemptuousness, defiance, insubordination, offensiveness, incivility; *Scot* snash
FORMAL hubris, effrontery, contumely
COLLOQ. cheek, cheekiness, sauce, sauciness, attitude, nerve, lip, mouth, chutzpah; *N Am* sass
E3 politeness, respect

insolent adj
rude, abusive, insulting disrespectful, ill-mannered, impertinent, impudent, bold, audacious, brazen, brash, forward, presumptuous, arrogant, defiant, contemptuous, insubordinate
COLLOQ. cheeky, saucy, fresh, lippy, mouthy; *N Am* sassy
E3 polite, respectful

SYNONYM NUANCES

Rude can be used of someone displaying appalling manners or of a deliberate attempt to offend, while **abusive** and **insulting** specifically suggest a deliberately offensive verbal assault. **Disrespectful** has more to do with not showing a proper level of courtesy: *his intimate form of address seemed very disrespectful.*

Ill-mannered returns to the idea of generally not conducting yourself correctly, whereas **impertinent** and **impudent** are milder terms, more suggestive of less severe insolence, or of not exhibiting the acceptable levels of restraint: *the boy gave an impertinent reply; he was greeted by impudent stares.* Both **bold** and **audacious** also suggest insolence based on overfamiliarity; **brazen** and **brash** have implications of impetuosity and shamelessness at one's actions: *I was shocked by the brazen way she spoke to her parents.* The terms **forward** and **presumptuous** also suggest overstepping the bounds of propriety: *it was presumptuous of him to offer me advice.*

Arrogant has more to do with an undue assumption of importance. **Defiant** could be used where conventions or demands are being flouted: *he's reached that defiant toddler stage.* You can use **contemptuous** where insolence is driven by a total lack of regard for propriety, and **insubordinate** where authority has been rejected: *you are on a training course – don't be rude or insubordinate.*

insoluble adj
unsolvable, unexplainable, inexplicable, incomprehensible, unfathomable, impenetrable, inscrutable, enigmatic, indecipherable, complex, intricate, involved, obscure, mysterious, mystifying puzzling perplexing baffling
E3 explicable

insolvency n
bankruptcy, default, failure, liquidation, ruin, indebtedness, destitution, impoverishment, pennilessness
FORMAL impecuniosity
COLLOQ. queer street
E3 solvency

insolvent adj
bankrupt, failed, in debt, liquidated, ruined, penniless, impoverished, destitute
FORMAL impecunious
COLLOQ. bust, broke, skint, strapped (for cash), on your beam ends, gone to the wall, gone under, in the red, on the rocks, in queer street
E3 solvent

insomnia n
sleeplessness, restlessness, wakefulness
FORMAL insomnolence
E3 sleep

insouciance n
nonchalance, unconcern, carefreeness, heedlessness, indifference, light-heartedness, flippancy, airiness, breeziness, jauntiness, ease
E3 anxiety, care

insouciant adj
nonchalant, unconcerned, untroubled, unworried, indifferent, heedless, carefree, casual, free and easy, flippant, happy-go-lucky, airy, breezy, buoyant, jaunty, light-hearted, easy-going
E3 anxious, careworn

inspect v
check, vet, look into, look over, go over, pore over, examine, search, investigate, appraise, assess, audit, scrutinize, study, scan, survey, view, eye, review, superintend, supervise, oversee, visit, reconnoitre, see over, tour
COLLOQ. check out, give something the once-over
SLANG case

inspection n
check, check-up, examination, scrutiny, scan, study, survey, review, search, investigation, vetting analysis, appraisal, assessment, audit, supervision, visit, tour
COLLOQ. once-over, look-over, recce, dekko

inspector n
supervisor, superintendent, overseer, surveyor, controller, appraiser, assessor, auditor, scrutineer, scanner, checker, tester, examiner, investigator, reviewer, critic, visitor, officer, searcher, viewer, conner
TECHNICAL exarch
OLD proveditor

inspiration n
1 CREATIVITY, originality, imagination, genius, inventiveness, muse, influence, encouragement, stimulation, incitement, stirring, arousing, motivation, spur, goad, stimulus, fillip, infusion, revelation, *duende*, *estro*; *Scot* taghairm; *Welsh* hwyl
TECHNICAL theopneusty, afflation, afflatus, Aganippe
OLD inflation, *inflatus*

2 IDEA, bright idea, stroke of genius, brainwave, brainstorm, insight, illumination, revelation, enlightenment, awakening
COLLOQ. lightbulb moment

inspirational adj
encouraging heartening inspiring motivating suggestive, influential, emotional, spiritual, devotional, psychological, instinctive

inspire v
encourage, hearten, influence, impress, animate, breathe, enliven, quicken, energize, galvanize, fire, kindle, inflame, stir, arouse, rouse, trigger, instigate, inject, produce, bring about, spark off, touch off, prompt, spur, goad, motivate, provoke, stimulate, excite, exhilarate, thrill, enthral, enthuse, imbue, infuse, inform, infatuate, enamour, embrave

inspired adj
brilliant, impressive, superlative, wonderful, outstanding exciting dazzling memorable, thrilling enthralling marvellous, exceptional, splendid, remarkable, creative, imaginative, talented
E3 dull, uninspired

inspiring adj
encouraging heartening uplifting invigorating stirring rousing interesting enthusiastic, inspirational, stimulating exciting exhilarating thrilling enthralling moving affecting memorable, impressive
E3 uninspiring dull

inspirit v
encourage, inspire, move, stimulate, nerve, hearten, invigorate, quicken, refresh, reinvigorate, enliven, exhilarate, fire, galvanize, incite, animate, rouse, cheer, gladden, embolden

instability n
unsteadiness, shakiness, vacillation, wavering oscillation, irresolution, uncertainty, impermanence, transience, unpredictability, changeableness, variability, fluctuation, volatility, capriciousness, flightiness, fitfulness, fickleness, inconstancy, unreliability, insecurity, precariousness, unsafeness, unsoundness, flimsiness, frailty
E3 stability

install v
1 *install a new phone system*
fix, fit, lay, put (in), plumb in, insert, place, position, locate, lodge, site, situate, station, plant, settle, establish, set up, introduce
2 *install her as president*
institute, inaugurate, invest, induct, ordain, swear in, consecrate, instate
3 ENSCONCE, settle, establish, entrench, nestle, put, place, lodge, locate

installation n
1 FITTING, insertion, positioning location, placing siting
2 EQUIPMENT, machinery, plant, system
3 *her installation as president*
inauguration, investiture, instatement, induction, consecration, ordination, swearing-in
4 *a military installation*
base, station, post, centre, site, settlement, establishment, headquarters, HQ, camp

instalment n
1 *pay in instalments*
payment, part payment, repayment, portion, tranche, hire purchase, HP
COLLOQ. the never-never
2 EPISODE, chapter, part, section, division, portion, segment

instance n, v
♦ n
1 *several instances of bullying*
case, example, illustration, exemplification, case in point, citation, occurrence, occasion, sample

2 *at his instance*
request, urging incitement, demand, initiative, insistence, entreaty, instigation, pressure, prompting solicitation
FORMAL behest, exhortation, importunity
♦ v
mention, quote, refer to, specify, give, name, cite, point to, exemplify
FORMAL adduce

instant n, adj
♦ n
flash, twinkling trice, moment, split second, second, minute, time, occasion, juncture; *Scot* whip
COLLOQ. tick, jiffy, jiff, sec, twinkling of an eye, two shakes of a lamb's tail, mo
♦ adj
1 INSTANTANEOUS, immediate, on-the-spot, direct, prompt, urgent, unhesitating quick, fast, rapid, swift
2 *instant food*
quickly prepared, easily prepared, pre-prepared, ready mixed, convenience, fast
E3 1 slow

instantaneous adj
immediate, instant, direct, prompt, rapid, unhesitating sudden, on-the-spot
COLLOQ. snappy
E3 eventual

instantaneously adv
at once, directly, forthwith, immediately, right away, instantly, on the spot, promptly, speedily, quickly, rapidly, straight away, there and then, unhesitatingly, without hesitation, without delay, in the twinkling of an eye
OLD anon
COLLOQ. pronto, in a jiffy, before you can say Jack Robinson, in two shakes of a lamb's tail, ASAP
E3 eventually

instantly adv
immediately, instantaneously, at once, right away, straight away, there and then, forthwith, now, on the spot, without delay, directly
COLLOQ. pronto, in a jiffy, before you can say Jack Robinson, in two shakes of a lamb's tail, ASAP
E3 eventually

instead adv
alternatively, preferably, rather, else, by/in contrast, as an alternative, substitute, replacement
■ **instead of**
as opposed to, in contrast to, in place of, in lieu of, on behalf of, in preference to, in favour of, as an alternative to, rather than

instigate v
initiate, set on, start, begin, cause, bring about, induce, press, generate, inspire, move, influence, persuade, encourage, urge, spur, prod, goad, prompt, provoke, stimulate, kindle, incite, stir up, whip up, foment, rouse, excite

instigation n
initiation, incitement, initiative, encouragement, prompting urging inducement, insistence, incentive, bidding
FORMAL behest

instigator n
leader, motivator, prime mover, initiator, provoker, ringleader, spur, goad, incendiary, inciter, mischief-maker, troublemaker, *agent provocateur*, agitator, fomenter, firebrand

instil v
infuse, imbue, insinuate, introduce, inject, implant, inculcate, impress, teach, drill
COLLOQ. din into

instinct n
1 NATURAL RESPONSE, inbred response, intuition, sixth sense, impulse, urge, drive, feeling hunch, tendency
FORMAL predisposition
COLLOQ. gut feeling/reaction

2 FLAIR, knack, gift, talent, bent, feel, faculty, ability, aptitude

> **QUOTATIONS**
> We only trust our own instincts / And only believe the worst when it comes true
> JEAN DE LA FONTAINE, *Fables*, 'L'hirondelle et les petits oiseaux'

instinctive *adj*
natural, native, inborn, innate, inherent, intuitive, impulsive, involuntary, unintentional, automatic, mechanical, reflex, spontaneous, immediate, unlearned, untaught, unthinking unpremeditated, visceral
COLLOQ. gut, knee-jerk
ℱ conscious, voluntary, deliberate

instinctively *adv*
intuitively, naturally, spontaneously, unthinkingly, without thinking automatically, involuntarily, mechanically
ℱ consciously, deliberately, voluntarily

institute *v, n*
♦ *v*
1 START, originate, initiate, introduce, enact, begin, create, establish, develop, set up, organize, found, inaugurate, open, launch, put/set in motion
FORMAL commence
2 APPOINT, install, invest, induct, ordain, initiate
ℱ **1** cancel, abolish; *formal* discontinue
♦ *n*
1 *an institute for advanced research*
school, college, academy, conservatory, seminary, foundation, institution, organization
2 LAW, principle, rule, custom, regulation, decree

institution *n*
1 ORGANIZATION, association, society, guild, league, club, concern, corporation, foundation, establishment, institute, hospital, home, centre
2 CUSTOM, tradition, usage, practice, ritual, convention, rule, law, system
3 INITIATION, starting introduction, enactment, creation, establishment, setting-up, formation, founding foundation, installation
FORMAL commencement, inception

institutional *adj*
established, organized, establishment, accepted, customary, conventional, formal, methodical, orderly, systematic, orthodox, regimented, set, routine, uniform, ritualistic, bureaucratic, clinical, impersonal, cold, unwelcoming dreary, dull, drab, forbidding monotonous, cheerless
ℱ individualistic, unconventional

instruct *v*
1 TEACH, educate, tutor, coach, train, drill, ground, school, discipline, prime, prepare, inspire, guide, indoctrinate, lecture, show, catechize
OLD lesson; (Shakesp) study
2 ORDER, command, direct, demand, require, charge, mandate, tell, inform, notify, make known, warn, advise, counsel, guide, enlighten, brief, call out
FORMAL enjoin, bid

instruction *n*
1 *give someone instructions*
order, direction, recommendation, advice, guidance, information, charge, command, requirement, injunction, mandate, directive, ruling briefing
2 EDUCATION, schooling lesson(s), classes, lecture(s), tuition, tutoring tutelage, teaching training coaching drilling grounding preparation, priming guidance, enlightenment, indoctrination
3 *read the instructions carefully*
directions, orders, recommendations, rules, brief, information, advice, key, legend, guidance, guidelines, book of words, handbook, manual

instructive *adj*
informative, educational, educative, doctrinal, uplifting edifying enlightening illuminating helpful, useful
ℱ unenlightening

instructor *n*
teacher, lecturer, educator, master, mistress, tutor, coach, trainer, demonstrator, exponent, adviser, mentor, guide, pedagogue, counsellor, guru, preceptor
TECHNICAL maharishi, swami
OLD institutor

instrument *n*
1 TOOL, implement, utensil, appliance, gadget, contraption, device, contrivance, apparatus, mechanism
COLLOQ. gismo
2 GAUGE, meter, measure, indicator, rule, guideline, yardstick
3 AGENT, agency, vehicle, organ, medium, factor, cause, channel, way, means
See also panels at **measuring instruments, musical instruments**.

instrumental *adj*
active, involved, contributory, conducive, influential, important, significant, useful, helpful, auxiliary, subsidiary
ℱ obstructive, unhelpful

insubordinate *adj*
disobedient, rebellious, defiant, ungovernable, unruly, disorderly, undisciplined, rude, riotous, seditious, insurgent, mutinous, turbulent, impertinent, impudent
FORMAL contumacious, recalcitrant, refractory
ℱ docile, obedient, compliant

insubordination *n*
disobedience, defiance, rebellion, insurrection, mutinousness, mutiny, revolt, riotousness, sedition, rudeness, ungovernability, indiscipline, impertinence, impudence
FORMAL recalcitrance
ℱ docility, obedience, compliance

insubstantial *adj*
1 FLIMSY, frail, feeble, weak, tenuous, poor, slight, thin
2 UNREAL, false, illusory, fanciful, imaginary, idle, vaporous, intangible, immaterial, incorporeal, moonshine
FORMAL chimerical, ephemeral
ℱ **1** solid, strong **2** real

insufferable *adj*
intolerable, unbearable, unendurable, detestable, loathsome, revolting repugnant, dreadful, shocking outrageous, impossible, too much to bear, more than you can bear
ℱ pleasant, tolerable

insufferably *adv*
unbearably, intolerably, outrageously, shockingly, impossibly, repugnantly

insufficiency *n*
inadequacy, shortage, deficiency, lack, scarcity, dearth, need, poverty, short supply
FORMAL want
ℱ sufficiency, excess

insufficient *adj*
inadequate, not enough, short, deficient, lacking wanting meagre, sparse, scanty, scant, scarce, in short supply
ℱ sufficient, enough, excessive

insular *adj*
parochial, provincial, cut off, detached, isolated, remote, withdrawn, separate, solitary, insulated, inward-looking short-sighted, blinkered, closed, narrow-minded, narrow, limited, restricted, petty, bigoted, biased, prejudiced, xenophobic
ℱ open-minded

insularity *n*
isolation, detachment, narrow-mindedness, short-sightedness, solitariness, pettiness, parochiality, parochialness, bigotry, bias, prejudice, xenophobia
ℱ open-mindedness, openness

insulate *v*
insulate water pipes; people insulated from outside influences
cushion, pad, lag cocoon, protect, wrap, cover, shield, shelter, isolate, separate, cut off, exclude, detach, segregate, encase, envelop
FORMAL sequester

insulation *n*
cushioning padding lagging cladding cocooning protection, wrapping cover, covering stuffing shield, shelter, isolation, separation, exclusion, detachment, segregation

insult *v, n*
♦ *v*
abuse, call names, taunt, ridicule, bait, rebuff, libel, slander, malign, slight, slur, snub, injure, hurt, wound, offend, outrage, mortify, trample, triumph over
OLD fly in the face of
FORMAL affront, disparage, revile, impugn, calumniate, traduce
COLLOQ. kick in the teeth, slap in the face
F3 compliment, praise
♦ *n*
abuse, rudeness, insolence, gibe, taunt, defamation, libel, slander, slight, slur, barb, snub, indignity, offence, outrage, aspersions
OLD contumely, injury, insultment; (*Spenser*) repriefe
FORMAL affront, disparagement, revilement
COLLOQ. put-down, backhanded compliment, kick in the teeth, slap in the face, verbal, mud pie
F3 compliment, praise

SYNONYM NUANCES

verb
Abuse can be widely applied to mental maltreatment, unlike **taunt** which suggests deliberate provocation: *they taunted the beaten team with chants of 'easy'.* **Ridicule**, on the other hand, would be reserved for making someone appear absurd, while **bait** has more to do with constant harassment or goading: *on his way home he was being continually baited by a drunk.*

While **malign** has to do with speaking badly of someone, it would imply it is not done in that person's presence: *he was much maligned by the critics.* Both **libel** and **slander** could be used of writing or saying injurious things about someone, but only where it is serious enough to be contested in a court of law.

If you want to refer to disrespectfully overlooking or rejecting someone, you can use **rebuff**, **slight** or **snub**: *he felt slighted when he was passed over for promotion.* The terms **injure**, **hurt** and **wound** may all be used to put the emphasis on mental or emotional harm caused by an insult. **Offend** implies a more moral indignation, and **outrage** is suggestive of great indignation: *they were outraged at the blanket smoking ban.* **Mortify** is appropriate where severe embarrassment has resulted: *I was mortified by the things you said about me.*

---

insulting *adj*
offensive, abusive, rude, hurtful, injurious, contemptuous, degrading slighting outrageous, insolent, scurrilous, libellous, slanderous
OLD contumelious
FORMAL affronting disparaging reviling
F3 complimentary, respectful

insuperable *adj*
insurmountable, formidable, overwhelming invincible, unconquerable, unassailable, impassable
F3 surmountable

insupportable *adj*
intolerable, unbearable, unendurable, insufferable, dreadful, loathsome, hateful, detestable, unacceptable, untenable, unjustifiable, indefensible
F3 bearable

insuppressible *adj*
irrepressible, lively, unstoppable, uncontrollable, ungovernable, unruly, unsubduable, obstreperous, incorrigible, energetic
COLLOQ. go-getting
F3 suppressible

insurance *n*
cover, protection, assurance, safeguard, security, surety, provision, indemnity, guarantee, indemnification, warranty, policy, premium

insure *v*
cover, protect, assure, underwrite, indemnify, guarantee, warrant, overinsure, reinsure
OLD ensure

insurer *n*
assurer, underwriter, protector, indemnifier, guarantor, warrantor
TECHNICAL abandonee

insurgence *n*
insurrection, rising uprising riot, rebellion, mutiny, revolt, revolution, sedition, coup, coup d'état, putsch

insurgent *n, adj*
♦ *n*
rebel, revolter, revolutionary, rioter, insurrectionist, seditionist, mutineer, partisan, revolutionist, resister
♦ *adj*
rebellious, revolting revolutionary, mutinous, riotous, seditious, disobedient, insubordinate, insurrectionary, partisan

insurmountable *adj*
insuperable, unconquerable, invincible, unassailable, overwhelming hopeless, impossible
F3 surmountable

insurrection *n*
rising uprising insurgency, riot, rebellion, mutiny, revolt, revolution, sedition, coup, coup d'état, putsch

intact *adj*
unbroken, (all) in one piece, whole, complete, integral, entire, perfect, faultless, flawless, sound, undamaged, unharmed, unhurt, uninjured, unscathed
F3 broken, incomplete, damaged

intangible *adj*
insubstantial, imponderable, elusive, fleeting airy, unclear, shadowy, vague, subtle, obscure, indefinite, indefinable, undefinable, indescribable, abstract, unreal, invisible, immeasurable, impalpable
F3 tangible, real

integer *n*
number, whole number, numeral, figure, digit, unit

integral *adj*
1 *an integral part*
intrinsic, constituent, component, inherent, built-in, inbuilt, elemental, basic, fundamental, necessary, essential, indispensable
FORMAL requisite
2 COMPLETE, entire, full, whole, total, undivided, intact, integrated
F3 **1** extra, additional, unnecessary

integrate *v*
assimilate, merge, join, unite, combine, amalgamate, co-ordinate, consolidate, incorporate, coalesce, fuse, knit, mesh, mix, intermix, mingle, blend, homogenize, harmonize, desegregate, mainstream
F3 divide, separate, segregate

integrated *adj*
mixed, desegregated, assimilated, merged, joined, unified, unseparated, united, combined, amalgamated, consolidated, incorporated, coalesced, fused, meshed, mingled, blended, harmonized, harmonious, cohesive, connected, tight-knit, tightly-knit, interrelated, hybrid, mongrel

COLLOQ. part and parcel
☞ unintegrated, segregated

integration n
assimilation, merger, unity, unification, combination, amalgamation, consolidation, incorporation, fusion, blend, harmony, mix, desegregation, homogenization
☞ separation, segregation

integrity n
1 HONESTY, uprightness, incorruptibility, purity, morality, principle, sincerity, honour, decency, virtue, goodness, fairness, righteousness, justice, impartiality, truthfulness
FORMAL probity, rectitude
2 COMPLETENESS, wholeness, unity, entirety, entireness, totality, coherence, cohesion, unification
☞ 1 dishonesty 2 incompleteness

intellect n
1 *a person of considerable intellect*
mind, brain(s), brainpower, brilliance, intelligence, genius, reason, thought, understanding comprehension, sense, wisdom, judgement
TECHNICAL noesis, noology
COLLOQ. nous
2 THINKER, academic, highbrow, mastermind, genius, intellectual
COLLOQ. egghead, brainbox
☞ 1 stupidity

intellectual adj, n
♦ adj
academic, scholarly, intelligent, studious, learned, thoughtful, mental, logical, highbrow, bookish, cultural, well-educated, well-read
TECHNICAL noetic, noematical
FORMAL cerebral, erudite
☞ low-brow
♦ n
thinker, academic, highbrow, mastermind, genius, intellect, good mind, titan
COLLOQ. egghead, brainbox, rocket scientist; *N Am* brainiac
☞ low-brow

intellectually adv
mentally, academically, studiously, conceptually, culturally
TECHNICAL noematically
FORMAL cerebrally

intelligence n
1 INTELLECT, reason, wit(s), brainpower, cleverness, brightness, brilliance, aptitude, quickness, alertness, sharpness, acumen, discernment, perception, thought, understanding comprehension
COLLOQ. brain(s), grey matter, little grey cells, nous
2 INFORMATION, facts, data, knowledge, findings, notification, news, report, notice, account, rumour, warning advice
COLLOQ. low-down, tip-off, gen, dope
3 SURVEILLANCE, spying espionage, observation
☞ 1 stupidity, foolishness

> QUOTATIONS
> Truths discovered by intelligence are sterile
> ANATOLE FRANCE, *La Vie littéraire*

intelligent adj
clever, bright, smart, brilliant, quick, alert, quick-witted, sharp, acute, discerning perceptive, knowing knowledgeable, well-informed, informed, thinking educated, rational, sensible
OLD apprehensive
FORMAL perspicacious, sagacious
COLLOQ. brainy, quick on the uptake, no flies on someone, knowing a thing or two, knowing how many beans make five, using your loaf, all there
See Synonym nuances panel at **clever**.
☞ unintelligent, stupid, foolish

intelligently adv
knowingly, rationally, sensibly, cleverly, quickly, discerningly, perceptively
FORMAL perspicaciously, sagaciously
COLLOQ. quick on the uptake, knowing a thing or two, knowing how many beans make five, using your loaf, all there
☞ stupidly, foolishly

intelligentsia n
academics, intellectuals, cognoscenti, literati, highbrows, illuminati
COLLOQ. brains, eggheads

intelligibility n
comprehensibility, comprehensibleness, clearness, clarity, plainness, lucidity, lucidness, explicitness, distinctness, legibility, precision, simplicity
FORMAL exotericism
☞ unintelligibility

intelligible adj
comprehensible, understandable, clear, plain, lucid, distinct, open, explicit, legible, decipherable, fathomable, penetrable
FORMAL exoteric, exoterical
☞ unintelligible

intemperance n
excess, immoderation, self-indulgence, overindulgence, unrestraint, extravagance, drunkenness, intoxication, insobriety, licence
FORMAL crapulence, inebriation
☞ temperance

intemperate adj
extreme, immoderate, inordinate, unrestrained, unbridled, uncontrolled, uncontrollable, irrestrainable, ungovernable, severe, violent, wild, tempestuous, passionate, excessive, unreasonable, extravagant, self-indulgent, drunken, intoxicated, dissolute, incontinent, prodigal, licentious, profligate
FORMAL inebriated
COLLOQ. over the top, OTT
☞ temperate

intend v
aim, have a mind, have in mind, contemplate, mean, think, meditate, be going be looking propose, choose, plan, project, scheme, devise, plot, design, expect, purpose, determine, be determined, resolve, destine, mark out, earmark, set apart; *Scot* ettle; *N Am* calculate
OLD foremean; (*Spenser*) hight
FORMAL purport

intended adj, n
♦ adj
designated, destined, deliberate, intentional, planned, proposed, designate, future, prospective, betrothed
☞ accidental
♦ n
fiancé, fiancée, husband-to-be, wife-to-be, future husband, future wife, betrothed

intense adj
1 EXTREME, great, deep, profound, strong powerful, vigorous, potent, forceful, fierce, harsh, severe, acute, sharp, keen, enthusiastic, zealous, eager, earnest, ardent, fervent, excited, passionate, impassioned, vehement, consuming burning energetic, violent, intensive, concentrated, heightened
FORMAL fervid
2 *an intense person*
serious, thoughtful, impassioned, emotional, tense, nervous, heavy
☞ 1 moderate, mild, weak 2 easy-going

> ❗ **intense** or **intensive**?
> *Intense* means 'very great': *the intense heat from the furnace; intense bitterness. Intensive* means 'concentrated, thorough, taking great care': *an intensive search; the intensive care ward of a hospital.*

SYNONYM NUANCES

sense 1

Great can be widely applied to describe magnitude, while **extreme** could be reserved for something of the greatest possible degree: *extreme grief led to his suicide.* **Deep** and **profound** tend to suggest being deeply rooted psychologically or intellectually: *deep sympathy; a profound influence.*

Vigorous and **energetic** have associations with liveliness and movement: *vigorous political campaigning*, while **violent** implies furiously unrestrained: *a violent coughing fit.* **Potent** conveys the idea of strength, as does **forceful**, while **fierce** shares similar implications but tends to be used in the contexts of competition or fighting.

The terms **harsh** and **severe** imply something unpleasant: *harsh winter; severe pain*, whereas **acute** and **sharp** have a more penetrative effect: *sharp criticism.* **Keen** has similar connotations, but along with **enthusiastic** and **zealous** may also be suggestive of a strong personal interest: *zealous commitment.* **Ardent**, **fervent**, **passionate** and **impassioned** go further by implying a heartfelt involvement.

Vehement, on the other hand, suggests intellectual conviction: *a vehement speech on workers' rights.* **Consuming** would be appropriate for an all-engrossing intensity: *horse-riding became her consuming passion*, while **heightened** could be used for something that has grown notably stronger: *heightened public awareness of crime; heightened tension.*

---

intensely *adv*
extremely, deeply, very, strongly, greatly, profoundly, fiercely, ardently, fervently, passionately
COLLOQ. with a vengeance
▸ mildly

intensification *n*
increase, stepping-up, strengthening reinforcement, magnification, escalation, heightening building-up, build-up, boost, aggravation, acceleration, worsening deepening concentration, emphasis, enhancement
FORMAL augmentation, exacerbescence
▸ lessening

intensify *v*
increase, step up, build up, escalate, heighten, maximize, fire, boost, fuel, fan, aggravate, worsen, add to, broaden, widen, strengthen, reinforce, magnify, sharpen, whet, quicken, deepen, concentrate, emphasize, enhance
FORMAL augment, exacerbate
COLLOQ. hot up, bump up, hike up, add fuel to the flames, bring to a head
▸ reduce, weaken

intensity *n*
greatness, extremity, intenseness, depth, profundity, fullness, strength, power, vigour, potency, force, fierceness, severity, acuteness, keenness, eagerness, earnestness, ardour, enthusiasm, zeal, fanaticism, fervency, fervour, fire, emotion, passion, concentration, energy, vehemence, strain, tension

intensive *adj*
concentrated, thorough, exhaustive, comprehensive, detailed, in-depth, rigorous, full, total, thoroughgoing all-out, intense
▸ superficial

> **⚠ intensive** or **intense**?
> *See panel at* **intense**.

intensively *adv*
thoroughly, exhaustively, comprehensively, rigorously, completely, totally, fully, closely, intensely, extensively
▸ superficially, on the surface

---

intent *adj, n*
♦ *adj*
1 *intent on doing something*
determined, resolved, set, bent, eager, keen, committed, firm
2 *an intent look*
attentive, alert, concentrating fixed, close, hard, keen, absorbed, occupied, wrapped up, focused, engrossed, preoccupied, steady, rapt, enrapt, searching watchful
▸ **2** absent-minded, distracted
♦ *n*
intention, purpose, meaning objective, plan, aim, goal, target, point, idea, view, design, object, end
■ **to all intents and purposes**
almost, nearly, practically, in effect, effectively, in essence, virtually, more or less, just about, as good as, pretty much, pretty well

intention *n*
aim, purpose, object, end, point, target, goal, objective, idea, plan, design, view, intent, meaning ambition, wish, aspiration

intentional *adj*
designed, wilful, conscious, planned, purposeful, purposed, set, deliberate, prearranged, premeditated, preconceived, considered, calculated, studied, systematic, systematical, voluntary, intended, weighed-up, meant, on purpose
TECHNICAL prepense
OLD willing
▸ unintentional, accidental

intentionally *adv*
deliberately, on purpose, wilfully, by design, designedly, meaningly, with malice aforethought, in cold blood
TECHNICAL prepensely
OLD willingly
▸ accidentally

intently *adv*
attentively, watchfully, carefully, closely, steadily, searchingly, staringly, fixedly, hard, keenly
▸ absent-mindedly

inter *v*
bury, lay to rest, entomb, inearth, sepulchre, inhume
FORMAL inurn
▸ exhume

interbreed *v*
cross, crossbreed, cross-fertilize, mongrelize, hybridize, reproduce together
FORMAL miscegenate

interbreeding *n*
cross-breeding crossing hybridization
FORMAL miscegenation

intercede *v*
mediate, arbitrate, intervene, plead, speak, petition, negotiate, moderate
FORMAL entreat, beseech, interpose

intercept *v*
head off, ambush, interrupt, deflect, cut off, stop, arrest, catch, commandeer, take, seize, check, block, impede, waylay, obstruct, delay, frustrate, thwart

interception *n*
ambush, deflection, heading-off, cutting-off, stopping seizure, checking blocking obstruction

intercession *n*
mediation, arbitration, negotiation, intervention, plea, pleading advocacy, agency, solicitation, prayer, good offices
FORMAL beseeching entreaty, supplication, interposition

intercessor *n*
mediator, arbitrator, negotiator, moderator, intermediary, agent, go-between, middleman, broker, prayer

interchange n, v

♦ n

1 EXCHANGE, trading barter, swap, alternation, reciprocation, interplay, crossfire
COLLOQ. give-and-take

2 INTERSECTION, junction, crossroad(s), crossing

♦ v

exchange, swap, switch, alternate, reciprocate, replace, substitute, trade, barter, transpose, reverse

interchangeability n

comparability, similarity, transposability, exchangeability, interaction, reciprocation, exchange, barter, swap, equivalence, correspondence, synonymy, parallelism
FORMAL congruence, reciprocity

interchangeable adj

reciprocal, exchangeable, transposable, equivalent, corresponding comparable, similar, identical, the same, synonymous, standard
E3 different

interconnect v

link, interlink, interrelate, interlock, interweave, communicate, intercommunicate

intercourse n

1 *sexual intercourse*
sex, sexual relations, intimacy, intimate relations, making love, love-making copulation, sleeping with someone, going to bed with someone, the sex act
OLD embraces
FORMAL carnal knowledge, coition, coitus, congress
COLLOQ. it, how's your father; *Aust & NZ* naughty
SLANG nooky, bonk, bang lay, greens, jig-a-jig knee-trembler, pussy, rumpy-pumpy, tail, leg-over, wham bam thank you ma'am, quickie, roll in the hay, get one's oats; *N Am* jazz, poontang; (*taboo*) fuck, screw, shag hole
2 ASSOCIATION, communication, communion, contact, connection, dealings, çonversation, converse, correspondence, commerce, trade, intercommunication, congress, traffic
COLLOQ. truck

> **QUOTATIONS**
> Sexual intercourse began / In nineteen sixty-three / (Which was rather late for me) – / Between the end of the Chatterley ban / And the Beatles' first LP
> PHILIP LARKIN, 'Annus Mirabilis'

interdependent adj

interconnected, interlinked, interrelated, interlocking reciprocal, correlated, complementary, mutual, two-way

interdict v, n

♦ v

ban, bar, debar, forbid, prohibit, prevent, embargo, rule out, veto, outlaw
FORMAL disallow, preclude, proscribe
E3 allow

♦ n

ban, injunction, prohibition, bar, embargo, taboo, veto
FORMAL disallowance, interdiction, proscription, preclusion
E3 permission

interest n, v

♦ n

1 *have an interest in dance*
curiosity, inquisitiveness, concern, care, attention, attentiveness, notice, regard, heed, charm, allure, appeal, attraction, fascination, involvement, engagement
2 IMPORTANCE, significance, consequence, concern, moment, consideration, magnitude, relevance, prominence, weight, value, note, urgency, priority, seriousness, gravity

3 *leisure interests*
activity, pursuit, pastime, hobby, diversion, recreation, amusement
4 ADVANTAGE, good, benefit, profit, gain
5 *business interests*
share, stake, concern, business, claim, involvement, participation, portion, investment, stock, equity
6 *earn interest*
dividend, return, profit, gain, receipts, revenue, proceeds, credits, bonus, premium, percentage
E3 **1** lack of interest **2** meaninglessness **4** loss

♦ v

concern, involve, touch, move, attract, appeal to, divert, amuse, occupy, engage, rivet, absorb, engross, fascinate, intrigue, captivate, grip
E3 bore

■ **in the interests of**
for the sake of, on behalf of, to the advantage of, for the benefit of

interested adj

1 ATTENTIVE, curious, absorbed, engrossed, engaged, fascinated, intent, captivated, gripped, enthralled, riveted, intrigued, enthusiastic, keen, attracted, devoted
COLLOQ. hot on, into, having the ... bug
2 CONCERNED, involved, affected, implicated
E3 **1** uninterested, indifferent, apathetic **2** disinterested, unaffected

interesting adj

attractive, appealing entertaining engaging absorbing engrossing exciting fascinating captivating intriguing compelling compulsive, gripping riveting stimulating thought-provoking readable, viewable, amusing curious, unusual
COLLOQ. unputdownable
E3 uninteresting boring monotonous, tedious

> **SYNONYM NUANCES**
>
> **Attractive** describes anyone or anything to which you are drawn, while **appealing** may be similarly enticing but perhaps with a more emotional element: *an appealing study of a lovable eccentric*. If you describe something as **entertaining** you merely suggest it provides a diversion, while **engaging**, **absorbing** and **engrossing** are stronger terms, all suggestive of completely capturing the attention: *an absorbing book*.
> **Fascinating** and **captivating** have suggestions of being spellbinding and suggest interest that has less specific, worldly causes: *he was a captivating scene-stealer as Puck*. You can use **intriguing** and the more explicit **curious** to suggest that an element of puzzlement has stirred interest.
> **Compelling** and **compulsive** have implications of being irresistibly drawn: *a drama that makes compelling TV viewing*. With **gripping** and **riveting** we return to the idea of being enthralled, whereas **stimulating** and **thought-provoking** are more appropriate for exciting an intellectual interest: *a stimulating public debate*.

interestingly adv

curiously, intriguingly, poignantly, ingeniously

interfere v

1 INTRUDE, pry, interrupt, intervene, meddle, tamper, intermeddle, trespass
TECHNICAL intromit
OLD mar
FORMAL interpose
COLLOQ. barge in, mess about/around, poke/stick your nose in, stick/put your oar in, put in your two pennyworth, muscle in on, butt in; *N Am* put in your two cents' worth; *Aust* stick/poke/put your bib in
2 HINDER, hamper, obstruct, block, check, impede, handicap, cramp, inhibit, trammel, balk, thwart, conflict, clash, choke, jam, upset

COLLOQ. get in the way of
3 MOLEST, abuse, assault, sexually assault, attack, touch sexually, rape
COLLOQ. grope, touch up, feel up
1 *colloq.* mind your own business **2** assist

SYNONYM NUANCES

sense 1
Intrude is critical in tone in that it suggests an uninvited or unwelcome encroachment. **Pry** is similar in tone, although it has more to do with invading someone's privacy: *her parents never pried into her affairs.* The term **interrupt** is less marked, although it also implies an element of disruption: *the speaker was interrupted by a question from the audience.* **Intervene** is more positive in that it suggests stepping in to assume a controlling role: *the government has intervened in environmental issues.*

The term **meddle**, however, expresses a critical attitude and suggests unhelpful involvement, while **tamper** similarly has suggestions of causing damage: *someone had tampered with the brakes.* **Trespass** is more formal, even legal in tone, and suggests literal or figurative encroachment on someone else's territory: *trespassing on railway property; parliament must refrain from trespassing upon the province of the courts.*

---

interference *n*
1 INTRUSION, prying interruption, intervention, meddling meddlesomeness
TECHNICAL intromission
FORMAL interposition
2 OBSTRUCTION, hindrance, hampering blocking checking impediment, handicap, inhibiting trammel(s), thwarting opposition, conflict, clashing
2 assistance

interfering *adj*
meddlesome, meddling prying intrusive, intruding
COLLOQ. nos(e)y

interim *adj, n*
♦ *adj*
temporary, provisional, stopgap, makeshift, improvised, stand-in, acting caretaker, pro tem
♦ *n*
meantime, meanwhile, interval, interregnum

interior *adj, n*
♦ *adj*
1 INTERNAL, inside, inner, innermost, central, inward, intrinsic
2 *interior thoughts*
inner, mental, personal, private, intimate, spiritual, emotional, psychological, secret, hidden, involuntary, spontaneous, impulsive, intuitive, instinctive, innate
3 HOME, domestic, central, local, inland, up-country, remote
1 exterior, external **3** external, coastal
♦ *n*
inside, inside part, centre, middle, core, heart, nucleus, depths
exterior, outside

interject *v*
cry, shout, call, utter, introduce, interrupt, exclaim
FORMAL ejaculate, interpose, interpolate

interjection *n*
exclamation, cry, shout, call, utterance, interruption
FORMAL ejaculation, interpolation, interposition

interlace *v*
entwine, braid, twine, knit, plait, cross, enlace, interweave, interlock, intertwine, intermix, intersperse, interwreathe
FORMAL reticulate

interlink *v*
link, link together, interconnect, lock together, interlock, mesh, knit, intergrow, intertwine, interweave, clasp together
separate, divide

interlock *v*
lock together, interconnect, link, link together, mesh, engage, clasp together, intertwine, tooth, pitch
FORMAL interdigitate
disengage

interloper *n*
intruder, uninvited guest, trespasser, encroacher, invader
COLLOQ. gatecrasher, third wheel, gooseberry

interlude *n*
interval, intermission, break, breathing space, pause, rest, recess, stop, stoppage, respite, wait, delay, halt, spell
FORMAL hiatus
COLLOQ. breather, let-up

intermediary *n*
mediator, go-between, negotiator, arbitrator, middleman, broker, agent

intermediate *adj*
midway, halfway, in-between, middle, mid, median, medial, mean, intermediary, intervening transitional
extreme

interment *n*
burial, burying funeral
FORMAL inhumation, exequies, obsequies, obsequy, sepulture
exhumation

interminable *adj*
endless, never-ending perpetual, limitless, boundless, unlimited, ceaseless, without end, everlasting eternal, long long-winded, long-drawn-out, dragging wearisome, tedious, boring dull, monotonous
FORMAL prolix, loquacious
limited, brief

intermingle *v*
mix, mix together, merge, blend, amalgamate, combine, fuse, intermix, interlace, interweave, mix up
FORMAL commingle, commix, intermix
separate

intermission *n*
interval, interlude, break, recess, rest, respite, breathing space, pause, lull, remission, suspension, interruption, halt, stop, stoppage
FORMAL cessation
COLLOQ. breather, let-up

intermittent *adj*
occasional, periodic, sporadic, spasmodic, fitful, erratic, irregular, cyclic, broken, off and on, on and off
FORMAL discontinuous
continuous, constant

intermittently *adv*
occasionally, periodically, sporadically, spasmodically, erratically, irregularly, from time to time, sometimes, off and on, on and off, in/by fits and starts
FORMAL discontinuously
continuously, regularly

intern *v, n*
♦ *v*
confine, detain, hold, hold in custody, jail, imprison
free, release
♦ *n*
trainee, apprentice, graduate, probationer, student, pupil, learner, novice, beginner, starter, recruit, newcomer, tiro, cadet, prentice

internal *adj*
1 INSIDE, inner, interior, inward
2 HOME, domestic, civil, interior, in-house, local

3 *internal processes of the mind*
subjective, intimate, private, personal, spiritual, mental, emotional, psychological
F3 1 external

internally *adv*
1 *known internally as 'B3'*
domestically, locally
2 SUBJECTIVELY, inwardly, inside, to yourself, within, at heart, in your heart of hearts, deep down, deep inside you, privately, secretly

international *adj*
global, worldwide, intercontinental, cosmopolitan, universal, general
F3 national, local, parochial

internecine *adj*
fierce, violent, bloody, deadly, mortal, fatal, destructive, ruinous, murderous, exterminating family, civil, internal

Internet *n*
the Net, the cloud
TECHNICAL broadband, WiFi
SLANG interweb

interplay *n*
exchange, interchange, interaction, reciprocation, alternation, transposition
COLLOQ. give-and-take

interpolate *v*
insert, add, put in, introduce, interject
FORMAL interpose, intercalate

interpolation *n*
insert, insertion, addition, introduction, aside, interjection
FORMAL intercalation

interpose *v*
insert, introduce, interject, add, put in, thrust in, interrupt, intrude, interfere, come between, put/place between, intervene, step in, mediate, arbitrate, intercede
FORMAL interpolate
COLLOQ. barge in, butt in, muscle in, poke your nose in, put your oar in

interpret *v*
explain, clarify, make clear, throw/shed light on, define, paraphrase, translate, render, decode, decipher, solve, make sense of, understand, read, take, construe, open up, rationalize
OLD aread, interpretate; (*Shakesp*) scan
FORMAL expound, elucidate, explicate
COLLOQ. read between the lines

interpretation *n*
explanation, clarification, analysis, translation, rendering version, paraphrase, performance, reading understanding sense, meaning opinion, decoding deciphering
TECHNICAL anagogy
FORMAL expounding exposition, elucidation, exegesis, explication, construe
COLLOQ. spin, take

interpretative *adj*
explanatory, clarificatory, interpretive
TECHNICAL hermeneutic
FORMAL exegetic, explicatory, expository

interpreter *n*
translator, linguist, commentator, annotator, interpretress, dragoman, dobhash, munshi, moonshee; *N Am* linguister
TECHNICAL hermeneutist, lawyer, textualist, oneirocritic, oneiroscopist
OLD Latiner, truchman
FORMAL elucidator, exegete, exponent, expositor

interrelate *v*
link, interlink, interconnect, interlock, interweave, communicate, intercommunicate

interrogate *v*
question, quiz, examine, cross-examine, cross-question, debrief
COLLOQ. grill, give a going-over, give the third degree, pump, give a roasting

interrogation *n*
questioning quizzing cross-questioning examination, cross-examination, inquisition, inquiry, inquest
COLLOQ. grilling going-over, the third degree, pumping

interrogative *adj*
questioning quizzical, curious, inquisitive, probing inquiring interrogatory
FORMAL inquisitional, inquisitorial, catechetical, erotetic

interrupt *v*
1 *interrupt a conversation*
cut in, intrude, break in, disturb, punctuate, cut short, cut off, heckle, barrack, take (up) short, snap up, take up
FORMAL interpolate, interpose, interject, interjaculate
COLLOQ. barge in, butt in, chip in, chop in, put your oar in
2 *interrupt an event*
disturb, disrupt, hold up, stop, halt, end, suspend, delay, postpone, cancel, cut off, disconnect, break, block, punctuate, intercept, intervene
FORMAL interlude
3 *interrupt a view*
obstruct, block, cut off, disturb, interfere with, chequer

interruption *n*
1 *work without interruption*
intrusion, interference, disturbance, cutting-in, disruption, suspension, breaking-off, delay, disconnection
FORMAL discontinuance, cessation
COLLOQ. barging-in, butting-in
2 *no interruptions are allowed*
question, remark, interjection, obstruction, impediment, obstacle, hitch, cutting-in, blocking
OLD interpellation
FORMAL interpolation
3 PAUSE, break, halt, stop, interval, intermission, recess, interlude, cut
OLD (*Spenser*) cesure
FORMAL hiatus
COLLOQ. breather, let-up

intersect *v*
cross, criss-cross, cut across, bisect, divide, meet, converge, overlap

intersection *n*
junction, interchange, crossroads, crossing meeting

intersperse *v*
scatter, distribute, spread, dispense, pepper, sprinkle, dot, intermix, diversify
FORMAL interpose, interlard

interstice *n*
space, gap, opening blank, void, hole, cavity, aperture, crack, chink, crevice, cleft, cranny, breach, rift, fracture, rent, divide, gulf
FORMAL orifice, lacuna

intertwine *v*
entwine, interweave, interlace, interlink, link together, connect, interwind, twirl, twist, twine, coil, cross, weave, blend, mix

interval *n*
1 BREAK, interlude, intermission, rest, pause, space, lull, gap, delay, wait, interim, period, time, recess, meantime, meanwhile
COLLOQ. breathing space, breather
2 SPACE, gap, opening distance, period, spell, time, season

intervene *v*
1 STEP IN, mediate, arbitrate, intercede, negotiate, involve yourself in, interfere, interrupt, intrude
2 OCCUR, happen, pass, arise, come to pass
FORMAL elapse, befall

intervening *adj*
between
FORMAL interposing intervenient, interjacent, mediate

intervention *n*
involvement, stepping-in, mediation, arbitration, negotiation, agency, intercession, interference, interruption, intrusion

interview *n, v*
♦ *n*
discussion, audience, consultation, talk, dialogue, meeting conference, press conference, encounter, tête-à-tête, evaluation, appraisal, assessment, oral examination, viva
♦ *v*
question, interrogate, examine, talk to, sound out, cross-examine, cross-question, evaluate, assess, vet
COLLOQ. grill, give the third degree to

interviewer *n*
examiner, questioner, investigator, reporter, correspondent, evaluator, appraiser, assessor, interrogator, inquisitor
FORMAL interlocutor, interrogant

interweave *v*
intertwine, entwine, interlace, interlink, interwind, interlock, twist, twine, coil, knit, cross, criss-cross, weave, intertangle, intertwist, interwork, interwreathe, braid, splice, blend, link together, interconnect, intermingle, connect, mix
FORMAL reticulate

intestinal *adj*
internal, abdominal, gastric, duodenal, visceral
TECHNICAL coeliac, ileac, enteric
FORMAL stomachic

intestines *n*
bowels, guts, entrails, insides, colon, offal, viscera, vitals
COLLOQ. innards

intimacy *n*
1 CLOSENESS, close relationship, friendship, familiarity, confidence, confidentiality, privacy, warmth, affection, love, understanding
2 SEXUAL INTERCOURSE, sexual relations, intimate relations, love-making copulation, sleeping with someone, going to bed with someone
FORMAL carnal knowledge, coition, coitus
COLLOQ. it, how's your father; *Aust & NZ* naughty
SLANG nooky, bonk, bang lay, greens, jig-a-jig knee-trembler, pussy, rumpy-pumpy, tail, leg-over, wham bam thank you ma'am, quickie, roll in the hay, get one's oats; *N Am* jazz, poontang; *(taboo)* fuck, screw, shag hole
Ⅎ distance

intimate[1] *adj, n*
♦ *adj*
1 an intimate friend
close, near, dear, bosom, cherished, friendly, informal, familiar, affectionate, boon; *Scot* chief
OLD privy, strict, gremial
COLLOQ. thick, mat(e)y, pally, chummy, tight
2 an intimate atmosphere
warm, welcoming cosy, friendly, snug *gemütlich; Scot* tosh; *intime*, throng
3 an intimate conversation
confidential, secret, private, personal, internal, innermost, heart-to-heart; *Scot* pack
4 intimate knowledge of art
deep, profound, in-depth, penetrating detailed, exhaustive, thorough, special, well-acquainted
Ⅎ 1 unfriendly, cold, distant 4 superficial
♦ *n*
friend, close friend, best friend, bosom friend, confidant(e), associate, boon companion, comrade, alter ego, better half, Achates, *fidus Achates*
OLD belamy, cater-cousin, inward
COLLOQ. mate, pal, chum, buddy, crony
OLD SLANG china
Ⅎ stranger

intimate[2] *v*
intimated that he'd be willing to help
hint, insinuate, imply, suggest, indicate, signal, communicate, impart, tell, state, declare, announce, make known, let it be known, give notice, allude

intimately *adv*
1 CLOSELY, affectionately, personally, tenderly, warmly, familiarly, hand and/in glove
2 CONFIDENTIALLY, confidingly, privately
3 DEEPLY, fully, in detail, exhaustively, thoroughly, inside out
Ⅎ 1 coldly, distantly 3 superficially

intimation *n*
hint, inkling insinuation, implication, suggestion, innuendo, indication, announcement, communication, signal, declaration, notice, statement, reference, warning reminder, allusion

intimidate *v*
daunt, cow, overawe, domineer, appal, dismay, alarm, scare, frighten, terrify, subdue, threaten, extort, blackmail, menace, tyrannize, terrorize, bully, browbeat, bulldoze, coerce, compel, pressure, pressurize, warn off, bullyrag
COLLOQ. get at, lean on, twist someone's arm, put the screws on, psych out, put the frighteners on, turn the heat on

intimidation *n*
frightening terrifying menaces, threats, threatening threatening behaviour, terrorization, terrorizing domineering tyrannization, bullying browbeating coercion, compulsion, pressure, fear, terror, scare tactics
COLLOQ. arm-twisting screws, frighteners, big stick, sabre-rattling
Ⅎ persuasion

intolerable *adj*
unbearable, unendurable, insupportable, unacceptable, insufferable, loathsome, detestable, impossible, more than you can bear
COLLOQ. too bad, awful, dreadful, the limit, the end, the last straw, the straw that broke the camel's back
Ⅎ tolerable

intolerably *adv*
unbearably, insufferably, outrageously, shockingly, impossibly, repugnantly

intolerance *n*
impatience, prejudice, discrimination, narrowness, narrow-mindedness, small-mindedness, insularity, bigotry, opinionativeness, dogmatism, fanaticism, extremism, illiberality, uncharitableness, chauvinism, jingoism, racialism, racism, sexism, ageism, xenophobia, anti-Semitism
Ⅎ tolerance

intolerant *adj*
impatient, prejudiced, biased, discriminating partisan, one-sided, bigoted, narrow, narrow-minded, small-minded, provincial, parochial, insular, opinionated, dogmatic, fanatical, extremist, illiberal, uncharitable, redneck, chauvinistic, jingoistic, racist, racialist, sexist, ageist, xenophobic, anti-Semitic
Ⅎ tolerant

intonation *n*
modulation, tone, accentuation, emphasis, stress, inflection, pitch, timbre, lilt, cadence

intone *v*
chant, croon, intonate, monotone, enunciate, pronounce, recite, sing say, speak, voice, utter
FORMAL declaim, incant

intoxicate *n*
1 MAKE DRUNK, befuddle, fuddle, stupefy
FORMAL inebriate

2 EXCITE, elate, exhilarate, stimulate, thrill, animate, enthuse, inspire, inflame

intoxicated adj
1 DRUNK, drunken, under the influence
FORMAL inebriated, crapulent, ebriose
COLLOQ. merry, tight, tipsy, tiddly, tiddled, well-oiled, blotto, drunk as a lord/newt, drunk as a piper, sloshed, stewed, blind drunk, roaring drunk, the worse for drink, soused, squiffy, happy, legless, plastered, sozzled, pickled, bibulous, woozy, one over the eight, under the table, bevvied, having had a few, tired and emotional, high, footless, full, half-cut, obfuscated, pie-eyed, sow-drunk, under the weather, the worse for wear, steaming; *Irish* jarred; *Scot & Irish* stocious
SLANG stoned, tanked up, loaded, lit up, canned, paralytic, smashed, pissed, bombed, wasted, ripped, hammered, wrecked, trolleyed, stinko, whiffled, whistled, bonkers, bottled, Brahms and Liszt, juiced (up), in liquor, liquored, maggoty, mortal, up the pole; (*vulgar*) arseholed, rat-arsed; *N Am* crocked, moon-eyed; *Aust* inky, inked; *Aust & NZ* shickered
OLD SLANG corked, moppy
2 EXCITED, elated, exhilarated, thrilled, moved, stirred, stimulated, enthusiastic, worked up, in high spirits
COLLOQ. carried away
E3 1 sober, abstinent

intoxicating adj
1 *intoxicating liquor*
alcoholic, strong stimulant
FORMAL inebriant
COLLOQ. going to your head
2 EXCITING, stimulating heady, exhilarating thrilling stirring dramatic, rousing moving enthralling inspiring
E3 1 sobering

intoxication n
1 DRUNKENNESS, intemperance, alcoholism, hard/serious drinking debauchery, dipsomania
TECHNICAL methysis
FORMAL inebriation, inebriety, insobriety, crapulence
COLLOQ. bibulousness, tipsiness
2 EXCITEMENT, elation, exhilaration, thrill, pleasure, animation, enthusiasm, stimulation, euphoria, rapture
E3 1 sobriety

intractability n
unmanageableness, uncontrollableness, ungovernability, unco-operativeness, unamenability, waywardness, stubbornness, obstinacy, perverseness, perversity, awkwardness, pig-headedness, indiscipline, incorrigibility, cantankerousness, contrariness
FORMAL obduracy
E3 amenability

intractable adj
unmanageable, uncontrollable, unyielding unbending unco-operative, undisciplined, ungovernable, unamenable, wild, unruly, obstinate, perverse, self-willed, wilful, wayward, pig-headed, stubborn, disobedient, awkward, difficult, fractious, headstrong cantankerous, contrary
FORMAL intransigent, obdurate, refractory
E3 amenable

intransigence n
stubbornness, obstinacy, relentlessness, irreconcilability, implacability, determination, toughness, tenacity, inflexibility, pig-headedness
FORMAL intractability, obduracy
COLLOQ. bloody-mindedness
E3 amenability, flexibility

intransigent adj
stubborn, obstinate, uncompromising unamenable, unbending unpersuadable, unyielding unbudgeable, unrelenting relentless, inexorable, immovable, irreconcilable, implacable, inflexible, pig-headed, hardline, determined, rigid, tenacious, tough
FORMAL intractable, obdurate

COLLOQ. uppity, bloody-minded
E3 amenable, flexible

intrepid adj
bold, daring brave, courageous, plucky, valiant, audacious, lion-hearted, fearless, dauntless, undaunted, undismayed, unafraid, unflinching stout-hearted, spirited, stalwart, gallant, heroic
FORMAL doughty, valorous
COLLOQ. gutsy, spunky, gritty
E3 cowardly, timid, afraid

intrepidness n
boldness, bravery, daring intrepidity, audacity, valour, courage, heroism, dauntlessness, fearlessness, gallantry, lion-heartedness, stout-heartedness, undauntedness, pluck, prowess, spirit, nerve
FORMAL doughtiness, fortitude
COLLOQ. guts, grit
E3 cowardice, timidity

intricacy n
complexity, complexness, complexedness, complication, intricateness, elaborateness, entanglement, sophistication, involvement, knottiness, obscurity, enigma, involution
FORMAL convolution(s)
E3 simplicity, straightforwardness

intricate adj
complex, complicated, elaborate, sophisticated, involved, tortuous, tangled, entangled, ravelled, knotty, twisty, perplexing baffling puzzling difficult, enigmatic, fancy, ornate, rococo
FORMAL convoluted
E3 simple, plain, straightforward

intrigue n, v
♦ *n*
1 PLOT, scheme, conspiracy, conniving manoeuvre, stratagem, artifice, ruse, wile, trickery, cabal, double-dealing junta, web
OLD consult, courtcraft, brigue
FORMAL collusion, machination
COLLOQ. sharp practice, dodge, dirty trick
2 ROMANCE, liaison, affair, love affair, amour, intimacy, *affaire*, gallantry
♦ *v*
1 FASCINATE, arouse your curiosity, rivet, tantalize, attract, pull, draw, charm, captivate, absorb, interest, puzzle
2 PLOT, scheme, conspire, connive, manoeuvre, manipulate, work the oracle, traffic, undermine
OLD collogue, pack, brigue, practise against
FORMAL machinate
E3 1 bore

> **QUOTATIONS**
> Everything is done by intrigue, not by loyalty
> VICTOR HUGO, *Ruy Blas*

intriguer n
plotter, schemer, conspirator, collaborator, conniver, Machiavellian, intrigant(e)
FORMAL machinator
COLLOQ. wangler, wheeler-dealer, wire-puller

intriguing adj
fascinating appealing charming absorbing riveting compelling captivating diverting exciting interesting beguiling attractive, tantalizing titillating puzzling
E3 boring uninteresting dull

intrinsic adj
basic, central, essential, fundamental, natural, underlying built-in, in-built, inborn, inbred, interior, inherent, inward, native, indigenous, congenital, constitutional, elemental, genuine
E3 extrinsic

intrinsically *adv*
inherently, basically, fundamentally, centrally, essentially, inwardly, constituently, integrally, constitutionally

introduce *v*
1 INSTITUTE, begin, start, establish, found, originate, organize, develop, inaugurate, launch, usher in, open, bring in, initiate, put/set in motion, instigate
FORMAL commence
2 PUT FORWARD, advance, submit, offer, propose, suggest, float
3 PRESENT, announce, acquaint, familiarize
4 PREFACE, precede, begin, start, lead in, lead into, open
FORMAL commence
1 end, conclude **2** remove, take away **4** conclude, end, finish

introduction *n*
1 INSTITUTION, beginning start, establishment, origination, organization, development, inauguration, launch, presentation, debut, initiation, baptism
FORMAL commencement
2 FOREWORD, preface, preamble, prologue, preliminaries, front matter, overture, prelude, lead-in, opening
FORMAL prolegomenon, exordium, proem
COLLOQ. intro
3 PRESENTATION, announcement, familiarization, acquainting
COLLOQ. *Aust* knock-down
4 BASICS, fundamentals, essentials, rudiments, first principles
1 removal, withdrawal, termination **2** appendix, conclusion

introductory *adj*
preliminary, preparatory, opening inaugural, first, beginning starting initial, early, elementary, basic, fundamental, essential, rudimentary
FORMAL prefatory, initiatory, precursory, exordial, isagogic

introspection *n*
self-examination, contemplation, pensiveness, thoughtfulness, brooding self-analysis, self-centredness, self-observation, soul-searching heart-searching introversion
COLLOQ. navel-gazing navel-contemplation

introspective *adj*
inward-looking contemplative, meditative, pensive, thoughtful, brooding musing introverted, subjective, self-centred, self-absorbed, self-examining self-analysing self-observing reserved, withdrawn
outward-looking

introverted *adj*
introspective, inward-looking self-centred, self-absorbed, self-examining withdrawn, shy, reserved, quiet
extroverted

intrude *v*
interrupt, meddle, interfere, violate, invade, infringe, impinge, encroach, trespass; *Scot* sorn
FORMAL interject, obtrude, interlope
COLLOQ. gatecrash, barge in, chip in, butt in
withdraw, stand back

intruder *n*
trespasser, prowler, burglar, raider, housebreaker, robber, pilferer, thief, unwelcome guest, invader, infiltrator
FORMAL interloper
COLLOQ. gatecrasher

intrusion *n*
interruption, interference, meddling violation, infringement, encroachment, trespass, invasion
FORMAL incursion, obtrusion
COLLOQ. gatecrashing
withdrawal

intrusive *adj*
disturbing interfering irritating annoying troublesome, invasive, obtrusive, interrupting trespassing meddlesome, uncalled-for, unwanted, unwelcome, uninvited, forward, impertinent, officious, presumptuous, prying pushy
FORMAL importunate
COLLOQ. nos(e)y, snooping go-getting
unintrusive, welcome

intuition *n*
instinct, sixth sense, perception, discernment, insight, hunch, feeling extrasensory perception, ESP, premonition, belief, anticipation, light of nature
FORMAL presentiment
COLLOQ. gut feeling feeling in your bones
reasoning

intuitive *adj*
instinctive, intuitional, spontaneous, involuntary, automatic, innate, inborn, unlearned, untaught
reasoned

intuitively *adv*
instinctively, by instinct, spontaneously, automatically, innately, by the seat of your pants

inundate *v*
flood, deluge, swamp, engulf, submerge, soak, immerse, drown, saturate, bury, overwhelm, overburden, overrun, overflow

inundation *n*
flood, deluge, swamp, overflow, torrent, spate, tidal wave, excess, surplus, glut
trickle

inure *v*
accustom, familiarize, acclimatize, harden, temper, strengthen, desensitize, toughen, train
FORMAL habituate

invade *v*
1 *invade a country*
enter (by force), penetrate, infiltrate, burst in, descend on, attack, assault, raid, seize, storm, maraud, plunder, pillage, occupy, take over, march into, conquer, overrun, swarm over, infest, pervade
2 *invade someone's privacy*
intrude, encroach, infringe, violate, trespass, interrupt
FORMAL obtrude
withdraw, evacuate

SYNONYM NUANCES

sense 1
Penetrate can be widely used of breaking through defences, whereas **infiltrate** has more to do with gradually permeating and has connotations of stealth or underhandedness: *microchips have infiltrated the home and the office.* **Pervade** also suggests a gradual, subtle invasion and diffusion: *a depressing atmosphere pervaded the small room.*

The term **burst in** is suggestive of force but also of an element of surprise, whereas **descend on** is appropriate to suggest overwhelming by force of numbers: *the press descended on the town.* The terms **overrun** and **swarm over** also imply uncontrollably large numbers: *the Mediterranean is overrun with tourists*, while **infest** is an even more marked term with its connotations of harmful pests: *a mite that infests various animals.* The verb **storm** also suggests large numbers of invaders, but returns to the idea of a sudden and forced entry.

Raid might be used of making a swift incursion, usually for the purpose of procurement, but **seize** would be appropriate for taking control: *they seized three military bases.* **Occupy** is similar in sense, but has less inherent implication of force: *the occupied territories*, while **conquer** would again imply force and an element of subjugation. The terms **maraud**, **plunder** and **pillage** would be reserved for invading in search of loot: *marauding bandits.*

invader n

aggressor, attacker, assailant, raider, plunderer, marauder, pillager, intruder, trespasser, infringer

invalid[1] n, adj

♦ n

visit an invalid in hospital

patient, sufferer, convalescent, chronic

FORMAL valetudinarian

♦ adj

sick, ill, unwell, poorly, ailing sickly, weak, feeble, frail, infirm, disabled, bedridden

FORMAL debilitated, valetudinarian

✷ healthy

invalid[2] adj

1 an invalid argument

false, unsound, ill-founded, unfounded, baseless, groundless, unjustified, unsubstantiated, untenable, unacceptable, unwarranted, illogical, irrational, unscientific, wrong incorrect, weak, mistaken, erroneous

FORMAL fallacious

2 ILLEGAL, null, void, null and void, worthless, abolished, cancelled, quashed, overturned, expired; Aust informal

FORMAL inoperative, revoked, rescinded, nullified

✷ **1** valid, sound **2** legal, binding

invalidate v

annul, cancel, quash, void, veto, discredit, negate, undo, overrule, overthrow, undermine, weaken

FORMAL abrogate, nullify, rescind, vitiate, revoke, terminate

✷ validate

invalidity n

incorrectness, falsity, irrationality, unsoundness, sophism, speciousness, illogicality, inconsistency, voidness

FORMAL fallaciousness, fallacy

invaluable adj

priceless, inestimable, incalculable, indispensable, critical, crucial, precious, valuable, costly, useful

✷ worthless, cheap

invariable adj

fixed, set, unvarying unchanging unchangeable, unalterable, changeless, permanent, constant, steady, consistent, stable, unwavering uniform, rigid, inflexible, habitual, regular

FORMAL immutable, invariant

✷ variable, changeable

invariably adv

always, without exception, without fail, unfailingly, consistently, regularly, repeatedly, constantly, habitually, inevitably

✷ never

invasion n

1 an invasion of a country

attack, offensive, onslaught, raid, foray, breach, occupation, storming penetration, infiltration

FORMAL incursion

2 invasion of privacy

interference, interruption, intrusion, encroachment, infringement, violation

✷ **1** withdrawal, evacuation

invective n

abuse, denunciation, reproach, scolding reprimand, rebuke, tirade, diatribe, recrimination, sarcasm, tongue-lashing

FORMAL censure, revilement, fulmination, berating castigation, obloquy, philippic, vilification, vituperation, contumely

✷ praise

inveigh v

criticize, blame, condemn, upbraid, denounce, scold, rail, recriminate, reproach, sound off, tongue-lash

FORMAL censure, fulminate, castigate, berate, lambast, expostulate, vituperate

✷ praise

inveigle v

cajole, persuade, beguile, coax, allure, lure, seduce, entrap, ensnare, entice, wile, decoy, manipulate, manoeuvre, lead on, wheedle

COLLOQ. bamboozle, con, sweet-talk

invent v

1 CONCEIVE, think up, design, discover, create, plan, originate, innovate, be the brainchild of, pioneer, formulate, frame, devise, contrive, improvise, coin, come up with, hit upon, dream up, fabricate, mint

2 invent an excuse

make up, concoct, cook up, trump up, imagine, dream up, manufacture, fable

TECHNICAL confabulate

FORMAL feign

SLANG swing the lead

invention n

1 her latest invention

design, creation, brainchild, innovation, discovery, development, idea, concept, construction, device, machine, system, contrivance, gadget

COLLOQ. baby

2 the invention of the steam engine

design, creation, discovery, development, innovation, contriving origination, coinage, contrivance

FORMAL excogitation

3 LIE, falsehood, falsification, untruth, deceit, fabrication, concoction, fake, forgery, fiction, fantasy, myth, figment, figment of your imagination

COLLOQ. tall story, fib

4 INVENTIVENESS, imagination, creativity, innovation, originality, ingenuity, resourcefulness, skill, artistry, talent, gift, inspiration, genius

OLD wit

✷ **3** truth

inventive adj

imaginative, creative, innovative, original, ingenious, resourceful, fertile, skilful, inspired, artistic, talented, gifted, clever

inventiveness n

creativity, imaginativeness, imagination, innovation, innovativeness, originality, resourcefulness, skill, enterprise, inspiration, power, gift, talent

inventor n

designer, discoverer, creator, originator, innovator, deviser, author, architect, developer, maker, producer, framer, scientist, engineer, father, mother

inventory n

list, listing checklist, record, register, catalogue, tally, file, account, description, schedule, roll, roster, equipment, supply, stock

inverse adj, n

♦ adj

inverted, upside down, transposed, reversed, opposite, other, contrary, counter, reciprocal, reverse, retrograde, converse, obverse

TECHNICAL antistrophic

♦ n

opposite, contrary, reverse, converse, obverse

COLLOQ. the other side of the coin

inversion n

opposite, reversal, reverse, converse, transposal, transposition, contrary

TECHNICAL hysteron-proteron

FORMAL antithesis, contrariety, contraposition

invert v

upturn, turn upside down, turn back to front, turn inside out, turn around, overturn, capsize, turn turtle, upset, transpose, reverse

✷ right

invertebrate

Invertebrates include:

SPONGES:	WORMS:	brine shrimp
calcareous	annelid worm	crayfish
glass	arrow worm	daphnia
horny	blood fluke	fairy shrimp
JELLYFISH, CORALS	bristle worm	fiddler crab
AND SEA	earthworm	fish louse
ANEMONES:	eelworm	goose barnacle
box jellyfish	flatworm	hermit crab
dead-men's	fluke	krill
fingers	hookworm	lobster
Portuguese	leech	mantis shrimp
man-of-war	liver fluke	mussel shrimp
sea cucumber	lugworm	pill bug
sea gooseberry	peanut worm	prawn
sea pansy	pinworm	sand hopper
sea wasp	ragworm	seed shrimp
Venus's girdle	ribbonworm	spider crab
	roundworm	spiny lobster
ECHINODERMS:	sea mouse	tadpole shrimp
brittle star	tapeworm	water flea
crown-of-thorns	threadworm	whale louse
feather star	velvet worm	woodlouse
sand dollar		
sea lily	**CRUSTACEANS:**	**ARTHROPODS:**
sea urchin	acorn barnacle	centipede
starfish	barnacle	millipede

See also **butterfly; insect; mollusc; moth.**

invest *v*
1 SPEND, lay out, put in, sink, subsidize, fund, tie up, lock up
2 *invest time/energy in something*
spend, put in, devote, dedicate, give, place, contribute
3 PROVIDE, supply, give, endow, grant, entrust, vest, imbue, endue, empower, authorize, sanction, mandate, create, dignify, clothe, gown, robe
OLD beglamour
FORMAL confer, bestow, enrobe
4 *invest a person in authority*
induct, install, inaugurate, ordain, admit, crown, swear in, belt
OLD frock

investigate *v*
inquire into, look into, consider, examine, study, inspect, scrutinize, analyse, research, go into, delve into, probe, explore, search, sift, comb, trawl, pry out, spy
COLLOQ. check out, suss out, give the once-over, see how the land lies, see which way the wind is blowing get to the bottom of, go over with a fine-tooth(ed) comb

investigation *n*
inquiry, inquest, hearing consideration, examination, study, research, survey, review, inspection, scrutiny, analysis, probe, exploration, dissection, search, sifting fact-finding mission/visit

investigative *adj*
fact-finding investigating inspecting research, researching analytical, exploratory
FORMAL heuristic, zetetic

investigator *n*
examiner, researcher, inquirer, reviewer, inspector, searcher, scrutineer, scrutinizer, analyst, analyser, explorer, prober, questioner, detective, private detective
COLLOQ. sleuth, private eye

investiture *n*
installation, induction, inauguration, investing investment, ordination, coronation, enthronement, swearing-in, admission, instatement

investment *n*
asset, speculation, venture, stake, risk, contribution, outlay, expenditure, capital, venture capital, cash, savings, wealth, resources, money, funds, finance, principal, property, stock, reserve, transaction

inveterate *adj*
chronic, habitual, hardened, diehard, dyed-in-the-wool, entrenched, confirmed, established, hard-core, obstinate, incorrigible, incurable, irreformable, inured, addicted, long-standing
F3 impermanent

invidious *adj*
awkward, difficult, undesirable, unpleasant, objectionable, hateful, obnoxious, offensive, slighting odious, repugnant, discriminating discriminatory
FORMAL
F3 desirable, pleasant

invigilate *v*
supervise, oversee, watch (over), look after, keep an eye on, inspect, superintend, direct, be in charge of, be responsible for, be in control of, monitor

invigilation *n*
supervision, surveillance, care, charge, superintendence, oversight, running direction, control, guidance, inspection

invigilator *n*
examiner, supervisor, overseer, inspector, superintendent, director, monitor

invigorate *v*
vitalize, energize, animate, enliven, liven up, quicken, strengthen, brace, motivate, stimulate, inspire, exhilarate, excite, rouse, renew, refresh, freshen, revitalize, rejuvenate
FORMAL fortify
COLLOQ. perk up, pep up, buck up, soup up, give a new lease of life to
F3 tire, weary, dishearten

invigorating *adj*
energizing stimulating refreshing animating exhilarating fresh, bracing uplifting rejuvenating quickening vivifying restorative, tonic, healthful, generous
FORMAL fortifying inspiriting salubrious
F3 tiring disheartening wearying

invincibility *n*
insuperability, impregnability, impenetrability, invulnerability, indestructibility, inviolability, unassailability, power, strength, force

invincible *adj*
unbeatable, unconquerable, insuperable, unsurmountable, undefeatable, unassailable, impregnable, impenetrable, invulnerable, indestructible, unyielding unshak(e)able, all-powerful
FORMAL indomitable
F3 beatable, surmountable

inviolability *n*
inalienability, inviolableness, inviolacy, invulnerability, sacrosanctness, sanctity, sacredness, holiness
F3 violability

inviolable *adj*
inalienable, unalterable, untouchable, sacred, sacrosanct, holy, hallowed
FORMAL intemerate
F3 violable, alienable

inviolate *adj*
entire, intact, complete, whole, undisturbed, unbroken, unhurt, undamaged, unharmed, uninjured, untouched, unpolluted, unprofaned, undefiled, unstained, unsullied, unspoiled, stainless, pure, sacred, virgin
FORMAL intemerate
F3 sullied

invisible *adj*
unseen, unseeable, out of sight, hidden, concealed, blind, disguised, unnoticed, unobserved, inconspicuous, indiscernible, imperceptible, imperceivable, undetectable,

indistinguishable, infinitesimal, microscopic, imaginary, non-existent, occulting dematerialized, evaporated
OLD viewless; (*Shakesp*) sightless
E3 visible

invitation *n*
request, call, summons, bidding petition, appeal, temptation, enticement, allurement, lure, bait, draw, attraction, encouragement, inducement, provocation, incitement, challenge, welcome, overture
FORMAL solicitation
COLLOQ. invite, come-on, come-hither, proposition

invite *v*
1 ASK, have round/over, entertain, call, summon, bid, press, will, petition, appeal, welcome, encourage, bring on, provoke, ask for, seek, look for
FORMAL request, solicit, request the pleasure of someone's company
2 ATTRACT, lead, draw, tempt, entice, allure, solicit, woo
COLLOQ. give the come-on to

inviting *adj*
welcoming appealing attractive, tempting seductive, enticing alluring pleasing pleasant, agreeable, delightful, captivating fascinating enchanting entrancing intriguing beguiling bewitching tantalizing engaging winning irresistible
E3 uninviting unappealing

invocation *n*
call, appeal, petition, prayer
TECHNICAL benediction, epiclesis
FORMAL request, supplication, solicitation, beseeching entreaty, conjuration, imploration

invoice *n*
account, bill, statement of account, charges, reckoning

invoke *v*
1 *invoke God for help*
call upon, appeal to, petition, implore, beg pray to
FORMAL request, supplicate, beseech, entreat, solicit, imprecate, conjure
2 *invoke a law*
turn to, resort to, have recourse to, make use of, cite, refer to

involuntary *adj*
1 SPONTANEOUS, unconscious, automatic, mechanical, reflex, instinctive, conditioned, impulsive, unthinking blind, uncontrolled, unintentional
COLLOQ. knee-jerk
2 FORCED, compulsory, obligatory, compelled, coerced, reluctant, unwilling against your wishes
FORMAL mandatory
E3 1 deliberate, intentional

involve *v*
1 REQUIRE, mean, assume, presuppose, imply, entail, necessitate, include, incorporate, encompass, cover, take in, affect, concern, cost
FORMAL denote, embrace, comprehend, connote
2 IMPLICATE, incriminate, draw in, let yourself in for, mix up, embroil, associate, connect, include, count in, cause to take part, compromise, embarrass, entangle, walk into; *Scot* wind someone a bonny pirn
OLD wrap
FORMAL inculpate
COLLOQ. mess with/in
3 ENGAGE, interest, occupy, absorb, engross, immerse, preoccupy, hold, grip, rivet, concern, commit
COLLOQ. dip into
E3 1 exclude

SYNONYM NUANCES

sense 1
Require suggests that the involvement of something is necessary: *a level of precision was required*, while **mean** and **entail** would be more appropriate for something resultant: *taking complete power meant silencing more*

---

liberal voices; the changes in housing policy entailed steep rent rises. Both **assume** and **presuppose** are suggestive of taking certain things for granted: *this plan presupposes public support*, unlike **imply** which suggests a resultant insinuation.

Incorporate, like **include** and **take in**, suggests being a part of, usually by design: *a demanding schedule which took in several matches and the World Cup; the provisions were incorporated into the act*. **Cover** and **encompass** also suggest total inclusion: *the extensive and diverse behaviour encompassed by the term 'crime'*.

The word **affect** would be appropriate to refer to influencing or touching on: *moving house affects many areas of your life*. You might use **concern** to suggest personal involvement: *much of my work has been concerned with bereavement counselling; these problems do not concern you*. **Cost** is inherently negative in that it suggests loss is involved: *his addiction to work cost him his marriage*.

involved *adj*
1 CONCERNED, associated, taking part, implicated, incriminated, mixed up, participating complicit
OLD (*Shakesp*) plighted
FORMAL inculpated
COLLOQ. in on
2 OCCUPIED, engaged, interested, absorbed, engrossed, preoccupied, immersed, caught up, held, gripped, riveted
3 *an involved explanation*
complicated, complex, intricate, difficult, elaborate, tangled, jumbled, knotty, tortuous, confusing confused
FORMAL convoluted
E3 1 uninvolved **3** simple

involvement *n*
concern, interest, responsibility, association, connection, participation, contribution, action, share, part, implication, entanglement, attachment

invulnerability *n*
safety, security, strength, unassailability, impenetrability, invincibility, impregnability, inviolability, insusceptibility
E3 vulnerability

invulnerable *adj*
safe, secure, unassailable, impenetrable, impervious, invincible, indestructible
E3 vulnerable

inward *adj*
turned-in, incoming entering inside, interior, internal, inner, innermost, inmost, hidden, intrinsic, personal, private, intimate, secret, confidential, heartfelt, homefelt, infelt
TECHNICAL involute
FORMAL incurrent, introrse
E3 outward, external

inwardly *adv*
inside, to yourself, within, at heart, in your heart of hearts, deep down, deep inside you, privately, secretly
OLD inly
E3 externally, outwardly

inwards *adv*
inside, within, inward, inwardly, indoors, towards the interior

iota *n*
scrap, bit, mite, jot, whit, speck, trace, hint, grain, morsel, fraction, particle, atom
COLLOQ. tad

irascibility *n*
snappishness, bad temper, cantankerousness, irritability, irritation, petulance, impatience, ill-temper, crossness, shortness, testiness, touchiness, fieriness
COLLOQ. crabbiness, edginess
E3 placidness

irascible *adj*
quick-tempered, short-tempered, bad-tempered, ill-natured, ill-tempered, hot-tempered, cantankerous, petulant, irritable, prickly, testy, touchy, choleric, cross, hasty
FORMAL querulous, iracund, iracundulous
COLLOQ. crabbed, crabby, narky, ratty
Ⅎ placid

irate *adj*
annoyed, irritated, indignant, up in arms, angry, enraged, furious, infuriated, incensed, worked up, fuming raging ranting livid, exasperated, vexed
COLLOQ. mad, hopping mad, hot under the collar, steamed up, up in arms
SLANG pissed off
Ⅎ calm, composed

irately *adv*
angrily, crossly, indignantly, furiously, reproachfully, acrimoniously, resentfully, bitterly
COLLOQ. in a huff

ire *n*
anger, wrath, exasperation, annoyance, fury, rage, indignation, passion, displeasure, choler
Ⅎ calmness

iridescent *adj*
shimmering sparkling multicoloured, rainbow, rainbow-coloured, rainbow-like, prismatic, dazzling glittering shot, pearly, polychromatic
FORMAL opalescent, variegated

irk *v*
annoy, anger, exasperate, incense, infuriate, irritate, provoke, put out, ruffle, get, get to, vex, weary, nettle, distress, gall, disgust, rile
COLLOQ. aggravate, wind up, get at, bug drive mad, drive crazy, drive bananas, drive up the wall, drive round the bend/twist, miff, needle, make someone's blood boil, make someone see red, rattle someone's cage, ruffle someone's feathers, raise someone's dander, make someone's hackles rise, make sparks fly, get under someone's skin, get up someone's nose, get on someone's wick
SLANG piss someone off
Ⅎ please

irksome *adj*
annoying irritating infuriating exasperating vexing vexatious, wearisome, bothersome, burdensome, disagreeable, tiresome, troublesome, trying tedious, boring
COLLOQ. aggravating confounded, infernal
Ⅎ pleasing

iron *n, adj, v*
Related adjectives: ferrous, ferreous
♦ *adj*
rigid, inflexible, adamant, determined, hard, steely, tough, strong firm, uncompromising
Ⅎ pliable, weak
♦ *v*
press, smooth, flatten
■ **iron out**
resolve, settle, sort out, straighten out, clear up, put right, reconcile, harmonize, deal with, get rid of, eradicate, eliminate

> **PROVERBS**
> Strike while the iron is hot

ironic, ironical *adj*
sarcastic, sardonic, scornful, contemptuous, derisive, sneering scoffing ridiculing ridiculous, mocking satirical, wry, paradoxical
COLLOQ. rich

irons *n*
chains, bonds, fetters, shackles, trammels, manacles

irony *n*
sarcasm, mockery, ridicule, scorn, satire, paradox, contrariness
TECHNICAL asteism, antiphrasis, enantiosis
FORMAL incongruity
COLLOQ. sting in the tail

irradiate *v*
brighten, enlighten, light up, lighten, illume, illuminate, illumine, expose, radiate, shine on

irrational *adj*
unreasonable, unreasoning unsound, illogical, inconsistent, invalid, groundless, implausible, arbitrary, ridiculous, absurd, crazy, wild, foolish, silly, senseless, beastlike, brute, brutish, nonsensical, unwise, paranoid, phobic, beside yourself, taken leave of your senses
Ⅎ rational, reasonable

irrationality *n*
unreasonableness, unreason, unsoundness, illogicality, groundlessness, absurdity, ridiculousness, senselessness, preposterousness, madness, lunacy, insanity
Ⅎ rationality

irreconcilable *adj*
incompatible, opposed, contrary, opposite, at odds, conflicting clashing contradictory, inconsistent, uncompromising hardline, inflexible, implacable, inexorable
FORMAL incongruous, intransigent
Ⅎ reconcilable

irrecoverable *adj*
irretrievable, lost, unrecoverable, unsavable, irredeemable, irreclaimable, irremediable, irreparable, unsalvageable
Ⅎ recoverable

irredeemable *adj*
incurable, incorrigible, irreparable, irrevocable, irretrievable, beyond hope, past hope

irrefutable *adj*
undeniable, incontrovertible, indisputable, incontestable, unquestionable, beyond doubt/question, indubitable, unanswerable, certain, sure, definite, positive, decisive

irregular *adj, n*
♦ *adj*
1 ROUGH, bumpy, lumpy, uneven, pitted, crooked, ragged, jagged, asymmetric, lopsided
2 VARIABLE, fluctuating wavering unsteady, uneven, shaky, erratic, fitful, intermittent, sporadic, spasmodic, occasional, random, haphazard, disorganized, fragmentary, disorderly, unmethodical, unsystematic, inconsistent
3 ABNORMAL, unconventional, unorthodox, unofficial, improper, unusual, exceptional, anomalous, out of order, aberrant, extraordinary, freak, odd, strange, peculiar
4 DISHONEST, lawless, against the law/rules, deceitful, fraudulent, false, cheating unprincipled, immoderate, indecent, improper, unscrupulous, corrupt, disreputable, dishonourable, devious
FORMAL perfidious, mendacious, duplicitous
COLLOQ. crooked, shady, bent, shifty, fishy, iffy
Ⅎ 1 smooth, level, uniform **2** regular **3** conventional **4** honest
♦ *n*
guerrilla, freedom fighter, terrorist, resistance fighter, partisan, sniper, guerrillero, *franc-tireur*, haiduk, bushwhacker, *maquisard*

irregularity *n*
1 ROUGHNESS, bumpiness, unevenness, raggedness, jaggedness, crookedness, asymmetry, lopsidedness, lumpiness
2 VARIABILITY, fluctuation, wavering fitfulness, intermittence, spasm, occasionalness, randomness, haphazardness, disorderliness, unpunctuality, inconsistency, unsteadiness, uncertainty, inconstancy, disorganization, patchiness

3 ABNORMALITY, unconventionality, unusualness, unorthodoxy, anomaly, deviation, breach, aberration, oddity, peculiarity, eccentricity, freak
FORMAL singularity
4 DISHONESTY, lawlessness, deceit, fraudulence, fraud, cheating malpractice, impropriety, misconduct, falsehood, falsity, criminality, insincerity, untruthfulness, treachery, double-dealing corruption, unscrupulousness, trickery, chicanery, sharp practice
FORMAL duplicity, improbity, perfidy
COLLOQ. crookedness, shadiness, dirty trick
E3 1 smoothness, levelness **2** regularity **3** conventionality

irregularly adv
occasionally, now and again, off and on, unevenly, spasmodically, haphazardly, intermittently, jerkily, unmethodically, anyhow, disconnectedly, eccentrically, erratically, fitfully, by/in fits and starts
E3 regularly

irrelevance n
inappropriateness, inaptness, unimportance, unrelatedness, inconsequence, irrelevancy, inapplicability, digression, tangent
FORMAL inappositeness, extraneousness, inconsequence
COLLOQ. red herring
E3 relevance, bearing

irrelevant adj
immaterial, beside/off the point, inapplicable, inappropriate, inapt, unimportant, out of place, inept, having no bearing unrelated, unconnected, peripheral, tangential, beside the mark/question
FORMAL inapposite, extraneous, inconsequent, ungermane, irrelative
COLLOQ. neither here nor there, not coming into it, making no difference, not matter, going off at a tangent
E3 relevant

irreligious adj
atheistic, unbelieving ungodly, unreligious, godless, undevout, unholy, unrighteous, agnostic, sceptical, heathenish, pagan, heathen, heretical, sacrilegious, iconoclastic, impious, irreverent, blasphemous, free-thinking profane, rationalistic, sinful, wicked
FORMAL nullifidian
E3 pious, religious

SYNONYM NUANCES

Atheistic is a fairly straightforward synonym for not believing in a god, while **unbelieving** is perhaps more suggestive of not being convinced by a particular religion: *although his family was Catholic, he remained unbelieving*. **Ungodly** and **godless** are more judgemental, suggesting a lack of moral guidance and virtue: *her ungodly want of duty*; *their godless pleasures*, while the more old-fashioned **unrighteous** conveys this idea more explicitly. **Unholy** can literally suggest a lack of sanctity: *unholy ground*, but is used more generally to imply something is unconscionable: *an unholy alliance*.

Agnostic and **sceptical** are uncritical terms relating to a tendency not to believe in unseen phenomena, while **rationalistic** can be applied to those who ascribe a practical explanation to any apparent miraculous phenomena. **Free-thinking**, on the other hand, would be used of someone who rejects religious authority, and the tone may depend on the viewpoint of the speaker.

The terms **pagan**, **heathen** and **heathenish**, although literally meaning irreligious, can all be implicative of being primitive or uncultured: *marauding heathen tribes*. **Heretical**, which would appropriately refer to holding a belief which is at odds with an authorized religion, also tends to have negative connotations.

Impious, **irreverent** and **blasphemous** make the inherent accusation of a lack of, or even contempt for, religious veneration: *I had no wish to indulge in such blasphemous, heretical talk*. Similarly, **sacrilegious**

implies a display of extreme disrespect for anything holy. **Iconoclastic** might be used to describe an attack on established beliefs: *the book may be iconoclastic but it is not just a parody of faith*. **Profane**, although literally meaning secular: *the sacred and the profane*, can also contain the idea of being contemptuous: *profane songs*.

---

irremediable adj
irreparable, irretrievable, irrecoverable, irreversible, remediless, irredeemable, incurable, inoperable, incorrigible, terminal, unmedicinable, deadly, fatal, final, hopeless, mortal
E3 remediable

irremovable adj
durable, immovable, indestructible, ineradicable, ingrained, inoperable, fast, fixed, set, stuck, permanent, persistent, rooted, obstinate
FORMAL obdurate
E3 removable

irreparable adj
irreversible, irreclaimable, irrecoverable, irremediable, irretrievable, incurable, unrepairable
E3 recoverable, remediable

irreplaceable adj
indispensable, essential, vital, unique, priceless, precious, peerless, matchless, unmatched, special
E3 replaceable

irrepressible adj
lively, energetic, uninhibited, buoyant, effervescent, animated, vivacious, resilient, boisterous, uncontrollable, unrestrainable, ungovernable, unstoppable, insuppressible, uncontainable
FORMAL ebullient
COLLOQ. bubbly

irreproachable adj
irreprehensible, blameless, unblamable, innocent, beyond reproach, unimpeachable, faultless, guiltless, flawless, impeccable, perfect, unblemished, immaculate, stainless, spotless, sinless, pure
E3 blameworthy; *formal* culpable

irresistible adj
1 *irresistible desire*
overwhelming overpowering forceful, unavoidable, inevitable, inescapable, inexorable, unpreventable, uncontrollable, irrepressible, potent, compelling imperative, pressing urgent
OLD (*Shakesp*) opposeless
2 *irresistible beauty*
tempting enticing alluring captivating tantalizing seductive, ravishing enchanting charming fascinating
E3 1 resistible, avoidable **2** unattractive, repulsive

irresolute adj
indecisive, hesitating hesitant, unsure, uncertain, doubtful, dubious, ambivalent, wavering fluctuating shifting dithering variable, weak, faint-hearted, fickle, undecided, unsettled, undetermined, unstable, unsteady, half-hearted, tentative
FORMAL vacillating
COLLOQ. shilly-shallying pussyfooting in two minds, (sitting) on the fence
E3 resolute, decisive

irrespective
■ **irrespective of**
regardless of, disregarding no matter, without considering ignoring not affecting however, whatever, whichever, whoever, never mind
FORMAL notwithstanding

irresponsible adj
unreliable, untrustworthy, careless, negligent, thoughtless, unwise, heedless, ill-considered, rash,

reckless, wild, carefree, flighty, fly-by-night, erratic, scatterbrained, light-hearted, immature
FORMAL injudicious
F3 responsible, dependable, cautious

> **QUOTATIONS**
> Perhaps it is better to be irresponsible and right than to be responsible and wrong
> SIR WINSTON CHURCHILL

irretrievable *adj*
irreparable, irrecoverable, irreversible, irredeemable, irremediable, unrecoverable, unrecallable, lost, hopeless, unsalvageable, damned
FORMAL irrevocable
F3 recoverable, reversible

irretrievably *adv*
irreparably, irrecoverably, irreversibly, irredeemably, hopelessly
FORMAL irrevocably

irreverence *n*
1 IMPIETY, godlessness, ungodliness, irreligion, heresy, profanity, sacrilege, blasphemy
2 DISRESPECT, disrespectfulness, discourtesy, rudeness, impoliteness, insolence, impudence, impertinence, mockery, flippancy, levity
COLLOQ. sauce, cheek, cheekiness
F3 **1, 2** reverence

irreverent *adj*
1 IMPIOUS, godless, ungodly, irreligious, heretical, profane, sacrilegious, blasphemous
OLD unreverend
2 DISRESPECTFUL, discourteous, rude, impolite, impudent, impertinent, insolent, mocking flippant
COLLOQ. cheeky, saucy
F3 **1** reverent **2** respectful, deferential

irreversible *adj*
irrevocable, unalterable, final, permanent, lasting irreparable, irremediable, irretrievable, incurable, unrectifiable, hopeless
F3 reversible, remediable, curable

irrevocable *adj*
unalterable, unchangeable, changeless, invariable, final, fixed, settled, predetermined, irreversible, irretrievable
FORMAL immutable
F3 alterable, flexible, reversible

irrevocably *adv*
irreparably, insuperably, unavoidably, inevitably, inescapably, hopelessly

irrigate *v*
water, flood, inundate, wet, soak, deluge, moisten, dampen, spray, sprinkle

irritability *n*
crossness, bad temper, ill-temper, impatience, grumpiness, prickliness, touchiness, fretfulness, edge, edginess, hypersensitivity, testiness, tetchiness, irascibility, peevishness, petulance, fractiousness
COLLOQ. rattiness, crabbiness, stroppiness
F3 cheerfulness, complacence, good humour, bonhomie

irritable *adj*
cross, bad-tempered, ill-tempered, quick-tempered, grumpy, crusty, cantankerous, testy, tetchy, short-tempered, hot-blooded, snappish, snappy, short, impatient, touchy, thin-skinned, hypersensitive, prickly, peevish, fretful, fractious, irascible, out of temper, splenetic, sore, fiery, peppery, hasty, nettlesome, spiky, on edge; *Scot* capernoity; *N Am* scratchy
OLD gustful, liverish, livery
COLLOQ. edgy, crotchety, crabby, arsey, ratty, stroppy, shirty, feisty, humpy, narky, riley; *Can* chippy

SLANG snarky; *N Am* peckish
F3 good-tempered, cheerful

irritant *n*
annoyance, nuisance, trouble, bother, menace, provocation, vexation, goad
COLLOQ. pain, thorn in the flesh
F3 pleasure, sweetness

irritate *v*
1 ANNOY, bother, harass, rouse, provoke, rile, irk, vex, goad, nettle, anger, enrage, infuriate, incense, exasperate, put out, grate, jar
COLLOQ. aggravate, wind up, get at, bug drive mad, drive crazy, drive bananas, drive up the wall, drive round the bend/twist, miff, needle, make someone's blood boil, make someone see red, rattle someone's cage, ruffle someone's feathers, raise someone's dander, make someone's hackles rise, make sparks fly, get up someone's skin, get up someone's nose, get on someone's wick
SLANG piss someone off
See Synonym nuances panel at **annoy**.
2 INFLAME, chafe, rub, fret, hurt, tickle, itch
F3 **1** please, gratify

irritated *adj*
annoyed, bothered, angry, cross, exasperated, irked, irritable, nettled, vexed, ruffled, roused, riled, impatient, uptight, harassed, flustered, discomposed, displeased, piqued
FORMAL exacerbated
COLLOQ. aggravated, ratty, edgy, mad, hopping mad, raving mad, seeing red, in a lather, disgruntled, up in arms, hot under the collar, stroppy, in a strop, choked, fit to be tied, on the warpath, in a paddy; *N Am* ticked off; *Aust* spewy, ropable; *Aust & NZ* crooked
SLANG pissed off; *N Am* pissed
F3 composed, gratified, pleased

irritating *adj*
1 ANNOYING, infuriating maddening troublesome, bothersome, irksome, tiresome, grating worrisome, vexatious, vexing disturbing upsetting nagging displeasing galling provoking thorny, trying
COLLOQ. aggravating pesky, confounded, infernal
2 ABRASIVE, rubbing chafing sore, ticklish, itchy
F3 **1** pleasant, pleasing

irritation *n*
1 *express your irritation*
displeasure, dissatisfaction, annoyance, aggravation, provocation, anger, vexation, pique, indignation, fury, exasperation, irritability, crossness, testiness, snappiness, impatience
COLLOQ. aggravation
2 NUISANCE, annoyance, disturbance, bother, trouble, pest
COLLOQ. pain, pain in the neck, thorn in the flesh, drag bind
F3 pleasure, satisfaction, delight

island *n*
isle, islet, atoll, archipelago, eyot, holm, cay, key, skerry; *Scot & Irish* inch
Related adjective: insular

isolate *v*
set apart, seclude, keep apart, segregate, quarantine, insulate, abstract, cut off, strand, maroon, detach, remove, disconnect, separate, divorce, alienate, shut out/away, ostracize, exclude, marginalize
FORMAL island, sequester, enisle
COLLOQ. cold-shoulder, send to Coventry
F3 assimilate, incorporate, integrate

isolated *adj*
1 REMOTE, out-of-the-way, outlying god-forsaken, deserted, unfrequented, secluded, detached, cut off, lonely, solitary, alone, separated, segregated, apart, single
COLLOQ. off the beaten track, in the sticks

2 *an isolated occurrence*

unique, special, exceptional, atypical, untypical, solitary, single, unusual, uncommon, freak, abnormal, anomalous, unrelated

E3 1 populous, accessible **2** typical, common

isolation *n*

quarantine, solitude, solitariness, loneliness, aloneness, remoteness, seclusion, retirement, withdrawal, exile, segregation, insulation, separation, separateness, detachment, disconnection, dissociation, alienation, marginalization, abstraction

FORMAL sequestration

E3 contact

issue *n, v*

♦ *n*

1 MATTER, affair, concern, problem, point, subject, topic, question, debate, argument, dispute, controversy

2 PUBLICATION, release, distribution, supply, supplying delivery, circulation, broadcast, announcement

FORMAL promulgation, dissemination

3 *last week's issue*

copy, number, instalment, edition, impression, version, printing

4 RESULT, consequence, upshot, outcome, conclusion, effect, finale

COLLOQ. pay-off

5 OFFSPRING, descendants, children, family, progeny, heirs, successors, seed, young

FORMAL scions

6 OUTFLOW, discharge, rush, jet, spurt, gush, emission

FORMAL effusion, effluence

♦ *v*

1 PUBLISH, announce, broadcast, proclaim, spread, put out, send out, release, deliver

FORMAL promulgate, disseminate

2 SUPPLY, provide, give out, distribute, equip, fit out/up, rig out, kit out, deal out

3 EMERGE, emanate, come, proceed, burst forth, gush, flow, exude, ooze, seep

4 RESULT, come, follow, originate, stem, spring rise, develop, ensue

■ **at issue**

being discussed, under discussion, in question, being debated

■ **take issue**

disagree, argue, challenge, quarrel, fight, dispute, contest, protest, be at odds with, object, take exception, call into question

itch *v, n*

♦ *v*

1 TICKLE, irritate, tingle, prickle, crawl; *dialect* yuke

2 *be itching to do something*

die, long burn, pine, crave, hanker, yearn, ache

♦ *n*

1 ITCHINESS, tickle, irritation, prickling tingling;
dialect yuke

TECHNICAL pruritis

OLD TECHNICAL psora

Related adjective: pruritic

2 EAGERNESS, keenness, desire, ache, hunger, thirst, longing yearning hankering craving burning passion

FORMAL cacoethes

itching *adj*

dying longing burning hankering aching eager, greedy, impatient, inquisitive, avid, prurient, raring

item *n*

1 OBJECT, article, thing piece, component, ingredient, element, factor, point, detail, particular, aspect, feature, consideration, matter, circumstance, issue

2 *an item in the local paper*

article, piece, feature, report, story, account, notice, entry, paragraph, bulletin

itemize *v*

list, record, catalogue, specify, detail, document, instance, particularize, count, mention, overname, number, enumerate, tabulate, make an inventory

itinerant *adj, n*

♦ *adj*

travelling peripatetic, running roving roaming wandering strolling journeying wayfaring drifting rambling nomadic, migratory, vagrant, rootless, unsettled, vagabond

E3 stationary, settled

♦ *n*

traveller, Gypsy, Romany, Romani, Roma, itinerary, peripatetic, wanderer, roamer, rover, rambler, hawker, huckster, nomad, tzigany, Zigeuner, Zincalo, Zingaro, Bohemian, tinker, diddicoy, faw, gitano, roadman, vagrant, chapman, minstrel, muffin man, preacher, evangelist, revivalist; *Scot* caird; *N Am* hobo

OLD strolling player, piepowder, Scotch draper

COLLOQ. *N Am* gandy dancer

itinerary *n*

route, course, journey, tour, way, circuit, plan, arrangements, programme, schedule, timetable

The Word Lover's Gallimaufry

At Chambers we love words. We enjoy browsing, discovering, collecting and using them as much as people who use our thesaurus do. With this in mind, we have brought together lists of some of the many words that we have come across and recorded over many decades. These range from the highly practical to the downright quirky. From established words that fulfil a need to newer coinages that fulfil a void, these words will usually be met with a nod of recognition, sometimes with a shake of the head, but often, we hope, with a smile.

The Word Lover's Gallimaufry

15 words to sound like a foodie

Contemporary cuisine has a language of its own. Here are some terms to help you hold your own in conversations with today's foodies.

aromatic accompaniment an aromatic vapour captured from an ingredient and trapped in a container, used when serving food

dirt tasting tasting soil for its quality and judging how it might affect the taste of foods that grow in it

emulsion a combination of ingredients that would not normally mix together, like oil and vinegar

flavour encapsulation any technique that makes the flavour of a food more distinct and helps differentiate it from other flavours with which it might be combined

foam a natural flavour combined with a gelling agent so it can be released from a canister as a foam

foodpairing combining foods based on their key flavours, which may be similar or dissimilar

gel any flavoured accompaniment presented in the form of a gel, for example balsamic vinegar or liquorice

ice cream any flavoured accompaniment presented in the form of ice cream, for example mustard or Parmesan

molecular gastronomy food preparation using methods that are scientifically justified to enhance flavour

nitro-poaching poaching a flavoured foam in liquid nitrogen so it hardens on the outside

shocking plunging blanched vegetables into iced water to prevent them cooking further, thus retaining colour and texture

slow food a movement encouraging local sourcing and traditional cooking of food

sous vide a method of cooking in which food is sealed in plastic bags and immersed in water at a lower than normal cooking temperature for a long time, sometimes facetiously referred to as 'boil-in-the-bag'

spherification forming and presenting foods in the form of small balls, as caviar

supreming removing the peel and membrane from citrus fruit so it can be served in clean segments

32 words to sound like an oenophile

An oenophile is someone with a love and knowledge of wines. These words will help you keep company with them.

aroma the smells associated with a variety of grape

attack the first impression of a wine on the palate

balance how well the various flavours, aromas, etc combine, without one overpowering the other (also **harmony**)

blend a wine made from more than one variety of grape

body the relative fullness of a wine's flavour on the palate

bouquet the smells developed by a wine after it has been bottled

breed denotes a wine from the best varieties of grape

character the combination of the various qualities of a wine

complexity how many flavours and aromas are perceptible

depth the relative concentration of flavours

evolution the wine's taste as it develops on the palate

finesse elegance and sophistication in a wine

finish the flavour that remains in the mouth after tasting (also **aftertaste**)

legs streaks of wine that form on the side of a glass, taken as an indicator of relative alcohol content (also **tears**)

length how long a wine stays in the mouth after tasting

maderization the heating and oxidation of a wine, resulting in a darker colour

mouthfeel the physical impression of a wine on the palate (also **texture**)

nose the overall odour of a wine, including aroma and bouquet

oxidation the deterioration of wine that has come into contact with air

palate the taste of a wine

prickle a slightly sparkling quality (also **spritz**)

residual sugar sugar that has not been converted to alcohol, determining the relative sweetness of a wine

structure the relative proportions of alcohol, tannins, acid and sugar in a wine

tannin a bitter substance derived from vegetable matter which gives a distinctive astringent quality to a wine

varietal a wine made from a single variety of grape

vintage the year the grapes used in wine were harvested

weight the relative heaviness of a wine on the palate

In addition, there are a multitude of words you can use to describe the wine you taste:

acetic	complex	grapefruit
acidic or **tart**	confected	grapey
aggressive	corked	grassy
angular	creamy	green
appley	crisp	grip
apricot	delicate	hard
astringent or **puckery**	developed	harsh
austere	dry	hay
backbone	dull	hazy
backward	dumb	heady
baked or **cooked**	earthy	hearty
berry	elegant	herbaceous or **herby**
big	eucalyptus	hollow
bitter	farmyard or **barnyard**	honey
blackberry	fat	hot
black cherry	fig	inky
blackcurrant or **cassis**	firm	intense
brawny or **powerful**	flabby	jammy
briary	flat	juicy
brilliant	fleshy	leafy
buttery	flinty	lean
caramel	flowery or **floral**	leather
cardboard	forward	leesy
cedar or **cigar box**	foxy	lemony
chewy	fragrant	light or **light-bodied**
chocolate	fresh	lingering
citrus	fruitcake	liquorice
clean	fruity	lively
closed	full-bodied	lush
cloudy	gamey	matchstick
cloying	geranium	mature
coarse	gooseberry	meaty

medicinal	raisiny	sweet
medium-bodied	raspberry	tarry or tarlike
mellow	raw	thin
melon	refined	tight
mineral	rich	toasty
minty	ripe	tobacco
musk	robust	tropical fruit
musty	rough or rustic	truffles
nose	round	unctuous
nutty	sharp	underripe
oaky	short	vanilla
oily	silky	vegetal
oxidized	simple	velvety
peach	smoky	vinegary
pear	smooth	violet
peppery	soft	volatile
perfumed	sour	walnut
petrolly	spicy	warm
pineapple	stalky or stemmy	watery
plummy	steely	well-balanced
plump	stony	woody
ponderous	sturdy	yeasty
pruney	stylish	zesty
racy	supple	

33 words to understand cocktail culture

Here are some essential terms for aspiring mixologists.

back a non-alcoholic drink served with an alcoholic drink

box to mix a drink by pouring ingredients once in and out of a shaker

build to pour ingredients into a glass one at a time

call drink a drink with a named brand of beverage, for example *Bacardi® and Coke®*

chaser a drink of a complementary or contrasting type that is drunk immediately after another

dirty with olive juice, making a drink look cloudy

dry with less vermouth

dry shake to mix a drink by first shaking it without ice, then with ice

flair bartending preparing and serving drinks in entertaining ways, for example by juggling bottles (sometimes shortened to **flairtending**; also called **extreme bartending**)

float to pour some liquid on top of a drink which should then appear as a layer

lace to pour a final ingredient on top of a drink

mixology the art of mixing drinks

molecular mixology cocktail preparation using methods that are scientifically justified to enhance them

muddle to combine ingredients in the bottom of a glass using a pestle-like instrument called a muddler (also **mash**)

neat without ice or a mixer added

on the rocks with ice

part a measure of beverage that is roughly equal to one of a different beverage

perfect with equal parts dry and sweet vermouth

pony a small measure, smaller than a jigger

roll to mix a drink by pouring ingredients from one glass into another and back again

shake to mix a drink by pouring the ingredients in a shaker and shaking vigorously

shooter a short drink designed to be drunk in one gulp

shot a measure of around 1.5 fluid ounces of a beverage (also **jigger**)

stir to mix a drink by stirring with a long spoon

straight up shaken with ice then strained to remove the ice

supercall a more aged, strong, expensive, etc version of a branded alcoholic drink

swizzle to mix a drink by inserting a swizzle stick and rotating it quickly between the palms

well drink a drink without a named brand of beverage, for example *gin and tonic*

wet with extra vermouth

50 words to understand café culture

Here are some essential terms for aspiring baristas.

Americano espresso with hot water added

babycino a cup of frothed milk (also called **steamer**, **fluffy**)

barista a person who has been specially trained to make coffee in a coffee shop

breve made with semi-skimmed milk or cream rather than full-fat milk

chai latte spiced tea, rather than coffee, blended with hot milk

cheapuccino a cheap coffee drink, such as from a vending machine

crema brown froth on top of espresso

dead eye three shots of espresso in a regular coffee (sometimes called **green eye**)

demitasse a small cup for serving espresso

doppio an espresso comprising two shots

dose the amount of coffee per cup

double (containing) a double shot of espresso

dry (of a cappuccino) with frothed milk but no hot milk

flat white one or two espresso shots with a layer of frothed milk

frappé an instant coffee drink mixed to form a froth and with ice added

half-and-half made up of one part caffeinated coffee and one part decaffeinated coffee (also **half-caf**, **split shot**)

harmless with no caffeine

latte espresso topped up with steamed milk

latte art pouring steamed milk on top of espresso in a way that creates an image in the froth

lazy eye a shot of espresso in a decaffeinated coffee

long black hot water with espresso added

lungo an espresso pulled so there is more fluid in the drink (also **pulled long**)

macchiato espresso 'marked' with a drop of milk

macrofoam steamed milk in a dry, frothy form for making cappuccinos

microfoam steamed milk in a creamy form for making espresso drinks

misto made with half coffee and half steamed milk

no-fun made with decaffeinated coffee

perked percolated

pull to create (an espresso drink) by passing water through espresso grounds

quad an espresso comprising four shots

red eye one or two shots of espresso in a regular coffee (variously called **black eye**, **Canadiano**, **hammerhead**, **shot in the dark**)

ristretto an espresso pulled so there is less fluid in the drink (also **pulled short**)

skinny made with skimmed milk

solo (containing) two shots of espresso
soy latte latte made with soy milk
tamp to press ground coffee into a filter basket
wet (of a cappuccino) with hot milk and frothed milk
with legs prepared in a disposable cup to take away (same as **to go**)

10 words to understand celebrity culture

Our obsession with celebrities has given rise to a whole new area of vocabulary as we pry into every detail of the looks, loves and lives of our favourite – and not so favourite – celebrities.

bromance a close, but not romantic or sexual, relationship between two men: *One of the first celebrity bromances was Matt Damon and Ben Affleck.*
celeblog a blog written by a celebrity or a blog focusing on a particular celebrity: *a Justin Bieber celeblog*
celebutante a young woman who achieves celebrity as a result of her inherited wealth and lifestyle: *that famed celebutante, Paris Hilton*
celesbian a celebrity who is, or is reputed to be, a lesbian: *Lindsay Lohan talked openly about her celesbian affair with DJ Samantha Ronson.*
fauxmance a pretended romantic relationship between two celebrities used to generate media interest: *Their off-screen romance is just a publicity stunt – it's a fauxmance.*
pap to photograph (a famous person) as a paparazzo: *As she waited outside the hotel, she was papped by a newspaper photographer.*
sex tape a recording of a celebrity involved in sexual activity: *I think some celebrities deliberately release sex tapes just to get attention.*
sleb a celebrity: *another sleb demanding an injunction over an alleged affair*
super-injunction an injunction which prevents the media not only from revealing the details of a story, but also from revealing the existence of the injunction: *Another well-known footballer has taken out a super-injunction in the High Court.*
Z-list the least important or famous group of (would-be) celebrities: *The channel was accused of hiring only Z-list celebrities for its latest quiz show.*

12 words to sound like a body fascist

It may be our obsession with celebrities and their looks that make us intolerant of – or should that be gleeful about? – any physical imperfection or wardrobe malfunction. Many informal terms have been coined for the problems we've identified in others.

bingo wings flaps of loose skin that hang down from the upper arms (known in the US as **bat wings**)
cankles shapeless ankles in which the calves seem to join straight to the feet
celebulite cellulite spotted on a celebrity
chub rub the chafing of plump inner thighs caused by friction when walking
love handles a deposit of fat on either side of the back just below the waist
menopot a layer of fat around a woman's belly that becomes more pronounced during and after the menopause
muffin top a roll of fatty flesh that spills out over the top of a pair of low-cut trousers
saddlebags excess fat on the hips and outer thighs

trout pout excessively swollen lips resulting from an enhancement procedure
whale tail the top part of a thong visible above the back of a low-cut pair of trousers
wobbly bits any areas of excess fat

38 ways to tell someone to go away

There are many slang and informal ways to tell someone to go away.

away!
away with you!
beat it!
be off!
bugger off!
buzz off!
choof off ! (Australian)
clear off!
clear out!
do one!
get knotted!
get lost!
get out!
get out of here!

get the hell out of here!
go and jump in the lake!
go fly a kite!
go to hell!
jog on!
naff off!
never darken my door
  again!
off with you!
off you go!
on your way!
out of my sight!
push off!
rack off ! (Australian)

run along!
scarper!
scat!
scram!
shoo!
shove off!
sling your hook!
sod off!
take a hike!
take a running jump!
vamoose! (chiefly US)

39 words to influence and persuade

Words are the most effective tool we have to influence and persuade people into sharing our point of view (or, more cynically, into doing what we would like them to!). Here are the techniques you can use, and some words to help you to use them.

Use personal pronouns, especially the inclusive pronouns **we** and **us**:
*It is the government's priority to sort out **our** nation's finances.*

Use words that elicit an emotional response, for example *the terrible economic mess we inherited*
astonishing
incredible
offensive
outrageous
terrible
tremendous

Use words with moral overtones, for example *the shameful silence of our politicians on this issue*
decent
disgraceful
immoral
indefensible
just
moral
shameful

Use words that appeal to your audience's aspirations, whatever they may be, for example *You can achieve online business mastery in a matter of days*.

achievement
intelligence
mastery
power
recognition

Be the voice of reason – no one likes to be preached to, ranted at or railroaded. Balance your statements, for example *It is fair to say that he's worked hard, but it is simply not enough*.

fair
logically
objectively
reasonable
understandable

Use imperatives, for example *We really must do something about it*.

have to
imperative that
must
need to
will

Use rhetorical questions:
That can't be right, can it?

A final influential technique is to present your opinion as fact. A good way to do this is to use an intensifying adverb, for example *This is clearly wrong*.

certainly
clearly
indeed
in fact
naturally
obviously
of course
patently
undoubtedly

50 words to sell something

Many of the words and techniques that can be used to influence and persuade can also be used to sell something. There are a few additional things to bear in mind.

For immediacy, use simple constructions and words, and avoid using any jargon that applies to the product you are trying to sell.

Avoid	Use
alleviate	**lessen, reduce**
ascertain	**find out, discover**
attain	**reach, achieve**
avail yourself of	**use**
demonstrate, illustrate	**show**

desire	**want**
discover	**find out**
necessitate	**need, call for**
purchase	**buy**
residence	**home**

Use direct address with the personal pronoun **you** to show you are thinking about the customer's individual needs.
*I thought of **you** when I heard about this.*

Use occasional personal statements with the pronouns **I** and **we** to link yourself directly to the customer, show your personal commitment to the product and even reinforce your credentials. Just be careful not to talk about yourself *too* much …

I'll share this with you.
I love this …
I invested three years in …
We discovered that people need …
We put a lot of care into …

The product you want to sell should offer a solution to a problem that the customer might not even know they had. Use and repeat words that reinforce the benefit to the buyer and make them want this solution.

benefit
help
need
solve
useful
worth

Use words that reinforce the idea of saving the buyer's effort and time.

as soon as
easy
just
right away
simple
simply
support

Use words that create a sense of conviction and certainty.

absolutely
assure
certain
definite
ensure
recommend
surely
understand

Use words that suggest you are sharing something of value with the customer.

discover
find
opportunity
secret
share

Use words that create an image in the customer's mind in which they own the product.

imagine
just think
suppose

Do not use negative words too often. Use words with positive connotations to create positive images in the customer's mind.

Avoid	Use
but	**and**
contract	**agreement**
free of errors	**perfect**
inexpensive	**economical**

36 words to put someone off

Just as you can use words skilfully to sell, you can also use them to repel, and the techniques of selling can also be used to convince someone they don't want something. Here are some key words to put people off an idea.

Use words that reinforce the idea of something troublesome or restrictive.

effort
mired
prevent
problem
struggle
stuck

Use words that create a sense of uncertainty.

caution
doubt
insecure
threat
uncertain
unsure

Use words that elicit a negative emotional response.

dreadful
grievous
horrific
outrageous

shocking
terrifying

Use words with negative moral overtones.

disgraceful
disreputable
immoral
indefensible
offensive
shameful

Use words that elicit a negative physical response.

disgusting
foul
nauseating
repulsive
revolting
sickening

Throw in emotive words that appeal to your audience's fears, whatever they may be.

embarrassment
failure
fear
grief
humiliation
misery

34 words to understand male culture

In recent years, it seems men have been claiming a few things for their own – even some of the ways traditionally regarded as those of women. The following are examples of what we mean.

andropause the period in a man's life when testosterone levels decline
Boyzilian the male version of the 'Brazilian' wax treatment to remove pubic hair
bromance a close, but not romantic or sexual, relationship between two men
guyliner eyeliner as worn by men
hevage a man's chest as seen under a buttoned shirt (from *he* and *cleavage*)
himbo a man who is excessively concerned with his appearance and seems dim
lad lit a type of fiction designed to appeal to young men
man bag a handbag designed for men
mancation a holiday involving male-oriented activities
mancession a recession that affects men more than women
mancessories fashion accessories for men
mandals sandals for men
man date an arranged social meeting of two heterosexual men
mandigan a man's cardigan
mandle a candle with a scent designed to appeal to men
man flu a heavy cold
man hug a handshake with a pat on the back

mankini a revealing one-piece posing garment for a man

manny a male nanny

manscaping removing excess body hair to create a more groomed appearance

manscara mascara for men

manther a middle-aged man who seeks out younger women; the male equivalent of a cougar (from *man* and *panther*)

manties snug male briefs

mantrum a tantrum thrown by a fully grown male

mantyhose tights for men

man up to accept responsibility in a mature fashion

meggings leggings for men

mengagement ring an engagement ring for a man

metrosexual a heterosexual man who takes an interest in traditionally non-male interests such as fashion and personal grooming (from *metropolitan* and *heterosexual*)

mewelry men's jewellery

mirdle a male girdle

moobs large male breasts (from *man boobs*)

murse a man's purse or handbag

omega male a man who does not want responsibility or feel the need to dominate the others in his social group

18 words to understand female culture

Men may have been encroaching on women's territory of late, but women have been making their own claims on certain areas of culture. Here are some examples of this.

alpha girl a young woman who dominates the others in her social group

boy briefs women's full briefs similar in design to those worn by men

boyfriend blazer, cardigan, shirt, etc an oversized blazer, cardigan, shirt, etc similar to one a woman might borrow from her boyfriend

bro-bra a girl who takes part in activities typical of young males, such as skateboarding (also **chick-bro, chick-dude**)

chick flick a film likely to appeal mainly to women

chick lit a type of fiction designed to appeal to young women

chickspeak the language females use with each other

femivore a woman who looks after the home and grows and produces her own food

geezerbird a mannish woman

girl geek a woman interested in technology, computer games, etc

guyatus a self-imposed break from dating men

herstory history from a feminist viewpoint

ladette a young woman who enjoys social activities associated with young men

lady guns well-toned female arms

she-pee an enclosed area, for example at a music festival, containing urinals for women

Shewee® a funnel-like device that allows a woman to urinate while standing up and/or without undressing

24 words to avoid sexism

Avoid sexism creeping into your language with these tips and alternative words.

Don't use *he* as a generic pronoun. Use **he or she**, or even **they**, if appropriate.

Avoid describing women in terms of appearance, age and family status where this is not relevant ('Mrs Jones, an attractive blonde mother of two, is expected to become Chancellor.').

Likewise, avoid describing men in terms of appearance and age where this is not relevant ('The diminutive 28-year-old will publish his paper on Austen later this month.').

Avoid adjectives that enforce stereotypes and have been traditionally applied to women.

blowzy
bossy
demure
feisty
headstrong
vivacious

Likewise, avoid adjectives that are generally only applied to men.

brawny
charismatic
creepy
stocky
weedy

Avoid gender-specific references to professions, for example:

Gender-specific	Gender-neutral
actress	**actor**
barmaid	**bartender**
businessman	**businessperson**
chairman	**chairperson** or **chair**
comedienne	**comedian**
policeman/policewoman	**police officer**
proprietress	**proprietor**
waitress	**server**

Be careful of gender-specific expressions that might sound incongruous in context.

| any Tom, Dick or Harry | **any person** |
| Joe Bloggs | **an ordinary person** |

79 words to sound more global

To bring a bit of variety to your English, try out these alternatives from English-speaking countries.

British	US	South African	Australian
alcohol	liquor	dop	grog
barbecue	barbecue	braai	barbie
bumpkin	hayseed	gomgat	bushie
chap	cove	ou	bloke
cinema	movie theater	bioscope	cinema
clobber	whale	donner	job
cool box	cooler	cooler box	esky
crisps	chips	skyfies	chips
Englishman	limey	khaki	pom
flip-flops	flip-flops	slip-slops	thongs
get lost!	vamoose!	voetsak!	choof off!
great	swell	lekker	bonzer
mate	dude	boet	cobber
off-licence	liquor store	bottle store	bottle shop
pickup truck	pickup	bakkie	ute
plastered	loaded	gesuip	full as a boot
plimsolls	sneakers	tackies	sandshoes
sweets	candy	lekkers	lollies
trainers	sneakers	tackies	joggers
tramp	hobo	bergie	dero
trousers	pants	pants	strides

51 ways to express surprise

Here are some of the many ways to express surprise.

bless my soul!	I ask you!	OMG!
blimey!	I don't know!	stone me!
blow me down!	I'll be blessed!	stone the crows!
by Jove!	I'll be blowed!	(Australian)
come off it!	I'll be damned!	strewth! (Australian)
did you ever!	imagine that!	that's news to me!
fancy that!	in heaven's name!	the (very) idea!
for goodness sake!	Mama Mia!	to think!
for heaven's sake!	musha! (Irish)	well I never!
good grief!	my eye!	what the … !
good heavens!	my foot!	wonders will never cease!
good lord!	my goodness!	would you believe!
Gordon Bennett!	my word!	you could have knocked
gosh!	no kidding!	me down with a feather!
great Scott!	no way!	you don't say!
heavens above!	of all the …!	you're joking!
holy smoke!	oh mother!	you're kidding!
how about that then!	oh my!	

25 words to understand mobile culture

From the technical to the facetious, a wide range of words are required if you want to understand the pervasive culture of the mobile communication device.

bling kit a set of shiny stickers with which to customize your mobile phone
crackberry a handheld computer that is used obsessively; a person who seems addicted to using their handheld computer
dead zone a place with no mobile phone signal
distracted driving driving while texting or while browsing on a smartphone
dumphone a mobile phone that does not have the technological features of a smartphone
fauxcellarm the momentary false perception of a sound as your mobile phone ringing
intexticated distracted while driving because you are sending a text
mob a group of people gathered using mobile contact (a **flash mob**), sometimes to achieve a particular aim (a **smart mob**), for example to mobilize a group of voters (a **vote mob**)
mobisode an episode of a TV show made for downloading and viewing on mobile phones
notspot an area that has no 3G mobile phone coverage
ping to use a facility allowing you to send a message quickly to a contact, or a number of contacts, on a smartphone
pocket dial an accidental call to a stored contact number caused by an unlocked mobile moving around in a pocket or bag
ringxiety the anxiety caused by hearing a mobile phone ringtone that is the same as your own; the momentary false perception of a sound as your mobile phone ringing
sexting the sending and receiving of text messages with sexual content
swarming gathering your acquaintances together quickly by contacting them through mobile technologies
textese or **textspeak** the language used in text messages
textism a typical texting usage, for example an abbreviation
text-walking walking without taking due care because you are texting
thumb culture or **thumb generation** people who are highly skilled in their use of mobile devices
thumbo a typographical error made while using the thumbs to type on a mobile device
vibranxiety the momentary false perception that your phone is vibrating
yellular a loud speaking voice adopted while using a mobile phone

34 words to understand social networking

Use of social networking sites is almost as ubiquitous as that of mobile phones. Here are some words you need to understand the culture of social networking.

add an instance of adding a friend to your circle (as in 'thanks for the add')
avatar a graphic image you use to represent yourself
Beboer a user of the site Bebo®
circle your set of friends on a social networking site
death tweet an apparent death threat posted on Twitter®

defriend to remove someone from your circle of friends (also **unfriend**)

Facebooker a user of the site Facebook®

follow to have the posts of (someone) appear in your page on Twitter®

follower someone who follows another person in their page on Twitter®

friend to add someone to your circle of friends

geosocial networking a form of social networking in which location data can be used to connect users to local people or events

hashtag on Twitter®, a word with a hash (#) in front of it to link it to a particular topic, for example *#politics*

like a feature on Facebook® that allows a user to show that they enjoyed or appreciated something that another user has posted

meformer someone who uses a social networking site mainly to post information about themselves and their activities, rather than to post more general information

nudge a greeting constituting a reminder from a Twitter® user to another to update their status

oversharing sharing too much personal information on social networking sites

pity friend a person whose friend request you accept out of pity

poke a greeting constituting a reminder from a Facebook® user to another to update their status

profile a site on Facebook® where a user gives information about themselves and their friends

retweet a repeated or forwarded message on Twitter®

social notworking reading and posting on social networking websites when you should be working

sofalizing socializing from home by using social networking websites

status a feature which allows users to tell friends about what they are currently doing or thinking

tag to link a status update, person in a photograph, etc to another Facebook® user to identify them, include them, etc

timeline on Twitter®, a list of Tweets® in chronological order; on Facebook®, a chronological record of your life and likes

trend a hashtag on Twitter® that has been searched most frequently

Tweet® a message posted on Twitter®

tweeter a user of the site Twitter®

tweetheart a sweetheart on Twitter®

tweetup an online meeting of individuals arranged on Twitter®

twitterati popular and influential Twitter® users collectively; sometimes used to refer to all Twitter® users collectively

twittersphere Twitter® users collectively

wall a space on a Facebook® user's page on which they and their friends post messages

28 words to be more flattering

For those occasions when you want to butter someone up, you need some flattering alternatives for everyday words.

Use words that turn potential negatives into positives.

old	**experienced, wise**
overweight	**curvy, well-built**
strange	**charming, quaint**
thin	**slender, slim**

Instead of using a mildly positive word, choose a stronger alternative.

attractive	**beautiful, gorgeous**
good	**excellent, superb**
interesting	**fascinating, captivating**
new	**fresh, novel**

Tell the listener what they want to hear. Use words that suggest personal qualities and abilities.

busy	**hard-working, diligent**
fashionable	**stylish, well-dressed**
suggestion	**insight, observation**

Most people like to think they have a positive effect on other people.

happy	**sunny, cheering**
interfering	**helpful, caring**
talkative	**friendly, communicative**

15 words to be less flattering

There may be occasions where it does not pay to put the most positive spin on something, so you need some terms and techniques to describe someone or something in a less flattering light.

Instead of using a word with very positive connotations, choose a word with less positive force.

attractive	**okay-looking, not bad looking**
funny	**diverting, amusing**
good	**acceptable, passable**

Instead of using a positive word, use negation of its negative equivalent. This immediately reduces the positive force of a statement.

attractive	**not unattractive**
competent	**not incompetent**
impressive	**not unimpressive**

Use words that convey the negative aspects of a potential positive.

cheerful	**irritating, smug**
confident	**conceited, big-headed**
young	**immature, inexperienced**

14 words to be blunt to the point of insult

If you are really tired of pussyfooting around, here are some blunt ways of expressing dislike.

Instead of using an everyday negative word, choose something with more negative force.

boring	**soporific, soul-destroying**
dislike	**abhor, revile**

Use words that focus strongly on any potentially negative aspects of a positive.

attractive	**empty-headed, vacuous**
clever	**smart-alecky, conceited**

Use words that present some characteristic as someone's fault.

unhappy	**self-pitying, whingeing**
overweight	**salad-dodging, gluttonous**

To be particularly insulting, use words that create a striking image.

miserable	**face like a torn melodeon**
ugly	**face like a bag of spanners**

43 words to decipher menus

Restaurants often use bizarre or exaggerated descriptions on menus when, in fact, the preparation is pretty simple. Look out for the more florid terms – some of which border on the meaningless – used to refer to some ordinary techniques and tastes.

It's dressed with:
anointed
caressed
drizzled
embellished
flourish
graced
kissed
swirled

It's covered with or wrapped in:
bound
cuddled
encrusted
enrobed
enveloped
smothered

It's filled with:
exploding
loaded

It's on top of:
atop
nestling
on a pillow (of)
resting

It's a mixture:
fusion
medley
mélange
symphony

There is more than one:
duet
profusion
trio

Overstated preparations:
gently simmered
hand picked
hand rolled
lovingly prepared
oven roasted

pan fried

Exaggerated adjectives:
famous
fragrant
indulgent
luscious
potent (fusion)
silken
special
sumptuous
traditional
zesty

41 words to sound like an estate agent

Just like menus, descriptions of properties in estate agents' literature can be a bit exaggerated. Here are some commonly used terms and what you can read into them.

It's small:
comfortable
compact
cosy
starter home

It's average in size:
ample
generous
spacious

It's weird:
characterful
charming
individual
unusual

It's dilapidated:
degree of modernization
  required
fixer-upper
flexible
potential

It looks okay:
fabulous
impressive
outstanding
stunning

It looks bad on the outside:
deceptively spacious
internal viewing
  recommended/essential

You'll want to change it:
beautifully presented
good decorative order
stylish décor
walk-in condition
well-maintained

It's in a run-down area:
popular locale
up-and-coming area

We're appealing to your sense of snobbery:
admired
exclusive
executive
prestigious
private
sought-after location

We can't think of much to recommend it:
refurbished
well laid-out
well placed
well proportioned

It's cheap, so don't complain:
priced to sell
reasonably priced
sold as seen

24 ways to avoid indirectness and tautology

Why use several words where one would do? Avoiding these expressions will help keep your style lean.

added extra an extra
advance warning warning
audible gasp, groan, etc a gasp, groan, etc
be of the opinion to think
blue, red, etc in colour blue, red, etc
close proximity proximity
end result result
few/many in number few/many
forward planning planning
future prospects prospects
in all probability probably
in excess of over

in the very near future soon
large/small in size large/small
mutual co-operation co-operation
nothing if not very
past history history
pre-plan to plan
pre-position to position
pre-prepare to prepare
revert back to revert
until such time as until
viable alternative alternative
wide/huge gulf gulf

70 words to identify phobias

Phobias can range from the natural to the downright incomprehensible, and while some are so common that their names have become firmly established in English, others have yet to gain widespread currency. The following is a guide to the vocabulary of our fears.

acrophobia high places
aerophobia flying
agliophobia pain
agoraphobia open spaces
aichomophobia sharp objects
ailurophobia cats
apiphobia bees
arachibutyrophobia peanut butter sticking to the roof of the mouth
arachnophobia spiders
astraphobia lightning
autophobia loneliness
bacillophobia microbes
bacteriophobia bacteria
bathophobia falling from a high place
belonephobia needles
brontophobia thunder
canophobia or **cynophobia** dogs
claustrophobia confined spaces
consecotaleophobia chopsticks
cyberphobia computers
dendrophobia trees
didaskaleinophobia going to school
dromophobia crossing streets

entomophobia insects
epistemophobia knowledge
ereuthrophobia blushing
euphobia good news
geliophobia laughter
genophobia sex
genuphobia knees and kneeling
graphophobia writing
herpetophobia reptiles
hierophobia sacred objects
hippophobia horses
hydrophobia water
hypsophobia (falling from) high places
kenophobia empty spaces
linonophobia string
monophobia being alone
mysophobia contamination
necrophobia corpses
neophobia novelty
nosocomephobia hospitals
nosophobia contacting disease
nyctophobia night, darkness
ochlophobia crowds
ophiophobia snakes

panophobia any groundless cause
pantophobia everything
paraskavedekatriaphobia Friday the 13th
phagophobia eating
phasmophobia ghosts
phengophobia daylight
phonophobia noise or speaking
photophobia light
pognophobia beards
pteronophobia feathers
pyrophobia fire
scopophobia being looked at
scotophobia or **achluophobia** darkness
sitophobia food
tachophobia speed
taphephobia being buried alive
technophobia technology
toxicophobia poison
triskaidekaphobia thirteen
trypophobia clusters of holes, cuts, etc
xenophobia foreigners
zelophobia jealousy
zoophobia animals

21 words to understand a recession

A number of terms become unsettlingly familiar in an 'economic downturn'. Knowledge of these words can give us a fix on what is happening in the economic world.

bad bank a bank set up to administer unprofitable (toxic) assets (also **toxic bank**)
bank run the withdrawal of money and closure of accounts by a large number of a bank's customers in a short space of time, the result of a belief the bank could become insolvent
credit easing government underwriting of bank borrowing so the banks can then lend more money to businesses

crunch creep social and economic trends suggested to be consequences of a credit crunch, for example a decline in the divorce rate because couples cannot pay for the divorce process

debt storm a large national debt with effects that can spread to other countries

deleveraging reducing the amount of a business's debt, often by selling its assets

double dip describes a recession in which a brief period of growth is followed by another decline

flash crash an extremely rapid stock market decline

funt financially untouchable

ghost estate (in Ireland) an unfinished and unoccupied housing estate, the construction of which started during the period of economic growth and stopped when the economy fell into decline

green shoots hoped-for signs of economic recovery

municide the economic or political death of a city with budget deficits that are untenable

ninja loan a loan given to someone with *no* *i*ncome, *no* *j*ob or *a*ssets, and who is therefore not well placed to pay it back

overleveraged having borrowed too much money and unable to pay it back

quantitative easing increasing the amount of money in circulation in order to stimulate economic activity

recapitalization helping a struggling bank to restore its capital

shovel ready denotes jobs that are created to be ready for people to start immediately

silent run a bank run that takes place without customers entering the bank, for example through online transactions

toxic asset a financial asset that is liable to cause a loss

zombie bank a financial institution that has negative net worth but continues to operate through financial support from the government

17 words to deal with a recession

While some words help you understand the economic jargon of a financial crisis, other words give it a different, more human, perspective.

accidentally retired having been made redundant in late middle age, and facing the possibility of not working again

austerication downgrading a holiday destination in order to make it more affordable

chiconomics the art of staying fashionable without having much cash available

daycation a holiday for a day; a daytrip viewed as some compensation for a lack of longer trips

funemployment the active enjoyment of your free time while unemployed

Generation Rent a generation of people who cannot afford to buy a home

glamping camping using upmarket sites, facilities, etc, considered more glamorous than traditional camping but still cheaper than hotel holidays

greycation holidaying with grandparents to help spread the cost across generations

paliday holidaying with friends and family to help spread the cost

paycation a break from your job taken to do different work and make extra money

precariat a social group comprising people who have little or no job security

recessionista a woman who wears fashionable clothes without spending too much on them (also **frugalista**)

reluctant breadwinner a person who is forced to be the main breadwinner in a household because a previous earner has lost his or her job

reluctant landlord a person who is forced to rent out his or her house because he or she is unable to sell it

staycation a holiday period spent at home or in your native country

stealth shopping shopping in secret so as not to reveal how much you are spending

28 ways to tell someone to be quiet

Here are some of the many very blunt ways to tell someone to be quiet.

belt up!	hold your peace!	shut it!
button it!	keep shtoom!	shut up!
can it!	mum!	shut your face!
cut the cackle!	not another word!	shut your gob!
drop dead!	one more word out of … !	shut your mouth!
dry up!	pack it in!	shut your trap!
enough said!	pipe down!	wrap up!
get knotted!	put a sock in it!	zip it!
give it a rest!	say no more!	
give over!	shhh!	

15 words to be more tactful

Brutal honesty is all very well, but there are occasions that demand we express something diplomatically or delicately. There are words and ways you can use to express disapproval tactfully.

Instead of using a word with negative force, choose something more neutral.

old	**mature**
ugly	**plain**
weird	**different**

Choose words that focus on any positive aspects of a potential negative.

boring	**relaxing, leisurely**
lacking	**shows potential/possibility**
odd	**unique, unusual**

Use words that suggest the problem arises partly from your own point of view.

I'm not very fond of …
not my cup of tea
not my taste

When describing a person's behaviour, use words that suggest the problem is partly with the person's situation rather than their character.

inappropriate
unhelpful
unsuitable

75 words to understand drug culture

With illegal drug use apparently widespread, it is worth knowing a few of the many slang names for common drugs.

Amyl nitrite:
amies
animal
boppers
pearls
poppers

Amphetamines:
amp
bennies
black beauties
bumblebees
co-pilot
dexies
footballs
hearts
hot ice
pep pills
speed
uppers

Methamphetamine:
crank
Cristina
crystal
crystal meth
meth
redneck cocaine

MDMA:
E
Ecstasy

love drug
Scooby snacks
X
XTC

Barbiturates:
barbs
blue angels
downers
goofballs
red devils
reds
yellowjackets

Cannabis:
bhang
blow
grass
jive
kif
Mary Jane
pot
reefer
wacky baccy
weed

Cocaine:
base
Big C
C
Charlie
coke

crack
crystal
snow
white horse

Heroin:
black tar
brown
brown sugar
diesel
horse
skag or **scag**
smack

LSD:
acid
microdots

PCP:
angel dust
dust
embalming fluid
ozone
rocket fuel
wack

Rohypnol:
forget pills
rib
roofies
rophies
R2

16 words to identify foodie factions

It seems we really are what we eat, judging by the number of words that classify people according to clearly defined food preferences.

breatharian someone who claims to gain nutrition from air
ecotarian someone who eats only food that is in season, and sustainably and locally produced (also **ecovore**)
ethical eater a person who eats only food produced according to ethical guidelines
femivore a woman who looks after the home and grows and produces her own food
flexitarian a vegetarian who sometimes eats meat or fish

freegan a person who eats food they have scavenged, for example from bins outside shops and restaurants
locapour a person who will drink only beer or wine produced locally
locavore a person who will eat only food produced locally
nutritarian someone who strives to eat only food of high nutritional value
opportunivore a person who eats food that has been discarded by others
orthorexic someone overly concerned with eating the kind of food that is health-inducing, sustainably produced, etc
pescatarian a person who excludes meat from their diet but will eat fish
rawist a person who will eat only unprocessed and uncooked food
vegangelical a vegan who pontificates about the correctness of veganism
vegivore a person who prefers eating vegetarian food but is not necessarily a vegetarian

21 words to make sense of rhetoric

There are rhetorical techniques you can use to put words in unexpected combinations and create a striking effect in your writing or speech.

An **allusion** involves using a form of words that makes the reader think of a particular person, object or event:
Never in the field of interior design have I seen anything like it.
Here, the words *never in the field* are an allusion to a famous wartime speech made by Winston Churchill (*Never in the field of human conflict ...*).

Anaphora is the repetition of an initial word or phrase to connect otherwise unattached clauses:
We shall fight on the beaches, we shall fight on the landing grounds, we shall fight in the fields and in the streets, we shall fight in the hills; we shall never surrender. (Winston Churchill)

Anastrophe is the reversal of normal word order:
Far have I travelled, and much have I seen. (Paul McCartney)
Into the valley of death rode the six hundred. (Alfred Tennyson)

Antithesis is the balancing, usually symmetrically, of contrasted clauses, phrases or words:
feared by the bad, loved by the good

Apophasis is the device of expressing something by saying you will not do so:
I wouldn't dream of mentioning that you failed your driving test!

Apostrophe involves speaking directly to an absent person, inanimate object or abstract idea that would normally be referred to in the third person:
O death, where is thy sting? (Bible)

Hyperbole is the use of extreme exaggeration to make a particular point:
there are a thousand and one reasons
not for all the tea in China

Irony is the expression of a meaning opposite to the one apparently expressed:
I can't wait!
Oh, very funny!

Litotes is the use of extreme understatement to make a particular point, for example by denying the opposite:
She is not unattractive.
It is a bit of a disappointment.

A **metaphor** involves using a word or phrase to describe something that it does not literally apply to. This unusual use of the word has the effect of making a comparison, although – unlike a simile – a metaphor does not use words such as *like* or *as*:
Annie sailed into the room.

NB: if you use two metaphors in the same sentence, the result can be a mixed metaphor – a combination that creates an illogical or ludicrous image. This is often regarded as a sign of bad writing:
There are concrete steps in the pipeline.

Metonymy is the use of a term to refer to something that is closely associated with it:
an oath of allegiance to the crown (instead of to the monarch)

An **oxymoron** is a phrase composed of words that have contradictory meanings:
a bitter-sweet love story

A **paradox** is a statement that, although apparently self-contradictory, contains an element of truth:
You've got to be cruel to be kind.
Expect the unexpected.
Less is more.

Personification involves attributing human qualities to inanimate objects or abstract ideas:
The computer won't be happy if you don't log out properly.
Fear stalks the corridors of the building.

Pleonasm is the use of words which are not strictly required, usually for emphasis:
I saw it with my very own eyes.

A **rhetorical question** is a question that is asked to emphasize a point, without expecting an answer:
Is the Pope a Catholic?
Do I have to do everything myself?

A **simile** involves making a comparison between two unlike things, introduced by words such as *like* or *as*:
She eyed the food like a hungry lion.
He was trembling like a leaf.
For a simile to be truly effective it should be both original and appropriate.

Syllepsis is the use of a word (usually a transitive verb or a preposition) which relates to two others, creating a different sense with each:
She went home in a flood of tears and a taxi.

Synecdoche is the use of a word denoting a part of something or someone to refer to the whole:
a safe pair of hands
a new set of wheels

Tmesis involves inserting a word into another word:
Oh, abso-blinking-lutely!

Zeugma is similar to syllepsis, except that one word relates to two nouns but can only normally be used with one of these:
He hung up his coat and his bad mood in the hallway.

27 words to self-diagnose

If you want to put your finger on what is causing those feelings of angst or ennui, it might be one of these contemporary conditions and modern maladies.

affluenza mental illness resulting from the need to spend money and have possessions

always-on syndrome the compulsion to access social networking sites, 24-hour news coverage, etc even at inappropriate times

apocalypse fatigue loss of interest in dire warnings of environmental catastrophe as a result of over-exposure to them

automatic eating eating without doing so consciously, or eating when not hungry

bagmata lines on the hands caused by carrying heavy bags of shopping

Blackberry thumb inflammation of the thumb muscles caused by heavy use of a PDA or smartphone

blogorrhoea verbosity in a blog

blogstipation writers' block for bloggers

busy brain syndrome the inability to clear your thoughts

cosmophobia the fear that Earth will be destroyed by a catastrophic event in the cosmos

cyberchondria checking symptoms of a perceived illness on the Internet and believing you have one, or many, of the ailments you have investigated

eco-anxiety anxiety caused by concerns about the state of the environment

email apnoea unconsciously stopping breathing while checking email

email bankruptcy having too many emails to deal with, so simply deleting them all and declaring to your contacts that you have done so

frugality fatigue being fed up with having to be careful in your spending

infomania the seemingly constant need to check social networking sites, emails, etc

iPod oblivion lack of awareness of your surroundings when listening to a mobile device

juvenoia paranoia about children and young people being corrupted by online influences

nature-deficit disorder the collective negative effects in urban dwellers caused by alienation from nature

password fatigue a sense of tiredness and frustration caused by the need to remember a large number of computer passwords

qwerty tummy a stomach upset caused by bacteria on computer keyboards

range anxiety the fear that an electric car does not have sufficient charge to reach its destination

ringxiety the anxiety caused by hearing a mobile phone ringtone that is the same as your own; (also **fauxcellarm**) the momentary false perception of a sound as your mobile phone ringing

solastalgia pining for a lost environment, such as one changed by global warming

toasted skin syndrome damage to the skin on the thighs as a result of long periods sitting with a laptop computer on the lap

white coat syndrome a condition in which anxiety at being in a medical environment causes an increase in blood pressure

63 ways to express disbelief

Here are some of the many ways you can express disbelief.

a good one!
a likely story!
come, come!
come off it!
do me a favour!
don't give me that!
don't make me laugh!
don't tell me!
do you mean to say?
excuses, excuses!
fancy that!
get along (with you)!
get away (with you)!
good heavens!
good Lord!
goodness gracious me!
goodness me!
go on!
go on with you!
heavens above!
I ask you!
I bet!

I don't think!
if you believe that you'd believe anything!
I'll eat my hat!
I've heard that one before!
just fancy!
make me laugh!
my (giddy) aunt!
my foot!
my goodness!
my hat!
no kidding!
no way!
oh yeah!
promises, promises!
pull the other one, it's got bells on!
says who?
says you!
sez who?
sez you!

stone me!
stone the crows!
strike a light!
strike me dead!
strike me pink!
stuff and nonsense!
tell it to the marines!
tell me another!
that's a tall story!
that's news to me!
that's rich!
the devil you do!
the hell you say!
what a load of cobblers!
you can't be serious!
you don't say!
you'll be lucky!
you must be joking!
you must be kidding!
you're kidding!
you're pulling my leg!
you what!

35 words and phrases to avoid in journalism

These are some of the stock words, collocations and phrases you hear so often that they might not even register on your consciousness.

acceptable/unacceptable face of ...
blitz
bone of contention
chorus of approval
crisis situation
dead in the water
glowing tribute
leading light

mood of cautious optimism
new high/low
no stranger to controversy
outpouring of grief
pale into insignificance
probe
reliable source
slam
sorely needed
sugar the pill
the acid test
the final analysis
tireless campaigner
track record
vote with their feet
woefully inadequate
worst-case scenario

Football reporting has its own language.

bad boy player who misbehaves on and/or off the pitch
bruising encounter a dirty match
chorus of boos booing
crash out to be beaten in a knockout competition
pledge a promise you will try to win a competition, play well, etc
snub to turn down an offer made by (someone), for example that of a new contract
swoop to (try to) buy a player from another club
the axe the sack
the drop relegation from a higher league division to a lower one
vow a promise you will try to win a competition, play well, etc

23 words and phrases to avoid in politics

Politicians can be guilty of overusing certain words, soundbites and slogans that they (or their spin doctors) have decided are catchy and succinct enough to get the message across. Here are a few potential bugbears.

big society a policy of civic engagement, with individuals actively involved in the provision of facilities, services, etc
broken society the notion of a society characterized by unemployment, crime, substance abuse, etc
clear and present danger a danger
consensus agreement
fit for purpose able to do the job
lessons to be learned mistakes that shouldn't be made again
let me say this listen to me
let's be clear precedes a statement: this is what I think, therefore it must be true
perfect storm a combination of circumstances that results in a catastrophic situation
proper debate, inquiry, etc a debate, inquiry, etc
quantum leap an advance
reach out to try to communicate with people who feel alienated or are disadvantaged, usually in an attempt to gain support

sea change a major change

silver bullet a straightforward solution to a problem

social cohesion more mutual respect and coordination in communities

step change a change in procedure

thank you for/we appreciate your honesty I wish you hadn't said or asked that

the reality is… the situation as I see it is …

three strikes and you're out describes any policy where a third instance of defiance results in more severe punishment

transparency openness

vision an intention or hope

we're listening we want you to think that we care what you think

with all due respect used to precede a statement of disagreement

49 words and phrases to avoid at work

These are the words and phrases that are intended to show you are in control, but are more likely to alienate your colleagues or, worse still, make them laugh.

bandwidth available time and resources: *Do we have the bandwidth for this project?*

be on the same page to be in agreement

big ask a request that will be difficult to fulfil

blue-sky thinking creative thought that is not constrained by traditional thinking

bring to the table to bring (a skill etc) to a job or activity

bring your A-game to perform at your best

cascade to disseminate from the top down: *Please cascade this information through your teams.*

circle back to come back to a topic later

come onstream of a product: to be released

comfort zone the limits within which you feel at ease

diarize to arrange a date for something: *Let's diarize a meeting.*

disincentivize to take away the incentive from someone to do something

empower to give individuals the power to take decisions in matters relating to themselves, especially (in an organization) in relation to self-development

event horizon a turning point

eventize to make an event of

face time face-to-face interaction

get your ducks in a row to make sure all the elements are in place before starting a new project

going forward in future

high-altitude view an overview

impactful having impact

incentivize to give, have or be given an incentive, especially to work more efficiently, productively, etc. Sometimes shortened to **incent**.

interface to speak face to face: *He is anxious to interface with you.*

joined-up of thinking: coherent, co-ordinated

low-hanging fruit the tasks or aims that are easiest to fulfil

mission-critical critical

on your radar describes something you are aware of and intend to deal with

own have responsibility for

paradigm shift any change in methods

park leave aside (a discussion, issue, etc) to return to later

peel the onion to look at each aspect of a problem

productionize to put into production
push the envelope to challenge the limits
quantum leap an advance
retask to give someone or something a different task
shared vision the idea that everyone working for the company has the same goals
shoot the puppy to do something that should be unthinkable
sing from the same hymn sheet to be in agreement
solution anything that has a function; what businesses sell: *all your storage solutions*
solutionize to work out solutions
step up to the plate to take on responsibility
synergy co-ordinated action
take offline to not speak about (something) until later
task to give someone a particular task
think outside the box to disregard conventional thinking
360-degree thinking a wide view
touch base with to contact
transition to change
walk the talk to do what you say you will
win-win (supposedly) advantageous to both parties involved in something

19 words to impress in job interviews

Whether or not you can 'walk the talk', these are the words and phrases you might use to show that you can, at least, talk the talk. Be wary, though – as far as your potential new colleagues are concerned, some of the terms in this list might well qualify for the previous list …

best practice the most appropriate way of doing something
champion to show support for: *I can champion this aspect of the business.*
change management planning and implementing changes in a company
collaborative consumption businesses using the Web to share services and goods
competencies abilities
-driven having as a stimulus or aim, for example, *profit-driven*, *task-driven*
grow as in 'grow the business'
ideation having new ideas
interpersonal skills the ability to work with people harmoniously
key driver an important stimulus
-oriented having a specific focus, for example *profit-oriented*, *task-oriented*
overarching purpose the main purpose for business partners working together
partnership working collaboration
proactive acting in anticipation of developments, rather than reacting to them as they happen
shared commitment a partnership
skillset a set of skills
soft skills personal qualities or aptitudes that indirectly qualify you to do a particular job
strategic fit how far an organization can meet its aims with its current resources
value proposition a selling point

72 words to impress anywhere

There are lots of precise and expressive words which, if used appropriately, will add colour and conviction to your expression.

abstruse difficult to understand
alacrity a willingness or eagerness to act quickly
apposite particularly appropriate under the circumstances or for the purpose
axiomatic so obviously true that it does not need to be proved or explained
cataclysmic revolutionary; catastrophic
caveat a warning that something is only true within certain limitations
circumspect cautious; prudent
circumvent to get round, outwit, avoid
clandestine concealed, done in secret
cognizant aware of or knowing all about something
contumacious opposing lawful authority with contempt; obstinate
corollary a natural or obvious consequence or result of something
coruscating (of wit) sparkling, flashing
deleterious harmful, damaging, or destructive
dilatory slow to act
draconian extremely severe
effulgent shining
effusive showing positive feelings in an open way
egregious exceptionally and shockingly bad
empirical known through practical experience
endemic regularly found among a particular people or in a particular district
ephemeral short-lived or fleeting
esoteric understood only by a few people who have the necessary knowledge
exculpate to absolve; to vindicate
execrable appallingly bad
expedient profitable or convenient rather than fair or just
foment to foster; to encourage or provoke
fulminate to issue decrees with violence or threats
hegemony leadership; predominant influence
heterogeneous composed of people or things that are not related to one another
homogeneous composed of people or things that are related to one another
hubris over-confidence; arrogance that brings about disaster
iconoclastic opposed to or attacking traditional beliefs or customs
incipient just beginning to happen
intractable impossible to solve, cure or deal with
inveigle to persuade using cajolery or trickery
invidious likely to cause envy, resentment or indignation
laconic using very few words
loquacious talkative
mercurial tending to change suddenly and unpredictably
meretricious superficially attractive but of no real value or merit; insincere
mordant sarcastic or critical in a clever, but sometimes cruel way
nebulous vague, not having been clearly defined or developed
obfuscate make unclear, confusing, or too complicated to understand
obloquy reproachful language; censure; slander; disgrace
obstreperous noisy; unruly
opprobrium severe public criticism or disapproval
peremptory arrogantly commanding; abrupt and direct

perfidious faithless; treacherous
perspicacity the ability to analyse and understand people and situations
prescient seeming to have foresight
profligate irresponsibly extravagant with money or resources
promulgate to spread or promote
pusillanimous lacking determination; mean-spirited; cowardly
putative commonly supposed to be, but not necessarily
salient prominent, striking
salubrious pleasant, respectable, clean
sanguine confident and inclined to hopefulness
sententious laden with meaning; tending to moralize
specious plausible, but wrong or inaccurate in reality
stochastic random
symbiosis a mutually beneficial relationship between two people or groups
tangential involving only a slight connection and relatively unimportant
tendentious deliberately and forcefully biased and controversial
trenchant forceful, direct, and effective
truculence discourtesy; aggression
unconscionable outrageous and completely unacceptable
unctuous offensively suave and smug
vertiginous dizzying
virulent with extremely rapid and harmful effects
visceral appealing to basic human instincts as opposed to the intellect
vituperate to attack with violently abusive criticism

50 words to identify manias

Like phobias, manias can range from the understandable to the bizarre. The following is a guide to the vocabulary of our obsessions, compulsions and cravings.

ablutomania personal cleanliness
aboulomania indecisiveness
ailuromania cats
anthomania flowers
bibliomania books
bruxomania grinding your teeth
cacoethes loquendi giving speeches (Latin, literally 'an itch for speaking')
clinomania staying in bed
cynomania dogs
demomania crowds
demonomania the obsessive belief that you are possessed by devils
dipsomania alcohol
egomania yourself
empleomania holding public office
ergomania work
erotomania the obsessive belief that someone is in love with you
gamomania making extravagant proposals of marriage
graphomania writing
hanatomania death
hedonomania pleasure
hippomania horses
infomania gathering (especially electronic) information

kleptomania stealing
logomania talking
megalomania power
melomania music
methomania alcohol
metromania writing verse
monomania any single idea or thing
mythomania lying and exaggerating
narcomania drugs
necromania dead bodies
nostomania going back to familiar places
oenomania wine
oniomania shopping and buying
onomatomania a particular word
onychotillomania picking or tearing your nails
plutomania wealth
polemomania war
potichomania imitating Oriental porcelain
pyromania fire-raising
rhinotillexomania picking your nose
sophomania the deluded belief that you are highly intelligent
technomania technology
theomania religion
tomomania surgery
toxicomania poisons
trichotillomania pulling out tufts of your own hair
typomania having your work published
xenomania foreign things

13 words and phrases to avoid in elegant English

Some people flinch at clumsy or even unnecessary uses of certain words and phrases. Here are some uses to avoid if you want to keep your language polished.

absolutely to mean 'yes'
actually to mean 'in fact', often without adding anything to the statement
like to introduce what someone has said, for example *I was like 'no!' and she was like 'yes!'.*
literally in connection with something unlikely or impossible, for example *I literally hit the roof.*
sort of to qualify anything, for example *The phrase was quite, sort of, catchy.*
to be fair when not giving balance to a statement , for example *It was a good goal, to be fair.*
to be honest or **to tell you the truth** without saying anything potentially dishonest or controversial, for example *I'm quite tired, to be honest.*
totally to mean 'yes'
unique to mean 'unusual' or 'special' rather than 'sole', giving rise to constructions such as 'very unique' and 'rather unique'
whatever! when used as a dismissive statement
you know or **you know what I mean** when added to various statements

40 words to sound more poetic

If you want to sound more poetic in your references to common concepts, there are many poetic-sounding words to help you.

agrin in the act of grinning
argent silver
Auster the south wind
brobdingnagian immense
brume fog
darkle to grow dark
day-peep dawn
day-spring dawn
daystar the sun
Dulcinea a sweetheart
enrheum to give the cold to
ever and anon from time to time
fire-flag a flash of fire, lightning, etc
frore frozen or frosty
fuliginous sooty; dusky
gasconade boasting talk
Hesperian western
horrent bristling
intempestive untimely, inopportune
joyance gaiety, festivity
marble-constant constant or firm as marble
niveous snowy
outward-sainted appearing outwardly to be a saint
overcrow to crow or triumph over
owl-light dusk, twilight
periculous dangerous
raven to devour hungrily or greedily
reboant loudly resounding
redivivus resuscitated
rident laughing or smiling radiantly, beaming
roscid dewy
rubescent growing red; blushing
rubies the lips
sea-girt surrounded by sea
sempiternal everlasting
sheathe the sword to end war
sheen glistening attire
temerarious rash, reckless
vivers food
wailful sorrowful

46 words to make yourself immediately understood

A formal or literary word is not always preferable to a plain, simple one. There will always be situations where a simple word is called for, especially when it is important that your audience immediately understands what you have to say.

Here are some formal words to look out for, and some simple alternatives to use.

Formal word	Simple alternative
accentuate	stress
alleviate	lessen, reduce
acquiesce	agree
acquire	buy, get
ascertain	find out, discover
attain	reach, achieve
avail yourself of	use
bestow	give
cessation	end
circumspect	cautious
desirous of	wanting, wishing for
desist	stop
effrontery	cheek
endeavour	try
eschew	avoid
evince	show, display
henceforth	from now on
heretofore	formerly
initiate	start, begin
latitude	freedom
manifest	show, display
multiplicity	lot
necessitate	need, involve, call for
opine	suppose
parameter	limit
proceed	go
proclivity	liking, preference
propensity	liking
purchase	buy
replete	full
reside	live, stay
residence	home
salubrious	healthy
veracity	truth

15 ways to express enthusiasm

Here are some of the many ways to express your enthusiasm and approval.

ace!

awesome!

boom!

bravo! or brava!

brilliant!

cool!

great!

hooray!

hurray!

huzzah!

woohoo!

woot!

yahoo!

yay!

yippee!

45 words to refer to contemporary characters

New technologies, activities and concerns have given rise to new breeds of people. There are words for them: here are just a few of the characters who have emerged in recent years.

armchair general a person who writes authoritatively and opinionatedly about a topic, especially online, without having genuine expertise

biohacker someone who experiments with DNA and genetics

bleachorexic someone who is obsessed with whitening their teeth

bossnapper a worker who detains a manager in the workplace as a form of industrial action

climate-sceptic a person who disputes the link between human activity and global warming

competitive commuter a cyclist who races another cyclist while commuting to or from work on a bicycle

couch hopper or **couch surfer** someone who moves between the homes of different acquaintances in order to receive temporary accommodation

cougar a middle-aged woman who seeks relationships with younger men

cyber-Cyrano a person who writes your online dating profile for you to show you in the best possible light

digital native a person who doesn't remember a time when computer use was not widespread

downager a person who acts younger than his or her age

drunkorexic someone who limits their food intake to allow for calories consumed in alcoholic drinks

eco-geek someone who is excessively enthusiastic about protecting the environment

ecosexual a person whose interest in the environment helps to attract, or affects their choice of, a romantic partner

freegan someone who expresses opposition to consumerism by retrieving and using discarded food, clothes, etc (also **dumpster diver**)

frenemy a person who pretends to be a friend but is actually an enemy

gastrosexual a person, especially a man, who uses his culinary skills to impress potential partners

hacktivist someone who hacks into computer systems as a form of protest

helicopter parent a parent who hovers over their offspring and does not give them enough independence

jargonaut someone who uses jargon excessively

jihobbyist someone who is sympathetic to radical Islam, but who is not a member of a radical group

lawnmower parent a parent who solves all their offspring's problems and smooths their way through life

lifecaster someone who broadcasts their daily activities over the Internet using a webcam

lycra lout an aggressive road (or pavement) hogging cyclist

meh-sayer someone who expresses indifference towards something

metrollectual an urban-dwelling man with a strong aesthetic sense who spends a great deal of time and money pontificating on the greatness of urban areas

mindcaster someone who broadcasts their thoughts using the Internet

mini-Madoff a con artist who has run a Ponzi scheme (see under 'scams and tricks') similar to one of the most notorious of the type, which was run by broker Bernard Madoff

mumpreneur a mother running a business from home

national treasure someone or something regarded as a cultural asset to a nation

nevertiree someone who works well beyond the accepted age of retirement

nonliner a person who never, or very rarely, uses the Internet

off-gridder someone who does not use public utilities but generates their own energy

putpocket someone who secretly puts things in another person's bag or pocket as a gift

rate tart a person who frequently changes their savings account or credit card in order to get the best interest rates on offer

recessionista someone who wears fashionable clothes without spending too much on them

reluctant landlord a person who is forced to rent out his or her house because he or she is unable to sell it

robosigner someone who signs a document without reading it

slacktivist someone who expresses support online for a cause, rather than using any physical, more effective method of protest

sock puppet a false identity used to comment positively on your own Web postings

tanorexic a person who is addicted to tanning his or her skin

12 o'clock flasher a person who is not very familiar with technology or who does not bother to read technical instructions (from the image of a clock on an electronic device always flashing '00:00' because it has not been set properly)

urban miner someone who takes valuable metals from discarded electronic devices

wagabee a girl or young woman who aspires to be a wealthy sportsman's partner

30 words to sound more posh

Some words and phrases seem to be the preserve of the posh. If you weren't born with a silver spoon in your mouth but would like to sound as if you were, then try using these.

awfully or **dreadfully** or **frightfully** very

bally euphemism for 'bloody', used as an intensifier

beastly or **ghastly** disagreeable

botheration! interjection expressing irritation

deffo definitely

drawing room or **sitting room** living room, lounge

good/bad show well/not well done

How do you do? a way of greeting someone

I say! exclamation calling attention or expressing surprise, protest, joy, etc

jolly very (especially in *jolly good*)

lavatory or **loo** not 'toilet'

looking glass mirror

my good fellow a term of address

napkin not 'serviette'

one you (ie generic 'you', as in *One gets very tired when one has to do some work.*)

pip pip! goodbye!

pudding not 'sweet' or 'dessert'

quite indeed; yes

rather! (with stress on *ther*): yes, indeed!

rich not 'wealthy' (which suggests aspiration)

sofa not 'settee' or 'couch'

What? not 'Pardon?'

… what … wouldn't you say? (used for emphasis, as in *Good show, what?*)

writing paper notepaper

21 words to understand Blinglish

Blinglish (from *bling*, the showy jewellery worn by some black rappers + *English*), is Jamaican patois or African-American slang as used by young white English people. (The language of Afro-Caribbean immigrants as adopted by young white people has also been called *Jafaikan*.) Here are just a few examples.

allow it let it be
bare lots of; very
blinging showy, shiny, excellent
blood or **blud** mate
boom! exclamation of approval or agreement
boss good
brethren or **bredren** family or close friends
bruv mate
butters or **butter** ugly (from 'everything but 'er face')
chong or **choong** attractive
diss insult, treat with disrespect
innit tag used generally at the end of a sentence: *I can't be bothered innit.*
man tag used generally at the beginning or end of a sentence: *Man, I can't be bothered.*
minging horrible, ugly
nang good
peng attractive
safe good
sick good
ting similar to 'thing' and used in various situations: *I can't be bothered and ting.*
vex to annoy: *Don't vex me man.*
you get me? tag question similar to 'do you know what I mean?'

45 words to sound archaic

If the language of youth is too much for you, you might find archaic words sound charmingly old-fashioned. If you fancy using some of the fine words of a bygone area, here are a few examples to get you started.

Abraham-man an unruly beggar
adry thirsty
alas! exclamation of grief or misfortune
alebench a bench in or in front of an alehouse
all-hid hide-and-seek
avaunt! go away!
bantling a young child, a brat
barm-cloth an apron
barmkin a battlement, or a turret, on the outer wall of a castle
brangle a brawl
brewis beef broth
bub strong drink
cap-à-pie (dressed) from head to foot
cramoisy crimson
cullion a mean or base person; a wretch, rascal
eftsoons soon afterwards
egad! a mild oath

embrangle to confuse or perplex
fain glad or joyful
fardel anything cumbersome or irksome
fetch-candle a nocturnal light, supposed to portend a death
forsooth certainly
gadzooks! a mild oath
hilding a mean, cowardly person
holus-bolus all at once; altogether
inclip to embrace
ladrone a robber
level-coil an old Christmas game in which the players changed seats; any hubbub
mammock a broken or torn piece, a shred
mayhap perhaps
mundungus a rank-smelling tobacco
napery household linen
oft often
prithee please
raiment clothing
rampick a dead tree
rouncy a riding horse
rumfustian a hot drink
sirrah sir (used in anger or contempt)
skimble-skamble wild, rambling, incoherent
swink to toil
to-fall a beginning, incidence
verily truly
wittol a man who knows his wife's unfaithfulness, and accepts it
zounds! exclamation of anger or astonishment

26 words to understand scams and tricks

From politicians to the press, from brokers to onliners, everyone seems to have a few dodgy tricks up their sleeves. These words will help you stay aware of the ways you can be played.

ambush marketing attaching your product to a major event without paying a sponsorship fee
antisocial networking using social networking sites for malicious purposes
bait advertising advertising a product at a low price to encourage buyers to come to the shop or visit the website when the company does not actually plan to sell at that price
ball-tampering the practice by a fielder in a cricket match of deliberately manipulating the condition of the ball in order to make it travel differently
blagging an overall term for deliberately obtaining or disclosing personal information without the consent of the owner of the data
boiler room an operation involving the fraudulent sale by a broker of shares that are overpriced or worthless
bullet dodging a practice whereby a company delays the granting of share options until a piece of negative market news is known to the public and the stock's price falls
carousel fraud an operation in which a fraudster charges VAT on the sale of goods, then absconds before paying the VAT to the government (also **missing trader fraud**)

clickjacking tricking a Web user into clicking on links disguised as innocuous buttons or options

click-laundering a scheme in which an automated script generates a huge number of clicks on website adverts (and for which advertisers have to pay), but which also has real users concealing the source of the clicks so they seem genuine

cybercasing using digital location data to find out when a building is unoccupied with a view to breaking into it

flipping (carried out by a member of parliament) switching from one property to another its official designation as a second home required for the fulfilment of parliamentary duties, especially to exploit tax advantages and claim upkeep allowances for which the property is eligible

pharming the covert redirection of users from legitimate websites to counterfeit sites in order to gain confidential information about them

phishing sending counterfeit emails in an attempt to get the recipients to divulge confidential information, for example bank account details

pinging locating a mobile phone by satellite, a technique theoretically restricted to police and security services, but possibly exploited by sections of the press

policy-based evidence making commissioning and undertaking research that will support a policy which has already been decided

Ponzi scheme (in the stock exchange) an operation in which a broker uses funds raised by new investors, rather than actual profits, to pay high returns to current shareholders

pretexting lying in order to obtain confidential data about another person and assume their identity

smishing sending counterfeit texts in an attempt to get the recipients to divulge confidential information (from *SMS phishing*)

spot-fixing the illegal manipulation of an incident in a sporting fixture by a participant

tab napping replacing an inactive tab in a user's browser with a false tab linked to a page that looks the same, tricking the user into thinking that it is a legitimate page and logging in as normal, so supplying their login details

typosquatting registering a variant of a well-known name, for example one that incorporates a common typographical error, as a domain name, so that a user making the error when looking for the well-known name may be led to your website (also **URL hijacking**)

vishing calling a telephone with a counterfeit recorded message in an attempt to get the recipient to divulge confidential information, for example bank account details

war-texting hacking into the software by which drivers unlock or start a car with a mobile phone, and using SMS to send commands to unlock or start the car

27 words to understand digital culture

The ubiquity of computers has resulted in a constantly and rapidly expanding area of vocabulary. Here are just a few of the interesting phenomena that have appeared with the widespread use of digital communication.

augmented reality an environment in which computer-generated elements are added in real time to the real environment, such as graphic effects being applied to live television coverage of events

bacn email that is neither spam nor personal, for example communications you have signed up to receive but often don't bother reading

blegging raising money by making your case on your blog

blog carnival a blog with many links to related articles

blogfade the phenomenon of a blogger gradually failing to update their blog

blogswarm the posting on a single story or issue by a number of bloggers in order to draw attention to it

citizen journalism the reporting of news by non-professional journalists, especially online via blogs etc

crowdsourcing attempting to solve a problem, improve a system, etc by getting suggestions from members of the public or the wider online community, using the Internet as a medium

data exhaust the large amount of digitally traceable actions and preferences that people generate when using computers and electronic devices

data furnace a group of servers used to warm a building with the heat they produce

data smog electronic information which, by its sheer volume, confuses people and increases stress

digisode a short episode of a show broadcast only on the Internet

exergaming video games that involve physical activity and constitute a form of exercise

fraudband low quality broadband

friendsourcing gathering information, recommendations, etc from trusted friends online

geek chic a style that deliberately emulates the stereotypical look and habits of computer obsessives, for example T-shirts bearing in-jokes, glasses, etc

immersive reality a computer-generated space in which a user can be projected, giving the impression of reality

lifecasting broadcasting your daily activities over the Internet using a webcam

meme an image or idea that spreads through the Web

mindcasting broadcasting your thoughts using the Internet

semantic web a development of the World Wide Web by means of which computer programs are enabled to understand human semantic input without further instructions, and with data in a form that machines themselves can process helpfully for the user

sousveillance informal networks of citizens who use digital devices to observe and, if necessary, reveal the behaviour of people in authority

splinternet the idea that the Internet is being fragmented by the existence of different social networking sites, different means of access, etc

splog a blog which the author uses to promote other websites (from *spam blog*)

transliteracy the ability to communicate using a variety of tools and media

virtual volunteering undertaking volunteer work using the Internet

web rage anger arising from problems using the Internet

19 ways to tell someone to hurry up

These are some of the many ways you can tell someone to hurry up.

chop-chop!	**look sharp!**
come along!	**look smart!**
come on!	**make it snappy!**
get a move on!	**pull your finger out!**
get a wiggle on!	**put your foot down!**
get cracking!	**shake a leg!**
get your skates on!	**show your heels!**
jump to it!	**step on it!**
look alive!	**step on the gas!**
look lively!	

60 words to understand wares

The widespread use of computers also brings with it a plethora of 'ware' words, in which the suffix -*ware* indicates a type of software or, occasionally, published data.

abandonware is no longer distributed or maintained by its original publisher (also **orphanware**)

adware is bundled with another program and displays advertising while the other program is running

beerware is released with a liberal licence that allows you to do what you want with the software

bloatware has more facilities than most users need, making correspondingly large demands on system resources

brochureware is pages on a company's website produced by converting printed marketing materials directly into an online format

cardware is freeware or shareware in return for which the author asks you to send him or her a postcard (also **postcardware**)

careware is freeware or shareware for which the author suggests a donation to charity as payment (also **charityware**, **donateware**)

censorware controls the content that can be downloaded from the Internet to your machine

cloudware runs on Internet servers rather than your hard drive

courseware is designed to be used in educational courses

crapware is superfluous and useless

crimeware is malware that facilitates cybercrime

crippleware has been partly disabled to provide a limited demonstration of its use, often as shareware (also **demoware**, **liteware**)

crudware is a slang term for low-quality freeware

dribbleware has to be maintained with frequently released patches

emailware is freeware or shareware in return for which the author asks you to send him or her an email

expireware has an inbuilt expiry date or usage limit

firmware forms a more or less permanent and unerasable part of a computer's memory

freeware can be copied without charge (but not sold)

fritterware has more facilities than most users need and which have no important purpose

greyware is in a 'grey area' between software and virus, for example spyware and adware

griddleware sends a single problem to multiple computers and collates the results

groupware supports group activity

guiltware is shareware for which the author makes a plea for you to buy it, emphasizing the hard work involved in it

hyperware is software with hypertext links

kruegerware is spyware that is hard to get rid of and can also damage the computer (named after the malicious character Freddy Krueger in the film *Nightmare on Elm Street*)

liveware is all the people working with a computer system (also **meatware**, **peopleware**)

malware is designed to cause damage to a computer system (also **badware**)

middleware allows two otherwise incompatible programs or networks to operate together

nagware sometimes pops up in shareware to encourage the user to register the product (also **annoyware**)

obnoxiousware is any malicious or intrusive software

payware has to be paid for

poachware copies sensitive information such as passwords

ransomware encrypts a computer's hard drive and the attacker demands a ransom to decrypt it

registerware requires you to register before you can use it

requestware is freeware or shareware in return for which the author asks you to do something

scareware is presented as anti-virus software but is actually harmful when downloaded

scumware can be downloaded to your computer without your consent or knowledge

shareware is available on free trial, often with restricted features or for a limited time, before the user has to register and pay for the product (also **trialware**)

shelfware is purchased and not used

shovelware is data published in electronic form without appropriate adaptation from its original format

snoopware monitors activity on a particular computer, for example that of an employee or spouse

spamware is designed for sending out spam

spyware gathers information about the user and transmits it to another user

stealthware can be installed on your computer without your knowledge

thiefware secretly takes information from your computer

treeware is data on paper

vapourware is loudly heralded but not yet (and possibly never to be) available

wetware is the living human brain

17 words to understand extreme sports

Here are terms for a few of the more bizarre sports which have emerged as thrill-seeking is taken to new levels.

adventure racing racing involving a combination of sporting disciplines, such as orienteering, rock climbing, and mountain biking

aggressive inline skating inline skating involving stunts, slides, etc

barefooting or **barefoot skiing** water-skiing without using water skis

bouldering rock climbing without a rope – usually at low levels and above a crash-pad

crocodile bungee bungee jumping into a body of water containing crocodiles

octopush a form of hockey played underwater

skysurfing skydiving involving the performance of stunts in free fall while riding on a board similar to a surfboard

slacklining walking across a nylon rope stretched across two anchor points and left relatively slack so that it moves more

street luge an activity involving riding a board similar to a sledge at high speed down along a paved street or course (also called **land luge**, **road luge**)

subway surfing standing on top of a train as it moves through an underground railway system

tombstoning jumping in a vertically straight position from a cliff into water

ultrarunning running very long distances, often over testing terrain such as mountains and jungle

volcano boarding sliding down an active volcano on a board similar to a sledge

wingsuit flying flying in the air wearing a special jumpsuit with extra material between the arms and torso and between the legs, which increases the surface area of the body and the amount of lift

zorbing rolling downhill while enclosed in a sphere of transparent plastic

15 words to sound more elegant

Words chosen for their beautiful sound as well as their meaning can add a mellifluous quality to a work, especially one in a spoken medium.

antelucan before dawn or daylight

benison a benediction, blessing

chatoyant iridescent, shimmering

chersonese a peninsula

coquelicot the poppy

grandiose grand or imposing; bombastic

greensward land covered with grass

labyrinthine full of intricate twists and turns

martellato played with a hammering touch (*music*)

mausolean grand, stately, imposing

nepenthe a drink or drug causing sorrow to be forgotten

serendipity the faculty of making fortunate discoveries by accident

suaveolent fragrant

susurrus a murmuring; a whisper; a rustling

zephyr a soft, gentle breeze

33 words to understand green culture

Our concerns for the environment have given us another new vocabulary. Among the more technical terms that have become widely understood are expressions for some intriguing ideas and concepts.

carrotmob an organized gathering of people at an environmentally friendly business in order to demonstrate support by buying its products

climate canary something, such as an animal or plant, whose poor health is an indicator of potential environmental damage

close the loop to buy a recycled item which has been reused or reprocessed more than once

cookprint the amount of energy and other resources used in preparing meals

daylighting locating and designing a building to allow optimal use of natural light and so reduce consumption of fuel

eco-bling household gadgets marketed as eco-friendly but which in reality do not save much energy

eco-driving driving in a manner that minimizes fuel consumption and exhaust emissions

ecological rucksack the amount of raw material used in the manufacture of a product measured against the lifespan of the end product

ecosexual a person whose interest in the environment helps to attract, or affects their choice of, a romantic partner

ecotarian someone who eats only food that is in season, and sustainably and locally produced (also **ecovore**)

freecycling recycling an unwanted product by giving it free to someone who can use it

garden-to-fork cooking food you have grown yourself

gas-sipper a car which does not use a lot of fuel (by analogy with *gas-guzzler*)

green anarchy a form of anarchism that focuses on environmental concerns

green collar relating to jobs in the environmental sector

green roof a roof that is covered with deliberately planted vegetation (also **eco-roof, living roof**)

greentailing selling environmentally friendly products

greenwash the extolling by a company of eco-friendly credentials that have little basis in reality

hypermiling driving using techniques that maximize a vehicle's fuel economy

off-grid or **off-the-grid** not using one or more public utilities

pay-as-you-throw a rubbish collection fee calculated on the basis of how much rubbish a household or business generates

precycling avoiding unnecessary waste by buying products with minimal packaging

season creep changes in the timing of the seasons, especially the earlier onset of spring, as a result of global warming

slow travel travelling long distances over land and sea rather than by plane in an attempt to reduce your carbon footprint

swishing swapping unused or unwanted clothes with family and friends as a means of recycling

trashion fashion items made from used and recycled items

upcycling turning waste products into higher value products

vertical garden a wall covered with deliberately planted vegetation (also called **green wall**, **living wall**)

18 words to refer to eccentric enthusiasts

Most of us are aware of gamers, philatelists and bibliophiles, but there are some curious collections and odd obsessions out there. These are a few of the collectors and enthusiasts with less widely recognized hobbies.

aerophilatelist a collector of airmail stamps

brandophilist a collector of cigar bands

brolliologist a collector of umbrellas

copoclephilist a collector of key rings

cosplayer someone who regularly dresses up as a fictional character, for example from science fiction or animé

errinophilist someone who collects stamps other than postage stamps

helixophile a collector of corkscrews

leaf-peeper a person who seeks out places where the leaves have changed to autumnal colours

lotologist a collector of lottery tickets

noodler someone who catches fish using their bare hands

photobomber someone who jumps into other people's photographs as they are being taken

planker someone who lies like a plank, straight and face down, in public places and posts pictures of the activity on the Internet

sleevefacer someone who holds a record sleeve featuring an image against an appropriate background and foreground to the image, creating an illusion which they post on the Internet
sucrologist a collector of sugar sachets
taphophile someone enthusiastic about cemeteries and gravestones
telegerist a collector of telephone calling cards
umbraphile a person who is enthusiastic about, and seeks out, eclipses
vecturist a collector of transport tickets and tokens

14 words to sound like an armchair general

An armchair general can be defined as, among other things, someone who speaks with an authoritative tone on military strategy, usually from the safety of their computer at home. If you want to join today's armchair militia, here are a few words to set you on your way.

asymmetric warfare conflict between two sides with significantly different military resources
blue-on-blue involving accidental firing on your allies in a military situation
collateral damage civilian casualties or damage to non-military targets
complex terrain terrain that restricts the use of weapons
decapitation removal of the leader of a regime
effects-based warfare warfare involving strategies intended to achieve a particular effect
exit strategy a planned method of withdrawal from a military situation
friendly fire accidental firing upon your allies rather than your enemies
human terrain populated terrain
hybrid threat the dangers of traditional warfare combined with those of terrorism and insurgency
optics how the public perceives a military action
pre-emptive self-defence attack
targets of opportunity military targets that are additional to primary targets but deemed legitimate
unlawful enemy combatant a terrorist, considered not subject to the conventional rights of prisoners of war

56 ways to avoid cliché

Many phrases have been so overused that they have become clichés. Here are some examples, with expressions to use instead.

Cliché	Use
at the end of the day	**ultimately; in the end**
at this moment in time	**at this moment; just now; right now**
can of worms	**complex problem; difficult situation; unpredictable situation**
cause a headache	**cause a problem; cause a difficulty**
come to terms with	**cope with; accept**
do the math	**work it out; make the calculation**
emotional rollercoaster	**difficult/trying/emotional experience**
go figure	**it's easy to work out/see**
hold your hands up	**admit/take responsibility**

in a very real sense	This can be omitted without loss of meaning.
in the fullness of time	later; after a while
in this day and age	now; these days
… is the new…	… has become fashionable/widespread
move the goalposts	change the conditions/requirements
not rocket science	simple; easy; requiring little intelligence
prodigious talent	exceptional ability; extraordinary talent
reach out to	attempt to contact; communicate with
score an own goal	make a move to your own disadvantage; make a mistake
set out your stall	make your aims/intentions clear
sing from the same hymn sheet	be in agreement
take your eye off the ball	lose focus; lose sight of your priorities; become distracted from your aims
the big picture	all the possibilities
the bottom line	what is most important
the complete package	have all the necessary talents
the fact of the matter	the fact; the truth; the reality
the jury is still out	it's not decided/clear yet
tick all the boxes	fulfil the requirements
years young	years old (or simply state the person's age)

18 ways to tell someone to wait

Here are some of the many ways to tell someone to wait.

all in good time
bear with me
half a mo
half a moment
half a tick
hang in there
hang on
hold on
hold the bus (*Scottish*)

hold your horses
I'll be right with you
just a jiffy
just a minute
just a moment
just a second
just a tick
wait a minute
wait a moment

18 words to sound like a muso

If you aspire to enter the world of music journalism, there are a few terms you should know. Beware – most come with a cliché warning.

angular with leaps between intervals: *angular guitar riffs*
-esque suffix denoting similarity: *chiming, Byrds-esque guitars*
listen as a noun: *It's an essential listen.*
meets denotes a combination of styles: *sounds as if Elvis meets Marilyn Manson*
muscular strong: *The band delivers muscular riffs.*
new level doing something slightly advanced or different: *Their sound takes emocore to a new level.*
on acid denotes a more energetic, bizarre, etc version of an established artist: *sounds like Coldplay on acid*

outing recording: *The band's latest outing is a departure from their previous efforts.*
pyrotechnics flashy performance: *a display of rock pyrotechnics*
return to form used when any artist releases good music again after a dip in quality: *U2's new album is a real return to form.*
songsmith a songwriter
soundscape the impression created by a sound: *a lush digital soundscape*
spiky edgy: *spiky, soulful post-punk*
stripped-down describes a sound with little production or embellishment (also **pared-down**)
stylings style of singing, playing, etc: *easygoing vocal stylings*
tunesmith a musician
wunderkind any successful young musician

25 words to sound like a gamer

The terminology of video games is extensive and ever-changing, but here are just some of the best examples of gamer language.

AI an artificial intelligence: a computer-controlled character in a game
BFG a big, powerful gun
boomstick a shotgun
boss a powerful enemy who appears at the end of a game, or at the end of a level
bot an element of a game controlled by computer
brick a character who is a powerful fighter but does not have any other abilities
camp to wait at a 'spawn point' for a character to appear again so as to kill that character immediately
cheat a hidden feature programmed into a game and revealed, for example, on a related web page, which allows a character to gain an additional advantage
dungeon crawl a situation within a game in which a character has to battle opponents in an enclosed, often labyrinthine, area
easter egg a hidden feature programmed into a game, often one which is amusing but does not affect the course of a game
frag to blow up (another character)
gameplay the way in which elements can behave and interact in a game, sometimes used as a measure of how satisfying a game is to play
griefer someone who takes part in an online game simply to cause trouble
grind to repeat tasks simply in order to improve a character, augment their ability, etc
level up to go up a level in a game (and improve a character's ability)
lurk to hide in a game
mini-boss a powerful enemy who appears during a level of a game
NPC a non-player character: a character controlled by the computer but not actively involved in a game
PvE player versus environment: a conflict between two or more online players
PvP player versus player: a conflict between two or more online players
pwn to kill or destroy (from a mistyping of *own*)
spawn (of a character) to appear again after dying
spawn point a location where a character appears again after dying
taunt to send a message to an opponent to gloat over a victory
walkthrough a guide that virtually 'walks' you through the environment and playing features of a game

18 words to sound like a fashionista

To be part of the fashion in-crowd, there are some words you simply have to know.

channel show as an influence: *a style that channels Audrey Hepburn*
fashion 2.0, 3.0, etc fashion sold on or connected in some way with the latest digital technology
fast fashion copies of clothes that appear in high street shops very soon after appearing in designers' catwalk shows
ferosh impressive (short for *ferocious*)
fierce impressive
frow in the front row at an influential fashion show
I'm loving I love: *I'm loving this look.*
investment piece a more expensive item that is durable and will survive fashion trends
lust-have an item of clothing, accessory, etc that you really want
now in fashion
on-trend in fashion
over out of fashion
pop to be brightened with colour: *A yellow bag will make the look pop.*
rock (the catwalk, a look, etc): to wear, carry off, etc very successfully
trendlet a minor or passing trend
statement piece an eye-catching item
swag style; stylish
tribe the group you belong to as determined by your style

11 words to identify quirks of language

We've all noticed those little quirks of language that can often be entertaining. These are some of the intriguing aspects of language and the little-known names for them.

anancronym an acronym that is so familiar that few people know that it is an acronym or what the letters stand for, for example *laser*, *radar* (from *anachronism* and *acronym*)
aptonym a coincidentally fitting name for your occupation, for example *Mr Read the librarian* (from *apt* and *onoma,* meaning 'name')
backronym or **bacronym** an acronym formed using the initial letters of an existing word, sometimes for humorous effect, for example *golf = gentlemen only, ladies forbidden* (from *back* and *acronym*)
eggcorn the substitution of a word or phrase for a word or words that sound similar and which also have some semantic connection (from the use of *eggcorn* to mean *acorn*, based on an acorn's egg-like shape)
mondegreen a phrase that results from mishearing the lyric of a song (coined in 1954 by Sylvia Wright, from the mistaken perception of the lyric *laid him on the green* for *Lady Mondegreen*)
mononym a single name by which a person is known, for example *Shakespeare, Madonna, Ronaldo* (from *mono* meaning 'single' and *onoma* meaning 'name')
paranym a word with a meaning that has been slightly altered from its original meaning, designed to evade or conceal an unpleasant truth, for example *efficiencies* used to mean 'cutbacks' (from *para* meaning 'beside, beyond'). Note that a **paronym**, which is occasionally spelt **paranym**, is a word from the same root as, or sounding like, another (and is therefore a paronym of paranym).

phantonym a word that looks like it should mean one thing, but actually means another thing, for example *fulsome*, which many people think means 'lavish', but strictly means 'sickeningly obsequious' (coined in this sense in 2009 by Jack Rosenthal, from *phantom*).

Phantonym has also been used to refer to an invented antonym, for example *overstand* as an antonym of *understand*.

recursive acronym an acronym in which one of the words in the full-out form is the acronym itself, for example *Visa = Visa International Service Association*

retronym a new word referring to a concept for which a word already exists, used to distinguish it from a newer concept, for example *snail mail*, which was coined after the development of email (from *retro* meaning 'backwards, behind')

snowclone a well-known phrase which you can adapt by substituting your own words, for example *In X, no one can hear you Y* (coined in 2004 by Glen Whitman, recognizing the then-overused phrase 'If Eskimos have N words for snow, X must have Y words for Z.')

J

jab *v, n*

♦ *v*

poke, prod, dig nudge, stab, push, elbow, lunge, punch, box, tap, thrust

♦ *n*

poke, prod, dig nudge, stab, push, punch, box, tap, shot, injection

jabber *v*

chatter, gab, gabble, prattle, rabbit, ramble, tattle, babble, jaw, prate, rattle, mumble, witter, yap, sputter; *dialect & N Am* blather; *Scot* yatter, blether; *Aust* yabber

jack

■ **jack up**

1 LIFT, raise, hoist, elevate

2 *jack up prices*

increase, inflate, put up, push up, hike (up), raise

jacket *n*

casing cover, covering wrapping wrap, wrapper, case, sheath, shell, skin, envelope, folder

See panel at **coat**.

jackpot *n*

prize, first prize, winnings, kitty, pool, pot, reward, award, bonanza, stakes

COLLOQ. big time

■ **hit the jackpot**

succeed, make it, arrive, score, get rich

COLLOQ. make a packet/bundle/pile, rake it in, hit the big time, clean up

jaded *adj*

fatigued, exhausted, dulled, played-out, tired, tired out, weary, wearied, worn out, spent, done, bored, unenthusiastic; *Scot* disjaskit

COLLOQ. fagged, done in, all in, ready to drop, shattered, knackered, whacked, jiggered, bushed, fed up, cheesed off; *N Am* pooped (out), tuckered out

F3 fresh, refreshed

jag *n*

barb, point, projection, protrusion, snag notch, spur, nick, tooth

TECHNICAL denticle, dentil

jagged *adj*

uneven, irregular, notched, indented, rough, serrated, saw-edged, toothed, ragged, pointed, ridged, craggy, snagged, snaggy, barbed, spiked, nicked, broken

TECHNICAL denticulate

F3 even, smooth

jaggedness *n*

unevenness, irregularity, roughness, brokenness, serration, raggedness

FORMAL serrature

F3 evenness, smoothness

jail, gaol *n, v*

♦ *n*

prison, jailhouse, custody, lock-up, penitentiary, detention centre, guardhouse, house of correction

OLD kitty

COLLOQ. inside, nick; *N Am* pen, poky

SLANG porridge, clink, cooler, slammer, quod, jug can, choky; *N Am* hoosegow, big house

♦ *v*

imprison, lock up, put away, send down, send to prison, confine, detain, intern, impound, immure

FORMAL incarcerate

jailer, gaoler *n*

prison officer, warden, warder, guard, keeper, captor

OLD turnkey, under-turnkey

SLANG screw

jam¹ *n*

bread and jam

conserve, preserve, jelly, spread, marmalade, confiture; *S Afr* konfyt

jam² *v, n*

♦ *v*

1 CRAM, pack, wedge, squash, squeeze, press, crush, crowd, congest, ram, stuff, insert, confine, force, thrust, push

2 BLOCK, clog obstruct, close (off), stall, stick

♦ *n*

1 CRUSH, crowd, press, congestion, pack, herd, swarm, mob, throng horde, multitude

2 *a traffic jam*

bottleneck, congestion, gridlock, hold-up, obstruction

3 PREDICAMENT, trouble, quandary, plight, straits

COLLOQ. fix, hole, (tight) spot, bind, pickle, scrape, stew, the soup

jamb *n*

post, shaft, pole, pillar, frame, support, prop, upright, stanchion

jamboree *n*

celebration, party, rally, festivity, festival, carnival, jubilee, junket, fête, frolic, revelry, spree, carouse, merriment, field day, gathering get-together, convention

COLLOQ. shindig

jammy *adj*

lucky, fortunate, favoured, charmed, successful, prosperous, timely, opportune, expedient, providential

FORMAL auspicious, fortuitous, propitious

F3 unlucky

jangle *v, n*

♦ *v*

1 CLANK, clash, jar, clang clatter, clink, jingle, chime, rattle, vibrate

2 *jangle someone's nerves*

upset, irritate, disturb, bother, trouble, make anxious

♦ *n*

clang clash, rattle, clatter, jar, jarring cacophony, clink, din, discord, racket, reverberation, clangour, stridor

FORMAL dissonance

F3 euphony

janitor *n*

caretaker, doorkeeper, doorman, custodian, concierge, porter; *Scot* servitor

TECHNICAL ostiary

jar¹ *n*

a jam jar

pot, container, vessel, receptacle, crock, pitcher, urn, vase, flask, flagon, carafe, jug mug cruet, caddy, canister, terrine, tureen, olla, pithos, tinaja, water monkey, greybeard, amphora, dolium, stamnos

jar² v

1 JOLT, agitate, rattle, shake, jerk, vibrate
2 GRATE, upset, disturb, trouble, jangle, irritate, rasp, grind, annoy, offend, irk
COLLOQ. nettle
3 CLASH, conflict, be in conflict, be at odds, be at variance, quarrel, disagree, bicker, jostle

jargon n

1 SPECIALIST LANGUAGE, technical language, journalese, computerese, computerspeak, legalese, psychobabble, buzz words, officialese, telegraphese, parlance, slang cant, argot, vernacular, idiom, usage
COLLOQ. Greek
2 NONSENSE, gibberish
COLLOQ. gobbledygook, mumbo-jumbo

SYNONYM NUANCES

sense 1

Both **specialist language** and **technical language** would be used without implication of language that has been tailored for its market audience, while **journalese** suggests less structured language and can imply bad or lazy journalism. **Computerese** and **computerspeak**, on the other hand, somewhat facetiously refer to language used by computer buffs, while **legalese** suggests the parallel term of the legal profession, and all hint at a deliberate arcaneness and exclusivity. **Officialese** is again fairly derogatory and conveys the idea of unnecessarily overblown bureaucratic language, whereas **telegraphese** is more straightforwardly suggestive of stark, clipped language. **Psychobabble**, while suggesting the language of psychologists, may often be used derogatively of any analytical or pseudo-psychological terms: *psychobabble portrays many criminals as the victims*.

Parlance is a more neutral term for a manner of speaking: *in medical parlance*, while **idiom** and **usage** have to do with the everyday mode of expression: *a term in current usage*. **Buzz words** refers to the current trends in any given field, and so has positive overtones of fun and fashionability. **Slang** is also fairly unmarked, and suggests informal language that falls outside of standard language; **argot** is used of informal, but perhaps slovenly language, and **vernacular** is more suggestive of pertaining to a particular group: *a speech in the cockney vernacular*. **Cant** is more disapproving in its implication of talk that lacks sincerity or meaningful content: *the prevalent cant and humbug about political reform*.

---

jarring adj

clashing discordant, jangling harsh, grating irritating cacophonous, rasping strident, upsetting disturbing troubling jolting

jaundiced adj

1 BITTER, cynical, pessimistic, sceptical, distrustful, disbelieving biased, prejudiced, bigoted, envious, jealous, hostile, jaded, suspicious, resentful, unenthusiastic, misanthropic
2 DISTORTED, biased, prejudiced, bigoted, preconceived

jaunt n

trip, outing excursion, holiday, tour, ride, drive, spin, ramble, stroll

jauntily adv

cheerfully, brightly, energetically, airily, self-confidently, cheekily, smartly, perkily

jaunty adj

1 CHEERFUL, sprightly, lively, perky, breezy, energetic, bouncy, buoyant, high-spirited, self-confident, carefree, airy, cheeky
2 DEBONAIR, dapper, smart, trim, showy, flashy, spruce, stylish
E₃ 1 depressed **2** dowdy

javelin n

spear, dart, harpoon, handstaff, jerid, gavelock, pilum, pile

jaw n, v

♦ *n*
1 *the lower jaw*
mandible, mouth, muzzle
TECHNICAL maxilla
COLLOQ. chops, trap
Related adjectives: maxillary, gnathic, gnathal
2 TALK, gossip, chat, conversation, discussion
COLLOQ. chinwag natter, confab, rap; *N Am* visit; *Aust* wongi
SLANG schmooze
3 *the jaws of death*
clutches, grasp, control, power, claws, threshold
♦ *v*
chat, chatter, gossip, talk, gabble, jabber, babble
COLLOQ. natter, rabbit (on)

jazz v, n

■ **jazz up**
liven up, enliven, smarten up, brighten up, ginger up

Kinds of jazz include:

acid jazz	free-form	neo-classic
Afro-Cuban	fusion	New Orleans
avant-garde	groove	post-bop
bebop	hard bop	ragtime
blues	hot jazz	soul jazz
boogie-woogie	improvised jazz	spiel
bop	jazz-funk	swing
bossa nova	jive	third stream
classic	mainstream	West Coast
cool	modal	
Dixieland	modern	

---

jazzy adj

lively, smart, spirited, stylish, bright, bold, wild, fancy, gaudy, vivacious, zestful
COLLOQ. flashy, snazzy, swinging
E₃ conservative, square

jealous adj

1 ENVIOUS, covetous, desirous, grudging begrudging resentful, jaundiced
OLD (*Spenser*) gealous
COLLOQ. green, green-eyed
2 SUSPICIOUS, wary, doubting distrustful, anxious, possessive, insecure
3 PROTECTIVE, watchful, mindful, careful, vigilant, wary, defensive
E₃ 1 contented, satisfied

jealously adv

with envy, enviously, covetously, desirously, resentfully, possessively, distrustfully

jealousy n

1 ENVY, covetousness, grudge, grudgingness, resentment, bitterness, spite, ill-will
OLD yellowness, emulation, zelotypia; (*Spenser*) gealousy, gelosy
COLLOQ. green-eyed monster
2 SUSPICION, distrust, mistrust, doubt, possessiveness, insecurity
3 PROTECTIVENESS, watchfulness, mindfulness, carefulness, vigilance, wariness, defensiveness

---

QUOTATIONS
O, beware, my lord, of jealousy, / It is the green-eyed monster which doth mock / The meat it feeds on
WILLIAM SHAKESPEARE, *Othello*

jeer *v, n*

♦ *v*

mock, scoff, taunt, gibe, ridicule, sneer, make fun of, scorn, chaff, barrack, tease, twit, heckle, shout down, hiss, boo, banter, jest, laugh to scorn, flout, fleer; *dialect* gird

FORMAL deride

COLLOQ. knock; *N Am* razz; *Aust* chiack, have a shot at; *Aust & NZ* sling off at

SLANG *N Am* goof; *Aust & NZ* poke borak at

♦ *n*

mockery, ridicule, banter, taunt, gibe, sneer, scoff, teasing abuse, catcall, hiss, boo, hoot, jest, flout, fleer

OLD frump, gird

FORMAL derision

COLLOQ. dig

jejune *adj*

1 UNSOPHISTICATED, simple, naive, immature, childish, juvenile, puerile, silly, callow
2 DULL, uninteresting boring unoriginal, arid, trite, banal, senseless, barren, empty, colourless, vapid, insipid, prosaic, wishy-washy, dry, spiritless

E3 1 mature 2 meaningful

jell

see **gel, jell.**

jeopardize *v*

endanger, expose to danger, risk, put at risk, put in jeopardy, hazard, venture, gamble, chance, take a chance, threaten, menace, expose, stake

FORMAL imperil

E3 protect, safeguard

jeopardy *n*

danger, risk, hazard, endangerment, venture, vulnerability, precariousness, menace, threat, insecurity, exposure, liability

FORMAL peril

E3 safety, security

jerk *v, n*

♦ *v*

jolt, tug twitch, jog yank, wrench, pull, jiggle, lurch, pluck, thrust, shrug throw, bounce

♦ *n*

1 JOLT, tug twitch, jar, jog yank, wrench, pull, pluck, lurch, throw, thrust, shrug
2 IDIOT, fool

COLLOQ. nincompoop, ass, chump, ninny, neddy, clot, dope, twit, nitwit, nit, sucker, mug twerp, birdbrain, silly-billy, berk, (proper) Charlie, gubbins, sap, saphead, wazzock, dum-dum, coot, goat, headbanger

SLANG wally, dumbo, pillock, prat, dork, geek, plonker, git, nerd, dweeb, nerk, goop, josser, nig-nog sawney, schlemiel, turkey, cloth head, dipstick, goof, kook, tosspot; (*taboo*) dickhead, prick

jerkily *adv*

fitfully, spasmodically, jumpily, bumpily, roughly, unevenly

E3 smoothly

jerky *adj*

fitful, twitchy, spasmodic, jumpy, jolting lurching convulsive, disconnected, bumpy, bouncy, shaky, shaking rough, uneven, unco-ordinated, uncontrolled, incoherent

E3 smooth

jerry-built *adj*

insubstantial, ramshackle, thrown together, quickly built, built on the cheap, rickety, unstable, cheap, shoddy, defective, faulty, flimsy, unsubstantial, slipshod, cheapjack

E3 firm, stable, substantial

jersey *n*

sweater, jumper, pullover, sweatshirt, top, woolly

jest *n, v*

♦ *n*

joke, quip, witticism, banter, fooling prank, practical joke, trick, hoax

OLD bourd

COLLOQ. wisecrack, crack, gag kidding leg-pull

♦ *v*

joke, tell jokes, quip, fool, tease, mock, jeer

COLLOQ. kid

■ **in jest**

in fun, as a joke, jokingly, to tease, playfully, mischievously

jester *n*

clown, fool, court-fool, comic, buffoon, comedian, humorist, joker, wag zany, wit, prankster, quipster, gagman, juggler, joculator, pantaloon, harlequin, mummer, merry-andrew, droll

OLD patch, merryman, bourder, scop, Jack-pudding; (*Shakesp*) motley

jet¹ *n, v*

♦ *n*

a jet of water

gush, spurt, spout, spray, spring sprinkler, sprayer, fountain, flow, stream, rush, squirt

♦ *v*

1 GUSH, spurt, spray, spring flow, stream, rush, squirt
2 FLY, zoom, rush, shoot, career

jet² *adj*

jet black

black, pitch-black, ebony, sable, raven, sooty, inky

jetsam

See **flotsam.**

jettison *v*

discard, scrap, throw away, get rid of, abandon, offload, unload, drop, eject, expel, heave

COLLOQ. ditch, dump, chuck

E3 load, take on

jetty *n*

breakwater, pier, dock, harbour, groyne, mole, quay, wharf, landing-place, landing-stage

jewel *n*

1 GEM, precious stone, gemstone, ornament

COLLOQ. rock, sparkler

2 TREASURE, gem, find, prize, masterpiece, showpiece, rarity, paragon, pearl, jewellery, pride and joy, crème de la crème, *pièce de résistance*

jewellery *n*

jewels, gems, ornaments, trinkets, regalia, treasure, bijoux, bijouterie, finery, gemmery, gauds

---

Types of jewellery include:

amulet	cufflink	pendant
anklet	diadem	power beads
bangle	ear cuff	ring
beads	earring	rivière
belly chain	eternity ring	signet ring
bindi	friendship bracelet	solitaire ring
body jewel	hatpin	stud
bracelet	hoop	tiara
brooch	locket	tiepin
cameo	nail jewel	toe ring
chain	navel ring	tooth jewel
charm bracelet	necklace	torque
choker	necklet	
coronet	nose ring	

Jezebel *n*

seductress, temptress, *femme fatale*, hussy, scarlet woman, loose woman, Delilah, wanton, whore, harlot, jade, man-eater, witch

COLLOQ. vamp

SLANG scrubber, tart

jib *v*

balk, shrink, recoil, back off, stall, refuse, retreat, stop, stop short

jibe
see **gibe**, **jibe**.

jiffy *n*
instant, moment, second, sec, split second, flash,
twinkling twinkling of an eye, minute, tick, two ticks,
trice, no time
COLLOQ. two shakes of a lamb's tail; *dialect* whiff
E3 age

jig *v*
jerk, prance, caper, hop, jump, leap, twitch, skip,
bounce, bob, wiggle, shake, wobble

jigger *v*
wreck, destroy, break, ruin, spoil, undermine
FORMAL vitiate
COLLOQ. botch up, kibosh, louse up, make a pig's ear of,
scupper
SLANG balls up, bugger up

jiggery-pokery *n*
deceit, trickery, dishonesty, fraud, deception, mischief,
subterfuge, chicanery, funny business, hanky-panky
COLLOQ. monkey business

jiggle *v*
jerk, jump, bounce, twitch, fidget, shift, shake, agitate,
jig jog joggle, waggle, wiggle, wobble

jilt *v*
abandon, reject, desert, walk out on, discard, brush off,
leave, drop, spurn, betray, cast aside; *Scot* begunk
OLD throw over
COLLOQ. ditch, chuck, dump, pack in

jingle *v, n*
♦ *v*
clink, tinkle, ring ding chime, chink, jangle, clatter, rattle
FORMAL tintinnabulate
♦ *n*
1 CLINK, tinkle, ringing chime, ring ding clang rattle,
jangle, clangour
FORMAL tintinnabulation
2 RHYME, verse, song carol, tune, ditty, doggerel, melody,
poem, chant, slogan, chorus, refrain

jingoism *n*
chauvinism, flag-waving patriotism, nationalism,
imperialism, sabre-rattling insularity

jinx *n, v*
♦ *n*
spell, curse, bad luck, evil eye, hex, voodoo, hoodoo,
Indian sign, black magic, charm, plague
FORMAL malediction, affliction
COLLOQ. gremlin
SLANG *Aust* moz, mozz
♦ *v*
curse, bewitch, bedevil, cast a spell on, doom, plague

jitters *n*
nerves, nervousness, tenseness, anxiety, fidgets,
agitation, trembling uneasiness
COLLOQ. edginess, heebie-jeebies, habdabs, the creeps,
the shakes, the shivers, the willies, jimjams

jittery *adj*
nervous, anxious, agitated, uneasy, on edge, flustered,
quivering shaky, shivery, trembling jumpy, fidgety,
quaking panicky
FORMAL perturbed
COLLOQ. edgy, nervy, twitchy, het up, keyed up,
wound up, climbing the walls, uptight, with butterflies in
your stomach, on pins and needles, shaking like a
leaf/jelly, with your heart in your mouth, in a sweat,
in a stew, in a tizzy
SLANG screwed-up
E3 calm, composed, confident

job *n*
1 *she has a good job*
work, employment, occupation, position, post, pursuit,
situation, profession, line of work/business, career, calling

vocation, trade, métier, capacity, business, (means of)
livelihood
2 *it's a difficult job*
task, piece of work, chore, duty, responsibility, charge,
commission, assignment, mission, activity, affair, concern,
business, proceeding project, enterprise, office, capacity,
pursuit, role, undertaking venture, province, part, place,
share, errand, function, contribution, stint, consignment
■ **have a job doing something**
find something difficult, find it a problem, have a problem
with, have a hard time doing something find something
(to be) troublesome
■ **just the job**
exactly what is needed/wanted, just the thing
COLLOQ. just the ticket, just what the doctor ordered

jobless *adj*
unemployed, out of work, without work, workless, laid
off, inactive, idle, redundant
COLLOQ. on the dole
E3 employed

jockey *n, v*
♦ *n*
equestrian, horseman, horsewoman, rider, jump-jockey
COLLOQ. jockette
♦ *v*
manipulate, manoeuvre, engineer, negotiate, wheedle,
cajole, coax, induce, ease, edge, manage
FORMAL inveigle

jocose *adj*
humorous, playful, funny, jesting mischievous,
pleasant, teasing comical, droll, facetious, witty,
zsportive, waggish, jovial, joyous, merry, mirthful
FORMAL lepid
E3 morose

jocular *adj*
joking jesting funny, humorous, jovial, amusing hilarious,
comical, comic, entertaining facetious, droll, whimsical,
teasing playful, witty, waggish, roguish
FORMAL jocose
E3 serious

jocularity *n*
jesting funniness, humour, joviality, amusement,
entertainment, laughter, hilarity, merriment, gaiety,
jolliness, comicality, drollery, wit, whimsicality,
waggishness, pleasantry, facetiousness, playfulness,
sportiveness, sport, roguishness, fooling teasing
FORMAL jocosity, jocoseness, desipience

jog *v, n*
♦ *v*
1 JOLT, jar, bump, jostle, jerk, joggle, nudge, poke, shake,
prod, bounce, push, rock, elbow; *dialect* shog; *Scot*
dunch, dunsh, hod, hotch, whig
2 PROMPT, remind, stir, arouse, activate, stimulate
3 RUN, trot, canter
COLLOQ. mosey
♦ *n*
1 JOLT, bump, jerk, nudge, shove, push, poke, prod, shake,
jig-jog joggle; *dialect* shog
2 RUN, trot, canter

joie de vivre *n*
cheerfulness, enjoyment, buoyancy, joyfulness, joy,
enthusiasm, merriment, mirth, pleasure, relish, zest, gaiety,
gusto
FORMAL blitheness, ebullience
COLLOQ. bounce, get-up-and-go
E3 depression

join *v*
1 UNITE, connect, combine, attach, link, amalgamate, ally,
unify, fasten, merge, converge, marry, couple, yoke, tie,
splice, knit, weld, fuse, bind, cement, glue, add, adhere,
annex
OLD (*Shakesp*) injoint, interjoin
FORMAL conjoin

2 BORDER (ON), verge on, touch, meet, coincide, march with
FORMAL abut, adjoin, conjoin
3 ASSOCIATE, affiliate, become a member of, accompany, co-operate, collaborate, ally, enlist, enrol, enter, sign up, team up with
COLLOQ. hook into
F3 1 divide, separate **3** leave
■ **join in**
take part in, participate, partake, co-operate, pitch in, lend a hand, help, contribute, chip in
COLLOQ. muck in
■ **join up**
enlist, sign up, enrol, enter

joint *n, adj, v*
♦ *n*
1 JUNCTION, connection, union, coupling juncture, join, intersection, hinge, knot, articulation, seam
FORMAL nexus
2 CLUB, bar, nightclub, pub, haunt, place, dive
3 CIGARETTE
COLLOQ. reefer, spliff, stick, roach
♦ *adj*
combined, common, communal, joined, shared, united, collective, amalgamated, mutual, co-operative, co-ordinated, consolidated, concerted
♦ *v*
1 JOIN, connect, couple, unite, fasten, fit, articulate
2 CUT UP, carve, divide, sever, dismember, dissect

jointly *adv*
in agreement, in harmony, in co-operation, co-operatively, in collaboration, in partnership, together
COLLOQ. in cahoots

joke *n, v*
♦ *n*
1 JEST, quip, crack, wisecrack, witticism, funny story, pun, hoot, whimsy, yarn, banter, repartee, (old) chestnut, throwaway, jape; *Scot* bar
OLD guy
COLLOQ. gag one-liner, funny, rib-tickler, wheeze, josh
2 TRICK, jape, lark, prank, practical joke, hoax, spoof, fun, play, sport, stunt
COLLOQ. leg-pull
3 FARCE, absurdity, nonsense, ridiculousness, mockery, parody, travesty
COLLOQ. shambles
♦ *v*
jest, tell jokes, quip, clown, fool (about/around), pun, tease, banter, mock, laugh, frolic, gambol, crack a joke, break a jest, jape, whip the cat
COLLOQ. kid, wisecrack, pull someone's leg
have someone on, pull a fast one on
SLANG cod, josh, take for a ride

SYNONYM NUANCES

noun sense 1
Jest, although now a little old-fashioned, can be used of anything that is spoken, or done, in fun; **jape** is similar and might be used facetiously to convey the notion of something done for amusement, although often at someone else's expense: *throwing his glasses under a bus was considered a jolly jape*.
The terms **quip** and **witticism** would be used, perhaps with a hint of admiration, of a short, clever remark. The term **pun** would be reserved for a play on words that is intended to be amusing.
The word **hoot** could be applied to any person or episode that gives rise to hilarity: *your mum's a real hoot*, while **whimsy** is more suggestive of mildly quaint and fanciful behaviour: *a film characterized by Ealingesque whimsy*. **Yarn** suggests a long rambling but amusing tale. **Banter** has to do with teasing and humorous chat: *he covered his shyness with a good deal of banter*, and **repartee** is appropriate for a series of sharp and witty retorts.

Chestnut, on the other hand, is rather more pejorative in its implication of a rather aged, and therefore stale, joke. **Throwaway** suggests a deliberately casual delivery of a line to increase its effect.

joker *n*
comedian, comic, wit, humorist, jester, trickster, quipster, teaser, gagman, prankster, hoaxer, practical joker, jokester, wag clown, buffoon, kidder, droll, character, sport, farceur, funster
COLLOQ. wisecracker, card, laugh

jollity *n*
cheerfulness, gladness, happiness, light-heartedness, merriment, merrymaking, high spirits
F3 sadness, unhappiness

jolly *adj, adv, v*
♦ *adj*
1 *a jolly person*
jovial, merry, glad, cheerful, cheery, playful, hearty, happy, exuberant, lively, gay, joyful, gleeful, mirthful
2 ENJOYABLE, happy, delightful, pleasurable, convivial, festive
F3 1 sad, unhappy
♦ *adv*
extremely, very, exceptionally, intensely, greatly, highly, certainly, extraordinarily
COLLOQ. ever so, dead, well, awfully, terribly
♦ *v*
encourage, urge, spur, prompt, coax, persuade, influence
COLLOQ. egg on

jolt *v, n*
♦ *v*
1 JAR, jerk, jog bump, jounce, jostle, push, knock, bounce, lurch, shake, shove, bang nudge
2 UPSET, startle, shock, shake (up), surprise, stun, amaze, astound, astonish, discompose, disconcert, disturb
FORMAL perturb
COLLOQ. floor, knock for six
♦ *n*
1 JAR, jerk, jog bump, blow, bang knock, push, shove, hit, impact, lurch, shake, start
2 SHOCK, surprise, reversal, setback, start, upset, blow, fright of your life
COLLOQ. bombshell, thunderbolt, bolt from the blue, turn-up for the book

jostle *v*
1 PUSH, shove, jog bump, elbow, hustle, jolt, crowd, shoulder, joggle, shake, squeeze, throng bang collide
2 COMPETE, vie, contend, fight, battle, struggle, jockey

jot *n, v*
♦ *n*
iota, glimmer, trace, fraction, scrap, atom, gleam, grain, hint, speck, trifle, whit, bit, particle, mite, morsel, scintilla, tittle, ace, detail
COLLOQ. smidgen
■ **jot down**
write down, take down, note (down), put down, list, record, scribble, register, enter

jotting *n*
note(s), scribble, line(s), message, reminder, comment
COLLOQ. memo

journal *n*
1 MAGAZINE, periodical, newspaper, paper, publication, review, weekly, monthly, fanzine, e-zine, webzine
2 DIARY, gazette, daybook, log logbook, record, account, register, chronicle, e-journal

journalism *n*
reporting, writing news, news coverage, reportage, feature-writing, press, Fleet Street, fourth estate, copy-writing, correspondence, media, broadcasting, radio, television, telejournalism, photojournalism, e-journalism, web journalism, citizen journalism, sportswriting, gutter press
COLLOQ. churnalism

journalist *n*
reporter, news-writer, correspondent, man, newspaperman, newspaperwoman, pressman, presswoman, columnist, feature-writer, sportswriter, gossip-writer, commentator, broadcaster, contributor, reviewer, editor, subeditor, newshound, paparazzo, freelance, stringer, telejournalist, e-journalist, web journalist
OLD diurnalist, gazetteer
COLLOQ. hack, hackette, sub, journo, scribe, hatchet man, thunderer, wireman, sob sister, ink-slinger
SLANG *N Am* ink-jerker

> QUOTATIONS
> The making of a journalist: no ideas and the ability to express them
> KARL KRAUS

journey *n, v*
 ♦ *n*
voyage, trip, travel(s), expedition, passage, trek, tour, ramble, roving outing excursion, jaunt, wanderings, cruise, ride, crossing flight, drive, safari, progress, globetrotting
FORMAL odyssey, peregrination
 ♦ *v*
travel, voyage, go, cruise, sail, trek, hike, tour, roam, rove, proceed, wander, tramp, ramble, range, fly, gallivant
FORMAL peregrinate

journeyer *n*
tourist, traveller, tripper, voyager, wanderer, wayfarer, rambler, pilgrim, trekker
FORMAL peregrinator

joust *v, n*
 ♦ *v*
fight, spar, vie, compete, contest, quarrel, wrangle, skirmish, tilt
 ♦ *n*
fight, encounter, contest, tournament, trial, engagement, skirmish, tilt, tourney

jovial *adj*
jolly, happy, cheerful, glad, cheery, merry, affable, animated, cordial, genial, lively, buoyant, mirthful, gleeful, gay, in good spirits, sociable
E3 gloomy, sad, depressed

joviality *n*
jollity, happiness, cheerfulness, cheeriness, gladness, merriment, mirth, glee, ebullience, fun, gaiety, affability, buoyancy, hilarity
E3 moroseness, sadness

joy *n*
1 HAPPINESS, gladness, delight, pleasure, bliss, ecstasy, elation, joyfulness, enjoyment, exultation, cheer, jubilation, rejoicing gratification, rapture, glee
OLD dream, list
FORMAL felicity, entrancement, transport
COLLOQ. seventh heaven, cloud nine
2 *the joys of childhood*
treasure, delight, pleasure, thrill, treat, prize, gem
COLLOQ. nuts
3 *get no joy from the inquiry desk*
satisfaction, achievement, success, successful/positive result, victory, accomplishment
E3 1 despair, grief

joyful *adj*
happy, pleased, delighted, glad, elated, ecstatic, overjoyed, euphoric, thrilled, gratified, pleasing triumphant, gleeful, merry, cheerful, jubilant
OLD gleesome
FORMAL exhilarant
COLLOQ. tickled pink, over the moon, on top of the world, on cloud nine, in seventh heaven
E3 sorrowful, mournful

joyfully *adv*
happily, gladly, cheerfully, ecstatically, euphorically, triumphantly, gleefully, jubilantly
E3 mournfully

joyless *adj*
miserable, discouraging depressing sad, unhappy, sombre, serious, sober, downcast, dreary, forlorn, gloomy, glum, grim, despondent, dejected, cheerless, bleak, dismal, dispirited, doleful, dour
E3 joyful

joyous *adj*
happy, joyful, cheerful, glad, gleeful, merry, jubilant, rapturous, ecstatic, festal, festive, gladsome
E3 sad

joyously *adv*
happily, joyfully, cheerfully, gladly, merrily, jubilantly, ecstatically, rapturously
E3 sadly

jubilant *adj*
joyful, rejoicing overjoyed, delighted, elated, triumphant, exuberant, exultant, excited, ecstatic, euphoric, thrilled, rhapsodic
COLLOQ. tickled pink, over the moon, on top of the world, on cloud nine, in seventh heaven

jubilation *n*
euphoria, ecstasy, elation, triumph, excitement, exultation, jollification, joy, celebration, festivity, jamboree, jubilee
E3 depression, lamentation

jubilee *n*
celebration, commemoration, anniversary, festival, festivity, holiday, gala, fete, carnival, feast day

Judas *n*
traitor, betrayer, deceiver, renegade, quisling turncoat
FORMAL tergiversator
COLLOQ. backstabber

judder *v*
shake, vibrate, shudder, tremble, quiver, quake

judge *n, v*
 ♦ *n*
1 JUSTICE, Law Lord, magistrate, sheriff, recorder, coroner, judiciary, procurator fiscal, district attorney, seneschal, arbiter, adjudicator, arbitrator, mediator, ombudsman, moderator, referee, umpire, assessor
SLANG beak, his/her nibs
Related adjectives: judicial, judiciary
See panel at **legal**.
2 CONNOISSEUR, authority, expert, evaluator, assessor, critic, reviewer
 ♦ *v*
1 ADJUDICATE, arbitrate, try, sit in judgement, deliver/pronounce a verdict, referee, umpire, decree, mediate, examine, sentence, pass sentence, give a sentence, review, rule, find
FORMAL adjudge
2 ASCERTAIN, determine, decide, assess, appraise, evaluate, estimate, value, weigh (up), gauge, review, examine, distinguish, discern, reckon, believe, think, form an opinion, consider, conclude, rate
3 CONDEMN, criticize, doom, convict, damn

judgement *n*
1 VERDICT, sentence, ruling adjudication, decree, conclusion, decision, arbitration, finding result, mediation, order, opinion
Related adjective: judiciary
2 DISCERNMENT, discrimination, understanding wisdom, common sense, good sense, sense, prudence, intelligence, taste, shrewdness, perception, penetration, acumen, enlightenment
FORMAL judiciousness, sagacity, perspicacity
3 OPINION, assessment, evaluation, appraisal, estimate, view, belief, diagnosis, conviction

4 CONVICTION, damnation, punishment, doom, fate, misfortune
FORMAL retribution

judgemental *adj*
critical, condemnatory, disapproving censorious, fault-finding scathing carping hypercritical, derogatory
FORMAL disparaging

judicial *adj*
legal, judiciary, magistral, forensic, official, discriminating critical, impartial

> **! judicial** or **judicious**?
> *Judicial* is a formal word meaning 'relating to judges and lawcourts'. *Judicious* means 'showing wisdom and good sense': *a judicious choice of words.*

judicially *adv*
legally, forensically, officially, impartially

judiciary *n*
judges, legal system, court system, magistracy, the law, justice, the bench

judicious *adj*
wise, careful, cautious, prudent, astute, discerning informed, discriminating shrewd, thoughtful, reasonable, sensible, clever, intelligent, smart, sound, well-judged, well-advised, considered, common-sense
FORMAL sagacious, circumspect
E3 injudicious

judiciously *adv*
wisely, carefully, cautiously, prudently, thoughtfully, sensibly, astutely, discerningly, shrewdly
FORMAL sagaciously, circumspectly
E3 injudiciously

jug *n*
pitcher, carafe, crock, ewer, flagon, urn, jar, decanter, vessel, Toby jug container, receptacle

juggle *v*
alter, change, manipulate, falsify, tamper with, fake, rearrange, balance, equalize, adjust, misrepresent, massage, rig disguise
COLLOQ. fiddle, doctor, cook

juice *n*
liquid, fluid, extract, essence, sap, secretion, nectar, liquor, serum

juicy *adj*
1 SUCCULENT, moist, wet, lush, watery, flowing sappy
OLD (*Shakesp*) moist
2 INTERESTING, colourful, vivid, thrilling exciting sensational, racy, risqué, suggestive, scandalous, lurid, spicy
COLLOQ. hot
E3 **1** dry

jumble *v, n*
♦ *v*
disarrange, confuse, disorganize, mix (up), muddle, shuffle, tangle, mingle, tumble, garble; *Scot* jabble; *N Am* wuzzle
E3 order
♦ *n*
1 DISORDER, disarray, confusion, mess, chaos, mix, mix-up, mixture, muddle, clutter, hotchpotch, miscellany, medley, potpourri, pastiche, huddle, mingle-mangle, praiseach, printer's pie, raffle
FORMAL conglomeration
COLLOQ. mishmash, shambles
2 *a jumble sale*
junk, clutter, oddments, bric-à-brac, rummage, cast-offs

jumbled *adj*
muddled, confused, chaotic, disorganized, disordered, disarrayed, mixed-up, tangled, unsorted, untidy, shuffled, tumbled, garbled, miscellaneous
E3 orderly, tidy

jumbo *adj*
gigantic, colossal, giant, extra-large, mammoth, massive, huge, enormous, immense, vast, Titanic

COLLOQ. whopping walloping ginormous
SLANG mega

jump *v, n*
♦ *v*
1 LEAP, spring bound, vault, clear, go over/across, hurdle, bounce, skip, hop, caper, cavort, frisk, romp, sport, prance, frolic, gambol
2 START, flinch, jerk, recoil, shake, quiver, twitch, jump out of your skin, wince, quail
3 OMIT, leave out, miss, skip, pass over, cut out, bypass, disregard, overlook, ignore, avoid, digress
4 RISE, increase, go up, gain, appreciate, ascend, shoot (up), leap (up), escalate, mount, advance, surge, spiral
5 POUNCE ON, attack, assault, spring on, swoop on, set upon
COLLOQ. mug beat up, do over
♦ *n*
1 LEAP, spring bound, vault, hop, skip, bounce, prance, frisk, frolic, pounce
2 START, flinch, jerk, jolt, jar, lurch, shock, spasm, quiver, shiver, shake, twitch
3 BREAK, gap, space, interruption, lapse, omission, interval, breach, switch
FORMAL hiatus, lacuna
4 RISE, increase, escalation, leap, boost, advance, increment, upsurge, elevation, upturn, mounting
COLLOQ. hike
5 HURDLE, fence, gate, hedge, barricade, barrier, obstacle, rail
Related adjective: saltatorial

■ **jump at**
accept eagerly/quickly, agree to, fall for, leap at, grab, welcome with both/open arms, seize (on), pounce on, snatch, swallow

■ **jump on**
criticize, blame, reprimand, rebuke, censure, reprove, scold, chide, fly at, tick off, reproach, upbraid
FORMAL berate, castigate, revile

■ **jump the gun**
act prematurely, act hastily, act too soon, start too early, anticipate

> **SYNONYM NUANCES**
>
> *verb sense 1*
> **Leap** and **bound** can be used of jumping that takes you quickly from one point to another, and connotes great height or distance, while **spring** has further connotations of a sudden jump, made as if by elastic force: *the tiger sprang from the long grass.* **Vault**, **hurdle** and **clear** also suggest high movement, but over an obstacle: *he vaulted the gate; he cleared the stream.* **Bounce** is more suggestive of short, rapid and repetitive upward movements.
> You might use **skip** and **hop** to suggest carefree, casual movement. The verbs **caper**, **cavort** and **romp** are suggestive of undisciplined jumping about, while **frisk**, **frolic** and **gambol** suggest playfulness, and rather unco-ordinated jumping movements. **Prance** suggests a graceful but perhaps exaggerated action: *she pranced in little pirouettes around the kitchen.*

jumper *n*
sweater, jersey, pullover, sweatshirt, woolly

jumpy *adj*
1 NERVOUS, anxious, agitated, apprehensive, uneasy, nervy, jittery, tense, panicky, fidgety, shaky, on edge, keyed up, wound up, climbing the walls
FORMAL restive
COLLOQ. twitchy, edgy, het up, uptight, with butterflies in your stomach, on pins and needles, shaking like a leaf/jelly, with your heart in your mouth, in a sweat, in a stew, in a tizzy

2 FITFUL, twitchy, spasmodic, jerky, jolting lurching convulsive, disconnected, bumpy, bouncy, shaky, shaking rough, unco-ordinated, uncontrolled, incoherent
F3 1 calm, composed

junction *n*
1 *a road junction*
intersection, crossing crossroads, T-junction, box junction, circus, interchange, meeting-point, confluence; *Scot* toll
2 JOINT, join, joining connection, meeting bond, seam, juncture, union, intersection, link, linking coupling welding close, cornice, knitting
TECHNICAL interface, abutment, cove, graft, collar, crown, node, raphe, suture, symphysis
FORMAL infall

> **!** **junction** or **juncture**?
> A *junction* is a point or place where things meet: *a road junction; a junction box for wires*. A *juncture* is a point in time: *at this/that juncture*.

juncture *n*
point, period, stage, time, occasion, minute, moment, crisis, emergency, crux, predicament

jungle *n*
1 *tigers in the dense jungle*
tropical forest, rainforest, equatorial rainforest, bush, growth, shola
2 *a jungle of building regulations*
mass, heap, tangle, confusion, disorder, disarray, chaos, snarl, clutter, hotchpotch, mishmash, miscellany, medley, maze, labyrinth, web

junior *adj, n*
♦ *adj*
younger, young minor, lesser, lower, subordinate, secondary, subsidiary, inferior, assistant, associate, chota
OLD puisne
F3 senior
♦ *n*
minor, subordinate, inferior, subsidiary, minion, servant, associate, assistant, under-boy, fils
COLLOQ. dogsbody, underling

junk *n, v*
♦ *n*
rubbish, refuse, trash, debris, garbage, waste, scrap, litter, clutter, oddments, bric-à-brac, rummage, cast-offs, leftovers, leavings, dregs, wreckage
♦ *v*
throw out, throw away, get rid of, ditch, jettison, discard, dispose of
COLLOQ. dump, chuck

junket *n*
trip, journey, visit, outing celebration, spree
COLLOQ. do, beano, bash

junta *n*
faction, clique, gang group, ring set, party, cartel, coterie, council, league, conclave, confederacy, cabal, camarilla

jurisdiction *n*
1 *under the council's jurisdiction*
power, authority, control, influence, dominion, province, sovereignty, administration, leadership, mastery, command, domination, rule, right, way
TECHNICAL competence
FORMAL prerogative, capacity
2 AREA, field, orbit, bounds, scope, range, reach, sphere, district, territory, region, province, zone

jury *n*
jurors, panel, jurymen, jurywomen, party-jury, petit jury, petty jury; *Scot* assize; *N Am* grand jury

just *adj, adv*
♦ *adj*
1 *a just ruler*
fair, equitable, impartial, unbiased, unprejudiced, fair-minded, even-handed, neutral, objective, disinterested,

righteous, upright, virtuous, moral, ethical, truthful, sincere, honourable, good, honest, irreproachable, upstanding principled
See Synonym nuances panel at **fair**[1].
2 *a just punishment*
deserved, merited, earned, fitting well-deserved, appropriate, suitable, apt, due, justified, valid, sound, well-grounded, well-founded, proper, reasonable, rightful, lawful, legitimate, legal
F3 1 unjust **2** undeserved
♦ *adv*
1 *he's just left*
a short time ago, a moment ago, recently, lately
2 *that's just like him*
exactly, precisely, perfectly, completely, absolutely, quite
COLLOQ. bang on, spot-on, to a T
3 *she's just a child*
only, merely, simply, purely, nothing but, barely, hardly, scarcely
■ **just about**
practically, almost, virtually, nearly, as good as, all but, well-nigh, more or less, to all intents and purposes

justice *n*
1 FAIRNESS, equity, fair play, impartiality, objectivity, neutrality, equitableness, fair-mindedness, even-handedness, justness, legitimacy, honesty, honour, uprightness, integrity, right, rightfulness, rightness, righteousness, morals, ethics, justifiableness, lawfulness, validity, soundness, reasonableness
FORMAL rectitude, propriety
2 LEGALITY, law, penalty, punishment, recompense, amends, redress, reparation, satisfaction, compensation
3 JUDGE, Justice of the Peace, JP, magistrate, sheriff
F3 1 injustice, unfairness, bias

> QUOTATIONS
> Justice is superior to injustice
> PLATO, *Republic*

justifiable *adj*
defensible, excusable, warranted, warrantable, reasonable, within reason, sustainable, supportable, justified, lawful, legal, legitimate, acceptable, explainable, forgivable, pardonable, understandable, plausible, valid, well-founded, sound, sensible, right, proper, fit, tenable
FORMAL explicable
F3 unjustifiable, inexcusable

justifiably *adv*
rightly, properly, validly, acceptably, understandably, plausibly, defensibly, excusably, reasonably, within reason, lawfully, legally, legitimately
F3 unjustifiably, inexcusably

justification *n*
defence, plea, mitigation, apology, explanation, excuse, vindication, verification, confirmation, warrant, rationalization, reason, grounds, basis

justify *v*
vindicate, warrant, defend, acquit, absolve, clear, excuse, forgive, explain, pardon, validate, uphold, authorize, show to be right/reasonable, sustain, support, give reasons for, give grounds for, stand up for, maintain, establish, prove, rationalize, verify, confirm, bear out, make good, deserve
TECHNICAL aver, avow
OLD darraign
FORMAL exculpate, exonerate, substantiate

justly *adv*
1 EQUITABLY, even-handedly, properly, fairly, honestly, impartially, lawfully, objectively, equally
2 JUSTIFIABLY, duly, rightfully, rightly, with reason, legitimately
F3 1, 2 unjustly

jut (out) *v*

project, protrude, stick out, overhang extend, beetle, extrude

▣ recede

juvenile *n, adj*

♦ *n*

child, youth, minor, young person, youngster, adolescent, teenager, boy, girl, infant

COLLOQ. kid

♦ *adj*

young youthful, minor, junior, immature, inexperienced, childish, puerile, infantile, teenage, adolescent, babyish, unsophisticated, callow

COLLOQ. green, wet behind the ears

SLANG *N Am* juvie

▣ mature

juxtapose *v*

put/place together, put/place side by side, put next to each other

TECHNICAL impale

juxtaposition *n*

proximity, nearness, closeness, contact, vicinity, immediacy

TECHNICAL impalement

FORMAL contiguity

K

kaleidoscopic *adj*
1 MANY-COLOURED, multicoloured, many-splendoured, variegated, motley, parti-coloured
TECHNICAL poikilitic
FORMAL polychromatic, polychrome
2 EVER-CHANGING, changeable, fluctuating manifold, fluid
FORMAL multifarious
E₃ 1 dull, monochrome, monotonous

kaput *adj*
broken, finished, ruined, wrecked, smashed, undone, defunct, destroyed, extinct
COLLOQ. bust, phut, conked out

karate

Shotokan karate belts include:

JUNIOR GRADES (KYU):
white belt (beginner)
orange belt (9th Kyu)
red belt (8th Kyu)
yellow belt (7th Kyu)
green belt (6th Kyu)

purple belt (5th–4th Kyu)
brown belt (3rd–1st Kyu)

SENIOR GRADES (DANS):
black belts (1st–8th Dan)

---

keel *n, v*
♦ *n*
base, bottom, back, centreboard, stabilizer
TECHNICAL keelson, carina, cheesecutter, skeg
■ **keel over**
1 OVERTURN, capsize, turn upside down, turn turtle, founder, collapse, upset
2 FAINT, pass out, lose consciousness, black out, fall, drop, stagger, topple over
OLD swoon

keen¹ *adj*
1 EAGER, avid, fervent, enthusiastic, earnest, devoted, diligent, industrious, conscientious, assiduous, intent, anxious, impatient
COLLOQ. keen as mustard
2 ASTUTE, sharp, shrewd, clever, perceptive, wise, discerning discriminating quick, quick-witted, sharp-witted, penetrating piercing acute, hawkish, fine, double-eyed, quick-eyed, deep, sensitive, razor-sharp, razor-like, smart; *Scot* gleg
OLD (*Shakesp*) hawking
FORMAL perspicacious, sagacious, argute
COLLOQ. wide awake
3 SHARP, piercing penetrating incisive, acute, pointed, intense, pungent, acid, biting shrill
FORMAL trenchant, mordant
4 *keen competition*
fierce, intense, strong wild, acute, ruthless, cut-throat
COLLOQ. dog-eat-dog
5 *keen on something/someone*
fond of, devoted to, liking attached to, enamoured, loving caring
COLLOQ. wild, mad, crazy, potty, nuts, having a soft spot for, heavily into

6 *a keen wind*
biting cold, sharp, severe, penetrating piercing nipping stinging; *Scot* snell
E₃ 1 apathetic **2** superficial **3** dull

keen² *v*
mourners keened over the body
wail, moan, cry, howl, lament, weep, sob, groan, grieve, mourn
FORMAL ululate
COLLOQ. yowl

keenly *adv*
1 INTENSELY, strongly, acutely, fiercely
2 EAGERLY, fervently, enthusiastically, earnestly, diligently, assiduously
3 ASTUTELY, sharply, acutely, shrewdly, perceptively, quickly, deeply, cleverly, sensitively, penetratingly, incisively

keenness *n*
1 ENTHUSIASM, eagerness, diligence, earnestness, industriousness, industry, sedulity
2 ASTUTENESS, sharpness, shrewdness, cleverness, discernment, penetration, sensitivity, wisdom, incisiveness
FORMAL sagacity, sapience, trenchancy
E₃ 1 apathy **2** bluntness, dullness

keep *v, n*
♦ *v*
1 RETAIN, hold, preserve, hold on to, hang on to, not part with, save, store (up), stock, deal in, carry, possess, keep possession of, amass, hoard, accumulate, collect, stack, conserve, deposit, heap, pile (up), place, maintain, furnish, sustain
2 CARRY ON, keep at/on, continue, persevere, persist, remain, stay, maintain
3 LOOK AFTER, tend, care for, keep in good order, have charge of, have custody of, maintain, provide for, subsidize, support, sustain, be responsible for, foster, superintend, mind, protect, shelter, guard, defend, watch (over), shield, safeguard, feed, nurture, manage
4 DETAIN, delay, keep waiting check, hinder, hold (up), hold back, impede, obstruct, prevent, block, curb, interfere with, restrain, limit, inhibit, deter, hamper, keep back, control, constrain, arrest, withhold, confine
FORMAL retard
5 OBSERVE, comply with, respect, obey, fulfil, adhere to, abide by, carry out, recognize, keep up, keep faith with, commemorate, celebrate, hold, maintain, perform, perpetuate, mark, honour, solemnize
FORMAL effectuate
6 *keep pets*
own, look after, take care of, support, breed, raise, rear
7 *keep a shop*
own, run, manage, be in charge of
♦ *n*
1 SUBSISTENCE, board, board and lodgings, livelihood, living maintenance, support, upkeep, means, food, nourishment, sustenance, nurture
2 FORT, fortress, tower, castle, citadel, stronghold, dungeon, donjon

keeper

■ **keep at**

persevere, stick at, be steadfast, continue, carry on, complete, endure, finish, last, maintain, remain, stay, persist, toil, grind, drudge, labour, beaver away at
COLLOQ. slog at, plug away at
E3 abandon, neglect

■ **keep back**

1 RESERVE, set/lay aside, retain, save, store, hold back, stockpile, hoard, accumulate
2 HOLD BACK, restrict, suppress, restrain, check, constrain, curb, impede, limit, prohibit, stop, control, delay, withhold, conceal, censor, hide, hush up, stifle, keep secret
FORMAL retard

■ **keep from**

prevent, resist, stop, restrain, halt
FORMAL forbear, desist, refrain

■ **keep in**

1 REPRESS, keep back, inhibit, bottle up, conceal, stifle, suppress, hide, control, restrain, quell, stop up
2 CONFINE, detain, shut in, coop up
E3 1 declare 2 release

■ **keep off**

avoid, stay away from, stay off, keep away, avoid going near, not go near, keep at a distance from, steer clear of, keep at arm's length
COLLOQ. give a wide berth to, body-swerve

■ **keep on**

1 CONTINUE, carry on, go on, endure, persevere, persist, keep at it, last, remain, stay, stay the course, hold on, retain, maintain
COLLOQ. soldier on, stick at it
2 *keep an employee on*
retain, keep, continue to employ, continue to engage/hire, keep in employment, keep on the payroll, retain the services of

■ **keep on at**

go on at, nag pester, plague, pursue, badger, chivvy, harass, harry
FORMAL importune

■ **keep secret**

hide, conceal, keep back, keep dark, suppress
FORMAL dissemble
COLLOQ. keep under your hat, keep under wraps, your lips be sealed

■ **keep to**

observe, comply with, respect, obey, fulfil, adhere to, stick to

■ **keep track of**

follow, grasp, keep up with, monitor, oversee, plot, record, trace, track, understand, watch

■ **keep up**

1 CONTINUE, maintain, persevere, persist, go along with, support, sustain, preserve, keep pace, equal, contend, compete, vie, rival, match, emulate
2 *keep up with the latest developments*
keep up to date with, keep abreast of, keep in touch with, stay familiar with
COLLOQ. keep tabs on, keep your finger on the pulse
E3 1 fall behind 2 lose touch

■ **for keeps**

for ever, for good, always, for all time

keeper n

guard, custodian, curator, caretaker, attendant, guardian, overseer, steward, warder, jailer, gaoler, warden, supervisor, proprietor, bodyguard, escort, inspector, defender, governor, superintendent, administrator, surveyor
FORMAL conservator
COLLOQ. minder

keeping n

1 CUSTODY, guardianship, supervision, care, charge, safe-keeping retention, protection, maintenance, surveillance, trust, tutelage, ward, cure, patronage
FORMAL auspices, aegis

2 *in keeping with the architecture*
agreement, harmony, conformity, correspondence, consistency, balance, proportion
FORMAL accord, congruity

keepsake n

memento, souvenir, remembrance, relic, reminder, token, pledge, emblem

keg n

barrel, butt, cask, drum, tun, vat, firkin, hogshead

ken n

knowledge, understanding perception, awareness, appreciation, comprehension, realization, field, grasp, notice, range, reach, scope, acquaintance, compass
FORMAL cognizance

kerfuffle n

fuss, bother, commotion, palaver, furore, ado, fluster, flurry, bustle, brouhaha
COLLOQ. to-do, hoo-ha, flap, carry-on, ballyhoo, tizzy

kernel n

core, crux, grain, seed, stone, nut, nucleus, centre, heart, nub, essence, germ, marrow, substance, gist
FORMAL quintessence
COLLOQ. nitty-gritty, nuts and bolts, innards

key n, adj

♦ n

1 CLUE, cue, indicator, pointer, explanation, guide, gloss, sign, answer, solution, interpretation, means, secret
FORMAL explication
2 GUIDE, glossary, translation, legend, code, table, index
3 *in a low key*
pitch, tone, style, character, mood
TECHNICAL timbre

♦ adj

important, essential, vital, crucial, necessary, principal, decisive, central, chief, main, major, leading basic, fundamental

keynote n

core, centre, heart, substance, point, theme, gist, pith, marrow, essence, emphasis, accent, stress

keystone n

cornerstone, core, crux, base, basis, foundation, ground, linchpin, principle, root, mainspring source, spring motive

kick v, n

♦ v

1 BOOT, hit, strike, knee, jolt, foot, toe, shoot, shin, project, fling hack, hoof, lash out, spur; *dialect* pause, punch, punce, yerk
TECHNICAL back-heel, chip, heel, punt
OLD let out, recalcitrate, spurn at/against
2 GIVE UP, stop, leave off, abandon, desist from, break
COLLOQ. pack in, jack in, quit
3 RECOIL, move back, jump back, spring back, rebound, react, falter, misfire, boomerang

♦ n

1 BLOW, recoil, jolt, striking boot
TECHNICAL penalty, chip, cross-kick, drop-kick, fly-kick, free kick, goal kick, place kick, point after, punt, set piece, spot kick, tap-kick, high kick, garryowen, grub kick, grubber, pile-driver
OLD spurn, wince
2 STIMULATION, thrill, excitement, fun, pleasure
COLLOQ. buzz, lift, lark, high
3 *a drink with a kick*
power, strength, potency, effect, tang stimulus
COLLOQ. punch, pep, bite, zing zip

■ **kick against**

resist, rebel, oppose, spurn, defy, withstand, protest, hold out against

■ **kick around**

1 DISCUSS, talk about, play with, toy with
2 TAKE ADVANTAGE OF, exploit, use, abuse, ill-treat, maltreat, push about/around, trample on, mess about/around

■ kick off
begin, start, open, get under way, open the proceedings, introduce, inaugurate, initiate
FORMAL commence
COLLOQ. set/start the ball rolling

■ kick out
eject, evict, expel, oust, remove, discharge, dismiss, get rid of, throw out, reject
COLLOQ. chuck out, sack, boot out, turf out, show someone the door, give the sack/push/boot/elbow to

kickback n
1 RECOIL, rebound, backlash, reaction
2 BRIBE, incentive, inducement
COLLOQ. back-hander, sweetener, pay-off

kick-off n
beginning start, outset, opening introduction
FORMAL commencement, inception
COLLOQ. word go

kid¹ n
she has three kids
child, young one, little one, littling littl 'un, young 'un, toddler, youngster, young person, youth, juvenile, infant, girl, little girl, boy, little boy, adolescent, teenager, lad; *Scot* littlin, littleane, bairn, wean
COLLOQ. nipper, tot, kiddy, kiddywink, tiny tot
SLANG sprog ankle-biter, rug rat

kid² v
1 *I was only kidding*
tease, joke, hoax, fool, pretend, trick, jest
COLLOQ. have on, rib, pull someone's leg wind up
2 *don't kid yourself*
delude, dupe, hoodwink, deceive, humbug gull
COLLOQ. con, bamboozle, lead up the garden path, pull the wool over someone's eyes

kidnap v
abduct, capture, seize, hold to ransom, snatch, hijack, take/hold as hostage, steal

kill v, n
♦ v
1 SLAUGHTER, murder, take someone's life, slay, put to death, exterminate, assassinate, stab to death, finish off, massacre, destroy, put down, put to sleep, do away with, butcher, annihilate, execute, hang, guillotine, behead, shoot, electrocute, send to the electric chair
FORMAL smite, decapitate
COLLOQ. do in, eliminate, dispatch, wipe out, decimate, polish off, take out, zap
SLANG bump off, knock off, rub out, waste, blow away, liquidate, zot
2 *kill a project*
end, destroy, put an end to, ruin, abolish, devastate, eradicate
COLLOQ. axe, scupper, put a spanner in the works
3 *my feet are killing me*
hurt, ache, cause pain, be painful, be sore, suffer, throb, pound, twinge, sting, smart
4 *don't kill yourself with all this work*
strain, exhaust, tire out, weary, fatigue, sap, drain
COLLOQ. do in, fag out, whack, knacker, take it out of
5 *kill time*
pass, spend, occupy, fill, use (up), while away
6 *kill noise*
stifle, deaden, dull, smother, quash, quell, suppress, muffle
7 *kill pain*
alleviate, relieve, soothe, ease, deaden, moderate
♦ n
death, shoot-out, death-blow, end, finish, climax, conclusion, *coup de grâce*, dénouement, dispatch, mop-up

---

SYNONYM NUANCES

verb sense 1
Slaughter can refer to the large-scale killing of animals, but when applied to humans it is a more marked term which tends to suggest wanton killing of defenceless victims. The term **massacre** also conveys this idea of killing large numbers, particularly in a brutal manner. **Annihilate** would suggest totally ending the existence of someone or something: *the Native Americans were virtually annihilated.* **Exterminate** also very starkly suggests bringing about someone's or something's end: *the dissidents, unable to defend themselves, were rounded up and exterminated.*

 Slay is more poetic in tone and tends to be used in a poetic or dramatic context: *slay the dragons.* **Butcher** is an emotive term which suggests a bloody and brutal death: *they were dragged from their cars and butchered by the angry mob.*

 Destroy can be used of killing an animal, especially one that is fatally ill or injured, although it is very detached in tone, while **put down** and **put to sleep** are rather more euphemistic and gentler in tone: *we had to tell the children that the old dog had been put to sleep.* **Assassinate** is reserved for the organized killing of a prominent person, while **execute** also suggests a cold, dispassionate action, and has connotations of punishment or retribution, either official or unofficial: *the terrorist was executed in a tit-for-tat killing.*

 Hang, **guillotine**, **behead**, **electrocute** and **shoot**, on the other hand, are all specific terms for the means by which someone is killed or executed.

---

killer n
murderer, assassin, executioner, destroyer, slayer, slaughterer, exterminator, cut-throat, gunman, homicide
COLLOQ. butcher, hatchet man, hit-man, liquidator

killing n, adj
♦ n
1 SLAUGHTER, murder, massacre, butchery, genocide, homicide, assassination, execution, slaying manslaughter, extermination, carnage, bloodshed, elimination, destruction, fatality
FORMAL patricide, matricide, infanticide, fratricide, sororicide, uxoricide
2 GAIN, fortune, windfall, booty, profit, lucky break, coup, success, stroke of luck, hit, big hit
COLLOQ. clean-up, bonanza
♦ adj
1 FUNNY, hilarious, comical, amusing uproarious, ludicrous, absurd, hysterical, rib-tickling
COLLOQ. side-splitting a scream
2 EXHAUSTING, hard, taxing arduous, tiring fatiguing wearing draining gruelling
FORMAL debilitating enervating
COLLOQ. back-breaking

killjoy n
spoilsport, moaner, complainer, dampener, damper, misery, cynic, pessimist, sceptic, grouch, whiner, prophet of doom, Weary Willie
COLLOQ. wet blanket, buzzkill
E∃ enthusiast, optimist, sport

kilter
■ out of kilter
awry, askew, misaligned, confused, out of balance, unbalanced, lopsided
COLLOQ. skew-whiff

kin n
relatives, relations, family, people, flesh and blood, cousins, blood, lineage, extraction, clan, stock, tribe
OLD kindred
FORMAL consanguinity

kind n, adj
♦ n
sort, type, class, category, set, order, variety, character, genus, genre, style, brand, family, breed, race, nature, persuasion, description, species, strain, stamp, temperament, manner

♦ *adj*
benevolent, kind-hearted, kindly, good-hearted,
good-natured, helpful, obliging humane, generous,
big-hearted, compassionate, merciful, forbearing pitying
charitable, benign, philanthropic, altruistic, humanitarian,
amiable, friendly, amicable, congenial, soft-hearted,
thoughtful, warm, warm-hearted, genial, cordial,
considerate, courteous, sympathetic, patient,
tender-hearted, loving affectionate, understanding lenient,
mild, gentle, indulgent, tolerant, unselfish, selfless,
neighbourly, tactful, giving nice, good, gracious
FORMAL magnanimous, bounteous
F3 cruel, inconsiderate, unhelpful
■ **kind of**
rather, moderately, relatively, slightly, a bit, a little,
somewhat, fairly, quite, to a limited degree/extent, to
some degree/extent, pretty
COLLOQ. sort of
■ **in kind**
in like manner, in return, in exchange, similarly, tit for tat

---

SYNONYM NUANCES

adjective
Benevolent may be used of someone predisposed to
doing good deeds, whereas **humane**, **compassionate**
and **merciful** have more to do with showing pity or
empathy: *he fought to establish humane conditions for
prisoners*. You can use **benign** of someone who has a
kind and sympathetic attitude: *a benign old uncle who
would listen to what you had to say*, whereas
philanthropic, **altruistic** and **humanitarian** all go
somewhat further by implying actively working for the
benefit of mankind. **Charitable** is similar, but can also
suggest empathy and leniency: *his charitable works; be
charitable, she's only young.*
  Forbearing, on the other hand, puts the emphasis on
the element of patient endurance: *we are not required to
be forbearing until there is a problem*. The terms
amiable, **friendly**, **amicable** and **congenial** suggest
being welcoming and outgoing while **warm**, **genial** and
cordial suggest an affectionate or friendly nature. You
can use **lenient**, **indulgent** and **tolerant** of someone
who is less severe than possible or warranted.
  The terms **unselfish**, the stronger **selfless**, and **giving**,
all emphasize the quality of putting others before
yourself. **Neighbourly** is milder in that it is more
suggestive of a dutiful helpfulness, while **tactful** is simply
being skilful in dealing with the feelings of others.
Gracious suggests that someone's kindness lends them
dignity: *our gracious queen.*

---

kind-hearted *adj*
kind, warm, warm-hearted, sympathetic, tender-hearted,
kindly, generous, considerate, compassionate, amicable,
good-hearted, good-natured, obliging gracious, benign,
big-hearted, helpful, philanthropic, altruistic, humanitarian,
humane
F3 ill-natured

kindle *v*
1 IGNITE, light, set alight, set on fire, set fire to
2 INFLAME, fire, stir, thrill, stimulate, rouse,
arouse, awaken, excite, fan, incite, inspire,
induce, provoke

kindliness *n*
kindness, benevolence, compassion, friendliness,
sympathy, warmth, generosity, charity, amiability
OLD loving-kindness
FORMAL beneficence, benignity
F3 cruelty, meanness, unkindness

kindly *adj, adv*
♦ *adj*
benevolent, kind, kind-hearted, compassionate, charitable,
good, good-natured, helpful, considerate, thoughtful,
warm, generous, big-hearted, cordial, genial, favourable,
giving indulgent, pleasant, nice, agreeable, sympathetic,
understanding tender, gentle, mild, humane, natural,
patient, friendly, neighbourly, avuncular, grandfatherly,
benign, fond, amicable, polite; *Scot* couthie
FORMAL magnanimous, benefic
F3 cruel, uncharitable
♦ *adv*
benevolently, kind-heartedly, helpfully, humanely,
compassionately, mercifully, generously, charitably,
benignly, philanthropically, altruistically, thoughtfully,
considerately, tolerantly, unselfishly, selflessly, tactfully,
courteously, sympathetically, patiently, warmly, gently,
lovingly, affectionately
OLD goodly
FORMAL magnanimously

kindness *n*
1 BENEVOLENCE, kindliness, charity, magnanimity,
compassion, fellow feeling generosity, hospitality,
humanity, humaneness, courtesy, friendliness,
pleasantness, goodwill, philanthropy, altruism,
humanitarianism, niceness, goodness, grace, patience,
indulgence, tolerance, leniency, understanding sympathy,
considerateness, consideration, warmth, warm-heartedness,
love, affection, helpfulness, thoughtfulness, gentleness,
mildness
OLD loving-kindness
FORMAL benignancy
2 FAVOUR, good turn, good deed, assistance, help, aid,
service
F3 1 cruelty, inhumanity **2** disservice

QUOTATIONS
For auld lang syne, my jo, / For auld lang syne, / We'll
tak a cup o' kindness yet / For auld lang syne
  ROBERT BURNS, 'Auld Lang Syne'

---

kindred *n, adj*
♦ *n*
relatives, relations, flesh and blood, family,
people, folk, connections, clan, relationship,
kinsfolk, lineage
OLD kin
FORMAL consanguinity
♦ *adj*
similar, common, related, matching like, corresponding
affiliated, connected, allied, akin
FORMAL cognate

king *n*
1 MONARCH, ruler, head of state,
sovereign, majesty, emperor, chief, chieftain,
prince, lord, supremo
Related adjective: regal
2 *the king of football*
supremo, kingpin, star, chief, leader, master
COLLOQ. leading light, top dog big cheese/shot/noise,
bigwig the greatest

kingdom *n*
monarchy, sovereignty, reign, realm, empire, dominion,
commonwealth, nation, principality, state, country,
domain, dynasty, province, sphere, territory, land,
grouping division

kingly *adj*
sovereign, majestic, royal, regal, imperial, imperious,
lordly, noble, stately, supreme, sublime, splendid,
glorious, grand, imposing grandiose, dignified
FORMAL august, monarchical

kink *n, v*
♦ *n*
1 CURL, twist, twirl, bend, dent, indentation,
knot, loop, crimp, coil, tangle, entanglement, crinkle,
wrinkle
2 QUIRK, eccentricity, idiosyncrasy, whim, foible,
peculiarity, deviation, perversion, fetish
FORMAL caprice

3 *iron out all the kinks*
defect, flaw, hitch, blemish, imperfection, deficiency, shortcoming weak point, weakness, failing foible
COLLOQ. bug glitch
♦ *v*
bend, curl, twist, curve, coil, tangle, crimp, wrinkle

kinky *adj*
1 STRANGE, odd, abnormal, unusual, unconventional, freakish, eccentric, outlandish, queer, quirky, idiosyncratic, peculiar, perverted, deviant, unnatural, warped, weird, bizarre, whimsical, degenerate, depraved, licentious
FORMAL capricious
2 CURLED, coiled, twisted, crumpled, tangled, curly, wavy, wrinkled, crimped, frizzy
Ea **1** normal

kinsfolk *n*
relatives, relations, family, clan, cousins, connections
OLD kin, kindred

kinship *n*
1 KIN, family, blood, relation, relationship, ties, lineage, ancestry
FORMAL consanguinity
2 AFFINITY, similarity, association, alliance, connection, correspondence, equivalence, relationship, tie, community, likeness, kindred, conformity

kiosk *n*
booth, stall, stand, news-stand, bookstall, cabin, box, counter

kismet *n*
destiny, fate, doom, fortune, lot, portion, providence, karma
FORMAL predestiny

kiss *v, n*
♦ *v*
1 CARESS, lip, smack; *dialect* smouch; *Welsh* buss
OLD (*Shakesp*) mouth
FORMAL osculate
COLLOQ. peck, give someone a peck, smooch, neck, canoodle, bill and coo
SLANG snog; *N Am* suck face
2 TOUCH, touch gently/lightly, graze, glance off, brush, lick, scrape, fan
♦ *n*
French kiss, deep kiss, butterfly kiss; *dialect* smouch; *Welsh* buss
OLD baisemain
FORMAL osculation, pax
COLLOQ. peck, smack, smacker, plonker
SLANG snog

kit *n, v*
♦ *n*
1 EQUIPMENT, gear, apparatus, supplies, tackle, provisions, outfit, implements, set, tools, trappings, rig instruments, paraphernalia, utensils, effects, luggage, baggage
FORMAL accoutrements, appurtenances
COLLOQ. things, stuff
2 *football kit*
tackle, clothing clothes, outfit, rig colours
COLLOQ. rig-out, gear, strip, togs, things, get-up, clobber
■ **kit out**
equip, fit out, outfit, supply, provide, fix up, furnish, prepare, arm, deck out, dress, rig out

kitchen utensils

Kitchen utensils include:

asparagus cooker	blowtorch	butter dish
bain marie	bottle opener	cake tin
baking sheet	breadbin	can-opener
baster	breadboard	casserole
biscuit press	brochette	cheese board
blender	bun tin	cheese slicer
blini pan	butter curler	chestnut pan

chopping-board	mixing bowl	terrine
cocotte	mortar and pestle	thermometer
colander	mouli	toast rack
corer	muffin tin	tongs
corkscrew	nutcracker	tureen
crêpe pan	nutmeg grater	vegetable brush
croquembouche mould	oil drizzler	vegetable steamer
	omelette pan	waffle iron
cruet set	paella pan	whisk
deep-fat fryer	pasta maker	wine cooler
dough hook	pastry board	wine rack
egg coddler	pastry brush	wok
egg poacher	pastry cutter	yoghurt maker
egg separator	peeler	zester
egg slicer	pepper mill	
egg-timer	pie funnel	**TYPES OF KNIFE:**
fish kettle	pie plate	boning knife
fish slice	potato masher	bread knife
fish tweezers	potato ricer	butter knife
flan tin	preserving pan	canelle knife
flour dredger	pressure cooker	carving knife
fondue set	pudding basin	cheese knife
food processor	pudding mould	cleaver
fork	punch bowl	cocktail knife
frying pan	quiche dish	cook's knife
garlic press	ramekin	fish knife
grater	rice cooker	grapefruit knife
gravy separator	roasting pan	Kitchen Devil®
grill pan	rolling pin	mezzaluna
ham stand	salad spinner	oyster knife
heat diffuser	sandwich tin	palette knife
herb mill	saucepan	paring knife
ice-cream scoop	scissors	steak knife
icing syringe	sharpening steel	table knife
jelly mould	shears	tomato knife
juicer	sieve	vegetable knife
karahi	sifter	
kitchen scales	skewer	**TYPES OF SPOON:**
knife block	skillet	dessert spoon
lemon reamer	slow cooker	draining spoon
lemon squeezer	soufflé dish	ladle
liquidizer	spatula	measuring spoon
loaf tin	spice rack	pasta ladle
madeleine tin	steamer	serving spoon
mandolin	stockpot	skimmer
measuring jug	stoner	soupspoon
meat thermometer	storage jar	straining spoon
melon baller	tea caddy	tablespoon
milk pan	tea infuser	teaspoon
mincer	tea strainer	wooden spoon

See also **cook**; **cutlery**; **domestic appliances**.

kittenish *adj*
playful, sportive, ludic, frolicsome, frisky, cute, fun-loving coquettish, flirtatious
Ea staid

knack *n*
flair, faculty, facility, bent, skill, competence, proficiency, talent, genius, gift, trick, ability, capability, adroitness, expertise, skilfulness, aptitude, forte, capacity, handiness, dexterity, quickness, turn
OLD (*Shakesp*) quirk
FORMAL propensity
COLLOQ. hang

knapsack *n*
bag pack, haversack, rucksack, backpack, duffel bag holdall, kitbag

knave *n*
rogue, scoundrel, villain, swindler, rascal, cheat, reprobate, scamp, scallywag swine
OLD boy, blighter, bounder, dastard, rotter, custrel, drôle, *fripon*, varlet; (*Shakesp*) coistrel, coistril

knavery n
knavishness, mischief, roguery, trickery, villainy, devilry, corruption, deceit, deception, dishonesty, double-dealing fraud, chicanery, imposture
OLD (*Shakesp*) patchery
FORMAL duplicity
COLLOQ. hanky-panky, monkey business

knavish adj
roguish, mischievous, rascally, fiendish, wicked, contemptible, corrupt, fraudulent, deceitful, deceptive, dishonest, dishonourable, unprincipled, unscrupulous, reprobate, scoundrelly, villainous, devilish
OLD dastardly
E3 honest, honourable, scrupulous

knead v
manipulate, press, massage, work, pummel, pound, ply, squeeze, shape, rub, form, mould, knuckle, conche, masticate, puddle
FORMAL malax, malaxate

kneel v
fall to your knees, bow (down), get down on your knees, stoop, bend, curtsy, revere, defer to, kowtow
FORMAL genuflect, make obeisance

knell n
toll, ringing ring chime, peal, sound, end
OLD knoll

knickers n
pants, underpants, panties, briefs, underwear, lingerie, bikini briefs, g-string camiknickers, knickerbockers, Directoire knickers, bloomers
COLLOQ. drawers, smalls, frillies, scanties

knick-knack n
trinket, trifle, bauble, gewgaw, gimcrack, bagatelle, ornament, bric-à-brac, plaything

knife n, v
♦ n
blade, cutter
SLANG chiv
♦ v
cut, rip, slash, stab, pierce, wound, lacerate, bayonet

Knives include:

automatic knife	dagger	paper knife
belt-buckle knife	dirk	penknife
boot knife	flick-knife	pocket knife
Bowie knife	gravity knife	scalpel
N Am box-cutter	jackknife	skene-dhu
butterfly knife	Kitchen Devil®	Stanley knife®
carver	lancet	Swiss Army knife
craft knife	machete	switchblade

See also **dagger**; **kitchen utensils**.

---

knight n
cavalier, horseman, equestrian, cavalryman, man-at-arms, soldier, warrior, chevalier, gallant, champion, knight-errant, Bayard, carpet-knight, *preux chevalier*
OLD kemper, kempery-man, banneret, bachelor, ritter, vavasour, douzeper; (*Spenser*) doucepere, freelance, younker

knightly adj
chivalrous, bold, courageous, valiant, dauntless, gallant, heroic, noble, honourable, intrepid, soldierly, courtly, gracious
FORMAL valorous
E3 cowardly, ignoble, ungallant

knit v
1 JOIN, unite, secure, bind, ally, connect, tie, fasten, link, draw together, mend, interlace, intertwine
2 KNOT, loop, crotchet, purl, weave
3 WRINKLE, furrow, crease, gather, tighten

Types of knitting stitch include:

basketweave	fisherman's rib	pavilion
box stitch	garter rib	plain stitch
braided cable	garter stitch	purl
cable stitch	honeycomb	rice stitch
chain cable	lattice cable	roman stripe
chain stitch	layette	seed stitch
chevron	mistake rib	stocking stitch
diagonal rib	moss panels	Swiss check
double seed stitch	moss stitch	twin rib

---

knob n
1 HANDLE, doorhandle, switch, button, push-button, tuner, stop
2 LUMP, ball, boss, protrusion, bump, projection, protuberance, nub, knot, knurl, gnarl, swell, knub, swelling tumour, boll, burr, tuber, eminence, node, stud, heel, snub; *Scot* plouk
TECHNICAL umbo, tubercle
OLD knop, noop, pommel

knock v, n
♦ v
1 *knock on the door*
tap, hit, strike, rap, thump, bang pound, slap, smack
2 *knock someone down*
hit, strike, collide with, bump into, smack, slap, punch, box, clout, cuff, clip, swipe, bang batter
COLLOQ. wallop, whack, belt
3 *knocked her head against the wall*
bang bump, hit, strike, collide, bash, pound, thump, stamp, dash, crash, jolt
4 CRITICIZE, condemn, run down, find fault with, slate, attack
FORMAL disparage, deprecate, censure
COLLOQ. slam, pan, rubbish, pick holes in, pull/tear to pieces, pull apart
SLANG slag (off)
E3 4 boost, praise
♦ n
1 *a knock at the door*
tap, rap, hit, pounding banging hammering
2 BLOW, bump, bang bash, box, rap, thump, clout, cuff, clip, pounding hammering slap, smack
COLLOQ. whack, belt, wallop
3 MISFORTUNE, blow, setback, failure, rejection, reversal, rebuff, defeat, bad experience/luck
COLLOQ. whammy
■ **knock about**
1 WANDER, travel, roam, rove, saunter, traipse, ramble, gad, gallivant, range
2 ASSOCIATE, go around
FORMAL consort
COLLOQ. hang around/about
3 BEAT UP, batter, abuse, mistreat, hurt, hit, strike, punch, bash, damage, maltreat, injure, wound, manhandle, bruise, buffet
■ **knock back**
swallow, devour, drink, gulp (down)
COLLOQ. guzzle, down, scoff, swig
■ **knock down**
1 DEMOLISH, destroy, fell, pull down, take down, floor, level, wreck, raze, pound, batter, clout, smash, wallop
2 RUN OVER, hit, knock over, run down
3 *knocked down prices*
reduce, lower, decrease, bring down
■ **knock off**
1 FINISH, finish/stop work, stop, cease, clock off, clock out
FORMAL terminate
COLLOQ. pack (it) in
2 STEAL, rob, pilfer, filch
COLLOQ. pinch, nick, lift, whip, snaffle, snitch, swipe
SLANG rip off

3 DEDUCT, take away
4 KILL, murder, slay, assassinate, get rid of, do away with
COLLOQ. bump off, polish off, do in
SLANG waste

■ **knock out**
1 *knock someone out*
make unconscious, floor, strike down, fell, level, prostrate
COLLOQ. KO
2 *knocked out of a competition*
defeat, eliminate, beat, overcome, get the better of, overwhelm, rout, crush
COLLOQ. thrash, hammer, run rings round
3 STUN, astound, impress, amaze, surprise, startle, astonish, shock, overwhelm, take your breath away
COLLOQ. bowl over, knock for six
E3 1 bring round

■ **knock up**
1 BUILD QUICKLY, jerry-build, make quickly, put together hurriedly, improvise
2 WAKE UP, waken, awake, awaken, rouse, stir, call
3 MAKE PREGNANT, impregnate
COLLOQ. put in the (pudding) club, put in the family way
E3 1 demolish

knockout *n*
success, triumph, sensation, attraction, coup, hit, winner
COLLOQ. smash, smash-hit, stunner
E3 flop, loser

knoll *n*
hill, hillock, mound, rise, barrow, elevation, hummock, koppie; *Scot* knowe

knot *v, n*
♦ *v*
tie, secure, bind, loop, tether, leash, lash, entangle, tangle, knit, entwine, ravel, weave
♦ *n*
1 TIE, bond, joint, fastening, loop, splice, twist, ligature
See panel below
2 BUNCH, cluster, clump, group, circle, ring, band, gathering, crowd
3 *a knot on a tree*
knob, lump, gnarl, knurl, swelling, nodule, knub

knotty *adj*
1 COMPLICATED, complex, intricate, difficult, hard, perplexing, thorny, tricky, troublesome, puzzling, baffling, mystifying, problematical, Byzantine
FORMAL anfractuous
2 GNARLED, knobby, knotted, rugged, rough, bumpy, nodose, nodous, nodular

know *v*
1 *know French*
understand, comprehend, apprehend, perceive, sense, notice, be aware, be conscious of, fathom, be well-versed in, be conversant with, be au fait with, experience, realize, see, undergo, go through
FORMAL be cognizant of
COLLOQ. be clued up, have at your fingertips, know like the back of your hand, have taped

2 *I know George*
be acquainted with, be familiar with, be friends with, associate with, be on good terms with, recognize, know by sight, identify
3 *know a good wine*
distinguish, discriminate, discern, differentiate, identify, make out, tell (apart)

> **QUOTATIONS**
> The person who knows 'how' will always have a job. The person who knows 'why' will always be his boss
> DIANE SILVERS RAVITCH

know-all *n*
know-it-all, pedant, wiseacre
COLLOQ. clever clogs, clever dick, wise guy, smart alec, smartypants
SLANG smartass, smartarse

knowhow *n*
expertise, knowledge, experience, proficiency, competence, gumption, savoir-faire, ability, capability, skill, ingenuity, dexterity, aptitude, adroitness, adeptness, talent, faculty, bent, flair, knack
COLLOQ. savvy

knowing *adj*
meaningful, expressive, perceptive, shrewd, significant, discerning conscious, cunning astute, aware
COLLOQ. sussed

knowingly *adj*
intentionally, willingly, on purpose, purposely, consciously, studiedly, wilfully, wittingly, deliberately, designedly, by design, calculatedly

knowledge *n*
1 LEARNING, scholarship, education, schooling letters, instruction, wisdom, tuition, enlightenment, information, data, facts
FORMAL erudition
COLLOQ. knowhow
2 ACQUAINTANCE, familiarity, awareness, intimacy, consciousness
FORMAL cognizance
3 UNDERSTANDING, comprehension, apprehension, recognition, judgement, discernment, wisdom, intelligence, ability, grasp, skill, expertise, proficiency, conversance, savoir-faire
FORMAL cognition
COLLOQ. knowhow
E3 1 ignorance **2** unawareness

> **PROVERBS**
> A little knowledge is a dangerous thing

> **SYNONYM NUANCES**
> *sense 1*
> **Learning** may be widely used of anything which has been retained from experience or study, while **scholarship** is more suggestive of intense academic research and expertise: *new standards of art history*

Types of knot include:

bend	double Cairnton	Flemish eye (or	loop knot	seizing	surgeon's knot
Blackwall hitch	double-overhand	double figure of	marling hitch	sheepshank	thief knot
blood knot	double-slipped	eight)	Matthew Walker's	sheet bend (or	tie
bow	reefknot	granny knot	overhand knot (or	common	timber hitch
bowline	drummer's chain	half hitch	thumb knot)	bend or swab	Turk's head
carrick bend	Englishman's tie	highwayman's	reef knot (or	hitch)	turle knot
chain knot	(or knot)	hitch (or donkey	square knot)	simple sennit (or	wall knot
clove hitch	figure of eight	hitch)	rolling hitch	plait knot)	weaver's
common whipping	fisherman's bend	hitch	round turn and	slipknot	knot
Domhof knot	fisherman's knot	Hunter's bend	two half hitches	slippery hitch	Windsor
double blood	flat knot	lark's head	running bowline	spade-end knot	knot

scholarship. **Education** usually refers to the general instruction and culture to which a person is subject, while **schooling** suggests a more narrow training received in a formal setting: *poor standards of secondary schooling*.

   Instruction and **tuition** are also straightforward synonyms that put the emphasis on teaching and **information**, **data** and **facts** are the basic components for building knowledge. **Letters** implies literary culture and suggests a degree of reverence: *a man of letters*. You can use **wisdom** simply of accrued knowledge: *conventional wisdom*, but it can also imply inherent good sense: *they have the wisdom to know themselves*, and it can have connotations of gravitas: *an ancient Chinese book of wisdom*. **Enlightenment** is also very positive in tone, and implies a more internal revelation brought about by learning: *learning about history brings enlightenment*.

knowledgeable *adj*
1 EDUCATED, scholarly, learned, informed, well-informed, well-read, lettered, intelligent, enlightened
FORMAL erudite
COLLOQ. a mine of information
2 AWARE, acquainted, conscious, familiar, au fait, conversant, experienced, expert, well-versed

COLLOQ. well up in, in the know, savvy, clued-up, up to speed
⊟ 1 ignorant

known *adj*
acknowledged, recognized, well-known, noted, obvious, patent, plain, admitted, revealed, familiar, avowed, commonplace, published, proclaimed, confessed, celebrated, famous

knuckle
■ **knuckle down**
buckle down, start to work hard, begin to study
■ **knuckle under**
submit, yield, give way, give in, succumb, surrender, capitulate, defer, buckle under
FORMAL accede, acquiesce

kowtow *v*
defer, cringe, fawn, grovel, pander, curry favour, pay court, flatter, kneel
COLLOQ. suck up, toady, bow and scrape

kudos *n*
fame, glory, applause, praise, honour, laurels, prestige, renown, repute, reputation, distinction, acclaim, esteem, regard, cachet, plaudits
FORMAL laudation

L

label n, v
♦ n
1 TAG, ticket, docket, tab, mark, marker,
sticker, stamp, seal, flash, trademark, number, tally,
bookplate, crowner
TECHNICAL address, identifier
2 DESCRIPTION, categorization, identification,
characterization, classification, designation, tag badge,
brand, name, title, nickname, epithet
3 TRADEMARK, make, logo, brand, brand name, proprietary
name
♦ v
1 TAG, mark, stamp, attach a label to, ticket
2 DESCRIBE, brand, classify, categorize, characterize,
identify, class, designate, define, term, call, dub, name

laboratory apparatus

Laboratory apparatus includes:

autoclave	electron	retort
beaker	microscope	separating funnel
bell jar	evaporating dish	slide
boiling tube	filter flask	spatula
Büchner funnel	filter paper	stand
Bunsen burner	flask	still
burette	fume cupboard	stirrer
centrifuge	funnel	stop clock
clamp	glove box	test tube
condenser	Kipp's apparatus	test tube rack
conical flask	Liebig condenser	thermometer
crucible	measuring	top-pan balance
cylinder	cylinder	tripod
desiccator	microscope	trough
distillation appara-	mortar	U-tube
tus	pestle	volumetric flask
dropper	Petri dish	Woulfe bottle
	pipette	

laborious adj
1 HARD, arduous, difficult, strenuous, tough, heavy,
backbreaking wearisome, wearying tiresome, tiring
fatiguing uphill, onerous, tedious, toilsome, slavish,
Sisyphean
OLD operose, painful; (Shakesp) laboursome
2 HARD-WORKING, industrious, painstaking indefatigable,
diligent, careful, assiduous
F3 1 easy, effortless **2** lazy

laboriously adv
with difficulty, arduously, strenuously, wearisomely,
tiresomely, toilsomely, drudgingly, slavishly
OLD operosely

labour n, v
♦ n
1 WORK, task, job, employment, chore, toil, effort, hard
work, exertion, drudgery, industriousness, diligence
COLLOQ. grind, slog sweat
2 WORKERS, employees, workforce, labourers, workmen,
hands
3 CHILDBIRTH, birth, delivery, labour pains, pangs, throes,
contractions

TECHNICAL parturition
F3 1 ease, leisure **2** management
♦ v
1 WORK, toil, work hard, drudge, slave, strive, exert
yourself, endeavour, struggle, plod
FORMAL travail
COLLOQ. grind, sweat, kill yourself
2 OVERDO, overemphasize, dwell on, elaborate, overstress,
put too much emphasis on, strain
3 *labour hard to get results*
struggle, strive, endeavour, work hard, try hard
COLLOQ. do your best, give your all, go all out, give it
your best shot
4 *labour under a mistaken belief*
suffer, be misled, be deceived, be blinded
5 *labour a point*
belabour, harp on about, keep talking about,
dwell on, reiterate
COLLOQ. go on and on about, flog to death,
do to death
6 TOSS, pitch, roll, turn
F3 1 laze, idle, lounge

laboured adj
awkward, unnatural, forced, difficult, complicated, heavy,
overdone, overwrought, stiff, stilted, strained, ponderous,
studied, contrived
FORMAL affected
F3 easy, natural

labourer n
manual worker, blue-collar worker, unskilled worker,
navvy, hand, worker, workman, drudge, menial, hireling
operative, boy, jack, pioneer, roustabout, hobbler, hod
carrier, hodman, docker, cottager, field hand; *Aust* (derog)
Kanaka
OLD churl
COLLOQ. *Irish* (derog) culchie; *N Am* gandy dancer
SLANG (offensive) coolie; *N Am* bohunk, grunt, (derog)
redneck
OLD SLANG Grecian

labyrinth n
maze, winding warren, complexity, intricacy,
complication, network, puzzle, riddle, enigma, tangle,
entanglement, jungle, confusion, web

labyrinthine adj
complex, intricate, complicated, perplexing puzzling
involved, knotty, tangled, tortuous, winding mazelike,
confused, mazy, Byzantine
FORMAL convoluted
F3 simple, straightforward

lace n, v
♦ n
1 NETTING, mesh-work, open work, tatting crochet, filigree
2 STRING, cord, twine, thong tie, shoelace, bootlace, lacing
♦ v
1 TIE, do up, fasten, secure, thread, close, bind, attach,
string twine, intertwine, interweave
2 ADD TO, mix in, flavour, blend, strengthen
FORMAL fortify
COLLOQ. spike

lacerate v
tear, rip, rend, cut (open), gash, slash, wound, claw, mangle, maim, injure, mutilate, torture, torment, harrow, hurt, distress
FORMAL afflict

laceration n
tear, cut, gash, rip, rent, slash, wound, injury, mutilation, maim

lachrymose adj
tearful, crying weeping weepy, mournful, sad, melancholy, sobbing teary, woeful
FORMAL dolorous, lugubrious
₣₴ happy, laughing

lack n, v
♦ n
need, scarcity, shortage, insufficiency, dearth, deficiency, absence, scantiness, vacancy, void, deprivation, destitution, emptiness
FORMAL want, paucity, privation
₣₴ abundance, profusion
♦ v
need, have need of, not have, not have enough of, miss, be deficient in, require
FORMAL want
COLLOQ. be clean/fresh out of

SYNONYM NUANCES

noun
Need can be used of a requirement: *there is a need for home care for the elderly*, while **scarcity** would be reserved for where there is a serious shortfall. The terms **shortage** and **insufficiency** simply say there is not enough, but **dearth** goes further by suggesting there are hardly any of something and the effects are detrimental: *a dearth of written records from that time means we cannot get a clear picture.* **Deficiency**, on the other hand, suggests a missing amount that detracts from completeness: *she was suffering from an iron deficiency.* You can use **absence** if nothing is present at all, while **vacancy**, like **emptiness** and **void**, suggests an unfilled space, although **vacancy** also often applies to an unfilled job. The more emotive **deprivation** suggests inadequate supplies for physical or emotional nourishment, while **destitution** takes that to extremes by implying being entirely without such things: *the venture failed, leaving the family in destitution.*

---

lackadaisical adj
apathetic, lazy, lethargic, inert, limp, spiritless, listless, indifferent, idle, dreamy, dull, lukewarm, half-hearted, abstracted, careless
FORMAL enervated, indolent, languorous, languid
₣₴ active, dynamic, energetic, vigorous

lackey n
1 FAWNER, sycophant, toady, flatterer, hanger-on, parasite, minion, pawn, poodle, instrument, tool
COLLOQ. yes-man, doormat
2 ATTENDANT, steward, servant, manservant, footman, menial, valet, page, retainer, guide, equerry, vassal
OLD skip-kennel

lacking adj
1 NEEDING, without, short of, missing absent, minus
2 DEFICIENT, inadequate, defective, flawed
FORMAL wanting

lacklustre adj
drab, dull, flat, boring tedious, dry, leaden, lifeless, spiritless, uninteresting unimaginative, uninspired, commonplace, dim, insipid, vapid
COLLOQ. run-of-the-mill
₣₴ brilliant, inspired, lively, bright

laconic adj
terse, succinct, pithy, concise, incisive, crisp, taciturn, short, curt, brief, economical, blunt, abrupt, to the point
₣₴ verbose, wordy

laconically adv
briefly, tersely, succinctly, pithily, concisely, incisively, bluntly, abruptly, in brief, in a word, to the point
₣₴ verbosely, at (great) length

lacuna n
gap, omission, space, void, break, blank, cavity
FORMAL hiatus

lad n
1 BOY, youth, youngster, stripling juvenile, schoolboy, son; *Scot* callant, chield, chiel; *Irish* bucko, gossoon, spalpeen
OLD *Scot* gillie-wetfoot, gillie-white-foot
COLLOQ. kid, nipper, whippersnapper; *Welsh & Irish* boyo; *N Am* tad
2 CHAP, fellow, individual, character, sort, type
COLLOQ. guy, bloke

ladder n
1 STEPS, set of steps, stairs, rungs
Related adjective: scalar
2 RANK, ranking level, rung point, hierarchy, grading scale, series, echelons, pecking order

---

Types of ladder include:

accommodation ladder	library steps	scale
companion ladder	loft ladder	side ladder
étrier	multipurpose ladder	stepladder
extension ladder	platform ladder	stepstool
folding ladder	quarter ladder	stern ladder
fruit-picking ladder	ratline	stile
gangway ladder	rolling ladder	straight ladder
hook ladder	roof ladder	tower scaffold
kitchen steps	rope ladder	

---

laden adj
loaded, charged, weighed down, burdened, oppressed, packed, stuffed, weighted, full, chock-full, fraught, encumbered, hampered, taxed, jammed
₣₴ empty

la-di-da adj
pretentious, posh, conceited, snobbish, snooty, mannered, over-refined, foppish
FORMAL affected
COLLOQ. highfalutin, put-on, stuck-up, toffee-nosed

ladle v
shovel, spoon, lade, dish, scoop, bail, dip
■ **ladle out**
hand out, distribute, disburse, dish out, dole out

lady n
woman, young woman, female, matron, noblewoman, dame, countess, grande dame, begum, khanum, sheikha, Señora, Señorita, duenna, Signora, Signorina
OLD damsel, gentlewoman, demoiselle, miss, ladykin, lakin, burd
SLANG old dear

ladylike adj
refined, well-bred, well-mannered, polite, courteous, proper, respectable, polished, modest, cultured, elegant, courtly, queenly, genteel, matronly
FORMAL decorous

lag v
dawdle, loiter, hang back, linger, fall behind, straggle, trail, bring up the rear, saunter, delay, shuffle, idle, dally
FORMAL tarry
COLLOQ. shilly-shally, lounge, drag your feet, kick your heels
₣₴ hurry, lead, keep up

laggard n
dawdler, loiterer, lingerer, straggler, sluggard, idler, saunterer, snail, loafer
COLLOQ. slowcoach, lounger
F3 dynamo, live wire; *colloq.* go-getter

lagoon n
pool, pond, shallows, lake, marsh, bog fen, swamp; *N Am* bayou

laid-back adj
relaxed, at ease, casual, leisurely, easy-going unhurried, untroubled, unworried, calm, cool, free and easy
FORMAL imperturbable
COLLOQ. unflappable
F3 tense; *colloq.* uptight

laid up adj
housebound, bedridden, confined to bed, ill, sick, incapacitated, disabled, *hors de combat*, immobilized, injured, out of action, on the sick list

lair

Lairs and homes of creatures include:

hill (*ant*)	earth (*fox*)	burrow (*rabbit*)
sett (*badger*)	form (*hare*)	warren (*rabbit*)
den (*bear*)	den (*lion*)	pen (*sheep*)
lodge (*beaver*)	fortress (*mole*)	fold (*sheep*)
hive (*bee*)	hole (*mouse*)	shell (*snail*)
nest (*bird*)	nest (*mouse*)	drey (*squirrel*)
byre (*cow*)	holt (*otter*)	mound (*termite*)
eyrie (*eagle*)	sty (*pig*)	nest (*wasp*)
coop (*fowl*)	dovecote (*pigeon*)	vespiary (*wasp*)

laissez-faire adj
permissive, non-interfering, non-interventionist, free-enterprise, free-market, free-trade
COLLOQ. hands-off, live and let live

laity n
1 THE NON-ORDAINED, unordained, parishoners, lay people
2 NON-PROFESSIONALS, amateurs, outsiders
F3 1 the clergy **2** experts, professionals, specialists

lake n
pond, pool, lagoon, sea, water, reservoir, dam, basin, mere, tarn, everglade, playa, salina, shott, nyanza; *Scot* loch; *Irish* lough; *N Am* bayou; *Can* saltchuck; *Aust* cowal
Related adjective: lacustrine

lam v
beat, batter, bash, hit, knock, pound, thump, clout, strike, thrash, leather, pelt, pummel
COLLOQ. wallop, whack, belt

lambast v
1 CRITICIZE, reprimand, rebuke, scold, upbraid
FORMAL berate, castigate, censure, reprove
COLLOQ. roast, rubbish, badmouth
SLANG slag (off)
2 BEAT, whip, flog thrash, strike, drub, clout, thump, batter, flay, leather
COLLOQ. wallop, whack, belt, clobber, tan

lame adj
1 DISABLED, handicapped, crippled, cripple, hurt, injured, maimed, limping hobbling halting game, hamstrung
TECHNICAL spavined
OLD halt, mained
FORMAL incapacitated
COLLOQ. gammy, poorly
2 WEAK, feeble, flimsy, inadequate, unsatisfactory, defective, poor, thin, unconvincing tame
F3 1 able-bodied **2** convincing

lamely adv
1 *halted lamely down the path*
with a limp, hobblingly, weakly, unsteadily, shakily

2 *'It wasn't my fault,' he said lamely*
feebly, weakly, unconvincingly, tamely, inadequately, unsatisfactorily

lament v, n
♦ v
mourn, grieve, sorrow, cry, weep, sob, wail, keen, complain, groan, moan, deplore, regret; *dialect* yammer
OLD bewail, bemoan, plain, beweep, mean, mein, repine; (*Spenser*) wayment
FORMAL ululate
F3 rejoice, celebrate
♦ n
lamentation, dirge, elegy, keen, requiem, complaint, moan, groan, wail, grieving crying weeping sobbing tears, howl
TECHNICAL dumka
FORMAL threnody

lamentable adj
1 DEPLORABLE, regrettable, mournful, distressing sorrowful, tragic, unfortunate, terrible, wretched, grievous, woeful
2 MEAGRE, low, inadequate, insufficient, mean, unsatisfactory, pitiful, miserable, niggardly, poor, disappointing
COLLOQ. measly, lousy, grotty

lamentably adv
deplorably, regrettably, pitifully, miserably, disappointingly, tragically, woefully, inadequately, insufficiently

lamentation n
dirge, elegy, lament, wailing mourning weeping moan, sobbing sorrow, grief, grieving keen, keening jeremiad
FORMAL ululation, deploration, threnody, plaint
F3 celebration, rejoicing

laminate v
cover, layer, overlay, plate, stratify, veneer, coat, face, flake, separate, split
TECHNICAL foliate
FORMAL exfoliate

lamp n
light, lantern, torch, bulb, light bulb
See panel at **light¹**.

lampoon n, v
♦ n
satire, skit, caricature, parody, spoof, burlesque, travesty, pasquinade
COLLOQ. send-up, take-off
♦ v
satirize, caricature, parody, spoof, make fun of, ridicule, mock, burlesque, pasquinade
COLLOQ. send up, take off

lampooner n
satirist, caricaturist, parodist, pasquinader, pasquilant, pasquiler

lance v, n
♦ v
pierce, slit, cut (open), puncture, prick, incise
♦ n
spear, javelin, pike, harpoon, bayonet, lancet, shaft

land n, v
♦ n
1 EARTH, ground, soil, loam, terrain, dry land, terra firma
Related adjective: terrestrial
2 PROPERTY, grounds, estate, real estate, country, countryside, fields, rural area, open space, farmland, are, agricultural land, tract, acres, acreage, manor
Related adjectives: agrarian, praedial
3 COUNTRY, nation, region, area, district, territory, province, domain, realm, state, fatherland, motherland, native country
♦ v
1 ALIGHT, disembark, dismount, dock, berth, anchor, moor, unload, arrive, touch down, come/bring in to land, bring/take down, go ashore, come to rest; *N Am* deplane

2 ARRIVE, deposit, reach, get, find yourself, drop, finish up, settle, turn up
COLLOQ. wind up, end up
3 OBTAIN, secure, gain, get, get hold of, acquire, net, capture, achieve, win
FORMAL procure
COLLOQ. bag nab
4 *land you with another bill*
saddle, weigh down, burden, oppress, trouble, tax, encumber
COLLOQ. lumber
5 *land a blow on the ear*
hit, deal, give, catch, deliver, administer, direct, inflict
COLLOQ. fetch

> **QUOTATIONS**
> Land of Hope and Glory, Mother of the Free, / How shall we extol thee who are born of thee? / Wider still and wider shall thy bounds be set; / God who made thee mighty, make thee mightier yet
>   A C BENSON, 'Land of Hope and Glory'
>
> Breathes there the man, with soul so dead, / Who never to himself hath said, / This is my own, my native land!
>   SIR WALTER SCOTT, *The Lay of the Last Minstrel*

landing *n*
1 TOUCHDOWN, coming in, coming in to land, coming to ground, arrival, disembarkation, putting ashore, alighting; *N Am* deplaning
2 LANDING-STAGE, landing-place, jetty, pier, dock, harbour, quay, wharf

landlady, landlord *n*
1 PUBLICAN, innkeeper, hotelier, hotel-keeper, host, mine host, restaurateur
2 OWNER, landowner, lessor, proprietor, proprietress, freeholder; *N Am* slumlord

landmark *n*
1 FEATURE, monument, signpost, milestone, milepost, boundary, beacon, cairn; *Scot* meith
2 TURNING-POINT, crisis, watershed

landscape *n*
scene, scenery, view, panorama, outlook, vista, prospect, perspective, countryside, aspect

landslide *n, adj*
♦ *n*
landslip, earthfall, rockfall, avalanche
♦ *adj*
overwhelming decisive, emphatic, runaway

lane *n*
way, track, passage(way), alley(way), footpath, footway, path(way), towpath, byroad, byway, driveway, avenue, channel; *Irish* boreen

language *n*
1 SPEECH, tongue, vocabulary, terminology, communication, speaking uttering verbalizing vocalizing
FORMAL parlance
2 TALK, conversation, utterance
FORMAL discourse, converse
3 WORDING, style, phraseology, phrasing expression, utterance, rhetoric
FORMAL diction
Related adjective: linguistic

Languages of the world include:

Aborigine	Belorussian	Croat
Afghan	Bengali	Czech
Afrikaans	British Sign	Danish
American Sign	Language (BSL)	Dutch
Language (ASL)	Burmese	Ebonics
Arabic	Catalan	English
Balinese	Celtic	Eskimo
Bantu	Chinese	Esperanto
Basque	Cornish	Estonian
Ethiopian	Kurdish	Shelta
Farsi	Lapp	Siamese
Finnish	Latin	Sinhalese
Flemish	Latvian	Slavonic
French	Lithuanian	Slovak
Gaelic	Magyar	Slovenian
German	Malay	Somali
Greek	Maltese	Spanish
Haitian	Mandarin	Swahili
Hawaiian	Manx	Swedish
Hebrew	Maori	Swiss
Hindi	Mexican	Tamil
Hindustani	Norwegian	Thai
Hottentot	Persian	Tibetan
Hungarian	Polish	Turkish
Icelandic	Portuguese	Ukrainian
Indonesian	Punjabi	Urdu
Inuit (or Inuktitut)	Romanian	Vietnamese
Iranian	Romany	Volapük
Iraqi	Russian	Welsh
Irish	Sanskrit	Yiddish
Italian	Scottish	Zulu
Japanese	Serbian	

Language terms include:

argot	patois	phonetics
brogue	*colloq.* patter	semantics
buzz word	pidgin	sociolinguistics
cant	regionalism	syntax
cockney rhyming	slang	usage
slang	textspeak (or	
colloquialism	textese)	**ARTIFICIAL INTELLI-**
creole	tongue	**GENCE:**
dialect	vernacular	automatic speech
doublespeak	vocabulary	recognition (ASR)
gobbledygook		language engineer-
idiom	**LANGUAGE STUDY:**	ing
jargon	etymology	machine transla-
journalese	grammar	tion
colloq. lingo	lexicography	natural language
lingua franca	linguistics	processing (NLP)
localism	orthography	

languid *adj*
listless, sluggish, lethargic, slow, inactive, lazy, feeble, heavy, uninterested, unenthusiastic, spiritless, indifferent, inert, lackadaisical, drooping dull, weak, faint, weary, pining limp, sickly
FORMAL debilitated, enervated, languorous, torpid
E3 alert, lively, vivacious

languidly *adv*
listlessly, lethargically, slowly, inactively, lazily, feebly, heavily, inertly, weakly, dully, unenthusiastically
FORMAL torpidly

languish *v*
1 WILT, droop, fade, fail, flag wither, waste away, rot, deteriorate, weaken, sink, faint, decline, mope, waste, grieve, sorrow, sigh, brood, sicken
2 PINE, yearn, want, long desire, hanker, hunger, sigh
E3 1 flourish, rise

languor *n*
lethargy, listlessness, laziness, faintness, fatigue, weariness, silence, inertia, drowsiness, dreaminess, sleepiness, feebleness, weakness, frailty, calm, lull, relaxation, oppressiveness, heaviness, ennui, sloth, stillness
FORMAL debility, enervation, indolence, lassitude, torpor
E3 gusto; *formal* alacrity

languorous *adj*
lazy, relaxed, lethargic, listless, weary, dreamy, sleepy, feeble, weak
FORMAL torpid
E3 lively, energetic

lank *adj*
1 *lank hair*
limp, straggling scraggy, drooping lifeless, lustreless
2 *lank young people*
tall, thin, long emaciated, skinny, gaunt, lanky, lean,
slender, slim, scrawny, rawboned; *N Am* slab-sided
F3 burly

lanky *adj*
gaunt, gangling gangly, scrawny, tall, thin, lean, slender,
slim, rangy, scraggy, weedy
F3 short, squat

lap[1] *n, v*
♦ *n*
1 *sat on her lap*
knees, thighs
Related adjective: (old) gremial
2 CIRCUIT, round, orbit, ambit, tour, loop, course, circle,
compass, distance
3 *a lap on a journey*
stage, section, leg stretch
♦ *v*
wrap, fold, wind, twine, envelop, enfold, swathe, encase,
surround, cover, swaddle, overlap

lap[2] *v*
1 *animals lapping milk*
drink, sip, sup, lick, lip, scoop up
2 *the sea lapping against the boat*
splash, wash, rush, flow, roll, swish, slop, slosh, break,
beat, dash
■ **lap up**
accept eagerly, take in enthusiastically, listen in, absorb,
relish, delight in, savour

lapse *n, v*
♦ *n*
1 ERROR, slip, mistake, negligence, omission, oversight,
fault, blunder, trip, failing indiscretion, backsliding relapse
FORMAL aberration, dereliction
2 FALL, descent, decline, drop, stumble, downturn,
deterioration, worsening degeneration, backslide, slipping
3 BREAK, gap, interval, lull, interruption, intermission,
pause, blank, course, passage
FORMAL hiatus
♦ *v*
1 DECLINE, fall, sink, drop, deteriorate, slide, slip, drift,
stumble, fail, worsen, degenerate, backslide, fall from
grace
COLLOQ. go downhill, go to pot, go to the dogs, go to rack
and ruin, go down the tubes
2 EXPIRE, run out, end, stop, become void/invalid
TECHNICAL prescribe, resolve
FORMAL terminate, cease
3 PASS, elapse, go by, go on, slip, slip away, slip by, drift,
fall
F3 2 continue

lapsed *adj*
1 EXPIRED, ended, run out, finished, out of date, outdated,
invalid, void, obsolete, unrenewed
FORMAL discontinued
2 *a lapsed Catholic*
once, former, non-practising backslidden
F3 1 renewed, continued

larceny *n*
stealing theft, burglary, robbery, pilfering piracy
FORMAL misappropriation, purloining expropriation
SLANG heist

larder *n*
pantry, storeroom, storage room, scullery

large *adj*
1 BIG, huge, immense, massive, vast, siz(e)able, great,
giant, gigantic, bulky, heavy, ample, enormous, colossal,
king-sized, broad, considerable, monumental, prodigious,
stupendous, mammoth, substantial, high, tall,
Brobdingnagian

FORMAL commodious, voluminous
COLLOQ. jumbo, whopping bumper, ginormous, dirty
great, humungous
SLANG mega
2 FULL, extensive, generous, liberal, ample, roomy,
plentiful, spacious, grand, far-reaching wide-ranging
sweeping broad, comprehensive, exhaustive, grandiose
F3 1 small, tiny
■ **at large**
1 GENERALLY, in general, by and large, on the whole,
chiefly, mainly, in the main
2 FREE, at liberty, on the loose, on the run, independent,
unconfined
■ **by and large**
on the whole, generally, mostly, mainly, generally
speaking as a rule, for the most part, all things
considered

largely *adv*
mainly, in the main, principally, chiefly, generally,
primarily, predominantly, mostly, for the most part,
considerably, by and large, to a large extent, widely,
extensively, greatly

largeness *n*
greatness, immensity, vastness, size, heaviness, bulk,
ampleness, enormousness, broadness, wideness,
expansiveness, siz(e)ableness, voluminousness, grandness,
stupendousness

large-scale *adj*
extensive, far-reaching broad, nationwide, country-wide,
wide, wide-ranging wide-reaching expansive, wholesale,
global, universal, vast, sweeping epic
F3 minor

largesse *n*
generosity, kindness, liberality, philanthropy, benefaction,
open-handedness, bounty, donation, gift, present, aid,
grant, handout, endowment, bequest, charity, allowance,
alms
FORMAL munificence
F3 meanness

lark *n, v*
♦ *n*
1 ESCAPADE, antic, fling prank, romp, revel, mischief,
fooling horseplay, tomfoolery, frolic, caper, cavorting play,
game; *dialect* gammock
OLD guy
COLLOQ. skylark
2 *this writing lark*
activity, task, job, chore
COLLOQ. business, thing
♦ *v*
play, play tricks, have fun, fool around/about, mess about,
cavort, frolic, caper, romp, sport, rollick, gambol; *dialect*
gammock
COLLOQ. skylark

lascivious *adj*
lecherous, lewd, licentious, lustful, ribald, sensual,
obscene, pornographic, crude, vulgar, coarse, bawdy,
wanton, dirty, indecent, offensive, suggestive, salacious,
scurrilous, unchaste
FORMAL libidinous, prurient
COLLOQ. blue, horny, randy, smutty

lash *n, v*
♦ *n*
blow, whip, stroke, swipe, hit, stripe, thong welt, belt
OLD wire
♦ *v*
1 WHIP, flog beat, hit, thrash, strike, scourge, flail, batter,
slash, switch, welt, bullwhip, horse, cat, flick
OLD swinge
COLLOQ. wallop, whack
2 ATTACK, criticize, lay into, scold, reprove, rebuke,
censure
FORMAL fulminate, berate
COLLOQ. bawl out, tear a strip off, tear to shreds

3 TIE, bind, fasten, secure, make fast, join, affix, rope, tether, strap
TECHNICAL seize
4 *waves lashing the shore*
strike, smash, dash, break, beat, pound, buffet
5 *an animal lashing its tail*
flick, swish, whip, switch, wag
■ **lash out**
1 *lash out at someone*
hit out at, thrash, yerk, attack strongly, speak out against, criticize fiercely, run down, have a go at
COLLOQ. lay into, tear a strip off, tear to pieces/shreds
2 *lash out on new clothes*
spend a lot of money, spend extravagantly
COLLOQ. splash out on, spend a fortune on, spend money like water

lashings *n*
lots, great quantity, large amount
COLLOQ. oodles, loads, masses, heaps, piles, stacks, tons

lass *n*
girl, young woman, schoolgirl, lassie, miss; *Scot* Jenny
OLD damsel, maiden, popsy
COLLOQ. hen
OLD COLLOQ. filly
SLANG bird, chick

lassitude *n*
sluggishness, tiredness, weariness, lethargy, listlessness, drowsiness, apathy, dullness, exhaustion, fatigue, heaviness
FORMAL enervation, languor, torpor
E3 energy, vigour

lasso *n*
rope, lariat, noose

last[1] *adj, adv, n*
♦ *adj*
1 *last Sunday*
most recent, latest, previous
2 FINAL, ultimate, closing latest, rearmost, hindmost, terminal, furthest, concluding finishing ending remotest, utmost, extreme
3 *the last house on the street*
coming at the end, back, hind, hindmost, tail-end, furthest, farthest, remotest, endmost, final
4 *the last person to expect help from*
least likely, least suitable, most unlikely, most improbable, most unsuitable
E3 **1** next **2** first, initial **3** first **4** most likely
♦ *adv*
finally, ultimately, behind, after, at the end, at the back/rear
E3 first, firstly
♦ *n*
finish, close, end, ending conclusion, completion
■ **at last**
eventually, finally, in the end, in conclusion, ultimately, in due course, at length
COLLOQ. at the end of the day
■ **last word**
1 final decision, final say, final statement, concluding remark, conclusive/definite comment, ultimatum
2 latest, best, pick, cream, ultimate, vogue, rage, perfection, crème de la crème, *dernier cri, ne plus ultra*
FORMAL quintessence

last[2] *v*
1 *it lasts six hours*
continue, go on, take, endure, remain, persist, carry on, keep (on), survive, hold out, hold on, exist, wear, stay, stand up
FORMAL abide, subsist
2 GET THROUGH, survive, manage to cope with, endure, keep going through
COLLOQ. stick it out
E3 **1** cease, stop, fade

last-ditch *adj*
final, desperate, frenzied, wild, last-chance, straining struggling frantic, heroic
COLLOQ. all-out, eleventh-hour, last-gasp

lasting *adj*
enduring unchanging unceasing ceaseless, unending abiding surviving continuing persisting permanent, durable, perpetual, external, everlasting undying never-ending lifelong long-lived, long-standing long-term
FORMAL interminable
E3 brief, fleeting short-lived

lastly *adv*
finally, ultimately, in conclusion, in the end, to sum up
E3 firstly

last-minute *adj*
late, overdue, hasty, rushed, forced, superficial
COLLOQ. eleventh-hour

latch *n, v*
♦ *n*
fastening catch, bar, bolt, lock, hook, hasp, clicket; *dialect* sneck
OLD (*Spenser*) clink
♦ *v*
fasten, bar, bolt, lock, hook, catch, make secure
■ **latch on to**
1 ATTACH YOURSELF TO, not want to leave, follow
2 UNDERSTAND, comprehend, grasp, learn, realize
FORMAL apprehend
COLLOQ. twig

late *adj, adv*
♦ *adj*
1 OVERDUE, behind, behindhand, behind schedule, behind time, slow, unpunctual, delayed, last-minute
FORMAL tardy
2 FORMER, previous, departed, dead, deceased, past, preceding old, defunct
3 RECENT, up-to-date, current, fresh, new, up-to-the-minute, latest
E3 **1** early, punctual
♦ *adv*
1 UNPUNCTUALLY, behindhand, behind schedule, behind time, in arrears, slowly, belatedly, formerly, recently
FORMAL dilatorily, tardily
2 *work late*
after hours, overtime
E3 **1** punctually **2** early
■ **of late**
recently, lately, not long ago, newly, latterly

> **PROVERBS**
> Better late than never

> **SYNONYM NUANCES**
>
> *adjective sense 1*
> **Overdue** can be used of anything not turning up by the expected time or to suggest something has not been fulfilled by the desired time: *a change of leadership is overdue*, while **behind**, **behindhand**, **behind schedule** and **behind time** would be used of actions that should already have been carried out: *your rent payments are behind*.
>   **Slow** suggests taking a longer than average time. **Unpunctual** is more disapproving in that it suggests an inability to keep to allotted times. **Delayed** would be used of something put off until a later time: *the delayed flight will now take off at 5.30*, and **last-minute** describes something done at the latest possible moment: *last minute check-ins are common at airports*.

lately *adv*
recently, of late, not long ago, newly, latterly
OLD alate, now of late

lateness *n*
belatedness, delay, unpunctuality
FORMAL dilatoriness, retardation, tardiness
E∃ earliness

latent *adj*
potential, possible, dormant, inactive, undeveloped,
undiscovered, unrealized, lurking unexpressed, unseen,
unrevealed, secret, concealed, hidden, invisible,
underlying veiled, passive
FORMAL quiescent
E∃ active, conspicuous, apparent

later *adv, adj*
♦ *adv*
next, afterwards, subsequently, eventually, after,
successively, in the (near) future, at a future
time/date, at a later time, later on, in due course,
in a while, some other time
E∃ earlier
♦ *adj*
next, subsequent, following succeeding

lateral *adj*
1 SIDEWAYS, side, oblique, indirect, slanting sideward,
edgeways, marginal, flanking
2 *lateral thinking*
creative, ingenious, fresh, alternative, original,
imaginative, inspired, clever, brilliant, unorthodox,
unconventional, illogical
COLLOQ. outside the box

laterally *adv*
1 SIDEWAYS, edgeways, obliquely
2 *think laterally*
creatively, ingeniously, originally, imaginatively,
unconventionally, illogically
COLLOQ. outside the box

latest *adj*
modern, newest, last, most recent, ultimate, up-to-date,
current, now, fashionable
COLLOQ. in, with it, up-to-the-minute, hip,
trendy, now
SLANG funky
E∃ earliest

lather *n, v*
♦ *n*
1 FOAM, suds, soapsuds, froth, bubbles, soap, shampoo
2 AGITATION, fluster, anxiety, panic, fuss, dither, flutter,
fever
COLLOQ. state, flap, tizzy, sweat, stew
♦ *v*
foam, froth, rub, soap, shampoo, whip up

latitude *n*
freedom, liberty, unrestrictedness, laxity,
indulgence, carte blanche, licence, leeway, flexibility,
scope, range, room, space, play, clearance, breadth,
width, spread, sweep, reach, span, field, extent

latter *adj*
last-mentioned, last, later, closing final, end, concluding
ensuing succeeding successive, second
E∃ former

latter-day *adj*
modern, contemporary, current, present-day

latterly *adv*
lately, recently, most recently, of late
FORMAL hitherto
E∃ formerly

lattice *n*
latticework, openwork, fretwork, mesh, web, grate, grating
network, espalier, grid, grille, tracery, trellis
FORMAL reticulation

laud *v*
praise, admire, approve, magnify,
acclaim, applaud, celebrate, glorify, extol,
honour, hail
E∃ blame, condemn, curse, damn

laudable *adj*
praiseworthy, commendable, estimable, of note,
excellent, exemplary, worthy, admirable, creditable,
sterling
FORMAL meritorious
E∃ damnable, execrable

laudation *n*
praise, acclaim, acclamation, reverence, adulation,
blessing accolade, celebrity, commendation,
devotion, extolment, glorification, glory, kudos,
homage, tribute
FORMAL encomium, encomion, eulogy, panegyric,
paean, veneration
E∃ condemnation, criticism

laudatory *adj*
complimentary, commendatory, adulatory, acclamatory,
approving congratulatory, celebratory, glorifying
FORMAL approbatory, encomiastic(al), eulogistic,
panegyrical
E∃ damning

laugh *v, n*
♦ *v*
chuckle, burst out laughing dissolve into laughter,
roar/shriek with laughter, cackle, giggle,
guffaw, snigger, snicker, titter, chortle, hoot,
roar, peal, scream, haw-haw, ha-ha, he-he, tee-hee;
dialect nicker; *Scot* snirtle
FORMAL cachinnate
COLLOQ. split/shake your sides, fall about,
crease up, break up, howl, be rolling in the aisles,
be in stitches, laugh like a drain, laugh
your head off
SLANG yok, yock
♦ *n*
1 *have a good laugh*
giggle, chuckle, snigger, snicker, titter, guffaw, chortle,
lark, roar, peel, cackle, hoot, belly-laugh, horse laugh,
he-he, tee-hee, haw-haw, ha-ha; *dialect* nicker;
Scot snirt
FORMAL cachinnation, irrision, risus
COLLOQ. scream, hoot; *N Am* boff
SLANG yok, yock
Related adjective: gelastic
2 JOKE, jest, prank, hoax, trick, sport, fun, play
3 *he's a great laugh*
joker, comedian, comic, wit, humorist, jester, trickster,
quipster, prankster, hoaxer, practical joker, wag clown,
buffoon, character, sport
COLLOQ. wisecracker, card
■ **laugh at**
mock, ridicule, make jokes about, jeer, make fun of,
scoff at, disparage, scorn, taunt, make a fool of,
poke fun at
FORMAL deride
■ **laugh off**
dismiss, disregard, ignore, brush aside, belittle,
shrug off, make little of, minimize
COLLOQ. pooh-pooh

PROVERBS
He who laughs last, laughs longest

QUOTATIONS
The most wasted day is that in which we have not
laughed
SEBASTIEN ROCH NICOLAS CHAMFORT, *Maximes
et pensées*

laughable *adj*

1 FUNNY, amusing comical, comic, humorous, hilarious, uproarious, droll, farcical, diverting entertaining
COLLOQ. side-splitting
2 RIDICULOUS, absurd, ludicrous, preposterous, nonsensical, derisory, derisive
❌ **1** serious

laughably *adv*

ridiculously, ludicrously, absurdly, preposterously, farcically

laughing-stock *n*

figure of fun, butt, dupe, victim, target, object of ridicule, fair game, stooge, Aunt Sally

laughter *n*

laughing giggling chuckling chortling cackling hooting guffawing sniggering tittering hilarity, amusement, merriment, happiness, cheerfulness, glee, convulsions, *fou rire*, hysterics, paroxysm, haw, ha-ha
OLD mirth
FORMAL cachinnation, irrision, risibility
Related adjective: gelastic

launch *v*

1 PROPEL, dispatch, discharge, hurl, fire, send off, project, float, set afloat, set in motion, throw
2 BEGIN, start, embark on, set up, establish, found, open, initiate, inaugurate, institute, introduce, organize, instigate, set in motion, roll out
FORMAL commence
COLLOQ. set/start the ball rolling

laundry *n*

1 WASHING, dirty washing (dirty) clothes, wash
2 LAUNDERETTE, dry cleaner's; *N Am* Laundromat®

lavatory *n*

toilet, WC, bathroom, cloakroom, washroom, gents', ladies', water closet, public convenience, convenience, urinal, latrine, privy, powder room, facilities, earth-closet, Elsan®, Portaloo®, lavabo, office; *N Am* rest room, comfort station
OLD reredorter, necessary
COLLOQ. loo, lav, dunny, smallest room, throne, superloo, little boys' room, little girls' room
SLANG kazi, bog crapper, can, cottage, rears, heads, thunderbox; *Scot* cludgie; *N Am* john; *Aust* toot
OLD SLANG dike

lavish *adj, v*

♦ *adj*
1 ABUNDANT, copious, lush, luxuriant, plentiful, profuse, unlimited, prolific, splendid, grand, gorgeous, rich, sumptuous

2 GENEROUS, liberal, open-handed, free, bountiful, extravagant, wasteful, thriftless, prodigal, profligate, immoderate, excessive, wild, intemperate, unsparing unstinting
❌ **1** scant, paltry **2** frugal, thrifty, mean
♦ *v*
spend, expend, heap, pour, give freely, shower, deluge, squander, waste, dissipate
FORMAL bestow

lavishly *adv*

1 *lavishly decorated*
grandly, richly, splendidly, sumptuously, luxuriously, lushly, abundantly, profusely
2 *pour cream lavishly over the pudding*
generously, liberally, freely, extravagantly, excessively, wildly, unsparingly, intemperately

law *n*

1 RULE, act, legislation, constitution, decree, edict, order, directive, statute, regulation, command, commandment, pronouncement, ordinance, charter, code, enactment
2 PRINCIPLE, axiom, maxim, criterion, standard, precept, rule, formula, tenet, code, direction, instruction, canon, guideline
3 JURISPRUDENCE, legislation, lawsuit, litigation, legal action, legal proceedings
Related adjective: legal
4 THE POLICE, the police force, police officers
COLLOQ. the force, cops, coppers, rozzers, boys in blue
SLANG the Bill, the fuzz, pigs

law-abiding *adj*

obedient, upright, orderly, lawful, complying honest, honourable, decent, virtuous, good, righteous, upstanding dutiful
❌ lawless

lawbreaker *n*

offender, wrongdoer, criminal, felon, miscreant, culprit, delinquent, convict, outlaw, sinner, trespasser
FORMAL infractor, transgresser
COLLOQ. crook

lawcourt *n*

court, court of law, bench, bar, judiciary, tribunal, trial, session, assizes
See panel at **court**

lawful *adj*

legal, legitimate, permissible, legalized, constitutional, authorized, recognized, allowable, sanctioned, warranted, valid, just, proper, rightful
FORMAL licit
COLLOQ. legit
❌ illegal, unlawful, illicit

lawfully *adv*

by law, according to the law, by rights, rightfully, legally, legitimately, permissibly, validly, properly, constitutionally

lawless *adj*

disorderly, anarchic(al), unruly, ungoverned, riotous, mutinous, insurgent, insurrectionary, rebellious, revolutionary, seditious, unrestrained, chaotic, illegal, wrongdoing lawbreaking criminal, wild, reckless
❌ law-abiding

lawlessness *n*

anarchy, disorder, chaos, insurgency, insurrection, rebellion, revolution, sedition, mob rule, mob law, piracy, racketeering
FORMAL ochlocracy
COLLOQ. mobocracy, rent-a-mob
❌ order

lawsuit *n*
litigation, suit, action, legal action, proceedings, legal proceedings, case, prosecution, dispute, process, trial, argument, contest, cause
TECHNICAL indictment

lawyer *n*
solicitor, barrister, advocate, attorney, counsel, QC, legal adviser, legal representative
SLANG brief

lax *adj*
1 CASUAL, careless, heedless, slack, lenient, indulgent, permissive, tolerant, easy-going negligent, neglectful, remiss, slipshod, sloppy, inattentive
COLLOQ. laid-back
2 IMPRECISE, inexact, indefinite, loose, inaccurate, vague, general, broad
🖃 **1** strict, careful **2** exact, rigorous, specific

laxative *n*
loosener, purgative, evacuant, lenitive, purge, salts, senna, ipecacuanha
TECHNICAL aperient, cathartic, eccoprotic

laxity *n*
1 CARELESSNESS, neglect, heedlessness, indulgence, negligence, slovenliness, slackness, sloppiness, tolerance, permissiveness, softness, leniency, freedom, indifference, nonchalance, latitude, latitudinarianism, laissez-faire
2 IMPRECISION, inexactness, indefiniteness, looseness
🖃 **1** severity, strictness **2** exactness, precision

lay¹ *v*
1 PUT, place, deposit, set down, settle, lodge, plant, set, establish, leave
FORMAL posit
COLLOQ. stick, bung plonk
2 ARRANGE, position, set out, locate, work out, devise, make, prepare, plan, design, present, submit, offer, put forward
FORMAL dispose
3 ATTRIBUTE, ascribe, assign, charge, impute, allot
4 *lay a burden on someone*
impose, put, burden, inflict, apply, thrust, encumber, saddle, oppress, weigh down
5 *lay a bet*
place, bet, wager, gamble, risk, chance, hazard
6 *lay eggs*
produce, bear, deposit, give birth to, breed, engender
TECHNICAL oviposit
OLD beget
7 HAVE SEX WITH, make love with, go to bed with
SLANG make it with, have, have it off with, bonk, bang (*taboo*) screw, shag fuck
■ **lay aside**
1 PUT ASIDE, save, keep, store
2 REJECT, set aside, put out of your mind, abandon, discard, dismiss, shelve, defer, postpone, put off, cast aside
■ **lay bare**
disclose, divulge, explain, expose, reveal, show, uncover, unveil, exhibit
FORMAL manifest
■ **lay down**
1 SURRENDER, yield, give up, give, discard, drop
FORMAL relinquish
2 STIPULATE, assert, postulate, affirm, state, establish, formulate, prescribe, ordain
■ **lay down the law**
dictate, crack down, emphasize, dogmatize
FORMAL pontificate
COLLOQ. read the riot act, throw your weight about, rule the roost
■ **lay hands on**
1 ATTACK, assault, beat up, lay into, seize, set on, grab, clasp, clutch, get, catch, lay hold of, grip

2 FIND, get hold of, locate, bring to light, obtain, acquire, discover, grasp, unearth
3 BLESS, consecrate, ordain, confirm
■ **lay in**
store (up), stock up, amass, accumulate, hoard, stockpile, gather, collect, build up, glean
■ **lay into**
attack, assail, pitch into, set about, tear into, let fly at, hit out at, have a go at, lash out at
■ **lay it on**
exaggerate, overdo it, flatter, overpraise
COLLOQ. butter up, soft-soap, sweet-talk
■ **lay off**
1 DISMISS, discharge, make redundant, pay off, let go
COLLOQ. sack
2 GIVE UP, drop, stop, leave off, leave alone, let up, refrain, cease
FORMAL desist, discontinue
COLLOQ. quit
■ **lay on**
provide, supply, cater, furnish, give, set up, organize
■ **lay out**
1 DISPLAY, set out, put out, spread out, exhibit, arrange, plan, design
2 KNOCK OUT, fell, floor, flatten, demolish
3 SPEND, pay, give, contribute, invest
FORMAL expend, disburse
COLLOQ. shell out, fork out
■ **lay up**
store up, hoard, accumulate, amass, keep, save, put away
■ **lay waste**
desolate, ravage, destroy, devastate, raze, ruin, sack, spoil, pillage, rape, vandalize
FORMAL depredate, despoil

> 🛈 **lay** or **lie**?
> *Lay* means 'to place in a flat, prone or horizontal position'. It is a transitive verb, ie, it requires an object: *If you lay the pen down there, it will roll off the table.* *Lie* means 'to be or move into a flat, prone or horizontal position'. It is an intransitive verb, ie, it does not have an object. The past tense is *lay: She went into the bedroom and lay on the bed.*

lay² *adj*
1 LAIC, secular
2 AMATEUR, non-professional, non-specialist, non-qualified
🖃 **1** clergy, ordained, clerical **2** expert, professional

lay³ *n*
heavenly lays
song poem, ballad, lyric, madrigal, ode

layabout *n*
good-for-nothing ne'er-do-well, waster, idler, laggard, lounger; *Irish* corner-boy
COLLOQ. loafer, shirker, skiver, lazybones
SLANG *N Am* goof-off

layer *n*
1 COVER, coating coat, covering film, blanket, mantle, sheet, lamina
2 STRATUM, seam, vein, band, deposit, thickness, tier, bed, plate, row, ply

layman, laywoman or **layperson** *n*
1 PARISHIONER, unordained man/woman/person
2 AMATEUR, outsider, non-professional
🖃 **1** clergyman, clergywoman, the clergy **2** expert, professional

lay-off *n*
redundancy, discharge, dismissal, unemployment
COLLOQ. the sack, sacking jotters, cards, papers, firing the push, the boot, the elbow

layout *n*
arrangement, design, outline, plan, blueprint, organization, format, sketch, draft, map, geography

laze v
idle, lounge, sit around, lie around, loll, relax, unwind
OLD lusk
COLLOQ. loaf, chill (out), veg (out), bum around, not pull your weight
SLANG *Aust & NZ* bludge
≠ work

lazily adv
idly, slowly, slackly, lethargically, sluggishly

laziness n
idleness, sloth, slothfulness, inactivity, slowness, sluggishness, lethargy, slackness, Oblomovism
FORMAL dilatoriness, fainéance, indolence, tardiness, langour
≠ industriousness

lazy adj
idle, slothful, slack, work-shy, inactive, inert, slow, slow-moving good-for-nothing lethargic, sluggish
OLD laesie, lither, lusk, luskish
FORMAL indolent, torpid, languid, languorous, tardy, fainéant
COLLOQ. bone-idle
See Synonym nuances panel at **inactive**.
≠ industrious, hard-working

lazybones n
idler, slouch, laggard, sluggard, good-for-nothing sleepyhead, layabout, ne'er-do-well, do-nought, do-nothing slug drone, lubber, lubbard
OLD bedpresser, lusk, slowback
FORMAL fainéant
COLLOQ. loafer, lounger, shirker, skiver, slob, mollusc
SLANG *N Am* goof-off

leach v
drain, extract, filter, strain, seep, filtrate, percolate
TECHNICAL osmose
FORMAL lixiviate

lead¹ v, n, adj
♦ v
1 GUIDE, conduct, escort, show, steer, pilot, usher
2 RULE, govern, head, be at the head of, be in charge of, preside over, direct, supervise, command, manage, regulate
COLLOQ. call the shots
3 CAUSE, result in, produce, bring about, bring on, contribute to, call forth, tend towards, prompt, induce, provoke
4 INFLUENCE, persuade, incline, sway, prompt, induce, move, dispose
5 SURPASS, outdo, excel, outstrip, outrun, outdistance, exceed, eclipse, transcend, be in the lead, be in front, come first
6 PASS, spend, live, have, undergo, experience
≠ **1** follow
♦ n
1 PRIORITY, precedence, first place, advance position, leading position, start, van, vanguard, forefront, advantage, supremacy, pre-eminence, edge, interval, gap, margin
2 LEADERSHIP, guidance, direction, example, model, pattern
3 CLUE, hint, indication, indicator, guide, pointer, tip, suggestion
COLLOQ. tip-off
4 TITLE ROLE, starring part, star role, principal, principal part, leading role, leading man/lady
5 LEASH, tether, rein, hold, cord, slip, string line, chain
♦ adj
leading first, principal, chief, main, foremost, head, premier, primary, prime, star, top

■ **lead off**
begin, open, get going start (off), inaugurate, initiate
FORMAL commence
COLLOQ. kick off, start the ball rolling
■ **lead on**
entice, lure, seduce, tempt, draw on, beguile, persuade, string along deceive, trick, mislead, dupe
COLLOQ. pull a fast one on, put one over on, lead up the garden path
SLANG take for a ride
■ **lead the way**
1 GO IN FRONT, go first, show, show the way, guide
2 TAKE THE INITIATIVE, blaze a trail, pave the way, set a trend, be a pioneer, break new ground
■ **lead up to**
prepare (the way) for, approach, introduce, make overtures, pave/open the way

lead² n
1 BULLETS, shot, ammunition, pellets, balls, slugs
2 WEIGHT, heavy weight, plumb, sinker

leaden adj
1 GREY, overcast, cloudy, gloomy, dingy, dismal, dreary, ashen, greyish, oppressive, sombre
2 DULL, heavy, boring burdensome, onerous, laboured, lifeless, lacklustre, listless, spiritless, sluggish, humdrum, inert, stilted
FORMAL languid
3 CUMBERSOME, wooden, stiff, heavy, laboured, sluggish, plodding lead

leader n
1 HEAD, chief, figurehead, director, ruler, principal, manager, governor, superintendent, overseer, supervisor, commander, captain, superior, chieftain, ringleader, guide, conductor, skipper, mover and shaker
COLLOQ. boss, gov, guv, top dog bigwig big cheese/noise/shot
2 GUIDE, courier, escort, usher
3 PIONEER, innovator, developer, expert, authority, leading light, guiding light, discoverer, inventor, founder, architect, trailblazer, pathfinder, groundbreaker, front-runner
≠ **1** follower

leadership n
direction, control, command, management, authority, rule, guidance, supervision, superintendency, domination, pre-eminence, premiership, captaincy, administration, sway, directorship, governorship, headship

lead-in n
introduction, opening foreword, preface, preamble, prologue, preliminaries, front matter, overture, prelude, beginning start, inauguration, launch, presentation, debut
FORMAL prolegomenon, exordium, proem
COLLOQ. intro
≠ conclusion, appendix

leading adj
main, principal, chief, primary, first, front, supreme, outstanding foremost, dominant, ruling directing guiding superior, greatest, highest, top, governing paramount, top-rank, pre-eminent, number one
≠ subordinate

leaf n, v
♦ n
1 *the leaves of a tree*
blade, bract, frond, pad, calyx, needle, sepal, leaflet
TECHNICAL cotyledon, foliole
Related adjectives: foliaceous, foliar, foliose
2 PAGE, sheet, folio
♦ v
thumb (through), browse, flip, glance, skim
■ **turn over a new leaf**
improve yourself, better yourself, mend/change your ways, pull your socks up, make a fresh start, start/begin again, start afresh, wipe the slate clean, turn over a new page

Leaf parts include:

axillary bud	leaf cells	stipule
blade	margin	stomata
chloroplasts	midrib	tip
epidermis	petiole	vein
leaf axil	sheath	

Leaf shapes include:

abruptly pinnate	falcate	peltate
acerose	hastate	pinnate
ciliate	lanceolate	pinnatifid
cordate	linear	reniform
crenate	lobed	runcinate
dentate	lyrate	sagittate
digitate	obovate	spathulate
doubly dentate	orbicular	subulate
elliptic	ovate	ternate
entire	palmate	trifoliate

leaflet *n*
pamphlet, booklet, brochure, circular, handout, bill, handbill, flier, tract; *N Am* dodger

leafy *adj*
green, leafed, leaved, wooded, woody, shady, shaded, bosky, frondescent, frondose, bowery
TECHNICAL dasyphyllous, foliose
FORMAL verdant

league *n, v*
♦ *n*
1 ASSOCIATION, confederation, confederacy, alliance, union, federation, coalition, affiliation, group, combination, band, syndicate, conglomerate, corporation, guild, consortium, cartel, combine, partnership, co-operative, fellowship, compact, *Bund*
2 *a football league*
championship, tournament, division, group, band, contest, competition, cup
3 CATEGORY, class, level, group
♦ *v*
amalgamate, associate, band together, co-operate, collaborate, combine, confederate, conspire, join forces, unite, link, ally, consort
■ **in league**
allied, in co-operation, co-operating linked, in partnership, in alliance, in collusion, in tandem, collaborating conspiring
COLLOQ. hand in glove, in cahoots
ЕЭ at odds

leak *n, v*
♦ *n*
1 CRACK, hole, opening puncture, crevice, chink, fissure, break, cut
2 LEAKAGE, leaking seeping seepage, spill, spillage, drip, oozing discharge, escape, percolation
3 DISCLOSURE, divulgence, revelation, exposure, exposé, uncovering bringing to light
♦ *v*
1 SEEP, drip, ooze, escape, overflow, run, let out, let in, make water, spill, trickle, percolate, exude, discharge, secrete, weep
2 DISCLOSE, reveal, let slip, let out, make known, make public, tell, relate, give away, pass on
FORMAL divulge, impart
COLLOQ. blab, squeal, let on, let the cat out of the bag blow the gaffe, spill the beans

leaky *adj*
leaking holey, perforated, punctured, dripping split, cracked, porous, permeable

lean¹ *v*
1 SLANT, slope, incline, bend, tilt, list, bank, be at an angle
2 RECLINE, prop, rest
FORMAL repose
3 INCLINE, favour, prefer, tend, gravitate, have an inclination/preference for
FORMAL have a propensity for
■ **lean on**
1 RELY ON, depend on, trust in, have confidence in, not manage without
COLLOQ. bank on
2 FORCE, persuade, pressurize, coerce, intimidate, put pressure on
COLLOQ. twist someone's arm, put the screws on

lean² *adj*
1 THIN, skinny, bony, gaunt, lank, angular, slim, slender, scraggy, scrawny, emaciated
COLLOQ. all skin and bones
2 SCANTY, inadequate, insufficient, meagre, bare, barren, sparse, poor, arid
3 *lean years*
unproductive, unfruitful, unsuccessful, unprofitable, poor, hard, difficult, tough, unpleasant, uncomfortable, austere
ЕЭ **1** fat, flabby **2** abundant

leaning *n*
tendency, inclination, preference, partiality, liking fondness, attraction, bent, bias, disposition, aptitude
FORMAL propensity, proclivity, penchant, predilection

leanness *n*
thinness, slimness, slenderness, boniness, gauntness, scragginess, scrawniness, lankiness, lankness
ЕЭ fat, flabbiness

lean-to *n*
shed, garage, lock-up, hut, outhouse, shack, penthouse; *Aust* skillion

leap *v, n*
♦ *v*
1 JUMP (OVER), bound, spring vault, clear; *Irish* lep; skip, hop, dance, jeté, bounce, caper, gambol, romp, frisk, frolic, cavort
2 SOAR, surge, mount, increase, rocket, skyrocket, escalate, rise, spring
ЕЭ **2** drop, fall
♦ *n*
1 JUMP, bound, spring vault, hop, skip, caper
TECHNICAL entrechat
2 INCREASE, upsurge, upswing surge, rise, soaring escalation
■ **leap at**
jump at, accept eagerly, agree to, fall for, grab, seize, pounce on, snatch, swallow
■ **by/in leaps and bounds**
rapidly, swiftly, quickly
COLLOQ. in no time (at all)

learn *v*
1 GRASP, comprehend, understand, master, acquire, train, study, pick up, take in, get, digest, gather, glean, read, receive, assimilate, absorb, discern, familiarize yourself in, gain knowledge of, acquire skill in, cram; *dialect* larn
OLD (*Spenser*) lear
COLLOQ. get the hang of, gen up on
2 MEMORIZE, learn by heart, commit to memory, have off pat, remember
OLD con
3 DISCOVER, find out, ascertain, understand, detect, determine, hear, see, gather, glean, realize, become aware of, become informed about
COLLOQ. get wind of, suss out

SYNONYM NUANCES

sense 1
Grasp can sometimes imply that there has been some difficulty in learning something: *they hadn't fully grasped the significance of what I said*, while **comprehend**,

along with **understand** and **get**, suggests also being able to follow the meaning: *I don't get what you're saying.* **Acquire** might be used of simply gaining knowledge which perhaps requires further application: *we acquired a knowledge of the tides*, whereas **master** suggests also attaining skill and proficiency: *he'd mastered the basics of sailing.*

  Glean and **gather** are more suggestive of accidental gaining of information along the way: *new ideas which he had gleaned from his trips to Europe*, while **pick up** implies a gradual improvement, perhaps again with little effort: *he picked up some French when he lived in Paris.* **Discern** implies a little more mental effort in finding something out: *from the remaining evidence I tried to discern what had happened.*

  The terms **take in** and **absorb** suggest learning something and retaining it, while **assimilate** and **digest** have added suggestions of classifying and using the information learned: *I assimilated all the facts of the situation and tried to reach a decision.*

learned *adj*
scholarly, erudite, well-informed, well-read, well-educated, knowledgeable, cultured, academic, lettered, literary, studious, literate, widely read, intellectual, versed, pedantic
F3 uneducated, illiterate

learner *n*
novice, beginner, student, trainee, pupil, scholar, apprentice, tiro, neophyte, intern
OLD conner
COLLOQ. rookie, greenhorn

learning *n*
scholarship, erudition, education, schooling knowledge, information, letters, study, wisdom, tuition, culture, edification, intellect, research, pedantry; *Scot* lear
OLD conning

lease *v, n*
♦ *v*
1 *lease a flat from the council*
rent, hire, charter, loan
2 *lease a field to a farmer*
rent, rent out, let, let out, loan, hire, hire out, sublet
♦ *n*
agreement, contract, chapter, rental, tenancy

leash *n*
lead, tether, rein, hold, cord, slip, string check, control, curb, restraint, discipline; *dialect* trash
OLD lyam
■ **strain at the leash**
be champing at the bit, be impatient, be eager, be anxious, be longing
COLLOQ. be itching be dying

least *adj*
smallest, lowest, minimum, fewest, slightest, poorest
F3 most
■ **at least**
1 *it'll cost at least £500*
as a minimum, at the (very) least, no less than
2 *my car may be old but at least it goes*
in any event, in any case, anyhow, however, nevertheless, at any rate, for all that, in spite of everything whatever happens, no matter what

■ **to say the least**
to put it mildly, at the very least, without any exaggeration, without exaggerating

leathery *adj*
hard, hardened, durable, rough, rugged, tough, wrinkled, wizened, leathern
TECHNICAL coriaceous, corious

leave[1] *v*
1 DEPART, go, go away, set out, take your leave, pull out, decamp, exit, move, retire, withdraw, retreat, emigrate, disappear
COLLOQ. push off, push along, quit, scoot, split, take off, clear off, shove off, make tracks, do a bunk, do one, up sticks, take French leave, vamoose, sling your hook, hook it; *Aust* shoot through
SLANG *Aust* choof off
See Synonym nuances panel at **depart**.
2 ABANDON, cease, desert, give up, drop, pull out, forego, surrender
FORMAL relinquish, renounce, forsake, desist
COLLOQ. quit, run out on, ditch, jilt, chuck, dump, turn your back on, leave high and dry
3 ASSIGN, commit, entrust, allot, consign, make over, hand over, deliver, transmit
4 *leave property in your will*
will, hand down, leave behind, endow, give over
TECHNICAL devise
FORMAL bequeath
5 *I must have left the tickets at home*
forget, mislay, miss, lose, drop, misplace
6 *the experience left a lasting impression on me*
cause, give rise to, lead to, result in, occasion, bring about, produce, generate, create
F3 3 receive
■ **leave off**
stop, refrain, lay off, break off, end, halt, cease
FORMAL discontinue, desist, abstain, terminate
COLLOQ. quit, give over, knock off
■ **leave out**
omit, exclude, overlook, ignore, miss out, except, disregard, pass over, count out, cut (out), eliminate, neglect, reject, cast aside, bar
F3 include

leave[2] *n*
1 PERMISSION, authorization, consent, allowance, sanction, warrant, concession, indulgence, liberty, freedom
FORMAL dispensation
COLLOQ. say-so, OK, green light
2 HOLIDAY, time off, day off, break, leave of absence, vacation, sabbatical, furlough, sick leave, compassionate leave
COLLOQ. vac
F3 1 refusal, rejection

leaven *n, v*
♦ *n*
yeast, ferment, zyme, raising agent, barm
♦ *v*
1 RAISE, cause to rise, puff up, ferment, work, expand, swell
2 INSPIRE, stimulate, lighten, quicken, enliven, pervade, permeate, imbue, suffuse

leavings *n*
remains, remainder, residue, remnants, leftovers, dregs, detritus, dross, fragments, bits, pieces, oddments, sweepings, scraps, refuse, rubbish, debris, waste, spoil

lecher *n*
womanizer, adulterer, seducer, sensualist, debauchee, libertine, profligate, libidinist, rake, roué, fornicator,

wanton, whoremonger, satyr, Casanova, Don Juan, Lothario, Romeo, Lovelace
COLLOQ. dirty old man, flasher, goat, wolf, lech
SLANG perv, masher

lecherous *adj*
lewd, womanizing carnal, promiscuous, lustful, leering salacious, lascivious, degenerate, debauched, dissolute, dissipated, unchaste, wanton, libidinous
OLD lickerish, rammish; *(Shakesp)* codding
FORMAL concupiscent, licentious, prurient
COLLOQ. randy, raunchy, horny
SLANG pervy

lechery *n*
lewdness, womanizing carnality, libertinism, debauchery, rakishness, lust, lustfulness, libidinousness, licentiousness, salaciousness, salacity, sensuality, wantonness, lasciviousness
OLD lickerishness
FORMAL concupiscence, prurience
COLLOQ. randiness, raunchiness

lectern *n*
desk, reading-desk, table, stand, eagle, oratory
OLD lettern

lecture *n, v*
♦ *n*
1 SPEECH, lesson, talk, instruction, sermon, address, extender, travelogue, *conférence*
OLD act
FORMAL discourse, disquisition, homily, prelection
COLLOQ. *N Am* chalk talk
2 REPRIMAND, rebuke, reproof, scolding harangue, censure, upbraiding chiding reproach, curtain lecture
FORMAL berating
COLLOQ. telling-off, talking-to, dressing-down, rocket, jaw, rollicking
♦ *v*
1 TALK, give a talk, teach, hold forth, speak, make a speech, expound, address, instruct, read, give lessons in
FORMAL prelect
2 REPRIMAND, reprove, rebuke, scold, admonish, harangue, chide, censure
FORMAL berate
COLLOQ. tell off, haul over the coals, tear/pull to pieces, pick holes in, jaw

lecturer *n*
teacher, tutor, talker, speechmaker, speechifier, orator, expounder, speaker, instructor, academic, professor, reader, don, scholar, preceptor, pedagogue, sermonizer, preacher, haranguer, extensionist, *conférencier*; *N Am* docent
FORMAL declaimer, prelector

ledge *n*
shelf, shelve, sill, mantel, mantelpiece, mantelshelf, ridge, projection, overhang step, bench, berm, offset, altar, gradin, buttery-bar; *dialect* linch, stock; *Scot* scarcement
OLD settle, fire-step, firing-step

ledger *n*
account book, books, accounts, record book, journal, register, inventory

lee *n*
shelter, refuge, protection, cover, sanctuary

leech *n*
hanger-on, parasite, sycophant, clinger, toady, bloodsucker, freeloader, extortioner, usurer
COLLOQ. sponger, scrounger

leer *v, n*
♦ *v*
eye, ogle, look lecherously at, stare, wink, squint, gloat, goggle, grin, smirk, sneer
♦ *n*
ogle, lecherous look, stare, wink, squint, grin, smirk, sneer
COLLOQ. glad eye

leery *adj*
wary, careful, cautious, guarded, uncertain, unsure, chary, suspicious, on your guard, distrustful, doubting dubious, sceptical

lees *n*
deposit, dregs, grounds, residue, sediment, refuse, settlings, draff
FORMAL precipitate

leeway *n*
space, room, latitude, elbow-room, play, scope, freedom, slack, margin, flexibility
COLLOQ. wiggle room

left *adj*
1 LEFT-HAND, port
FORMAL sinistral
2 LEFT-WING, left-leaning liberal, progressive, socialist, radical, revolutionary, communist, collectivist, revisionist, Bolshevist, Leninist, Marxist, Stalinist, Trotskyist, Trotskyite, Maoist, Spartakist
COLLOQ. red
F3 1 right **2** right-wing

left-handed *adj*
1 *a left-handed person*
Scot corrie-fisted
FORMAL sinistral
COLLOQ. cack-handed, southpaw
2 AWKWARD, clumsy, gauche
3 DUBIOUS, ambiguous, equivocal, insincere, hypocritical
COLLOQ. backhanded

left-over *adj*
remaining settled, excess, surplus, superfluous, unused, uneaten

leftovers *n*
leavings, remainder, remains, remnants, residue, surplus, scraps, sweepings, refuse, dregs, excess

left-wing *adj*
left, left-leaning socialist, radical, progressive, revolutionary, liberal, communist, collectivist, revisionist, Bolshevist, Leninist, Marxist, Stalinist, Trotskyist, Trotskyite, Maoist, Spartakist

leg *n, v*
♦ *n*
1 LIMB, member, shank
TECHNICAL crus
COLLOQ. pin, stump, peg
Related adjective: crural
2 SUPPORT, prop, upright, brace, underpinning
3 STAGE, part, bit, section, portion, stretch, segment, lap
■ **leg it**
run, hurry, walk, go by foot
COLLOQ. hoof it
■ **not have a leg to stand on**
be unjustified, be unproved, lack support, lack an excuse
■ **on its last legs**
weak, failing fading fast, ailing nearing collapse, about to fail/collapse, near to ruin, near to death
COLLOQ. at death's door
■ **pull someone's leg**
tease, trick, joke, play a joke on, make fun of, fool, deceive
COLLOQ. kid, rib, have on, wind up, lead up the garden path
SLANG take for a ride

legacy *n*
bequest, endowment, gift, heritage, inheritance, birthright, estate, heirloom, heritance
FORMAL bequeathal, patrimony

legal *adj*
1 LAWFUL, legitimate, within the law, permissible, permitted, sanctioned, allowed, authorized, licensed, allowable, legalized, constitutional, valid, warranted, above-board, right, sound, proper, rightful, acceptable, admissible
FORMAL licit
COLLOQ. legit
2 JUDICIAL, forensic
3 JUDICIARY, statutory, constitutional
⊟ 1 illegal
See panel below

SYNONYM NUANCES

sense 1
Lawful would be used specifically of something that is allowed within the constraints of law, while **legitimate**, along with **valid** and **warranted**, may be used more widely of anything that is deemed acceptable or justified: *the player's claims for a penalty were legitimate*. **Permissible** and **permitted**, like **allowable** and **allowed**, **acceptable** and **admissible**, similarly suggest anything that is likely to be tolerated, considered or consented to: *admissible evidence.*
  The terms **sanctioned** and **authorized** go further by implying official backing. **Licensed**, likewise, suggests the stamp of officialdom but has fairly specific contexts where licences are granted: *licensed to carry firearms*. **Legalized**, on the other hand, would be reserved for something previously illegal now being encompassed by the law: *legalized abortion*, whereas **constitutional** has more to do with laws of state: *the abdication represented a constitutional crisis.*
  Above-board has more judgemental but positive connotations of a lack of deceit, as do both **right** and

sound, which similarly suggest being trustworthy, while **proper** is also a fairly approving term for something conforming to the correct procedures. **Rightful**, on the other hand, is suggestive of legal entitlement: *the rightful heir to the throne.*

legality *n*
lawfulness, legitimacy, validity, rightness, rightfulness, soundness, admissibleness, permissibility, constitutionality
⊟ illegality

legalize *v*
legitimize, make legal, license, permit, sanction, allow, decriminalize, authorize, warrant, validate, approve, ratify, accept, admit

legally *adv*
lawfully, by law, according to the law, by rights, rightfully, legitimately, permissibly, validly, properly, constitutionally

legate *n*
representative, ambassador, delegate, deputy, emissary, envoy, agent, commissioner, messenger, nuncio

legatee *n*
beneficiary, recipient, receiver, inheritor, heir, co-heir(ess), devisee, inheritrix

legation *n*
mission, diplomatic mission, commission, consulate, embassy, ministry, deputation, delegation, representation

legend *n*
1 MYTH, story, traditional story, tale, folk tale, fable, fiction, romance, narrative, saga
2 INSCRIPTION, caption, motto, key, cipher, explanation, underline
3 *he has become a legend in his own lifetime*
celebrity, star, personality, name, dignitary, famous person, superstar, living legend, household name

---

Legal terms include:

CRIMINAL LAW:	MARRIAGE AND DIVORCE:	judge	endowment	brief	legal aid
acquittal	adultery	juror	estate	by-law	liability
age of consent	alimony	jury	exchange of	charter	mandate
alibi	annulment	justice of the	contracts	civil law	misadventure
arrest	bigamy	peace (JP)	fee simple	claim	miscarriage of
bail	decree absolute	juvenile	foreclosure	codicil	justice
caution	decree nisi	Law Lord	freehold	common law	oath
charge	divorce	lawyer	inheritance	constitution	party
confession	maintenance	Lord Advocate	intestacy	contract	penalty
contempt of court	settlement	Lord Chancellor	lease	county court	power of attorney
dock		Lord Chief Justice	leasehold	judgement (CCJ)	precedent
fine		liquidator	legacy	court case	probate
guilty	PEOPLE:	magistrate	local search	court martial	proceedings
indictment	accessory	notary public	mortgage	covenant	proof
innocent	accomplice	offender	patent	cross-examine	proxy
malice	accused	plaintiff	tenancy	custody	public inquiry
aforethought	advocate	procurator fiscal	title	damages	repeal
pardon	Attorney General	receiver	trademark	defence	sanction
parole	barrister	Queen's Counsel	will	demand	settlement
plea	*colloq.* brief	(QC)		equity	statute
plea bargain	clerk of the court	sheriff	MISCELLANEOUS:	eviction	subpoena
plead guilty	client	solicitor	act of God	evidence	sue
plead not guilty	commissioner for	solicitor advocate	Act of Parliament	extradition	summons
prisoner	oaths	witness	adjournment	grant	superinjunction
probation	convict	young offender	affidavit	hearing	testimony
Queen's	coroner		agreement	hung jury	trial
(or King's)	criminal	PROPERTY OR	allegation	indemnity	tribunal
evidence	defendant	OWNERSHIP:	amnesty	injunction	verdict
remand	Director of Public	asset	appeal	inquest	waiver
reprieve	Prosecutions	conveyance	arbitration	inquiry	ward of court
sentence	(DPP)	copyright	bar	judgement	warrant
suspended	executor	deed	bench	judiciary	will
sentence	felon	easement	Bill of Rights	lawsuit	writ

See also **court**; **crime**.

FORMAL personage, notable, luminary, worthy
COLLOQ. VIP, big name, bigwig big shot, celeb

legendary adj
1 MYTHICAL, fabulous, fabled, storybook, fictitious, fictional, fanciful, traditional
2 FAMOUS, celebrated, renowned, well-known, illustrious, glorious, acclaimed, honoured, remembered, popular, immortal
🖃 2 unknown

legerdemain n
trickery, sleight of hand, deception, cunning craftiness, chicanery, artifice, artfulness, subterfuge, contrivance, manipulation, manoeuvring feint
FORMAL prestidigitation, thaumaturgics, sophistry
COLLOQ. hocus-pocus

legibility n
readability, readableness, clarity, clearness, plainness, lucidity, lucidness, intelligibility, comprehensibility, comprehensibleness, explicitness, distinctness, precision, simplicity
🖃 illegibility

legible adj
readable, easy to read, intelligible, decipherable, clear, lucid, distinct, neat, plain, comprehensible, explicit, precise, simple
🖃 illegible

legibly adv
readably, intelligibly, clearly, lucidly, plainly, easily read, comprehensibly, explicitly, precisely, simply
🖃 illegibly

legion n, adj
♦ n
1 *Roman legions*
army, battalion, brigade, company, division, regiment, unit, cohort, troop, force
2 *legions of foreign tourists*
host, number, multitude, myriad, swarm, throng drove, mass, horde
♦ adj
countless, numerous, myriad, numberless, innumerable, illimitable, multitudinous

legislate v
enact, ordain, decree, order, pass/make laws, authorize, codify, establish, formulate
FORMAL constitutionalize, prescribe

legislation n
1 LAW, statute, regulation, bill, act, charter, enactment, ordinance, code, authorization, ruling rules, measure
2 LAWMAKING, enactment, codification, formulation
FORMAL prescription

legislative adj
lawmaking lawgiving judicial, parliamentary, congressional, senatorial
TECHNICAL jurisdictive

legislator n
lawmaker, lawgiver, member of parliament, MP, parliamentarian, congressman, congresswoman, senator

legislature n
assembly, chamber, house, parliament, congress, senate

legitimacy n
1 LEGALITY, lawfulness, validity, rightness, rightfulness, soundness, admissibility, permissibility, constitutionality
2 REASONABLENESS, sensibleness, soundness, fairness, validity, rationality, admissibility, plausibility, acceptability, justifiability, credibility
🖃 1 illegality 2 invalidity

legitimate adj
1 LEGAL, lawful, authorized, warranted, sanctioned, statutory, rightful, proper, correct, real, genuine, acknowledged
FORMAL licit
COLLOQ. legit

2 REASONABLE, sensible, rational, logical, admissible, plausible, acceptable, justifiable, justified, warranted, well-founded, sound, fair, valid, true, credible
🖃 1 illegal 2 invalid

legitimize v
sanction, authorize, permit, allow, warrant, license, validate, charter, entitle, legalize, decriminalize
FORMAL legitimate

leisure n
relaxation, rest, spare time, free time, time, time off, ease, freedom, liberty, recreation, retirement, holiday, vacation, break, time out; N Am off-hours
OLD leisure, by-time, respite
COLLOQ. space, R and R
🖃 work

■ **at your leisure**
when you want to, at your convenience, unhurriedly, in your own time, in your spare time, when it suits you, when you get round to it

leisurely adj
unhurried, slow, relaxed, comfortable, easy, easy-going unhasty, tranquil, restful, gentle, carefree, lazy, loose
OLD leasurable
COLLOQ. laid-back
🖃 rushed, hectic

lend v
1 LOAN, advance, credit, put forth, allow to have, allow to use, let someone use, on-lend, overlend
OLD prest
COLLOQ. sub
2 *lend your support to something*
give, grant, provide, supply, contribute, donate, add
FORMAL bestow, furnish, confer, impart
🖃 1 borrow

■ **lend an ear**
listen, pay attention, take notice, heed, give ear
FORMAL hearken

■ **lend a hand**
help, help out, assist, give assistance, aid, give a helping hand
COLLOQ. do your bit, pitch in

■ **lend itself to**
be suitable for, be appropriate for, be easily/readily used for

length n
1 EXTENT, distance, measure, reach, span
2 DURATION, period, term, stretch, space, span
3 PIECE, portion, section, segment

■ **at length**
1 THOROUGHLY, in great detail, fully, comprehensively, exhaustively, for a long time
2 EVENTUALLY, after a long time, finally, in due course, at last

■ **go to any lengths**
be very determined, try very hard, do anything go to extremes

lengthen v
stretch, extend, draw out, grow longer, prolong protract, spin out, eke (out), pad out, increase, expand, continue
FORMAL elongate
🖃 reduce, shorten

lengthwise adv
lengthways, endways, endwise, endlong horizontally, vertically

lengthy adj
long prolonged, extended, lengthened, overlong long-drawn-out, long-winded, rambling diffuse, wordy, verbose, drawn-out, interminable, tedious
FORMAL protracted, prolix
🖃 brief, concise

leniency n
lenience, tolerance, forbearance, permissiveness, indulgence, mercy, forgiveness, soft-heartedness, softness,

kindness, mildness, tenderness, gentleness, compassion, humaneness, generosity, magnanimity, moderation
FORMAL clemency
E∃ severity

lenient *adj*
tolerant, forbearing sparing indulgent, liberal, merciful, forgiving soft-hearted, kind, mild, tender, gentle, compassionate, humane, generous, magnanimous, moderate
E∃ strict, severe

lenitive *adj*
alleviating calming easing palliative, relieving soothing assuaging mollifying
FORMAL mitigating
E∃ irritant

lens
See panel at **spectacles**.

leper *n*
outcast, social outcast, undesirable, untouchable, pariah, lazar

leprechaun *n*
goblin, imp, brownie, fiend, hobgoblin, gnome, elf, sprite, spirit, gremlin, nixie, red-cap, bogey, kelpie, kobold, demon, troll, puck; *Irish* pooka

lesbian *n, adj*
♦ *n*
gay, homosexual, sapphist, tribade
COLLOQ. butch
SLANG (*offensive*) dyke, les, lez, lezzy, lesbo, queer
♦ *adj*
gay, homosexual, Sapphic, tribadic, lesbic
COLLOQ. butch
SLANG (*offensive*) dykey

lesion *n*
injury, wound, abrasion, sore, scratch, scrape, bruise, cut, gash, laceration, impairment, hurt, trauma
TECHNICAL contusion

less *n, adv, prep*
♦ *n*
fewer, smaller amount, not as/so much, not as/so many
E∃ more
♦ *adv*
to a lesser degree/extent, to a smaller extent, not as/so much
E∃ more
♦ *prep*
minus, without, short of, excluding except, with the exception of, excepting save, bar

lessen *v*
decrease, go/come down, reduce, diminish, decline, dip, plunge, plummet, curtail, lower, ease (off), tail off/away, peter out, contract, die down, let up, dwindle, lighten, slow down, weaken, shrink, allay, cut, abridge, de-escalate, erode, minimize, narrow, moderate, extenuate, mitigate, subside, ebb, wane, slack, slacken, flag fail, dull, deaden, relieve, impair
OLD bate
FORMAL abate, derogate
COLLOQ. nosedive
E∃ grow, increase

lessening *n*
decrease, reduction, decline, dip, curtailment, easing contraction, dwindling weakening shrinkage, cutting de-escalation, erosion, minimization, extenuation, mitigation, moderation, ebbing waning slackening flagging failure, deadening let-up
OLD batement, imminution
FORMAL abatement, diminution, derogation
COLLOQ. petering out
E∃ increase

lesser *adj*
lower, secondary, inferior, less important, smaller, subordinate, slighter, tinier, minor
E∃ greater

lesson *n*
1 CLASS, period, instruction, lecture, seminar, workshop, masterclass, sermon, tutorial, teaching coaching course
2 ASSIGNMENT, exercise, homework, schoolwork, practice, task, drill
3 EXAMPLE, model, warning deterrent, moral
4 *read the lesson at church*
Bible reading reading passage from the Bible, Scripture, text

lest *conj*
in case, in order to avoid, for fear that

let[1] *v*
1 PERMIT, allow, give permission, authorize, agree to, sanction, grant, enable, tolerate
FORMAL give leave, consent to, assent to
COLLOQ. OK, give the OK, give the go-ahead, greenlight, give the green light to, give the nod, say the magic word
2 *let something happen*
allow, cause, enable, make
3 LEASE, hire, hire out, rent, rent out, let out
E∃ 1 prohibit, forbid
■ **let alone**
not to mention, not forgetting never mind, apart from, also, as well as
■ **let down**
fail, disappoint, disillusion, dissatisfy, disenchant, fall short, abandon, betray, desert
COLLOQ. leave in the lurch
E∃ satisfy
■ **let fly**
fly at, attack, assault, go for, fall upon, hit, strike, lay into, charge, lash out at
COLLOQ. bite someone's head off, have a go at, jump down someone's throat, let someone have it
■ **let go**
release, give up, set free, stop holding free, liberate, unhand
FORMAL manumit
E∃ catch, imprison
■ **let in**
admit, allow to enter, accept, receive, take in, include, incorporate, greet, welcome
E∃ prohibit, bar, forbid
■ **let in on**
allow to know, allow to share in, tell, inform, let know, include
■ **let off**
1 EXCUSE, absolve, pardon, exempt, discharge, reprieve, forgive, acquit, spare, ignore, liberate, release
FORMAL exonerate
2 DISCHARGE, detonate, fire, explode, emit, give off, release
E∃ 1 punish
■ **let on**
disclose, reveal, let slip, make known, make public, tell, relate, give away, pass on
FORMAL divulge, impart
COLLOQ. blab, squeal, give the game away, let the cat out of the bag spill the beans
■ **let out**
1 FREE, release, let go, discharge
COLLOQ. leak
2 REVEAL, disclose, make known, utter, betray, let slip
COLLOQ. blab, squeal, let the cat out of the bag spill the beans
E∃ 1 keep in
■ **let up**
subside, ease (off), lessen, moderate, slacken, diminish, decrease, stop, cease, end, halt, die down
FORMAL abate
E∃ continue

let² n

without let or hindrance
check, constraint, impediment, hindrance, obstacle, obstruction, prohibition, restriction, restraint, interference
E₃ assistance

let-down n
disappointment, anticlimax, disillusionment, setback, betrayal, desertion
COLLOQ. washout

lethal adj
fatal, deadly, deathly, death-dealing mortal, dangerous, venomous, poisonous, toxic, murderous, ruinous, disastrous, destructive, devastating
FORMAL noxious
E₃ harmless, safe

lethally adv
fatally, mortally, dangerously, toxically, disastrously, destructively, devastatingly
FORMAL noxiously
E₃ harmlessly, safely

lethargic adj
listless, sluggish, dull, lifeless, inert, slow, lazy, inactive, idle, slothful, apathetic, drowsy, heavy, sleepy, weary
FORMAL debilitated, enervated, hebetant, languid, somnolent, torpid
E₃ lively

lethargically adv
listlessly, sluggishly, dully, lifelessly, inertly, slowly, lazily, inactively, idly, slothfully, apathetically, drowsily, heavily, sleepily, wearily
FORMAL languidly, somnolently, torpidly
E₃ energetically

lethargy n
listlessness, sluggishness, dullness, lifelessness, inertia, slowness, laziness, idleness, sloth, apathy, inactivity, inaction, indifference, sleepiness, drowsiness, weariness, stupor
FORMAL lassitude, torpor, langour, somnolence
E₃ liveliness

let-out n
excuse, escape, means/way of escape, way out, cure, remedy, safety valve, loophole, error in the law, legal flaw, technicality, escape clause
COLLOQ. get-out

letter n
1 NOTE, message, line, correspondence, dispatch, communication, chit, acknowledgement, reply, circular
FORMAL missive, epistle
2 CHARACTER, symbol, sign, figure
TECHNICAL grapheme
FORMAL device
3 *a woman of letters*
literature, books, culture, education, learning humanities, writing scholarship, academia, belles-lettres
FORMAL erudition

■ to the letter
exactly, strictly, strictly speaking accurately, precisely, word for word, literally, religiously, punctiliously, in every detail, by the book

lettered adj
learned, scholarly, educated, informed, knowledgeable, academic, well-educated, well-read, widely read, cultivated, cultured, literary, literate, studied, versed, accomplished
FORMAL erudite
COLLOQ. highbrow
E₃ ignorant

let-up n
break, interval, lessening pause, recess, remission, slackening respite, lull
FORMAL abatement, cessation
COLLOQ. breather
E₃ continuation

level adj, n, v
♦ adj
1 FLAT, smooth, even, flush, plane, uniform, horizontal, aligned, abreast
2 EQUAL, balanced, aligned, drawn, even, on a par, neck and neck, matching uniform, level pegging
3 STEADY, stable, constant, unchanging regular, uniform
4 CALM, unemotional, steady, composed, self-possessed
COLLOQ. unflappable
E₃ 1 uneven 2 unequal 3 unsteady 4 emotional
♦ n
1 HEIGHT, elevation, altitude, highness
2 POSITION, point, rank, status, class, degree, grade, mark, standard, standing station, plane, layer, stratum, storey, stage, zone
FORMAL echelon
3 MEASURE, degree, extent, quantity, size, magnitude, amount, volume
♦ v
1 DEMOLISH, destroy, devastate, flatten, knock down, raze, raze to the ground, make level, pull down, bulldoze, tear down, lay waste
2 EVEN OUT, flush, plane, smooth, equalize, even up, stabilize, make level, make flat
3 DIRECT, point, aim, train, focus, concentrate, zero in on
4 *level with someone*
admit, open up, confess, divulge, tell, tell all, speak plainly, be frank, keep nothing back
FORMAL avow
COLLOQ. come clean, put your cards on the table, be upfront, give it to someone straight, tell it like it is, bring out in the open

■ on the level
honest, open, candid, fair, straight
COLLOQ. fair and square, straight-up, up-front, above board

level-headed adj
calm, balanced, even-tempered, sensible, steady, reasonable, rational, composed, cool, cool-headed, practical, prudent, sane, self-possessed, dependable
FORMAL circumspect, imperturbable
COLLOQ. unflappable

lever n, v
♦ n
1 HANDLE, bar, pull, switch, joystick, crank, brake, key, pedal, tiller, trigger
OLD whipstaff
2 CROWBAR, bar, jemmy, handspike, crossbar
♦ v
force, prise, pry, raise, lift, hoist, dislodge, jemmy, shift, move, heave, pinch

leverage n
1 *apply economic leverage*
force, strength, power, advantage, authority, influence, rank, weight
FORMAL ascendancy, purchase
COLLOQ. clout, pull
2 *the leverage of the straps*
grip, hold, grasp, force
FORMAL purchase

leviathan n
giant, mammoth, hulk, colossus, monster, sea monster, behemoth, whale, Titan

levitate v
float, glide, waft, drift, fly, hover, suspend, hang

levitation n
hovering floating hanging gliding wafting drifting flying suspension

levity n
light-heartedness, light-mindedness, frivolity, carefreeness, facetiousness, flippancy, irreverence, hilarity, triviality, silliness, fun
E₃ seriousness

levy *v, n*
♦ *v*
tax, impose, exact, demand, charge, raise,
gather, collect; *Scot* stent
TECHNICAL estreat
OLD leave, tallage
♦ *n*
tax, toll, subscription, contribution, duty,
customs, excise, duties, due, fee, tariff, collection,
assessment, precept, tithe
TECHNICAL impost

lewd *adj*
obscene, indecent, suggestive, bawdy,
pornographic, salacious, licentious, lascivious, impure,
unclean, sensual, vulgar, unchaste, lustful, lecherous,
carnal, promiscuous, degenerate, debauched,
dissolute, wanton, harlot
OLD lubricious
FORMAL concupiscent, libidinous
COLLOQ. smutty, blue, raunchy, randy
E3 decent, chaste

lewdly *adv*
obscenely, indecently, pornographically, vulgarly,
impurely, lustfully, lecherously, promiscuously,
degenerately, dissolutely
COLLOQ. smuttily, raunchily, randily

lewdness *n*
obscenity, smut, smuttiness, indecency,
bawdiness, pornography, salaciousness, licentiousness,
lasciviousness, impurity, unchastity, lustfulness, lechery,
vulgarity, wantonness, carnality, crudity, debauchery,
depravity
FORMAL concupiscence
COLLOQ. randiness
E3 chasteness, politeness

lexicon *n*
dictionary, glossary, vocabulary, wordbook, word-list,
phrase book, encyclopedia

liability *n*
1 ACCOUNTABILITY, duty, obligation, responsibility,
answerability, blameworthiness
FORMAL culpability
2 DEBIT, arrears, obligation, dues, indebtedness
3 DRAWBACK, disadvantage, inconvenience, hindrance,
impediment, burden, onus, nuisance, encumbrance
COLLOQ. drag millstone around your neck
E3 1 unaccountability **2** asset **3** advantage

liable *adj*
1 INCLINED, likely, apt, disposed, prone, tending
susceptible, vulnerable, exposed, subject, open
FORMAL predisposed
2 RESPONSIBLE, answerable, accountable, amenable,
changeable, to blame, at fault
E3 1 unlikely **2** unaccountable

liaise *v*
contact, communicate, intercommunicate, co-operate,
work together, collaborate, exchange information, relate
to, network, interface

liaison *n*
1 CONTACT, connection, communication, interchange, co-
operation, collaboration, working together, exchange of
information
2 INTERMEDIARY, link, go-between, mediator, negotiator,
arbitrator, middleman, broker, agent
3 LOVE AFFAIR, affair, relationship, romance, intrigue,
amour, flirtation, entanglement
COLLOQ. bit on the side, fling carry-on, two-timing

liar *n*
falsifier, perjurer, deceiver, prevaricator, false witness
COLLOQ. fibber

libation *n*
drink offering sacrifice
FORMAL oblation

libel *n, v*
♦ *n*
defamation, false report, untrue statement, slur, smear,
slander, denigration
FORMAL disparagement, vilification, aspersion, calumny
COLLOQ. muck-raking mudslinging
♦ *v*
defame, slander, malign, abuse, denigrate
FORMAL cast aspersions on, vilify, revile, disparage,
calumniate, traduce
COLLOQ. slur, smear, drag someone's name through the
mud, throw mud at, badmouth

> **!** **libel** or **slander**?
> In English law, *libel* is an untrue defamatory statement
> made in a permanent form such as print, writing or
> pictures or broadcast on radio or television, whereas
> *slander* is one made by means of the spoken word (not
> broadcast) or gesture. In Scots law, both are *slander*.

libellous *adj*
defamatory, abusive, slanderous, derogatory, maligning
injurious, scurrilous, false, untrue, denigratory
FORMAL vilifying disparaging calumniatory, traducing

liberal *adj*
1 BROAD-MINDED, open-minded, enlightened, tolerant,
lenient, unprejudiced, unbiased, impartial, flexible, broad,
broad-based, wide-ranging catholic, libertarian,
latitudinarian
2 PROGRESSIVE, reformist, forward-looking advanced,
radical, moderate, left, left-wing leftish
3 GENEROUS, giving ample, bountiful, lavish, plentiful,
abundant, copious, profuse, handsome, open-handed,
open-hearted, large-hearted, big-hearted, unsparing
philanthropic, altruistic
OLD frank, handsome
FORMAL magnanimous, munificent
E3 1 narrow-minded, exclusive **2** conservative **3** mean,
miserly

liberalism *n*
progressivism, radicalism, free-thinking leftism,
humanitarianism, libertarianism, latitudinarianism
E3 conservatism, narrow-mindedness

liberality *n*
1 GENEROSITY, benevolence, free-handedness, large-
heartedness, kindness, open-handedness, open-
heartedness, largesse, charity, bounty, philanthropy,
altruism
FORMAL magnanimity, beneficence, munificence
2 BROAD-MINDEDNESS, liberalism, impartiality, open-
mindedness, permissiveness, breadth, tolerance, toleration,
progressivism, flexibility, catholicity, libertarianism,
latitudinarianism
E3 1 meanness **2** illiberality

liberalize *v*
relax, deregulate, lift controls on, loosen, reduce, slacken,
moderate, soften, ease (off)

liberate *v*
free, emancipate, release, let loose, set loose, let go, let
out, set free, deliver, unchain, unfetter, uncage, unshackle,
discharge, rescue, ransom
FORMAL redeem, manumit, disimmure
E3 imprison, enslave, restrict

liberation *n*
freedom, freeing liberating liberty, emancipation, release,
deliverance, loosing unchaining uncaging unfettering
unshackling unpenning ransoming enfranchisement
FORMAL manumission, redemption
COLLOQ. lib
E3 enslavement, imprisonment, restriction

liberator *n*
rescuer, deliverer, freer, saviour, ransomer, redeemer,
emancipator

FORMAL manumitter
🖃 enslaver, jailer

libertine n, adj
♦ n
debauchee, reprobate, seducer, sensualist, womanizer, rake, profligate, lecher, voluptary, roué, Don Juan, Casanova, Lothario, Romeo, Lovelace
♦ adj
debauched, degenerate, womanizing lecherous, reprobate, dissolute, promiscuous, lustful, salacious
FORMAL licentious

liberty n
1 FREEDOM, emancipation, deliverance, release, liberation, independence, autonomy, self-government, self-rule, self-determination, sovereignty, discretion, leave
FORMAL manumission
2 LICENCE, permission, sanction, right, privilege, prerogative, entitlement, authorization, dispensation, franchise, indulgence
3 FAMILIARITY, disrespect, overfamiliarity, boldness, presumption, impertinence, impudence, insolence
FORMAL impropriety
🖃 1 imprisonment 3 respect, politeness
■ **at liberty**
free, allowed, permitted, entitled, unconstrained, unrestricted, unhindered, without restraint, unrestrained, loose, not confined, at large
■ **take the liberty**
be so bold as to, make bold, be impertinent, be impudent, show disrespect, act presumptuously, behave overfamiliarly

libidinous adj
lustful, debauched, impure, promiscuous, loose, lascivious, lecherous, carnal, lewd, salacious, unchaste, sensual, wanton, wicked
FORMAL concupiscent, cupidinous, prurient, ruttish
COLLOQ. randy, horny
🖃 modest, temperate

libido n
sexual desire, sex drive, sexual appetite, sexual urge, erotic desire, passion, ardour, lust, eroticism
COLLOQ. randiness, the hots

libretto n
words, text, lines, lyrics, script, book

licence n
1 PERMIT, warrant, certificate, charter, document, pass, authority, grant, imprimatur
2 PERMISSION, warranty, authorization, authority, sanction, consent, certification, right, franchise, entitlement, prerogative, privilege, dispensation, carte blanche, freedom, liberty, approval, exemption, independence
FORMAL leave, accreditation
3 ABANDON, dissipation, excess, immoderation, indulgence, self-indulgence, intemperance, lawlessness, unruliness, anarchy, disorder, debauchery, decadence, dissoluteness, licentiousness, immorality, impropriety, irresponsibility
4 *poetic licence*
imaginativeness, exaggeration, fancifulness, creativity, inspiration, originality, freedom, exemption, deviation
🖃 2 prohibition, restriction 3 decorum, moderation, restraint, control

license v
permit, give permission, consent, allow, authorize, certify, warrant, entitle, empower, sanction, commission, franchise, privilege
FORMAL accredit
🖃 ban, prohibit

licentious adj
debauched, dissolute, dissipated, depraved, decadent, profligate, lascivious, immoral, abandoned, lewd, lecherous, promiscuous, libertine, impure, lax, lustful, disorderly, wanton, unchaste

COLLOQ. randy, raunchy
🖃 modest, chaste

licentiousness n
debauchery, dissoluteness, immorality, abandon, lewdness, lechery, promiscuity, libertinism, impurity, lust, lustfulness, salaciousness, salacity, wantonness, dissipation
FORMAL cupidinousness, prurience
COLLOQ. randiness, raunchiness
🖃 modesty, temperance

licit adj
legitimate, legal, lawful, authorized, warranted, sanctioned, statutory, rightful, proper, correct, real, genuine, acknowledged
COLLOQ. legit

lick v, n
♦ v
1 *lick the chocolate*
tongue, wet, moisten, lap, taste, wash, clean, fawn; *Scot* slake
2 FLICKER, dart, play over, touch, flick, ripple
3 DEFEAT, beat, conquer
FORMAL vanquish
COLLOQ. thrash, hammer, trounce, slaughter, demolish, make mincemeat (out) of, run rings round
♦ n
bit, dab, little, speck, spot, touch, tad, taste, stroke, sample, brush, smidgeon, hint
■ **lick your lips**
enjoy, savour, drool over, relish, anticipate

licking n
thrashing whipping flogging hiding smacking spanking tanning beating defeat, drubbing

lid n
top, cover, covering cap, stopper

lie¹ n, v
♦ n
tell lies
falsehood, untruth, perjury, falsification, fabrication, invention, fiction, half-truth, deceit, falsity, white lie, prevarication
FORMAL dissimulation
COLLOQ. fib, whopper, porky, tall story, made-up story, cock-and-bull story
SLANG (*vulgar*) crap, bullshit
🖃 truth
♦ v
perjure, misrepresent, tell a lie, fabricate, falsify, invent, make up a story, equivocate, prevaricate
FORMAL forswear yourself, dissemble, dissimulate
COLLOQ. fib, lie through your teeth
■ **give the lie to**
disprove, rebut, contradict, invalidate, prove false

SYNONYM NUANCES

noun
Falsehood and **untruth** can be used for untrue statements, whereas the use of **perjury** is restricted to giving dishonest evidence under oath. **Falsification** can be used to imply deliberate alteration or forgery: *the falsification of the company's accounts*, while **fabrication** suggests making something up for one's own ends. Similarly, **invention** has to do with devising something and **fiction** suggests a tale that is a work of the imagination, but with less implication of selfish motives.

    Half-truth suggests an element of truth is involved but an important element has been hidden, whereas **deceit** suggests a deliberate attempt to mislead, while **prevarication** has more to do with deliberate deviation from and avoidance of the truth: *the minister's speech contained falsehoods and prevarications*. **White lie** is more approving in that it suggests a tactful evasion of the truth to save someone's feelings.

lie² v

1 BE, exist, be located, be placed, be positioned, be found, belong extend, remain, stay, keep, stretch, reach, stand, continue
FORMAL dwell
2 *lie down for a rest*
rest, recline, stretch out, sprawl out, lounge, couch, laze
FORMAL repose
■ **lie in wait for**
ambush, waylay, lay a trap for, trap, attack, surprise, lurk
OLD lie at lurch
FORMAL ambuscade
■ **lie low**
go into hiding hide, hide away, hide out, conceal yourself, go to earth, take cover, lurk, skulk
COLLOQ. hole up, lie doggo, keep a low profile

> ! **lie** or **lay**?
> See panel at **lay¹**.

liege n
lord, liege-lord, feudal lord, overlord, master, king nobleman, superior, chief

lieutenant n
assistant, second-in-command, deputy, subordinate, right-hand man/woman

life n
1 BEING, existence, animation, breath, viability, aliveness, entity, soul
Related adjectives: vital, zoetic
2 LIVING THINGS, human life, animal life, plant, fauna, flora, fauna and flora
3 *the loss of many lives*
person, individual, human being man, woman, child
4 DURATION, lifetime, existence, life expectancy, course, span, lifespan, career
5 *the machine has a limited life*
duration, continuance, span, lifespan, time, course, period of usefulness, time of being active, lifetime
6 *see life*
(wide) experience, varied activities, travelling meeting people
7 LIFE STORY, biography, autobiography, diary, diaries, memoirs, journal
8 LIVELINESS, vigour, vitality, vivacity, animation, high spirits, exuberance, enthusiasm, excitement, verve, zest, energy, élan, spirit, sparkle, effervescence, activity, cheerfulness
COLLOQ. oomph, pep, zip, zing pizzazz
⊟ **1** death
■ **come to life**
become active, become interesting become lively, become exciting come alive, wake up
■ **give your life**
sacrifice yourself for, give up/sacrifice your life, offer up/surrender your life, die for, dedicate yourself to, devote yourself to

> **QUOTATIONS**
> Life is the greatest of blessings, and death the worst of evils
>   HEINRICH HEINE, *Idéen, Das Buch Le Grand*
>
> Life is first boredom, then fear
>   PHILIP LARKIN, 'Dockery and Son'
>
> Cold – cold as truth, cold as life. No, nothing can be as cold as life
>   JEAN RHYS, *Voyage in the Dark*
>
> Life, like a dome of many-coloured glass, / Stains the white radiance of Eternity
>   PERCY BYSSHE SHELLEY, *Adonais*
>
> What is this life if, full of care, / We have no time to stand and stare?
>   W H DAVIES, 'Leisure'

life-and-death adj
important, all-important, crucial, vital, serious, critical

lifeblood n
essential part/factor, life-force, spirit, soul, core, centre, heart, inspiration

lifeless adj
1 DEAD, deceased, defunct, cold, unconscious, gone, inanimate, insensible, stiff, stone-dead, clay-cold
OLD (*Shakesp*) key-cold
2 LETHARGIC, listless, sluggish, lacklustre, dull, apathetic, passive, insipid, uninspired, uninspiring unemotional, bloodless, colourless, slow, flat, wooden, stiff; *Scot* cauldrife
OLD (*Shakesp*) key-cold
FORMAL exanimate
3 BARREN, bare, empty, desolate, stark, uninhabited, arid, sterile, unproductive, soulless
⊟ **1** alive, exciting **2** lively

lifelike adj
realistic, true-to-life, real, true, vivid, natural, authentic, faithful, exact, graphic
⊟ unrealistic, unnatural

lifelong adj
lifetime, for all your life, long-lasting long-standing persistent, lasting enduring abiding permanent, constant
⊟ impermanent, temporary

lifestyle n
way of life, life, way of living manner of living living conditions, position, situation

lifetime n
duration, existence, life, lifespan, span, period, time, course, day(s), career

lift v, n
♦ v
1 *she lifted the chair*
raise, pick up, elevate, hoist, heave, uplift, upraise, hold up, hold high
2 *he lifted their spirits*
uplift, exalt, buoy up, boost, raise, elevate
3 *the ban has been lifted*
cancel, end, stop, relax, remove, withdraw, annul
FORMAL revoke, rescind, terminate
4 *lift people out of the war zone*
fly, transport, move, transfer, airlift, convey, shift
5 *the fog lifted*
clear, disperse, vanish, disappear, scatter, dissolve, thin out
6 DIG UP, dig out of the ground, pull up, pick, root out, unearth
7 *lift someone else's material*
copy, plagiarize, steal, borrow
COLLOQ. crib, nick
⊟ **1** drop, put down **2** lower, depress **3** start, apply **5** come down, gather **6** plant, sow
♦ n
1 ELEVATOR, escalator, hoist, paternoster
2 *give you a lift home*
drive, hitch, ride, run, transport
3 BOOST, fillip, encouragement, pick-me-up, uplift, spur, reassurance
COLLOQ. shot in the arm
⊟ **3** discouragement
■ **lift off**
take off, blast off, ascend, climb, depart
⊟ touch down

lift-off n
take-off, blast-off, ascent, climb, departure
⊟ touchdown

ligature n
band, binding bond, link, tie, connection, cord, rope, string thong strap, bandage, tourniquet, ligament
TECHNICAL deligation, funicle

light[1] *n, v, adj*

♦ *n*

1 ILLUMINATION, brightness, brilliance, radiance, glow, ray, beam, shaft, shine, glare, gleam, glint, lustre, flash, blaze
FORMAL luminescence, effulgence, lux, lambency
Related adjective: photic
2 LAMP, lantern, lighter, match, torch, candle, taper, bulb, beacon
TECHNICAL luminosity, incandescence; *N Am* flashlight
3 DAY, daybreak, daylight, daytime, dawn, sunrise, first light, crack of dawn, cockcrow
4 ENLIGHTENMENT, illumination, explanation, understanding comprehension, insight, knowledge
FORMAL elucidation
5 *presented in a different light*
aspect, way, approach, manner, style, slant, angle, side, dimension, point of view
F3 1 darkness **3** night

♦ *v*

1 IGNITE, fire, set alight, set fire to, set burning kindle
COLLOQ. torch
2 ILLUMINATE, light up, lighten, floodlight, brighten, animate, cheer (up), make cheerful, switch on, turn on, put on
FORMAL irradiate
F3 1 extinguish **2** darken

♦ *adj*

1 ILLUMINATED, bright, brilliant, luminous, glowing shining well-lit, sunny
2 PALE, pastel, fair, blond, blonde, bleached, faded, whitish, faint
F3 1 dark **2** black

■ **bring to light**
make known, notice, reveal, expose, discover, uncover, disclose

■ **come to light**
become obvious, be made known, be noticed, be discovered, be uncovered, be exposed

■ **in the light of**
considering taking into consideration, taking into account, because of, in view of, bearing/keeping in mind, being mindful of, remembering

■ **shed/throw/cast light on**
clarify, make clear, explain, make plain, illuminate
OLD enlight
FORMAL elucidate

> **QUOTATIONS**
> More light!
> JOHANN WOLFGANG VON GOETHE, last words

Sources of light include:

NATURAL LIGHT:	halogen light	tail-light
aurora borealis	headlamp	torch
daylight	headlight	traffic light
infrared	indicator light	wand
lightning	laser	
moonlight	light bulb	FIRELIGHT:
starlight	light buoy	bonfire
sunlight	lighthouse	candle
ultraviolet	navigation light	candlelight
	neon light	fire
ELECTRIC LIGHT:	night light	firework
Belisha beacon	pedestrian light	flame
brake light	range light	flare
chandelier	runway light	gaslight
courtesy light	searchlight	hurricane lamp
fairy light	sidelight	lighter
flashgun	spotlight	match
N Am flashlight	standard lamp	oil lamp
floodlight	streetlight	pilot light
fluorescent light	strip light	spark
fog lamp	strobe light	taper
footlight	sun-lamp	tealight

light[2] *adj*

1 WEIGHTLESS, insubstantial, lightweight, delicate, fine, airy, buoyant, flimsy, thin, feathery, floaty, slight
2 *light rain; light winds*
slight, mild, gentle, soft, weak, faint
3 *light machinery*
small, portable, easily moved, easy to carry around
4 *light work*
easy, effortless, moderate, undemanding unexacting untaxing
5 *a light punishment*
mild, lenient, slight, moderate
6 *light movements*
graceful, quick, gentle, nimble, agile, deft
7 TRIVIAL, inconsiderable, trifling superficial, unimportant, inconsequential, worthless, petty
8 CHEERFUL, cheery, carefree, light-hearted, lively, happy, merry, gay
FORMAL blithe
9 ENTERTAINING, diverting amusing funny, humorous, frivolous, light-hearted, witty, pleasing
10 *light food*
easy to digest, digestible, modest, delicately flavoured
11 *light soil*
easily dug porous, loose, crumbly
FORMAL friable
F3 1 heavy, weighty, thick **2, 3, 4** heavy **5** severe, harsh **7** important, serious **8** solemn **9** serious **10** heavy, rich **11** solid, dense

---

> **SYNONYM NUANCES**
>
> *sense 1*
> **Weightless** suggests being unrestrained by gravity and so is fairly technical in tone, whereas **insubstantial**, while still fairly technical, is more suggestive of a lack of solidity: *an insubstantial trail of smoke.* **Lightweight** can be used similarly, or may be applied more figuratively to imply a lack of authority: *he's a lightweight political figure.* **Delicate** and **fine** are more suggestive of physical fragility: *delicate fabrics should be washed by hand.*
> **Airy** can be used literally or figuratively to imply a lack of tangibility or substance: *airy speculation*, whereas **buoyant** has implications of lightness with particular regard to your spirits as well as its literal meaning: *in buoyant mood.* You can use **feathery** to suggest something rather wispy: *the ferns' feathery fronds*, or **floaty** to suggest light movement: *floaty skirts.*
> **Flimsy**, **thin** and **slight**, on the other hand, are vaguely pejorative and suggest not being solid or strong enough: *flimsy clothes that do not keep out the cold; flimsy arguments.*

light[3]

■ **light on/upon**
find, come across, discover, notice, hit on, spot, stumble on
FORMAL chance on, encounter, happen upon

lighten[1] *v*

the sky lightened
illuminate, illumine, make lighter, brighten, make brighter, light up, shine, glow
F3 darken

lighten[2] *v*

1 EASE, lessen, make lighter, unload, lift, relieve, reduce, calm
OLD levigate
FORMAL mitigate, alleviate, allay, assuage
2 BRIGHTEN, cheer (up), encourage, hearten, uplift, lift, gladden, restore, revive, elate, buoy up, inspire
FORMAL inspirit
COLLOQ. perk up
F3 1 burden **2** depress

■ **lighten up**
relax, unwind, calm down
COLLOQ. take it easy, let yourself go, put your feet up, cool, chill (out), hang loose

light-fingered *adj*
dishonest, pilfering stealing thieving thievish, shoplifting crafty, furtive, shifty, sly
COLLOQ. crooked, filching
F3 honest

light-footed *adj*
agile, active, nimble, sprightly, spry, swift, deft, lithe, graceful
F3 clumsy, slow

light-headed *adj*
1 FAINT, giddy, dizzy, unsteady, airy, delirious
FORMAL vertiginous
COLLOQ. woozy
2 FLIGHTY, foolish, frivolous, silly, superficial, shallow, empty-headed, flippant, vacuous, trifling
COLLOQ. scatter-brained, feather-brained, airheaded
F3 2 level-headed, solemn

light-hearted *adj*
cheerful, joyful, jolly, happy, happy-go-lucky, bright, in good spirits, in high spirits, carefree, untroubled, merry, sunny, glad, elated, gay, jovial, playful, frolicsome, amusing entertaining
FORMAL blithe
COLLOQ. chirpy, bouncy, high
F3 sad, unhappy, serious

lighthouse *n*
beacon, tower, danger/warning signal, fanal, pharos

lightly *adv*
1 SLIGHTLY, gently, faintly, delicately, gingerly, softly, thinly, sparingly, sparsely, slightingly
2 EASILY, effortlessly, readily, airily, breezily, gaily, facilely
3 FRIVOLOUSLY, flippantly, carelessly, heedlessly, thoughtlessly, casually
4 LENIENTLY, mildly, easily
F3 1 heavily **3** soberly

lightness *n*
1 *lightness of the clothes*
weightlessness, slightness, airiness, buoyancy, crumbliness, porosity, porousness, sandiness, delicacy, delicateness, flimsiness, thinness
2 *lightness of movement*
grace, gracefulness, agility, gentleness, litheness, deftness, nimbleness, mildness
3 *lightness of spirit*
cheerfulness, cheeriness, light-heartedness, liveliness, gaiety, animation
FORMAL blitheness
4 FICKLENESS, triviality, frivolity, levity
F3 1 heaviness, solidity **2** clumsiness **3** sadness, heaviness **4** seriousness, severity, sobriety

lightning *n*
forked lightning sheet lightning ball lightning chain lightning zigzag lightning summer lightning lightning strike, thunderbolt, thunderclap, clap of thunder, thunderdart, thunderstorm, electric storm, wildfire
OLD fire, levin
FORMAL fulguration
Related adjective: fulgural
■ **like lightning**
speedily, quickly, rapidly, hastily, immediately;
COLLOQ. wildfire, a rocket

lightweight *adj*
1 LIGHT, insubstantial, delicate, flimsy, thin, feathery, weightless
2 UNIMPORTANT, insignificant, inconsequential, insubstantial, trivial, worthless, negligible, trifling petty, slight, paltry
FORMAL nugatory
F3 1 heavy, thick, strong **2** important, major, heavyweight

likable *adj*
lov(e)able, pleasing appealing nice, agreeable, charming engaging winsome, winning pleasant, friendly, genial, amiable, congenial, attractive, sympathetic
F3 unpleasant, disagreeable

like¹ *adj, n, prep*
♦ *adj*
like minds
similar, resembling alike, same, much the same, having an affinity, identical, equivalent, akin, comparable, corresponding related, relating parallel, allied, approximating of a kind
FORMAL analogous
F3 unlike, dissimilar
♦ *n*
equal, match, counterpart, equivalent, opposite number, fellow, mate, twin, parallel, peer
♦ *prep*
1 *he was shaking like a leaf*
in the same way/manner as, along/on the lines of, similar to
2 *sports like running or climbing*
such as, for example, for instance, by way of example
3 *it's just like him to change his mind*
typical, characteristic, true, usual, normal

like² *v*
1 ENJOY, delight in, find enjoyable/interesting find pleasant, take pleasure in, take to, appeal to, care for, admire, esteem, appreciate, be fond of, find attractive, be keen on, love, adore, hold dear, cherish, prize, relish, revel in, approve, welcome, take (kindly) to, be someone's liking
COLLOQ. have a soft spot for, dig
2 PREFER, choose, select, decide on, feel inclined, desire, want, wish, would rather, would sooner, would more willingly/readily
COLLOQ. go for, fancy, go a bundle on, take a shine to
F3 1 dislike **2** reject

likelihood *n*
likeliness, probability, possibility, chance, prospect, liability
F3 improbability, unlikeliness

likely *adj, adv*
♦ *adj*
1 PROBABLE, possible, anticipated, expected, to be expected, liable, prone, tending inclined, predictable, foreseeable
COLLOQ. odds-on, on the cards, in the wind
2 CREDIBLE, believable, plausible, feasible, reasonable, acceptable
3 PROMISING, appropriate, acceptable, proper, fitting fit, right, promising hopeful, pleasing
F3 1 unlikely **3** unsuitable
♦ *adv*
probably, presumably, in all probability, no doubt, doubtlessly, (as) likely as not

like-minded *adj*
agreeing in agreement, of one mind, of the same mind, unanimous, in harmony, in rapport, compatible, harmonious
FORMAL in accord
F3 disagreeing

liken *v*
compare, equate, match, parallel, link, relate, juxtapose, associate, set beside
OLD (*Shakesp*) like
FORMAL correlate, analogize, similize

likeness *n*
1 SIMILARITY, resemblance, comparison, affinity, correspondence, parallelism
FORMAL semblance, similitude, analogy, simulacrum
2 REPRESENTATION, image, expression, copy, reproduction, replica, facsimile, statue, bust, sculpture, effigy, drawing painting picture, sketch, portrait, study, depiction, photograph, icon, counterpart, caricature, guise

FORMAL personation
3 SEMBLANCE, guise, appearance, form, shape
≡ 1 dissimilarity, unlikeness

likewise adv
1 SIMILARLY, in the same way/manner, by the same token, in like manner, as also
COLLOQ. same here
2 ALSO, moreover, furthermore, in addition, further, besides, too
OLD to boot, eke

liking n
fondness, love, affection, preference, partiality, affinity, taste, attraction, appreciation, proneness, inclination, tendency, bias, leaning bent, desire, weakness, fancy
FORMAL predilection, penchant, propensity, proclivity
COLLOQ. soft spot, thing
≡ dislike, aversion, hatred

lilt n
rise and fall, rhythm, sway, swing song measure, beat, cadence, air

lily-white adj
faultless, pure, spotless, virtuous, virgin, blameless, chaste, incorrupt, innocent, irreproachable, uncorrupt, uncorrupted, unsullied, untainted, untarnished, milk-white
≡ corrupt

limb n
1 *stretch your limbs*
arm, leg member, appendage, extremity, quarter, flipper; *Scot* spauld
TECHNICAL pterygium
Related adjective: membral
2 BRANCH, projection, offshoot, wing fork, extension, section, part, spur, bough
■ **out on a limb**
exposed, isolated, in a weak position, vulnerable, in a risky/precarious situation

limber adj, v
♦ *adj*
flexible, supple, pliant, plastic, elastic, agile, graceful, lithe, loose-jointed, loose-limbed, pliable, lissom
≡ stiff
■ **limber up**
loosen up, warm up, work out, exercise, prepare

limbo
■ **in limbo**
in a state of uncertainty, awaiting action, left hanging left in the air
FORMAL in abeyance
COLLOQ. up in the air, on the back burner

limelight n
fame, celebrity, spotlight, stardom, recognition, renown, attention, focus of attention, notice, eminence, notability, prominence, publicity, public eye

limit n, v
♦ *n*
1 EXTREMITY, ultimate, utmost, extreme, maximum, terminus, greatest extent, greatest amount, lid, ceiling cut-off point, saturation point, deadline
2 BOUNDARY, confines, parameters, bound(s), brim, border, frontier, edge, brink, threshold, verge, end, perimeter, rim, compass, demarcation, termination
3 CHECK, curb, restraint, restriction, constraint, limitation
♦ *v*
restrict, check, curb, restrain, constrain, hold/keep in check, confine, demarcate, delimit, control, contain, bound, hem in, rein, bridle, ration, reduce, specify, hinder, impede
FORMAL circumscribe
■ **the limit**
enough, intolerable, too much, the end, the worst
COLLOQ. the final blow, the last straw

limitation n
1 CHECK, restriction, curb, control, constraint, restraint, delimitation, demarcation, block, hindrance, impediment
2 INADEQUACY, shortcoming incapability, inability, imperfection, weakness, weak point, defect, disadvantage, drawback, snag condition, qualification, reservation
≡ 1 freedom, extension **2** advantage, strong point

limited adj
restricted, constrained, controlled, confined, checked, defined, finite, qualified, fixed, minimal, small, basic, narrow, inadequate, insufficient, scanty, incomplete, stinted, imperfect
FORMAL circumscribed
≡ limitless, boundless

limitless adj
unlimited, unbounded, boundless, illimited, undefined, immeasurable, measureless, incalculable, infinite, countless, endless, never-ending unending interminable, inexhaustible, untold, vast, unspecified
≡ limited

limp[1] v, n
♦ *v*
limp down the road
hobble, falter, stumble, hop, shuffle, shamble, stagger, totter, walk with a limp, walk unevenly, hitch; *dialect* hamble
OLD halt, dot
COLLOQ. *N Am* gimp
♦ *n*
hobble, lameness, hitch, shuffle, flop, uneven walk, hop; *Scot* hilch
TECHNICAL claudication
OLD halt

limp[2] adj
1 FLABBY, drooping flaccid, floppy, loose, slack, relaxed, lax, soft, flexible, pliable, limber, flaggy, lank
2 TIRED, weary, exhausted, fatigued, spent, weak, frail, feeble, worn out, lethargic, out of energy
FORMAL debilitated, enervated
≡ 1 stiff, firm **2** vigorous, energetic

limpid adj
1 CLEAR, crystal-clear, transparent, translucent, pure, glassy, bright, still, unruffled, untroubled
FORMAL pellucid
2 INTELLIGIBLE, comprehensible, clear, plain, flowing coherent, lucid
≡ 1 muddy, ripply; *formal* turbid **2** unintelligible

limply adv
loosely, slackly, flabbily, softly, flexibly, flaccidly
≡ stiffly, firmly

limpness n
flabbiness, looseness, slackness, laxity, flexibility
FORMAL flaccidness, flaccidity, claudication
≡ stiffness, firmness

line[1] n, v
♦ *n*
1 STROKE, band, bar, stripe, mark, strip, rule, dash, slash, strand, streak, seam, belt, underline, score, underscore, scratch
2 ROW, rank, queue, file, column, sequence, series, procession, parade, chain, string trail, tier, bank
3 LIMIT, boundary, border, borderline, edge, perimeter, periphery, frontier, demarcation, margin
4 STRING, rope, cord, cable, thread, strand, filament, wire, twine
5 PROFILE, contour, outline, silhouette, figure, shape, appearance, pattern, style, formation
FORMAL configuration, delineation
6 CREASE, wrinkle, furrow, groove, crow's feet, corrugation
7 COURSE, path, direction, track, route, channel, way, trajectory, axis

8 APPROACH, avenue, course (of action), belief, ideology, attitude, policy, system, position, practice, procedure, method, way, scheme, technique, modus operandi
9 OCCUPATION, business, trade, profession, vocation, work, job, line of business/work, career, activity, interest, employment, department, calling field, province, forte, area, pursuit, specialization, specialty, specialism, speciality
10 *chat-up line*
spiel, patter, talk, sales talk, story, pitch
11 *drop you a line*
note, letter, card, postcard, message, email, word, report, memo, memorandum, information
12 WORDS, part, role, text, script, book, libretto
13 *a shipping line*
company, business, firm, transport business
14 *enemy lines*
defences, position, front, front line, firing-line, battleground, battlefield, battle zone
FORMAL formation
15 *a line of products*
brand, make, kind, sort, variety, type
16 ANCESTRY, family, descent, extraction, parentage, heritage, lineage, strain, pedigree, stock, race, breed
♦ *v*
1 BORDER, skirt, verge, edge, bound, fringe, rim
2 CREASE, score, furrow, mark, draw, hatch, inscribe, rule
■ **line up**
1 ALIGN, range, straighten, marshal, order, group, regiment, queue up, form a queue, stand in line, wait in line, form ranks, fall in, assemble
FORMAL array
2 ORGANIZE, arrange, prepare, produce, secure, obtain
FORMAL procure
COLLOQ. lay on
■ **draw the line**
refuse, say no to, exclude, limit, reject, rule out, stop short of, stand firm
COLLOQ. put your foot down
■ **in line**
1 IN A ROW, in a queue, in a column, in series
2 *bring the two systems in line with each other*
in agreement, in step, in harmony
FORMAL in accord
3 *in line for promotion*
due, likely, being considered, in the running
COLLOQ. on the cards
■ **lay/put on the line**
risk, put in jeopardy, jeopardize, endanger, imperil
■ **toe the line**
conform, keep/follow the rules, be conventional

line² *v*
line a box with paper
encase, panel, cover, fill, inlay, pad, back, face, stuff, reinforce

lineage *n*
ancestry, descent, extraction, genealogy, family, line, pedigree, race, stock, birth, breed, house, heredity, ancestors, forebears, descendants, offspring succession
OLD (*Shakesp*) descending progeny; lignage, parage

lineaments *n*
features, face, lines, outline(s), appearance, aspect, profile, traits
FORMAL countenance, visage, physiognomy, configuration

lined *adj*
1 RULED, feint
2 WRINKLED, furrowed, creased, wizened, worn
E3 1 unlined, blank **2** smooth

linen *n*
bed linen, sheets, pillowcases, tablecloths, table linen, napkins, tea towels, white goods
FORMAL napery

liner *n*
ship, cruise ship, ocean-going vessel, steamer, boat

line-up *n*
array, arrangement, queue, row, line, selection, cast, team, bill, list

linger *v*
1 LOITER, delay, dally, wait, remain, stay, hang on, hang around, lag dawdle, idle, stop, take your time, hover, lurk, straggle; *dialect* hanker; *Scot* taigle
OLD tarry; (*Spenser*) hove
FORMAL procrastinate
COLLOQ. stick around, dilly-dally, let the grass grow under your feet
2 CONTINUE, endure, hold out, last, persist, survive, remain
E3 1 leave, rush

lingerie *n*
underclothes, underwear, underclothing undergarments, panties, knickers, camiknickers, camisole, slip, half-slip, teddy, body stocking panty girdle, brassiere, bra, suspender belt, unmentionables, inexpressibles
COLLOQ. frillies, undies, smalls, scanties

lingering *adj*
persistent, remaining surviving persisting slow, dragging long-drawn-out, prolonged
FORMAL protracted
E3 quick

lingo *n*
language, tongue, patois, speech, talk, jargon, idiom, vernacular, terminology, vocabulary, parlance, dialect, argot, cant, patter
COLLOQ. mumbo-jumbo

liniment *n*
cream, lotion, salve, ointment, embrocation, emollient, balm, balsam, wash
FORMAL unguent

lining *n*
inlay, interfacing facing padding backing casing encasement, stiffening panelling reinforcement

link *n, v*
♦ *n*
1 CONNECTION, bond, tie, association, joint, relationship, tie-up, union, knot, liaison, attachment, communication, partnership
FORMAL concatenation
2 RING, loop, bond, tie, knot, joint, shackle, swivel
TECHNICAL karabiner
3 PART, piece, element, member, constituent, component, division
♦ *v*
connect, join, attach, couple, tie, fasten, unite, bind, amalgamate, merge, associate, ally, bracket, interlink, identify, relate, liaise, yoke, hook up, join forces, team up, bridge, network; *Scot* cleek
OLD enchain
FORMAL concatenate
E3 separate, unfasten
■ **link up**
connect, join (up), ally, amalgamate, meet up, join forces, merge, team up, unify, hook up, dock, bridge
E3 separate

linkage *n*
connection, bond, tie, tie-in, tie-up, association, joint, relationship, union, knot, liaison, attachment, communication, partnership, alliance, amalgamation, merger

link-up *n*
connection, alliance, amalgamation, association, relationship, partnership, merger, tie-in, union
E3 separation

lion
■ **lion's share**
most, main part, majority, bulk, mass, greatest/largest part, preponderance, almost/nearly all

lion-hearted *adj*
bold, brave, courageous, heroic, daring gallant, intrepid, stout-hearted, valiant, fearless, dauntless, resolute, stalwart, dreadless
FORMAL valorous
E3 cowardly

lionize *v*
glorify, hero-worship, treat as a hero, honour, idolize, magnify, fête, exalt, celebrate, praise, sing the praises of, acclaim, adulate
FORMAL aggrandize, eulogize
COLLOQ. put on a pedestal
E3 vilify

lip *n*
1 mouth, underlip; *dialect* fipple
TECHNICAL labium, labrum, flew, hare-lip, ligula, muffle, submentum
Related adjective: labial
2 EDGE, brim, border, brink, rim, margin, verge, spout
TECHNICAL helmet, corolla
3 IMPERTINENCE, impudence, insolence, rudeness, effrontery, backchat
COLLOQ. cheek, sauce, attitude
E3 politeness

lippy *adj*
cheeky, impertinent, impudent, insolent, disrespectful, forward, brazen, pert, audacious, overfamiliar
COLLOQ. fresh, saucy, mouthy; *N Am* sassy
E3 respectful, polite

liquefaction *n*
dissolution, dissolving fusion, liquefying melting thawing
FORMAL deliquescence
E3 solidification

liquefy *v*
dissolve, fuse, liquidize, melt, smelt, run, thaw, flux, fluidize
FORMAL liquesce, deliquesce
E3 solidify

liqueur

Liqueurs include:

absinthe	Drambuie®	ouzo
advocaat	Frangelico®	Parfait Amour
amaretto	Galliano®	pastis
Amarula®	Glayva®	Pernod®
anisette	Goldschlager®	Ponche
Aurum®	Grand Marnier®	pousse-café
Averna	Irish Mist®	prunelle
Bailey's®	Izarra®	ratafia
Benedictine	Jägermeister	Ricard®
Chartreuse®	Kahlúa®	sambuca
cherry brandy	kirsch	Southern
Cherry Heering	kümmel	Comfort®
Cointreau®	limoncello	Strega®
crème de cacao	Malibu®	Tia Maria®
crème de cassis	maraschino	Triple sec
crème de menthe	Midori®	Vana Tallinn
Cuarenta y Tres	mirabelle	Van der Hum
(or Licor 43)	Nocino	
curaçao	noyau	

---

liquid *n, adj*
♦ *n*
liquor, fluid, juice, drink, sap, solution, lotion
♦ *adj*
1 FLUID, flowing liquefied, watery, wet, running runny, sloppy, thin, melted, molten, thawed, clear
FORMAL aqueous, hydrous
2 SMOOTH, flowing steady, even, regular, unbroken, uninterrupted, pure, clear, mellow, melodious
E3 1 solid, gas

liquidate *v*
1 PAY (OFF), close down, dissolve, break up, clear, discharge, wind up, sell (off), disband, cash in, convert to cash; *N Am* shutter
2 ANNIHILATE, terminate, do away with, put an end to, dissolve, kill, murder, massacre, assassinate, destroy, dispatch, abolish, eliminate, exterminate, remove, finish off
COLLOQ. rub out, wipe out

liquidize *v*
process, blend, crush, purée, cream, mix, synthesize

liquor *n*
1 ALCOHOL, intoxicant, strong drink, spirits, drink
OLD (*Shakesp*) tickle-brain
COLLOQ. hard stuff, hoo(t)ch, juice, Dutch courage, sauce, firewater, tipple, the bottle, stiffener, the creature, tiddly, tinct; *Aust & NZ* grog
SLANG booze, gnat's piss, jungle juice, rotgut; *Aust & NZ* shicker; *N Am* juice
2 LIQUID, juice, gravy, essence, extract, stock, broth, infusion

lissom *adj*
graceful, supple, pliable, flexible, pliant, light, nimble, agile, limber, lithe, lithesome, loose-jointed, loose-limbed, willowy
E3 stiff, awkward

list¹ *n, v*
♦ *n*
a shopping list
catalogue, roll, inventory, register, enumeration, schedule, programme, agenda, index, contents, listing record, manifest, file, directory, table, tabulation, tally, series, syllabus, calendar, recipe, roster, rota, checklist, invoice
♦ *v*
enumerate, register, itemize, classify, catalogue, alphabetize, index, tabulate, record, programme, file, schedule, enrol, enter, note, bill, book, set down, write down, compile

list² *v*
the ship is listing
lean (over), incline, tilt, slope, slant, keel (over), tip, cant

listen *v*
attend, pay attention, hear, heed, hang on someone's words/lips, prick up your ears, take notice, mind, lend an ear, eavesdrop, monitor
TECHNICAL auscultate
OLD hark, hearken, give ear, intend, list, lithe
SLANG get a load of

■ **listen in**
eavesdrop, overhear, tap, wiretap, monitor, pin back your ears, prick up your ears
COLLOQ. bug

> **QUOTATIONS**
> We listen to others to discover what we ourselves believe
> GEORGE P GRANT

listless *adj*
sluggish, lethargic, spiritless, languishing lackadaisical, limp, lifeless, dull, passive, inert, inactive, impassive, indifferent, uninterested, vacant, apathetic, depressed, bored, heavy
FORMAL languid, torpid, enervated, indolent
E3 energetic, enthusiastic

listlessly *adv*
sluggishly, lethargically, spiritlessly, apathetically, lifelessly, dully, limply, passively, inertly, inactively, impassively, lacking energy, lacking enthusiasm
E3 energetically, enthusiastically

listlessness *n*
lethargy, sluggishness, spiritlessness, lifelessness, sloth, inattention, indifference, ennui, apathy

FORMAL enervation, indolence, languidness, languor, torpidity, torpor, supineness

E3 liveliness

litany *n*

1 PRAYER, petition, procession, devotion

TECHNICAL eirenicon, synapte

FORMAL supplication, invocation

2 CATALOGUE, account, enumeration, list, repetition, recital, recitation

literacy *n*

ability to read, ability to write, proficiency, education, culture, cultivation, intelligence, knowledge, learning scholarship, learnedness, articulacy, articulateness

FORMAL erudition

E3 illiteracy

literal *adj, n*

♦ *adj*

1 VERBATIM, word-for-word, verbal, strict, close, actual, plain, clear, precise, faithful, exact, accurate, factual, true, genuine, undistorted, unexaggerated, unembellished, unvarnished

2 PROSAIC, unimaginative, uninspired, colourless, matter-of-fact, down-to-earth, humdrum, boring dull, tedious

E3 1 imprecise, loose, deviating free **2** imaginative

♦ *n*

misprint, mistake, error, printing error, typographical error

FORMAL corrigendum, erratum

COLLOQ. typo

literalism *n*

exact rendering textualism, letter (of the law), fundamentalism, biblicism, scripturalism

literally *adv*

1 *many people in Africa are literally starving*

actually, really, truly, certainly

2 *translate literally*

exactly, faithfully, to the letter, strictly, strictly speaking precisely, closely, plainly, word for word, verbatim

E3 2 imprecisely, loosely

literary *adj*

1 EDUCATED, well-read, bookish, learned, scholarly, lettered, literate, widely-read, cultured, cultivated, refined

FORMAL erudite

2 *literary phrases*

formal, poetic, written, old-fashioned

E3 1 ignorant, illiterate **2** everyday, colloquial, informal

literate *adj*

able to read, able to write, proficient, educated, well-educated, cultured, intelligent, learned, intellectual, knowledgeable

literati *n*

the learned, the scholarly, the erudite, the well-informed, men/women of letters, the studious, intelligentsia, academics, intellectuals, cognoscenti, highbrows, illuminati

COLLOQ. brains, eggheads

literature *n*

1 WRITINGS, printed works, published works, letters, paper(s)

See panel below

2 INFORMATION, facts, data, leaflet(s), pamphlet(s), circular(s), brochure(s), hand-out(s), printed matter, advertising material

COLLOQ. bumf

lithe *adj*

agile, supple, flexible, pliable, pliant, lissom, limber, lithesome, double-jointed, loose-jointed, loose-limbed

E3 stiff

litigant *n*

contender, contestant, disputant, opponent, claimant, complainant, litigator, plaintiff, party

litigation *n*

lawsuit, law, action, legal action, dispute, suit, case, legal proceedings, legal case, prosecution, process, contention

litigious *adj*

argumentative, quarrelsome, contentious, disputatious, disputable, belligerent

E3 easy-going

litter *n, v*

♦ *n*

1 RUBBISH, debris, refuse, odds and ends, waste, mess, disorder, clutter, confusion, disarray, untidiness, muck, jumble, fragments, shreds; *N Am* trash, garbage

FORMAL detritus

COLLOQ. junk, shambles, grot

2 OFFSPRING, young brood, family

TECHNICAL farrow

OLD kindle, team

FORMAL progeny, issue

♦ *v*

1 strew, scatter, mess up, make a mess of, disorder, clutter, make untidy

2 *litter for cattle*

bedding straw, bed, hay, bracken, chaff

3 LIGHT COUCH, sedan, palanquin, palankeen, doolie, wagon

E3 tidy

little *adj, adv, n*

♦ *adj*

1 SMALL, short, tiny, minute, diminutive, miniature, infinitesimal, mini, microscopic, petite, baby, midget, dwarf, Lilliputian, slender, slight, younger, junior

COLLOQ. wee, teeny, pint-size(d)

2 SHORT-LIVED, brief, short, fleeting passing momentary, transient, transitory

FORMAL ephemeral

3 INSUFFICIENT, sparse, scant, meagre, paltry, skimpy

FORMAL exiguous

4 INSIGNIFICANT, unimportant, inconsiderable, negligible, trivial, petty, minor, paltry, nominal, trifling

FORMAL nugatory

COLLOQ. peanuts

Types of literature include:

Aga saga	classic novel	fiction	novel	postil	steampunk
allegory	crime fiction	Gothic novel	novelization	prose	thesis
anti-novel	criticism	graphic novel	novella	pulp fiction	thriller
autobiography	dirty realism	hint fiction	parody	roman à clef	tragedy
formal	drama	historical novel	pastiche	roman novel	travelogue
belles-lettres	epic	horror	*colloq.* penny	saga	travel writing
Bildungsroman	epistle	interactive fiction	dreadful	satire	treatise
biography	epistolary novel	lampoon	picaresque	science	triad
colloq.	essay	libretto	novel	fiction	trilogy
bodice-ripper	*colloq.* fanfic	magnum opus	poetry	*colloq.*	verse
colloq. chick lit	fan fiction	misery memoir	polemic	sex-and-shopping	
children's literature	fantasy	non-fiction	police procedural	slash fiction	

See also **poem**; **story**.

5 *a nice little house*
pleasant, attractive, nice, sweet, cute
E3 1 big **2** long lengthy **3** ample **4** considerable, serious
♦ *adv*
barely, hardly, scarcely, slightly, faintly, rarely, seldom, infrequently, not much, next to nothing a drop in the ocean
E3 frequently
♦ *n*
bit, dash, pinch, small amount, spot, trace, drop, dab, speck, touch, taste, soupçon, smattering particle, hint, fragment, modicum, trifle, trickle; *N Am, Aust & NZ dialect* skerrick
E3 lot

■ **little by little**
gradually, bit by bit, progressively, slowly, step by step, by degrees, imperceptibly, piecemeal
E3 all at one go, quickly

> **PROVERBS**
> Many a little makes a mickle

liturgical *adj*
ceremonial, ritual, solemn, sacramental, formal, eucharistic
FORMAL sacerdotal, hieratic
E3 secular

liturgy *n*
service, office, form, formula, rite, usage, worship, ceremony, ritual, observance, sacrament, ordinance, celebration

live[1] *v*
1 BE, be alive, have life, exist, breathe, draw breath
2 LAST, endure, continue, remain, persist, stay, survive, support yourself, earn your living
FORMAL abide
3 *live in Leeds*
have your home, be settled, inhabit, lodge, stay, squat
FORMAL reside, abide, dwell
4 PASS, spend, lead, experience, undergo, behave
FORMAL comport, conduct
5 *live while you're young*
enjoy life, enjoy yourself, have fun, enjoy life to the full, see life, make the most of your life
COLLOQ. live it up
E3 1 die **2** cease

■ **live it up**
revel, celebrate, live extravagantly, go on a spree
COLLOQ. have a ball, make merry, make whoopee, push the boat out, paint the town red

■ **live on**
live on fruit and vegetables
feed, live off, depend for nourishment, rely on, exist
FORMAL subsist on

live[2] *adj*
1 ALIVE, living having life, existent, breathing animate
2 LIVELY, vital, active, energetic, dynamic, alert, vigorous
3 BURNING, glowing blazing flaming hot, red hot, ignited, alight
4 *a live appearance*
personal, in person, in the flesh, bodily, public
5 *a live TV programme*
not prerecorded, not recorded, real-time, with an audience
6 *live cables*
connected, charged, electrified, electrically charged, active
7 *a live bomb*
unexploded, explosive, unstable, volatile
8 *a live issue*
relevant, current, topical, controversial, active, important, vital, lively, urgent, pressing
FORMAL pertinent
COLLOQ. hot
E3 1 dead **2** apathetic **5** prerecorded **6** disconnected **7** defused **8** irrelevant

■ **live wire**
self-starter

COLLOQ. life and soul of the party; ball of fire, dynamo, go-getter, eager beaver, whizz kid
E3 wet blanket

liveable, livable *adj*
1 INHABITABLE, habitable
2 BEARABLE, tolerable, supportable, comfortable, endurable, acceptable, adequate, satisfactory, worthwhile
E3 1 uninhabitable **2** unbearable

■ **liveable with**
companionable, sociable, *gemütlich*, compatible, congenial, harmonious, passable, tolerable, bearable
E3 impossible, unbearable

livelihood *n*
occupation, employment, job, work, profession, trade, living means of living means, means of support, income, source of income, maintenance, daily bread, existence, support, subsistence, sustenance, upkeep, keep
OLD livelod, livelood, livelihead
COLLOQ. bread-and-butter, crust

liveliness *n*
animation, energy, quickness, spirit, life, vigour, vitality, vivacity, vivaciousness, dynamism, activity, boisterousness, briskness, smartness, sprightliness, refreshment, *esprit*, *entrain*
OLD livelihead
COLLOQ. brio, oomph, pizzazz
E3 apathy, inactivity

livelong *adj*
complete, entire, full, whole, enduring long protracted
E3 partial

lively *adj*
1 ANIMATED, alert, active, energetic, alive, spirited, high-spirited, enthusiastic, dynamic, vivacious, vigorous, sprightly, brisk, spry, agile, nimble, quick, keen; *dialect* wick
2 CHEERFUL, blithe, merry, frisky, perky, playful, ludic, jaunty, breezy, frolicsome, buoyant
COLLOQ. chirpy, bouncy
3 *a lively discussion*
animated, enthusiastic, heated, interesting exciting stimulating vigorous
4 BUSY, bustling quick, brisk, rapid, crowded, eventful, vibrant, exciting buzzing teeming swarming hectic
5 VIVID, bright, strong colourful, graphic, striking vibrant, exciting imaginative, stimulating stirring invigorating racy, refreshing sparkling
E3 1 moribund, apathetic **3** dull **4** inactive **5** dull

liven *v*
enliven, vitalize, put life into, rouse, invigorate, animate, energize, brighten, stir (up), spice (up), cheer (up)
COLLOQ. buck up, pep up, perk up, hot up, jazz up
E3 dishearten

liverish *adj*
irritable, snappy, testy, tetchy, crusty, grumpy, disagreeable, ill-humoured, quick-tempered, irascible, peevish, splenetic
COLLOQ. crabbed, crabby, crotchety
E3 calm, easy-going

livery *n*
uniform, costume, regalia, dress, clothes, clothing garments, vestments, suit, garb, habit
FORMAL apparel, attire, habiliments
COLLOQ. get-up, gear, clobber, togs

livid *adj*
1 ANGRY, furious, infuriated, irate, outraged, enraged, raging seething fuming indignant, incensed, exasperated
COLLOQ. mad
2 LEADEN, black-and-blue, blue, bruised, discoloured, greyish, purple, purplish; *Scot* blae
3 PALE, deathly pale, pallid, ashen, blanched, white, bloodless, wan, waxy, ghastly, pasty
OLD Hippocratic
E3 1 calm

living *adj, n*
+ *adj*
1 ALIVE, breathing existing live, animate
2 CURRENT, surviving continuing active, operative, in use, strong vigorous, lively, vital, animated
FORMAL extant
COLLOQ. going strong
3 *a living likeness*
close, exact, identical, precise, faithful, true, genuine
F3 **1** dead **2** dead, sluggish **3** inexact
+ *n*
1 BEING, life, animation, existence
2 LIVELIHOOD, maintenance, support, means of living/support, income, source of income, subsistence, daily bread, sustenance, work, job, occupation, profession, trade, way of life, lifestyle
TECHNICAL benefice
COLLOQ. bread, bread-and-butter, crust

living room *n*
lounge, sitting room, drawing room, day room, front room, reception room, parlour

load *n, v*
+ *n*
1 CARGO, consignment, shipment, goods, lading, freight, contents, burden, charge
2 BURDEN, onus, responsibility, duty, obligation, commitment, encumbrance, weight, pressure, charge, trouble, worry, strain, oppression, millstone, albatross
FORMAL tribulation
3 *loads of money*
a lot, lots, large amount, great deal, heaps, dozens, scores, hundreds, thousands, a million, millions, gazillions, hordes, tons
COLLOQ. masses, piles, stacks, bucketloads, shedloads, lashings, oodles, scads, miles
SLANG shitloads
+ *v*
1 PACK, pile, heap, freight, fill (up), cram, stuff, stack, lade, charge
2 *load a film into a camera*
put (in/into), insert, enter, slide, slot
3 *load a gun*
charge, prime, arm, prepare, equip, fill, plug, prepare to fire
4 BURDEN, weigh down, encumber, overburden, oppress, overwhelm, worry, trouble, weight, strain, tax, saddle with

loaded *adj*
1 BURDENED, charged, laden, full, filled, weighted, packed, piled, heaped, stacked
COLLOQ. snowed under
2 WEIGHTED, biased, to your disadvantage
COLLOQ. fixed, rigged, set up
3 RICH, wealthy, well-off, affluent
COLLOQ. well-heeled, flush, in the money, made of money, on easy street, rolling in it
4 DRUNK, under the influence, drunken, incapable, tipsy, mellow, merry, foxed; *dialect* fairish; *Scot* capernoity, fou; *Scot & Irish* stotious; *N Am* jagged
OLD overseen; (*Shakesp*) fap, paid
FORMAL inebriated, intoxicated, crapulent, ebriose
COLLOQ. a sheet in the wind, three sheets in/to the wind, tight, tiddly, tiddled, well-oiled, blotto, drunk as a lord/newt, drunk as a piper, sloshed, stewed, blind drunk, roaring drunk, the worse for drink, soused, squiffy, happy, legless, plastered, sozzled, pickled, bibulous, woozy, one over the eight, under the table, bevvied, having had a few, tired and emotional, high, footless, full, half-cut, obfuscated, pie-eyed, sow-drunk, under the weather, the worse for wear
OLD COLLOQ corked, moppy, overshot
SLANG stoned, tanked up, lit up, canned, paralytic, smashed, pissed, bombed, wasted, wrecked, trashed, trolleyed, stinko, whiffled, whistled, bonkers, bottled, Brahms and Liszt, juiced (up), in liquor, liquored, maggoty, mortal, up the pole, ripped; arseholed, rat-arsed, shitfaced; *Scot* blootered; *N Am* crocked, moon-eyed; *Aust* inky, inked; *Aust & NZ* shickered

loaf¹ *n*
1 *a loaf of bread*
block, slab, brick, mass, lump, cube, cake
2 *use your loaf*
common sense, sense, head, mind
COLLOQ. brains, gumption, nous, noddle

> **PROVERBS**
> Half a loaf is better than no bread

loaf² *v*
loafing about/around
stand about, idle, laze, loiter
COLLOQ. take it easy, hang around, lounge, lounge around, sit around, lie around, mooch, loll, relax, unwind, veg (out)
SLANG *Aust & NZ* bludge
F3 toil

loafer *n*
idler, shirker, sluggard, wastrel, lounger, ne'er-do-well; *Irish* corner-boy
COLLOQ. slob, layabout, skiver, lazybones
SLANG *N Am* goof-off

loam *n*
earth, soil, clay, sand, core
TECHNICAL brickclay, malm

loan *n, v*
+ *n*
advance, credit, mortgage, allowance, lending
OLD prest
+ *v*
lend, advance, credit, allow, put forth, on-lend, overlend
OLD prest
COLLOQ. sub

loath *adj*
reluctant, unwilling resisting disinclined, opposed, grudging hesitant, indisposed, against
FORMAL averse
F3 willing

loathe *v*
hate, detest, abhor, despise, dislike, not stand, recoil from, have an aversion to, nauseate, feel revulsion at
OLD ug
FORMAL abominate, execrate
F3 adore, love

loathing *n*
hatred, hate, detestation, abhorrence, repugnance, revulsion, repulsion, dislike, contempt, disgust, aversion, odium, ill-will, horror
FORMAL abomination, antipathy, execration
F3 affection, love

loathsome *adj*
detestable, odious, repulsive, hateful, abhorrent, repugnant, repellent, offensive, horrible, disgusting nauseating vile, revolting nasty, obnoxious, despicable, contemptible, disagreeable, abominable
OLD lothefull
FORMAL execrable

lob *v*
throw, toss, hurl, pitch, fling heave, launch, lift, shy, loft
COLLOQ. chuck; *Irish* puck

lobby *v, n*
+ *v*
campaign for, press for, demand, persuade, call for, urge, influence, solicit, pressure, promote
COLLOQ. push for
+ *n*
1 VESTIBULE, foyer, porch, anteroom, hall, hallway, waiting room, entrance hall, entrance, entry, corridor, passage, passageway, box-lobby

2 PRESSURE GROUP, campaign, faction, ginger group, lobbyists

local adj, n
♦ adj
regional, provincial, community, district, neighbourhood, municipal, city, urban, town, village, parish, parochial, vernacular, small-town, limited, narrow, restricted, hyperlocal, parish-pump
E3 national
♦ n
1 INHABITANT, citizen, resident, native
2 PUB, bar, inn, public house, tavern, saloon
COLLOQ. hostelry, watering-hole
SLANG boozer

locale n
place, position, scene, setting site, spot, venue, area, locality, location, neighbourhood, environment, zone
FORMAL locus

locality n
neighbourhood, vicinity, district, area, locale, environment, region, position, place, site, spot, scene, setting surrounding area

localize v
1 IDENTIFY, specify, narrow down, pinpoint, ascribe, assign
COLLOQ. zero in on
2 RESTRAIN, limit, restrict, confine, contain, concentrate, delimit, delimitate
FORMAL circumscribe

locate v
1 FIND, discover, uncover, unearth, come across, track down, detect, pinpoint, identify, spot, pick out, access
COLLOQ. run to earth, lay your hands on, hit upon
2 SITUATE, settle, fix, establish, place, allocate, plant, position, put, lay, set, site, station, seat, build

location n
position, situation, place, whereabouts, venue, site, locale, bearings, spot, point, zone, setting scene
FORMAL locus

loch n
lake, pond, pool, sea, water, reservoir, dam, basin, mere, tarn; *Irish* lough

lock¹ n, v
♦ n
fit locks to windows
fastening bolt, clasp, catch, padlock, mortise lock, combination lock, spring lock, Chubb® lock, Yale® lock
♦ v
1 FASTEN, secure, bolt, latch, bar, seal, shut, padlock
2 JOIN, unite, engage, link, mesh, entangle, entwine, clench, interlock, jam, stick
3 CLASP, hug embrace, grasp, encircle, enclose, clutch, grapple
E3 1 unlock

■ **lock out**
shut out, refuse admittance/entrance to, keep out, exclude, bar, debar

■ **lock up**
imprison, jail, confine, shut in, shut up, put behind bars, put under lock and key, secure, cage, pen, detain, wall in, close up
FORMAL incarcerate
COLLOQ. put away
E3 free

Parts of a lock include:

barrel	dead bolt	key
bolt	escutcheon	key card
cylinder	face plate	keyhole
cylinder hole	hasp	keyway

knob	pin	spindle hole
latch	push button	spring
latch bolt	rose	strike plate
latch follower	sash	staple
latch lever	sash bolt	
mortise bolt	spindle	

---

lock² n
locks of hair
strand, tress, tuft, plait, ringlet, curl

locker n
cupboard, container, cabinet, compartment

lock-up n
1 JAIL, gaol, prison, penitentiary, cell
SLANG can, clink, cooler, jug slammer, quod
2 GARAGE, storeroom, depository, warehouse

locomotion n
movement, motion, moving progress, progression, travel, travelling headway, action, walking
FORMAL ambulation, perambulation

locus n
place, location, position, situation, whereabouts, venue, site, locale, point

locution n
1 STYLE, diction, articulation, accent, intonation, inflection
2 WORDING, term, phrase, phrasing cliché, turn of phrase, expression, idiom, collocation

lodge n, v
♦ n
1 HUT, cabin, cottage, chalet, gatehouse, house, hunting-lodge, box
2 BRANCH, chapter, section, group, club, society, association, meeting-place, habitation, campfire
3 HAUNT, retreat, shelter, nest, lair, den
♦ v
1 ACCOMMODATE, quarter, board, billet, shelter, harbour
OLD inn
COLLOQ. put up
2 LIVE, stay, have your home, be settled, lie, nest, shelter, room, barrack, keep
OLD (*Spenser*) bower; (*Shakesp & Spenser*) host
FORMAL reside, dwell, sojourn
COLLOQ. hang out, dig
3 FIX, imbed, implant, get stuck, get caught
4 DEPOSIT, place, put, put in, hand in, show up, stow, lay, submit, register, bank
5 *lodge a complaint*
register, make, submit, record, file, put forward

lodger n
boarder, paying guest, resident, tenant, roomer, inmate, guest

lodgings n
accommodation, quarters, billet, board, boarding house, rooms, place, bedsit, bedsitter, bedsitting-room
FORMAL dwelling abode, residence
COLLOQ. digs, pad, a roof over your head, flea-bag

loftily adv
proudly, arrogantly, haughtily, disdainfully, superciliously
COLLOQ. snootily
E3 humbly, modestly

lofty adj
1 *lofty ideals*
noble, grand, exalted, esteemed, distinguished, illustrious, majestic, sublime, stately, imposing dignified, imperial, renowned
2 HIGH, tall, sky-high, elevated, raised, towering soaring
OLD (*Shakesp*) skyish
3 ARROGANT, proud, haughty, condescending disdainful, patronizing supercilious, superior, lordly
COLLOQ. snooty, high and mighty, toffee-nosed
E3 2 low **3** humble, lowly, modest

log *n, v*
* *n*

1 TIMBER, trunk, block, chunk, piece
2 RECORD, diary, journal, logbook, daybook, account, tally, register, chart
* *v*

record, register, write up, note, set down, book, chart, tally, file

logbook *n*
log record, diary, journal, daybook, account, tally, register, chart

loggerheads
■ **at loggerheads**
disagreeing in conflict, at odds, in opposition, quarrelling
COLLOQ. at daggers drawn, at each other's throats, like cat and dog

logic *n*
reasoning reason, sense, judgement, deduction, rationale, coherence, argument, argumentation
TECHNICAL dialectics
FORMAL ratiocination

logical *adj*
reasonable, rational, reasoned, well-reasoned, well-founded, well-thought-out, coherent, consistent, relevant, valid, sound, clear, sensible, wise, intelligent, thinking deducible, methodical, consecutive, well-organized
TECHNICAL Boolean, convergent, dialectic, dialectical, syllogistic
FORMAL deductive, inductive, cogent, judicious, sequacious
E3 illogical, irrational

logically *adv*
rationally, coherently, consistently, relevantly, validly, clearly, sensibly, intelligently, methodically, consecutively
TECHNICAL dialectically
FORMAL deductively, inductively

logistics *n*
organization, co-ordination, management, masterminding arrangement, orchestration, strategy, tactics, planning plans, direction, engineering

logo *n*
symbol, sign, trademark, representation, insignia, emblem, device, mark, badge, figure, image

loiter *v*
dawdle, hang about/around, idle, waste time, take your time, linger, dally, delay, mooch, lag saunter
FORMAL tarry
COLLOQ. dilly-dally, loaf, lounge

loll *v*
1 RELAX, slouch, slump, sprawl
FORMAL recline
COLLOQ. loaf, lounge
2 HANG, flop, droop, drop, dangle, flap, sag

lollop *v*
run, lope, bound, spring stride, canter, gallop

lone *adj*
1 BY YOURSELF, single, sole, alone, one, only, isolated, solitary, separate
2 *a lone parent*
by yourself, on your own, single, unmarried, unattached, divorced, separated, without a partner
3 ISOLATED, uninhabited, remote, out-of-the-way, unfrequented, secluded, abandoned, deserted, forsaken, desolate, barren
E3 1 accompanied

loneliness *n*
aloneness, isolation, lonesomeness, solitariness, solitude, seclusion, desolation

lonely *adj*
1 ALONE, friendless, lone, lonesome, solitary, abandoned, forsaken, companionless, reclusive, unaccompanied, destitute, rejected, outcast, sad, unhappy, miserable, wretched

See Synonym nuances panel at **alone**.
2 ISOLATED, uninhabited, remote, out-of-the-way, unfrequented, secluded, abandoned, deserted, forsaken, desolate, barren, god-forsaken
FORMAL solitudinous
COLLOQ. off the beaten track
E3 1 popular, content 2 crowded, populous

loner *n*
individualist, recluse, solitary, hermit, introvert
FORMAL solitudinarian
COLLOQ. lone wolf

lonesome *adj*
1 ALONE, lonely, friendless, lone, solitary, abandoned, forsaken, companionless, reclusive, unaccompanied, destitute, rejected, outcast, sad, unhappy, miserable, wretched
2 ISOLATED, lonely, uninhabited, remote, out-of-the-way, unfrequented, secluded, abandoned, deserted, forsaken, desolate, barren

long *adj, v*
* *adj*
lengthy, extensive, extended, expanded, elongated, prolonged, stretched (out), spread out, sustained, expansive, far-reaching long-drawn-out, verbose, overlong spun out, marathon, interminable, slow
FORMAL protracted, tardy
E3 short, brief, fleeting abbreviated
* *v*
yearn, crave, want, wish, desire, hope, dream, aspire, hanker, pine, thirst, hunger, lust, covet, itch, ache
COLLOQ. yen
■ **before long**
soon, presently, shortly, in a short time, in a moment, in a minute or two, in the near future

long-drawn-out *adj*
lengthy, long-winded, spun out, overlong prolonged, interminable, tedious, marathon, overextended, long-drawn
FORMAL protracted, prolix
COLLOQ. dragging on
E3 brief, curtailed

longing *n, adj*
* *n*
craving desire, yearning hunger, hungering hankering pining thirst, wish, wanting dream, hope, urge, coveting itch, aspiration, ambition
COLLOQ. yen
* *adj*
wishful, eager, craving pining yearning wistful, languishing hungry, anxious, avid, ardent
FORMAL desirous

longingly *adv*
wishfully, eagerly, yearningly, wistfully, anxiously, avidly, ardently
OLD (*Shakesp*) wistly

long-lasting *adj*
permanent, imperishable, enduring unchanging unfading continuing abiding chronic, lingering long-standing prolonged
FORMAL protracted
E3 short-lived, transient; *formal* ephemeral

long-lived *adj*
enduring lasting durable, long-lasting long-standing
TECHNICAL macrobian, macrobiotic
FORMAL longevous
E3 brief, short-lived; *formal* ephemeral

long-standing *adj*
established, long-established, well-established, long-lived, long-lasting enduring abiding time-honoured, traditional

long-suffering *adj*
uncomplaining forbearing forgiving tolerant, indulgent, easy-going patient, stoical, resigned
E3 complaining

long-winded *adj*
lengthy, overlong prolonged, long-drawn-out, diffuse, verbose, wordy, garrulous, discursive, repetitious, rambling tedious
FORMAL prolix, protracted, voluble
E3 brief, terse

long-windedness *n*
lengthiness, verbosity, wordiness, diffuseness, discursiveness, repetitiousness, tediousness, garrulity
FORMAL volubility, prolixity, longueur, macrology
E3 brevity, curtness

loo *n*
toilet, lavatory, WC, bathroom, cloakroom, washroom, gents', ladies', water closet, public convenience, convenience, urinal, latrine, privy, powder room, facilities, Elsan®, Portaloo®; *N Am* rest room, comfort station
COLLOQ. lav, dunny, smallest room, superloo, throne, little boys' room, little girls' room
SLANG bog kazi, crapper; *N Am* john; *Aust* toot

look *v, n*
♦ *v*
1 WATCH, see, take a look, observe, view, survey, regard, gaze, eye, study, stare, examine, inspect, focus, check, take in, consider, scrutinize, glance, contemplate, scan, peep, gape
COLLOQ. gawp, run your eyes over, give the once-over, give a going-over, get a load of, get an eyeful of, take a squint at, take a dekko at, take a gander at, take a butcher's at, take a shufti at; *N Am* eyeball
2 SEEM, appear, give the appearance of, show, exhibit, display
3 *the house looks onto the fields*
face, front, front on, give on (to), overlook, be opposite, look onto
♦ *n*
1 VIEW, survey, inspection, examination, study, contemplation, observation, sight, review, glance, glimpse, stare, gaze, gape, peek, peep
COLLOQ. once-over, squint, eyeful, dekko, gander, butcher's, shufti
SLANG *Aust & NZ* squiz
2 APPEARANCE, aspect, manner, air, effect, impression, semblance, expression, face, guise, features, façade, complexion
FORMAL countenance, mien, bearing

■ **look after**
take care of, mind, care for, attend to, take charge of, maintain, tend, keep an eye on, watch over, nurse, protect, supervise, guard, babysit, sit, childmind
E3 neglect, disregard, ignore

■ **look back**
remember, recall, think back, reminisce, reflect on the past

■ **look down on**
despise, scorn, sneer at, hold in contempt, disdain, spurn, think of as inferior/unimportant, patronize, talk down to, act/speak condescendingly
FORMAL disparage
COLLOQ. look down your nose at, turn your nose up at, pooh-pooh
E3 esteem, approve

■ **look for**
try to find, search for, seek, quest, hunt for, hunt out, forage for

■ **look forward to**
anticipate, await, expect, hope for, long for, envisage, envision, count on, wait for, look for

■ **look into**
investigate, probe, research, study, go into, search into, examine, inquire about, ask about, explore, inspect, scrutinize, look over, plumb, fathom, dig delve
COLLOQ. check out

■ **look like**
resemble, take after, be similar (in appearance) to, have the appearance of, remind you of

■ **look on/upon**
consider, regard, think, judge, count, hold
FORMAL deem

■ **look out**
pay attention, watch out, beware, be careful, be alert, be on your guard, guard yourself, keep your eyes open/peeled/skinned, be on the qui vive, keep an eye out, look/mind where you're going

■ **look over**
inspect, examine, check, cast an/your eye over, look through, go through, scan, read through, view, monitor
COLLOQ. check out, give a once-over

■ **look to**
1 *look to your parents for support*
turn to, reckon on, rely on, count on, resort to, fall back on
2 *look to the future*
consider, think about, give thought to, anticipate, await

■ **look up**
1 SEARCH FOR, research, seek, consult, hunt for, find, track down
2 VISIT, call on, drop in on, look in on, pay a visit to, stop by, drop by
3 IMPROVE, get better, pick up, progress, make progress, develop, advance, make headway, come on/along
FORMAL ameliorate
COLLOQ. perk up

■ **look up to**
admire, respect, regard highly, esteem, revere, honour, have a high opinion of, think highly of

> **PROVERBS**
> Look before you leap

> **SYNONYM NUANCES**
>
> *verb sense 1*
> **Watch**, **view**, **observe**, **take in** and **regard** can be used to suggest prolonged, attentive looking. **Survey**, however, suggests a sweeping movement of the eyes to see everything: *surveying the landscape from the cliff top*, while **scan** also suggests quickly running the eyes over, but often to pick out something specific: *he scanned the rows of seats to see if she was there*. **Study**, **examine**, **scrutinize** and **inspect** share the idea of a close and lengthy look for the purpose of assessment and appraisal.
>
> The terms **consider** and **contemplate** can be used to suggest weighing up what is seen: *I contemplated the scene of carnage before me*. **Gaze**, on the other hand, can imply an element of abstraction, or even stupefaction: *he gazed at the wall*, while **gape** suggests wide-eyed amazement: *they gaped at her as if she were an alien*. A different implication is made with **eye**, which suggests looking with a degree of suspicion: *they eyed the stranger*, while **focus** has more to do with deliberately directing your eyes: *I focused on the incident unfolding in the street below*.
>
> The verb **check** suggests a quick movement seeking confirmation: *he checked his watch*, while **glance** is suggestive of a short but more uninterested glimpse: *he just glanced at the photos*, and **peep** suggests taking a surreptitious look: *neighbours peeping through the curtains*.

lookalike *n*
double, replica, twin, image, living image, exact likeness, clone, *doppelgänger*
COLLOQ. spitting image, spit, (dead) ringer

lookout n

1 GUARD, sentry, watch, watch-tower, watchman, sentinel, tower, post, observation post
2 CONCERN, responsibility, worry, affair, business, problem
COLLOQ. pigeon

■ **keep a lookout**
remain alert, watch, keep guard, be vigilant, be on the qui vive

loom v

appear, emerge, take shape, become visible, menace, threaten, impend, be imminent, hang over, dominate, tower, overhang rise, soar, mount, overshadow, overtop

loony adj, n

♦ adj
mad, crazy, insane, lunatic, unbalanced, disturbed, deranged, demented, crazed, wild, berserk, frantic, unhinged, distracted, distraught, maniac, eccentric, strange, silly, foolish, idiotic, stupid
COLLOQ. daft, loopy, barmy, potty, bonkers, nutty
♦ n
madman, madwoman, lunatic, psychotic, psychopath, maniac, imbecile
COLLOQ. nutter, nut, crackpot, crank, headcase, nutcase, fruitcake, screwball, oddball, basket case; N Am hook
SLANG psycho

loop n, v

♦ n
hoop, ring circle, noose, coil, eye, eyelet, loophole, spiral, curve, curl, oval, kink, twist, whorl, twirl, turn, bend, runner, sling stitch, tab, purl, hank, knop, lug grommet, picot
TECHNICAL becket, cannon, jubilee clip
OLD latchet
FORMAL convolution
♦ v
coil, encircle, surround, roll, bend, circle, curve round, turn, curl, twist, spiral, wind, connect, join, tie, knot, fasten, fold, braid

loophole n

let-out, escape, omission, escape clause, evasion, excuse, pretext, plea, ambiguity, pretence, mistake
COLLOQ. get-out

loose adj, v

♦ adj
1 FREE, unfastened, untied, at large, unconfined, released, undone, untethered, uncoupled, unlocked, let go, escaped, off, movable, unattached, insecure, wobbly, unsteady
2 SLACK, lax, baggy, hanging loose-fitting sagging flowing shapeless, unbound, untied
3 IMPRECISE, vague, inexact, ill-defined, indefinite, inaccurate, indistinct, general, broad, rambling
4 *loose morals*
promiscuous, dissolute, lax, unchaste, fast, debauched, disreputable, immoral, corrupt, wanton, degenerate, abandoned
E3 **1** firm, fixed, secure **2** tight, fitting **3** exact, precise, specific, literal **4** chaste, pure
♦ v
1 RELEASE, set free, free, let go, liberate, loosen, unbind, unclasp, unfasten, untie, disconnect, disengage, detach, unleash, unhook, uncouple, undo, unlock, unmoor, unpen
2 RELAX, slacken, ease, moderate, lessen, loosen, weaken, diminish, reduce
E3 **1** bind, fasten, fix, secure **2** tighten

■ **at a loose end**
with nothing to do, bored, out of action, idle, aimless, purposeless, off duty
COLLOQ. fed up, twiddling your thumbs, with time to kill

■ **on the loose**
escaped, at large, on the run, free, at liberty, unconfined

loosely adv

1 FREELY, insecurely, unsteadily, movably
2 SLACKLY, baggily, shapelessly
3 IMPRECISELY, inexactly, vaguely, inaccurately, generally, broadly
E3 **1** firmly, securely **2** tightly **3** exactly, precisely, specifically

loosen v

1 EASE, relax, loose, slacken, moderate, weaken, diminish, undo, unbind, untie, unfasten
2 FREE, set free, release, let go, set loose, let out, deliver
E3 **1** tighten

■ **loosen up**
1 RELAX, unwind, let up, go easy, lessen, ease up
COLLOQ. hang loose, cool it, chill out
2 LIMBER UP, warm up, warm down, work out, exercise, prepare

loot n, v

♦ n
spoils, booty, plunder, stolen money, stolen goods, pickings, riches, haul, prize
COLLOQ. swag
♦ v
steal (from), plunder, pillage, rob, burgle, sack, rifle, raid, maraud, ransack, ravage
FORMAL despoil

lop v

chop, cut (off), dock, prune, sever, trim, clip, crop, hack, shorten, curtail, detach, remove, take off, reduce, truncate

lope v

run, lollop, bound, spring stride, canter, gallop

lopsided adj

asymmetrical, unbalanced, askew, off balance, uneven, unequal, crooked, squint, tilting sloping slanted, one-sided
COLLOQ. skew-whiff
E3 balanced, symmetrical

loquacious adj

talkative, chatty, chattering babbling blathering gossipy, wordy, garrulous
FORMAL voluble, multiloquent, multiloquous
COLLOQ. gabby, gassy
E3 succinct, taciturn, terse, reserved

loquacity n

talkativeness, chattiness, garrulity, effusiveness
FORMAL volubility, multiloquence, multiloquy
COLLOQ. gassiness
E3 succinctness, taciturnity, terseness

lord n

1 PEER, noble, nobleman, earl, duke, count, viscount, baron, aristocrat, patrician
2 MASTER, ruler, superior, overlord, leader, chief, captain, commander, governor, king prince, sovereign, monarch, emperor
3 *God, the Lord*
God, Creator, Maker, King Almighty, Holy One, Jehovah, Yahweh, Father, Eternal, Christ, Jesus Christ, Messiah, the Word, Redeemer, Saviour, Son of God, Son of Man, King of kings

■ **lord it over**
domineer, tyrannize, be overbearing order around, queen it over, oppress, repress, pull rank, swagger
FORMAL put on airs
OLD (*Shakesp*) overoffice
COLLOQ. act big throw your weight around, boss around

lordliness n

1 NOBLENESS, magnificence, splendidness, majesty, grandness, imperiality, impressiveness
2 PRIDE, arrogance, disdain, imperiousness, haughtiness, condescension, superciliousness, high-handedness, overconfidence
COLLOQ. big-headedness
E3 **1** lowliness **2** humility

lordly *adj*
1 NOBLE, dignified, aristocratic, magnificent, splendid, majestic, grand, grandiose, stately, imperial, impressive, lofty
2 PROUD, arrogant, disdainful, haughty, imperious, condescending patronizing supercilious, dictatorial, high-handed, domineering overbearing overconfident
FORMAL peremptory, hubristic
COLLOQ. big-headed, stuck-up, high and mighty, uppity, toffee-nosed, hoity-toity, too big for your boots
F3 **1** lowly **2** humble

lore *n*
knowledge, wisdom, learning scholarship, traditions, folklore, teaching beliefs, legends, stories, sayings, superstitions, myths, mythology
FORMAL erudition

lorry *n*
truck, trailer, articulated lorry, pantechnicon, removal van, vehicle, wagon, juggernaut, pick-up, float

lose *v*
1 MISLAY, misplace, forget, miss, not find, forfeit, drop
2 FAIL, fall short, suffer defeat, be defeated, be beaten, be conquered, go down, be unsuccessful
COLLOQ. come to grief, come a cropper, throw in the towel
3 ELUDE, escape from, evade, throw off, shake off, leave behind, outrun
4 BE DEPRIVED OF, no longer have, stop having
have taken away, be bereaved of, be dispossessed of, be divested of
5 *lose an opportunity*
not take advantage of, fail to grasp, neglect, miss, disregard, ignore, waste, squander, fritter
6 *lose your way*
wander from, stray from, depart from, go astray, get lost, lose your bearings
7 WASTE, squander, spend, consume, use up, exhaust, expend, drain
FORMAL dissipate, deplete
F3 **1** find, keep, gain **2** win **5** grasp, take advantage of **6** find **7** make
■ **lose out**
suffer, miss out, be unsuccessful, be beaten, be at a disadvantage, be disadvantaged
■ **lose yourself in something**
be absorbed in, be preoccupied in, be occupied in, be taken up with, be engrossed in, be fascinated by, be enthralled by, be captivated by, be riveted by

loser *n*
failure, runner-up, the defeated
COLLOQ. also-ran, flop, no-hoper, washout, non-starter, write-off, has-been, dead loss
F3 winner

loss *n*
1 MISLAYING, misplacement, missing forfeiture, forgetting dropping
2 DEPRIVATION, disappearance, bereavement, dispossession, disadvantage, harm, hurt, impairment, undoing waste
FORMAL privation
3 *losses in war*
casualty, fatality, death toll, dead, missing wounded
4 *the business made a loss*
deficit, debt, deficiency
F3 **1** finding **2** gain **4** profit
■ **at a loss**
puzzled, perplexed, bewildered, baffled, mystified, not knowing what to do/say

lost *adj*
1 MISLAID, missing vanished, disappeared, misplaced, stray, astray, strayed, disoriented, disorientated, off course
2 CONFUSED, disoriented, bewildered, puzzled, baffled, perplexed, nonplussed, at a loss

3 WASTED, squandered, ruined, destroyed, wrecked, demolished, neglected, missed, frittered away, unrecoverable
4 *a lost civilization*
past, dead, defunct, extinct, bygone, former, long-forgotten, vanished, untraceable
5 *lost souls*
damned, fallen, condemned, doomed, cursed, irredeemable
6 *lost in thought*
absorbed, preoccupied, occupied, taken up with, engrossed, fascinated, enthralled, captivated, riveted, spellbound, absent-minded, dreamy
F3 **1** found
■ **lost cause**
hopeless case, hopeless situation, hopeless person
COLLOQ. also-ran, flop, no-hoper, washout, non-starter, write-off, has-been, dead loss

lot *n*
1 *lots of food; a lot of people*
large amount, great number, many, a quantity, a good/great deal
COLLOQ. oodles, tons, loads, bucketloads, shedloads, masses, heaps, piles, stacks, lashings, scads, dozens, hundreds, thousands, millions, miles; *N Am* gobs
SLANG shitloads
2 COLLECTION, batch, bundle, assortment, quantity, group, set, consignment, crowd, gathering
COLLOQ. bunch, shower
3 SHARE, portion, allowance, ration, quota, percentage, part, piece, parcel
COLLOQ. cut
4 *content with your lot in life*
destiny, fate, fortune, luck, circumstances, situation
FORMAL portion
5 PLOT, allotment, parcel, piece of land, piece of ground; *S Afr* erf
■ **a lot**
much, to a great extent/degree, a great deal, often, frequently, for a long time
■ **throw in your lot with**
join forces with, align yourself with, team up with, combine with, pitch in, take part in
COLLOQ. muck in

lotion *n*
ointment, balm, balsam, cream, salve, emollient, embrocation, liniment, cleanser, wash, hairdressing sunscreen, toner, aftershave, astringent, witch-hazel, blackwash, fomentation
TECHNICAL collyrium
OLD arquebusade, lavatory

lottery *n*
1 DRAW, raffle, sweepstake, bingo, tombola, gambling game, lotto
2 SPECULATION, venture, risk, gamble, chance, hazard, luck; *N Am* crapshoot

loud *adj*
1 NOISY, deafening booming resounding resonant, reverberating roaring ear-piercing ear-splitting piercing penetrating thundering blaring clamorous, insistent, emphatic, vehement, vociferous, strident, shrill, raucous, rowdy, aggressive, brazen, loud-mouthed, full-mouthed
FORMAL stentorian
2 GARISH, gaudy, glaring flashy, flamboyant, brash, showy, bold, obtrusive, ostentatious, tasteless, vulgar
COLLOQ. flash
F3 **1** quiet, soft **2** subdued, subtle

SYNONYM NUANCES

sense 1
Noisy is mildly disapproving in tone in that it suggests anyone or anything that is creating too much sound, while **deafening** goes further by making the negative suggestion that such a din affects your ears. **Booming,**

resounding, **reverberating** and **resonant** have more to do with the quality of the loudness, in this instance a deep echoing sound: *a booming baritone voice*, while **roaring** and **thundering** similarly emphasize certain qualities in the sound, but again suggest great volume. **Blaring**, like deafening implies excessive volume, with further implications of harshness: *blaring car radios*.

The terms **ear-piercing**, **ear-splitting**, **piercing** and **penetrating**, as well as **strident** and **shrill**, convey the notion of exceedingly high-pitched and jarring noise, whereas **raucous** is suggestive of loud, harsh voices: *raucous cheering*. **Rowdy**, on the other hand, is more suggestive of the loudness that comes with being disorderly: *rowdy football fans*. Terms such as **clamorous**, **insistent**, **vehement** and **vociferous** also focus on the cause of loud noise, and have to do with a persistent and disturbing outcry: *clamorous criticism of capital punishment; a vociferous protest*.

loudly *adv*
noisily, strongly, deafeningly, resoundingly, clamorously, vehemently, shrilly, vigorously, uproariously, vociferously, lustily, stridently, at the top of your voice
TECHNICAL fortissimo
FORMAL streperously, strepitantly
F3 quietly, softly

loudmouth *n*
boaster, braggart, brag blusterer, braggadocio, swaggerer
COLLOQ. windbag gasbag big mouth, blowhard

loud-mouthed *adj*
noisy, aggressive, bold, brazen, boasting blustering bragging coarse, vulgar

lounge *v, n*
◆ *v*
relax, loll (about), idle, laze, waste time, kill time, lie about/around, sprawl, recline, lie back, slump
FORMAL repose
COLLOQ. take it easy
◆ *n*
sitting room, living room, drawing room, day room, reception room, front room, parlour

lour, lower *v*
1 DARKEN, blacken, cloud over, threaten, menace, loom, impend, be brewing
2 SCOWL, frown, glare, glower
COLLOQ. give a dirty look, look daggers

louring lowering *adj*
menacing threatening forbidding ominous, grim, impending foreboding gloomy, cloudy, overcast, dark, darkening grey, black, heavy

lousy *adj*
1 BAD, rotten, poor, second-rate, no good, inferior, unsatisfactory, inadequate, contemptible, miserable, low
COLLOQ. awful, terrible, mingy, rop(e)y, pathetic, rubbish
SLANG crap, pants
2 ILL, unwell, sick, poorly, off-colour, seedy, queasy
COLLOQ. awful, rough, rotten, out of sorts, under the weather, below par
F3 1 excellent, superb **2** well, fine

lout *n*
oaf, boor, dolt, barbarian, yahoo, gawk, lubber, calf, bull-calf, hob, lob, hallion, lumpkin, chuckle-head; *dialect* loblolly, swad; *Scot* coof, cuif; *N Am* jake
OLD (*Spenser*) loord
COLLOQ. clod, clodhopper, hick, hobbledehoy, slob, yob, yobbo, bumpkin, oik; *N Am* roughneck; *Aust* hoon

loutish *adj*
uncouth, oafish, boorish, doltish, ill-mannered, ill-bred, gawky, rude, coarse, rough, crude, vulgar, churlish, unmannerly, unrefined, uncivilized, gruff, impolite, rustic, uneducated, ignorant
COLLOQ. clodhopping yobbish
F3 polite, refined, cultured, genteel

lovable, loveable *adj*
adorable, endearing winsome, appealing captivating enchanting bewitching taking dear, charming engaging attractive, fetching sweet, lovely, pleasing delightful, lik(e)able, cute
F3 detestable, hateful

love *v, n*
◆ *v*
1 *he loves his wife*
be fond of, like very much, adore, cherish, dote on, treasure, hold dear, be attracted to, feel affection for, be devoted to, care for, prize, desire, long for, be infatuated with, idolize, worship, think the world of, mean the world to someone
COLLOQ. be mad on, be sweet on, be daft/nuts on, be sold on, have a crush on
SLANG have the hots for
2 *I love macaroons*
take pleasure in, enjoy, delight in, like very much, appreciate, desire, fancy, have a liking for, be partial to, savour, relish
F3 detest, hate
◆ *n*
1 FONDNESS, affection, adoration, attachment, care, regard, concern, compassion, liking amorousness, ardour, intimacy, desire, devotion, adulation, passion, rapture, tenderness, warmth, inclination, infatuation, lust, delight, enjoyment, weakness, taste, friendship, brotherhood, sympathy, kindness, *tendresse*
COLLOQ. soft spot
Related adjective: amatory
2 *a love of power*
pleasure, enjoyment, delight, liking appreciation, weakness, partiality, relish
COLLOQ. soft spot
3 *come here, my love*
darling beloved, dear, dear one, dearest, favourite, sweetheart, honey, angel, pet, treasure, poppet, precious; *Irish* machree, mavourneen, acushla, asthore
COLLOQ. sweetie, sugar
F3 1 hate, hatred, dislike **2** detestation, loathing
■ **love affair**
affair, romance, liaison, relationship, love, intrigue, passion
OLD amour
COLLOQ. fling carry-on
■ **fall in love with**
fall for, become infatuated with, burn with passion for, take to, lose your heart to
COLLOQ. fall head over heels in love with, have a thing for, fancy, be crazy about, have a crush on, take a shine to, have it bad
■ **in love with**
attracted to, smitten, sweet/soft on, besotted, charmed, doting enamoured, infatuated
COLLOQ. mad/crazy/wild about, have a crush on, hooked, nuts about, potty about, stuck on
■ **make love**
have sex with
COLLOQ. sleep with, sleep together, go to bed with
SLANG have it off with, get your leg over, bang bonk; (*taboo*) fuck, screw, shag; *N Am* make out

---

QUOTATIONS

But love's a malady without a cure
  JOHN DRYDEN, *Palamon and Arcite*

But love is blind, and lovers cannot see / The pretty follies that themselves commit
  WILLIAM SHAKESPEARE, *The Merchant of Venice*

SYNONYM NUANCES

verb sense 1
Be fond of and **care for** can be used to suggest a cosy, fairly mild affection, whereas **dote on** implies an excessive, even foolish, love: *being an only child, her*

parents doted on her. **Be devoted to** is also suggestive of deep attachment, often with a degree of subservience, while **adore** could refer to extreme love, with implications of reverence: *she adored her son, and admired everything he did.* **Idolize** and **worship** give emphasis to this idea of reverence and exaltation: *the doctor was worshipped by the islanders.*

You can use **treasure** and **prize** to suggest placing a high value on someone or something while **cherish** and **hold dear** also suggest a high estimation, as well as protectiveness: *she cherished her cat and looked after her well.* **Desire** and **long for**, on the other hand, suggest a yearning unfulfilled love, while **be infatuated with** has implications of obsession, and perhaps also of being short-lived: *he was infatuated with Marilyn for a time, seeing all her films.*

loveless *adj*
cold, cold-hearted, hard, icy, insensitive, unresponsive, unloved, unloving passionless, unfeeling unfriendly, unappreciated, friendless, disliked, frigid, forsaken, unvalued, heartless, uncherished
F3 passionate

lovelorn *adj*
infatuated, desiring longing pining yearning languishing lovesick, unrequited in love

lovely *adj*
1 ATTRACTIVE, beautiful, charming delightful, enchanting pleasing pleasant, good-looking pretty, handsome, fair, adorable, sweet, winning exquisite
2 MARVELLOUS, wonderful, enjoyable, pleasing pleasant, delightful, agreeable
F3 1 ugly, hideous **2** unpleasant, disagreeable

lovemaking *n*
sexual intercourse, intercourse, sex, sexual relations, sexual union, copulation, intimacy, sleeping with someone, going to bed with someone, foreplay, mating
OLD embraces
FORMAL carnal knowledge, coition, coitus, congress
SLANG lay, pussy, rumpy-pumpy, tail, bonk, bang quickie; (*taboo*) fuck, screw, shag; *N Am* making out

lover *n*
1 BELOVED, loved one, admirer, boyfriend, man friend, girlfriend, woman friend, lady friend, date, sweetheart, partner, live-in partner, suitor, mistress, lady love, fiancé(e), other man, other woman, significant other
COLLOQ. flame, bit on the side, bird, fella, toy boy
2 ENTHUSIAST, devotee, admirer, fan, supporter, follower, fanatic
COLLOQ. buff, freak, fiend

lovesick *adj*
infatuated, desiring longing pining yearning languishing lovelorn, unrequited in love

loving *adj*
amorous, affectionate, devoted, doting fond, adoring ardent, passionate, warm, warmhearted, kind, tender, caring friendly, sympathetic
OLD lovely; (*Shakesp*) beloving

lovingly *adv*
affectionately, fondly, tenderly, ardently, passionately, sympathetically, warmly

low[1] *adj, n*
♦ *adj*
1 SHORT, small, squat, stunted, little, shallow
2 INADEQUATE, insufficient, deficient, poor, sparse, scarce, inferior, unsatisfactory, meagre, paltry, trifling scant, scanty, little, insignificant, reduced
3 *low land*
close to the ground, sea-level, ground-level, low-lying depressed, deep, sunken, flat
4 LOWLY, humble, low-born, obscure, poor, plebeian, plain, simple, common, modest, ordinary, inferior, junior,

low-ranking peasant, meek, mild, mean, submissive, subordinate, unimportant
5 *have a low opinion of someone*
poor, unfavourable, bad, negative, adverse, hostile, opposing antagonistic
6 *low notes*
deep, low-pitched, bass, resonant, sonorous, rich
7 *low achiever*
unintelligent, foolish, slow, dull, mediocre, inadequate, deficient, below standard
8 UNHAPPY, depressed, down, downcast, gloomy, low-spirited, miserable, despondent, sad, downhearted, disheartened, glum
FORMAL disconsolate
COLLOQ. down in the dumps, blue, fed up, cheesed off
9 BASE, coarse, vulgar, bad, evil, wicked, mean, contemptible, nasty, despicable, dishonourable, depraved, immoral, obscene, indecent, smutty
OLD dastardly
FORMAL heinous
10 CHEAP, inexpensive, reasonable, moderate, modest, reduced, slashed, sale, rock-bottom
COLLOQ. a snip, a steal, going for a song dirt-cheap, dog-cheap, ten a penny
11 SUBDUED, muted, soft, quiet, quietened, gentle, hushed, muffled, whispered
F3 1, 2, 3 high **4** high, important **5** high, good **6** high **8** cheerful, happy **9** honourable, decent **10** high, exorbitant **11** loud, noisy
♦ *n*
all-time low, lowest point, nadir, bottom, low point, low-watermark
F3 high

low[2] *v*
cattle lowing
bellow, moo

low-born *adj*
humble, poor, mean-born, plebeian, unexalted, lowly, low-ranking peasant, obscure
F3 high-born, noble

lowbrow *adj*
ignorant, uncultivated, uncultured, unrefined, uneducated, unlearned, unscholarly, unlettered, mass-market, downmarket, tabloid, crude, rude
F3 highbrow, intellectual

lowdown *n, adj*
♦ *n*
information, news, facts, data, inside information, inside story, intelligence
COLLOQ. dope, gen, info
♦ *adj*
despicable, contemptible, vile, worthless, detestable, disgusting mean, degrading wretched, disgraceful, disreputable, shameful, abominable, loathsome, reprobate
OLD dastardly, caitiff
FORMAL reprehensible
F3 admirable, noble

lower[1] *adj, v*
♦ *adj*
1 *the lower jaw*
under, bottom, undermost, nether
2 INFERIOR, lesser, subordinate, secondary, minor, second-class, low-level, lowly, junior
F3 1 upper **2** higher
♦ *v*
1 DROP, depress, sink, descend, let down, let fall, move down, take down
2 REDUCE, decrease, cut, lessen, diminish, curtail, slash, bring down, cow, cheapen
FORMAL abate
3 *lower your eyes*
look down, move downwards, set down, bring low
4 *lower your voice*
speak (more) quietly, quieten, hush

5 *not lower yourself by doing something*
debase, belittle, degrade, demean, disgrace, dishonour, abase
FORMAL disparage
E3 1 raise **2** increase **3** raise

lower²
see **lour, lower.**

lowering
see **louring, lowering.**

low-grade *adj*
bad, inferior, poor, poor-quality, substandard, below standard, second-class, second-rate, third-rate, cheap-jack
COLLOQ. not up to scratch, awful, terrible, botched, lousy, crummy, pathetic, rop(e)y, useless, a load of rubbish, a load of garbage
SLANG the pits, pants, poxy, naff, crappy; (*vulgar*) a load of crap/shit
E3 good, quality

low-key *adj*
muted, quiet, restrained, subdued, understated, easy-going relaxed, subtle, slight, soft
E3 showy, impressive

lowliness *n*
humility, modesty, ordinariness, inferiority, meekness, mildness, submissiveness, simplicity, commonness, poverty, obscurity, unimportance, subordinateness
E3 nobility

lowly *adj*
humble, low-born, obscure, poor, plebeian, plain, simple, common, modest, ordinary, inferior, junior, low-ranking peasant, meek, mild, mean, submissive, subordinate, unimportant
OLD base
E3 lofty, noble, pretentious

low-pitched *adj*
deep, low, bass, resonant, sonorous, rich
E3 high, high-pitched

low-spirited *adj*
depressed, gloomy, heavy-hearted, low, down, downhearted, despondent, dejected, discouraged, sad, unhappy, miserable, moody, glum
COLLOQ. fed up, cheesed off, down in the dumps
E3 high-spirited, cheerful

loyal *adj*
true, faithful, steadfast, staunch, devoted, constant, firm, unchanging trustworthy, true-hearted, trusty, reliable, dependable, dedicated, committed, sincere, supportive, well-affected, patriotic
OLD feal, leal
E3 disloyal, treacherous

loyalty *n*
allegiance, faithfulness, fidelity, devotion, dedication, commitment, staunchness, steadfastness, constancy, trustworthiness, reliability, dependability, sincerity, patriotism
OLD fealty, lealty
E3 disloyalty, treachery

> QUOTATIONS
> An ounce of loyalty is worth a pound of cleverness
>   ELBERT HUBBARD, *The Note Book*

lozenge *n*
pastille, gumdrop, tablet, cough drop, jujube
TECHNICAL troche, trochiscus, trochisk

lubber *n*
oaf, boor, dolt, barbarian, yahoo, gawk, lout
COLLOQ. clod, clodhopper, hick, hobbledehoy, slob, yob, yobbo, bumpkin

lubberly *adj*
clumsy, awkward, blundering gawky, ungainly, heavy-handed, bungling churlish, loutish, oafish, uncouth, doltish, lumbering clownish, lumpish, coarse, dense, crude
COLLOQ. clodhopping

lubricant *n*
oil, grease, lubrication, fat, lard
COLLOQ. *N Am & Aust* lube

lubricate *v*
1 OIL, grease, smear, wax, polish, make smooth, lard
2 FACILITATE, ease, make easier, help, assist, encourage, further, smooth, smooth the way, promote, advance, forward, accelerate, speed up
FORMAL expedite
COLLOQ. *N Am & Aust* lube

lucid *adj*
1 *lucid writing*
clear, comprehensible, plain, explicit, distinct, intelligible, obvious, evident
FORMAL perspicuous
2 CLEAR-HEADED, sane, rational, reasonable, intelligible, sensible, sober, sound, of sound mind, *compos mentis*
3 SHINING, bright, brilliant, beaming transparent, translucent, gleaming radiant, glassy, luminous, resplendent, crystalline, pure
FORMAL diaphanous, effulgent, limpid, pellucid
E3 1 unclear, unintelligible **2** confused, irrational **3** dark, murky

lucidity *n*
1 CLARITY, comprehensibility, plainness, intelligibility
2 CLEAR-HEADEDNESS, sanity, rationality, reasonableness, soundness, *compos mentis*
E3 1 unintelligibility **2** irrationality

lucidly *adv*
clearly, comprehensibly, plainly, explicitly, intelligibly, obviously, evidently
E3 unclearly, unintelligibly

luck *n*
1 CHANCE, fortune, accident, providence, fate, the stars, hazard, destiny, predestination
FORMAL fortuity
COLLOQ. fluke
See Synonym nuances panel at **chance.**
2 GOOD FORTUNE, good luck, success, prosperity, godsend
FORMAL serendipity
COLLOQ. break
E3 1 design, manipulation **2** misfortune, bad luck
■ **in luck**
fortunate, happy, favoured, successful, advantaged, timely, opportune
FORMAL auspicious
COLLOQ. jammy
■ **out of luck**
unlucky, unfortunate, luckless, hapless, unsuccessful, disadvantaged
FORMAL inauspicious
COLLOQ. down on your luck

> QUOTATIONS
> I am a great believer in luck, and I find the harder I work the more I have of it
>   STEPHEN LEACOCK, *Literary Lapses*

luckily *adv*
as luck would have it, by good luck, by chance, by accident, fortunately, happily, providentially
FORMAL fortuitously, propitiously
E3 unfortunately

luckless *adj*
unlucky, unfortunate, hopeless, ill-fated, ill-starred, jinxed, cursed, doomed, hapless, star-crossed, miserable, unhappy, unsuccessful, disastrous, calamitous, catastrophic

FORMAL unpropitious
🖪 lucky, fortunate

lucky adj
fortunate, in luck, promising favoured, happy, charmed, successful, prosperous, timely, opportune, expedient, providential, just as well; Scot canny, chancy
FORMAL auspicious, fortuitous, propitious
COLLOQ. jammy; Aust & NZ tinny
SLANG spawny
See Synonym nuances panel at **fortunate**.
🖪 unlucky

lucrative adj
profitable, well-paid, remunerative, profit-making moneymaking high-paying gainful, productive, financially rewarding advantageous, worthwhile
🖪 unprofitable

lucratively adv
profitably, gainfully, remuneratively, productively, advantageously
🖪 unprofitably

lucre n
money, cash, riches, wealth, profit(s), gain(s), proceeds, winnings, pay, income, remuneration, spoils, mammon
SLANG dough, dosh, bread, lolly, spondulicks, brass, readies, ready, greenies

ludicrous adj
absurd, ridiculous, preposterous, nonsensical, laughable, farcical, silly, comical, comic, humorous, amusing hilarious, funny, droll, burlesque, grotesque, outlandish, zany, odd, eccentric
FORMAL risible
COLLOQ. crazy
🖪 serious

ludicrously adv
absurdly, ridiculously, laughably, hilariously, outlandishly, grotesquely, nonsensically, preposterously

lug v
pull, drag haul, carry, bear, lift, tow, tote, heave, tug hump

luggage n
baggage, belongings, paraphernalia, traps
FORMAL impedimenta
COLLOQ. gear, things, stuff, clobber

Types of luggage include:

attaché case	Gladstone bag	portmanteau
backpack	grip	rucksack
bag	hamper	satchel
basket	hand-luggage	suitcase
bergen	haversack	travel bag
box	holdall	trunk
briefcase	kitbag	valise
case	knapsack	vanity-case
chest	overnight bag	
flight bag	portfolio	

See also **bag**.

---

lugubrious adj
melancholy, morose, gloomy, glum, sad, woeful, woebegone, sorrowful, sombre, serious, dismal, doleful, dreary, mournful, funereal, sepulchral
🖪 cheerful, jovial, merry

lukewarm adj
1 *lukewarm water*
tepid, slightly warm, warmish, coolish
2 HALF-HEARTED, cool, apathetic, tepid, indifferent, unenthusiastic, uninterested, unresponsive, unconcerned, impassive, Laodicean

lull n, v
♦ n
calm, calmness, peace, quiet, tranquillity, stillness, let-up, pause, hush, silence
🖪 agitation
♦ v
soothe, subdue, calm, silence, hush, pacify, quieten down, quiet, quell, still, allay, ease, compose
FORMAL assuage, abate
🖪 agitate

lullaby n
cradle song berceuse, hushaby
OLD dialect & Scot baloo

lumber[1] n, v
♦ n
1 *store away lumber*
clutter, jumble, rubbish, refuse, bits and pieces, odds and ends, junk, trash
2 TIMBER, wood
♦ v
burden, encumber, saddle, land, load, hamper, impose, charge

lumber[2] v
lumber round the house
clump, shamble, plod, shuffle, stump, stamp, trundle, trudge, stumble

lumbering adj
awkward, clumsy, heavy-footed, ungainly, unwieldy, heavy, blundering bumbling lumpish, ponderous, hulking massive, elephantine, bovine
COLLOQ. like a bull in a china shop
🖪 agile, nimble

luminary n
expert, authority, leader, leading light, celebrity, VIP, dignitary, worthy, notable, personage, star, superstar
COLLOQ. big name, bigwig celeb

luminescent adj
glowing bright, luminous, fluorescent, radiant, shining
FORMAL effulgent, luciferous, phosphorescent

luminosity n
glow, brightness, light, illumination, brilliance, radiance, lustre, fluorescence

luminous adj
glowing illuminated, lit, lighted, radiant, shining dazzling fluorescent, brilliant, lustrous, bright
FORMAL luminescent, effulgent

lump[1] n, v
♦ n
1 MASS, block, cluster, clump, clod, ball, dab, wad, bunch, piece, chunk, chuck, chump, cake, hunk, nugget, wedge, slug pat, knot, node, nut, lob, gnarl, gob, knub, nub, slub; dialect dad, daud, hunch, lunch; Scot claut, nirl, slump, plouk; N Am rock
TECHNICAL bolus, concretion, pustule
OLD loaf
COLLOQ. dollop, wedge
2 SWELLING, growth, bulge, bump, protuberance, bruise, protrusion, tumour, carbuncle, burr
TECHNICAL bunion, tuber
OLD bunch
FORMAL tumescence
♦ v
collect, mass, gather, put together, cluster, combine, pool, blend, fuse, coalesce, group, crowd, consolidate, unite, mix together, conglomerate; Scot slump

lump[2] v
like it or lump it
put up with, bear (with), endure, tolerate, stand, suffer, swallow, take, brook; Scot thole
COLLOQ. stomach

lumpish *adj*
awkward, heavy, clumsy, ungainly, hulking gawky, bungling lumbering lethargic, elephantine, stupid, dull-witted, oafish, boorish, doltish, obtuse, stolid

lumpy *adj*
clotted, congealed, coagulated, curdled, bunched, bumpy, cloggy, knobbly, grainy, granular
FORMAL nodous, nodose
⊟ even, smooth

lunacy *n*
madness, insanity, aberration, derangement, dementia, dementedness, mania, idiocy, imbecility, folly, foolishness, absurdity, nonsense, stupidity, preposterousness, outrageousness, irresponsibility, silliness, inanity, ridiculousness, illogicality, irrationality, senselessness
COLLOQ. craziness
⊟ sanity

lunatic *n, adj*
♦ *n*
psychotic, psychopath, madman, madwoman, insane person, imbecile, maniac, neurotic
COLLOQ. nutcase, nutter, fruitcake, headcase, oddball
SLANG loony, psycho, mentalist
♦ *adj*
mad, insane, deranged, unbalanced, disturbed, demented, irrational, foolish, idiotic, absurd, stupid, illogical, nonsensical, senseless, silly, inane, moonstruck
COLLOQ. crazy, bonkers, loopy, nuts, nutty, daft, barmy, potty, hare-brained, crackpot, round the bend/twist
SLANG loony, off your rocker
⊟ sane

lunch *n*
midday meal, luncheon, light lunch, ploughman's lunch, packed lunch, snack, brunch, Sunday lunch, dinner

lunge *v, n*
♦ *v*
thrust, jab, stab, pounce, plunge, pitch into, charge, dart, dash, dive, poke, strike (at), fall upon, grab (at), hit (at), leap, spring bound
♦ *n*
thrust, stab, pounce, charge, jab, poke, pass, cut, spring plunge, leap, bound

lurch *v*
roll, rock, pitch, sway, swerve, veer, stagger, totter, stumble, reel, list
■ **leave in the lurch**
abandon, desert, disappoint, let down, fail, leave stranded, leave high and dry

lure *v, n*
♦ *v*
tempt, entice, draw, attract, allure, induce, decoy, seduce, ensnare, beguile, lead on, take a rise out of; *N Am* tole
TECHNICAL stool
OLD trepan
FORMAL inveigle
♦ *n*
temptation, enticement, attraction, draw, allurement, bait, decoy, inducement, seduction, train, honey-trap
TECHNICAL jig spoonbait, spoonhook, trolling-bait, trolling-spoon, trout-spoon, Devon minnow
OLD stale, trepan
COLLOQ. carrot

lurid *adj*
1 SENSATIONAL, shocking startling explicit, graphic, exaggerated, melodramatic, macabre, gruesome, gory, ghastly, grisly, horrific, revolting
2 BRIGHTLY COLOURED, garish, glaring loud, showy, vivid, brilliant, dazzling intense
⊟ 1 restrained, tame **2** pale, subdued

luridly *adv*
1 SHOCKINGLY, explicitly, graphically, melodramatically, gruesomely, revoltingly
2 GARISHLY, brilliantly, vividly, intensely

lurk *v*
skulk, prowl, slink, lie in wait, crouch, lie low, hide, conceal yourself, snoop, sneak

luscious *adj*
1 *luscious food*
delicious, juicy, succulent, appetizing mouthwatering sweet, tasty, savoury
FORMAL delectable
COLLOQ. scrumptious, yummy, mor(e)ish
2 *a luscious blonde*
attractive, beautiful, voluptuous, desirable, gorgeous, sensuous, stunning ravishing sexy
COLLOQ. smashing

lush *adj, n*
♦ *adj*
1 FLOURISHING, luxuriant, abundant, prolific, teeming dense, overgrown, green, profuse
FORMAL verdant
2 SUMPTUOUS, opulent, ornate, plush, rich, luxurious, grand, lavish, extravagant, palatial
COLLOQ. posh, glitzy, classy, swanky, ritzy
♦ *n*
drunk, drunkard, alcoholic, inebriate, drinker, hard drinker, heavy drinker, dipsomaniac, wine-bibber, bloater, fuddler, habitual; *N Am* souse
COLLOQ. tippler
SLANG boozer, wino, alkie, dipso, soak, piss artist, pisshead, toper, sot, tosspot, sponge; *Aust & NZ* shicker

lust *n, v*
♦ *n*
1 SENSUALITY, sexual desire, libido, sexual drive, lechery, licentiousness, lewdness, lasciviousness
FORMAL concupiscence, prurience
COLLOQ. randiness, raunchiness, horniness, the hots
2 CRAVING, desire, appetite, longing passion, will, greed, greediness, covetousness, hunger, yearning avidity
FORMAL cupidity
■ **lust after**
desire, crave, yearn for, want, need, hunger for, thirst for, covet, long for, lecher, slaver

lustful *adj*
sensual, passionate, licentious, lewd, lascivious, lecherous, carnal, unchaste, wanton, craving hankering salacious
OLD lickerish; (*Shakesp*) rank, ruttish
FORMAL concupiscent, libidinous, prurient, cupidinous
COLLOQ. horny, randy, raunchy

lustily *adv*
loudly, hard, heartily, robustly, strongly, vigorously, forcefully, powerfully, stoutly, with all your might
FORMAL with might and main
⊟ weakly, feebly

lustiness *n*
power, robustness, sturdiness, vigour, health, healthiness, strength, energy, haleness, hardiness, toughness, stoutness, virility

lustre *n*
1 SHINE, gloss, sheen, gleam, glow, brilliance, brightness, radiance, sparkle, shimmer, resplendence, glare, burnish, glitter, glint; *dialect* gaum
FORMAL refulgence, lambency
2 GLORY, honour, prestige, renown, distinction, fame, illustriousness, merit, credit

lustrous *adj*
bright, shiny, shining brilliant, glossy, glowing dazzling gleaming glistening glittering shimmering sparkling twinkling burnished, luminous, radiant
FORMAL lambent
⊟ dull, lacklustre, matt

lusty *adj*
robust, strong sturdy, vigorous, tough, hale, hearty, hale and hearty, healthy, fit, blooming energetic, lively, strapping rugged, forceful, powerful, virile

COLLOQ. beefy, gutsy

E∃ weak, feeble

luxuriance *n*

abundance, copiousness, lushness, denseness, rankness, fertility, lavishness, profusion, sumptuousness, richness, excess, exuberance

FORMAL fecundity

luxuriant *adj*

1 ABUNDANT, prolific, lush, superabundant, sumptuous, profuse, plentiful, plenteous, overflowing ample, lavish, teeming thriving rich, riotous, rank, copious, dense, productive, fertile

FORMAL fecund

2 ELABORATE, extravagant, fancy, ornate, flamboyant, flowery, opulent, excessive, rococo, baroque

FORMAL florid

E∃ barren, infertile

> ⚠ **luxuriant** or **luxurious**?
>
> *Luxuriant* means 'abundant, prolific, growing vigorously': *the luxuriant growth of the jungle plants*. *Luxurious* means 'relating to luxury and riches, expensive': *a luxurious house*.

luxuriate *v*

delight, enjoy, revel, relish, savour, thrive, bask, abound, wallow, relax in, indulge, prosper, flourish, grow, bloom, burgeon

COLLOQ. live in the lap of luxury, live off the fat of the land, live the life of Riley, live in clover, live on easy street, have a ball

luxurious *adj*

sumptuous, opulent, lavish, de luxe, magnificent, splendid, rich, expensive, costly, affluent, self-indulgent, pampered, comfortable, grand, well-appointed

COLLOQ. plush, posh, cushy, glitzy, swanky, ritzy

E∃ austere, spartan

> ⚠ **luxurious** or **luxuriant**?
>
> See panel at **luxuriant.**

luxuriously *adv*

sumptuously, lavishly, opulently, magnificently, affluently, comfortably

COLLOQ. poshly, plushly, swankily, glitzily

luxury *n*

1 SUMPTUOUSNESS, opulence, hedonism, splendour, affluence, richness, expensiveness, costliness, magnificence, grandness, grandeur, pleasure, indulgence, self-indulgence, gratification, comfort, milk and honey, *luxe, grand luxe*

COLLOQ. lap of luxury

2 *life's little luxuries*

extravagance, indulgence, satisfaction, extra, treat

OLD delicate

COLLOQ. pie

E∃ **1** austerity **2** essential

lying *adj, n*

♦ *adj*

deceitful, dishonest, false, untruthful, double-dealing

FORMAL mendacious, dissembling dissimulating

COLLOQ. two-faced, crooked

E∃ honest, truthful

♦ *n*

dishonesty, untruthfulness, deceit, falsity, perjury, falsification, fabrication, invention, double-dealing

FORMAL duplicity

COLLOQ. fibbing white lies, crookedness

E∃ honesty, truthfulness

lynch *v*

hang hang by the neck, execute, put to death, kill

COLLOQ. string up

lyric *adj*

emotional, passionate, personal, subjective, poetic, musical, melodic

lyrical *adj*

1 POETIC, musical, romantic

2 ENTHUSIASTIC, emotional, rapturous, rhapsodic, ecstatic, effusive, passionate, carried away, expressive, impassioned, inspired

lyrically *adv*

1 POETICALLY, romantically, musically

2 ENTHUSIASTICALLY, emotionally, rapturously, passionately, expressively, effusively, ecstatically

lyrics *n*

text, words, book, libretto

M

macabre *adj*
gruesome, chilling grisly, grim, horrible, gory, horrific, frightful, frightening terrifying shocking dreadful, morbid, ghostly, eerie, hideous, ghastly, sick
COLLOQ. Gothic

mace *n*
rod, stick, staff, club, cudgel

macerate *v*
soak, steep, marinade, soften, liquefy, mash, blend, pulp, squash

Machiavellian *adj*
devious, crafty, designing scheming shrewd, sly, cunning wily, artful, astute, calculating deceitful, double-dealing guileful, underhand, opportunist, foxy, intriguing unscrupulous
FORMAL perfidious

machination *n*
scheme, intrigue, plot, design, manoeuvre, conspiracy, tactic, wile, ruse, ploy, stratagem, trick, device, dodge, cabal
FORMAL artifice
COLLOQ. shenanigans

machine *n*
1 INSTRUMENT, device, contrivance, tool, contraption, mechanism, engine, motor, apparatus, appliance, gadget, hardware
2 AGENCY, organization, structure, instrument, tool, organ, vehicle, influence, catalyst, system, workings
3 AUTOMATON, robot, mechanical person, tool, mechanism, zombie, android

machine-gun
See panels at **gun**; **weapon**.

machinery *n*
1 INSTRUMENTS, mechanism, tools, apparatus, equipment, tackle, gear, gadgetry
2 ORGANIZATION, channel(s), structure, system, procedure, workings, agency

---

Types of heavy machinery include:

all-terrain fork lift	fertilizer spreader	road roller
bulldozer	fire appliance	road-sweeping
caterpillar tractor	fork-lift truck	lorry
combine harvester	gantry crane	Rotovator®
concrete mixer	grader	silage harvester
concrete pump	grapple	snowplough
crane	gritter	straw baler
crawler crane	hydraulic bale	threshing machine
crawler tractor	loader	tower crane
digger	hydraulic shovel	tracklayer
dragline excavator	JCB®	tractor
dredger	muck spreader	tractor-scraper
dumper	pick-up loader	truck crane
dump truck	pile-driver	wheel loader
dustcart	platform hoist	
excavator	riding mower	

machinist *n*
worker, operator, operative, factory hand, mechanic

machismo *n*
masculinity, maleness, manliness, virility, toughness, strength

macrocosm *n*
universe, solar system, cosmos, creation, world, planet, society, civilization, community, culture, humanity, totality, (single) entity, system, structure
F3 microcosm

mad *adj*
1 INSANE, lunatic, unbalanced, psychotic, disturbed, deranged, maniacal, out of your mind, out of your senses, of unsound mind, unhinged, crazed, unstable, *non compos mentis*, frenzied, wild, berserk, manic, maniac, distracted, distraught, fey, frenetic, frantic, stone-crazy, queer; *Scot* gyte, red-mad
OLD frantic-mad, lymphatic, bestraught
COLLOQ. crazy, demented, nuts, nutty, nutty as a fruitcake, wacky, mad as a hatter, barmy, bonkers, batty, cracked, crackers, dippy, daffy, dotty, loopy, potty, off your nut, off your head, wrong in the head, out of your head, off the wall, out to lunch, round the bend, round the twist, bats, having bats in the belfry, cuckoo, off the rails, screwy, up the wall, raving not all there; *N Am* buggy, flaky, fruity; *Aust & NZ* dingbats
SLANG loony, mental, bananas, barking wacko, doolally, off your rocker, off your chump, off your trolley, out of your tree, needing your head examined, having lost your marbles, having a screw loose, having a tile loose, having several cards short of a full deck, with one sandwich short of a picnic, meshuga; *N Am* gonzo, loco, wiggy
2 ANGRY, furious, enraged, raging infuriated, incensed, irate, blazing fuming livid
COLLOQ. aggravated, cross, ratty, uptight, hopping mad, raving mad, seeing red, in a lather, disgruntled, up in arms, hot under the collar, stroppy, in a strop, flipped, choleric, choked, fit to be tied, on the warpath, in a paddy; *N Am* ticked off; *Aust* spewy, ropable; *Aust & NZ* crooked
SLANG pissed off, hairless, ape, apeshit; *N Am* burned up
3 IRRATIONAL, illogical, unreasonable, absurd, ludicrous, preposterous, foolish, foolhardy, idiotic, insane, stupid, silly, nonsensical, wild
COLLOQ. crazy, daft, barmy, potty, hare-brained, crackbrained, crackpot
4 FANATICAL, enthusiastic, infatuated, ardent, zealous, devoted, fond, keen, avid, passionate
COLLOQ. crazy, daft, nuts, potty, wild
5 UNCONTROLLED, wild, frantic, furious, reckless, violent, energetic, intense, rapid, hasty, hurried, unrestrained, frenzied, abandoned, excited
F3 **1** sane **2** calm **3** sensible **4** apathetic **5** controlled
■ **like mad**
energetically, quickly, furiously, wildly, frantically, hurriedly, enthusiastically, fanatically, zealously, avidly

---

SYNONYM NUANCES

sense 1
You can use **insane** as a more clinical term for someone or something displaying complete mental unsoundness, while **lunatic** may be used more generally and more offensively of hugely abnormal or irrational behaviour, and **psychotic** would be reserved for a serious mental

disorder with untypical thought patterns. **Unbalanced**, however, has far less strong implications of a lack of mental equilibrium, and **unstable** is used of a variable psychological state.

Deranged again suggests more severe mental disorder, but **distracted**, on the other hand, can suggest a more temporary confusion or, more usually, lack of concentration, while **distraught** is more suggestive of being frantic with grief or worry. The term **demented** can be used of mental deterioration due to illness or age, but is often used to suggest distraction through worry, unlike **unhinged** and **crazed** which are more suggestive of wildly unpredictable behaviour, and **frenzied**, **manic**, **maniac** and **maniacal**, which are suggestive of wild and unrestrained behaviour: *a frenzied attack*; *police described the killing as maniacal*. **Frenetic** suggests hurried and chaotic activity: *the frenetic bustle of the metropolis*.

You can use **fey** if you wish to convey a slight madness or eccentricity: *she was a strange, fey woman who had become odder since her husband's death*, while **queer** simply suggests strangeness.

madcap *adj, n*
♦ *adj*
foolhardy, rash, reckless, impulsive, silly, thoughtless, wild, lively, flighty, heedless, ill-advised, imprudent, hotheaded, crazy
COLLOQ. birdbrained, hare-brained
♦ *n*
adventurer, tearaway, hothead, daredevil, firebrand, fury, desperado, eccentric
COLLOQ. crackpot

madden *v*
anger, enrage, infuriate, incense, annoy, upset, agitate, exasperate, provoke, irritate, inflame, irk, vex, distract
OLD bemad
COLLOQ. aggravate, bug hassle, rub up the wrong way, get someone's blood up, make your blood boil, get on your nerves, get up your nose, get under your skin, get someone's goat, get on your wick, drive crazy/nuts, drive up the wall, drive round the bend/twist, get your back up, get your dander up
F∃ calm, pacify

maddening *adj*
infuriating exasperating annoying troublesome, irritating vexatious, galling upsetting disturbing
COLLOQ. aggravating

made-up *adj*
1 INVENTED, make-believe, unreal, untrue, false, fictional, imaginary, specious, fabricated, fairytale, mythical
COLLOQ. trumped-up
2 WEARING MAKE-UP, painted, powdered, done up
F∃ 1 real, factual, true

madhouse *n*
1 BEDLAM, chaos, disarray, disorder, uproar, turmoil, mayhem, pandemonium, Babel
2 MENTAL HOSPITAL, lunatic asylum, asylum, mental institution, psychiatric hospital
COLLOQ. funny farm, loony bin, nuthouse

madly *adv*
1 *he rolled his eyes madly*
insanely, dementedly, hysterically, frenziedly, deliriously, wildly, distractedly
COLLOQ. crazily
2 *madly cleaning up*
wildly, excitedly, frantically, furiously, recklessly, violently, energetically, intensely, rapidly, hastily, fast, hurriedly
3 *madly in love*
intensely, wildly, fervently, devotedly, completely
4 EXTREMELY, very, wildly, exceedingly, exceptionally, utterly, unreasonably

madman, madwoman *n*
lunatic, psychotic, psychopath, maniac, imbecile, furioso
OLD bedlam, frenetic, gelt, Tom o' Bedlam
COLLOQ. nutter, nut, crackpot, crank, headcase, nutcase, fruitcake, screwball, oddball, kook
SLANG loony, psycho, basket case; *N Am* cupcake

madness *n*
1 INSANITY, insaneness, lunacy, dementia, psychosis, mental instability, mania, derangement, distraction, delusion, frenzy, deliration, *folie*, furiosity
COLLOQ. craziness, meshugaas
2 FURY, rage, raving frenzy, hysteria, anger, agitation, exasperation, wrath, ire
3 FOLLY, craziness, irrationality, unreasonableness, insanity, stupidity, silliness, inanity, absurdity, nonsense, foolishness, foolhardiness, preposterousness, wildness
COLLOQ. daftness
4 KEENNESS, enthusiasm, ardour, craze, abandon, zeal, wildness, unrestraint, uproar, riot, passion, excitement, fanaticism, infatuation, intoxication
F∃ 1 sanity 2 calmness 3 reasonableness

maelstrom *n*
confusion, disorder, turmoil, mess, pandemonium, tumult, uproar, bedlam, chaos, turbulence, vortex, whirlpool, Charybdis

maestro *n*
expert, master, genius, prodigy, virtuoso, director, conductor
COLLOQ. wizard, ace

magazine *n*
1 JOURNAL, periodical, publication, paper, weekly, monthly, quarterly, supplement, colour supplement, fanzine, e-zine, webzine
2 ARSENAL, storehouse, ammunition dump, depot, ordnance

magic *n, adj*
♦ *n*
1 SORCERY, enchantment, supernatural, occult, occultism, black magic, black art, witchcraft, wizardry, wicca, wonder-working voodoo, hoodoo, magical powers, spell, curse, incantation
FORMAL necromancy, thaumaturgy
2 CONJURING, illusion, sleight of hand, deception, trickery, legerdemain
FORMAL prestidigitation
3 CHARM, fascination, glamour, enticement, allure, allurement, enchantment, magnetism, pull, wonder, mystery
SLANG *N Am* mojo
♦ *adj*
1 SUPERNATURAL, occult, mysterious, demonic, spellful
OLD hermetic
COLLOQ. metaphysical
2 CHARMING, enchanting bewitching fascinating spellbinding entrancing captivating irresistible, magnetic, romantic, stardust
3 WONDERFUL, excellent, great, tremendous, marvellous
COLLOQ. terrific, smashing brill, ace
SLANG mega, cool, wicked

> **QUOTATIONS**
> He did not, even in his extremity, quite abandon his faith in the magic of official forms. In bumf lay salvation
> EVELYN WAUGH, *Officers and Gentlemen*

magical *adj*
1 MAGIC, mysterious, supernatural, occult, demonic
2 WONDERFUL, marvellous, charming enchanting fascinating spellbinding captivating

magician *n*
1 SORCERER, miracle-worker, enchanter, wizard, witch, warlock, spellbinder, spellworker, wonder-worker, magus, witch doctor; *dialect* wise man; *N Am* powwow

OLD archimage
FORMAL necromancer, thaumaturge
2 CONJURER, illusionist, juggler
3 GENIUS, maestro, expert, master, virtuoso
COLLOQ. wizard, ace

magisterial adj
authoritative, commanding masterful, assertive,
authoritarian, domineering imperious, high-handed,
dictatorial, lordly, overbearing arrogant, despotic
FORMAL peremptory
COLLOQ. bossy

magistrate n
judge, justice, justice of the peace, JP, stipendiary,
bailiff, tribune, Scot reeve, bailie
COLLOQ. beak
OLD tribune
Related adjective: magisterial

magnanimity n
generosity, liberality, open-handedness, benevolence,
selflessness, unselfishness, charity, charitableness, big-
heartedness, bountifulness, kindness, high-mindedness,
nobility, philanthropy, altruism, mercy, forgiveness,
largesse
FORMAL beneficence, munificence
F3 meanness, vindictiveness

magnanimous adj
generous, liberal, open-handed, benevolent, selfless,
charitable, big-hearted, bountiful, kind, kindly, noble,
philanthropic, altruistic, unselfish, ungrudging merciful,
forgiving
FORMAL beneficent, munificent
COLLOQ. big
F3 mean

magnate n
tycoon, captain of industry, industrialist, mogul,
entrepreneur, financier, plutocrat, baron, executive,
personage, notable, leader
COLLOQ. fat cat, moneybags, bigwig big shot, big noise,
big timer, big cheese

magnet n
draw, bait, lure, allurement, charm, enticement,
appeal, attraction, centre of attraction, focus, focal point,
lodestone
TECHNICAL solenoid
F3 repellent

magnetic adj
attractive, alluring fascinating appealing enthralling
charming engaging mesmerizing hypnotic, seductive,
tempting tantalizing irresistible, entrancing
bewitching enchanting captivating gripping
absorbing charismatic
F3 repellent, repulsive

magnetism n
attraction, allure, fascination, enchantment, captivation,
charm, temptation, seductiveness, lure, appeal, drawing
power, draw, pull, hypnotism, mesmerism, charisma, grip,
magic, power, spell

magnification n
1 ENLARGEMENT, amplification, increase, expansion,
intensification, enhancement, inflation, heightening
deepening dilation, build-up, boost, extolment,
lionization
FORMAL aggrandizement, augmentation
2 EXAGGERATION, dramatization, overemphasis,
overstatement, overdoing embellishment, embroidery,
hyperbole
F3 **1** diminution, reduction

magnificence n
splendour, grandeur, impressiveness, glory, gorgeousness,
brilliance, excellence, majesty, sumptuousness, nobility,
luxuriousness, luxury, lavishness, pomp, stateliness
FORMAL resplendence, opulence, sublimity
F3 modesty, plainness, simplicity

magnificent adj
splendid, grand, imposing grandiose, impressive, striking
elegant, glorious, gorgeous, brilliant, dazzling excellent,
marvellous, wonderful, majestic, superb, sumptuous,
noble, exalted, fine, lavish, luxurious, rich, royal, stately
FORMAL resplendent, opulent, august, sublime
F3 modest, humble, poor

magnify v
1 ENLARGE, amplify, increase, expand, intensify,
enhance, boost, extend, greaten, heighten, broaden,
deepen, dilate, build up
2 EXAGGERATE, dramatize, overemphasize, overplay,
overstate, overdo, embellish, embroider
COLLOQ. blow up, blow up out of all proportion, make a
mountain out of a molehill
F3 **1** reduce, diminish **2** belittle, play down

magniloquence n
pomposity, pretentiousness, bombast, loftiness, rhetoric,
euphuism, turgidity, fustian
FORMAL grandiloquence, orotundity
F3 simplicity, straightforwardness

magniloquent adj
pompous, high-sounding lofty, overblown, elevated,
exalted, bombastic, fustian, high-flown, pretentious,
rhetorical, declamatory, euphuistic, sonorous,
turgid, stilted
FORMAL grandiloquent, orotund
F3 simple, straightforward

magnitude n
1 SIZE, extent, measure, amount, expanse, dimensions,
mass, proportions, quantity, weight, volume, capacity,
bulk, largeness, greatness, space, strength, amplitude
2 IMPORTANCE, consequence, significance, weight,
greatness, eminence, fame, distinction, moment, note,
intensity
FORMAL import, moment

magnum opus n
masterpiece, masterwork, chef d'oeuvre, pièce de
résistance

maid n
servant, domestic, waitress, kitchenmaid, chambermaid,
housemaid, girl, au pair, maidservant, serving-maid, lady's
maid, dresser, handmaiden, soubrette, abigail,
maid-of-all-work, maiden, suivante, daily, charlady,
charwoman
OLD bonnibell, bowerwoman, may, pucelle
COLLOQ. skivvy, slavey, Mrs Mop

maiden n, adj
♦ n
girl, young girl, young lady, young woman, virgin, lass,
lassie, miss, nymph; N Am bachelorette
OLD damsel, popsy
♦ adj
1 a maiden voyage
first, inaugural, new, introductory, initial, initiatory
2 CHASTE, decent, demure, gentle, girlish, female, modest,
proper, pure, celibate, reserved, undefiled, unsullied,
unbroached, vestal, virgin, unmarried, unwed, virginal,
virtuous
OLD seemly
FORMAL decorous
F3 **2** defiled, deflowered, unchaste

maidenhood n
purity, chastity, chasteness, virtue, honour
OLD maidenhead

maidenly adj
becoming chaste, decent, demure, gentle, girlish, female,
modest, proper, pure, reserved, undefiled, immaculate,
unsullied, unbroached, vestal, virgin, unmarried, unwed,
virginal, virtuous
OLD seemly
FORMAL decorous
F3 immodest

maidservant n

maid, servant, domestic, waitress, kitchenmaid, chambermaid, housemaid, girl, au pair, serving-maid, lady's maid, dresser, handmaiden, soubrette, abigail, maid-of-all-work, maiden, suivante, daily, charlady, charwoman, Mrs Mopp

OLD bonnibell, bowerwoman, may, pucelle

COLLOQ. skivvy, slavey

mail[1] n, v

♦ n

1 *deliver the mail*

post, general post, letters, correspondence, communications, packages, parcels, packets, delivery, registered mail, recorded mail, special delivery, direct mail, airmail, all-up service, surface mail, international mail, electronic mail, email, first-class mail, second-class mail, fan mail, hate mail

COLLOQ. junk mail, snail mail, spam, junk fax

2 POSTAL SERVICE, postal system, post, Post Office

♦ v

post, send, dispatch, forward

Related adjective: postal

> **QUOTATIONS**
> This is the Night Mail crossing the border / Bringing the cheque and the postal order
> W H AUDEN, 'Night Mail'

mail[2] n

protected by a coat of mail

armour, chain mail, chain armour, iron-cladding panoply, protective covering

OLD cataphract, habergeon

maim v

mutilate, disfigure, wound, incapacitate, injure, disable, hurt, impair, mar, cripple, lame, put out of action, truncate; *dialect* main

OLD scotch

main adj, n

♦ adj

principal, chief, leading first, foremost, major, key, predominant, dominant, pre-eminent, primary, most important, prime, premier, supreme, paramount, central, head, cardinal, outstanding essential, critical, crucial, necessary, vital, fundamental, pivotal

See Synonym nuances panel at **dominant**.

E3 minor, unimportant, insignificant

♦ n

pipe, duct, conduit, channel, cable, line

■ **in the main**

chiefly, mostly, on the whole, for the most part, generally, in general, especially, as a rule, by and large, commonly, usually, largely

mainly adv

primarily, principally, chiefly, first and foremost, in the main, mostly, on the whole, for the most part, generally, in general, especially, as a rule, by and large, commonly, usually, above all, largely, overall, predominantly

mainspring n

motive, motivation, cause, reason, driving force, impulse, incentive, inspiration, origin, prime mover, generator, source, fountainhead, wellspring

mainstay n

support, buttress, bulwark, linchpin, prop, pillar, anchor, backbone, cornerstone, foundation, basis, base, key player, right-hand man/woman, tower of strength

mainstream adj

normal, average, central, general, typical, regular, standard, conventional, established, orthodox, received, accepted, mainline

E3 heterodox, peripheral, marginal

maintain v

1 CARRY ON, continue, keep (up), keep going sustain, preserve, perpetuate, conserve, retain

2 CARE FOR, conserve, look after, keep (up), take care of, preserve, keep in good condition/repair

3 PROVIDE FOR, keep, support, finance, supply, feed, sustain, nourish, nurture

4 ASSERT, claim, profess, contend, declare, announce, affirm, hold, state, insist, believe, stand by, fight for, support, defend, uphold

FORMAL avow, aver, asseverate

E3 **2** neglect **4** deny

maintenance n

1 CONTINUATION, continuance, carrying-on, preservation, conservation, perpetuation

2 CARE, conservation, preservation, support, repairs, protection, upkeep, running

3 KEEP, subsistence, feeding sustenance, nourishment, nurture, living livelihood, financing support, financial support, upkeep, allowance, alimony, traineeship

TECHNICAL altarage, appanage, title

OLD aliment

E3 **2** neglect

majestic adj

magnificent, grand, glorious, dignified, distinguished, noble, royal, queenly, kingly, princely, lordly, stately, splendid, imperial, marvellous, impressive, elevated, exalted, awesome, imposing regal, superb, lofty, monumental, pompous

FORMAL resplendent, sublime, august

E3 lowly, unimpressive, unimposing

majestically adv

magnificently, grandly, gloriously, splendidly, marvellously, impressively, superbly, pompously, nobly, royally, regally, imperially

TECHNICAL maestoso

FORMAL resplendently, sublimely

majesty n

grandeur, grandness, glory, dignity, magnificence, beauty, awesomeness, nobility, nobleness, royalty, regality, splendour, stateliness, pomp, exaltedness, impressiveness, loftiness

OLD majesticalness, majesticness

FORMAL resplendence, sublimity

major adj

greater, greatest, chief, main, larger, largest, bigger, higher, highest, best, leading outstanding notable, supreme, prime, paramount, uppermost, significant, crucial, important, serious, key, keynote, great, senior, older, superior, pre-eminent, vital, weighty

E3 minor, unimportant, trivial

majority n

1 MASS, bulk, preponderance, (the) many, most, greater/larger part, greater/larger number, more than half, nearly all, plurality

COLLOQ. lion's share

2 ADULTHOOD, maturity, manhood, womanhood, legal age, coming of age, reaching full age, age of consent, years of discretion

E3 **1** minority

make v, n

♦ v

1 CREATE, manufacture, mass-produce, fabricate, construct, assemble, build, erect, produce, turn out, put together, put up, originate, compose, form, shape, fashion, mould, model

2 CAUSE, bring about, produce, accomplish, occasion, create, give rise to, engender, generate, render, perform

FORMAL effect

3 CARRY OUT, accomplish, achieve, do, perform, undertake, discharge

FORMAL effect, execute

COLLOQ. deliver (the goods), get down to, wrap up

4 COERCE, force, urge, oblige, constrain, compel, impel, prevail upon, pressure, pressurize, press, drive, require, dragoon

COLLOQ. bulldoze, strongarm, put the screws on

5 APPOINT, vote in, elect, select, designate, nominate, name, ordain, install, create, vote
6 COMPOSE, create, write, arrange, prepare, produce, devise, think up, form, formulate, frame, construct, draw up
7 EARN, gain, net, gross, obtain, acquire, get, bring in, secure, win, take home, clear
FORMAL realize
8 CONSTITUTE, compose, comprise, add up to, amount to, come to, total
9 SCORE, gain, chalk up
COLLOQ. notch up
10 PREPARE, get ready, put together, cook
COLLOQ. *N Am* fix
11 CALCULATE, work out, compute, reckon (up), add up (to), estimate
12 SERVE AS, have the qualifications for, become, act as, function as, play the role/part of, achieve
13 *make a decision*
reach, come to, arrive at, settle, determine
14 *make a mistake*
commit, carry out, be responsible for, be to blame for
FORMAL perpetrate
15 *make a speech*
give, communicate, convey, tell, declare, deliver, state, pronounce, set forth
FORMAL impart
E3 1 dismantle, demolish 7 spend, lose
♦ *n*
brand, sort, type, style, variety, manufacture, model, mark, kind, marque, form, structure

■ **make away with**
1 STEAL, run off with, walk off with, snatch, seize, carry off, kidnap
COLLOQ. pinch, lift, nick, nab, swipe
2 KILL, do away with, murder, slaughter, assassinate
COLLOQ. do in, knock off, bump off

■ **make believe**
pretend, play, play-act, imagine, dream, enact, fantasize, act
FORMAL feign
COLLOQ. make castles in the air

■ **make do**
cope, manage, survive, get along get by, improvise, make out, muddle through
COLLOQ. scrape by, make the best of a bad job, keep your head above water

■ **make for**
1 HEAD FOR, aim for, go towards, move towards
2 PRODUCE, lead to, promote, contribute to, facilitate, favour, forward, further, be conducive to

■ **make it**
succeed, be successful, get on, come through, arrive, pull through, reach, survive, prosper
E3 fail

■ **make of**
assess, consider, regard, think of, evaluate, weigh up, judge, rate

■ **make off**
run off, run away, depart, bolt, leave, fly
COLLOQ. cut and run, beat a hasty retreat, clear off, make a getaway, take to your heels, skedaddle, scarper, beat it

■ **make off with**
run off with, carry off, steal, take, swipe, walk off with, pilfer, kidnap, abduct
FORMAL appropriate, purloin
COLLOQ. filch, knock off, nab, nick, pinch

■ **make out**
1 DISCERN, manage to see/hear, perceive, decipher, distinguish, recognize, see, detect, discover
FORMAL espy
2 UNDERSTAND, work out, grasp, comprehend, follow, fathom
3 DRAW UP, complete, fill in, write out

4 MAINTAIN, imply, claim, assert, affirm, declare, describe, demonstrate, prove, establish
FORMAL aver
5 MANAGE, get on, get along get by, cope, progress, succeed
FORMAL fare
6 WRITE OUT, fill in/out, complete
7 MAKE LOVE, have sex with someone, sleep with someone, sleep together, go to bed with someone
SLANG have it off with someone, get your leg over, bang bonk; (*taboo*) fuck, screw, shag

■ **make over**
transfer, sign over, convey, assign, bequeath, leave

■ **make up**
1 CREATE, invent, devise, fabricate, construct, originate, formulate, frame, dream up, compose, think up, concoct, spin, hatch
2 COMPLETE, fill, supply, provide, meet, supplement, round off
3 COMPRISE, constitute, compose, form
4 BE RECONCILED, make peace, settle differences, become friends again, shake hands, repent
COLLOQ. bury the hatchet, forgive and forget, call it quits
5 PUT MAKE-UP ON, powder, rouge, perfume, paint
COLLOQ. put on your face, doll up, tart up

■ **make up for**
compensate for, make amends for, make recompense for, offset, redress
FORMAL atone for

■ **make up to**
curry favour with, toady to, court, fawn on, butter up, make overtures to
COLLOQ. chat up, suck up to; *N Am* cozy up (with)

■ **make up your mind**
decide, choose, determine, resolve, settle
E3 waver

■ **make way**
allow to pass, make room/space for, stand back for, not stand in the way of, clear the way, allow to succeed

make-believe *n, adj*
♦ *n*
pretence, imagination, fantasy, unreality, fabrication, play-acting role-play, dream, dreaming daydreaming masquerade, charade
E3 reality
♦ *adj*
imaginary, imagined, made-up, imitated, pretended, fantasy, fantasized, dream, simulated, unreal, mock, sham
FORMAL feigned
COLLOQ. pretend
E3 real

maker *n*
creator, manufacturer, constructor, builder, producer, director, deviser, architect, author, fabricator, repairer

makeshift *adj*
temporary, improvised, rough and ready, thrown together, cobbled together, provisional, substitute, stopgap, stand-by, expedient, make-do
E3 permanent

make-up *n*
1 COSMETICS, paint, powder, greasepaint, maquillage
COLLOQ. war paint
SLANG slap
See also panel at **cosmetics**.
2 CONSTITUTION, nature, composition, character, construction, form, format, formation, arrangement, organization, style, structure, assembly
FORMAL configuration
3 PERSONALITY, temperament, temper, nature, character, disposition, style

making *n*
1 PRODUCTION, producing creation, creating manufacture, assembly, building composition, construction, fabrication, modelling moulding forging

2 POTENTIAL, qualities, potentiality, promise, capability, capacity, possibilities, beginnings, materials, ingredients
3 EARNINGS, income, profits, proceeds, revenue, returns, takings
F3 **1** dismantling
■ **in the making**
budding potential, promising coming developing emergent, up and coming
FORMAL nascent, burgeoning incipient

maladjusted *adj*
disturbed, unstable, confused, alienated, disordered, neurotic
FORMAL estranged
COLLOQ. dotty, round the bend, screwed-up
SLANG schizo, psycho, gaga
F3 well-adjusted; *colloq.* together

maladministration *n*
inefficiency, incompetence, mismanagement, mishandling misrule, blundering bungling misgovernment, misconduct, corruption, dishonesty, malpractice, stupidity
TECHNICAL malfeasance, misfeasance
FORMAL malversation

maladroit *adj*
clumsy, awkward, bungling unskilful, unhandy, gauche, graceless, inelegant, inept, inexpert, tactless, insensitive, thoughtless, inconsiderate, undiplomatic, ill-timed
FORMAL untoward
COLLOQ. cack-handed, ham-fisted
F3 skilful, adroit, tactful

maladroitness *n*
clumsiness, awkwardness, unskilfulness, ineptitude, inelegance, gracelessness, tactlessness, insensitivity, thoughtlessness
F3 skilfulness

malady *n*
illness, disease, sickness, complaint, infirmity, ailment, disorder, breakdown
FORMAL affliction, malaise, indisposition
F3 health

malaise *n*
uneasiness, unease, discontent, depression, discomfort, disquiet, restlessness, weariness, anxiety, unhappiness, anguish, doldrums, angst, illness, disease, sickness, weakness
FORMAL lassitude, melancholy, indisposition, enervation
F3 happiness, wellbeing

malapropism *n*
wrong word, misuse, slip of the tongue, misapplication
FORMAL solecism, infelicity

malapropos *adj, adv*
♦ *adj*
inappropriate, unsuitable, untimely, ill-timed, inopportune, misapplied, inapt, uncalled-for, tactless
FORMAL inapposite, unseemly
F3 appropriate, tactful
♦ *adv*
inappropriately, unsuitably, inaptly, unseasonably, tactlessly, inopportunely
FORMAL inappositely
F3 appropriately, tactfully

malcontent *n, adj*
♦ *n*
grumbler, complainer, moaner, rebel, agitator, mischief-maker, troublemaker
COLLOQ. grouch, grouser, nit-picker, whinger
SLANG bellyacher
♦ *adj*
dissatisfied, unhappy, unsatisfied, discontented, disgruntled, ill-disposed, disaffected, morose, rebellious, fault-finding resentful
FORMAL restive, dissentious

COLLOQ. fed up
SLANG cheesed off, bellyaching
F3 contented

male *adj*
masculine, manly, virile, boyish, he-, manlike
COLLOQ. laddish
F3 female

SYNONYM NUANCES

Male can be used to suggest anything living that is not female: *groin guards are mandatory for all male competitors*, whereas **manlike** suggests having the appearance of an adult human male: *I saw the shadow of a manlike creature*. **Manly**, however, may be used to refer favourably to the positive attributes associated with men: *his manly shoulders*, unlike **mannish**, which is more likely to be used, often of women, to suggest having properties normally attributed to a man: *a rather mannish woman doctor*. **Virile** has very positive implications of sexual potency: *an imposing specimen of virile manhood*.

---

malediction *n*
curse, cursing denunciation, oath, anathema, anathematization, damnation, damning
FORMAL execration, imprecation, malison
F3 blessing praise

malefactor *n*
lawbreaker, criminal, offender, felon, convict, outlaw, delinquent, wrongdoer, evildoer, culprit, villain
TECHNICAL misfeasor
FORMAL miscreant, transgressor
COLLOQ. crook

malevolence *n*
malice, malignancy, malignity, maliciousness, spite, spitefulness, vindictiveness, vengefulness, ill-will, hostility, unfriendliness, hate, hatred, bitterness, venom, viciousness, fierceness, cruelty
FORMAL rancour
F3 benevolence

malevolent *adj*
malicious, malign, spiteful, vindictive, sinister, vengeful, ill-natured, hostile, unfriendly, bitter, rancorous, resentful, vicious, fierce, cruel, ruthless, venomous, pernicious, evil-minded
FORMAL baleful, maleficent
F3 benevolent, kind

malevolently *adv*
maliciously, spitefully, vindicatively, vengefully, bitterly, resentfully, viciously, cruelly, fiercely, venomously
F3 benevolently

malformation *n*
deformity, misshapenness, disfigurement, irregularity, distortion, warp

malformed *adj*
deformed, misshapen, irregular, disfigured, distorted, twisted, warped, crooked, bent
F3 perfect

malfunction *v, n*
♦ *v*
break down, go wrong fail, stop working
COLLOQ. crash, go kaput, go phut, pack up
SLANG conk out
♦ *n*
fault, defect, failure, breakdown, flaw
COLLOQ. crash

malice *n*
maliciousness, enmity, hostility, animosity, ill-will, hatred, hate, bad blood, spite, vindictiveness, malevolence, venom, spleen, bitterness, resentment
OLD despite
FORMAL animus, rancour

COLLOQ. bone to pick, bloody-mindedness, bitchiness
≣ love

malicious *adj*
ill-natured, hostile, malign, malevolent, spiteful,
venomous, snide, vicious, vengeful, evil, evil-minded,
pernicious, bitter, rancorous, resentful
FORMAL baleful
≣ friendly, kind

maliciously *adv*
spitefully, malevolently, venomously, viciously, bitterly,
resentfully, perniciously

malign *v, adj*
◆ *v*
defame, slander, libel, abuse, run down, harm, injure,
insult, bait, envenom
OLD misintend
FORMAL disparage, calumniate, vilify, traduce
COLLOQ. smear, slur, badmouth, stab in the back, kick in
the teeth, drag through the mud
≣ praise
◆ *adj*
harmful, malignant, malevolent, bad, evil, hurtful,
injurious, destructive, sinister, hostile
≣ benign, kind

malignancy *n*
fatality, mortality, lethality, incurability, virulence,
uncontrollability

malignant *adj*
1 EVIL, devilish, hostile, malicious, vicious, venomous,
spiteful, destructive, harmful, hurtful, pernicious, injurious,
viperous, malign, malevolent, rancorous, black, cankered,
sullen, poisonous; *dialect* swart
FORMAL baleful
2 FATAL, deadly, lethal, incurable, dangerous,
life-threatening cancerous, uncontrollable,
virulent
≣ 1 kind **2** benign, innocent

malignity *n*
malice, maliciousness, harmfulness, malevolence, hate,
hurtfulness, ill-will, hatred, bad blood, bitterness,
deadliness, perniciousness, gall, destructiveness, hostility,
wickedness, vengefulness, vindictiveness, spite, venom,
viciousness, animosity
OLD taking
FORMAL animus, balefulness, rancour
≣ harmlessness, kindness

malinger *v*
pretend, pretend to be ill, slack, dodge, shirk
COLLOQ. loaf, skive, put it on, swing the lead
SLANG *N Am* gold-brick
≣ work

malingerer *n*
slacker, dodger, shirker
COLLOQ. loafer, skiver, lead-swinger
≣ worker

mall *n*
arcade, shopping centre, shopping complex,
shopping precinct, precinct, galleria, plaza

malleability *n*
1 SUPPLENESS, flexibility, softness, plasticity, pliancy,
pliability
FORMAL ductileness
2 IMPRESSIONABILITY, receptiveness, flexibility, susceptibility,
pliancy, pliability, adaptability, manageability, compliance
FORMAL tractableness

malleable *adj*
1 SUPPLE, plastic, pliable, pliant, flexible, soft, yielding
workable
FORMAL ductile
2 IMPRESSIONABLE, manageable, receptive, flexible,
susceptible, persuadable, pliant, pliable, adaptable,
biddable, governable, compliant

FORMAL tractile, tractable
≣ 1 rigid **2** *formal* intractable

malnourished *adj*
undernourished, underfed, starved, hungry, anorexic,
anorectic

malnutrition *n*
starvation, undernourishment, underfeeding hunger,
unhealthy diet, anorexia (nervosa)
FORMAL inanition
≣ nourishment

malodorous *adj*
foul-smelling evil-smelling f(o)etid, nauseating niffy,
offensive, putrid, rank, reeking smelly, stinking
FORMAL noisome, mephitic, miasmal, miasmatic,
miasmatous, miasmic, miasmous
≣ sweet-smelling

malpractice *n*
misconduct, unethical behaviour, unprofessional conduct,
mismanagement, negligence, carelessness, impropriety,
wrongdoing offence, abuse, misdeed
FORMAL dereliction of duty

maltreat *v*
mistreat, ill-treat, treat badly, mishandle, misuse, abuse,
injure, harm, damage, hurt, bully, hound, victimize,
torture, maul, rough-house
OLD assassinate
≣ care for

maltreatment *n*
mistreatment, ill-treatment, ill-usage, ill-use, abuse, misuse,
injury, harm, damage, hurt, bullying victimization, torture
≣ care

mammal

___

Mammals include:

aardvark	gibbon	orang-utan
African elephant	giraffe	otter
anteater	goat	pig
antelope	gopher	polar bear
armadillo	gorilla	porcupine
baboon	grizzly bear	porpoise
Bactrian camel	guinea pig	rabbit
badger	hamster	raccoon
bat	hare	rat
bear	hedgehog	rhinoceros
beaver	hippopotamus	sea cow
bushbaby	horse	seal
camel	human being	sea lion
cat	hyena	sheep
chimpanzee	Indian elephant	shrew
chipmunk	kangaroo	sloth
cow	koala	squirrel
deer	lemming	tamarin
dog	lemur	tapir
dolphin	leopard	tiger
duck-billed	lion	vole
platypus	manatee	wallaby
dugong	marmoset	walrus
echidna	marmot	weasel
elephant	marsupial mouse	whale
ferret	mole	wolf
fox	mouse	zebra
gerbil	opossum	

See also **cat**; **cattle**; **dog**; **horse**; **marsupial**; **monkey**;
rodent.

___

mammoth *adj*
enormous, huge, vast, colossal, gigantic, giant,
massive, immense, stupendous, monumental, mighty,
prodigious, gargantuan, herculean, leviathan,
Brobdingnagian
COLLOQ. whopping jumbo, bumper, ginormous
≣ tiny, minute

man *n, v*

♦ *n*

1 MALE, gentleman

COLLOQ. guy, chap, bloke, boy, lad, fellow, geezer;
S Afr ou
Related adjective: male

2 HUMAN BEING, person, individual, adult, human, mortal

3 HUMANITY, human race, human beings, humankind,
mankind, people, mortals
TECHNICAL Homo sapiens
Related adjective: human

4 MANSERVANT, servant, worker, workman, labourer,
employee, helper, hand, soldier, valet, houseman,
houseboy, page, attendant, factotum, man-of-all-work,
jack-of-all-trades, odd-jobman

5 PARTNER, husband, lover, boyfriend, fiancé, spouse,
sweetheart
COLLOQ. fellow, bloke, guy, toy boy

♦ *v*

staff, crew, take charge of, be in charge of, work,
operate, occupy

■ **to a man**
without exception, with no exceptions, unanimously, as
one, with one voice, one and all, bar none

> QUOTATIONS
> What a piece of work is a man!
> WILLIAM SHAKESPEARE, *Hamlet*
>
> A woman needs a man like a fish needs a bicycle
> GLORIA STEINEM

manacle *v*
handcuff, shackle, restrain, secure, tie, fetter, chain, put in
chains, bind, curb, check, hamper, inhibit
🔁 free, unshackle

manacles *n*
handcuffs, chains, fetters, cuffs, shackles, wristlets,
irons, bonds
OLD gyves
COLLOQ. bracelets, darbies, mittens, nippers
OLD SLANG snitchers

manage *v*

1 ADMINISTER, direct, run, organize, command, govern, be
in charge of, be responsible for, head (up), be head of,
lead, guide, preside over, rule, superintend, supervise,
control, oversee, conduct, negotiate, navigate

2 ACCOMPLISH, succeed, achieve, bring about, bring off,
engineer
FORMAL effect

3 CONTROL, influence, deal with, master, handle,
keep, operate, manipulate, work, guide, play, manoeuvre,
use, wield

4 COPE, deal with, survive, get by, get along get on,
carry on, make do, shift
FORMAL fare
COLLOQ. make out
🔁 **1** mismanage **2** fail

manageable *adj*

1 *a manageable amount of work*
reasonable, doable, feasible, attainable, practicable,
acceptable, viable, tolerable

2 CONTROLLABLE, governable, amenable, accommodating
yielding submissive, compliant, docile, pliant, pliable,
flexible
FORMAL tractable

3 *manageable blocks of ice*
handy, functional, practicable, easy-to-use, wieldy
🔁 **1, 2** unmanageable **3** unmanageable, unwieldy,
awkward

management *n*

1 ADMINISTRATION, direction, control, government,
command, leadership, organization, running ruling
overseeing superintendence, supervision, charge, care,
handling conduct

2 MANAGERS, directors, directorate, executive, executives,
governors, board, owners, employers, proprietors,
supervisors
COLLOQ. bosses
🔁 **1** mismanagement **2** workers

manager *n*
director, executive, employer, businessman,
businesswoman, manageress, president, chairman,
chairwoman, chair, chairperson, chief executive,
managing director, administrator, controller,
superintendent, supervisor, commissioner, overseer,
governor, organizer, head, chief, head of department,
comptroller, landlord, landlady, *maître d'hôtel*, hotelier,
manufacturer, procurator, proctor, agent, amildar,
husband, contriver, conductor, impresario, *régisseur*,
intendant
COLLOQ. boss, gaffer, guv, suit; *Scot* head-bummer;
N Am honcho

managerial *adj*
supervisory, superintendent, executive, administrative,
organizational, departmental, governmental, legislative,
industrial, entrepreneurial

mandate *n, v*

♦ *n*
order, command, decree, edict, injunction, dictate, charge,
directive, direction, ordinance, ruling law, statute, bidding
warrant, authorization, authority, instruction, commission,
sanction

♦ *v*
authorize, legalize, make legal, validate, ratify, confirm,
license, entitle, empower, give authority to, enable,
commission, warrant, permit, give permission to, allow,
let, consent to, sanction, approve
COLLOQ. OK, okay, give the go-ahead to, greenlight, give
the green light to, give the thumbs-up to

mandatory *adj*
obligatory, compulsory, binding required, necessary,
essential, imperative
FORMAL requisite
🔁 optional

manful *adj*
brave, manly, gallant, courageous, heroic, intrepid,
bold, lion-hearted, determined, resolute, stalwart, stout,
stout-hearted, valiant, strong powerful, indomitable,
hardy, daring unflinching vigorous, noble, noble-minded
🔁 half-hearted, timid

manfully *adv*
bravely, courageously, valiantly, heroically, intrepidly,
boldly, gallantly, pluckily, determinedly, hard, vigorously,
strongly, powerfully, unflinchingly, desperately, resolutely,
stalwartly, stoutly, steadfastly, nobly
🔁 half-heartedly, timidly

manger *n*
trough, feeding trough, feeder, crib

mangle *v*

1 MUTILATE, disfigure, mar, maim, butcher, destroy,
deform, wreck, twist, maul, distort, crush, cut, hack, tear,
lacerate, rend

2 SPOIL, butcher, ruin, bungle
COLLOQ. botch, mess up, make a mess of, make a hash of
SLANG screw up

mangy *adj*
seedy, shabby, scruffy, scabby, shoddy, moth-eaten,
worn, filthy, dirty, mean
COLLOQ. tatty

manhandle *v*

1 *the porters manhandled the baggage*
haul, heave, pull, push, shove, tug
COLLOQ. hump

2 *the police manhandled the demonstrators*
maul, mistreat, maltreat, misuse, abuse, handle roughly,
push, shove, jostle
COLLOQ. knock about, rough up

manhood *n*
1 ADULTHOOD, maturity
2 MASCULINITY, virility, manliness, manfulness, maleness
COLLOQ. machismo

mania *n*
1 MADNESS, insanity, lunacy, dementia, psychosis, derangement, disorder, aberration, frenzy, wildness, raving hysteria
COLLOQ. craziness
2 PASSION, craze, rage, obsession, compulsion, fetish, preoccupation, enthusiasm, infatuation, fixation, craving urge, desire, fascination
COLLOQ. fad, thing

Manias include:

dipsomania (*alcohol*)	anthomania (*flowers*)	nymphomania (*sex*)
bibliomania (*books*)	hippomania (*horses*)	monomania (*single idea or thing*)
ailuromania (*cats*)	mythomania (*lying and exaggerating*)	kleptomania (*stealing*)
demomania (*crowds*)	ablutomania (*personal cleanliness*)	tomomania (*surgery*)
necromania (*dead bodies*)	hedonomania (*pleasure*)	logomania (*talking*)
thanatomania (*death*)	megalomania (*power*)	ergomania (*work*)
cynomania (*dogs*)	theomania (*religion*)	egomania (*yourself*)
narcomania (*drugs*)		
pyromania (*fire-raising*)		

See also **phobia**.

---

maniac *n*
1 LUNATIC, madman, madwoman, psychotic, psychopath, deranged person
COLLOQ. nutter, nut, nutcase, fruitcake, crackpot, crank, headcase, kook
SLANG loony, screwball, oddball, psycho, mentalist; N Am cupcake
2 ENTHUSIAST, fan, fanatic
COLLOQ. fiend, freak, buff

manic *adj*
1 INSANE, mad, deranged, demented, crazed
COLLOQ. crazy, barmy, batty, dippy, daffy, loopy
2 FRENZIED, frantic, frenetic, hectic, feverish, desperate, furious, overwrought, distraught, distracted, crazed, wild, uncontrolled, mad, berserk, amok, raving demented, hysterical, panic-stricken, beside yourself, obsessive
F3 1 sane 2 calm, composed

manically *adv*
frenetically, hectically, wildly, excitedly, intensely, madly, hysterically

manifest *adj, v*
♦ *adj*
obvious, evident, clear, apparent, plain, open, patent, distinct, noticeable, conspicuous, perceptible, glaring blatant, unmistak(e)able, visible, unconcealed, transparent
F3 unclear
♦ *v*
show, exhibit, display, demonstrate, reveal, appear, set forth, present, express, declare, indicate, expose, make clear/plain, prove, illustrate, establish, be evidence of, extrovert
OLD confess
FORMAL evince, attest
F3 conceal, hide

manifestation *n*
display, exhibition, demonstration, show, presentation, declaration, revelation, exposure, disclosure, appearance, expression, representation, reflex, illustration, exemplification, evidence, mode, sign, indication, token, mark
TECHNICAL incarnation
FORMAL exposition

manifesto *n*
statement, declaration, announcement, proclamation, publication, policies, programme, platform

manifold *adj*
many, several, numerous, varied, various, diverse, multiple, kaleidoscopic, abundant, copious
FORMAL multifarious, multitudinous

manipulate *v*
1 MANOEUVRE, influence, control, exploit, work, milk, engineer, guide, direct, steer, use/turn to your advantage, negotiate, capitalize on, finesse
COLLOQ. wangle, cash in on, pull strings, have in the palm of your hand, twist round your little finger, have over a barrel, wheel and deal, frame, fit up
2 FALSIFY, rig juggle with, massage, tamper with, gerrymander, shuffle, thimblerig cog
COLLOQ. doctor, cook, fiddle
3 HANDLE, control, manage, wield, operate, work, knead, massage, use, utilize, employ, process, ply, nurse; N Am tong
OLD hand

manipulation *n*
1 MANOEUVRING, influence, exploitation, control, working guidance, directing steering negotiation, milking
COLLOQ. wheeling and dealing wangling pulling strings
2 FALSIFICATION, rigging juggling massaging
COLLOQ. doctoring fiddling cooking the books
3 HANDLING, control, wielding operation, kneading using utilization

manipulative *adj*
scheming crafty, cunning deceitful, sly, underhand, unscrupulous, wily, devious, artful, calculating conniving designing insidious, tricky, slippery, foxy, Machiavellian
FORMAL duplicitous
F3 artless, honest, open, transparent

manipulator *n*
1 EXPLOITER, controller, manoeuvrer, influencer, schemer, engineer, director, negotiator
COLLOQ. wheeler-dealer, smoothy, smart guy
2 HANDLER, operator, user, worker, controller, wielder

mankind *n*
human race, humanity, human beings, humankind, man, people, mortals
TECHNICAL Homo sapiens

manliness *n*
masculinity, maleness, virility, manfulness, bravery, boldness, courage, valour, fearlessness, heroism, intrepidity, resoluteness, resolution, stout-heartedness, stalwartness, hardihood, independence, manhood, strength, vigour, mettle, firmness
FORMAL fortitude
COLLOQ. machismo
F3 timidity, unmanliness

manly *adj*
masculine, male, virile, manful, brave, courageous, bold, intrepid, fearless, heroic, determined, strong powerful, firm, tough, rugged, vigorous, sturdy, robust
COLLOQ. macho

man-made *adj*
synthetic, manufactured, simulated, imitation, artificial, mock, faux
COLLOQ. ersatz
F3 natural

manner *n*
1 WAY, method, means, fashion, style, variety, procedure, technique, approach, practice, process, routine, form
FORMAL mode

2 BEHAVIOUR, conduct, appearance, look, character, attitude, posture, stance
FORMAL bearing demeanour, air, mien, aspect, deportment
3 good manners
behaviour, conduct, way of behaving etiquette, politeness, courtesy, protocol, good form, formalities, social graces
FORMAL decorum, propriety, demeanour, bearing
COLLOQ. p's and q's, the done thing

mannered adj
artificial, posed, pretentious, stilted, precious
FORMAL affected, euphuistic
COLLOQ. pseudo, put-on
E3 natural

mannerism n
idiosyncrasy, peculiarity, characteristic, quirk, trait, feature, foible, habit

mannerly adj
polite, courteous, refined, well-behaved, well-bred, well-mannered, gentlemanly, ladylike, respectful, civil, civilized, deferential, gracious, formal, genteel, polished
FORMAL decorous
E3 unmannerly

mannish adj
masculine, unfeminine, unladylike, unwomanly, tomboyish, viraginian, viraginous, viragoish, Amazonian
OLD (Shakesp) mankind
FORMAL virilescent
COLLOQ. butch, laddish
E3 womanish

mannishness n
masculinity, unfemininity, unladylikeness, unwomanliness, virilism
FORMAL virilescence
COLLOQ. butchness
E3 womanishness

manoeuvre v, n
♦ v
1 MOVE, manipulate, handle, guide, pilot, steer, navigate, dock, berth, negotiate, jockey, direct, drive, turn, cut in, ease, exercise
TECHNICAL chandelle
2 CONTRIVE, engineer, plot, scheme, intrigue, manipulate, manage, plan, devise, negotiate
COLLOQ. wangle, pull strings, jockey for position
♦ n
1 EXERCISE, move, movement, turn, roll, operation, deployment, action
OLD decursion
2 MANIPULATION, skilful plan, ploy, plot, ruse, stratagem, device, gambit, tactic, trick, scheme, subterfuge, stall
FORMAL machination, artifice
COLLOQ. dodge, wangle

manor n
house, country house, seat, hall, villa, barony, château, Schloss, Hof
Related adjective: manorial

manpower n
workers, skilled workers, workforce, staff, employees, human resources, personnel

manse n
vicarage, rectory, parsonage, deanery, glebe-house

manservant n
butler, gentleman's gentleman, valet, attendant, retainer

mansion n
home, hall, house, manor, manor-house, castle, château, Schloss, villa, seat, place, casa
FORMAL abode, dwelling habitation, residence

manslaughter n
killing slaughter, murder, massacre, butchery, genocide, homicide, assassination, execution, slaying extermination, carnage, bloodshed, elimination, destruction, fatality

FORMAL patricide, matricide, infanticide, fratricide, sororicide, uxoricide
COLLOQ. liquidation

mantle n, v
♦ n
1 CLOAK, cape, hood, shawl, veil, wrap, shroud, screen
2 COVER, covering veil, shroud, blanket, layer, cloak, mask, cloud, envelope
♦ v
cover, cloak, veil, mask, wrap, blanket, shroud, cloud, envelop, hide, disguise, conceal

manual n, adj
♦ n
handbook, guide, guidebook, instruction book, instructions, ABC, companion, bible, prospectus, vade-mecum, directions
COLLOQ. book of words
♦ adj
hand-operated, by hand, (done) with your hands, physical, human
E3 mental, automatic

manually adv
by hand, with your hands, done/operated with your hands, physically

manufacture v, n
♦ v
1 MAKE, produce, construct, build, fabricate, create, assemble, mass-produce, put together, turn out, fashion, process, forge, model, form
2 INVENT, make up, devise, construct, frame, concoct, fabricate, think up, dream up
♦ n
production, making construction, building fabrication, mass-production, assembly, processing creation, formation, fashioning modelling forming

manufacturer n
maker, producer, industrialist, constructor, factory-owner, builder, creator
OLD fabricant

manure n
fertilizer, compost, muck, dung animal excrement, droppings, guano, ordure, top-dressing; dialect vraic; Scot hen-pen, police-manure
TECHNICAL biosolids
FORMAL animal faeces

manuscript n
document, text, typescript, paper, parchment, scroll, vellum

many adj, n
♦ adj
a lot of, a large number of, several, numerous, innumerable, countless, various, multiple, copious, varied, sundry, diverse
FORMAL manifold, multitudinous
COLLOQ. umpteen
E3 few
♦ n
a lot, a large number, a mass, a multitude, plenty, scores
COLLOQ. lots, loads, hundreds, thousands, millions, billions, zillions, gazillions, masses, piles, heaps, stacks, oodles, scads, wads, tons

map n, v
♦ n
chart, plan, projection, town plan, street plan, street guide, road-map, atlas, gazetteer, graph, plot, inset, cartogram, card, carte du pays, horoscope
TECHNICAL hypsography, planisphere
OLD mappemond
♦ v
chart, plot, plan, mark, sketch
FORMAL delineate
■ **map out**
sketch, draw (up), draft, outline, work out

mar *v*
spoil, impair, harm, hurt, damage, blemish, deface,
deform, disfigure, mutilate, injure, maim, scar, detract
from, mangle, ruin, wreck, taint, tarnish, contaminate,
stain
⊟ enhance

maraud *v*
plunder, raid, ravage, ransack, loot, pillage, harry, forage,
foray, sack
FORMAL despoil, spoliate, depredate

marauder *n*
bandit, brigand, robber, raider, plunderer, looter, pillager,
pirate, buccaneer, freebooter, outlaw, highwayman,
ravager, predator, rustler, rover
COLLOQ. mugger

march *v, n*
♦ *v*
walk, file, parade, pace, step, tread, stride,
tramp, hike, footslog stalk, strut, swagger, forward,
advance, progress, make headway, countermarch,
debouch, defile
♦ *n*
1 STEP, pace, stride, walk, gait
2 WALK, route-march, trek, hike, tramp, footslog *étape*
COLLOQ. yomp
3 PROCESSION, parade, demonstration, protest
TECHNICAL walk-around
COLLOQ. demo
4 ADVANCE, development, progress, evolution, passage,
headway

marches *n*
boundary, border, border district, borderland,
frontier

margin *n*
1 BORDER, edge, boundary, bound, periphery, perimeter,
frontier, demarcation line, rim, brim, brink, limit(s),
confine(s), verge, side, skirt
2 ALLOWANCE, play, leeway, latitude, scope,
room, room for manoeuvre, difference, differential, space,
surplus, extra

marginal *adj*
borderline, doubtful, peripheral, on the edge, negligible,
minute, minimal, insignificant, minor, slight, tiny,
low, small
⊟ central, core, mainstream

marginalization *n*
isolation, separation, separateness, detachment,
disconnection, dissociation, alienation, abstraction,
solitude, solitariness, loneliness, aloneness, remoteness,
seclusion, retirement, withdrawal, exile, segregation
FORMAL sequestration
⊟ assimilation, integration

marginalize *v*
isolate, set apart, seclude, keep apart, segregate, abstract,
cut off, detach, remove, disconnect, separate, divorce,
alienate, shut out/away, ostracize, exclude, strand, maroon
FORMAL sequester
COLLOQ. cold-shoulder
⊟ assimilate, integrate

marijuana *n*
cannabis, hemp, hashish, ganja, bhang kef,
kaif, kif, sinsemilla
COLLOQ. joint, bifter, dope, pot, gage, puff, wacky baccy
SLANG hash, blow, blaze, weed, grass, reefer, spliff, roach,
toke, blunt, bomber, skunk, leaf, greens, shit;
N Am locoweed, Mary Jane, splay; *S Afr* dagga
OLD SLANG *N Am* tea

marina *n*
dock, harbour, mooring port, yacht station

marinade *v*
steep, soak, immerse, marinate, souse, saturate, imbue,
permeate, infuse

marine *adj*
sea, maritime, naval, nautical, seafaring seagoing
ocean-going oceanic, saltwater, seawater,
aquatic
FORMAL pelagic, thalassian, thalassic

mariner *n*
sailor, seaman, seafarer, deckhand, navigator
COLLOQ. tar, Jack Tar, matlo, matlow, matelot,
sea dog salt, limey

marital *adj*
married, marriage, wedding wedded
FORMAL matrimonial, conjugal, nuptial, connubial,
spousal

maritally *adv*
in/by marriage
OLD in/by wedlock
FORMAL matrimonially, conjugally, nuptially, connubially

maritime *adj*
marine, nautical, naval, seafaring sea, seaside, sea-trade,
sea-coast, seagoing oceanic, coastal
FORMAL littoral, pelagic

mark *n, v*
♦ *n*
1 SPOT, stain, blemish, patch, pimple, freckle, birthmark,
blot, blotch, smudge, smear, dent, impression, trace,
fingerprint(s), track(s), imprint, speck, notch, chip, cut,
scar, scratch, bruise, score, line, nick
FORMAL stigma
COLLOQ. zit
2 SIGN, indication, character, symbol, stamp, token,
characteristic, feature, quality, attribute, symptom, clue,
proof, hint, evidence, impression, print, imprint
3 SYMBOL, emblem, brand, stamp, seal, badge, device,
logo, trademark, motto, monogram
4 SCORE, grade, percentage, tick, assessment, evaluation
5 *inflation reaching the 5% mark*
point, level, stage, norm, standard, criterion, gauge, scale,
measure, yardstick
6 TARGET, goal, aim, objective, object, purpose, end,
intention, bull's-eye
♦ *v*
1 STAIN, blemish, blot, smudge, discolour, dent, scar,
scratch, bruise, chip, cut, score, nick
2 BRAND, label, stamp, tag flag characterize, indicate,
scribe, put your name on, identify, distinguish
3 EVALUATE, assess, correct, grade
FORMAL appraise
4 WRITE DOWN, note (down), indicate, name, label,
specify, designate, jot down
5 CHARACTERIZE, identify, stamp, brand, typify, distinguish
6 *mark an event/occasion*
observe, remember, celebrate, commemorate, keep,
honour, recognize, acknowledge, pay tribute to
7 *the war marked a turning point in the city's history*
represent, indicate, signify, denote, designate
8 *mark my words*
listen, mind, note, spot, observe, regard, see,
notice, take note of, discern, pay attention to, bear in
mind, take to heart
FORMAL heed, take heed of
■ **mark down**
reduce, lower, decrease, cut
COLLOQ. slash
⊟ mark up
■ **mark out**
1 *mark out a football pitch*
draw lines, demarcate, show the boundaries of,
fix, delimit
FORMAL delineate
2 DISTINGUISH, differentiate, tell apart, set apart,
discriminate, single out, tell the difference between
■ **mark up**
increase, raise, put up
COLLOQ. hike up, jack up

■ **make your mark**
succeed, be successful, prosper, get on
COLLOQ. make it, make the grade, hit/make the big time
■ **up to the mark**
good enough, satisfactory, acceptable
COLLOQ. up to scratch, OK
■ **wide of the mark**
incorrect, inaccurate, imprecise, irrelevant, beside the
point, off target

marked *adj*
1 SPOTTED, spotty, stained, blemished, blotched, blotchy,
scarred, pimply, freckled, bruised, scratched
2 NOTICEABLE, obvious, conspicuous, prominent, signal,
evident, clear, pronounced, distinct, noted, decided,
emphatic, considerable, remarkable, apparent, glaring
striking blatant, unmistakable
3 SUSPECTED, watched, doomed, condemned
F3 1 unnoticeable, slight

markedly *adv*
noticeably, obviously, conspicuously, prominently,
signally, evidently, clearly, distinctly, decidedly,
emphatically, considerably, remarkably, glaringly,
strikingly, blatantly, unmistakably

market *n, v*
♦ *n*
1 *buy goods at the market*
mart, market-place, shopping centre, mall, bazaar, fair,
exchange, outlet, farmers' market, souk
OLD agora
Related adjective: nundinal
2 *no market for these goods*
demand, call, requirement, need, occasion, want, desire
3 BUSINESS, trade, trading, buying, selling, industry, dealings
♦ *v*
sell, retail, hawk, peddle, offer for sale
F3 buy
■ **on the market**
for sale, on sale, up for sale, available

marketable *adj*
in demand, sought after, wanted, saleable, sellable,
merchantable
FORMAL vendible
F3 unsaleable

marketing *n*
sales, promotion, publicity, advertising merchandizing
distribution
COLLOQ. hype, pushing plugging
See panel on next page

marksman, markswoman *n*
crack shot, dead shot, sharpshooter, sniper

mark-up *n*
increase, price increase, rise, escalation, leap, upsurge
COLLOQ. hike

maroon *v*
abandon, strand, cast away, desert, put ashore, leave
(behind), isolate, turn your back on
FORMAL forsake
COLLOQ. leave in the lurch, leave high and dry

marriage *n*
1 *the marriage ceremony*
union, married relationship, married state, wedding
OLD wedlock
FORMAL matrimony, nuptials, spousage, espousals
Related adjectives: marital, matrimonial, conjugal,
connubial
2 UNION, alliance, partnership, merger, coupling fusion,
amalgamation, unification, combination, link, connection,
association, confederation, affiliation
F3 1 divorce **2** separation

QUOTATIONS
All weddings are similar but every marriage is different
JOHN PETER BERGER, *The White Bird,* 'The Storyteller'

married *adj*
marital, wedded, united, wed, joined, husbandly,
wifely, wived, yoked
FORMAL conjugal, connubial, matrimonial, nuptial,
spousal
COLLOQ. hitched, spliced
F3 divorced, single, widowed

marrow *n*
essence, heart, nub, kernel, core, nucleus, centre, pith,
soul, spirit, substance, quick, stuff, gist
FORMAL quintessence
COLLOQ. nitty-gritty, nuts and bolts
Related adjective: myeloid

marry *v*
1 WED, get married, become husband and wife,
intermarry, unite, elope; *Scot* cleek
OLD spouse, take to wife, wive; *(Shakesp)* go to the world
FORMAL join in matrimony, become espoused
COLLOQ. tie the knot, get hitched, hitch up, get spliced,
take the plunge, lead to the altar, lead up the aisle, make
an honest woman of
2 UNITE, ally, join (together), merge, combine,
amalgamate, couple, affiliate, match, link, connect,
associate, pair, weld, fuse, knit
F3 1 divorce **2** separate

marsh *n*
marshland, bog swamp, fen, morass, mire, quagmire,
slough; *N Am* bayou
Related adjective: paludal

marshal *v*
1 ARRANGE, dispose, order, line up, align, array, rank,
organize, put in order, assemble, gather (together), muster,
group, collect, draw up, deploy
2 GUIDE, lead, take, escort, conduct, usher, shepherd

marshy *adj*
boggy, fenny, fennish, swampy, quaggy, waterlogged, wet,
muddy, squelchy, miry, slumpy, spongy
FORMAL paludal, paludinal, paludine, paludinous
F3 solid, firm, dry

marsupial

Marsupials include:

bandicoot	marsupial rat	rock wallaby
cuscus	numbat	Tasmanian Devil
kangaroo	opossum	Tasmanian wolf
koala	pademelon	tree kangaroo
kowari	phalanger	wallaby
marsupial anteater	possum	wallaroo
marsupial mole	quoll	wombat
marsupial mouse	rat kangaroo	

mart *n*
market, market-place, shopping centre, bazaar,
mall, fair, exchange, outlet, souk

martial *adj*
warlike, military, army, soldierly, militant, heroic, brave,
belligerent, combative, aggressive, hawkish
FORMAL pugnacious, bellicose

martial arts

Martial arts include:

UNARMED:		WITH WEAPONS:
aikido	kempo	bandesh
Brazilian	kickboxing	bojutsu
jujitsu (BJJ)	kung fu	jojutsu
capoeira	muay thai	kendo
judo	tae kwon do	kenjutsu
jujitsu	t'ai chi	kumdo
karate	vale tudo	kyodo
	wushu	

Terms used in marketing include:

PEOPLE IN MARKETING:
account executive
commando salesman
media buyer
media planner

SELLING METHODS:
cold call
cross selling
door-to-door
face-to-face
field selling
hard sell
high-pressure selling
house-to-house
inertia selling
low-pressure selling
mailshot
missionary selling
party selling
personal selling
pyramid selling
telephone selling
upselling

ADVERTISING AND PROMOTION TECHNIQUES:
above-the-fold advertising
above-the-line advertising
advergaming
adware
bait advertising
banner ads
below-the-line advertising
blanket coverage
blind advertisement
BOGO(F)F (buy one get one (for) free)
BOGOL (buy one get one later)
classified advertising
commercial
comparative advertising
co-operative advertising
flash pack
free gift (or sample)
gimmick
giveaway
industrial advertising
institutional advertising
interstitial web page
island display
jingle
loyalty card
outdoor advertising
personality promotion
piggyback promotion
pop-under
pop-up
predatory pricing
sales campaign
sales drive

slogan
spot advertising
subliminal advertising

BRANDING:
brand awareness
brand image
brand loyalty
corporate identity
corporate image
dealer brand
family brand
market leader
multi-brand strategy
own-brand
own-label
recognition

MARKET RESEARCH:
aided (or prompted) recall
area sampling
attitude research
audience research
buying motives
canvass
cluster sampling
concept testing
consumer panel
consumer research
filter question
focus group survey
Gallup poll
group discussion
leading question
motivation research
random sampling
reference group
unaided recall
unprompted response

BUYERS:
adopter
angel customer
captive audience
demon customer
early adopter
heavy user
late adopter
target audience

PRODUCTS:
articles of ostentation
cash cow
dog
FMCGs (fast-moving consumer goods)
heterogenous products
homogenous products
loss-leader
low-involvement products

masstige product
prestige product
problem children (or wildcats)
star

MISCELLANEOUS:
ACORN (a classification of residential neighbourhoods)
after-sales service
AIDA (Attention Interest Desire Action)
ambush marketing
ASA (Advertising Standards Authority)
B2B (business-to-business)
buyers' market
call rate
campaign
cannibalism
captive market
churn
competitive market
concentrated marketing
consumer sovereignty
corner a market
coverage
credibility gap
customer orientation
customer profile
DAGMAR (defining advertising goals for measured advertising results)
demarketing
demographic
elasticity of demand
family life cycle
footfall
four p's (Product, Price, Promotion and Place)
freemium
frequency
gap analysis
generic
geographical concentration
Giffen good
green marketing
growth-share matrix
guerilla marketing
halo effect
harvesting strategy
hierarchy of effects
hierarchy of needs
high-involvement products
hit rate
horizontal marketing
impulse buying
incentive marketing
infomediary
international marketing

journey planning
key prospects
launch
macro marketing
market demand
marketing audit
marketing board
marketing concept
marketing intelligence
marketing mix
market orientation
market penetration
market potential
market profile
market segmentation
market share
matched sample
media independent
merchandizing
micro marketing
mock-up
necessity good
Nielsen index
normal good
observation
opinion leaders
opportunity to see
paired comparisons
pay-per-click
perceptual map
perfect competition
product differentiation
product orientation
product positioning
psychographic measurement
P2P (peer-to-peer marketing)
response rate
retail audit
rolling launch
sales aid
saturation point
skimming pricing
social marketing
socio-economic groups
solus position
static market
tachistoscope
Target Group Index
test marketing
tribal marketing
undifferentiated marketing
up-market
USP (unique selling proposition)
vertical marketing
viral marketing
visualizer

---

martinet *n*
dsciplinarian, stickler, tyrant, taskmaster, taskmistress, formalist
COLLOQ. slave-driver

martyr *v*
put to death, make a martyr of, crucify, stone, persecute, torture, torment, burn at the stake, throw to the lions, put on the rack
COLLOQ. give the works, give the third degree

martyrdom *n*
death, suffering torture, torment, persecution, excruciation, ordeal, agony, anguish, witness

marvel *v, n*
♦ *v*
wonder, gape, gaze, stare, goggle, not expect, be amazed, be astonished, stand in amazement
COLLOQ. gawp, be flabbergasted, not believe your eyes, not know what to say

♦ *n*

wonder, miracle, surprise, something amazing/incredible, phenomenon, prodigy, spectacle, sensation, genius
COLLOQ. eye-opener, quite something

marvellous *adj*

1 WONDERFUL, excellent, splendid, superb, great, magnificent, terrific, super, fantastic
COLLOQ. ace, neat, brill, sensational, magic
SLANG awesome, wicked, bad, def, phat, mean, crucial, rad, radical, cool, mega
2 EXTRAORDINARY, amazing surprising astonishing astounding sensational, spectacular, miraculous, remarkable, awesome, unbelievable, incredible, stupendous, glorious
E₃ 1 terrible, awful **2** ordinary, run-of-the-mill

marvellously *adv*

extremely, exceedingly, excessively, very, really, exceptionally, extraordinarily, intensely, thoroughly, remarkably, utterly, greatly, highly, unusually, uncommonly, inordinately, acutely, severely, decidedly
COLLOQ. awfully, terribly, dreadfully, frightfully, terrifically

masculine *adj*

1 MALE, manlike, manly, mannish, virile
COLLOQ. macho, butch
2 VIGOROUS, strong strapping robust, powerful, muscular, rugged, red-blooded, virile, bold, brave, gallant, fearless, heroic, determined, confident, resolute, stout-hearted
E₃ 1 feminine

masculinity *n*

manliness, maleness, virility, manfulness, bravery, boldness, courage, valour, fearlessness, heroism, intrepidity, resolution, stout-heartedness, stalwartness, hardihood, independence, manhood, strength, vigour, mettle, firmness
FORMAL fortitude
COLLOQ. machismo
E₃ femininity

mash *v, n*

♦ *v*

crush, pulp, beat, pound, purée, pulverize, pummel, grind, smash, squash

♦ *n*

mush, pulp, crush, purée, squash, pap, paste

mask *n, v*

♦ *n*

disguise, camouflage, façade, front, concealment, cover-up, cover, guise, pretence, semblance, cloak, veil, blind, screen, show, veneer, visor, goggles, vizard, false face, domino
TECHNICAL matte, persona
OLD masque

♦ *v*

disguise, camouflage, cover (up), conceal, cloak, veil, hide, obscure, screen, shield
OLD vizard; (*Shakesp*) immask
FORMAL dissemble
E₃ expose, uncover

masquerade *n, v*

♦ *n*

1 MASQUE, masked ball, costume ball, fancy dress ball/party
2 DISGUISE, counterfeit, cover-up, cover, deception, front, pose, pretence, guise, cloak

♦ *v*

disguise, impersonate, pose, pass yourself off, mask, play, pretend, profess
FORMAL dissimulate

mass¹ *n, adj, v*

♦ *n*

1 HEAP, pile, load, accumulation, collection, combination, entirety, whole, total, totality, sum, lot, group, batch, stack, bunch
FORMAL aggregate, conglomeration, assemblage

2 QUANTITY, abundance, multitude, large number, throng troop, crowd, band, horde, mob
COLLOQ. loads, heaps, bags, piles, lots, tons, scores, oodles
3 MAJORITY, body, bulk, greater part, most, preponderance
4 SIZE, dimension, magnitude, immensity, bulk, weight, capacity
5 LUMP, piece, chunk, block, hunk
COLLOQ. wodge
6 *the masses*
crowd, herd, mob, lower classes, working class(es), common people, proletariat, rabble, hoi polloi, the rank and file
COLLOQ. plebs, riff-raff

♦ *adj*

widespread, large-scale, extensive, comprehensive, general, universal, indiscriminate, popular, across-the-board, sweeping wholesale, blanket
FORMAL pandemic
E₃ limited, small-scale

♦ *v*

collect, gather, assemble, congregate, amass, accumulate, draw together, come/bring together, crowd, rally, cluster, muster, swarm, throng
E₃ separate

mass² *n*

go to mass
Eucharist, Communion, Holy Communion, Lord's Supper, Lord's Table

massacre *n, v*

♦ *n*

slaughter, murder, homicide, extermination, carnage, butchery, wholesale slaughter, indiscriminate killing holocaust, bloodbath, annihilation, killing genocide, ethnic cleansing pogrom, liquidation, decimation, purge

♦ *v*

slaughter, butcher, murder, mow down, exterminate, annihilate, kill (off), slay, decimate, liquidate
COLLOQ. wipe out

massage *n, v*

♦ *n*

manipulation, kneading rub, rubbing rub-down, pummelling reflexology, aromatherapy, acupressure, shiatsu, Jacuzzi®, tripsis, osteopathy, physiotherapy, Reichian therapy, reiki

♦ *v*

1 *massaged her thigh*
manipulate, knead, rub (down), pummel, shampoo
2 *massage statistics*
alter, tamper with, interfere with, falsify, misrepresent, manipulate
COLLOQ. doctor, fiddle, cook

massive *adj*

huge, immense, enormous, vast, colossal, mammoth, gigantic, big, bulky, monumental, solid, hulking, hefty, weighty, substantial, heavy, large, large-scale, great, extensive, mighty
COLLOQ. XXL, whopping, jumbo, ginormous
E₃ tiny, small

massively *adv*

immensely, greatly, very much, substantially, heavily, extensively, enormously, vastly, monumentally

mast *n*

pole, shaft, rod, bar, spar, boom, yard, heel, post, staff, stick, upright, support

master *n, adj, v*

♦ *n*

1 RULER, chief, governor, head, lord, captain, employer, commander, controller, director, manager, superintendent, overseer, principal, overlord, owner; *S Afr* baas
COLLOQ. boss, gaffer, skipper, guv; *N Am* honcho
2 EXPERT, genius, professional, pundit, virtuoso, past master, grand master, maestro, adept
COLLOQ. dab hand, ace, pro, buff, egghead, wise guy; *N Am* mavin

3 TEACHER, tutor, mentor, instructor, schoolteacher, schoolmaster, schoolmistress, guide, guru
FORMAL pedagogue, preceptor
E3 **1** servant, underling **2** amateur, beginner **3** learner, pupil

♦ *adj*
1 CHIEF, principal, main, leading foremost, most important, prime, predominant, controlling great, grand
2 EXPERT, masterly, skilled, skilful, experienced, proficient, practised, adept, dexterous
E3 **1** subordinate **2** inept

♦ *v*
1 CONQUER, defeat, subdue, triumph over, overcome, overpower, quell, suppress, rule, control, govern, tame, bridle, check, curb
FORMAL subjugate, vanquish
2 LEARN, grasp, acquire, manage, pick up
COLLOQ. get the hang of

masterful *adj*
arrogant, authoritative, domineering overbearing controlling high-handed, despotic, dictatorial, autocratic, tyrannical, powerful, dominating imperious
FORMAL peremptory
COLLOQ. bossy
E3 humble, downtrodden; *colloq.* hen-pecked

> **⚠ masterful** or **masterly**?
> *Masterful* means 'showing power, authority or determination': *The directors show a masterful approach to their employees. Masterly* means 'showing the skill of a master': *a masterly display of swordsmanship.*

masterly *adj*
expert, professional, accomplished, polished, skilled, skilful, dexterous, adept, adroit, first-rate, excellent, superb, superior, supreme
FORMAL consummate
COLLOQ. ace, crack, top-notch
E3 inept, clumsy

mastermind *v, n*
♦ *v*
devise, think up, contrive, engineer, direct, control, organize, manage, originate, plan, conceive, design, dream up, frame, hatch, forge, inspire, be behind
♦ *n*
organizer, initiator, manager, planner, creator, director, originator, authority, genius, intellect, mind, engineer, architect, prime mover, virtuoso
COLLOQ. brains

masterpiece *n*
masterwork, *pièce de résistance*, *chef d'oeuvre*, magnum opus, work of art, creation, jewel

masterstroke *n*
superior performance, triumph, victory, success, achievement, accomplishment, attainment, feat, coup

mastery *n*
1 PROFICIENCY, skill, ability, capability, command, expertise, virtuosity, knowledge, understanding comprehension, knowhow, dexterity, familiarity, grasp
FORMAL prowess
2 CONTROL, command, domination, supremacy, superiority, victory, triumph, dominion, authority, sovereignty, rule, direction
FORMAL ascendancy
COLLOQ. upper hand
E3 **1** incompetence **2** subjugation

masticate *v*
champ, chew, munch, chomp, crunch, eat, ruminate, knead
FORMAL manducate

mastication *n*
chewing champing munching eating rumination
FORMAL manducation

masturbate *v*
stimulate yourself, gratify yourself
COLLOQ. jerk off, jack off, toss (it) off, play with yourself, enjoy yourself
SLANG wank, frig

masturbation *n*
self-gratification, self-stimulation, autoeroticism, onanism, self-abuse, tribadism, tribady
COLLOQ. playing with yourself, enjoying yourself, hand relief
SLANG wank, wanking frig frigging frottage

mat *n*
1 CARPET, doormat, felt, rug underfelt, underlay, drugget, table mat, place mat, coaster
2 TANGLE, knot, twist, cluster, mass

match¹ *n, v*
♦ *n*
1 CONTEST, competition, bout, game, test, trial, event, meet, tournament
2 EQUAL, equivalent, peer, counterpart, fellow, mate, rival, competitor, one of a pair, copy, double, companion, complement, replica, lookalike, twin, duplicate
COLLOQ. dead ringer
3 MARRIAGE, alliance, union, combination, partnership, affiliation, pairing merger, coupling
♦ *v*
1 EQUAL, compare, measure up to, rival, parallel, compete, oppose, contend, vie, keep up with, pit against
OLD (*Spenser*) amate
2 FIT, go with, agree, suit, harmonize, tally, co-ordinate, blend, complement, adapt, go together, correspond, be in agreement, relate, tone with, accompany, connect
OLD (*Shakesp*) besort, pattern
FORMAL accord
3 JOIN, marry, unite, mate, link, couple, combine, ally, pair (up), yoke, team
COLLOQ. hitch up
E3 **2** clash, conflict **3** separate, divorce
■ match up to
come up to, reach, meet, measure up to, live up to, make the grade, compare with, approach, bear comparison with

match² *n*
light the fire with matches
light, safety match, spill, taper, fuse, vesta

matching *adj*
corresponding comparable, complementing equivalent, parallel, like, identical, co-ordinating blending harmonizing complementary, correlative, similar, duplicate, same, twin, paired, double, coupled
FORMAL analogous
E3 clashing conflicting

matchless *adj*
unequalled, without equal, peerless, incomparable, beyond compare, unmatched, unparalleled, unsurpassed, unexcelled, unrivalled, inimitable, perfect, unique
E3 ordinary

mate *n, v*
♦ *n*
1 FRIEND, companion, comrade, colleague, partner, fellow worker, co-worker, workmate, associate, mucker; *dialect* marrow, wack; *Welsh* wus
OLD (*Shakesp*) co-mate; (*Spenser*) paragon
FORMAL compeer
COLLOQ. chum, crony, buddy, pal; *Aust & NZ* cobber
SLANG china, fere
OLD SLANG cully
2 PARTNER, husband, wife, spouse, boyfriend, girlfriend, companion; *Scot* maik
OLD make, fere, paragon
COLLOQ. better half, other half, hubbie, missis, missus, Mr Right, opposite number

3 ASSISTANT, helper, subordinate, apprentice, accomplice, partner
COLLOQ. sidekick
4 MATCH, fellow, twin, equivalent, counterpart
♦ v
1 COUPLE, pair, breed, copulate, line, leap, nick
OLD gender
2 JOIN, match, marry, wed

material n, adj
♦ n
1 STUFF, substance, body, matter, medium
2 FABRIC, textile, cloth, stuff
3 INFORMATION, facts, facts and figures, numbers, data, details, particulars, ideas, evidence, constituents, work, notes
COLLOQ. low-down, gen, info
♦ adj
1 PHYSICAL, bodily, concrete, tangible, palpable, substantial, earthly, worldly
FORMAL corporeal
2 RELEVANT, significant, important, momentous, consequential, meaningful, essential, vital, key, indispensable, serious, weighty
FORMAL pertinent, germane, apposite
E₃ 1 spiritual, abstract **2** irrelevant, insignificant

materialism n
1 CORPOREALISM, hylicism, hylism, somatism
2 CONSUMERISM, worldliness, greed, acquisitiveness
E₃ 1 spiritualism

> **QUOTATIONS**
> Without war the world would deteriorate into materialism
> COUNT HELMUTH VON MOLTKE

materialistic adj
consumerist, worldly, acquisitive, mercenary, money-grabbing mammonist, mammonistic

materialize v
appear, arise, become visible, show/reveal yourself, take shape, turn up, happen, occur, take place, come into being
E₃ disappear

materially adv
significantly, essentially, fundamentally, substantially, basically, considerably, seriously, gravely, greatly, much
E₃ insignificantly

maternal adj
motherly, motherlike, nurturing nourishing loving caring affectionate, warm, tender, gentle, fond, kind, protective, comforting understanding vigilant, doting

matey
see **maty, matey.**

mathematics
See panel below

mating n
breeding copulating sexual intercourse, copulation, coupling fusing uniting pairing joining matching twinning
FORMAL coition

Mathematical terms include:

acute angle	complement	even number	mapping	plane figure	side
addition	complementary	exponent	matrix	plus	simultaneous
algebra	angle	exponential	maximum	point	equation
algorithm	complex number	face	mean	positive number	sine
analysis	concave	factor	measure	prime number	speed
angle	concentric circles	factorial	median	probability	spiral
apex	congruent	Fibonacci	minimum	product	square
approximate	conjugate angles	sequence	minus	proportion	square root
arc	constant	formula	mirror image	protractor	standard deviation
area	continuous	fraction	mirror symmetry	Pythagoras's	statistics
argument	distribution	function	mixed fraction	theorem	straight line
arithmetic	converse	geometric	Möbius strip	quadrant	subset
arithmetic	convex	progression	mode	quadratic equation	subtractor
progression	coordinate	geometry	modulus	quadrilateral	supplementary
asymmetrical	correlation	gradient	multiple	quartile	angles
average	cosine	graph	multiplication	quotient	symmetry
axis	covariance	greater than	natural logarithm	radian	tangent
axis of	cross section	group	natural number	radius	three-dimensional
symmetry	cube	harmonic	negative	random sample	total
bar chart	cube root	progression	number	ratio	transcendental
bar graph	curve	height	number	rational number	number
base	decimal	helix	numerator	real number	transformation
bearing	degree	histogram	oblique	reciprocal	triangulation
binary	denominator	horizontal	obtuse angle	recurring decimal	trigonometry
binomial	depth	hyperbola	odd number	reflection	unit
breadth	derivative	hypotenuse	operation	reflex angle	universal set
calculus	determinant	identity	ordinal number	regression	variable
capacity	diagonal	infinity	origin	remainder	variance
cardinal number	diameter	integer	parabola	right-angle	vector
Carroll diagram	differentiation	integration	parallel lines	right-angled	velocity
Cartesian	directed number	irrational number	parallel planes	triangle	Venn diagram
coordinates	distribution	latitude	parameter	root	vertex
chance	dividend	length	percentage	rotation	vertical
chord	division	less than	percentile	rotational	volume
circumference	divisor	line	perimeter	symmetry	vulgar fraction
coefficient	edge	linear	permutation	sample	whole number
combination	enlargement	locus	perpendicular	scalar segment	width
common fraction	equal	logarithm	pi	secant	zero
commutative	equation	longitude	pie chart	sector	
operation	equidistant	magic square	place value	set	

See also **shape.**

matrimonial *adj*
marital, marriage, wedding married, wedded
FORMAL nuptial, conjugal, spousal

matrimony *n*
marriage, married relationship/state, union
OLD wedlock
FORMAL espousals, nuptials, spousage

matrix *n*
1 TABLE, arrangement, analysis, context, frame, framework
TECHNICAL array
2 MOULD, cast, form, template, frame, framework
OLD plasm

matted *adj*
knotted, tangled, entangled, tangly, tousled, dishevelled, uncombed
F3 tidy, untangled

matter *n, v*
♦ *n*
1 SUBJECT, issue, topic, question, affair, business, case, point, concern, event, occurrence, happening situation, proceeding circumstance, episode, incident, thing
2 IMPORTANCE, significance, consequence, momentousness, interest, value, note, weight
FORMAL import
3 *What's the matter?*
trouble, problem, difficulty, distress, upset, worry, bother, nuisance, inconvenience, shortcoming weakness
4 SUBSTANCE, stuff, material, medium, physical elements, body, content
5 DISCHARGE, pus, secretion
FORMAL purulence, suppuration
♦ *v*
count, be important, be of importance, be relevant, have influence, carry weight, make a difference, mean something
COLLOQ. make a stir, make waves, cut a lot of ice
■ **as a matter of fact**
in fact, actually, as it happens, really, truly, in actual fact
■ **no matter**
never mind, it does not matter, it is unimportant

matter-of-fact *adj*
unemotional, prosaic, down-to-earth, emotionless, unsentimental, straightforward, practical, sober, pedestrian, unimaginative, lifeless, dry, dull, flat
COLLOQ. deadpan
F3 emotional

mattress *n*
bed, feather bed, Lilo®, airbed, futon, water bed, crash-mat, pallet, palliasse
SLANG biscuit

maturation *n*
ripening seasoning development, growth

mature *adj, v*
♦ *adj*
1 ADULT, grown-up, grown, full-grown, of age, sensible, responsible, balanced, experienced, wise, fully fledged, complete, finished, finalized, perfect, perfected, well-developed, precocious, well-thought-out
2 RIPE, ripened, seasoned, mellow, ready
F3 **1** childish **2** immature
♦ *v*
grow up, become adult, become sensible, come of age, develop, be fully developed, become ripe, become mellow, mellow, ripen, perfect, age, bloom, prepare, concoct, draw to a head, season, evolve, fall due
OLD maturate

maturity *n*
1 ADULTHOOD, full growth, majority, age, coming of age, womanhood, manhood, wisdom, experience, responsibility, sensibleness, age/years of discretion
2 RIPENESS, readiness, mellowness, perfection
F3 **1** childishness **2** immaturity

maty, matey *adj*
friendly, affable, genial, convivial, cordial, kind, warm, neighbourly, helpful, sympathetic, affectionate, familiar, intimate, inseparable, close, companionable, sociable, outgoing approachable, receptive, comradely, amicable, peaceable, well-disposed, favourable, agreeable, good-natured
COLLOQ. pally, chummy, thick, tight, folksy

maudlin *adj*
sentimental, mawkish, emotional, tearful, half-drunk, drunk, fuddled, tipsy
FORMAL lachrymose
COLLOQ. gushy, schmaltzy, mushy, sickly, slushy, soppy, weepy
F3 pleasant

maul *v*
attack, abuse, ill-treat, mutilate, mangle, batter, manhandle, maltreat, assault, molest, savage, paw, beat (up), claw, lacerate, thrash
COLLOQ. wallop, belt, do over, mug knock about, rough up, knock someone's block off

maunder *v*
1 MUTTER, ramble, babble, blather, chatter, jabber, gabble
COLLOQ. prattle, witter, natter, waffle, rabbit (on)
2 WANDER, meander, stray, amble, ramble, stroll, roam, rove, ease, shuffle, inch
COLLOQ. laze, mosey, mooch

mausoleum *n*
tomb, crypt, vault, burial chamber, catacomb, sepulchre, undercroft

maverick *n*
outsider, rebel, agitator, nonconformist, individualist
COLLOQ. fish out of water

maw *n*
mouth, jaws, throat, stomach, gullet, gulf, abyss, chasm

mawkish *adj*
sentimental, maudlin, emotional, offensive, nauseous, nauseating feeble, flat, disgusting foul, loathsome
COLLOQ. soppy, gushy, schmaltzy, mushy, sickly, slushy
F3 matter-of-fact, pleasant

mawkishly *adv*
sentimentally, emotionally, nauseatingly, loathsomely, feebly
COLLOQ. soppily, mushily

maxim *n*
saying proverb, adage, axiom, aphorism, saw, epigram, motto, byword, precept, rule
TECHNICAL apothegm, apophthegm
FORMAL gnome

maximize *v*
increase, raise, boost, add to, enhance, advance, further, step up, intensify, strengthen, heighten, develop, build up, accumulate, enlarge, magnify, broaden, widen, deepen, extend, prolong expand, spread, breed, propagate, scale up
FORMAL augment
COLLOQ. hike up, bump up
F3 decrease, reduce

maximum *adj, n*
♦ *adj*
greatest, highest, largest, biggest, most, utmost, supreme, top, topmost
F3 minimum
♦ *n*
most, top (point), utmost, uttermost, upper limit, peak, pinnacle, summit, zenith, apogee, acme, height, ceiling extremity
F3 minimum

maybe *adv*
perhaps, possibly, conceivably, for all you know
FORMAL perchance, peradventure
F3 definitely

mayhem *n*
chaos, disorder, confusion, disorganization, tumult, disruption, uproar, riot, bedlam, madhouse, mess, anarchy, lawlessness

maze *n*
labyrinth, network, tangle, jungle, web, mesh, complex, confusion, puzzle, intricacy

meadow *n*
field, grassland, grass, pasture, pastureland, paddock, green, lea, saeter; *dialect* leasow; *Scot* haugh; *Scot & Irish* inch
OLD mead

meagre *adj*
1 SCANTY, sparse, inadequate, insufficient, deficient, skimpy, paltry, negligible, small, poor, slight, stingy, niggardly
FORMAL exiguous
COLLOQ. measly
2 THIN, puny, insubstantial, bony, emaciated, skinny, scraggy, gaunt, scrawny, slight
E3 1 ample, generous **2** fat, plump

meagreness *n*
scantiness, sparseness, inadequacy, insufficiency, deficiency, smallness, slightness, stinginess, puniness
COLLOQ. measliness

meal *n*
NZ kai
FORMAL repast

Meals include:

afternoon tea	dinner party	*colloq.* slap-up
banquet	*colloq.* elevenses	meal
barbecue	evening meal	snack
colloq. barbie	feast	spread
colloq. bite	fork supper	supper
colloq. blow-out	harvest supper	takeaway
breakfast	high tea	tea
brunch	lunch	tea break
buffet	luncheon	tea party
cold table	midday meal	tiffin
cream tea	*slang* nosh-up	TV dinner
dinner	picnic	wedding breakfast

---

mealy-mouthed *adj*
hestitant, indirect, mincing over-squeamish, overdelicate, reticent, plausible, equivocal, flattering smooth-tongued, euphemistic, prim, glib

mean¹ *v*
1 SIGNIFY, represent, stand for, symbolize, show, designate, convey, express, suggest, indicate, imply, intimate
FORMAL denote, betoken, purport, connote
2 INTEND, aim, propose, design, purpose, plan, aspire, wish, wont, have in mind, think of
3 CAUSE, give rise to, lead to, bring about, produce, involve, entail, result in, necessitate
FORMAL effect
4 *it was meant to happen*
destine, predestine, fate, design, intend, appoint, ordain
5 *your approval means a lot to me*
matter, be important, have influence, carry weight, make a difference

mean² *adj*
1 MISERLY, niggardly, selfish, grasping close-fisted/handed
FORMAL parsimonious
COLLOQ. tight, tight-fisted, stingy, penny-pinching mingy
2 UNKIND, unpleasant, nasty, bad-tempered, cruel, disagreeable, unfriendly, cross, spiteful
COLLOQ. beastly, crotchety, crabby, grouchy
3 LOWLY, base, poor, humble, ordinary, common, obscure, wretched, shabby, dirty, miserable, dismal, squalid

4 *she makes a mean rice salad*
excellent, wonderful, brilliant, marvellous, fantastic, first-class/rate, high-quality, very good, prime, superlative, unequalled, unparalleled, matchless, rare, exceptional, outstanding surpassing remarkable, perfect, superb, admirable, magnificent, splendid, fine
COLLOQ. top-notch, smashing stunning terrific, neat, ace, brill, boffo, out of this world, second to none, divine, heavenly, fabulous, sensational, crack, not half bad
SLANG mega, cool, radical, rad, crucial, way-out
E3 1 generous, liberal **2** kind **3** noble, splendid **4** inferior, second-rate

> **SYNONYM NUANCES**
>
> *sense 1*
> Naturally, the synonyms tend to be disapproving in tone. **Miserly** can be used disapprovingly of someone with an antipathy to spending money, whereas **niggardly** has more to do with undertaking expenditure grudgingly: *niggardly payouts*. **Selfish**, on the other hand, emphasizes self-interest, and therefore a reluctance to give to others, while **grasping** has the negative implication of greed: *the grasping acquisitiveness of an affluent society*. Both **tight-fisted** and the less common **close-fisted** can be used more informally, and sometimes more jocularly, to suggest an unwillingness to spend money: *being tight-fisted, we bypassed the museums with entrance fees*.

mean³ *adj, n*
♦ *adj*
the mean score
average, intermediate, middle, medium, middling halfway, median, normal
E3 extreme
♦ *n*
average, middle, mid-point, norm, median, mode, compromise, middle course, middle way, medium, happy medium, golden mean
E3 extreme

meander *v*
1 WIND, zigzag turn, twist, snake, bend, curve; *Scot* wimple
2 WANDER, stray, amble, ramble, stroll, roam, rove, ease, shuffle, inch
COLLOQ. laze, mosey, mooch

meandering *adj*
wandering winding twisting turning rambling tortuous, circuitous, snaking serpentine, sinuous, indirect, roundabout, meandrous
FORMAL convoluted
E3 straight, direct

meaning *n*
1 SIGNIFICANCE, sense, implication, message, expression, gist, drift, substance, essence, thrust, trend, definition, explanation, interpretation
FORMAL import, signification, connotation, explication, elucidation
Related adjective: semantic
2 AIM, intention, purpose, plan, goal, object, objective, aspiration, wish, idea
3 VALUE, worth, point, significance, purpose, usefulness

> **QUOTATIONS**
> The meanings of words are not in the words; they are in us
>   S I HAYAKAWA, *Language in Thought and Action*

meaningful *adj*
1 IMPORTANT, significant, relevant, valid, useful, worthwhile, material, purposeful, effective, serious
2 EXPRESSIVE, speaking suggestive, eloquent, pregnant, warning pointed, telling
E3 1 unimportant, worthless

meaningfully adv
1 SIGNIFICANTLY, effectively, importantly, relevantly, usefully, purposefully
2 EXPRESSIVELY, suggestively, eloquently, pointedly

meaningless adj
1 SENSELESS, pointless, purposeless, useless, insignificant, incomprehensible, unintelligible, aimless, motiveless, irrational, futile, insubstantial, trifling trivial
2 EMPTY, hollow, vacuous, vain, worthless, nonsensical, absurd
E3 1 important, meaningful 2 worthwhile, productive

meaninglessly adv
pointlessly, purposelessly, aimlessly, senselessly, uselessly, incomprehensibly, unintelligibly, irrationally, futilely, vainly, in vain, without rhyme or reason

meanly adv
1 SELFISHLY, niggardly, graspingly, ungenerously
2 UNKINDLY, unpleasantly, nastily, cruelly, spitefully, contemptibly
3 *a meanly furnished flat*
poorly, commonly, beggarly, shabbily, miserably, scurvily
E3 1 generously 2 kindly 3 splendidly

meanness n
mean-spiritedness, miserliness, narrow-mindedness, beastliness, niggardliness, close-fistedness/handedness, illiberality
FORMAL parsimony, penuriousness
COLLOQ. stinginess, tight-fistedness
E3 generosity, kindness

means n
1 METHOD, way, manner, medium, course, agency, process, instrument, avenue, channel, vehicle
FORMAL mode
2 RESOURCES, funds, money, income, wealth, capital, riches, substance, wherewithal, fortune, affluence, assets, property
■ **by all means**
of course, naturally, certainly, surely, with pleasure
■ **by means of**
using with, through, via, with the help of, with the aid of, as a result of
FORMAL by dint of
■ **by no means**
certainly not, not at all, never, in no way
COLLOQ. no way

meantime, meanwhile adv
at the same time, for the time being for now, for the moment, in the meantime, in the meanwhile, in the interim, in the interval, simultaneously
FORMAL concurrently

measly adj
mean, miserable, paltry, meagre, pitiful, scanty, skimpy, petty, poor, puny, trivial, ungenerous, miserly, niggardly, beggarly, contemptible
COLLOQ. stingy, piddling pathetic, mingy
E3 generous

measurable adj
perceptible, significant, quantifiable, noticeable, appreciable, determinable, assessable, computable, gaugeable, fathomable, material, quantitative
FORMAL mensurable
E3 measureless

measure n, v
♦ n
1 SIZE, quantity, magnitude, amount, degree, extent, range, scope, proportion(s), dimension(s), area, expanse, capacity, height, depth, length, width, weight, volume, mass, bulk
2 RULE, gauge, ruler, scale, level, standard, system, unit(s), criterion, norm, touchstone, yardstick, benchmark, test, meter, barometer, litmus test, acid test
3 STEP, course, action, act, deed, expedient, procedure, proceeding means, method, bill, statute, resolution
4 PORTION, ration, share, piece, part, allocation, quota, division, lot, allotment
COLLOQ. rake-off, cut
♦ v
quantify, evaluate, assess, weigh, value, gauge, judge, sound, fathom, read, record, meter, time, determine, calculate, estimate, size (up), be, rate, plumb, survey, compute, measure out, measure off
FORMAL appraise
Related adjective: mensural
■ **measure off**
mark out, measure (out), determine, fix, lay down, limit, pace out, delimit, demarcate
FORMAL circumscribe
■ **measure out**
share out, divide, distribute, proportion, dispense, deal out, dole out, allot, apportion, hand out, mete out, parcel out, pour out, issue, assign
■ **measure up**
do, come up to standard, make the grade, pass muster, fit/fill the bill
FORMAL suffice
COLLOQ. come up to scratch, shape up
■ **measure up to**
equal, meet, live up to, come up to, match, match up to, compare with, touch, rival, satisfy, make the grade
■ **beyond measure**
beyond belief, immensely, infinitely, endlessly, limitlessly, incalculably, inestimably

---

Units of measurement include:

acre	coulomb	fresnel	kilometre	nautical mile	square inch
ampere	cubic centimetre	furlong	knot	newton	square kilometre
angstrom	cubic foot	gallon	league	ohm	square metre
atmosphere	cubic inch	gill	litre	ounce	square mile
bar	cubic metre	gram (or gramme)	lumen	pascal	square yard
barrel	cubic yard	hand	metre	peak	steradian
becquerel	day	hectare	micrometre	pint	stone
bushel	decade	hertz	mile	pound	therm
cable	decibel	horsepower	millennium	pound per square	ton
calorie	degree	hour	millibar	inch	tonne
candela	dyne	hundredweight	milligram (or	radian	volt
centigram (or	erg	inch	milligramme)	rod	watt
centigramme)	farad	joule	millilitre	second	week
centilitre	fathom	kelvin	millimetre	siemens	yard
centimetre	fluid ounce	kilogram (or	minute	span	year
century	foot	kilogramme)	mole	square centimetre	
chain	foot-pound	kilolitre	month	square foot	

Gauges include:

cutting gauge	gauge rod	paper gauge	ring gauge	taper gauge
drill gauge	gauge wheel	pressure gauge	snap gauge	tide gauge
feeler gauge	marking gauge	radius gauge	steam gauge	vacuum gauge
gauge glass	mortise gauge	rain gauge	strain gauge	water gauge

Measuring instruments include:

altimeter	colorimeter	meter	pyrometer	stopwatch
ammeter	cyclometer	micrometer	quadrant	tachometer
anemometer	densitometer	multimeter	radiosonde	tachymeter
audiometer	galvanometer	octant	rheometer	tape measure
balance	gauge	optometer	rule	tensiometer
barometer	Geiger counter	pedometer	saccharometer	theodolite
bathometer	gravimeter	photometer	salinometer	thermometer
Breathalyser®	hourglass	pipette	seismograph	vinometer
burette	hydrometer	planimeter	sextant	voltmeter
callipers	hygrometer	plumb line	speedometer	weighbridge
calorimeter	hypsometer	protractor	spherometer	Wheatstone bridge
chronometer	manometer	psychrometer	sphygmomanometer	
clinometer	measuring cylinder	pyranometer	steelyard	

■ **for good measure**
as well, besides, in addition, furthermore, over and above, as a bonus
■ **get/take the measure of**
get a handle on, evaluate, value, assess, estimate, reckon, calculate, gauge, judge, determine, rate, size up, handle
FORMAL appraise
COLLOQ. get a handle on

measured *adj*
deliberate, planned, reasoned, slow, unhurried, steady, regular, studied, well-thought-out, calculated, careful, considered, premeditated, precise

measureless *adj*
endless, immeasurable, inestimable, incalculable, innumerable, limitless, unbounded, infinite, boundless, bottomless, immense, vast
E∃ measurable

measurement *n*
1 DIMENSION, size, extent, amount, proportion(s), amplitude, unit, magnitude, area, range, expanse, capacity, height, depth, length, width, weight, volume, mass, bulk, quantity
2 ASSESSMENT, evaluation, estimation, computation, calculation, calibration, quantification, sizing weighing reading gauging judgement, appraisal, appreciation, survey
See panel on previous page

measuring instruments
See panels above

meat *n*
1 FLESH
See panels below
2 FOOD, rations, provisions, nourishment, sustenance, subsistence, fare, comestibles
FORMAL viands, victuals
COLLOQ. eats, eatables, tuck, scran
SLANG grub, nosh; *Aust & NZ* tucker
3 ESSENCE, substance, fundamentals, heart, kernel, marrow, core, crux, nub, nucleus, pith, point, gist

> **PROVERBS**
> One man's meat is another man's poison

meaty *adj*
1 FLESHY, hearty, solid, heavy, brawny, beefy, burly, muscular, strapping sturdy
COLLOQ. hunky
2 SUBSTANTIAL, interesting significant, meaningful, profound, rich, pithy

mechanic *n*
engineer, repairman, operative, operator, technician, machinist, mechanician, artificer

mechanical *adj*
1 *a mechanical device*
automatic, automated, mechanized, machine-powered, power-driven, electric
2 AUTOMATIC, involuntary, instinctive, routine, machine-like, unthinking habitual, impersonal, emotionless, unemotional, unconscious,

Meats and meat products include:

bacon	faggot	heart	mutton	pig's knuckle	sweetbread
beef	gammon	kidney	offal	pork	tongue
beefburger	goose	lamb	oxtail	quail	tripe
black pudding	grouse	liver	partridge	rabbit	trotters
brains	haggis	Lorne sausage	pastrami	rissole	turkey
brawn	ham	(square sausage)	pâté	salami	venison
chicken	hamburger	mince	pheasant	sausage	
duck	hare	minced beef	pigeon	steak	

Cuts of meat include:

breast	cutlet	hock	rib	shoulder
brisket	escalope	knuckle	rump	silverside
chine	fillet	leg	saddle	sirloin
chop	flank	loin	scrag	spare-rib
collar	hand	neck	shin	topside

Medical and surgical equipment includes:

aspirator	dilator	instrument table	oxygen cylinder	stethoscope
audiometer	disposable enema pack	iron lung	oxygen mask	stomach pump
aural speculum	ear syringe	isolator tent	rectoscope	surgical mask
auriscope	ECG (electro-	kidney dish	respirator	surgical suture
autoclave	cardiograph)	laparoscope	resuscitator	materials
body scanner	electroencephalograph	laryngoscope	retractor	swabs
bronchoscope	endoscope	microscope	rhinoscope	syringe
ca(n)nula	first aid kit	MRI (magnetic	scales	thermometer
catheter	forceps	resonance imaging)	scalpel	tracheostomy tube
CAT scanner	haemodialysis unit	scanner	sliding-weight scales	traction apparatus
clamp	hypodermic needle	nebulizer	specimen glass	tweezers
CT (computed	hypodermic syringe	obstetrical forceps	speculum	ultrasound
tomography) scanner	incubator	oesophagoscope	sphygmomanometer	urethroscope
curette	inhalator	operating table	sterile donor-pack	vaginal speculum
defibrillator	inhaler	ophthalmoscope	sterilizer	X-ray unit

cold, matter-of-fact, unfeeling perfunctory, lifeless, dead, dull
F3 2 conscious

mechanically adv
1 *mechanically sorted letters*
as/by a machine, automatically, electronically
2 *waved his arm mechanically*
involuntarily, automatically, instinctively, intuitively, habitually, unconsciously, unthinkingly, routinely, as a matter of routine, on autopilot
F3 2 consciously

mechanism n
1 MACHINE, machinery, engine, appliance, instrument, tool, contraption, motor, works, workings, action, movement, system, gadget, device, apparatus, contrivance, gears, components
COLLOQ. guts
2 MEANS, method, agency, process, procedure, system, technique, medium, channel, structure, workings, operation, functioning performance

mechanize v
automate, computerize, program

medal n
award, medallion, prize, trophy, decoration, honour, ribbon, reward, gold medal, silver medal, bronze medal, cross, contorno, vernicle
OLD model
SLANG gong
See panel at **honour**.

meddle v
interfere, intervene, pry, intrude, butt in, tamper
COLLOQ. fiddle, poke/stick your nose in, stick/put your oar in, snoop

meddlesome adj
interfering meddling prying snooping intrusive, intruding mischievous
COLLOQ. nos(e)y

mediaeval
See **medieval, mediaeval**.

mediate v
arbitrate, conciliate, intervene, referee, umpire, intercede, intermediate, moderate, reconcile, act as mediator/intermediary/peacemaker, negotiate, resolve, settle, step in
OLD stickle
FORMAL interpose

mediation n
arbitration, reconciliation, negotiation, conciliation, intercession, peacemaking good offices, intervention
FORMAL interposition

mediator n
arbitrator, referee, umpire, intermediary, negotiator, go-between, interceder, judge, arbiter, reconciler, middleman, intervener, moderator, intercessor, conciliator, peacemaker, Ombudsman

medical equipment
See panel above

medical specialists

Medical specialists include:

anaesthetist	gerontologist	osteopath
audiologist	gynaecologist	paediatrician
bacteriologist	haematologist	pathologist
cardiologist	hom(o)eopath	pharmacist
chiropodist	immunologist	pharmacologist
chiropractor	microbiologist	physiotherapist
dentist	neurologist	proctologist
dermatologist	obstetrician	psychiatrist
dietician	oncologist	psychologist
embryologist	ophthalmologist	radiologist
endocrinologist	optician (or	rheumatologist
forensic	optometrist)	toxicologist
pathologist	orthodontist	vaccinologist
gastroenterologist	orthopaedist	
geriatrician	orthoptist	

See also **doctor**; **nurse**; **surgeon**.

medical terms
See panel on next page

medicinal adj
therapeutic, healing remedial, health-giving curative, restorative, medical

medicinally adv
therapeutically, remedially, curatively, restoratively, medically

medicine n
medication, drug cure, remedy, medicament, prescription, pharmaceutical, panacea
TECHNICAL analeptic
See panels on next page

medieval, mediaeval adj
1 *medieval history*
of the Middle Ages, of the Dark Ages, historic, old, archaic
2 OLD-FASHIONED, obsolete, primitive, antiquated, archaic, antique, antediluvian, old-world, outmoded, unenlightened

mediocre adj
ordinary, average, middling medium, indifferent, unexceptional, undistinguished, commonplace, pedestrian, insignificant, second-rate, passable, adequate, inferior, uninspired, tolerable

Medical terms include:

abortion	case history	dislocate	implantation	post-mortem	splint
allergy	casualty	dissection	incubation	pregnancy	sterilization
amniocentesis	cauterization	doctor	infection	prescription	surgery
amputation	cervical smear	donor	inflammation	prognosis	suture
assisted	check-up	dressings	injection	prosthesis	symptom
conception	chemotherapy	enema	injury	psychosomatic	syndrome
bandage	childbirth	examination	inoculation	quarantine	therapy
barium meal	circulation	gene	intensive care	radiotherapy	tourniquet
biopsy	circumcision	genetic	in-vitro fertilization	recovery	transfusion
blood bank	clinic	counselling	(IVF)	rehabilitation	transplant
blood count	complication	health	keyhole surgery	relapse	trauma
blood donor	compress	screening	labour	remission	treatment
blood group	consultant	home visit	laser treatment	respiration	tumour
blood pressure	consultation	hormone	microsurgery	resuscitation	ultrasound
blood test	contraception	replacement	miscarriage	scan	scanning
Caesarean (section)	convulsion	therapy (HRT)	mouth-to-mouth	side effect	vaccination
cardiopulmonary	cure	hospice	nurse	sling	vaccine
resuscitation	diagnosis	hospital	operation	smear test	virus
(CPR)	dialysis	immunization	paraplegia	specimen	X-ray

See also **therapy**.

COLLOQ. so-so, run-of-the-mill, bog standard, fair to middling not up to much, not all that it is cracked up to be, nothing much to write home about, no great shakes, not much cop
F3 exceptional, extraordinary, distinctive

mediocrity n
1 ORDINARINESS, unimportance, averageness, unexceptionableness, adequacy, passableness, insignificance, poorness, inferiority, indifference
2 NONENTITY, nobody, nothing
COLLOQ. non-starter, no-hoper, dead loss
F3 1 distinction, exceptionableness

meditate v
reflect, ponder, ruminate, chew, contemplate, muse, brood, think (over), consider, deliberate, mull over, study, concentrate, speculate, scheme, plan, design, intend, have in mind
OLD devise
FORMAL cogitate
COLLOQ. put on your thinking cap, chew the cud

meditation n
contemplation, reflection, pondering musing thought, ruminating rumination, deliberation, brooding mulling over, speculation, study, reverie, concentration, brown study
FORMAL cerebration, cogitation, excogitation

meditative adj
contemplative, deliberative, reflective, thoughtful, studious, museful, pensive, ruminant, ruminative, prayerful
FORMAL cogitative

medium adj, n
♦ adj
average, middle, median, mean, medial, intermediate, middling midway, midpoint, standard, fair
♦ n
1 AVERAGE, middle, median, mean, mode, intermediate point, midpoint, norm, compromise, centre, middle ground/way, happy medium, golden mean
2 MEANS, means of expression, means of communication, way of expressing agency, channel, vehicle, instrument, way, form, substance, material, stuff, avenue, organ
FORMAL instrumentality, mode
3 ENVIRONMENT, element, setting surroundings, atmosphere, conditions, habitat, circumstances, influences, ambience, milieu
4 PSYCHIC, spiritualist, spiritist, clairvoyant, fortune-teller, necromancer

medley n
assortment, mixture, mix, miscellany, variety, melange, potpourri, hotchpotch, hodgepodge, helter-skelter, confusion, farrago, salmagundi, smorgasbord, collection, pastiche, patchwork, gallimaufry, jumble, mess, mingle, olio, macaroni, *macédoine*

Types of medicine include:

analgesic	capsule	eye drops	lozenge	pellet	syrup
anodyne	cough medicine	gargle	nasal spray	penicillin	tablet
antacid	diuretic	gripe-water	nebulizer	pessary	tonic
antibiotic	dragee	implant	ointment	pill	tranquillizer
anti-histamine	ear drops	inhaler	painkiller	polypill	Ventolin®
anti-inflammatory	elixir	laxative	paregoric	sedative	
antiseptic	emetic	linctus	pastille	steroid	
arnica	enema	liniment	patch	suppository	

See also **drug**.

Forms of alternative medicine include:

acupressure	Chinese medicine	herbal medicine	kinesiology	reiki
acupuncture	chiropractic	hom(o)eopathy	naturopathy	rolfing
aromatherapy	craniosacral	hypnotherapy	osteopathy	shiatsu
Ayurveda	therapy	iridology	reflexology	

FORMAL conglomeration
COLLOQ. mixed bag mishmash, omnium-gatherum

meek *adj*
modest, long-suffering forbearing humble, docile, patient,
unassuming quiet, lowly, mild, unpretentious, resigned,
gentle, peaceful, tame, timid, submissive, yielding
compliant, deferential, weak, spiritless
COLLOQ. spineless
ⴹ arrogant, assertive, rebellious

meekly *adv*
humbly, mildly, gently, modestly, patiently, quietly,
submissively, deferentially, like a lamb to the
slaughter
ⴹ arrogantly, assertively, rebelliously

meekness *n*
modesty, long-suffering forbearance, humility, docility,
patience, unpretentiousness, lowliness, mildness,
gentleness, humbleness, peacefulness, submission,
submissiveness, compliance, deference, tameness, softness,
self-abasement, self-disparagement, self-effacement,
timidity, spiritlessness, resignation, weakness
FORMAL acquiescence
COLLOQ. spinelessness, wimpishness
ⴹ arrogance, assertiveness, rebelliousness

meet *v, n*
♦ *v*
1 ENCOUNTER, come across, run across, run into, make
contact with, join up with, chance on
FORMAL happen upon
COLLOQ. bump into
2 GATHER, get together, collect, come together, muster,
assemble, congregate, rally, rendezvous
FORMAL convene, convoke, for(e)gather
3 FULFIL, fill, satisfy, match, answer, come up to,
measure up to, equal, comply with, discharge, perform,
execute
4 EXPERIENCE, encounter, face, come across, go through,
undergo, bear, endure, suffer
5 *meet a challenge*
deal with, manage, handle, tackle, look after, cope with,
get to grips with
6 *meet the cost*
pay (for), settle, discharge, honour
7 JOIN, converge, come together, connect, link (up), cross,
intersect, touch, unite
FORMAL abut, adjoin
8 *the reports were met with disbelief*
receive, give, greet, get, take, react to, respond to, hear,
listen to
ⴹ **2** scatter, disperse **7** diverge, separate
♦ *n*
event, game, match, fixture, competition, contest, round,
race, tournament, engagement, meeting

meeting *n*
1 ENCOUNTER, confrontation, rendezvous, appointment,
date, engagement, contact, assignation, introduction
FORMAL tryst
2 ASSEMBLY, gathering session
3 CONVERGENCE, confluence, junction, intersection,
union, venue, (point of) contact, interface,
watersmeet
FORMAL concourse, abutment, conjunction

Types of meeting include:

AGM (annual	committee	council
general meeting)	*formal* conclave	debate
assignation	conference	discussion
audience	congregation	EGM (extra-
audition	congress	ordinary general
board	consultation	meeting)
brainstorming	convention	*Welsh* eisteddfod
briefing	*formal*	*Irish* feis
cabinet	convocation	forum

general meeting	panel	service
colloq.	party	social
get-together	press conference	soirée
Welsh gorsedd	rally	summit
NZ hui	rendezvous	symposium
inaugural meeting	reunion	talk-in
interview	review	teleconference
meet	seminar	workshop

See also **committee**.

megalomania *n*
overestimation, self-importance, exaggerated sense of
power, delusions of grandeur, *folie de grandeur*,
conceitedness

melancholy *adj, n*
♦ *adj*
melancholic, depressed, dejected, down, downhearted,
downcast, gloomy, glum, low, low-spirited, heavy-hearted,
sad, unhappy, despondent, dispirited, miserable, mournful,
dismal, sombre, sorrowful, doleful, rueful, moody,
hypochondriac, *pensieroso*
OLD adust, allicholy, hipped
FORMAL disconsolate, lugubrious, woeful, woebegone
COLLOQ. blue, down in the dumps, in the doldrums
ⴹ cheerful, elated, joyful
♦ *n*
depression, dejection, gloom, despondency, low spirits,
sadness, unhappiness, sorrow, misery, pessimism, the
black dog
OLD tristesse
COLLOQ. blues, doldrums, dumps
ⴹ cheerfulness, elation, joy

melange *n*
assortment, mixture, mix, miscellany, variety, potpourri,
hotchpotch, hodgepodge, confusion, farrago, salmagundi,
smorgasbord, collection, pastiche, patchwork, gallimaufry,
jumble
FORMAL conglomeration
COLLOQ. mixed bag mishmash, omnium-gatherum

mêlée *n*
1 BRAWL, rumpus, scuffle, set-to, fight, tussle, ruckus,
ruction, broil, affray, fracas, fray, free-for-all, scrum; *Scot*
stramash
2 MUDDLE, confusion, chaos, disorganization, disorder,
mess, mix-up, jumble, clutter, tangle

mellifluous *adj*
smooth, sweet-sounding sweet, soothing soft, tuneful,
harmonious, dulcet, mellow, honeyed, silvery
FORMAL canorous, euphonious
ⴹ discordant, grating harsh

mellow *adj, v*
♦ *adj*
1 MATURE, ripe, juicy, soft, tender, full-flavoured, sweet,
luscious, mild
2 GENIAL, cordial, affable, pleasant, relaxed, easy-going
good-natured, amiable, amicable, placid, gentle, serene,
tranquil, cheerful, happy, jolly, jovial, kind, kind-hearted
3 SMOOTH, melodious, tuneful, harmonious, smooth, rich,
rounded, full, soft, sweet, fruity, resonant, pear-shaped,
dulcet
FORMAL euphonious
ⴹ **1** unripe **2** cold **3** harsh
♦ *v*
mature, ripen, improve, sweeten, soften, temper,
make/become less extreme, season, perfect

melodic *adj*
melodious, tuneful, musical, harmonious, dulcet, sweet,
sweet-sounding silvery
FORMAL euphonious
ⴹ discordant, grating harsh

melodically *adv*
melodiously, tunefully, musically, harmoniously, sweetly
ⴹ discordantly, harshly

melodious *adj*
tuneful, musical, melodic, harmonious, dulcet, sweet, sweet-sounding silvery, listenable
FORMAL euphonious
⊟ discordant, grating harsh

melodrama *n*
histrionics, overacting theatricality, staginess, dramatics, performance, tragedy, tragicomedy, high drama

melodramatic *adj*
histrionic, theatrical, overdramatic, exaggerated, extravagant, overemotional, sensational, overdone, stag(e)y
COLLOQ. hammy, over-the-top, OTT

melody *n*
1 TUNE, music, song refrain, harmony, rhythm, theme, air, strain, chant, part, carillon
TECHNICAL counterpoint, canto, cantus, plainsong aria, augmentation, cabaletta, cantilena, cavatina, melisma, musette
OLD ayre
2 TUNEFULNESS, musicality, musicalness, harmony, harmoniousness, sweetness
FORMAL euphony

> **QUOTATIONS**
> Melody is the very essence of music. When I think of a good melodist I think of a fine race horse
> WOLFGANG AMADEUS MOZART

melt *v*
1 LIQUEFY, dissolve, thaw, defrost, unfreeze, fuse
FORMAL deliquesce
2 *melt someone's heart*
soften, move, affect, touch, make/become tender, moderate, calm
⊟ **1** freeze, solidify **2** harden, inure
■ **melt away**
disappear, vanish, fade (away), evaporate, dissolve, disperse
FORMAL evanesce
COLLOQ. disappear into thin air

meltdown *n*
failure, defeat, collapse, breakdown, downfall, miscarriage, disaster, calamity, fiasco, debacle, abortion, frustration, coming to nothing

member *n*
1 *members of a club*
adherent, associate, subscriber, representative, comrade, fellow
2 PART, limb, arm, leg appendage, extremity, organ, element

membership *n*
1 *membership of a club*
affiliation, adherence, allegiance, participation, enrolment, fellowship
2 MEMBERS, associates, body, adherents, subscribers, representatives, comrades, fellows, fellowship

membrane *n*
sheet, film, skin, tissue, layer, veil, partition, diaphragm
TECHNICAL integument, septum, velum, hymen

memento *n*
souvenir, keepsake, remembrance, reminder, token, memorial, trophy, record, vestige, relic

memo *n*
memorandum, message, note, reminder, aide-mémoire, email, fax, letter
COLLOQ. memory-jogger

memoir *n*
account, biography, autobiography, essay, journal, life, monograph, narrative, chronicle, record, register, report

memoirs *n*
reminiscences, recollections, memories, autobiography, life story, diary, diaries, chronicles, annals, journals, records, confessions, experiences

memorable *adj*
unforgettable, remarkable, significant, impressive, striking notable, noteworthy, historic, extraordinary, important, consequential, distinguished, distinctive, special, outstanding momentous, unique
⊟ forgettable, trivial, unimportant

memorandum *n*
message, note, reminder, aide-mémoire, email, fax, letter
COLLOQ. memo, memory-jogger

memorial *n, adj*
♦ *n*
remembrance, monument, statue, stone, plaque, shrine, cenotaph, mausoleum, record, souvenir, memento
♦ *adj*
commemorative, celebratory, monumental

memorize *v*
learn, learn by heart, learn by rote, commit to memory, remember
⊟ forget

memory *n*
1 RECALL, powers of recall, retention, recollection, remembrance, reminiscence
2 COMMEMORATION, remembrance, tribute, honour, observance, recognition
⊟ **1** forgetfulness

menace *n, v*
♦ *n*
1 THREAT, intimidation, terrorism, ominousness, threatening behaviour, terrorizing tyrannization, bullying browbeating coercion, pressure, warning; *Scot* shore
COLLOQ. screws, frighteners, big stick
2 DANGER, peril, hazard, jeopardy, risk, threat
3 NUISANCE, annoyance, pest, bother, public enemy, troublemaker
COLLOQ. pain, thorn in your side/flesh
♦ *v*
threaten, frighten, alarm, daunt, dismay, appal, intimidate, scare, terrorize, terrify, browbeat, coerce, press, pressure, pressurize, bully, loom, lour; *Scot* shore

menacing *adj*
threatening intimidating intimidatory, warning ominous, alarming frightening dangerous, looming sinister, grim, louring Damoclean
FORMAL impending portentous, minacious, minatory

mend *v*
1 REPAIR, fix, renovate, restore, renew, refit, patch (up), put back together, run up, solder, cobble, darn, toe, stick, sew, cure, heal, make whole, clout, plash, solution; *N Am* bushel
OLD beet
2 RECOVER, get better, improve, recuperate
3 REMEDY, correct, rectify, reform, revise, amend, improve, put right, put in order, mend your fences
FORMAL ameliorate, emend
⊟ **1** break **2** deteriorate **3** destroy
■ **mend your ways**
reform, improve yourself, make a fresh start, turn over a new leaf, come/get back onto the straight and narrow, see the error of your ways, wipe the slate clean
■ **on the mend**
convalescing convalescent, recovering improving recuperating reviving healing

mendacious *adj*
untruthful, untrue, false, fictitious, insincere, deceitful, deceptive, dishonest, lying perjured, fraudulent
FORMAL fallacious, perfidious, duplicitous
⊟ honest, truthful; *formal* veracious

mendacity *n*
untruthfulness, untruth, lie, lying misrepresentation, distortion, falsehood, falsification, insincerity, deceit, deceitfulness, dishonesty, fraudulence, perjury
FORMAL inveracity, duplicity, perfidy
⊟ honesty, truthfulness; *formal* veracity

mendicant *adj, n*

♦ *adj*
begging scrounging
FORMAL petitionary, supplicant
COLLOQ. cadging

♦ *n*
beggar, supplicant, pauper, down-and-out, tramp, vagabond, vagrant, beachcomber, craver, canter, *besognio*; *N Am* hobo, panhandler
OLD whipjack
COLLOQ. bum, cadger, scrounger, sponger, freeloader; *N Am* moocher
SLANG blighter, toerag; *Aust & NZ* bludger
OLD SLANG jarkman

menial *adj, n*

♦ *adj*
low, lowly, humble, base, dull, humdrum, routine, boring degrading demeaning ignominious, unskilled, subservient, servile, slavish

♦ *n*
servant, domestic, labourer, minion, attendant, drudge, slave, underling
COLLOQ. skivvy, dogsbody

menstruation *n*
period, time of the month, menstrual cycle, monthly flow, courses, flow, menses
TECHNICAL menorrhoea
COLLOQ. monthlies, the usual, the curse
Related adjective: menstrual

mensuration *n*
measurement, measuring calibration, computation, estimation, calculation, assessment, evaluation, survey, surveying valuation
TECHNICAL metage

mental *adj*
1 INTELLECTUAL, abstract, unconscious, conceptual, theoretical, rational
FORMAL cognitive, cerebral
2 MAD, insane, lunatic, unbalanced, psychotic, disturbed, deranged, maniacal, out of your mind/senses, of unsound mind, unhinged, crazed, unstable, *non compos mentis*, frenzied, wild, berserk, manic, maniac, distracted, distraught, fey, frenetic, frantic, stone-crazy, queer; *Scot* gyte, red-mad
OLD frantic-mad, lymphatic, bestraught
COLLOQ. crazy, demented, nuts, nutty, nutty as a fruitcake, wacky, mad as a hatter, barmy, bonkers, batty, cracked, crackers, dippy, daffy, dotty, loopy, potty, off your nut/head, wrong in the head, out of your head, off the wall, out to lunch, round the bend/twist, bats, having bats in the belfry, cuckoo, off the rails, screwy, up the wall, raving not all there; *N Am* buggy, flaky, fruity; *Aust & NZ* dingbats
SLANG loony, bananas, barking wacko, doolally, off your rocker, off your chump, off your trolley, out of your tree, needing your head examined, having lost your marbles, having a screw loose, having a tile loose, having several cards short of a full deck, with one sandwich short of a picnic, meshuga, ape, apeshit; *N Am* gonzo, loco, wiggy
See Synonym nuances panel at **mad**.
1 physical **2** sane

mentality *n*
1 FRAME OF MIND, mind, way of thinking (mental) attitude, make-up, character, disposition, personality, psychology, outlook, mindset
2 INTELLECT, intelligence, understanding mind, comprehension, faculty, rationality
COLLOQ. brains, little grey cells, grey matter

mentally *adv*
intellectually, in the mind, inwardly, psychologically, rationally, temperamentally, subjectively, emotionally

mention *v, n*

♦ *v*
1 SPEAK OF, refer to, say, name, namecheck, acknowledge, report, make known, impart, introduce, declare, note, notice, communicate, divulge, disclose, broach, cite, reveal, state, quote, specify, instance, particular
OLD bename, remember, hight
FORMAL nominate, condescend upon
2 TOUCH ON, allude to, cite, refer to, speak about briefly, bring up, hint at, intimate, point out, exhume, drag up, cast up

♦ *n*
reference, allusion, hint, citation, observation, recognition, remark, speech, talk, statement, acknowledgement, announcement, notification, notice, tribute, indication
OLD mind

■ **don't mention it**
not at all, don't worry, forget it, it was nothing it's a pleasure, think nothing of it, *bitte*

■ **not to mention**
not including to say nothing of, besides, as well as, let alone, not forgetting much less

mentioned *adj*
quoted, reported, stated, cited
FORMAL above-mentioned, aforementioned, forementioned, forenamed, fore-quoted, foresaid, aforesaid, fore-cited

mentor *n*
teacher, tutor, adviser, counsellor, guru, swami, guide, confidant(e), coach, instructor, pedagogue, therapist

menu *n*
bill of fare, tariff, list, card, *carte du jour*

mercantile *adj*
trade, trading commercial, merchantable, marketable, sal(e)able

mercenary *adj, n*

♦ *adj*
1 GREEDY, covetous, grasping acquisitive, money-orientated, materialistic, mammonistic, sordid
FORMAL avaricious
COLLOQ. money-grubbing on the make
2 HIRED, paid, professional, venal

♦ *n*
soldier of fortune, hired soldier, freelance, free companion, hireling *condottiere*, galloglass, *landsknecht*, lansquenet
COLLOQ. merc

merchandise *n*
goods, commodities, stock, produce, products, wares, cargo, freight, shipment
FORMAL vendibles

merchandize *v*
1 TRADE, deal in, market, retail, sell, buy and sell, carry, distribute, supply, traffic in, peddle
FORMAL vend
2 PROMOTE, publicize, advertise, market, sell
COLLOQ. push, plug hype

merchant *n*
trader, dealer, broker, agent, trafficker, wholesaler, distributor, retailer, seller, salesperson, salesman, saleswoman, sales executive, shopkeeper, vendor, factor, jobber, bourgeois, *négociant*, *bunnia*
OLD (*Shakesp*) marcantant
Related adjective: mercantile

merciful *adj*
compassionate, forgiving forbearing humane, lenient, sparing tender-hearted, soft-hearted, pitying gracious, humanitarian, kind, liberal, tolerant, sympathetic, generous, mild
hard-hearted, merciless

QUOTATIONS
Blessed are the merciful: for they shall obtain mercy
Bible, St Matthew

mercifully *adv*
1 COMPASSIONATELY, graciously, kindly, generously, tender-heartedly, sympathetically, tolerantly
2 THANKFULLY, fortunately, luckily
E₃ 1 hard-heartedly, mercilessly

merciless *adj*
pitiless, relentless, unmerciful, ruthless, barbarous, hard-hearted, hard, heartless, implacable, inexorable, intolerant, inhumane, unforgiving remorseless, unpitying unsympathetic, unfeeling unsparing severe, rigid, stern, cruel, callous, harsh, inhuman
E₃ compassionate, merciful

mercilessly *adv*
ruthlessly, hard-heartedly, cruelly, severely, sternly, callously, harshly, heartlessly, pitilessly, relentlessly, implacably, inexorably, remorselessly
E₃ compassionately, mercifully

mercurial *adj*
volatile, temperamental, unpredictable, unstable, variable, changeable, inconstant, erratic, fickle, impetuous, impulsive, irrepressible, flighty, light-hearted, lively, spirited, sprightly, active, mobile
FORMAL capricious
E₃ saturnine

mercy *n*
1 COMPASSION, grace, forgiveness, forbearance, leniency, pity, humaneness, humanitarianism, kindness, tender-heartedness, tenderness, mildness, sympathy, generosity, quarter
OLD loving-kindness, misericord
FORMAL clemency
2 BLESSING, godsend, boon, favour, good luck, stroke of good luck, relief
E₃ 1 cruelty, harshness
■ **at the mercy of**
in the control of, in the power of, in someone's clutches, defenceless against, unarmed against, exposed to, vulnerable to, unprotected against, at the whim of, prostrate

> **SYNONYM NUANCES**
>
> *sense 1*
> **Compassion** is a fairly strong term for having mercy towards others, whereas **grace** suggests a divine reprieve: *there but for the grace of God go I.*
> **Forbearance** has more to do with patience: *it requires the forbearance of a saint to keep making allowances for others.* **Leniency**, however, is more suggestive of displaying perhaps too much tolerance, while **sympathy** and **pity** would be appopriate synonyms for mercy springing from feeling sorry for someone.
> The term **humaneness** suggests the essential nature of mankind, and so fellow feeling whereas **humanitarianism** is less abstract in its reference to benevolence to your fellow man: *his humanitarianism led him to work for children's charities abroad.*
> **Tender-heartedness** and **tenderness** too suggest a condition whereby you are sensitive and easily moved: *an unexpected tenderness towards the misfortunes of others.* **Mildness** is less marked in that it simply suggests gentleness. **Quarter** has narrower implications of clemency granted to an antagonist, and is usually used in the negative: *expect no quarter to be given when the sides meet again.*

mere *adj*
sheer, plain, simple, pure and simple, no more than, bare, utter, pure, absolute, complete, stark, unadulterated, common, paltry, petty

merely *adv*
simply, just, only, purely, nothing but, barely, hardly, scarcely

meretricious *adj*
flashy, flash, showy, ostentatious, flamboyant, glamorous, bold, loud, garish, gaudy, jazzy, pretentious, tawdry, cheap, vulgar, tasteless, kitsch, showing poor taste
COLLOQ. tacky, glitzy
E₃ plain, tasteful

merge *v*
join, unite, combine, come/bring together, join forces, team up, converge, amalgamate, blend, coalesce, mix, intermix, mingle, melt into, run into, fuse, meet, meld, be swallowed up in, be assimilated in, become lost in, be engulfed, incorporate, consolidate

merger *n*
amalgamation, union, fusion, combination, coalition, alliance, consolidation, confederation, incorporation, convergence, blend, assimilation

merit *n, v*
♦ *n*
1 GOODNESS, worth, excellence, value, quality, high quality, good, virtue, worthiness
2 STRONG POINT, virtue, asset, credit, advantage, talent, justification, reward, recompense, due, deserts, claim
COLLOQ. plus
E₃ 1 fault, drawback; *colloq.* minus
♦ *v*
deserve, be worthy of, be worth, earn, justify, have a right to, be entitled to, warrant

merited *adj*
deserved, earned, justified, entitled, fitting appropriate, warranted, worthy, due, just, rightful
FORMAL condign
E₃ inappropriate, unjustified

meritorious *adj*
commendable, deserving right, righteous, virtuous, excellent, good, honourable, praiseworthy, worthy, estimable, admirable, creditable, exemplary
FORMAL laudable
E₃ unworthy

mermaid *n*
sea nymph, water-spirit, water sprite, undine, siren
OLD seamaid

merrily *adv*
happily, jovially, cheerfully, gladly, pleasantly
FORMAL blithely
COLLOQ. chirpily

merriment *n*
fun, jollity, hilarity, laughter, conviviality, high spirits, joyfulness, cheerfulness, gaiety, festivity, amusement, revelry, frolic, liveliness, joviality, buoyance, carefreeness
FORMAL mirthfulness, mirth, jocundity, blitheness
E₃ gloom, seriousness

merry *adj*
1 JOLLY, light-hearted, jovial, joyful, happy, high-spirited, in good spirits, convivial, festive, cheerful, cheery, amusing carefree, glad
FORMAL mirthful, blithe
COLLOQ. chirpy
2 TIPSY, slightly drunk, happy, tiddly
COLLOQ. squiffy
E₃ 1 gloomy, melancholy **2** sober
■ **make merry**
have fun, enjoy yourself, celebrate, have a party, sing dance, drink, carouse

merry-go-round *n*
roundabout, carousel, joy-wheel, whirligig

merrymaking *n*
merriment, celebration, fun, gaiety, jollification, rejoicings, conviviality, festivity, party, carousal, carousing revel, revelry

mesh *n, v*
♦ *n*
net, network, netting lattice, latticework, tracery, gauze, trellis, web, tangle, entanglement, snare, trap
♦ *v*
engage, interlock, dovetail, fit together (closely), connect, harmonize, match, co-ordinate, combine, go/come together, entangle, enmesh, inmesh

mesmerize *v*
transfix, hypnotize, magnetize, spellbind, hold spellbound, captivate, enthral, fascinate, grip, entrance, stupefy, benumb

mess *n, v*
♦ *n*
1 CHAOS, untidiness, disorder, disarray, confusion, muddle, jumble, clutter, litter, turmoil, disorganization, midden, mix-up, dirt, dirtiness, filth, filthiness, squalor
COLLOQ. shambles, hole, dump, tip, dog's breakfast, pig's breakfast, dog's dinner
2 DIFFICULTY, trouble, predicament, plight, dilemma, quandary
COLLOQ. fix, (tight) spot, jam, pickle, hiccup, hole, stew, hot/deep water, pretty pass
3 BOTCH, bungle, muddle, failure
COLLOQ. farce, shambles, hash
SLANG cock-up, balls-up, screw-up
F3 1 order, tidiness
■ **mess about/around**
fool around, play, play around, play about, potter about, fiddle around; *N Am* putter
COLLOQ. muck about, faff about/around
SLANG frig about/around, piss about/around; *N Am* goof about/around; *(taboo)* fuck about/around
■ **mess about/around with**
interfere with, treat badly, upset, bother, trouble, inconvenience, meddle with, play (about/around) with, fool about/around with, tamper with
■ **mess up**
1 DISARRANGE, jumble, untidy, clutter up, throw into disorder, disrupt, confuse, muddle, tangle, dishevel, dirty, foul
2 BOTCH, bungle, spoil, ruin, make a mess of
COLLOQ. muck up, bodge, fluff, muff, foul up, make a hash of
SLANG louse up, cock up, screw up
F3 1 order, tidy

message *n*
1 COMMUNICATION, bulletin, dispatch, communiqué, report, news, piece of information, word, signal, intimation, errand, task, letter, memorandum, note, notice, fax, cable
FORMAL missive, tidings, epistle
COLLOQ. memo
2 MEANING, idea, sense, significance, point, theme, implication, gist, drift, essence, thrust, moral
FORMAL purport, import
■ **get the message**
understand, comprehend, take in, follow, see, grasp
COLLOQ. get it, get the point, get the picture, get the idea, get the hang catch the drift, catch on, latch on, cotton on (to), tumble to, twig

messenger *n*
courier, envoy, go-between, herald, runner, errand-boy, errand-girl, express, carrier, bearer, dispatch, forerunner, agent, ambassador, angel, nuncio, page, commissionaire, footpost, pursuivant, *valet de place*, Mercury, Hermes, chaprassi, internuncio, peon; *Scot* send, corbie messenger, shellycoat
OLD post, beadle; *(Shakesp)* missive; *Scot* caddie, gillie-wetfoot
FORMAL emissary, harbinger

messy *adj*
1 DIRTY, sloppy, slovenly, grubby, filthy

2 DISORGANIZED, untidy, unkempt, dishevelled, disordered, in disarray, chaotic, confused, muddled, cluttered, littered
COLLOQ. shambolic, slobbish
F3 1 clean **2** neat, ordered, tidy

metallic *adj*
1 *metallic elements*
copper, iron, tin, lead, nickel, steel, gold, silver, shiny, polished, gleaming
2 *metallic sounds*
harsh, grating jarring unpleasant, rough, dissonant, jangling tinny

metamorphose *v*
change, alter, transform, remake, remodel, reshape, convert, modify, translate
TECHNICAL mutate, transubstantiate
FORMAL transmute, transfigure
COLLOQ. transmogrify

metamorphosis *n*
change, alteration, rebirth, regeneration, transfiguration, conversion, modification, changeover
TECHNICAL mutation
FORMAL transformation, transmutation
COLLOQ. transmogrification

metaphor *n*
figure of speech, allegory, analogy, symbol, emblem, emblematic, visual, picture, image, representation
FORMAL trope

metaphorical *adj*
figurative, allegorical, symbolic, analogical, emblematic, visual, representational
F3 literal

metaphysical *adj*
philosophical, theoretical, abstract, unreal, essential, fundamental, basic, subjective, spiritual, supernatural, transcendental, unsubstantial, insubstantial, general, immaterial, speculative, intellectual, ideal, high-flown, intangible, deep, profound, universal, eternal
FORMAL abstruse, esoteric, impalpable, incorporeal, recondite

mete *v*
■ **mete out**
allot, apportion, deal out, dole out, hand out, measure out, share out, ration out, portion, distribute, dispense, divide out, assign, administer

meteor *n*
falling star, meteorite, meteoroid, comet, shooting star, fireball, aerolite, aerolith, bolide

meteoric *adj*
rapid, speedy, swift, quick, fast, sudden, lightning overnight, instantaneous, momentary, brief, transient, spectacular, brilliant, dazzling flashing

meteorologist *n*
weather forecaster, climatologist, weatherman, weathergirl, weatherlady, met man, weather prophet

method *n*
1 WAY, approach, means, course, manner, fashion, form, process, procedure, system, practice, route, technique, style, plan, arrangement, scheme, rule, programme, modus operandi
FORMAL mode
2 ORGANIZATION, order, structure, system, pattern, arrangement, form, design, plan, planning regularity, orderliness, routine

methodical *adj*
systematic, structured, organized, ordered, orderly, well-ordered, logical, tidy, regular, planned, efficient, formal, disciplined, businesslike, deliberate, neat, scrupulous, precise, meticulous, painstaking
F3 chaotic, irregular, confused

methodically adv
systematically, logically, tidily, uniformly, regularly, efficiently, formally, as planned, in place, neatly, scrupulously, precisely, meticulously, painstakingly, by the book, according to the rules, to the rule
F3 chaotically, irregularly

meticulous adj
precise, scrupulous, careful, conscientious, rigorous, exact, punctilious, fussy, particular, detailed, accurate, thorough, fastidious, painstaking strict
F3 careless, slapdash

meticulously adv
accurately, thoroughly, precisely, exactly, carefully, scrupulously, painstakingly, conscientiously, rigorously, punctiliously, strictly
F3 chaotically

métier n
calling vocation, line, line of business, business, job, occupation, profession, sphere, field, forte, trade, pursuit, speciality, craft; N Am specialty

metropolis n
capital city, main city, large city, municipality, megalopolis, cosmopolis, industrial/cultural centre

mettle n
1 CHARACTER, temperament, disposition, nature, calibre, personality, personal qualities, make-up
2 SPIRIT, courage, bravery, vigour, nerve, boldness, daring intrepidity, indomitability, fearlessness, pluck, resolve, determination, endurance, valour, gallantry, fortitude
COLLOQ. guts, backbone, spunk

mettlesome adj
high-spirited, spirited, bold, daring intrepid, brave, courageous, fearless, resolute, unflinching gallant, plucky, valiant, lion-hearted, stout-hearted
COLLOQ. spunky
F3 cowardly, afraid, fearful

mew v
miaow, meow, mewl, caterwaul, whine

mewl v
whine, whimper, whinge, cry, blubber, grizzle, snivel

miaow v
mew, meow, mewl, caterwaul, whine

miasma n
odour, smell, stench, stink, pollution, reek
FORMAL fetor, effluvium, mephitis

miasmal adj
foul, foul-smelling noxious, putrid, reeking smelly, stinking polluted, unwholesome
FORMAL f(o)etid, malodorous, noisome, mephitic, miasm(at)ic, miasm(at)ous

microbe n
micro-organism, bacterium, bacillus, germ, virus, pathogen
COLLOQ. bug

microscopic adj
minute, tiny, extremely small, minuscule, infinitesimal, indiscernible, imperceptible, negligible
F3 huge, enormous

microscopically adv
minutely, extremely, infinitesimally, imperceptibly
F3 hugely, gigantically

midday n
noon, twelve, twelve o'clock, twelve noon, lunchtime
FORMAL noonday, noontide
Related adjective: meridian

middle adj, n
  ♦ adj
central, mid, midway, halfway, mean, medium, medial, median, equidistant, intermediate, inner, inside, intervening

  ♦ n
1 CENTRE, halfway point, midpoint, mean, median, heart, core, midst, inside
COLLOQ. bull's eye
2 MIDRIFF, waist, stomach, belly, paunch
COLLOQ. tummy
SLANG bread basket
F3 extreme, end, edge, beginning border
■ **in the middle of**
busy with, during engaged in, in the process of, occupied with, surrounded by, while, in the midst of, among

middle-class adj
conventional, suburban, professional, white-collar, gentrified, bourgeois

middleman n
intermediary, go-between, negotiator, entrepreneur, distributor, retailer, broker, fixer

middling adj
mediocre, medium, ordinary, moderate, average, fair, unexceptional, unremarkable, run-of-the-mill, indifferent, modest, adequate, passable, tolerable
COLLOQ. so-so, OK, fair to middling not up to much, no great shakes, not much cop, nothing much to write home about

midget n, adj
  ♦ n
person of restricted growth, small person, pygmy, dwarf, Lilliputian, Tom Thumb, gnome, man(n)ikin, homunculus
F3 giant
  ♦ adj
tiny, small, minute, diminutive, dwarf, miniature, little, baby, pocket, pocket-sized, toy, pygmy, Lilliputian
COLLOQ. teeny, itsy-bitsy, teeny-weeny
F3 giant

midpoint n
middle point, central point, halfway point

midst n
middle, centre, midpoint, heart, core, bosom, nucleus, hub, depths, thick, interior
■ **in the midst**
during in the middle/thick of, among surrounded by

midway adv
halfway, in the middle, at the midpoint, in the centre, equidistant between, betwixt and between

mien n
appearance, look, manner, aspect, expression, air, complexion, presence, semblance, aura
FORMAL bearing carriage, countenance, demeanour, deportment

miffed adj
annoyed, irritated, displeased, aggrieved, nettled, hurt, offended, put out, resentful, upset, vexed, irked, disgruntled, chagrined, piqued
COLLOQ. in a huff, peeved
SLANG cheesed off, narked
F3 delighted, pleased; *colloq.* chuffed

might n
power, strength, force, forcefulness, energy, powerfulness, ability, capability, capacity, sway, vigour, stamina, heftiness, muscularity, potency, valour, prowess
FORMAL efficacy, puissance
COLLOQ. clout, muscle

mightily adv
exceedingly, very, very much, much, extremely, greatly, highly, hugely, decidedly, intensely, powerfully, strongly, vigorously, energetically, forcefully, lustily, manfully, strenuously

mighty adj, adv
  ♦ adj
1 STRONG, powerful, almighty, potent, forceful, vigorous, hefty, robust, tough, stalwart, stout, strapping muscular,

dominant, influential, doughty, grand, hardy, indomitable, lusty, manful
OLD puissant; (*Shakesp*) mightful
2 LARGE, enormous, colossal, huge, immense, vast, massive, gigantic, great, tremendous, towering titanic, stupendous, monumental, bulky, prodigious; *Scot* fell
OLD *Scot* felon
E3 1 frail, weak **2** small
♦ *adv*
extremely, very, really, exceedingly, excessively, exceptionally, extraordinarily, intensely, thoroughly, remarkably, utterly, greatly, highly, unusually, unreasonably
COLLOQ. awfully, terribly, dreadfully, frightfully, terrifically

migrant *n, adj*
♦ *n*
traveller, wanderer, itinerant, emigrant, immigrant, economic migrant, *Gastarbeiter*, transmigrant, rover, nomad, transient, globetrotter, drifter, Gypsy, tinker, vagrant
♦ *adj*
travelling wandering peripatetic, itinerant, immigrant, roving nomadic, shifting transient, globetrotting drifting Gypsy, migratory, vagrant

migrate *v*
move, resettle, relocate, wander, roam, rove, journey, emigrate, travel, voyage, hike, trek, drift

migration *n*
movement, travel, journey, voyage, wandering roving emigration, shift, trek
TECHNICAL diaspora
FORMAL transhumance

migratory *adj*
travelling wandering peripatetic, itinerant, immigrant, roving nomadic, shifting transient, globetrotting drifting Gypsy, migrant, vagrant

mild *adj*
1 *a mild form of the disease*
slight, faint, feeble, weak, gentle, modest, subtle, vague, imperceptible
2 *mild manners*
gentle, calm, peaceable, placid, tender, tender-hearted, sensitive, soft, soft-hearted, good-natured, easy-going kind, sympathetic, warm, warm-hearted, meek, amiable, lenient, humane, compassionate, merciful, forbearing
3 *mild weather*
calm, temperate, warm, balmy, clement, fair, moderate, pleasant
4 *mild food*
bland, mellow, smooth, subtle, soothing tasteless, flavourless, insipid
E3 1 strong severe, extreme **2** harsh, aggressive, fierce **3** cold, stormy **4** strong sharp, spicy

mildewy *adj*
rotten, fusty, musty
FORMAL f(o)etid, mucedinous, mucid

mildly *adv*
1 SLIGHTLY, faintly, weakly, vaguely, gently, subtly, imperceptibly
2 GENTLY, calmly, tenderly, sensitively, softly, warmly, meekly, compassionately, mercifully
E3 1 strongly, severely, extremely **2** harshly, aggressively, fiercely

mildness *n*
1 GENTLENESS, calmness, placidity, tenderness, softness, docility, kindness, sympathy, warmth, meekness, indulgence, leniency, lenity, compassion, mercy, forbearance, tranquillity, passivity
2 TEMPERATENESS, calmness, warmth, clemency, moderation
3 BLANDNESS, mellowness, smoothness, tastelessness, insipidness
E3 1 harshness, aggressiveness, violence **2** storminess, chilliness **3** sharpness, spiciness

milieu *n*
environment, location, scene, setting surroundings, background, locale, medium, arena, element, sphere

militancy *n*
aggressiveness, belligerence, extremism, assertiveness, activism, vigorousness

militant *adj, n*
♦ *adj*
aggressive, belligerent, vigorous, fighting combative, embattled, warring assertive, activist
FORMAL pugnacious
E3 pacifist, peaceful
♦ *n*
activist, combatant, fighter, struggler, soldier, warrior, aggressor, belligerent, partisan

militantly *adv*
aggressively, belligerently, vigorously, assertively

military *adj, n*
♦ *adj*
martial, armed, army, soldierly, warlike, service, disciplined
♦ *n*
army, armed forces, soldiers, forces, services, militia, air force, navy
See panel on next page

militate *v*
■ **militate against**
oppose, discourage, counter, counteract, go/count against, act/tell against, work against, weigh against, be detrimental/harmful/disadvantageous to, damage, hurt, prejudice, be a decisive factor against, contend, resist
■ **militate for**
help, promote, speak for, back, further, advance, aid

militia *n*
reserve, reservists, Territorial Army, yeomanry, National Guard, home guard, minutemen
OLD fencibles, trainband

milk *v*
1 DRAIN, bleed, tap, extract, draw (off), exploit, use, express, press, pump, siphon, squeeze, wring
2 EXPLOIT, use, squeeze, wring pump, take advantage of, oppress, impose on, manipulate
COLLOQ. bleed
SLANG screw, rip off

> **PROVERBS**
> It's no use crying over spilt milk

milksop *n*
coward, weakling namby-pamby, pansy, cissy
COLLOQ. wimp, mummy's boy; *Scot* jessie
SLANG wuss

milky *adj*
white, milk-white, snow-white, chalky, opaque, clouded, cloudy

mill *n, v*
♦ *n*
1 FACTORY, plant, processing plant, works, workshop, shop, foundry
2 GRINDER, crusher, quern, roller
♦ *v*
grind, pulverize, powder, pound, crush, crunch, roll, press, grate
FORMAL comminute
■ **mill around**
move about, crowd around, throng swarm, stream, press around

millstone *n*
1 GRINDSTONE, quernstone
2 BURDEN, load, encumbrance, weight, dead-weight, obligation, duty, onus, trouble, affliction
COLLOQ. cross to bear

Military terms include:

about turn	brevet	depot	insignia	operational com-	route march
absent without	bridgehead	desertion	inspection	mand	salute
leave (AWOL)	briefing	detachment	installation	operational fleet	sentry
action	brigade	detail	insubordination	operations	shell
action stations	bugle call	disarmament	intelligence	orders	shell-shock
adjutant	call up	discharge	invasion	ordnance	signal
aide-de-camp	camouflage	dispatches	kit bag	outpost	skirmish
(ADC)	camp	division	landing	padre	slow march
Airborne Warning	campaign	draft	last post	parade	sniper
and Control	canteen	drill	latrine	parade ground	sortie
System (AWACS)	ceasefire	duty	leave	parley	squad
air cover	charge	encampment	left wheel	parole	squadron
air-drop	chemical warfare	enemy	liaison	patrol	*slang*
air force	citation	enlist	lines	pincer movement	square-bashing
allies	close ranks	ensign	logistics	platoon	standard
ambush	collateral damage	epaulette	manoeuvres	posting	stores
arm	colours	evacuation	march	prisoner of war	strategy
armed forces	combat	excursion	marching orders	(POW)	supplies
armistice	command	expedition	march past	quartermaster	surrender
army	commission	fall out	married quarters	quarters	tactics
arsenal	company	fatigues	martinet	quick march	tank
artillery	conquest	firing line	mess	radar	target
assault course	conscript	first post	minefield	range	task force
atomic warfare	conscription	flank	mission	rank	tattoo
attack	corps	fleet	mission creep	ration	the front
attention	counter-attack	flight	mobilize	rearguard	training
barracks	court-martial	flotilla	munitions	*colloq.* recce	trench
base	crossfire	foe	muster	reconnaissance	trench warfare
battle	debriefing	foray	mutiny	recruit	troop
battle fatigue	decamp	forced march	national service	regiment	truce
beachhead	decoration	friendly fire	navy	reinforcements	unit
billet	defeat	front line	Navy, Army and	requisition	van
biological warfare	defence	fusillade	Air Force	retreat	vanguard
bivouac	demilitarize	garrison	Institutes (NAAFI)	reveille	victory
blockade	*colloq.* demob	guard	nuclear warfare	rifle range	white flag
bomb	demobilize	incursion	observation post	roll-call	wing
bombardment	demotion	infantry	offensive	rout	

See also **armed services**; **rank¹**; **sailor**; **soldier**.

---

mime *n, v*

♦ *n*

dumb show, pantomime, gesture, mimicry, mummery, charade

♦ *v*

gesture, signal, indicate, act out, represent, simulate, impersonate, mimic, imitate

mimic *v, n*

♦ *v*

imitate, parody, caricature, copy, ape, monkey, parrot, impersonate, echo, mirror, resemble, simulate, mime, mock, play, look like

FORMAL emulate, personate

COLLOQ. take off, send up

♦ *n*

imitator, impersonator, impressionist, mimicker, caricaturist, parrot, ape, mime, starling copy, copyist

COLLOQ. copycat

mimicry *n*

imitation, imitating impersonation, copying parody, mockery, simulation, impression, caricature, aping burlesque

TECHNICAL mimesis

COLLOQ. take-off

minatory *adj*

threatening menacing intimidatory, warning cautionary, ominous, foreboding sinister, grim, looming

FORMAL inauspicious, impending minacious

mince *v*

1 CHOP, cut, cut into very small pieces, hash, dice, grind, crumble

2 WALK AFFECTEDLY, attitudinize, pose, strike a pose, posture, ponce, simper, walk in an effeminate/a dainty way, prance

■ **not mince your words**

talk plainly, speak directly, not hold anything back

COLLOQ. call a spade a spade, not beat about the bush, not pull any punches

mincing *adj*

dainty, effeminate, nice, precious, foppish, pretentious, minikin, niminy-piminy, coxcombic(al)

FORMAL affected

COLLOQ. la-di-da, poncy, cissy

mind *n, v*

♦ *n*

1 INTELLIGENCE, intellect, reason, powers of reasoning judgement, sense, understanding comprehension, wits, mentality, thinking thoughts, subconscious, head, genius, concentration, application, attention, spirit, psyche

FORMAL ratiocination

COLLOQ. brains, brainbox, grey matter, little grey cells

Related adjective: mental

2 MEMORY, remembrance, recollection, recall, retention

3 OPINION, view, viewpoint, point of view, way of thinking belief, attitude, judgement, outlook, feeling sentiment

4 INCLINATION, disposition, tendency, will, wish, intention, desire, fancy, urge, notion

5 THINKER, intellect, intellectual, genius, academic, mastermind, scholar, expert

COLLOQ. egghead, brain, brainbox

■ **be in two minds**
be uncertain, hesitate, be hesitant, be unsure, be
undecided, waver, vacillate, dither
COLLOQ. shilly-shally, dilly-dally, sit on the fence
■ **bear/keep in mind**
consider, remember, note, take note of, make
a mental note of, take into account/consideration, give
thought to
■ **cross your mind**
think of, remember, occur to, come to, strike, hit
■ **have in mind**
plan, design, aim, think of, contemplate,
want, intend
■ **make up your mind**
decide, come to/arrive at a decision, reach/make a
decision, choose, determine, settle, resolve
■ **mind's eye**
imagination, mind, head, contemplation, memory,
recollection, remembrance
■ **out of your mind**
mad, insane, lunatic, unbalanced, psychotic, deranged,
maniacal, demented, out of your senses, of unsound mind,
unhinged, crazed, unstable, *non compos mentis*, frenzied,
manic, maniac, distracted, distraught
COLLOQ. crazy, nuts, nutty, nutty as a fruitcake, barmy,
bonkers, batty, crackers, dippy, daffy, loopy, off your
head, wrong in the head, off the wall, round the bend,
round the twist, having bats in the belfry, mad as a hatter,
barking mad, cuckoo, flipped, off the rails, screwy, up the
wall, potty, raving not all there
SLANG bananas, loony, off your rocker, off your chump, off
your trolley, needing your head examined, having lost
your marbles, having a screw loose, having a tile loose,
mental, doolally
See Synonym nuances panel at **mad.**
■ **put you in mind of**
remind, prompt, bring to mind, call to mind, make you
think of
■ **put your mind to**
concentrate on, persevere, exert yourself, rise to the
occasion, take pains, buckle down
■ **speak your mind**
talk plainly, not mince your words, give it to someone
straight
COLLOQ. tell it like it is, call a spade a spade
■ **to my mind**
in my opinion, in my view, personally, personally
speaking according to what I think, I think/believe,
as I see it
♦ *v*
1 OBJECT (TO), take offence (at), be offended by, be
bothered by, be annoyed by, be troubled by, care about,
resent, disapprove, dislike
2 *mind the traffic*
watch, watch out, be careful, heed, pay attention, pay
heed to, regard, note, obey, respect, listen to, concentrate
on, comply with, follow, mark, observe
3 MAKE SURE, ensure, make certain, take care, remember,
not forget, note
4 LOOK AFTER, take care of, watch over, keep an eye on,
guard, have charge of, attend to
■ **mind out**
be careful, take care, look out, watch out,
watch, pay attention, beware, be on your guard, keep
your eyes open
■ **never mind**
1 TAKE NO NOTICE OF, not bother about, don't worry,
forget it
2 LET ALONE, not to mention, not forgetting apart from,
also, as well as, too

> **QUOTATIONS**
> The pendulum of the mind oscillates between sense and
> nonsense, not between right and wrong
> CARL JUNG, *Memories, Dreams and Reflections*

> **SYNONYM NUANCES**
> *noun sense 1*
> **Intelligence** may be used straightforwardly of mental
> skill or knowledge: *I didn't have the intelligence to
> become a doctor,* while **intellect** implies a person's
> capacity for developed thought: *his was a heavyweight
> intellect with a lightweight judgement.* **Reason**, although
> similar, is more appropriate for processing thought to
> draw conclusions, whereas **judgement** has more to do
> with assessment and discernment. **Wits**, however, is
> suggestive of alertness and ingenuity: *you need your wits
> about you in this place.*
> **Subconscious** puts the emphasis on innate mental
> influences rather than formulated thought, while **head**
> suggests the overall concept of the brain: *for goodness'
> sake, use your head; a good head for figures.* **Genius** is
> a highly approbatory term reserved for a unique inborn
> ability. **Concentration** and **attention** would be
> appropriate where the mind is focused on something
> while **application** implies a level of diligence.
> To suggest the essential nature of a person, you can
> use **spirit**, whereas **mentality** or **psyche** might be used
> of their mental make-up or a particular, set way of
> thinking: *this country is entrenched in a litigation
> mentality; staking a claim to a piece of land is deeply
> rooted in the American psyche.*

mind-boggling *adj*
incredible, unbelievable, impossible, inconceivable,
unthinkable, unimaginable, extraordinary, amazing
surprising astonishing astounding formidable, exceptional

mindful *adj*
aware, conscious, alive (to), alert, attentive, paying
attention to, careful, watchful, wary, chary, heedful
FORMAL cognizant, sensible
F∃ heedless, inattentive

mindless *adj*
1 THOUGHTLESS, senseless, illogical, irrational, stupid,
foolish, witless, dull, unintelligent, gratuitous, negligent
COLLOQ. dumb, dopey, thick, birdbrained
2 MECHANICAL, automatic, robotic, tedious, routine,
involuntary, instinctive
COLLOQ. knee-jerk
F∃ **1** thoughtful, intelligent

mindlessly *adv*
1 THOUGHTLESSLY, senselessly, foolishly, stupidly,
irrationally, illogically
2 MECHANICALLY, automatically, routinely, involuntarily,
instinctively
F∃ **1** thoughtfully

mine *n, v*
♦ *n*
1 PIT, colliery, coalfield, excavation, quarry, well, vein,
lode, seam, shaft, trench, deposit
2 SUPPLY, source, stock, store, storehouse, reserve,
reservoir, quarry, fund, repository, hoard, treasury, wealth
3 LANDMINE, explosive, depth charge, bomb
♦ *v*
excavate, dig for, dig up, delve, quarry, extract, search,
unearth, tunnel, remove, undermine

Parts of a mine include:

air lock	coal seam	main shaft
bord-and-pillar	fan drift	overburden
bunker	fault line	pan
cage	gallery	pithead frame
cage-winding sys-	goaf/gob/waste	pithead gear
tem	hydraulic pit prop	pit prop
capping	jib coal-cutter	plough coal-cutter
charging conveyor	lateral	powered support
coal-bearing rock	long-wall	retreat long-wall
coal-cutter	long-wall face	scraper chain

shaft	spoil	tunnelling
shearer loader		machine
skip winding	staple shaft	ventilation shaft
system	sump/sink	winding engine

miner n

coalminer, mineworker, collier, pitman, digger, faceman, faceworker, tributer; *Aust* hatter

mineral

Minerals include:

alabaster	fluorite	microcline
albite	fluorspar	montmorillonite
anhydrite	fool's gold	olivine
asbestos	French chalk	orthoclase
aventurine	galena	peridot
azurite	graphite	plumbago
bentonite	gypsum	pyrites
blacklead	haematite	quartz
bloodstone	halite	rock salt
blue john	haüyne	rutile
borax	hornblende	saltpetre
cairngorm	hyacinth	sanidine
calamine	idocrase	silica
calcite	jacinth	smithsonite
calcspar	jargoon	sodalite
cassiterite	jet	spar
chalcedony	kandite	sphalerite
chlorite	kaolinite	spinel
chrysoberyl	lapis lazuli	talc
cinnabar	lazurite	uralite
corundum	magnetite	uranite
dolomite	malachite	vesuvianite
emery	meerschaum	wurtzite
feldspar	mica	zircon

---

mingle v

1 MIX, intermingle, intermix, combine, blend, merge, unite, alloy, fuse, amalgamate, coalesce, join, compound
2 ASSOCIATE, socialize, circulate
FORMAL commingle
COLLOQ. hobnob, rub shoulders

mingy adj

1 NIGGARDLY, mean, miserly, close, ungenerous, ungiving sparing grudging hard-fisted, close-fisted/handed
FORMAL parsimonious
COLLOQ. stingy, tight-fisted, cheese-paring
2 *a mingy amount*
paltry, meagre, pitiful, miserable, scanty, skimpy, poor, puny, trivial
COLLOQ. measly, piddling pathetic
E3 **1** generous, liberal **2** great, large

miniature adj

tiny, small, small-scale, scaled-down, minute, reduced, diminutive, midget, toy, dwarf, baby, pocket-sized, little, cameo, microcosmic; *Scot* wee
COLLOQ. pint-size(d), mini, young
E3 giant

minimal adj

least, smallest, minimum, slightest, littlest, negligible, minute, token, nominal

minimize v

1 REDUCE, decrease, diminish, cut, curtail, shrink
COLLOQ. slash
2 BELITTLE, make light of, make little of, deprecate, discount, play down, underestimate, underrate, trivialize, laugh off
FORMAL disparage, decry
COLLOQ. soft-pedal
E3 **1** maximize **2** emphasize, play up

minimum n, adj

♦ n
least, lowest, lowest point, nadir, lowest number, smallest quantity, slightest, bottom
E3 maximum
♦ adj
minimal, least, lowest, slightest, smallest, littlest, tiniest
E3 maximum

minion n

1 ATTENDANT, follower, underling lackey, flunkey, henchman/woman/person, hireling servant, menial, drudge
2 DEPENDANT, hanger-on, favourite, darling sycophant, fawner, parasite, leech
COLLOQ. yes-man, bootlicker

minister n, v

♦ n
1 OFFICIAL, office-holder, politician, dignitary, diplomat, ambassador, delegate, legate, envoy, emissary, representative, consul, leader, cabinet minister, chancellor, agent, aide, administrator, executive, department secretary
2 CLERGYMAN/WOMAN, churchman, cleric, parson, priest, dean, pastor, vicar, rector, verger, curate, deacon, elder, chaplain, preacher, divine, padre
FORMAL ecclesiastic
♦ v
attend, serve, tend, take care of, look after, administer, wait on, cater to, accommodate, nurse
Related adjective: ministerial

ministration n

help, aid, assistance, care, service, relief, supervision, backing support, favour, patronage
FORMAL succour

ministry n

1 GOVERNMENT, cabinet, department, office, bureau, administration
2 THE CHURCH, holy orders, the priesthood, the clergy, the cloth
Related adjective: ministerial

minor adj, n

♦ adj
lesser, secondary, small, smaller, inferior, subordinate, subsidiary, junior, younger, unimportant, insignificant, inconsiderable, unknown, little known, negligible, petty, trivial, trifling second-class, unclassified, slight, light
E3 major, significant, important
♦ n
child, boy, girl, son, daughter, youngster, young person, juvenile, infant, junior, little one, young one, baby, toddler
COLLOQ. tot, tiny tot, kid, nipper

minstrel n

singer, musician, troubadour, bard, rhymer, joculator, jongleur

mint v, adj, n

♦ v
1 COIN, stamp, strike, cast, forge, punch, make, manufacture, produce, construct, devise, fashion
2 INVENT, make up, coin, fabricate, forge, falsify, fake, trump up, concoct, hatch
♦ adj
perfect, brand-new, new, as new, mint-new, fresh, immaculate, undamaged, unblemished, unused, excellent, first-class
♦ n
fortune, wealth, riches
COLLOQ. pile, packet, bomb, bundle, heap, stack, million(s), billion(s), king's ransom
SLANG megabucks, loadsamoney

minus prep

less, without, short of, excluding except, with the exception of, excepting save, bar

minuscule *adj*
tiny, fine, little, very small, minute, miniature, microscopic, infinitesimal, diminutive, Lilliputian
COLLOQ. teeny, teeny-weeny, itsy-bitsy
F3 gigantic, huge

minute[1] *n*
1 *ten minutes*
moment, second, instant, short (length of) time, flash
COLLOQ. jiffy, tick, sec, mo
2 *the minute something happens*
the moment, immediately, the instant, the point, directly, no sooner, as soon as
■ **in a minute**
soon, very soon, shortly, in a moment, in a flash, before long in the near future
COLLOQ. pronto, in a jiffy/tick, in two shakes of a lamb's tail, before you can say Jack Robinson
■ **this minute**
this instant, immediately, now, then, straight away, right away, right now, at once, next, there and then, instantly, instantaneously, directly, speedily, quickly, without delay, no sooner ... than, as soon as, promptly, unhesitatingly, without hesitation, without question, without further/more ado
FORMAL forthwith
COLLOQ. pronto, yesterday, before you know it, before you can say Jack Robinson, in two shakes of a lamb's tail, like a shot
■ **up to the minute**
latest, most modern, newest, most recent, fashionable, on-trend
COLLOQ. with it, in, all the rage, now

minute[2] *adj*
1 TINY, very small, infinitesimal, minuscule, microscopic, diminutive, miniature, inconsiderable, insignificant, negligible, slight, trifling trivial, Lilliputian
2 DETAILED, precise, accurate, exact, meticulous, painstaking close, strict, critical, exhaustive, punctilious
F3 1 gigantic, huge **2** cursory, superficial

minutely *adv*
closely, in detail, meticulously, painstakingly, scrupulously, systematically, precisely, exactly, exhaustively, critically
COLLOQ. with a fine-tooth comb

minutes *n*
proceedings, record(s), notes, memorandum, transcript, transactions, details, tapes

minutiae *n*
details, fine details, finer points, intricacies, complexities, particulars, niceties, subtleties, trifles, trivialities
COLLOQ. small print

miracle *n*
wonder, marvel, sign, prodigy, phenomenon
Related adjective: miraculous

miraculous *adj*
1 WONDERFUL, marvellous, phenomenal, extraordinary, remarkable, incredible, amazing surprising astounding astonishing unbelievable, unexpected
2 SUPERNATURAL, inexplicable, unaccountable, phenomenal, unnatural, extraordinary, remarkable, unbelievable, superhuman, monstrous
F3 2 natural, normal

miraculously *adv*
1 WONDERFULLY, remarkably, incredibly, amazingly, surprisingly, unbelievably, unexpectedly
2 SUPERNATURALLY, extraordinarily, remarkably, superhumanly, inexplicably, unaccountably
F3 2 naturally, normally

mirage *n*
illusion, optical illusion, hallucination, loom, fantasy, phantasm, phantasmagoria
TECHNICAL fata Morgana

mire *n, v*
♦ *n*
1 QUAGMIRE, quag marsh, marshland, morass, bog fen, swamp, slough; *Scot* glaur
2 MUCK, mud, dirt, slime, ooze
3 DIFFICULTIES, trouble, mess
COLLOQ. spot, jam, pickle, fix, hole, stew
♦ *v*
sink, bog down, overwhelm, deluge

mirror *n, v*
♦ *n*
1 GLASS, looking-glass, reflector, driving-mirror, rear-view mirror, wing mirror, hand-glass, pier-glass, cheval-glass; *dialect* keeking-glass
TECHNICAL condenser, laryngoscope, siderostat, Claude Lorraine glass
OLD (*Shakesp*) stone
FORMAL speculum
Related adjective: specular
2 REFLECTION, likeness, exact likeness, image, double, twin, copy, clone
COLLOQ. dead ringer, spitting image
♦ *v*
reflect, echo, imitate, copy, follow, represent, show, depict, mimic, parrot, ape, image
FORMAL emulate

mirth *n*
merriment, hilarity, gaiety, fun, laughter, enjoyment, pleasure, jollity, jocularity, amusement, frolics, revelry, glee, cheerfulness, light-heartedness, high spirits, buoyancy
FORMAL blitheness
F3 gloom, melancholy

mirthful *adj*
merry, hilarious, laughing laughable, uproarious, pleasurable, jolly, jovial, amusing funny, amused, happy, gay, cheerful, cheery, glad, gladsome, light-hearted, light-spirited, vivacious, buoyant, playful, ludic, sportive, frolicsome, festive
FORMAL blithe, jocund
F3 gloomy, glum, melancholy, mirthless

mirthless *adj*
glum, gloomy, unhappy, humourless, unamused, sad, miserable, depressed, despondent, moody, dejected, morose, pessimistic, doleful, crestfallen, sour, sulky, sullen, surly, grumpy, gruff, ill-humoured, churlish
F3 happy, cheerful

miry *adj*
marshy, swampy, boggy, fenny, muddy, mucky, dirty, oozy, slimy; *Scot* glaury

misadventure *n*
bad luck, hard luck, accident, ill fortune, ill luck, misfortune, mischance, calamity, catastrophe, tragedy, mishap, disaster, failure, problem, debacle, cataclysm, reverse, setback

misanthrope *n*
solitary, loner, recluse, hermit, unsocial person, cynic, miser
COLLOQ. meanie

misanthropic *adj*
antisocial, unfriendly, surly, unsociable, unsympathetic, malevolent, egoistic, inhumane
F3 philanthropic

misanthropy *n*
antisociality, unsociableness, malevolence, egoism, inhumanity
F3 philanthropy

misapply *v*
misuse, use unwisely/unsuitably, pervert, misappropriate, misemploy, abuse, exploit

misapprehend v
misunderstand, misinterpret, miscomprehend, misconceive, misconstrue, mistake, misread, get the wrong idea, get a false impression
COLLOQ. get hold of the wrong end of the stick
⊨ apprehend

misapprehension n
misunderstanding misconception, misinterpretation, misreading error, mistake, wrong idea, false impression, fallacy, delusion, mix-up

misappropriate v
steal, embezzle, pocket, thieve, pilfer, rob, swindle, misspend, misuse, misapply, abuse, pervert
FORMAL peculate, defalcate
COLLOQ. filch, pinch, nab, nick, have your fingers/hand in the till

misappropriation n
embezzlement, stealing theft, pilfering robbing pocketing misapplication, misuse
FORMAL defalcation, peculation

misbegotten adj
1 DISHONEST, disreputable, contemptible, stolen, unlawful, illicit, ill-gotten, shady
FORMAL purloined
2 ILL-CONCEIVED, ill-advised, unadvised, imprudent, ill-judged, poorly thought-out, abortive
COLLOQ. hare-brained
3 ILLEGITIMATE, natural, bastard, born out of wedlock

misbehave v
behave unacceptably/badly, behave improperly, be naughty, be rude, mess about, fool about/around, be beyond the pale, get up to mischief, offend, disobey, lapse, trespass
FORMAL transgress, misdemean
COLLOQ. muck about, play up, act up, carry on

misbehaviour n
unacceptable/bad behaviour, misconduct, bad manners, disobedience, naughtiness, mischief, insubordination
FORMAL misdemeanour, impropriety
COLLOQ. mucking about, carrying-on

misbelief n
wrong belief, delusion, illusion, error, mistake, misapprehension, misunderstanding misconception, fallacy, heresy, unorthodoxy, heterodoxy

miscalculate v
misjudge, get wrong go wrong make a mistake, slip up, blunder, err, miscount, overestimate, underestimate
COLLOQ. boob

miscalculation n
misjudgement, mistake, blunder, overestimate, underestimate, error, inaccuracy, slip, oversight, aberration, lapse, gaffe, fault, misunderstanding misapprehension
COLLOQ. slip-up, boob, booboo, bloomer, howler, clanger

miscarriage n
1 *have a miscarriage*
spontaneous abortion
2 FAILURE, breakdown, abortion, aborting mishap, mismanagement, error, perversion, ruination, disappointment
⊨ 2 success, fulfilment

miscarry v
1 *she miscarried*
abort, lose the baby, have a spontaneous abortion
2 FAIL, abort, come to nothing fall through, go wrong go amiss, misfire, founder, come to grief
COLLOQ. flop, fold, not come off, come a cropper, bite the dust
⊨ 2 succeed

miscellaneous adj
mixed, varied, various, assorted, diverse, diversified, eclectic, sundry, motley, mingled, jumbled, chow, farraginous
FORMAL heterogeneous, multifarious, variegated

miscellany n
assortment, mixture, mix, variety, collection, anthology, medley, potpourri, hotchpotch, jumble, diversity, pastiche, patchwork, olio, olla, gallimaufry, farrago, salmagundi, smorgasbord
FORMAL conglomeration, collectanea, miscellanea
COLLOQ. mixed bag mishmash, omnium-gatherum

mischance n
accident, misfortune, bad break, ill-chance, ill fortune, ill luck, misadventure, disaster, tragedy, calamity, mishap, blow, contretemps
FORMAL infelicity

mischief n
1 TROUBLE, harm, hurt, evil, damage, injury, disruption
OLD bale
2 MISBEHAVIOUR, bad behaviour, naughtiness, impishness, roguishness, devilment, pranks, tricks, escapade, wrongdoing; *Scot* pliskie
COLLOQ. monkey business, shenanigans, carry-on, lark, hanky-panky, jiggery-pokery, funny business; *Scot* barnsbreaking; *N Am* dido
SLANG *N Am* monkey shine
3 IMP, elf, puck, monkey, wag rascal, rogue, stirrer, scallywag scamp, nuisance, terror, pest, tyke, urchin, villain, devil, limb (of Satan), flibbertigibbet, gamin(e), varmint, *esprit follet*; *Scot* cutty, nickum; *Irish* spalpeen
OLD makebate
COLLOQ. cockatrice; *N Am* hellion

mischievous adj
1 MALICIOUS, evil, spiteful, vicious, wicked, malignant, pernicious, destructive, harmful, hurtful, injurious, detrimental, pestilent
OLD litherly, shrewd; *Scot* ill-deedly
2 NAUGHTY, badly-behaved, bad, disobedient, misbehaving up to no good, impish, rascally, roguish, playful, teasing waggish, frolicsome, troublesome, tricksy, arch, elfish, elfin; *dialect* gallows
OLD unhappy
⊨ 1 kind 2 well-behaved, good

mischievously adv
1 MALICIOUSLY, spitefully, wickedly, viciously, harmfully, injuriously, destructively
2 NAUGHTILY, disobediently, roguishly, playfully, impishly, teasingly, waggishly

misconceive v
misunderstand, misapprehend, misinterpret, misread, misjudge, misconstrue, mistake
COLLOQ. get hold of the wrong end of the stick

misconception n
misapprehension, misunderstanding misreading misinterpretation, error, mistake, fallacy, delusion, wrong idea, false impression
COLLOQ. the wrong end of the stick

misconduct n
misbehaviour, bad/unacceptable behaviour, malpractice, unethical/unprofessional behaviour, mismanagement, wrongdoing
FORMAL impropriety, misdemeanour

misconstrue v
misinterpret, misjudge, misread, misunderstand, misconceive, misapprehend, mistranslate, misreckon, mistake, take the wrong way
COLLOQ. get hold of the wrong end of the stick

miscreant n
wrongdoer, criminal, evildoer, sinner, rogue, rascal, scoundrel, scamp, scallywag villain, vagabond, wretch, reprobate, profligate, mischief-maker, knave, dastard, troublemaker

FORMAL malefactor
Ⅲ worthy

misdeed n
wrong wrongdoing crime, felony, offence, peccadillo,
delinquency, error, fault, misconduct, villainy,
sin, trespass
FORMAL misdemeanour, transgression

misdemeanour n
wrongdoing wrong misdeed, offence, infringement, lapse,
fault, error, indiscretion, misbehaviour, misconduct,
trespass, peccadillo
FORMAL malfeasance, transgression

misdirect v
divert, avert, misuse, misapply, misguide, mislead,
misaddress, misinform, misappropriate
COLLOQ. throw off the scent
SLANG give a bum steer

miser n
niggard, skinflint, cheeseparer, Scrooge, save-all,
curmudgeon, muckworm, hunks; *Scot* carl
OLD scrapegood
COLLOQ. penny-pincher, cheapskate, meanie, tightwad,
money-grubber
SLANG tight arse
Ⅲ spendthrift

miserable adj
1 UNHAPPY, sad, sorrowful, sorry, dejected, despondent,
depressed, down, downcast, downhearted, heartbroken,
low-spirited, wretched, distressed, crushed, desolate,
forlorn, gloomy, glum
FORMAL disconsolate, melancholic
COLLOQ. down in the dumps, blue
See Synonym nuances panel at **sad**.
2 *miserable weather*
cheerless, depressing dreary, gloomy, dismal, disagreeable,
unpleasant, forlorn, joyless
COLLOQ. lousy
3 *miserable living conditions*
impoverished, shabby, squalid, poor, wretched, rotten,
punk
4 CONTEMPTIBLE, despicable, ignominious, detestable, vile,
base, mean, disgraceful, deplorable, low, shameful,
pitiable
5 MEAGRE, paltry, niggardly, scanty, poor, worthless,
pathetic, pitiful
COLLOQ. measly
6 GRUMPY, bad-tempered, ill-tempered, irritable, surly,
sullen
COLLOQ. grouchy, crotchety
Ⅲ **1** cheerful, happy **2** pleasant, fair **3** comfortable **5**
generous, liberal

> **QUOTATIONS**
> The secret of being miserable is to have leisure to bother
> about whether you are happy or not. The cure for it is
> occupation
>   GEORGE BERNARD SHAW, *Parents and Children*

miserably adv
1 UNHAPPILY, sadly, sorrowfully, despondently, desolately,
gloomily, glumly
FORMAL disconsolately
2 NIGGARDLY, poorly, scantily, paltrily, pathetically, pitifully
COLLOQ. stingily
3 *fail miserably*
greatly, very much, desperately, dangerously, markedly

miserliness n
meanness, niggardliness, tightness, close-fistedness,
frugality, parsimony, penny-pinching cheeseparing
covetousness, avarice
FORMAL penuriousness
COLLOQ. tight-fistedness, minginess, stinginess
Ⅲ generosity, lavishness; *formal* prodigality

miserly adj
mean, niggardly, close, close-fisted/handed, sparing
parsimonious, cheeseparing beggarly, chintzy, candle-
paring; *Scot* gare
FORMAL penurious
COLLOQ. tight, tight-fisted, stingy, penny-pinching mingy,
money-grubbing
Ⅲ generous, spendthrift

misery n
1 UNHAPPINESS, sadness, suffering sorrow, distress,
desolation, depression, melancholy, melancholia,
discomfort, despair, anguish, agony, gloom, grief,
wretchedness, adversity, misfortune, living death, hell,
perdition
OLD bale
FORMAL woe, affliction
2 DEPRIVATION, hardship, poverty, want, oppression,
destitution
FORMAL privation, penury, indigence
3 SPOILSPORT, pessimist, killjoy, moaner, complainer,
prophet of doom, Jeremiah
COLLOQ. wet blanket, grouch, whiner, whinger, sourpuss,
dog in the manger, buzzkill
Ⅲ **1** contentment **2** comfort

misfire v
miscarry, go wrong go amiss, go awry, abort, fail, fall
through, founder, fizzle out, come to grief
COLLOQ. flop, not come off, come a cropper, bite the dust
Ⅲ succeed

misfit n
individualist, nonconformist, eccentric, maverick, dropout,
loner, lone wolf
COLLOQ. oddball, weirdo, freak, odd one out, fish out of
water, square peg in a round hole
Ⅲ conformist

misfortune n
bad luck, mischance, mishap, ill luck, hard luck,
misadventure, setback, reverse, failure, calamity,
catastrophe, disaster, blow, accident, tragedy, trouble,
adversity, evil, sorrow, hardship, trial
FORMAL tribulation, affliction, woe
Ⅲ luck, success

> **SYNONYM NUANCES**
>
> The less common synonym **mischance** suggests any
> unfortunate happening and the term **mishap**, although
> similar, is more appropriate for an unhappy accident: *his
> death was a million-to-one mishap.* **Ill-luck** again
> suggests the general concept of chance conspiring
> against you, and **hard luck** echoes this suggestion, with
> a hint of sympathy: *you've had your share of hard luck.*
> **Adversity** and **evil** imply particular circumstances
> working against you to a more serious degree: *we all
> need support in times of adversity;* similarly both
> **hardship** and **trial** are suggestive of a period of suffering.
>   **Misadventure**, on the other hand, is now most
> commonly applied to an accidental cause of death,
> unlike **setback** which is appropriate where there is an
> element of disappointing delay, while **reverse** could be
> used of a complete regression of fortune: *a reverse in the
> profits of the company.*
>   To refer to a sudden and dreadful occurrence, you might
> choose **calamity**, **catastrophe** or **disaster**, while **tragedy**
> is liable to suggest more dire human consequences:
> *neighbours were shocked by the tragedy.* **Blow**, although
> similar, would be a less serious impediment: *losing the
> match was a bit of a blow.* **Sorrow** can be used to put
> more emphasis on the grief caused.

misgiving n
doubt, uncertainty, unease, hesitation, qualm, reservation,
apprehension, scruple, suspicion, distrust, second thoughts,
niggle, anxiety, worry, fear
Ⅲ confidence

misguided *adj*

misled, misconceived, ill-considered, ill-advised, ill-judged, imprudent, rash, misdirected, inapposite, misinformed, misplaced, deluded, foolish, erroneous, wrong mistaken
FORMAL fallacious, injudicious
E3 sensible, wise

mishandle *v*

mismanage, make a mess of, bungle, misjudge, mess up
COLLOQ. botch, make a hash of, make a pig's ear of, fluff, muff
SLANG balls up, make a balls(-up) of, screw up
E3 cope, manage

mishap *n*

misfortune, ill fortune, stroke of bad luck, misadventure, accident, reverse, setback, calamity, catastrophe, disaster, adversity, blow, incident, trouble, trial
FORMAL tribulation

mishmash *n*

hotchpotch, hodgepodge, jumble, medley, potpourri, pastiche, mess, muddle, salad, hash, farrago, gallimaufry, salmagundi, olla, olio
FORMAL conglomeration

misinform *v*

mislead, misdirect, misguide, deceive, bluff, hoodwink
COLLOQ. lead up the garden path
SLANG give a bum steer, take for a ride

misinformation *n*

disinformation, misleading deception, misdirection, nonsense, bluff, lies, baloney
COLLOQ. dope, eyewash, guff, hype
SLANG bum steer

misinterpret *v*

misconstrue, misread, misunderstand, mistake, misjudge, misconceive, misapprehend, distort, garble, take the wrong way
COLLOQ. get hold of the wrong end of the stick

misinterpretation *n*

misunderstanding misconception, misjudgement, misapprehension, misreading misconstruction, false impression

misjudge *v*

miscalculate, mistake, misinterpret, misconstrue, misunderstand, overestimate, underestimate, get the wrong idea about, have a wrong opinion about

misjudgement *n*

miscalculation, misinterpretation, misunderstanding mistake, wrong opinion/idea/conclusion
COLLOQ. the wrong end of the stick

mislay *v*

lose, misplace, miss, forget where you have put, lose sight of, lose track of, be unable to find, misfile

mislead *v*

misinform, misdirect, misguide, misrepresent, deceive, fool into, delude, lead astray, blindfold, lead into error, put on, impose on/upon, fool, hoodwink
COLLOQ. send on a wild-goose chase, lead up the garden path, pull a fast one on, pull the wool over someone's eyes, put/throw off the scent
SLANG give a bum steer, take for a ride; N Am snow

misleading *adj*

deceptive, deceiving confusing unreliable, equivocal, ambiguous, biased, loaded, evasive, delusive, illusory
FORMAL fallacious
COLLOQ. tricky
E3 unequivocal, authoritative, informative

mismanage *v*

mishandle, botch, bungle, make a mess of, mess up, misrule, misspend, misjudge, foul up, mar, waste
COLLOQ. make a hash of, make a pig's ear of, muff
SLANG balls up, make a balls(-up) of, screw up

mismanagement *n*

mishandling misjudgement, failure, muddle, bungling mess
COLLOQ. hash, pig's ear, pig's breakfast, shambles, farce
SLANG balls-up, cock-up

mismatched *adj*

clashing discordant, ill-assorted, incompatible, unmatching misallied, mismated, unsuited, unreconcilable, irregular
FORMAL incongruous, disparate, antipathetic
E3 compatible, matching

misogynist *n*

woman-hater, anti-feminist, male chauvinist, male supremacist, sexist
COLLOQ. male chauvinist pig (MCP)
E3 feminist

misogyny *n*

anti-feminism, male chauvinism, male supremacy, sexism, sexual discrimination

misplace *v*

lose, mislay, miss, misapply, misassign, misfile, forget where you have put, lose sight of, lose track of, be unable to find

misprint *n*

mistake, error, literal (error), printing error, typographical error
FORMAL corrigendum, erratum
COLLOQ. typo

misquote *v*

misrepresent, misreport, muddle, misstate, twist, distort, pervert, falsify, garble, misremember

misread *v*

misinterpret, misconstrue, misunderstand, mistake, misjudge, misconceive, misapprehend, distort, garble, take the wrong way
COLLOQ. get hold of the wrong end of the stick

misrepresent *v*

distort, falsify, slant, pervert, manipulate, twist, garble, misquote, exaggerate, minimize, misconstrue, misinterpret, misreport, misstate, give a false/wrong account of

misrepresentation *n*

distortion, perversion, falsification, twisting manipulation, exaggeration, misreporting misconstruction, misinterpretation

misrule *n*

disorder, disorganization, maladministration, misgovernment, mismanagement, chaos, confusion, indiscipline, lawlessness, anarchy, riot, tumult, turmoil, turbulence, unreason

miss[1] *v, n*

♦ *v*

1 *miss a target*
fail, lose, let slip, let go, omit, fail to hit/get/catch, miscarry, overlook, pass over, slip, leave out, mistake, trip, misunderstand, err
COLLOQ. blow, muff

2 *miss a meeting*
be absent from, be away from, fail to attend, not take part in, not go to, not go to see, not see, not be part of, be too late for

3 *miss an opportunity*
let go, let slip, fail to seize, not take advantage of, neglect, disregard, overlook, pass up

4 NOT NOTICE, not spot, fail to notice, fail to notice the absence of, overlook, disregard, pass over

5 AVOID, escape, evade, beat, dodge, for(e)go, skip, bypass, sidestep
FORMAL circumvent

6 PINE FOR, long for, yearn for, regret, feel the loss of, grieve for, mourn, sorrow for, ache for, want, wish, need, lament

E3 1 hit, get, catch **2** take part in, attend **3** seize, grab **4** notice, spot

♦ *n*
failure, error, blunder, mistake, omission, oversight, fault, slip, fiasco
COLLOQ. flop; *N Am* flub

■ **miss out**
bypass, dispense with, disregard, ignore, jump, leave out, exclude, omit, pass over, skip

> **PROVERBS**
> A miss is as good as a mile

miss² *n*
Miss Bancroft
girl, schoolgirl, young lady, young woman, teenager, Ms, mademoiselle, damsel, lass, maid, maiden

missal *n*
breviary, formulary, mass-book, office-book, prayerbook, servicebook, euchologion, Triodion

misshapen *adj*
deformed, distorted, twisted, malformed, warped, contorted, crooked, crippled, bent, misproportioned, grotesque, ugly, monstrous
F3 regular, shapely

missile *n*
projectile, shot, guided missile, ballistic missile, arrow, shaft, dart, rocket, bomb, shell, flying bomb, grenade, torpedo, weapon

missing *adj*
absent, lost, lacking gone, mislaid, unaccounted-for, wanting disappeared, astray, gone astray, strayed, misplaced, nowhere to be found
F3 found, present

mission *n*
1 TASK, undertaking assignment, operation, commission, campaign, crusade, business, errand, work, duty, chore
2 CALLING, duty, purpose, vocation, *raison d'être*, aim, goal, quest, pursuit, charge, office, job, work
3 DEPUTATION, ministry, delegation, commission, task force, legation, embassy
4 *a bombing mission*
operation, raid, sortie, campaign, exercise, manoeuvre, action

missionary *n*
evangelist, campaigner, preacher, converter, proselytizer, apostle, minister, crusader, propagandist, champion, promoter, emissary, envoy, ambassador

missive *n*
communication, dispatch, letter, line, message, report, note, bulletin, communiqué, memorandum
FORMAL epistle
COLLOQ. memo

misspent *adj*
wasted, frittered away, squandered, thrown away, idle, idled away, misused, profitless, misapplied, dissipated, unprofitable
FORMAL prodigal
F3 profitable

misstate *v*
misreport, misrepresent, misquote, misrelate, pervert, twist, distort, falsify, garble, misremember

mist *n, v*
♦ *n*
haze, fog vapour, smog cloud, murk, condensation, film, spray, drizzle, mizzle, dew, steam, veil, dimness

■ **mist over/up**
cloud over, become cloudy, become hazy, fog (up), dim, blur, become blurred, steam up, obscure, veil, glaze
F3 clear

mistake *n, v*
♦ *n*
error, inaccuracy, omission, oversight, aberration, lapse, slip, slip of the tongue, mix-up, blunder, gaffe, fault, flaw,

fallacy, faux pas, indiscretion, misjudgement, miscalculation, misunderstanding, misapprehension, misprint, misspelling, misreading, mispronunciation, miscommunication, misstep, boss, miscue, misprise, misprision
TECHNICAL domino
OLD misprize; (*Spenser*) mesprize
FORMAL solecism, erratum, corrigendum
COLLOQ. bloomer, howler, clanger, slip-up, muff, fluff, botch-up, boob, booboo, bad move, cardinal sin, blooper, bish, foul-up, own goal; *Scot* stumer
SLANG goof
♦ *v*
1 MISUNDERSTAND, misapprehend, misconstrue, misjudge, misread, miscalculate, misconceive, get wrong, go wrong, slip up, make a slip, blunder, err, misstep, miscue
OLD misprise; (*Spenser*) mesprize
COLLOQ. muff, boob, duff it, mess up, make a booboo, foul up, put your foot in it, get your wires crossed, bark up the wrong tree, get hold of the wrong end of the stick, drop a clanger, come a cropper; *N Am* flub
SLANG louse up, balls up, cock up, screw up, goof (up)
2 *mistake a person for another*
confuse, mix up, confound, muddle (up), take for

> **QUOTATIONS**
> The man who makes no mistakes does not usually make anything
> EDWARD JOHN PHELPS

> **SYNONYM NUANCES**
>
> *noun*
> **Error** can be widely applied to anything that has been done wrong while **fault** suggests a flaw: *a simple technical fault*. **Inaccuracy** has more to do with a lack of precision, but suggests a less obvious mistake; **slip** is also suggestive of a smaller mistake but one made through a degree of carelessness. The word **oversight**, similarly, suggests an inadvertent omission: *an administrative oversight*, whereas **aberration** and **lapse** are appropriate for a deviation from normal practices or expectations: *Vichy was an aberration in French history*. **Blunder** and **gaffe** are more suggestive of stupidity and more contemptuous in tone.
> **Indiscretion** is a gentler term which has more to do with a misdeed through lack of judgement: *a youthful indiscretion*. This more tolerant tone is continued by **misjudgement** and **miscalculation** which both simply imply an incorrect assessment, while **misunderstanding** and **misapprehension** suggest taking the wrong meaning.

mistaken *adj*
wrong incorrect, in error, erroneous, inaccurate, inexact, untrue, unfounded, inappropriate, ill-judged, inauthentic, false, deceived, deluded, misguided, misinformed, misled, faulty, at fault, misprised
FORMAL fallacious
COLLOQ. having got hold of the wrong end of the stick, got the wrong idea, wide of the mark
F3 correct, right

mistakenly *adv*
wrongly, by mistake, erroneously, in error, incorrectly, falsely, inaccurately, inappropriately, misguidedly, unfairly, unjustly
FORMAL fallaciously
F3 appropriately, correctly, fairly, justly

mistimed *adj*
inconvenient, unfortunate, untimely, ill-timed, inopportune, unseasonable, unsynchronized, tactless
FORMAL infelicitous, malapropos
F3 opportune

mistreat v
abuse, misuse, ill-treat, ill-use, maltreat, treat badly, mishandle, harm, hurt, bully, batter, injure, molest, maul
COLLOQ. knock about, beat up, walk (all) over
F∃ cosset, pamper

mistreatment n
maltreatment, abuse, ill-treatment, ill-use, harm, hurt, battering injury, molestation, bullying cruelty, unkindness, manhandling mauling mishandling misuse, ill-usage, brutalization
F∃ cosseting pampering

mistress n
1 LOVER, live-in lover, partner, girlfriend, woman, lady, kept woman, concubine, courtesan, paramour, lady-love, inamorata, hetaera, *amie*, *belle amie*, canary-bird
OLD miss, wench; (*Shakesp*) doxy
COLLOQ. bit on the side, fancy woman
OLD SLANG stepney
2 TEACHER, schoolteacher, governess, tutor

mistrust n, v
◆ n
distrust, doubt, suspicion, wariness, misgiving reservations, qualm, hesitancy, chariness, caution, uncertainty, scepticism, apprehension
F∃ trust
◆ v
distrust, doubt, have doubts about, have no faith in, suspect, be suspicious of, be wary of, beware, have reservations, have misgivings, fear
F∃ trust

mistrustful adj
distrustful, doubtful, dubious, hesitant, sceptical, suspicious, uncertain, wary, cautious, apprehensive, fearful, shy, chary, cynical
COLLOQ. leery
F∃ trustful

misty adj
hazy, foggy, cloudy, blurred, fuzzy, murky, smoky, unclear, dim, indistinct, obscure, opaque, vague, nebulous, veiled
F∃ clear, distinct

misunderstand v
misapprehend, misconstrue, misinterpret, misread, misjudge, mistake, get wrong get the wrong idea, get a false impression, miss the point, mishear
COLLOQ. get hold of the wrong end of the stick, not make head or tail of, get your wires crossed
F∃ understand

misunderstanding n
1 MISTAKE, error, misapprehension, misconception, misjudgement, misinterpretation, wrong idea, false impression, misreading mix-up
COLLOQ. the wrong end of the stick, crossed wires
2 DISAGREEMENT, argument, dispute, conflict, clash, difference, difference of opinion, breach, quarrel, rift, row, squabble
FORMAL discord
COLLOQ. falling-out, tiff
F∃ **1** understanding right idea **2** agreement, accord

misunderstood adj
misappreciated, misconstrued, misjudged, misread, misrepresented, mistaken, unappreciated, unrecognized, misheard, misinterpreted, ill-judged

misuse n, v
◆ n
mistreatment, maltreatment, mishandling injury, abuse, wrong use, harm, ill-treatment, misapplication, misemployment, misappropriation, waste, squandering perversion, corruption, exploitation
◆ v
abuse, misapply, misemploy, ill-use, ill-treat, treat badly, harm, mistreat, wrong distort, injure, hurt, corrupt, pervert, waste, squander, misappropriate, exploit, dissipate

⚠ misuse or **abuse**?
See panel at **abuse**.

mite n
bit, trace, spark, whit, touch, atom, morsel, scrap, grain, jot, iota, modicum, ounce
COLLOQ. smidgen, tad

mitigate v
moderate, temper, alleviate, relieve, reduce, lessen, calm, pacify, soften, soothe, still, subdue, tone down, weaken, placate, quiet, decrease, diminish, dull, check, ease, mollify, lighten, sweeten, modify, qualify, help, blunt;
Scot mease
OLD aslake, slake
FORMAL abate, allay, appease, assuage, extenuate, palliate, remit, lenify
F∃ increase, exacerbate, aggravate

mitigating adj
extenuating justifying vindicating tempering modifying lenitive, qualifying vindicatory, mitigant
FORMAL palliative, assuasive

mitigation n
moderation, lessening tempering reduction, relief, easement, alleviation, decrease, diminution, qualification, mollification
FORMAL abatement, allaying appeasement, assuagement, extenuation, palliation, remission
F∃ increase, exacerbation, aggravation

mix v, n
◆ v
1 COMBINE, blend, mingle, put together, intermingle, intermix, amalgamate, compound, homogenize, synthesize, merge, join, unite, coalesce, fuse, alloy, incorporate, stir, whisk, mash, emulsify, infiltrate, introduce, fold in
FORMAL interpolate
2 ASSOCIATE, consort, fraternize, socialize, meet others, mingle, join
COLLOQ. hobnob
3 BE COMPATIBLE, harmonize, get along/on, agree, complement, go well with, suit
COLLOQ. be on the same wavelength
F∃ **1** divide, separate
◆ n
mixture, blend, amalgam, amalgamation, assortment, combination, union, compound, merger, coalition, alloy, fusion, synthesis, medley, hotchpotch, hodgepodge, composite, jumble, potpourri, pastiche, hash, farrago, gallimaufry, salmagundi, olla-podrida, olio
FORMAL conglomerate
COLLOQ. mishmash

■ mix in
add in, blend, merge, introduce, incorporate, infiltrate
FORMAL interpolate
F∃ extract, isolate

■ mix up
confuse, bewilder, muddle (up), mistake, perplex, puzzle, confound, mix, jumble, get jumbled up, complicate, garble, involve, implicate, disturb, upset, snarl up

mixed adj
1 *of mixed race*
combined, hybrid, mingled, crossbred; (*offensive*) half-caste; mongrel, interbred, blended, composite, compound, incorporated, united, alloyed, amalgamated, fused
2 *mixed biscuits*
assorted, varied, miscellaneous, diverse, diversified, motley
3 *mixed feelings*
ambivalent, equivocal, conflicting contradicting uncertain, unsure

■ **mixed up**

1 *a mixed-up person*
maladjusted, disturbed, disordered, disoriented, distracted, distraught, confused, bewildered, muddled, perplexed, puzzled, upset, chaotic, complicated, *désorienté*
COLLOQ. messed up, hung up
SLANG screwed up
2 *mixed up in a crime*
INVOLVED, embroiled, incriminated, caught up, entangled, implicated
FORMAL inculpated
COLLOQ. in on

mixer *n*

1 *a food mixer*
blender, food processor, liquidizer, beater, whisk
2 EXTROVERT, joiner, socializer, everybody's friend
COLLOQ. life and soul of the party
3 INTERFERER, busybody, disrupter, meddler, mischief-maker, subversive, troublemaker
OLD makebate
COLLOQ. stirrer
2 introvert, loner, recluse **3** peacemaker

mixing *n*

1 AMALGAMATION, combination, synthesis, intermingling coalescence, blending union, fusion, hybridization, interbreeding interflow
FORMAL minglement
2 ASSOCIATION, fraternization, socializing mingling
1 separation

mixture *n*
mix, blend, combination, amalgamation, amalgam, compound, composite, coalescence, alloy, brew, synthesis, union, fusion, concoction, cross, hybrid, assortment, variety, miscellany, medley, melange, farrago, smorgasbord, pastiche, patchwork, potpourri, jumble, hotchpotch, hodgepodge, olio, olla-podrida
FORMAL conglomeration
COLLOQ. mixed bag mishmash

mix-up *n*
mess, mistake, misunderstanding muddle, nonsense, chaos, confusion, jumble, disorder, complication, snarl-up, tangle
COLLOQ. foul-up
SLANG balls-up; *N Am* snafu

moan *n, v*
♦ *n*
1 GROAN, lament, lamentation, sob, wail, howl, whimper, whine
2 COMPLAINT, grumble, grievance, groan, dissatisfaction, annoyance, fault-finding criticism, carping censure, accusation, charge, representation
COLLOQ. beefing beef, grouse, gripe, bleating whingeing whinge
SLANG bellyaching
♦ *v*
1 GROAN, wail, sob, weep, howl, whimper, mourn, lament, sigh, grieve; *dialect* hone; *Scot* mean
2 COMPLAIN, grumble, whine, carp; *Scot* mean
COLLOQ. whinge, gripe, grouse, bleat, beef, kick up a fuss
SLANG bellyache
1 rejoice

moaner *n*
complainer, grumbler, niggler, fault-finder
COLLOQ. whinger, grouser, fusspot, nit-picker, whiner; *N Am* fussbudget
SLANG bellyacher

mob *n, v*
♦ *n*
1 CROWD, mass, throng multitude, horde, rabble, host, swarm, gathering group, collection, body, flock, herd, drove, brood, pack, press, set, tribe, troop, company, crew, gang ribble-rabble
FORMAL assemblage

2 POPULACE, rabble, masses, proletariat, hoi polloi, rank and file, common people, common herd, great unwashed, ribble-rabble, king mob, many-headed beast/monster, *canaille, faex populi*
OLD mobile, rabble rout
COLLOQ. plebs, riff-raff, proles
SLANG mobility
♦ *v*
crowd, crowd round, surround, swarm round, gather round, jostle, overrun, set upon, fall upon, besiege, descend on, throng pack, fill, pester, attack, charge

mobile *adj*

1 MOVING, movable, able to move, portable, transportable, travelling roaming roving itinerant, wandering migrant
FORMAL peripatetic, motile, locomotive, ambulatory
2 FLEXIBLE, adjustable, adaptable, supple, agile, active, energetic, nimble
3 CHANGING, changeable, ever-changing expressive, suggesting revealing lively
1 immobile

mobility *n*
movability, movableness, portability, flexibility, motion, expressiveness, vivacity, agility, animation, suppleness
FORMAL locomobility, locomotion, locomotivity, motility, motivity
immobility, inflexibility, rigidity

mobilization *n*
activation, organization, preparation, summoning assembly, marshalling mustering

mobilize *v*
assemble, marshal, rally, conscript, muster, call up, enlist, call into action, activate, cause to take action, galvanize, organize, prepare, get ready, make ready, ready, summon, animate

mob rule *n*
mob law, lynch law, kangaroo court, Reign of Terror
FORMAL ochlocracy
COLLOQ. mobocracy

mobster *n*
gangster, desperado, hoodlum, ruffian, rough, tough, thug terrorist, racketeer, bandit, brigand, robber, criminal, bovver boy, hooligan, skinhead
COLLOQ. crook
SLANG heavy

mock *v, adj*
♦ *v*
1 RIDICULE, jeer, make fun of, poke fun at, laugh at, scoff, sneer, taunt, gibe, scorn, insult, tease, chaff, laugh in someone's face, flout, fleer; *dialect* geck; *Scot* murgeon; *Aust* poke mullock at
OLD bemock, dor, jape, scout
FORMAL disparage, deride
COLLOQ. kid, rib, rag knock, take the mickey out of
SLANG slag (off), take the piss out of; *N Am* goof; *Aust & NZ* poke borak at
2 IMITATE, simulate, mimic, ape, caricature, parody, burlesque, lampoon, satirize
FORMAL emulate
COLLOQ. send up, take off
♦ *adj*
imitation, imitative, counterfeit, artificial, sham, mimic, simulated, synthetic, substitute, ersatz, false, fake, forged, fraudulent, bogus, pseudo, spurious, feigned, faked, pretended, dummy
COLLOQ. phoney, pretend
SLANG cod

mocker *n*
jeerer, ridiculer, scoffer, scorner, sneerer, satirist, tease, tormentor, flouter, lampooner, lampoonist, critic, detractor, pasquinader
FORMAL derider, reviler, vilifier, iconoclast
SLANG piss-taker
flatterer, supporter

mockery n

1 RIDICULE, jeering scoffing scorn, sneer, sneering taunting teasing contempt, disdain, disrespect, sarcasm, sport, fleer, banter, raillery, quiz
OLD dor, gab
FORMAL derision, disparagement, contumely
COLLOQ. kidding ribbing ragging mickey-taking
SLANG piss-taking; *Aust* serve
2 PARODY, satire, sham, travesty, caricature, farce, burlesque, lampoon, apology, charivari, horning
FORMAL emulation
COLLOQ. send-up, take-off, spoof

mocking adj

scornful, derisive, derisory, contemptuous, sarcastic, satirical, taunting scoffing sardonic, sneering insulting irreverent, impudent, disrespectful, disdainful, cynical
COLLOQ. snide

mock-up n

model, copy, replica, representation, facsimile, image, imitation, dummy

mode n

1 WAY, style, manner, approach, condition, method, form, plan, practice, procedure, process, technique, system, convention
2 FASHION, style, custom, trend, vogue, fad, look
COLLOQ. craze, latest thing rage, *dernier cri*

model n, adj, v

♦ n
1 COPY, replica, representation, facsimile, image, imitation, mock-up, dummy
2 EXAMPLE, pattern, design, standard, ideal, epitome, paragon, perfect example, embodiment, byword, mould, original, type, prototype, sample, template, specimen, version
TECHNICAL stereotype
FORMAL exemplar, archetype, paradigm
3 DESIGN, style, form, sort, kind, variety, type, version, mark
FORMAL mode
4 MANNEQUIN, fashion model, artist's model, photographer's model, dummy, sitter, subject, poser
♦ adj
1 EXEMPLARY, perfect, typical, optimum, ideal
FORMAL archetypal, prototypical
2 *a model railway*
miniature, small-scale, reduced, replica, reproduction, toy
♦ v
1 MAKE, form, fashion, mould, sculpt, carve, cast, shape, work, create, design, plan, base
2 DISPLAY, wear, sport, pose, show off

moderate adj, v, n

♦ adj
1 MEDIOCRE, medium, modest, ordinary, fair, fairish, indifferent, average, middling adequate, tolerable, passable, middle-of-the-road
COLLOQ. so-so, fair to middling not up to much, no great shakes, not much cop, nothing much to write home about
2 REASONABLE, restrained, fair, just, modest, sensible, calm, steady, sober, controlled, temperate, cool, mild, well-regulated
Eꟻ 1 exceptional, extreme **2** immoderate, excessive
♦ v
1 CONTROL, regulate, decrease, lessen, slacken, die down, soften, restrain, tone down, play down, diminish, ease, curb, calm, check, keep in check, keep under control, modulate, repress, subdue, assuage, tame, subside, pacify, dwindle
FORMAL attenuate, mitigate, allay, alleviate, abate, appease, palliate
COLLOQ. soft-pedal
2 *moderate a debate*
chair, act as chair/chairperson/chairman/chairwoman at, preside over, direct, supervise

♦ n
nonextremist, centrist, liberal, neutral person, don't know
Eꟻ extremist, hardliner

moderately adv

reasonably, somewhat, quite, rather, fairly, slightly, passably, within reason, to some extent, to a certain degree, conservatively, within measure
Eꟻ extremely

moderation n

1 RESTRAINT, self-control, self-restraint, caution, control, composure, sobriety, abstemiousness, temperance, temperateness, reasonableness
2 DECREASE, reduction, lessening regulation, curbing subsidence, relaxation
FORMAL attenuation, mitigation, alleviation, abatement
Eꟻ 1 (over-)indulgence, self-indulgence
■ **in moderation**
within limits, within bounds, within reason, moderately, with self-control
Eꟻ to excess

modern adj

current, contemporary, up-to-date, existing new, fresh, latest, late, novel, present, present-day, recent, up-to-the-minute, advanced, avant-garde, progressive, modernistic, innovative, inventive, state-of-the-art, go-ahead, forward-looking futuristic, fashionable, in fashion, stylish, in vogue, in style, voguish, modish
COLLOQ. newfangled, in, now, trendy, with it, spanking new, faddish, all the rage, the latest, hot off the press(es), hip, cool
Eꟻ old-fashioned, old, out-of-date, antiquated, traditional, oldfangled

---

SYNONYM NUANCES

Current, **contemporary**, **up-to-date** and **up-to-the-minute** can be used with overtones of fashionability: *pubs of the 1950s adopted a contemporary 'Festival of Britain' look*, while **existing**, **present** and **present-day** straightforwardly refer to what is presently available or happening: *present-day standards; customer needs are being met by existing products*, whereas **fresh** has positive implications of not being stale: *we need a fresh outlook*. **Novel** too has suggestions of newness as well as originality.

The terms **advanced** and **avant-garde** would actually suggest something is ahead of its time, the latter often in a shocking way, and **progressive**, **go-ahead** and **forward-looking** too echo the idea of pushing old boundaries: *progressive thinking leads to scientific advance*. **Innovative** and **inventive** are also more positively suggestive of being imaginatively creative. The term **modernistic**, however, can be used to imply a stylized representation and is not necessarily approving: *the car was given a modernistic design, intended to look like a space ship*; **futuristic** is similar but indicates looking to the imagined future for inspiration: *futuristic houses with labour-saving gadgets*. **State-of-the-art**, on the other hand, is more approbatory in its suggestion of being unsurpassed at a given time: *state-of-the-art technology*.

The various terms **in vogue**, **voguish** and **modish** all return to the idea of the present and its prevailing trends, while **fashionable** and **stylish** express approval of them.

---

modernity n

innovation, innovativeness, newness, novelty, originality, contemporaneity, fashionableness, freshness, recentness
Eꟻ antiquatedness, antiquity

modernization n

renovation, refurbishment, regeneration, renewal, revamping updating redesign, remodelling transformation, modification, improvement

modernize _v_
renovate, refurbish, rejuvenate, regenerate, streamline, revamp, renew, make modern, update, bring up-to-date, improve, do up, redesign, reform, remake, remodel, refresh, transform, modify, progress
COLLOQ. do over, fix up, move with the times, get with it
≠ regress

modest _adj_
1 UNASSUMING, humble, self-effacing self-deprecating quiet, reserved, retiring lowly, unpretentious, unpretending, discreet, bashful, shy, self-conscious, coy, timid, diffident, shamefaced
FORMAL verecund
2 MODERATE, ordinary, unexceptional, fair, satisfactory, reasonable, tolerable, passable, decent, adequate, limited, small
3 _a modest house_
unassuming unpretentious, simple, ordinary, plain, small, inexpensive
4 _modest behaviour_
proper, prudent, discreet, pure, chaste, virtuous, demure, maidenly
OLD seemly
FORMAL decorous
≠ 1 immodest, conceited, arrogant **2** exceptional, excessive **3** pretentious, expensive, extravagant **4** immoral, indecent

modestly _adv_
1 HUMBLY, unassumingly, quietly, bashfully, shyly, self-consciously, coyly, timidly, diffidently, unpretentiously
2 MODERATELY, reasonably, satisfactorily, adequately, decently
3 _behave modestly_
discreetly, purely, chastely, virtuously, demurely
≠ 1 arrogantly **2** excessively **3** immorally

modesty _n_
1 HUMILITY, humbleness, self-effacement, self-deprecation, reticence, reserve, quietness, shyness, bashfulness, coyness, self-consciousness, timidity
2 _modesty of behaviour_
decency, propriety, demureness, chasteness
OLD seemliness
FORMAL decorum
3 UNPRETENTIOUSNESS, simplicity, plainness, inexpensiveness
≠ 1 immodesty, vanity, conceit **3** extravagance

modicum _n_
little, bit, small amount, little bit, particle, molecule, fragment, grain, scrap, shred, speck, touch, degree, trace, tinge, atom, crumb, dash, drop, pinch, ounce, hint, suggestion, inch, iota, mite
COLLOQ. tad

modification _n_
adaptation, adjustment, alteration, change, revision, tweak, variation, improvement, transformation, mutation, refinement, reformation, reorganization, remoulding reworking recasting limitation, moderation, qualification, restriction, tempering
FORMAL modulation

modify _v_
1 CHANGE, alter, redesign, revise, vary, adapt, adjust, transform, reform, convert, improve, reorganize, reshape, remould, rework, recast, sculpt, retrofit, diversify, temper, touch, tweak, invert, overrule, explain away, trim your sails
TECHNICAL assimilate, dash, vowel, vowelize, umlaut
2 MODERATE, reduce, lessen, decrease, diminish, temper, tone down, limit, soften, dull, qualify
OLD attemper
FORMAL abate, mitigate

modish _adj_
fashionable, stylish, smart, vogue, voguish, contemporary, current, modern, modernistic, avant-garde, fashion-forward, chic, _à la mode_
COLLOQ. cool, all the rage, hip, in, jazzy, latest, mod, trendy, on-trend, up-to-the-minute, with it, now
≠ dowdy, old-fashioned

modulate _v_
modify, adjust, balance, alter, soften, temper, moderate, lower, regulate, change, vary, harmonize, inflect, tune

modulation _n_
modification, adjustment, balance, alteration, softening lowering moderation, regulation, change, variation, harmonization, tuning tone, shift, inflection, inflexion, intonation, accent, shade

module _n_
component, unit, part, section, element, factor, item, piece

modus operandi _n_
method, way, operation, plan, practice, procedure, process, manner, technique, system, rule, rule of thumb
FORMAL praxis

mogul _n_
magnate, tycoon, baron, potentate, notable, personage, supremo
COLLOQ. big cheese, big gun, big noise, big pot, big shot, big wheel, bigwig, Mr Big, top dog, VIP
≠ nobody

moist _adj_
damp, clammy, dank, humid, wet, wettish, liquid, dewy, rainy, muggy, marshy, drizzly, drizzling watery, washy, soggy, dripping
FORMAL humectant, hydric, hygrophil, hygrophilous
≠ dry, arid

moisten _v_
moisturize, dampen, damp, wet, make wet, soak, water, humidify, humify, lick, irrigate, slake; _Scot_ sparge, spairge
FORMAL humect, humectate
≠ dry

moisture _n_
water, liquid, wetness, wet, wateriness, damp, dampness, dankness, humidity, vapour, rain, drizzle, dew, mugginess, condensation, soaking steam, spray, perspiration, sweat
TECHNICAL precipitate, precipitation
OLD humour
FORMAL humectation
≠ dryness

mole[1] _n_
a mole on the skin
spot, blemish, blotch, mark, speckle, freckle

mole[2] _n_
a mole in the organization
agent, infiltrator, secret agent, spy, double agent

mole[3] _n_
a mole stretching out to sea
barrier, breakwater, pier, causeway, dyke, groyne, jetty, embankment

molest _v_
1 ANNOY, disturb, bother, harass, irritate, agitate, vex, exasperate, persecute, pester, nag chivvy, harry, plague, tease, torment, hound, upset, fluster, worry, trouble, provoke, badger
COLLOQ. aggravate, needle, hassle, bug
2 ATTACK, accost, assail, hurt, ill-treat, maltreat, mistreat, abuse, interfere with, (sexually) assault, rape, harm, injure
FORMAL ravish

molestation _n_
abuse, interference, harm, injury, attack, assault, rape

molester _n_
abuser, attacker, assaulter, rapist
FORMAL ravisher

mollify v
placate, appease, calm, pacify, compose, conciliate, cushion, ease, relax, relieve, lessen, moderate, temper, modify, quell, soften, soothe, lull, quieten, quiet, blunt, sweeten, mellow
FORMAL abate, allay, mitigate, assuage, propitiate
Ea aggravate, anger

mollusc

Molluscs include:

abalone	limpet	scallop
clam	marine snail	sea slug
cockle	mussel	slug
conch	nautilus	squid
cowrie	nudibranch	tusk shell
cuttlefish	octopus	whelk
freshwater snail	oyster	
land snail	periwinkle	

---

mollycoddle v
pamper, coddle, indulge, spoil, overprotect, pander to, cosset, spoon-feed, mother, pet, baby, ruin
Ea ill-treat, neglect

molten adj
melted, liquefied, flowing fusil
TECHNICAL magmatic

moment n
1 *stop for a moment*
second, instant, (very) short time, little while, less than no time, point in time, minute, split second, flash, twinkling of an eye, trice
COLLOQ. mo, sec, jiffy, tick, two ticks, two shakes of a lamb's tail
2 *the moment something happens*
the minute, immediately, the instant, the point, directly, no sooner ..., as soon as
3 IMPORTANCE, significance, substance, note, interest, value, worth, concern, consequence, gravity, seriousness, weight, weightiness
FORMAL import
Ea **3** insignificance

momentarily adv
briefly, for a moment, for a short time, for a second, for an instant, instantaneously, fleetingly, temporarily

momentary adj
brief, short, short-lived, temporary, transient, transitory, fleeting hasty, quick, passing spasmodic, instantaneous, momentaneous
OLD (*Shakesp*) momentany
FORMAL ephemeral, evanescent
Ea lasting permanent

momentous adj
significant, important, of importance, of great consequence, of significance, critical, crucial, decisive, weighty, grave, serious, vital, consequential, fateful, historic, pivotal, earth-shaking earth-shattering world-shattering epoch-making eventful, major, pregnant
Ea insignificant, unimportant, trivial

momentum n
impetus, force, energy, impulse, drive, power, driving-power, thrust, propulsion, speed, velocity, impact, incentive, stimulus, urge, strength, push

monarch n
sovereign, the Crown, crowned head, ruler, king queen, emperor, empress, prince, princess, Caesar, tsar, potentate, autocrat

monarchy n
1 KINGDOM, empire, principality, realm, sovereign state, domain, dominion

2 ROYALISM, sovereignty, kingship, autocracy, absolutism, despotism, tyranny
FORMAL monocracy

monastery n
friary, priory, nunnery, convent, abbey, cloister, charterhouse, religious community
FORMAL coenobium

monastic adj
reclusive, withdrawn, secluded, cloistered, anchoritic, canonical, austere, ascetic, celibate, meditative, contemplative
FORMAL sequestered, eremitic, coenobitic
Ea secular, worldly
See panel **religious orders** *at* **religious**.

monasticism n
asceticism, austerity, recluseness, reclusion, seclusion, monkhood
FORMAL monachism, eremitism, coenobitism

monetary adj
financial, money, fiscal, budgetary, economic, capital, cash
FORMAL pecuniary

money n
currency, cash, legal tender, banknotes, coin, mammon, funds, finances, assets, means, savings, resources, capital, riches, wealth, prosperity, affluence
COLLOQ. the necessary
SLANG loot, readies, bucks, ready, megabucks, dough, dosh, bread, lolly, spondulicks, brass, gravy, greens, shekels, moolah, greenies, scratch, smash, stumpy, chink; *N Am* Benjamins; *Aust & NZ* Oscar
OLD SLANG blunt, rhino
Related adjectives: monetary, pecuniary
■ **in the money**
rich, wealthy, affluent, prosperous, well-off, well-to-do
COLLOQ. rolling in it, well-heeled, stinking rich, flush
SLANG loaded
Ea poor

> **QUOTATIONS**
> I will admit that money does not bring happiness, but it must be admitted that it facilitates much
> CHODERLOS DE LACLOS, *Les Liaisons dangereuses*

> **SYNONYM NUANCES**
> **Currency** refers to money in circulation, with an exchangeable value: *foreign currency*. **Legal tender**, likewise, is a more formal term for a country's legitimate units of payment. **Cash** can be used to put the emphasis on the physical nature of money: *you can pay by cash or cheque*.
> **Funds** and **finances**, on the other hand, have more to do with the money available for a particular project, or to a particular person or group: *the party has started raising funds for its campaign; the company's finances are strong*. **Capital** is also appropriate for available money, but more suggestive of that provided by an initial investment. **Assets**, **means** and **resources** are similar, but can also refer to anything owned that is of monetary value and which you can use to support yourself: *she tried to make the most of her limited resources*.
> While **riches** and **wealth** have more to do with an abundance of money and valuable possessions, **prosperity** and **affluence** suggest potential for increase in monetary wealth.

money-box n
cash box, chest, safe, coffer, piggy-bank

moneyed *adj*
wealthy, rich, affluent, comfortable, well-off, prosperous, well-to-do
FORMAL opulent
COLLOQ. flush, well-heeled, rolling in it
SLANG loaded
F3 poor, impoverished

money-grubbing *adj*
acquisitive, grasping miserly, mercenary, mammonish, mammonistic
FORMAL quaestuary

moneymaking *adj*
profitable, profit-making lucrative, commercial, remunerative, paying successful

mongrel *n, adj*
♦ *n*
cross, crossbreed, hybrid, half-breed, mixed breed, cur; *NZ* kuri
♦ *adj*
crossbred, hybrid, half-bred, bastard, mixed, of mixed breed, ill-defined
F3 pure-bred, pedigree

monicker *n*
name, alias, nickname, pseudonym, assumed/false name, so(u)briquet, pen name, stage name

monitor *v, n*
♦ *v*
check, watch, keep track of, keep under surveillance, keep an eye on, follow, track, supervise, oversee, observe, note, survey, trace, scan, record, plot, detect
♦ *n*
1 SCREEN, display, VDU, recorder, scanner, detector, security camera, CCTV
2 SUPERVISOR, watchdog observer, overseer, invigilator, adviser, regulator, prefect, head boy/girl

monk *n*
brother, religious, friar, frater, prior, abbot, hermit, monastic, mendicant, contemplative, cloisterer, beguin, conventual, *religieux*, religionary, religioner, anchorite, possessionate, *talapoin*, abbey-lubber
OLD gyrovague
FORMAL coenbite
Related adjectives: monastic, monasterial

monkey *n, v*
♦ *n*
1 PRIMATE, simian
Related adjective: simian
2 SCAMP, imp, urchin, brat, rogue, rascal, mischief-maker, scallywag tyke
♦ *v*
play, fool, tinker, tamper, trifle, fiddle, fidget, interfere, meddle, mess, potter
COLLOQ. muck, clown, footle
■ **monkey business**
mischief, tomfoolery, trickery, chicanery, clowning pranks, dishonesty, skulduggery, legerdemain, sleight-of-hand, foolery
COLLOQ. carry-on, hanky-panky, jiggery-pokery, monkey tricks, shenanigans, funny business

Monkeys include:

ape	langur	rhesus monkey
baboon	leaf monkey	saki
capuchin monkey	macaque	spider monkey
colobus	mandrill	squirrel monkey
drill	mangabey	tamarin
guenon	marmoset	titi
guereza	night monkey (or	toque
howler	douroucouli)	uakari (or cacajou)
kipunji	proboscis monkey	woolly monkey

monochrome *adj*
black-and-white, monotone, sepia, monochromatic, monotonous
FORMAL monochroic, unicolor, unicolorate, unicolorous, unicolour, unicoloured
F3 kaleidoscopic, multicoloured

monocle *n*
eyeglass, glass

monogamous *adj*
having only one marriage partner
FORMAL monandrous, monogamic, monogynous
F3 bigamous, polygamous

monogamy *n*
FORMAL monandry, monogyny
F3 bigamy, polygamy

monolingual *adj*
FORMAL monoglot, unilingual
F3 polyglot

monolith *n*
megalith, standing stone, shaft, menhir, sarsen

monolithic *adj*
massive, vast, colossal, gigantic, huge, monumental, giant, immovable, immobile, rigid, solid, unmoving unchanging inflexible, faceless, undifferentiated, fossilized, hidebound, intractable, unvaried

monologue *n*
speech, soliloquy, lecture, sermon, address, oration, homily
COLLOQ. spiel
F3 conversation, dialogue, discussion

monomania *n*
obsession, fixation, ruling passion, fanaticism, *idée fixe*, mania, neurosis, fetish
COLLOQ. bee in your bonnet, hobby-horse, thing

monopolize *v*
dominate, take over, keep to yourself, have (all) to yourself, corner, control, not share with others, have exclusive/sole rights, engross, occupy, preoccupy, take up, tie up
FORMAL appropriate
COLLOQ. hog
F3 share

monopoly *n*
domination, control, corner, exclusive right(s), sole right(s), privilege, franchise, *appalto*, *régie*
TECHNICAL monopsony
FORMAL ascendancy

monotonous *adj*
boring dull, tedious, uninteresting unexciting tiresome, wearisome, unchanging uneventful, unvarying unvaried, all the same, uniform, toneless, flat, colourless, repetitive, repetitious, routine, mechanical, plodding humdrum, soul-destroying
COLLOQ. run-of-the-mill, samey, deadly, ho-hum
F3 lively, varied, colourful

monotony *n*
tedium, dullness, boredom, sameness, tiresomeness, uneventfulness, flatness, wearisomeness, uniformity, routine, routineness, repetitiveness, repetition
F3 liveliness, colour, variety, excitement, interest

monster *n, adj*
♦ *n*
1 *sea monsters*
frightening creature, imaginary creature, mythical creature, mythological creature, Frankenstein, chimera, prodigy, bandersnatch, jabberwock
TECHNICAL wivern, satyral, teratism
OLD mooncalf, wasserman, whirlpool
See panel at **mythical**.
2 BEAST, fiend, brute, barbarian, savage, villain, dragon, Frankenstein, giant, ogre, ogress, devil, troll

3 FREAK, freak of nature, monstrosity, mutant, malformation, miscreation
TECHNICAL teratism
4 MAMMOTH, jumbo, giant, colossus, leviathan, behemoth, cyclops, Brobdingnagian
♦ adj
huge, gigantic, giant, colossal, enormous, immense, massive, monstrous, jumbo, mammoth, vast, tremendous
COLLOQ. whopping ginormous, mega
⊟ tiny, minute

monstrosity n
1 EYESORE, blot on the landscape, atrocity, abnormality, enormity, freak, monster, mutant, miscreation, obscenity
TECHNICAL teras
2 DREADFULNESS, frightfulness, hideousness, loathsomeness, horror, hellishness, evil
FORMAL heinousness

monstrous adj
1 WICKED, evil, vicious, savage, cruel, criminal, outrageous, scandalous, shocking disgraceful, abominable, atrocious, abhorrent, dreadful, frightful, horrible, horrifying grisly, terrible, vile, foul, nasty, inhuman
FORMAL heinous
2 UNNATURAL, inhuman, freakish, abnormal, grotesque, hideous, gruesome, deformed, malformed, misshapen
TECHNICAL teratoid
3 HUGE, enormous, colossal, gigantic, vast, immense, tremendous, massive, mammoth

monstrously adv
1 OUTRAGEOUSLY, shockingly, atrociously, scandalously, dreadfully, frightfully, terribly
2 IMMENSELY, hugely, enormously, colossally, gigantically, vastly, massively, tremendously

monument n
memorial, cenotaph, headstone, gravestone, tombstone, shrine, mausoleum, cairn, barrow, cross, marker, obelisk, pillar, column, statue, relic, remembrance, commemoration, witness, testament, reminder, record, memento, evidence, token

monumental adj
1 IMPRESSIVE, imposing striking awe-inspiring awesome, overwhelming significant, important, epoch-making historic, magnificent, remarkable, majestic, memorable, unforgettable, notable, outstanding abiding permanent, enduring immortal, lasting classic
2 HUGE, immense, enormous, colossal, vast, tremendous, extraordinary, massive, great, exceptional
3 COMMEMORATIVE, celebratory, memorial
⊟ **1** insignificant, unimportant

monumentally adv
immensely, hugely, enormously, colossally, gigantically, vastly, massively, tremendously

mood n
1 DISPOSITION, frame of mind, state of mind, temper, humour, vein, spirit, tenor, whim
2 BAD TEMPER, bad mood, sulk, the sulks, pique, melancholy, low spirits, depression, doldrums
COLLOQ. blues, dumps
3 ATMOSPHERE, feeling feel, spirit, tenor, tone, climate, ambience
■ **in the mood for**
wanting to do/have, feeling like, willing to, eager to, keen on/to, inclined to, ready for, in the right frame of mind to
FORMAL disposed to

moody adj
changeable, temperamental, unpredictable, volatile, unstable, irritable, short-tempered, bad-tempered, crotchety, testy, touchy, morose, angry, broody, irascible, cantankerous, petulant, mop(e)y, sulky, sullen, gloomy, melancholy, miserable, downcast, in a huff, in a (bad) mood, doleful, glum, impulsive, fickle, flighty
FORMAL capricious

COLLOQ. crabby, crusty
⊟ equable, cheerful

moon v
idle, loaf, languish, pine, mope, brood, daydream, dream, fantasize
COLLOQ. mooch
■ **once in a blue moon**
very rarely, seldom, not often, hardly ever, almost never
■ **over the moon**
ecstatic, elated, blissful, joyful, jubilant, rapturous, enraptured, overjoyed, euphoric, delirious, frenzied, fervent
FORMAL rhapsodic
COLLOQ. jumping for joy, on top of the world, on cloud nine, in seventh heaven, tickled pink, high as a kite

moonlike adj
lunar, moon-shaped, crescent, crescentic, moony
TECHNICAL lunate
FORMAL lunular, meniscoid, selenic

moonshine n
1 NONSENSE, rubbish, fantasy, stuff; dialect & N Am blathers; Scot blethers
COLLOQ. hot air, guff, hogwash, baloney, bosh, bunk, bunkum, claptrap, eyewash, tommyrot, tosh, tripe, twaddle, piffle, rot
SLANG (vulgar) shit, bullshit, crap
2 SPIRITS, liquor, bootleg hoo(t)ch, pot(h)een
⊟ **1** sense

moor[1] v
to moor a boat
fasten, secure, tie up, drop anchor, anchor, berth, dock, make fast, fix, fix firmly, hitch, lash, bind
⊟ loose

moor[2] n
the Yorkshire moors
moorland, heath, fell, upland

moot v, adj
♦ v
put forward, propose, suggest, submit, advance, bring up, raise, broach, introduce, pose, discuss, argue, debate
FORMAL propound
♦ adj
controversial, problematic, difficult, questionable, vexed, unsettled, unresolved, unresolvable, undecided, undetermined, disputed, disputable, arguable, doubtful, insoluble, knotty, open, open to debate, debatable, crucial, contestable, academic

mop n, v
♦ n
1 a floor mop
sponge, wiper, swab, squeegee
2 a mop of hair
head of hair, shock, mane, tangle, thatch, mat, mass
♦ v
swab, sponge, wipe, clean, wash, absorb, soak
■ **mop up**
1 WIPE UP, wash, absorb, soak up, sponge, swab, clean up, tidy up
2 FINISH OFF, deal with, wipe up, dispose of, account for, round up, neutralize, eliminate, secure, take care of

mope v, n
♦ v
brood, fret, sulk, pine, languish, droop, despair, be miserable, grieve
♦ n
melancholic, misery, depressive, pessimist, killjoy, melancholiac, moaner, introvert
COLLOQ. grouch, grump, moper
■ **mope about**
idle, wander, moon, languish
COLLOQ. mooch, lounge, loll

moral *adj, n*
◆ *adj*
1 ETHICAL, virtuous, good, right, principled, honourable, decent, upright, upstanding straight, righteous, high-minded, honest, incorruptible, proper, blameless, chaste, clean-living pure, just, noble
2 *give moral support*
encouraging emotional, psychological
E3 1 immoral
◆ *n*
lesson, message, significance, teaching point, dictum, meaning maxim, adage, precept, saying proverb, aphorism, epigram

> **SYNONYM NUANCES**
>
> *adjective sense 1*
> **Ethical** can be used to suggest anything that conforms to acceptable forms of human conduct: *the ethical dilemma of cloning*, while **virtuous** and **good** are more judgemental, suggesting an inherent goodness. **Decent**, **principled** and **upstanding** similarly suggest adherence to conventions of social morality: *fine, upstanding young men*, but **honourable** is stronger in that it further implies integrity, while **upright** implies strong moral rectitude. **Righteous** and **high-minded** are similar, but can on occasion imply a degree of self-satisfaction or arrogance: *a school with high-minded staff and prissy pupils*.
>   **Proper**, although it is rather prim in tone, might be used in a variety of contexts to suggest behaving appropriately: *I didn't feel her forwardness was quite proper*. **Chaste**, **pure** and **clean-living**, however, more specifically suggest an avoidance of wrong-doing and debauchery. **Straight** tends to suggest an adherence to the law, whereas **just** is more suggestive of fairness or sometimes simply validity: *a just cause*, and **noble** suggests morality with an element of dignity: *enlightened, noble thoughts*.

morale *n*
confidence, spirit(s), *esprit de corps*, self-esteem, self-confidence, state of mind, heart, mood, optimism, hopefulness

moralistic *adj*
self-righteous, smug complacent, superior, priggish, pious, sanctimonious, holier-than-thou, pietistic, hypocritical, pharisaical
COLLOQ. goody-goody
E3 humble

morality *n*
ethics, morals, moral values, moralism, ideals, principles, principles of behaviour, principles of right and wrong standards, virtue, righteousness, decency, purity, chastity, goodness, honesty, integrity, justice, uprightness, conduct, manners, *Sittlichkeit*
OLD morale
FORMAL rectitude, propriety
E3 immorality

moralize *v*
preach, lecture, pontificate, edify, sermonize
FORMAL discourse, ethicize

morally *adv*
ethically, honourably, properly, justly, nobly, socially, behaviourally

morals *n*
morality, moral values, moral code, ethics, principles, principles of behaviour, right and wrong standards, ideals, integrity, scruples, behaviour, conduct, habits, manners

morass *n*
1 QUAGMIRE, bog moss, marsh, marshland, swamp, slough, mire, fen, quag quicksand
2 CONFUSION, clutter, chaos, mess, jam, jumble, muddle, mix-up, tangle
COLLOQ. can of worms

moratorium *n*
delay, postponement, halt, freeze, suspension, stay, standstill, stoppage, respite, ban, embargo
E3 *colloq.* go-ahead, green light

morbid *adj*
1 GHOULISH, obsessed with death, ghastly, gruesome, grisly, macabre, hideous, horrible, horrid, dreadful, grim
2 GLOOMY, pessimistic, melancholy, dejected, down, morose, sombre
FORMAL lugubrious
COLLOQ. down in the dumps
3 SICK, ailing diseased, unhealthy, unwholesome
FORMAL insalubrious

morbidly *adv*
ghoulishly, gruesomely, horribly, horridly, grimly, dreadfully, hideously

mordant *adj*
biting acid, caustic, bitter, acrimonious, astringent, critical, scathing sharp, harsh, incisive, waspish, stinging wounding vicious, venomous, cutting sarcastic, pungent, edged
FORMAL acerbic, trenchant
E3 gentle, mild, sparing

more *adj, adv, pron*
◆ *adj*
further, extra, additional, added, new, fresh, increased, other, another, supplementary, repeated, alternative, spare
E3 less
◆ *adv*
further, longer, to a greater extent/degree, again, better
E3 less
◆ *pron*
greater number/quantity, additional people/things, extra
■ **more or less**
generally, in general, by and large, for the most part, on the whole, mostly, in most cases, predominantly, mainly, broadly

moreover *adv*
furthermore, further, besides, in addition, as well, also, additionally, what is more

mores *n*
custom, traditions, habits, procedures, practices, ways, manners, ways of life, ways of behaving conventions, usages, etiquette

morgue *n*
mortuary, funeral parlour, deadhouse, charnel house

moribund *adj*
1 DYING, failing fading expiring declining wasting away, senile, in extremis
TECHNICAL comatose
COLLOQ. on your last legs, on the way out, with one foot in the grave, not long for this world
2 WEAK, feeble, lifeless, declining wasting away, waning ebbing stagnating stagnant, obsolescent, doomed, dwindling collapsing crumbling
E3 1 alive, lively; *formal* nascent **2** flourishing

morning *n*
before noon, a.m., dawn, sunrise, first light, daybreak, break of day, cock-crow, crack of dawn, daylight, forenoon
OLD morn; (*Shakesp*) matin
Related adjectives: matutinal, antemeridian

moron *n*
fool, blockhead, fat-head, dolt, dunce, dimwit, simpleton, halfwit, idiot, cretin, imbecile, ignoramus, dupe, stooge, butt, laughing-stock, clown, comic, buffoon, jester
COLLOQ. nincompoop, ass, chump, ninny, neddy, clot, dope, twit, nitwit, nit, sucker, mug twerp, birdbrain, silly-billy, berk, (proper) Charlie
SLANG wally, jerk, dumbo, muppet, pillock, prat, dork, geek, plonker, git, nerd, dweeb, nerk, cloth head, dipstick, goof, kook, tosspot; (*taboo*) dickhead, knobhead, prick

moronic adj
foolish, stupid, senseless, silly, absurd, ridiculous, ludicrous, nonsensical, unwise, ill-advised, ill-considered, shortsighted, half-baked, crazy, mad, insane, idiotic, hare-brained, half-witted, simple-minded, simple, ignorant, unintelligent, inept, inane, pointless, unreasonable
COLLOQ. daft, crack-brained, gormless, dumb, dotty, wacky, potty, batty, barmy, nutty, not in your right mind, out of your mind
SLANG with a screw/tile loose, needing your head examined

morose adj
ill-tempered, bad-tempered, moody, sombre, sullen, sulky, surly, gloomy, grim, gruff, sour, taciturn, glum, saturnine, depressed, mournful, melancholic, pessimistic
FORMAL lugubrious
COLLOQ. grouchy, crabby
E3 cheerful, communicative

morosely adv
sullenly, gloomily, moodily, gruffly, sourly, mournfully
FORMAL lugubriously
E3 cheerfully

morsel n
bit, scrap, piece, fragment, crumb, bite, mouthful, nibble, taste, soupçon, titbit, slice, segment, fraction, modicum, grain, atom, part, particle

mortal adj, n
♦ adj
1 WORLDLY, earthly, bodily, fleshly, human, perishable, transient, temporal
FORMAL corporeal, ephemeral
2 FATAL, lethal, dying deadly, killing murderous, deathful
3 EXTREME, great, severe, intense, grave, awful, dire, terrible, unbearable
4 mortal enemies
implacable, relentless, unrelenting deadly, cruel, bitter, vengeful
5 a mortal sin
unforgivable, unpardonable, irremissible
E3 1 immortal **5** venial
♦ n
human being human, individual, person, man, woman, being body, creature, earthling
OLD worldling
E3 immortal, god

> **QUOTATIONS**
> For in that sleep of death what dreams may come /
> When we have shuffled off this mortal coil / Must give us pause
>   WILLIAM SHAKESPEARE, *Hamlet*

mortality n
1 HUMANITY, impermanence, worldliness, earthliness, perishability, transience
FORMAL ephemerality
2 FATALITY, death, death rate, killing slaughter, carnage, casualty, loss of life
E3 1 immortality

mortally adv
1 mortally wounded
fatally, lethally, finally, terminally destructively, disastrously
2 EXTREMELY, greatly, severely, intensely, gravely, awfully, terribly

mortgage n
loan, pledge, security, bond, debenture; *Scot* wadset
FORMAL lien

mortification n
1 EMBARRASSMENT, humiliation, confounding shame, disgrace, dishonour, loss of face, abasement, annoyance, chastening vexation
FORMAL chagrin, discomfiture, ignominy

2 DISCIPLINE, punishment, asceticism, control, self-control, denial, self-denial, conquering
FORMAL subjugation

mortified adj
humiliated, horrified, shamed, ashamed, disgraced, dishonoured, humbled, embarrassed, crushed, confounded, defeated, sick

mortify v
1 HUMILIATE, horrify, shame, put to shame, embarrass, offend, disgrace, dishonour, chastise, chasten, abash, confound, humble, bring low, crush, deflate, affront, annoy, disappoint, wither
FORMAL discomfit, chagrin
COLLOQ. take down a peg or two
2 DISCIPLINE, restrain, suppress, deny, die, control, conquer, subdue

mortifying adj
embarrassing humbling humiliating salutary, shaming ignominious, overwhelming crushing chastening punishing thwarting
FORMAL discomfiting

mortuary n
morgue, funeral parlour, deadhouse, charnel house

most n
bulk, mass, majority, overwhelming majority, preponderance, greatest/largest part, almost all, nearly all
COLLOQ. lion's share
■ **for the most part**
mostly, mainly, on the whole, principally, especially, chiefly, generally, in general, usually, largely, predominantly, overall, in the main, as a rule, above all

mostly adv
mainly, on the whole, principally, especially, chiefly, generally, in general, usually, largely, predominantly, overall, for the most part, in the main, as a rule, above all

moth

Types of moth include:

brown-tail	hawk moth	privet hawk moth
buff-tip	Kentish glory	puss
burnet	lackey	red underwing
carpet	lappet	silkworm
cinnabar	leopard	silver-Y
clearwing	lobster	six-spot burnet
clothes	magpie	swallowtail
death's-head moth	oak hook-tip	turnip
emperor	pale tussock	wax
garden tiger	peach blossom	winter
gypsy	peppered	

See also **butterfly**.

moth-eaten adj
old, worn, worn-out, old-fashioned, obsolete, outdated, outworn, ragged, tattered, threadbare, dated, ancient, antiquated, archaic, decrepit, dilapidated, decayed, musty, shabby, stale, mouldy, mangy, moribund, seedy
E3 fresh, new

mother n, v
♦ n
1 PARENT, birth mother, dam, matriarch, ancestor, matron
FORMAL procreator, progenitress, materfamilias, mater
COLLOQ. mum, mummy, ma, mam, mumsy, ma(m)ma, old woman, old lady, yummy mummy; *N Am* mom, mommy, soccer mom
Related adjective: maternal
2 ORIGIN, source, spring, fount, foundation, base, cause, derivation, roots, wellspring
♦ v
1 BEAR, give birth to, produce, bring forth, nurture, raise, rear, tend, nurse, care for, take care of, look after, cherish

2 PAMPER, spoil, baby, indulge, overprotect, fuss over, nanny

motherly adj
motherlike, maternal, caring comforting affectionate, kind, loving protective, nurturing warm, tender, gentle, fond
🔁 neglectful, uncaring

motif n
theme, idea, topic, concept, pattern, design, figure, form, logo, shape, device, emblem, ornament, decoration

motion n, v
♦ n
1 MOVEMENT, action, mobility, moving activity, locomotion, travelling travel, transit, going changing place(s), passage, passing progress, change, flow, inclination
FORMAL motility
Related adjective: kinetic
2 GESTURE, gesticulation, movement, act, action, indication, signal, sign, wave, nod
3 PROPOSAL, suggestion, recommendation, proposition, plan, scheme, project, manifesto, presentation, bid, offer
♦ v
signal, gesture, gesticulate, sign, wave, nod, beckon, direct, usher
■ **in motion**
under way, moving on the move, going on the go, travelling in progress, functioning running operational
🔁 stationary, at rest
■ **set in motion**
begin to happen, begin, start, set about, embark on, get going launch into, activate, actuate, set off, initiate, introduce, found, institute, open, instigate
FORMAL commence
COLLOQ. kick off, get cracking set the ball rolling take the plunge, set the wheels turning

motionless adj
unmoving still, stationary, static, immobile, immovable, unmovable, moveless, at a standstill, stock-still, fixed, set, halted, at rest, resting sleeping standing paralysed, inanimate, inert, lifeless, frozen, transfixed, rigid, stagnant
OLD becalmed
🔁 active, moving

motivate v
prompt, incite, impel, spur, provoke, stimulate, drive, lead, stir, urge, goad, push, propel, persuade, move, inspire, encourage, cause, trigger, actuate, activate, induce, kindle, draw, excite, arouse, bring initiate
COLLOQ. kick-start
🔁 deter, discourage, prevent, inhibit

motivation n
reason, incitement, inducement, prompting spur, stimulus, provocation, drive, push, hunger, desire, wish, urge, impulse, incentive, ambition, inspiration, instigation, momentum, motive, persuasion, interest
🔁 discouragement, prevention

motive n
ground(s), cause, reason, basis, purpose, motivation, aim, occasion, object, intention, influence, rationale, thinking incentive, impulse, stimulus, inspiration, incitement, inducement, urge, goad, spur, encouragement, design, desire, attraction, lure, consideration, persuasion, pretext, mainspring propellant
TECHNICAL sanction
OLD instance, moment
🔁 deterrent, disincentive

> **QUOTATIONS**
> We must judge a man's motives from his overt acts
> LORD KENYON, judgement in Rex v. Waddington

> **SYNONYM NUANCES**
> **Grounds** and **basis** can be used to suggest sufficient foundation or justification: *an appeal for clemency on the grounds of ill health*; *he was elected on the basis of his local reputation*, whereas **purpose** and **motivation**, **object** and **intention** put the emphasis on a desired outcome. **Occasion**, on the other hand, has more to do with a specific set of circumstances: *the family gathering afforded the occasion to reveal a few home truths*, unlike **influence** which suggests an external force: *the influence of religion on lifestyle is on the decline*.
>   The words **rationale**, **thinking** and **consideration** imply the application of constructive thought to a motive: *what is the rationale behind this seemingly impetuous move?*. **Design** is similar but also implies a degree of contrivance. The word **pretext** would be reserved for a false objective: *I went uninvited to the party, on the pretext of helping with the food*. The terms **impulse** and **urge**, conversely, imply a sudden inclination. **Incentive** and **inducement** suggest an encouraging or rewarding element: *what is my incentive to do this for you?*, while **attraction** and **lure** imply an element of temptation.
>   **Stimulus**, **inspiration** and **spur** have suggestions of a response that has been provoked: *hunger was the main spur for our hunting*, as does **incitement**, though perhaps with less desirable consequences: *the incitement of racial hatred*. The terms **encouragement** and **inspiration** suggest a very positive infusion with spirit or enthusiasm. The less common **propellant** and **mainspring** might be used of a powerful, driving motive: *being a supreme athlete was the mainspring of his life*.

motley adj
1 ASSORTED, varied, mixed, miscellaneous, diverse, diversified, multifarious
FORMAL heterogeneous
2 MULTICOLOURED, variegated, particoloured, colourful, many-hued, pied, piebald, tabby, dappled, brindled, mottled, spotted, striped, streaked
🔁 **1** uniform, homogeneous **2** monochrome

motor vehicle
See **car**.
See panel on next page

mottled adj
speckled, dappled, blotchy, blotched, flecked, piebald, stippled, streaked, marbled, splotchy, tabby, spotted, freckled, brinded, brindled, brindle, variegated
TECHNICAL poikilitic
🔁 monochrome, uniform

motto n
saying slogan, maxim, watchword, cry, catchword, byword, precept, proverb, aphorism, saw, axiom, adage, formula, rule, golden rule, dictum, truism
FORMAL epigram, gnome

mould¹ n, v
♦ n
1 CAST, form, shape, die, template, pattern, matrix, frame, framework, blister pack
2 SHAPE, form, format, pattern, structure, style, type, build, construction, formation, cast, cut, figure, design, kind, model, sort, stamp, arrangement, brand, frame, framework, character, nature, quality, calibre, line, outline, make
FORMAL configuration
♦ v
1 FORGE, cast, shape, stamp, make, form, fashion, create, design, construct, sculpt, carve, model, work, frame
2 INFLUENCE, affect, form, shape, direct, control

Parts of a motor vehicle include:

ABS (anti-lock braking system)
accelerator
airbag
air brake
air-conditioner
air inlet
antidazzle mirror
antiglare switch
anti-roll bar
antitheft device
ashtray
axle
N Am backup light
battery
bench seat
bezel
bodywork
bonnet
boot
brake drum
brake light
brake pad
brake shoe

bumper
car radio
car phone
catalytic converter
central locking
centre console
chassis
child-safety seat
cigarette-lighter
clock
clutch
courtesy light
crankcase
cruise control
dashboard
differential gear
dimmer
disc brake
door
door-lock
drive shaft
drum brake
electric window
emergency light
engine

exhaust pipe
N Am fender
filler cap
flasher switch
fog light (or lamp)
folding seat
four-wheel drive
fuel gauge
N Am gas tank
gear
gearbox
gear-lever (or gear-stick)
N Am gearshift
glove compartment
grill
handbrake
hazard warning light
headlight
headrest
heated rear window
heater

N Am hood
horn
hub-cap
hydraulic brake
hydraulic suspension
ignition
ignition key
indicator
instrument panel
jack
jump lead
kingpin
N Am license plate
lift gate
monocoque
number plate
oil gauge
overrider
parcel shelf
parking-light
petrol tank
pneumatic tyre
power brake

prop shaft
quarterlight
rack and pinion
radial-ply tyre
rear light
rear-view mirror
reclining seat
reflector
Aust & NZ registration plate
colloq. rev counter
reversing light
roof rack
screen-washer bottle
seat belt
shaft
shock absorber
sidelight
side-impact bar
side mirror
silencer
sill
solenoid
spare tyre

speedometer
spoiler
steering-column
steering-wheel
N Am stick shift
stoplight
sunroof
sun visor
suspension
temperature gauge
towbar
track rod
transmission
N Am trunk
tyre
vent
wheel
wheel arch
windscreen
windscreen-washer
windscreen-wiper
N Am windshield
wing
wing mirror

See also **engine**.

---

mould² *n*

a smell of mould

mildew, must, fungus, mouldiness, mustiness, fust, blight, rot

moulder *v*

decay, decompose, perish, rot, waste, corrupt, crumble, disintegrate, turn to dust, humify

mouldy *adj*

mildewed, blighted, musty, muggy, decaying corrupt, rotten, fusty, putrid, bad, spoiled, stale, vinewed; *dialect* foughty; *Scot* fousty, mochie

OLD hoar

FORMAL mucedinous, mucid

E3 fresh, wholesome

mound *n*

1 HILL, hillock, hummock, mount, rise, knoll, bank, dike, dune, dun, elevation, ridge, embankment, whaleback, earthwork, rampart, tumulus, barrow, cairn, kurgan, tell; *dialect* tump; *Scot* barp

TECHNICAL butt

OLD agger, motte, tuffet

FORMAL monticule

2 HEAP, pile, stack, accumulation, collection, supply, store, hoard, abundance, mountain, lot, bundle, stockpile; *dialect* hog

TECHNICAL mogul, pingo, termitarium

mount *v, n*

♦ *v*

1 ORGANIZE, produce, put on, set up, prepare, stage, exhibit, display, launch, arrange, install

2 INCREASE, grow, build (up), accumulate, pile up, tot up, multiply, rise, intensify, escalate, soar, swell, accrue

3 CLIMB (UP), ascend, get up, go up, get on, clamber up, scale, step up, climb on (to), jump on (to), get astride, ride, horse, escalade; *S Afr* saddle up

OLD back, sty

E3 **2** decrease, descend **3** descend, dismount, go down

♦ *n*

1 HORSE, steed

2 SUPPORT, mounting backing base, fixture, stand, frame

mountain *n*

1 HEIGHT, elevation, mount, peak, pinnacle, hill, fell, mound, alp, tor, massif; *S Afr* berg

2 HEAP, pile, mound, stack, mass, abundance, accumulation, lot, backlog

> **PROVERBS**
> If the mountain won't come to Mahomet, Mahomet must go to the mountain

> **QUOTATIONS**
> Mountains are the beginning and the end of all natural scenery
> JOHN RUSKIN, *Modern Painters*

mountaineering

See panel on next page

mountainous *adj*

1 CRAGGY, rocky, hilly, high, highland, upland, alpine, soaring lofty, towering steep

2 HUGE, towering enormous, immense, vast, colossal, massive, gigantic, giant, mammoth

COLLOQ. jumbo, ginormous, humongous

SLANG mega

E3 **1** flat **2** tiny

mountebank *n*

charlatan, swindler, cheat, fake, fraud, impostor, pretender, rogue, trickster

COLLOQ. con man, phoney, pseud, quack

mourn *v*

grieve, lament, sorrow, miss, regret, deplore, weep, wail, keen

OLD bemoan, bewail

E3 rejoice

mourner *n*

griever, bereaved, sorrower, mute, keener

mournful *adj*

sorrowful, sad, unhappy, desolate, doleful, rueful, grief-stricken, heavy-hearted, heartbroken, broken-hearted, cast-down, downcast, miserable, tragic, melancholy, melancholic, plaintive, funereal, sombre, depressed, dejected, gloomy, dismal, *funèbre*

Mountaineering and climbing terms include:

abseiling	cam	crevasse	ice piton	ringed piton	snow gaiters
abseil piton	carabiner (or	debolting	ice ridge	rock	snow
abseil sling	karabiner)	descender	ice screw	rock face	goggles
abseil station	chalk bag	descent	ice slope	rock spike	solo ascent
N Am adz	chalk cliff	drive-in ice piton	ice step	rock wall	spike
adze	climbing	Dülfer seat	kernmantel rope	rope	sport
Alpinism	chimney	dynamic rope	Munro	rope sling	climbing
arête	chock	étrier	non-belayer	saddle	spur
ascender	chockstone	fissure	nut	scree	stack
ascent	cleft	glacier	on the rope	sea stack	standing
avalanche	climbing harness	gully	overhang	self-belaying	rope
N Am ax	climbing wall	hammer axe	pick	sérac	summit
axe	col	hand hold	piolet	Sherpa	top out
base camp	corkscrew	harness	pitch	shunt	trad route
belay	piton	helmet	piton	sit harness	traverse
belayer	cornice	helmet lamp	prusik knot	sling	tying in
bivouac	corrie	hut	prusik loop	sling seat	unrope
bolting	crag	ice axe	rappelling	snow bridge	wallnut
bouldering	crampon	ice climbing	ridge	snow cornice	wrist sling

OLD dernful
FORMAL woeful, lugubrious, disconsolate, elegiac
E3 happy, joyful, cheerful

mournfully *adv*
sadly, unhappily, sorrowfully, desolately, dolefully,
ruefully, plaintively, broken-heartedly, miserably,
sombrely, gloomily, dismally
E3 happily, joyfully, cheerfully

mourning *n*
grief, grieving bereavement, lamentation, sadness, sorrow,
sorrowing desolation, weeping wailing keening
E3 rejoicing

mousey, mousy *adj*
1 BROWNISH, greyish, colourless, drab, dull, plain,
uninteresting diffident
2 SHY, quiet, timid, withdrawn, unassertive, unforthcoming
shrinking self-effacing meek, timorous
E3 2 assertive, bright, extrovert, irrepressible

moustache *n*
whiskers, mustachio, handlebar moustache, toothbrush
moustache, zapata moustache, walrus, Charlie
OLD excrement
COLLOQ. tache, tash, face fungus

mouth *n, v*
♦ *n*
1 LIPS, jaws, embouchure
COLLOQ. chops, kisser
SLANG trap, gob, traphole, cakehole; N Am bazoo
Related adjectives: oral, stomatic
2 OPENING, aperture, cavity, vent, entrance, door,
doorway, gateway, hatch, portal, inlet, estuary, outlet,
delta
TECHNICAL stoma
FORMAL orifice
3 BOASTING, bragging blustering babble, empty/idle talk
COLLOQ. hot air, gas
4 CHEEK, nerve, gall, impudence, impertinence, insolence,
disrespect, rudeness, backchat
FORMAL effrontery
COLLOQ. sauce, lip, brass neck
♦ *v*
enunciate, articulate, utter, say, pronounce,
whisper, form
■ **keep your mouth shut**
keep quiet, shut up, say nothing not breathe a word, hold
your tongue, cover up
COLLOQ. pipe down, clam up, keep mum
SLANG keep your trap shut

Parts of the mouth include:

alveolar ridge	labial commissure	superior dental
gum	lower lip	arch
hard palate	palatoglossal arch	tongue
inferior dental	palato-pharyngeal	tonsil
arch	arch	upper lip
isthmus of fauces	soft palate	uvula

See also **tooth**.

mouthful *n*
sample, morsel, spoonful, swallow, taste, bite, nibble, bit,
gulp, sip, titbit, drop, forkful, slug sup, bonne-bouche

mouthpiece *n*
spokesperson, spokesman, spokeswoman, representative,
agent, delegate, propagandist, journal, periodical,
publication, voice, organ

movable *adj*
mobile, portable, transportable, changeable, alterable,
adjustable, flexible, transferable
FORMAL portative
E3 fixed, immovable

movables *n*
belongings, possessions, goods, furniture, property
FORMAL chattels, effects, impedimenta, plenishings
COLLOQ. gear, stuff, things, clobber

move *v, n*
♦ *v*
1 GO, advance, travel, walk, shift, stir, change, pass, act,
take action, proceed, progress, develop, make strides
COLLOQ. budge
2 TRANSPORT, carry, bring take, fetch, relocate, transfer,
shift, switch, shunt, swing
FORMAL transpose
3 DEPART, go away, leave, transfer, decamp, migrate,
remove, move house, move away, relocate
4 STIMULATE, prompt, incline, urge, impel, drive, cause,
lead, propel, actuate, motivate, incite, excite, rouse,
arouse, push, persuade, induce, inspire, influence, provoke
5 AFFECT, touch, agitate, stir, impress, strike, excite, disturb,
upset
6 PROPOSE, put forward, request, suggest, advocate,
recommend, submit
7 FRATERNIZE, circulate, mix, mingle, associate,
keep company, go around
FORMAL consort
COLLOQ. hang about, hang out, hobnob, pal up, gang up,
rub shoulders

♦ *n*

1 MOVEMENT, motion, manoeuvre, gesture, gesticulation, activity

2 REMOVAL, relocation, migration, transfer, repositioning change of address

3 MEASURE, initiative, step, act, manoeuvre, action, activity, device, stratagem, tack

■ **get a move on**
hurry up, speed up, make haste
COLLOQ. get cracking shake a leg put your foot down, step on it/the gas

■ **make a move**
1 GO, depart, leave, get going take your leave
COLLOQ. make tracks, push/clear off, split
2 TAKE A COURSE OF ACTION, do something take the initiative
COLLOQ. get cracking take the plunge, get the show on the road

■ **on the move**
moving travelling journeying progressing advancing
moving forward, making progress, active, on the go, astir, under way

movement *n*
1 REPOSITIONING, move, moving gesture, gesticulation, relocation, activity, act, action, agitation, stirring shifting transfer, transportation, passage
2 CHANGE, development, variation, advance, improvement, breakthrough, evolution, passage, current, drift, flow, fall, rise, swing shift, progress, progression, trend, tendency
3 CAMPAIGN, crusade, drive, group, organization, party, coalition, faction, wing
4 MECHANISM, works, workings, machinery, system, action
COLLOQ. guts
5 *a movement in a symphony*
section, part, division, piece, bit, portion, passage

movie *n*
1 FILM, motion picture, picture, feature film, video, silent film, talkie
OLD flick
2 *What's on at the movies?*
cinema, film theatre, movie theatre, entertainment centre, multiplex, picture-house, picture-palace
COLLOQ. fleapit

moving *adj*
1 MOBILE, active, dynamic, in motion, astir, manoeuvrable
TECHNICAL kinetic
FORMAL motile
2 TOUCHING, affecting poignant, impressive, emotive, arousing stirring emotional, inspiring inspirational, exciting thrilling persuasive, stimulating disturbing upsetting worrying pathetic
3 *the moving force/spirit*
driving motivating leading influential, dynamic, stimulating inspiring urging
E3 1 immobile, fixed **2** unemotional

movingly *adv*
touchingly, with feeling/emotion, poignantly, inspirationally, expressively, pathetically

mow *v*
cut, trim, crop, clip, shear, scythe
■ **mow down**
butcher, slaughter, massacre, kill, shoot down, decimate, gun down, cut down, cut to pieces

much *adv, adj, n*
♦ *adv*
greatly, to a great extent, to a great degree, a great deal, considerably, a lot, frequently, often
♦ *adj*
copious, plentiful, ample, considerable, a lot, abundant, great, substantial, a great number of, extensive, widespread
COLLOQ. lots, masses, piles, stacks, scads, lashings, oodles
♦ *n*
plenty, a great deal, a lot

COLLOQ. lots, loads, heaps, lashings
E3 little

muck *n, v*
♦ *n*
1 DIRT, mire, filth, mud, slime, grime, scum, sludge; *Aust & NZ* scunge
COLLOQ. gunge, yuck; *N Am* guck
SLANG grunge, crud
2 EXCREMENT, dung manure, ordure, sewage
TECHNICAL guano
FORMAL faeces

■ **muck about/around**
1 FOOL ABOUT/AROUND, play around, play about
COLLOQ. mess about/around, lark about/around
SLANG *N Am* goof about/around
2 INCONVENIENCE, upset, bother, trouble
COLLOQ. lead a merry dance, lead up the garden path, send on a wild goose chase, make life hell for
3 INTERFERE, tamper, meddle, untidy, disorder, disarrange, dishevel, mess up

■ **muck up**
ruin, wreck, spoil, mess up, make a mess of, botch, bungle
SLANG cock up, screw up, louse up

mucky *adj*
begrimed, bespattered, dirty, filthy, grimy, messy, miry, mud-caked, muddy, oozy, slimy, soiled, sticky; *Aust & NZ* scungy
COLLOQ. *N Am* gucky
E3 clean

mucous *adj*
gelatinous, glutinous, gummy, viscous, viscid, slimy, snotty
FORMAL mucilaginous

mud *n*
clay, mire, ooze, dirt, soil, sludge, silt, slab; *Scot & Irish* clabber

muddle *n, v*
♦ *n*
chaos, confusion, disorganization, disorder, disarray, mess, mix-up, jumble, clutter, tangle
♦ *v*
1 DISORGANIZE, disorder, throw into disorder, mix up, mess up, jumble (up), scramble, tangle
2 CONFUSE, bewilder, bemuse, perplex, daze, puzzle, confound, befuddle

■ **muddle through**
get by, get along cope, manage, make do

muddled *adj*
confused, chaotic, disorganized, disordered, jumbled, mixed-up, tangled, scrambled, disarrayed, messy, loose, higgledy-piggledy, disorient(at)ed, bewildered, perplexed, unclear, vague, woolly, befuddled, stupefied, dazed, incoherent
COLLOQ. at sea, addle-headed

muddy *adj, v*
♦ *adj*
1 DIRTY, filthy, foul, miry, mucky, grimy, grubby, slimy, slushy, oozy, marshy, boggy, swampy, quaggy, sludgy, sloppy, splashy, dreggy, slabby, waterlogged; *dialect* grouty; *Scot* drumly
OLD limous
2 CLOUDY, indistinct, obscure, opaque, murky, turbid, hazy, smoky, blurred, fuzzy, dull, dingy; *Scot* drumly
E3 1 clean **2** clear
♦ *v*
1 DIRTY, soil, make muddy, puddle, smear, smirch, cloud
FORMAL begrime, bespatter, bedash, bedaub
2 CONFUSE, cloud, make unclear, muddle, mix up, jumble (up), disorganize, scramble, tangle, trouble
E3 1 clean **2** clarify

muff _v_
botch, bungle, mess up, mismanage, mishandle, miss,
spoil, mishit
COLLOQ. fluff

muffle _v_
1 WRAP, wrap up, envelop, cloak, swathe, swaddle,
cover (up)
2 DEADEN, dull, quieten, soften, mute, hush, silence, stifle,
dampen, muzzle, suppress, smother, gag
E3 2 amplify

mug¹ _n_
drink coffee from a mug
cup, beaker, pot, tankard, stein, noggin, sconce, _bock_
COLLOQ. tinny

mug² _v_
mugged on his way home
set upon, attack, assault, waylay, steal from, rob, beat up,
batter, bash, jump (on), knock about
COLLOQ. do over, rough up, knock someone's block off,
knock into the middle of next week

mug³ _n_
like a mug I agreed
fool, simpleton, gull, dupe
COLLOQ. sucker, chump, muggins, soft touch

mug⁴ _n, v_
♦ _n_
his ugly mug
face, features
FORMAL countenance, visage, physiognomy
COLLOQ. kisser, mush, clock, phiz
■ **mug up**
bone up, con, cram, get up, study, swot

muggy _adj_
humid, sticky, stuffy, sultry, close, clammy, oppressive,
airless, sweltering moist, damp; _Scot_ mochie
E3 dry

mulish _adj_
obstinate, stubborn, defiant, difficult, headstrong inflexible,
self-willed, stiff-necked, unreasonable, wilful, perverse,
rigid, wrong-headed
FORMAL intractable, intransigent, recalcitrant, refractory
COLLOQ. pig-headed

mull
■ **mull over**
reflect on, ponder, contemplate, think over,
think about, consider, weigh up, muse on,
chew over, meditate, study, examine,
deliberate
FORMAL ruminate

multicoloured _adj_
variegated, particoloured, colourful, kaleidoscopic,
motley, pied, piebald, dappled, brindled,
spotted, striped
COLLOQ. psychedelic

multifarious _adj_
diverse, diversified, different, miscellaneous, varied,
sundry, variegated, numerous, many, multiple,
multitudinous, legion
FORMAL manifold, multiform

multiple _adj_
many, numerous, various, several, sundry,
collective
FORMAL manifold

multiplicity _n_
abundance, array, number, numerousness, profusion,
variety, diversity, mass, host, lot, myriad
FORMAL manifoldness
COLLOQ. heaps, loads, lots, oodles, piles, scores,
stacks, tons

multiply _v_
increase, proliferate, expand, grow, spread, reproduce,
propagate, breed, accumulate, intensify, extend,
build up, boost
FORMAL augment, manifold
E3 decrease, lessen

multipurpose _adj_
versatile, adaptable, flexible, all-round, all-purpose,
multifaceted, adjustable, many-sided, general-purpose,
functional, resourceful, handy, variable
E3 inflexible

multitude _n_
1 CROWD, throng horde, swarm, mob, mass, herd,
congregation, assembly, host, lot, legion
COLLOQ. lots
2 PUBLIC, people, populace, crowd, mob, common people,
rank and file, rabble, hoi polloi, herd, common herd, great
unwashed, _canaille_
COLLOQ. plebs, riff-raff
E3 1 few, scattering

multitudinous _adj_
numerous, many, profuse, swarming copious,
considerable, abundant, abounding teeming innumerable,
countless, great, infinite, legion, myriad
FORMAL manifold
COLLOQ. umpteen

mum _adj_
quiet, mute, dumb, silent, reticent, secretive,
tight-lipped, close-lipped, close-mouthed,
uncommunicative, unforthcoming

mumble _v_
murmur, rumble, talk to yourself, talk
under your breath, mutter, stutter, splutter,
speak unclearly, speak softly, speak in a
low voice, slur

mumbo-jumbo _n_
nonsense, claptrap, gibberish, incantation, jargon,
magic, superstition, spell, chant, cant, charm, ritual,
rite, mummery, rigmarole, abracadabra
FORMAL conjuration
COLLOQ. double talk, gobbledygook, hocus-pocus,
humbug

munch _v_
eat, chew, crunch, champ, chomp
FORMAL masticate

mundane _adj_
1 ORDINARY, banal, hackneyed, boring dull, stale, trite,
everyday, common, commonplace, usual, normal,
typical, regular, customary, prosaic, humdrum,
workaday, routine
2 WORLDLY, secular, earthly, terrestrial, fleshly, temporal
FORMAL terrene
E3 1 extraordinary 2 spiritual

municipal _adj_
civic, city, civil, town, metropolitan, urban, borough,
community, public

municipality _n_
city, town, township, borough, department, district,
precinct, council, local government, burgh,
département

munificence _n_
generosity, generousness, liberality, magnanimousness,
open-handedness, bounty, benevolence, philanthropy,
charitableness, altruism, hospitality
FORMAL largesse, beneficence, bounteousness
E3 meanness

munificent _adj_
generous, open-handed, big-hearted, bountiful,
free-handed, magnanimous, lavish, liberal, hospitable,
benevolent, philanthropical, charitable, altruistic, rich,
unstinting princely

FORMAL beneficent, bounteous
◼ mean

munitions n
equipment, supplies, apparatus, gear,
tackle, kit, tools, materials, provisions, bombs,
shells, guns

murder n, v
♦ n
1 KILLING, homicide, manslaughter, slaying slaughter,
assassination, execution, massacre, butchery, bloodshed,
blood, foul play, dispatch
OLD murther, petty treason
FORMAL patricide, matricide, infanticide, fillicide, fratricide,
sororicide, uxoricide, parricide, femicide
COLLOQ. liquidation, removal, rubout
2 *driving in town is murder*
hell, torment, torture, agony, ordeal, nightmare, misery,
wretchedness, suffering anguish
♦ v
1 KILL, slaughter, slay, put to death, execute, assassinate,
butcher, massacre, rid, burke
COLLOQ. do in, wipe out
SLANG bump off, eliminate, liquidate, knock off,
hit, rub out, take out, waste, blow away, fill in,
stiff, whack
2 RUIN, spoil, destroy, botch, mess up, wreck,
make a mess of
3 DEFEAT EASILY, beat, overwhelm, rout, annihilate, outplay,
outwit, outsmart, trounce
COLLOQ. slaughter, hammer, clobber, lick, thrash,
wipe the floor with

murderer n
killer, homicide, slayer, slaughterer, assassin, butcher,
cut-throat
OLD murtherer

murderous adj
1 HOMICIDAL, brutal, barbarous, bloodthirsty, bloody,
cut-throat, killing lethal, fatal, mortal, cruel, savage,
ferocious, deadly
2 DIFFICULT, exhausting strenuous, arduous, punishing
gruelling unpleasant, dangerous
COLLOQ. killing

murderously adv
dangerously, alarmingly, menacingly, threateningly,
ominously, sinisterly, fatally, homicidally, unpleasantly,
grimly, bloodthirstily
FORMAL portentously

murk n
murkiness, dark, darkness, dimness, blackness,
gloom gloominess, night, dusk, twilight,
half-light, shadows, shade, shadiness, sunlessness,
cloudiness
FORMAL tenebrity, tenebrosity

murky adj
1 DARK, dismal, gloomy, dreary, cheerless, dull, overcast,
misty, foggy, dim, cloudy, obscure, veiled, grey
FORMAL tenebrose, tenebrious, tenebrous
2 *murky water*
dirty, dark, dingy, cloudy, turbid
3 MYSTERIOUS, shady, dark, secret, suspicious,
questionable
COLLOQ. fishy, shady
SLANG sus
◼ **1** bright, clear, fine **2** clear

murmur n, v
♦ n
1 MUMBLE, muttering whisper, undertone, humming
rumble, drone, grumble
2 *the murmur of voices*
hum, buzz, drone, purring thrum, rumbling
3 GRUMBLE, complaint, moan, grievance,
protest, objection, dissatisfaction, annoyance, fault-finding
criticism, carping censure

COLLOQ. grouse, gripe, beefing whingeing
SLANG bellyaching
♦ v
1 MUTTER, mumble, whisper, intone, buzz,
drone, hum, rustle, rumble, purr, purl,
burble, babble
2 COMPLAIN, criticize, find fault, object, protest, grumble,
carp, fuss, whine
COLLOQ. beef, grouse, gripe, whinge
SLANG bellyache

murmuring adj, n
♦ adj
mumbling murmurous, muttering rumbling whispering
humming buzzing droning purring
♦ n
drone, mumble, mumbling muttering rumble, rumbling
whisper(ing), buzz(ing), purr(ing)
FORMAL murmuration, susurrus

muscle n, v
♦ n
1 *strong muscles*
sinew, tendon, ligament
Related adjective: muscular
2 FORCE, brawn, beef, power, forcefulness, strength,
stamina, potency, sturdiness, weight
FORMAL might
COLLOQ. clout
◼ **muscle in**
butt in, push in, shove, strongarm, impose yourself, force
your way in, interfere with, elbow your way in, jostle

Muscles include:

abdominal	latissimus dorsi	rectus
biceps	(or lat)	rhomboideus
buccinator	masseter	risorius
cardiac	omohyid	sartorius
ciliary body	pectoralis major	scalenus
complexus	pectoralis minor	soleus
deltoid	perforans	splenius
detrusor	peroneal muscles	stapedius
eye-string	platysma	supinator
gastrocnemius	pronator	trapezius
gluteus	psoas	triceps
iliacus	quadriceps	xiphihumeralis

---

muscular adj
brawny, sinewy, fibrous, athletic, strong powerfully built,
strapping hefty, burly, powerful, husky, robust, stalwart,
rugged, sturdy, vigorous, potent
COLLOQ. beefy
◼ puny, flabby, weak

muse v
ponder, think, think over, meditate, mull over,
weigh, contemplate, consider, brood, reflect, review,
study, chew over, dream, deliberate, speculate
FORMAL cogitate, ruminate

mush n
1 PASTE, pulp, pap, dough, corn, slush, swill, mash,
cream, purée
2 SENTIMENTALITY, mawkishness
COLLOQ. schmaltz

mushroom v
proliferate, shoot up, grow, increase, expand, flourish,
boom, spread, spring up, sprout, luxuriate
FORMAL burgeon

mushrooms and toadstools
See panel on next page

mushy adj
1 PULPY, pappy, pulpous, squashy, squelchy, squidgy,
soft, doughy, wet
2 SENTIMENTAL, maudlin, mawkish, saccharine, sugary,
syrupy, weepy
COLLOQ. schmaltzy, soppy, sloppy, slushy

Types of mushroom and toadstool include:

amanita	common morel	fairy ring	meadow	satan's mushroom	velvet shank
beefsteak fungus	copper trumpet	false morel	mushroom	shaggy milk cap	verdigris
blewit	cramp ball	fly agaric	mower's	shaggy parasol	agaric
boletus	cultivated	gypsy mushroom	mushroom	shiitake	winter
button mushroom	mushroom	honey fungus	oyster mushroom	slippery jack	mushroom
cep	death cap	horn of plenty	panther cap	stinking parasol	wood
champignon	destroying angel	horse mushroom	parasol mushroom	sulphur tuft	hedgehog
chanterelle	devil's boletus	lawyer's wig	penny bun	sweetbread	woolly milk cap
chestnut boletus	dingy agaric	man on	porcini	mushroom	yellow-staining
clouded agaric	earth ball	horseback	purple boletus	truffle	mushroom
common ink cap	elf cup	march mushroom	saffron milk cap	trumpet agaric	

music n

tune, melody, harmony

> **QUOTATIONS**
> Music is the universal language of mankind
> HENRY WADSWORTH LONGFELLOW, *Outre Mer*

Types of music include:

acid house	easy listening	northern soul
adult-orientated	electronic	nu-metal
rock (AOR)	electropop	old-time
alt.country	emo	operatic
alternative	filk	orchestral
ambient	folk	pop
Americana	folk rock	popera
antifolk	folktronica	post-punk
art rock	funk	power pop
ballet	fusion	progressive (or
ballroom	gangsta	prog) rock
Baltimore club	garage	psychedelic
(or Bmore)	glam rock	psychobilly
baroque	gospel	pub rock
bashment	goth	punk rock
beatboxing	grime	ragga (or
bebop	grunge	ragamuffin)
bhangra	hardcore	ragtime
big band	hard rock	rap
Big Beat	heavy metal	reggae
big-room	hip-hop	reggaeton
bluegrass	honky-tonk	rhythm and blues
blues	house	(R&B)
boogie-woogie	incidental	rock
breakbeat	indie	rockabilly
Britpop	industrial	rock and roll
cajun	instrumental	sacred
calypso	jazz	salsa
chamber	jazz fusion	samba
chamber pop	jazz-rock	screamo
choral	jive	shoegazer
classical	J-pop	ska
contemporary	jumpstyle	skiffle
R&B (RnB)	jungle	soca
country	karaoke	soft rock
country-	krautrock	soul
and-western	lo-fi	surf
country rock	lounge	swing
crunk	lovers' rock	symphonic
dance	mallcore	techno
dancehall	mariachi	technopop
death metal	metal	thrash metal
desi	middle-of-the-road	trance
disco	(MOR)	trip-hop
Dixieland	minimalist	urban
doo-wop	Motown	world
drum and bass	muzak	zydeco
dub	New Age	
dubstep	new wave	

See also **jazz**.

musical adj

tuneful, melodious, melodic, harmonious, mellow, dulcet, sweet-sounding lyrical
FORMAL euphonious, mellifluous
E3 discordant, unmusical

musical composition

Musical compositions include:

arabesque	fugue	prelude
aubade	gavotte	requiem
bagatelle	humoresque	rhapsody
berceuse	impromptu	rondo
bourrée	intermezzo	round
canon	lied	scherzo
capriccio	march	serenade
cavatina	minuet	sinfonietta
chaconne	nocturne	sonata
concerto	opus	sonatina
concerto grosso	overture	suite
divertimento	partita	symphony
étude	pastorale	toccata
extravaganza	pavane	voluntary
fanfare	polka	waltz
fantasia	polonaise	

See also **song**.

musical instruments

Musical instruments include:

STRINGED INSTRU-	ukulele	bassoon
MENTS:	viola	bugle
balalaika	violin	clarinet
bandore	zither	cor anglais
banjo		cornet
bouzouki	**KEYBOARD**	didgeridoo
cello	**INSTRUMENTS:**	euphonium
cembalo	accordion	fife
clarsach	clavichord	flugelhorn
crwth	concertina	flute
double-bass	grand piano	French horn
erhu	harmonium	gaita
colloq. fiddle	harpsichord	harmonica
guitar	mbira	horn
gusla	Mellotron®	kazoo
harp	melodeon	mouth-organ
hurdy-gurdy	organ	oboe
kaval	piano	Pan-pipes
lute	Pianola®	piccolo
lyre	player-piano	recorder
mandolin	*colloq.*	saxophone
oud	squeeze-box	sousaphone
sarangi	synthesizer	Swanee
saz	virginals	whistle
sitar	Wurlitzer®	tin whistle
spinet		trombone
surbahar	**WIND INSTRU-**	trumpet
tambura	**MENTS:**	tuba
	bagpipes	

uillean pipes
vuvuzela

PERCUSSION INSTRUMENTS:
bass-drum
bodhran
bongo
castanets
cymbal

gamelan
glockenspiel
kettle drum
maracas
marimba
rainstick
snare drum
steel pan
tabla

tambour
tambourine
tassa
tenor drum
timpani
tom-tom
triangle
tubular bells
xylophone

musical terms
See panel below

musician
See panel on next page

musing *n*
thinking meditation, introspection, dreaming daydreaming wool-gathering abstraction, absent-mindedness, contemplation, study, studying reflection, reverie, brown study
FORMAL cerebration, cogitation, ponderment, rumination

muss *v*
ruffle, make untidy, dishevel, tousle, disarrange, make a mess of

must *n*
necessity, prerequisite, obligation, requirement, stipulation, essential, fundamental, imperative, duty, basic, provision
FORMAL requisite, sine qua non

muster *v, n*
♦ *v*
assemble, convene, gather (together), call together, mobilize, round up, marshal, bring/come together, congregate, collect, group, meet, rally, mass, throng call up, summon (up), enrol
FORMAL convoke
♦ *n*
gathering assembly, collection, congregation, convention, mass, mobilization, rally, round-up, turnout, meeting parade, review, march past, throng concourse
OLD hosting
FORMAL assemblage, convocation

■ **pass muster**
be acceptable, be accepted, come up to standard, be good enough, measure up, fit/fill the bill, make the grade, muster
COLLOQ. come up to scratch, shape up

musty *adj*
mouldy, mildewy, mildewed, stale, stuffy, fusty, damp, dank, airless, decayed, decaying, smelly, vinewed; *dialect* foughty; *Scot* fousty, mochie; *N Am* funky
OLD frowy
FORMAL mucid

mutability *n*
changeableness, interchangeability, alterability, variability, permutability, variation

mutable *adj*
changing, interchangeable, changeable, adaptable, alterable, vacillating, variable, volatile, wavering,

---

Musical terms include:

accelerando	cantilena	expression	metre	rallentando	sul ponticello
acciaccatura	chord	fifth interval	mezza voce	recital	supertonic
accidental	chromatic	finale	mezzo forte	refrain	swell
accompaniment	clef	fine	microtone	resolution	syncopation
acoustic	coda	fingerboard	middle C	rest	tablature
adagio	col canto	flat	minim	rhythm	tacet
ad lib	compound time	forte	minor	rinforzando	tanto
a due	con brio	fortissimo	minor interval	ritenuto	tempo
affettuoso	concert	four-four time	mode	root	tenor
agitato	con fuoco	fourth interval	moderato	scale	tenor clef
al fine	con moto	fret	modulation	score	tenuto
alla breve	consonance	glissando	molto	second interval	theme
alla cappella	contralto	grave	mordent	semibreve	third interval
allargando	counterpoint	harmonics	movement	semiquaver	three-four time
allegretto	crescendo	harmony	mute	semitone	tie
allegro	cross-fingering	hemi-	natural	semplice	timbre
al segno	crotchet	demisemiquaver	non troppo	sempre	time signature
alto	cue	hold	note	senza	tone
alto clef	da capo	imitation	obbligato	sequence	tonic sol-fa
amoroso	decrescendo	improvisation	octave	seventh interval	transposition
andante	demisemiquaver	interval	orchestra	sextuplet	treble
animato	descant	intonation	orchestration	sforzando	treble clef
appoggiatura	diatonic	key	ostinato	shake	tremolo
arco	diminished interval	key signature	part	sharp	triad
arpeggio	diminuendo	langsam	pause	simple time	trill
arrangement	dissonance	larghetto	pedal point	six-eight time	triplet
a tempo	dolce	largo	pentatonic	sixth interval	tune
attacca	doloroso	leading note	perdendo	slur	tuning
augmented interval	dominant	ledger line	perfect interval	smorzando	turn
bar	dotted note	legato	phrase	solo	tutti
baritone	dotted rest	lento	pianissimo	soprano	two-two time
bar line	double bar line	lyric	piano	sostenuto	unison
bass	double flat	maestoso	piece	sotto voce	upbeat
bass clef	double sharp	major	pitch	spiritoso	vibrato
beat	double trill	major interval	pizzicato	staccato	vigoroso
bis	downbeat	manual	presto	staff	virtuoso
breve	drone	marcato	quadruplet	stave	vivace
buffo	duplet	mediant	quarter tone	subdominant	
cadence	encore	medley	quaver	subito	
cantabile	ensemble	melody	quintuplet	submediant	

Musicians include:

GENERAL:	clarinettist	piper	GROUPS:	quartet
accompanist	clarsair	soloist	backing group	quintet
busker	drummer	trombonist	band	sextet
instrumentalist	flautist	trumpeter	chamber	trio
minstrel	fiddler	violinist	orchestra	
performer	guitarist	SINGERS:	choir	OTHER:
player	harpist	balladeer	duet	composer
virtuoso	lutenist	bard	duo	conductor
PARTICULAR	oboist	diva	ensemble	maestro
INSTRUMENTS:	organist	minstrel	nonet	
bugler	percussionist	prima donna	octet	
cellist	pianist	vocalist	orchestra	

inconsistent, uncertain, undependable, unreliable, unsettled, inconstant, fickle, flexible, irresolute, unstable, unsteady, permutable
E3 constant, invariable, permanent

mutate v
metamorphose, change, alter, transform, remake, remodel, reshape, convert, modify, evolve, translate
TECHNICAL transubstantiate
FORMAL transmute, transfigure
COLLOQ. transmogrify, morph

mutation n
change, alteration, variation, modification, adaptation, transformation, deviation, anomaly, evolution
FORMAL metamorphosis
COLLOQ. transmogrification

mute adj, v
♦ adj
silent, dumb, voiceless, uncommunicative, taciturn, wordless, speechless, unspoken, noiseless, unexpressed, unpronounced
TECHNICAL aphasic
COLLOQ. mum, shtoom
E3 vocal, talkative
♦ v
tone down, subdue, muffle, lower, moderate, dampen, deaden, dull, smother, quieten, stifle, suppress, soften, silence
COLLOQ. soft-pedal
E3 intensify

muted adj
quiet, soft, softened, low-key, subtle, discreet, subdued, restrained, faint, dull, muffled, suppressed, dampened, stifled

mutely adv
silently, in silence, dumbly, voicelessly, speechlessly, noiselessly, taciturnly

mutilate v
1 MAIM, injure, dismember, disable, disfigure, lame, cripple, mangle, lacerate, cut to pieces, cut up, butcher, hack (up)
2 SPOIL, mar, damage, impair, ruin, distort, mangle, cut, censor
FORMAL bowdlerize
COLLOQ. hack, butcher

mutilation n
amputation, maiming disfigurement, dismembering damage
FORMAL detruncation

mutinous adj
rebellious, insurgent, insubordinate, disobedient, disorderly, uncontrollable, ungovernable, seditious, revolutionary, riotous, anarchistic, subversive, unruly
FORMAL refractory, contumacious
COLLOQ. bolshie
E3 obedient, compliant

mutiny n, v
♦ n
rebellion, insurrection, revolt, revolution, rising uprising insurgence, insubordination, disobedience, defiance, resistance, riot, strike, protest
♦ v
rebel, revolt, rise up, resist, protest, disobey, defy, strike

mutt n
1 MONGREL, dog cur, hound, bitch
COLLOQ. pooch
2 FOOL, idiot, imbecile, ignoramus, moron, dolt
COLLOQ. dunderhead, thickhead

mutter v
1 MUMBLE, murmur, talk to yourself, talk under your breath, stutter, splutter, rumble, drone, witter; *dialect* mump; *Scot* whittie-whattie
OLD mussitate; (*Spenser*) royne
COLLOQ. chunter
2 COMPLAIN, grumble, criticize, find fault, object, protest, carp, fuss, whine
OLD maunder
COLLOQ. grouse, beef, gripe, whinge, chunter
SLANG bellyache

mutual adj
reciprocal, shared, common, joint, collective, interchangeable, interchanged, exchanged, complementary

muzzle v
restrain, inhibit, check, stifle, suppress, gag fetter, mute, silence, censor, choke

muzzy adj
1 GROGGY, tipsy, confused, dazed, befuddled, addled, muddled, bewildered
2 FUZZY, blurred, unfocused, unclear, indistinct, faint, hazy
E3 2 clear

myopic adj
1 *myopic vision*
short-sighted, near-sighted, purblind, half-blind
2 *myopic attitudes*
short-sighted, unwise, ill-considered, imprudent, thoughtless, narrow, narrow-minded, localized, parochial, unimaginative, unadventurous, short-term
FORMAL uncircumspect
E3 2 far-sighted

myriad adj, n
♦ adj
countless, innumerable, limitless, immeasurable, incalculable, untold, boundless
FORMAL multitudinous
♦ n
multitude, throng horde, army, flood, host, swarm, sea
COLLOQ. scores, thousands, millions, zillions, mountain

mysterious *adj*
1 ENIGMATIC, cryptic, mystifying inexplicable, incomprehensible, puzzling perplexing obscure, shadowy, sinister, shady, strange, unfathomable, unsearchable, inscrutable, mystical, baffling curious, hidden, insoluble
FORMAL abstruse, arcane, recondite, esoteric
2 SECRET, as if by magic, occult, weird, secretive, veiled, dark, furtive, obscure, strange, creepy, mystic, mystical, baffling curious, hidden, surreptitious, reticent
F≡ 1 straightforward, comprehensible

SYNONYM NUANCES

sense 1
Enigmatic can be used of people or things that are complex and therefore not readily understood by other people, and can have a vaguely romantic tone: *an enigmatic stranger*, while **cryptic** can be used with implications of secret meanings: *cryptic crossword clues; a cryptic code*. **Mystifying** and **baffling**, on the other hand, are more suggestive of creating confusion in the mind, and both **puzzling** and **perplexing** suggest someone or something that elicits many unanswered questions in the mind: *the perplexing phenomenon of racism in Europe*.

Obscure could be used straightforwardly to suggest a lack of clarity, especially of something that can never be known or deciphered: *obscure ancient languages*. To use **shadowy**, however, would suggest an element of furtiveness: *shadowy figures hiding in doorways*, and **sinister** and **shady** go further with their implication of being underhand: *shady dealings not declared to the taxman*. **Inscrutable** and the rarer **unsearchable** have implications of foiling attempts at analysis: *the inscrutable workings of providence*.

To suggest an element of sacred mystery, the term **mystical** is appropriate, whereas **curious** is more suitable for something that deviates a little from what is expected, and so elicits interest: *that was a curious thing for him to say, don't you think?*

---

mysteriously *adv*
1 ENIGMATICALLY, cryptically, puzzlingly, inexplicably, incomprehensibly, curiously, strangely, inscrutably
FORMAL abstrusely, arcanely, esoterically
2 SECRETLY, in secret, magically, obscurely, strangely, mystically, surreptitiously

mystery *n*
1 ENIGMA, puzzle, secret, riddle, problem, conundrum, closed book, question, question mark
OLD concealment
FORMAL arcanum
2 OBSCURITY, mystique, secrecy, ambiguity, curiosity, strangeness, weirdness, incomprehensibility, inexplicability, inscrutability, unfathomability, furtiveness, surreptitiousness, reticence

mystic *n*
esotericist, psychic, supernaturalist, metaphysicist, spiritist, spiritualist, transcendentalist, swami, Sufi, occultist

mystical *adj*
occult, mystic, esoteric, spiritual, supernatural, paranormal, other-worldly, transcendental, metaphysical, hidden, mysterious, obscure, incomprehensible, inexplicable, unfathomable, strange, weird, baffling
FORMAL preternatural, abstruse, arcane, recondite
F≡ rational, logical

mysticism *n*
spirituality, deism, theism, spiritism, supernaturalism, transcendentalism, esotericism, occultism, mystery, mysteriousness, incomprehensibility, inexplicability
FORMAL arcaneness

mystification *n*
bewilderment, perplexity, confusion, uncertainty, daze, disconcertion, disorientation, puzzlement, stupefaction, surprise, awe, muddle, fog

mystify *v*
puzzle, bewilder, baffle, perplex, confound, confuse
COLLOQ. bamboozle

mystique *n*
mystery, secrecy, fascination, glamour, magic, spell, charm, appeal, adventure, romance, charisma, awe

myth *n*
1 LEGEND, fable, fairy tale, fairy story, allegory, parable, saga, story, tale, folk tale, bestiary
2 FICTION, fancy, fallacy, delusion, fantasy, invention, fabrication, lie, untruth, pretence, misconception
COLLOQ. fib, tall story

QUOTATIONS
A myth is, of course, not a fairy story. It is the presentation of facts belonging to one category in the idioms appropriate to another. To explode a myth is accordingly not to deny the facts but to re-allocate them
GILBERT RYLE, *The Concept of Mind*

---

mythical *adj*
1 MYTHOLOGICAL, legendary, fabled, fairytale, fictitious
FORMAL chimerical, fabulous, fantastic
2 FICTITIOUS, imaginary, made-up, invented, non-existent, unreal, untrue, fantasy, fabricated, pretended, make-believe, fanciful
COLLOQ. pretend, put-on, phoney
F≡ 1 historical **2** actual, real, true

Mythical creatures and spirits include:

abominable	Gigantes	ogre
snowman	gnome	ogress
(or yeti)	goblin	orc
afrit	golem	oread
basilisk	Gorgon	Pegasus
Bigfoot	Grendel	phoenix
brownie	griffin	pixie
bunyip	hamadryad	roc
Cecrops	Harpies	salamander
centaur	hippocampus (or	sasquatch
Cerberus	seahorse)	satyr
Charybdis	hippogriff	Scylla
Chimera	hobgoblin	sea serpent
cockatrice	imp	selkie
Cyclops	kelpie	Siren
dragon	kraken	Sphinx
dryad	lamia	sylph
dwarf	leprechaun	taniwha
Echidna	Lilith	troll
elf	lindworm	Typhoeus
Erinyes (or Furies)	Loch Ness	unicorn
Fafnir	monster	vampire
fairy	Medusa	werewolf
faun	mermaid	windigo
Frankenstein's	merman	wivern
monster	Minotaur	yaksha
genie	naiad	yowie
Geryon	nereid	
giant	nymph	

---

mythological *adj*
legendary, mythical, traditional, mythic, fabled, fairytale, fictitious
FORMAL fabulous, folkloric

mythology *n*
legend, myths, lore, tradition(s), stories, folklore, folk tales, tales

nab *v*
catch, arrest, capture, grab, seize, snatch
FORMAL apprehend
COLLOQ. collar, pull in, run in, nail, nick, nobble

nabob *n*
celebrity, magnate, personage, tycoon, VIP, millionaire, multimillionaire, billionaire, financier
FORMAL luminary .
COLLOQ. bigwig celeb, zillionaire

nadir *n*
low point, lowest point, minimum, zero, bottom, depths, all-time low, low-watermark
COLLOQ. rock bottom
F3 zenith, peak, acme, apex

nag¹ *v*
1 SCOLD, pester, badger, plague, torment, harass, harry, vex, upbraid, pick on, keep on at, moan, complain
FORMAL berate
COLLOQ. henpeck, hassle, grouse, earbash
2 NIGGLE, tease, worry, bother, trouble, annoy, irritate
COLLOQ. bug aggravate, get someone's back up

nag² *n*
ride a nag
horse, stallion, hack, jade, rip, Rosinante; *Welsh* keffel
COLLOQ. plug
SLANG *Aust & NZ* moke

nagging *adj*
1 *a nagging pain*
continuous, critical, distressing upsetting worrying irritating niggling painful, aching persistent
2 SCOLDING, shrewish, critical, tormenting moaning
COLLOQ. nit-picking

nail *v, n*
♦ *v*
1 FASTEN, attach, secure, pin, tack, fix, join, hammer
2 CATCH, arrest, capture, grab, seize, trap, snatch, corner, pin down
FORMAL apprehend
COLLOQ. collar, nick, nab, nobble
3 EXPOSE, detect, identify, reveal, uncover, unearth, unmask
♦ *n*
1 FASTENER, pin, tack, rivet, brad, sprig clout, sparable, spike, skewer, screw
2 FINGERNAIL, toenail, nipper, pincer, claw, talon
■ **hit the nail on the head**
be accurate, be exactly/precisely right, score a bull's eye

naive *adj*
unsophisticated, ingenuous, innocent, naif, artless, guileless, simple, simplistic, unrealistic, natural, frank, childlike, inexperienced, immature, primitive, open, candid, trusting born yesterday, having no idea, unsuspecting unsuspicious, unaffected, unworldly, gullible, unpretentious, bread-and-butter, credulous, wide-eyed, pollyannaish
FORMAL jejune
COLLOQ. green, wet behind the ears
F3 experienced, sophisticated

Unsophisticated may be widely applied to anything displaying a lack of artifice, and **ingenuous** to someone or something without wiles. **Innocent**, on the other hand, suggests an endearing vulnerability brought about by lack of exposure to the ways of the world, and while **unaffected** and **unpretentious** have more to do with a lack of pretension, they also suggest positive qualities. Both **artless** and **guileless** would suggest a complete lack of ability to deceive, but can occasionally hint at lack of intelligence: *artless prattle*.

The term **simple** can be used in many contexts to describe a lack of complexity, unlike **simplistic** which, like **unrealistic**, more negatively implies a shallow reduction of complexities: *she rejected the simplistic connection between unemployment and rioting*.

The term **childlike** again suggests a more endearing outlook comparable to that of a child, whereas **immature** is a rather more disapproving term, suggestive of retarded development, and **primitive** can have additional, negative connotations of a lack of advancement: *the primitive mores of the rustics*.

Like **innocent**, **unworldly** suggests a vulnerability arising from lack of experience: *a schoolgirl who was unworldly in the extreme*, whereas both **gullible** and **credulous** further imply a tendency to be duped and are rather more contemptuous in tone: *he treated her as a credulous imbecile*.

naively *adv*
artlessly, guilelessly, simply, simplistically, naturally, ingenuously, without affectation, innocently, unsuspiciously, gullibly, immaturely

naivety *n*
ingenuousness, innocence, inexperience, immaturity, naturalness, artlessness, guilelessness, childlikeness, simplicity, openness, frankness, candidness, gullibility, credulity
F3 experience, sophistication

naked *adj*
1 NUDE, bare, with nothing on, undressed, unclothed, uncovered, exposed, stripped, stark-naked, disrobed, denuded, raw, mother-naked, Adamic, skyclad, undraped, *in puris naturalibus*; *dialect* start-naked; *Scot* in the scud
COLLOQ. in the altogether, starkers, in your birthday suit, in the raw, in the buff, not a stitch on, naked as the day you were born
SLANG bollock-naked
2 OPEN, unadorned, undisguised, unqualified, unvarnished, plain, stark, bald, simple, evident, overt, patent, blatant, flagrant, glaring exposed
3 DEFENCELESS, exposed, unprotected, unguarded, uncovered, weak, vulnerable, helpless, powerless
4 *a naked landscape*
denuded, stripped, grassless, treeless, exposed, barren, bare, stark
F3 **1** clothed, covered **2** concealed, veiled

nakedness *n*
1 NUDITY, bareness, undress, starkness
COLLOQ. the altogether, the buff

2 PLAINNESS, openness, simplicity, baldness, barrenness, bareness, starkness

namby-pamby *adj*
sentimental, feeble, spineless, weak, weedy, wet, wishy-washy, mawkish, vapid, maudlin, insipid, colourless, anaemic, pretty-pretty, prim, prissy
COLLOQ. soppy, cissy, wimpish
SLANG wussy

name *n, v*
♦ *n*
1 TITLE, designation, label, tag style, eponym, term, epithet, nickname
FORMAL appellation, denomination, cognomen
COLLOQ. handle
SLANG monicker
Related adjective: nominal
2 REPUTATION, character, repute, renown, eminence, prominence, fame, honour, prestige, distinction, note, esteem, standing popularity, celebrity
3 STAR, expert, authority, leading light, celebrity, dignitary, VIP, luminary, hero
COLLOQ. big noise, big name, celeb, bigwig somebody
♦ *v*
1 CALL, christen, baptize, give name to, term, title, entitle, dub, label, tag style, identify
FORMAL denominate
2 DESIGNATE, nominate, mention, cite, choose, pick, select, specify, classify, commission, appoint

> **QUOTATIONS**
> What's in a name? That which we call a rose / By any other word would smell as sweet
>   WILLIAM SHAKESPEARE, *Romeo and Juliet*

> **SYNONYM NUANCES**
>
> *noun sense 1*
> The term **title** tends to be reserved for a form of address conferred on a person, whereas **designation** more widely encompasses any term indicating who or what someone or something is: *his designation as a 'comic' novelist; the area's designation as an enterprise zone.*
>   **Label**, likewise, suggests a descriptive name, but a more informal one given for purposes of classification, and **tag** has further implications of this being an unwelcome summary: *he had to live up to the tag of anti-hero that the media gave him.* **Term** is a more neutral, widely applicable word for a way of referring to something: *the technical term is 'codification'.*
>   **Epithet**, however, is a more formal-sounding word which returns to the idea of description through a name: *the epithet 'Clyde-built' was a badge of quality*, but **nickname**, while perhaps similarly descriptive, is an informal name which usually suggests affection: *Martinique deserves its nickname 'island of flowers'*, but could be a taunt: *his nickname is Mouse because he is small and weedy.*

Kinds of name include:

agnomen	first name	place name
alias	full name	proper name
assumed name	given name	pseudonym
baptismal name	last name	second name
brand name	maiden name	so(u)briquet
Christian name	middle name	stage-name
code name	nickname	surname
diminutive	*nom-de-plume*	term of
false name	pen-name	endearment
family name	pet name	trademark

named *adj*
called, known as, by the name of, labelled, termed, titled, entitled, dubbed, styled, baptized, christened, identified, designated, mentioned, chosen, picked, selected, singled out, specified, classified, commissioned, cited, nominated, appointed, *dit*
FORMAL denominated
E3 nameless

nameless *adj*
1 UNNAMED, anonymous, unidentified, untitled, unlabelled, unspecified, undesignated, unknown, obscure
OLD (*Shakesp*) titleless
FORMAL innominate
2 INEXPRESSIBLE, indescribable, unutterable, unspeakable, unmentionable, unheard-of
E3 **1** named

namely *adv*
that is, ie, specifically, viz, that is to say, in other words
FORMAL to wit

nanny *n, v*
♦ *n*
nurse, nursemaid, governess, nursery-governess, childminder, au pair, amah, ayah
♦ *v*
mollycoddle, pamper, coddle, indulge, spoil, overprotect, pander to, cosset, spoon-feed, mother, pet, baby

nap[1] *n, v*
♦ *n*
have a nap
rest, lie-down, doze, sleep, light sleep, siesta, catnap
COLLOQ. snooze, forty winks, kip
♦ *v*
doze (off), sleep, sleep lightly, drop off, catnap, lie down, rest
COLLOQ. nod off, snooze, kip, have forty winks, get some shut-eye

nap[2] *n*
the nap of the carpet
down, pile, weave, shag surface, texture, fibre, grain, fuzz, downiness

nappy *n*
diaper, napkin, towel, serviette

narcissism *n*
self-love, egotism, egomania, egocentricity, self-centredness, self-obsession, self-regard, self-conceit, conceit, vanity

narcissistic *adj*
self-loving egotistic, egomaniacal, egocentric, self-centred, self-obsessed, self-absorbed, conceited, vain

narcotic *n, adj*
♦ *n*
drug opiate, sedative, tranquillizer, sleeping pill, painkiller, analgesic, anodyne, anaesthetic, palliative, soporific
SLANG upper, downer
♦ *adj*
soporific, sleep-inducing hypnotic, sedative, analgesic, anaesthetic, tranquillizing opiate, painkilling numbing dulling pain-dulling calming stupefying
FORMAL somnolent, stupefacient

narked *adj*
annoyed, bothered, irritated, piqued, irked, exasperated, provoked, riled, vexed, galled
COLLOQ. bugged, miffed, nettled, peeved, cheesed off, brassed off, got the hump, in a huff, in a paddy, hot under the collar
SLANG pissed off

narrate *v*
tell, read, report, describe, portray, unfold, recite, state, explain, set out, detail, chronicle, record
FORMAL relate, recount, rehearse, set forth

narration n

account, story, tale, description, explanation, telling report, statement, history, chronicle, detail, sketch, portrayal, reading recital, storytelling voice-over
FORMAL rehearsal, recountal

narrative n

story, tale, chronicle, account, history, report, description, sketch, portrayal, reading detail, statement, relation, saga, novel, allegory, fable, anecdote
OLD prose; (*Shakesp*) process
FORMAL récit

narrator n

storyteller, chronicler, reporter, raconteur, tale-teller, anecdotist, commentator, writer, author, describer, relater, relator, annalist
TECHNICAL mythographer, sagaman
FORMAL recounter

narrow adj, v

♦ adj
1 TIGHT, confined, constricted, cramped, small, slim, slender, thin, fine, spare, tapering close
FORMAL attenuated
2 LIMITED, restricted, cramped, squeezed, tight, close, meagre, scant
FORMAL circumscribed, incommodious, exiguous
3 NARROW-MINDED, biased, bigoted, prejudiced, dogmatic, intolerant, illiberal, reactionary, hidebound, strait-laced, dyed-in-the-wool, close-minded, set, rigid, conservative, small-minded, insular, petty
4 *in the narrow sense of the word*
strict, literal, exact, precise, true, original
Ea 1 wide **2** broad **3** broad-minded, tolerant **4** broad
♦ v
constrict, limit, tighten, confine, restrict, cramp, reduce, diminish, taper, simplify
FORMAL attenuate, circumscribe
Ea broaden, widen, increase

narrowing n

compression, constriction, curtailment, contraction, reduction, tapering thinning emaciation, constipation
TECHNICAL stenosis
FORMAL attenuation
Ea broadening widening

narrowly adv

1 BARELY, scarcely, just, only just
COLLOQ. by a hair's breadth, by a whisker
2 CAREFULLY, closely, strictly, scrutinizingly, attentively, precisely, exactly, painstakingly

narrow-minded adj

illiberal, biased, bigoted, prejudiced, reactionary, hidebound, strait-laced, dyed in the wool, opinionated, diehard, small-minded, close-minded, set, rigid, inflexible, entrenched, conservative, ultra-conservative, blimpish, intolerant, insular, provincial, parochial, twisted, warped, jaundiced, petty, petty-minded, exclusive, unreasonable
Ea broad-minded, liberal, tolerant

narrow-mindedness n

bigotry, bias, prejudice, small-mindedness, close-mindedness, petty-mindedness, conservativeness, parochialism, exclusiveness, inflexibility, rigidity
Ea broadmindedness, tolerance

narrowness n

1 THINNESS, tightness, slenderness, limitation, restrictedness, nearness, constriction, closeness, meagreness
FORMAL attenuation
2 NARROW-MINDEDNESS, insularity, parochialism, exclusiveness, bias, bigotry, prejudice, intolerance, pettiness, small-mindedness, rigidity, conservatism
Ea 1 breadth, width **2** broad-mindedness, tolerance

narrows n

straits, sound, channel, passage, waterway

nascent adj

budding developing growing rising young embryonic, beginning evolving advancing
FORMAL burgeoning incipient, naissant
Ea dying

nastily adv

unpleasantly, disagreeably, offensively, obnoxiously, objectionably, repulsively, disgustingly
Ea kindly, pleasantly

nastiness n

1 UNPLEASANTNESS, repulsiveness, horribleness, disagreeableness, offensiveness, filth, dirtiness, defilement, filthiness, foulness, impurity, pollution, squalor, uncleanliness, unsavouriness
2 OBSCENITY, indecency, filth, pornography
COLLOQ. porn, smuttiness
3 MALICE, spitefulness, spite, malevolence, viciousness, meanness

nasty adj

1 UNPLEASANT, awful, repulsive, hateful, loathsome, objectionable, disagreeable, offensive, distasteful, disgusting obnoxious, repellent, repugnant, revolting sickening horrible, horrid, dirty, filthy, squalid, foul, mucky, vile, odious, polluted, rank
FORMAL noisome, malodorous
COLLOQ. grotty, yucky, rough; *Aust & NZ* crook
SLANG ribby
2 OBSCENE, offensive, indecent, dirty, filthy, pornographic, ribald
COLLOQ. blue, smutty
3 MALICIOUS, mean, malevolent, spiteful, vicious, cruel, unkind, bad-tempered, disagreeable, unpleasant
4 SERIOUS, grave, critical, dangerous, worrying alarming disquieting unpleasant, difficult, tricky
5 *a nasty situation*
difficult, tricky, awkward, annoying exasperating delicate, ticklish
COLLOQ. dodgy
6 *nasty weather*
stormy, wet, rainy, foggy, foul, disagreeable, unpleasant, vile, wild, rough, dirty, filthy, awful
Ea 1 agreeable, nice, pleasant **2** decent **3** benevolent, kind **6** fine

nation n

country, people, race, tribe, state, kingdom, land, realm, republic, population, community, society, folk, vassal; *S Afr* volk
OLD public

> **QUOTATIONS**
> Even if I die in the service of this nation, I would be proud of it
> INDIRA GANDHI

national adj, n

♦ adj
countrywide, civil, civic, domestic, nationwide, state, internal, native, general, governmental, federal, public, widespread, comprehensive, social
♦ n
citizen, native, subject, inhabitant, resident

nationalism n

patriotism, allegiance, loyalty, chauvinism, xenophobia, jingoism

nationalist n

patriot, loyalist, chauvinist, jingoist, flag-waver, xenophobe

nationalistic adj

patriotic, loyal, chauvinistic, jingoistic, xenophobic
FORMAL ethnocentrist

nationality n

race, nation, ethnic group, birth, citizenship, tribe, clan

nationally adv

generally, comprehensively, countrywide, nationwide, throughout all the country, across the whole country

nationwide adj

national, countrywide, general, overall, extensive, widespread, comprehensive, state, coast-to-coast

native adj, n

♦ adj

1 INDIGENOUS, local, domestic, vernacular, home, home-grown, aboriginal, mother, original
FORMAL autochthonous
2 INHERENT, inborn, innate, inbred, ingrained, hereditary, inherited, congenital, instinctive, intuitive, natural, built-in, intrinsic
FORMAL natal, connate

♦ n

inhabitant, resident, national, citizen, dweller, aborigine
FORMAL autochthon
E3 foreigner, outsider, stranger, alien

SYNONYM NUANCES

adj sense 1

Indigenous is a straightforward, fairly technical term to refer to something originating from the place indicated: *gibbons are indigenous to Burma*, whereas **local** has to do with being a more immediate vicinity: *local customs in this part of Spain*. **Vernacular** tends to be reserved for language to suggest being particular to an area.

Domestic is also a fairly technical term for pertaining to one's native place, and can be used in political contexts: *domestic and foreign policy*, while **home** is perhaps more affectionate in tone, and **home-grown** has overtones of pride at something being created in one's native land: *home-grown talent*.

Original is widely used to suggest being there at the start: *the original settlements found by discoverers*, while **aboriginal** would be appropriate for an original inhabitant of a country, though the term is now strongly associated with Australia. **Mother**, with its connotations of nurture, is a more affectionate-sounding term for something belonging to your land: *mother tongue*.

---

nativity n

birth, childbirth, delivery
FORMAL parturition

natter v, n

♦ v

chat, chatter, gabble, jabber, gossip, talk, confabulate; *dialect & N Am* blather; *Scot* blether
COLLOQ. confab, gab, jaw, prattle, rabbit (on), chinwag witter, chew the fat, shoot the breeze

♦ n

chat, conversation, talk, gossip, prattle, chit-chat; *dialect & N Am* blather; *Scot* blether
COLLOQ. chinwag confab, gab, jaw

nattily adv

smartly, neatly, elegantly, fashionably, stylishly

natty adj

smart, neat, dapper, chic, elegant, well-dressed, fashionable, spruce, stylish, trim
COLLOQ. ritzy, snazzy, swanky

natural adj

1 ORDINARY, normal, common, regular, standard, everyday, routine, run-of-the-mill, usual, typical
2 INNATE, inborn, inbred, ingrained, built-in, normal, instinctive, intuitive, inherent, inherited, congenital, native, indigenous
FORMAL connate
3 *natural fibres*
genuine, pure, authentic, additive-free, chemical-free, organic, raw, virgin, unrefined, unprocessed, unmixed, plain, real, whole

4 SINCERE, unaffected, genuine, artless, ingenuous, guileless, simple, unpretentious, unsophisticated, frank, open, candid, spontaneous, relaxed
E3 1 unnatural **2** acquired **3** artificial, man-made, synthetic **4** affected, disingenuous, contrived

naturalist n

life scientist, plant scientist, botanist, biologist, zoologist, ecologist, evolutionist, Darwinist, creationist

naturalistic adj

natural, realistic, true-to-life, representational, lifelike, graphic, real-life, photographic, factual
E3 idealistic, unrealistic

naturalize v

introduce, adopt, incorporate, familiarize, acclimatize, accept, assimilate, accustom, adapt, enfranchise, give citizenship to, domesticate
FORMAL acclimate, acculturate, endenizen, habituate

naturally adj

1 OF COURSE, obviously, clearly, as a matter of course, simply, logically, typically, certainly, absolutely, as you would expect, as might be expected
SLANG natch
2 NORMALLY, genuinely, sincerely, instinctively, spontaneously, artlessly, ingenuously, candidly, frankly

naturalness n

sincerity, genuineness, artlessness, ingenuousness, simpleness, simplicity, plainness, pureness, purity, wholeness, candidness, frankness, openness, realism, unpretentiousness, unaffectedness, unselfconsciousness, spontaneousness, spontaneity, informality

nature n

1 ESSENCE, quality, character, essential quality/character, identity, features, disposition, attributes, personality, stamp, make-up, characteristic(s), complexion, constitution, temperament, mood, outlook, humour, temper
COLLOQ. chemistry
2 KIND, sort, type, description, category, variety, style, species, class
3 UNIVERSE, world, creation, cosmos, earth, mother earth/nature, Gaia, environment
4 COUNTRYSIDE, country, landscape, scenery, natural history

QUOTATIONS

I have a terrible lucidity at moments when nature is so beautiful. I am not conscious of myself any more, and the pictures come to me as if in a dream
VINCENT VAN GOGH

---

naught n

nothing nothingness, zero, nought, nil; *dialect* nowt
COLLOQ. zilch, sweet Fanny Adams, sweet FA

naughtily adv

1 BADLY BEHAVED, mischievously, disobediently, waywardly, defiantly, perversely, playfully
2 INDECENTLY, obscenely, bawdily, vulgarly, coarsely, lewdly

naughtiness n

1 BAD BEHAVIOUR, misbehaviour, mischief, disobedience, waywardness, defiance, lack of discipline, playfulness
2 INDECENCY, obscenity, bawdiness, vulgarity, coarseness, lewdness
COLLOQ. smuttiness

naughty adj

1 BAD, badly behaved, misbehaving mischievous, disobedient, wayward, defiant, undisciplined, unruly, exasperating playful, roguish, perverse, incorrigible
FORMAL refractory
2 INDECENT, obscene, bawdy, risqué, end-of-the-pier, vulgar, off-colour, coarse, ribald, lewd
COLLOQ. blue, smutty
E3 1 good, well-behaved **2** decent

nausea *n*
1 VOMITING, sickness, retching gagging queasiness, biliousness, morning sickness, travel sickness, motion sickness, seasickness, carsickness, airsickness, sick headache; *dialect* wamble
COLLOQ. throwing up, puking
2 DISGUST, revulsion, loathing aversion, distaste, hatred
FORMAL repugnance, detestation

nauseate *v*
sicken, make sick, disgust, revolt, repel, offend, make your gorge rise, turn your stomach
COLLOQ. turn off; *N Am* gross out

nauseating *adj*
sickening disgusting stomach-churning stomach-turning repulsive, offensive, distasteful, repellent, repugnant, odious, loathsome, abhorrent, nauseous, revolting
FORMAL detestable
SLANG *Aust* chunderous

nauseous *adj*
queasy, nauseated, sick, ill, travel sick, seasick, carsick, airsick
COLLOQ. under the weather, about to throw up

nautical *adj*
naval, maritime, seagoing seafaring sailing oceanic, boating yachting

Nautical terms include:

afloat	harbour	reef
aft	harbour-bar	refit
air-sea rescue	harbour dues	ride out
amidships	harbour-master	riptide
ballast	haven	roll
beam	head to wind	row
bear away	heave to	run
beat	heavy swell	run aground
becalmed	heel	run before the
bow-wave	helm	wind
breeches-buoy	high tide	salvage
broach	inflatable life-raft	seafaring
capsize	jetsam	sea lane
cargo	jetty	sea legs
cast off	knot	seamanship
chandler	launch	seasick
circumnavigate	lay a course	seaworthy
coastguard	lay up	set sail
compass bearing	lee	sheet in
convoy	lee shore	shipping
course	leeward	shipping lane
cruise	life buoy	ship's company
current	life-jacket	ship water
Davy Jones's	life-rocket	shipwreck
locker	list	shipyard
dead reckoning	low tide	shore leave
deadweight	make fast	sink
disembark	marina	slip anchor
dock	marine	slipway
dockyard	maroon	stevedore
dry dock	mayday	stowaway
ebb tide	moor	tack
embark	mooring	tide
ferry	mutiny	trim
fleet	navigation	voyage
float	neap tide	wake
flotilla	on board	wash
flotsam	pitch and toss	watch
foghorn	plane	wave
fore	put in	weather
foreshore	put to sea	weigh anchor
go about	quay	wharf
gybe	reach	wreck

See also **navigation**; **sail**; **sailing**; **ship**.

naval *adj*
marine, maritime, nautical, sea, seagoing seafaring

navel *n*
umbilicus, centre, middle, hub
FORMAL omphalos
COLLOQ. belly-button, tummy-button
Related adjective: umbilical

navigable *adj*
passable, crossable, negotiable, open, clear, unblocked, unobstructed, surmountable
FORMAL traversable

navigate *v*
steer, drive, direct, pilot, guide, plan a course, handle, manoeuvre, negotiate, cruise, sail, voyage, journey, cross, helm, plot, plan
COLLOQ. skipper

navigation *n*
sailing steering piloting pilotage, directing direction, guiding guidance, cruising voyaging seamanship, helmsmanship, manoeuvring
Related adjective: nautical

Navigational aids include:

astronavigation	echo-sounder	marker buoy
bell buoy	flux-gate compass	nautical table
channel-marker	Global Positioning	parallel ruler
buoy	System (GPS)	pilot
chart	gyrocompass	radar
chronometer	lighthouse	sectored
conical buoy	lightship	leading-light
Decca® navigator	log	sextant
system	loran (long-range	VHF radio
depth gauge	radio navigation)	
dividers	magnetic compass	

navigator *n*
pilot, seaman, helmsman, steersman, mariner

navvy *n*
labourer, common labourer, worker, manual worker, workman, digger, ganger

navy *n*
fleet, naval fleet, naval force, ships, flotilla, armada, warships, merchant navy, merchant service, mercantile marine

nay *adv*
1 NO, not at all, not really, of course not, absolutely not, certainly not, most certainly not, under no circumstances; *Scot* nae
2 INDEED, actually, in fact, in truth, in point of fact, or rather

near *adj, adv, prep, v*
♦ *adj*
1 NEARBY, close, close-range, close by, within reach, within range, at hand, accessible, convenient, bordering adjacent, alongside, local, neighbouring surrounding; *Scot* ewest
FORMAL adjoining contiguous
COLLOQ. a stone's throw from; *Aust & NZ* within cooee
2 IMMINENT, close, impending forthcoming coming looming immediate, approaching in the offing
FORMAL proximate
3 DEAR, familiar, close, related, closely related, intimate, akin
4 SIMILAR, close, like, alike, comparable, corresponding
F3 1 far, far off, far-away **2** distant **3** remote
♦ *adv*
nearby, close, close by, not far away, at close quarters, alongside, within reach, at hand, within close range; *Scot* ewest
OLD forby
COLLOQ. a stone's throw away; *Aust & NZ* within cooee
See Synonym nuances panel at **close**[1].

♦ *prep*

nearby, close to, next to, bordering on, adjacent to, alongside, in the neighbourhood of, within reach of
OLD forby
FORMAL adjoining contiguous to

♦ *v*

approach, get closer to, come nearer/closer, advance towards, come/move towards, draw near to, draw nearer to, close in on, cling to
E∃ withdraw, keep your distance

■ near thing

near miss, narrow escape, nasty moment, close call
COLLOQ. close shave, narrow squeak

nearby *adj, adv*

♦ *adj*

near, close, neighbouring adjoining adjacent, accessible, convenient, handy, within reach
E∃ faraway

♦ *adv*

near, within reach, at close quarters, close by, close at hand, not far away, a short distance away, in the vicinity
COLLOQ. on your doorstep, in your own backyard

nearly *adv*

almost, practically, virtually, as good as, closely, close to, approximately, more or less, all but, just about, roughly, verging on, well-nigh

nearness *n*

1 CLOSENESS, vicinity, handiness, accessibility, availability, immediacy, imminence
FORMAL proximity, contiguity, propinquity
2 INTIMACY, dearness, familiarity, closeness, chumminess

near-sighted *adj*

short-sighted, myopic, half-blind, purblind

neat *adj*

1 TIDY, orderly, ordered, well-ordered, organized, well-organized, well-groomed, straight, tight, smart, smug spruce, dapper, trim, dainty, clean, clean-cut, shipshape; *dialect* jemmy; *Scot* dink, jimpy, snod, tosh, trig genty; *N Am* band-box
OLD net, featous; *Scot* donsie
COLLOQ. dinky, natty, spick-and-span, in apple-pie order, shipshape and Bristol fashion
2 DEFT, clever, adroit, nimble, skilful, practised, dexterous, expert
OLD (*Shakesp*) feat
COLLOQ. nifty
3 COMPACT, handy, dainty, convenient, efficient, well-designed, well-made, user-friendly
4 a neat solution
clever, convenient, nice, simple, apt, sensible, ingenious, elegant, slick, clean, crisp
COLLOQ. nifty
5 GREAT, excellent, wonderful, marvellous, superb, admirable, tremendous, fantastic, fabulous
COLLOQ. super, terrific, smashing
SLANG cool, mega, wicked
6 UNDILUTED, unmixed, unadulterated, straight, pure
COLLOQ. short
E∃ 1 untidy, scruffy, shabby, slovenly **2** clumsy **6** diluted

neaten *v*

tidy (up), straighten, smarten (up), spruce up, clean (up), arrange, trim, edge, round off, groom, put to rights; *N Am* square away

neatly *adv*

1 TIDILY, smartly, stylishly, sprucely, methodically, systematically, efficiently
2 CLEVERLY, conveniently, handily, aptly, nicely, daintily, elegantly
3 DEFTLY, skilfully, adeptly, adroitly, agilely, nimbly, dexterously, effortlessly, expertly, precisely, accurately, gracefully
OLD (*Shakesp*) featly; (*Spenser*) feateously
E∃ 1 untidily **2** inelegantly **3** unskilfully, inexpertly

neatness *n*

1 TIDINESS, smartness, trimness, spruceness, stylishness, style, orderliness, straightness, efficiency, methodicalness
2 CLEVERNESS, aptness, handiness, elegance, daintiness, niceness, nicety
3 SKILFULNESS, skill, adeptness, deftness, adroitness, agility, dexterity, gracefulness, grace, nimbleness, expertness, preciseness, precision, accuracy
E∃ 1 untidiness, disorderliness **2** inelegance

nebulous *adj*

vague, hazy, imprecise, indefinite, indistinct, cloudy, misty, shadowy, obscure, uncertain, unclear, dim, ambiguous, confused, fuzzy, abstract, shapeless, unformed
FORMAL amorphous, indeterminate
E∃ clear

necessarily *adv*

inevitably, unavoidably, incontrovertibly, certainly, compulsorily, by definition, inescapably, of necessity, indispensably, inexorably, of course, naturally, consequently, automatically, therefore, thus, accordingly, axiomatically, willy-nilly, *nolens volens*
TECHNICAL obligate
OLD no remedy
FORMAL ineluctably, perforce

necessary *adj*

needed, required, essential, compulsory, indispensable, vital, crucial, de rigueur, obligatory, needful, unavoidable, sure, inevitable, inescapable, inexorable, certain
OLD needful; (*Shakesp*) needy
FORMAL mandatory, imperative, requisite, ineluctable
E∃ unnecessary, inessential, unimportant

necessitate *v*

require, involve, entail, make necessary, need, take, mean, call for, demand, oblige, exact, force, constrain, compel

necessity *n*

1 REQUIREMENT, obligation, prerequisite, essential, fundamental, indispensable, need, want, compulsion, demand
OLD extremes
FORMAL exigency, requisite, desideratum, sine qua non
COLLOQ. must
2 INDISPENSABILITY, inevitability, certainty, inescapability, inexorability, destiny, fate, obligation, need, needfulness; *Scot* mister
3 POVERTY, destitution, hardship, want, need, deprivation
FORMAL penury, privation, indigence
E∃ luxury

■ of necessity

inevitably, unavoidably, incontrovertibly, certainly, compulsorily, indispensably, by definition, inescapably, inexorably, automatically
OLD no remedy

> **PROVERBS**
> Necessity is the mother of invention

neck *n, v*

♦ *n*

nape, scruff, scrag halse
TECHNICAL cervix
Related adjective: cervical

♦ *v*

kiss, pet, caress
COLLOQ. smooch, canoodle
SLANG snog

■ neck and neck

level, equal, balanced, aligned, drawn, even, on a par, matching uniform, level pegging

necklace *n*

chain, string band, pearls, beads, jewels, choker, locket, pendant, *lavallière*, negligee, torque, torc, gorget, carcanet, *rivière*

necromancer n
magician, conjurer, diviner, sorcerer, sorceress, witch, wizard, warlock, spiritist, spiritualist
FORMAL thaumaturge, thaumaturgist

necromancy n
divination, enchantment, wonder-working magic, magical powers, black magic, black art, sorcery, witchcraft, witchery, spiritism, spiritualism, wizardry, demonology, voodoo, hoodoo
FORMAL conjuration, thaumaturgy

necropolis n
cemetery, graveyard, burial ground, burial place, burial site, churchyard, God's acre, charnel house

need v, n
♦ v
miss, lack, want, require, demand, call for, have need of, necessitate, be necessary to have, have occasion for, have to, must, be compelled/obliged to, desire, crave, pine for, yearn for, be desperate for, cry out for, be dependent on, depend on, be reliant on, rely on
OLD mister
♦ n
1 *a need for caution*
call, demand, obligation, necessity, want, wish, justification, requirement; *Scot* mister
FORMAL exigency
2 *the country's needs*
essential, necessity, prerequisite
FORMAL requisite, desideratum
3 *a need for equipment*
want, lack, insufficiency, inadequacy, neediness, demand, shortage
■ **in need**
poor, impoverished, needy, penniless, disadvantaged, deprived, poverty-stricken, underprivileged
FORMAL destitute, penurious, indigent, impecunious
COLLOQ. on the breadline, hard up, dirt-poor, unable to keep the wolf from the door

needed adj
called for, desired, required, wanted, lacking compulsory, necessary, obligatory, essential
FORMAL requisite
ᴱᴬ unnecessary, unneeded

needful adj
required, needed, necessary, essential, indispensable, vital, stipulated, needy
FORMAL requisite
ᴱᴬ excess, needless, superfluous

needle n, v
♦ n
1 *needle and thread*
knitting needle, pin, sharp, stylus, nib, bodkin, darner, darning-needle, packing-needle, hypodermic needle, syringe
TECHNICAL spud, dry-point, microneedle
SLANG hype, hypo
2 POINTER, indicator, arrow, marker, hand
3 THORN, prickle, spike, splinter, barb, spine, quill, briar, bristle, bramble
FORMAL spicule
♦ v
annoy, irritate, harass, pester, goad, spur, provoke, ruffle, prick, rile, bait, prod, nag irk, taunt, torment, sting
COLLOQ. aggravate, wind up, get at, bug drive mad, drive crazy, drive bananas, drive up the wall, drive round the bend/twist, miff, make someone's blood boil, make someone see red, rattle someone's cage, ruffle someone's feathers, raise someone's dander, make someone's hackles rise, make sparks fly, get under someone's skin, get up someone's nose, get on someone's wick
SLANG nark, piss off
OLD SLANG get someone's shirt out

needless adj
unnecessary, gratuitous, uncalled-for, unwanted, undesired, redundant, dispensable, superfluous, expendable, useless, pointless, purposeless, luxury
ᴱᴬ necessary, essential, indispensable
■ **needless to say**
of course, naturally, certainly, surely, by all means, definitely, without a doubt, no doubt, undoubtedly, doubtlessly, indubitably

needlessly adv
unnecessarily, superfluously, redundantly, pointlessly, uselessly, dispensably
ᴱᴬ necessarily, indispensably

needlework n
embroidery, fancywork, stitching sewing crocheting tapestry, tatting needlepoint

needy adj
poor, impoverished, in need, needful, penniless, disadvantaged, deprived, poverty-stricken, underprivileged
OLD strait, wanting
FORMAL destitute, penurious, indigent, impecunious
COLLOQ. on the breadline, hard up, dirt-poor, unable to keep the wolf from the door
ᴱᴬ affluent, wealthy, well-off

ne'er-do-well n
good-for-nothing idler, layabout, loafer, slacker, lounger, shirker, wastrel, waster, do-nothing
COLLOQ. black sheep, skiver, dodger, spiv
SLANG *Irish* dosser; *N Am* goof-off; *Aust & NZ* bludger

nefarious adj
wicked, detestable, dreadful, evil, foul, loathsome, vile, vicious, shameful, outrageous, horrendous, terrible, odious, monstrous, villainous, abominable, atrocious, base, sinful, unholy, criminal, depraved, infamous, horrible, satanic, infernal
FORMAL execrable, heinous, iniquitous, opprobrious
ᴱᴬ exemplary

negate v
1 CANCEL, annul, invalidate, undo, neutralize, quash, reverse, wipe out, void, repeal
FORMAL nullify, countermand, abrogate, retract, revoke, rescind
2 DENY, contradict, oppose, disprove, repudiate, reject, discredit
FORMAL renounce, refute, gainsay
COLLOQ. explode, squash
ᴱᴬ **2** affirm

negation n
1 CANCELLATION, repeal, neutralization, veto
FORMAL disavowal, nullification, abrogation, countermanding
2 DENIAL, contradiction, rejection, renunciation, disclaimer
3 OPPOSITE, reverse, contrary
FORMAL inverse, antithesis, converse
ᴱᴬ **2** affirmation

negative adj, n
♦ adj
1 *a negative impact*
adverse, bad, unfavourable, disadvantageous, hostile, antagonistic, opposing opposite, counter, contrary, conflicting counter-productive, negative, unfortunate, unlucky, detrimental, harmful, injurious, hurtful, unfriendly, uncongenial
FORMAL inauspicious, unpropitious
2 *a negative attitude*
pessimistic, defeatist, gloomy, unenthusiastic, uninterested, unwilling unco-operative, unhelpful, cynical, critical, weak, spineless
3 *a negative reply*
contrary, denying saying no, refusing opposing opposed, invalidating neutralizing annulling
FORMAL nullifying dissenting gainsaying
ᴱᴬ **1** positive **2** constructive, positive **3** affirmative

♦ *n*
contradiction, denial, opposite, refusal,
rejection
FORMAL dissension

negativity *n*
pessimism, defeatism, gloominess, lack of
interest/enthusiasm, unco-operativeness, cynicism,
unwillingness, unhelpfulness, criticalness

neglect *v, n*
♦ *v*
1 DISREGARD, ignore, overlook, leave alone, leave out,
abandon, pass by, pass up, rebuff, scorn, disobey, infringe,
disdain, slight, spurn, pigeon; *dialect* mislippen
FORMAL forsake
2 FORGET, fail (in), omit, overlook, let slide, shirk, skimp,
be lax about
E∃ 1 cherish, appreciate **2** remember, pay attention to,
attend to
♦ *n*
negligence, disregard, carelessness, shortcoming failure,
abuse, non-performance, inattention, disuse, disrepair,
rack and ruin, indifference, slackness, laxity, forgetfulness,
ignoring rebuff, scorn, disdain, slight, spurning oversight,
disrespect
TECHNICAL incivism, misprision
FORMAL remissness, default, dereliction of duty,
heedlessness, desuetude
E∃ care, attention, concern

neglected *adj*
1 *they feel neglected*
uncared-for, disregarded, unheeded, unnoticed,
abandoned, undervalued, unappreciated, deserted,
stranded, forsaken
2 *a neglected garden*
derelict, overgrown, uncultivated, unmaintained,
untended, untilled, unweeded, unhusbanded, dilapidated
COLLOQ. run-down
E∃ 1 cherished, treasured **2** tended, cared for

neglectful *adj*
uncaring careless, sloppy, inattentive, disregardful,
forgetful, thoughtless, unmindful, indifferent, lax, negligent,
oblivious
FORMAL heedless, remiss
E∃ attentive, careful

negligence *n*
inattentiveness, inattention, carelessness, sloppiness, laxity,
neglect, slackness, thoughtlessness, forgetfulness,
indifference, omission, oversight, disregard, shortcoming
failure
FORMAL default, remissness, dereliction of duty,
heedlessness
E∃ attentiveness, care, regard

negligent *adj*
neglectful, inattentive, thoughtless, casual, lax, cursory,
careless, indifferent, offhand, nonchalant, slack, uncaring
unmindful, forgetful
FORMAL remiss, heedless, dilatory
COLLOQ. sloppy
E∃ attentive, careful, scrupulous

negligible *adj*
unimportant, insignificant, small, imperceptible,
inappreciable, minimal, trifling trivial, petty, paltry,
minor, minute, tiny, not worth bothering about, off the
map
OLD neglectable
E∃ significant

negotiable *adj*
1 DEBATABLE, arguable, questionable, contestable, open to
discussion/question, undecided, unsettled
2 NAVIGABLE, passable, crossable, open, clear, unblocked,
unobstructed, surmountable
FORMAL traversable
E∃ 1 non-negotiable, fixed, definite

negotiate *v*
1 *negotiate an agreement*
deal, mediate, arbitrate, intervene, intercede, debate,
haggle, bargain, arrange, agree, come to an agreement,
resolve, hammer out, thrash out, pull off, transact, work
out, manage, complete, settle, fulfil, consult, contract, talk,
discuss, broker, treat, reach a compromise
FORMAL confer, execute, conclude
COLLOQ. parley, wheel and deal
2 GET ROUND, cross, clear, surmount, pass (over/through)
FORMAL traverse

negotiation *n*
mediation, arbitration, debate, conference, discussion,
diplomacy, bargaining haggling parleying transaction,
reaching an agreement, thrashing-out, hammering-out,
pulling-off, talks
COLLOQ. parley, wheeling and dealing

negotiator *n*
arbitrator, go-between, mediator, intermediary, bargainer,
haggler, moderator, intercessor, adjudicator, broker,
ambassador, diplomat
COLLOQ. parleyer, wheeler-dealer

neigh *v*
whinny, hinny, bray, nicker

neighbourhood *n*
district, locality, vicinity, community, locale, quarter, part,
precinct, environs, confines, surroundings, area, region,
presence
OLD convicinity, voisinage
FORMAL proximity, purlieus, vicinage
COLLOQ. *N Am* hood
■ **in the neighbourhood of**
near, close to, about, roughly, almost, approximately,
nearby, next to, round, around, up to

neighbouring *adj*
adjacent, bordering near, nearby, nearest, near at hand,
close at hand, local, connecting next, surrounding
FORMAL adjoining abutting contiguous
E∃ distant, remote, far away

neighbourly *adj*
sociable, friendly, amiable, kind, generous,
helpful, genial, warm, cordial, easy to get
on/along with, affable, hospitable, obliging considerate,
companionable

nemesis *n*
retribution, vengeance, punishment, just punishment,
destruction, ruin, downfall, destiny, fate

neologism *n*
new word/term, new expression, new phrase, innovation,
coinage, novelty, vogue word

neophyte *n*
beginner, learner, novice, newcomer, apprentice,
probationer, trainee, recruit, raw recruit, new member,
tiro, rookie
FORMAL noviciate, novitiate
COLLOQ. greenhorn, newbie

nepotism *n*
favouritism, bias, partiality, preferential treatment, keeping
it in the family, looking after your own
COLLOQ. jobs for the boys, Old Boy network, old school
tie

nerve *n, v*
♦ *n*
1 COURAGE, bravery, mettle, pluck, spirit, vigour,
intrepidity, valour, daring fearlessness, cool-headedness,
hardihood, firmness, self-confidence, resolution,
steadfastness, will, determination, endurance, force
FORMAL fortitude
COLLOQ. guts, spunk, grit, bottle
2 AUDACITY, impudence, effrontery, brazenness, gall,
boldness, impertinence, insolence, presumption, temerity

COLLOQ. cheek, chutzpah, face, neck, brass neck, sauce, mouth, lip
E3 1 weakness **2** timidity
♦ *v*
steel, strengthen, invigorate, encourage, bolster, prepare, brace, hearten, embolden
FORMAL fortify
E3 unnerve

nerveless *adj*
feeble, weak, flabby, inert, slack, nervous, spineless, timid, unnerved, afraid, cowardly
FORMAL debilitated, enervated
E3 bold, brave, strong

nerve-racking *adj*
harrowing distressing trying stressful, tense, maddening worrying anxious, disquieting difficult, frightening
COLLOQ. nail-biting

nerves *n*
nervousness, tension, nervous tension, stress, anxiety, worry, shock, strain, fretfulness, apprehensiveness, twitter, *crise de nerfs*
COLLOQ. jitters, butterflies (in your stomach), collywobbles, wobbly, willies, heebie-jeebies
Related adjective: neural

■ **get on someone's nerves**
annoy, irritate, rile, displease, anger, vex, irk, madden, exasperate, tease, provoke, ruffle, gall, trouble, nag disturb, bother, pester, plague, harass, molest; *Scot* fash
COLLOQ. aggravate, bug wind up, hassle, rub up the wrong way, get someone's blood up, make someone's blood boil, get up someone's nose, get under someone's skin, get someone's goat, get on someone's wick, drive crazy/nuts, drive bananas, drive up the wall, drive round the bend/twist, get someone's back up, brass off, cheese off, make someone's hackles rise, make sparks fly, give someone the hump, get your dander up; *N Am* tick/hack off

nervous *adj*
highly-strung, excitable, anxious, agitated, on edge, tense, strained, fidgety, apprehensive, neurotic, overwrought, shaky, uneasy, worried, flustered, disquieted, fretful, quaking, on tenterhooks, fearful, afraid, timid, timorous
FORMAL perturbed
COLLOQ. edgy, nervy, twitchy, het up, keyed up, wound up, jumpy, jittery, uptight, trepidatious, with/having butterflies in your stomach, on pins and needles, having kittens, shaking like a leaf/jelly, with your heart in your mouth, in a sweat, in a stew, in a tizzy
SLANG screwed-up
E3 calm, relaxed

nervous breakdown *n*
mental breakdown, nervous disorder, nervous exhaustion, neurosis, crisis, depression, clinical depression, melancholia
COLLOQ. cracking-up

nervously *adv*
anxiously, apprehensively, uneasily, on edge, fretfully, fearfully, timidly
COLLOQ. twitchily, edgily, with/having butterflies in your stomach, having kittens, shaking like a leaf/jelly, with your heart in your mouth, in a sweat, in a stew, in a tizzy
E3 calmly

nervousness *n*
anxiety, tension, strain, stress, edginess, worry, uneasiness, disquiet, apprehensiveness, agitation, restlessness, fluster, excitability, timidity, timorousness, tremulousness
FORMAL perturbation
COLLOQ. habdabs, heebie-jeebies, touchiness, willies
E3 calmness, coolness

nervy *adj*
highly-strung excitable, anxious, agitated, on edge, tense, strained, fidgety, apprehensive, neurotic, shaky, uneasy, worried, flustered, fearful

COLLOQ. edgy, twitchy, het up, keyed up, wound up, jumpy, jittery, uptight, with/having butterflies in your stomach, on pins and needles, having kittens, shaking like a leaf/jelly, with your heart in your mouth
E3 calm, relaxed

nescient *adj*
ignorant, uneducated, illiterate, innumerate, backward, unread, untaught, untrained, inexperienced, unschooled, unlearned, stupid, uninitiated, unenlightened, uninformed, ill-informed, unwitting unaware, unfamiliar, unacquainted
COLLOQ. clueless, dense, thick, thick as two short planks
E3 educated, knowledgeable, learned, clever; *formal* conversant

nest *n*
1 *a bird's nest*
breeding-ground, den, roost, perch, lair, cote, nesting-box, hive-nest; *N Am* bird-house
OLD (*Shakesp*) cabinet
FORMAL nidus, nidification
Related adjective: nidal
2 RETREAT, refuge, shelter, haunt, hideaway, hideout, hiding-place, den, mew

---

Nests of creatures include:

formicarium (or formicary) (*ants*)	dialect cage (*squirrel*)	*Scot* bike (*wasps, wild bees*)
hive (*bees*)	drey (*squirrel*)	*Scot* bink (*wasps, wild bees*)
eyrie (*eagle*)	termitarium (*termites*)	
nid (*pheasant*)		
Aust wurley (*rat*)	vespiary (*wasps*)	

See also **lair**.

---

nest egg *n*
fund(s), reserve(s), savings, store, cache, deposit, bottom drawer
COLLOQ. money saved for a rainy day

nestle *v*
snuggle (up), huddle (together), cuddle (up), nuzzle, curl up

nestling *n*
fledgling chick, suckling weanling baby

net¹ *n, v*
♦ *n*
a fishing net
mesh, meshwork, web, webbing network, netting open work, tracery, lattice, latticework, filigree, lace, fishnet, drag dragnet, drift, drift-net, drop-net, seine, seine net, snare, trap
FORMAL reticulum
Related adjectives: retiary, reticular
♦ *v*
catch, trap, capture, take captive, bag ensnare, snare, enmesh, entangle
COLLOQ. nab, collar, nick

net² *adj, v*
♦ *adj*
1 *net salary*
nett, clear, after tax(es), after deductions, take-home, final, lowest
2 OVERALL, general, broad, total, inclusive, final, end, ultimate
E3 1 gross
♦ *v*
bring in, clear, earn, take, take home, raise, get, make, receive, gain, pocket, obtain, accumulate
FORMAL realize
COLLOQ. pull in, rake in

nether *adj*
1 LOWER, under, lower-level, bottom, below, beneath, underground, low
FORMAL basal, inferior
2 INFERNAL, hellish, underworld, Plutonian, Stygian

netherworld *n*
hell, underworld, inferno, infernal regions, lower regions, abyss, fire, fire and brimstone, bottomless pit, pit, Hades, Sheol, Acheron, Gehenna, Tophet, Abaddon, Tartarus, Malebolge, Erebus
FORMAL perdition, abode of the devil
COLLOQ. below, down there, other place

nettle *v*
annoy, chafe, discountenance, exasperate, fret, goad, harass, incense, irritate, rile, pique, provoke, ruffle, sting tease, torment, vex, upset
COLLOQ. aggravate, wind up, get at, bug needle, drive mad, drive crazy, drive bananas, drive up the wall, drive round the bend/twist, miff, make someone's blood boil, make someone see red, rattle someone's cage, ruffle someone's feathers, make sparks fly, get under someone's skin, get up someone's nose, get on someone's wick, make someone's hackles rise
SLANG nark, piss off

nettled *adj*
annoyed, offended, irritated, angry, aggrieved, incensed, exasperated, cross, harassed, provoked, piqued, riled, ruffled, stung vexed, galled, goaded, huffy, irritable
COLLOQ. aggravated, wound up, got at, bugged, driven mad, driven crazy, driven bananas, driven up the wall, driven round the bend/twist, miffed, needled, rattled
SLANG narked, pissed off

network *n*
1 NET, maze, mesh, labyrinth, circuitry, grill, meshwork, web, webbing network, netting open work, tracery, lattice, latticework, filigree, lace
FORMAL convolution
2 SYSTEM, organization, arrangement, structure, interconnections, complex, grid, matrix, web, channels, tracks
FORMAL nexus
COLLOQ. grapevine, bush telegraph, Old Boy network, old school tie

neurosis *n*
(mental) disorder, psychological disorder, affliction, abnormality, disturbance, instability, maladjustment, derangement, deviation, fixation, obsession, mania, phobia

neurotic *adj*
paranoid, irrational, disturbed, maladjusted, deranged, anxious, overanxious, nervous, overwrought, hysterical, unstable, unhealthy, deviant, abnormal, compulsive, obsessive, manic, phobic

> **QUOTATIONS**
> Everything great in the world is done by neurotics; they alone founded our religions and created our masterpieces
> MARCEL PROUST, *The Perpetual Pessimist*

neuter *adj, v*
♦ *adj*
sexless, asexual, agamic, agamous
TECHNICAL clonal, conidial, monogenetic
♦ *v*
castrate, emasculate, doctor, geld, spay, dress, caponize, sterilize
COLLOQ. fix

neutral *adj*
1 IMPARTIAL, uncommitted, unbiased, unprejudiced, non-aligned, disinterested, undecided, non-partisan, non-combatant, non-committal, objective, detached, indifferent, dispassionate, uninvolved, even-handed, open-minded
2 DULL, bland, inoffensive, unexceptional, unremarkable, unassertive, ordinary, uninteresting nondescript, colourless, grey, insipid, drab, expressionless, indistinct, anodyne, anaemic, anonymous

3 *a neutral colour*
pale, pastel, indefinite, indistinct, grey, fawn, beige, white, colourless
Ð 1 biased, prejudiced, partisan **2** remarkable, exciting **3** colourful

neutrality *n*
unbiasedness, impartiality, impartialness, detachment, disinterest, disinterestedness, non-alignment, non-intervention, non-involvement
COLLOQ. sitting on the fence
Ð bias, partiality

neutralize *v*
counteract, counterbalance, offset, balance, compensate for, make up for, negate, cancel (out), invalidate, annul, undo, frustrate, incapacitate
FORMAL nullify

never *adv*
at no time, not ever, not for a moment, under no circumstances, not at all, on no account
COLLOQ. not on your life, not on your nellie, when pigs fly, no way, not in a month of Sundays, not in a million years
Ð always

never-ending *adj*
everlasting eternal, non-stop, endless, unending without end, perpetual, unceasing uninterrupted, continuous, unbroken, unremitting interminable, incessant, permanent, persistent, constant, unchanging relentless, infinite, boundless, limitless
Ð fleeting transitory

nevertheless *adv*
nonetheless, still, anyway, even so, yet, however, in spite of everything though, after all, by any means, in any case/event, by some means, anyhow, but, regardless, for all that, all/just the same, at the same time, *tout de même*, *quand même*, *malgré tout*
OLD algate, none but what, withal
FORMAL notwithstanding
COLLOQ. at that

new *adj*
1 MODERN, contemporary, current, latest, recent, state-of-the-art, present-day, up-to-date, up-to-the-minute, topical, modish, ultra-modern, futuristic, advanced, avant-garde
COLLOQ. trendy, newfangled, way out
See Synonym nuances panel at **modern**.
2 NOVEL, original, fresh, different, creative, resourceful, imaginative, innovative, pioneering revolutionary, ground-breaking experimental, ingenious, unfamiliar, strange, unconventional, unusual, brand-new, mint, unknown, unused, newly discovered, virgin, newborn
3 CHANGED, altered, modernized, improved, renewed, refreshed, reinvigorated, restored, remodelled, redesigned
COLLOQ. born-again
4 *new or used cars*
fresh, unused, brand-new, spanking-new
5 ADDED, additional, another, further, extra, more, supplementary
6 *new to the work*
unfamiliar, unacquainted, unknown, inexperienced, unversed, unaccustomed, ignorant, a stranger, alien
Ð 1 out-of-date, old-fashioned, outdated **2** usual, ordinary, just another **3** old **4** used **6** familiar

> **SYNONYM NUANCES**
>
> *sense 2*
> **Novel** and **original** have positive connotations and can be used of something perhaps a bit quirky, that has not been previously encountered: *an entirely novel perspective*; *original thoughts*. **Fresh**, however, implies replacing something or someone jaded: *fresh ideas*; *a fresh investigation*.
>
> The similarly positive **creative**, **imaginative** and **resourceful** emphasize the initiative behind something new, as does **ingenious**, which would appropriately

describe something that cleverly meets its requirements: *ingenious booby-traps*.

The terms **innovative**, **pioneering** and *ground-breaking* are appropriate for something that initiates further developments: *pioneering medical work*, but **revolutionary** would be reserved for some radical change: *revolutionary farming methods that hugely increase crop yields*. **Experimental**, although similar, is more suggestive of varying degrees of success and less inherently positive.

Less complimentary terms for something that deviates from the usual are **unfamiliar** and **strange**, while **unconventional** and **unusual** would be more neutral terms to use.

If you want to refer to a more physical newness, the term **mint** can be used to suggest that something is in a perfect condition, while **virgin** is appropriate for something so far untainted by use or experience: *virgin green grass*.

newcomer n
1 IMMIGRANT, alien, foreigner, incomer, colonist, settler, (new) arrival, outsider, intruder, stranger
2 NOVICE, beginner, learner, pupil, trainee, recruit, probationer, apprentice, tiro
FORMAL neophyte
COLLOQ. greenhorn, rookie, newbie

newfangled adj
modern, new, recent, state-of-the-art, contemporary, ultra-modern, futuristic, fashionable, modernistic, novel, gimmicky
COLLOQ. trendy
F3 old-fashioned

newly adv
recently, lately, latterly, just, freshly, of late, afresh, anew

newness n
freshness, innovation, novelty, originality, oddity, uniqueness, unusualness, strangeness, unfamiliarity
FORMAL recency
F3 oldness, ordinariness

news n
report, account, information, data, facts, intelligence, dispatch, message, communication, announcement, press release, communiqué, bulletin, news item, newsflash, newscast, gossip, hearsay, rumour, statement, story, word, latest, developments, scandal, revelation, exposé, disclosure, advice
FORMAL tidings
COLLOQ. lowdown, gen, info, dope

> **PROVERBS**
> No news is good news

newspaper n
daily, paper, publication, broadsheet, tabloid, sheet, journal, periodical, magazine, weekly, local paper, local, regional paper, regional, provincial paper, provincial, national paper, national, morning paper, evening paper, press, gazette, organ
COLLOQ. rag

> **QUOTATIONS**
> One of the virtues, perhaps almost the chief virtue, of a newspaper is its independence. Whatever its position or character, at least it should have a soul of its own
> C P SCOTT

newsreader n
newscaster, journalist, newsman/woman, reporter, correspondent, announcer, commentator, presenter, anchor, anchorman/woman

newsworthy adj
reportable, hitting/making the headlines, important, significant, interesting remarkable, stimulating notable, noteworthy, topical, arresting unusual

next adj, adv
♦ adj
1 ADJACENT, neighbouring bordering along alongside, beside, nearest, closest
FORMAL adjoining contiguous, tangential
2 FOLLOWING, succeeding successive, ensuing later
FORMAL subsequent
F3 **2** previous, preceding
♦ adv
afterwards, after that time, later, then
FORMAL subsequently, thereafter

nibble n, v
♦ n
bite, peck, gnaw, munch, morsel, taste, titbit, bit, crumb, snack, piece
♦ v
bite, eat, peck, pick at, munch, gnaw; *dialect* chumble
COLLOQ. snack
SLANG nosh

nice adj
1 *have a nice time*
pleasant, agreeable, enjoyable, lovely, good, delightful, satisfying acceptable, pleasurable, fine, appealing amusing entertaining welcome
FORMAL delectable
COLLOQ. decent
2 *he seems a nice man*
pleasant, agreeable, delightful, charming lik(e)able, attractive, good, good-natured, good-humoured, kind, kindly, friendly, genial, sweet, amiable, sympathetic, understanding endearing well-mannered, polite, respectable, civil, courteous; *dialect* canny
3 SUBTLE, delicate, fine, minute, fastidious, refined, particular, discriminating scrupulous, meticulous, precise, exact, accurate, careful, strict, close, ticklish
OLD tickle
F3 **1** unpleasant, horrible **2** nasty, disagreeable, unpleasant **3** careless

nicely adv
1 SATISFACTORILY, well, agreeably, delightfully, pleasurably, pleasantly, pleasingly, attractively, respectably, properly
2 POLITELY, respectably, civilly, courteously
F3 **1** unpleasantly, disagreeably, nastily **2** rudely, impolitely, disrespectfully

niceness n
pleasantness, kindness, agreeableness, friendliness, delightfulness, lik(e)ableness, attractiveness, charm, amiability, politeness, respectability
F3 unpleasantness, disagreeableness, nastiness

nicety n
1 SUBTLETY, refinement, delicacy, distinction, nuance, fine point
2 PRECISION, accuracy, meticulousness, exactness, scrupulousness, minuteness, finesse

niche n
1 POSITION, place, vocation, calling métier, slot, specialized/specialist area
2 RECESS, alcove, hollow, nook, cranny, cubbyhole, corner, opening

nick n, v
♦ n
1 NOTCH, indentation, chip, cut, groove, dent, scar, scratch, mark
2 PRISON, jail, jailhouse, police station
COLLOQ. inside
SLANG porridge, clink, cooler, slammer, quod, jug can, choky
3 *in good nick*
condition, shape, form, state, health, fettle

♦ *v*

1 NOTCH, cut, dent, indent, chip, score, scratch, scar, mark, damage, snick
2 STEAL, pilfer, take, pocket
COLLOQ. knock off, pinch, swipe, lag snitch
3 ARREST, catch, capture, pick up
FORMAL apprehend
COLLOQ. bust, nab, collar, run in, pull in, pick up, do, nail

nickname *n*
pet name, familiar name, so(u)briquet, epithet, diminutive, byname, to-name
FORMAL cognomen
SLANG monicker

nifty *adj*
slick, neat, clever, pleasing enjoyable, excellent, quick, skilful, deft, chic, smart, stylish, spruce, sharp, adroit, agile, nippy, apt

niggardliness *n*
1 MEANNESS, miserliness, closeness, grudgingness, ungenerousness
FORMAL parsimony
COLLOQ. stinginess, tight-fistedness, cheeseparing
2 MEAGRENESS, paltriness, smallness, scantiness, skimpiness, inadequacy, insufficiency
E3 **1** generosity **2** bountifulness

niggardly *adj*
1 MEAN, miserly, close, ungenerous, ungiving sparing grudging illiberal, hard, hard-fisted, penny-wise, nippy; *Scot* near-begaun, near-gaun, nirly
OLD nithing
FORMAL parsimonious, penurious
COLLOQ. mingy, stingy, tight-fisted, cheeseparing
2 MEAGRE, small, miserable, scanty, skimpy, paltry, inadequate, insufficient
COLLOQ. measly, mingy
E3 **1** generous, liberal **2** bountiful, abundant

niggle *v, n*
♦ *v*
1 BOTHER, worry, trouble, annoy, irritate, upset
COLLOQ. bug
2 NAG, criticize, keep on at, pick on, complain, moan, carp, quibble
COLLOQ. nit-pick, hassle, henpeck
♦ *n*
quibble, complaint, objection, criticism, query, protest, cavil, equivocation, prevarication
OLD pettifogging
COLLOQ. nit-picking

night *n*
night-time, darkness, hours of darkness, dark, dead of night
E3 day, daytime
Related adjective: nocturnal

nightclub *n*
club, disco, discotheque, cabaret, nightspot
COLLOQ. niterie, nitery

nightfall *n*
sunset, dusk, twilight, dark, evening sundown
FORMAL gloaming crepuscule
E3 dawn, sunrise

nightly *adv*
every night, each night, night after night, at night, after dark, nocturnally

nightmare *n*
1 BAD DREAM, hallucination, *cauchemar*
OLD ephialtes; (*Shakesp*) cacodemon
FORMAL incubus, oneirodynia
2 ORDEAL, horror, torment, torture, trial, calamity, agony, anguish, awful experience

nightmarish *adj*
terrifying alarming dreadful, frightening ghostly, harrowing horrible, horrific, agonizing disturbing scaring unreal
COLLOQ. creepy

night-time *n*
night, darkness, hours of darkness, dark, dead of night
E3 day, daytime

nihilism *n*
rejection, repudiation, negation, denial, pessimism, scepticism, nothingness, oblivion, emptiness, non-existence, lawlessness, anarchy, terrorism, disorder, agnosticism, atheism, cynicism, disbelief, negativism
FORMAL abnegation, nullity, renunciation

nihilist *n*
pessimist, revolutionary, extremist, agitator, anarchist, terrorist, negationist, negativist, agnostic, atheist, disbeliever, cynic, sceptic, antinomian

nil *n*
nothing zero, none, nought, naught, love, cipher
COLLOQ. duck, zilch

nimble *adj*
1 AGILE, active, lively, sprightly, spry, smart, graceful, lithe, quick, quick-moving brisk, deft, light-footed, light, lissome, prompt, ready, swift, sure-footed; *dialect* wandle; *Scot* swack, yauld
OLD fleet, flippant, wight, deliver; (*Shakesp*) fleet-foot, quiver; (*Spenser*) wimble
FORMAL volant
COLLOQ. nippy
2 ALERT, quick-witted, quick, quick-thinking clever, smart, sharp-witted, sharp-eyed
E3 **1** clumsy, slow **2** slow

nimbleness *n*
agility, adroitness, dexterity, grace, lightness, deftness, finesse, sprightliness, spryness, smartness, skill, alertness
FORMAL alacrity
COLLOQ. niftiness, nippiness

nimbly *adv*
smartly, agilely, fast, sharply, snappily, speedily, swiftly, spryly, quickly, readily, promptly, actively, lightly, proficiently, dexterously, deftly, briskly, easily, alertly, quick-wittedly
E3 awkwardly, clumsily

nincompoop *n*
fool, idiot, dunce, dimwit, simpleton, ignoramus, dolt
COLLOQ. blockhead, nitwit, numskull, chump, clot, twit, twerp
SLANG nerd, plonker, wally

nip¹ *v*
1 BITE, pinch, squeeze, snip, clip, dock, lop, tweak, catch, grip, nibble
2 DASH, go, hurry, rush, fly, tear, dart, run
COLLOQ. pop
■ **nip in the bud**
halt, arrest, stop, stem, check, curb, block, frustrate, obstruct, impede

nip² *n*
a nip of brandy
dram, draught, shot, swallow, mouthful, drop, sip, taste, portion

nipple *n*
teat, udder, breast, dug
TECHNICAL mamilla, papilla
COLLOQ. *dialect* diddy, pap
SLANG tit

nippy *adj*
1 CHILLY, cold, biting sharp, raw, nipping piercing icy, stinging
2 FAST, quick, speedy, nimble, brisk, active, agile, sprightly, spry
E3 **1** warm **2** slow

nirvana *n*
enlightenment, paradise, heaven, tranquillity, bliss, joy, peace, ecstasy, exaltation, serenity

nit-picking *adj*
quibbling carping finicky, fussy, hair-splitting
hypercritical, pedantic, captious, pettifogging cavilling

nitty-gritty *n*
basics, essentials, fundamentals, main points, key points
COLLOQ. bottom line, nuts and bolts, brass tacks

nitwit *n*
fool, idiot, dimwit, simpleton
COLLOQ. nincompoop, ass, chump, ninny, neddy, clot,
dope, twit, birdbrain, silly-billy
SLANG wally, jerk, dumbo, pillock, prat, plonker

no *adv, interj*
not at all, not really, of course not, absolutely not,
certainly not, most certainly not, no thanks, under no
circumstances; *Scot* nae
COLLOQ. no way, nope, not on your life,
over my dead body

nob *n*
VIP, aristocrat, personage
COLLOQ. big shot, bigwig fat cat, toff

nobble *v*
1 BRIBE, buy (off), influence, warn off, threaten,
intimidate
2 DOPE, drug interfere with, disable, incapacitate,
hamstring
COLLOQ. get at
3 CATCH, arrest, grab, seize
COLLOQ. nab, collar, nick, bust, run in, pull in, pick up,
do, nail
4 STEAL, grab, take, pilfer, pinch
COLLOQ. nick, knock off, snitch, swipe
5 THWART, frustrate, foil, check, defeat, hinder

nobility *n*
1 NOBLENESS, dignity, grandeur, grandness, illustriousness,
stateliness, majesty, magnificence, splendour,
impressiveness, glory, eminence, excellence, superiority,
uprightness, integrity, honour, virtue, worthiness,
generosity
FORMAL magnanimity
2 ARISTOCRACY, peerage, peers, nobles, gentry, élite, lords,
high society, family, rank
COLLOQ. nobs, toffs
Related adjective: nobiliary
1 baseness **2** proletariat

Members of the nobility include:

baron	governor	nawab
baroness	jarl	patrician
baronet	Junker	peer
count	knight	peeress
countess	lady	seigneur
daimio	laird	squire
dame	liege	starosta
dowager	liege lord	thane
duchess	life peer	toiseach
duke	lord	vavasour
earl	magnifico	*vicomte*
grand duchess	marchioness	*vidame*
grand duke	marquess	viscount
grand seigneur	marquis	viscountess

---

noble *n, adj*
♦ *n*
aristocrat, peer, lord, lady, nobleman, noblewoman,
magnate
OLD grandee, atheling; (*Spenser*) douzeper
commoner
♦ *adj*
1 ARISTOCRATIC, high-born, titled, landed, high,
high-ranking patrician
OLD (*Spenser*) gent
COLLOQ. blue-blooded, born with a silver spoon in your
mouth

2 MAGNIFICENT, glorious, splendid, stately, generous,
dignified, distinguished, fine, eminent, grand, great,
exalted, lofty, honoured, honourable, venerated,
imposing impressive, majestic, illustrious
FORMAL magnanimous
3 VIRTUOUS, unselfish, honourable, worthy, excellent,
elevated, fine, gentle, generous, great-hearted,
self-sacrificing noble-minded, brave, gallant, manful
OLD handsome
FORMAL magnanimous
1 low-born, common **3** ignoble, base, contemptible

nobly *adv*
worthily, unselfishly, honourably, virtuously, gallantly,
manfully, bravely, generously
contemptibly

nobody *pron, n*
no one, nothing nonentity, menial, cipher, mediocrity;
Scot naebody
COLLOQ. lightweight
somebody

nocturnal *adj*
night, night-time, occurring at night, active at night

nod *v, n*
♦ *v*
1 GESTURE, indicate, sign, signal, salute, acknowledge,
beckon, beck, incline, dip, bow, nid-nod, noddle
FORMAL nutate
2 AGREE, approve, support, accept, say yes to
FORMAL assent
♦ *n*
gesture, indication, sign, signal, salute, greeting beck,
acknowledgement
■ **nod off**
sleep, fall asleep, doze (off), drop off, drowse, nap
FORMAL slumber
■ **give the nod to**
approve, agree to, assent to, consent to, allow, permit,
pass, sanction, authorize, mandate, ratify, validate,
endorse, support, hold with, uphold, second, back,
accept, adopt, carry, confirm
COLLOQ. give the go-ahead to, give the green light to,
greenlight, OK, rubber-stamp, give the thumbs-up to, buy

node *n*
swelling protuberance, lump, knob, knot, growth, bud,
bump, nodule, carbuncle, junction, convergence

noise *n, v*
♦ *n*
sound, din, racket, row, clamour, clash, clatter,
commotion, outcry, hubbub, uproar, cry, blare, talk,
pandemonium, tumult, babble
quiet, silence
♦ *v*
report, rumour, publicize, announce, circulate

noiseless *adj*
silent, inaudible, soundless, quiet, mute, still, soft, hushed
loud, noisy

noiselessly *adv*
silently, inaudibly, soundlessly, quietly, softly
noisily

noisily *adv*
loudly, deafeningly, resoundingly, tumultuously,
boisterously, rowdily, at the top of your voice
TECHNICAL fortissimo
FORMAL vociferously
COLLOQ. so loud you can't hear yourself think
quietly, softly

noisome *adj*
disgusting offensive, repulsive, disagreeable, obnoxious,
nauseating harmful, hurtful, injurious, pernicious, bad,
unhealthy, unwholesome, smelly, stinking foul, putrid,
reeking poisonous

FORMAL deleterious, f(o)etid, malodorous, mephitic, noxious, pestiferous, pestilential
🔄 balmy, pleasant, wholesome

noisy *adj*
booming roaring thundering loud, deafening blasting blaring ear-splitting clamorous, piercing vocal, tumultuous, rowdy, rackety, rumbustious, boisterous, obstreperous, turbulent
FORMAL vociferous
COLLOQ. so loud you can't hear yourself think
🔄 quiet, silent, peaceful

nomad *n*
traveller, wanderer, itinerant, transient, rambler, roamer, rover, migrant, vagabond, vagrant

nomadic *adj*
travelling itinerant, wandering roaming migrant, migratory, drifting roving Gypsy, unsettled, vagrant
FORMAL peregrinating peripatetic

nom-de-plume *n*
pseudonym, pen-name, assumed name, alias

nomenclature *n*
naming classification, vocabulary, terminology, phraseology
TECHNICAL taxonomy
FORMAL codification, locution

nominal *adj*
1 TITULAR, in name only, supposed, professed, ostensible, so-called, theoretical, formal, self-styled, puppet, symbolic
FORMAL purported
2 TOKEN, minimal, trifling trivial, insignificant, small, tiny, peppercorn, symbolic
🔄 1 actual, genuine, real

nominally *adv*
in name only, ostensibly, theoretically, symbolically, formally

nominate *v*
1 PROPOSE, designate, submit, suggest, recommend, present
COLLOQ. put up
2 APPOINT, choose, select, name, elect, assign, commission, elevate, term
TECHNICAL postulate, present
OLD voice

nomination *n*
1 PROPOSAL, submission, suggestion, recommendation
2 APPOINTMENT, choice, selection, designation, election

nominee *n*
candidate, entrant, contestant, appointee, runner, assignee

non-aligned *adj*
neutral, independent, impartial, non-partisan, uncommitted, undecided, uninvolved, disinterested

nonchalance *n*
calm, calmness, cool, composure, aplomb, equanimity, indifference, detachment, unconcern, self-possession
FORMAL imperturbability, insouciance, sangfroid, pococurant(e)ism
🔄 anxiousness, worriedness

nonchalant *adj*
unconcerned, detached, dispassionate, offhand, blasé, indifferent, casual, easy-going cool, calm, collected, apathetic, careless
FORMAL insouciant, imperturbable
COLLOQ. laid-back, cool and collected, cool as a cucumber
🔄 concerned, careful

non-combatant *adj, n*
♦ *adj*
non-fighting non-violent, non-belligerent, unaggressive, civilian, neutral, non-aligned, pacifist, conciliatory, peacemaking dovish
♦ *n*
pacifist, passive resister, conscientious objector
COLLOQ. conchie

non-committal *adj*
guarded, unrevealing cautious, wary, reserved, ambiguous, discreet, equivocal, evasive, careful, prudent, neutral, indefinite, tactful, diplomatic, tentative, vague
FORMAL circumspect, politic
COLLOQ. sitting on the fence, playing your cards close to your chest

non compos mentis *adj*
insane, mad, lunatic, unbalanced, psychotic, disturbed, deranged, maniacal, out of your mind, out of your senses, of unsound mind, unhinged, crazed, unstable, frenzied, wild, berserk, manic, maniac, distracted, distraught, fey, frenetic, frantic, stone-crazy, queer; *Scot* gyte, red-mad
OLD frantic-mad, lymphatic, bestraught
COLLOQ. crazy, demented, nuts, nutty, nutty as a fruitcake, wacky, mad as a hatter, barmy, bonkers, batty, cracked, crackers, dippy, daffy, dotty, loopy, potty, off your nut, off your head, wrong in the head, out of your head, off the wall, out to lunch, round the bend, round the twist, bats, having bats in the belfry, cuckoo, off the rails, screwy, up the wall, raving not all there; *N Am* buggy, flaky, fruity; *Aust & NZ* dingbats
SLANG loony, mental, bananas, barking wacko, doolally, off your rocker, off your chump, off your trolley, out of your tree, needing your head examined, having lost your marbles, having a screw loose, having a tile loose, having several cards short of a full deck, with one sandwich short of a picnic, meshuga, ape, apeshit; *N Am* gonzo, loco, wiggy
See Synonym nuances panel at **mad**.

nonconformist *n, adj*
♦ *n*
dissenter, rebel, individualist, dissident, radical, protester, heretic, iconoclast, eccentric, maverick, seceder, secessionist
FORMAL dissentient
COLLOQ. fish out of water, square peg in a round hole
🔄 conformist
♦ *adj*
rebel, dissident, unco-operative, radical, heretical, eccentric, individualist
FORMAL dissentient

nonconformity *n*
unconventionality, originality, eccentricity, dissent, deviation, heterodoxy, heresy, secession
🔄 conformity, conventionality

nondescript *adj*
featureless, indeterminate, undistinctive, undistinguished, indistinguishable, unexceptional, ordinary, commonplace, plain, dull, vague, bland, anaemic, insipid, uninspiring uninteresting unattractive, unremarkable, unclassified
COLLOQ. run of the mill, common or garden, vanilla, nothing much to write home about, no great shakes, not going to set the Thames on fire; *N Am* cookie-cutter
🔄 distinctive, remarkable

none *pron*
no one, not any, not one, not even one, not a single one, nothing nobody, not a soul, nil, zero
■ **none the ...**
no, not at all, to no extent, not a bit

nonentity *n*
nobody, nothing menial, cipher, mediocrity
COLLOQ. lightweight
🔄 somebody

non-essential *adj*
unnecessary, unimportant, superfluous, redundant, unneeded, inessential, peripheral, dispensable, excessive, extraneous, expendable, supplementary
🔄 essential, necessary

nonetheless *adv*
nevertheless, still, anyway, even so, yet, however, in spite of everything though, after all, by any means,

in any case/event, by some means, anyhow, but, regardless, for all that, all/just the same, at the same time
FORMAL notwithstanding

non-event n
anticlimax, comedown, let-down, disappointment, fiasco
COLLOQ. damp squib, not all that it was cracked up to be

non-existence n
unreality, fancy, illusion, illusiveness, insubstantiality, unbeing
FORMAL chimera
F₃ existence, reality

non-existent adj
missing unreal, null, legendary, mythical, fictitious, fictional, fancied, fanciful, hallucinatory, illusory, hypothetical, imaginary, imagined, fantasy, immaterial, insubstantial
FORMAL chimerical, incorporeal, suppositional
F₃ actual, existing real

non-flammable adj
not flammable, fireproof, fire-resistant, flame-resistant, incombustible, uninflammable
F₃ flammable, inflammable

non-intervention n
non-involvement, non-participation, non-alignment, non-interference, laissez-faire, inaction, inertia, passivity, apathy
COLLOQ. hands-off policy

nonpareil adj
unparalleled, incomparable, beyond compare, without equal, unequalled, matchless, unrivalled, unique, inimitable

non-partisan adj
unbiased, unprejudiced, impartial, independent, neutral, objective, even-handed, detached, dispassionate
F₃ partisan, biased, prejudiced

nonplus v
puzzle, perplex, take aback, stagger, baffle, bewilder, confound, confuse, dumbfound, stun, astonish, astound, dismay, embarrass, disconcert, mystify
FORMAL discomfit, discountenance
COLLOQ. stump, flabbergast, flummox, faze, sew up

nonplussed adj
disconcerted, confounded, taken aback, at a loss, stunned, bewildered, astonished, astounded, dumbfounded, perplexed, puzzled, baffled, dismayed, embarrassed, blank
COLLOQ. stumped, flabbergasted, flummoxed, fazed, floored, out of your depth

nonsense n
rubbish, trash, drivel, balderdash, gibberish, gobbledygook, senselessness, stupidity, silliness, foolishness, folly, twaddle, ridiculousness, codology, blague, doggerel; *dialect* faddle, havers; *dialect & N Am* blathers; *Scot* blethers, clamjamphrie
OLD galimatias
COLLOQ. stuff and nonsense, double Dutch, mumbo-jumbo, bunk, bunkum, claptrap, cobblers, poppycock, piffle, waffle, flannel, rot, tripe, tosh, bosh, tommyrot, codswallop, baloney, humbug hooey, bilge, bull, blah, eyewash, hogwash, rhubarb, guff, malarkey, moonshine
SLANG (*vulgar*) crap, cack, shit, balls, bollocks, bullshit; *N Am* jazz; *Aust & NZ* borak
F₃ sense, wisdom

> **QUOTATIONS**
> Natural rights is simple nonsense: natural and imprescriptable rights, rhetorical nonsense – nonsense upon stilts
> JEREMY BENTHAM, *Anarchical Fallacies*

nonsensical adj
ridiculous, meaningless, senseless, foolish, stupid, inane, irrational, silly, incomprehensible, unintelligible, gibberish, ludicrous, preposterous, absurd, fatuous

COLLOQ. crazy, crackpot, potty, nutty, dotty, barmy, hare-brained, wacky
F₃ reasonable, sensible, logical

non-stop adj, adv
♦ adj
never-ending uninterrupted, continuous, unceasing ceaseless, incessant, constant, endless, interminable, persistent, relentless, unending unbroken, without interruption, unfaltering round-the-clock, ongoing
F₃ intermittent, occasional
♦ adv
uninterruptedly, continuously, constantly, incessantly, unceasingly, ceaselessly, endlessly, interminably, unendingly, unbrokenly, round-the-clock, unfalteringly, steadily, relentlessly, unrelentingly, unremittingly
F₃ intermittently, occasionally

non-violent adj
peaceable, peaceful, pacifist, passive, dovish
FORMAL irenic
F₃ violent

nook n
1 RECESS, alcove, corner, cranny, niche, cubbyhole
2 SHELTER, retreat, hideout, hideaway, den, refuge, cavity, opening

noon n
midday, twelve o'clock, twelve p.m., twelve noon, lunchtime

norm n
average, mean, standard, rule, usual rule, pattern, type, criterion, gauge, model, yardstick, benchmark, touchstone, measure, scale, reference

normal adj
usual, standard, general, commonplace, common, ordinary, conventional, popular, average, regular, routine, everyday, accepted, typical, mainstream, natural, habitual, accustomed, well-adjusted, straight, rational, reasonable
COLLOQ. run of the mill, bog standard
F₃ abnormal, irregular, peculiar, deviant

normality n
usualness, commonness, ordinariness, regularity, routine, conventionality, balance, adjustment, averageness, typicality, naturalness, reason, reasonableness, rationality
FORMAL normalcy
F₃ abnormality, irregularity, peculiarity

normally adv
ordinarily, usually, as usual, as a rule, generally, typically, commonly, conventionally, characteristically, naturally, regularly, routinely
F₃ abnormally, exceptionally

northern adj
north, northerly, polar, Arctic
OLD septentrional
FORMAL boreal, hyperborean
F₃ southern

nose n, v
♦ n
1 the animal's nose
beak, bill, neb
FORMAL proboscis
COLLOQ. boko, hooter, snitch, snout, snoot
SLANG conk, schnozzle, schnoz
Related adjectives: nasal, rhinal
2 a nose for a good story
sense, flair, feel, perception, instinct
♦ v
nudge, inch, edge, ease, move slowly, push
■ **nose around**
poke around, search, pry
COLLOQ. snoop, rubberneck, poke your nose in
■ **nose out**
discover, detect, find out, uncover, reveal, inquire
COLLOQ. sniff out

■ **get up your nose**
irritate, rile, displease, anger, vex, irk, madden, exasperate, tease, provoke, ruffle, gall, trouble, nag disturb, bother, pester, plague, harass, molest; *Scot* fash
COLLOQ. aggravate, bug wind up, hassle, rub up the wrong way, get your blood up, make your blood boil, get on your nerves, get under your skin, get your goat, get on your wick, drive crazy/nuts, drive bananas, drive up the wall, drive round the bend/twist, get your back up, brass off, cheese off, make your hackles rise, make sparks fly, give you the hump, get your dander up; *N Am* tick/hack off
F3 please, gratify, comfort

■ **poke your nose into**
interfere, intervene, pry, intrude, butt in, tamper
COLLOQ. fiddle, stick your nose into, stick/put your oar in, snoop

■ **under your nose**
in front of you, right in front of you, plainly, obviously, clearly, staring you right in the face, plain to see, plain as a pikestaff, for all to see

PROVERBS
Don't cut off your nose to spite your face

nosedive *v, n*
♦ *v*
plummet, dive, drop, plunge, decline, get worse, go down, submerge, swoop
♦ *n*
plummet, dive, drop, plunge, swoop, header, purler

nosegay *n*
bouquet, posy, spray, bunch

nosey, nosy *adj*
inquisitive, meddlesome, prying interfering curious, eavesdropping probing
COLLOQ. snooping

nosh *n*
food, foodstuffs, comestibles, provisions, meals, stores, rations, refreshments, sustenance, nourishment, nutrition, nutriment, subsistence, feed, fodder, diet, fare, dish, speciality, delicacy, cooking cuisine, menu, board, table
FORMAL viands, victuals
COLLOQ. eatables, eats, tuck, scran
SLANG grub

nosiness *n*
inquisitiveness, curiousness, meddlesomeness, interference, intrusiveness, prying
COLLOQ. snooping

nostalgia *n*
yearning longing wistfulness, regretfulness, regret(s), remembrance, recollection(s), reminiscence(s), homesickness, pining *mal du pays*

nostalgic *adj*
yearning longing pining wistful, emotional, regretful, sentimental, homesick, reminiscent

nostrum *n*
medicine, pill, drug potion, cure, remedy, elixir, panacea, cure-all, cure for all ills, universal cure/remedy

notability *n*
1 NOTEWORTHINESS, impressiveness, importance, significance, distinction, fame, eminence, esteem, renown, observableness
2 CELEBRITY, dignitary, magnate, worthy, luminary
FORMAL notable, personage
COLLOQ. somebody, VIP, bigwig big shot, big noise, big cheese, heavyweight, top brass, someone, celeb
F3 nonentity

notable *adj, n*
♦ *adj*
noteworthy, remarkable, noticeable, observable, particular, striking extraordinary, signal, impressive, outstanding special, important, significant, marked, unusual,
uncommon, celebrated, distinguished, famous, great, illustrious, eminent, pre-eminent, well-known, momentous, notorious, memorable, renowned, unforgettable, rare
F3 ordinary, commonplace, usual
♦ *n*
celebrity, notability, personage, dignitary, luminary, star, worthy
COLLOQ. somebody, VIP, bigwig big shot, big noise, big cheese, heavyweight, top brass, someone, celeb
F3 nobody, nonentity

notably *adv*
markedly, noticeably, particularly, in particular, significantly, remarkably, strikingly, signally, conspicuously, distinctly, especially, impressively, outstandingly, extraordinarily, eminently, uncommonly

notation *n*
symbols, characters, code, cipher, signs, alphabet, system, script, hieroglyphics, noting record, shorthand

notch *n, v*
♦ *n*
1 CUT, nick, indentation, incision, dent, indent, score, groove, gouge, cleft, gash, scratch, mark, snip, nail-hole, nock, hack, jag kerf
TECHNICAL joggle, sinus, swan-mark
FORMAL crena, insection
2 DEGREE, grade, step, level, stage
♦ *v*
cut, nick, score, dent, gouge, groove, indent, mark, gash, scratch, serrate, tally, vandyke, nock, raffle; *dialect* gap, gimp; *Scot* lip, mush
■ **notch up**
achieve, gain, attain, make, score, record, register
COLLOQ. chalk up

notched *adj*
jagged, jaggy, pinked, serrate(d), serrulate(d), eroded
TECHNICAL emarginate
FORMAL crenellate(d), erose

note *n, v*
♦ *n*
1 MESSAGE, letter, communication, memorandum, reminder, line, jotting account, record, entry, comment, email
FORMAL epistle, missive
COLLOQ. memo
2 ANNOTATION, comment, commentary, explanation, gloss, footnote, remark
FORMAL explication, marginalia
3 INDICATION, signal, element, tone, inflection, token, mark, symbol
4 EMINENCE, distinction, importance, significance, consequence, fame, renown, greatness, illustriousness, reputation, pre-eminence, prestige
5 HEED, attention, attentiveness, care, mindfulness, regard, notice, observation, consideration
♦ *v*
1 NOTICE, observe, perceive, become aware of, heed, detect, mark, remark, mention, allude to, refer to, touch on, see, witness
2 RECORD, register, log write down, mark, enter, put in writing put down, jot down

notebook *n*
notepad, pocket-book, exercise book, jotter, logbook, log record, diary, journal, daybook, address book, table-book, field book, *cahier*, *index rerum*

noted *adj*
famous, well-known, renowned, notable, celebrated, eminent, pre-eminent, prominent, great, of note, acclaimed, illustrious, distinguished, respected, recognized
F3 obscure, unknown

notes *n*
jottings, record, impressions, report, commentary, sketch, outline, synopsis, transcript, minutes, draft

noteworthy *adj*
remarkable, significant, important, notable, memorable, striking exceptional, impressive, extraordinary, unusual, outstanding marked
F∃ commonplace, unexceptional, ordinary

nothing *n*
1 NOUGHT, zero, not a thing naught, nothingness; *dialect* nowt; *Scot* naething; *S Afr* nix-nie
COLLOQ. zilch, nil, sweet Fanny Adams, sweet FA; diddly-squat, squat
SLANG bugger all, sod all; *(taboo)* fuck all
2 NON-EXISTENCE, emptiness, void, vacuum, oblivion
FORMAL nullity
3 NOBODY, nonentity, menial, cipher, mediocrity
COLLOQ. lightweight
F∃ something
■ **nothing but**
only, simply, just, merely, solely, exclusively
■ **for nothing**
1 FREE, gratis, without charge, free of charge, at no cost, complimentary
COLLOQ. on the house
2 IN VAIN, unsuccessfully, futilely, needlessly, with no result, to no avail

> **PROVERBS**
> Nothing ventured, nothing gained

nothingness *n*
non-existence, oblivion, vacuum, void, emptiness
FORMAL nihilism, nihility, nullity
F∃ life, existence

notice *v, n*
◆ *v*
note, remark, perceive, observe, mind, see, discern, distinguish, make out, mark, detect, spot, become aware of, take note of, pay attention to
FORMAL heed, take heed of, behold, espy
F∃ ignore, overlook, miss
◆ *n*
1 ANNOUNCEMENT, notification, information, declaration, communication, intimation, intelligence, news, warning, instruction, advice, order
COLLOQ. heads-up
FORMAL apprisal
2 ADVERTISEMENT, ad, poster, sign, bill, handbill, bulletin, leaflet, pamphlet, circular, information sheet
3 REVIEW, comment, criticism, critique, write-up
COLLOQ. crit
4 ATTENTION, observation, awareness, note, regard, thought, interest, watchfulness, consideration
FORMAL heed, cognizance
■ **give/hand in your notice**
quit, leave, resign, stand down, step down, walk out
COLLOQ. chuck/pack in your job
■ **give someone notice**
fire, dismiss, discharge, eject, get rid of
COLLOQ. sack, axe, boot out, kick out, show someone the door, give someone their cards/jotters, give someone the sack/push/boot/elbow

noticeable *adj*
perceptible, observable, appreciable, unmistakable, conspicuous, visible, discernible, evident, clear, distinct, significant, striking plain, patent, obvious, manifest, marked, pronounced, bold, notable, predominant, detectable, distinguishable, measurable, impressive, powerful
COLLOQ. sticking out like a sore thumb
F∃ inconspicuous, unnoticeable

noticeably *adv*
perceptibly, unmistakably, evidently, clearly, distinctly, significantly, strikingly, plainly, patently, obviously, notably, conspicuously, visibly, discernibly

notification *n*
announcement, information, notice, declaration, advice, warning telling informing intelligence, message, publication, statement, communication, divulgence, disclosure

notify *v*
inform, tell, make known, advise, announce, declare, communicate, broadcast, warn, acquaint, caution, alert, publish, disclose, reveal, divulge
FORMAL apprise

notion *n*
1 IDEA, thought, concept, conception, belief, impression, view, opinion, conviction, theory, hypothesis, assumption, understanding apprehension
FORMAL conceptualization
2 INCLINATION, desire, wish, impulse, whim, fancy, caprice

notional *adj*
theoretical, abstract, imaginary, hypothetical, illusory, conceptual, speculative, fanciful, fancied, unfounded, unreal, visionary, thematic, classificatory
FORMAL ideational
F∃ real

notionally *adv*
theoretically, in theory, hypothetically, conceptually
FORMAL conjecturally, putatively

notoriety *n*
infamy, disrepute, dishonour, disgrace, scandal
FORMAL ignominy, obloquy, opprobrium

notorious *adj*
infamous, disreputable, scandalous, dishonourable, ill-famed, of ill repute, disgraceful, flagrant, blatant, noted, glaring well-known, proverbial, arrant
TECHNICAL *Scot* notous
FORMAL ignominious, egregious, opprobrious

> **QUOTATIONS**
> If you can't be famous, at least you can be notorious
> MOHAMAD MAHATHIR

notoriously *adv*
infamously, disreputably, scandalously, dishonourably, disgracefully, flagrantly, blatantly, glaringly, overtly, notably, obviously, openly, particularly, patently, arrantly, spectacularly
FORMAL egregiously, opprobriously, ignominiously

notwithstanding *adv, prep*
nevertheless, nonetheless, although, though, even so, however, yet, despite, in spite of, regardless of

nought *n*
zero, nil, naught, nothing nothingness
COLLOQ. zilch

nourish *v*
1 NURTURE, feed, foster, care for, provide for, take care of, sustain, support, attend to, tend, nurse, bring up, rear, maintain, have, cherish
2 STRENGTHEN, encourage, promote, cultivate, stimulate, foster, further, forward, advance, boost, help, aid, assist

nourishing *adj*
nutritious, wholesome, healthful, health-giving good, beneficial, substantial, strengthening invigorating
TECHNICAL alimentative
FORMAL nutritive

nourishment *n*
nutrition, food, sustenance, diet, nutriment, subsistence
TECHNICAL ingesta
OLD aliment, nouriture, pabulum
COLLOQ. eats, tuck, scran
SLANG grub, nosh

nouveaux riches *n*
the new rich, upstarts, parvenus, arrivistes

novel *adj, n*
♦ *adj*
new, original, fresh, innovative, unfamiliar, unique, rare, unusual, uncommon, different, creative, imaginative, resourceful, ingenious, inventive, unconventional, unorthodox, modern, unprecedented, pioneering ground-breaking strange
See Synonym nuances panel at **new**.
E3 hackneyed, familiar, ordinary
♦ *n*
story, tale, narrative, romance, book, paperback, hardback, fiction

novelist *n*
writer, author, storyteller, man/woman of letters, creative writer, fabler, fiction writer

novelty *n*
1 NEWNESS, originality, freshness, innovation, unfamiliarity, unusualness, uniqueness, rareness, difference, creativity, imaginativeness, unconventionality, strangeness
2 GIMMICK, gadget, trifle, memento, knick-knack, curiosity, souvenir, trinket, bauble, gimcrack

novice *n*
beginner, tiro, learner, student, pupil, trainee, probationer, recruit, raw recruit, apprentice, amateur, newcomer
FORMAL acolyte, neophyte, noviciate
COLLOQ. greenhorn, rookie, newbie, noob
E3 expert

noviciate *n*
novitiate, apprenticeship, trainee period, training initiation, probationary period, trial period

now *adv*
1 AT PRESENT, right now, just now, at the moment, for the time being at the present time, at this moment in time, at this time, currently, nowadays, today, these days; *N Am* presently
2 IMMEDIATELY, at once, directly, instantly, straight away, right away, promptly, without delay, next
■ **now and then**
at times, sometimes, from time to time, now and again, occasionally, on and off, on occasion, once in a while, periodically, infrequently, fitfully, intermittently, spasmodically, sporadically
FORMAL desultorily

nowadays *adv*
at present, today, at the present time, at the moment, at this moment in time, at this time, currently, these days, in this day and age; *N Am* presently

noxious *adj*
harmful, poisonous, pernicious, toxic, injurious, unhealthy, deadly, destructive, ruinous, damaging detrimental, malignant, foul, disgusting threatening menacing
FORMAL noisome, deleterious
E3 innocuous, wholesome

nozzle *n*
sprinkler, sprinkler head, rose, sprayer, jet, nose, sparger, adjutage, twyer; *Scot* stroup

nuance *n*
subtlety, suggestion, shade, shading hint, suspicion, gradation, (fine) distinction, overtone, refinement, touch, trace, tinge, degree, nicety

> **QUOTATIONS**
> No colour, only nuance!
> PAUL VERLAINE, *Jadis et naguère*, 'Art poétique'

nub *n*
centre, central point, heart, core, nucleus, kernel, crux, gist, pith, marrow, meat, pivot, focus, point, essence

nubile *adj*
mature, adult, marriageable, attractive, desirable, voluptuous
COLLOQ. sexy

nucleus *n*
centre, heart, nub, core, kernel, basis, marrow, meat, pivot, focus, crux

nude *adj*
naked, bare, with nothing on, undressed, unclothed, uncovered, exposed, stripped, disrobed, denuded, raw, mother-naked, Adamic, skyclad, undraped, *in puris naturalibus*; *dialect* start-naked; *Scot* in the scud
COLLOQ. in the altogether, starkers, in your birthday suit, in the raw, in the buff, not a stitch on, naked as the day you were born
SLANG bollock-naked
E3 clothed, dressed

nudge *v, n*
poke, prod, jab, shove, dig jog prompt, push, elbow, bump; *Scot* dunch, dunsh

nudity *n*
nakedness, bareness, undress, state of undress, nudism, dishabille, *déshabillé*
COLLOQ. in the altogether

nugatory *adj*
worthless, futile, useless, vain, valueless, unavailing null and void, invalid, inoperative, insignificant, negligible, inconsequential, trifling trivial, inadequate
FORMAL ineffectual
E3 important, significant

nugget *n*
lump, mass, piece, chunk, clump, hunk, wad, wodge

nuisance *n*
annoyance, inconvenience, bother, irritation, irritant, vexation, pest, bore, difficulty, problem, trial, trouble, weight, burden, plague, drawback
FORMAL affliction, tribulation
COLLOQ. pain, drag thorn in your side/flesh
SLANG chizz; *N Am* hoop

null *adj*
void, invalid, invalidated, annulled, revoked, cancelled, useless, vain, worthless, powerless, inoperative
FORMAL ineffectual, nullified, abrogated
E3 valid

nullify *v*
annul, revoke, cancel, invalidate, declare null and void, abolish, rescind, quash, repeal, void, set aside, bring to an end, reverse, offset, counteract
FORMAL abrogate, negate, countermand, renounce, discontinue
E3 validate

nullity *n*
non-existence, voidness, characterlessness, immateriality, invalidity, powerlessness, uselessness, worthlessness
FORMAL incorporeality, ineffectualness
E3 validity

numb *adj, v*
♦ *adj*
benumbed, insensible, unfeeling dead, deadened, insensitive, without feeling sleeping drugged, anaesthetized, stunned, dazed, frozen, paralysed, immobilized, in shock
FORMAL insensate, torpid
E3 sensitive
♦ *v*
deaden, benumb, anaesthetize, drug freeze, immobilize, paralyse, dull, daze, stupefy, stun
FORMAL torpefy
E3 sensitize

number *n, v*
♦ *n*
1 FIGURE, numeral, digit, integer, unit, character, cipher, fraction, decimal, statistics, data
2 TOTAL, sum, aggregate, tally, score, count, collection, amount, quantity, several, many, company, crowd, group, multitude, throng horde

3 COPY, issue, edition, impression, imprint, volume, printing
4 PIECE OF MUSIC, song dance, item, track, turn, act, sketch, routine, performance
♦ v
1 COUNT, calculate, enumerate, reckon, total, add (up to), compute, estimate, include
2 *your days are numbered*
limit, restrict, restrain, delimit, specify

numberless *adj*
innumerable, countless, endless, uncounted, without number, many, unnumbered, unsummed, infinite, untold, myriad, immeasurable
FORMAL multitudinous

numbness *n*
deadness, paralysis, anaesthetization, unfeelingness, dullness, insensitivity, stupefaction, stupor, torpor
FORMAL insensateness, insensibility
F∃ sensitivity

numeral *n*
number, figure, digit, integer, unit, character, cipher

numerical *adj*
integral, digital, whole, figural, computational, statistical, in numerical order, ranked, graded, hierarchical

numerically *adv*
arithmetically, algebraically, digitally, mathematically, in numerical order, in ascending order, in order, measurably, quantifiably, exponentially

numerous *adj*
many, innumerable, countless, endless, abundant, several, great (in number), strong quite a few, a lot of, legion, plentiful, copious, profuse, various, sundry
OLD (*Shakesp*) populous
FORMAL manifold, multitudinous
COLLOQ. a good few
F∃ few, scarce, rare

numerousness *n*
plentifulness, abundance, copiousness, countlessness, plurality, profusion
FORMAL manifoldness, multiplicity, multitudinousness, multeity
F∃ scantiness, scarcity

numinous *adj*
spiritual, mystical, supernatural, religious, holy, sacred, divine, transcendent, mysterious

numskull *n*
fool, dimwit, dunce, simpleton
COLLOQ. nincompoop, ass, chump, ninny, neddy, clot, dope, twit, nitwit, nit, sucker, mug twerp, birdbrain, silly-billy, berk, (proper) Charlie, gubbins, sap, saphead, wazzock, dum-dum, coot, goat, headbanger; *Scot* bampot; *N Am* lunkhead, chowderhead, putz, doofus; *Aust* dill, boofhead
SLANG wally, jerk, dumbo, pillock, prat, dork, geek, plonker, git, nerd, dweeb, nerk, goop, josser, nig-nog sawney, schlemiel, turkey, yo-yo, cloth head, dipstick, muppet, goof, kook, tosspot; (*taboo*) prick, dickhead; *N Am* jughead, schmo, dingbat; *Aust* galah, nana; *Aust & NZ* nong

nun *n*
sister, abbess, prioress, mother superior, anchoress, ancress, canoness, vestal, deaconess, religieuse, conventual, zelatrix
OLD vowess; (*Shakesp*) cloistress

nuncio *n*
representative, envoy, ambassador, legate

nunnery *n*
convent, priory, cloister, abbey

nuptial *adj*
wedding wedded, marital, bridal
FORMAL matrimonial, conjugal, connubial, hymeneal, epithalamial, epithalamic

nuptials *n*
wedding celebrations, wedding marriage, bridal
FORMAL matrimony, spousals, espousal

nurse *v*
1 TEND, care for, look after, treat, attend to, take care of, cradle
2 BREAST-FEED, feed, suckle, wet-nurse, nurture, nourish
3 PRESERVE, sustain, support, nourish, cherish, harbour, entertain, encourage, keep, foster, boost, promote, advance, further, nurture, help, aid, assist

---

Nurses include:

auxiliary nurse	matron	Registered General
charge nurse	midwife	Nurse (RGN)
children's nurse	nanny	school nurse
community nurse	night nurse	sicknurse
dental nurse	night sister	sister
district nurse	nurse consultant	staff nurse
dry-nurse	nursemaid	State Enrolled
healthcare	nurse practitioner	Nurse (SEN)
assistant	nursery nurse	State Registered
health visitor	nurse tutor	Nurse (SRN)
home nurse	occupational	theatre sister
Iain Rennie nurse	health nurse	ward sister
locality manager	psychiatric nurse	wet nurse
Macmillan nurse		

---

nurture *n, v*
♦ n
1 FOOD, nourishment, nutrition, sustenance, diet, subsistence, nouriture
COLLOQ. eats, tuck, scran
SLANG grub, nosh
2 REARING, upbringing training care, cultivation, stimulation, encouragement, fostering promotion, help, aid, assistance, furtherance, advance, boosting development, education, tending feeding schooling discipline
FORMAL nouriture
♦ v
1 FEED, nourish, nurse, tend, care for, foster, support, sustain, cherish
2 BRING UP, rear, cultivate, develop, stimulate, promote, foster, help, aid, assist, further, advance, boost, educate, instruct, train, school, coach, tutor, discipline

nut *n*
1 *a bag of mixed nuts*
kernel, pip, seed, stone
2 MANIAC, insane person, lunatic, psychopath, madman, madwoman
COLLOQ. oddball, nutcase, nutter, fruitcake, crackpot, crank, headcase, basket-case
SLANG loony, psycho, screwball
3 ENTHUSIAST, fan, fanatic, follower, supporter, devotee, zealot, admirer
FORMAL aficionado
COLLOQ. buff, freak, fiend
■ **do your nut**
explode, blow up, blow a fuse, blow your top/cool, boil over, burst a blood vessel, flip your lid, fly into a rage, fly off the handle, foam at the mouth, freak out, go ballistic, go berserk, go mad, go off the deep end, go up the wall, have kittens, hit the ceiling lose your cool, lose your rag lose it, raise hell, see red, throw a tantrum/wobbly

---

Varieties of nut include:

almond	coconut	peanut (or
beech nut	filbert	groundnut)
brazil nut	hazelnut	pecan
cashew	macadamia	pine nut
chestnut	monkey nut	pistachio
cobnut		walnut

nutriment *n*
food, nourishment, nutrition, sustenance, diet, subsistence
COLLOQ. eats, tuck, scran
SLANG grub, nosh

nutrition *n*
food, nourishment, sustenance, diet, nutriment, subsistence
TECHNICAL eutrophy
COLLOQ. eats, tuck, scran
SLANG grub, nosh
Related adjective: trophic

nutritious *adj*
nourishing wholesome, healthful, health-giving good, beneficial, strengthening body-building substantial, sustaining invigorating
FORMAL nutritive
E₃ bad, unwholesome

nuts *adj*
1 MAD, crazy, insane, lunatic, unbalanced, disturbed, deranged, demented, crazed, wild, berserk, unhinged, out of your mind
COLLOQ. loopy, bonkers, barmy, batty, dippy, daffy, potty, nutty, nutty as a fruitcake, out to lunch, round the bend, round the twist
SLANG loony, doolally, with one sandwich short of a picnic, off your rocker, off your trolley

2 *nuts about computers*
crazy, enthusiastic, fanatical, zealous, devoted, fond, keen, avid, ardent, passionate, infatuated, enamoured, smitten, mad, wild
COLLOQ. daft, potty
E₃ 1 sane **2** indifferent

nuts and bolts *n*
basics, essentials, fundamentals, details, components, bits and pieces, practicalities
COLLOQ. nitty-gritty

nutty *adj*
mad, crazy, insane, lunatic, unbalanced, disturbed, deranged, demented, crazed, wild, berserk, unhinged, out of your mind
COLLOQ. loopy, bonkers, barmy, batty, dippy, daffy, potty, nuts, nutty as a fruitcake, out to lunch, round the bend, round the twist
SLANG loony, doolally, with one sandwich short of a picnic, off your rocker, off your trolley

nuzzle *v*
snuggle, cuddle, pet, nestle, fondle, nudge, nose, burrow

nymph *n*
sprite, sylph, dryad, hamadryad, naiad, oread, maelid, mermaid, oceanid, undine, girl, damsel, lass, maid, maiden, houri, Tethys

o

oaf *n*
lout, boor, dolt, yahoo, barbarian, gawk, lubber
COLLOQ. clod, clodhopper, hick, hobbledehoy, slob, yobbo, bumpkin, oik; *N Am* roughneck; *Aust* hoon

oafish *adj*
boorish, churlish, doltish, lumpish, lubberly, stolid, swinish, uncouth, unmannerly, bungling rough, coarse, gross, ill-bred, ill-mannered, gawky, lumpen
COLLOQ. clodhopping yobbish

oar *n*
paddle, scull, blade, spoon, sweep, bow-oar, stroke oar, stroke

oasis *n*
1 SPRING, watering-hole
2 REFUGE, haven, island, sanctuary, retreat, hideaway, hideout
FORMAL sanctum

oath *n*
1 VOW, pledge, promise, bond, word, assurance, affirmation, word of honour
FORMAL avowal, attestation
2 CURSE, swear-word, obscenity, profanity, expletive, bad language, blasphemy; *N Am* curse-word
FORMAL imprecation
COLLOQ. four-letter word
SLANG cuss; *N Am* cussword

obduracy *n*
obstinacy, stubbornness, inflexibility, hard-heartedness, persistence, perseverance, resoluteness, tenacity, wilfulness, wrongheadedness, perversity, firmness, doggedness, relentlessness, mulishness
FORMAL frowardness, intransigence, pertinacity
COLLOQ. pigheadedness
EA co-operativeness, flexibility, submissiveness

obdurate *adj*
obstinate, stubborn, inflexible, hard-hearted, implacable, iron, stiff-necked, stony, unfeeling immovable, unyielding unbending unrelenting persistent, dogged, headstrong strong-minded, self-willed, steadfast, firm, determined, adamant, wilful
FORMAL intractable, intransigent
COLLOQ. pigheaded, bloody-minded
EA submissive, tender

obedience *n*
submissiveness, submission, respect, reverence, amenableness, amenability, malleability, allegiance, conformability, compliance, accordance, agreement, deference, duty, dutifulness, passivity, subservience, observance, docility
FORMAL acquiescence, tractability
EA disobedience, rebellion

obedient *adj*
submissive, docile, yielding conforming pliable, compliant, malleable, amenable, dutiful, duteous, biddable, law-abiding deferential, respectful, well-trained, disciplined, subservient, observant; *N Am* bridle-wise
OLD (*Spenser*) bent
FORMAL acquiescent, tractable, obsequious
EA disobedient, rebellious, wilful

Submissive and **yielding** can be used of someone who habitually gives in to others, and have negative suggestions of weakness, whereas **docile** implies a willingness to comply, and is more connotative of gentleness. **Conforming**, which has more to do with falling in with the plans of others, is not so marked by approval or disapproval.

The terms **pliable**, **malleable** and **biddable** again have implications of weakness making someone suggestible to whatever is proposed, while **amenable** is suggestive of not being obstructive, and is more positive in tone: *he was quite amenable to her suggestion*.

Both **dutiful** and the less common **duteous** are suggestive of strict obligations of responsibility and also tend to convey approval, as does **law-abiding**. **Deferential**, on the other hand, has more to do with humbly resigning yourself to the wishes of others and has overtones of criticism: *the prince's fawning and deferential friends*, and **subservient** echoes this idea of ingratiating humility.

While **respectful** is similar, it suggests a less extreme aspect and perhaps a more admirable quality. **Observant** is more suggestive of careful adherence to ritual, especially with regard to religion: *I married a traditional, observant Jew.*

obeisance *n*
respect, reverence, submission, deference, homage, bow, curtsy, kowtow, salaam, salute
FORMAL genuflection, salutation, veneration

obelisk *n*
pillar, column, monument, memorial, needle

obese *adj*
fat, overweight, tubby, stout, big large, portly, fleshy, round, well-endowed, paunchy, ponderous, plump, podgy, chubby, roly-poly, heavy, bulky, outsize, Falstaffian
FORMAL corpulent, rotund
COLLOQ. gross, flabby, beefy, porky, well-upholstered
EA skinny, slender, thin

obesity *n*
fatness, overweight, stoutness, plumpness, portliness, chubbiness, podginess, tubbiness, bulk
FORMAL corpulence, rotundity
COLLOQ. grossness, flabbiness
EA thinness, slenderness, skinniness

obey *v*
1 *obey an order*
follow, observe, abide by, adhere to, conform, comply, consent to, heed, keep (to), mind, respond, submit, surrender, yield, be ruled by, bow to, take orders from, do as you are told, defer (to), respect, give way
FORMAL acquiesce in
COLLOQ. stick to the rules, go by the book, toe the line

2 CARRY OUT, discharge, execute, act upon, fulfil, perform
E3 1 disobey

obfuscate v
obscure, cover, blur, confuse, muddle, complicate, conceal, cloud, hide, disguise, mask, overshadow, shadow, shade, cloak, veil, shroud
E3 clarify

obfuscation n
confusion, muddle, obscurity, concealment, complication, disguise
E3 clarification

obituary n
death notice, eulogy
OLD necrology
COLLOQ. obit

object¹ n
1 THING, article, item, entity, body, something device, gadget, artefact, phenomenon
2 AIM, objective, purpose, goal, target, intention, point, idea, motive, end, reason, ambition, design
FORMAL intent
3 TARGET, focus, recipient, butt, victim

object² v
object to something
protest, oppose, take exception, disapprove, refuse, complain, rebut, repudiate, withstand, resist, argue, challenge, beg to differ, take issue, take a stand against, cavil, jib
OLD recuse
FORMAL demur, expostulate, remonstrate, recalcitrate
E3 agree, approve; *formal* acquiesce, accede, assent

objection n
protest, dissent, disapproval, opposition, complaint, dissatisfaction, argument, challenge, grievance, scruple, difficulty, question, exception, but, boggle, cavil
TECHNICAL recusation
OLD quarrel
FORMAL demur, expostulation, remonstration, recalcitrance
E3 agreement, approval, assent

objectionable adj
unacceptable, unpleasant, offensive, obnoxious, disagreeable, hateful, detestable, deplorable, despicable, contemptible, intolerable, loathsome, abhorrent, revolting repugnant, repellent, repulsive, nauseating sickening
FORMAL reprehensible
E3 acceptable, pleasant, delightful

objective adj, n
♦ adj
1 IMPARTIAL, unbiased, detached, unprejudiced, open-minded, equitable, dispassionate, even-handed, neutral, disinterested, uninvolved, just, fair
2 *objective information*
factual, real, true, actual, authentic, genuine
E3 1 subjective
♦ n
object, aim, goal, end, purpose, ambition, mark, target, intention, point, idea, design
FORMAL intent

objectively adv
impartially, equitably, dispassionately, disinterestedly, even-handedly, neutrally, justly, fairly, with an open mind

objectivity n
impartiality, detachment, disinterest, disinterestedness, equitableness, even-handedness, justness, justice, fairness, open-mindedness, open mind
E3 subjectivity, bias, prejudice

objector n
protester, demonstrator, opposer, opponent, complainer, agitator, striker, rebel, dissident, dissenter

obligate v
oblige, compel, constrain, coerce, require, make, necessitate, force, impel, pressurize, pressure, press, bind

obligation n
duty, responsibility, onus, charge, task, function, assignment, job, commitment, tie, liability, accountability, requirement, agreement, bond, deed, covenant, contract, debt, indebtedness, burden, trust, compulsion, demand, command, pressure, duress

obligatory adj
1 COMPULSORY, statutory, required, binding essential, necessary, unavoidable, enforced
FORMAL mandatory, imperative, requisite
2 CUSTOMARY, traditional, conventional, accepted, established, set, habitual, routine, regular, usual, normal, ordinary, familiar, fashionable
E3 1 optional

oblige v
1 COMPEL, constrain, coerce, require, make, necessitate, force, impel, pressurize, pressure, press, bind, tie, leave/be given no option
OLD astringe
FORMAL obligate
2 HELP, assist, accommodate, do someone a favour, serve, do someone a service, put yourself out for, gratify, please

obliged adj
under an obligation, indebted, in debt (to), grateful, thankful, gratified, appreciative, bound, forced, compelled, constrained, duty-bound, honour-bound, required, having (got) to, under compulsion
OLD debted
FORMAL obligated, beholden

obliging adj
accommodating co-operative, helpful, considerate, willing generous, pleasant, agreeable, friendly, kind, good-natured, polite, courteous, civil, indulgent
OLD officious
FORMAL complaisant
E3 unhelpful, unkind, rude

obligingly adv
helpfully, considerately, willingly, generously, agreeably, politely, courteously, civilly
E3 unhelpfully, rudely

oblique adj, n
♦ adj
1 SLANTING, sloping inclined, angled, skew, cross, sidelong sideways, squint, traverse, tilted
TECHNICAL bevelled
OLD awkward
COLLOQ. skew-whiff
2 INDIRECT, roundabout, circuitous, divergent, devious, rambling winding meandering zigzag tortuous, discursive
FORMAL periphrastic, circumlocutory
E3 2 direct
♦ n
diagonal, slant, slash, forward slash, stroke, solidus
FORMAL virgule

obliquely adv
1 DIAGONALLY, at an angle, aslant, aslope, askance, askant, slantwise, askew
2 INDIRECTLY, in a roundabout way, circuitously, evasively, not in so many words
E3 2 directly

obliterate v
eradicate, destroy, eliminate, annihilate, strike out, delete, blot out, wipe out, rub out, erase
FORMAL efface, expunge, extirpate

obliteration n
eradication, destruction, elimination, annihilation, blotting out, deletion, erasure
FORMAL effacement, expunction, extirpation

oblivion *n*
1 UNCONSCIOUSNESS, blankness, darkness, stupor, void, limbo, inattentiveness, unmindfulness, absent-mindedness, carelessness, blindness, deafness, ignorance
FORMAL insensibility, Lethe
2 OBSCURITY, nothingness, non-existence, disuse
Ea 1 awareness
Related adjective: lethean

oblivious *adj*
unaware, unconscious, inattentive, unmindful, preoccupied, absent-minded, careless, forgetful, heedless, unheeding blind, deaf, ignorant, negligent, unconcerned
FORMAL insensible
Ea aware, conscious

obliviousness *n*
ignorance, unintelligence, illiteracy, unawareness, unconsciousness, unfamiliarity, inexperience, innocence, naivety, stupidity
COLLOQ. greenness, thickness

obloquy *n*
disgrace, dishonour, discredit, disfavour, shame, reproach, humiliation, criticism, attack, abuse, blame, censure, defamation, slander, detraction, bad press
FORMAL animadversion, aspersion, calumny, contumely, ignominy, invective, odium, opprobrium, stigma, vilification

obnoxious *adj*
unpleasant, disagreeable, disgusting offensive, objectionable, unacceptable, loathsome, nasty, horrid, horrible, odious, vile, repulsive, repugnant, repellent, revolting sickening nauseating hateful, detestable, abhorrent, contemptible, deplorable, intolerable
Ea pleasant

obscene *adj*
1 INDECENT, rude, improper, immoral, immodest, shameless, unchaste, impure, coarse, vulgar, filthy, dirty, foul, gross, vile, bawdy, fruity, lewd, licentious, X-rated, pornographic, hard-core, scurrilous, suggestive, sexy, risqué, smutty, disgusting nasty, greasy
OLD paw, pawpaw
FORMAL carnal, lubricious, prurient
COLLOQ. blue, near the knuckle/bone, raunchy, sleazy, off-colour
2 SHOCKING, shameless, offensive, outrageous, disgraceful, immoral, scandalous
Ea 1 decent, wholesome

obscenity *n*
1 INDECENCY, immodesty, immorality, impurity, impropriety, unchasteness, lewdness, licentiousness, bawdiness, suggestiveness, eroticism, pornography, dirt, dirtiness, filth, filthiness, foulness, coarseness, grossness, indelicacy, vulgarity, shamelessness, scurrilousness, salaciousness, lasciviousness, ribaldry, scatology; *dialect* balderdash
FORMAL carnality, prurience, lubricity
COLLOQ. raunchiness, sleaze, smut
2 ATROCITY, evil, outrage, offence, wickedness, vileness
FORMAL heinousness
3 SWEAR-WORD, curse, profanity, expletive, bad language
FORMAL imprecation
COLLOQ. four-letter word
SLANG cuss; *N Am* cussword

obscure *adj, v*
♦ *adj*
1 UNKNOWN, unimportant, insignificant, little-known, unheard-of, remote, out-of-the-way, god-forsaken, undistinguished, nameless, unsung unrecognized, inconspicuous, humble, minor
COLLOQ. off the beaten track
2 INCOMPREHENSIBLE, unclear, complex, involved, enigmatic, cryptic, opaque, mysterious, unexplained, inexplicable, unfathomable, impenetrable, deep, hidden, concealed, confusing puzzling perplexing
FORMAL recondite, esoteric, arcane, abstruse

3 INDISTINCT, unclear, indefinite, uncertain, doubtful, shadowy, blurred, cloudy, faint, hazy, fuzzy, dim, misty, shady, vague, murky, dark, gloomy, dusky
Ea 1 famous, renowned **2** intelligible, straightforward **3** clear, definite
♦ *v*
conceal, cloud, hide, cover, blur, confuse, muddle, complicate, disguise, mask, overshadow, shadow, shade, cloak, veil, shroud, darken, dim, eclipse, screen, block out
FORMAL obfuscate
Ea clarify, illuminate

obscurity *n*
1 UNIMPORTANCE, insignificance, lowliness, namelessness, inconspicuousness, lack of fame/recognition
2 INCOMPREHENSIBILITY, impenetrability, unclearness, complexity, intricacy, ambiguity, mystery, depth, night, fog murkiness, shade, confusion, mysticism
FORMAL abstruseness, reconditeness
Ea 1 fame, renown **2** intelligibility, clarity, lucidity

obsequies *n*
funeral, burial, cremation, wake
FORMAL interment, entombment, inhumation, exequies

obsequious *adj*
servile, ingratiating grovelling fawning menial, sycophantic, cringing toadying toadyish, deferential, flattering oily, fulsome, submissive, subservient, slavish, abject, knee-crooking
FORMAL unctuous
COLLOQ. smarmy, bootlicking crawling creepy
SLANG (*vulgar*) arse-licking; *N Am* kiss-ass

observable *adj*
noticeable, perceptible, discernible, appreciable, detectable, recognizable, measurable, significant, visible, apparent, clear, obvious, evident, open, patent

observance *n*
1 ADHERENCE, performance, execution, discharge, obedience, compliance, keeping following fulfilment, honouring notice, attention
FORMAL heeding
2 RITUAL, custom, ceremony, rite, practice, tradition, formality, service, celebration, festival

observant *adj*
1 ATTENTIVE, alert, vigilant, on guard, seeing watchful, mindful, perceptive, sharp, sharp-eyed, hawk-eyed, eagle-eyed, wide-awake, on the lookout, on the qui vive
FORMAL heedful, percipient, observative
COLLOQ. with your eyes skinned/peeled, with eyes like a hawk
2 DUTIFUL, committed, devoted, obedient, practising orthodox
COLLOQ. card-carrying
Ea 1 unobservant

observation *n*
1 ATTENTION, notice, noticing seeing viewing examination, inspection, scrutiny, monitoring study, review, watching consideration, discernment, perception
2 REMARK, comment, utterance, thought, statement, pronouncement, declaration, reflection, opinion, finding result, description, note, information, data
FORMAL annotation

observatory *n*
planetarium, planisphere, orrery

observe *v*
1 WATCH, see, view, spot, study, notice, note, contemplate, inspect, examine, monitor, keep an eye on, discern, perceive, detect, catch sight of, keep watch on, keep under surveillance
FORMAL behold, espy
COLLOQ. keep tabs on, miss nothing keep your eyes skinned/peeled, watch like a hawk
2 REMARK, comment, say, mention, utter, state, declare

3 *observe a law/custom*
abide by, honour, keep, follow, obey, adhere to, fulfil, celebrate, mark, commemorate, remember, recognize, perform, conform to, respect, execute, discharge
FORMAL comply with
E3 1 miss, ignore **3** break, violate

SYNONYM NUANCES

sense 3

Abide by can be used of being governed by: *they abided by the umpire's decision*, whereas **honour** and **respect** additionally imply showing due deference.

    Keep, however, is suggestive of maintaining something usually a ritual or a faith, while **follow** and **adhere to** can be used more widely: *he faithfully followed the cabinet's line*. The terms **obey** and **conform to** suggest compliance but not necessarily willingness, while **fulfil**, along with **perform** and **execute**, has more to do with carrying something out: *they fulfilled the conditions of the pact; the will had been duly executed*.

    Celebrate is more suggestive of performing with appropriate ceremony: *celebrating the seasonal festivals*, and **mark** similarly implies making distinct in some way, although not necessarily as a cause for celebration: *we must mark the occasion*. **Commemorate**, however, is appropriate for remembrance of something that has happened in the past: *commemorating the deeds of our war heroes*, while you could use **recognize** to simply suggest acknowledgement: *we must recognize the multicultural nature of our society*.

---

observer *n*
watcher, spectator, viewer, witness, reporter, looker-on, onlooker, sightseer, eyewitness, commentator, bystander
FORMAL beholder

obsess *v*
preoccupy, dominate, rule, control, monopolize, haunt, hound, torment, bedevil, grip, have a grip/hold on, plague, prey on, possess, engross, consume, be uppermost in your mind
COLLOQ. eat up

obsessed *adj*
preoccupied, dominated, gripped, in the grip of, immersed in, haunted, hounded, plagued, infatuated, bedevilled, beset
COLLOQ. hung up on, having ... on the brain
E3 detached, indifferent, unconcerned

obsession *n*
preoccupation, fixation, *idée fixe*, ruling passion, compulsion, fetish, infatuation, mania, complex, phobia, enthusiasm, fascination, hobby-horse, neurosis
COLLOQ. hang-up, thing bug bee in your bonnet, one-track mind

obsessive *adj*
consuming all-consuming compulsive, gripping fixed, haunting tormenting maddening

obsolescence *n*
redundancy, obsoleteness, disuse, rejection, scrapping disappearance, failure

obsolescent *adj*
out of date, old-fashioned, outdated, dated, dying out, disappearing declining fading waning ag(e)ing redundant, on the way out, past its prime, on the decline, on the wane
FORMAL moribund
COLLOQ. past its sell-by date, old hat, on the shelf, out of the ark, antediluvian

obsolete *adj*
outmoded, disused, in disuse, discarded, out of date, old-fashioned, out of fashion, passé, dated, outworn, old, ancient, antiquated, antique, superannuated, dead, extinct, bygone, behind the times, on the way out, past its prime
FORMAL discontinued

COLLOQ. past its sell-by date, old hat, on the shelf, out of the ark, antediluvian
E3 modern, current, up-to-date, in use

obstacle *n*
barrier, bar, obstruction, blockade, barricade, impediment, hurdle, jump, hindrance, check, snag stumbling-block, blockage, drawback, handicap, difficulty, hitch, catch, stoppage, stop, curb, interference, interruption, deterrent, drag entanglement, rock, boyg remora
OLD stay
COLLOQ. hiccup, fly in the ointment, spanner in the works
E3 advantage, help

obstinacy *n*
stubbornness, inflexibility, hard-heartedness, persistence, perseverance, resoluteness, tenacity, wilfulness, wrongheadedness, perversity, firmness, doggedness, relentlessness, mulishness
FORMAL frowardness, intransigence, obduracy, pertinacity
COLLOQ. pigheadedness
E3 co-operativeness, flexibility, submissiveness

obstinate *adj*
stubborn, inflexible, hard-hearted, immovable, unyielding unbending unrelenting persistent, dogged, headstrong strong-minded, self-willed, steadfast, firm, persevering determined, adamant, wilful, diehard, hidebound, dour, hard-set, restive, wrongheaded, stiff-necked, mulish, bullish, camelish, rusty, sturdy; *Scot* kittle, thrawart, thrawn
OLD stomachful, pervicacious, stiff-hearted, stoor; *(Shakesp)* high-stomached
FORMAL intractable, intransigent, refractory, recalcitrant, contumacious, pertinacious
COLLOQ. pigheaded, bloody-minded, obstinate as a mule, cussed
E3 flexible, tractable

obstreperous *adj*
disorderly, unruly, tumultuous, unmanageable, undisciplined, wild, uncontrolled, out of hand, noisy, loud, boisterous, clamorous, raucous, riotous, rip-roaring tempestuous, rowdy, rough, turbulent, uproarious, vociferous
FORMAL refractory, restive, intractable
COLLOQ. stroppy, bolshie, bloody-minded
E3 calm, disciplined, quiet

obstruct *v*
block, impede, hinder, prevent, check, frustrate, hamper, clog choke, bar, barricade, stop, halt, bridle, stall, restrict, limit, thwart, encumber, hamstring inhibit, hold up, brake, curb, arrest, slow down, delay, interrupt, interfere with, shut off, cut off, obscure, cross, hedge, blanket, stuff, sandbag crab, foul, portcullis
OLD stap, waylay
FORMAL retard, arrest
COLLOQ. stymie
E3 assist, further

obstruction *n*
barrier, blockage, bar, barricade, hindrance, impediment, obstacle, stumbling-block, check, stop, stoppage, restriction, embargo, sanction, difficulty, deterrent
E3 help

obstructive *adj*
hindering delaying blocking stalling unhelpful, unco-operative, awkward, difficult, restrictive, inhibiting interrupting
E3 co-operative, helpful

obtain *v*
1 ACQUIRE, get, gain, gain possession of, come by, attain, secure, seize, earn, achieve
FORMAL procure
COLLOQ. get your hands on
2 PREVAIL, exist, hold, be in force, be the case, be effective, be in use, hold sway, stand, reign, rule, be prevalent

obtainable *adj*
available, at hand, ready, to be had, accessible,
achievable, attainable, realizable, on call
FORMAL procurable
COLLOQ. on tap
▣ unobtainable, unavailable

obtrude *v*
impose, intrude, foist, force yourself,
thrust yourself, butt in, break in, encroach,
presume, exploit, put upon, abuse, mislead, take
advantage of

obtrusive *adj*
1 PROMINENT, protruding projecting noticeable,
obvious, conspicuous, blatant, flagrant, bold,
forward
2 INTRUSIVE, interfering forward, pushy, prying
meddling
COLLOQ. nos(e)y
▣ **1** unobtrusive

obtuse *adj*
slow, slow-witted, stupid, unintelligent,
dull, dense, crass, stolid, dull-witted, thick-skinned
COLLOQ. thick, dumb, dim, dim-witted, dopey, dozy,
slow on the uptake
▣ bright, sharp

obverse *n*
reverse, opposite, inverse, contrary, converse
FORMAL antithesis

obviate *v*
avert, prevent, divert, forestall, remove, counter,
counteract, anticipate
FORMAL preclude

obvious *adj*
evident, self-evident, manifest, patent, clear,
crystal clear, plain, visible, distinct, transparent,
undeniable, unmistakable, conspicuous,
glaring apparent, open, unconcealed, noticeable,
detectable, perceptible, pronounced,
recognizable, self-explanatory, straightforward, clear-cut,
prominent
COLLOQ. as plain as a pikestaff, as plain as the nose on
your face, as clear as daylight, staring you in the face,
sticking out a mile, right under your nose, shouting from
the rooftops
▣ unclear, indistinct, obscure

> **QUOTATIONS**
> Familiar things happen, and mankind does not bother
> about them. It requires a very unusual mind to
> undertake the analysis of the obvious
> ALFRED NORTH WHITEHEAD, *Science and the
> Modern World*

obviously *adv*
plainly, clearly, evidently, noticeably,
patently, manifestly, undeniably, unmistakably,
without doubt, undoubtedly, certainly, distinctly,
of course

occasion *n, v*
♦ *n*
1 EVENT, occurrence, incident, episode, experience,
situation, circumstance, happening affair,
time, instance, point, chance, case, opportunity,
juncture
2 REASON, cause, excuse, justification, call, ground(s)
3 CELEBRATION, function, affair, party,
(social) event
COLLOQ. do, get-together, bash
♦ *v*
cause, bring about, bring on, make, produce, create, give
rise to, generate, induce, lead to, provoke, prompt, evoke,
elicit, influence, inspire, persuade, originate, engender
FORMAL effect

occasional *adj*
periodic, intermittent, irregular, sporadic,
infrequent, uncommon, incidental, odd,
rare, casual, off and on, on and off, fugitive;
Scot daimen, orra
▣ frequent, regular, constant

occasionally *adv*
sometimes, on occasion, from time to time,
at times, at intervals, now and then, now and again,
irregularly, periodically, every so often, once in a while,
off and on, on and off, infrequently, intermittently,
sporadically
OLD once in a way
▣ frequently, often, always

occlude *v*
block, stop (up), choke, clog (up), plug dam up, close,
seal, bar, obstruct, impede, hinder, fill, check, arrest, halt,
thwart
COLLOQ. bung up

occlusion *n*
blockage, obstruction, blocking stoppage, block, clot, jam,
log jam, congestion, hindrance, impediment

occult *adj, n*
♦ *adj*
mystical, supernatural, magical, magic, mysterious,
concealed, obscure, secret, hidden, veiled
FORMAL esoteric, arcane, recondite, abstruse,
transcendental, preternatural, metaphysical
♦ *n*
the supernatural, black arts, mysticism, supernaturalism,
art(s)

Terms associated with the occult include:

amulet	hallucination	relic
astral projection	hoodoo	rune
astrologer	horoscope	satanic
astrology	horseshoe	Satanism
bewitch	hydromancer	Satanist
black cat	hydromancy	séance
black magic	illusion	second sight
black mass	incantation	shaman
cabbala	influence	shamrock
charm	jinx	sixth sense
chiromancer	juju	sorcerer
chiromancy	magic	sorcery
clairvoyance	magician	spell
clairvoyant	mascot	spirit
conjure	medium	spiritualism
coven	necromancer	spiritualist
crystal ball	necromancy	supernatural
curse	obi	superstition
déjà vu	omen	talisman
divination	oneiromancer	tarot card
diviner	oneiromancy	tarot reading
divining-rod	Ouija board®	telepathist
dream	palmist	telepathy
ectoplasm	palmistry	totem
evil eye	paranormal	trance
evil spirit	pentagram	vision
exorcism	planchette	voodoo
exorcist	poltergeist	Walpurgis Night
extrasensory	possession	warlock
perception (ESP)	prediction	white magic
familiar	premonition	witch
fetish	psychic	witchcraft
fortune-teller	psychometer	witch doctor
garlic	psychometry	witch's broomstick
Hallowe'en	rabbit's foot	witch's sabbath

occupancy *n*
tenancy, residence, tenure, term, occupation,
owner-occupancy, ownership, possession, holding use
FORMAL domiciliation, habitation, inhabitancy

Occupations include:

accountant
account executive
actor/actress
actuary
administrator
advertising executive
air traffic controller
animator
anthropologist
archaeologist
architect
archivist
art director
artist
arts administrator
astronomer
athlete
author
baker
banker
bank teller
barista
barperson
barrister
blacksmith
biologist
biotechnologist
bodyguard
bookbinder
bookkeeper
botanist
bricklayer
broadcaster
bus driver
business analyst
butcher
buyer
camera operator
carpenter
cashier
chauffeur
chef
chemist
chiropractor
choreographer
civil engineer
civil servant
claims assessor
cleaner
coach
commercial artist
composer
computer analyst

computer engineer
computer programmer
computer support
  specialist
conductor
conservationist
construction manager
construction worker
consultant
costume designer
counsellor
crane operator
criminologist
critic
curator
customer services
  representative
dancer
data entry operator
dental hygienist
dentist
dietician
director
DJ
doctor
draughtsperson
ecologist
economist
editor
electrician
engineer
environmental health
  officer
environmental scientist
estate agent
event manager
farmer
fashion designer
financial advisor
financial analyst
financial controller
firefighter
fisherman
fitness instructor
fitter
flight attendant
florist
food scientist
forensic scientist
forester
fund manager
fundraiser
funeral director

game warden
gardener
general practitioner
  (GP)
geneticist
geologist
glazier
graphic designer
groundskeeper
historian
home economist
horticulturalist
hotel manager
human resource
  manager
illustrator
industrial designer
insurance underwriter
interior designer
interpreter
IT consultant
janitor
joiner
journalist
judge
keyboarder
laboratory technician
landscape architect
landscape gardener
lawyer
lecturer
librarian
life coach
lighting technician
linguist
machinist
management
  consultant
marine biologist
marketing manager
massage therapist
mathematician
mechanic
media planner
meteorologist
microbiologist
midwife
military member (or
  officer)
minister
model
MP
musician

music therapist
nurse
nutritionist
occupational therapist
oceanographer
office administrator
operations research
  analyst
optician
optometrist
orthodontist
osteopath
painter/decorator
panel beater
paralegal
paramedic
personal assistant (PA)
personal trainer
pharmacist
pharmacologist
philosopher
photographer
physicist
physiotherapist
pilot
plasterer
plumber
podiatrist
poet
police officer
political scientist
postal worker
potter
printing-press operator
prison officer
private investigator
producer
proofreader
property developer
psychologist
publicist
public relations (PR)
  consultant
publishing manager
purchasing manager
radiographer
railwayman
receptionist
recruitment consultant
refuse collector
restaurant manager
retail manager
roofer

sales and marketing
  manager
sales representative
scriptwriter
sculptor
secretary
security guard
set designer
shop assistant
shopkeeper
signalman
singer
social worker
sociologist
sound engineer
speech therapist
spokesperson
stage manager
statistician
stenographer
stockbroker
stock controller
stonemason
streetcleaner
subeditor
surgeon
surveyor
systems analyst
tailor
taxi driver
teacher
tourism development
  officer
toxicologist
traffic warden
trainer
translator
travel agent
truck driver
upholsterer
urban planner
van driver
veterinarian
waiter/waitress
weaver
web designer
welder
writer
youth worker
zookeeper
zoologist

See also **medical specialists**.

occupant *n*
occupier, owner, owner-occupier, homeowner,
holder, inhabitant, resident, householder,
tenant, user, renter, leaseholder, lessee, squatter,
inmate
FORMAL incumbent

occupation *n*
1 JOB, profession, work, career, vocation,
employment, employ, trade, post, calling business,
field, line, province, pursuit, craft, walk of life,
activity, interest, métier
See panel above
2 INVASION, seizure, conquest, control, possession,
capture, overthrow, foreign rule, foreign domination,
takeover
FORMAL subjugation

3 OCCUPANCY, possession, holding tenancy, tenure,
residence, residency, use
FORMAL habitation

SYNONYM NUANCES

sense 1
Job can be used widely to suggest any task, or used
more particularly to suggest a task undertaken on a daily
basis for payment, whereas **profession** tends to be used
more generally of a skilled occupation: *the medical
profession.* **Post** has the narrower referent of a particular
appointment: *he was appointed to the post of Managing
Director.*
    Work and **employment**, again, can be used to imply a
specific task or more generally that done regularly for
money: *he's been out of work for a year now,* and

employ usually implies the state of being employed: *in the employ of local government.*

Career, on the other hand, suggests the progress charted throughout your working life and implies an impressive or skilled occupation: *a career in law*, while the terms **vocation** and **calling** particularly suggest an occupation one feels drawn to by principles or religion: *a vocation to the priesthood.*

To refer more generally to a form of skilled livelihood you could use **trade**: *the building trade*, while **business** has more commercial implications: *the freight business.* The terms **field**, **line** and **province** are appropriate for a wider referent of a particular area of expertise: *his line of research*, and **métier** further implies a particular aptitude. **Craft** conveys the involvement of highly specialized, even artistic skills.

More personal occupations can be referred to with the terms **interest**, **activity** or **pursuit**: *horticultural work supplanted his pursuit of agriculture.*

occupational *adj*
job-related, professional, vocational, career, work, employment, trade, business

occupied *adj*
1 UNAVAILABLE, in use, taken, busy, full, engaged, tenanted
2 ABSORBED, engrossed, taken up, employed, engaged, preoccupied, immersed, busy, working tied up
COLLOQ. hard at it
E3 1 unoccupied, vacant

occupier *n*
occupant, owner-occupier, homeowner, holder, inhabitant, resident, householder, tenant, user, renter, leaseholder, lessee, squatter, inmate
FORMAL incumbent

occupy *v*
1 INHABIT, live in, possess, reside in, stay in, make your home in, settle, people, tenant, take possession of, move in, own, rent, nest
OLD occupate, manure; *N Am* improve
FORMAL dwell in
2 ABSORB, take up, engross, employ, engage, hold, involve, possess, fill in, preoccupy, immerse, amuse, entertain, busy, overbusy, interest, stimulate, divert, obsess
OLD tire, trade; (*Spenser*) entreat, embusy
3 INVADE, seize, capture, overrun, take over, take possession of
OLD beset
4 FILL, take up, use (up), hold, have
OLD obtain

occur *v*
1 HAPPEN, come about, take place, chance, come to pass, turn out, materialize, develop, crop up, turn up, result
FORMAL transpire, befall, eventuate
2 EXIST, be present, be found, have its being arise, appear
FORMAL obtain, manifest itself
3 *the idea occurred to me*
come to you, dawn on, strike, hit, suggest itself, come to mind, cross your mind, enter your head, present itself, spring to mind, sink in

occurrence *n*
1 INCIDENT, event, happening affair, proceedings, circumstance, episode, instance, case, development, action
2 INCIDENCE, existence, appearance, arising springing-up, development
FORMAL manifestation

ocean *n*
main, profound, sea, the deep
COLLOQ. briny, the drink
Related adjective: pelagic

ocean-going *n*
seafaring seagoing sailing marine, maritime, nautical, naval

odd *adj*
1 UNUSUAL, strange, uncommon, peculiar, funny, exceptional, curious, quaint, atypical, abnormal, different, queer, bizarre, eccentric, deviant, singular, idiosyncratic, remarkable, original, unconventional, uncanny, droll, drôle, freakish, weird, irregular, wild, extraordinary, outlandish, quirky, whimsical, whimsy, rare; *Scot* orra, odd-like
OLD rum
COLLOQ. out of the ordinary, freaky, kinky, wacky, oddball, zany, barmy, crackers, off the wall
SLANG rum, far-out, way-out
2 OCCASIONAL, incidental, haphazard, irregular, periodic, seasonal, random, casual, part-time, temporary
FORMAL fortuitous
3 UNMATCHED, unpaired, single, spare, surplus, superfluous, left-over, remaining mismatched, sundry, various, miscellaneous
E3 1 normal, usual 2 regular

■ **odd one out**
nonconformist, eccentric,
odd man/woman out
COLLOQ. freak, oddball, weirdo, case, odd bod, odd/queer fish, fish out of water, square peg in a round hole
SLANG cure

oddball *n*
eccentric, nonconformist, oddity, crank
OLD rum
COLLOQ. freak, character, case, card, nut, nutter, weirdo, crackpot, loon, kook, odd/queer fish, square peg in a round hole, fish out of water;
N Am flake
SLANG geek; *N Am* dingbat, wack, cupcake; *Aust* dag

oddity *n*
1 ABNORMALITY, strangeness, peculiarity, queerness, rarity, eccentricity, idiosyncrasy, phenomenon, twist, quirk
2 CURIOSITY, anomaly, rarity, phenomenon, misfit
OLD rum
COLLOQ. oddball, freak, character, case, card, nut, nutter, weirdo, crackpot, loon, kook, odd/queer fish, square peg in a round hole, fish out of water; *N Am* flake
SLANG geek; *N Am* dingbat, wack, cupcake; *Aust* dag

oddly *adv*
strangely, curiously, unusually, abnormally, remarkably, unconventionally, irregularly, weirdly
E3 normally, usually, regularly

oddment *n*
bit, scrap, piece, leftover, fragment, offcut, end, remnant, shred, snippet, patch; *dialect* fent

odds *n*
1 LIKELIHOOD, probability, chances, the line, price
2 ADVANTAGE, edge, lead, superiority, supremacy
FORMAL ascendancy

■ **odds and ends**
bits and pieces, bits, oddments, junk, remnants, bric-à-brac, job-lot, rubbish, litter, scraps, cuttings, snippets, tatt, debris, flotsam and jetsam, leavings
OLD odd-come-shorts
COLLOQ. odds and sods, this and that

■ **at odds**
disagreeing in disagreement, in conflict, at variance, differing clashing quarrelling arguing at loggerheads, out of step; *N Am* at outs

odious *adj*
offensive, loathsome, unpleasant, disagreeable, obnoxious, disgusting hateful, objectionable, repulsive, repugnant, revolting foul, detestable, abhorrent, horrible, horrid, abominable, vile, contemptible, despicable
FORMAL execrable, heinous
E3 pleasant

odium *n*
dislike, hatred, abhorrence, disapproval, disrepute, dishonour, shame, disgrace, disfavour, discredit, censure, condemnation, contempt
FORMAL detestation, disapprobation, animosity, antipathy, obloquy, opprobrium, infamy, reprobation, execration

odorous *adj*
scented, sweet-smelling balmy, aromatic, fragrant, perfumed, pungent
FORMAL odoriferous, redolent
F3 odourless

odour *n*
smell, scent, aroma, fragrance, bouquet, perfume, stench
FORMAL redolence
COLLOQ. stink, pong niff, whiff

odourless *adj*
having no smell, without smell, unscented, deodorized
FORMAL inodorous

odyssey *n*
journey, voyage, trek, travels, wandering adventure
FORMAL peregrination

off *adv, adj*
♦ *adv*
1 AWAY, elsewhere, out, at a distance, apart, aside
2 ILL, out of sorts, unwell, sick, seedy, queasy, off form, off-colour, poorly
FORMAL indisposed
COLLOQ. rough, under the weather
♦ *adj*
1 AWAY, absent, gone, unavailable, unobtainable
2 CANCELLED, postponed, called off, abandoned, dropped
COLLOQ. shelved, scrapped
3 ROTTEN, bad, sour, turned, high, spoilt, rancid, mouldy, decomposed
4 SUBSTANDARD, below par, disappointing unsatisfactory, slack, wrong incorrect

offbeat *adj*
unorthodox, weird, unconventional, untraditional, abnormal, strange, unusual, bizarre, out of the ordinary
COLLOQ. oddball, freaky, kooky, wacky
SLANG far-out, way-out

off-colour *adj*
1 ILL, out of sorts, unwell, sick, seedy, queasy, off form, poorly
FORMAL indisposed
COLLOQ. under the weather, run down, rough, crummy
2 RUDE, indecent, improper, immoral, immodest, indelicate, coarse, crude, foul, gross, vulgar, impure, filthy, dirty, obscene, pornographic, lewd, perverted, depraved, degenerate, licentious, offensive, suggestive, sexy, risqué, smutty
COLLOQ. blue, sleazy

off-duty *adj*
off, off work, not at work, on holiday, free, at leisure
F3 on-duty

offence *n*
1 *a criminal offence*
infringement, crime, trespass, wrong wrongdoing illegal act, breach of the law, sin
FORMAL misdemeanour, transgression, violation, misdeed, infraction
2 AFFRONT, insult, injury, hurt, outrage, snub, slight, indignity, atrocity, ire
3 RESENTMENT, indignation, anger, annoyance, exasperation, disapproval, pique, umbrage, outrage, hurt, hard feelings
FORMAL antipathy
■ **take offence**
resent, be indignant, be angry, be annoyed, be exasperated, be hurt, be offended, be insulted, be upset,

be/feel put out, take exception, take personally, take umbrage
COLLOQ. be miffed, get huffy, go into a huff, get the hump, get/have your nose put out of joint

offend *v*
1 HURT, insult, injure, affront, wrong wound, displease, snub, upset, annoy, anger, outrage, exasperate, incense, provoke; *Scot* kittle
OLD distaste, umbrage, hip
FORMAL disoblige
COLLOQ. miff, needle, put out, put someone's back up, rub someone up the wrong way, put someone's nose out of joint, raise someone's hackles, rattle someone's cage, ruffle someone's feathers, tread on someone's toes, give someone the pip
2 DISGUST, repel, sicken, revolt, nauseate, put off
3 BREAK THE LAW, do wrong sin, err, go astray
FORMAL transgress, violate
F3 1 please

offended *adj*
upset, hurt, resentful, disgruntled, affronted, displeased, angered, annoyed, exasperated, incensed, outraged, wounded, smarting stung piqued, pained, disgusted
COLLOQ. huffy, in a huff, miffed, put out
F3 pleased, happy

offender *n*
wrongdoer, culprit, criminal, miscreant, guilty party, lawbreaker, delinquent
FORMAL malefactor, transgressor

offensive *adj, n*
♦ *adj*
1 DISAGREEABLE, unpleasant, objectionable, displeasing disgusting odious, obnoxious, revolting repellent, repugnant, abhorrent, loathsome, vile, sickening nauseating nasty, foul, detestable, abominable
2 INSOLENT, abusive, rude, insulting affronting upsetting hurtful, wounding annoying exasperating impolite, disrespectful, discourteous, impertinent
3 ATTACKING, hostile, antagonistic, aggressive, invading belligerent
F3 1 pleasant 2 polite
♦ *n*
attack, assault, onslaught, invasion, raid, drive, thrust, push, sortie, charge
FORMAL incursion

offensively *adv*
unpleasantly, disagreeably, objectionably, disgustingly, detestably, nauseatingly
F3 pleasantly

offer *v, n*
♦ *v*
1 PRESENT, make available, advance, extend, put forward, submit, suggest, propose, posit, introduce, recommend, hold out
FORMAL propound, proffer
2 PROVIDE, give, supply, sell, put on the market
FORMAL afford
3 *offer £100*
propose, bid, put in a bid, tender
4 VOLUNTEER, come forward, make yourself available, be at someone's service
COLLOQ. show willing
5 *offer prayers/a sacrifice*
offer up, sacrifice, dedicate, present, worship, give, consecrate, celebrate
6 *offer resistance*
show, express, give, present, try, attempt
♦ *n*
proposal, bid, submission, tender, suggestion, proposition, overture, approach, attempt, presentation, oblation

offering *n*
1 GIFT, present, donation, handout, contribution, subscription

2 SACRIFICE, dedication, consecration, tithe, celebration
FORMAL oblation

offhand *adj, adv*
♦ *adj*
casual, unconcerned, uninterested, indifferent, unceremonious, discourteous, rude, brusque, abrupt, curt, snap, terse, airy, perfunctory, cursory, informal, cavalier, careless, blasé, nonchalant
COLLOQ. take-it-or-leave-it, happy-go-lucky, free-and-easy, laid-back, couldn't-care-less
♦ *adv*
impromptu, immediately, ad lib, without thinking about it, without preparation, without checking at the first blush
FORMAL extempore
COLLOQ. off the cuff, off the top of your head
E3 calculated, planned

office *n*
1 RESPONSIBILITY, duty, obligation, charge, commission, occupation, tenure, situation, post, position, employment, function, work, appointment, business, role, place, service
2 WORKPLACE, workroom, place of business, base, bureau
3 *our Edinburgh office*
branch, department, local/regional office, agency, bureau, part, section, division, subsidiary, subsection, subdivision, affiliate, wing
4 *through the offices of someone*
support, advocacy, help, aid, assistance, favour, recommendation, word, back-up, backing patronage, mediation, intervention, referral
FORMAL auspices, aegis, intercession

office equipment and furniture
See panels below

officer *n*
official, office-holder, office-bearer, public servant, functionary, dignitary, bureaucrat, committee member, administrator, representative, executive, board member, agent, appointee, envoy, messenger, deputy

official *adj, n*
♦ *adj*
1 AUTHORIZED, authoritative, legal, lawful, legitimate, formal, accepted, recognized, licensed, certified, validated, endorsed, sanctioned, approved, authenticated, authentic, bona fide, proper
FORMAL accredited
COLLOQ. kosher
2 *official activities*
formal, ceremonial, stately, dignified, solemn, ritual
E3 1 unofficial
♦ *n*
office-bearer, office-holder, officer, functionary
See panel on next page

> **!** official or **officious**?
> *Official* means 'done by someone in authority; relating to authority': *We think she has won, but we're still waiting for the official result of the race. Officious* means 'too eager to meddle, offering unwanted advice or assistance' or, more often, 'holding too rigidly to rules and regulations': *An officious little man told us that we would have to move our bicycles.*

officialdom *n*
officials, bureaucracy, administration, administrator, government, central/national/regional/local government, ministry, civil service, civil servants, the authorities, the system, the establishment, mandarins
COLLOQ. them

officialese *n*
gobbledygook, gibberish, jargon, journalese, computerese, psychobabble, buzz words, nonsense, rubbish

officially *adv*
authoritatively, formally, authentically, properly, correctly, on the record, procedurally, bureaucratically, administratively, managerially
E3 unofficially, off the record

officiate *v*
preside, superintend, conduct, chair, take the chair, manage, oversee, run, be in charge, take charge

officious *adj*
obtrusive, domineering dictatorial, intrusive, interfering prying meddlesome, meddling inquisitive, over-zealous, overbusy, self-important, forward, pushy, opinionated, superserviceable, bustling

---

Office equipment includes:

acoustic hood	dictation machine	intercom	mouse mat	scanner	textphone
adhesive binder	disk storage-system	keyboard	noticeboard	screen	thermal binder
answering	diskette mailer	laminator	overhead projector	screen filter	time clock
machine	duplicator	laptop computer	(OHP)	share certificate	trimmer
calculator	dust cover	letter-folding	paper-folding	book	typewriter
cash box	electric typewriter	machine	machine	shredder	visitors' book
collating machine	electronic	letter opener	paper punch	slide projector	visual display unit
comb binder	organizer	letter scales	parcel scales	stapler	(VDU)
comb binding	electronic	letter tray	photocopier	staple-remover	wages book
computer	typewriter	message board	plan file	switchboard	waste-paper bin
copy holder	facsimile machine	microcassette	planner	tacker	wire-binding
data cartridge	(or fax)	microcassette	planning board	telephone	machine
date-stamp	flip-chart easel	recorder	printer	telephone	wire bindings
desk organizer	guillotine	microfiche reader	printwheel	directory	word processor
desk-top display	hole puncher	monitor	projection screen	telephone index	
calculator	information board	monitor arm	reference book	telex machine	
Dictaphone®	inkpad	mouse	rotary filing-system	terminal trolley	

Office furniture includes:

boardroom table	draughtsman's	filing cupboard	partition	stationery	workstation
computer desk	chair	filing trolley	plan chest	cupboard	work table
conference table	drawing-board	fire cupboard	printer stand	stepstool	
desk	executive chair	fire-extinguisher	reception chair	storage unit	
desk lamp	executive desk	fire safe	safe	swivel chair	
display cabinet	filing cabinet	lectern	secretarial desk	typist's chair	

See also **computer**; **stationery**.

Officials include:

administrator	civil	delegate	governor	member of	proprietor
agent	servant	diplomat	hakim	parliament (MP)	public prosecutor
ambassador	clerk	director	inspector	minister	*Scot* reeve
bailiff	commander	elder	justice of the	monitor	registrar
bureaucrat	commissar	envoy	peace (JP)	notary	representative
captain	commissioner	equerry	magistrate	ombudsman	*N Am* senator
chairman (or	congressman	Eurocrat	manager	overseer	sheriff
chairwoman or	congresswoman	Euro-MP	mandarin	prefect	steward
chairperson)	consul	executive	marshal	president	superintendent
chancellor	coroner	executor	mayor	principal	supervisor
chief	councillor	Gauleiter	mayoress	proctor	usher

OLD spoffish, pragmatical
FORMAL importunate
COLLOQ. bossy

> **!** **officious** or **official**?
> *See panel at* **official**.

officiously *adv*
dictatorially, over-zealously, self-importantly
FORMAL with importunity
COLLOQ. bossily, pushily

offing
■ **in the offing**
imminent, near, coming/happening soon, coming up,
(close) at hand, just round the corner, in sight, on the
way, on the horizon
COLLOQ. on the cards
🔁 far off

offish *adj*
standoffish, aloof, cool, haughty,
unsociable
COLLOQ. stuck-up
🔁 friendly, sociable

off-key *adj*
out of tune, discordant, unsuitable, inappropriate, out of
keeping inharmonious, jarring
FORMAL dissonant
🔁 in tune

offload *v*
unburden, unload, jettison, dump, drop, deposit, get rid of,
shift, discharge
FORMAL disburden
COLLOQ. chuck

off-putting *adj*
intimidating daunting frightening unpleasant, disconcerting
discouraging disheartening deterring dispiriting formidable,
unnerving unsettling unappealing demoralizing disturbing
upsetting
FORMAL discomfiting

offset *v*
counterbalance, compensate for, cancel out, counteract,
make up for, balance (out), neutralize
FORMAL counterpoise, countervail

offshoot *n*
1 BRANCH, outgrowth, limb, arm
2 SPIN-OFF, by-product, product, result, consequence,
outcome, development, branch, appendage

offspring *n*
child, children, son(s), daughter(s), infant(s), young young
one(s), youngster(s), family, brood, baby, babies, little
one(s), heirs, successors, descendants
FORMAL issue, progeny, fruit of your loins
COLLOQ. kid(s), nipper(s)
🔁 parent(s), ancestor(s)

often *adv*
frequently, repeatedly, regularly, generally, again and
again, over and over again, time after time, time and

(time) again, day in day out, week in week out, month in
month out, many times, many a time, much
🔁 rarely, seldom, never

ogle *v*
eye, eye up, leer, make eyes at, look, stare
COLLOQ. give someone the glad eye

ogre *n*
1 GIANT, monster, devil, demon, troll, fiend, bogey,
bogeyman, boyg
2 *his father is a bit of an ogre*
monster, beast, brute, villain, savage, barbarian, fiend

oil *v, n*
♦ *v*
lubricate, grease, make smooth, anoint
♦ *n*
lubricant, grease, ointment, lotion, liniment, cream, balm,
salve
FORMAL unguent

> **QUOTATIONS**
> The oil can is mightier than the sword
> EVERETT MCKINLEY DIRKSEN

Types of oil include:

INDUSTRIAL:	peanut (or	coconut
benzaldehyde	groundnut)	cod-liver
biodiesel	peppermint	croton
diesel	rapeseed	eucalyptus
kerosene	safflower	evening primrose
mineral	sesame	jojoba
neat's foot	soybean	lavender
palm	sunflower	lemon grass
paraffin	vegetable	macassar
rapeseed	walnut	neroli
rosin		nim (or neem)
sperm	**AROMATIC,**	orange
tung	**COSMETIC AND**	patchouli
	MEDICINAL:	peppermint
EDIBLE:	attar (rose)	rose
canola	avocado	sandalwood
coconut	baby oil	sassafras
corn	bergamot	savin
grapeseed	cajeput	tea tree
lemon grass	camphor	vetiver
maize	castor	wheatgerm
nut	chaulmoogra	wintergreen
olive	cinnamon	ylang ylang
palm	citronella	
	clove	

oily *adj*
1 GREASY, fatty, buttery, slippery
FORMAL oleaginous
2 SMOOTH-TALKING, smooth, ingratiating glib, slippery,
suave, urbane, flattering servile, subservient
FORMAL unctuous, obsequious
COLLOQ. smarmy, slimy

ointment n

salve, balm, cream, gel, lotion, liniment, preparation, Vaseline®, basilicon
TECHNICAL emollient, cerate, collyrium, pomade, pomatum
FORMAL embrocation, unction, unguent

OK adj, adv, n, v, interj

♦ adj
acceptable, all right, fine, permitted, in order, fair, satisfactory, reasonable, tolerable, passable, good, adequate, convenient, correct, accurate
COLLOQ. not bad, so-so, up to par, up to scratch; N Am A-OK; N Am & Aust jake
♦ adv
fine, all right, in order, well, satisfactorily, reasonably, tolerably, passably
♦ n
authorization, approval, endorsement, permission, agreement, consent, sanction
FORMAL approbation
COLLOQ. go-ahead, green light, thumbs-up
♦ v
approve, authorize, pass, rubber-stamp, consent to, agree to, say yes to
COLLOQ. give the go-ahead to, give the green light to, greenlight, give the thumbs-up to
♦ interj
all right, fine, very well, very good, agreed, right, yes

old adj

1 AGED, ag(e)ing elderly, advanced in years, mature, sensible, wise, past your prime, grey, senile
FORMAL senescent
COLLOQ. silver, getting on, past it, no spring chicken, not as young as you were, not getting any younger, over the hill, (a bit) long in the tooth, not long for this world, gaga
2 ANCIENT, age-old, bygone, antique, classic, vintage, veteran, original, primitive, early, earlier, earliest, antiquated, prehistoric, primal
FORMAL pristine, prim(a)eval, primordial
3 LONG-STANDING, long-established, long-lived, enduring lasting time-honoured, traditional, age-old
COLLOQ. old as the hills
4 OBSOLETE, old-fashioned, unfashionable, out of date, behind the times, outdated, passé, archaic
COLLOQ. on the way out, past it, past its sell-by date, Dickensian, out of the ark, antediluvian
5 WORN OUT, cast-off, torn, shabby, decayed, decaying decrepit, broken down, crumbling ramshackle, tumbledown
COLLOQ. have seen better days
6 HACKNEYED, stale, overworked, overused, tired, worn-out, time-worn, threadbare, wearing thin, unoriginal, cliché-ridden, clichéed, stereotyped, stock, banal, trite, commonplace, common, pedestrian, uninspired, unimaginative
FORMAL platitudinous
COLLOQ. corny, run-of-the-mill, yawn-making
7 TRADITIONAL, conventional, customary, habitual, usual, routine, accustomed, ceremonial, established, fixed, set, long-established, time-honoured, age-old, historic, folk, oral, unwritten
8 FORMER, previous, earlier, one-time, sometime, ex-
FORMAL erstwhile, quondam
E3 1 young youthful **2** new, recent **4** modern, contemporary, state-of-the-art, up-to-date, fashionable, new **5** new **6** original, new, fresh **7** innovative, new, modern, contemporary **8** current, present

■ **old age**
age, agedness, oldness, elderliness, advancing years, declining years, second childhood, senility, dotage, twilight of your life
FORMAL senescence
E3 youth
Related adjective: geriatric

■ **old man**
father, grandfather, husband, elder, old-age pensioner, OAP, pensioner, senior citizen, employer, greybeard, white-beard, patriarch, elder statesman
COLLOQ. old codger, old stager, old-timer, oldster, boss, gaffer, geezer, fuddy-duddy; N Am golden ager
SLANG (offensive) coffin-dodger

■ **old woman**
mother, grandmother, granny, wife, old-age pensioner, OAP, pensioner, senior citizen, old dear, complainer, grumbler
COLLOQ. bag fusspot, grouch, trout, hag; N Am golden ager
SLANG (offensive) coffin-dodger

QUOTATIONS
The old – like children – talk to themselves, for they have reached that hopeless wisdom of experience which knows that though one were to cry it in the streets to multitudes, or whisper it in the kiss to one's beloved, the only ears that can ever hear one's secrets are one's own!
EUGENE O'NEILL, *Lazarus Laughed*

SYNONYM NUANCES
sense 1
Aged can refer to someone or something of advanced years: *his aged parents*, unlike **ag(e)ing** which is more appropriate for the process of getting older: *an ageing population*. **Elderly**, on the other hand, is reserved for people who have passed their middle age.
The term **mature** has more to do with development, and when used of humans, and particularly of the emotions, it has positive associations: *mature judgement*. **Sensible**, too, is suggestive of good reasoning brought about by experience, and **wise** goes further by emphasizing inherent prudence.
The term **past your prime**, however, disrespectfully suggests physical and mental decline, and **grey**, while literally reflecting hair colour, can also have connotations of the dullness of old age. **Senile**, while used technically of a medical condition, can also be used rather offensively to suggest that someone's mental faculties are diminished through age.

---

old-fashioned adj

outmoded, out of date, outdated, dated, old, unfashionable, out of fashion, obsolete, past, bygone, ancient, old-time, dead, moth-eaten, written off, behind the times, antiquated, antique, archaic, passé, obsolescent, primitive, quaint, schmaltzy, fusty, *arriéré*, *vieux jeu*
OLD auld-farrant, auld-farand, rococo
COLLOQ. antediluvian, out of the ark, fuddy-duddy, old hat, past it, square, past its sell-by date, on the way out, Neanderthal, steam, oldfangled, uncool, mumsy; N Am rinky-dink
E3 modern, up-to-date

old-time adj

old-fashioned, outmoded, out of date, outdated, dated, old, unfashionable, out of fashion, obsolete, past, bygone, behind the times, antiquated, archaic, passé

old-world adj

old-fashioned, quaint, traditional, picturesque, antiquated, past, archaic, bygone
COLLOQ. olde-worlde

omen n

sign, warning token, premonition, foreboding indication, forecast, prediction, harbinger, forerunner, prognosis, presage, boding bodement; *Scot* freit

OLD abodement, presagement, soothsay
FORMAL portent, augury, auspice, presentiment, prodrome, prodromus
Related adjective: ominous

ominous *adj*
menacing foreboding sinister, fateful, unpromising unlucky, unfavourable, threatening bodeful
FORMAL portentous, inauspicious, unpropitious, minatory
E3 favourable; *formal* auspicious

ominously *adv*
alarmingly, dangerously, frighteningly, grimly
E3 favourably

omission *n*
exclusion, gap, exception, leaving-out, erasure, oversight, failure, lack, neglect, negligence, disregard, default, deletion, avoidance
FORMAL lacuna, expunction, dereliction
E3 inclusion

omit *v*
leave out, exclude, miss (out), pass (over), except, overlook, drop, skip, eliminate, forget, neglect, leave undone, fail, fail to mention, disregard, overskip, edit out, erase, delete, cross out, rub out, white out
OLD let, pretermit
FORMAL expunge
E3 include, mention

omnibus *adj, n*
♦ *adj*
comprehensive, inclusive, wide-ranging all-embracing compendious, encyclopedic
E3 selective
♦ *n*
anthology, collection, compilation, compendium, encyclopedia

omnipotence *n*
absolute/total power, complete authority, all-powerfulness, almightiness, divine right, invincibility, mastery, sovereignty, supremacy
FORMAL plenipotence
E3 impotence

omnipotent *adj*
all-powerful, almighty, invincible, supreme
FORMAL plenipotent
E3 impotent

omnipresent *adj*
universal, all-present, present everywhere, pervasive, all-pervasive, limitless, infinite, ubiquitous
FORMAL ubiquitary

omniscient *adj*
all-knowing all-seeing all-wise
FORMAL pansophic

omnivorous *adj*
all-devouring eating anything gluttonous, indiscriminate, undiscriminating

on *prep, adv*
♦ *prep*
1 *on the shelf*
touching resting on, in contact with, attached to, stuck to, being supported by
2 *a book on China*
on the subject of, about, concerning relating to, connected with, concerned with, regarding as regards, referring to, with regard to, with respect to, with reference to, in the matter of, re, dealing with
FORMAL apropos of
■ **on and off**
now and then, occasionally, on occasion, off and on, periodically, sometimes, from time to time, now and again, every so often, irregularly, at intervals, intermittently, spasmodically, sporadically, fitfully
FORMAL discontinuously
■ **on and on**

continually, constantly, perpetually, incessantly, ceaselessly, interminably, ever, forever, eternally, everlastingly, always, endlessly, non-stop, regularly, frequently, recurrently, repeatedly, persistently, habitually, all the time
E3 occasionally, intermittently

once *adv, prep*
♦ *adv*
1 FORMERLY, previously, in the past, at one time, long ago, in times past, in times gone by, once upon a time, in the old days
2 ON ONE OCCASION, at one point, one time
♦ *conj*
after, immediately after, as soon as, when
■ **once and for all**
permanently, decisively, definitively, conclusively, positively, finally, for good, for the last time
■ **once in a while**
now and again/then, at times, sometimes, from time to time, occasionally, on and off, on occasion, periodically, infrequently, intermittently, sporadically, off and on
■ **at once**
1 IMMEDIATELY, instantly, directly, right away, straightaway, without delay, now, right now, promptly, on the spot
FORMAL forthwith
COLLOQ. pronto, before you know it, before you can say Jack Robinson, in two shakes of a lamb's tail, like a shot, yesterday
2 SIMULTANEOUSLY, together, at the same time, at the same moment

once-over *n*
checkup, check, look, examination, inspection, scrutiny, investigation, inquiry, audit, test, research, monitoring analysis, probe, confirmation, verification, glance, glimpse, stare, gaze, gape, peek, peep
COLLOQ. squint, eyeful, dekko, gander, butcher's, shufti

oncoming *adj*
approaching advancing upcoming looming nearing onrushing gathering

one *adj*
1 SINGLE, solitary, lone, individual, only, sole, ace
2 UNITED, joined, fused, bound, married, wedded, harmonious, like-minded, whole, entire, complete, equal, identical, alike

oneness *n*
singleness, unity, completeness, wholeness, identity, individuality, identicalness, sameness, consistency

onerous *adj*
oppressive, burdensome, demanding tiring wearying laborious, arduous, strenuous, back-breaking crushing hard, taxing difficult, troublesome, exacting fatiguing exhausting heavy, weighty
FORMAL exigent

oneself
■ **by oneself**
1 ALONE, by yourself, on your own, lonely, lonesome, deserted, isolated, abandoned, forsaken, forlorn, desolate, unaccompanied, unescorted, unattended, solo
2 ON YOUR OWN, independently, unaided, unassisted, without help, without assistance, singly, single-handed, unaccompanied

one-sided *adj*
1 UNBALANCED, unequal, uneven, lopsided
2 UNFAIR, unjust, prejudiced, biased, bigoted, partial, partisan, narrow-minded, discriminatory, inequitable
3 UNILATERAL, independent, one-way, separate, separated, disconnected
E3 **1** balanced **2** impartial **3** bilateral, multilateral

one-time *adj*
former, previous, old, ex-, late, sometime
FORMAL erstwhile, quondam

ongoing *adj*
1 CONTINUING, continuous, unending unbroken, uninterrupted, non-stop, constant, incessant
2 DEVELOPING, evolving progressing advancing growing in progress, current, unfinished, unfolding

onlooker *n*
bystander, observer, spectator, looker-on, eyewitness, witness, sightseer, watcher, viewer
COLLOQ. rubberneck, gawper

only *adv, adj*
♦ *adv*
just, at most, merely, simply, purely, barely, not more than, no more than, nothing but, exclusively, solely
FORMAL but
♦ *adj*
sole, single, one and only, solitary, lone, unique, exclusive, individual

onrush *n*
surge, rush, push, stream, flood, flow, charge, cascade, career, onset, onslaught, stampede

onset *n*
1 BEGINNING, start, outset, outbreak
FORMAL commencement, inception
COLLOQ. kick-off
2 ASSAULT, attack, onslaught, onrush, charge
E∃ 1 end, finish

onslaught *n*
attack, assault, offensive, charge, onrush, storming raid, drive, push, thrust, foray, bombardment, blitz

onus *n*
burden, responsibility, weight, load, obligation, duty, charge, encumbrance, liability, task
COLLOQ. millstone, albatross

onwards *adv*
forward(s), on, ahead, in front, beyond
FORMAL forth
E∃ backward(s)

oodles *n*
lots, masses, abundance
COLLOQ. bags, heaps, lashings, loads, tons
E∃ scarcity

oomph *n*
vitality, sparkle, vigour, energy, vivacity, enthusiasm, exuberance, animation
COLLOQ. bounce, get-up-and-go, pep, pizzazz, zing sexiness

ooze *v, n*
♦ *v*
seep, exude, leak, percolate, escape, dribble, drip, trickle, drop, discharge, bleed, secrete, emit, flow, overflow with, pour forth, filter, drain
FORMAL filtrate, excrete
♦ *n*
sludge, silt, slime, muck, mire, mud, sediment, deposit, seepage
FORMAL alluvium

oozy *adj*
sludgy, muddy, slimy, mucky, miry, dripping dewy, moist, weeping sweaty, sloppy
FORMAL uliginous

opacity *n*
1 CLOUDINESS, opaqueness, dullness, unclearness, impermeability, milkiness, murkiness, filminess, density
2 OBSCURITY, impenetrability, incomprehensibility, unintelligibility
FORMAL obfuscation
E∃ 1 transparency **2** clarity

opalescence *n*
multicolour, shimmering sparkling dazzling glitter, glittering rainbow, rainbow colours, prism
FORMAL iridescence

opalescent *adj*
shimmering sparkling multicoloured, rainbow, rainbow-coloured, rainbow-like, prismatic, dazzling glittering shot, pearly, polychromatic
FORMAL iridescent, variegated

opaque *adj*
1 CLOUDY, clouded, murky, unclear, dull, dim, hazy, misty, muddied, muddy, dingy, blurred, dense, thick, turbid
2 OBSCURE, unclear, impenetrable, unfathomable, incomprehensible, unintelligible, enigmatic, cryptic, difficult, dense, confusing baffling puzzling
FORMAL abstruse, recondite, esoteric
COLLOQ. as clear as mud
E∃ 1 transparent, see-through **2** clear, obvious

open *adj, v*
♦ *adj*
1 UNCLOSED, ajar, gaping wide open, uncovered, unfastened, unbolted, unlocked, unsealed, unbarred, unlatched, unfolded, spread out, yawning lidless, topless, coverless
2 UNRESTRICTED, free, unobstructed, unblocked, passable, navigable, unenclosed, unfenced, clear, accessible, exposed, unprotected, unsheltered, vacant, wide, obtainable, available, unoccupied
3 OVERT, obvious, manifest, plain, clear, visible, patent, evident, noticeable, apparent, flagrant, blatant, conspicuous, unhidden, unconcealed, undisguised
4 UNDECIDED, unresolved, unsettled, debatable, arguable, problematic, moot
COLLOQ. up in the air
5 FRANK, candid, honest, guileless, natural, simple, ingenuous, unreserved, forthright, blunt, direct
6 LOOSELY WOVEN, airy, holey, openwork, porous, honeycombed, cellular, spongelike
7 *an open secret*
widely known, well known, public, general, accessible, unrestricted
8 *open to misinterpretation*
liable, vulnerable, susceptible, subject, open to the risk of, receptive, exposed, disposed, accessible
E∃ 1 shut, closed **2** restricted, exclusive **3** hidden, concealed **4** decided, resolved **5** reserved **6** close, dense, compact **7** private, closed, exclusive
♦ *v*
1 UNFASTEN, undo, unlock, unlatch, uncover, unseal, untie, unbolt, unblock, uncork, crack, broach, break open, burst open, slide open, push open, force open, prise open, clear, expose
2 EXPLAIN, divulge, expose, disclose, bare, lay bare, uncover, reveal
3 EXTEND, spread (out), unroll, unfold, unfurl, flower, come apart, separate, split
4 BEGIN, start, commence, inaugurate, initiate, set in motion, launch
COLLOQ. set the ball rolling kick off, get cracking take the plunge
E∃ 1 close, shut **2** hide, cover up **4** end, finish
■ **open onto**
give onto, overlook, lead to, command a view of, face

open-air *adj*
outdoor, out-of-doors, outside, afield, alfresco
E∃ indoor

open-and-shut *adj*
straightforward, obvious, simple, clear, easily decided, easily solved

open-handed *adj*
generous, free, liberal, large-hearted, lavish, bountiful, unstinting
FORMAL bounteous, eleemosynary, magnanimous, munificent
E∃ *colloq.* tight-fisted

opening *n, adj*
♦ *n*
1 APERTURE, breach, gap, space, break, chink, crack, fissure, cleft, crevice, chasm, hole, entry, cave, slot, split, inlet, outlet, vent, rupture
FORMAL orifice, interstice
2 START, onset, beginning outset, inauguration, birth, dawn, launch
FORMAL inception
COLLOQ. the word go, square one, kick-off, first base
3 OPPORTUNITY, chance, occasion, place, possibility, vacancy, job, position
COLLOQ. break
⊟ 2 close, end
♦ *adj*
first, beginning starting introductory, initial, early, primary
FORMAL commencing inaugural
⊟ closing

openly *adv*
overtly, frankly, candidly, directly, forthrightly, bluntly, honestly, blatantly, flagrantly, plainly, unashamedly, brazenly, unreservedly, glaringly, publicly, in public, in full view, immodestly, shamelessly
COLLOQ. with no holds barred
⊟ secretly, slyly

open-minded *adj*
unprejudiced, unbiased, broad-minded, broad, impartial, tolerant, liberal, receptive, reasonable, objective, free, catholic, dispassionate, enlightened
FORMAL latitudinarian
⊟ bigoted, intolerant, prejudiced, narrow-minded

open-mindedness *n*
impartiality, neutrality, non-partisanship, objectivity, unbiasedness, fairness, justice, even-handedness, detachment, disinterest, disinterestedness, dispassion, equality, equity
⊟ bias, prejudice, favouritism, discrimination

open-mouthed *adj*
amazed, astounded, astonished, spellbound, dumbfounded, shocked, clamorous, thunderstruck, expectant, wide-eyed
COLLOQ. flabbergasted

operate *v*
1 *it operates on batteries*
function, act, perform, run, work, go, make go, serve, set, trip, actuate
OLD play
2 *she can operate that machine*
control, handle, manage, direct, work, run, be in charge of, drive, pilot, fly, use, utilize, employ, manoeuvre

operation *n*
1 FUNCTIONING, action, running motion, movement, performance, working
2 INFLUENCE, manipulation, handling control, working running management, use, using utilization
3 UNDERTAKING, enterprise, affair, procedure, proceeding process, exercise, action, activity, business, deal, job, task, transaction, effort
4 CAMPAIGN, action, task, manoeuvre, exercise, attack, assault, charge, raid
5 SURGERY, surgical operation, surgical intervention
COLLOQ. op
■ in operation
operational, in force, functioning active, effective, efficient, in action, in effect, taking effect, working workable, viable, serviceable, functional, valid

operational *adj*
working in working order, in use, usable, functioning functional, in action,

going running up and running viable, workable, ready, prepared, in service
⊟ out of order

operative *adj, n*
♦ *adj*
1 OPERATIONAL, in operation, in force, functioning active, effective, efficient, in action, working workable, viable, serviceable, functional, valid
2 KEY, crucial, important, relevant, significant, vital
⊟ 1 inoperative, out of service
♦ *n*
1 WORKER, workman, employee, labourer, hand, mechanic, machinist, operator, artisan
2 DETECTIVE, private detective, (private) investigator
COLLOQ. private eye, sleuth, gumshoe, shamus, dick
3 SECRET AGENT, agent, spy, double agent
COLLOQ. mole

operator *n*
1 OPERATIVE, worker, mechanic, machinist, technician, mover, driver, practitioner
2 TRADER, contractor, dealer, manager, director, administrator, handler
3 MANIPULATOR, machinator, punter, manoeuvrer, speculator
COLLOQ. wheeler-dealer, shyster

opiate *n*
drug narcotic, sedative, pacifier, anodyne, tranquillizer, soporific, stupefacient, depressant, bromide
FORMAL nepenthe
COLLOQ. downer

opine *v*
think, believe, suppose, suggest, guess, say, volunteer, presume, declare, judge, conceive, conclude, suspect, venture
FORMAL conjecture, surmise

opinion *n*
belief, judgement, view, point of view, viewpoint, idea, perception, stance, standpoint, theory, impression, feeling(s), sentiment, assumption, assessment, conception, mind, notion, way of thinking thought(s), school of thought, conviction, persuasion, attitude
FORMAL estimation
■ in my opinion
I think, I believe, in my view, from my point of view, from my standpoint, as I see it, (according) to my way of thinking personally (speaking)
COLLOQ. in my book, if you ask me, for my money

> **QUOTATIONS**
> Nobody holds a good opinion of a man who has a low opinion of himself
> ANTHONY TROLLOPE, *Orley Farm*

> **SYNONYM NUANCES**
> **Belief** can be used of something that you are sure is true, while **conviction** further implies an unshakable confidence in it. **Judgement** has more to do with your evaluation, a suggestion made even more explicit with the term **assessment**. **Idea**, however, suggests something less well formulated: *his own ideas of democracy*, while **theory** suggests a hypothetical explanation: *I have no theory as to how this happened.*
>   **Perception**, **conception** and **impression** have more to do with a personal interpretation of events: *I had the impression he was frightened of me; one's conception of the world.* **Feeling(s)** likewise has suggestions of personal sensitivities, whereas **sentiment** hints at an emotional reaction: *public sentiment turned against the war.*
>   You can use **mind** to suggest your current opinion: *he was of a mind to sack them*, whereas **notion** is more suggestive of a passing whim. **Persuasion** is again

suggestive of assured opinion, often relating to a creed: *voters of every political persuasion*. **Attitude** could be used of the particular position someone has adopted on an issue, and both **stance** and **standpoint** imply a view that is firmly held: *I have urged him to reconsider his stance on the issue*.

opinionated *adj*
dogmatic, doctrinaire, dictatorial, arrogant, inflexible, obstinate, stubborn, pigheaded, uncompromising with preconceived ideas, single-minded, adamant, prejudiced, biased, bigoted, self-important, pompous, cocksure, pontifical
E3 open-minded

opponent *n*
adversary, enemy, antagonist, foe, competitor, contestant, challenger, opposer, opposition, rival, contender, objector, dissenter, dissident
FORMAL dissentient
E3 ally, friend, supporter

opportune *adj*
suitable, proper, convenient, appropriate, advantageous, apt, fit, seasonable, timely, well-timed, favourable, providential, fitting fortunate, good, lucky, happy
FORMAL auspicious, felicitous, pertinent, propitious
E3 unsuitable; *formal* inopportune

opportunism *n*
exploitation, expediency, pragmatism, realism, taking advantage, unscrupulousness, Machiavellianism
COLLOQ. making hay while the sun shines

opportunity *n*
chance, opening occasion, possibility, hour, moment, room, scope, power, privilege, pick, overture, turn
OLD (*Shakesp*) vantage
COLLOQ. break, look-in, space, a bite of the cherry, crack of the whip

oppose *v*
1 RESIST, withstand, counter, attack, combat, contest, challenge, contradict, disapprove of, argue against, disagree with, stand up to, take a stand against, be against, take issue with, confront, defy, face, fight, hinder, obstruct, bar, check, prevent, thwart
COLLOQ. fly in the face of
2 COMPARE, contrast, match, offset, balance, counterbalance, set against, play off
FORMAL juxtapose
E3 1 defend, support

SYNONYM NUANCES

sense 1
Resist and **withstand** are suggestive of opposition while under pressure: *the party is resisting calls for modernization*. **Counter**, on the other hand, implies a positive retaliation, unlike **attack**, which suggests the initial incursion. The term **combat** has implications of an organized struggle against something: *combating drug abuse*, while **contest** and **challenge** are appropriate for disputing something verbally: *many anthropologists challenged his conclusions*. **Take issue with** a bit more forceful: *local scientists took issue with some of his evidence*.
   The term **disapprove of** likewise suggests a lack of accord, though not a vociferous one and without necessarily involving any active steps, whereas **stand up to**, **confront** and **face** are more suggestive of bravely encountering your opponents. **Defy** also suggests a degree of boldness in actively resisting: *I defied my father's wishes*, and the term **fight** is appropriate if you want to suggest a more fierce struggle against adversity.

---

opposed *adj*
in opposition, against, hostile, conflicting disagreeing opposing opposite, antagonistic, clashing contrary, incompatible
FORMAL averse, inimical
COLLOQ. anti
E3 in favour
■ **as opposed to**
rather than, instead of, in contrast to, as against, versus

opposing *adj*
opposite, contrary, differing at odds, at variance, rival, clashing conflicting irreconcilable, incompatible, opposed, contentious, enemy, hostile, antagonistic, fighting contending warring combatant
FORMAL antipathetic, disputatious, oppugnant

opposite *adj, n*
♦ *adj*
1 FACING, face to face, fronting corresponding
2 OPPOSED, antagonistic, conflicting contrary, hostile, contradictory, clashing irreconcilable, unlike, reverse, inconsistent, different, contrasted, differing at odds, at variance, opposing
FORMAL adverse, antithetical, dissident
COLLOQ. poles apart
E3 2 same
♦ *n*
reverse, converse, contrary, contradiction, inverse
FORMAL antithesis
COLLOQ. flip side, the other side of the coin, the other side of the fence
E3 same

opposition *n*
1 ANTAGONISM, hostility, resistance, confrontation, obstructiveness, unfriendliness, dislike, disapproval
2 OPPONENT, adversary, enemy, contender, antagonist, rival, foe, opposing side, other side, competition
E3 1 co-operation, support **2** ally, supporter

oppress *v*
1 OVERWHELM, subjugate, suppress, subdue, overpower, crush, trample, tyrannize, repress, enslave, quell, quash, persecute, maltreat, abuse, ride, grind, gripe, tread on the neck of
COLLOQ. bully, bring someone to their knees, treat like dirt, use as a doormat, walk all over
SLANG (*vulgar*) treat like shit
2 BURDEN, afflict, lie heavy on, bear hard upon, bear heavily upon, weigh down, weight, hang on/over, crush, harass, depress, press, sadden, discourage, dishearten, deject, dispirit, torment, vex, tread
FORMAL desolate

oppressed *adj*
tyrannized, burdened, persecuted, downtrodden, enslaved, subject, crushed, repressed, harassed, abused, maltreated, misused, troubled, disadvantaged, underprivileged
FORMAL subjugated
E3 free

oppression *n*
tyranny, overwhelming overpowering subjection, repression, despotism, suppression, injustice, cruelty, brutality, ruthlessness, abuse, persecution, maltreatment, harshness, hardship
FORMAL subjugation

oppressive *adj*
1 TYRANNICAL, tyrannous, despotic, overbearing overwhelming repressive, iron-fisted, domineering crushing harsh, unjust, inhuman, extortionate, cruel, brutal, ruthless, pitiless, merciless, burdensome, onerous, intolerable, Draconian
2 AIRLESS, stuffy, close, stifling suffocating sultry, muggy, heavy, sweltry, leaden
OLD faint
E3 1 just, gentle **2** airy

oppressor *n*
tyrant, bully, (hard) taskmaster, slave-driver, despot, dictator, persecutor, tormentor, torturer, intimidator, autocrat
FORMAL subjugator

opprobrious *adj*
contemptuous, insulting offensive, scandalous, abusive, damaging defamatory, derogatory, insolent, scurrilous, vitriolic, venomous
FORMAL calumniatory, calumnious, contumelious, invective, vituperative

opprobrium *n*
censure, disgrace, dishonour, reproach, disrepute, disfavour, discredit, degradation, debasement, shame, infamy, scurrility, stigma
FORMAL calumny, contumely, ignominy, obloquy, odium
COLLOQ. slur

opt *v*
choose, pick, decide (on), elect, prefer, go for, select, settle on, single out
COLLOQ. plump for

optical instrument

Optical instruments and devices include:

astronomical	laser	sextant
telescope	magnifying glass	simple microscope
binoculars	opera-glass	slide projector
camera	periscope	spyglass
compound	photomicroscope	stereocamera
microscope	reflecting	telescope
endoscope	telescope	telescopic sight
field-glasses	refracting	theodolite
film projector	telescope	

See also **spectacles**.

---

optimism *n*
cheerfulness, cheer, confidence, hopefulness, brightness, morale, buoyancy, idealism, expectancy, sanguineness
COLLOQ. feel-good factor
Fꓱ pessimism

optimistic *adj*
confident, assured, sanguine, hopeful, positive, cheerful, buoyant, bright, idealistic, expectant, bullish, pollyann(a)ish, Panglossian, Panglossic
COLLOQ. upbeat, happy-go-lucky, looking on the bright side, through rose-coloured spectacles
Fꓱ pessimistic

optimum *adj*
best, ideal, model, perfect, optimal, flawless, supreme, highest, superlative, top, choice, most favourable, utopian
Fꓱ worst

option *n*
choice, alternative, preference, possibility, selection

optional *adj*
voluntary, discretionary, elective, free, unforced
Fꓱ compulsory, required; *formal* mandatory

opulence *n*
1 RICHES, fortune, wealth, prosperity, affluence
COLLOQ. easy street
2 SUMPTUOUSNESS, lavishness, richness, luxury, plenty
3 ABUNDANCE, fullness, copiousness, profusion, superabundance, luxuriance
FORMAL cornucopia
Fꓱ **1** poverty; *formal* penury

opulent *adj*
1 RICH, wealthy, prosperous, affluent, well-to-do, well-off, moneyed
COLLOQ. well-heeled, rolling in it
2 SUMPTUOUS, lavish, luxurious
COLLOQ. plush, posh

3 ABUNDANT, copious, prolific, plentiful, profuse, superabundant, luxuriant
Fꓱ **1** poor; *formal* penurious

opus *n*
work, piece, production, composition, creation, oeuvre, brainchild

or *conj*
as an alternative, alternatively, conversely, in preference to, on the other hand

oracle *n*
1 SEER, prophet, prophetess, sage, soothsayer, wizard, sibyl, high priest, augur, fortune teller, forecaster
2 AUTHORITY, adviser, mentor, expert, specialist
COLLOQ. guru, mastermind, pundit
3 PROPHECY, vision, divination, prediction, forecast, revelation, answer, augury
FORMAL prognostication

oracular *adj*
prophetic, wise, significant, positive, authoritative, dogmatic, dictatorial, grave, predictive, obscure, mysterious, cryptic, Delphic, venerable, ominous, portentous, ambiguous, equivocal, two-edged
FORMAL arcane, abstruse, auspicious, haruspical, prescient, sage

oral *adj*
verbal, spoken, said, uttered, unwritten, vocal
Fꓱ written

orally *adv*
verbally, vocally, in spoken language, by mouth, *viva voce*
Fꓱ in written language

orate *v*
speak, talk, hold forth, lecture, sermonize, pontificate, discourse, harangue, speechify
FORMAL declaim

oration *n*
address, speech, lecture, sermon, discourse, harangue, homily
FORMAL declamation
COLLOQ. spiel

orator *n*
public speaker, speaker, lecturer, rhetorician, demagogue, declaimer, spellbinder, phrasemonger
COLLOQ. spieler

oratorical *adj*
rhetorical, eloquent, sonorous, high-flown, elocutionary, silver-tongued, smooth-tongued, Ciceronian, Demosthenic
FORMAL bombastic, declamatory, grandiloquent, magniloquent

oratory *n*
rhetoric, eloquence, public speaking speech, speechifying speechmaking diction, elocution, declamation
FORMAL grandiloquence

orb *n*
ball, sphere, globe, circle, ring mound, round, globule, spherule

orbit *n, v*
♦ *n*
1 CIRCUIT, cycle, circle, course, path, trajectory, track, revolution, rotation, orb
FORMAL circumgyration
2 RANGE, scope, reach, domain, influence, sphere of influence, sweep, ambit, compass
♦ *v*
revolve, circle, encircle, circumnavigate

orchestrate *v*
arrange, co-ordinate, organize, stage-manage, put together, prepare, present, mastermind, fix, integrate, score, compose

orchestration n

1 *orchestration of the event*
organization, arrangement, management,
running planning preparation, co-ordination,
stage-managing masterminding engineering

2 *orchestration of the music*
arrangement, adaptation, interpretation, setting score,
instrumentation, harmonization, version

ordain v

1 CONSECRATE, invest, appoint, call, elect, anoint,
frock, lay hands on
OLD ordinate
OLD SLANG japan

2 DECREE, order, require, instruct, rule, set,
lay down, fix, dictate, establish, pronounce, will, fate,
destine, predestine, preordain, predetermine
OLD ordinate, foresay
FORMAL dispose, foreordain, prescribe

ordeal n

trial, test, trouble(s), suffering anguish, distress, agony,
pain, torment, persecution, torture, nightmare, gruelling
baptism of fire
FORMAL tribulation(s), affliction

order n, v

♦ n

1 COMMAND, directive, decree, injunction, summons, writ,
warrant, instruction, direction, edict, dictate, ordinance,
stipulation, mandate, regulation, rule, precept, law

2 REQUISITION, request, requirement, booking commission,
reservation, application, demand, call, notification

3 ARRANGEMENT, organization, grouping sequence, cycle,
categorization, classification, codification, method, form,
pattern, plan, system, rota, regularity, uniformity,
symmetry, array, layout, line-up, set-up, structure
FORMAL disposition
Related adjective: ordinal

4 ORDERLINESS, neatness, tidiness, method, system

5 PEACE, quiet, calm, tranquillity, harmony,
law and order, lawfulness, discipline, control

6 ASSOCIATION, society, club, community, fellowship,
fraternity, brotherhood, sisterhood, sorority, lodge,
guild, league, company, organization, denomination,
sect, union, secret society

7 CONDITION, state, shape, form, order, working order,
fettle, kilter
COLLOQ. nick

8 CLASS, kind, sort, type, group, set, variety, species, genus,
rank, position, level, grade, degree, station, hierarchy,
family, caste
COLLOQ. pecking order
E3 **3** disorder **4** confusion, chaos **5** anarchy

♦ v

1 COMMAND, instruct, direct, bid, decree, rule, legislate,
require, authorize
FORMAL prescribe, enjoin

2 REQUEST, reserve, book, apply for, call for,
send away for, write off for
FORMAL requisition

3 ARRANGE, organize, systematize, dispose, classify,
group, marshal, tidy up, sort out, lay out,
manage, control, regulate, catalogue, codify

■ **order around**
order about, domineer, dominate, tyrannize, bully,
bulldoze, browbeat, boss around
COLLOQ. push about/around, throw your weight
about/around, lay down the law

■ **in order**

1 WORKING, functioning operative, mended

2 ORDERED, orderly, organized, tidy, neat, shipshape,
arranged, well-organized, systematic, regular,
methodical, categorized, classified, in sequence, in
alphabetical order

3 ACCEPTABLE, proper, correct, right, lawful, allowed,
permitted, suitable, appropriate, fitting all right, done
COLLOQ. OK

■ **in order to**
with the purpose, with the intention of, intending to, to,
with a view to, so that, with the result

■ **out of order**

1 BROKEN, broken down, not working not functioning
inoperative, out of commission
COLLOQ. gone phut, haywire, on the blink, bust, kaput
SLANG conked out

2 DISORDERED, disorganized, untidy, messy, confused,
muddled, out of sequence

3 UNACCEPTABLE, improper, un-called-for, incorrect,
wrong irregular, inappropriate, unsuitable, unlawful
OLD unseemly

orderliness n

neatness, tidiness, smartness, organization, straightness,
methodicalness, regularity, trimness, spruceness
E3 untidiness, disorderliness

orderly adj

1 ORDERED, systematic, neat, tidy, regular, methodical,
efficient, businesslike, in order, well-organized,
well-regulated, trim
COLLOQ. in apple-pie order

2 WELL-BEHAVED, controlled, disciplined, restrained, law-
abiding ruly
E3 **1** chaotic **2** disorderly, unruly

ordinance n

1 REGULATION, law, rule, ruling command,
decree, dictum, directive, injunction, canon,
statute, edict, enactment, fiat

2 SACRAMENT, ceremony, order, practice, observance, rite,
ritual, institution

ordinarily adv

as a rule, usually, commonly, normally, in general,
generally, familiarly, customarily, habitually,
conventionally

ordinary adj

normal, usual, customary, common, commonplace,
regular, routine, standard, mainstream, average, everyday,
workaday, quotidian, unexceptional, unremarkable, fair,
typical, plain, familiar, habitual, simple, conventional,
modest, mediocre, indifferent, uninteresting dull,
mundane, banal, bland, nondescript, pedestrian, prosaic,
undistinguished, unpretentious, unmemorable
COLLOQ. run-of-the-mill, common-or-garden, bog standard;
N Am garden-variety
E3 extraordinary, unusual

■ **out of the ordinary**
unusual, exceptional, remarkable, memorable, noteworthy,
extraordinary, different, unique, rare, outstanding surprising
unexpected

ordnance n

munitions, weapons, military supplies, arms, artillery,
cannon, guns
COLLOQ. big guns

ordure n

dirt, dung excrement, excretion, waste matter, droppings,
filth
TECHNICAL egesta, frass, scats, guano
FORMAL faeces, stool
SLANG poo, poop; (*vulgar*) crap, shit

organ n

1 DEVICE, instrument, implement, tool, element,
constituent, part, component, process, structure, unit,
member
See panel on next page

2 MEDIUM, agency, forum, vehicle, voice, mouthpiece,
publication, newspaper, paper, magazine, periodical,
journal

organic adj

1 *organic matter*
biological, living animate, natural
TECHNICAL biotic

Major organs of the body include:

DIGESTIVE SYSTEM:
bowel
colon
gall bladder
intestines
large intestine
liver
oesophagus
pancreas
rectum
small intestine
stomach

ENDOCRINE SYSTEM:
adrenal glands
hypothalamus

ovaries
pancreas
parathyroid glands
pituitary
testes
thymus glands
thyroid gland

LYMPHATIC/IMMUNE SYSTEM:
adenoids
appendix
lymph
lymph nodes and
 vessels
spleen

thymus
tonsils

NERVOUS SYSTEM:
brain
peripheral nerves
spinal cord

REPRODUCTIVE SYSTEM:
cervix
clitoris
ejaculatory duct
epididymis
fallopian tubes
ovaries
oviduct

penis
prostate
scrotum
seminal vesicles
testes
uterus
vagina
vas deferens
vulva

RESPIRATORY SYSTEM:
bronchus
diaphragm
lungs
nose

throat (or pharynx)
windpipe
 (or trachea)

SENSORY:
ear
eye
nose
skin
taste buds

URINARY SYSTEM:
bladder
kidneys
ureter
urethra

---

2 *organic vegetables*
natural, not artificial, non-chemical, chemical-free, pesticide-free, additive-free, GM-free
3 *an organic whole*
structured, organized, ordered, harmonious, coherent

organism *n*
1 LIVING THING, being creature, entity, body, structure, cell, animal, plant, bacterium
2 SYSTEM, structure, entity, whole, unity, organization, set-up

organization *n*
1 ASSOCIATION, institution, institute, society, company, firm, corporation, concern, operation, federation, group, body, union, league, club, confederation, consortium, conglomeration, syndicate, authority, council, outfit
2 ARRANGEMENT, management, running co-ordination, administration, development, planning regulation, establishment
3 SYSTEM, classification, methodology, order, formation, grouping method, plan, structure, arrangement, unity, whole, set-up, pattern, composition, design
FORMAL configuration

organize *v*
1 ARRANGE, co-ordinate, structure, manage, run, see to, administer, be in charge of, be responsible for, order, standardize, group, marshal, dispose, orchestrate, rationalize, put in order, sort out, classify, systematize, regiment, tabulate, catalogue
OLD embody
TECHNICAL lemmatize
2 ESTABLISH, found, set up, create, originate, start, begin, institute, prepare, develop, form, mould, frame, construct, assemble, put together, shape
1 disorganize

organized *adj*
arranged, neat, tidy, orderly, planned, ordered, well-ordered, structured, systematic, efficient, regular, methodical, businesslike, in order, well-organized, well-regulated
disorganized

orgiastic *adj*
bacchanalian, orgic, Dionysiac, Bacchic, debauched, wild

orgy *n*
1 PARTY, wild party, debauch, carousal, revelry, revel(s), bout, bacchanalia, Saturnalia, Dionysia
COLLOQ. binge, splurge
2 INDULGENCE, excess, spree, frenzy, bout
COLLOQ. binge, splurge

orient *v*
accustom, accommodate, familiarize, acclimatize, adapt, adjust, orientate, attune, align, get your bearings, find your bearings
FORMAL habituate

oriental *adj*
Eastern, Far Eastern, Asian, Asiatic

orientation *n*
1 SITUATION, bearings, location, direction, position, positioning alignment, placement, attitude, inclination
2 INDUCTION, initiation, training guiding leading acclimatization, familiarization, adaptation, adjustment, getting your bearings, finding your bearings, SYN> settling-in

orifice *n*
opening hole, gap, space, aperture, breach, break, inlet, pore, rent, slit, slot, vent, mouth, cleft, crack, rift, crevice, fissure, perforation
FORMAL aperture

origin *n*
1 SOURCE, spring fount, foundation, basis, base, cause, derivation, root(s), fountain, fountainhead, well-spring
TECHNICAL etymology
FORMAL provenance
2 BEGINNING, start, inauguration, foundation, launch, birth, dawn, dawning creation, conception, emergence
FORMAL commencement, inception, genesis
3 ANCESTRY, descent, line of descent, line, extraction, heritage, family, lineage, parentage, pedigree, birth, paternity, stock
2 end, termination
Related adjective: genetic

original *adj, n*
♦ *adj*
1 FIRST, early, earliest, initial, primary, archetypal, rudimentary, embryonic, starting opening commencing first-hand, primitive, primal
FORMAL indigenous, autochthonous, prim(a)eval, primordial
2 CREATIVE, innovative, new, novel, fresh, imaginative, ingenious, inventive, resourceful, unconventional, unorthodox, unusual, unique, pioneering ground-breaking
3 GENUINE, real, authentic, true, actual
1 latest **2** hackneyed, unoriginal **3** copied
♦ *n*
prototype, master, paradigm, model, pattern, archetype, standard, type
copy

originality *n*
inventiveness, creativeness, creativity, imaginativeness, imagination, freshness, boldness, cleverness, creative spirit, daring innovativeness, innovation, ingenuity, individuality, resourcefulness, newness, novelty, unconventionality, unorthodoxy, singularity, eccentricity

> **QUOTATIONS**
> Talent comes from originality which has a special manner of thinking of seeing of understanding and of judging
> GUY DE MAUPASSANT, *Pierre et Jean*

originally adv
initially, at first, at the start, at the outset, in the beginning
first, to begin with, in origin, by derivation, by birth

originate v
1 RISE, arise, spring stem, issue, flow, emanate, proceed,
derive, result, come, evolve, emerge, be born
2 CREATE, invent, inaugurate, introduce, give birth to,
develop, discover, establish, begin, start, set up, set in
motion, launch, pioneer, conceive, form, produce,
generate, be the father/mother of, seed, plant
FORMAL commence
⊟ 1 end, terminate

origination n
creation, development, forming production, conception,
generation, invention

originator n
architect, author, creator, designer, father, mother,
founder, generator, developer, establisher, innovator,
discoverer, inventor, initiator, pioneer, prime mover
COLLOQ. the brains

ornament n, v
♦ n
1 ADORNMENT, decoration, embellishment, garnish,
trimming accessory, frill, pattern
2 TRINKET, decoration, bauble, jewel, knick-knack,
accessory, gewgaw, furbelow, fallal
♦ v
decorate, adorn, embellish, garnish, trim, beautify,
brighten, dress up, deck, gild

> **QUOTATIONS**
> The evolution of culture is synonymous with the
> removal of ornament from utilitarian objects
> ADOLF LOOS, *Trotzdem*

ornamental adj
decorative, embellishing adorning embroidering attractive,
showy, fancy

ornamentation n
decoration, adornment, embellishment, embroidery,
ornateness, elaboration, garniture, frills, fallalery

ornate adj
elaborate, ornamented, decorated, elegant, fine, fancy,
embellished, showy, ostentatious, baroque, rococo, florid,
flowery, flamboyant, fussy, busy, grandiose, sumptuous
OLD adorn
COLLOQ. flash
⊟ plain, simple

orotund adj
1 *orotund voices*
full, loud, round, powerful, strong deep, rich, sonorous,
booming resonating
2 *orotund speaking*
dignified, imposing ornate, pompous, strained, pretentious
FORMAL magniloquent

orthodox adj
1 CONFORMIST, conventional, accepted, correct, official,
traditional, usual, regular, well-established, established,
received, customary, conservative, recognized,
authoritative, *bien pensant*
COLLOQ. square
2 *orthodox religious views*
sound, conservative, correct, true, faithful, devout,
traditional, strict, canonic, canonical, fundamentalist,
hardshell
⊟ 1 nonconformist, unorthodox

orthodoxy n
1 CONVENTIONALITY, conformity, conformism, correctness,
properness, authoritativeness, received wisdom
2 TRADITIONALISM, soundness, conservatism, devoutness,
devotion, trueness, faithfulness, inflexibility, strictness,
fundamentalism

3 DOCTRINE, dogma, creed, belief, tenet, principle, teaching
precept, conviction, canon, credo

oscillate v
fluctuate, vary, waver, sway, swing vacillate, move
backwards and forwards, move to and fro, vibrate,
wigwag go from one extreme to the other
COLLOQ. seesaw, yo-yo

oscillation n
fluctuation, wavering variation, vacillation, swinging swing
instability
COLLOQ. shilly-shallying seesawing

ossify v
fossilize, harden, solidify, make/become fixed,
make/become hard
FORMAL indurate, petrify, rigidify

ostensible adj
alleged, apparent, presumed, seeming supposed,
so-called, professed, claimed, outward, pretended,
superficial, specious
FORMAL feigned, purported, ostensive
⊟ real, genuine

ostensibly adv
allegedly, apparently, professedly, supposedly, seemingly,
reputedly, outwardly, superficially, on the surface,
to all intents and purposes
FORMAL purportedly

ostentation n
showiness, showing-off, flamboyance, pretension,
pretentiousness, show, flaunting vaunting pomp, dash,
éclat, pride, puff, exhibitionism, boasting display, flourish,
pageantry, parade, trappings, pretence, vanity, window-
dressing splash, fuss, fanfaronade, peacockery
TECHNICAL phylactery
OLD ostent
FORMAL affectation
COLLOQ. flash, flashiness, swank, tinsel, dog
⊟ unpretentiousness

ostentatious adj
showy, pretentious, vulgar, loud, obtrusive, flaunting
demonstrative, garish, gaudy, flamboyant, conspicuous,
outré, extravagant, splashy, barbarous
OLD fastuous
FORMAL affected
COLLOQ. flashy, flash, kitsch, glitzy, over the top, OTT
⊟ restrained, modest

ostentatiously adv
showily, flamboyantly, pretentiously, loudly, obtrusively,
demonstratively, garishly, extravagantly, conspicuously
COLLOQ. flashily, over the top, OTT
⊟ modestly

ostracism n
exclusion, isolation, rejection, barring avoidance,
banishment, boycott, exile, expulsion, excommunication
FORMAL disfellowship, proscription
COLLOQ. cold-shoulder
⊟ acceptance, reinstatement, welcome

ostracize v
exclude, banish, exile, expel, excommunicate, reject,
segregate, isolate, send to Coventry, shun, snub, boycott,
bar, outlaw, avoid
COLLOQ. cold-shoulder, cut
⊟ accept, welcome

other adj
1 DIFFERENT, dissimilar, unlike, variant, separate, distinct,
contrasting
FORMAL disparate
2 MORE, further, extra, additional, supplementary, spare,
alternative

otherwise adv
1 UNLESS, if not, or, or else, failing that
2 DIFFERENTLY, in a different way, in another way,
along different lines, in other respects

otherworldly *adj*
dreamy, absent-minded, ethereal, preoccupied, rapt, bemused, fey
F3 worldly, mundane, solid, substantial

otiose *adj*
redundant, superfluous, extra, spare, excess, surplus, remaining to spare, unnecessary, unneeded, needless, gratuitous, unwanted, unwarranted, uncalled-for, excessive
FORMAL supernumerary
F3 necessary, needed, required, wanted

ounce *n*
particle, scrap, speck, spot, trace, touch, tad, iota, jot, shred, whit, atom, crumb, drop, grain, modicum, morsel
Related adjective: uncial

oust *v*
expel, eject, depose, displace, supplant, turn out, throw out, overthrow, evict, drive out, thrust out, force out, put out, get rid of, dismiss, unseat, dislodge, dispossess, disinherit, replace, topple
COLLOQ. sack, fire, kick out, boot out, show the door to, give someone the boot/elbow
F3 install, settle

out *adj*
1 AWAY, absent, elsewhere, not at home, gone, outside, abroad
2 UNCONSCIOUS, knocked out, out cold
TECHNICAL comatose
FORMAL insensible
COLLOQ. KO'd
3 *the book is out*
published, available, obtainable, ready, in print
4 REVEALED, exposed, known, disclosed, divulged, public, evident, manifest, in the open
5 FORBIDDEN, unacceptable, impossible, excluded, inadmissible, unwelcome, undesirable, inappropriate, unsuitable
FORMAL disallowed
6 OUT-OF-DATE, unfashionable, old-fashioned, dated, passé, antiquated, *démodé*
COLLOQ. old hat
7 EXTINGUISHED, finished, expired, dead, not burning doused, not shining used up
8 *the flowers are out*
in bloom, in full bloom, blooming blossoming in flower
9 *out to make money*
determined, bent, insistent, intent, set
F3 **1** in, here, at home **2** conscious **3** out of print, unavailable **4** hidden, concealed **5** allowed, permitted **6** in fashion, up-to-date; *colloq.* in **7** burning

out-and-out *adj*
absolute, thorough, total, complete, utter, outright, perfect, downright, inveterate, thoroughgoing unmitigated, unqualified, uncompromising
FORMAL arrant, consummate
COLLOQ. dyed-in-the-wool

outbreak *n*
eruption, outburst, explosion, flare-up, clash, upsurge, sudden start, flash, rash, burst, epidemic, storm, upbreak
FORMAL recrudescence, ebullition, excrescence

outburst *n*
outbreak, eruption, explosion, flare-up, salvo, outpouring outcry, burst, fit, gush, surge, storm, spasm, seizure, gale, attack, fit of temper, paroxysm

outcast *n*
castaway, exile, pariah, outsider, untouchable, leper, refugee, evacuee, reject, *persona non grata*

outclass *v*
surpass, outshine, beat, excel over, be much better than, outrival, transcend, top, eclipse, outdo, exceed, outdistance, outrank, outstrip, overshadow, leave standing put in the shade

outcome *n*
result, consequence, upshot, conclusion, effect, after-effect, product, issue, sequel, end result, answer, proceeds, dénouement, pay-off, outspring upcome
OLD proof
SLANG *Aust* wash-up

outcry *n*
protest, complaint, protestation, objection, dissent, indignation, uproar, cry, exclamation, clamour, row, fuss, commotion, noise, tumult, hue and cry, outburst
COLLOQ. hullaballoo, racket

outdated *adj*
out of date, old-fashioned, out of fashion, dated, unfashionable, outmoded, behind the times, obsolete, obsolescent, superseded, antediluvian, antiquated, antique, archaic, passé, *démodé*
COLLOQ. out of the ark, fuddy-duddy, old-fogeyish, old hat, past it, square, past its sell-by date, on the way out, steam, oldfangled, uncool, mumsy
F3 modern, up-to-date, fashionable

outdistance *v*
outstrip, outpace, outrun, pass, overtake, pull ahead of, shake off, overhaul, surpass, leave behind, leave standing

outdo *v*
surpass, exceed, beat, excel, outstrip, outshine, get the better of, have the advantage over, come first, overcome, defeat, outclass, outdistance, eclipse, transcend
COLLOQ. cap, gain the upper/whip hand over, stand/be head and shoulders above, run rings/circles round

outdoors *adv*
out, outside, in the open air, out-of-doors, alfresco, *en plein air*
F3 indoors

outer *adj*
1 EXTERNAL, exterior, outside, outermost, outward, surface, superficial, peripheral
2 OUTLYING, distant, remote, further, fringe, peripheral, faraway
F3 **1** internal **2** inner

outface *v*
brave, confront, defy, stand up to, outstare, stare down, brazen out, beard
F3 capitulate; *formal* succumb

outfit *n, v*
♦ *n*
1 CLOTHES, dress, suit, costume, ensemble, separates, turnout, setout
OLD weed
FORMAL accoutrements
COLLOQ. get-up, togs, garb, gear
2 EQUIPMENT, kit, tools, apparatus, rig trappings, paraphernalia, layout
OLD fit-out
COLLOQ. gear, bag of tricks
3 ORGANIZATION, firm, business, company, corporation, group, team, unit, set, set-up, clique, coterie, crew, gang squad
♦ *v*
fit out, furnish, provide, supply, equip, stock, turn out, fit up, kit out, appoint, provision
FORMAL accoutre, apparel, attire

outfitter *n*
tailor, clothier, costumer, costumier, dressmaker, sartor, modiste, haberdasher, couturier, *couturière*

outflow *n*
discharge, rush, spout, gush, jet, emergence, effusion, emanation, outrush, outpouring drainage, ebb, outfall
FORMAL debouchment, disemboguement, effluence, effluent, effluvium, efflux, effluxion
F3 inflow

outflowing *adj*
discharging gushing leaking rushing spurting effluent, emanant
FORMAL debouching

outfox *v*
outsmart, outwit, outperform, outmanoeuvre, best, out-think, beat, get the better of, deceive, trick, dupe
COLLOQ. kid, con, have on, pull a fast one on
SLANG take for a ride

outgoing *adj*
1 SOCIABLE, friendly, unreserved, uninhibited, affable, amiable, warm, affectionate, approachable, expansive, open, talkative, extrovert, gregarious, cordial, genial, easy-going communicative, demonstrative, sympathetic
2 DEPARTING, retiring leaving former, last, past, ex-, emissary
F3 1 reserved 2 incoming

outgoings *n*
costs, expenditure, outlay, overheads, spending expenses
FORMAL disbursal, disbursement
F3 income

outgrowth *n*
1 CONSEQUENCE, effect, product, offshoot, by-product, spin-off, emanation
2 SWELLING, shoot, sprout
FORMAL protuberance, excrescence

outing *n*
excursion, expedition, jaunt, trip, pleasure trip, tour, mystery tour, spin, picnic, hike, sally, junket; *dialect* out
COLLOQ. jolly

outlandish *adj*
unconventional, unfamiliar, unheard-of, unknown, bizarre, strange, odd, unusual, peculiar, weird, eccentric, alien, exotic, curious, quaint, barbarous, grotesque, foreign, extraordinary, preposterous, unreasonable
COLLOQ. freaky, oddball, wacky
SLANG way-out, far-out
F3 familiar, ordinary

outlandishness *n*
bizarreness, oddness, unusualness, strangeness, weirdness, queerness, eccentricity, exoticness, quaintness, grotesqueness
F3 commonplaceness, familiarity

outlast *v*
survive, come through, outlive, outstay, ride, weather

outlaw *n, v*
♦ *n*
fugitive, bandit, brigand, robber, desperado, highwayman, criminal, marauder, pirate, outcast, exile, Robin Hood; *N Am* badman
♦ *v*
ban, disallow, forbid, prohibit, exclude, embargo, bar, debar, banish, excommunicate, condemn
OLD TECHNICAL *Scot* horn
FORMAL proscribe, interdict
F3 allow, legalize

outlay *n*
expenditure, expenses, outgoings, payment, charge, cost, price, spending
FORMAL disbursement
F3 income

outlet *n*
1 RETAILER, retail outlet, shop, store, market, supplier
2 EXIT, way out, vent, duct, escape, issue, let-off, outfall, opening port, sea gate, release, valve, safety valve, sluice, nozzle, channel, culvert, conduit, *débouché*, emissary
TECHNICAL femerall
OLD going forth
FORMAL egress

3 *an outlet for your feelings*
channel, means of release, means of expression, safety valve
F3 2 entry, inlet

outline *n, v*
♦ *n*
1 SUMMARY, sketch, synopsis, précis, résumé, main points, prospectus, programme, scenario, rough idea, bare facts, bare bones, framework, skeleton, thumbnail sketch, abstract, aperçu, *croquis, esquisse*
2 PROFILE, sketch, tracing form, shape, design, figure, layout, plan, contour, silhouette, keyline, skyline, waterline, chart, diagram, map, schema, ground plan, underdrawing balloon
TECHNICAL trick
FORMAL configuration, delineation, lineament, contorno
♦ *v*
1 SKETCH (OUT), summarize, draft, trace, rough out, give a rough idea of, chalk out
FORMAL delineate, adumbrate
2 EDGE, trim, fringe, dress, braid

outlive *v*
survive, outlast, come through, live through, weather
F3 predecease

outlook *n*
1 VIEW, viewpoint, point of view, attitude, mindset, perspective, frame of mind, interpretation, angle, slant, standpoint, opinion, world-view, *Weltanschauung*
2 EXPECTATIONS, future, forecast, prospect(s), prognosis
3 *a house with a pleasant outlook*
view, prospect, aspect, panorama

outlying *adj*
distant, remote, isolated, far-off, far-away, far-flung outer, out-of-the-way, inaccessible, provincial
COLLOQ. off the beaten track
F3 inner

outmanoeuvre *v*
outdo, outthink, outwit, outsmart, outfox, beat, outflank, outgeneral, get the better of
FORMAL circumvent

outmoded *adj*
out of date, old-fashioned, out of fashion, dated, unfashionable, behind the times, obsolete, obsolescent, superseded, antediluvian, antiquated, archaic, passé, démodé
COLLOQ. out of the ark, fuddy-duddy, old-fogeyish, old hat, past it, square, past its sell-by date, on the way out, steam, oldfangled, uncool
F3 modern, new, fashionable, fresh

out of date *adj*
old-fashioned, outdated, outmoded, out of fashion, dated, unfashionable, behind the times, obsolete, obsolescent, superseded, antediluvian, antiquated, archaic, passé, démodé
COLLOQ. out of the ark, fuddy-duddy, old-fogeyish, old hat, past it, square, past its sell-by date, on the way out, steam, oldfangled, uncool
F3 modern, new, fashionable, fresh

out-of-the-way *adj*
remote, isolated, far-flung far-off, far-away, distant, outlying outer, inaccessible, lonely, little-known, obscure, unfrequented, peripheral, god-forsaken
COLLOQ. off the beaten track

out of work *adj*
unemployed, redundant, out of a job, jobless, idle, laid off, workless
COLLOQ. on the dole, resting between jobs
F3 employed, occupied, busy

outpace *v*
outstrip, outrun, outdistance, outdo, beat, pass, overtake, surpass, overhaul

outpouring *n*
flood, deluge, torrent, stream, spate, spurt, flow, outflow, flux, cascade, effusion, emanation
FORMAL debouchment, disemboguement, effluence, efflux

output *n*
production, productivity, product, manufacture, achievement, performance, accomplishment, gain, yield, fruits, harvest, return, outturn, turnout, throughput

outrage *n, v*
♦ *n*
1 ANGER, fury, rage, indignation, shock, affront, horror, dudgeon, wrath
2 ATROCITY, offence, injury, enormity, barbarism, brutality, crime, violation, evil, scandal, horror, affront
♦ *v*
1 APPAL, anger, infuriate, affront, incense, enrage, madden, disgust, injure, offend, shock, horrify, scandalize
2 ASSAULT, violate, abuse, desecrate, defile, ravish, ravage

outrageous *adj*
1 ATROCIOUS, abominable, shocking scandalous, offensive, disgraceful, dreadful, terrible, monstrous, unspeakable, flagrant, diabolical, horrible, ghastly, gruesome, vile, foul, unacceptable, intolerable, unbearable, insufferable
OLD enormous
FORMAL heinous, egregious
COLLOQ. unchristian, ungodly, unholy, infernal
2 EXCESSIVE, exorbitant, immoderate, unreasonable, extortionate, scandalous, obscene, inordinate, preposterous
🖅 **2** acceptable, reasonable

outrageously *adv*
scandalously, disgracefully, obscenely, unspeakably, unacceptably, intolerably, unbearably, terribly, dreadfully, horribly

outré *adj*
unconventional, unusual, strange, odd, extraordinary, eccentric, weird, bizarre, shocking outrageous
COLLOQ. oddball, freaky
SLANG way-out, far-out

outrider *n*
advance guard, escort, attendant, guard, bodyguard, vanguard, herald, precursor

outright *adj, adv*
♦ *adj*
1 TOTAL, utter, absolute, complete, downright, out-and-out, unqualified, unconditional, unmitigated, perfect, pure, thorough, direct
2 CLEAR, definite, categorical, unequivocal, unmistakable, undeniable, straightforward
🖅 **2** ambiguous, indefinite
♦ *adv*
1 TOTALLY, absolutely, completely, wholly, entirely, categorically, utterly, thoroughly, openly, without restraint, straightforwardly, positively, directly, explicitly
2 *killed outright*
instantaneously, at once, there and then, instantly, immediately, straight away

outrun *v*
outstrip, outpace, outdistance, overtake, outdo, shake off, pass, overhaul, surpass, exceed, excel, beat, lose, run faster than, leave behind

outset *n*
start, beginning opening inauguration
FORMAL inception, commencement
COLLOQ. kick-off
🖅 end, conclusion

outshine *v*
outclass, outstrip, outdo, overshadow, transcend, eclipse, surpass, beat, best, upstage, excel, dwarf, outrank, top, put in the shade, put to shame

outside *adj, n*
♦ *adj*
1 EXTERNAL, exterior, outer, surface, superficial, outward, extraneous, outdoor, outermost, extreme
2 *an outside chance*
remote, marginal, distant, small, faint, slight, slim, slender, vague, negligible, improbable, unlikely
3 *outside examiners*
external, independent, consulting non-resident, casual, temporary, visiting self-employed, extramural, peripatetic, subcontracted, neutral, objective, impartial, unbiased
🖅 **1** inside, internal **2** likely, real, substantial **3** resident, internal
♦ *n*
exterior, façade, front, surface, outer surface, face, appearance, cover
🖅 inside

outsider *n*
stranger, intruder, alien, non-member, non-resident, foreigner, newcomer, visitor, emigrant, émigré, immigrant, outlander, interloper, misfit, gatecrasher, outlier
COLLOQ. odd one out, gooseberry, third wheel
SLANG N Am ringer

outsize *adj*
huge, immense, vast, enormous, massive, colossal, titanic, giant, gigantic, mammoth, tremendous, stupendous, great, very big very large, extensive, monstrous, gargantuan
FORMAL prodigious
COLLOQ. jumbo, frightful, ginormous, humongous
SLANG mega
🖅 tiny, minute

outskirts *n*
suburbs, suburbia, vicinity, neighbourhood, environs, periphery, edges, fringes, borders, boundary, limit, frontier, edge, margin, perimeter
🖅 centre

outsmart *v*
outwit, outperform, outmanoeuvre, best, out-think, beat, get the better of, deceive, trick, dupe, outfox
COLLOQ. kid, con, have on, pull a fast one on
SLANG take for a ride

outsource *v*
contract out, farm out, delegate, pass/give to others
🖅 insource

outspoken *adj*
candid, frank, forthright, free, unreserved, unequivocal, unceremonious, plain-spoken, plain, direct, straightforward, bluff, broad, straight, vocal, explicit, blunt, brusque, rude, Rabelaisian
🖅 diplomatic, reserved

outspokenness *n*
candidness, frankness, plainness, directness, forthrightness, straightforwardness, bluntness, bluffness, brusqueness, rudeness

outspread *adj*
spread out, outstretched, open, opened, wide, wide-open, unfolded, unfurled, stretched, extended, fanned out, flared, expanded

outstanding *adj*
1 EXCELLENT, distinguished, eminent, pre-eminent, famous, famed, well-known, renowned, celebrated, exceptional, superior, remarkable, prominent, superb, great, notable, extraordinaire, impressive, striking salient, superlative, important, noteworthy, memorable, special, extraordinary, arresting golden, chief, uber-
FORMAL prosilient
COLLOQ. ace, top-notch, smashing brill, out of this world; N Am some
SLANG cool, wicked, radical
2 OWING, unpaid, due, unsettled, unresolved, uncollected, pending payable, remaining unfinished, to be done, ongoing left-over
🖅 **1** ordinary, unexceptional **2** paid, settled

outstandingly adv
exceptionally, remarkably, greatly, notably, extremely, especially, extraordinarily, impressively, strikingly, amazingly

outstrip v
surpass, exceed, better, outdo, beat, top, transcend, outshine, pass, gain on, go/travel faster than, leave behind, leave standing outrun, outdistance, overtake, eclipse

outward adj
external, exterior, outer, outside, outermost, surface, superficial, visible, apparent, perceptible, noticeable, discernible, observable, evident, supposed, professed, public, obvious, ostensible
▣ inner, private

outwardly adv
apparently, externally, to all appearances, visibly, superficially, supposedly, seemingly, on the surface, on the outside, at first sight, as far as you can see, on the face of it

outweigh v
exceed, surpass, be greater than, be more than, be superior to, override, prevail over, overcome, take precedence over, cancel out, make up for, compensate for, predominate
FORMAL preponderate

outwit v
outsmart, outthink, outmanoeuvre, get the better of, be cleverer than, trick, better, beat, dupe, cheat, deceive, defraud, swindle
COLLOQ. kid, con, have on, pull a fast one on
SLANG take for a ride

outworn adj
outdated, out of date, outmoded, ancient, antiquated, archaic, stale, discredited, defunct, old-fashioned, behind the times, hackneyed, rejected, obsolete, obsolescent, disused, exhausted, abandoned
COLLOQ. old hat, moth-eaten, past it, past its sell-by date
▣ fresh, new

oval adj
egg-shaped, elliptical, ovoid, ovate, ellipsoidal
TECHNICAL obovate, oviform
FORMAL vulviform

ovation n
applause, acclaim, acclamation, praise(s), tribute, clapping handclapping cheering cheers, accolade, bravos
FORMAL plaudits, laudation
COLLOQ. bouquet
▣ abuse, catcalls

oven n
cooker, stove, microwave (oven), kiln

over adj, adv, prep
♦ adj
finished, ended, at an end, done with, past, gone, no more, completed, closed, in the past, settled, up, forgotten, accomplished
FORMAL concluded, terminated
COLLOQ. over and done with, ancient history
♦ adv
1 ABOVE, beyond, overhead, on high
FORMAL aloft
2 EXTRA, remaining surplus, superfluous, left, left over, unclaimed, unused, unwanted, in excess, in addition
♦ prep
1 ABOVE, on, on top of, upon, in charge of, in command of, higher than, superior to

2 EXCEEDING, more than, in excess of
3 ON THE SUBJECT OF, about, on, concerning relating to, connected with, concerned with, regarding as regards, referring to, with regard to, with respect to, with reference to, on the subject of, in the matter of, re, dealing with
FORMAL apropos of

■ **over and above**
in addition to, on top of, together with, plus, along with, as well as, besides, added to, let alone, not to mention

■ **over and over (again)**
again and again, repeatedly, frequently, often, continually, endlessly, time and (time) again, ad infinitum, ad nauseam

overabundance n
surplus, surfeit, excess, glut, profusion, oversupply, embarras de choixembarras de richesses
FORMAL superfluity, superabundance, plethora
COLLOQ. too much of a good thing
▣ lack, dearth

overact v
overplay, exaggerate, overdo
COLLOQ. ham, lay/pile it on, lay/pile it on thick, lay/pile it on with a trowel
▣ underact, underplay

overall adj, adv
♦ adj
total, all-inclusive, all-embracing comprehensive, inclusive, complete, sweeping general, universal, global, broad, all-over, out to out
COLLOQ. blanket, umbrella
▣ narrow, specific
♦ adv
in general, on the whole, by and large, broadly, broadly/generally speaking altogether

overalls n
dungarees, coverall, boiler suit, workwear, dust-coat, pinafore, crawler, tablier; dialect save-all
OLD jumper
COLLOQ. pinnie

overawe v
intimidate, daunt, dismay, disconcert, abash, frighten, scare, terrify, petrify, alarm, awe, impress, unnerve, browbeat, cow
▣ reassure, comfort

overbalance v
lose your balance, fall over, tip over, topple over, trip, slip, tumble, upset, somersault, lose your footing capsize, keel over, overturn, turn turtle

overbearing adj
imperious, domineering arrogant, officious, dictatorial, despotic, lordly, tyrannical, high-handed, haughty, proud, cavalier, autocratic, dogmatic, oppressive, presumptuous, contemptuous, disdainful
COLLOQ. bossy, la-di-da, snobby, snooty, snotty, stuck-up, toffee-nosed, too big for your boots
SLANG smartarse, smartass
▣ meek, unassertive

overblown adj
overstated, overdone, overestimated, overcharge, excessive, extravagant, pretentious, embellished, amplified, bombastic, inflated, caricatured, burlesqued, exalted, self-important
COLLOQ. over the top, OTT

overcast adj
cloudy, clouded (over), grey, dull, dark, darkened, sombre, gloomy, dreary, dismal, sunless, hazy, misty, foggy, leaden, louring
▣ bright, clear

overcharge v
surcharge, short-change, cheat, extort, fleece, swindle
COLLOQ. do, diddle, rook

SLANG rip off, sting
F3 undercharge

overcoat
See panel at **coat**.

overcome *v, adj*
♦ *v*
conquer, defeat, beat, surmount, prevail,
triumph over, get the better of, be victorious over,
rise above, master, overpower, overwhelm,
overthrow, subdue, trounce, best, worst, rout,
break, knock out, outdo, outplay, outwit, outsmart,
be more than a match for, have the edge on, wear down,
put on the foil
OLD convince, evince, fordo, superate; (*Spenser*)
underfong
FORMAL vanquish, subjugate, expugn
COLLOQ. hammer, slaughter, clobber, lick, thrash, wipe the
floor with, hit/knock for six
♦ *adj*
overwhelmed, overpowered, exhausted, broken, moved,
speechless, choked up
COLLOQ. dead-beat, bowled over, swept off your feet,
lost for words
FORMAL affected

over-confident *adj*
arrogant, brash, cocksure, self-assured, blustering
swaggering presumptuous, overweening foolhardy, rash,
incautious, over-optimistic, sanguine
FORMAL hubristic, temerarious
COLLOQ. cocky, uppity, uppish
F3 cautious, diffident

overcritical *adj*
overparticular, fault-finding hypercritical, hard to please,
pedantic, over-nice, purist, captious, carping cavilling
Zoilean
FORMAL ultra-crepidarian
COLLOQ. nit-picking pernickety, hair-splitting; *N Am*
persnickety
F3 easy-going tolerant, uncritical

overcrowded *adj*
congested, packed (out), crammed full,
chock-full, chock-a-block, overpopulated,
overloaded, swarming teeming overrun,
full to overflowing
COLLOQ. jam-packed, packed like sardines
SLANG chocker
F3 deserted, empty

overdo *v*
exaggerate, go too far, carry to excess, overindulge,
overstate, overact, overplay
COLLOQ. ham it up, go overboard, camp it up, lay/pile it
on, lay/pile it on thick, lay/pile it on with a trowel, stretch
a point
■ **overdo it**
overwork, work too hard, do too much, overstretch
yourself, strain yourself, overreach yourself, overexert
yourself
COLLOQ. sweat blood, burn yourself out, bite off more
than you can chew, run yourself into the ground, burn the
candle at both ends, work your fingers to the bone, crack
up

overdone *adj*
1 OVERCOOKED, burnt, spoiled, dried up, overbaked,
charred
COLLOQ. burnt to a cinder, burnt to a frazzle
2 EXAGGERATED, overstated, overelaborate, undue,
unnecessary, overplayed, excessive, immoderate, fulsome,
effusive, gushing inordinate, histrionic
COLLOQ. over the top, OTT
F3 **1** underdone, raw **2** underplayed, understated

overdraft *n*
overdrawn account, debt, arrears, liabilities, borrowings,
unpaid amounts, deficit, insufficient funds

overdue *adj*
late, behindhand, behind schedule, delayed, owing
unpaid, due, unsettled, pending payable, unpunctual, slow
FORMAL tardy, belated
F3 early

overeat *v*
gorge, overindulge, guzzle, eat too much, go on a binge,
stuff yourself, gormandize
COLLOQ. binge, make a pig of yourself, pig out, have eyes
bigger than your stomach
F3 abstain, starve

overeating *n*
guzzling overindulgence, gluttony, bulimia, hyperphagia,
gourmandism, gormandism, gourmandise, gormandise
COLLOQ. bingeing
F3 abstemiousness, abstention

overemphasize *v*
exaggerate, overstress, lay/put too much emphasis on,
attach too much importance to, make too much of,
labour, belabour, overdramatize
COLLOQ. make a mountain out of a molehill, blow up out
of all proportion
F3 minimize, play down, underplay, understate, belittle

overexert
■ **overexert yourself**
overdo it, overstrain yourself, overtax yourself, overtire
yourself, overwork, strain yourself, wear yourself out,
drive yourself too hard, work too hard, run yourself into
the ground, fatigue, work yourself to death, push yourself
too hard
COLLOQ. burn the candle at both ends, knock yourself out
F3 idle, laze

overflow *v, n*
♦ *v*
spill (over), overrun, run over, pour over, well over,
flow over, brim over, bubble over, surge, discharge,
flood, cover, inundate, deluge, shower, submerge, soak,
swamp, teem
♦ *n*
overspill, spill, inundation, flood, spillage, overabundance,
surplus

overflowing *adj*
crowded, filled, full, swarming teeming thronged,
bountiful, abounding superabundant, brimful, plentiful,
copious, profuse, rife
FORMAL inundant, plenteous
F3 lacking scarce

overgrowth *n*
escalation, overabundance, overdevelopment,
superabundance
TECHNICAL hypertrophy
F3 decline, failure, shrinkage, wasting

overhang *v*
jut (out), project, bulge (out), protrude, stick out,
poke (out), stand out, extend, beetle

overhanging *adj*
projecting protruding jutting (out), bulging (out), sticking
out, standing out, beetling prominent
FORMAL pensile

overhaul *v, n*
♦ *v*
1 RENOVATE, repair, service, recondition, revamp, mend,
examine, inspect, investigate, check, check over/up,
survey, go over, re-examine, fix
OLD rummage
2 OVERTAKE, pull ahead of, outpace, outstrip, outdistance,
gain on, pass, get ahead of
♦ *n*
reconditioning repair, renovation, check, check-up,
service, examination, inspection
COLLOQ. going-over

overhead *adv, adj*
♦ *adv*
above, up above, on high, upward
OLD aloft
⊟ below, underfoot
♦ *adj*
elevated, aerial, overhanging raised, air

overheads *n*
running costs, outgoings, operating costs, regular costs,
fixed costs, expenses, expenditure, burden, oncost(s)
FORMAL disbursement
⊟ income, profit

overheated *adj*
angry, agitated, inflamed, fiery, flaming overwrought,
passionate, roused, impassioned, excited,
overexcited
⊟ calm, cool, impassive, dispassionate

overindulge *v*
1 GORGE, gormandize, gluttonize, guzzle, debauch,
eat/drink too much, satiate, sate
COLLOQ. binge, pig out, make a pig of yourself
SLANG booze, get pissed, lush
2 PAMPER, mollycoddle, spoil, cosset, pander, pet
COLLOQ. spoon-feed
⊟ 1 abstain

overindulgence *n*
excess, immoderation, overeating intemperance, surfeit,
debauch
COLLOQ. binge
⊟ abstemiousness, abstention

overjoyed *adj*
delighted, elated, euphoric, ecstatic, in raptures, joyful,
enraptured, rapturous, thrilled, jubilant, in transports of
delight
COLLOQ. over the moon, tickled pink, on cloud nine,
in seventh heaven, on top of the world, like a child
with a new toy, pleased as Punch, high as a kite
⊟ sad, disappointed

overlap *v*
coincide, cover, overlay, overlie, flap over
TECHNICAL imbricate, shingle

overlay *v*
cover, wrap, envelop, blanket, inlay, face,
surface, line, decorate, ornament, adorn, veneer, varnish,
laminate

overload *v, n*
♦ *v*
burden, overburden, oppress, strain, tax, overtax, weigh
down, overcharge, encumber, saddle, lumber
♦ *n*
overabundance, surplus, surfeit, excess, glut, oversupply
FORMAL superfluity, superabundance, plethora
⊟ lack, dearth

overlook *v*
1 FRONT ONTO, face, look onto, open onto, look over,
command/have a view of
2 MISS, disregard, ignore, omit, neglect, pass over,
pass by, leave, forget, take no notice of, let pass, let ride,
slight, take no account of; *dialect* mislippen
3 EXCUSE, forgive, pardon, condone, wink at, turn a blind
eye to, pass over
⊟ 2 notice, observe **3** penalize, condemn

overlooked *adj*
unhonoured, unvalued, unregarded, unnoted,
unremarked, unprized, unconsidered, unheeded
⊟ appreciated, prized, sought-after, valued

overly *adv*
too, over, unduly, excessively, exceedingly,
immoderately, unreasonably, inordinately, unnecessarily
⊟ inadequately, insufficiently

overmuch *adv*
too much, unduly, excessively, unreasonably,
immoderately, inordinately, unnecessarily

overnice *adj*
overfastidious, over-meticulous, overparticular,
overprecise, oversensitive, overscrupulous, oversubtle,
finical
COLLOQ. nit-picking pernickety; *N Am* persnickety
⊟ casual, uncritical

overplay *v*
exaggerate, overstate, overdo, magnify, overemphasize,
emphasize, stress, make too much of, dramatize,
overdramatize, embellish, embroider, colour,
stretch the truth, enlarge, amplify, enhance, oversell
FORMAL aggrandize
COLLOQ. lay/pile it on, lay/pile it on thick, lay/pile it on
with a trowel, make a mountain out of a molehill, blow
something up out of all proportion, shoot a line
⊟ understate, play down

overpopulated *adj*
overcrowded, congested, packed (out), crammed full,
chock-full, overloaded, swarming teeming overrun, full to
overflowing
COLLOQ. jam-packed, packed like sardines
⊟ deserted, empty

overpower *v*
1 OVERWHELM, overcome, conquer, defeat, beat,
trounce, rout, subdue, overthrow, quash, quell, crush,
immobilize, overbear, master, gain mastery over,
gain the upper hand over
OLD evince, whelm, swelt
FORMAL vanquish, subjugate
2 *overpowered by a feeling*
move, affect deeply/strongly, touch, confuse, perplex,
daze, stagger, dumbfound, leave speechless, hypnotize,
take aback, dazzle
OLD bedazzle
COLLOQ. bowl over, floor, flabbergast, hit/knock for six

overpowering *adj*
overwhelming powerful, strong forceful, irresistible,
undeniable, irrefutable, uncontrollable, compelling
extreme, oppressive, suffocating stifling unbearable,
nauseating sickening

overrate *v*
overestimate, overvalue, overpraise, magnify,
overprize, make too much of, attach too much
importance to
COLLOQ. blow up
⊟ underrate

overreach
■ **overreach yourself**
overstretch yourself, try to do too much, overdo it, go too
far, strain yourself
COLLOQ. bite off more than you can chew, spread yourself
too thinly, burn yourself out

overreact *v*
get upset over nothing make a lot of fuss about nothing
lose your sense of proportion
COLLOQ. blow something up out of all proportion, make a
mountain out of a molehill

override *v*
1 OUTWEIGH, be more important than, exceed, surpass, be
greater than, be superior to, prevail over, overcome
2 OVERRULE, cancel, annul, set aside, supersede, quash,
reverse, disregard, ignore, trample over
FORMAL abrogate, countermand, nullify, rescind, vanquish
COLLOQ. ride roughshod over

overriding *adj*
most important, most significant, principal, first, major,
predominant, primary, prime, supreme, compelling
dominant, essential, final, ultimate, overruling prior,

prevailing ruling paramount, pivotal, cardinal, determining number one
⊟ insignificant, unimportant

overrule v
overturn, override, revoke, set aside, disallow, reject, reverse, invalidate, cancel, annul, vote down
FORMAL countermand, abrogate, rescind, nullify

overrun v
1 INVADE, occupy, besiege, attack, storm, infest, overwhelm, inundate, permeate, penetrate, spread over, swamp, swarm over, surge over, ravage, overgrow
OLD depopulate
COLLOQ. run riot, spread like wildfire
2 EXCEED, go over, overshoot, overstep, overreach
TECHNICAL bleed, lip

overseas adj, adv
♦ adj
foreign, international, external, exotic, faraway, distant, remote, ultramarine
⊟ domestic, home
♦ adv
abroad, in/to a foreign country, out of the country, in/to foreign parts, in/to foreign climes, far and wide, widely

oversee v
supervise, watch (over), look after, keep an eye on, inspect, superintend, run, manage, administer, direct, guide, conduct, preside over, be in charge of, be responsible for, be in control of, control

overseer n
supervisor, chief, foreman, forewoman, manager, manageress, superintendent, steward, captain, surveyor, workmaster, workmistress, overman; Scot grieve; S Afr baas, induna
OLD decurion
COLLOQ. boss, gaffer, guv, guv'nor

overshadow v
1 OBSCURE, cloud, darken, dim, mar, spoil, blight, veil, take the edge off, put a damper on
2 OUTSHINE, eclipse, excel, surpass, be superior to, dominate, dwarf, put in the shade, rise above, tower above

oversight n
1 LAPSE, omission, fault, error, slip-up, mistake, blunder, carelessness, neglect
FORMAL dereliction
COLLOQ. howler, boob; N Am flub
2 SUPERVISION, responsibility, care, charge, control, custody, superintendence, handling keeping administration, management, surveillance, direction

oversize adj
huge, immense, vast, enormous, massive, colossal, giant, gigantic, mammoth, monumental, tremendous, stupendous, great, very big very large, extensive, titanic, monstrous, gargantuan
FORMAL prodigious
COLLOQ. jumbo, frightful, ginormous, humongous
SLANG mega
⊟ tiny, minute

overstate v
exaggerate, overdo, magnify, overemphasize, emphasize, stress, make too much of, dramatize, overdramatize, embellish, embroider, colour, stretch the truth, enlarge, amplify, enhance, oversell
FORMAL aggrandize
COLLOQ. lay/pile it on, lay/pile it on thick, lay/pile it on with a trowel, make a mountain out of a molehill, blow something up out of all proportion, shoot a line, sex up
⊟ understate, play down

overstatement n
exaggeration, overemphasis, emphasis, magnification, overestimation, excess, extravagance, embellishment, enlargement, pretentiousness, amplification, burlesque, caricature, parody

FORMAL hyperbole
⊟ meiosis, understatement

overt adj
open, plain, evident, patent, observable, obvious, manifest, noticeable, visible, conspicuous, apparent, public, professed, unconcealed, undisguised
⊟ covert, secret

overtake v
1 PASS, go past, drive/run past, catch up with, outdistance, leave behind, outstrip, draw level with, gain on, come up with, pull ahead of, ride down, overhaul
OLD overcatch
2 COME UPON, happen to, happen suddenly/unexpectedly to, take by surprise, catch unawares, strike, overwhelm, engulf
FORMAL befall

overthrow v, n
♦ v
1 DEPOSE, oust, bring down, put down, bear down, down, topple, unseat, displace, dethrone, conquer, beat, defeat, crush, confound, overcome, overpower, overwhelm, overcast, subvert, quash, quell, trounce, best, worst, subdue, master, abolish, upset, lay low
FORMAL vanquish
OLD smite, supplant
SLANG stonker
2 OVERTURN, upset, upturn, tip over, topple, tumble, overbalance, keel over, knock over, spill, turn over, invert, prostrate, run over/down, ride down, trip up someone's heels; dialect whemmle
⊟ **1** install, protect, reinstate, restore
♦ n
ousting unseating defeat, deposition, dethronement, fall, rout, undoing suppression, downfall, end, humiliation, upsetting destruction, ruin, subversion, confusion; dialect whemmle
FORMAL vanquishing bouleversement, labefactation, labefaction

overtly adv
plainly, clearly, obviously, manifestly, openly, noticeably, conspicuously, in full view, for all to see, patently
⊟ covertly, secretly

overtone n
suggestion, intimation, nuance, hint, undercurrent, insinuation, innuendo, connotation, hidden meaning indirect reference, association, feeling implication, sense, flavour

overture n
1 APPROACH, advance(s), feeler(s), offer, invitation, proposal, proposition, suggestion, signal, move(s), motion
2 PRELUDE, opening introduction, opening move, (opening) gambit

overturn v
1 CAPSIZE, upset, upturn, tip over, topple, overbalance, keel over, knock over, spill, turn over, invert, skittle
2 OVERRULE, repeal, override, reverse, cancel, annul, abolish, destroy, quash, set aside, veto
FORMAL abrogate, nullify, rescind, revoke
3 OVERTHROW, depose, oust, bring down, topple, unseat, displace, dethrone, confound, subvert, conquer, beat, defeat, crush, overcome, overpower, overwhelm
FORMAL vanquish

overused adj
overworked, hackneyed, trite, stereotyped, worn, tired, unoriginal, stale, played out, commonplace, bromidic, cliché(e)d, threadbare
FORMAL platitudinous
⊟ fresh, original, new

overview n
survey, review, examination, inspection, consideration, study, appraisal, scrutiny, assessment, measurement, valuation

overweening *adj*
arrogant, conceited, haughty, proud, self-confident,
over-confident, supercilious, vain, presumptuous,
overblown, high-handed, cocksure, excessive,
immoderate, inflated, extravagant, swollen, opinionated,
lordly, egotistical, cavalier, pompous, insolent
FORMAL hubristic, vainglorious
COLLOQ. cocky
E3 unassuming modest, diffident

overweight *adj*
fat, plump, stout, massive, huge, chunky, obese, ample,
hefty, bulky, outsize, podgy, portly, pot-bellied, fleshy,
heavy, tubby, chubby, buxom, voluptuous
FORMAL corpulent
COLLOQ. flabby, gross, well-padded, well-upholstered
E3 underweight, thin, skinny, emaciated

overwhelm *v*
1 OVERCOME, overpower, overthrow, destroy, defeat, beat,
trounce, worst, best, subdue, oppress, overbear, quash,
quell, prevail, get the better of, be victorious over,
outplay, outwit, outsmart, be more than a match for,
have the edge on, crush, rout, devastate
FORMAL vanquish, subjugate
COLLOQ. hammer, slaughter, clobber, lick, thrash, wipe the
floor with
2 OVERRUN, deluge, inundate, bury, submerge, overburden,
swamp, engulf
COLLOQ. snow under
3 CONFUSE, stagger, move, affect deeply/strongly, amaze,
daze, touch
COLLOQ. bowl over, floor, kill, knock out, knock sideways,
knock/hit for six

overwhelming *adj*
1 OVERPOWERING, powerful, strong forceful, irresistible,
undeniable, irrefutable, uncontrollable, compelling
extreme, oppressive, suffocating stifling unbearable,
nauseating sickening
2 *an overwhelming majority*
great, large, enormous, massive, vast, immense, huge,
formidable
E3 1 resistible **2** insignificant, negligible

overwork *v*
overstrain, overload, exploit, exhaust, overuse, overtax,
strain, wear out, oppress, burden, weary, work too hard,
overdo it, do too much, overstretch yourself, strain
yourself, overreach yourself, overexert yourself
COLLOQ. sweat blood, burn yourself out, bite off
more than you can chew, run yourself into the ground,
burn the candle at both ends, work your fingers to the
bone, crack up

overworked *adj*
1 *overworked employees*
overstrained, exhausted, worn out, overtaxed
COLLOQ. stressed out

2 *an overworked expression*
hackneyed, trite, stereotyped, worn, tired, unoriginal, stale,
played out, commonplace, bromidic, cliché(e)d,
threadbare
FORMAL platitudinous
E3 2 fresh, original, new

overwrought *adj*
tense, on edge, distraught, agitated, worked up, wound
up, nervous, highly, strung frantic, overcharged,
overexcited, excited, beside yourself
COLLOQ. edgy, uptight, nervy, keyed up
E3 calm

owe *v*
be in debt to, be overdrawn, get into debt, run up debts,
be indebted to, be in arrears to, be under an obligation to
COLLOQ. be in the red, be up to your ears in debt

owing *adj*
unpaid, due, owed, in arrears, outstanding payable,
unsettled, overdue
■ **owing to**
because of, as a result of, on account of, thanks to, in
consequence of, due to

own *adj, v*
♦ *adj*
personal, individual, private, particular, idiosyncratic
♦ *v*
possess, be the owner of, have, have got, have as your
belongings/property, have in your possession, have (all) to
yourself, monopolize, hold, retain, keep, enjoy, use,
occupy
■ **own up**
admit, confess, tell the truth, acknowledge, plead guilty
COLLOQ. come clean, make a clean breast of it
■ **on your own**
alone, isolated, by yourself, singly, unaccompanied,
unaided, unassisted, independently
COLLOQ. off your own bat, on your tod

> **QUOTATIONS**
> Who owns the whole rainy, stony earth? Death / Who
> owns all of space? Death
>   TED HUGHES, 'Examination at the Womb-door'

owner *n*
possessor, holder, keeper, householder, homeowner,
landlord, landlady, proprietor, proprietress, master,
mistress, freeholder

ownership *n*
possession, proprietary rights, right of possession,
proprietorship, rights, freehold, dominion
TECHNICAL title

ox *n*
bull, bullock, steer, buffalo, bison, yak
Related adjective: bovine

P

pace *n, v*

♦ *n*

1 STEP, stride, walk, gait, tread
2 SPEED, movement, motion, progress, rate, rate of progress, velocity, quickness, rapidity, swiftness, tempo, measure
FORMAL celerity

♦ *v*

step, stride, walk, walk up and down, march, tramp, pound, patrol, mark out, measure

pacific *adj*

peaceable, peaceful, peace-loving, mild, peacemaking, pacifist, appeasing, friendly, gentle, equable, placid, still, unruffled, quiet, serene, tranquil, smooth, calm, conciliatory, non-belligerent, non-violent, diplomatic, dovelike, dovish
FORMAL irenic, complaisant, pacificatory, placatory, propitiatory, halcyon
E3 belligerent, aggressive, contentious; *formal* pugnacious

pacification *n*

conciliation, soothing, calming, moderation, moderating, quietening (down), silencing
FORMAL appeasement, placating, propitiation

pacifism *n*

non-violence, pacificism, peacemaking, passive resistance, satyagraha

pacifist *n*

peacemaker, pacificist, peace-lover, conscientious objector, peace-monger, dove
COLLOQ. conchy
E3 warmonger, hawk

pacify *v*

conciliate, mollify, calm, calm down, compose, soothe, assuage, allay, defuse, moderate, soften, lull, still, quiet, quieten, silence, quell, crush, put down, tame, subdue
FORMAL appease, placate, propitiate
E3 anger

pack *n, v*

♦ *n*

1 PACKET, box, carton, container, parcel, package, blister card, bundle, truss, bale, burden, load
OLD fardel
2 BAG, backpack, rucksack, haversack, knapsack, kitbag
3 GROUP, company, set, troop, crew, herd, flock, drove, band, bunch, crowd, gang, mob, rout

♦ *v*

1 WRAP, wrap up, tie up, parcel, package, bundle, put in, cover, crate, stow, store, prepack
2 FILL, load, charge, cram, stuff, crowd, throng, mob, jam, press, squeeze, ram, wedge, compact, compress, crate, stow, tin, canister, canisterize
TECHNICAL steeve

■ **pack in**

1 CRAM IN, fill, load, charge, stuff, crowd, throng, mob, jam, press, squeeze, ram, wedge
2 STOP, end, give up, leave, resign
COLLOQ. throw in, jack in, chuck

■ **pack off**

send, dismiss, dispatch, bundle off

■ **pack up**

1 TIDY UP, tidy away, clear up, put things away, bundle, break camp
OLD empacket, truss
2 STOP, finish, end, give up
COLLOQ. throw in, jack in, wrap up, call it a day
3 BREAK DOWN, stop working, fail
FORMAL malfunction
COLLOQ. seize up, go phut, go kaput, crash; *N Am* go on the fritz
SLANG conk out

package *n, v*

♦ *n*

1 PARCEL, pack, packet, box, container, carton, bale, consignment
2 WHOLE, unit, group, collection, set, entity, lot, bundle, package deal

♦ *v*

parcel (up), wrap (up), pack (up), gift-wrap, box, batch

packaging *n*

container, box, packet, packing, wrapping(s), wrapper(s), presentation

packed *adj*

filled, full, crammed, jammed, crowded, congested, brimful, overflowing, overloaded
COLLOQ. jam-packed, chock-a-block, chocker, chockfull, packed like sardines
E3 empty, deserted

packet *n*

1 PACK, carton, box, bag, package, parcel, case, container, sachet, wrapper, wrapping, envelope, packing, padded bag, padded envelope, Jiffy bag®
2 *cost a packet*
a lot, lots, fortune, small fortune, king's ransom
COLLOQ. mint, pile, pots, pretty penny, a bob or two, bomb, bundle, tidy sum
SLANG loadsamoney, megabucks

pact *n*

treaty, convention, covenant, bond, alliance, cartel, contract, deal, bargain, settlement, agreement, arrangement, entente, understanding
FORMAL compact, concordat
E3 disagreement, quarrel

pad¹ *n, v*

♦ *n*

1 CUSHION, pillow, bolster, squab, wad, wadding, buffer, padding, pack, stuffing, compress, dressing, protection
2 WRITING PAD, notepad, jotter, notebook, block
COLLOQ. memo pad
3 *an animal's pad*
foot, paw, sole, print, footprint
4 HOME, place, room, rooms, quarters, penthouse, flat, apartment
COLLOQ. hang-out

♦ *v*

fill, stuff, wad, pack, wrap, line, cushion, protect

■ **pad out**

expand, inflate, fill out, amplify, elaborate, increase, flesh out, lengthen, stretch, spin out
FORMAL augment, protract

pad² *v*
to pad softly
walk, move, step, run, tread, trudge, tramp, tiptoe, lope

padding *n*
1 FILLING, stuffing, wadding, packing, cushioning, lining, protection
2 VERBOSITY, verboseness, wordiness, bombast, hot air
FORMAL verbiage, prolixity
COLLOQ. waffle

paddle¹ *n, v*
♦ *n*
the paddles of a canoe
oar, scull, sweep
♦ *v*
row, oar, scull, propel, pull, punt, steer, canoe

paddle² *v*
children paddling in the water
wade, splash, slop, dabble, plunge

paddock *n*
enclosure, field, pen, fold, yard, pound, compound, stockade, corral

paddy *n*
rage, tiff, temper, tantrum, fit of temper, fury, passion, taking, pet, bate
COLLOQ. strop

padlock *n, v*
♦ *n*
lock, mortise lock, spring lock, fastening, bolt, clasp, catch
♦ *v*
lock, fasten, secure, bolt, latch, bar, seal, shut

padre *n*
chaplain, minister, priest, pastor, vicar, cleric, curate, reverend, father, parson, rector, deacon, deaconess, clergyman, churchman

paean *n*
eulogy, song of praise, ode to joy, hymn, doxology, anthem, psalm, ovation
FORMAL dithyramb, encomium, panegyric
E₃ denunciation, satire

pagan *n, adj*
♦ *n*
heathen, atheist, unbeliever, non-believer, infidel, idolater
TECHNICAL Gentile
OLD paynim
FORMAL nullifidian
E₃ believer
♦ *adj*
heathen, irreligious, atheistic, godless, ungodly, infidel, idolatrous, pantheistic
FORMAL nullifidian

page¹ *n*
1 *write on a new page*
leaf, sheet, folio, side, recto, verso
2 *start a new page of your life*
episode, incident, event, period, stage, chapter, phase, era, epoch

page² *n, v*
♦ *n*
a page at a wedding
pageboy, attendant, servant, messenger, bellboy, courtier, footman; *N Am* bellhop
♦ *v*
call, ask for, send for, summon, bid, announce

pageant *n*
procession, parade, show, tattoo, display, tableau, scene, play, representation, cavalcade, spectacle, extravaganza, triumph
OLD antic

pageantry *n*
pomp, ceremony, grandeur, magnificence, splendour, glamour, glitter, flourish, spectacle, parade, display, show, showiness, extravagance, theatricality, drama, melodrama

pageboy *n*
page, attendant, servant, messenger, bellboy, footman; *N Am* bellhop

paid-up *adj*
committed, active, dedicated, devoted, loyal, involved, enthusiastic, zealous, fervent, red-hot, evangelical
COLLOQ. card-carrying
E₃ apathetic, uncommitted

pail *n*
bucket, can, tub, bail, scuttle, pitcher, vessel, churn, piggin

pain *n, v*
♦ *n*
1 HURT, ache, throb, cramp, stitch, spasm, twinge, pang, stab, sting, smart, smarting, soreness, irritation, aching, throbbing, tenderness, discomfort, distress, suffering, trouble, anguish, agony, torment, torture
OLD teen
FORMAL affliction
2 ANGUISH, grief, sorrow, agony, anxiety, desolation, distress, suffering, torment, torture, heartache, heartbreak, broken-heartedness, misery, pang, rack, woe, wretchedness
FORMAL tribulation
3 NUISANCE, bother, pest, annoyance, vexation, burden
COLLOQ. bore, drag, headache, pain in the neck/backside
SLANG pain in the arse, bummer
♦ *v*
1 HURT, ache, be sore, sting, smart, irritate, be tender
2 AFFLICT, torment, torture, agonize, distress, worry, trouble, upset, make miserable, make anxious, sadden, grieve
E₃ **2** please, delight, gratify

> **QUOTATIONS**
> O that 'twere possible / After long grief and pain / To find the arms of my true love / Round me once again!
> ALFRED, LORD TENNYSON, *Maud*

> **SYNONYM NUANCES**
>
> *noun sense 1*
> **Hurt** can be used to suggest any painful feeling, but more usually an emotional one, while **ache** is likely to imply one that is continuous. **Throb** is also suggestive of the form pain takes, in this instance occurring in waves, whereas **cramp** suggests muscular contractions.
>   **Spasm** implies a sudden convulsive movement, unlike **twinge** which is a shorter, shooting pain. **Pang** and **stab** on the other hand, though similarly short and sharp, suggest a more violent pain. The terms **sting**, **smart** and **smarting** would be used of a tingling or nipping pain. **Irritation** suggests a reaction, and **tenderness** suggests something painful to the touch, but neither suggest an extreme pain.
>   While you could also use **discomfort** to suggest minor degrees of pain, **distress**, **suffering** and **anguish** would suggest a more extreme experience. **Agony** is similar, but tends to be used of more concentrated pain. Both **torment** and **torture** are best reserved to refer to enduring extreme physical or mental pain.

pained *adj*
hurt, injured, wounded, stung, offended, aggrieved, reproachful, distressed, upset, worried, unhappy, sad, saddened, grieved, piqued, vexed
E₃ pleased, gratified

painful *adj*
1 SORE, tender, hurting, irritating, inflamed, aching, throbbing, smarting, stabbing, agonizing, excruciating
OLD baleful, poignant, pungent; (*Shakesp*) panging
2 *a painful experience*
unpleasant, disagreeable, distressing, upsetting, bad, bitter, saddening, wretched, miserable, agonizing, disturbing, harrowing, traumatic, grievous

OLD baleful, poignant, pungent
FORMAL disquieting
COLLOQ. tortured
3 EMBARRASSING, awkward, touchy, uncomfortable, disconcerting, distressing, upsetting, sensitive, mortifying, humiliating, shameful, shaming, guilty
FORMAL discomfiting
4 HARD, difficult, tough, trying, exacting, laborious, tedious, arduous, rigorous, strenuous
⊟ 1 painless, soothing **2** pleasant, agreeable **4** easy, simple

painfully adv
distressingly, dreadfully, terribly, excessively, clearly, markedly, alarmingly, pitiably, pitifully, sadly, unfortunately, wretchedly, agonizingly, excruciatingly, woefully, deplorably

painkiller n
analgesic, anodyne, anaesthetic, palliative, sedative, drug, remedy, lenitive

painless adj
pain-free, trouble-free, comfortable, effortless, easy, simple, undemanding
COLLOQ. cushy, a piece of cake, child's play, like falling off a log, plain sailing
⊟ painful, difficult

painlessly adv
effortlessly, simply, easily, undemandingly, comfortably
⊟ painfully

pains n
trouble, bother, effort, labour, care, diligence, assiduousness
■ be at pains
be anxious, be concerned, make every effort, try hard, put yourself out, take care, bother, go to great lengths

painstaking adj
careful, meticulous, scrupulous, thorough, conscientious, attentive, diligent, assiduous, industrious, hardworking, laborious, dedicated, devoted, persevering, searching
FORMAL punctilious, sedulous
⊟ careless, negligent

paint n, v
♦ n
colour, colouring, pigment, colorant, vinyl wash, dye, tint, stain
♦ v
1 COLOUR, dye, tint, stain, lacquer, varnish, glaze, apply, daub, wash, whitewash, coat, plaster, smear, cover, spray, respray, decorate, redecorate
2 PORTRAY, depict, tell, describe, narrate, draw, sketch, picture, evoke, represent
FORMAL recount, delineate
■ paint the town red
celebrate, have/throw a party, rejoice, enjoy yourself, have fun, go out
COLLOQ. rave, binge, have a ball, live it up, whoop it up, go out on the town, go on the razzle, have a night on the tiles, push the boat out, kill the fatted calf, put the flags out

Paints include:

acrylic paint	gloss paint	poster paint
colourwash	gouache	primer
distemper	lacquer	stencil paint
eggshell	masonry paint	undercoat
emulsion	matt paint	varnish
enamel	oil paint	watercolour
fabric paint	oils	whitewash
glaze	pastel	

painter n
artist, colourist, oil painter, watercolourist, miniaturist, dauber, limner, depicter
FORMAL delineator

painting n
oil painting, oil, watercolour, picture, portrait, landscape, portrayal, representation, likeness, still life, miniature, illustration, fresco, mural
FORMAL delineation
Related adjective: pictorial

> **QUOTATIONS**
> Painting, n. The art of protecting flat surfaces from the weather and exposing them to the critic
> AMBROSE BIERCE, *The Cynic's Word Book*

Painting terms include:

abstract	frottage	pigment
alla prima	gallery	pochade box
aquarelle	genre painting	pointillism
aquatint	gesso	portrait
art gallery	gouache	primer
bleeding	grisaille	round brush
bloom	grotesque	sable brush
brush	hair-pencil	scumble
brush strokes	hard edge	seascape
canvas	icon	secco
canvas board	illustration	sfumato
capriccio	impasto	sgraffito
cartoon	landscape	silhouette
charcoal	maulstick (or	sketch
chiaroscuro	mahlstick)	skyscape
collage	miniature	still life
composition	monochrome	stipple
craquelure	montage	tempera
diptych	mural	thinners
drawing	oil painting	tint
easel	paint	tondo
encaustic	palette	tone
facture	palette knife	triptych
fête champêtre	pastels	trompe l'oeil
fête galante	pastoral	turpentine
figurative	paysage	underpainting
filbert brush	pencil sketch	vignette
flat brush	pentimento	wash
foreshortening	perspective	watercolour
fresco	picture	
frieze	pieta	

See also **art**; **paint**; **picture**.

pair n, v
♦ n
couple, couplet, brace, two, twosome, duo, twins, two of a kind, set
♦ v
match (up), twin, team (up), mate, marry, wed, unite, splice, join (up), couple, link (up), bracket, put together, arrange in pairs
⊟ separate, part

paired adj
coupled, joined, linked, matched, double, twinned, in twos, yoked, mated, associated, bracketed
⊟ single

pal n, v
♦ n
friend, comrade, companion, partner, confidant(e), intimate, soul mate
COLLOQ. buddy, chum, crony, mate, sidekick; *Aust & NZ* cobber
⊟ enemy, opponent

■ pal up
get together, become friends, make friends, join up
COLLOQ. gang up, chum up

palace n
castle, château, *schloss*, mansion, stately home, basilica, dome, court, Savoy, *hôtel*, *alcázar*, Alhambra, *palazzo*, seraglio
Related adjectives: palatial, palatine

palatable adj
1 TASTY, appetizing, eatable, edible, flavoursome, flavorous, succulent, mouthwatering, delicious, savoury
FORMAL delectable
COLLOQ. yummy, mor(e)ish, scrumptious, scrummy, delish, done to a turn
2 ACCEPTABLE, satisfactory, pleasant, pleasing, nice, agreeable, enjoyable, attractive
F3 1 unpalatable **2** unacceptable, unpleasant, disagreeable

palate n
taste, sense of taste, taste buds, appreciation, liking, relish, gout, enjoyment, enthusiasm, appetite, stomach, heart

palatial adj
grand, magnificent, splendid, majestic, regal, stately, grandiose, imposing, luxurious, de luxe, sumptuous, opulent, spacious
COLLOQ. plush, posh, ritzy

palaver n
fuss, bother, fuss about nothing, rigmarole, procedure, carry-on, activity, business, bustle, commotion, fluster
COLLOQ. song and dance, kerfuffle, hoo-ha, to-do, flap

pale[1] adj, v
♦ *adj*
1 PALLID, livid, ashen, ashy, white, whitish, colourless, chalky, pasty, pasty-faced, waxen, waxy, wan, peaky, sallow, anaemic, drained, lurid, complexionless, whey-faced, bloodless; *Scot* peelie-wally
OLD pallescent; (*Shakesp*) maid-pale
COLLOQ. washed out
2 *pale blue*
light, pastel, lily, faded, bleached, colourless, insipid, vapid, weak, muted, feeble, thin, faint, dim, restrained, low-key, delicate
TECHNICAL etiolated, high-key
COLLOQ. washed-out
F3 1 ruddy, florid **2** dark, strong, intense
♦ *v*
1 WHITEN, blanch, bleach, fade, dim, grow white, grow pale, change colour
TECHNICAL etiolate
OLD appal, blank, pall
2 *pale into insignificance*
fade, dim, lessen, diminish, melt, dwindle
OLD stain
F3 1 colour, blush

SYNONYM NUANCES

adjective sense 1
Pallid can be used to suggest weakness of colour or, sometimes, a lack of vigour: *his pallid cheeks*; *their pallid apathy*. **Livid** occasionally refers to an extreme lack of colour: *his scar became a livid white*; **lurid** is similar, though this usage is not common.
  Ashen and **ashy** are more suggestive of being tinged with grey, and have overtones of unhealthiness. **Whey-faced** is a similar, if more poetic, way of conveying paleness. **Chalky** suggests not only paleness but also a powdery texture; **pasty** and **pasty-faced** suggest an unhealthy sheen, but with a more derogatory tone: *the pasty complexion of a kid raised in institutions*. Similarly, **waxen** and **waxy** connote an unnatural, deathly lustre. **Wan** returns to the idea of a lack of colour, while **peaky** suggests an aura of sickliness: *he looked a bit peaky and green around the gills.*

The term **sallow** is often used to suggest a yellowy complexion, while **anaemic**, **bloodless**, the uncommon **complexionless** and **drained** more straightforwardly refer to lack of blood: *thin bloodless lips*.

pale[2] n
the pales of the fence
post, pole, stake, fence, column, shaft, upright
■ beyond the pale
unacceptable, intolerable, unreasonable, improper, unsuitable, inappropriate, inadmissible
FORMAL unseemly

paleness n
pallor, pale, whiteness, colourlessness, pastiness, wanness, sallowness, anaemia
OLD pallescence
F3 ruddiness

palisade n
fence, paling, defence, enclosure, barricade, bulwark, fortification, stockade

pall[1] n
a pall over a coffin; a pall of smoke
shroud, veil, mantle, cloak, cloud, shadow, gloom, damper
■ cast a pall over
spoil, mar, upset, impair, harm, ruin, destroy, wreck

pall[2] v
interest began to pall
wear off, tire, weary, become tired, become bored, lose its attraction, jade, sate, satiate, cloy, sicken

palliate v
ease, diminish, moderate, mollify, relieve, soften, soothe, temper, lessen, lighten, allay, alleviate, excuse, minimize, mitigate, cover, conceal, cloak
FORMAL abate, assuage, extenuate, lenify

palliative adj, n
♦ *adj*
sedative, soothing, mollifying, alleviative, calming, lenitive, calmative, anodyne
TECHNICAL demulcent, paregoric
FORMAL mitigative, mitigatory, assuasive
F3 irritant
♦ *n*
analgesic, anodyne, painkiller, sedative, tranquillizer, calmative, lenitive
TECHNICAL demulcent, paregoric

pallid adj
1 PALE, pasty, whitish, sallow, colourless, pasty-faced, ashen, ashy, bloodless, anaemic, wan, waxen, waxy, whey-faced, lurid, complexionless, bloodless; *Scot* peelie-wally
TECHNICAL etiolated
OLD pallescent
2 UNEXCITING, weak, dull, boring, uninteresting, bland, uninspired, tame, sterile, tired, lifeless, insipid, spiritless, vapid
F3 1 vigorous, ruddy, high-complexioned **2** lively, exciting

pallor n
paleness, whiteness, pallidness, wanness, sallowness, bloodlessness, anaemia, chalkiness
TECHNICAL etiolation
OLD pallescence
F3 ruddiness

pally adj
friendly, close, affectionate, familiar, intimate, warm
COLLOQ. chummy, thick, tight, folksy
F3 unfriendly

palm n, v
♦ *n*
hand
TECHNICAL thenar

COLLOQ. paw
SLANG mitt
Related adjectives: palmar, volar

♦ v
take, grab, snatch, appropriate

■ **palm off**
foist, impose, fob off, thrust, offload, unload, pass off, get rid of

■ **have someone in the palm of your hand**
have power/control/authority over, have someone at your mercy
COLLOQ. have someone in your clutches, have someone eating out of your hand, be able to twist someone round your little finger

palmist *n*
fortune-teller, clairvoyant, palm reader

palmistry *n*
fortune-telling, clairvoyancy, palm reading, chirognomy, chiromancy

palmy *adj*
carefree, thriving, prosperous, flourishing, successful, fortunate, happy, glorious, triumphant, joyous, luxurious, golden
FORMAL halcyon

palpable *adj*
1 SOLID, substantial, material, concrete, real, touchable, tangible
2 OBVIOUS, visible, apparent, clear, plain, evident, patent, manifest, conspicuous, glaring, blatant, unmistak(e)able, staring you in the face
COLLOQ. plain as a pikestaff
E3 **1** intangible, insubstantial **2** impalpable, imperceptible, elusive

palpably *adv*
obviously, clearly, apparently, visibly, plainly, evidently, patently, manifestly, conspicuously, blatantly, glaringly, unmistak(e)ably
E3 imperceptibly

palpitate *v*
flutter, quiver, tremble, shiver, vibrate, quake, shake, beat, pulse, pulsate, pound, thump, thud, throb

palpitation *n*
pounding, vibration, trembling, shaking, shake(s), flutter(ing), quiver(ing), throbbing, throb

paltry *adj*
meagre, miserly, derisory, contemptible, mean, low, miserable, wretched, poor, sorry, small, slight, trifling, inconsiderable, negligible, trivial, minor, petty, unimportant, insignificant, puny, worthless
COLLOQ. measly, piddling
E3 substantial, significant, valuable

pamper *v*
spoil, cosset, coddle, mollycoddle, baby, featherbed, humour, gratify, indulge, overindulge, pander, pet, fondle, cocker; *dialect* cosher; *Scot* cuiter
OLD pompey
COLLOQ. spoon-feed, wait on someone hand and foot
E3 neglect, ill-treat

pampered *adj*
spoilt, cosseted, coddled, mollycoddled, indulged, overfed, high-fed, petted
COLLOQ. spoon-fed
E3 abused, neglected

pamphlet *n*
leaflet, brochure, booklet, folder, circular, handout, flyer, notice

pan[1] *n, v*
♦ n
1 *pots and pans*
saucepan, frying-pan, fryer, pot, skillet, casserole, wok, container, vessel, pancheon

2 *a salt pan*
hollow, basin, bowl, hole, pit, well, cavity, crater, excavation, cavern, cave, depression, channel
FORMAL concavity
♦ v
criticize, censure, flay, slate, find fault with, hammer
COLLOQ. knock, pull to pieces, roast, rubbish, slam
SLANG slag (off)
E3 praise

■ **pan out**
work out, turn out, result, happen, yield, culminate, come to an end, be exhausted
FORMAL eventuate

pan[2] *v*
pan the camera
sweep, scan, move, turn, follow, track, swing, circle
FORMAL traverse

panacea *n*
cure-all, universal remedy, elixir, nostrum
FORMAL catholicon, diacatholicon, panpharmacon

panache *n*
flourish, flamboyance, ostentation, style, flair, élan, dash, spirit, enthusiasm, zest, brio, energy, vigour, verve

pancake *n*
crêpe, waffle, wafer, blini, griddle-cake, tortilla, taco, crumpet, omelette, spring roll, blintz, latke, drop scone, froise, fraise; *Scot* bannock; *N Am* battercake, flapjack
OLD flawn, flaune, flam

pandemic *adj*
widespread, extensive, general, common, prevalent, far-reaching, rife, pervasive, universal, global

pandemonium *n*
chaos, disorder, confusion, commotion, rumpus, turmoil, turbulence, tumult, uproar, din, bedlam, hubbub, hullaballoo, hue and cry
COLLOQ. to-do, shemozzle, all hell breaking loose
E3 order, calm, peace

pander *v*
■ **pander to**
humour, indulge, pamper, please, gratify, satisfy, fulfil, provide, cater to

pane *n*
window, windowpane, glass

panegyric *n, adj*
♦ n
eulogy, praise, speech of praise, tribute, commendation, homage, accolade, citation
FORMAL paean, encomium, eulogium
E3 censure, criticism
♦ adj
eulogistic, favourable, flattering, glowing, praiseful, praising, complimentary, commendatory
FORMAL encomiastic, laudatory, panegyrical
E3 censorious, critical, damning

panel *n*
1 *a wooden panel*
board, sheet, table, tablet, sign, slab, plank, beam, timber, cartouche, pane, plate, faceplate, headboard, valance
2 *a panel of judges*
board, committee, council, jury, team, commission, directorate, trustees, advisory group, focus group
3 *a control panel*
board, console, unit, dashboard, instrument panel, instruments, controls, switches, knobs, dials, buttons, levers, patchboard

panelling *n*
panelwork, wainscot, wainscot(t)ing, dado, coffer, lacunar

pang *n*
pain, ache, twinge, stab, sting, prick, stitch, gripe, spasm, throe, misgiving, scruple, qualm, agony, anguish, uneasiness, discomfort, distress

panic n, v

♦ n

agitation, alarm, dismay, fright, fear, scare, horror, terror, frenzy, hysteria, *sauve qui peut*

OLD amaze, amazedness

FORMAL consternation, disquiet, trepidation, perturbation

COLLOQ. flap, funk, flat spin, tailspin

☲ calmness, confidence

♦ v

lose your nerve, lose your head, overreact, unnerve

COLLOQ. flap, freak out, go to pieces, lose your cool, have kittens, get the jitters, get the shakes, get the willies, get into a flat spin, lose your bottle, feel your hair stand on end, run round like a headless chicken

☲ relax

panic-stricken adj

alarmed, frightened, horrified, terrified, terror-stricken, petrified, scared, scared stiff, aghast, in a cold sweat, panicky, frantic, frenzied, hysterical

FORMAL perturbed

COLLOQ. in a tizzy, in a blue funk, in a flat spin

☲ relaxed, confident

panoply n

array, range, equipment, show, regalia, insignia, armour, dress, raiment, trappings

FORMAL attire

COLLOQ. garb, gear, get-up, turn-out

panorama n

view, wide-broad view, bird's-eye view, vista, prospect, scenery, landscape, scene, spectacle, perspective, overview, survey, cyclorama

panoramic adj

scenic, wide, broad, sweeping, extensive, far-reaching, wide-ranging, widespread, overall, comprehensive, general, universal

☲ narrow, restricted, limited

pant v, n

♦ v

1 PUFF, blow, gasp, wheeze, breathe, sigh, heave, throb, palpitate

COLLOQ. huff and puff

2 LONG, pine, desire, want, yearn, covet, crave, hanker, sigh, ache, thirst

COLLOQ. yen

♦ n

gasp, puff, huff, throb, wheeze

panting adj

1 PUFFED OUT, breathless, out of breath, gasping, short-winded, winded, puffing, puffed

2 ANXIOUS, eager, impatient, longing, craving, hankering

pantomime n

show, charade, farce, commedia dell'arte, harlequinade, masque

COLLOQ. panto

pantry n

larder, storeroom, scullery

pants n

1 UNDERPANTS, drawers, panties, briefs, knickers, camiknickers, teddy, panty girdle, Y-fronts, boxer shorts, trunks, shorts

COLLOQ. undies, smalls, frillies

SLANG *Aust* budgie smugglers

2 TROUSERS, slacks, jeans

pap n

1 MUSH, pulp, purée, soft food, semi-liquid food

COLLOQ. goo

2 RUBBISH, drivel, trash, nonsense, twaddle, gibberish

COLLOQ. poppycock, hot air, rot, claptrap

SLANG crap

paper n, v

♦ n

1 NEWSPAPER, daily, broadsheet, tabloid, magazine, periodical, weekly, journal, organ

COLLOQ. rag

Related adjective: papyraceous

2 *a paper on alternative medicine*

essay, composition, dissertation, thesis, treatise, article, study, report, work, examination, analysis

FORMAL monograph

■ **paper over**

hide, conceal, cover up, obscure, put out of sight, disguise, camouflage

■ **on paper**

1 IN WRITING, written down, officially, on the record, recorded, in black and white

2 IN THEORY, hypothetically, ideally, theoretically, supposedly, seemingly, in your mind's eye

Types of paper include:

acid-free paper	greaseproof paper	silver paper
art paper	handmade paper	sugar paper
bank	manila	tissue paper
blotting paper	notepaper	toilet paper
bond	papyrus	tracing paper
carbon paper	parchment	vellum
card	pasteboard	wallpaper
cardboard	printer paper	wrapping paper
cartridge paper	rag paper	writing-paper
crêpe paper	recycled paper	
graph paper	rice paper	

papers n

documentation, document, records, certificates, evidence, qualifications, driving licence, birth certificate, marriage certificate, deeds, credentials, authorization, identification, identity card, ID, passport; *S Afr* passbook

papery adj

thin, paper-thin, light, lightweight, delicate, insubstantial, flimsy, fragile, frail, translucent

par n

level, standard, norm, usual, correspondence, similarity, equivalence, equal footing, equality, balance, equilibrium, accordance, average, mean

TECHNICAL median

FORMAL parity

■ **below par**

1 UNSATISFACTORY, inadequate, inferior, below average, not up to par

COLLOQ. not up to scratch

2 UNWELL, under par, tired, rough, out of sorts

COLLOQ. lousy, under the weather

■ **on a par with**

equal to, equivalent to, as good as, the same standard as

■ **par for the course**

typical, normal, standard, usual, predictable, only to be expected

■ **up to par**

satisfactory, adequate, acceptable, fine

COLLOQ. OK, up to scratch

parable n

fable, allegory, lesson, moral tale, story, story with a moral

parade n, v

♦ n

1 PROCESSION, cavalcade, motorcade, march, column, file, train, line-up, progression, review, ceremony, stand-to

OLD decursion

2 SPECTACLE, pageant, show, display, demonstration, exhibition

FORMAL array

♦ v

1 MARCH, process, file past

2 SHOW, display, exhibit, show off, vaunt, flaunt, brandish, prance

paradigm n
pattern, model, example, original, ideal, framework, prototype
FORMAL archetype, exemplar

paradise n
1 HEAVEN, home of God, bliss, next world, hereafter, life to come, afterlife, utopia, Elysium, Elysian Fields, happy hunting ground, Shangri-La, Eden, Garden of Eden, Swarga
2 ECSTASY, rapture, bliss, happiness, complete happiness, joy, delight, transports of delight
FORMAL felicity
COLLOQ. seventh heaven, cloud nine
🖃 **1** hell, Hades

paradox n
contradiction, inconsistency, absurdity, oddity, mystery, enigma, riddle, puzzle
FORMAL incongruity, anomaly

paradoxical adj
self-contradictory, contradictory, conflicting, inconsistent, absurd, illogical, improbable, impossible, mysterious, enigmatic, puzzling, baffling
FORMAL incongruous, anomalous

paragon n
ideal, epitome, model, pattern, perfect example, crème de la crème, masterpiece, prototype, standard, criterion
FORMAL exemplar, quintessence, archetype, nonpareil
COLLOQ. the bee's knees

paragraph n
passage, section, part, portion, segment, subsection, subdivision, article, piece, clause, item

parallel adj, n, v
♦ adj
1 ALIGNED, equidistant, alongside, side by side, coextensive, collateral
2 SIMILAR, like, matching, resembling, equivalent, comparable, uniform, corresponding, co-existing
FORMAL analogous, homologous
🖃 **2** divergent, different
♦ n
1 MATCH, equal, twin, duplicate, equivalent, counterpart
FORMAL analogue
2 SIMILARITY, resemblance, likeness, correspondence, equivalence, analogy, comparison
FORMAL correlation
♦ v
match, echo, be similar to, resemble, be like, be equivalent, equal, conform, agree, correspond, compare, liken
FORMAL be analogous, correlate
🖃 diverge, differ

paralyse v
1 *paralysed his leg*
cripple, lame, disable, incapacitate, debilitate, immobilize, palsy, anaesthetize, numb, dull, deaden, freeze, shock, terrify, transfix, torpefy; *dialect* scram
OLD benumb
2 *paralyse the transport system*
bring to a standstill, immobilize, cripple, halt, stop, disable, deactivate

paralysed adj
paralytic, paraplegic, quadriplegic, crippled, lame, disabled, incapacitated, immobilized, numb
🖃 able-bodied

paralysis n
1 *paralysis in the legs*
paraplegia, quadriplegia, palsy, numbness, deadness, immobility, powerlessness, debilitation
TECHNICAL paresis

2 *paralysis of the transport system*
standstill, halt, stoppage, shutdown, breakdown, immobility

paralytic adj
1 CRIPPLED, disabled, paralysed, incapacitated, lame, immobilized, immobile, numb, palsied, quadriplegic, monoplegic, hemiplegic
2 DRUNK, inebriated, intoxicated, incapable
COLLOQ. a sheet in the wind, three sheets in/to the wind, legless, plastered, pie-eyed, blotto, sloshed, soused, sozzled, stewed
SLANG wasted, wrecked, trolleyed, stoned, pissed, canned, smashed; (*vulgar*) arseholed, rat-arsed, shitfaced
🖃 **2** (stone-cold) sober

parameter n
variable, guideline, indication, criterion, specification, factor, limiting factor, limitation, restriction, framework, limit, boundary

paramount adj
supreme, highest, topmost, predominant, pre-eminent, prime, principal, main, chief, outstanding, cardinal, primary, first, foremost, first and foremost, most important, of greatest importance
🖃 lowest, last

paramour n
lover, beloved, beau, courtesan, mistress, woman, kept woman, inamorato, inamorata, concubine, hetaera
COLLOQ. fancy man, fancy woman, bit on the side, bit of fluff

paranoia n
obsession, delusions, psychosis, megalomania, monomania, persecution complex

paranoid adj
suspicious, distrustful, bewildered, confused, afraid, fearful, fazed

paranormal adj
supernatural, unnatural, abnormal, otherworldly, metaphysical, spiritual, psychic, mystic, mystical, occult, hidden, mysterious, miraculous, magical, magic, phantom, ghostly, eerie, weird
FORMAL preternatural
🖃 natural, normal

parapet n
1 WALL, railing, fence, rail, paling, balustrade, barrier
2 EMBANKMENT, defence, guard, battlement, bulwark, fortification, rampart, barricade, barbican, bastion

paraphernalia n
equipment, gear, tackle, apparatus, tools, implements, materials, accessories, trappings, belongings, possessions, stuff, things, baggage
FORMAL effects, accoutrements
COLLOQ. bits and pieces, odds and ends

paraphrase v, n
♦ v
reword, rephrase, restate, put in other words, express differently, interpret, render, translate, gloss
COLLOQ. rehash
♦ n
rewording, rephrasing, restatement, different expression, other form of words, version, interpretation, rendering, translation, gloss

parasite n
1 LEECH, bloodsucker
TECHNICAL endophyte, entozoon, endozoon, epiphyte, epizoon, epizoan
2 *parasites in society*
hanger-on, passenger, leech, drone, bloodsucker
COLLOQ. sponger, scrounger, cadger, freeloader, ligger, bum, moocher

parasitic *adj*
1 *parasitic animals*
parasitical, biogenous, leechlike
TECHNICAL epizoan, epizoic
2 *a parasitic person*
bloodsucking, freeloading
COLLOQ. cadging, scrounging, sponging

parasol *n*
sunshade, shade, umbrella, shelter, protection, shield, veil

parcel *n, v*
♦ *n*
1 PACKAGE, packet, pack, box, carton, bundle, *dak*
2 *a parcel of land*
plot, patch, area, piece, portion, lot, allotment, tract
3 GROUP, company, troop, herd, flock, band, crowd, gang, mob, crew, bunch, collection
OLD sort
4 LOT, deal, transaction, package, pack, collection
♦ *v*
package, pack (up), wrap (up), gift-wrap, bundle (up), make up, put up, tie up
■ **parcel out**
divide (out), carve up, apportion, allocate, allot, share out, distribute, hand out, dispense, dole out, deal out, mete out
COLLOQ. whack

parch *v*
dry (up), dehydrate, bake, burn, scorch, sear, blister, wither, shrivel
FORMAL desiccate

parched *adj*
1 ARID, waterless, dry, dried up, dehydrated, baked, burned, seared, blistered, scorched, withered, shrivelled
FORMAL desiccated, sear, sere
COLLOQ. dry as a bone
2 THIRSTY, dry, dehydrated
COLLOQ. gasping

parchment *n*
scroll, vellum, document, certificate, charter, diploma, palimpsest
Related adjective: pergameneous

pardon *v, n, interj*
♦ *v*
forgive, condone, overlook, excuse, absolve, let off, reprieve, free, liberate, release
FORMAL vindicate, acquit, remit, exonerate, exculpate
COLLOQ. let off the hook
E3 punish, discipline
♦ *n*
forgiveness, mercy, clemency, indulgence, forbearance, lenience, amnesty, excuse, absolution, reprieve, release, discharge, act of grace
OLD grace, oblivion
FORMAL acquittal, condonation, exoneration, exculpation, remission
E3 punishment, condemnation
♦ *interj*
sorry, I beg your pardon, what did you say?, excuse me, *bitte*
OLD cry you mercy
COLLOQ. come again?, say again?, you what?, what?, eh?

SYNONYM NUANCES

verb
Forgive can be used to suggest a charitable readiness to forget about someone's misdeeds, while **condone** implies an element of acceptance: *society by its silence is condoning racism*. **Overlook** is appropriate for letting someone's misdemeanours go unpunished, and **excuse** further suggests making allowances for them. **Absolve** goes further with its suggestion of completely discharging from blame, whereas **let off** has more to do with allowing someone to get away with something, for which they were responsible. **Reprieve**, on the other hand, is more suggestive of overturning the proposed

---

punishment or fate: *many rail projects facing the axe have been reprieved*.
    Free and **liberate** suggest the removal of restraints or confinement, literally or figuratively: *Paris has been liberated by the Allies; his new direction liberated his art*. **Release** has narrower associations of setting someone free from imprisonment.

pardonable *adj*
forgivable, excusable, justifiable, warrantable, understandable, allowable, permissible, slight, minor, venial, condonable
E3 inexcusable

pare *v*
peel, skin, shear, clip, trim, crop, cut, dock, lop, prune, cut back, whittle, reduce, decrease

parent *n, v*
♦ *n*
1 *a single parent*
father, mother, biological/birth parent, bioparent, single parent, guardian, step-parent, adoptive parent, foster parent, custodial parent, dam, sire;
Aust & NZ solo parent
OLD begetter, generant, genitor
FORMAL progenitor, procreator
COLLOQ. folks, dad, daddy, pop, pa, papa, old man, mum, mummy, ma, mam, mumsy, mamma, old woman, empty-nester; *N Am* mom, mommy
2 SOURCE, origin, root, cause, creator, originator, author, architect, prototype, forerunner
OLD begetter
♦ *v*
be the father/mother of, bring into the world, create, look after, take care of, nurture, bring up, raise, foster, educate, teach, train
OLD beget
FORMAL rear, procreate
Related adjective: parental

QUOTATIONS
All the same, you know parents – especially step-parents – are sometimes a disappointment to their children. They don't fulfil the promise of their early years
  ANTHONY DYMOKE POWELL, *A Buyer's Market*

---

parentage *n*
family, birth, origin(s), source, stock, extraction, filiation, affiliation, ancestry, lineage, derivation, descent, line, race, pedigree, paternity
FORMAL stirps

parenthetical *adj*
in parenthesis, incidental, as an aside, qualifying, explanatory, bracketed, inserted, extraneous
FORMAL elucidative, interposed, intervening
E3 basic, original

parenthetically *adv*
incidentally, by the way, secondarily, as a digression, as an aside
COLLOQ. btw

par excellence *adj*
first-class, first-rate, excellent, wonderful, brilliant, marvellous, fantastic, superior, high-quality, very good, prime, superlative, unequalled, unparalleled, matchless, rare, exceptional, outstanding, surpassing, remarkable, distinguished, great, eminent, flawless, faultless, perfect, best, exemplary, select, superb, magnificent, shining, commendable, splendid, pre-eminent, praiseworthy, noteworthy, notable, noted, fine, A1
COLLOQ. top-notch, smashing, stunning, terrific, neat, ace, brill, out of this world, second to none, divine, heavenly, fabulous, sensational
SLANG wicked, cool, mean
E3 inferior, second-rate

pariah n

outcast, outlaw, exile, castaway, leper, undesirable, unperson, untouchable, *persona non grata*, Ishmael
COLLOQ. black sheep

paring n

peel, peeling, skin, shaving, shred, clipping, trimming, fragment, cutting, flake, rind, slice, sliver, snippet, flaught

parish n

1 DISTRICT, community, village, town
2 PARISHIONERS, church, churchgoers, congregation, community, flock, fold
Related adjective: parochial

parity n

equality, equivalence, parallelism, consistency, conformity, analogy, agreement, correspondence, similarity, resemblance, likeness, sameness, uniformity, unity, semblance, affinity, par
FORMAL congruence, congruity, consonance, similitude

park n, v

♦ n
grounds, woodland, grassland
♦ v
1 *park your car*
stop, pull up, draw up, leave
2 *park your bag down*
put, position, place, deposit, set, leave
COLLOQ. bung, plonk

Types of park include:

amusement park	municipal park	reserve
arboretum	national park	safari park
botanical garden	parkland	sanctuary
business park	play area	science park
caravan site/park	playground	theme park
estate	pleasance	wildlife park
fun park	pleasure garden	zoological
game reserve	pleasure ground	garden/park
industrial park	recreation ground	

---

parlance n

phraseology, language, talk, speech, tongue, idiom, jargon, diction, argot, cant
COLLOQ. lingo

parley n, v

♦ n
talk(s), negotiation, meeting, conference, council, deliberation, discussion, get-together, dialogue, tête-à-tête
FORMAL colloquy
COLLOQ. confab, powwow
♦ v
talk, speak, discuss, get together, negotiate, consult, deliberate
FORMAL confer
COLLOQ. powwow

parliament n

legislature, senate, congress, house, lower house, upper house, assembly, chamber, convocation, council, diet

parliamentary adj

governmental, senatorial, congressional, legislative, lawmaking, lawgiving, elected, democratic, popular, representative, official, republican
FORMAL legislatorial

parlour n

sitting room, lounge, living room, front room, drawing room, morning room

parlous adj

dire, disastrous, dreadful, terrible, frightful, awful, appalling, calamitous, catastrophic, horrible, atrocious, shocking, alarming, distressing, desperate, grave

parochial adj

insular, provincial, parish-pump, small-town, petty, small-minded, narrow-minded, narrow, inward-looking, blinkered, limited, restricted, confined
COLLOQ. hick
F3 national, international

parochialism n

insularity, provincialism, small-mindedness, pettiness, narrow-mindedness, narrowness

parody n, v

♦ n
caricature, lampoon, burlesque, satire, pasquinade, skit, mimicry, imitation, travesty, distortion, corruption, misrepresentation, perversion
COLLOQ. send-up, spoof, take-off
♦ v
caricature, lampoon, burlesque, satirize, mimic, imitate, ape
COLLOQ. send up, spoof, take off

paroxysm n

fit, seizure, spasm, convulsion, attack, eruption, flare-up, outbreak, outburst, explosion

parrot v, n

♦ v
repeat, copy, imitate, mimic, echo, rehearse, reiterate, ape
♦ n
mimic, repeater, imitator, copycat, phraser, ape
Related adjective: psittacine

parrot-fashion adv

by rote, mechanically, mindlessly, unthinkingly, automatically

parry v

ward off, fend off, repel, repulse, rebuff, field, deflect, stave off, block, avert, turn aside, avoid, evade, keep/hold at bay, sidestep, steer clear of, shun
FORMAL circumvent
COLLOQ. duck, dodge, bodyswerve

parsimonious adj

mean, niggardly, miserly, stinting, sparing, scrimpy, saving, close, cheeseparing, close-fisted, close-handed, frugal, grasping
FORMAL penurious
COLLOQ. mingy, penny-pinching, stingy, tight, tight-fisted
F3 generous, liberal, open-handed

parsimony n

meanness, miserliness, frugality, niggardliness
COLLOQ. minginess, penny-pinching, stinginess, tightness, tight-fistedness
F3 generosity, liberality

parson n

vicar, rector, priest, minister, pastor, deacon, preacher, clergyman, reverend, curate, cleric, churchman

part n, v, adj

♦ n
1 COMPONENT, constituent, module, element, factor, ingredient, side, dimension, aspect, facet, piece, bit, particle, fragment, slice, scrap, segment, fraction, proportion, percentage, portion, extract, excerpt, share, section, division, department, branch, sector, wing
2 ROLE, character, portrayal, representation, persona
3 INVOLVEMENT, duty, job, work, charge, task, responsibility, chore, office, function, capacity, participation
4 SECTION, chapter, volume, book, passage, scene, episode, instalment
5 AREA, district, sector, region, neighbourhood, territory, locality, quarter
6 *a person of many parts*
skill, gift, talent, ability, capability, attribute, accomplishment, faculty, endowment, expertise, genius, intellect, intelligence, calibre
F3 **1** whole, totality

♦ *v*

1 SEPARATE, detach, disconnect, sever, split, tear, break, break up, take apart, dismantle, come apart, split up, divide
FORMAL disjoin, cleave
2 PART COMPANY WITH, split up from, separate from, divorce from, get divorced from, leave, withdraw from, go away from, go your separate ways, depart from, take your leave, say goodbye, get going
COLLOQ. push along/off, split, scarper, clear off, take off, hit the road/trail, make tracks
3 DISPERSE, separate, diverge, disband, scatter, split up, break up
≣ 1, 2 join
♦ *adj*
partial, half, not complete, limited, restricted, imperfect, fragmentary, unfinished
■ **part with**
relinquish, let go of, give up, yield, surrender, for(e)go, abandon, discard, jettison
FORMAL renounce
≣ hold onto
■ **for the most part**
by and large, on the whole, generally, usually, mostly, mainly, in the main, chiefly, largely, commonly
■ **in part**
to some degree, partly, somewhat, to some extent, to a certain extent, to a certain degree, up to a point, slightly
■ **on the part of**
by, caused by, carried out by, on behalf of, from the side of
■ **take part in**
join in, opt in, be involved in, participate in, share in, engage in, help with, assist in, play a part in, play a role in, contribute to
FORMAL partake

> **SYNONYM NUANCES**
>
> *verb sense 2*
> The phrase **part company with** can be used where someone has opted to take a different direction from their previous associates, while **split up from** is generally used of a marital or familial rift: *she split up from her husband*. **Separate from** can refer to any type of severance, as can **divorce from**, but **get divorced from** is generally appropriate only for marital break-ups. **Withdraw from** is appropriate for ending an association with someone or something: *he withdrew from politics*, while **go away from** suggests removing yourself from a person or place: *they went away from the conference, convinced by his argument*.
> The phrase **go your separate ways** implies two or more parties have mutually decided to follow their individual choices, unlike **depart from**, which again implies only one party is diverging. **Take your leave**, along with **say goodbye**, suggests a definite ending of contact on a specific occasion: *we said goodbye at the station*, whereas **get going**, although similarly suggesting parting, also implies embarking on a fresh activity.

partake *v*
take part, share, participate, be involved, engage, enter
■ **partake of**
1 *partake of food*
consume, eat, drink
2 *partake of the divine nature*
receive, share, have, show, demonstrate, take, suggest, evoke
FORMAL evince, manifest

partial *adj*
1 *a partial victory*
incomplete, in part, part, limited, restricted, imperfect, fragmentary, unfinished
2 BIASED, prejudiced, partisan, one-sided, discriminatory, preferential, unfair, unjust, inequitable, coloured, affected

FORMAL predisposed
≣ 1 complete, total **2** impartial, disinterested, unbiased, fair
■ **partial to**
fond of, liking, loving, keen on, taken with, with a weakness for
FORMAL with a penchant for
COLLOQ. crazy about, mad about, with a soft spot for

partiality *n*
1 BIAS, prejudice, discrimination, unfairness, injustice, inequity, inequitableness, partisanship, favour, respect
2 LIKING, fondness, love, inclination, preference
FORMAL predilection, predisposition, proclivity

partially *adv*
incompletely, not fully, to a limited degree/extent, fractionally, somewhat, in part, partly

participant *n*
entrant, competitor, contestant, contributor, participator, member, party, co-operator, helper, associate, partner, worker, sharer, shareholder

participate *v*
take part, join in, contribute, engage, be involved, be associated, enter, opt in, share, play a part, play a role, co-operate, help, assist
FORMAL partake
COLLOQ. muck in, be in

participation *n*
involvement, sharing, partnership, co-operation, contribution, assistance, association
FORMAL partaking
COLLOQ. mucking in

particle *n*
bit, piece, fragment, scrap, trace, touch, shred, sliver, speck, morsel, mite, crumb, iota, whit, jot, tittle, atom, molecule, nanoparticle, grain, drop, spot
COLLOQ. smidgen, tad
See panel at **atom**.

parti-coloured *adj*
motley, variegated, piebald
FORMAL polychromatic, polychromic, versicoloured
≣ monochromatic, plain

particular *adj, n*
♦ *adj*
1 *on that particular day*
specific, precise, exact, distinct, certain, individual, special, peculiar
2 EXCEPTIONAL, remarkable, notable, marked, special, outstanding, thorough, unusual, uncommon, peculiar, noteworthy
FORMAL especial
3 FUSSY, discriminating, finicky, fastidious, selective, meticulous, painstaking, exacting
COLLOQ. choosy, pernickety, picky, faddy; *N Am* persnickety
4 EXACT, detailed, thorough, precise, faithful, accurate
≣ 1 general
♦ *n*
detail, specific, point, feature, item, fact, circumstance
■ **in particular**
particularly, especially, specifically, exactly, precisely, to be specific, in detail

particularity *n*
feature, trait, detail, instance, fact, item, circumstance, characteristic, idiosyncrasy, individuality, point, property, distinctiveness, uniqueness, peculiarity, quirk, singularity

particularize *v*
detail, specify, itemize, stipulate, individualize, enumerate
FORMAL individuate

particularly *adv*
especially, exceptionally, remarkably, notably, markedly, extraordinarily, unusually, uncommonly, surprisingly, in particular, specifically, explicitly, distinctly, expressly

parting *n, adj*

♦ *n*

1 DEPARTURE, going, leaving, leave-taking, farewell, goodbye, adieu
FORMAL valediction

2 DIVERGENCE, separation, divorce, division, partition, rift, split, rupture, breaking, breaking-up

F3 1 meeting **2** convergence

♦ *adj*

departing, leaving, farewell, goodbye, last, dying, final, closing, concluding
FORMAL valedictory

F3 first, arriving, opening

partisan *n, adj*

♦ *n*

1 SUPPORTER, devotee, adherent, follower, party man, disciple, backer, upholder, champion, fan, votary, stalwart

2 GUERRILLA, irregular, freedom fighter, resistance fighter

♦ *adj*

biased, prejudiced, unfair, unjust, inequitable, partial, predisposed, discriminatory, one-sided, factional, sectarian

F3 impartial

partisanship *n*

bias, prejudice, partiality, partyism, sectarianism, factionalism

F3 impartiality

partition *n, v*

♦ *n*

1 DIVIDER, barrier, wall, dividing wall, panel, screen, room-divider, dividing screen, separator
TECHNICAL diaphragm

2 DIVISION, break-up, splitting, separation, segregation, parting, severance, subdivision
Related adjectives: septiform, septiferous

♦ *v*

1 SEPARATE, separate off, divide, subdivide, bar, wall off, fence off, screen (off)

2 SHARE, divide (up), split up, break up, segregate, sever, parcel out

partly *adv*

somewhat, to some extent, to some degree, a little, to a certain extent, to a certain degree, (up) to a point, slightly, fractionally, in some measure, moderately, relatively, in part, partially, incompletely, half

F3 completely, totally, fully, wholly

partner *n*

1 ASSOCIATE, ally, confederate, colleague, co-worker, teammate, opposite number, collaborator, co-operator, accomplice, helper, mate, companion, comrade, consort, pair, yoke-fellow; *dialect* butty
OLD copesmate, copemate; (*Shakesp*) rival
COLLOQ. sidekick, oppo, pal
SLANG *N Am* pard, pardner

2 *bring your partner to the party*
spouse, husband, man, wife, woman, lady, boyfriend, girlfriend, fiancé, fiancée, friend, common-law wife/husband, cohabitee, live-in lover, significant other, SOP (significant other person), companion, consort, cavalier, catch
COLLOQ. other half, better half, bit on the side, kept man/woman

---

SYNONYM NUANCES

sense 1
The term **associate** is appropriate for someone you are involved with in a business sense, while **confederate** suggests someone you are in league with. **Ally** suggests a slightly closer relationship and someone who will stand up for you.

Colleague, **co-worker** and **teammate** are more suggestive of a person whom you work alongside, whereas **opposite number** would be reserved for someone with equivalent status in a different

---

organization: *the Foreign Minister met his Chinese opposite number.*

Collaborator is more suggestive of someone who works in association with you: *his musical collaborator*, and may be used in a narrower sense, and with connotations of underhandedness, of people who assist the enemy: *a Nazi collaborator.* The less common **co-operator** similarly suggests mutual support. **Accomplice** has strong connotations of illegality: *an accomplice to murder.* A person you are closer to could be described as a **mate**, which could also be used of either a friend or a fellow worker, or **companion**, if they are someone who often accompanies you. **Comrade** is more suggestive of someone you have shared experiences with and so have forged a bond with: *old war comrades.* **Consort** is a more formal term which tends to be reserved for a spouse: *the queen's consort.*

partnership *n*

1 *the partnership between teachers and parents*
association, alliance, co-operation, collaboration, participation, sharing, confederation, affiliation, combination, union, fellowship, fraternity, brotherhood
OLD consort

2 *a business partnership*
company, firm, corporation, syndicate, co-operative, association, society, conglomerate

party *n, v*

♦ *n*

1 CELEBRATION, festivity, social, get-together, gathering, reunion, function, reception, at-home
COLLOQ. do, bash, thrash, beanfeast, beano, blow-out, bunfight, knees-up, rave, rave-up, shindig; *Irish* hooley; *Aust* shivoo; *S Afr* jol

2 *a search party*
team, squad, crew, gang, band, group, body, company, unit, contingent, detachment
SLANG posse

3 *a political party*
faction, side, league, cabal, alliance, association, affiliation, grouping, camp, combination

4 *the parties in a contract*
person, individual, litigant, plaintiff, defendant

♦ *v*

celebrate, have/throw a party, enjoy yourself, have fun, go out
COLLOQ. rave, binge, have a ball, live it up, whoop it up, go out on the town, go on the razzle, have a night on the tiles, paint the town red, kill the fatted calf, put the flags out, push the boat out
COLLOQ. large it, have it large

■ **be a party to**
be involved in, be associated with, know about, share in the responsibility for

---

Kinds of party include:

after-party	fiesta	picnic
baby shower	flatwarming	*N Am* potluck
barbecue	garden party	party
colloq. beanfeast	*colloq.* gathering	pyjama party
birthday party	of the clan	sleepover
N Am bridal	*Aust colloq.* grog-	slumber party
shower	on	social
ceilidh	Hallowe'en party	soirée
cheese and wine	NZ hangi	stag night
party	hen party	stag party
Christmas party	hoedown	supper party
cocktail party	*N Am colloq.*	tea party
dinner party	hootenanny	toga party
disco	housewarming	welcoming party
discotheque	leaving party	wrap party
fancy dress party	new year party	
farewell party	orgy	

parvenu *n*
upstart, pretender, climber, social climber, arriviste, *nouveau riche*, new rich, vulgarian

pass[1] *v, n*
♦ *v*
1 GO, move, proceed, travel, progress, flow, run, drive, make your way
2 OVERTAKE, go past, drive/run past, outdistance, outstrip, beat, lose, lap, leave behind, draw level with, pull ahead of, overhaul
3 GO THROUGH, go across, go over, get across, get over, run, move, traverse
4 *pass the salt*
hand, give, reach, let someone have, transfer, transmit
5 *time passes quickly*
go by, go past, elapse, proceed, advance, slip by, slip away, drag
6 *pass time wisely*
spend, fill, occupy, employ, use up, take up, devote, while away
7 EXCEED, surpass, go beyond, go over, outdo, outstrip
8 *pass an exam*
succeed, be successful in, get through, qualify, graduate, pass with flying colours, sail/breeze through, scrape through
9 *the examiner passed him*
declare successful, approve, accept, declare satisfactory
10 *pass a new law*
enact, ratify, validate, adopt, authorize, sanction, approve, vote for, agree to, accept
11 *pass from one state to another*
change, go, move, turn, become, develop, transfer, evolve
12 HAPPEN, take place, occur, come about
FORMAL transpire, befall
13 *the estate passed to her daughter*
be left, be willed, be bequeathed, be inherited, be made over, be given, be handed down, be transferred, be endowed, be granted, be consigned, transfer
14 *pass the ball*
throw, kick, hit, move, swing, lunge
15 *pass comment*
make, say, speak, voice, utter, express, declare
16 *pass judgement*
pronounce, deliver, issue, announce, proclaim, decree, assert
17 *we let her attempt at humour pass*
go unnoticed, stand, go without comment
18 *pass urine*
discharge, expel, emit, let out, release
FORMAL excrete
F3 2 fall behind, trail 7 fail to reach, miss 8, 9 fail
♦ *n*
1 THROW, kick, move, hit, lunge, swing
2 PERMIT, passport, visa, identification, ticket, licence, authorization, warrant, permission
3 *make a pass at someone*
advances, approach, overture, suggestion, proposition, play
■ **pass as/for**
appear to be, be taken for, be mistaken for, be regarded as
■ **pass away**
die, pass on, go, depart this life, breathe your last
FORMAL expire, decease
COLLOQ. give up the ghost, go the way of all flesh, peg out, pop off, kick the bucket
■ **pass off**
1 HAPPEN, occur, take place, go off
2 *the effects passed off quickly*
wear off, fade away, die down, disappear, vanish
3 FEIGN, misrepresent, counterfeit, fake, palm off
■ **pass out**
1 FAINT, lose consciousness, black out, collapse, drop

OLD swoon
COLLOQ. flake out, keel over
2 GIVE OUT, hand out, distribute, deal out, allocate, allot, share out, dole out
■ **pass over**
disregard, ignore, overlook, miss, omit, leave, neglect, forget, take no notice of, not take into consideration, turn a blind eye to, turn a deaf ear to
■ **pass up**
not take advantage of, ignore, miss, refuse, neglect, reject, let slip

pass[2] *n*
a pass through the mountains
way, route, path, col, defile, gorge, ravine, canyon, gap, passage

passable *adj*
1 SATISFACTORY, acceptable, allowable, tolerable, average, ordinary, unexceptional, moderate, fair, adequate, all right, mediocre
COLLOQ. OK, run of the mill, so-so, nothing to write home about, not much cop, no great shakes
2 CLEAR, unobstructed, unblocked, open, navigable, traversable
F3 1 unacceptable, excellent 2 obstructed, blocked, impassable

passably *adv*
fairly, rather, quite, somewhat, tolerably, relatively, reasonably, moderately, after a fashion

passage *n*
1 PASSAGEWAY, aisle, corridor, hall, hallway, lobby, vestibule, doorway, opening, entrance, exit
2 THOROUGHFARE, way, route, road, avenue, path, track, lane, alley
3 CHANNEL, duct, conduit, main, groove, furrow, trough, gutter, gully, canal, flume, watercourse, waterway, strait, neck, sound
TECHNICAL orifice
4 MOVEMENT, passing, flow, running, course, advance
5 TRANSITION, progress, advance, change, transfer, turning, development
TECHNICAL mutation, metamorphosis
6 *the passage of a bill*
acceptance, approval, passing, adoption, authorization, validation, sanction, enactment, ratification
7 *grant passage through a country*
access, entry, admission, permission to travel through, safe conduct
8 EXTRACT, excerpt, quotation, text, paragraph, section, piece, clause, verse
FORMAL citation
9 JOURNEY, voyage, trip, crossing, tour, trek

passageway *n*
passage, corridor, hall, hallway, lobby, entrance, exit, aisle, lane, path, way, track, alley, gangway, arcade, runway

passé *adj*
outdated, old-fashioned, out-of-date, dated, obsolete, outmoded, unfashionable, outworn, démodé, antiquated, past its best
COLLOQ. old hat, out, on the way out, past it, past its sell-by date
F3 fashionable, in

passenger *n*
1 TRAVELLER, voyager, commuter, rider, fare, fare-payer, strap-hanger, hitchhiker
2 *get rid of passengers who don't work*
hanger-on, drone, shirker
COLLOQ. freeloader

passer-by *n*
bystander, looker-on, onlooker, observer, spectator, witness, eyewitness
COLLOQ. rubberneck, gawper

passing adj, n

♦ adj
1 SHORT-LIVED, temporary, momentary, transitional, fleeting, brief, short
FORMAL ephemeral, transient
2 CASUAL, incidental, cursory, hasty, quick, rapid, slight, superficial, shallow
F3 1 lasting, permanent
♦ n
1 *the passing of time*
passage, flow, march, course, advance, movement
2 DEATH, departure, passing away, perishing, end, finish, loss
FORMAL decease, demise, expiration, quietus, termination
■ **in passing**
incidentally, by the way, parenthetically, *en passant*
COLLOQ. by the by(e)

passion n

1 FEELING, emotion, ardour, zeal, fervour, warmth, heat, spirit, intensity, fire, vehemence
2 OUTBURST, explosion, anger, indignation, wrath, rage, fit, temper, fury, tantrum
3 LOVE, desire, sexual desire, ardour, lust, adoration, infatuation, fondness, affection, craving
4 *a passion for football*
enthusiasm, obsession, mania, craze, fascination, eagerness, keenness, avidity, zest, fanaticism, zeal
F3 1 coolness, indifference

passionate adj

1 ARDENT, fervent, eager, keen, avid, enthusiastic, fanatical, zealous, warm, hot, fiery, inflamed, aroused, excited, impassioned, intense, strong, fierce, vehement, violent, stormy, tempestuous, wild, frenzied
COLLOQ. crazy, mad, nuts, potty
2 EMOTIONAL, excitable, hotheaded, intense, warm, impetuous, impulsive, frenzied, quick-tempered, irritable, stormy, headstrong, wilful, self-willed, obstinate, choleric, Latin, torrid
OLD affectionate; (*Shakesp*) waspish-headed
3 LOVING, affectionate, ardent, aroused, lustful, erotic, sexy, sensual, sultry
COLLOQ. turned on, randy, horny, gutsy
F3 1 phlegmatic; *colloq.* laid-back **3** frigid, cold

> **QUOTATIONS**
> The passionate heart of the poet is whirled into folly and vice
> ALFRED, LORD TENNYSON, *Maud*

passionately adv

1 ENTHUSIASTICALLY, ardently, fervently, keenly, fanatically, zealously, intensely, strongly, hotly, violently, fiercely
2 LOVINGLY, affectionately, ardently, lustfully, sensually, erotically
F3 1 apathetically **2** coldly

passionless adj

emotionless, unfeeling, unemotional, unloving, impassive, calm, cold, cold-hearted, frigid, callous, frosty, icy, cold-blooded, apathetic, restrained, unresponsive, uncaring, indifferent, insensible, uninvolved, detached, dispassionate, impartial, neutral, withdrawn
F3 passionate, caring, sensitive, sympathetic

passive adj

1 DOCILE, receptive, unassertive, yielding, submissive, unresisting, non-violent, patient, resigned, compliant, long-suffering
2 UNEMOTIONAL, apathetic, lifeless, emotionless, unmoved, indifferent, detached, distant, uninvolved, unenterprising, non-participating, remote, aloof, dispassionate, inert, inactive
F3 1 involved, lively, active **2** responsive

passively adv

submissively, unassertively, patiently, emotionlessly, lifelessly
F3 actively

passport n

1 *show your passport at the border*
travel documents, papers, identity card, ID, visa, permit, pass, authorization, laissez-passer
2 *the passport to success*
key, entry, door, doorway, avenue, path, way, route, admission, means of access

password n

watchword, signal, key, word, open sesame, parole, shibboleth, countersign

past adj, n, prep

♦ adj
1 OVER, ended, finished, completed, done, over and done with
2 FORMER, previous, preceding, foregoing, foregone, late, sometime, last, latter, recent
FORMAL erstwhile
3 ANCIENT, bygone, olden, early, gone, gone by, elapsed, long ago, no more, extinct, defunct, forgotten
F3 2 future, next
♦ n
1 *in the past*
history, former times, olden days, olden times, days gone by, bygone times/days, good old days, antiquity
FORMAL days of yore
2 LIFE, background, experience, record, track record
F3 1 future
♦ prep
1 *walking past the trees*
by, near, beside, beyond
OLD forby
2 *past childish jokes*
after, over, beyond, too old for, too mature for

> **QUOTATIONS**
> I tell you the past is a bucket of ashes
> CARL SANDBURG, *Cornhuskers*, 'Prairie'

pasta

Forms and shapes of pasta include:

agnolotti	fiochetti	penne
anelli	fusilli	pennine
angel's hair	gnocchi	ravioli
bombolotti	lasagne	rigatoni
bucatini	lasagne verde	ruoti
cannelloni	linguini	spaghetti
capelletti	lumache	stelline
casarecci	macaroni	strangozzi
conchiglie	mafalde	tagliatelle
crescioni	manicotti	taglierini
ditali	maruzze	tortellini
elbow macaroni	mezzani	trofie
farfalle	noodle	vermicelli
farfalline	noodle farfel	ziti
fedelini	orecchiette	
fettuccine	pappardelle	

paste n, v

♦ n
1 ADHESIVE, glue, gum, mastic, putty, cement
2 *fish paste*
pap, pulp, mush, blend, pâté, purée, spread, mixture
♦ v
stick, glue, gum, cement, fix, fasten

pastel adj, n

♦ adj
soft, soft-hued, light, light-coloured, pale, delicate, subtle, discreet, muted, low-key, subdued, faint

♦ *n*
1 CHALK, crayon, pastille
2 DRAWING, sketch, vignette

pastiche *n*
assortment, mixture, mix, miscellany, variety, melange, potpourri, hotchpotch, hodgepodge, olio, olla-podrida, confusion, farrago, salmagundi, smorgasbord, collection, medley, patchwork, gallimaufry, jumble
FORMAL conglomeration
COLLOQ. mixed bag, mishmash, omnium-gatherum

pastille *n*
lozenge, pastel, sweet, tablet, cough sweet, cough drop, confection, jujube, troche

pastime *n*
hobby, activity, leisure activity, leisure pursuit, game, sport, recreation, play, fun, amusement, entertainment, diversion, distraction, relaxation, avocation, *Zeitvertreib*
OLD pastance; (*Shakesp*) abridgement, suppliance
🖾 work, employment

past master *n*
expert, proficient, virtuoso, adept, artist
COLLOQ. ace, old hand, dab hand, wizard
🖾 incompetent

pastor *n*
minister, clergyman, priest, rector, vicar, parson, deacon, cleric, churchman, canon, prebendary, divine, ecclesiastic
Related adjective: pastoral

pastoral *adj*
1 RURAL, country, rustic, agricultural, agrarian, simple, idyllic
FORMAL bucolic
2 ECCLESIASTICAL, clerical, priestly, ministerial
🖾 **1** urban

pastry

Types of pastry include:

American crust	hot-water crust	puff
biscuit-crumb	one-stage	rich shortcrust
cheese	pâte à savarin	rough-puff
choux	pâte brisée	short
Danish	pâte frolle	shortcrust
filo	pâte sablée	suetcrust
flaky	pâte sucrée	sweet
flan	plain pastry	wholewheat

---

pasture *n*
grass, grassland, meadow, field, paddock, pasturage, grazing, grazing land; *N Am* range
Related adjective: pastoral

pasty *adj*
sallow, pale, pallid, wan, anaemic, pasty-faced, sickly, unhealthy
🖾 ruddy, healthy

pat *v, n, adj, adv*
♦ *v*
tap, dab, slap, touch, stroke, caress, fondle, pet, patter, burp; *Scot* clap
OLD bepat, tick
♦ *n*
1 *gave the dog a pat*
tap, dab, slap, touch, stroke, caress; *Scot* clap
OLD tick
2 *a pat of butter*
dab, lump, mass, chunk, ball, coquille, print
♦ *adj*
glib, fluent, smooth, slick, ready, easy, facile, simple, simplistic
♦ *adv*
precisely, exactly, perfectly, flawlessly, faultlessly, fluently, word-for-word
🖾 imprecisely, inaccurately, wrongly

■ **pat someone on the back**
congratulate, praise, compliment, say well done to
COLLOQ. take your hat off to

patch *n, v*
♦ *n*
1 *a patch of land*
bed, plot, lot, parcel, tract, area, piece, spot
2 COVER, material, cloth, covering, shield, protection
3 *go through a bad patch*
phase, period, stretch, time, term, spell
♦ *v*
mend, repair, sew, stitch, fix, cover, reinforce

patchwork *n*
medley, jumble, mixture, assortment, farrago, gallimaufry, hash, hotchpotch, pastiche
COLLOQ. mishmash

patchy *adj*
uneven, irregular, inconsistent, varying, variable, random, fitful, erratic, sketchy, bitty, spotty, blotchy
🖾 even, uniform, regular, consistent

patent *adj, n*
♦ *adj*
obvious, manifest, evident, self-evident, conspicuous, clear, crystal clear, plain, transparent, apparent, visible, undeniable, unmistak(e)able, palpable, unequivocal, open, overt, blatant, flagrant, glaring
COLLOQ. plain as a pikestaff, plain as the nose on your face, clear as daylight, staring you in the face
🖾 hidden, opaque
♦ *n*
privilege, right, certificate, charter, licence, invention, copyright, registered trademark

patently *adv*
clearly, manifestly, plainly, visibly, conspicuously, unmistak(e)ably, unequivocally, palpably, blatantly, glaringly

paternal *adj*
fatherly, fatherlike, protective, benevolent, concerned, vigilant

path *n*
1 FOOTPATH, pathway, bridleway, trail, towpath, track, walk
2 ROUTE, course, direction, approach, way, circuit, passage, road, avenue, lane

pathetic *adj*
1 PITIABLE, poor, sorry, lamentable, miserable, wretched, sad, dismal, distressing, moving, affecting, touching, pitiful, poignant, plaintive, heart-rending, heartbreaking, woeful
2 FEEBLE, poor, sorry, miserable, useless, worthless, inadequate, unsatisfactory, meagre, contemptible, derisory, deplorable, woeful
🖾 **1** cheerful **2** admirable, excellent, valuable

pathetically *adv*
1 PITIABLY, lamentably, wretchedly, sadly, dismally, pitifully, woefully
2 INADEQUATELY, unsatisfactorily, miserably, deplorably, contemptibly, woefully
🖾 **1** happily **2** admirably

pathological *adj*
compulsive, habitual, inveterate, obsessive, confirmed, chronic, hardened, addicted, dependent, persistent

pathos *n*
poignancy, misery, sadness, tragedy, pitiableness, pitifulness, plaintiveness, inadequacy

patience *n*
calmness, composure, self-control, equanimity, even-temperedness, restraint, tolerance, forbearance, endurance, fortitude, long-suffering, submission, resignation, stoicism, tranquillity, serenity, inexcitability, persistence, perseverance, diligence, doggedness, tenacity
OLD sufferance
FORMAL imperturbability

COLLOQ. unflappability, cool, stickability
E3 impatience, intolerance, exasperation

patient adj, n
♦ adj
calm, composed, serene, self-possessed, self-controlled, restrained, even-tempered, mild, unhurried, leisurely, easy-going, lenient, indulgent, kind, tender, understanding, forgiving, tolerant, accommodating, forbearing, long-suffering, uncomplaining, submissive, resigned, philosophical, stoical, persistent, persevering, resolute
OLD forbearant
FORMAL imperturbable
COLLOQ. patient as Job, unflappable, cool, laid-back, hanging in there
E3 impatient, restless, intolerant, exasperated
♦ n
invalid, sufferer, case, client, subject, out-patient
OLD ambulant

SYNONYM NUANCES

adjective
Calm and **serene** can be used to suggest being in a fairly constant tranquil state. **Composed**, **self-possessed** and **self-controlled** are more suggestive of having your emotions under control, while **restrained** implies a greater difficulty in achieving this: *restrained enthusiasm*.

You can use **lenient** to suggest being influenced by mercy, but **indulgent** goes further by implying an excessive tolerance: *a rather indulgent parent who was never put out by anything*. **Understanding** has added associations of empathy, whereas **forgiving** implies compassion in the face of trying behaviour, and both **tolerant** and **forbearing** suggest an element of permissiveness. **Accommodating**, however, suggests being more actively obliging: *he is a most accommodating interviewee, talking freely about his projects*.

Uncomplaining, **submissive** and **resigned** have more to do with yielding to the wishes of others, while **long-suffering** is suggestive of martyred endurance: *a long-suffering mother of four*. Both **philosophical** and **stoical** have implications of acceptance: *he was philosophical about their defeat*, while **resolute** is less connotative of gentleness, and suggests intractability.

---

patiently adv
calmly, unhurriedly, leisurely, mildly, considerately, tenderly, kindly, tolerantly, enduringly, resolutely, persistently, perseveringly
COLLOQ. unflappably, through thick and thin

patois n
dialect, vernacular, local parlance, local speech, argot, cant, lingo, lingua franca, patter, slang, jargon

patriarch n
elder, father, grandfather, paterfamilias, greybeard, founder, sire
COLLOQ. grand old man

patrician n, adj
♦ n
aristocrat, noble, nobleman, gentleman, grandee, peer
COLLOQ. nob
E3 commoner, plebeian
♦ adj
aristocratic, noble, lordly, high-class, high-born, blue-blooded, gentle, thoroughbred, well-born
COLLOQ. upper-crust
E3 common, humble

patrimony n
inheritance, legacy, bequest, heritage, estate, property, possessions, birthright, revenue, share, portion

patriot n
nationalist, loyalist, chauvinist, flag-waver, jingoist, jingo

patriotic adj
nationalistic, nationalist, chauvinistic, jingoistic, loyal, loyalist, flag-waving

patriotism n
chauvinism, flag-waving, jingoism, loyalty, nationalism

QUOTATIONS
Patriotism is the last refuge of a scoundrel
SAMUEL JOHNSON

---

patrol v, n
♦ v
police, guard, keep guard on, protect, defend, keep watch on/over, monitor, go the rounds, make your/do the rounds, be on the beat, tour, inspect
♦ n
1 GUARD, patrolman, patrolwoman, sentry, sentinel, police officer, security guard, defender, night-watchman, watchman
2 on patrol
watch, guard, vigil, surveillance, policing, patrolling, protection, defence, round, beat

patron n
1 BENEFACTOR, philanthropist, sponsor, backer, supporter, friend, promoter, sympathizer, advocate, upholder, champion, defender, protector, guardian, guardian angel, helper, Maecenas; *Scot* stoop, stoup
OLD fautor
COLLOQ. angel, fairy godmother
2 CUSTOMER, client, frequenter, shopper, buyer, purchaser, subscriber
COLLOQ. regular

patronage n
1 SPONSORSHIP, funding, backing, support, promotion, financial help/aid/assistance, encouragement, protection, aegis, auspices
2 CUSTOM, business, trade, commerce, buying, purchasing, shopping, subscription

patronize v
1 LOOK DOWN ON, talk down to, despise, scorn, act/speak condescendingly towards
FORMAL disparage
COLLOQ. look down your nose at, turn your nose up at
2 SPONSOR, fund, finance, back, support, maintain, protect, help, assist, aid, promote, champion, foster, encourage
OLD (*Shakesp*) empatron
3 FREQUENT, shop at, buy from, deal with
COLLOQ. be a regular at

patronizing adj
condescending, stooping, overbearing, high-handed, haughty, lofty, superior, snobbish, supercilious, scornful, contemptuous, disdainful
COLLOQ. snooty, toffee-nosed, stuck up, high-and-mighty, on your high horse
E3 humble, lowly

patter¹ v, n
♦ v
rain pattering on the window
tap, pat, pitter-patter, drum, pound, beat, pelt, trip, scuttle, scurry
♦ n
pattering, tapping, pitter-patter, beating

patter² n
a salesman's patter
chatter, gabble, jabber, line, pitch, jargon, monologue
COLLOQ. spiel, lingo, yak

pattern n, v
♦ n
1 SYSTEM, method, order, plan, arrangement
2 DECORATION, ornamentation, ornament, figure, motif, device, design, style, markings

3 MODEL, template, stencil, guide, plan, design, instruction, original, prototype, blueprint, standard, criterion, norm, ideal, example
4 *a book of fabric patterns*
sample, swatch
♦ v
model, style, order, form, follow, imitate, match, stencil, emulate, copy, decorate, design, shape, mould, influence, trim

patterned *adj*
decorated, ornamented, figured, printed, watered, moiré
⊟ plain

paucity *n*
lack, shortage, insufficiency, scarcity, scantiness, poverty, rarity, fewness, sparseness, sparsity, want, dearth, deficiency, smallness, slightness, slenderness, meagreness, paltriness
FORMAL exiguousness
⊟ abundance

paunch *n*
fat stomach, abdomen, belly, pot-belly, beer belly, beer gut
COLLOQ. corporation

paunchy *adj*
pot-bellied, fat, podgy, pudgy, portly, tubby
TECHNICAL adipose
FORMAL corpulent, rotund

pauper *n*
insolvent, down-and-out, have-not, bankrupt, beggar, mendicant, church mouse
FORMAL indigent

pause *v, n*
♦ v
halt, stop, cease, break (off), interrupt, adjourn, take a break, rest, sit down, stay, wait, delay, hold back, hesitate, breathe
FORMAL discontinue, desist
COLLOQ. let up, take a breather, take a rest, take five
♦ n
halt, stoppage, stop, close, interruption, break, rest, lull, stay, respite, gap, interval, interlude, intermission, wait, delay, hesitation, hold
TECHNICAL caesura, diaeresis, limma, fermata, dwell
OLD demur
FORMAL cessation
COLLOQ. breather, breathing space, let-up, time out

pave *v*
flag, tile, floor, surface, cover, asphalt, tar, macadamize, tarmac, concrete
■ **pave the way for**
get/make ready for, prepare for, lead up to, introduce, take steps/measures, clear the ground, lay/do the groundwork for, do the spadework for

pavement *n*
footpath, footway, walkway, path, way, floor, bed, causeway; *N Am* sidewalk

paw *n, v*
♦ n
foot, pad, forefoot, hand
♦ v
maul, touch, stroke, manhandle, mishandle, poke, molest
COLLOQ. touch up

pawn¹ *n*
mere pawns in the power struggle
dupe, puppet, tool, instrument, toy, plaything
COLLOQ. cat's paw, stooge

pawn² *v*
pawn your watch
deposit, pledge, stake, mortgage, dip;
Scot wadset
OLD impawn, lumber, pignorate, oppignorate;
(*Shakesp*) fine

FORMAL impignorate
COLLOQ. hock, pop, lay in lavender
OLD SLANG spout

pawnbroker *n*
pawnshop, lender, money-lender, usurer, gombeen-man, *mont-de-piétémonte di pietà*
OLD lumberer; (*offensive*) sheeny
COLLOQ. pop-shop
SLANG uncle

pay *v, n*
♦ v
1 *pay money to someone*
spend, pay out, meet the cost of, lay out, outlay, hand over, recompense, invest, reimburse, repay, refund, settle, settle up, discharge, reward
FORMAL remunerate, remit, expend, disburse, indemnify
COLLOQ. dip (your hand) into your pocket, foot the bill, pick up the tab, fork out, shell out, cough up, stump up; *N Am* ante up
2 BENEFIT, profit, pay off, bring in, produce, yield, return, be beneficial to, be advantageous to, be worthwhile to
COLLOQ. rake in
3 *pay attention/a compliment/a visit*
give, make, do, let someone have, offer, extend, grant, supply
FORMAL afford, proffer, bestow
4 ATONE, make amends, compensate, avenge yourself on, pay back, answer, suffer, be punished
♦ n
wages, salary, earnings, income, gross/net pay, take-home pay, commission, fee, stipend, honorarium, payment, reward, recompense, compensation, reimbursement
FORMAL remuneration, emoluments
■ **pay back**
1 REPAY, refund, return, reimburse, recompense, settle, pay off, give back, square
2 RETALIATE, get your own back, take revenge, get your revenge on, avenge yourself on, get even with, punish, repay, reciprocate, counter-attack, give someone a taste of their own medicine
■ **pay for**
answer for, atone, be punished for, compensate, make amends, suffer, pay a penalty for, pay the price for, count the cost (of), cost dearly
COLLOQ. face the music, get your deserts
■ **pay off**
1 DISCHARGE, settle, square, clear, meet, honour, repay, pay in full
2 DISMISS, discharge, make redundant, lay off
COLLOQ. fire, sack
3 *the preparations paid off*
succeed, be successful, work, get results
4 BRIBE, buy off, suborn, take care of
COLLOQ. fix, grease, grease someone's palm
■ **pay out**
spend, hand over, part with, lay out
FORMAL disburse, remit, expend
COLLOQ. fork out, shell out, cough up; *N Am* ante up

> **PROVERBS**
> He that pays the piper calls the tune

> **SYNONYM NUANCES**
>
> *verb sense 1*
> **Pay out** generally suggests a financial payment made from duty or necessity, whereas **meet the cost** implies taking on the responsibility of payment: *it was the government, rather than the UN, which met the cost.* Both **settle** and **settle up** suggest the final payment of accumulated costs, while **discharge** would be appropriate for meeting a debt. You can use **hand over** to suggest the actual transference of money, but it has connotations of unwillingness: *forced to hand over the money at gunpoint.*

Invest implies devoting money or time to a project in the hope of an augmented return: *they had invested heavily in new technology*; *she invested a great deal of time in the project*. **Lay out**, on the other hand, implies an element of extravagance, whilst **outlay** is again more suggestive of necessary costs incurred, though is less common in its verbal form.

Recompense and **repay** have suggestions of an equable return for something proffered: *he was adequately recompensed for his loyalty*, whereas **reimburse** and **refund** are more specifically to do with compensating someone for their expenses. **Reward** would suggest giving something in recognition of merit.

payable *adj*
owed, owing, unpaid, to be paid, outstanding, in arrears, due, mature

payload *n*
cargo, freight, load, haul, lading, tonnage, shipment, consignment, contents, goods, merchandise, baggage

payment *n*
settlement, discharge, clearance, premium, outlay, advance, deposit, instalment, amount, contribution, donation, allowance, reward, pay, fee, hire, fare, toll
FORMAL remittance, remuneration

pay-off *n*
1 RESULT, outcome, benefit, advantage, reward, settlement, consequence, upshot
COLLOQ. crunch, moment of truth, punchline
2 BRIBE, inducement, allurement, enticement
COLLOQ. back-hander, sweetener, hush money, slush fund, protection money
3 PAYMENT, pay, wages, salary, earnings, income, gross/net pay, take-home pay, commission, fee, stipend, honorarium, reward, recompense, compensation, reimbursement
FORMAL remuneration, emoluments

peace *n*
1 CALM, quiet, quietness, peacefulness, hush, silence, still, stillness, rest, restfulness, relaxation, tranquillity, calmness, serenity, composure, contentment, placidity
FORMAL repose
2 ARMISTICE, truce, ceasefire, peace treaty, non-violence, non-aggression, law and order, conciliation, harmony, pax, friendship, amicableness, goodwill, agreement, pact, treaty
FORMAL concord, amity, accord
E3 **1** noise, disturbance **2** war, disagreement, discord
Related adjective: irenic

QUOTATIONS
When will the world know that peace and propagation are the two most delightful things in it?
HORACE WALPOLE

Peace, n. In international affairs, a period of cheating between two periods of fighting
AMBROSE BIERCE, *The Cynic's Word Book*

peaceable *adj*
pacific, peace-loving, unwarlike, dovish, non-violent, non-aggressive, conciliatory, friendly, cordial, easy-going, even-tempered, good-natured, amicable, harmonious, inoffensive, gentle, placid, mild
FORMAL irenic
E3 aggressive, violent, quarrelsome, belligerent

peaceably *adv*
amicably, harmoniously, pacifically, inoffensively, gently, placidly, mildly, cordially
E3 aggressively, violently

peaceful *adj*
quiet, still, restful, relaxing, tranquil, serene, calm, placid, sleepy, unruffled, undisturbed, untroubled, friendly, harmonious, amicable, peaceable, pacific, gentle

FORMAL halcyon, irenic, reposeful, in repose
E3 noisy, disturbed, troubled, violent

peacefully *adv*
quietly, calmly, serenely, gently, sleepily, restfully, harmoniously, amicably, placidly
E3 noisily

peacemaker *n*
appeaser, conciliator, mediator, arbitrator, intercessor, broker, peace-monger, pacifier, pacifist, dove
OLD (*Shakesp*) make-peace

peacemaking *adj*
appeasing, conciliatory, pacific, mediating, mediative, mediatorial, mediatory
FORMAL irenic

peak *n*, *v*
♦ *n*
top, summit, pinnacle, crest, crown, zenith, apogee, height, high point, elevation, mountain, mount, hill, maximum, climax, culmination, apex, tip, point, rise, spire, pin, summer, aiguille, nib, crise; *Scot & Irish* ben
OLD (*Spenser*) prick
E3 trough, nadir
♦ *v*
climax, culminate, come to a head, reach the highest point, spike

peaky *adj*
pale, pallid, wan, ill, sick, unwell, off-colour, sickly, poorly, out of sorts, seedy, queasy
COLLOQ. under the weather, washed-out, dicky, crummy, green about the gills
E3 healthy; *colloq.* in the pink

peal *n*, *v*
♦ *n*
chime, carillon, toll, knell, ring, clang, ringing, reverberation, resounding, triple, rumble, boom, roar, crash, clap, firing
FORMAL tintinnabulation
♦ *v*
chime, toll, ring (out), clang, resonate, reverberate, resound, rumble, boom, roll, roar, crash

peasant *n*
rustic, provincial, country person, yokel, bumpkin, oaf, lout, churl, campesino, contadino, Cossack, kulak, muzhik, fellah, jungli, kisan, ryot; *Scot* cottar, blue-bonnet
OLD boor, carlot, kern, swain
COLLOQ. country bumpkin, clodhopper, hick

pebble *n*
stone, agate, chip, gallet

peccadillo *n*
error, fault, indiscretion, lapse, slip, minor offence, misdeed, misdemeanour, delinquency
FORMAL infraction
COLLOQ. boob, slip-up

peck *v*
nip, jab, tap, rap, hit, strike, bite, prick, kiss

peculiar *adj*
1 *a peculiar sound*
strange, odd, curious, funny, queer, weird, bizarre, quaint, extraordinary, unusual, abnormal, exceptional, unconventional, offbeat, droll, eccentric, outlandish, freakish, grotesque, exotic
SLANG way-out
2 CHARACTERISTIC, distinctive, distinguishing, specific, particular, special, distinct, remarkable, individual, individualistic, personal, idiosyncratic, unique
FORMAL singular
3 *feel peculiar*
unwell, ill, sick, poorly, out of sorts, dizzy, queasy
COLLOQ. under the weather
E3 **1** ordinary, normal **2** general

■ peculiar to
unique to, characteristic of, like, belonging to, in keeping with, typical of, representative of
FORMAL indicative of

peculiarity n
oddity, bizarreness, weirdness, abnormality, exception, eccentricity, quirk, foible, mannerism, feature, trait, mark, hallmark, quality, attribute, property, characteristic, distinctiveness, particularity, idiosyncrasy
FORMAL singularity
COLLOQ. jimjam

peculiarly adv
1 STRANGELY, oddly, bizarrely, quaintly, curiously, extraordinarily, unusually, exceptionally, unconventionally
2 CHARACTERISTICALLY, distinctively, uniquely, particularly, remarkably, distinctly
FORMAL singularly
E3 1 ordinarily, normally **2** generally

pecuniary adj
monetary, financial, fiscal, commercial
FORMAL nummary, nummulary

pedagogic adj
educational, teaching, instructional, tuitional, academic, scholastic, didactic

pedagogue n
teacher, instructor, educator, master, mistress, educationalist, educationist, schoolteacher, schoolmaster, schoolmistress, don, pedant, dogmatist, preceptor, dominie

pedagogy n
teaching, instruction, training, tuition, tutelage, didactics, pedagogics

pedant n
purist, formalist, literalist, perfectionist, precisionist, precisian, dogmatist, quibbler, casuist, doctrinaire, academic, intellectual, pettifogger, Dryasdust, scholastic
FORMAL academe
COLLOQ. hair-splitter, nit-picker, egghead, highbrow, schoolmarm

pedantic adj
stilted, fussy, purist, perfectionist, literalist, formalist, particular, precise, exact, meticulous, punctilious, scrupulous, quibbling, finical, pompous, pretentious, academic, scholastic, intellectual, bookish, heavy, inkhorn, stuffy, erudite
TECHNICAL sesquipedalian, sesquipedal
OLD blue
COLLOQ. hair-splitting, nit-picking, schoolmarmish
E3 imprecise, informal, casual

pedantry n
punctiliousness, exactness, meticulousness, dogmatism, cavilling, finicality, quibbling, pomposity, pretentiousness, academicness, intellectualism, bookishness, stuffiness, pedagogism, pedagoguishness, pedantism
COLLOQ. hair-splitting, nit-picking

peddle v
sell, sell from house to house, sell from door to door, sell from place to place, vend, hawk, tout, push, trade, traffic, market, offer/present for sale, huckster; S Afr smouch
COLLOQ. flog

pedestal n
plinth, pillar, column, stand, support, mounting, foot, base, foundation, platform, podium
■ put on a pedestal
idolize, hero-worship, exalt, revere, admire, look up to, adulate

pedestrian n, adj
♦ n
walker, foot-traveller, hiker; S Afr voetganger
♦ adj
dull, boring, flat, uninspired, unexciting, unimaginative, banal, mundane, commonplace, humdrum, ordinary, mediocre, indifferent, prosaic, stodgy, plodding, turgid

COLLOQ. run-of-the-mill, not up to much, no great shakes, nothing much to write home about
E3 exciting, imaginative

pedigree n, adj
♦ n
genealogy, family tree, lineage, ancestry, descent, line, line of descent, bloodline, family, parentage, derivation, extraction, race, breed, stock, strain, blood
FORMAL stirps
♦ adj
pure-bred, pedigree, full-blooded, thoroughbred, aristocratic

pedlar n
seller, house-to-house salesman, door-to-door salesman, hawker, huckster, vendor, walker, street-trader, colporteur, chapman, gutter-man, gutter-merchant, boxwallah, cheap-jack, camelot; dialect bodger, jagger; Scot yagger, pedder, pether; S Afr smouch, smouser
OLD cadger

peek v, n
♦ v
peep, glance, peer, spy, look
COLLOQ. have a gander, have a look-see
♦ n
peep, glance, glimpse, look, blink
COLLOQ. dekko, look-see, shufti
SLANG gander; Aust & NZ squiz

peel v, n
♦ v
pare, skin, strip, scale, shell, flake (off), take off, remove; dialect pill; N Am shuck
FORMAL decorticate, desquamate
♦ n
skin, rind, zest, peeling
TECHNICAL epicarp, exocarp, integument
■ keep your eyes peeled
watch closely, observe, monitor, keep a lookout for, be alert, keep your eyes skinned

peep[1] v, n
♦ v
1 *peep through the keyhole*
look, peek, glimpse, spy, squint, peer, blink, pink, pry; Scot cook, kook, keek
OLD (Spenser) toot
2 *the sun peeped through the clouds*
emerge, issue, appear
♦ n
look, quick look, peek, glimpse, glance, squint; Scot keek
COLLOQ. dekko, look-see, shufti, gander

peep[2] v, n
♦ v
birds peeping
chirp, cheep, chirrup, pipe, tweet, chatter, twitter, warble, squeak
♦ n
chirp, cheep, chirrup, pipe, tweet, chatter, twitter, warble, squeak, cry, utterance, sound, noise, word

peephole n
spyhole, keyhole, pinhole, hole, opening, aperture, slit, chink, slink, crack, fissure, cleft, crevice, Judas hole, Judas window
FORMAL interstice

peer[1] v
peer through the window
look, gaze, scan, scrutinize, examine, inspect, spy, pry, snoop, peep, squint, pink; Scot styme
OLD squinny; (Shakesp) twire; (Spenser) toot
SLANG dick

peer[2] n
1 ARISTOCRAT, peeress, noble, nobleman, lady, lord, Law Lord, duke, marquess, marquis, earl, count, viscount, baron, patrician, trier, backwoodsman

2 EQUAL, counterpart, equivalent, like, match, fellow, confrère, compeer

peerage n
aristocracy, nobility, lords and ladies
COLLOQ. upper crust, top drawer

peeress n
aristocrat, noble, noblewoman, lady, dame, duchess, marchioness, countess, viscountess, baroness

peerless adj
matchless, without equal, unequalled, unexcelled, unmatched, incomparable, beyond compare, unparalleled, unrivalled, unsurpassed, unbeatable, unique, supreme, excellent, paramount, outstanding, superlative
FORMAL nonpareil
COLLOQ. second to none

peeve v
annoy, exasperate, irritate, vex, irk, gall, rile
COLLOQ. aggravate, bug, wind up, hassle, rub up the wrong way, get someone's blood up, make someone's blood boil, get on someone's nerves, get up someone's nose, get under someone's skin, get someone's goat, get on someone's wick, drive crazy/nuts, drive up the wall, drive round the bend/twist, get someone's back up, brass off, cheese off, make someone's hackles rise, make sparks fly, give someone the hump, get someone's dander up; N Am tick/hack off
SLANG drive bananas

peeved adj
annoyed, irritated, exasperated, put out, upset, vexed, irked, galled, riled, sore, piqued, nettled
COLLOQ. miffed, narked, bugged, stroppy, shirty, hassled, driven crazy, driven nuts, cheesed off, brassed off, got the hump, in a huff, in a paddy, hot under the collar; N Am ticked off

peevish adj
petulant, querulous, fractious, fretful, touchy, complaining, irritable, cross, grumpy, ill-tempered, in a bad mood, cantankerous, crusty, snappy, short-tempered, moody, testy, tetchy, churlish, surly, sullen, sulky
COLLOQ. crotchety, crabbed, ratty, grouchy
🔁 good-tempered

peevishly adv
irritably, crossly, grumpily, churlishly, sullenly, fractiously, fretfully, petulantly, in a bad mood

peevishness n
ill-temper, irritability, perversity, petulance, querulousness, testiness, pique, pet, captiousness, acrimony
FORMAL protervity

peg n, v
♦ n
pin, nail, screw, spike, brad, dowel, hook, knob, marker, post, stake, picket, plug, tap, hatpeg, knag, nog, thole, key
TECHNICAL cheville, piton, spigot, soft spile
OLD perch
♦ v
1 FASTEN, secure, fix, attach, join, mark
2 peg prices
control, stabilize, hold down, limit, freeze, fix, set
■ **peg away**
apply yourself, work away, work hard, persevere, persist, plug away, plod along
COLLOQ. beaver away, hang in, keep at it, stick at it
■ **take/bring down a peg or two**
humiliate, humble, bring/cut down to size, put someone in their place, take the wind out of someone's sails

pejorative adj
derogatory, disparaging, belittling, slighting, unflattering, uncomplimentary, unpleasant, bad, negative
FORMAL deprecatory
🔁 complimentary

pellet n
ball, shot, bullet, pill, drop, capsule, lozenge
COLLOQ. slug

pell-mell adv
hurriedly, hastily, feverishly, precipitously, posthaste, recklessly, rashly, heedlessly, impetuously, at full tilt
COLLOQ. helter-skelter, hurry-scurry

pellucid adj
clear, limpid, transparent, translucent, pure, glassy, bright

pelt¹ v
1 THROW, hurl, bombard, shower, attack, assail, batter, beat, hit, strike
2 POUR, teem
COLLOQ. bucket (down), rain cats and dogs
3 RUSH, hurry, charge, tear, race, dash, run, speed, sprint, career
COLLOQ. belt, scoot, zip

pelt² n
a beaver pelt
skin, coat, fur, fleece, hide, fell

pen¹ n, v
♦ n
write with a pen
fountain pen, ballpoint, ballpoint pen, Biro®, felt-tip pen, felt-tip, felt pen, Sharpie®, self-filler, highlighter, marker pen, Rollerball®, stylograph, Magic Marker®, J-pen, quill
♦ v
write (down), note (down), take down, compose, draft, scribble, jot down, dash off

> **PROVERBS**
> The pen is mightier than the sword

pen² n, v
♦ n
a sheep pen
enclosure, fold, pound, compound, stall, sty, coop, cage, hutch, mew, corral, crawl, kraal, cruive
♦ v
enclose, fence, hedge, hem in, confine, cage, coop, shut (up), corral, kraal

penal adj
punitive, disciplinary, corrective, retaliatory, retributive, vindictive

penalize v
punish, discipline, correct, fine, disadvantage, handicap
FORMAL castigate, chastise
🔁 reward

penal servitude n
hard labour, stretch, time
SLANG bird, lag, porridge

penalty n
1 PUNISHMENT, retribution, sentence, fine, forfeit, chastisement
FORMAL mulct, castigation
2 DISADVANTAGE, handicap, drawback, snag, weak point
COLLOQ. downside, minus
🔁 **1** reward **2** advantage, benefit

penance n
atonement, reparation, punishment, penalty, self-punishment, self-abasement, mortification, penitence, sackcloth and ashes
Related adjective: penitentiary

penchant n
fondness, liking, tendency, taste, preference, affinity, bent, inclination, leaning, bias, partiality, weakness, soft spot, proneness
FORMAL disposition, predilection, predisposition, proclivity, propensity
🔁 dislike

pendant n
medallion, locket, necklace

pendent *adj*
hanging, suspended, dangling, drooping, swinging
FORMAL pendulous, pensile, nutant

pending *adj, prep*
♦ *adj*
imminent, impending, in the offing, forthcoming, coming, approaching, nearing, near, undecided, unresolved, unsettled, awaiting settlement, uncertain
COLLOQ. in the balance, up in the air
F3 finished, settled
♦ *prep*
until, till, to, before, so long as, while, whilst, throughout

pendulous *adj*
sagging, hanging, suspended, dangling, drooping, droopy, swaying, swinging
FORMAL pendent

penetrable *adj*
clear, open, passable, permeable, pervious, porous, fathomable, understandable, intelligible, accessible, comprehensible, explicable
F3 impenetrable

penetrate *v*
1 PIERCE, stab, prick, perforate, puncture, spike, probe, sink, bore
2 GET INTO, enter, infiltrate, make your way, permeate, fill, seep, saturate, pervade, suffuse, imbue
3 GRASP, understand, fathom, comprehend, make out, work out, see, register, sink in
COLLOQ. crack, cotton on, suss out, twig, get to the bottom of

penetrating *adj*
1 PIERCING, stinging, biting, incisive, sharp, keen, cutting
2 *a penetrating sound*
loud, clear, strident, shrill, piercing, carrying
3 *a penetrating mind*
keen, acute, shrewd, discerning, discriminating, wise, perceptive, observant, profound, deep, searching, insightful, probing
F3 1 blunt

penetration *n*
1 PIERCING, puncturing, perforation, stabbing, pricking, incision
2 ENTRANCE, entry, inroad, infiltration, permeation, pervasion, invasion
FORMAL interpenetration
3 DISCERNMENT, perception, insight, acumen, astuteness, sharpness, keenness, acuteness, shrewdness, wit
FORMAL perspicacity

peninsula *n*
cape, point, mull, tongue, chersonese, doab

penis *n*
male organ of copulation/urination, pizzle; *dialect* jock
OLD pillicock, pintle, yard
FORMAL phallus, *membrum virile*
COLLOQ. willy; *N Am* putz
SLANG pecker, chopper, John Thomas, schmuck, tail, todger, winkle, joystick; *N Am* dork; *Aust* tonk, *(taboo)* dick, cock, prick, knob, tool, rod, cory, dong, plonker, roger, shaft, whang, wang
Related adjective: penile

penitence *n*
repentance, contrition, sorrow, shame, remorse, regret, self-reproach
FORMAL compunction, ruefulness

penitent *adj*
repentant, contrite, sorry, sorrowful, apologetic, remorseful, ashamed, regretful, conscience-stricken, shamefaced, humble
FORMAL rueful
F3 unrepentant, hard-hearted, callous

pen-name *n*
assumed name, pseudonym, stage-name, *nom de plume*, false name
FORMAL allonym

pennant *n*
flag, banner, ensign, standard, streamer, colours, banderol, gonfalon, jack

penniless *adj*
poor, poverty-stricken, impoverished, destitute, bankrupt, ruined
FORMAL indigent
COLLOQ. dirt-poor, broke, stony-broke, down and out, on the breadline, cleaned out, strapped for cash, on your beam-ends, on your uppers, bust
SLANG skint
F3 rich, wealthy, affluent

penny-pincher *n*
miser, niggard, skinflint, cheeseparer, Scrooge
COLLOQ. meanie, cheapskate, money-grubber

penny-pinching *adj*
miserly, mean, close, niggardly, scrimping, cheeseparing, ungenerous, frugal
FORMAL parsimonious
COLLOQ. tight, tight-fisted, mingy, stingy
F3 generous, open-handed

pension *n*
old-age pension, retirement pension, state pension, personal pension, company pension, index-linked pension, stakeholder pension, annuity, superannuation, support, welfare, social assistance, income, allowance, benefit, corrody

pensioner *n*
retired person, old-age pensioner, OAP, senior citizen, out-pensioner
SLANG *(offensive)* coffin-dodger

pensive *adj*
thoughtful, reflective, contemplative, meditative, thinking, pondering, musing, ruminative, absorbed, preoccupied, absent-minded, dreamy, wistful, solemn, serious, sober
FORMAL cogitative
F3 carefree

pensively *adv*
thoughtfully, contemplatively, meditatively, absent-mindedly, wistfully, dreamily, seriously

pent-up *adj*
repressed, inhibited, restrained, bridled, curbed, suppressed, stifled, held in
COLLOQ. bottled-up

penurious *adj*
1 POOR, impoverished, destitute, poverty-stricken, beggarly, penniless, hard up, in straitened circumstances, inadequate
FORMAL impecunious, indigent
COLLOQ. bust, flat broke, on your beam-ends, on your uppers
2 MISERLY, mean, niggardly, close, close-fisted, grudging, ungenerous
FORMAL parsimonious
COLLOQ. cheeseparing, tight-fisted, tight, mingy, stingy
F3 1 wealthy, generous

penury *n*
poverty, destitution, pauperism, impoverishment, insolvency, straitened circumstances, straits, deficiency, need, want, dearth, beggary
FORMAL indigence, mendicity
F3 prosperity

people *n, v*
♦ *n*
1 PERSONS, individuals, humans, human beings, the human race, mankind, humankind, humanity, mortals, folk(s)

2 CITIZENS, ordinary citizens, public, general public, populace, rank and file, hoi polloi, population, men women and children, inhabitants, community, society, electorate, masses, mob, rabble, great unwashed, riff-raff
COLLOQ. punters, plebs, proles
3 NATION, race, tribe, clan, ethnic group
OLD *Irish* tuath
4 *his people are from Wales*
parents, relations, relatives, folks, family, kith and kin
♦ *v*
populate, inhabit, occupy, settle, colonize

pep *n, v*
♦ *n*
energy, vigour, verve, spirit, sparkle, vitality, life, liveliness, dynamism, exuberance, effervescence, high spirits
FORMAL ebullience
COLLOQ. get-up-and-go, oomph, pizzazz, zing, zip
■ **pep up**
invigorate, vitalize, liven up, quicken, improve, stimulate, animate, excite, exhilarate, inspire, energize
E3 tone down

pepper *v*
1 BOMBARD, attack, assail, pelt, blitz, bomb
2 SPRINKLE, shower, scatter, spatter, bespatter, strew, dot, stud

peppery *adj*
1 SPICY, hot, pungent, seasoned, piquant
2 QUICK-TEMPERED, hot-tempered, irritable, irascible, choleric, testy, touchy, fiery, grumpy, snappish
3 INCISIVE, sharp, sarcastic, biting, stinging, astringent, caustic, waspish
FORMAL trenchant

peppy *adj*
lively, energetic, alive, spirited, high-spirited, animated, alert, active, enthusiastic, dynamic, vivacious, vigorous, sprightly, brisk, spry, agile, nimble, quick
E3 inactive, apathetic

perceive *v*
1 SEE, discern, make out, detect, discover, spot, catch sight of, glimpse, notice, observe, view, remark, note, distinguish, recognize
FORMAL espy, behold
2 SENSE, feel, apprehend, learn, realize, appreciate, be aware of, discern, recognize, see, know, grasp, understand, gather, deduce, conclude, comprehend
FORMAL be cognizant of
COLLOQ. get wind of

perceptible *adj*
perceivable, discernible, detectable, appreciable, distinguishable, observable, noticeable, obvious, evident, manifest, conspicuous, clear, plain, distinct, patent, apparent, tangible, visible
E3 imperceptible, inconspicuous

perception *n*
1 VIEW, interpretation, understanding, sense, feeling, impression, idea, conception, knowledge, apprehension
2 DISCERNMENT, awareness, consciousness, observation, recognition, insight, understanding, grasp, discrimination, sensitivity, responsiveness
FORMAL cognizance

> **QUOTATIONS**
> If the doors of perception were cleansed everything would appear to man as it is, infinite
> WILLIAM BLAKE, *The Marriage of Heaven and Hell*, 'A Memorable Fancy'

perceptive *adj*
discerning, observant, sensitive, responsive, aware, alert, quick, quick-witted, keen, sharp, acute, sharp-eyed, astute, penetrating, discriminating, shrewd, understanding, deep, insightful

FORMAL perspicacious, percipient
E3 unobservant

perceptively *adv*
astutely, observantly, sensitively, keenly, sharply, discriminatingly, insightfully
FORMAL perspicaciously

perch *n, v*
♦ *n*
rod, pole, bar, roost
♦ *v*
land, alight, settle, sit, roost, balance, rest, overperch; *dialect* perk

perchance *adv*
perhaps, maybe, possibly, conceivably, feasibly

percipience *n*
perception, discernment, astuteness, awareness, insight, intuition, understanding, sensitivity, penetration, judgement, alertness, acuteness
FORMAL perspicacity, sagacity

percipient *adj*
perceptive, observant, discerning, discriminating, sharp, aware, alive, astute, alert, penetrating, quick-witted, knowing, intelligent, wide-awake
FORMAL judicious, perspicacious
E3 unaware, obtuse

percolate *v*
filter, strain, seep, ooze, leach, leak, drip, drain, sift, sieve, penetrate, pass through, spread (slowly) through, trickle through, permeate, pervade

perdition *n*
damnation, hell, everlasting punishment, condemnation, hellfire, destruction, doom, downfall, ruin, ruination, annihilation

peregrination *n*
travel, travelling, voyage, wandering, roaming, roving, journey, tour, expedition, exploration, trek, trekking, trip, excursion, globetrotting, wayfaring, odyssey

peremptory *adj*
imperious, commanding, dictatorial, autocratic, tyrannical, lordly, authoritative, assertive, high-handed, overbearing, domineering, dogmatic, absolute, irrefutable, abrupt, curt, summary, arbitrary
COLLOQ. bossy

perennial *adj*
lasting, enduring, abiding, everlasting, eternal, immortal, undying, imperishable, unceasing, ceaseless, endless, unending, incessant, never-ending, constant, continual, unchanging, uninterrupted, unfailing, perpetual, persistent, permanent

perfect *adj, v*
♦ *adj*
1 FAULTLESS, impeccable, flawless, immaculate, sinless, unmarred, unblemished, spotless, mint, blameless, pure, superb, wonderful, excellent, matchless, peerless, incomparable, superlative
2 IDEAL, model, textbook, exemplary, ultimate, expert, accomplished, finished, completed, experienced, skilful
FORMAL consummate
COLLOQ. just the job
3 EXACT, precise, accurate, right, correct, true, faithful
4 *perfect strangers*
utter, absolute, sheer, complete, entire, total, thorough, downright, out-and-out
E3 **1** imperfect, flawed, blemished **2** inexperienced, unskilled **3** inaccurate, wrong
♦ *v*
fulfil, complete, finish, better, improve, polish, refine, mature, elaborate
FORMAL consummate
E3 spoil, mar

perfection n
1 EXCELLENCE, faultlessness, flawlessness, superiority, immaculateness, impeccability
2 IMPROVEMENT, betterment, polishing, refinement, completion, realization, maturity, ripeness, roundedness
FORMAL consummation
3 IDEAL, model, paragon, crown, pinnacle, peak of perfection, prime, best, flower, bloom, ultimate, *ne plus ultra*, acme
COLLOQ. one in a million

perfectionism n
1 PEDANTRY, formalism
2 IDEALISM, purism, Utopianism

perfectionist n
1 PEDANT, formalist, stickler, precisionist
2 IDEALIST, purist

perfectly adv
1 UTTERLY, absolutely, quite, thoroughly, very, completely, entirely, wholly, totally, fully, altogether
2 FAULTLESSLY, flawlessly, immaculately, without blemish, impeccably, ideally, wonderfully, superbly, exactly, correctly, to perfection
COLLOQ. *N Am* down pat
Fꓱ 1 partially **2** imperfectly, badly

perfidious adj
treacherous, untrustworthy, deceitful, dishonest, disloyal, double-dealing, double-faced, false, traitorous, two-faced, unfaithful, faithless, corrupt, Machiavellian, treasonous, Punic
FORMAL duplicitous
Fꓱ faithful, honest, loyal

perfidy n
treachery, betrayal, deceit, falsity, faithlessness, infidelity, disloyalty, double-dealing, traitorousness, treason
FORMAL duplicity, perfidiousness
Fꓱ faithfulness, honesty, loyalty

perforate v
hole, make holes in, punch, drill, bore, pierce, prick, puncture, spike, stab, gore, burst, rupture, tear, split, penetrate
TECHNICAL trephine

perforated adj
pierced, holed, bored, drilled, punctured, punched, porous
TECHNICAL ethmoid, fenestrate(d), fenestrial, foraminous

perforation n
hole, bore, prick, pierce, puncture, dotted line
TECHNICAL fenestra, fenestration, foramen

perforce adv
unavoidably, inevitably, necessarily, of necessity, willy-nilly

perform v
1 DO, carry out, discharge, fulfil, satisfy, complete, achieve, accomplish, conduct, bring off, pull off, bring about
FORMAL execute, effect
2 *perform a play*
stage, put on, present, enact, represent, act, do, play, appear as, portray, recite
3 FUNCTION, work, operate, go, run, behave, produce

performance n
1 SHOW, appearance, presentation, production, interpretation, rendering, rendition, representation, portrayal, acting, recital
2 ACTION, deed, doing, carrying-out, implementation, discharge, fulfilment, conducting, completion, achievement, accomplishment
FORMAL execution, effecting
3 FUNCTIONING, operation, working, running, going, behaviour, conduct

Types of performance include:

act	farewell	production
audition	performance	read-through
benefit	first house	recital
N Am colloq.	first night	rehearsal
bomb	*colloq.* flop	rendition
cabaret	full house	review
charity concert	gala night	revue
command	*colloq.* gig	run-through
performance	*colloq.* hit	second house
concert	last night	sell-out
debut	last night of the	short run
dress rehearsal	Proms	show
dry run	matinée	sketch
encore	one-night stand	*colloq.* smash hit
entertainment	opening night	sneak preview
exhibition	play	song and dance
extended run	première	theatre
	preview	turn

See also **theatrical**.

performer n
1 *circus performer*
actor, actress, player, musician, singer, dancer, comic, comedian, clown, artiste, entertainer, trouper, Thespian
See panels at **entertainer**; **musician**; **singer**.
2 ACHIEVER, doer, operator, author
FORMAL executor

perfume n
scent, fragrance, smell, odour, aroma, bouquet, sweetness, balm, essence, cologne, eau-de-cologne, eau-de-toilette, toilet water, incense
FORMAL redolence

perfunctorily adv
quickly, carelessly, superficially, cursorily, hurriedly, inattentively
Fꓱ carefully

perfunctory adj
quick, careless, superficial, cursory, negligent, offhand, slipshod, slovenly, inattentive, hurried, heedless, automatic, mechanical, routine, indifferent, brief, wooden
FORMAL desultory
Fꓱ careful, enthusiastic

perhaps adv
maybe, possibly, conceivably, feasibly
FORMAL perchance

peril n
danger, hazard, risk, jeopardy, uncertainty, insecurity, threat, menace
Fꓱ safety, security

perilous adj
dangerous, unsafe, hazardous, risky, high-risk, chancy, precarious, insecure, unsure, vulnerable, fraught with danger, exposed, menacing, threatening, dire
COLLOQ. dicey, hairy, dodgy
Fꓱ safe, secure

perimeter n
circumference, edge, border, boundary, frontier, limit(s), outer limits, bounds, confines, circuit, fringe, margin, periphery
Fꓱ middle, centre, heart

period n
1 TIME, season, stretch, duration, space, span, spell, stint, shift, term, while, turn, session, interval, cycle
COLLOQ. *Aust & NZ* spin
2 STAGE, phase, era, epoch, age, eon, generation, date, years
3 CLASS, lesson, lecture, session, seminar, tutorial, instruction

4 *a woman's monthly period*
menstruation, menstrual flow, menstrual cycle, time of the month, monthlies
FORMAL menses
COLLOQ. the curse
5 *a period at the end of the sentence*
full stop, stop, full point, point
6 *you may not go, period*
full stop, stop, end, end of story, finish, conclusion

periodic *adj*
occasional, infrequent, sporadic, intermittent, once in a while, recurrent, recurring, repeated, regular, periodical, seasonal, cyclical, cyclic

periodical *n*
magazine, journal, publication, weekly, monthly, quarterly, review, organ

periodically *adv*
occasionally, sometimes, on occasion, from time to time, at times, at intervals, now and then, now and again, irregularly, every so often, once in a while, off and on, on and off, infrequently, intermittently, sporadically
E3 frequently, often, always

peripatetic *adj*
travelling, itinerant, journeying, mobile, roaming, roving, migrant, migratory, nomadic, wandering, vagabond, vagrant
FORMAL ambulant, ambulatory
E3 fixed

peripheral *adj*
1 MINOR, secondary, lesser, incidental, unimportant, irrelevant, subsidiary, ancillary, unnecessary, marginal, sidelined, tangential, borderline, surface, superficial
COLLOQ. beside the point, neither here nor there
2 OUTLYING, outer, outermost, surrounding
3 *peripheral devices*
additional, add-on, auxiliary, computer, input, output, storage
E3 **1** major, crucial **2** central, inner

periphery *n*
edge, boundary, border, circumference, fringe, perimeter, brim, brink, rim, skirt, outskirts, outer regions, margin, verge, hem, circuit, ambit
E3 centre, nub, middle

periphrastic *adj*
roundabout, indirect, circuitous, wandering, oblique, discursive, tortuous, rambling, long-drawn-out
FORMAL circumlocutory
E3 direct

perish *v*
1 DIE, pass away, pass on, pass, depart, depart this life, breathe your last, draw your last breath, lose your life, fail, go, drown, starve, go west, succumb, close your eyes, go over to the majority
OLD exit, famish, be gathered to your fathers, give up the ghost, go the way of all flesh, go the way of the earth, pip out, sterve, swelt; (*Shakesp*) go off; (*Spenser*) quell, tine, vade
FORMAL expire, decease
COLLOQ. peg out, bite the dust, pop off, have had it, meet your maker, push up daisies, shuffle off this mortal coil; *Aust* go bung; slip the cable, turn up your toes
SLANG snuff it, cash in your chips, cash/pass in your checks, kick the bucket, kick off, kiss off, spark out, choke, croak, flatline, hop the twig, pop your clogs; *N Am* go belly up; *Aust* cark
2 COLLAPSE, disintegrate, crumble, fail, fall, come to an end, disappear, vanish, die away, rot, decay, decompose, go off

perishable *adj*
destructible, biodegradable, decomposable, short-lived
E3 imperishable, durable

perjure *v*
■ **perjure yourself**
lie, lie under oath, commit perjury, bear false witness/testimony, make false statements, give false evidence
FORMAL forswear yourself

perjury *n*
false evidence, false testimony, false witness, false swearing, false oath, false statement, lying under oath, falsification, hard swearing
TECHNICAL *crimen falsi*
OLD (*Shakesp*) oath-breaking
FORMAL forswearing, mendacity

perk *n, v*
♦ *n*
fringe benefit, soft benefit, benefit, bonus, advantage, dividend, gratuity, tip, extra, baksheesh
FORMAL perquisite
COLLOQ. plus, freebie, golden handshake
■ **perk up**
brighten (up), cheer up, take heart, revive, rally, liven up, make/become lively, recover, revitalize, improve, look up
COLLOQ. buck up, pep up

perky *adj*
lively, jaunty, spirited, vivacious, sprightly, cheerful, cheery, gay, bright, animated, bouncy, buoyant, bubbly, effervescent, sunny
FORMAL ebullient
COLLOQ. peppy
E3 cheerless, dull, gloomy

permanence *n*
fixedness, stability, imperishability, indestructibility, perpetuity, constancy, endurance, steadfastness, persistence, durability
E3 impermanence, transience

permanent *adj*
1 LASTING, enduring, durable, imperishable, indestructible, unfading, eternal, everlasting, lifelong, perpetual, constant, steadfast, immutable, invariable, unchangeable, indelible, perennial, long-lasting
2 FIXED, stable, unchanging, constant, solid, firm, established
E3 **1** temporary, fleeting; *formal* ephemeral

permanently *adv*
always, continually, constantly, ceaselessly, endlessly, eternally, perpetually, in perpetuity, incessantly, unceasingly, unremittingly, unendingly, once and for all, indelibly, everlastingly, ever more, for ever, for ever and ever, for all time
COLLOQ. for keeps, till doomsday, till kingdom come, till the cows come home, till hell freezes over
E3 temporarily

permeable *adj*
porous, absorbent, absorptive, penetrable, pervious, passable, spongy
E3 impermeable, watertight

permeate *v*
pass through, soak through, filter through, seep through, spread through, penetrate, infiltrate, percolate, pervade, imbue, saturate, impregnate, fill, diffuse

permissible *adj*
permitted, allowable, allowed, admissible, all right, tolerable, acceptable, proper, authorized, sanctioned, lawful, legal, legitimate
COLLOQ. OK, kosher, legit
E3 prohibited, banned, forbidden

permission *n*
consent, assent, agreement, approval, allowance, clearance, authorization, sanction, leave, warrant, permit, licence, dispensation, freedom, liberty
FORMAL approbation
COLLOQ. green light, thumbs-up, go-ahead
E3 prohibition

permissive *adj*
liberal, broad-minded, tolerant, forbearing, easy-going, lenient, indulgent, overindulgent, lax, free
FORMAL latitudinarian
⊟ strict, rigid, narrow-minded

permit *v, n*
♦ *v*
allow, let, consent, agree, admit, grant, authorize, give, enable, empower, sanction, warrant, license, indulge, tolerate
OLD suffer
COLLOQ. give the go-ahead to, give the green light to, greenlight, give the thumbs up to, give the nod to
⊟ prohibit, forbid
♦ *n*
pass, passport, visa, licence, warrant, authorization, sanction, permission, safe-conduct, docket, *carnet*, green card, laissez-passer, *permis de séjour*
OLD placard
⊟ prohibition

permutation *n*
alteration, change, shift, transformation, variation
FORMAL transposition, configuration, transmutation, commutation

pernicious *adj*
harmful, damaging, dangerous, destructive, ruinous, detrimental, bad, hurtful, injurious, offensive, malicious, poisonous, venomous, pestilent, toxic, wicked, evil, malevolent, malignant, fatal, deadly, unhealthy, unwholesome
FORMAL deleterious, maleficent, noisome, noxious
⊟ innocuous

pernickety *adj*
fussy, particular, over-particular, over-precise, carping, nice, punctilious, fastidious, difficult to please, fiddly, finical, finicky, exacting, detailed, careful, painstaking, fine, tricky
COLLOQ. choosy, picky, hair-splitting, nit-picking; *N Am* persnickety

peroration *n*
1 SUMMING-UP, summary, conclusion, closing remarks, reiteration, recapitulation
COLLOQ. recapping
2 SPEECH, lecture, talk, address
FORMAL oration, diatribe, declamation

perpendicular *adj, n*
♦ *adj*
vertical, upright, erect, straight, right, at right angles, sheer, steep, abrupt, precipitous, plumb
TECHNICAL anticlinal, normal
OLD downright
⊟ horizontal
♦ *n*
TECHNICAL apothem, cathetus, offset, sine

perpetrate *v*
commit, carry out, execute, do, accomplish, be responsible for, be to blame for, perform, inflict, wreak
FORMAL effect, effectuate

perpetration *n*
carrying-out, implementation, execution, doing, performance, achievement, accomplishment, commitment, committal

perpetrator *n*
doer, committer, offender, agent
FORMAL executor, executant
COLLOQ. *N Am* perp

perpetual *adj*
eternal, everlasting, infinite, endless, unending, never-ending, interminable, ceaseless, unceasing, incessant, continuous, unbroken, uninterrupted, unremitting, constant, persistent, continual, repeated, recurrent, perennial, permanent, lasting, enduring, abiding,
persisting, unchanging, unfailing, undying, unvarying, intermittent
⊟ temporary; *formal* ephemeral, transient

perpetually *adv*
eternally, endlessly, interminably, ceaselessly, unceasingly, incessantly, unremittingly, constantly, persistently, continually, permanently

perpetuate *v*
continue, keep up, maintain, sustain, preserve, keep alive, keep going, immortalize, commemorate, eternalize, memorialize

perpetuation *n*
continuation, prolongation, maintenance, preservation, commemoration, sustaining, keeping alive, lengthening, extension
FORMAL protraction
⊟ *formal* cessation, termination

perpetuity
■ **in perpetuity**
for ever, for ever and ever, for all time, always, endlessly, eternally, perpetually, ever more
COLLOQ. till the cows come home

perplex *v*
puzzle, baffle, mystify, stump, confuse, confound, muddle, bemuse, bewilder, dumbfound, tickle, bother, pother, embarrass, entangle, gravel, hobble, beset; *Scot* bumbaze, fickle
OLD distrouble, embrangle, feague, pose
COLLOQ. throw, bamboozle, flummox, nonplus

perplexed *adj*
puzzled, baffled, bewildered, mystified, stumped, confused, muddled, confounded, disconcerted, fuddled, worried, at a loss
COLLOQ. bamboozled, flummoxed, nonplussed

perplexing *adj*
puzzling, baffling, bewildering, confusing, mystifying, amazing, complex, complicated, intricate, inexplicable, hard, strange, weird, paradoxical, difficult, taxing, involved, knotty, thorny, enigmatic, mysterious
FORMAL labyrinthine
⊟ easy, simple

perplexity *n*
1 PUZZLEMENT, bafflement, bewilderment, confusion, incomprehension, mystification, nonplus; *Scot* fickleness
2 COMPLEXITY, complication, difficulty, intricacy, involvement, dilemma, enigma, mystery, puzzle, paradox, obscurity, labyrinth
FORMAL obfuscation

perquisite *n*
fringe benefit, soft benefit, benefit, bonus, advantage, dividend, gratuity, tip, extra, baksheesh, plus
COLLOQ. freebie, perk

persecute *v*
1 ILL-TREAT, abuse, mistreat, maltreat, oppress, tyrannize, victimize, martyr, distress, afflict, torment, torture, crucify
2 HARASS, hound, pursue, hunt (down), bother, worry, annoy, pester, badger, bait, molest
COLLOQ. hassle
⊟ 1 pamper, spoil

persecution *n*
ill-treatment, mistreatment, abuse, maltreatment, discrimination, oppression, harassment, molestation, suppression, tyranny, victimization, punishment, torture, martyrdom, crucifixion
FORMAL subjugation

perseverance *n*
persistence, determination, resolution, resolve, doggedness, tenacity, diligence, application, assiduity, dedication, commitment, purpose, purposefulness, constancy, steadfastness, stamina, endurance, indefatigability
FORMAL pertinacity, intransigence
COLLOQ. stickability; *N Am* stick-to-it-iveness

persevere v
continue, carry on, go on, keep going, struggle on, soldier on, persist, remain, be persistent, be determined, be resolute, stand firm, stand fast, hold on, hang on
OLD prosecute
COLLOQ. stick at it, plug away, hang in there, hammer away, bash on, truck, go the whole distance, stick to your guns, leave no stone unturned, mean business; *Scot* stick in
⊟ give up, stop; *formal* discontinue

persist v
1 CONTINUE, carry on, go on, keep on, keep going, soldier on, keep at it, persevere, stand firm, stand fast, hold on, hang on, be persistent, be determined, be resolute, insist
COLLOQ. stick at it, hang in, plug away
2 REMAIN, keep on, hold, linger, last, endure, continue
FORMAL abide
⊟ **1** stop, give up; *formal* desist

persistence n
perseverance, determination, endurance, doggedness, diligence, assiduousness, assiduity, constancy, resolution, tenacity, steadfastness, tirelessness, stamina, indefatigableness
FORMAL pertinacity, sedulity
COLLOQ. grit, stickability; N Am stick-to-it-iveness

persistent adj
1 INCESSANT, endless, never-ending, interminable, continual, unceasing, ceaseless, lasting, unrelenting, relentless, unremitting, constant, steady, repeated, perpetual, enduring, continuous
2 *persistent effort*
persevering, determined, resolute, purposeful, diligent, assiduous, dogged, tenacious, stubborn, obstinate, steadfast, zealous, tireless, unflagging, indefatigable
FORMAL intractable, obdurate, pertinacious
COLLOQ. N Am stick-to-it-ive

persistently adv
1 CONTINUALLY, incessantly, interminably, unceasingly, ceaselessly, relentlessly, constantly, continuously
2 RESOLUTELY, diligently, assiduously, obstinately, stubbornly, tenaciously, tirelessly

person n
individual, human being, human, being, man, woman, mortal, body, soul, character, type, someone, somebody
■ **in person**
personally, face to face, actually, bodily
COLLOQ. in the flesh, as large as life

persona n
image, face, public face, role, part, character, personality, front, façade, mask

personable adj
pleasant, pleasing, likeable, presentable, nice, agreeable, amiable, affable, attractive, good-looking, handsome, charming, warm, winning, outgoing
⊟ unpleasant, disagreeable, unattractive

personage n
celebrity, name, notable, worthy, public figure, personality, luminary, dignitary, headliner
COLLOQ. VIP, celeb, big shot, somebody, big noise, big cheese, bigwig

personal adj
1 *give you my personal attention*
individual, special, particular, exclusive
2 *a personal appearance*
live, in person, in the flesh, bodily
3 *your personal style*
individual, idiosyncratic, peculiar, characteristic, distinctive, unique, own, subjective
4 PRIVATE, confidential, intimate, secret
5 *personal remarks*
offensive, insulting, critical, rude, abusive, hurtful, wounding, disrespectful, derogatory, upsetting
⊟ **3** general, universal **4** public, official

personality n
1 CHARACTER, nature, disposition, temperament, temper, identity, individuality, mind, self, selfhood, psyche, traits, make-up, charm, charisma, magnetism
COLLOQ. the real you
2 CELEBRITY, notable, personage, (public) figure, person, dignitary, worthy, star
COLLOQ. VIP

personalize v
customize, adapt, convert, modify, tailor, alter, adjust, suit, fit, transform

personally adv
1 *personally, I don't approve*
from my point of view, in my opinion, I think, I believe, in my view, from my standpoint, the way I see it, as I see it, (according) to my way of thinking
COLLOQ. if you ask me, in my book, for my money
2 INDIVIDUALLY, in person, specially, particularly, exclusively, solely, alone, independently, subjectively, idiosyncratically, distinctively, characteristically, uniquely, privately, confidentially
3 *take something personally*
directed against you, as personal criticism, as hurtful comments, as a slight, insultingly, offensively

personification n
essence, embodiment, incarnation, likeness, image, representation, recreation, portrayal, semblance
FORMAL delineation, manifestation, quintessence

personify v
embody, epitomize, typify, exemplify, symbolize, represent, mirror, incarnate, be the incarnation of, personize, personalize
OLD impersonate
FORMAL hypostatize

personnel n
staff, workforce, workers, employees, crew, human resources, labour force, manpower, people, members
COLLOQ. liveware

perspective n
1 VIEW, point of view, viewpoint, aspect, angle, slant, attitude, frame of mind, vantage point, standpoint, vista, scene, prospect, outlook
COLLOQ. take
2 *get things into perspective*
proportion, relation, balance, equilibrium

perspicacious adj
discerning, observant, sensitive, responsive, aware, alert, quick, quick-witted, keen, sharp, sharp-eyed, astute, penetrating, discriminating, shrewd, understanding
FORMAL sagacious, percipient, judicious
⊟ unobservant, obtuse

perspicacity n
discernment, astuteness, perceptiveness, discrimination, insight, acuteness, cleverness, sharpness, keenness, acumen, shrewdness, penetration, wit
FORMAL percipience, perspicaciousness, perspicuity, sagaciousness, sagacity
COLLOQ. brains

perspicuity n
clarity, clearness, plainness, precision, lucidity, straightforwardness, distinctness, explicitness, intelligibility, comprehensibility, comprehensibleness, penetrability, transparency
FORMAL limpidity, limpidness

perspicuous adj
clear, crystal-clear, unambiguous, plain, obvious, manifest, self-evident, transparent, understandable, lucid, straightforward, apparent, explicit, distinct, intelligible, comprehensible
FORMAL limpid

perspiration n
sweat, secretion, moisture, wetness, foam

TECHNICAL sudor, diaphoresis, hidrosis
FORMAL exudation

perspire *v*
sweat, secrete, swelter, drip
TECHNICAL sudate
FORMAL exude

persuadable *adj*
amenable, agreeable, compliant, flexible, persuasible, malleable, pliable, receptive, susceptive, impressionable
FORMAL acquiescent
▣ firm, inflexible, stubborn

persuade *v*
coax, prevail upon, cajole, wheedle, talk into, argue (into), induce, bring round, win over, convince, satisfy, convert, lobby, sway, influence, tempt, lure, lead on, incite, prompt, urge, coerce, move, get round, bring yourself
OLD perswade
FORMAL inveigle
COLLOQ. lean on, sweet-talk, fast-talk, soft-soap, swing it, pull strings, twist someone's arm, put the screws on, con, nobble, moody; N Am snow
▣ dissuade, deter, discourage, talk out of, put off

> **QUOTATIONS**
> Eloquence should persuade gently, not by force or like a tyrant or king
> BLAISE PASCAL, *Pensées*

> **SYNONYM NUANCES**
>
> **Coax** or **induce** would be appropriate to refer to enticing someone with an element of flattery or encouragement, while **prevail upon** is more suggestive of successfully convincing someone: *he was prevailed upon to become chairman*. **Cajole** and **wheedle**, however, both have slight implications of deception or trickery, whereas **get round**, **talk into**, **bring round** and **win over** suggest convincing someone to do something they were originally opposed to. **Convince** and **satisfy** have similar connotations but with suggestions of supplying evidence rather than just encouragement to effect the change, while the term **convert** further implies getting someone to turn from one viewpoint to another.
>
>   **Lobby** is generally used in the context of persuading public officials, while **sway** and **influence** are suggestive of the use of power in persuasion: *the Home Secretary denied influencing the Prime Minister in his decision*. Both **tempt** and **lure** imply a degree of enticement with promises of a favourable result, whereas **lead on** implies delusion: *you led me on into taking part – now we shall both go to prison*.
>
>   **Incite** suggests rousing into action, often with undesirable or dramatic results: *opposition incited him to drastic methods*. You could use **prompt** to suggest a causal effect, although a less dramatic one: *what happened recently has prompted me to write to you*. Meanwhile **urge** has more to do with persuasion through persistence, and **coerce** implies a degree of compulsion.

persuasion *n*
1 COAXING, prevailing, cajolery, wheedling, talking into, winning over, inducement, enticement, pull, power, influence, sway, conviction, conversion, incitement, prompting, urging, coercion
COLLOQ. clout, sweet-talking, arm-twisting
2 OPINION, school (of thought), party, faction, side, camp, affiliation, philosophy, conviction, faith, belief, view, point of view, viewpoint, denomination, sect

persuasive *adj*
convincing, plausible, sound, valid, influential, forceful, pushy, weighty, effective, slick, telling, potent, compelling, moving, touching
FORMAL cogent, effectual

COLLOQ. smooth-talking
▣ unconvincing

persuasively *adv*
convincingly, plausibly, influentially, powerfully, forcefully, effectively, compellingly
FORMAL cogently, effectually
▣ unconvincingly

pert *adj*
impudent, cheeky, presumptuous, impertinent, insolent, bold, cocky, brash, gay, forward, fresh, flippant, lively, spirited, brisk, daring, sprightly, jaunty, tossy
COLLOQ. perky, saucy; N Am sassy
▣ coy, shy

pertain *v*
relate, apply, be appropriate, be part of, be relevant, bear on, have a bearing on, befit, belong, come under, concern, refer, regard
FORMAL appertain

pertinacious *adj*
persistent, persevering, determined, dogged, purposeful, tenacious, relentless, resolute, uncompromising, unyielding, wilful, headstrong, inflexible, obstinate, stubborn, self-willed, strong-willed, perverse, mulish
FORMAL intractable, obdurate

pertinent *adj*
relevant, suitable, appropriate, fitting, apt, apposite, to the point, material, applicable
FORMAL germane, apropos, ad rem
▣ inappropriate, unsuitable, irrelevant

pertness *n*
impudence, cheek, cheekiness, impertinence, insolence, presumption, rudeness, effrontery, forwardness, freshness, boldness, brashness, audacity, brazenness
COLLOQ. sauciness, brass, cockiness, face, chutzpah; N Am sass, sassiness

perturb *v*
worry, alarm, disturb, bother, trouble, upset, make anxious, disconcert, unsettle, discompose, disquiet, ruffle, fluster, confuse, agitate, vex
COLLOQ. put the wind up, rattle
▣ reassure, compose

perturbation *n*
worry, fright, scare, alarm, fear, terror, panic, horror, shock, consternation, dismay, distress, anxiety, nervousness, apprehension, trepidation, uneasiness
COLLOQ. flap

perturbed *adj*
worried, anxious, alarmed, upset, fearful, shaken, troubled, nervous, restless, disturbed, unsettled, discomposed, disconcerted, flustered, agitated, uncomfortable, uneasy, harassed, flurried
▣ calm, composed

perusal *n*
read, reading, look, scrutiny, study, examination, inspection, check, browse, glance, skim, run-through

peruse *v*
study, pore over, read, scan, scrutinize, examine, inspect, check, browse, look through, run through, leaf through, glance through, skim

pervade *v*
affect, penetrate, permeate, percolate, charge, fill, pass through, spread through, be disseminated through, imbue, infuse, suffuse, diffuse, infiltrate, saturate, impregnate

pervasive *adj*
prevalent, common, extensive, widespread, general, universal, inescapable, rife, diffuse, ubiquitous
FORMAL omnipresent, immanent

perverse *adj*
contrary, wayward, wrong-headed, wilful, headstrong, stubborn, obstinate, unyielding, disobedient, awkward, unruly, difficult, rebellious, troublesome, worrying, alarming, obstructive, unhelpful, unco-operative,

uncontrollable, unmanageable, pig-headed, ill-tempered, cantankerous, unreasonable, senseless, incorrect, improper, deviant, cross-grained, thwart, balky; *Scot* thrawn, camstairy
OLD overthwart, cussed, froward, wry; (*Shakesp*) peevish; *Scot* donsie
FORMAL intransigent, obdurate, refractory, intractable
COLLOQ. crabbed, stroppy, bolshie, bloody-minded
E3 obliging, co-operative, reasonable

perversely *adv*
waywardly, stubbornly, obstinately, worryingly, alarmingly, obstructively, unhelpfully, unco-operatively
E3 obligingly, reasonably

perversion *n*
1 CORRUPTION, depravity, debauchery, immorality, vice, wickedness, deviance, abnormality, irregularity
COLLOQ. kinkiness
2 TWISTING, distortion, misrepresentation, travesty, misinterpretation, deviation, misuse, misapplication, falsification
FORMAL aberration

perversity *n*
contrariness, waywardness, wrong-headedness, wilfulness, stubbornness, obstinacy, disobedience, awkwardness, unruliness, rebelliousness, troublesomeness, uncontrollability, unreasonableness, senselessness, contradictoriness, frowardness, gee
OLD cussedness
FORMAL contumacy, intransigence, obduracy, refractoriness

pervert *v, n*
♦ *v*
1 *pervert the truth*
twist, warp, distort, misrepresent, falsify, garble, misinterpret, misdirect, turn aside, deflect, avert, wrest
OLD prevaricate, wry
2 CORRUPT, lead astray, deprave, debauch, debase, degrade, subvert, warp, abuse, misuse, misapply
OLD wry
FORMAL vitiate
♦ *n*
deviate, deviant, debauchee, degenerate
COLLOQ. weirdo, oddball; *N Am* sicko
SLANG perv

perverted *adj*
corrupt, depraved, debauched, debased, immoral, evil, wicked, corrupted, deviant, unnatural, abnormal, unhealthy, twisted, warped, distorted
FORMAL vitiated
COLLOQ. kinky
SLANG pervy
E3 natural, normal

pesky *adj*
irritating, annoying, infuriating, maddening, troublesome, bothersome, irksome, tiresome, grating, worrisome, vexatious, vexing, disturbing, upsetting, nagging, displeasing, galling, provoking, thorny, trying
COLLOQ. aggravating, confounded, infernal

pessimism *n*
defeatism, fatalism, hopelessness, cynicism, depression, dejection, despair, gloom, gloominess, glumness, despondency, doomwatch, melancholy, negative thinking, distrust, *Weltschmerz*
COLLOQ. looking on the black side
E3 optimism, hopefulness

pessimist *n*
defeatist, fatalist, alarmist, doubter, cynic, melancholic, worrier, prophet of doom, gloom-monger, doomster, doomwatcher, doubting Thomas
OLD saturnist
COLLOQ. dismal Jimmy, gloom and doom merchant, doom merchant, killjoy, wet blanket, no-hoper, crapehanger
E3 optimist, hopeful

pessimistic *adj*
negative, cynical, fatalistic, defeatist, resigned, distrustful, suspicious, doubting, hopeless, alarmist, discouraging, depressing, off-putting, despairing, despondent, dejected, downhearted, glum, cheerless, morose, melancholy, depressed, dismal, gloomy, bleak
COLLOQ. looking on the black side, doomy
E3 optimistic

pest *n*
nuisance, bother, annoyance, irritation, irritant, vexation, trial, curse, scourge, bane, blight, bug
COLLOQ. pain, pain in the neck, thorn in the flesh

pester *v*
nag, badger, hound, harass, plague, torment, provoke, worry, irk, fret, bother, disturb, annoy, irritate, pick on
COLLOQ. hassle, get at, get on someone's nerves, drive round the bend, drive up the wall

pestilence *n*
plague, epidemic, disease, sickness, infection, contagion, infestation, cholera
OLD lues
FORMAL pandemic
Related adjective: luetic

pestilent *adj*
1 HARMFUL, destructive, ruinous, diseased, disease-ridden, plague-ridden, poisonous, contaminated, contagious, infectious, infected, communicable, catching, corrupting, detrimental, pernicious
FORMAL deleterious
2 INFURIATING, troublesome, annoying, bothersome, irritating, tiresome, vexing, irksome

pestilential *adj*
1 HARMFUL, destructive, ruinous, diseased, disease-ridden, plague-ridden, poisonous, contaminated, contagious, infectious, infected
2 INFURIATING, annoying, troublesome, bothersome, irritating, tiresome, vexing, irksome, pernicious

pet[1] *n, adj, v*
♦ *n*
teacher's pet
favourite, darling, idol, treasure, jewel
COLLOQ. teacher's pet, apple of your eye, blue-eyed boy/girl
♦ *adj*
1 *my pet rabbit*
tame, domesticated, trained, house-trained, manageable, subdued
See also panel at **animal**.
2 *her pet project*
favourite, favoured, preferred, dear, dearest, cherished, prized, chosen, special, particular, personal
♦ *v*
stroke, caress, fondle, cuddle, embrace, kiss
COLLOQ. neck, canoodle, smooch
SLANG snog

pet[2] *n*
in a pet
bad mood, bad temper, temper, sulk(s), tantrum
COLLOQ. paddy, hump, huff, stew, strop, grumps, the pits

peter *v*
■ **peter out**
dwindle, taper off, fade, wane, evaporate, ebb, diminish, fail, cease, stop, die away, come to an end, come to nothing
COLLOQ. fizzle out

petite *adj*
dainty, small, slight, little, delicate, bijou, dinky
E3 big, large

petition *n, v*
♦ *n*
appeal, round robin, e-petition, protest, application, request, representation, solicitation, plea, entreaty, prayer, supplication

TECHNICAL supplicat
OLD boon, suit
FORMAL invocation
♦ v
appeal, call upon, ask, crave, solicit, bid, urge, press, implore, beg, plead, entreat, beseech, pray, request, memorialize
OLD sue
FORMAL supplicate, adjure

pet name n
diminutive, endearment, term of endearment, nickname
FORMAL hypocorisma

petrified adj
terrified, terror-stricken, aghast, horrified, horror-stricken, appalled, stunned, dumbfounded, shocked, speechless, stupefied, transfixed, numb, benumbed, dazed, frozen
COLLOQ. scared stiff, scared out of your wits, scared to death, having kittens, in a blue funk, shaking like a leaf, with your heart in your mouth

petrify v
1 TERRIFY, horrify, frighten, alarm, panic, appal, paralyse, numb, stupefy, stun, dumbfound
COLLOQ. rattle, spook, boggle, scare someone out of their wits, make someone's blood run cold, scare the living daylights out of, make someone's hair stand on end, make someone jump out of their skin, put the frighteners on, put the wind up
SLANG scare the shit out of
2 TURN TO STONE, ossify, fossilize

petticoat n
slip, underskirt, jupon, kirtle

pettifogging adj
mean, petty, quibbling, paltry, captious, niggling, over-refined, subtle, sophistical, cavilling, casuistic, equivocating
COLLOQ. hair-splitting, nit-picking

pettiness n
small-mindedness, narrow-mindedness, meanness, quibbling, spitefulness
COLLOQ. nit-picking

pettish adj
peevish, sulky, irritable, petulant, thin-skinned, tetchy, touchy, grumpy, bad-tempered, ill-humoured, fractious, cross, fretful, querulous, snappish, waspish, splenetic
COLLOQ. huffy

petty adj
1 MINOR, unimportant, insignificant, inconsequential, inessential, trivial, secondary, lesser, small, in a small way, little, slight, trifling, paltry, inconsiderable, negligible, pimping, poking, twopenny-halfpenny; N Am shoestring
OLD puisne, scantle
COLLOQ. measly, grotty, piffling, piddling, potty; N Am picayune
2 SMALL-MINDED, small, narrow-minded, mean, ungenerous, grudging, niggling, quibbling, parochial, spiteful
COLLOQ. nit-picking, parish-pump
1 important, significant **2** generous, open-minded

petulance n
bad temper, irritability, ill-temper, ill-humour, sulkiness, sullenness, waspishness, peevishness, pique
FORMAL procacity, querulousness, spleen
COLLOQ. crabbedness, crabbiness

petulant adj
fretful, peevish, touchy, cross, irritable, snappish, bad-tempered, ill-humoured, complaining, impatient, moody, sullen, sulky, sour, ungracious
FORMAL querulous
COLLOQ. crotchety, crabby, crabbed, ratty, browned off, in a paddy, in a stew

phantasmagorical adj
phantasmagoric, dreamlike, surreal, illusory, unreal, trance-like, hallucinatory, insubstantial, unsubstantial, visionary, chimerical, fantastic, Alice-in-Wonderland
FORMAL ethereal

phantom n
ghost, spectre, spirit, apparition, wraith, vision, hallucination, illusion, figment
FORMAL revenant
COLLOQ. spook

pharisaical adj
sanctimonious, self-righteous, holier-than-thou, formal, hypocritical, insincere, pietistic, preachy, moralizing
COLLOQ. goody-goody

Pharisee n
hypocrite, fraud, pietist, whited sepulchre
FORMAL dissembler, dissimulator
COLLOQ. phoney, humbug

phase n, v
♦ n
stage, step, time, juncture, period, spell, season, chapter, position, part, point, aspect, form, shape, state, condition, development
■ **phase in**
introduce, ease in, bring in, start, start using, initiate
■ **phase out**
wind down, run down, ease off, taper off, wind up, eliminate, dispose of, get rid of, remove, withdraw, close, stop, stop using
FORMAL terminate

phenomenal adj
unbelievable, incredible, wonderful, fantastic, sensational, stupendous, amazing, astounding, astonishing, marvellous, breathtaking, remarkable, extraordinary, exceptional, unprecedented, unparalleled, unique, singular, unheard of, unusual
COLLOQ. mind-blowing, mind-boggling, too good to be true

phenomenally adv
incredibly, unbelievably, remarkably, extraordinarily, exceptionally, amazingly, astoundingly, astonishingly, wonderfully, marvellously, sensationally

phenomenon n
1 OCCURRENCE, happening, event, incident, episode, circumstance, fact, experience, appearance, sight
2 WONDER, marvel, miracle, prodigy, rarity, curiosity, spectacle, sensation
SLANG phenom

philander v
womanize, flirt, dally, play/fool around, have an affair
COLLOQ. sleep around, play the field

philanderer n
womanizer, ladies' man, lady-killer, flirt, dallier, libertine, rake, playboy, Casanova, Don Juan
COLLOQ. stud, wolf

philanthropic adj
humanitarian, public-spirited, altruistic, unselfish, selfless, benevolent, kind, kind-hearted, humane, charitable, alms-giving, generous, liberal, open-handed
FORMAL munificent, bounteous, bountiful
misanthropic

philanthropist n
humanitarian, benefactor, patron, sponsor, giver, donor, helper, backer, contributor, alms-giver, altruist
misanthrope

philanthropy n
humanitarianism, public-spiritedness, altruism, unselfishness, selflessness, social concern/awareness, social conscience, benevolence, kind-heartedness, kindness,

charity, alms-giving, giving, patronage,
sponsorship, help, backing, generosity, liberality,
open-handedness
FORMAL beneficience, munificence, bounteousness,
bountifulness
E= misanthropy

philippic n
diatribe, tirade, abuse, harangue, attack, onslaught,
denunciation, criticism, insult, reviling, upbraiding,
reproof, reprimand, rebuke
FORMAL invective, vituperation

philistine n, adj
♦ n
lowbrow, ignoramus, barbarian, bourgeois,
vulgarian, yahoo
COLLOQ. boor, lout
♦ adj
uncultivated, uncultured, uneducated, unrefined, unread,
unlettered, ignorant, lowbrow, tasteless, boorish,
bourgeois, crass

philosopher n
philosophizer, thinker, theorist, theorizer,
analyser, scholar, expert, guru, metaphysicist,
sage, logician
TECHNICAL epistemologist, dialectician
FORMAL deipnosophist

philosophical adj
1 *a philosophical discussion*
metaphysical, abstract, theoretical, analytical, rational,
logical, erudite, learned, wise, thoughtful, pensive,
reflective, contemplative, meditative
COLLOQ. unflappable
2 RESIGNED, patient, stoic, stoical, self-possessed,
dispassionate, serene, unruffled, calm, composed,
unemotional, impassive, collected, cool, placid, rational,
logical, realistic
FORMAL phlegmatic, imperturbable

philosophically adv
1 METAPHYSICALLY, theoretically, abstractly, analytically,
logically
2 *they accepted their fate philosophically*
stoically, calmly, patiently, resignedly, unemotionally,
impassively, placidly
COLLOQ. unflappably

philosophy n
1 *study philosophy*
reason, thought, thinking, wisdom, knowledge
See panels below
2 IDEOLOGY, world-view, doctrine, beliefs, convictions,
tenets, values, principles, attitude, viewpoint, point of
view, view

> **QUOTATIONS**
> The problems are solved, not by giving new information,
> but by arranging what we have always known.
> Philosophy is a battle against the bewitchment of our
> intelligence by means of language
> LUDWIG WITTGENSTEIN, *Philosophical Investigations*

phlegmatic adj
placid, stolid, impassive, calm, tranquil, cool,
unemotional, unconcerned, indifferent,
matter-of-fact, self-controlled, stoical,
dispassionate, saturnine
FORMAL imperturbable
COLLOQ. unflappable, cool and collected
E= emotional, passionate, nervous

phobia n
fear, irrational fear, terror, dread, anxiety, neurosis,
obsession, aversion, dislike, hatred, horror, loathing,
revulsion, repulsion
FORMAL antipathy, detestation
COLLOQ. hang-up, thing
E= love, liking
See panel on next page

Philosophical schools, doctrines and theories include:

absolutism	critical rationalism	experimentalism	Kantianism	Platonism	sensationalism
agnosticism	cynicism	fatalism	libertarianism	pluralism	solipsism
altruism	deism	feminism	logical positivism	positivism	Stoicism
analytic philoso-	descriptivism	fideism	Marxism	post-structuralism	structuralism
phy	determinism	Frankfurt School	materialism	pragmatism	subjectivism
antinomianism	dialectical materi-	gnosticism	monism	prescriptivism	Taoism
Aristotelianism	alism	hedonism	naturalism	Pyrrhonism	theism
ascetism	dogmatism	Hegelianism	neo-Kantianism	Pythagoreanism	Thomism
atheism	dualism	historicism	Neoplatonism	rationalism	transcendentalism
atomism	egoism	humanism	nihilism	realism	utilitarianism
behaviourism	Eleaticism	idealism	nominalism	reductionism	Vedanta-Mimamsa
Cartesianism	empiricism	immaterialism	Nyaya-Vaisesika	relativism	
conceptualism	Epicureanism	instrumentalism	objectivism	Sankhya-Yoga	
Confucianism	essentialism	interactionism	pantheism	scepticism	
consequentialism	existentialism	intuitionism	phenomenalism	scholasticism	

Philosophical terms include:

a posteriori	deontology	identity	jurisprudence	sense data	teleology
a priori	entailment	induction	ontology	substance	
deduction	falsafa	intuition	phenomenology	syllogism	

Branches of philosophy include:

aesthetics	ethics	philosophy of	philosophy of	philosophy of	philosophy of
AI and cognitive	history of	biology	informatics	mathematics	psychology
science	philosophy	philosophy of	philosophy of	philosophy of	philosophy of
applied ethics	logic	economics	language	medicine	religion
axiology	metaphysics	philosophy of	philosophy of law	philosophy of	philosophy of
bioethics	moral philosophy	education	(jurisprudence)	mind	science
eastern philosophy	ontology	philosophy of	philosophy of	philosophy of	semiotics
epistemology	phenomenology	history	literature	politics	

Phobias (by name of fear) include:

zoophobia (*animals*)
bacteriophobia (*bacteria*)
apiphobia (*bees*)
ailurophobia (*cats*)
cyberphobia (*computers*)
necrophobia (*corpses*)
scotophobia (or achluophobia) (*darkness*)
cynophobia (*dogs*)
claustrophobia (*enclosed places*)
panphobia (*everything*)
pyrophobia (*fire*)

xenophobia (*foreigners*)
phasmophobia (*ghosts*)
acrophobia (*high places*)
hippophobia (*horses*)
entomophobia (*insects*)
astraphobia (*lightning*)
autophobia (*loneliness*)
bacillophobia (*microbes*)
belonephobia (*needles*)

agoraphobia (*open spaces*)
toxiphobia (*poison*)
herpetophobia (*reptiles*)
ophiophobia (*snakes*)
tachophobia (*speed*)
arachnophobia (*spiders*)
triskaidekaphobia (*thirteen*)
brontophobia (*thunder*)
hydrophobia (*water*)

phone *n, v*

♦ *n*
1 TELEPHONE, receiver, handset, mobile phone, cordless phone, car phone, cell phone
COLLOQ. blower
2 *give me a quick phone*
ring, call, phone call
COLLOQ. buzz, tinkle, bell
♦ *v*
telephone, ring (up), call (up), dial, contact, get in touch, give someone a call, make a call
COLLOQ. buzz, give a buzz, give a tinkle, give a bell

phonetic alphabet

The NATO phonetic alphabet code words for letters are:

Alpha	Juliet	Sierra
Bravo	Kilo	Tango
Charlie	Lima	Uniform
Delta	Mike	Victor
Echo	November	Whiskey
Foxtrot	Oscar	Xray
Golf	Papa	Yankee
Hotel	Quebec	Zulu
India	Romeo	

phoney *adj, n*

♦ *adj*
fake, counterfeit, forged, fraudulent, bogus, trick, false, mock, spurious, assumed, feigned, simulated, affected, put-on, contrived, sham, imitation, ersatz
COLLOQ. pseudo
E₃ real, genuine
♦ *n*
impostor, pretender, fraud, sham, fake, faker, forgery, counterfeit, mountebank
COLLOQ. humbug, pseud, quack

phosphorescent *adj*

glowing, bright, luminescent, luminous, radiant
TECHNICAL noctilucent, noctilucous
FORMAL refulgent

photocopy *v, n*

♦ *v*
copy, duplicate, Photostat®, Xerox®, print, run off
♦ *n*
copy, duplicate, facsimile, Photostat®, Xerox®

photograph *n, v*

♦ *n*
photo, snap, snapshot, print, shot, still, slide, transparency, picture, image, likeness, visual aid, retake, close-up,
enlargement, blow-up, exposure, abstract, composition, montage, landscape, portrait, seascape, centrefold, panel, pinhole, sepia, hologram, headshot, heliochrome, microdot, microgram, micrograph, microphotograph, nephogram, pyrophotograph, skiagram, wirephoto
TECHNICAL angiogram, cathodograph, encephalogram, karyotype, mammogram, radiogram, radiograph, X-ray, röntgenogram, chlorobromide, chromatype, daguerreotype, ferro-print, rotograph, spectrogram, spectroheliogram
OLD ferrotype, photogene, platinotype, sun picture, sun print
COLLOQ. pic, piccy, mug shot
♦ *v*
snap, take, take a picture of, take a photograph of, take a snapshot of, film, shoot, video, record, capture on film/videotape, blow up, enlarge
TECHNICAL X-ray, daguerreotype, rotograph
OLD Kodak®
SLANG pap

photographer *n*

camera operator, cameraman, camerawoman, paparazzo

photographic *adj*

1 *photographic equipment*
filmic, graphic, cinematic, pictorial
See panels on next page
2 *photographic memory*
accurate, exact, detailed, faithful, precise, realistic, retentive, vivid, minute, visual, lifelike, natural, naturalistic, representational

Photostat® *n, v*

♦ *n*
copy, duplicate, facsimile, photocopy, Xerox®
♦ *v*
copy, duplicate, photocopy, Xerox®, print, run off

phrase *n, v*

♦ *n*
construction, clause, idiom, expression, group of words, saying, utterance, remark, comment, language, phraseology, usage, way/style of speaking
♦ *v*
word, formulate, frame, couch, present, put, put into words, express, say, utter, pronounce

phraseology *n*

terminology, phrase, phrasing, wording, expression, idiom, language, parlance, speech, writing, style, syntax, diction, argot, cant, patois

phrasing *n*

wording, words, choice of words, language, expression, idiom, phraseology, terminology, style, diction, wordage, verbiage

physical *adj*

1 BODILY, corporeal, fleshy, fleshly, carnal, incarnate, mortal, earthly, unspiritual
FORMAL somatic
2 MATERIAL, concrete, solid, substantial, tangible, palpable, visible, real, actual, spatial
E₃ 1 mental, spiritual **2** abstract, theoretical

physically *adv*

1 *physically fit*
in your body, bodily, physiologically
2 *the school is physically unable to expand*
materially, substantially, concretely, tangibly, actually, really, visibly
E₃ 1 mentally, spiritually

physician *n*

doctor, medical practitioner, general practitioner, GP, houseman, intern, internist, registrar, consultant, specialist, healer, external, hakim, Paean
OLD leech, mediciner, physicianer; (*Shakesp*) medicine
COLLOQ. medic, doc, quack, medico

Photographic equipment includes:

boom arm	developing tank	film-drying cabinet	light-box	print washer	stand
camcorder	dry mounting press	film projector	monopod	safelight	stop bath
camera	easel	fixing bath	negative carrier	screen	tripod
contact printer	enlarger	flash umbrella	paper drier	slide projector	Vertoscope®
developer bath	enlarger timer	focus magnifier	print-drying rack	slide viewer	viewer

Photographic accessories include:

afocal lens	cartridge film	film	heat filter	memory card	supplementary lens
air-shutter release	cassette adaptor	film pack	honeycomb diffu-	memory reader	tele-cine converter
auxiliary lens	cassette film	filter	ser	parabolic reflector	teleconverter
barn doors	close-up lens	fish-eye lens	hot shoe	polarizing filter	telephoto lens
battery	colour filter	flashbulb	light meter	remote control	video editor
cable release	diffuser	flash card	lens	right-angle finder	video light
camcorder battery	disc film	flashcube	lens cap	sepia filter	video mixer
charger/dischar-	exposure meter	flash drive	lens hood	skylight filter	viewfinder
ger/tester	eye-cup	flashgun	lens shield	slide mount	wide-angle lens
camera bag	eyepiece magnifier	flash unit	macro lens	spot meter	zoom lens

See also **camera**.

physics *n*
natural philosophy
See panel on next page

physiognomy *n*
face, features, look
OLD visnomy; (*Shakesp*) fisnomie
FORMAL countenance, visage
COLLOQ. clock, dial, mug, phiz, phizog, kisser

physique *n*
body, figure, shape, form, build, frame, structure,
constitution, make-up

pick *v, n*
♦ *v*
1 SELECT, choose, go for, opt for, decide on, settle on, fix
on, single out, prefer, favour, make up your mind
COLLOQ. plump for
2 GATHER, collect, pluck, pull, harvest, cull, take in
3 *pick a lock/safe*
open, crack, break open, prise open, force open
4 *pick a quarrel*
cause, start, begin, provoke, produce, lead to,
prompt, give rise to
♦ *n*
1 CHOICE, selection, option, decision, preference, favour
2 BEST, cream, choicest, prize, flower, élite, elect, crème
de la crème
■ **pick at**
nibble, peck, play with, toy with, eat small amounts of
■ **pick off**
1 SHOOT, hit, kill, remove, strike, fire at, gun down, take
out
2 REMOVE, detach, take away, pull off
■ **pick on**
bully, torment, victimize, persecute, criticize, blame, find
fault with, nag, bait
COLLOQ. get at, needle
■ **pick out**
1 CHOOSE, select, go for, opt for, decide on, settle on, fix
on, single out, prefer, favour, make up your mind
2 DISCERN, make out, spot, notice, perceive, recognize,
distinguish, tell apart, discriminate, separate, single out,
hand-pick
■ **pick up**
1 LIFT, raise, hoist, take up
2 *I'll pick you up at eight*
call for, fetch, collect, give a lift/ride
3 LEARN, master, grasp, acquire, get to know,
gather
4 IMPROVE, get better, rally, recover, make progress, make
headway
COLLOQ. perk up

5 ARREST, take into custody, apprehend
COLLOQ. nick, nab, collar, pinch, bust, run in, take in
6 RESUME, begin again, start again, continue, go on, carry on
7 OBTAIN, acquire, gain, learn, hear, find, discover, come
across, buy, purchase
FORMAL chance upon
8 *pick up an infection*
catch, contract, get, become ill with, become infected
with, go down with
9 *pick up a girl at a party*
COLLOQ. get off with, pull, cop off with
10 *pick up a radio signal*
receive, detect, get, hear

picket *n, v*
♦ *n*
1 PICKETER, protester, objector, rebel, dissident,
demonstrator, striker
2 GUARD, sentry, watch, patrol, lookout, outpost, blockade
3 STAKE, post, spike, upright, peg, pike, stanchion, pale,
paling
♦ *v*
protest, demonstrate, boycott, blockade, go on a picket
line, enclose, surround

pickings *n*
proceeds, profits, returns, rewards, earnings, yield, take,
spoils, booty, loot, plunder
SLANG gravy

pickle *n, v*
♦ *n*
1 *cheese and pickle*
chutney, relish, vinegar, sauce, flavouring, seasoning,
condiment, piccalilli
2 MESS, difficulty, dilemma, predicament, plight, crisis,
quandary, straits
FORMAL exigency
COLLOQ. bind, fix, hot water, jam, pinch, scrape, spot,
tight spot
♦ *v*
preserve, conserve, souse, marinade, steep, cure, salt;
dialect put down

pick-me-up *n*
tonic, boost, refreshment, restorative, fillip, stimulant,
stimulus, cordial
TECHNICAL roborant
COLLOQ. shot in the arm

pickpocket *n*
thief, snatcher, pick-purse, bagsnatcher
OLD file, cutpurse; (*Shakesp*) bung
COLLOQ. dip, diver, wire, nipper, whizzer
OLD SLANG cly-faker

Terms used in physics include:

absolute zero	electric discharge	hydrodynamics	Mach number	principle	specific heat
acceleration	electricity	hydrostatics	magnetic field	process	capacity
acoustics	electrodynamics	incandescence	magnetism	proton	spectroscopy
alpha particle	electromagnetic	indeterminacy	mass	quantum	spectrum
analogue signal	spectrum	principle	mechanics	chromodynamics	speed
applied physics	electromagnetic	inertia	microwaves	(QCD)	states of matter
Archimedes	waves	infrared	mirror	quantum	statics
principle	electron	interference	Mohs scale	electrodynamics	substance
area	energy	ion	molecule	(QED)	superstring theory
atom	engine	Kelvin effect	moment	quantum	supersymmetry
beta particle	entropy	kinetic energy	momentum	mechanics	surface tension
Big Bang theory	equation	kinetic theory	motion	quantum theory	temperature
boiling point	equilibrium	laser (light	neutrino	quark	tension
bubble-chamber	evaporation	amplification by	neutron	radiation	theory
capillary action	field	stimulated	nuclear	radioactive	theory of relativity
centre of gravity	flash point	emission of	nuclear fission	element	thermodynamics
centre of mass	force	radiation)	nuclear fusion	radioactivity	Thomson effect
centrifugal force	formula	latent heat	nuclear physics	radioisotope	transverse wave
chain reaction	freezing point	law	nucleus	radio wave	ultrasound
charge	frequency	laws of motion	optical centre	ratio	ultraviolet
charged particle	friction	laws of reflection	optics	reflection	uncertainty
circuit	fundamental con-	laws of refraction	oscillation	refraction	principle
circuit-breaker	stant	laws of	parallel motion	relativity	velocity
couple	gamma ray	thermodynamics	particle	resistance	viscosity
critical mass	gas	lens	periodic law	resonance	visible spectrum
cryogenics	gate	lever	perpetual motion	rule	volume
density	Grand Unified	light	phonon	semiconductor	wave
diffraction	Theory (GUT)	light emission	photon	sensitivity	wave property
digital	gravity	light intensity	photosensitivity	separation	weight
dynamics	half-life	light source	polarity	SI unit	white heat
efficiency	heat	liquid	potential energy	sound	work
elasticity	heavy water	longitudinal wave	power	sound wave	X-ray
electric current	hydraulics	luminescence	pressure	specific gravity	

See also **atom**; **electricity and electronics**.

---

pick-up *n*
1 IMPROVEMENT, betterment, enhancement, rectification, rectifying, correction, amendment, revision, reform, reformation, rehabilitation, upgrading, modernizing, increase, rise, upswing, gain, development, advance, growth, progress, headway, furtherance, recovery, rally
FORMAL amelioration
2 *load boxes into a pick-up*
truck, lorry, van, wagon, float
E3 **1** deterioration, decline, worsening

picky *adj*
fussy, choosy, selective, discriminating, particular, finicky, fastidious, exacting, faddy
COLLOQ. pernickety; *N Am* persnickety

picnic *n*
1 *a picnic lunch*
outing, excursion, outdoor meal, *fête champêtre*, junket
OLD a kettle of fish, wayzgoose
2 *minding young children is no picnic*
COLLOQ. child's play, cinch, doddle, piece of cake, pushover, walkover, a fine/pretty kettle of fish

pictorial *adj*
graphic, diagrammatic, schematic, representational, vivid, striking, expressive, illustrated, picturesque, scenic, in pictures, in photographs

picture *n, v*
♦ *n*
1 DESCRIPTION, portrayal, depiction, account, report, story, narrative, tale, semblance, impression
FORMAL delineation, similitude
Related adjective: pictorial
2 *the picture of health*
embodiment, personification, epitome, essence
FORMAL archetype, exemplar, quintessence
3 FILM, motion picture

COLLOQ. movie
OLD COLLOQ. flick
4 *go to the pictures*
cinema, movies, picture-house, film theatre, entertainment centre, multiplex, picture-palace
OLD COLLOQ. flicks
♦ *v*
1 IMAGINE, envisage, envision, conceive, visualize, call to mind, see, see in your mind's eye
2 DEPICT, describe, represent, reproduce, show, portray, draw, sketch, paint, photograph, illustrate, appear
FORMAL delineate
■ **get the picture**
understand, comprehend, grasp, take in, follow, see
COLLOQ. get the message, get it, get the idea, get the point, catch on, cotton on, latch on, tumble to
■ **put someone in the picture**
inform, tell, notify, communicate, explain, update
COLLOQ. fill in, clue up, keep posted

QUOTATIONS
The scenes of our life resemble pictures in rough mosaic; they are ineffective from close up, and have to be viewed from a distance if they are to seem beautiful
ARTUR SCHOPENHAUER, *Parerga und Paralipomena*

Kinds of picture include:

abstract	collage	etching
bitmap	design	fresco
bricolage	digital image	graffiti
cameo	doodle	graphics
canvas	drawing	icon
caricature	effigy	identikit
cartoon	engraving	illustration

image	passport photo	snap
kakemono	Photofit®	snapshot
landscape	photograph	still
likeness	photogravure	still life
miniature	pin-up	study
montage	plate	tableau
mosaic	portrait	tapestry
colloq. mugshot	print	tracing
mural	representation	transfer
negative	reproduction	transparency
oil painting	self-portrait	triptych
old master	silhouette	trompe l'oeil
painting	sketch	vignette
panorama	slide	watercolour

picturesque *adj*

1 ATTRACTIVE, beautiful, pretty, lovely, delightful, charming, pleasant, pleasing, quaint, idyllic, romantic, scenic, picture-book
2 DESCRIPTIVE, depictive, graphic, vivid, colourful, striking, impressive
F3 **1** unattractive **2** dull, boring

piddling *adj*

paltry, meagre, derisory, contemptible, mean, low, miserable, wretched, poor, sorry, small, slight, trifling, inconsiderate, negligible, trivial, minor, petty, unimportant, insignificant, puny, worthless
COLLOQ. measly, piffling
F3 substantial, significant, valuable

pie *n*

pastry, flan, tart
See also **food.**

■ **pie in the sky**
daydream, dream, delusion, fantasy, reverie, romance, mirage, notion
COLLOQ. jam tomorrow, hot air, castle in Spain, castle in the air

piebald *adj*

black and white, dappled, flecked, mottled, pied, spotted, speckled, variegated, brindled, skewbald

piece *n, v*

♦ *n*
1 FRAGMENT, bit, scrap, crumb, morsel, flake, speck, fleck, titbit, mouthful, bite, lump, chunk, wedge, hunk, dollop, block, slab, bar, slice, sliver, snippet, chip, splinter, shred, offcut, length, sample, component, constituent, element, part, segment, section, unit, division, fraction, share, allocation, allotment, percentage, quota, portion, quantity; *N Am* tidbit
COLLOQ. smithereen, cut, slice
2 ARTICLE, item, study, work, opus, story, review, composition, report, illustration, creation, specimen, example, instance

■ **piece together**
assemble, join, put together, unite, attach, compose, fit, mend, fix, repair, patch, restore

■ **all in one piece**
intact, unbroken, whole, complete, integral, entire, undamaged, unharmed, unhurt, uninjured
F3 broken, incomplete, damaged

■ **go to pieces**
lose control, break down, have a breakdown, be overcome, collapse
COLLOQ. crack up

■ **in pieces**
in bits, broken, damaged, disintegrated, ruined, shattered, smashed
COLLOQ. kaput, in smithereens

■ **pull/tear to pieces**
criticize, condemn, disapprove of, find fault with, denounce, attack, censure, slate, snipe, run down, come down on, pick holes in, blame
COLLOQ. nag, slam, knock, give someone some stick, go to town on, haul over the coals, pan, tear to shreds, tear a

strip off, do a hatchet job on, badmouth, rubbish, put the boot in
SLANG slag (off)

pièce de résistance *n*

masterpiece, masterwork, prize, showpiece, magnum opus, *chef-d'oeuvre*, jewel

piecemeal *adv, adj*

♦ *adv*
little by little, intermittently, parcel-wise, partially, at intervals, slowly, bit by bit, by degrees, fitfully
COLLOQ. in dribs and drabs
F3 completely, entirely, wholly
♦ *adj*
fragmentary, intermittent, interrupted, partial, unsystematic, scattered, patchy, sporadic
FORMAL discrete
F3 complete, entire, whole, wholesale

pied *adj*

flecked, irregular, motley, mottled, multicoloured, particoloured, piebald, dappled, brindle(d), spotted, streaked, skewbald, varicoloured, variegated

pier *n*

1 JETTY, breakwater, landing-stage, dock, quay, wharf
2 SUPPORT, upright, pile, pillar, post, column

pierce *v*

1 PENETRATE, enter, pass through, stick into, puncture, drill, bore, probe, perforate, punch, prick, stab, lance, bayonet, pike, stake, run through, spear, skewer, spike, barb, pink, impale, transfix, transpierce, needle, thrust, gore, pith, broach, tap, jag, peg, gimlet, spile, drift; *dialect* thirl; *Scot* slap, steek
OLD pearce, perse, perce, cleave, engore, gride, launch, nail, prog, rive, thrill (through); *(Spenser)* empierce
FORMAL lancinate
2 *pierce someone's spirit*
stab, sting, pain, hurt, move, prick, cut to the quick
3 *pierce the darkness*
burst through, penetrate, fill, enter, light up

pierced *adj*

perforated, perforate, impaled, punctured, pinked, stung
TECHNICAL foraminated, foraminous
OLD pearst, pierst
FORMAL pertusate, pertuse(d), fenestrate

piercing *adj*

1 *a piercing cry*
shrill, high-pitched, loud, ear-splitting, ear-piercing, penetrating, sharp, acute, keen
OLD perceant
2 PENETRATING, probing, searching, discerning, perceptive, shrewd, alert, astute, sharp, sharp-witted
OLD perceant; *(Spenser)* thrillant
3 COLD, bitter, raw, biting, numbing, keen, fierce, severe, wintry, frosty, freezing, Arctic
4 PAINFUL, agonizing, excruciating, extreme, severe, intense, stabbing, lacerating, shooting

piercingly *adv*

1 *shriek piercingly*
shrilly, loudly, sharply, keenly
2 *look piercingly*
penetratingly, discerningly, sharply, alertly, astutely
3 *piercingly cold*
bitterly, numbingly, fiercely, keenly, severely
4 *piercingly poignant*
intensely, extremely, severely, painfully, agonizingly, excruciatingly, bitterly

piety *n*

piousness, devoutness, godliness, saintliness, holiness, sanctity, spirituality, religiousness, religion, faith, devotion, reverence, respect, fear of God, deference
F3 impiety, irreligion

piffle *n*

nonsense, rubbish, trash, tripe, drivel, balderdash, rot, tarradiddle

COLLOQ. bunk, bunkum, codswallop, guff, hooey, poppycock, cock, tommyrot, tosh, twaddle, baloney, blah, bosh, eyewash, hogwash, rhubarb, malarkey, moonshine
SLANG bull; (*vulgar*) balls, shit, bullshit

piffling *adj*
trifling, small, paltry, slight, negligible, inadequate, insufficient, inconsiderable, unimportant, insignificant, minor, trivial, superficial, petty, silly, foolish, frivolous, idle, empty, shallow, worthless
FORMAL inconsequential
F3 important, significant, serious

pig *n, v*
◆ *n*
1 SWINE, hog, sow, boar, grunter, piglet
COLLOQ. piggy
Related adjective: porcine
2 ANIMAL, beast, brute, monster, boor
3 GLUTTON, gormandizer, gourmand
COLLOQ. greedy guts, guzzler
◆ *v*
gorge, feast, gobble, guzzle, cram, stuff
COLLOQ. wolf, scoff, snarf

pigeonhole *n, v*
◆ *n*
1 COMPARTMENT, niche, slot, cubby-hole, cubicle, locker, box, place, section
2 CATEGORY, class, classification, compartment
◆ *v*
1 LABEL, compartmentalize, categorize, classify, sort, file, tag, slot, catalogue, alphabetize
2 SHELVE, defer, postpone, put off
COLLOQ. put on the back burner

pig-headed *adj*
stubborn, obstinate, perverse, self-willed, stiff-necked, inflexible, contrary, mulish, stupid, unyielding, wilful, wrong-headed, headstrong, bull-headed
OLD froward
FORMAL intractable, intransigent
F3 flexible, tractable

pigment *n*
colour, hue, tint, dye, stain, paint, colouring, tincture

pile¹ *n, v*
◆ *n*
1 STACK, heap, bundle, mound, mountain, mass, accumulation, collection, assortment, hoard, stockpile, store
FORMAL assemblage
2 LARGE QUANTITY, a great deal, a lot, quantities
COLLOQ. loads, lots, lashings, stacks, heaps, masses, oodles, millions, thousands, hundreds, tons
3 *make a pile*
fortune, wealth, riches
COLLOQ. mint, packet, bundle, bomb
SLANG megabucks, big bucks, loadsamoney
4 *a pile in the country*
large building, imposing/impressive building, edifice, mansion
◆ *v*
1 STACK (UP), heap (up), mass, amass, accumulate, build up, gather, assemble, collect, hoard, stockpile, store, load
2 PACK, jam, crush, squeeze, crowd, flock, flood, stream, rush, charge
■ **pile it on**
exaggerate, overstate, overdo, magnify, overemphasize, emphasize, stress, make too much of, overplay, dramatize, overdramatize
COLLOQ. lay it on, lay/pile it on thick, lay/pile it on with a trowel, make a mountain out of a molehill, blow something up out of all proportion
F3 understate, play down
■ **pile up**
mount up, increase, grow, accumulate, multiply, escalate, soar

pile² *n*
houses built on piles
post, piling, column, upright, support, bar, beam, foundation

pile³ *n*
the pile of a carpet
nap, shag, plush, fur, hair, fluff, fuzz, down, wool, fibres, threads, (soft) surface, texture
Related adjectives: villose, villous

pile-up *n*
crash, accident, collision, bump, wreck
COLLOQ. smash, smash-up, prang

pilfer *v*
steal, filch, shoplift, rob, thieve, make away with, run off with; *dialect* mag; *N Am* boost
FORMAL purloin, peculate
COLLOQ. pinch, nick, knock off, lift, snaffle, nobble, have sticky fingers, snitch, swipe, whip, bag
SLANG heist, hoist, pull, lag, blag, mill, smug, sneak

pilgrim *n*
crusader, traveller, wanderer, wayfarer, worshipper, devotee, palmer, hadji
OLD peregrine

> **QUOTATIONS**
> Who would true valour see, / Let him come hither; / One here will constant be, / Come wind, come weather. / There's no discouragement / Shall make him once relent / His first avow'd intent / To be a pilgrim
> JOHN BUNYAN, *The Pilgrim's Progress*, 'Shepherd Boy's Song in the Valley of Humiliation'

pilgrimage *n*
crusade, mission, expedition, journey, trip, tour, hadj
FORMAL peregrination

pill *n*
tablet, capsule, lozenge, pellet, ball, bolus, caplet

pillage *v, n*
◆ *v*
plunder, raid, sack, vandalize, maraud, loot, spoil, ransack, ravage, raze, freeboot, rifle, rob, strip
FORMAL depredate, despoil, spoliate
◆ *n*
plunder, sack, devastation, marauding, harrying, seizure, spoils, robbery, loot, booty
FORMAL depredation, rapine, spoliation

pillar *n*
1 COLUMN, shaft, pole, post, mast, pier, upright, pile, support, prop, stanchion, obelisk, baluster, pilaster, stack, lat, man, monolith, trumeau, lamppost, standard, lamp-standard; *dialect* stoop
TECHNICAL cippus, telamon
OLD goal
2 *a pillar of society*
mainstay, bastion, support, rock, stalwart, tower of strength

pillory *v*
ridicule, mock, pour scorn on, laugh at, denounce, attack, criticize, lash, hold up to shame, show up, brand, cast a slur on, stigmatize

pillow *n*
cushion, bolster, rest, headrest, bed

pilot *n, v, adj*
◆ *n*
1 FLYER, aviator, airman, airwoman, captain, commander, first officer, flight engineer, crew, aircrew
2 NAVIGATOR, steersman, helmsman, coxswain, captain, leader, director, guide
◆ *v*
fly, drive, steer, direct, control, handle, manoeuvre, manage, operate, run, conduct, lead, guide, navigate
◆ *adj*
experimental, trial, test, model, sample

pimp *n*
pander, panderer, procurer, fancy man, fleshmonger, whoremonger, solicitor
OLD bawd, broker, mackerel
SLANG hustler, ponce, mack; *Aust* hoon

pimple *n*
spot, blackhead, boil, swelling, papula, papule, pustule, whitehead, carbuncle, whelk, button, milium, rum-blossom, rum-bud; *dialect* quat; *Scot* plouk
OLD botch, bubukle
COLLOQ. zit
Related adjectives: papulose, papulous

pin *v, n*
♦ *v*
1 TACK, nail, fix, stick, affix, attach, join, staple, clip, fasten, secure
2 HOLD DOWN, hold, hold fast, restrain, constrain, press, immobilize
3 *pin the blame on someone*
attach, put, place, lay, attribute, ascribe
FORMAL impute
♦ *n*
tack, nail, screw, spike, rivet, bolt, peg, dowel, fastener, clip, staple, skewer, brooch
■ **pin down**
1 PINPOINT, identify, define, determine, specify
COLLOQ. nail down, put your finger on
2 FORCE, make, compel, press, pressurize, hold down, hold fast, restrain, constrain
COLLOQ. nail down

pincers *n*
forceps, tweezers, forfex

pinch *v, n*
♦ *v*
1 SQUEEZE, compress, crush, press, tweak, nip, hurt, confine, cramp, grip, gripe, grasp, twinge, twitch, shut, pincer, sneap, check, lace; *Scot* chack, pook
OLD wring
2 STEAL, pilfer, filch, snatch
FORMAL appropriate, purloin, peculate
COLLOQ. nick, walk off with, knock off, lift, swipe, whip, bag; *Aust & NZ* souvenir
3 ECONOMIZE, save, cut back, budget, keep costs down, live on the cheap, scrimp and save, eke out
COLLOQ. tighten your belt, cut your coat according to your cloth, scrape a living
4 ARREST, capture, catch, seize, detain
COLLOQ. bust, nick, collar, nab, book, run in, pull in, pick up, nail
♦ *n*
1 SQUEEZE, tweak, nip, twinge; *Scot* chack
2 DASH, soupçon, trace, taste, bit, touch, speck, spot, jot, mite, pugil, snuff; *Scot* tate, sneesh
COLLOQ. smidgen, tad
3 EMERGENCY, crisis, predicament, difficulty, hardship, pressure, stress
■ **at a pinch**
if necessary, if absolutely necessary, in an emergency, with great difficulty
■ **feel the pinch**
have a hard time, hit/strike a bad patch, not have enough money, be short of money, be poor, scratch a living, tighten your belt

pinched *adj*
pale, thin, drawn, strained, haggard, gaunt, peaky, careworn, worn, narrowed, straightened, starved

pine *v*
1 YEARN, long, ache, sigh, wish, desire, crave, hanker, hunger, thirst
2 *pine away from grief*
grieve, mourn, fret, weaken, fade, languish, waste away

pinion *v*
pin down, tie, fasten, confine, bind, chain, fetter, manacle, shackle, hobble, immobilize, truss

pink[1] *adj, n*
♦ *adj*
pink flowers
reddish, flushed, rose, rosy, salmon, roseate
♦ *n*
perfection, height, peak, acme, extreme, best, flower, prime, summit, top, tiptop
■ **in the pink**
fit, healthy, well, very well, in good shape, trim, in fine fettle, in good/perfect health, in the best of health
COLLOQ. right as rain, in good nick, on good form

pink[2] *v*
to pink cloth
cut, notch, serrate, perforate, score, incise, prick, punch, scallop
FORMAL crenellate

pinnacle *n*
1 PEAK, summit, top, cap, crown, crest, apex, vertex, acme, zenith, apogee, height, eminence, culmination
2 SPIRE, steeple, turret, minaret, pyramid, cone, obelisk, needle

pinpoint *v, adj*
♦ *v*
identify, spot, distinguish, locate, place, home in on, pin down, discover, determine, specify, define
COLLOQ. zero in on, nail down, put your finger on
♦ *adj*
precise, exact, accurate, right, scrupulous, punctilious, meticulous, rigorous

pint-size *adj*
pint-sized, little, small, pocket, pocket-sized, tiny, diminutive, miniature, dwarf, midget, pygmy; *Scot* wee
COLLOQ. mini, teeny, teeny-weeny, dinky
E3 giant, huge, enormous

pioneer *n, v*
♦ *n*
1 SETTLER, colonist, frontiersman, frontierswoman, explorer
2 *a pioneer in science*
developer, pathfinder, trailblazer, groundbreaker, leader, innovator, inventor, discoverer, founder, founding father
♦ *v*
invent, discover, originate, create, initiate, instigate, begin, start, launch, institute, introduce, found, establish, set up, develop, open up, prepare the way for, lead the way, spearhead, break new ground, blaze a trail, make the first move
COLLOQ. set/start the ball rolling, pave the way

pious *adj*
1 DEVOUT, godly, saintly, holy, spiritual, religious, reverent, sanctified, faithful, dedicated, devoted, good, virtuous, righteous, moral, wise, *pia*
2 SANCTIMONIOUS, self-righteous, hypocritical, insincere, priggish
FORMAL unctuous
COLLOQ. holier-than-thou, goody-goody, pi
E3 **1** impious, irreligious, irreverent

piously *adv*
1 DEVOUTLY, religiously, spiritually, reverently, faithfully, morally, righteously, virtuously
2 SELF-RIGHTEOUSLY, sanctimoniously, insincerely, hypocritically, priggishly

pipe *n, v*
♦ *n*
1 TUBE, hose, piping, tubing, pipeline, line, main, flue, duct, conduit, drainpipe, channel, passage, cylinder, conveyor, overflow, tap, faucet, jet, manifold, blast-pipe, blow pipe, feed-pipe, stopcock, standpipe, service pipe, gas-bracket, goose-neck, dip-pipe, exhaust pipe, tailpipe, stovepipe, throttle-pipe, uptake, chimney pot, dry riser, riser, wastepipe, crane, worm, dead-end, soil pipe, aqueduct, ventiduct
TECHNICAL kill/injection string, kelly
OLD clyster-pipe

2 *pipe and tobacco*
tabacco-pipe, clay, claypipe, hookah, hubble-bubble, kalian, water pipe, brier, dudeen, meerschaum, narghile, calumet, peace-pipe, chibouk, churchwarden, cob-pipe; *Scot* cutty
3 *play music on a pipe*
recorder, flute, fife, whistle, penny whistle, bagpipes, reed, quill, aulos, chanter, cornpipe, drone, pitch-pipe, tibia
OLD oat
♦ *v*
1 CHANNEL, funnel, siphon, carry, bring, take, convey, conduct, duct, transmit, supply, deliver
2 WHISTLE, chirp, tweet, cheep, chirrup, peep, twitter, sing, warble, trill, shrill, tweedle, play, sound, pule
OLD shrike
■ **pipe down**
be quiet, stop talking
COLLOQ. shut up

pipe dream *n*
daydream, dream, delusion, fantasy, reverie, romance, false hope, mirage, notion
FORMAL chimera, vagary
COLLOQ. castle in Spain, castle in the air, pie in the sky

pipeline *n*
passage, pipe, tube, line, conduit, channel, duct, conveyor
■ **in the pipeline**
in preparation, planned, already started, on the way, under way

pipsqueak *n*
nobody, nonentity, nothing
COLLOQ. upstart, squirt, twerp, whippersnapper, creep, hobbledehoy
Ⓕ somebody

piquancy *n*
1 SPICINESS, pungency, tang, pepperiness, spice, relish, flavour, strong flavour, sharpness, ginger, bite
2 LIVELINESS, excitement, interest, vigour, vitality, spirit, zest, colour, raciness, punch
COLLOQ. edge, kick, oomph, pep, pizzazz, zip

piquant *adj*
1 *piquant sauce*
spicy, tangy, savoury, salty, peppery, seasoned, highly seasoned, pungent, zesty, sharp, biting, tart, stinging
2 LIVELY, spirited, stimulating, provocative, interesting, sparkling, intriguing, fascinating, sharp, racy, colourful
COLLOQ. juicy
Ⓕ **1** bland, insipid **2** dull, banal

pique *n, v*
♦ *n*
annoyance, anger, irritation, gall, vexation, displeasure, offence, resentment, grudge, umbrage
COLLOQ. huff
♦ *v*
1 AROUSE, stimulate, excite, goad, rouse, provoke, stir, spur, whet, kindle, galvanize
2 ANNOY, anger, irritate, affront, displease, gall, irk, get, put out, rile, incense, offend, mortify, vex, wound, sting
COLLOQ. aggravate, wind up, get at, bug, drive mad, drive crazy, drive up the wall, drive round the bend/twist, miff, needle, peeve, nettle, make someone's blood boil, make someone see red, rattle someone's cage, ruffle someone's feathers, make sparks fly, get under someone's skin, get up someone's nose, get on someone's wick, make someone's hackles rise
SLANG drive bananas, nark, piss off
OLD SLANG get someone's shirt out

piqued *adj*
annoyed, irritated, vexed, riled, angry, cross, displeased, offended, put out, resentful
COLLOQ. miffed, peeved, aggravated, ratty, uptight, mad, hopping mad, raving mad, seeing red, in a lather, disgruntled, up in arms, hot under the collar, stroppy, choked, fit to be tied, on the warpath, in a paddy
SLANG narked, pissed off

piracy *n*
buccaneering, freebooting, bootlegging, robbery, stealing, theft, hijacking, infringement, plagiarism
FORMAL rapine

pirate *n, v*
♦ *n*
1 BUCCANEER, brigand, freebooter, filibuster, corsair, marauder, raider, picaroon, sea robber, sea rover, sea dog, sea wolf, sea rat, water rat, marque, viking, arch-pirate
OLD sallee-man, rover, algerine; (*Shakesp*) water-thief
2 INFRINGER, plagiarist, plagiarizer
♦ *v*
copy, reproduce illegally, steal, pinch, plagiarize, poach
FORMAL appropriate
COLLOQ. borrow, crib, lift, nick, knock off

pirouette *n, v*
♦ *n*
gyration, spin, turn, twirl, whirl, pivot
♦ *v*
gyrate, spin, turn, twirl, whirl, pivot

pistol *n*
gun, handgun, revolver, sidearm, six-shooter, Luger®, Colt®, puffer; *N Am* derringer
OLD dag, pistole
COLLOQ. gat, iron, piece
SLANG pop, barking iron
OLD SLANG barker; *N Am* heater, rod

pit *n, v*
♦ *n*
1 *dig a pit*
hole, cavity, crater, pothole, gulf, chasm, abyss, mine, coalmine, quarry, diggings, trench, ditch, excavations, workings
2 HOLLOW, depression, dent, indentation, pockmark
♦ *v*
pockmark, blemish, scar, mark, dent, notch, depress, indent, dimple, pothole
■ **pit against**
compete, match, oppose, set against
■ **the pits**
awful, very poor, abysmal, inferior, dreadful, unsatisfactory, inadequate, second-rate, third-rate
COLLOQ. terrible, lousy, pathetic, crummy, a load of rubbish
SLANG pants, naff, cruddy; (*vulgar*) crap, shit; *Aust* spewy

pitch[1] *v, n*
♦ *v*
1 THROW, fling, toss, cast, lob, bowl, hurl, heave, sling, fire, launch, aim, direct
COLLOQ. chuck
2 PLUNGE, dive, plummet, drop, fall, fall headlong, topple, tumble
3 *pitch camp*
erect, put up, set up, place, station, settle, plant, fix
4 MOVE UP AND DOWN, lurch, sway, roll, toss, reel, keel, list, flounder, wallow
♦ *n*
1 *a cricket pitch*
ground, field, sports field, playing-field, park, arena, stadium
2 SOUND, tone, timbre, tonality, modulation, frequency, level
3 GRADIENT, incline, slope, slant, tilt, angle, degree, inclination, steepness, cant
4 *reach a high pitch*
level, degree, extent, height, point, position, intensity, grade, mark
5 THROW, fling, toss, lob, cast, hurl
COLLOQ. chuck
6 TALK, patter, line, gabble, chatter, jargon
COLLOQ. spiel, yak

■ **pitch in**
join in, co-operate, be involved, participate, help (out), lend a hand
COLLOQ. muck in, do your bit

■ **make a pitch for**
bid for, try to sell, put in for, try to get/obtain, offer, tender, submit, put up, put forward, advance, propose
FORMAL proffer

pitch² n
to coat a surface with pitch
tar, bitumen, asphalt
Related adjective: piceous

pitch-black adj
pitch-dark, black, dark, jet-black, inky, coal-black, unilluminated, unlit

pitcher n
jug, ewer, jar, vessel, crock, bottle, can, container, urn

PROVERBS
Little pitchers have large ears

piteous adj
poignant, moving, touching, distressing, heartbreaking, heart-rending, plaintive, mournful, sad, sorrowful, woeful, wretched, lamentable, pitiful, pitiable, pathetic

❗ piteous, pitiable or **pitiful**?
Pitiful means 'very sad, arousing or deserving pity': *She was a pitiful sight*; and also 'arousing or deserving contempt, very bad, very poor': *a pitiful attempt at catching the ball. Pitiable* means the same as *pitiful* but is less common: *He was in a pitiable condition; That was a pitiable attempt you made. Piteous* is a rather formal word meaning 'arousing or deserving pity': *She gave a piteous cry.*

pitfall n
danger, peril, hazard, risk, trap, snare, stumbling-block, catch, snag, drawback, difficulty

pith n
gist, essence, essential part, salient point, point, crux, nub, heart, core, meat, kernel, importance, significance, moment, weight, value, consequence, substance, forcefulness, vigour, matter
TECHNICAL medulla
OLD marrow, papyrus
FORMAL import, quintessence

pithily adv
concisely, succinctly, compactly, tersely, in brief, in a few words, in a word, to the point, meaningfully
COLLOQ. in a nutshell
E3 wordily, verbosely

pithy adj
succinct, concise, compact, terse, short, brief, condensed, summary, pointed, expressive, meaningful, forceful, incisive, telling
FORMAL trenchant, cogent
E3 wordy, verbose

pitiable adj
contemptible, distressed, distressful, distressing, doleful, grievous, lamentable, miserable, mournful, piteous, poor, sad, sorry, woeful, woesome, wretched
COLLOQ. pathetic

❗ pitiable, piteous or **pitiful**?
See panel at **piteous.**

pitiful adj
1 PITEOUS, doleful, mournful, distressing, heartbreaking, heart-rending, affecting, moving, pathetic, pitiable, sad, miserable, wretched, lamentable, poor, sorry; *Scot* waeful
OLD ruthful, seely
2 CONTEMPTIBLE, meagre, despicable, low, base, mean, poor, vile, shabby, miserable, deplorable, lamentable,

woeful, inadequate, hopeless, insignificant, paltry, worthless
COLLOQ. pathetic, lousy, terrible, crummy
SLANG the pits

❗ pitiful, piteous or **pitiable**?
See panel at **piteous.**

pitifully adv
1 *pitifully thin*
piteously, distressingly, sadly, miserably, lamentably, pathetically
2 *pitifully inadequate*
deplorably, lamentably, woefully, contemptibly, despicably, hopelessly
COLLOQ. terribly, pathetically

pitiless adj
merciless, cold-hearted, unsympathetic, unfeeling, uncaring, heartless, hard-hearted, callous, cruel, inhuman, inhumane, brutal, cold-blooded, ruthless, relentless, unremitting, inexorable, harsh, severe
E3 merciful, compassionate, kind, gentle

pitilessly adv
mercilessly, cruelly, callously, harshly, brutally, ruthlessly, hard-heartedly, cold-heartedly, cold-bloodedly
E3 mercifully, compassionately

pittance n
modicum, crumb, drop (in the ocean), trifle
COLLOQ. chickenfeed
SLANG peanuts

pitted adj
dented, holey, potholed, pockmarked, blemished, scarred, marked, notched, depressed, indented, rough

pity n, v
♦ n
1 SYMPATHY, commiseration, regret, sorrow, sadness, distress, understanding, fellow-feeling, feeling, emotion, condolence, compassion, kindness, tenderness, mercy, forgiveness, grace
OLD piety, bowels, misericord, rue, ruth; (*Spenser*) remorse
FORMAL forbearance
2 *What a pity!*
shame, disappointment, misfortune, unfortunate thing, bad luck
COLLOQ. crying shame
OLD COLLOQ sin
E3 1 cruelty, anger, scorn
♦ v
feel sorry for, feel for, sympathize with, be sympathetic towards, empathize with, show understanding towards, feel/have compassion for, commiserate with, grieve for, weep for, have a heart, bleed
OLD bemoan, bepity, compassion; (*Spenser*) mercify

■ **take pity on**
feel sorry for, feel for, sympathize with, be sympathetic towards, empathize with, show understanding towards, feel/have compassion for, commiserate with, show mercy, have mercy on, pardon, spare, rue

QUOTATIONS
And if you are wise you will never pity the past for what it did not know, but pity yourself for what it did
JOHN ROBERT FOWLES, *The Magus*

SYNONYM NUANCES
noun sense 1
Sympathy can be used to suggest having concern for another's predicament, while **commiseration** would be used more appropriately of expressing that concern to them: *I offered my commiserations on her loss.*
Condolence, is similar, but is more narrowly used in cases of bereavement: *he gave his condolences to the widow.*

Regret, sorrow and sadness, on the other hand, imply a heartfelt upset and unhappiness at the suffering of another, while **distress** goes further by suggesting extreme feeling.

Understanding and **fellow-feeling** have more to do with empathy and an ability to appreciate how others are feeling. Both **kindness** and **tenderness** also suggest a condition in which you are sensitive and easily moved, as well as displays of thoughtful attention: *an unexpected tenderness towards the misfortunes of others*, while **compassion** is a fairly strong term for caring about the suffering of others, combined with a desire to alleviate it.

Mercy is more suggestive of pity and consequent leniency when one is in a superior position.
Forgiveness, although similar, would be appropriate where pity prompts forgetting or overlooking a misdemeanour; likewise **grace**, although its usage is less common, and tends to connote divine mercy.

pivot *n, v*
♦ *n*
the wheel turns on a pivot; the pivot of her life
axis, hinge, axle, spindle, fulcrum, kingpin, linchpin, swivel, hub, central point, focal point, focus, centre, heart
♦ *v*
1 SWIVEL, turn, spin, revolve, rotate, swing
2 DEPEND, rely, revolve, hinge, hang, lie
FORMAL turn, be contingent

pivotal *adj*
vital, important, focal, central, critical, crucial, decisive, determining, climactic, axial

pixie *n*
elf, brownie, goblin, leprechaun, fairy, imp, sprite

pizzazz *n*
liveliness, animation, energy, quickness, spirit, life, vigour, vitality, vivacity, vivaciousness, dynamism, activity, boisterousness, briskness, smartness, sprightliness, refreshment, *esprit, entrain*
COLLOQ. brio, oomph
F3 apathy, inactivity

placard *n*
poster, bill, notice, sticker, sign, advertisement
COLLOQ. ad, advert

placate *v*
appease, pacify, conciliate, win over, mollify, calm (down), assuage, soothe, lull, quiet
FORMAL propitiate
F3 anger, enrage, incense, infuriate

placatory *adj*
appeasing, calming, soothing, mollifying, conciliatory, peace-making
FORMAL pacificatory, propitiatory, propitiative

place *n, v*
♦ *n*
1 SITE, venue, location, locus, scene, setting, situation, station, spot, point, position, locale, part, whereabouts, seat, space, room
2 *a place name*
city, town, village, hamlet, locality, neighbourhood, whereabouts, district, area, region, state, country
3 BUILDING, establishment, hotel, restaurant, institution, property, accommodation, house, flat, apartment, home
FORMAL dwelling, residence, abode, domicile
COLLOQ. pad, digs
4 JOB, position, appointment, situation, role, part, niche, status, standing, grade, rank, footing
5 *not your place to comment*
role, function, task, duty, responsibility, right, concern, business

♦ *v*
1 PUT, put down, set, set down, plant, fix, position, locate, situate, station, rest, settle, install, establish, lay, lay down, stand, deposit, lodge, leave
2 ARRANGE, put, class, sort, classify, categorize, order, group, rank, grade
3 *I can't quite place her*
recognize, know, remember, identify, establish, pinpoint
4 *place graduates in companies*
find a job for, find employment for, find accommodation for, allocate, assign
■ **in place**
arranged, in order, in position, in the correct position, set up, working
■ **in place of**
instead of, in lieu of, as a replacement for, as an alternative to, in exchange for, as a substitute for, taking the place of
■ **out of place**
inappropriate, unsuitable, unfitting, improper, tactless, unbecoming
FORMAL unseemly, inapposite
■ **put someone in their place**
humble, humiliate, shame, crush, deflate, bring low, bring/take someone down a peg or two, take the wind out of someone's sail
■ **take place**
happen, occur, come about, be held, come off, fall
OLD befall, betide
FORMAL transpire, come to pass
■ **take the place of**
replace, substitute for, supersede, stand in for, take over from, act for

placement *n*
locating, location, installation, ordering, arrangement, deployment, appointment, positioning, ranking, stationing, distribution, classification, job, assignment, disposition, engagement, employment
FORMAL emplacement

placid *adj*
1 *a placid person*
calm, composed, unmoved, undisturbed, unruffled, untroubled, unexcitable, cool, self-possessed, level-headed, imperturbable, easy-going, mild, gentle, equable, serene, unemotional, even-tempered, peaceable, tranquil
COLLOQ. unflappable
2 *live in placid surroundings*
tranquil, still, quiet, calm, peaceful, restful
FORMAL pacific
F3 1 excitable, agitated, disturbed

placidly *adv*
calmly, gently, mildly, imperturbably, peacefully, restfully, serenely
COLLOQ. unflappably
F3 excitably

plagiarism *n*
infringement, copying, reproduction, counterfeiting, piracy, theft
FORMAL appropriation
COLLOQ. borrowing, cribbing, lifting

plagiarist *n*
copier, robber, thief, pirate, imitator

plagiarize *v*
crib, copy, reproduce, imitate, counterfeit, pirate, infringe copyright, poach, steal, borrow
FORMAL appropriate
COLLOQ. lift, nick

plague *n, v*
♦ *n*
1 PESTILENCE, epidemic, disease, sickness, infection, contagion, infestation, cholera, bubonic plague, pneumonic plague, Black Death
FORMAL pandemic

2 *a plague of rats*
infestation, influx, swarm, invasion, huge number, epidemic
3 NUISANCE, annoyance, curse, scourge, trial, affliction, torment, calamity, bane
COLLOQ. thorn in the flesh, pain in the neck
♦ *v*
annoy, vex, bother, disturb, trouble, distress, upset, irritate, worry, cause problems for, pester, harass, hound, dog, hamper, hinder, haunt, bedevil, afflict, torment, torture, persecute
COLLOQ. bug, hassle, aggravate, cause headaches to

The ten Biblical plagues are:

Nile Waters Turn to Blood	Boils
Frogs	Hailstorm
Lice	Locusts
Flies	Darkness
Disease of Livestock	Death of the Firstborn

---

plain *adj, adv, n*
♦ *adj*
1 *plain cookery*
ordinary, basic, simple, unpretentious, unsophisticated, modest, unadorned, unelaborate, restrained, stark, austere, spartan
2 *plain fabric*
undecorated, unadorned, unembellished, unpatterned, unvariegated, uncoloured, self-coloured, restrained, muted
3 OBVIOUS, evident, patent, manifest, clear, understandable, apparent, noticeable, perceptible, discernible, visible, overt, unmistakable, transparent
COLLOQ. plain as a pikestaff, plain as the nose on your face, clear as daylight
4 UNATTRACTIVE, ordinary, ugly, unprepossessing, unlovely; *N Am* homely
5 *plain language*
clear, intelligible, understandable, lucid, unambiguous, uncomplicated, simple, direct, straightforward, accessible
6 FRANK, candid, blunt, outspoken, direct, forthright, straightforward, unambiguous, plain-spoken, open, honest, sincere, truthful, simple, unassuming
E3 1 fancy, elaborate **2** patterned, ornate **3** unclear, obscure **4** attractive, beautiful, good-looking **5** complicated, obscure **6** devious, deceitful
♦ *adv*
completely, utterly, totally, thoroughly, undeniably, simply, quite, downright
♦ *n*
grassland, prairie, steppe, lowland, pampas, flat, flatland, plateau, tableland, savannah, tundra

plain-spoken *adj*
candid, frank, open, honest, blunt, outspoken, straightforward, direct, truthful, unequivocal, outright, explicit, forthright, downright, round

plaintive *adj*
doleful, mournful, melancholy, wretched, woeful, wistful, sad, unhappy, sorrowful, grief-stricken, heartbroken, piteous, pitiful, heart-rending, high-pitched
FORMAL disconsolate

plaintively *adv*
mournfully, sadly, unhappily, pitifully, wistfully, dolefully, wretchedly, woefully
FORMAL disconsolately

plan *n, v*
♦ *n*
1 IDEA, suggestion, intention, aim, arrangement, proposal, proposition, project, scheme, plot, system, method, means, way, policy, procedure, strategy, ploy, formula, programme, roadmap, schedule, scenario
COLLOQ. *Aust* dart

2 BLUEPRINT, layout, diagram, chart, map, drawing, scale drawing, sketch, representation, illustration, design
FORMAL delineation
♦ *v*
1 PLOT, scheme, design, invent, think of, devise, contrive, develop, formulate, frame, shape, draft, outline, sketch, map out, work out, prepare, organize, arrange, schedule, programme, mastermind
See Synonym nuances panel at **devise.**
2 AIM, intend, want, wish, propose, purpose, mean, resolve, seek, contemplate, envisage, foresee

plane¹ *n, adj*
♦ *n*
1 FLAT SURFACE, level surface, flat, level
2 LEVEL, stage, position, class, condition, degree, rank, footing, rung, stratum, echelon
♦ *adj*
level, smooth, uniform, regular, plain, flat, flush, even, horizontal
TECHNICAL homaloidal
FORMAL planar

plane² *n, v*
♦ *n*
travel by plane
aeroplane, aircraft, jet, jumbo jet, jumbo, airliner, glider, bomber, fighter, seaplane, swing-wing, VTOL; *N Am* airplane
See also panel at **aircraft.**
♦ *v*
skim, skate, fly, glide, sail, volplane, wing

plank *n*
board, sheet, panel, slab, beam, timber, slat

planner *n*
designer, deviser, originator, maker, stylist, inventor, creator, contriver, producer, fashioner, architect, author, arranger, developer, organizer, mastermind

planning *n*
organization, arrangement, management, preparation, design, running, co-ordination, administration, development, regulation, establishment, control

plant *n, v*
♦ *n*
1 *garden plants*
flower, tree, shrub, herb, bush, vegetable
Related adjective: botanical
2 FACTORY, works, foundry, mill, shop, yard, workshop, machinery, apparatus, equipment, gear
♦ *v*
1 SOW, seed, scatter, implant, put into the ground, bury, transplant
2 INSERT, put, place, set, position, situate, fix, lodge, imbed, root, settle, found, establish
3 HIDE, put secretly, conceal, bury, disguise, put out of sight
FORMAL secrete

Types of plant include:

air-plant	fern	sapling
algae	flower	seedling
annual	fungus	shrub
biennial	grass	succulent
bulb	herb	tree
bush	herbaceous plant	vegetable
cactus	house plant	vine
cereal	hybrid	water plant
climber	lichen	weed
corm	moss	wild flower
cultivar	perennial	
evergreen	pot plant	

See also **flower; grass; leaf; poisonous; shrub; weed; wild flower.**

plaque *n*
plate, slab, tablet, panel, sign, plaquette, brass, shield, plateau, medal, medallion, badge, brooch
TECHNICAL cartouche

plaster *n, v*
♦ *n*
1 *apply plaster to walls*
stucco, mortar, plasterwork, gypsum, plaster of Paris, gesso, plasterboard, grout, Polyfilla®, laying, rendering, scratchcoat, screed, roughcast, pugging
2 *put a plaster on a wound*
sticking-plaster, patch, dressing, adhesive dressing, bandage, Band-aid®, Elastoplast®, butterfly clip/plaster
TECHNICAL cataplasm, peloid
FORMAL emplastron, emplastrum
OLD plaister, emplaster
♦ *v*
daub, smear, coat, cover, cover thickly, overlay, spread, mortar, render, mud, parget, parge, leep; *dialect* smarm; *Scot* clatch
TECHNICAL teer
OLD bedaub, beplaster, emplaster

plastic *adj*
1 *plastic toys*
soft, pliable, flexible, supple, malleable, mouldable, ductile, shapeable
2 EASILY INFLUENCED, receptive, compliant, malleable, pliable, pliant, impressionable, manageable, mouldable
FORMAL tractable
3 ARTIFICIAL, unnatural, false, synthetic, man-made
COLLOQ. phoney
E3 **1** rigid, inflexible **2** inflexible; *formal* intractable **3** natural

---

Types of plastic include:

Bakelite®	polymethyl metha-	PVC (polyvinyl
bioplastic	crylate	chloride)
Biopol®	polynorbornene	silicone
celluloid®	polypropylene	Teflon®
epoxy resin	polystyrene	transpolyisoprene
Perspex®	polythene	uPVC
phenolic resin	polyurethane	urea formaldehyde
plexiglass	PTFE (polytetra-	vinyl
polyester	fluoroethylene)	
polyethylene		

---

plasticity *n*
flexibility, softness, suppleness, pliancy, pliableness, pliability, malleability
FORMAL tractability
E3 inflexibility, rigidity

plate *n, v*
♦ *n*
1 DISH, bowl, platter, salver, helping, serving, portion, ashet
2 SHEET, layer, slab, pane, panel, sign, plaque, tablet
FORMAL lamina
3 ILLUSTRATION, photograph, picture, print, lithograph
♦ *v*
coat, cover, overlay, veneer, laminate, electroplate, anodize, galvanize, platinize, gild, silver, tin

plateau *n*
1 *a grassy plateau*
plane, highland, tableland, table, upland, mesa
2 STABILITY, level, grade, stage

platform *n*
1 STAGE, podium, dais, rostrum, stand
COLLOQ. soapbox
2 POLICY, party line, principles, tenets, manifesto, programme, objectives, aims, ideas, intentions, strategy

platitude *n*
banality, generality, commonplace, truism, cliché, bromide, inanity, stereotype, hackneyed statement, trite expression, overworked phrase; *N Am* glittering generality
COLLOQ. chestnut

platitudinous *adj*
banal, commonplace, truistic, trite, clichéd, hackneyed, overworked, stale, stereotyped, set, stock, inane, tired, dull, flat, well-worn, vapid
COLLOQ. corny

platonic *adj*
non-physical, spiritual, non-romantic, non-sexual, intellectual, ideal, idealistic, transcendent
FORMAL incorporeal
E3 sexual

platoon *n*
company, group, patrol, troop, unit, battery, team, squad, squadron, outfit

platter *n*
plate, dish, salver, tray, charger, trencher

plaudits *n*
commendation, approval, praise, acclaim, acclamation, applause, congratulations, hurrahs, accolade, ovation, standing ovation, clapping
FORMAL approbation
COLLOQ. hand, bouquet, pat on the back, rave review, good press
E3 criticism

plausible *adj*
credible, believable, reasonable, logical, likely, fair, possible, probable, imaginable, conceivable, convincing, persuasive, smooth-talking, glib, soft-spoken, silver-tongued, colourable
FORMAL cogent, specious
E3 implausible, unlikely, improbable

plausibly *adv*
reasonably, logically, probably, possibly, conceivably, convincingly, persuasively, imaginably
E3 implausibly, improbably

play *v, n*
♦ *v*
1 AMUSE YOURSELF, have fun, enjoy yourself, play games, occupy yourself, divert yourself, revel, sport, romp, frolic, caper, gambol, frisk, cavort
2 PARTICIPATE IN, take part in, join in, be involved in, do, compete
3 *France played Italy*
oppose, compete against, vie with, rival, challenge, take on
4 ACT, perform, play the part of, portray, represent, impersonate
5 *light playing on the water*
dance, move lightly, flicker, twinkle, flash, gleam, glance
E3 **1** work
♦ *n*
1 FUN, amusement, enjoyment, entertainment, diversion, leisure, recreation, sport, game, hobby, pastime, merrymaking
2 DRAMA, tragedy, comedy, farce, show, melodrama, plot, performance, work
3 MOVEMENT, action, flexibility, give, freedom of movement, slack, looseness, leeway, latitude, freedom, liberty, free rein, margin, scope, range, licence, room, space
COLLOQ. give
4 ACTION, operation, exercise, interaction, interplay, transaction
5 JEST, fun, joking, teasing, laugh
COLLOQ. kicks
E3 **1** work
■ **play around with**
1 FIDDLE WITH, toy with, fidget with, meddle with, tamper with, interfere with

2 DALLY WITH, mess around with, flirt with, fool with, trifle with, womanize with, philander with

■ **play at**
pretend (to be), put on an act, make out
FORMAL affect
COLLOQ. go through the motions

■ **play down**
minimize, make light of, gloss over, underplay, downplay, understate, undervalue, underestimate
🖃 exaggerate, emphasize, play up

■ **play on**
exploit, take advantage of, turn to account, profit by, trade on, capitalize on

■ **play out**
continue, go on, carry on, unfold, be revealed, act, enact

■ **play up**
1 EXAGGERATE, highlight, spotlight, accentuate, emphasize, stress, underline, point up, call attention to
2 MISBEHAVE, be mischievous, be naughty, give trouble, be difficult to control, trouble, bother, annoy, hurt
3 MALFUNCTION, not work, go wrong
COLLOQ. go/be on the blink
🖃 **1** play down, underplay **3** work properly

■ **play up to**
flatter, ingratiate yourself, suck up to, curry favour with, blandish, fawn, toady
COLLOQ. bootlick, butter up, soft-soap; *N Am* cozy up

play-act *v*
pretend, put on, assume, feign, sham, counterfeit, fake, fabricate, simulate, bluff, impersonate, pass yourself off, act, put on an act, mime, go through the motions
FORMAL affect, dissemble
COLLOQ. keep up appearances

playboy *n*
philanderer, womanizer, ladies' man, lady-killer, rake, libertine, roué, debauchee
COLLOQ. man about town, socialite

player *n*
1 CONTESTANT, competitor, participant, sportsman, sportswoman
2 PERFORMER, entertainer, artiste, actor, actress, artist, comedian, trouper, player, musician, instrumentalist, accompanist

playful *adj*
1 *as playful as a kitten*
frisky, sportive, frolicsome, ludic, lively, fun-loving, spirited, mischievous, roguish, impish, puckish, kittenish
2 *a playful remark*
humorous, funny, friendly, light-hearted, tongue-in-cheek, jesting, joking, facetious, waggish, teasing
🖃 **2** serious

playfully *adv*
light-heartedly, jokingly, humorously, facetiously, in jest
🖃 seriously

playground *n*
park, playing-field, play area, adventure playground, amusement park, pleasure ground, recreation ground

playmate *n*
friend, companion, comrade, neighbour, playfellow
COLLOQ. buddy, chum, pal, mate

plaything *n*
toy, trifle, amusement, game, puppet, trinket, pastime, bauble, gewgaw, gimcrack

playwright *n*
dramatist, writer, scriptwriter, screen writer, dramaturge, dramaturgist, tragedian

plea *n*
1 APPEAL, petition, request, entreaty, supplication, prayer
FORMAL invocation, imploration
2 DEFENCE, justification, excuse, explanation, claim, pretext, alibi
TECHNICAL declinature, demurrer, *nolo contendere*
FORMAL vindication, placitum

plead *v*
1 BEG, implore, entreat, appeal, petition, ask, request, urge, intercede (for), moot
OLD persuade
FORMAL beseech, solicit, make supplication
2 *plead ignorance*
assert, state, argue, maintain, claim, allege, put forward
FORMAL adduce

pleasant *adj*
1 *a pleasant chat*
enjoyable, agreeable, nice, fine, lovely, delightful, charming, amusing, pleasing, gratifying, satisfying, acceptable, welcome, entertaining, refreshing; *S Afr* lekker
2 *a pleasant person*
friendly, amiable, affable, likeable, cheerful, congenial, good-humoured, charming, nice, lovely, winsome
🖃 **1, 2** unpleasant, nasty **2** unfriendly

pleasantly *adv*
enjoyably, delightfully, pleasingly, entertainingly, refreshingly

pleasantry *n*
1 *exchange pleasantries about the weather*
friendly remark, polite comment, casual remark
2 JOKE, jest, banter, badinage, quip, sally, witticism, *bon mot*

please *v, interj*
♦ *v*
1 DELIGHT, make happy, give pleasure to, charm, attract, appeal to, captivate, entertain, amuse, divert, cheer (up), gladden, humour, flatter, indulge, gratify, satisfy, fulfil, content, suit
OLD aggrate, agree, arride; (*Spenser*) queme
COLLOQ. tickle
2 WANT, will, wish, desire, like, prefer, choose, think fit, see fit
OLD list
🖃 **1** displease, annoy, anger, sadden
♦ *interj*
if you please, *bitte, je vous en prie*
OLD prithee, I'll trouble you to

pleased *adj*
contented, satisfied, gratified, glad, happy, cheerful, delighted, thrilled, euphoric, elated
COLLOQ. chuffed, over the moon, tickled pink; *Aust & NZ* rapt
🖃 displeased, annoyed

pleasing *adj*
gratifying, satisfying, acceptable, good, pleasant, pleasurable, agreeable, nice, fine, delightful, enjoyable, amusing, entertaining, charming, attractive, engaging, winning, taking
🖃 unpleasant, disagreeable

pleasurable *adj*
enjoyable, delightful, fun, good, lovely, nice, pleasant, gratifying, welcome, entertaining, amusing, diverting, agreeable, congenial
OLD COLLOQ. groovy
🖃 bad, disagreeable

pleasure *n*
1 HAPPINESS, contentment, joy, delight, gladness, enjoyment, satisfaction, gratification
FORMAL solace
2 *the pleasure of playing a sport*
joy, delight, enjoyment, thrill, glory, treasure, prize, gem
3 *combine business with pleasure*
recreation, amusement, entertainment, leisure, fun
4 PREFERENCE, wish, will, desire, choice, inclination
🖃 **1** sorrow, pain, trouble, displeasure **2** disappointment, sadness

■ **it's a pleasure**
my pleasure, you're welcome, not at all, it's no trouble, any time, don't mention it, forget it, it was nothing, it's all right, that's all right, think nothing of it, no problem

■ **with pleasure**
gladly, willingly, of course, happily, readily
OLD fain

> QUOTATIONS
> But pleasures are like poppies spread, / You seize the flower, its bloom to shed; / Or like the snow falls in the river, / A moment white – then melts for ever
>   ROBERT BURNS, 'Tam o'Shanter. A Tale'

pleat *n*
tuck, fold, crease, flute, crimp, gather, pucker
FORMAL plication

plebeian *adj, n*
♦ *adj*
1 LOWER-CLASS, working-class, proletarian, low-born, peasant, mean
2 COMMON, uncultured, unrefined, uncultivated, coarse, base, ignoble, low
COLLOQ. non-U
SLANG chavvy
F3 1 aristocratic, noble, patrician **2** refined, sophisticated
♦ *n*
common person, commoner, person in the street, proletarian, worker, peasant
COLLOQ. pleb, prole
F3 aristocrat, noble, patrician

plebiscite *n*
vote, referendum, ballot, poll, straw poll

pledge *n, v*
♦ *n*
1 PROMISE, vow, word of honour, word, oath, bond, hand, covenant, guarantee, warrant, commitment, committal, dedication, assurance, undertaking
OLD plight, band, sacrament, wager
2 DEPOSIT, security, surety, bail, guarantee, pawn
OLD gage, earnest, borrow, wed; *Scot* wad
FORMAL collateral
♦ *v*
1 PROMISE, vow, give your word, swear, take an oath, commit, contract, dedicate, engage, undertake, give an undertaking, vouch, guarantee, secure, pass
OLD plight, betroth, propine
FORMAL impignorate
2 GUARANTEE, mortgage, secure
OLD impawn, pignorate, wage; (*Shakesp*) fine
FORMAL put up as collateral, impledge

plenary *adj*
full, complete, entire, open, absolute, unrestricted, whole, general, integral, unconditional, unlimited, unqualified, thorough, sweeping

plenipotentiary *n*
ambassador, envoy, minister, dignitary, diplomat, emissary, legate, nuncio

plenitude *n*
abundance, plenty, plentifulness, profusion, fullness, completeness, copiousness, bounty, excess, wealth, entireness
FORMAL amplitude, plenteousness, plethora, cornucopia, repletion
F3 scarcity

plenteous *adj*
abundant, plentiful, bountiful, copious, fruitful, lavish, abounding, ample, generous, liberal, productive, fertile, profuse, prolific, overflowing, inexhaustible, infinite
FORMAL bounteous, luxuriant
COLLOQ. bumper
F3 scarce, paltry

plentiful *adj*
ample, abundant, profuse, copious, overflowing, lavish, generous, liberal, bountiful, fruitful, productive, inexhaustible, infinite
FORMAL bounteous

COLLOQ. bumper
F3 scarce, scanty, rare

plentifully *adv*
abundantly, amply, profusely, copiously, generously, lavishly, liberally, bountifully, fruitfully
F3 scarcely

plenty *n*
1 ABUNDANCE, profusion, copiousness, enough, fullness, sufficiency, quantity, mass, volume, fund, mine, store, milk and honey; *Scot* scouth, scowth
OLD foison; *Scot* stouth and routh
FORMAL plethora, plenteousness, cornucopia
2 AFFLUENCE, wealth, wealthiness, riches, fortune, substance, prosperity
F3 1 scarcity, lack, want **2** need
■ **plenty of**
many, large amount, large number, enough, more than enough, more than is needed
COLLOQ. bags, lots, loads, masses, heaps, piles, stacks, shedloads
SLANG shitloads

plethora *n*
surfeit, surplus, excess, glut, abundance, overabundance, profusion, overfullness, superabundance
FORMAL superfluity

pliability *n*
1 BENDABILITY, elasticity, flexibility, plasticity, ductility
2 ADAPTABILITY, amenability, susceptibility, malleability, suggestibility, impressionableness, compliance, docility
FORMAL tractableness
F3 1, 2 inflexibilty, rigidity

pliable *adj*
1 *pliable pieces of wood*
pliant, flexible, bendable, supple, lithe, malleable, elastic, plastic, superplastic, cheverel
COLLOQ. bendy
2 *a pliable person*
yielding, adaptable, flexible, accommodating, manageable, docile, biddable, compliant, persuadable, responsive, receptive, impressionable, susceptible
FORMAL tractable
F3 1 rigid, inflexible **2** headstrong, stubborn

pliant *adj*
1 *pliant pieces of wood*
pliable, flexible, bendable, supple, lithe, malleable, elastic, plastic
COLLOQ. bendy
2 *a pliant person*
yielding, adaptable, flexible, accommodating, manageable, docile, biddable, compliant, persuadable, responsive, receptive, impressionable, susceptible
FORMAL tractable
F3 1 rigid, inflexible **2** headstrong, stubborn

plight[1] *n*
the plight of starving children
predicament, quandary, dilemma, extremity, trouble, difficulty, difficult/distressing situation, straits, dire straits, state, condition, situation, circumstances, case; *Scot* pliskie
OLD liking, point; (*Spenser*) taking
COLLOQ. jam, hole, tight spot, scrape, fix, pickle

plight[2] *v*
plight your troth
promise, pledge, vow, swear, contract, covenant, engage, guarantee, propose, vouch, secure
OLD affiance

plod *v*
1 TRUDGE, tramp, stump, clump, stomp, lumber, walk heavily, plough through
2 DRUDGE, labour, toil, grind, slog, persevere, peg away, plug away, soldier on

plodder *n*
drudge, dullard, toiler, slogger, mug, sap
F3 high-flier

plot *n, v*

♦ *n*

1 CONSPIRACY, intrigue, scheme, plan, ruse, stratagem, cabal

FORMAL machination

2 STORY, narrative, action, subject, theme, storyline, thread, outline, scenario

3 *plot of land*

patch, piece, tract, area, allotment, lot, parcel; *S Afr* erf

♦ *v*

1 CONSPIRE, intrigue, collude, connive, scheme, hatch, lay, devise, contrive, plan, project, design, draft, concoct, frame

FORMAL machinate

COLLOQ. cook up

2 CHART, map (out), mark, locate, draw, sketch, plan, calculate

plotter *n*

conspirator, intriguer, schemer, planner

FORMAL machinator

plough *n, v*

♦ *n*

tractor, drill-plough, ridger, beam, sill, subsoiler, swing-plough, wheel plough; *N Am* plow, lister, scooter

OLD ard

♦ *v*

cultivate, dig, till, work, ridge, spade, break (up), turn up, furrow, fallow, rafter, rib, thwart; *Scot* rive; *N Am* plow, list

OLD ear

■ **plough into**

crash into, drive into, smash into, run/go into, hit, collide, bump into

■ **plough through**

plod through, move through laboriously, trudge through, wade through

ploy *n*

manoeuvre, stratagem, tactic, move, device, contrivance, scheme, game, trick, artifice, dodge, wile, ruse, subterfuge

See Synonym nuances panel at **trick**.

pluck *v, n*

♦ *v*

1 PULL, draw, tug, snatch, pull off, remove, extract, pick, collect, gather, take in, harvest

COLLOQ. yank

2 *pluck a guitar*

pick, twang, strum, finger, thrum

♦ *n*

courage, bravery, daring, boldness, spirit, intrepidity, audacity, fearlessness, mettle, backbone, resolution, determination

FORMAL fortitude, valour

COLLOQ. nerve, guts, grit

Ｅ∃ cowardice

pluckily *adv*

bravely, daringly, courageously, confidently, boldly, fearlessly, audaciously, valiantly, intrepidly, heroically, adventurously

Ｅ∃ cowardly, cautiously, timidly

plucky *adj*

brave, courageous, bold, daring, audacious, fearless, intrepid, heroic, valiant, spirited, determined

COLLOQ. gutsy, spunky, gritty, feisty

Ｅ∃ cowardly, weak, feeble

plug *n, v*

♦ *n*

1 STOPPER, bung, cork, seal, spigot, spile, dossil; *Scot* dook

TECHNICAL access eye, neck, fipple, tampion

OLD stopple

2 ADVERTISEMENT, publicity, commercial, promotion, recommendation, blurb, mention, puff, good word

COLLOQ. hype, ad, push, promo

3 *a plug of tobacco*

chew, wad, twist, cake, dottle

♦ *v*

1 STOP (UP), stopper, bung, cork, block, choke, close, seal, fill, pack, stuff

TECHNICAL tampon, stem

OLD stopple

2 ADVERTISE, publicize, promote, market, tout, mention

COLLOQ. hype, push

■ **plug away**

keep trying, persevere, plod on, slog away, peg away, toil (away), soldier on

plum *adj*

first-class, best, choice, prize, especially valued, excellent

COLLOQ. cushy

plumb *adv, v*

♦ *adv*

1 VERTICALLY, perpendicularly, sheer, straight up, straight down, up and down

2 PRECISELY, right, exactly, dead

COLLOQ. slap, bang, spot-on

♦ *v*

sound (out), fathom, measure, gauge, penetrate, delve into, probe, search (out), examine, investigate, explore

■ **plumb in**

install, fix, fit, put (in), place, position, set up

■ **plumb the depths of**

experience the worst extremes of, experience fully, hit the lowest point/level, reach the nadir, reach rock bottom

plumbing

Plumbing fittings and equipment include:

auger	gate valve	shower
back boiler	geyser	shower attach-
ballcock	hopper	ment
ball valve	hose	shower head
basin	immersion heater	sink
basin spanner	joint	siphon washer
bath	jointing com-	soil vent
bend	pound	solder
bidet	lavatory	Stillson® wrench
blowtorch	lavatory chain	stopcock
boiler	lever tap	stop end
bottle trap	lockshield valve	sump pump
bowl	mains pipe	tank
ceiling joint	mixer tap	tap
check valve	monkey wrench	tee
cistern	motorized zone	Teflon® tape
compression fitting	valve	thermostat
copper pipe	nipple	thermostatic valve
copper tube	nipple key	toilet
coupler	overflow bend	trap
cylinder	pan	tube (or pipe)
deburring tool	pedestal	cutter
draincock	pipe	tube flaring tool
drain rod	pipe bender	U-bend
elbow joint	pipe clip	union
electric water	pipe coupling	urinal
heater	pipe wrench	valve
expansion (or	plug	valve key
header) tank	plunger	washer
N Am faucet	programmer	waste disposal
flare joint	P-trap	unit
float	pump	waste pipe
flux	radiator	water closet
gasket	reducer	WC
gas water heater	septic tank	Y-branch

plume *n*

feather, crest, pinion, quill, tuft, aigrette, streamer, marabou, osprey, plumule

TECHNICAL pappus

OLD panache

plume yourself on
congratulate yourself, boast about, pride yourself, preen
yourself, exult in
COLLOQ. pat yourself on the back

plummet *v*
plunge, dive, nose-dive, descend, drop, fall, drop/fall
rapidly, decrease quickly, tumble, hurtle
F3 soar

plummy *adj*
high-class, aristocratic, upper-class, affected, refined
COLLOQ. posh, U

plump[1] *adj*
a plump person
fat, obese, dumpy, tubby, stout, round, well-rounded,
portly, chubby, podgy, fleshy, full, ample, buxom
FORMAL rotund, corpulent
COLLOQ. well-upholstered, beefy, flabby, gross
F3 thin, skinny

plump[2] *v*
plump the sacks on the floor
put down, set down, deposit, drop, flop, sink, slump,
collapse, descend, fall
COLLOQ. dump

plump for
choose, select, prefer, opt for, back, side with, support,
favour

plumpness *n*
fatness, fat, fleshiness, chubbiness, stoutness, portliness,
tubbiness, podginess, obesity, pudginess
FORMAL corpulence, rotundity
F3 thinness, skinniness

plunder *v, n*
♦ *v*
loot, pillage, ravage, lay waste, devastate, sack, raid,
ransack, maraud, rifle, forage, steal, rob, strip, fleece
FORMAL despoil, depredate
♦ *n*
loot, pillage, booty, spoils, pickings, ill-gotten gains, prize
SLANG swag
Related adjective: predatory

plunge *v, n*
♦ *v*
1 DIVE, jump, nose-dive, swoop, dive-bomb, plummet,
crash, descend, go down, sink, drop, fall, drop/fall rapidly,
decrease quickly, throw, pitch, tumble, hurtle, career,
launch, charge, dash, rush, tear, bull (into), enew yourself
COLLOQ. go in at the deep end
2 THRUST, push, drive, stick, stab, shove, ram, jab, pitch,
lunge
3 IMMERSE, submerge, dip, sink, douse, mire, plump, souse
TECHNICAL enew
OLD beduck, merge, demerge, demerse, immerge,
implunge, whelm; (*Shakesp*) emplonge
♦ *n*
dive, nose-dive, dip, duck, jump, swoop, descent, drop,
fall, tumble, charge, rush, hurtle, immersion, submersion

take the plunge
decide to do something, commit yourself
COLLOQ. bite the bullet, go for it

plurality *n*
diversity, variety, number, numerousness, profusion, mass,
bulk, majority, most
FORMAL multiplicity, multitudinousness, preponderance
COLLOQ. galaxy

plus *n, prep*
♦ *n*
advantage, benefit, bonus, good point, asset, credit, gain,
extra, surplus
COLLOQ. perk
F3 disadvantage, drawback; *colloq.* minus
♦ *prep*
and, with, together with, as well as, in addition to, added
to, over and above

COLLOQ. not to mention
F3 minus

plush *adj*
luxurious, luxury, lavish, de luxe, palatial, stylish, affluent,
sumptuous, costly, rich
FORMAL opulent
COLLOQ. ritzy, glitzy, posh, swanky

plutocrat *n*
rich man, capitalist, millionaire, tycoon, magnate,
billionaire, multimillionaire, Dives, Croesus
COLLOQ. fat cat, moneybags, zillionaire

ply[1] *v*
1 KEEP SUPPLYING, provide, supply, furnish, feed, lavish,
assail, beset, bombard, harass, importune
2 TRAVEL, go, ferry, make regular journeys between/along
3 *ply a trade*
practise, carry on, follow, pursue, engage in, exercise,
work at
4 *ply a tool*
use, employ, utilize, wield, handle, manipulate

ply[2] *n*
three-ply wool
thickness, strand, leaf, layer, sheet, fold

poach *v*
1 STEAL, pilfer, copy, take
FORMAL appropriate
COLLOQ. lift, borrow, nick
2 TRESPASS, encroach, infringe, intrude, catch/hunt illegally

pocket *n, adj, v*
♦ *n*
1 *a pocket on the back of the seat*
pouch, bag, envelope, receptacle, compartment, hollow,
cavity; *Scot* plaid-neuk
OLD placket, bin, poke
2 *the fees are a drain on my pocket*
resources, funds, means, money, finances, budget, assets,
capital, wherewithal
3 *pocket of resistance/unemployment*
patch, small area, isolated area, small group
♦ *adj*
small, little, concise, abridged, potted, compact, portable,
miniature
COLLOQ. mini, pint-size
♦ *v*
take, gain, win unfairly, help yourself to, pilfer, filch, steal
OLD fob
FORMAL appropriate, purloin
COLLOQ. lift, nick, pinch, trouser, whip; *Aust
& NZ* souvenir

pockmark *n*
blemish, pock, pit, scar, pockpit

pod *n*
shell, husk, case, hull
TECHNICAL legume

podgy *adj*
fat, chubby, paunchy, plump, fleshy, roly-poly, squat,
chunky, dumpy, stout, tubby, stubby, stumpy
FORMAL corpulent, rotund
F3 thin, skinny

podium *n*
dais, platform, stage, stand, rostrum

poem

Types of poem include:

ballad	elegy	idyll
bucolic	epic	lay
cinquain	epigram	limerick
clerihew	epithalmium	lipogram
concrete poem	epode	lyric
couplet	epopee	madrigal
ditty	georgic	monody
eclogue	haiku	nursery rhyme

ode	roundelay	triolet
palinode	sestina	verse
pantoum	shape poem	verselet
pastoral	song	versicle
prothalamion	sonnet	villanelle
rhyme	tanka	virelay
rondeau	thin poem	

See also **prosody**; **song**; **verse**.

poet *n*

versifier, verse-maker, rhymer, rhymester, rhymist, lyricist, idyllist, sonneteer, balladeer, elegist, bard, minstrel, beat poet, performance poet, poetaster, poeticule

> **QUOTATIONS**
> The worst tragedy for a poet is to be admired through being misunderstood
> JEAN COCTEAU, *Le Coq et l'Arlequin*

poetic *adj*

poetical, lyrical, moving, artistic, graceful, flowing, expressive, sensitive, beautiful, creative, imaginative, metrical, rhythmical, rhyming, figurative, symbolic
F3 prosaic

poetry *n*

verse, lyrics, rhyme, rhyming, versing, poems, poesy, free verse, versification, vers libre, pennill, iambics, muse, Parnassus

> **QUOTATIONS**
> Poetry is the supreme fiction
> WALLACE STEVENS, *Harmonium*

pogrom *n*

slaughter, murder, homicide, extermination, carnage, massacre, butchery, wholesale slaughter, indiscriminate killing, holocaust, bloodbath, annihilation, killing, genocide, ethnic cleansing, liquidation, decimation

poignancy *n*

pathos, feeling, sentiment, emotion, evocativeness, intensity, keenness, painfulness, piquancy, tenderness, piteousness, sharpness, pungency, sadness, pain, distress, tragedy, misery, wretchedness, bitterness

poignant *adj*

moving, touching, affecting, emotional, tender, distressing, tragic, upsetting, heartbreaking, heart-rending, heartfelt, piteous, pathetic, sorrowful, sad, tearful, painful, agonizing, miserable, wretched
OLD poynant

poignantly *adv*

movingly, emotionally, tenderly, sadly, sorrowfully, pathetically, tearfully, painfully, miserably, wretchedly, tragically

point *n, v*

♦ *n*
1 *the main points of the argument*
issue, matter, subject, topic, question, item
2 FEATURE, attribute, quality, aspect, characteristic, trait, property, facet, detail, particular, item, subject, topic
3 *What's the point?*
use, sense, purpose, motive, reason, object, objective, intention, aim, end, goal
4 ESSENCE, main point, crux, core, central point, heart, heart of the matter, pith, gist, nub, meat, marrow, thrust, meaning, significance, importance, theme, vein, tenor, drift, burden, keynote
5 PLACE, position, situation, location, locality, area, site, spot
6 MOMENT, instant, juncture, stage, time, period, position
7 DOT, spot, mark, speck, full stop, stop, full point, period, decimal point
8 *the point of a needle*
sharp end, end, extremity, tip, top, taper, spike, tine, nib

9 HEADLAND, head, foreland, promontory, cape, ness
10 MARK, score, goal, run, hit, total
♦ *v*
1 *point a gun*
aim, direct, train, level
2 INDICATE, signal, gesture at/towards, show, signify, designate, suggest
FORMAL denote, evidence
■ **point out**
show, indicate, draw/call attention to, point to, reveal, identify, specify, mention, bring up, allude to, remind
■ **point up**
emphasize, stress, underline, highlight, flag up, call attention to
■ **beside the point**
irrelevant, immaterial, unrelated, unconnected, out of place
COLLOQ. neither here nor there
■ **in point of fact**
actually, in fact, as a matter of fact, in reality, really
■ **on the point of**
on the verge of, (just) about to, going to, ready to, preparing to
■ **point of view**
1 OPINION, view, belief, judgement, attitude, feeling, sentiment, position, standpoint, viewpoint
2 PERSPECTIVE, outlook, approach, angle, slant, aspect
■ **to the point**
relevant, related, connected, germane, applicable, appropriate
FORMAL apposite, pertinent
■ **up to a point**
partly, somewhat, to some extent/degree, slightly

point-blank *adv, adj*

♦ *adv*
outright, directly, forthrightly, straightforwardly, straight, plainly, explicitly, openly, bluntly, frankly, candidly, rudely, abruptly, unequivocally
♦ *adj*
1 OUTRIGHT, direct, forthright, straightforward, plain, explicit, open, unreserved, blunt, frank, candid
2 AT CLOSE RANGE, closely, close to, near, touching

pointed *adj*

1 SHARP, keen, edged, tapering, barbed
TECHNICAL acicular, cuspidate(d)
FORMAL aculeate(d), fastigiate, lanceolate(d), mucronate(d)
2 *a pointed comment*
cutting, incisive, biting, forceful, penetrating, telling, striking, clear, obvious
FORMAL mordant, trenchant

pointedly *adv*

intentionally, on purpose, plainly, provocatively, defiantly, explicitly, bluntly

pointer *n*

1 ARROW, indicator, needle, hand
2 TIP, recommendation, suggestion, sign, hint, guide, guideline, clue, indication, indicator, advice, piece of advice, warning, caution
3 STICK, rod, cane, pole

pointless *adj*

useless, futile, vain, fruitless, unproductive, unprofitable, worthless, senseless, valueless, absurd, ridiculous, nonsensical, foolish, inane, meaningless, insignificant, a waste of time/effort, aimless, to no avail, unavailing
COLLOQ. a mug's game
F3 useful, profitable, meaningful

pointlessly *adv*

senselessly, in vain, meaninglessly, aimlessly, unproductively, unprofitably
F3 usefully, profitably, meaningfully

poise *n, v*

♦ *n*
calmness, composure, self-control, self-possession, presence of mind, assurance, self-assurance, dignity,

elegance, grace, serenity, balance, equanimity, equilibrium, aplomb
COLLOQ. cool, coolness
♦ v
balance, position, steady, hover, hang, suspend, support

poised adj
1 DIGNIFIED, graceful, calm, composed, collected, self-possessed, self-controlled, self-confident, assured, serene, suave, urbane
COLLOQ. cool, cool calm and collected, unruffled, unflappable
2 poised for action
prepared, ready, set, all set, waiting, expectant

poison n, v
♦ n
1 poison such as arsenic
toxin, venom
2 a poison spreading through society
bane, blight, cancer, malignancy, contagion, pollution, contamination, corruption, canker
♦ v
kill by poison, envenomate, infect, contaminate, pollute, taint, adulterate, corrupt, deprave, defile, pervert, warp, spoil, blight
OLD (Shakesp) bane

poisonous adj
1 TOXIC, venomous, mephitic, lethal, deadly, fatal, mortal
2 HARMFUL, noxious, pernicious, malicious, vicious, spiteful, virulent, malignant, contaminating, corrupting, cancerous, cankerous

---

Poisonous plants include:

aconite	dwale	naked boys
amanita	foxglove	naked lady
anemone	giant hogweed	oleander
banewort	helmet flower	poison ivy
belladonna	hemlock	stinkweed
black nightshade	hemlock water	stramonium
castor oil plant	dropwort	thorn apple
common night-	jimson weed	wake-robin
shade	laburnum	wild arum
cowbane	lantana	windflower
cuckoo pint	lords-and-ladies	wolfsbane
deadly nightshade	meadow saffron	
digitalis	monkshood	

See also **mushrooms and toadstools**.

---

poke v, n
♦ v
prod, stab, jab, stick, thrust, push, shove, nudge, nuzzle, pick, elbow, dig, butt, hit, punch; *dialect* poach, pote, proke, snuzzle; *Scot* powter; *N Am* scuffle
OLD prick, prog
♦ n
prod, jab, thrust, shove, nudge, dig, butt, punch; *dialect* peg
■ **poke around**
grope around, search for, look (all over) for, rummage around, rake through, root, rout
■ **poke fun at**
ridicule, mock, jeer, make fun of, tease, parody, joke, quiz; *Aust* poke mullock at
COLLOQ. rag, rib, send up, spoof, take the mickey; *Aust & NZ* poke borak at
■ **poke out**
stick out, jut out, protrude, project, overhang, extend, beetle, extrude
■ **poke your nose into**
meddle in, interfere in, tamper with, pry in
COLLOQ. put/stick your oar in, stick/thrust your nose into, butt in

poker-faced adj
blank, expressionless, stone-faced, deadpan, impassive, emotionless, without feeling, lifeless, apathetic, uninterested, indifferent, glazed, empty, vacant, vacuous, inscrutable, uncomprehending

poky adj
confined, restricted, cramped, small, tight, tiny, narrow, crowded
FORMAL incommodious
F∃ spacious, roomy

polar adj
1 COLD, freezing, frozen, icy, glacial, arctic, Siberian, Antarctic
2 OPPOSITE, completely/utterly different, diametrically opposed, conflicting, ambivalent, contradictory
FORMAL antithetical, dichotomous

polarity n
opposition, oppositeness, contradiction, ambivalence, separation, difference, contrariety, duality, paradox
FORMAL antithesis, dichotomy

polarize v
divide, disunite, separate, alienate, split (up), segregate, break up, drive apart, come between, set someone against another
FORMAL estrange
F∃ unite

pole[1] n
a telegraph pole
bar, rod, stick, shaft, spar, upright, pillar, support, post, stake, mast, staff, stanchion

pole[2] n
views that represent opposite poles
extremity, extreme, limit
■ **poles apart**
completely different, extremely different, incompatible, irreconcilable, worlds apart
COLLOQ. like chalk and cheese

polemic n, adj
♦ n
argument, controversy, debate, dispute
FORMAL diatribe, invective
♦ adj
argumentative, contentious, controversial, polemical
FORMAL disputatious, eristic(al)

polemicist n
debater, controversialist, arguer, contender, disputer, disputant, polemist
FORMAL logomachist

polemics n
debate, dispute, argument, controversy, contention, argumentation
FORMAL disputation, logomachy

police n, v
♦ n
police force, police officers, constabulary; *Scot & Irish* polis
COLLOQ. the law, the force, cops, coppers, boys in blue
SLANG the Bill, bizzies, the fuzz, rozzers, pigs
♦ v
1 PATROL, guard, protect, defend, keep watch, keep the peace
2 CHECK, control, keep under control, regulate, monitor, watch, observe, supervise, oversee

police officer n
officer, policeman, policewoman, constable, PC, WPC; *Scot & Irish* polis
COLLOQ. cop, copper, bobby
SLANG pig, nark, rozzer, flat-foot, bluebottle; *Aust & NZ* John Hop
OLD SLANG *N Am* bull

policy _n_
1 CODE OF PRACTICE, rules, guidelines, procedure, method, system, practice, custom, protocol
2 COURSE OF ACTION, line, course, plan, programme, scheme, schedule, stance, position, guideline(s), approach, strategy

polish _v, n_
♦ _v_
1 SHINE, brighten, smooth, rub (up), buff, burnish, clean, wax, brilliant, slick, beeswax, furbish, sand, scour, supercalender, glaciate, rottenstone
OLD glass, lap
FORMAL planish
COLLOQ. posh up
SLANG bull
2 IMPROVE, enhance, brush up, touch up, finish, perfect, refine, cultivate, file
E3 1 tarnish, dull
♦ _n_
1 _a tin of polish_
wax, varnish
2 SHINE, gloss, sheen, lustre, brightness, brilliance, sparkle, smoothness, finish, glaze, veneer, burnish
3 REFINEMENT, cultivation, class, breeding, sophistication, finesse, style, elegance, grace, poise
E3 2 dullness **3** clumsiness
■ **polish off**
1 EAT UP, consume, devour, put away, bolt, gobble, finish, complete, dispose of, down, stuff
COLLOQ. wolf
2 MURDER, kill, destroy
COLLOQ. do in, eliminate, dispatch, wipe out, take out, zap
SLANG bump off, knock off, rub out, waste, blow away, liquidate

polished _adj_
1 SHINING, shiny, waxed, burnished, glossy, lustrous, gleaming, smooth, sleek, glassy, slippery
2 FAULTLESS, flawless, impeccable, perfect, outstanding, superlative, remarkable, excellent, masterly, expert, professional, skilful, accomplished, proficient, adept, perfected
FORMAL consummate
3 REFINED, cultivated, genteel, well-bred, well-mannered, polite, sophisticated, civilized, urbane, suave, elegant, graceful
E3 1 tarnished, dull **2** inexpert, unskilful **3** gauche, awkward

polite _adj_
1 COURTEOUS, well-mannered, respectful, civil, well-bred, well-behaved, deferential, refined, cultured, gentlemanly, ladylike, gallant, chivalrous, gracious, obliging, thoughtful, considerate, tactful, diplomatic, suave, courtlike, delicate, humane, bland, Grandisonian
2 _in polite society_
refined, cultured, genteel, well-bred, well-mannered, polite, sophisticated, civilized, urbane, suave, elegant
E3 1 impolite, rude, discourteous

SYNONYM NUANCES

sense 1
Courteous may be used to describe paying someone due regard and attention, although it suggests a rather formal manner, and while **well-mannered** describes similarly formal behaviour, it is more suggestive of adhering to social conventions.
You can use **respectful** to imply displaying an attentive regard for someone; **deferential** goes further by implying an element of submissiveness: _the media are deferential to Prime Ministers._ **Civil**, however, generally implies showing the minimum courtesy required to avoid rudeness: _it was an effort to remain civil to her._
Well-bred puts the emphasis on someone's upbringing, while **refined** and **cultured** further imply tastefulness and a complete lack of vulgarity. **Gallant** and **chivalrous**

would be reserved for a man's attentive conduct towards women, while **suave** also tends to be used of men, but conveys an ease of manner.
Gracious has implications of dignity: _she accepted his gift with a gracious smile._ The terms **tactful** and **diplomatic** put the emphasis on skill in dealing with people's feelings: _I showed a diplomatic interest in his inane ramblings._ **Delicate** has more negative suggestions of tentativeness. More critical is the term **bland**, which quite pointedly suggests an absence of personality.

politely _adv_
courteously, respectfully, thoughtfully, considerately, diplomatically, tactfully, graciously, obligingly, chivalrously, gallantly
E3 impolitely, rudely, discourteously

politeness _n_
courtesy, manners, good manners, deference, cordiality, gentility, mannerliness, polish, refinement, elegance, courtliness, culture, thoughtfulness, cultivation, civility, considerateness, graciousness, grace, gentlemanliness, good breeding, respect, respectfulness, diplomacy, tact, discretion, attention, savoir-vivre
FORMAL complaisance
E3 impoliteness, rudeness, discourtesy

politic _adj_
wise, prudent, shrewd, sensible, tactful, diplomatic, advisable, advantageous, opportune, expedient
FORMAL judicious, sagacious, sage
E3 impolitic

❗ politic or **political**?
Politic is a rather formal word meaning 'wise, sensible': _He considered it politic to leave before there was any further trouble. Political_ means 'relating to politics': _the political system of the USA; party political broadcasts._

political _adj_
governmental, parliamentary, constitutional, ministerial, administrative, executive, bureaucratic, civil, public, judicial, party political

political ideology

**Political ideologies include**:

absolutism	holism	pluralism
anarchism	imperialism	republicanism
authoritarianism	individualism	social democracy
Bolshevism	liberal democracy	socialism
Christian	liberalism	syndicalism
democracy	Maoism	Thatcherism
collectivism	Marxism	theocracy
communism	nationalism	third way
conservatism	Nazism	totalitarianism
democracy	neocolonialism	Trotskyism
egalitarianism	neoconservatism	unilateralism
fascism	neo-fascism	Whiggism
federalism	neo-nazism	

political party _n_
faction, side, league, cabal, alliance, association, affiliation, grouping, camp, combination

politics _n_
1 _go into politics_
public affairs, civics, affairs of state, statecraft, government, national government, regional government, local government, diplomacy, statesmanship, political science, party politics, political views/beliefs
2 _office politics_
power struggle, power game, power politics, manipulation, manoeuvring, jockeying for position/power

FORMAL machination(s)

COLLOQ. wheeler-dealing

> QUOTATIONS
> Politics is too important to be left to the politicians
> CHARLES DE GAULLE

People in politics include:

activist	lawmaker	president
AM (Assembly Member)	left-winger	presiding officer
	colloq. lefty	prime minister
ambassador	legislator	radical
backbencher	Liberal	colloq. red
Black Rod	Liberal Democrat (Lib Dem)	Republican
capitalist		revolutionary
colloq. commie	loyalist	right-winger
Communist	Marxist	secretary of state
comrade	Marxist-Leninist	senator
congressman	MEP (Member of the European Parliament)	Social Democrat
congresswoman		Socialist
Conservative		speaker
crossbencher	minister	spin doctor
Democrat	moderate	statesman
Deputy Speaker	MP (Member of Parliament)	stateswoman
dictator		Tánaiste
dissident	MSP (Member of the Scottish Parliament)	Taoiseach
colloq. dry		TD (Member of the Dáil)
Eurosceptic		
extremist	party chairman	Tory
first minister	party member	Trotskyite
frontbencher	party worker	true-blue
Green	colloq. pinko	colloq. wet
high commissioner	politician	Whig
independent	premier	

Terms used in politics include:

alliance	ginger group	proportional repre- sentation
apartheid	go to the country	
ballot	government	rainbow coalition
big tent	green paper	referendum
bill	Hansard	right wing
blockade	hung parliament	sanction
cabinet	judiciary	shadow cabinet
campaign	left wing	sovereignty
civil service	lobby	state
coalition	local government	summit
constitution	majority	summit con- ference
council	mandate	
coup d'état	manifesto	term of office
cross-party	nationalization	three-line whip
détente	parliament	trade union
devolution	party	veto
election	party line	vote
electoral register	prime minister's question time	welfare state
first-past-the-post		whip
focus group	privatization	white paper
general election	propaganda	

poll n, v

♦ n

ballot, ballot-box, vote, voting, plebiscite, referendum, straw poll, straw vote, head count, show of hands, sampling, canvass, opinion poll, market research, Gallup poll, survey, returns, census, count, tally

♦ v

1 WIN, net, get, receive, return, gain, obtain

2 BALLOT, survey, canvass, sample, question, interview, solicit, electioneer, campaign

3 CLIP, cut, trim, shear, pollard, dod, dishorn

pollute v

contaminate, infect, poison, taint, adulterate, debase, corrupt, dirty, make dirty, foul, befoul, soil, defile, deprave, warp, sully, stain, tarnish, blacken, mar, spoil; *Scot* file

FORMAL vitiate

pollution n

impurity, contamination, infection, taint, adulteration, corruption, dirtiness, filthiness, foulness, fouling, defilement, debasement, depravity, sullying, staining, tarnishing, blackening

OLD soilure

COLLOQ. muckiness

E∃ purification, purity, cleanness

polychromatic adj

multicoloured, many-coloured, kaleidoscopic, many-hued, mottled, motley, rainbow, variegated, varicoloured, polychrome, parti-coloured

E∃ monochromatic, monochrome, black and white

polyglot adj, n

♦ adj

multilingual, cosmopolitan, international, multiracial

FORMAL polyglottal, polyglottic

E∃ monoglot

♦ n

linguist, multilinguist

polymath n

all-rounder, oracle, mine of information

FORMAL pansophist, polyhistor

COLLOQ. know-all, walking encyclopaedia

E∃ ignoramus

pomp n

ceremony, ceremonial, ritual, solemnity, formality, ceremoniousness, state, grandeur, splendour, magnificence, pageantry, show, display, parade, spectacle, ostentation, flourish, brilliance, glory, majesty

OLD triumph

COLLOQ. glitter

E∃ austerity, simplicity

pomposity n

1 SELF-IMPORTANCE, arrogance, vanity, pride, haughtiness, loftiness, presumption, pretension, pretentiousness, imperiousness, superciliousness, condescension, airs

FORMAL affectation

2 *his annoying pomposities*

turgidity, rhetoric, stuffiness, preachiness

FORMAL bombast, euphuism, fustian, grandiloquence, magniloquence

E∃ **1** modesty **2** simplicity, economy

pompous adj

1 SELF-IMPORTANT, arrogant, proud, haughty, lofty, conceited, vain, presumptuous, grandiose, supercilious, patronizing, condescending, overbearing, imperious, solemn, magisterial, aldermanlike, aldermanly, pretentious, ostentatious, magnificent, portentous, budge

OLD magnific

FORMAL affected

COLLOQ. snooty, big

2 *pompous language/occasions*

elaborate, grant, high-flown, overblown, windy, stilted, flowery, ostentatious, turgid, stuffy, state, inflated, fustian

FORMAL euphuistic, magniloquent, bombastic, orotund

COLLOQ. heavy, preachy, la-di-da

E∃ **1** unassuming, modest, unaffected **2** simple, unpretentious

pond n

pool, puddle, lake, mere, tarn, watering-hole, waterhole, rink, stew, oceanarium, seaquarium; *Scot* pound; *Irish* turlough; *N Am* tank

OLD flash

FORMAL piscary

ponder v

deliberate, give thought to, reflect, reason, think, contemplate, meditate, consider, brood, examine, analyse, study, ruminate over, turn over, weigh, muse (on), puzzle over, mull over, pore (over), revolve, incubate
OLD poise, volve
FORMAL cerebrate, cogitate, excogitate, ratiocinate, ponderate

ponderous adj

1 *ponderous writing*
dull, serious, dreary, tedious, stilted, long-winded, plodding, verbose, laborious, pedantic, pedestrian, stodgy, stolid, humourless, laboured, lifeless
FORMAL prolix
2 CLUMSY, unwieldy, awkward, cumbersome, graceless, heavy, bulky, weighty, heavy-handed, heavy-footed, huge, massive, hefty, slow-moving, lumbering, elephantine
F3 **1** light, simple **2** delicate, nimble

ponderously adv

1 TEDIOUSLY, seriously, laboriously, verbosely, pedantically, stodgily
2 CLUMSILY, awkwardly, cumbersomely, heavily, slowly, gracelessly
F3 **1** simply **2** delicately

ponderousness n

seriousness, tedium, heaviness, laboriousness, stodginess, stolidity, weightiness, humourlessness, gravitas
F3 delicacy, lightness, subtlety

pontifical adj

1 PAPAL, apostolic, ecclesiastical, prelatic
2 SELF-IMPORTANT, pompous, overbearing, condescending, imperious, pretentious, magisterial, dogmatic, didactic, portentous, sermonizing
COLLOQ. snooty, preachy
F3 **2** reticent, unassuming

pontificate v

preach, hold forth, lecture, expound, pronounce, sermonize, sound off, harangue, dogmatize, moralize
FORMAL declaim, perorate
COLLOQ. lay down the law, spiel

pony

See panel at **horse**.

pooh-pooh v

dismiss, scorn, make little of, belittle, brush aside, ridicule, disdain, disregard, slight, sneer, sniff at, scoff, spurn, reject, play down, minimize
FORMAL deride, disparage
COLLOQ. turn up your nose at
F3 exaggerate, magnify

pool¹ n

a pool of water
puddle, pond, lake, mere, tarn, watering-hole, waterhole, paddling-pool, swimming-pool, swimming-bath(s)
OLD flash; (*Spenser*) plesh

pool² n, v

♦ *n*
1 FUND, reserve, supply, accumulation, bank, kitty, purse, pot, jackpot, ante
2 SYNDICATE, cartel, ring, combine, consortium, collective, group, team
♦ *v*
share, merge, put together, combine, amalgamate, contribute
COLLOQ. chip in, muck in

poor adj

1 IMPOVERISHED, poverty-stricken, badly off, in need, hard-up, bankrupt, penniless, as poor as a church mouse, without means, without the wherewithal, destitute, deprived, underprivileged, disadvantaged, reduced, humble, lowly, mean, miserable, wretched, distressed, straitened, beggared, needy
FORMAL penurious, impecunious, exiguous, obolary, indigent

COLLOQ. dirt-poor, broke, stony, stony-broke, flat broke, skint, strapped (for cash), cash-strapped, cleaned-out, on your uppers, on your beam ends, not having two pennies to rub together, not having a penny to your name, on the breadline, in Queer Street
2 BAD, substandard, unsatisfactory, inferior, mediocre, below standard, below par, low, low-quality, low-grade, low-rent, second-rate, third-rate, shoddy, imperfect, defective, faulty, jerry, weak, feeble, sorry, worthless, fruitless, unproductive, barren
COLLOQ. pathetic, rubbish, rop(e)y, rotten, duff, measly, crumm; *Aust* cronk; *Aust & NZ* crook
SLANG cruddy, naff, pants
3 LACKING, deficient, inadequate, insufficient, scanty, skimpy, meagre, sparse, paltry, depleted, exhausted
4 UNFORTUNATE, unlucky, luckless, ill-fated, ill-starred, unhappy, miserable, wretched, sorry, sad, spiritless, pathetic, pitiable, pitiful
FORMAL hapless
F3 **1** rich, wealthy, affluent **2** good, superior, impressive **3** sufficient, ample **4** fortunate, lucky

> **QUOTATIONS**
> No society can surely be flourishing and happy, of which the far greater part of the members are poor and miserable
> ADAM SMITH, *The Wealth of Nations*

SYNONYM NUANCES

sense 1
While both **bankrupt** and **penniless** emphasize the idea of having absolutely no money, **impoverished**, **poverty-stricken** and **distressed** suggest a complete lack of any resources, and suffering as a result. Likewise **destitute** suggests being entirely bereft of money or possessions.
  The terms **badly off** and **hard-up** suggest having very little rather than nothing, while **in need** and **needy** put the emphasis on what you do not have but require: *cash grants for those in need*. **Deprived**, likewise, implies being without, while **underprivileged** and **disadvantaged** suggest financial misfortunes arising from a lack of opportunity: *the unemployed and other disadvantaged groups*. Similarly, **straitened** can be used to suggest limitations through reduced resources.
  You can use **reduced** and **impoverished** where there has been a deterioration in circumstances, whereas **humble** and **lowly** are more suggestive of being modest or basic: *lowly accommodation in run-down areas*. The terms **mean**, **miserable** and **wretched** could be used to suggest an element of pitiable shabbiness: *the mean little houses; poor immigrants in their wretched clothes*.
  You can use **without means** or **without the wherewithal** to refer to a lack of pecuniary resources for something in particular: *we were without the wherewithal for private health care*.

---

poorly adj, adv

♦ *adj*
ill, sick, unwell, ailing, sickly, off colour, below par, seedy, groggy
FORMAL indisposed
COLLOQ. out of sorts, under the weather, rotten
F3 well, healthy
♦ *adv*
badly, inadequately, unsatisfactorily, unsuccessfully, faultily, incompetently, inexpertly, insufficiently, inferiorly, rottenly, shabbily, shoddily, meanly, feebly
F3 well

pop v, n

♦ *v*
1 BURST, explode, go off, bang, crack, snap
2 RUSH, dash, hurry, go quickly, leave quickly, go for a short time
COLLOQ. nip

3 PUT, push, insert, slide, slip, thrust, drop, shove
♦ *n*
1 BANG, crack, snap, burst, explosion, boom
FORMAL report
2 FIZZY DRINK, fizzy lemonade, cola, soda
■ **pop off**
die, pass away, pass on
COLLOQ. peg out, have had it
SLANG snuff it, kick the bucket, flatline
■ **pop up**
appear, occur, materialize, crop up, turn up,
show up, come along

pope *n*
pontiff, sovereign pontiff, Bishop of Rome, Holy Father,
Vicar of Christ, His Holiness, *Il Papa*
Related adjectives: papal, pontifical

popinjay *n*
dandy, fop, beau, coxcomb, peacock, pansy,
swell, dude
COLLOQ. toff
E3 he-man, macho

poppycock *n*
nonsense, rubbish, trash, drivel, balderdash, gibberish,
gobbledygook, stupidity, silliness, foolishness, folly,
twaddle; *Scot* blether; *dialect & N Am* blathers
COLLOQ. stuff and nonsense, bunk, rot, claptrap, cobblers,
piffle, waffle, flannel, tripe, tosh, bosh, tommyrot,
codswallop, baloney, humbug, hooey, bilge, hogwash,
blah, guff, rhubarb
SLANG bull; (*vulgar*) crap, shit, balls, bollocks, bullshit
E3 sense

populace *n*
inhabitants, natives, residents, citizens, occupants,
community, society, people, folk, general public, crowd,
masses, proletariat, public, common people, mob,
multitude(s), canaille, hoi polloi, third estate, rabble, rank
and file, herd, common herd, great unwashed, riff-raff
COLLOQ. punters, plebs, proles
E3 aristocracy, élite, nobility

popular *adj*
1 WELL-LIKED, favourite, liked, favoured, in favour, admired,
wanted, desired, approved, in demand, sought-after,
fashionable, modish
COLLOQ. trendy, in, now, hip, cool, big, all the rage
2 FAMOUS, famed, well-known, celebrated, renowned,
acclaimed, noted, idolized
3 PREVAILING, current, accepted, usual, customary,
conventional, standard, stock, common, prevalent,
widespread, universal, general, generally recognized,
household
4 *a popular history of science*
general, non-specialist, non-technical, amateur,
understandable, accessible, simple, simplified, ordinary,
mass-market, lay
E3 **1** unpopular, disliked, out of favour **2** unheard of,
obscure, unknown **3** rare, unusual **4** specialist, technical,
expert, professional

popularity *n*
approval, acceptance, recognition, reputation, favour,
vogue, kudos, mass appeal, regard, fame, renown, esteem,
currency, repute, acclaim, adoration, adulation, glory,
worship, idolization, lionization
FORMAL approbation
E3 unpopularity

popularize *v*
spread, propagate, familiarize, universalize, democratize,
generalize, give currency to, simplify, make
understandable, make accessible

popularly *adv*
commonly, widely, universally, generally, usually,
customarily, non-technically, ordinarily, regularly,
conventionally, traditionally

populate *v*
people, occupy, settle, colonize, inhabit, live in,
overrun
FORMAL dwell

population *n*
inhabitants, natives, residents, citizens, occupants,
community, society, people, folk
FORMAL populace

populous *adj*
crowded, packed, swarming, teeming, crawling, densely
populated, overpopulated, overpeopled
E3 deserted, empty

porcelain

Types of porcelain include:

biscuit	copper red	Kakiemon
bisque	eggshell	Kraak
blue and white	faience	nankeen
bone china	famille-rose	Parian
Canton	famille-verte	saltglazed
Capodimonte	First Period	soapstone paste
chinoiserie	Worcester	soft paste
Compagnie des	hard paste	Yingqing
Indes	Imari	

Famous makers of porcelain include:

Arita	Copeland	Rockingham
Belleek	Derby	Royal Doulton
Bow	Dresden	Royal Worcester
Bristol	Limoges	Satsuma
Caughley	Meissen	Sèvres
Chantilly	Ming	Vienna
Chelsea	Minton	Wedgwood®
Coalport	Nanking	Worcester

porch *n*
vestibule, hall, hallway, entrance-hall, lobby, foyer; *N Am*
stoop; *S Afr* stoep
TECHNICAL galilee

pore[1] *v*
■ **pore over**
study, study intensely, examine, examine closely,
scrutinize, go over, read, scan, contemplate, ponder, dwell
on, brood
OLD con
FORMAL peruse

pore[2] *n*
sweating from every pore
hole, opening, perforation, aperture, outlet, vent
TECHNICAL foramen, micropore, stoma, stigma, lenticel
FORMAL orifice

pornographic *adj*
obscene, indecent, dirty, filthy, X-rated, pink, adult, risqué,
bawdy, coarse, gross, lewd, salacious, erotic, titillating
FORMAL prurient
COLLOQ. blue, off-colour, porn

pornography *n*
indecency, obscenity, filth, dirt, smut, erotica, grossness,
bawdiness, facetiae, curiosa, peep-show, snuff
film/movie/video
COLLOQ. porn, porno, sexploitation, girlie magazines,
(video) nasty, skinflick

porous *adj*
permeable, pervious, penetrable, absorbent, spongy,
spongelike, honeycombed, cellular, holey, open, airy
TECHNICAL foraminous, foveate
E3 impermeable, impervious

port *n*
seaport, harbour, jetty, dock, anchorage, harbourage,
haven, roads, roadstead, hithe

portability *n*
movability, transportability, manageability, handiness, convenience, compactness

portable *adj*
movable, transportable, compact, lightweight, manageable, conveyable, handy, convenient
▣ fixed, immovable

portal *n*
gateway, opening, entrance, access, way in, door, doorway

portend *v*
indicate, point to, be a sign of, be an indication of, warn of, announce, forecast, predict, foretell, promise, signify, threaten, herald
FORMAL augur, bode, forebode, foreshadow, foreshow, forewarn, harbinger, foretoken, prognosticate, adumbrate, presage, purport, betoken, bespeak

portent *n*
sign, indication, warning, threat, omen, precursor, forecast, foreboding, forerunner, prefiguration, premonition
FORMAL augury, signification, prognostication, foreshadowing, forewarning, prognostic, presage, presentiment, prodrome, harbinger

portentous *adj*
1 FOREBODING, ominous, sinister, menacing, threatening, momentous, fateful
2 REMARKABLE, significant, important, amazing, astounding, extraordinary, awe-inspiring, earth-shaking, epoch-making, miraculous, crucial
3 POMPOUS, self-important, arrogant, proud, haughty, conceited, vain, presumptuous, grandiose, supercilious, patronizing, condescending, overbearing, imperious, magisterial, pretentious, ostentatious
FORMAL affected
COLLOQ. snooty
▣ **2** insignificant, unimportant, unimpressive

portentously *adv*
pompously, self-importantly, arrogantly, haughtily, conceitedly, superciliously, condescendingly, patronizingly
COLLOQ. snootily

porter¹ *n*
a porter at a hotel
bearer, carrier, baggage-attendant, baggage-handler, baggage-carrier, out-porter, ticket-porter, bellhop, page, bummaree, hammal; *N Am* redcap
OLD caddie
COLLOQ. humper

porter² *n*
a porter at a college
doorman, commissionaire, door-keeper, gatekeeper, door attendant, janitor, caretaker, concierge, night-porter, dvornik
OLD doorsman

portion *n, v*
♦ *n*
1 SHARE, allocation, tranche, allotment, parcel, quantity, allowance, ration, quota, measure, part, section, division, fraction, percentage, bit, fragment, morsel, piece, segment, slice, wedge, serving, helping
COLLOQ. cut, whack, rake-off
2 DESTINY, fate, lot, kismet, fortune, luck, chance
♦ *v*
distribute, divide, deal, share out, allocate, allot, apportion, assign, slice up, parcel, partition
COLLOQ. carve up, dole out

portliness *n*
ampleness, stoutness, roundness, plumpness, fatness, paunchiness, obesity, heaviness, fullness, dumpiness, tubbiness, chubbiness, fleshiness
FORMAL corpulence, rotundity
COLLOQ. beefiness

portly *adj*
stout, round, fat, plump, obese, overweight, stocky, ample, heavy, large
FORMAL corpulent, rotund
▣ slim, thin, slight

portrait *n*
picture, painting, drawing, sketch, caricature, miniature, carte-de-viste, icon, photograph, likeness, image, representation, self-portrait, pin-up, full-length, whole-length, half-length, profile, Kit-Cat, vignette, study, thumbnail sketch, characterization, description, depiction, portrayal, story, account; *N Am* composite
OLD pourtray; (*Spenser*) retrate, retraitt
▣ landscape

portray *v*
1 DRAW, sketch, paint, illustrate, picture, represent
OLD pourtray, portrait
2 DESCRIBE, depict, picture, represent, present, take, characterize, self-portrait, illustrate, evoke
OLD pourtray, portrait
3 PLAY, act, play/act the part of, perform, impersonate, characterize, image, personify
OLD pourtray, portrait

portrayal *n*
representation, characterization, depiction, description, picture, painting, drawing, sketch, study, evocation, presentation, acting, performance, interpretation, rendering
FORMAL delineation

pose *v, n*
♦ *v*
1 MODEL, sit, position, arrange
2 PRETEND, feign, act, put on an act, put on airs, masquerade, pass yourself off, impersonate, attitudinize
FORMAL affect
3 *pose a question*
put forward, ask, submit, suggest, propose, put, set, advance
FORMAL posit, postulate, propound
4 *pose a problem/threat*
create, present, cause, produce, give rise to, lead to, result in
FORMAL constitute
♦ *n*
1 POSITION, stance, air, posture, attitude
FORMAL bearing, carriage, deportment
2 PRETENCE, sham, façade, front, masquerade, airs, role, act, pretence
FORMAL affectation

poser¹ *n*
he's a poser
poseur, poseuse, posturer, attitudinizer, exhibitionist, show-off, play-actor, charlatan, sham, impostor
COLLOQ. pseud, phoney

poser² *n*
this is a poser
puzzle, riddle, conundrum, mystery, enigma, problem, dilemma, vexed question, brainteaser, mind-bender; *N Am* brain-twister

poseur *n*
poser, poseuse, posturer, attitudinizer, exhibitionist, show-off, play-actor, charlatan, sham, impostor
COLLOQ. pseud, phoney

posh *adj*
smart, stylish, fancy, fashionable, elegant, high-class, upper-class, grand, luxurious, lavish, sumptuous, luxury, de-luxe, rich, up-market, exclusive, select
FORMAL opulent
COLLOQ. la-di-da, swanky, classy, swish, plush, snazzy
▣ inferior, cheap

posit *v*
put forward, pose, advance, state, submit, assert, assume, presume
FORMAL postulate, predicate, propound

position *n, v*

♦ *n*

1 PLACE, situation, location, site, spot, scene, setting, area, locality, whereabouts, point

2 POSTURE, stance, pose, attitude, arrangement, disposition

FORMAL bearing

3 JOB, post, occupation, employment, situation, appointment, office, duty, function, role, capacity

4 RANK, grade, level, place, status, standing, ranking, influence, prestige

5 SITUATION, state, condition, state of affairs, circumstances, case, factor(s), background, plight, predicament

6 OPINION, point of view, belief, view, outlook, viewpoint, attitude, stance, standpoint, stand

♦ *v*

put, place, set, settle, fix, stand, arrange, dispose, lay out, deploy, station, locate, situate, site, install, establish

FORMAL array

positive *adj*

1 SURE, certain, convinced, confident, assured

2 OPTIMISTIC, hopeful, confident, encouraged, good, favourable, cheerful, promising, encouraging

COLLOQ. upbeat

3 *positive criticism*

helpful, constructive, practical, useful, productive, affirmative

4 DEFINITE, decisive, conclusive, real, actual, concrete, clear, clear-cut, unmistakable, explicit, precise, unequivocal, express, direct, firm, emphatic, categorical, undeniable, indisputable, incontestable, incontrovertible

FORMAL irrefutable

5 ABSOLUTE, utter, sheer, complete, rank, perfect, unmitigated, outright, out-and-out, thorough, veritable

FORMAL consummate

E3 **1** uncertain, doubtful **2** negative, pessimistic **3** negative, unhelpful **4** indefinite, vague

positively *adv*

absolutely, definitely, categorically, firmly, finally, decisively, emphatically, expressly, conclusively, certainly, assuredly, surely, unmistakably, unquestionably, incontestably, incontrovertibly, indisputably, unequivocally, undeniably, uncompromisingly

possess *v*

1 OWN, have, hold, be in possession of, acquire, gain, get, enjoy, be endowed with, be gifted with, be blessed with, boast

OLD wield

2 SEIZE, take, obtain, acquire, take over, take possession of, take control of, get, occupy; *dialect* overget

3 INFLUENCE, control, dominate, bewitch, haunt, enchant, infatuate, obsess, demonize

possessed *adj*

dominated, controlled, mesmerized, enchanted, berserk, bedevilled, demonized, bewitched, haunted, cursed, hag-ridden, frenzied, demented, crazed, mad, maddened, raving, consumed, infatuated, obsessed, besotted

possession *n*

1 OWNERSHIP, title, tenure, occupation, holding, tenancy, custody, proprietorship, control, hold, grip

2 OBSESSION, infatuation, domination, control, haunting, craze

possessions *n*

lose your possessions

belongings, property, baggage, luggage, paraphernalia, effects, goods, chattels, personal effects, goods and chattels, movables, assets, estate, wealth, riches, temporalities, temporalties, ana

OLD aver, worth

FORMAL accoutrements

COLLOQ. things, stuff, gear, clobber, (all your) worldly wealth

possessive *adj*

selfish, clinging, overprotective, domineering, dominating, controlling, jealous, covetous, acquisitive, grasping, greedy

E3 unselfish, sharing

possessiveness *n*

selfishness, jealousy, exclusiveness, greed, covetousness, acquisitiveness

possibility *n*

1 LIKELIHOOD, probability, odds, chance, risk, danger, hazard, hope, prospect, potentiality, conceivability, practicability, feasibility, attainability

2 *a place with possibilities*

promise, potential, prospects, advantages, capabilities, expectations, talent

FORMAL potentiality

3 OPTION, alternative, choice, preference, recourse

E3 **1** impossibility, impracticability **2** disadvantages, liabilities

possible *adj*

likely, probable, promising, potential, imaginable, conceivable, practicable, feasible, that can be done, viable, tenable, credible, workable, achievable, attainable, doable, accomplishable, realizable

COLLOQ. on the cards, odds-on

E3 impossible, unthinkable, impracticable, unattainable

possibly *adv*

perhaps, maybe, conceivably, by any means, at all, by any chance

FORMAL peradventure

COLLOQ. hopefully

post¹ *n, v*

♦ *n*

a fence post

pole, stake, picket, pale, pillar, column, shaft, standard, support, prop, baluster, banister, palisade, upright, newel, stanchion, jamb, strut, leg

♦ *v*

1 DISPLAY, stick up, pin (up), put up, attach, affix

2 ANNOUNCE, advertise, publicize, make known, circulate, report, publish, broadcast

post² *n, v*

♦ *n*

a teaching post

office, job, employment, position, situation, place, vacancy, appointment, assignment, station, beat

♦ *v*

station, locate, situate, position, place, put, put on duty, appoint, assign, second, transfer, move, send

post³ *n, v*

♦ *n*

1 *deliver the post*

mail, letters, correspondence, communications, packages, parcels, packets, delivery, registered mail, recorded mail, special delivery, direct mail, airmail, all-up service, first-class mail, second-class mail, surface mail, international mail, electronic mail, email

COLLOQ. junk mail, snail mail

2 POSTAL SERVICE, postal system, mail, Post Office

♦ *v*

mail, send, dispatch, transmit, forward

■ **keep someone posted**

inform, keep up to date, keep informed, give the latest information

COLLOQ. fill in, keep in the picture, keep in the loop

poster *n*

notice, bill, sign, placard, sticker, advertisement, bulletin, announcement, show bill

COLLOQ. ad, advert

posterior *adj, n*

♦ *adj*

rear, rearward, behind, back, hind, hinder, after, ensuing, following, subsequent, succeeding, later, latter

TECHNICAL dorsal, posticous
⊟ anterior, front, previous
♦ *n*
bottom, rear, behind, buttocks, rump, seat, haunches, hinder end, hindquarters
COLLOQ. backside, bum, tail; *N Am* butt; *Scot* bahookie
SLANG (*vulgar*) arse; *N Am* ass
Related adjective: pygal

posterity *n*
descendants, successors, future generations, succeeding generations, heirs, offspring, seed, children
FORMAL progeny, issue

posthaste *adv*
quickly, speedily, straightaway, immediately, at once, as quickly as possible, directly, promptly, hastily, swiftly, with all speed
COLLOQ. double-quick, full tilt, pronto
⊟ eventually, gradually, slowly

postman, postwoman *n*
delivery officer, letter-carrier, mail-carrier, mail handler, postal worker; *N Am* mailman
COLLOQ. postie

post-mortem *n*
autopsy, dissection, necropsy, analysis, examination, review

postpone *v*
put off, defer, put back, do later, hold over, carry over, delay, adjourn, suspend, reschedule, roll back, shelve, pigeonhole, freeze, mothball, waive, stand over; *N Am* table
OLD frist, protract, refer, rejourn, retard, withhold; (*Shakesp & Spenser*) prolong
FORMAL prorogue, procrastinate
COLLOQ. put on ice, put/place on the back burner, sleep on it, wait, take a raincheck on
⊟ advance, forward, bring forward

postponed *adj*
put off, adjourned, deferred, carried over, held over, shelved, suspended, pigeonholed, frozen
FORMAL in abeyance
COLLOQ. on ice, on the back burner
⊟ advanced

postponement *n*
adjournment, put-off, deferment, delay, deferral, moratorium, freeze, suspension, stay, respite
FORMAL prorogation

postscript *n*
addition, supplement, afterthought, addendum, appendix, afterword, epilogue
TECHNICAL codicil
COLLOQ. PS
⊟ introduction, prologue

postulate *v*
theorize, suppose, assume, presume, presuppose, hypothesize, propose, advance, put forward, lay down, stipulate
FORMAL posit

posture *n, v*
♦ *n*
1 POSITION, stance, pose, attitude, disposition, set, motion, counter-view, defensive, guard, offensive, sprawl
TECHNICAL decubitus, mudra, pike
OLD gesture, site
FORMAL bearing, carriage, deportment
2 ATTITUDE, opinion, point of view, belief, view, outlook, viewpoint, stance, standpoint, stand

♦ *v*
pose, put on airs, show off, strike attitudes, attitudinize, strut
FORMAL affect

posy *n*
bouquet, spray, buttonhole, nosegay, corsage

pot *n*
1 RECEPTACLE, vessel, teapot, coffee pot, urn, jar, vase, bowl, basin, pan, cauldron, crucible, cruse, can, box, caster, crock, casserole, *pot-au-feu*, marmite, pipkin, flowerpot, planter, lota, tajine, chamberpot; *Scot* pat
TECHNICAL aludel, test, gallipot
OLD boughpot, bowpot, crewe, pottle; (*Shakesp & Spenser*) stew
2 KITTY, purse, pool, bank, fund, reserve

potable *adj*
drinkable, clean, safe, fit to drink

pot-bellied *adj*
bloated, distended, fat, gor-bellied, obese, overweight, paunchy, portly, tubby
FORMAL corpulent

pot-belly *n*
belly, beer belly, paunch, gut, pot
COLLOQ. corporation, spare tyre

potency *n*
power, strength, force, influence, potential, vigour, powerfulness, control, authority, effectiveness, persuasiveness, energy, sway, capacity
FORMAL cogency, efficaciousness, efficacy, might, puissance
COLLOQ. headiness, kick, muscle, punch
⊟ weakness, impotence

potent *adj*
effective, powerful, mighty, strong, intoxicating, pungent, impressive, convincing, persuasive, eloquent, compelling, forceful, dynamic, energetic, active, vigorous, authoritative, commanding, dominant, influential, overpowering, virile
OLD puissant
FORMAL cogent, efficacious
COLLOQ. still having a shot in your locker
⊟ impotent, weak

potentate *n*
ruler, monarch, sovereign, autocrat, head of state, king, queen, despot, dictator, tyrant, emperor, empress, prince, chief, chieftain, mogul, leader, dynast, overlord

potential *adj, n*
♦ *adj*
possible, likely, probable, prospective, future, aspiring, would-be, promising, budding, developing, embryonic, inherent, implicit, undeveloped, dormant, latent, hidden, concealed, unrealized, virtual
♦ *n*
possibility, ability, capability, capacity, aptitude, gift, flair, talent, promise, powers, resources

potentiality *n*
likelihood, possibilities, potential, promise, prospect, virtuality, ability, capability, aptitude, capacity

potentially *adv*
possibly, probably, in all likelihood, virtually, inherently, implicitly, dormantly, latently
FORMAL in potentia

potion *n*
mixture, concoction, brew, beverage, drink, draught, dose, medicine, tonic, elixir, philtre, potation

potpourri *n*
medley, mixture, assortment, jumble, hotchpotch, miscellany, collection, melange, confusion, smorgasbord,

pastiche, patchwork, gallimaufry, hodgepodge, olla-podrida, olio
COLLOQ. mishmash

potter v
dawdle, amble, loiter; N Am putter
COLLOQ. mess about, toddle, dilly-dally, pootle
■ **potter about**
tinker about/around, fiddle about/around, fool about/around, play about/around, do nothing much
COLLOQ. mess about/around, muck about/around
SLANG fart about/around

pottery n
ceramics, crockery, china

Terms used in pottery include:

armorial	figure	overglaze
art pottery	firing	porcelain
basalt	flambé	raku
blanc-de-chine	flatback	sagger
bronzing	glaze	scratch blue
celadon	grotesque	sgraffito
ceramic	ground	slip
china clay	ironstone	slip-cast
cloisonné	jasper	spongeware
crackleware	kiln	Staffordshire
crazing	lustre	stoneware
creamware	majolica (or	terracotta
delft	maiolica)	tin-glazed
earthenware	maker's mark	earthenware
enamel	mandarin palette	transfer printing
faience	model	underglaze
fairing	monogram	Willow pattern

See also **porcelain**.

potty adj
1 MAD, insane, lunatic, unbalanced, psychotic, disturbed, deranged, maniacal, out of your mind, out of your senses, of unsound mind, unhinged, crazed, unstable, *non compos mentis*, frenzied, wild, berserk, manic, maniac, distracted, distraught, fey, frenetic, frantic, stone-crazy, queer; Scot gyte, red-mad
OLD frantic-mad, lymphatic, bestraught
COLLOQ. crazy, demented, nuts, nutty, nutty as a fruitcake, wacky, mad as a hatter, barmy, bonkers, batty, cracked, crackers, dippy, daffy, dotty, loopy, off your nut, off your head, wrong in the head, out of your head, off the wall, out to lunch, round the bend, round the twist, bats, having bats in the belfry, cuckoo, off the rails, screwy, up the wall, raving, not all there; N Am buggy, flaky, fruity; Aust & NZ dingbats
SLANG loony, mental, bananas, barking, wacko, doolally, off your rocker, off your chump, off your trolley, out of your tree, needing your head examined, having lost your marbles, having a screw loose, having a tile loose, having several cards short of a full deck, with one sandwich short of a picnic, meshuga, ape, apeshit; N Am gonzo, loco, wiggy
2 FANATICAL, enthusiastic, infatuated, ardent, zealous, devoted, fond, keen, avid, passionate, mad, wild
COLLOQ. crazy, daft, nuts
F3 1 sane **2** apathetic

pouch n
bag, purse, pocket, container, receptacle, sack, wallet, sporran, poke; Scot gaberlunzie; Scot & Irish spleuchan
TECHNICAL marsupium, sac, bursa, diverticulum, spur
OLD scrip, codpiece
FORMAL reticule
Related adjectives: marsupial, saccate

pounce v, n
♦ v
fall (on), dive (on), swoop (on), drop, descend (on), attack, strike, ambush, spring, jump (on), leap, bound, lunge,

snatch, grab, take by surprise, catch/take unawares, catch off guard
♦ n
attack, assault, bound, dive, grab, jump, leap, swoop, lunge, spring

pound¹ n
it cost 100 pounds
pound coin, £, pound sterling
OLD Irish punt
COLLOQ. quid
SLANG nicker, smacker, smackeroo, oncer, sov, squid
OLD SLANG bar, jimmy-o'goblin; Aust iron man

> **PROVERBS**
> Take care of the pennies and the pounds will take care of themselves
> In for a penny, in for a pound

pound² n
keep animals in a pound
enclosure, compound, corral, yard, pen, fold, penfold, pinfold

pound³ v
1 STRIKE, thump, beat, drum, pelt, hammer, batter, bang, bash, smash, pummel, knead, bruise; Scot nevel
TECHNICAL contuse
OLD contund, pun
2 PULVERIZE, powder, grind, mash, bray, pestle, crush, beat, smash, granulate, stamp
OLD pun
FORMAL levigate, comminute, triturate
3 *his heart was pounding*
throb, pulsate, palpitate, thump, thud, hammer
OLD pownd
4 *pound the streets*
tread, tramp, walk, pace, trudge, plod, stomp

pour v
1 *pour a drink*
make flow, let flow, serve, pour out, decant, tip, spill, sprinkle
2 SPILL, issue, come out, discharge, flow, emit, leak, ooze, stream, run, rush, spout, spew, jet, spurt, gush, course, cascade, flood, crowd, throng, swarm
FORMAL disgorge, disembogue
3 RAIN, teem down, pelt down
COLLOQ. rain cats and dogs, bucket down, come down in buckets/stair rods/torrents
SLANG piss down

pout v, n
♦ v
scowl, glower, lour, grimace, pull a face, make a moue, sulk, mope, boody; Scot tout
OLD (Shakesp) make a lip
F3 grin, smile
♦ n
scowl, glower, grimace, long face, moue
F3 grin, smile

poverty n
poorness, impoverishment, insolvency, bankruptcy, pennilessness, destitution, deprivation, beggary, distress, hardship, need, necessity, want, lack, deficiency, shortage, inadequacy, insufficiency, depletion, scarcity, meagreness, paucity, dearth, narrow circumstances, shabbiness, locust-years; Scot poortith
FORMAL penury, impecuniosity, indigence, privation
F3 wealth, richness, affluence, plenty

> **SYNONYM NUANCES**
> **Impoverishment** suggests having lost what you once owned: *the north is an area of progressive impoverishment*. **Insolvency** means being unable to meet one's debts, and **bankruptcy** also suggests being at the mercy of your creditors. Similarly, **pennilessness** suggests a total absence of funds, while **destitution**

would further refer to a lack of possessions, and **beggary** has clear connotations of being reduced to asking for handouts.

Both **distress** and **hardship** again have implications of a lack of money and its potential effects: *they are in dire distress financially*. **Deprivation** too implies a state of being without, while **need** and **necessity** emphasize a condition requiring aid. The terms **want**, **lack**, **deficiency** and **shortage** are less forceful, and concentrate on what is absent: *the want of funding; a shortage of science teachers*. **Inadequacy** and **insufficiency**, **meagreness** and **paucity** do suggest a presence, but have implications of being somewhat insubstantial: *a paucity of research*. **Scarcity** and **dearth**, on the other hand, suggest a more serious lack: *a dearth of skilled applicants is damaging industry*.

poverty-stricken *adj*
poor, penniless, impoverished, needy, destitute, distressed, bankrupt, beggared
FORMAL impecunious, obolary, indigent, penurious
COLLOQ. dirt-poor, broke, skint, stony, stony-broke, cleaned-out, flat broke, strapped, on your beam-ends, on your uppers, in Queer Street
Ⅎⅎ rich, affluent

powder *n, v*
♦ *n*
dust, grains, pounce, bran, talc
TECHNICAL triturate, pulvil, pulville, pulvil(l)io
FORMAL efflorescence
♦ *v*
1 PULVERIZE, grind, mash, bray, pestle, crush, beat, smash, granulate
FORMAL levigate, comminute, triturate
2 SPRINKLE, scatter, cover, dust, strew

Kinds of powder include:

baking powder	flea powder	plate-powder
black powder	fly powder	polishing-powder
bleaching powder	giant powder	priming-powder
calamine powder	Goa powder	projecting-powder
chilli powder	Gregory's powder	putty-powder
coffee powder	gunpowder	Rochelle-powder
curry powder	hair-powder	Seidlitz powder
custard powder	insect powder	soap powder
diamond-powder	itching powder	talcum powder
Dover's powder	medicated powder	tea powder
dusting powder	pearl-powder	tooth powder
egg powder	pebble-powder	washing powder
emery powder	percussion-powder	worm powder
face powder	Persian powder	yeast powder

---

powdery *adj*
dusty, sandy, grainy, granular, granulated, powdered, pulverized, ground, fine, loose, dry, floury, crumbly, chalky, mealy
FORMAL friable, pulverulent, pulverous, efflorescent, levigate

power *n*
1 COMMAND, authority, sovereignty, rule, dominion, domination, control, say, influence, mastery, supremacy, sway
FORMAL ascendancy
COLLOQ. clout, pull, muscle, teeth, clutches
2 RIGHT, authority, privilege, prerogative, authorization, licence, warrant
3 POWERFULNESS, strength, intensity, energy, force, forcefulness, effectiveness, vigour, potency
FORMAL might
COLLOQ. juice, oomph
4 ABILITY, capability, capacity, potential, faculty, competence

FORMAL potentiality
5 *the western powers*
nation, state, country, people, superpower
Ⅎⅎ **1** subjection, servitude **3** weakness, impotence **4** inability, incapacity
■ **the powers that be**
the establishment, the authorities, the system
COLLOQ. them

> **QUOTATIONS**
> Power tends to corrupt, and absolute power corrupts absolutely. Great men are almost always bad men. There is no worse heresy than that the office sanctifies the holder of it
> JOHN EMERICH EDWARD DALBERG, 1ST BARON ACTON
>
> Power corrupts, but lack of power corrupts absolutely
> ADLAI STEVENSON

powerful *adj*
1 INFLUENTIAL, dominant, prevailing, leading, high-powered, authoritative, commanding, potent, effective, energetic, forceful, telling, impressive, convincing, persuasive, compelling, winning, overwhelming, all-powerful
FORMAL cogent
2 STRONG, mighty, robust, tough, muscular, brawny, strapping, burly, hardy
OLD puissant; (*Shakesp*) mightful
See Synonym nuances panel at **strong**.
Ⅎⅎ **1** powerless, ineffective, impotent **2** weak, puny

powerfully *adv*
strongly, strong, vigorously, hard, high, highly, forcefully, forcibly, potently, convincingly, persuasively, impressively, tellingly
FORMAL cogently, mightily, with might and main

powerless *adj*
helpless, unfit, unable, impotent, incapable, ineffective, weak-handed, weak, having a say, feeble, toothless, frail, infirm, incapacitated, debilitated, disabled, paralysed, vulnerable, defenceless, unarmed, hamstrung, numb, castrated
OLD benumbed, impuissant
FORMAL ineffectual
COLLOQ. with your hands tied, had by the short and curlies
Ⅎⅎ powerful, influential, able, potent

practicability *n*
possibility, feasibility, practicality, viability, workability, workableness, handiness, operability, use, usefulness, value, utility
Ⅎⅎ impracticability

practicable *adj*
possible, feasible, performable, achievable, doable, attainable, viable, workable, practical, realistic
Ⅎⅎ impracticable

> **!** **practicable** or **practical**?
> *Practicable* means 'able to be done, used, carried out, etc': *a practicable plan*. *Practical*, when applied to things, suggestions, etc also means 'able to be done, used, or carried out' but has the further connotation of 'efficient, sensible, useful': *Both these suggested courses of action are practicable, but John's is certainly the more practical of the two; High heels aren't very practical for hill-walking*. Applied to people, *practical* means 'able to do, make, or deal with things well or efficiently': *He's not a very practical person: he has lots of ideas for redesigning the bathroom but he doesn't have a clue how to put up a shelf*.

practical *adj*
1 *put knowledge to practical use*
applied, hands on, real, actual

2 *a practical person*
down-to-earth, matter-of-fact, sensible, realistic, pragmatic, hard-headed, businesslike, efficient, experienced, trained, qualified, skilled, accomplished, proficient
COLLOQ. hard-nosed, having both feet on the ground
3 *practical ideas*
realistic, workable, feasible, sensible, commonsense, applied, workaday, practicable
4 *wear practical shoes*
sensible, strong, suitable, utilitarian, functional, working, everyday, ordinary, serviceable, useful, handy
5 *a practical walkover*
virtual, effective, in effect, essential
E3 **1** theoretical **2** impractical, unskilled **3, 4** impractical
■ **practical joke**
trick, hoax, joke, prank, antic, caper, frolic, gag, jape, feat, stunt
COLLOQ. leg-pull, frame-up, fast one, scam

practicality *n*
sense, common sense, realism, basics, experience, practicability, pragmatism, practicalness, serviceability, soundness, usefulness, utility, workability, feasibility, practice
COLLOQ. nitty-gritty, nuts and bolts

practically *adv*
1 ALMOST, nearly, well-nigh, virtually, all but, just about, in principle, in effect, essentially, fundamentally, to all intents and purposes
COLLOQ. pretty much, pretty well
2 REALISTICALLY, sensibly, reasonably, rationally, pragmatically, matter-of-factly

practice *n*
1 CUSTOM, tradition, convention, usage, habit, routine, way, method, system, procedure, policy
FORMAL wont
2 REHEARSAL, run-through, dry run, dummy run, try-out, training, drill, exercise, work-out, study, preparation, warm-up, experience
3 *in practice*
effect, reality, actuality, action, operation, performance, use, exercise, application
4 *the practice of medicine*
business, work, profession, career, occupation, employment, job, following, pursuit
5 *a lawyer's practice*
business, partnership, establishment, company, firm
E3 **3** theory, principle
■ **out of practice**
unpractised, disused, out of (the) habit, rusty
FORMAL disaccustomed
■ **put into practice**
apply, put into effect/operation, put into action, use, make use of, put to use, exercise, perform

> **PROVERBS**
> Practice makes perfect

practise *v*
1 DO, perform, implement, carry out, apply, put into practice, observe, follow, pursue, engage in, undertake
FORMAL execute
2 REHEARSE, run through, go through, go over, repeat, drill, exercise, train, study, work on, work at, prepare, perfect, refine, polish

practised *adj*
experienced, seasoned, veteran, trained, qualified, accomplished, skilled, skilful, versed, knowing, knowledgeable, able, adept, proficient, expert, masterly, finished, old
OLD experimented; (*Shakesp*) traded
FORMAL consummate
E3 unpractised, inexperienced, inexpert

practitioner *n*
expert, specialist, authority, professional, pundit, master, maestro, virtuoso, crack, proficient, doer
COLLOQ. pro, dab hand, old hand, ace, buff

pragmatic *adj*
practical, realistic, sensible, matter-of-fact, businesslike, efficient, utilitarian, hard-headed, unsentimental
COLLOQ. hard-nosed
E3 unrealistic, idealistic, romantic

pragmatism *n*
practicality, realism, utilitarianism, hard-headedness, humanism, practicalism, opportunism, unidealism
E3 idealism, romanticism

pragmatist *n*
realist, utilitarian, opportunist, practicalist
E3 idealist, romantic

praise *v, n*
♦ *v*
commend, congratulate, express approval of, speak highly of, speak well of, admire, compliment, flatter, sing the praises of, wax lyrical, extol, promote, applaud, cheer, acclaim, hail, recognize, acknowledge, pay tribute to, honour, glorify, magnify, exalt, worship, adore, bless
FORMAL eulogize, laud
COLLOQ. talk up, rave over
E3 criticize, revile
♦ *n*
approval, admiration, commendation, congratulation, compliment, flattery, adulation, applause, plaudits, ovation, cheering, acclaim, recognition, testimonial, tribute, accolade, homage, honour, glory, worship, adoration, devotion, thanks, thanksgiving, hallelujah, hosanna
FORMAL approbation, eulogy, encomium, laudation, panegyric
COLLOQ. bouquets, puff
E3 criticism, revilement

> **SYNONYM NUANCES**
>
> *verb*
> **Commend** can be used of singling someone out for an honourable mention: *I commend you for arriving early*, while **congratulate** conveys more enthusiasm in extending recognition for something well done. **Admire**, on the other hand, suggests holding someone in high regard, and **compliment** might be used of expressing that regard. **Flatter**, although similar, has more negative implications of insincerity.
> While you can use **promote** to suggest praise bringing to the attention of others, the term **extol** would be appropriate for paying a more lavish tribute: *the poem extolled his achievements*.
> **Acclaim**, often used in the passive, suggests enthusiastic public recommendation: *the acclaimed violinist*. **Recognize** and **acknowledge**, on the other hand, are less effusive, much less so than the term **honour**, which again suggests paying tribute; the terms **glorify**, **magnify**, **exalt** and **worship** go much further by attributing with the highest status: *life in Britain may be glorified by ex-pats*.
> **Adore** similarly suggests having feelings of reverence, whereas **bless** has more to do with giving thanks, and has strong religious connotations.

praiseworthy *adj*
commendable, fine, excellent, admirable, exemplary, worthy, deserving, honourable, reputable, estimable, sterling
FORMAL laudable
E3 blameworthy, dishonourable, ignoble

praising *adj*
approving, complimentary, congratulatory, favourable, flattering, commendatory, adulatory, recommendatory, promotional, worshipful

FORMAL approbatory, eulogistic, encomiastic, laudative, laudatory, panegyric, plauditory
᠊ condemnatory, critical

pram n
buggy, Baby Buggy®, pushchair; N Am baby carriage, stroller
FORMAL perambulator

prance v
1 LEAP, jump, spring, skip, dance, frisk, frolic, gambol, cavort, caper, bound, romp, vault
OLD (*Shakesp*) jaunce
2 SHOW OFF, strut, swagger, stalk, parade, curvet
COLLOQ. swank

prank n
trick, practical joke, joke, stunt, caper, frolic, lark, antic, escapade
SLANG N Am monkey shine

prankster n
joker, jester, trickster, quipster, hoaxer, practical joker, jokester

prat n
idiot, fool, imbecile, fat-head, dunce, dimwit, simpleton, halfwit, cretin, clown, ignoramus, oaf, innocent
COLLOQ. thickhead, numskull, nincompoop, ass, chump, ninny, clot, dope, twit, nitwit, nit, sucker, mug, twerp, birdbrain, berk, dum-dum, knuckle-head, lamebrain
SLANG jerk, nerd, wally, muppet, dumbo, pillock, dork, geek, plonker; (*taboo*) prick, dickhead

prattle v, n
♦ v
chat, chatter, gabble, babble, jabber, rattle, twitter, twaddle, twattle, patter, drivel, gossip; *Scot* blether; *dialect & N Am* blather
COLLOQ. blabber, witter
♦ n
chat, chatter, gossip, talk, babble, jaw, gab, tattle, nonsense, prating, gibberish, foolishness, drivel; *Scot* blether; *dialect & N Am* blather
COLLOQ. hot air

prattler n
chatterer, talker, gossip, gabbler, babbler, tatler, tattler, magpie; *Scot* blether
COLLOQ. blabbermouth, chatterbox, loudmouth, windbag
᠊ clam

pray v
1 *pray to God*
invoke, call on, commune with, talk to, speak to, say a prayer, be at prayer, say your prayers, praise, worship, adore, confess, thank
TECHNICAL daven
OLD beseech, bid, wrestle with God
FORMAL imprecate, supplicate
2 ENTREAT, implore, plead, beg, petition, ask, request, crave, solicit
OLD beseech
FORMAL supplicate

prayer n
1 *prayer to God*
collect, litany, devotion, doxology, communion, invocation, fellowship, intercession, praise, worship, adoration, confession, thanksgiving, mantra, novena
FORMAL imprecation, supplication, orison
2 ENTREATY, plea, appeal, petition, request
FORMAL supplication

Prayers include:

Act of Contrition	Ave Maria	Habdalah (or
adhan	Benedictus	Havdalah)
Agnus Dei	Confiteor	Hail Mary
Amidah	Divine Office	Kaddhish
Angelus	Gloria	khutbah (or
Ardas	grace	khotbah)
Kol Nidre	Om	shahadah
Kyrie eleison	Our Father	Shema
Lord's Prayer	Paternoster	Sursum Corda
Lychnapsia	requiescat	Yizkor
Magnificat	Rosary	
Nunc Dimittis	salat	

---

prayer-book n
ordinal, service-book, Book of Common Prayer, Alternative Service Book, liturgy, missal, breviary, mahzor, euchologion, euchology, formulary, Triodion

preach v
address, lecture, teach, proclaim, harangue, pontificate, sermonize, evangelize, give a sermon, spread the gospel, moralize, exhort, advise, admonish, urge, advocate
OLD prophesy, sermon, predicate
COLLOQ. preachify

preacher n
minister, clergyman, parson, evangelist, televangelist, missionary, apostle, revivalist, lay preacher, local preacher, sermonizer, moralizer, licentiate, predicant, predikant, ranter, homilist, pontificater, gospeller, prophet, itinerant, open-air preacher, field preacher, tent preacher, spintext, mullah, Boanerges; *Scot* probationer
OLD circuit rider, pulpit(e)er, martext
COLLOQ. Bible-pounder, Bible-thumper, Bible-basher, tub-thumper, holy Joe, Holy Roller
SLANG devil-dodger

preaching n
teaching, instruction, doctrine, precepts, message, homiletics, homilies, dogma, gospel, sermons, sermonizing, pulpit, open-air/tent preaching, evangelism, pontificating
TECHNICAL evangel, kerygma
OLD prophecy
FORMAL exhortation
COLLOQ. Bible-bashing, tub-thumping
Related adjective: homiletic

preachy adj
moralizing, moralistic, pontificating, sermonizing, religiose, pietistic, pharisaic, pontifical, sanctimonious, self-righteous, pious, dogmatic, didactic, edifying, homiletic
FORMAL exhortatory, hortatory
COLLOQ. holier-than-thou, pi

preamble n
introduction, lead-in, preliminaries, preparation, prelude, foreword, preface, prologue, overture
FORMAL exordium, proem, prolegomenon
᠊ postscript, epilogue

prearrange v
arrange in advance, arrange beforehand, plan ahead, pre-plan, prepare, prepare beforehand, prepare in advance, organize, schedule, diarize
FORMAL predetermine

precarious adj
unsafe, dangerous, treacherous, risky, hazardous, chancy, uncertain, unsure, unsettled, dubious, doubtful, unpredictable, unreliable, undependable, unsteady, unstable, shaky, wobbly, insecure, vulnerable
COLLOQ. dicey, dodgy, hairy, iffy, dicky
᠊ safe, certain, stable, secure

precariously adv
dangerously, riskily, unsafely, hazardously, insecurely, unsteadily, unstably, shakily, unpredictably, unreliably
᠊ safely, securely

precaution n
safeguard, security, preventive/preventative measure, protection, insurance, providence, forethought, care, caution, prudence, attentiveness, foresight, farsightedness, anticipation, preparation, provision
FORMAL circumspection

precautionary *adj*
safety, protective, preventive, preventative,
provident, prudent, cautious, far-sighted, preparatory,
preliminary
FORMAL judicious

precede *v*
come before, lead, come first, go before,
go ahead of, take precedence, introduce,
herald, usher in, head, forego, preface,
prelude
OLD anticipate, prevent, prevene
FORMAL antecede, antedate
E3 follow, succeed

precedence *n*
priority, preference, pride of place, superiority,
supremacy, eminence, pre-eminence, lead, first place,
seniority, rank, right of way
FORMAL ascendancy
■ **take precedence over**
take priority over, come before, be more important than

precedent *n*
example, instance, case, parallel, pattern, model, standard,
criterion, yardstick
FORMAL paradigm, exemplar

preceding *adj*
above, earlier, former, past, previous, prior, precedent,
foregoing, antecedent
FORMAL aforementioned, aforesaid, supra, precursive,
anterior
E3 following, later

precept *n*
principle, axiom, command, commandment, charge,
direction, directive, ordinance, regulation, guideline, order,
injunction, institute, law, instruction, decree, dictum,
mandate, doctrine, rule, statute, convention, canon,
maxim, motto, saying, sentence, rubric

precinct *n*
1 ZONE, area, district, quarter, sector, division, section,
shopping centre, mall, galleria, food court
2 BOUNDARY, limit, bound, confine, enclosure, close,
court, neighbourhood, surrounds, locality, vicinity,
environs, milieu, verge, purlieus
3 *the precinct of a cathedral*
close, enclosure, land(s), building(s)
TECHNICAL temenos, vihara

preciosity *n*
artificiality, pretentiousness, floweriness, over-refinement,
affectation, tweeness, chichi

precious *adj*
1 VALUED, treasured, prized, cherished, beloved,
dear, dearest, darling, favourite, loved, revered, adored,
idolized
2 VALUABLE, expensive, costly, high-priced, dear, priceless,
inestimable, rare, choice, fine
3 AFFECTED, overrefined, simulated, contrived, artificial,
mannered, pretentious, flowery, twee, chichi

precipice *n*
cliff, cliff face, bluff, brink, steep, escarpment,
crag, drop, sheer drop, height, escarp,
scarp, krantz

precipitate *v, adj*
♦ *v*
1 HASTEN, hurry, speed (up), accelerate, quicken, expedite,
advance, further, bring about, bring on, induce, trigger,
cause, occasion
2 THROW, plunge, hurl, shoot, heave, thrust, fling
♦ *adj*
sudden, unexpected, abrupt, quick, swift, speedy, rapid,
brief, hasty, hurried, headlong, breakneck, frantic, violent,
impatient, hot-headed, impetuous, impulsive, rash,
reckless, heedless, indiscreet
OLD precipitant, precipitous
E3 cautious, careful

⚠ **precipitate** or **precipitous**?
Precipitate means 'hasty or too hasty': *precipitate
decision. Precipitous* means 'very steep, like a
precipice': *The path through the mountains is narrow
and precipitous.*

---

precipitately *adv*
suddenly, unexpectedly, abruptly, quickly, rapidly, hastily,
frantically, violently, recklessly, rashly, impulsively,
impetuously
E3 carefully, cautiously

precipitous *adj*
steep, sheer, perpendicular, vertical, abrupt, sharp,
high, sudden
E3 gradual

⚠ **precipitous** or **precipitate**?
See panel at **precipitate**.

---

précis *n, v*
♦ *n*
summary, abridgement, contraction, abbreviation,
condensation, synopsis, abstract, digest, epitome, outline,
résumé, sketch, compendium, run-down, table
FORMAL conspectus, encapsulation
♦ *v*
summarize, shorten, sum up, outline, abstract, abridge,
condense, synopsize, digest, abbreviate, encapsulate,
epitomize, contract, compress
E3 amplify, expand

precise *adj*
exact, accurate, right, punctilious, correct, factual, faithful,
authentic, literal, word-for-word, actual, express, definite,
explicit, very, specific, particular, unequivocal,
unambiguous, clear-cut, distinct, detailed, blow-by-blow,
minute, nice, fixed, rigid, strict, tight, careful, scrupulous,
meticulous, conscientious, rigorous, fastidious, finical,
formal, starchy, narrow, prim, priggish, ceremonious, dry,
razor, surgical, buckram; *Scot* preceese
OLD punctual
E3 imprecise, inexact, indefinite, ambiguous, careless

precisely *adv*
1 *one o'clock precisely; speak precisely*
exactly, absolutely, just so, accurately, on the dot, dead
on, correctly, literally, verbatim, word for word, strictly,
minutely, clearly, distinctly; *N Am* on the button
COLLOQ. bang on, spot-on, plumb, slap, smack, to a T
2 YES, exactly, quite, of course, just so, indeed, absolutely,
agreed, certainly, right, that's right, true
COLLOQ. you got it

precision *n*
preciseness, exactness, exactitude, accuracy,
correctness, faithfulness, explicitness, distinctness, detail,
particularity, rigour, care, reliability, meticulousness,
scrupulousness, punctiliousness, conscientiousness,
neatness, fastidiousness
E3 imprecision, inaccuracy

preclude *v*
prevent, exclude, eliminate, rule out, hinder,
inhibit, prohibit, restrain, stop, avoid, check, debar,
forestall
FORMAL obviate
E3 incur, involve

precocious *adj*
forward, ahead, far ahead, advanced,
advanced/old for your age, early, premature, mature,
developed, gifted, talented, clever, bright, brilliant, smart,
quick, fast
E3 backward, slow, stupid

preconceive *v*
presuppose, presume, assume, anticipate, project, imagine,
conceive, envisage, expect, visualize, picture
FORMAL predetermine, ideate

preconception n
presupposition, presumption, assumption, notion, idea, anticipation, expectation, prejudgement, bias, prejudice
FORMAL conjecture, predisposition

precondition n
condition, stipulation, requirement, prerequisite, essential, necessity
FORMAL sine qua non
COLLOQ. must

precursor n
forerunner, antecedent, sign, indication, prelude, herald, messenger, usher, morning star, pioneer, trailblazer, way-maker, curtain-raiser, ancestor, forebear
FORMAL progenitor, harbinger
🗷 follower, successor

precursory adj
preceding, warning, introductory, antecedent, preliminary, preparatory, previous, prior, prefatory, anterior
FORMAL preambulatory, precursive, preludial, prelusive, prevenient, prodromal
🗷 following, resulting, subsequent

predatory adj
hunting, preying, voracious, carnivorous, greedy, acquisitive, avaricious, covetous, despoiling, thieving, ravaging, plundering, marauding, pillaging, wolfish, lupine, vulturine, vulturous
FORMAL predacious, predative, rapacious, raptatorial, raptorial

predecessor n
ancestor, forefather, forebear, antecedent, forerunner, precursor
FORMAL progenitor
🗷 successor, descendant

predestination n
destiny, fate, lot, doom, foreordination
FORMAL predetermination

predestine v
intend, mean, destine, fate, preordain, predetermine, pre-elect, doom, foredoom
FORMAL foreordain, predestinate

predetermined adj
1 PREDESTINED, destined, fated, doomed, ordained
FORMAL foreordained
2 PREARRANGED, arranged, agreed, fixed, set, settled

predicament n
situation, plight, trouble, mess, pass, quandary, dilemma, impasse, crisis, emergency, box
OLD taking
COLLOQ. spot, tight spot, scrape, pickle, jam, fix, hiccup, hole, stew, hot/deep water, kettle of fish, how-d'ye-do, cart, chancery, praemunire

predicate v
1 ASSERT, affirm, state, declare, proclaim, contend
FORMAL aver, avouch, avow, posit, postulate, premise
2 BE DEPENDENT, rest, base, build, found, establish, maintain, ground

predict v
forecast, foretell, prophesy, foresee, bet, project
TECHNICAL cast
OLD warrant
FORMAL prognosticate, vaticinate, augur, portend, presage, divine, auspicate
COLLOQ. second-guess

predictable adj
foreseeable, expected, anticipated, likely, probable, imaginable, foreseen, foregone, certain, sure, reliable, dependable, unsurprising, usual, customary
COLLOQ. on the cards, odds-on
🗷 unpredictable, unforeseeable, uncertain

prediction n
prophecy, forecast, prognosis, fortune-telling, soothsaying
FORMAL augury, divination, prognostication, auspication

predictive adj
prophetic, foretelling, diagnostic
FORMAL augural, divinatory, prognostic

predilection n
fondness, preference, inclination, leaning, liking, affection, love, partiality, tendency, bent, bias, enthusiasm, fancy, taste, affinity, soft spot, weakness
FORMAL penchant, predisposition, proclivity, propensity
🗷 dislike, disinclination; formal antipathy

predispose v
dispose, incline, prompt, induce, make, make liable, sway, move, influence, persuade, affect, bias, prejudice

predisposed adj
inclined, liable, prepared, ready, susceptible, willing, disposed, well-disposed, minded, not unwilling, subject, agreeable, amenable, favourable, prone, biased, prejudiced
🗷 unwilling, reluctant, loath

predisposition n
likelihood, inclination, leaning, tendency, preference, disposition, bent, proneness, willingness, liability, susceptibility, vulnerability, bias, prejudice
FORMAL penchant, potentiality, predilection, proclivity, propensity

predominance n
dominance, dominion, power, control, leadership, mastery, prevalence, superiority, supremacy, influence, sway, weight, hold, numbers
FORMAL hegemony, ascendancy, paramountcy, preponderance, prepotence, prepotency, prepollence, prepollency
COLLOQ. edge, upper hand
🗷 ineffectiveness, weakness

predominant adj
dominant, prevailing, chief, main, principal, primary, capital, paramount, supreme, sovereign, ruling, controlling, in control, leading, powerful, potent, prime, important, most important, influential, forceful, strong, most noticeable, most obvious
FORMAL preponderant, ascendant, in the ascendancy
🗷 minor, lesser, weak

predominantly adv
mainly, primarily, principally, chiefly, in the main, mostly, on the whole, for the most part, generally, in general, especially, as a rule, by and large, commonly, usually, above all, largely, overall

predominate v
prevail, dominate, outnumber, be in the majority, outweigh, override, overrule, overshadow, transcend, tell, reign, rule
FORMAL obtain, preponderate

pre-eminence n
supremacy, distinction, excellence, fame, prestige, renown, repute, predominance, prominence, superiority, incomparability, peerlessness, matchlessness, paramountcy, transcendence

pre-eminent adj
supreme, unsurpassed, unrivalled, unequalled, unmatched, matchless, incomparable, inimitable, chief, first, most important, foremost, leading, eminent, distinguished, renowned, famous, prominent, outstanding, exceptional, excellent, superlative, transcendent, superior
🗷 inferior, unknown

pre-eminently adv
especially, notably, particularly, exceptionally, eminently, signally, superlatively, singularly, strikingly, surpassingly, par excellence, exclusively, supremely, primarily, principally, emphatically, conspicuously, incomparably, inimitably, matchlessly, peerlessly

pre-empt *v*
prevent, forestall, anticipate, assume, acquire, secure, seize, usurp
FORMAL appropriate, arrogate

preen *v*
1 CLEAN, smooth, groom, plume, trim, spruce up, dress up, trick out, slick, prettify, adorn, beautify, deck, primp, prink; *N Am* trick up
FORMAL array
COLLOQ. do up, doll up, tart up
2 CONGRATULATE, pride, exult, bask, plume, gloat, pique
COLLOQ. pat yourself on the back

preface *n, v*
♦ *n*
foreword, introduction, preamble, prologue, prelude, frontmatter, preliminaries
FORMAL proem, prolegomenon, exordium
COLLOQ. prelims
☒ epilogue, postscript
Related adjective: prefatory
♦ *v*
precede, prefix, lead up to, introduce, launch, open, begin, start
☒ end, finish, complete

prefatory *adj*
introductory, opening, preparatory, preliminary, explanatory, antecedent
FORMAL exordial, preambulatory, precursory, prefatorial, preludial, prelusive, prelusory, proemial, prolegomenal
☒ closing, final

prefect *n*
monitor, administrator, supervisor, praeposter, prepositor, praefect

prefer *v*
1 *I prefer tea to coffee*
favour, like better, would rather, would sooner, be partial to, want, wish, desire, choose, select, pick (out), opt (for), go for, single out, advocate, recommend, back, support, elect, adopt
FORMAL elect
COLLOQ. plump for, fancy
2 PROMOTE, favour, advance, move up, raise, elevate, exalt, honour
FORMAL aggrandize
3 *prefer charges*
bring, file, lodge, press, present, place
☒ **1** reject **2** demote

preferable *adj*
better, superior, nicer, preferred, favoured, more desired, chosen, desirable, advantageous, advisable, recommended
☒ inferior, undesirable

preferably *adv*
rather, much rather, if possible, ideally, sooner, much sooner, from choice, for choice, by/for preference, first

preference *n*
1 FAVOURITE, first choice, choice, pick, selection, option, wish, desire
COLLOQ. cup of tea; *N Am* druthers
2 LIKING, fancy, inclination, will, bent, leaning, bias, discrimination, partiality, favouritism, priority, precedence, preferential treatment, fad, forehand
OLD pre-election
FORMAL predilection
COLLOQ. kink
OLD SLANG mark
■ **in preference to**
rather than, instead of, in place of, before, by/for/from choice

preferential *adj*
better, superior, favoured, privileged, special, favourable, advantageous, partial, partisan, biased
☒ equal

preferment *n*
promotion, advancement, furtherance, improvement, rise, step up, betterment, dignity, elevation, exaltation, upgrading
FORMAL aggrandizement
☒ demotion

preferred *adj*
favoured, selected, approved, choice, chosen, desired, recommended, authorized, sanctioned
FORMAL predilect
☒ rejected, undesirable

prefigure *v*
foreshadow, signal, indicate, signify, mean, suggest, promise, predict, prophesy
FORMAL bode, presage, augur, portend, prognosticate

pregnancy *n*
child-bearing, conception, fertilization, impregnation, gestation
TECHNICAL parturition
OLD being with child
FORMAL gravidity
COLLOQ. family way

pregnant *adj*
1 *a pregnant woman*
expectant, expecting, big-bellied
TECHNICAL parturient, gravid
OLD with child, great, quick, in an interesting condition/state/situation; (*Shakesp*) great-bellied
FORMAL enceinte
COLLOQ. in the family way, in the club, in a certain condition, in trouble
SLANG preggers, with a bun in the oven, up the spout, in the pudding club, up the duff
2 *a pregnant pause*
meaningful, significant, eloquent, rich, expressive, suggestive, telling, pointed, charged, loaded, heavy, full, filled, fraught
FORMAL replete

prehistoric *adj*
primitive, earliest, early, ancient, archaic, antiquated, antediluvian, old, obsolete, out-of-date, outmoded
FORMAL prim(a)eval, primordial
COLLOQ. out of the ark, before the flood
☒ modern

prejudge *v*
judge prematurely, anticipate, presume, assume, presuppose, forejudge
FORMAL predetermine, prejudicate

prejudice *n, v*
♦ *n*
1 BIAS, partiality, partisanship, discrimination, preference, one-sidedness, unfairness, injustice, intolerance, narrow-mindedness, bigotry, chauvinism, racism, sexism, misogyny, ageism, xenophobia, misanthropy, anti-Semitism
2 HARM, damage, impairment, hurt, injury, detriment, disadvantage, loss, ruin
☒ **1** fairness, tolerance **2** benefit, advantage
♦ *v*
1 BIAS, incline, sway, influence, condition, colour, jaundice, slant, distort, load, weight
FORMAL predispose
2 HARM, damage, impair, be detrimental to, be disadvantageous to, hinder, undermine, hurt, injure, mar, spoil, ruin, wreck
☒ **2** benefit, help, advance

> **QUOTATIONS**
> Drive out prejudices through the door, and they will return through the window
> FREDERICK THE GREAT

prejudiced adj

biased, partial, subjective, partisan, one-sided, slanted, discriminatory, unfair, unjust, loaded, weighted, intolerant, narrow-minded, bigoted, blinkered, chauvinist, chauvinistic, xenophobic, anti-Semitic, racist, sexist, ageist, jaundiced, distorted, warped, influenced, conditioned, insular, parochial, illiberal, prepossessed

TECHNICAL ex parte
OLD prejudicial
FORMAL predisposed
E3 impartial, fair, tolerant

prejudicial adj

harmful, damaging, hurtful, injurious, detrimental, disadvantageous, counter-productive, unfavourable, inimical
FORMAL deleterious, noxious
E3 beneficial, advantageous

preliminary adj, n

• adj
preparatory, prior, advance, exploratory, experimental, trial, test, pilot, early, earliest, first, initial, beginning, primary, qualifying, inaugural, introductory, opening, prefatory
FORMAL precursory, exordial
E3 final, closing

• n
preparation, groundwork, foundations, basics, rudiments, formalities, introduction, preface, foreword, prelude, preamble, opening, beginning, start
FORMAL proem, exordium, prolegomenon, prodrome

prelude n

overture, introduction, preface, foreword, preamble, prologue, opening, opener, preliminary, preparation, beginning, start, forerunner, herald, precursor, curtain-raiser
FORMAL proem, exordium, prolegomenon, prodrome, commencement, harbinger
E3 finale, epilogue
Related adjectives: preludial, preludious, proemial

premature adj

1 a premature baby
COLLOQ. prem; N Am preemie
2 her premature death
early, soon, too early, too soon, untimely
3 it is premature to dismiss the suggestion
hasty, ill-considered, rash, impetuous, impulsive, precipitate, inopportune, untimely, ill-timed
COLLOQ. jumping the gun
E3 **1** overdue, late **2** timely, overdue **3** well-timed, timely

prematurely adv

1 born prematurely
early, too early, too soon
2 a decision taken prematurely
early, too early, too soon, incompletely, hastily, impulsively, rashly, impetuously

premeditated adj

planned, intended, intentional, deliberate, wilful, conscious, cold-blooded, calculated, considered, contrived, preplanned, prearranged, predetermined
E3 unpremeditated, spontaneous

premeditation n

planning, prearrangement, purpose, intention, deliberation, deliberateness, determination, forethought, design, scheming, plotting
TECHNICAL malice aforethought
OLD aforethought
FORMAL predetermination
E3 impulse, spontaneity

premier n, adj

• n
head of government, prime minister, chief minister, first minister, chancellor, secretary of state

• adj
principal, leading, highest, top, head, foremost, chief, primary, prime, main, supreme, paramount, pre-eminent, first, cardinal, earliest, original, initial

première n

first performance, first showing, opening, opening night, first night, debut

premise n, v

• n
proposition, statement, assertion, thesis, argument, basis, supposition, hypothesis, assumption
FORMAL presupposition, postulate

• v
lay down, state, assert, assume, stipulate, take as true, presuppose, hypothesize
FORMAL posit, postulate, predicate

premises n

building, property, establishment, office, grounds, estate, site, place

premium n

1 pay an insurance premium
regular payment, instalment
2 SURCHARGE, extra sum/charge, overcharging, bonus
COLLOQ. an arm and a leg, daylight robbery
■ **at a premium**
scarce, rare, hard to come by, in short supply, in great demand, few and far between
COLLOQ. like gold dust
■ **put a premium on**
value greatly, treasure, appreciate, favour, hold dear, attach great/special importance to, regard highly, set great store by

premonition n

feeling, intuition, sixth sense, hunch, idea, suspicion, sneaking suspicion, foreboding, misgiving, fear, apprehension, anxiety, worry, warning, omen, sign
OLD prevention
FORMAL presentiment, presage, portent
COLLOQ. feeling in your bones, funny feeling, gut feeling

preoccupation n

1 OBSESSION, fixation, concern, interest, enthusiasm, hobby-horse
COLLOQ. hang-up, thing, bee in your bonnet, one-track mind
2 DISTRACTION, absent-mindedness, daydreaming, reverie, abstraction, heedlessness, obliviousness, oblivion, inattentiveness, wool-gathering, pensiveness, absorption, engrossment

preoccupied adj

1 OBSESSED, intent, immersed, engrossed, absorbed, engaged, fixated, taken up, wrapped up, involved, pensive, deep in thought
2 DISTRACTED, abstracted, absent-minded, daydreaming, absorbed, faraway, heedless, oblivious
FORMAL distrait

preoccupy v

occupy, absorb, engage, take up, involve, obsess, fixate, prepossess, occupy the attention of
COLLOQ. eat (up)

preordain v

destine, prearrange, foreordain, doom, fate
FORMAL predestine, predetermine

preparation n

1 preparations for the wedding; in preparation for the event
planning, plan, arrangement, organization, development, basics, rudiments, preliminaries, readiness, provision, supply, equipping, assembly, composition, construction, production, homework, foundation, groundwork, spadework
2 TRAINING, coaching, study, revision, practice
3 MIXTURE, compound, composition, concoction, potion, medicine, lotion, application, cosmetic

preparatory adj
preliminary, introductory, opening, initial, primary, basic, fundamental, rudimentary, elementary
FORMAL precursory, prefatory
■ **preparatory to**
before, in advance of, in anticipation of, in expectation of, previous to, prior to, in preparation for, as a preparation for

prepare v
1 GET READY, make ready, make preparations for, set up, plan, organize, arrange, adjust, provide, supply, equip, fit out, rig out, prime, put together, construct, assemble, concoct, contrive, devise, draft, fashion, draw up, compose, pave the way, do your homework for, lay the foundations for, lay the groundwork for, do the spadework for, take the necessary steps for, set the scene for
COLLOQ. gear up, psych up, tee up
2 TRAIN, teach, instruct, exercise, coach, study, practise, prime, warm up, get into shape, make ready
3 *prepare a meal*
make, produce, concoct, put together, throw together, get ready; N Am fix
■ **prepare yourself**
brace yourself, steel yourself, gird yourself
FORMAL fortify yourself, gird up your loins

prepared adj
ready, willing, disposed, waiting, set, fit, inclined, arranged, planned, organized, in order, fixed
FORMAL predisposed
ⅎ unprepared, unready

preparedness n
readiness, preparation, order, fitness, alertness, anticipation, expectancy
ⅎ unreadiness

preponderance n
dominance, supremacy, greater number, superiority, majority, bulk, mass, extensiveness, prevalence, predominance, domination, dominion, power, force, sway, weight
FORMAL ascendancy
COLLOQ. lion's share

preponderant adj
greater, larger, superior, predominant, dominant, prevailing, overriding, overruling, controlling, foremost, important, significant

preponderate v
dominate, predominate, prevail, be in the majority, outnumber, override, overrule, rule, tell, weigh with, turn the balance, turn the scales

prepossessing adj
attractive, charming, good-looking, winning, winsome, appealing, beautiful, likeable, lov(e)able, amiable, delightful, fair, handsome, pleasing, striking, captivating, bewitching, enchanting, engaging, inviting, alluring, magnetic, fascinating, fetching, taking
ⅎ unattractive, unprepossessing

preposterous adj
incredible, unbelievable, absurd, ridiculous, ludicrous, foolish, farcical, crazy, nonsensical, irrational, unreasonable, senseless, monstrous, shocking, outrageous, asinine, intolerable, unthinkable, impossible
ⅎ sensible, reasonable, acceptable

preposterously adv
absurdly, ludicrously, ridiculously, incredibly, unbelievably, unreasonably, shockingly, outrageously, intolerably

prerequisite n, adj
♦ n
condition, proviso, qualification, requirement, imperative, necessity, essential
FORMAL precondition, requisite, sine qua non
COLLOQ. must
ⅎ extra

♦ adj
indispensable, necessary, obligatory, required, needed, needful, essential, basic, fundamental, vital, imperative
FORMAL mandatory, requisite
ⅎ unnecessary, superfluous

prerogative n
privilege, right, authority, advantage, choice, sanction, exemption, immunity, liberty, due, claim, entitlement, licence, carte blanche, birthright, royalty
TECHNICAL droit
OLD purvey

presage v, n
♦ v
indicate, point to, be a sign of, be an indication of, warn of, announce, forecast, predict, foretell, promise, signify, threaten, herald, foretoken
FORMAL augur, portend, bode, forebode, foreshadow, forewarn, harbinger, bespeak, betoken, adumbrate, prognosticate
♦ n
sign, indication, warning, threat, omen, precursor, forecast, foreboding, forerunner, prefiguration, premonition
FORMAL augury, portent, signification, prognostication, foreshadowing, forewarning, prognostic, presentiment, harbinger

prescience n
foreknowledge, foresight, far-sightedness, second sight, prophecy, clairvoyance, propheticness
FORMAL precognition, prevision

prescient adj
foreknowing, far-sighted, far-seeing, prophetic, foresighted, perceptive, discerning, clairvoyant, divinatory, divining, psychic
FORMAL previsional
ⅎ imperceptive

prescribe v
1 *prescribe medicine*
advise, specify, stipulate
2 *prescribe a duty*
ordain, decree, dictate, rule, command, order, require, direct, specify, stipulate, lay down, set, appoint, impose, fix, define, limit

> **⚠ prescribe or proscribe?**
> To *prescribe* is to advise or order: *The doctor prescribed a course of antibiotics; The law prescribes severe penalties for such offences.* To *proscribe* is to ban, outlaw or forbid: *This book was formerly proscribed by the church; Such actions are proscribed by law.*

prescribed adj
laid down, specified, stipulated, set, ordained, assigned, decreed
FORMAL formulary

prescription n
1 INSTRUCTION, direction, formula, recipe, advice, recommendation, guideline(s)
2 MEDICINE, drug, preparation, mixture, remedy, treatment, concoction
TECHNICAL optometry
OLD leechdom

prescriptive adj
dictatorial, legislating, prescribing, didactic, dogmatic, rigid, authoritarian, customary
FORMAL preceptive

presence n
1 ATTENDANCE, company, companionship, occupancy, residence, existence, being
2 AURA, air, appearance, dignity, poise, self-confidence, self-assurance, attraction, personality, charisma, appeal, magnetism
FORMAL demeanour, bearing, carriage
3 NEARNESS, closeness, proximity, neighbourhood, vicinity

FORMAL propinquity
4 SPIRIT, ghost, phantom, spectre, apparition, visitant, shadow
▣ **1** absence **3** remoteness, distance
■ **presence of mind**
calmness, self-possession, composure, coolness, self-assurance, self-command, level-headedness, alertness, aplomb, equanimity, poise
FORMAL imperturbability, sangfroid
COLLOQ. cool, unflappability
▣ agitation, confusion

present[1] *adj*
1 ATTENDING, in attendance, here, there, near, nearby, at hand, close at hand, to hand, available, ready, existing
2 *at the present time*
current, contemporary, present-day, immediate, instant, existent, existing
▣ **1** absent, far away **2** past, out-of-date
■ **the present day**
today, now, nowadays, at this time, currently, here and now
■ **at present**
at the moment, now, just now, at this time, today, currently
■ **for the present**
for the time being, for the moment, for now, in the meantime, pro tem

present[2] *v*
1 AWARD, grant, give, donate, hand over, entrust, extend, hold out
FORMAL confer, bestow
2 OFFER, tender, submit, put forward
FORMAL proffer
3 SHOW, display, put on display, exhibit, demonstrate, organize, mount, stage, perform, put on, introduce, host, make known
4 *present a television show*
introduce, compère, host, announce
5 *the story presents her sympathetically*
describe, depict, represent, portray, characterize, picture
FORMAL delineate
■ **present yourself**
1 *present yourself somewhere*
appear, arrive, attend, show up, turn up
COLLOQ. pop up
2 *an idea presents itself*
occur, arise, crop up, emerge, materialize, come to light, happen

present[3] *n*
Christmas presents
gift, offering, donation, contribution, handout, award, grant, endowment, bounty, largesse, gratuity, tip, favour
FORMAL benefaction
COLLOQ. prezzie, freebie, perk, sweetener

> **QUOTATIONS**
> Christmas won't be Christmas without any presents
> LOUISA MAY ALCOTT, *Little Women*

presentable *adj*
1 NEAT, tidy, clean, smart, smartly dressed, spruce, respectable, decent
2 QUITE GOOD, satisfactory, tolerable, passable, acceptable
▣ **1** untidy, shabby

presentation *n*
1 APPEARANCE, arrangement, organization, structure, system, layout, form, format, packaging
2 AWARD, awarding, presenting, granting, donating, investiture
FORMAL conferral, bestowal
3 TALK, address, lecture, speech, seminar, demonstration
FORMAL disquisition
4 SHOW, performance, production, staging, showing, mounting, representation, rendition, recital, display,

exhibition, demonstration, introduction, making known, launch

present-day *adj*
current, present, existing, living, contemporary, modern, up-to-date, fashionable, latest
▣ past, future

presenter *n*
host, announcer, compère, anchor, anchorman, anchorwoman, frontman, master of ceremonies, MC
COLLOQ. emcee

presentiment *n*
premonition, intuition, apprehension, fear, feeling, misgiving, hunch, anticipation, foreboding, expectation, forecast, forethought
OLD bodement
FORMAL forebodement, presage, presension
COLLOQ. bad vibes

presently *adv*
1 SOON, shortly, in a short time, in a short while, in a minute, in a moment, in a second, before long, by and by
COLLOQ. in a jiffy, pronto, in a mo, in a tick, in two shakes of a lamb's tail, before you can say Jack Robinson
2 CURRENTLY, at present, now, at the moment, at the present time, these days, at this moment in time

preservation *n*
protection, defence, maintenance, keeping, guarding, safeguarding, safekeeping, safety, security, conservation, storage, upkeep, support, retention, upholding, continuation, perpetuation, reservation
▣ destruction, ruin

preserve *v, n*
♦ *v*
1 PROTECT, safeguard, guard, defend, shield, shelter, care for, look after, take care of, maintain, uphold, secure, sustain, continue, perpetuate, commemorate, keep, retain, conserve, reserve, save, store, lay up, cocoon, embalm; *Scot* hain
OLD salve
2 *preserve food*
bottle, tin, can, chill, freeze, freeze-dry, quick-freeze, pickle, salt, cure, dry, desiccate, smoke, kipper, candy, corn; *dialect* put down
OLD confect
3 *preserve timber*
season, creosote, kyanize, powellize
▣ **1** destroy, ruin
♦ *n*
1 *home made preserves*
conserve, jam, marmalade, jelly, pickle, sweetmeat, chow-chow; *S Afr* konfyt
2 DOMAIN, realm, sphere, area, field, speciality
3 RESERVATION, sanctuary, reserve, game reserve, nature reserve, safari park, chase, forest

preside *v*
chair, be in the chair, be the chairman/chairwoman/chairperson of, officiate, conduct, direct, manage, administer, control, run, head, lead, govern, rule, be responsible for, be in charge of
COLLOQ. head up, call the shots

president *n*
head of state, ruler, leader, controller, governor, head, director, manager, principal, chief
COLLOQ. prez, boss
Related adjective: presidial

press *v, n*
♦ *v*
1 CRUSH, squash, squeeze, mash, pinch, knead, compress, stuff, jam, cram, crowd, push (down), depress, surge, swarm, throng, trample
2 *press clothes*
iron, smooth (out), flatten, roll
3 HUG, embrace, clasp, enfold, hold close, grasp, squeeze, caress, cuddle, crush

4 URGE, plead, petition, campaign, demand, call for, insist on, exhort, entreat, implore, push for, push forward, compel, constrain, force, coerce, pressure, pressurize, put pressure on, harass, besiege, afflict, vex, worry, trouble
FORMAL supplicate
COLLOQ. sweet-talk, fast-talk, soft-soap, twist someone's arm, lean on, put/turn/tighten the screws on, swing it, pull strings
♦ *n*
1 CROWD, throng, multitude, mob, horde, troop, swarm, pack, crush, flock, push
2 JOURNALISTS, reporters, correspondents, photographers, paparazzi, newspapermen, newspaperwomen, pressmen, presswomen, the media, news media, newspapers, papers, Fleet Street, journalism, fourth estate
COLLOQ. hacks
3 PRINTING PRESS, printing-machine, rotary press
4 get a good/bad press
coverage, treatment, articles, reports, reviews, praise, criticism
■ **press on**
press ahead, continue, carry on, go on, keep going, persevere, go ahead, proceed, keep trying, plod on, slog away, peg away, toil (away)
COLLOQ. plug away, soldier on, stick at it

pressed *adj*
1 FORCED, pressured, pressurized, coerced, bullied, browbeaten, constrained, hurried, pushed, rushed, harassed
COLLOQ. bludgeoned, railroaded
2 be pressed for time
short of, having too little, not having enough, lacking, deficient in
☲ **1** unhurried **2** well-off

pressing *adj*
urgent, needing to be dealt with immediately, high-priority, burning, crucial, demanding, vital, essential, imperative, serious, important, critical, key
FORMAL exigent
☲ unimportant, trivial

pressure *n, v*
♦ *n*
1 FORCE, power, load, burden, weight, heaviness, compression, crushing, squeezing, stress, strain
2 COMPULSION, force, constraints, coercion, duress, bullying, harassment
3 STRESS, tension, strain, difficulty, problem, demand, adversity, burden, trouble, constraint, obligation
COLLOQ. hassle, aggro
♦ *v*
force, compel, constrain, oblige, drive, bulldoze, dragoon, coerce, press, pressurize, put pressure on, browbeat, bully
COLLOQ. lean on, put the screws on, sweet-talk, fast-talk, soft-soap, swing it, pull strings, twist someone's arm, railroad, bludgeon

pressurize *v*
force, compel, constrain, oblige, drive, bulldoze, dragoon, coerce, press, pressure, put pressure on, browbeat, bully
COLLOQ. lean on, put the screws on, sweet-talk, fast-talk, soft-soap, swing it, pull strings, twist someone's arm, railroad, bludgeon; *Aust & NZ* put the acid on

prestige *n*
status, reputation, standing, stature, eminence, distinction, regard, importance, authority, influence, fame, renown, esteem, kudos, credit, honour, izzat
☲ humbleness, unimportance

prestigious *adj*
respected, reputable, important, influential, distinguished, high-ranking, great, eminent, prominent, illustrious, esteemed, renowned, celebrated, famous, well-known, exalted, imposing, impressive, up-market
COLLOQ. blue-chip
☲ humble, modest, down-market

presumably *adv*
most likely, very likely, in all likelihood, in all probability, I presume, I guess, doubtless, doubtlessly, no doubt, probably, apparently, seemingly

presume *v*
1 ASSUME, take it, think, believe, imagine, suppose, surmise, infer, presuppose, hypothesize, deduce, take for granted, take as read
2 presume to criticize
dare, make so bold, have the audacity, take the liberty, go so far, venture, undertake, take upon yourself
■ **presume on**
count on, rely on, depend on, bank on, trust, take (unfair) advantage of, exploit

presumption *n*
1 ASSUMPTION, belief, opinion, surmise, deduction, inference, hypothesis, presupposition, supposition, conjecture, guess, likelihood, probability
2 PRESUMPTUOUSNESS, boldness, arrogance, effrontery, temerity, audacity, cheek, impertinence, impudence, insolence, forwardness, assurance
COLLOQ. nerve, sauce, gall, lip, mouth, neck, brass neck, chutzpah
☲ **2** humility

presumptive *adj*
expected, assumed, believed, designate, prospective, likely, possible, probable, reasonable, supposed, understood, believable, conceivable, hypothetical, credible, inferred, plausible
FORMAL conjectural
☲ known, unlikely

presumptuous *adj*
bold, audacious, impertinent, impudent, insolent, over-familiar, forward, arrogant, pushy, over-confident, conceited, cocky, cocksure
COLLOQ. cheeky, fresh, saucy, lippy, mouthy, bigheaded, too big for your boots
☲ humble, modest

presuppose *v*
assume, presume, necessitate, suppose, accept, consider, imply, take for granted
FORMAL posit, postulate, premise

presupposition *n*
assumption, presumption, belief, supposition, hypothesis, theory, preconception
FORMAL premise, premiss

pretence *n*
show, display, appearance, cover, front, charade, façade, veneer, cloak, veil, mask, masquerade, guise, sham, feigning, faking, false show, false colours, semblance, hypocrisy, simulation, deception, trickery, wile, ruse, excuse, pretext, bluff, falsehood, deceit, lie, fabrication, invention, acting, play-acting, make-believe, posturing, posing, showiness, ostentation, pretentiousness, profession, humbug, feint, daubery
FORMAL affectation, dissimulation, dissembling, pretension
☲ honesty, openness

SYNONYM NUANCES

Show and **display** can be used to suggest a false image, especially one projected for public consumption.
Charade has an element of the absurd about it: *they have finally ended their charade of a marriage;*
masquerade is similar, although more suggestive of an elaborate deception. **Façade** suggests a carefully contrived image and **veneer** an outward gloss which may be more easily seen through: *underneath her veneer of kindness there lay a devious imp.*

Both **cover** and **front** have stronger implications of keeping something undesirable hidden, as do **cloak**, **veil** and **mask**, which make this more explicit, while **guise** also implies presenting something in another form: *promoting his ambitions under the guise of revenge.*

Semblance is a straightforward term for appearing to be like, while **sham** implies a hollow display: *the country's democracy is a sham.* **Humbug** shares this idea of hollowness: *the humbug of suburban life.*

Simulation is a fairly neutral term for a recreation of something. **Feigning** and **faking** are far more disapproving in tone, like **deception**, **trickery**, **wile** and **ruse**, which all imply deliberate misleading. While you might use **invention** for something devised, **bluff** and **falsehood** would convey the same idea with more disapprobation.

The terms **acting**, **posturing** and **posing** return to the idea of presenting a false image, and again suggest mild disapproval, while the more negative terms **showiness**, **ostentation** and **pretentiousness** all make suggestions of vulgar affectation.

Hypocrisy is a strongly critical term, particularly relevant where someone's real views or actions belie the beliefs they profess.

pretend *v*
1 *pretend to be asleep*
put on, assume, feign, sham, counterfeit, fake, fabricate, simulate, bluff, impersonate, pass yourself off, act, play-act, put on an act, mime, go through the motions
OLD pass the bottle of smoke
FORMAL affect, dissemble
COLLOQ. keep up appearances
2 CLAIM, allege, profess
FORMAL purport
3 IMAGINE, make believe, suppose

pretended *adj*
artificial, put on, alleged, ostensible, professed, supposed, spurious, bogus, fake, false, feigned, sham, fictitious, counterfeit, so-called, imaginary, specious
FORMAL affected, avowed, purported, supposititious
COLLOQ. phoney, pretend, pseudo
☒ real

pretender *n*
claimant, aspirant, claimer, candidate

pretension *n*
1 PRETENTIOUSNESS, pomposity, self-importance, airs, conceit, vanity, snobbishness, hypocrisy, pretence, show, showiness, floweriness, ostentation
FORMAL affectation, magniloquence
2 CLAIM, profession, demand, aspiration, ambition
FORMAL purporting
☒ **1** modesty, humility, simplicity

pretentious *adj*
pompous, self-important, conceited, immodest, snobbish, mannered, flaunting, showy, ostentatious, extravagant, flamboyant, elaborate, exaggerated, high-sounding, uppish, chichi, twee, artificial, inflated, grandiose, ambitious, overambitious, kitschy; *Scot* fantoosh
OLD fine
FORMAL affected, magniloquent, vainglorious, bombastic
COLLOQ. over-the-top, OTT, pseud, pseudo, big
☒ modest, humble, simple, straightforward

pretentiously *adv*
pompously, self-importantly, snobbishly, ostentatiously, uppishly, showily, artificially, flamboyantly
☒ modestly, humbly

pretentiousness *n*
ostentation, posing, pretension, show, theatricality, floweriness, floridness, flamboyance, attitudinizing, ambitiousness, overambitiousness, uppishness, chichi, kitsch; *Scot* paraffle
FORMAL posturing
COLLOQ. pseudery, side
☒ humbleness, modesty, simplicity, straightforwardness

preternatural *adj*
extraordinary, unusual, exceptional, abnormal

pretext *n*
excuse, alleged/ostensible reason, ploy, ruse, cover, cloak, mask, veil, guise, sham, semblance, appearance, pretence, show
COLLOQ. red herring

> QUOTATIONS
> Tyrants seldom want pretexts
> EDMUND BURKE

prettify *v*
decorate, smarten up, ornament, adorn, beautify, bedeck, deck, deck out, embellish, gild, garnish, trick out, trim; *N Am* trick up
COLLOQ. do up, doll up, tart up
☒ mar, uglify

prettily *adv*
attractively, charmingly, beautifully, nicely, delightfully, pleasantly, engagingly, winsomely, gracefully, daintily, elegantly
☒ plainly, unattractively

pretty *adj, adv*
♦ *adj*
attractive, good-looking, beautiful, fair, lovely, delightful, nice, cute, pleasant, pleasing, engaging, personable, prepossessing, winsome, appealing, charming, handsome, dainty, graceful, elegant, fine, delicate, chocolate-box, twee; *dialect* purty; *Scot* bonny
OLD comely; *(Shakesp)* incony
☒ plain, unattractive, ugly
♦ *adv*
fairly, somewhat, rather, quite, reasonably, moderately, tolerably
COLLOQ. not half

prevail *v*
1 WIN, triumph, be victorious, succeed, overcome, overrule, override, conquer, reign, rule, gain mastery, have it
FORMAL gain ascendancy
COLLOQ. carry the day
2 PREDOMINATE, abound, hold sway, occur, be common, be customary, be present, be normal, be accepted, be current
FORMAL preponderate; obtain
☒ **1** lose

■ **prevail upon**
persuade, talk into, prompt, induce, incline, sway, influence, convince, urge, win over, bring round, pressure, pressurize
COLLOQ. sweet-talk, lean on, soft-soap, pull strings, twist someone's arm

prevailing *adj*
predominant, preponderant, main, principal, chief, supreme, dominant, controlling, powerful, compelling, influential, reigning, ruling, current, fashionable, in fashion, in style, in vogue, popular, mainstream, accepted, established, set, usual, most usual, customary, general, common, most common, average, prevalent, widespread
FORMAL prepotent, ascendant
☒ minor, subordinate

prevalence *n*
commonness, currency, frequency, order of the day, pervasiveness, acceptance, popularity, predominance, universality, regularity, rule, hold, mastery, sway, profusion
FORMAL ascendancy, omnipresence, preponderance, primacy, ubiquity
☒ uncommonness

prevalent *adj*
widespread, extensive, rampant, rife, pervasive, epidemic, frequent, general, customary, usual, universal, established, accepted, set, ubiquitous, common, vulgar, everyday, popular, current, prevailing, dominant
TECHNICAL enzootic

FORMAL endemic, regnant
⊟ uncommon, rare

prevaricate v
equivocate, quibble, evade, be evasive, shift,
shuffle, lie, deceive, stonewall
FORMAL cavil, tergiversate
COLLOQ. hedge, dodge, shilly-shally, waffle, pussyfoot,
beat about the bush, sit on the fence

> **❗ prevaricate or procrastinate?**
> To *prevaricate* is 'to talk evasively in order to avoid
> telling the truth, coming to the point, or answering a
> question': *When faced with difficult questions,
> politicians usually prevaricate.* To *procrastinate* is to put
> off until later things that should be done immediately.

prevarication n
evasion, equivocation, pretence, quibbling, lie, falsehood,
untruth, falsification, fibbing, fib(s), half-truth,
misrepresentation, deception, deceit
FORMAL cavilling, tergiversation
COLLOQ. shilly-shallying, pussyfooting, beating about the
bush, sitting on the fence

prevaricator n
evader, equivocator, quibbler, liar, hypocrite,
deceiver
OLD pettifogger
FORMAL casuist, caviller, dissembler, sophist
COLLOQ. dodger, fibber

prevent v
stop, avert, avoid, keep from, halt, arrest, hold back,
inhibit, head off, ward off, fend off, stave off, intercept,
forestall, anticipate, frustrate, thwart, restrain, hinder,
hamper, impede, obstruct, block, check, hold in check,
foil, balk, deter, bar
FORMAL preclude, obviate
⊟ cause, help, foster, encourage, allow

> **SYNONYM NUANCES**
>
> Both **avert** and **avoid** might be used of taking action to
> escape something unwanted: *full-scale civil war was
> averted.* The term **keep from** is also a fairly restrained
> one, which usually implies the intervention of another
> party: *her youthful outlook kept him from becoming
> staid.*
> **Head off** and **ward off** are more appropriate for
> keeping something at bay, as are **fend off** and **stave off**,
> which have further implications of deflecting an
> onslaught: *he fended off all challenges to his leadership.*
> **Intercept**, on the other hand, suggests a less defensive
> action, interrupting something before it can continue:
> *she was about to strike him but he intercepted her,
> taking the stick from her hand.* **Forestall** and **anticipate**
> are more appropriate for pre-emptive action: *he
> anticipated her punch and ducked.*
> The terms **hinder** and **hamper** can be used of
> interfering with the progress of something, but **impede**,
> **block**, **balk** and **obstruct** suggest more effectively, and
> perhaps more deliberately, handicapping: *his refusal to
> talk obstructed the police inquiry.* **Frustrate**, **foil** and
> **thwart** imply putting paid to the plans of others in a
> definite fashion: *bad weather frustrated the attack.*
> **Deter**, on the other hand, is more relevant to providing
> discouragement: *alarms help deter burglars.*

prevention n
avoidance, halting, arresting, heading off, warding off,
fending off, staving off, frustration, check, hindrance,
impediment, obstruction, obstacle, bar, elimination,
exclusion, precaution, safeguard, deterrence, hampering,
foiling, balking
TECHNICAL contraception, prophylaxis
OLD impeach
FORMAL preclusion, obviation
⊟ cause, help

> **PROVERBS**
> Prevention is better than cure

preventive adj, n
♦ adj
preventative, anticipatory, pre-emptive, inhibitory,
obstructive, precautionary, protective, counteractive,
deterrent
TECHNICAL prophylactic
OLD prevenient
⊟ causative, fostering
♦ n
prevention, protection, precautionary measure, protective,
impediment, hindrance, deterrent, block, obstruction,
obstacle, safeguard, remedy, shield, neutralizer
TECHNICAL prophylactic
⊟ cause, encouragement, incitement

previous adj
preceding, foregoing, earlier, prior, past, former,
ex-, one-time, sometime, antecedent
FORMAL erstwhile, quondam
⊟ following, subsequent, later

previously adv
formerly, once, earlier, earlier on, until now, before,
beforehand, already, at one time, in the past
OLD afore, fore
FORMAL heretofore, hitherto, erst, erstwhile
⊟ later

prey n, v
♦ n
quarry, game, kill, victim, target, spreagh
OLD (*Spenser*) soyle, ravin
FORMAL rapine
COLLOQ. mug, fall guy
■ **prey on**
1 HUNT, kill, seize, catch, pounce on, prowl, devour, eat,
feed on, moth-eat, raven on, vampire, live off, exploit,
fleece, take advantage of
FORMAL deprecate, predate
COLLOQ. con, bleed
2 *prey on your mind*
haunt, trouble, distress, worry, burden, weigh down, hang
over, oppress, plague, torment

price n, v
♦ n
1 *the price of the car*
value, worth, cost, expense(s), outlay, expenditure, fee,
charge, levy, toll, rate, bill, assessment, valuation,
estimate, quotation, figure, amount, sum,
payment, reward
2 *publicity is the price of fame*
penalty, forfeit, sacrifice, consequence(s), result
♦ v
value, rate, cost, evaluate, assess, estimate,
set/fix the price at
FORMAL appraise, valorize
■ **at a price**
expensive, at a high price, at a high cost
■ **at any price**
at any cost, whatever it takes, whatever the cost, no
matter what it costs

priceless adj
1 INVALUABLE, inestimable, incalculable, expensive,
costly, dear, precious, valuable, prized, treasured,
cherished, irreplaceable, incomparable, rare
COLLOQ. worth its weight in gold
2 FUNNY, amusing, comic, hilarious, riotous,
side-splitting
COLLOQ. killing, rich, a scream
⊟ 1 cheap, run-of-the-mill

pricey adj
costly, dear, excessive, exorbitant, expensive, extortionate,
high-priced

COLLOQ. steep, over the odds, sky-high, costing an arm and a leg, costing the earth, costing a bomb, daylight robbery
☞ cheap

prick *v, n*
♦ *v*
1 PIERCE, puncture, perforate, point, punch, jab, jag, nick, slit, gash, wound, spike, prod, thorn, rowel, bore, stab, sting, bite, prickle, itch, tingle, smart; *Scot* brog
OLD prog, accloy, cloy
2 *prick your conscience*
trouble, distress, worry, torment, plague, harass, harry, gnaw at, prey on
♦ *n*
puncture, perforation, pinhole, hole, stab, pierce, prickle, jab, jag, nick, wound, pang, twinge, sting, pain, smarting, tingle, bite; *dialect* brod
■ **prick up your ears**
listen eagerly, listen expectantly, listen carefully, attend, lend an ear, pay attention, pin back your ears, take note/notice of

prickle *n, v*
♦ *n*
1 THORN, spine, barb, spur, point, spike, needle, prong, tine
TECHNICAL aculeus
FORMAL spicula, acantha
2 *feel a prickle of fear*
sensation, sting, stinging, itching, smarting, twinge, pang, tingle
TECHNICAL paraesthesia
FORMAL formication
COLLOQ. pins and needles
♦ *v*
tingle, itch, smart, sting, prick, nip

prickly *adj*
1 THORNY, brambly, spiny, barbed, spiky, spiked, armed, pronged, bristly, bearded, rough, scratchy; *Scot* jaggy
TECHNICAL acanaceous, acanthaceous, aculeate, echinate
2 IRRITABLE, on edge, touchy, grumpy, short-tempered, bad-tempered
COLLOQ. stroppy, ratty, crabby, crotchety, edgy, shirty, grouchy
3 *a prickly subject*
complicated, difficult, hard, thorny, problematic(al), tough, troublesome, tricky, delicate, sensitive
☞ **1** smooth **2** relaxed, easy-going

pride *n, v*
♦ *n*
1 SATISFACTION, gratification, sense of achievement, pleasure, delight, joy, elation, triumphalism
2 DIGNITY, self-respect, self-esteem, self-image, self-worth, ego, honour
3 CONCEIT, vanity, egotism, boastfulness, smugness, disdain, arrogance, self-importance, self-conceit, presumption, haughtiness, superciliousness, snobbery, pretentiousness
COLLOQ. bigheadedness
☞ **1** shame, embarrassment **3** humility, modesty
■ **pride and joy**
glory, joy, delight, apple of your eye, beloved/treasured possession, darling, best, pick, élite, flower, choice/select part, finest, pick of the bunch, crème de la crème
■ **pride yourself on**
take satisfaction in, congratulate yourself, flatter yourself, take pride in, revel in, glory in, exult in, vaunt, crow about, boast about, brag about, plume yourself, preen yourself
COLLOQ. pat yourself on the back for
☞ belittle, humble

priest *n*
minister, vicar, parson, pastor, padre, father, man/woman of God, man/woman of the cloth, apostle, clergyman, clergywoman, churchman, churchwoman, deacon, deaconess, chaplain, cleric, clerk, neophyte, orator, concelebrant, high priest, pontiff, prelate, presbyter, secular, seminarian, seminarist, hierarch, hierophant, ecclesiastic, arch-priest, redemptorist; (*derog*) hedge-parson, hedge-priest
OLD masspriest; (*derog*) lack-Latin, Sir John Lack-Latin
Related adjective: sacerdotal

Priests include:

arch-flamen & flamen (*Ancient Rome*)	corybant & Pythian (*Ancient Greece*)	mambo (*voodoo*)
bacchant & bacchanal (*Bacchus*)	druid (*Celtic*) Levite & rabbi (*Judaism*)	papa & pope (*Greek Orthodox*) presbyter (*Episcopal churches*)
bonze & lama (*Buddhism*)	lucumo (*Etruscan*)	tohunga (*Maori*)
Brahman (*Hindu*)	magus (*Ancient Persia*)	

priestess *n*
clergywoman, canoness, deaconess, nun, prioress, sister, abbess, religious, vestal, beguine, mambo

priesthood *n*
holy orders, the church, the ministry, the pastorate, the cloth, full orders, priestship, hierocracy, sacerdotalism

priestly *adj*
clerical, ecclesiastical, canonical, pastoral, priestlike, sacerdotal, Aaronic(al)
FORMAL hieratic

prig *n*
prude, puritan, killjoy, precisian, old maid, Mrs Grundy
COLLOQ. goody-goody, holy Joe, holy Willie

priggish *adj*
smug, self-righteous, sanctimonious, puritanical, prim, prudish, narrow-minded, starchy, stuffy, strait-laced
COLLOQ. goody-goody, holier-than-thou
☞ broad-minded

prim *adj*
prudish, strait-laced, formal, demure, proper, smug, priggish, prissy, fussy, particular, stuffy, starchy, puritanical, precise, fastidious, old-maidish, governessy; *dialect* mimsy; *Scot* mim, perjink, primsie
OLD (*Spenser*) quaint
COLLOQ. fuddy-duddy, schoolmarmish
☞ relaxed, easy-going

primacy *n*
supremacy, greatest importance, dominance, paramouncy, pre-eminence, sovereignty, superiority, command, seniority, dominion, leadership
FORMAL ascendancy
☞ inferiority

prima donna *n*
1 LEADING LADY, female lead, leading female singer, leading soprano, diva
2 TEMPERAMENTAL PERSON, over-sensitive person, moody person, unpredictable person

primal *adj*
original, basic, earliest, fundamental, primitive, first, primary, initial, major, greatest, highest, main, central, chief, paramount, principal, prime
FORMAL prim(a)eval, primordial
☞ later, minor

primarily adv

chiefly, principally, mainly, mostly, basically, first, firstly, first and foremost, fundamentally, especially, particularly, predominantly, essentially, in essence, in the main, in the first place

primary adj

1 CHIEF, principal, main, dominant, leading, foremost, supreme, prime, predominant, cardinal, capital, paramount, greatest, highest, ultimate
2 FIRST, basic, fundamental, essential, radical, rudimentary, elementary, simple, earliest, original, initial, introductory, beginning, opening
FORMAL elemental, prim(a)eval, primordial
F3 1 secondary, subsidiary, minor

prime[1] adj, n

♦ adj
1 BEST, choice, select, quality, first-class, first-rate, excellent, top, top-grade, supreme, highest, pre-eminent
2 CHIEF, principal, main, leading, foremost, supreme, predominant
3 CLASSIC, typical, standard, characteristic
FORMAL paradigmatic, quintessential, prototypical
F3 second-rate, secondary
♦ n
height, peak, pinnacle, acme, zenith, heyday, flower, blossom, bloom, culmination, best part, maturity, perfection

prime[2] v

1 PREPARE, equip, get ready, make ready, gear up, coach, train
2 BRIEF, inform, notify, prepare, fill, fill in
COLLOQ. clue up, gen up

prime minister n

premier, head of government, chief minister, first minister, chancellor, secretary of state

primer n

introduction, manual, textbook
OLD (Shakesp) absey-book
FORMAL prodrome, prodromus

primeval, primaeval adj

1 EARLIEST, first, original, early, old, ancient, prehistoric, primitive
FORMAL primordial, autochthonal
2 INSTINCTIVE, basic, intuitive, natural, innate, inherent, inborn, primal
F3 1 modern

primitive adj

1 CRUDE, rough, unsophisticated, uncivilized, simple, natural, uncultured, undeveloped, barbarian, wild, savage
2 EARLY, elementary, rudimentary, primary, first, original, earliest, ancient
FORMAL prim(a)eval, primordial
F3 1 advanced, sophisticated, civilized

primly adv

prudishly, prissily, fussily, stuffily

primordial adj

earliest, first, original, early, old, ancient, prehistoric, primitive, instinctive
FORMAL prim(a)eval, autochthonal
F3 modern

primp v

groom, smarten, tidy, dress up, spruce up, brush up, beautify, preen
COLLOQ. titivate, doll up, tart up, put on your best bib and tucker, put on your glad rags

prince n

lord, ruler, monarch, potentate, sovereign, duke, prince consort, princekin, princelet, princeling, khan, ras, sherif, Tunku
OLD archduke, atheling, infante, hospodar, raja(h), maharaja(h), nizam, rana, Upper Roger, nawab, porphyrogenite, tetrarch, lucumo; (Shakesp) potent

princely adj

1 SOVEREIGN, imperial, royal, regal, majestic, stately, grand, imposing, magnificent, splendid, glorious, impressive, superb, noble, en prince
2 princely sum
handsome, generous, liberal, lavish, sumptuous, magnificent, enormous, huge, immense, vast, massive, colossal, large-scale, mammoth, considerable, tremendous, stupendous
FORMAL bounteous, magnanimous

princess n

lady, ruler, monarch, potentate, sovereign, crown princess, begum
OLD archduchess, infanta

principal adj, n

♦ adj
main, chief, key, major, essential, cardinal, primary, first, foremost, leading, controlling, dominant, in charge, prime, paramount, pre-eminent, most important, supreme, highest, uppermost, arch
F3 minor, subsidiary, lesser, least
♦ n
1 HEAD, head teacher, headmaster, headmistress, rector, chief, leader, director, manager, superintendent, controller, ruler
COLLOQ. boss
2 MONEY, capital, capital sum, capital funds, assets

> ⚠ **principal** or **principle**?
> As an adjective, *principal* means 'most important': *Shipbuilding and coal-mining were two of Britain's principal industries*. As a noun, *principal* means 'the head of a school, college or university'. *Principle* can only be used as a noun. It means 'a general rule' or 'the theory underlying a method or way of working': *the principles of economic theory*.

principality n

princedom, principate, duchy, dukedom, grand duchy, archduchy, archdukedom, earldom, palatinate, sultanate, protectorate, kingdom, realm, dominion, empire, dependency, federation, confederation

principally adv

mainly, mostly, chiefly, primarily, predominantly, above all, particularly, especially, in the main, for the most part, first and foremost, capitally

principle n

1 RULE, formula, law, canon, axiom, dictum, precept, maxim, truth, tenet, doctrine, creed, dogma, code, theory, idea, standard, criterion, proposition, basis, fundamental, essential
FORMAL postulate
2 a man of principle
honour, integrity, uprightness, virtue, decency, morality, morals, ethics, standards, scruples, conscience
FORMAL rectitude, probity
■ **in principle**
theoretically, in theory, ideally, en principe, in essence

> **QUOTATIONS**
> Man cannot make principles, he can only discover them
> THOMAS PAINE, *The Age of Reason*

> ⚠ **principle** or **principal**?
> See panel at **principal**.

principled adj

upright, virtuous, moral, ethical, high-minded, honourable, conscientious, decent, respectable, righteous, just, right-minded, scrupulous
F3 unprincipled

print *v, n*
* *v*

mark, stamp, imprint, impress, engrave, etch, record, register, copy, reproduce, run off, publish, issue
COLLOQ. put to bed
See panels below

* *n*

1 LETTERS, characters, lettering, type, typescript, typeface, fount, font
2 MARK, impression, fingerprint, footprint
3 COPY, reproduction, replica, facsimile, design, picture, engraving, lithograph, photograph, photo, snapshot
COLLOQ. snap

■ **in print**
published, available, obtainable, in stock, in circulation
ЕӬ out of print

■ **out of print**
no longer available, unavailable, unobtainable, out of stock, sold out, off the market, out of/withdrawn from circulation
ЕӬ in print

prior *adj*
earlier, preceding, foregoing, previous, former
ЕӬ later

■ **prior to**
before, preceding, earlier than, up to, until, till, in advance of
ЕӬ after, following

priority *n*
1 *a top priority*
most important thing, most urgent matter, matter of highest/greatest importance, main thing, supreme matter, first concern, primary issue, essential, requirement, pole position
COLLOQ. top of the tree

2 PRECEDENCE, right of way, seniority, rank, superiority, pre-eminence, supremacy, paramouncy, the lead, greater/greatest importance, first/highest place
ЕӬ 2 inferiority

priory *n*
monastery, abbey, cloister, friary, priorate, convent, nunnery, religious community, religious house, béguinage

prise *v*
lever, force, jemmy, pry, raise, lift, hoist, dislodge, shift, move, winkle

prison *n*
jail, jailhouse, guardhouse, penitentiary, cell, lock-up, cage, dungeon, imprisonment, confinement, detention centre, custody
OLD kitty; (*Shakesp*) confine
COLLOQ. nick, inside
SLANG porridge, clink, cooler, slammer, jug, can, choky, quod; *N Am* big house, hoosegow

> **QUOTATIONS**
> Stone walls do not a prison make, / Nor iron bars a cage
> RICHARD LOVELACE, *Lucasta*

prisoner *n*
captive, hostage, convict, prisoner of war, POW, inmate, internee, detainee, recidivist, prisoner of conscience, political prisoner, Rule 43, state prisoner, trust, *détenu(e)*
TECHNICAL culprit
COLLOQ. jailbird, con, lifer, (old) lag, yardbird
OLD SLANG passman

prissily *adv*
prudishly, primly, fussily, stuffily

Printing methods include:

bubble-jet printing	copper engraving	etching	letterpress	photoengraving	twin-etching
collotype	die-stamping	flexography	lino blocking	rotary press	xerography
colour-process printing	duplicating	gravure	litho	screen printing	
computer-to-plate (CTP)	electrostatic printing	ink-jet printing	lithography	silk-screen printing	
	engraving	intaglio	offset lithography	stencilling	
		laser printing	offset printing	thermography	

Printing terms include:

anodized plate	colour control bar	font	literal	phototypesetting	take in
author's proof	colour separation	forme	logotype	planographic	take over
backing-up	column inch/centimetre	galley	lower-case	printing press	text
back margin		gutter	machine composition	progressive proofs	thermal printer
bad break	compose	hard hyphen		proof	tint
base alignment	composing room	hot-metal typesetting	machine proof	quoin	trim marks
batter	composition size		mackle	ragged right/left	type
bi-directional printing	compositor	image printing	makeready	registration	typeface
	condensed	imposition	manuscript	relief printing	type scale
black printer	copy	impression	margin	reprint	typescript
blanket-to-blanket press	cylinder press	indent	matrix	roman	typesetting
	dampers	initial caps	misprint	run-around	type spec
bold face	dot-etching	inking roller	moiré	running head	typo
bromide	dot gain	Intertype®	Monophoto®	running text	typographer
camera-ready copy	drum printer	italic	Monotype®	sans serif	upper-case
carding	electrotype	justification	mottling	see-through	web-fed
caret	em	keep standing	newsprint	signature	web offset
cast-off	en	kern	non-image area	small capitals	widow
catchword	end even	kiss impression	non-impact printing	soft hyphen	woodcut
centre	expanded type	large print		specimen page	wood engraving
character set	feathering	leaders	offprint	spoilage	zinco
chase	finishing	leading	orphan	stereotype	
cliché	first proof	letterset	overprint	stet	
cold composition	flat-bed press	line printer	Ozalid®	strike-on	
collograph	flong	Linotype®	perfecting	strip in	

prissy *adj*
prim, squeamish, prudish, strait-laced, formal, demure, proper, priggish, fussy, particular, stuffy, starchy, puritanical, precise, fastidious, old-maidish
COLLOQ. finicky, po-faced, schoolmarmish

pristine *adj*
1 IMMACULATE, undefiled, uncorrupted, untouched, virgin, unspoiled, unsullied
2 ORIGINAL, earliest, first, initial, former, primary, primitive, primal
FORMAL prim(a)eval, primordial, primigenial
E3 **1** spoiled, defiled **2** developed, later

privacy *n*
secrecy, confidentiality, independence, solitude, quietness, isolation, seclusion, privateness, concealment, retirement, retreat
FORMAL sequestration
E3 publicness, interruption, interference

private *adj, n*
♦ *adj*
1 *private discussions*
confidential, classified, secret, top secret, privileged, unofficial, off the record
COLLOQ. hush-hush
2 *your private life/feelings*
personal, confidential, intimate, innermost, secret, hidden, individual
3 *a private bathroom*
exclusive, particular, own, special, individual, personal
4 *a private person*
quiet, reserved, withdrawn, independent, solitary, retiring, separate, self-contained, introverted
5 *a private place*
secluded, isolated, hidden, concealed, closed, secret, remote, undisturbed, quiet, out-of-the-way
FORMAL sequestered
6 *private industries*
independent, commercial, free-enterprise, free-market, privatized, non-governmental, denationalized, self-governing, self-determining
E3 **1** official, public **5** public, open **6** public, state-controlled, state-run, nationalized
♦ *n*
enlisted man, private soldier, Tommy, squaddy, swad, swaddy, gunner
COLLOQ. Tommy Atkins
■ **in private**
privately, in confidence, confidentially, secretly, in secret, with no one else present, behind closed doors, in camera, *sub rosa*
E3 publicly, openly
■ **private detective**
private eye, private investigator, pinkerton
COLLOQ. sleuth, shamus, dick
■ **private parts**
genitals, sexual organs, reproductive organs, vagina, womb, uterus, penis, scrotum, testicles
TECHNICAL pudenda, vulva
FORMAL genitalia
COLLOQ. privates
SLANG (*taboo*) fanny, pussy, muff, cunt, cock, prick, dick, balls

privateer *n*
buccaneer, pirate, brigand, filibuster, freebooter, corsair, marque, sea robber, sea wolf

privately *adv*
1 *we need to talk privately*
in private, in confidence, confidentially, secretly, in secret, with no one else present, behind closed doors, in camera, *sub rosa*
2 *privately, I'm worried about him*
personally, inwardly, inside, to yourself, within, at heart, in your heart of hearts, deep down, deep inside you, secretly

privation *n*
hardship, destitution, deprivation, affliction, neediness, poverty, suffering, lack, need, austerity, loss, misery, distress
FORMAL indigence, penury, want
E3 affluence, wealth

privilege *n*
advantage, benefit, concession, birthright, title, due, right, prerogative, entitlement, honour, freedom, liberty, franchise, licence, sanction, dispensation, authority, immunity, exemption, priority, status symbol, patent, faculty
TECHNICAL octroi
OLD commodity; (*Shakesp*) prise
E3 disadvantage

privileged *adj*
1 FAVOURED, advantaged, special, indulgent, sanctioned, authorized, immune, excepted, exempt, élite, honoured, ruling, powerful, rich, wealthy
2 CONFIDENTIAL, private, classified, secret, top secret, unofficial, off the record
COLLOQ. hush-hush
E3 **1** disadvantaged, under-privileged **2** public, common

privy *n*
toilet, lavatory, water closet, WC, public convenience, washroom, cloakroom, latrine, gents', ladies', urinal, powder room; *N Am* rest room, comfort station
COLLOQ. bog, loo, lav, dunny, smallest room
SLANG kazi, crapper, can, cottage, heads, thunderbox
■ **privy to**
aware of, cognizant of, informed about, wise to
FORMAL apprised of
COLLOQ. genned up on, clued up on, in on, in the know about
E3 unaware of

prize *n, adj, v*
♦ *n*
1 REWARD, trophy, medal, award, winnings, jackpot, purse, premium, stake(s), honour, accolade, laurels, pennant
2 AIM, goal, gain, hope, desire, honour
3 BOOTY, loot, spoils, plunder, pickings, capture, pillage, trophy
♦ *adj*
best, top, first-rate, excellent, outstanding, champion, winning, prize-winning, award-winning
COLLOQ. top-notch, terrific, smashing, out of this world
E3 second-rate
♦ *v*
treasure, value, appreciate, revere, cherish, love, hold dear, think highly of, hold in high regard, set great store by, esteem
E3 despise, undervalue

prize-winner *n*
winner, champion, cup-winner, medallist, prizeman, prizewoman, dux
COLLOQ. champ

pro[1] *n*
a tennis pro
professional, expert, authority, specialist, consultant, practitioner, master, past master, old hand, virtuoso
COLLOQ. dab hand, wizard, ace
E3 amateur

pro[2] *prep*
♦ *prep*
pro democracy
in favour of, for, supporting, backing
E3 against
■ **pros and cons**
advantages and disadvantages, reasons for and reasons against, arguments for and arguments against, strengths and weaknesses, pluses and minuses

probability n
likelihood, likeliness, odds, chance(s), expectation, prospect, possibility
F3 improbability

probable adj
likely, expected, to be expected, anticipated, credible, believable, plausible, feasible, forseeable, predictable, possible, apparent, seeming
COLLOQ. odds-on, on the cards, a fair bet
F3 improbable, unlikely

probably adv
in all likelihood, in all probability, likely, it looks like, the chances are, most likely, as likely as not, doubtless, presumably, arguably, possibly, perhaps, maybe
COLLOQ. (as) like as not, a fair bet
F3 improbably

probation n
trial period, experimental period, trial, test, test period, apprenticeship, supervision

probationer n
trainee, apprentice, novice, beginner, learner, student, pupil, recruit, raw recruit, amateur, newcomer, tiro
FORMAL neophyte, noviciate
COLLOQ. greenhorn, rookie

probe v, n
◆ v
1 INVESTIGATE, scrutinize, examine, study, inquire, analyse, research, go into, look into, search, sift, test
2 PROD, poke, pierce, penetrate, sound, plumb, check, explore, examine, feel
◆ n
1 INQUIRY, inquest, investigation, exploration, examination, test, scrutiny, scrutinization, study, analysis, research
2 *examine with a probe*
instrument, bore, drill, device
OLD tent

probity n
uprightness, righteousness, integrity, honour, honourableness, virtue, morality, worth, honesty, goodness, equity, fairness, justice, truthfulness, trustworthiness, sincerity
FORMAL fidelity, rectitude
F3 *formal* improbity

problem n, adj
◆ n
1 TROUBLE, worry, predicament, quandary, plight, dilemma, difficulty, complication, snag; *S Afr* indaba
COLLOQ. hassle, hole, pickle, fix, mess, tight spot, dire straits, no-win situation, catch-22
2 QUESTION, issue, matter, poser, puzzle, conundrum, riddle, enigma, brainteaser, mind-bender; *N Am* brain-twister
3 NUISANCE, annoyance, inconvenience, bother, irritation, irritant, vexation, pest, bore
COLLOQ. pain, pain in the neck, drag, thorn in your side/flesh
◆ adj
difficult, unmanageable, uncontrollable, unruly, troublesome, disobedient, delinquent
FORMAL recalcitrant, intransigent
F3 well-behaved, manageable

SYNONYM NUANCES

noun sense 1
Trouble and **difficulty** can be widely used to refer to anything that is hard to deal with, while **worry** has a narrower suggestion of causing mental anguish.
Predicament can be used of physical problems: *he was in a bit of a predicament when he missed his plane*, as can **plight**, but this is far more suggestive of a position of danger.
  Both **predicament** and **quandary** can appropriately refer to being in an awkward situation, especially one requiring action: *the government is in a quandary trying to reconcile the conflicting demands*; **dilemma** would specifically suggest being faced with two equally undesirable choices.
  The term **complication** can be used to suggest something that increases the complexity of a situation, and **snag**, although similar, often implies something that is not initially evident: *another unexpected snag.*

problematic adj
1 DIFFICULT, fraught with difficulties, troublesome, awkward, hard, puzzling, perplexing, intricate, involved, tricky, thorny, problematical, enigmatic, moot
COLLOQ. a can of worms, a minefield
2 UNCERTAIN, questionable, debatable, doubtful, dubious
F3 **1** easy, straightforward **2** certain

procedure n
routine, process, method, methodology, system, technique, custom, practice, means, measure, policy, formula, way, course, course of action, scheme, strategy, plan of action, move, step, action, conduct, operation, modus operandi, performance

proceed v
1 *the permission to proceed*
advance, go ahead, move on, go on, go forward, progress, continue, carry on, press on, make your way
2 START, begin, make a start, take steps, get under way, set in motion
3 ORIGINATE, derive, flow, start, stem, spring, arise, issue, emanate, result, ensue, follow, come
F3 **1** stop, retreat

proceedings n
1 MATTERS, affairs, business, dealings, transactions, report(s), account, minutes, records, archives, annals
2 EVENTS, activities, happenings, deeds, doings, moves, steps, measures, action, course of action, operations, procedures, manoeuvres
3 *legal proceedings*
lawsuit, case, trial, action, process, litigation

proceeds n
revenue, income, returns, receipts, takings, earnings, gain, profit(s), yield, produce
F3 expenditure, outlay

process n, v
◆ n
1 PROCEDURE, operation, practice, action, method, system, technique, means, manner, way, stage, step
FORMAL mode
2 COURSE, progression, advance, progress, development, change(s), evolution, formation, growth, movement, action, proceeding
◆ v
deal with, sort, attend to, handle, treat, prepare, refine, transform, convert, change, alter
■ **in the process of**
in the course of, in the middle of, being, in the making, in preparation

procession n
march, parade, cavalcade, motorcade, pageant, cortège, file, column, walk, funeral, train, succession, stream, series, sequence, course, run, progress, pomp, corso, demonstration, manifestation
TECHNICAL Moharram
OLD triumph
FORMAL exequy

proclaim v
announce, declare, pronounce, affirm, give out, publish, advertise, circulate, broadcast, make known, notify, profess, testify, blaze abroad, blazon, trumpet, show, indicate, bid, cry, herald, preach, show forth, summon, knell, ring, sing, sound, apostolize; *dialect* out-ask

TECHNICAL preconize
OLD ask, annuntiate, denounce; (*Shakesp*) protest
FORMAL promulgate, enounce

proclamation *n*
announcement, declaration, affirmation, pronouncement, publication, circulation, advertisement, notice, notification, preaching, broadcast, manifesto, order, order of the day, rule, command, decree, edict, banns
TECHNICAL kerygma
OLD proclaim, annunciation, indiction, hue and cry, placard; (*Shakesp*) oyez
FORMAL promulgation, pronunciamento

proclivity *n*
tendency, leaning, inclination, weakness, disposition, bent, bias, liability, proneness, liableness
FORMAL penchant, predilection, predisposition, propensity
E3 disinclination

procrastinate *v*
defer, put off, postpone, delay, stall, play for time, dally, drag your feet, prolong, protract
FORMAL retard, temporize
COLLOQ. dilly-dally
E3 advance, proceed

> **!** **procrastinate** or **prevaricate**?
> See panel at **prevaricate**.

procrastination *n*
delaying, deferral, stalling, delaying tactics
FORMAL temporizing, cunctation
COLLOQ. dilly-dallying

> **PROVERBS**
> Procrastination is the thief of time

procreate *v*
reproduce, produce, father, mother, breed, conceive, generate, propagate, multiply, engender, sire, spawn
OLD beget

procure *v*
1 ACQUIRE, buy, purchase, get, obtain, find, come by, pick up, lay hands on, earn, gain, win, secure, get hold of
FORMAL appropriate, requisition
2 *procure a prostitute*
pimp, pander, ponce, solicit, importune
COLLOQ. hook, hustle
E3 **1** lose

procurer *n*
procuress, pimp, pander, panderer, madam, fancy man, whoremonger, fleshmonger, solicitor
OLD bawd, broker, mackerel
SLANG hustler, ponce, mack; *Aust* hoon

prod *v, n*
♦ *v*
1 POKE, jab, dig, elbow, nudge, push, butt, thrust
COLLOQ. shove
2 URGE, goad, spur, prompt, stimulate, motivate, stir, move, encourage, incite
COLLOQ. egg on
♦ *n*
1 POKE, jab, dig, elbow, nudge, push
COLLOQ. shove
2 PROMPT, prompting, reminder, push, stimulus, spur, goad, motivation, encouragement

prodigal *adj, n*
♦ *adj*
wasteful, extravagant, squandering, excessive, improvident, intemperate, unsparing, unthrifty, unthrift, wanton, reckless, spendthrift, immoderate, lavish, profuse, sumptuous, exuberant, bountiful, copious
FORMAL bounteous, luxuriant, profligate
E3 modest, thrifty, parsimonious

♦ *n*
squanderer, waster, spendthrift, spendall, wastrel
FORMAL profligate
COLLOQ. big spender

prodigality *n*
wastefulness, extravagance, recklessness, squandering, waste, wantonness, unthriftiness, immoderation, intemperance, dissipation, excess, abandon, exuberance, richness, profusion, lavishness, sumptuousness, plenty, abundance
FORMAL luxuriance, plenteousness, profligacy, bounteousness, amplitude, copiousness
E3 modesty, thrift, parsimony

prodigious *adj*
1 ENORMOUS, gigantic, huge, massive, vast, immense, colossal, giant, mammoth, immeasurable
2 EXTRAORDINARY, marvellous, startling, amazing, astounding, staggering, fabulous, fantastic, flabbergasting, striking, impressive, miraculous, wonderful, monumental, inordinate, spectacular, remarkable, stupendous, tremendous, phenomenal, unusual, exceptional, abnormal
E3 **1** small **2** commonplace, unremarkable

prodigiously *adv*
vastly, massively, immensely, astoundingly, amazingly, wonderfully, staggeringly, fantastically, impressively, unusually, remarkably, phenomenally, exceptionally, spectacularly
E3 commonly, usually, unremarkably

prodigy *n*
genius, virtuoso, child genius, wonder child, wunderkind, gifted child, mastermind, wonder, marvel, miracle, phenomenon, sensation, freak, curiosity, rarity
OLD monster; (*Shakesp*) monument
FORMAL portent
COLLOQ. whizz kid
SLANG phenom

produce *v, n*
♦ *v*
1 CAUSE, occasion, give rise to, provoke, bring about, result in, create, evoke, originate, invent, develop, prepare, make, manufacture, fashion, fabricate, build, construct, put together, assemble, compose, generate, yield, bear, breed, grow, deliver
FORMAL effect
2 ADVANCE, put forward, present, offer, give, supply, provide, furnish, bring out, bring forward, bring forth, show, exhibit, demonstrate, come up with
FORMAL proffer
3 *produce a play*
direct, stage, present, perform, manage, organize, arrange, mount, put on
♦ *n*
crop, harvest, yield, output, product(s), food, foodstuffs, fruit, vegetables, dairy products, eggs

producer *n*
1 *the producer of a play*
director, presenter, impresario, manager, régisseur
2 *a producer of wine*
manufacturer, maker, farmer, grower

product *n*
1 COMMODITY, merchandise, goods, wares, end-product, artefact, work, article, item, creation, invention, production, output, yield, produce, fruit, return
2 RESULT, consequence, effect, outcome, issue, upshot, fruit, offshoot, spin-off, by-product, legacy
E3 **2** cause

production *n*
1 MAKING, manufacture, manufacturing, producing, building, fabrication, construction, assembly, creation, origination, preparation, formation, composition, development
2 OUTPUT, yield, harvest, fruit(s), return(s), productivity, manufacture, achievement, performance

3 *the production of a play*
staging, mounting, performance, presentation, direction, management, organization
4 SHOW, play, drama, concert, musical, opera, film, revue, presentation, performance
E3 1 consumption

productive *adj*
fruitful, profitable, rewarding, valuable, beneficial, worthwhile, useful, constructive, gainful, creative, inventive, fertile, prolific, rich, high-yielding, teeming, busy, energetic, vigorous, efficient, effective
FORMAL fecund, fructiferous
E3 unproductive, fruitless, useless

productivity *n*
productiveness, fruitfulness, yield, output, production, capacity, work rate, efficiency

profanation *n*
desecration, violation, abuse, misuse, defilement, debasement, dishonouring, sacrilege, blasphemy, perversion

profane *adj, v*
♦ *adj*
1 SACRILEGIOUS, irreligious, blasphemous, idolatrous, godless, ungodly, irreverent, disrespectful, abusive, crude, vulgar, coarse, foul, foul-mouthed, foul-spoken, filthy, unclean
2 SECULAR, temporal, lay, worldly, unconsecrated, unhallowed, unsanctified, unholy, impious
E3 1 religious, respectful **2** sacred, holy
♦ *v*
desecrate, pollute, contaminate, defile, debase, pervert, violate, abuse, misuse, misemploy
E3 revere, honour

profanity *n*
1 SACRILEGE, irreverence, profaneness, impiety, blasphemy, abuse
FORMAL execration, imprecation, malediction
2 OBSCENITY, swear-word, swearing, oath, expletive, curse, cursing
COLLOQ. four-letter word
E3 politeness, reverence

profess *v*
1 CLAIM, maintain, allege, lay claim to, make out, pretend
FORMAL dissemble, purport
2 DECLARE, admit, confess, acknowledge, own, confirm, certify, announce, proclaim, state, assert, affirm
FORMAL aver, avow

professed *adj*
1 SELF-ACKNOWLEDGED, self-confessed, self-styled, so-called, soi-disant, confirmed, declared, certified, acknowledged, proclaimed
FORMAL avowed
2 PRETENDED, supposed, ostensible, alleged, apparent, would-be
FORMAL purported

profession *n*
1 CAREER, job, occupation, employment, business, line (of work), walk of life, craft, trade, vocation, calling, métier, office, appointment, post, position, situation
2 ADMISSION, confession, acknowledgement, declaration, announcement, statement, testimony, assertion, affirmation, claim
FORMAL averment, avowal

> **QUOTATIONS**
> The most important thing in life is to choose a profession: chance arranges for that
>   BLAISE PASCAL, *Pensées*

professional *adj, n*
♦ *adj*
qualified, licensed, trained, experienced, practised, dexterous, skilful, skilled, educated, knowledgeable,

specialist, expert, masterly, adept, able, accomplished, proficient, competent, businesslike, efficient
E3 amateur, unprofessional
♦ *n*
expert, authority, specialist, consultant, practitioner, master, past master, maestro, old hand, virtuoso
COLLOQ. pro, dab hand, wizard, whizz, ace;
N Am mavin, maven
E3 amateur

professor *n*
head of department, chair, head of faculty, vice chancellor, dean, principal, provost, don, fellow, reader, academic, lecturer, intellectual

proffer *v*
offer, tender, advance, extend, hold out, hand, suggest, present, propose, submit, volunteer

proficiency *n*
skill, skilfulness, expertise, experience, mastery, talent, knack, dexterity, finesse, aptitude, accomplishment, capability, ability, competence, aptness, adeptness
E3 incompetence

proficient *adj*
able, capable, skilled, qualified, trained, experienced, accomplished, expert, masterly, gifted, talented, clever, skilful, competent, efficient, effective, apt, adept, keeping your eye in
OLD wise
E3 unskilled, incompetent

profile *n*
1 SIDE VIEW, outline, contour, silhouette, cameo, description, shape, form, line(s), figure, sketch, drawing, diagram, chart, graph, template
TECHNICAL thalweg
OLD half-cheek, purfle
2 BIOGRAPHY, curriculum vitae, CV, thumbnail sketch, vignette, portrait, sketch, study, analysis, examination, survey, review
COLLOQ. biog
■ **high profile**
exposure, prominence, public attention, visibility, conspicuous position, noticeable position, the limelight, the spotlight
■ **keep a low profile**
blend/merge into the background, be/keep/stay in the background, lie low, escape notice, hide yourself, avoid publicity, escape the limelight

profit *n, v*
♦ *n*
1 *the company's profits*
revenue, return, yield, proceeds, receipts, takings, earnings, winnings, dividend, interest, bonus, gain, surplus, excess, windfall, bottom line
COLLOQ. fast buck, gravy, killing, rake-off
2 ADVANTAGE, benefit, gain, use, usefulness, avail, value, worth
E3 1, 2 loss
♦ *v*
gain, make money, pay, serve, avail, benefit
COLLOQ. line your pockets
SLANG make megabucks, make loadsamoney
E3 lose
■ **profit by/from**
exploit, take advantage of, use, utilize, turn to advantage, put to good use, gain a benefit from, gain an advantage from, capitalize on, reap the benefit of
COLLOQ. cash in on, milk

> **QUOTATIONS**
> The smell of profit is clean / And sweet, whatever the source
>   JUVENAL, *Satires*

profitable *adj*
1 *a profitable business*
cost-effective, economic, commercial, moneymaking, lucrative, remunerative, fat, paying, rewarding, successful, juicy, plummy, expedient
FORMAL gainful
COLLOQ. in the black
2 *a profitable discussion*
helpful, useful, valuable, worthwhile, fruitful, productive, advantageous, beneficial
OLD advantageable, available, behovely, utile
F∃ 1 unprofitable, loss-making, non-profit-making **2** unhelpful, useless

profitably *adv*
1 *a business operating profitably*
economically, commercially, successfully
2 *spend your leisure time profitably*
usefully, productively, beneficially, valuably, fruitfully
F∃ 1 unprofitably **2** uselessly

profiteer *n, v*
♦ *n*
racketeer, exploiter, extortioner, extortionist
♦ *v*
exploit, extort, racketeer, fleece, overcharge
COLLOQ. make a fast/quick buck, make a quick killing

profiteering *n*
exploitation, extortion, racketeering, Rachmanism

profitless *adj*
useless, worthless, fruitless, futile, vain, pointless, thankless, ineffective, idle, unavailing, unproductive, unprofitable, unremunerative, gainless, to no purpose, to no avail
FORMAL ineffectual
F∃ profitable

profligacy *n*
1 WASTE, wastefulness, extravagance, excess, unrestraint, lavishness, unthriftiness, recklessness, squandering, improvidence, prodigality
2 IMMORALITY, promiscuity, corruption, debauchery, degeneracy, depravity, libertinism, licentiousness, wantonness, dissipation, dissoluteness
F∃ morality, parsimony, thrift, uprightness

profligate *adj, n*
♦ *adj*
1 WASTEFUL, extravagant, squandering, immoderate, excessive, improvident, reckless, spendthrift, prodigal
2 IMMORAL, corrupt, dissolute, unprincipled, wicked, loose, dissipated, depraved, degenerate, debauched, iniquitous, promiscuous, licentious, wanton, libertine
F∃ 1 thrifty; *formal* parsimonious **2** upright, moral
♦ *n*
1 WASTER, wastrel, squanderer, spendthrift, prodigal
2 REPROBATE, debauchee, libertine, degenerate, wanton, rake, roué

profound *adj*
1 DEEP, great, intense, extreme, heartfelt, sincere, marked, thorough, complete, absolute, thoroughgoing, far-reaching, radical, extensive, exhaustive
2 *a profound remark*
serious, weighty, deep, penetrating, discerning, thoughtful, philosophical, wise, learned, impenetrable
FORMAL sagacious, erudite, esoteric, abstruse, recondite
F∃ 1 shallow, slight, mild **2** shallow, superficial

profoundly *adv*
deeply, intensely, extremely, seriously, acutely, greatly, heartily, thoroughly, keenly, sincerely
F∃ slightly

profundity *n*
depth, profoundness, extremity, intensity, severity, strength, seriousness, penetration, learning, insight, intelligence, wisdom, perceptiveness, acumen

FORMAL abstruseness, erudition, perspicuity, perspicacity, sagacity
F∃ shallowness

profuse *adj*
ample, abundant, plentiful, copious, generous, liberal, lavish, rich, excessive, immoderate, extravagant, large-handed, fulsome, unsparing, unstinting, overabundant, superabundant, overflowing
TECHNICAL colliquative
FORMAL luxuriant, inordinate
COLLOQ. over the top
F∃ inadequate, sparse

profusely *adv*
abundantly, copiously, liberally, lavishly, immoderately, extravagantly, unstintingly, unsparingly
F∃ inadequately, sparsely

profusion *n*
abundance, copiousness, plenty, wealth, multitude, glut, riot, excess, surplus, superfluity, superabundance, extravagance, unsparingness
FORMAL plethora, plenitude
COLLOQ. loads, lots, heaps, tons
F∃ inadequacy, scarcity

progenitor *n*
1 ANCESTOR, forebear, forefather, father, mother, parent
OLD begetter
FORMAL procreator, primogenitor
2 ORIGINATOR, forerunner, founder, instigator, precursor, predecessor, antecedent, source

progeny *n*
offspring, children, young, descendants, family, issue, lineage, race, breed, seed, stock, quiverful
FORMAL posterity, scions

prognosis *n*
diagnosis, expectation, forecast, prediction, outlook, projection, assessment, evaluation, prospect, speculation, surmise
FORMAL prognostication

prognosticate *v*
forecast, foreshadow, foretell, predict, prophesy, herald, indicate, soothsay, divine
FORMAL augur, betoken, harbinger, portend, presage

prognostication *n*
prediction, projection, forecast, expectation, speculation, surmise, horoscope, prophecy
FORMAL prognosis

programme *n, v*
♦ *n*
1 SCHEDULE, timetable, agenda, calendar, order of events, listing, list, line-up, plan, plan of action, scheme, project, syllabus, course, prospectus, curriculum
2 *radio programme*
broadcast, transmission, show, performance, production, presentation, episode, simulcast
♦ *v*
arrange, plan, schedule, work out, formulate, itemize, lay on, line up, design, list, map out, book, prearrange

progress *n, v*
♦ *n*
movement, progression, passage, going, journey, way, advance, headway, step(s) forward, forward movement, breakthrough, development, evolution, growth, increase, improvement, upgrading, betterment, promotion
FORMAL advancement
F∃ recession, deterioration, decline
♦ *v*
proceed, advance, go forward, move forward, forge ahead, make progress, make headway, make your way, make strides, continue, go on, come on, develop, grow, mature, blossom, bloom, flourish, thrive, improve, better, recover, prosper, increase
COLLOQ. be getting there, shape up
F∃ deteriorate, decline

■ **in progress**
under way, proceeding, going on, happening,
occurring, continuing, in preparation, not finished, not
completed
COLLOQ. in the pipeline, on the stocks

progression n
cycle, chain, string, succession, series, sequence, process,
stream, train, order, course, advance, headway, passage,
progress, development, forward movement
TECHNICAL movement, motion, direct motion, resolution,
paraphonia
OLD precession
FORMAL advancement

progressive adj, n
♦ adj
1 MODERN, avant-garde, advanced, forward-looking,
forward-thinking, enlightened, liberal, radical,
revolutionary, reformist, innovative, dynamic, enterprising,
go-ahead, up-and-coming
2 ADVANCING, continuing, developing, growing, increasing,
escalating, intensifying, accelerating, gradual
E3 1 conservative **2** regressive
♦ n
reformer, modernizer, innovator, originator, fresh thinker,
creator, pioneer, deviser, developer, trailblazer

progressively adv
gradually, increasingly, step by step, by degrees, by/in
stages, little by little, piecemeal, bit by bit

prohibit v
forbid, ban, bar, veto, outlaw, rule out, prevent, exclude,
stop, hinder, hamper, impede, obstruct, restrict
OLD defend, injunct
FORMAL proscribe, preclude, interdict, enjoin
E3 permit, allow, authorize

prohibited adj
forbidden, banned, barred, taboo, vetoed,
embargoed, verboten
FORMAL disallowed, interdicted, proscribed
E3 permitted, allowed

prohibition n
forbidding, forbiddance, ban, bar, constraint, veto,
restriction, obstruction, exclusion, prevention, negation,
embargo
TECHNICAL injunction
FORMAL disallowance, forbiddal, interdict, interdiction,
proscription
E3 permission

prohibitionist n
teetotaller, abolitionist, dry, pussyfoot

prohibitive adj
forbidding, preposterous, excessive, exorbitant,
extortionate, impossible, restrictive, restraining,
suppressive, repressive, prohibiting, prohibitory
FORMAL proscriptive
COLLOQ. sky-high, steep
E3 encouraging, reasonable

project n, v
♦ n
scheme, campaign, plan, venture, programme, design,
proposal, assignment, contract, task, job, work,
occupation, activity, enterprise, undertaking, idea,
conception
♦ v
1 PREDICT, forecast, plan, propose, intend, extrapolate,
estimate, reckon, calculate, gauge, expect,
design, map out
FORMAL predetermine
2 THROW, fling, hurl, cast, launch, propel, discharge
COLLOQ. chuck
3 PROTRUDE, stick out, stand out, extend, bulge, jut out,
overhang
FORMAL obtrude

projectile n
missile, rocket, shell, shot, grenade, bullet, ball, bomb,
mortar

projecting adj
overhanging, protruding, sticking out, protrusive, beetling
FORMAL exsertile, extrusive, extrusory, protrudent

projection n
1 PREDICTION, forecast, expectation, extrapolation, estimate,
estimation, reckoning, calculation, computation, plan,
design
2 PROTUBERANCE, bulge, jutting, overhang, ledge, sill,
shelf, ridge

proletarian adj
working-class, ordinary, common, plebeian

proletariat n
working class, common people, masses, mob, lower
classes, rabble, herd, hoi polloi, rank and file, canaille,
commoners, commonalty, third estate, great unwashed,
riff-raff
COLLOQ. plebs, proles

proliferate v
multiply, reproduce, grow quickly, breed, increase,
increase rapidly, build up, intensify, extend, escalate,
mushroom, snowball, rocket, spread, expand, flourish,
thrive
FORMAL burgeon
E3 dwindle

proliferation n
multiplication, increase, rapid increase, intensification,
escalation, expansion, spread, extension, build-up,
concentration, duplication, mushrooming, snowballing,
rocketing
TECHNICAL ecblastesis
E3 decrease

prolific adj
productive, fruitful, fertile, profuse, copious, plentiful,
abundant, rank
OLD broody
FORMAL fecund, luxuriant
E3 unproductive

prolix adj
long-winded, verbose, lengthy, prolonged, prosy,
discursive, digressive, long, diffuse, rambling, tedious,
tiresome, wordy
TECHNICAL pleonastic
FORMAL protracted
E3 succinct

prolixity n
long-windedness, verboseness, verbiage, wordiness,
prosiness, rambling, discursiveness, diffuseness, wandering,
verbosity, boringness, tediousness
TECHNICAL pleonasm
E3 succinctness

prologue n
introduction, foreword, preface, preamble, preliminary,
prelude
FORMAL exordium, proem, prolegomena, prooemion,
prooemium

prolong v
lengthen, extend, elongate, stretch (out),
draw out, spin out, drag out, delay, continue,
perpetuate, sustain
OLD prorogue; (Shakesp) linger, respite
FORMAL protract
E3 shorten

prolongation n
extension, lengthening, stretching, continuation,
perpetuation
FORMAL protraction
E3 shortening

promenade *n, v*
♦ *n*
1 SEAFRONT, walkway, front, parade, esplanade, prom, boulevard, terrace
2 WALK, stroll, breather, airing, saunter, turn, walkabout
FORMAL constitutional
♦ *v*
walk, stroll, saunter, strut, swagger, sally forth, parade
FORMAL perambulate
COLLOQ. mosey

prominence *n*
1 FAME, celebrity, renown, eminence, pre-eminence, illustriousness, distinction, greatness, note, importance, conspicuousness, reputation, name, standing, stature, rank, prestige, weight, emphasis, top billing, pride of place
OLD prominency
2 BULGE, protuberance, swelling, jutting, protruding, bump, hump, lump, mound, rise, rising, elevation, projection, rib, boss, embossment, process, headland, promontory, pinnacle, crest, height, cliff, crag
TECHNICAL antitragus, tragus, mastoid, cusp, colliculus, torus
OLD prominency
F∃ 1 unimportance, insignificance

prominent *adj*
1 *a prominent writer*
famous, well-known, celebrated, renowned, noted, notable, eminent, pre-eminent, distinguished, respected, illustrious, leading, foremost, chief, main, important, popular, outstanding, top, acclaimed
COLLOQ. A-list
2 NOTICEABLE, conspicuous, obvious, unmistak(e)able, striking, eye-catching
3 BULGING, protuberant, projecting, jutting (out), standing out, sticking out, protruding, obtrusive, protrusive
F∃ 1 unknown, unimportant, insignificant **2** inconspicuous

promiscuity *n*
looseness, laxity, permissiveness, wantonness, immorality, dissoluteness, dissipation, licentiousness, debauchery, depravity
FORMAL profligacy, protervity
COLLOQ. sleeping around
F∃ chastity, morality

promiscuous *adj*
loose, immoral, licentious, dissolute, debauched, dissipated, abandoned, wanton, fast, of easy virtue, sluttish, casual, random, haphazard, indiscriminate, mixed
FORMAL profligate
COLLOQ. swinging, slack, sleeping around
F∃ chaste, moral

promise *v, n*
♦ *v*
1 VOW, pledge, swear, take an oath, contract, give an undertaking, undertake, give your word, vouch, warrant, guarantee, assure, give an assurance
OLD plight, betroth
2 *clouds that promise rain*
indicate, suggest, hint at, signify, denote, be a sign of
FORMAL augur, presage, betoken
♦ *n*
1 VOW, pledge, oath, word, word of honour, bond, hand, betrothal, guarantee, assurance, contract, undertaking, engagement, commitment, committal
FORMAL compact, covenant
2 POTENTIAL, ability, capability, aptitude, talent, flair
3 *a promise of autumn sunshine*
sign, hint, suggestion, indication, evidence
■ **promised land**
paradise, heaven, land of milk and honey, Zion, Canaan, Elysium, Elysian fields, Shangri-la, El Dorado, Utopia

---

SYNONYM NUANCES

verb sense 1
Vow can be used to suggest a firm resolve, particularly one binding you to a person or a cause, and **pledge** or **take an oath** are similar, though often given more formally or ritually. **Swear** suggests an assertion made in earnest: *she swore she would behave*. You might choose to use **contract** of a more legally binding commitment.
   Give an undertaking and **undertake** suggest a less officially binding but serious expression of intent. **Vouch**, **warrant** and **guarantee** are generally used for affirming something is true or will happen: *her colleagues vouched for her good character*. **Assure** and **give an assurance** are perhaps least suggestive of strongly expressed promise, but have added implications of instilling, or attempting to instil, confidence: *the tutor assured me that my exam results would be fine*.

---

promising *adj*
favourable, rosy, bright, encouraging, optimistic, hopeful, talented, able, gifted, budding
FORMAL auspicious, propitious
COLLOQ. up-and-coming
F∃ unpromising, inauspicious, discouraging

promontory *n*
cliff, headland, head, foreland, bluff, precipice, point, projection, prominence, ridge, spur, cape, naze, ness, peninsula

promote *v*
1 UPGRADE, advance, move up, raise, elevate, exalt, honour
FORMAL aggrandize, prefer
2 ENCOURAGE, recommend, advocate, champion, endorse, sponsor, support, back, help, aid, assist, advance, foster, nurture, further, forward, boost, stimulate, urge, contribute to
FORMAL espouse
3 ADVERTISE, publicize, popularize, market, merchandize, sell
COLLOQ. plug, hype, push, puff up
F∃ 1 demote, relegate **2** discourage, hinder; *formal* disparage

promoter *n*
supporter, upholder, champion, advocate, campaigner, pleader, vindicator, proponent, exponent, evanglist, speaker, spokesman, spokeswoman, spokesperson

promotion *n*
1 ADVANCEMENT, upgrading, rise, elevation, exaltation, move-up
TECHNICAL remove
FORMAL preferment, aggrandizement, prelation
2 ENCOURAGEMENT, support, recommendation, advocacy, urging, fostering, contribution, backing, furtherance, development, speeding, boosting
FORMAL espousal
3 ADVERTISING, publicity, campaign, propaganda, marketing, payola, puff, puffery
COLLOQ. plugging, hype, pushing, promo
F∃ 1 demotion **2** discouragement, obstruction; *formal* disparagement

prompt *adj, adv, v, n*
♦ *adj*
punctual, on time, immediate, instantaneous, instant, sudden, direct, quick, swift, rapid, speedy, unhesitating, willing, ready, alert, eager, responsive, timely, early; *Scot* frack
OLD expedite, pernicious
FORMAL expeditious
F∃ slow, hesitant, late
♦ *adv*
promptly, punctually, exactly, on time, on the dot, to the minute, sharp
COLLOQ. dead on, bang on, spot-on

◆ v
cause, give rise to, result in, lead, occasion, produce, make, instigate, call forth, elicit, provoke, induce, incite, urge, encourage, inspire, move, stimulate, motivate, spur, impel, prod, remind
OLD premove
FORMAL expedite
E3 deter, dissuade
◆ n
reminder, cue, refresher, encouragement, hint, help, jolt, prod, spur, stimulus

prompting n
encouragement, reminder, reminding, advice, assistance, hint, influence, jogging, prodding, pushing, suggestion, urging, persuasion, incitement, pressing, pressure
FORMAL admonition, protreptic
E3 dissuasion

promptly adv
1 IMMEDIATELY, instantly, directly, unhesitatingly, quickly, speedily, swiftly, without further ado, smartly
FORMAL forthwith
COLLOQ. pronto, yesterday, before you know it, before you can say Jack Robinson, in two shakes of a lamb's tail, like a shot
2 PUNCTUALLY, on time, on target, exactly, on the dot, to the minute, sharp, as soon as possible, posthaste
COLLOQ. bang on, spot-on, dead on, pronto, asap, pdq, pretty damn quick

promptness n
punctuality, quickness, readiness, speed, swiftness, willingness, briskness, dispatch, eagerness, alertness, haste
FORMAL alacrity, expedition, promptitude
E3 formal tardiness

promulgate v
announce, proclaim, declare, decree, promote, circulate, notify, communicate, make known, make public, publish, spread, publicize, broadcast, advertise, issue
FORMAL disseminate

promulgation n
announcement, communication, declaration, proclamation, publication, publicizing, issuance, promulgating
FORMAL dissemination

prone adj
1 LIKELY, given, inclined, disposed, bent, apt, liable, subject, tending, susceptible, vulnerable
OLD proclive
FORMAL predisposed
2 *she lay prone*
face down, prostrate, flat, horizontal, full-length, stretched
OLD proclive
FORMAL recumbent, procumbent
E3 **1** unlikely, immune **2** upright, supine

proneness n
inclination, leaning, tendency, susceptibility, aptness, bent, bias, disposition, liability, weakness
FORMAL penchant, proclivity, propensity
E3 dislike

prong n
point, spike, projection, spur, tine, tip, fork, grain

pronounce v
1 SAY, utter, speak, express, voice, vocalize, sound, enunciate, articulate, stress
2 DECLARE, announce, proclaim, decree, judge, affirm, assert

pronounceable adj
speakable, utterable, sayable, vocable, articulable, enunciable, expressible
E3 unpronounceable

pronounced adj
clear, distinct, definite, positive, decided, marked, noticeable, conspicuous, evident, obvious, striking, unmistak(e)able, strong, broad, thick
E3 faint, vague

pronouncement n
declaration, statement, announcement, judgement, notification, proclamation, assertion, decree, edict, manifesto, dictum
FORMAL pronunciamento, *ipse dixit*, promulgation

pronunciation n
speech, diction, elocution, enunciation, articulation, saying, uttering, voicing, vocalization, delivery, accent, stress, inflection, intonation, modulation

proof n, adj
◆ n
evidence, documentation, demonstration, verification, confirmation, corroboration, certification, validation, substantiation, authentication
FORMAL attestation
COLLOQ. smoking gun
◆ adj
impenetrable, impervious, proofed, repellent, resistant, strong, tight, treated, fireproof, weatherproof, waterproof, rainproof, leakproof, windproof, bombproof, bulletproof, childproof, foolproof, tamperproof, soundproof
E3 permeable, untreated

> **PROVERBS**
> The proof of the pudding is in the eating

prop v, n
◆ v
1 SUPPORT, sustain, uphold, hold up, maintain, shore (up), stay, brace, buttress, bolster (up), underpin, set, underwrite
2 *propped against the wall*
lean, rest, stand, balance, steady
◆ n
1 *a clothes prop*
support, stick, post, column, shaft, stay, mainstay, strut, buttress, upright, bolster, brace, truss, stanchion
2 *drink is the prop in his life*
mainstay, support, pillar, column, supporter, anchor

propaganda n
advertising, publicity, promotion, information, indoctrination, brainwashing, disinformation, Agitprop
COLLOQ. hype, ballyhoo

propagandist n
promoter, advocate, canvasser, publicist, pamphleteer, evangelist, proselytizer, indoctrinator
FORMAL proponent
COLLOQ. plugger

propagandize v
1 *propagandize communism*
champion, advocate, promote, uphold, campaign for, argue for, press for, preach
2 BRAINWASH, indoctrinate, pressurize, re-educate, persuade, talk into, win over

propagate v
1 SPREAD, transmit, broadcast, communicate, distribute, proclaim, diffuse, circulate, publish, publicize, promote
FORMAL disseminate, promulgate
2 INCREASE, multiply, proliferate, grow, generate, produce, breed, spawn, reproduce
OLD beget
FORMAL procreate

propagation n
1 COMMUNICATION, spread, spreading, transmission, promotion, distribution, circulation, diffusion
FORMAL dissemination, promulgation
2 INCREASE, generation, breeding, multiplication, proliferation, spawning, reproduction
OLD procreation

propel *v*
move, drive, impel, force, thrust, push (forward), project, launch, shoot, send, wheel, leg, row, oar, paddle, scull, punt, pole, pump, sail, swim, waft, frogmarch, loft; *Scot* ca'
COLLOQ. power, shove
F3 stop

propeller *n*
screw, airscrew, rotor, vane, prop

propensity *n*
tendency, liability, susceptibility, inclination, leaning, disposition, aptness, proneness, bent, bias, readiness, foible, weakness
FORMAL penchant, predisposition, proclivity
F3 disinclination

proper *adj*
1 RIGHT, correct, accurate, exact, precise, true, genuine, real, actual
2 ACCEPTED, correct, suitable, appropriate, fitting, acceptable, conventional, orthodox, established, decent, respectable, polite, refined, genteel, strict, gentlemanly, ladylike, prim, prudish, formal
F3 **1** wrong, incorrect **2** improper, indecent

properly *adv*
1 ACCEPTABLY, appropriately, suitably, fittingly, conventionally, correctly, respectably
2 CORRECTLY, accurately, rightly, right, exactly, precisely, actually, faultlessly, flawlessly, unerringly
F3 **1** unacceptably, rudely **2** incorrectly, wrongly, inaccurately

property *n*
1 ESTATE, land, real estate, acres, premises, buildings, house(s), wealth, riches, resources, means, capital, assets, holding(s), belongings, possessions, goods, chattels, paraphernalia
FORMAL effects
COLLOQ. gear, things, clobber
2 FEATURE, trait, quality, attribute, characteristic, idiosyncrasy, quirk, peculiarity, mark

> **QUOTATIONS**
> Property is theft
> PIERRE JOSEPH PROUDHON, *Qu'est-ce que la propriété?*

prophecy *n*
prediction, forecast, prognosis, second sight, fortune-telling, divination, soothsaying, message
FORMAL augury, prognostication, vaticination
Related adjective: vatic

prophesy *v*
predict, foresee, foretell, forewarn, forecast
FORMAL prognosticate, augur, vaticinate

prophet, prophetess *n*
seer, soothsayer, foreteller, forecaster, oracle, clairvoyant, fortune-teller
FORMAL prognosticator, vaticinator
■ **prophet of doom**
pessimist, doomwatcher, Jeremiah, Cassandra
COLLOQ. doom merchant, doomster

prophetic *adj*
forecasting, predictive, prognostic, foreshadowing, oracular, fey
FORMAL sibylline, presaging, prescient, augural, divinatory, fatidical, mantic, vatic, vaticidal
F3 unprophetic

prophylactic *adj, n*
◆ *adj*
preventive, preventative, anticipatory, pre-emptive, inhibitory, obstructive, precautionary, protective, counteractive, deterrent
F3 causative, fostering

◆ *n*
1 PREVENTIVE, preventative, preservative, precaution, immunization
2 CONDOM, sheath, contraceptive, female condom, Femidom®; *N Am* protective
SLANG French letter, johnnie, rubber; *N Am* scumbag, safe

propinquity *n*
nearness, closeness, connection, tie, vicinity, neighbourhood, proximity, adjacency, relation, relationship, blood, kinship, affiliation, affinity
FORMAL consanguinity, contiguity, kindredness, kindredship
F3 remoteness

propitiate *v*
reconcile, pacify, placate, satisfy, appease, conciliate, mollify, soothe
F3 anger, provoke

propitiation *n*
reconciliation, peacemaking, appeasement, conciliation, mollification, pacification, placation, pacifying
F3 angering, provocation

propitiatory *adj*
reconciliatory, peacemaking, soothing, pacifying, pacificatory, appeasing, conciliatory, mollifying, assuaging
FORMAL placative, placatory, propitiative
F3 provocative

propitious *adj*
favourable, fortunate, advantageous, happy, friendly, gracious, opportune, timely, promising, prosperous, encouraging, reassuring, well-disposed, bright, lucky, kindly, rosy, benign, beneficial, benevolent
FORMAL auspicious
F3 inauspicious

proponent *n*
advocate, supporter, backer, proposer, subscriber, apologist, partisan, defender, enthusiast, exponent, upholder, vindicator, champion, friend, patron
FORMAL propounder
F3 opponent, enemy

proportion *n*
1 PERCENTAGE, fraction, part, segment, portion, measure, division, share, quota, amount
COLLOQ. cut, split, whack, slice of the cake, piece of the action
2 RATIO, relationship, correspondence, symmetry, balance, distribution, quotient
3 *a task/building of huge proportions*
dimensions, measurements, size, magnitude, extent, volume, capacity, bulk, mass, height, length, depth, breadth, width, scale
F3 **2** disproportion, imbalance

proportional *adj*
proportionate, relative, equivalent, commensurate, consistent, corresponding, analogous, comparable, equitable, even
F3 disproportionate

proportionally *adv*
proportionately, relatively, correspondingly, comparably, commensurately, evenly, pro rata
F3 disproportionately

proposal *n*
plan, scheme, project, design, programme, manifesto, presentation, proposition, suggestion, recommendation, motion, bid, offer, tender, terms

propose *v*
1 SUGGEST, recommend, move, advance, put forward, introduce, bring up, advocate, plan, table, place, submit, present, offer, tender, slate; *Scot* propone
FORMAL proffer, propound, moot, motion, put forth
COLLOQ. vote
2 INTEND, mean, aim, purpose, plan, design, have in mind
OLD bethink
3 NOMINATE, put up, name, recommend, suggest

4 *propose marriage*
ask to marry, ask for someone's hand in marriage
OLD plight your troth
COLLOQ. pop the question, go down on bended knee
F3 1 withdraw

proposition *n, v*
♦ *n*
1 PROPOSAL, suggestion, deal, theory, plan, project,
programme, recommendation, scheme, manifesto, motion,
tender
FORMAL hypothesis, theorem
2 TASK, activity, undertaking, venture, job
3 *a sexual proposition*
advance, overture, approach, indirect proposal/suggestion,
pass
COLLOQ. come-on
♦ *v*
accost, solicit, make sexual advances/overtures to, make
an indecent proposal to, make a pass at

propound *v*
put forward, suggest, propose, advance, set forth,
advocate, contend, lay down, present, submit
FORMAL move, postulate
F3 oppose

proprietor, proprietress *n*
landlord, landlady, title-holder, freeholder, leaseholder,
landholder, landowner, owner, possessor, deed holder,
entrepreneur, patron
OLD proprietrix

propriety *n*
1 MODESTY, decorum, decency, civility, etiquette, protocol,
delicacy, respectability, refinement, rightness, correctness,
manners, good manners, politeness, courtesy, breeding,
appropriateness, aptness, becomingness, suitableness,
fitness, gentlemanliness, ladylikeness
OLD seemliness
FORMAL punctilio, rectitude
2 *observe proprieties*
civility, standard, etiquette, convention, decency, social
graces, social niceties
COLLOQ. the done thing, p's and q's
F3 1, 2 impropriety

propulsion *n*
drive, driving force, power, pressure, push, thrust, motive
force, momentum, impetus, impulse, impulsion

pro rata *adv*
proportionally, proportionately, relatively, correspondingly,
comparably, commensurately, evenly
F3 disproportionately

prosaic *adj*
mundane, ordinary, routine, dull, stale, boring,
commonplace, humdrum, matter-of-fact, unimaginative,
uninspired, uninspiring, monotonous, bland, tame, trite,
banal, vacuous, vapid, pedestrian, workaday, flat, dry,
hackneyed, everyday
F3 imaginative, interesting

prosaically *adv*
mundanely, ordinarily, unimaginatively, uninspiringly,
monotonously, blandly, dully
F3 imaginatively, interestingly

proscribe *v*
forbid, prohibit, ban, outlaw, bar, banish, condemn,
embargo, reject, exclude, boycott, censure, damn, doom,
black, blackball, denounce, deport, expel, exile,
excommunicate, expatriate, ostracize
FORMAL interdict, disallow
F3 allow, permit

> ⚠ **proscribe** or **prescribe**?
> *See panel at* **prescribe.**

proscription *n*
prohibition, ban, bar, barring, embargo, outlawry, censure,
condemnation, damning, denunciation, ostracism,
rejection, banishment, boycott, deportation, expulsion,
ejection, eviction, exclusion, exile, excommunication,
expatriation
FORMAL interdict
F3 admission, allowing

prosecute *v*
accuse, sue, charge, bring charges, bring an action against,
prefer charges, take to court, litigate, summon, put on trial,
try, proceed, process; *Scot* pursue
FORMAL arraign, indict
F3 defend

prosecution *n*
accusation, bringing charges, charging, trial, taking to
court, litigation, indictment, impeachment

proselyte *n*
convert, neophyte, new believer, changed person, new
person, recruit, catechumen

proselytize *v*
convert, evangelize, make converts, persuade, win over,
propagandize, spread the gospel, bring into the fold, bring
to God

prosody
See panel on next page

prospect *n, v*
♦ *n*
1 *the prospect of rain*
chance(s), odds, probability, likelihood, likeness,
possibility, hope, expectation, anticipation, outlook, future,
promise
2 *a prospect of the bay*
outlook, vista, view, scene, panorama, aspect, spectacle,
perspective, landscape, opening
F3 1 unlikelihood
♦ *v*
explore, search, look for, seek, survey, examine, inspect,
quest, fossick
COLLOQ. nose

prospective *adj*
future, -to-be, would-be, intended, designate, destined,
forthcoming, approaching, coming, imminent, awaited,
expected, anticipated, hoped-for, likely, possible,
probable, potential, aspiring

prospectus *n*
syllabus, manifesto, outline, synopsis, pamphlet, leaflet,
brochure, catalogue, list, literature, announcement,
description, plan, scheme, programme
FORMAL conspectus

prosper *v*
boom, thrive, flourish, flower, bloom, succeed, be
successful, get on, get on well, do well, turn out well,
advance, progress, make progress, grow rich
FORMAL burgeon
COLLOQ. get ahead, get on in the world, go up in the
world, make your pile, hit the big time, hit the jackpot,
live on easy street
F3 fail

prosperity *n*
boom, plenty, affluence, wealth, riches, fortune, wellbeing,
welfare, luxury, success, good fortune
COLLOQ. the good life, the life of Riley, easy street,
bed of roses, land of milk and honey, clover,
lap of luxury
F3 adversity, poverty

prosperous *adj*
booming, thriving, flourishing, blooming, successful,
fortunate, lucky, rich, wealthy, affluent, well-off, well-to-do
FORMAL burgeoning, opulent
COLLOQ. well-heeled, rolling in it
F3 unfortunate, poor

Terms used in prosody include:

abstract verse	caesura	epitrite	Ionic	Pindaric	sprung rhythm
Alcaic verse	canto	epode	internal rhyme	poulters' measure	strophe
alexandrine	catalexis	eye rhyme	kyrielle	pyrrhic	substitution
alliteration	choliamb	false quantity	laisse	Pythian verse	synaphea
amphibrach	choree	feminine caesura	Leonine rhyme	quatorzain	tetrameter
amphimacer	choriamb	feminine ending	linked verse	quatrain	tetrapody
Anacreontic verse	cinquain	feminine rhyme	long-measure	reported verses	tetrastich
anacrusis	consonance	foot	macaronic	rhopalic	tribrach
analysed rhyme	couplet	free verse	masculine ending	rhyme royal	trimeter
anapaest	dactyl	galliambic	masculine rhyme	rime riche	triolet
antibacchius	decastich	glyconic	metre	rime suffisante	tripody
antispast	dipody	half-rhyme	miurus	rondeau	triseme
Archilochian verse	dispondee	heptameter	monometer	rondel	trochee
asclepiad	distich	heptapody	monorhyme	rove-over	villanelle
assonance	ditrochee	heroic couplet	paeon	Sapphic	virelay
asynartete	dizain	hexameter	pantoum	senarius	
ballade	dochmius	hexastich	pentameter	septenarius	
blank verse	elision	hypermetrical	pentastich	sonnet	
bouts rimés	enjambment	iamb	Petrarchan sonnet	Spenserian stanza	
broken rhyme	envoy	ictus	Pherecratean	spondee	

prostitute *n, v*

♦ *n*

harlot, call-girl, rent-boy, woman of the streets, woman of the town, woman of ill repute, loose woman, fallen woman, scarlet woman, whore, trollop, street-walker, cocotte, courtesan, bawd, *fille de joie*, *fille des rues*, drab, grande cocotte, lorette, lady of the night, geisha, hetaera, hierodule, loose fish, magdalen, night-walker, vizard-mask
OLD bulker, convertite, trull, moll, strumpet, cockatrice, public woman, wench, pug, punk, stew, stale; (*Shakesp*) quail, bona-roba, callet, polecat, road, venture
COLLOQ. hooker, hustler, pro, hostess, fancy woman; *N Am* working girl
SLANG *poule de luxe*, quiff, rough trade, tart, tom, tramp, brass, floozie; *N Am* ho, broad
OLD SLANG dell, mutton, dolly-mop, plover; (*Shakesp*) laced mutton

♦ *v*

cheapen, degrade, debase, demean, devalue, pervert, betray, sacrifice, misapply, misuse, profane

prostitution *n*

harlotry, whoredom, whoring, street-walking, vice, meretriciousness
OLD social evil
COLLOQ. the game, the oldest profession
Related adjective: meretricious

prostrate *adj, v*

♦ *adj*

1 FLAT, horizontal, prone, lying down, lying flat, fallen
2 OVERCOME, overwhelmed, devastated, crushed, paralysed, powerless, helpless, defenceless, laid low, brought to your knees, exhausted, worn out, tired out
COLLOQ. bushed, whacked, all-in, dead beat; *N Am* pooped (out), tuckered out
E₃ 1 erect **2** triumphant

♦ *v*

lay low, flatten, level, knock down, overcome, overwhelm, crush, overthrow, bring to your knees, tire, wear out, fatigue, exhaust, sap, drain, ruin
E₃ strengthen

■ **prostrate yourself**

bow down, kneel, kowtow, submit, grovel, cringe, abase yourself

prostration *n*

collapse, abasement, kneeling, kowtow, submission, depression, desolation, despair, despondency, dejection, grief, helplessness, weakness, weariness, exhaustion, paralysis, bow
FORMAL slough of despond, obeisance, genuflection
E₃ elation, exaltation, happiness, triumph

protagonist *n*

hero, heroine, lead, principal, leader, main/chief/leading character, leading figure/player, title role, prime mover, champion, advocate, supporter, banker, adherent, mainstay, standard-bearer, exponent, moving spirit
FORMAL proponent
E₃ critic, opponent

protean *adj*

ever-changing, changeable, versatile, inconstant, many-sided, variable, volatile, mercurial, multiform, mutable
TECHNICAL polymorphic, polymorphous, amoebic
E₃ stable, unchanging

protect *v*

safeguard, defend, guard, escort, cover, screen, shield, secure, watch over, look after, care for, take care of, support, shelter, harbour, keep, keep safe, conserve, preserve, save, ring-fence
See Synonym nuances panel at **defend**.
E₃ attack, neglect

protection *n*

1 *protection of the environment*
care, custody, charge, guardianship, safekeeping, conservation, preservation, safety, security, safeguard, defence
2 BARRIER, buffer, bulwark, defence, guard, shield, armour, screen, cover, shelter, safeguard, refuge, security, insurance
E₃ 1 neglect, attack

protective *adj*

1 *protective clothing*
waterproof, fireproof, windproof, insulating, covering, shielding, defensive
2 POSSESSIVE, defensive, motherly, maternal, fatherly, paternal, watchful, vigilant, careful, wary, over-protective
E₃ 2 aggressive, threatening

protector *n*

1 DEFENDER, benefactor, advocate, guardian, patron, champion, counsel, bodyguard, minder, keeper, father-figure
OLD (*Shakesp*) guardant
FORMAL protectress, protectrix
2 GUARD, safeguard, shield, cushion, bolster, pad, buffer, buckler, screen
E₃ 1 attacker, threat

protégé, protégée *n*

pupil, student, ward, charge, dependant, disciple, follower, discovery
COLLOQ. blue-eyed boy
E₃ guardian

protest *v, n*

♦ *v*

1 OBJECT, make/raise an objection to, speak out, take exception, complain, appeal, demonstrate, march, go on strike, down tools, sit in, work to rule, picket, oppose, disapprove, disagree, argue, reject, take issue
OLD abhor, obtest, reclaim
FORMAL remonstrate, demur
COLLOQ. gripe, whinge, kick up a fuss

2 *protest your innocence*
assert, maintain, contend, insist (on), profess, proclaim, announce, declare, affirm, testify
FORMAL attest, avow
1 accept

♦ *n*

1 OBJECTION, disapproval, disagreement, opposition, outcry, scruple, dissent, complaint, exception, protestation, fuss, appeal, demonstration, mass meeting, march, boycott, strike, hunger strike, sit-in, work-in, industrial action, work-to-rule, riot, civil disobedience
FORMAL demurral, remonstration, remonstrance
COLLOQ. demo, squawk

2 ASSERTION, contention, declaration, affirmation, proclamation, announcement
FORMAL attestation, avowal
1 acceptance

protestation *n*

1 STATEMENT, declaration, profession, affirmation, pledge, vow, assurance, oath
FORMAL asseveration, avowal, expostulation

2 OBJECTION, complaint, outcry, disagreement, protest, dissent
FORMAL remonstrance, remonstration

protester *n*
demonstrator, opposer, opponent, objector, complainer, agitator, striker, picket, rebel, mutineer, dissident, dissenter

protocol *n*
procedure, formalities, convention, custom, etiquette, manners, code of behaviour, civilities, good form
FORMAL propriety, decorum
COLLOQ. p's and q's

prototype *n*
original, model, mock-up, example, standard, type, pattern, precedent
FORMAL archetype, exemplar, paradigm

protract *v*
continue, draw out, extend, keep going, lengthen, prolong, make longer, spin out, stretch out, sustain
COLLOQ. drag out
shorten

protracted *adj*
long, lengthy, prolonged, extended, drawn-out, long-drawn-out, stretched out, spun out, overlong, endless, interminable
brief, shortened

protrude *v*
stick out, poke out, come through, bulge, jut out, project, extend, stand out, goggle, poke, pout, pop, beetle; *dialect* strout
OLD peer, strut
FORMAL protract, obtrude, extrude, exsert

protruding *adj*
jutting (out), prominent, protuberant, sticking out, proud
FORMAL exsertive, extrusive, extrusory, protrudent, protrusive
flat, flush

protrusion *n*
lump, bulge, knob, bump, outgrowth, projection, protuberance, swelling, jut
FORMAL obtrusion, process

protuberance *n*
lump, bump, bulge, bulging-out, bulb, knob, outgrowth, swelling, prominence, protrusion, projection, tumour, wart, welt, tuber, tubercle, paunch, beer belly, ball; *dialect* wame
TECHNICAL apophysis
OLD wallet
FORMAL excrescence, process
COLLOQ. pot-belly

protuberant *adj*
swelling, swollen, jutting, prominent, popping, full, bulging, bulbous, protruding, proud, beetling, bunched, gibbous
OLD astrut
FORMAL protrusive, exsertive, extrusive, extrusory, protrudent, rotund
flat

proud *adj*

1 CONCEITED, vain, egotistical, boastful, smug, complacent, arrogant, self-important, self-satisfied, cocky, presumptuous, haughty, full of yourself, scornful, high-handed, imperious, lordly, pompous, overweening, puffed up, overbearing, supercilious, snobbish; *dialect* proudful
OLD cockhorse, misproud, stout, sublime, superb, top-proud; (*Spenser*) brag
FORMAL hubristic
COLLOQ. high and mighty, snooty, toffee-nosed, stuck-up, jumped-up, too big for your boots, bigheaded
SLANG *N Am* dicty

2 SATISFIED, contented, gratified, pleased, delighted, happy, glad, content, thrilled, honoured

3 DIGNIFIED, noble, honourable, worthy, self-respecting, walking tall

4 *a proud moment*
satisfying, gratifying, pleasing, memorable, notable, splendid, marvellous, wonderful
COLLOQ. red-letter

5 *a proud sight*
splendid, grand, imposing, glorious, magnificent, outstanding, notable, honourable, worthy

6 *the surface stands proud*
projecting, jutting, prominent, protuberant, sticking out, jutting out
1 humble, modest, unassuming **2** ashamed, abashed **3** deferential, ignoble

---

SYNONYM NUANCES

sense 1
Many of the synonyms, for example **conceited**, **bigheaded** and **vain**, are very disapproving in tone. **Egotistical** suggests a selfish concern for your own interests as well as a high opinion of yourself. **Boastful** is appropriate for bragging about your own perceived accomplishments, while both **smug** and **complacent** suggest a more internalized feeling of being very pleased with yourself, with the latter having further implications of blinkeredness: *a complacent belief in his own abilities lost him the match.*

Arrogant and **cocky** can be used to suggest a visibly over-confident attitude, while **presumptuous**, although similar, further implies taking things for granted: *the way I have been treated by people has been patronizing and presumptuous.*

Haughty and **supercilious** suggest someone has belief in their own superiority and acts with disdain, whereas **scornful** goes further and would describe someone who openly displays their contempt for others. Meanwhile **high-handed**, **lordly**, **imperious** and **overweening** are appropriate terms for someone who adopts a dominant role. **Pompous** and **puffed up**, although similar, have further implications of affectation, while **snobbish** tends to be reserved for someone's awareness of their own and others' social standing.

proudly adv
1 *she smiled proudly at her son*
with satisfaction, with delight, contentedly, delightedly,
appreciatively
2 ARROGANTLY, vainly, boastfully, smugly, conceitedly,
haughtily
COLLOQ. bigheadedly, snootily

provable adj
demonstrable, establishable, confirmable, verifiable,
testable
FORMAL attestable, corroborable, evincible
⊟ unprovable

prove v
1 SHOW, demonstrate, verify, confirm, bear out, bear
witness to, document, certify, authenticate, validate,
justify, establish, determine, ascertain, try (out), test, check,
examine, analyse
FORMAL attest, corroborate, substantiate
2 TURN OUT, come about, be the case
FORMAL transpire, eventuate
COLLOQ. pan out
⊟ 1 disprove, discredit, falsify

proven adj
proved, confirmed, certified, checked, established,
accepted, dependable, reliable, tested, tried, definite,
authentic, trustworthy, valid, verified, undoubted
FORMAL attested, corroborated
⊟ unproven

provenance n
source, origin, derivation, birthplace, spring
FORMAL provenience

provender n
food, provisions, foodstuffs, eats, supplies, stores, rations,
sustenance, groceries, edibles, comestibles, fare, feed,
fodder, forage
OLD aliment, pabulum; (*Spenser*) pasture; (*Shakesp*)
repasture
FORMAL viands, victuals
COLLOQ. eatables, tuck
SLANG grub, nosh, chow, scoff; *Aust & NZ* tucker

proverb n
saying, adage, aphorism, maxim, byword, motto, dictum,
axiom, precept, saw, gnome
FORMAL apophthegm, paroemia

proverbial adj
axiomatic, accepted, conventional, traditional, customary,
time-honoured, famous, famed, well-known, renowned,
acknowledged, legendary, notorious, infamous, typical,
archetypal

provide v
1 SUPPLY, furnish, stock, equip, outfit, kit out, prepare for,
cater, serve, present, give, offer, contribute, yield, lend,
add, bring, lay on, put on
FORMAL afford, impart
2 PLAN FOR, make plans for, allow, make provision,
accommodate, arrange for, anticipate, take precautions,
take measures/steps
3 STATE, specify, stipulate, lay down, require
⊟ 1 take, remove

■ **provide for**
support, maintain, sustain, look after, take care of, keep,
endow, fend
⊟ ignore, neglect

provided conj
given, as/so long as, on condition, on the understanding,
presuming, assuming, in the event, with the proviso

providence n
1 FATE, destiny, divine intervention, God's will, fortune,
luck
2 PRUDENCE, far-sightedness, foresight, forethought,
judgement, wisdom, caution, care, thrift, economy
FORMAL sagacity, circumspection, judiciousness
⊟ 2 improvidence

provident adj
prudent, far-sighted, cautious, careful, thrifty, economical,
frugal
FORMAL sagacious, circumspect, judicious
⊟ improvident

providential adj
fortunate, lucky, opportune, timely, happy, convenient,
welcome, heaven-sent
FORMAL fortuitous
⊟ unfortunate, untimely

providentially adv
fortunately, luckily, coveniently, happily, opportunely
FORMAL fortuitously
⊟ unfortunately

provider n
supplier, supporter, sponsor, patron, benefactor, wage-
earner, breadwinner, earner, giver, donor, funder, source,
mainstay
COLLOQ. angel

providing conj
provided, given, as long as, on condition, on the
understanding, presuming, assuming, in the event, with
the proviso

province n
1 REGION, area, district, zone, county, shire, department,
territory, state, colony, dependency
2 *live out in the provinces*
backwater, backwoods
COLLOQ. middle of nowhere, the sticks, dorp; *N Am* the
boondocks, the boonies
3 RESPONSIBILITY, concern, duty, office, business, role,
function, charge, field, sphere, area, domain, department,
line
COLLOQ. pigeon

provincial adj, n
♦ adj
1 *a provincial theatre*
regional, local, rural, rustic, country, mofussil
OLD presidial
2 *provincial attitudes*
parochial, insular, inward-looking, limited, intolerant,
narrow, narrow-minded, small-minded, naive, suburban,
unsophisticated, home-grown, small-town, outlying,
parish-pump
COLLOQ. hick
⊟ 1 national, metropolitan, capital, cosmopolitan, urban
2 sophisticated, urbane
♦ n
country bumpkin, yokel, rustic, peasant
COLLOQ. hillbilly, hick, hayseed

provincialism n
parochialism, provinciality, regionalism, sectionalism,
insularity, localism, narrow-mindedness
⊟ sophistication

provision n
1 SUPPLY, giving, equipping, furnishing, preparation,
service, contribution, outfitting
2 FACILITIES, amenities, services, resources
3 PLAN, arrangement, preparation, measure, step,
allowance, contingency, concession, precaution
4 STIPULATION, specification, proviso, condition, term,
requirement, clause, qualification, rider
5 FOOD, foodstuff, groceries, sustenance, rations, supplies,
stocks, stores
OLD victuals, viands
COLLOQ. eatables

provisional *adj*
temporary, interim, transitional, stopgap, makeshift,
conditional, tentative, pencilled in, subject to confirmation
COLLOQ. pro tem
☒ permanent, fixed, definite, confirmed

provisionally *adv*
temporarily, tentatively, for the time being, interim,
meanwhile
COLLOQ. pro tem

proviso *n*
condition, term, requirement, stipulation, qualification,
reservation, restriction, limitation, provision, clause, rider
COLLOQ. strings

provocation *n*
1 ANNOYANCE, enraging, angering, irritation, exasperation,
vexation, grievance, offence, insult, affront, injury, taunt,
challenge, dare
COLLOQ. aggravation
2 CAUSE, grounds, justification, reason, motive, stimulus,
stimulation, motivation, incitement, inducement,
inspiration, eliciting, production, generation, instigation

provocative *adj*
1 ANNOYING, irritating, infuriating, exasperating, galling,
outrageous, offensive, insulting, abusive
COLLOQ. aggravating
2 STIMULATING, exciting, challenging
3 EROTIC, titillating, arousing, sexy, sexually arousing,
seductive, alluring, tempting, inviting, tantalizing, teasing,
suggestive
☒ **1** conciliatory

provocatively *adv*
1 ANNOYINGLY, infuriatingly, exasperatingly, offensively,
outrageously
2 EROTICALLY, sexily, sexually, seductively, suggestively,
temptingly, alluringly, invitingly

provoke *v*
1 ANNOY, irritate, rile, offend, insult, anger, enrage,
infuriate, incense, madden, exasperate, tease, taunt, pique,
vex, nettle, harass
FORMAL exacerbate
COLLOQ. aggravate, get at, bug, needle, hassle, miff, wind
up, make someone's blood boil, get someone's back up,
rattle someone's cage, ruffle someone's feathers, drive
mad, drive crazy, drive up the wall, drive round the
bend/twist, make someone see red, make sparks fly, get
under someone's skin, get under someone's nose, get on
someone's wick, make someone's hackles rise
SLANG drive bananas, nark, piss off
OLD SLANG get someone's shirt out
2 GOAD, stir, spur, prod, move, prompt, stimulate,
motivate, incite, rouse, inflame, kindle, instigate, entice
COLLOQ. egg on
SLANG N Am sound
3 CAUSE, occasion, give rise to, produce, generate, induce,
elicit, evoke, call forth, engender, promote, excite, inspire,
move
☒ **1** please, pacify **3** result

provoking *adj*
annoying, exasperating, infuriating, irritating, offensive,
maddening, obstructive, tiresome, vexatious, vexing,
irking, irksome, galling
COLLOQ. aggravating
☒ pleasing

prow *n*
bow(s), fore, stem, front, head, nose, forepart,
cut-water
☒ stern

prowess *n*
1 ACCOMPLISHMENT, attainment, ability, capability, aptitude,
skill, skilfulness, expertise, facility, mastery, command,
proficiency, talent, genius, dexterity, adeptness, adroitness,
vassalage

2 BRAVERY, courage, dauntlessness, fearlessness,
daring, heroism, gallantry, pluck, valour, audacity,
intrepidity
COLLOQ. grit, nerve, guts, bottle, spunk

prowl *v*
creep, hunt, rove, roam, move stealthily, slink, sneak,
stalk, lurk, skulk, steal, range, search, scavenge, cruise,
patrol, nose, snoop, mouse; *dialect* ratch
OLD prole, proll, proul, lurch

prowler *n*
stalker, scavenger, patrol, roamer, nighthawk, tenebrio
OLD proler, proller, prouler

proximity *n*
closeness, nearness, vicinity, neighbourhood, adjacency,
juxtaposition
FORMAL contiguity, propinquity
☒ remoteness

proxy *n*
agent, deputy, stand-in, substitute, surrogate,
representative, delegate, attorney, factor

prude *n*
prig, old maid, puritan, Mrs Grundy
COLLOQ. goody-goody, schoolmarm

prudence *n*
wisdom, judgement, good sense, common sense, care,
foresight, forethought, far-sightedness, economy,
heedfulness, preparedness, discretion, caution,
cautiousness, vigilance, wariness, planning, providence,
precaution, policy, happy medium, canniness, frugality,
saving, thrift, husbandry
FORMAL circumspectness, circumspection, judiciousness,
sagacity, advisedness
☒ imprudence, rashness, improvidence

SYNONYM NUANCES

Many of these synonyms are approving in tone; both
good sense and **common sense** share suggestions of
everyday practicality, while **care**, **heedfulness** and the
more active **vigilance** have more to do with being
aware of possible eventualities. Similarly, **foresight**,
forethought and **far-sightedness** imply consideration of
future possibilities, and **preparedness** and **precaution**
further suggest being ready for them.

   Economy, on the other hand, is more appropriate for
careful management of resources: *she attempted to
combine good living with economy*, and the less
common **husbandry** would describe careful financial
management. The terms **canniness**, **frugality** and **thrift**
could also all be used of shrewdness in handling
financial resources, although they may have slight but
unpleasant connotations of meanness.

   Discretion is more approving and implies due reserve
in someone's conduct, while both **caution** and
cautiousness, along with **wariness**, return to the
general idea of exercising restraint, and do not suggest
approval or disapproval.

   Providence and **policy** are positive terms to convey
the notion of skilful management or timely organization:
a scheme of forward planning and providence.

---

prudent *adj*
wise, sensible, politic, shrewd, discerning,
careful, well-advised, cautious, wary, vigilant,
discreet, provident, far-sighted, frugal,
economical, thrifty
OLD considerative, ware and wise
FORMAL judicious, circumspect, sagacious
☒ imprudent, unwise, careless, rash, improvident

prudently *adv*
sensibly, wisely, carefully, shrewdly,
discreetly, far-sightedly, warily, vigilantly, economically,
providently
☒ imprudently, rashly, unwisely, carelessly

prudery *n*
overmodesty, primness, squeamishness, starchiness, strictness, stuffiness, priggishness, prissiness, old-maidishness, puritanism, Grundyism
🖅 laxness

prudish *adj*
overmodest, overnice, proper, prim, narrow-minded, squeamish, demure, starchy, strait-laced, stuffy, puritanical, old-maidish, prissy, priggish, po-faced, ultra-virtuous, Victorian, mimsy
FORMAL pudibund
COLLOQ. goody-goody, schoolmarmish
🖅 lax, easy-going

prune *v*
clip, trim, snip, cut, cut back, cut off, dock, lop, pare, shape, reduce, shorten

prurient *adj*
salacious, lewd, dirty, obscene, indecent, lustful, desirous, itching, erotic, pornographic, lascivious, lecherous, voyeuristic
FORMAL concupiscent, cupidinous, libidinous
COLLOQ. smutty, blue
🖅 decent

pry *v*
meddle, interfere, intrude, peep, peer, nose, ferret, dig, delve
OLD prodnose; (*Spenser*) toot
COLLOQ. snoop, poke/stick your nose in, put your oar in
SLANG *N Am* gumshoe
🖅 mind your own business

prying *adj*
meddlesome, meddling, interfering, intrusive, nos(e)y, curious, inquisitive, spying, peering, peery
COLLOQ. snooping, snoopy
🖅 uninquisitive

psalm *n*
hymn, song, poem, prayer, chant, canticle, paean, paraphrase

pseud *n*
poser, poseur, trendy, fraud, humbug
COLLOQ. phoney

pseudo *adj*
false, sham, mock, pretended, imitation, fake, counterfeit, bogus, artificial, spurious, ersatz, quasi-, ungenuine
COLLOQ. phoney, pseud
🖅 genuine, real, authentic

pseudonym *n*
false name, assumed name, alias, incognito, pen-name, *nom de plume*, stage name
FORMAL allonym

psych *v*
■ **psych out**
intimidate, daunt, cow, overawe, domineer, appal, dismay, upset, unsettle, put off balance, alarm, scare, frighten, terrify, menace, tyrannize, terrorize, bully, browbeat, bulldoze, coerce, compel, pressure, pressurize, warn off
COLLOQ. throw, rattle, get to, lean on, twist someone's arm, put the screws on, put the frighteners on, turn the heat on
■ **psych yourself up**
prepare yourself mentally, get yourself prepared, work yourself up, gear yourself up, nerve yourself, steel yourself, brace yourself, pluck up courage
SLANG man up

psyche *n*
spirit, soul, anima, mind, self, inner self, inmost self, innermost self, deepest feelings, heart of hearts, consciousness, personality, awareness, individuality, subconscious, intellect, intelligence, understanding
TECHNICAL pneuma

psychiatrist *n*
analyst, psychoanalyst, therapist, psychotherapist, psychologist, psychoanalyser
COLLOQ. headshrinker, shrink, trick cyclist, head doctor, man in a white coat

psychic *adj, n*
♦ *adj*
1 *psychic power*
spiritual, supernatural, occult, mystic(al), clairvoyant, extrasensory, telepathic, telekinetic
2 MENTAL, psychological, intellectual, emotional, cognitive, spiritual
♦ *n*
clairvoyant, fortune-teller, prophet, prophetess, visionary, seer, soothsayer, augur, oracle, diviner, telepath

psychological *adj*
mental, intellectual, cognitive, emotional, subjective, subconscious, unconscious, psychosomatic, irrational, unreal, imaginary, theoretical, conceptual
FORMAL cerebral
COLLOQ. all in the mind
🖅 physical, real

psychologically *adv*
mentally, emotionally, intellectually, cognitively, unconsciously, subjectively, theoretically, conceptually

psychology *n*
1 *study psychology*
science of the mind, study of the mind, study of mental processes, science of human/animal behaviour
TECHNICAL metapsychology
See panels on next page
2 *the psychology of crowds*
mind, mental characteristics, behavioural characteristics, mental chemistry, make-up, attitudes, habits, motives, mindset
TECHNICAL conation
COLLOQ. what makes someone tick

psychopath *n*
lunatic, mad person, madman, madwoman, maniac, sociopath, psychotic
COLLOQ. psycho

psychopathic *adj*
lunatic, mad, insane, maniacal, psychotic, deranged, unbalanced, mentally disturbed, demented

psychosomatic *adj*
psychological, irrational, subjective, unreal, imaginary
COLLOQ. all in the mind

psychotic *adj*
insane, lunatic, unbalanced, disturbed, deranged, maniacal, out of your mind, out of your senses, of unsound mind, unhinged, crazed, unstable, *non compos mentis*, frenzied, wild, berserk, manic, maniac, distracted, distraught, fey, frenetic, frantic, stone-crazy, queer; *Scot* gyte, red-mad
OLD frantic-mad, lymphatic, bestraught
COLLOQ. crazy, demented, nuts, nutty, nutty as a fruitcake, wacky, mad as a hatter, barmy, bonkers, batty, cracked, crackers, dippy, daffy, dotty, loopy, potty, off your nut, off your head, wrong in the head, out of your head, off the wall, out to lunch, round the bend, round the twist, bats, having bats in the belfry, cuckoo, off the rails, screwy, up the wall, raving, not all there; *N Am* buggy, flaky, fruity; *Aust & NZ* dingbats
SLANG loony, mental, bananas, barking, wacko, doolally, off your rocker, off your chump, off your trolley, out of your tree, needing your head examined, having lost your marbles, having a screw loose, having a tile loose, having several cards short of a full deck, with one sandwich short of a picnic, meshuga; *N Am* gonzo, loco, wiggy

Psychological conditions and disorders include:

abreaction	antisocial	blindsight	kleptomania	postpartum	schizophrenia
acatamathesia	personality	bulimia	manias	depression	separation anxiety
addiction	disorder	dementia	Munchausen	post traumatic	sociopathy
affective disorders	Asperger's	depression	neurosis	stress disorder	Tourette's
agnosia	syndrome	dysmorphia	paranoia	psychopathy	syndrome
Alzheimer's	autism	Huntington's	personality	psychosexual	
anhedonia	battle fatigue	disease	disorder	dysfunctions	
anorexia nervosa	bipolar disorder	hypochondria	phobias	psychosis	

Forms of psychological therapy include:

art therapy	cognitive beha-	drama therapy	Gestalt therapy	person-centred	psychotherapy
aversion therapy	viour therapy	electroconvulsive	group therapy	therapy	regression therapy
behavioural	cognitive therapy	(or electroshock)	hypnotherapy	psychoanalysis	
therapy	colour therapy	therapy	interpersonal	psychodynamic	
	counselling	expressive therapy	therapy	therapy	

Branches of psychology include:

abnormal	criminal	evolutionary	industrial and	psychoanalysis	social psychology
psychology	psychology	psychology	organizational	psychobiology	sport psychology
behaviour analysis	depth psychology	experimental	psychology	psychogeriatrics	structural
biospsychology	developmental	psychology	narrative	psycholinguistics	psychology
child psychology	psychology	forensic	psychology	psychometrics	transpersonal
clinical psychology	educational	psychology	neuropsychology	psychopathology	psychology
cognitive	psychology	health psychology	occupational	psychopharmacol-	
psychology	environmental	hedonics	psychology	ogy	
	psychology		parapsychology	psychophysiology	

Terms used in psychology include:

affect	complex	escape mechanism	limen	projection	subconscious
anal stage	conditioning	externalization	mechanism	psychosexual	superego
anima/animus	configuration	extrovert	metacognition	psychosomatic	superiority
anxiety	consciousness	fixation	Oedipus complex	puerilism	complex
body image	cue	horme	over-compensation	reality principle	symbol
bonding	death wish	id	paragnosis	regression	transference
catharsis	delusion	identification	passive-aggressive	repression	unconscious
cathexis	denial	illusion	penis envy	role reversal	wish fulfilment
chunking	displacement	image	perception	Rorschach test	word salad
co-dependency	dissociation	imago	Phaedra complex	schema	Zener cards
cognitive map	ego	inferiority complex	phallic	self	
collective uncon-	ego ideal	introvert	preconscious	Stockholm	
scious	Electra complex	libido	primal therapy	syndrome	

Theories of psychology include:

Adlerian	behavioural theory	Freudian	humanistic theory	Pavlovian	Skinnerian
associationism	cognitive theory	functional theory	Jamesian	personality theory	structural theory
atomism	connectionism	(or functionalism)	Jungian	psychoanalytic	(or structuralism)
attachment theory	environmentalism	Gestalt theory	Lacanian	theory	

pub *n*

public house, inn, tavern, wine bar, free house, bar, saloon, taproom, lounge, lounge bar, cocktail bar, style bar, grill, brasserie, counter, table, brewpub, jerry-shop; *Scot* howf; *S Afr* canteen

COLLOQ. local, hostelry, watering-hole
SLANG boozer

puberty *n*

pubescence, adolescence, teens, teenage years, youth, young adulthood, growing up, maturity

E3 childhood, immaturity, old age

public *adj, n*

♦ *adj*

1 *public buildings*

state, government, national, nationalized, federal, official, civil, community, social, civic, collective, communal, common, general, popular, universal, open, available, accessible, unrestricted

2 KNOWN, well-known, famous, important, influential, respected, eminent, prominent, illustrious, celebrated, popular, widespread, recognized, acknowledged, plain, overt, obvious, open, exposed, published

E3 1 private, privatized, personal **2** secret, exclusive

♦ *n*

people, nation, country, population, populace, masses, citizens, society, everyone, community, voters, electorate, multitude, crowd, followers, supporters, fans, audience, spectators, patrons, clientèle, customers, buyers, consumers

■ **in public**

publicly, openly, in the open, in full view, for all to see

E3 in secret

■ **public house**

bar, saloon, inn, tavern, taproom, lounge, lounge bar, grill, brasserie, counter, table; *Scot* howf

COLLOQ. pub, local, hostelry, watering-hole

SLANG boozer

publican n

landlord, landlady, barman, barmaid, barperson, hotelier, hotel-keeper, innkeeper, taverner, licensed victualler, tapster, host, mine host; *N Am* saloon-keeper

publication n

1 *the publication of a book*

publishing, production, printing, distribution, circulation, release, issue

2 BOOK, volume, title, paperback, hardback, newspaper, magazine, mag, fanzine, journal, periodical, newsletter, weekly, monthly, daily, quarterly, booklet, leaflet, pamphlet, brochure, handbill

3 ANNOUNCEMENT, declaration, notification, reporting, proclamation, disclosure, broadcasting

publicity n

advertising, promotion, marketing, puff, propaganda, build-up, boost, attention, limelight, splash, air, notoriety, réclame

COLLOQ. plug, hype

> **QUOTATIONS**
> Without publicity there is no prosperity
> YAKOV ZEL'DOVICH

publicize v

advertise, promote, market, spotlight, broadcast, make known, announce, make public, bring to the public's attention, blaze

FORMAL disseminate, promulgate

COLLOQ. plug, hype, push

public-spirited adj

community-minded, humanitarian, philanthropic, altruistic, charitable, unselfish, generous, conscientious

E3 selfish

publish v

1 *publish a book*

produce, print, issue, bring out, release, distribute, circulate, gazette, paperback, paragraph, spread, diffuse

FORMAL disseminate, promulgate

COLLOQ. pirate

2 ANNOUNCE, declare, communicate, broadcast, report, notify, make known, carry, run, serialize, syndicate, put about, make public, proclaim, celebrate, diffuse, import, divulge, disclose, reveal, sound, release, publicize, advertise, notice, poster, placard

OLD evulgate, delate, vent

FORMAL give forth, set forth, fulminate

pucker v, n

♦ v

gather, ruffle, wrinkle, pleat, ruckle, ruck, shrivel, crinkle, crumple, crease, furrow, purse, screw up, contract, compress

♦ n

crinkle, crumple, fold, crease, ruck, wrinkle, ruckle, shirr

puckered adj

creased, gathered, rucked, ruckled, wrinkled, pursy

E3 smooth

puckish adj

impish, mischievous, naughty, playful, roguish, sly, waggish, whimsical, teasing, frolicsome, sportive

E3 serious, solemn

pudding n

dessert, sweet, tart, pie, pastry

COLLOQ. afters, pud

See panel at **dessert**.

puddle n

pool, sop, plash, slop, plashet; *dialect* dub, pant, soss, sump

OLD flush; (*Spenser*) plesh

puerile adj

childish, babyish, infantile, juvenile, immature, adolescent, irresponsible, silly, foolish, inane, trivial

E3 mature

puff n, v

♦ n

1 BREATH, waft, whiff, draught, flurry, gust, blast, waff, waif; *Scot* fuff, pluff

OLD huff, whift

FORMAL flatus

2 *a puff on a cigarette*

pull, drag

SLANG *N Am* toke

3 ADVERTISEMENT, publicity, promotion, marketing, commendation

COLLOQ. plug, push

♦ v

1 BREATHE, pant, gasp, gulp, wheeze, blow, waft, whiff, inflate, expand, swell; *Scot* flaff, fuff, pluff, skiff

OLD huff

2 *puff a cigarette*

smoke, pull, drag, draw, suck

3 ADVERTISE, praise, publicize, promote, market, commend

COLLOQ. plug, push

■ **puff out**

bulge, balloon, swell, hump, expand, enlarge, bulb, project, protrude, bag, belly, billow, bloat, blouse, heave

OLD bepuff

FORMAL dilate, distend

COLLOQ. sag

puffed adj

out of breath, breathless, panting, winded, exhausted, gasping

COLLOQ. done in

■ **puffed up**

arrogant, proud, swollen-headed, self-important, full of yourself, prideful

COLLOQ. bigheaded, high and mighty, too big for your boots

E3 modest

puffy adj

puffed up, inflated, swollen, bloated, enlarged

TECHNICAL oedematous

FORMAL distended, dilated

pugilism n

boxing, fighting, prize-fighting, the noble art, the noble science, the ring, the prize-ring

COLLOQ. the fancy, fistiana

pugilist n

boxer, fighter, prize-fighter

COLLOQ. bruiser

pugnacious adj

hostile, aggressive, belligerent, contentious, combative, antagonistic, argumentative, quarrelsome, bad-tempered, hot-tempered

FORMAL disputatious, bellicose

E3 peaceable

puke v, n

♦ v

vomit, retch, regurgitate, bring up, disgorge, heave, cat; *dialect* boke

OLD egurgitate, parbreak

COLLOQ. spew, throw up, sick up, chuck up, fetch up

SLANG honk; *N Am* barf, upchuck; *Aust* chunder

♦ n

vomit, sick, spew, retch(ing); *dialect* boke

TECHNICAL emesis

OLD parbreak

COLLOQ. spew

SLANG technicolour yawn

pull v, n

♦ v

1 TOW, drag, haul, trail, heave, draw, tug, jerk

COLLOQ. yank

2 REMOVE, take out, draw out, extract, root out, pull out, pluck, uproot, pull up, rip, tear, wrench

3 ATTRACT, draw, bring in, pull in, lure, allure, charm, entice, tempt, magnetize

4 DISLOCATE, sprain, wrench, strain, turn, damage, tear
⊟ 1 push, press **3** repel, deter, discourage
♦ *n*
1 TOW, drag, tug, haul, jerk, power, forcefulness, exertion
COLLOQ. yank
2 ATTRACTION, lure, allurement, draw, drawing power, magnetism, influence, weight, sway
COLLOQ. clout, muscle

■ **pull apart**
1 SEPARATE, part, dismember, demolish, dismantle, take to pieces, tear apart
2 CRITICIZE, take apart, run down, slate, attack
COLLOQ. slam, pan, tear to shreds, pick holes in, pull to pieces, do a hatchet job on
⊟ 1 join

■ **pull back**
draw back, withdraw, retreat, fall back, retire, disengage, back out

■ **pull down**
destroy, demolish, knock down, dismantle, bulldoze, raze to the ground
⊟ build, erect, put up

■ **pull in**
1 STOP, arrive, draw in, pull up, halt, park
2 ATTRACT, draw, bring in, lure, allure, entice
3 ARREST, capture, seize, apprehend, detain, take into custody
COLLOQ. bust, nick, collar, nab, book, run in
4 EARN, receive, be paid, make, clear, collect, bring in, take home
COLLOQ. rake in
⊟ 1 pull away **2** repel **4** lose

■ **pull off**
1 ACCOMPLISH, achieve, bring off, succeed, manage, fulfil, carry off, carry out
2 DETACH, remove, separate, take off, tear off, rip off
⊟ 1 fail **2** attach

■ **pull out**
retreat, withdraw, leave, depart, quit, move out, back out, evacuate, desert, scratch, abandon
⊟ join, arrive

■ **pull through**
recover, come through, improve, get better, get well again, rally, recuperate, survive, weather

■ **pull together**
co-operate, work together, collaborate, team up
⊟ fight

■ **pull up**
1 STOP, halt, come to a halt, park, draw up, pull in, pull over, brake
2 REPRIMAND, take to task, rebuke, scold, criticize, reprove, chide, lecture, censure, blame
FORMAL admonish, berate, castigate
COLLOQ. tell off, tick off, carpet, give someone a ticking-off, give someone a dressing-down, haul over the coals, read the riot act, rap over the knuckles, give someone a rap over the knuckles, give someone a flea in their ear

■ **pull yourself together**
control yourself, regain your self-control, get a grip on yourself
COLLOQ. get your act together, get yourself together, snap out of it, buck up your ideas

---

SYNONYM NUANCES

verb sense 1
Tow is usually reserved for an act of assistance, often aided by the attachment of a rope, while **drag** may suggest reluctance or resistance from the object: *she dragged him round the shops.* **Haul** and **heave** suggest exertion on the part of the subject: *I hauled my luggage to the nearest hotel*, whereas **trail** has connotations of weariness or inertia: *he stumbled along, trailing his bag behind him.*

If you want to suggest short and sudden movements, the terms **tug** and **jerk** would be appropriate: *she tugged at the zip*, while **draw** suggests a more gradual, deliberate action: *he pushed the notebook aside and drew the typewriter to him.*

pullover *n*
jersey, sweater, jumper, sweatshirt, top, woolly

pulp *n, v*
♦ *n*
1 *crushed to a pulp*
paste, purée, cream, mash, mush, pap, flesh, pith, must, pomace
TECHNICAL chyme, furnish
OLD marrow
FORMAL triturate
2 SENTIMENTALITY, tenderness, sentimentalism, emotionalism, romanticism, mawkishness, nostalgia
FORMAL bathos
COLLOQ. corniness, gush, mush, schmaltz, sloppiness, slush, gloop
♦ *v*
crush, squash, pulverize, mash, purée, liquidize, shred, beat, pound

pulpit *n*
platform, rostrum, stand, lectern, dais, podium
OLD ambo
COLLOQ. soapbox

pulpy *adj*
soft, sloppy, pappy, mushy, crushed, squashy, fleshy, succulent
⊟ hard

pulsate *v*
pulse, beat, throb, pound, hammer, drum, thud, thump, vibrate, oscillate, quiver, palpitate

pulsating *adj*
vibrating, oscillating, pulsing, palpitating
FORMAL pulsatile, pulsative, pulsatory, vibrative, vibratile

pulsation *n*
vibration, oscillation, palpitation, vibratiuncle
TECHNICAL ictus

pulse[1] *n, v*
♦ *n*
felt his pulse
beat, stroke, rhythm, throb, pulsation, beating, throbbing, thud, thudding, thump, thumping, pounding, drumming, vibration, oscillation, flutter
TECHNICAL sphygmus
♦ *v*
beat, drum, pulsate, vibrate, pound, thud, throb, tick, flutter

pulse[2] *n*
beans and pulses
bean, legume, gram, dal
TECHNICAL calavance, caravance
Related adjective: leguminous
See panel at **bean**.

pulverize *v*
1 CRUSH, pound, grind, mill, powder, crumble, pulp, squash
FORMAL triturate
2 DEFEAT, destroy, demolish, annihilate, smash
FORMAL vanquish
COLLOQ. thrash, hammer, wipe the floor with

pummel *v*
hit, knock, hammer, beat, batter, pound, punch, strike, thump, bang

pump *v*
1 PUSH, drive, force, send, inject, siphon, draw, drain, jet, surge, spurt, spout, gush

2 CROSS-EXAMINE, cross-question, interrogate, quiz
COLLOQ. grill, give someone the third degree, put the screws on

■ **pump out**
bail out, drain, draw off, empty, force out, siphon

■ **pump up**
blow up, inflate, puff up, fill

pun *n*
play on words, *double entendre*, double meaning, witticism, quip
TECHNICAL paronomasia

punch[1] *v, n*
♦ *v*
hit, strike, pummel, jab, bash, knock, clout, cuff, box, slug, thump, thwack, wind, black, fib, counter-punch
COLLOQ. sock, wallop, bop, biff, plug; *N Am* boff, bust, sucker-punch; *Aust* job
♦ *n*
1 BLOW, jab, bash, knock, hit, clout, thump, thwack, plug, bolo punch, roundhouse, *coup de poing*; *dialect* pounce
COLLOQ. sock, wallop, bop, biff, whammy; *N Am* boff, bust, sucker-punch
OLD SLANG fourpenny one
2 FORCE, strength, power, energy, impact, effectiveness, drive, vigour, forcefulness, verve, panache, zap
COLLOQ. bite, pizzazz, stingo

punch[2] *v*
punch a hole
perforate, pierce, puncture, make a hole in, prick, bore, drill, hole, stamp, cut, clip, check, keypunch

punch-drunk *adj*
dazed, confused, befuddled, stupefied, unsteady, reeling, staggering, dizzy, groggy, woozy

punch-up *n*
stand-up fight, brawl, fight, row, scuffle, fracas, free-for-all, argument, ruckus
COLLOQ. scrap, set-to, ding-dong, dust-up, shindy

punchy *adj*
incisive, effective, forceful, aggressive, dynamic, lively, powerful, strong, spirited, vigorous
COLLOQ. zappy
🗲 feeble, weak

punctilio *n*
1 SCRUPULOUSNESS, strictness, exactness, ceremony, finickiness, formality, convention, punctiliousness, precision, meticulousness, refinement, preciseness
2 FINE POINT, detail, nicety, particular, exactitude, delicacy, distinction, particularity
🗲 **1** informality

punctilious *adj*
scrupulous, conscientious, meticulous, careful, exact, precise, strict, formal, proper, particular, finicky, fussy
COLLOQ. pernickety, choosy, picky, nit-picking; *N Am* persnickety
🗲 lax, informal

punctiliously *adv*
conscientiously, meticulously, scrupulously, carefully, exactly, precisely

punctual *adj*
prompt, on time, exact, precise, well-timed, early, in good time
COLLOQ. on the dot, dead on time, bang on time, on cue
🗲 unpunctual, late

punctuality *n*
promptness, promptitude, regularity, readiness, strictness
🗲 unpunctuality

punctually *adv*
on time, prompt, promptly, precisely, exactly, sharp, to the minute
COLLOQ. dead on, bang on, spot-on, on the dot, on the button, on the stroke (of), up to time
🗲 unpunctually, late

punctuate *v*
interrupt, sprinkle, break (up), intersperse, pepper, emphasize, point, accentuate
FORMAL interject

punctuation

Punctuation marks include:

apostrophe	exclamation mark	quotation marks
asterisk	full stop	*colloq.* quotes
backslash	hyphen	semicolon
brackets	inverted commas	solidus
colon	oblique stroke	speech marks
comma	parentheses	square brackets
dash	period	star
ellipsis	question mark	

---

puncture *n, v*
♦ *n*
1 FLAT TYRE, blow-out
COLLOQ. flat
2 LEAK, hole, holing, piercing, perforation, cut, rupture, prick, nick, slit
♦ *v*
1 PRICK, pierce, penetrate, perforate, hole, make a hole in, bore, spike, cut, nick, burst, rupture
2 DEFLATE, flatten, let down, humiliate
COLLOQ. put down

pundit *n*
authority, expert, master, teacher, adviser, maestro, guru, sage, savant
COLLOQ. buff

pungency *n*
1 *the pungency of the herbs*
spiciness, strong flavour, tang, pepperiness, sharpness, bite
2 *writing that lacks pungency*
incisiveness, sharpness, power, strength, bite, causticity, sarcasm
FORMAL trenchancy, mordancy
COLLOQ. oomph, kick, pizzazz
🗲 **1** mildness, blandness, tastelessness **2** blandness

pungent *adj*
1 *a pungent taste/smell*
strong, powerful, hot, peppery, fiery, spicy, aromatic, tangy, tart, piquant, sharp, keen, acute, sour, bitter, acid, acrid, caustic, stinging, burning, biting
2 *pungent comments*
cutting, incisive, pointed, piercing, penetrating, sarcastic, scathing, caustic, stinging, burning, biting
FORMAL trenchant, mordant
🗲 **1** mild, bland, tasteless **2** bland

punish *v*
1 PENALIZE, discipline, correct, scold, beat, make someone pay, smack, slap, flog, whip, scourge, lash, cane, spank, knee-cap, crucify, hang, fine, imprison, strafe, make an example of, log, gate, bring to justice, pay out, serve out, scour, trounce; *Scot* give it laldie
OLD justify, shend, visit, wreak
FORMAL chastise, chasten, castigate, amerce
COLLOQ. teach someone a lesson, bring to book, throw the book at, come down (heavily) on, give someone stick, ground, sort, give someone hell
2 BEAT, defeat, trounce, batter
COLLOQ. hammer, thrash, rough up
3 MISUSE, maltreat, harm, damage, abuse
🗲 **1** reward

sense 1

Penalize suggests imposing a penalty on someone for their misdeeds or mistakes: *councils spending too much are penalized by a reduction in grants*, unlike **discipline**, which is more suggestive of training for the prevention of undesirable behaviour: *it's up to the parents to discipline their children*. **Correct** suggests showing someone the error of their ways as well as punishing them: *can criminals be corrected by prison sentences?*

  Crucify used literally refers to a form of capital punishment, but used figuratively it is an emotive term for subjecting someone to extremely humiliating or severe treatment: *his infidelities crucified his wife*. The rarely used **pay out** and **serve out** suggest retaliation and revenge, and while **scour** and **trounce** also suggest punishing severely, they do not have such strong implications of avenging a previous misdeed.

punishable *adj*
criminal, convictable, chargeable, unlawful, illegal, blameworthy
FORMAL culpable, indictable

punishing *adj*
arduous, strenuous, crippling, crushing, burdensome, taxing, grinding, demanding, hard, harsh, severe, cruel, gruelling, fatiguing, tiring, wearying, exhausting, backbreaking
E₃ easy

punishment *n*
1 *corporal punishment*
discipline, correction, chastisement, castigation, penalty, sentence, deserts, retribution, revenge
COLLOQ. short sharp shock
Related adjective: penal
2 *punishment from the wind*
damage, harm, injury, ill-use, maltreatment, rough handling, force, turbulence, storminess, ferocity
E₃ 1 reward

Forms of punishment include:

banishment	expulsion	the rack
beating	fine	rap across the
belting	flaying	knuckles
the birch	flogging	scourging
borstal	gaol	sending to
breaking upon the	gating	Coventry
wheel	grounding	sequestration
the cane	hiding	slapping
capital	hitting	the slipper
punishment	horsewhipping	smacking
cashiering	house arrest	solitary
chain gang	imprisonment	confinement
confinement	incarceration	spanking
confiscation	internment	the stocks
corporal	jail	strappado
punishment	jankers	suspension
decimation	keelhauling	tarring and
defrocking	knee-capping	feathering
demotion	*colloq.* larruping	thrashing
deportation	lashing	torturing
detention	leathering	transportation
dressing-down	lines	unfrocking
exclusion	mastheading	walking the plank
excommunication	penal colony	whipping
execution	prison	
exile	probation	

See also **execution**.

punitive *adj*
1 PENAL, disciplinary, retributive, retaliatory, vindictive
FORMAL chastising, castigatory

2 CRIPPLING, crushing, burdensome, demanding, hard, harsh, severe, cruel, gruelling, stiff, punishing, corrective

punter *n*
1 GAMBLER, better, backer, wagerer
2 CUSTOMER, client, consumer, person, individual, fellow, chap
COLLOQ. guy, bloke

puny *adj*
weak, feeble, frail, sickly, undeveloped, underdeveloped, stunted, small, undersized, diminutive, little, tiny, insignificant, minor, inconsequential, trifling, petty, trivial
COLLOQ. measly, piddling
E₃ strong, sturdy, large, important

pupil *n*
student, scholar, schoolboy, schoolgirl, learner, apprentice, beginner, novice, disciple, protégé(e), class-fellow, classmate, monitor, prefect, boarder, day-boarder, parlour-boarder, gymnasiast, bluecoat, grey-coat, alumnus, old boy/girl, pupil teacher, abiturient; *Scot* academical; *Scot & NZ* bursar; *N Am* kindergartener
TECHNICAL ashrama
COLLOQ. prep; *N Am* preppy; *Aust* schoolie; St Trinian
Related adjective: pupillary
E₃ teacher

puppet *n*
1 MARIONETTE, finger puppet, glove puppet, hand puppet, doll, rod puppet, Guignol, *fantoccino, fantoccio; dialect* puppy
OLD poppet, Jack of Lent; *(Shakesp)* mammet, motion, motion generative
2 *a mere puppet of a government*
pawn, tool, instrument, dupe, cat's-paw, quisling, stooge, gull, figurehead, mouthpiece, creature, dependant

puppy *n*
pup, young dog, whelp

purchase *v, n*
♦ *v*
buy, pay for, invest in, acquire, obtain, get, pick up, shop for, go shopping, secure, gain, earn, win
FORMAL procure
COLLOQ. snap up, splash out on
E₃ sell
♦ *n*
1 ACQUISITION, gain, buy, bargain, deal, investment, asset(s), possession(s), property, goods, holdings
FORMAL emption
2 GRASP, foothold, grip, hold, advantage, leverage
E₃ 1 sale

purchaser *n*
buyer, consumer, shopper, customer, client, hirer, patron
FORMAL vendee, emptor
E₃ seller; *formal* vendor

pure *adj*
1 *pure gold*
unadulterated, unalloyed, unmixed, undiluted, 100%, flawless, perfect, neat, straight, solid, simple, natural, real, authentic, genuine, true
2 STERILE, uncontaminated, unpolluted, uninfected, germ-free, aseptic, antiseptic, disinfected, sterilized, hygienic, sanitary, clean, immaculate, spotless, clear, fresh, natural
3 SHEER, utter, complete, total, thorough, absolute, perfect, unqualified, unmitigated, downright
4 CHASTE, virgin, virginal, virtuous, undefiled, unsullied, moral, unblemished, upright, honourable, honest, good, righteous, decent, noble, worthy, blameless, innocent
5 *pure mathematics*
theoretical, abstract, conjectural, speculative, academic
E₃ 1 impure, adulterated **2** contaminated, polluted **4** immoral, corrupt, defiled **5** applied, practical

pure-bred *adj*
pedigree, pedigreed, pure-blood, pure-blooded, thoroughbred, full-blooded, blooded
E₃ cross-bred, hybrid, mixed, mongrel

purely *adv*
1 UTTERLY, completely, totally, entirely, wholly, thoroughly, absolutely
2 ONLY, simply, merely, just, solely, exclusively

purgative *n, adj*
♦ *n*
laxative, enema, evacuant, purge
TECHNICAL emetic, aperient, cathartic, eccoprotic
FORMAL depurative
♦ *adj*
cleansing, laxative, purging, evacuant
TECHNICAL aperient, cathartic, cathartical, eccoprotic
FORMAL abstersive, depurative

purgatory *n*
torment, torture, hell, agony, ordeal, anguish, misery, wretchedness, hopelessness

purge *v, n*
♦ *v*
1 PURIFY, cleanse, clean out, scour, clear (out), expurgate, absolve; *dialect* work
TECHNICAL absterge, soil
FORMAL catharize
2 OUST, remove, get rid of, rid, eject, expel, depose, root out, clear (out), dismiss, eradicate, exterminate, wipe out, kill
♦ *n*
removal, ejection, expulsion, witch hunt, eradication, rooting-out, extermination, cleansing, disposal, ousting

purification *n*
1 DECONTAMINATION, refinement, cleaning, cleansing, disinfection, filtration, sanitization, fumigation, deodorization, desalination
TECHNICAL sublimation, elution, reverse osmosis
FORMAL depuration, epuration
2 SANCTIFICATION, redemption, absolution, purge, cleansing
FORMAL lustration, purgation, catharsis
⊟ 1 contamination, defilement, pollution

purify *v*
1 DECONTAMINATE, refine, filter, distil, clarify, clean, cleanse, sanitize, freshen, disinfect, sterilize, fumigate, deodorize, filtrate, fine, expurgate
TECHNICAL clay, defecate, rectify, retort, scrub, sublime
OLD chastise, chasten, mundify, try
FORMAL depurate, epurate, furbish
2 SANCTIFY, redeem, absolve, purge, cleanse, shrive
FORMAL catharsize, lustrate
⊟ 1 contaminate, pollute, defile

purifying *adj*
cleansing, purificatory, refining, purging, purgative
TECHNICAL cathartic
FORMAL depurative, lustral, mundificative
⊟ contaminating, defiling, polluting

purism *n*
fastidiousness, formalism, fussiness, over-precision, pedantry, restraint, strictness, orthodoxy, austerity, classicism, Atticism
⊟ liberality, open-mindedness, tolerance

purist *n, adj*
♦ *n*
pedant, literalist, formalist, precisionist, dogmatist, stickler, quibbler
COLLOQ. nit-picker
♦ *adj*
fastidious, over-exact, over-fastidious, over-meticulous, over-particular, over-precise, pedantic, quibbling, uncompromising, strict, captious, finicky, fussy, hypercritical, puristic
COLLOQ. nit-picking
⊟ liberal, open-minded, tolerant

puritan *n*
pietist, rigorist, disciplinarian, zealot, fanatic, moralist, killjoy, prig, spoilsport, prude

COLLOQ. goody-goody
⊟ hedonist, libertarian

puritanical *adj*
puritan, moralistic, disciplinarian, ascetic, abstemious, austere, severe, stern, strict, strait-laced, prim, proper, prudish, disapproving, stuffy, stiff, rigid, narrow-minded, bigoted, fanatical, zealous
COLLOQ. goody-goody
⊟ hedonistic, liberal, indulgent, broad-minded

puritanism *n*
rigorousness, self-discipline, self-denial, strictness, uncompromisingness, austerity, propriety, sternness, severity, stiffness, rigidity, zealotry, fanaticism, bigotry, narrow-mindedness, narrowness, priggishness, primness, prudishness, abstemiousness, abstinence, asceticism
⊟ broad-mindedness, hedonism, indulgence, liberality

purity *n*
1 CLEARNESS, clarity, cleanness, cleanliness, pureness, freshness, untaintedness, flawlessness, wholesomeness
TECHNICAL chiarezza, orient
OLD pure
2 SIMPLICITY, authenticity, genuineness, truth, perfection
3 CHASTITY, virginity, decency, morality, integrity, rectitude, uprightness, goodness, virtue, virtuousness, honour, honesty, nobility, worthiness, innocence, blamelessness, sanctity
OLD candour
⊟ 1 impurity, pollution, contamination **3** immorality

purlieus *n*
neighbourhood, surroundings, vicinity, suburbs, environs, precincts, periphery, borders, bounds, confines, limits, fringes, perimeter, outskirts

purloin *v*
steal, rob, remove, take, pilfer, make away with, run off with
FORMAL appropriate
COLLOQ. swipe, nick, pinch, filch, finger, lift, nobble, pocket, snaffle, snitch, thieve, bag, whip; *Aust & NZ* souvenir
SLANG rip off

purport *v, n*
♦ *v*
claim, allege, profess, seem, pose as, pretend, imply, proclaim, show, mean, intend, indicate, denote, signify, suggest, express, convey, declare, assert, maintain
FORMAL import, portend, betoken
♦ *n*
meaning, significance, point, gist, drift, idea, spirit, substance, theme, tendency, tenor, thrust, bearing, direction, implication
FORMAL import

purportedly *adv*
allegedly, supposedly, apparently, reportedly, by all accounts, doubtfully, dubiously
FORMAL ostensibly, putatively

purpose *n, v*
♦ *n*
1 INTENTION, aim, objective, end, goal, target, plan, design, vision, idea, ambition, hope, wish, desire, aspiration, point, object, function, reason, motive, motivation, rationale, justification, principle, result, outcome, basis
2 DETERMINATION, resolve, resolution, drive, single-mindedness, firmness, dedication, devotion, constancy, backbone, steadfastness, perseverance, persistence, doggedness, tenacity, zeal
3 USE, function, application, good, advantage, benefit, gain, effect, value, usefulness
♦ *v*
intend, mean, plan, propose, resolve, decide, determine, settle, design, aspire, aim, desire, contemplate, meditate

■ **on purpose**
deliberately, intentionally, consciously, knowingly, wittingly, wilfully, purposely, by design, premeditatedly
⊟ accidentally, impulsively, spontaneously

purposeful *adj*
determined, decided, purposed, resolved, resolute, single-minded, constant, steadfast, persistent, persevering, unwavering, unfaltering, tenacious, dogged, strong-willed, positive, firm, deliberate
⊟ purposeless, aimless

purposefully *adv*
resolutely, steadfastly, single-mindedly, persistently, perseveringly, unwaveringly, unfalteringly, tenaciously

⚠ purposefully or purposely?
Purposefully means 'obviously, or apparently, having some purpose': *She stole purposefully towards him, clearly intent on settling things once and for all. Purposely* means 'intentionally, on purpose': *She didn't want to go to college so she purposely failed her exams.*

purposeless *adj*
pointless, senseless, aimless, objectless, empty, unmeaning, goalless, thoughtless, gratuitous, unasked-for, uncalled-for, unnecessary, useless, needless, motiveless, nonsensical, vain, wanton, vacuous
OLD (*Shakesp*) shapeless
⊟ purposeful

purposely *adv*
on purpose, intentionally, deliberately, consciously, calculatedly, by design, specifically, wilfully, knowingly, premeditatedly, designedly, expressly, with malice aforethought
⊟ unintentionally, by accident, impulsively, spontaneously

⚠ purposely or purposefully?
See panel at **purposefully**.

purse *n, v*
♦ *n*
1 MONEY-BAG, wallet, pouch, burse, *porte-monnaie*; *Scot & Irish* spleuchan; *N Am* pocketbook
OLD (*Spenser*) crumenal
OLD SLANG bung
2 MONEY, means, resources, finances, funds, coffers, treasury, exchequer
OLD fisc
3 REWARD, award, prize, present, gift
♦ *v*
pucker, wrinkle, draw together, press together, close, tighten, contract, compress, prim

pursuance *n*
discharge, pursuit, pursuing, performance, fulfilment, following, accomplishment, achievement, completion
FORMAL effecting, effectuation, execution, prosecution

pursue *v*
1 CHASE, go after, run after, follow, give chase, make after, track, stalk, trail, shadow, tail, dog, harass, harry, hound, hunt, seek, search for, investigate, inquire into
OLD persue, poursew, pursew, prosecute, sue

2 *pursue an activity*
perform, engage in, practise, conduct, follow, carry on, continue, keep on, keep up, maintain, persevere in, persist in, apply yourself to, hold to, whore after
3 STRIVE FOR, aspire to, aim for, seek, search for, try for, work towards, have your goal

pursuit *n*
1 CHASE, hue and cry, tracking, pursuing, stalking, trail, tailing, shadowing, hunt
OLD poursuit
2 SEARCH, quest, aim, aspiration, goal, investigation, following, continuance, persistence, perseverance
3 ACTIVITY, interest, hobby, pastime, occupation, trade, craft, line, speciality, vocation

purvey *v*
1 SUPPLY, cater, deal in, provide, furnish, stock, sell, retail, trade in
FORMAL provision, victual
2 TRANSMIT, spread, communicate, publicize, publish, put about, pass on
FORMAL propagate, disseminate

purveyor *n*
1 SUPPLIER, stockist, trader, dealer, seller, provider, provisor, retailer
FORMAL victualler, vendor
2 TRANSMITTER, communicator
FORMAL disseminator, propagator

pus *n*
discharge
TECHNICAL matter, diapyesis, seropus
OLD quitter
FORMAL suppuration
Related adjective: purulent

push *v, n*
♦ *v*
1 PROPEL, thrust, ram, shove, jostle, hustle, manhandle, butt, jolt, elbow, prod, nudge, poke, press, depress, squeeze, plunge, squash, cram, drive, force, constrain
2 PRESS (FOR), encourage, urge, incite, impel, spur, prod, goad, force, influence, persuade, press, pressurize, coerce, bully
COLLOQ. egg on, twist someone's arm, put the screws on
3 PROMOTE, advertise, market, publicize, boost
COLLOQ. hype, plug
⊟ **1** pull **2** discourage, dissuade
♦ *n*
1 KNOCK, shove, nudge, jolt, prod, poke, thrust, ram, jostle, butt
2 OFFENSIVE, assault, advance, charge, drive, invasion, incursion, raid, onslaught, foray
3 ENERGY, vigour, vitality, drive, effort, force, forcefulness, dynamism, enterprise, initiative, ambition, determination
COLLOQ. go, get-up-and-go
4 *get/be given the push*
dismissal, discharge, your cards, notice, marching orders
COLLOQ. the boot, the elbow, the axe, the chop, papers, sacking, firing
■ **push around**
bully, torment, terrorize, intimidate, victimize, pick on
■ **push off**
go away, depart, leave, run along, move
COLLOQ. push along, shove off, beat it, buzz off, scarper, scat, scram, clear off/out, make a move, make tracks
■ **push on**
press on, advance, continue, go on, carry on, keep going, persevere, go ahead, proceed, keep trying, plod on, slog away, peg away, toil (away)
COLLOQ. plug away, soldier on, stick at it

SYNONYM NUANCES

verb sense 1
Propel can be used of causing something to move forward, usually briskly: *I propelled myself through the doorway and rushed down the corridor*, while **thrust**

and **drive** have implications of greater force: *he thrust his way through the crowds; he was driven by his commitment.* **Ram** also suggests the use of great force, resulting in a collision, while **shove** is more suggestive of a rough physical push by another person. **Manhandle** and **jostle** also have suggestions of treating roughly, although they tend to suggest more continual pushing.

The word **jolt** is appropriate for a short, sudden action: *the crowd suddenly jolted forwards and he fell over.* **Nudge** too suggests a sudden action, although a more gentle one, whereas **prod** and **poke** have more painful connotations of a stab with, for example, a finger. **Press** and **squeeze** are appropriate for pushing with continuous force, while **depress**, although similar, generally implies a downward movement. Likewise, **plunge** suggests a downwards action, but a more sudden and dramatic one: *he missed his footing and plunged to the ground.*

pushed *adj*
short of, stretched, under pressure, harassed, rushed, hard-pressed, hard-up, hurried, in difficulties, strapped, pinched, pressed, harried

pushover *n*
1 *he's a pushover*
sucker, dupe, mug, weakling, stooge, gull
COLLOQ. fall guy, sitting duck, sitting target, soft touch, easy touch
2 *the job's a pushover*
COLLOQ. child's play, cinch, doddle, picnic, piece of cake, walkover
SLANG (*vulgar*) piece of piss
F3 **2** challenge, labour

pushy *adj*
assertive, self-assertive, ambitious, forceful, aggressive, over-confident, forward, bold, brash, arrogant, presumptuous, impertinent, assuming
COLLOQ. bossy
F3 unassertive, unassuming

pusillanimity *n*
cowardliness, faint-heartedness, fearfulness, feebleness, timidity, timorousness, weakness, spinelessness, cravenness
FORMAL poltroonery
COLLOQ. gutlessness

pusillanimous *adj*
cowardly, faint-hearted, craven, fearful, timorous, scared, weak, weak-kneed, chicken-hearted, spineless, lily-livered, feeble, timid
COLLOQ. chicken, gutless, yellow, wimpish
F3 brave, courageous, strong

pussyfoot *v*
1 PREVARICATE, equivocate, hedge
FORMAL tergiversate
COLLOQ. mess about, beat about the bush
2 CREEP, slink, tiptoe, prowl, pad, steal

pustule *n*
boil, pimple, abscess, carbuncle, eruption, fester, whitehead, blotch, ulcer, pock, whitlow, blister, papule
TECHNICAL uredosorus

put *v*
1 PLACE, lay (down), deposit, set (down), fix, settle, rest, establish, stand, position, dispose, situate, locate, station, post
COLLOQ. plonk, dump
2 ARRANGE, place, class, sort, classify, categorize, group, rank, grade
3 APPLY, impose, inflict, levy, assign, subject, exact, demand, require
4 *put the blame on someone*
place, attribute, attach, fix, ascribe, assign, lay, pin, charge, impute

5 EXPRESS, word, phrase, formulate, frame, couch, say, speak, voice, pronounce, utter, state
6 *put a suggestion*
submit, present, offer, suggest, propose, tender, set/lay before, set forth, bring forward
FORMAL proffer
7 *put money/energy into a project*
invest, spend, sink, devote, dedicate, give, contribute
8 TRANSLATE, transcribe, turn, render, convert
9 *put money on a horse*
bet, gamble, place, lay, risk, chance
10 *put the number of casualties at 50*
estimate, reckon, calculate roughly, work out, gauge, guess
COLLOQ. guesstimate

■ **put about**
tell, spread, make known, circulate, announce
FORMAL disseminate

■ **put across**
put over, get across/over, communicate, convey, express, explain, clarify, make clear, make understood, spell out, bring home to, get through to

■ **put aside**
put by, set aside, lay aside/by, keep, retain, save, reserve, keep in reserve, store, stow, stockpile, hoard, shelve, salt away, put to one side
COLLOQ. stash

■ **put away**
1 CONSUME, devour, eat (up), drink, swallow, down
COLLOQ. wolf, tuck in, guzzle, scoff, snarf, polish off
2 IMPRISON, jail, lock up, confine, commit, certify
FORMAL incarcerate
COLLOQ. send down
SLANG bang up
3 SAVE, put aside/by, set aside, lay aside/by, keep, retain, reserve, keep in reserve, store, stow, stockpile

■ **put back**
1 DELAY, defer, postpone, reschedule, adjourn, suspend, shelve, freeze
FORMAL procrastinate
COLLOQ. put on ice
2 REPLACE, return, restore, reinstate, return to its place, clear away/up, tidy away/up
F3 **1** bring forward

■ **put down**
1 WRITE DOWN, note down, jot down, transcribe, enter, log, register, list, record
2 CRUSH, quash, suppress, defeat, quell, stop, stamp out, silence
3 *put down a sick dog*
kill, destroy, put to sleep, put out of its misery
4 ASCRIBE, attribute, blame, charge, set down, fix, attach, lay
5 HUMILIATE, snub, slight, squash, belittle, deflate, humble, crush, shame, mortify
FORMAL disparage, deprecate
COLLOQ. take down a peg

■ **put forward**
advance, suggest, recommend, nominate, propose, move, table, introduce, present, pose, submit, propound, offer, tender
FORMAL proffer

■ **put in**
insert, enter, input, submit, present, install, fit

■ **put in for**
apply for, request, ask for, fill in a form for, write off for, order
FORMAL requisition

■ **put off**
1 DELAY, defer, postpone, reschedule, adjourn, suspend, shelve
FORMAL procrastinate
COLLOQ. put on ice, put on the back burner
2 DETER, dissuade, talk out of, discourage, dishearten, demoralize, daunt, dismay, intimidate, disconcert, confuse, distract, sicken, nauseate

3 DISTRACT, divert, sidetrack, deflect, turn away/aside
⊟ 2 encourage
■ **put on**
1 *put on new clothes*
get dressed in, dress in, change into, get into, slip into, wear, don, try on
COLLOQ. throw on, get dolled up in
2 SWITCH ON, turn on, start up, activate, plug in, connect
3 ATTACH, affix, apply, place, add, impose
4 *put on a service*
lay on, provide, supply, give, add
5 PRETEND, feign, sham, fake, simulate, make believe, affect, assume
6 STAGE, mount, organize, produce, present, do, perform
⊟ 1 take off
■ **put out**
1 PUBLISH, announce, broadcast, circulate, issue, disclose, make known, bring out
2 EXTINGUISH, quench, douse, smother, stamp out
3 INCONVENIENCE, cause inconvenience to, impose on, bother, disturb, trouble, disconcert, upset, hurt, offend, annoy, irritate, irk, anger, exasperate, provoke, infuriate, unsettle
FORMAL perturb, discommode
COLLOQ. faze
⊟ 2 light
■ **put through**
accomplish, achieve, complete, conclude, finalize, execute, manage, bring off
■ **put together**
assemble, join, build, construct, fit/piece together
⊟ take apart
■ **put up**
1 ERECT, build, construct, assemble, raise
2 ACCOMMODATE, give accommodation to, house, lodge, shelter, give a room to, provide with board and lodging
3 *put up prices*
raise, increase, escalate
COLLOQ. jack up, hike up, bump up
4 PAY, invest, give, advance, float, provide, supply, pledge, offer
5 *put up a candidate*
nominate, put forward, propose, suggest, recommend, choose
⊟ 1 take down, pull down **3** bring down
■ **put up to**
prompt, incite, encourage, urge, persuade, goad
COLLOQ. egg on
⊟ discourage, dissuade
■ **put up with**
stand, bear, abide, stomach, endure, suffer, tolerate, allow, accept, stand for, take, brook
COLLOQ. swallow, wear, take lying down
⊟ object to, reject
■ **put upon**
impose on, exploit, take advantage of, take for granted, take liberties, inconvenience

putative *adj*
supposed, assumed, presumed, alleged, reported, reputed, hypothetical, theoretical, suppositional, reputative
FORMAL conjectural, supposititious

put-down *n*
affront, humiliation, insult, slight, sneer, snub, rebuff, sarcasm, gibe
FORMAL disparagement
COLLOQ. slap in the face, dig

put-off *n*
deterrent, discouragement, disincentive, hindrance, constraint, curb, damper, obstacle, restraint
⊟ encouragement, incentive

putrefaction *n*
decay, decomposition, rot, rotting, going bad, perishing, mould, fungus, mildew
FORMAL putrescence, putridity

putrefy *v*
rot, perish, go bad, decay, corrupt, mould, spoil, stink, taint, gangrene, decompose, deteriorate, fester, addle

putrescent *adj*
rotting, perishing, decaying, decomposing, putrefying, stinking, festering
FORMAL mephitic

putrid *adj*
rotten, decayed, decaying, decomposed, decomposing, mouldy, off, bad, rancid, addled, addle, turned, corrupt, contaminated, tainted, polluted, foul, rank, f(o)etid, stinking
⊟ fresh, wholesome

put-upon *adj*
imposed on, taken advantage of, exploited, used, inconvenienced, abused, maltreated, persecuted

puzzle *v, n*
♦ *v*
1 BAFFLE, mystify, perplex, confound, confuse, stagger, bewilder, intrigue, fascinate, riddle, gravel, metagrobolize; *Scot* bumbaze, fickle, kittle
OLD bemuse, pose
COLLOQ. stump, floor, flummox, beat, nonplus, bamboozle
2 THINK, ponder, meditate, consider, brood, mull over, muse over, deliberate, think hard about, figure, rack your brains, beat your brains (out)
♦ *n*
question, poser, anagram, riddle, conundrum, mystery, enigma, dilemma, paradox, tickler, crux, brainteaser, mind-bender; *N Am* brain-twister
■ **puzzle out**
solve, work out, figure out, think out, decipher, decode, unravel, untangle, find the answer to, piece together, sort out, resolve, clear up
COLLOQ. crack, get, suss (out)

Types of puzzle include:

acrostic	jigsaw puzzle	Rubik's Cube®
alphametic	kakuro	sorites
anagram	magic pyramid	Sudoku
crossword	maze	tangram
cryptogram	quiz	wordgame
hangman	rebus	wordsearch

---

puzzled *adj*
baffled, mystified, perplexed, confounded, at a loss, beaten, confused, bewildered, lost, in a haze
COLLOQ. stumped, nonplussed, at sea, flummoxed, floored, bamboozled
⊟ clear

puzzlement *n*
bafflement, perplexity, bewilderment, confusion, disorientation, astonishment, mystification, surprise, wonder, uncertainty, doubt, doubtfulness
FORMAL incertitude
COLLOQ. bamboozlement
⊟ certainty, clarity, lucidity

puzzling *adj*
baffling, bewildering, confusing, perplexing, unclear, hard to understand, difficult to understand, queer, peculiar, strange, bizarre, mystifying, mysterious, arcane, mystical, misleading, unaccountable, unfathomable, impenetrable, inexplicable, intricate, involved, ambiguous, equivocal, mind-bending, mind-boggling, curious, enigmatic, cryptic, tortuous, knotty, Sphinx-like
FORMAL abstruse, labyrinthine

pygmy *n, adj*
- ♦ *n*

person of restricted growth, dwarf, midget, Tom Thumb, Lilliputian, manikin, thumbling, fingerling, hop-o'-my-thumb, Negrito

OLD (*Shakesp*) atomy

FORMAL homunculus

▣ giant

♦ *adj*

miniature, small, tiny, baby, diminutive, half-pint, undersized, minuscule, minute, pint-sized, pocket, elfin, stunted, dwarf, midget, dwarfish, toy, Lilliputian; *Scot* wee

▣ gigantic

pyromaniac *n*
arsonist, incendiary, fire-raiser

COLLOQ. firebug

Q

quack *n, adj*
♦ *n*
charlatan, impostor, fraud, mountebank, pretender, masquerader, humbug, sham, fake, cowboy, swindler, trickster
OLD quacksalver
COLLOQ. phoney, pseud
♦ *adj*
false, bogus, counterfeit, fake, pretended, fraudulent, spurious, supposed, sham, so-called, unqualified
COLLOQ. phoney
F3 genuine, real

quackery *n*
charlatanism, mountebankery, mountebankism, fraud, fraudulence, sham, imposture
COLLOQ. humbug, phoniness

quadrangle *n*
courtyard, court, square, cloister, enclosure, plaza, esplanade, piazza
COLLOQ. quad

quaff *v*
down, drink, gulp, knock back, swallow, swig, toss off, swill, carouse, drain
FORMAL imbibe
COLLOQ. booze, guzzle, tipple

quagmire *n*
1 BOG, marsh, quag, fen, swamp, morass, mire, slough, quicksand
OLD (*Spenser*) wagmoire
2 MESS, problem, dilemma, quandary, perplexity
COLLOQ. fix, hole, pickle, tight spot, hot/deep water

quail *v*
recoil, back away, shy away, shrink, flinch, pull back, draw back, cringe, cower, tremble, quake, shake, shiver, blench, shudder, falter

quaint *adj*
picturesque, charming, attractive, sweet, old-fashioned, antiquated, old-world, unusual, strange, odd, queer, curious, droll, bizarre, fanciful, whimsical, whimsy; *Scot* auld-farand
OLD queint
COLLOQ. twee, olde-worlde, funky
F3 modern

quaintly *adv*
charmingly, attractively, strangely, oddly, curiously, unusually, picturesquely, whimsically

quaintness *n*
charm, attractiveness, picturesqueness, old-fashionedness, unusualness, whimsicalness

quake *v*
shake, tremble, shudder, quiver, shiver, quail, vibrate, throb, pulsate, wobble, rock, sway, move, convulse, heave, dither; *dialect* wamble

qualification *n*
1 CERTIFICATE, diploma, degree, training, certification, skill, competence, proficiency, ability, capability, capacity, aptitude, suitability, fitness, accomplishment, eligibility
2 RESTRICTION, limitation, reservation, exception, allowance, exemption, condition, caveat, rider, provision, proviso, stipulation, modification, adjustment, adaptation

qualified *adj*
1 CERTIFIED, chartered, licensed, professional, trained, experienced, practised, skilled, accomplished, expert, knowledgeable, skilful, talented, proficient, competent, efficient, able, capable, adept, fit, fitted, equipped, prepared, eligible
2 *qualified praise*
reserved, guarded, cautious, restricted, limited, bounded, modified, conditional, provisional, equivocal
FORMAL contingent, circumscribed
F3 1 unqualified, untrained **2** unconditional, wholehearted

qualify *v*
1 TRAIN, prepare, make ready, teach, instruct, equip, fit, coach, ground, pass, graduate, certify, empower, entitle, authorize, license, sanction, permit, allow, warrant, capacitate, be allowed, be eligible, fit/meet the requirements
TECHNICAL habilitate
2 MODERATE, reduce, lessen, diminish, temper, soften, weaken, ease, adjust, modify, restrain, restrict, limit, delimit, make conditional, define, classify, alloy
TECHNICAL contemper
FORMAL mitigate, alleviate
F3 1 disqualify

quality *n*
1 *of poor quality*
standard, grade, class, kind, sort, type, make, variety, calibre, status, rank, level, value, worth, merit, condition
2 EXCELLENCE, superiority, eminence, pre-eminence, distinction, merit, value, worth, refinement
3 CHARACTERISTIC, property, attribute, aspect, feature, trait, peculiarity, mark, nature, character, make-up

qualm *n*
misgiving, apprehension, fear, anxiety, worry, concern, disquiet, uneasiness, scruple, hesitation, hesitancy, disinclination, reluctance, reservation, uncertainty, doubt
FORMAL compunction

quandary *n*
dilemma, predicament, impasse, perplexity, confusion, bewilderment, muddle, mess, problem, difficulty
COLLOQ. fix, hole, pickle, jam, tight spot

quantify *v*
measure, calculate, number, count, weigh, enumerate, calibrate, evaluate, determine, specify

quantity *n*
1 AMOUNT, number, sum, total, aggregate, mass, lot, share, portion, quota, allotment, measure, dose, proportion, part, content, capacity, volume, weight, bulk, size, magnitude, expanse, extent, area, length, breadth
2 *quantities of food*
much, many, lots
COLLOQ. loads, heaps, stacks, oodles, tons, masses

quarantine *n*
detention, isolation, segregation, lazaretto

quarrel *n, v*
♦ *n*
row, argument, wrangle, squabble, tiff, misunderstanding, disagreement, dispute, dissension, controversy, difference, difference of opinion, conflict, clash, contention, strife, fight, brawl, fracas, feud, vendetta, schism

FORMAL altercation, disputation
COLLOQ. barney, broil, spat, miff, bust-up, punch-up, slanging match, scrap, set-to, dust-up
E3 agreement, harmony
♦ v
1 ROW, argue, bicker, squabble, wrangle, be at loggerheads, fall out, disagree, dispute, dissent, differ, be at variance, clash, contend, fight, feud, spat, have words; *Scot* cast out, flyte
OLD jangle
COLLOQ. scrap
SLANG part brass rags
2 FIND FAULT WITH, fault, slate, criticize, dispute, censure
COLLOQ. pick holes in, knock, slam, pull to pieces
E3 1 agree

quarrelling *n, adj*
♦ *n*
bickering, contention, dissension, feuding, rowing, variance, strife, wrangling, disharmony, argumentation
FORMAL altercation, discord, disputation, vitilitigation
COLLOQ. argy-bargying
E3 concord, harmony
♦ *adj*
bickering, contending, fighting, squabbling, wrangling, warring, feuding, rowing, at odds, at variance, at loggerheads
FORMAL discordant, dissentient
COLLOQ. scrapping
E3 amicable, friendly

quarrelsome *adj*
argumentative, disputatious, contentious, irascible, belligerent, ill-tempered, hot-tempered, irritable, ready for a fight
FORMAL bellicose, pugnacious
E3 peaceable, placid

quarry *n*
prey, victim, object, goal, target, game, kill, prize

quarter *n, v*
♦ *n*
1 DISTRICT, sector, zone, neighbourhood, locality, vicinity, area, region, province, territory, division, section, part, place, spot, point, direction, side
COLLOQ. digs
2 MERCY, leniency, favour, pardon, pity, compassion, grace, indulgence, forgiveness, clemency
3 *living quarters*
accommodation, lodgings, billet, residence, rooms, barracks, station, post
FORMAL dwelling, habitation, domicile
COLLOQ. digs, pad
♦ *v*
station, post, billet, accommodate, put up, lodge, board, house, shelter

quash *v*
1 ANNUL, revoke, rescind, cancel, repeal, void, invalidate, reverse, set aside, overturn, overrule, override
FORMAL nullify, abrogate, countermand
2 CRUSH, squash, quell, suppress, scotch, put an end to, subdue, defeat, overthrow
E3 1 confirm, vindicate, reinstate

quaver *v, n*
♦ *v*
shake, tremble, quake, waver, shudder, quiver, wobble, vibrate, pulsate, oscillate, flutter, flicker, trill, warble
♦ *n*
tremble, trembling, tremor, trill, break, quiver, shake, throb, sob, quaveriness, vibration, vibrato, warble, tremolo

quay *n*
wharf, pier, jetty, dock, harbour

queasiness *n*
nausea, vomiting, sickness, retching, gagging, biliousness, morning sickness, travel sickness, motion sickness, seasickness, carsickness, airsickness, sick headache

queasy *adj*
sick, ill, unwell, queer, groggy, green, nauseous, nauseated, sickened, bilious, squeamish, faint, dizzy, giddy
COLLOQ. rough, under the weather, out of sorts

queen *n*
1 MONARCH, sovereign, ruler, head of state, majesty, princess, empress, consort
OLD prince
FORMAL regina
Related adjectives: royal, regal, reginal
2 BEAUTY, belle, idol, Venus

queenly *adj*
sovereign, majestic, regal, royal, imperial, imperious, noble, stately, splendid, dignified, gracious, grand
FORMAL reginal, august, monarchical, sublime
E3 undignified

queer *adj, v*
♦ *adj*
1 ODD, mysterious, strange, unusual, uncommon, weird, unnatural, extraordinary, bizarre, eccentric, outlandish, peculiar, funny, puzzling, curious, unconventional, unorthodox, abnormal, deviant, remarkable; *dialect* quare
OLD rum
FORMAL singular
2 *I feel queer*
unwell, ill, sick, queasy, light-headed, faint, giddy, dizzy
COLLOQ. rough, under the weather, out of sorts
3 SUSPICIOUS, suspect, shifty, dubious, doubtful, irregular, peculiar, strange
COLLOQ. shady, fishy, iffy
4 HOMOSEXUAL, gay, lesbian, bisexual
COLLOQ. camp, butch
E3 1 ordinary, usual, common **2** well, fine **4** heterosexual; *colloq.* straight
♦ *v*
spoil, harm, ruin, upset, wreck, mar, botch, thwart, impair, foil, frustrate, endanger, jeopardize, stymie

queerness *n*
oddity, peculiarity, strangeness, unusualness, uncommonness, unconventionality, unnaturalness, bizarreness, anomalousness, curiousness, abnormality, irregularity, eccentricity, unorthodoxy
FORMAL singularity

quell *v*
subdue, quash, crush, squash, suppress, rout, put down, put an end to, overcome, conquer, defeat, overpower, moderate, allay, soothe, calm, pacify, appease, hush, quiet, silence, stifle, extinguish
FORMAL mitigate, alleviate, vanquish

quench *v*
1 *quench your thirst*
slake, satisfy, sate, cool; *Scot* slocken
OLD stanch
FORMAL satiate
2 EXTINGUISH, stifle, smother, douse, put out, snuff out, stamp out; *Scot* slocken

querulous *adj*
peevish, fretful, fractious, cross, irritable, complaining, grumbling, sour, testy, petulant, discontented, dissatisfied, critical, carping, captious, fault-finding, fussy, irascible
FORMAL cantankerous
COLLOQ. grouchy, shirty, ratty
E3 placid, uncomplaining, contented

query *v, n*
♦ *v*
ask, inquire, question, challenge, dispute, quarrel with, doubt, throw doubts on, suspect, be sceptical of, have suspicions about, distrust, mistrust, disbelieve
E3 accept

♦ *n*
question, inquiry, problem, uncertainty, doubt, suspicion, scepticism, reservation, hesitation, uneasiness, qualm(s), quibble

quest *n*
search, seeking, hunt, pursuit, investigation, inquiry, purpose, aim, goal, mission, crusade, enterprise, undertaking, venture, journey, voyage, expedition, exploration, pilgrimage, adventure
■ **in quest of**
searching for, seeking after, trying to find, trying to obtain, in pursuit of, for, out for, hunting for, harking after, questing

question *n, v*
♦ *n*
1 QUERY, inquiry, poser, problem, difficulty
2 ISSUE, matter, problem, subject, theme, topic, point, point at issue, proposal, proposition, motion, debate, dispute, controversy
3 DOUBT, query, debate, dispute, argument, controversy, uncertainty
♦ *v*
1 INTERROGATE, quiz, grill, pump, interview, examine, cross-examine, cross-question, debrief, ask, inquire, investigate, probe, catechize
COLLOQ. give the third degree to
2 QUERY, challenge, dispute, have doubts about, zhave reservations/qualms about, doubt, disbelieve
■ **in question**
at issue, being discussed, under discussion, concerned
■ **out of the question**
impossible, unthinkable, unbelievable, absurd, ridiculous, unacceptable, not worth considering
COLLOQ. not by any stretch of the imagination
■ **without question**
without arguing, immediately, unhesitatingly, unquestionably, without a shadow of doubt

---

SYNONYM NUANCES

verb sense 1
Interrogate can be used to suggest a thorough questioning, often in official circumstances, and **quiz** likewise implies a detailed investigation. **Grill**, too, has connotations of pressure, or even harassment: *he was grilled by detectives for two hours*, while **pump** is more suggestive of persistently trying to extract particular information: *she pumped me about his movements*.

The word **interview**, while suggesting a formal situation, suggests a less intense questioning, but both **cross-examine** and **cross-question** return to the idea of close questioning in minute detail, and are usually associated with court cases. The term **debrief** has the specific use of questioning someone on their return from business or a mission: *the aircrews had yet to be debriefed as to the operations.*

Inquire is not a particularly marked term, and can be generally used of seeking information, but the terms **investigate** and **examine** return to the idea of looking more carefully into a matter. To suggest an even deeper scrutiny, you could use **probe**: *police probed allegations of assault and arrests were made.*

The uncommon **catechize** is reserved for a systematic questioning, usually regarding religious tenets.

---

questionable *adj*
debatable, disputable, unsettled, undetermined, unproven, uncertain, arguable, controversial, vexed, doubtful, dubious, suspicious, suspect, at question, problematic(al), equivocal

COLLOQ. shady, fishy, iffy
E3 unquestionable, indisputable, certain

questioner *n*
1 INTERVIEWER, examiner, inquirer, question-master, quizmaster, inquisitor, interrogator, investigator, catechizer, catechist
FORMAL interlocutor
2 DISBELIEVER, doubter, sceptic, agnostic

questionnaire *n*
quiz, test, form, survey, opinion poll, market research

queue *n, v*
♦ *n*
line, tailback, tail, file, row, column, crocodile, procession, train, string, chain, succession, series, sequence, order, breadline
FORMAL concatenation
♦ *v*
line up, form a queue, form a line, stand in line, wait in line, fall in, tail back; *N Am* back up

quibble *v, n*
♦ *v*
carp, cavil, split hairs, find fault with, equivocate, avoid the issue, prevaricate, dodge, haggle, peck at
OLD pettifog
COLLOQ. nit-pick, split hairs
♦ *n*
complaint, objection, criticism, query, protest, cavil, niggle, equivocation, prevarication, dodge, quip, quirk
OLD quiblin, pettifogging, brabble, carriwitchet; (*Shakesp*) snatch
FORMAL quiddity, equivoke, quillet
COLLOQ. nit-picking

quibbler *n*
caviller, niggler, sophist, equivocator, casuist
OLD pettifogger
COLLOQ. hair-splitter, nit-picker

quibbling *adj*
niggling, critical, overnice, carping, captious, ambiguous, cavilling, evasive, casuistic, equivocating, logic-chopping
OLD pettifogging
COLLOQ. hair-splitting, nit-picking

quick *adj*
1 FAST, swift, rapid, speedy, express, hurried, hasty, cursory, fleeting, brief, perfunctory, prompt, ready, immediate, without delay, instant, instantaneous, sudden, brisk, nimble, sprightly, agile
FORMAL expeditious
COLLOQ. like greased lightning, nifty, nippy, zippy, pdq, pretty damn quick
2 CLEVER, intelligent, quick-witted, smart, sharp, sharp-witted, keen, shrewd, astute, discerning, perceptive, responsive, alive, receptive, quick off the mark, quick on the uptake
E3 **1** slow, sluggish, lethargic **2** unintelligent, dull

SYNONYM NUANCES

sense 1
Swift can imply not lasting long: *the swift burst of curiosity flickered out*, while **rapid** is appropriate for something accomplished within a short time: *the patient has made rapid progress.* Both **speedy** and **nippy** can be used to suggest agility and mobility: *a nippy little car.* Similarly **nimble**, **sprightly** and **agile** can suggest both speed and lightness or suppleness of movement.

Express, however, implies the fastest of various set options: *express delivery*, unlike the more critical **hurried**, **hasty** and **cursory**, which suggest not being apportioned enough time or attention: *a cursory examination of an important issue.* You can use **brief** or **fleeting** fairly neutrally of something transitory, whereas **perfunctory** returns to the idea of merely going through the motions and is more disapproving.

> **Prompt** and **ready** have connotations of efficiency, when referring to something quickly achieved or available: *prompt payment of bills will help you to budget.* **Brisk** can have similar connotations of efficiency but can also suggest brusqueness in manner: *a brisk retort,* or purposeful movement: *a brisk walk.*

quicken v
1 ACCELERATE, speed (up), hurry (up), hasten, dispatch, advance
FORMAL precipitate, expedite
2 ANIMATE, enliven, invigorate, energize, galvanize, activate, incite, instigate, rouse, arouse, stimulate, stir (up), excite, kindle, inspire, whet, revive, refresh, reinvigorate, strengthen, revitalize, reactivate
FORMAL revivify
🖅 **1** slow, retard **2** dull, enervate

quickly adv
rapidly, quick, fast, speedily, swiftly, express, briskly, apace, hurriedly, hastily, immediately, instantaneously, readily, smartly, soon, abruptly, instantly, promptly, unhesitatingly, cursorily, posthaste
TECHNICAL presto, prestissimo
FORMAL expeditiously, perfunctorily
COLLOQ. pronto, lickety-split, at a rate of knots, at the double, before you can say Jack Robinson, by leaps and bounds, hell for leather, like a bat out of hell, like the clappers, like greased lightning, a mile a minute
🖅 slowly; *formal* tardily

quickness n
1 SPEED, speediness, rapidity, swiftness, hastiness, immediacy, briskness, promptness, readiness, suddenness, instantaneousness, agility, nimbleness
OLD nimblesse
FORMAL expedition, precipitation, promptitude, celerity
2 INTELLIGENCE, shrewdness, sharpness, penetration, acuteness, astuteness, keenness, quick-wittedness, alertness
FORMAL acumen
🖅 **1** slowness; *formal* tardiness **2** dullness; *colloq.* dim-wittedness

quick-tempered adj
fiery, impatient, impulsive, hot-tempered, irascible, testy, touchy, irritable, explosive, volcanic, waspish, choleric, excitable, quarrelsome, shrewish, snappy, temperamental, splenetic, petulant
🖅 cool, dispassionate

quick-witted adj
intelligent, clever, resourceful, keen, bright, sharp, shrewd, penetrating, acute, perceptive, smart, wide-awake, alert, astute, crafty, ingenious, witty, ready-witted, nimble-witted, quick off the mark, quick on the uptake
🖅 dull, slow, stupid

quid pro quo n
exchange, swap, trade-off, give-and-take, equivalent, equivalence, co-operation, compensation, remuneration, damages
FORMAL reciprocity, reciprocation, mutuality
COLLOQ. tit for tat

quiescent adj
quiet, at rest, resting, calm, peaceful, serene, placid, tranquil, undisturbed, untroubled, still, passive, silent, motionless, inactive, inert, sleeping, asleep, latent, dormant
FORMAL in abeyance, reposeful
🖅 active

quiet adj, n
♦ adj
1 SILENT, soundless, without a sound, noiseless, inaudible, hushed, soft, faint, indistinct, muffled, low
COLLOQ. you could hear a pin drop
2 PEACEFUL, still, tranquil, serene, calm, mild, gentle, restrained, composed, undisturbed, untroubled, placid

3 SHY, reserved, reticent, uncommunicative, taciturn, placid, unforthcoming, undemonstrative, retiring, withdrawn, introvert, unexcitable, stoic, thoughtful, discreet, subdued, meek
FORMAL imperturbable, phlegmatic
COLLOQ. unflappable
4 *have a quiet word with you*
secret, private, confidential, discreet, off-the-record, personal, man-to-man, woman-to-woman
5 *a quiet spot*
isolated, unfrequented, lonely, secluded, undisturbed, private, sleepy, peaceful
FORMAL sequestered
COLLOQ. off the beaten track
6 *quiet colours*
muted, subdued, soft, subtle, faint, pale, restrained, low-key
🖅 **1** noisy, loud **2** excitable, animated **3** extrovert, talkative **4** public **5** noisy, busy **6** loud, ostentatious
♦ n
quietness, silence, hush, peace, lull, stillness, peacefulness, soundlessness, noiselessness, tranquillity, serenity, calm, rest
FORMAL repose
🖅 noise, loudness, disturbance, bustle

quieten v
1 SILENCE, hush, shush, mute, soften, lower, diminish, reduce, stifle, muffle, deaden, dull
COLLOQ. shut up
2 SUBDUE, pacify, quell, quiet, still, smooth, calm (down), tranquillize, soothe, compose, sober
🖅 **2** disturb, agitate

quietly adv
calmly, noiselessly, inaudibly, mutely, silently, softly, soundlessly, surreptitiously, placidly, tranquilly, peacefully, gently, mildly, meekly, unobtrusively, unostentatiously, undemonstratively, modestly, secretly, privately
🖅 noisily, obtrusively

quietness n
calm, quiet, silence, serenity, tranquillity, calmness, hush, peace, peacefulness, placidity, lull, still, stillness, composure, inactivity, inertia, uneventfulness, dullness
FORMAL quiescence, quietude, repose
🖅 activity, bustle, commotion, disturbance, noise, racket

quietude n
tranquillity, calm, peace, peacefulness, serenity, calmness, composure, quiet, quietness, rest, restfulness, stillness, hush, silence, imperturbability, coolness, equanimity, sedateness, placidity
TECHNICAL ataraxia, ataraxy
FORMAL repose
🖅 disturbance, agitation, noise

quietus n
release, end, silencing, discharge, dispatch, acquittance, death, death-blow, death-stroke, finishing stroke, *coup de grâce*, extinction
FORMAL decease, demise

quilt n
bedcover, coverlet, bedspread, counterpane, eiderdown, duvet, continental quilt, patchwork quilt, kantha; *N Am* comforter; *Aust* doona
OLD counterpoint
COLLOQ. *N Am* comfort

quintessence n
embodiment, personification, essence, core, distillation, marrow, pith, soul, spirit, extract, gist, heart, kernel, pattern, sum and substance
FORMAL exemplar, quiddity

quintessential adj
typical, essential, ideal, perfect, ultimate, complete, definitive, entire
FORMAL archetypical, consummate, prototypical

quip n, v

♦ n
joke, jest, crack, wisecrack, witticism, riposte, retort, gibe, epigram, pleasantry
COLLOQ. gag, one-liner
♦ v
jest, joke, retort, riposte, gibe, quirk, gag, wisecrack

quirk n

freak, eccentricity, curiosity, oddity, peculiarity, idiosyncrasy, mannerism, habit, trait, characteristic, feature, foible, whim, vagary, caprice, obsession, turn, twist, kink
COLLOQ. thing, hang-up, fluke

quirkiness n

eccentricity, unconventionality, strangeness, unorthodoxy, peculiarity, nonconformity, abnormality, oddity, bizarreness, weirdness, idiosyncrasy, singularity, freakishness, anomaly
FORMAL aberration, capriciousness
COLLOQ. freakiness, wackiness, zaniness
E3 conventionality, ordinariness

quirky adj

odd, unusual, strange, eccentric, idiosyncratic, uncommon, peculiar, funny, abnormal, exceptional, curious, atypical, different, queer, bizarre, deviant, singular, remarkable, original, unconventional, uncanny, droll, drôle, freakish, weird, irregular, wild, extraordinary, outlandish, whimsical, whimsy
FORMAL aberrant, capricious
COLLOQ. out of the ordinary, freaky, kinky, wacky, oddball, zany, barmy, crackers, off the wall
SLANG far-out, way-out, funky

quisling n

betrayer, traitor, turncoat, collaborator, renegade, fifth columnist, puppet, Judas
FORMAL collaborationist

quit v

1 *quit smoking*
give up, stop, end, cease, abandon, drop, leave off
FORMAL discontinue, desist, abstain
COLLOQ. pack in
2 LEAVE, depart, go (away), exit, decamp, desert, abandon, relinquish, surrender, give up, resign, retire, withdraw
FORMAL renounce, forsake

quite adv

1 MODERATELY, rather, somewhat, reasonably, fairly, relatively, comparatively, to some extent/degree
2 UTTERLY, absolutely, totally, completely, entirely, wholly, fully, perfectly, exactly, precisely

quits adj

equal, even, level, square
■ **call it quits**
stop, cease, break off, make peace, stop fighting
FORMAL discontinue
COLLOQ. call it a day, bury the hatchet, lay down your arms

quitter n

defector, delinquent, renegade, shirker, deserter, apostate
OLD recreant
COLLOQ. rat, skiver

quiver v, n

♦ v
shake, tremble, shudder, shiver, quake, quaver, vibrate, pulsate, tingle, thrill, palpitate, flutter, flicker, oscillate, wobble, tremor, bicker; *Scot* flichter
♦ n
shake, tremble, shudder, shiver, tremor, throb, vibration, palpitation, quaver, pulsation, flutter, flicker, oscillation, wobble, twinkle

quixotic adj

unrealistic, unworldly, idealistic, impracticable, visionary, extravagant, fanciful, Utopian, fantastical, romantic, starry-eyed, impetuous, impulsive, chivalrous
E3 hard-headed, practical, realistic

quiz n, v

♦ n
questionnaire, test, examination, competition, questioning, cross-examination, cross-questioning
♦ v
question, interrogate, examine, cross-examine, cross-question
OLD smoke
COLLOQ. grill, pump, give the third degree to, trail

quizzical adj

questioning, inquiring, curious, amused, humorous, teasing, mocking, satirical, sardonic, sceptical, mystified, perplexed, puzzled, baffled

quizzically adv

questioningly, inquiringly, curiously, mockingly, sceptically

quota n

ration, allowance, allocation, assignment, share, portion, part, slice, percentage, proportion, contingent
TECHNICAL numerus clausus
FORMAL quotum
COLLOQ. cut, whack, slice of cake

quotation n

1 CITATION, extract, excerpt, line, passage, selection, piece, cutting, reference, allusion
COLLOQ. quote
2 ESTIMATE, tender, figure, price, cost, charge, rate, bid
COLLOQ. quote

> **QUOTATIONS**
> In the dying world I come from, quotation is a national vice. No one would think of making an after-dinner speech without the help of poetry. It used to be classics, now it's lyric verse
> EVELYN WAUGH, *The Loved One*

quote v

cite, refer to, mention, name, reproduce, echo, repeat, recite, recall, recollect, allude to

quoted adj

cited, referred to, reported, reproduced, stated, above-mentioned
FORMAL forementioned, instanced

quotidian adj

everyday, normal, ordinary, routine, workaday, regular, daily, day-to-day, repeated, common, commonplace, customary, recurrent, habitual
FORMAL diurnal
COLLOQ. run-of-the-mill, bog-standard

R

rabbit *n, v*

♦ *n*

bunny, cony, bunny rabbit, daman, hyrax, dassie, buck, doe; *N Am* cottontail
COLLOQ. bun
Related adjective: oryctolagine, lagomorphic

■ **rabbit on**

chatter, babble, go on (and on), maunder (on); *Scot* blether; *dialect & N Am* blather
COLLOQ. natter, witter (on), waffle, gab

Breeds of rabbit and hare include:

Alaska	Harlequin	sable
Angora	Havana	sage rabbit
Arctic hare	Himalayan	satin
Argente	hotot	silver
Belgian hare	jack rabbit	snowshoe hare (or
black silver	lop	rabbit)
brown hare	New Zealand	swamp (or water)
chinchilla	oar-lap	rabbit
cottontail	pika	tan
Dutch	Polish	tapeti
English spot	Rex	Van Beveren
European	Rhinelander	Vienna
Flemish	riverine rabbit	
fox	rock rabbit	

---

rabble *n*

1 CROWD, throng, horde, herd, mob
2 MASSES, populace, crowd, herd, mob, common people, proletariat, hoi polloi, rank and file, riff-raff, great unwashed
COLLOQ. plebs, proles

rabble-rouser *n*

agitator, troublemaker, incendiary, firebrand, demagogue, ringleader
COLLOQ. tub-thumper

rabble-rousing *n*

stirring up, troublemaking
COLLOQ. tub-thumping

Rabelaisian *adj*

satirical, exuberant, extravagant, coarse, bawdy, earthy, gross, vulgar, uninhibited, unrestrained, indecent, lewd, racy, ribald, risqué

rabid *adj*

1 FANATICAL, ferocious, extreme, burning, ardent, raging, fervent, frantic, unreasoning, intolerant, irrational, furious, obsessive, zealous, overzealous, bigoted, narrow-minded
2 MAD, hydrophobic, maniacal, wild, berserk, frenzied, crazed, violent, hysterical

rabies *n*

hydrophobia, rabidity, rabidness

race¹ *n, v*

♦ *n*

a horse race

competition, contest, contention, rivalry, chase, pursuit, quest

♦ *v*

run, sprint, dash, tear, fly, gallop, speed, career, dart, bolt, zoom, rush, hurry, hasten, accelerate, take part in a race
COLLOQ. get a move on, go all out, get cracking, scoot, zip, zap, run like hell

---

Types of race include:

CYCLING:	MOTOR-RACING:	SKIING:
criterium	Formula One	downhill
cyclo-cross	scramble	slalom
keirin race	stock car race	**FUN RACES:**
road race	**SAILING:**	egg-and-spoon
time trial	regatta	race
HORSE RACING:	yacht race	pancake race
N Am harness	**RUNNING:**	sack race
race	cross-country	three-legged race
steeplechase	dash	wheelbarrow race
trotting	hurdles	**OTHER:**
race	marathon	greyhound race
MOTORCYCLING:	relay	swimming race
motocross	sprint	walkathon
scramble	steeplechase	walking race
speedway	track event	

---

race² *n*

a race of people

nation, people, ethnic group, racial group, colour, tribe, clan, house, dynasty, family, kindred, ancestry, line, lineage, blood, extraction, stock, parentage, strain, stirps, genus, species, breed
Related adjective: ethnic

racecourse *n*

racetrack, course, track, circuit, lap, turf, speedway

racial *adj*

national, tribal, ethnic, folk, ethnological, genealogical, ancestral, inherited, genetic

raciness *n*

1 RIBALDRY, indecency, indelicacy, bawdiness, naughtiness, lewdness, smuttiness, suggestiveness, vulgarity, crudeness, coarseness
2 LIVELINESS, animation, zest, zestfulness, energy, exhilaration, freshness, dynamism
FORMAL ebullience
COLLOQ. pep, pizzazz

racism *n*

racialism, xenophobia, chauvinism, jingoism, discrimination, racial discrimination, prejudice, racial prejudice, apartheid, bias

racist *n, adj*

♦ *n*

racialist, discriminator, bigot, chauvinist

♦ *adj*

racialist, discriminatory, bigoted, intolerant

rack *n, v*

♦ *n*

1 HOLDER, shelf, stand, support, structure, frame, framework, trestle, flake, hack; *dialect* heck
OLD portmanteau

2 SUFFERING, pain, misery, affliction, agony, anguish, distress, pangs, torment, torture, persecution

♦ *v*

afflict, oppress, distress, agonize, pain, harass, convulse, shake, strain, stress, tear, stretch, wrench, wrest, wring, excruciate, harrow, lacerate, torment, torture, crucify

OLD touse

■ **rack your brains**

think hard, think deeply, concentrate, study, put your mind to

■ **on the rack**

suffering, in distress, under pressure/stress, in difficulties, in trouble, in agony, in pain

racket *n*

1 NOISE, din, uproar, row, fuss, outcry, clamour, shouting, yelling, tumult, commotion, disturbance, hullabaloo, pandemonium, hurly-burly, hubbub

2 SWINDLE, fraud, fiddle, deception, trick, dodge, scheme, business

COLLOQ. scam, con, game

SLANG *N Am* gold brick

racketeering *n*

cheating, swindling, fraud, defrauding, extortion, stealing, overcharging, fleecing, fiddling

COLLOQ. cooking the books

SLANG ripping off, stinging, chiselling, taking for a ride, taking to the cleaners

raconteur *n*

narrator, storyteller, chronicler, reporter, anecdotist, commentator, describer, relater

racy *adj*

1 RIBALD, bawdy, risqué, vulgar, crude, rude, coarse, dirty, naughty, indecent, indelicate, suggestive, off-colour, smutty

COLLOQ. blue

2 LIVELY, animated, spirited, vigorous, vivacious, fast-moving, energetic, dynamic, buoyant, enthusiastic, boisterous, sparkling, piquant, witty, spicy

FORMAL ebullient

COLLOQ. peppy, zippy

raddled *adj*

haggard, drawn, gaunt, wasted, worn out, unkempt, dishevelled, in a mess, the worse for wear

radiance *n*

1 LIGHT, luminosity, radiation, brightness, brilliance, shine, lustre, gleam, glow, glitter, resplendence, splendour

TECHNICAL incandescence

FORMAL effulgence, refulgence

2 JOY, happiness, pleasure, delight, elation, ecstasy, bliss, rapture

radiant *adj*

1 BRIGHT, luminous, shining, illuminated, gleaming, glowing, beaming, glittering, sparkling, brilliant, splendid, magnificent, glorious, beamish, beamy

TECHNICAL incandescent

FORMAL resplendent, effulgent, refulgent, lambent, profulgent

2 JOYFUL, happy, delighted, elated, pleased, blissful, ecstatic, in raptures

COLLOQ. in seventh heaven, on top of the world, on cloud nine, over the moon

F3 **1** dull **2** miserable

radiate *v*

1 *radiate light/an emotion*

shine, gleam, glow, beam, shed, pour, send out/forth, give off, emit, emanate, diffuse, issue

2 SPREAD (OUT), scatter, disperse, diverge, branch

FORMAL disseminate, divaricate

radiation *n*

emanation, emission, rays, waves, transmission

TECHNICAL insolation

Types of radiation include:

alpha radiation	cosmic radiation	microwaves
background	electromagnetic	radio waves
radiation	radiation	soft radiation
beta radiation	gamma radiation	synchrotron
black body	hard radiation	radiation
radiation	Hawking radiation	ultraviolet
bremsstrahlung	infrared radiation	radiation
Cerenkov	insolation	visible radiation
radiation	ionizing	X-rays

radical *adj, n*

♦ *adj*

1 BASIC, fundamental, rudimentary, primary, elementary, elemental, essential, natural, native, innate, intrinsic, deep-seated, profound

2 *radical changes*

drastic, comprehensive, thorough, sweeping, far-reaching, exhaustive, thoroughgoing, profound, complete, absolute, total, entire, utter

3 FANATICAL, militant, extreme, extremist, rebellious, revolutionary

F3 **1** superficial **3** conservative, moderate

♦ *n*

fanatic, militant, extremist, revolutionary, rebel, reformer, reformist, fundamentalist

raffish *adj*

disreputable, dissipated, dissolute, cheap, tawdry, vulgar, uncouth, trashy, bohemian, rakish, showy, sporty, jaunty, casual, careless, devil-may-care, improper, gross, flamboyant, flashy, garish, gaudy, tasteless, loud, coarse

OLD dashing

FORMAL meretricious

F3 proper, sedate, staid; *formal* decorous

raffle *n*

draw, lottery, sweepstake, sweep, tombola

rag[1] *n*

1 *an old clothes rag*

cloth, flannel, floorcloth, duster, towel; *S Afr* lap, lappie

OLD slut

2 *dressed in rags*

remnant, shred, raggedness, tatter, tat, clout, tagrag; *Scot* wallop

COLLOQ. duddery, duds, schmutter

rag[2] *v*

rag the new boy

tease, badger, jeer, mock, ridicule, taunt, torment, bait, haze

OLD row

COLLOQ. rib, kid, take the mickey out of

SLANG *N Am* goof

ragamuffin *n*

urchin, guttersnipe, waif, street arab, gamin

ragbag *n*

confusion, miscellany, assortment, mixture, mix, jumble, medley, pastiche, hotchpotch, hodgepodge, salad, potpourri, olio, olla-podrida

FORMAL assemblage

COLLOQ. omnium-gatherum, mishmash

rage *n, v*

♦ *n*

anger, wrath, fury, frenzy, raving, madness, tumult, tantrum, temper, paroxysm

♦ *v*

fume, seethe, rant, rave, storm, thunder, explode, rampage

COLLOQ. blow a fuse, blow a gasket, blow your cool, blow your top, boil over, burst a blood vessel, do your nut, flip your lid, fly off the handle, go mad, foam at the mouth, go off the deep end, go up the wall, hit the roof, lose your cool, lose your rag, raise hell, see red

■ **all the rage**
fashionable, popular, the craze, in vogue, stylish
COLLOQ. cool, in, the in thing, trendy, now

> **QUOTATIONS**
> Rage is the only quality which has kept me, or anybody
> I have ever studied, writing columns for newspapers
> JIMMY BRESLIN

ragged adj
1 *ragged clothes*
frayed, torn, ripped, tattered, in tatters, worn-out,
in holes, holey, threadbare, falling to pieces, tatty,
shabby
OLD rent
2 *ragged children*
scruffy, untidy, unkempt, poor, destitute, down and out,
down-at-heel
FORMAL indigent
3 JAGGED, serrated, indented, notched, rugged, rough,
uneven, irregular
4 *a ragged group of people*
fragmented, erratic, disorganized, straggling

raging adj
1 VIOLENT, wild, stormy, turbulent, tumultuous
2 ANGRY, furious, enraged, infuriated, ireful, irate, fuming,
incensed, raving, seething, wrathful, frenzied, mad
FORMAL fulminating, furibund

raid n, v
♦ n
attack, onset, assault, charge, onslaught, inroad, invasion,
descent, excursion, incursion, foray, sortie, sally, strike,
blitz, air raid, Baedeker raid, swoop, robbery, break-in,
hold-up, smash-and-grab raid, dawn raid, ram-raid,
sneak-raid, spreagh
OLD (*Shakesp & Spenser*) road; (*Spenser*) bodrag
SLANG bust
♦ v
loot, pillage, plunder, sack, ransack, forage, rifle, maraud,
break into, attack, assail, rush, set upon, descend on,
invade, storm, foray, ram-raid
SLANG bust, do, pull

raider n
attacker, invader, looter, plunderer, pillager, ransacker,
marauder, robber, thief, criminal, brigand,
villain, pirate
COLLOQ. crook, shark

rail v
censure, criticize, attack, abuse, protest, decry, upbraid,
vociferate, mock, jeer, revile, ridicule, scoff
FORMAL arraign, castigate, denounce, fulminate, inveigh,
vituperate

railing n
fence, fencing, paling, barrier, parapet, rail(s), balustrade

raillery n
mockery, teasing, jeering, jesting, banter, chaff, badinage,
repartee, irony, joke, joking, ridicule, satire, sport,
pleasantry, persiflage
OLD dicacity
FORMAL diatribe, invective
COLLOQ. kidding, ragging, ribbing; *Aust* chiacking

railway n
track, line, rail(s); *N Am* railroad

Types of railway include:

branch line	freight	marshalling yard
broad gauge	funicular railway	metro
cable railway	garden railway	model railway
cutting	goods line	monorail
electric railway	high-speed line	mountain railway
elevated railway	InterCity®	narrow gauge
express	light railway	passenger line
feeder line	main line	

rack-and-pinion railway	siding	*colloq.* tube
rack railway	standard gauge	underground
rapid transit system	subway	
	tramway	
	trunk line	

rain n, v
♦ n
1 RAINFALL, precipitation, raindrops, drizzle, mizzle,
shower, cloudburst, downpour, deluge, torrent, storm,
rainstorm, thunderstorm, squall
Related adjectives: pluvial, hyetal
2 *a rain of stones*
torrent, volley, shower, deluge
♦ v
spit, drizzle, mizzle, sprinkle, shower, pour (down), tipple
down, teem, pelt, deluge
COLLOQ. bucket (down), rain cats and dogs, come down
in buckets/sheets/stair rods/torrents, the floodgates/clouds
open
SLANG piss down

> **PROVERBS**
> It never rains but it pours

> **QUOTATIONS**
> It is impossible to live in a country which is continually
> under hatches … Rain! Rain! Rain!
> JOHN KEATS

rainbow n, adj
♦ n
arc, arch, bow, spectrum, prism, iris, fog-bow, moon-bow,
weather gall, *arc-en-ciel*; *Scot* weather gaw
OLD water gall
♦ adj
rainbow-like, kaleidoscopic, prismatic, variegated, spectral,
opalescent
FORMAL iridescent, irisated, irised
 monochrome

rainy adj
wet, damp, moist, watery, showery, drizzly; *dialect* soft
FORMAL inclement, pluvial, pluviose, pluvious, hyetal
 dry

raise v
1 LIFT, lift up, elevate, hoist, uplift, heave up, jack up, put
up, set up, erect, build, construct, weigh
2 INCREASE, escalate, put up, magnify, heighten, strengthen,
step up, push up, intensify, amplify, boost, enhance,
upgrade
FORMAL augment
COLLOQ. jack up, bump up, hike up
3 *raise funds*
get, obtain, collect, gather, get together, amass,
accumulate, assemble, rally, muster, recruit
4 BRING UP, rear, breed, propagate, grow, cultivate,
educate, produce, develop, nurture
5 *raise a subject*
bring up, broach, introduce, present, put forward, moot,
suggest
6 PROVOKE, cause, create, arouse, rouse, activate, give rise
to, evoke, excite, stir
 1 lower, drop **2** decrease, reduce **5** suppress

raised adj
embossed, relief, applied, appliqué, cameo, relievo
 engraved, incised, intaglio

rake¹ v, n
♦ v
1 *rake the grass*
scratch, hoe, scrape, graze, comb, level, smooth
2 SEARCH, scour, hunt, ransack, rifle, rummage, comb
3 GATHER, collect, amass, accumulate

♦ *n*

harrow, muck-rake, buckrake, stubble rake, horse rake

rake² *n, v*

♦ *n*

DEGENERATE, debauchee, playboy, roué, wanton, dissolute, libertine, hedonist, lecher, sensualist, pleasure-seeker, spendthrift, swinger, rakehell, Lothario, gay dog
FORMAL profligate, prodigal
E3 ascetic, puritan

■ **rake in**

earn, receive, get paid, make, fetch, haul in, net, gross, reap
COLLOQ. bring in, pull in

■ **rake up**

remind, bring up, raise, mention, revive, introduce, drag up, dredge up, dig up

rake-off *n*

cut, share, slice, part, portion, proportion, percentage

rakish *adj*

1 STYLISH, sporty, smart, dapper, sharp, flamboyant, flashy, jaunty, debonair, nonchalant, adventurous, casual, breezy, devil-may-care
OLD dashing
COLLOQ. natty, snazzy
2 DEBAUCHED, dissolute, dissipated, abandoned, libertine, loose, lecherous, raffish, sinful, depraved, degenerate, immoral, licentious
FORMAL prodigal, profligate

rally *n, v*

♦ *n*

1 GATHERING, assembly, convention, convocation, conference, meeting, mass meeting, jamboree, reunion, march, demonstration
FORMAL assemblage
2 RECOVERY, recuperation, revival, comeback, improvement, resurgence, renewal

♦ *v*

1 GATHER, collect, come/bring together, get together, assemble, congregate, group, band together, muster, summon, round up, unite, marshal, organize, mobilize, reassemble, regroup, reorganize, reform
OLD really, rely; (*Shakesp*) re-enforce
FORMAL convene
2 RECOVER, recuperate, revive, improve, pick up, get well, get better, gain strength, pull through
COLLOQ. perk up, bounce back, get back on your feet, be on the mend

ram *v*

1 HIT, strike, beat, butt, hammer, pound, drive, drum, bump, crash, smash, dash, slam, stem
OLD pun
2 FORCE, drive, thrust, cram, stuff, pack, crowd, jam, squeeze, compress, wedge
TECHNICAL tamp

ramble *v, n*

♦ *v*

1 WALK, hike, trek, tramp, traipse, stroll, amble, saunter, stray, straggle, wander, roam, range, jaunt, rove, diverge, meander, wind, zigzag
2 CHATTER, babble, digress, wander, drift; *Scot* blether; *dialect & N Am* blather
FORMAL expatiate
COLLOQ. rabbit (on), witter (on), gas, jaw, natter, waffle, go off at a tangent

♦ *n*

walk, hike, trek, tramp, stroll, saunter, wander, roam, amble, jaunt, tour, trip, excursion

rambler *n*

hiker, walker, traveller, stroller, rover, roamer, saunterer, wanderer, drifter, wayfarer

rambling *adj*

1 SPREADING, sprawling, straggling, trailing

2 ROUNDABOUT, digressive, wandering, wordy, verbose, long-winded, long-drawn-out, disjointed, disconnected, incoherent
FORMAL circuitous, periphrastic, errant
E3 2 direct

ramification *n*

1 RESULT, consequence, effect, upshot, outcome, sequel
2 BRANCH, offshoot, limb, outgrowth, development, implication, complication
FORMAL divarication

ramp *n*

slope, incline, gradient, rise, grade
FORMAL acclivity, declivity

rampage *v, n*

♦ *v*

run wild, run amok, run riot, go berserk, rush, rush violently/wildly, charge, tear, storm, rage, rant, rave

♦ *n*

rage, fury, frenzy, turmoil, mayhem, storm, uproar, violence, destruction, furore

■ **on the rampage**

wild, amok, berserk, frenzied, in a frenzy, violent(ly), wild(ly), out of control

rampant *adj*

unrestrained, uncontrolled, out of control, out of hand, unbridled, unchecked, wanton, excessive, fierce, violent, raging, wild, riotous, rank, profuse, rife, widespread, prevalent, epidemic, pandemic
COLLOQ. spreading like wildfire

rampart *n*

earthwork, embankment, bank, fence, barricade, bastion, bulwark, defence, stronghold, guard, wall, security, parapet, fort, fortification, breastwork, vallum

ramshackle *adj*

dilapidated, tumbledown, broken-down, run-down, crumbling, ruined, neglected, derelict, jerry-built, unsafe, rickety, shaky, flimsy, unsteady, tottering, decrepit, gone to rack and ruin
E3 solid, stable

ranch *n*

farm, estate, plantation, fazenda, hacienda, estancia, dude ranch; *N Am* range, spread; *Aust & NZ* station

rancid *adj*

sour, off, bad, turned, high, overripe, unpleasant, musty, stale, rank, foul, f(o)etid, putrid, rotten
FORMAL noxious, noisome, malodorous
E3 sweet

rancorous *adj*

resentful, bitter, acrimonious, acerbic, hostile, spiteful, malevolent, malignant, vindictive, venomous, vengeful, implacable, virulent, splenetic

rancour *n*

resentfulness, resentment, spite, hate, hatred, animosity, malevolence, malice, malignity, ill-feeling, ill-will, hostility, bitterness, acrimony, enmity, grudge, venom, vindictiveness, spleen
FORMAL animus, antipathy

random *adj*

arbitrary, chance, casual, incidental, haphazard, irregular, sporadic, unsystematic, unarranged, unplanned, unmethodical, accidental, aimless, purposeless, indiscriminate, stray
FORMAL fortuitous, serendipitous
COLLOQ. hit-or-miss
E3 systematic, deliberate

■ **at random**

randomly, haphazardly, incidentally, fortuitously, arbitrarily, sporadically, irregularly, unsystematically, unmethodically, aimlessly, purposelessly, indiscriminately
E3 systematically, deliberately

randomly *adv*

at random, haphazardly, incidentally, arbitrarily, sporadically, irregularly, unsystematically, unmethodically, aimlessly, purposelessly, indiscriminately

Ⅎ systematically, deliberately

randy *adj*

horny, sexy, raunchy, amorous, aroused, hot, lustful, goatish, lascivious, lecherous, satyric

FORMAL concupiscent

COLLOQ. turned-on

range *n, v*

♦ *n*

1 *a range of fittings*
variety, diversity, assortment, selection, array, sort, kind, type, class, order, species, genus, series, string, chain, line, row, file
2 SCOPE, compass, scale, gamut, spectrum, radius, sweep, spread, extent, distance, reach, span, confines, limits, bounds, parameters, area, field, domain, province, sphere, orbit
3 *a mountain range*
line, row, chain, string, sierra, cordillera
4 PASTURE, grass, grassland, meadow, field, paddock, pasturage, grazing, grazing land
5 *a cooking range*
stove, cooker, oven
♦ *v*
1 EXTEND, stretch, reach, go, run, cover, spread, vary, fluctuate
2 ALIGN, arrange, draw up, line up, order, rank, class, classify, catalogue, group, categorize, grade, pigeonhole, compartmentalize
FORMAL dispose
3 ROAM, wander, stroll, stray, drift, amble, ramble, rove

rangy *adj*

long-legged, leggy, lanky, gangling, long-limbed, skinny, weedy, rawboned

Ⅎ compact, dumpy

rank¹ *n, v*

♦ *n*

1 GRADE, degree, class, caste, status, standing, position, station, condition, estate, mark, echelon, level, stratum, tier, classification, sort, type, group, division
COLLOQ. place in the pecking order
See panel below
2 ARISTOCRACY, nobility, peerage, peers, nobles, gentry, élite, lords, high society, family
COLLOQ. nobs, toffs
3 ROW, line, range, column, file, string, series, order, formation
♦ *v*
1 GRADE, class, rate, place, position, range, sort, classify, categorize, order, arrange, organize, marshal
2 ALIGN, arrange, order, draw up, line up
FORMAL dispose

■ **rank and file**

1 ORDINARY SOLDIERS, ordinary men, soldiers, private soldiers
2 RABBLE, masses, populace, crowd, herd, mob, common people, proletariat, hoi polloi, riff-raff
COLLOQ. proles, plebs

rank² *adj*

1 UTTER, total, complete, absolute, unmitigated, unqualified, thorough, sheer, downright, out-and-out, arrant, gross, flagrant, glaring, blatant, outrageous
2 FOUL, repulsive, disgusting, unpleasant, offensive, disagreeable, revolting, stinking, evil-smelling, acrid, pungent, putrid, f(o)etid, rancid, stale
FORMAL malodorous, mephitic, graveolent
3 *rank disobedience*
gross, coarse, shocking, outrageous, vile
4 OVERGROWN, lush, abundant, dense, profuse, vigorous
FORMAL luxuriant

rankle *v*

annoy, irritate, rile, nettle, gall, irk, vex, peeve, fester, cause bitterness/resentment in/to, embitter, anger

COLLOQ. bug, get your blood up, get your back up, make your blood boil, get on your nerves, get up your nose, get under your skin, get your goat, get on your wick

---

Ranks in the armed services include:

UK AIR FORCE:			UK NAVY:		US STATE POLICE:
aircraftsman/	first-lieutenant	general	able seaman	chief petty officer	superintendent/
aircraftswoman	captain	field marshal	rating	senior chief petty	detective
corporal	major		petty officer	officer	superintendent
sergeant	lieutenant-colonel	US ARMY:	chief petty officer	master chief petty	chief
master aircrew	colonel	private	midshipman	officer	superintendent/
warrant officer	brigadier-general	private first class	sublieutenant	ensign	detective chief
pilot officer	major-general	corporal	lieutenant	lieutenant junior	superintendent
flying officer	lieutenant-general	sergeant	lieutenant-	grade	commander
flight lieutenant	general	staff sergeant	commander	lieutenant	deputy assistant
squadron leader	general of the air	sergeant first class	commander	lieutenant	commissioner
wing commander	force	first sergeant	captain	commander	assistant
group captain		master sergeant	commodore	commander	commissioner
air-commodore	UK ARMY:	sergeant major	rear admiral	captain	deputy
air vice-marshal	private	command sergeant	vice-admiral	rear admiral	commissioner
air-marshal	lance-corporal	major	admiral	vice-admiral	commissioner
air-chief-marshal	corporal	second lieutenant	admiral of the fleet	admiral	
marshal of the	sergeant	first lieutenant		fleet admiral	US STATE POLICE:
Royal Air Force	warrant officer	captain	US NAVY:		Trooper (or
	second	major	seaman recruit/	UK POLICE:	Trooper Second
US AIR FORCE:	lieutenant	lieutenant colonel	apprentice	constable/detective	Class)
airman	lieutenant	colonel	seaman	constable	Trooper First Class
airman first class	captain	brigadier general	petty officer third	sergeant/detective	Corporal
senior airman	major	major general	class	sergeant	Sergeant
staff sergeant	lieutenant-colonel	lieutenant general	petty officer	inspector/detective	Lieutenant
chief master	colonel	general	second class	inspector	Captain
sergeant	brigadier	general of the	petty officer first	chief inspector/	Major
second-lieutenant	major general	army	class	detective chief	Lieutenant Colonel
	lieutenant-general			inspector	Colonel

See also **soldier**.

ransack v
1 PLUNDER, rifle, raid, sack, strip, ravage, devastate, maraud, harry, loot, pillage
FORMAL deprecate
2 SEARCH, scour, comb, rake, hunt, fish, rummage through, go through, turn inside out, turn upside down; Scot ripe
OLD ranshackle
FORMAL despoil

ransom n, v
♦ n
1 PAYMENT, price, money, pay-off
2 REDEMPTION, deliverance, rescue, freedom, setting free, liberation, restoration, release
♦ v
buy off, buy/purchase the freedom of, redeem, deliver, rescue, liberate, free, set free, release

rant v, n
♦ v
shout, cry, yell, roar, bellow, bluster, rave, harangue, rant and rave
FORMAL declaim, vociferate, hold forth
COLLOQ. tub-thump
♦ n
storm, shouting, crying, yelling, roaring, bluster, tirade, oration, harangue, rhetoric, bombast
FORMAL declamation, diatribe, philippic, vociferation

rap v, n
♦ v
1 KNOCK, hit, strike, tap, clout, clip, cuff, hammer, thump, bang, batter, flick, flirt, knap
COLLOQ. whack
2 REPROVE, reprimand, criticize, pick holes in, pull/tear to pieces, slate, run down, come down on, censure, punish, blame, scold
FORMAL castigate
COLLOQ. rail, slam, knock, pan, haul over the coals, tear to shreds
♦ n
1 KNOCK, hit, blow, tap, clout, clip, cuff, hammer, thump, bang, batter; Scot yanker
COLLOQ. whack
2 REBUKE, reprimand, censure, blame, punishment
FORMAL castigation
COLLOQ. flak, slating, slamming, knocking, stick
■ **take the rap**
take the blame, be punished, suffer the consequences, pay for it, face the music, get it in the neck, lay your head on the block

rapacious adj
uncaring, greedy, grasping, extortionate, preying, ravening, ravenous, voracious, plundering, predatory, marauding, insatiable, wolfish, wolvish, vulturish, vulturous, usurious
FORMAL avaricious, esurient

rapacity n
greed, greediness, graspingness, avarice, insatiableness, predatoriness, rapaciousness, ravenousness, voraciousness, voracity, wolfishness, usury
FORMAL avidity, esurience, esuriency
COLLOQ. shark's manners

rape v, n
♦ v
1 rape a woman
violate, ravish, assault, assault sexually, abuse, maltreat, defile, deflower, gang-rape
OLD vitiate
2 rape the land
ravage, sack, ransack, strip, raid, loot, rob, pillage, plunder, devastate, violate, defile
FORMAL despoil, deprecate, spoliate
♦ n
1 the rape of a young girl
violation, assault, sexual assault, violence, ravishment, abuse, outrage, maltreatment, date rape, gang rape; N Am statutory rape

2 rape of the countryside
ravaging, sacking, ransacking, stripping, raid, looting, plundering, devastation, violation, defilement
FORMAL rapine, despoliation, depredation, spoliation

rapid adj
swift, speedy, quick, fast, express, prompt, lively, brisk, hurried, hasty, headlong
FORMAL precipitate, expeditious
COLLOQ. like lightning, like greased lightning, nifty, zippy, pdq, pretty damn quick
🗲 slow, leisurely, sluggish; formal tardy

rapidity n
quickness, hurry, speed, speediness, rush, haste, briskness, swiftness, velocity, fleetness, promptness, dispatch
FORMAL alacrity, celerity, expedition, expeditiousness, precipitateness, promptitude
🗲 slowness

rapidly adv
fast, quickly, speedily, swiftly, hastily, hurriedly, briskly, promptly
FORMAL expeditiously, precipitately
COLLOQ. pronto, lickety-split, at a rate of knots, at the double, before you can say Jack Robinson, by leaps and bounds, hell for leather, like a bat out of hell, like the clappers, like greased lightning, a mile a minute
🗲 slowly

rapine n
ravaging, sacking, ransacking, rage, stripping, raid, looting, plundering, devastation, violation, defilement
FORMAL despoliation, depredation, spoliation

rapport n
bond, link, affinity, relationship, empathy, sympathy, understanding, good understanding, friendship, harmony

rapprochement n
increased friendliness, agreement, reconciliation, reunion, détente, softening, harmonization, reconcilement

rapt adj
engrossed, absorbed, preoccupied, intent, gripped, spellbound, enthralled, bewitched, captivated, concentrated, fascinated, entranced, charmed, enchanted, ecstatic, delighted, thrilled, ravished, enraptured, transported

rapture n
delight, happiness, joy, bliss, ecstasy, elation, exhilaration, enchantment, euphoria, exaltation, transport
OLD (Spenser) enragement
FORMAL delectation, felicity
COLLOQ. seventh heaven, cloud nine, top of the world
■ **go into raptures**
enthuse, praise, rave, wax lyrical, gush, drool, excite, inspire, motivate, fire, bubble over, effervesce

rapturous adj
joyful, joyous, overjoyed, happy, delighted, enthusiastic, blissful, ecstatic, entranced, euphoric, exalted, ravished, transported, rhapsodic
COLLOQ. over the moon, on cloud nine, in seventh heaven, tickled pink, on top of the world

rare adj
1 UNCOMMON, unusual, exceptional, scarce, sparse, sporadic, infrequent
COLLOQ. thin on the ground, few and far between, like gold dust
2 EXQUISITE, superb, excellent, superlative, superior, outstanding, unparalleled, incomparable, matchless, exceptional, remarkable, precious, choice
COLLOQ. one in a million
🗲 **1** common, abundant, frequent, ordinary, typical

rarefied adj
exclusive, select, private, esoteric, refined, high, noble, sublime, special

rarely *adv*
seldom, hardly ever, scarcely ever, infrequently, occasionally, little, scarcely, hardly, intermittently, sporadically, spasmodically
COLLOQ. once in a blue moon
E3 often, frequently

raring *adj*
eager, keen, enthusiastic, ready, willing, impatient, longing, itching, desperate

rarity *n*
1 CURIOSITY, curio, gem, pearl, treasure, find, collector's item, marvel, wonder, nonpareil
2 UNCOMMONNESS, unusualness, strangeness, scarcity, shortage, sparseness, infrequency
E3 2 commonness, frequency

rascal *n*
rogue, scoundrel, scamp, scallywag, imp, devil, villain, good-for-nothing, ne'er-do-well, mischief-maker, wastrel, vagabond, loon, rascallion, rapscallion, hallion, scapegrace; *dialect* skellum; *Scot* smaik; *Irish* spalpeen; *N Am* skeesicks; *S Afr* skelm
OLD rascaille, cullion, varlet
COLLOQ. tinker, toerag
SLANG son of a gun, a bad hat

rascally *adj*
dishonest, wicked, mischievous, scoundrelly, unscrupulous, villainous, good-for-nothing, evil, vicious, disreputable, base, crooked, bad, knavish, low, mean, reprobate
COLLOQ. furciferous

rash[1] *adj*
a rash action
impulsive, impetuous, hasty, over-hasty, fast, reckless, ill-considered, inconsiderate, foolhardy, ill-advised, inadvisable, madcap, hare-brained, hot-headed, headstrong, headlong, unguarded, unwary, indiscreet, imprudent, adventurous, audacious, careless, premature, heedless, unthinking, dare-devil, harum-scarum
OLD furthersome, hasty-witted, temerarious; (*Shakesp*) madbrain(ed)
FORMAL precipitate, temerous
E3 cautious, wary, careful

rash[2] *n*
1 *a rash on the skin*
eruption, outbreak, hives, nettlerash, heat rash, epidemic, plague, itch, irritation
TECHNICAL pompholyx, urticaria, rosacea
2 *a rash of burglaries*
spate, flood, deluge, torrent, run, series, rush, wave

rashly *adv*
impulsively, on impulse, impetuously, hastily, over-hastily, recklessly, heedlessly, carelessly, without thinking, unwarily, indiscreetly, imprudently, audaciously
E3 cautiously, carefully

rashness *n*
impulsiveness, incaution, hastiness, foolhardiness, carelessness, incautiousness, imprudence, recklessness, thoughtlessness, adventurousness, audacity, heedlessness, brashness, indiscretion
FORMAL precipitance, precipitation, precipitancy, temerity
E3 carefulness, cautiousness, wariness

rasp *n, v*
♦ *n*
grating, scrape, grinding, scratch, harshness, hoarseness, croak
♦ *v*
1 GRATE, scrape, grind, file, sand, scour, scratch, abrade, rub; *Scot* risp
FORMAL excoriate
2 IRRITATE, grate, jar
COLLOQ. peeve, bug, get on your nerves
3 CROAK, screech, squawk, cackle; *Scot* risp

rasping *adj*
harsh, hoarse, creaking, croaking, grating, jarring, raspy, gravelly, gruff, husky, croaky, scratchy, rough, raucous
FORMAL stridulant

rat *n, v*
♦ *n*
informer, informant, betrayer, traitor, Judas, tell-tale, sneak, spy, squeaker, whisperer
OLD approver, discoverer, promoter, sycophant
COLLOQ. mole, finger, squealer, whistle-blower, snitch, snitcher, canary, fink, nose
SLANG grass, supergrass, stool pigeon, nark, peacher, snout; *N Am* stoolie; *Aust* fizgig
OLD SLANG stag
♦ *v*
inform, betray, incriminate, denounce, blab
COLLOQ. tell on, squeal, blow, blow the whistle on, sell down the river, split, snitch; *N Am* sing; *Aust* put someone's pot on, dob on
SLANG peach, grass, shop, rumble

rate *n, v*
♦ *n*
1 SPEED, velocity, tempo, time, ratio, proportion, percentage, relation, degree, grade, rank, rating, standard, basis, measure, scale
2 CHARGE, fee, hire, toll, tariff, price, cost, value, evaluate, assess, worth, pay, payment, tax, duty, amount, figure, percentage
♦ *v*
1 JUDGE, regard, consider, deem, esteem, count, reckon, figure, estimate, evaluate, value, assess, weigh (up), sum (up), measure, grade, rank, categorize, class, classify
FORMAL appraise, adjudge
2 ADMIRE, respect, value, prize, have a high opinion of, esteem
3 DESERVE, merit, be worthy of, have a right to, warrant, justify, be entitled to
■ **at any rate**
in any case, anyway, anyhow, in any event, nevertheless, regardless, at all

rather *adv*
1 MODERATELY, relatively, slightly, a bit, a little, somewhat, fairly, quite, to some degree/extent, pretty, noticeably, significantly, very
2 PREFERABLY, sooner, much rather, much sooner, instead, by/for preference, by/for/from choice

ratification *n*
approval, endorsement, corroboration, authorization, affirmation, confirmation, certification, validation, authentication, seal/stamp of approval
E3 rejection

ratify *v*
approve, uphold, endorse, corroborate, sign, countersign, legalize, sanction, authorize, warrant, establish, affirm, agree to, confirm, certify, validate, authenticate, seal, strike, amen
TECHNICAL preconize
FORMAL homologate
E3 repudiate, reject

rating *n*
assessment, classification, category, score, mark, evaluation, class, rank, degree, status, standing, position, placing, order, grade, grading
FORMAL appraisal, adjudging

ratio *n*
proportion, percentage, fraction, index, relation, relationship, correspondence, correlation, symmetry, balance

ration *n, v*
♦ *n*
1 QUOTA, allowance, allocation, allotment, share, proportion, percentage, portion, helping, part, measure, lot, amount

2 rations in times of shortage
food, foodstuffs, provisions, supplies, stores, iron ration
TECHNICAL compo ration
FORMAL viands, victuals
♦ v
allot, allocate, apportion, budget, share, deal out,
distribute, hand out, divide out, measure out, mete out,
dole out, dispense, supply, issue, control, restrict, limit,
conserve, save, point
FORMAL apportion

rational adj
logical, reasonable, sound, well-founded, realistic,
sensible, prudent, clear-headed, wise, sane, normal,
balanced, in your right mind/senses, lucid, reasoning,
thinking, intelligent, intellectual, enlightened, Apollonian;
Scot wice
TECHNICAL discursive
OLD sober
FORMAL judicious, sagacious, circumspect, philosophical,
cognitive, cerebral, ratiocinative
☲ irrational, unreasonable, illogical, insane, crazy

> QUOTATIONS
> Appeals to rationality are mostly bluff. There is no good
> theory of what it is nor of how to recognize it
> D H MELLOR, Social Theory and Practice

rationale n
logic, reasoning, philosophy, thesis, principle, basis,
grounds, explanation, reason(s), purpose, raison d'être,
motive, motivation, hypothesis, theory

rationalization n
1 JUSTIFICATION, excuse, excusing, vindication, explanation
2 REORGANIZATION, modernization, streamlining, updating

rationalize v
1 JUSTIFY, excuse, vindicate, explain, account for, make
allowances for, explain away
2 REORGANIZE, streamline, trim, modernize, update, make
more efficient, cut back on, cut out waste

rationally adv
logically, reasonably, sensibly, prudently, sanely, lucidly,
thinkingly, intelligently, without bias/prejudice
FORMAL judiciously, sagaciously, philosophically
☲ irrationally, illogically, insanely

rattle v, n
♦ v
1 CLATTER, jingle, jangle, clang, clank, clink, shake, vibrate,
jolt, jar, bounce, bang, rap, bump, knock
2 UNNERVE, disconcert, unsettle, disturb, confuse, upset,
put off/out, shake, alarm, throw off balance
COLLOQ. faze, put someone's nose out of joint
♦ n
clatter, jingle, jangle, clank, clanking, clink, clinking,
shaking, vibration, jolting, jarring
■ **rattle off**
reel off, list, list quickly, run through, recite, repeat
■ **rattle on**
chatter, gabble, jabber, prate, prattle, blether, cackle
COLLOQ. gab, rabbit on, witter, yack, chunter

ratty adj
irritable, annoyed, angry, cross, impatient, testy, touchy,
short, snappy, short-tempered
COLLOQ. crabbed, peeved, grouchy
☲ calm, patient

raucous adj
harsh, rough, hoarse, husky, scratching, rasping, grating,
jarring, screeching, piercing, ear-piercing, discordant,
strident, shrill, sharp, noisy, loud

raunchy adj
sexy, alluring, desirable, attractive, sensual, voluptuous,
nubile, seductive, inviting, flirtatious, arousing, stimulating,
slinky, provoking, provocative, titillating, pornographic,
erotic, salacious, suggestive

ravage v, n
♦ v
destroy, devastate, lay waste, demolish, level, raze, wreck,
ruin, leave in ruins, spoil, damage, loot, harry, maraud,
pillage, plunder, sack, depredate
FORMAL despoil
♦ n
destruction, devastation, havoc, damage, ruin, ruination,
looting, ransacking, desolation, wreckage, pillage, plunder
FORMAL despoliation, depredation, spoliation

ravaged adj
devastated, destroyed, desolate, wrecked, ransacked,
spoilt, shattered, war-worn, war-torn, battle-torn, war-
wasted
☲ unspoilt

rave v, adj, n
♦ v
1 TALK WILDLY, rant and rave, shout, cry, yell, roar, bellow,
babble, jabber, ramble
2 RAGE, storm, thunder, roar, rant, rant and rave, fume,
seethe, explode, lose your temper
COLLOQ. lose your cool, boil over, flip your lid, hit the
roof, blow up, blow a fuse, blow a gasket, blow your
cool, blow your top, burst a blood vessel, do your nut, fly
into a rage, fly off the handle, foam at the mouth, freak
out, go berserk, go mad, go off the deep end, go up the
wall, have kittens, lose your rag, raise hell, see red, sizzle,
throw a tantrum, throw a wobbly, get all steamed up
SLANG go bananas, go ape, go apeshit
3 ENTHUSE, sing the praises of, wax lyrical, go into
raptures, extol, acclaim, hail
COLLOQ. be mad about
♦ adj
enthusiastic, praising, rapturous, favourable, excellent,
ecstatic, wonderful
FORMAL laudatory
♦ n
party, disco, celebration, carousal, orgy, acid-house party
COLLOQ. do, knees-up, rave-up, bash, blow-out

raven adj
black, jet-black, coal-black, jet, ebony, sable, inky, dusky

ravenous adj
hungry, very hungry, starving, starved, famished, greedy,
voracious, insatiable, wolfish

rave-up n
party, celebration, carousal, debauch, orgy
COLLOQ. bash, blow-out, do, shindig, thrash

ravine n
canyon, gorge, deep narrow valley, gully, abyss, gap, pass,
chine, gill, khor, linn, nulla, flume; dialect clough, grike,
gullet; Scot heuch; N Am arroyo, coulée, gulch, purgatory;
S Afr kloof

raving adj
mad, insane, hysterical, delirious, deranged, demented,
unbalanced, wild, frenzied, furious, berserk, irrational, out
of your mind
COLLOQ. crazy, barmy, batty, loopy, round the bend/twist
SLANG loony, mental
☲ rational, sane, balanced

ravings n
gibberish, nonsense, rubbish, drivel, twaddle, balderdash,
prattle, yammer
COLLOQ. gobbledygook, mumbo-jumbo
☲ sense

ravish v
1 DELIGHT, enrapture, overjoy, enchant, charm, captivate,
enthral, entrance, fascinate, spellbind, bewitch
OLD rape
2 RAPE, violate, assault, assault sexually, abuse, maltreat,
defile, force yourself on, outrage
OLD stuprate, constuprate, oppress; (Spenser) suppress

ravishing *adj*
delightful, enchanting, bewitching, enthralling, charming, lovely, beautiful, gorgeous, stunning, radiant, dazzling, alluring, seductive

raw *adj*
1 *raw vegetables*
uncooked, fresh
2 UNPROCESSED, unrefined, untreated, unprepared, unfinished, rough, crude, natural
3 PLAIN, bare, naked, basic, harsh, brutal, strong, intense, realistic, true-to-life, candid, blunt, outspoken, frank, forthright
4 SCRATCHED, grazed, scraped, abraded, chafed, open, bloody, red, sore, exposed, tender, sensitive
FORMAL excoriated
5 COLD, chilly, chill, bitter, biting, nippy, piercing, freezing, bleak, wintry, wet, damp
6 *a raw recruit*
inexperienced, new, green, immature, callow, ignorant, naive, untrained, untutored, unpractised, unskilled
COLLOQ. wet behind the ears
F3 **1** cooked, done **2** processed, refined, treated **5** warm, mild **6** experienced, skilled

ray *n*
beam, shaft, flash, streak, stream, gleam, flicker, glimmer, twinkle, glint, spark, trace, hint, suggestion, indication

raze *v*
demolish, pull down, tear down, knock down, bulldoze, flatten, level, wreck, ruin, destroy, fell

razor

Types of razor include:

battery shaver	electric razor	shaver
cut-throat	Ladyshave®	wet-and-dry sha-
disposable razor	razor blade	ver
double-edged	rechargeable razor	wet razor
razor	safety razor	

re *prep*
about, concerning, regarding, with regard to, with reference to, on the subject of

reach *v, n*
  ♦ *v*
1 ARRIVE AT, get to, attain, achieve, make, make it to, amount to, come to, touch
COLLOQ. hit
2 *reach for a pen*
stretch (out), extend, spread, touch, contact, grasp, hold, hit, strike
3 EXTEND, stretch, spread, project, continue, come to, go as far as, go down/up to, come down/up to
4 CONTACT, get in touch with, get hold of, communicate with, get through to, write to, speak to, get onto, telephone, phone, ring, call, fax
  ♦ *n*
range, scope, compass, distance, span, spread, extent, extension, stretch, ambit, latitude, grasp, command, power, influence, authority, control, jurisdiction

react *v*
1 RESPOND, retaliate, reciprocate, reply, answer, acknowledge, act, behave
2 *react against something*
rebel, rise up, oppose, defy, resist
FORMAL dissent

reaction *n*
response, reply, answer, acknowledgement, repercussion, counteraction, reflex, recoil, reciprocation, counterbalance, reversal, reversion, retaliation
COLLOQ. feedback, backlash, kickback

reactionary *adj, n*
  ♦ *adj*
conservative, ultraconservative, right-wing, rightist, diehard, counter-revolutionary, traditional
F3 progressive, revolutionary
  ♦ *n*
conservative, ultraconservative, right-winger, rightist, diehard, counter-revolutionary, traditionalist
F3 progressive, revolutionary

> **QUOTATIONS**
> All the so-called powerful reactionaries are paper tigers, for they are cut off from their people
> MAO ZEDONG

read *v, n*
  ♦ *v*
1 STUDY, look at, pore over, scan, examine, scrutinize, skim, glance
FORMAL peruse
COLLOQ. dip into, browse through, leaf through, thumb through, flick through
2 INTERPRET, understand, comprehend, decipher, decode
FORMAL construe
3 RECITE, deliver, speak, utter
FORMAL declaim
4 *the gauge read zero*
indicate, show, display, register, record, measure
  ♦ *n*
study, look, perusal, scan, scanning, skimming, scrutiny, browsing
■ **read into**
interpret, deduce, infer, reason, misinterpret, take out of context
FORMAL construe
COLLOQ. read between the lines, get hold of the wrong end of the stick

readable *adj*
1 LEGIBLE, decipherable, intelligible, clear, easy to read, understandable, comprehensible
2 INTERESTING, enjoyable, worth reading, entertaining, stimulating, captivating, enthralling, gripping
COLLOQ. unputdownable
F3 **1** illegible **2** unreadable

reader *n*
addressee, listener, hearer, audience

readership *n*
audience, following, regulars, subscribers

readily *adv*
willingly, unhesitatingly, happily, gladly, eagerly, enthusiastically, promptly, quickly, swiftly, rapidly, speedily, freely, smoothly, with ease, easily, effortlessly
F3 unwillingly, reluctantly, with difficulty

readiness *n*
willingness, preparedness, skill, preparation, aptitude, fitness, eagerness, keenness, inclination, quickness, rapidity, ease, promptness, facility, availability, handiness
COLLOQ. gameness
■ **in readiness**
in preparation, available, prepared, ready, on standby, standing by, on call, on full alert

reading *n*
1 STUDY, perusal, scrutiny, scan, browsing, examination, inspection
2 INTERPRETATION, understanding, decoding, deciphering, rendering, version, edition, rendition, recital
3 *the reading on a meter*
indication, display, register, record, measurement, figure
4 *a reading from the Bible*
passage, lesson, text, recitation, piece, section

ready *adj, v*

♦ *adj*

1 *ready to go*
prepared, waiting, set, all set, fit, fitted out, equipped, rigged out, arranged, organized, completed, finished
COLLOQ. geared up

2 WILLING, inclined, disposed, happy, pleased, eager, enthusiastic, keen
FORMAL predisposed
COLLOQ. game, psyched up

3 AVAILABLE, to hand, on hand, present, near, close, accessible, convenient, handy, within reach
COLLOQ. at your fingertips

4 ABOUT TO, on the point of, likely to, liable to, on the verge of

5 PROMPT, immediate, quick, swift, rapid, speedy, easy, sharp, astute, perceptive, clever, discerning, alert, resourceful

E3 1 unprepared **2** unwilling, reluctant, disinclined **3** unavailable, inaccessible **5** slow

♦ *v*

prepare, organize, arrange, equip, order, prime, set, alert

■ **at the ready**
prepared, ready, set, all set, mobilized, poised

real *adj*

1 *in the real world*
actual, existing, physical, material, substantial, tangible, concrete

2 *real leather*
genuine, authentic, bona fide, official, rightful, legitimate, valid, true, factual, occurring, certain, sure, positive, veritable

3 SINCERE, honest, truthful, genuine, true, from the heart, fervent, heartfelt, unfeigned, unaffected

4 *this is a real mess*
right, complete, absolute, utter, thorough

E3 1 unreal, imaginary **2** false, imitation **3** insincere, feigned

---

SYNONYM NUANCES

sense 2
Genuine can be widely used to suggest a lack of artificiality, while **authentic** is more suggestive of being an original rather than a modification or derivative: *an authentic Spanish galleon*. The phrase **bona fide** may be used to imply being absolutely as presented: *a bona fide charity*, while **official** could be used where there is an element of authorization.

Rightful, on the other hand, has implications of entitlement: *the rightful Scottish queen*. Similarly, both **legitimate** and **valid** echo the idea of being justified: *he has a legitimate claim to the throne*. The word **factual** is appropriate for real events that can be verified: *a factual account of the war*.

Certain could be used to suggest there is a lack of any doubt, or in some instances suggests an inevitability, and both **sure** and **positive** share similar connotations of dependability: *this job requires a positive commitment*. **Veritable** implies being undeniably as described, and can be used in a rather tongue-in-cheek way: *a veritable explosion of laughter*.

---

realism *n*

1 ACTUALITY, practicality, pragmatism, sanity, saneness, sensibleness, rationality

2 LIFELIKENESS, faithfulness, truthfulness, authenticity, naturalness, genuineness

realistic *adj*

1 PRACTICAL, down-to-earth, commonsense, sensible, matter-of-fact, level-headed, clear-sighted, businesslike, hard-headed, pragmatic, rational, logical, objective, detached, unsentimental, unromantic
COLLOQ. hard-boiled, hard-nosed

2 LIFELIKE, faithful, truthful, true, true-to-life, vivid, genuine, authentic, natural, close, real, real-life, graphic, representational, figurative

E3 1 unrealistic, impractical, irrational, idealistic **2** fake, imitation, unrealistic, unfaithful, abstract

---

SYNONYM NUANCES

sense 1
Practical can be used to suggest looking at things in the most straightforward way: *we need some practical thinking on what to do next*, while **down-to-earth** implies an absence of fanciful ideas. Both **commonsense** and **sensible** are more suggestive of exhibiting sound judgement: *he has tackled these issues with a commonsense approach*, whereas **matter-of-fact** is best used to suggest an absence of personal input or bias: *a matter-of-fact analysis*.

The term **level-headed** suggests an ability to keep calm in a crisis: *any hiccups in the relationship are best addressed in level-headed discussion*, while **clear-sighted** has more to do with discerning the reality of a situation. **Businesslike** implies a brisk effectiveness coupled with emotional detachment, but **hard-headed**, although similar, has further connotations of shrewdness: *hard-headed investigators examined the data*.

Pragmatic suggests accepting the actual rather than theory: *pragmatic compromises*, while **rational** implies the use of reason, and **logical** similarly suggests deduction and analysis.

You might use **objective** to suggest a lack of emotional involvement, and **detached** implies a similar absence of subjectivity, whereas both **unsentimental** and **unromantic** put the emphasis more firmly on a lack of emotion.

---

realistically *adv*

1 PRACTICALLY, sensibly, pragmatically, rationally, logically, objectively, unsentimentally, unromantically

2 *the film follows the book's storyline realistically*
faithfully, truly, truthfully, vividly, genuinely, authentically, graphically, representationally, figuratively

E3 1 impractically, idealistically **2** unfaithfully

reality *n*

truth, fact, certainty, realism, actuality, real world, real life, existence, materiality, tangibility, substantiality, genuineness, authenticity, validity
FORMAL corporeality

E3 fiction, fantasy

■ **in reality**
in fact, actually, in actual fact, in point of fact, as a matter of fact, in practice, really, indeed, truly, in truth

---

QUOTATIONS
The ethical reality of the individual is the only reality
SÖREN AABYE KIERKEGAARD, *Concluding Unscientific Postscript*

---

realization *n*

1 UNDERSTANDING, comprehension, grasp, recognition, discernment, perception, acceptance, appreciation, awareness, consciousness
FORMAL cognizance, apprehension

2 ACHIEVEMENT, accomplishment, fulfilment, completion, implementation, performance
FORMAL actualization, consummation

3 EARNING, selling, fetching, making, gain, clearing

realize *v*

1 UNDERSTAND, grasp, comprehend, discover, learn, ascertain, catch on, take in, become aware/conscious of, recognize, perceive, discern, accept, register, appreciate, glean
FORMAL apprehend
COLLOQ. cotton on, twig, tumble to, get

2 ACHIEVE, accomplish, fulfil, complete, implement, perform, bring about
FORMAL effect, effectuate, consummate
3 SELL FOR, fetch, make, earn, gain, produce, get, obtain, net, clear, bring in, encash

really *adv*
1 ACTUALLY, in fact, truly, honestly, sincerely, genuinely, positively, surely, certainly, undoubtedly, absolutely, categorically
2 VERY, extremely, exceptionally, intensely, thoroughly, remarkably, highly, severely, indeed

realm *n*
1 *defence of the realm*
kingdom, queendom, monarchy, royalty, principality, empire, country, state, land, territory, area, region, province, domain
OLD reame, reign
2 *the realm of politics*
sphere, area, region, province, domain, world, orbit, field, department

reap *v*
1 HARVEST, cut, crop, gather, mow; *dialect* swap;
Scot shear
FORMAL garner
2 GAIN, obtain, secure, acquire, get, derive, collect, receive, realize, win

rear *n, adj, v*
♦ *n*
back, stern, end, hind, tail, rump, buttocks, posterior, behind, bottom
COLLOQ. backside
☒ front
♦ *adj*
back, hind, hindmost, rearmost, last, tail-end
☒ front
♦ *v*
1 *rear a child*
bring up, care for, look after, raise, breed, grow, cultivate, foster, nurse, nurture, instruct, train, educate, parent
2 RISE, rise up, loom, tower, soar, raise, elevate, lift (up), hoist

rearrange *v*
change, adjust, alter, shift, vary, reorder, reschedule, reposition, rejig

reason *n, v*
♦ *n*
1 CAUSE, motive, motivation, incentive, impetus, inducement, explanation, excuse, justification, defence, warrant, ground(s), basis, case, argument, aim, intention, purpose, object, end, goal
FORMAL rationale, *raison d'être*
See Synonym nuances panel at **motive**.
2 SENSE, logic, reasoning, rationality, sanity, mind, thought, wit, brain, intellect, intellectuality, intelligence, understanding, comprehension, wisdom, judgement, common sense, gumption
FORMAL ratiocination
COLLOQ. nous
♦ *v*
work out, solve, reckon, resolve, conclude, deduce, infer, think, use your brain
FORMAL cerebrate, ratiocinate, cogitate, syllogize
■ **reason with**
urge, persuade, coax, move, argue with, debate with, discuss with, plead with
FORMAL remonstrate with
■ **within reason**
within limits, in moderation, moderately, within bounds, with self-control
☒ to excess

reasonable *adj*
1 SENSIBLE, wise, well-advised, sane, intelligent, rational, logical, practical, sound, fair, reasoned, understandable,

well-thought-out, plausible, credible, possible, viable, justifiable
OLD (*Shakesp*) wholesome
FORMAL sagacious, judicious
2 *a reasonable price*
acceptable, satisfactory, moderate, average, fair, just, modest, competitive, inexpensive, low
3 *a reasonable standard of work*
tolerable, acceptable, satisfactory, moderate, average, fair
COLLOQ. OK, not a lot to write home about, no great shakes, not to be sneezed at
☒ **1** unreasonable, irrational **2** exorbitant, expensive **3** poor, bad

reasonably *adv*
1 SENSIBLY, wisely, rationally, intelligently, fairly, plausibly
2 *a reasonably large crowd*
fairly, quite, rather, somewhat, tolerably, passably, moderately, adequately
☒ **1** unreasonably, irrationally

reasoned *adj*
clear, logical, methodical, organized, rational, sensible, sound, systematic, well-thought-out
FORMAL judicious
☒ illogical, unsystematic

reasoning *n*
logic, thinking, thought, analysis, interpretation, deduction, supposition, hypothesis, rationalization, argument, case, proof
FORMAL rationale, ratiocination, cerebration
Related adjective: logistical

reassurance *n*
comfort, encouragement, inspiration, motivation, cheer, cheering, heartening, incitement, urging, coaxing, persuasion, stimulation, consolation
FORMAL exhortation, succour

reassure *v*
comfort, cheer (up), encourage, hearten, inspire, brace, bolster, buoy up, nerve, rally
FORMAL inspirit
☒ alarm, unnerve

rebate *n*
refund, repayment, reduction, decrease, discount, deduction, allowance

rebel *n, v, adj*
♦ *n*
1 REVOLUTIONARY, agitator, insurgent, insurrectionary, guerrilla, freedom fighter, mutineer, revolter, paramilitary
OLD (*Shakesp*) mutine, revolt
2 DISSENTER, nonconformist, schismatic, apostate, heretic
OLD recusant
COLLOQ. aginner
♦ *v*
revolt, mutiny, rise up, riot, run riot, dissent, disobey, oppose, turn against, defy, resist, recoil, shy away, pull back, shrink, flinch
OLD mutine
☒ conform, obey
♦ *adj*
revolutionary, insurgent, insurrectionary, mutinous, rebellious, defiant, disobedient, malcontent(ed)
FORMAL insubordinate

> QUOTATIONS
> What is a rebel? A man who says no
> ALBERT CAMUS, *L'Homme révolté*

rebellion *n*
revolt, revolution, rising, uprising, insurrection, insurgence, insurgency, mutiny, riot, military takeover, coup, coup d'état, resistance, opposition, defiance, disobedience, civil disobedience, dissent, unrest, heresy
OLD mutine
FORMAL insubordination

rebellious _adj_
rebelling, resistant, defiant, disobedient, unruly,
disorderly, ungovernable, unmanageable, obstinate,
revolutionary, insurrectionary, insurgent, seditious,
mutinous, rioting
FORMAL contumacious, insubordinate, intractable,
recalcitrant
F3 obedient, submissive

rebirth _n_
restoration, revival, renewal, regeneration, renaissance,
revitalization, reawakening, rejuvenation, resurrection,
reincarnation

rebound _v, n_
♦ _v_
recoil, backfire, return, bounce (back), spring (back),
ricochet, boomerang, fail, defeat itself, be self-defeating
COLLOQ. come home to roost, score an own goal
♦ _n_
recoil, backfiring, return, bounce, spring, ricochet,
repercussion, reverberation, reflection

> **!** **rebound** or **redound**?
> To _rebound_ is 'to bounce back', in either a neutral, a
> good, or a bad sense: _She was throwing the ball_
> _against the wall and catching it as it rebounded; His_
> _overweening ambition rebounded on him, as, having_
> _displaced his father from the throne, he was in turn_
> _ousted by those who would not accept him as the_
> _legitimate ruler._ To _redound_ (now a rather old-
> fashioned or formal word) is 'to have advantageous or
> disadvantageous consequences': _His actions redounded_
> _to the credit of the regiment; A child's bad behaviour_
> _in public inevitably redounds on the parents._

rebuff _v, n_
♦ _v_
spurn, reject, refuse, decline, repudiate, turn down,
repulse, discourage, snub, slight, cut, counterbuff, put
someone's nose out of joint
COLLOQ. cold-shoulder, give the cold shoulder to, put
down, knock back
♦ _n_
rejection, refusal, repulse, check, discouragement,
spurning, repudiation, snub, slight, counterbuff, noser,
rubber, set-down, squelch
COLLOQ. brush-off, put-down, cold shoulder,
slap in the face, kick in the teeth, one in the eye,
a flea in your ear

rebuild _v_
restore, remake, remodel, renovate, reassemble,
reconstruct, refashion, re-edify
F3 demolish, destroy

rebuke _v, n_
♦ _v_
reprove, chide, scold, reprimand, upbraid, rate, censure,
blame, reproach, snub, speak to, talk to, take someone to
task, trim, trounce, slap, keelhaul, countercheck; _dialect_
threap; _N Am_ score
OLD lesson, objurgate; _(Shakesp)_ sauce
FORMAL castigate, admonish, remonstrate
COLLOQ. tell off, tick off, dress down, carpet, read the riot
act to, throw the book at, give an earful, tear off a strip,
give someone some stick, go to town on, lash out, take to
task, haul over the coals, come down on like a ton of
bricks, give someone hell, rollick, pin back someone's
ears, talk like a Dutch uncle; _N Am_ call down; _Aust & NZ_
go crook on/at
F3 praise, compliment
♦ _n_
reproach, reproof, reprimand, scolding, lecture, censure,
blame, countercheck
FORMAL admonition, castigation, remonstration
COLLOQ. dressing-down, telling-off, ticking-off, carpeting,
earful, rollicking, stick, comeuppance
F3 praise, commendation

rebut _v_
refute, quash, defeat, discredit, disprove, invalidate,
negate, overturn, give the lie to
FORMAL confute
COLLOQ. explode

rebuttal _n_
refutation, negation, defeat, disproof, invalidation,
overthrow
FORMAL confutation

recalcitrance _n_
disobedience, defiance, waywardness, wilfulness,
stubbornness, obstinacy, unwillingness
FORMAL insubordination
F3 amenability

recalcitrant _adj_
disobedient, defiant, uncontrollable, ungovernable,
unmanageable, unruly, wayward, wilful, contrary,
obstinate, stubborn, unsubmissive, unwilling, unco-
operative
OLD renitent
FORMAL contumacious, insubordinate, intractable,
refractory
F3 amenable, tractable

recall _v, n_
♦ _v_
1 REMEMBER, think of, call to mind, recollect, reminisce,
think back to, cast your mind back, evoke, call up,
summon up, bring back
2 ORDER BACK, summon (back), call back, order to return
3 CANCEL, revoke, withdraw, repeal, annul
FORMAL rescind, retract, countermand, abrogate, nullify
♦ _n_
1 REMEMBRANCE, memory, recollection
2 CANCELLATION, annulment, repeal, withdrawal
FORMAL abrogation, nullification, countermanding,
retraction, revocation, recision

recant _v_
deny, disown, repudiate, rescind, apostatize, retract,
revoke, withdraw, recall, unsay, renounce
FORMAL abjure, abrogate, disavow, disclaim, forswear

recantation _n_
denial, renunciation, repudiation, apostasy, withdrawal,
revocation, revoke, disownment
FORMAL abjuration, disavowal, disclaimer, retractation

recapitulate _v_
recap, summarize, sum up, review, repeat, reiterate,
restate, recount, run over, go over

recapitulation _n_
summarizing, summary, review, repetition, reiteration,
restatement

recce _v, n_
♦ _v_
reconnoitre, explore, survey, scan, spy out, inspect,
examine, scrutinize, investigate, patrol, observe, probe
COLLOQ. check out, see how the land lies, see the lie of
the land
♦ _n_
reconnaissance, exploration, reconnoitring, scouting,
survey, expedition, examination, inspection, probe,
observation, scrutiny, scan, investigation, search, patrol

recede _v_
1 GO BACK, return, retire, withdraw, move away, retreat
2 DIMINISH, decline, fade, dwindle, decrease, lessen, fall
off, drop, shrink, slacken, subside, ebb, wane, sink
FORMAL abate
F3 **1** advance, approach **2** grow, increase

receipt _n_
1 VOUCHER, ticket, slip, proof of purchase, counterfoil,
stub, acknowledgement, paper, chit, deposit-receipt
TECHNICAL warrant, dock-warrant
OLD note, quittance
FORMAL acquittance

2 RECEIVING, reception, acceptance, getting, obtaining, deriving, gaining, delivery
3 MONEY RECEIVED, takings, income, earnings, pay, proceeds, profits, gains, return(s), turnover

receive v
1 TAKE, take up, accept, get, be given, obtain, derive, gain, acquire, come by, pick up, collect, gather, inherit
2 *receive guests*
admit, let in, greet, welcome, entertain, take, contain, hold, accommodate
3 EXPERIENCE, undergo, go through, suffer, bear, sustain, meet with, encounter
4 REACT TO, respond to, hear, find out about, be informed of, learn about, perceive
FORMAL apprehend
F3 1 give, donate

receiver n
1 RECIPIENT, beneficiary, donee, assignee, grantee, legatee
2 RADIO, tuner, wireless, apparatus, handset
F3 1 donor

recent adj
late, latest, current, present-day, contemporary, modern, up-to-date, up-to-the-minute, new, novel, fresh, young
F3 old, out-of-date

recently adv
lately, of late, newly, freshly, in the last few days/weeks/months, in the past few days/weeks/months, not long ago, a short time ago, a little while back
F3 long ago

receptacle n
container, vessel, holder
FORMAL repository, reservatory
See panel at **container**.

reception n
1 ACCEPTANCE, admission, greeting, recognition, welcome, entertaining, treatment, response, reaction, acknowledgement, receipt
2 PARTY, function, social, get-together, gathering, reunion, at-home, occasion, entertainment
COLLOQ. do, bash, beano, shindig, rave-up

receptive adj
open-minded, open to reason, amenable, accommodating, suggestible, susceptible, flexible, willing, quick, sensitive, responsive, open, accessible, approachable, friendly, hospitable, welcoming, sympathetic, favourable, interested
F3 narrow-minded, resistant, unresponsive

recess n
1 BREAK, breaktime, playtime, interval, intermission, rest, respite, time off, holiday, vacation
COLLOQ. time out
2 ALCOVE, niche, nook, corner, bay, cavity, hollow, depression, indentation, indent, cupboard, closet, press, cove, bower, bunk, bunker; *Scot* bole, ingo, outshot
TECHNICAL apse, confessional, ambry, sepulchre, columbarium, embrasure, oriel, exedra, loculus, corrie, hitch, mortise
3 *in the recesses of your mind*
innards, heart, depths, interior, reaches, bowels
FORMAL penetralia

recession n
slump, depression, downturn, decline, economic decline, slide, trough, collapse, crash, failure
F3 boom, upturn

recherché adj
refined, select, choice, rare, far-fetched, obscure, exotic
FORMAL esoteric, abstruse, arcane
F3 commonplace

recipe n
formula, prescription, ingredients, instructions, directions, method, system, way, means, procedure, guide, process, technique
OLD receipt

recipient n
receiver, addressee, beneficiary, assignee, donee, grantee, legatee
F3 donor, giver

reciprocal adj
mutual, joint, exchanged, shared, give-and-take, returned, requited, complementary, alternating, corresponding, equivalent, interchangeable, interdependent, reflex
FORMAL correlative, commutual
F3 irreciprocal

reciprocate v
respond, reply, return, give in return, exchange, swap, repay, trade, match, equal, correspond, interchange, alternate
FORMAL requite
COLLOQ. do the same, give as good as you get, give an eye for an eye

reciprocity n
exchange, mutuality, give-and-take, alternation, correspondence, equivalence, interchangeability, interdependence
F3 irreciprocity

recital n
1 *a music recital*
performance, show, concert
2 RECITATION, reading, narration, report, telling, account, description, rendition, rendering, interpretation, repetition, enumeration
FORMAL declamation

recitation n
passage, reading, piece, party piece, poem, verse, monologue, narration, story, tale, recital, rendering, telling, performance

recite v
repeat, repeat from memory, tell, narrate, relate, recount, speak, say aloud, deliver, articulate, perform, reel off, rattle off, itemize, enumerate, improvise, chant, chime, rhapsodize
TECHNICAL daven, scan
FORMAL declaim

reckless adj
heedless, thoughtless, mindless, careless, negligent, inattentive, irresponsible, imprudent, incautious, ill-advised, indiscreet, rash, hasty, foolhardy, desperate, daredevil, devil-may-care, wild, madcap, tearaway
FORMAL precipitate
F3 cautious, wary, careful, prudent

SYNONYM NUANCES

Many of these synonyms are inherently disapproving in tone.
  Heedless can be used to suggest a disregard for consequences: *warriors, heedless of the dangers*, while **thoughtless** suggests a more general lack of concern. **Mindless** has implications of stupidity: *a brutal and mindless sport*, while **careless** is more appropriately used to imply either a lack of concern or an element of clumsiness: *careless disposal of toxic waste*.
  Negligent is more suggestive of a deliberate dereliction of duty, and is very negative in tone. Similarly, **irresponsible** implies casualness, often verging on the dangerous, while **incautious** more straightforwardly suggests a failure to consider risks: *the wine made her incautious*, and **indiscreet** has more to do with divulging confidences. **Ill-advised**, meanwhile, appropriately describes an erroneous choice: *you would be ill-advised to go out on your own*.
  Both **rash** and **hasty** could be used to suggest something done quickly without proper consideration, while the term **foolhardy** can be used to more explicitly express unwise recklessness. **Desperate** would suggest actions that have to do with a loss of hope, whereas **daredevil** implies those motivated by absence of fear

and even a sense of adventure. While **madcap** is more suggestive of exuberant eccentricity, **tearaway** implies a lack of restraint, usually a characteristic of youth: *his tearaway son*.

recklessly *adv*
carelessly, negligently, irresponsibly, rashly, mindlessly, thoughtlessly, hastily, desperately
≠ carefully, cautiously

recklessness *n*
carelessness, heedlessness, inattention, irresponsibility, irresponsibleness, negligence, rashness, thoughtlessness, incaution, imprudence, foolhardiness, mindlessness, madness
≠ carefulness, caution, prudence

reckon *v*
1 THINK, believe, imagine, fancy, suppose, assume, guess
FORMAL surmise, conjecture
2 CONSIDER, regard, esteem, think of, look upon, value, rate, judge, make, put down, count, evaluate, assess, figure, estimate, gauge, designate, call
OLD vogue
FORMAL deem, appraise, impute
3 CALCULATE, compute, figure out, work out, add up, total, tally, count, sum (up), number, enumerate, account
■ **reckon on**
rely on, depend on, bank on, count on, take for granted, trust in, hope for, expect, anticipate, foresee, plan for, bargain for, figure on, trade on, take into account, face
■ **reckon with**
anticipate, bargain for, consider, take into account, plan for, expect, foresee, handle, cope, deal, face, treat
■ **reckon without**
not expect, fail to think of, ignore, disregard, overlook, not notice, not take into consideration/account
■ **to be reckoned with**
strong, powerful, influential, forceful, great, important, significant, considerable, formidable, weighty
FORMAL mighty

reckoning *n*
1 ***by my reckoning***
calculation, computation, addition, working-out, total, tally, score, number, enumeration, estimate
2 BILL, account, charge, due, score, paying, payment, settlement
3 JUDGEMENT, opinion, estimation, evaluation, assessment
FORMAL appraisal
4 ***the day of reckoning***
judgement, punishment, retribution, doom, damnation

reclaim *v*
recover, regain, get back, claim back, take back, recapture, retrieve, salvage, rescue, redeem, restore, reinstate, regenerate

reclamation *n*
salvage, recovery, regaining, retrieval, rescue, restoration, reinstatement, regeneration

recline *v*
rest, lean back, lie (down), lounge, loll, sprawl, stretch out
FORMAL repose

recluse *n*
ascetic, hermit, solitary, loner, monk, eremite, stylite, solitarian, solitaire, anchorite, anchoret, anchoress

reclusive *adj*
isolated, solitary, withdrawn, secluded, retiring, recluse, cloistered, monastic, ascetic, eremitic, hermitical, anchoritic
FORMAL sequestered

recognition *n*
1 IDENTIFICATION, detection, discovery, recollection, recall, remembrance, awareness, knowing, knowledge, consciousness, perception, realization, admission, confession, understanding, placing, spotting
FORMAL cognizance
2 ACCEPTANCE, allowing, admittance, endorsement, grating, approval, acknowledgement, validation, sanction
3 ***receive recognition for your work***
appreciation, honour, reward, respect, credit, salute, gratitude, thankfulness, thanks

recognize *v*
1 IDENTIFY, know, remember, recollect, recall, call to mind, pick out, tell, place, see, notice, spot, perceive, not miss, not mistake
2 ***recognize your faults***
accept, acknowledge, admit, grant, concede, allow, endorse, appreciate, discern, perceive, understand, realize, confess, own, be aware of, be conscious of
FORMAL apprehend
3 ***recognize a qualification***
accept, allow, admit, endorse, grant, approve, acknowledge, adopt, validate, sanction
4 APPRECIATE, be thankful for, honour, respect, salute, show your gratitude/thankfulness
COLLOQ. take your hat off to

recoil *v, n*
♦ *v*
move back, draw back, jump back, spring back, shy away, withdraw, flinch, shrink, quail, rebound, react, redound, reverberate, falter, kick, backfire, boomerang, misfire, come home to roost
TECHNICAL resile
OLD requoyle; (*Spenser*) recuile, rebut
♦ *n*
rebound, reaction, resilience, spring, kick, backlash, repercussion
TECHNICAL undertow
OLD requoyle

recollect *v*
recall, remember, call to mind, cast your mind back, reminisce

recollection *n*
memory, recall, remembrance, souvenir, reminiscence, (mental) impression

recommend *v*
commend, approve, endorse, praise, vouch for, advocate, urge, advise, counsel, preach, guide, suggest, propose, put forward, advance, move, tout, put in a good word for
OLD wish
FORMAL exhort, set forth
COLLOQ. plug
≠ disapprove

recommendation *n*
commendation, endorsement, approval, advice, counsel, guidance, suggestion, urging, proposal, advocacy, sanction, blessing, praise, tip, good word, special mention, reference, testimonial
TECHNICAL coupon
FORMAL exhortations
COLLOQ. plug
≠ disapproval

recompense *n, v*
♦ *n*
compensation, indemnification, damages, reparation, restitution, amends, requital, satisfaction, repayment, reward, payment, remuneration, pay, wages
FORMAL guerdon
♦ *v*
compensate, indemnify, remunerate, pay, reward, repay, redress, reimburse, make up for, requite, satisfy
FORMAL guerdon

reconcile *v*
1 ***be reconciled with someone***
reunite, conciliate, pacify, appease, placate, mollify, bring together, make (your) peace, put on friendly terms
OLD agree, atone
FORMAL propitiate

COLLOQ. make up, bury the hatchet, become friends again, shake hands, forgive and forget
2 *reconcile different aims*
harmonize, accommodate, adjust, resolve, settle, mend, remedy, put right, rectify, square, accord
OLD (*Spenser*) upknit
COLLOQ. patch up
3 *reconcile yourself to an unpleasant situation*
resign yourself to, face up to, accept, come to accept, submit, wean
Ea 1 estrange, alienate

reconciliation *n*
reunion, conciliation, pacification, peace, mollification, appeasement, rapprochement, détente, settlement, agreement, harmony, harmonizing, accommodation, resolution, squaring, adjustment, compromise
FORMAL propitiation, accord
Ea estrangement, separation

recondite *adj*
obscure, difficult, involved, complicated, intricate, mysterious, mystical, deep, profound, dark, concealed, hidden, secret
FORMAL abstruse, arcane, esoteric
Ea simple, straightforward

recondition *v*
renovate, repair, restore, renew, refurbish, overhaul, fix, remodel, revamp

reconnaissance *n*
exploration, reconnoitring, scouting, survey, expedition, examination, inspection, probe, observation, scrutiny, scan, investigation, search, patrol
COLLOQ. recce
SLANG *N Am* recon

reconnoitre *v*
explore, survey, scan, spy out, inspect, examine, scrutinize, investigate, patrol, observe, probe
COLLOQ. recce, check out, see how the land lies, see the lie of the land

reconsider *v*
think over, rethink, review, revise, re-examine, think twice, modify, reassess, think better of, have second thoughts

reconsideration *n*
review, rethink, re-examination, reassessment, further reflection, fresh look, second thoughts

reconstruct *v*
remake, rebuild, reassemble, re-establish, refashion, remodel, recondition, revamp, reform, reorganize, redo, recreate, restore, renovate, regenerate

record *n, v, adj*
♦ *n*
1 REGISTER, log, chart, report, account, minutes, memorandum, note(s), entry, document(s), file, dossier, diary, logbook, journal, chronicle, memoir, memorial, history, annals, archives, documentation, data, evidence, photography, testimony, reminder, trace
2 RECORDING, disc, single, CD, compact disc, DVD, MiniDisc®, album, release, LP, 45, 78, cassette, microcassette, tape, audio tape, DAT, digital audio tape
COLLOQ. vinyl
3 *break the record*
fastest time, best performance, furthest distance, personal best, world record
4 BACKGROUND, history, previous performance, track record, curriculum vitae, career
♦ *v*
1 NOTE, enter, inscribe, write down, transcribe, register, log, chart, put down, take down, put on record, enrol, report, list, catalogue, minute, chronicle, document, keep, preserve
2 TAPE-RECORD, make a recording of, tape, videotape, video, burn, cut, edit, make, produce
3 *the gauge records electrical activity*
show, register, indicate, display, read, express

4 ACHIEVE, accomplish, obtain, manage, complete, produce
COLLOQ. notch up, chalk up
♦ *adj*
best, best ever, fastest, record-breaking, world-beating, unsurpassed, unequalled, unparalleled, without equal, supreme, superlative, top-ranking
■ **off the record**
unofficial, unofficially, confidential, confidentially, private, privately
FORMAL sub rosa
Ea officially
■ **on record**
1 *the wettest April on record*
noted, documented, written down
2 *to go on record as saying*
officially recorded, publicly known, documented

recorder *n*
1 REGISTRAR, archivist, annalist, chronicler, diarist, historian, chronologer, secretary, clerk, stenographer, scribe, scorer, score-keeper
2 TAPE RECORDER, cassette recorder, cassette-player, CD burner, DVD recorder, video recorder, digital video recorder, DVR, VCR, video cassette recorder
COLLOQ. video

recount *v*
tell, relate, impart, communicate, report, narrate, describe, depict, portray, unfold, detail, repeat, rehearse, recite

recoup *v*
recover, retrieve, regain, get back, win back, claw back, make good, repossess, repay, refund, indemnify, reimburse, recompense, compensate
OLD recruit

recourse *n*
appeal, resort, access, turning to, choice, option, alternative, possibility, remedy, refuge, way out
■ **have recourse to**
resort to, turn to, use, utilize, make use of, avail yourself of, fall back on, employ, exercise

recover *v*
1 *recover from illness*
get better, feel better, get well, improve, pick up, rally, mend, heal, respond to treatment, get over, recuperate, feel yourself again, revive, convalesce, gain strength, get stronger, come round
FORMAL ameliorate
COLLOQ. pull through, bounce back, turn the corner, get back on your feet, be on the mend
2 REGAIN, get back, win back, recoup, retrieve, rescue, salvage, retake, recapture, repossess, reclaim, recycle, restore
OLD (*Spenser*) recure
Ea 1 worsen, fail **2** lose, forfeit

recovery *n*
1 RECUPERATION, convalescence, rehabilitation, mending, healing, improvement, upturn, rally, rallying, revival, restoration
OLD convalescency, reconvalescence, recure, recover
FORMAL amelioration
2 *recovery in a country's economy*
improvement, rally, comeback, upturn, upswing, pick-up, *Wirtschaftswunder*
TECHNICAL amelioration
SLANG dead-cat bounce
3 RETRIEVAL, salvage, rescue, reclamation, recouping, regaining, repossession, recapture, recycling, revival
TECHNICAL regeneration
Ea 1, 2 worsening **3** loss, forfeit

recreation *n*
fun, enjoyment, pleasure, amusement, diversion, distraction, entertainment, hobby, pastime, game, sport, play, leisure pursuit, leisure activity, leisure, relaxation, refreshment
COLLOQ. R & R

recrimination *n*

accusation, countercharge, counter-attack, reprisal, retaliation, retort, bickering, quarrel

recruit *v, n*

♦ *v*

enlist, draft, conscript, enrol, sign up, levy, engage, take on, mobilize, raise, muster, gather, assemble, put together, obtain, acquire, unionize, talent-spot, headhunt
FORMAL procure

♦ *n*

beginner, newcomer, novice, new entrant, initiate, learner, trainee, apprentice, tiro, conscript, draftee, convert
COLLOQ. greenhorn, rookie
SLANG nozzer, sprog, yob, nig-nog; *N Am* swabby, yardbird

recruitment *n*

enrolment, enlisting, drafting, conscription, signing-up, engaging, engagement, mobilization

rectification *n*

correction, improvement, amendment, putting/setting right, making good, adjustment, reformation

rectify *v*

correct, put right, right, set right, make good, remedy, cure, repair, fix, mend, reform, improve, better, amend, adjust
FORMAL emend, ameliorate, redress

rectitude *n*

integrity, uprightness, virtue, honesty, honour, goodness, justice, morality, incorruptibility, irreproachability, exactness, decency, correctness, righteousness, scrupulousness
FORMAL probity

recumbent *adj*

lying down, lying, flat, horizontal, resting, reclining, leaning, lounging, prostrate, prone, sprawling
FORMAL supine
F3 erect, upright

recuperate *v*

recover, get better, get well, get stronger, regain your strength, improve, pick up, rally, revive, mend, convalesce
COLLOQ. pull through, bounce back, turn the corner, get back on your feet, be on the mend
F3 worsen, weaken

recuperation *n*

recovery, convalescence, rehabilitation, mending, healing, improvement, upturn, rally, rallying, revival, restoration
OLD convalescency, reconvalescence, recure
FORMAL amelioration

recur *v*

repeat itself, happen again, persist, return, reappear, run, come round (again), revert
TECHNICAL perseverate

recurrence *n*

repetition, return, appearance, reversion, regularity, persistence, continuation

recurrent *adj*

recurring, chronic, persistent, repeated, repetitive, continual, habitual, regular, periodic, cyclical, frequent, intermittent

recycle *v*

re-use, reprocess, reclaim, recover, salvage, save, freecycle, upcycle, precycle

red *adj*

1 SCARLET, vermilion, cherry, ruby, crimson, rose, maroon, russet, pink, reddish, bloodshot, inflamed
2 RUDDY, florid, glowing, rosy, flushed, feverish, blushing, embarrassed, shamefaced
TECHNICAL rufescent
FORMAL rubicund
3 *red hair*
flaming red, ginger, carroty, auburn, chestnut, Titian
4 COMMUNIST, socialist, leftist, Bolshevik, revolutionary

■ in the red

overdrawn, insolvent, bankrupt, in debt, in arrears, owing money, penniless, impoverished
COLLOQ. on the rocks, broke, bust, gone to the wall, on your beam ends, on your uppers
F3 in the black

■ see red

become angry, lose your temper
COLLOQ explode, blow your cool, blow your top, boil over, burst a blood vessel, hit the roof, do your nut, fly into a rage, fly off the handle, go mad, lose your cool, lose your rag

> QUOTATIONS
> When in doubt wear red
> BILL BLASS

red-blooded *adj*

virile, strong, vigorous, manly, masculine, robust, hearty, lively, lusty

redden *v*

blush, flush, colour, go red, crimson, suffuse

reddish *adj*

red, bloodshot, rosy, ruddy, russet, ginger, sandy, pink
TECHNICAL rufescent
FORMAL rubicund, rufous

redeem *v*

1 BUY BACK, repurchase, cash (in), convert, trade in, exchange, give in exchange, change, trade, ransom, reclaim, regain, get back, repossess, recoup, recover, recuperate, retrieve, salvage
2 COMPENSATE FOR, make up for, offset, outweigh
3 *a saviour who redeems sinners*
atone for, absolve, acquit, remove guilt from, discharge, release, liberate, emancipate, free, set free, deliver, rescue, save, reprieve; *Scot* lowse
TECHNICAL buy
FORMAL ransom, expiate

redemption *n*

1 REPURCHASE, repossession, reclamation, recovery, reparation, retrieval, exchange, reinstatement, trade-in, fulfilment, compensation
2 ATONEMENT, deliverance, expiation, emancipation, freedom, rescue, salvation, ransom, liberation, release

red-handed *adv*

in the act, in the very act, by surprise, unawares, off-guard, napping
FORMAL in flagrante delicto
COLLOQ. on the hop, with your trousers down

redolent *adj*

1 EVOCATIVE, reminiscent, suggestive, remindful
2 AROMATIC, fragrant, perfumed, scented, sweet-smelling
FORMAL odorous

redoubtable *adj*

formidable, fearsome, strong, terrible, powerful, resolute, mighty, awful, dreadful, fearful

redound *v*

contribute, ensue, reflect, result, tend
FORMAL conduce, effect

> **!** redound or rebound?
> See panel at **rebound**.

redress *v, n*

♦ *v*

1 RIGHT, put right, rectify, remedy, avenge, requite, recompense, make compensation for, compensate
2 ADJUST, amend, correct, balance, regulate

♦ *n*

compensation, recompense, indemnification, remedy, relief, assistance, help, aid, correction, requital, restitution, satisfaction, reparation, payment, justice, atonement

reduce v
1 LESSEN, make less, make smaller, decrease, contract, shrink, slim, shorten, abbreviate, curtail, trim, minimize, downsize, lower, moderate, weaken, diminish, impair, deplete, beat down, clip, bring/come down, condense, cut back/down, deduct, restrict, step down, take down, wind down, dock, de-escalate, scant, take the edge off, water down, dilute
OLD slake
FORMAL mitigate
COLLOQ. axe
2 DRIVE, force, degrade, bring down, lower, downgrade, demote, humble, humiliate, impoverish, subdue, overcome, overpower, conquer, master
FORMAL vanquish
3 *reduce prices*
lower, decrease, cut, slash, knock down, discount, rebate, halve, deduct, deflate, devalue
COLLOQ. axe
4 SLIM, diet, go on a diet, lose weight
COLLOQ. weight-watch
⊟ **1** increase, raise **2** boost

reduction n
decrease, drop, fall, decline, lessening, moderation, weakening, contraction, abbreviation, compression, shrinkage, downsizing, narrowing, shortening, minimization, curtailment, restriction, limitation, cutback, cut, discount, discounting, rebate, concession, allowance, devaluation, depreciation, deduction, subtraction, loss, clipping, condensation
FORMAL diminution
⊟ increase, rise, enlargement

redundancy n
1 DISMISSAL, notice, laying-off, discharge, removal, expulsion, marching-orders, downsizing, outplacement
COLLOQ. papers, cards, jotters, sacking, firing, sack, push, boot, elbow
2 SUPERFLUITY, surplus, uselessness, wordiness, excess, repetition, tautology
TECHNICAL pleonasm, cheville
FORMAL prolixity, verbosity, exuberance
⊟ **1** appointment, hiring

redundant adj
1 UNEMPLOYED, out of work, jobless, laid off, dismissed
COLLOQ. sacked, fired
2 SUPERFLUOUS, surplus, excess, extra, unneeded, unnecessary, unwanted, inessential
FORMAL supernumerary, otiose
3 WORDY, verbose, padded, repetitious, tautological
TECHNICAL pleonastic
FORMAL periphrastic
⊟ **2** necessary, essential, required **3** concise, pithy

reef n
sandbank, sandbar, ridge, shoal, cay, key, motu, scar, skerry; *Aust* bombora

reek v, n
♦ v
smell, stink, fume, whiff
FORMAL exhale
COLLOQ. hum, pong; *Scot* ming
SLANG honk, niff
♦ n
smell, odour, whiff, stink, stench, vapour, fume(s)
FORMAL exhalation, effluvium, malodour, mephitis, fetor
COLLOQ. pong; *Scot* ming

reel v
stagger, totter, wobble, rock, sway, waver, falter, stumble, fling, lurch, pitch, swim, roll, revolve, gyrate, spin, wheel, twirl, whirl, swirl
■ **reel off**
rattle off, list, list quickly, run through, recite, repeat

refer v
1 MENTION, allude, touch on, speak of, bring up, recommend, cite, quote, hint at

2 *refer to a catalogue*
consult, look up, turn to, look at, resort to
3 SEND, direct, point, guide, pass on, hand on, transfer, commit, deliver
FORMAL remit
4 APPLY, concern, be relevant, relate, belong, mean, describe, indicate
FORMAL pertain

referee n, v
♦ n
umpire, judge, adjudicator, arbitrator, mediator
COLLOQ. ref
SLANG N Am zebra
♦ v
umpire, judge, adjudicate, mediate, intercede, arbitrate

reference n
1 MENTION, remark, allusion, hint, citation, quotation, illustration, source, authority, instance, note, footnote
2 TESTIMONIAL, recommendation, endorsement, credentials, character
3 RELATION, applicability, regard, respect, connection, bearing
FORMAL pertinence
■ **with reference to**
referring to, concerning, about, regarding, with regard to, as regards, respecting, with respect to, relating to, relevant to, in the matter of, on the subject of, re
FORMAL apropos

referendum n
poll, vote, voting, plebiscite, survey

referral n
transfer, sending, direction, pointing, passing/handing on, handover

refine v
1 PURIFY, process, treat, clarify, filter, sift, strain, distil, clear, cleanse
2 IMPROVE, polish, brush up, hone, perfect, elaborate, civilize, elevate, exalt

refined adj
1 CIVILIZED, cultured, cultivated, polished, sophisticated, stylish, urbane, genteel, gentlemanly, ladylike, well-bred, well-mannered, polite, civil, elegant, gracious, courtly, fine, delicate, subtle, precise, exact, sensitive, discriminating
2 PURIFIED, processed, treated, distilled, filtered, clear
⊟ **1** coarse, vulgar, rude

refinement n
1 MODIFICATION, alteration, amendment, addition, improvement
FORMAL amelioration
2 CULTIVATION, sophistication, culture, urbanity, gentility, breeding, style, elegance, grace, civility, good manners, polish, taste, discrimination, subtlety, finesse
⊟ **1** deterioration, degeneration **2** coarseness, vulgarity

reflect v
1 MIRROR, echo, glass, imitate, reproduce, image, send back, throw back, bounce off, shine, glint, reverberate
TECHNICAL scatter
OLD repercuss
2 SHOW, portray, depict, reveal, display, exhibit, demonstrate, indicate, express, communicate
FORMAL manifest, bespeak
3 THINK, ponder, consider, mull (over), dwell, brood, deliberate, contemplate, meditate, muse, speculate, study, chew
OLD advise
FORMAL ruminate, cogitate, cerebrate
COLLOQ. chew the cud
4 *his behaviour reflects badly on the school*
discredit, disgrace, tarnish, put in a bad light, give a bad name to
OLD redound

reflection *n*
1 IMAGE, likeness, echo, mirror image
2 INDICATION, impression, expression, display,
demonstration, portrayal, observation, view
FORMAL manifestation
3 THINKING, thought, study, consideration, deliberation,
contemplation, meditation, musing, view, opinion,
impression, belief, viewpoint, idea, feeling(s)
FORMAL rumination, cogitation, cerebration
4 DISCREDIT, slur, disgrace, shame, criticism, disrepute,
blame, reproach
FORMAL aspersion

reflective *adj*
thoughtful, contemplative, pondering, deliberative,
meditative, pensive, reasoning, absorbed, dreamy
FORMAL cogitating, ruminative

reflex *adj*
automatic, spontaneous, without thinking, unwilled,
uncontrollable, involuntary, natural, instinctive,
mechanical
TECHNICAL re-entrant, re-entering
COLLOQ. knee-jerk

reform *v, n*
♦ *v*
change, amend, improve, better, rectify, correct, mend,
repair, revise, refashion, rehabilitate, rebuild, reconstruct,
remodel, revamp, renovate, restore, regenerate,
reconstitute, reorganize, revolutionize, purge
FORMAL ameliorate
COLLOQ. shake up, turn over a new leaf
♦ *n*
change, amendment, improvement, betterment,
rectification, correction, rehabilitation, renovation,
reorganization, revision, rebuilding, reconstruction,
remodelling, restoration, purge
COLLOQ. shake-up

reformation *n*
improvement, amendment, revision, rehabilitation,
progress, renovation, restoration, rectification
FORMAL amelioration

reformer *n*
revolutionary, progressive, liberal; (*derog*) do-gooder,
bleeding heart
COLLOQ. whistle-blower

refractory *adj*
stubborn, obstinate, headstrong, unmanageable,
uncontrollable, naughty, unruly, wilful, unco-operative,
perverse, mulish, difficult, disobedient, resistant, defiant,
cantankerous, contentious
FORMAL intractable, contumacious, recalcitrant,
disputatious, restive
Ⓔ co-operative, malleable, obedient

refrain¹ *v*
refrain from smoking
stop, cease, give up, do without, leave off, hold off, avoid,
keep
FORMAL desist, abstain, forbear, for(e)go, renounce, eschew
OLD withhold, spare, supersede, surcease, restrain
COLLOQ. quit

refrain² *n*
sing the refrain twice
chorus, response, burden, strain, melody, song, tune, tag,
falderal, overture
TECHNICAL epistrophe, faburden, hemistich, ritornello
OLD undersong, bob, wheel, fading, tirra-lirra, turnagain
FORMAL repetend

refresh *v*
1 COOL, freshen, energize, stimulate, enliven, invigorate,
revive, brace, restore, renew, rejuvenate, reanimate,
revitalize, reinvigorate
FORMAL fortify, revivify
COLLOQ. breathe new life into

2 *refresh your memory*
jog, stimulate, stir, prompt, prod, arouse, activate, remind
Ⓔ **1** tire, exhaust

refreshing *adj*
1 *a refreshing bath/drink*
invigorating, energizing, stimulating, exhilarating, reviving,
cool, thirst-quenching, bracing
2 *a refreshing change from routine*
different, fresh, freshening, stimulating, inspiring, new,
novel, original, welcome, unexpected
COLLOQ. not another

refreshment *n*
sustenance, food, food and drink, drink(s), snack,
freshening, stimulation, revival, restoration, renewal,
reanimation, invigoration, reinvigoration, revitalization

> QUOTATIONS
> The unexempt condition / By which all mortal frailty
> must subsist, / Refreshment after toil / Ease after pain
> JOHN MILTON, *Comus, A Mask*

refreshments *n*
aliment, drinks, food, food and drink, provisions, snacks,
elevenses, sustenance, titbits
COLLOQ. eats, eatables
SLANG nosh, grub; *Aust* tucker

refrigerate *v*
chill, cool, keep cold, freeze
Ⓔ heat, warm

refuge *n*
sanctuary, asylum, shelter, protection, security, retreat,
place of safety, hideout, hideaway, resort, harbour, haven,
bolthole, island

refugee *n*
exile, émigré, displaced person, stateless person, asylum
seeker, asylee, fugitive, runaway, escapee
OLD contraband
SLANG *Aust* reffo

refulgent *adj*
brilliant, shining, beaming, bright, radiant, gleaming,
glistening, glittering
FORMAL irradiant, lambent, lustrous, resplendent

refund *v, n*
♦ *v*
repay, pay back, reimburse, rebate, return, give back,
restore
♦ *n*
repayment, reimbursement, rebate, return

refurbish *v*
renovate, redecorate, re-equip, refit, remodel, revamp,
repair, mend, overhaul, restore, recondition
COLLOQ. do up

refurbishment *n*
renovation, redecoration, restoration, recondition,
revamping, refitting, repairing
COLLOQ. doing-up

refusal *n*
rejection, turning-down, no, rebuff, spurning, repudiation,
repulse, denial, negation, withholding
OLD nay-say
FORMAL incompliance
Ⓔ acceptance, agreement
■ **first refusal**
option, choice, consideration, opportunity, right of
purchase

refuse¹ *v*
refuse to go; refuse permission
reject, turn down, say no, spurn, repudiate, rebuff, repel,
deny, withhold
FORMAL decline
COLLOQ. pass up, knock back, shake your head, draw the
line at, dig your heels in
Ⓔ accept, agree, allow, permit, grant

refuse² n

piles of refuse
rubbish, waste, garbage, sewage, junk, litter, debris, dregs, dross, scum, offscum; N Am trash
TECHNICAL scoria, draff

refutation n

disproof, negation, rebuttal, overthrow
TECHNICAL elenchus
FORMAL confutation

refute v

disprove, rebut, give the lie to, discredit, counter, negate, overthrow, silence, deny (strongly)
FORMAL confute

regain v

recover, get back, win back, recoup, reclaim, repossess, retake, take back, recapture, retrieve, return to

SYNONYM NUANCES

Recover and **get back** can be widely used to suggest taking or finding something previously yours: *she's got back her figure.* **Win back**, however, suggests that a contest or at least some kind of effort has been involved. **Recoup**, is more suggestive of compensation or making up for losses: *basic costs must be recouped for the retailer to stay in business.*
   Reclaim is appropriate for reasserting ownership of something that is rightfully yours, while **repossess** tends to be used of items taken back as a debt: *failure to meet mortgage payments will result in your house being repossessed.* The term **recapture** has implications of effort or even force: *trying to recapture the magic of those days; government forces recaptured the towns.* **Retrieve**, meanwhile, is appropriate for successfully bringing something back that may have been lost: *we finally retrieved our lost luggage.*

regal adj

majestic, kingly, queenly, princely, imperial, royal, sovereign, stately, magnificent, noble, lordly

regale v

amuse, entertain, delight, divert, captivate, fascinate, feast, ply, gratify, serve, refresh

regard v, n

♦ v
1 CONSIDER, judge, rate, value, gauge, estimate, think, believe, suppose, imagine, contemplate, weigh up
FORMAL deem, appraise
2 LOOK AT, look upon, see, view, observe, watch, gaze at, scrutinize, eye
FORMAL behold
COLLOQ. give the once-over
3 HEED, listen to, observe, follow, note, bear in mind, take notice of, pay attention to, take into account/consideration
♦ n
1 CARE, concern, consideration, attention, notice, heed, respect, deference, esteem, honour, admiration, affection, love, sympathy, approval
FORMAL approbation
2 *in this regard*
matter, subject, aspect, respect, point, detail, particular
3 *send her my regards*
best wishes, good wishes, greetings, respects, compliments, love
FORMAL salutations
E≡ **1** disregard, contempt
■ **with/in regard to**
as regards, concerning, with reference to, with respect to, in relation to, in connection with, re, about, as to, on the subject of
FORMAL apropos

SYNONYM NUANCES

noun sense 1
Care and **concern** can widely be used to suggest feeling for the situation of others. **Consideration**, however, conveys a less intense feeling, more suggestive of modifying your behaviour to take account of others, whereas **attention** implies a more focused concentration: *children need a great deal of attention.* Both **notice** and **heed** have similar implications, though to a less intense degree.
   Respect has further connotations of looking up to someone, while **deference** goes further by implying submission: *in deference to his elders.* **Honour**, on the other hand, has more to do with veneration, whereas **admiration** implies high esteem. You could use **affection** to suggest fond feelings, and **love**, although similar, suggests something much stronger.

regardful adj

attentive, mindful, thoughtful, noticing, observant, aware, careful, considerate, watchful, respectful, dutiful, heedful
FORMAL circumspect
E≡ heedless, inattentive, regardless, unobservant

regarding prep

with regard to, in regard to, as regards, concerning, with reference to, with respect to, in relation to, in connection with, re, about, as to, on the subject of, vis-à-vis
FORMAL apropos

regardless adj, adv

♦ adj
disregarding, heedless, unmindful, neglectful, negligent, inattentive, careless, unconcerned, indifferent
E≡ heedful, mindful, attentive
♦ adv
anyway, nevertheless, nonetheless, no matter what, despite everything, come what may, anyhow
COLLOQ. at any price/cost, irregardless

regenerate v

revive, reinvigorate, revitalize, reawaken, rekindle, renew, restore, reconstitute, reconstruct, re-establish, renovate, refresh, uplift, change, invigorate, rejuvenate, reproduce
FORMAL inspirit, revivify

regeneration n

renewal, renovation, restoration, re-establishment, reinvigoration, reconstruction, reconstitution, rejuvenation, reproduction
FORMAL homomorphosis

regime n

1 GOVERNMENT, rule, administration, management, leadership, command, control, direction, reign, establishment, system
2 *a daily regime of training*
routine, system, procedure, way, method, order, pattern, schedule, programme, formula, practice
3 REGIMEN, diet, fast, abstinence

regiment n

army, brigade, cohort, battery, band, company, platoon, squadron, group, crew, gang, body, pultun
OLD tercio
See panel on next page

regimented adj

strict, disciplined, controlled, regulated, standardized, ordered, methodical, systematic, organized, systematized
E≡ free, lax, disorganized

region n

1 LAND, terrain, expanse, tract, place, area, territory, reservation, country, continent, subcontinent, hemisphere, time zone
2 DISTRICT, neighbourhood, estate, area, quarter, zone, belt, borough, burgh, county, shire, state, bailiwick, postal district, catchment area, diocese, parish, mission, municipality, territory, domain, dominion, duchy, manor,

Regiments include:

Army Air Corps	King's Royal	Queen's Dragoon	Royal Engineers	Royal Military	Royal Welsh
Blues and Royals	Hussars	Guards	Royal Gibraltar	Police	Regiment
Coldstream Guards	King's Troop Royal	Queen's Royal	Regiment	Royal Regiment of	Scots Guards
Duke of	Horse Artillery	Hussars	Royal Green	Artillery	Special Air Service
Lancaster's	Life Guards	Queen's Royal	Jackets	Royal Regiment of	(SAS)
Regiment (King's	Light Dragoons	Lancers	Royal Gurkha	Fusiliers	Special
Lancashire and	London Regiment	Rifles	Rifles	Royal Regiment of	Reconnaissance
Border)	Mercian Regiment	Royal Anglian	Royal Horse	Scotland	Welsh Guards
Grenadier Guards	Parachute	Regiment	Artillery	Royal Scots	Yorkshire
Household Cavalry	Regiment	Royal Corps of	Royal Irish	Dragoon Guards	Regiment
Intelligence Corps	Princess of Wales's	Signals	Regiment	Royal Tank	
Irish Guards	Royal Regiment	Royal Dragoon	Royal Lancers	Regiment	
		Guards	— 9th/12th		

emirate, empire, kingdom, realm, principality, province, riding, heartland, interior, inner city, ghetto, red-light district, outskirts, suburbs
OLD hundred; (*Shakesp*) climate, climature
3 SECTOR, division, section, part
4 *a region of influence*
range, scope, expanse, sphere, world, field, ambit, orbit, domain
■ **in the region of**
approximately, roughly, around, about, some, something like, odd, circa, more or less, loosely, round about, or thereabouts, approaching, close to, nearly, just about, not far off, in the neighbourhood/vicinity of, in round numbers, rounded up/down
COLLOQ. give or take
E∃ exactly

Types of geographical region include:

Antarctic	jungle	savannah
Arctic	lowlands	scrubland
basin	marshland	seaside
coast	midlands	steppe
countryside	occident	Third World
desert	orient	tropics
developed world	outback	tundra
developing world	pampas	urban district
forest	plain	veld
grassland	prairie	wasteland
green belt	riviera	wilderness
heath	rural district	woodland

See also **park**.

regional *adj*
district, local, localized, provincial, sectional, zonal, parochial
E∃ national, international, worldwide

register *n, v*
♦ *n*
1 *a doctor's register*
roll, roster, list, listing, index, catalogue, directory, log, diary, journal, record, chronicle, annals, archives, file(s), ledger, schedule, almanac, enrolment, muster, poll
TECHNICAL obituary, patent-rolls, transfer book, cadastre, cartulary, diptych, menology, docket, matricula
OLD album, regest, terrier
FORMAL notitia
Related adjective: matricular
2 *a musical register*
range, voice, tone, note(s)
♦ *v*
1 RECORD, note, log, enter, put in writing, put down, set down, take down, inscribe, mark, list, catalogue, chronicle, enrol, enlist, sign on, check in, book in, turn in, cast, clock
TECHNICAL matriculate, tax
FORMAL enregister

2 SHOW, reveal, betray, display, exhibit, indicate, demonstrate, express, say
FORMAL manifest
3 *the gauge registers a measurement*
read, indicate, record, show, display

registrar *n*
official, recorder, secretary, clerk, administrator, cataloguer, annalist, archivist, chronicler, protocolist

registration *n*
enrolment, record, recording, inscription, list, noting, logging, entering, signing-on, checking-in

regress *v*
deteriorate, recede, relapse, retreat, return, revert, wane, backslide, degenerate, lapse, ebb
FORMAL retrocede, retrogress
E∃ progress

regret *v, n*
♦ *v*
feel/be sorry, wish that you had not done, be disappointed, be distressed, rue, repent, lament, bemoan, weep, mourn, grieve, deplore
♦ *n*
remorse, contrition, repentance, penitence, self-reproach, shame, sorrow, grief, disappointment, bitterness
OLD rue, had-I-wist
FORMAL compunction

> **QUOTATIONS**
> My one regret in life is that I am not someone else
> WOODY ALLEN

> **SYNONYM NUANCES**
>
> *noun*
> **Remorse** can refer to a strong feeling of being extremely upset by your actions, while **contrition** goes further by implying more deeply felt pain for your deeds. **Repentance**, although similar, has further implications of seeking to change: *he was released as he had shown repentance*, whereas **penitence** is more appropriate where there is atonement. **Self-reproach** is a more restrained term for blaming yourself, while **shame** is stronger, with the implication of humiliation.
> **Sorrow** can be used to cover a wide range of sad feelings, not just where one blames oneself, while **grief** is generally associated with loss or bereavement: *the grief of a child's death*. You can use **disappointment** of feelings of being let down either by oneself or by others, but **bitterness** would further imply resentment: *he spoke of his loss without bitterness or self-pity*.

regretful *adj*
remorseful, rueful, repentant, contrite, penitent, conscience-stricken, ashamed, sorry, apologetic, sad, sorrowful, disappointed
E∃ impenitent, unashamed

> **⚠ regretful** or **regrettable**?
> *Regretful* means 'full of regret, sad, sorry'; *regrettable* means 'causing regret, to be regretted': *It is regrettable that you have behaved so foolishly, and I feel regretful that I must now ask you to leave.*

regrettable *adj*
unfortunate, unlucky, unhappy, sad, disappointing, upsetting, distressing, lamentable, deplorable, disgraceful, shameful, sorry, wrong, ill-advised
FORMAL reprehensible
⊟ fortunate, happy

regrettably *adv*
unfortunately, unhappily, unluckily, sadly, alas, sad to say, sad to relate
COLLOQ. worse luck
⊟ fortunately

regular *adj*
1 ROUTINE, habitual, typical, usual, customary, time-honoured, classic, conventional, established, orthodox, correct, official, approved, proper, standard, normal, average, ordinary, common, commonplace, daily, everyday
2 PERIODIC, rhythmic, frequent, recurring, hourly, daily, weekly, monthly, yearly, steady, constant, fixed, set, unchanging, unvarying, uniform, consistent, even, level, flat, evenly spread, smooth, balanced, symmetrical, orderly, systematic, methodical, well-organized
COLLOQ. regular as clockwork
⊟ 1 unusual, unconventional **2** irregular, intermittent

regulate *v*
1 CONTROL, direct, guide, govern, rule, administer, oversee, superintend, supervise, manage, handle, conduct, run, organize, order, arrange, settle, square, monitor
2 ADJUST, set, synchronize, control, tune, moderate, balance

regulation *n, adj*
♦ *n*
1 RULE, statute, law, act, ordinance, by-law, edict, decree, order, ruling, directive, command, supervision, commandment, principle, precept, dictate, dictum, pronouncement, requirement, procedure, curfew
2 CONTROL, direction, guidance, rule, administration, superintendence, supervision, management
FORMAL dispensation
♦ *adj*
standard, official, statutory, obligatory, required, fixed, set, orthodox, accepted, customary, usual, normal
FORMAL prescribed, mandatory
SLANG pusser

regurgitate *v*
1 VOMIT, bring up, spew, retch, heave
FORMAL disgorge
COLLOQ. puke, throw up, sick up, fetch up
2 REPEAT, say/tell again, restate, recapitulate
FORMAL reiterate

rehabilitate *v*
reintegrate, restore, renew, reinvigorate, normalize, reform, reinstate, reconstitute, re-establish, renovate, recondition, rebuild, convert, adjust, clear, mend, reconstruct, save, redeem
COLLOQ. rehab

rehash *n, v*
♦ *n*
reworking, rearrangement, rejig, rejigging, restatement, reshuffle, rewrite
♦ *v*
rework, change, alter, rearrange, rejig, rejigger, restate, reshuffle, refashion, rewrite

rehearsal *n*
practice, drill, exercise, trial run, run-through, walk-through, preparation, reading, recital
COLLOQ. dry run, dummy run

rehearse *v*
1 PRACTISE, drill, train, go over, run through, prepare, try out, block (out)
2 REPEAT, recite, recount, relate, narrate, go over, enumerate, pour forth/out

reign *v, n*
♦ *v*
1 RULE, be king/queen, sit on the throne, be in power, be in charge, be in control, govern, be in government, command, be in command
2 *silence reigns*
prevail, predominate, occur, hold sway, be present, exist, influence
FORMAL obtain
♦ *n*
rule, sway, monarchy, empire, sovereignty, supremacy, government, power, command, dominion, control, influence
FORMAL ascendancy

reigning *adj*
1 *the reigning king*
ruling, governing, in power, in command, in control, current
FORMAL regnant
2 *the reigning champion*
present, current, presiding, victorious, world
FORMAL incumbent

reimburse *v*
refund, repay, pay back, give back, return, restore, recompense, compensate, indemnify, remunerate

reimbursement *n*
refund, repayment, recompense, compensation, idemnity

rein *n, v*
♦ *n*
check, control, curb, restraint, hold, overcheck, restriction, brake, bridle, harness
♦ *v*
check, control, curb, restrain, restrict, limit, hold back, stop, hold, halt, arrest, bridle
■ **free rein**
carte blanche, blank cheque, free hand, free-for-all, liberty, freedom, laissez-faire; *Aust & NZ* open slather

reincarnation *n*
rebirth
TECHNICAL samsara
FORMAL palingenesis, metempsychosis

reinforce *v*
1 STRENGTHEN, toughen, harden, stiffen, steel, brace, support, buttress, shore, prop, stay, supplement, increase
FORMAL fortify, augment
2 EMPHASIZE, stress, underline, consolidate
⊟ 1 weaken, undermine

reinforcement *n*
1 STRENGTHENING, supplement, support, addition, increase, enlargement, prop, shore, stay, brace, buttress, emphasis, hardening, amplification
OLD re-enforcement
FORMAL fortification, augmentation
2 *send reinforcements*
auxiliaries, reserves, additional soldiers/troops/police officers, supplementaries, back-up, support, help
OLD recruit

reinstate *v*
restore, return, give back, replace, recall, reappoint, reinstall, re-establish

reinstatement *n*
restoration, return, giving-back, replacement, recall, re-establishment

reiterate *v*
repeat, recapitulate, resay, restate, retell,
emphasize, stress
FORMAL iterate, rehearse
COLLOQ. recap

reject *v, n*
♦ *v*
1 *reject a proposal*
refuse, deny, decline, turn down, say no to, veto, disallow,
condemn, despise, spurn, rebuff, recuse, jilt, exclude,
repudiate, repel
TECHNICAL athetize
FORMAL renounce
COLLOQ. have nothing to do with, take a raincheck on,
wash your hands of, turn your back on, turn your nose up
at, not touch with a bargepole, kick into touch
2 DISCARD, scrap, jettison, eliminate, cast off,
throw away, set aside
FORMAL forsake
COLLOQ. give the brush-off to, give the cold shoulder to
◪ **1** accept, agree **2** choose, select
♦ *n*
failure, second, discard, outcast, cast-off

SYNONYM NUANCES

verb sense 1
The term **refuse** gives a impression of a strong or
definite rejection, while **deny** is more suggestive of
refuting: *the anger of those who were denied passports*.
Decline and **turn down**, however, would be appropriate
for a rejection of an offer or proposal.
 Veto, on the other hand, suggests forbidding, often
with official overtones: *the government vetoed the
proposal*, whereas **disallow** implies a failure to grant
legitimacy: *his confession was disallowed*. You can use
condemn to suggest censure, while **despise** is more
implicative of contempt, and **spurn** is similarly
disdainful, but further implies an element of discarding.
Likewise, **rebuff** suggests a snub, often unexpectedly: *his
suggestions were constantly rebuffed by the Prime
Minister*. **Jilt** too shares connotations of abruptness or
unexpectedness: *on his wedding day, he was afraid of
being jilted at the altar*.
 Repudiate implies disowning or rejecting completely:
*previous theories have been thoroughly repudiated by
latest research*.

---

rejection *n*
refusal, turning-down, denial, declining, veto, dismissal,
rebuff, exclusion, discarding, jettisoning, repudiation,
elimination
TECHNICAL athetesis
FORMAL renunciation, reprobation
COLLOQ. brush-off, cold shoulder, Dear John letter, push,
heave-ho
◪ acceptance, choice, selection

rejig *v*
reorganize, restructure, rearrange, shake up, modernize,
streamline, rationalize

rejoice *v*
celebrate, revel, delight, be delighted/pleased, be joyful/
happy, take pleasure, glory, exult, triumph
OLD make merry
COLLOQ. jump for joy, whoop it up

rejoicing *n*
celebration, revelry, festivity, happiness, gladness, joy,
delight, pleasure, euphoria, elation, jubilation, glory,
exultation, triumph
OLD merrymaking

rejoin *v*
retort, answer, reply, respond, quip, repartee, riposte

rejoinder *n*
retort, answer, reply, response, quip, repartee, riposte

rejuvenate *v*
revitalize, reinvigorate, reanimate, revive,
renew, freshen up, refresh, restore, rekindle, recharge,
regenerate
FORMAL revivify

rejuvenation *n*
reinvigoration, revival, renewal, restoration, regeneration,
revitalization

relapse *v, n*
♦ *v*
worsen, deteriorate, degenerate, weaken, sink, fail, lapse,
revert, regress, fall away, backslide
FORMAL retrogress
♦ *n*
worsening, deterioration, setback, recurrence,
weakening, lapse, decline, reversion, regression,
backsliding
FORMAL retrogression

relate *v*
1 LINK, connect, join, couple, ally, associate, compare
FORMAL correlate
2 REFER, apply, concern, have a bearing on, be relevant
OLD respect
FORMAL pertain, appertain
3 *relate an anecdote*
tell, recount, narrate, report, describe, recite,
present, communicate, detail, make known,
impart, fable
OLD story
FORMAL delineate
4 IDENTIFY, sympathize, empathize, understand, have a
rapport, feel for, get on (well) with
COLLOQ. hit it off, speak the same language, be on the
same wavelength

related *adj*
kindred, of the same family, akin, affiliated, allied,
associated, connected, linked, interrelated, interconnected,
accompanying, joint, mutual, relevant
FORMAL concomitant, correlated, cognate,
consanguineous, agnate
◪ unrelated, unconnected

relation *n*
1 LINK, linking, connection, bond, relationship,
comparison, similarity, affiliation, alliance, interrelation,
interconnection, interdependence
FORMAL correlation
2 REGARD, reference, relevance, bearing, application
FORMAL pertinence
3 RELATIVE, family, kin, kinsman, kinswoman, kinsfolk,
kindred

relations *n*
1 RELATIVES, family, kin, kinsman, kinswoman, kinsfolk,
kindred
COLLOQ. folks
2 RELATIONSHIP, terms, rapport, liaison, interaction, affairs,
dealings, connections, communications, contact(s),
associations
FORMAL intercourse
3 *sexual relations*
intercourse, sex, union, intimacy, intimate relations,
sleeping with someone, going to bed with someone,
love-making, copulation
FORMAL coition, coitus, carnal knowledge,
consummation

relationship *n*
1 CONNECTION, bond, link, tie(s), tie-up, association,
alliance, liaison, rapport, friendship, affinity, closeness,
similarity, parallel, ratio, proportion
FORMAL correlation
COLLOQ. chemistry
2 AFFAIR, love affair, romance, intimacy, liaison, friendship,
flirtation
COLLOQ. fling, thing

relative *adj, n*
♦ *adj*
1 COMPARATIVE, proportional, proportionate, moderate, comparable, corresponding, respective, parallel, reciprocal
FORMAL commensurate, correlative
2 APPROPRIATE, relevant, applicable, related, connected, interrelated, dependent
FORMAL apposite, germane, pertinent
♦ *n*
relation, family, kin, kinsman, kinswoman, kinsfolk, kindred

relatively *adv*
comparatively, in/by comparison, fairly, quite, rather, somewhat

relax *v*
1 *relax on holiday*
calm (down), rest, unwind, wind down, loosen up, de-stress, tranquillize, sedate, unbend, slump, unknit, unpurse
COLLOQ. take it/things easy, let yourself go, make yourself at home, let your hair down, put your feet up, hang loose, cool it, chill (out), veg (out), lighten up
SLANG chillax
2 *relax the rules*
moderate, soften, ease (off), liberalize, lessen, reduce, diminish, weaken, lower, slacken, loosen, loose, unrein, mollify
OLD relent
FORMAL abate, remit, resolve
2 tighten

relaxation *n*
1 REST, unwinding, loosening up, refreshment, leisure, recreation, fun, amusement, entertainment, enjoyment, pleasure
FORMAL repose
COLLOQ. R & R
2 SLACKENING, loosening, weakening, lessening, abatement, reduction, softening, easing, moderation, détente
FORMAL abatement
COLLOQ. let-up
2 tension, intensification

relaxed *adj*
1 *feel relaxed*
at ease, comfortable, uninhibited, carefree, happy-go-lucky, cool, calm, composed, restful, collected, unhurried, rested, leisurely, easy-going
2 *a relaxed situation*
informal, casual, restful
COLLOQ. laid-back, chilled-out
1 tense, nervous, worried **2** formal, tense

relay *n, v*
♦ *n*
1 BROADCAST, transmission, programme, communication, message, dispatch
2 *work in relays*
shift, turn, stint, time, spell, period
♦ *v*
broadcast, transmit, communicate, pass on, hand on, send, circulate, spread, carry, supply

release *v, n*
♦ *v*
1 SET FREE, free, liberate, deliver, emancipate

2 LOOSEN, loose, unloose, let go, untie, undo, unlock, unfasten, unchain, unbind, unshackle, unclasp, unleash
3 EXCUSE, exempt, discharge, let go, let off, acquit, absolve
FORMAL exonerate
4 ISSUE, publish, make available, make known, make public, announce, disclose, reveal, circulate, distribute, present, launch, divulge, unveil
1 imprison **3** detain
♦ *n*
1 FREEDOM, liberty, liberation, deliverance, emancipation
FORMAL manumission
2 ACQUITTAL, absolution, exoneration, exemption, discharge
COLLOQ. let-off
3 ISSUE, publication, publishing, disclosure, revelation, declaration, bulletin, announcement, proclamation
1 imprisonment, detention

relegate *v*
demote, downgrade, degrade, sideline, reduce, consign, entrust, assign, refer, dispatch, delegate, transfer, banish, expatriate, deport, eject, exile, expel
promote

relent *v*
1 GIVE IN, give way, come round, yield, allow, change your mind, capitulate
2 *the storm relented*
ease (off), let up, die down, slacken, soften, weaken, unbend, relax
FORMAL abate

relentless *adj*
unrelenting, unremitting, incessant, persistent, unflagging, unceasing, ruthless, remorseless, implacable, merciless, pitiless, cold-hearted, hard-hearted, unforgiving, cruel, harsh, fierce, grim, hard, punishing, uncompromising, inflexible, unyielding, inexorable
merciful, yielding

relevance *n*
suitability, aptness, appropriateness, appositeness, significance, applicability
FORMAL pertinence
irrelevance

relevant *adj*
material, significant, related, to the point, applicable, live, apposite, apt, appropriate, suitable, fitting, proper, admissible, relative, appertains, to the purpose
OLD german
FORMAL pertinent, germane, congruous, apropos
irrelevant, inapplicable, inappropriate, unsuitable

reliability *n*
dependability, trustworthiness, constancy, steadiness, responsibility, faithfulness, honesty, integrity, conscientiousness, certainty
unreliability, fickleness

reliable *adj*
unfailing, certain, sure, dependable, responsible, trusty, trustworthy, dutiful, honest, true, devoted, conscientious, faithful, constant, staunch, solid, safe, sound, well-grounded, well-founded, stable, tested, predictable, regular
unreliable, doubtful, untrustworthy

reliance *n*
dependence, trust, faith, belief, conviction, credit, confidence, assurance

relic *n*
memento, souvenir, keepsake, token, reminder, monument, remembrance, survival, remains, artefact, heirloom, antique, remnant, scrap, fragment, vestige, trace; N Am holdover
TECHNICAL fossil
OLD relique, relict
Related adjective: reliquary

relief n

1 *relief from pain*
respite, alleviation, easing, lessening, reduction, soothing, release, cure, remedy, deliverance, remission
FORMAL mitigation, abatement, allaying, assuaging, palliation
2 COMFORT, reassurance, happiness, relaxation, calmness, consolation
3 REST, refreshment, diversion, relaxation, respite, break, interruption
FORMAL repose
COLLOQ. breather, let-up
4 *famine relief*
aid, help, assistance, rescue, saving, support, back-up, sustenance
FORMAL succour
5 SUBSTITUTE, replacement, reserve, stand-by, stand-in, supply, locum, understudy, proxy, surrogate

relieve v

1 *relieve the pain*
alleviate, soothe, lessen, soften, slacken, reduce, cure, heal, comfort, console, reassure
FORMAL mitigate, abate, allay, assuage, palliate
2 DELIVER, set free, free, liberate, release, unburden, discharge
3 SUBSTITUTE, replace, stand in for, take the place of, take over from
4 HELP, aid, assist, rescue, save, support, sustain
FORMAL succour
5 DISCHARGE, exempt, excuse, dismiss, expel, remove, free, release
6 *relieve the tedium*
break (up), interrupt, pause, stop, bring to an end, punctuate
FORMAL discontinue
E₃ **1** aggravate, intensify

relieved adj
happy, glad, pleased, thankful, cheered, encouraged, refreshed, eased

religion n
faith, belief system, beliefs, creed, code, doctrine, dogma
See panels below and on next page

> QUOTATIONS
> Religion is what a man does with his solitariness
> ALFRED NORTH WHITEHEAD, *Religion in the Making*

Religions include:

BUDDHISM:
Theravada
Mahayana

CHRISTIANITY:
Anglicanism
Baptists
Calvinism
Catholicism
Church of England (C of E)
Congregationalism
evangelicalism
Jehovah's Witnesses
Lutheranism
Methodism
Mormonism
Pentecostalism

Presbyterianism
Protestantism
Quakerism

ISLAM:
Ismaili
Shi'ah
Sufi
Sunni
Wahhabi

JUDAISM:
Conservative
Orthodox
Reform

OTHER:
Amish
Bahaism
Candomblé

Confucianism
druidism
Hare Krishna
Hinduism
Jainism
New Age
paganism
Rastafari
Santeria
Scientology
Shintoism
Sikhism
Taoism
voodoo
Zen
Zoroastrianism

See also **sacred writings**; **worship**.

---

religious adj

1 SACRED, holy, divine, spiritual, devotional, scriptural, theological, doctrinal

2 *a religious person*
believing, having a living faith, devout, godly, pious, God-fearing, church-going, practising, committed, reverent, righteous
3 CONSCIENTIOUS, scrupulous, rigorous, meticulous, strict
E₃ **1** secular **2** irreligious, ungodly

Religious festivals include:

BUDDHIST:	Id-al-Adha	Samhain
Buddha Purnima	Id-al-Fitr	Yule
Dhamma	Laylat al-Miraj	
Sangha	Laylat al-Qadr	**SHINTO:**
Vesak	Milad-un-Nabi	Ohinamatsuri
		Oshogatsu
CHRISTIAN:	**JEWISH:**	Tanabata Matsuri
All Saints' Day	Hanukkah	Tango no Sekku
Ascension	Pesach (Passover)	
Christmas	Purim	**SIKH:**
Corpus Christi	Rosh Hashanah	Baisakhi
Easter	Shavuot	Birthday of Guru
Epiphany	Simchat Torah	Gobind Singh
Good Friday	Sukkoth (Feast of	Birthday of Guru
Pentecost	Tabernacles)	Nanak (Prakash
HINDU:	Yom Kippur	Utsav)
Basant		Martyrdom of
Diwali	**PAGAN:**	Guru Arjan Dev
Ganesh Chaturthi	Beltane	Martyrdom of
Holi	Imbolc	Guru Teg
Navaratri	Lammas (Lughna-	Bahadur
Vaisakhi	sadh)	
ISLAMIC:	Litha	**ANCIENT ROMAN:**
Al-Hijra	Mabon	Bacchanalia
	Ostara	Saturnalia
		Vulcanalia

See also **celebration**.

---

religiously adv

1 CONSCIENTIOUSLY, strictly, rigorously, scrupulously, meticulously
2 *he converted religiously*
spiritually, theologically, doctrinally

relinquish v
let go, release, hand over, surrender, yield, cede, give up, resign, repudiate, waive, for(e)go, part with, retreat, abandon, desert, drop, discard; *Scot* demit
OLD (*Shakesp*) give out, cease
FORMAL renounce, forsake, discontinue, desist, abstain, abdicate
COLLOQ. quit
E₃ keep, retain

> SYNONYM NUANCES
>
> **Let go** is a synonym which can be generally applied, while **release** has added implications of setting free, or relinquishing something firmly held: *he agreed to release his claims on the estate for a one-off payment.* **Hand over** implies placing in someone else's care, whereas **surrender** has the added suggestion of defeat: *the trade unions retained influence in negotiations, but surrendered control.* The terms **give up**, **yield** and **cede** are also suggestive of a degree of reluctance, with **cede** generally used of political situations: *a region ceded to Russia.*
> The terms **renounce** and **repudiate**, on the other hand, imply a more heartfelt disowning, and **waive** and **for(e)go** describe a conscious refraining from exercising your rights or claims: *some celebrities waive their appearance fees for charity.* **Retreat** has a more military tone and implies moving back, thereby giving ground to the enemy, while **abandon** and **desert** suggest leaving behind something that is no longer profitable or productive: *the artist abandoned her old palette in favour of bolder colours.* **Drop** is more suggestive of a loss of interest or willingness: *he dropped friends at the bat of an eye*, and **discard** is similarly dismissive.

Religious orders include:

Augustinians	Celestines	Loreto (The	Marists (Society of	Oratorians	Sisters of Mercy
Benedictines	Cistercians	Institute of the	Mary)	(Congregation of	Trappists
Capuchins	Dominicans	Blessed Virgin	Missionary Sisters	the Oratory)	Ursulines
Carmelites	Franciscans	Mary)	of Charity	Poor Clares	
Carthusians	Jesuits			Salesians	

Religious officers include:

abbess	cardinal	deacon	imam	mullah	prelate
abbot	chancellor	deaconess	kohen	nun	priest
archbishop	chaplain	dean	minister	Pachen Lama	prior
archdeacon	clergyman	elder	monk	padre	proctor
ayatollah	clergywoman	father	Monsignor	parson	rabbi
bishop	curate	friar	mother superior	pastor	rector
canon	Dalai Lama	guru	muezzin	pope	vicar

See also **priest**.

relish v, n
* v
like, enjoy, savour, appreciate, taste, adore, love, revel in, delight in
OLD degust; (Shakesp) palate
* n
1 SEASONING, flavouring, condiment, sauce, pickle, chutney, garnish, spice, flavour, piquancy, tang, palate, savour, gout, goût; Scot kitchen
OLD gust, lust
FORMAL opsonium
2 ENJOYMENT, pleasure, enthusiasm, delight, appreciation, satisfaction, taste, appetite, stomach, tooth, gusto, zest, liveliness, vivacity, vigour, charm

relocate v
move, move house, move away, remove, transfer, go (away), leave, change address
COLLOQ. up sticks

reluctance n
unwillingness, hesitancy, hesitation, disinclination, indisposition, dislike, distaste, repugnance, loathing, aversion, backwardness
OLD renitency
FORMAL recalcitrance
F3 eagerness, enthusiasm, willingness

reluctant adj
unwilling, indisposed, hesitant, slow, backward, loath, averse, disinclined, unenthusiastic, grudging, shy, squeamish, loathful
OLD renitent
F3 willing, ready, eager, enthusiastic

rely v
depend, lean, be sure, count, bank, reckon, trust, swear by

remain v
stay, rest, stand, last, endure, survive, stay behind, be left over, prevail, persist, continue, linger, wait
OLD bide; (Shakesp) climate
FORMAL dwell, abide, tarry
F3 go, leave, depart

remainder n
rest, balance, surplus, excess, residue, leftovers, carry-over, remnant, remains, vestiges; Scot lave
OLD remanent, remanet
FORMAL superfluity, residuum

remaining adj
left, left over, spare, unused, unspent, unfinished, residual, last, outstanding, surviving, persisting, lingering, lasting, abiding

remains n
1 REST, remainder, residue, dregs, leavings, leftovers, scraps, crumbs, fragments, remnants, oddments, traces, vestiges, relics

FORMAL detritus, reliquiae
COLLOQ. odds and ends
2 CORPSE, body, dead body, cadaver, carcase, ashes, debris

remark v, n
* v
comment, observe, note, notice, mention, say, state, assert, pronounce, declare
* n
comment, observation, opinion, reflection, mention, reference, utterance, statement, assertion, pronouncement, acknowledgement, declaration, notice

remarkable adj
striking, impressive, noteworthy, surprising, amazing, strange, odd, unusual, uncommon, rare, extraordinary, phenomenal, exceptional, memorable, momentous, outstanding, notable, considerable, conspicuous, prominent, important, significant, pre-eminent, signal, surpassing, distinguished
FORMAL singular
F3 average, ordinary, commonplace, usual

remarkably adv
surprisingly, unusually, uncommonly, significantly, signally, extraordinarily, exceptionally, outstandingly, considerably

remedy n, v
* n
cure, antidote, countermeasure, corrective, restorative, medicine, medication, treatment, therapy, relief, solution, answer, panacea
FORMAL medicament, physic, nostrum
* v
correct, put right, redress, control, counteract, cure, heal, restore, treat, help, relieve, soothe, ease, mend, repair, sort (out), fix, solve
FORMAL rectify, mitigate

SYNONYM NUANCES

noun
The word **antidote** and the less clinical-sounding **countermeasure** are suggestive of counteraction: *rules are the only antidote to chaos*, whereas **corrective** is appropriate for putting right: *the book provides a much-needed corrective to the film's lack of atmosphere*. **Restorative** has stronger implications of returning to a previous state or full strength: *restorative sleep*.

   While **medicine** and **medication** tend to be reserved for chemical preparations, **treatment** can be used more generally of a medical remedy, and **therapy** can be used for any non-surgical practice. To emphasize the alleviation of suffering you can use **relief**, whereas the terms **solution** and **answer** could be used of anything that satisfactorily addresses a problem: *the solution to most problems is anticipation*. **Panacea** would be reserved for an almost hypothetical remedy, effective against all ills: *there is no panacea for economic problems*.

remember *v*

1 RECALL, recollect, summon up, think back, think of, look back, hark back, cast your mind back, call to mind, reminisce, recognize, place
2 MEMORIZE, learn, learn by heart, commit to memory, make a mental note of, retain
3 COMMEMORATE, honour, mark, keep, recognize, celebrate, pay tribute to
4 *remember me to your parents*
send good/best wishes, send greetings, send your regards/respects
E3 1 forget

> **QUOTATIONS**
> Remember me when I am gone away, / Gone far away into the silent land
> CHRISTINA GEORGINA ROSSETTI, *Goblin Market and other Poems*, 'Remember'

remembrance *n*

1 MEMORY, recollection, mind, reminder, recall, reminiscence, thought, testimonial, retrospect, nostalgia
2 COMMEMORATION, memorial, monument, souvenir, memento, token, keepsake, relic, recognition

remind *v*

prompt, nudge, hint, jog your memory, refresh your memory, bring to mind, call to mind, put you in mind of, make you think of, call up, evoke, take back

reminder *n*

prompt, nudge, hint, suggestion, note, memorandum, aide-mémoire, souvenir, memento, token, remembrance, keepsake, phylactery
TECHNICAL prompt-note
COLLOQ. memo

reminisce *v*

remember, recall, recollect, think back, look back, hark back, review, retrospect

reminiscence *n*

memory, remembrance, memoir, anecdote, recollection, recall, retrospection, review, reflection

reminiscent *adj*

suggestive, evocative, nostalgic
FORMAL redolent

remiss *adj*

careless, negligent, neglectful, forgetful, unmindful, heedless, lackadaisical, inattentive, indifferent, lax, slack, slipshod, sloppy, slow, thoughtless, casual, wayward
FORMAL culpable, tardy, dilatory
E3 careful, scrupulous

remission *n*

1 LESSENING, moderation, slackening, relaxation, release, weakening, decrease, reduction, respite, reprieve, ebb, lull
FORMAL abatement, alleviation, diminution
COLLOQ. let-up
2 CANCELLATION, repeal, annulment, suspension
TECHNICAL acceptilation
FORMAL rescinding, abrogation, revocation
3 PARDON, forgiveness, acquittal, excuse, absolution, exemption, discharge, indulgence, amnesty
TECHNICAL baptismal regeneration, plenary indulgence
OLD remitment
FORMAL exoneration, remittal

> **⚠ remission or remittance?**
> *Remission* means 'a lessening in force or effect': *Remissions in that form of cancer are not unknown*, 'the shortening of a prison sentence', 'the cancelling of a debt or punishment', and, in Christian theology, 'the forgiveness (of sins)'. *Remittance* is a formal word for the sending of money in payment for something, or for the money itself: *We are grateful for your remittance of the correct sum of money.*

remit *v, n*

♦ *v*
1 SEND, transmit, dispatch, post, mail, forward, pay, settle
2 REFER, transfer, direct, pass on
3 CANCEL, set aside, hold over, suspend, repeal
FORMAL rescind, abrogate, revoke
♦ *n*
brief, orders, instructions, guidelines, terms of reference, scope, authorization, (area of) responsibility

remittance *n*

sending, dispatch, payment, fee, allowance, consideration

> **⚠ remittance or remission?**
> See panel at **remission**.

remnant *n*

scrap, piece, bit, fragment, end, offcut, leftover, remainder, oddment, balance, residue, remains, shred, trace, vestige, butt, rump; *dialect* fent
TECHNICAL outlier, witness
OLD odd-come-short, wrack
FORMAL remanent

remonstrance *n*

grievance, complaint, objection, opposition, protest, protestation, reprimand, reproof, exception, petition
FORMAL expostulation

remonstrate *v*

protest, argue, challenge, oppose, take exception to, take issue with, complain, object, dispute
FORMAL dissent, expostulate
COLLOQ. gripe

remorse *n*

regret, ruefulness, repentance, penitence, contrition, contriteness, self-reproach, shame, guilt, bad conscience, sorrow, grief, worm
OLD rue, ruth, ayenbite, had-I-wist
FORMAL compunction
See Synonym nuances panel at **regret**.

remorseful *adj*

guilty, regretful, repentant, ashamed, penitent, conscience-stricken, guilt-ridden, sorrowful, sorry, sad, apologetic, rueful, contrite
FORMAL chastened, compunctious
COLLOQ. on a guilt trip
E3 impenitent, remorseless

remorseless *adj*

relentless, unrelenting, unremitting, unstoppable, undeviating, inexorable, implacable, pitiless, unforgiving, merciless, hard, hard-hearted, harsh, ruthless, savage, unmerciful, unremorseful, callous, cruel, stern, inhumane
E3 sorry, remorseful

remorselessly *adv*

relentlessly, unremittingly, inexorably, implacably, callously, cruelly, mercilessly, harshly, ruthlessly, savagely

remote *adj*

1 DISTANT, far, faraway, far-off, outlying, out-of-the-way, inaccessible, god-forsaken, isolated, secluded, lonely
COLLOQ. off the beaten track
2 DETACHED, aloof, distant, standoffish, unapproachable, uncommunicative, unconcerned, uninvolved, reserved, withdrawn

3 *a remote possibility*
slight, small, slim, poor, meagre, slender, faint,
inconsiderable, negligible, doubtful, dubious, unlikely,
improbable, insignificant, outside
4 *official policies remote from everyday experience*
irrelevant, immaterial, beside/off the point, inapplicable,
inappropriate, inapt, unimportant, out of place, having no
bearing, unrelated, unconnected, peripheral, tangential,
beside the mark/question
FORMAL inapposite, extraneous, inconsequent, ungermane,
irrelative
COLLOQ. neither here nor there, not coming into it, making
no difference, not matter, going off at a tangent
F3 1 close, nearby, accessible 2 friendly, warm,
approachable 3 strong, distinct 4 relevant, pertinent

removable *adj*
detachable, movable, separable, eradicable, transferable

removal *n*
1 MOVE, transferral, departure, relocation, uprooting, shift,
shifting, transporting, conveyance
2 WITHDRAWAL, taking away, detachment, extraction,
deletion, obliteration, abolition, purging
3 DISMISSAL, discharge, departure, riddance, ejection,
ousting, eviction, expulsion, relegation, disposal
FORMAL dislodgement
COLLOQ. firing, sacking, sack, push, boot, elbow

remove *v*
1 MOVE, transfer, relocate, take away, shift, dislodge,
transport, carry, convey
2 TAKE AWAY, withdraw, take off, detach, tear off, pull off,
amputate, destroy, cut off, lop off, take out, cut out,
extract, excise, pull out, get out, strip, shed, doff
TECHNICAL deaccession
3 ELIMINATE, get rid of, erase, rub out, delete, strike out,
cross out, obliterate, abolish, purge, blue-pencil,
elbow out
FORMAL expurge, efface
4 DISMISS, discharge, eject, throw out, get rid of, oust,
evict, expel, dislodge, unseat, depose, cast out, cashier,
relegate
COLLOQ. fire, sack, boot out

remunerate *v*
pay, reimburse, recompense, compensate, reward,
indemnify, redress, repay

remuneration *n*
pay, payment, wages, salary, emolument, stipend, fee,
honorarium, retainer, earnings, income, profit, reward,
recompense, remittance, repayment, reimbursement,
compensation, indemnity
OLD (*Spenser*) sold

remunerative *adj*
profitable, lucrative, moneymaking, paying,
rewarding, rich, (financially) worthwhile, gainful,
fruitful

renaissance *n*
revival, renewal, rebirth, reawakening, awakening,
resurrection, rejuvenation, regeneration, re-emergence,
restoration, new birth, new dawn, reappearance,
resurgence
FORMAL recrudescence, renascence

renascent *adj*
revived, resurgent, renewed, re-emergent, reborn,
resurrected, reawakened, reanimated
FORMAL redivivus
COLLOQ. born again

rend *v*
tear (apart), split, break, burst, divide, separate, rupture,
sever, rip, fracture, pierce, shatter, smash, splinter, stab,
lacerate, wring
OLD dilacerate, cleave, rent, rive, to-rend

render *v*
1 *they rendered it harmless*
make, cause to be, leave, change, turn

2 GIVE, provide, supply, tender, present, contribute, furnish,
submit, hand over, deliver
FORMAL proffer
3 TRANSLATE, transcribe, interpret, explain, clarify,
represent, perform, play, sing
4 SHOW, describe, represent, display, exhibit, depict
FORMAL manifest

rendering *n*
1 PERFORMANCE, rendition, show, appearance,
presentation, production, interpretation, representation,
portrayal, acting
2 TRANSLATION, version, rendition, explanation,
interpretation, gloss, crib, rewording, rephrasing,
paraphrase, simplification, transliteration, transcription
FORMAL metaphrasis

rendezvous *n, v*
♦ *n*
1 MEETING, appointment, engagement,
assignation, date
OLD tryst
2 MEETING-PLACE, venue, haunt, resort
OLD trysting-place
♦ *v*
meet, come together, gather, collect, assemble, rally,
muster, converge
FORMAL convene

rendition *n*
1 PERFORMANCE, presentation, version, rendering,
portrayal, reading, translation, arrangement, construction,
delivery
FORMAL execution
2 TRANSLATION, version, interpretation, explanation,
transcription, gloss, rewording, rephrasing, paraphrase,
simplification, transliteration, depiction

renegade *n, adj*
♦ *n*
deserter, defector, traitor, turncoat, dissident, mutineer,
outlaw, rebel, betrayer, apostate, backslider, runaway,
runagate
OLD recreant
FORMAL tergiversator
COLLOQ. rat
F3 adherent, disciple, follower
♦ *adj*
disloyal, rebel, rebellious, traitorous, treacherous,
unfaithful, apostate, backsliding, dissident, mutinous,
outlaw, runaway
OLD recreant
FORMAL perfidious
F3 loyal, faithful

renege *v*
default, repudiate, go back on your promise, backslide,
apostatize, welsh, cross the floor

renew *v*
1 RENOVATE, modernize, refurbish, refit, recondition,
innovate, mend, repair, overhaul, remodel, reform,
transform, recreate, reconstitute, re-establish, regenerate,
revive, resuscitate, refresh, rejuvenate, reinvigorate, boost,
brush up, revitalize, restore, replace, replenish, restock
OLD new, renforce
2 RESUME, repeat, restate, reaffirm, extend, prolong,
continue, recommence, restart
FORMAL reiterate, reprise

renewal *n*
1 RENOVATION, reconditioning, re-creation, repair,
refurbishment, reconstitution, reconstruction,
reinvigoration, rejuvenation, revitalization, replenishment,
resurrection, resuscitation
OLD recruit, recruital
FORMAL revivification
COLLOQ. kiss of life
2 RESUMPTION, repetition, restatement, reaffirmation,
continuance, recommencement
FORMAL reiteration

renounce *v*
abandon, give up, resign, relinquish, surrender, waive, sign away, discard, reject, spurn, shun, disown, for(e)go, disinherit, repudiate, deny, refuse, revolt, cut, declare off, swear off, pass up, put away, recede
TECHNICAL disgown, forisfamiliate
OLD renay; (*Spenser*) forsay
FORMAL forsake, disclaim, desist, abstain, eschew, abnegate, recant, abjure, abdicate, renege, disprofess, forswear
COLLOQ. wash your hands of

renovate *v*
restore, renew, recondition, repair, overhaul, modernize, refurbish, refit, redecorate, remodel, reform, rehabilitate, revamp, improve
COLLOQ. do up, give a facelift

renovation *n*
refurbishment, improvement, modernization, repair, restoration, renewal, reconditioning, refit
COLLOQ. facelift

renown *n*
fame, celebrity, stardom, acclaim, glory, eminence, pre-eminence, illustriousness, distinction, prestige, esteem, prominence, note, mark, reputation, repute, honour
E3 obscurity, anonymity

renowned *adj*
famous, well-known, celebrated, acclaimed, famed, noted, eminent, pre-eminent, distinguished, prestigious, prominent, illustrious, notable, of repute
E3 unknown, obscure

rent[1] *n, v*
♦ *n*
pay the rent
rental, lease, hire, payment, cost, rate, fee
♦ *v*
1 *rent a television*
hire, lease
2 LET (OUT), rent out, sublet, lease, hire (out), charter

rent[2] *adj*
a world rent by conflict
torn apart, split, ripped apart, ruptured, divided, severed
OLD riven

renunciation *n*
abandonment, giving up, relinquishment, surrender, waiving, discarding, rejection, spurning, shunning, disowning, disinheriting, repudiation, denial
FORMAL forsaking, disclaiming, desistance, abstinence, abnegation, abdication

reorganize *v*
restructure, rearrange, shake up, modernize, streamline, rationalize, rejig

repair[1] *v, n*
♦ *v*
repair a faulty machine
mend, fix, patch up, sew, darn, overhaul, refit, service, maintain, put right, rectify, adjust, redress, restore, make good, heal, renovate, renew
♦ *n*
1 MEND, patch, darn, overhaul, service, refit, maintenance, restoration, adjustment, improvement
2 *in good/bad repair*
condition, shape, state, form, (working) order, fettle, kilter
COLLOQ. nick

repair[2] *v*
repair to a place
go, move, turn, withdraw, retire, resort, remove, wend your way

reparable *adj*
recoverable, rectifiable, remediable, restorable, retrievable, salvageable, savable, corrigible, curable
E3 irreparable

reparation *n*
amends, redress, requital, restitution, satisfaction, renewal, compensation, recompense, damages, indemnity, atonement
TECHNICAL solatium
FORMAL propitiation

repartee *n*
banter, bantering, badinage, jesting, wit, witticism, word play, riposte, retort

repast *n*
meal, snack, food, nourishment, spread, board, table, feed
FORMAL refection, collation, victuals

repatriate *v*
deport, expel, banish, exile, extradite, transport, oust, ostracize

repay *v*
1 REFUND, reimburse, pay back, compensate, recompense, reward, remunerate, pay, settle, settle up with, square
OLD yield
2 GET EVEN WITH, get back at, retaliate, return, reciprocate, revenge, avenge
OLD apay, quit
COLLOQ. get your own back on, settle the score, give as good as you get, not take it lying down

repayment *n*
1 REFUND, reimbursement, compensation, recompense, reward, remuneration, payment, reparation, redress, restitution, amends, requital, rebate
2 VENGEANCE, revenge, retribution, reciprocation, retaliation
COLLOQ. tit for tat, eye for an eye

repeal *v, n*
♦ *v*
quash, annul, void, invalidate, cancel, set aside, lift, recall, withdraw, reverse, abolish
FORMAL revoke, rescind, abrogate, nullify, abjure, retract, countermand, recant
E3 enact
♦ *n*
cancellation, invalidation, quashing, reversal, withdrawal, abolition, annulment
FORMAL abrogation, nullification, rescinding, rescindment, rescission, revocation
E3 enactment, establishment

repeat *v, n*
♦ *v*
restate, say again, go over, recapitulate, reiterate, echo, parrot, quote, recite, relate, retell, reproduce, duplicate, renew, rebroadcast, reshow, replay, rerun, redo
FORMAL iterate, rehearse
COLLOQ. recap
♦ *n*
repetition, restatement, recapitulation, echo, reproduction, copy, duplicate, duplication, rebroadcast, reshowing, replay, rerun, ditto

repeated *adj*
frequent, constant, continual, regular, recurrent, periodic, rhythmical, persistent, recurring

repeatedly *adv*
time after time, time and (time) again, again and again, over and over (again), frequently, often

repel *v*
1 DRIVE BACK, repulse, check, hold off, ward off, parry, resist, keep at bay, oppose, fight (off), beat off, force back, beat back, push back, refuse, decline, reject, spurn, rebuff, rebut
2 DISGUST, revolt, nauseate, sicken, make you sick, offend
FORMAL be repugnant to
COLLOQ. turn off, turn your stomach
E3 **1** attract **2** delight

repellent *adj*
repulsive, revolting, disgusting, nauseating, sickening, offensive, shocking, distasteful, gruesome, objectionable,

off-putting, obnoxious, foul, vile, nasty, repugnant, loathsome, abominable, abhorrent, noisome, contemptible, despicable, hateful, horrid, unpleasant, disagreeable
F3 attractive, pleasant, delightful

repent v
regret, rue, feel remorse, sorrow, be sorry, be ashamed, be contrite, confess, lament, deplore, reproach yourself, turn, be converted
OLD (Spenser) relent
FORMAL recant
COLLOQ. go down on your knees, beat your breasts, see the error of your ways, see the light, do a U-turn, wipe the slate clean

repentance n
penitence, confession, penance, contrition, remorse, regret, sorrow, grief, guilt, shame, conversion
FORMAL compunction, recantation
COLLOQ. U-turn

repentant adj
penitent, contrite, sorry, sorrowful, apologetic, remorseful, regretful, guilty, rueful, chastened, ashamed, conscience-stricken
F3 unrepentant, impenitent

repercussion n
result, consequence, effect, side-effect, spin-off, reverberation, echo, rebound, recoil, backwash
COLLOQ. blowback, backlash, ripple, shock wave

repertoire n
collection, list, range, repertory, reserve, reservoir, stock, store, supply
FORMAL repository

repetition n
restatement, reiteration, recapitulation, quoting, copying, echo, echoing, return, reappearance, recurrence, duplication, redundancy, superfluity, tautology
TECHNICAL echolalia
FORMAL iterance, iteration, rehearsal, reprise

repetitious adj
tedious, monotonous, boring, dull, unchanging, unvaried, redundant, tautological, long-winded, verbose, wordy, windy
TECHNICAL pleonastic(al)
FORMAL prolix

repetitive adj
recurrent, monotonous, tedious, boring, dull, mechanical, automatic, unchanging, unvaried
COLLOQ. samey, soul-destroying

rephrase v
paraphrase, reword, put in other/different words, put another way, ask/express/say differently, rewrite, recast

repine v
grumble, complain, murmur, fret, lament, grieve, languish, moan, brood, sulk, mope
COLLOQ. beef, grouse, grouch

replace v
1 replace the lid
put back, return, restore, make good, reinstate, re-establish, hang up
2 SUPERSEDE, take the place of, succeed, come after, follow, supplant, relieve, oust, deputize, substitute, stand in for, act for, fill in for, displace, exchange, change, pre-empt, refund
TECHNICAL replant

SYNONYM NUANCES

sense 2
While the terms **succeed**, **come after** and **follow** are suggestive of a time sequence, and natural or expected progression: *Reagan succeeded Carter as president*, **supersede** generally suggests replacing something due to its obsolescence: *sheep netting has been superseded by electric fencing.*

Supplant and **displace** imply a more marked removal by a rival person or cause: *a sense of Britishness has been supplanted by Scottish and Welsh nationalism; he displaced the long-time title holder*, while **oust** would more clearly convey a forcible ejection: *Allende was ousted in a military coup.*
Relieve is appropriate where replacement gives respite: *they were relieved by the morning shift*. **Substitute** suggests a straightforward replacing of a person or thing for practical reasons: *substitute skimmed milk for full fat milk if you are on a diet*; you could use **deputize**, **act for**, **stand in for** or **fill in for** if you want to suggest a more temporary arrangement: *Mr Smith will deputize for the manager while he is in hospital.*
Where a replacement is made in advance you may use the term **pre-empt**: *the latest episode of the soap will be pre-empted for the prime ministerial address.*

---

replaceable adj
1 DISPOSABLE, throwaway, expendable, non-returnable, biodegradable
2 he thinks he's not replaceable
substitutable, exchangeable, interchangeable
F3 1 returnable **2** irreplaceable

replacement n
substitute, stand-in, reserve, understudy, fill-in, supply, proxy, surrogate, successor, spare part

replenish v
refill, restock, reload, recharge, replace, restore, renew, supply, provide, furnish, stock, fill, fill up, top up, make up

replenishment n
restocking, recharging, replacement, restoration, renewal, provision, supply, filling, refilling

replete adj
1 FILLED, full, full up, charged, abounding, brimful, brimming, teeming, well-provided, well-stocked, jammed, stuffed, crammed
COLLOQ. chock-a-block, chock-full, chocker, jam-packed
2 WELL-FED, gorged, sated, glutted
FORMAL satiated
COLLOQ. full, full up, stuffed

repletion n
fullness, overfullness, glut, completeness, superabundance, superfluity
FORMAL plethora, satiation, satiety

replica n
model, imitation, reproduction, facsimile, copy, duplicate, dummy, clone

replicate v
repeat, duplicate, copy, mimic, follow, reduplicate, reproduce, recreate, clone, ape

reply v, n
♦ v
answer, respond, retort, rejoin, react, acknowledge, return, come back, write back, echo, reciprocate, counter, retaliate, riposte
♦ n
answer, response, retort, rejoinder, riposte, repartee, reaction, comeback, acknowledgement, return, echo, retaliation
COLLOQ. comeback

SYNONYM NUANCES

verb
The term **respond** implies that something has been directly prompted: *she responded to the cheering with a curtsy*. **Return**, **come back**, **retort** and **rejoin** are similar but suggest swift verbal retaliation for a perceived taunt, and **riposte** too suggests speed and wit.
React, however, can be used of a more instinctive reply brought about by a stimulus: *he reacted angrily to*

their proposal, whereas **acknowledge** is more suggestive of replying through courtesy, and **reciprocate** could be used of any verbal interchange.

While **echo** would suggest a remark made in agreement, **counter** suggests a contradictory or retaliatory reply. **Retaliate** more explicitly returns to the idea of requital of a perceived insult.

report *n, v*

♦ *n*

1 ACCOUNT, article, piece, item, write-up, record, relation, narrative, description, story, tale, statement, communiqué, press release, bulletin, register, chronicle, minutes, declaration, announcement, communication, information, news, word, message, note, brief, file, dossier
FORMAL delineation
2 *a school report*
evaluation, assessment, inspection, appraisal, examination, judgement
3 GOSSIP, hearsay, rumour, talk, whisper
4 REPUTATION, honour, character, standing, stature, opinion, credit, esteem, repute, fame, renown, celebrity, distinction, name
5 EXPLOSION, shot, bang, crack, boom, crash, blast, reverberation, noise

♦ *v*

1 STATE, announce, declare, proclaim, air, broadcast, relay, publish, circulate, pass on, communicate, notify, tell, recount, relate, narrate, describe, detail, set forth, disclose, divulge, cover, document, chronicle, record, note
FORMAL delineate
2 COMPLAIN, inform on
COLLOQ. tell on, squeal, rat, split, blow the whistle on
SLANG shop, grass; *N Am* stool on

QUOTATIONS
I can only report on what I know
MAX RUDOLPH FRISCH, *Homo Faber*

reportedly *adv*
allegedly, supposedly, apparently, by all accounts
FORMAL ostensibly, putatively

reporter *n*
journalist, correspondent, columnist, newspaperman, newspaperwoman, newscaster, anchor, commentator, announcer, cub
COLLOQ. hack

repose¹ *n, v*

♦ *n*

moments of repose
rest, calm, peace, restfulness, ease, relaxation, respite, stillness, tranquillity, serenity, calmness, composure, inactivity, quietness, quiet, poise, equanimity, dignity, self-possession, sleep, night-rest, kef
FORMAL slumber, aplomb, quietude
E∃ activity, strain, stress

♦ *v*

lie, lay, lean, rest, recline, relax, sleep
FORMAL slumber
COLLOQ. laze

repose² *v*
repose confidence in someone
place, put, set, rest, store, lodge, deposit, confide, entrust, invest
OLD affy

repository *n*
store, storehouse, depository, depot, warehouse, safe, bank, treasury, vault, archive, container, receptacle, magazine

reprehensible *adj*
disgraceful, deplorable, discreditable, objectionable, shameful, unworthy, blamable, blameworthy, bad, ill,

remiss, censurable, condemnable, delinquent, erring, errant, ignoble, base
FORMAL culpable, opprobrious
E∃ creditable, good, praiseworthy

represent *v*
1 STAND FOR, symbolize, designate, denote, mean, mark, be, amount to, constitute, correspond to, be equivalent to
2 ACT FOR, stand for, speak for, act/speak on behalf of, act as representative of, act as spokesperson for, act/speak in the name of, appear for/on behalf of, deputize for
3 EXEMPLIFY, typify, stand for, epitomize, embody, personify, show
4 DEPICT, portray, describe, picture, display, exhibit, draw, sketch, illustrate, evoke, characterize
OLD refer
5 ACT AS, enact, perform, appear as

representation *n*
1 LIKENESS, image, icon, picture, portrait, drawing, illustration, sketch, model, statue, bust, tableau, depiction, portrayal, description, account, explanation
FORMAL delineation
2 REPRESENTATIVE, delegate, delegation, deputy, deputation, proxy, stand-in, spokesperson, spokesman, spokeswoman, envoy, ambassador, mouthpiece, MP, member of parliament, Congressman, Congresswoman, councillor
3 PERFORMANCE, production, presentation, play, show, spectacle
4 *make representations*
request, report, account, statement, allegation, protest, complaint

representative *n, adj*

♦ *n*

1 DELEGATE, delegation, deputy, deputation, proxy, stand-in, spokesperson, spokesman, spokeswoman, envoy, ambassador, mouthpiece, MP, member of parliament, councillor
2 *a sales representative*
salesman, saleswoman, salesperson, traveller, commercial traveller, travelling salesman, commissioner, agent; *N Am* drummer
OLD bagman, rider
COLLOQ. rep, knight of the road

♦ *adj*

1 TYPICAL, illustrative, exemplary, characteristic, usual, normal, symbolic, indicative
FORMAL archetypal
2 DELEGATED, chosen, elected, elective, nominated, appointed, commissioned, authorized, decentralized, devolved
E∃ unrepresentative, atypical

repress *v*
1 INHIBIT, check, control, curb, restrain, suppress, bottle up, hold back, stifle, smother, muffle, silence, keep back, swallow, cork (up)
COLLOQ. sit on, bite your lip
2 *repress a revolt*
quell, put down, crush, quash, subdue, overpower, overcome, master, dominate, domineer, oppress, stifle, sneap
OLD reprime; (*Spenser*) repeal
FORMAL subjugate, vanquish

repressed *adj*
frustrated, inhibited, withdrawn, introverted, self-restrained
COLLOQ. hung-up, uptight
E∃ uninhibited, relaxed

repression *n*
1 OPPRESSION, suppression, quashing, quelling, crushing, suffocation, gagging, censorship, authoritarianism, dictatorship, despotism, tyranny, domination, control, constraint, coercion
FORMAL subjugation

2 *repression of your feelings*
suppression, inhibition, restraint, control, holding-back, stifling, smothering, muffling

repressive *adj*
oppressive, authoritarian, despotic, tyrannical, dictatorial, dominating, autocratic, totalitarian, absolute, harsh, cruel, severe, strict, tough, coercive

reprieve *v, n*
♦ *v*
pardon, forgive, acquit, show mercy/pity, spare, rescue, redeem, relieve, respite
OLD repreeve, reprive
COLLOQ. let off, let off the hook, forgive and forget
♦ *n*
pardon, amnesty, suspension, postponement, deferment, stay of execution, remission, respite, relief
OLD (*Shakesp*) repreeve; (*Spenser*) reprive
FORMAL abatement, abeyance
COLLOQ. let-up

reprimand *v, n*
♦ *v*
rebuke, reprove, reproach, scold, chide, lecture, criticize, censure, slate, blame, lambast, bring/call to account, lace into, jobe; *Scot* targe; *Aust* rouse on
FORMAL admonish, berate, castigate
COLLOQ. tell off, tick off, take/pull apart, bawl out, bounce, carpet, catch it, chew out, see off, give someone a ticking-off, dress down, give someone a dressing-down, haul over the coals, read the riot act to, rap over the knuckles, give someone a rap over the knuckles, give someone a flea in their ear, give someone an earful, give someone a piece of your mind, shoot down in flames, tear a strip off someone; *Scot* give someone their kale through the reek
SLANG bollock; *Aust* go off at
♦ *n*
rebuke, reproof, reproach, lecture, censure, blame, schooling, tongue-lashing
FORMAL upbraiding, admonition, castigation
OLD check
COLLOQ. telling-off, ticking-off, talking-to, dressing-down, slap/smack on the wrist, rap over the knuckles, a flea in someone's ear, rocket, wigging, carpeting, earful

reprisal *n*
retaliation, counter-attack, retribution, requital, revenge, vengeance, recrimination, redress
OLD ultion
COLLOQ. tit for tat, eye for an eye, a taste of someone's own medicine

reprise *n, v*
♦ *n*
repetition, restatement, recapitulation, quoting, copying, echoing
FORMAL reiteration, iterance, iteration, rehearsal
♦ *v*
play, sing, put on, perform, act, relate, narrate

reproach *v, n*
♦ *v*
rebuke, reprove, reprimand, upbraid, scold, chide, reprehend, blame, censure, condemn, slate, criticize, find fault with, defame
FORMAL disparage, admonish
COLLOQ. tell off, tick off, take/pull apart, bawl out, bounce, carpet, catch it, chew out, see off, give someone a ticking-off, dress down, give someone a dressing-down, haul over the coals, read the riot act to, rap over the knuckles, give someone a rap over the knuckles, give someone a flea in their ear, give someone an earful, give someone a piece of your mind, shoot down in flames, tear a strip off someone

♦ *n*
1 REBUKE, reproof, reprimand, scolding, blame, censure, condemnation, criticism, disapproval, scorn, contempt
FORMAL admonition
COLLOQ. telling-off, ticking-off, talking-to, dressing-down, slap/smack on the wrist, rap over the knuckles, a flea in someone's ear, rocket, wigging, carpeting, earful
2 DISGRACE, shame, disrepute, disrespect, discredit, stigma, dishonour, degradation, blemish, blot, smear, stain, slur
FORMAL ignominy, opprobrium, obloquy

reproachful *adj*
reproving, upbraiding, scolding, censorious, critical, fault-finding, disapproving, disappointed, scornful
FORMAL castigating, disparaging, opprobrious
F3 complimentary

reprobate *adj, n*
♦ *adj*
immoral, corrupt, depraved, sinful, unprincipled, vile, wicked, bad, shameless, incorrigible, dissolute, degenerate, base, abandoned, hardened, damned
FORMAL profligate, reprobative, reprobatory
F3 upright, virtuous
♦ *n*
degenerate, miscreant, rake, *roué*, wrongdoer, criminal, evildoer, sinner, rogue, rascal, scoundrel, scamp, scallywag, villain, vagabond, wretch, mischief-maker, ne'er-do-well, knave, dastard, troublemaker
FORMAL profligate

reproduce *v*
1 COPY, transcribe, print, duplicate, photocopy, Xerox®, Photostat®, mirror, echo, repeat, imitate, emulate, match, follow, cline, ape, mimic, simulate, recreate, remake, redo, reconstruct, enlarge, facsimile, express, reflect, render, pirate
TECHNICAL autotype, phototype, hectograph
OLD (*Shakesp*) refigure
FORMAL replicate
2 BREED, spawn, bear young, give birth, generate, propagate, multiply, proliferate, clone, regenerate
TECHNICAL gemmate
FORMAL procreate, replicate

reproduction *n*
1 COPY, print, picture, duplicate, photocopy, Xerox®, Photostat®, facsimile, replica, clone, imitation
2 BREEDING, generation, propagation, multiplication
FORMAL procreation
F3 1 original
Related adjective: genital

reproductive *adj*
generative, sexual, sex, genital, propagative
FORMAL procreative, progenitive

reproof *n*
rebuke, reproach, reprimand, scolding, censure, condemnation, criticism
FORMAL upbraiding, admonition, castigation, disapprobation, berating
COLLOQ. telling-off, ticking-off, talking-to, dressing-down, slap/smack on the wrist, rap over the knuckles, a flea in someone's ear, rocket, wigging, carpeting, earful
F3 praise

reprove *v*
rebuke, reproach, reprimand, scold, chide, reprehend, censure, slate, condemn, criticize; *Aust* rouse on
FORMAL upbraid, admonish, berate, castigate
COLLOQ. tell off, tick off, take/pull apart, bawl out, bounce, carpet, catch it, chew out, see off, give someone a ticking-off, dress down, give someone a dressing-down, haul over the coals, read the riot act to, rap over the knuckles, give someone a rap over the knuckles, give someone a flea in their ear, give someone an earful, give someone a piece of your mind, shoot down in flames, tear a strip off someone
F3 praise

reptile

Reptiles include:

alligator	green turtle	slowworm (or
chameleon	hawksbill turtle	blindworm)
crocodile	iguana	snake
frilled lizard	lizard	terrapin
gecko		tortoise
giant tortoise	skink	turtle

See also **dinosaur**; **snake**.

repudiate *v*
reject, denounce, deny, disown, discard, retract, reverse, revoke, cast off, desert, abandon, repel, divorce
TECHNICAL notchel
FORMAL abjure, disaffirm, disavow, disclaim, disprofess, forsake, rescind, renounce
COLLOQ. not touch with a barge pole, have nothing to do with, turn your back on
E3 admit, own

repudiation *n*
rejection, denial, disclaimer, disowning
FORMAL renunciation, abjuration, disaffirmance, disaffirmation, disavowal, recantation, retraction
E3 acceptance

repugnance *n*
reluctance, distaste, dislike, aversion, hatred, loathing, abhorrence, horror, repulsion, revulsion, nausea, disgust
OLD reluctation, repugnancy
FORMAL odium, antipathy
COLLOQ. allergy
E3 liking, pleasure, delight

repugnant *adj*
repellent, objectionable, obnoxious, offensive, unacceptable, antagonistic, antipathetic, hostile, alien, averse, opposed, distasteful, inconsistent, incompatible, contradictory, adverse, disgusting, foul, vile, hateful, horrid, abhorrent, abominable, revolting, sickening, nauseating, loathsome, odious
FORMAL inimical
E3 acceptable, consistent, pleasant

repulse *v, n*
♦ *v*
repel, drive back, defeat, beat off, check, rebuff, reject, refuse, disregard, disdain, snub, spurn
♦ *n*
check, defeat, disappointment, failure, rebuff, refusal, rejection, repudiation, reverse, snub, spurning
E3 acceptance, success

repulsion *n*
revulsion, disgust, distaste, hatred, aversion, repugnance, abhorrence, loathing
FORMAL detestation, disrelish, repellence, repellency
E3 liking

repulsive *adj*
repellent, revolting, disgusting, nauseating, sickening, offensive, shocking, distasteful, objectionable, off-putting, obnoxious, foul, vile, nasty, loathsome, abominable, abhorrent, contemptible, odious, repugnant, despicable, hateful, horrid, unpleasant, disagreeable, ugly, hideous, unattractive, forbidding
OLD evil-favoured, loth
FORMAL reprehensible, heinous
COLLOQ. gross, icky
E3 attractive, pleasant, delightful

repulsively *adv*
unpleasantly, disagreeably, disgustingly, shockingly, abominably, objectionably, despicably, obnoxiously, nauseatingly
E3 attractively, delightfully

reputable *adj*
respectable, respected, reliable, dependable, trustworthy, upright, honourable, honest, creditable, admirable, of high/ good repute, well-thought-of, esteemed, worthy, good, virtuous, excellent, irreproachable
FORMAL estimable
E3 disreputable, infamous

reputation *n*
1 NAME, good name, opinion, credit, repute, character, standing, stature, status, rank, position, infamy, notoriety
FORMAL estimation
2 FAME, renown, celebrity, distinction, prestige, esteem, image, character, good name, good standing, honour, respect, respectability

> **QUOTATIONS**
> Reputation, reputation, reputation! O – I ha' lost my reputation, I ha' lost the immortal part of myself, and what remains is bestial
> WILLIAM SHAKESPEARE, *Othello*
>
> Reputation is fine but you have to keep justifying it. In a sense, it makes it harder because people's expectations of you are higher. So, you have to fulfil those expectations. Or, try to exceed those expectations. But, it becomes more difficult as time goes on
> SIR DEREK JACOBI

repute *n*
reputation, name, standing, stature, renown, fame, good name, celebrity, distinction, esteem, estimation
E3 infamy

reputed *adj*
alleged, supposed, said, rumoured, believed, thought, considered, regarded, reckoned, estimated, held, judged, seeming, assumed, presumed, apparent
FORMAL ostensible
E3 actual, true

reputedly *adv*
allegedly, apparently, seemingly, supposedly, by all accounts, reputatively
FORMAL ostensibly
E3 actually

request *v, n*
♦ *v*
ask for, demand, require, seek, desire, beg, petition, apply for, call for, appeal, invite, order, send for, wish, write in/off for
OLD bespeak, require
FORMAL solicit, entreat, requisition, supplicate, beseech, adjure, impetrate
COLLOQ. put in for; *N Am* hit
♦ *n*
appeal, call, demand, desire, application, suit, petition, petitioning, plea, pleading, prayer, invitation
OLD boon, behest
FORMAL requisition, solicitation, entreaty, supplication, imploration

require *v*
1 NEED, want, wish, desire, crave, lack, miss, be short of, be deficient in
2 *you are required to attend*
oblige, force, compel, necessitate, make, ask, request, call on, instruct, direct, command, order, demand, entail, insist on, take, involve
FORMAL constrain, enjoin

required *adj*
compulsory, essential, obligatory, recommended, advised, demanded, necessary, stipulated, set, needed, unavoidable, vital
FORMAL mandatory, prescribed, requisite
E3 optional, inessential

requirement n

need, necessity, essential, sine qua non, demand, lack, want, stipulation, condition, term, specification, proviso, prerequisite, qualification, provision, obligation, occasion
FORMAL requisite, precondition, desideratum
COLLOQ. must

requisite adj, n

♦ adj
required, needed, needful, necessary, essential, indispensable, obligatory, compulsory, set, prerequisite, vital
FORMAL prescribed, mandatory
♦ n
requirement, essential, due, necessity, need, condition, prerequisite, stipulation, specification, qualification, sine qua non
FORMAL desideratum, precondition, desiderative
COLLOQ. must
☒ inessential

requisition v, n

♦ v
commandeer, take, take over, take possession of, use, confiscate, seize, occupy, request, put in for, demand, summons
FORMAL appropriate
♦ n
commandeering, confiscation, seizure, takeover, occupation, order, use, application, summons, request, call, demand
FORMAL appropriation

requital n

amends, redress, restitution, satisfaction, recompense, compensation, indemnification, indemnity, repayment, payment, pay-off, reparation
FORMAL quittance

requite v

repay, reciprocate, respond, retaliate, return, pay, pay off, recompense, reimburse, remunerate, reward, satisfy, redress, even up on, compensate, avenge
OLD requight, apay, quit

rescind v

cancel, set aside, overturn, quash, reverse, recall, repeal, annul, invalidate, void, negate
FORMAL revoke, abrogate, countermand, nullify, retract
☒ enforce

rescission n

cancellation, negation, reversal, invalidation, annulment, recall, repeal
FORMAL abrogation, nullification, rescindment, retraction, revocation, voidance
☒ enforcement

rescue v, n

♦ v
save, recover, salvage, deliver, free, set free, liberate, emancipate, extricate, release, relieve, bring off, pluck, redeem, ransom, reprieve, retrieve, come/go to someone's rescue
OLD reskew
COLLOQ. throw a lifeline to, pull the chestnuts out of the fire
☒ capture, imprison
♦ n
saving, recovery, salvage, deliverance, liberation, freeing, release, emancipation, relief, redemption, salvation
☒ capture

research n, v

♦ n
investigation, inquiry, fact-finding, groundwork, examination, analysis, assessment, scrutiny, inspection, testing, test(s), study, review, search, probe, exploration, experiment, experimentation

♦ v
investigate, examine, look into, analyse, scrutinize, study, inspect, search, probe, test, assess, review, explore, experiment

researcher n

investigator, student, analyst, inspector, inquirer, field worker, boffin

resemblance n

likeness, similarity, sameness, conformity, nearness, closeness, affinity, uniformity, parallel, parallelism, comparison, comparability, agreement, analogy, correspondence, image, facsimile
FORMAL parity, similitude, congruity
☒ dissimilarity

resemble v

be like, look like, be similar to, bear resemblance to, take after, favour, mirror, echo, duplicate, parallel, approach
☒ differ from

resent v

grudge, begrudge, envy, feel bitter about, feel aggrieved at, be angry at, take offence at, take umbrage at, take amiss, object to, grumble at, take exception to, dislike
SLANG Aust & NZ have a derry on
☒ accept, like

resentful adj

grudging, envious, jealous, bitter, embittered, hurt, wounded, offended, aggrieved, put out, piqued, incensed, in high dudgeon, indignant, angry, irritated, irked, vindictive, malicious, spiteful
COLLOQ. miffed, peeved
☒ satisfied, contented

resentment n

grudge, envy, jealousy, bitterness, spite, malice, ill-will, ill-feeling, bad feeling, hard feelings, (high) dudgeon, bad blood, ill blood, animosity, hostility, hurt, umbrage, pique, offence, displeasure, irritation, indignation, annoyance, ire, vexation, anger, vindictiveness, snuff
COLLOQ. miff
SLANG Aust derry
☒ contentment, happiness

reservation n

1 DOUBT(S), scepticism, misgiving(s), qualm(s), scruple(s), hesitancy, hesitation, second thoughts, arrière-pensée
FORMAL demur
2 BOOKING, advance booking, engagement, appointment, arrangement, order, prearrangement
3 RESERVE, preserve, park, sanctuary, homeland, enclave, tract
COLLOQ. N Am res
4 PROVISO, stipulation, qualification, condition, limitation
TECHNICAL salvo
5 PRESERVATION, keeping, storage, protection, defence, maintenance, guarding, safeguarding, safekeeping, safety, security, conservation, upkeep, support, retention, upholding, continuation, perpetuation
☒ destruction, ruin

■ without reservation

unreservedly, completely, entirely, utterly, wholeheartedly, outright, unhesitatingly, without hesitation, without qualification
COLLOQ. gloves-off; Aust & NZ boots and all

reserve v, n, adj

♦ v
1 SET ASIDE, earmark, keep, retain, hold back, keep back, save, store, lay aside, put on one side, put to one side, set apart, stockpile, hoard, accumulate, ring-fence
2 reserve a seat
book, engage, order, arrange for, secure, prearrange
3 DELAY, postpone, defer, put off, suspend, shelve, hold over, adjourn
☒ 1 use up

♦ *n*
1 STORE, stock, supply, fund, stockpile, pool, reservoir, bank, cache, hoard, accumulation, savings
2 SUBSTITUTE, replacement, stand-in, understudy, fill-in, supply, proxy, surrogate, successor
3 RESERVATION, preserve, park, area, sanctuary, tract, enclave
4 SHYNESS, reticence, unresponsiveness, secretiveness, coldness, coolness, aloofness, detachment, modesty, restraint, self-restraint, distance, remoteness, unapproachability
5 *military reserves*
backup, auxiliaries, support, help, reinforcements, additional soldiers/troops/police officers, supplementaries
E₃ 4 friendliness, openness, approachability
♦ *adj*
spare, substitute, additional, auxiliary, alternative, extra, stand-in, secondary
■ in reserve
for use when needed, available, to hand, in hand, unused, stored, spare, set aside

reserved *adj*
1 BOOKED, engaged, ordered, arranged, prearranged, taken, spoken for, set aside, earmarked, meant, intended, designated, destined, saved, held, kept, retained
2 SHY, retiring, backward, reticent, unresponsive, unforthcoming, uncommunicative, secretive, silent, taciturn, introverted, unsociable, cool, cold, aloof, standoffish, unapproachable, modest, diffident, restrained, cautious, distant, remote
E₃ 1 unreserved, free, available **2** friendly, open

reservoir *n*
1 LAKE, pond, pool, cistern; *Scot* loch; *Aust* gilgai
OLD reservatory
2 TANK, cistern, vat, basin, container, receptacle, holder, header, header tank
TECHNICAL sump, hot well, steam chest, wind chest
OLD TECHNICAL urinary
3 STORE, stockpile, stock, supply, source, reserves, accumulation, fund, holder, bank, well, fountain
FORMAL repository, reservatory

reshuffle *n, v*
♦ *n*
reorganization, upheaval, redistribution, regrouping, rearrangement, realignment, restructuring, revision, change, interchange
COLLOQ. shake-up
♦ *v*
reorganize, restructure, shake up, change, interchange, shift, shuffle, revise, rearrange, regroup, realign, redistribute

reside *v*
1 LIVE, inhabit, lodge, stay, board, occupy, settle, remain
FORMAL dwell, sojourn
2 BE PRESENT, exist, lie, rest, be inherent, be contained
FORMAL dwell, abide

residence *n*
home, house, flat, apartment, seat, place, lodgings, quarters, hall, manor, mansion, mansionary, palace, villa, country house, country seat, stay, lodging
FORMAL dwelling, habitation, domicile, abode, sojourn
COLLOQ. pad, digs

resident *n, adj*
♦ *n*
inhabitant, citizen, local, householder, occupant, occupier, tenant, lodger, guest, patient, inmate, client, transient
OLD ledger, resiant
FORMAL resider, dweller, sojourner
E₃ non-resident
♦ *adj*
live-in, living-in, dwelling, local, permanent, inhabiting, inhabitant, neighbourhood, settled, stationary, ledger
TECHNICAL commorant
OLD gremial, resiant

FORMAL *en poste*
E₃ non-resident

residential *adj*
commuter, suburban, dormitory
FORMAL exurban

residual *adj*
remaining, left-over, unused, unconsumed, net, excess, surplus

residue *n*
remainder, remains, remnant, rest, surplus, excess, extra, overflow, balance, difference, lees, dregs, leftovers, carry-over
FORMAL residuum
E₃ core

resign *v*
stand down, retire, step down, leave, abdicate, vacate, give up, throw up, hand in your notice, give in your notice, for(e)go, waive, surrender, yield, withdraw, abandon, submit; *Scot* demit
OLD forelend
FORMAL renounce, relinquish, forsake
COLLOQ. quit
E₃ join
■ resign yourself
reconcile yourself, accept, comply, bow, submit, yield, come to terms, put something behind you, turn your face to the wall
FORMAL acquiesce
E₃ resist

resignation *n*
1 STANDING-DOWN, stepping-down, abdication, retirement, departure, notice, letter of resignation, surrender, giving-up, waiving
FORMAL renunciation, relinquishment
2 ACCEPTANCE, reconciliation, submission, non-resistance, passivity, patience, stoicism, yielding, compliance, defeatism
FORMAL acquiescence
E₃ 2 resistance

> **QUOTATIONS**
> Please accept my resignation. I don't want to belong to any club that will accept me as a member
> GROUCHO MARX

resigned *adj*
reconciled, philosophical, stoical, patient, long-suffering, unprotesting, uncomplaining, unresisting, passive, submissive, yielding, defeatist
FORMAL acquiescent
E₃ resistant, protesting

resignedly *adv*
stoically, philosophically, submissively, uncomplainingly, patiently

resilience *n*
1 FLEXIBILITY, elasticity, springiness, spring, pliability, plasticity, suppleness, give, bounciness, bounce, recoil
2 STRENGTH, toughness, hardiness, adaptability, buoyancy, irrepressibility, unshockability
E₃ inflexibility, rigidity

resilient *adj*
1 *resilient material*
flexible, pliable, supple, plastic, elastic, springy, bouncy, rubbery
2 STRONG, tough, hardy, adaptable, buoyant, springing, irrepressible, unshockable
E₃ 1 rigid, brittle **2** weak

resist *v*
oppose, defy, confront, face, fight (off), struggle, contend, battle, combat, weather, withstand, defend, buck, stand up to, stand against, stick out, hold out against, obstruct, repel, counter, counteract, check, stop, halt, avoid, refuse, prevent, hinder, thwart, impede, restrain, curb, stem, wear

TECHNICAL deforce
OLD gainstrive
SLANG *Aust* jack up
⊟ submit, accept

resistance *n*
opposition, defiance, confrontation, fight, fighting, struggle,
combat, contention, counteraction, battle, withstanding,
repulsion, avoidance, refusal, prevention, thwarting,
hindrance, obstruction, impedance, impediment, restraint
FORMAL intransigence
⊟ acceptance, submission

resistant *adj*
1 OPPOSED, antagonistic, defiant, unyielding, unwilling
OLD renitent
FORMAL intransigent
2 PROOF, impervious, waterproof, immune, unaffected,
invulnerable, unsusceptible, tough, strong, windproof,
shellproof, shockproof
⊟ 1 compliant, yielding

resolute *adj*
determined, resolved, intent, decided, dedicated, constant,
serious, earnest, adamant, stalwart, set, strong, fixed,
unwavering, unyielding, unswerving, inflexible, staunch,
firm, steadfast, steady, relentless, single-minded,
persevering, dogged, tenacious, stubborn, obstinate, strong-
willed, undaunted, dauntless, unflinching, bold, diehard,
granite, hardy; *N Am* flat-footed
FORMAL obdurate
⊟ irresolute, weak-willed, half-hearted

resolutely *adv*
firmly, steadily, strongly, with determination,
unwaveringly, unswervingly, steadfastly, relentlessly,
single-mindedly, unflinchingly, adamantly, inflexibly,
seriously, earnestly, staunchly, obstinately, stubbornly,
dauntlessly
⊟ irresolutely, half-heartedly

resolution *n*
1 DECISION, judgement, finding, declaration, proposition,
motion, decree, verdict
2 DETERMINATION, resolve, willpower, commitment,
dedication, devotion, constancy, firmness, intentness,
seriousness, earnestness, steadfastness, persistence,
perseverance, doggedness, inflexibility, tenacity, zeal,
courage, boldness
3 SOLVING, answer, solution, unravelling, disentangling,
working out, sorting out
⊟ 2 half-heartedness, uncertainty, indecision

resolve *v, n*
♦ *v*
1 DECIDE, make up your mind, determine, fix, settle (on),
conclude, talk out, patch
2 SOLVE, answer, unravel, untie, disentangle, sort out,
straighten out, work out
OLD dissolve
3 BREAK UP, break down, analyse, reduce, divide, separate,
dissolve, disintegrate, detail, convert, anatomize, itemize
TECHNICAL decompose, factorize, sublate
♦ *n*
determination, willpower, commitment, dedication,
devotion, constancy, firmness, intentness, seriousness,
earnestness, steadfastness, persistence, perseverance,
doggedness, inflexibility, tenacity, zeal, courage, boldness,
sense of purpose, vow
COLLOQ. bottle, pecker
⊟ indecision

resonance *n*
depth, strength, richness, vibrancy, fullness, reverberation
FORMAL canorousness, plangency

resonant *adj*
deep, strong, sonorous, ringing, booming, rich, fruity,
vibrant, full, plummy, resounding, reverberant,
reverberating, echoing, pear-shaped

FORMAL canorous, plangent
⊟ weak, faint, tinny

resonate *v*
resound, reverberate, echo, re-echo, ring, sound, boom,
thunder

resort *v, n*
♦ *v*
go, visit, frequent, patronize, haunt
FORMAL repair
♦ *n*
1 HOLIDAY CENTRE, centre, holiday destination, spot, health
resort, spa
2 RECOURSE, refuge, course (of action), measure, step,
alternative, option, chance, possibility
■ **resort to**
turn to, use, utilize, make use of, avail yourself of, fall
back on, have recourse to, employ, exercise
■ **in the last resort**
ultimately, finally, eventually, at last, in the end, after all,
sooner or later, fundamentally
COLLOQ. at the end of the day

resound *v*
resonate, reverberate, echo, re-echo, ring, sound, boom,
thunder

resounding *adj*
1 RESONANT, reverberating, echoing, ringing, loud,
sonorous, booming, resonating, thunderous, full, rich,
vibrant
2 *a resounding victory*
decisive, conclusive, impressive, striking, outstanding,
roaring, great, memorable, remarkable, notable, emphatic,
thorough
⊟ 1 faint

resource *n*
1 *a shortage of resources*
materials, supplies, reserves, holdings, funds, money,
wealth, riches, capital, assets, property, means, power,
wherewithal
2 SUPPLY, reserve, pool, accumulation, stockpile, store,
fund, source, contrivance, device, course, resort, expedient
3 RESOURCEFULNESS, initiative, enterprise, ingenuity,
inventiveness, wit, imagination, talent, ability, capability
OLD artifice, chevisance

resourceful *adj*
ingenious, imaginative, creative, inventive, enterprising,
innovative, original, versatile, clever, bright, sharp, quick-
witted, witty, with your wits about you, able, capable,
talented, adroit; *Scot* fendy

resourceless *adj*
inadequate, useless, hopeless, helpless, feeble, feckless,
shiftless
⊟ unimaginative

respect *v, n*
♦ *v*
1 ADMIRE, regard, have a good opinion of, think highly of,
hold in high regard, set great store by, appreciate, value,
praise, honour, approve of, revere, esteem
FORMAL venerate
See Synonym nuances panel at **admire**.
2 OBEY, observe, heed, comply with, follow, adhere to,
honour, fulfil
3 CONSIDER, show consideration for, pay attention to, take
into account, show regard for
FORMAL take cognizance of
⊟ 1 despise, scorn 2 ignore, disobey
♦ *n*
1 ADMIRATION, appreciation, recognition, honour,
deference, reverence, high opinion, esteem, regard, high
regard, homage
FORMAL veneration, approbation, obeisance
2 CONSIDERATION, attention, attentiveness, notice, regard,
heed, thoughtfulness, politeness, courtesy
FORMAL cognizance

3 GREETINGS, compliments, regards, salutations, best wishes, good wishes
FORMAL devoirs
4 *in every respect*
point, aspect, facet, feature, characteristic, particular, detail, sense, matter, way, regard, reference, bearing, relation, connection
E∃ 1 disrespect
■ **with respect to**
with regard to, in regard to, as regards, concerning, with reference to, in relation to, in connection with, re, about, as to, on the subject of
FORMAL apropos

respectability *n*
worthiness, trustworthiness, integrity, honesty, uprightness, decency, gentility

respectable *adj*
1 REPUTABLE, honourable, worthy, respected, dignified, upright, honest, above-board, trustworthy, decent, superior, good, presentable, neat, tidy, clean, clean-living, clean-cut; *dialect* sponsible; *Scot* menseful
FORMAL decorous, salubrious
2 ACCEPTABLE, tolerable, passable, adequate, fair, fairly good, nice, reasonable, all right, appreciable, considerable
COLLOQ. not bad, OK
E∃ 1 dishonourable, disreputable **2** inadequate, paltry

respected *adj*
admired, valued, esteemed, highly esteemed, highly regarded, highly valued, held in high regard, thought highly of

respectful *adj*
deferential, reverent, reverential, humble, polite, well-mannered, courtly, dutiful, courteous, civil, subservient
E∃ disrespectful

respectfully *adv*
courteously, civilly, politely, deferentially, reverently, reverentially
E∃ disrespectfully

respecting *prep*
about, concerning, considering, in respect of, with regard to, regarding, with respect to, vis-à-vis

respective *adj*
corresponding, relevant, various, several, separate, individual, personal, own, specific, particular, special

respectively *adv*
correspondingly, in the order stated/given/listed, in turn, one by one, individually, specifically, particularly, specially

respite *n*
1 PAUSE, rest, relief, break, adjournment, intermission, recess, relaxation, interval, interruption, halt, gap, lull, reprieve, truce
FORMAL cessation, hiatus
COLLOQ. breather, let-up
2 DELAY, reprieve, postponement, deferment, remission, stay, suspension, moratorium
OLD frist
FORMAL abatement

resplendent *adj*
glorious, magnificent, splendid, dazzling, shining, radiant, brilliant, bright, irradiant, luminous, beaming, gleaming, glittering
FORMAL effulgent, fulgent, lustrous, refulgent
COLLOQ. splendiferous
E∃ dull

respond *v*
answer, reply, acknowledge, retort, rejoin, answer back, react, return, counter, reciprocate
See Synonym nuances panel at **reply.**

response *n*
answer, reply, acknowledgement, retort, rejoinder, riposte, return, reaction, feedback

OLD *(Spenser)* respondence
COLLOQ. comeback
E∃ query

responsibility *n*
1 DUTY, obligation, burden, onus, charge, care, role, task, authority, power, trust, business, affair, concern
COLLOQ. baby, pidgin
2 FAULT, blame, guilt, answerability, accountability
FORMAL culpability
3 DEPENDABILITY, reliability, conscientiousness, trustworthiness, honesty, soundness, maturity, adulthood, stability

> **QUOTATIONS**
> In dreams begins responsibility
>   W B YEATS, *Responsibilities*

responsible *adj*
1 IN CHARGE OF, in control of, controlling, managing, leading, accountable, answerable
2 TO BLAME, guilty, at fault, blameworthy, liable, answerable, accountable
FORMAL culpable
3 DEPENDABLE, reliable, conscientious, trustworthy, honest, sound, steady, sober, mature, adult, stable, reasonable, sensible, rational, sane, level-headed
4 IMPORTANT, authoritative, powerful, executive, decision-making
COLLOQ. high-level
E∃ 3 irresponsible, unreliable, untrustworthy

> **SYNONYM NUANCES**
>
> *sense 3*
> Most of these synonyms are, naturally, approbatory in tone.
>   Both **dependable** and **reliable** suggest someone who can be counted on, while **trustworthy** and **honest** clearly suggest someone morally deserving of peoples' confidence. **Conscientious** is suggestive of a high degree of diligence; the terms **sound**, **steady** and **stable** are more appropriate if you want to suggest firmness of character, and **mature** and **adult** have suggestions of emotional responsibility: *women show a more adult approach to driving, and tend not to show off.*
>   The terms **reasonable**, **rational** and **sane** put more emphasis on intellectual responsibility and judiciousness: *he had a sane approach to the controversy, seeing both sides,* while **sensible** and **level-headed** emphasize the use of common sense: *he is sensible enough to become a nurse: as it was raining, he drove at a sensible speed.*

responsibly *adv*
sensibly, reasonably, steadily, dependably, reliably, honestly, conscientiously, rationally
E∃ irresponsibly

responsive *adj*
alert, aware, sensitive, awake, open, sharp, quick, reactive, amenable, receptive, susceptible, sympathetic, perceptive, forthcoming, impressionable, alive, respondent, teachable, stimulable
TECHNICAL excitable
FORMAL responsorial, sentient
COLLOQ. on the ball, with it, swinging, switched on
E∃ unresponsive

responsiveness *n*
alertness, awareness, openness, receptiveness, susceptibility, sensitivity

rest[1] *n, v*
 ♦ *n*
1 LEISURE, relaxation, lie-down, sleep, snooze, nap, siesta, idleness, inactivity, ease, motionlessness, standstill, stillness, tranquillity, calm
FORMAL repose, quietude, slumber
COLLOQ. R & R

2 BREAK, pause, breathing space, intermission, interlude, interval, recess, holiday, vacation, time off, halt, lull, respite
FORMAL cessation
COLLOQ. breather
3 SUPPORT, prop, stand, base, holder
⊟ **1** action, activity, work
♦ v
1 PAUSE, halt, stop, cease
2 RELAX, sit (down), recline, lounge, laze, lie down, sleep, snooze, doze
FORMAL repose
COLLOQ. put your feet up, take it easy, recharge your batteries, veg (out)
3 DEPEND, rely, hinge, hang, lie, be based
4 LEAN, prop, support, stand, steady
⊟ **1** continue **2** work

rest² n, v
♦ n
the rest of us stayed behind
remainder, others, balance, surplus, excess, residue, remains, leftovers, remnant(s)
FORMAL residuum
♦ v
continue, remain, stay, last, endure, persist

restaurant

Types of restaurant include:

bistro	eating-house	pizzeria
brasserie	fast food restaurant	pull-in
buffet	fish-and-chip shop	refectory
burger bar	slang greasy spoon	rotisserie
café	grill	sandwich bar
cafeteria	grill room	self-service restau-
canteen	health food	rant
carvery	restaurant	snack-bar
Irish colloq.	ice-cream parlour	steakhouse
chipper	Internet café	sushi bar
colloq. chippy	N Am	taqueria
coffee bar	luncheonette	taverna
creperie	mess room	teahouse
curry house	milk bar	tea room
N Am diner	motorway café	tea shop
dining-car	NAAFI (Navy	transport café
dining room	Army and Air	trattoria
drivethrough	Force Institutes)	

---

restful adj
relaxing, soothing, calming, calm, tranquil, serene, peaceful, quiet, still, placid, undisturbed, relaxed, comfortable, leisurely, unhurried
FORMAL languid
⊟ tiring, restless

restitution n
amends, reparation, requital, restoration, restoring, return, satisfaction, redress, repayment, damages, compensation, recompense, remuneration, refund, reimbursement, indemnification, indemnity

restive adj
1 UNRULY, impatient, wayward, wilful, turbulent, uncontrollable, undisciplined, unmanageable
FORMAL recalcitrant, refractory
2 RESTLESS, agitated, fidgety, fidgeting, unsettled, nervous, uneasy, anxious, fretful, tense, on edge
COLLOQ. edgy, jumpy, uptight
⊟ **2** calm, relaxed

restiveness n
unruliness, waywardness, wilfulness, uncontrollableness, unmanageableness, restlessness, turbulence
⊟ calmness

restless adj
1 FIDGETY, fidgeting, unruly, turbulent, impatient, changeable; Scot wanrestful

FORMAL restive
COLLOQ. having ants in your pants
2 AGITATED, nervous, anxious, worried, uneasy, fretful, troubled, unsettled, on edge, unquiet
TECHNICAL agitato
OLD disquiet
COLLOQ. edgy, jittery, jumpy, uptight
SLANG Aust toey
3 SLEEPLESS, uncomfortable, broken, disturbed, tossing and turning
⊟ **1** still, motionless **2** calm, relaxed **3** restful, comfortable

restlessly adv
nervously, anxiously, fretfully, impatiently, turbulently
⊟ calmly

restlessness n
agitation, disturbance, unsettledness, uneasiness, unrest, turbulence, turmoil, worriedness, anxiety, nervousness, fermentation, fitfulness, insomnia, fretfulness, bustle, disquiet, hurry, activity, dynamism, instability, movement, inconstancy, transience
TECHNICAL jactitation
FORMAL inquietude, restiveness
COLLOQ. edginess, jitters, jumpiness, heebie-jeebies
SLANG gate fever
⊟ calmness, relaxation

restoration n
1 RENOVATION, repair, refurbishing, rebuilding, reconstruction, renewal, rehabilitation
OLD instauration
2 REVIVAL, refreshment, rejuvenation, revitalization, recovery
OLD recruit, recruital
COLLOQ. kiss of life
3 RETURN, replacement, reinstallation, restitution, reinstatement, re-establishment, reconstitution
TECHNICAL restitutio in integram
⊟ **1** damage **2** weakening **3** removal

restore v
1 **restore a building**
renovate, renew, rebuild, reconstruct, redecorate, refurbish, retouch, recondition, rehabilitate, revamp, repair, mend, fix
COLLOQ. do up
2 REVIVE, refresh, recover, rejuvenate, revitalize, reinvigorate, strengthen, build up
FORMAL revivify
3 REPLACE, return, give back, hand back, reinstate, re-establish, reintroduce, re-impose, re-enforce
⊟ **1** damage **2** weaken **3** remove

restrain v
restrain your feelings; restrain a prisoner
hold back, keep back, suppress, subdue, repress, inhibit, check, hold in check, curb, chasten, bridle, stop, arrest, prevent, hinder, obstruct, impede, bind, tie, chain, fetter, manacle, imprison, detain, jail, confine, hold captive, restrict, regulate, control, keep under control, govern
COLLOQ. bottle up
⊟ encourage, liberate

SYNONYM NUANCES

Hold back, **keep back** and **detain** are fairly unmarked terms which suggest preventing progress. **Control** and **keep under control** have connotations of dominance, and **subdue** is similar but implies something has been overcome, while **suppress** is more suggestive of forcibly quashing. **Repress** would also suggest preventing using a more forcible control: *she repressed a shudder*.

The idea of curtailing something can be conveyed in a fairly neutral way by **inhibit**, **check** and **hold in check**, but **restrict**, **curb** and **bridle** imply subjecting to rigid limitations: *the government must curb spending*. **Arrest** and **prevent** could be used of bringing completely to a standstill. **Hinder** implies interfering with progress in a way that is unwelcome: *there is a difference between* *not helping and actually hindering our plans*; both **obstruct** and **impede** suggest even more effective handicaps: *the doctor did not make it on time, as he was impeded by the weather conditions*.

The terms **bind**, **tie**, **chain**, **fetter** and **manacle** all suggest physical restraints, though they may also be used figuratively to imply powerful and perhaps frustrating restrictions: *she is not fettered by preconceptions*.

The term **regulate** would be appropriate where restraining involves the application of rules, whereas **govern**, although similar, has perhaps a more democratic and less strict element: *a contract which regulates the rights of the parties*; *our upbringing can govern how we think*.

restrained *adj*
1 CALM, controlled, steady, self-controlled, self-restrained, unemotional, formal, cold, aloof, uncommunicative, sober, measured, ordered, reserved, abstemious, chaste, relaxed, cool
TECHNICAL ritenuto
2 *restrained decorations*
tasteful, moderate, temperate, mild, subdued, subtle, muted, quiet, soft, low-key, unobtrusive, discreet, refined, modest, dry, severe
E3 1 emotional, demonstrative **2** garish, ostentatious; *colloq.* loud

restraint *n*
behave with restraint; no restraints in modern life
moderation, prudence, inhibition, self-control, self-discipline, hold, grip, check, curb, rein, bridle, suppression, bondage, captivity, confinement, imprisonment, bonds, chains, fetters, straitjacket, control, constraint, limit(s), restriction(s), duress, block, barrier, stint, limitation, tie, hindrance, prevention
FORMAL judiciousness
E3 liberty

restrict *v*
limit, bound, demarcate, control, keep under control, keep within limits, regulate, tighten, confine, contain, localize, cramp, constrict, strangle, constrain, gate, hold, impede, hinder, hamper, handicap, tie, restrain, curtail, curb, inhibit, pinch, bind, condition, peg down, go slow, fast, ration, scant
TECHNICAL astrict
OLD stint, straiten, thirl; (*Shakesp*) combine
COLLOQ. hem in, cramp someone's style, draw/pull in your horns
E3 broaden, free

restricted *adj*
1 SMALL, narrow, cramped, confined, constricted, tight
2 SECRET, private, limited, exclusive, closed, controlled, regulated

restriction *n*
limit, bound, confine, limitation, constraint, handicap, check, curb, restraint, ban, stint, embargo, control, regulation, rule, stipulation, qualification, condition, proviso
E3 freedom

restructure *v*
reorganize, rearrange, shake up, modernize, streamline, rationalize, rejig

result *n, v*
♦ *n*
effect, consequence, sequel, repercussion, reaction, implication, outcome, upshot, end, issue, end-product, by-product, side effect, fruit(s), score, grade, mark, answer, verdict, judgement, decision, conclusion
COLLOQ. pay-off, spin-off
E3 cause

♦ *v*
follow, ensue, happen, occur, issue, emerge, arise, spring, derive, stem, flow, evolve, emanate, proceed, come out of, develop, end, finish, terminate, culminate
FORMAL eventuate
E3 cause

resultant *adj*
ensuing, consequent, resulting, subsequent, following

resume *v*
restart, start again, begin again, recommence, reopen, reconvene, re-occupy, continue, carry on, go on, proceed, take up (again)
TECHNICAL rejuvenesce
E3 cease

résumé *n*
summary, précis, synopsis, outline, sketch, breakdown, abstract, digest, recapitulation, review, overview, run-down, epitome; *N Am* wrap-up
COLLOQ. recap

resumption *n*
restart, recommencement, reopening, re-establishment, renewal, resurgence, continuation, proceeding
E3 cessation

resurgence *n*
re-appearance, re-emergence, resumption, return, rebirth, resurrection, revival, renaissance
FORMAL renascence, recrudescence, revivification, risorgimento
E3 decrease

resurrect *v*
1 *Jesus Christ was resurrected*
bring back to life, raise from the dead, restore, restore to life, revive
2 *resurrect an old idea*
restore, revive, resuscitate, reactivate, bring back, reintroduce, re-establish, re-install, renew, revitalize
E3 1 kill, bury

resurrection *n*
1 *the resurrection of Jesus Christ*
bringing back to life, raising/rising from the dead, restoration to life, return from the dead
TECHNICAL anastasis
2 *resurrection of former procedures*
restoration, revival, resuscitation, renaissance, rebirth, renewal, revitalization, re-establishment, resurgence, reappearance, return, comeback

resuscitate *v*
revive, bring round, resurrect, save, rescue, reanimate, quicken, reinvigorate, breathe new life into, revitalize, restore, renew
FORMAL revivify
COLLOQ. give the kiss of life to

resuscitated *adj*
restored, revived, resurrected
FORMAL redivivus, redintegrate(d)

resuscitation *n*
revival, restoration, renewal, reinvigoration, revitalizing, quickening
FORMAL revivification

retain *v*
1 KEEP, hold, keep hold of, grasp, grip, reserve, hold back, hold fast to, save, continue, maintain, preserve
COLLOQ. hang on to
2 *retain information*
remember, recall, recollect, memorize, bear in mind, keep in mind, call to mind
3 EMPLOY, engage, hire, pay, contract, commission
E3 1 release **2** forget **3** dismiss

retainer *n*
1 FEE, retaining fee, deposit, advance

2 SERVANT, lackey, footman, domestic, attendant, supporter, follower, valet, dependant, vassal, menial, jackman
OLD galloglass, samurai

retaliate v
reciprocate, counter-attack, get back at, pay someone back, hit back, strike back, fight back, avenge, take revenge
COLLOQ. get your own back, get even with, give as good as you get, return like for like, give someone a taste of their own medicine

retaliation n
reprisal, counter-attack, revenge, vengeance, retribution, reciprocation, retort
OLD talion
FORMAL ultion, quid pro quo, *lex talionis*
COLLOQ. tit for tat, like for like, an eye for an eye (and a tooth for a tooth), a taste of your own medicine

retard v
slow down, delay, hold up, decelerate, brake, put a/the brake on, handicap, incapacitate, obstruct, hinder, impede, check, curb, restrict
E3 speed up, accelerate

retardation n
slowness, slowing, incapability, mental handicap, deficiency, incapacity, impeding, hindering, hindrance, delay, lag, obstruction, dullness
FORMAL retardment
E3 advancement

retch v
vomit, spew, heave, disgorge, regurgitate, gag, disgorge; *dialect* reach
COLLOQ. puke, throw up, chuck up, fetch up, sick up
SLANG *N Am* barf

retching n
vomiting, nausea, reaching, gagging
FORMAL vomiturition
COLLOQ. puking, spewing

retention n
keeping, holding, keeping hold, holding (on), saving, continuance, maintenance, preservation
COLLOQ. hanging-on

rethink v
reconsider, think over, review, revise, re-examine, think twice, modify, reassess, think better of, have second thoughts

reticence n
reserve, restraint, quietness, uncommunicativeness, unforthcomingness, secretiveness, silence, taciturnity, muteness, diffidence
E3 communicativeness, forwardness, frankness

reticent adj
reserved, shy, restrained, uncommunicative, unforthcoming, tight-lipped, close-lipped, close-mouthed, secretive, taciturn, silent, quiet, diffident, boutonné
E3 communicative, forward, frank

retinue n
entourage, following, followers, personnel, staff, suite, train, attendants, escort, cortège, aides, servants, tail, sowarry
TECHNICAL comitatus
OLD attendancy, equipage, port; (*Shakesp*) meinie; (*Spenser*) many

retire v
1 STOP WORK, stop working, leave work, give up work, resign
COLLOQ. bow out, be put out to pasture
2 LEAVE, depart, go away, withdraw, retreat, recede, move, go, decamp, go aside, step, scratch, den, lick your wounds
E3 **1** join **2** enter, advance

retired adj
former, ex-, emeritus, past

retirement n
withdrawal, retreat, exit, departure, resignation, solitude, loneliness, seclusion, privacy, obscurity

> **QUOTATIONS**
> Retirement at sixty-five is ridiculous. When I was sixty-five, I still had pimples
> GEORGE BURNS

retiring adj
shy, bashful, timid, shrinking, quiet, reticent, reserved, self-effacing, unassertive, diffident, coy, modest, unassuming, humble
E3 bold, forward, assertive

retort v, n
♦ v
answer, reply, respond, rejoin, return, counter, retaliate, repartee, throw back, turn upon
COLLOQ. give as good as you get
♦ n
answer, reply, response, rejoinder, riposte, repartee, quip, wisecrack, comeback, backword, clinch, outfling, sally, squelch
COLLOQ. floorer; *N Am* zinger

retract v
1 *retract criticism*
take back, withdraw, recant, reverse, cancel, repeal, repudiate, disown, disclaim, deny, renege
OLD (*Shakesp*) unspeak
FORMAL renounce, revoke, rescind, disavow, abjure, abrogate
2 *retract like cat's claws*
pull back, move back, move in, draw in, withdraw
E3 **1** assert, maintain

retreat v, n
♦ v
draw back, pull back, fall back, turn back, shrink, withdraw, decamp, give ground, climb down, give way, retire, leave, depart, flee, beat a retreat
OLD disadvance, recoil, retrate
COLLOQ. turn tail, quit, back-pedal; *N Am* bug out, crawfish
E3 advance
♦ n
1 WITHDRAWAL, drawing-back, pulling-back, pull-back, falling-back, climb-down, departure, evacuation, flight, katabasis
OLD recoil, retraict, retrate
2 SECLUSION, privacy, solitude, retirement, hideaway, hideout, den, refuge, asylum, sanctuary, shelter, harbour, haven, tower, lair, lodge, mew, nest, nook, hermitage, ivory tower, arbour, ashram
TECHNICAL redoubt, hibernaculum, reduit, interglacial, interstadial
OLD alcove, growlery
COLLOQ. sanctum sanctorum
SLANG funkhole
E3 **1** advance, charge

retrench v
cut back, economize, cut, slim down, live more economically, save, reduce, lessen, limit, decrease, diminish, curtail, trim, pare, prune, husband
COLLOQ. tighten your belt
E3 increase

retrenchment n
cutback, cutting back, cut, economy, reduction, pruning, curtailment, cost-cutting, run-down, contraction, shrinkage
COLLOQ. tightening your belt, tightening/pulling the purse strings
E3 increase

retribution *n*
punishment, reckoning, justice, satisfaction, retaliation, requital, reward, reprisal, redress, repayment, payment, compensation, recompense, revenge, vengeance, Nemesis, utu
TECHNICAL karma
OLD talion, vengement
COLLOQ. just deserts

retrieve *v*
recover, get back, fetch, bring back, regain, recapture, repossess, recoup, reclaim, put to rights, make good, salvage, save, rescue, redeem, restore, remedy, return, mend, repair
Ⅎ lose

retro *adj*
old, old-time, old-fashioned, antique, olde-worlde, former, past, bygone, passé, period, in period style

retrograde *adj*
backward, reverse, retrogressive, negative, downward, worsening, declining, deteriorating
Ⅎ progressive

retrogress *v*
regress, retrograde, return, revert, relapse, withdraw, recede, drop, ebb, fall, sink, wane, retire, retreat, backslide, decline, deteriorate, worsen, degenerate
Ⅎ progress, advance

retrogression *n*
regression, regress, return, relapse, decline, worsening, deterioration, drop, ebb, fall
FORMAL recidivism, retrogradation
Ⅎ increase, progress

retrospect *n*
hindsight, afterthought, thinking back, reflection, re-examination, review, survey, recollection, remembrance
Ⅎ prospect
■ **in retrospect**
retrospectively, with hindsight, looking back, thinking back, on reflection, with the wisdom of hindsight
FORMAL retroactively

retrospective *adj*
backward-looking, retro-active, retro-operative

retrospectively *adv*
in retrospect, with hindsight, looking back, thinking back, on reflection, with the wisdom of hindsight
FORMAL retroactively

return *v, n*
♦ *v*
1 COME BACK, reappear, recur, go back, get back, come home, come again, happen again, backtrack, regress, revert
2 GIVE BACK, hand back, pay back, send back, take back, deliver, put back, replace, reinstate, restore
FORMAL remit
3 *return a favour*
reciprocate, repay, refund, reimburse, recompense, exchange, match, equal, correspond
FORMAL requite
COLLOQ. do the same
4 ANSWER, reply, respond, rejoin, retort, riposte, counter
5 *return a verdict*
announce, pronounce, declare, deliver, bring in, hand down
Ⅎ **1** leave, depart **2** take, keep
♦ *n*
1 REAPPEARANCE, recurrence, home-coming
COLLOQ. comeback
2 REPAYMENT, recompense, replacement, restoration, reinstatement, reciprocation
3 REVENUE, income, proceeds, takings, yield, gain, profit, interest, reward, advantage, benefit
4 *the return of the books*
giving-back, handing-back, taking-back, reinstatement, restoration, delivery, replacement

5 *a tax return*
form, statement, document, account, report, record, data
Ⅎ **1** departure, disappearance **2** removal **3** payment, expense, loss
■ **in return for**
in exchange for, in response to, in consideration of, equivalently, mutually, reciprocally

re-use *v*
recycle, reconstitute

revamp *v*
renovate, recondition, rebuild, reconstruct, repair, restore, revise, refit, refurbish, modernize, rehabilitate, overhaul, recast
COLLOQ. do up, pimp

reveal *v*
expose, bring to light, make aware, uncover, unveil, unmask, unearth, unfold, unshadow, expose to view, show, display, exhibit, lay bare, manifest, disclose, declare, divulge, give away, betray, leak, tell, let out, let slip, impart, communicate, express, publicize, broadcast, publish, make public, make known, announce, proclaim, confess, undeceive, unbosom, disbosom, throw up
OLD discover, bewray, decipher, descry;
(*Spenser*) presage
COLLOQ. take the wraps off, let on, blow someone's cover, take/lift/blow the lid on, tell tales out of school
Ⅎ hide, conceal, mask

SYNONYM NUANCES

Expose and **bring to light** can be used of bringing something into view or making others aware of it, particularly something underhand or unwelcome: *a drugs ring exposed by investigative journalists*. Both **uncover** and **unveil** are similar, and have implications of prior secrecy, while **unmask** is more appropriate for making known someone's true identity: *the trial unmasked him as a charlatan*.

The archaeological image of **unearth** suggests an element of perseverance, and has connotations of finding something valuable or useful: *the club unearthed a prodigious talent in this young player*, whereas **throw up** implies something produced incidentally: *the medical detective work threw up new uncertainties*. **Unfold** suggests gradually opening out, without any element of effort involved: *the Watergate drama unfolded*. **Manifest**, likewise, can be used of something becoming apparent: *the crisis manifested itself in a variety of ways*, while **display** and **exhibit** could be used to suggest a more deliberate element of presentation.

A lack of intention is conveyed by **give away**, and **betray** has further implications of an unwanted revelation: *his expression betrayed how he really felt*, while both **let out** and **let slip** could be used of accidentally passing on information. **Leak** can convey being deliberately indiscreet, while both **disclose** and **divulge** suggest revelations of an intimate nature, without the same connotations of stealth or secrecy.

Express is appropriate for deliberately revealing your feelings: *he expressed his concern*, while **confess** has more to do with admission. **Announce** and **proclaim** would be appropriate for a strong verbal gesture bringing something to public attention, while **publicize**, **broadcast** and **publish** could be used where such a gesture is aimed at a wider audience, often through the media.

---

revealing *adj*
1 *a revealing interview*
indicative, significant, revelatory, giveaway
2 *a revealing dress*
low-cut, daring, see-through, diaphanous, sheer

revel *v, n*

♦ *v*

1 *revel in an experience*
enjoy, delight, take delight, take pleasure, relish, glory, joy, indulge, thrive, wallow, savour, bask, rejoice, lap up, gloat, crow, luxuriate
2 *revelling through the night*
celebrate, carouse, have a party, make merry, riot, roist, roister
OLD wake
COLLOQ. live it up, whoop it up, paint the town red, push the boat out, raise the roof, large it, have it large
F3 1 dislike

♦ *n*
celebration, party, carousal, carouse, festivity, spree, gala, merrymaking, jollification, bacchanal, orgy, debauch, saturnalia, comus
OLD night-rule
COLLOQ. rave, rave-up, do, knees-up

revelation *n*

1 UNCOVERING, unveiling, unearthing, exposure, unmasking, show, display, exhibition, disclosure, divulgence, expression, vision, confession, admission, betrayal, giveaway, broadcasting
OLD revealment
FORMAL manifestation, apocalypse, epiphany
COLLOQ. reveal
2 NEWS, fact, detail, information, secreted/confidential information, communication, giveaway, publication, announcement, proclamation, leak
COLLOQ. eye-opener

reveller *n*
celebrator, party-goer, raver, pleasure-seeker, merrymaker, carouser, roisterer, wassailer, bacchanal

revelry *n*
celebration(s), festivity, festivities, party, merrymaking, fun, carousal, jollity, jollification, debauchery
F3 sobriety

revenge *n, v*

♦ *n*
vengeance, satisfaction, reprisal, retaliation, requital, retribution, redress, vendetta, revanche
OLD avenge, avengement, ultion
COLLOQ. tit for tat, eye for an eye (and a tooth for a tooth), a dose/taste of your own medicine

♦ *v*
avenge, take vengeance on, repay, pay off, retaliate, settle a score/an old score, pay someone back, put someone back in their own court, get back at, hit back, fight back, settle accounts with, square an account with, serve out
OLD wreak of
COLLOQ. get, get your own back, get even with, give as good as you get

---

SYNONYM NUANCES

noun
Vengeance is an emotive word which suggests a deeply felt need for revenge, while **satisfaction** puts more emphasis on reparation: *he demanded satisfaction for his losses.* **Reprisal** conveys the more clinical idea of a deliberate action striking back at the actions of another: *the hostages were executed in reprisal for the bombing raid.* **Retaliation** likewise suggests a fairly immediate return in kind, but one made more instinctively.
   Both **requital** and **retribution** imply an element of punishment, with **retribution** in particular suggesting a large-scale or dramatic action, unlike **redress**, which implies restoration as an important element: *the farmers' best hope of redress lay in court action.* **Vendetta** is appropriate for a continued state of hostility and acts of revenge between two parties, while the uncommon **revanche** more narrowly refers to recovery of territory.

---

revengeful *adj*
bitter, resentful, implacable, vengeful, vindictive, malignant, malevolent, spiteful, malicious, merciless, unmerciful, pitiless, unforgiving
F3 forgiving, merciful

revenue *n*
income, return, yield, interest, profit(s), gain, proceeds, receipts, rewards, takings
F3 expenditure

reverberate *v*
echo, re-echo, resound, resonate, ring, boom, vibrate
COLLOQ. repercuss

reverberation *n*

1 ECHO, re-echoing, resounding, resonance, ringing, vibration, wave, rebound, recoil, reflection
2 *reverberations following the resignation*
repercussion, effect, consequence, result
COLLOQ. shock wave, ripple

revere *v*
respect, admire, esteem, honour, look up to, think highly of, pay homage to, worship, reverence, adore, exalt
FORMAL venerate
F3 despise, scorn

reverence *n, v*

♦ *n*
respect, deference, honour, (high) esteem, homage, admiration, awe, worship, exaltation, adoration, devotion, idolism
OLD obeisance
FORMAL veneration
F3 irreverence, contempt, scorn

♦ *v*
admire, respect, honour, acknowledge, revere, adore, worship, hallow, fear, dread, overawe, prostrate yourself
FORMAL venerate
F3 despise, scorn

reverent *adj*
reverential, respectful, admiring, deferential, humble, dutiful, devoted, awed, solemn, pious, devout, adoring, worshipping, loving
OLD obeisant
F3 irreverent, disrespectful

reverie *n*
daydream, daydreaming, musing, trance, abstraction, absent-mindedness, inattention, preoccupation, brown study, woolgathering

reversal *n*

1 NEGATION, cancellation, annulment, nullification, countermanding, repeal, reverse, turnabout, turnaround, exchange, swap, volte-face, upset
FORMAL revocation, rescinding
COLLOQ. U-turn
2 MISFORTUNE, mishap, misadventure, adversity, affliction, hardship, trial, blow, disappointment, upset, setback, check, delay, problem, difficulty, failure, defeat
F3 1 advancement, progress

reverse *v, n, adj*

♦ *v*

1 *reverse a car*
back, move backwards, drive backwards, retreat, backtrack, withdraw
FORMAL regress
2 *reverse a decision*
undo, negate, set aside, cancel, annul, invalidate, overrule, repeal, quash, overthrow
FORMAL countermand, revoke, rescind, retract
3 TRANSPOSE, turn round, invert, up-end, overturn, turn upside-down, put back to front, upset, change, change round, exchange, swap, alter
F3 1 go forwards, progress **2** advance, enforce

♦ *n*

1 UNDERSIDE, other side, back, rear, inverse, verso, counter, converse, contrary, opposite
FORMAL antithesis
2 MISFORTUNE, mishap, misadventure, adversity, affliction, hardship, trial, blow, disappointment, upset, setback, check, delay, problem, difficulty, failure, defeat, reversal
FORMAL vicissitude

♦ *adj*

opposite, contrary, converse, inverse, inverted, backward, back, rear, verso

reversion *n*

return, restoration, reinstatement, handing-back, giving-back, taking-back, throwback

revert *v*

return, go back, resume, lapse, relapse, regress

review *n, v*

♦ *n*

1 ASSESSMENT, criticism, critique, evaluation, appraisal, judgement, report, commentary, examination, scrutiny, analysis, study, survey, rating, recapitulation, reassessment, re-evaluation, re-examination, revision, notice, reviewal, revise, summing-up, write-up, *tour d'horizon*
FORMAL recension
COLLOQ. rethink
2 MAGAZINE, periodical, journal

♦ *v*

1 ASSESS, criticize, evaluate, judge, weigh (up), discuss, examine, view, inspect, scrutinize, analyse, study, survey, recapitulate, write up, comment on
FORMAL appraise
2 *review the situation*
reassess, re-evaluate, re-examine, reconsider, rethink, revise, take stock of, go over; *N Am* appeal
COLLOQ. size up

reviewer *n*

commentator, critic, judge, observer, connoisseur, arbiter, essayist

revile *v*

despise, hate, scorn, slander, libel, defame, abuse, smear, reproach, malign, blackguard, rail; *dialect* miscall
FORMAL calumniate, denigrate, traduce, vituperate, vilify, inveigh
OLD missay
☒ praise

revise *v*

1 *revise your opinion*
change, alter, modify, amend, correct, update, edit, rewrite, reword, redraft, recast, rework, revamp, reconsider, re-examine, review, go over, peruse, think better of, have second thoughts about, expurgate
FORMAL emend, recense
2 STUDY, learn, memorize
COLLOQ. swot up, cram, bone up on, mug up

revision *n*

1 CHANGE, amendment, editing, modification, alteration, correction, recast, recasting, reworking, re-examination, reconstruction, review, rewriting, rereading
FORMAL emendation
2 STUDYING, memorizing, homework, learning, updating
COLLOQ. swotting

revitalize *v*

revive, renew, restore, refresh, reactivate, reanimate, rejuvenate, resurrect, reinvigorate
FORMAL revivify
☒ dampen, suppress

revival *n*

resuscitation, revitalization, restoration, re-establishment, reintroduction, renewal, renaissance, rebirth, resurrection, reawakening, resurgence, upsurge, upturn
COLLOQ. the kiss of life, comeback

revive *v*

resuscitate, bring round, reanimate, revitalize, restore, renew, refresh, animate, invigorate, reinvigorate, quicken, rouse, awaken, recover, rally, comfort, cheer up, reawaken, breathe new life into, rekindle, reactivate, re-establish, reintroduce, wake, resurrect
OLD relive
FORMAL revivify
COLLOQ. give the kiss of life to, rake up
☒ weary

revivify *v*

revive, revitalize, invigorate, restore, resuscitate, refresh, renew, reactivate, reanimate
FORMAL inspirit
☒ dampen, depress

reviving *adj*

refreshening, invigorating, reinvigorating, exhilarating, bracing, stimulating, tonic, reanimating, enheartening, regenerating
FORMAL revivescent, revivifying, reviviscent
☒ disheartening, exhausting

revocation *n*

revoking, repeal, repealing, quashing, reversal, withdrawal, annulment, nullification, invalidation, negation, cancellation, abolition, repudiation
FORMAL countermanding, rescinding, rescission, retractation, retraction
☒ enforcement

revoke *v*

repeal, quash, annul, nullify, invalidate, negate, cancel, abolish, reverse, withdraw, recall, recant, lift, unpray, unshout
FORMAL rescind, abrogate, countermand, retract, renege
☒ enforce

revolt *n, v*

♦ *n*

revolution, rebellion, mutiny, rising, uprising, insurrection, putsch, coup (d'état), secession, defection
TECHNICAL apostasy, expressionism

♦ *v*

1 REBEL, mutiny, rise, rise up, riot, resist, defect, take up arms, take to the streets, fall away
FORMAL dissent
2 DISGUST, sicken, nauseate, repel, turn your stomach, offend, shock, outrage, scandalize
☒ **1** submit **2** please, delight

revolting *adj*

disgusting, sickening, nauseating, repulsive, repellent, obnoxious, nasty, horrible, vile, hateful, foul, loathsome, abhorrent, repugnant, abominable, distasteful, off-putting, offensive, shocking, appalling
FORMAL reprehensible, heinous
☒ pleasant, delightful, attractive, palatable

revolution *n*

1 REVOLT, rebellion, mutiny, rising, uprising, insurrection, insurgence, putsch, coup (d'état)
2 CHANGE, reformation, transformation, innovation, upheaval, cataclysm
TECHNICAL metamorphosis
COLLOQ. sex change
3 ROTATION, turn, spin, wheel, whirl, cycle, circuit, round, circle, orbit, gyration

> **QUOTATIONS**
> A revolution is not a dinner party
>   MAO ZEDONG
>
> The blood-red flower of revolution
>   DUDLEY RANDALL, *Cities Burning*, 'Roses and Revolutions'

revolutionary *n, adj*

♦ *n*

rebel, mutineer, insurgent, insurrectionist, anarchist, revolutionist, Leninist, Bolshevik, Sandinista, filibuster, sansculotte
OLD Menshevik
COLLOQ. red

♦ *adj*

1 REBEL, rebellious, mutinous, insurgent, insurrectionary, subversive, seditious, extremist, anarchistic, Leninist, Bolshevik
OLD Menshevik
COLLOQ. red

2 *revolutionary ideas*
new, innovative, novel, progressive, ground-breaking, experimental, avant-garde, different, drastic, radical, thoroughgoing, complete
≡ 1 conservative

revolutionize *v*
transform, reform, restructure, cause radical changes in, reorganize, transfigure, turn upside-down

revolve *v*
1 ROTATE, turn, go, move, pivot, swivel, spin, wheel, whirl, gyrate, circle, orbit, run, twist, rev
TECHNICAL circumduct
FORMAL circumvolve

2 *his life revolves around sport*
centre on, focus on, concentrate on, be preoccupied with, turn on, hinge on, hang on

revolver *n*
gun, handgun, firearm, pistol, rifle, shotgun, airgun, six-shooter, bulldog, Colt®
OLD peacemaker
COLLOQ. shooter
SLANG iron, shooting iron; *N Am* gat, rod

revolving *adj*
rotating, turning, spinning, whirling, gyrating, gyratory
≡ stationary

revulsion *n*
disgust, distaste, dislike, repulsion, repugnance, aversion, hatred, hate, loathing, nausea, abhorrence, recoil, abomination
FORMAL detestation
≡ delight, pleasure, approval

reward *n, v*

♦ *n*

1 *a reward for long service*
present, prize, honour, medal, decoration, bounty, pay-off, bonus, premium, payment, remuneration, recompense, repayment, compensation, gain, profit, return, benefit, merit, desert

2 REQUITAL, punishment, retribution
COLLOQ. just deserts

♦ *v*

pay, remunerate, recompense, repay, requite, compensate, honour, decorate

OLD yield; (*Shakesp*) reguerdon
≡ punish

rewarding *adj*
worthwhile, satisfying, gratifying, pleasing, fulfilling, enriching, profitable, remunerative, lucrative, productive, fruitful, valuable, advantageous, beneficial, edifying
≡ unrewarding

rewording *n*
rephrasing, rewriting, paraphrase, revision
TECHNICAL metaphrase, metaphrasis

rework *v*
revise, rewrite, reword, redraft, recast, revamp, reconsider, re-examine, review, change, alter, modify, amend, correct, update, edit, go over, peruse, think better of, have second thoughts about, expurgate
FORMAL emend, recense

rewrite *v*
revise, rework, reword, redraft, recast, correct, edit
FORMAL emend

rhetoric *n*
eloquence, oratory, bombast, pomposity, hyperbole, verbosity, wordiness, long-windedness, fustian
FORMAL grandiloquence, magniloquence, prolixity

rhetorical *adj*
oratorical, bombastic, pompous, high-sounding, long-winded, verbose, wordy, stylistic, grand, high-flown, flowery, florid, flamboyant, showy, pretentious, artificial, insincere
FORMAL grandiloquent, magniloquent, declamatory, prolix
≡ simple
See panel below

rhyme *n*
poetry, verse, poem, ode, limerick, jingle, song, ditty, couplet, chime, tink, crambo
OLD rhime, rhythm
See panel on next page

rhythm *n*
beat, pulse, time, throb, tempo, metre, measure, movement, harmony, flow, lilt, swing, accent, cadence, pattern

rhythmic *adj*
rhythmical, metric, metrical, pulsating, pulsing, throbbing, flowing, lilting, periodic, regular, repeated, steady

rib *n*
bone, band, bar, support, vein, moulding, ribbing, ridge, shaft, welt, wale
FORMAL costa
Related adjective: costal

ribald *adj*
rude, obscene, risqué, racy, off-colour, bawdy, earthy, coarse, smutty, vulgar, filthy, foul-mouthed, gross, base, scurrilous, low, mean, lewd, disrespectful, licentious, indecent, irreverent, satirical, jeering, mocking, derisive, Rabelaisian
COLLOQ. blue, naughty
≡ polite

Rhetorical devices include:

abscission	apostrophe	ellipsis	euphemism	metaphor	simile
alliteration	asyndeton	enantiosis	figure of speech	metonymy	syllepsis
amplification	auxesis	enumeration	hendiadys	mixed metaphor	symploce
anacoluthon	bathos	epanadiplosis	hypallage	onomatopoeia	synchoresis
anadiplosis	catachresis	epanalepsis	hyperbole	oxymoron	synchrysis
anaphora	cataphora	epanaphora	hypostrophe	parabole	synecdoche
anastrophe	chiasmus	epanodos	hypotyposis	paradox	synoeciosis
anticlimax	climax	epanorthosis	hysteron-proteron	paraleipsis	tautology
antimetabole	diallage	epigram	increment	parenthesis	transferred epithet
antimetathesis	diegesis	epiphonema	innuendo	pathetic fallacy	trope
antiphrasis	dissimile	epistrophe	irony	personification	vicious circle
antithesis	double entendre	epizeuxis	litotes	prolepsis	zeugma
antonomasia	dramatic irony	erotema	meiosis	pun	
aporia	dysphemism	erotetic	metalepsis	rhetorical question	

Forms of rhyme include:

apocopated rhyme	end rhyme	identical rhyme	rich rhyme (or rime riche)
assonance (or vowel-rhyme)	eye-rhyme	internal rhyme	riding-rhyme
consonance	female (or feminine) rhyme	male (or masculine) rhyme	rime suffisant
cynghanedd	half-rhyme (or near-rhyme)	pararhyme	slant rhyme
dactylic rhyme	head-rhyme	rhyme royal	tail(ed) rhyme

See also **prosody**.

---

ribaldry *n*
rudeness, obscenity, bawdiness, raciness, vulgarity, smut, smuttiness, sauciness, earthiness, coarseness, filth, grossness, lowness, baseness, licentiousness, indecency, scurrility, jeering, derision, mockery
COLLOQ. naughtiness

ribbing *n*
teasing, mocking, taunting, ridicule, banter, provocation, baiting, goading, annoying, badgering
COLLOQ. ragging, kidding

ribbon *n*
band, cord, cloth, line, sash, strip, braid, shred, tatter, jag, hair-band, headband, fillet, taenia
Related adjectives: taeniate, taenioid

rich *adj*
1 WEALTHY, affluent, moneyed, prosperous, well-to-do, well-off
COLLOQ. flush, well-heeled, made of money, in the money, rolling in it, with money to burn
OLD COLLOQ. oofy
SLANG loaded, filthy rich, stinking rich
2 EXPENSIVE, precious, valuable, priceless, costly, lavish, magnificent, sumptuous, luxurious, lush, splendid, grand, gorgeous, palatial, fine, elaborate, ornate
FORMAL opulent
3 PLENTIFUL, abundant, abounding, copious, profuse, prolific, ample, full, high, packed, steeped, overflowing, well-provided, well-supplied
FORMAL replete, plenteous
4 FERTILE, fruitful, productive, lush
FORMAL fecund
5 *rich food*
creamy, fatty, oily, full-bodied, heavy, full-flavoured, strong, spicy, savoury, tasty, delicious, luscious, juicy, sweet
6 *rich colours*
deep, intense, vivid, strong, bright, brilliant, vibrant, warm
7 IRONIC, laughable, ridiculous, outrageous, unreasonable, preposterous, absurd
8 *a rich voice*
deep, mellow, full, sonorous, resonant
FORMAL mellifluous
9 *a rich life*
full, eventful, active, busy, lively, exciting
E3 **1** poor, impoverished **2** plain, basic **4** barren, infertile **5** plain, bland **6** dull, soft **9** dull, empty

> QUOTATIONS
> If you aren't rich, you should always look useful
> LOUIS-FERDINAND CÉLINE, *Journey to the End*

> SYNONYM NUANCES
> *sense 1*
> **Wealthy** and **affluent** can be used to suggest having an abundance of money and possessions, whereas **well-to-do** and **well-off** suggest a more moderate degree of wealth. **Moneyed** puts the focus solely on pecuniary riches. **Prosperous** is suggestive of being continually financially successful: *the prosperous southern half of Britain.*

riches *n*
wealth, affluence, prosperity, money, gold, treasure, fortune, assets, property, substance, resources, means
OLD (filthy) lucre
FORMAL opulence
COLLOQ. the necessary
SLANG loot, readies, ready, megabucks, dough, dosh, bread, lolly, spondulicks, brass, gravy, greens, shekels, moolah, greenies, scratch, smash, stumpy
E3 poverty

richly *adv*
1 LAVISHLY, splendidly, gorgeously, sumptuously, elegantly, elaborately, expensively, exquisitely, luxuriously, palatially
FORMAL opulently, floridly
2 FULLY, thoroughly, completely, well, strongly, suitably, appropriately, properly
E3 **1** poorly, scantily

richness *n*
1 *the richness of mineral deposits*
plentifulness, abundance, fullness, provision
2 *the richness of the pudding*
fattiness, creaminess, oiliness, heaviness, taste, juiciness
3 *the richness of the furnishings*
lavishness, magnificence, splendour, luxuriousness, luxuriance, sumptuousness, elegance, exquisiteness
4 *Japan's cultural richness*
depth, fullness, eventfulness, business, liveliness, excitement
5 RESONANCE, mellowness, fullness, intensity, loudness

rickety *adj*
unsteady, wobbly, shaky, unstable, insecure, flimsy, jerry-built, decrepit, ramshackle, broken-down, dilapidated, derelict
E3 stable, strong

ricochet *v, n*
♦ *v*
bounce (back), rebound, spring back, bob, recoil, throw, dap; *Scot* stoit, stot
♦ *n*
bounce, rebound, bound, spring, jump, leap; *Scot* stot

rid *v*
free, deliver, relieve, unburden, clear, purge, cleanse, purify
■ **get rid of**
throw away, throw out, dispose of, discard, dump, scrap, jettison, abolish, put an end to, eliminate, do away with
COLLOQ. chuck (out), get shot of, ditch, junk

riddance *n*
deliverance, release, relief, removal, freedom, elimination, clearance, disposal, ejection, expulsion, extermination, purgation
E3 burdening

riddle[1] *n*
tell me a riddle
enigma, mystery, conundrum, puzzle, poser, problem, teaser, charade, brainteaser, mind-bender; *Scot* guess; *N Am* brain-twister
TECHNICAL koan, logograph
OLD (*Shakesp*) conclusion

**riddle² ** v

1 PERFORATE, pierce, puncture, pepper, fill, permeate, pervade, infest
2 SIFT, sieve, strain, filter, mar, winnow
OLD cribble

ride v, n

♦ v

sit, move, go, progress, travel, journey, gallop, trot, pedal, drive, steer, control, dominate, handle, manage
FORMAL bestride

♦ n

journey, trip, outing, jaunt, spin, drive, lift

rider n

horseman, horsewoman, equestrian, jockey, cavalryman, horse soldier, hussar, dragoon, knight

ridge n

band, escarpment, hill, hummock, lump, arête, drum, drumlin, hog's back, reef, ripple, saddle, knurl, wale, welt, crinkle
TECHNICAL esker, yardang, sastruga
FORMAL costa

ridicule n, v

♦ n

mockery, jeering, laughter, scorn, derision, taunting, teasing, chaff, banter, badinage, satire, irony, sarcasm, jest, depreciation
🔁 praise

♦ v

laugh at, mock, make fun of, poke fun at, jeer, scorn, gibe, scoff, deride, sneer, tease, humiliate, taunt, satirize, send up, caricature, lampoon, burlesque, parody, jest, mimic, have a game with, make a game of, pillory, crucify; *Aust* poke mullock at
OLD smoke
COLLOQ. rib, kid, rag, pull someone's leg, pooh-pooh, take the mickey out of, guy, josh, queer
SLANG *N Am* goof
🔁 praise

SYNONYM NUANCES

verb
You can use **laugh at** as a fairly general synonym, while **mock** and **deride** have greater implications of disparagement and contempt: *intellectuals who deride romance novels*. **Jeer** is more suggestive of expressing this contempt: *the team's performance was jeered by fans*. You could use **scoff** or **sneer** to imply a degree of superciliousness in the expression, while **scorn** also implies rejection: *he scorned my attempts to humour him*.
  Tease is a fairly mild term, which can even suggest affection, whereas **gibe** and **taunt** are more suggestive of hurtful provocation: *Bremner was taunted mercilessly by rival fans*. **Humiliate** is a strong term to use, appropriately describing belittling someone to their extreme embarrassment. **Crucify** is similarly extreme, especially referring to holding up to public derision: *the press crucified him for the affair*.
  Other synonyms relate to ridicule as a source of humour, for example **satirize**, which suggests the use of witty invective, and **lampoon**, which might be used of a more concentrated assault on an individual. **Mimic**, **parody**, and the less common verb **burlesque** can be used to suggest impersonating in a ridiculous way: *every movement was ridiculed and parodied*, while **caricature** is appropriate for the use of gross exaggeration: *scientists caricatured as absent-minded professors*. **Send up** suggests similar activity, but perhaps to a less sophisticated degree.

---

ridiculous adj

ludicrous, absurd, nonsensical, silly, foolish, stupid, contemptible, derisory, laughable, facetious, farcical,

comical, funny, humorous, droll, hilarious, outrageous, shocking, preposterous, incredible, unbelievable
FORMAL risible
🔁 sensible

ridiculously adv

absurdly, ludicrously, laughably, shockingly, unreasonably, unbelievably, incredibly, outrageously, surprisingly, preposterously
🔁 sensibly

rife adj

abundant, abounding, rampant, teeming, swarming, overflowing, raging, epidemic, prevalent, widespread, predominant, extensive, general, common, frequent, ubiquitous
🔁 scarce

riff-raff n

mob, rabble, hoi polloi, scum, dregs, undesirables, *canaille*
COLLOQ. rent-a-mob

**rifle¹ ** n

shoot with a rifle
gun, firearm, shotgun, weapon
SLANG bundook
See also **gun**.

**rifle² ** v

rifle through some files
search, rummage, sack, pillage, plunder, ransack, rob, maraud, loot, strip, burgle, gut
FORMAL despoil

rift n

1 SPLIT, breach, break, fracture, crack, fault, chink, cleft, fissure, slit, cavity, cranny, crevice, gap, space, opening, hole
2 DISAGREEMENT, difference, fight, split, row, feud, argument, conflict, breach, separation, division, schism, alienation
FORMAL estrangement, altercation
🔁 **2** unity

rig n, v

♦ n

equipment, kit, outfit, gear, tackle, apparatus, structure, machinery, fittings, fixtures
FORMAL accoutrements

♦ v

falsify, tamper with, doctor, fiddle, distort, twist, pervert, manipulate, massage, misrepresent, forge, fake
COLLOQ. cook

■ **rig out**
1 EQUIP, kit out, outfit, fit (out), supply, provide, furnish, make ready
2 CLOTHE, dress (up), wear, put on, get into, garb, robe, trim, turn out; *N Am* trick up
FORMAL array, accoutre, attire
COLLOQ. get up, trick out

■ **rig up**
arrange, build, assemble, construct, erect, fit up, fix up, put together, improvise
COLLOQ. knock up, throw together, cobble together
🔁 dismantle

right adj, adv, n, v

♦ adj

1 *the right answer*
correct, accurate, exact, precise, true, factual, actual, real, genuine, authentic, valid
COLLOQ. spot on, bang-on
2 PROPER, fitting, correct, accepted, approved, becoming, appropriate, suitable, fit, admissible, acceptable, satisfactory, reasonable, desirable, favourable, preferable, advantageous, convenient, opportune
OLD seemly
FORMAL propitious, auspicious
COLLOQ. the done thing

3 FAIR, just, equitable, lawful, legal, honest, upright, good, virtuous, righteous, moral, ethical, proper, principled, honourable, impartial

4 RIGHT-WING, conservative, Tory, reactionary, true-blue

5 *he's a right fool*
complete, absolute, utter, real, thorough

E3 **1** wrong, incorrect, erroneous **2** improper, unsuitable **3** unfair, wrong **4** left-wing, liberal

♦ *adv*

1 CORRECTLY, accurately, exactly, precisely, factually, properly, satisfactorily, well, favourably, fairly
COLLOQ. by the book

2 *right to the bottom*
straight, in a straight line, directly, as the crow flies, completely, utterly, entirely, absolutely, exactly, wholly, totally, all the way
COLLOQ. slap bang

3 *I'll be right back*
straight, immediately, without delay
COLLOQ. pronto, yesterday, before you know it, before you can say Jack Robinson, in two shakes of a lamb's tail, like a shot

E3 **1** wrongly, incorrectly, unfairly

♦ *n*

1 JUSTICE, legality, lawfulness, good, goodness, virtue, righteousness, morality, ethics, honour, honesty, integrity, uprightness, truthfulness, impartiality, fairness
FORMAL rectitude, propriety

2 PRIVILEGE, prerogative, due, claim, entitlement, birthright, business, authority, power, permission, warrant, freedom, opportunity, licence, charter, sanction, title deed
TECHNICAL droit
FORMAL lien

E3 **1** wrong

♦ *v*

rectify, correct, put right, put in order, fix, repair, redress, vindicate, avenge, settle, straighten (out), stand up

■ **right away**
straight away, immediately, at once, now, instantly, directly, forthwith, without delay, promptly
COLLOQ. from the word go, pronto, yesterday, before you know it, before you can say Jack Robinson, in two shakes of a lamb's tail, in a jiffy, like a shot
E3 later, eventually

■ **right-hand man/woman**
assistant, PA, personal assistant, executive assistant, secretary, helper, helping hand, aide, deputy, lieutenant, second-in-command, number two, subordinate, understudy, man/girl Friday, backroom boy/girl

■ **right of way**
precedence, priority, preference, superiority, supremacy, eminence, pre-eminence, lead, first place, seniority, rank

■ **by rights**
rightfully, correctly, properly, rightly, in fairness, justifiably, justly, lawfully, legally, legitimately;
TECHNICAL de jure

■ **in the right**
justified, right, warranted, vindicated
E3 in the wrong, at fault

■ **put/set to rights**
rectify, correct, put in order, fix, remedy, settle, straighten (out)

■ **within your rights**
justified, entitled, permitted, allowed, reasonable, right

QUOTATIONS
Always do right. This will gratify some people, and astonish the rest
  Mark Twain

I am not interested in picking up crumbs of compassion thrown from the table of someone who considers himself my master. I want the full menu of rights
  DESMOND TUTU

SYNONYM NUANCES
adjective sense 1
Correct may be widely used to suggest an absence of error, while **accurate**, **exact** and **precise** suggest a complete lack of deviation: *the precise measurements.* **True** has implications of depth, and can be used to suggest an absolute: *the true meaning of the word*, whereas **factual** more narrowly refers to correctness based on actual events and proof: *factual news stories.* **Actual** and **real**, although similar, go further by suggesting the validity of the existence of something: *the actual words that were said.* The terms **genuine** and **authentic** are more suggestive of being right, in the sense of being as perceived and therefore not fraudulent, while **valid** appropriately describes something that can be ratified: *a valid marriage*, or is justifiable: *valid suggestions.*

righteous *adj*
1 *a righteous person/action*
just, good, virtuous, moral, worthy, honourable, upright, fair, ethical, equitable, honest, law-abiding, blameless, irreproachable, incorrupt, guiltless, God-fearing, saintly, pure, sinless
2 *righteous anger*
justifiable, defensible, excusable, warranted, reasonable, supportable, justified, lawful, legal, legitimate, acceptable, explainable, valid, well-founded, proper
E3 **1** unrighteous **2** unjustifiable

righteousness *n*
goodness, honesty, honour, virtue, uprightness, morality, integrity, justice, blamelessness, faithfulness, equity, ethicalness, purity, holiness, sanctification
TECHNICAL dharma
FORMAL probity, rectitude
E3 unrighteousness

rightful *adj*
legitimate, lawful, legal, just, bona fide, true, real, genuine, valid, authorized, correct, proper, suitable, due
E3 wrongful, unlawful

rightfully *adv*
correctly, properly, rightly, by rights, justifiably, justly, lawfully, legally, legitimately
TECHNICAL de jure
E3 incorrectly, unjustifiably

rightly *adv*
1 CORRECTLY, properly, rightly, by rights, justifiably, justly, lawfully, legally, legitimately, fairly, equitably, morally
2 PROPERLY, fittingly, correctly, appropriately, reasonably
E3 **1** wrongly, unfairly, incorrectly **2** improperly, unsuitably

rigid *adj*
1 STIFF, inflexible, inelastic, unbending, cast-iron, hard, firm, set, fixed, unyielding, unalterable, invariable
2 *a rigid political system*
austere, harsh, severe, inflexible, unrelenting, strict, rigorous, stringent, stern, uncompromising, unyielding, spartan
FORMAL intransigent
E3 **1** flexible, elastic, bending, malleable **2** variable, weak

rigidity *n*
inflexibility, hardness, stiffness, fixity, immovability, immutability, immutableness, inelasticity, obstinacy, stubbornness, stringency, unsuppleness
FORMAL intractability, intransigence, obduracy
E3 flexibility

rigmarole *n*
process, bother, performance, fuss, palaver, nonsense, jargon, gibberish, twaddle, riddle-me-ree
OLD *Scot* ragman
COLLOQ. carry-on, hassle, to-do

rigorous *adj*
1 EXACT, precise, accurate, meticulous, painstaking, scrupulous, conscientious, punctilious, laborious, thorough
2 STRICT, stringent, rigid, firm, tough, harsh, hard, severe, stern, austere, exacting, uncompromising, spartan
FORMAL intransigent
F3 1 lax, superficial

rigorously *adv*
meticulously, painstakingly, scrupulously, thoroughly, accurately, exactly, precisely, punctiliously
F3 carelessly, superficially

rigour *n*
1 *the rigours of war*
trial, hardship, severity, suffering, ordeal
FORMAL privation
2 THOROUGHNESS, exactness, meticulousness, accuracy, preciseness, precision, conscientiousness, punctiliousness, inflexibility
3 STRICTNESS, stringency, rigidity, firmness, toughness, harshness, hardship, hardness, severity, sternness, austerity
FORMAL intransigence
F3 3 leniency, mildness

rig-out *n*
clothing, clothes, garments, outfit, kit, uniform, dress, costume, habit, livery
FORMAL apparel, raiment
COLLOQ. clobber, garb, gear, get-up, togs, things

rile *v*
annoy, irritate, nettle, pique, put out, upset, taunt, irk, vex, anger, exasperate
COLLOQ. peeve, aggravate, bug, wind up, hassle, rub up the wrong way, get your blood up, make your blood boil, get on your nerves, get up your nose, get under your skin, get your goat, get on your wick, drive crazy/nuts, drive bananas, drive up the wall, drive round the bend/twist, get your back up, brass off, cheese off, make your hackles rise, make sparks fly, give you the hump, get your dander up; *N Am* tick/hack off
F3 calm, soothe

rim *n*
lip, edge, brim, brink, verge, margin, border, circumference, ring, skirt, apron, shoe, strake
TECHNICAL felloe, helix, velum, bezel, wood, chime, fiddle, girdle
OLD rymme
F3 centre, middle

rind *n*
peel, zest, skin, husk, crust, shell, bark, gourd, crackling
OLD rine
FORMAL epicarp, integument

ring[1] *n, v*
♦ *n*
1 CIRCLE, round, loop, hoop, disc, halo, band, circlet, belt, girdle, collar, circuit, area, arena, enclosure, atoll
2 GROUP, cartel, syndicate, association, organization, league, alliance, combine, society, club, fraternity, sorority, gathering, circle, gang, crew, mob, band, cell, clique, coterie
♦ *v*
surround, encircle, gird, loop, encompass, enclose, cage in, hem in
FORMAL circumscribe

ring[2] *v, n*
♦ *v*
1 CHIME, peal, toll, knell, ding, ding-dong, tinkle, clink, jingle, clang, sound, resound, resonate, echo, reverberate, buzz
2 TELEPHONE, phone, call (up), ring up, reach, dial
COLLOQ. buzz, give a buzz, give a tinkle, give a bell

♦ *n*
1 CHIME, peal, toll, knell, tinkle, clink, jingle, clang, ding-dong
2 PHONE CALL, call
COLLOQ. buzz, tinkle, bell

ringleader *n*
leader, spokesman, spokeswoman, spokesperson, mouthpiece, chief, fugleman, bell-wether
COLLOQ. brains

rinse *v*
swill, bathe, wash (out), wash clean, clean, cleanse, flush (away), wet, dip

riot *n, v*
♦ *n*
1 *a riot in the streets*
insurrection, rising, uprising, revolt, rebellion, insurgence, anarchy, lawlessness, fight, brawl, fray, fracas, mêlée, affray, disturbance, race riot, turbulence, disorder, confusion, commotion, tumult, turmoil, uproar, row, quarrel, strife, breach of the peace, rout, hubbub
2 REVELRY, feasting, partying, indulgence, debauchery, orgy
OLD merrymaking
COLLOQ. rave, rave-up
3 *a riot of colour*
display, show, flourish, exhibition, extravaganza
4 LAUGH
COLLOQ. scream, hoot
F3 1 order, calm
♦ *v*
revolt, rebel, mutiny, rise up, run riot, run wild, run amok, go berserk, rush wildly, charge, tear, storm, rage, rant, rave, rampage, go on the rampage
■ **run riot**
rampage, go on the rampage, run wild, run amok, go berserk, rush wildly, charge, tear, storm, rage, rant, rave

riotous *adj*
1 WILD, violent, uncontrollable, unrestrained, unruly, rebellious, lawless, insurrectionary, insubordinate, disorderly, mutinous, ungovernable, wanton
2 NOISY, loud, rowdy, roaring, tumultuous, boisterous, uproarious
F3 1 orderly, restrained

riotously *adv*
wildly, uncontrollably, noisily, loudly, tumultuously, ariot

rip *v, n*
♦ *v*
tear, rend, split, separate, rupture, burst, cut, shred, slit, slash, gash, lacerate, hack
♦ *n*
tear, rent, split, cleavage, rupture, cut, ladder, slit, slash, gash, hole
■ **rip off**
overcharge, swindle, defraud, fleece, cheat, diddle, trick, dupe, exploit
COLLOQ. do, con
SLANG sting; *N Am* gold-brick

ripe *adj*
1 RIPENED, mature, mellow, seasoned, grown, fully-grown, developed, fully-developed, complete, finished, perfect, in season, forward, rare-ripe, drop-ripe, premature, under-ripe
OLD ratheripe
2 READY, suitable, fit, right, advantageous, favourable, timely, opportune
FORMAL auspicious, propitious
COLLOQ. spoiling (for)
F3 2 untimely, inopportune; *formal* inauspicious

ripen *v*
develop, mature, bring/come to maturity, mellow, season, age

rip-off n

robbery, exploitation, cheat, swindle, theft, fraud, diddle
COLLOQ. scam, con, con trick, daylight robbery
SLANG sting, swiz; *N Am* gold brick

riposte n, v

♦ *n*

retort, rejoinder, repartee, quip, answer, reply, response,
return, sally, comeback

♦ *v*

retort, rejoin, quip, reciprocate, answer, reply,
respond, return

ripple n, v

♦ *n*

1 WAVE, disturbance, eddy, gurgle, lapping, ripplet,
wavelet, undulation, burble, babble, purl, wimple
2 REPERCUSSION, effect, result, consequence, reverberation
COLLOQ. shock wave

♦ *v*

ruffle, wrinkle, flow, undulate, purl, wimple, crease,
pucker, crumple

rise v, n

♦ *v*

1 GO UP, move upwards, ascend, climb (up), mount, slope
(up), soar, tower, loom, grow, get higher, increase,
escalate, swell, intensify, rocket
2 STAND UP, get up, arise, jump up, leap up, spring up, get
to your feet, get out of bed
3 ADVANCE, progress, make progress, approach, improve,
prosper, be promoted
4 ORIGINATE, spring, flow, issue, emanate, emerge, appear,
start, begin
FORMAL commence
5 REBEL, revolt, mutiny, riot, resist, defect, take up arms,
take to the streets
FORMAL dissent
6 *rise to the challenge*
attempt, try, do your best, respond, react to, exert yourself
E≡ **1** fall, descend **2** sit down, lie down **3** decline, fall
back

♦ *n*

1 ASCENT, climb, slope, upward slope, soaring, towering,
incline, hill, elevation
FORMAL acclivity
2 INCREASE, growth, escalation, leap, increment, upsurge,
upturn, advance, progress, improvement, advancement,
promotion; *N Am* raise
FORMAL amelioration, aggrandizement
COLLOQ. hike, bounce
E≡ **1** descent, valley **2** fall, descent

■ **give rise to**
cause, bring about, bring on, make, produce, create,
generate, induce, lead to, provoke, prompt, evoke, elicit,
influence, inspire, persuade, originate, engender
FORMAL effect

SYNONYM NUANCES

verb sense 1
Go up can be widely applied as a synonym of rise:
house prices went up; the curtain went up. **Ascend**
generally describes the action of making your way up
something, while both **climb (up)** and **mount** have
suggestions of overcoming a slope or height with a
degree of difficulty. **Slope (up)** would be reserved for
simply increasing in gradient. **Tower** suggests a
superiority of height: *horse and rider towered
above her*, while **loom** has perhaps more menacing
implications.
   To refer to a rise in size or amount, **grow**, **get higher**
and **increase** can be widely used, while **escalate**
implies a rapid rise and possibly a loss of control, and
rocket implies rising at an incredible rate: *exports
rocketed*. You can use **swell** to suggest inflating or a
more lateral growth: *holiday-makers swelled the local
population*, and **intensify** to imply building in strength:
the new, extreme policy intensified opposition.

---

risible adj

ridiculous, ludicrous, funny, hilarious, humorous,
laughable, absurd, amusing, comic, comical, droll,
farcical
COLLOQ. rib-tickling, side-splitting
E≡ serious, unfunny

rising n, adj

♦ *n*

riot, revolution, revolt, uprising, insurrection

♦ *adj*

ascending, growing, increasing, intensifying,
mounting, soaring, swelling, advancing, emerging,
approaching
E≡ decreasing

risk n, v

♦ *n*

danger, peril, jeopardy, hazard, threat, chance,
possibility, uncertainty, gamble, speculation, venture,
adventure
COLLOQ. throw, flier
E≡ safety, certainty

♦ *v*

endanger, imperil, jeopardize, put in jeopardy, hazard,
chance, take a chance, gamble, venture, dare
COLLOQ. chance it, put on the line, go for broke, stick
your neck out, play with fire

QUOTATIONS
Without risk there is no faith
   SÖREN AABYE KIERKEGAARD, *Concluding Unscientific
   Postscript*

---

risky adj

dangerous, unsafe, perilous, hazardous, chancy, uncertain,
touch-and-go, touchy, high-risk, tricky, precarious,
venturesome
COLLOQ. dicey, dodgy, iffy, hairy
E≡ safe

risqué adj

indecent, improper, rude, immodest, indelicate, suggestive,
coarse, crude, earthy, dirty, bawdy, racy, smutty, naughty,
adult, ribald, off-colour
COLLOQ. blue, saucy, fruity, near the knuckle
E≡ decent, proper

rite n

ceremony, custom, act, usage, office, form, formality,
ceremonial, ordinance, practice, procedure, ritual, service,
worship, liturgy, sacrament, observance

ritual n, adj

♦ *n*

custom, tradition, convention, usage, practice, habit, wont,
routine, procedure, ordinance, prescription, form,
formality, ceremony, ceremonial, solemnity, rite,
sacrament, service, liturgy, celebration, observance, act,
mumbo-jumbo, trumpery
TECHNICAL cultus
OLD sacring
FORMAL consuetude

♦ *adj*

ceremonial, prescribed, set, formal, customary, traditional,
conventional, habitual, routine, procedural
FORMAL formulary

ritualistic adj

ritual, ceremonial, formulaic, traditional, formal, official,
solemn, dignified, stately, customary, festive
FORMAL formulary

ritzy adj

sumptuous, luxurious, opulent, lavish, de luxe,
magnificent, splendid, rich, expensive, costly,
affluent, self-indulgent, pampered, comfortable, grand,
well-appointed
COLLOQ. plush, posh, cushy, glitzy, swanky
E≡ austere, spartan

rival *n, adj, v*

♦ *n*

competitor, contestant, contender, challenger, opponent, opposition, adversary, antagonist, vier, fellow, match, equal, peer, collateral, nemesis
OLD corrival, paragon
E3 colleague, associate

♦ *adj*

competitive, competing, in competition, in conflict, conflicting, opposed, opposing, in opposition
OLD corrival
E3 associate

♦ *v*

compete with, contend with, vie with, oppose, compare with, measure up to, emulate, match, equal, parallel, touch
OLD mate
E3 co-operate

rivalry *n*

competitiveness, competition, contest, contention, conflict, struggle, strife, vying, opposition, antagonism
OLD corrivalry, corrivalship; (*Shakesp*) rivality
E3 co-operation

riven *adj*

torn apart, split, ripped apart, ruptured, divided, severed
OLD rent

river *n*

waterway, watercourse
Related adjectives: fluvial, potamic

Forms of river or watercourse include:

beck	creek	rill
billabong	cut	rillet
bourn	delta	rivulet
broads	estuary	runnel
brook	firth	source
burn	frith	stream
canal	inlet	tributary
channel	mountain stream	wadi
confluence	mouth	waterway

rivet *v*

fascinate, absorb, intrigue, interest very much, excite, grip, captivate, engross, enthral, arrest
E3 bore

riveting *adj*

fascinating, absorbing, interesting, exciting, gripping, arresting, captivating, engrossing, enthralling, spellbinding, magnetic, hypnotic
E3 boring

road *n*

route, way, roadway

PROVERBS
The road to hell is paved with good intentions

roam *v*

wander, rove, range, travel, traverse, walk, tramp, trek, ramble, meander, stroll, amble, prowl, raven, drift, stray; *dialect* rake, stroam
OLD squander; (*Shakesp*) wheel
FORMAL ambulate, perambulate, peregrinate
E3 stay

roar *v, n*

♦ *v*

1 BELLOW, yell, shout, cry, scream, shriek, bawl, howl, hoot, guffaw, thunder, crash, blare, rumble, boom, bell; *dialect* rout
OLD (*Spenser*) royne
2 LAUGH, shriek with laughter, guffaw, hoot
COLLOQ. split your sides, fall about, break up, crease up, laugh like a drain
E3 1 whisper

♦ *n*

bellow, yell, shout, cry, scream, shriek, bawl, howl, hoot, guffaw, thunder, crash, blare, boom, rumble

roaring *adj*

1 RESONANT, reverberating, echoing, ringing, loud, sonorous, booming, resounding, resonating, thunderous, full, rich, vibrant
2 CONCLUSIVE, resounding, decisive, impressive, striking, outstanding, roaring, great, memorable, remarkable, notable, emphatic, thorough

rob *v*

steal from, hold up, raid, burgle, loot, pillage, plunder, sack, rifle, ransack, swindle, cheat, defraud, deprive, bereave, despoil, pluck, ramp, fake, hijack, pirate, steal someone's thunder; *Scot* rub; *N Am* bunko
OLD pad, reave; (*Spenser*) berob
FORMAL depredate
COLLOQ. do, mug, knock off, nick
SLANG rip off, sting, heist, screw, stiff, turn over, blag, flimp, mill; *N Am & NZ* roll

robber *n*

thief, burglar, stealer, bandit, swindler, embezzler, fraud, cheat, plunderer, raider, pirate, highwayman, looter, brigand
COLLOQ. con man, mugger

robbery *n*

theft, stealing, larceny, break-in, housebreaking, hold-up, pilferage, raid, burglary, pillage, plunder, fraud, embezzlement, swindle
COLLOQ. mugging
SLANG rip-off, stick-up, heist

robe *n, v*

♦ *n*

costume, gown, vestment, habit, bathrobe, dressing-gown, nightgown, housecoat, peignoir, wrap, wrapper, talar, cassock, dolman, kimono
TECHNICAL chimer, purple, chrisom, killut
OLD palliament, vest, parament, peplos; (*Spenser*) camis

Types of road include:

A-road	byroad	course	freeway	path	terrace
alley	byway	crescent	grove	pathway	thoroughfare
arterial road	carriageway	cul-de-sac	high street	primary route	toll road
autobahn	cartroad	dead end	highway	ring road	towpath
avenue	cart-track	dirt road	lane	service road	track
B-road	cartway	dirt track	main road	side road	trail
boulevard	causeway	drive	motorway	side street	trunk road
bridle path	circle	driveway	one-way street	single-track road	turnpike
bridle way	circus	dual carriageway	overpass	slip road	unadopted road
broadway	clearway	*N Am* expressway	parade	square	underpass
bypass	close	flyover	passage	street	walk

♦ *v*
clothe, dress, drape, garb, vest
FORMAL apparel, attire

robot *n*
automaton, machine, android, zombie

robust *adj*
1 STRONG, sturdy, tough, hardy, energetic, vigorous, powerful, muscular, well-built, strapping, stalwart, athletic, fit, healthy, well
2 *robust opinions*
strong, forceful, vigorous, straightforward, direct, down-to-earth, no-nonsense
3 COARSE, earthy, rude, crude, ribald, risqué, raw
E3 **2** weak, feeble, unhealthy

rock¹ *n*
rocks rolling down the hill
boulder, stone, pebble, crag, outcrop
■ **on the rocks**
in a bad way, failing, in difficulty, in difficulties, unstable, hopeless, slipping, doomed, in a mess, in pieces, in shreds, at an impasse
COLLOQ. in a fix/scrape/hole/jam

Rocks include:

basalt	granite	porphyry
breccia	gravel	pumice stone
chalk	lava	sandstone
coal	limestone	schist
conglomerate	marble	serpentine
flint	marl	shale
gabbro	obsidian	slate
gneiss	ore	

rock² *v*
1 SWAY, swing, tilt, tip, shake, wobble, roll, undulate, pitch, toss, lurch, reel, stagger, totter, oscillate, move to and fro
2 *news that rocked the nation*
shock, stun, stagger, bewilder, daze, dumbfound, astound, astonish, surprise, startle, take back

rocket *n, v*
♦ *n*
projectile, missile, guided missile, ballistic missile, flying bomb
♦ *v*
soar, tower, increase quickly/suddenly, escalate, shoot up

rocky¹ *adj*
rocky moorland
stony, pebbly, craggy, rugged, rough, hard, flinty
E3 smooth, soft

rocky² *adj*
a rocky marriage
unsteady, shaky, wobbly, wobbling, staggering, tottering, unstable, unreliable, uncertain, weak
E3 steady, stable, dependable, strong

rococo *adj*
flamboyant, baroque, florid, extravagant, elaborate, ornate, flowery, embellished, exuberant, vigorous, bold, convoluted, decorated, overelaborate, overdecorated, overwrought, showy, fanciful, fantastic, whimsical, grotesque
TECHNICAL churrigueresque
E3 plain, simple, unadorned, austere

rod *n*
bar, shaft, strut, pole, stick, baton, wand, cane, switch, staff, mace, sceptre
Related adjective: rhabdoid

> **PROVERBS**
> Spare the rod and spoil the child

rodent

Kinds of rodent include:

agouti	fieldmouse	mouse
bandicoot	gerbil	muskrat
beaver	gopher	musquash
black rat	grey squirrel	pika
brown rat	groundhog	porcupine
cane rat	guinea pig	prairie dog
capybara	hamster	rabbit
cavy	hare	rat
chinchilla	harvest mouse	red squirrel
chipmunk	hedgehog	sewer rat
cony	jerboa	squirrel
coypu	kangaroo rat	vole
degu	lemming	water rat
dormouse	marmot	water vole
ferret	meerkat	woodchuck

rogue *n*
scoundrel, rascal, scamp, villain, miscreant, deceiver, swindler, fraud, fraudster, cheat, reprobate, good-for-nothing, wastrel, ne'er-do-well, rascallion, scallywag, drôle, hedge-creeper; *dialect* skellum; *Scot* hempy, limmer
OLD knave, palliard, slip-string, varlet, Greek, gypsy
COLLOQ. terror, wrong 'un, crook, con man, nasty piece of work
SLANG son of a gun, bugger; *S Afr* donder
OLD SLANG dummerer

roguish *adj*
mischievous, playful, cheeky, impish, knavish, rascally, waggish, frolicsome, coquettish, swindling, villainous, deceiving, deceitful, dishonest, criminal, crooked, fraudulent, shady, unprincipled, unscrupulous, rascal-like, hempy
OLD slip-string
E3 honest, serious

roister *v*
revel, rollick, celebrate, carouse, frolic, romp, strut, swagger, brag, bluster, boast
OLD make merry
COLLOQ. paint the town red, whoop it up, have it large, large it

roisterer *n*
reveller, carouser, ranter, roister, swaggerer, boaster, braggart, blusterer

roisterous *adj*
loud, noisy, wild, rowdy, uproarious, disorderly, exuberant, boisterous, clamorous, obstreperous
COLLOQ. laddish
E3 orderly, restrained

role *n*
part, character, representation, portrayal, impersonation, function, capacity, task, duty, job, post, position, situation, place

roll *v, n*
♦ *v*
1 ROTATE, revolve, turn (round), go round, spin, wheel, twirl, whirl, gyrate, move, go, run, pass, elapse
2 WIND, coil, furl, twist, curl, wrap, envelop, fold, enfold, bind
3 *the ship rolled*
rock, sway, swing, pitch, toss, lurch, reel, billow, tumble, stagger, wallow, undulate
4 PRESS, press down, flatten, crush, smooth, level
5 RUMBLE, grumble, roar, thunder, boom, resound, reverberate, echo
♦ *n*
1 *a bread roll*
bap, bun, bagel, bridge roll, finger roll, petit pain, brioche, burger bun, burger, hamburger, hot dog, submarine

sandwich, crescent, croissant, twist; *dialect* barm cake;
N Am hoagie
2 ROLLER, cylinder, drum, reel, spool, bobbin, scroll
3 REGISTER, roster, census, list, inventory, index,
catalogue, directory, schedule, record, file, chronicle,
annals
4 ROTATION, revolution, cycle, turn, spin, wheel, twirl,
whirl, gyration, undulation
5 RUMBLE, roar, thunder, boom, resonance,
reverberation
6 SWELL, pitching, tossing, rocking, reeling, billowing,
undulation
■ **roll in**
1 *money is rolling in*
be received, pour in, come in, flow in, rush in, flood in
2 *he rolled in an hour late*
turn up, appear, come, arrive, put in an appearance, be
present
COLLOQ. show up, blow in
■ **roll up**
arrive, assemble, gather, congregate, convene
E3 leave
■ **rolling in it**
rich, wealthy, affluent, moneyed, prosperous, well-to-do,
well-off
COLLOQ. flush, well-heeled, made of money, in the
money, with money to burn
SLANG loaded, filthy rich, stinking rich

rollicking¹ *adj*
a rollicking story
lively, noisy, light-hearted, hearty, romping, sprightly,
exuberant, frolicsome, jovial, carefree, boisterous, joyous,
merry, spirited, sportive, jaunty, cavorting, devil-may-care,
roisterous, roisting, frisky, playful, rip-roaring,
swashbuckling
E3 restrained, serious

rollicking² *n*
given a rollicking by the boss
reprimand, rebuke, reproof, scolding, harangue, censure,
upbraiding, chiding, reproach, lecture
FORMAL berating
COLLOQ. telling-off, talking-to, dressing-down, rocket

rolling *adj*
heaving, surging, waving, rippling, undulating,
undulant
E3 flat

roly-poly *adj*
fat, plump, chubby, overweight, rounded, tubby, buxom,
podgy, pudgy
FORMAL rotund
E3 slim

romance *n, v*
♦ *n*
1 LOVE AFFAIR, affair, relationship, liaison, attachment,
intrigue, amour, passion
COLLOQ. fling, thing
2 LOVE STORY, romantic fiction, novel, story, tale, fairy
story, fairytale, legend, idyll, fiction, fantasy, whimsy,
bodice-ripper
3 ADVENTURE, excitement, melodrama,
mystery, charm, fascination, glamour, colour,
sentiment, crusade
♦ *v*
1 LIE, fantasize, exaggerate, overstate
2 GO OUT WITH, court, woo, chase, see, date,
go steady with

romantic *adj, n*
♦ *adj*
1 IMAGINARY, fictitious, fanciful, fantastic, legendary,
fairytale, idyllic, utopian, optimistic, idealistic, quixotic,
visionary, starry-eyed, dreamy, unrealistic, impractical,
improbable, unlikely, wild, extravagant, exciting,
fascinating, mysterious, stardust
2 SENTIMENTAL, loving, amorous, passionate, tender, fond

COLLOQ. soppy, sloppy, lovey-dovey
E3 1 real, practical **2** unromantic, unsentimental
♦ *n*
sentimentalist, dreamer, visionary, idealist, utopian
E3 realist

> **QUOTATIONS**
> Men are so romantic, don't you think? They look for a
> perfect partner when what they should be looking for is
> perfect love
> FAY WELDON

romantically *adv*
1 *dance romantically*
lovingly, tenderly, fondly, sentimentally, amorously,
passionately
2 *as they romantically call it*
fancifully, optimistically, idealistically, unrealistically,
impractically, extravagantly, excitingly, mysteriously

Romeo *n*
lover, ladies' man, Don Juan, Casanova, Lothario,
lady-killer, gigolo

romp *v, n*
♦ *v*
gambol, frolic, skip, play, sport, frisk, caper, cavort, revel,
rollick, roister
♦ *n*
caper, frolic, lark, rig, spree

roof *n*
covering, canopy, vault; *dialect & Scot* rigging
Related adjective: tectiform
■ **hit the roof**
COLLOQ. explode, fly off the handle, blow up, blow your
cool/top, boil over, burst a blood vessel, do your nut, flip
your lid, freak out, go mad, go off the deep end, go up
the wall, lose your cool/rag, see red

Types of roof include:

bell roof	gable roof	pavilion roof
conical broach roof	gambrel roof	pendentive dome
	geodesic dome	pitched roof
cupola	helm roof	saddle roof
dome	hip roof	saucer dome
eco-roof (or green roof or living roof)	imbricated roof	sawtooth roof
	imperial roof	sloped turret
	lean-to roof	span roof
flat roof	mansard roof	thatched roof
French roof	monitor roof	
gable-and-valley roof	ogee roof	
	onion dome	

---

rook *v*
cheat, swindle, defraud, fleece, overcharge
COLLOQ. do, diddle, con, bilk
SLANG rip off, sting, take for a ride, take to the cleaners;
N Am gold-brick

room *n*
space, volume, capacity, area, headroom, legroom,
elbow-room, *Lebensraum*, scope, range, extent,
expanse, leeway, latitude, margin, allowance, chance,
opportunity
See panel on next page

roomy *adj*
spacious, large, sizeable, broad, wide, extensive, ample,
generous
FORMAL capacious, voluminous, commodious
E3 cramped, small, tiny

root¹ *n, v*
♦ *n*
1 TUBER, rhizome, stem, radical, radicle, radix
Related adjective: radical
2 ORIGIN, source, derivation, reason, cause, starting point,
fount, fountainhead, seed, germ, kernel, nucleus, heart,

Types of room include:

anteroom	changing room	en suite bathroom	lecture room	playroom	storeroom
assembly room	classroom	family room	library	porch	strongroom
atrium	cloakroom	fitting-room	living room	reading-room	studio
attic	common room	foyer	lobby	reception room	study
basement	computer room	front room	locker room	recreation room	sun lounge
bathroom	conservatory	games room	loft	*N Am* restroom	tack room
bedroom	consulting room	greenroom	*colloq.* loo	rumpus room	toilet
billiard room	control room	guardroom	lounge	saddleroom	TV room
boardroom	courtroom	guest room	lounge-diner	salon	utility room
boudoir	cubicle	hall	lumber room	scullery	waiting-room
box-room	darkroom	kitchen	meeting room	seminar room	washroom
breakfast room	day room	kitchen-diner	mezzanine	sick-room	WC
buttery	*colloq.* den	kitchenette	morning room	sitting room	wet room
cabin	dining-room	laboratory	music-room	smoking room	workroom
cell	dormitory	landing	nursery	spare room	workshop
cellar	drawing room	larder	office	staffroom	
chamber	dressing-room	laundry	pantry	stateroom	
chambers	engine-room	lavatory	parlour	stockroom	

core, nub, essence, seat, base, bottom, basis, foundation, fundamental

3 tracing your family roots
beginning(s), origins, family, heritage, background, birthplace, home
 ♦ *v*
anchor, moor, fasten, fix, set, stick, implant, embed, entrench, establish, ground, base

■ **root out**
unearth, dig out, uncover, discover, uproot, eradicate, eliminate, put an end to, exterminate, destroy, abolish, clear away, remove, get rid of
FORMAL extirpate

■ **put down roots**
settle down, establish yourself, make your home, set up home

■ **root and branch**
completely, entirely, wholly, totally, utterly, thoroughly, radically, finally
E3 not at all, slightly

■ **take root**
become established, become fixed, become entrenched, take hold, establish itself, become acceptable

root²
■ **root around**
rummage, ferret, poke, pry, nose, dig, delve, burrow, forage, hunt

root³ *v*
root for your team
support, shout, cheer (on), encourage, applaud, hail; *N Am* pull

rooted *adj*
entrenched, established, felt, firm, fixed, deep, deeply, deep-seated, ingrained, confirmed, rigid, radical
E3 superficial, temporary

rootless *adj*
unsettled, homeless, free, carefree, transient, of no fixed abode, moving, wandering, drifting, floating, nomadic, itinerant
E3 settled, established

rope *v, n*
 ♦ *v*
tie, bind, lash, fasten, hitch, moor, tether

■ **rope in**
enlist, engage, involve, persuade, talk into
FORMAL inveigle
Related adjective: funicular

■ **know the ropes**
understand what should be done, learn, master, get the hang of what to do, know what's what
COLLOQ. know the score, know the drill

Kinds of rope include:

bobstay	guy	noose
bowline	guy-rope	outhaul
brace	hackamore	painter
bridle	halter	ratline
buntline	halyard	runner
cable	hawser	stay
clew-line	head rope	strand
cord	hobble	string
cordage	lanyard	tack
cringle	lariat	tackle
dockline	lashing	tether
downhaul	lasso	towrope
dragline	line	vang
dragrope	marline	warp
gantline	mooring rope	widdy

ropy, ropey *adj*
poor, substandard, deficient, inadequate, inferior, unsatisfactory, rough, unwell, off colour
COLLOQ. duff, not up to scratch, below par
E3 good, well

roster *n*
rota, schedule, register, roll, list, listing, index, directory

rostrum *n*
platform, stage, dais, podium, bema

rosy *adj*
1 PINK, reddish, red, rose, rose-coloured, rose-hued, roselike, rose-pink, rose-red, rose-scented, roseate, glowing, fresh, sunny, healthy-looking, blooming, blushing, ruddy, flushed, florid, inflamed, bloodshot
FORMAL rubicund
2 PROMISING, cheerful, bright, encouraging, optimistic, hopeful, reassuring, favourable
FORMAL auspicious
E3 2 depressing, sad, unhappy

rot *v, n*
 ♦ *v*
decay, decompose, fester, perish, corrode, spoil, go bad, go off, degenerate, go sour, deteriorate, crumble, disintegrate, taint, corrupt, ret
FORMAL putrefy
 ♦ *n*
1 DECAY, decomposition, deterioration, corruption, disintegration, corrosion, rust, mould
FORMAL putrefaction
2 NONSENSE, rubbish, drivel, claptrap
COLLOQ. poppycock, bunk, bunkum, baloney, humbug, piffle, tosh, bosh, codswallop, cobblers, kibosh, blah, hogwash, rhubarb, hooey, malarkey, moonshine

rota n
roster, schedule, register, roll, list, listing, index, directory

rotary adj
rotating, revolving, turning, spinning, whirling,
gyrating, gyratory
▣ fixed

rotate v
1 REVOLVE, turn (round), spin (round), go round, move
round, reel, whirl, gyrate, pivot, swivel, roll
2 ALTERNATE, take (it) in turns, interchange, reciprocate

rotation n
revolution, turn, turning, spin, spinning, swivel, swivelling,
whirl, whirling, gyration, orbit, cycle, alternation,
sequence, succession

rote
■ **learn by rote**
memorize, commit to memory, learn from memory, learn
off by heart, learn off pat, learn word for word, learn
parrot-fashion

rotten adj
1 DECAYED, decomposed, putrid, addled, bad, off,
gone off, sour, spoilt, tainted, mouldy, f(o)etid, stinking,
rank, foul, rotting, decaying, rancid, disintegrating,
mouldering
OLD putid
FORMAL putrescent
2 INFERIOR, bad, poor, inadequate, low-grade, terrible,
dreadful, mean
COLLOQ. lousy, crummy, rop(e)y
SLANG manky, poxy, punk, putrid
3 NASTY, evil, wicked, horrible, beastly, dirty, despicable,
contemptible, dishonourable, dishonest, immoral, corrupt,
unprincipled
4 ILL, sick, unwell, poorly, awful, off colour, guilty
COLLOQ. grotty, rough, rop(e)y
5 *I'm fed up with your rotten questions*
damned, confounded, wretched, horrible,
unpleasant
COLLOQ. blasted, blooming, blinking, flipping, flaming,
darned, dashed, infernal, dratting
SLANG bloody; (*taboo*) fucking, frigging
▣ **1** fresh **2, 3** good **4** well

rotter n
scoundrel, rogue, cad, blackguard, dastard, cur
COLLOQ. bounder, blighter, stinker, swine, beast, pig, rat,
fink, louse
SLANG (*vulgar*) scrote; N Am (*vulgar*) douchebag

rotund adj
1 FAT, round, stout, tubby, full, fleshy, plump, podgy,
portly, chubby, roly-poly, heavy, obese, spherical,
globular, spheric, spheral, spherular, bulbous
FORMAL corpulent, rotundate, orbicular
2 RESONANT, rich, sonorous, full, rounded
FORMAL grandiloquent, magniloquent, orotund
▣ **1** flat, slim, gaunt

roué n
rake, lecher, libertine, profligate, wanton, debauchee,
sensualist, rakehell

rough adj, n, v
♦ adj
1 UNEVEN, bumpy, lumpy, stony, rugged, craggy, jagged,
irregular, gnarled, coarse, bristly, hairy, shaggy, scaly,
prickly, scratchy
2 BOISTEROUS, forceful, energetic, lively, disorderly, violent,
aggressive, belligerent, wild, noisy, rowdy, raucous,
discordant
3 HARSH, severe, stern, tough, hard, difficult, insensitive,
unfeeling, merciless, cruel, unkind, brutal, drastic,
extreme, vulgar, impolite, coarse, brutish, brusque, curt,
sharp
4 *in a rough voice*
husky, throaty, gruff, harsh, hoarse, rasping, croaking,
guttural, raucous, discordant, strident

5 APPROXIMATE, estimated, imprecise, inexact, hazy, vague,
general, quick, cursory, hasty, sketchy, incomplete,
unfinished, unpolished, unrefined, crude, plain, basic,
rudimentary
6 *rough sea*
choppy, agitated, turbulent, stormy, tempestuous,
violent, wild
7 ILL, sick, unhealthy, unwell, poorly,
off colour
COLLOQ. below par, rotten, grotty, lousy, under the
weather
▣ **1** smooth, level **2** gentle, sensitive **3** kind, mild
5 accurate, exact **6** calm, smooth **7** well
♦ n
1 SKETCH, mock-up, outline, draft, model
2 THUG, hooligan, bully, rowdy, ruffian, bruiser,
roughneck, tough
SLANG yob, yobbo
■ **rough out**
sketch, draft, draw in rough, outline, mock up, give
a summary of
■ **rough up**
beat up, maltreat, manhandle, mistreat
COLLOQ. do in, knock about, bash, mug

> **SYNONYM NUANCES**
>
> *adjective sense 1*
> **Uneven** and **irregular** are very general terms to describe
> a surface that is not flat, while **bumpy**, **lumpy** and **stony**
> are more descriptive of the physical appearance. The
> terms **rugged** and **craggy** are suggestive of broken rock
> and have connotations of rough beauty: *the craggy
> coastline*, but **jagged** suggests a more dangerous outline.
> **Gnarled** is suggestive of a twisted and knotted
> appearance.
>   **Coarse** suggests being in need of refining and is mildly
> pejorative: *a coarse woollen coat*, while both **bristly** and
> **hairy** again describe the finish in more detail and have
> similar connotations of discomfort, connotations which
> are made more explicit with **prickly** and **scratchy**.
> **Shaggy** is usually associated with hair, and has
> implications of being unkempt.

rough-and-ready adj
approximate, crude, sketchy, simple, basic, plain,
makeshift, make-do, provisional, stop-gap, hurried,
unpolished, unrefined
▣ exact, refined

rough-and-tumble n
scuffle, struggle, fight, fracas, rumpus, affray,
brawl, mêlée
COLLOQ. dust-up, punch-up, scrap

roughen v
abrade, asperate, coarsen, granulate, graze, harshen,
rough, chafe, chap, rasp, ruffle, scuff
▣ smooth

roughly adv
1 *speak to someone roughly*
harshly, toughly, cruelly, unkindly, brutally, insensitively,
mercilessly
2 *hustled roughly*
forcefully, energetically, violently, wildly,
noisily, rowdily, boisterously
3 *roughly £5million*
approximately, around, about, something like, circa, more
or less, loosely, round about, or thereabouts, approaching,
close to, nearly, just about, not far off, in the region/
neighbourhood/vicinity of, somewhere in the region of, in
round numbers, rounded up/down
COLLOQ. give or take
▣ **1, 2** gently **3** exactly

roughneck n
tough, thug, rough, rowdy, ruffian, hooligan, lout, bully
boy, bruiser; Scot keelie

round *prep, adv, adj, n, v*

♦ *prep, adv*

1 SURROUNDING, around, encircling, encompassing, enclosing, on all sides (of), on every side (of), about, framed by

2 EVERYWHERE (IN), to all parts (of), all over, in all directions, on all sides (of), throughout, about, around, here and there, to and fro

♦ *adj*

1 SPHERICAL, globular, ball-shaped, circular, ring-shaped, disc-shaped, disclike, globelike, hooplike, cylindrical, rounded, curved

FORMAL spheroid, discoid, discoidal, orbicular, globate

2 CHUBBY, fat, plump, stout, portly, ample

FORMAL corpulent, rotund

3 APPROXIMATE, rough, imprecise, estimated

♦ *n*

1 CIRCLE, ring, band, hoop, circlet, disc, sphere, cylinder, globe, ball, orb

2 CYCLE, series, sequence, succession, period, bout, session, heat, game, level, stage

3 BEAT, circuit, route, path, lap, course, routine

♦ *v*

go round, move past, circle, skirt, travel round, flank, bypass

■ **round off**

finish (off), complete, end, close, conclude, cap, crown, top off

 begin

■ **round on**

turn on, set upon, attack, lay into, abuse

■ **round up**

bring together, herd, marshal, assemble, gather, rally, muster, collect, group

 disperse, scatter

■ **round about**

approximately, roughly, around, about, something like, circa, more or less, loosely, or thereabouts, approaching, close to, nearly, just about, not far off, in the region/neighbourhood/vicinity of, somewhere in the region of, in round numbers, rounded up/down

COLLOQ. give or take

roundabout *adj*

indirect, circuitous, tortuous, twisting, winding, meandering, oblique, devious, evasive

FORMAL periphrastic, circumlocutory

 straight, direct

roundly *adv*

completely, thoroughly, forcefully, violently, vehemently, fiercely, intensely, rigorously, severely, sharply, bluntly, openly, frankly, outspokenly

 mildly

round-up *n*

1 SUMMARY, survey, overview, précis, collation, collection, assembly

2 GATHERING, herding, marshalling, muster, rally

 2 dispersal

rouse *v*

1 WAKE (UP), waken, awake, awaken, arouse, call, stir, get up, raise, look alive, unbed;
dialect rear

TECHNICAL flush

OLD abraid

2 EXCITE, arouse, awake, awaken, waken, move, start, disturb, agitate, anger, provoke, stimulate, instigate, incite, fire, inflame, impel, induce, kindle, enkindle, evoke, call up, galvanize, whip up, work up, stir, raise, summon, send, yerk, roust, irritate, put someone on their mettle

OLD firk; (*Spenser*) amove

FORMAL suscitate

COLLOQ. turn on, shake

 2 calm

rousing *adj*

stirring, exciting, inspiring, lively, moving, stimulating, spirited, vigorous, exhilarating, brisk, electrifying

 dull, boring, calming

rout *n, v*

♦ *n*

defeat, conquest, overthrow, beating, trouncing, drubbing, flight, retreat, stampede

OLD hurricane

FORMAL subjugation

COLLOQ. thrashing

 win

♦ *v*

defeat, conquer, overthrow, crush, beat, trounce, put to flight, chase, dispel, scatter, shoot down

FORMAL vanquish, subjugate, discomfit

COLLOQ. hammer, thrash, lick, slaughter, clobber, walk all over, wipe the floor with

route *n, v*

♦ *n*

course, run, path, road, avenue, way, flight path, direction, itinerary, journey, passage, circuit, round, beat

♦ *v*

direct, send, forward, convey, dispatch

routine *n, adj*

♦ *n*

1 PROCEDURE, way, method, system, order, pattern, schedule, programme, formula, practice, usage, custom, wont, habit, regime, rut, groove, rota, round, mechanics, treadmill, jogtrot, journey-work, heigh;
Scot heich-how

TECHNICAL chain, run

COLLOQ. drill; *N Am* milk run

2 *comedy routine*

act, piece, programme, performance, lines

COLLOQ. patter, spiel, yak

SLANG shtick

♦ *adj*

customary, habitual, usual, typical, ordinary, run-of-the-mill, normal, standard, common, wonted, workaday, conventional, unoriginal, predictable, familiar, everyday, banal, humdrum, dull, boring, monotonous, tedious, tiresome, hackneyed, institutional, bread-and-butter, day-to-day, perfunctory

COLLOQ. ho-hum

 unusual, different, exciting, inspiring

routinely *adv*

regularly, usually, normally, commonly, conventionally, typically, customarily, habitually

 surprisingly, irregularly, unusually

rove *v*

roam, wander, ramble, range, meander, drift, cruise, stroll, stray, gallivant, traipse; *Scot* stravaig

 stay

rover *n*

rambler, wanderer, transient, vagrant, traveller, drifter, itinerant, ranger, nomad, Gypsy, gadabout;
Scot stravaiger

 stay-at-home

row[1] *n*

a row of seats

line, tier, bank, rank, range, column, file, queue, string, chain, series, sequence, arrangement

■ **in a row**

consecutively, successively, sequentially, continuously, uninterruptedly, one after the other, in turn

COLLOQ. on the trot, back to back

row[2] *n, v*

♦ *n*

1 ARGUMENT, quarrel, disagreement, dispute, controversy, squabble, tiff, fight, conflict, fracas, brawl

FORMAL altercation

COLLOQ. slanging match, falling-out, set-to, scrap, dust-up

2 NOISE, racket, din, uproar, commotion, clamour, disturbance, rumpus, hubbub, tumult
F3 2 calm

♦ *v*
argue, quarrel, wrangle, bicker, squabble, fight
COLLOQ. scrap, be at each other's throats

rowdy *adj, n*
♦ *adj*
noisy, loud, rough, boisterous, disorderly, unruly, unrestrained, riotous, wild, obstreperous, blowzy
COLLOQ. stroppy; *Aust* rorty
F3 quiet, peaceful, restrained
♦ *n*
rough, ruffian, tough, tearaway, hooligan, lout, brawler, apache; *Scot* keelie; *Aust* larrikin
COLLOQ. hoodlum
SLANG yahoo, yob, yobbo, brat packer, bovver boy

royal *adj*
regal, majestic, kingly, kinglike, queenly, queenlike, princely, imperial, monarchical, sovereign, august, grand, impressive, imposing, stately, magnificent, splendid, superb

royally *adv*
impressively, grandly, greatly, wonderfully, tremendously, magnificently, splendidly, superbly

rub *v, n*
♦ *v*
1 STROKE, caress, fondle, pat, massage, scratch, knead
FORMAL embrocate
2 CLEAN, smooth, polish, buff (up), burnish, shine
3 SCOUR, scratch, scrape, scrub, wipe, clean, abrade
4 PUT ON, apply, work in, spread, smear
5 CHAFE, grate, scrape, pinch
♦ *n*
1 MASSAGE, stroke, caress, kneading, rub-down
2 POLISH, shine, wipe, clean
3 DIFFICULTY, drawback, hindrance, trouble, impediment, problem, obstacle, hitch, catch
COLLOQ. snag
■ **rub along**
get along/on, cope, manage, get by
■ **rub down**
clean, smooth, wash (down), sponge, dry, massage
■ **rub in**
emphasize, stress, underline, highlight, make much of, insist on, keep going on about, harp on
■ **rub off on**
influence, affect, have an effect on, change, alter, transform
■ **rub out**
1 ERASE, obliterate, delete, cancel
FORMAL efface
2 KILL, assassinate, murder, put to death, finish off, do away with
SLANG do in, bump off, eliminate, liquidate
■ **rub up the wrong way**
annoy, anger, irk, irritate, get, vex, niggle, get to
COLLOQ. bug, wind up, get your goat, get under your skin, needle, peeve
F3 calm

rubberneck *v*
gape, stare, look at, watch, view, goggle
COLLOQ. gawp, gawk

rubbish *n*
1 REFUSE, junk, litter, scrap, waste, dross, debris, rubble, flotsam and jetsam; *N Am* garbage, trash
FORMAL detritus
2 NONSENSE, drivel, twaddle, gibberish, gobbledegook, balderdash
COLLOQ. stuff and nonsense, claptrap, poppycock, rot, cobblers, bunk, bunkum, piffle, tripe, tosh, bosh, baloney, blah, eyewash, hogwash, rhubarb, guff, hooey, malarkey, moonshine; *Aust & NZ* bulldust; *Aust* bull's wool

SLANG bull; (*vulgar*) crap, cack, shit, bullshit, balls, bollocks
F3 2 sense

rubbishy *adj*
worthless, valueless, trashy, cheap, tawdry, low-quality, inferior, unsatisfactory, second-rate, third-rate, grotty, paltry, petty, shoddy, throw-away, gimcrack, tatty, twopenny-halfpenny
COLLOQ. crummy
SLANG cruddy
F3 high-quality, classy

rubble *n*
debris, remains, ruins, waste, wreck, wreckage, fragments

ruction *n*
protest, quarrel, trouble, fracas, fuss, row, rout, rumpus, disturbance, noise, din, hue and cry, dispute, commotion, racket, uproar, storm, brawl, rookery, ruffle
FORMAL altercation
COLLOQ. scrap, to-do, carry-on, kerfuffle
F3 calm

ruddy *adj*
1 *a ruddy complexion*
red, reddish, scarlet, crimson, blushing, flushed, rosy, glowing, healthy, blooming, florid, fresh, sunburnt, apple-cheeked
FORMAL rubicund
2 *the ruddy machine has broken down again*
annoying, infernal, confounded
COLLOQ. blasted, blooming, flipping, flaming, darned, dashed
F3 1 pale, unhealthy

rude *adj*
1 IMPOLITE, discourteous, disrespectful, bad-tempered, bad-mannered, impertinent, impudent, cheeky, insolent, offensive, insulting, abusive, ill-mannered, ill-bred, unpleasant, uncouth, uncivilized, unrefined, unpolished, uneducated, untutored, uncivil, curt, brusque, abrupt, sharp, short; *Scot* goustrous
OLD giant rude
See Synonym nuances panel at **insolent**.
2 *a rude joke*
obscene, vulgar, coarse, smutty, crude, offensive, improper, indecent, indelicate, dirty, filthy, risqué, ribald, lewd, bawdy, salacious, naughty, gross
COLLOQ. blue, near the bone, near the knuckle
3 *get a rude shock*
unpleasant, harsh, disagreeable, nasty, unexpected, sudden, startling
4 SIMPLE, rough, crude, primitive, rudimentary, basic, makeshift, rough-and-ready
5 IGNORANT, illiterate, uncivilized, unrefined, uneducated, untutored, unpolished, uncouth, rough, coarse, peasant, barbaric, bestial, boorish, churlish, heathenish
F3 1 polite, courteous, civil **2** clean, decent **3** pleasant, welcome **4** advanced, well-developed **5** educated, sophisticated

rudely *adv*
1 IMPOLITELY, discourteously, disrespectfully, impudently, insolently, abusively, curtly, brusquely, abruptly
2 *be made rudely aware*
harshly, unexpectedly, suddenly, unpleasantly, disagreeably
F3 1 politely, courteously, civilly, respectfully **2** pleasantly, agreeably

rudeness *n*
discourtesy, disrespect, impoliteness, bad manners, impertinence, impudence, insolence, abuse, ill manners, incivility, unpleasantness, uncouthness
F3 politeness, courtesy, civility, respect

rudimentary *adj*
1 BASIC, primary, initial, introductory, elementary, fundamental, essential

2 PRIMITIVE, undeveloped, embryonic, crude, unsophisticated, rough and ready, simple, rough
3 VESTIGIAL, remaining, surviving, undeveloped, imperfect, incomplete, reduced, functionless
F3 **1** advanced **2** developed

rudiments *n*
basics, fundamentals, essentials, principles, first principles, elements, ABC, beginnings, foundations

rue *v*
regret, be regretful, be sorry, mourn, grieve, lament, deplore, feel remorse for, reproach yourself, repent
OLD bemoan, bewail
F3 rejoice

rueful *adj*
regretful, remorseful, penitent, sad, melancholy, repentant, sorrowful, sorry, mournful, dismal, apologetic, grievous, conscience-stricken, doleful, pitiable, pitiful, plaintive, self-reproachful
FORMAL contrite, lugubrious, woebegone, woeful
F3 glad, joyful

ruffian *n*
villain, scoundrel, bully, bully-boy, brute, thug, lout, rowdy, rogue, cut-throat, rascal, roughneck, hooligan, bruiser, desperado, Apache; *N Am* highbinder, plug-ugly
· OLD sweater, trailbastion
FORMAL miscreant
COLLOQ. hoodlum, rough, tough, toerag, yobbo
SLANG yob, bovver boy, lager lout; *Scot* ned

ruffle *v, n*
♦ *v*
1 RUMPLE, dishevel, tangle, tousle, wrinkle, crease, pucker, crumple, ripple
FORMAL disarrange
2 ANNOY, upset, irritate, anger, put out, vex, irk, exasperate, fluster, rile, nettle, discompose, confuse, trouble
FORMAL perturb
COLLOQ. aggravate, bug, hassle, rattle, wind up, rub up the wrong way, get someone's blood up, make someone's blood boil, get on someone's nerves, get up someone's nose, get under someone's skin, get someone's goat, get on someone's wick, drive crazy/nuts, drive bananas, drive up the wall, drive round the bend/twist, get someone's back up, brass off, cheese off, make someone's hackles rise, make sparks fly, give someone the hump, get someone's dander up
F3 **1** smooth **2** pacify
♦ *n*
fold, tuck, pleat, gather, crease, flounce, frill, fringe, trimming, valance, falbala, line, wrinkle, crinkle, pucker, furrow

rug *n*
mat, carpet, floor-covering, covering, matting, kali, kilim, Persian carpet, doormat, felt, underfelt, underlay

rugged *adj*
1 ROUGH, bumpy, uneven, irregular, jagged, rocky, stony, craggy, stark
2 STRONG, robust, hardy, tough, sturdy, stalwart, vigorous, burly, well-built, muscular, sinewy, weather-beaten, furrowed
3 DETERMINED, strong, robust, tough, resolute, firm, tenacious, unflinching, unwavering
F3 **1** smooth

ruggedly *adv*
1 ROUGHLY, unevenly, irregularly, rockily, starkly
2 STRONGLY, toughly, vigorously, muscularly

ruin *n, v*
♦ *n*
1 DESTRUCTION, devastation, wreckage, havoc, damage, disrepair, decay, disintegration, breakdown, collapse, fall, downfall, failure, defeat, overthrow, ruination, undoing
2 *financial ruin*
insolvency, bankruptcy, loss, failure, crash, disaster

FORMAL indigence, penury
3 *the ruins of the castle*
remains, debris, rubble, fragments, traces, vestiges, relics, remnants, chaos, devastation, havoc, shambles
FORMAL detritus
F3 **1** development, reconstruction
♦ *v*
1 DAMAGE, harm, spoil, mar, botch, break, smash, shatter, injure, wreck, wreak havoc, destroy, demolish, raze, devastate, lay waste, overwhelm, overthrow, defeat, cripple, crush
COLLOQ. mess up
SLANG screw up
See Synonym nuances panel at **destroy**.
2 IMPOVERISH, bankrupt, make bankrupt, make insolvent, cripple
F3 **1** develop, restore
■ **in ruins**
ruined, damaged, dilapidated, broken-down, ramshackle, decrepit, destroyed, devastated, wrecked, falling apart, tumbledown

ruination *n*
destruction, devastation, wreckage, havoc, damage, disrepair, decay, disintegration, breakdown, collapse, fall, downfall, failure, defeat, overthrow, undoing

ruinous *adj*
1 *ruinous costs*
exorbitant, extortionate, excessive, unreasonable, immoderate, crippling
2 RUINED, in ruins, damaged, dilapidated, broken-down, ramshackle, decrepit, destroyed, devastated, wrecked, shattered, catastrophic, calamitous, disastrous, devastating, cataclysmic
OLD tottered, waste
F3 **1** low **2** beneficial

ruinously *adv*
exorbitantly, extortionately, unreasonably, immoderately, excessively

rule *n, v*
♦ *n*
1 REGULATION, law, statute, ordinance, decree, ruling, order, command, commandment, guide, corrective, restriction, precept, tenet, canon, maxim, axiom, truth, truism, principle, formula, guideline, direction, instruction, standard, criterion
2 REIGN, sovereignty, supremacy, kingship, queenship, dominion, mastery, influence, sway, power, authority, command, direction, control, regime, administration, government, leadership, jurisdiction
3 CUSTOM, convention, practice, standard, routine, procedure, protocol, form, habit, wont
♦ *v*
1 *rule a country*
reign, govern, command, lead, preside over, officiate, administer, manage, direct, guide, control, be in control, regulate, prevail, dominate
COLLOQ. call the shots, sit in the driving seat
2 JUDGE, adjudicate, decide, find, settle, determine, resolve, establish, decree, direct, order, lay down, pronounce
■ **rule out**
exclude, eliminate, reject, dismiss, prevent, ban, prohibit, forbid, disallow
FORMAL preclude
■ **as a rule**
usually, normally, mainly, in the main, ordinarily, generally, in general, on the whole, by and large, for the most part

> **QUOTATIONS**
> The golden rule is that there are no golden rules
> GEORGE BERNARD SHAW, *Man and Superman*,
> 'Maxims for Revolutionists: The Golden Rule'

noun sense 1
You can use **regulation** of a strict rule controlling various organizations or procedures, whereas **law** and **statute** are appropriate for a legal constitution devised by a corporation or body. **Ordinance**, likewise, implies the legal guidelines of an authority: *the German Drinking Water Ordinance*, while **decree** and **ruling**, although similar, suggest a judicial decision.

   Order or **command** can be used of a direction issued by anyone in a superior position, whereas **commandment** tends to suggest a divine or religious element. **Instruction** suggests a dictatorial element; the term **direction** suggests a less strict rule advising on how to proceed, and **guide** is even more suggestive of a helping hand. **Corrective** would be appropriate to refer to a rule that has been issued to put something right: *this policy could prove a strong corrective to inefficient practices*, whereas a **restriction** would refer to one which applies limitations.

   Principle, **precept** and **tenet** suggest a rule that is part of a moral code or belief system, while **canon** has ecclesiastical connotations. Both **maxim** and **axiom** would be appropriate to refer to a generally accepted adage, and **truism** used for something that is self-evident: *the truism that you get what you pay for*. The terms **principle**, **formula** and **guideline**, along with **standard** and **criterion**, can be used of fundamental truths, laws or norms that can be used as rules in doing something: *we will work on the principle of first come, first served*.

ruler

Titles of rulers include:

Aga	kaiser	princess
begum	khan	queen
caesar	king	rajah
caliph	leader	rani
commander	lord	regent
consul	maharajah	satrap
controller	maharani	shah
duce	mikado	sheikh
emir	monarch	shogun
emperor	nawab	sovereign
empress	nizam	sultan
Führer	overlord	sultana
governor	pharaoh	suzerain
governor-general	potentate	tsar (or czar)
head	president	tsarina (or czarina)
head of state	prince	viceroy

ruling *n, adj*
 ♦ *n*
judgement, adjudication, verdict, decision, finding, resolution, decree, pronouncement
 ♦ *adj*
1 REIGNING, sovereign, on the throne, supreme, governing, controlling, in control, in charge, commanding, leading
2 MAIN, chief, leading, principal, dominant, predominant, most influential

rum *adj*
strange, unusual, odd, peculiar, abnormal, bizarre, curious, weird, funny, freakish, queer, suspect, suspicious
FORMAL singular
COLLOQ. funny-peculiar

rumble *v, n*
 ♦ *v*
roar, thunder, boom, roll, reverberate
 ♦ *n*
roar, thunder, boom, roll, reverberation

rumbustious *adj*
boisterous, loud, noisy, rowdy, disorderly, clamorous, exuberant, unmanageable, unruly, uproarious, wild, rough, wayward, wilful, robust, roisterous, roisting
FORMAL obstreperous, refractory
 ✷ quiet, restrained, sensible

ruminate *v*
ponder, think, reflect, meditate, mull over, muse, brood, consider, contemplate, deliberate, chew over
FORMAL cogitate

rummage *v, n*
 ♦ *v*
root (around), search (through), turn over, poke around, hunt, explore, examine, delve, ransack, forage, rifle
 ♦ *n*
jumble, junk, tat, bric-à-brac, odds and ends

rumour *n, v*
 ♦ *n*
hearsay, gossip, talk, speculation, whisper, scandal, word, information, news, report, story, the word on the street, say-so, underbreath, cry, kite, canard, on-dit, sough; *dialect* tittle-tattle; *Scot* fama clamosa; *Aust* furphy
OLD noise, speech, voice, fame, bruit; *(Shakesp)* murmur
FORMAL tidings
COLLOQ. goss, grapevine, bush telegraph, buzz, breeze; *N Am* scuttlebutt
 ♦ *v*
say, tell, hint, put about, noise abroad, report, publish, gossip, circulate, whisper, bruit (about/abroad)

rump *n*
1 BUTTOCKS, bottom, behind, rear, seat, dock, hindquarters, breech, haunches, nache, croup, *derrière*
COLLOQ. backside, bum, posterior, fundament, tail; *N Am* butt, heinie, booty
SLANG duff, prat; *(vulgar)* arse; *N Am* ass, can, fanny, keister, tush; *Aust* coit, quoit
2 LEFTOVERS, remains, remainder, residue, trace, vestige

rumple *v*
wrinkle, crease, pucker, crumple, ruffle, dishevel, disorder, tousle, crinkle, crush, derange, scrunch
 ✷ smooth

rumpus *n*
disturbance, noise, uproar, confusion, commotion, disruption, furore, rout, row, tumult, fuss, fracas, brawl, brouhaha, ruction, bagarre, ruckus
COLLOQ. kerfuffle, shindy, rhubarb, shemozzle
 ✷ calm

run *v, n*
 ♦ *v*
1 SPRINT, jog, race, charge, career, tear, dash, hurry, rush, speed, run away, flee, bolt, dart, gallop, trot, scuttle, scamper, scurry
COLLOQ. step on it, scoot, scarper
2 GO, pass, move, travel, proceed, issue, flow
3 FUNCTION, work, go, operate, be in operation, perform, progress
4 CARRY OUT, do, perform, execute, fulfil, implement, undertake
5 *run a company*
head, lead, administer, direct, operate, own, carry on, carry out, conduct, manage, superintend, supervise, organize, co-ordinate, oversee, control, be in control of, regulate, be in charge of
6 COMPETE, contend, stand, enter, take part in, put yourself forward, challenge
7 LAST, continue, go, go on, extend, reach, stretch, proceed, spread, range
8 FLOW, stream, glide, roll, course, pour, gush, issue, jet, spurt, cascade, drip, trickle
9 *run your hand over something*
move, pass, spread, slide, cross
10 *run you to the station*
drive, take, convey, transport, give a lift; *N Am* give a ride

11 *run a car*
own, possess, have, drive, use, keep, maintain
12 *run for president*
stand, be a candidate in the election of, offer yourself as a candidate for
13 *that train doesn't run on a Sunday*
travel regularly, go, ply, shuttle
14 *the contract runs for three years*
be valid, be in effect, last, continue, operate, be in operation
15 *the play ran for four years*
be performed, be presented, be produced, be staged, be mounted, be played, last, go on
16 *the newspaper ran a story*
publish, print, carry, feature, include, communicate, broadcast
♦ *n*
1 JOG, gallop, race, sprint, spurt, dash, rush, hurry
2 DRIVE, ride, jaunt, excursion, outing, trip, journey
COLLOQ. spin
3 SERIES, sequence, string, cycle, chain, course, round, succession, spell, stretch, period
4 COURSE, route, way, line, track, road, flight path
5 ENCLOSURE, coop, pen, pound, fold, sty, paddock, yard
6 *a run on a currency*
demand, need, call, rush, clamour, pressure
7 POINT, goal, hit, mark, score
8 *gave us the run of their apartment*
free use of, permission to go anywhere in, permission to use anythig in, unrestricted access to
9 *different from the average run of things*
sort, kind, type, class, set, variety, category
10 *a run in a stocking*
ladder, rip, tear, cut, hole, split, slit, slash, snag, gash
■ **run across**
meet, encounter, come across, meet by chance, meet unexpectedly, run into
FORMAL chance upon
COLLOQ. bump into
■ **run after**
chase, pursue, follow, tail
Ⓕ flee
■ **run along**
go away, away with you, off with you, off you go, be off, on your way
COLLOQ. buzz off, clear off, scarper, scat
■ **run away**
1 ESCAPE, flee, abscond, decamp, bolt, run off, make off
COLLOQ. scarper, beat it, clear off, make a run for it, vamoose
2 *run away from problems*
avoid, ignore, disregard, evade, neglect, overlook, take no notice of, brush aside, dodge
COLLOQ. shut your eyes to, turn your back on
3 *run away with your neighbour's wife*
run off, elope, make off, leave
4 *run away with the money*
make off with, walk off with, steal, filch, pocket
FORMAL appropriate, purloin
COLLOQ. pinch, nick, lift
5 *run away with a competition*
win easily, win hands down, coast home
Ⓕ **1** stay **2** deal with
■ **run down**
1 CRITICIZE, slate, denounce, attack, pull/tear to pieces, belittle, defame
FORMAL disparage, denigrate
COLLOQ. slam, knock, pan, rubbish
SLANG slag (off)
2 RUN OVER, knock down, knock over, knock to the ground, hit, strike
3 TIRE, weary, exhaust, weaken
4 *run down production*
reduce, decrease, drop, cut, cut back on, trim, curtail
Ⓕ **1** praise **4** increase

■ **run for it**
escape, flee, fly, make off, retreat, bolt
COLLOQ. scarper, scram, do a bunk, skedaddle
Ⓕ stay
■ **run in**
arrest, jail
FORMAL apprehend
COLLOQ. nick, pick up, nab, lift, pinch, bust, nail, collar
■ **run into**
1 MEET, encounter, run across, meet by chance, meet unexpectedly
FORMAL chance upon
COLLOQ. bump into
2 HIT, strike, collide with, bump into, crash, ram
3 *run into difficulties*
encounter, meet, face, experience, come up against
4 *debts running into thousands of pounds*
amount to, come to, equal, add up to
Ⓕ **2** miss
■ **run off**
1 RUN AWAY, escape, make off, abscond, bolt, decamp, elope
COLLOQ. scarper, skedaddle
2 DUPLICATE, print, produce, copy, photocopy, Xerox®, Photostat®
Ⓕ **1** stay
■ **run off with**
1 *run off with your neighbour's wife*
run away with, make off with, elope with
2 *run off with the money*
run away with, make off with, walk off with, steal, filch, pocket
FORMAL appropriate, purloin
COLLOQ. pinch, nick, lift
■ **run on**
continue, go on, carry on, last, extend, reach
■ **run out**
expire, terminate, cease, end, close, finish, be used up, be finished, exhaust, be exhausted, dry up, give out, fail
■ **run out on**
abandon, leave, strand, desert, maroon
FORMAL forsake
COLLOQ. walk out on, jilt, ditch, chuck, dump, leave in the lurch
■ **run over**
1 HIT, knock down, run down, strike
2 REPEAT, go over, run through, practise, rehearse, review, recapitulate, reiterate, survey
COLLOQ. recap
■ **run through**
1 REHEARSE, go through, run over, practise, read, read through, review, survey, examine
2 SPEND, waste, squander, exhaust, fritter away
FORMAL dissipate
■ **run to**
amount to, add up to, total, come to, equal, afford, have enough of
■ **run together**
join, mix, unite, blend, combine, fuse, merge, mingle, amalgamate, coalesce
FORMAL commingle
Ⓕ separate
■ **in the long run**
eventually, ultimately, at last, in the end
COLLOQ. when all is said and done, at the end of the day
■ **on the run**
trying to escape, running away, on the loose, escaped, at large, free, at liberty, unconfined
SLANG N Am on the lam

+---+
| **SYNONYM NUANCES** |
| |
| *verb sense 1* |
| While **jog** suggests a comparatively slow, |
| regular pace, **sprint** and **race** can be |
| used of covering a short distance |
| at speed. The term **charge** usually implies a fixed |
+---+

purpose: *she charged off in search of her mother*, while **career** implies a degree of wildness and lack of direction. The terms **tear**, **dash** and **speed** have suggestions of a rather sudden, fleeting action: *she grabbed her mobile phone and dashed out into the street; something sped past me*. **Rush** is similar, but with overtones of impetuosity: *Why are you rushing from room to room?* **Dart** also suggests quick and sudden movement, although perhaps more brief in duration: *he darted across the road*.

The terms **run away** and **flee** are appropriate words for running to escape, and **bolt** likewise implies a hurried departure made to escape: *the gate was left open and the animals bolted*. **Gallop** returns to the idea of moving at a fast rhythmic pace, while **trot** is more suggestive of a quickened walk. While the association of these terms with horses lend suggestions of almost exaggerated movements, the terms **scuttle**, **scurry** and **scamper** are connotative of the short rapid steps of small animals, especially those taken nervously or playfully: *the blast sent people scurrying for cover; the boy scampered away, pleased with himself.*

runaway *n, adj*

♦ *n*

escaper, escapee, fugitive, absconder, truant, deserter, refugee

♦ *adj*

escaped, fugitive, loose, out of control, uncontrolled, wild

run-down *n, adj*

♦ *n*

1 REDUCTION, decrease, curtailment, decline, drop, cut, cutback
2 SUMMARY, résumé, synopsis, analysis, outline, sketch, briefing, review, run-through
COLLOQ. recap

♦ *adj*

1 WEAK, ill, unwell, tired, weary, drained, exhausted, fatigued, debilitated, worn-out, unhealthy, seedy, peaky
FORMAL enervated
2 NEGLECTED, uncared-for, dilapidated, tumble-down, ramshackle, broken-down, decrepit, dingy, shabby
COLLOQ. grotty
E3 1 healthy **2** well-kept

run-in *n*

fight, quarrel, argument, dispute, wrangle, skirmish, tussle, confrontation, difference of opinion, brush, contretemps
FORMAL altercation
COLLOQ. dust-up, set-to

runner *n*

1 JOGGER, sprinter, athlete, competitor, participant
2 COURIER, messenger, racer, dispatch rider, bearer
3 STEM, shoot, offshoot, sprout, tendril, sprig, sarmentum, stolon
TECHNICAL flagellum

■ **do a runner**

depart, go, go away, set out, take your leave, pull out, decamp, exit, disappear
COLLOQ. push off, push along, quit, scoot, take off, clear off, shove off, make tracks, do a bunk, up sticks, take French leave, vamoose, sling your hook, hook it

running *n, adj*

♦ *n*

1 SPRINTING, jogging, racing, rushing
2 ADMINISTRATION, direction, management, organization, co-ordination, superintendency, supervision, leadership, charge, control, controlling, regulation
3 FUNCTIONING, working, operation, performance, conduct
4 *out of the running*
contention, contest, competition, shortlist, candidacy

♦ *adj*

1 UNBROKEN, uninterrupted, continuous, ongoing, constant, perpetual, ceaseless, incessant, moving, flowing
FORMAL unceasing

2 IN SUCCESSION, successive, consecutive, in a row
COLLOQ. on the trot
E3 1 broken, occasional

runny *adj*

flowing, fluid, liquid, liquefied, melted, molten, watery, diluted
E3 solid

run-of-the-mill *adj*

ordinary, common, normal, everyday, average, unexceptional, mediocre, middling, tolerable, fair, unremarkable, undistinguished, unimpressive
COLLOQ. OK, so-so, bog standard, common-or-garden, not up to much, no great shakes
E3 exceptional, remarkable

rupture *n, v*

♦ *n*

1 SPLIT, tear, burst, puncture, break, breaking, breach, fracture, crack
TECHNICAL hernia, scissure, rhexis, amniotomy, cerebral haemorrhage
2 DIVISION, separation, split, schism, rift, disagreement, quarrel, falling-out, scissure
OLD rent
FORMAL estrangement
COLLOQ. bust-up

♦ *v*

split, tear, burst, puncture, break, fracture, crack, sever, separate, divide, cut off
OLD rend

rural *adj*

country, rustic, countryside, pastoral, agricultural, agrarian, bucolic, sylvan
E3 urban

SYNONYM NUANCES

Country can be used to suggest anything that is not urbanized, and **countryside**, less usual in its adjectival form, suggests the general area: *the Countryside Commission*. **Rustic** can be used to describe something characteristic of a rural way of life, usually with connotations of old-fashionedness or simplicity: *a rustic kitchen with wooden floors*. Both **agricultural** and **agrarian**, on the other hand, are appropriate for a more practical view of farming life, unlike **bucolic** and **pastoral**, which are literary in tone and often imply an idealized image: *a romantic, pastoral scene*. **Sylvan** is similar, but is suggestive of a wooded area: *beautiful trees, and vistas of sylvan charm.*

---

ruse *n*

plan, trick, deception, dodge, hoax, imposture, stratagem, tactic, manoeuvre, ploy, plot, scheme, wile, subterfuge, artifice, device, blind, sham, stall

rush *v, n*

♦ *v*

1 HURRY, dash, hasten, quicken, accelerate, speed (up), press, push, dispatch, bolt, dart, shoot, hurtle, fly, tear, career, race, run, sprint, scramble, gallop, stampede, charge
OLD make haste
COLLOQ. belt, bomb, pelt, get a move on, run like hell
2 ATTACK, charge, assault, storm, raid, strike, run at

♦ *n*

1 HURRY, haste, urgency, speed, rapidity, swiftness, dash, race, scramble, stampede, charge, flow, flood, surge, stream, gush
2 BUSTLE, activity, hustle and bustle, stir, commotion, excitement, flurry, hurry, hurly-burly
COLLOQ. hive of activity, comings and goings
3 ATTACK, charge, onslaught, assault, storm, raid, strike
4 DEMAND, call, need, run, clamour, pressure

rushed *adj*
busy, hurried, emergency, careless, cursory, superficial, quick, fast, rapid, swift, brisk, hasty, prompt, urgent
FORMAL expeditious

rust *n, v*
♦ *n*
corrosion, oxidation, verdigris, stain, decay, dross
TECHNICAL uredo, ferrugo
♦ *v*
corrode, oxidize, tarnish, deteriorate, decline, decay, rot

rust-coloured *adj*
rusty, reddish-brown, brown, red, reddish, copper, auburn, chestnut, russet, ginger, sandy, tawny, titian
FORMAL ferruginous, ferrugineous, rubiginous, rubiginose

rustic *adj, n*
♦ *adj*
1 PASTORAL, sylvan, bucolic, countrified, country, countryside, rural
2 PLAIN, simple, rough, crude, coarse, rude, clumsy, awkward, artless, homespun, ingenuous, unsophisticated, unrefined, uncultured, provincial, uncouth, graceless, indelicate, boorish, clodhopping, oafish
FORMAL maladroit
E3 1 urban **2** urbane, sophisticated, cultivated, polished
♦ *n*
bumpkin, countryman, countrywoman, oaf, peasant, provincial, yokel, boor, churl, clodhopper, clod, country cousin
COLLOQ. hayseed, hick, hillbilly
E3 sophisticate , dandy

rustle *v, n*
♦ *v*
crackle, whoosh, swish, whisper, sigh; *Scot* fissle
FORMAL susurrate
♦ *n*
crackle, crinkling, rustling, swish, whoosh, whisper, whispering
FORMAL crepitation, crepitus, susurration, susurrus

■ **rustle up**
prepare quickly, get/provide quickly, make, get/put together
COLLOQ. scare up

rusty *adj*
1 CORRODED, rusted, rust-covered, oxidized, tarnished, discoloured, dull
TECHNICAL aeruginous
2 RUST-COLOURED, reddish-brown, brown, red, reddish, coppery, copper, auburn, chestnut, russet, ginger, gingery, sandy, tawny, titian
FORMAL ferruginous, ferrugineous, rubiginous, rubiginose
3 *my German is a bit rusty*
unpractised, out of practice, weak, poor, impaired, deficient, dated, old-fashioned, outmoded, antiquated, stale, stiff, creaking

rut *n*
1 DITCH, channel, furrow, groove, gutter, indentation, trough, track, gouge, pothole, wheel track
2 ROUTINE, habit, pattern, system, humdrum, grind, daily grind, treadmill, same old round/place, no change of scenery

ruthless *adj*
merciless, pitiless, hard-hearted, hard, heartless, unforgiving, unmerciful, unfeeling, unsparing, callous, cruel, inhuman, grim, stern, vicious, brutal, savage, barbarous, fierce, ferocious, relentless, remorseless, unrelenting, inexorable, implacable, harsh, severe, Draconian, stopping at nothing, hard-bitten, third-degree
OLD fell; (*Spenser*) felonous
COLLOQ. cut-throat, dog-eat-dog
E3 merciful, compassionate

ruthlessly *adv*
hard-heartedly, unmercifully, mercilessly, pitilessly, callously, unfeelingly, fiercely, cruelly, brutally, savagely, harshly, severely, inexorably, remorselessly
E3 compassionately

S

sable *adj*
dark, black, coal-black, pitch-black, pitch-dark, pitchy, ebony, inky, jet, raven, dusky, sombre, midnight

sabotage *v, n*
♦ *v*
damage, spoil, mar, disrupt, vandalize, wreck, destroy, thwart, ruin, scupper, cripple, incapacitate, disable, undermine, impair, weaken
OLD ratten
♦ *n*
vandalism, damage, impairment, disruption, wrecking, destruction, ruin, spoiling, crippling, disabling, weakening
OLD rattening

sac *n*
bag, pocket, pouch, pod, bladder, capsule, follicle, cyst, saccule, vesicle
TECHNICAL bursa, theca, vesica, vesicula
Related adjective: thecal

saccharine *adj*
sickly, sweet, sentimental, honeyed, cloying, maudlin, mawkish, nauseating, oversweet, sugary, syrupy, sickly-sweet
COLLOQ. soppy, sloppy, mushy, gushy, schmaltzy
E3 bitter, tart

sachet *n*
packet, pack, bag, package, container, wrapping, envelope

sack¹ *v, n*
♦ *v*
sack 100 workers
dismiss, fire, discharge, lay off, make redundant, give notice, give someone their papers, remove
COLLOQ. axe, send packing, boot out, give someone their cards, give someone their jotters, give someone the sack/push/boot/elbow/heave-ho, show someone the door
COLLOQ. *N Am* can, select out
♦ *n*
1 BAG, pocket, pouch, pack, satchel, mat
OLD budget
2 DISMISSAL, discharge, notice, marching orders
COLLOQ. the boot, the push, the elbow, the axe, the chop, the heave-ho, papers, cards, jotters, sacking, firing

sack² *v, n*
♦ *v*
the army sacked the town
destroy, raid, plunder, ravage, raze, lay waste, waste, level, devastate, desecrate, demolish, maraud, pillage, rifle, rob, loot, ruin, rape, spoil, strip
FORMAL depredate, despoil
♦ *n*
destruction, devastation, ravage, razing, ruin, waste, levelling, looting, plunder, plundering, marauding, desecration, rape, pillage
FORMAL depredation, despoliation, rapine

sacrament *n*
ordinance, ceremony, order, practice, observance, rite, ritual, institution

sacred *adj*
1 HOLY, divine, heavenly, blessed, hallowed, sanctified, consecrated, dedicated

2 RELIGIOUS, spiritual, devotional, ecclesiastical, priestly, saintly, godly
3 REVERED, venerable, respected, sacrosanct, inviolable, defended, protected, hallowed, untouchable, impregnable, secure
E3 1 profane, secular **2** temporal

sacredness *n*
holiness, divinity, godliness, sanctity, solemnity, saintliness, sacrosanctity, invulnerability, inviolability
E3 profaneness, worldliness

sacred writings

Sacred writings of religions include:

BAHAI:	**CONFUCIANISM:**	**JAINISM:**
Most Holy Book	Shih Ching	Svetambara canon
The Seven	Li Ching	Digambara texts
Valleys	Shu Ching	
The Hidden	Ch'un Ch'iu	**JUDAISM:**
Words	I Ching	Hebrew Bible
The Bayan	Lun Yu	Torah (Pentateuch)
BUDDHISM:	Chung Yung	Talmud
Tipitaka	Ta Hsueh	Zohar
Mahayana Sutras	Meng Tzu	**MORMONISM:**
Milindapandha		Book of Mormon
Bardo Thodol	**HINDUISM:**	
	the Vedas (Rig,	**SHINTOISM:**
CHRISTIANITY:	Yajur, Sama,	Kojiki
The Bible	Atharva)	Nihon Shoki
Old Testament	Upanishads	
New Testament	Ramayana	**SIKHISM:**
Pentateuch	Mahabharata	Adi Granth
Gospels	Bhagavad-Gita	**TAOISM:**
Acts of the	Puranas	Chuang Tzu
Apostles	**ISLAM:**	Lao Tzu (Tao Te
Epistles	Koran	Ching)
Apocrypha	Hadith	**ZOROASTRIANISM:**
		Avesta

sacrifice *v, n*
♦ *v*
1 *sacrifice an animal in a religious ceremony*
offer, offer up, slaughter, martyrize
TECHNICAL molochize
OLD sacrify; (*Spenser*) sacrifide
FORMAL immolate, lustrate
2 GIVE UP, surrender, forfeit, relinquish, let go, abandon, for(e)go
TECHNICAL gambit
FORMAL renounce
♦ *n*
1 OFFERING, slaughter, victim, blood-sacrifice
TECHNICAL burnt-offering, heave-offering, heave-shoulder, sin-offering, propitiation, acceptilation, hecatomb
OLD suovetaurilia, taurobolium
FORMAL oblation, immolation, lustration, holocaust, juggernaut
2 GIVING-UP, destruction, surrender, abandonment, loss
TECHNICAL gambit
FORMAL renunciation

sacrificial *adj*
atoning, votive
TECHNICAL propitiatory, expiatory, piacular
FORMAL oblatory, reparative

sacrilege *n*
blasphemy, profanity, heresy, desecration, profanation, violation, outrage, irreligion, impiety, irreverence, disrespect, mockery
E3 piety, reverence, respect

sacrilegious *adj*
blasphemous, profane, heretical, desecrating, disrespectful, irreverent, impious, irreligious, godless, ungodly, unholy
FORMAL profanatory
E3 pious, reverent, respectful

sacrosanct *adj*
sacred, hallowed, untouchable, inviolable, impregnable, respected, protected, secure

sad *adj*
1 UNHAPPY, sorrowful, tearful, grief-stricken, heavy-hearted, upset, distressed, miserable, low-spirited, in low spirits, downcast, glum, long-faced, crestfallen, dejected, downhearted, despondent, melancholy, depressed, mournful, doleful, wistful, joyless, gloomy, dismal, wretched
FORMAL woebegone, disconsolate
COLLOQ. fed up, blue, low, down, down in the dumps, (at) rock bottom; *N Am* in a funk
2 *sad news*
upsetting, distressing, painful, depressing, touching, poignant, heart-rending, heartbreaking, tragic, grievous, lamentable, regrettable, miserable, sorry, sorrowful, unfortunate, unhappy, serious, grave, calamitous, disastrous
3 *in a sad state*
grievous, lamentable, regrettable, deplorable, disgraceful, shameful, sorry, unfortunate, wretched, pitiful, pitiable
COLLOQ. pathetic
E3 1 happy, cheerful **2** fortunate, lucky **3** good, healthy

> **QUOTATIONS**
> For all sad words of tongue or pen, / The saddest are, 'It might have been'
> JOHN GREENLEAF WHITTIER, 'Maud Muller'

> **SYNONYM NUANCES**
>
> *sense 1*
> **Unhappy** can be widely used as a synonym for sad, while **sorrowful** implies a more intense feeling, often with further implications of regret: *a homesick and sorrowful refugee*, and **grief-stricken** has suggestions of a crushing loss. **Upset** can suggest various depths of emotional disturbance, while **distressed** suggests acute mental anguish.
> **Miserable** and the stronger **wretched** have connotations of a pitiful state, whilst **downcast** and **glum** often suggest a sad appearance. Similarly, **crestfallen** suggests a facial expression, implying disappointment as the cause: *her crestfallen countenance revealed her feelings at the news*. Both **dejected** and **downhearted** are appropriate to convey a slump in spirits, and **despondent** suggests a lack of hope: *many people who have lost their jobs become despondent, fearing they will never work again.*
> **Melancholy** implies a lingering condition, often tinged with self-indulgence: *a melancholy reverie*, while **wistful** suggests sadness tinged with yearning. The term **depressed** may be used to describe a persistent, clinical state. **Mournful** suggests bereavement or loss, while **doleful** is more suggestive of a heavy heart. **Gloomy** and **dismal** suggest a more pervasive feeling of darkness or lack of hope: *don't look so gloomy, I am sure there are good times coming.*

sadden *v*
upset, distress, grieve, depress, deject, dismay, discourage, dishearten, cast down, dispirit, break your heart, drive to despair
OLD attrist, contrist
COLLOQ. get someone down
E3 cheer, please, gratify, delight

saddle *n, v*
♦ *n*
See panel at **tack**.
♦ *v*
burden, encumber, lumber, land, impose, tax, charge, load

sadism *n*
cruelty, inhumanity, brutality, savagery, viciousness, heartlessness, ruthlessness, unnaturalness, sado-masochism, spite, malevolence, callousness, barbarity, bestiality
FORMAL schadenfreude

sadist *n*
torturer, abuser, molester, monster, brute, savage, barbarian
COLLOQ. terror

sadistic *adj*
cruel, inhuman, brutal, savage, vicious, merciless, pitiless, barbarous, bestial, unnatural, perverted

sadly *adv*
1 UNHAPPILY, sorrowfully, gloomily, dismally, tearfully, weepingly, heavy-heartedly, dejectedly, despondently, miserably
2 UNFORTUNATELY, regrettably, unhappily, unluckily, alas, sad to say, sad to relate
COLLOQ. worse luck
E3 1 happily, cheerfully **2** fortunately, luckily

sadness *n*
unhappiness, sorrow, sorrowfulness, grief, misery, misfortune, despondency, desolation, depression, dejection, cheerlessness, bleakness, joylessness, dolefulness, dismalness, poignancy, sombreness, mournfulness, distress, low spirits, glumness, gloominess, tearfulness, wretchedness, tragedy, pain, regret, pathos
OLD contristation
FORMAL disconsolateness, lugubriousness, melancholy, woe
COLLOQ. heartache
E3 happiness, cheerfulness, delight

safe *adj, n*
♦ *adj*
1 HARMLESS, innocuous, non-toxic, non-poisonous, uncontaminated
2 UNHARMED, undamaged, unscathed, uninjured, out of danger, unhurt, intact, secure, sound, protected, sheltered, defended, guarded, impregnable, invulnerable, unassailable, immune
COLLOQ. out of harm's way, safe and sound, safe as houses, in good hands
3 DEPENDABLE, reliable, trustworthy, responsible, honest, honourable, sure, proven, tried, tested, sound, upright
4 UNADVENTUROUS, unenterprising, cautious, prudent, timid, conservative
FORMAL circumspect
E3 1 dangerous, harmful **2** vulnerable, at risk, exposed **3** risky, uncertain **4** adventurous, reckless
♦ *n*
cash box, deposit box, safety-deposit box, strongbox, chest, coffer, vault, depository, repository

> **PROVERBS**
> Better safe than sorry

safe-conduct *n*
authorization, pass, passport, permit, safeguard, warrant, licence, convoy, *laissez-passer*
OLD SLANG jark

safeguard v, n
- v

protect, preserve, defend, look after, take care of, guard, shield, screen, shelter, secure
Ｅ endanger, jeopardize
- n

protection, defence, shield, security, surety, guarantee, assurance, insurance, cover, precaution, preventive, preventative

safekeeping n
protection, care, custody, keeping, charge, trust, guardianship, surveillance, supervision, ward, wardship

safely adv
securely, out of danger, without injury, without risk, without harm, impregnably
COLLOQ. out of harm's way

safety n, adj
- n

1 PROTECTION, security, safeguard, immunity, welfare, sanctuary, impregnability, safeness, harmlessness, soundness, reliability, dependability, trustworthiness
2 SANCTUARY, refuge, shelter, cover
Ｅ 1 danger, jeopardy, risk
- adj

precautionary, preventive, preventative, protective, fail-safe

> **PROVERBS**
> There is safety in numbers

sag v, n
- v

1 HANG LOOSELY, bend, give, bag, droop, hang, swag
2 *prices/her spirits started to sag*
fall, drop, sink, dip, decline, slump, subside, flop, fail, flag, falter, weaken, wilt
Ｅ 1 bulge 2 rise
- n

drop, fall, low, low point, reduction, slump, slip, slide, dip, decline, depression, downturn, dwindling
Ｅ peak, rise

saga n
chronicle, epic, history, narrative, adventure, story, tale, yarn, romance, soap opera, *roman fleuve*
FORMAL epopee, epopeia, epos

sagacious adj
wise, discerning, insightful, penetrating, perceptive, far-sighted, able, intelligent, knowing, acute, sharp, astute, canny, quick, shrewd, prudent, smart, wary, wide-awake, wily, fly
FORMAL judicious, percipient, perspicacious, sage, sapient
Ｅ foolish, obtuse

sagacity n
wisdom, discernment, understanding, judgement, insight, foresight, penetration, sense, sharpness, shrewdness, prudence, acumen, knowingness, astuteness, acuteness, canniness, wariness, wiliness
FORMAL judiciousness, percipience, perspicacity, sapience
Ｅ folly, foolishness, obtuseness

sage n, adj
- n

wise person, wise man, wise woman, teacher, master, expert, authority, pundit, savant, guru, maharishi, oracle, elder, philosopher, wiseacre, Solomon, mahatma, hakam, rishi, Solon
Ｅ ignoramus
- adj

wise, intelligent, discerning, knowing, learned, knowledgeable, astute, canny, politic, prudent, sensible
FORMAL judicious, perspicacious, sagacious, sapient
Ｅ foolish

sagely adv
wisely, perceptively, discerningly, ably, intelligently, knowingly, sharply, quickly, acutely, astutely, prudently, shrewdly
FORMAL judiciously, perspicaciously

saggy adj
sagging, droopy, drooping, limp, floppy, falling, dropping, slack, loose, lax, weak, feeble

sail v
1 *sail for France*
embark, set sail, leave port, weigh anchor, put to sea, put off, go/travel by sea, cruise, yacht, boat, ship, voyage
2 CAPTAIN, skipper, pilot, navigate, steer
3 GLIDE, plane, sweep, float, drift, coast, skim, scud, fly, wing, soar
■ **sail into**
attack, let fly, set about, turn on, assault
COLLOQ. lay into, tear into
■ **sail through**
deal with successfully, succeed in/pass easily, romp through
Ｅ scrape through

Types of sail include:

Bermuda rig	headsail	royal
canvas	jib	skysail
course	jigger	spanker
fore-and-aft rig	jury rig	spinnaker
foreroyal	kite	spritsail
foresail	lateen sail	square sail
forestaysail	lugsail	staysail
foretop	main course	studdingsail
fore-topgallant	mainsail	topgallant
fore-topsail	maintopsail	topsail
gaff sail	mizzen	trysail
gaff-topsail	moonraker	
genoa	rig	

---

sailing n
boating, yachting

Terms used in sailing include:

abaft	going about	running goose-
across the wind	gybe	winged
alongside	handing (a sail)	sailing by the lee
astern	hard on the wind	sail trimming
backing	heeling (to the	sheeting in a sail
beam reach	wind)	spilling wind
bearing	in irons/in stays	standing on
beat	knockdown (by	starboard
beating	the wind)	starboard tack
bending (on a sail)	laying off (a	steerage way
blanketing effect	course)	stepping/unstep-
breaking out (the	lay up	ping (the mast)
anchor)	lee helm	tacking
broad reach	lee-oh!	taking soundings
casting off/letting	leeway	unbending (a sail)
go	lift	under way
close-hauled	points of sailing	upwind
close reach	port	veer (the anchor)
coming about	port tack	weather helm
downwind	reaching	weathering
fetch	ready about!	windward
fitting-out	running	yawing
fixing a position		

---

sailor n
seafarer, mariner, seaman
OLD (*Shakesp*) canvas-climber
COLLOQ. hearty, tar, Jack, Jack tar, sea dog, water rat; *Scot* tarry-breeks
SLANG limey, matlo, matelot, salt
See panel on next page

Types of sailor include:

AB	crewman	oarsman
able seaman	deck hand	pilot
bargee	fisherman	pirate
bluejacket	galiongee	purser
boatman	*N Am slang* gob	rating
boatswain (or	helmsman	rower
bosun)	lascar	sculler
buccaneer	leatherneck	skipper
cabin boy	*N Am* marine	Wren
captain	master	yachtsman
cox	mate	yachtswoman
coxswain	navigator	

saint *n*

sant, santon, patron saint, guardian saint, tutelar; *Scot* saunt

OLD hallow

See panel below

saintliness *n*

godliness, piety, devoutness, holiness, spirituality, blessedness, purity, spotlessness, faith, innocence, blamelessness, sinlessness, virtue, selflessness, morality, goodness, righteousness, sanctity, chastity, self-denial, self-sacrifice, asceticism, uprightness, unselfishness

E3 godlessness, unholiness, wickedness

saintly *adj*

saintlike, godly, pious, devout, God-fearing, holy, religious, spiritual, believing, blessed, angelic, pure, spotless, innocent, blameless, sinless, virtuous, moral, ethical, good, upright, worthy, righteous

E3 godless, unholy, wicked

sake *n*

benefit, advantage, good, welfare, wellbeing, gain, profit, behalf, interest, account, regard, respect, purpose, aim, goal, object, objective, cause, reason, consideration

salacious *adj*

prurient, bawdy, indecent, improper, obscene, scurrilous, pornographic, lecherous, lewd, carnal, coarse, erotic, horny, ribald, wanton, randy, lustful, raunchy, fruity, ruttish

OLD salt

FORMAL concupiscent, lascivious, libidinous, lubricious

COLLOQ. blue, smutty, steamy

E3 clean, decent, proper

salaciousness *n*

prurience, lewdness, obscenity, bawdiness, lustfulness, indecency, pornography, lecherousness

FORMAL concupiscence, lasciviousness

COLLOQ. smuttiness, steaminess

salaried *adj*

paid, remunerated, waged, stipendiary

FORMAL emolumental, emolumentary

E3 unpaid, voluntary, honorary

salary *n*

pay, remuneration, stipend, honorarium, wages, earnings, income, fee, allowance, weighting allowance

FORMAL emolument

SLANG screw

sale *n*

selling, marketing, vending, bargaining, disposal, trade, market, traffic, transaction, deal

See panel on next page

■ **for sale**

on sale, up for sale, available, obtainable, on the market, for purchase, in the shops

COLLOQ. up for grabs

saleable *adj*

marketable, merchantable, sought-after, desirable

FORMAL vendible

E3 unmarketable, unsaleable

salesperson *n*

salesman, saleswoman, saleslady, sales assistant, shop assistant, shop-boy, shop-girl, salesgirl, shopkeeper, representative; *N Am* clerk, salesclerk

COLLOQ. rep

Groups of people with a patron saint include:

Accountants (*Matthew*)	Book trade (*John of God*)	Glassworkers (*Luke; Lucy*)	Miners (*Anne; Barbara*)	Sailors (*Christopher; Erasmus; Francis of Paola*)	Tax collectors (*Matthew*)
Actors (*Genesius; Vitus*)	Brewers (*Amand; Wenceslas*)	Gravediggers (*Joseph of Arimathea*)	Motorists (*Christopher*)		Taxi drivers (*Fiacre*)
Advertisers (*Bernardino of Siena*)	Builders (*Barbara; Thomas Apostle*)	Grocers (*Michael*)	Musicians (*Cecilia; Gregory the Great*)	Scholars (*Thomas Aquinas*)	Teachers (*Gregory the Great; John Baptist de la Salle*)
Architects (*Thomas Apostle*)	Butchers (*Luke*)	Hotelkeepers (*Amand; Julian the Hospitaler*)	Nurses (*Camillus de Lellis; John of God*)	Scientists (*Albert the Great*)	Television workers (*Gabriel*)
Artists (*Luke; Angelico*)	Carpenters (*Joseph*)			Sculptors (*Luke; Louis*)	
Astronauts (*Joseph of Cupertino*)	Chemists (*Cosmas and Damian*)	Housewives (*Martha*)	Philosophers (*Thomas Aquinas; Catherine of Alexandria*)	Secretaries (*Genesius*)	Theologians (*Augustine; Alphonsus Liguori; Thomas Aquinas*)
Astronomers (*Dominic*)	Comedians (*Vitus*)	Jewellers (*Eligius*)		Servants (*Martha; Zita*)	
Athletes (*Sebastian*)	Cooks (*Lawrence; Martha*)	Journalists (*Francis de Sales*)	Poets (*Cecilia; David*)	Shoemakers (*Crispin; Crispinian*)	Undertakers (*Dismas; Joseph of Arimathea*)
Authors (*Francis de Sales*)	Dancers (*Vitus*)	Labourers (*James; John Bosco*)	Police (*Michael*)		Waiters (*Martha*)
Aviators (*Our Lady of Loreto*)	Dentists (*Apollonia*)	Lawyers (*Ivo; Thomas More*)	Postal workers (*Gabriel*)	Singers (*Cecilia; Gregory*)	Widows (*Monica; Paula*)
Bakers (*Honoratus*)	Doctors (*Cosmas and Damian; Luke*)	Librarians (*Jerome; Catherine of Alexandria*)	Pregnant women (*Margaret of Antioch*)	Soldiers (*George; Joan of Arc; Martin of Tours; Sebastian*)	Workers (*Joseph*)
Bankers (*Bernardino (Feltre)*)	Editors (*Francis de Sales*)		Priests (*Jean-Baptiste Vianney*)		Writers (*Lucy*)
Barbers (*Cosmas and Damian*)	Farmers (*Isidore*)	Merchants (*Francis of Assisi*)		Students (*Thomas Aquinas*)	
Blacksmiths (*Eligius*)	Firemen (*Florian*)	Messengers (*Gabriel*)	Printers (*John of God*)	Surgeons (*Luke; Cosmas and Damian*)	
	Fishermen (*Andrew; Peter*)	Metalworkers (*Eligius*)	Prisoners (*Leonard*)		
Bookkeepers (*Matthew*)	Florists (*Dorothy; Thérèse of Lisieux*)	Midwives (*Raymond Nonnatus*)	Radio workers (*Gabriel*)	Tailors (*Homobonus*)	
	Gardeners (*Adam; Fiacre*)				

Types of sale include:

auction	clearance sale	fleamarket	online auction	sale of bankrupt	telesales
autumn sale	*Aust* clearing sale	forced sale	online sale	stock	trade show
bargain offer	closing-down sale	garage sale	on-promotion	sale of the century	trash and treasure
bazaar	cold call	grand opening sale	open market	sale of work	sale
bazumble	e-auction	introductory offer	pre-season sale	second-hand sale	warrant sale
boot-sale	end-of-line sale	January sale	private sale	special offer	winter sale
bring-and-buy	end-of-season sale	jumble sale	public sale	spring sale	
car-boot sale	exhibition	mail order	pyramid selling	stocktaking sale	
charity sale	exposition	market	remainder sale	summer sale	
church bazaar	fair	mid-season sale	rummage sale	tabletop sale	

salient *adj*
important, significant, chief, main, principal, striking, arresting, conspicuous, noticeable, obvious, prominent, pronounced, outstanding, signal, remarkable
TECHNICAL saltant

saliva *n*
spit, spittle, slaver, drool, dribble, sputum, phlegm
FORMAL expectoration

sallow *adj*
yellowish, pale, pallid, wan, waxen, pasty, sickly, jaundiced, unhealthy, anaemic, colourless, ashen
E∃ rosy, healthy

sally¹ *v, n*
♦ *v*
1 RUSH, surge, attack, sortie, charge, breeze, venture, erupt, foray, issue
2 SAUNTER, stroll, wander, promenade, amble
COLLOQ. mosey
E∃ 1 retire, retreat
♦ *n*
1 RUSH, raid, assault, attack, foray, incursion, offensive, surge, sortie, thrust, venture, dash
2 EXCURSION, jaunt, wander, trip, drive, frolic, escapade

sally² *n*
RETORT, riposte, witticism, wisecrack, joke, jest, crack, quip, *bon mot, jeu d'esprit*

salt *n, adj, v*
♦ *n*
1 *add a pinch of salt*
seasoning, taste, flavour, savour, relish, piquancy, pungency, smack, punch, rock-salt, sea-salt
TECHNICAL sodium chloride
Related adjective: saline
2 LIVELINESS, zest, interest, wit, vigour, zip
FORMAL trenchancy, mordancy
3 SAILOR, seafarer, mariner, seaman, marine, rating
♦ *adj*
salted, saltish, salty, saline, brackish, briny
E∃ fresh
■ **salt away**
store up, hoard, save, stash, stockpile, collect, cache, bank, accumulate, amass, put/set aside, put away, hide
E∃ spend, squander
■ **take with a pinch/grain of salt**
have reservations, have hesitations, have misgivings, disbelieve, not fully believe, hesitate, question

salty *adj*
1 SALT, salted, saline, briny, brackish, savoury, spicy, piquant, tangy
2 LIVELY, vigorous, witty, exciting, stimulating, animated
FORMAL trenchant, mordant
E∃ fresh, sweet

salubrious *adj*
sanitary, hygienic, health-giving, healthy, healthful, wholesome, pleasant, beneficial, salutary, refreshing, invigorating

salutary *adj*
1 GOOD, beneficial, advantageous, profitable, valuable, helpful, useful, practical, timely
2 HEALTHY, sanitary, hygienic, health-giving, refreshing, invigorating

salutation *n*
greeting, address, welcome, salute, reverence, respects, homage
FORMAL obeisance

salute *v, n*
♦ *v*
1 GREET, acknowledge, recognize, wave, hail, address, nod, bow, cap, honour, present arms
OLD halse, move, make your manners, salue
2 HONOUR, acknowledge, recognize, mark, celebrate, pay tribute to
♦ *n*
1 GREETING, acknowledgement, recognition, welcome, wave, gesture, hail, address, handshake, nod, bow, reverence, banzai
TECHNICAL coupé
OLD half-cap
2 HONOUR, celebration, recognition, acknowledgement, tribute, homage, salvo

salvage *v, n*
♦ *v*
save, preserve, conserve, rescue, recover, recuperate, retrieve, get back, reclaim, redeem, repair, restore, retain, salve
E∃ waste, abandon
♦ *n*
rescue, saving, recovery, retrieval, reclamation, raising, restoration, reinstatement, regeneration, regaining

salvation *n*
deliverance, liberation, rescue, saving, preservation, lifeline, redemption, reclamation
TECHNICAL soteriology
Related adjective: soterial
E∃ loss, damnation

salve *n, v*
♦ *n*
ointment, lotion, cream, balm, liniment, medication, preparation, application
FORMAL embrocation
♦ *v*
ease, lighten, relieve, calm, comfort, soothe

salver *n*
plate, dish, platter, tray, charger, trencher

same *adj, n*
♦ *adj*
1 IDENTICAL, twin, indistinguishable, equal, selfsame, the very same, one and the same, very, alike, like, similar, duplicate, carbon copy, comparable, equivalent, matching, corresponding, mutual, reciprocal, interchangeable, unchanging, substitutable, synonymous
COLLOQ. samey
2 UNCHANGING, consistent, uniform, unvarying, unvariable, changeless, unchanged

COLLOQ. samey
E3 1 different **2** inconsistent, variable, changeable
♦ *n*
the above-mentioned, the above-named, ditto
FORMAL the aforementioned, the aforesaid
■ **all the same**
nevertheless, nonetheless, still, anyway, even so, yet, however, by any means, in any case/event, by some means, anyhow, but, regardless, for all that, in spite of everything
FORMAL notwithstanding

sameness *n*
changelessness, invariability, consistency, monotony, predictability, repetition, tedium, uniformity, standardization, resemblance, similarity, indistinguishability, likeness, identicalness, identity, oneness, duplication, déjà vu
E3 variety, difference

samey *adj*
same, similar, identical, uniform, indistinguishable, unchanging, monotonous, tedious, predictable
COLLOQ. identikit; *N Am* cookie-cutter

sample *n, v, adj*
♦ *n*
specimen, example, cross-section, representative, model, pattern, type, test, sampling, swatch, piece, demonstration, illustration, instance, sign, indication, foretaste
♦ *v*
try (out), test, taste, sip, inspect, examine, experience
♦ *adj*
representative, specimen, demonstrative, illustrative, typical, dummy, trial, test, pilot

sanatorium *n*
clinic, medical centre, health centre, hospital, infirmary

sanctification *n*
holiness, sacredness, piety, godliness, purity, righteousness, blessedness, devotion, spirituality

sanctify *v*
1 HALLOW, consecrate, make holy, make sacred, bless, anoint, dedicate, set apart, cleanse, purify, wash, absolve, exalt, canonize
2 SANCTION, authorize, allow, permit, approve, ratify, confirm, support, back, endorse, underwrite, accredit, license, warrant, legitimize
E3 1 desecrate, defile **2** veto, forbid, disapprove

sanctimonious *adj*
self-righteous, holier-than-thou, holy, pious, pietistic, moralizing, smug, superior, hypocritical, priggish, pharisaical
FORMAL unctuous
COLLOQ. goody-goody, pi
E3 humble

sanctimoniousness *n*
self-righteousness, moralizing, righteousness, hypocrisy, self-satisfaction, priggishness, pietism, preachiness, complacency, cant, smugness, humbug, pharisaism
FORMAL unctuousness
E3 humility

sanction *n, v*
♦ *n*
1 AUTHORIZATION, permission, agreement, approval, ratification, confirmation, support, backing, endorsement, licence, authority, suffrage
OLD approof
FORMAL approbation, accreditation, subscription, countenance
COLLOQ. OK, go-ahead, green light, thumbs-up
2 *impose sanctions on a country*
restriction, boycott, embargo, ban, prohibition, penalty, deterrent, punishment, sentence

♦ *v*
authorize, allow, permit, approve, ratify, confirm, support, back, endorse, underwrite, accredit, license, warrant, legitimize, sustain
TECHNICAL royalize
OLD sanctify
FORMAL fiat
COLLOQ. OK, give the go-ahead to, give the green light to, give the thumbs-up to
E3 veto, forbid, disapprove

sanctity *n*
holiness, sacredness, inviolability, piety, godliness, saintliness, blessedness, religiousness, devotion, grace, spirituality, purity, goodness, virtue, righteousness, sanctification
FORMAL sacrosanctity
E3 unholiness, secularity, worldliness, godlessness, impurity

sanctuary *n*
1 CHURCH, temple, tabernacle, shrine, altar, place of worship, holy place, holy of holies
TECHNICAL oracle, nymphaeum
FORMAL sacrarium, sanctum, sanctum sanctorum, delubrum
2 ASYLUM, refuge, protection, shelter, haven, retreat, hideout, hideaway
OLD grith
3 SAFETY, protection, security, safeguard, immunity
OLD privilege, frith
4 RESERVE, reservation, park, area, enclave, tract, preserve

sanctum *n*
1 HOLY PLACE, holy of holies, shrine, sanctuary
FORMAL sanctum sanctorum
2 REFUGE, retreat, den, hideaway, hideout, study, cubbyhole

sand *n*
beach, shore, strand, sands, seashore, desert, wilderness, grit, rock
Related adjectives: arenaceous, sabulous

sandbank *n*
dune, reef, sand bar, sandhill, bar, spit, hurst, key, yardang

sandy *adj*
gritty, ginger, rusty, tawny, reddish, reddish-yellow, yellow, yellowish, yellowy, gingerous, gingery, auburn, coppery, red, Titian
TECHNICAL arenaceous, psammitic

sane *adj*
normal, rational, right-minded, balanced, well-balanced, lucid, in your right mind, of sound mind, stable, sound, sober, level-headed, yourself, herself, himself, sensible, responsible, wise, reasonable, moderate, *compos mentis*; *Scot* wice
OLD (*Shakesp*) formal
FORMAL judicious, *mens sana in corpore sano*
COLLOQ. all there
E3 insane, mad, crazy, foolish

QUOTATIONS
Show me a sane man and I will cure him for you
CARL GUSTAV JUNG

sangfroid *n*
composure, aplomb, self-control, poise, self-possession, indifference, equanimity, assurance, calmness, dispassion, cool-headedness, nonchalance, coolness, imperturbability
FORMAL phlegm
COLLOQ. nerve, cool, unflappability
E3 discomposure, excitability, hysteria, panic

sanguinary *adj*
bloody, bloodied, gory, grim, bloodthirsty, brutal, cruel, merciless, murderous, savage, pitiless, ruthless

sanguine *adj*
1 CHEERFUL, confident, hopeful, lively, expectant, optimistic, over-confident, over-optimistic, assured, animated, ardent, buoyant, spirited, roseate, unabashed, unbowed
2 RUDDY, rosy, florid, red, pink, fresh-complexioned, fresh, flushed, roseate
FORMAL rubicund
⊟ 1 cynical, depressive, gloomy, melancholy, pessimistic
⊟ 2 pale, sallow

sanitary *adj*
clean, pure, uncontaminated, unpolluted, aseptic, antiseptic, germ-free, disinfected, sterile, hygienic, healthy, wholesome
FORMAL salubrious
⊟ insanitary, unwholesome

sanitize *v*
1 PURIFY, sterilize, decontaminate, refine, filter, clean, cleanse, freshen, disinfect, fumigate, deodorize
2 MAKE ACCEPTABLE, make presentable, expurgate, make palatable

sanity *n*
normality, rationality, reason, sense, common sense, good sense, balance of mind, soundness of mind, lucidity, right-mindedness, stability, soundness, level-headedness, prudence, wisdom, responsibility
FORMAL judiciousness
⊟ insanity, madness

sap *v, n*
♦ *v*
bleed, drain, exhaust, weaken, wear down/away, erode, enfeeble, debilitate, undermine, deplete, reduce, diminish, impair
FORMAL enervate
⊟ strengthen, build up, increase
♦ *n*
1 *sap in a plant*
lifeblood, vital fluid, plant fluid, juice, essence, vigour, energy
2 FOOL, idiot, imbecile, moron
COLLOQ. clot, twit, nit, nitwit
SLANG jerk, prat, git, fink

sarcasm *n*
irony, satire, mockery, sneering, ridicule, scoffing, derision, scorn, contempt, gibing, cynicism, resentment, acidity, acrimony, spitefulness, bitterness
OLD wipe
FORMAL invective, trenchancy, mordancy

sarcastic *adj*
ironical, ironic, satirical, satiric, mocking, snide, taunting, sneering, derisive, derisory, scornful, sardonic, jeering, scoffing, scathing, cynical, incisive, cutting, sharp, witty, biting, caustic, acid, pungent, back-handed, Juvenalian, Voltairian
FORMAL disparaging, acerbic, mordant, invective
COLLOQ. sarky, snarky

sarcastically *adv*
ironically, satirically, scornfully, cynically, jeeringly, tauntingly, scathingly

sardonic *adj*
mocking, jeering, sneering, derisive, scornful, contemptuous, sarcastic, dry, biting, cruel, heartless, malicious, cynical, acrimonious, bitter
FORMAL acerbic, mordant

sash *n*
belt, girdle, scarf, waistband, cummerbund, cincture, lungi, obi, baldric
OLD shash, burdash

sassy *adj*
cheeky, impertinent, impudent, insolent, disrespectful, forward, brazen, pert, audacious, overfamiliar
COLLOQ. fresh, saucy, lippy, mouthy
⊟ respectful, polite

Satan *n*
the Devil, the Enemy, the Adversary, the Evil One, the Tempter, the serpent, Beelzebub, Lucifer, Old Nick, Prince of Darkness, prince of this world, Mephistopheles, Belial, Apollyon, Abaddon, arch-enemy, Shaitan
OLD leviathan

satanic *adj*
satanical, diabolical, diabolic, devilish, demonic, fiendish, hellish, infernal, damned, accursed, inhuman, wicked, malevolent, sulphurous, evil, sinful, abominable, black, dark
FORMAL iniquitous
⊟ holy, divine, godly, saintly, benevolent

sate *v*
satisfy, overfill, saturate, surfeit, fill, glut, gorge, gratify, cloy, sicken, slake
FORMAL satiate
⊟ deprive, dissatisfy, starve

satellite *n*
1 ORBITING BODY, natural/artificial satellite, spacecraft, moon, planet, spaceship, space station, sputnik
2 *the USSR and its former satellites*
dependency, colony, province, protectorate, dominion
3 DEPENDANT, hanger-on, parasite, sycophant, subordinate, follower, attendant, aide, adherent, disciple, minion, lackey, sidekick, retainer, vassal
COLLOQ. puppet

satiate *v*
sate, overfill, fill, overfeed, satisfy, gorge, slake, glut, cloy, engorge, stuff, surfeit, jade, nauseate
⊟ deprive, dissatisfy, underfeed

satiety *n*
satiation, saturation, satisfaction, gratification, fullness, over-fullness, overindulgence, surfeit
OLD (Shakesp) cloyment
FORMAL repleteness, repletion

satire *n*
ridicule, irony, sarcasm, wit, burlesque, lampoon, skit, parody, caricature, travesty, jeer, comedy of manners
OLD glance
FORMAL invective
COLLOQ. send-up, spoof, take-off, mickey-taking
SLANG piss-taking

satirical *adj*
ironical, sarcastic, mocking, ridiculing, irreverent, taunting, derisive, sardonic, incisive, cutting, biting, caustic, cynical, bitter, Swiftian, Archilochian
FORMAL trenchant, acerbic, mordant, invective

satirist *n*
cartoonist, mocker, parodist, ridiculer, caricaturist, lampooner, lampoonist, pasquilant, pasquiler, pasquinader

satirize *v*
ridicule, mock, make fun of, poke fun at, burlesque, lampoon, parody, caricature, criticize
FORMAL deride
COLLOQ. send up, take off, take the mickey out of
SLANG take the piss out of
⊟ acclaim, honour

satisfaction *n*
1 GRATIFICATION, contentment, happiness, pleasure, enjoyment, delight, comfort, ease, wellbeing, fulfilment, self-satisfaction, pride, sense of achievement
2 SETTLEMENT, compensation, reimbursement, indemnification, indemnity, damages, reparation, amends, redress, recompense, requital, vindication, restitution
⊟ 1 dissatisfaction, displeasure

satisfactorily *adv*
acceptably, passably, adequately, competently, sufficiently, favourably, nicely
⊟ unsatisfactorily, unacceptably, inadequately

satisfactory *adj*
acceptable, passable, up to the mark, all right, fair,
average, competent, adequate, fine, sufficient, suitable,
proper, well, favourable, nice
COLLOQ. OK, up to scratch, tickety-boo; *N Am* copacetic,
A-OK; *Aust* sweet
unsatisfactory, unacceptable, inadequate

satisfied *adj*
1 HAPPY, contented, pleased, self-satisfied, content, smug
2 CONVINCED, reassured, persuaded, sure, certain, positive,
pacified
3 FULL, sated, satiated
FORMAL replete
1 dissatisfied; *colloq.* disgruntled **2** unconvinced,
unsure **3** hungry

satisfy *v*
1 GRATIFY, indulge, content, please, delight, appease,
quench, slake, sate, satiate, surfeit
OLD agree, pay, apay
FORMAL assuage
2 *satisfy requirements*
meet, fulfil, discharge, settle, answer, fill, be sufficient for,
be adequate for, comply with, supply, serve, qualify
FORMAL suffice
3 ASSURE, reassure, convince, persuade
4 COMPENSATE FOR, indemnify, make reparation for, stay
OLD defray
FORMAL appease, placate, requite
1 dissatisfy **2** fail

satisfying *adj*
pleasing, fulfilling, gratifying, cheering, pleasurable,
satisfactory, convincing, persuasive, filling, cool, refreshing,
harmonious, enough, square
dissatisfying, frustrating, unsatisfactory

saturate *v*
1 SOAK, make wet through, wet, steep, flood, souse,
drench, waterlog
2 IMPREGNATE, permeate, imbue, pervade, suffuse, fill,
overfill, sate, glut, surfeit

saturated *adj*
1 SOAKED, soaking, sopping, dripping, soused, steeped,
drenched, flooded, wringing, waterlogged, sodden
2 IMBUED, impregnated, permeated, suffused

saturation *n*
filling, flooding, soaking, pervading, permeation, suffusion,
glutting, sating, satiation

saturnine *adj*
morose, gloomy, unfriendly, sombre, severe, austere,
dismal, dour, dull, grave, melancholy, moody, glum, stern,
heavy, withdrawn, taciturn, uncommunicative, phlegmatic
cheerful, jovial

sauce *n*
1 DRESSING, relish, condiment, flavouring, dip, mayonnaise
2 CHEEKINESS, cheek, impudence, impertinence,
presumption, presumptuousness, audacity, freshness,
flippancy, pertness, backchat, brazenness, insolence,
disrespectfulness, disrespect, irreverence, rudeness, sass
FORMAL malapertness
COLLOQ. brass, lip, nerve, sauciness, mouth
2 politeness, respectfulness

PROVERBS
What's sauce for the goose is sauce for the gander

saucepan *n*
pan, pot, skillet, casserole, wok, container, vessel, frying-
pan, fryer, pancheon

saucy *adj*
impertinent, impudent, insolent, brazen, presumptuous,
disrespectful, irreverent, rude, cheeky, pert, forward,
flippant
COLLOQ. fresh, lippy; *N Am* sassy
polite, respectful

saunter *v, n*
♦ *v*
stroll, amble, wander, ramble, meander; *dialect* dander,
shool; *Scot* dacker
OLD promenade
COLLOQ. mosey, mooch, knock about/around, toddle
♦ *n*
stroll, amble, walk, constitutional, ramble
OLD promenade
COLLOQ. mosey, mooch

savage *adj, n, v*
♦ *adj*
wild, untamed, undomesticated, uncivilized, primitive,
barbaric, barbarous, fierce, ferocious, vicious, beastly,
cruel, terrible, inhuman, grim, brutal, sadistic, bloodthirsty,
bloody, murderous, pitiless, merciless, ruthless, harsh,
catamountain, warrigal
OLD salvage, fell, immane
FORMAL feral
COLLOQ. cut-throat, dog-eat-dog
tame, civilized, humane, mild
♦ *n*
brute, boor, churl, beast, monster, barbarian, wild person,
wild man, wild woman
OLD salvage
♦ *v*
1 *savaged by a dog*
attack, bite, claw, tear, tear to pieces, lacerate, maul,
mangle
2 *savaged by the critics*
attack, slate, run down, denounce
COLLOQ. slam, rubbish, pull/tear to pieces, pull/tear to
shreds, go to town on, pick holes in, do a hatchet job on

QUOTATIONS
Birds feed on birds, beasts on each other prey, / But
savage man alone does man betray
JOHN EILMOT, 2ND EARL OF ROCHESTER, 'A Satyr
Against Mankind'

savagely *adv*
viciously, brutally, cruelly, ruthlessly, harshly, mercilessly,
pitilessly, fiercely, ferociously, barbarically, barborously

savagery *n*
cruelty, fierceness, ferocity, viciousness, wildness,
roughness, barbarity, bestiality, brutality, inhumanity,
ruthlessness, mercilessness, pitilessness, murderousness,
bloodthirstiness, brutishness, sadism, primitiveness
FORMAL ferity
civilization, civility, humanity

savant *n*
authority, scholar, intellectual, pundit, guru, mastermind,
man/woman of letters, master, philosopher
FORMAL sage
amateur, ignoramus

save *v, prep*
♦ *v*
1 RESCUE, come to the rescue of, deliver, liberate, free, set
free, release, get someone out of, redeem, salvage,
recover, reclaim
COLLOQ. bail out
2 *save food*
conserve, preserve, keep, retain, hold, reserve, store, lay
up, set aside, put by, put aside, hoard, stockpile, collect,
gather
COLLOQ. stash
3 ECONOMIZE, cut back, cut costs, use less, budget, buy
cheaply, live on the cheap, be thrifty, scrimp and save
COLLOQ. tighten your belt, cut your coat according to your
cloth
4 PROTECT, guard, screen, keep, shield, safeguard, keep
safe, preserve, spare, prevent, hinder
FORMAL obviate
2 waste, discard **3** spend, squander

♦ *prep*
apart from, except (for), not counting, excepted, aside from, excluding, with the exception of, but for

---

SYNONYM NUANCES

verb sense 1
You can use **rescue** to suggest removal from a dangerous or disagreeable situation, while **deliver** likewise has connotations of removing from potential harm or evil: *people delivered from fear, oppression and famine.* **Liberate**, on the other hand, suggests restoring freedom, and the terms **free**, **set free** and **release** all echo this suggestion of getting someone out of captivity.
   Redeem, however, might be used with a more figurative sense of undoing damage: *her performance redeemed the show*, though it may also be used more literally to imply getting back in return for money: *redeem a debt.* It can also have religious connotations of being saved from sin. **Salvage** and **recover** can be used for retrieving whatever you can from being lost: *stained glass windows salvaged from ruined churches.*

---

saving *adj, n*
♦ *adj*
1 ECONOMICAL, careful, sparing, thrifty, frugal
2 *a saving grace*
redeeming, compensating, qualifying, compensatory, extenuating, mitigating
♦ *n*
1 ECONOMY, thrift, discount, reduction, bargain, cut, conservation, preservation
2 *put your savings in the bank*
capital, investments, nest egg, fund, store, reserves, resources
E3 1 expense, loss, waste **2** expenditure, outgoings

saviour *n*
1 RESCUER, deliverer, redeemer, liberator, emancipator, guardian, protector, defender, champion, messiah
2 *Jesus Christ, the Saviour*
Redeemer, Deliverer, Lamb of God, Mediator, Emmanuel, Christ, Messiah
E3 1 destroyer

savoir-faire *n*
capability, ability, accomplishment, confidence, assurance, discretion, expertise, finesse, poise, diplomacy, tact, urbanity, social grace(s)
COLLOQ. knowhow
E3 awkwardness, clumsiness, incompetence, inexperience

savour *n, v*
♦ *n*
1 TASTE, flavour, smack, tang, piquancy, salt, spice, relish, zest; *Scot* sair
2 SMELL, aroma, bouquet, fragrance, perfume, scent, odour
3 TRACE, hint, suggestion, touch, smattering
♦ *v*
1 RELISH, taste to the full, enjoy, enjoy to the full, delight in, take pleasure in, revel in, like, appreciate; *Scot* sar, sair
2 SMACK, suggest, speak, smell, seem like, have all the signs of, have the hallmarks of
OLD resent
E3 1 shrink from

savoury *adj, n*
♦ *adj*
1 TASTY, flavoursome, appetizing, delicious, mouthwatering, umami, luscious, palatable, sapid; *Scot* gustie
OLD gustful
COLLOQ. yummy, scrumptious, scrummy
2 *savoury pancakes*
salty, spicy, aromatic, piquant, tangy
E3 1 unappetizing, unsavoury, tasteless, insipid **2** sweet, sugary

♦ *n*
appetizer, snack, *hors d'œuvre*, bonne-bouche, canapé, tapas

savvy *adj*
shrewd, astute, well-advised, calculated, far-sighted, smart, clever, intelligent, sharp, keen, acute, alert, perceptive, observant, discerning, discriminating, knowing, calculating, cunning, crafty, wily, canny, artful, sly
FORMAL callid, judicious, sagacious, perspicacious
E3 unwise, obtuse, naive, unsophisticated

saw¹

Kinds of saw include:

band-saw	fretsaw	rabbet saw
bench saw	hacksaw	radial-arm saw
chainsaw	handsaw	ripsaw
circular saw	jigsaw	scroll saw
compass saw	panel saw	tenon saw
coping-saw	power-driven saw	
crosscut saw	pruning saw	

---

saw² *n*
SAYING, byword, proverb, maxim, aphorism, adage, axiom, dictum, epigram, commonplace, gnome, mot
FORMAL apophthegm

say *v, n*
♦ *v*
1 EXPRESS, phrase, put, put into words, mention, render, utter, voice, articulate, enunciate, pronounce, deliver, speak, rehearse, recite, repeat, perform, read, indicate
FORMAL orate
2 ANSWER, reply, respond, rejoin, retort, exclaim, comment, remark, observe, mention, add, drawl, mutter, grunt
FORMAL ejaculate
3 TELL, instruct, order, communicate, convey, intimate, report, announce, declare, state, assert, affirm, maintain, claim, allege, rumour, suggest, imply, signify, reveal, disclose, divulge
4 GUESS, estimate, reckon, judge, imagine, suppose, assume, presume, surmise
♦ *n*
1 *have a say in something*
voice, word, opinion, vote, right to express yourself, opportunity to speak, turn/chance to speak
2 *have no say in the matter*
influence, power, authority, sway, weight
COLLOQ. clout
■ *that is to say*
ie, that is, in other words, to put it another way

saying *n*
adage, proverb, dictum, precept, axiom, aphorism, maxim, motto, slogan, phrase, catch phrase, cliché, platitude, expression, quotation, epigram, statement, remark, word/pearl of wisdom
FORMAL apophthegm

say-so *n*
authorization, permission, agreement, approval, consent, affirmation, authority, backing, assertion, assurance, word, guarantee, ratification, sanction
FORMAL asseveration, dictum
COLLOQ. OK, go-ahead, green light, thumbs-up

scaffold *n*
1 PLATFORM, framework, scaffolding, gantry, stage, tower
2 GALLOWS, gibbet, the rope
OLD catasta

scald *v*
burn, sear, brand, scorch, blister
FORMAL cauterize

scalding *adj*
extremely hot, burning, boiling, blistering, piping hot, steaming

scale¹ *n, v*

♦ *n*

1 *the Richter scale*
graduation, calibration, system of measurement, measuring system, calibrated system, register
2 EXTENT, level, degree, measure, spread, reach, range, scope, compass, spectrum, gamut
3 *What is the scale of the map?*
ratio, proportion, relative size
4 SEQUENCE, series, gamut, progression, hierarchy, ranking, order, ladder
COLLOQ. pecking order

♦ *v*

climb, go up, ascend, mount, clamber, scramble, shin up, conquer, surmount

■ **scale down**
decrease, make less, lessen, reduce, cut back/down, drop, contract, shrink

■ **scale up**
increase, expand, raise, boost, improve, enhance, further, step up, intensify, strengthen, develop, build up, accumulate
FORMAL augment
COLLOQ. hike up, bump up

scale² *n*

scale in a kettle; scales on a fish
encrustation, deposit, crust, layer, coat, coating, limescale, tartar, plaque, film, lamina, plate, flake, scurf, furfur
FORMAL squama
Related adjective: squamose

scaliness *n*

dandruff, flakiness, furfur, scurfiness, scabrousness
FORMAL squamosity

scaly *adj*

flaky, scurfy, scabby, scabrous, rough, branny
FORMAL lepidote, furfuraceous, furfurous, squamose, squamous, squamulose, desquamative, desquamatory

scam *n*

racket, swindle, fraud, fiddle, deception, trick, dodge, scheme, business
COLLOQ. con, game
SLANG rip-off; *N Am* gold brick

scamp *n*

rogue, rascal, scallywag, monkey, mischief-maker, troublemaker, imp, devil, wretch, good-for-nothing, reprobate, vagabond, losel, *fripon*; *dialect* skellum; *Irish* spalpeen
COLLOQ. whippersnapper, blighter, bugger

scamper *v*

scuttle, scurry, dart, dash, run, sprint, rush, hurry, race, scramble, fly, romp, frolic, gambol
FORMAL hasten
COLLOQ. scoot

scan *v, n*

♦ *v*

1 EXAMINE, scrutinize, inspect, study, search, survey, sweep, investigate, check, spell
OLD con
2 SKIM, have a quick look at, browse through, run through, run over, go over, glance at, flick through, flip through, thumb through, leaf through, run your eye over

♦ *n*

screening, examination, scrutiny, inspection, search, probe, check, study, investigation, test, survey, review
TECHNICAL scintilliscan, sector scan, CAT scan

scandal *n*

1 OUTRAGE, offence, outcry, uproar, furore, discredit, dishonour, disgrace, shame, embarrassment, ignominy, -gate
FORMAL obloquy, opprobrium
2 GOSSIP, rumours, libel, slander, smear, dirt, *chronique scandaleuse*

FORMAL defamation, calumny
COLLOQ. dirty linen/washing/laundry, skeleton in the cupboard
3 DISGRACE, shame, pity, reproach, blot, slur, smear, stain, black mark
COLLOQ. crying shame

scandalize *v*

shock, horrify, appal, dismay, disgust, repel, revolt, offend, insult, affront, outrage

scandalmonger *n*

gossip, gossip-monger, tattler, tattle, talebearer, busybody, quidnunc
FORMAL calumniator, defamer, traducer
COLLOQ. muck-raker, Nosey Parker

scandalous *adj*

shocking, appalling, atrocious, abominable, monstrous, unspeakable, outrageous, blatant, flagrant, disgraceful, shameful, disreputable, dishonourable, infamous, improper, malicious, scurrilous, sensational, gamey, slanderous, libellous, untrue
FORMAL unseemly, defamatory, opprobrious
COLLOQ. juicy

scant *adj*

little, sparse, limited, little or no, bare, deficient, minimal, hardly any, inadequate, insufficient
FORMAL exiguous
COLLOQ. measly
E∃ adequate, ample, sufficient

scantily *adv*

poorly, meagerly, inadequately, insufficiently, deficiently, skimpily, barely, sparsely
E∃ adequately, sufficiently

scanty *adj*

deficient, short, inadequate, insufficient, scant, little, limited, restricted, narrow, poor, meagre, insubstantial, thin, skimpy, sparse, bare
E∃ adequate, sufficient, ample, plentiful, substantial

scapegoat *n*

victim, whipping-boy, sucker
COLLOQ. fall guy; *Aust* bunny
SLANG *N Am* patsy

scar *n, v*

♦ *n*

mark, lesion, wound, injury, shock, trauma, defacement, disfigurement, discolouration, blemish, blotch, stigma, pockmark, pockpit, sword-cut, cicatrice
TECHNICAL desmoid, hilum, leaf-cushion, keloid, ulosis
OLD (*Shakesp*) wipe
FORMAL cicatricula

♦ *v*

mark, deface, disfigure, discolour, spoil, damage, injure, shock, traumatize, brand, stigmatize

scarce *adj*

few, rare, infrequent, uncommon, unusual, sparse, scanty, scant, meagre, in short supply, too little, not enough, insufficient, inadequate, deficient, lacking, dear
COLLOQ. few and far between, like gold dust
E∃ plentiful, common

■ **make yourself scarce**
leave quickly, go fast, dash off, rush away, take to your heels
COLLOQ. scoot, make tracks, run for it

scarcely *adv*

1 *I can scarcely hear you*
hardly, barely, only just
2 *that is scarcely a reason to hit him*
hardly, not, not at all, certainly not, definitely not
3 *scarcely had I put the phone down when it rang again*
hardly, barely, only just, no sooner

scarcity n
lack, shortage, dearth, deficiency, insufficiency, rareness, rarity, infrequency, uncommonness, sparseness, scantness, scantiness
FORMAL paucity, want, exiguity
F3 glut, plenty, abundance, sufficiency, enough

scare v, n
♦ v
frighten, startle, alarm, make afraid, make frightened, dismay, daunt, intimidate, unnerve, threaten, menace, terrorize, shock, appal, panic, terrify, petrify
FORMAL perturb
COLLOQ. rattle, scare someone out of their wits, make someone's blood run cold, scare silly, scare the living daylights out of, make someone's hair stand on end, make someone's flesh creep, make someone jump out of their skin, put the frighteners on, put the wind up
SLANG scare the shit out of
F3 reassure, calm
♦ n
fright, start, shock, alarm, panic, hysteria, horror, terror, fearfulness
F3 reassurance, comfort

scared adj
afraid, frightened, fearful, nervous, anxious, worried, startled, alarmed, cowed, shaken, panic-stricken, panicky, quivery, terrified, petrified, terrorized, terror-stricken, unnerved, jittery
COLLOQ. scared out of your wits, scared to death, with your heart in your mouth, shaking like a leaf, having kittens, in a blue funk
F3 confident, reassured

scaremonger n
alarmist, pessimist, prophet of doom, doom and gloom merchant, doomwatcher, jitterbug, Cassandra

scarf n
headscarf, headsquare, kerchief, neckerchief, muffler, necktie, shawl, stole, cravat, babushka, sash, comforter, pagri, vexillum
TECHNICAL orarium, tippet
OLD screen, nightingale

scarper v
leave, depart, go, run away, vanish, disappear, abscond, bolt, escape, flee, decamp, flit
COLLOQ. clear off, beat it, bunk off, run for it, make a run for it, scram, skedaddle, vamoose, hightail it, do a bunk

scary adj
frightening, alarming, daunting, formidable, fearsome, forbidding, intimidating, disturbing, shocking, horrifying, terrifying, petrifying, hair-raising, bloodcurdling, spine-chilling, chilling, creepy, eerie
COLLOQ. spooky, hairy, white-knuckle

scathing adj
withering, sarcastic, scornful, critical, cutting, biting, stinging, caustic, acid, vitriolic, ferocious, fierce, severe, bitter, harsh, brutal, savage, unsparing, devastating
FORMAL trenchant, mordant
F3 complimentary

scatter v
disperse, dispel, dissipate, disband, disunite, separate, divide, break up, disintegrate, diffuse, broadcast, spread, sprinkle, sow, strew, fling, shower, spatter, splutter, shake, dot, intersperse, litter, blind, cast/fling/throw to the winds; *dialect* scamble; *Scot* skail
TECHNICAL backscatter
OLD bescatter, flurr, shatter, squander
FORMAL disseminate, disject
F3 gather, collect

scatterbrained adj
forgetful, absent-minded, empty-headed, feather-brained, hare-brained, careless, inattentive, thoughtless, unreliable, impulsive, irresponsible, wool-gathering, frivolous, slaphappy, carefree

COLLOQ. scatty, dizzy, having your head in the clouds, airheaded; *N Am* ditsy
F3 sensible, sober, efficient, careful

scattering n
sprinkling, few, handful, smattering, break-up
F3 mass, abundance

scavenge v
forage, rummage, rake, search, look for, hunt, scrounge

scavenger n
rummager, scavager, forager, scrounger, raker

scenario n
1 SITUATION, scene, circumstances, state, state of affairs, sequence of events, plan, programme
2 OUTLINE, synopsis, summary, résumé, storyline, script, screenplay, plot, scheme, plan, programme, projection, sequence

scene n
1 PLACE, area, spot, location, locale, site, situation, position, whereabouts, locality, environment, milieu, setting, context, background, backdrop, arena, set, stage
2 LANDSCAPE, scenery, panorama, view, vista, outlook, prospect, sight, spectacle, picture, tableau, pageant
3 EPISODE, incident, proceeding, part, division, act, clip
4 *don't make a scene*
fuss, commotion, outburst, tantrum, furore, performance, drama, exhibition, display, show
COLLOQ. to-do, kerfuffle
5 *not my scene*
area of interest, area of activity, field, area, speciality
■ **behind the scenes**
secretly, not in public, out of the public eye, privately, in private, behind closed doors, surreptitiously, on the quiet, out of sight, backstage

scenery n
landscape, terrain, panorama, view, vista, outlook, prospect, scene, background, setting, surroundings, backdrop, set, *mise-en-scène*

scenic adj
panoramic, picturesque, attractive, pretty, beautiful, grand, striking, impressive, spectacular, breathtaking, awe-inspiring
F3 dull, dreary

scent n, v
♦ n
1 FRAGRANCE, aroma, perfume, bouquet, smell, odour
FORMAL redolence
2 PERFUME, essence, cologne, eau-de-cologne, eau-de-toilette, toilet water
3 *follow the scent*
track, trail, trace, spoor
F3 1 stink
♦ v
1 SMELL, sniff (out), nose (out), track, trail, trace
2 SENSE, become aware of, become conscious of, perceive, detect, discern, recognize

> QUOTATIONS
> The first scent you pour in a jar lasts for years
>   HORACE, *Epistulae*

scented adj
perfumed, fragrant, sweet-smelling, aromatic
F3 malodorous, stinking

sceptic n
doubter, unbeliever, disbeliever, agnostic, atheist, rationalist, questioner, scoffer, cynic, doubting Thomas
F3 believer

sceptical adj
doubting, doubtful, unconvinced, unbelieving, disbelieving, incredulous, questioning, distrustful, mistrustful, hesitating, hesitant, dubious, suspicious, scoffing, cynical, academic, pessimistic, infidel, Voltairian
F3 convinced, confident, trusting

scepticism *n*
doubt, unbelief, disbelief, hesitancy, agnosticism, atheism, rationalism, distrust, doubtfulness, dubiety, suspicion, incredulity, cynicism, pessimism
🢂 belief, faith

schedule *n, v*
♦ *n*
timetable, programme, agenda, diary, calendar, itinerary, plan, scheme, list, syllabus, inventory, catalogue, table, form
♦ *v*
timetable, time, table, programme, plan, organize, arrange, appoint, assign, book, list; *N Am* slate
OLD (*Shakesp*) enschedule
■ **behind schedule**
behind time, behindhand, late, running late, overdue
■ **on schedule**
on time, on target, according to plan, on course, on track

schema *n*
outline, profile, sketch, tracing, form, shape, design, figure, layout, plan, chart, diagram, map
FORMAL configuration, delineation, lineament

schematic *adj*
diagrammatic, representational, symbolic, simplified, illustrative, graphic

scheme *n, v*
♦ *n*
1 PROGRAMME, schedule, plan, project, strategy, tactics, system, method, procedure, course of action, idea, proposal, proposition, suggestion, draft, outline, blueprint, schema, diagram, chart, map, layout, sketch, pattern, design, shape, arrangement
OLD practice
FORMAL configuration, disposition, delineation
COLLOQ. *Aust & NZ* dart
2 INTRIGUE, plot, conspiracy, device, stratagem, ruse, ploy, shift, manoeuvre, tactic(s), strategy
FORMAL machinations
♦ *v*
plot, conspire, connive, collude, intrigue, manoeuvre, manipulate, pull strings, mastermind, plan, project, contrive, devise, frame, work out
FORMAL machinate

schemer *n*
plotter, intriguer, politician, conniver, deceiver, mastermind, intrig(u)ant(e), Machiavelli, Machiavellian, éminence grise, fox, contriver
FORMAL machinator
COLLOQ. wangler, wheeler-dealer, wire-puller

scheming *adj*
crafty, cunning, deceitful, sly, underhand, unscrupulous, wily, devious, artful, manipulative, calculating, conniving, designing, insidious, tricky, slippery, foxy, Machiavellian
FORMAL duplicitous
🢂 artless, honest, open, transparent

schism *n*
1 DIVISION, split, rift, rupture, break, breach, disunion, separation, severance, discord
FORMAL estrangement, scission
2 SPLINTER, group, faction, sect, detachment

schismatic *adj*
breakaway, rebel, dissenting, separatist, renegade, heretical
FORMAL apostate, seceding, secessionist

schmaltz *n*
sentimentality, emotionalism, romanticism, mawkishness
COLLOQ. slush, mush, gush, pulp, soppiness, sloppiness

scholar *n*
1 STUDENT, pupil, learner, schoolchild, schoolboy, schoolgirl, day-scholar, day-boy, day-girl
COLLOQ. schoolie
2 ACADEMIC, intellectual, authority, expert, philosopher, mastermind, pundit, bookman, man/woman/person of letters, savant, scholastic, schoolman

OLD artsman, clerk
COLLOQ. egghead, bookworm

scholarly *adj*
learned, erudite, lettered, academic, scholastic, school, intellectual, highbrow, bookish, studious, knowledgeable, well-read, conscientious, analytical, scientific
🢂 uneducated, illiterate

scholarship *n*
1 LEARNING, learnedness, knowledge, wisdom, education, schooling, academic achievements/attainments
FORMAL erudition
2 *a scholarship to a public school*
grant, award, bursary, endowment, fellowship, exhibition

scholastic *adj*
academic, scholarly, educational, pedagogic, learned, lettered, literary, bookish, analytical, pedantic, precise

school *n, v*
♦ *n*
1 *go to school*
college, academy, institute, institution, university, seminary, faculty, department, division, discipline, class, group, pupils, students, yeshiva(h)
See also **educational establishments** *at* **educational**.
2 *a school of artists*
group, set, circle, clique, coterie, faction, association, club, society, guild, league, company
♦ *v*
educate, teach, instruct, tutor, coach, train, discipline, drill, verse, prime, prepare, indoctrinate

schooling *n*
education, learning, book-learning, teaching, instruction, tuition, coaching, training, drill, preparation, grounding, guidance, indoctrination

schoolteacher *n*
teacher, instructor, educator, schoolmaster, master, schoolmistress, mistress, schoolmarm, pedagogue; *Scot* dominie
COLLOQ. *Aust* schoolie

science *n*
technology, discipline, specialization, knowledge, skill, proficiency, expertise, technique, dexterity, art
See panel on next page

> **QUOTATIONS**
> The grand aim of all science is to cover the greatest number of empirical facts by logical deduction from the smallest number of hypotheses or axioms
> ALBERT EINSTEIN
>
> That is the essence of science: ask an impertinent question and you are on the way to a pertinent answer
> JACOB BRONOWSKI, *The Ascent of Man*

scientific *adj*
methodical, systematic, controlled, regulated, orderly, analytical, mathematical, exact, precise, accurate, scholarly, thorough

scientific instruments
See panel on next page

scientist *n*
experimenter, researcher, investigator, research worker, technologist, doctor, analyst, expert, engineer, designer, planner, inventor, mastermind, genius, brain, intellect, intellectual, thinker
COLLOQ. boffin, backroom-boy

scintilla *n*
shred, scrap, snippet, bit, piece, fragment, remnant, particle, modicum, speck, spot, jot, iota, atom, grain, mite, whit, trace; *N Am, Aust & NZ* skerrick

scintillate *v*
sparkle, spark, shine, flash, gleam, glint, glisten, glitter, twinkle, blaze, wink
FORMAL coruscate

Sciences include:

acoustics	bioorganic	economics	graphology	metallurgy	radiochemistry
aerodynamics	chemistry	electrodynamics	hydraulics	meteorology	robotics
aeronautics	biophysics	electronics	information	microbiology	seismology
agricultural science	botany	engineering	technology	mineralogy	sociology
(or agriscience)	chemistry	entomology	inorganic	morphology	space technology
anatomy	chemurgy	environmental	chemistry	natural science	telecommunica-
anthropology	climatology	science	life science	nuclear physics	tions
archaeology	computer science	food science	linguistics	organic chemistry	thermodynamics
astronomy	cybernetics	genetics	macrobiotics	ornithology	toxicology
astrophysics	diagnostics	geoarchaeology	materials science	pathology	ultrasonics
behavioural	dietetics	geochemistry	mathematics	pharmacology	veterinary science
science	domestic science	geographical	mechanical	physics	zoology
biochemistry	dynamics	science	engineering	physiology	
biology	earth science	geology	mechanics	political science	
	ecology	geophysics	medical science	psychology	

scintillating adj
sparkling, glittering, flashing, bright, shining, brilliant, dazzling, exciting, stimulating, lively, animated, vivacious, witty, exhilarating, invigorating
FORMAL ebullient
◼ dull

scion n
1 CHILD, descendant, offspring, heir, successor
2 OFFSHOOT, shoot, branch, sprout, graft, twig

scoff¹ v
scoff at something
mock, ridicule, laugh at, poke fun, taunt, tease, jeer, sneer, gibe, scorn, despise, revile, belittle, rail; *dialect* geck at
OLD dor; (*Shakesp*) gall at
FORMAL deride, disparage
COLLOQ. rib, pooh-pooh, knock
◼ praise, compliment, flatter

scoff² v, n
♦ v
scoff food
eat, consume, devour, finish off, gobble, guzzle, bolt, gulp, binge
COLLOQ. put away, wolf, snarf
♦ n
food, foodstuffs, comestibles, provisions, meal, refreshments, sustenance, nourishment, nutrition, nutriment, subsistence; *Scot* scaff
COLLOQ. eatables, eats, tuck, scran; *N Am* chow down
SLANG grub, nosh, nosh-up

scoffing adj
mocking, taunting, sneering, derisive, scathing, cynical, sarcastic, fiendish, Mephistophelian
FORMAL disparaging

scold v, n
♦ v
reprimand, reprove, rebuke, chide, take to task, reproach, blame, censure, lecture, nag, rant, row, speak to, rate; *Scot* flyte, rage, yaff; *Aust* rouse on

OLD clapperclaw, rattle
FORMAL admonish, upbraid, castigate, berate, lambast, objurgate
COLLOQ. tell off, tick off, start on, take apart, tear into, yap, blow up, give it to someone, give someone a piece of your mind, give a dressing-down, read the riot act to, haul over the coals, rap over the knuckles, jaw, slang, wig; *Aust & NZ* go crook at
SLANG *Aust* go off at
◼ praise, commend
♦ n
shrew, dragon, nag, termagant, virago, vixen, harridan, henpecker, spitfire, Fury, Xantippe; *Scot* yankie
OLD brimstone, callet, trimmer

scolding n
telling-off, reprimand, reproof, rebuke, lecture, talking-to
FORMAL castigation, upbraiding
COLLOQ. a piece of your mind, ticking-off, dressing-down, carpeting, wigging, earful, earbashing
◼ praise, commendation

scoop n, v
♦ n
1 LADLE, spoon, dipper, bailer, bucket, shovel
2 PORTION, helping, ladleful, spoonful
3 EXCLUSIVE, coup, inside story, revelation, exposé, sensation
COLLOQ. latest
♦ v
gouge, scrape, hollow, empty, excavate, dig, shovel, remove, ladle, spoon, dip, bail

scoot v
rush, hurry, dash, dart, career, bolt, shoot, run, sprint, zip, scurry, scud, scuttle, tootle
COLLOQ. belt, tear, vamoose, skedaddle, beat it, scarper

scope n
1 RANGE, compass, field, area, sphere, ambit, terms of reference, realm, confines, limits, reach, orbit, extent, span, sweep, breadth, coverage

Types of scientific instrument include:

absorptiometer	dipleidoscope	hydrophone	optical character	rheostat	telethermoscope
barostat	electromyograph	hydroscope	reader	slide rule	tesla coil
cathode ray	electrosonde	hydrostat	oscillograph	spectroscope	thermostat
oscilloscope	eudiometer	hygrograph	oscilloscope	stactometer	thyratron
centrifuge	fluoroscope	hygrostat	pantograph	stauroscope	torsion balance
chronograph	Fresnel lens	iconoscope	parametric	strobe	transformer
coherer	Geissler tube	image converter	amplifier	stroboscope	transponder
collimator	heliograph	image tube	phonendoscope	tachistoscope	tunnel diode
cryostat	heliostat	interferometer	radarscope	tachograph	vernier
decoherer	hodoscope	microtome	radiosonde	teinoscope	zymoscope
dephlegmator	humidistat	nephograph	rheocord	telemeter	

See also **laboratory apparatus**; **measuring instruments**; **medical equipment**.

2 ***scope for improvement***
room, space, capacity, elbow-room, latitude, leeway, freedom, liberty, opportunity
COLLOQ. wiggle room

scorch *v*
burn, singe, char, blacken, discolour, scald, roast, sear, parch, shrivel, wither, dry up, fry, frizzle, sizzle, blast, scathe; *dialect* plot, sweal; *Scot* birsle, scouther
OLD adust
FORMAL torrefy

scorching *adj*
burning, roasting, sizzling, blistering, sweltering, torrid, tropical, searing, extremely hot, red-hot
COLLOQ. boiling, baking

score *n, v*
♦ *n*
1 RESULT, goals, runs, hits, total, sum, tally, points, marks, record, outcome
2 SCRATCH, line, groove, mark, cut, gouge, incision, nick, notch, gash, slit, scrape
3 ***scores of people***
crowds, lots, masses, multitudes, hundreds, thousands, millions, myriads, swarms, shoals, droves, hosts, legions
4 REASON, grounds, basis, motives, explanation, case, argument
5 ***no worries on that score***
matter, subject, question, issue, concern, aspect
6 ***know the score***
state of affairs, situation, facts, truth
COLLOQ. what's what, the (whole) picture, the gen
7 ***settle old scores***
grievance, grudge, complaint, dispute, quarrel, argument, bone of contention
♦ *v*
1 RECORD, register, get, count, total, keep a tally, make, earn, gain, achieve, attain, win, be successful, have the advantage, have the edge, be one up
COLLOQ. chalk up, notch up, hit the jackpot
2 SCRATCH, scrape, graze, mark, groove, gouge, cut, incise, engrave, indent, nick, slit, gash, slash, notch
3 ***score a piece of music***
set, arrange, adapt, write, orchestrate, instrument

■ **score off**
gain an advantage over, make a clever reply to, humiliate, have the edge
COLLOQ. get one over on

■ **score out**
cross out, cancel, remove, strike out, erase, delete
FORMAL efface, expunge, obliterate
≠ reinstate, restore

scorn *n, v*
♦ *n*
contempt, scornfulness, disdain, sneering, derision, mockery, haughtiness, ridicule, sarcasm, disgust; *dialect* geck
OLD misprise
FORMAL disparagement, contumely
≠ admiration, respect
♦ *v*
despise, look down on, disdain, sneer at, sniff at, scoff at, mock, laugh at, slight, rebuff, spurn, refuse, shun, reject, dismiss, crucify, scorch, spit
OLD blurt, misprise
FORMAL deride, disparage
SLANG *N Am* zing
≠ admire, respect

> **!** **scorn** or **spurn**?
> In *scorn*, the main focus is on contempt for someone or something: *Courbet had little formal art training and scorned the rigid classical outlook of the time.* In *spurn*, the emphasis is on the rejection rather than the contempt: *Spurned by her family, she moved to London; He spurned their offer of help.*

scornful *adj*
contemptuous, disdainful, supercilious, haughty, arrogant, sneering, scoffing, derisive, mocking, jeering, sarcastic, scathing, insulting, slighting, dismissive
FORMAL disparaging
≠ admiring, respectful

scornfully *adv*
contemptuously, disdainfully, superciliously, haughtily, arrogantly, scathingly, slightingly, sneeringly, derisively, dismissively, witheringly
FORMAL disparagingly
≠ admiringly, respectfully

scotch *v*
put an end to, put a stop to, bring to an end, stop, halt, ruin, wreck, scupper, scuttle
COLLOQ. pull the plug on, put the lid on

scot-free *adj*
clear, unpunished, unrebuked, unreprimanded, unreproached, unharmed, unhurt, unscathed, undamaged, safe, uninjured, without a scratch

scoundrel *n*
rogue, rascal, villain, vagabond, ruffian, ne'er-do-well, good-for-nothing, miscreant, scamp, scallywag, cheat, reprobate, dog, cur, hound; *Irish* spalpeen
OLD blighter, bounder, dastard, rotter, stinker, blackguard
COLLOQ. rat, swine; *Irish* louser
SLANG louse, scab; *S Afr* donder

scour[1] *v*
scour pots and pans
scrub, scrape, clean, wash, cleanse, purge, flush, rub, polish, wipe, burnish
TECHNICAL full
FORMAL abrade

scour[2] *v*
scour the hillside
search, hunt, comb, drag, ransack, rummage, turn upside-down, forage, rake, skirt, *battre la campagne*; *Scot* skirr

scourge *n, v*
♦ *n*
1 AFFLICTION, misfortune, torment, terror, torture, bane, evil, curse, menace, plague, trial, penalty, nuisance, punishment, thorn in your side
2 WHIP, lash, strap, flail, birch, cat-o'-nine-tails, switch, disciplinarium, scorpion
OLD flagellum
≠ **1** blessing, godsend, boon
♦ *v*
1 AFFLICT, torment, torture, burden, curse, plague, devastate, punish, chastise, discipline
2 WHIP, flog, beat, lash, strap, birch, cane, flail, thrash

scout *v, n*
♦ *v*
spy out, reconnoitre, explore, investigate, check out, survey, inspect, spy, snoop, search, seek, hunt, probe, look (for), watch, observe
COLLOQ. recce
SLANG case
♦ *n*
spy, reconnoitre, vanguard, advance guard, outrider, escort, lookout, recruiter, spotter, talent spotter, A & R person

scowl *v, n*
♦ *v*
frown, glower, glare, grimace, pout, lour, look daggers at
OLD gloom, overgloom
≠ smile, grin, beam
♦ *n*
frown, glower, glare, grimace, lour, pout; *Scot* gloom
COLLOQ. dirty/black look
≠ smile, grin, beam

scrabble *v*
clamber, scramble, scrape, scratch, claw, grope, grub, paw, dig, root

scraggy *adj*
scrawny, skinny, thin, lean, lanky, bony, raw-boned, angular, gaunt, undernourished, emaciated, wasted
F3 plump, sleek

scram *v*
go away, leave, depart, disappear, flee
COLLOQ. take to your heels, get out, clear out, clear off, quit, beat it, shove off, skedaddle, vamoose, do a bunk, scarper, scoot, bolt, buzz off, scat

scramble *v, n*
♦ *v*
1 CLIMB, scale, clamber, crawl, shuffle, scrabble, grope, grabble
OLD scamble
2 RUSH, hurry, run, push, jostle, jockey, struggle, tussle, strive, vie, contend, compete, battle; *Scot* sprattle
FORMAL hasten
3 MIX, jumble, mix up, infuse, disturb, disorganize, shuffle
♦ *n*
1 CLAMBER, climb, scrabble, shuffle, scaling
2 RUSH, hurry, race, dash, hustle, bustle, scurry, commotion, confusion, muddle, struggle, tussle, vying, competition, free-for-all, mêlée, stampede
OLD (*Shakesp*) muss
COLLOQ. rat race

scrap[1] *n, v*
♦ *n*
1 *a scrap of paper*
bit, piece, fragment, part, fraction, crumb, morsel, bite, mouthful, sliver, shred, shard, snippet, tatter, patch, atom, iota, grain, particle, mite, trace, vestige, remnant, leftover, waste, junk, snap, stitch, rag, scrip; *Scot* glim; *N Am, Aust & NZ* skerrick
OLD quantity
2 *scraps of meat*
leftovers, bits, scrapings, leavings, remains, residue
COLLOQ. bits and pieces, odds and ends
SLANG odds and sods
♦ *v*
discard, throw away, get rid of, jettison, shed, abandon, drop, dump, cancel, axe, demolish, break up, write off
COLLOQ. chuck out, ditch, junk
F3 recover, restore
■ **on the scrap heap**
discarded, forgotten, jettisoned, redundant, rejected, written off
COLLOQ. ditched, dumped

scrap[2] *n, v*
♦ *n*
a scrap in the school playground
fight, scuffle, brawl, quarrel, row, argument, squabble, wrangle, dispute, disagreement, tiff, fracas; *Scot* splore
COLLOQ. dust-up, set-to, punch-up
SLANG bundle
F3 peace, agreement
♦ *v*
fight, brawl, quarrel, argue, fall out, squabble, bicker, row, wrangle, disagree
F3 agree

scrape *v, n*
♦ *v*
1 GRATE, grind, rasp, file, scour, rub, clean, remove, erase, scrabble, claw, shave, descale, flesh, hoe, shred
TECHNICAL curette
OLD scalp
FORMAL abrade
2 SCRATCH, graze, skin, cut, bark, scuff, rake, raze, paw; *Scot* claut, scart
OLD scrab
♦ *n*
1 GRAZE, scratch, rub, abrasion, scuff, shave
TECHNICAL curettage
2 DIFFICULTY, dilemma, predicament, trouble, plight, distress; *Scot* snapper

OLD hobble
COLLOQ. fix, hole, mess, pickle, tight spot, pretty kettle of fish, wrong box, shemozzle, praemunire
■ **scrape by**
just manage to live, get by, scrimp, skimp, scarcely have enough to live on, muddle through, eke out
COLLOQ. keep the wolf from the door, keep your head above water
■ **scrape through**
just pass, only just/barely win, just succeed in
COLLOQ. get through by a whisker
■ **scrape together**
get together, round up, pool together, get with difficulty, collect with difficulty, obtain with difficulty, just manage to get, scuffle

scrappy *adj*
bitty, disjointed, piecemeal, fragmentary, incomplete, untidy, disorganized, sketchy, superficial, slapdash, slipshod
F3 complete, finished

scratch *v, n, adj*
♦ *v*
claw, gouge, score, mark, cut, nick, incise, etch, engrave, scrape, rub, scuff, graze, gash, skin, tear, lacerate, curry, race; *dialect* scram, scrawm; *Scot* claut, rit, scart
TECHNICAL tease
OLD clapperclaw, scrab, scrat
FORMAL abrade
♦ *n*
mark, line, scrape, scuff, abrasion, graze, gash, wound, laceration, score, streak, race; *Scot* claut, rit, scart
♦ *adj*
improvised, impromptu, unrehearsed, rough-and-ready, rough, haphazard
F3 polished
■ **up to scratch**
good enough, satisfactory, adequate, acceptable, up to the mark, reasonable, tolerable, competent
COLLOQ. OK, up to snuff
F3 unsatisfactory

scrawl *v, n*
♦ *v*
scribble, write quickly, pen, jot (down), dash off, doodle
♦ *n*
scribble, squiggle, writing, handwriting, bad/illegible handwriting, scratch, scrabble
FORMAL cacography

scrawny *adj*
scraggy, skinny, thin, lean, lanky, angular, bony, raw-boned, underfed, undernourished, emaciated
F3 fat, plump

scream *v, n*
♦ *v*
shriek, screech, cry, shout, yell, bawl, roar, howl, wail, squeal, yelp, squawk
COLLOQ. holler, shout/cry blue murder; *N Am* yawp
F3 whisper
♦ *n*
1 SHRIEK, screech, cry, shout, yell, bawl, roar, howl, wail, squeal, yelp, squawk
COLLOQ. holler; *N Am* yawp
2 *he's a scream*
joker, comic, comedian, wit
COLLOQ. character, hoot, laugh, riot
OLD SLANG yell
F3 1 whisper 2 bore

screech *v, n*
♦ *v*
squeal, cry, scream, shriek, howl, yell, squawk, yelp
F3 whisper
♦ *n*
squeal, cry, scream, shriek, howl, yell, squawk, yelp
F3 whisper

screen *n, v*

♦ *n*

1 PARTITION, divider

2 SHIELD, guard, protection, cover, mask, veil, cloak, shroud, concealment, front, façade, disguise, camouflage, shelter, shade, curtain, blind, awning, canopy, net, netting, mesh

♦ *v*

1 *screen a film*

show, present, broadcast

2 SHIELD, protect, safeguard, defend, guard, cover, mask, veil, cloak, shroud, hide, conceal, disguise, camouflage, shelter, shade

3 SORT, grade, sift, sieve, riddle, filter, process, evaluate, test, check, investigate, gauge, examine, scan, vet

F3 2 uncover, expose

■ **screen off**

partition (off), separate (off), divide (off), fence off, hide, conceal

screw *n, v*

♦ *n*

fastener, pin, tack, nail, rivet, brad, bolt

♦ *v*

1 FASTEN, adjust, tighten, clamp, fix, contract, compress, squeeze, turn, wind, twist, wring, distort, wrinkle

2 *screw money out of him*

extract, extort, force, constrain, pressurize

COLLOQ. bleed, milk

F3 1 unscrew

■ **screw up**

1 *screw up your face*

wrinkle, distort, tighten, knot, crumple, contract, pucker, contort; *Can* squinch

2 MESS UP, spoil, botch, bungle, mishandle, mismanage

COLLOQ. make a hash of

SLANG louse up, cock up

F3 2 manage

■ **screwed up**

mixed up, disturbed, disordered, disoriented, distracted, distraught, confused, bewildered, muddled, perplexed, puzzled, upset, maladjusted

COLLOQ. messed up, hung up

■ **put the screws on**

pressurize, force, strongarm, compel, constrain, dragoon, coerce

COLLOQ. lean on

screwy *adj*

crazy, eccentric, mad, odd, weird, queer

COLLOQ. daft, dotty, nutty, batty, crackers, round the twist, round the bend

F3 sane

scribble *v, n*

♦ *v*

write, pen, jot (down), dash off, scrawl, doodle

OLD bescrawl, bescribble

♦ *n*

squiggle, writing, handwriting, bad/illegible handwriting, scratch, scrabble

FORMAL cacography

scribbler *n*

writer

COLLOQ. hack, pen-pusher, pot-boiler

scribe *n*

writer, author, reporter, copyist, transcriber, amanuensis, secretary, clerk, recorder, mallam

TECHNICAL hierographer

OLD scrivener

COLLOQ. hack, pen-pusher

scrimmage *n*

brawl, fight, riot, row, struggle, scuffle, skirmish, squabble, disturbance, fray, free-for-all, affray, shindy, mêlée

COLLOQ. bovver, dust-up, scrap, set-to

scrimp *v*

skimp, save, economize, cut back on, limit, reduce, restrict, scrape, curtail, shorten, stint, pinch

COLLOQ. tighten your belt, cut your coat according to your cloth

F3 spend

script *n*

1 *a film script*

text, lines, words, manuscript, dialogue, screenplay, shooting script, libretto, book

2 WRITING, handwriting, hand, longhand, running-hand, calligraphy, letters, manuscript, copy

scripture

See **sacred writings**.

scroll *n*

paper, parchment, roll, volume, list, inventory

Scrooge *n*

miser, skinflint, niggard

COLLOQ. cheapskate, meanie, money-grubber, penny-pincher, tightwad

F3 spendthrift

scrounge *v*

cadge, beg, borrow

COLLOQ. sponge, bum

SLANG *Aust & NZ* bludge

scrounger *n*

cadger, parasite, beggar, borrower; *dialect* scunge

COLLOQ. sponger, bum, freeloader, moocher

SLANG *Aust & NZ* bludger

scrub[1] *v*

1 *scrub the floor*

rub, brush, clean, wash, cleanse, wipe, scour

2 ABOLISH, cancel, delete, abandon, give up, drop, forget

FORMAL discontinue

COLLOQ. axe, wipe

scrub[2] *n*

an area of scrub

scrubland, bush, backwoods, brush, undergrowth, thicket

scruffy *adj*

untidy, messy, unkempt, dishevelled, bedraggled, ungroomed, run-down, tattered, shabby, down-at-heel, disreputable, slatternly, worn-out, ragged, seedy, squalid, slovenly, sloppy

COLLOQ. grotty; *Aust & NZ* daggy

SLANG sluttish

F3 tidy, well-dressed

scrumptious *adj*

delicious, appetising, tasty, mouthwatering, succulent, luscious, delightful, gorgeous, exquisite, magnificent

FORMAL delectable

COLLOQ. mor(e)ish, yummy, scrummy

F3 unappetizing; *colloq.* yucky

scrunch *v*

crunch, crumple (up), twist, crush, grate, grind, screw (up), mash, squash, chew, champ

scruple *n, v*

♦ *n*

1 RELUCTANCE, hesitation, doubt, qualm, reservation, misgiving, second thoughts, uneasiness, difficulty, perplexity, objection, boggle, point of honour

FORMAL vacillation, compunction

2 *has no scruples*

standards, principles, morals, ethics

♦ *v*

hesitate, be reluctant, think twice, hold back, shrink, balk, doubt

OLD stick, stickle

FORMAL vacillate

scrupulous *adj*

1 PAINSTAKING, meticulous, conscientious, careful, rigorous, thorough, strict, exact, precise, minute, fastidious, nice

FORMAL punctilious

2 PRINCIPLED, high-principled, moral, ethical, honourable, honest, upright
E3 1 superficial, careless, reckless **2** unscrupulous, unprincipled

scrutinize *v*
examine, inspect, study, scan, go over, go through, look over, look through, run over, run through, analyse, sift, investigate, probe, search, explore
FORMAL peruse

scrutiny *n*
examination, inspection, study, analysis, investigation, inquiry, search, exploration, probe
FORMAL perusal

scud *v*
sail, skim, race, blow, fly, speed, shoot, dart

scuff *v*
scrape, scratch, graze, rub, brush, drag
FORMAL abrade

scuffle *v, n*
♦ *v*
fight, quarrel, tussle, brawl, come to blows, grapple, struggle, contend, clash
OLD cuffle, pull caps
COLLOQ. scrap
♦ *n*
fight, tussle, brawl, fray, rumpus, commotion, disturbance, affray, row, quarrel, rough-and-tumble, *bagarre*
COLLOQ. scrap, punch-up, set-to, dust-up

sculpt *v*
sculpture, carve, chisel, hew, cut, model, mould, cast, form, shape, fashion, represent

sculptor *n*
sculptress, carver, stone-carver, chiseller, hewer, mason, modeller, caster, moulder, figurist, artist, craftsman, craftswoman

sculpture

Types of sculpture include:

bas-relief	figurine	moulding
bronze	group	plaster cast
bust	head	relief
carving	herm	statue
caryatid	high-relief	statuette
cast	kinetic	telamon
effigy	maquette	waxwork
figure	marble	

---

scum *n*
1 *scum floating on a liquid*
froth, foam, film, layer, covering, impurities, dross, dregs
2 *they're the scum of the earth*
rabble, dregs of society, dirt, undesirables, lowest of the low, rubbish, trash, great unwashed, riff-raff
COLLOQ. plebs

scupper *v*
1 *scupper a plan*
foil, wreck, ruin, mess up, scuttle, disable, demolish, defeat, destroy, overthrow, overwhelm
COLLOQ. axe, kill, put a spanner in the works
SLANG louse up, cock up, screw up
2 *scupper a ship*
sink, destroy, submerge, torpedo
E3 1 advance, promote

scurf *n*
scale, scaliness, dandruff, flakiness, furfur, scruff, scabrousness
OLD scald
Related adjective: furfuraceous

scurfy *adj*
scaly, flaky, scabby, scabrous
OLD scaberulous, scabrid, scald
FORMAL furfuraceous, furfurous, lepidote

scurrility *n*
scurrilousness, rudeness, offensiveness, vulgarity, nastiness, obscenity, coarseness, foulness, indecency, grossness, abuse, abusiveness
FORMAL invective, obloquy, vituperation
E3 politeness

scurrilous *adj*
rude, vulgar, coarse, foul, obscene, indecent, salacious, offensive, abusive, insulting, slanderous, libellous, scandalous, Fescennine, Sotadic, Sotadean
FORMAL disparaging, defamatory, vituperative
E3 polite, courteous, complimentary

scurry *v, n*
♦ *v*
dash, rush, hurry, bustle, scramble, scuttle, scamper, dart, run, sprint, trot, race, fly, skim, scud
FORMAL hasten
COLLOQ. scoot
♦ *n*
rush, bustling, hurry, flurry, scampering, whirl
COLLOQ. hustle and bustle
E3 calm

scurvy *adj*
contemptible, vile, dirty, shabby, worthless, dishonourable, sorry, ignoble, despicable, rotten, pitiful, mean, low, bad, base
FORMAL abject
COLLOQ. low-down
E3 good, honourable

scuttle *v*
scurry, hurry, rush, scutter, bustle, scamper, scramble, scud, run
FORMAL hasten

sea *n, adj*
♦ *n*
1 OCEAN, waves, main, deep
COLLOQ. briny
See also **ocean**.
Related adjectives: marine, maritime, thalassic, pelagic
2 *a sea of faces*
large number, multitude, abundance, profusion, host, mass, expanse
♦ *adj*
marine, maritime, ocean, oceanic, salt, saltwater, aquatic, seafaring, afloat
E3 land, air
■ **at sea**
adrift, lost, confused, bewildered, baffled, puzzled, perplexed, mystified, disoriented, disorientated

> **QUOTATIONS**
> I must down to the seas again, to the lonely sea and the sky, / And all I ask is a tall ship and a star to steer her by, / And the wheel's kick and the wind's song and the white sail's shaking, / And a grey mist on the sea's face and a grey dawn breaking
> JOHN MASEFIELD, 'Sea Fever'
>
> The bottom of the sea is cruel
> HART CRANE, *White Buildings*

seafaring *adj*
sea-going, ocean-going, oceanic, sailing, nautical, naval, marine, maritime

seal *v, n*
♦ *v*
1 *seal a jar*
close (up), shut, stop (up), plug, cork, stopper, waterproof, fasten, secure, tighten, make airtight/watertight
TECHNICAL plumb, tar-seal

2 SETTLE, conclude, finalize, confirm, ratify, stamp, shake hands
OLD consign, counterseal, enseal, obsign, obsignate
COLLOQ. clinch
EЭ 1 unseal
◆ n
stamp, signet, insignia, imprimatur, authentication, assurance, confirmation, ratification
TECHNICAL cachet, bulla
FORMAL attestation, sigil
OLD SLANG jark
Related adjectives: sigillary, sphragistic
■ **seal off**
block up, cordon off, close off, shut off, fasten, fence off, cut off, segregate, isolate, quarantine, cap
EЭ open up

sealed *adj*
closed, shut, corked, plugged, hermetic
EЭ unsealed

seam *n*
1 JOIN, joint, junction, weld, closure, line, stitching
2 *a coal seam*
layer, stratum, vein, lode

seaman *n*
sailor, rating, seafarer, steersman, AB, tar, deck hand, Jack tar, sea dog
SLANG matelot

seamy *adj*
disreputable, sordid, squalid, unsavoury, rough, dark, low, nasty, unpleasant
COLLOQ. sleazy
EЭ respectable, wholesome, pleasant

sear *v*
burn, scorch, char, singe, brown, fry, sizzle, seal, brand, parch, shrivel, wither, wilt, dry up
OLD sere
FORMAL cauterize

search *v, n*
◆ v
1 SEEK, look for, look through, go through, hunt, rummage, rifle, ransack, forage, scour, comb, sift
COLLOQ. go through with a fine-tooth comb, turn upside-down/inside-out
2 EXAMINE, probe, explore, scrutinize, inspect, check, investigate, inquire, pry
COLLOQ. frisk
◆ n
1 HUNT, quest, pursuit, rummage, rifling, forage, ransacking
2 EXAMINATION, exploration, probe, scrutiny, inspection, investigation, inquiry, research, survey
■ **search me**
I don't know
COLLOQ. I've no idea, I haven't got a clue, it beats me, I haven't got the faintest/foggiest, you've got me there, dunno, ask me another
■ **in search of**
searching for, looking for, seeking, in pursuit of, in quest of, on the lookout for

SYNONYM NUANCES

verb sense 1
The terms **seek** and **look for** can be employed widely for attempting to find someone or something. **Look through**, however, suggests cursorily riffling through papers or such like, whereas **go through** implies a greater degree of systematic attention. **Hunt**, on the other hand, implies an element of desperation, while **rummage** and **rifle** convey the idea of a haphazard execution: *she rifled through her wardrobe in an attempt to find a decent dress.* **Ransack** goes further by suggesting resultant disarray.

You can use **forage** of scrabbling about to retrieve anything useful, whereas **scour** could be used for a wide-ranging quest: *she scoured all the antique shops for authentic pieces.* The terms **comb** and **sift** are both suggestive of a close and thorough examination: *he methodically sifted through the files, papers and notebooks.*

searching *adj*
penetrating, piercing, alert, discerning, observant, keen, sharp, close, intent, probing, thorough, minute, inquisitional, trying, home
EЭ vague, superficial

searing *adj*
1 *searing pain/heat*
extreme, severe, intense, fierce, unbearable, insufferable, blazing, burning, scorching
2 *a searing personal attack on the politician*
savage, fierce, ferocious, cruel, brutal, devastating, scathing, vitriolic
FORMAL trenchant, mordant

seaside *n*
coast, shore, seashore, beach, sands, strand
Related adjective: littoral

season *n, v*
◆ n
period, spell, phase, term, time, span, interval
◆ v
1 *season food*
flavour, spice, salt, add flavouring, add pepper to, add herbs to, add relish/sauce to
COLLOQ. pep up
2 AGE, mature, ripen, mellow, harden, toughen, train, prime, prepare, condition, treat
3 TEMPER, moderate, tone down
■ **in season**
available, obtainable, growing plentifully, growing, on the market

seasonable *adj*
timely, well-timed, welcome, opportune, providential, convenient, suitable, appropriate, fitting
EЭ unseasonable, inopportune

seasoned *adj*
mature, experienced, practised, established, well-versed, veteran, long-serving, battle-scarred, old, hardened, toughened, conditioned, acclimatized, weathered
FORMAL habituated
EЭ inexperienced, novice

seasoning *n*
flavouring, spice, condiment, salt, pepper, herbs, relish, sauce, dressing

seat *n, v*
◆ n
1 CHAIR, bench, pew, stool, sofa, throne, stall, form, settle
2 *country seat*
residence, house, mansion, stately home
FORMAL abode
3 PLACE, site, situation, location, headquarters, centre, heart, hub, axis, source, cause, origin, reason, bottom, base, foundation, footing, ground
◆ v
1 SIT, place, put, position, deposit, set, locate, install, fit, fix, settle
2 *the theatre seats 1000*
accommodate, hold, contain, take, have room for

seating *n*
seats, chairs, places, room, accommodation

seaweed *n*
alga, seaware, kelp, varec(h), vraic
Related adjective: fucoid
See panel on next page

Seaweed species include:

bladderwrack	gulfweed	sargasso
carrageen	Irish moss	sea moss
channelled wrack	laver	tangle
coral weed	oarweed	thongweed
dulse	peacock's tail	wrack

---

secede *v*
separate, split off, withdraw, break away, break, resign,
retire, leave, disaffiliate, turn your back on
FORMAL apostatize
COLLOQ. quit
F3 join, unite with

secession *n*
seceding, split, withdrawal, defection, break, breakaway,
disaffiliation, schism
FORMAL apostasy
F3 amalgamation, unification

secluded *adj*
private, secret, withdrawn, cloistered, shut away, cut off,
isolated, lonely, unfrequented, solitary, remote, out-of-the-
way, sheltered, hidden, concealed, close, recluse, retired,
shadowy, shy, in purdah, purdahed
FORMAL sequestered, claustral, cloistral, umbratic
F3 public, accessible

seclusion *n*
privacy, retirement, withdrawal, retreat, isolation, solitude,
remoteness, shelter, secrecy, hiding, concealment,
hermitage, nook, recess, byplace, bypath, bolt hole
FORMAL sequestration

second¹ *adj, n, v*
♦ *adj*
1 NEXT, following, subsequent, succeeding
2 ADDITIONAL, further, extra, supplementary, alternative,
other, alternate, back-up, spare
3 DUPLICATE, twin, double, repeated, another
4 SECONDARY, subordinate, lower, inferior, lesser,
supporting
♦ *n*
helper, assistant, backer, supporter, attendant, second-in-
command, right-hand man/woman, deputy
♦ *v*
approve, agree with, endorse, back, back up, support,
help, assist, aid, further, advance, forward, promote,
encourage
■ **second to none**
incomparable, matchless, beyond compare, without equal,
without parallel, unrivalled, unsurpassed, peerless,
inimitable, nonpareil, paramount, supreme, superlative,
superb, brilliant
F3 ordinary, run-of-the-mill, poor

second² *n*
in ten seconds
minute, moment, instant, flash, split second, twinkling,
twinkling of an eye, trice
COLLOQ. tick, mo, jiff, jiffy, two shakes of a lamb's tail

second³ *v*
seconded to Australia for a year
transfer, relocate, change, move, shift,
assign, send

secondary *adj*
subsidiary, subordinate, lower, inferior, lesser, minor,
unimportant, non-essential, ancillary, auxiliary, supporting,
relief, back-up, reserve, spare, extra, second, alternative,
indirect, derived, derivative, resulting
F3 primary, main, major, essential

second-class *adj*
second-best, second-rate, mediocre, inferior, unimportant,
indifferent, uninspiring, undistinguished, uninspired
F3 valuable

second-hand *adj, adv*
♦ *adj*
used, old, formerly owned, pre-owned, nearly-new, worn,
hand-me-down, borrowed, derivative, secondary, indirect,
vicarious
F3 brand-new
♦ *adv*
indirectly, in a roundabout way, obliquely, incidentally
COLLOQ. on the grapevine
F3 directly

second-in-command *n*
deputy, helper, assistant, backer, supporter, attendant,
right-hand man/woman

secondly *adv*
furthermore, moreover, in addition, further, next, besides,
also, too, as well, additionally
COLLOQ. what's more, into the bargain

second-rate *adj*
inferior, substandard, lesser, unimportant, second-class,
second-best, poor, low-grade, shoddy, cheap, tawdry,
mediocre, undistinguished, uninspired, uninspiring
COLLOQ. rop(e)y, tacky, lousy, tinpot, grotty; *Aust & NZ*
crook
F3 first-rate

secrecy *n*
privacy, seclusion, confidentiality, confidence, disguise,
covertness, concealment, camouflage, furtiveness,
surreptitiousness, stealthiness, stealth, mystery
F3 openness

secret *adj, n*
♦ *adj*
1 PRIVATE, discreet, covert, hidden, concealed, unseen,
shrouded, covered, disguised, camouflaged, undercover,
furtive, surreptitious, stealthy, sly, underhand, under-the-
counter, underground, backstairs, back-door
FORMAL clandestine
COLLOQ. cloak-and-dagger, hole-and-corner, closet
2 CLASSIFIED, restricted, confidential, sensitive, unpublished,
undisclosed, unrevealed, unknown
COLLOQ. hush-hush, top secret, between you and me,
between you me and the gatepost
3 CRYPTIC, mysterious, occult, deep
FORMAL arcane, recondite, abstruse
4 CONCEALED, private, cloistered, shut away, cut off,
isolated, lonely, unfrequented, solitary, remote, close,
sheltered, hidden, retired, secluded, out-of-the-way
FORMAL sequestered
F3 1 public, open **2** well-known, widely-known **4** public,
accessible
♦ *n*
1 CONFIDENTIAL MATTER, confidence, private matter,
mystery, enigma
COLLOQ. inside story
2 *the secret of eternal youth*
code, key, answer, solution, formula, recipe
■ **in secret**
confidentially, in confidence, in private, secretly, under
cover, privately, quietly, surreptitiously, stealthily,
unobserved, covertly, furtively, on the quiet
FORMAL clandestinely, in camera, privily
COLLOQ. on the q.t., on the sly, behind closed doors,
hugger-mugger
F3 openly
■ **secret agent**
spy, undercover agent, foreign agent, enemy agent, double
agent, fifth columnist, scout, snooper
COLLOQ. mole

SYNONYM NUANCES

adjective sense 1
Private can be used to suggest something of a personal,
intimate nature, while **discreet** implies being rather low-
key: *the discreet intervention of the bank*. **Covert**, on the
other hand, would be used of something being kept

from the knowledge of others: *covert payments to amateur players*. **Unseen** has suggestions of protecting identity: *an unseen associate*, while **shrouded** and **covered** both have connotations of mystery: *the writer's sensitive and shrouded lyrics*.

The term **undercover** conveys the idea of false representation, often to undertake sensitive work, and **underground** also has connotations of confidential activity which, if not illegal, is outside of the mainstream: *she worked for an underground movement, forging passports and papers*. The more negative term **furtive** suggests an element of shiftiness, and **surreptitious** and **stealthy** share the idea of being deliberately unobtrusive, although again with connotations of being up to no good. The term **sly** clearly implies an element of craftiness, and you might use **underhand** to imply a degree of deception.

secretary *n*
personal assistant, PA, assistant, office administrator, executive assistant, administrative assistant, typist, stenographer, clerk, scribe, man/girl/person Friday, amanuensis
OLD chancellor, famulus, prothonotary

secrete¹ *v*
secrete a weapon
hide, conceal, bury, cover, cover up, cache, screen, shroud, veil, disguise, take, appropriate
FORMAL sequester
COLLOQ. stash away
E3 uncover, reveal, disclose

secrete² *v*
secrete a liquid
exude, discharge, release, excrete, give off, emit, send out, emanate, produce, leach, leak, ooze
TECHNICAL water, lactate, salivate
OLD secern

secretion *n*
exudation, discharge, release, production, emission, emanation, leakage, oozing
TECHNICAL osmosis, lactation
OLD secernment

secretive *adj*
tight-lipped, close, uncommunicative, unforthcoming, reticent, taciturn, reserved, withdrawn, intent, quiet, deep, cryptic, enigmatic
COLLOQ. cagey, playing your cards close to your chest
E3 open, communicative, forthcoming

secretively *adv*
quietly, silently, enigmatically, uncommunicatively, reticently, taciturnly
E3 openly, communicatively

secretly *adv*
confidentially, in confidence, in private, in secret, under cover, privately, quietly, surreptitiously, stealthily, unobserved, covertly, furtively, on the quiet
FORMAL clandestinely, in camera, privily
COLLOQ. on the q.t., on the sly, behind closed doors, between you me and the gatepost
E3 openly

sect *n*
denomination, cult, division, subdivision, group, splinter group, order, faction, camp, wing, party, school, tradition

sectarian *adj, n*
♦ *adj*
factional, partisan, cliquish, exclusive, narrow, hidebound, limited, parochial, insular, narrow-minded, bigoted, prejudiced, fanatical, extreme, doctrinaire, dogmatic, rigid
E3 non-sectarian, broad-minded
♦ *n*
bigot, fanatic, partisan, zealot, dogmatist, extremist, separatist, fractionalist

section *n*
division, subdivision, chapter, paragraph, passage, instalment, part, component, fraction, fragment, bit, piece, slice, portion, segment, sector, zone, district, area, region, department, branch, wing
E3 whole

sectional *adj*
separate, divided, exclusive, factional, separatist, individual, regional, local, localized, partial, class, racial, sectarian
E3 general, universal

sector *n*
zone, district, quarter, area, precinct, region, branch, field, category, section, division, subdivision, part
E3 whole

secular *adj*
lay, temporal, worldly, earthly, civil, state, non-religious, non-spiritual, profane
E3 religious, spiritual

secure *adj, v*
♦ *adj*
1 SAFE, unharmed, undamaged, protected, sheltered, shielded, immune, impregnable, fast, tight, closed, sealed, fastened, locked
FORMAL fortified
COLLOQ. out of harm's way
2 CONFIDENT, self-confident, assured, self-assured, reassured, certain, safe, comfortable, relaxed, happy, contented
3 FIXED, immovable, stable, steady, sturdy, solid, firm
4 CERTAIN, sure, well-founded, reliable, dependable, steadfast, conclusive, definite, established, settled
E3 **1** insecure, vulnerable **2** uneasy, ill at ease, embarrassed, uncomfortable
♦ *v*
1 OBTAIN, acquire, gain, get, get hold of
FORMAL procure
COLLOQ. come by, land
2 FASTEN, attach, fix, make fast, tie (up), moor, lash, tether, leash, strap, anchor, chain, lock (up), shut, close, padlock, bolt, batten down, nail, rivet
3 PROTECT, make safe, strengthen, guard, safeguard, defend, cover, shield, screen
4 GUARANTEE, assure, ensure, establish, confirm, sponsor, underwrite, endorse
E3 **1** lose **2** unfasten

securely *adv*
firmly, tightly, steadily, stably, sturdily, strongly, robustly, safely, impregnably, out of danger, immovably, steadfastly
E3 uncertainly, unsoundly

security *n*
1 SAFETY, immunity, asylum, sanctuary, refuge, cover, protection, defence, invulnerability, surveillance, safe-keeping, preservation, care, custody
2 *security for a loan*
collateral, surety, pledge, guarantee, warranty, assurance, insurance, precaution(s), safeguard(s), protection, defence
OLD gage
3 CONFIDENCE, assurance, ease, peace of mind, conviction, certainty, positiveness
E3 **1** insecurity, danger **3** anxiety, worry, embarrassment

sedate *adj, v*
♦ *adj*
staid, dignified, solemn, grave, stiff, serious, earnest, sober, proper, noble, worthy, demure, composed, unruffled, serene, tranquil, calm, quiet, unexciting, dull, cool, collected, deliberate, slow-moving
OLD seemly
FORMAL decorous, imperturbable
COLLOQ. unflappable
E3 undignified, lively, agitated
♦ *v*
tranquillize, calm, calm down, quieten down, soothe, relax, pacify

sedately adv

calmly, quietly, serenely, deliberately, seriously, earnestly, soberly, with dignity, nobly, worthily, demurely
FORMAL decorously, imperturbably

sedative adj, n

♦ adj

calming, soothing, anodyne, lenitive, quietive, tranquillizing, relaxing, soporific, depressant
E∃ rousing

♦ n

tranquillizer, sleeping-pill, narcotic, barbiturate, opiate, calmative, depressant, quietive
COLLOQ. downer

Sedatives and tranquillizers include:

amobarbital	diazepam	pentobarbitone
Amytal ®	dichlor-	phenobarbitone
Ativan ®	alphenazone	promethazine
barbitone	laurel-water	Rohypnol ®
chloral hydrate	Librium ®	scopalamine
clonazepam	lorazepam	Temazepam
clozapine	lupulin	tetronal
codeine	meprobramate	thalidomide
cyclobarbitone	methaqualone	thridace
deserpidine	Nembutal ®	Valium ®

---

sedentary adj

sitting, seated, desk-bound, inactive, still, stationary, immobile, unmoving
E∃ active

sediment n

deposit, residue, grounds, lees, dregs, silt
FORMAL precipitate, residuum

sedition n

agitation, rabble-rousing, subversion, disloyalty, treachery, treason, mutiny, rebellion, revolt
FORMAL insubordination, fomentation, incitement to riot
E∃ calm, loyalty

seditious adj

agitating, inciting, rabble-rousing, subversive, disloyal, traitorous, mutinous, rebellious, revolutionary
FORMAL insubordinate, dissident, insurrectionist, fomenting, refractory
E∃ calm, loyal

seduce v

entice, lure, allure, attract, tempt, charm, beguile, ensnare, lead astray, mislead, deceive, corrupt, dishonour, deprave, ruin, betray, debauch
OLD jape, undo, wrong
FORMAL inveigle
COLLOQ. get into bed, chat up, vamp, make a play for
SLANG pull
E∃ repel

seducer n

charmer, philanderer, rake, womanizer, flirt, deceiver, libertine, Romeo, Don Juan, Casanova, Lothario
COLLOQ. wolf, goat

seduction n

enticement, lure, allure, allurement, attraction, appeal, temptation, charm, beguilement, corruption, deception, misleading, ruin
COLLOQ. come-on

seductive adj

enticing, alluring, luring, attractive, appealing, tempting, tantalizing, inviting, flirtatious, sexy, provocative, arousing, beguiling, charming, captivating, bewitching, deceiving, misleading, irresistible, sultry
COLLOQ. come-hither
E∃ unattractive, repulsive

seductress n

femme fatale, temptress, siren, Delilah, Lorelei, Circe
COLLOQ. vamp

sedulous adj

diligent, industrious, conscientious, painstaking, persevering, persistent, laborious, busy, constant, assiduous, tireless, untiring, unflagging, unremitting, resolved, determined
E∃ half-hearted

see v

1 PERCEIVE, catch sight of, set eyes on, glimpse, discern, spot, make out, recognize, distinguish, identify, sight, notice, observe, watch, view, look at, get a look at, witness, mark, note
FORMAL espy, behold
2 *I see your point*
understand, grasp, comprehend, fathom, follow, know, take in, make out, realize, recognize, appreciate, think, regard, consider, reflect, deem
COLLOQ. get, get it, latch onto, cotton onto
3 IMAGINE, picture, visualize, envisage, forecast, foresee, predict, anticipate
4 DISCOVER, find out, ask, learn, ascertain, investigate, inquire, determine, decide
5 ACCOMPANY, usher, lead, show, take, escort
6 VISIT, consult, speak to, interview, meet, encounter
FORMAL chance upon, confer with
COLLOQ. bump into, run into, come across
7 GO OUT WITH, court, date, take out, keep company with, go with

■ **see about**
arrange, attend to, deal with, take care of, look after, organize, manage, be responsible for, do, fix, repair, sort out

■ **see through**
1 *see through a trick*
realize, understand, fathom, penetrate, not be deceived by, not be taken in by
COLLOQ. rumble, get wise to
2 *see a task through*
stick out, continue, persist, persevere, not give up
COLLOQ. hang in
3 *she saw me through the difficult times*
sustain, get through, encourage, support, keep going

■ **see to**
attend to, deal with, take care of, look after, arrange, organize, manage, be responsible for, do, fix, repair, sort out, mind, ensure, make sure, make certain

---

SYNONYM NUANCES

sense 1

You can use **perceive** to suggest becoming visually aware, while **catch sight of** or **glimpse** suggests a brief and unexpected look. The phrase **set eyes on** tends to be used for emphasis: *I tell you, I've never set eyes on him before.* **Discern** and **make out** imply an ability to make visual sense of something despite possible obstacles: *she could no longer make out the hills through the mist.* **Spot** and **notice** are more suggestive of suddenly detecting, or you can use **sight** to suggest seeing a rare occurrence: *he sighted a herd of whales.*

  Recognize suggests previous familiarity, whereas **distinguish** suggests differentiation from surrounding items, and **identify** takes this further by suggesting an ability to name what is seen. Both **observe** and **watch** suggest prolonged attentiveness. **View** and **look at**, on the other hand, are more appropriate for focusing on a particular image. **Get a look at** implies managing to overcome some difficulty: *did you manage to get a look at the new museum?*

  Witness has implications of being able to testify to what has been seen, especially something significant: *he had witnessed the actual event.* The terms **mark** and **note**, meanwhile, both have suggestions of carefully heeding what is seen: *I noted her flushed countenance.*

seed *n*

1 *the seeds of a plant*

pip, stone, kernel, nut, pit, nucleus, grain, germ, sperm, ovum, egg, ovule, spawn, embryo, semen, spermatozoon

Related adjective: seminal

2 *the seeds of rebellion*

source, start, beginning, root, origin, cause, reason(s)

FORMAL genesis

3 OFFSPRING, child, children, young, young one(s), family, heirs, successors, descendants

■ **go/run to seed**

deteriorate, decay, decline, degenerate, get worse

COLLOQ. go downhill, go to pot, go to the dogs, go down the tubes, go to hell

seediness *n*

shabbiness, dirtiness, untidiness, squalidness, dilapidation, decay

seedy *adj*

1 SHABBY, dirty, untidy, scruffy, tatty, mangy, squalid, run-down, dilapidated, decaying

COLLOQ. grotty, crummy, sleazy, ribby

2 UNWELL, ill, sick, poorly, ailing, off-colour, chippy

COLLOQ. groggy, rough, under the weather, out of sorts

E∃ **2** well

seek *v*

look for, search for, try to find, hunt for, pursue, follow, inquire, ask, invite, request, beg, petition, want, desire, aim, try, attempt, endeavour, strive

FORMAL solicit, entreat, aspire

seeker *n*

inquirer, searcher, student, disciple, novice

FORMAL chela, zetetic

seem *v*

appear, look, have/give the appearance of being, look like, come across as, have the look of, show signs of, give the impression of being, strike you as, feel, sound, pretend to be

seeming *adj*

apparent, outward, external, superficial, surface, supposed, pretended, quasi-, pseudo, specious

FORMAL ostensible, assumed

E∃ real

seemingly *adv*

apparently, superficially, on the surface, on the face of it, as far as you can see, outwardly, allegedly

FORMAL ostensibly

E∃ really

seemly *adj*

appropriate, proper, suitable, suited, befitting, fit, fitting, decent, nice, attractive, handsome, maidenly, becoming, *comme il faut*

OLD comely, meet

FORMAL decorous

E∃ unseemly

seep *v*

ooze, leak, exude, well, trickle, drip, dribble, percolate, drain, permeate, soak; *dialect* sipe

seepage *n*

leak, leakage, dripping, oozing, exudation, percolation

TECHNICAL osmosis

seer *n*

seeress, augur, prophet, prophetess, soothsayer, sibyl, wise man, spaeman, spaewife

seesaw *v*

alternate, swing, go from one extreme to the other, fluctuate, oscillate, teeter, pitch

COLLOQ. yo-yo

seethe *v*

1 BOIL, simmer, bubble, effervesce, fizz, foam, froth, ferment, rise, swell, surge, teem, swarm; *Scot* buller

2 RAGE, be angry, fume, smoulder, storm, be furious, be outraged, be livid, be incensed

COLLOQ. explode, boil over, see red, foam at the mouth, blow up, blow a fuse, blow a gasket, blow your cool, burst a blood vessel, fly off the handle, go off the deep end, lose your cool

SLANG go ape, go ballistic

see-through *adj*

transparent, translucent, sheer, filmy, gauzy, gossamer(y), flimsy

E∃ opaque

segment *n*, *v*

♦ *n*

section, division, compartment, part, bit, piece, joint, link, slice, portion, wedge; *Scot* scliff

TECHNICAL ring, urite, somite, arthromere, metamere, uromere

OLD article, lith

SLANG pig

E∃ whole

♦ *v*

cut up, separate, divide, split, slice, halve, anatomize

segregate *v*

separate, keep apart, cut off, isolate, dissociate, ostracize, quarantine, set apart, exclude

FORMAL sequester

E∃ unite, join

segregation *n*

separation, setting apart, isolation, quarantine, dissociation, apartheid, discrimination, separate development

FORMAL sequestration

E∃ unification, desegregation

seize *v*

1 GRAB, snatch, grasp, clutch, grip, hold, get/take hold of, grab hold of

2 *seize property/a plane*

take, confiscate, impound, usurp, appropriate, commandeer, hijack, annex, kidnap, abduct

FORMAL sequestrate

3 *seize a criminal*

catch, capture, arrest, apprehend

COLLOQ. nab, collar, nail, nobble

E∃ **1, 2** let go, release, hand back

■ **seize on**

grab, grasp eagerly, grasp with both hands, exploit

■ **seize up**

stop, break down, stop working

FORMAL malfunction

COLLOQ. pack up, go phut, conk out

seizure *n*

1 FIT, attack, convulsion, paroxysm, spasm

2 TAKING, confiscation, commandeering, hijack, annexation, abduction, snatching, capture, arrest, apprehension

FORMAL appropriation, sequestration

E∃ **2** release, liberation

seldom *adv*

rarely, infrequently, occasionally, hardly ever, scarcely ever

COLLOQ. once in a blue moon

E∃ often, usually

select *v*, *adj*

♦ *v*

choose, pick, single out, decide on, settle on, appoint, elect, favour, prefer, opt for, invite

COLLOQ. cherry-pick

♦ *adj*

selected, choice, top, prime, first-class, first-rate, best, finest, supreme, high-quality, hand-picked, élite, exclusive, limited, privileged, special, excellent, superior

COLLOQ. posh

E∃ second-rate, ordinary, general

selection *n*

1 CHOICE, pick, option, preference

2 ASSORTMENT, variety, choice, range, line-up, miscellany, medley, potpourri, collection, anthology

selective *adj*
particular, careful, fussy, finicky, fastidious, discerning, discriminating
COLLOQ. choosy, picky, pernickety; *N Am* persnickety
⊟ indiscriminate

selectively *adv*
carefully, particularly, discerningly, by choice, preferentially, discriminatingly, differentially

self *n*
ego, personality, identity, I, person, inner being, soul
COLLOQ. the real me, heart of hearts

self-assembly *adj*
DIY, flat-pack, kit-form, prefabricated

self-assertive *adj*
forceful, pushing, pushy, aggressive, authoritarian, commanding, dictatorial, overbearing, heavy-handed, high-handed, overweening, domineering
FORMAL peremptory
COLLOQ. bossy, not backward in coming forward
⊟ compliant

self-assurance *n*
confidence, overconfidence, belief in yourself, self-confidence, assurance, self-possession, positiveness, aplomb, cocksureness
COLLOQ. cockiness
⊟ humility, unsureness

self-assured *adj*
self-confident, confident, assured, sure of yourself, self-collected, self-possessed, overconfident, cocksure, cocky
⊟ humble, unsure

self-centred *adj*
selfish, self-seeking, self-serving, self-interested, egotistic(al), narcissistic, self-absorbed, egocentric, thinking only of yourself, wrapped up in yourself
⊟ altruistic

self-confidence *n*
assurance, self-assurance, confidence, belief in yourself, self-reliance, positiveness, composure, aplomb
⊟ insecurity, self-consciousness

self-confident *adj*
confident, self-reliant, self-assured, assured, self-possessed, composed, cool, bold, fearless, positive, unabashed
⊟ unsure, insecure, self-conscious

self-conscious *adj*
uncomfortable, ill at ease, awkward, embarrassed, blushing, shamefaced, sheepish, shy, diffident, bashful, coy, retiring, timid, timorous, shrinking, self-effacing, nervous, insecure
⊟ natural, unaffected, confident

self-contained *adj*
1 *a self-contained person*
independent, self-reliant, self-sufficient, private, quiet, secretive
2 *a self-contained flat*
separate, independent, free-standing
FORMAL discrete

self-control *n*
calmness, composure, patience, self-restraint, restraint, self-denial, temperance, self-discipline, self-mastery, willpower
COLLOQ. cool

self-denial *n*
moderation, temperance, abstemiousness, asceticism, self-sacrifice, unselfishness, selflessness
FORMAL self-abnegation, self-renunciation
⊟ self-indulgence

self-discipline *n*
willpower, self-control, self-mastery, persistence, resolve, determination, single-mindedness

self-employed *adj*
independent, freelance, out-of-house, consultant, casual, temporary, part-time

self-esteem *n*
ego, self-respect, self-regard, self-assurance, self-image, self-confidence, pride, self-pride, dignity, *amour-propre*
⊟ inferiority complex

self-evident *adj*
obvious, clear, plain, manifest, undeniable, axiomatic, unquestionable, incontrovertible, inescapable

self-explanatory *adj*
easy-to-understand, easy-to-read, easy-to-follow, self-evident, obvious, clear, plain, understandable, intelligible, approachable, accessible, comprehensible

self-glorification *n*
self-exaltation, self-aggrandizement, self-admiration, self-advertisement, egotism, egotheism
⊟ humility

self-governing *adj*
independent, autonomous, free, sovereign, self-determining

self-government *n*
autonomy, independence, home rule, democracy, self-sovereignty, self-determination
FORMAL autarchy
⊟ subjection

self-importance *n*
arrogance, cockiness, pushiness, pompousness, conceit, conceitedness, vanity, pomposity, self-opinion, donnism, self-consequence
COLLOQ. bigheadedness, bumptiousness
⊟ humility

self-important *adj*
arrogant, pompous, conceited, egoistic, vain, proud, overbearing, swaggering, strutting, cocky, pushy, self-consequent, swollen-headed, swell-headed
COLLOQ. bigheaded, bumptious
⊟ humble

self-indulgence *n*
extravagance, excess, self-gratification, sensualism, dissoluteness, intemperance, high living, hedonism
FORMAL dissipation, profligacy
⊟ self-denial

self-indulgent *adj*
hedonistic, pleasure-seeking, dissolute, extravagant, intemperate, immoderate
FORMAL dissipated, profligate
⊟ abstemious

self-interest *n*
selfishness, self-love, self-regard, self-serving, self
⊟ selflessness

selfish *adj*
self-interested, self-seeking, self-serving, mean, miserly, mercenary, greedy, covetous, self-centred, inconsiderate, egocentric, egotistic(al)
COLLOQ. thinking of nobody except yourself, looking after number one
⊟ unselfish, selfless, generous, considerate

selfishly *adv*
thinking only of yourself, only for yourself, from personal motives, inconsiderately, ungenerously, greedily, egotistically, egocentrically
⊟ unselfishly, generously

selfishness *n*
self-centredness, self-seeking, self-serving, self-love, self-interest, self-regard, greed, meanness, egotism
⊟ selflessness

selfless *adj*
unselfish, altruistic, self-denying, self-sacrificing, generous, philanthropic
FORMAL magnanimous
E3 selfish, self-centred

selflessness *n*
unselfishness, generosity, consideration of others, thinking of others first, altruism, philanthropy, self-denial, self-sacrifice
FORMAL magnanimity
E3 selfishness, self-centredness

self-possessed *adj*
self-assured, assured, self-collected, calm, collected, composed, confident, unruffled, poised
COLLOQ. cool, unflappable, together
E3 worried

self-possession *n*
self-assurance, assurance, calmness, confidence, composure, aplomb, self-confidence, coolness, self-command, poise
FORMAL sangfroid
COLLOQ. cool, unflappability

self-reliance *n*
independence, self-support, self-sufficiency, self-sustenance, self-sustainment
TECHNICAL autarky
FORMAL self-sustentation
E3 dependence

self-reliant *adj*
independent, self-supporting, self-sufficient, self-sustaining
TECHNICAL autarkic(al)
E3 dependent

self-respect *n*
pride, dignity, self-esteem, self-assurance, self-confidence, self-regard, *amour-propre*
E3 inferiority complex

> QUOTATIONS
> Self-respect … comes to us when we are alone, in quiet moments in quiet places when we suddenly realize that, knowing the good, we have done it; knowing the beautiful, we have served it; knowing the truth, we have spoken it
> ALFRED WHITNEY GRISWOLD

self-restraint *n*
self-discipline, self-denial, self-control, patience, forbearance, moderation, abstemiousness, self-government, temperance, self-command, willpower
FORMAL encraty
E3 licence

self-righteous *adj*
smug, complacent, superior, priggish, pious, sanctimonious, holier-than-thou, pietistic, hypocritical, pharisaical, moralistic
COLLOQ. goody-goody, pi
E3 humble

self-righteousness *n*
priggishness, piousness, goodiness, sanctimoniousness, pharisaicalness, pharisaism
COLLOQ. goody-goodiness
E3 humility

self-sacrifice *n*
self-denial, selflessness, altruism, unselfishness, generosity
FORMAL self-abnegation, self-renunciation
E3 selfishness

self-satisfaction *n*
smugness, complacency, contentment, pride, self-appreciation, self-approval
FORMAL self-approbation
E3 humility

self-satisfied *adj*
smug, complacent, self-congratulatory, self-righteous, proud
COLLOQ. puffed up
E3 humble

self-seeking *adj*
mercenary, self-interested, selfish, self-loving, self-serving, self-endeared, opportunistic, acquisitive, calculating, careerist, fortune-hunting, gold-digging
COLLOQ. on the make
E3 altruistic

self-styled *adj*
self-appointed, self-titled, professed, so-called, *soi-disant*, would-be, pretended

self-sufficient *adj*
independent, self-contained, self-supporting, self-reliant, self-sustaining
E3 dependent

self-supporting *adj*
self-sufficient, self-financing, independent, self-reliant, self-sustaining
E3 dependent

self-willed *adj*
stubborn, obstinate, stiff-necked, opinionated, self-opinionative, self-opinionated, headstrong, pig-headed, ungovernable, wilful, bloody-minded, perverse
FORMAL intractable, refractory
COLLOQ. cussed
E3 complaisant

sell *v*
1 *sell cars*
exchange, trade, barter, auction, dispose of, vend, retail, hawk, peddle, tout; *S Afr* smouch
COLLOQ. flog
2 *it sold for £10,000*
be priced at, go for, retail at
3 STOCK, handle, deal in, carry, market, trade in, traffic in, merchandize, import, export
4 PROMOTE, advertise, market, get support/approval for, persuade, win over, bring round
COLLOQ. push, hype
E3 **1** buy
■ **sell out**
1 *sell out of fruit*
run out of, have none left, be out of stock, be exhausted
2 BETRAY, fail, double-cross
COLLOQ. rat on, sell down the river, stab in the back
SLANG fink on; *N Am* stool on

seller *n*
vendor, merchant, trader, supplier, stockist
E3 buyer, purchaser

Types of seller include:

agent	huckster	saleswoman
auctioneer	jobber	shop assistant
bagman	knight of the road	shopkeeper
barrow-boy	market trader	*S Afr* smouch
broker	merchandizer	*S Afr* smouser
cold caller	milklady	store clerk
colporteur	milkman	storekeeper
commercial	*N Am* peddler	street trader
traveller	pedlar	tallyman
costermonger	*colloq.* rep	telephone
dealer	representative	sales-person
demonstrator	retailer	ticket agent
door-to-door	sales assistant	tout
salesman/	sales clerk	tradesman
saleswoman	sales executive	tradeswoman
estate agent	saleslady	traveller
factor	salesman	wholesaler
hawker	salesperson	

See also **shop**.

selling *n*
dealing, marketing, trading, transactions, traffic, trafficking, merchandizing, salesmanship, promotion
FORMAL vending, vendition
⊟ buying

semblance *n*
appearance, air, show, pretence, guise, mask, front, façade, veneer, look, aspect, image, resemblance, likeness, similarity
FORMAL apparition

semen *n*
seminal fluid, sperm, ejaculate
OLD seed
SLANG come, cum; *Aust* spoof; (*taboo*) jism, spunk

seminal *adj*
influential, major, important, original, innovative, productive, creative, formative, imaginative, seminary
⊟ derivative

seminar *n*
1 *a business seminar*
meeting, discussion, workshop, conference, convention, forum, symposium, colloquy
2 *a seminar at a university*
tutorial, lecture, class, session, workshop, study group

seminary *n*
college, institute, institution, training college, academy, school, theological college

send *v*
1 POST, mail, get off, address, put in the post/mail, dispatch, consign, forward, redirect, convey, deliver, courier; *N Am* Fed-Ex
FORMAL remit
2 TRANSMIT, broadcast, beam, relay, communicate, convey, radio, televise
3 PROPEL, drive, move, throw, cast, fling, hurl, launch, fire, shoot, discharge, project, emit, direct
4 *the heat sent him to sleep*
make, cause to be, drive
5 THRILL, stimulate, excite, arouse, give pleasure to
COLLOQ. turn on, give a buzz/kick
■ **send for**
summon, call for, request, order, command
⊟ dismiss
■ **send off**
order to leave, order off, tell to leave the field
■ **send up**
satirize, mock, ridicule, parody, mimic, imitate
COLLOQ. take off, take the mickey out of
SLANG take the piss out of

send-off *n*
goodbye, farewell, leave-taking, departure, start
⊟ arrival

send-up *n*
mockery, parody, skit, satire, imitation, burlesque
COLLOQ. mickey-take, spoof, take-off

senile *adj*
old, aged, doddering, decrepit, failing, confused; *Scot* doited
FORMAL senescent
COLLOQ. gaga

senility *n*
old age, infirmity, dotage, second childhood, senile dementia, decrepitude, anility
FORMAL paracme, caducity, senescence

senior *adj*
older, elder, higher, superior, high-ranking, first, major, chief
FORMAL doyen(ne), âiné(e)
⊟ junior
■ **senior citizen**
pensioner, retired person, old-age pensioner, OAP

COLLOQ. *N Am* golden ager
SLANG (*offensive*) coffin-dodger

seniority *n*
priority, precedence, rank, standing, status, age, superiority, importance

sensation *n*
1 FEELING, sense, impression, perception, awareness, consciousness, emotion
COLLOQ. vibes
2 *the report caused a sensation*
commotion, stir, agitation, excitement, thrill, furore, outrage, scandal
3 SUCCESS, hit, triumph
COLLOQ. winner, wow

sensational *adj*
1 EXCITING, thrilling, electrifying, galvanic, breathtaking, startling, stirring, amazing, astounding, staggering, incredible, dramatic, spectacular, impressive, exceptional, excellent, wonderful, superb, marvellous, fantastic, gorgeous
COLLOQ. smashing, terrific, fabulous, drop-dead, shock
2 SCANDALOUS, shocking, horrifying, revealing, melodramatic, lurid, gamy
COLLOQ. juicy, pulp
⊟ **1** ordinary, run-of-the-mill

sense *n*, *v*
♦ *n*
1 FEELING, sensation, impression, perception, awareness, consciousness, appreciation, faculty, ability
FORMAL sensibility
2 REASON, logic, mind, brain(s), wit(s), wisdom, common sense, intelligence, cleverness, understanding, comprehension, apprehension, discernment, prudence, judgement, appreciation, intuition
FORMAL judiciousness
COLLOQ. gumption, nous, savvy
3 MEANING, significance, definition, interpretation, implication, drift, tenor, nuance, point, purpose, substance
FORMAL denotation, import, purport
⊟ **2** foolishness **3** nonsense
♦ *v*
feel, suspect, be aware of, be conscious of, discern, perceive, detect, experience, notice, observe, recognize, realize, appreciate, understand, comprehend, grasp
FORMAL intuit, divine
COLLOQ. pick up
■ **make sense of**
understand, grasp, comprehend, make out
COLLOQ. figure out, fathom, make head or tail of

senseless *adj*
1 FOOLISH, stupid, unwise, silly, idiotic, mad, crazy, moronic, ridiculous, ludicrous, absurd, meaningless, nonsensical, fatuous, irrational, illogical, unreasonable, mindless, pointless, purposeless, futile, inane
OLD surd
COLLOQ. daft, dotty, batty, load of nonsense/rubbish
2 UNCONSCIOUS, stunned, anaesthetized, deadened, numb, unfeeling
FORMAL insensible, insensate
COLLOQ. out, out cold
⊟ **1** sensible, meaningful, intelligent **2** conscious, aware

sensibility *n*
1 *show sensibility*
sensitiveness, sensitivity, susceptibility, discernment, perceptiveness, appreciation, awareness, responsiveness, insight, intuition, delicacy, taste
2 *offend someone's sensibilities*
feelings, emotions, sentiments, susceptibilities, sensitivities
⊟ **1** insensibility

sensible *adj*
1 WISE, well-advised, prudent, shrewd, sharp, far-sighted, intelligent, clever, mature, level-headed, clear-headed, down-to-earth, commonsense, commonsensical, sober,

sane, rational, logical, reasonable, realistic, practical, pragmatic, functional, sound
FORMAL judicious, sagacious
COLLOQ. with both feet on the ground, with your head screwed on (the right way)
See Synonym nuances panel at **realistic**.
2 SENSITIVE, responsive, aware, perceptive, discerning, susceptible, vulnerable
3 *wear sensible shoes*
practical, ordinary, everyday, working, serviceable, hard-wearing, strong, tough, functional
☒ **1** senseless, foolish, unwise **2** insensitive, unresponsive **3** impractical, fashionable, decorative
■ **sensible of**
sensitive to, understanding, conscious of, aware of, acquainted with, mindful of, observant of, alive to, convinced of
FORMAL cognizant of
☒ unaware of

sensibly *adv*
1 WISELY, prudently, shrewdly, cleverly, rationally, logically, reasonably, realistically, practically
FORMAL judiciously, sagaciously
2 *sensibly dressed*
practically, strongly, suitably, usefully, handily, functionally, serviceably
☒ **1** foolishly, unwisely **2** impractically, fashionably

sensitive *adj*
1 SUSCEPTIBLE, vulnerable, impressionable, tender, emotional, thin-skinned, temperamental, touchy, irritable, sensitized, responsive, reactive, aware, perceptive, discerning, appreciative
FORMAL sentient
2 DELICATE, fine, fragile, soft, exact, precise
3 *a sensitive issue*
delicate, tricky, controversial, difficult, problematic, awkward, touchy
4 *needs sensitive handling*
tactful, delicate, diplomatic, careful, considerate, sympathetic, discerning, discreet, well-thought-out
☒ **1** insensitive, thick-skinned **2** imprecise, approximate

sensitivity *n*
1 SUSCEPTIBILITY, vulnerability, responsiveness, awareness, perceptiveness, receptiveness, reactiveness, discernment, appreciation, sympathy
2 DELICACY, fineness, fragility, softness
☒ **1** insensitivity

sensual *adj*
self-indulgent, voluptuous, voluptuary, sultry, worldly, physical, animal, carnal, fleshly, bodily, embodied, brute, gross, sexual, erotic, sexy, lustful, lecherous, lewd, licentious
OLD swinish
FORMAL encarnalized, pandemian
COLLOQ. randy, horny
☒ ascetic

> **⚠ sensual** or **sensuous**?
> *Sensual* means 'of or concerning the physical senses and the body rather than the mind', and is used especially with a connotation of sexuality or sexual arousal: *a full, sensual mouth; a strong desire for sensual pleasure. Sensuous* means 'perceived by or affecting the senses, especially in a pleasant way', as in *I find his music very sensuous; Her sculptures have a certain sensuous quality to them.*

sensuality *n*
pleasure, voluptuousness, lewdness, lustfulness, salaciousness, sexiness, licentiousness, libertinism, eroticism, carnality, animalism, lasciviousness, debauchery, lecherousness, gourmandise
FORMAL profligacy, prurience
☒ asceticism, Puritanism

sensuous *adj*
pleasurable, gratifying, pleasing, pleasant, voluptuous, rich, lush, luxurious, sumptuous, aesthetic
☒ ascetic, plain, simple

> **⚠ sensuous** or **sensual**?
> *See panel at* **sensual**.

sensuously *adv*
pleasurably, gratifyingly, voluptuously, richly, lushly, sumptuously, luxuriously
☒ plainly

sentence *n, v*
♦ *n*
judgement, decision, verdict, condemnation, pronouncement, ruling, decree, order, punishment
♦ *v*
judge, pass judgement on, impose a sentence on, condemn, doom, punish, penalize

sententious *adj*
1 MORALIZING, moralistic, judgemental, sanctimonious, canting, pompous colloq. preachy
2 BRIEF, concise, compact, pithy, short, terse, succinct, pointed, epigrammatic, aphoristic, laconic, axiomatic, gnomic
COLLOQ. preachy
☒ **1** humble **2** verbose

sentient *adj*
conscious, aware, sensitive, responsive, feeling, live, living, reactive
☒ *formal* insentient

sentiment *n*
1 THOUGHT, idea, feeling, opinion, view, point of view, judgement, belief, persuasion, attitude
2 EMOTION, sensibility, tenderness, soft-heartedness, softness, romance, romanticism, sentimentality, mawkishness

sentimental *adj*
tender, soft-hearted, emotional, loving, gushing, sugary, touching, pathetic, tear-jerking, maudlin, mawkish, nostalgic, romantic, affectionate
COLLOQ. soppy, weepy, lovey-dovey, slushy, mushy, schmaltzy, corny, sickly, gushy, sloppy, gooey, gloopy, yucky
☒ unsentimental, realistic, cynical

> **SYNONYM NUANCES**
> You can use **tender** to suggest having a sensitive nature, while **soft-hearted** implies generosity, although perhaps to a fault: *James cursed himself for being a soft-hearted fool.* **Emotional** can be widely used to suggest exaggerated sensibilities, while **gushing** is disapproving in tone, implying over-effusiveness, often tinged with insincerity: *the gushing praise of the critics.* **Sugary** is similarly critical in its implication that something is cloyingly sweet: *sugary heroines in old movies.*
>   If you want to express approval of sentimentality, you might use **touching** to suggest that something is positively affecting. **Pathetic**, however, would imply a degree of being pitiable, and while **tear-jerking** literally suggests prompting crying, it is often used facetiously. You can use **maudlin** to imply being foolishly lachrymose, while **mawkish**, although similar, implies a more nauseating or embarrassing aspect: *he wrote a mawkish poem when his father died, an attempt to suggest feelings that had never existed.*
>   Whereas **nostalgic** straightforwardly suggests a hankering for the past, **romantic** has connotations, mostly positive, of idealized love. The terms **sloppy** and **soppy**, by contrast, share negative implications of causing embarrassment: *soppy love songs that make us cringe.*

sentimentality *n*
tenderness, sentimentalism, sentiment, emotionalism, feeling, sensibility, romanticism, mawkishness, nostalgia, treacle
FORMAL bathos
COLLOQ. corniness, gush, mush, pulp, schmaltz, sloppiness, slush, goo, gloop, yuck

sentry *n*
sentinel, guard, picket, watchman, watch, lookout, out-sentry, vedette
OLD centry

separable *adj*
divisible, detachable, removable, distinguishable, distinct, independent, different, particular
OLD (Shakesp) dividant
FORMAL partible
E3 inseparable

separate *v, adj*
♦ *v*
divide, sever, take/come apart, keep apart, break off, break up, part, split (up), divorce, part company, diverge, dismantle, disconnect, uncouple, disunite, disaffiliate, disentangle, single out, segregate, isolate, cut off, partition, abstract, remove, detach, withdraw, secede
OLD sunder
FORMAL disjoin, become estranged
E3 join, unite, combine
♦ *adj*
different, distinct, unattached, unconnected, unrelated, single, individual, particular, independent, alone, solitary, segregated, isolated, apart, divorced, divided, disunited, disconnected, disjointed, detached, sundry
FORMAL disparate, discrete, several, autonomous
E3 together, attached

separated *adj*
separate, split up, divided, disconnected, parted, isolated, disunited, disassociated, apart, segregated
OLD sundered
E3 attached, together

separately *adv*
independently, individually, singly, one by one, apart, discriminately, discretely, alone, personally
FORMAL severally
E3 together

separating *adj*
divisive, isolating, dividing, intervening, partitioning, segregating
E3 unifying

separation *n*
division, parting, parting of the ways, leave-taking, farewell, split-up, break-up, divorce, split, rift, schism, gap, divergence, disconnection, uncoupling, disunion, disjunction, disengagement, dissociation, segregation, isolation, apartheid, detachment
FORMAL severance, estrangement, disseverment
E3 unification

separatist *adj*
breakaway, rebel, dissenting, renegade, heretical
FORMAL apostate, schismatic, seceding, secessionist

septic *adj*
infected, poisoned, festering, putrefying, putrid
FORMAL putrefactive, suppurating

sepulchral *adj*
gloomy, grave, melancholy, sombre, cheerless, mournful, sad, solemn, dismal, funereal, morbid, deep, hollow
FORMAL lugubrious, sepulchrous, woeful
E3 happy, cheerful

sepulchre *n*
tomb, grave, burial place, vault, mausoleum

sequel *n*
follow-up, continuation, development, result, consequence, outcome, issue, upshot, pay-off, end, conclusion

sequence *n*
succession, series, run, progression, chain, string, train, line, procession, order, arrangement, consequence, course, track, cycle, set
FORMAL seriatim

sequester *v*
1 ISOLATE, set apart, seclude, insulate, detach, remove, alienate, shut away, shut off
2 CONFISCATE, seize, impound, take, commandeer
FORMAL sequestrate, appropriate

sequestered *adj*
isolated, secluded, lonely, outback, out-of-the-way, private, remote, quiet, retired, unfrequented, cloistered
E3 public, busy, frequented

sequestrate *v*
seize, confiscate, impound, take, commandeer, sequester
FORMAL appropriate

seraphic *adj*
seraphical, angelic, heavenly, celestial, holy, divine, pure, saintly, innocent, blissful
FORMAL beatific, sublime
E3 demonic

serendipitous *adj*
chance, lucky, happy, accidental, unexpected, fortunate
FORMAL fortuitous

serendipity *n*
chance, coincidence, happy coincidence, accident, luck, fortune, good fortune
FORMAL fortuity

serene *adj*
calm, tranquil, cool, composed, placid, untroubled, undisturbed, unclouded, unruffled, still, quiet, peaceful, seraphic
FORMAL halcyon, imperturbable
COLLOQ. unflappable
E3 troubled, disturbed

serenely *adv*
calmly, placidly, quietly, peacefully, tranquilly
FORMAL imperturbably

serenity *n*
calm, calmness, stillness, tranquillity, cool, composure, placidity, peace, peacefulness, quietness
FORMAL quietude
COLLOQ. unflappability
E3 anxiety, disruption

serf *n*
slave, servant, thrall, villein, bondservant, bond-slave, bond(s)man, bond(s)woman, bondmaid, helot, thirl, thete, adscript
E3 master

series *n*
set, cycle, succession, sequence, run, progression, row, chain, string, line, train, stream, order, arrangement, course
FORMAL concatenation

serious *adj*
1 IMPORTANT, significant, weighty, momentous, crucial, critical, urgent, pressing, acute, grave, worrying, difficult, life-and-death, grim, severe, deep, far-reaching
FORMAL of consequence, consequential
COLLOQ. no joke, no laughing matter
2 UNSMILING, long-faced, humourless, unlaughing, grim, dour, solemn, sober, sombre, grave, stern, thoughtful, quiet, pensive, preoccupied, earnest, genuine, honest, sincere
COLLOQ. heavy

3 *serious injuries*
severe, acute, critical, grave, bad, dangerous, precarious, life-and-death, grievous
FORMAL perilous
4 *serious money*
considerable, great, large, big, siz(e)able, substantial, ample, plentiful, abundant, lavish, generous, significant
COLLOQ. tidy
⊟ 1 trivial, unimportant, insignificant **2** smiling, laughing, joking, light-hearted, facetious, frivolous **3** slight, mild **4** small, slight, insignificant

---

SYNONYM NUANCES

sense 2
Unsmiling and **unlaughing** can be used to suggest facial expressions that show you will brook no nonsense, but **long-faced** can have further implications of deeper sadness. **Humourless**, on the other hand, has more to do with temperament, implying an inability to enjoy levity, while the equally negative **grim** suggests a forbidding manner or countenance: *a grim look on his face*; *grim resolve*. **Dour** is similar, but further implies a degree of moroseness.

Sober implies a restrained and quiet persona, and the term **solemn** too has connotations of quiet dignity: *a solemn funeral ceremony*. **Sombre** can be more suggestive of gloominess: *a sombre death-haunted melancholic*, while **grave** suggests significance.

Stern carries suggestions of being slightly fearsome, while **quiet**, **thoughtful** and **pensive** suggest an introspective nature. **Preoccupied** suggests a somewhat abstracted air, while **earnest** implies being rather focused in intent: *earnest conviction*. To suggest an absence of affectation or pretence, you could use **genuine**, **honest** and **sincere**, which are all approving in tone.

---

seriously *adv*
1 SOLEMNLY, thoughtfully, earnestly, sincerely, joking apart, *au sérieux*
COLLOQ. for real
2 ACUTELY, gravely, badly, severely, critically, dangerously, sorely, distressingly, grievously
3 EXTREMELY, exceedingly, excessively, very, really, exceptionally, extraordinarily, intensely, thoroughly, remarkably, utterly, greatly, highly, unusually, unreasonably, immoderately, uncommonly, inordinately, acutely, severely, decidedly
OLD jolly
COLLOQ. awfully, terribly, dreadfully, frightfully, terrifically
⊟ 1 casually, in fun **3** slightly

seriousness *n*
1 IMPORTANCE, significance, urgency, weight, gravity
FORMAL moment
2 SOLEMNITY, earnestness, humourlessness, sternness, staidness, sedateness
FORMAL sobriety, gravitas
⊟ 1 triviality, slightness **2** casualness

sermon *n*
address, discourse, lecture, talk, message, harangue, homily, khutbah
FORMAL oration, exhortation, declamation
COLLOQ. talking-to, preach, nagging

serpentine *adj*
winding, twisting, tortuous, meandering, coiling, crooked, sinuous, snakelike, snaking, snaky
FORMAL serpentiform
⊟ straight

serrated *adj*
toothed, notched, indented, jagged, sawlike, saw-toothed, saw-edged
FORMAL serratulate, serrulated
⊟ smooth

serried *adj*
dense, close, close together, close-set, crowded, compact, massed
⊟ scattered

servant *n*
attendant, retainer, hireling, help, helper, assistant, ancillary
Related adjectives: menial, servile
⊟ master, mistress

Servants and servers include:

au pair	domestic	livery-servant
barista	domestic help	maid
barmaid	drudge	manservant
barman	equerry	menial
batman	errand boy	nanny
bellboy	factotum	ostler
N Am bellhop	fag	page
body servant	flunkey	pageboy
boot-catcher	footman	parlour-maid
boots	garçon	retainer
butler	*Irish* gossoon	scullery maid
care assistant	governess	scullion
carer	groom	seneschal
chambermaid	*haiduk*	*old* servitor
colloq. char	*old* handmaid(en)	*colloq.* skivvy
charlady	henchman	slave
chauffeur	henchperson	steward
chauffeuse	henchwoman	stewardess
chef	home help	tapsman
chokra	house boy	*colloq.* tweeny
cleaner	housekeeper	valet
coachman	housemaid	waiter
commissionaire	kitchen-maid	waitress
cook	lackey	wench
colloq. daily	lady-in-waiting	wet nurse
dogsbody	lady's maid	

---

serve *v*
1 WAIT ON, attend, minister to, be employed by, work for, help, aid, assist, be of assistance to, benefit, be of benefit to, be of service to, further, support, be of use to
FORMAL succour
COLLOQ. do a good turn to
2 *serve a purpose*
fulfil, complete, answer, satisfy, perform, carry out, go through, act, function, do the work of
FORMAL discharge, suffice
3 DISTRIBUTE, give out, dish up, dish out, wait, dole out, present, deliver, take care of, provide, supply

service *n, v*
♦ *n*
1 EMPLOYMENT, work, labour, business, duty, duties, job, function, performance, activity, assistance
2 USE, usefulness, usage, utility, advantage, benefit, help, assistance
COLLOQ. turn
3 SERVICING, maintenance, repair(s), overhaul, check
4 *church service*
worship, observance, ceremony, rite, ritual, sacrament, ordinance
5 *armed services*
forces, military, air force, navy, army
See also panel at **armed services**.
6 *railway/postal services*
facility, amenity, resource, utility
♦ *v*
maintain, overhaul, check, repair, go over, recondition, tune
■ **in service**
in use, in regular use, in working order, working, in operation, functional, operative

■ **of service**
useful, helpful, profitable, advantageous, beneficial, of benefit

■ **out of service**
out of use, no longer in service, out of order, not working, not in working order, defective, faulty
COLLOQ. on the blink, packed up, conked out, kaput, phut; *N Am* on the fritz

> QUOTATIONS
> Small service is true service, while it lasts
> WILLIAM WORDSWORTH, 'To a Child, Written in her Album'

serviceable *adj*
usable, useful, helpful, profitable, advantageous, beneficial, utilitarian, simple, plain, unadorned, strong, tough, durable, hard-wearing, dependable, efficient, functional, practical, sensible, convenient
Ⅎ3 unserviceable, unusable

servile *adj*
sycophantic, toadying, cringing, fawning, grovelling, bootlicking, slavish, subservient, subject, submissive, humble, abject, low, lowly, mean, base, menial, vassal
FORMAL obsequious, unctuous
COLLOQ. slimy
Ⅎ3 assertive, aggressive

servility *n*
sycophancy, toadyism, grovelling, fawning, bootlicking, self-abasement, slavishness, submissiveness, subservience, meanness, abjection, abjectness, baseness
FORMAL obsequiousness, unctuousness
Ⅎ3 aggressiveness, boldness

serving *n*
helping, portion, share, amount, plateful, bowlful, spoonful, ration

servitude *n*
slavery, enslavement, bondage, obedience, bonds, chains, serfdom, thrall, thraldom, vassalage, villeinage
FORMAL subjugation
Ⅎ3 freedom, liberty

session *n*
1 MEETING, sitting, hearing, assembly, conference, discussion; *Scot* down-sitting
TECHNICAL séance
COLLOQ. talkathon
2 PERIOD, stretch, spell, time, term, semester, year, drill, clinic, scrimmage, shoot
TECHNICAL church court
COLLOQ. bevvy, sesh; *Aust* grog-on, grog-up

set *v, n, adj*
♦ *v*
1 PUT, place, lay (down), locate, situate, position, station, arrange, prepare, make ready, install, lodge, insert, fix, stick, park, deposit, rest
COLLOQ. plonk, dump
2 SCHEDULE, appoint, arrange, organize, designate, specify, name, prescribe, ordain, assign, allocate, impose, fix, establish, determine, stipulate, decide, conclude, confirm, settle, agree on, resolve
3 ADJUST, regulate, synchronize, co-ordinate, harmonize, put right
4 *set the table*
lay, prepare, get ready, make ready, arrange, set out
5 *set something in motion*
cause, start, begin, occasion, bring about, produce, prompt, set off, give rise to, lead to, result in, trigger (off)
6 *set someone a task*
assign, allocate, give, grant, delegate, choose, select, consign
7 *set a record/precedent*
establish, provide, inaugurate, start, begin, create, bring into being

8 *set a trap*
prepare, arrange, organize, lay, set up, plan, devise
9 *set words to music*
arrange, score, adapt, write, orchestrate, harmonize
10 *the sun sets*
go down, go below the horizon, sink, dip, decline, subside, disappear, vanish
11 CONGEAL, thicken, gel, stiffen, become firm/hard, solidify, harden, cake, coagulate, crystallize
Ⅎ3 **10** rise
♦ *n*
1 COLLECTION, batch, series, sequence, kit, outfit, compendium, assortment, class, category
FORMAL array, assemblage
2 *a set of people*
group, band, gang, crowd, circle, clique, faction
3 *the set of a film*
setting, background, scene, scenery, stage, backdrop, wings, *mise-en-scène*
4 *the set of someone's face/body*
expression, turn, look, position, posture
FORMAL bearing
♦ *adj*
1 FIXED, established, scheduled, appointed, arranged, prearranged, ordained, specified, decided, agreed, settled, firm, strict, rigid, inflexible, ingrained, entrenched
FORMAL predetermined, prescribed
2 REGULAR, routine, usual, customary, everyday, traditional, habitual, standard, stock, stereotyped, conventional
3 READY, prepared, equipped, arranged, organized, completed, finished, all set
Ⅎ3 **1** undecided, movable **2** spontaneous **3** unprepared

■ **set about**
begin, start, get down to, embark on, undertake, tackle, attack
FORMAL commence
COLLOQ. set the ball rolling

■ **set against**
1 BALANCE, compare, contrast, weigh
FORMAL juxtapose
2 OPPOSE, divide, disunite, alienate
FORMAL estrange

■ **set apart**
distinguish, make different, differentiate, mark off, put aside, separate

■ **set aside**
1 PUT ASIDE, lay aside, lay by, keep (back), put away, save, give over to, keep in reserve, reserve, set apart, separate, select, earmark, mothball
COLLOQ. stash away
2 ANNUL, cancel, reverse, overturn, overrule, reject, ignore, discount, discard
FORMAL abrogate, revoke

■ **set back**
delay, hold up, slow, thwart, check, hinder, impede
FORMAL retard

■ **set down**
1 LAY DOWN, record, stipulate, assert, affirm, state, establish, formulate, prescribe
2 WRITE DOWN, note (down), record, put in writing

■ **set forth**
1 EXPLAIN, expound, describe, present, set out, clarify
FORMAL delineate, elucidate, explicate
2 *set forth on a journey*
depart, set out, set off, leave, start out

■ **set in**
begin, start, come, arrive
FORMAL commence

■ **set off**
1 LEAVE, depart, set out, start (out), set forth, begin
2 DETONATE, blow up, light, ignite, touch off, trigger off, explode
3 ACTIVATE, trigger (off), touch off, prompt, encourage, initiate, set in motion
4 DISPLAY, show off, enhance, contrast, throw into relief, heighten, intensify

■ **set on**

1 set upon, attack, assault, turn on, go for, fall upon, lay into, mug
COLLOQ. beat up
2 determined, resolved, fixed, bent, decided, resolute, firm, purposeful, strong-willed, single-minded, persevering, persistent, strong, strong-minded, steadfast, tenacious, dogged, insistent, intent, unflinching, unwavering, uncompromising, stubborn
COLLOQ. hell-bent, dead set, out

■ **set out**

1 LEAVE, depart, set off, start (out), begin
2 ARRANGE, lay out, display, exhibit, present, describe, explain

■ **set up**

1 BUILD, raise, elevate, erect, construct, assemble, compose
FORMAL dispose, array
2 START, form, create, establish, institute, found, inaugurate, initiate, begin, introduce, bring into being, organize, arrange, prepare
3 FRAME, trap, incriminate, accuse falsely
COLLOQ. fit up

setback n

delay, problem, difficulty, hitch, hiccup, reverse, reversal, stumbling-block, impediment, hindrance, obstruction, misfortune, upset, disappointment, defeat, rebuff, throwback, blight
COLLOQ. hold-up, snag, blow, body blow, whammy, knock
E3 boost, advance, help, advantage

settee n

sofa, couch, chesterfield, davenport, lounge, canapé, day-bed, bed-settee, sofa bed, futon, dos-à-dos, squab, tête-à-tête, bergère

setting n

mounting, frame, surroundings, milieu, environment, background, context, perspective, period, position, location, locale, site, scene, scenery, *mise-en-scène*

setting-up n

start, establishment, institution, initiation, inauguration, foundation, founding, introduction, creation
FORMAL inception
E3 abolition, termination

settle v

1 AGREE (ON), decide (on), resolve, reconcile, solve, compromise, fix, establish, determine, accept, choose, confirm, appoint, arrange
COLLOQ. patch up, clinch
2 ARRANGE, order, put in order, organize, adjust, complete, conclude
3 *the dust settled*
sink, subside, drop, go down, fall, come down, descend, land, alight, light upon
FORMAL repose
4 COLONIZE, occupy, populate, people, inhabit, live, make your home, put down roots
FORMAL reside
5 *settle a bill*
pay, clear, discharge, settle up, square (up)
COLLOQ. fork out, cough up, foot; *N Am* ante up

■ **settle down**

1 CALM DOWN, make comfortable, quieten, still, soothe, compose
2 CONCENTRATE ON, apply yourself to, get down to, knuckle/buckle down to
3 *time to settle down*
put down roots, get married, buy a house, start a family

settlement n

1 RESOLUTION, agreement, arrangement, decision, satisfaction, conclusion, reconciliation, contract, treaty
FORMAL termination
COLLOQ. patching up
2 ARRANGEMENT, ordering, organization, completion, conclusion

3 PAYMENT, clearance, clearing, liquidation, discharge
FORMAL defrayal
4 COLONY, outpost, community, kibbutz, camp, encampment, hamlet, village, plantation, establishment, colonization, occupation, population

settler n

colonist, colonizer, pioneer, frontiersman, frontierswoman, planter, immigrant, incomer, newcomer, squatter, pilgrim, beachcomber; *Aust & NZ* bushman
OLD inhabiter, Cromwellian, Varangian; *NZ* shagroon
E3 native

set-to n

argument, quarrel, conflict, fight, row, squabble, wrangle, disagreement, exchange, fracas, brush, contest, slanging-match
FORMAL altercation
COLLOQ. argy-bargy, barney, bust-up, dust-up, scrap, spat

set-up n

system, structure, organization, composition, arrangement, format, framework, business, conditions, circumstances
FORMAL disposition

sever v

1 CUT, split, part, separate, divide, break off, tear off, lop off, chop (off), hack, cut off, amputate, detach, disconnect, disjoin, disunite, divorce, dissever, disbranch, hew, nip off
TECHNICAL pith
OLD rend, cleave
2 *sever a relationship*
dissociate, alienate, break (off), make a clean break with, divorce, dissolve, cease, end
TECHNICAL cut the painter
FORMAL terminate, estrange
E3 **1** join, combine, attach, unite

several adj

some, many, a number of, (quite) a few, various, assorted, sundry, diverse, different, distinct, separate, particular, individual
FORMAL disparate

severally adv

separately, individually, singly, discretely, particularly, respectively, specifically, seriatim, apiece
E3 simultaneously, together

severe adj

1 EXTREME, acute, intense, fierce, violent, strong, forceful, powerful, cruel, pitiless, merciless, relentless, inexorable, harsh, tough, hard, difficult, grim, forbidding, rigorous, stringent, drastic, Draconian, tyrannical, iron-handed, iron-fisted
2 STRICT, rigid, unbending, stern, grim, dour, cold, unsympathetic, disapproving, sober, serious, unsmiling, strait-laced
3 AUSTERE, ascetic, plain, simple, modest, stark, spartan, undecorated, unembellished, unadorned, functional
4 *a severe illness*
serious, grave, critical, acute, dangerous, intense, unbearable, agonizing, excruciating, perilous
5 HARD, difficult, demanding, rigorous, arduous, burdensome, taxing, exacting, punishing
E3 **1** mild, kind, compassionate, sympathetic **2** lenient **3** decorated, ornate **4** minor **5** easy, simple

severely adv

1 EXTREMELY, acutely, intensely, badly, critically, dangerously, gravely
2 STRICTLY, rigorously, disapprovingly, sternly, hard, harshly, sharply, sorely, grimly, bitterly, coldly, unsympathetically, dourly

severity n

1 EXTREMITY, acuteness, severeness, intensity, strength, forcefulness, fierceness
2 HARSHNESS, hardness, toughness, sharpness, ungentleness, ruthlessness, pitilessness, mercilessness, grimness, wrath, stringency, coldness, sternness, strictness, seriousness, gravity

3 AUSTERITY, plainness, rigour, asceticism, simplicity, bareness, spartanism

⊟ 1 mildness **2** compassion, kindness, leniency

sew *v*

stitch, tack, baste, hem, darn, mend, seam, embroider
Related adjectives: sutorial, sutorian

sex *n*

1 GENDER, sexuality, sex appeal, sexual desire, libido, sexual attraction, sensuality, desirability, allure, seductiveness, glamour, sexiness, magnetism, voluptuousness
FORMAL nubility
COLLOQ. it
2 SEXUAL INTERCOURSE, intercourse, sexual relations, copulation, lovemaking, fornication, reproduction, union, intimacy, intimate relations, sleeping with someone, going to bed with someone
OLD congress, commixtion, embraces
FORMAL carnal knowledge, consummation, coitus, coition
COLLOQ. how's your father, it; *Aust & NZ* naughty
SLANG lay, bang, greens, jig-a-jig, knee-trembler, nooky, bonk, leg-over, wham bam thank you ma'am, pussy, rumpy-pumpy, tail; *N Am* jazz, poontang; (*taboo*) fuck, fucking, screw, screwing, shag, shagging
Related adjective: sexual

■ **have sex with**

make love to, sleep with, go to bed with
OLD know, lie with
FORMAL copulate with
COLLOQ. do it, go all the way
SLANG lay, get your leg over, have it off with, bonk, bang; (*taboo*) fuck, screw, shag; *Aust & NZ* root

> **QUOTATIONS**
> If sex is such a natural phenomenon, how come there are so many books on how to?
>   BETTE MIDLER

sexless *adj*

asexual, unsexual, unsexed, unfeminine, unmasculine, undersexed, neuter
TECHNICAL parthenogenetic

sexton *n*

caretaker, verger, grave-digger, fossor, sacristan
OLD (*Shakesp*) grave-maker

sexual *adj*

sex, reproductive, procreative, genital, coital, venereal, carnal, sensual, erotic

sexuality *n*

sexual instincts, sexual urge, sexual orientation, sexual desire, sexiness, sensuality, desire, carnality, eroticism, virility, lust, voluptuousness

---

Sexual orientations include:

asexual	homosexual
bi-curious	pansexual
bisexual	polysexual
heterosexual	transsexual

---

sexy *adj*

alluring, desirable, attractive, sensual, voluptuous, nubile, seductive, inviting, flirtatious, arousing, stimulating, slinky, provoking, provocative, titillating, pornographic, erotic, salacious, suggestive
COLLOQ. raunchy, beddable
⊟ sexless

shabbily *adv*

1 *dressed shabbily*
unfashionably, inelegantly, scruffily, disreputably
2 *he's been treated shabbily*
unfairly, unacceptably, dishonourably, shamefully, despicably, contemptibly, rottenly
⊟ 1 smartly **2** fairly, honourably

shabby *adj*

1 RAGGED, tattered, frayed, threadbare, worn, worn-out, mangy, moth-eaten, faded, scruffy, tatty, dowdy, disreputable
2 DILAPIDATED, run-down, broken-down, tumbledown, ramshackle, seedy, dirty, squalid, dingy, poky, in disrepair
COLLOQ. tacky
3 *a shabby trick*
unfair, unacceptable, contemptible, despicable, rotten, mean, low, cheap, shoddy, unworthy, shameful, dishonourable
⊟ 1 , **2** smart **3** honourable, fair

shack *n*

hut, cabin, shanty, hovel, shed, hutch, lean-to
COLLOQ. dump, hole

shackle *v, n*

♦ *v*
1 HAMPER, inhibit, impede, encumber, limit, restrict, restrain, secure, thwart, bind, tie, constrain, obstruct, handicap, hamstring
OLD gyve
2 CHAIN, handcuff, bind, restrain, manacle, fetter, trammel, tether
TECHNICAL hamshackle
OLD gyve
⊟ 1 free **2** unshackle
♦ *n*
1 BOND, tether, chain, fetter, iron, handcuff, rope, manacle, trammel, hamper
TECHNICAL fetterlock
OLD gyve
COLLOQ. bracelets, darbies
2 *throw off the shackles of tyranny*
restriction, restraint, constraint, tie, encumbrance, obstruction, trammel

shade *n, v*

♦ *n*
1 SHADINESS, shadow(s), darkness, obscurity, semi-darkness, dimness, gloom, gloominess, murkiness, twilight, dusk, gloaming
2 AWNING, canopy, cover, covering, shelter, protection, screen, blind, curtain, veil, shield, visor, umbrella, parasol, sunshade
3 COLOUR, hue, tint, tone, tinge
4 TRACE, dash, hint, suggestion, suspicion, touch, memory, reminder, nuance, gradation, degree, difference, amount, variety
COLLOQ. tad
5 GHOST, spectre, phantom, spirit, apparition, semblance
♦ *v*
shield, screen, protect, cover, shroud, veil, hide, conceal, obscure, block light from, cloud, dim, darken, shadow, overshadow

■ **a shade**
a little, a bit, rather, slightly, a touch, a trace, a trifle

■ **put in the shade**
outshine, outclass, surpass, beat, excel, eclipse, outrank, top, dwarf

shadow *n, v*

♦ *n*
1 SHADE, darkness, obscurity, inconspicuousness, semi-darkness, dimness, gloom, twilight, dusk, gloaming, cloud, cover, protection
FORMAL tenebrosity
2 SILHOUETTE, shape, outline, image, representation
3 *cast a shadow over the proceedings*
cloud, gloom, sadness, blight, pall, foreboding
4 FOLLOWER, companion, inseparable companion, pal, detective, sleuth
COLLOQ. sidekick
5 TRACE, hint, suggestion, suspicion, vestige, remnant, remainder

♦ *v*

1 OVERSHADOW, overhang, shade, shield, screen, obscure, darken

2 FOLLOW, tail, dog, stalk, trail, watch

■ **a shadow of your former self**

vestige, remnant, apology, weaker version, poor imitation

■ **without a shadow of a doubt**

doubtless, certainly, without doubt, undoubtedly, unquestionably, indisputably, no doubt, clearly, surely, of course, truly, most likely, assuredly, indubitably

shadowy *adj*

1 DARK, gloomy, murky, obscure, dim

FORMAL crepuscular, tenebrous, tenebrose, tenebrious

2 VAGUE, faint, indistinct, ill-defined, indistinguishable, indeterminate, unclear, hazy, nebulous, intangible, unsubstantial, ethereal, ghostly, spectral, phantom, illusory, dreamlike, imaginary, unreal, mysterious

shady *adj*

1 SHADED, shadowy, shielded, screened, protected, covered, shrouded, veiled, dim, dark, obscure, clouded, cool, leafy, bowery, opaque, bosky

OLD caliginous

FORMAL umbrageous, umbratile, umbratilous, umbriferous, umbrose, umbrous, tenebrous, tenebrose, tenebrious

2 DUBIOUS, questionable, suspect, suspicious, dishonest, crooked, unreliable, untrustworthy, disreputable, unscrupulous, unethical, underhand, shifty, louche

COLLOQ. fishy, slippery, iffy

🖛 **1** sunny, sunlit, bright **2** honest, trustworthy, honourable

shaft *n*

1 PASSAGE, duct, tunnel, well, flue

2 HANDLE, shank, stem, hilt, butt, stock, upright, pillar, pole, rod, bar, stick, arrow

3 *a shaft of light*

ray, dart, pencil, beam, duct, passage

TECHNICAL winze

shaggy *adj*

hairy, long-haired, hirsute, bushy, woolly, unshorn, dishevelled, unkempt

FORMAL crinose

🖛 bald, shorn, close-cropped

shake *v, n*

♦ *v*

1 *the windows are shaking in the wind*

rattle, jolt, jerk, bump, roll, bounce, judder, wag, agitate, twitch, convulse, heave, throb, vibrate, oscillate

2 TREMBLE, quiver, quake, wobble, totter, sway, rock, shiver, shudder, judder, convulse

3 WAVE, swing, flourish, brandish, wield

4 *the news shook her*

upset, distress, alarm, shock, shake up, frighten, unnerve, intimidate, disturb, discompose, unsettle, agitate, stir, rouse

FORMAL perturb

COLLOQ. rattle, faze

5 *shake someone's confidence*

weaken, undermine, reduce, diminish, lower, lessen

♦ *n*

1 JOLT, rattle, roll, bounce, rocking, jerk, judder, jiggle, twitch, throbbing, vibration, oscillation

2 TREMBLING, convulsion, quiver, quake, quaking, shiver, shivering, shudder, shuddering

3 SHOCK, upset, alarm, disturbance, jolt, unsettling

■ **shake a leg**

hurry, get a move on

COLLOQ. get cracking, step on it, look lively, get your skates on

■ **shake off**

1 *shake someone off*

get rid of, dislodge, lose, elude, escape, give the slip, get away from, leave behind, outdistance, outstrip

2 *shake off an illness*

recover from, get better, feel better, get well, improve, pick up, rally, mend, heal, respond to treatment, get over, recuperate, revive, convalesce, gain strength

COLLOQ. pull through, bounce back, turn the corner, get back on your feet, be on the mend

■ **shake up**

1 *the accident shook me up*

upset, distress, alarm, shock, unnerve, unsettle

COLLOQ. rattle

2 *shake up an organization*

reorganize, rearrange, restructure

COLLOQ. reshuffle

shake-up *n*

reorganization, rearrangement, restructuring, disturbance, upheaval

COLLOQ. reshuffle

shaky *adj*

1 TREMBLING, quivering, quavery, faltering, unsteady, wobbly, tottering, tottery, staggering, doddering, tentative, uncertain

FORMAL tremulous

2 UNSTABLE, unsteady, insecure, precarious, wobbly, rocky, tottery, rickety, weak

3 DUBIOUS, questionable, suspect, weak, flimsy, unreliable, unsound, unfounded, ungrounded, unsupported, untrustworthy

🖛 **2** firm, strong

shallow *adj*

1 *shallow water/containers*

superficial, surface, skin-deep

2 *a shallow person*

superficial, slight, flimsy, trivial, frivolous, foolish, idle, empty, petty, trifling, meaningless, unscholarly, ignorant, simple, insincere, one-dimensional

COLLOQ. rattle-brained

🖛 **1** deep, profound **2** deep, profound, serious, careful

sham *n, adj, v*

♦ *n*

1 PRETENCE, fraud, counterfeit, imposture, forgery, fake, copy, imitation, simulation, feigning, hoax

COLLOQ. humbug

SLANG *N Am* gold brick

2 IMPOSTOR, fraud, fake, charlatan, impersonator, pretender, deceiver, cheat, swindler

COLLOQ. phoney, con man

♦ *adj*

false, fake, counterfeit, spurious, bogus, pretended, feigned, make-believe, put-on, simulated, artificial, mock, imitation, synthetic

COLLOQ. phoney

🖛 genuine, authentic, real

♦ *v*

pretend, feign, put on, make believe, simulate, imitate, fake, counterfeit

FORMAL affect, dissemble

shaman *n*

magician, sorcerer, witch doctor, medicine man, medicine woman, healer, powwow, pawaw, angekok

shamble *v*

shuffle, scrape, drag, falter, limp, toddle, doddle, hobble

shambles *n*

mess, chaos, muddle, confusion, disorganization, disorder, havoc, anarchy, bedlam, wreck

FORMAL disarray

COLLOQ. madhouse, pigsty

shambling *adj*

awkward, clumsy, unsteady, ungainly, lumbering, lurching, shuffling, unco-ordinated, disjointed, loose

🖛 agile, neat, nimble, spry

shambolic *adj*
chaotic, messy, muddled, in disarray, disorganized, confused
COLLOQ. at sixes and sevens, all over the shop

shame *n, v*
♦ *n*
1 HUMILIATION, degradation, shamefacedness, remorse, guilt, embarrassment, mortification, modesty, confusion, *aidos*
OLD pudor; (*Spenser*) repriefe
FORMAL compunction
2 DISGRACE, dishonour, discredit, stain, stigma, disrepute, infamy, scandal, reproof, reproach
FORMAL ignominy, opprobrium
3 *it's a shame*
pity, disappointment, misfortune, unfortunate thing, bad luck
COLLOQ. too bad
OLD COLLOQ. sin
E⦁ **1** pride **2** honour, credit, distinction
♦ *v*
embarrass, mortify, abash, confound, humiliate, ridicule, humble, put to shame, disgrace, dishonour, discredit, debase, degrade, sully, taint, stain
OLD ashame, beshame, rebuke, shend
■ **put to shame**
humiliate, humble, embarrass, mortify, disgrace, upstage, outshine, outclass, outstrip, surpass, eclipse
COLLOQ. show up

> QUOTATIONS
> Shame is the most violent of all the passions
> MARIE MADELEINE PIOCHE DE LA VERGNE LA FAYETTELA PRINCESSE DE CLEVES

shamefaced *adj*
ashamed, conscience-stricken, guilty, regretful, penitent, remorseful, contrite, apologetic, sorry, red-faced, blushing, embarrassed, mortified, abashed, humiliated, uncomfortable
COLLOQ. sheepish
E⦁ unashamed, proud

shameful *adj*
1 *a shameful waste of money*
disgraceful, outrageous, shocking, scandalous, indecent, abominable, atrocious, wicked, mean, base, foul, poor, low, vile, reprehensible, dishonourable, discreditable, inglorious, contemptible, unworthy, ignoble
OLD pudendous
FORMAL heinous
2 EMBARRASSING, mortifying, shaming, humiliating
FORMAL ignominious
E⦁ **1** honourable, creditable, worthy

shamefully *adv*
shockingly, scandalously, atrociously, embarrassingly, disgracefully, outrageously, reprehensibly
FORMAL ignominiously

shameless *adj*
1 UNASHAMED, unabashed, unshamed, unrepentant, unregretful, impenitent, barefaced, bald-faced, flagrant, blatant, brazen, brash, audacious, unblushing, insolent, impudent, defiant, hardened, incorrigible
OLD browless, frontless; (*Shakesp*) unbashful
2 IMMODEST, indecent, improper, unprincipled, wanton, dissolute, corrupt, depraved
FORMAL unbecoming, indecorous, unseemly
E⦁ **1** ashamed, shamefaced, contrite **2** modest

shamelessly *adv*
unashamedly, blatantly, defiantly, incorrigibly, immodestly, indecently, improperly

shanty *n*
hut, cabin, shed, shack, lean-to, hovel, bothy, hutch

shape *n, v*
♦ *n*
1 FORM, outline, outward appearance, silhouette, profile, model, mould, pattern, cut, lines, contours, figure, physique, build, structure, frame, design, format
FORMAL configuration
2 APPEARANCE, guise, likeness, form, look, aspect, image, air, semblance
3 *in good shape*
condition, state, form, health, trim, fettle, kilter
4 PATTERN, mould, model, format, structure, character
FORMAL configuration
♦ *v*
form, fashion, model, mould, cast, forge, sculpt, sculpture, carve, whittle, make, guide, influence, develop, produce, construct, create, design, define, determine, devise, frame, block, plan, prepare, organize, adapt, adjust, regulate, accommodate, alter, modify, remodel
■ **shape up**
develop, come on, take shape, progress, make progress, move forward, make headway, improve, flourish
■ **take shape**
become clear, become recognizable, become definite, gel, come together, form

---

Geometrical shapes include:

circle	kite	quadrilateral
cone	nonagon	rectangle
crescent	oblong	rhombus
cube	octagon	right-angled trian-
cuboid	octahedron	gle
cylinder	oval	scalene triangle
decagon	parallelogram	semicircle
diamond	pentagon	sphere
ellipse	pentahedron	square
equilateral triangle	polygon	tetrahedron
hemisphere	polyhedron	trapezium
heptagon	prism	triangle
hexagon	pyramid	
isosceles triangle	quadrant	

---

shapeless *adj*
formless, amorphous, unformed, unfashioned, undeveloped, unframed, nebulous, unstructured, chaotic, irregular, misshapen, badly proportioned, ill-proportioned, deformed, dumpy
OLD unfashionable
FORMAL indigest

shapely *adj*
elegant, pretty, attractive, well-formed, well-proportioned, well-turned, trim, neat, graceful, gainly, curvaceous, voluptuous, clean-limbed; *dialect* tidy, gainly; *Scot* trig
TECHNICAL forehanded
OLD comely, featous

shard *n*
fragment, piece, bit, part, chip, particle, splinter, shiver, sherd

share *v, n*
♦ *v*
divide, split, go halves, partake, participate, have a share in, share out, distribute, dole out, give out, hand out, deal out, allot, allocate, assign
OLD (*Shakesp*) common
FORMAL apportion
COLLOQ. go fifty-fifty, go Dutch, go halvesies, carve up
♦ *n*
portion, ration, quota, allowance, allocation, allotment, lot, part, division, proportion, percentage, dividend, due, contribution
OLD (*Shakesp*) allottery
COLLOQ. cut, whack, rake-off, slice of the cake, piece/slice of the action

■ **share out**
give out, distribute, hand out, mete out, divide up, parcel out, allot, apportion, assign
🗲 monopolize

shark n
CROOK, extortioner, swindler, parasite, slicker
COLLOQ. fleecer, sponger, wheeler-dealer

Types of shark include:

angelfish	great white	sand tiger
basking	Greenland	saw
beagle	grey reef	school
blacktip	hammerhead	sea cat
blind	lemon	sevengill
blue	leopard	sharpnose
bramble	mackerel	shovelhead
bull	mako	sleeper
carpet	man-eating	smooth-hound
cat	night	soupfin
Colclough's	nurse	swell
dogfish	porbeagle	thresher
dusky	Portuguese	tiger
epaulette	ragged-tooth	whale
fox	requiem	whitetip
ghost	sagre	wobbegong
goblin	salmon	zebra

---

sharp adj, adv
♦ adj
1 *a sharp needle*
pointed, keen, edged, knife-edged, razor-edged, razor-sharp, needle-like, cutting, serrated, jagged, barbed, spiky
2 QUICK-WITTED, quick, clever, bright, intelligent, alert, shrewd, astute, perceptive, observant, discerning, penetrating
COLLOQ. on the ball, all there
3 HARSH, brusque, curt, incisive, cutting, biting, bitter, cruel, hurtful, malicious, acrimonious, caustic, sarcastic, sardonic, scathing, vitriolic, venomous
FORMAL trenchant
4 CLEAR, clear-cut, well-defined, definite, distinct, crisp, stark, marked
5 SUDDEN, abrupt, unexpected, violent, fierce, rapid, tight, intense, extreme, severe, keen, acute, piercing, stinging, shooting, stabbing
6 PUNGENT, strong, piquant, tangy, sour, tart, vinegary, bitter, biting, acerbic, acid, acidic, burning, acrid
7 *a sharp bend*
tight, sudden, hairpin, abrupt
8 *a sharp wind*
biting, cold, freezing, bitter, harsh, severe, penetrating, piercing, nipping, stinging
9 CRAFTY, clever, shrewd, deceptive, dishonest, cunning, artful, wily, sly
10 *a sharp dresser*
neat, tidy, smart, elegant, stylish, fashionable
COLLOQ. snappy, natty
🗲 **1** blunt **2** slow, stupid **3** mild **4** blurred **5** gentle **6** bland **7** gentle **8** gentle, mild **10** shabby
♦ adv
1 *six o'clock sharp*
punctually, promptly, on the dot, exactly, precisely
2 *pull up sharp*
abruptly, suddenly, unexpectedly
🗲 **1** approximately, roughly

sharpen v
edge, whet, hone, grind, file, keen, strop
FORMAL acuminate
🗲 blunt, blur

sharp-eyed adj
observant, perceptive, noticing, eagle-eyed, hawk-eyed, keen-sighted
🗲 short-sighted, unobservant

sharply adv
1 *prices rose sharply*
suddenly, abruptly, unexpectedly, rapidly, quickly, acutely
2 *speak to someone sharply*
harshly, brusquely, curtly, bitterly, acrimoniously, fiercely, sarcastically, vitriolically, venomously
3 *the road turns sharply*
abruptly, tightly, suddenly
4 *opinions are sharply divided*
clearly, distinctly, starkly, definitely, markedly
🗲 **1** slowly **2** gently

sharpness n
1 DISCERNMENT, penetration, acuteness, keenness, astuteness, shrewdness, observation, perceptiveness, incisiveness, eagerness
2 INTENSITY, fierceness, severity
3 HARSHNESS, brusqueness, cruelty, incisiveness, sarcasm, vitriol, venom
4 CLARITY, definition, precision, crispness

shatter v
1 BREAK, smash, splinter, shiver, crack, split, burst, explode, blast, crush, demolish, smash/blow to smithereens, star
OLD craze, smithereen
FORMAL pulverize
COLLOQ. bust
2 *shatter your hopes*
destroy, devastate, dash, crush, wreck, ruin, disappoint, overturn
3 *shattered by her death*
upset, devastate, crush, overwhelm, break your heart

shattered adj
1 OVERWHELMED, devastated, crushed, broken
2 WORN OUT, exhausted, weary, tired out
COLLOQ. all in, dead beat, dog-tired, done in, fagged out, ready to drop, knackered, zonked; *N Am* pooped (out), tuckered out

shattering adj
devastating, damaging, crushing, overwhelming, paralysing, severe

shave v, n
♦ v
cut, trim, barber, shear, crop, fleece, graze, brush, touch, pare, plane, scrape
OLD barb
♦ n
■ **close shave**
narrow miss, narrow escape, lucky escape, close thing, close call, near touch

shawl n
wrap, scarf, stole, blanket, afghan, zephyr, tonnag, dopatta, tallith, prayer shawl, Kashmir shawl, India shawl, Paisley shawl, pashmina, shahtoosh; *dialect* whittle
OLD turnover, tozie

sheaf n
bundle, bunch, armful, truss

shear v
shave, fleece, trim, cut, crop, barber

sheath n
1 SCABBARD, case, sleeve, envelope, shell, wrapping, casing, covering
Related adjective: thecal
2 CONDOM, protective contraceptive; *N Am* prophylactic
SLANG rubber, French letter, johnnie

shed[1] v
1 DROP, let fall, remove, cast (off), moult, discard, get rid of, slough, spill
2 SEND OUT, pour, spill, scatter, diffuse, emit, shower, throw, radiate, shine
■ **shed tears**
weep, sob, be in tears, blubber, wail, howl, bawl, whimper, whine, snivel
COLLOQ. burst into tears, cry your eyes out, turn on the waterworks

shed[2] *n*
  a garden shed
  hut, outhouse, lean-to, building, shack; *Aust* skillion

sheen *n*
  lustre, gloss, shine, gleam, sparkle, shimmer, brightness, brilliance, shininess, polish, varnish, burnish
  OLD shine
  FORMAL patina
  F3 dullness, tarnish, lacklustre

sheep *n*
  ram, ewe, lamb, wether, tup, teg, bell-wether
  COLLOQ. *Aust* jumbuck
  Related adjective: ovine
  See panel below

> **PROVERBS**
> As well be hanged for a sheep as a lamb

sheepish *adj*
  ashamed, shamefaced, embarrassed, mortified, chastened, abashed, uncomfortable, self-conscious, silly, foolish
  F3 unabashed, brazen, bold

sheer[1] *adj*
  1 UTTER, complete, total, absolute, thorough, full, pure, mere, simple, perfect, unadulterated, downright, out-and-out, flat, stark, rank, veritable, thoroughgoing, unconditional, unqualified, blank, plumb
  FORMAL unmitigated
  2 a sheer drop
  vertical, perpendicular, precipitous, abrupt, steep, sharp
  3 THIN, fine, light, delicate, flimsy, gauzy, gossamer, translucent, transparent, see-through
  FORMAL diaphanous
  F3 2 gentle, gradual **3** thick, heavy

sheer[2] *v*
  sheer away to the right
  swerve, turn, bend, veer, swing, shift, drift, deviate, diverge, deflect

sheet *n*
  1 cotton sheets
  cover, blanket, bed linen

2 COVERING, coating, coat, film, layer, stratum, skin, membrane, veneer, overlay, plate, piece, panel, slab, pane
  FORMAL lamina
  3 a sheet of paper
  leaf, page, folio
  4 a sheet of ice
  expanse, stretch, reach, sweep, surface

shelf *n*
  1 put books on the shelf
  ledge, mantelpiece, mantelshelf, sill, step, bench, bracket, counter, bar, shelve, shelving, stage, rack, chimney piece; *Scot* bink
  TECHNICAL credence, retable, shrine
  2 the shelf on the seabed
  bank, sandbank, reef, ledge, terrace, continental shelf, sand bar, bar, step, shoal
  ■ **on the shelf**
  unmarried, unattached, single, on your own, without a partner, spouseless

shell *n, v*
  ♦ *n*
  1 COVERING, hull, husk, pod, rind, crust, case, carapace, casing, body, chassis, frame, framework, structure, skeleton; *N Am* shuck
  TECHNICAL integument
  Related adjective: conchoidal
  2 EXPLOSIVE, bullet, shot, pellet, bomb, projectile, missile, grenade
  ♦ *v*
  1 shell nuts
  hull, husk, pod; *N Am* shuck
  2 BOMB, bombard, fire on, barrage, blitz, attack
  ■ **shell out**
  pay out, spend, lay out, give, contribute, donate, expend
  FORMAL disburse
  COLLOQ. cough up, fork out; *N Am* ante up

shelter *n, v*
  ♦ *n*
  cover, roof, shade, shadow, protection, shield, screen, defence, guard, security, safety, sanctuary, asylum, haven, refuge, harbour, retreat, accommodation, lodging
  F3 exposure

Breeds of sheep include:

Arcott	Charollais	Galway	Meatlinc	Scotch Mule	Welsh Mule
Awassi	Cheviot	German	Merino	Scottish Blackface	Wensleydale
Badger Face	Clun Forest	Blackheaded	Montadale	Scottish Greyface	White Face
Welsh Mountain	Colbred	Mutton	Morada Nova	Shetland	Dartmoor
Balwen	Columbia	Gotland	Navajo-Churro	Shetland-Cheviot	White Faced
Barbados Black-	Coopworth	Greenland	Norfolk Horn	Shropshire	Marsh
belly	Corriedale	Greyface	North Country	Soay	White Faced
Beltex	Cotentin	Dartmoor	Cheviot	Southdown	Woodland
Berrichon du Cher	Cotswold	Gute	North of England	South Wales	Wicklow Cheviot
Beulah Speckled	Dala	Hampshire Down	Mule	Mountain	Wiltshire Horn
Face	Dalesbred	Hebridean	North Ronaldsay	St Croix	Zwartbles
Blackface	Danish Landrace	Herdwick	Ouessant	Steigar	
Blackfaced	Derbyshire	Hill Radnor	Oxford Down	Suffolk	**WILD SHEEP**:
Mountain	Gritstone	Icelandic	Peliquey	Swaledale	argali
Blackheaded	Devon Closewool	Ile de France	Perendale	Swiss Black-Brown	barbary (or aodad)
Persian	Devon and	Jacob	Poll Dorset	Mountain	bighorn
Black Welsh	Cornwall	Karakul	Polwarth	Swiss White	blue sheep
Mountain	Longwool	Karaman	Portland	Alpine	Dall Sheep
Bleu du Marine	Dorper	Katahdin	Rambouillet	Teeswater	Desert Bighorn
Bluefaced Leicester	Dorset Down	Kerry Hill	Romanov	Texel	mouflon
Borderdale	Dorset Horn	Leicester Longwool	Romney	Tibetan	Rocky Mountain
Border Leicester	East Friesian	Lincoln	Rouge de l'Ouest	Troender	Bighorn
Brecknock Hill	English Leicester	Llanwenog	Rough Fell	Tunis	snow sheep
Cheviot	Est A Laine Merino	Lleyn	Roussin	Tyrol Mountain	stone sheep
British Milksheep	Exmoor Horn	Lonck	Rya	Vendeen	thinhorn
Cambridge	Faroe Islands	Manx Loghtan	Ryeland	Welsh Halfbred	urial
Castlemilk Moorit	Finn Sheep	Masai	Rygja	Welsh Hill	
Charmoise	Fuglestad	Masham	Scotch Halfbred	Speckled Face	

sheltered

♦ *v*

cover, shroud, screen, shade, shadow, protect, defend, guard, safeguard, shield, harbour, hide, conceal, accommodate, put up

F3 expose

sheltered *adj*

covered, shaded, shady, shielded, protected, screened, cosy, snug, warm, quiet, secluded, isolated, retired, withdrawn, reclusive, cloistered, unworldly

F3 exposed

shelve *v*

postpone, defer, put off, suspend, halt, put aside, lay aside, pigeonhole, mothball

COLLOQ. put on ice, put on the back burner

F3 expedite, implement

shepherd *n, v*

♦ *n*

shepherdess, herdess, shepherdling, herdsman, pastor, protector, shepherd boy, herdboy, guardian, flockmaster, tar-box

OLD feeder, herd-groom

Related adjective: pastoral

♦ *v*

guide, lead, conduct, convoy, escort, usher, steer, pastor, marshal, herd

shield *n, v*

♦ *n*

buckler, defence, bulwark, rampart, support, screen, guard, cover, shelter, protection, protector, safeguard, targe

TECHNICAL escutcheon

♦ *v*

defend, guard, protect, safeguard, keep safe, screen, shade, shadow, cover, shelter

OLD (*Shakesp*) buckle

F3 expose

shift *v, n*

♦ *v*

1 CHANGE, vary, fluctuate, alter, adjust, modify, move, budge, relocate, reposition, rearrange, transfer, carry, switch, swerve, veer

FORMAL transpose

2 REMOVE, dislodge, displace, get rid of

♦ *n*

1 CHANGE, variation, fluctuation, alteration, modification, move, movement, removal, switch, displacement, relocation, rearrangement, transfer

FORMAL transposition

COLLOQ. U-turn

2 *work shifts*

period, spell, time, stretch, span, stint

shiftless *adj*

lazy, idle, unambitious, unenterprising, resourceless, aimless, directionless, goalless, incompetent, inefficient, irresponsible, inept, feckless

FORMAL indolent, ineffectual, slothful

COLLOQ. good-for-nothing, lackadaisical

F3 enterprising, ambitious, aspiring, eager

shifty *adj*

untrustworthy, dishonest, deceitful, scheming, contriving, tricky, wily, crafty, cunning, devious, evasive, furtive, underhand, dubious

FORMAL duplicitous

COLLOQ. shady, slippery, iffy

F3 dependable, honest, open

shilly-shally *v*

dither, hesitate, vacillate, be indecisive, waver, fluctuate, falter, teeter, seesaw

FORMAL prevaricate

COLLOQ. dilly-dally, hem and haw, sit on the fence, mess about

shimmer *v, n*

♦ *v*

glisten, gleam, sparkle, glimmer, glint, glitter, scintillate, glow, play, flicker, twinkle

♦ *n*

lustre, gleam, sparkle, glint, glimmer, glitter, glistening, glow, haze, flicker, twinkle

FORMAL iridescence

shimmering *adj*

glittering, glowing, glistening, gleaming, shining, shiny, lustrous, luminous

TECHNICAL aventurine

FORMAL incandescent, iridescent

F3 dull, matt

shin *v*

climb, mount, soar, scramble, scrabble, ascend, clamber, scale, shoot, swarm

shine *v, n*

♦ *v*

1 BEAM, radiate, glow, flash, glare, dazzle, gleam, glint, glitter, flicker, sparkle, twinkle, shimmer, glisten, glimmer, give off, emit

FORMAL incandesce

See Synonym nuances panel at **flash**.

2 POLISH, burnish, gloss, buff, brush, rub (up), wax

3 *shine at athletics*

excel, stand out, be brilliant, be excellent, be outstanding, be pre-eminent

♦ *n*

1 LIGHT, radiance, glow, brightness, glare, dazzle, flash, gleam, sparkle, shimmer, glitter, glint, flicker, twinkle

FORMAL effulgence, luminescence, incandescence, lambency

2 GLOSS, polish, burnish, gleam, sheen, lustre, glaze

FORMAL patina

shininess *n*

brightness, gleam, glitter, shine, sheen, polish, lustre, glossiness, burnish

FORMAL effulgence

F3 dullness

shining *adj*

1 BRIGHT, radiant, glowing, beaming, flashing, gleaming, glittering, glinting, glistening, shimmering, twinkling, sparkling, flickering, luminous, brilliant, splendid, glorious

FORMAL phosphorescent, resplendent, effulgent, incandescent

2 *a shining example*

conspicuous, outstanding, splendid, magnificent, glorious, brilliant, leading, eminent, pre-eminent, perfect, celebrated, distinguished, illustrious

F3 1 dark

shiny *adj*

polished, burnished, shining, sheeny, lustrous, glossy, silky, sleek, bright, gleaming, glistening, glassy, shimmering

F3 dull, matt

ship *n*

vessel, craft, liner, steamer, tanker, trawler, ferry, boat, yacht

See panel on next page

shipshape *adj*

tidy, neat, orderly, spruce, trim, well-organized, well-planned, businesslike, well-regulated, spick and span; *Scot* trig

F3 disorderly, untidy

shirk *v*

dodge, get out of, evade, avoid, shun, shrink from, play truant, wriggle out of, balk, slack, soldier

COLLOQ. duck, skive, funk; *Aust & NZ* duckshove

SLANG *N Am* gold-brick, goof off; *Aust & NZ* bludge

shirker *n*

dodger, slacker, idler, layabout, loafer, absentee, truant, malingerer, shirk

Parts of a ship include:

afterdeck	cabin	flight deck	head	port	stanchion
anchor	capstan	forecastle (fo'c'sle)	hold	porthole	starboard
berth	chain locker	funnel	keel	promenade deck	stateroom
bilge	chart room	galley	landing	prow	stern
boat deck	cleat	gangplank	lower deck	quarter	superstructure
boiler room	companion ladder	gangway	main deck	quarter deck	tiller
bollard	companionway	gun deck	mast	radio room	top deck
bridge	crow's nest	gunwale (gunnel)	oar	rigger	transom
brig	davit	hammock	paddle wheel	rowlock	wardroom
bulkhead	deck	hatch	pilot house	rudder	waterline
bulwarks	engine room	hatchway	Plimsoll line	sail	wheel
bunk	figurehead	hawser	poop deck	stabilizer	winch

See also **boat**; **sail**.

COLLOQ. quitter, skiver; *Aust & NZ* duckshover
SLANG *N Am* gold brick, goof-off; *Aust & NZ* bludger

shiver¹ *v, n*

♦ *v*
shivering with cold
shudder, tremble, quiver, quake, shake, vibrate, palpitate, flutter, dither; *dialect* chitter
OLD shrug

♦ *n*
shudder, quiver, shake, tremor, twitch, start, vibration, flutter, frisson; *Scot* grue

shiver² *n, v*

♦ *n*
shivers of light
splinter, piece, bit, fragment, shred, sliver, shaving, chip, shard
COLLOQ. smithereen(s)

♦ *v*
shatter, break, smash, splinter, crack, split
OLD disshiver

shivery *adj*
cold, chilly, trembly, trembling, shuddery, shaking, quivery, quaking, chilled, nervous, fluttery; *Scot* ourie

shoal *n*
group, mass, multitude, mob, throng, swarm, horde, flock
FORMAL assemblage

shock¹ *v, n*

♦ *v*
his attitude shocked her
disgust, revolt, repel, sicken, offend, nauseate, appal, outrage, scandalize, horrify, startle, astound, stagger, amaze, stun, daze, stupefy, numb, paralyse, traumatize, jolt, jar, shake, agitate, unsettle, upset, distress, disquiet, unnerve, bewilder, take aback, confound, dumbfound, dismay
FORMAL perturb
COLLOQ. bowl over
E3 delight, please, gratify, reassure

♦ *n*
1 FRIGHT, start, jolt, surprise, blow, trauma, upset, distress, dismay, disgust, outrage, horror
FORMAL consternation, perturbation
COLLOQ. bombshell, thunderbolt, bolt from the blue, whammy, rude awakening
2 IMPACT, crash, collision, blow, shake, jolt, jarring, jerk
E3 1 delight, pleasure, reassurance

shock² *n*
a shock of hair
mop, head, mane, tangle, thatch, mat, mass

shocking *adj*
appalling, outrageous, scandalous, offensive, horrifying, disgraceful, deplorable, intolerable, unbearable, atrocious, abominable, monstrous, vile, foul, unspeakable, egregious, obscene, detestable, abhorrent, dreadful, loathsome, awful, terrible, frightful, ghastly, hideous, horrible, horrific, disgusting, revolting, repulsive, repugnant, sickening, nauseating, unsettling, disquieting, distressing
FORMAL perturbing
E3 acceptable, satisfactory, pleasant, delightful

shockingly *adv*
outrageously, appallingly, scandalously, disgracefully, deplorably, unbearably, abominably, disgustingly, revoltingly, repulsively, sickeningly, atrociously, dreadfully, terribly, frightfully

shoddy *adj*
inferior, second-rate, cheap, tawdry, tatty, trashy, rubbishy, poor, poor-quality, careless, slipshod, slapdash, cheapjack, third-rate
COLLOQ. rop(e)y, tacky, rubbish; *Aust & NZ* crook
E3 superior, well-made

shoe *n*
See **footwear**.

shoemaker *n*
cobbler, bootmaker, snob, snab

shoemaking *n*
bootmaking, cobblery, cobbling

shoot *v, n*

♦ *v*
1 FIRE, discharge, launch, propel, kick, hit, throw, hurl, fling, lob, project, let off, aim, direct
2 HIT, kill, injure, wound, open fire, blast, bombard, gun down, mow down, shell, snipe at, pick off
COLLOQ. zap
3 DART, bolt, dash, tear, rush, race, sprint, speed, hurry, charge, fly, hurtle, streak, whisk, whiz
COLLOQ. scoot, zip, zap, belt, get a move on, go all out
4 *shoot a film*
film, photograph, take photographs of, video
COLLOQ. snap
5 GROW, germinate, shoot up, sprout, burgeon, bolt, bud, stretch

♦ *n*
sprout, bud, offshoot, branch, twig, sprig, cutting, slip, scion, graft, tendron

shop *n, v*

♦ *n*
store, retail outlet
FORMAL emporium
See panel on next page

♦ *v*
1 *shop for clothes*
go shopping, buy, buy things, do the shopping, stock up on, get, pick up, purchase
2 INFORM ON, betray
COLLOQ. tell on, tell tales on, split, squeal, rat, blow the whistle on
SLANG grass; *N Am* stool on

Types of shop include:

auction house	chain store	*N Am* drugstore	haberdasher	off-licence	second-hand shop
baker	charity shop	electrical shop	hairdresser	*colloq.* offie	shoe shop
barber	chemist	e-shop	hardware shop	online shop (or	stall
bazaar	*Irish colloq.*	farmers' market	health-food shop	store)	stationer
betting shop	chipper	farm shop	hypermarket	*Aust & NZ*	*Aust & N Am*
bookmaker	*colloq.* chippy	fish and chip shop	indoor market	opportunity shop	superette
colloq. bookie	clothes shop	fishmonger	internet auction	(or op-shop)	supermarket
bookshop	computer store	*N Am* five-and-	site	outfitter	superstore
Aust & NZ bottle	confectioner	dime	ironmonger	pawnbroker	sweet shop
shop (or store)	corner shop	florist	jeweller	pharmacy	tailor
boutique	dairy	general store	launderette	phone shop	takeaway
butcher	delicatessen	greengrocer	market	post office	tobacconist
candy store	department store	grocer	milliner	radio and TV shop	toy shop
car dealership	draper	*Aust & NZ* grog-	mini-market	record shop	tuck shop
cash-and-carry	dress shop	shop	newsagent	saddler	video shop

shopkeeper *n*
dealer, salesman, saleswoman, retailer, stockist, trader, tradesman, manager, owner, proprietor, storekeeper, merchant

shopper *n*
buyer, purchaser, client, customer, consumer

shore[1] *n*
walk along the shore
seashore, beach, sand(s), shingle, strand, waterfront, waterside, front, promenade, coast, seaside, seaboard, foreshore, lakeside, bank
OLD rivage
FORMAL littoral
Related adjective: littoral

shore[2] *v*
shore up a building
support, hold (up), prop (up), stay, underpin, buttress, brace, strengthen, reinforce

shorn *adj*
cut, cropped, shaved, shaven, stripped, polled, bald, beardless, crew-cut, deprived

short *adj, adv*
♦ *adj*
1 *a short visit*
brief, short-lived, cursory, hasty, quick, swift, fleeting, passing, momentary, transitory, transient, temporary, limited
FORMAL ephemeral, evanescent, fugacious
2 CONCISE, brief, succinct, terse, crisp, pithy, to the point, compact, compressed, shortened, condensed, truncated, curtailed, abbreviated, abridged, summarized, summary
FORMAL aphoristic
3 SMALL, little, low, petite, slight, minuscule, diminutive, squat, dumpy, stubby, Lilliputian; *Scot* wee
COLLOQ. teeny, teensy, pint-size(d)
SLANG shortarsed
4 INADEQUATE, insufficient, deficient, lacking, wanting, low, poor, meagre, scarce, scanty, scant, sparse
COLLOQ. tight
5 BRUSQUE, curt, gruff, snappy, sharp, abrupt, terse, blunt, direct, rude, impolite, discourteous, uncivil
E3 **1** long, lasting **3** tall, big **4** adequate, ample **5** polite, civil
♦ *adv*
unexpectedly, suddenly, abruptly
■ **short of**
1 DEFICIENT IN, lacking, missing, short on, less than, low on, other than
FORMAL wanting
COLLOQ. pushed for
2 EXCEPT FOR, apart from, excepting, but, but for, other than, with the exception of, aside from, save, omitting, not counting, leaving out, excluding, besides, bar, barring

■ **fall short**
be less than required, be lacking, be insufficient, be inadequate
■ **in short**
in brief, briefly, in a word, in a few words, in conclusion, summarizing, concisely, to sum up, in fine
COLLOQ. in a nutshell, to cut a long story short

SYNONYM NUANCES

adjective sense 1
You can use **short-lived** of something lasting only for a little time, with an intimation of regret at this: *my joy was short-lived*. **Temporary** and **limited**, however, may be used to show that something, in addition to lasting a short time, is also known from the outset to be impermanent: *a temporary repair; the seasonal positions they seek to fill are of limited duration*. **Momentary** suggests something of exceedingly limited duration, likewise **ephemeral**, which also carries the added suggestion that its brevity is expected: *statistics, ephemeral though they may be*. Similarly **fleeting**, **transient**, **passing** and **transitory** all describe restricted existence, though the first emphasizes great speed: *a fleeting glimpse of the star*.
Quick and **swift** are not particularly marked terms, although the second may be used to hint that the speed is desirable. **Cursory** presents a more negative aspect, often implying superficiality: *the book is similarly cursory in its treatment of style*, and **hasty** might appropriately be used of a brief act not thought to be well done: *a hasty transition from one system to another*.

---

shortage *n*
inadequacy, insufficiency, deficiency, shortfall, deficit, lack, want, need, scarcity, poverty, absence, dearth; *N Am* wantage
TECHNICAL skills gap
FORMAL paucity
E3 sufficiency, abundance, surplus

shortcoming *n*
defect, imperfection, fault, flaw, drawback, failing, weak point, weakness, frailty, foible

shorten *v*
cut (down), trim, prune, crop, dock, pare (down), make/ become shorter, curtail, truncate, abbreviate, abridge, condense, compress, contract, sum up, reduce, lessen, decrease, diminish, take up
E3 lengthen, enlarge, amplify

shortened *adj*
abridged, condensed, summarized, abbreviated, abstracted
FORMAL abbreviatory
E3 amplified

shortfall *n*
deficit, shortage, deficiency, loss, arrears, lack, default
F3 excess

short-lived *adj*
brief, momentary, passing, short, temporary, transient, transitory, fleeting, impermanent
TECHNICAL caducous
FORMAL ephemeral, evanescent, fugacious
F3 abiding, enduring, lasting, long-lived

shortly *adv*
1 SOON, in a little while, in a while, before long, presently, by and by
2 BRUSQUELY, curtly, gruffly, sharply, abruptly, tersely, bluntly, directly, rudely, impolitely, discourteously, uncivilly

short-sighted *adj*
1 MYOPIC, near-sighted
2 IMPROVIDENT, imprudent, unwise, unthinking, impolitic, ill-advised, thoughtless, careless, rash, heedless, hasty, ill-considered
FORMAL injudicious, uncircumspect
F3 1 long-sighted, far-sighted

short-staffed *adj*
shorthanded, understaffed, with insufficient staff, below strength

short-tempered *adj*
bad-tempered, impatient, irritable, hot-tempered, quick-tempered, fiery, irascible, choleric, crusty, touchy
COLLOQ. ratty, testy, grouchy
F3 calm, patient, placid

short-winded *adj*
breathless, gasping, panting, puffing

shot¹ *n*
1 GUNFIRE, discharge, blast, bang, crack, explosion
2 BULLET, ammunition, missile, projectile, ball, pellet
COLLOQ. slug
3 *he's a good shot*
shooter, marksman, markswoman, gunner, sniper, hunter
4 *have a shot at goal*
kick, hit, throw, stroke, fling, lob
5 PHOTOGRAPH, photo, snap, snapshot, print, picture, image, slide, transparency
6 ATTEMPT, try, effort, endeavour, guess, turn
COLLOQ. go, bash, whack, crack, stab; *Aust & NZ* burl
7 INJECTION, inoculation, immunization, vaccination, dose
COLLOQ. jab
SLANG fix
■ **shot in the arm**
encouragement, stimulus, boost, fillip, lift, uplift, impetus, fresh talent
■ **shot in the dark**
guess, guesswork, wild guess, blind guess, conjecture, speculation
■ **call the shots**
be in charge, lead, give a lead, head (up), manage, direct, supervise, command
COLLOQ. be in the driving seat, wear the trousers
■ **like a shot**
without delay, without hesitation, unhesitatingly, immediately, instantly, at once, eagerly, enthusiastically, willingly
■ **not by a long shot**
by no means, never, certainly not, not at all, not in the least, in no way
COLLOQ. no way

shot² *adj*
shot fabric
variegated, mottled, watered, moiré, iridescent

shoulder *v*
1 ACCEPT, assume, take on, take upon yourself, bear, carry, sustain, support
2 PUSH, shove, jostle, thrust, press, force, elbow

■ **shoulder to shoulder**
side by side, hand in hand, united, together, co-operatively, working together, closely, in alliance
■ **give someone the cold shoulder**
snub, rebuff, shun, spurn, insult, disregard, ignore, brush off, cut, slight, rebuke, put down, squash, humble, shame, humiliate, mortify
COLLOQ. slap in the face, kick in the teeth, blank
■ **rub shoulders with**
meet with, associate with, socialize with, mix with, fraternize with
COLLOQ. hang/knock about/around with, hobnob with

shout *v, n*
♦ *v*
call (out), cry (out), scream, shriek, yell, raise your voice, rant and rave, squawk, roar, bellow, bawl, howl, bay, cheer
COLLOQ. holler; *N Am* yawp
♦ *n*
call, cry, scream, shriek, yell, squawk, roar, bellow, bawl, howl, bay, cheer
COLLOQ. holler; *N Am* yawp

> **QUOTATIONS**
> When in doubt, shout – that's the motto
> SIR CEDRIC HARDWICKE, Advice given to him as a young actor

> **SYNONYM NUANCES**
> *verb*
> You can use **call** (**out**) of deliberately projecting your voice so your words may be heard, whereas **cry** (**out**) is more suggestive of instinctively emitted sounds: *he cried out in pain*. **Scream** suggests a loud, high-pitched emission, with connotations of negative emotions such as pain, fear or anger, while **shriek** suggests an even more piercing sound: *children shrieking in the playground*. **Yell**, too, implies sounding loud and sharp, as well as implying a degree of effort, and is often used in the context of anger: *he yelled at them to keep quiet*, whereas **rant and rave** is more suggestive of an inarticulate tirade.
> More instinctive, animal-like sounds are suggested by **squawk**: *she squawked in surprise*, and **roar** and **bellow**, which could be used to describe a deeper and hoarser sound. The term **bay** may be used to suggest vengeful jeers like the prolonged wailing of hounds in pursuit of quarry: *the crowd bayed for the referee's blood*. **Bawl** returns to the idea of loudness, often with an element of anger, whereas **howl** is more connotative of being in distress.
> In comparison, **raise your voice** suggests a far more restrained increase in volume.

shove *v, n*
♦ *v*
push, thrust, drive, propel, force, barge, jolt, jostle, elbow, shoulder, press, crowd
♦ *n*
push, thrust, jolt, jostle, elbow, shoulder
■ **shove off**
leave, depart
COLLOQ. beat it, clear off, push off, get lost, scram, scarper, clear out, skedaddle, vamoose, do a bunk, scoot, run for it, buzz off, scat
SLANG *Aust* choof off

shovel *n, v*
♦ *n*
spade, scoop, bucket, backhoe, backhoe loader, excavator, dust-pan, peel; *dialect* shool
TECHNICAL van
OLD main

♦ *v*

dig, excavate, scoop, dredge, clear, move, shift, spade, heap; *dialect* shool

show *v, n*

♦ *v*

1 REVEAL, expose, uncover, disclose, divulge, make visible, make clear, make plain, make known
FORMAL manifest
2 EXPRESS, mean, indicate, signify, register, record, portray, depict, make it clear, prove, demonstrate, be evidence, bear witness to, suggest
FORMAL manifest
3 TEACH, instruct, clarify, make clear, elucidate, point out, explain, demonstrate, prove, illustrate, exemplify
FORMAL expound
4 DISPLAY, exhibit, demonstrate, present, televise, produce, set out, offer
5 *show him out*
lead, guide, direct, conduct, steer, take, usher, escort, accompany, attend
6 *he didn't show*
appear, arrive, come, turn up
F3 1 hide, cover (up)

♦ *n*

1 ENTERTAINMENT, performance, programme, production, staging, showing, spectacle, extravaganza
2 EXHIBITION, fair, parade, presentation, demonstration, display, spectacle, cabaret
FORMAL exposition
COLLOQ. expo
3 DISPLAY, representation, demonstration, presentation, sign, indication, arrangement
FORMAL manifestation, array
4 PRETENCE, semblance, façade, front, illusion, ostentation, parade, flamboyance, panache, showiness, exhibitionism, pose
FORMAL affectation
COLLOQ. window dressing, play-acting, pizzazz
5 APPEARANCE, air, impression, guise, display, profession
6 *Who's running the show?*
affair, proceedings, organization, undertaking, operation

■ **show off**
1 BOAST, parade, strut, swagger, brag, flaunt, brandish
COLLOQ. swank; *S Afr* pronk
2 DISPLAY, exhibit, demonstrate, show to advantage, advertise, set off, enhance

■ **show up**
1 REVEAL, show, make visible, expose, unmask, lay bare, highlight, pinpoint
2 HUMILIATE, embarrass, mortify, shame, put to shame, disgrace, let down
3 ARRIVE, come, turn up, appear
COLLOQ. materialize

showdown *n*

confrontation, clash, crisis, climax, moment of truth, culmination, dénouement, face-off

shower *n, v*

♦ *n*

rain, drizzling, stream, torrent, sprinkling, deluge, hail, volley, barrage, drift, scud, thunder-shower; *dialect* scat, skit; *Scot* scouther
TECHNICAL avalanche, pelter
OLD (*Shakesp*) aspersion

♦ *v*

spray, sprinkle, rain, pour, fall, deluge, inundate, overwhelm, load, heap, lavish, pelt, pepper, play, hail
OLD (*Spenser*) pound

showiness *n*

flamboyance, pretentiousness, glitter, ostentation, razzle-dazzle
COLLOQ. flashiness, pizzazz, razzmatazz, glitz, swank, ritziness
F3 restraint

showing *n, adj*

♦ *n*

display, evidence, impression, representation, record, presentation, performance, exhibition, show, staging, account, statement, appearance, past performance
COLLOQ. track record

♦ *adj*

explanatory, demonstrative, descriptive, illustrative, indicative, representative, significant, symbolic
FORMAL explicatory, elucidative, revelatory

showing-off *n*

boasting, self-advertisement, bragging, exhibitionism, swagger, egotism, peacockery
FORMAL braggadocio, vainglory
COLLOQ. swank
F3 modesty

showman *n*

performer, entertainer, impresario, publicist, ring-master, self-advertiser
COLLOQ. show-off

show-off *n*

swaggerer, braggart, boaster, exhibitionist, peacock, poser, poseur, egotist
COLLOQ. swanker, know-all

showy *adj*

flashy, flamboyant, ostentatious, gaudy, garish, glittering, loud, conspicuous, tawdry, fancy, ornate, pretentious, pompous
COLLOQ. swanky, flash, ritzy, glitzy
SLANG bling, blingy
F3 quiet, restrained

shred *n, v*

♦ *n*

1 SCRAP, ribbon, tatter, rag, snippet, sliver, bit, piece, fragment, remnant, particle, modicum, speck, vestige, peeling, clipping, snip, tag, wisp, frazzle, screed, hangnail, agnail; *dialect* mammock, mummock; *Scot* taver
2 JOT, iota, atom, spot, grain, mite, whit, trace, wisp

♦ *v*

cut (up), tear (up), rip (up), chop, slice, julienne
OLD mammock

shrew *n*

dragon, nag, scold, termagant, virago, vixen, Xanthippe, harridan, henpecker, spitfire, Fury
OLD shrow
SLANG bitch

shrewd *adj*

astute, prudent, well-advised, calculated, far-sighted, smart, clever, intelligent, sharp, keen, acute, alert, perceptive, observant, discerning, discriminating, knowing, calculating, cunning, crafty, wily, canny, artful, sly, wise, hard-headed, long-headed, sharp-sighted, arch, cut-and-thrust, argute, gnostic
OLD callid
FORMAL judicious, sagacious, perspicacious
COLLOQ. savvy, knowing a thing or two
F3 unwise, obtuse, naive, unsophisticated

SYNONYM NUANCES

Astute can be used to suggest having an insightful ability to understand: *an astute awareness of the way events are unfolding*. **Sharp**, **keen**, **perceptive** and **acute** echo this idea of being able to deftly assess a situation: *with her sharp pen and keen observation*. **Alert**, on the other hand, is more suggestive of being attentive, while **observant** implies being deliberately watchful.
  Discerning, again, has implications of insight but further suggests an element of good taste; **discriminating**, likewise, implies an ability to distinguish between options: *make a discriminating selection from your range of reference materials*. **Calculated** is more

suggestive of having weighed up the pros and cons: *a calculated bid for media coverage*.

You can use **knowing** to imply having the advantage of privileged information: *with a knowing look*, whereas **calculating** has rather more negative implications of scheming. Similarly, **cunning**, **crafty**, **wily** and **sly** are more disapproving, and suggest an underhand element, but **canny** is merely suggestive of being prudent: *canny investors*, like the approbatory **wise**, which implies innate knowledge and judgement. **Artful** suggests a degree of mental dexterity, again with overtones of deception. **Arch** would be reserved for someone with expertise, but again in deception and cunning: *an arch manipulator*.

shrewdly adv
astutely, cleverly, far-sightedly, wisely, knowingly, perceptively, craftily, cannily, artfully, slyly, argutely
FORMAL judiciously, sagaciously, perspicaciously

shrewdness n
discernment, intelligence, perceptiveness, sharpness, acuteness, astuteness, grasp, judgement, penetration, wisdom, acumen, canniness, prudence
FORMAL perspicacity, astucity, sagacity
OLD callidity
COLLOQ. smartness
E3 foolishness, naivety, obtuseness

shrewish adj
scolding, bad-tempered, ill-tempered, ill-humoured, ill-natured, nagging, peevish, quarrelsome, complaining, discontented, fault-finding, henpecking, petulant, captious, sharp-tongued, vixenish
FORMAL querulous
E3 affectionate, peaceable, placid, supportive

shriek v, n
♦ v
scream, screech, squawk, squeal, cry (out), shout, yell, wail, howl, yelp
♦ n
scream, screech, squawk, squeal, cry, shout, yell, wail, howl, yelp

shrill adj
high, high-pitched, treble, sharp, acute, piercing, penetrating, screaming, screeching, strident, ear-splitting
E3 deep, low, soft, gentle

shrine n
holy place, sacred place, chapel, sanctuary, church, tabernacle, pagoda, temple, martyry, fane, dome, delubrum, dagoba, stupa, tope, darga, vimana

shrink v
1 CONTRACT, shorten, grow/become smaller, narrow, decrease, lessen, reduce, diminish, drop off, fall off, dwindle, shrivel, wrinkle, wither, atrophy
2 RECOIL, draw back, back away, shy away, withdraw, retire, balk, quail, cower, cringe, wince, flinch, start back, shun, have scruples/qualms about
E3 1 expand, stretch 2 accept, embrace

shrivel v
wrinkle, pucker (up), wither, wilt, shrink, dwindle, parch, dry (up), dehydrate, desiccate, scorch, sear, burn, frizzle; *Scot* gizzen

shrivelled adj
wrinkled, puckered, shrunken, withered, emaciated, wizened, dried up, dry, desiccated; *Scot* gizzen
OLD writhled
FORMAL sere

shroud v, n
♦ v
wrap, envelop, swathe, cloak, veil, screen, cloud, hide, conceal, enshroud, blanket, cover, fog
E3 uncover, expose

♦ n
winding-sheet, cloth, graveclothes, cerecloth, cerement, pall, mantle, cloak, veil, screen, cloud, blanket, covering
OLD sindon

shrouded adj
wrapped, enveloped, swathed, cloaked, enshrouded, hidden, concealed, covered, clouded, blanketed, veiled
E3 exposed, uncovered

shrub

Shrubs include:

azalea	fuchsia	mallow
berberis	heather	mimosa
broom	hebe	mock orange
buddleia	holly	musk rose
camellia	honeysuckle	peony
clematis	hydrangea	phlomis
cotoneaster	ivy	privet
daphne	japonica	rhododendron
dogwood	jasmine	rose
eucryphia	laburnum	spiraea
euonymus	laurel	viburnum
firethorn	lavender	weigela
flowering currant	lilac	wistaria
forsythia	magnolia	witch hazel

See also **flower**; **plant**.

shrug v
■ **shrug off**
brush off, ignore, disregard, dismiss, neglect, take no notice of

shrunken adj
reduced, shrunk, shrivelled, contracted, emaciated, gaunt
FORMAL cadaverous
E3 full, generous, rounded, sleek

shudder v, n
♦ v
shiver, shake, tremble, quiver, quake, heave, convulse, judder
♦ n
shiver, quiver, tremble, quake, heave, tremor, spasm, convulsion, judder

shuffle v
1 MIX (UP), intermix, jumble (up), confuse, disorder, rearrange, reorganize, move around, shift around, switch, reshuffle
OLD pack
2 *shuffle across the room*
shamble, scuffle, scrape, drag, falter, limp, toddle, doddle, hobble, dodge, hedge

shun v
avoid, evade, elude, steer clear of, shy away from, keep away from, spurn, ignore, snub, ostracize
OLD evite
FORMAL eschew
COLLOQ. give a wide berth to, cold-shoulder, avoid like the plague
E3 accept, embrace

shunt v
move, transport, carry, bring, take, fetch, relocate, transfer, shift, switch, swing
FORMAL transpose
COLLOQ. budge

shut v
1 close, slam, seal, fasten, secure, put the lid on, lock, latch, bolt, bar
E3 open
2 CONFINE, lock up, cage in, coop up, imprison, jail, intern
FORMAL incarcerate, immure

■ **shut down**
close (down), stop, cease, halt, suspend, switch off, inactivate
FORMAL terminate, discontinue

■ **shut in**
enclose, box in, hem in, fence in, confine, imprison, cage (in), keep in, restrain
FORMAL immure

■ **shut off**
seclude, isolate, cut off, separate, segregate

■ **shut out**
1 EXCLUDE, bar, debar, lock out, ostracize, banish, outlaw, exile
2 HIDE, conceal, cover (up), block out, mask, screen, veil

■ **shut up**
SILENCE, gag, quiet, quieten, hush (up),
hold your tongue
COLLOQ. pipe down, clam up, keep mum

shutter *n*
screen, shade, blind, louvre, jalousie

shuttle *v*
go to and fro, travel, ply, run, alternate, commute, shunt, shuttlecock, seesaw

shy *adj, v*
♦ *adj*
timid, timorous, bashful, reticent, reserved, demure, diffident, introverted, retiring, coy, self-conscious, embarrassed, inhibited, modest, self-effacing, shrinking, withdrawn, hesitant, cautious, chary, suspicious, nervous, backward, squab, farouche; *Scot* skeigh, willyard
COLLOQ. mous(e)y, backward in coming forward
F⊒ bold, assertive, confident

■ **shy away**
avoid, balk, shrink, recoil, wince, back away, flinch, swerve, start, quail, rear, buck, jib, startle, spook

■ **fight shy of**
avoid, steer clear of, shun, spurn
FORMAL eschew
COLLOQ. give a wide berth to, keep at arm's length

SYNONYM NUANCES

adjective
You might use **timid** to suggest a slightly fearful aspect to someone's shyness, while **diffident** would suggest an deeper lack of confidence. **Bashful** is more suggestive of a restraining modesty rather than fear, while **demure** suggests primness, and hints at a more affected modesty. **Coy** also implies a degree of affectedness: *a coy smile of invitation*, but can also be used to suggest evasion: *the company is coy about revealing its profits.*
   Reticent is more straightforwardly suggestive of a disinclination to talk: *he was reticent about the perks of his job*, while **reserved**, too, implies an uncommunicative element more explicitly expressed by **withdrawn**. The term **introverted** may be used to suggest an inward-looking nature, and while **retiring** is more suggestive of being deliberately unobtrusive, the term **inhibited** implies being more subconsciously restrained: *Charles felt inhibited in mixed company, and found it difficult to talk*. The term **self-effacing** is suggestive of someone who prefers to keep their presence or achievements hidden, and **backward** and **shrinking** similarly suggest keeping a low profile.
   Both **hesitant** and **cautious** put more focus on the cause of shyness and suggest a degree of apprehension, whereas **chary** and **suspicious** put more emphasis on mistrust. **Self-conscious** would be used specifically of shyness brought about by being overly concerned about how you are perceived.

---

shyly *adv*
timidly, bashfully, reticently, diffidently, coyly, self-consciously, hesitantly, cautiously, cagily, charily
F⊒ boldly, assertively, confidently

shyness *n*
timidity, timidness, timorousness, hesitancy, diffidence, bashfulness, reticence, self-consciousness, inhibition, embarrassment, modesty, constraint, introversion, nervousness, coyness, caginess, chariness
COLLOQ. mousiness
F⊒ boldness, assertiveness, confidence

sibling *n*
brother, sister, twin
OLD german

sibyl *n*
wise woman, oracle, prophetess, seer, seeress, sorceress, Pythia, pythoness

sick *adj*
1 ILL, unwell, laid up, poorly, ailing, sickly, weak, feeble
FORMAL indisposed
COLLOQ. under the weather, rough, groggy, seedy, off colour, out of sorts
See Synonym nuances panel at **ill**.
2 VOMITING, retching, heaving, nauseous, queasy, bilious, travel-sick, carsick, seasick, airsick
COLLOQ. throwing up, spewing up, puking
3 *sick of waiting*
bored, tired, weary, disgusted, nauseated
COLLOQ. fed up
4 DISGUSTED, annoyed, disappointed, angry, enraged, disgruntled
COLLOQ. fed up, sick and tired, cheesed off, browned off, hacked off
SLANG pissed off
5 *a sick joke*
cruel, black, tasteless, vulgar, gross, macabre, in bad taste
F⊒ **1** well, healthy

■ **be sick**
vomit, retch, heave, gag, feel nauseous, feel queasy
COLLOQ. throw up, spew, puke, fetch up
SLANG *N Am* barf

QUOTATIONS
A sick society must think much about politics, as a sick man must think about his digestion
C S LEWIS, *The Weight of Glory*

---

sicken *v*
1 NAUSEATE, revolt, disgust, repel, appal, put off
COLLOQ. turn off, turn your stomach
2 BECOME ILL, catch, develop, pick up, get, go down with, come down with, become infected with, become ill with
FORMAL contract, succumb to
F⊒ **1** delight, attract

sickening *adj*
nauseating, revolting, disgusting, offensive, appalling, shocking, distasteful, off-putting, foul, vile, loathsome, nauseous, repulsive, repellent, stomach-turning
SLANG *Aust* chunderous
F⊒ delightful, pleasing, attractive

sickly *adj*
1 UNHEALTHY, infirm, delicate, weak, feeble, frail, wan, pale, pallid, insipid, ailing, sick, bilious, faint, languid
FORMAL indisposed
COLLOQ. washed out
2 NAUSEATING, revolting, sweet, syrupy, cloying, mawkish
COLLOQ. soppy, schmaltzy, gushy, mushy, slushy
F⊒ **1** healthy, robust, sturdy, strong

sickness *n*
1 ILLNESS, disease, ailment, complaint, ill-health, disorder, infirmity
FORMAL malady, affliction, indisposition
COLLOQ. bug, virus
2 VOMITING, retching, heaving, nausea, queasiness, biliousness, travel sickness, motion sickness, morning sickness, carsickness, seasickness, airsickness
COLLOQ. throwing up, spewing up, puking
F⊒ **1** health

side *n, adj, v*

♦ *n*

1 the side of an object
face, facet, surface, end, profile
2 EDGE, margin, fringe, periphery, border, boundary, limit, end, verge, rim, brink, bank, shore, flank, hand
TECHNICAL jamb
Related adjective: lateral
3 the other side of the city
district, quarter, area, region, sector, neighbourhood, section, zone
4 draw the figure from all sides
aspect, angle, slant, facet, standpoint, view, viewpoint, point of view, profile
5 hear one side of the story
standpoint, viewpoint, point of view, view, aspect, angle, slant
6 TEAM, party, faction, wing, camp, sect, splinter group, cause, interest

♦ *adj*

1 LATERAL, flanking, wing
2 MINOR, marginal, secondary, subsidiary, subordinate, lesser, incidental
3 OBLIQUE, sideward, sideways, sidelong

■ **side-effect**
spin-off, repercussion, result, consequence, effect, outcome, reverberation, echo, rebound, recoil, backwash, aftermath
COLLOQ. ripple

■ **side with**
agree with, team up with, take someone's side, be on the side of, support, give your support to, back, give your backing to, join with, vote for, favour, prefer

■ **side by side**
next to each other, close to each other, alongside each other, shoulder to shoulder

■ **take someone's side**
be on the side of, support, give your support to, back, give your backing to, join with, vote for, favour, prefer, encourage, help, motivate, sympathize with

sideline *n, v*

♦ *n*

second job, subsidiary activity, hobby, pastime, interest, diversion, recreation, relaxation, pursuit, leisure activity/pursuit, game, sport, entertainment, amusement, divertissement

♦ *v*

exclude, demote, downgrade, degrade, relegate, transfer, banish, expatriate, deport, eject, exile, expel

sidelong *adj*
indirect, oblique, sideward, sideways, secret, covert, surreptitious
F∃ direct, overt

side-splitting *adj*
hilarious, funny, amusing, comical, humorous, farcical, laughable, riotous, uproarious
COLLOQ. hysterical, killing, a scream
F∃ serious, grave

sidestep *v*
avoid, find a way around, dodge, evade, elude, skirt, bypass
FORMAL circumvent
COLLOQ. duck, shirk, give a miss
F∃ tackle, deal with

sidetrack *v*
deflect, head off, lead away from, divert, distract

sideways *adv, adj*

♦ *adv*

from side to side, sidewards, to the side, edgeways, edgewise, crabwise, laterally, obliquely, askance, athwart

♦ *adj*

sideward, side, lateral, slanted, oblique, indirect, sidelong

sidle *v*
slink, edge, inch, creep, sneak

siege *n*
blockade, encirclement, besiegement, beleaguerment
Related adjective: obsidional

siesta *n*
rest, sleep, relaxation, nap, afternoon nap, doze
FORMAL repose
COLLOQ. catnap, forty winks, snooze

sieve *v, n*

♦ *v*

sift, strain, filter, screen, riddle, separate, remove, sort, winnow; *dialect* sye, temse
OLD cribble, searce

♦ *n*

colander, strainer, filter, sifter, riddle, screen, boulter, cribble, trommel; *dialect* sye, temse
OLD searce
Related adjectives: cribrate, cribrose, coliform, cribriform, ethmoid

sift *v*

1 SIEVE, strain, filter, riddle, screen, winnow, separate, sort
OLD cribble, garble, searce
2 EXAMINE, scrutinize, investigate, analyse, study, pore over, probe, review, search

sigh *v*

1 BREATHE, moan, complain, lament, grieve
OLD suspire, besigh, sithe
FORMAL exhale
2 the wind sighing through the valley
rustle, whisper, crackle, swish, sough
FORMAL susurrate

■ **sigh for**
grieve, lament, languish, long, mourn, pine, weep, yearn, cry, cry for the moon

sight *n, v*

♦ *n*

1 VISION, eyesight, seeing, ability to see, faculty/sense of sight, observation, perception
2 VIEW, look, glance, glimpse, range, field of vision, range of vision, visibility
3 APPEARANCE, spectacle, show, display, exhibition, scene, monstrosity
COLLOQ. eyesore, fright
4 see the sights of London
place of interest, landmark, amenity, beauty, feature, curiosity, wonder, splendour, marvel

♦ *v*

see, observe, spot, glimpse, perceive, discern, distinguish, make out
FORMAL espy, behold
Related adjective: visual

■ **catch sight of**
see, perceive, notice, note, watch, view, look at, mark, glimpse, discern, make out, recognize, spot, identify

■ **lose sight of**
forget, omit, fail to remember, neglect, overlook, disregard, ignore, put aside, slip your mind

■ **set your sights on**
aim at, plan for, seek to, intend to, strive for, aspire towards, work towards

> **PROVERBS**
> Out of sight, out of mind

sightless *adj*
blind, visually impaired, unsighted, unseeing, visionless, eyeless
F∃ sighted

sightseer *n*
tourist, visitor, holidaymaker, tripper, excursionist; *N Am* rubberneck

sign *n, v*

♦ *n*

1 SYMBOL, token, character, figure, code, cipher, representation, emblem, badge, insignia, logo

2 INDICATION, mark, signal, gesture, evidence, proof, clue, pointer, token, hint, suggestion, trace, symptom
FORMAL manifestation
3 GESTURE, signal, movement, motion, wave, indication, act, action, gesticulation
4 NOTICE, poster, board, placard, signpost, marker, indicator
5 PORTENT, omen, forewarning, foreboding
FORMAL augury, prognostication, harbinger, presage
♦ v
1 *sign your name*
autograph, countersign, initial, endorse, write
FORMAL inscribe, attest, ratify, witness
2 SIGNAL, wave, gesticulate, gesture, beckon, wink, motion, nod, indicate, express, show, mark, communicate
3 RECRUIT, enlist, draft, conscript, enrol, sign up, levy, engage, take on, mobilize, raise, muster, gather, assemble, put together, obtain, acquire, talent-spot, headhunt
■ **sign over**
make over, transfer, turn over, surrender, entrust, deliver, convey, consign
■ **sign up**
enlist, enrol, join (up), join the services, volunteer, register, sign on, put your name down for, recruit, take on, hire, engage, employ

signal *n, v, adj*
♦ n
sign, indication, mark, gesture, evidence, clue, message, symptom, pointer, token, hint, light, alert, warning, tip-off
COLLOQ. shot across the bows
See panel below
♦ v
wave, gesticulate, gesture, beckon, wink, motion, nod, sign, indicate, express, show, mark, communicate
FORMAL signify, presage
♦ adj
significant, important, exceptional, notable, noteworthy, outstanding, extraordinary, impressive, memorable, momentous, remarkable, striking, eminent, distinguished, conspicuous, glorious, famous

signature *n*
autograph, name, initials, mark, endorsement, inscription, subscription, hand, countersignature, frank, sheet, tag
COLLOQ. *N Am* John Hancock

significance *n*
importance, relevance, consequence, seriousness, status, solemnity, magnitude, matter, interest, consideration, weight, force, meaning, implication(s), sense, essence, gist, point, message
FORMAL import, purport
🞬 insignificance, unimportance, pettiness

significant *adj*
1 IMPORTANT, relevant, consequential, momentous, memorable, weighty, serious, noteworthy, material, critical, vital, crucial, key, fateful, marked, considerable, appreciable

2 MEANINGFUL, symbolic, expressive, suggestive, indicative, symptomatic, eloquent, pregnant, ominous
🞬 **1** insignificant, unimportant, trivial **2** meaningless

significantly *adv*
1 VITALLY, crucially, considerably, appreciably, remarkably, notably, noticeably, perceptibly, critically, materially
2 MEANINGFULLY, eloquently, meaningly, expressively, knowingly, suggestively

signify *v*
1 MEAN, symbolize, be a sign of, represent, stand for, indicate, mark, show, exhibit, signal, express, convey, transmit, communicate, declare, proclaim, intimate, imply, suggest
FORMAL denote, betoken, portend
2 MATTER, count, be of importance, be important, be relevant, have influence, carry weight
FORMAL be of consequence
COLLOQ. make waves

signpost *n*
sign, pointer, marker, indicator, placard, guidepost, fingerpost, handpost, waypost, clue

silence *n, v*
♦ n
quiet, quietness, hush, peace, peacefulness, stillness, still, calm, calmness, tranquillity, lull, noiselessness, soundlessness, muteness, dumbness, speechlessness, wordlessness, voicelessness, taciturnity, uncommunicativeness, reticence, reserve, secretiveness
TECHNICAL quiescence
COLLOQ. mum
🞬 noise, sound, din, uproar
♦ v
quiet, quieten, hush, mute, strike dumb, deaden, muffle, stifle, gag, muzzle, suppress, subdue, quell, still, dumbfound
FORMAL abate

> **PROVERBS**
> Speech is silver, but silence is golden

> **QUOTATIONS**
> For words divide and rend; / But silence is most noble till the end
>   ALGERNON SWINBURNE, *Atlanta in Calydon*, 'Who hath given man speech'

silent *adj*
inaudible, noiseless, soundless, quiet, peaceful, still, calm, hushed, muted, mute, dumb, speechless, tongue-tied, tight-lipped, taciturn, reticent, reserved, secretive, tacit, unspoken, implicit, implied, unexpressed, understood, unvoiced, voiceless, wordless, dummy, sulking, sullen
TECHNICAL quiescent
OLD hush, conticent, creepmouse, tuneless, whisht, whist; (*Shakesp*) languageless
FORMAL obmutescent

Kinds of signal and warning include:

alarm	car horn	gong	Lutine bell	semaphore signal	tattoo
alarm-bell	cue	green light	mayday	a shot across the	time signal (pips)
alarm clock	curfew bell	hand signal	Morse code	bows	tocsin
amber light	distress signal	heliograph	pager	shout	toot
beacon	drumbeat	honk	password	signal box	trafficator
Belisha beacon	final warning	hooter	personal alarm	signal letters	traffic lights
bell	fire	horn	police whistle	siren	Very light
bicycle bell	fire alarm	hurricane warning	red alert	smoke alarm	vigia
bleeper	flag	indicator	red card	smoke signal	warning light
bugle	flare	klaxon	red flag	SOS	whistle
buoy	flashing light	knell	red light	starter's gun	winker
burglar alarm	foghorn	larum	reveille	storm cone	written warning
buzzer	gale warning	larum-bell	rocket	storm signal	yellow card
car alarm	go-ahead	lighthouse beacon	security alarm	storm warning	yellow flag

COLLOQ. mum, shtoom
◼ noisy, loud, talkative

silently adv
noiselessly, quietly, calmly, inaudibly, soundlessly, speechlessly, wordlessly, without a word, unheard, dumbly, mutely, tacitly
TECHNICAL quiescently

silhouette n, v
♦ n
outline, contour, shape, form, profile, shadow, shadow figure, skyline
FORMAL delineation, configuration
♦ v
outline, shadow, shape, profile, stand out
FORMAL delineate, configurate, configure

silky adj
silken, fine, sleek, lustrous, glossy, satiny, smooth, soft, velvety
FORMAL diaphanous

silliness n
foolishness, folly, stupidity, absurdity, ridiculousness, ludicrousness, preposterousness, idiocy, frivolousness, frivolity, childishness, inaneness, fatuousness, immaturity, irresponsibility, senselessness, pointlessness, meaninglessness, irrationality, foolhardiness, recklessness, rashness
COLLOQ. daftness, looniness, loopiness, barminess, pottiness
◼ sense, sensibleness, wisdom, maturity

silly adj, n
♦ adj
foolish, stupid, unintelligent, unwise, senseless, pointless, thoughtless, idiotic, ridiculous, ludicrous, preposterous, absurd, meaningless, unreasonable, irrational, illogical, frivolous, childish, puerile, inane, fatuous, immature, irresponsible, imprudent, foolhardy, rash, reckless, scatterbrained, feather-brained
FORMAL injudicious
COLLOQ. airheaded, daft, dizzy, soft, dotty, loopy, barmy, potty, nutty
See Synonym nuances panel at **stupid**.
◼ wise, sensible, sane, mature, clever, intelligent
♦ n
fool, idiot, ignoramus, simpleton, ninny, halfwit
COLLOQ. dumbo, silly-billy, nincompoop, clot, dope, duffer, berk, nit, twit, wally, goose; Aust bunny

silt n, v
♦ n
sediment, deposit, residue, sludge, mud, ooze, sullage
FORMAL alluvium, illuvium
◼ **silt up**
block (up), clog (up), dam, choke, congest

silvan adj
leafy, tree-covered, wooded, woodland
FORMAL arboreous, forestal, forested, forestine
◼ treeless

silver adj
greyish-white, whitish-grey, pale grey, snowy
OLD argent
Related adjective: argentine

similar adj
like, alike, close, much the same, related, akin, corresponding, equivalent, coincident, comparable, uniform, cut from the same cloth
TECHNICAL homologous
FORMAL analogous, homogeneous
COLLOQ. samey
◼ dissimilar, different

similarity n
likeness, resemblance, sameness, closeness, relation, kinship, correspondence, parallelism, equivalence, comparability, compatibility, agreement, affinity, uniformity

FORMAL similitude, congruence, analogy, homogeneity, concordance
◼ dissimilarity, difference, clash

similarly adv
in the same way, likewise, correspondingly, uniformly, by the same token, by analogy
◼ differently

similitude n
similarity, likeness, resemblance, sameness, closeness, relation, correspondence, parallelism, equivalence, comparability, compatibility, agreement, affinity, uniformity
FORMAL congruence, analogy

simmer v
1 BOIL GENTLY, bubble, cook gently, seethe, stew
2 *simmer with anger*
fume, rage, boil, seethe, burn, smoulder
◼ **simmer down**
calm down, cool down, subside, lessen, become less angry, control yourself, collect yourself

simpering adj
self-conscious, silly, coy, giggling, smirky, missish, schoolgirlish
FORMAL affected

simple adj
1 *a simple question; in simple language*
easy, elementary, straightforward, uncomplicated, uninvolved, effortless, clear, lucid, plain, understandable, comprehensible
COLLOQ. cushy, easy-peasy, easy as pie, rough and ready, a cinch, a doddle, a piece of cake, a pushover, a walkover, a cakewalk, as easy as falling off a log, not rocket science
2 BASIC, plain, crude, primitive, natural, undecorated, unadorned, unembellished, unsophisticated, ordinary, mere, unpretentious, unfussy, classic, rudimentary, stark, austere, spartan
COLLOQ. low-tech, no-frills
3 *the simple fact is ...*
plain, basic, straightforward, bald, stark, direct, unambiguous, open, honest, sincere, candid, blunt
4 UNSOPHISTICATED, unpretentious, natural, innocent, artless, guileless, ingenuous, naive, green
5 FOOLISH, stupid, silly, idiotic, half-witted, simple-minded, feeble-minded, slow, backward, retarded
◼ **1** difficult, hard, complicated, intricate **2** elaborate, fancy, luxurious **4** sophisticated, worldly, artful **5** clever, sharp, intelligent

simple-minded adj
unsophisticated, simple, natural, artless, stupid, foolish, idiot, idiotic, imbecile, moronic, cretinous, brainless, backward, retarded, feeble-minded, addle-brained; Welsh twp
COLLOQ. dim-witted, dopey, goofy
◼ bright, clever

simpleton n
idiot, fool, moron, ninny, imbecile, dolt, dullard, dunce, dupe, jackass, flathead, softhead, noddy, spoon, wiseacre, Johnny, Gothamite, Abderite; dialect gaby, zany; Scot gomeril, sumph
OLD simple, rook, cokes, daw, dawcock, woodcock, hoddy-doddy, shot-clog, Gothamist
COLLOQ. mug, dope, nincompoop, numskull, nitwit, stupid, twerp, clot, twit, greenhorn, goose, gander, blockhead, booby, noodle, flat, mafflin; Aust bunny
SLANG juggins, patsy
OLD SLANG green goose, tony
◼ brain

simplicity n
simpleness, ease, easiness, facility, straightforwardness, uncomplicatedness, elementariness, clarity, purity, plainness, lucidity, intelligibility, restraint, starkness,

naturalness, clean lines, innocence, guilelessness, naivety, artlessness, unpretentiousness, directness, frankness, candour, openness, sincerity, honesty

F3 difficulty, complexity, intricacy, sophistication, elaborateness

> **QUOTATIONS**
> Simplicity, without variety, is wholly insipid
> WILLIAM HOGARTH, *The Analysis of Beauty*

simplification n
explanation, clarification, paraphrase, abridgement, reduction, interpretation, popularization
F3 complication, elaboration

simplify v
disentangle, untangle, unravel, decipher, make easy/easier, make easier to understand, make (more) comprehensible, make (more) accessible, popularize, remove complexities in, explain, interpret, clarify, paraphrase, abridge, reduce, sort out, streamline
F3 complicate, elaborate

> **QUOTATIONS**
> The ability to simplify means to eliminate the unnecessary so that the necessary may speak
> HANS HOFFMAN, *Search for the Real*

simplistic adj
oversimplified, superficial, shallow, sweeping, facile, simple, oversimple, naive, pat
F3 analytical, detailed

simplistically adv
superficially, shallowly, simply, facilely, naively

simply adv
1 MERELY, just, only, solely, purely, utterly, completely, totally, wholly, altogether, absolutely, positively, quite, really, undeniably, unquestionably, without doubt, unreservedly, unconditionally, clearly, plainly, obviously
2 EASILY, straightforwardly, directly, intelligibly, plainly, clearly, lucidly, naturally

simulate v
pretend, make believe, assume, put on, act, feign, sham, fake, mock, counterfeit, reproduce, duplicate, copy, imitate, mimic, parrot, echo, reflect, parallel
FORMAL affect

simulated adj
pretended, feigned, artificial, assumed, imitation, put-on, sham, fake, faux, mock, make-believe, bogus, spurious, substitute, synthetic, man-made, inauthentic, insincere
COLLOQ. phoney, pseudo
F3 real, genuine

simultaneous adj
happening at the same time, existing at the same time, done at the same time, synchronous, synchronic, coexistent, coinciding, parallel
FORMAL concurrent, contemporaneous, concomitant
F3 asynchronous

simultaneously adv
at the same time, at once, all at once, together, all together, in parallel, in unison, synchronically, synchronously

sin n, v
♦ n
wrong, offence, misdeed, lapse, fault, error, trespass, crime, wrongdoing, sinfulness, wickedness, badness, evil, impiety, immorality, ungodliness, unrighteousness, irreligiousness, guilt
FORMAL transgression, misdemeanour, iniquity
♦ v
offend, commit a sin, lapse, err, trespass, misbehave, go wrong, do wrong, stray, go astray, fall, fall from grace
FORMAL transgress

The seven deadly sins are:

pride	lust
envy	gluttony
anger/wrath	greed/avarice
sloth	

---

since adv, prep, conj
♦ adv, prep, conj
from that time, from the time (that/of), until (now), after, following, subsequent to, ago
♦ conj
as, because, seeing that, considering that, inasmuch as, being, the reason is..., through, on account of, as a result of, owing to, in view of the fact that

sincere adj
genuine, true, real, honest, truthful, bona fide, trustworthy, candid, frank, open, direct, straightforward, no-nonsense, plain-spoken, plain-hearted, serious, fervent, earnest, heartfelt, wholehearted, hearty, pure, unadulterated, unmixed, undesigning, unfeigned, natural, artless, ingenuous, guileless, simple, cordial; *Scot* aefald
OLD simple-hearted, single
FORMAL unaffected
COLLOQ. above board, up front
F3 insincere, hypocritical, affected

> **SYNONYM NUANCES**
> Many of these synonyms are marked by a note of approval.
> **Genuine** and **real** can be used to suggest being exactly as you seem, while **true** implies being correct in all aspects. **Honest** and **truthful** have more to do with virtue, whilst **trustworthy** suggests someone honourable. The term **bona fide** suggests authenticity or a lack of intention to deceive: *a bona fide money-back guarantee.*
> The less marked terms **candid** and **frank** describe someone who is simply forthright, and **direct**, **straightforward** and **plain-spoken** are similarly uncompromising. **Open** has further suggestions of being unrestrained: *an open exchange of views.*
> **Serious** and **earnest** suggest commitment: *a serious foray into acting*, and both **fervent** and **heartfelt**, although similar, perhaps suggest an even greater degree of passion. **Wholehearted**, too, remains with the idea of unreserved involvement, while **hearty** and **cordial** convey extra enthusiasm and an element of affability: *hearty congratulations were sent to the trophy winners.*
> Both **pure** and **unadulterated** put the emphasis on a lack of defilement or distraction, and **natural** and **simple**, likewise, imply an absence of artificiality or complexity. The terms **artless**, **ingenuous** and **guileless** suggest sincerity that stems from basic innocence: *the artless writing style of a child.*

sincerely adv
genuinely, honestly, earnestly, in earnest, seriously, really, simply, truly, truthfully, wholeheartedly, unfeignedly
FORMAL unaffected

sincerity n
genuineness, honour, integrity, probity, uprightness, honesty, truth, truthfulness, candour, frankness, openness, directness, straightforwardness, seriousness, earnestness, wholeheartedness, trustworthiness, artlessness, ingenuousness, guilelessness
F3 insincerity

> **QUOTATIONS**
> A little sincerity is a dangerous thing, and a great deal of it is absolutely fatal
> OSCAR WILDE, *Intentions*, 'The Critic as Artist'

sinecure *n*
soft option
COLLOQ. plum job, picnic, doddle, cinch, cushy job, money for jam, money for old rope, gravy train

sinewy *adj*
muscular, burly, brawny, strapping, stalwart, strong, sturdy, robust, vigorous, athletic, wiry, stringy

sinful *adj*
wrong, wrongful, criminal, evil, bad, wicked, erring, fallen, immoral, corrupt, depraved, impious, ungodly, unholy, unrighteous, irreligious, guilty
FORMAL iniquitous
EA sinless, righteous, godly

sinfulness *n*
immorality, wickedness, sin, ungodliness, unrighteousness, impiety, corruption, guilt
FORMAL iniquity, depravity, peccability, peccancy, transgression
EA righteousness

sing *v*
chant, intone, vocalize, burst into song, chorus, croon, serenade, yodel, trill, warble, chirp, quaver, pipe, whistle, hum
■ **sing out**
shout, yell, cry (out), call, bawl, bellow, cooee
COLLOQ. holler

singe *v*
scorch, char, blacken, burn, sear

singer

Singers include:

balladeer	pop singer	warbler
carol-singer	pop star	**REGISTERS:**
chanteuse	precentor	alto
choirboy	prima donna	baritone
choirgirl	rapper	bass
chorister (or	rock singer	castrato
chorist)	soloist	coloratura soprano
crooner	songster	contralto
diva	songstress	soprano
folk-singer	torch singer	tenor
minstrel	troubadour	treble
opera singer	vocalist	

---

single *adj, v*
◆ *adj*
1 ONE, unique, singular, individual, particular, exclusive, sole, only, one and only, by yourself/itself, lone, solitary, isolated, separate, distinct, unshared, undivided, unbroken, simple, one-to-one, person-to-person, man-to-man, woman-to-woman
2 UNMARRIED, unwed, free, unattached, celibate, on your own, by yourself, available
EA **1** multiple **2** married
■ **single out**
choose, select, pick, hand-pick, distinguish, identify, separate (out), set apart, decide on, isolate, highlight, pinpoint

single-handed *adj, adv*
by yourself, on your own, alone, solo, independent(ly), without help, unaided, unassisted, unaccompanied

single-minded *adj*
determined, resolute, dogged, persevering, tireless, unwavering, fixed, set, unswerving, undeviating, steadfast, dedicated, committed, devoted, obsessive, onefold, monomaniacal; *Scot* aefald

singly *adv*
one by one, on their own, one at a time, individually, separately, distinctly, solely, independently

singular *adj*
1 REMARKABLE, exceptional, unusual, extraordinary, noteworthy, unique, unparalleled, pre-eminent, outstanding, eminent, conspicuous
2 PECULIAR, odd, queer, unusual, strange, uncommon, curious, eccentric, atypical
EA **1** usual **2** normal

singularity *n*
peculiarity, strangeness, queerness, quirk, particularity, oddness, oddity, abnormality, curiousness, eccentricity, idiosyncrasy, irregularity, extraordinariness, uniqueness, oneness, twist
EA normality

singularly *adv*
remarkably, exceptionally, extraordinarily, notably, outstandingly, particularly, uncommonly, unusually, especially, surprisingly, signally, conspicuously, prodigiously, bizarrely

sinister *adj*
ominous, menacing, threatening, disturbing, disquieting, terrifying, frightening, unlucky, evil, dark, forbidding, Gothic, louche, harmful, cruel, malevolent, wicked, vicious
FORMAL inauspicious, portentous
COLLOQ. shady
EA harmless, innocent; *formal* auspicious

sink *v*
1 DESCEND, slip, fall, drop, go down, slump, lower, go lower, plummet, plunge, stoop, succumb, lapse, droop, sag, dip, set, disappear, vanish
2 DECREASE, lessen, subside, abate, dwindle, diminish, ebb, fade, flag, weaken, fail, decline, worsen, degenerate, degrade, decay, collapse, fall (in)
FORMAL abate
COLLOQ. go downhill, go to pot
3 FOUNDER, dive, plunge, plummet, go under, capsize, submerge, immerse, engulf, drown
4 *sink a well*
bore, drill, penetrate, dig, excavate, drive, put down, embed, lay, conceal
5 *sink money into a project*
invest, put in, lay out, fund, risk, venture, plough
6 RUIN, destroy, wreck, devastate, demolish, foil, scupper, scuttle
COLLOQ. put a spanner in the works
EA **1** rise **2** increase, improve **3** float

sinless *adj*
innocent, virtuous, faultless, guiltless, immaculate, pure, unblemished, uncorrupted, undefiled, unsullied, unspotted, impeccable
EA sinful

sinner *n*
wrongdoer, offender, trespasser, criminal, backslider, reprobate, evil-doer
FORMAL malefactor, miscreant, transgressor

sinuous *adj*
lithe, slinky, curved, curving, wavy, undulating, weaving, tortuous, twisting, winding, bending, turning, meandering, serpentine, coiling, curling, wriggly, ogee
FORMAL sinuate
EA straight

sip *v, n*
◆ *v*
taste, sample, drink, drink slowly, sup
◆ *n*
taste, drop, drink, spoonful, mouthful

siren *n*
1 ALARM, tocsin, burglar alarm, car alarm, horn, fire alarm, personal alarm, security alarm
2 SEDUCTRESS, *femme fatale*, temptress, vamp, charmer, Lorelei, Circe, Delilah

sissy, cissy *n, adj*

♦ *n*

baby, coward, weakling, pansy, softy, mummy's boy, milksop

COLLOQ. wimp, namby-pamby, wet

SLANG wuss; *Aust & NZ* tonk

♦ *adj*

unmanly, weak, soft, cowardly, effeminate, feeble, pansy

COLLOQ. wimpish, namby-pamby, wet

sister *n*

1 *brothers and sisters*

sibling, blood-sister, full sister, twin-sister, half-sister, relation, relative, sib

OLD german

COLLOQ. sis

2 *sisters in the struggle against injustice*

comrade, friend, partner, colleague, associate, fellow, companion

3 *sisters in a convent*

nun, abbess, prioress, vowess

Related adjective: sororal

sit *v*

1 SETTLE, sit down, take your seat, be seated, lie, hang, rest, squat (down), place, put, deposit, position, situate, locate, stand, perch, roost, brood, pose

2 SEAT, accommodate, hold, contain, have room/space for

3 MEET, assemble, gather, convene, consult, deliberate, be in session

4 *sit an exam*

take, do, study for

5 *sit for an artist*

pose, model

6 *sit on a committee*

be a member (of), serve, take part (in)

■ **sit back**

relax, do nothing, not be involved in/with

■ **sit in on**

be present at, attend, observe, watch

site *n, v*

♦ *n*

1 LOCATION, place, spot, position, situation, locality, station, setting, scene

2 PLOT, lot, ground, area

♦ *v*

locate, place, position, situate, station, put, set, install

sitting *n*

session, period, spell, meeting, assembly, hearing, consultation

sitting room *n*

living room, lounge, drawing room, day room, front room, reception room, parlour

situate *v*

locate, place, position, site, station, put, set, install

situation *n*

1 SITE, location, position, place, spot, seat, locality, locale, setting, environment, milieu, scenario

2 STATE OF AFFAIRS, case, circumstances, predicament, affairs, environment, climate, set-up, state, state of play, condition(s), status, rank, station

COLLOQ. scenario, lie of the land, picture, what's going on, score

3 JOB, post, office, position, appointment, place, employment

sizable, sizeable *adj*

substantial, fairly large, considerable, respectable, goodly, largish, biggish, decent, generous

F3 small, tiny

size *n, v*

♦ *n*

magnitude, measurement(s), dimensions, proportions, volume, bulk, mass, expanse, height, length, area, extent, range, scale, amount, greatness, largeness, bigness, vastness, immensity

■ **size up**

gauge, assess, evaluate, judge, weigh up, estimate, rate, measure

FORMAL appraise

COLLOQ. suss out

sizzle *v*

hiss, crackle, spit, sputter, fry, frizzle

skeletal *adj*

skin-and-bone, wasted, drawn, emaciated, gaunt, haggard, hollow-cheeked, shrunken, fleshless, unfleshed

FORMAL cadaverous

skeleton *n, adj*

♦ *n*

bones, frame, structure, framework, support, bare bones, outline, blueprint, plan, draft, sketch

TECHNICAL endoskeleton, coenosteum, corallum

OLD anatomy; (*Shakesp*) atomy

♦ *adj*

smallest, lowest, minimum, reduced, basic

sketch *v, n*

♦ *v*

draw, depict, portray, represent, pencil, paint, outline, delineate, draft, rough out, block out, line, platform

♦ *n*

1 DRAWING, vignette, design, plan, diagram, outline, skeleton, abstract, draft, representation, description, rough, visual, memoir, cartoon, pencilling, thumbnail; *Scot* skiff

TECHNICAL bozzetto, modello, trick

FORMAL delineation, prosopography

2 SUMMARY, synopsis, précis, résumé, main points, prospectus, programme, scenario, rough idea, bare facts, bare bones, framework, skeleton, thumbnail sketch, abstract, *aperçu, croquis, ébauche, esquisse*

3 SKIT, satire, parody, caricature, burlesque, scene, act, turn

COLLOQ. spoof, take-off, send-up, mickey-taking

SLANG piss-taking

sketchily *adv*

roughly, vaguely, incompletely, inadequately, imperfectly, patchily, cursorily, perfunctorily, hastily

F3 fully

sketchy *adj*

rough, vague, incomplete, unpolished, unfinished, scrappy, crude, provisional, patchy, bitty, imperfect, inadequate, insufficient, defective, deficient, slight, superficial, cursory, meagre, perfunctory, hasty

F3 full, complete

skew *v*

distort, slant, twist, bias, weigh, falsify, misrepresent, colour

skilful *adj*

able, capable, adept, competent, proficient, efficient, good, dexterous, deft, adroit, handy, expert, (well-) versed, masterly, clever, smart, accomplished, skilled, gifted, talented, practised, experienced, trained, professional, technical, tactical, cunning

F3 inept, clumsy, awkward

skilfully *adv*

ably, capably, competently, proficiently, deftly, cleverly, handily, expertly

F3 ineptly, awkwardly

skill *n*

skilfulness, ability, aptitude, facility, handiness, adeptness, deftness, adroitness, talent, knack, art, technique, training, experience, expertise, expertness, professionalism, finesse, mastery, artistry, proficiency, competence, efficiency, accomplishment, cleverness, smartness, intelligence

skilled *adj*

trained, schooled, qualified, professional, experienced, practised, accomplished, gifted, talented, expert, masterly,

proficient, competent, efficient, able, capable, good, adept, skilful
E3 unskilled, inexperienced

skim v
1 BRUSH, touch, skate, plane, hydroplane, float, sail, glide, graze, fly, skip, bounce, skiff, skitter
2 SCAN, look through, glance at, skip, read (through) quickly, run through/over, have a quick look at, browse through, flick through, flip through, thumb through, leaf through
COLLOQ. graze
3 CREAM, separate, take off; *Scot* ream
FORMAL despumate

skimp v
economize, be economical, cut back on, scrimp, pinch, stint, be mean with, withhold
COLLOQ. cut corners, tighten your belt, cut your coat according to your cloth
E3 squander, waste

skimpy adj
small, scanty, short, sparse, thin, tight, sketchy, meagre, miserly, niggardly, inadequate, insufficient, insubstantial, beggarly
FORMAL exiguous
COLLOQ. measly
E3 generous

skin n, v
♦ n
hide, fleece, fell, pelt, membrane, film, coating, layer, surface, covering, cover, complexion, outside, peel, rind, husk, hull, pod, casing, crust
TECHNICAL corium, derma, dermis, cutis, integument, tegument, epidermis
FORMAL cuticle
Related adjectives: dermatoid, cutaneous
♦ v
flay, fleece, strip, peel, scrape, graze
■ **by the skin of your teeth**
narrowly, barely, only just
COLLOQ. by a whisker, a near/close thing

skin-deep adj
shallow, superficial, surface, external, outward, artificial, empty, meaningless

skinflint n
miser, niggard, cheeseparer, Scrooge
COLLOQ. meanie, penny-pincher, tightwad
E3 spendthrift

skinny adj
thin, lean, scrawny, scraggy, skin-and-bone, skeletal, emaciated, underfed, undernourished
E3 fat, plump

skip v
1 HOP, jump, leap, dance, spring, bounce, bob, bound, cavort, gambol, frisk, caper, prance, scamper, ricochet, tittup; *dialect* trounce; *Scot* flisk
See Synonym nuances panel at **jump**.
2 *skip a page*
miss (out), omit, leave out, overskip
COLLOQ. dodge, cut
3 *skip from one thing to another*
move quickly, jump, rush, pass, dart, tear, race

skirmish n, v
♦ n
fight, combat, battle, engagement, encounter, confrontation, conflict, clash, brush, affray, fracas, mêlée, tussle, argument, dispute, difference of opinion
FORMAL altercation
COLLOQ. scrap, set-to, dust-up, punch-up
♦ v
clash, fight, tussle, brawl, scuffle, combat, battle, contend, argue, quarrel, wrangle
COLLOQ. scrap, fall out, be at each other's throats

skirt v
1 CIRCLE, move/go round, border, edge, flank
FORMAL circumnavigate
2 AVOID, evade, bypass, find a way round
FORMAL circumvent

skit n
satire, parody, caricature, burlesque, sketch, scene, act, turn
COLLOQ. spoof, take-off, send-up, mickey-taking
SLANG piss-taking

skittish adj
nervous, excitable, fidgety, lively, playful, jumpy, highly-strung, frivolous, fickle
FORMAL restive

skittles n
ninepins, pins, tenpin bowling, tenpins, skittle-pins, kettle-pins

skive v
dodge, laze, idle, shirk, avoid work, malinger, skulk, slack
COLLOQ. bunk off, swing the lead
SLANG N Am goof off

skiver n
dodger, idler, do-nothing, shirker, slacker, loafer, malingerer
SLANG N Am goof-off

skulduggery n
trickery, swindling, fraudulence, double-dealing, underhandedness, unscrupulousness, chicanery
FORMAL duplicity, machinations
COLLOQ. jiggery-pokery, shenanigans, hanky-panky

skulk v
lurk, hide, prowl, sneak, creep, slink, lie in wait, steal, slide, pad, pussyfoot, loiter

sky n
space, atmosphere, air, heavens, the blue
OLD firmament, empyrean, welkin
FORMAL vault of heaven
Related adjectives: celestial, supernal, empyreal

skyscraper n
high-rise building, tower block, splinter building, sliver building

slab n
piece, block, lump, chunk, hunk, brick, briquette, wedge, slice, portion
COLLOQ. wodge

slack adj, n, v
♦ adj
1 LOOSE, relaxed, flexible, limp, hanging, sagging, flapping, flabby, nerveless, baggy
OLD lash
FORMAL flaccid
2 *a slack period*
sluggish, slow, quiet, idle, lazy, inactive, languid
3 NEGLECTFUL, negligent, careless, sloppy, slapdash, inattentive, permissive, lax, remiss, relaxed, easy-going
OLD lash
FORMAL tardy
E3 1 tight, taut, stiff, rigid **2** busy **3** diligent
♦ n
looseness, give, play, room, leeway, excess, spare capacity
♦ v
1 IDLE, shirk, dodge, malinger, neglect
COLLOQ. skive
2 SLACKEN, ease, moderate, reduce, lessen, get less, decrease, diminish, slow (down), become slower, become less intense/active

slacken
■ **slacken off**
loosen, release, relax, ease, moderate, reduce, lessen, get less, decrease, diminish, abate, slow (down), become slower, become less intense/active
OLD forslack

FORMAL abate
COLLOQ. take it easy
⊞ tighten, increase, intensify, quicken

slacker n
idler, shirker, dawdler, loafer, malingerer, clock-watcher, good-for-nothing, layabout
COLLOQ. skiver

slag v
■ **slag off**
criticize, slate, abuse, mock, malign, berate, run down, lambast, insult
FORMAL deride
COLLOQ. slam, knock

slake v
satisfy, satiate, quench, moisten, sate, gratify, allay, reduce, extinguish, moderate
FORMAL abate, assuage, mitigate

slam v
1 BANG, crash, dash, smash, thump, slap, throw, hurl, fling
2 CRITICIZE, attack, slate, denounce, run down, find fault with
COLLOQ. pan, rubbish, pull/tear to pieces, tear to shreds, do a hatchet job on
SLANG slag (off)

slander n, v
♦ n
defamation, misrepresentation, libel, scandal, smear, smear campaign, slur, denigration, backbiting, character assassination, mudslinging, evil-speaking, detraction
OLD sclaunder
FORMAL aspersion, disparagement, calumny, vilification, traducement, obloquy
COLLOQ. muck-raking, mudslinging
♦ v
defame, malign, libel, smear, blacken the name of, slur, backbite, speak evil of
OLD missay
FORMAL vilify, cast aspersions on, asperse, disparage, denigrate, vilipend, calumniate, traduce
COLLOQ. sling/throw mud at, drag someone's name through the mud; N Am badmouth
⊞ praise, compliment

> ⚠ **slander** or **libel**?
> See panel at **libel**.

slanderous adj
defamatory, false, untrue, libellous, damaging, malicious, abusive, insulting, backbiting
OLD venom'd-mouth'd
FORMAL aspersory, aspersive, calumniatory, calumnious

slang n
cant, jargon, argot, patois, patter, cockney, cockney rhyming slang, vulgarism, doublespeak, gobbledygook, colloquialism, informal expressions
COLLOQ. lingo, mumbo-jumbo

slanging match n
argument, row, quarrel, dispute, shouting match
FORMAL altercation
COLLOQ. argy-bargy, barney, set-to, spat

slant v, n
♦ v
1 TILT, slope, incline, lean, list, oblique, dip, skew, bevel, be askew, angle, shelve; Scot sklent
TECHNICAL splay
2 DISTORT, twist, warp, bend, weight, bias, skew, colour; Scot sklent
♦ n
1 SLOPE, incline, inclination, bevel, leaning, gradient, ramp, camber, pitch, tilt, dip, angle, diagonal, oblique, slash, forward slash; Scot sklent
TECHNICAL embrasure, splay

2 BIAS, prejudice, distortion, twist, one-sidedness, emphasis, attitude, angle, opinion, view, viewpoint, point of view

slanting adj
sloping, tilting, tilted, inclining, leaning, listing, dipping, on an incline, at a slant, aslant, askew, oblique, diagonal; Scot asklent

slap n, v, adv
♦ n
smack, spank, cuff, blow, buffet, hit, bang, clap, clout, thump, punch; dialect skelp, twank; Scot scud, yank, clatch, sclaff
OLD spat
COLLOQ. whack, wallop, biff, sock, clobber
SLANG paddy-whack
♦ v
1 SMACK, spank, hit, strike, thump, punch, clout, cuff, bang, clap, strike hands; dialect skelp; Scot scud
OLD spat
COLLOQ. whack, wallop, biff, sock, clobber, pandy
2 PUT DOWN, set (down), plump, plonk, slam, stick; dialect swap
3 DAUB, plaster, spread, apply
♦ adv
right, directly, straight, exactly, precisely, dead, plumb
COLLOQ. bang, slap-bang, smack
■ **slap in the face**
insult, humiliation, blow, affront, rejection, repulse, snub, rebuke, rebuff, indignity
COLLOQ. put-down
■ **slap on the wrist**
rebuke, reprimand, punishment, censure, blame
FORMAL castigation
COLLOQ. flak, slating, slamming, knocking, stick, dressing-down, telling-off, ticking-off, carpeting, earful, rollicking, comeuppance

slapdash adj
careless, thoughtless, haphazard, slovenly, sloppy, disorderly, clumsy, offhand, negligent, messy, slipshod, thrown-together, untidy, hurried, last-minute, hasty, rash, perfunctory
⊞ careful, orderly

slap-happy adj
casual, irresponsible, boisterous, haphazard, reeling, happy-go-lucky, nonchalant, reckless, slapdash, hit-or-miss, dazed, giddy, punch-drunk, woozy

slapstick n
comedy, farce, buffoonery, tomfoolery, knockabout, horseplay, custard pie

slap-up adj
excellent, splendid, lavish, elaborate, first-class, first-rate, magnificent, superb, sumptuous, luxurious, princely, superlative

slash v, n
♦ v
1 **slash your wrists**
cut, slit, gash, lacerate, knife, rip, tear, hack, score, rend
2 **slash costs**
cut, reduce, decrease, curb, curtail, prune
COLLOQ. axe
♦ n
1 CUT, incision, slit, gash, laceration, score, rip, tear, rent
2 OBLIQUE, diagonal, forward slash, solidus, stroke
FORMAL virgule

slate v
scold, rebuke, reprimand, berate, censure, blame, criticize, run down, pull apart, pull/tear to pieces
COLLOQ. slam, pan, knock, rubbish, tear to shreds, do a hatchet job on
SLANG slag (off)
⊞ praise

slatternly adj
slovenly, sloppy, dirty, slipshod, untidy, unkempt, unclean, dowdy, bedraggled, frowzy, frumpish, frumpy, sluttish

slaughter v, n
♦ v
1 KILL, put to death, slay, butcher, murder, massacre, exterminate, liquidate, annihilate
2 DEFEAT, beat, trounce, best, worst, conquer, overcome, overwhelm, overpower, subdue, rout, annihilate, outplay, outwit, outsmart, be more than a match for, get the better of, have the edge on, drub
FORMAL vanquish, subjugate
COLLOQ. hammer, clobber, lick, thrash, wipe the floor with
♦ n
killing, putting to death, murder, massacre, extermination, liquidation, annihilation, butchery, carnage, bloodbath, bloodshed

slaughterhouse n
abattoir, butchery, shambles

slave n, v
♦ n
servant, drudge, menial, lackey, vassal, serf, villein, captive, thrall, bondservant, bond-slave, bond(s)man, bond(s)woman, bondmaid, abject, galley slave, maroon, praedial
TECHNICAL odalisque
OLD sclave, boy, contraband, esne, theow, Mameluke, Gibeonite
COLLOQ. skivvy
SLANG gimp, bitch
Related adjective: servile
♦ v
toil, labour, drudge, sweat, grind, slog, work your fingers to the bone, work your guts out

slave-driver n
taskmaster, tyrant, dictator, despot, autocrat, bully, oppressor, martinet

slaver v
dribble, drivel, slobber, drool
FORMAL salivate

slavery n
servitude, bondage, yoke, captivity, enslavement, serfdom, vassalage, thrall, thraldom
FORMAL subjugation
⊟ freedom, liberty

slavish adj
1 UNORIGINAL, imitative, unimaginative, uninspired, literal, strict
2 SERVILE, abject, submissive, meek, sycophantic, deferential, grovelling, cringing, fawning, menial, low, mean
FORMAL obsequious
⊟ **1** original, imaginative **2** independent, assertive

slavishly adv
unimaginatively, unoriginally, strictly, submissively, meekly, unresistingly
⊟ imaginatively

slay v
kill, butcher, massacre, murder, dispatch, destroy, eliminate, execute, slaughter, annihilate, assassinate, exterminate
COLLOQ. rub out

slaying n
murder, killing, butchery, slaughter, assassination, massacre, destruction, dispatch, elimination, annihilation, extermination
FORMAL mactation

sleazy adj
disreputable, low, seedy, sordid, corrupt, squalid
COLLOQ. crummy, tacky

sledge n
sleigh, toboggan, slide, luge, bobsled, bobsleigh, skeleton bob, Ski-doo®, dray, kibitka, pulka; Scot hurly-hacket; N Am dogsled, travois; Can train
TECHNICAL slipe

sleek adj
shiny, glossy, lustrous, smooth, silky, silken, soft, well-groomed, stylish, thriving, prosperous, slick, smug
⊟ rough, unkempt

sleep v, n
♦ v
be asleep, get some sleep, fall asleep, doze, drowse, hibernate, drop off, go off, drift off, nap, rest
OLD slumber
FORMAL repose
COLLOQ. snooze, have a snooze, have forty winks, nod off, be in the land of Nod, sleep like a log, flake out, go out like a light
SLANG kip, doss (down), crash out
♦ n
doze, nap, catnap, hibernation, rest, siesta
OLD slumber
FORMAL repose
COLLOQ. snooze, forty winks, shut-eye
SLANG kip
Related adjectives: hypnic, hypnoid, hypnoidal
■ **go to sleep**
fall asleep, drift off, drop off, doze (off), go off, catnap
COLLOQ. crash out, nod off, snooze, have forty winks
SLANG kip
■ **put to sleep**
put down, destroy, put out of its misery

> QUOTATIONS
> To die, to sleep. / To sleep, perchance to dream
> WILLIAM SHAKESPEARE, Hamlet
>
> The greatest asset that a head of state can have is the ability to get a good night's sleep
> SIR WINSTON CHURCHILL

sleepily adv
drowsily, wearily, heavily, inactively, lethargically, quietly, slowly, sluggishly
FORMAL languidly, torpidly

sleepiness n
drowsiness, doziness, heaviness, lethargy, torpor
FORMAL languor, oscitancy, oscitation, somnolence
⊟ alertness, wakefulness

sleeping adj
asleep, daydreaming, idle, inactive, unaware, becalmed, passive, off guard, inattentive, dormant, hibernating
FORMAL slumbering
⊟ alert, awake

sleepless adj
unsleeping, awake, wide-awake, alert, vigilant, watchful, wakeful, restless, disturbed, insomniac

sleeplessness n
insomnia, wakefulness
FORMAL insomnolence

sleepwalker n
somnambulist, noctambulist

sleepwalking n
somnambulism, somnambulation, noctambulism, noctambulation

sleepy adj
1 DROWSY, tired, weary, heavy, slow, sluggish, lethargic, inactive, quiet, dull, soporific, hypnotic; Scot sleepery
TECHNICAL comatose, soporose
OLD slumberous
FORMAL somnolent, languid, languorous, torpid
2 a sleepy little village
quiet, dull, peaceful, still, tranquil, isolated, lonely, unfrequented, undisturbed

FORMAL sequestered
COLLOQ. off the beaten track
⊞ **1** awake, alert, wakeful, restless **2** bustling, lively

sleigh *n*
sledge, toboggan, slide, luge, bobsled, bobsleigh, skeleton bob, Ski-doo®, dray, kibitka, pulka; *Scot* hurly-hacket; *N Am* dogsled, travois; *Can* train
TECHNICAL slipe

sleight of hand *n*
trickery, skill, artifice, dexterity, legerdemain, deception, magic, adroitness, manipulation
FORMAL prestidigitation

slender *adj*
1 SLIM, thin, lean, slight, svelte, graceful, trim, sylphlike, willowy, willowish
2 *a slender chance*
faint, remote, small, little, slim, slight, inconsiderable, tenuous, flimsy, feeble, deficient, inadequate, insufficient, meagre, scant, scanty
⊞ **1** fat, plump, overweight **2** appreciable, considerable, ample

sleuth *n*
detective, private investigator, shadow, tail, tracker, Pinkerton
COLLOQ. private eye, bloodhound, dick, gumshoe

slice *n, v*
♦ *n*
piece, sliver, wafer, rasher, tranche, slab, wedge, segment, section, hunk, chunk, part, share, portion, allocation, allotment, helping
COLLOQ. cut, whack, slice of the cake
♦ *v*
carve, cut (up), chop, sever, divide, separate, segment

slick *adj*
1 GLIB, plausible, easy, simplistic, deft, adroit, sharp, dexterous
2 SMOOTH, sleek, glossy, shiny, polished, quick, streamlined, well-oiled, well-organized, skilful, smooth, professional, efficient, masterly
3 INSINCERE, glib, smarmy, smooth-speaking, smooth-talking, persuasive, polished, sophisticated, urbane, suave
FORMAL unctuous

slide *v, n*
♦ *v*
1 MOVE SMOOTHLY, go smoothly, slip, slither, skid, skate, ski, toboggan, glide, plane, coast, skim
2 DETERIORATE, lessen, decrease, decline, fall, descend, drop, plummet, plunge, lapse, worsen, get worse, depreciate
♦ *n*
decrease, decline, fall, drop, descent, plunge, depreciation

slight *adj, v, n*
♦ *adj*
1 MINOR, unimportant, insignificant, inconsequential, negligible, inappreciable, imperceptible, trivial, petty, scant, paltry, subtle, modest, small, little, minute, inconsiderable, insubstantial
2 SLENDER, slim, small, dainty, diminutive, petite, frail, fragile, delicate, elfin
⊞ **1** major, significant, noticeable, considerable **2** large, muscular, burly
♦ *v*
scorn, despise, disdain, insult, affront, offend, snub, rebuff, spurn, slur, cut, ignore, disregard, neglect
FORMAL disparage
COLLOQ. give the cold shoulder to, cold-shoulder, give someone the brush-off
⊞ respect, praise, compliment, flatter

♦ *n*
insult, affront, scorn, slur, snub, rebuff, rudeness, discourtesy, disrespect, contempt, disdain, indifference, disregard, neglect
COLLOQ. cold shoulder, slap in the face, kick in the teeth, brush-off

slighting *adj*
disdainful, disrespectful, belittling, insulting, scornful, offensive, defamatory, derogatory, slanderous, abusive, supercilious, uncomplimentary
FORMAL disparaging
⊞ complimentary

slightly *adv*
rather, quite, a little, a bit, somewhat, to some degree, to some extent, to a certain extent

slim *adj, v*
♦ *adj*
1 SLENDER, thin, slight, lean, svelte, trim, graceful, sylphlike, willowy, willowish, leggy
See Synonym nuances panel at **thin**.
2 SLIGHT, remote, faint, poor, small, little, scant, scanty, meagre, inconsiderable, tenuous, flimsy, insufficient, inadequate
⊞ **1** fat, chubby **2** strong, considerable
♦ *v*
1 LOSE WEIGHT, diet, go on a diet, reduce
2 *slim down the workforce*
lessen, make less, make smaller, reduce, decrease, contract, shrink, curtail, trim, minimize, downsize, lower, moderate, weaken, bring down, cut back/down, restrict, wind down
COLLOQ. axe

slime *n*
mud, ooze, muck, sludge, mess; *dialect* slake
COLLOQ. goo, gunk, yuck

slimy *adj*
1 MUDDY, miry, sludgy, oozy, sticky, mucous, viscous, oily, greasy, slippery
2 SERVILE, sycophantic, toadying, ingratiating, grovelling, creeping, oily
FORMAL obsequious, unctuous
COLLOQ. smarmy

sling *v, n*
♦ *v*
1 THROW, hurl, fling, catapult, heave, pitch, lob, toss, shy
COLLOQ. chuck
2 HANG, suspend, dangle, swing
♦ *n*
bandage, loop, strap, support, band, catapult
TECHNICAL parbuckle, prusik
OLD scarf

slink *v*
sneak, steal, creep, sidle, slip, lurk, prowl, skulk

slinky *adj*
tight-fitting, close-fitting, figure-hugging, body-con, clinging, tight, skin-tight, sleek, sinuous

slip[1] *v, n*
♦ *v*
1 SLIDE, glide, skate, skid, stumble, lose your balance, trip, lose your footing, fall, slither, slink, sneak, steal, creep
2 *slip into/out of clothes*
put on, get dressed in, change into, get into, take off, change out of, pull on, wear, don
3 *standards are slipping*
fall, drop, sink, decrease, decline, plummet, plunge, slump, deteriorate, worsen, lapse, get worse
COLLOQ. go to the dogs, go to pot, go down the tubes
♦ *n*
1 MISTAKE, error, blunder, fault, indiscretion, omission, oversight, failure
COLLOQ. slip-up, bloomer, boob, booboo, howler, clanger; *N Am* flub
SLANG cock-up, goof

2 PETTICOAT, underskirt, jupon, kirtle

■ **slip up**
make a mistake, go wrong, get wrong, miscalculate, bungle, blunder, err, stumble
COLLOQ. boob, botch, fluff
SLANG cock up, screw up, goof (up)

■ **give someone the slip**
escape from, run away from, get away from, flee from, break loose from, shake off
COLLOQ. slip through someone's fingers, dodge, duck

■ **let slip**
let out, reveal, divulge, disclose, give away, betray, leak, tell
COLLOQ. blab, squeal, give the game away, let the cat out of the bag, spill the beans

slip² n

a slip of paper
piece, strip, scrap, paper, note, voucher, chit, coupon, certificate

■ **a slip of a**
small, thin, slender, slim, slight, delicate, fragile, young

slipper n
houseshoe, moccasin, mule, flip-flop, sandal, pump, loafer, pabouche, pantof(f)le, pantoufle, pantable, carpet-slipper, babouche; *Scot* panton
OLD slip-shoe

slippery adj
1 SLIPPY, icy, wet, greasy, oily, slimy, slithery, glassy, smooth, dangerous, treacherous, perilous
COLLOQ. skiddy
2 *a slippery character*
dishonest, untrustworthy, unreliable, false, two-faced, crafty, cunning, devious, clever, shifty, deceitful, foxy, evasive, smooth, smarmy
FORMAL duplicitous, perfidious
E3 2 trustworthy, reliable

slipshod adj
careless, slapdash, sloppy, slovenly, untidy, disorganized, negligent, lax, casual
E3 careful, fastidious, neat, tidy, methodical, organized

slip-up n
slip, mistake, error, blunder, fault, indiscretion, omission, oversight, failure
COLLOQ. bloomer, boob, booboo, howler, clanger; *N Am* flub
SLANG cock-up, goof

slit v, n
♦ v
cut, gash, slash, slice, split, pierce, lance, knife, rip, tear; *Scot* rit, speld
OLD rend
♦ n
opening, aperture, fissure, vent, cut, incision, gash, slash, split, rip, tear, slot, snip, peep, rent, fent, loop, race, buttonhole; *Scot* rit, spare
TECHNICAL sipe
FORMAL pertusion

slither v
slide, skid, slip, glide, slink, creep, snake, worm

sliver n
flake, shaving, paring, slice, wafer, shred, fragment, piece, bit, scrap, chip, splinter, shiver, shard

slob n
lout, oaf, layabout, good-for-nothing, sloven, churl, boor, philistine
COLLOQ. yob

slobber v
drool, dribble, drivel, slaver, foam at the mouth
FORMAL salivate

slog v, n
♦ v
1 HIT, strike, thump, belt, clout

FORMAL smite
COLLOQ. bash, slosh, slug, sock, wallop
2 PERSEVERE, labour, slave, work, work hard, plough through, toil, plod, trudge, trek, tramp
COLLOQ. plug away at, peg away at, sweat blood, work your fingers to the bone, work till you drop
♦ n
struggle, effort, exertion, grind, labour, hike, trek, trudge, tramp
COLLOQ. sweat, graft

slogan n
jingle, motto, catch phrase, catchword, watchword, cry, battle-cry, rallying cry, war cry, chant, logo, splash; *N Am* tag line
OLD slughorn
FORMAL shibboleth

slop v
spill, overflow, slosh, splash, splatter, spatter; *dialect* slattern; *N Am* slather

slope v
slant, lean, tilt, tip, dip, pitch, incline, rise, fall (away), drop

■ **slope off**
slip away, sneak off, steal away, go away, leave quietly

Words used for slopes include:

UP:	dip	gradient
acclivity	downgrade	hill
ascent	downhill	inclination
climb	downward	pitch
elevation	drop	ramp
incline	fall	scarp
rise	**UP AND DOWN:**	slant
uphill	bajada	staircase
upward	brae	stairs
DOWN:	cant	stairway
decline	escalator	steps
declivity	escarp	tilt
descent	glacis	versant

---

sloping adj
inclined, inclining, at a slant, slanting, leaning, oblique, tilting, askew, angled, canting, bevelled
FORMAL acclivitous, acclivous, declivitous, declivous
E3 level

sloppily adv
carelessly, hurriedly, hastily, untidily, messily, lackadaisically, haphazardly
E3 carefully, precisely, methodically

sloppy adj
1 WATERY, wet, liquid, runny, soggy, splashy, mushy, slushy
2 *sloppy work*
careless, hit-or-miss, slapdash, slipshod, hurried, hasty, slovenly, slack, lackadaisical, haphazard, untidy, disorganized, messy, clumsy, amateurish
3 SENTIMENTAL, romantic, gushing, mawkish, maudlin
COLLOQ. mushy, soppy, schmaltzy, gushy, gooey, slushy, sickly, corny
E3 1 solid **2** careful, exact, precise, organized, methodical

slosh v
1 SPLASH, wade, slop, slog, pour, shower, flounder, spray, swash
2 HIT, strike, thump, clout, thwack, slap, swipe, punch
COLLOQ. bash, biff, slug, sock, wallop

slot n, v
♦ n
1 HOLE, opening, aperture, crack, slit, vent, notch, groove, channel

2 *a slot in your schedule*
gap, space, time, vacancy, place, opening, spot, position, niche
COLLOQ. window

♦ v

insert, fit, put, install, place, position, assign, pigeonhole

sloth n
laziness, idleness, inactivity, slackness, listlessness, slothfulness, sluggishness, torpor, inertia
FORMAL indolence, acedia, accidie, fainéance
F3 diligence, industriousness; *formal* sedulity

slothful adj
lazy, idle, inactive, inert, slack, listless, sluggish, workshy, torpid, do-nothing
FORMAL indolent, fainéant
COLLOQ. skiving
F3 diligent, industrious; *formal* sedulous

slouch v
stoop, hunch, bend, droop, slump, lounge, mooch, loll, shuffle, shamble

slovenly adj
sloppy, careless, slipshod, untidy, messy, disorganized, scruffy, unclean, dirty, unkempt, slatternly, sluttish
F3 careful, tidy, neat, smart

slow adj, v
♦ adj
1 LEISURELY, unhurried, lingering, loitering, lagging, dawdling, lazy, sluggish, slow-moving, slow-motion, ponderous, creeping, gradual, deliberate, measured, plodding, at a snail's pace, delayed, late
FORMAL tardy, dilatory
2 STUPID, unintelligent, slow-witted, dim, dull, dull-witted, dense, retarded, daft; *Welsh* twp
FORMAL obtuse
COLLOQ. thick, dumb, dopey, slow off the mark, slow on the uptake
3 PROLONGED, time-consuming, protracted, long-drawn-out, tedious, boring, dull, tiresome, wearisome, uninteresting, uneventful
4 QUIET, sleepy, dull, slack, sluggish, stagnant, dead
5 *slow to anger*
unwilling, reluctant, hesitant, averse, disinclined, loath, indisposed
F3 1 fast, quick, swift, rapid, speedy **2** bright, clever, intelligent **3** brief, exciting **4** brisk, lively, exciting

■ **slow down**
1 BRAKE, decelerate, ease up, reduce speed, put the brakes on, delay, hold up, handicap, check, curb, detain, keep/hold back, restrict
FORMAL retard
2 BECOME LESS ACTIVE, relax, do less, take it easy, ease up, calm down
COLLOQ. chill out, hang loose
F3 1 speed, accelerate

SYNONYM NUANCES

adjective sense 1
The term **leisurely** suggests taking your time in a relaxed way, and **unhurried** could describe similarly dilatory action. **Loitering** and **dawdling**, however, are more negative in that they are suggestive of wasting time, and **lagging** also suggests falling behind: *conversation was lagging and everyone wanted to go home*. **Lazy**, on the other hand, although it implies a reluctance to exert oneself, is not necessarily disapproving in tone: *happy, lazy summer days*. **Sluggish** could be used to describe more undesirable inactivity: *the sluggish economy*. **Ponderous** and **plodding** also have more unpleasant implications of a lumbering slowness.
   The terms **creeping** and **gradual** would appropriately describe a slow but stealthy progress: *creeping privatization of the health service*, whereas **deliberate**

and **measured** have vaguely positive connotations of a more careful consideration: *she slowed her words to a more measured pace so we could understand her.*

slowly adv
leisurely, at a leisurely pace, slowly but surely, unhurriedly, gradually, little by little, by degrees, steadily, lazily, ploddingly, ponderously, sluggishly, at a snail's pace
TECHNICAL lento, adagio, largo, larghetto
F3 fast, quickly

sludge n
mud, ooze, mire, muck, residue, sediment, silt, slime, slush, swill, slop, slob, slag, dregs
COLLOQ. gunge, gunk, mudge

sluggish adj
lethargic, listless, torpid, heavy, dull, slow, slow-moving, slothful, languid, lazy, idle, inactive, apathetic, lifeless, unresponsive, phlegmatic
FORMAL languorous, indolent, somnolent
F3 brisk, vigorous, lively, dynamic

sluggishness n
lethargy, listlessness, torpor, phlegm, heaviness, inertia, dullness, slowness, slothfulness, apathy, drowsiness, stagnation, lassitude
FORMAL indolence, languor, somnolence, fainéance
F3 dynamism, eagerness, quickness

sluice n, v
♦ n
1 DRAIN, channel, passage, conduit, outlet, inlet
TECHNICAL penstock
OLD sasse
2 FLOODGATE, lock gate, water gate
♦ v
wash, cleanse, drain, flush, swill, drench, irrigate, slosh, slush

slum n
ghetto, shanty town, hovel, favela; *Can* cabbagetown
OLD rookery
COLLOQ. the wrong side of the tracks

slumber n, v
♦ n
sleep, rest, doze, nap
FORMAL repose
COLLOQ. snooze, forty winks, shut-eye
SLANG kip
♦ v
doze, drowse, nap, rest, sleep
FORMAL repose
COLLOQ. snooze

slummy adj
run-down, squalid, dirty, decayed, seedy, sordid, ramshackle, overcrowded, wretched
COLLOQ. sleazy

slump v, n
♦ v
1 COLLAPSE, fall, go down, decrease, drop, plunge, plummet, sink, subside, nosedive, decline, deteriorate, worsen, crash, fail
COLLOQ. go downhill
2 DROOP, sag, bend, stoop, slouch, loll, lounge, flop
COLLOQ. flump
♦ n
recession, depression, stagnation, devaluation, downturn, slide, low, lowering, trough, downswing, decline, deterioration, worsening, fall, drop, decrease, plunge, collapse, crash, failure
F3 boom, upturn

slur n, v
♦ n
smear, slight, insult, disgrace, discredit, reproach, slander, libel, affront, stain, blot, innuendo, insinuation, stigma
FORMAL aspersion, calumny

♦ *v*
mumble, speak unclearly, splutter, stumble

slush *n*
1 SNOW, melting snow, wet snow
2 SENTIMENTALITY, emotionalism, romanticism, mawkishness, soppiness, sloppiness
COLLOQ. mush, gush, pulp, schmaltz

slut *n*
1 LOOSE WOMAN, hussy, drab, prostitute
OLD pucelle; (*Shakesp*) pussel
COLLOQ. hooker
SLANG tart, floozie, scrubber, slag, skank
OLD SLANG dolly-mop
2 SLATTERN, sloven, trollop, draggle-tail; *dialect* dratchell, drazel, slummock; *Scot* clatch

sly *adj*
wily, foxy, crafty, cunning, artful, guileful, clever, canny, shrewd, smart, astute, knowing, subtle, devious, shifty, tricky, furtive, stealthy, surreptitious, insidious, underhand, covert, secret, secretive, scheming, conniving, mischievous, impish, roguish, peery, sleeky, weaselly; *dialect* carny; *Scot* slee, sleekit
FORMAL clandestine
COLLOQ. sneaky
SLANG fly
E∃ honest, frank, candid, open

■ **on the sly**
in secret, secretly, in private, under cover, privately, stealthily, surreptitiously, underhandedly, furtively, covertly
FORMAL clandestinely
COLLOQ. on the q.t.
E∃ openly

slyly *adv*
cunningly, artfully, cannily, shrewdly, deviously, stealthily, surreptitiously, underhandedly, furtively, covertly
E∃ openly

smack[1] *v, n, adv*
♦ *v*
Do you ever smack your children?
hit, strike, slap, spank, clap, box, thump, punch, bang, crash, thud, clout, cuff, pat, tap
COLLOQ. whack, thwack, belt, wallop, biff, sock, clobber, put over your knee, give a hiding to
♦ *n*
1 BLOW, slap, spank, box, thump, punch, bang, crash, thud, clout, cuff, pat, tap
COLLOQ. whack, thwack, belt, wallop, biff, sock, clobber
SLANG paddy-whack
2 KISS, smacker; *dialect* smouch
♦ *adv*
bang, slap-bang, right, plumb, straight, directly, exactly, precisely

■ **smack your lips**
enjoy, relish, savour, drool over, delight in, anticipate

smack[2] *v, n*
♦ *v*
1 *his attitude smacks of hypocrisy*
suggest, savour of, hint at, give the impression of, intimate, evoke, bring to mind, remind you of
2 SAVOUR, relish, taste, enjoy, delight in, take pleasure in, revel in, like, appreciate
OLD smatch
♦ *n*
1 TASTE, flavour, savour, tang, spice, relish, piquancy, zest; *dialect* tack
OLD smatch
2 SUGGESTION, hint, trace, impression, intimation, tinge, touch, dash, speck, smell, whiff, nuance; *dialect* twang

small *adj*
1 LITTLE, tiny, minute, minuscule, short, slight, puny, petite, diminutive, compact, pocket, cramped, poky, miniature, microscopic, infinitesimal, mini, pocket-sized, young, peewee; *Scot* wee

COLLOQ. pint-size(d), knee-high to a grasshopper, teeny, teensy, teensy-weensy
2 PETTY, trifling, trivial, unimportant, insignificant, minor, inconsiderable, inappreciable, negligible
3 INADEQUATE, insufficient, scanty, meagre, paltry, mean, limited
4 *make you feel small*
humiliated, ashamed, embarrassed, foolish, crushed, broken, deflated, degraded, disgraced, stupid, unimportant, insignificant
E∃ **1** big, large, tall, huge **2** great, major, considerable **3** ample, generous, liberal

┌───┐
SYNONYM NUANCES

sense 1
Little can be widely applied as a synonym of small, although it can have overtones of cuteness: *a little boy*; *a little kitten*. **Tiny** and **minute** would be reserved for something extremely small, with **minute** having the more scientific tone: *minute quantities of uranium*. **Minute** also tends to be used when implying something is not enough: *she poured a minute amount of milk on my cereal*. **Teeny** can be used with a suggestion of amused affection: *she has such teeny hands*.

  Minuscule goes further by suggesting another step down in size, suggesting something hardly visible: *a minuscule particle*, while **microscopic** would be the more scientific term. Likewise, **infinitesimal** is reserved for something immeasurable: *an infinitesimal speck*. **Miniature** and **mini**, while still suggesting something very small, are usually applied to a scaled-down version of something: *a miniature railway*; *a mini disc*; *a mini riot*.

  Short, on the other hand, is more often associated with a lack of height, whereas **slight** suggests a lightness of build. However, this is more flattering than **puny**, which further implies weakness. **Petite** is more complimentary in tone, and suggests a neat, dainty frame.

  Compact suggests convenience and manageability, whereas **cramped** and **poky** obviously have more claustrophobic implications when applied to spaces.
└───┘

small-minded *adj*
petty, mean, ungenerous, illiberal, intolerant, bigoted, narrow-minded, prejudiced, biased, parochial, insular, rigid, hidebound
E∃ liberal, generous, tolerant, broad-minded, open-minded

smallness *n*
small size, littleness, tininess, slightness, compactness, diminutiveness, minuteness
E∃ largeness, bigness

small-time *adj*
unimportant, minor, insignificant, small-scale, petty, piddling, inconsequential, no-account
E∃ important, major, big-time

smarminess *n*
oiliness, servility, sycophancy, toadying, suavity
FORMAL obsequiousness, unctuousness, unctuosity

smarmy *adj*
smooth, oily, servile, sycophantic, bootlicking, suave, toadying, ingratiating, crawling, fawning
FORMAL obsequious, unctuous

smart *adj, v*
♦ *adj*
1 *smart clothes*
elegant, stylish, snappy, chic, fashionable, modish, neat, tidy, spruce, trim, presentable, dapper, well-dressed, well-groomed, well-turned-out
COLLOQ. natty, cool, snazzy, suited and booted
2 CLEVER, intelligent, bright, sharp, acute, shrewd, astute
COLLOQ. on the ball, all there
3 *a smart hotel*
fashionable, elegant, expensive, stylish, chic, modish

COLLOQ. posh, glitzy, ritzy
E≥ 1 dowdy, unfashionable, untidy, scruffy **2** stupid, slow
3 cheap, shabby, down-at-heel
♦ *v*
sting, hurt, prick, burn, nip, ache, tingle, twinge,
throb
■ **smart alec**
know-all, wise guy, wiseacre
COLLOQ. clever clogs, clever dick, smartypants,
smartyboots
SLANG smartarse

smarten *v*
neaten, make neat, tidy (up), make tidy, spruce up, groom,
clean, polish, beautify

smartly *adv*
1 *dress smartly*
stylishly, elegantly, fashionably, neatly, tidily, presentably
COLLOQ. snazzily, nattily
2 *move away smartly*
quickly, promptly, immediately, instantly, directly,
unhesitatingly, speedily, swiftly, rapidly, briskly,
hurriedly, hastily, instantaneously, readily, abruptly,
without further ado
E≥ 1 unfashionably, untidily **2** slowly, later

smash *v, n*
♦ *v*
1 *smash a window*
break, shatter, crack, splinter, disintegrate, shiver, ruin,
wreck, demolish, destroy, dash, defeat, crush; *Scot*
stramash
FORMAL pulverize
2 CRASH, collide, wreck, strike, bang, bump, drive, go, run,
knock, hit, plough, bash, thump
COLLOQ. prang
♦ *n*
1 ACCIDENT, crash, collision, pile-up, bump, wreck
COLLOQ. smash-up, prang
SLANG *Aust* bingle
2 SUCCESS, smash hit, sensation, triumph, winner
COLLOQ. knockout, wow

smashing *adj*
excellent, wonderful, marvellous, superb, tremendous,
great, fantastic, magnificent, sensational, superlative,
stupendous, super, exhilarating, first-class, first-rate
COLLOQ. fabulous, terrific

smattering *n*
bit, modicum, dash, sprinkling, basics, rudiments,
elements
OLD smatch

smear *v, n*
♦ *v*
1 DAUB, plaster, spread, cover, slap, coat, rub, smudge,
mire, streak
2 SULLY, blacken, stain, tarnish, slur, taint
FORMAL defame, malign, vilify, calumniate
COLLOQ. drag someone's name through the mud; *N Am*
badmouth
♦ *n*
1 STREAK, smudge, blot, spot, patch, blotch, splodge,
splotch, daub
2 *a smear campaign against a politician*
taint, slur, stain, false report, slander, libel
FORMAL defamation, aspersion, vilification, obloquy
COLLOQ. mudslinging, muck-raking

smell
Related adjective: olfactory

Words used for types of smell include:

PLEASANT:	nose	scent
aroma	odour	
bouquet	pot pourri	UNPLEASANT:
fragrance	perfume	b.o. (body odour)
incense	redolence	fetor

N Am funk	niff	stench
hum	pong	stink
malodour	pungency	whiff
mephitis	reek	
miasma	sniff	

---

smelly *adj*
stinking, reeking, foul, foul-smelling, bad, off, putrid, high,
strong-smelling
FORMAL malodorous, f(o)etid, mephitic, noisome
COLLOQ. pongy, humming; *Scot* mingin
SLANG honking

smile *v, n*
♦ *v*
grin, beam, simper, smirk, leer, sneer, laugh, chuckle,
giggle, snigger, titter
♦ *n*
grin, beam, simper, smirk, leer, sneer, laugh, chuckle,
giggle, snigger, titter
COLLOQ. someone's face lights up, be all smiles

> **QUOTATIONS**
> A smile is often the key thing. One is paid with a smile.
> One is rewarded with a smile. One is brightened by a
> smile. And the quality of a smile can make one die
> ANTOINE DE SAINT-EXUPÉRY, *Lettre à un otage*

> **SYNONYM NUANCES**
> *verb*
> You can use **grin** to suggest the wideness of a smile,
> while **beam** suggests brightness and underlying
> enthusiasm. **Simper**, on the other hand, is a pejorative
> term, and implies affectation or weakness, whereas
> **smirk** carries a negative suggestion of smugness: *he
> smirked in triumph*, and **sneer** is strongly associated
> with contempt: *he sneered at her bookish tastes*. **Leer**,
> however, would be reserved for smiling lecherously.

smirk *v, n*
grin, sneer, snigger, leer, simper

smitten *adj*
obsessed, bewitched, beguiled, charmed, attracted,
enthusiastic, captivated, infatuated, enamoured, afflicted,
plagued, struck, troubled, burdened, beset
COLLOQ. bowled over

smog *n*
fog, pea-souper, smoke, pollution, exhaust, fumes, haze,
mist, vapour

smoke *n, v*
♦ *n*
fumes, exhaust, gas, vapour, mist, fog, smog
♦ *v*
fume, draw (on), puff (on), light up, smoulder, preserve,
cure, dry

> **PROVERBS**
> There's no smoke without fire

smoky *adj*
sooty, black, grey, dark, grimy, murky, cloudy, hazy,
foggy, smoggy, smudgy, reechy, reeky, fuggy, peaty

smooch *v*
cuddle, hug, embrace, clasp, hold, enfold, nurse, nestle,
snuggle, pet, fondle, caress
COLLOQ. snog, canoodle, neck

smooth *adj, v*
♦ *adj*
1 LEVEL, plane, even, flat, horizontal, flush
2 *a smooth sauce*
even, creamy, velvety, rich, thick
3 *a smooth wine*
full-flavoured, mellow, sweet, mature, soft, mild

4 STEADY, even, unbroken, uninterrupted, continuous, flowing, regular, uniform, rhythmic, easy, simple, straightforward, effortless, problem-free, trouble-free
COLLOQ. plain sailing
5 SHINY, polished, burnished, glossy, silky, silken, velvety, sleek, like a mirror, glassy
6 CALM, still, undisturbed, serene, tranquil, peaceful
7 SUAVE, agreeable, smooth-talking, urbane, sophisticated, over-confident, glib, plausible, persuasive, slick, ingratiating, crawling, fawning
FORMAL unctuous
COLLOQ. smarmy
🔁 **1** rough, coarse **2** lumpy **3** sharp, bitter **4** troublesome, irregular, erratic, unsteady **6** bumpy, rough, choppy
◆ v
1 IRON, press (down), roll, flatten, plaster (down), slick, rub down, level, plane, even (out), file, sand, grind, polish
2 EASE, alleviate, pacify, soothe, allay, calm (down), palliate, mollify
FORMAL assuage, mitigate, appease
3 *smooth the way*
make easier, facilitate, ease, help, assist, aid, encourage, clear the way for
🔁 **1** roughen, wrinkle, crease

smoothly adv
evenly, calmly, steadily, soothingly, peacefully, tranquilly, serenely, pleasantly, mildly, easily, effortlessly, equably, fluently

smoothness n
1 LEVELNESS, evenness, flatness
2 STEADINESS, evenness, flow, regularity, rhythm, unbrokenness, ease, efficiency, effortlessness, facility, fluency, finish
3 SHINE, polish, silkiness, velvetiness, sleekness, glassiness, serenity, calmness, stillness, softness
🔁 **1** roughness, coarseness

smooth-talking adj
persuasive, plausible, slick, suave, silver-tongued, facile, glib, bland
COLLOQ. smooth

smother v
suffocate, asphyxiate, strangle, throttle, choke, stifle, put out, extinguish, snuff, smoulder, damp (down), dampen, muffle, inundate, overwhelm, overlie, suppress, repress, keep back, hide, conceal, cover, shroud, cocoon, envelop, surround, wrap; Scot smore
OLD oppress

smoulder v
burn, smoke, fume, rage, foam, boil, seethe, fester, simmer

smudge n, v
◆ n
(dirty) mark, blot, blotch, stain, spot, blemish, blur, smear, streak, smutch
◆ v
blur, smear, streak, daub, mark, spot, stain, dirty, make dirty, soil, blacken, besmirch

smug adj
complacent, self-satisfied, superior, smirking, holier-than-thou, self-righteous, pleased with yourself, priggish, conceited
FORMAL unctuous
🔁 humble, modest

smuggler n
runner, contrabandist, moonshiner, free-trader, courier
OLD owler
COLLOQ. bootlegger, mule

smutty adj
dirty, crude, coarse, rude, filthy, indecent, improper, indelicate, obscene, pornographic, risqué, racy, bawdy, suggestive, vulgar, gross, lewd, salacious, ribald
FORMAL prurient
COLLOQ. blue, off colour, raunchy, sleazy
🔁 clean, decent

snack n
refreshment(s), light meal, sandwich, bite, nibble(s), titbit, buffet, bar lunch/meal, snap, snatch, nacket, supper, hors d'œuvre, appetizer, tapas, meze, zakuska; dialect bever, butty; Scot chack; N Am gorp
OLD lunch
COLLOQ. elevenses, fours, bite to eat, pick-me-up

snaffle v
grab, seize, steal, make off with, take, take/get hold of, pluck, pull, wrench, wrest, gain, win, clutch, pounce on, grasp, grip, secure
COLLOQ. nab, swipe, bag, collar, nail

snag n, v
◆ n
disadvantage, inconvenience, drawback, catch, problem, difficulty, complication, setback, hitch, obstacle, stumbling-block
◆ v
catch, rip, tear, hole, ladder

snake n, v
◆ n
serpent, naga
OLD worm
TECHNICAL ophidian
SLANG Aust Joe Blake
Related adjective: anguine, ophidian, serpentine
◆ v
wind, curve, bend, loop, spiral, zigzag, twine, deviate, meander, ramble

Types of snake include:

adder	diamondback	pipe snake
anaconda	diamond python	pit viper
asp	dipsas	puff adder
bandy-bandy	dugite	python
black snake	file snake	racer
blind snake	flying snake	rat snake
boa	gaboon snake	rattlesnake
boomslang	garter-snake	ribbon snake
brown snake	gopher snake	ringhals
bull snake	grass snake	ring snake
bushmaster	green snake	rock snake
carpet snake	hamadryad	sand snake
coachwhip	hognose	sea snake
cobra	hoop-snake	sidewinder
colubrid	indigo snake	smooth snake
constrictor	jararaca	taipan
copperhead	king snake	tiger snake
coral snake	krait	tree snake
corn snake	langaha	viper
cottonmouth	mamba	water moccasin
cylinder snake	massasauga	water snake
death adder	milk snake	whip snake
dendrophis	pine snake	worm snake

snap v, n, adj
◆ v
1 *the twig snapped*
break, crack, split, splinter, fracture, separate, crackle, chop, give way, collapse, knap
FORMAL crepitate
2 CLICK, clink, snip, snick, tick, gnash
3 BITE, nip, bark, growl, snarl, retort, crackle; dialect snack; Scot hanch
4 SNATCH, seize, catch, grasp, grip
OLD snip
5 SPEAK ANGRILY TO, growl at, snarl at, lash out at, bark at, speak sharply/brusquely to
COLLOQ. jump down someone's throat
6 PHOTOGRAPH, take, film, shoot, record
◆ n
1 BREAK, crack, bite, nip, flick, fillip, crackle; Scot snack
2 CLICK, clink, snip, snick, tick, crackle, gnash

3 *a cold snap*
spell, period, time, stretch, span, stint
4 PHOTOGRAPH, photo, snapshot, print, shot, still, picture
♦ *adj*
sudden, immediate, instant, on-the-spot, abrupt
■ **snap up**
grab, grasp, seize, snatch, pounce on, buy quickly, pick up, pluck
COLLOQ. nab

snappy *adj*
1 SMART, stylish, chic, elegant, fashionable, up-to-date, up-to-the-minute, modish
COLLOQ. trendy, snazzy, natty
2 QUICK, hasty, brisk, lively, energetic
3 CROSS, irritable, brusque, bad-tempered, quick-tempered, short-tempered, ill-tempered, ill-natured, irascible, testy
COLLOQ. ratty, grouchy, stroppy, edgy, crabby, crabbed, touchy, crotchety
E3 1 dowdy **2** slow
■ **make it snappy**
hurry up
COLLOQ. get cracking, step on it, go all out, pull your finger out, shake a leg, buck up, come along, jump to it, look lively, look sharp, get your skates on

snare *v, n*
♦ *v*
trap, ensnare, entrap, catch, capture, seize, net
♦ *n*
trap, wire, net, noose, gin, springe, catch, pitfall

snarl¹ *v*
the dog snarled
growl, show your teeth, snap, bark, howl, yelp, lash out at, grumble, complain

snarl² *v*
the rope was snarled in the bushes
tangle, knot, ravel, twist, entangle, enmesh, entwine, embroil, confuse, muddle, jumble, complicate

snarl-up *n*
muddle, tangle, mess, mix-up, jumble, confusion, entanglement, traffic jam, gridlock

snatch *v, n*
♦ *v*
grab, seize, steal, kidnap, abduct, take as hostage, make off with, take, take/get hold of, pluck, pull, wrench, wrest, gain, win, clutch, pounce on, grasp, grip, secure
COLLOQ. nab, swipe, bag, collar, nail
♦ *n*
part, piece, bit, section, segment, fraction, fragment, smattering, snippet, spell

snazzy *adj*
stylish, showy, fashionable, smart, attractive, flamboyant, raffish, sporty, dashing, sophisticated
COLLOQ. flashy, jazzy, ritzy, snappy, swinging, with it
E3 drab, unfashionable

sneak *v, n, adj*
♦ *v*
1 CREEP, steal, slip, slink, sidle, slide, skulk, pad, lurk, prowl, snook, smuggle, spirit
OLD (*Shakesp*) peak
2 TELL TALES, inform on
COLLOQ. split, squeal, snitch, blow the whistle on, rat
SLANG shop, grass on; *N Am* stool on
♦ *n*
tell-tale, informer, stool pigeon
COLLOQ. squealer, mole, rat, whistle-blower
SLANG grass; *N Am* stoolie
♦ *adj*
secret, surprise, quick, covert, furtive, stealthy, surreptitious
FORMAL clandestine

sneaking *adj*
private, secret, furtive, surreptitious, hidden, lurking, suppressed, unvoiced, unexpressed, grudging, nagging, niggling, persistent, worrying, uncomfortable, intuitive

sneaky *adj*
shady, shifty, furtive, dishonest, devious, guileful, deceitful, unethical, unreliable, unscrupulous, untrustworthy, sly, snide, double-dealing, base, contemptible, cowardly, nasty, mean, low, low-down, malicious
FORMAL disingenuous
COLLOQ. slippery
E3 honest, open; *colloq.* up front

sneer *v, n*
♦ *v*
scorn, disdain, look down on, scoff, jeer, mock, ridicule, deride, insult, taunt, slight, gibe, laugh, snigger, snicker, smirk, twitch, curl your lips
♦ *n*
scorn, disdain, derision, jeer, mockery, ridicule, insult, taunt, barb, slight, gibe, snigger, snicker, smirk

snicker *v, n*
snigger, laugh, giggle, titter, chuckle, chortle, sneer

snide *adj*
derogatory, sarcastic, cynical, scornful, sneering, hurtful, mocking, taunting, jeering, scoffing, derisive, scathing, biting, caustic, unkind, nasty, mean, spiteful, malicious, ill-natured
FORMAL disparaging
COLLOQ. snarky
E3 complimentary

sniff *v, n*
♦ *v*
1 BREATHE, inhale, snuff, snuffle, snivel, snift, vent
2 SMELL, nose, scent, whiff, get a whiff of
♦ *n*
1 SNIFFLE, snivel, snuff, snuffle
2 SMELL, scent, whiff, aroma
3 HINT, whiff, suggestion, trace, impression, intimation
■ **sniff at**
look down on, disdain, sneer at, scoff at, scorn, mock, laugh at, slight, spurn, refuse, shun, reject, dismiss, disregard, overlook
FORMAL deride, disparage
E3 admire, respect

sniffy *adj*
snobbish, snobby, contemptuous, scoffing, sneering, scornful, condescending, superior, supercilious, disdainful, haughty

snigger *v, n*
snicker, laugh, giggle, titter, chuckle, chortle, sneer, smirk

snip *v, n*
♦ *v*
cut, clip, trim, crop, dock, prune, slit, nick, snick, notch, incise
♦ *n*
1 CUT, clip, trim, crop, prune, slit, clipping
2 BIT, fragment, piece, scrap, shred, snippet
3 BARGAIN, giveaway, special offer, good buy, discount, reduction, value for money
COLLOQ. steal

sniper *n*
guerrilla, freedom fighter, terrorist, irregular, resistance fighter, partisan, bushwhacker, *franc-tireur*, guerrillero, haiduk

snippet *n*
piece, scrap, bit, cutting, clipping, fragment, particle, shred, snatch, part, portion, segment, section

snivel *v*
cry, weep, bawl, sniff, sniffle, snuffle, sob, whimper, grizzle, moan, whinge, whine colloq. blub, blubber,

snivelling *adj*
crying, weeping, sniffling, snuffling, blubbering, whimpering, grizzling, moaning, whingeing, whining

snob *n*
élitist, social climber, swank, parvenu
COLLOQ. bighead, high-hat

snobbery *n*
snobbishness, superciliousness, airs, loftiness, arrogance, haughtiness, pride, pretension, pretentiousness, condescension, superiority, disdain, airs and graces
COLLOQ. snootiness, uppishness, side

snobbish *adj*
supercilious, disdainful, proud, haughty, snobby, superior, lofty, arrogant, pretentious, affected, condescending, patronizing
COLLOQ. snooty, stuck-up, toffee-nosed, uppity, jumped-up, hoity-toity, too big for your boots, high and mighty

snog *v*
cuddle, hug, embrace, clasp, hold, enfold, nurse, nestle, snuggle, pet, fondle, caress
COLLOQ. smooch, canoodle, neck

snoop *v, n*
♦ *v*
spy, sneak, pry, nose, interfere, meddle
COLLOQ. poke/stick your nose in, stick/put your oar in
♦ *n*
1 *have a snoop around*
sneak, pry, nose, interference, meddling
2 SNOOPER, spy, busybody, pry, meddler
COLLOQ. Nosey Parker, Paul Pry

snooper *n*
snoop, spy, busybody, pry, meddler, eavesdropper
COLLOQ. Nosey Parker, Paul Pry

snooty *adj*
supercilious, disdainful, proud, haughty, snobbish, snobby, superior, lofty, arrogant, pretentious, affected, condescending, patronizing
COLLOQ. stuck-up, toffee-nosed, uppity, jumped-up, hoity-toity, too big for your boots, high and mighty

snooze *v, n*
♦ *v*
nap, drop off, catnap, doze, sleep
OLD slumber
COLLOQ. have forty winks, nod off
SLANG kip
♦ *n*
nap, catnap, doze, siesta, sleep
OLD slumber
FORMAL repose
COLLOQ. forty winks, shut-eye
SLANG kip

snout *n*
nose, muzzle, neb, trunk
FORMAL proboscis
COLLOQ. schnozzle, snitch

snow *n*
snowfall, snowstorm, snowflakes, snowdrift, blizzard, snow flurries, sleet, slush, ice
Related adjective: niveous

> **QUOTATIONS**
> In the bleak mid-winter / Frosty wind made moan, / Earth stood hard as iron, / Water like a stone; / Snow had fallen, snow on snow, / Snow on snow, / In the bleak mid-winter, / Long ago
> CHRISTINA GEORGINA ROSSETTI, 'Mid-winter'

snub *v, n*
♦ *v*
rebuff, shun, spurn, insult, disregard, ignore, brush off, cut, slight, rebuke, put down, squash, humble, shame, humiliate, mortify, squelch, sneap; *Scot* snool
OLD frump, sneb, snib
FORMAL affront
COLLOQ. cold-shoulder, give the cold shoulder to, slap in the face, kick in the teeth, blank, give the heave-ho

♦ *n*
rebuff, brush-off, slight, affront, insult, rebuke, put-down, humiliation, slap, set-down, down-setting, sneap;
Scot sloan
OLD frump, snib
COLLOQ. slap in the face, kick in the teeth, cold shoulder, heave-ho

snuff
■ **snuff out**
1 *snuff out a candle*
put out, blow out, stifle, smother, choke, douse, quench, dampen down
2 CRUSH, eliminate, destroy, eradicate, erase, abolish, remove, end, suppress

snug *adj*
cosy, warm, comfortable, homely, friendly, intimate, sheltered, secure, tight, skintight, close-fitting, figure-hugging; *Scot* snod
COLLOQ. comfy, snug as a bug in a rug

snuggle *v*
nestle, nuzzle, curl up, cuddle, embrace, hug
COLLOQ. *N Am* cozy up

snugly *adv*
warmly, cosily, comfortably, securely, tightly

soak *v*
wet, drench, saturate, penetrate, permeate, infuse, bathe, marinate, souse, steep, submerge, immerse, mop, absorb, sop, sog, sponge, macerate, seethe, imbue, ret;
dialect sipe
TECHNICAL *dialect* buck

soaking *adj*
soaked, soaked to the skin, wet through, drenched, sodden, waterlogged, saturated, sopping, sopping wet, wringing, dripping, streaming
F3 dry

soar *v*
1 *the bird soared up into the air*
fly (up), wing, glide, plane, tower, rise, take off, ascend
2 *temperatures soared*
climb, mount, increase quickly, escalate, spiral, rocket, skyrocket
F3 **1** fall, descend **2** decrease, plummet

sob *v*
cry, weep, shed tears, bawl, howl, blubber, snivel
COLLOQ. boohoo, turn on the waterworks

sober *adj, v*
♦ *adj*
1 TEETOTAL, temperate, moderate, abstinent, abstemious, clear-headed
COLLOQ. sober as a judge, dry, drying out, stone-cold sober, on the wagon, off the bottle, having taken/signed the pledge
2 SOLEMN, dignified, serious, earnest, grave, thoughtful, staid, steady, sedate, quiet, serene, calm, composed, unruffled, unexcited, cool, dispassionate, level-headed, practical, realistic, reasonable, rational, clear-headed, self-controlled
3 *sober dress*
sombre, staid, drab, demure, dull, dark, plain, severe, austere, subdued, restrained
F3 **1** drunk, intemperate **2** frivolous, excited, unrealistic, irrational **3** flashy, garish
■ **sober up**
clear your head
COLLOQ. dry out, sleep it off

sobriety *n*
1 ABSTEMIOUSNESS, soberness, abstinence, moderation, temperance, teetotalism
2 SOLEMNITY, seriousness, staidness, steadiness, calmness, composure, level-headedness, coolness, sedateness, restraint, self-restraint, gravity
F3 **1** drunkenness **2** excitement, frivolity

sobriquet, soubriquet *n*
name, title, designation, label, tag, style, term, epithet, nickname
FORMAL appellation, denomination, cognomen
COLLOQ. handle
SLANG monicker

so-called *adj*
alleged, supposed, ostensible, nominal, self-styled, professed, would-be, pretended, soi-disant
FORMAL purported

sociability *n*
friendliness, companionability, congeniality, conviviality, cordiality, affability, neighbourliness, gregariousness
COLLOQ. chumminess

sociable *adj*
friendly, outgoing, gregarious, affable, companionable, genial, convivial, cordial, warm, hospitable, neighbourly, approachable, accessible, familiar, clubbable, extrovert, conversable; *N Am* folksy
COLLOQ. chummy, mat(e)y
F3 unsociable, withdrawn, unfriendly, hostile

> ⚠ **sociable** or **social**?
> *Sociable* is usually applied to people and means 'friendly, fond of the company of others': *Our new neighbours aren't very sociable; He's a cheerful, sociable sort of bloke. Social* means 'of or concerning society': *Problems such as this are social rather than medical in origin; social class. Social* also means 'concerning the gathering together or meeting of people for recreation and amusement': *a social club; His reasons for calling round were purely social.*

social *adj, n*
♦ *adj*
1 *social policies*
communal, public, community, civic, common, general, collective, group, organized
2 *social activities*
leisure, recreational, entertainment, amusement
♦ *n*
party, get-together, gathering, function, dance, at-home
COLLOQ. do, bash, blow-out, knees-up, rave-up, thrash

> ⚠ **social** or **sociable**?
> *See panel at* **sociable**.

socialism *n*
leftism, communism, welfarism, Leninism, Marxism, Stalinism, Trotskyism

socialist *adj, n*
♦ *adj*
left-wing, leftist, hard-left, communist, Trotskyist, Trotskyite
COLLOQ. commie, leftie, red, Trot
♦ *n*
left-winger, leftist, communist, welfarist, Trotskyist, Trotskyite
COLLOQ. commie, leftie, red, pink, pinko, Trot

socialize *v*
mix, mingle, be sociable, meet people, meet socially, fraternize, converse, get together, go out, entertain
COLLOQ. hobnob

society *n*
1 COMMUNITY, population, culture, civilization, nation, public, people, mankind, humanity, human race, humankind
2 CLUB, circle, group, band, body, association, organization, company, corporation, federation, alliance, league, union, guild, fellowship, fraternity, brotherhood, sisterhood, sorority
3 FRIENDSHIP, companionship, camaraderie, fellowship, company

4 UPPER CLASSES, high society, polite society, aristocracy, gentry, nobility, élite
COLLOQ. nobs, toffs, swells, top drawer, the smart set, the upper crust, Sloane Rangers

sodden *adj*
wet, soaking, soaked, drenched, saturated, sopping, waterlogged, soggy, marshy, boggy, miry; *Scot* drookit
F3 dry

sofa *n*
settee, couch, chesterfield, davenport, lounge, canapé, day-bed, bed-settee, futon, dos-à-dos, squab, tête-à-tête, bergère

soft *adj*
1 YIELDING, pliable, flexible, pliant, elastic, springy, plastic, supple, malleable, tender, spongy, squashy, mushy, squelchy, pulpy
FORMAL ductile
COLLOQ. squishy
2 *soft colours; speak in a soft voice*
pale, light, pastel, delicate, subdued, shaded, muted, restrained, quiet, low, low-key, whispered, hushed, dim, faint, diffuse, mild, bland, gentle, flowing, soothing, sweet, mellow, melodious, dulcet, pleasant
FORMAL mellifluous
3 FURRY, downy, fleecy, velvety, silky, silken, smooth
4 LENIENT, lax, easy-going, liberal, permissive, indulgent, tolerant, forgiving, forbearing, weak
COLLOQ. spineless
5 TENDER, kind, generous, sympathetic, affectionate, gentle, mild, merciful, soft-hearted, sensitive
6 *a soft life*
easy, comfortable, easy-going, luxurious, successful, prosperous
COLLOQ. cushy, a bed of roses, all beer and skittles
F3 **1** hard, firm **2** harsh, hard, sharp, bright, loud **3** rough, abrasive **4** hard, strict, severe **5** unsympathetic, cruel **6** hard
■ **soft in the head**
foolish, stupid, unintelligent, unwise, senseless, childish, puerile, immature, irresponsible
COLLOQ. daft, dotty, loopy, barmy, potty, nutty
■ **soft spot**
fondness, liking, partiality, weakness
FORMAL penchant, proclivity

soften *v*
1 MODERATE, temper, lessen, diminish, alleviate, ease, cushion, soothe, palliate, quell, subdue, mollify, appease, calm (down), still, relax
FORMAL abate, mitigate, assuage
2 MELT, liquefy, dissolve, reduce
3 CUSHION, pad, muffle, quicken, lower, lighten
■ **soften up**
persuade, conciliate, disarm, win over, weaken, melt
COLLOQ. butter up, soft-soap

soft-hearted *adj*
sympathetic, compassionate, gentle, kind, benevolent, charitable, generous, warm-hearted, tender, tender-hearted, affectionate, sentimental
F3 hard-hearted, callous

softly-softly *adj*
cautious, restrained, low-key, diplomatic, patient, tentative, indirect
FORMAL circumspect
F3 aggressive, direct, assertive

soft-pedal *v*
moderate, minimize, go easy, play down, subdue, tone down
F3 highlight, emphasize

soggy *adj*
wet, damp, moist, soaked, soaking, drenched, sodden, waterlogged, marshy, swampy, saturated, sopping, sopping wet, dripping, heavy, boggy, spongy, pulpy

soil[1] n

1 EARTH, clay, loam, humus, dirt, dust, ground
Related adjective: edaphic
2 LAND, region, country, territory
FORMAL terra firma

soil[2] v

1 DIRTY, begrime, stain, spot, smudge, smear, foul, bespatter, muddy, pollute, defile
2 *soil your reputation*
stain, smear, sully, tarnish, damage, defile
OLD besmirch

soiled adj

dirty, grimy, stained, spotted, sullied, polluted, tarnished
FORMAL maculate
COLLOQ. manky
E3 clean, immaculate

sojourn n, v

♦ *n*
stay, rest, visit, stop, stopover
FORMAL peregrination
♦ *v*
lodge, rest, stay, stop
FORMAL dwell, reside, abide, tarry, tabernacle

solace n, v

♦ *n*
comfort, consolation, relief, alleviation, support, condolence, cheer
FORMAL succour
♦ *v*
comfort, console, support, allay, alleviate, soften, soothe
FORMAL mitigate, succour

soldier

Related adjective: military
■ **soldier on**
continue, persevere, keep on, keep going, remain, hold on, hang on
COLLOQ. keep at it, stick at it, hang in there, plug away

Types of soldier include:

cadet	gunner	private
cavalryman	hussar	recruit
centurion	infantryman	regular
commando	lancer	rifleman
conscript	legionnaire	sapper
dragoon	marine	sentry
ensign	mercenary	serviceman
fighter	NCO	Territorial
fusilier	officer	*colloq.* terrier
N Am GI	orderly	tommy
guardsman	paratrooper	trooper
guerrilla	partisan	warrior

See also **rank**[1] .

sole adj

only, unique, exclusive, individual, single, singular, one, lone, solitary, alone
E3 shared, multiple

solecism n

error, mistake, blunder, lapse, gaucherie, impropriety, absurdity, faux pas
TECHNICAL anacoluthon
FORMAL cacology, incongruity, indecorum
COLLOQ. boob, booboo, howler, gaffe

solely adv

exclusively, only, singly, uniquely, merely, simply, just, completely, entirely, alone, single-handedly

solemn adj

1 *a solemn expression*
serious, grave, sober, sedate, sombre, glum, thoughtful, earnest, formal, awed, reverential, devout, pious
COLLOQ. po-faced
2 GRAND, stately, majestic, ceremonial, ritual, formal, ceremonious, pompous, dignified, august, venerable, awe-inspiring, impressive, imposing, momentous
3 *a solemn promise*
sincere, formal, earnest, genuine, wholehearted, committed, honest
E3 1 light-hearted **2** frivolous

solemnity n

1 SERIOUSNESS, earnestness, gravity, sacredness, sanctity, momentousness, dignity, impressiveness, grandeur, stateliness
FORMAL portentousness
2 CEREMONY, celebration, observance, rite, ritual, ceremonial, proceedings, formality
E3 1 frivolity

solemnize v

keep, honour, observe, commemorate, celebrate, perform, dignify

solemnly adv

seriously, gravely, soberly, earnestly, formally, in a dignified manner
E3 frivolously, light-heartedly

solicit v

1 *solicit advice*
ask (for), request, crave, beg, implore, plead, pray, apply (for), petition, canvass, woo, court;
N Am drum
OLD beseech
FORMAL seek, entreat, supplicate, sue, importune
COLLOQ. tout
2 *solicit as a prostitute*
accost, importune, proposition
SLANG hustle, bash

solicitor n

lawyer, advocate, attorney, barrister, QC, commissioner of oaths, recorder, barrister; *Scot* crown agent, law agent

solicitous adj

caring, attentive, considerate, concerned, anxious, worried, apprehensive, uneasy, troubled, eager, earnest, zealous

solicitude n

care, concern, attentiveness, considerateness, consideration, regard, worry, anxiety, uneasiness, disquiet, trouble

solid adj

1 HARD, firm, dense, thick, compact, compressed, strong, concrete, sturdy, substantial, stable, sound, well-built, durable, long-lasting, unshak(e)able
2 RELIABLE, dependable, trusty, trustworthy, worthy, decent, upstanding, upright, sensible, level-headed, steadfast, stable, serious, sober, respectable
3 *solid evidence*
reliable, sound, valid, strong, firm, authoritative, weighty, well-grounded, well-founded
FORMAL cogent
4 REAL, genuine, pure, concrete, tangible, unadulterated, unmixed, unalloyed
5 *a solid white line*
unbroken, continuous, undivided, uninterrupted
E3 1 liquid, gaseous, hollow **2** unreliable, unstable
3 unsound, unreliable **4** unreal **5** broken, dotted

solidarity n

unity, agreement, accord, unanimity, consensus, harmony, concord, cohesion, like-mindedness, single-mindedness, camaraderie, team spirit, *esprit de corps*, soundness, stability
E3 discord, division, schism

solidify v

harden, go/become hard, set, gel, jell, congeal, coagulate, clot, cake, crystallize
E3 soften, liquefy, dissolve

soliloquy *n*
monologue, speech, lecture, sermon, address, oration, homily
🔁 conversation, dialogue, discussion

solitary *adj, n*
♦ *adj*
1 LONELY, sole, single, lone, alone, lonesome, by yourself, friendless, companionless, unsociable, introverted, recluse, reclusive, hermitical, withdrawn, retired, monasterial
OLD dernful
2 REMOTE, lonely, separate, isolated, desolate, out-of-the-way, inaccessible, cloistered, secluded, unfrequented, unvisited, untrodden
FORMAL sequestered
COLLOQ. off the beaten track
🔁 **1** accompanied, gregarious, busy **2** accessible
♦ *n*
loner, individualist, hermit, recluse, ascetic, monk, anchorite, anchoress, ancress, eremite, stylite
COLLOQ. lone wolf; *Aust & NZ* Jimmy Woodser

solitude *n*
aloneness, loneliness, singleness, friendlessness, lonesomeness, introversion, unsociability, reclusiveness, retirement, privacy, seclusion, isolation, remoteness, desolation
🔁 companionship

solo *adj*
unaccompanied, alone, unescorted, unattended, by yourself, on your own, lone, single, single-handed
🔁 accompanied

solution *n*
1 ANSWER, result, explanation, resolution, key, remedy, way out, panacea, cure-all, clarification, decipherment, disentanglement, unfolding, unravelling
FORMAL elucidation
COLLOQ. (quick) fix
2 MIXTURE, blend, mix, compound, suspension, emulsion, liquid, solvent

solve *v*
work out, figure out, puzzle out, decipher, read, resolve, crack, disentangle, unravel, unfold, answer, put right, remedy, settle, clear up, clarify, explain, interpret, think out, riddle, unriddle, undo, untie, guess, get to the bottom of; *N Am* work, solution
OLD assoil; *(Spenser)* loose
FORMAL rectify, expound
COLLOQ. fathom

solvent *adj*
sound, financially sound, able to pay, creditworthy, out of debt, unindebted
COLLOQ. in the black
🔁 insolvent

sombre *adj*
1 SAD, serious, solemn, grave, melancholy, mournful, depressed, doleful, morose, joyless, sober
FORMAL lugubrious
2 *sombre colours*
dark, dull, gloomy, funereal, drab, dim, obscure, shady, shadowy, dismal, dingy
🔁 **1** happy, cheerful **2** bright, cheerful

somebody *n*
someone, celebrity, dignitary, name, personage, star, superstar, VIP, notable, luminary, magnate, mogul, heavyweight, nabob, panjandrum
COLLOQ. household name, bigwig, big noise, big shot, big wheel
🔁 nobody

someday *adv*
sometime, at some time in the future, one day, one of these (fine) days, sooner or later, later, later on, in due course, by and by, eventually, ultimately
🔁 never

somehow *adv*
by some means, one way or another, come what may
COLLOQ. by fair means or foul, by hook or by crook, come hell or high water

sometime *adv, adj*
♦ *adv*
someday, one day, at some time in the future, at some time in the past, another time, in the past, then, previously, earlier
♦ *adj*
former, previous, one-time, late, retired, emeritus
FORMAL erstwhile, quondam
COLLOQ. ex

sometimes *adv*
occasionally, on occasion(s), now and again, now and then, on and off, off and on, every so often, once in a while, at times, from time to time
🔁 always, never

somewhat *adv*
rather, moderately, relatively, slightly, a bit, a little, fairly, quite, to a limited degree/extent, to some degree/extent, pretty
COLLOQ. kind of, sort of

somnolent *adj*
sleepy, drowsy, dozy, half-awake, heavy-eyed, soporific, torpid
TECHNICAL comatose
FORMAL oscitant

son *n*
boy, child, lad(die), offspring, descendant, inhabitant, disciple
Related adjective: filial

song
■ **song and dance**
commotion, stir, fuss, bother, ado, to-do, tumult, furore, performance
COLLOQ. flap, hoo-ha, kerfuffle, pother, tizzy

Types of song include:

air	descant	penillion-singing
amoret	dirge	plainchant
anthem	dithyramb	plainsong
aria	ditty	pop song
art-song	elegy	power ballad
ballad	epinikion	psalm
barcarole	epithalamium	pub song
birdcall	folk song	recitative
birdsong	gospel song	refrain
blues	hymn	requiem
bothy ballad	jingle	rock and roll
calypso	lay	rock song
cantata	lied	roundelay
canticle	lilt	serenade
cantilena	love-song	shanty
canzone	lullaby	spiritual
canzonet	lyric(s)	threnody
carol	madrigal	torch song
catch	melody	tune
chanson	Negro spiritual	war song
chansonette	number	wassail
chant	nursery rhyme	yodel
chorus	ode	

See also **poem**.

songster *n*
singer, vocalist, chorister, balladeer, chanteuse, soloist, minstrel, troubadour, crooner, warbler

sonorous *adj*
resonant, resounding, ringing, rich, rounded, orotund, ororotund, full, full-mouthed, full-voiced, full-throated, loud, sounding, high-flown, high-sounding
FORMAL grandiloquent, plangent

soon adv

shortly, presently, in a little while, in no time (at all), in a short time, in a minute, in a moment (or two), any minute (now), just now, early, without delay, in a hurry, before long, in the near future

OLD anon, betimes, ere long, timely

COLLOQ. quick, pronto, in a jiffy, in a tick, in two shakes of a lamb's tail, before you can say Jack Robinson, (just) round the corner

■ **as soon as**

directly after, immediately after, once, when, no sooner ... than, right after, in the wake of

OLD eftsoons

sooner adv

1 EARLIER, before, in advance, beforehand

2 RATHER, preferably, much rather, instead, by/for preference, by/for/from choice

■ **sooner or later**

eventually, finally, ultimately, at last, in the end, at length, subsequently, after all, in the long run, in due course, in the fullness of time

COLLOQ. at the end of the day, when all is said and done, in the final analysis

■ **no sooner than**

scarcely, hardly, barely, only just

soothe v

alleviate, relieve, ease, salve, comfort, allay, calm (down), compose, tranquillize, settle (down), still, quiet, quieten (down), hush, lull, pacify, mollify, soften, palliate, temper

FORMAL appease, assuage, mitigate

■ aggravate, irritate, annoy, vex

soothing adj

relaxing, restful, calming, easeful, emollient, lenitive, balmy, palliative, balsamic

TECHNICAL anetic

FORMAL assuasive, demulcent

■ annoying, irritating, vexing

soothsayer n

prophet, prophetess, diviner, foreteller, seer, sibyl, augur

OLD Chaldaic

FORMAL haruspex

sophisticated adj

1 URBANE, cosmopolitan, worldly, worldly-wise, experienced, seasoned, cultured, cultivated, mature, civilized, stylish, elegant, refined, polished, suave, couth, slick

OLD (Shakesp) inland

COLLOQ. having been around, cool

2 *sophisticated technology*

advanced, highly-developed, high-tech, hi-tech, space-age, state-of-the-art, complicated, complex, intricate, elaborate, delicate, subtle, gold, expensive, executive

■ **1** unsophisticated, naive **2** primitive, simple

sophistication n

urbanity, worldliness, culture, experience, elegance, finesse, poise, savoir-faire, savoir-vivre

■ naivety, simplicity

sophistry n

false reasoning, casuistry, sophism, quibble, fallacy

TECHNICAL paralogism, elenchus

soporific adj, n

♦ adj

sleep-inducing, hypnotic, sedative, opiate, narcotic, tranquillizing, sleepy

FORMAL somnolent

■ stimulating, invigorating

♦ n

tranquillizer, sleeping pill, sleeping tablet, sedative, opiate, narcotic, hypnotic, anaesthetic, hypnic

■ stimulant

soppy adj

sentimental, overemotional, mawkish, maudlin, cloying, soft, crazy, wild, silly

COLLOQ. slushy, mushy, sloppy, lovey-dovey, weepy, schmaltzy, gooey, cheesy, corny, wet, wimpish, daft

sorcerer n

sorceress, wizard, warlock, witch, magician, enchanter, magus, mage, magian, reim-kennar, necromancer, voodoo, angek(k)ok

FORMAL thaumaturgist

Related adjective: magian

sorcery n

magic, black magic, witchcraft, wizardry, necromancy, wicca, obeah, voodoo, spell, incantation, charm, enchantment, pishogue

FORMAL thaumaturgy

sordid adj

1 DIRTY, filthy, unclean, foul, vile, squalid, grimy, stained, soiled, mucky, seamy, seedy, disreputable, shabby, tawdry; *Aust & NZ* scungy

COLLOQ. sleazy

2 CORRUPT, degraded, degenerate, immoral, debased, dishonest, dishonourable, disreputable, debauched, low, base, vile, foul, despicable, shameful, abhorrent, wretched, mean, miserly, niggardly, grasping, mercenary, self-seeking

FORMAL ignominious

■ **1** clean, pure **2** honourable, upright

sore adj, n

♦ adj

1 PAINFUL, hurting, aching, smarting, stinging, burning, chafed, tender, sensitive, inflamed, red, reddened, bruised, injured, raw, wounded, nasty; *Scot* sair

2 ANNOYED, irritated, vexed, angry, upset, hurt, wounded, afflicted, aggrieved, offended, bitter, resentful, distressed; *Scot* sair

COLLOQ. peeved, miffed, cheesed off

■ **2** pleased, happy

♦ n

wound, cut, graze, laceration, lesion, scrape, abrasion, chafe, swelling, inflammation, boil, abscess, ulcer, the raw, bite, felon, fester, gall, nerve; *Scot* sair

TECHNICAL anthrax, quittor

OLD botch

sorely adv

greatly, much, very much, highly, extremely, noticeably, significantly, remarkably, notably, substantially, markedly, powerfully, exceedingly

sorrow n, v

♦ n

1 SADNESS, unhappiness, grief, mourning, misery, woe, distress, suffering, desolation, pain, dejection, anguish, heartache, heartbreak, misfortune, wretchedness

FORMAL affliction, disconsolateness, dolour

2 TROUBLE, misfortune, hardship, worry, trial, regret, remorse

FORMAL tribulation, affliction

■ **1** happiness, joy **2** joy, delight

♦ v

grieve, lament, bewail, bemoan, be/feel sad, be/feel miserable, weep, agonize, moan, mourn, pine

■ rejoice

sorrowful adj

miserable, mournful, sad, unhappy, tearful, sorry, distressing, depressed, dejected, wretched, painful, lamentable, woeful, melancholy, grievous, doleful, heartbroken, heart-rending, heavy-hearted, piteous, rueful, *Scot* wae

OLD woe

FORMAL afflicted, disconsolate, lugubrious, plaintive, woebegone

■ happy, joyful

sorry *adj*
1 APOLOGETIC, regretful, ashamed, remorseful, contrite, penitent, repentant, rueful, conscience-stricken, guilt-ridden, shamefaced
SLANG SOZ
2 *sorry to hear the news*
sad, unhappy, upset, distressed
3 SYMPATHETIC, compassionate, understanding, pitying, concerned, moved
4 *in a sorry state*
pathetic, pitiful, poor, mean, simple, wretched, miserable, sad, unfortunate, unhappy, dismal, grievous, heart-rending, shameful
E3 1 impenitent, unashamed **2** happy, pleased **3** uncaring **4** happy, cheerful

sort *n, v*
♦ *n*
kind, type, ilk, family, race, breed, species, variety, order, class, set, category, group, denomination, style, make, brand, stamp, quality, nature, character, description
TECHNICAL genus
FORMAL genre
♦ *v*
class, group, categorize, distribute, divide, separate, segregate, sift, screen, grade, rank, order, classify, catalogue, arrange, put in order, organize, systematize
■ **sort out**
1 ARRANGE, order, put in order, organize, work out
2 CLASSIFY, class, group, categorize, rank, order, grade, separate, divide, segregate, choose, select
3 RESOLVE, clear up, work out, put right, solve
■ **sort of**
rather, moderately, relatively, slightly, a bit, a little, somewhat, fairly, quite, to a limited degree/extent, to some degree/extent, pretty
COLLOQ. kind of
■ **out of sorts**
1 UNWELL, ill, sick, poorly, laid up, ailing, off-colour, seedy, queasy, diseased, unhealthy, infirm, frail, weak, feeble, bedridden
COLLOQ. in a bad way, dicky, below par, down in the dumps, down in the mouth, under the weather, run-down, rough, groggy
2 BAD-TEMPERED, irritable, cross, snappy, quick-tempered, grumpy, fractious, in a (bad) mood, narky, impatient, choleric
COLLOQ. crotchety, crabbed, crabby, grouchy, stroppy, shirty, ratty, in a huff, in a sulk

sortie *n*
foray, raid, offensive, attack, charge, assault, sally, swoop, invasion, rush

so-so *adj*
average, middling, moderate, mediocre, indifferent, fair, adequate, ordinary, respectable, neutral, tolerable, unexceptional, undistinguished, passable, *comme ci comme ça*
COLLOQ. fair to middling, not bad, OK, no great shakes, run-of-the-mill

sought-after *adj*
in great demand, popular, well-liked, favourite, liked, favoured, in favour, admired, wanted, desired, approved, in demand, fashionable, modish
COLLOQ. trendy, now, in, hip, cool, big, all the rage
E3 unpopular, disliked, out of favour

soul *n*
1 SPIRIT, psyche, mind, reason, intellect, character, inner being, inner self, essence, life, life-giving principle, vital force
FORMAL anima
COLLOQ. heart of hearts
2 INDIVIDUAL, person, human being, man, woman, creature
COLLOQ. character

3 *a singer with no soul*
sensitivity, sympathy, compassion, feeling, humanity, understanding, appreciation, tenderness, inspiration, passion
4 *he's the soul of discretion*
epitome, personification, embodiment, essence, model, example
E3 1 body

QUOTATIONS
What of soul was left, I wonder, when the kissing had to stop?
ROBERT BROWNING, *Men and Women*, 'A Toccata of Galuppi's'

soulful *adj*
sensitive, emotional, expressive, heartfelt, moving, profound, mournful, meaningful, eloquent
E3 soulless

soulless *adj*
unfeeling, spiritless, unsympathetic, inhuman, lifeless, cold, callous, cruel, unkind, dead, uninteresting, characterless, ignoble, mean, mean-spirited, soul-destroying, mechanical
E3 soulful

sound[1] *n, v*
♦ *n*
1 *hear a tapping sound*
noise, din, report, resonance, reverberation, tone, timbre, tenor
Related adjectives: acoustic, audial, sonic
See panels on next page
2 *I don't like the sound of that idea*
impression, sense, notion, feeling, implication
COLLOQ. vibe
♦ *v*
1 RING, toll, chime, peal, resound, resonate, reverberate, echo, go off
2 ARTICULATE, enunciate, pronounce, voice, express, utter, say, declare, announce
3 *that sounds like an excellent idea*
seem, appear, look, give the impression

sound[2] *adj, adv*
♦ *adj*
1 FIT, well, healthy, in good health, in good condition/shape, vigorous, robust, sturdy, firm, solid, whole, sane, complete, intact, perfect, disease-free, unbroken, undamaged, unimpaired, unhurt, uninjured
COLLOQ. in fine fettle, sound as a bell
2 VALID, well-founded, well-grounded, reasonable, rational, logical, orthodox, authoritative, weighty, right, true, proven, reliable, dependable, trustworthy, secure, substantial, solid, sturdy, thorough, good, complete
FORMAL judicious, cogent
3 *a sound sleep*
deep, intense, serious, very great, extreme, severe, strong, vigorous, profound
E3 1 unfit, ill, shaky **2** unsound, unreliable, poor **3** light, shallow
♦ *adv*
deeply, intensely, extremely, completely, thoroughly, very much, greatly, severely, vigorously, seriously, profoundly

sound[3] *v*
to sound the depths
measure, plumb, fathom, probe, gauge, examine, test, inspect, investigate
■ **sound out**
ask, canvass, examine, investigate, research, survey, probe, pump, question
COLLOQ. suss out

sound[4] *n*
the Sound of Jura
channel, estuary, inlet, passage, strait, firth, fjord, voe

Sounds include:

bang	clatter	gurgle	pop	smack	thunder
beep	click	hiccup	rattle	snap	tick
blare	clink	hiss	report	sniff	ting
blast	crack	honk	reverberate	snore	tinkle
bleep	crackle	hoot	ring	snort	toot
boom	crash	hum	roar	sob	twang
bubble	creak	jangle	rumble	splash	wail
buzz	crunch	jingle	rustle	splutter	whimper
chime	cry	knock	scrape	squeak	whine
chink	drone	moan	scream	squeal	whirr
chug	echo	murmur	screech	squelch	whistle
clack	explode	patter	sigh	swish	whoop
clang	fizz	peal	sizzle	tap	yell
clank	grate	ping	skirl	throb	
clap	grizzle	pip	slam	thud	
clash	groan	plop	slurp	thump	

Animal sounds include:

bark	chirp	growl	miaow	snarl	woof
bay	chirrup	grunt	moo	squawk	yap
bellow	cluck	hiss	neigh	squeak	yelp
bleat	coo	hoot	purr	tweet	yowl
bray	croak	howl	quack	twitter	
cackle	crow	low	roar	warble	
caw	gobble	mew	screech	whinny	

soundly adv
  1 *soundly asleep*
  deeply, intensely, extremely, completely, thoroughly, very much, greatly, severely, vigorously, seriously, profoundly
  2 *soundly beaten in the finals*
  fully, perfectly, completely, absolutely, downright, entirely, quite, totally, utterly
  3 *a soundly based decision*
  validly, reasonably, logically, dependably, securely, solidly, authoritatively
  F3 1 lightly **2** partially

soup n
  broth, potage, consommé, stock, chowder, bisque, cockieleekie, borsch, gazpacho, mulligatawny, julienne

sour adj, v
  ♦ adj
  1 TART, sharp, acid, tangy, acidy, acidulous, acetic, pungent, vinegary, bitter, rancid, curdled, turned, verjuice, acerbic, acerb, subacid; *Scot* wersh
  OLD eager; (*Shakesp*) aygre
  FORMAL acetous
  COLLOQ. off, bad
  2 EMBITTERED, bad-tempered, surly, churlish, ill-tempered, peevish, crusty, resentful, unpleasant, acrimonious, nasty, disagreeable, austere, subacid, vinegary
  COLLOQ. crabbed, grouchy, shirty, ratty
  F3 1 sweet, sugary **2** good-natured, generous
  ♦ v
  disenchant, embitter, make bitter, exacerbate, exasperate, alienate, spoil, envenom, canker

source n
  origin, derivation, beginning, start, cause, root, rise, spring, wellspring, fountainhead, wellhead, supply, mine, originator, author, authority, informant
  TECHNICAL ylem
  FORMAL commencement, provenance, primordium, *fons et origo*

sourpuss n
  misery, grumbler, killjoy, shrew, whiner, kvetch
  COLLOQ. crosspatch, grouse, grump, whinger, dog in the manger, buzzkill

souse v
  douse, drench, dunk, sink, immerse, marinate, marinade, pickle, plunge, soak, saturate, steep, dip, submerge

souvenir n
  memento, reminder, remembrance, keepsake, relic, token, trophy

sovereign n, adj
  ♦ n
  ruler, monarch, king, queen, emperor, empress, tsar, chief
  FORMAL potentate
  ♦ adj
  1 RULING, royal, kingly, queenly, princely, imperial, majestic, absolute, unlimited, supreme, paramount, predominant, principal, chief, dominant, independent, autonomous, self-governing, self-ruling
  2 UNRIVALLED, outstanding, utmost, extreme, unequalled

sovereignty n
  autonomy, independence, supremacy, domination, sway, dominion, kingship, queenship, regality, primacy, raj
  FORMAL ascendancy, imperium, suzerainty

sow v
  plant, seed, scatter, strew, bestrew, spread, distribute, disperse, broadcast, lodge, implant
  FORMAL disseminate

space n, v
  ♦ n
  1 ROOM, place, seat, accommodation, capacity, area, volume, extent, expanse, sweep, stretch, expansion, latitude, scope, range, play, clearance, elbow-room, legroom, *Lebensraum*, leeway, margin
  FORMAL amplitude
  Related adjective: spatial
  2 BLANK, omission, gap, break, empty space, opening, interval, intermission, chasm
  FORMAL lacuna, interstice
  Related adjective: lacunary
  3 *in a short space of time*
  period, stretch, span, spell, time, shift, stint
  4 OUTER SPACE, the Milky Way, galaxy, universe, cosmos, solar system, deep space
  Related adjective: cosmic
  ♦ v
  arrange, order, put in order, range, be apart, set apart, space out, stretch out, string out, place at intervals
  FORMAL array, dispose

spaceman, spacewoman n
  astronaut, space traveller, cosmonaut, taikonaut

spacious adj
roomy, ample, big, large, siz(e)able, broad, wide, huge, vast, immense, extensive, expansive, open, uncrowded, palatial
FORMAL capacious, commodious
🔁 small, narrow, cramped, confined, poky

spadework n
foundation, groundwork, homework, preparation, preliminary work, labour, drudgery
COLLOQ. donkey-work

span n, v
♦ n
spread, stretch, reach, range, scope, compass, piece, extent, length, distance, duration, time, interval, term, period, spell
♦ v
arch, vault, bridge, link, cross, traverse, range, extend, stretch, last, cover, include
OLD overlay
FORMAL bestride

spank v
smack, slap, thrash, slipper, cane
COLLOQ. wallop, whack, thwack, tan, put over your knee

spanking adj, adv
♦ adj
brisk, fast, quick, lively, smart, speedy, swift, vigorous, energetic, snappy, invigorating, fine, gleaming
🔁 slow
♦ adv
absolutely, completely, utterly, totally, exactly, strikingly, positively, brand

spar v
argue, dispute, contest, fall out, contend, quarrel, wrangle, squabble, bicker, wrestle, box, skirmish
COLLOQ. scrap, spat, tiff

spare adj, v
♦ adj
1 RESERVE, emergency, extra, additional, supplementary, subsidiary, leftover, remaining, unused, over, surplus, surplus to requirements, superfluous, supernumerary, auxiliary, unwanted
OLD subsecive
SLANG buckshee, gash
2 spare time
free, unoccupied, leisure
3 LEAN, thin, skinny, bony, gaunt, lank, slim, slender, scraggy, scrawny
COLLOQ. all skin and bones
4 FRUGAL, scanty, scant, meagre, modest, sparing, skimpy
🔁 1 necessary, vital, used 3 fat, plump
♦ v
1 PARDON, let off, reprieve, show mercy to, forgive, release, free, forbear, withhold
2 GRANT, allow, provide, give, afford, part with, do without, manage without
FORMAL dispense with
3 NOT HARM, protect, save, guard, safeguard, secure, take care of, defend, reserve, stint; Scot hain
■ to spare
left over, remaining, extra, in reserve, unused, surplus

sparing adj
economical, thrifty, careful, prudent, frugal, meagre, miserly
FORMAL penurious
COLLOQ. stingy, mingy, tight-fisted, close-fisted
🔁 unsparing, liberal, lavish

sparingly adv
economically, carefully, prudently, meagrely, frugally
COLLOQ. stingily
🔁 unsparingly, lavishly

spark n, v
♦ n
1 FLASH, flare, gleam, glint, glimmer, flicker, sparkle, flame, flake, flaught, funk, bluette
2 not a spark of intelligence
flicker, hint, trace, vestige, scrap, bit, touch, suggestion, iota, atom, jot, scintilla; dialect spunk; N Am, Aust & NZ skerrick
■ spark off
kindle, set off, trigger (off), start (off), cause, touch off, occasion, prompt, give rise to, provoke, stimulate, stir, incite, excite, inspire
FORMAL precipitate

sparkle v, n
♦ v
1 TWINKLE, glitter, scintillate, flash, flicker, gleam, glint, glisten, glow, glimmer, shimmer, shine, beam
OLD glister
FORMAL coruscate, emicate
2 EFFERVESCE, fizz, bubble
3 BE LIVELY, be animated, be spirited, be enthusiastic, be witty, be vivacious, be effervescent
FORMAL be ebullient
COLLOQ. be bubbly
♦ n
1 TWINKLE, glitter, flash, shimmer, gleam, glow, shine, glint, flicker, spark, fire, radiance, brilliance, dazzle
FORMAL coruscation, emication
2 SPIRIT, vitality, life, animation, vivacity, liveliness, energy, dash, brio, zest, enthusiasm
FORMAL ebullience
COLLOQ. get-up-and-go, vim, pizzazz

> **QUOTATIONS**
> Take a pair of sparkling eyes
> SIR W S GILBERT, The Gondoliers

sparkling adj
1 EFFERVESCENT, fizzy, carbonated, bubbly
2 TWINKLING, flashing, glittering, glistening, gleaming, scintillating, scintillant
FORMAL coruscating
3 LIVELY, animated, scintillating, witty
🔁 1 flat 3 dull

sparse adj
scarce, scanty, meagre, slight, scattered, infrequent, sporadic
🔁 plentiful, thick, dense

sparsely adv
scarcely, scantily, meagrely, slightly, sporadically, few and far between
🔁 plentifully

spartan adj
austere, harsh, severe, rigorous, strict, disciplined, self-denying, ascetic, abstemious, stringent, temperate, frugal, plain, simple, bleak, joyless
🔁 luxurious, self-indulgent

spasm n
burst, eruption, outburst, frenzy, fit, bout, pang, convulsion, seizure, attack, paroxysm, contraction, cramp, crick, jerk, twitch, tic, start, grip, throe
TECHNICAL clonic spasm, clonus, tonic spasm, tonus, trismus
FORMAL access
Related adjective: spastic

spasmodic adj
sporadic, occasional, intermittent, erratic, periodic, irregular, fitful, jerky
🔁 continuous, uninterrupted

spasmodically adv
sporadically, occasionally, intermittently, periodically, now and again, off and on, on and off
🔁 continuously, uninterruptedly

spate *n*
flood, deluge, torrent, rush, series, outpouring, flow

spatter *v*
splatter, splash, splodge, spray, sprinkle, shower,
speckle, scatter, daub, bedaub, bestrew, besprinkle,
bespatter, dirty, soil

spawn *v*
give rise to, cause, bring about, bring on,
make, produce, create, generate, lead to, originate,
engender

spay *n*
neuter, sterilize, castrate, emasculate, doctor, geld

speak *v*
talk, say, state, declare, express, utter, voice, articulate,
enunciate, pronounce, tell, chat, communicate, address,
lecture, harangue, hold forth, argue, discuss
FORMAL converse, declaim
COLLOQ. have a word with, chatter, gab, witter, yak
■ **speak for**
speak on behalf of, represent, act for, stand for, act as
spokesperson for
■ **speak of**
refer to, make reference to, mention, make mention of,
discuss
■ **speak out/up**
say publicly, speak openly, defend, support, protest
COLLOQ. stand up and be counted
■ **speak to**
rebuke, reprimand, scold, warn, lecture, accost, address;
Aust rouse on
FORMAL admonish, upbraid
COLLOQ. bring to book, tell off, tick off, take/pull apart,
bawl out, bounce, carpet, give someone a ticking-off,
dress down, give someone a dressing-down, haul over the
coals, read the riot act to, throw the book at, rap over the
knuckles, give someone a rap over the knuckles, give
someone a flea in their ear, give someone an earful, give
someone a piece of your mind, shoot down in flames, tear
a strip off someone, give someone some stick, go to town
on, come down on like a ton of bricks, give someone
hell; *Aust & NZ* go crook at
■ **speak up**
talk (more) loudly, raise your voice, make yourself heard

SYNONYM NUANCES

State has added implications of emphasis and clarity:
everything I have stated in my report is accurate, and
declare also suggests an announcement. While **utter** is
merely to vocalize, **express** implies conveying meaning
or feeling: *a speech expressing grave misgivings*, and
voice could also be used of making your feelings
known: *he voiced his support for the proposal*.

Articulate, similarly, suggests the verbal conveying of a
precise meaning, whereas **enunciate** puts the emphasis
on the physical formation of words: *he enunciated his
words with clarity and force*. **Pronounce** can be
used similarly, but is also appropriate for making a
formal declaration: *a death sentence was
pronounced*.

Address would be used of directing words to an
audience, while **harangue** has suggestions of
forcefulness and aggression. **Lecture** can be used of
delivering a more specific talk, but can also describe
delivering a perhaps rather overbearing reproof: *he
lectured them on their appalling manners*. The term **hold
forth** suggests engaging an audience: *Asimov could hold
forth on almost any subject with lucidity*. However, it
may have overtones of pompousness: *a bulky woman
was holding forth in stentorian tones*.

---

speaker *n*
talker, lecturer, orator, spokesperson, spokesman,
spokeswoman, mouthpiece
FORMAL prolocutor

spear *n*
javelin, dart, harpoon, pike, trident, handstaff, assegai,
boar-spear, fish-spear, gig, leister, truncheon; *dialect*
gleave; *Scot* waster
OLD ash, demi-lance, gad, glaive, lancegay, gavelock,
pilum, pile

spearhead *v, n*
♦ *v*
lead, head, initiate, launch, front, pioneer
♦ *n*
vanguard, front line, leading position, pioneer, trailblazer,
leader, guide, overseer
COLLOQ. van, cutting edge

special *adj*
1 *a special occasion*
important, significant, momentous, major, noteworthy,
notable, distinguished, distinctive, memorable, remarkable,
extraordinary, outstanding, exceptional, unusual
COLLOQ. out of the ordinary, red-letter
2 DIFFERENT, distinctive, characteristic, peculiar, individual,
unique, exclusive, select, choice, particular, exact,
specific, precise, detailed
FORMAL singular
F3 **1** normal, ordinary, usual; *colloq.* run-of-the-mill **2**
general, common

specialist *n*
consultant, authority, expert, master, professional,
connoisseur
COLLOQ. brains

speciality *n*
strength, feature, forte, talent, gift, field/area of study, field,
pièce de résistance; *N Am* specialty

specialization *n*
special interest, special subject, specialist subject, special
study, concentration, focus, particularization

specialize *v*
concentrate on, focus on, study, follow, have as your
specialist subject; *N Am* major in

specially *adv*
for a special purpose, for a particular purpose, particularly,
exclusively, uniquely, in particular, specifically, explicitly,
distinctly, expressly

species *n*
class, kind, breed, sort, type, category, variety, group,
collection, description
TECHNICAL genus

specific *adj*
particular, precise, exact, fixed, set, limited, determined,
special, definite, well-defined, unequivocal, clear-cut,
detailed, explicit, express, unambiguous
F3 vague, approximate, unspecific

specifically *adv*
1 *designed specifically for the elderly*
particularly, specially, exclusively, in particular, for a
special purpose, for a particular purpose
2 *I specifically told you not to go there*
distinctly, exactly, clearly, plainly, unambiguously,
expressly, definitely

specification *n*
requirement, condition, qualification, stipulation,
instruction, description, listing, naming, statement,
designation, item, particular, detail
FORMAL delineation

specify *v*
stipulate, spell out, set out, define, particularize, detail,
itemize, enumerate, list, mention, state, cite, name,
designate, indicate, describe
FORMAL delineate

specimen *n*
sample, example, instance, illustration, model, pattern,
type, representative, copy, exhibit
FORMAL paradigm, exemplar

specious adj
false, misleading, unsound, untrue, deceptive, plausible
FORMAL fallacious, casuistic, sophistic, sophistical
☒ valid, true

speck n
mark, fleck, dot, speckle, shred, grain, particle, bit, blot,
defect, blemish, fault, flaw, stain, spot, atom, mite, iota,
jot, trace, whit, tittle, mote, peep, pip, spangle
TECHNICAL floater, sheave

speckled adj
spotted, spotty, flecked, dotted, dappled, mottled,
sprinkled, stippled, brinded, brindle(d), fleckered,
freckled
TECHNICAL lentiginous

spectacle n
show, performance, display, exhibition, parade, pageant,
extravaganza, scene, sight, picture, curiosity, wonder,
marvel, phenomenon

spectacles n
GLASSES, eyewear, lens, eyeglasses
COLLOQ. specs

Types of spectacles include:

aviators	monocle	shooting glasses
bifocals	pince-nez	sports spex
diving mask	Polaroid® glasses	sunglasses
eyeglass	quizzing glass	trifocals
goggles	Ray-ban® glasses	varifocals
half-glasses	reading glasses	
lorgnette	safety glasses	

---

spectacular adj, n
♦ adj
grand, splendid, magnificent, sensational, impressive,
glorious, striking, stunning, staggering, amazing,
astonishing, extraordinary, outstanding, remarkable,
dramatic, daring, breathtaking, dazzling, eye-catching,
colourful, ostentatious, flamboyant
FORMAL resplendent, opulent
☒ unimpressive, ordinary
♦ n
extravaganza, show, display, exhibition, pageant,
spectacle

spectacularly adv
amazingly, astonishingly, strikingly, stunningly,
staggeringly, extraordinarily, outstandingly,
remarkably, magnificently, sensationally,
impressively, gloriously
☒ ordinarily

spectator n
watcher, viewer, onlooker, looker-on, bystander,
passer-by, witness, eyewitness, observer,
ringsider
OLD groundling; (Shakesp) supervisor
FORMAL beholder
COLLOQ. wallflower
SLANG N Am rubberneck
☒ player, participant

spectral adj
ghostly, incorporeal, insubstantial, disembodied,
supernatural, unearthly, weird, uncanny, phantom,
shadowy, eerie; Scot eldritch
COLLOQ. spooky

spectre n
1 GHOST, phantom, phantasm, spirit, wraith, apparition,
vision, presence, shade, shadow, revenant, visitant, bogle,
Empusa; Scot bodach
OLD larva, phantosme
COLLOQ. spook
2 THREAT, menace, fear, dread

spectrum n
See **rainbow**.

speculate v
1 GUESS, wonder, imagine, contemplate, meditate, muse,
reflect, consider, deliberate, theorize, hypothesize, suppose
FORMAL conjecture, surmise, cogitate
2 GAMBLE, bet, risk, hazard, venture

speculation n
1 GUESS, guesswork, consideration, supposition, theory,
thinking, contemplation, deliberation, imagination, flight of
fancy
FORMAL conjecture, surmise, hypothesis
2 GAMBLE, gambling, bet, hazard, risk

speculative adj
hypothetical, theoretical, notional, indefinite, vague,
abstract, academic, tentative, risky, hazardous, uncertain,
unpredictable, unproven
FORMAL conjectural, suppositional
COLLOQ. iffy, chancy, dicey

speech n
1 COMMUNICATION, spoken communication, language,
dialogue, conversation, talk, articulation, pronunciation,
diction, enunciation, elocution, accent, delivery, utterance,
voice, tongue, parlance, dialect, jargon
COLLOQ. lingo
2 make a speech
oration, address, discourse, talk, lecture, homily, sermon,
message, harangue, patter, conversation, dialogue,
monologue, soliloquy, tirade
FORMAL diatribe, philippic
COLLOQ. spiel

> **QUOTATIONS**
> Human speech is like a cracked kettle on which we
> beat out tunes for bears to dance to, when all the time
> we are longing to move the stars to pity
>   GUSTAVE FLAUBERT, *Madame Bovary*
>
> Speeches in our culture are the vacuum that fills a
> vacuum
>   JOHN KENNETH GALBRAITH

speechless adj
dumbfounded, dumbstruck, lost for words, thunderstruck,
amazed, astounded, shocked, aghast, tongue-tied,
inarticulate, mute, dumb, struck dumb, silent, mum
FORMAL obmutescent
☒ talkative

speed n, v
♦ n
velocity, rate, pace, tempo, momentum, quickness,
swiftness, promptness, rapidity, haste, hurry, dispatch,
rush, acceleration
FORMAL alacrity, celerity, expeditiousness
☒ slowness, delay
♦ v
race, tear, zoom, career, bowl along, sprint, cruise, whisk,
gallop, hurry, rush, dash, accelerate, quicken
FORMAL hasten
COLLOQ. belt, hurtle, pelt, put your foot down, step on it/
the gas/the juice
☒ slow, delay
■ **speed up**
1 ACCELERATE, quicken, speed, drive faster, go faster, pick
up/gather speed, gain momentum
COLLOQ. open up, put your foot down, step on it/the gas/
the juice, put on a spurt
2 speed up a process
accelerate, hurry, step up, stimulate, facilitate, advance,
further, promote, spur on, forward
FORMAL hasten, expedite, precipitate

speedily adv
fast, quickly, rapidly, swiftly, hastily, hurriedly, promptly,
posthaste
FORMAL expeditiously
COLLOQ. pronto, lickety-split, at a rate of knots, at the
double, before you can say Jack Robinson, by leaps and

bounds, hell for leather, like a bat out of hell, like the clappers, like greased lightning, a mile a minute
🖃 slowly

speedy *adj*
fast, quick, swift, rapid, nimble, express, prompt, immediate, hurried, hasty, cursory, summary, posthaste
FORMAL precipitate, expeditious
COLLOQ. nippy, zippy, zappy, like greased lightning, pdq, pretty damn quick
🖃 slow, leisurely

spell[1] *v*
his expression spelt trouble
signal, suggest, mean, indicate, imply, promise, amount to, lead to, signify, herald
FORMAL augur, portend, presage

■ **spell out**
explain, clarify, make clear, elucidate, emphasize, detail, stipulate, specify

spell[2] *n*
a spell of sunny weather
period, time, bout, session, term, season, interval, extent, course, stretch, span, patch, turn, shift, stint

spell[3] *n*
1 CHARM, incantation, abracadabra, magic, sorcery, witchery, bewitchment, enchantment, trance, Indian sign
2 FASCINATION, charm, glamour, pull, attraction, influence, drawing power, allure, magnetism
SLANG N Am mojo

■ **cast a spell on**
fascinate, charm, attract, bewitch, enchant, enthral, captivate, mesmerize

spellbinding *adj*
gripping, fascinating, riveting, enthralling, captivating, enchanting, bewitching, entrancing, mesmerizing

spellbound *adj*
transfixed, hypnotized, mesmerized, fascinated, enthralled, gripped, entranced, riveted, captivated, bewitched, transported, enraptured, enchanted, charmed, rapt

spend *v*
1 *spend money*
pay out, invest, lay out, waste, squander, fritter, expend, consume, use up, exhaust, finish
FORMAL disburse
COLLOQ. fork out, shell out, splash out, stump up, cough up, spend like water, dip/dig into your pocket
SLANG blow
2 *spend time*
pass, fill, occupy, use (up), take up, while away, put in, employ, apply, devote
COLLOQ. do, kill
🖃 **1** save, hoard

QUOTATIONS
The workers spend what they get and the capitalists get what they spend
MICHAL KALECKI

SYNONYM NUANCES

sense 1
Pay out can be used to suggest spending a substantial amount of money from duty or necessity, while **invest** implies an expectation of increased returns, and has positive suggestions of prudent action. The term **lay out** has implications of more extravagant expenditure, while **waste**, **fritter** and **squander** more specifically and negatively suggest misuse.
    Expend is a term which might be used in more formal contexts: *resources expended on community programmes*. The terms **consume**, **use up** and **exhaust**, however, are more suggestive of depletion and carry the negative implication of lost resources: *the museum's funds were exhausted by its purchases*.

---

spendthrift *n, adj*
♦ *n*
squanderer, prodigal, wastrel
FORMAL profligate
🖃 miser, hoarder, saver
♦ *adj*
improvident, extravagant, prodigal, wasteful, squandering
FORMAL profligate

spent *adj*
1 USED (UP), finished, expended, exhausted, consumed, gone
2 TIRED OUT, exhausted, weary, wearied, drained, weakened, debilitated
FORMAL effete
COLLOQ. worn out, fagged (out), burnt out, all in, bushed, dead beat, dog-tired, done in, jiggered, knackered, shattered, whacked, zonked; N Am pooped (out), tuckered out

sperm *n*
germ cell, sex cell, semen, seminal fluid
TECHNICAL spermatozoon, gamete

spew *v*
vomit, bring up, spit out, spurt, gush, issue, emit, retch, regurgitate, disgorge, belch
COLLOQ. puke, throw up, sick up, chuck up, fetch up
SLANG barf; *Aust* chunder

sphere *n*
1 BALL, globe, orb, round, globule
2 DOMAIN, realm, province, department, territory, discipline, speciality, field, area, range, scope, compass, extent, rank, function, capacity
3 *a sphere of people*
circle, class, group, set, band, crowd, clique

spherical *adj*
round, ball-shaped, globe-shaped, globular
FORMAL rotund, globoid, globate, globose, orbicular

spice *n, v*
♦ *n*
1 FLAVOURING, seasoning, piquancy, relish, savour, tang
See also **herbs and spices**.
2 EXCITEMENT, life, colour, zest, gusto
COLLOQ. kick, pep, zap, zip
♦ *v*
liven (up), enliven, vitalize, put life into, rouse, invigorate, animate, energize, brighten, ginger up, stir (up)
COLLOQ. buck up, jazz up, pep up, perk up, hot up

spick and span *adj*
tidy, clean, polished, scrubbed, trim, well-kept, neat, immaculate, spotless, spruce, shipshape, uncluttered
🖃 dirty, untidy

spicy *adj*
1 PIQUANT, hot, peppery, pungent, sharp, tangy, tart, seasoned, well-seasoned, flavoured, strongly flavoured, flavoursome, aromatic, fragrant, picante
2 RACY, risqué, adult, ribald, suggestive, indelicate, indecent, improper, scandalous, sensational
FORMAL indecorous, unseemly
COLLOQ. raunchy, juicy, blue, near the bone/knuckle
🖃 **1** bland, insipid **2** clean, decent

spiel *n*
patter, pitch, sales patter, line, speech, recital
FORMAL oration

spike *n, v*
♦ *n*
point, prong, projection, tine, spine, barb, nail, stake, rowel, spick, tang, chape, nib, pricket, beard, catkin, spire; *dialect* brod
TECHNICAL spadix, strobilus
OLD gad
Related adjectives: spicate, spicated
♦ *v*
1 IMPALE, stick, prick, spear, skewer, spit

2 *spike a drink*
lace, drug, add, mix in, contaminate

spill *v, n*
♦ *v*
overturn, upset, slop, flow, overflow, disgorge, run (out/over), pour, tip, discharge, well, shed, scatter; *dialect* slatter, swatter; *Scot* skail
♦ *n*
1 LEAK, spillage, leakage, leaking, seeping, seepage, drip, oozing, discharge, escape, percolation
2 FALL, accident, tumble, overturn, upset
COLLOQ. cropper
■ **spill the beans**
inform, tell (on), tell all
COLLOQ. blab, rat, split, squeal, blow the gaff, give the game away, let the cat out of the bag
SLANG grass

spin *v, n*
♦ *v*
1 TURN (ROUND), go round, revolve, rotate, circle, twist, gyrate, twirl, swivel, pirouette, wheel, whirl, whirr, swirl, reel
2 *spin a story/yarn*
tell, narrate, relate, make up, invent, fabricate, dream up
♦ *n*
1 TURN, revolution, rotation, circle, twist, gyration, twirl, swivel, pirouette, wheel, whirl, swirl, reel
2 COMMOTION, agitation, panic
COLLOQ. flap, state, dither, fluster, tizzy, tizz
3 DRIVE, ride, run, trip, journey, outing, jaunt
■ **spin out**
prolong, extend, lengthen, keep going, amplify, pad out
FORMAL protract

spindle *n*
axis, pivot, pin, rod, axle, staff, verge, spit
TECHNICAL arbor, fusee
Related adjective: fusiform

spindly *adj*
long, thin, lanky, gangly, gangling, skinny, spidery, skeletal, spindle-shanked
FORMAL attenuate(d), fusiform
COLLOQ. weedy
F∃ stocky, thickset

spine *n*
1 BACKBONE, spinal column, vertebral column, vertebrae, dorsum, rachis
Related adjective: vertebral
2 THORN, barb, prickle, bristle, spike, needle, quill, rachis
3 STRENGTH OF CHARACTER, courage, bravery, determination, spirit, resolution, mettle, pluck
FORMAL fortitude
COLLOQ. guts, bottle, grit, spunk

spine-chilling *adj*
frightening, hair-raising, horrifying, scary, terrifying, bloodcurdling, eerie
COLLOQ. spooky

spineless *adj*
weak, feeble, irresolute, indecisive, ineffective, cowardly, faint-hearted, spiritless, lily-livered, soft, submissive, weak-kneed, timid, timorous
COLLOQ. chicken, cissy, yellow, wet, wimpish
SLANG wussy
F∃ strong, brave, courageous

spin-off *n*
repercussion, result, consequence, effect, side effect, reverberation

spiny *adj*
thorny, thistly, prickly, briery, spiky
FORMAL spinose, spinous, acanthaceous, acanthous, spinigerous, spiniferous, spicular, spiculate

spiral *adj, n, v*
♦ *adj*
winding, twisting, coiled, corkscrew, helical, whorled, scrolled, circular
TECHNICAL cochlear
FORMAL cochleate(d)
♦ *n*
coil, helix, corkscrew, screw, twist, whorl, convolution, wreath, curlicue
TECHNICAL cochlea
FORMAL gyre, volute, volution, volute(d)
Related adjective: helical
♦ *v*
1 WIND, twist, coil, circle, screw, whorl, wreathe, gyrate, gyre
2 *costs spiralling*
rise, increase, go up, soar, climb, escalate, rocket, skyrocket
3 *prices spiralling downwards*
fall/drop rapidly, decrease quickly, plunge, dive, plummet, nosedive, dive-bomb

spire *n*
steeple, belfry, tower, turret, pinnacle, peak, summit, crown, crest, top, tip, point, spike, broach, spear, flèche
OLD spyre

spirit *n, v*
♦ *n*
1 SOUL, psyche, inner being, inner self, mind, breath, life, life-giving principle, vital force, *élan vital*
FORMAL anima
2 GHOST, spectre, phantom, apparition, supernatural being, presence, poltergeist, wraith, shade, shadow, revenant, visitant, angel, demon, fiend, devil, fairy, sprite
COLLOQ. spook
3 MOOD, atmosphere, air, humour, temper, disposition, temperament, character, feeling(s), morale, make-up, quality, state/frame of mind, attitude, outlook, mindset
OLD complexion
4 DETERMINATION, strength of character, resolution, willpower, courage, bravery, backbone, mettle, pluck, dauntlessness, stout-heartedness
COLLOQ. guts, bottle, grit, spunk
5 TENDENCY, characteristic, principle, essence, essential quality, force
6 LIVELINESS, vivacity, animation, sparkle, vigour, energy, zest, fire, ardour, motivation, enthusiasm, zeal, enterprise
COLLOQ. pizzazz, zip, kick
7 *the spirit of the law*
meaning, sense, substance, essence, drift, gist, tenor, implication, character, quality
FORMAL purport
■ **spirit away**
remove, capture, carry, convey, abstract, seize, kidnap, abduct, steal, whisk
FORMAL purloin
COLLOQ. snaffle

spirited *adj*
lively, vivacious, animated, sparkling, high-spirited, vigorous, energetic, fiery, passionate, active, ardent, zealous, bold, determined, resolute, courageous, valiant, mettlesome, plucky, confident
FORMAL valorous
COLLOQ. feisty
F∃ spiritless, lethargic, cowardly

spiritless *adj*
apathetic, weak, lifeless, listless, dull, unenthusiastic, unmoved, lacklustre, anaemic, despondent, depressed, dejected, dispirited, low, melancholy, torpid, droopy
FORMAL languid
COLLOQ. wishy-washy
F∃ spirited

spirits *n*
1 LIQUOR, alcohol, strong drink, strong liquor, moonshine
COLLOQ. firewater, hooch, the hard stuff
2 FEELINGS, emotions, mood, temperament, temper,
attitude, humour

Spirits include:

añejo tequila	golden rum	rum
apple-jack	gold tequila	rye
armagnac	grappa	sambucca
Bacardi®	kahlua	schnapps
bitters	kir	Scotch
bourbon	kirsch	silver tequila
brandy	malt whisky	slivovitz
calvados	mezcal	sloe gin
cognac	mirabelle	spiced rum
cointreau	ouzo	tequila
dark rum	pastis	vodka
eau de vie	Pernod®	whiskey
framboise	poteen	whisky
genever	raki	white rum
gin	reposado tequila	

See also **drink**; **liqueur**.

---

spiritual *adj*
1 UNWORLDLY, transcendent, incorporeal, immaterial,
ethereal, otherworldly, intangible
FORMAL metaphysical
2 RELIGIOUS, devotional, heavenly, divine, holy, sacred,
ecclesiastical
E∃ 1 physical, material, temporal **2** secular

spit¹ *v, n*
♦ *v*
he spat at me
eject, discharge, issue, rasp, hawk, splutter, hiss, sputter;
Scot fuff, yex
OLD bespit, spawl, spet
FORMAL expectorate
SLANG gob; *Aust* slag
♦ *n*
spittle, saliva, slaver, drool, dribble, sputum, phlegm;
Scot yex
TECHNICAL emptysis
OLD spawl
FORMAL expectoration
SLANG *Aust* slag
■ **spitting image**
likeness, exact likeness, double, lookalike, picture, replica,
twin, clone
COLLOQ. spit, dead spit, dead ringer, ringer

spit² *n*
to roast meat on a spit
skewer, rotisserie, brochette, turnspit, broach, jack
OLD smoke-jack

spite *n, v*
♦ *n*
spitefulness, malice, maliciousness, malevolence, venom,
gall, bitterness, resentment, rancour, animosity, ill-feeling,
ill-will, grudge, vengeance, vindictiveness, ill nature,
hostility, evil, hate, hatred
OLD spight, maugre
FORMAL malignity
COLLOQ. hard feelings
E∃ goodwill, compassion, affection
♦ *v*
annoy, irritate, irk, vex, provoke, gall, hurt, upset, injure,
wound, offend, put out; *Scot* maugre
■ **in spite of**
despite, regardless of, undeterred by, against, defying, in
the face of, for, with, after all, be that as it may,
nevertheless, *malgré*
OLD malgrado, maugre
FORMAL notwithstanding

spiteful *adj*
malicious, venomous, snide, barbed, resentful, bitter,
cruel, hostile, rancorous, vindictive, vengeful, ill-natured,
ill-disposed, nasty, malevolent
FORMAL malignant
COLLOQ. catty, bitchy
E∃ charitable, affectionate

spitefully *adv*
maliciously, bitterly, resentfully, cruelly, vindictively,
venomously, malevolently
COLLOQ. bitchily

splash *v, n*
♦ *v*
1 BATHE, wallow, paddle, wade, lap, dabble, plunge, wet,
wash, shower, spray, squirt, sprinkle, spatter, splatter,
splodge, splotch, scatter, spread, daub, plaster, slop, slosh,
slush, plop, surge, break, dash, beat, strike, batter, buffet,
smack, swash, plash, squatter; *dialect* flouse, slatter,
swatter, sozzle; *Scot* jabble, jaup
OLD bedash
COLLOQ. splosh, splish
2 PUBLICIZE, show, display, exhibit, flaunt, blazon, trumpet,
plaster
♦ *n*
1 SPOT, patch, splatter, splodge, splotch, splurge, stain,
burst, touch, streak, dash, beating, spat; *Scot* blash, jaup;
Scot & N Am splatch
COLLOQ. splosh, splish
2 PUBLICITY, display, ostentation, blaze, effect, impression,
impact, stir, excitement, sensation
COLLOQ. splurge
■ **splash out**
invest in, lash out, spend, splurge, be extravagant
COLLOQ. push the boat out

spleen *n*
anger, bad temper, bitterness, resentment, hatred, hostility,
ill-will, ill-humour, spite, spitefulness, malice,
vindictiveness, peevishness, venom, malevolence, wrath,
pique, rancour, bile, biliousness, gall, acrimony, animosity
FORMAL animus, malignity

splendid *adj*
1 *splendid Georgian buildings*
impressive, great, fine, grand, stately, imposing, brilliant,
dazzling, glittering, lustrous, bright, radiant, glowing,
glorious, magnificent, gorgeous, sumptuous, luxurious,
lavish, rich, distinguished, illustrious, renowned, celebrated
FORMAL resplendent, opulent, refulgent
2 *have a splendid time*
marvellous, wonderful, superb, excellent, first-class,
outstanding, remarkable, exceptional, sublime, supreme,
admirable
COLLOQ. fabulous, terrific, super
E∃ 1 drab, ordinary, run-of-the-mill **2** poor, bad

splendidly *adv*
1 IMPRESSIVELY, brilliantly, magnificently, grandly
2 MARVELLOUSLY, wonderfully, remarkably, exceptionally,
superbly, admirably, outstandingly

splendour *n*
brightness, radiance, brilliance, dazzle, glow, gleam,
lustre, glory, luxury, sumptuousness, magnificence,
richness, grandeur, majesty, illustriousness, solemnity,
pomp, ceremony, display, show, spectacle
FORMAL resplendence, opulence
E∃ drabness, squalor

splenetic *adj*
angry, cross, bad-tempered, irritable, irascible, rancorous,
sullen, spiteful, choleric, morose, peevish, petulant,
churlish, fretful, bilious, envenomed, acid, sour, testy
OLD atrabilious
COLLOQ. bitchy, crabbed, crabby, touchy, ratty

splice *v*
join, fasten, connect, marry, bind, tie, plait, braid,
interweave, interlace, intertwine, entwine, mesh, knit, graft

■ **get spliced**
get married, wed, become husband and wife
OLD plight your troth
COLLOQ. get hitched, tie the knot, take the plunge

splinter *n, v*
♦ *n*
sliver, shiver, chip, shard, fragment, bit, piece, shred, flake, shaving, paring, splint, spall, spicula, spicule; *dialect* skelf, speel, spelk, spell; *Scot* spale
OLD flinders; (*Shakesp*) flaw
COLLOQ. smithereens
♦ *v*
split, break, break into pieces, fracture, smash, shatter, shiver, crumble, fragment, disintegrate, spall, spalt
FORMAL cleave

split *v, n, adj*
♦ *v*
1 *split the logs; the cloth split*
break, cut, splinter, shiver, crack, burst, rupture, tear, rip, chop, slit, slash, open
OLD rend
FORMAL cleave
2 *split in two*
divide, separate, partition, halve, bisect, share
3 *split the profits*
share, separate, divide, halve, allocate, allot, apportion, distribute, hand out, dole out, parcel out
COLLOQ. carve up
4 PART COMPANY, part, disunite, disband, break up, set apart, dissociate from, divide, separate, divorce, become estranged, become alienated
5 INFORM ON, betray, incriminate
COLLOQ. tell on, squeal, rat, blow the whistle on, stitch
SLANG shop, peach, grass, rumble; *N Am* stool on
♦ *n*
1 DIVISION, separation, partition, break, cut, breach, gap, cleft, crevice, crack, fissure, rupture, tear, rip, rift, slit, slash
OLD rent
2 SCHISM, disunion, dissension, discord, difference, division, separation, rupture, estrangement, alienation, divergence, break-up
♦ *adj*
divided, cleft, bisected, dual, twofold, broken, fractured, cracked, ruptured
FORMAL cloven
■ **split hairs**
find fault, quibble, pettifog, over-refine, cavil
COLLOQ. nit-pick
■ **split up**
part, part company, estrange, disband, break up, separate, divorce, get divorced

split-up *n*
break-up, separation, divorce, estrangement, alienation, parting, parting of the ways

spoil *v*
1 MAR, upset, wreck, ruin, destroy, damage, botch, bodge, butcher, impair, harm, hurt, injure, distort, mutilate, deface, disfigure, blemish, taint, contaminate, pollute, corrupt, foul, tarnish, cook, mangle, deform, obliterate, poison, ret; *Scot* bauchle, blunk; *N Am* mux
OLD wrong, distaste, prejudicate
FORMAL vitiate
COLLOQ. mess up, throw a spanner in the works, queer, pour cold water on, put a damper on, cast a shadow over, foul up, wash up, kill, murder
SLANG louse up, screw up, gum up, bitch up, bugger up
2 *spoil a child*
indulge, overindulge, pamper, cosset, coddle, mollycoddle, baby, spoon-feed
COLLOQ. wait on hand and foot
3 DETERIORATE, go bad, go off, go sour, sour, turn, curdle, decay, decompose, rot, go/become rotten
■ **spoil for**
be eager for, be keen on, be intent on, long for, yearn for

spoils *n*
plunder, loot, booty, haul, gain, benefit, profit, acquisitions, prizes, winnings, the game, boodle; *Scot* spulzie
OLD bribe
FORMAL spoliation, despoliation
COLLOQ. pickings
SLANG swag

spoilsport *n*
misery, killjoy, meddler, damper
COLLOQ. dog in the manger, party-pooper, wet blanket, buzzkill
SLANG *Aust & NZ* wowser, nark

spoken *adj*
verbal, oral, voiced, said, stated, told, uttered, phonetic, expressed, declared, unwritten, viva voce
E3 unspoken, unexpressed, written

spokesman, spokeswoman *n*
spokesperson, representative, delegate, agent, voice, negotiator, arbitrator, intermediary, mediator, go-between, broker, mouthpiece, propagandist

sponge *v*
1 WIPE, mop, clean, wash, swab
2 *sponge off/on other people*
cadge, beg, borrow, scrounge
COLLOQ. bum, freeload
SLANG *Aust & NZ* bludge

sponger *n*
cadger, scrounger, parasite, hanger-on, beggar, borrower
COLLOQ. freeloader, bum, moocher
SLANG *Aust & NZ* bludger

spongy *adj*
soft, cushioned, cushiony, yielding, elastic, resilient, springy, squashy, porous, absorbent, light

sponsor *n, v*
♦ *n*
patron, supporter, backer, friend, promoter, subsidizer, underwriter, guarantor, surety, godfather
OLD gossip, susceptor, undertaker
COLLOQ. angel
♦ *v*
finance, fund, bankroll, subsidize, patronize, be a patron of, back, support, promote, underwrite, guarantee, put up the money for, stand for
OLD promise, vouch

sponsorship *n*
(financial) backing, (financial) support, (financial) aid, (financial) assistance, endorsement, patronage, finance, funds, grant, subsidy, promotion

spontaneity *n*
naturalness, instinctiveness, instinct, impulse, improvisation, extemporization

spontaneous *adj*
1 UNPLANNED, voluntary, unprompted, uncompelled, impromptu, extempore, unrehearsed, unpremeditated, free, willing, unhesitating, reflex, automatic
COLLOQ. spur of the moment, knee-jerk
2 NATURAL, unforced, untaught, instinctive, impulsive
E3 1 planned, deliberate **2** forced, studied

spontaneously *adv*
voluntarily, willingly, freely, impromptu, extempore, impulsively, on impulse, unplanned, unprompted, instinctively, of your own accord, without being asked, on the spur of the moment
COLLOQ. off the cuff, off the top of your head

spoof *n*
joke, hoax, game, travesty, trick, prank, fake, deception, caricature, bluff, burlesque, parody, mockery, satire, lampoon
COLLOQ. send-up, take-off, con, leg-pull

spooky *adj*
creepy, chilling, eerie, frightening, hair-raising, ghostly, scary, mysterious, spine-chilling, supernatural, weird, unearthly, uncanny

spoon *n*
See panel at **kitchen utensils**.

spoon-feed *v*
indulge, overindulge, cosset, pamper, spoil, mollycoddle, baby, featherbed
COLLOQ. wait on hand and foot

sporadic *adj*
occasional, intermittent, infrequent, isolated, spasmodic, erratic, irregular, uneven, random, scattered
E₃ frequent, regular

sporadically *adv*
spasmodically, occasionally, intermittently, periodically, now and again, off and on, on and off
E₃ continuously, uninterruptedly

sport *n, v*
♦ *n*
1 GAME, exercise, activity, physical activity, pastime, amusement, entertainment, diversion, recreation, pleasure, fun, play
See panel below
2 FUN, mirth, humour, joking, joke, jesting, jest, banter, teasing, mockery, ridicule, sneering
COLLOQ. kidding
♦ *v*
wear, display, exhibit, show off

> **QUOTATIONS**
> Sports do not build character. They reveal it
> HEYWOOD CAMPBELL BROUN

sporting *adj*
sportsmanlike, decent, modest, considerate, fair, reasonable, respectable, just, honourable, gentlemanly, ladylike
E₃ unsporting, ungentlemanly, unfair

sportive *adj*
playful, lively, frisky, frolicsome, gamesome, gay, jaunty, merry, skittish, sprightly, prankish, rollicking, coltish, kittenish, ludic

sports equipment
See panel on next page

sporty *adj*
1 ATHLETIC, fit, energetic, outdoor
2 STYLISH, jaunty, showy, loud, flashy, casual, informal
COLLOQ. trendy, natty, snazzy

spot *n, v*
♦ *n*
1 DOT, speckle, fleck, mark, speck, blotch, blot, splodge, splotch, smudge, daub, splash, stain, discoloration, blemish, flaw
2 PIMPLE, blackhead, boil, pock, papula, papule, pustule
3 PLACE, point, position, situation, location, site, scene, setting, locality, locale, area
4 *have a spot of lunch*
bit, little, some, small amount, bite, morsel
5 *have a spot on television*
slot, niche, opening, position, place, time, airtime, show, programme
6 PLIGHT, predicament, quandary, difficulty, trouble, mess
COLLOQ. fix, hole, jam, scrape, pickle, fine/pretty kettle of fish
♦ *v*
1 NOTICE, see, observe, detect, discern, identify, recognize, make out, catch sight of, spy
FORMAL descry, espy
2 MARK, dot, speckle, fleck, soil, blemish, taint, stain

■ **spot-on**
exact, precise, accurate, correct, flawless, faultless, right, true, definite, explicit, detailed, specific, strict, unerring, close, factual
COLLOQ. on the nail, bang on, on the button

■ **on the spot**
immediately, straight away, right away, right now, at once, next, there and then, instantly, instantaneously, directly, speedily, quickly, without delay, promptly,

---

Sports include:

RACKET SPORTS:						EXTREME SPORTS:
badminton	pétanque	canoeing	snowboarding	jogging		bouldering
fives	pitch and putt	diving	speed skating	mountaineering		canyoning
lacrosse	polo	fishing	toboganing	Nordic walking		flowboarding
colloq. ping-pong	pool	kitesurfing (or	(luging)	orienteering		free running
squash	putting	kiteboarding)		pot-holing		heli-skiing
table-tennis	rounders	rowing	TARGET GAMES:	rock-climbing		ice climbing
tennis	rugby	sailing	archery	walking		sandboarding
	shinty	skin-diving	clay-pigeon			skysurfing
BALL GAMES:	snooker	surfing	shooting	RACING:		slacklining
American football	soccer	swimming	darts	cycle racing		street luge
Australian Rules	tenpin bowling	synchronized	quoits	drag-racing		tombstoning
football	volleyball	swimming	shooting	go-karting		ultrarunning
baseball		wakeboarding		greyhound-racing		volcano boarding
basketball	ATHLETICS:	water polo	COMBAT SPORTS:	horse racing		wingsuit flying
billiards	cross-country	water-skiing	boxing	motocross		
boules	decathlon	windsurfing	cage fighting	motor racing		MISCELLANEOUS:
bowls	discus	yachting	fencing	Nascar®		aerobics
camogie	high-jump		judo	speedway racing		chessboxing
Canadian football	hurdling	WINTER SPORTS:	jujitsu	stock-car racing		gymnastics
cricket	javelin	airboarding	karate			keep-fit
croquet	long-jump	bobsleigh	kung fu	ON HORSEBACK:		roller-skating
football	marathon	cross-country	lucha libre	horse-racing		spinning
futsal	pentathlon	skiing	mixed martial arts	hunting		trampolining
Gaelic football	pole vault	curling	(MMA)	show-jumping		weightlifting
golf	running	downhill skiing	tae kwon do	trotting		
handball	shot put	ice-hockey	wrestling			
hockey	triple-jump	ice-skating		IN THE AIR:		
hurling		ringette	OUTDOOR PUR-	gliding		
netball	WATER SPORTS:	skeleton bob	SUITS:	hang-gliding		
pelota	angling	skiing	adventure racing	paragliding		
	aqua aerobics	slalom	climbing	sky-diving		

Sports equipment includes:

ANGLING:
bait
disgorger
fishing-line
fishing-rod
float
fly
fly reel
fly rod
gaff
gang-hook
hook
jig
keep-net
lure
net
paternoster
priest
reel
spinning rod
trace

ARCHERY:
arrow
bolt
bow

crossbow

ATHLETICS:
discus
hammer
javelin
shot

BADMINTON:
badminton racket
net
shuttlecock

BASEBALL:
baseball
baseball bat
catcher's glove
mitt

BOWLING:
boule
bowl
jack
wood

BOXING:
boxing glove
gum shield

punch-bag
punch-ball

CRICKET:
bail
cricket ball
cricket bat
nets
stump
wicket

CURLING:
brush
curling stone

DEEP-SEA DIVING:
aqualung
snorkel

FENCING:
épée
face-guard
foil
mask
sabre

GOLF:
golfball

golf club
golfing glove
tee

GYMNASTICS:
asymmetrical bars
balance beam
beam
horizontal bar
isometric bar
mat
parallel-bars
pommel horse
rings
rope
springboard
trampoline
vaulting horse

HOCKEY:
hockey ball
hockey stick

ICE-HOCKEY:
hockey skate
ice-hockey stick
puck

SKATING:
ice-skate
in-line skate
Rollerblade®
roller boot
roller-skate
speed skate

SKIING:
ski
ski stick

**SNOOKER AND
BILLIARDS:**
billiard ball
bridge
chalk
cue
cue ball
rack
rest
snooker ball
spider
table

TENNIS:
net

racket press
tennis ball
tennis racket

TENPIN BOWLING:
bowling ball
pins

OTHER:
basketball
caman
football
hurley
netball
oar
rugby ball
sailboard
skateboard
snow board
surfboard
toboggan
volleyball
water-ski

See also **golf club**.

---

unhesitatingly, without hesitation, without question, this minute/instant, without further/more ado, straightforth
FORMAL forthwith
COLLOQ. pronto, before you know it, before you can say Jack Robinson, in two shakes of a lamb's tail, in a jiffy, like a shot

> **PROVERBS**
> A leopard doesn't change its spots

spotless *adj*
immaculate, clean, white, gleaming, shining, spick and span, unmarked, unstained, unblemished, unsullied, untainted, pure, chaste, virgin, virginal, untouched, innocent, blameless, faultless, irreproachable
E3 dirty, impure

spotlight *v, n*
♦ *v*
emphasize, stress, accentuate, focus on, highlight, underline, illuminate, feature, point up, draw attention to, give prominence to, throw into relief
E3 tone down, play down
♦ *n*
attention, public attention, public eye, fame, emphasis, notoriety, interest
COLLOQ. limelight

spotted *adj*
dotted, speckled, flecked, mottled, dappled, brindle(d), pied, piebald, polka-dot, spotty
FORMAL macular, guttate(d)

spotty *adj*
1 PIMPLY, pimpled, acned, blotchy, spotted, dotted, speckled, flecked, mottled, dappled, pied, piebald
2 PATCHY, uneven, inconsistent, varying, erratic, bitty

spouse *n*
husband, wife, partner, companion, consort, mate
OLD fere
COLLOQ. better half, other half, hubby, missus

spout *v, n*
♦ *v*
1 SPURT, jet, squirt, spray, shoot, gush, flow, stream, pour, surge, erupt, emit, discharge, disgorge, spew, blow
OLD bespout

2 *spouting poetry*
pontificate, go on, rant, hold forth, spout off/forth, mouth
OLD bespout
FORMAL expatiate, sermonize, orate
COLLOQ. spiel, rabbit on, waffle, witter (on)
♦ *n*
stream, jet, fountain, geyser, gargoyle, outlet, nozzle, rose, spray, waterspout; *Scot* stroup

sprain *v*
twist, wrench, turn, injure, dislocate, pull, rick, crick

sprawl *v*
1 *sprawl on the couch*
flop, slump, stretch, slouch, recline
FORMAL repose
COLLOQ. loll, lounge
2 STRAGGLE, spread, stretch, trail, ramble

spray¹ *n, v*
♦ *n*
1 MOISTURE, drizzle, mist, foam, froth, spume, shower, jet, spindrift, spoondrift, swish, waterspout, scud
OLD (*Shakesp*) aspersion
2 AEROSOL, atomizer, sprinkler, vaporizer, mister, sprayer, nebulizer, propellant, spray gun; *N Am* squirt gun
♦ *v*
shower, spatter, spout, sprinkle, scatter, diffuse, disperse, gush, jet, wet, drench, squirt, vaporize, mothball
FORMAL disseminate

spray² *n*
a spray of flowers/leaves
sprig, branch, corsage, posy, nosegay, bouquet, garland, wreath, aigrette

spread *v, n*
♦ *v*
1 STRETCH, extend, sprawl, broaden, widen, dilate, enlarge, develop, grow, increase, advance, expand, grow/become bigger, swell, mushroom, proliferate, escalate, spill over, open (out), unroll, unfurl, unfold, fan out, cover, lay (out), order, set, arrange
2 SCATTER, strew, diffuse, radiate, fan out, broadcast, transmit, communicate, propagate, make public, make known, publicize, advertise, publish, circulate, go/get round, distribute
FORMAL disseminate, promulgate

3 COAT, cover, put on, apply, smear, layer
1 close, fold **2** suppress
♦ *n*
1 STRETCH, reach, span, extent, expanse, sweep, compass
2 *the spread of disease*
advance, development, expansion, increase, proliferation, escalation, swelling, mushrooming, diffusion, dispersion, distribution, transmission, broadcasting, communication, propagation
FORMAL dissemination
3 LARGE MEAL, banquet, feast, party, dinner, dinner party, treat
FORMAL repast
COLLOQ. blow-out

spree *n*
bout, fling, orgy, revel, carouse, debauch
COLLOQ. binge, splurge, razzle, razzle-dazzle, bender

sprig *n*
twig, stem, spray, shoot, branch, bough

sprightly *adj*
agile, nimble, spry, active, energetic, lively, animated, spirited, vivacious, hearty, brisk, jaunty, playful, frolicsome, cheerful, light-hearted, blithe, airy
COLLOQ. perky
doddering, inactive, lifeless

spring *v, n*
♦ *v*
1 JUMP, leap, vault, bound, hop, bounce, rebound, recoil
2 ORIGINATE, derive, come, stem, arise, start, proceed, issue, descend, emerge, emanate, appear, sprout, grow, develop
3 *spring the news on someone*
tell/announce unexpectedly, reveal suddenly, present without warning
♦ *n*
1 JUMP, leap, vault, bound, hop, bounce, rebound, recoil
2 SPRINGINESS, resilience, give, flexibility, elasticity, bounciness, buoyancy
3 LIVELINESS, energy, spirit, briskness, cheerfulness, light-heartedness, animation
4 SOURCE, origin, beginning, basis, cause, root, fountainhead, wellhead, wellspring, well, geyser, spa
■ **spring up**
appear suddenly, come into existence, come into being, develop, grow, shoot up, sprout up, proliferate, mushroom

springy *adj*
bouncy, resilient, flexible, elastic, stretchy, rubbery, spongy, buoyant, tensible, tensile
hard, stiff, rigid

sprinkle *v*
shower, spray, spatter, splash, trickle, scatter, strew, dot, pepper, dust, powder

sprinkling *n*
few, handful, dash, scattering, scatter, smattering, sprinkle, trickle, touch, trace, dusting
FORMAL admixture

sprint *v*
run, race, dash, tear, fly, dart, career, shoot
COLLOQ. belt, scoot, zip

sprite *n*
gnome, spirit, elf, fairy, goblin, imp, kelpie, nymph, naiad, puck, pouke, pixie, sylph, brownie, leprechaun, dryad, apparition, bogy, bogle, spright
TECHNICAL apsaras
OLD pug

sprout *v*
shoot, bud, germinate, grow, develop, come up, put forth, spring up

spruce *adj, v*
♦ *adj*
smart, elegant, neat, trim, dapper, well-dressed, chic, well-turned-out, well-groomed, sleek

COLLOQ. natty, cool, snazzy, suited and booted
scruffy, untidy
■ **spruce up**
neaten, tidy (up), smarten up, groom, preen, primp, titivate
COLLOQ. tart up

spry *adj*
sprightly, quick, alert, agile, energetic, brisk, ready, nimble, active, supple
COLLOQ. nippy, peppy
doddering, inactive, lethargic

spume *n*
foam, froth, lather, suds, head, bubbles, fizz, effervescence

spunk *n*
courage, nerve, spirit, pluck, resolution, toughness, backbone, gameness, heart, mettle, chutzpah
COLLOQ. guts, grit, bottle
colloq. funk

spur *v, n*
♦ *v*
stimulate, prompt, incite, drive, propel, impel, urge, induce, encourage, motivate, goad, prod, poke, prick
OLD (*Spenser*) spurne
curb, discourage
♦ *n*
1 INCENTIVE, encouragement, inducement, motive, motivation, stimulus, stimulant, urge, incitement, impetus, prompt, fillip
2 SPIKE, prong, rowel, stud, projection, protuberance, protrusion, heel
TECHNICAL calcar, spica, star wheel
3 *a mountain spur*
limb, branch, offset, embranchment
1 curb, disincentive, discouragement
■ **on the spur of the moment**
on impulse, impulsively, impetuously, spontaneously, impromptu, extempore, unexpectedly, suddenly, thoughtlessly, unpremeditatedly, without planning
OLD (*Shakesp*) upon the gad
COLLOQ. on the spot

spurious *adj*
false, fake, counterfeit, forged, fraudulent, deceitful, contrived, bogus, mock, sham, feigned, pretended, simulated, imitation, artificial, make-believe
COLLOQ. pseudo, phoney, trumped-up; *Aust* cronk
genuine, authentic, real

spurn *v*
reject, turn down, turn away, say no to, scorn, condemn, despise, disdain, rebuff, repulse, repudiate, slight, snub, ignore, disregard
COLLOQ. cold-shoulder, look down on, turn up your nose at
accept, embrace

> **!** **spurn** or **scorn**?
> See panel at **scorn**.

spurt *v, n*
♦ *v*
gush, spray, squirt, jet, shoot, pour, stream, well, burst, erupt, issue, surge
♦ *n*
1 JET, gush, stream, spray, squirt, outpouring, welling, eruption
2 *a spurt of activity*
burst, rush, surge, increase, spate, fit, access

spy *n, v*
♦ *n*
secret agent, agent, undercover agent, foreign agent, enemy agent, double agent, fifth columnist, scout, snooper, shadow, emissary, setter, sleeper, *mouchard*
OLD spie, intelligencer, beagle, spial, under-espial, wait; (*Spenser*) spyal
COLLOQ. mole
SLANG plant, nark, spook

♦ v

spot, glimpse, notice, see, observe, discern, discover, make out, catch sight of, tout
OLD spie, survey
FORMAL descry, espy
SLANG nark

■ **spy on**

watch, observe (closely), keep an eye on, keep tabs on, keep under surveillance

squabble v, n

♦ v

bicker, wrangle, fight, quarrel, row, argue, dispute, have words, clash, brawl
COLLOQ. scrap, set to

♦ n

row, clash, dispute, fight, argument, quarrel, disagreement, spat
COLLOQ. barney, scrap, set-to, tiff

squad n

crew, team, gang, band, group, company, unit, side, brigade, platoon, troop, force, outfit

squalid adj

1 DIRTY, filthy, unclean, grimy, grubby, mucky, foul, disgusting, repulsive, sordid, seedy, dingy, untidy, slovenly, unkempt, broken-down, run-down, ramshackle, dilapidated, neglected, uncared-for, Dickensian
COLLOQ. sleazy, grotty, slummy
SLANG ribby
2 REPULSIVE, low, mean, nasty, sordid, unpleasant, wretched, vile, shameful, obscene, offensive, improper, disgraceful
F3 **1** clean, attractive **2** pleasant

squall n, v

♦ n

wind, storm, gale, gust, hurricane, blow, flurry, tempest, windstorm

♦ v

wail, yell, cry, howl, yowl, moan, groan

squally adj

windy, stormy, rough, wild, gusty, blowy, blustery, tempestuous, turbulent

squalor n

squalidness, dirtiness, dirt, filthiness, filth, uncleanness, grime, griminess, grubbiness, muckiness, foulness, dinginess, decay, neglect, meanness, wretchedness, slum, dung-heap, dung-hill; N Am skid row/road
COLLOQ. sleaziness

squander v

waste, misspend, misuse, lavish, fritter away, throw away, dissipate, scatter, spend, expend, consume, blue, fool away, muck, muddle away, gamble, plunge; dialect scamble; N Am slather
OLD bezzle, lash, sport away
COLLOQ. splash out on, splurge, throw/pour down the drain, spend money like water, spend money as if it grows on trees, spend money as if it's going out of style/fashion, spend money like there's no tomorrow, make/play ducks and drakes of/with
SLANG blow

square n, v, adj

♦ n

1 QUADRANGLE, market square, town square, marketplace, plaza
COLLOQ. quad
2 TRADITIONALIST, conservative, conventionalist, conformer, conformist, diehard
COLLOQ. fuddy-duddy, (old) fogey, stick-in-the-mud

♦ v

settle (up), reconcile, tally, agree, harmonize, conform, accord, correspond, match, be compatible with, balance, straighten, level, align, even, make equal, adjust, regulate, set/put right, adapt, tailor, fit, suit, resolve
FORMAL be congruous with

♦ adj

1 QUADRILATERAL, rectangular, right-angled, perpendicular, straight, true, even, level
2 FAIR, equitable, just, ethical, upright, straight, honourable, honest, genuine, above-board
COLLOQ. on the level; Aust & NZ dinkum
3 TRADITIONALIST, conservative, conventionalist, conformist, dated, diehard, old-fashioned, strait-laced
COLLOQ. fuddy-duddy; N Am buttoned-down

squarely adv

directly, straight, unswervingly, right, dead, just, exactly, precisely
COLLOQ. bang, smack, plumb

squash v

1 CRUSH, flatten, press, squeeze, compress, crowd, pack, jam, trample, stamp, pound, grind, pulp, mash, smash, distort, squidge
FORMAL macerate, pulverize
2 SUPPRESS, silence, quell, quash, crush, annihilate, put down, squelch, snub, humiliate
F3 **1** stretch, expand

squashy adj

soft, spongy, springy, squelchy, mushy, pappy, pulpy, squishy, yielding
F3 firm

squat v, adj

♦ v

crouch, stoop, bend, kneel, hunch, sit on your haunches, sit, hunker (down), ruck; dialect croup
COLLOQ. N Am absquatulate

♦ adj

short, stocky, thickset, dumpy, chunky, stubby, podgy, pudgy, squabby, Humpty-dumpty; dialect fubby
TECHNICAL pyknic
F3 slim, lanky, slender

squawk v, n

♦ v

1 SCREECH, shriek, cry, scream, yelp, croak, cackle, crow, hoot
2 COMPLAIN, criticize, find fault, kick up a fuss, object, protest, air your grievances, grumble, carp, fuss, moan, nag, whine, carry on, groan, growl
COLLOQ. beef, bellyache, grouse, grouch, gripe, grump, bleat, whinge, squeal, raise a stink, have a bone to pick
SLANG bitch

♦ n

screech, shriek, cry, scream, yelp, croak, cackle, crow, hoot

squeak v, n

squeal, whine, creak, peep, cheep, pipe

squeal v, n

♦ v

1 CRY, shout, yell, howl, yelp, wail, scream, screech, shriek, squawk
2 INFORM, tell tales, sneak, betray
COLLOQ. tell, sell out, sell down the river, snitch, split, rat
SLANG grass, shop; N Am stool

♦ n

cry, shout, yell, howl, yelp, wail, scream, screech, shriek, squawk

squeamish adj

queasy, nauseated, nauseous, sick, delicate, fastidious, finicky, particular, punctilious, prudish, strait-laced, scrupulous

squeeze v, n

♦ v

1 PRESS, squash, crush, pulp, mash, pinch, nip, tighten, compress, gripe, strain, twist, wring, extract, grip, clasp, clutch, hold tight, hug, embrace, enfold, cuddle, suck, chirt, squidge; dialect scruze, thrutch

2 *squeeze into a corner*
cram, stuff, pack, crowd, crush, squash, wedge, jam, force, ram, push, thrust, shove, jostle, shoe, sandwich; *dialect* scrouge, scrowdge
3 WRING, wrest, extort, milk, force, pressurize, pressure, extract, juice, mangle, sweat
COLLOQ. bleed, lean on, put the screws on
♦ *n*
1 PRESS, squash, crush, crowd, congestion, jam, chirt; *dialect* thrutch
2 HUG, embrace, cuddle, hold, grasp, grip, clutch, clasp

squint *n, v, adj*
♦ *n*
glance, side-glance, glimpse, sideways look, cast, cross-eye; *Scot* gley
TECHNICAL strabism
Related adjective: strabismal
♦ *v*
peer, look askance, blink, gaze, scan, peep, pink; *Scot* gledge, gley, skelly
OLD twire, squinny
♦ *adj*
crooked, indirect, oblique, off-centre, aslant, askew, awry, cockeyed, walleyed; *Scot* gleyed
TECHNICAL strabismic
COLLOQ. skew-whiff
E3 straight

squirm *v*
wriggle, twist, writhe, squiggle, move, shift, wiggle, fidget, agonize, flounder

squirrel
■ **squirrel away**
hoard, store, hide, conceal, lay up, save (up), set aside, put by, put away, lay in, stock up, stockpile, salt away
COLLOQ. stash away

squirt *v, n*
♦ *v*
spray, spurt, jet, shoot, spout, gush, stream, spew (out), ejaculate, discharge, issue, pour, well, surge, emit, eject, expel; *Scot* scoosh
♦ *n*
spray, spurt, jet, stream, gush, surge; *Scot* scoosh

stab *v, n*
♦ *v*
pierce, puncture, cut, wound, injure, gore, knife, spear, skewer, slash, bayonet, transfix, stick, push, jab, thrust, pink, fork, prong, kris, poniard, stilleto
OLD dirk
♦ *n*
1 ACHE, pang, pain, spasm, throb, twinge, prick
2 CUT, puncture, incision, slash, gash, injury, wound, jab, pierce, prick, pink, thrust
3 TRY, attempt, go, endeavour, venture
FORMAL essay
COLLOQ. bash, crack, shot, whirl
■ **stab in the back**
betray, deceive, let down, slander, double-cross, inform on, sell out
COLLOQ. sell down the river

stabbing *adj*
shooting, stinging, piercing, throbbing, painful, sharp, acute

stability *n*
steadiness, firmness, secureness, soundness, sturdiness, solidity, reliability, durability, uniformity, constancy, regularity, unchangeability
E3 instability, unsteadiness, insecurity, weakness

stabilize *v*
make stable, keep steady, steady, fix, secure, support, establish, firm up, balance, equalize, make uniform
TECHNICAL valorize

stable *adj*
1 *a stable structure*
balanced, fixed, static, steady, firm, secure, fast, sound, strong, sturdy, solid, sure, reliable
2 *a stable government/relationship*
established, well-founded, deep-rooted, lasting, long-lasting, durable, enduring, abiding, permanent, dependable, reliable, unchangeable, invariable, unwavering, unswerving
3 *the patient's condition is stable*
regular, uniform, steady, constant, unchanging, static
E3 1 wobbly, shaky, weak, unstable **2** unstable, changeable **3** irregular, erratic, unstable

stack *n, v*
♦ *n*
1 HEAP, pile, mound, mass, load, collection, accumulation, store, hoard, stock, stockpile, rick, ruck
COLLOQ. stash
2 *stacks of money*
a large amount, lot, great numbers, many, a good/great deal
COLLOQ. oodles, tons, loads, masses, heaps, piles
3 *a chimney stack*
chimney, clamp, funnel, shaft, vent, flue
TECHNICAL blow-out preventer
♦ *v*
heap, pile, load, amass, accumulate, assemble, gather, save, hoard, stockpile, rick
COLLOQ. stash

stadium *n*
sports ground, sports field, field, arena, bowl, ring, track, pitch

staff *n, v*
♦ *n*
1 *member of staff*
personnel, workforce, employees, workers, human resources, manpower, crew, team, teachers, officers
2 STICK, pole, cane, crook, rod, baton, crutch, wand, truncheon, alpenstock, prop, crosier
♦ *v*
man, work, operate, occupy, provide, supply, equip

stage *n, v*
♦ *n*
1 PHASE, point, juncture, step, time, period, division, lap, leg, length, level, floor
2 PLATFORM, podium, dais, rostrum, stand, apron
COLLOQ. soapbox
3 ARENA, setting, scene, sphere, field, realm, background, backdrop
♦ *v*
mount, put on, lay on, put together, present, produce, give, do, perform, direct, arrange, organize, stage-manage, orchestrate, engineer
■ **the stage**
theatre, drama, the play, dramatics, theatrics, show business
FORMAL Thespian art
COLLOQ. the boards, the footlights, rep

> **QUOTATIONS**
> All the world's a stage, / And all the men and women merely players. / They have their exits and their entrances, / And one man in his time plays many parts
> WILLIAM SHAKESPEARE, *As You Like It*

stagger *v*
1 LURCH, totter, teeter, wobble, bumble, blunder, sway, rock, roll, pitch, reel, recoil, falter, hesitate, waver, keel over, titubate; *Scot* daidle, stoit, stoiter, stot, wintle
OLD *N Am* step
2 SURPRISE, amaze, astound, astonish, stun, stupefy, dumbfound, shake, shock, confound, overwhelm
COLLOQ. flabbergast, nonplus, bowl over

staggered *adj*
astonished, surprised, startled, amazed, astounded, stunned, dazed, dumbfounded, taken aback, shocked, confounded, bewildered, open-eyed
COLLOQ. lost for words, knocked for six, bowled over, flabbergasted, gobsmacked

staggering *adj*
amazing, astounding, astonishing, surprising, dramatic, shocking, stunning, stupefying, unexpected, unforeseen
COLLOQ. mind-boggling

stagnant *adj*
1 *stagnant water*
still, motionless, unflowing, standing, brackish, stale, foul, dirty, filthy, smelly, unhealthy
2 *a stagnant economy*
inactive, slow, quiet, dull, sluggish, torpid, lethargic, dying, moribund
E3 **1** fresh, moving **2** busy, brisk, booming

stagnate *v*
vegetate, become stagnant, idle, languish, do nothing, decline, deteriorate, degenerate, decay, rot, putrefy, fester, rust

staid *adj*
sedate, calm, composed, sober, demure, solemn, serious-minded, serious, proper, formal, grave, sombre, quiet, steady, stiff, starchy, prim
FORMAL decorous
COLLOQ. *N Am* buttoned-down
E3 jaunty, debonair, frivolous, adventurous

stain *v, n*
♦ *v*
1 MARK, spot, blemish, blot, blotch, smear, smudge, discolour, dirty, soil, taint, contaminate, corrupt, sully, tarnish, blacken, disgrace, damage, injure
FORMAL besmirch
2 DYE, tint, tinge, colour, paint, varnish
♦ *n*
mark, spot, blemish, blot, blotch, smear, splodge, smudge, discoloration, slur, taint, disgrace, shame, dishonour, damage, injury
OLD mote

stake[1] *n, v*
♦ *n*
a stake supporting a young tree
post, pole, standard, picket, pale, paling, spike, stick, rod
♦ *v*
1 SUPPORT, fasten, brace, tie, tie up, prop (up), secure, hold (up), tether, pierce
2 *stake a claim*
establish, lay claim to, state, declare, demand, assert, put in
FORMAL requisition
■ **stake out**
demarcate, define, delimit, stake off, mark off/out, outline, reserve, survey, watch, keep an eye on

stake[2] *n, v*
♦ *n*
1 INVESTMENT, share, claim, involvement, concern, (financial) interest, bet, wager, pledge
COLLOQ. ante
2 *the leadership stakes*
contest, competition, race, prize, winnings
♦ *v*
risk, gamble, bet, wager, pledge, chance, hazard, venture
COLLOQ. ante

stale *adj*
1 *stale bread*
dry, hard, hardened, old, musty, mouldy, fusty, flat, insipid, tasteless, sour
COLLOQ. (gone) off
2 OVERUSED, hackneyed, corny, clichéd, cliché-ridden, stock, stereotyped, tired, jaded, worn-out, worthless,

blown, overfamiliar, unoriginal, uninspired, flat, trite, insipid, banal, commonplace
FORMAL platitudinous
COLLOQ. run-of-the-mill
E3 **1** crisp, fresh **2** new, original, imaginative

stalemate *n*
draw, tie, deadlock, impasse, standstill, halt, blockade, stand-off
TECHNICAL zugzwang
E3 progress

stalk[1] *n*
the stalk of a flower
stem, shoot, twig, branch, trunk
TECHNICAL peduncle, petiole
Related adjective: peduncular

stalk[2] *v*
1 *stalk a person/an animal*
trail, track, hunt, chase, give chase, follow, pursue, shadow, track down, tail, creep up on, haunt
2 STRIDE, walk, step, pace, march

stall[1] *v*
stall them to give you more time
temporize, play for time, delay, hold up, put off, slow (down), defer, postpone, hedge, equivocate, obstruct, stonewall
COLLOQ. beat about the bush, drag your feet, put on ice, put on the back burner

stall[2] *n*
1 STAND, table, booth, kiosk, counter, surface, place, platform
2 CUBICLE, compartment, enclosure, coop, pen, corral

stalwart *adj*
1 STAUNCH, loyal, faithful, devoted, committed, steady, trusty, steadfast, reliable, dependable, vigorous, valiant, daring, intrepid, indomitable, determined, resolute
2 STRONG, sturdy, robust, rugged, stout, hardy, strapping, muscular, athletic, brawny, burly
E3 **1** disloyal, unfaithful **2** weak, feeble, timid

stamina *n*
energy, vigour, strength, power, power to stay the course, force, grit, resilience, resistance, endurance, indefatigability, staying power, fibre, bottom
FORMAL fortitude
COLLOQ. guts
E3 weakness

stammer *v, n*
♦ *v*
stutter, stumble, falter, hesitate, splutter, lisp, mumble, gibber, babble, hum
♦ *n*
stutter, speech impediment, speech defect

stamp *v, n*
♦ *v*
1 TRAMPLE, tread, crush, beat, pound, pulp, mash, squash
2 IMPRINT, impress, print, inscribe, engrave, emboss, mark, brand, fix, label, categorize, designate, identify, characterize
♦ *n*
print, imprint, impression, seal, signature, authorization, mark, hallmark, tag, label, brand, cast, mould, cut, form, fashion, sort, kind, type, quality, variety, breed, character, description
FORMAL attestation
■ **stamp out**
eradicate, suppress, crush, quell, quash, curb, put down, scotch, destroy, eliminate, end, put an end to, extinguish, quench, kill
FORMAL extirpate

stampede *n, v*
♦ *n*
charge, rush, onrush, dash, sprint, flight, rout, scattering, debacle, *sauve qui peut*; *Aust* breakaway

◆ *v*

charge, rush, dash, tear, career, run, race, sprint, gallop, shoot, fly, flee, scatter

stance *n*

position, posture, deportment, carriage, bearing, stand, standpoint, viewpoint, policy, angle, slant, line, point of view, opinion, attitude

stanch *v*

stem, stop, check, block, arrest, stay, halt, plug, dam
F3 increase, promote

> **!** **stanch** or **staunch**?
> In the sense of 'to stop the flow of', either form is correct, but *staunch* is the commoner: *staunched the flow of blood from the wound; staunch the decline of royal authority; This helped to staunch the Danish invasion.* As an adjective, the form to use is *staunch*, meaning 'loyal, trusty, steadfast': *a staunch ally/ Catholic/opponent.*

stand *v, n*

◆ *v*

1 RISE, rise to your feet, get on/to your feet, get up, stand up, be on your feet, straighten up, be erect, be upright
2 PUT, place, set, erect, up-end, position, station, locate
3 *I can't stand it*
bear, tolerate, put up with, cope with, endure, allow, brook, suffer, experience, live with, undergo, withstand, weather
FORMAL abide
COLLOQ. stomach, swallow
4 *the offer still stands*
exist, be, remain, hold, be valid, be in effect, be in force
FORMAL prevail, obtain
◆ *n*
1 BASE, pedestal, support, shelf, case, frame, rack
2 STALL, booth, counter, table, stage, dais, platform, place
3 STANCE, position, standpoint, viewpoint, policy, angle, slant, line, point of view, opinion, attitude
■ **stand by**
support, back, champion, defend, stand up for, stick up for, uphold, side with, adhere to, hold to, stick by
F3 let down
■ **stand down**
step down, resign, abdicate, quit, give up, retire, withdraw
F3 join
■ **stand for**
1 REPRESENT, symbolize, mean, signify, denote, indicate
FORMAL betoken
2 *not stand for such nonsense*
put up with, tolerate, bear, endure, allow, brook
COLLOQ. stomach
■ **stand in for**
deputize for, cover for, understudy, replace, take the place of, substitute for
COLLOQ. hold the fort for
■ **stand out**
show, be noticeable, be obvious, be conspicuous, stick out, jut out, extend, project, poke out
COLLOQ. catch the eye, stick out a mile, jump out
■ **stand up**
1 RISE, rise to your feet, get up, get to your feet, straighten up, stand
2 REMAIN VALID, cohere, hold up, hold water, stand
COLLOQ. wash
3 *she stood me up*
fail to meet, not keep a date with, let down, jilt
■ **stand up for**
defend, stick up for, side with, fight for, stand by, support, remain loyal to, protect, champion, uphold, adhere
F3 attack
■ **stand up to**
defy, oppose, resist, withstand, challenge, endure, face, face up to, confront, brave
F3 give in to

standard *n, adj*

◆ *n*

1 NORM, average, type, model, pattern, example, sample, guide, guideline, benchmark, touchstone, yardstick, principle, rule, measure, gauge, criterion, requirement, specification, grade, level, quality
FORMAL archetype, paradigm, exemplar
2 PRINCIPLE, scruple, ethic, moral, code, ideal
3 FLAG, ensign, pennant, pennon, streamer, colours, banner, gonfalon
TECHNICAL vexillum
◆ *adj*
normal, average, typical, stock, classic, basic, staple, usual, ordinary, customary, habitual, popular, prevailing, regular, approved, accepted, recognized, official, authoritative, orthodox, conventional, set, fixed, established, definitive
F3 abnormal, unusual, irregular

standard-bearer *n*

ensign, standard, gonfalonier, cornet, vexillary

standardize *v*

normalize, equalize, systematize, regiment, regularize, homogenize, stereotype, mass-produce
F3 differentiate

stand-in *n*

deputy, representative, delegate, proxy, substitute, surrogate, second, second-in-command, understudy, locum
COLLOQ. *N Am* pinch-hitter

standing *n, adj*

◆ *n*

1 REPUTATION, status, rank, position, seniority, eminence, station, repute, experience, footing
2 DURATION, existence, continuance
◆ *adj*
1 UPRIGHT, erect, perpendicular, vertical, up-ended, on your feet
2 PERMANENT, perpetual, lasting, fixed, regular, repeated
3 *standing water*
stagnant, still, motionless, unflowing, brackish, stale, foul, dirty, filthy, smelly, unhealthy
F3 **1** horizontal, lying **2** temporary

stand-off *n*

deadlock, impasse, standstill, halt, blockade

standoffish *adj*

aloof, remote, distant, unapproachable, unsociable, unfriendly, uncommunicative, withdrawn, detached, reserved, cold, cool
F3 friendly, approachable

standpoint *n*

viewpoint, angle, slant, point of view, perspective, position, station, vantage point, stance

standstill *n*

stop, halt, pause, lull, rest, stoppage, jam, log jam, hold-up, tie-up, gridlock, stand, dead stop, impasse, deadlock, stalemate, dead-finish, stall, jib
OLD (*Shakesp*) still-stand
FORMAL cessation
F3 advance, progress

staple *adj*

basic, fundamental, primary, key, main, chief, major, important, foremost, principal, essential, indispensable, vital, necessary, standard
F3 minor, dispensable

star *n, adj*

◆ *n*

1 *the stars in the sky*
asteroid, planet, sun, moon, heavenly/celestial body, sphere, orb, satellite
Related adjectives: stellar, astral, sidereal

2 CELEBRITY, personage, luminary, idol, lead, leading man, leading lady, superstar, megastar, principal
COLLOQ. household name, big name, bigwig, big shot, leading light, celeb
♦ *adj*
brilliant, well-known, famous, leading, illustrious, celebrated, prominent, talented, principal, major, pre-eminent, paramount
E3 minor

Types of star include:

brown dwarf	North Star	red dwarf
comet	nova	red giant
falling star	Polaris	shooting star
Halley's comet	Pole Star	supergiant
meteor	pulsar	supernova
neutron star	quasar	white dwarf

See also **constellation**.

starchy *adj*
formal, stiff, prim, punctilious, ceremonious, conventional, stuffy, staid, strait-laced
E3 informal

stare *v, n*
♦ *v*
gaze, look, watch, gape, gawp, gawk, goggle, glare, glower, ogle, outface
OLD dare
SLANG rubberneck
♦ *n*
gaze, look, glare, gawp, glower, goggle
SLANG fisheye
■ **be staring you in the face**
be very obvious, be glaringly obvious, be blatant, be conspicuous
COLLOQ. stick out a mile

stark *adj, adv*
♦ *adj*
1 *faced with the stark reality*
bald, bare, plain, simple, blunt, harsh, grim, severe, undecorated, unembellished, unadorned
2 *a stark contrast*
sharp, clear, clear-cut, distinct, obvious
3 *a stark landscape*
bare, barren, desolate, bleak, austere, forsaken, empty, harsh, severe, grim, dreary, gloomy, depressing
4 UTTER, complete, unmitigated, unqualified, total, absolute, sheer, pure, downright, thorough, out-and-out, flagrant, arrant
FORMAL consummate
♦ *adv*
completely, entirely, wholly, totally, absolutely, altogether, quite, utterly, clean
E3 mildly, slightly

stark-naked *adj*
naked, nude, in the nude, stripped, undressed, stark, *in puris naturalibus, en cueros*
FORMAL unclad
COLLOQ. in the altogether, in the buff, in your birthday suit, in the raw, starkers
E3 clothed, dressed

start *v, n*
♦ *v*
1 BEGIN, originate, initiate, introduce, pioneer, create, embark on/upon, bring/come into being, bring/come into existence, get under way, found, establish, set up, institute, inaugurate, launch, open, instigate, activate, turn on, trigger (off), set off, get going, set out, leave, depart, appear, arise, issue
FORMAL commence
COLLOQ. kick in, kick off, set the ball rolling, get things moving, get cracking, fire away
See Synonym nuances panel at **begin**.

2 JUMP, jerk, leap, twitch, flinch, shrink, wince, recoil
E3 **1** stop, finish, end
♦ *n*
1 BEGINNING, outset, dawn, birth, break, outburst, onset, origin, origination, initiation, introduction, foundation, institution, inauguration, launch, opening, emergence; *N Am* get-go
FORMAL commencement, inception
COLLOQ. kick-off
2 JUMP, jerk, leap, twitch, flinch, wince, spasm, convulsion, fit
E3 **1** stop, finish, end

starter *n*
appetizer, first course, canapé, *hors d'œuvre*, meze, apéritif, cocktail, tapas, bhajee, whet, relish
OLD antepast

startle *v*
surprise, amaze, astonish, astound, shock, make you jump, scare, frighten, alarm, agitate, upset, unsettle, disturb
OLD start, affray
FORMAL perturb
COLLOQ. rock, spook
E3 calm

startling *adj*
surprising, astonishing, astounding, extraordinary, shocking, staggering, unexpected, sudden, dramatic, alarming, unforeseen, electrifying, galvanic
COLLOQ. eye-popping
E3 boring, calming, ordinary

starvation *n*
hunger, extreme hunger, undernourishment, malnutrition, famine, fasting, death, famishment
E3 plenty, excess

starve *v*
hunger, fast, diet, deprive, deny, die, perish, faint, famish, atrophy, pine, clem
OLD (*Spenser*) sterve
E3 feed, gorge

starving *adj*
(very) hungry, underfed, undernourished, ravenous, famished, faint, dying

stash *v, n*
♦ *v*
store, hide, conceal, hoard, squirrel away, closet, lay up, save up, stockpile, stow, cache
FORMAL secrete
COLLOQ. salt away
E3 bring out, uncover
♦ *n*
hoard, store, collection, accumulation, mass, heap, pile, fund, reservoir, reserve, stockpile, cache

state *n, v, adj*
♦ *n*
1 CONDITION, shape, situation, position, circumstances, case, predicament
2 NATION, country, land, territory, kingdom, republic, realm, government, federation
3 PANIC, bother, plight, predicament
COLLOQ. fluster, flap, tizzy, dither, tizwas
4 GOVERNMENT, administration, authorities, parliament, council, Establishment
5 POMP, ceremony, dignity, majesty, grandeur, glory, splendour, display
♦ *v*
say, declare, tell, announce, report, communicate, assert, affirm, specify, present, express, put, set out, make known, proclaim, formulate, articulate, voice, utter, reveal, divulge, disclose
FORMAL aver, promulgate
♦ *adj*
national, governmental, parliamentary, public, official, formal, ceremonial, pompous, stately
E3 private, commercial

■ **state of affairs**
case, situation, position, circumstances, condition, plight, predicament, crisis, juncture
COLLOQ. kettle of fish, lie of the land

■ **in a state**
agitated, anxious, worried, distressed, troubled, upset, worked up, panic-stricken, ruffled
COLLOQ. flustered, hassled, het up, in a stew, in a tizzy
☲ calm

stately *adj*
grand, imposing, impressive, splendid, glorious, magnificent, elegant, majestic, regal, royal, imperial, noble, lofty, pompous, dignified, measured, deliberate, solemn, ceremonial, ceremonious, graceful
FORMAL august
☲ informal, unimpressive

statement *n*
account, report, bulletin, communiqué, announcement, declaration, assertion, proclamation, communication, presentation, utterance, revelation, divulgence, disclosure, testimony, affirmation
FORMAL averment, promulgation

state-of-the-art *adj*
modern, up-to-the-minute, advanced, cutting-edge, bleeding-edge, highly-developed, high-tech, hi-tech, space-age, complicated, complex, progressive, modernistic, innovative, inventive, go-ahead, forward-looking, futuristic, contemporary, up-to-date, new, fresh, latest, novel, present, present-day, recent, in vogue, modish
COLLOQ. newfangled, in, trendy, with it, the latest, hip, cool
☲ old, old-fashioned, out-of-date, antiquated

statesman, stateswoman *n*
politician, leader, elder statesman, diplomat
COLLOQ. grand old man, GOM

> QUOTATIONS
> Some men are born kings; and some are born statesman.
> The two are seldom the same
> GEORGE BERNARD SHAW, *Saint Joan*

static *adj*
stationary, motionless, immobile, unmoving, still, at a standstill, inert, resting, fixed, constant, steady, changeless, unchanging, undeviating, unvarying, stable
☲ dynamic, mobile, varying

station *n, v*
♦ *n*
1 *a bus/railway station*
stop, stopping-place, halt, fare-stage, terminus, exchange, park-and-ride
2 OFFICE, base, depot, headquarters

3 *a pumping station*
establishment, base, centre, office, post
4 *a television station*
channel, wavelength, broadcasting company
5 *your station in life*
status, standing, position, rank, level, grade, class
6 PLACE OF DUTY, post, place, site, location, position
♦ *v*
locate, set, establish, install, garrison, post, send, appoint, assign

stationary *adj*
motionless, immobile, unmoving, still, at a standstill, static, constant, inert, standing, resting, parked, moored, sessile, fixed
☲ mobile, moving, active

stationery
See panel below

statue *n*
figure, head, bust, effigy, image, idol, statuette, figurine, carving, sculpture, bronze, representation, monument, torso, acrolith, polychrome, xoanon; *Scot* stookie
OLD colossus, ka, kore, kouros

statuesque *adj*
dignified, imposing, impressive, majestic, stately, regal, handsome, tall
☲ small

stature *n*
1 HEIGHT, tallness, elevation, attitude, loftiness, size, inches
2 IMPORTANCE, reputation, standing, prominence, prestige, fame, renown, eminence, rank, consequence, weight
☲ **2** unimportance

status *n*
1 POSITION, rank, grade, degree, level, class, station, standing, state, condition
2 IMPORTANCE, prestige, eminence, standing, distinction, reputation, consequence, weight
☲ **2** unimportance, insignificance

statute *n*
law, rule, regulation, act, decree, ordinance, edict, enactment, act of parliament, written law, ukase
TECHNICAL capitular, *lex scripta*
OLD assize
FORMAL interlocution
Related adjective: statutory

staunch[1] *adj*
a staunch supporter
steadfast, loyal, faithful, devoted, hearty, strong, stout, firm, resolute, sound, sure, constant, true, trusty, trustworthy, committed, reliable, dependable, zealous, yeomanly
☲ unfaithful, weak, unreliable

> ⚠ **staunch** or **stanch**?
> *See panel at* **stanch**.

Items of stationery include:

account book	correction fluid	file tab	memo pad	printer ribbon	stamp pad
address book	correction ribbon	filing tray	notepaper	reinforcement ring	staple
adhesive tape	desk diary	Filofax®	paper clip	reply-paid envel-	suspension file
blotter	diary	flip chart	paper fastener	ope	tape dispenser
Blu-Tack®	divider	floppy disk	paper knife	ring binder	Tipp-Ex®
bulldog clip	document folder	folder	pen	rubber	toner
calendar	document wallet	graph paper	pencil	rubber band	treasury tag
carbon paper	drawing pin	headed notepaper	pencil-sharpener	rubber stamp	typewriter ribbon
card index	dry-transfer letter-	index card	personal organizer	ruler	wall chart
cartridge ribbon	ing	ink	pin	scissors	window envelope
cash book	elastic band	Jiffy bag®	pocket calculator	self-seal envelope	writing paper
clipboard	envelope	label	pocket folder	Sellotape®	
computer disk	eraser	lever arch file	Post-it note®	shorthand	
copying paper	expanding file	manila envelope	printer label	notebook	
correcting paper	file	marker	printer paper	spiral notebook	

See also **paper**.

staunch² v

staunch the flow of blood
stanch, stem, stop, check, block, arrest, stay, halt, plug
E3 increase, promote

> **! staunch** or **stanch**?
> *See panel at* **stanch**.

staunchly adv
steadfastly, firmly, resolutely, unswervingly, unfalteringly, implacably, unflinchingly
E3 unfaithfully, unreliably

stave

■ **stave off**
fend off, ward off, avoid, avert, deflect, repel, repulse, turn aside, prevent, parry, foil, keep back, keep at bay
E3 cause, encourage

stay¹ v, n

♦ *v*
1 REMAIN, last, continue, endure, linger, persist, keep, stay put
FORMAL abide, tarry
2 *stay in a hotel*
live, settle, stop, board, lodge, put up, rest, halt, pause, wait, visit, be accommodated at, take a room at
FORMAL reside, dwell, sojourn
3 *stay judgement*
suspend, halt, postpone, put off, delay, defer, adjourn, reprieve
FORMAL prorogue
COLLOQ. put on ice
4 *stay your anger*
control, restrain, arrest, check, curb, stop, halt, prevent, hinder, block, obstruct
♦ *n*
1 VISIT, holiday, vacation, stopover
FORMAL sojourn
2 *a stay of execution*
suspension, postponement, deferment, delay, reprieve
FORMAL remission

stay² n

a stay supporting a mast
prop, brace, buttress, reinforcement, stanchion, support, wire, strut, shoring

staying power n
stamina, energy, vigour, strength, power, power to stay the course, force, grit, resilience, resistance, endurance, indefatigability, fibre, bottom
FORMAL fortitude
COLLOQ. guts

steadfast adj
firm, fixed, resolute, stable, steady, intent, single-minded, loyal, faithful, stout-hearted, sturdy, strong, dedicated, constant, dependable, staunch, reliable, fast, established, persevering, unswerving, unwavering, immovable, unfaltering, implacable, unflinching, perseverant
OLD sad
E3 unreliable, wavering, weak

steadily adv
1 *work away steadily*
constantly, uninterruptedly, regularly, evenly, on an even keel, round the clock, all year round
2 CALMLY, sensibly, rationally, seriously, soberly
E3 **1** sporadically, intermittently **2** excitably, impulsively

steady adj, v

♦ *adj*
1 *hold the camera steady*
stable, balanced, well-balanced, poised, fixed, secure, immovable, unmoving, motionless, firm
2 *make steady progress*
regular, even, uniform, on an even keel, consistent, unvarying, unvariable, unchanging, ceaseless, perpetual, constant, persistent, uninterrupted, unbroken, unfaltering, unwavering

FORMAL incessant, unremitting
3 CALM, stable, settled, controlled, self-controlled, well-balanced, still, imperturbable, unexcitable, unexcited
COLLOQ. unflappable
4 RELIABLE, dependable, balanced, well-balanced, serious, sober, sensible, steadfast
5 *a steady boyfriend*
regular, constant, usual, customary, established, habitual
E3 **1** unsteady, shaky, wobbly **2** uneven, irregular, variable, wavering **3** excitable, worried **4** unreliable
♦ *v*
1 STABILIZE, balance, fix, secure, brace, support
2 COMPOSE, control, soothe, relax, tranquillize, still, subdue, check, restrain

steal v, n

♦ *v*
1 *steal a car*
make off/away with, run off with, go/walk off with, thieve, pilfer, take, misappropriate, snatch, break in, pocket, shoplift, poach, embezzle, kidnap, abduct, plagiarize, rob, burgle, hijack, crib, knap, nap, twitch; *dialect* mag; *N Am* boost
OLD bribe, condiddle, purse
FORMAL appropriate, purloin, peculate
COLLOQ. pinch, nick, filch, lift, snaffle, knock up, nobble, loot, knock off, swipe, whip, bag, nip, liberate, relieve of, help yourself to, have your fingers in the till, scrump, *Aust & NZ* duckshove, souvenir
SLANG rip off, heist, hoist, pull, lag, blag, mill, smug, sneak; *N Am* glom
OLD SLANG cabbage, cly, nim
2 CREEP, tiptoe, slip, slink, slide, slither, sneak
E3 **1** return, give back
♦ *n*
bargain, giveaway, special offer, good buy, value for money, discount, reduction
COLLOQ. snip

> **SYNONYM NUANCES**
>
> *verb sense 1*
> The phrases **make off with**, **run off with** and **go off with** widely refer to taking something without the knowledge of the owner, whereas **thieve** more directly refers to illegal procurement and is more accusatory in tone.
>   **Pilfer**, although similar, suggests taking small quantities: *she regularly pilfered the office stationery*. **Misappropriate** refers to wrongly taking something for your own use, and may be used rather euphemistically: *the branch secretary had misappropriated funds*, whereas **embezzle** more directly refers to fraudulently acquiring large sums of money.
>   **Pocket** is appropriate for furtively taking possession of something small: *she pocketed his keys*, while **snatch** suggests elements of speed and surprise.

stealing n
theft, robbery, thieving, shoplifting, pilfering, pilferage, burglary, break-in, embezzlement, larceny, misappropriation, plagiarism, poaching, piracy, thievery, snatch
FORMAL peculation, appropriation, purloining
COLLOQ. filching, pinching, nicking, stick-up, mugging, swipe, smash-and-grab

stealth n
stealthiness, furtiveness, surreptitiousness, covertness, secrecy, slyness, sneakiness, unobtrusiveness
E3 openness

stealthily adv
by stealth, surreptitiously, covertly, secretly, furtively, slyly, cunningly, *à la dérobée*; *Scot* stownlins
OLD stolenwise

stealthy adj
surreptitious, covert, secret, unobtrusive, secretive, quiet, furtive, sly, cunning, sneaky, underhand

FORMAL clandestine
▣ open

steam *n, v*

♦ *n*

1 VAPOUR, water vapour, mist, haze, exhalation, condensation, moisture, dampness

2 *run out of steam*
energy, activity, enthusiasm, eagerness, liveliness, vigour, stamina, momentum

■ **steam up**
mist up, fog up, become covered with steam, become covered with mist

■ **let off steam**
let yourself go, release surplus energy, air your feelings, sound off

■ **under your own steam**
by your own efforts, independently, by yourself, alone, unaided, without (others') help

■ **get steamed up**
get annoyed, get angry, get flustered, get excited
COLLOQ. get het up, boil over, fly into a rage, blow a fuse, blow your cool, do your nut, explode, fly off the handle, have kittens, hit the roof, lose your cool, lose your rag

steamboat *n*
steamer, steamship, steam-packet, steam vessel, packet-boat, packet-ship, packet, paddle-boat, paddle steamer, vaporetto

steamy *adj*

1 HUMID, hot, steaming, sweltering, hazy, muggy, sticky, misty, sweaty, close, damp, sultry, stewy, vaporous, vapourish, vapoury, gaseous
FORMAL vaporiform

2 EROTIC, passionate, sensual, lustful, amorous, seductive
COLLOQ. sexy, raunchy, blue

steed *n*
horse, charger, hack, mount, nag, jade, Rosinante

steel *v*
brace, harden, toughen, nerve, prepare
FORMAL fortify
COLLOQ. psych
▣ weaken

steely *adj*

1 GREY, steel-coloured, steel-blue, blue-grey

2 DETERMINED, firm, resolute, strong, hard, harsh, inflexible, pitiless, merciless, unyielding

steep¹ *adj*

1 *a steep slope*
sheer, precipitous, headlong, abrupt, sudden, sharp, vertical, perpendicular, precipiced, bluff, bold, cragged, high-pitched, arduous, exponential; *dialect* stickle; *Scot* brent, stey
OLD steepy
FORMAL acclivitous, declivitous

2 EXCESSIVE, extreme, stiff, unreasonable, uncalled-for, high, exorbitant, extortionate, inordinate, expensive, costly, dear, overpriced
COLLOQ. over the top
▣ **1** gentle, gradual **2** moderate, low

steep² *v*

steep something in liquid
saturate, seethe, soak, moisten, damp, souse, submerge, suffuse, drench, fill, bathe, imbue, immerse, infuse, permeate, pervade, marinate, pickle, brine, macerate, imbrue, sop; *dialect* plot; *Scot* mask
OLD buck; (*Shakesp*) ensteep; (*Spenser*) embay

steeple *n*
spire, belfry, tower, turret, spire-steeple, rood-steeple

steeply *adv*
sharply, abruptly, rapidly, suddenly
▣ gradually

steer *v*
pilot, guide, direct, control, drive, govern, conduct, navigate, cox, lead, usher, helm, tack
OLD steare

■ **steer clear of**
avoid, keep away from, shun, evade, bypass, escape, skirt, dodge
FORMAL circumvent, eschew
COLLOQ. give a wide berth to
▣ seek

stem¹ *n, v*

♦ *n*

the stem of a plant
stalk, shoot, stock, branch, trunk
TECHNICAL peduncle
Related adjective: cauline

♦ *v*
come, develop, flow, originate, have its origins, derive, emanate, spring, issue, arise
▣ give rise to, cause

stem² *v*

stem the flow of blood
stop, halt, arrest, stanch, staunch, block, dam, check, curb, restrain, contain, resist, oppose
▣ encourage

stench *n*
stink, reek, smell, odour, whiff
FORMAL mephitis, miasma
COLLOQ. pong
SLANG niff

stentorian *adj*
loud, strong, booming, thunderous, thundering, resonant, sonorous, ringing, full, vibrant, reverberating, strident

step *n, v*

♦ *n*

1 PACE, stride, footstep, walk, gait, tread, tramp, footprint, print, impression, trace, track

2 MOVE, act, action, course of action, deed, measure, procedure, process, proceeding, progression, advance, development, movement, manoeuvre, expedient, effort, stage, rank, grade, level, phase, degree

3 RUNG, stair, tread, stage, level, rank, point

♦ *v*
pace, stride, tread, stamp, walk, move, advance, progress

■ **step down**
stand down, resign, abdicate, quit, leave, retire, withdraw, give up your post

■ **step in**
intervene, mediate, arbitrate, intercede, interfere, interrupt, intrude, involve yourself in

■ **step up**
increase, raise, boost, build up, intensify, escalate, accelerate, speed up
FORMAL augment
▣ decrease

■ **step by step**
gradually, slowly, progressively, one step at a time, bit by bit, gradatim

■ **in step**
together, in agreement, in harmony, in unison, in accord

■ **out of step**
in disagreement, not in step, having different opinions, at odds, at loggerheads

■ **watch your step**
be careful, look out, watch out, take care, be attentive, have your wits about you
COLLOQ. mind how you go

stereotype *n, v*

♦ *n*
formula, convention, mould, pattern, model, cliché, hackneyed expression, conventional/standardized image, fixed set of ideas

♦ v

typecast, cast, pigeonhole, standardize, formalize, tag, label, conventionalize, mass-produce, categorize
🖪 differentiate

stereotyped adj

conventional, stereotypical, standardized, standard, unoriginal, stock, overused, mass-produced, hackneyed, clichéed, cliché-ridden, banal, stale, trite, tired, threadbare, corny
FORMAL platitudinous
🖪 different, unconventional

sterile adj

1 GERM-FREE, germless, clean, pure, aseptic, sterilized, disinfected, antiseptic, uncontaminated, uninfected
2 INFERTILE, barren, arid, bare, unproductive, unprofitable, fruitless, unfruitful, moorish
TECHNICAL acarpous
FORMAL infecund
3 *a sterile argument*
dry, unimaginative, uninspired, lifeless, stale, unproductive, unfruitful, pointless, futile, vain, useless, unyielding, abortive
FORMAL ineffectual
🖪 **1** septic **2** fertile **3** fruitful

sterility n

1 CLEANNESS, purity, disinfection
TECHNICAL asepsis
2 INFERTILITY, barrenness, unfruitfulness, unproductiveness, impotence
TECHNICAL atocia
FORMAL unfecundity
3 UNPRODUCTIVENESS, fruitlessness, futility, pointlessness, uselessness, ineffectiveness, unfruitfulness, unimaginativeness
FORMAL inefficacy
🖪 **1** infection, contamination **2** fertility **3** fruitfulness

sterilize v

1 DISINFECT, fumigate, purify, clean, cleanse;
N Am retort
TECHNICAL autoclave
2 MAKE INFERTILE, castrate, neuter, doctor, geld, spay
🖪 **1** contaminate, infect

sterling adj

excellent, great, superlative, first-class, genuine, real, sound, standard, authentic, true, pure, worthy
COLLOQ. top-notch, smashing, terrific, neat, ace, brill, out of this world, second to none, mean
🖪 false, poor

stern[1] adj

a stern look/person
strict, severe, authoritarian, rigid, inflexible, unyielding, hard, tough, rigorous, demanding, exacting, stringent, harsh, cruel, tyrannical, Draconian, unsparing, relentless, unrelenting, unsmiling, grim, sombre, forbidding, stark, austere
🖪 kind, gentle, mild, lenient

stern[2] n

the stern of the ship
rear, back, tail, tail end, poop
🖪 bow

sternly adv

harshly, cruelly, grimly, forbiddingly, sombrely, strictly, severely, inflexibly, relentlessly
🖪 gently, kindly

stew v, n

♦ v
1 *stew the meat*
boil, simmer, braise, cook, casserole, ragout, jug; Scot stove
2 *let him stew in his own juice*
worry, sweat, fret, fuss, agonize

♦ n
1 *beef stew*
casserole, goulash, pot-au-feu, *daube*, ragout, hash, chowder, lobscouse, bouillabaisse, Irish stew, paella, zarzuela, ratatouille, haricot, matelote, carbonado, cassoulet, cholent, tzimmes, maconochie, salmi, navarin, potpourri, olla-podrida, succotash, tajine; Scot stovies;
N Am burgoo
COLLOQ. scouse; N Am mulligan
2 FLUSTER, worry, fuss, bother, agitation, pother, fret
COLLOQ. tizzy, tizwas

steward n

stewardess, attendant, flight attendant, air hostess, waiter, waitress, official, butler, supervisor, overseer, custodian, caretaker, marshal, bailiff, factor, chamberlain, manciple, major-domo, *homme d'affaires*, *maître d'hôtel*, commis, sommelier
OLD mormaor, reeve, seneschal
COLLOQ. trolley dolly

stick[1] v

1 THRUST, poke, stab, jab, push, pierce, prick, penetrate, insert, puncture, spear, impale, transfix
2 GLUE, gum, paste, cement, bond, fuse, weld, solder, tape, adhere, grip, cling, hold, attach, affix, fasten, secure, fix, pin, tack, join, bind
3 PUT, place, lay, position, site, locate, set (down), install, deposit, drop
4 *the car got stuck in the mud*
fix, jam, clog (up), get bogged down, trap, stop, come to a halt, come to a standstill
5 REMAIN, stay, linger, persist, continue, carry on, rest, last, endure
FORMAL dwell, abide
6 TOLERATE, bear, stand, endure, put up with
FORMAL abide
COLLOQ. stomach, swallow
■ **stick at**
1 PERSEVERE, persist, continue, keep at
COLLOQ. plug away
2 HESITATE, recoil, shrink from, stop at, doubt, pause, balk, scruple
FORMAL demur
COLLOQ. draw the line at
🖪 **1** give up
■ **stick by**
stand by, support, back, champion, defend, stand up for, stick up for, uphold, side with, adhere to, hold to
🖪 let down
■ **stick it out**
persevere, persist, continue
COLLOQ. plug away, see things through to the end, keep at it, grin and bear it, hang in there
■ **stick out**
protrude, jut out, poke out, bulge, project, extend, be noticeable, be obvious, be conspicuous
■ **stick to**
obey, observe, follow, go along with, carry out, stand by, abide by, hold to, keep to, agree to, accept, respect, uphold, fulfil, comply with, adhere to, conform to, submit to, discharge
COLLOQ. go by the book, toe the line
🖪 ignore, reject; colloq. flout
■ **stick up for**
stand up for, speak up for, fight for, stand by, defend, protect, champion, support, uphold, take the side/part of
🖪 attack

stick[2] n

1 BRANCH, twig, switch
2 CRITICISM, hostility, punishment, reproof, blame, abuse
COLLOQ. flak, rocket, dressing-down
🖪 praise

■ the sticks
remote areas, backwoods, bush, outback; *Aust & NZ* back-blocks; *S Afr* backveld
COLLOQ. middle of nowhere, end of the earth, hickdom, yokeldom; *N Am* boondocks, boonies; *Aust & NZ* scrub, beyond the black stump

---

Types of stick include:

alpeen	cudgel	shillelagh
alpenstock	drumstick	staff
baton	hockey stick	stake
billy	kierie	tripod stick
birch	knobkerrie	truncheon
bludgeon	lathi	waddy
cane	lug	walking stick
chopstick	pike	wand
club	pole	whip
cosh	post	woomera
crook	rod	
crutch	sceptre	

---

stickiness *n*
adhesiveness, gumminess, glueyness, tackiness, syrupiness
FORMAL glutinousness, viscidity
COLLOQ. goo, gooeyness

stick-in-the-mud *adj, n*
♦ *adj*
fuddy-duddy, unadventurous, conservative, fossilized, fogeyish, outmoded, antiquated, antediluvian, Victorian
COLLOQ. square; *N Am* buttoned-down
E3 adventurous, modern
♦ *n*
fuddy-duddy, conservative
COLLOQ. (old) fogey, back number, fossil

stickler *n*
fanatic, maniac, perfectionist, pedant, purist, precisian, fusspot; *N Am* fussbudget
COLLOQ. nut

sticky *adj*
1 ADHESIVE, gummed, tacky, gluey, gummy, viscous
FORMAL glutinous, viscoid
COLLOQ. gooey
2 *a sticky situation*
difficult, tricky, thorny, unpleasant, awkward, embarrassing, delicate, sensitive, ticklish
3 HUMID, clammy, muggy, close, oppressive, sweltering, sultry, sweaty
E3 1 dry **2** easy **3** fresh, cool

stiff *adj*
1 RIGID, unbending, unyielding, inflexible, hard, solid, hardened, solidified, firm, tight, taut, inelastic, tense
2 *stiff muscles/joints*
aching, arthritic, rheumatic, tight, tense, rheumaticky
3 DIFFICULT, hard, tough, tiring, harsh, arduous, laborious, awkward, demanding, exacting, challenging, rigorous
4 FORMAL, ceremonial, ceremonious, reserved, pompous, standoffish, cold, chilly, awkward, prim, priggish
FORMAL decorous
5 SEVERE, extreme, rigorous, hard, harsh, tough, demanding, austere, strict, drastic, stringent, Draconian
6 *a stiff breeze*
strong, fresh, brisk, windy, forceful, vigorous
7 *a stiff drink*
large, alcoholic, strong, intoxicating, potent
E3 1 flexible, supple **3** easy **4** informal, relaxed, friendly **5** lenient, easy-going **6** light, gentle **7** weak

stiffen *v*
1 HARDEN, solidify, tighten, tense (up), starch, thicken, congeal, coagulate, gel, jell, set
2 STRENGTHEN, steel, brace, harden, reinforce
FORMAL fortify

stiff-necked *adj*
proud, stubborn, obstinate, arrogant, haughty, uncompromising, pig-headed, opinionated
FORMAL contumacious
E3 humble, flexible

stifle *v*
1 *stifle opposition*
repress, silence, hush (up), suppress, quell, quash, check, curb, restrain, constrain, keep in, hold back, gulp back/down, smother, crush, subdue, extinguish, muffle, dampen, deaden
2 SMOTHER, suffocate, asphyxiate, strangle, choke, funk; *Scot* scomfish
E3 1 encourage

stigma *n*
brand, mark, stain, blot, spot, note, blemish, slur, taint, disgrace, shame, dishonour
E3 credit, honour

stigmatize *v*
stain, mark, blemish, disgrace, shame, condemn, denounce, demonize, discredit, brand, label
OLD note
FORMAL vilify, vilipend
E3 praise

still *adj, v, adv, n*
♦ *adj*
1 STATIONARY, motionless, immobile, unmoving, unstirring, static, stock-still, lifeless, stagnant, inert, inactive, sedentary
2 QUIET, undisturbed, unruffled, calm, smooth, tranquil, serene, mild, restful, peaceful, hushed, silent, noiseless
E3 1 moving, active **2** disturbed, agitated, noisy
♦ *v*
calm, soothe, allay, tranquillize, subdue, restrain, hush, quieten, silence, pacify, settle, moderate, smooth
FORMAL abate, assuage, appease
E3 agitate, stir up
♦ *adv*
1 UNTIL NOW, up to the present time, up to this time, yet
2 YET, but, even so, though, although, nevertheless, nonetheless, however, in spite of this/that, for all that
FORMAL notwithstanding
♦ *n*
stillness, quiet, quietness, hush, peace, peacefulness, silence, noiselessness, serenity, tranquillity
E3 agitation, disturbance, noise

stillness *n*
tranquillity, calm, peace, peacefulness, serenity, calmness, composure, quiet, quietness, rest, restfulness, hush, silence, imperturbability, coolness, equanimity, sedateness, placidity
FORMAL quietude, repose
E3 disturbance, agitation, noise

stilted *adj*
artificial, unnatural, laboured, stiff, wooden, forced, constrained
E3 natural, relaxed, fluent, flowing

stimulant *n*
tonic, restorative, whetstone
TECHNICAL analeptic
COLLOQ. pick-me-up, pep pill
SLANG reviver

> **! stimulant** or **stimulus**?
> *Stimulant* is normally used only of a drug or medicine which makes a person more alert or part of their body more active: *Tea and coffee contain stimulants; a powerful heart stimulant.* *Stimulus* is used to mean 'something which causes or encourages a person to make greater efforts': *Many people think that children need the stimulus of competition to make them work well at school.*

stimulate v

rouse, arouse, animate, quicken, kindle, fan, fire, inflame, excite, inspire, motivate, encourage, induce, fillip, urge, impel, spur, prompt, goad, provoke, incite, instigate, trigger (off)
COLLOQ. whip up, hype (up)
⊟ discourage, hinder, prevent

stimulating adj

stimulant, inspiring, rousing, stirring, interesting, exciting, exhilarating, intriguing, provoking, provocative, thought-provoking, piquant, suggestive, galvanic, excitant
⊟ uninspiring, boring, depressing, bland

stimulation n

animation, quickening, kindling, excitement, arousal, inspiration, motivation, encouragement, prompting, provocation, incitement, instigation
⊟ discouragement, prevention, hindrance

stimulus n

incentive, encouragement, impetus, inducement, spur, goad, prod, provocation, incitement, fillip, drive, push, jolt, jog
COLLOQ. shot in the arm
⊟ discouragement

> ❗ **stimulus** or **stimulant**?
> *See panel at* **stimulant**.

sting v, n

♦ v
1 *bees sting*
bite, prick, hurt, injure, wound; *Scot* stang
2 SMART, tingle, burn, pain, irritate
3 HURT, distress, wound, upset, offend, annoy, grieve, torment, provoke, exasperate, incense, needle, nettle
4 CHEAT, swindle, defraud, deceive, trick, fiddle, fleece
COLLOQ. do, con
SLANG rip off, take for a ride, take to the cleaners; *N Am* gold-brick
♦ n
1 PRICK, point, bite, nip, wound, injury, hurt, pain, smart, tingle, irritation, tang, piercer; *Scot* stang
TECHNICAL aculeus
OLD TECHNICAL stimulus
2 *the memory lost its sting*
sharpness, viciousness, spite, malice, pungency, incisiveness, sarcasm, causticness, causticity, edge, bite, heartache, barb
3 SWINDLE, fraud, fiddle, diddle, racket, sharp practice, double-dealing, trickery, deception
COLLOQ. con, scam
SLANG rip-off; *N Am* gold brick; *Aust* lurk

stinging adj

burning, smarting, tingling, irritating, hurtful, injurious, wounding, offensive, distressing
FORMAL urent, urticant, aculeate(d)
⊟ mild, soothing, comforting

stingy adj

mean, miserly, niggardly, cheeseparing
FORMAL parsimonious, penurious
COLLOQ. tight-fisted, tight, penny-pinching, mingy
⊟ generous, liberal

stink v, n

♦ v
1 SMELL, reek
COLLOQ. pong, hum; *Scot* ming
SLANG honk
2 *the whole set-up stinks*
be bad, be awful, be nasty, be unpleasant, be despicable
COLLOQ. suck
♦ n
1 SMELL, bad/foul smell, odour, stench
FORMAL malodour, mephitis
COLLOQ. pong; *Scot* ming, guff
SLANG niff

2 FUSS, trouble, bother, furore, row, commotion, stir, fluster
COLLOQ. hassle, hoo-ha, flap, song and dance

stinker n

1 PROBLEM, difficulty, predicament, plight, impediment, horror, shocker
2 SCOUNDREL, rogue, rascal, good-for-nothing, villain, vagabond, ruffian, ne'er-do-well, miscreant, scamp, scallywag, cheat, reprobate, dog, cur, hound
OLD blighter, bounder, dastard, rotter, blackguard
COLLOQ. rat, swine; *Irish* louser
SLANG louse, scab, (*vulgar*) scrote; *N Am* (*vulgar*) douchebag

stinking adj

bad, unpleasant, vile, awful, f(o)etid, stenchy, nasty, contemptible, disgusting, terrible, foul, rotten
COLLOQ. pongy, humming; *Scot* mingin
SLANG niffy
⊟ good, pleasant

stint n, v

♦ n
spell, stretch, period, time, shift, turn, bit, share, quota
♦ v
economize, save, withhold, pinch, begrudge, scrimp
COLLOQ. skimp on

stipend n

allowance, payment, grant, income, maintenance, subsistence allowance, expenses, expense allowance, contribution, benefit, pension, annuity, assistance, alimony

stipulate v

specify, lay down, set down, require, demand, insist on

stipulation n

specification, requirement, point, clause, rider, demand, condition, proviso, prerequisite
FORMAL precondition

stir v, n

♦ v
1 MOVE, budge, shift, rouse, disturb, agitate, shake, tremble, twitch, quiver, flutter, rustle, turn, riffle, jog, torment; *Scot* jee
OLD steer, stire, tempest, wag; (*Spenser*) quich, quinche
2 MIX, blend, whip, beat, agitate, churn, puddle; *N Am* muddle
3 AFFECT, touch, inspire, excite, thrill, provoke, pique
OLD tempest
♦ n
activity, movement, bustle, flurry, commotion, ado, fuss, uproar, tumult, disturbance, disorder, agitation, excitement, ferment; *dialect* clutter
OLD steer, stire
COLLOQ. to-do, hoo-ha, flap, kerfuffle, tizzy, song and dance
⊟ calm

■ stir up
encourage, rouse, arouse, awaken, waken, wake, awake, inspire, animate, quicken, kindle, fire, inflame, excite, stimulate, spur, motivate, drive, impel, prompt, provoke, incite, instigate, agitate, electrify, galvanize, raise, rummage, rustle, poke, disturb, racket, rattle someone's cage, put the cat among the pigeons; *dialect* poach, rear
OLD amove
⊟ calm, discourage

stirring adj

rousing, exciting, spirited, inspiring, stimulating, moving, animating, thrilling, exhilarating, heady, emotive, dramatic, lively, impassioned, intoxicating
⊟ calming, uninspiring

stitch v

sew, tack, darn, mend, repair, seam, embroider, hem
See panel at **embroidery**.

■ stitch up
trap, incriminate, plant, double-cross

COLLOQ. set up, con, stab in the back, fit up, sell down the river
SLANG shop, grass, rumble

> **PROVERBS**
> A stitch in time saves nine

stock *n, adj, v*
♦ *n*
1 GOODS, merchandise, wares, commodities, inventory, repertoire, quantity, collection, range, selection, variety, assortment, source, supply, fund, reservoir, store, reserve, cache, stockpile, hoard, heap, pile, amassment, accumulation
2 stocks and shares
investment, holding, shares, bonds, securities, equities, portfolio, money, capital, funds, assets
3 PARENTAGE, ancestry, genealogy, background, descent, extraction, family, relatives, line, lineage, pedigree, race, breed, strain, species, blood
4 REPUTATION, name, good name, opinion, credit, repute, standing
FORMAL estimation
5 LIVESTOCK, animals, farm animals, cattle, cows, pigs, horses, sheep, herds, flocks
♦ *adj*
standard, basic, regular, routine, ordinary, average, run-of-the-mill, usual, common, customary, essential, traditional, conventional, set, stereotyped, tired, worn-out, hackneyed, clichéd, overused, banal, trite
E3 original, unusual
♦ *v*
keep, carry, sell, market, trade in, traffic in, merchandize, deal in, handle, supply, provide, furnish, equip
FORMAL accoutre
COLLOQ. kit out
■ **stock up**
gather, accumulate, amass, lay in, fill (up), load, store (up), buy (up), put aside, put away, save, hoard, stockpile, stack up, pile up, heap (up)
FORMAL provision, replenish
COLLOQ. salt away, stash away
■ **in stock**
available, for sale, on sale, on the market, on the shelves
■ **take stock**
assess, reassess, estimate, review, survey, evaluate, re-evaluate, re-examine, size up, weigh up
FORMAL appraise

stockpile *v, n*
♦ *v*
hoard, stock, store (up), save, gather, accumulate, amass, pile up, heap (up), keep, put aside, put away
♦ *n*
store, stock, hoard, fund, reservoir, reserve, cache, pile, heap, amassment, accumulation

stock-still *adj*
motionless, unmoving, unstirring, static, still, immobile, inactive, inert, stationary

stocky *adj*
sturdy, solid, thickset, chunky, broad, short, squat, dumpy, stubby, stumpy
FORMAL mesomorphic
E3 tall, skinny

stodgy *adj*
1 stodgy food
solid, heavy, indigestible, filling, starchy, substantial
2 STUFFY, unimaginative, uninspired, unexciting, unenterprising, solemn, heavy, boring, dull, tedious, staid, formal, leaden, laboured, turgid, spiritless
COLLOQ. fuddy-duddy
E3 exciting, informal, light

stoical *adj*
patient, long-suffering, uncomplaining, accepting, resigned, philosophical, indifferent, impassive, unexcitable,

unemotional, dispassionate, self-disciplined, self-controlled, forbearing, cool, calm, imperturbable
FORMAL phlegmatic
E3 excitable, anxious

stoicism *n*
patience, long-suffering, resignation, indifference, dispassion, unexcitability, impassivity, calmness, acceptance, forbearance, imperturbability, stolidity, fatalism, philosophy
FORMAL fortitude, ataraxia, ataraxy
E3 anxiety, depression, fury

> **QUOTATIONS**
> 'Tis pride, rank pride, and haughtiness of soul; / I think the Romans call it stoicism
> JOSEPH ADDISON, *Cato*

stoke *v*
add fuel to, feed with fuel, add wood to, add coal to, keep burning, tend

stolen *adj*
ill-gotten, obtained dishonestly, obtained illegally, pilfered, taken
FORMAL purloined
COLLOQ. punched, swiped, nicked, nobbled, knocked off, ripped off
SLANG hot

stolid *adj*
slow, heavy, dull, bovine, wooden, blockish, lumpish, impassive, unemotional, uninspiring, unimaginative, solemn, indifferent, apathetic
FORMAL phlegmatic
E3 lively, interested

stomach *n, v*
♦ *n*
1 GUT, inside(s), belly, abdomen, paunch, pot-belly
COLLOQ. tummy, tum, corporation; *Aust* bingy
SLANG bread basket
Related adjective: gastric
2 have the stomach for food
desire, relish, hunger, appetite, taste, zest
3 not have the stomach for a fight
courage, determination, desire, inclination, liking, passion, appetite
COLLOQ. guts
♦ *v*
tolerate, bear, stand, endure, suffer, approve of, submit to, take, brook, put up with
FORMAL abide

stomachache *n*
colic, gripes, grass/stomach staggers
TECHNICAL dyspepsia
OLD hypochondria
COLLOQ. tummy ache, bellyache

stone *n*
1 ROCK, boulder, cobble, pebble
FORMAL concretion
Related adjectives: lapidarian, lithic
2 precious stones
jewel, gemstone, gem, lapis
3 GRAVESTONE, tombstone, headstone, slab, flagstone, set(t)
4 PIP, kernel, pit, seed
TECHNICAL endocarp

> **PROVERBS**
> A rolling stone gathers no moss

stonewall *v*
prevaricate, equivocate, quibble, evade, be evasive, shift, shuffle, lie, deceive
COLLOQ. hedge, dodge, shilly-shally, waffle, pussy-foot, beat about the bush, sit on the fence

stony *adj*
1 *stony beach*
pebbly, shingly, rocky, gravelly, gritty
2 BLANK, expressionless, deadpan, poker-faced, hard, cold, frigid, icy, frosty, chilly, indifferent, unfeeling, heartless, adamant, steely, unresponsive, callous, merciless, pitiless, severe, stern, unforgiving, inexorable, unfriendly, hostile
F3 2 warm, soft-hearted, friendly

stooge *n*
puppet, pawn, lackey, henchman, dupe, foil, butt
COLLOQ. cat's paw, fall guy

stool

Types of stool include:

bar stool	*technical* cutty-	music stool
dialect buffet	stool	piano stool
camp-stool	*old* ducking-stool	stillage
close-stool	faldstool	*Scot* sunk
dialect coppy	fender-stool	tabouret
creepie	footstool	*technical* tripod
dialect cricket	*old* joint-stool	
old cucking stool	milking-stool	

---

stoop *v, n*
♦ *v*
1 HUNCH, bow, bend, lower, incline, lean, poke, duck, squat, crouch, kneel
OLD courb, lout
2 *stoop to blackmail*
descend, sink, lower yourself, resort, go so far as, condescend, go so low as, deign, decline, cringe; *dialect* steep
FORMAL vouchsafe
♦ *n*
droop, hunch, hunching, round-shoulderedness, sag, slouch, slump, bending, inclination, lowering, ducking

stop *v, n*
♦ *v*
1 HALT, end, finish, conclude, cease, discontinue, abandon, bring/come to an end, bring/come to a rest, suspend, interrupt, pause, quit
FORMAL terminate, arrest, refrain, desist
COLLOQ. quit, wind up, pack in, kick, knock off, leave off, give over
2 PREVENT, bar, frustrate, thwart, intercept, hinder, impede, obstruct, block, check, restrain, stall
3 SEAL, close, plug, block, bung, stop up, cover, obstruct, arrest, stem, stanch, staunch
4 STAY, live, settle, lodge, board, visit, put up, rest, pause, break your journey
FORMAL reside, dwell, sojourn
F3 1 begin, start, continue
♦ *n*
1 HALT, standstill, stoppage, end, finish, close, conclusion
FORMAL cessation, termination, discontinuance, discontinuation, diapason
2 STATION, halt, bus stop, fare stage, stopping-place, terminus, destination
3 REST, break, stay, pause, stage, stopover, visit
FORMAL sojourn
F3 1 start, beginning, continuation

SYNONYM NUANCES

verb sense 1
You can use **halt** to suggest coming to a complete standstill, whereas **end**, **finish** and **conclude** imply a more permanent but less sudden cessation. **Discontinue** suggests putting a stop to an ongoing process: *the patient asked for his treatment to be discontinued.* **Abandon** suggests a degree of disenchantment, or loss of interest: *the party has now abandoned monetarism.*
    Suspend carries implications of being a temporary measure. Similarly, **interrupt** implies a short-term

intervention, while **pause** implies a brief break. However, **quit** has implications of a permanent departure from something, with overtones of resolve: *he quit smoking years ago.*

stopgap *n, adj*
♦ *n*
improvisation, makeshift, substitute, temporary substitute, expedient, resort, shift
♦ *adj*
improvised, makeshift, provisional, temporary, emergency, impromptu
FORMAL expediential
COLLOQ. rough-and-ready
F3 finished, permanent

stopover *n*
stop-off, stop, visit, rest, break, overnight stay; *N Am* layover
FORMAL sojourn

stoppage *n*
1 STOP, halt, standstill, arrest, blockage, obstacle, obstruction, check, hindrance, interruption
FORMAL cessation, termination, discontinuance, discontinuation, occlusion
2 STRIKE, shutdown, closure, walk-out, sit-in, industrial action; *S Afr* stayaway
3 DEDUCTION, subtraction, reduction, decrease, taking away/off, withdrawal, removal, discount, allowance
F3 1 start, continuation

stopper *n*
cork, bung, plug, seal, spigot
OLD stopple

store *v, n*
♦ *v*
save, keep, put aside, lay by, reserve, stock, stock up with, lay in, deposit, put down, lay down, lay up, squirrel away, bank, gather, collect, accumulate, pack, hoard, stockpile
COLLOQ. salt away, stash, save for a rainy day
F3 use
♦ *n*
1 STOCK, supply, provision, fund, reserve, mine, reservoir, hoard, cache, stockpile, heap, load, accumulation, amassment, deposit, quantity, abundance, plenty, lot
2 SHOP, retail outlet, supermarket, hypermarket, chain store, department store, corner shop, deli
See panel at **shop**.
3 STOREROOM, storehouse, warehouse, repository, depository, larder, buttery, barn
F3 1 scarcity
■ **set/lay store by**
value, think highly of, consider highly, admire, hold in high regard, esteem

storehouse *n*
repository, warehouse, treasury, wealth, vault, depository, depot, garner, granary, hold, cellar, armoury, arsenal, fund, entrepot, repertory, barn, buttery, larder, pantry, silo

storey *n*
floor, level, stage, tier, flight, deck
FORMAL stratum

storm *n, v*
♦ *n*
outburst, uproar, furore, outcry, row, rumpus, commotion, disturbance, clamour, tumult, brouhaha, turmoil, stir, agitation, rage, roar, outbreak, offensive, attack, assault, onslaught
COLLOQ. to-do, kerfuffle
F3 calm
♦ *v*
1 *storm a citadel*
charge, rush, attack, assault, assail
2 RAGE, roar, rant, rave, shout, fume, thunder, explode, seethe
COLLOQ. hit the roof, lose your cool, foam at the mouth

3 storm out of the room
charge, rush, stamp, tear, flounce

Kinds of storm include:

blizzard	firestorm	sand storm
buran	gale	snow storm
cloudburst	haboob	squall
cyclone	hailstorm	tempest
downpour	hurricane	thunderstorm
dust devil	ice storm	tornado
dust storm	monsoon	typhoon
electrical storm	rainstorm	whirlwind

See also **wind¹** .

stormy adj
tempestuous, squally, rough, choppy, turbulent, rainy, wild, raging, windy, gusty, blustery, foul, dirty, boisterous, unruly, gustful, stormful, wintry; N Am rugged
OLD oragious, wroth
FORMAL inclement
Ea calm, peaceful

story n
1 TALE, fiction, anecdote, episode, plot, storyline, narrative, history, chronicle, record, account, relation, recital, report, item, article, feature
2 LIE, falsehood, untruth
COLLOQ. rib

> **QUOTATIONS**
> Every fine story must leave in the mind of the sensitive reader an intangible residuum of pleasure, a cadence, a quality of voice that is exclusively the writer's own, individual, unique
> WILLA SIBERT CATHER, Not Under Forty, 'Miss Jewett'

Types of story include:

adventure story	fantasy	parable
Aga saga	folk tale	romance
anecdote	ghost story	saga
bedtime story	hint fiction	science fiction
black comedy	historical novel	colloq. sci-fi
colloq.	horror story	shaggy-dog story
blockbuster	interactive story	short story
colloq. bonkbuster	legend	spiel
colloq. chick lit	love story	spine-chiller
children's story	Mills & Boon®	spy story
comedy	misery memoir	supernatural tale
crime story	mystery	tall story
detective story	myth	thriller
fable	novel	western
fairy story	novelization	colloq. whodunnit
fairy tale	novella	yarn

storyteller n
narrator, writer, author, novelist, raconteur, raconteuse, anecdotist, chronicler, bard, romancer, tell-tale

stout adj
1 FAT, stocky, plump, fleshy, portly, obese, overweight, heavy, tubby, bulky, big, brawny, beefy, hulking, thickset, burly, muscular, athletic, lusty, chopping, embonpoint; dialect stuggy
FORMAL corpulent
2 stout packaging
strong, tough, durable, thick, solid, heavy, sturdy, substantial, robust, hardy, vigorous
3 BRAVE, courageous, valiant, plucky, tough, fearless, bold, gallant, heroic, intrepid, dauntless, resolute, stalwart, determined, strong, forceful, fierce, staunch, manful; dialect cobby; Scot stuffy
OLD tall
FORMAL valorous

COLLOQ. gutsy, spunky, gritty
Ea 1 thin, lean, slim **2** weak **3** cowardly, timid, afraid

stoutly adv
strongly, fiercely, toughly, fearlessly, boldly, resolutely, staunchly
Ea weakly, timidly, fearfully

stove n
cooker, oven, range, furnace, kiln, grill, aga, heater

stow v
put away, store, place, deposit, load, pack, cram, bundle, stuff
COLLOQ. stash
Ea unload
■ **stow away**
hide, travel secretly, conceal yourself

straggle v
stray, wander, drift, lag, amble, loiter, ramble, roam, rove, trail, range, scatter, spread, string out
COLLOQ. dilly-dally

straggly adj
untidy, rambling, drifting, straying, straggling, aimless, disorganized, irregular, random, spreading, loose, strung out
Ea tidy, organized, grouped

straight adj, adv
♦ adj
1 a straight line
direct, undeviating, unswerving, unbending, unbent, uncurving
2 LEVEL, even, flat, horizontal, upright, vertical, aligned, true, right
3 FRANK, honest, candid, blunt, forthright, direct, outspoken, straightforward
4 CONSECUTIVE, successive, continuous, unbroken, uninterrupted, one after the other
5 TIDY, neat, in order, orderly, shipshape, arranged, organized
6 HONOURABLE, honest, law-abiding, respectable, upright, trustworthy, reliable, upstanding, decent, straightforward, fair, just, faithful, sincere, conventional
7 straight whisky
undiluted, neat, pure, unadulterated, unmixed
Ea 1 bent, crooked, curved, wavy, curly **2** sloping **3** evasive **5** untidy **6** dishonest **7** diluted
♦ adv
1 DIRECTLY, with no changes of direction, without deviating, as the crow flies
2 IMMEDIATELY, directly, instantly, promptly, right away, without delay, at once, as soon as possible
COLLOQ. pronto
3 tell someone straight
frankly, honestly, candidly, bluntly, directly, plainly, clearly, forthrightly, straightforwardly, point-blank
COLLOQ. not pulling any punches, straight from the shoulder
4 CONSECUTIVELY, successively, continuously, uninterruptedly, one after the other
COLLOQ. on the trot
■ **straight away**
at once, immediately, instantly, right away, directly, without delay, now, there and then
COLLOQ. pronto
Ea later, eventually

straighten v
unbend, make/become straight, align, tidy (up), neaten, order, arrange, adjust, put in order, put right
Ea bend, twist
■ **straighten out**
clear up, sort out, settle, resolve, correct, realign, disentangle, regularize, tidy up, put in order, put right
FORMAL rectify
Ea confuse, muddle

■ **straighten up**
stand up, stand, stand erect, stand upright, straighten your
back/body

straightforward *adj*
1 EASY, simple, uncomplicated, clear, elementary,
unexacting, undemanding, plain, penny-plain,
point-blank, pukka
COLLOQ. child's play, a piece of cake, like falling off a log,
no frills
2 HONEST, truthful, sincere, genuine, open, frank, candid,
direct, forthright, outspoken, plain-speaking, undesigning,
on the level; *dialect* jannock
COLLOQ. up-front
1 difficult, complicated, complex, tricky **2** evasive,
devious, underhand

strain¹ *v, n*
♦ *v*
1 PULL, heave, tug, wrench, twist, sprain, hurt,
injure, wrick, tear, stretch, extend, elongate, tighten,
tauten
FORMAL distend
2 SIEVE, sift, screen, separate, filter, percolate, riddle, purify,
drain, wring, squeeze, compress, express
3 WEAKEN, tire, fatigue, tax, overtax, overwork, pressure,
labour, try, endeavour, struggle, strive, exert, force, drive,
push to/beyond the limit, make every effort, do your
utmost
COLLOQ. go all out, put your heart and soul into, pull out
all the stops
♦ *n*
1 SPRAIN, pull, wrench, twist, injury, wrick
2 PRESSURE, tension, stress, anxiety, worry, duress, effort,
struggle, exertion, pressure, force, burden, demand,
tiredness, weariness, fatigue, exhaustion, overwork
2 relaxation

strain² *n*
1 STOCK, ancestry, descent, extraction, breed, family,
lineage, pedigree, blood, variety, type, sort, kind
2 TRAIT, streak, quality, characteristic, vein, tendency, way,
trace, element, suggestion, suspicion
FORMAL disposition, proclivity
3 *the strains of music*
theme, tune, melody, music, sound, song, air

strained *adj*
forced, constrained, laboured, false, artificial, unnatural,
stiff, wooden, tense, unrelaxed, uneasy, uncomfortable,
awkward, embarrassed, self-conscious
**natural, relaxed

strainer *n*
sieve, colander, sifter, filter, screen, riddle

strait *n*
1 *the Straits of Gibraltar*
sound, narrows, inlet, channel, kyle
2 *in desperate straits*
crisis, difficulty, emergency, hardship, predicament, plight,
perplexity, distress, dilemma, embarrassment, extremity,
poverty
COLLOQ. hole, mess, fix, pickle, jam, pretty/fine kettle
of fish

straitened *adj*
poor, reduced, difficult, distressed, limited, restricted,
impoverished, embarrassed
**easy, well-off

strait-laced *adj*
prudish, stuffy, starchy, prim, prim and proper, priggish,
proper, strict, narrow, narrow-minded, puritanical,
moralistic
**broad-minded

strand¹ *n*
1 FIBRE, filament, wire, thread, string, piece, length
2 *the strands of a theory*
element, feature, component, factor, ingredient

strand² *n*
walk along the strand
shore, beach, seashore, foreshore, sand(s),
waterfront, front

stranded *adj*
marooned, high and dry, abandoned, forsaken, helpless,
penniless, aground, grounded, beached, shipwrecked,
wrecked
COLLOQ. (left) in the lurch

strange *adj*
1 ODD, peculiar, curious, queer, weird, bizarre, eccentric,
offbeat, abnormal, irregular, uncommon, unusual,
unexpected, exceptional, remarkable, fantastic,
extraordinary, unreal, surreal, mystifying, perplexing,
unexplained, inexplicable, uncanny; *dialect* unked;
Scot unco
OLD rum, selcouth
FORMAL singular
COLLOQ. funny, freaky, wacky, oddball, kinky, off the wall
2 NEW, novel, untried, unknown, unheard-of, unfamiliar,
unaccustomed, unacquainted, foreign, alien, exotic; *Scot*
fremd
OLD straunge
1 ordinary, common **2** well-known, familiar

SYNONYM NUANCES

sense 1
You can use **odd** and **peculiar** to suggest an element of
quirkiness: *a distinctly odd appearance; a peculiar brand
of humour*, and **curious** also suggests raising questions
in the mind: *a curious tale*. **Queer** and **weird** continue
the idea of singularity, but with a more negative or
slightly sinister tone: *I had a queer feeling we were
being watched*, while **bizarre** would be reserved for
something very outlandish. **Eccentric** suggests being
somewhat unconventional in a more endearing way:
eccentric old ladies.
   Abnormal more alarmingly and negatively implies
deviation from what is considered the norm: *abnormal
behaviour; abnormal cells*. **Irregular**, although negative
in its connotations, is more suggestive of being
unpredictable: *irregular behaviour*. The terms
uncommon and **unusual**, however, have
different connotations, and imply a degree of rarity,
and this is conveyed more positively by **exceptional**
and **remarkable**, which suggest outstanding
qualities.
   Both **fantastic** and **extraordinary** suggest something
beyond reality, in the realms of the imagination, and the
connotations tend to be positive. **Unreal** and **surreal**,
although more neutral in tone, echo these suggestions,
the first suggesting something unbelievable, and the latter
something akin to dreaming: *a surreal nightmare of fire
engines and police cars.*

---

strangely *adv*
peculiarly, oddly, curiously, weirdly, bizarrely,
abnormally, unusually, uncommonly, unexpectedly,
exceptionally, remarkably, inexplicably
**commonly, familiarly

strangeness *n*
oddity, oddness, peculiarity, bizarreness, extraordinariness,
irregularity, abnormality, queerness, eccentricity,
uncanniness, eeriness, exoticness
FORMAL singularity
**ordinariness

stranger *n*
newcomer, new arrival, visitor, guest, non-member,
outsider, incomer, foreigner, alien, pilgrim; *Scot* fremd,
unco
**local, native

■ **a stranger to**
unfamiliar with, inexperienced in, unversed in,
unacquainted with, unaccustomed to

strangle v

1 THROTTLE, choke, asphyxiate, suffocate, stifle, smother, strangulate, bowstring, thropple
2 SUPPRESS, gag, repress, inhibit, restrain, check, keep in, hold back, stifle, smother

strap n, v

♦ n
thong, tie, band, belt, cord, leash
♦ v
1 BEAT, lash, whip, flog, belt, scourge
2 FASTEN, secure, tie, bind, truss, lash, bandage

strapping adj

brawny, strong, sturdy, well-built, beefy, big, burly, hefty, robust, hulking, husky
COLLOQ. hunky
🖪 puny

stratagem n

plan, scheme, plot, intrigue, ruse, ploy, trick, deception, dodge, manoeuvre, device, tactic, artifice, wile, subterfuge
FORMAL machination

> ❗ **stratagem** or **strategy**?
> A *stratagem* is a plan or trick, intended to deceive someone or gain an advantage over them: *He was a master of the cunning stratagem and the bare-faced lie.* *Strategy* is used to describe tactics, especially in a long-term plan of campaign: *adopt a strategy of civil disobedience; guerrilla tactics were replaced by a strategy of conventional warfare.*

strategic adj

strategical, important, key, critical, decisive, crucial, vital, essential, tactical, planned, calculated, deliberate, politic, diplomatic, commanding
🖪 unimportant

strategy n

tactics, planning, policy, approach, procedure, plan, plan of action, roadmap, programme, schedule, design, scheme
TECHNICAL geostrategy, maximin, minimax
COLLOQ. blueprint, game plan

> ❗ **strategy** or **stratagem**?
> See panel at **stratagem**.

stratification n

division, classification, categorization, ranking, layering, hierarchy, graduation, sorting, gradation

stratum n

1 LEVEL, grade, class, rank, table, tier, category, bracket, caste, station, group, region
2 LAYER, seam, vein, lode, bed, stratification

stray v, adj, n

♦ v
wander (off), get lost, err, go astray, ramble, saunter, amble, roam, rove, range, meander, straggle, drift, diverge, deviate, digress, go wrong, go off the subject; *Scot* stravaig, traik
OLD estray, exorbitate, wilder; (*Spenser*) forwander
COLLOQ. go off at a tangent
♦ adj
1 LOST, abandoned, homeless, wandering, roaming, drifting; *Scot* waff
2 RANDOM, chance, occasional, accidental, freak, odd, erratic, scattered, isolated
♦ n
straggle, straggler, waif, tag, maverick, stray cat, alleycat, stray dog

streak n, v

♦ n
1 LINE, stroke, smear, band, stripe, strip, layer, vein, mark, stria, wave, wake, weal, waif
TECHNICAL vibex
OLD freak, strake
2 TRACE, dash, touch, element, strain

3 *on a lucky streak*
spell, time, period, stint, stretch, roll
♦ v
1 BAND, stripe, mark, fleck, smear, smudge, daub, ribbon, lace
OLD freak
FORMAL striate
2 SPEED, tear, rush, hurtle, sprint, race, gallop, fly, dart, dash, flash, whistle, zoom, whizz, sweep, scurry
COLLOQ. belt, vamoose, skedaddle, beat it, scarper

streaked adj

flecked, fleckered, streaky, lined, banded, barred, brinded, brindle(d)
FORMAL striate

stream n, v

♦ n
1 RIVER, creek, brook, beck, burn, rill, rillet, rivulet, watercourse, tributary
2 *a stream of traffic*
course, drift, flow, surge, current, outpouring, succession, jet, run, gush, rush, tide, flood, deluge, cascade, torrent, volley, burst
FORMAL influx, efflux
♦ v
1 ISSUE, well, surge, run, flow, course, pour, spout, gush, flood, cascade, crowd, spill, shed; *Irish* streel
2 *streaming in the wind*
float, trail, flap, fly, flutter

streamer n

ribbon, banner, pennant, pennon, flag, ensign, standard, gonfalon
FORMAL vexillum

streamlined adj

1 AERODYNAMIC, smooth, sleek, graceful
2 EFFICIENT, well-run, smooth-running, rationalized, time-saving, organized, modernized, slick
COLLOQ. up-to-the-minute
🖪 **2** clumsy, inefficient

street n

road, way, thoroughfare, avenue, lane
■ **man/woman in the street**
ordinary person, ordinary citizen, average person, Mr/Mrs Average, average punter
COLLOQ. Joe Bloggs, person/man/woman on the Clapham omnibus

strength n

1 POWER, force, energy, vigour, brawn, muscle, sinew, stoutness, toughness, stamina, fitness, health
COLLOQ. clout
2 TOUGHNESS, resilience, robustness, sturdiness, impregnability, durability, solidity, solidness, resistance, firmness, soundness, hardiness
3 DETERMINATION, resolution, forcefulness, firmness, assertiveness, persistence, spirit, bravery, courage
FORMAL fortitude
COLLOQ. guts, grit
4 INTENSITY, depth, vividness, graphicness, sharpness, keenness, pungency, passion, fervency, ardour, vehemence
5 FORCEFULNESS, effectiveness, power, force, potency, persuasiveness, influence, weight, validity, soundness, urgency
FORMAL cogency
6 STRONG POINT, talent, gift, aptitude, advantage, asset, bent, forte, specialty, speciality, métier
COLLOQ. thing
🖪 **1** weakness, frailty **2** weakness **3** weakness, feebleness **4** mildness, blandness, faintness **5** weakness, ineffectiveness **6** weakness
■ **on the strength of**
because of, because of the influence of, on account of, based on, on the basis of
FORMAL by virtue of

strengthen v

reinforce, brace, steel, buttress, build up, prop up, shore up, bolster, support, back up, protect, toughen, man, harden, stiffen, consolidate, substantiate, corroborate, confirm, encourage, hearten, refresh, restore, rally, invigorate, nourish, edify, increase, turn up, heighten, intensify, arm, stay, picket
TECHNICAL work-harden, anneal, cleat, fish, line, afforce
OLD munite, sinew, wharf; (*Shakesp*) force
FORMAL fortify
COLLOQ. beef up
E3 weaken, undermine

strenuous adj

1 *strenuous work*
hard, tough, demanding, gruelling, taxing, difficult, laborious, heavy, uphill, arduous, tiring, exhausting, warm, weighty
2 ACTIVE, energetic, vigorous, eager, keen, earnest, tenacious, determined, forceful, resolute, spirited, bold, tireless, indefatigable, blistering
E3 1 easy, effortless

strenuously adv

vigorously, boldly, actively, resolutely, tirelessly, tenaciously, forcefully

stress n, v

♦ n
1 PRESSURE, strain, tension, worry, uneasiness, apprehension, anxiety, distress, difficulty, trouble, weight, burden, trauma
COLLOQ. hassle
2 EMPHASIS, accent, accentuation, beat, force, weight, value, priority, importance, significance
TECHNICAL ictus
E3 1 relaxation
♦ v
emphasize, accentuate, highlight, underline, underscore, point up, spotlight, repeat, exaggerate
E3 understate, play down, moderate, downplay, tone down

stressed adj

tense, nervous, anxious, worried, strained, distraught, under pressure, jittery, uneasy, apprehensive, fidgety, restless, jumpy, overwrought, on edge
COLLOQ. edgy, uptight, keyed up, stressed out
SLANG screwed up
E3 relaxed, calm

stressful adj

tense, worrying, uneasy, strained, charged, fraught, nerve-racking, nail-biting
E3 easy, light, relaxing, calm

stretch v, n, adj

♦ v
1 LENGTHEN, extend, make/become longer, broaden, widen, make/become wider, expand, spread, elongate, prolong, draw out
FORMAL protract
2 *stretch from one point to another*
reach, extend, spread, unfold, unroll, continue, project, go as far as, go/come down/up to, last, range
3 TIGHTEN, pull, tauten, strain
4 REACH OUT, straighten, extend, hold out, present, offer
FORMAL proffer
5 *the job will stretch you*
challenge, extend, push, test, tax, try, stimulate, put demands on
E3 1 shorten, condense, compress
♦ n
1 EXPANSE, spread, sweep, reach, extent, distance, space, area, tract
2 PERIOD, time, term, spell, stint, run
♦ adj
elastic, pliable, flexible, stretchable, stretchy, supple, resilient, yielding, springy, rubbery, pliant, elasticated, plastic, bouncy, buoyant

■ stretch out

extend, relax, hold out, put out, lie down, sprawl, reach
FORMAL recline
E3 draw back

■ stretch your legs

exercise, go for a walk, move about, stroll, take a walk, take the air
FORMAL promenade
COLLOQ. take a breather

strew v

scatter, spread, disperse, bestrew, litter, sprinkle, toss
OLD bespread, besprinkle
E3 gather

stricken adj

affected, afflicted, hit, struck, injured, wounded, smitten
E3 unaffected

strict adj

1 *a strict teacher*
stern, authoritarian, no-nonsense, hard, firm, rigid, inflexible, uncompromising, stringent, rigorous, disciplinarian, iron-handed, iron-fisted, harsh, tough, severe, austere, narrow
2 EXACT, precise, accurate, clear, clear-cut, literal, faithful, close, true, absolute, utter, total, complete, thoroughgoing, meticulous, scrupulous, conscientious, particular, orthodox, religious
E3 1 liberal, soft, flexible, easy-going **2** loose

SYNONYM NUANCES

sense 1
You can use **stern** to suggest a rather fearsome attitude or manner, while **authoritarian** implies a dictatorial element: *the premier's authoritarian leadership*.
No-nonsense, however, is slightly more positive in its implication of being sensible, while **hard**, **firm** and **tough** have more to do with resolve.
The words **rigid** and **inflexible** imply an unyielding determination and are rather more negative in their connotations. **Uncompromising** also suggests complete resistance to concession, but tends to suggest that this is a strength: *a staunch defence of France's uncompromising stand on trade*.
Stringent implies being rigidly applied: *stringent airport checks*. **Rigorous**, too, has more positive overtones and suggests being scrupulous, but **harsh** and **severe** imply a degree of injustice. The synonym **austere** could be used of an absence of any ameliorating traits: *life was austere in the war years*, while **narrow** might be used critically to imply something rather limiting: *companies fail because of their narrow view of how profits are made*.

---

strictly adv

1 *he was brought up very strictly*
sternly, firmly, inflexibly, uncompromisingly, rigorously, severely, narrowly
2 *strictly forbidden*
absolutely, completely, totally, wholly, categorically, definitely, positively, in every way/respect, unequivocally, unambiguously, unquestionably
3 *strictly for the use of members*
only, purely, exclusively, uniquely
E3 1 liberally

■ strictly speaking

literally, strictly, exactly, precisely, to the letter

strictness n

1 STERNNESS, authoritarianism, firmness, harshness, rigidity, rigidness, severity, stringency, stringentness, austerity
2 EXACTNESS, precision, accuracy, meticulousness, rigorousness, rigour, scrupulousness
E3 1 flexibility, mildness

stricture n

1 CRITICISM, rebuke, reproof, blame, censure
FORMAL animadversion

COLLOQ. flak
2 RESTRICTION, limit, bound, confine, constraint, restraint, control, tightness
⊟ **1** praise

stride *v, n*
♦ *v*
walk, step, pace, tread, advance, progress, lope, overstride, stalk, galumph; *dialect* stroam; *Scot* lamp, stend
OLD bestride
♦ *n*
step, pace, walk, tread, movement, advance, progression; *Scot* stend

■ **take something in your stride**
deal with easily, cope with easily, make light of, do with both eyes shut, do blindfold, do with one hand tied behind your back, do standing on your head, think nothing of

strident *adj*
loud, thundering, roaring, booming, clamorous, vociferous, harsh, rough, raucous, grating, rasping, shrill, screeching, unmusical, discordant, clashing, jarring, jangling
FORMAL stentorian, stridulant
⊟ quiet, soft

strife *n*
conflict, disagreement, discord, dissension, controversy, animosity, hostility, friction, rivalry, contention, ill-feeling, ill-will, quarrel, quarrelling, row, argument, dispute, bickering, wrangling, struggle, fighting, combat, battle, warfare, trouble, contest, contestation, feud, mutiny, brigue; *Scot* sturt
OLD bargain, barrat, colluctation, conteck, debate; (*Spenser*) bate
⊟ peace

strike *n, v*
♦ *n*
1 INDUSTRIAL ACTION, work-to-rule, go-slow, stoppage, sit-in, walk-out, mutiny, revolt
2 HIT, blow, stroke, slap, smack, thump
COLLOQ. wallop, clobber, whack, thwack, belt, biff
3 ATTACK, charge, raid, storming, assault, rush, ambush, trap
♦ *v*
1 STOP WORK, down tools, take industrial action, work to rule, walk out, protest, mutiny, revolt
2 HIT, knock, collide with, crash, slap, smack, cuff, clout, thump, thrash, rap, beat, bang, pound, punch, box, hammer, buffet, batter
COLLOQ. wallop, sock, clock, clobber, swipe, whack, thwack, belt, biff
SLANG twat; *N Am* lam
3 ATTACK, charge, storm, assail, assault, raid, rush, set about, pounce on, ambush, trap
4 FIND, discover, come upon, unearth, uncover, encounter, reach
FORMAL chance upon, happen upon
5 *the idea suddenly struck me*
occur to, hit, come to, come to mind, dawn on, register
6 *it strikes me as odd*
seem, appear, look, look like, feel, sound, give the impression, impress, affect, touch, have the look of
7 *strike a particular pose*
adopt, take on, assume, embrace, affect
8 *strike a bargain*
reach, come to, agree on, come to an agreement on, settle on, arrive at, achieve
COLLOQ. clinch
■ **strike back**
retaliate, hit back, fight back, reciprocate, get back at, pay someone back
COLLOQ. get your own back, get even with
■ **strike down**
afflict, ruin, destroy, kill, murder, assassinate
FORMAL slay, smite

■ **strike out**
cross out, delete, rub out, erase, strike through, cancel, strike off, remove, obliterate
⊟ add
■ **strike up**
begin, start, initiate, instigate, introduce, establish
FORMAL commence
COLLOQ. kick off

striking *adj*
1 NOTICEABLE, conspicuous, obvious, evident, salient, outstanding, remarkable, extraordinary, memorable, distinct, visible, impressive, dazzling, arresting, astonishing, stunning
2 ATTRACTIVE, stunning, beautiful, good-looking, gorgeous, pretty, glamorous
SLANG drop-dead gorgeous
⊟ **1** unimpressive **2** ugly

string *n, v*
♦ *n*
1 *a piece of string*
twine, cord, rope, yarn, cable, line, strand, fibre
2 SERIES, succession, sequence, chain, line, row, column, file, queue, procession, stream, train
♦ *v*
thread, link, connect, fasten, tie up, sling, hang, suspend, festoon, loop
■ **string along**
deceive, mislead, fool, bluff, dupe, play (someone) false, hoax, humbug
COLLOQ. play fast and loose with, put one over on
SLANG take for a ride
■ **string out**
space out, spread out, stretch out, straggle, fan out, disperse, extend, lengthen, wander
FORMAL protract
⊟ gather, shorten
■ **string up**
hang, kill, lynch, send to the gallows/scaffold/gibbet
COLLOQ. top
■ **with no strings attached**
unconditional, without qualifications, without limitations, without stipulations, with no obligation

stringency *n*
strictness, rigour, rigorousness, toughness, firmness, inflexibility, exactness, demands
⊟ flexibility

stringent *adj*
binding, strict, severe, rigorous, tough, firm, rigid, inflexible, uncompromising, exacting, demanding, tight, hard, harsh
⊟ lax, flexible

stringy *adj*
tough, gristly, chewy, fibrous, sinewy, leathery, wiry, rop(e)y
⊟ tender

strip *v, n*
♦ *v*
1 UNDRESS, take your clothes off, unclothe, disrobe, remove your clothes, uncover, expose, lay bare
FORMAL denude
2 CLEAN OUT, clear, empty, divest, deprive, dispossess, gut, ransack, pillage, plunder, loot
OLD disfurnish
3 PEEL, skin, flay, flake off
FORMAL excoriate
4 DISMANTLE, take apart, disassemble, separate, pull apart, take to pieces
⊟ **1** clothe, dress, get dressed **2** cover, fill **4** assemble, put together
♦ *n*
1 *a strip of wood*
ribbon, thong, strap, belt, sash, band, bar, stripe, lath, slat, piece, bit, slip, shred

2 *a strip of land*
stretch, belt, expanse, extent, area, runway, tract, swathe, zone
3 *a football strip*
outfit, clothing, clothes, rig, colours
COLLOQ. rig-out, gear, togs, things, get-up, clobber

stripe *n*
band, line, bar, chevron, flash, streak, fleck, strip, belt, ribbon, slash, snip, list, pin-stripe, zone, whelk
TECHNICAL vitta, pale, endorse
OLD strake, laticlave

striped *adj*
banded, barred, streaky, stripy, variegated, striated, vittate
TECHNICAL endorsed
OLD bausond

stripling *n*
boy, fledgling, lad, teenager, adolescent, youth, youngster
COLLOQ. young 'un

strive *v*
1 TRY, attempt, endeavour, struggle, strain, work, toil, labour, try hard, campaign, exert yourself, give your all, do your best, do your utmost
2 FIGHT, battle, contend, engage, contest, combat, do battle, vie, compete

stroke *n, v*
♦ *n*
1 CARESS, pat, rub
2 BLOW, hit, knock, swipe, slap, thump, smack
COLLOQ. wallop, clobber, whack, thwack, belt, biff
3 SWEEP, flourish, movement, action, move, motion, line
4 ACCOMPLISHMENT, achievement, coup
5 COLLAPSE, shock, spasm, attack, seizure, thrombosis, cerebral haemorrhage
♦ *v*
caress, fondle, pet, touch, pat, rub, massage

> PROVERBS
> Little strokes fell great oaks

stroll *v, n*
♦ *v*
saunter, amble, dawdle, ramble, wander, meander, go for a walk
COLLOQ. stretch your legs
♦ *n*
walk, saunter, amble, constitutional, turn, ramble

stroller *n*
saunterer, rambler, walker, wanderer, dawdler

strong *adj*
1 POWERFUL, mighty, potent, lusty, strapping, sturdy, stout, burly, well-built, beefy, brawny, muscular, sinewy, athletic, fit, well, healthy
2 TOUGH, resilient, durable, hard-wearing, heavy-duty, industrial-strength, solid, long-lasting, well-built, well-protected, reinforced, secure, robust, hardy, sturdy, vigorous, stalwart, rugged
3 DETERMINED, forceful, firm, confident, resolute, assertive, aggressive, formidable, strong-willed, strong-minded, single-minded, persistent, brave, courageous
COLLOQ. gutsy
4 *a strong colour*
intense, deep, vivid, graphic, fierce, violent, powerful, sharp, heady, keen, pungent, piquant, biting, highly-flavoured, highly-seasoned, hot, spicy
5 *a strong impression*
marked, clear, clear-cut, obvious, evident, remarkable, pronounced
6 *take strong action*
decisive, firm, definite, positive, active, severe, resolute, forceful
7 *a strong interest in railways*
keen, enthusiastic, eager, devoted, committed, deep, passionate

8 *a strong case/argument*
convincing, persuasive, powerful, potent, plausible, valid, sound, effective, telling, forceful, weighty, compelling, urgent
FORMAL cogent, efficacious
9 *strong feelings*
intense, passionate, fervent, great, powerful, deep, profound, ardent, vehement
10 UNDILUTED, concentrated, potent
F3 **1** weak, frail, sickly, unhealthy **2** weak, insubstantial **3** feeble, weak **4** weak, faint, mild, bland **6** weak, indecisive **8** weak, unconvincing **9** weak, feeble **10** diluted

■ **strong point**
strength, talent, gift, aptitude, advantage, asset, bent, forte, speciality, specialty, métier
COLLOQ. thing

> **SYNONYM NUANCES**
>
> *sense 1*
> Most of the synonyms are positive in tone.
>   You can use **powerful** or **mighty** to suggest having great strength, while **potent** has further implications of effectiveness: *the most potent political force in the country.* **Lusty**, meanwhile, suggests vigour, while **strapping** conveys a picture of a tall, robust build.
>   Other synonyms make suggestions about appearance; **sturdy** and **stout** imply a firm, stocky body, while **burly** additionally suggests height: *burly bouncers on the door.* The term **beefy** has suggestions of fleshiness: *his great wide beefy back*, while **brawny** implies muscularity, and **sinewy** echoes this toned form: *his long sinewy body.* **Athletic** and **fit**, although similar, are more suggestive of concomitant physical prowess.

strongarm *adj*
forceful, physical, violent, oppressive, terror, aggressive, bullying, coercive, threatening, intimidatory, thuggish
COLLOQ. bully-boy
F3 gentle

strongbox *n*
safe, cash box, deposit box, safety-deposit box, chest, coffer, vault, depository, repository

stronghold *n*
citadel, bastion, fort, fortress, castle, tower, keep, hold, centre, refuge, fastness, outpost, eyrie, hill-fort
OLD holt

strongly *adv*
1 *a strongly built man*
powerfully, muscularly, athletically
2 *strongly-constructed apparatus*
durably, solidly, toughly, resiliently, substantially
3 *strongly opposed to the idea*
firmly, positively, resolutely, deeply, intensely, definitely, forcefully
4 *his breath smells strongly of garlic*
intensely, powerfully, markedly
F3 **1 2** insubstantially weakly **3** mildly **4** faintly

strong-minded *adj*
resolute, steadfast, strong-willed, tenacious, firm, determined, independent, iron-willed, uncompromising, unbending, unwavering
F3 weak-willed

strong-willed *adj*
stubborn, obstinate, intractable, wayward, inflexible, wilful, self-willed
FORMAL obdurate, refractory, recalcitrant, intransigent

stroppy *adj*
bad-tempered, difficult, unhelpful, unco-operative, perverse, awkward, bloody-minded, quarrelsome, rowdy, cantankerous, obstreperous
FORMAL refractory
COLLOQ. bolshie, ratty, shirty
F3 co-operative, sweet-tempered

structural *adj*
design, constructional, organizational
TECHNICAL tectonic
FORMAL configurational, formational, edificial

structure *n, v*
♦ *n*
1 the structure of society
framework, frame, construction, fabric, form, shape,
design, make-up, formation, arrangement, organization,
composition, constitution, system, set-up, chassis
FORMAL configuration, conformation
2 BUILDING, construction, edifice, erection
♦ *v*
construct, assemble, build, form, shape, design,
arrange, organize

struggle *v, n*
♦ *v*
1 STRIVE, work, toil, labour, strain, flounder, vie, try hard,
exert yourself, give your all, do your best, do your utmost,
agonize
2 FIGHT, battle, wrestle, grapple, engage, contest, combat,
contend, compete, vie
F3 2 yield, give in
♦ *n*
clash, conflict, strife, fight, battle, skirmish, encounter,
combat, scuffle, brawl, hostilities, contest, competition,
difficulty, problem, effort, exertion, trouble, pains, agony,
work, labour, toil
F3 ease, submission, co-operation

> **QUOTATIONS**
> I've never forgotten for long at a time that living is a
> struggle. I know that every good and excellent thing in
> the world stands moment by moment on the razor-edge
> of danger and must be fought for – whether it's a field,
> or a home, or a country
> THORNTON NIVEN WILDER, *The Skin of Our Teeth*

strut *v*
parade, prance, stalk, swagger, peacock; *S Afr* pronk
COLLOQ. swank

stub *n*
end, stump, remnant, butt, counterfoil
COLLOQ. fag end, dog-end

stubborn *adj*
obstinate, stiff-necked, mulish, pig-headed, rigid,
uncompromising, inflexible, unbending, unyielding,
dogged, persistent, tenacious, headstrong, self-willed,
strong-willed, adamant, hidebound, wilful, difficult,
unmanageable, stubborn as a mule, not listening/open to
reason, opinionated, overdetermined, stiff, inveterate,
perverse, cantankerous; *Scot* rigwiddie, thrawn
OLD stoor, stout; (*Shakesp*) obstacle
FORMAL obdurate, intransigent, refractory, intractable,
recalcitrant, contumacious
COLLOQ. *N Am* ornery
F3 compliant, flexible, yielding

> **SYNONYM NUANCES**
> You can use **obstinate** to suggest unreasonable
> determination, and **rigid**, **inflexible**, **stiff**, **unbending**
> and **unyielding** are also rather negative in their
> implication of being fixed in your ideas and not open to
> suggestion. **Uncompromising** suggests a refusal to allow
> any concessions, but can be more suggestive that this is
> a strength.
>   The terms **dogged** and **tenacious** suggest a refusal to
> give up, which can be interpreted as admirable: *a
> thorough and tenacious businesswoman*. **Persistent**,
> although similar, has implications of repetition and being
> a nuisance: *persistent demands*. The terms **headstrong**
> and **self-willed** suggest acting on your own wishes,
> regardless of others, and are rather disapproving;
> however, **strong-willed**, which also suggests

single-mindedness, is far more approbatory: *he is
strong-willed, and a great competitor*. **Wilful** suggests an
untamed element, and the terms **difficult** and
unmanageable make more explicit these problems of
control.
  Hidebound is a fairly critical term which implies
habitual behaviour and attitudes: *a liberator from
hidebound convention*, while **inveterate** has slightly less
criticism inherent in its tone: *an inveterate rebel who
would not be shifted*. **Opinionated** is also negative in its
implication of undue adherence to your own assertions:
entrenched, opinionated and bombastic idiots. You
might use the disapproving term **perverse** of being
deliberately provocative by championing the opposite
viewpoint, and **cantankerous**, too, has suggestions of
being deliberately contrary: *he can be a cantankerous
old fossil at times*.

stubbornly *adv*
obstinately, pig-headedly, inflexibly, uncompromisingly,
doggedly, persistently, tenaciously, perversely, wilfully
FORMAL intransigently
F3 compliantly

stubby *adj*
stumpy, dumpy, chunky, short, squat, thickset
F3 long, tall, thin

stuck *adj*
1 FAST, jammed, firm, fixed, embedded, rooted, fastened,
unmovable, immobile, joined, glued, cemented
COLLOQ. bogged down
2 BEATEN, perplexed, baffled
COLLOQ. stumped, at a loss, at your wits' end, nonplussed
F3 1 loose
■ **stuck on**
fond of, enthusiastic about, keen on, obsessed with,
infatuated with, wild about, crazy about
COLLOQ. dotty about, mad on, nuts on, sweet on
■ **get stuck into**
set about, tackle, get down to, start, begin, embark on
F3

stuck-up *adj*
snobbish, supercilious, haughty, patronizing,
condescending, proud, arrogant, conceited
COLLOQ. snooty, bigheaded, toffee-nosed, high and
mighty, hoity-toity, uppish, toploftical
F3 humble, modest

stud *n*
knob, boss, tack, rivet, doornail, press fastener,
seg; *Aust* stop

studded *adj*
dotted, flecked, set, spotted, speckled, sprinkled,
ornamented, spangled, scattered
OLD bejewelled, bespangled

student *n*
undergraduate, postgraduate, scholar, schoolboy,
schoolgirl, pupil, disciple, learner, probationer, trainee,
apprentice

studied *adj*
deliberate, conscious, wilful, intentional, premeditated,
planned, purposeful, calculated, contrived, forced,
affected, unnatural, artificial, over-elaborate
F3 unplanned, impulsive, natural

studio *n*
workshop, workroom, gallery, school, atelier,
bottega

studious *adj*
scholarly, academic, intellectual, bookish, serious,
thoughtful, reflective, diligent, hard-working, industrious,
meticulous, thorough, assiduous, careful, attentive,
earnest, eager
FORMAL sedulous
F3 lazy, idle, negligent

study v, n

♦ v

read, learn, train, revise, cram, read up, research, work, major in, investigate, analyse, survey, scan, examine, scrutinize, peruse, pore over, contemplate, meditate, ponder, consider, deliberate

COLLOQ. swot, mug up, bone up

♦ n

1 READING, homework, preparation, learning, scholarship, revision, cramming, research, investigation, inquiry, analysis, examination, scrutiny, inspection, contemplation, thought, consideration, attention

COLLOQ. swotting

See panel below

2 REPORT, essay, thesis, paper, monograph, article, work, survey, review, critique

3 OFFICE, studio, library, workplace, workroom

COLLOQ. den

stuff v, n

♦ v

1 PACK, stow, load, fill, pad, press, cram, crowd, force, push, ram, thrust, wedge, jam, squeeze, compress, block, obstruct, bung up

COLLOQ. shove

2 GORGE, gormandize, overindulge, guzzle, gobble, sate, satiate

COLLOQ. pig out, gross out, make a pig of yourself, binge

E3 1 unload, empty **2** nibble

♦ n

1 MATERIAL, fabric, matter, substance, essence

2 BELONGINGS, possessions, things, objects, articles, items, goods, luggage, paraphernalia, kit, tackle, equipment, materials

COLLOQ. gear, clobber

stuffing n

padding, wadding, quilting, packing, kapok, filling, forcemeat, farce

stuffy adj

1 *a stuffy room*

musty, stale, airless, unventilated, suffocating, stifling, oppressive, heavy, close, muggy, sultry, fuggy, fusty

2 STAID, strait-laced, prim, conventional, old-fashioned, pompous, dull, dreary, uninteresting, fusty, stodgy, stiff, starchy

COLLOQ. fuddy-duddy; *N Am* buttoned-down

E3 1 airy, well-ventilated **2** informal, modern, lively

stultify v

blunt, dull, stupefy, numb, smother, stifle, suppress, thwart, invalidate, negate, nullify

FORMAL hebetate

E3 prove, sharpen, electrify

stumble v

1 TRIP, slip, fall, falter, lurch, reel, stagger, flounder, founder, blunder, lose your balance, peck, titubate; *dialect* hamble; *Scot* snapper, stoit

2 STAMMER, stutter, hesitate, falter

■ stumble across/on

come across, find, discover, encounter

FORMAL chance upon, happen upon

stumbling-block n

obstacle, hurdle, barrier, bar, obstruction, hindrance, impediment, difficulty, snag

stump n, v

♦ n

end, remnant, trunk, stub, butt, remains

COLLOQ. fag end, dog-end

♦ v

defeat, outwit, confound, perplex, puzzle, baffle, mystify, confuse, bewilder, dumbfound, foil

COLLOQ. flummox, bamboozle, nonplus

E3 assist

■ stump up

pay, pay out/up, hand over, donate, contribute

COLLOQ. fork out, shell out, chip in, cough up; *N Am* ante up

E3 receive

stumped adj

perplexed, stuck, baffled

COLLOQ. floored, bamboozled, flummoxed, nonplussed, stymied

stumpy adj

chunky, heavy, short, squat, stocky, stubby, thickset, thick, dumpy

E3 long, tall, thin

stun v

amaze, astonish, astound, stagger, shock, daze, deafen, stupefy, dumbfound, overcome, overpower, confound, confuse, bewilder, settle; *Scot* devvel, dover; *N Am* Taser®

OLD stonn, bedeafen; (*Spenser*) stoun, stound

COLLOQ. flabbergast, knock out, knock for six, bowl over, take your breath away

stunned adj

amazed, astounded, devastated, dumbfounded, dazed, numb, shocked, staggered, stupefied

COLLOQ. flabbergasted, floored, gobsmacked

E3 indifferent

Subjects of study include:

accountancy	cosmology	eugenics	languages	oceanography	social sciences
agriculture	craft	fashion	law	ornithology	sociology
anatomy	creative writing	film studies	leisure studies	pathology	sport
anthropology	dance	fitness	lexicography	penology	statistics
archaeology	design	food technology	librarianship	personal and	surveying
architecture	design and	forensics	linguistics	social education	technology
art	technology	gender studies	literature	(PSE)	theology
astrology	(D & T)	genetics	logistics	personal social	tourism and
astronomy	development	geography	management	and health	hospitality
biology	studies	geology	studies	education (PSHE)	translation and
botany	drama	heraldry	marine studies	pharmacology	interpretation
building studies	dressmaking	history	marketing	philosophy	typewriting
business studies	driving	home economics	mathematics	photography	visual arts
calligraphy	ecology	horticulture	mechanics	physics	web design
chemistry	economics	hotel management	media studies	physiology	women's studies
citizenship	education	humanities	medicine	politics	word processing
civil engineering	electronics	information and	metallurgy	pottery	zoology
the Classics	engineering	communication	metaphysics	psychology	
commerce	environmenal	technology (ICT)	meteorology	publishing	
communication	studies	information tech-	music	religious studies	
studies	erotology	nology (IT)	mythology	science	
computer studies	ethnology	journalism	natural history	shorthand	

stunner n
beauty, charmer, good-looker, sensation, dazzler, heart-throb, looker, *femme fatale*, lovely, siren
COLLOQ. smasher, cracker, knock-out, peach, wow, eye-catcher

stunning adj
beautiful, lovely, gorgeous, ravishing, dazzling, brilliant, striking, impressive, spectacular, remarkable, extraordinary, amazing, phenominal, wonderful, marvellous, great, sensational, incredible, staggering
COLLOQ. smashing, fabulous, jaw-dropping
E3 ugly, awful

stunningly adv
brilliantly, strikingly, impressively, remarkably, spectacularly, amazingly, extraordinarily, staggeringly, marvellously, wonderfully, beautifully, gorgeously
COLLOQ. fabulously

stunt[1] n
a publicity stunt
feat, exploit, act, deed, action, enterprise, trick, turn, performance, ramp
COLLOQ. wheeze, hype

stunt[2] v
stunt someone's growth
stop, arrest, check, restrict, curb, slow, hinder, hamper, inhibit, impede, dwarf; *dialect* stock; *Scot* nirl
FORMAL retard
E3 promote, encourage

stunted adj
small, little, tiny, undersized, diminutive, dwarfed, dwarfish
OLD (*Shakesp*) scrubbed
E3 large, sturdy

stupefaction n
daze, numbness, state of shock, blackout, senselessness, bewilderment, wonder, bafflement, amazement, astonishment

stupefy v
daze, stun, numb, dumbfound, shock, devastate, stagger, dull, amaze, astound, fuddle, drowse, drug, etherize, hocus; *dialect* moider; *Scot* dozen
OLD bemuse, benumb, somniate; (*Shakesp*) mull
COLLOQ. knock out, knock for six, bowl over

stupendous adj
huge, enormous, immense, gigantic, colossal, vast, phenomenal, tremendous, breathtaking, wonderful, extraordinary, overwhelming, staggering, stunning, amazing, astounding, superb, marvellous, fantastic
FORMAL prodigious
COLLOQ. fabulous
E3 ordinary, unimpressive

stupid adj
1 SILLY, foolish, irresponsible, ill-advised, indiscreet, foolhardy, rash, senseless, mad, lunatic, brainless, mindless, half-witted, idiotic, imbecilic, moronic, feeble-minded, simple-minded, slow, dim, dull, dull-witted, dense, crass, inane, fatuous, puerile, futile, pointless, meaningless, nonsensical, absurd, ludicrous, laughable; *Welsh* twp
OLD (*Shakesp*) clay-brained, fatbrained, sodden-witted
FORMAL injudicious
COLLOQ. gormless, thick, dumb, dopey, not all there, loopy, barmy, potty, slow on the uptake, thick as a plank/two short planks
SLANG loony
2 DAZED, groggy, stupefied, stunned, sluggish, semiconscious, unconscious
E3 **1** sensible, wise, clever, intelligent **2** alert, sharp

---

SYNONYM NUANCES

sense 1
Many of the synonyms are disapproving in tone.
 Silly and **foolish** are fairly restrained terms to suggest a lack of good sense or wisdom. **Irresponsible**, on the other hand, makes the accusation of recklessness, and **foolhardy** also suggests an absence of caution: *an example of foolhardy daring*, while **rash** is appropriate to suggest a degree of impulsiveness in an action: *take your time rather than make rash decisions based on wishful thinking*. **Ill-advised** is more restrained, and has more to do with lack of judgement: *his ill-advised return to television failed miserably*.
 To emphasize the purposelessness of an action you might use **senseless**, **pointless**, **meaningless** or **futile**: *futile departmental infighting*. However, to convey the idea of a lack of mental sharpness or ability **slow**, **dim**, **dull** and **dense** are more useful. More strongly critical terms are **idiotic**, **imbecilic** and **moronic**, which suggest total intellectual incapacity.
 Crass suggests not just stupidity but also insensitivity or lack of taste: *crass comments made to try to cheer me up*, while **inane** is suggestive of being vacuous. **Fatuous** further implies cheerful complacency: *their fatuous optimism*, while **puerile** could be used to suggest that something is childish. **Absurd**, **ludicrous** and **laughable** all suggest an element of the ridiculous and so convey contempt: *the idea that these weapons deter anyone is laughable*.

---

stupidity n
silliness, folly, foolishness, foolhardiness, irresponsibility, indiscretion, rashness, senselessness, madness, lunacy, denseness, crassness, absurdity, dimness, asininity, feeble-mindedness, dullness, puerility, fatuousness, fatuity, futility, impracticality, brainlessness, idiocy, imbecility, inanity, ineptitude, naivety, obtuseness, pointlessness, ludicrousness, slowness
COLLOQ. dopiness, doziness, dumbness, thickness
E3 intelligence, alertness, cleverness

stupidly adv
foolishly, irresponsibly, unthinkingly, sillily, inanely, fatuously, absurdly, mindlessly
E3 sensibly

stupor n
daze, state of shock, stupefaction, lethargy, inertia, trance, blackout, coma, numbness, oblivion, insensibility, unconsciousness
FORMAL torpor
E3 alertness, consciousness

sturdy adj
strong, robust, durable, well-made, stout, substantial, solid, well-built, powerful, muscular, lubberly, burly, stocky, athletic, hardy, rugged, vigorous, flourishing, hearty, staunch, stalwart, steadfast, firm, resolute, determined, tenacious; *dialect* turnsick; *Scot* stuffy, steeve
FORMAL mighty
E3 weak, flimsy, puny

stutter v, n
♦ v
stammer, hesitate, splutter, falter, stumble, mumble, lisp
♦ n
stammer, speech impediment, speech defect

style n, v
♦ n
1 *style of working*
technique, approach, method, methodology, manner, fashion, way, custom
FORMAL mode
2 APPEARANCE, cut, design, pattern, shape, form, sort, type, kind, variety, category
FORMAL genre

3 ELEGANCE, smartness, chic, flair, panache, stylishness, dash, taste, polish, refinement, sophistication, urbanity, suaveness, fashion, vogue, trend, mode, dressiness, flamboyance, wealth, affluence, comfort, luxury, grandeur
4 WORDING, phrasing, expression, language, tone, tenor
F3 3 inelegance, tastelessness
♦ *v*
1 DESIGN, cut, tailor, fashion, make, shape, produce, adapt
2 DESIGNATE, term, name, call, address, title, dub, tag, label
FORMAL denominate

stylish *adj*
chic, fashionable, à la mode, modish, in vogue, voguish, snappy, dressy, smart, elegant, polished, refined, sophisticated, urbane
COLLOQ. trendy, natty, snazzy, classy, ritzy
F3 old-fashioned, shabby

stylus *n*
needle, pointer, pen, index, hand, style, probe
FORMAL graphium

stymie *v*
foil, frustrate, hinder, stump, thwart, hamper, impede, interfere, defeat, confound, baffle, balk, mystify, puzzle
COLLOQ. bamboozle, flummox, nonplus, snooker
F3 help, assist

suave *adj*
debonair, refined, polite, courteous, charming, civil, civilized, agreeable, affable, soft-spoken, smooth, polished, bland, glib, sophisticated, urbane, worldly
FORMAL unctuous
F3 rude, unsophisticated

suavity *n*
refinement, politeness, courtesy, sophistication, urbanity, charm, civility, agreeability, blandness, smoothness, worldliness
FORMAL unctuousness
F3 coarseness

sub *n*
1 SUBSTITUTE, reserve, stand-by, supply, locum, understudy, stand-in, replacement, relief, surrogate, proxy, agent, deputy, makeshift, stopgap
FORMAL *locum tenens*
COLLOQ. temp, fill-in; *N Am* pinch-hitter
2 SUBSCRIPTION, membership fee, dues, payment, donation, contribution, offering, gift

subaquatic *adj*
underwater, undersea, submersed, submarine
FORMAL subaqua, subaqueous, demersal

subconscious *adj, n*
♦ *adj*
subliminal, unconscious, intuitive, instinctive, inner, innermost, deep, hidden, latent, underlying, repressed, suppressed
F3 conscious
♦ *n*
psyche, mind, unconscious, unconscious self, inner self, inner being, ego, super-ego, id

subcontract *v*
contract out, pass/give to others, delegate, farm out, outsource

subdue *v*
overcome, quell, suppress, repress, oppress, overpower, crush, quash, defeat, conquer, overrun, subject, gain mastery over, get the better of, humble, bring under, cow, crucify, take in, break, tame, master, discipline, chasten, chastise, control, check, stifle, restrain, moderate, reduce, soften, quieten, damp, mellow, soft-pedal, step on, charm, daunt, mortify, starve; *Scot* daunton
OLD subdew, do down, quail, mate; (*Spenser*) accoy, adaw
FORMAL vanquish, subjugate, subact
SLANG settle someone's hash
F3 arouse, awaken

subdued *adj*
1 SAD, downcast, dejected, crestfallen, depressed, quiet, unexcited, lifeless, serious, grave, solemn
COLLOQ. down in the dumps
2 QUIET, muted, hushed, silent, noiseless, still, soft, softened, pastel, dim, shaded, sombre, sober, restrained, delicate, unobtrusive, low-key, subtle, toned-down
F3 1 lively, excited **2** bright, loud, striking, obtrusive

subject *n, adj, v*
♦ *n*
1 TOPIC, theme, matter, issue, question, aspect, point, substance, case, affair, business, discipline, area of study, field, field of study, motif
2 NATIONAL, citizen, native, inhabitant, resident
3 PARTICIPANT, client, patient, case, victim
COLLOQ. guinea pig
4 SUBORDINATE, vassal, liegeman, inferior, dependant, captive
COLLOQ. underling
F3 4 monarch, ruler, master
♦ *adj*
1 LIABLE, disposed, prone, susceptible, vulnerable, likely, apt, open, exposed
2 *subject to a law*
captive, bound, constrained, obedient, answerable, accountable, subordinate, inferior, subservient, submissive
FORMAL subjugated
3 DEPENDENT, depending, conditional, resting, hanging
FORMAL contingent
F3 1 invulnerable, immune **2** free, superior **3** unconditional
♦ *v*
expose, lay open, submit, subdue
FORMAL subjugate

subjection *n*
captivity, bondage, slavery, oppression, domination, mastery, defeat, enslavement, chains, shackles
FORMAL subjugation

subjective *adj*
biased, prejudiced, bigoted, personal, individual, idiosyncratic, emotional, intuitive, instinctive
F3 objective, unbiased, impartial

subjugate *v*
conquer, overpower, overcome, master, overthrow, gain mastery over, get the better of, crush, defeat, subdue, suppress, oppress, quell, reduce, enslave, tame, thrall
FORMAL vanquish
F3 free, liberate

sublimate *v*
channel, divert, transfer, redirect, turn, exalt, heighten, elevate, purify, refine
FORMAL transmute
F3 let out

sublime *adj*
1 GLORIOUS, exalted, elevated, high, lofty, noble, winged, august, majestic, great, grand, imposing, magnificent, transcendent, spiritual, heavenly, celestial, Dantean
FORMAL empyreal
2 SUPREME, great, intense, extreme, complete, utter
F3 1 lowly, base

subliminal *adj*
subconscious, hidden, concealed, unconscious

submerge *v*
submerse, immerse, plunge, plummet, duck, dip, dive, dunk, sink, go down, go/put under water, drown, engulf, overwhelm, swamp, overflow, flood, inundate, deluge, bury; *Scot* take
OLD whelm, implunge, indrench
F3 surface

submerged *adj*
submersed, immersed, underwater, sunk, sunken, drowned, swamped, inundated, hidden, concealed, cloaked, veiled, unseen

submission n
1 SURRENDER, giving in, capitulation, resignation, agreement, acquiescence, compliance, obedience, deference, submissiveness, meekness, passivity
FORMAL assent
2 PRESENTATION, offering, contribution, entry, introduction, tendering, tabling, tender, suggestion, proposal, statement, assertion
FORMAL averment
1 resistance, opposition, intransigence, intractability
2 withdrawal, retraction

submissive adj
yielding, passive, unresisting, resigned, patient, uncomplaining, accommodating, malleable, biddable, compliant, acquiescent, obedient, deferential, ingratiating, subservient, resisting, servile, humble, meek, self-effacing, docile, weak, weak-willed, downtrodden, subdued
FORMAL supine
intractable, assertive; *formal* intransigent

submissively adv
passively, patiently, uncomplainingly, obediently, deferentially, humbly, meekly, subserviently, weakly
assertively, intractably

submit v
1 YIELD, give in, give way, surrender, lay down your arms, capitulate, knuckle under, bow, bend, bend/bow the knee, stoop, succumb, agree, comply, defer, acquiesce, subject, resign, come to terms, expose, violate, bite the bullet, come to heel, kiss the rod
TECHNICAL passage
OLD permit; (*Shakesp*) subscribe
FORMAL accede
2 PRESENT, tender, offer, put forward, suggest, propose, posit, introduce, table, move, state, claim, assert, lay before, put, refer, render, argue, send in
TECHNICAL prefer
FORMAL proffer, propound, aver
1 resist, oppose **2** withdraw

subnormal adj
below normal, below average, low, backward, inferior, slow, retarded, feeble-minded
gifted

subordinate adj, n
♦ adj
secondary, auxiliary, ancillary, subsidiary, dependent, inferior, lower, lower in rank, lower-ranking, junior, minor, lesser, subservient, lowly
superior, senior
♦ n
inferior, junior, assistant, attendant, second, deputy, aide, dependant, menial, vassal
COLLOQ. underling, sidekick, skivvy, dogsbody, second fiddle
superior, boss

subordination n
inferiority, subjection, submission, dependence, servitude, subservience
superiority

subscribe v
1 *subscribe to a magazine*
pay for regularly, buy regularly, receive/take regularly, take, sign up to
2 DONATE, give, contribute, pledge
COLLOQ. chip in, shell out, fork out
3 *subscribe to a theory*
support, endorse, back, approve, agree
FORMAL advocate

subscriber n
regular reader, member, customer

subscription n
membership fee, dues, payment, donation, contribution, offering, gift

subsequent adj
following, later, future, next, succeeding, consequent, resulting, ensuing
previous, earlier, prior

subsequently adv
later, after, afterwards, consequently
previously

subservience n
servility, servitude, deference, submissiveness, obedience, acquiescence, dutifulness, humility, subjection, subordination

subservient adj
1 SERVILE, deferential, submissive, fawning, ingratiating, toadying, sycophantic
FORMAL obsequious, unctuous
COLLOQ. bootlicking
2 SUBORDINATE, less important, secondary, ancillary, auxiliary, subsidiary, dependent, inferior, lower, junior, minor, lesser
1 domineering, rebellious **2** superior, senior, more important

subside v
1 DECREASE, lower, get lower, lessen, diminish, dwindle, decline, wane, peter out, ebb, recede, moderate, die down, quieten, let up, fall, slacken, ease, lull, slake
OLD adaw, assuage, quell, quench
FORMAL abate
COLLOQ. pipe down
2 SINK, collapse, cave in, settle, descend, lower, fall, drop, founder, dissolve
OLD swoon
1 rise, increase

subsidence n
collapse, decline, decrease, descent, settlement, sinking, slackening, lessening, ebb, de-escalation, settling
FORMAL abatement, detumescence, diminution
increase

subsidiary adj, n
♦ adj
auxiliary, supplementary, additional, ancillary, assistant, supporting, contributory, secondary, subordinate, subservient, lesser, minor
primary, chief, major
♦ n
branch, offshoot, division, section, part, wing

subsidize v
support, back, endorse, underwrite, sponsor, finance, fund, invest in, give a subsidy to, pay part of the cost of, contribute to, aid, promote

subsidy n
grant, allowance, assistance, help, aid, contribution, sponsorship, finance, funding, investment, support, backing, endorsement, underwriting
FORMAL subvention

subsist v
exist, continue, endure, hold out, live, survive, remain, last, eke out an existence

subsistence n
living, survival, existence, continuance, livelihood, maintenance, support, keep, sustenance, nourishment, food, provisions, rations, aliment

substance n
1 MATTER, material, stuff, fabric, essence, mass, medium, entity, body, solidity, materiality, tangibility, concreteness, reality, actuality, ground, foundation
FORMAL corporeality
2 SUBJECT, subject matter, matter, topic, theme, text, burden, pith, gist, meaning, meaningfulness, significance, validity, truth, foundation, ground, basis, force, power, weight
FORMAL import

3 *a person of substance*
wealth, money, prosperity, riches, fortune, assets, means, resources, affluence, power, influence

substandard *adj*
second-rate, inferior, imperfect, damaged, shoddy, poor, inadequate, unacceptable
COLLOQ. below par, not up to scratch; *Aust & NZ* crook
F3 first-rate, superior, perfect

substantial *adj*
1 LARGE, big, siz(e)able, ample, fat, measurable, generous, great, considerable, significant, important, meaningful, notable, remarkable, weighty, worthwhile, valuable
COLLOQ. tidy, pretty
2 WELL-BUILT, solid, stout, sturdy, strong, tough, hard, durable, sound, cast-iron
3 TANGIBLE, material, existing, concrete, real, actual, true
FORMAL corporeal
4 BASIC, essential, central, primary, main, principal, fundamental, inherent, intrinsic
5 WEALTHY, prosperous, rich, successful, affluent, powerful, influential
F3 **1** small, insignificant **2** flimsy **3** insubstantial, imaginary **5** poor

substantially *adv*
1 SIGNIFICANTLY, largely, considerably, to a great extent
2 ESSENTIALLY, fundamentally, mainly, in the main, materially, to all intents and purposes, in effect, at heart
F3 **1** slightly

substantiate *v*
prove, verify, confirm, uphold, support, back up, bear out, authenticate, validate
FORMAL corroborate
F3 disprove, refute

substantive *adj*
real, substantial, material, factual, valid, concrete, solid, fundamental, intrinsic

substitute *v, n, adj*
♦ *v*
1 CHANGE, exchange, swap, switch, interchange, replace, use instead
2 STAND IN, cover, deputize, understudy, relieve, take over, take the place of, represent, double, act instead of
COLLOQ. fill in, sub
♦ *n*
reserve, stand-by, supply, locum, understudy, stand-in, replacement, relief, surrogate, proxy, agent, deputy, makeshift, stopgap
FORMAL *locum tenens*
COLLOQ. temp, sub, fill-in; *N Am* pinch-hitter
♦ *adj*
reserve, temporary, relief, acting, deputy, surrogate, proxy, replacement, alternative, stand-by, stand-in

substitution *n*
change, exchange, replacement, interchange, swap, swapping, switch, switching

subsume *v*
include, incorporate, embody, contain, enclose, hold, encompass, cover, take in, admit, insert, introduce, add, enter, put in, add in, count in
FORMAL comprehend, comprise, embrace
F3 exclude, omit

subterfuge *n*
trick, stratagem, scheme, ploy, ruse, wile, intrigue, expedient, manoeuvre, deviousness, evasion, deception, artifice, pretence, excuse, pretext
FORMAL machination, duplicity
COLLOQ. dodge
F3 openness, honesty

subtle *adj*
1 DELICATE, understated, implied, indirect, low-key, slight, minute, tenuous, elusive, faint, indistinct, indefinite, mild, toned-down, fine, nice, refined, sophisticated, deep, profound, scholastic

OLD subtil, suttle
2 ARTFUL, cunning, crafty, sly, devious, wily, indirect, shrewd, astute, discreet, discriminating, tactful, clever, strategic, intricate, complex
OLD subtil, suttle
F3 **1** blatant, obvious **2** artless, open, indiscreet, tactless

subtlety *n*
1 DELICACY, nicety, nuance, refinement, finesse, faintness, indistinctness, indefiniteness, mutedness, sophistication
OLD suttletie
2 ARTFULNESS, cunning, wiliness, guile, deviousness, craftiness, cleverness, discernment, astuteness, skill, discrimination, intricacy, slyness, acuteness, acumen
OLD suttletie
FORMAL sagacity

subtly *adv*
1 *subtly different*
indirectly, tenuously, mildly, faintly, indistinctly, indefinitely
OLD suttly
2 *subtly manipulate an audience*
deceitfully, deviously, artfully, cunningly, slyly, cleverly, astutely
OLD suttly
F3 **1** obviously **2** openly

subtract *v*
deduct, take away, remove, dock, withdraw, debit, detract, diminish
F3 add

suburb *n*
suburbia, outskirts, commuter belt, residential area, dormitory (town), *banlieue, faubourg*; *N Am* bedroom suburb
FORMAL purlieus
F3 centre, heart

suburban *adj*
1 *a suburban railway*
commuter, residential
2 *suburban attitudes*
conventional, dull, unimaginative, narrow, narrow-minded, parochial, provincial, insular, bourgeois, middle-class
COLLOQ. common-or-garden

subversive *adj, n*
♦ *adj*
seditious, treasonous, treacherous, traitorous, revolutionary, inflammatory, incendiary, disruptive, troublemaking, riotous, weakening, undermining, discrediting, destructive
F3 loyal
♦ *n*
seditionist, terrorist, dissident, traitor, quisling, troublemaker
COLLOQ. freedom fighter, fifth columnist

subvert *v*
undermine, destroy, ruin, pervert, corrupt, confound, overthrow, deprave, demoralize, contaminate, poison, overturn, upset, disrupt, invalidate, wreck, demolish, debase, raze, sabotage
FORMAL vitiate
F3 boost, uphold

subway *n*
1 UNDERGROUND RAILWAY, underground, metro
COLLOQ. tube
2 UNDERPASS, tunnel, pedestrian tunnel, underground passage

succeed *v*
1 TRIUMPH, do well, be successful, thrive, flourish, prosper, make good, manage, carry out, complete, achieve, accomplish, reach, realize, attain, fulfil, prevail, work, work out, get results
COLLOQ. make it, get on, bring off, pull off, turn up trumps, take over, steal the show, go places, win the day,

land/fall on your feet, bring home the bacon, strike gold, hit the jackpot
2 *winter succeeds autumn*
follow, come after, replace, take the place of, result, ensue
E3 **1** fail; *colloq.* flop **2** precede, come before
■ **succeed to**
come into, enter upon, inherit, replace, take over, supersede
FORMAL accede, assume
E3 abdicate, precede

succeeding *adj*
following, next, subsequent, ensuing, coming, to come, later, successive
TECHNICAL hereditary
E3 previous, earlier, prior

success *n*
1 TRIUMPH, victory, positive result, luck, fortune, prosperity, happiness, fame, eminence, completion, achievement, accomplishment, realization, attainment, fulfilment
2 CELEBRITY, star, winner, bestseller, hit, sensation
COLLOQ. somebody, VIP, celeb, big name, bigwig, big shot, wow, sell-out, box-office hit, smash hit, smash
E3 **1** failure, disaster **2** failure, loser; *colloq.* write-off, flop, dead loss

> **QUOTATIONS**
> Eighty percent of success is showing-up
> WOODY ALLEN
>
> The toughest thing about success is that you've got to keep on being a success
> IRVING BERLIN

successful *adj*
1 VICTORIOUS, triumphant, winning, lucky, fortunate, prosperous, wealthy, affluent, thriving, flourishing, booming, moneymaking, lucrative, profitable, rewarding, satisfying, fruitful, productive
2 *a successful writer*
famous, well-known, popular, leading, bestselling, top, unbeaten
E3 **1** unsuccessful, unprofitable, fruitless **2** unknown, little-known

successfully *adv*
fine, well, victoriously, beautifully, famously
COLLOQ. swimmingly
E3 unsuccessfully

succession *n*
1 SERIES, sequence, order, progression, run, chain, string, cycle, continuation, flow, course, line, train, procession
2 *the succession to the throne*
accession, attaining, elevation, inheritance
FORMAL assumption
■ **in succession**
successively, consecutively, sequentially, uninterruptedly, running, in a row, one after the other
COLLOQ. on the trot

successive *adj*
consecutive, sequential, following, succeeding, running, serial

successively *adv*
consecutively, in succession, sequentially, uninterruptedly, running, one after the other
COLLOQ. on the trot

successor *n*
replacement, substitute, relief, descendant, beneficiary, heir, co-heir, inheritor, next in line

succinct *adj*
concise, short, brief, terse, crisp, pithy, compact, condensed, summary, to the point, in a word, Laconian
E3 long, lengthy, wordy, verbose

succinctly *adv*
concisely, briefly, in brief, tersely, crisply, pithily, compactly, to the point, in a word
E3 wordily, verbosely

succour *n, v*
♦ *n*
help, aid, assistance, support, comfort, relief
FORMAL ministrations
COLLOQ. helping hand
♦ *v*
help, help out, aid, assist, comfort, encourage, support, relieve, foster, minister to, nurse, befriend
E3 undermine

succulent *adj*
fleshy, juicy, moist, luscious, mouthwatering, lush, rich, mellow
E3 dry

succumb *v*
1 GIVE IN, give way, yield, submit, knuckle under, surrender, capitulate, collapse, fall
2 *succumb to an illness*
catch, go down with, pick up, die of/from
FORMAL contract
E3 **1** overcome, overwhelm, master

suck *v*
draw (in), imbibe, absorb, blot up, soak up, extract, drain, pull, sponge, suckle, hoover
■ **suck up to**
fawn, flatter, ingratiate, toady, creep, grovel, curry favour, truckle
COLLOQ. lick someone's boots

sucker *n*
fool, victim, dupe, stooge, sap, leech
COLLOQ. pushover, mug, butt, cat's-paw

suckle *v*
breastfeed, feed, nurse

suction *n*
sucking, drawing-in, absorbing, extraction, draining

sudden *adj*
unexpected, unforeseen, unanticipated, surprising, startling, dramatic, abrupt, sharp, quick, fast, swift, rapid, speedy, meteoric, immediate, instantaneous, prompt, hurried, hasty, rash, impetuous, impulsive
COLLOQ. snap, spur-of-the-moment
E3 expected, predictable, gradual, slow

suddenly *adv*
unexpectedly, all of a sudden, quickly, abruptly, sharply, immediately, instantaneously, without warning, all at once
COLLOQ. out of the blue, from out of nowhere

suddenness *n*
unexpectedness, abruptness, hurriedness, haste, hastiness, impulsiveness
E3 slowness

suds *n*
bubbles, soapiness, lather, froth, foam

sue *v*
1 PROSECUTE, charge, bring charges against, take (legal) action against, indict, take to court, bring to trial
2 SUMMON, solicit, appeal, beg, petition, plead
FORMAL beseech

suffer *v*
1 HURT, ache, be in pain, be afflicted, agonize, grieve, sorrow
COLLOQ. go through the mill
2 UNDERGO, experience, go through, incur, feel, meet with, endure, sustain
3 BEAR, support, stand, put up with, allow, permit, tolerate, endure
FORMAL abide

suffering n
pain, discomfort, hurt, hurting, agony, anguish, affliction, distress, misery, hardship, wretchedness, plight, adversity, ordeal, torment, torture
F∃ ease, comfort

suffice v
do, satisfy, be sufficient, be enough, be adequate, answer, measure up, serve, content
COLLOQ. fit/fill the bill

sufficiency n
adequateness, adequacy, enough, plenty, satiety, competence
FORMAL sufficience
F∃ insufficiency, inadequacy

sufficient adj
enough, adequate, ample, plenty, satisfactory, effective
COLLOQ. decent
F∃ insufficient, inadequate

suffocate v
asphyxiate, smother, stifle, choke, strangle, throttle, be/make breathless, smoke; *dialect* stive; *Scot* smore

suffrage n
franchise, right to vote, right of representation
FORMAL enfranchisement

suffuse v
spread, imbue, infuse, permeate, pervade, steep, transfuse, cover, flood, mantle, bathe, colour, redden

sugar

Kinds of sugar include:

beet sugar	golden syrup	powdered sugar
brown sugar	granulated sugar	refined sugar
cane sugar	icing sugar	sucrose
caster sugar	invert sugar	sugar loaf
crystallized sugar	jaggery	sugar lump
demerara	lactose	syrup
dextrose	maltose	treacle
fructose	maple syrup	unrefined sugar
glucose	molasses	

Artificial sweeteners include:

acesulfame K	Hermesetas®	sorbitol
aspartame	neotame	Splenda®
Canderel®	NutraSweet®	sucralose
cyclamate	saccharin	Sweetex®

See also **sweet**.

sugary adj
1 sugary drinks
sweet, syrupy, sweetened, saccharine, sickly
2 SENTIMENTAL, emotional, gushing, touching, maudlin, mawkish
COLLOQ. soppy, lovey-dovey, slushy, mushy, schmaltzy, corny, sickly, gushy, sloppy

suggest v
1 PROPOSE, put forward, advocate, recommend, submit, advise, counsel, move, table, nominate, bring forward, come up with, envisage, present
COLLOQ. float, vote
2 IMPLY, insinuate, hint (at), intimate, evoke, bring to mind, indicate, give the impression, allude, connote, prompt, savour, smack (of), smell (of)

suggestion n
1 PROPOSAL, proposition, motion, recommendation, submission, idea, plan, hint, piece of advice, pointer
COLLOQ. wrinkle, kite
2 IMPLICATION, insinuation, intimation, innuendo, allusion, prompting
OLD (*Shakesp*) prompture

3 HINT, intimation, suspicion, trace, touch, indication, note, pointer, smack, wind, whiff; *dialect* twang

suggestive adj
1 EVOCATIVE, reminiscent, expressive, meaning, indicative
FORMAL redolent
2 a suggestive remark
indecent, immodest, improper, indelicate, titillating, off-colour, sexual, risqué, bawdy, dirty, smutty, ribald, lewd, provocative
COLLOQ. blue
F∃ 1 inexpressive **2** decent, clean

suicide n
killing yourself, self-destruction, self-murder, taking of your (own) life, self-slaughter, parasuicide, hara-kiri, suttee
FORMAL *felo de se*, self-immolation
COLLOQ. topping yourself, doing away with yourself, cutting your (own) throat, ending it all, hari-kari
■ **commit suicide**
kill yourself, take your (own) life
COLLOQ. top yourself, do yourself in, do away with yourself, end it all, commit hari-kari

suit n, v
♦ n
1 wear a suit
outfit, costume, dress, clothing, set of clothes, ensemble
OLD suite
2 LAWSUIT, action, case, cause, dispute, argument, contest, prosecution, litigation, proceedings, process, trial
OLD suite
♦ v
1 GO WELL WITH, complement, match, tally with, agree with, harmonize with, fit, befit, become, look good/attractive on, flatter
2 PLEASE, satisfy, answer, gratify
3 BE CONVENIENT FOR, be suitable for, be appropriate for, be applicable to, be acceptable to, be satisfactory to, qualify for
FORMAL suffice
COLLOQ. fit/fill the bill
F∃ 1 clash, jar **2** displease, dissatisfy **3** be unsuitable for, be inconvenient for

suitability n
appropriateness, aptness, fitness, fittingness, opportuneness, timeliness, convenience, rightness
FORMAL appositeness
F∃ unsuitability, inappropriateness

suitable adj
appropriate, fitting, convenient, opportune, suited, in keeping, right, compatible, well-suited, well-matched, due, apt, relevant, applicable, fit, adequate, satisfactory, acceptable, befitting, becoming, proper
OLD seemly; (*Shakesp*) liable
FORMAL apposite, pertinent
COLLOQ. (right/just) up someone's street
F∃ unsuitable, inappropriate

suitably adv
appropriately, fittingly, properly, fitly, acceptably, as well, accordingly, quite
F∃ unsuitably

suitcase n
case, vanity-case, bag, holdall, portmanteau, valise, overnight-bag, flight bag, hand-luggage, travel bag, attaché case, portfolio, trunk

suite n
1 APARTMENT, rooms, set of rooms, chambers, flat, household
2 SET, series, collection, sequence, train, furniture
TECHNICAL partita
3 ATTENDANTS, retinue, entourage, court, train, tail, escort, followers, retainers, servants

suitor n
admirer, boyfriend, lover, young man, wooer, beau, follower, pretendant
OLD swain

sulk v, n
♦ v
mope, brood, pout, grouse, grump, pull a long face
COLLOQ. be miffed, be in a huff
♦ n
mood, temper, bad mood, bad temper, pique
COLLOQ. huff, miff

sulkily adv
morosely, moodily, resentfully, grudgingly, sullenly, crossly
⊟ cheerfully

sulky adj
brooding, moody, morose, resentful, grudging, disgruntled, put out, cross, moping, grumpy, out of sorts, bad-tempered, sullen, aloof, unsociable
COLLOQ. miffed, ratty, huffy; dialect mardy
⊟ cheerful, good-tempered, sociable

sullen adj
1 SULKY, moody, morose, glum, gloomy, silent, uncommunicative, surly, sour, cross, churlish, perverse, obstinate, stubborn, resentful
2 DARK, gloomy, sombre, dismal, cheerless, dull, leaden, heavy
⊟ **1** cheerful, happy **2** fine, clear

sullenly adv
glumly, morosely, moodily, sulkily, gloomily, crossly, sourly, churlishly, stubbornly, resentfully, obstinately

sullenness n
moroseness, sulkiness, surliness, moodiness, brooding, glowering, sourness, glumness, heaviness
⊟ cheerfulness

sully v
dirty, soil, defile, pollute, contaminate, taint, spoil, mar, spot, blemish, besmirch, stain, tarnish, damage, disgrace, dishonour
OLD befoul
⊟ cleanse, honour

sultry adj
1 sultry weather
hot, sweltering, sweltry, stifling, stuffy, oppressive, suffocating, close, airless, humid, muggy, soggy, sticky
2 SENSUAL, voluptuous, passionate, attractive, sexy, provocative, seductive, tempting, alluring
⊟ **1** cool, cold

sum n, v
♦ n
total, sum total, aggregate, whole, entirety, number, quantity, amount, tally, reckoning, score, result, answer, summary, culmination
■ **sum up**
1 SUMMARIZE, review, recapitulate, conclude, close
COLLOQ. put in a nutshell, recap
2 EPITOMIZE, embody, encapsulate, exemplify
3 ASSESS, evaluate, gauge, review, consider, size up

summarily adv
immediately, promptly, speedily, swiftly, without delay, hastily, abruptly, arbitrarily
FORMAL expeditiously, peremptorily, forthwith

summarize v
outline, précis, condense, abridge, abbreviate, shorten, sum up, epitomize, encapsulate, review, sketch, synopsize, minute, abstract, resume, docket
COLLOQ. recap
⊟ expand (on)

summary n, adj
♦ n
synopsis, résumé, outline, main points, abstract, précis, condensation, digest, compendium, abridgement, summing-up, review, recapitulation, overview, plan,

summation, short, tabloid, argument, minutes, epitome, docket, aide-mémoire, aperçu, curriculum vitae; N Am wrap-up
TECHNICAL brief, memorandum, balance-sheet, bank statement, creed
FORMAL conspectus, summa
COLLOQ. rundown, recap
♦ adj
short, succinct, brief, curt, cursory, swift, speedy, hasty, prompt, without delay, immediate, instant, instantaneous, direct, unceremonious, offhand, without formality, arbitrary; Scot summar
FORMAL peremptory
⊟ lengthy, careful

summerhouse n
belvedere, gazebo, pavilion

summit n
1 TOP, peak, pinnacle, point, crest, crown, head, vertex, acme, apex, zenith, spire, apogee, climax, culmination, height
2 a NATO summit
meeting, conference, negotiation, talks, discussion, consultation
⊟ **1** bottom, foot, nadir

summon v
call, send for, order, demand, invite, bid, beckon, gather, assemble, convene, rally, muster (up), mobilize, rouse, arouse, challenge, warn, drum up, work up, pluck up, screw up, hail, recollect, cite, page, ring, buzz, gong, knell, toll, trumpet, whistle, whoop, throw the handkerchief
TECHNICAL conjure; Scot sist
OLD provoke, accite, history; (Shakesp & Spenser) convent
FORMAL convoke, preconize
COLLOQ. shake
⊟ dismiss
■ **summon up**
gather, assemble, convene, rally, muster, mobilize, rouse, arouse, evoke, revive, call to mind

summons n
writ, subpoena, citation, order, call, injunction

sumptuous adj
luxurious, plush, lavish, extravagant, rich, costly, expensive, dear, splendid, magnificent, gorgeous, superb, grand, de luxe
FORMAL opulent
⊟ plain, poor

sun n, v
♦ n
star, daystar, sunlight, light, daylight, sunshine
Related adjective: solar
♦ v
sunbathe, tan, brown, bake, bask
FORMAL insolate

sunbathe v
sun, bask, tan, brown, bake, sunbake
FORMAL insolate

sunburnt adj
burnt, red, weather-beaten, blistered, blistering, peeling, inflamed
⊟ pale

sunder v
split, separate, divide, part, cut, chop, sever
FORMAL cleave, dissever, dissunder
⊟ join

sundry adj
various, diverse, miscellaneous, assorted, varied, different, several, some, a few

sunk adj
failed, lost, ruined, finished, doomed
COLLOQ. done for, up the creek, up the spout, in a fix/jam

sunken adj

1 SUBMERGED, buried, recessed, lower, lowered, below ground level
2 *sunken eyes*
depressed, concave, hollow, hollowed, haggard, drawn

sunless adj

bleak, overcast, dark, cloudy, grey, hazy, gloomy, depressing, dismal, dreary, sombre, cheerless
FA sunny, bright

sunlight n

light, daylight, sun, sun's rays, natural light

sunny adj

1 FINE, cloudless, unclouded, clear, summery, sunshiny, sunlit, bright, brilliant
2 CHEERFUL, happy, joyful, smiling, cheery, glad, bright, merry, beaming, radiant, light-hearted, bubbly, bouncy, buoyant, optimistic, hopeful, pleasant
FORMAL blithe
FA 1 sunless, cloudy, dull 2 gloomy, pessimistic, glum

sunrise n

dawn, crack of dawn, break of day, daybreak, daylight, first light, sun-up, cock-crow, aurora

sunset n

sundown, dusk, twilight, gloaming, evening, close of day, nightfall

super adj

great, excellent, superb, wonderful, outstanding, marvellous, magnificent, glorious, incomparable, peerless, matchless, sensational
COLLOQ. smashing, terrific, top-notch, neat, ace, brill
SLANG mega, cool, wicked
FA poor; *colloq.* lousy

superannuated adj

antiquated, old, elderly, pensioned off, obsolete, senile, retired, aged, decrepit
FORMAL moribund
COLLOQ. past it, put out to grass
FA young

superb adj

excellent, first-rate, first-class, superior, superlative, choice, fine, exquisite, brilliant, gorgeous, magnificent, splendid, lavish, grand, wonderful, great, outstanding, remarkable, unrivalled, unsurpassed, marvellous, admirable, impressive, breathtaking, dazzling
COLLOQ. fabulous, smashing, terrific, neat, ace, brill
FA bad, poor, inferior

supercilious adj

arrogant, condescending, patronizing, overbearing, scornful, lofty, lordly, imperious, insolent, proud, disdainful, haughty, contemptuous
FORMAL vainglorious
COLLOQ. snooty, snotty, stuck-up, toffee-nosed, uppish, uppity, hoity-toity, jumped-up, too big for your boots
FA humble, self-effacing

superficial adj

surface, external, exterior, peripheral, outward, outer, apparent, alleged, seeming, cosmetic, skin-deep, shallow, one-dimensional, slight, trivial, facile, lightweight, insignificant, frivolous, casual, cursory, sketchy, careless, slapdash, perfunctory, hasty, hurried, passing
FORMAL ostensible
FA internal, deep, thorough

superficiality n

shallowness, slightness, triviality, lightness, worthlessness, frivolousness, simplicity
FA depth, seriousness

superficially adv

externally, on the surface, outwardly, apparently, seemingly, casually, carelessly, hurriedly
FORMAL ostensibly
FA in depth

superfluity n

redundancy, excess, surfeit, surplus, extra, exuberance, glut, superabundance, excessiveness
TECHNICAL pleonasm
FORMAL plethora
FA lack

superfluous adj

extra, spare, excess, surplus, remaining, redundant, waste, to spare, unnecessary, unneeded, needless, gratuitous, unwanted, unwarranted, uncalled-for, excessive, frilly, at a discount, fifth-wheel
OLD (*Shakesp*) prolixious
FORMAL supernumerary, otiose, *de trop*, excrescent
FA necessary, needed, required, wanted, essential

superhuman adj

great, immense, supernatural, herculean, heroic, extraordinary, stupendous, divine, paranormal, phenomenal
FORMAL preternatural, prodigious
FA average, ordinary

superimpose v

put on, add, overlay, lay over, lay on, transfer

superintend v

supervise, oversee, overlook, inspect, run, manage, administer, direct, be in charge of, be responsible for, control, be in control of, handle, steer

superintendence n

supervision, oversight, inspection, direction, control, government, charge, care, management, administration, running, guidance, surveillance

superintendent n

supervisor, overseer, director, governor, controller, conductor, administrator, manager, inspector, chief, curator, warden, intendant, steward, viewer
TECHNICAL provincial
COLLOQ. gaffer, boss, super

superior adj, n

♦ adj
1 EXCELLENT, first-class, first-rate, high-class, high-quality, good-quality, exclusive, prime, premium, quality, prize, choice, select, fine, de luxe, admirable, distinguished, exceptional, unrivalled, par excellence
COLLOQ. top-notch, top-flight, top-drawer
2 BETTER, preferred, greater, higher, beyond, higher in rank, senior
3 HAUGHTY, lordly, lofty, pretentious, snobbish, supercilious, disdainful, condescending, patronizing
COLLOQ. snooty, stuck-up, toffee-nosed, uppish, uppity, jumped-up, too big for your boots
FA 1 inferior, average 2 inferior, worse, lower 3 humble, self-effacing
♦ n
senior, elder, better, chief, principal, director, manager, foreman, supervisor
COLLOQ. boss
FA subordinate, inferior, junior, assistant

superiority n

advantage, lead, edge, supremacy, pre-eminence, eminence, dominance, predominance
FORMAL ascendancy
FA inferiority

superlative adj

best, greatest, highest, first-class, first-rate, supreme, unbeatable, unrivalled, unparalleled, matchless, peerless, unsurpassed, unbeaten, excellent, brilliant, magnificent, outstanding
FORMAL transcendent, consummate
COLLOQ. ace, brill
FA poor, average, mediocre

supermarket n

superstore, hypermarket, cash-and-carry

supernatural *adj*
paranormal, unnatural, abnormal, otherworldly, spiritual, miraculous, psychic, mystic, mystical, occult, daemonic, witchlike, hidden, mysterious, magical, magic, phantom, fey, ghostly, eerie, weird, uncanny; *Scot* eldritch
FORMAL metaphysical, transcendental, preternatural, hyperphysical
F3 natural, normal

supernumerary *adj*
superfluous, surplus, redundant, spare, excess, excessive, extra, extraordinary
F3 necessary

supersede *v*
succeed, replace, supplant, usurp, oust, displace, take the place of, take over from, remove
SLANG Stellenbosch

superstition *n*
myth, old wives' tale, fallacy, delusion, illusion, magic

> QUOTATIONS
> In all superstition wise men follow fools
> FRANCIS BACON, *Essays*, 'Of Superstition'

superstitious *adj*
mythical, false, fallacious, irrational, groundless, delusive, illusory
F3 rational, logical, factual

supervise *v*
oversee, watch (over), look after, keep an eye on, inspect, superintend, run, manage, administer, boss, direct, guide, conduct, preside over, be in charge of, be responsible for, be in control of, control, handle, monitor, invigilate, umpire, edit, nanny, bear-lead; *Scot* targe

supervision *n*
surveillance, care, charge, superintendence, oversight, running, management, administration, direction, control, guidance, inspection, instruction

supervisor *n*
overseer, inspector, superintendent, chief, director, administrator, manager, steward, foreman, forewoman, monitor, invigilator, umpire, governor, warden
COLLOQ. boss

supervisory *adj*
administrative, managerial, executive, overseeing, superintendent
FORMAL directorial

supine *adj*
1 PROSTRATE, flat, horizontal
FORMAL recumbent
2 LAZY, idle, inactive, lethargic, careless, heedless, resigned, bored, uninterested, apathetic, indifferent, weak, sluggish, slothful, inert, languid, negligent, passive, listless, spiritless, unresisting
FORMAL indolent, torpid
COLLOQ. spineless
F3 **1** upright **2** alert

supper *n*
dinner, evening meal, tea, snack
OLD rere-supper; (*Shakesp*) aftersupper

supplant *v*
replace, supersede, usurp, oust, displace, take the place of, take over from, remove, overthrow, topple, unseat

supple *adj*
flexible, bending, stretching, elastic, pliant, pliable, plastic, lithe, limber, graceful, loose-limbed, loose-jointed, double-jointed, willowish, agile, sinuous, whippy, lofty; *dialect* souple, wandle; *Scot* leish
F3 stiff, rigid, inflexible

supplement *n, v*
♦ *n*
addition, additive, extra, insert, pull-out, add-on, addendum, appendix, rider, postscript, sequel, annex, schedule, relay
TECHNICAL codicil
OLD sooterkin
♦ *v*
add to, boost, reinforce, increase, fill up, top up, complement, extend, eke out
FORMAL augment
F3 deplete, use up

> ❗ **supplement**, **complement** or **compliment**?
> *See panel at* **complement**.

supplementary *adj*
additional, extra, added, auxiliary, second, secondary, attached, complementary, accompanying, ancillary, bolt-on
TECHNICAL ripieno
OLD (*Shakesp*) suppliant
FORMAL expletory

> ❗ **supplementary**, **complementary** or **complimentary**?
> *See panel at* **complementary**.

suppliant *adj*
begging, entreating, imploring, supplicating, craving
FORMAL beseeching, importunate

supplicant *n*
petitioner, pleader, suitor, applicant, suppliant
FORMAL postulant

supplicate *v*
request, entreat, appeal, petition, plead, pray, solicit
FORMAL invoke, beseech

supplication *n*
request, appeal, entreaty, petition, plea, pleading, prayer, orison, suit
FORMAL invocation, imploration, solicitation, rogation

supplicatory *adj*
begging, petitioning, supplicating, imploring
FORMAL beseeching, imprecatory, precative, precatory

supplier *n*
dealer, seller, vendor, wholesaler, retailer, outfitter, provider, contributor, donor

supply *v, n*
♦ *v*
provide, furnish, equip, outfit, fit out, stock, fill, replenish, give, donate, grant, endow, contribute, yield, produce, sell
FORMAL endue, proffer
F3 take, receive
♦ *n*
1 STOCK, source, amount, quantity, fund, reservoir, store, reserve, heap, mass, pile, stockpile, hoard, cache
2 PROVISIONS, stores, food, rations, equipment, materials, necessities
F3 **1** lack

support *v, n*
♦ *v*
1 BACK, second, defend, champion, advocate, further, be in favour of, be in sympathy with, be behind/with, promote, foster, help, aid, assist, rally round
FORMAL espouse, give countenance to
COLLOQ. run with, throw your weight behind
2 HELP, encourage, comfort, motivate, befriend, care for, sympathize with, be kind to, give strength to, give moral support to, be supportive to
3 HOLD UP, bear, carry, take the weight of, sustain, brace, reinforce, strengthen, prop (up), shore up, buttress, underpin, bolster (up)
4 MAINTAIN, keep, look after, take care of, provide for, sustain, feed, nourish

5 *support a statement*
endorse, confirm, back up, bear out, verify, authenticate, substantiate, validate, ratify, document
FORMAL corroborate
6 FINANCE, fund, subsidize, underwrite, back, sponsor, contribute to, give a donation to
F3 1 oppose **4** live off **5** contradict
♦ *n*
1 BACKING, allegiance, loyalty, defence, protection, patronage, approval, encouragement, comfort, relief, help, aid, assistance
FORMAL espousal
2 PROP, stay, post, pillar, brace, buttress, bolster, crutch, foundation(s), base, underpinning, skeleton, substructure, trestle, bracket, mainstay, rest, easel
3 HELP, encouragement, comfort, care, sympathy, motivation, strength, friendship, moral support
COLLOQ. tower of strength
4 MAINTENANCE, keep, provision, sustenance, food, subsistence
5 FINANCE, funding, assistance, capital, sponsorship, grant, donation, subsidy, contribution, patronage
6 EVIDENCE, confirmation, backing, verification, authentication, substantiation, validation, ratification
F3 1 opposition, hostility

SYNONYM NUANCES

verb sense 2
Help can be widely used to suggest giving assistance, while **encourage** has more to do with inspiring with confidence, and **motivate** suggests providing the necessary incentive to achieve something.
   Comfort, however, would be specifically used of cheering or consoling someone: *he was comforted by her reassurances*, while **sympathize with** is more suggestive of identifying with another's problems. **Care for** also implies emotional concern and involvement: *he cared for his elderly parents at home*, and **befriend** could be used of a specific support born of compassion and given at a time of need: *numerous Czechoslovaks befriended the refugees.*

---

supporter *n*
fan, follower, adherent, advocate, champion, defender, upholder, promoter, sympathizer, seconder, second, apostle, patron, sponsor, donor, contributor, partner, co-worker, helper, ally, friend, voter, well-wisher, apologist, henchman, militant, prop, bottle-holder, ideologist, janizary; *N Am* booster; *Scot* stoop
OLD understander
COLLOQ. angel
F3 opponent

supportive *adj*
helpful, caring, attentive, sympathetic, understanding, comforting, reassuring, encouraging, affirmative, positive, sensitive, in someone's corner, on someone's side
F3 discouraging

suppose *v*
1 THINK, guess, believe, consider, imagine, reckon, fancy, judge, expect, infer, conclude, take for granted, perceive; *N Am* calculate
OLD *(Shakesp)* propose; *(Spenser)* devise
FORMAL conjecture, surmise, opine
COLLOQ. dare say
2 ASSUME, presume, imply, require, take, say, put (the) case, hypothesize, uphold, warrant, sepad
FORMAL postulate, posit, presuppose

supposed *adj*
alleged, reported, rumoured, assumed, presumed, reputed, so-called, believed, imagined, hypothetical
FORMAL putative
■ **supposed to**
meant to, intended to, expected to, required to, obliged to

supposedly *adv*
allegedly, apparently, reportedly, by all accounts
FORMAL ostensibly, putatively

supposition *n*
assumption, presumption, guess, speculation, theory, hypothesis, idea, notion
FORMAL conjecture, surmise, postulation, presupposition
F3 knowledge

suppress *v*
crush, stamp out, put an end to, quash, squash, quell, subdue, stop, silence, hush up, censor, stifle, smother, strangle, strangulate, throttle, choke, squelch, block out, blank out, conceal, withhold, hold back, control, keep under control, contain, restrain, check, keep in check, repress, inhibit, cancel, cushion, elide, black out, gulp back/down, mince, sink, submerge, vote down, burke
OLD stay
FORMAL vanquish
COLLOQ. crack/clamp down on, kill, knock on the head, put the tin lid/hat on
F3 encourage, incite

suppression *n*
crushing, quashing, quelling, elimination, prohibition, censorship, check, inhibition, dissolution, smothering, cover-up, termination, extinction
COLLOQ. clampdown, crackdown
F3 encouragement, incitement

suppurate *v*
gather, discharge, fester, ooze, weep
TECHNICAL maturate

suppuration *n*
festering, pus, mattering
TECHNICAL diapyesis

supremacy *n*
dominance, domination, dominion, mastery, lordship, rule, power, control, predominance, primacy, sovereignty, sway, pre-eminence
FORMAL ascendancy, hegemony, paramountcy

supreme *adj*
1 GREATEST, best, highest, excellent, top, crowning, culminating, first, first-rate, first-class, leading, foremost, chief, principal, head, sovereign, pre-eminent, predominant, prevailing, world-beating, unsurpassed, second-to-none, incomparable, peerless, matchless, consummate, transcendent, superlative, prime
2 *the supreme sacrifice*
utmost, extreme, ultimate, final, last, greatest, highest
F3 1 lowly, poor

supremely *adv*
extremely, exceedingly, excessively, very, really, exceptionally, extraordinarily, intensely, thoroughly, remarkably, utterly, greatly, highly, unusually, uncommonly, inordinately, acutely, severely, decidedly
COLLOQ. terrifically

sure *adj, interj*
♦ *adj*
1 CERTAIN, convinced, assured, confident, decided, positive, definite, doubtless, unmistakable, unfaltering, unwavering, clear, accurate, precise, unquestionable, indisputable, undoubted, undeniable, irrevocable, inevitable, guaranteed, bound
COLLOQ. pukka, as sure as eggs is eggs
2 SAFE, secure, fast, solid, firm, steady, stable, guaranteed, reliable, dependable, tested, loyal, faithful, trustworthy, steadfast, unwavering, unerring, unfailing, never-failing, infallible, effective, foolproof
FORMAL efficacious
COLLOQ. home and dry, sure-fire, sure-footed, safe as houses
F3 1 unsure, uncertain, hesitating, doubtful **2** unsafe, insecure

♦ *interj*

all right, fine, of course, right, indeed, agreed, very well
COLLOQ. OK, okay

■ **for sure**

definitely, for certain, positively, unquestionably, without question, absolutely, certainly, categorically, undeniably, clearly, undoubtedly, without doubt, unmistakably, plainly, obviously, indeed, indubitably

■ **make sure**

make certain, check, ensure, guarantee, confirm, verify

surely *adv*

certainly, without doubt, doubtlessly, undoubtedly, unquestionably, indubitably, definitely, assuredly, firmly, confidently, inevitably, inexorably

surety *n*

guarantee, indemnity, pledge, security, safety, warrant, warranty, certainty, bail, insurance, mortgagor, sponsor, bond, deposit, guarantor, hostage, bondsman

surface *n, v, adj*

♦ *n*

outside, outward appearance, exterior, façade, veneer, covering, skin, top, side, face, plane
E3 inside, interior

♦ *v*

rise, arise, come up, come to the surface, emerge, appear, reappear, materialize, come to light
E3 sink, disappear, vanish

♦ *adj*

superficial, outer, outside, outward, exterior, external, apparent
E3 interior

■ **on the surface**

superficially, externally, at first glance, apparently, seemingly
FORMAL ostensibly

surfeit *n, v*

♦ *n*

surplus, superfluity, excess, glut, satiation, satiety, superabundance, overindulgence, repleteness, repletion, stall; *Scot* staw
OLD (*Shakesp*) cloyment
FORMAL plethora
COLLOQ. bellyful; *Aust & NZ* gutful
E3 lack

♦ *v*

fill, overfill, overfeed, stuff, cram, glut, gorge, satiate, overcloy

surge *n, v*

♦ *n*

1 RUSH, gush, stream, sweep, pouring, flow, wave(s), billow, breaker, roller, swell, eddy; *Scot* jaw
OLD whelm
FORMAL efflux
2 INCREASE, upswing, upsurge, rise, escalation, intensification

♦ *v*

1 RUSH, gush, stream, sweep, pour, flow, break, swell, swirl, eddy, heave, roll, seethe, wallow
OLD welter; (*Spenser*) redound
2 INCREASE, rise, escalate, upsurge

surgeon *n*

COLLOQ. sawbones

Types of surgeon include:

brain surgeon	general surgeon	oral surgeon
cosmetic surgeon	heart surgeon	plastic surgeon
dental surgeon	house surgeon	tree surgeon
eye surgeon	neurosurgeon	veterinary surgeon

---

surly *adj*

gruff, brusque, churlish, ungracious, uncivil, ill-natured, bad-tempered, cross, crusty, grumpy, testy, cantankerous, irascible, sullen, sulky, morose

COLLOQ. crabbed, grouchy, crotchety
E3 friendly, polite

surmise *v, n*

♦ *v*

infer, suppose, presume, assume, conclude, deduce, imagine, fancy, guess, consider, speculate, suspect
FORMAL conjecture, opine
E3 know

♦ *n*

inference, conclusion, deduction, supposition, hypothesis, assumption, presumption, speculation, guess, idea, suspicion, thought, opinion, notion, possibility
FORMAL conjecture
E3 certainty

surmount *v*

overcome, get over, conquer, master, triumph over, prevail over, surpass, exceed
FORMAL vanquish

surpass *v*

beat, outdo, exceed, outstrip, outclass, better, excel, transcend, tower above, outshine, overshadow, eclipse, surmount, go beyond, put down, cap, top, outbrag; *dialect* overgo; *Scot* ding
OLD outrival, pass; (*Shakesp*) outpeer, paragon; (*Spenser*) underlay
COLLOQ. whop, leave for dead, knock (the) spots off, knock the socks off, beat to sticks, bang

surpassing *adj*

exceptional, incomparable, outstanding, matchless, unrivalled, unsurpassed, rare, inimitable, extraordinary, supreme, phenomenal, transcendent
E3 poor

surplus *n, adj*

♦ *n*

excess, residue, remainder, balance, carry-over, superfluity, glut, surfeit, leftovers
E3 lack, shortage

♦ *adj*

excess, superfluous, redundant, extra, spare, remaining, unused, left over

surprise *v, n*

♦ *v*

1 AMAZE, startle, astonish, astound, stagger, take aback, stun, bewilder, confuse, disconcert, dismay
COLLOQ. flabbergast, nonplus, bowl over, wow, blow away, knock for six, knock someone down with a feather, take someone's breath away
2 CATCH RED-HANDED, catch in the act, catch unawares, expose, unmask, startle, burst in on, find (out)
COLLOQ. catch someone with their pants/trousers down

♦ *n*

amazement, astonishment, incredulity, wonder, bewilderment, dismay, shock, start, revelation
FORMAL surprisal
COLLOQ. bombshell, thunderbolt, bolt from the blue, curveball
E3 composure

QUOTATIONS

Surprises are foolish things. The pleasure is not enhanced, and the inconvenience is often considerable
JANE AUSTEN, *Emma*

SYNONYM NUANCES

verb sense 1
You can use **amaze** to suggest filling with wonder as well as great surprise. The terms **astonish** and **astound** are even stronger, while **stagger** and **stun** suggest being overwhelmed, possibly even stupefied: *they were staggered by the distance he'd covered.*

Startle can be used where there is a degree of fright: *startled by a sudden noise*, but **take aback** has more to do with the unexpected causing dismay: *he was taken aback by their outburst.*

To use **bewilder** or **confuse** would put the emphasis on perplexity caused by the unexpected. Likewise, **disconcert** conveys a degree of disturbance at surprising events: *he was disconcerted by her sudden departure,* and **dismay** an element of alarm.

surprised *adj*
startled, amazed, astonished, astounded, staggered, thunderstruck, dumbfounded, speechless, lost for words, open-mouthed, shocked, stunned, jiggered, with raised eyebrows
COLLOQ. flabbergasted, nonplussed, gobsmacked
▪ unsurprised, composed

surprising *adj*
amazing, astonishing, astounding, staggering, stunning, incredible, extraordinary, remarkable, wonderful, startling, eyebrow-raising, funny, strange, unexpected, unforeseen, unlooked-for
COLLOQ. shocking, jaw-dropping, eye-popping
▪ unsurprising, expected

surprisingly *adv*
amazingly, astonishingly, incredibly, extraordinarily, remarkably, wonderfully, staggeringly, stunningly, funnily, strangely, unexpectedly
▪ unsurprisingly, as expected

surrender *v, n*
♦ *v*
capitulate, submit, resign, concede, yield, give in, lay down your arms, strike/lower the flag, render, strike, kamerad, sacrifice, cede, give up, leave behind, let go of, relinquish, abandon, abdicate, for(e)go, waive, release, turn in; *Aust* bail up
TECHNICAL remise
OLD enfeoff
FORMAL succumb, renounce
COLLOQ. quit, throw in the towel/sponge, throw in your hand
♦ *n*
capitulation, resignation, submission, yielding, relinquishment, renunciation, abandonment, abdication, waiving, sacrifice, rendition
TECHNICAL remise
OLD surrendry
FORMAL cession

surreptitious *adj*
furtive, stealthy, sly, covert, veiled, hidden, secret, underhand, unauthorized
FORMAL clandestine
COLLOQ. sneaky
▪ open, obvious

surrogate *n*
substitute, replacement, representative, stand-in, deputy, proxy

surround *v, n*
♦ *v*
encircle, ring, go round, gird, girdle, encompass, confine, envelop, encase, enclose, fence in, hem in, besiege, beset
OLD (*Shakesp*) enround
FORMAL environ
♦ *n*
border, edging, setting, edge, rim, brim, verge, margin, fringe, periphery, perimeter, circumference, bound, bounds, confine, confines, limit, brink

surrounding *adj*
encircling, bordering, adjacent, adjoining, neighbouring, nearby

surroundings *n*
neighbourhood, vicinity, locality, scene, setting, environment, habitat, environs, background, milieu, element, ambience

surveillance *n*
watch, observation, inspection, superintendence, supervision, vigilance, stewardship, guardianship, monitoring, spying, scrutiny, check, care, charge, control, direction, regulation

survey *v, n*
♦ *v*
1 VIEW, contemplate, observe, look at, look over, supervise, scan, scrutinize, examine, inspect, study, research, poll, review, consider, reconnoitre, prospect
TECHNICAL traverse, triangulate, plane-table
OLD overeye
FORMAL surview
COLLOQ. recce
2 ASSESS, estimate, evaluate, measure, plot, plan, map, chart
FORMAL appraise
COLLOQ. size up
♦ *n*
1 REVIEW, overview, view, scrutiny, examination, inspection, consideration, study, poll, appraisal, assessment, measurement, valuation, prospect, reconnaissance, *tour d'horizon*
TECHNICAL traverse, triangulation, level
OLD perambulation
FORMAL conspectus
COLLOQ. once-over
2 QUESTIONNAIRE, quiz, test, form, study, probe, opinion poll, market research

surveyor *n*
inspector, examiner, assessor
TECHNICAL geodesist

survival *n*
continuance, endurance, persistence, perseverance, existence, withholding, coping, managing, will to live, staying power

survive *v*
outlive, outlast, endure, last, continue, persist, stay, remain, live (on), exist, withstand, get/come through, live through, hold out, cope, manage, weather, die hard, recover, rally
FORMAL be extant
COLLOQ. pull through, make it, keep your head above water
▪ succumb, die

susceptibility *n*
liability, openness, vulnerability, defencelessness, weakness, proneness, responsiveness, sensitivity, suggestibility, gullibility, tendency
FORMAL predisposition, proclivity, propensity
▪ impregnability, resistance

susceptible *adj*
liable, prone, inclined, disposed, predisposed, given, capable, subject, receptive, responsive, impressionable, impressible, easily led, credulous, gullible, suggestible, weak, vulnerable, at risk, defenceless, open, sensitive, tender
▪ resistant, immune

suspect *v, adj*
♦ *v*
1 DOUBT, have doubts about, distrust, mistrust, fear, be wary of, have misgivings/qualms about, be uneasy about, call into question; *dialect* mislippen; *Scot* jalouse; *N Am* suspicion
OLD misdoubt
COLLOQ. smell a rat
2 *I suspect you're right*
believe, fancy, feel, guess, suppose, speculate, consider, conclude, infer, sniff, snuff; *Scot* jalouse; *N Am* suspicion
OLD misconceive, misdeem, smoke
FORMAL conjecture, surmise
COLLOQ. have a hunch, get it into your head, suss

♦ *adj*
suspicious, doubtful, dubious, questionable, debatable, unreliable, inadequate, insufficient
COLLOQ. iffy, dodgy, fishy
E3 acceptable, reliable

suspend *v*
1 HANG, dangle, swing
TECHNICAL disperse, entrain
2 ADJOURN, interrupt, delay, defer, postpone, put off, arrest, shelve, pigeonhole, side, cease; *N Am* hold
FORMAL discontinue, put in abeyance, prorogue, stay
COLLOQ. put on ice, put on the back burner, take a raincheck on
3 EXPEL, dismiss, exclude, remove, debar, keep out, shut out, unfrock
COLLOQ. ground, stand off
E3 2 continue, carry on **3** restore, reinstate

suspended *adj*
1 HANGING, dangling
FORMAL pendent, pensile
2 POSTPONED, delayed, deferred, put off, shelved, pending
COLLOQ. put on ice

suspense *n*
uncertainty, insecurity, doubt, doubtfulness, anxiety, tension, nervousness, apprehension, anticipation, expectation, expectancy, excitement
E3 certainty, knowledge
■ **in suspense**
expectantly, eagerly, anxiously, with bated breath, on edge, on tenterhooks
COLLOQ. keyed up

suspension *n*
1 ADJOURNMENT, interruption, break, intermission, respite, remission, stay, moratorium, delay, deferral, deferment, postponement
OLD inhibition
FORMAL cessation, abeyance
2 EXPULSION, dismissal, exclusion, removal, debarment, unfrocking
COLLOQ. grounding, standing-off
E3 1 continuation

suspicion *n*
1 DOUBT, scepticism, distrust, mistrust, chariness, wariness, qualm(s), caution, misgiving(s), apprehension, paranoia
OLD suspect, misdeeming, misdoubt, surmise
COLLOQ. suss
2 TRACE, hint, suggestion, soupçon, touch, tinge, shade, glimmer, shadow, scintilla, dash
3 IDEA, notion, intuition, feeling, belief, opinion, inkling, intimation, sniff
FORMAL conjecture, surmise
COLLOQ. hunch, sixth sense, funny feeling
E3 1 trust

suspicious *adj*
1 DOUBTFUL, sceptical, unbelieving, disbelieving, suspecting, unsure, distrustful, mistrustful, wary, chary, apprehensive, uneasy
OLD misdeeming, suspectful
2 DUBIOUS, questionable, suspect, irregular, equivocal, strange, queer, odd, funny, peculiar, dishonest, guilty, shifty
OLD smoky
COLLOQ. shady, dodgy, fishy, iffy
E3 1 trustful, confident **2** trustworthy, innocent

suspiciously *adv*
1 DOUBTFULLY, sceptically, unbelievingly, disbelievingly, distrustfully, mistrustfully, warily, apprehensively
2 DUBIOUSLY, questionably, strangely, oddly, dishonestly
COLLOQ. shadily
E3 1 confidently **2** trustworthily

sustain *v*
1 NOURISH, feed, provide for, nurture, foster, help, aid, assist, comfort, encourage, relieve, support, uphold, give strength to, endorse, bear, carry
OLD aliment, upbear
2 MAINTAIN, keep going, keep up, carry on, continue, prolong, hold, uphold, buoy (up), prop (up), ride out, stand, scaffold, upstay
FORMAL protract
3 SUFFER, go through, experience, undergo, endure, receive, happen to, face
OLD underbear
FORMAL abide

sustained *adj*
prolonged, long-drawn-out, steady, continuous, continuing, constant, ongoing, perpetual
FORMAL protracted, unremitting
E3 broken, interrupted, intermittent, spasmodic

sustenance *n*
nourishment, food, provisions, nutrients, fare, maintenance, subsistence, support, livelihood
FORMAL refection, aliment, comestibles, provender, viands, victuals
COLLOQ. grub, nosh, scoff

svelte *adj*
slender, slim, lithe, elegant, graceful, lissom, willowy, sylphlike, shapely, sophisticated, urbane, polished
E3 bulky, ungainly

swagger *v, n*
♦ *v*
bluster, boast, crow, brag, prance, parade, strut; *S Afr* pronk
COLLOQ. swank, show off, play to the gallery, make an exhibition of yourself, go over the top
♦ *n*
bluster, show, ostentation, arrogance, prancing, parading

swallow *v*
1 CONSUME, devour, eat, gobble up, drink, quaff, gulp (down)
FORMAL ingest
COLLOQ. guzzle, knock back, down, scoff, swig, polish off
2 ACCEPT, believe, trust, be certain of
COLLOQ. buy, fall for, swallow hook line and sinker
3 STIFLE, smother, repress, hold back, contain, suppress
4 TOLERATE, put up with, accept, endure, stand, take, bear; *Scot* thole
FORMAL abide
COLLOQ. stomach
■ **swallow up**
overwhelm, overrun, engulf, enfold, envelop, absorb, assimilate, take over

swamp *n, v*
♦ *n*
bog, marsh, fen, slough, quagmire, quag, quicksand, mire, morass, mud, swampland; *N Am* loblolly, purgatory; *Can* muskeg; *Aust* cowal; *S Afr* vlei
OLD Lerna; *N Am* Dismals
♦ *v*
flood, inundate, deluge, engulf, submerge, bog down, mire, sink, drench, saturate, waterlog, wash out, weigh down, overload, overwhelm, besiege, beset

swampy *adj*
boggy, marshy, wet, miry, fenny, soggy, quaggy, squelchy, waterlogged
FORMAL paludal, uliginous
E3 arid, dehydrated, dry

swank *v, n*
♦ *v*
brag, boast, show off, strut, swagger, parade, posture, preen yourself, attitudinize; *S Afr* pronk

♦ *n*

bragging, boastfulness, pretentiousness, showing-off, show, display, ostentation, conceit, conceitedness, swagger, self-advertisement
FORMAL vainglory
F3 modesty, restraint

swanky *adj*

glamorous, ostentatious, fashionable, expensive, luxurious, rich, lavish, smart, grand, stylish, showy, exclusive, de luxe, sumptuous, fancy, pretentious
COLLOQ. flash, flashy, plush, plushy, posh, ritzy, swish
F3 discreet, unobtrusive

swap, swop *v, n*

♦ *v*

exchange, transpose, switch, interchange, substitute, barter, trade, bandy, traffic

♦ *n*

exchange, switch, substitution, interchange, trade, trade-off, transposition

swarm *n, v*

♦ *n*

crowd, throng, mob, mass, stream, body, multitude, myriad, host, army, horde, pack, herd, flock, drove, shoal

♦ *v*

flock, flood, surge, stream, mass, congregate, crowd, throng

■ **be swarming with**

be crowded with, be teeming with, be overrun with, be crawling with, be bristling with, be thronged with, abound in; *Scot* be hotching with

swarthy *adj*

dark, dark-complexioned, dark-skinned, tanned, dusky, brown, black
F3 fair, pale

swashbuckling *adj*

daring, courageous, adventurous, bold, spirited, swaggering, exciting, gallant, flamboyant, dare-devil, dashing, robust
F3 tame, unadventurous, unexciting

swat *v, n*

♦ *v*

swipe, hit, strike, lash out, lunge
COLLOQ. whack, wallop, biff

♦ *n*

swipe, hit, strike, lunge
COLLOQ. whack, wallop, biff

swathe *v*

wrap, bandage, bind, wind, cloak, envelop, drape, enshroud, enwrap, fold, shroud, swaddle, lap, sheathe, furl
F3 unwind, unwrap

sway *v, n*

♦ *v*

1 ROCK, roll, reel, lurch, stagger, swing, wave, shake, wobble, oscillate, vacillate, fluctuate, bend, incline, lean, divert, veer, swerve, sally, swag, teeter, thraw, swale, titter, totter, waddle; *dialect* shog; *Scot* shoogie, shoogle, swee
2 INFLUENCE, affect, persuade, win over, bring round, induce, convince, convert, overrule, rule, direct, dominate, govern
OLD swinge
FORMAL prevail upon

♦ *n*

1 ROCKING, swing, roll, reeling, lurch, stagger, wave, shake, wobble, oscillation, fluctuation, swerve; *Scot* shoogie, shoogle, swee
2 CONTROL, command, authority, power, influence, leadership, government, rule, sovereignty, dominion, predominance, jurisdiction
TECHNICAL hegemony
OLD swinge
FORMAL ascendancy, preponderance
COLLOQ. clout

■ **hold sway**

have power, exercise/wield power, have influence, have authority, reign, rule, prevail, lay down the law

swear *v*

1 VOW, promise, promise solemnly, pledge, pledge yourself, take an oath, be on/under oath, take the oath, testify, affirm, assert, declare, insist, rap
OLD adjure, abjure, depose, objure
FORMAL avow, attest, asseverate, aver, forswear, overswear
2 CURSE, blaspheme, utter profanities, abuse, damn, use bad language, take the Lord's name in vain, turn the air blue
FORMAL imprecate, maledict
COLLOQ. damn and blast, eff, eff and blind, blind
SLANG cuss

■ **swear by**

believe in, trust in, depend on, rely on, have confidence in, have faith in, put your faith in

swearing *n*

bad language, foul language, cursing, profanity, expletives, blasphemy
TECHNICAL coprolalia
FORMAL imprecations, maledictions
COLLOQ. effing and blinding
SLANG cussing

swear-word *n*

expletive, four-letter word, curse, oath, obscenity, profanity, blasphemy, swearing, bad language, foul language
FORMAL imprecation
SLANG cuss; *N Am* cussword

sweat *n, v*

♦ *n*

1 PERSPIRATION, moisture, stickiness, lather, bloody-sweat, mucksweat, death-damp
TECHNICAL sudor, diaphoresis, hidrosis, osmidrosis
OLD sudation
Related adjective: sudatory
2 ANXIETY, worry, agitation, panic, fuss, dither, cold sweat
COLLOQ. fluster, flap, tizzy, tizwas
3 TOIL, labour, drudgery, chore, effort

♦ *v*

perspire, secrete, swelter, drip, break out in a sweat
OLD sudate, perspirate
FORMAL exude
COLLOQ. sweat like a pig, sweat buckets

> **QUOTATIONS**
> His brow is wet with honest sweat, / He earns whate'er he can, / And looks the whole world in the face, / For he owes not any man
> Henry Wadsworth Longfellow, 'The Village Blacksmith'

sweaty *adj*

damp, moist, clammy, sticky, sweating, perspiring
OLD forswatt
F3 dry, cool

sweep *v, n*

♦ *v*

1 *sweep the floor*
brush, dust, clean (up), clear (up), remove, vacuum, broom, besom (away/out), overrake; *Scot* soop
OLD ensweep
2 PUSH, thrust, drive, move quickly, spread quickly, force, shove, drag, jostle, elbow, poke
3 PASS, sail, fly, glide, scud, skim, glance, whisk, race, swing, whip, tear, hurtle, roll, wash
OLD swoop

♦ *n*
1 *give the room a good sweep*
brush, dust, clean, clear, wipe, vacuum
2 ARC, curve, bend, swing, stroke, move, movement,
action, gesture, sling, lash, scoop, swipe, sway
FORMAL curvature
3 SCOPE, compass, range, extent, span, stretch, vastness,
immensity, expanse, vista
■ **sweep under the carpet**
hide, conceal, cover up, hush up, suppress,
paper over, gloss over

sweeping *adj*
general, global, universal, all-inclusive, all-embracing,
broad, wide, wide-ranging, extensive, far-reaching,
comprehensive, thorough, thoroughgoing,
radical, wholesale, indiscriminate, oversimplified,
simplistic
COLLOQ. blanket, across-the-board
E3 specific, narrow

sweepstake *n*
draw, lottery, gambling, sweep, sweepstakes

sweet *adj, n*
♦ *adj*
1 SUGARY, syrupy, sickly, sickly sweet, sweetened,
honeyed, candied, glacé, saccharine, luscious,
delicious, ripe
OLD soot
2 AROMATIC, fragrant, perfumed, balmy,
sweet-scented
OLD soot
FORMAL ambrosial, odoriferous, odorous, redolent
3 *sweet music*
melodious, tuneful, harmonious, sweet-sounding,
euphonious, musical, dulcet, soft, mellow
OLD soot
FORMAL mellifluous
4 PLEASANT, delightful, pleasing, lovely, attractive, beautiful,
pretty, winsome, winning, cute, engaging, appealing,
likeable, lov(e)able, adorable, charming, agreeable,
amiable, affectionate, tender, kind, kindly, treasured,
precious, cherished, dear, darling
OLD soot
5 FRESH, clean, wholesome, pure, clear
E3 1 savoury, salty, sour, bitter **2** foul, off **3** discordant,
cacophonous **4** unpleasant, nasty, ugly **5** foul
♦ *n*
1 DESSERT, pudding
COLLOQ. afters, pud
2 BONBON, candy, sweetmeat, confectionery
FORMAL confection
COLLOQ. sweetie
■ **sweet on**
fond of, liking, keen on, having a soft spot for, infatuated
with, ravished with
COLLOQ. crazy about, mad about, far gone on

Sweets include:

alcorza	gumdrop	nougat
aniseed ball	halva	nougatine
barley sugar	humbug	pear drop
bonbon	jelly	peppermint
bull's eye	jelly baby	pineapple chunk
butterscotch	jelly bean	pomfret
caramel	*Aust* jujube (or	praline
cherry drop	jube)	rock
chewing-gum	lemon drop	sherbet
chocolate	liquorice	*Scot* tablet
dolly mixture	liquorice allsort	toffee
drumstick	lollipop	toffee apple
Edinburgh rock	lozenge	truffle
fondant	Mars®	Turkish delight
fruit pastille	marshmallow	wine gum
fudge	marzipan	
gobstopper	noisette	

sweeten *v*
1 SUGAR, add sugar to, honey
2 MELLOW, soften, soothe, mollify, appease
3 TEMPER, cushion, alleviate, ease, relieve
FORMAL mitigate
E3 2 sour, embitter

sweetheart *n*
darling, dear, boyfriend, beau, girlfriend, love, lover,
truelove, suitor, valentine, admirer, beloved, betrothed,
follower, inamorata, inamorato, Romeo
OLD swain
COLLOQ. flame, steady, sweetie

sweetly *adv*
1 *smile sweetly*
pleasantly, delightfully, kindly, affectionately, lovingly,
winsomely, tenderly, charmingly
2 *sing sweetly*
tunefully, in tune, melodiously, harmoniously,
euphoniously, softly, mellowly
3 *a machine working sweetly*
smoothly, easily, effortlessly, evenly, steadily

sweetness *n*
1 SUGARINESS, syrup, succulence, lusciousness, mellowness,
freshness
2 FRAGRANCE, balminess, aroma
3 KINDNESS, amiability, winsomeness, tenderness, sweet
temper, love, loveliness, pleasantness, charm
4 HARMONY, euphony
FORMAL dulcitude
E3 1 saltness, sourness, bitterness, acidity **2** foulness **3**
nastiness **4** cacophony

sweet-smelling *adj*
aromatic, fragrant, perfumed, balmy, sweet-scented
FORMAL ambrosial, odoriferous, odorous, redolent
E3 f(o)etid, malodorous

swell *v, n, adj*
♦ *v*
1 EXPAND, inflate, blow up, puff up, bloat, fatten, bulge,
balloon, billow, raise, bag, belly (out), berry, boll, bulb,
bulk, plump, bunch, hove; *dialect* blast, plim, strout
OLD blab, outswell, huff; (*Shakesp*) farce
FORMAL dilate, distend, intumesce, tumesce, tumefy
2 RISE, surge, mount, increase, enlarge, grow larger,
escalate, extend, grow, step up, accelerate, mushroom,
proliferate, snowball, skyrocket, heighten, intensify, heave
OLD hove, volume
FORMAL augment
E3 1 shrink, contract **2** decrease, dwindle
♦ *n*
1 BILLOW, wave, undulation, sea, roughness, surge, rise,
increase, enlargement, backwater
OLD wallow
2 DANDY, fop, beau, dude, cockscomb
COLLOQ. bigwig, toff, don
E3 2 down-and-out, scarecrow, tramp
♦ *adj*
wonderful, excellent, great, grand, smart, stylish, exclusive,
fashionable, de luxe
COLLOQ. flashy, posh, ritzy, swanky
E3 seedy, shabby

swelling *n*
lump, tumour, bump, bruise, blister, boil,
inflammation, bulge, node, protuberance, puffiness,
enlargement
FORMAL distension, tumescence, intumescence,
tumefaction

sweltering *adj*
hot, tropical, baking, boiling, roasting, scorching, torrid,
stifling, suffocating, airless, oppressive, sultry, clammy,
muggy, steamy, sticky, humid
COLLOQ. sizzling
E3 cold, cool, fresh, breezy, airy

swerve v

change direction suddenly, turn, bend, incline, veer, swing, twist, shift, deviate, stray, wander, diverge, deflect, skew, sheer

swift adj

fast, quick, rapid, brisk, speedy, express, flying, hurried, hasty, short, brief, sudden, abrupt, immediate, prompt, ready, agile, lively, nimble
OLD fleet; (Shakesp) flighty
FORMAL expeditious
COLLOQ. nippy
E3 slow, sluggish, unhurried

swiftly adv

quickly, posthaste, fast, rapidly, speedily, express, hurriedly, instantly, promptly, at full tilt
FORMAL expeditiously
COLLOQ. double-quick, hotfoot
E3 slowly; formal tardily

swiftness n

quickness, rapidity, speed, speediness, suddenness, velocity, immediacy, immediateness, instantaneity, readiness, promptness, dispatch
OLD fleetness
FORMAL alacrity, celerity, expedition
E3 delay, slowness; formal tardiness

swill v, n

♦ v
drink, swallow, swig, quaff, gulp, guzzle, drain, consume
FORMAL imbibe
COLLOQ. knock back, toss off
♦ n
1 DRINK, gulp, swallow, swig
2 WASTE, slops, hogwash, pigswill, scourings, refuse
■ **swill out**
wash out, wash down, rinse, clean, cleanse, drench, flush, sluice

swim v

bathe, take a dip, tread water, float, bob, snorkel, paddle, run, strike out; Scot soom
COLLOQ. swan
Related adjectives: natatorial, natant

The main swimming strokes include:

backstroke	crawl
breaststroke	doggy-paddle
butterfly	sidestroke

---

swimmingly adv

very well, smoothly, easily, without a hitch
COLLOQ. like clockwork, like a house on fire

swimming-pool n

swimming-bath(s), baths, leisure pool, lido, swimming-pond

swimsuit n

swimming costume, bathing costume, bathing suit, bikini, trunks

swindle v, n

♦ v
cheat, defraud, fiddle, diddle, overcharge, exploit, trick, deceive, dupe, nobble, fleece, skin, ramp, skelder, financier, mulct, chouse; N Am beat, bunko
OLD bucket, let in
COLLOQ. do, con, take, bamboozle, rook, stitch up, shaft, put one over on, pull the wool over someone's eyes, sell smoke
SLANG rip off, sting, gyp, pluck, tweedle, hand someone a lemon, sell a pup, take for a ride, take to the cleaners; N Am grift, gold-brick
♦ n
fraud, fiddle, diddle, racket, sharp practice, double-dealing, trickery, deception, conspiracy, clean-out, fake, chouse

COLLOQ. con, scam, do, rig
SLANG chizz, rip-off, gyp; N Am gold brick; Aust lurk

swindler n

cheat, fraud, fraudster, fiddler, impostor, trickster, rogue, rascal, charlatan, mountebank
COLLOQ. con man/woman, con artist, shark, rook, hustler, hood, hoodlum; N Am bunko-steerer
SLANG N Am grifter

swine n

1 PIG, beast, boar, hog
2 SCOUNDREL, rogue, rascal, good-for-nothing, brute, boor

swing v, n

♦ v
1 HANG, dangle, wave, spin, rotate, pivot, sway, rock
2 SWERVE, veer, turn, twist, wind, curve, bend, incline, lean, oscillate, fluctuate, change, vary
FORMAL pendulate
3 ARRANGE, achieve, get, set up, make, organize
COLLOQ. fix (up)
♦ n
sway, rock, oscillation, waving, vibration, fluctuation, variation, change, shift, move, movement, motion, stroke, rhythm

> **PROVERBS**
> What you lose on the swings you gain on the roundabouts

swingeing adj

harsh, severe, stringent, drastic, serious, extreme, punishing, devastating, excessive, extortionate, exorbitant, oppressive, heavy, Draconian
COLLOQ. thumping
E3 mild

swinging adj

lively, exciting, dynamic, fashionable, contemporary, modern, up-to-date, up-to-the-minute, stylish
COLLOQ. jet-setting, trendy, with it
SLANG hip
E3 old-fashioned, fuddy-duddy

swipe v, n

♦ v
1 HIT, strike, clout, lunge, lash out, slap, swat
COLLOQ. whack, wallop, sock, biff
2 STEAL, pilfer, lift
COLLOQ. pinch, whip, nick, filch
♦ n
stroke, strike, blow, clout, slap, smack, swat
COLLOQ. whack, wallop, biff

swirl v

churn, agitate, spin, revolve, circulate, twirl, whirl, wheel, eddy, twist, curl

swish[1] v

the horses swished their tails
flourish, whisk, swing, swirl, thrash, flog, lash, birch, whip, rustle, twirl, whizz, swoosh, wave, brandish, whirl, whistle, whoosh

swish[2] adj

a swish hotel
smart, grand, fashionable, exclusive, plush, stylish, elegant, sumptuous, de luxe
COLLOQ. flash, posh, ritzy, swanky, swell
E3 seedy, shabby

switch v, n

♦ v
change, exchange, swap, trade, barter, interchange, substitute, replace, shift, rearrange, turn, put, veer, deviate, divert, deflect, beat, scutch, twig, convert
FORMAL transpose
COLLOQ. chop and change

♦ *n*

1 BUTTON, control, on-off device, lever, circuit-breaker, relay, shunt, toggle
TECHNICAL cryotron
2 CHANGE, alteration, shift, exchange, swap, interchange, substitution, replacement, reversal, about-turn
3 TWIG, shoot, branch, cane, rod, birch, lash, twitch, whisk, whip, thong
■ **switch off**
turn off, close down, shut off, flick off, stop working, cut
■ **switch on**
turn on, put on, flick on, operate, activate, set off, trigger off

swivel *v*
pivot, spin, rotate, revolve, turn, twirl, pirouette, gyrate, wheel

swollen *adj*
bloated, inflated, tumid, puffed up, puffy, bulbous, bulging, inflamed, enlarged, expanded, engorged
FORMAL distended, dilated, tumescent
E∃ shrunken, shrivelled

swoop *v, n*
♦ *v*
dive, plunge, drop, fall, descend, stoop, pounce, lunge, rush, souse
♦ *n*
dive, plunge, drop, descent, pounce, stoop, lunge, rush, attack, onslaught
■ **at/in/with one fell swoop**
by a single action, by one complete action, by one decisive action, on one occasion, suddenly, by one blow, with one deadly blow

swop
see **swap, swop**.

sword *n*
blade, foil, rapier, sabre, scimitar, steel, épée, katana
■ **cross swords**
disagree, argue, quarrel, fight, contend, dispute, contest, wrangle, bicker, be at odds, be at loggerheads

sworn *adj*
devoted, confirmed, eternal, implacable, inveterate, relentless
FORMAL attested

swot *v*
study, work, learn, memorize, revise, cram
COLLOQ. mug up, bone up, burn the midnight oil

sybarite *n*
parasite, pleasurer, pleasure-seeker, sensualist, bon vivant, epicure, epicurean, hedonist, playboy, voluptuary
E∃ ascetic, toiler

sybaritic *adj*
easy, pleasure-loving, pleasure-seeking, self-indulgent, sensual, voluptuous, hedonistic, epicurean, luxurious, parasitic
E∃ ascetic

sycophancy *n*
cringing, fawning, flattery, toadyism, toad-eating, grovelling, servility, slavishness, kowtowing, backscratching, adulation, truckling, oleaginousness
FORMAL obsequiousness
COLLOQ. bootlicking
SLANG (*vulgar*) arse-licking

sycophant *n*
cringer, fawner, flatterer, groveller, backscratcher, slave, parasite, hanger-on, toady, truckler, claqueur
OLD placebo, toad-eater
COLLOQ. crawler, bootlicker, sponger, yes-man
SLANG (*vulgar*) arse-licker; *N Am* cookie-pusher

sycophantic *adj*
cringing, fawning, flattering, grovelling, servile, slavish, ingratiating, parasitical, backscratching, slimy, toad-eating, toadying, time-serving, truckling, oleaginous

OLD sycophantical
FORMAL obsequious, unctuous
COLLOQ. bootlicking, smarmy
SLANG (*vulgar*) arse-licking

syllabus *n*
curriculum, course, programme, schedule, plan, outline

syllogism *n*
deduction, argument, proposition
TECHNICAL epicheirema

sylph-like *adj*
slim, slight, slender, elegant, graceful, lithe, willowy, streamlined, svelte
E∃ bulky, plump

symbiotic *adj*
co-operative, interactive, interdependent
TECHNICAL endophytic, epizoan, epizoic, epizootic
FORMAL commensal, synergetic

symbol *n*
sign, token, representation, mark, emblem, badge, logo, character, ideograph, figure, image
FORMAL type

Symbols include:

badge	logo	TEXT SYMBOLS:
brand	logogram	ampersand
cipher	monogram	asterisk
coat of arms	motif	at sign
crest	pictograph	caret
emblem	swastika	dagger
hieroglyph	token	double-dagger
icon	totem	emoticon
ideogram	trademark	hash
insignia	watermark	obelus
		smiley

symbolic *adj*
symbolical, representative, typical, illustrative, emblematic, token, figurative, metaphorical, allegorical, meaningful, significant

symbolically *adv*
representationally, figuratively, representatively, characteristically, emblematically, as a symbol, as a sign, as an emblem, by this token

symbolize *v*
represent, stand for, denote, mean, signify, express, symbol, typify, exemplify, epitomize, personify, personate
TECHNICAL type
OLD betoken, emblem, figure, present

symmetrical *adj*
balanced, even, regular, well-proportioned, parallel, uniform, consistent, harmonious, corresponding, proportional
E∃ asymmetrical, irregular

symmetry *n*
balance, evenness, regularity, parallelism, correspondence, proportion(s), harmony, uniformity, consistency, agreement
FORMAL congruity
E∃ asymmetry, irregularity

sympathetic *adj*
understanding, appreciative, supportive, comforting, encouraging, consoling, commiserating, pitying, interested, concerned, caring, compassionate, tolerant, tender, kind, kindly, warm, warm-hearted, kind-hearted, well-disposed, affectionate, agreeable, favourable, considerate, friendly, pleasant, likeable, companionable, congenial, sociable, neighbourly, like-minded, compatible, feeling, genial, soft, commiserative
OLD sympathetical, social
FORMAL solicitous
COLLOQ. simpatico
E∃ unsympathetic, indifferent, callous, antipathetic

sympathetically *adv*
appreciatively, supportively, understandingly, compassionately, comfortingly, consolingly, responsively, sensitively, warmly, warm-heartedly, feelingly, kindly, pityingly

sympathize *v*
understand, comfort, console, encourage, be supportive, appreciate, show concern/interest, care for, offer condolences, commiserate, pity, feel sorry for, feel for, your heart goes out, empathize, identify with, respond to, condole
E3 ignore, disregard

sympathizer *n*
supporter, condoler, admirer, backer, adherent, well-wisher, fan, fellow-traveller, partisan
E3 enemy, opponent, adversary

sympathy *n*
1 UNDERSTANDING, comfort, encouragement, support, appreciation, consolation, condolences, commiseration, pity, compassion, tenderness, kindness, warmth, warm-heartedness, thoughtfulness, empathy, fellow-feeling, closeness, consideration, affinity, rapport, *Weltschmerz*
FORMAL solace
2 AGREEMENT, approval, correspondence, accord, harmony
FORMAL approbation
E3 1 indifference, insensitivity, callousness **2** disagreement

symptom *n*
sign, indication, signal, evidence, expression, display, demonstration, note, feature, characteristic, mark, token, warning, diagnostic
TECHNICAL prodrome, prodromus
FORMAL manifestation

symptomatic *adj*
indicative, typical, characteristic, associated, suggesting, suggestive

syndicate *n*
association, alliance, combination, group, bloc, cartel, ring, combine

synonymous *adj*
interchangeable, substitutable, the same, identical, similar, comparable, tantamount, equivalent, corresponding
E3 antonymous, opposite

synopsis *n*
outline, abstract, summary, sketch, résumé, précis, condensation, digest, abridgement, review, recapitulation, compendium, tabulation, schema
FORMAL summation, conspectus
COLLOQ. run-down, recap

synthesis *n*
amalgamation, combination, compound, fusion, integration, union, welding, blend, alloy, amalgam, coalescence, composite, pastiche
FORMAL unification

synthesize *v*
unite, combine, amalgamate, integrate, merge, blend, compound, alloy, fuse, weld, coalesce, unify
E3 separate, analyse, resolve

synthetic *adj*
manufactured, man-made, simulated, artificial, ersatz, imitation, fake, faux, bogus, mock, sham, pseudo
E3 genuine, real, natural

syrupy *adj*
1 SWEET, sugary, sickly sweet, oversweet, sweetened, honeyed, saccharine
2 SENTIMENTAL, emotional, loving, gushing, sugary, pathetic, tear-jerking, maudlin, mawkish, romantic, affectionate
COLLOQ. soppy, weepy, lovey-dovey, slushy, mushy, schmaltzy, sloppy, corny, sickly, gushy

system *n*
1 METHOD, technique, procedure, process, routine, practice, approach, way, means, usage, rule, modus operandi
FORMAL mode
2 ORGANIZATION, structure, set-up, systematization, co-ordination, orderliness, methodology, logic, classification, arrangement, network, framework, order, plan, scheme, apparatus, mechanism
3 THE ESTABLISHMENT, the government, the authorities, the powers that be
COLLOQ. them

systematic *adj*
methodical, methodic, logical, ordered, well-ordered, planned, well-planned, organized, well-organized, structured, systematized, standardized, scientific, orderly, businesslike, efficient
E3 unsystematic, unstructured, arbitrary, disorderly, inefficient

systematize *v*
arrange, order, structure, plan, organize, rationalize, methodize, standardize, schematize, regulate, regiment, classify, tabulate, make uniform
FORMAL dispose

T

tab *n*
flap, tag, marker, label, sticker, ticket, fob, strap, trimmer
■ **keep tabs on**
watch closely, keep an eye on, observe, keep a close watch on, keep a close check on

tabby *adj*
stripy, striped, streaked, wavy, mottled, variegated, banded, brindle(d)

table *n, v*
♦ *n*
1 BOARD, slab, counter, bar, worktop, desk, bench, stand
2 DIAGRAM, chart, figure, graph, timetable, schedule, programme, plan, list, inventory, catalogue, tabulation, index, register, record
3 FOOD, board, diet, fare, dish, speciality, menu
COLLOQ. tuck
SLANG grub, nosh; *N Am* chow
♦ *v*
propose, suggest, submit, put forward, move

tableau *n*
representation, picture, portrayal, scene, spectacle, vignette, diorama, *tableau vivant*

tablet *n*
1 PILL, capsule, lozenge, pellet, ball, bolus, caplet, purple heart
FORMAL troche
COLLOQ. sleeper
SLANG benny
2 SLAB, surface, plate, plaque, pad, medallion, monument, stele; *N Am* marker
TECHNICAL abacus, triglyph
OLD tablature

taboo *adj, n*
♦ *adj*
forbidden, prohibited, banned, ruled out, vetoed, sacrosanct, unacceptable, unmentionable, unthinkable
FORMAL proscribed
E3 permitted, acceptable
♦ *n*
ban, prohibition, veto, restriction, anathema, curse
FORMAL interdiction, proscription
E3 permission, acceptance

tabulate *v*
order, arrange, arrange in columns, chart, classify, list, sort, systematize, table, catalogue, categorize, range, index, codify, tabularize

tabulation *n*
arrangement, ordering, sorting, classification, listing, cataloguing, categorization, indexing

tacit *adj*
unspoken, unexpressed, unstated, unvoiced, silent, wordless, understood, implicit, implied, inferred
E3 express, explicit

taciturn *adj*
silent, quiet, uncommunicative, unforthcoming, untalkative, close-mouthed, tight-lipped, reticent, reserved, withdrawn, aloof, detached, distant, cold, dumb, mute
E3 talkative, communicative, forthcoming

tack[1] *n, v*
♦ *n*
1 NAIL, pin, drawing-pin, staple, tintack, tingle; *N Am* thumbtack
2 COURSE, path, bearing, heading, direction, line, line of action, course of action, approach, method, way, technique, procedure, process, policy, strategy, plan, tactic, attack
♦ *v*
1 ADD, append, attach, annex
2 FIX, fasten, affix, nail, pin, staple, tag, stitch, sew, baste
3 CHANGE COURSE, turn, change direction, go/come about, swerve
TECHNICAL club-haul

tack[2]

Parts of a horse's tack include:

alforja	girth	saddlebow
old arson	hackamore	saddlecloth
backband	halter	saddle-girth
bearing rein	hames	saddlepad
bellyband	*N Am* headstall	saddletree
bit	housing	*old* shabrack (or
N Am blinders	martingale	shabracque)
blinkers	noseband	stirrup
breeching	numnah	surcingle
bridle	pommel	throatlatch (or
cantle	reins	throatlash)
N Am cinch	saddle	traces
collar	saddlebag	
crupper	saddle blanket	

---

tackle *n, v*
♦ *n*
1 *a rugby tackle*
attack, challenge, interception, intervention, block
2 EQUIPMENT, tools, implements, apparatus, rig, outfit, gear, things, trappings, paraphernalia, harness
FORMAL accoutrements
COLLOQ. stuff, clobber, things
♦ *v*
1 BEGIN, embark on, set about, go about, try, attempt, undertake, take on, challenge, confront, encounter, face up to, grapple with, get to grips with, apply yourself to, address, deal with, attend to, handle, grab, seize, grasp, take hold of
2 INTERCEPT, block, take, halt, stop, deflect, catch, grapple with, challenge, obstruct
E3 1 avoid, sidestep

tacky[1] *adj*
tacky paint
sticky, wet, adhesive, gluey, gummy
COLLOQ. gooey

tacky[2] *adj*
1 SHABBY, scruffy, tatty, threadbare, shoddy, dingy, tattered, ragged, untidy, messy, sloppy
COLLOQ. grotty
2 TASTELESS, vulgar, tawdry, flashy, gaudy, kitschy
SLANG naff

tact *n*
tactfulness, diplomacy, discretion, prudence, delicacy, subtlety, sensitivity, perception, discernment, judgement, understanding, thoughtfulness, consideration, skill, dexterity, adroitness, finesse, savoir-faire
FORMAL judiciousness
F3 tactlessness, indiscretion

tactful *adj*
diplomatic, discreet, politic, prudent, careful, delicate, tender, subtle, sensitive, perceptive, discerning, thoughtful, understanding, considerate, polite, skilful, adroit, kid-glove
FORMAL judicious
F3 tactless, indiscreet, thoughtless, rude

tactfully *adv*
diplomatically, discreetly, carefully, sensitively, delicately, tenderly, thoughtfully, skilfully, politely, prudently
FORMAL judiciously
F3 tactlessly, thoughtlessly

tactic *n*
1 APPROACH, course, course of action, way, means, method, procedure, plan, stratagem, scheme, ruse, ploy, subterfuge, trick, device, shift, expedient, move, manoeuvre
2 *military tactics*
strategy, campaign, plan, policy, approach, line of attack, moves, manoeuvres
COLLOQ. game plan, hardball, soft sell

tactical *adj*
strategic, planned, calculated, artful, cunning, shrewd, adroit, skilful, clever, smart, prudent, politic
FORMAL judicious

tactician *n*
strategist, orchestrator, planner, politician, diplomat, director, campaigner, co-ordinator, mastermind
COLLOQ. brain

tactless *adj*
undiplomatic, indiscreet, indelicate, unsubtle, inappropriate, impolitic, imprudent, careless, clumsy, awkward, blundering, gauche, insensitive, unfeeling, hurtful, unkind, thoughtless, inconsiderate, rude, rough, impolite, discourteous
FORMAL injudicious, maladroit
F3 tactful, diplomatic, discreet

tactlessness *n*
insensitivity, impoliteness, indelicacy, indiscretion, thoughtlessness, discourtesy, rudeness, ineptitude, bad timing, clumsiness, gaucherie, boorishness
FORMAL maladroitness
F3 tact, tactfulness, diplomacy

tag *n, v*
♦ *n*
1 LABEL, sticker, tab, ticket, mark, identification, note, slip, docket, bracelet, anklet, strap, flap, tally, treasury tag, aglet, Kimball tag
OLD dag
2 IDENTIFICATION, label, description, name, title, nickname, epithet, identity disc, badge
3 QUOTATION, saying, expression, phrase, maxim, moral, motto, proverb, dictum, epithet, allusion, stock phrase, cliché, remnant
COLLOQ. quote
♦ *v*
1 LABEL, mark, identify, designate, term, title, entitle, call, name, christen, nickname, style, dub
2 ADD, attach, append, annex, adjoin, affix, fasten, tack
■ **tag along**
follow, shadow, tail, trail, accompany

tail *n, v*
♦ *n*
1 END, extremity, rear, rear end, bottom, back, rump, appendage, conclusion

FORMAL termination
COLLOQ. behind, posterior, backside
Related adjective: caudal, cercal
2 DETECTIVE, (private) investigator, shadow
COLLOQ. private eye, sleuth, gumshoe, shamus
♦ *v*
follow, pursue, shadow, dog, stalk, track, trail
■ **tail back**
queue, jam, line; *N Am* back up
■ **tail off**
decrease, decline, drop (off), fall away, fade, wane, dwindle, taper off, peter out, die (out)
F3 increase, grow
■ **turn tail**
run away, escape, flee, abscond, decamp, bolt
COLLOQ. skedaddle, scarper, beat it

tailback *n*
queue, line, tail, file, row, column, crocodile, procession, train; *N Am* backup

tailor *n, v*
♦ *n*
outfitter, dressmaker, costumer, costumier, couturier, seamster, seamstress, modiste, clothier, cutter, knight of the shears, whipcat, darzi; *dialect* teller; *Scot* prick-louse
COLLOQ. sartor
SLANG snip
OLD SLANG dung, flint
Related adjective: sartorial
♦ *v*
fit, suit, cut, trim, style, fashion, shape, mould, alter, modify, convert, adapt, adjust, accommodate, customize, personalize

tailor-made *adj*
made-to-measure, custom-built, bespoke, ideal, perfect, right, suited, tailored, fitted
F3 off-the-peg, ready-made

taint *v, n*
♦ *v*
contaminate, infect, pollute, adulterate, corrupt, deprave, stain, blemish, blot, smear, tarnish, blacken, dirty, soil, muddy, defile, sully, harm, damage, injure, blight, spoil, ruin, shame, disgrace, dishonour, envenom, mildew, smoke, poison
OLD attainder
FORMAL befoul
♦ *n*
contamination, infection, contagion, adulteration, pollution, corruption, stain, blemish, fault, flaw, defect, spot, blot, smear, stigma, shame, disgrace, dishonour

take *v, n*
♦ *v*
1 SEIZE, grab, snatch, clutch, grasp, hold, get/lay hold of, grip, catch, capture, get, obtain, acquire, secure, gain, receive, win, derive, adopt, assume, pick, choose, select, decide, settle on, accept
FORMAL procure
2 REMOVE, draw, eliminate, take away, subtract, deduct, extract, steal, seize, kidnap, abduct, carry off, confiscate
FORMAL purloin, appropriate
COLLOQ. filch, nick, pinch, lift, have your fingers in the till
3 *take me home*
convey, carry, bring, fetch, deliver, drive, transport, ferry, accompany, escort, show, lead, guide, conduct, help, usher, shepherd
FORMAL bear
COLLOQ. whisk
4 BEAR, tolerate, put up with, stand, endure, suffer, undergo, experience, withstand
FORMAL abide
COLLOQ. stomach
5 *the journey takes 6 hours*
need, necessitate, require, demand, call for, use (up), last

6 CAPTURE, win, seize, catch, conquer, occupy
FORMAL vanquish
7 *take pleasure in something*
derive, obtain, draw, gain, receive, attain, secure, achieve, be given, come by, get
FORMAL procure
8 *take the blame/responsibility*
accept, bear, be responsible for, admit, acknowledge, undertake
9 CONSIDER, believe, assume, presume, suppose, note, remember, examine, bear in mind
10 UNDERSTAND, comprehend, grasp, gather, apprehend, follow, fathom (out)
COLLOQ. cotton on, twig
11 *take the news badly*
react to, accept, respond to, cope with, deal with, handle
12 *take him for a fool*
believe, think, consider, regard, look upon, view, reckon, suppose, hold
FORMAL deem
13 *the hall takes 400 people*
hold, contain, accommodate, seat, have a capacity of, have room for, have space for
14 *take a measurement*
find out, discover, measure, establish, determine, ascertain
15 BUY, purchase, rent, hire, lease, pay for, book, receive, subscribe to
16 *take a subject at university*
study, learn, pursue, be taught, research, read, major in
17 *take the new road*
use, travel along, drive along, go along, follow
18 *take food/drink*
consume, swallow, eat, drink, devour
FORMAL imbibe, ingest
COLLOQ. tuck in, guzzle, scoff
19 *will the drug take?*
succeed, work, produce results, take effect, be effective
FORMAL be efficacious
E3 1 leave, refuse **2** replace, put back **6** lose
15 sell **19** fail
♦ *n*
1 CATCH, gate, haul, bag, yield
2 INCOME, revenue, takings, proceeds, profit(s), receipts, return(s), yield, gate, gate-money
3 PERSPECTIVE, view, point of view, viewpoint, aspect, angle, slant, attitude, frame of mind, vantage point, standpoint, interpretation
■ **take after**
resemble, look like, be like, be similar to, favour, mirror, echo
■ **take against**
dislike, object to, disapprove of, despise, regard with distaste
E3 take to
■ **take apart**
1 *take apart a machine*
pull/take to pieces, separate, dismantle, disassemble, analyse
2 CRITICIZE, condemn, carp, disapprove of, find fault with, snipe, pass judgement on, denounce, slate, attack, run down, censure, blame
FORMAL disparage
COLLOQ. nag, slam, knock, come down on, give someone some stick, go to town on, haul over the coals, pick holes in, pan, pull/take to pieces, tear to shreds, tear a strip off, nit-pick, do a hatchet job on, badmouth, rubbish, put the boot in
SLANG slag (off)
■ **take back**
1 WITHDRAW, retract, recant, repudiate, disclaim, deny
FORMAL renounce
COLLOQ. eat your words
2 REPOSSESS, reclaim, regain, get back
3 RETURN, replace, restore, give back, hand back, send back

4 REMIND, put you in mind of, make you think of, call up, evoke
■ **take down**
1 DISMANTLE, disassemble, remove, demolish, raze, level, lower
2 NOTE, make a note of, record, write down, put down, set down, get down, transcribe, put on paper
E3 1 put up
■ **take in**
1 ABSORB, assimilate, digest, realize, appreciate, understand, comprehend, grasp
2 ACCOMMODATE, admit, receive, shelter, welcome
3 INCLUDE, contain, comprise, incorporate, embrace, encompass, cover
4 DECEIVE, fool, dupe, mislead, trick, hoodwink, cheat, swindle
COLLOQ. con, bamboozle, pull the wool over someone's eyes, lead up the garden path
■ **take off**
1 *watch the plane take off*
depart, fly, lift off, ascend, climb, rise, soar, mount, become airborne
2 REMOVE, undress, get undressed, strip, divest, shed, discard, detach, pull off, throw off, tear off, drop, doff
3 SUBTRACT, take away, remove, deduct, discount
4 LEAVE, depart, go, run away, decamp, disappear, flee, abscond
COLLOQ. skedaddle, scarper, bunk off, do a runner
5 IMITATE, impersonate, mimic, parody, caricature, satirize, mock
COLLOQ. send up
6 *the project has really taken off*
succeed, work, do well, become fashionable, become popular, catch on, prosper, flourish
COLLOQ. make it, become all the rage, go places, hit the jackpot, strike gold
■ **take on**
1 ACCEPT, assume, acquire, undertake, tackle, face
2 COMPETE WITH, contend with, fight, oppose, vie with, tackle
3 *take on staff*
employ, hire, enlist, recruit, engage, enrol, retain
4 GET UPSET, get angry, make a fuss
■ **take out**
1 REMOVE, extract, get out, detach, excise, cut out, pull out
2 *take someone out to a restaurant*
go with, go out with, accompany, escort, see
3 *take out a loan*
arrange, organize, set up, settle on, work out
COLLOQ. fix
4 *take out a book from the library*
borrow, use temporarily, have a loan, be lent
5 KILL, murder, put to death, exterminate, assassinate, finish off, massacre, execute, destroy, do away with, butcher, shoot
COLLOQ. do in, bump off, eliminate, dispatch, liquidate, knock off, rub out, wipe out, polish off, waste, blow away, zap
■ **take over**
gain control of, take charge of, become responsible for, assume control/responsibility for, buy out
■ **take to**
1 LIKE, find pleasant, find attractive, become friendly with, become keen on, appreciate
2 BEGIN, start, launch into, undertake, set about
FORMAL commence
■ **take up**
1 OCCUPY, fill, engage, engross, absorb, become interested in, become involved in, monopolize, use (up), consume
2 RAISE, lift, pick up
3 *take up a hobby*
start, begin, embark on, pursue
FORMAL commence
4 RESUME, carry on, continue, pick up
COLLOQ. pick up the threads
5 ACCEPT, adopt, assume, agree to

6 *what made you take up with him?*
become friends with, become friendly with, hang/knock about with, get involved with
E₃ 5 refuse

take-off *n*
1 DEPARTURE, flight, flying, lift-off, ascent, climbing
2 IMITATION, mimicry, impersonation, parody, caricature, travesty
COLLOQ. spoof, send-up

takeover *n*
gaining of control, merger, amalgamation, combination, incorporation, buyout, coalition, coup

taking *adj, n*
◆ *adj*
catching, attractive, charming, pleasing, delightful, winning, winsome, appealing, fascinating, fetching, engaging, enchanting, compelling, alluring, beguiling, captivating, intriguing, prepossessing
E₃ repellent, repulsive, unattractive
◆ *n*
receipts, proceeds, profits, gain, returns, income, revenue, yield, earnings, winnings, pickings, gate, gate-money

tale *n*
1 STORY, yarn, anecdote, narrative, account, report, rumour, tall story, old wives' tale, superstition, fable, myth, legend, epic, saga, parable, allegory, fairy story, fairytale, novel, romance, roman, tradition, mystery, jeremiad, hair-raiser, traveller's tale, odyssey, sob story, toy, weird
TECHNICAL fabliau
OLD rede, gest
COLLOQ. spiel
2 LIE, falsehood, untruth, fabrication, hoax
COLLOQ. fib, whopper, porky, tall story, cock-and-bull story, fairy story, fairytale, bam

talent *n*
gift, endowment, genius, flair, feel, knack, bent, aptitude, faculty, facility, skill, ability, capacity, aptness, power, strength, strong point, forte, showmanship, long suit
OLD ingenium
COLLOQ. nous, shot in the arm
E₃ inability, weakness, limitation

> **QUOTATIONS**
> Talent comes from originality which is a special manner of thinking, of seeing, of understanding and of judging
> GUY DE MAUPASSANT, *Pierre et Jean*

talented *adj*
gifted, brilliant, well-endowed, versatile, accomplished, able, capable, proficient, adept, adroit, deft, artistic, clever, skilful
E₃ inept

talisman *n*
amulet, charm, fetish, mascot, totem, symbol, idol, ju-ju, phylactery, periapt, abraxas

talk *v, n*
◆ *v*
1 SPEAK, say, utter, articulate, voice, communicate, express, chat, chatter, babble; *Scot* blether
FORMAL converse, confer, orate
COLLOQ. natter, jabber, babble, prattle, chinwag, jaw
2 NEGOTIATE, discuss, bargain, haggle, work out an agreement
3 GOSSIP, spread rumours, chat, chatter, natter
4 *talk to the police*
tell, confess, give (secret) information to, inform on
COLLOQ. tell tales, squeal, blab, spill the beans, let the cat out of the bag, give the game away
SLANG grass
◆ *n*
1 CONVERSATION, dialogue, discussion, chat, chatter, tête-à-tête; *Scot* blether; *NZ* korero
COLLOQ. natter, confab, jaw, jaw-jaw, chinwag

2 *give a talk*
lecture, seminar, symposium, speech, address, discourse, sermon
FORMAL disquisition, oration
COLLOQ. spiel
3 GOSSIP, hearsay, rumour, tittle-tattle
4 *the two sides are holding talks*
negotiation, discussion, interview, meeting, consultation, debate, conference, summit conference, dialogue, seminar, symposium, bargaining, haggling
FORMAL conclave
5 LANGUAGE, dialect, slang, cant, jargon, speech, utterance, words
TECHNICAL idiolect
COLLOQ. lingo

■ **talk back**
answer back, answer rudely, be cheeky to, retort, riposte, retaliate
■ **talk big**
bluster, boast, brag, show off, crow, exaggerate, vaunt
COLLOQ. swank
■ **talk down to**
patronize, speak condescendingly towards, look down on, despise
■ **talk into**
persuade, encourage, coax, sway, convince, bring round, win over
E₃ dissuade, talk out of
■ **talk out of**
dissuade, discourage, deter, put off, prevent, stop
E₃ persuade, convince, talk into

talkative *adj*
garrulous, vocal, communicative, forthcoming, unreserved, expansive, chatty, gossipy, verbose, wordy, long-winded
FORMAL voluble, loquacious
COLLOQ. gabby, gassy, mouthy, can talk the hind legs off a donkey
SLANG gobby
E₃ taciturn, quiet, reserved

> **SYNONYM NUANCES**
> You can use **garrulous** of someone who talks excessively, but with the negative suggestion that what they say has little meaningful content, while **vocal** is more appropriate for someone who likes to make their opinions known, and is not particularly disapproving: *his most vocal critics*.
>   More positive-sounding synonyms include **communicative**, which is suggestive of an ability to impart meaning, and **forthcoming**, which further implies sociability. **Unreserved** suggests an element of wholeheartedness: *unreserved enthusiasm*, while **expansive** appropriately describes being able to talk extensively on a subject: *he was expansive on both himself and his future plans*.
>   The term **chatty**, again, returns to the idea of being friendly, but a more disapproving tone is discernible in **gossipy**, with its implications of idle speculation. The terms **verbose** and **wordy** suggest a propensity for using more words than are necessary and are also critical: *much academic language is obtuse and verbose*, and **long-winded** suggests a similarly tedious quality.

talker *n*
speaker, conversationalist, communicator, lecturer, orator, speechmaker
COLLOQ. chatterbox

talking-to *n*
lecture, scolding, reprimand, rebuke, reproof, reproach, criticism
COLLOQ. dressing-down, telling-off, carpeting, wigging, ticking-off, rocket
E₃ praise, commendation

tall *adj*
1 HIGH, lofty, elevated, soaring, towering, sky-high, lanky, big, great, giant, gigantic
2 *a tall story*
unlikely, unbelievable, incredible, improbable, remarkable, implausible, absurd, far-fetched, exaggerated, dubious, preposterous, overblown
3 *a tall order*
difficult, demanding, exacting, taxing, hard, challenging, trying
E3 1 short, low, small **2** reasonable **3** easy

tallness *n*
altitude, height, loftiness, stature

tally *n, v*
♦ *n*
1 RECORD, count, total, sum, score, enumeration, reckoning, account, register, list, roll, stick
OLD stock, nickstick
2 COUNTERFOIL, counterpart, duplicate, ticket, tag, tab, stub; *N Am* tab
♦ *v*
1 AGREE, concur, tie in, square, harmonize, coincide, correspond, match, conform, suit, fit
OLD nick
FORMAL accord, concur
2 ADD (UP), total, count, reckon, figure
E3 1 disagree, differ

tame *adj, v*
♦ *adj*
1 *a tame rabbit*
pet, domesticated, domestic, broken in, trained, disciplined, manageable, tractable, amenable, gentle, docile, meek, subdued, submissive, unresisting, obedient, biddable
OLD mansuete
2 DULL, boring, tedious, uninteresting, unexciting, humdrum, flat, bland, insipid, weak, feeble, lame, uninspired, unadventurous, unenterprising, wearisome, lifeless, spiritless, vapid
COLLOQ. kids' stuff
E3 1 wild, unmanageable, rebellious **2** exciting, adventurous
♦ *v*
domesticate, house-train, break (in), train, discipline, master, overcome, conquer, bring to heel, bridle, curb, repress, suppress, quell, subdue, temper, soften, mellow, calm, pacify, humble
OLD *(Shakesp)* entame; *(Spenser)* amenage
FORMAL subjugate

tamper *v*
interfere, meddle, tinker, fiddle, manipulate, juggle, alter, damage
COLLOQ. mess about, muck about, monkey, fix, rig, poke/stick your nose in, stick/put your oar in

tan *adj, v*
♦ *adj*
brown, light brown, yellowish brown
♦ *v*
1 BROWN, go/turn brown, make/become darker, bronze
2 BEAT, flog, lash, thrash, whip, flay, cane, birch, strap, spank, clout
COLLOQ. wallop, whack, belt

tang *n*
1 SHARPNESS, piquancy, spice, pungency, taste, flavour, savour, smack, smell, aroma, scent, whiff
COLLOQ. bite, edge, kick, pep, punch
2 TINGE, touch, trace, hint, suggestion, overtone

tangible *adj*
touchable, palpable, solid, concrete, material, substantial, physical, real, actual, hard, perceptible, discernible, visible, evident, definite, well-defined, unmistakable, positive
FORMAL tactile, manifest
E3 intangible, abstract, unreal

tangle *n, v*
♦ *n*
1 KNOT, snarl-up, snarl, twist, coil, mesh, mat, web, maze, ravel, skein, wilderness; *Scot* fank
FORMAL convolution
2 MESS, muddle, jumble, mix-up, confusion, entanglement, embroilment, complication, labyrinth, imbroglio, raffle, skein, perplexity; *Scot* burble, fankle
♦ *v*
1 ENTANGLE, knot, snarl, ravel, twist, coil, interweave, interlace, intertwine, intertwist, intertangle, catch, ensnare, entrap, enmesh, mat; *Scot* fankle, taut
FORMAL convolve
2 INVOLVE, embroil, ensnare, entrap, enmesh, implicate, muddle, confuse, perplex, come into conflict
COLLOQ. mess with
E3 1, 2 disentangle

tangled *adj*
1 *tangled hair*
knotty, knotted, twisted, snarled, matted, tousled, dishevelled, messy, entangled
2 CONFUSED, muddled, jumbled, twisted, tortuous, involved, mixed up, complicated, complex, intricate
FORMAL convoluted

tangy *adj*
sharp, biting, acid, tart, spicy, piquant, pungent, strong, fresh
E3 tasteless, insipid

tank *n*
1 *a hot-water tank*
container, reservoir, header, receptacle, cistern, flush-box, aquarium, stew, vat, basin, gasometer, septic tank
TECHNICAL sponson, shield pond
2 *anti-tank missiles*
armoured car, armoured vehicle, panzer, whippet, Valentine

tantalize *v*
tease, taunt, torment, torture, provoke, lead on, titillate, tempt, allure, entice, beguile, bait, balk, frustrate, thwart, disappoint
E3 gratify, satisfy, fulfil

tantamount *adj*
as good as, equivalent, equal, synonymous, the same as
FORMAL commensurate

tantrum *n*
temper, rage, fury, storm, outburst, fit, fit of temper, flare-up, blow-up, pet, scene, paroxysm
COLLOQ. paddy, hissy fit

tap¹ *v, n*
♦ *v*
tap someone on the shoulder
hit, strike, knock, rap, beat, drum, pat, touch, blip, bob, chuck, broach, percuss, pitapat, tat
OLD tick
♦ *n*
knock, rap, beat, pat, touch, light blow, blip, chuck, tack, tip, tat; *dialect* tit, tuck
OLD tick

tap² *n, v*
♦ *n*
1 STOPCOCK, valve, faucet, spigot, spout, cock, bibcock, petcock; *Scot* stroup
2 STOPPER, plug, bung
3 BUG, listening device, hidden microphone, receiver
♦ *v*
1 *tap a supply*
use, make use of, utilize, exploit, draw on, take advantage of, mine, quarry, siphon, bleed, milk, drain
2 *tap someone's telephone*
monitor, listen in on, listen to, eavesdrop on, bug, wiretap

■ **on tap**
available, ready, on/at hand, handy, accessible

tape *n, v*
- *n*
1 BAND, strip, string, binding, ribbon
2 VIDEO, videotape, cassette, video cassette, recording, tape-recording, video recording, audio cassette, audiotape, magnetic tape
3 *with tape over their mouths*
adhesive tape, Sellotape®, Scotch tape®, masking tape, gaffer tape, sticky tape
- *v*
1 BIND, secure, tie, fasten, stick, seal, Sellotape®
2 RECORD, tape-record, video, video-record

taper *v, n*
- *v*
narrow, make/become narrow, thin, thin out, make/ become thin, slim, decrease, reduce, lessen, diminish, dwindle, fade, wane, peter out, tail off, die away/off
FORMAL attenuate
⊟ widen, flare, swell, increase
- *n*
spill, candle, wick

tardily *adv*
late, slowly, unpunctually, sluggishly, late in the day, at the last minute
FORMAL belatedly
COLLOQ. at the eleventh hour
⊟ promptly, punctually

tardiness *n*
lateness, delay, slowness, unpunctuality, sluggishness, dawdling
FORMAL procrastination, dilatoriness, belatedness
⊟ promptness, punctuality

tardy *adj*
slow, slack, sluggish, late, unpunctual, overdue, delayed, dawdling, loitering, behindhand, backward, last-minute, eleventh-hour
FORMAL belated, dilatory, procrastinating, retarded
⊟ prompt, punctual

target *n, v*
- *n*
1 MARK, aim, goal, bull's eye, victim, butt, game, prey, quarry
COLLOQ. sitter, sitting duck
2 AIM, object, objective, end, purpose, intention, ambition, goal, destination
- *v*
aim for, try for, seek, have as your goal
■ **on target**
1 ACCURATE, precise, exact
COLLOQ. spot-on, bang on
2 ON SCHEDULE, on time, on course, according to plan

tariff *n*
1 TOLL, tax, levy, customs, excise, duty, *zabeta*
2 PRICE LIST, schedule, (list of) charges, menu, bill of fare, rate

tarnish *v, n*
- *v*
discolour, corrode, rust, dull, dim, darken, blacken, sully, taint, stain, blemish, spot, blot, mar, spoil
FORMAL befoul, besmirch
⊟ polish, brighten
- *n*
blemish, spot, stain, taint, blot, discoloration, blackening, film, rust, patina
⊟ brightness, polish

tarry *v*
linger, remain, stay, stop, rest, wait, pause, delay, lag, dally, dawdle, loiter
FORMAL abide, bide, sojourn

tart[1] *n, v*
- *n*
1 *cherry tart*
pie, flan, pastry, tartlet, patty, quiche, strudel
2 PROSTITUTE, call girl, loose woman, fallen woman, slut, street-walker, whore, harlot, scarlet woman, trollop, drab, *fille de joie*, woman of the streets, rent-boy, woman of the town, woman of ill repute, cocotte, courtesan, bawd, *fille des rues*, grande cocotte, lorette, lady of the night, geisha, hetaera, hierodule, loose fish, magdalen, night-walker, vizard-mask
OLD strumpet, wench
COLLOQ. hooker, hustler, moll, pro, hostess, fancy woman; *N Am* working girl
SLANG floozie, scrubber, tramp, *poule de luxe*, quiff, rough trade, tom, brass; *N Am* broad
■ **tart up**
smarten (up), dress up, renovate, decorate, redecorate, embellish
COLLOQ. doll up

tart[2] *adj*
1 *the food tastes tart*
sharp, acid, sour, bitter, vinegary, tangy, acidulous, piquant, pungent
2 *tart remarks*
biting, sharp, cutting, sarcastic, incisive, caustic, acid, acerbic, scathing, sardonic
FORMAL trenchant, astringent
⊟ **1** bland, sweet **2** kind

task *n*
job, chore, duty, charge, imposition, assignment, commission, exercise, mission, engagement, errand, undertaking, enterprise, business, occupation, activity, employment, work, piece of work, labour, toil, burden
■ **take to task**
reprimand, rebuke, criticize, blame, scold, reproach, reprove, censure, lecture
FORMAL upbraid
COLLOQ. tell off, tick off, give someone a dressing-down, slate, slam, knock, give someone stick
⊟ commend, praise

taste *n, v*
- *n*
1 FLAVOUR, savour, relish, smack, tang
Related adjective: gustative, gustatory
See panel on next page
2 SAMPLE, bit, piece, morsel, titbit, bite, nibble, mouthful, specimen, sip, drop, dash, soupçon
3 *a taste for adventure*
liking, fondness, partiality, preference, inclination, bent, leaning, hankering, desire, hunger, thirst, appetite
FORMAL penchant, predilection
4 DISCRIMINATION, discernment, judgement, perception, appreciation, sensitivity, refinement, polish, culture, cultivation, breeding, decorum, stylishness, etiquette, finesse, style, grace, elegance, tastefulness, propriety
⊟ **1** blandness **3** distaste **4** tastelessness
- *v*
1 SAMPLE, nibble, sip, try, test
2 SAVOUR, smack, relish
3 EXPERIENCE, undergo, feel, encounter, meet, know
4 DIFFERENTIATE, distinguish, discern, make out, perceive

SYNONYM NUANCES

noun sense 1
While **taste** can be used to refer to both pleasant and unpleasant sensations, the associations of **flavour** tend to be positive: *a delicious flavour.* While still positive, **savour** is more suggestive of a distinctive quality: *the salt has lost its savour.* **Relish** could be used of an appetizing element that enhances, whereas **smack** suggests an identifiable trace of something: *a beer with a modest smack of hops,* but **tang** is more suggestive of a strong, sharp ingredient: *the tang of fresh lemons.*

Ways of describing taste include:

acid(ic)	meaty	sharp
acrid	*colloq.* mor(e)ish	sour
appetizing	mouthwatering	spicy
bitter	peppery	sugary
bittersweet	piquant	sweet
citrus	pungent	tangy
creamy	salty	tart
delicious	sapid	tasty
flavoursome	savoury	umami
fruity	*colloq.*	vinegary
hot	scrumptious	*colloq.* yummy

tasteful *adj*
refined, polished, cultured, cultivated, elegant, pleasing, charming, smart, stylish, aesthetic, artistic, harmonious, beautiful, pretty, exquisite, delicate, dainty, gracious, graceful, restrained, well-judged, correct, fastidious, discriminating
FORMAL judicious
COLLOQ. tasty
F3 tasteless, garish, tawdry

tastefully *adv*
elegantly, graciously, smartly, stylishly, artistically, harmoniously, beautifully, charmingly, exquisitely, delicately
FORMAL judiciously
F3 tastelessly

tasteless *adj*
1 FLAVOURLESS, insipid, bland, mild, weak, thin, watery, watered-down, flat, plain, stale, dull, boring, uninteresting, vapid
2 INELEGANT, graceless, unseemly, improper, unfitting, indiscreet, crass, rude, tactless, crude, vulgar, kitsch, cheap, tawdry, flashy, showy, gaudy, garish, loud, uncouth
COLLOQ. tacky
SLANG naff
F3 1 tasty **2** tasteful, elegant

tasting *n*
testing, sampling, trial, assay, assessment
FORMAL gustation

tasty *adj*
luscious, palatable, appetizing, mouthwatering, delicious, flavoursome, toothsome, succulent, tangy, spicy, piquant, savoury, umami, sweet
FORMAL flavorous, delectable
COLLOQ. mor(e)ish, scrumptious, yummy
See Synonym nuances panel at **delicious**.
F3 tasteless, insipid

tatter
■ **in tatters**
1 IN RAGS, ragged, in shreds, in ribbons, in pieces, in bits
2 DESTROYED, ruined, in ruins, wrecked, broken, shattered, devastated

tattered *adj*
ragged, frayed, threadbare, ripped, torn, tatty, shabby, scruffy
F3 smart, neat

tattler *n*
gossip, busybody, tell-tale, scandalmonger, tale-teller, newsmonger, rumour-monger, talebearer

taunt *v, n*
♦ *v*
tease, torment, provoke, bait, goad, jeer, mock, ridicule, make fun of, poke fun at, gibe, deride, sneer, insult, revile, reproach, dig, twit, cast/throw/fling in someone's teeth
OLD gird
COLLOQ. rib

♦ *n*
jeer, catcall, gibe, dig, barb, fling, jest, sneer, insult, reproach, taunting, teasing, provocation, mockery, ridicule, sarcasm, derision, censure
OLD gird
COLLOQ. brickbat

taut *adj*
tight, stretched, tightened, contracted, strained, tense, tensed, unrelaxed, worried, anxious, fraught, stiff, rigid
F3 slack, loose, relaxed

tautological *adj*
repetitive, superfluous, redundant, wordy
TECHNICAL pleonastic
FORMAL verbose
F3 succinct, economical

tautology *n*
repetition, repetitiveness, duplication, superfluity, redundancy
TECHNICAL pleonasm, perissology
FORMAL iteration, verbosity

tavern *n*
public house, local, inn, bar, alehouse, tap-house, roadhouse, trust-house, *Kneipe, fonda*
OLD public, bush, night-cellar
COLLOQ. dive, hostelry, joint, pub
SLANG boozer

tawdry *adj*
cheap, vulgar, tasteless, fancy, showy, flashy, gaudy, garish, tinselly, glittering, chintzy, tatty, gingerbread
COLLOQ. tacky, cheapo
F3 fine, tasteful

tawny *adj*
golden, golden brown, khaki, sandy, yellow, tan, fawn
FORMAL fulvous, fulvid, xanthous

tax *n, v*
♦ *n*
1 LEVY, charge, rate, duty, tariff, customs, contribution
FORMAL imposte
Related adjective: fiscal
2 BURDEN, load, strain, stress, pressure, imposition, weight
♦ *v*
1 LEVY, charge, demand, exact, assess, impose
2 BURDEN, weigh (down), load, overload, strain, stretch, encumber, impose, exact, try, test, tire, wear out, weary, exhaust, drain, sap, weaken, make demands on
FORMAL enervate

> **QUOTATIONS**
> In this world nothing can be said to be certain, except death and taxes
> BENJAMIN FRANKLIN

Taxes include:

airport tax	environmental tax	property tax
capital gains tax	estate duty	rates
capital transfer tax	excise	road tax
capitation	*colloq.* fat tax	sales tax
carbon tax	fuel duty	stamp duty land
climate change	*Can & Aust* goods	tax
levy	and services tax	surtax
community charge	(GST)	tithe
congestion charge	income tax	Tobin tax
corporation tax	inheritance tax	toll
council tax	insurance tax	value added tax
customs	landfill tax	(VAT)
death duty	PAYE (pay as you	vehicle excise
emission tax	earn)	duty
energy tax	poll tax	

taxi n
cab, minicab, taxicab, hansom-cab, hackney carriage, fiacre, samlor
OLD hackney cab, hackney coach

taxing adj
burdensome, exacting, demanding, exhausting, punishing, stressful, heavy, tough, hard, tiring, trying, onerous, draining, wearing, wearying, wearisome
FORMAL enervating
🖅 easy, gentle, mild

tea n
infusion, tisane, cha
SLANG char

> **QUOTATIONS**
> There are few hours in life more agreeable than the hour dedicated to the ceremony known as afternoon tea
> HENRY JAMES, *The Portrait of a Lady*

Types of tea include:

Assam	fruit tea	Nilgiri
black tea	green tea	oolong
camomile tea	herbal tea	orange pekoe
Ceylon	iced tea	pekoe
chai	instant tea	peppermint tea
China tea	Irish Breakfast	pu'erh tea
CTC (crush, tear,	Jasmine	red bush (rooibos)
curl)	Keemun	rosehip tea
Darjeeling	Lapsang Souchong	Russian Caravan
decaffeinated tea	lemon tea	Scottish Breakfast
Dragon Well	Macha	Sencha
Earl Grey	masala chai	white tea
English Breakfast	mint tea	Yunnanchai

teach v
instruct, train, coach, tutor, lecture, drill, give lessons, ground, verse, discipline, school, educate, enlighten, edify, inform, impart, indoctrinate, condition, brainwash, advise, counsel, guide, direct, show, demonstrate, read, perfect, preach, take, cram, parrot; *dialect* larn
OLD disciple, foreteach, lear
FORMAL inculcate, pedagogue
COLLOQ. hammer in/into, din in/into
🖅 learn

> **QUOTATIONS**
> He who can, does. He who cannot, teaches
> GEORGE BERNARD SHAW, *Man and Superman*, 'Maxims for Revolutionists: Education'

> **SYNONYM NUANCES**
> **Instruct** is a synonym with fairly general application, while **train** would suggest a more structured process, to pass on a skill. **Coach**, however, might also be used of preparing someone for a specific test: *coaching for my French exam*. **Tutor** similarly suggests individual attention.
> **Drill**, on the other hand, suggests physical training, while **ground** and **verse** suggest instilling a rudimentary but thorough knowledge: *in his day, students were grounded in spelling*. **Discipline**, meanwhile, implies a more rigid application: *disciplined in dance from a young age*, whereas **school** and **educate** both suggest a lengthy and structured formal programme.
> While these synonyms are fairly neutral in tone, **enlighten** has very positive overtones of enhanced awareness or comprehension, and **edify**, likewise, suggests a beneficial outcome: *an edifying lesson in self-sufficiency*. Negative ideas are conveyed by **indoctrinate**, which suggests a forceful and narrow practice of imbuing with your own opinions. Similarly,

condition and **brainwash** have unhealthy suggestions of controlling another's mind.
> The terms **advise** and **counsel** convey the more positive suggestion of supplying help. The terms **guide** and **direct** echo this, while **show** and **demonstrate** suggest the provision of a practical example. The more disapproving **preach**, however, suggests overbearing proclamations, usually with a religious or moralistic tone: *we ignored his pompous preaching on his favourite topics*.

teacher n
schoolteacher, educator, guide; *Scot* dominie
COLLOQ. *Aust* schoolie
🖅 pupil

Kinds of teacher include:

adviser	housemaster	professor
coach	housemistress	pundit
college lecturer	instructor	reader
counsellor	lecturer	reception teacher
crammer	maharishi	*N Am*
dean	master	schoolmarm
demonstrator	mentor	schoolmaster
deputy head	middle school	schoolmistress
doctor	teacher	schoolteacher
don	mistress	secondary school
duenna	nursery school	teacher
fellow	teacher	senior lecturer
form teacher	pastoral head	student teacher
governess	pedagogue	subject
guru	pedant	co-ordinator
headmaster	preceptor	supply teacher
headmistress	preceptress	trainer
head of	primary school	tutor
department	teacher	university lecturer
head of year	principal	upper school
headteacher	private tutor	teacher

teaching n
1 INSTRUCTION, tuition, education, pedagogy, didactics
2 DOGMA, doctrine, tenet, precept, principle
Related adjective: doctrinal

Methods of teaching include:

apprenticeship	hands-on training	role-play
briefing	home-learning	rote learning
coaching	indoctrination	schooling
computer-aided	induction training	seminar
learning	in-service training	shadowing
correspondence	instruction	special tuition
course	job training	theory
counselling	lecturing	training
demonstration	lesson	tuition
distance learning	master-class	tutelage
drilling	on-the-job training	tutorial
familiarization	practical	vocational training
grounding	preaching	work experience
guidance	private tuition	

team n, v
♦ n
side, line-up, squad, shift, crew, gang, band, group, set, troupe, bunch, company, stable
■ **team up**
join, join forces, unite, couple, combine, come together, band together, co-operate, collaborate, work together, match, yoke

teamwork n
collaboration, co-operation, co-ordination, joint effort, team spirit, interplay, fellowship, *esprit de corps*
🖅 disharmony, disunity

tear¹ *v, n*

♦ *v*

1 RIP, rend, divide, pull apart, break apart, split, ladder, rupture, sever, shred, scratch, claw, gash, wound, injure, lacerate, slash, mutilate, mangle
OLD sunder
2 PULL, snatch, grab, seize, pluck, wrest
COLLOQ. yank
3 *tear down the street*
dash, rush, hurry, speed, race, run, sprint, fly, shoot, dart, bolt, career, gallop, charge
COLLOQ. belt, nip, rip, bomb, scoot, whizz, vroom, zap, zing, zip, zoom, step on it

♦ *n*

rip, rent, slit, hole, split, run, rupture, scratch, gash, wound, injury, laceration, slash, mutilation
■ **tear down**
destroy, demolish, pull down, knock down, dismantle

tear²

■ **in tears**
crying, weeping, tearful, sobbing, wailing, whimpering, blubbering, sad, sorrowful, upset, distressed, emotional
COLLOQ. weepy
Related adjective: lachrymal

tearaway *n*
rough, tough, rowdy, ruffian, rascal, daredevil, delinquent, hooligan, hoodlum, hothead, madcap, roughneck
COLLOQ. good-for-nothing

tearful *adj*
crying, in tears, weeping, sobbing, whimpering, blubbering, sad, sorrowful, upset, distressed, emotional, upsetting, distressing, mournful, doleful
FORMAL lachrymose
COLLOQ. weepy
E3 happy, smiling, laughing

tease *v*
taunt, provoke, bait, make fun of, poke fun at, goad, annoy, vex, irritate, badger, bother, worry, pester, plague, torment, tantalize, mock, ridicule, gibe, banter, chaff, perplex, grig; *dialect* mag
OLD teaze
COLLOQ. aggravate, needle, wind up, rag, kid, rib, have a go at, take the mickey out of, pull someone's leg, chip; *Aust* chiack
SLANG nark, josh, take the piss out of; *N Am* sound, goof

technical *adj*
mechanical, scientific, technological, electronic, computerized, specialist, specialized, practical, applied, expert, professional

technically *adv*
technologically, mechanically, scientifically, electronically, practically, professionally

technician *n*
operator, operative, mechanic, engineer, fitter, mechanical engineer, machinist, mechanician

technique *n*
1 METHOD, system, procedure, manner, fashion, style, way, means, approach, course, performance, execution, modus operandi
FORMAL mode
2 SKILL, skilfulness, ability, capability, delivery, artistry, mastery, craftsmanship, dexterity, facility, proficiency, expertise, art, craft, knack, touch
COLLOQ. knowhow

tedious *adj*
boring, monotonous, uninteresting, unexciting, dull, dreary, uninspired, unvaried, lifeless, flat, drab, banal, routine, humdrum, tiresome, wearisome, wearying, weary, tiring, laborious, long, long-winded, long-drawn-out, irksome
OLD operose
FORMAL prosaic
COLLOQ. run-of-the-mill, samey, a drag

SLANG balls-aching, dragsville
E3 lively, interesting, exciting

tedium *n*
boredom, tediousness, monotony, monotonousness, dullness, dreariness, lifelessness, drabness, irksomeness, banality, sameness, routine, prosiness, ennui, vapidity
COLLOQ. rut
E3 excitement, interest

> **QUOTATIONS**
> Tedium is the worst disease in schools, the corrupting tedium that comes equally from monotony, work or leisure
> RAUL D'AVILA POMPÉIA, *The Atheneum*

teem¹ *v*
streets teeming with tourists
swarm, bristle, crawl, burst, proliferate, abound, be full, increase, multiply, overflow, produce, bear, brim
FORMAL pullulate
E3 lack, want

teem² *v*
it was teeming with rain
pour, rain, pelt down
COLLOQ. rain cats and dogs, bucket down, come down in buckets/stair rods/torrents
SLANG piss down, chuck it down

teeming *adj*
swarming, crawling, alive, bristling, seething, full, packed, brimming, overflowing, bursting, numerous, abundant, fruitful, thick
FORMAL replete, pullulating
COLLOQ. chock-a-block, chock-full
E3 lacking, sparse, rare

teenage *adj*
teenaged, adolescent, young, youthful, juvenile, immature

teenager *n*
young person, young adult, adolescent, youth, boy, girl, minor, juvenile, emerging adult
COLLOQ. teen, teeny-bopper, bobbysoxer

teeny *adj*
tiny, minute, minuscule, miniature, diminutive, microscopic; *Scot* wee
COLLOQ. titchy, teeny-weeny, teensy-weensy

teeter *v*
sway, rock, roll, reel, stagger, totter, shake, tremble, waver, wobble, balance, lurch, pitch, pivot, seesaw

teetotal *adj*
temperate, abstinent, abstemious, sober
COLLOQ. on the wagon, TT, tee-tee

teetotaller *n*
non-drinker, abstainer, nephalist, Rechabite, water-drinker
COLLOQ. tee-tee

telegram *n*
Telemessage®, cable, telex, fax, telegraph
COLLOQ. wire

telegraph *n, v*

♦ *n*

cable, teleprinter, telex, telegram, radiotelegraph
COLLOQ. wire

♦ *v*

send, transmit, signal, cable, telex
COLLOQ. wire

telepathy *n*
mind-reading, thought transference, sixth sense, ESP, extrasensory perception, second sight, clairvoyance

telephone *n, v*

♦ *n*

phone, handset, receiver
COLLOQ. blower, hot line

♦ v
phone, ring (up), call (up), dial, contact, get in touch, give someone a call, make a call
COLLOQ. buzz, give a buzz, give a tinkle, give a bell

Types of telephone include:

Android® phone	4G phone	swivel phone
Ansaphone®	hands-free phone	system phone
answering machine	hazardous area phone	textphone
Blackberry®	iPhone®	3G phone
Bluetooth® phone	landline	3.5G phone
caller display phone	Minicom®	tone-dialling phone
camera phone	mobile phone	Touchtone®
camphone	netphone	tri-band phone
cardphone	1G phone	2G phone
carphone	pager	2.5G phone
cashphone	payphone	2.75G phone
cellphone	picture mobile	Uniphone®
cellular phone	push-button tele- phone	videophone
corded phone	quad-band phone/ world phone	VOIP (Voice Over Internet Protocol) phone
cordless phone	satellite phone	WAP (Wireless Application Protocol) phone
dual-band phone colloq. dumbphone	SIP (Session Initiation Protocol) phone	weather-resistant phone
fax	Skype phone	webphone
fax-phone	smartphone	
feature phone	speakerphone	
flip phone		

telescope v
contract, shrink, compress, condense, abridge, squash, squeeze, crush, shorten, compact, curtail, truncate, abbreviate, reduce, cut, trim, concertina

televise v
broadcast, screen, show, put on, transmit, air, beam, relay, cable

television n
TV, receiver, set, small screen
COLLOQ. telly, the box, goggle-box, idiot box, the tube, tele; N Am boob tube

> **QUOTATIONS**
> Television? No good will come of this device. The word is half Greek and half Latin
> **C P SCOTT**

Television genres include:

action	educational	shockumentary
animation	television	colloq. sitcom
award show	edutainment	situation comedy
breakfast television	game show	sketch show
chat show	home shopping	soap opera
children's television	infotainment	sports
comedy	medical drama	colloq. tabloid television
current affairs magazine	mockumentary music TV	talent show
daytime television	nature show	talk show
docudrama	news	telethon
documentary	quiz show	TV movie
docutainment	reality television	variety show
drama	religious program- ming	
dramedy	science fiction	

tell v
1 INFORM, notify, let know, brief, mention, acquaint, impart, communicate, make known, report, speak, utter, say, state, confess, divulge, show, disclose, reveal, announce, broadcast, declare, proclaim

FORMAL apprise
COLLOQ. give the low-down
2 tell a story
narrate, recount, relate, recite, report, announce, describe, sketch, portray, mention
FORMAL delineate
3 ORDER, command, direct, instruct, require, charge, bid, dictate, advise, authorize, decree
4 DIFFERENTIATE, distinguish, discriminate, tell apart, discern, recognize, identify, discover, see, perceive, make out, understand, comprehend
5 AFFECT, have an effect on, take its toll of, exhaust, drain, change, transform, alter
6 INFORM ON, talk, betray, denounce
COLLOQ. rat, squeal, tell tales, blab, blow the whistle on, spill the beans, let the cat out of the bag, give the game away, blow the gaff
SLANG grass, shop
■ tell off
scold, chide, reprimand, rebuke, reprove, lecture, reproach, censure
FORMAL upbraid, berate
COLLOQ. tick off, dress down, slate, slam, knock, bawl out, bounce, carpet, catch it, chew out, see off, take/pull apart, give a talking-to, give someone a ticking-off/a dressing-down, haul over the coals, read the riot act to, (give someone a) rap over the knuckles, give someone a flea in their ear/an earful/a piece of your mind, shoot down in flames, tear a strip off someone

teller n
cashier, clerk, bank clerk, banker, treasurer

telling adj
revealing, significant, impressive, marked, effective, powerful, convincing, persuasive
FORMAL cogent

telling-off n
scolding, chiding, rebuke, reprimand, reproach, reproof, lecture, row
FORMAL castigation, upbraiding
COLLOQ. dressing-down, ticking-off, bawling-out, talking-to, slap/smack on the wrist, rap over the knuckles, flea in someone's ear, rocket, wigging, carpeting, earful

tell-tale adj, n
♦ adj
revealing, suggestive, meaningful, revelatory, noticeable, perceptible, unmistakable
COLLOQ. give-away
♦ n
informer, secret agent, sneak, spy, tale-teller; Scot clype; N Am tattle-tale
OLD (Shakesp) buzzer
COLLOQ. squealer, snake in the grass, snitch, snitcher
SLANG grass; N Am stoolie

temerity n
presumption, impudence, impertinence, effrontery, gall, audacity, boldness, daring, rashness, recklessness, impulsiveness
COLLOQ. cheek, nerve
E3 caution, prudence

temper n, v
♦ n
1 MOOD, humour, nature, temperament, character, attitude, disposition, constitution, frame/state of mind
2 ANGER, bad mood, rage, fury, passion, tantrum, fit of temper, flare-up, scene, storm, annoyance, resentment, irritability, petulance, ill-humour
COLLOQ. paddy, wax
3 CALM, calmness, composure, self-control, tranquillity
SLANG cool
E3 2 calmness, self-control **3** anger, rage
♦ v
1 MODERATE, lessen, weaken, reduce, calm, soothe, allay, alleviate, palliate, modify, soften

FORMAL mitigate, assuage
COLLOQ. tone down
2 HARDEN, roughen, toughen, inure, strengthen
TECHNICAL anneal
FORMAL fortify

■ **lose your temper**
lose your patience, get aggravated, get angry
COLLOQ. boil over, get all steamed up, foam at the mouth, fly off the handle, go mad, see red, get up in arms, blow a fuse, blow a gasket, blow your cool, blow your top, burst a blood vessel, do your nut, explode, flip your lid, fly into a rage, go off the deep end, go up the wall, hit the ceiling, hit the roof, lose your cool, lose your rag, raise hell, freak out, throw a tantrum, throw a wobbly

temperament n
1 CHARACTER, temper, nature, personality, disposition, tendency, bent, constitution, make-up, complexion, soul, spirit, mood, humour, frame/state of mind, attitude, outlook, mettle, idiosyncrasy, kidney
OLD composure, complexion
2 MOODINESS, excitability, sensitivity, touchiness, irritability, impatience, fieriness, explosiveness, hot-headedness, red-headedness, volatility

temperamental adj
1 MOODY, emotional, over-emotional, neurotic, highly-strung, sensitive, over-sensitive, hypersensitive, touchy, irritable, impatient, passionate, fiery, excitable, explosive, hot-blooded, hot-headed, petulant, volatile, mercurial, capricious, artistic, unpredictable, unreliable
2 NATURAL, inborn, innate, inherent, constitutional, ingrained, congenital
E3 1 calm, level-headed, steady

temperamentally adv
naturally, constitutionally, innately, inherently, basically, fundamentally

temperance n
1 TEETOTALISM, prohibition, abstinence, abstemiousness, sobriety
2 MODERATION, restraint, self-restraint, self-control, self-discipline, self-denial, austerity, continence
E3 2 intemperance, excess

temperate adj
1 *temperate climate*
mild, clement, balmy, fair, equable, balanced, stable, moderate, gentle, pleasant, agreeable
2 TEETOTAL, abstinent, abstemious, self-denying, sober, continent, moderate, restrained, self-restrained, controlled, self-controlled, even-tempered, calm, composed, reasonable, sensible
E3 2 intemperate, extreme, excessive

tempest n
1 STORM, gale, squall, tornado, typhoon, hurricane, cyclone
2 FURORE, upheaval, uproar, ferment, disturbance, commotion, turmoil, tumult

tempestuous adj
stormy, windy, gusty, blustery, squally, turbulent, tumultuous, rough, wild, uncontrolled, violent, furious, raging, heated, boisterous, impassioned, fierce, feverish, passionate, intense
E3 calm, peaceful, quiet

template n
prototype, model, pattern, form, frame, mould, matrix, blueprint, profile, jig, master
TECHNICAL strickle

temple n
place of worship, shrine, sanctuary, church, tabernacle, mosque, pagoda
See also **worship.**

tempo n
time, rhythm, metre, measure, beat, cadence, pulse, throb, speed, velocity, rate, pace

temporal adj
secular, profane, worldly, earthly, terrestrial, material, carnal, fleshly, mortal
E3 spiritual

temporarily adv
for the time being, momentarily, for now, in the interim, pro tem, transiently, transitorily, briefly, fleetingly
E3 permanently

temporary adj
impermanent, provisional, interim, short-term, fill-in, makeshift, stopgap, pro tem, temporal, transient, transitory, passing, fleeting, brief, short-lived, momentary
FORMAL ephemeral, evanescent, fugacious
E3 permanent, everlasting

temporize v
delay, hang back, pause, stall, equivocate, play for time
FORMAL procrastinate, tergiversate
COLLOQ. hum and haw

tempt v
1 ENTICE, coax, cajole, persuade, woo, bait, lure, induce, educe, provoke, incite, egg on
OLD assay, attempt; (Shakesp) suggest
FORMAL inveigle
2 ALLURE, attract, draw, invite, tantalize
COLLOQ. make someone's mouth water
E3 1 discourage, dissuade **2** repel

temptation n
enticement, inducement, incitement, coaxing, cajolery, persuasion, urging, bait, snare, lure, allure, allurement, appeal, attraction, influence, draw, pull, trial, seduction, invitation, suggestion
OLD tentation, attempt, invitement, cloven hoof

tempting adj
attractive, inviting, alluring, tantalizing, enticing, appetizing, mouthwatering, seductive
E3 unattractive, uninviting

temptress n
enchantress, seductress, siren, vamp, flirt, sorceress, femme fatale, coquette, Delilah, Lorelei, Circe

tenable adj
credible, defensible, justifiable, reasonable, rational, sound, arguable, believable, defendable, plausible, maintainable, supportable, viable, feasible
E3 untenable, indefensible, unjustifiable

tenacious adj
1 DETERMINED, persistent, dogged, firm, single-minded, adamant, resolute, purposeful, steadfast, relentless, persevering, unyielding, unshak(e)able, unswerving, obstinate, stubborn
FORMAL intransigent, obdurate
2 ADHESIVE, cohesive, sticky, clinging, secure, firm, tight, fast
E3 1 loose, slack, weak

tenacity n
determination, persistence, single-mindedness, firmness, fastness, perseverance, doggedness, resoluteness, resolution, resolve, steadfastness, staunchness, toughness, diligence, power, solidity, solidness, strength, force, forcefulness, inflexibility, indomitability, application, stubbornness, obstinacy
FORMAL intransigence, obduracy, pertinacity
E3 looseness, slackness, weakness

tenancy n
occupancy, possession, renting, residence, tenure, holding, lease, leasehold, occupation, incumbency

tenant n
renter, lessee, leaseholder, occupier, occupant, resident, inhabitant, landholder
FORMAL incumbent

tend[1] _v_

tends to arrive late
incline, be inclined, lean, show a tendency, be liable, bend, bear, head, aim, point, lead, go, move, gravitate

tend[2] _v_

tend someone who is ill
look after, take care of, care for, cultivate, keep, maintain, see to, manage, handle, guard, protect, watch (over), keep an eye on, mind, nurture, nurse, minister to, serve, attend (to), wait on
F3 neglect, ignore

tendency _n_
trend, drift, movement, course, direction, bearing, heading, bias, partiality, readiness, liability, susceptibility, proneness, inclination, leaning, bent, aptness, disposition
FORMAL predisposition, propensity, proclivity, conatus

tendentious _adj_
controversial, contentious, polemical, disputed, doubtful, questionable, debatable, disputable, at issue
F3 uncontroversial

tender[1] _adj_
1 KIND, gentle, caring, humane, generous, benevolent, considerate, compassionate, merciful, sympathetic, warm, kindly, fond, affectionate, loving, amorous, romantic, sentimental, emotional, evocative, sensitive, vulnerable, tender-hearted, soft-hearted
TECHNICAL affetuoso, amoroso
OLD (_Spenser_) frail
2 YOUNG, youthful, immature, green, raw, new, early, callow, inexperienced, impressionable, vulnerable
3 SOFT, easy to chew/cut, succulent, fleshy, juicy, dainty, delicate, fragile, frail, sensitive, weak, feeble; _dialect_ nesh
4 SORE, painful, aching, smarting, bruised, throbbing, inflamed, red, raw, sensitive, footsore
F3 1 hard-hearted, callous **2** mature **3** tough, hard

tender[2] _v, n_
♦ _v_
tender an apology
offer, extend, give, present, submit, propose, suggest, advance, volunteer, bid, render
FORMAL proffer
♦ _n_
1 _legal tender_
currency, money, coins, banknotes
2 OFFER, bid, estimate, quotation, price, proposal, proposition, suggestion, submission

tender-hearted _adj_
caring, gentle, kind, kind-hearted, kindly, mild, warm, warm-hearted, sympathetic, soft-hearted, feeling, considerate, compassionate, benevolent, loving, fond, affectionate, responsive, sensitive, humane, merciful, pitying, sentimental, benign
F3 callous, cruel, hard-hearted, unfeeling

tenderly _adv_
gently, warmly, generously, benevolently, considerately, compassionately, sympathetically, sensitively, lovingly, affectionately, fondly, romantically, sentimentally, emotionally
F3 cruelly, hard-heartedly, unfeelingly

tenderness _n_
1 KINDNESS, gentleness, warmth, warm-heartedness, tender-heartedness, sympathy, sweetness, sensitivity, loving-kindness, humaneness, benevolence, attachment, devotion, affection, fondness, amorousness, love, liking, mercy, pity, care, compassion, consideration, humanity, sentimentality, soft-heartedness, vulnerability
2 YOUTH, youthfulness, immaturity, callowness, greenness, inexperience
3 SOFTNESS, succulence, juiciness, weakness, delicateness, frailness, fragility, feebleness

4 SORENESS, rawness, bruising, sensitiveness, ache, aching, inflammation, irritation, pain, painfulness
F3 1 cruelty, hardness, harshness **2** maturity **3** toughness, hardness

tenet _n_
principle, belief, precept, presumption, conviction, opinion, teaching, rule, thesis, view, doctrine, dogma, maxim, creed, credo, canon, article of faith

tennis

**Terms used in tennis include**:

ace	eastern grip	passing shot
advantage	En-Tout-Cas®	racket (or racquet)
advantage court	exhibition match	rally
All England Lawn	fault	real tennis
Tennis and	Flushing Meadows	retrieve
Croquet Club	follow-through	return
N Am alley	foot fault	Roland Garros
approach shot	forecourt	royal tennis
Association of	forehand	runback
Tennis	French Open	second serve
Professionals	game	seeding
(ATP)	game point	serve
Australian Open	Grand Slam	serve and volley
backcourt	grass court	service court
backhand	grip	service line
backspin	ground stroke	set
ball	half volley	set point
ball-boy	hard court	shot
ball-girl	hit	singles
baseline	kick serve	slice
baseliner	kill	smash
baseline rally	knock-up	sphairistike
break (of service)	lawn tennis	spin
break point	Lawn Tennis	straight sets
bye	Association (LTA)	stringing
call	let	stroke
Centre Court	line judge	sweet spot
centre mark	linesman	tie-break
change of ends	lob	topspin
clay court	love	tournament
continental grip	love game	tramlines
court	match	umpire
cross-court	match point	unforced error
cut	Melbourne Park	US Open
Davis Cup	mini-break	volley
deuce	mixed doubles	western grip
deuce court	moon-ball	whites
double fault	net	wild card
doubles	net cord	Wimbledon
down the line	not up	Women's Tennis
drive	overhead	Association
drop-shot	overrule	(WTA)

---

tenor _n_
meaning, tendency, theme, trend, essence, substance, gist, aim, point, direction, drift, purpose, sense, spirit, intent, course, path, way, burden
FORMAL purport

tense _adj, v_
♦ _adj_
1 TIGHT, taut, stretched, strained, stiff, rigid
2 NERVOUS, anxious, worried, strained, distraught, under pressure, jittery, uneasy, apprehensive, on edge, fidgety, restless, jumpy, overwrought, keyed up
COLLOQ. edgy, uptight, stressed out
SLANG screwed up
3 STRESSFUL, exciting, worrying, uneasy, strained, charged, fraught, nerve-racking, nail-biting
F3 1 loose, slack **2** calm, relaxed
♦ _v_
tighten, contract, brace, stretch, strain, stiffen, work
F3 loosen, relax

tensely *adv*
worriedly, anxiously, nervously, apprehensively, uneasily, restlessly
COLLOQ. stressed out, in a state, with butterflies in your stomach
⊟ calmly, in a relaxed manner

tension *n*
1 TIGHTNESS, tautness, stiffness, rigidity, strain, straining, stretching, stress, pressure
2 NERVOUSNESS, anxiety, worry, strain, stress, pressure, uneasiness, apprehension, edginess, restlessness, agitation, disquiet, distress, suspense, hypertension
COLLOQ. nerves, jitters, butterflies, butterflies in your stomach, collywobbles, wobbly, willies, heebie-jeebies
3 CONFLICT, disagreement, friction, quarrel, dissension, dispute, opposition, antagonism, hostility, strife, unrest, confrontation, feud, discord, contention, ill-will, difference of opinion, variance, clash
FORMAL antipathy
⊟ **1** looseness **2** calm(ness), relaxation **3** harmony

tent

Types of tent include:

barrel-vaulted tent	double-A pole	sloping wedge
bell tent	mountain tent	tent
big top	frame tent	tabernacle
bivvy	hooped bivvy	tepee
black tent	kata	touring tent
box tent	lodge	trailer tent
canopy	marquee	tunnel tent
canvas	mat tent	tupik
conical tent	ridge tent	wigwam
crossover pole tent	single hoop tent	yaranga
dome tent	sloping ridge tent	yurt

---

tentative *adj*
1 PROVISIONAL, experimental, exploratory, speculative, test, trial, pilot, indefinite, unconfirmed, to be confirmed, unproven
FORMAL conjectural, peirastic
2 HESITANT, wavering, faltering, cautious, unsure, uncertain, timid, doubtful, undecided
⊟ **1** definite, conclusive, final, firm **2** decisive, confident

tentatively *adv*
1 PROVISIONALLY, experimentally, indefinitely, speculatively, on spec
FORMAL peirastically
2 HESITANTLY, cautiously, doubtfully, timidly, gingerly
⊟ **1** definitely, firmly **2** decisively, confidently

tenterhooks
■ **on tenterhooks**
anxious, in suspense, impatient, nervous, excited, waiting, watchful, expectant, eager, with bated breath
COLLOQ. keyed up

tenuous *adj*
thin, slim, slender, fine, slight, insubstantial, flimsy, fragile, delicate, weak, vague, hazy, shaky, indefinite, subtle, recherché, doubtful, dubious, questionable
⊟ strong, substantial

tenure *n*
possession, proprietorship, residence, tenancy, term, time, holding, occupancy, occupation
FORMAL habitation, incumbency

tepid *adj*
lukewarm, cool, lew, warmish, half-hearted, indifferent, unenthusiastic, apathetic
⊟ cold, hot, passionate

term *n, v*
♦ *n*
1 WORD, name, title, epithet, phrase, expression
FORMAL designation, denomination, appellation, locution
2 TIME, period, course, duration, spell, span, stretch, interval, space, semester, session, season
3 *on good terms*
relations, relationship, footing, standing, position
4 *the terms of the contract*
condition, point, detail, specification, stipulation, clause, proviso, provision, qualification, restriction, particular
5 CHARGES, rates, fees, prices, costs, tariff
6 END, interval, conclusion, limit, finish, duration, period, culmination, close, bound, boundary, fruition, terminus
♦ *v*
call, name, dub, style, designate, label, tag, title, entitle
FORMAL denominate

terminal *adj, n*
♦ *adj*
1 LAST, final, concluding, ultimate, extreme, utmost, ending, confining, limiting
2 *terminal illness*
fatal, deadly, lethal, mortal, incurable, untreatable, dying, killing
⊟ **1** initial, first
♦ *n*
1 END, extremity, limit, termination, boundary, station, last stop, end of the line, garage, depot, terminus
2 *a computer terminal*
VDU, computer workstation, input-output device, keyboard, console, monitor

terminally *adv*
incurably, fatally, mortally, malignantly, lethally

terminate *v*
finish, bring/come to an end, cease, complete, conclude, end, stop, close, cut off, result, put an end to, wind up, close the book on, leave off, dismiss, abort, lapse, run out, expire, dissolve, issue
FORMAL discontinue
⊟ begin, start, initiate

termination *n*
end, ending, finish, conclusion, close, abortion, completion, boundary, issue, result, consequence, effect, dénouement, expiry, finale, success, finis
FORMAL demise, cessation, discontinuation
⊟ beginning, initiation, start

terminology *n*
language, jargon, phraseology, vocabulary, words, expressions, terms, nomenclature

terminus *n*
end, close, termination, extremity, limit, boundary, destination, goal, target, depot, station, garage, end of the line, terminal

terrain *n*
land, ground, territory, country, countryside, landscape, topography

terrestrial *adj*
earthly, worldly, global, mundane
⊟ cosmic, heavenly

terrible *adj*
1 BAD, awful, frightful, dreadful, shocking, appalling, outrageous, disgusting, revolting, repulsive, nasty, offensive, abhorrent, heinous, hateful, horrid, horrible, unpleasant, obnoxious, foul, vile, monstrous, hideous, gruesome, horrific, harrowing, grim, distressing, unspeakable, fearful, pokerish
COLLOQ. abortional
2 EXTREME, serious, severe, great, intense, exceptional, big, large
COLLOQ. frightful, awful
3 *my arithmetic is terrible*
poor, bad, inferior, inadequate, weak, mediocre, substandard, imperfect, faulty, defective, deficient, unsatisfactory, unacceptable, second-rate, third-rate, useless, hopeless, incompetent, ineffective
COLLOQ. awful, lousy, crummy, pathetic, rop(e)y, a load of rubbish, a load of garbage; *N Am* hellacious

SLANG the pits, pants, poxy, naff, crappy; (*vulgar*) a load of crap/shit
4 GUILTY, bad, sorry, ashamed, shamefaced, apologetic, conscience-stricken, remorseful, contrite
5 ILL, unwell, sick, poorly, diseased, painful, in pain, aching, unhappy, despondent, gloomy
FORMAL indisposed
COLLOQ. under the weather
F3 **1** excellent, wonderful, superb **3** good **5** well, happy

terribly *adv*
very, much, greatly, extremely, exceedingly, thoroughly, desperately, decidedly, seriously
COLLOQ. frightfully, awfully

terrific *adj*
1 EXCELLENT, wonderful, great, marvellous, fantastic, super, remarkable, outstanding, brilliant, magnificent, superb, sensational, amazing, stupendous, breathtaking
COLLOQ. smashing, fabulous, neat, ace, brill, crack, out of this world, hell of a, wild
SLANG mega, cool, wicked, awesome, crucial, triff
2 HUGE, enormous, gigantic, tremendous, great, intense, extreme, excessive, extraordinary
F3 **1** awful, terrible, appalling

terrifically *adv*
extremely, exceedingly, excessively, very, really, exceptionally, extraordinarily, intensely, thoroughly, remarkably, utterly, greatly, highly, unusually, unreasonably, immoderately, uncommonly, inordinately, acutely, severely, decidedly
OLD jolly
COLLOQ. awfully, terribly, dreadfully, frightfully

terrified *adj*
frightened, petrified, scared, scared stiff, panic-stricken, intimidated, horrified, horror-struck, dismayed, appalled, alarmed, awed, aghast
COLLOQ. scared out of your wits, scared to death, having kittens, in a blue funk

terrify *v*
petrify, horrify, appal, shock, terrorize, intimidate, frighten, scare, scare stiff, panic, alarm, dismay, paralyse, numb
OLD fear, grise, affright; (*Shakesp & Spenser*) gast, ghast; (*Spenser*) agrise
COLLOQ. rattle, scare someone out of their wits, make someone's blood run cold, scare the living daylights out of, make someone's hair stand on end, make someone jump out of their skin, put the frighteners on, put the wind up
SLANG scare the shit out of

territorial *adj*
geographical, area, district, zonal, regional, sectional, topographic, localized
FORMAL domainal

territory *n*
country, land, state, dependency, province, domain, preserve, jurisdiction, sector, region, area, district, county, zone, tract, terrain, field

terror *n*
1 FEAR, panic, dread, trepidation, horror, shock, fright, alarm, dismay, terrorism, intimidation
OLD affright, amazedness
FORMAL consternation
COLLOQ. blue funk, cold sweat
2 *that child's a terror*
rascal, rogue, horror, tearaway
3 FIEND, monster, devil, demon, bogy, scarecrow, bugbear, bogle, poker
OLD bug

terrorist *n*
revolutionary, gunman, guerrilla, urban guerrilla, militant, anarchist, butcher, seditionist, freedom fighter, bomber, attacker, aggressor, agitator, assailant, assassin, fundamentalist

terrorize *v*
threaten, menace, intimidate, oppress, coerce, bully, browbeat, frighten, scare, alarm, terrify, petrify, horrify, shock
COLLOQ. strongarm, put the frighteners on, put the wind up

terse *adj*
short, brief, succinct, concise, to the point, compact, crisp, condensed, pithy, incisive, snappy, curt, blunt, brusque, abrupt, laconic
FORMAL epigrammatic, elliptical, gnomic
F3 long-winded, verbose

test *v, n*
♦ *v*
1 *test them on spelling*
try (out), experiment, examine, assess, evaluate, check, scrutinize, inspect, investigate, study, analyse, screen, sample, prove, verify
FORMAL appraise, assay
COLLOQ. probe
2 *test someone's patience*
strain, burden, load, overload, stretch, encumber, impose, exact, try, test, tire, wear out, weary, exhaust, drain, sap, weaken, make demands on
FORMAL enervate
♦ *n*
trial, try-out, experiment, examination, audition, pilot study, assessment, evaluation, questions, questionnaire, quiz, check, check-up, scrutinization, investigation, inspection, analysis, exploration, proof, probation, ordeal

testament *n*
testimony, witness, demonstration, proof, evidence, exemplification, tribute, will, earnest
FORMAL attestation

testicles *n*
SLANG goolies, nuts; (*vulgar*) balls, bollocks, rocks
Related adjective: testicular

testify *v*
give evidence, state, declare, assert, swear, vouch, affirm, certify, confirm, verify, establish, demonstrate, substantiate, show, bear witness, back up, support, endorse, speak to, rap
TECHNICAL *Scot* depone
FORMAL avow, attest, corroborate

testimonial *n*
reference, character, credential, certificate, (letter of) recommendation, endorsement, commendation, tribute

> **⚠ testimonial** or **testimony**?
> A *testimonial* is a letter describing a person's character and abilities. A *testimony* is a statement of evidence, for example that of a witness at a trial: *he was convicted mainly by the testimony of his former partner; her book is a remarkable testimony to her vision for the future of her country.*

testimony *n*
evidence, statement, submission, declaration, profession, assertion, support, proof, verification, confirmation, affirmation, witness, demonstration, indication
TECHNICAL affidavit, deposition
OLD (*Shakesp*) attest
FORMAL attestation, corroboration, manifestation

testy *adj*
bad-tempered, cross, quarrelsome, crusty, quick-tempered, short-tempered, irritable, impatient, touchy, grumpy, irascible, snappish, snappy, waspish, sullen, fretful, peevish, splenetic, petulant, captious
FORMAL cantankerous
COLLOQ. crabbed, tetchy, crotchety, stroppy, shirty, ratty
F3 even-tempered, good-humoured

tetchy *adj*
irritable, irascible, peevish, bad-tempered, crusty, grumpy, touchy, short-tempered, snappish
COLLOQ. grouchy, crotchety, shirty, ratty

tête-à-tête *n*
conversation, chat, talk, heart-to-heart, dialogue
COLLOQ. jaw, chitchat, confab, natter

tether *n, v*
♦ *n*
chain, rope, cord, line, lead, leash, bond, fetter, shackle, restraint, fastening
♦ *v*
tie, fasten, secure, restrain, chain, rope, leash, bind, lash, fetter, shackle, manacle

text *n*
1 WORDS, wording, content, matter, main matter, body
2 SUBJECT, subject matter, topic, theme, issue, point
3 READING, passage, verse, chapter, paragraph, sentence
4 BOOK, set book, textbook, source

texture *n*
consistency, feel, touch, surface, finish, grain, appearance, weave, tissue, fabric, structure, composition, constitution, character, quality

thank *v*
say thank you to, be grateful, show/express your gratitude, express your thanks, appreciate, show your appreciation, acknowledge, recognize, credit, owe
OLD aggrate; (*Spenser*) remercy

thankful *adj*
grateful, appreciative, obliged, indebted, pleased, contented, relieved
FORMAL beholden
E₃ ungrateful, unappreciative

thankfulness *n*
gratitude, appreciation, obligation, indebtedness

thankless *adj*
unrecognized, unappreciated, ungrateful, unacknowledged, unrequited, unrewarded, unrewarding, unprofitable, useless, fruitless
E₃ rewarding, worthwhile

thanks *n, interj*
♦ *n*
gratitude, gratefulness, appreciation, acknowledgement, recognition, credit, thanksgiving, thank-offering
♦ *interj*
thank you, many thanks, bless you, much obliged, that's very kind of you, that's very good of you, you shouldn't have
COLLOQ. cheers, ta
■ **thanks to**
because of, owing to, due to, on account of, as a result of, through

thaw *v*
1 MELT, defrost, defreeze, unfreeze, de-ice, soften, liquefy, dissolve, warm, heat up
2 BECOME FRIENDLIER, become more relaxed, relax, loosen up
E₃ **1** freeze

theatre *n*
1 *go to the theatre*
auditorium, hall, playhouse, amphitheatre, lyceum, odeon, opera house
2 DRAMA, the stage, dramatics, theatrics, show business
FORMAL Thespian art
COLLOQ. the boards, the footlights, rep

> QUOTATIONS
> I go to the theatre to be entertained. I don't want to see plays about rape, sodomy and drug addiction – I can get all that at home
> PETER COOK

Parts of a theatre include:

apron	footlights	pit
auditorium	forestage	prompt side
backstage	fourth wall	proscenium
balcony	gallery	proscenium arch
border	*colloq.* the gods	revolving stage
box	green room	rostrum
bridge	grid	safety curtain
catwalk	leg drop	scruto
circle	lights	set
coulisse	loge	spots
cut drop	loggia	stage
cyclorama	logum	stalls
decor	mezzanine	tormentor
downstage	open stage	trapdoor
flat	opposite prompt	upper circle
flies	orchestra pit	upstage
floats	picture-frame	wings
floods	stage	

theatrical *adj*
1 DRAMATIC, thespian
2 MELODRAMATIC, histrionic, dramatic, mannered, affected, unreal, artificial, forced, pompous, ostentatious, showy, extravagant, emotional, exaggerated, overdone
COLLOQ. over the top, OTT

Theatrical forms include:

ballet	Grand Guignol	operetta
burlesque	kabuki	pageant
cabaret	kitchen-sink	pantomime
circus	legitimate drama	play
comedy	masque	Punch and Judy
black comedy	melodrama	puppet theatre
comedy of	mime	revue
humours	miracle play	street theatre
comedy of	monologue	tableau
manners	morality play	theatre-in-the-
comedy of	mummery	round
menace	musical	Theatre of Cruelty
commedia del-	musical comedy	Theatre of the
l'arte	music hall	Absurd
duologue	mystery play	tragedy
farce	Noh	variety show
fringe theatre	opera	

See also **performance**.

theft *n*
robbery, thieving, burglary, stealing, pilfering, larceny, shoplifting, kleptomania, fraud, swindling, embezzlement, walk-in, autocrime
OLD mainor, pilferage, plagiary; *Scot* stouth, stouthrie, stouthrief
FORMAL purloining
COLLOQ. pinching, nicking, swiping, lifting, nobbling, filching, mugging, steal, job, stick-up, swipe, smash-and-grab
SLANG heist, touch, blag, sting, rip-off

thematic *adj*
conceptual, notional, classificatory
FORMAL taxonomic

theme *n*
1 SUBJECT, topic, subject matter, thread, motif, keynote, idea, gist, essence, burden, argument, text, story, talk
TECHNICAL subtext, topos
FORMAL leitmotif, lemma, mythus
COLLOQ. the name of the game, peg
2 THESIS, paper, dissertation, composition, essay, text, matter
3 MELODY, tune, motif, song
TECHNICAL leitmotiv

then *adv*
1 AT THAT TIME, at that point, at that moment, in those days, by that time
FORMAL whereupon
2 AFTERWARDS, after, next, soon, subsequently, at a later date
3 IN ADDITION, additionally, also, as well, moreover, besides, too, further, furthermore
4 THEREFORE, and so, accordingly, consequently, as a result
FORMAL thus

theological *adj*
religious, divine, doctrinal, ecclesiastical, scriptural
TECHNICAL hierological

theorem *n*
formula, principle, rule, statement, deduction, proposition
FORMAL dictum, postulate, hypothesis

theoretical *adj*
hypothetical, speculative, abstract, conceptual, notional, academic, doctrinaire, pure, ideal
TECHNICAL a priori
FORMAL conjectural, suppositional
COLLOQ. on paper, armchair
🖅 practical, applied, concrete, hands-on

theoretically *adv*
in theory, in principle, hypothetically, notionally, conceptually, ideally, seemingly
TECHNICAL a priori
COLLOQ. on paper
🖅 in practice

theorize *v*
suppose, guess, speculate, formulate, hypothesize
FORMAL conjecture, postulate, propound

theory *n*
hypothesis, supposition, assumption, presumption, guess, speculation, idea, view, opinion, notion, abstraction, rationale, philosophy, thesis, plan, proposal, scheme, system, principle, law
FORMAL conjecture, surmise, postulation
🖅 certainty, practice; *formal* praxis
■ **in theory**
theoretically, in principle, hypothetically, notionally, conceptually, ideally, seemingly
TECHNICAL a priori
COLLOQ. on paper
🖅 in practice

therapeutic *adj*
remedial, curative, healing, curing, restorative, tonic, medicinal, corrective, good, advantageous, beneficial, salutary, health-giving
FORMAL ameliorative, sanative
🖅 harmful, detrimental

therapy *n*
treatment, remedy, cure, healing, tonic
See panel below

thereabouts *adv*
about, approximately, roughly, near that number, near that date

thereafter *adv*
subsequently, afterwards, after that, after that time, next

therefore *adv*
and so, then, accordingly, consequently, as a result, for that reason
FORMAL thus, ergo

thesaurus *n*
dictionary, lexicon, wordbook, wordfinder, vocabulary, synonymy, encyclopedia, storehouse, repository, treasury

thesis *n*
1 *a doctoral thesis*
dissertation, essay, composition, treatise, paper, monograph
FORMAL disquisition
2 SUBJECT, topic, theme, idea, opinion, view, theory, hypothesis, proposal, proposition, premise, statement, argument, contention, position
🖅 **2** antithesis

thick *adj, n*
♦ *adj*
1 WIDE, broad, fat, stout, chunky, heavy, bulky, deep, big, substantial, stiff, solid, dense, impenetrable, close, compact
2 FULL, packed, crowded, filled, overflowing, swarming, teeming, bristling, brimming, crawling, bursting, numerous, abounding, abundant
COLLOQ. chock-a-block, chocker
3 *a thick soup*
semi-solid, heavy, concentrated, condensed, viscous, coagulated, creamy, lumpy, clotted
4 *thick clothes*
heavy, warm, woollen, chunky, bulky
5 *thick fog*
impenetrable, dense, heavy, murky, smoggy, soupy, opaque, concentrated
6 *a thick voice*
husky, rough, unclear, indistinct, throaty, guttural, hoarse, croaky, croaking, gruff, gravelly, rasping
7 *a thick accent*
strong, pronounced, broad, marked, definite, obvious, noticeable, striking
8 STUPID, foolish, slow, unintelligent, dense, dull, brainless, simple
COLLOQ. dim-witted, dumb, gormless, dopey, daft, dippy, thick as a plank/two short planks
🖅 **1** thin, slim, slender, slight **2** sparse **3** clear, watery **4** thin, light, lightweight **6** clear, distinct **7** faint, vague **8** clever, intelligent; *colloq.* brainy
♦ *n*
middle, centre, focus, midst, hub, heart

thicken *v*
1 *thicken a soup*
make/become more solid, solidify, stiffen, condense, congeal, coagulate, curdle, clot, cake, gel, jell, set, reduce;
Scot meal
TECHNICAL upset
OLD incrassate, inspissate

Types of therapy include:

acupressure	cognitive therapy	expressive therapy	horticulture	osteopathy	reminiscence
acupuncture	confrontation	faith healing	therapy	phototherapy	therapy
Alexander	therapy	family therapy	hydrotherapy	physiotherapy	*colloq.* retail
technique	craniosacral	Gestalt therapy	hypnotherapy	play therapy	therapy
aromatherapy	therapy (CST)	group therapy	irradiation	primal therapy	Rolfing
art therapy	drama therapy	heat treatment	lymphatic drainage	psychoanalysis	sex therapy
aversion therapy	dream analysis	herbalism	therapy (LDT)	psychotherapy	shiatsu
beauty therapy	drug therapy	homeopathy	moxibustion	radiotherapy	speech therapy
behaviour therapy	electroconvulsive	hormone-	music therapy	reflexology	ultrasound
biofeedback	(or electroshock)	replacement	naturopathy	regression therapy	zone therapy
chemotherapy	therapy	therapy (HRT)	occupational	reiki	
chiropractic	electrotherapy		therapy		

2 *the plot thickens*
become more mysterious/complicated/involved/intricate
🖃 **1** thin

thicket *n*
wood, copse, coppice, grove, spinney, maquis

thickhead *n*
fool, idiot, dunce, imbecile
COLLOQ. nitwit, twit, numskull, fathead, blockhead, dimwit, dope, clot, dummy, pinhead, chump, moron, nincompoop, ninny, twerp, oaf, halfwit, buffoon
SLANG prat, dork, geek, git, berk; (*taboo*) dickhead

thick-headed *adj*
stupid, foolish, dense, slow, brainless, obtuse, dull-witted, idiotic, imbecilic, moronic, asinine, doltish, slow-witted
COLLOQ. dim-witted, blockheaded, dopey, thick, gormless, dumb, not all there, loopy, barmy, potty, slow on the uptake, thick as a plank/two short planks
SLANG loony
🖃 clever, intelligent, sharp; *colloq.* brainy

thickness *n*
1 WIDTH, breadth, diameter, extent, density, viscosity, consistency, bulk, bulkiness, body, solidness, closeness
2 LAYER, stratum, seam, vein, band, deposit, bed, ply, sheet, coat, film, lamina
🖃 **1** thinness

thickset *adj*
stocky, heavy, heavily built, well-built, sturdy, powerful, strong, muscular, burly, beefy, brawny, solid, bulky, squabby, squat, dense
🖃 lanky

thick-skinned *adj*
insensitive, unfeeling, callous, tough, invulnerable, hardened, case-hardened, inured, impervious
COLLOQ. hard-boiled, hard-nosed, tough as old boots
🖃 thin-skinned, sensitive, vulnerable

thief *n*
robber, bandit, pickpocket, shoplifter, burglar, housebreaker, crook, highwayman, plunderer, poacher, stealer, pilferer, kleptomaniac, fraud, fraudster, swindler, embezzler, brigand, larcener, snatch-purse, sneak, coon, knight of industry, land-rat, river-rat, area-sneak, Autolycus, nut-hook; *dialect* limmer
OLD abactor, footpad, water thief, bulker; (*Shakesp*) lifter
COLLOQ. mugger, filcher, nicker, nobbler, hotter
SLANG tea leaf, chummy, kiddy; *N Am* ice man
OLD SLANG snow-dropper, snow-gatherer; (*Shakesp*) prig

thieve *v*
steal, rob, pinch, cheat, swindle, make/run off with, misappropriate, burgle, embezzle, pilfer, plunder, poach, abstract
FORMAL peculate, purloin
COLLOQ. nobble, snaffle, filch, knock off, lift, nick, swipe, whip, bag
SLANG rip off, heist, hoist, pull, blag, lag

thieving *n, adj*
◆ *n*
stealing, theft, robbery, burglary, pilferage, pilfering, shoplifting, plundering, embezzlement, larceny, thievery, banditry, crookedness, piracy
FORMAL peculation
COLLOQ. mugging, knocking off, ripping off, lifting, nicking, filching
◆ *adj*
dishonest, fraudulent, crooked, light-fingered, larcenous, predatory
OLD furacious; (*Shakesp*) pugging
FORMAL rapacious
COLLOQ. sticky-fingered

thievish *adj*
dishonest, fraudulent, crooked, light-fingered, thieving, larcenous, predatory
OLD furacious

FORMAL rapacious
COLLOQ. sticky-fingered

thin *adj, v*
◆ *adj*
1 LEAN, slim, slender, fine, light, svelte, narrow, paper-thin, wafer-thin, attenuated, slight, skinny, bony, skeletal, scraggy, scrawny, spindly, lanky, gaunt, spare, anorexic, wasted, shrunken, underweight, undernourished, emaciated
COLLOQ. thin as a rake, size-zero
2 *thin fabric*
fine, delicate, light, lightweight, flimsy, filmy, gauzy, gossamer, sheer, see-through, transparent, translucent
FORMAL diaphanous
3 SPARSE, scarce, scattered, scant, paltry, meagre, poor, inadequate, deficient, scanty, skimpy, straggly, wispy
4 WEAK, feeble, runny, watery, diluted, dilute
COLLOQ. wishy-washy
5 *the evidence is thin*
weak, flimsy, unconvincing, implausible, insubstantial, feeble, lame, inadequate, inconclusive, untenable, defective, deficient
6 *a thin voice/sound*
high-pitched, soft, quiet, weak, faint
🖃 **1** fat, broad **2** substantial, thick, dense, solid **3** thick, plentiful, abundant **4** strong, thick **5** strong, convincing, substantial
◆ *v*
1 DIMINISH, reduce, dwindle, decrease, lessen, make/become less in number, trim, narrow, weed out
FORMAL attenuate
2 WEAKEN, dilute, make more watery, water down, rarefy, refine
■ **on thin ice**
precarious, unsafe, at risk, vulnerable, insecure, in jeopardy, open to attack

---

SYNONYM NUANCES

adjective sense 1
Lean can be used positively to suggest an athletic thinness. Also complimentary-sounding, but usually used of women, are **slim** and **slender**, which suggest an attractively shaped figure, and **svelte**, which suggests sleekness. **Narrow**, on the other hand, is more straightforwardly descriptive of width: *a narrow waist*, while **attenuated** is more appropriate to suggest being elongated: *an attenuated El Greco face*.
   Slight returns to the idea of a dainty build, and is not particularly suggestive of any point of view, but **skinny**, **bony** and **skeletal** all suggest an extreme and unattractive lack of flesh, and are uncomplimentary in tone: *his skeletal fingers*. **Scraggy** and **scrawny** are similar, but more suggestive of resultant stretched skin: *her scrawny neck*. You can use **spindly** and **lanky** to suggest an awkward ungainliness, whereas **gaunt** creates an unattractive image of a pinched face.
   Spare returns to the idea of having no excess flesh and is not judgemental: *a spare man, in middle age*, unlike **underweight** and **undernourished**, which are more technical in tone and suggest an unhealthy look. This is more explicit in the rather more emotive terms **anorexic**, **wasted** and **emaciated**, implying seriously debilitating conditions. **Shrunken** has more to do with having contracted, and again is associated with ill health: *his grey and shrunken face dwarfed by the pillow.*

---

thing *n*
1 ARTICLE, item, object, entity, creature, body, substance
2 DEVICE, contrivance, gadget, tool, implement, instrument, apparatus, machine, mechanism, waldo
COLLOQ. gismo, doodah, thingy, thingummy, thingamy, thingummyjig, thingummybob, what-d'you-call-it, whatsit, what's-its-name; *S Afr* dinges

3 *take your things with you*
clothes, clothing, garments, belongings, possessions, paraphernalia, goods, luggage, baggage, equipment, tools, apparatus, tackle, oddments, odds and ends, bits and pieces
FORMAL apparel, attire, effects
COLLOQ. stuff, gear, togs, bits and bobs, clobber
4 ASPECT, detail, particular, characteristic, trait, feature, quality, property, factor, element, attribute, point, fact, concept, notion, thought, idea
5 ACT, deed, feat, exploit, action, activity, undertaking, job, chore, task, responsibility, problem
6 CIRCUMSTANCE, situation, eventuality, happening, occurrence, event, episode, matter, incident, phenomenon, affair, proceeding, arrangement, condition
7 OBSESSION, preoccupation, fixation, *idée fixe*, fetish, mania, phobia, dislike, fear, horror, aversion
COLLOQ. hang-up, one-track mind
8 LIKING, fondness, love, affection, preference, partiality, affinity, taste, attraction, appreciation, proneness, inclination, tendency, bias, leaning, bent, desire, weakness, fancy
FORMAL predilection, penchant, propensity, proclivity
COLLOQ. soft spot
9 *computers are his thing*
speciality, what you like, what interests you
COLLOQ. cup of tea, baby, bag, what turns you on, what floats your boat, what lights your candle
■ **the thing**
fashionable, popular, in fashion, in vogue, current, latest, modish
COLLOQ. the latest, all the rage, hip, cool

> **PROVERBS**
> You can have too much of a good thing
> Little things please little minds

think *v, n*
♦ *v*
1 BELIEVE, hold, consider, regard, judge, esteem, estimate, reckon, calculate, determine, conclude, reason
FORMAL deem, opine
COLLOQ. figure, reckon
2 CONCEIVE, imagine, suppose, guess, presume, expect, foresee, envisage, visualize, anticipate
OLD conceit
FORMAL surmise, conjecture
3 *think it over*
ponder, mull over, chew over, brood, ruminate, meditate, contemplate, muse, reflect, concentrate, deliberate, weigh up, recall, review, take stock, recollect, remember
FORMAL cogitate, cerebrate
COLLOQ. sleep on it
♦ *n*
consideration, contemplation, deliberation, muse, ponder, reflection, meditation, assessment, evaluation
FORMAL cogitation
■ **think better of**
change your mind about, think again, think twice, reconsider, rethink, revise, have second thoughts about, decide not to do
COLLOQ. get cold feet
■ **think much of**
think highly of, admire, esteem, prize, respect, value, set store by, rate
E3 abominate
■ **think nothing of**
consider normal, consider usual, take in your stride, have no qualms about
■ **think over**
reflect upon, consider, weigh up, contemplate, meditate, ponder, chew over, ruminate, mull over
■ **think up**
devise, contrive, dream up, imagine, conceive, visualize, invent, design, create, concoct

> **SYNONYM NUANCES**
>
> *verb sense 3*
> You can use **ponder**, **mull over** and **chew over** to suggest turning a matter over in your mind, while **brood** implies less focused thought, and a degree of moroseness. **Ruminate**, **meditate** and **contemplate**, on the other hand, suggest intense thought and consideration, while **muse** and **reflect** would be appropriate of a mental aside: *what a daft world this is, he mused.*
> **Concentrate**, however, suggests focusing strongly on a particular matter, whereas **deliberate** has implications of lengthy and careful thought with the purpose of arriving at an answer: *the jury deliberated for five days.* Similarly, **weigh up** suggests looking at the benefits and disadvantages of a situation, and **take stock** and **review** also suggest careful judgement, but after looking back over past events.

thinkable *adj*
likely, imaginable, possible, feasible, reasonable, supposable, conceivable
FORMAL cogitable
E3 unthinkable

thinker *n*
philosopher, scholar, theorist, ideologist, intellect, sage, mastermind
FORMAL theoretician
COLLOQ. brain

thinking *n, adj*
♦ *n*
reasoning, philosophy, thought(s), conclusion(s), theory, idea, opinion, view, outlook, position, judgement, assessment, evaluation, appraisal
♦ *adj*
reasoning, rational, sensible, intellectual, intelligent, cultured, sophisticated, philosophical, analytical, logical, reflective, contemplative, meditative, thoughtful

thin-skinned *adj*
sensitive, easily upset, snappish, soft, susceptible, tender, vulnerable, hypersensitive, irritable, touchy
E3 thick-skinned, unfeeling, callous

third-rate *adj*
low-grade, low-quality, poor, poor-quality, bad, awful, inferior, substandard, unsatisfactory, mediocre, indifferent, slipshod, shoddy, cheap and nasty
COLLOQ. not up to scratch, terrible, botched, lousy, crummy, pathetic, rop(e)y, useless, a load of rubbish/garbage
SLANG the pits, pants, poxy, naff, crappy; *(vulgar)* a load of crap/shit
E3 first-rate

thirst *n, v*
♦ *n*
1 THIRSTINESS, dryness, drought, parchedness, aridity, drouth, drouthiness
OLD thrist
2 DESIRE, longing, yearning, hankering, craving, hunger, appetite, lust, passion, eagerness, keenness
COLLOQ. yen
♦ *v*
hunger, desire, want, long, yearn, hanker, crave, lust
COLLOQ. have a yen for

thirsty *adj*
1 DRY, dehydrated, arid, droughty, drouthy
OLD athirst, hydropic
COLLOQ. parched, gasping
2 *thirsty for knowledge*
desirous, longing, yearning, hankering, craving, hungry, thirsting, burning, itching, dying, eager, keen, avid, greedy, athirst

thong *n*
band, strip, belt, cord, lash, strap

thorn *n*
spike, point, barb, prickle, spine, bristle, needle, acantha; *S Afr* doorn
TECHNICAL aculeus
OLD prick
Related adjective: spiniform

thorny *adj*
1 SPIKY, pointed, sharp, barbed, prickly, spiny, bristly, armed, briery
FORMAL acanthous, spinous, spinose
2 *a thorny problem*
difficult, troublesome, irksome, vexed, worrying, trying, upsetting, problematic, knotty, complex, intricate, tough, awkward, delicate, tricky, ticklish
FORMAL convoluted
COLLOQ. dicey, sticky

thorough *adj*
1 *a thorough person*
painstaking, scrupulous, meticulous, careful, conscientious, efficient, methodical
2 *thorough research*
sweeping, all-embracing, comprehensive, rigorous, in-depth, all-inclusive, exhaustive, scrupulous, meticulous, extensive, deep, thoroughgoing, intensive, widespread
3 *a thorough waste of time*
full, complete, total, entire, utter, absolute, perfect, pure, sheer, unqualified, unmitigated, out-and-out, downright
E∃ **1** superficial, careless **2** partial

thoroughbred *adj*
pedigree, pedigreed, pure-blood, pure-blooded, full-blooded, blooded
E∃ cross-bred, hybrid, mixed, mongrel

thoroughfare *n*
road, street, roadway, way, highway, avenue, motorway, passage, passageway, access, turnpike, boulevard, concourse

thoroughgoing *adj*
1 *a thoroughgoing Socialist*
full, complete, total, entire, utter, absolute, perfect, pure, sheer, unqualified, unmitigated, out-and-out, downright, uncompromising
2 *thoroughgoing reform/research*
sweeping, all-embracing, comprehensive, rigorous, in-depth, all-inclusive, exhaustive, scrupulous, extensive, deep, thoroughgoing, intensive, widespread, meticulous, painstaking, careful, methodical

thoroughly *adv*
1 CAREFULLY, painstakingly, meticulously, scrupulously, intensively, conscientiously, assiduously, efficiently, comprehensively, sweepingly, exhaustively, root and branch, inside out
2 FULLY, perfectly, completely, absolutely, downright, entirely, quite, totally, utterly, soundly
OLD throughly
COLLOQ. every inch, with a fine-tooth comb
E∃ **1** carelessly, haphazardly **2** partially

though *conj, adv*
♦ *conj*
although, even if, while, allowing, granted
FORMAL notwithstanding
♦ *adv*
however, but, nevertheless, nonetheless, yet, still, even so, for all that
COLLOQ. all the same

thought *n*
1 THINKING, attention, care, heed, regard, consideration, reasoning, study, scrutiny, introspection, meditation, pondering, contemplation, musing, rumination, reflection, deliberation
OLD conceit
FORMAL cogitation, cerebration

2 IDEA, notion, concept, conception, belief, conviction, opinion, view, point of view, feeling, judgement, theory, assessment, estimation, appraisal, conclusion, plan, design, intention, purpose, reason, aim, hope, dream, prospect, expectation, anticipation, aspiration
OLD conceit
3 THOUGHTFULNESS, consideration, kindness, care, concern, regard, compassion, sympathy, tenderness, gesture, touch
FORMAL solicitude

> **QUOTATIONS**
> To be able to be caught up into the world of thought –
> that is educated
>   EDITH HAMILTON

thoughtful *adj*
1 PENSIVE, wistful, dreamy, abstracted, reflective, contemplative, introspective, thinking, absorbed, studious, serious, solemn, quiet, lost in thought, deep, profound, sobering, *pensieroso*
OLD (*Spenser*) conceitful
FORMAL cogitative
COLLOQ. in a brown study
2 CONSIDERATE, kind, unselfish, helpful, caring, compassionate, sympathetic, tender, attentive, mindful, careful, methodical, prudent, cautious, wary
FORMAL heedful, solicitous
E∃ **2** thoughtless, insensitive, selfish

thoughtfully *adv*
1 PENSIVELY, wistfully, dreamily, reflectively, contemplatively, introspectively, seriously, quietly, deeply, profoundly
2 CONSIDERATELY, unselfishly, helpfully, compassionately, sympathetically, carefully, methodically, mindfully, cautiously
E∃ **2** inconsiderately, thoughtlessly

thoughtless *adj*
1 INCONSIDERATE, unthinking, insensitive, unfeeling, tactless, undiplomatic, indiscreet, unkind, rude, impolite, selfish, uncaring
OLD (*Shakesp*) unweighing
FORMAL incogitant
2 ABSENT-MINDED, inattentive, heedless, mindless, foolish, stupid, silly, rash, hasty, reckless, ill-considered, ill-advised, unwise, imprudent, careless, negligent, remiss, vain, improvident, frivolous, giddy-headed, light-headed, blindfold, *étourdi(e)*
FORMAL precipitate
E∃ **1** thoughtful, considerate **2** careful

thoughtlessly *adv*
inconsiderately, insensitively, unfeelingly, tactlessly, undiplomatically, indiscreetly, impolitely, rudely, inattentively, foolishly, stupidly, carelessly, recklessly, rashly
E∃ thoughtfully, carefully

thrall *n*
thraldom, power, control, bondage, enslavement, servitude, slavery, subjection, serfdom, vassalage, hands, grip, clutches
FORMAL subjugation
E∃ freedom

thrash *v*
1 PUNISH, beat, whip, lash, flog, scourge, cane, spank, clobber, lay into
COLLOQ. wallop, tan, whack, belt
SLANG *N Am* lam; *S Afr* donder
2 DEFEAT, beat, trounce, drub, be more than a match for, have the edge on, crush, overwhelm, rout
FORMAL vanquish
COLLOQ. hammer, slaughter, clobber, lick, pound, demolish, wipe the floor with, walk all over
SLANG take to the cleaners
3 THRESH, flail, hit, flog, toss, jerk, swish, writhe

■ **thrash out**
discuss, debate, negotiate, hammer out, settle, resolve, clear the air

thrashing n
1 PUNISHMENT, flogging, lashing, caning, hiding, beating, tanning, whipping, leathering, pasting
FORMAL chastisement
COLLOQ. belting
2 DEFEAT, drubbing, beating, rout, crushing, trouncing, lamming
COLLOQ. hammering, clobbering, licking

thread n, v
♦ n
1 YARN, strand, fibre, filament, string, line, strip, streak
Related adjective: fibrillary, fibrillous
2 COURSE, direction, drift, tenor, theme, subject, motif, plot, storyline, train of thought
♦ v
pass, ease, move, push, inch, meander, wind, string, weave

Types of thread and wool include:

THREAD:	mercerized cotton	chunky wool
button thread	metallic thread	crewel wool
coton à broder	pearl cotton	double-knitting
cotton	polyester	wool
embroidery silk	purl	embroidery wool
embroidery	quick-match	knitting wool
thread	silk	Persian wool
floss	stranded cotton	tapestry wool
machine		2-ply
embroidery	**WOOL:**	3-ply
thread	Arran wool	4-ply
machine twist	baby wool	

---

threadbare adj
1 *threadbare clothes*
worn, frayed, ragged, moth-eaten, scruffy, tatty, tattered, shabby
2 HACKNEYED, overused, old, stale, tired, trite, worn-out, well-worn, cliché-ridden, commonplace, stock, stereotyped
COLLOQ. corny
🖪 **1** new **2** fresh

threat n
menace, warning, ultimatum, omen, foreboding, danger, risk, hazard, peril, blackmail, denunciation, enemy at the door, gunboat diplomacy, war drum, *brutum fulmen*
FORMAL portent, presage, commination
COLLOQ. stick, big stick

threaten v
1 MENACE, intimidate, browbeat, cow, pressurize, bully, extort, blackmail, terrorize, warn (off), endanger, jeopardize, imperil, flank, lift a/your hand to; *Scot* shore
OLD comminate
COLLOQ. push around, lean on, put the frighteners on, put the screws on
2 BE IMMINENT, be in the offing, approach, loom (up), forebode, foreshadow, impend, hang over, look like
FORMAL portend, presage, augur, comminate

threatening adj
menacing, intimidatory, warning, cautionary, ominous, foreboding, sinister, grim, looming
FORMAL inauspicious, impending, minacious, minatory, comminative

threesome n
trio, trilogy, triple, triplet, triumvirate, triad, triune, troika, trinity, triptych

thresh v
thrash, flail, hit, flog, toss, jerk, swish, writhe

threshold n
doorstep, sill, doorway, door, entrance, entry, brink, verge, starting-point, dawn, beginning, start, commencement, outset, opening
FORMAL inception

thrift n
economy, husbandry, prudence, saving, conservation, frugality, carefulness
FORMAL parsimony
COLLOQ. scrimping and saving
🖪 extravagance, waste

thriftless adj
extravagant, lavish, spendthrift, unthrifty, imprudent, wasteful, prodigal
FORMAL improvident, dissipative, profligate
🖪 thrifty

thrifty adj
economical, saving, frugal, sparing, prudent, careful, conserving, provident, husbandly;
Scot fendy
OLD wary
FORMAL parsimonious
🖪 extravagant, profligate, prodigal, wasteful, thriftless, unthrifty

thrill n, v
♦ n
excitement, adventure, pleasure, delight, joy, stimulation, charge, sensation, feeling, glow, tingle, throb, frisson, shudder, flutter, vibration, quiver, tremor, bang, pulse;
Scot dinnle
COLLOQ. kick, buzz, the shivers
SLANG charge; *N Am* gas
♦ v
excite, exhilarate, rouse, arouse, move, stir, stimulate, electrify, galvanize, flush, glow, tingle, throb, shudder, flutter, vibrate, tremble, shiver, quiver, shake, pulsate;
dialect thirl; *Scot* dirl
COLLOQ. give a buzz/kick to
🖪 bore

thrilling adj
exciting, stimulating, stirring, rousing, riveting, sensational, exhilarating, gripping, electrifying, rip-roaring, heart-stirring, soul-stirring, shaking, shuddering, shivering, trembling, vibrating, quaking, tinglish
COLLOQ. hair-raising, action-packed

thrive v
flourish, prosper, boom, grow, increase, advance, develop, bloom, blossom, gain, profit, succeed, do well, make progress, make headway
FORMAL burgeon
🖪 languish, stagnate, fail, die

thriving adj
prosperous, successful, blossoming, booming, developing, flourishing, growing, healthy, wealthy, affluent, well, comfortable, blooming
FORMAL burgeoning
🖪 ailing, failing, languishing, stagnating, dying

throat n
throttle, windpipe, gullet, gorge, oesophagus, craw, thropple, fauces, halse; *Scot* thrapple
TECHNICAL trachea, pharynx
OLD weasand
COLLOQ. the Red Lane
Related adjectives: guttural, pharyngeal, jugular

throaty adj
guttural, hoarse, rasping, raucous, low, husky, deep, gruff, thick

throb v, n
♦ v
pulse, pulsate, beat, palpitate, vibrate, pound, thump, drum, jump, tingle, stound
OLD quop

♦ *n*
pulse, pulsation, beat, heartbeat, palpitation, vibration, pant, pounding, thumping, drumming

throe *n*
convulsion, fit, pain, pang, paroxysm, seizure, spasm, stab, suffering, distress, agony, anguish, torture
FORMAL travail
■ **in the throes of**
struggling with, wrestling with, deeply involved in, busy with, preoccupied with, in the process of, in the middle of, in the midst of

thrombosis *n*
heart attack, coronary, coronary thrombosis, blood clot, apoplexy

throng *n, v*
♦ *n*
crowd, mass, mob, multitude, pack, press, crush, jam, swarm, flock, congregation, herd, bevy, horde, host; *Scot* thrang
FORMAL assemblage, *grex venalium*
♦ *v*
flock, fill, crowd, cram, converge, herd, press, swarm, pack, bunch, congregate, jam, besiege; *Scot* thrang
OLD press
COLLOQ. mill around

throttle *v*
1 STRANGLE, strangulate, choke, asphyxiate, suffocate, smother, stifle, scrag, thropple
2 SUPPRESS, gag, silence, inhibit, restrain, check, keep in, hold back, strangle, stifle, smother

through *prep, adv, adj*
♦ *prep*
1 ACROSS, all the way across, from one side of to the other, from one end of to the other
2 BETWEEN, by, with the help of, via, by way of, by means of, using, through the agency of
FORMAL through the good offices of, by virtue of
3 *all through the night*
throughout, during, in, to/until the end of, from the beginning to the end of, without a break/interruption in
4 BECAUSE OF, as a result of, owing to, due to, thanks to, on account of, by virtue of
♦ *adv*
1 ALL THE WAY ACROSS, from one side to the other, from one end to the other
OLD throughly
2 FROM BEGINNING TO END, from start to finish, from wire to wire, during the whole time, continuously, uninterruptedly
OLD throughly
3 *warmed/soaked through*
thoroughly, completely, fully, entirely, totally
♦ *adj*
1 FINISHED, ended, completed, done, no longer having anything to do with, no longer involved with
FORMAL terminated
2 *through train*
direct, express, non-stop
■ **through and through**
completely, totally, thoroughly, utterly, wholly, entirely, fully, unreservedly, in every respect, altogether, to the core, from top to bottom

throughout *adv, prep*
♦ *adv*
everywhere, in every part, extensively, widely, completely, from beginning to end
FORMAL ubiquitously
♦ *prep*
1 DURING, during/in the whole of, all through, in the course of, for the duration of
2 IN ALL PARTS, in every part of, all over, all round, everywhere

throughput *n*
output, production, productivity, product, manufacture, yield, fruits, harvest, return, outturn, turnout

throw *v, n*
♦ *v*
1 HURL, heave, lob, pitch, sling, cast, fling, flip, toss, shy, launch, project, propel, catapult, send
COLLOQ. chuck; *Irish* puck
2 MOVE QUICKLY, fling, turn, force, put, cast
3 *throw light*
shed, cast, project, send, direct, cause to fall, emit, radiate, give off
4 BRING DOWN, floor, fell, prostrate, upset, overturn, dislodge, unseat, unsaddle, unhorse
5 *throw a switch*
put on, switch on, operate, work
6 PERPLEX, baffle, confound, disturb, put out, confuse, disconcert, surprise, astonish, dumbfound
FORMAL discomfit
COLLOQ. floor, faze, rattle
7 *throw a party*
arrange, organize, give, put on, lay on, host
♦ *n*
heave, lob, pitch, sling, fling, flip, toss, cast
COLLOQ. chuck
■ **throw away**
1 DISCARD, jettison, get rid of, reject, scrap, dispose of, throw out
FORMAL dispense with
COLLOQ. dump, ditch, chuck away/out
2 WASTE, lose, squander, fritter away
SLANG blow
E∃ 1 keep, preserve, salvage, rescue **2** exploit, make use of, capitalize on
■ **throw off**
shed, cast off, drop, abandon, shake off, free yourself from, get rid of, discard, divest, jettison, buck, elude, escape from
■ **throw out**
1 EVICT, turn out, expel, eject
COLLOQ. turf out
2 REJECT, discard, dismiss, turn down, jettison, throw away, scrap
FORMAL dispense with
COLLOQ. dump, ditch
3 EMIT, radiate, give off, emanate, exude, send out, diffuse, produce
4 MENTION, speak about, refer to, bring up, point out, introduce
■ **throw over**
abandon, desert, discard, drop, finish with, jilt, leave, reject
FORMAL forsake
COLLOQ. chuck, quit
■ **throw up**
1 VOMIT, bring up, spew, regurgitate, disgorge, retch, heave, gag
COLLOQ. puke, sick up, chuck up, fetch up
SLANG barf, upchuck; *Aust* chunder
2 ABANDON, resign, quit, leave
FORMAL relinquish, renounce
COLLOQ. chuck in, pack in, jack in

SYNONYM NUANCES

verb sense 1
You can use **hurl** to suggest a violent movement, while **heave** suggests the movement of something heavy and implies a degree of effort involved. **Lob**, on the other hand, implies a slow but effective underhand motion, whereas **pitch** often suggests a specific target. **Sling**, however, implies a much more casual aspect, and **fling** is equally haphazard: *she flung the cutlery on to the table.* **Cast** has overtones of a decisive or powerful action: *the die is cast; Adam and Eve were cast from Eden.*

The term **flip** is appropriate where a throw sends something spinning, while **toss** implies an upward movement, and again a casual one: *let's toss a coin*. You can use **launch** to suggest the provision of an initial force, and **project**, **propel** and **catapult** likewise suggest strongly driving something forward: *he propelled me off the terrace*.

throwaway *adj*
1 *throwaway comments*
careless, casual, offhand, passing, unemphatic, undramatic
2 *a throwaway product*
disposable, cheap, expendable, non-returnable, biodegradable

throwback *n*
reversion, return, retrogression, restoration, reinstatement, taking back

thrust *v, n*
♦ *v*
1 PUSH, shove, butt, ram, jam, wedge, stick, poke, prod, jab, lunge, pierce, stab, plunge, drive, press, force, impel, propel
2 IMPOSE, press, urge, force, inflict, burden, saddle, encumber, foist
♦ *n*
1 PUSH, shove, poke, prod, lunge, jab, ram, stab
2 DRIVE, motive, power, force, pressure, impetus, momentum
3 *the thrust of an argument*
gist, essence, drift, tenor, theme, message, point, force, substance

thud *n, v*
thump, clump, knock, clunk, clonk, smack, bash, crash, bang, thunder, bounce, dump, plod
COLLOQ. wallop, wham, flump

thug *n*
ruffian, tough, rough, roughneck, robber, bandit, killer, murderer, cut-throat, assassin, hoodlum, gangster, hooligan, villain, goonda; *N Am* plug-ugly; *S Afr* tsotsi
OLD phansigar
COLLOQ. mugger, yobbo
SLANG gorilla, cosh boy; *N Am* goon

thuggery *n*
violence, hooliganism, vandalism, brutality, abuse, viciousness, inhumanity, atrocity, foul play, murder, killing, butchery

thumb
■ **thumb through**
glance at, scan, skim, peruse, browse through, flick through, flip through, leaf through

thumbnail *adj*
short, brief, concise, pithy, quick, small, compact, succinct, miniature

thumbs-down *n*
refusal, rejection, disapproval, negation, rebuff, no, turn down
E3 thumbs-up

thumbs-up *n*
approval, affirmation, encouragement, acceptance, yes, sanction
COLLOQ. go-ahead, green light, OK
E3 thumbs-down

thump *v, n*
♦ *v*
1 HIT, strike, knock, punch, box, cuff, clout, smack, thrash, slap, rap, crash, bang, thud, batter, pound, cob, dump, pummel; *dialect* dad; *Scot* daud, dunt, paik
OLD bethump, ding, tund
COLLOQ. whack, thwack, wallop, bonk, whop
2 THROB, pound, hammer, beat, pulsate, palpitate

♦ *n*
knock, blow, punch, box, cuff, clout, smack, rap, crash, bang, thud, beat, throb, bump, clunk, souse; *dialect* dad, dunt; *Scot* paik
COLLOQ. whack, thwack, wallop, bonk

thumping *adj, adv*
♦ *adj*
big, enormous, great, intense, extreme, severe, immense, massive, huge, colossal, monumental, terrific, thundering, tremendous, impressive, mammoth, excessive, exorbitant, gigantic, towering, gargantuan, titanic
COLLOQ. whopping
E3 insignificant, petty, trivial; *colloq.* piddling
♦ *adv*
extremely, very, intensely, really, greatly, severely, unusually, remarkably, tremendously, highly
COLLOQ. seriously
SLANG mega

thunder *n, v*
♦ *n*
boom, reverberation, crash, crashing, bang, crack, clap, peal, rumble, roll, roar, outburst, blast, explosion
♦ *v*
1 BOOM, resound, reverberate, crash, bang, crack, clap, peal, rumble, roll, roar, blast
OLD intonate, upthunder; (*Spenser*) foulder
FORMAL fulminate
2 BELLOW, roar, yell, shout, bawl, cry, scream, shriek, howl, clamour, raise your voice
COLLOQ. holler

thundering *adj, adv*
♦ *adj*
great, enormous, excessive, remarkable, monumental, tremendous, unmitigated
FORMAL tonant, altitonant
♦ *adv*
extremely, very, intensely, really, greatly, severely, unusually

thunderous *adj*
booming, resounding, reverberating, roaring, rumbling, loud, noisy, deafening, tumultuous, ear-splitting

thunderstruck *adj*
stunned, shocked, staggered, amazed, astonished, astounded, dazed, dumbfounded, open-mouthed, paralysed, aghast, agape, petrified
COLLOQ. flabbergasted, floored, flummoxed, nonplussed, bowled over, knocked for six

thus *adv*
1 THEREFORE, so, consequently, then, accordingly
FORMAL hence, ergo
2 LIKE THIS, in this way, so, as follows
■ **thus far**
up to/till now, until now, so far, up to the present, up to this point

thwack *v, n*
♦ *v*
beat, strike, bash, hit, flog, smack, thump, slap, buffet, clout, cuff
COLLOQ. wallop, whack
♦ *n*
blow, bash, slap, thump, smack, cuff, buffet
COLLOQ. wallop, whack

thwart *v*
frustrate, foil, defeat, hinder, hamper, impede, obstruct, block, balk, check, baffle, stop, prevent, oppose, cross, nobble, forestall, pre-empt, snooker, spite, transverse, traverse, hogtie, thraw, clip someone's wings, put a spoke in someone's wheel, put the skids on/under; *N Am* crimp
COLLOQ. stymie
SLANG pip, stonker
E3 help, assist, aid

tic *n*
jerk, spasm, twitch, tic douloureux

tick *n, v*
 • *n*
1 CLICK, tap, stroke, beat, tock, tick-tock
OLD (*Shakesp*) jar
2 *wait a tick*
moment, instant, flash, second, minute, twinkling
COLLOQ. jiffy, mo, sec, trice
3 MARK, line, stroke; *N Am* check
 • *v*
1 MARK, indicate, choose, select; *N Am* check
2 CLICK, tap, beat
OLD jar
■ **tick off**
1 *tick off items on a list*
put a tick against, mark, indicate, select, pick; *N Am*
check (off)
2 SCOLD, chide, reprimand, rebuke, reproach, reprove
FORMAL upbraid
COLLOQ. tell off, take/pull apart, bawl out, bounce, carpet,
catch it, chew out, see off, give someone a ticking-off,
dress down, give someone a dressing-down, haul over the
coals, read the riot act to, give someone a rap over the
knuckles, give someone a flea in their ear, give someone
an earful, give someone a piece of your mind, shoot
down in flames, tear a strip off someone, throw the book
at, give someone some stick, go to town on, come down
on like a ton of bricks, give someone hell, rollick, pin
back someone's ears, talk like a Dutch uncle; *N Am* call
down; *Aust & NZ* go crook on/at
F3 2 praise, compliment

ticket *n*
pass, card, certificate, authorization, warrant, permit,
token, voucher, coupon, docket, stub, counterfoil, slip,
label, tag, sticker

tickle *v*
touch, stroke, excite, thrill, delight, please, gratify, amuse,
entertain, divert, interest, stimulate

ticklish *adj*
sensitive, touchy, delicate, thorny, awkward, problematic,
difficult, tricky, knotty, critical, risky, hazardous, precarious
COLLOQ. dodgy
F3 easy, simple, straightforward

tide *n, v*
 • *n*
1 CURRENT, ebb, flow, stream, flux, movement, sea, water,
flood
2 COURSE, movement, run, direction, drift, trend, tendency,
tenor, rising tide
■ **tide over**
help (through), assist, aid, see through, keep going, sustain,
help out

tidily *adv*
neatly, orderly, just so, systematically, methodically,
smartly, immaculately, in order, in place
F3 untidily, in a muddle, in a mess

tidings *n*
news, communication, report, bulletin, message, advice,
word, information, intelligence, greetings
COLLOQ. dope, gen

tidy *adj, v*
 • *adj*
1 NEAT, orderly, methodical, efficient, businesslike,
systematic, organized, in order, well-ordered, ordered,
uncluttered, clean, spick, spick-and-span, immaculate,
shipshape, smart, spruce, trim, well-groomed, well-kept,
kempt; *N Am* band-box,
COLLOW. tiddley
2 *a tidy sum*
large, substantial, siz(e)able, considerable, fair, respectable,
good, generous, ample
F3 1 untidy, messy, disorganized **2** small, insignificant
 • *v*
neaten, straighten (out), clear out, clear the decks,
declutter, do, straighten up, order, arrange, clean (up),

clear up, smarten, spruce up, groom, trim, brush up,
primp, slick; *dialect* fettle; *Scot* redd (up);
N Am square away

tie *v, n*
 • *v*
1 FASTEN, knot, fix, secure, moor, tether, attach, join,
connect, link, couple, unite, rope, lash, strap, lace, chain,
bind
2 RESTRAIN, restrict, confine, limit, curb, constrain, hamper,
impede, hinder, cramp, shackle
3 DRAW, be equal, be even, be neck and neck
COLLOQ. be all square
 • *n*
1 KNOT, fastening, link, band, bond, ribbon, lace, tape,
clip
2 CONNECTION, link, liaison, relationship, bond, friendship,
affiliation, allegiance, kinship
3 OBLIGATION, commitment, duty, restraint, constraint,
restriction, limit, limitation, hindrance
4 DRAW, dead heat, stalemate, deadlock
■ **tie down**
restrain, constrain, restrict, confine, limit, hamper, hinder
■ **tie in with**
be consistent with, be connected with, fit in with, relate
to, be associated with, agree with, correlate with
■ **tie up**
1 MOOR, tether, attach, fasten, secure, rope, lash, chain,
bind, connect, truss, wrap up, restrain
COLLOQ. do up
2 CONCLUDE, settle, finalize
FORMAL terminate
COLLOQ. wind up, wrap up
3 OCCUPY, engage, engross, keep busy
4 *tie up your money*
reserve, make unavailable, commit

tie-in *n*
connection, relationship, link, relation, co-ordination,
association, liaison, tie-up, affiliation
COLLOQ. hook-up

tier *n*
floor, storey, level, stage, layer, stratum, belt, zone, band,
echelon, rank, row, line, bank, deck, gradin; *N Am*
bleachers

tie-up *n*
connection, link, tie-in, association, bond, alliance,
relation, relationship, interrelation, parallel, correlation,
analogy, correspondence, reference

tiff *n*
disagreement, squabble, row, difference, difference of
opinion, quarrel, words, dispute, temper, ill-humour, sulk,
tantrum
COLLOQ. falling-out, huff, scrap, set-to, dust-up, pet,
barney, spat

tight *adj*
1 TAUT, stretched, tense, strained, rigid, stiff, firm, fixed,
fast, secure, close, cramped, clenched, constricted,
compressed, limited, restricted, narrow, compact, snug,
close-fitting, skin-tight, body-con, figure-hugging
2 SEALED, hermetic, soundproof, impervious, impenetrable,
airtight, watertight
3 *tight security*
strict, tough, firm, severe, stringent, rigorous, hard, harsh,
rigid, inflexible
4 *money is tight; a tight budget*
scarce, limited, insufficient, inadequate, scanty, too little,
not enough, in short supply
5 *a tight contest*
close, evenly matched, well-matched, even, hard-fought
COLLOQ. neck and neck
6 *in a tight corner/spot*
difficult, awkward, problematic, tricky, delicate
COLLOQ. dodgy
7 MEAN, stingy, miserly, niggardly, penny-pinching
FORMAL parsimonious

COLLOQ. tight-fisted
8 DRUNK, intoxicated, tipsy, under the influence
COLLOQ. sloshed, sozzled, plastered, tiddly, merry, well-oiled, legless
SLANG pissed, stoned, tanked up, smashed
F3 **1** loose, slack **2** open **3** lax **4** plentiful **6** easy **7** generous **8** sober

tighten v
1 *tighten a rope/hold*
tauten, stretch, pull tight, tense, stiffen, fix, fasten, make fast, secure, narrow, close, cramp, constrict, crush, squeeze, take in, wind up, pull up, screw, brace; *N Am* cinch
TECHNICAL swift, swig
OLD strait, straiten; (*Shakesp*) restrain
FORMAL rigidify, constringe
2 *tighten up the security/rules*
make stricter, make more rigorous, increase, heighten, toughen up, firm up, strengthen
COLLOQ. beef up
F3 **1** loosen **2** relax

tight-fisted adj
mean, stingy, miserly, niggardly, penny-pinching, sparing, grasping
FORMAL parsimonious
COLLOQ. mingy, tight
F3 generous, charitable

tight-lipped adj
silent, uncommunicative, unforthcoming, close-lipped, close-mouthed, quiet, reticent, taciturn, reserved, secretive, mum, mute
F3 talkative, forthcoming, garrulous

till[1] prep
till the end of June
until, up to, to, up to the time of, all through; *N Am* through

till[2] n
take money from the till
cash register, cash box, cash drawer, checkout

till[3] v
till the land
cultivate, work, plough, dig, farm

tilt v, n
♦ v
1 SLOPE, incline, slant, pitch, list, tip, lean, cant, bank, careen, cock, heel, rock, toss, trip
TECHNICAL peak
2 ATTACK, charge, rush, fight, contend, encounter, clash, duel, spar, joust
OLD jostle
♦ n
1 SLOPE, incline, angle, inclination, slant, pitch, list, bank
TECHNICAL attitude
2 ATTACK, charge, fight, contest, encounter, combat, clash, duel, spar, joust, tournament, *pas d'armes*
■ **at full tilt**
very quickly, very fast, at full speed, at top speed, at full blast, at full pelt, with full force
COLLOQ. all out, flat out

timber n
1 WOOD, trees, forest; *N Am* lumber
2 BEAM, lath, plank, pole, spar, board, log

timbre n
quality, voice quality, tone, tonality, sound, resonance, ring, colour
TECHNICAL klang

time n, v
♦ n
1 SPELL, stretch, period, term, season, session, span, duration, interval, space, while
2 TEMPO, beat, rhythm, metre, measure
3 MOMENT, point, juncture, stage, instance, instant, occasion, date

4 AGE, era, epoch, life, lifetime, lifespan, generation, heyday, peak
Related adjective: temporal
♦ v
1 ARRANGE, set, schedule, programme, timetable, fix
2 MEASURE, clock, calculate, count, meter, regulate, control, adjust
■ **time after time**
repeatedly, frequently, often, recurrently, many times, on many occasions, time and (time) again, again and again, over and over again
■ **ahead of time**
in advance, early, beforehand, previously, earlier, sooner, ahead, in front
COLLOQ. up front
F3 later, behind
■ **ahead of your time**
new, innovative, novel, progressive, experimental, revolutionary, avant-garde, radical
■ **all the time**
continually, constantly, perpetually, incessantly, interminably, always, forever, all along
F3 never
■ **at one time**
once, formerly, previously, at one point, long ago, in times past
■ **at the same time**
1 SIMULTANEOUSLY, all together, in parallel
FORMAL concurrently
2 NEVERTHELESS, nonetheless, still, but, however, anyway, even so, for all that
■ **at times**
sometimes, on occasions, occasionally, from time to time, now and again, now and then, off and on, every so often
■ **behind time**
late, overdue, unpunctual, delayed, behind, behind schedule
FORMAL tardy
F3 early
■ **behind the times**
old-fashioned, oldfangled, out of date, dated, old, unfashionable, out of fashion, obsolete, past
COLLOQ. fuddy-duddy, old hat, past its sell-by date
F3 up to date
■ **for the time being**
at present, for now, right now, just now, at the moment, for the moment, for the present, at the present time, temporarily, (in the) meantime, meanwhile, pro tem
■ **from time to time**
now and again, now and then, at times, sometimes, occasionally, on occasion, once in a while, periodically, intermittently, spasmodically, sporadically, every now and then, every so often
F3 constantly, always
■ **in good time**
early, with time to spare, ahead of time, ahead of schedule, punctually, on time
F3 late
■ **in time**
not too late, early enough, punctually, on time
■ **on time**
punctually, promptly, exactly, precisely, sharp, on the dot
COLLOQ. dead on, bang on, spot-on
F3 late
■ **play for time**
delay, hesitate, stall, temporize, stonewall, hang fire, filibuster
FORMAL procrastinate
COLLOQ. drag your feet

PROVERBS
Time and tide wait for no man

Times and periods of time include:

afternoon	hour	p.m.
age	instant	quarter
a.m.	lifetime	quinquennium
autumn	light-year	season
bedtime	long-weekend	second
century	microsecond	spring
chiliad	midday	summer
dawn	midsummer	sunrise
day	midweek	sunset
daytime	millennium	sun-up
decade	millisecond	teatime
decennium	minute	today
dusk	moment	tomorrow
the early hours	month	tonight
eon	morn	twilight
epoch	morning	week
era	morrow	weekday
eternity	nanosecond	weekend
evening	night	*colloq.* wee small
N Am fall	nightfall	hours
fortnight	night-time	winter
generation	noon	year
high noon	period	yesteryear

---

time-honoured *adj*
age-old, traditional, long-established, usual, accustomed, conventional, customary, established, fixed, old, ancient, historic, venerable

timeless *adj*
ageless, immortal, deathless, everlasting, eternal, endless, permanent, lasting, enduring, changeless, unchanging, unending, indestructible, imperishable
FORMAL immutable, abiding

timely *adj*
well-timed, at the right time, seasonable, suitable, appropriate, convenient, opportune, prompt, punctual
FORMAL propitious, felicitous
E3 ill-timed, unsuitable, inappropriate

timetable *n, v*
♦ *n*
schedule, programme, agenda, calendar, diary, rota, roster, list, listing, curriculum
♦ *v*
schedule, programme, diarize, set (up), fix, arrange, list

time-worn *adj*
worn, old, aged, dog-eared, out of date, passé, outworn, worn out, ruined, well-worn, tired, trite, stock, stale, threadbare, bromidic, cliché(e)d, hackneyed, weathered, dated, decrepit, ancient, broken-down, run-down, shabby, ragged, hoary, wrinkled, lined
E3 fresh, new

timid *adj*
shy, bashful, modest, shrinking, retiring, nervous, apprehensive, timorous, afraid, scared, frightened, fearful, cowardly, faint-hearted, spineless, irresolute, mousey, lily-livered, chicken-hearted, chicken-livered, pigeon-hearted, hen-hearted, pavid
OLD meticulous
FORMAL pusillanimous

COLLOQ. chicken, yellow, gutless, wimpish, wimpy, cissy, afraid of your own shadow
E3 brave, bold, confident

timidity *n*
shyness, bashfulness, apprehensiveness, fear, fearfulness, cowardice
FORMAL pusillanimity
E3 braveness, boldness, confidence

timorous *adj*
shy, timid, bashful, afraid, fearful, scared, frightened, apprehensive, shrinking, retiring, faint-hearted, nervous, diffident, coy, tentative, irresolute, modest, unadventurous, cowardly, trembling
OLD aspen
FORMAL pusillanimous
COLLOQ. mous(e)y
E3 assertive, assured, bold

tincture *n, v*
♦ *n*
trace, flavour, touch, tinge, tint, colour, hint, hue, dash, suggestion, shade, stain, seasoning, smack, aroma
♦ *v*
flavour, scent, season, stain, tinge, tint, colour, dye, infuse, permeate, imbue, suffuse

tinge *n, v*
♦ *n*
1 TRACE, touch, suggestion, hint, smack, flavour, pinch, drop, dash, bit, sprinkling, smattering, tang
2 TINT, dye, colour, shade, wash, tincture, cast, tinct
OLD taint; (*Shakesp*) eye
♦ *v*
tint, dye, stain, colour, flavour, shade, suffuse, imbue, touch, encolour, tincture
OLD taint, tinct

tingle *v, n*
♦ *v*
sting, prickle, tickle, itch; prick, thrill, throb, tremble, quiver, vibrate
♦ *n*
stinging, prickling, tickle, tickling, itch, itching, thrill, tremor, throb, quiver, shiver, gooseflesh, goosepimples
COLLOQ. pins and needles

tinker *v, n*
♦ *v*
fiddle, play, toy, trifle, potter, dabble, meddle, fool about/around, tamper, tink
COLLOQ. mess about/around
♦ *n*
itinerant, Gypsy, traveller, fixer, mender, botcher, bungler, diddicoy, pedlar, hawker; *Scot* caird, (*derog*) tinkler, tink
OLD SLANG prig

tinkle *v, n*
♦ *v*
ring, ding, jingle, jangle, clink, chink, peal, chime
♦ *n*
1 *the tinkle of the bell*
ring, ding, jingle, jangle, clink, chink, peal, chime
2 *give you a tinkle*
ring, phone call, call
COLLOQ. buzz, bell

tinny *adj*
1 *tinny sounds*
metallic, jangling, jingly, harsh, jarring, high-pitched
2 *his tinny old car*
flimsy, insubstantial, thin, cheap, poor-quality, cheapjack

tinpot *adj*
inferior, substandard, second-rate, low-quality, mediocre, bad, poor, awful, unsatisfactory, insignificant, imperfect, defective, incompetent, slipshod, shoddy
COLLOQ. crummy, rop(e)y, useless, pathetic
E3 excellent

tinsel *adj, n*
* *adj*

showy, ostentatious, cheap, gaudy, tawdry, trashy, superficial, specious, gimcrack, sham
FORMAL meretricious
COLLOQ. flashy
* *n*

glitter, spangle, frippery, show, triviality, display, ostentation, flamboyance, garishness, gaudiness, sham, worthlessness, artificiality, meaninglessness, insignificance, pretension

tint *n, v*
* *n*

dye, stain, rinse, wash, colour, hue, shade, tincture, tinge, tone, cast, streak, trace, touch
* *v*

dye, colour, tinge, streak, stain, taint, affect

tiny *adj*

minute, microscopic, infinitesimal, minuscule, small, little, slight, trifling, negligible, insignificant, diminutive, petite, dwarfish, midget, pocket, miniature, Lilliputian; *Scot* wee
COLLOQ. pint-sized, mini, teensy, teeny, teeny-weeny, itsy-bitsy
🔁 huge, enormous, immense

tip¹ *n, v*
* *n*

the tip of a finger
end, extremity, point, nib, apex, peak, pinnacle, summit, acme, top, cap, crown, head
* *v*

cap, crown, top, surmount

tip² *v, n*
* *v*

tip your head
lean, incline, slant, list, tilt, cant, topple (over), capsize, upset, overturn, spill, pour (out), empty, unload, dump
* *n*

dump, rubbish-heap, refuse-heap, slag heap, midden

tip³ *n, v*
* *n*

1 HINT, pointer, clue, suggestion, advice, recommendation, warning, tip-off, information, inside information, forecast
2 GRATUITY, gift, bonus, reward, present, baksheesh, *pourboire*
FORMAL perquisite
COLLOQ. perk
* *v*

1 ADVISE, suggest, warn, caution, forewarn, tip off, inform, nap, tell
2 *tip the driver*
reward, remunerate

tip-off *n*

hint, pointer, clue, suggestion, warning, information, inside information

tipple *v, n*
* *v*

drink, imbibe, indulge, quaff, bib
COLLOQ. swig, booze, down, knock back
* *n*

drink, regular drink, favourite drink, alcohol, liquor
COLLOQ. booze, poison, usual

tippler *n*

drinker, hard drinker, drunk, drunkard, dipso(maniac), bibber, inebriate, winebag
COLLOQ. boozer, sponge
SLANG lush, soak, sot, toper, wino, alkie, dipso, piss artist, tosspot

tipsy *adj*

drunk, under the influence, mellow, merry, totty, muzzy, nappy, rocky, top-heavy, a peg too low, a pip out
COLLOQ. happy, squiffy, tiddly, tight, tiddled, woozy, the worse for wear, oiled, well-oiled, bosky, cockeyed, sprung, pleasant

OLD COLLOQ. glorious
SLANG lushy, moony, wet, screwed, slewed
🔁 sober

tirade *n*

harangue, diatribe, denunciation, abuse, lecture, admonishment, outburst, rant
FORMAL fulmination, invective, philippic

tire *v*

weary, fatigue, wear out, tire out, exhaust, tax, strain, drain, drop, flag, bore
FORMAL enervate
🔁 enliven, invigorate, refresh

tired *adj*

1 WEARY, drowsy, sleepy, flagging, fatigued, wearied, worn out, exhausted, dog-tired, drained, jaded, blown, outspent; *Scot* forjeskit, wabbit
OLD wappend; *(Shakesp)* fatigate
FORMAL enervated
COLLOQ. fagged out, bushed, whacked, shattered, beat, dead-beat, all in, knackered, clapped-out, rough, ready to drop, washed-out, hardly able to keep your eyes open, zonked; *N Am* pooped (out), tuckered out
SLANG *(taboo)* shagged out
2 *tired of waiting*
bored, sick; *Aust* jack
COLLOQ. fed up, sick and tired
3 HACKNEYED, old, stale, worn-out, trite, cliché(e)d
COLLOQ. corny, past its sell-by date
🔁 1 lively, energetic, rested, refreshed 3 new, original

SYNONYM NUANCES

sense 1
You can use **weary** to suggest having depleted reserves of vigour, while **drowsy** and **sleepy** are more appropriate for having an inclination to sleep. **Flagging**, on the other hand, suggests being unable to maintain your levels of energy: *even in old age he showed no signs of flagging*, whereas **fatigued** suggests that your physical or mental resources are almost expended.

Similarly, both **worn out** and **exhausted** imply having used up your strength, but perhaps more completely, while **drained** has also to do with being physically or emotionally spent: *she felt quite drained by the whole experience*. **Jaded**, however, has implications of suffering from over-indulgence or over-exposure to something: *after three years in the job she felt jaded*.

---

tireless *adj*

untiring, unwearied, unflagging, indefatigable, energetic, vigorous, diligent, industrious, resolute, determined
🔁 tired, lazy, unenthusiastic

tirelessly *adv*

untiringly, indefatigably, energetically, vigorously, diligently, resolutely
🔁 lazily, idly, unenthusiastically

tiresome *adj*

troublesome, trying, annoying, irritating, exasperating, irksome, vexatious, wearisome, dull, boring, routine, humdrum, tedious, monotonous, uninteresting, unexciting, tiring, fatiguing, laborious
🔁 interesting, stimulating, easy

tiring *adj*

wearying, wearisome, fatiguing, exhausting, draining, demanding, hard, tough, difficult, exacting, taxing, arduous, strenuous, laborious
FORMAL enervating

tiro, tyro *n*

beginner, novice, apprentice, freshman, learner, pupil, starter, student, trainee, tenderfoot, greenhorn, initiate, neophyte, novitiate, catechumen
🔁 veteran; *colloq.* old hand

tissue *n*

1 MATTER, substance, material

2 *a box of tissues*
paper handkerchief, disposable handkerchief, Kleenex®, facial tissue, toilet paper, toilet tissue
3 *tissue paper*
fabric, stuff, gauze, gossamer
4 *a tissue of lies*
web, mesh, network, structure, texture

titan *n*
colossus, giant, superman, Hercules, Atlas, leviathan

titanic *adj*
colossal, huge, enormous, massive, vast, immense, giant, gigantic, jumbo, mammoth, monumental, prodigious, stupendous, towering, mountainous, monstrous, herculean, cyclopean
FORMAL mighty
E3 insignificant, small

titbit *n*
morsel, scrap, appetizer, snack, delicacy, dainty, treat, bonne-bouche

tit for tat *n*
blow for blow, retaliation, revenge, requital, reprisal, measure for measure, counterblow, counterbuff, countercharge
FORMAL quid pro quo, *lex talionis*
COLLOQ. like for like, an eye for an eye (and a tooth for a tooth), a taste of your own medicine

tithe *n, v*
♦ *n*
tenth, tax, levy, duty, tariff, toll, tribute, rent, assessment, impost
♦ *v*
give, hand over, pay, take in, tax, assess, charge, levy, rate

titillate *v*
stimulate, arouse, excite, thrill, tickle, provoke, tease, tantalize, intrigue, interest
COLLOQ. turn on

titillating *adj*
stimulating, arousing, exciting, sexy, erotic, seductive, lewd, lurid, thrilling, provocative, sensational, suggestive, intriguing, interesting, teasing, captivating

titivate *v*
smarten up, touch up, refurbish, preen, make up, groom, primp, prink
COLLOQ. doll up, tart up

title *n, v*
♦ *n*
1 NAME, term, designation, form of address, label, epithet, nickname, so(u)briquet, pseudonym, *nom-de-plume*, rank, status, office, position
FORMAL appellation, denomination
COLLOQ. handle
SLANG monicker
Related adjective: titular
2 PUBLICATION, book, work
3 HEADING, headline, caption, legend, inscription, credit(s)
4 RIGHT, prerogative, privilege, claim, entitlement, ownership, proprietorship, deeds
5 CHAMPIONSHIP, match, contest, competition, game, prize, trophy, stakes, laurels, crown
♦ *v*
entitle, name, call, dub, style, term, designate, tag, label

titter *v, n*
♦ *v*
giggle, snigger, snicker, chuckle, cackle, laugh, chortle, mock
♦ *n*
giggle, snigger, snicker, chuckle, cackle, laugh, chortle

tittle-tattle *n, v*
♦ *n*
gossip, rumour, hearsay, chatter, babble, cackle, prattle; *Scot* blether; *dialect & N Am* blather
COLLOQ. chitchat, jaw, natter, twaddle, ya(c)k, yackety-yak

♦ *v*
gossip, chat, chatter, babble, cackle, prattle; *Scot* blether; *dialect & N Am* blather
COLLOQ. chitchat, tell tales, witter, jaw, rabbit on, natter, ya(c)k, yack-yack, yackety-yak

titular *adj*
nominal, in name only, token, so-called, self-styled, honorary, formal, official
FORMAL putative
COLLOQ. puppet

toadstool
See panel at **mushrooms and toadstools**.

toady *n, v*
♦ *n*
fawner, flatterer, sycophant, groveller, lackey, minion, parasite, flunkey, jackal
COLLOQ. yes-man, sucker, bootlicker, crawler, creep, hanger-on, truckler
SLANG (*vulgar*) arse-licker; *Aust* suck-hole; *N Am* suck-up
♦ *v*
curry favour, crawl, flatter, grovel, fawn, creep, cringe, kowtow
COLLOQ. bootlick, bow and scrape, butter up, kiss the feet, suck up, truckle

toast *v, n*
♦ *v*
1 *toast bread*
grill, brown, roast, crisp, bake, heat (up), warm (up), barbecue, scorch; *Scot* birsle, scouther
2 *toast the bride and groom*
drink to, drink the health of, honour, salute, pledge
♦ *n*
drink, pledge, tribute, salute, salutation, compliment(s), best wishes, health, sentiment, *brindisi*

Toasts include:

all the best!	good health!	here's to ...!
auf Ihre	good luck!	here's to you!
Gesundheit!	happy landings!	*prosit!*
à votre santé!	here's how!	skoal!
bottoms up!	here's looking at	*slàinte!*
cheers!	you!	to absent friends!
chin-chin!	here's mud in	your health!
down the hatch!	your eye!	

---

tobacco *n*
COLLOQ. baccy, the weed

Tobacco accessories include:

ashtray	cigarette roller	petrol lighter
box of matches	cigar holder	pipe
chibouk	clay pipe	pipe-cleaner
church-warden	gas lighter	pipe-light
cigar box	hookah	pipe rack
cigar case	humidor	pipe rest
cigar cutter	match	smoker's
cigarette box	matchbook	companion
cigarette case	match striker	snuffbox
cigarette holder	meerschaum	tobacco pipe
cigarette lighter	narghile	tobacco pouch
cigarette machine	peace pipe (pipe	vesta
cigarette paper	of peace)	

---

toboggan *n*
sledge, sleigh, slide, luge, bobsled, bobsleigh, skeleton bob, Ski-doo®, dray, kibitka, pulka; *Scot* hurly-hacket; *N Am* dogsled, train, travois
TECHNICAL slipe

today *n, adv*
♦ *n*
THIS DAY, the present day, this very day, the present time, this morning, this afternoon, this evening
♦ *adv*
AT THIS MOMENT, at this moment in time, now, right now, just now, at the present time, these days, nowadays

> **PROVERBS**
> Don't put off till tomorrow what you can do today

> **QUOTATIONS**
> Never do today what you can put off till tomorrow
> *Punch*

toddle *v*
walk/move unsteadily, totter, wobble, stagger, waddle, reel, lurch, stumble, falter, waver, teeter, sway, rock, shake

to-do *n*
commotion, fuss, furore, bother, disturbance, flurry, stir, tumult, turmoil, uproar, unrest, excitement, bustle, agitation, rumpus, ruction, quarrel
COLLOQ. performance, brouhaha, flap, hullabaloo, hoo-ha, stew

together *adv, adj*
♦ *adv*
1 UNITED, collectively, jointly, mutually, in concert, in unison, in company, working together, in collaboration, in conjunction, as one, as a partnership, as a team
2 *travel together*
side by side, shoulder to shoulder, hand in hand, in a row
3 SIMULTANEOUSLY, at the same time, at one time, all at once
FORMAL concurrently
4 CONTINUOUSLY, consecutively, successively, in succession, without a break, without interruption, on end
COLLOQ. on the trot, back to back
E3 1 separately, individually **2** alone
♦ *adj*
well-balanced, well-adjusted, stable, well-organized, organized, level-headed, sensible, down-to-earth, composed, calm, commonsensical
COLLOQ. cool, unflappable

toil *n, v*
♦ *n*
labour, hard work, slog, drudgery, sweat, slaving, industry, application, effort, exertion
COLLOQ. donkey-work, graft, elbow grease
♦ *v*
labour, work, slave, drudge, sweat, grind, push yourself, slog, persevere, strive, struggle
COLLOQ. graft, plug away, work like a Trojan, work your fingers to the bone

toiler *n*
worker, workaholic, drudge, grafter, slogger, struggler, slave, workhorse, labourer, menial, navvy
E3 idler, loafer, shirker

toilet *n*
lavatory, WC, bathroom, cloakroom, washroom, water closet, public convenience, convenience, urinal, latrine, powder room, the ladies', the gents', facilities, earth-closet, Elsan®, Portaloo®, lavabo; *N Am* rest room, comfort station
OLD reredorter, necessary
COLLOQ. loo, lav, dunny, smallest room, superloo, throne, little boys' room, little girls' room
SLANG bog, kazi, crapper, can, cottage, heads, thunderbox; *Scot* cludgie; *N Am* john; *Aust* toot
OLD SLANG dike

toilsome *adj*
difficult, hard, laborious, arduous, burdensome, backbreaking, fatiguing, painful, tough, wearisome, severe, strenuous, taxing, tedious, tiresome, uphill, herculean

token *n, adj*
♦ *n*
1 SYMBOL, emblem, representation, mark, sign, indication, demonstration, expression, evidence, proof, recognition, clue, warning, signal, index, reminder, remembrance, memorial, memento, souvenir, keepsake
FORMAL manifestation
2 *gift token*
voucher, coupon, counter, disc
♦ *adj*
symbolic, emblematic, nominal, slight, minimal, perfunctory, superficial, cosmetic, hollow, insincere

tolerable *adj*
1 BEARABLE, endurable, sufferable, acceptable
2 ACCEPTABLE, satisfactory, passable, adequate, reasonable, fair, fairly good, average, all right, mediocre, indifferent, unexceptional, ordinary, middling
COLLOQ. OK, so-so, run-of-the-mill, not bad, nothing (much) to write home about, no great shakes, not much cop
E3 1 intolerable, unbearable, insufferable

tolerably *adv*
reasonably, fairly, ordinarily, adequately, sufficiently, bearably, acceptably

tolerance *n*
1 TOLERATION, patience, forbearance, open-mindedness, broad-mindedness, liberalism, sympathy, good-humour, understanding, leniency, lenity, laxness, indulgence, permissiveness
FORMAL magnanimity
2 VARIATION, fluctuation, allowance, clearance
COLLOQ. play, give, swing
3 RESISTANCE, resilience, toughness, endurance, stamina
FORMAL fortitude
E3 1 intolerance, prejudice, bias, bigotry, narrow-mindedness

tolerant *adj*
patient, forbearing, long-suffering, open-minded, fair, unprejudiced, broad-minded, catholic, liberal, charitable, kind-hearted, sympathetic, understanding, forgiving, lenient, compliant, indulgent, permissive, easy-going, lax, soft, mellowed
FORMAL magnanimous
COLLOQ. decent
E3 intolerant, biased, prejudiced, bigoted, unsympathetic

tolerate *v*
endure, suffer, put up with, bear, stand, take, have, receive, accept, admit, allow, permit, warrant, sanction, condone, indulge, pardon; *dialect* abear; *Scot* thole
FORMAL abide, countenance
COLLOQ. stomach, swallow, wear

toleration *n*
1 PATIENCE, forbearance, open-mindedness, broad-mindedness, liberalism, sympathy, understanding, leniency, lenity, laxness, indulgence, permissiveness
FORMAL magnanimity
2 RESISTANCE, resilience, toughness, endurance, stamina
FORMAL fortitude
3 ACCEPTANCE, allowance, endurance, sufferance, sanction, indulgence

toll[1] *v*
the bell tolls
ring, peal, chime, knell, sound, strike, clang, announce, call, signal, warn, herald; *dialect* jowl; *Scot* jow

toll[2] *n*
1 *motorway tolls*
charge, fee, payment, levy, tax, duty, tariff, rate, cost, penalty, demand, tollage, due, pike; *N Am* streetage
TECHNICAL pontage, pierage, octroi
OLD scavage, tallage
2 *the casualty toll*
cost, loss, damage, injury, death

3 *take its toll*
adverse effect, cost, price, harm, damage, suffering, hardship

tomb *n*
grave, burial-place, vault, crypt, sepulchre, catacomb, mausoleum, cenotaph, shrine, marble, monument, sarcophagus, speos, tholus, heroon, hypogeum, mastaba, sacellum
TECHNICAL cist
OLD burial, reposit; *(Spenser)* funeral
Related adjective: sepulchral

tombstone *n*
gravestone, headstone, stone, memorial, memorial stone, monument, marble; *Scot* through-stone

tome *n*
book, volume, work, opus

tomfoolery *n*
mischief, horseplay, silliness, stupidity, messing about, carrying on, foolishness, childishness, idiocy, inanity, skylarking, clowning, buffoonery, hooey
COLLOQ. larking about, larks, shenanigans

tone *n, v*
◆ *n*
1 *tone of voice*
note, timbre, pitch, sound, quality, volume, expression, intonation, modulation, inflection, accent, accentuation, stress, emphasis, force, strength
2 TINT, tinge, colour, hue, shade, cast, tonality, tincture
3 AIR, manner, attitude, mood, spirit, humour, temper, character, quality, feel, style, effect, vein, tenor, drift
Related adjective: tonal
◆ *v*
match, co-ordinate, suit, blend, harmonize, go (well) with

■ **tone down**
moderate, temper, subdue, restrain, soften, lighten, dim, dampen, play down, reduce, alleviate
FORMAL assuage, mitigate
COLLOQ. soft-pedal

■ **tone up**
shape up, touch up, trim, tune up, sharpen up, limber up, freshen, invigorate, brighten

toneless *adj*
tuneless, unmelodious, unmusical, dull, colourless, neutral, grey, faded, dim, unexpressive, listless
F3 tuneful, melodious, musical, bright

tongue *n*
language, speech, discourse, talk, utterance, articulation, vernacular, idiom, dialect, patois, jargon, slang, argot, cant
FORMAL parlance
COLLOQ. lingo
Related adjective: lingual, glottic

tongue-tied *adj*
speechless, dumbstruck, inarticulate, silent, mute, dumb, wordless, voiceless, lost for words
F3 talkative, garrulous, voluble

tonic *n*
1 *a herbal tonic*
cordial, pick-me-up, restorative, refresher, bracer, stimulant, analeptic, boost, fillip, roborant
OLD saloop
COLLOQ. shot in the arm
2 *a tonic of a musical scale*
keynote, fundamental note, final, home key

too *adv*
1 ALSO, as well, in addition, furthermore, besides, moreover, likewise
2 EXCESSIVELY, inordinately, unduly, over, overly, unreasonably, ridiculously, extremely, very

tool *n, v*
◆ *n*
1 IMPLEMENT, instrument, utensil, gadget, device, contrivance, contraption, apparatus, artefact; *Irish* yoke;

appliance, machine, means, vehicle, medium, agency, agent, intermediary
COLLOQ. gismo
See Synonym nuances panel at **device**.
2 PUPPET, pawn, dupe, stooge, flunkey, minion, hireling, cat's-paw
◆ *v*
work, machine, cut, shape, decorate, fashion, ornament, chase

---

Types of tool include:

auger	hod	rasp
awl	hoe	rule
axe	jack	sander
bevel	jackhammer	saw
billhook	jack-plane	scalpel
bodkin	jig-saw	scissors
bolster	jointer	screwdriver
brace and bit	level	scriber
bradawl	mace	scythe
caulking-iron	mallet	secateurs
chainsaw	mattock	set-square
chaser	mortar	shears
chisel	needle	shovel
chopper	paper-cutter	sickle
clamp	paper-knife	sledgehammer
cleaver	penknife	snips
crochet hook	pestle	socket-wrench
crowbar	pick	soldering-iron
dibber	pick-axe	spade
dividers	pincers	spirit level
dolly	pinking-shears	spraygun
drill	pitchfork	stapler
file	plane	steel
forceps	pliers	tenon-saw
fork	plough	thresher
fretsaw	plumb-line	tommy bar
gimlet	pocket-knife	tongs
grass-rake	protractor	trowel
hacksaw	pruning-knife	T-square
hammer	pruning-shears	tweezers
handsaw	punch	vice
hay fork	rake	wrench

---

tooth *n*
cog, denticle, denticulation, dentil, fang, incisor, jag, masticator, molar, prong, tush, tusk

---

Types of tooth include:

baby tooth	first molar	snaggletooth
back tooth	first premolar	third molar
bicuspid	first tooth	tush
bucktooth	gold tooth	tusk
canine	grinder	wisdom tooth
carnassial	incisor	
central incisor	lateral incisor	**FALSE TEETH:**
denture	milk tooth	bridge
dog-tooth	molar	cap
eye tooth	premolar	crown
false tooth	second molar	plate
fang	second premolar	

---

toothsome *adj*
appetizing, delicious, tasty, tempting, mouthwatering, palatable, nice, agreeable, flavoursome, sweet, luscious, savoury, dainty
FORMAL delectable
COLLOQ. scrumptious, yummy, scrummy, mor(e)ish
F3 disagreeable, unpleasant

top *n, adj, v*

♦ *n*

1 HEAD, tip, highest point, apex, crest, crown, peak, pinnacle, summit, vertex, acme, zenith, apogee, climax, culmination, height

2 LID, cap, cover, cork, stopper

3 *a sleeveless top*
blouse, shirt, sweatshirt, T-shirt, tee shirt, jumper, jersey, sweater, pullover, tank top, smock

1 bottom, base, nadir **3** bottoms

♦ *adj*

highest, topmost, upmost, uppermost, upper, superior, head, chief, leading, main, first, foremost, premier, principal, sovereign, ruling, pre-eminent, dominant, prime, paramount, utmost, greatest, maximum, best, finest, premium, supreme, crowning, culminating, uber-

bottom, lowest, inferior

♦ *v*

1 TIP, cap, crown, cover, finish (off), decorate, garnish

2 BEAT, exceed, outstrip, better, excel, best, surpass, eclipse, outshine, outdo, surmount, transcend

3 HEAD, lead, be first in, rule, command

■ **top up**
refill, recharge, reload, add to, supplement, increase, boost
FORMAL replenish, augment

■ **on top of the world**
thrilled, happy, overjoyed, ecstatic, elated, exhilarated, exultant
COLLOQ. on cloud nine, over the moon

■ **over the top**
excessive, immoderate, inordinate, extreme, too much, undue, uncalled-for, disproportionate, unreasonable, lavish, exorbitant, extravagant
COLLOQ. OTT, a bit much

SYNONYM NUANCES

noun sense 1
You can use **head** to refer to the uppermost part of anything, while **tip** suggests something that tapers up to a point. **Apex**, likewise, implies the high point, literally or figuratively: *the apex of the pyramid*; *the apex of military command*. **Crown** can also be used of the highest extremity: *the crown of the hill*; *the crown of his head*, but **crest** tends to be reserved for the top edge of something: *the crest of a wave*.

Other synonyms lend themselves more to figurative uses. **Peak** can either suggest a pointed end or, like **pinnacle** and **summit**, suggest the highest position: *the pinnacle of his career*. You can use the terms **climax** and **culmination** if you want to refer to the highest that is achievable, or the defining point: *the culmination of a lifetime's dream*.

---

topic *n*
subject, subject matter, theme, issue, question, argument, matter, point, talking point, thesis, text, hobby-horse, *cheval de bataille*, touch-me-not; *N Am* hot button
TECHNICAL topos
OLD commonplace, place
COLLOQ. hardy annual, old chestnut

topical *adj*
current, contemporary, up-to-date, up-to-the-minute, recent, newsworthy, relevant, popular, familiar

topmost *adj*
uppermost, highest, loftiest, top, upper, supreme, first, leading, foremost, principal, maximum, paramount, dominant
TECHNICAL apical
bottom, bottommost, lowest

top-notch *adj*
first-rate, first-class, second-to-none, matchless, peerless, top, top-flight, leading, supreme, superior, prime, excellent, outstanding, superlative, premier, exceptional, splendid, superb, fine, admirable

COLLOQ. super, A1, ace, crack, out of this world
SLANG wicked, way-out, cool, radical, mega

topple *v*

1 OVERBALANCE, totter, tumble, fall (over), collapse, upset, pitch, tip over, knock over/down, keel over, overturn, capsize

2 OVERTHROW, oust, bring down, unseat, displace, dethrone

top-secret *adj*
confidential, highly confidential, secret, classified, restricted, off-the-record, private, personal, intimate, sensitive
COLLOQ. hush-hush

topsy-turvy *adj*
confused, in confusion, jumbled, chaotic, inside out, upside down, disorganized, disarranged, disorderly, in disorder, untidy, mixed-up, messy
ordered, tidy

torch *n, v*

♦ *n*
light, firebrand, brand, flambeau; *N Am* flashlight
OLD cresset

♦ *v*
ignite, set fire to, set on fire, set alight, burn, put a match to

torment *n, v*

♦ *n*

1 ANGUISH, distress, misery, affliction, suffering, pain, agony, ordeal, worry, torture, persecution, martyrdom, furnace, Gehenna

2 ANNOYANCE, provocation, irritation, vexation, bane, scourge, curse, pest, trouble, bother, nuisance, harassment, worry
COLLOQ. thorn in the flesh, pain in the neck

♦ *v*

1 AFFLICT, plague, distress, trouble, harrow, pain, torture, persecute, crucify, grill, wrack
OLD pine

2 ANNOY, tease, provoke, irritate, vex, trouble, worry, harass, hound, pester, bother, plague, badger, bedevil, tantalize

torn *adj*

1 CUT, ragged, ripped, slit, split, rent, lacerated

2 DIVIDED, uncertain, undecided, unsure, in two minds, irresolute, conflicted, vacillating, wavering, dithering

tornado *n*
storm, cyclone, gale, hurricane, whirlwind, typhoon, monsoon, tempest, squall
COLLOQ. twister

torpid *adj*
sluggish, lethargic, slow, dull, lifeless, inert, inactive, apathetic, lazy, passive, listless, drowsy, sleepy, dead, deadened, numb, nerveless, insensible
FORMAL languorous, somnolent, supine, indolent
active, lively, vigorous

torpor *n*
torpidity, sluggishness, lethargy, listlessness, slowness, dullness, lifelessness, inactivity, inertia, inertness, drowsiness, sleepiness, numbness, apathy, laziness, passivity, sloth
FORMAL indolence, languor, somnolence, hebetude
activity, vigour, enthusiasm

torrent *n*

1 *torrent of water*
stream, gush, rush, flood, storm, outburst, volley, barrage, inundation, spate, deluge, cascade, downpour

2 *a torrent of abuse*
outburst, volley, barrage, stream, gush, rush, flood, storm, inundation, spate, deluge; *Scot* blatter
1 trickle

torrential *adj*
heavy, persistent, pouring down, pelting, driving, teeming, inundating
COLLOQ. raining cats and dogs, bucketing down, coming down in stair rods
SLANG pissing

torrid *adj*
1 HOT, blazing, sweltering, blistering, boiling, sizzling, scorching, tropical, stifling, arid, parched, scorched, waterless, desert
2 PASSIONATE, erotic, red-hot, sexy, amorous
COLLOQ. steamy

tortuous *adj*
1 *a tortuous road*
twisting, winding, meandering, curving, serpentine, snaking, zigzag, circuitous, roundabout, indirect
FORMAL sinuous
2 COMPLICATED, involved, serpentine, zigzag, circuitous, roundabout, indirect
FORMAL convoluted
E3 1 straight **2** straightforward

torture *v, n*
♦ *v*
pain, agonize, excruciate, crucify, rack, martyr, persecute, abuse, ill-treat, mistreat, torment, harrow, plague, punish, afflict, worry, distress, trouble
♦ *n*
pain, agony, suffering, affliction, distress, punishment, misery, anguish, torment, abuse, ill-treatment, mistreatment, martyrdom, persecution

Forms and instruments of torture include:

Austrian ladder	gridirons	scavenger's
ball and chain	harrow	daughter
bastinado	head crusher	scold's bridle
bilboes	heretic's forks	scourge
boiling	hooding	shabeh
boot (or bootikin)	impalement	shin vice
branding	iron collar	shrew's fiddle
brank	iron maiden	skull crusher
brazen bull	irons	sleep deprivation
cage	jougs	Spanish chair
carcan	Judas cradle (or	spider
cat-o'-nine-tails	scale)	spiked hare
cat's paw	keelhauling	squassation
cattle prod	knee-capping	starvation
cave of roses	knotting	stocks
confession chair	pear	stoning
devil-on-the-neck	peine forte et dure	strappado
disembowelment	pendulum	suspension
drunkard's cloak	picana	thumbscrews
(or Spanish	picketing (or	treadmill (or
mantle)	picquet)	treadwheel)
ducking-stool	pilliwinks	turcas
electric shock	pillory	waterboarding
flesh tearers	pincers	water torture
forcipation	pressing	wheel
garrotte	rack	wooden horse
gauntlets	saw	
German chair	scarpines	

toss *v, n*
♦ *v*
1 FLIP, cast, fling, throw, pitch, heave, sling, hurl, lob, shy, loft, tip, cant; *Scot* birl, bum
COLLOQ. chuck; *Irish* puck
2 ROLL, heave, sway, pitch, lurch, jolt, shake, jerk, agitate, rock, thrash, squirm, writhe, wriggle, tumble, welter, bandy, dandle
♦ *n*
flip, cast, fling, throw, pitch, cant
COLLOQ. chuck

tot¹ *n*
1 TODDLER, child, infant, mite, baby; *Scot* bairn
2 *a tot of whisky*
dram, measure, nip, shot, slug, swallow, swig, finger

tot²
■ **tot up**
add (up), calculate, compute, count (up), reckon, mount (up), sum, tally, total

total *n, adj, v*
♦ *n*
sum, whole, entirety, grand total, subtotal, totality, all, lot, mass, amount
FORMAL aggregate
♦ *adj*
full, complete, entire, whole, comprehensive, integral, all-out, utter, absolute, unconditional, unqualified, outright, undisputed, perfect, thoroughgoing, rank, sheer, downright, out-and-out, thorough
FORMAL consummate, unmitigated
E3 partial, limited, restricted
♦ *v*
add (up), sum (up), tot (up), count (up), reckon, amount to, come to, reach, make

totalitarian *adj*
authoritarian, one-party, despotic, dictatorial, oppressive, tyrannous, monolithic, undemocratic
FORMAL omnipotent, monocratic
E3 democratic

totality *n*
total, sum, whole, wholeness, entirety, entireness, everything, fullness, completeness, all, cosmos, universe
FORMAL aggregate, pleroma

totally *adv*
completely, fully, wholly, entirely, perfectly, utterly, quite, thoroughly, wholeheartedly, absolutely, unconditionally, comprehensively, undividedly, unqualifiedly, undisputedly
FORMAL consummately, unmitigatedly
COLLOQ. *Aust & NZ* boots and all
E3 partially

totter *v*
1 STAGGER, waddle, move unsteadily, reel, lurch, stumble, falter, waver, teeter, sway, roll, rock, shake, wobble, quiver, tremble, dodder, titter, topple; *dialect* daddle; *Scot* hotter
2 *the economy is tottering*
be unstable, be unsteady, be insecure, be shaky, teeter, be precarious, be about to collapse
COLLOQ. wobble

touch *v, n*
♦ *v*
1 FEEL, handle, hold, finger, run your finger over, brush, skim, graze, stroke, caress, fondle, pet, tickle, pat, tap, hit, strike, contact
2 ADJOIN, bring/come into contact, meet, abut, border, impinge
FORMAL be contiguous to
3 MOVE, stir, upset, sadden, disturb, impress, inspire, influence, affect, have an effect on, have an influence/impact on, involve, concern, regard
4 EQUAL, match, rival, better, come near, approach
COLLOQ. hold a candle to
5 REACH, attain, make, come to
COLLOQ. hit
6 *not touch alcohol*
consume, use, eat, drink, take, devour
7 MENTION, broach, speak of, remark on, refer to, allude to, cover, deal with
♦ *n*
1 FEEL, brush, stroke, caress, pat, tap, blow, hit, contact, tactility
Related adjective: tactile, haptic
2 TEXTURE, feel, surface, finish, grain, weave

3 SKILL, art, knack, flair, craftsmanship, dexterity, style, method, manner, technique, approach, way, direction, influence
4 *finishing touches*
detail, feature, point, addition, aspect, nicety, minutia
5 *keep/lose touch*
contact, communication, correspondence, connection, association
6 *a touch of garlic*
trace, spot, dash, pinch, taste, soupçon, suspicion, hint, suggestion, bit, speck, jot, tinge, smack
COLLOQ. whiff
■ **touch down**
land, come in, come in to land, come to earth
■ **touch off**
spark off, trigger (off), detonate, begin, cause, set off, initiate, provoke, foment, fire, ignite, inflame, light, arouse
FORMAL actuate
■ **touch up**
renovate, improve, brush up, retouch,
revamp, enhance, finish off, round off, patch up, perfect, polish up

touch-and-go *adj*
close, critical, dangerous, uncertain, hazardous, near, nerve-racking, offhand, perilous, dire, precarious, risky, sticky, tricky
FORMAL parlous
COLLOQ. dodgy, hairy

touchdown *n*
landing, coming in, coming in to land, arrival
E3 take-off

touched *adj*
1 MOVED, stirred, inspired, influenced, affected, impressed, disturbed, upset
2 MAD, crazy, insane, deranged, disturbed, eccentric, unbalanced
COLLOQ. dotty, daft, barmy, nutty, bonkers, batty, loopy

touchiness *n*
bad temper, irritability, grumpiness, irascibility, peevishness, pettishness, surliness, testiness, tetchiness, petulance, captiousness
COLLOQ. crabbedness, grouchiness

touching *adj*
moving, stirring, impressive, affecting, upsetting, disturbing, poignant, pitiable, pitiful, heartbreaking, heart-rending, pathetic, sad, emotional, tender
FORMAL piteous

touchstone *n*
criterion, standard, test, norm, proof, measure, gauge, guide, model, pattern, template, benchmark, yardstick

touchy *adj*
1 IRRITABLE, bad-tempered, quick-tempered, grumpy, cross, prickly, over-sensitive, thin-skinned, peevish, captious, irascible
COLLOQ. grouchy, crabbed, edgy; *Can* chippy
2 *a touchy subject*
delicate, sensitive, tricky, difficult, problematic, awkward, controversial
E3 **1** calm, imperturbable

tough *adj, n*
♦ *adj*
1 STRONG, durable, resilient, resistant, firm, hardy, sturdy, solid, rigid, stiff, inflexible, hard, leathery
2 *tough criminal*
rough, violent, disorderly, rowdy, vicious, callous, hardened, obstinate
3 HARSH, severe, strict, stern, firm, resolute, adamant, determined, tenacious, unyielding, uncompromising, hard-faced
4 ARDUOUS, strenuous, laborious, exacting, hard, taxing, grim, difficult, puzzling, perplexing, baffling, knotty, thorny, troublesome
COLLOQ. uphill

5 FIT, muscular, hardy, burly, well-built, robust, sturdy, rugged, vigorous, stalwart
6 *the meat is tough*
rubbery, chewy, fibrous, gristly
COLLOQ. tough as leather
7 *tough luck*
hard, unpleasant, unfortunate, unlucky, uncomfortable, distressing
E3 **1** fragile, delicate, weak, tender **2** gentle, soft **3** gentle, easy-going **4** easy, simple **5** weak, frail **6** tender **7** good, fortunate
♦ *n*
brute, thug, bully, ruffian, hooligan, lout, rowdy, roughneck
COLLOQ. rough, yobbo
SLANG yob, bovver boy, lager lout

toughen *v*
strengthen, harden, reinforce, brace, stiffen, considerate, substantiate, make stricter
TECHNICAL anneal
FORMAL fortify

toughness *n*
strength, resilience, resistance, firmness, hardiness, sturdiness, tenacity, determination, inflexibility, ruggedness, obduracy
COLLOQ. grit
E3 weakness, vulnerability, softness, liberality

toupee *n*
hairpiece, wig, postiche, scratch-wig, spencer, bobwig, Brutus, buzz-wig, tie-wig; *Scot* gizz, jiz
OLD periwig, peruke, transformation, bagwig, caxon, major, Ramilie
OLD COLLOQ. jasey

tour *n, v*
♦ *n*
circuit, round, visit, expedition, journey, trip, outing, excursion, inspection, drive, ride, jaunt, course, hike
FORMAL peregrination
COLLOQ. walkabout, road
♦ *v*
visit, go round, sightsee, explore, travel round, journey through, drive through, ride, tramp, barnstorm
COLLOQ. do

tourist *n*
holidaymaker, visitor, sightseer, tripper, day-tripper, tourer, excursionist, traveller, voyager, globetrotter
OLD emmet
FORMAL sojourner
COLLOQ. *dialect* (*derog*) grockle
SLANG *N Am* rubberneck

tournament *n*
championship, series, competition, contest, match, event, meeting, meet, joust, round robin
OLD tourney

tousled *adj*
dishevelled, ruffled, unkempt, untidy, messed up, disordered, in disarray, disarranged, tangled, rumpled, tumbled

tout *v*
1 SELL, hawk, peddle, trade
2 ADVERTISE, promote, market, endorse, commend, solicit, petition, ask, appeal, seek
COLLOQ. plug, hype, push

tow *v, n*
♦ *v*
pull, tug, draw, trail, drag, lug, haul, transport
♦ *n*
pull, tug, haul, trail, lug
■ **in tow**
following closely, accompanying, by your side, in convoy

towards *prep*
1 TO, in the direction of, on the way to, approaching, nearing, close to, nearly, almost, -wards

2 *his feelings towards her*
regarding, with regard to, with respect to, concerning,
about, for
3 *£500 towards the cost of the project*
to help pay for, as a contribution to, for

tower *v*
rise, rear, ascend, mount, soar, loom, overlook, dominate,
surpass, transcend, overshadow, eclipse, exceed, excel,
top, cap
■ **tower of strength**
supporter, support, pillar, pillar of the community, prop,
mainstay, friend in need

Types of tower include:

barbican	fort	peel-tower
bastille	fortification	scaffold tower
bastion	fortress	skyscraper
belfry	gate-tower	smock mill
bell tower	high-rise building	spire
belvedere	hill-fort	steeple
campanile	keep	stronghold
castle	Leaning Tower of	tower block
church tower	Pisa	tower mill
citadel	lookout tower	Tower of London
column	Martello tower	turret
cooling tower	minar	watchtower
demi-bastion	minaret	water tower
donjon	mirador	
Eiffel Tower	pagoda	

towering *adj*
1 HIGH, soaring, tall, lofty, elevated, monumental, colossal,
gigantic, great
2 MAGNIFICENT, imposing, impressive, outstanding, sublime,
supreme, incomparable, unrivalled, surpassing,
overpowering, extraordinary, extreme, inordinate
E3 1 low, small, tiny **2** minor, trivial

town *n*
borough, village, municipality, burgh, market town,
county town, new town, city, suburbs, outskirts,
conurbation, metropolis, urban district, urban area,
settlement, township, pueblo; *Scot* burgh
Related adjective: urban
E3 country

town-dweller *n*
citizen, townsman, townswoman, burgher, urbanite
FORMAL oppidan
COLLOQ. towny
E3 country-dweller, rustic

toxic *adj*
poisonous, harmful, noxious, unhealthy, dangerous,
deadly, lethal, baneful
E3 harmless, safe

toy *n, v, adj*
♦ *n*
plaything, knick-knack, trinket, trifle, bauble
See panel on next page
♦ *v*
play, tinker, fiddle, sport, trifle, dally, flirt
COLLOQ. mess about/around
♦ *adj*
model, miniature, small-scale, reduced, replica,
reproduction

trace *n, v*
♦ *n*
1 *leave traces of blood*
hint, suggestion, suspicion, soupçon, dash, pinch, drop,
spot, bit, jot, touch, tinge, shadow, smack, thought,
scintilla, whiff, dreg
2 MARK, token, sign, indication, impression, scar, evidence,
record, relic, remains, monument, remnant, vestige, trail,
track, spoor, footprint, footmark, scent, fossil

TECHNICAL engram
OLD (*Shakesp & Spenser*) tract
COLLOQ. hide nor/or hair
♦ *v*
1 FIND, discover, detect, unearth, track (down), uncover,
dig up, trail, track, stalk, hunt, seek, follow, pursue, dog,
shadow, analyse, derive
OLD (*Shakesp & Spenser*) tract
COLLOQ. run down
2 COPY, draw, draft, sketch, outline, show, depict, mark
(out), record, map, chart, describe, chalk out,
counterdraw
TECHNICAL generate
FORMAL delineate

track *n, v*
♦ *n*
1 WAY, rail, path, route, orbit, line, trail, trajectory, slot,
groove, course, drift, sequence, argument
OLD sleuth; (*Shakesp & Spenser*) tract
2 FOOTPRINT, footstep, footmark, scent, spoor, trail, wake,
mark, trace
♦ *v*
stalk, trail, hunt, trace, follow, pursue, chase, dog, tail,
shadow
■ **track down**
find, discover, trace, detect, hunt down, run to earth, nose
out, sniff out, ferret out, turn up, dig up, uncover, unearth,
expose, catch, capture
COLLOQ. run down
■ **keep track of**
monitor, check, watch, follow, observe, record, keep an
eye on
E3 lose track of
■ **lose track of**
forget, misplace, miss, lose touch/contact with
■ **make tracks**
leave, go, depart, make off, dash (off), disappear
COLLOQ. scram, beat it, hit the road
■ **on track**
on course, on schedule, on target, on time

tract *n*
1 *a tract of land*
stretch, extent, expanse, plot, lot, territory, area, region,
terrain, zone, district, quarter
2 *a religious tract*
booklet, leaflet, brochure, pamphlet, treatise,
sermon, essay, dissertation, homily, discourse,
monograph
FORMAL disquisition

tractable *adj*
pliant, pliable, manageable, obedient, persuadable,
willing, submissive, docile, controllable, amenable,
biddable, governable, malleable, compliant, yielding,
workable, tame, tractile
FORMAL complaisant
E3 headstrong, intractable, obstinate, refractory, stubborn,
unruly, wilful

traction *n*
drawing, pull, pulling, haulage, propulsion, drag, draught,
grip, friction, adhesion

trade *n, v*
♦ *n*
1 COMMERCE, traffic, trafficking, business, dealing,
buying, selling, buying and selling, marketing,
shopkeeping, barter, exchange, switch, swap,
transactions, custom
Related adjective: mercantile
2 OCCUPATION, employment, job, work, business,
line (of work), profession, career, calling, vocation, métier,
craft, skill
♦ *v*
do business, deal, transact, buy, sell, run, traffic, peddle,
market, merchandize, barter, exchange, swap, switch,
bargain

Kinds of toy include:

action figure	catapult	guitar	Moxie Girlz®	rocker	Super Mario®
Action Man®	climbing-frame	gun	Mr Potato Head®	rocking-horse	swing
activity centre	computer game	gyroscope	musical box	Rollerblades®	swingball
aeroplane	crayons	Hello Kitty®	Nintendo®	roller skates	Sylvanian
baby-bouncer	doll	hobby-horse	ocarina	Rubik's Cube®	Families®
baby-walker	doll's buggy	Hot Wheels®	paddling-pool	sandpit	tea set
ball	doll's cot	hula-hoop	paints	Scalextric®	teddy bear
balloon	doll's house	jack-in-the-box	pantograph	scooter	toy soldier
Barbie doll®	doll's pram	jigsaw puzzle	peashooter	seesaw	train set
bicycle	dreidel	kaleidoscope	pedal-car	sewing machine	trampoline
colloq. bike	drum set	kewpie doll	Plasticene®	shape-sorter	Transformers®
blackboard and	electronic game	kite	Play-Doh®	skipping-rope	tricycle
easel	executive toy	Lego®	playhouse	slide	trike
Bob the Builder®	farm	marbles	Playmobil®	soft toy	typewriter
Bop It®	fivestones	Meccano®	PlayStation®	Sonic the	video game
boxing-gloves	football	Miko Cat®	pogo stick	Hedgehog®	walkie-talkie
box-kite	fort	model car	Pokémon®	spacehopper	water pistol
Bratz®	Frisbee®	model kit	pop-gun	Space Invaders®	Wendy house
building-blocks	game	modelling clay	Power Rangers®	spinning top	Wii®
building-bricks	garage	model railway	puzzle	Spongebob Squar-	XBox®
Buzz Lightyear®	glove puppet	Moshi Monsters®	rag doll	epants®	yo-yo
cap-gun	go-kart	mountain bike	rattle	Subbuteo®	Zhu Zhu Pets®

See also **game**¹.

---

trademark *n*
1 *a registered trademark*
brand, brand name, brand label, tradename, proprietary name, proprietary brand, label, name, sign, symbol, logo, insignia, crest, emblem, badge
2 HALLMARK, stamp, mark, speciality, typical quality, (distinctive) feature, attribute, characteristic, idiosyncrasy, peculiarity, quirk

trader *n*
merchant, tradesman, tradeswoman, exporter, importer, broker, dealer, buyer, seller, marketeer, marketer, vendor, supplier, wholesaler, retailer, shopkeeper, trafficker, peddler
OLD plier

tradesman, tradeswoman *n*
1 SHOPKEEPER, retailer, buyer, seller, merchant, dealer, trader, vendor
2 ARTISAN, craftsman, craftswoman, worker, mechanic, journeyman

tradition *n*
convention, custom, belief, ceremony, usage, way, habit, routine, practice, observance, ritual, rite, institution, folklore, legend
FORMAL praxis
See Synonym nuances panel at **custom**.

traditional *adj*
conventional, classic, customary, habitual, usual, routine, accustomed, conservative, ceremonial, established, fixed, set, long-established, time-honoured, old, age-old, historic, folk, oral, unwritten; *N Am* old-line
Ⅎ unconventional, innovative, new, modern, contemporary

traditionalist *n*
conventionalist, conservative, formalist, reactionary, diehard, old guard, one of the old school; *N Am* old-liner
COLLOQ. old fogey, stick-in-the-mud

traduce *v*
misrepresent, slander, run down, revile, decry, defame, blacken, abuse, insult, malign, smear
FORMAL disparage, detract, asperse, denigrate, deprecate, depreciate, calumniate, vilify
COLLOQ. knock
SLANG slag (off)

traducer *n*
defamer, slanderer, abuser, smearer

FORMAL disparager, asperser, calumniator, denigrator, deprecator, detractor, vilifier
COLLOQ. knocker, mud-slinger

traffic *n, v*
♦ *n*
1 VEHICLES, cars, shipping, transport, transportation, freight, passengers
2 CONGESTION, traffic jam, queue, tailback, gridlock, hold-up
3 TRADE, commerce, business, dealing, trading, trafficking, buying and selling, peddling, barter, exchange
4 COMMUNICATION, dealings, relations, contact
FORMAL intercourse
♦ *v*
peddle, buy, sell, trade, do business, deal, bargain, barter, exchange

trafficker *n*
dealer, merchant, trader, seller, supplier, distributor, marketer, agent, broker, peddler, merchandizer, monger

tragedy *n*
adversity, misfortune, unhappiness, affliction, blow, calamity, disaster, catastrophe
Ⅎ success, triumph

tragic *adj*
calamitous, disastrous, catastrophic, deadly, fatal, sad, sorrowful, miserable, terrible, unhappy, wretched, unfortunate, unlucky, ill-fated, pitiable, pathetic, heartbreaking, shocking, appalling, dreadful, awful, deplorable, dire
Ⅎ happy, comic, successful

tragically *adv*
catastrophically, terribly, most unfortunately, awfully, dreadfully, appallingly, shockingly, wretchedly
Ⅎ happily, fortunately

trail *n, v*
♦ *n*
track, path, footpath, road, route, way, wake, piste, runway, footprints, footmarks, marks, scent, spoor, sign, trace
TECHNICAL abature
OLD sleuth; (*Spenser*) trade
♦ *v*
1 DRAG, pull, tow, haul, draw, droop, dangle, hang, extend, reach, stream, sweep, straggle, dawdle, lag, loiter,

linger, fall, draggle, ramble, traipse; *Scot* trauchle;
Irish streel
OLD train
2 TRACK, stalk, hunt, follow, pursue, chase, dog, shadow,
tail, tag along
■ **trail away**
decrease, die away, diminish, disappear, dwindle, fade
(away), fall/melt away, lessen, peter out, shrink, sink,
subside, tail/taper/trail off, weaken

trailblazer *n*
pioneer, ground-breaker, leader, pathfinder, developer,
innovator, founder, discoverer

train *n, v*
  ♦ *n*
1 *a train of events*
sequence, succession, series, progression, order, set, suite,
string, chain, trail, line, path, track, stream, file,
procession, column, convoy, cortège, caravan
FORMAL concatenation
2 RETINUE, entourage, attendants, court, household, staff,
followers, following, cortège
  ♦ *v*
1 TEACH, instruct, coach, tutor, educate, improve, school,
indoctrinate, discipline, prepare, reskill, drill, ground,
exercise, work out, practise, rehearse, groom
FORMAL inculcate
2 LEARN, study, be trained, be taught, be prepared
3 POINT, direct, aim, focus, level

trainee *n*
probationer, apprentice, novice, beginner, learner, student,
pupil, tiro

trainer *n*
teacher, instructor, coach, tutor, handler, educator

training *n*
teaching, instruction, coaching, tuition, tutoring, education,
schooling, learning, lessons, discipline, preparation,
grounding, drill, exercise, workout, working-out, practice,
apprenticeship

traipse *v, n*
  ♦ *v*
trudge, tramp, plod, slouch, trail
  ♦ *n*
trudge, trek, slog, plod, tramp

trait *n*
feature, attribute, quality, property, characteristic,
idiosyncrasy, peculiarity, quirk

traitor *n*
betrayer, informer, deceiver, double-crosser, double-dealer,
turncoat, renegade, deserter, defector, quisling,
collaborator, fifth columnist, Judas, proditor
OLD traditor, treacher, treachetour, nithing
COLLOQ. backstabber, two-timer
Ea loyalist, supporter, defender

traitorous *adj*
disloyal, unfaithful, faithless, false, untrue, treasonable,
dishonourable, double-crossing, double-dealing, renegade,
treacherous, apostate
FORMAL perfidious, seditious
Ea faithful, loyal, patriotic

trajectory *n*
line, orbit, path, route, flight, flight path, course,
track, trail

trammel *n, v*
  ♦ *n*
bar, block, bond, fetter, rein, shackle, check, clog, chain,
hamper, curb, handicap, hindrance, impediment, restraint,
obstacle, stumbling-block
  ♦ *v*
bar, block, clog, restrict, restrain, fetter, catch, check, tie,
enmesh, ensnare, entrap, shackle, inhibit, impede, hinder,
handicap, hamper, curb, capture, net

tramp *n, v*
  ♦ *n*
1 VAGRANT, vagabond, down-and-out, beggar, derelict,
piker, *clochard*, floater, straggle, stroller; *dialect* walker;
Scot caird, gangrel, hallan-shaker, landloper, rinthereout,
(*derog*) tinkler; *Aust* sundowner
OLD cursitor, rogue, scatterling, truant, vagrom
OLD COLLOQ. Weary Willie
SLANG dosser, bum, toerag, knight of the road, gook; *Scot*
jakey; *N Am* dingbat
2 TRUDGE, march, tread, step, walk, trek, hike, ramble
3 LOOSE WOMAN, prostitute, wench, trollop, whore,
slattern, sloven
COLLOQ. hooker
SLANG floozie, slut, tart, scrubber, slag, skank
  ♦ *v*
walk, march, tread, stamp, stomp, stump, plod, trudge,
traipse, trail, trek, hike, ramble, roam, rove, footslog; *N
Am* tromp

trample *v*
tread, stamp, crush, squash, flatten, tramp, poach, potch,
override, ride down, hobnail; *Scot* stramp; *N Am* tromp
OLD foil

trance *n*
dream, reverie, daze, stupor, unconsciousness, catalepsy,
spell, ecstasy, rapture

tranche *n*
part, piece, section, segment, length, cut, slice, wedge,
instalment

tranquil *adj*
calm, peaceful, quiet, serene, composed, cool,
imperturbable, unexcited, even-tempered, placid, sedate,
relaxed, easy, restful, still, undisturbed, untroubled,
hushed, silent, pacific, unimpassioned, disimpassioned
FORMAL reposeful
COLLOQ. laid-back, unflappable
Ea agitated, disturbed, troubled, noisy

tranquillity *n*
calm, peace, peacefulness, serenity, calmness, composure,
quiet, quietness, rest, restfulness, stillness, hush, silence,
imperturbability, coolness, equanimity, sedateness,
placidity
TECHNICAL ataraxia, ataraxy
FORMAL quietude, repose
Ea disturbance, agitation, noise

tranquillize *v*
calm, quiet, pacify, relax, sedate, soothe, quell, lull,
compose
TECHNICAL narcotize, opiate
Ea disturb, agitate, upset

tranquillizer *n*
sedative, calmative, sleeping pill, opiate, narcotic,
barbiturate, depressant, quietive, bromide
COLLOQ. downer

transact *v*
carry out, conduct, do, perform, settle, handle, manage,
carry on, accomplish, negotiate, conclude, dispatch,
discharge, enact, execute
FORMAL prosecute

transaction *n*
1 *bank transactions*
deal, bargain, agreement, arrangement, negotiation,
business, affair, matter, proceeding, enterprise,
undertaking, deed, action, handling, settlement,
enactment, execution, discharge
2 *the transactions of a learned society*
reports, proceedings, record, minutes, publications,
concerns, annals, affairs, doings
COLLOQ. goings-on

transcend *v*
surpass, excel, outshine, eclipse, outdo, outstrip, leave
behind, beat, surmount, exceed, go beyond, rise above,
overstep

transcendence n

transcendency, superiority, supremacy, pre-eminence, predominance, incomparability, matchlessness, paramoun(t)cy, excellence, greatness
FORMAL ascendancy, sublimity

transcendent adj

1 SURPASSING, supreme, sublime, superlative, excelling, excellent, magnificent, incomparable, matchless, peerless, unparalleled, unsurpassable
2 SUPERHUMAN, supernatural, spiritual
FORMAL ineffable, numinous

transcendental adj

supernatural, spiritual, otherworldly, metaphysical, mystical, mysterious
FORMAL preternatural

transcribe v

write out, write up, copy out, copy up, reproduce, rewrite, transliterate, translate, render, take down, note, record

transcript n

transcription, copy, reproduction, duplicate, transliteration, translation, version, note, record, manuscript

transcription n

writing-out, reproduction, transliteration, translation, version

transfer v, n

♦ v
1 CHANGE, transpose, move, shift, remove, relocate, transplant, transport, carry, take, convey
2 *transfer land*
assign, convey, transmit, consign, grant, hand over
♦ n
change, changeover, transposition, move, movement, shift, removal, relocation, displacement, transmission, handover, assignment, transference
TECHNICAL conveyance

transfigure v

transform, change, alter, convert, exalt, glorify, idealize
FORMAL transmute, translate, metamorphose, apotheosize
COLLOQ. morph

transfix v

1 FASCINATE, spellbind, mesmerize, hypnotize, paralyse, stun, hold, engross, rivet, petrify
2 IMPALE, pierce, run through, spear, skewer, spike, stick

transform v

change, alter, adapt, convert, turn, mutate, remodel, rebuild, reform, resolve, reconstruct, renew, transfigure, revolutionize, transverse
TECHNICAL transmute, decentralize, absorb, receive
OLD disclose, trans-shape; (*Shakesp*) transpose
FORMAL commute, translate, metamorphose
COLLOQ. transmogrify, morph
E3 preserve, maintain

transformation n

change, alteration, conversion, transfiguration, revolution, turning, reformation
TECHNICAL metastasis, reaction, metaplasia, anthropomorphosis, theriomorphosis
FORMAL mutation, transmutation, metamorphosis
COLLOQ. sea change, transmogrification
E3 preservation, conservation

transfuse v

transfer, imbue, pervade, instil, permeate, suffuse

transgress v

break, offend, sin, contravene, disobey, misbehave, overstep, exceed, violate, breach, defy, infringe, encroach, lapse, err, trespass
E3 keep, obey

transgression n

wrong, wrongdoing, offence, infringement, lapse, trespass, crime, sin, violation, disobedience, fault, error, iniquity, misdeed, peccadillo, misbehaviour, misdemeanour, breach, contravention, encroachment, debt
FORMAL infraction

transgressor n

lawbreaker, offender, wrongdoer, evil-doer, criminal, culprit, delinquent, debtor, trespasser, miscreant, felon, sinner, villain
FORMAL malefactor

transience n

transitoriness, shortness, briefness, brevity, temporariness, impermanence, deciduousness
TECHNICAL caducity
FORMAL ephemerality, evanescence, fugacity, fugitiveness
COLLOQ. fleetingness
E3 permanence

transient adj

transitory, passing, flying, fleeting, brief, short, momentary, short-lived, temporary, short-term, impermanent, volatile, bubble
OLD fleet; (*Shakesp*) summer-seeming
FORMAL ephemeral, evanescent, fugacious
COLLOQ. here today gone tomorrow
E3 lasting, permanent

transit n

passage, journey, journeying, travel, crossing, route, movement, transfer, transportation, conveyance, carriage, haulage, shipment
■ **in transit**
en route, on the way, travelling, by road, by rail, by air, by sea

transition n

passage, passing, progress, progression, development, evolution, move, movement, flux, change, changeover, alteration, conversion, transformation, shift, switch, leap, rite of passage
TECHNICAL composition, metabasis, metastasis, transitional, unbecoming
FORMAL metamorphosis, transmutation

transitional adj

provisional, temporary, passing, intermediate, interim, developmental, evolutionary, changing, fluid, unsettled
E3 initial, final

transitory adj

transient, passing, flying, fleeting, brief, short, momentary, short-lived, temporary, short-term, impermanent
OLD fleet
FORMAL ephemeral, evanescent, fugacious
COLLOQ. here today gone tomorrow
E3 lasting, permanent

translate v

1 *translate into German*
put, render, paraphrase, reword, turn, explain, interpret, simplify, encode, decode, decipher, transliterate, transcribe, reduce
OLD traduce
FORMAL construe
2 CHANGE, alter, convert, turn, transform, improve, move, transfer, relocate, shift
FORMAL transmute
COLLOQ. transmogrify

translation n

1 *a translation from Spanish*
rendering, version, rendition, explanation, interpretation, gloss, crib, rewording, rephrasing, paraphrase, simplification, transliteration, transcription
OLD traduction
FORMAL metaphrasis
2 CHANGE, alteration, conversion, transformation, move, transfer, shift
FORMAL transmutation, metamorphosis
COLLOQ. transmogrification

translator *n*
linguist, polyglot, paraphraser, interpreter, glosser,
dragoman
FORMAL exegete, exegetist, glossarist, glossator, metaphrast,
paraphrast

translucent *adj*
transparent, clear, see-through, pellucid, translucid, limpid
FORMAL diaphanous
F3 opaque

transmigration *n*
transformation, rebirth, reincarnation
FORMAL metempsychosis, Pythagoreanism

transmission *n*
1 BROADCASTING, diffusion, spread, communication,
conveyance, carriage, transport, shipment, sending,
dispatch, relaying, beaming, transfer, consignment,
transference, imparting, trajection
FORMAL dissemination
2 *a live transmission*
broadcast, programme, show, performance, production,
presentation, episode, simulcast, signal
F3 1 reception

transmit *v*
communicate, impart, convey, carry, bear, transport,
conduct, hand down/on, send, pass (on), dispatch,
forward, consign, mediate, relay, beam, remit, transfer,
broadcast, televise, telecast, radio, network, diffuse,
spread, report, propagate, buzz, fax, message, modem,
radiate, pipe, satellite
OLD traduce, traject
FORMAL disseminate, remit
F3 receive

transmute *v*
transform, alter, change, convert, remake, transfigure,
transverse
FORMAL metamorphose, translate
COLLOQ. transmogrify
F3 retain

transparency *n*
1 CLEARNESS, clarity, translucence, translucency, sheerness,
gauziness, filminess, pellucidity, pellucidness,
perspicuousness, limpidity, limpidness, translucidity, water
FORMAL diaphanousness
2 PLAINNESS, clearness, clarity, obviousness, apparentness,
distinctness, unambiguousness, straightforwardness,
directness, openness, patentness, frankness, forthrightness,
explicitness, candidness
3 *holiday transparencies*
slide, photograph, photo, picture
F3 1 opacity 2 ambiguity, unclearness

transparent *adj*
1 *transparent plastic*
clear, see-through, translucent, sheer, pellucid,
diaphanous, gauzy, filmy
2 PLAIN, distinct, clear, lucid, explicit, unambiguous,
unequivocal, unmistakable, apparent, visible, obvious,
noticeable, discernible, perceptible, evident, patent,
manifest, undisguised, open, direct, forthright, candid,
straightforward
F3 1 opaque 2 unclear, ambiguous

transparently *adv*
plainly, clearly, distinctly, obviously, evidently, patently,
explicitly, unambiguously, unequivocally, unmistakably,
noticeably, perceptibly, discernibly
F3 unclearly, ambiguously

transpire *v*
1 BECOME KNOWN, turn out, come to light, come out, be
disclosed, become apparent, appear, prove
2 HAPPEN, occur, take place, ensue, arise, come about,
come to pass
FORMAL befall

transplant *v*
move, shift, displace, remove, uproot, graft, transfer,
relocate, resettle, repot, replant
F3 leave

transport *v, n*
♦ *v*
1 CONVEY, carry, bear, take, fetch, bring, move, run, shift,
transfer, ship, haul, remove, deport, exile
OLD traject
2 DELIGHT, enrapture, thrill, ravish, entrance, captivate,
electrify, spellbind
COLLOQ. carry away
♦ *n*
1 CONVEYANCE, transit, vehicle, carriage, transfer,
transportation, shipment, shipping, haulage, freight,
removal
2 *transports of delight*
rapture, ecstasy, bliss, euphoria, elation, exhilaration,
frenzy, fit
COLLOQ. seventh heaven

transportation *n*
conveyance, transit, carriage, transfer, shipment, shipping,
haulage, freight

transpose *v*
swap, exchange, switch, interchange, transfer, shift, invert,
rearrange, reorder, change, convert, alter, move, substitute

transverse *adj*
cross, crossways, crosswise, transversal, diagonal, oblique

trap *n, v*
♦ *n*
1 SNARE, net, mesh, noose, springe, gin, pit, hook, toils,
booby-trap, pitfall, danger, hazard, ambush, trick, wile,
ruse, stratagem, device, trickery, ploy, artifice, subterfuge,
deception; *dialect* grin, weel
TECHNICAL mantrap, mouse-trap, rat-trap, dead-fall,
fall-trap, flytrap, gin trap, pot, putcher
OLD snaphaunce
SLANG sting, plant
2 *Shut your trap!*
mouth
SLANG gob, traphole, cakehole, potato trap; *N Am* bazoo
♦ *v*
snare, net, entrap, ensnare, pin, enmesh, confine, catch,
capture, take, ambush, lure, beguile, corner, trick, deceive,
dupe, decoy, tangle, gin, lime, dig a pit for; *dialect* grin
TECHNICAL mist-net
FORMAL inveigle

trapped *adj*
caught, beguiled, cornered, ensnared, ambushed, snared,
stuck, netted, surrounded, tricked, deceived, duped
FORMAL inveigled
F3 free

trapper *n*
hunter, huntsman, backwoodsman, frontiersman, voyageur

trappings *n*
ornaments, accompaniments, clothes, adornments, dress,
decorations, fripperies, accessories, equipment,
paraphernalia, fixtures, fittings, furnishings, housings,
finery, livery, gear, trimmings
FORMAL accoutrements, panoply, raiment
COLLOQ. things, bells and whistles

trash *n, v*
♦ *n*
1 RUBBISH, garbage, refuse, junk, waste, litter, sweepings,
offscourings, scum, dregs, kitsch, trashery; *Scot* trashtrie
SLANG dreck; *N Am* grunge

2 NONSENSE, rubbish, garbage, junk, drivel, balderdash, gibberish, gobbledygook
COLLOQ. bunk, rot, tripe, bull, baloney, blah, bosh, eyewash, hogwash, rhubarb, guff, hooey, malarkey, moonshine
SLANG (*vulgar*) balls, bollocks, shit, bullshit
3 UNDESIRABLES, riff-raff, rabble, scum, dregs, *canaille*
♦ *v*
1 WRECK, destroy, ruin, demolish, devastate, shatter, smash, break, sink, spoil, mar, play havoc with, torpedo, ravage, write off
2 CRITICIZE, condemn, carp, snipe, disapprove of, find fault with, pass judgement on, denounce, attack, slate, run down, censure, blame
FORMAL disparage, excoriate, decry, denigrate, vituperate
COLLOQ. slam, knock, badmouth, rubbish, come down on, give someone some stick, go to town on, haul over the coals, pick holes in, pan, pull to pieces, tear to shreds, tear a strip off, do a hatchet job on, put the boot in
E3 1 build, repair **2** praise, commend

trashy *adj*
rubbishy, worthless, shabby, tawdry, tinsel, flimsy, third-rate, cheap, cheap-jack, kitschy, shoddy, inferior
FORMAL meretricious
SLANG naff, crappy
E3 first-rate

trauma *n*
injury, wound, hurt, lesion, damage, pain, suffering, grief, anguish, agony, torture, distress, ordeal, shock, disorder, jolt, upset, disturbance, upheaval, strain, stress
E3 healing

traumatic *adj*
painful, harmful, hurtful, injurious, wounding, shocking, agonizing, upsetting, distressing, disturbing, unpleasant, frightening, stressful
E3 healing, relaxing

traumatize *v*
shock, upset, distress, dismay, appal, outrage, horrify, startle, astound, stagger, amaze, stun, daze, stupefy, numb, paralyse, offend, hurt, grieve

travail *n*
1 TOIL, hardship, exertion, effort, drudgery, slog, strain, stress, suffering, distress, grind, tears, sweat
FORMAL tribulation
2 LABOUR PAINS, childbirth, birth-pangs, labour, throes
E3 rest

travel *v, n*
♦ *v*
journey, voyage, tour, make a trip, explore, go, go abroad/overseas, wend, make your way, move, advance, proceed, progress, wander, ramble, roam, rove, coast, cover, cross, traverse
OLD wayfare
COLLOQ. see the world
E3 stay, remain
♦ *n*
1 TRAVELLING, touring, journeying, tourism
OLD wayfare
COLLOQ. globetrotting
2 *travels abroad*
voyage, expedition, passage, journey, trip, excursion, sightseeing, tour, wanderings
COLLOQ. globetrotting

> **QUOTATIONS**
> To travel hopefully is a better thing than to arrive, and the true success is to labour
> ROBERT LOUIS STEVENSON, *Virginibus Puerisque*, 'El Dorado'

Methods of travel include:

aviate	hike	ride
backpack	hitch-hike	row
colloq. bike	jog	run
bus	march	sail
commute	motor	shuttle
cruise	orienteer	skate
cycle	paddle	ski
drive	pilot	steam
fly	punt	trek
freewheel	ramble	walk

Forms of travel include:

circumnavigation	jaunt	safari
cruise	journey	sail
drive	march	tour
excursion	migration	trek
expedition	mission	trip
exploration	outing	visit
flight	pilgrimage	voyage
hike	ramble	walk
holiday	ride	

traveller *n*
1 TOURIST, explorer, voyager, globetrotter, sightseer, holidaymaker, tourer, excursionist, passenger, commuter, wanderer, rambler, hiker, wayfarer, viator, seafarer, spacer
OLD roadster, peregrine
COLLOQ. tripper
2 WANDERER, wayfarer, migrant, nomad, Gypsy, itinerant, tinker, vagrant, tramp, drifter; *Aust & NZ* bushman
3 SALES REPRESENTATIVE, salesman, saleswoman, representative, commercial traveller, agent, commercial, knight of the road; *N Am* drummer
OLD bagman, rider
COLLOQ. rep

travelling *adj*
touring, wandering, roaming, roving, wayfaring, migrating, migrant, migratory, nomadic, itinerant, mobile, moving, vagrant, homeless, unsettled
FORMAL peripatetic
E3 fixed, settled

travel-worn *adj*
weary, tired, jet-lagged, saddle-sore, travel-weary, footsore, waygone, wayworn
E3 fresh

traverse *v*
cross, pass over/through, go across/through, travel across/through, negotiate, bridge, span, ford, ply, range, roam, wander
FORMAL peregrinate

travesty *n*
mockery, parody, burlesque, farce, caricature, perversion, corruption, distortion, misrepresentation, sham, apology
COLLOQ. take-off, send-up, wind-up, spoof, tall story

trawl *v*
search, hunt, look for, investigate, sift, wade, comb

treacherous *adj*
1 TRAITOROUS, disloyal, unfaithful, faithless, unreliable, untrustworthy, false, untrue, deceitful
FORMAL duplicitous, perfidious
COLLOQ. double-crossing, backstabbing, two-timing
2 *treacherous roads*
dangerous, hazardous, risky, perilous, precarious, unsafe, icy, slippery
E3 1 loyal, faithful, dependable **2** safe, stable

treacherously *adv*
deceitfully, falsely, disloyally, faithlessly
FORMAL perfidiously
E3 loyally

treachery *n*
treason, betrayal, sabotage, unfaithfulness, faithlessness, disloyalty, infidelity, falseness, deceitfulness, double-dealing, double-crossing, backstabbing, traitorhood, bad faith, hollowness, Judas kiss, Punic faith, *fides Punica*, *trahison*
FORMAL duplicity, perfidity
COLLOQ. two-timing
E3 loyalty, dependability

tread *v, n*
♦ *v*
walk, step, pace, stride, march, go, hike, trek, tramp, trudge, plod, stamp, trample, walk on, press (down), crush, squash, flatten
♦ *n*
walk, footstep, step, pace, stride, tramp, gait, footprint, footmark, footfall
■ **tread on someone's toes**
offend, hurt, upset, vex, irk, annoy, infringe, injure, affront, bruise, inconvenience
FORMAL discommode
COLLOQ. disgruntle
E3 soothe

treason *n*
treachery, disloyalty, subversion, mutiny, rebellion, disaffection, lese-majesty, traitorhood, *trahison*
OLD perduellion
FORMAL perfidy, duplicity, sedition, *crimen laesae majestatis*
E3 loyalty

treasonable *adj*
traitorous, disloyal, false, unfaithful, faithless, subversive, seditious, mutinous, rebellious
FORMAL perfidious
E3 loyal

treasure *n, v*
♦ *n*
1 FORTUNE, wealth, valuables, riches, money, cash, gold, jewels, gems, hoard, cache
2 *she's a real treasure*
gem, angel, prize, masterpiece, pride and joy, pet, darling, *pièce de résistance*, *crème de la crème*
♦ *v*
prize, value, hold dear, cherish, revere, worship, love, adore, idolize, dote on, think highly of, preserve, guard, esteem
E3 belittle; *formal* disparage

treasurer *n*
bursar, cashier, purser

treasury *n*
bank, exchequer, repository, resources, revenues, finances, capital, money, funds, assets, coffers, cache, hoard, vault, store, storehouse, thesaurus, corpus

treat *n, v*
♦ *n*
indulgence, gratification, pleasure, delight, enjoyment, fun, entertainment, amusement, celebration, excursion, outing, party, feast, banquet, gift, present, surprise, thrill
♦ *v*
1 DEAL WITH, manage, handle, use, attend to, behave towards, view, regard, consider, study, discuss, cover, review
2 TEND, nurse, minister to, attend to, care for, look after, heal, cure, medicate
3 PAY FOR, buy, stand, give, pay/foot the bill, provide, take out, entertain, amuse, delight, regale, feast
4 *wood treated with creosote*
put on, apply, spread on, lay on, cover with, paint, smear, rub, prime

treatable *adj*
curable, remediable, operable, medicable, reparable, rectifiable, reformable
E3 incurable

treatise *n*
essay, dissertation, thesis, monograph, paper, pamphlet, tract, study, discourse
FORMAL exposition, disquisition, prodrome

treatment *n*
1 HEALING, cure, remedy, medication, medicament, therapy, surgery, care, nursing, manipulation, therapeutics
2 MANAGEMENT, handling, dealing(s), use, usage, conduct, behaviour, action, discussion, coverage

treaty *n*
pact, convention, agreement, covenant, negotiation, bargain, contract, deal, pledge, bond, alliance, concord, peace, pacification
TECHNICAL protocol
OLD assiento, engagement
FORMAL concordat, compact
Related adjective: federal

treble *adj*
1 HIGH, high-pitched, shrill, sharp, piping
2 TRIPLE, threefold
E3 1 deep

tree *n*
bush, shrub, evergreen, conifer
Related adjective: arboreal

> **PROVERBS**
> The tree is known by its fruit

Trees include:

acacia	gum	sandalwood
acer	hawthorn	sapele
alder	hazel	sequoia
almond	hickory	shea
apple	hornbeam	silver birch
ash	horse chestnut	silver maple
aspen	jacaranda	spruce
balsa	Japanese maple	sycamore
bay	larch	tamarisk
beech	laurel	teak
birch	lime	walnut
blackthorn	linden	weeping willow
blue gum	mahogany	whitebeam
box	maple	willow
cedar	melaleuca	witch hazel
cherry	monkey puzzle	yew
chestnut	mountain ash	yucca
coconut palm	oak	
cottonwood	palm	**TYPES OF TREE:**
cypress	pear	bonsai
date palm	pine	conifer
dogwood	plane	deciduous
Dutch elm	plum	evergreen
ebony	poplar	fruit
elder	prunus	hardwood
elm	pussy willow	ornamental
eucalyptus	redwood	palm
fig	rowan	
fir	rubber tree	

trek *v, n*
♦ *v*
hike, journey, walk, march, tramp, traipse, trudge, plod, slog, ramble, rove, roam
COLLOQ. yomp
♦ *n*
hike, walk, march, tramp, ramble, journey, trip, expedition, safari, odyssey

trellis *n*
framework, mesh, grid, net, network, lattice, latticework, grate, grating, grille
FORMAL reticulation

tremble v, n

♦ v

shake, vibrate, quake, shiver, shudder, judder, wobble, rock, quaver, quiver, dither, dodder; *Scot* hotter

♦ n

shake, vibration, quake, shiver, shudder, judder, quiver, tremor, wobble, dither, quaver; *dialect* wuther

E3 steadiness

trembling n

shaking, vibration, quaking, quavering, quivering, shuddering, juddering, shivering, heart-quake, oscillation, rocking

COLLOQ. shakes

E3 steadiness

tremendous adj

1 WONDERFUL, marvellous, stupendous, remarkable, sensational, spectacular, exceptional, extraordinary, great, amazing, incredible, impressive

COLLOQ. terrific, smashing, out of this world

SLANG wicked

2 HUGE, immense, vast, great, enormous, massive, colossal, gigantic, towering, formidable

E3 1 ordinary, unimpressive

tremendously adv

extremely, exceedingly, excessively, very, really, exceptionally, extraordinarily, intensely, thoroughly, remarkably, utterly, greatly, highly, unusually, unreasonably, immoderately, uncommonly, inordinately, acutely, severely, decidedly

COLLOQ. awfully, frightfully, terrifically

tremor n

shake, quiver, tremble, trembling, shiver, quake, quaver, wobble, vibration, agitation, thrill, shock, earthquake; *N Am* temblor

E3 steadiness

tremulous adj

unsteady, shaky, shaking, wavering, vibrating, trembling, shivering, jumpy, jittery, quavering, quivering, quivery, agitated, trembly, afraid, scared, frightened, fearful, nervous, anxious, excited, timid

OLD aspen

E3 steady, firm, calm

trench n

ditch, channel, excavation, trough, waterway, earthwork, furrow, gutter, pit, cut, drain, rill, sap, entrenchment, fosse

trenchant adj

1 INCISIVE, pungent, caustic, biting, scathing, acerbic, penetrating, acute, astute, sharp, clear, perceptive, effective, clear-cut

FORMAL mordant, perspicacious

2 FORTHRIGHT, vigorous, forceful, emphatic, blunt, terse, unequivocal, no-nonsense

E3 woolly

trend n

1 TENDENCY, course, flow, current, drift, direction, bearing, inclination, leaning, tide, bent, rising tide, consensus

2 FASHION, craze, vogue, mode, style, look, mainstream, bandwagon

COLLOQ. rage, fad, latest, name of the game

trendsetter n

leader, model, pioneer, trailblazer, groundbreaker, innovator, modernist, new/modern man/woman, avant-gardist(e)

trendy adj

fashionable, latest, modish, stylish, on-trend, up-to-the-minute, fashion-forward, voguish

COLLOQ. all the rage, natty, hip, cool, funky, in, snazzy, groovy, with it, now

E3 unfashionable

trepidation n

fear, apprehension, alarm, dread, anxiety, worry, unease, qualms, disquiet, misgivings, dismay, uneasiness,

excitement, emotion, trembling, nervousness, shaking, agitation, quivering, tremor, palpitation, fright

FORMAL consternation, perturbation

COLLOQ. butterflies (in your stomach), cold sweat, jitters, nerves

E3 calm

trespass v, n

♦ v

invade, intrude, encroach, impinge, poach, infringe, violate, offend, sin, wrong

FORMAL obdurate, transgress

E3 obey, keep to

♦ n

invasion, intrusion, encroachment, poaching, infringement, violation, wrong, wrongdoing, contravention, offence, sin, misdemeanour

FORMAL transgression

trespasser n

intruder, encroacher, burglar, poacher, offender, criminal, delinquent, evil-doer, sinner

FORMAL transgressor

tress n

hair, curl, lock, braid, bunch, plait, pigtail, ringlet, tail

trial n, adj, v

♦ n

1 LITIGATION, case, lawsuit, hearing, inquiry, examination, tribunal, appeal, retrial

2 EXPERIMENT, test, examination, check, dummy run, try-out, practice, rehearsal, audition, contest, competition, selection, probation

FORMAL assay

COLLOQ. dry run

3 SUFFERING, grief, misery, distress, adversity, hardship, ordeal, trouble, nuisance, annoyance, burden, vexation, bother, bane, cross, cross to bear

FORMAL affliction, tribulation

COLLOQ. hassle, pest, pain in the neck, thorn in the flesh

E3 3 relief, happiness

♦ adj

experimental, test, testing, pilot, exploratory, provisional, probationary, dummy

COLLOQ. dry

♦ v

try out, pilot, experiment with, examine, assess, evaluate, check, investigate, study, analyse, screen, sample, put through its paces

FORMAL appraise, assay

COLLOQ. probe

triangle

Types of triangle include:

acute-angled	obtuse-angled
congruent	right-angled
equilateral	scalene
isosceles	similar
oblique	

---

triangular adj

triangle-shaped, three-sided, three-cornered, trilateral

TECHNICAL trigonous

FORMAL trigonal, trigonic

tribal adj

ethnic, family, native, indigenous, class, group, sectional

tribe n

race, nation, people, clan, sept, family, house, dynasty, blood, stock, group, ethnic group, caste, class, division, branch; *NZ* iwi

tribulation n

suffering, grief, pain, sorrow, vexation, ordeal, misery, unhappiness, misfortune, wretchedness, worry, care, anxiety, woe, burden, blow, distress, heartache, trial, reverse, adversity, hardship, trouble, curse

FORMAL affliction, travail
⊟ happiness, rest

tribunal *n*
court, committee, hearing, examination, inquisition, trial, bar, bench, kangaroo court

tributary *n*
stream, river, branch, feeder; *N Am* bogan
TECHNICAL head-stream
FORMAL confluent, influent

tribute *n*
1 PRAISE, commendation, compliment, high/good opinion, good word, accolade, present, gift, homage, respect, honour, applause, testimonial, credit, acknowledgement, evidence, proof, recognition, gratitude
FORMAL eulogy, paean, panegyric, enconium
2 PAYMENT, levy, charge, fee, toll, due, tax, tariff, duty, gift, offering, contribution
OLD pension, cain, gavel, scat, drift-land, Peter's pence, Rome-penny, Rome-scot

trice *n*
moment, minute, second, instant, flash, twinkling
COLLOQ. jiffy, sec, shake, tick, mo

trick *n, adj, v*
♦ *n*
1 FRAUD, swindle, deception, deceit, artifice, stratagem, ploy, ruse, dodge, subterfuge, trap, device, manoeuvre
COLLOQ. con, scam, diddle; *Aust & NZ* slinter
SLANG rip-off; *N Am* gold brick
2 HOAX, practical joke, joke, prank, antic, caper, frolic, gag, jape, feat, stunt
COLLOQ. leg-pull, frame-up, fast one, cod, wheeze, scam, curveball
SLANG *N Am* monkey shine
3 ILLUSION, apparition, mirage, fantasy, trick of light, sleight of hand, legerdemain
4 KNACK, gift, talent, technique, skill, art, flair, ability, capability, faculty, facility, capacity, secret, genius
COLLOQ. knowhow, hang
♦ *adj*
false, mock, artificial, imitation, ersatz, fake, forged, counterfeit, feigned, sham, bogus
⊟ real, genuine
♦ *v*
deceive, delude, dupe, fool, hoodwink, beguile, mislead, take in, bluff, hoax, cheat, swindle, diddle, defraud, trap, outwit, palter
COLLOQ. con, pull someone's leg, kid, fix, rook, have on, do, pull a fast one on, pull one over, lead up the garden path, pull the wool over someone's eyes; *N Am* pull/yank someone's chain
SLANG take for a ride
■ **trick out**
decorate, spruce up, ornament, adorn, dress up; *N Am* trick up
FORMAL array, attire, bedeck
COLLOQ. do up, doll up, tart up

SYNONYM NUANCES

noun sense 1
You might use the terms **fraud** and **swindle** to refer to the intent to trick someone for financial gain, with **fraud** more suggestive of a criminal practice. **Deception** can be widely used of any attempt to mislead, and **deceit** also implies misrepresentation, but has greater connotation of malicious intent. **Artifice** is less disapproving, and is more suggestive of a false display: *ventriloquism is a kind of artifice*.
  Both **stratagem** and **ruse** may be used of a premeditated plan for fooling an enemy, while **ploy** has stronger implications of mischievous intent, and **dodge** usually implies a devious motive in avoiding something. **Subterfuge**, on the other hand, suggests complex tactics in order to obscure the truth: *anorexics use all manner of subterfuge to avoid eating*.

While **trap** would be used specifically of a scheme to ensnare someone, and **manoeuvre** is more suggestive of calculated trickery, the term **device** can be widely applied to any kind of contrivance.

trickery *n*
deception, deceit, cunning, illusion, sleight, sleight of hand, smoke and mirrors, pretence, contrivance, conveyance, dodgery, jugglery, legerdemain, practice, artifice, guile, wiliness, subterfuge, dishonesty, cheating, swindling, fraud, imposture, double-dealing, monkey business, chicanery, skulduggery; *Scot* joukery, joukery-pawkery, cantrip
OLD ropery
FORMAL duplicity
COLLOQ. funny business, hanky-panky, jiggery-pokery, hocus-pocus, shenanigans
SLANG trap
⊟ straightforwardness, honesty

trickle *v, n*
♦ *v*
dribble, run, leak, seep, ooze, flow slowly, drizzle, exude, drip, drop, filter, percolate
⊟ stream, gush
♦ *n*
dribble, drip, drop, leak, seepage
⊟ stream, gush

trickster *n*
cheat, swindler, deceiver, fraud, fraudster, hoaxer, impostor, joker, pretender, tricker, cozener, rogue, rascal, charlatan, mountebank
OLD tregetour
FORMAL dissembler
COLLOQ. con man/woman, con artist, diddler, shark, rook, hustler, hood, hoodlum

tricky *adj*
1 *a tricky problem*
difficult, awkward, problematic, complicated, knotty, thorny, nasty, sensitive, delicate, ticklish
COLLOQ. dodgy
2 CRAFTY, artful, cunning, sly, wily, foxy, subtle, devious, slippery, scheming, deceitful, shifty
COLLOQ. dodgy
⊟ **1** easy, simple **2** honest

tried *adj*
tested, proven, proved, reliable, dependable, trusted, trustworthy, established

trifle *n, v*
♦ *n*
1 LITTLE, bit, small amount, spot, drop, dash, touch, trace
2 TOY, plaything, trinket, bauble, knick-knack, gewgaw, geegaw, triviality, nothing, trivia, inessential, minor consideration
OLD flamflew
♦ *v*
toy, play, sport, flirt, treat frivolously, dally, dabble, fiddle, meddle, fool, potter
COLLOQ. mess about/around

QUOTATIONS
You know my method. It is founded upon the observance of trifles
  SIR ARTHUR CONAN DOYLE, *The Adventures of Sherlock Holmes*, 'The Boscombe Valley Mystery'

---

trifling *adj*
small, paltry, slight, negligible, inconsiderable, unimportant, insignificant, minor, trivial, superficial, petty, silly, foolish, frivolous, idle, empty, shallow, worthless
OLD (*Shakesp*) baubling, immoment
FORMAL inconsequential
COLLOQ. piffling
⊟ important, significant, serious

trigger v, n

♦ v

cause, start, initiate, activate, bring about, set off, spark off, touch off, provoke, prompt, elicit, generate, produce, set in motion/action

COLLOQ. set/start the ball rolling

♦ n

lever, catch, switch, spur, stimulus

trill v

sing, warble, flute, pipe, lilt

trim adj, v, n

♦ adj

1 NEAT, tidy, orderly, shipshape, in good order, spick-and-span, spruce, smart, well-turned-out, well-groomed, well-dressed, presentable, dapper; Scot snod

COLLOQ. natty, cool, snazzy

2 SLIM, slender, svelte, streamlined, fit, compact

Ｅ **1** untidy, scruffy

♦ v

1 CUT, clip, crop, dock, snip, prune, pare, shave, shear, chop

2 DECREASE, reduce, cut (down), cut back on, diminish, curtail, contract, scale down

3 DECORATE, ornament, embellish, garnish, adorn, festoon, dress, fringe, edge, adjust, arrange, order, neaten, tidy (up)

FORMAL array

♦ n

1 CONDITION, state, order, form, shape, fitness, health, fettle

2 TRIMMING, braid, border, edging, fringe, frill, decoration

trimming n

1 ADORNMENT, decoration, braid, border, edging, fringe, frill, embellishment, garnish, ornamentation, trim, extra, accompaniment, accessory, piping, falbala, frou-frou, passement, passementerie

TECHNICAL fimbriation

OLD furbelow

COLLOQ. bells and whistles

2 CUTTING, clipping, paring, end

trinket n

bauble, jewel, ornament, charm, knick-knack, trifle, gimcrack, gewgaw, geegaw, bagatelle, whim-wham, seal, trick, bijou, doodah, kickshaw(s); Scot whigmaleerie

OLD flamflew, trankum

trio n

threesome, triad, trinity, triune, triunity, triplet, triplicity, trilogy

FORMAL triumvirate, troika

trip n, v

♦ n

1 OUTING, excursion, tour, jaunt, ride, drive, spin, run, journey, voyage, expedition, sail, cruise, flip, whirl, foray; Scot hurl

COLLOQ. daycation, jolly, tootle

2 FALL, slip, stumble, tumble, false step

3 ERROR, blunder, mistake, inaccuracy, slip, gaffe, faux pas

COLLOQ. howler, bloomer, clanger, booboo

4 HALLUCINATION, illusion, vision, apparition, fantasy, dream, experience

COLLOQ. high, bummer

SLANG freak-out, buzz

♦ v

1 STUMBLE, slip, slide, fall, tumble, stagger, totter, lose your footing

OLD spurn

2 DANCE, waltz, skip, gambol, hop, spring, caper, tiptoe; Scot link

OLD kilt

■ **trip up**

catch (out), trap, disconcert, wrongfoot, throw off balance, snare, ensnare, ambush, waylay, outsmart, outwit, surprise, trick

tripe n

rubbish, nonsense, bunkum, drivel, garbage, inanity, claptrap, trash

COLLOQ. balderdash, hogwash, twaddle, tosh, rot, poppycock, blah, bosh, baloney, eyewash, rhubarb, guff, hooey, malarkey, moonshine

SLANG (vulgar) balls, shit, bullshit, bollocks

Ｅ sense

triple adj, v, n

♦ adj

treble, three times, triplicate, threefold, three-ply, three-way, tripartite

♦ v

treble, triplicate

♦ n

trio, threesome, triad, trinity, triune, triunity, triplet, triplicity, trilogy

FORMAL triumvirate, troika

tripper n

tourist, sightseer, traveller, voyager, holidaymaker, excursionist

COLLOQ. grockle

trite adj

banal, commonplace, common, ordinary, run-of-the-mill, stale, tired, worn, well-worn, worn-out, threadbare, unoriginal, uninspired, dull, routine, hackneyed, overdone, overused, overworn, stock, stereotyped, cliché(e)d, predictable, beaten, novelettish, truistic, tritical; N Am cornball

FORMAL platitudinous

COLLOQ. corny, Mickey Mouse

SLANG N Am rinky-dink

Ｅ original, new, fresh, imaginative, inspired

SYNONYM NUANCES

You can use the adjectives **banal** or **commonplace** to suggest that something is without distinctive traits; **common**, **ordinary** and **routine** are even more widely used to describe something frequent and thereby unremarkable.

Stale, **tired**, **worn** and **well-worn** are more marked by disapproval, and have further connotations of having been seen or used too often: *the stale routines of life; tired old excuses*, and **worn-out** and **threadbare**, **overdone**, **overused** and **overworn** even more markedly suggest this loss of effectiveness through constant employment. **Hackneyed** and **clichéd** are also highly critical, and applied particularly to verbal expressions that have become meaningless or tedious through excessive use: *clichéd phrases used every day in the papers*.

Unoriginal and **uninspired** are equally critical, but make the accusation of a lack of new thinking, rather than of overuse. **Stock** could describe something conventionally used in certain situations: *he gave his stock reply*, while **stereotyped** has more to do with fixed, standardized images: *homeless people stereotyped as drug addicts*. The word **predictable** puts the emphasis on an inability to surprise: *a predictable plot where all the usual events unfold*.

---

triumph n, v

♦ n

1 WIN, victory, conquest, success, mastery, achievement, accomplishment, attainment, feat, coup, masterstroke, hit, sensation, flying colours

COLLOQ. walkover

2 EXULTATION, jubilation, rejoicing, celebration, elation, joy, happiness, glory, paean

Ｅ **1** failure

♦ v

1 WIN, succeed, prosper, conquer, defeat, beat, overcome, overwhelm, gain mastery, dominate

FORMAL vanquish, prevail

COLLOQ. win the day

2 CELEBRATE, rejoice, glory, gloat, exult, revel, swagger, crow

OLD overcrow
FORMAL jubilate
▣ 1 lose, fail

triumphant adj
winning, victorious, conquering, successful, prize-winning,
exultant, jubilant, rejoicing, celebratory, glorious, elated,
joyful, proud, boastful, gloating, swaggering, crowing
COLLOQ. cock-a-hoop
▣ defeated, humble

trivia n
details, trifles, trivialities, irrelevancies, technicalities,
minutiae
COLLOQ. pap
▣ essentials

trivial adj
unimportant, insignificant, incidental, minor, petty, paltry,
trifling, flimsy, small, little, inconsiderable, negligible,
worthless, meaningless, frivolous, banal, trite,
commonplace, everyday, frothy, gimcrack, quibbling,
footling, pettifogging, snippety, peppercorn
OLD bald
FORMAL inconsequential, of no consequence
COLLOQ. measly, piddling, piffling, no great shakes, cutting
no ice; N Am dinky
SLANG N Am rinky-dink
▣ important, significant, profound, substantial

> **SYNONYM NUANCES**
>
> **Unimportant** can be used of anything that has a lack of
> consequence, and **insignificant** of something not being
> worthy of note, while **incidental** is more suggestive of
> something, often unforeseen, accompanying a major
> issue: *incidental expenses.* **Minor**, however, might be
> used of anything inferior in size or importance: *the
> police ignored the minor details of the incident*, whereas
> **petty**, **paltry** and **trifling** are dismissive terms, suggesting
> something is unworthy of consideration: *trifling details
> are of no interest to me.* **Flimsy**, on the other hand, puts
> the emphasis on a lack of substance: *flimsy evidence.*
>
> **Inconsiderable** suggests literally that something is
> unworthy of notice, but is usually used in the negative to
> mean the opposite: *using his not inconsiderable bulk*,
> and **negligible** can be used in a less judgemental way of
> something which can be safely ignored: *the hazards
> were negligible.* **Worthless**, meanwhile, does suggest
> more of a judgement that something has no inherent
> value, and **frivolous** and **frothy** again imply a
> judgement, suggesting an inappropriate lack of gravity,
> or excessive concern with inconsequential things: *a
> frothy chat show.*
>
> To describe something, such as an opinion or phrase,
> that has lost all significance through overuse, you might
> use **banal** or **trite**, **commonplace** or **everyday**. The
> terms **quibbling** and **pettifogging** have more to do with
> an excessive concern for irrelevant detail.

triviality n
1 UNIMPORTANCE, insignificance, pettiness, smallness,
worthlessness, meaninglessness, nonsense, nothingism,
pretence, foolishness, frivolity, banality, frippery, puerility
2 TRIFLE, detail, technicality, nothing
▣ 1 importance 2 essential

trivialize v
minimize, play down, underestimate, underplay,
undervalue, devalue, belittle, depreciate, scoff at
▣ exalt

troll n
goblin, dwarf, elf, gnome, jinn; Scot trow, drow; Irish
pooka

trollop n
prostitute, harlot, callgirl, rent-boy, woman of the streets,
woman of the town, woman of ill repute, loose woman,
fallen woman, scarlet woman, whore, street-walker,

cocotte, courtesan, bawd, *fille de joie, fille des rues*, drab,
grande cocotte, lorette, lady of the night, geisha, hetaera,
hierodule, loose fish, magdalen, night-walker, vizard-mask
OLD bulker, convertite, trull, strumpet, cockatrice, public
woman, wench, pug, punk, stew, stale; (*Shakesp*) quail,
bona-roba, callet, polecat, road, venture
COLLOQ. hooker, hustler, moll, pro, hostess, fancy woman;
N Am working girl
SLANG *poule de luxe*, quiff, rough trade, tart, tom, tramp,
brass, floozie; N Am broad
OLD SLANG dell, mutton, dolly-mop, plover; (*Shakesp*)
laced mutton

troop n, v
♦ n
1 *send in troops*
army, military, soldiers, armed forces, servicemen,
servicewomen, fighters, cavalry, gunners, infantrymen,
fusiliers, platoons, brigades, regiments, commandos,
squadrons, paratroopers, paratroops, militia, convoys
OLD kern, turm
2 *a troop of soldiers/children*
contingent, squadron, unit, division, company, squad,
team, crew, gang, band, bunch, group, body, pack, herd,
flock, school, horde, crowd, throng, mob, gathering,
multitude
FORMAL assemblage
♦ v
go, march, parade, walk, stream, flock, swarm, throng,
traipse, trudge

trophy n
cup, prize, laurels, award, spoils, souvenir, memento,
silverware

tropical adj
hot, very hot, torrid, sultry, boiling (hot), sweltering,
stifling, steamy, humid
▣ arctic, cold, cool, temperate

trot v, n
♦ v
jog, canter, run, pace, scamper, scuttle, bustle, scurry; S
Afr tripple
♦ n
jog, canter, run, dogtrot, jogtrot; S Afr tripple
TECHNICAL passage
■ **trot out**
bring out, bring up, drag up, relate, repeat, bring forward,
exhibit, reiterate
FORMAL adduce, recite, rehearse
■ **on the trot**
in a row, consecutively, successively, sequentially,
continuously, uninterruptedly, one after the other, in turn
COLLOQ. back to back

troubadour n
singer, minstrel, balladeer, cantabank, jongleur, poet,
trouvère, trouveur, Minnesinger

trouble n, v
♦ n
1 PROBLEM, difficulty, struggle, annoyance, irritation,
vexation, bother, nuisance, inconvenience, hardship,
misfortune, adversity, trial, torment, burden, pain,
suffering, distress, grief, woe, heartache, concern, unease,
uneasiness, worry, anxiety, agitation
FORMAL tribulation, affliction, disquiet
COLLOQ. hassle, headache, hot water, mess, corner, fix,
scrape, jam, pickle, tight spot
See Synonym nuances panel at **problem**.
2 UNREST, strife, fighting, tumult, commotion, disturbance,
disorder, bother, upheaval
3 *back trouble*
disorder, complaint, ailment, illness, disease, disability,
defect
4 *engine trouble*
problem(s), failure, breakdown, cutting-out, shutdown,
stopping, stalling
FORMAL malfunction

COLLOQ. packing-up
SLANG conking-out
5 EFFORT, exertion, pains, care, attention, thought, thoughtfulness, bother, fuss, ado, inconvenience
COLLOQ. hassle
F3 **1** relief, calm **2** order, peace **3** health
♦ v
annoy, vex, harass, torment, bother, distract, make the effort, inconvenience, disturb, upset, distress, sadden, pain, afflict, weigh (down), burden, worry, agitate, irritate, disconcert, perplex
FORMAL discommode, perturb
COLLOQ. put out, hassle
F3 reassure, help

> **PROVERBS**
> Trouble shared is trouble halved

troubled adj
worried, anxious, uneasy, ill at ease, apprehensive, concerned, bothered, upset, fearful, afraid, frightened, overwrought, tense, strained, nervous, disturbed, distraught, distracted, disquieted, dismayed, fretful, distressed, agonized
FORMAL perturbed
COLLOQ. on edge, uptight, (all) hot and bothered
F3 calm, unworried, unconcerned

troublemaker n
agitator, rabble-rouser, incendiary, instigator, inciter, ringleader, agent provocateur, mischief-maker
COLLOQ. stirrer, mixer
SLANG bovver boy; (taboo) shit-stirrer
F3 peacemaker

troublesome adj
1 ANNOYING, irritating, vexatious, irksome, bothersome, worrisome, disturbing, inconvenient, difficult, hard, awkward, tricky, thorny, taxing, demanding, exacting, laborious, tiresome, wearisome
FORMAL perturbing
2 UNRULY, mischievous, rowdy, turbulent, trying, unco-operative, insubordinate, rebellious
F3 **1** easy, simple **2** helpful

trough n
1 MANGER, feeding trough, feeder, crib, watering-trough, sluice; Scot backet
2 GUTTER, conduit, drain, trench, ditch, gully, channel, chute, duct, groove, furrow, flame, hollow, valley, depression, trunk, hopper, launder; N Am gum
TECHNICAL sand table, tye, sheep-dip

trounce v
defeat, rout, beat, thrash, overwhelm, paste, punish, best, crush
COLLOQ. wallop, slaughter, hammer, clobber, lick, drub, wipe the floor with
SLANG take to the cleaners, pwn

troupe n
company, group, set, band, cast, troop

trouper n
actor, performer, player, theatrical, artiste, entertainer, veteran
FORMAL thespian
COLLOQ. old hand

trousers n
slacks, jeans, denims, Levis®, flannels, chinos, corduroys, cords, dungarees, breeches, shorts; Scot trews; N Am pants
OLD (Shakesp) strossers; Irish trouse
COLLOQ. Aust daks
SLANG Irish trouses

truancy n
absence, absenteeism, shirking, malingering, French leave
COLLOQ. skiving
F3 attendance

truant n, adj, v
♦ n
absentee, deserter, runaway, idler, shirker, dodger, malingerer
COLLOQ. skiver
♦ adj
absent, missing, runaway
♦ v
play truant, desert, dodge, shirk, malinger
COLLOQ. skive, skive off, play hooky
SLANG N Am goof off

truce n
ceasefire, peace, armistice, pacification, cessation, moratorium, suspension, stay, respite, lull, rest, break, interval, intermission; dialect barley
OLD (Spenser) treague
COLLOQ. let-up
F3 war, hostilities

truck¹ n
heavy trucks on the road
lorry, articulated lorry, heavy goods vehicle (HGV), juggernaut, van, wagon, float

truck² n
have no truck with someone
contact, communication, connection, assocation, relations, dealings, business, trade, commerce, traffic, exchange
FORMAL intercourse

truculence n
aggressiveness, belligerence, defiance, disobedience, quarrelsomeness, hostility, violence, rudeness, bad-temperedness, obstreperousness
FORMAL bellicosity, pugnacity

truculent adj
aggressive, belligerent, defiant, disobedient, quarrelsome, antagonistic, contentious, hostile, violent, savage, combative, fierce, argumentative, rude, bad-tempered, ill-tempered, sullen, cross, obstreperous, discourteous, disrespectful
FORMAL bellicose, pugnacious
F3 co-operative, good-natured

trudge v, n
♦ v
tramp, plod, clump, stump, lumber, traipse, slog, toil, labour, trek, hike, walk, march, shuffle
♦ n
tramp, traipse, slog, haul, trek, hike, walk, march

true adj, adv
♦ adj
1 REAL, genuine, authentic, actual, veritable, exact, precise, accurate, close, correct, right, factual, truthful, sincere, honest, legitimate, faithful, unerring, valid, rightful, proper
FORMAL veracious
2 FAITHFUL, loyal, constant, steadfast, fast, staunch, firm, dependable, reliable, true-hearted, trustworthy, trusty, honourable, sincere, dedicated, devoted
F3 **1** false, wrong, untrue, incorrect, inaccurate **2** unfaithful, faithless
♦ adv
accurately, exactly, correctly, faithfully, honestly, precisely, rightly, truly, truthfully, unerringly, properly, perfectly, veritably
FORMAL veraciously
F3 falsely, inaccurately

true-blue adj
card-carrying, committed, confirmed, constant, dedicated, devoted, diehard, dyed-in-the-wool, faithful, loyal, orthodox, staunch, true, trusty, uncompromising, unwavering
F3 superficial, wavering

truism n
platitude, self-evident truth, truth, commonplace, cliché, bromide, axiom

truly *adv*
very, greatly, extremely, exceptionally, really, genuinely, sincerely, honestly, constantly, steadfastly, truthfully, on my word/honour, surely, definitely, certainly, undoubtedly, without a doubt, undeniably, indubitably, indeed, true, in fact, in reality, in truth, actually, exactly, precisely, correctly, rightly, properly, quite; *dialect* fegs
OLD certes; (*Spenser*) soothly, soothlich
E3 slightly, falsely, incorrectly

trump *v*
outdo, outshine, surpass, top, cap, eclipse, upstage
COLLOQ. knock spots off
■ **trump up**
invent, fake, fabricate, falsify, create, devise, make up, concoct, contrive
COLLOQ. cook up

trumped-up *adj*
false, fabricated, fake, faked, falsified, invented, made-up, untrue, bogus, cooked-up, concocted, contrived, spurious
COLLOQ. phoney
E3 genuine, real, true

trumpery *adj*
worthless, useless, valueless, shabby, trifling, showy, cheap, flashy, nasty, rubbishy, shoddy, tawdry, trashy
FORMAL meretricious
E3 first-rate

trumpet *n, v*
♦ *n*
bugle, horn, cornet, trombone, ram's horn, clarion, clarino, shell, conch, blare, blast, roar, bellow, cry, call, clang, tantara, taratantara, tucket, last trump
OLD trump, tuba, alchemy, buccina, lituus, lure, salpinx, sennet
♦ *v*
blare, blast, roar, bellow, bay, shout, proclaim, announce, call, sound, herald, broadcast, advertise, taratantara, chide
OLD trump
COLLOQ. toot, parp
■ **blow your own trumpet**
boast, crow, brag, show off, sing your own praises
COLLOQ. swank, talk big, loudmouth; *N Am* blow your own horn; *Aust* skite

truncate *v*
shorten, abbreviate, curtail, reduce, diminish, cut short, cut, lop, dock, prune, pare, clip, trim, crop
E3 lengthen, extend

truncheon *n*
baton, club, cudgel, cosh, stick, staff, shillelagh, knobkerrie; *N Am* billy, billystick

trundle *v*
roll, bowl, chug, cruise, freewheel

trunk *n*
1 STEM, shaft, stock, stalk
2 CASE, suitcase, chest, coffer, box, crate, portmanteau
3 SNOUT, nose
TECHNICAL proboscis
4 TORSO, body, frame

truss *v, n*
♦ *v*
tie, strap, bind, pinion, fasten, tether, secure, bundle, wrap, pack
E3 untie, loosen
♦ *n*
binding, bandage, pad, support, brace, prop, stay, shore, buttress, strut, joist; *Scot* dorlach

trust *n, v*
♦ *n*
1 FAITH, belief, credence, credit, hope, expectation, reliance, confidence, assurance, conviction, certainty

2 CARE, charge, custody, safekeeping, guardianship, trusteeship, protection, obligation, responsibility, duty, commitment
E3 1 distrust, mistrust, scepticism, doubt
Related adjective: fiduciary
♦ *v*
1 RELY ON, depend on, put your confidence in, put your trust in, have confidence in, believe in, be sure of, count on, bank on, swear by
2 BELIEVE, imagine, assume, presume, suppose, hope, expect
FORMAL surmise
3 ENTRUST, commit, consign, confide, give, assign, turn over, delegate
E3 2 distrust, mistrust, doubt, disbelieve

trustee *n*
keeper, administrator, agent, custodian, guardian, executor, executrix, fiduciary, depositary, assignee

trusting *adj*
trustful, credulous, gullible, naive, innocent, ingenuous, unquestioning, unsuspecting, unguarded, unwary
E3 distrustful, suspicious, cautious

trustworthiness *n*
honesty, integrity, consistency of character, honourableness, reliability, dependability, steadfastness, stability, commitment, devotion, faithfulness, loyalty, responsibility, sensibleness, level-headedness
E3 irresponsibility, unreliability

trustworthy *adj*
honest, upright, honourable, principled, ethical, dependable, reputable, reliable, steadfast, stable, staunch, true, safe, sound, committed, devoted, faithful, loyal, responsible, sensible, level-headed, creditable, authentic
COLLOQ. (as) good as your word
E3 untrustworthy, dishonest, unreliable, irresponsible

trusty *adj*
faithful, dependable, reliable, responsible, strong, supportive, firm, honest, loyal, staunch, trustworthy, true, solid, straightforward, steady, upright
E3 unreliable

truth *n*
1 TRUTHFULNESS, candour, frankness, honesty, sincerity, genuineness, authenticity, realism, exactness, precision, correctness, accuracy, validity, legitimacy, rightness, honour, honourableness, integrity, uprightness, faithfulness, loyalty, constancy
FORMAL verity, veracity, fidelity
2 *tell the truth*
facts, reality, actuality, fact, the gospel truth, axiom, maxim, principle, truism
OLD sooth
COLLOQ. home truth
E3 1 deceit, dishonesty, falseness **2** lie, falsehood
■ **in truth**
in fact, indeed, really, in reality, surely, actually, as a matter of fact, in actual fact, in point of fact, to tell you the truth, truth to tell, if truth be told, to be honest
OLD forsooth, insooth, soothly, soothlich

> **QUOTATIONS**
> The truth is rarely pure, and never simple
> OSCAR WILDE, *The Importance of Being Earnest*
>
> Truth is tough. It will not break, like a bubble, at a touch; nay, you may kick it about all day like a football, and it will be round and full at evening
> OLIVER WENDELL HOLMES, *The Autocrat of the Breakfast Table*

truthful *adj*
frank, candid, straight, honest, open, forthright, true, sincere, veritable, exact, precise, right, factual, accurate, correct, valid, realistic, faithful, trustworthy, reliable
OLD sooth, soothfast

FORMAL veracious
E3 untruthful, deceitful, false, untrue

truthfully adv
honestly, openly, truly, sincerely, precisely, factually, accurately, correctly, faithfully, reliably
E3 falsely, deceitfully

truthfulness n
frankness, candour, honesty, openness, sincerity, straightness, uprightness, righteousness
FORMAL veracity
E3 untruthfulness

try v, n
♦ v
1 ATTEMPT, endeavour, venture, undertake, seek, search, strive, aim
FORMAL assay
COLLOQ. have a go, have a bash/crack/shot/stab, give something your best shot, give something a whirl
2 HEAR, judge
3 EXPERIMENT, test, try out, sample, taste, inspect, examine, investigate, evaluate
FORMAL appraise
4 *try someone's patience*
tax, make demands on, strain, stress, tire, wear out, weary, exhaust, drain, sap, weaken, stretch
♦ n
1 ATTEMPT, endeavour, effort
COLLOQ. go, bash, crack, shot, stab, whirl
2 EXPERIMENT, test, trial, evaluation, ample, taste
FORMAL appraisal
■ **try out**
test, evaluate, try on, check out, inspect, sample, taste
FORMAL appraise

trying adj
annoying, irritating, vexatious, exasperating, troublesome, tiresome, wearisome, bothersome, difficult, hard, tough, arduous, taxing, stressful, demanding, testing
COLLOQ. aggravating
E3 easy

tub n
bath, bathtub, washtub, basin, vat, tun, butt, cask, barrel, container, keg, hogshead, lucky dip, bran tub, stand, back, swill-tub, keeve, kid; *dialect* cowl, dan, kit
TECHNICAL kier
OLD bran-pie
COLLOQ. *Aust* bucket

tubby adj
chubby, plump, portly, podgy, paunchy, stout, pudgy, roly-poly, fat, overweight, obese, buxom, well-upholstered
FORMAL corpulent, rotund
E3 slim

tube n
hose, pipe, tubing, cylinder, duct, conduit, spout, channel, shaft, inlet, outlet

tubular adj
tubelike, pipelike, pipy
FORMAL tubulous, tubulate, tubiform, tubate, vasiform

tuck v, n
♦ v
1 INSERT, push, ease, thrust, stuff, cram, gird yourself
2 FOLD, pleat, gather, crease, ruffle, kilt
♦ n
1 FOLD, pleat, gather, pucker, crease
2 FOOD, comestibles, meals, snack(s)
COLLOQ. eats, scrab
SLANG grub, nosh, scoff, chow
■ **tuck away**
stash away, save (up), store, hide, conceal, hoard
■ **tuck in/into**
eat, eat up, eat heartily, gorge, devour, dine, feast
COLLOQ. gobble, scoff, wolf down

■ **tuck in/up**
put to bed, make comfortable, make snug, cover up, wrap up, fold in/under, truss

tuft n
crest, beard, tassel, truss, knot, clump, cluster, bunch, wisp
FORMAL flocculus

tug v, n
♦ v
pull, draw, tow, haul, drag, lug, heave, wrench, jerk, pluck
COLLOQ. yank
♦ n
pull, tow, haul, heave, wrench, jerk, pluck
COLLOQ. yank

tuition n
teaching, instruction, coaching, training, guidance, lessons, schooling, education

tumble v, n
♦ v
1 FALL, fall over, trip (up), topple, stumble, drop, flop, knock down, unseat, overthrow
2 PITCH, roll, toss, lurch, sway, reel, heave, welter
3 *prices are tumbling*
decrease, fall, decline, collapse, slide, plummet, dive, nosedive, plunge, fall headlong
4 TOUSLE, rumple, dishevel, disarrange, disorder
♦ n
1 FALL, stumble, trip, drop, roll, toss
2 DECREASE, fall, decline, collapse, slide, dive, nosedive
■ **tumble to**
understand, realize, grasp, perceive, become aware of, comprehend
COLLOQ. cotton on to, twig, suss, get, get the picture, latch on to; *N Am* savvy

tumbledown adj
broken-down, ramshackle, rickety, dilapidated, unstable, unsteady, shaky, unsafe, ruinous, ruined, crumbling, crumbly, disintegrating, decrepit, tottering
E3 well-kept

tumbler n
1 ACROBAT, gymnast, contortionist
2 DRINKING-GLASS, glass, beaker, cup, goblet, mug

tumid adj
1 SWOLLEN, enlarged, bulging, protuberant, bloated, puffed up, bulbous
FORMAL distended, tumescent
2 BOMBASTIC, pompous, affected, overblown, grandiose, high-flown, inflated, pretentious, fulsome, flowery, stilted, turgid
FORMAL euphuistic, grandiloquent, magniloquent
E3 1 flat 2 simple

tummy n
stomach, gut, inside(s), belly, abdomen, paunch, pot-belly
COLLOQ. corporation
SLANG bread basket

tumour n
cancer, growth, malignancy, lump, swelling
TECHNICAL carcinoma, melanoma, lymphoma, myeloma, sarcoma, polyp, neoplasm

tumult n
commotion, turmoil, disturbance, upheaval, stir, agitation, unrest, disorder, confusion, chaos, pandemonium, bedlam, babel, noise, clamour, shouting, din, racket, hubbub, hullaballoo, row, rumpus, uproar, riot, fracas, brawl, affray, strife, mutiny, rout, bustle, hurricane, ferment, surge, whirl, hurly, hurly-burly, rabblement, ruffle, stour, williwaw; *Scot* brattle, stramash
OLD coil, deray, rore; (*Shakesp*) romage
FORMAL disarray
E3 peace, calm, composure

tumultuous *adj*
turbulent, stormy, raging, frenzied, fierce, violent, wild, vehement, fervent, hectic, boisterous, rowdy, noisy, loud, deafening, clamorous, disorderly, unruly, riotous, uncontrolled, restless, agitated, troubled, disturbed, excited
OLD troublous, tumultuary
F3 calm, peaceful, quiet

tune *n, v*
♦ *n*
melody, theme, motif, song, air, strain, serenade, chorus, dance, spring, lilt, round, folk-tune, signature, signature tune, theme song, jingle, port, rant, melisma
OLD ayre, dump, note, loure, hunt's-up, light-o'-love, maggot
♦ *v*
pitch, harmonize, set, regulate, adjust, adapt, temper, synchronize
FORMAL attune
■ **change your tune**
change your mind, change your attitude/opinions, change your approach
■ **in tune with**
in agreement with, in sympathy with, agreeing with, in harmony with, on the same wavelength as, true, *d'accord*
FORMAL in accord with
■ **out of tune**
jarring, false, disagreeing, at odds
TECHNICAL off-key, out of key, untuned, mistuned, scordato
OLD ajar, distuned

> **PROVERBS**
> There's many a good tune played on an old fiddle

tuneful *adj*
melodious, melodic, catchy, musical, euphonious, harmonious, pleasant, agreeable, mellow, sonorous
FORMAL mellifluous
F3 tuneless, discordant

tuneless *adj*
unmelodic, unmelodious, unmusical, unpleasant, disagreeable, harsh, clashing, discordant, cacophonous, dissonant
FORMAL atonal, horrisonant
F3 tuneful

tunnel *n, v*
♦ *n*
passage, underground passage, passageway, gallery, subway, underpass, burrow, hole, mine, shaft, chimney
♦ *v*
burrow, dig, excavate, mine, bore, penetrate, undermine, sap

turbid *adj*
cloudy, clouded, hazy, dense, dim, foggy, fuzzy, muddy, murky, unclear, thick, muddled, opaque, confused, disordered, turbulent, unsettled, impure, incoherent, foul
FORMAL feculent
F3 clear

turbulence *n*
roughness, storm, unrest, boiling, upheaval, agitation, turmoil, tumult, confusion, commotion, chaos, disorder, disruption, instability, pandemonium
F3 calm

turbulent *adj*
rough, choppy, foaming, stormy, blustery, tempestuous, raging, furious, violent, wild, tumultuous, unbridled, boisterous, noisy, rowdy, disorderly, unruly, undisciplined, obstreperous, rebellious, mutinous, riotous, agitated, in turmoil, unsettled, unstable, confused, disordered, outrageous, factious
OLD combustious
F3 calm, composed

turf *n, v*
♦ *n*
grass, clod, sod, divot, sward, green, lawn, glebe

■ **turf out**
discharge, dismiss, eject, turn out, throw out, evict, banish, remove, fling out, expel, oust
FORMAL dispossess
COLLOQ. kick out, chuck out, elbow, fire, sack, give the elbow to

turgid *adj*
pompous, bombastic, flowery, fulsome, grandiose, high-flown, inflated, ostentatious, extravagant, overblown, pretentious, stilted, affected
FORMAL grandiloquent, magniloquent
F3 simple

turmoil *n*
confusion, disorder, tumult, commotion, disturbance, trouble, disquiet, agitation, turbulence, stir, ferment, flurry, bustle, chaos, pandemonium, bedlam, noise, din, hubbub, row, uproar, upheaval
FORMAL disarray
F3 calm, peace, quiet

turn *v, n*
♦ *v*
1 REVOLVE, circle, spin, go round (and round), go round in circles, twirl, whirl, spiral, wind, reel, twist, gyrate, pivot, hinge, swivel, rotate, roll, move, shift, invert, reverse, bend, veer, swing, swerve, pass, point, direct, aim, focus, divert
2 MAKE, transform, change, alter, modify, convert, develop, adapt, adjust, fit, mould, shape, cast, form, fashion, remodel
FORMAL mutate, transmute, metamorphose
3 *turn cold*
go, become, grow, come to be
4 RESORT, have recourse, apply, appeal, take up, become involved with, attend
5 SOUR, curdle, spoil, go off, go bad, make/become rancid
♦ *n*
1 REVOLUTION, cycle, round, circle, rotation, spin, twirl, whirl, twist, swivel, gyration, bend, curve, corner, loop, reversal
2 CHANGE, alteration, shift, variation, difference, deviation, divergence
3 *it's your turn*
go, chance, opportunity, occasion, time, stint, period, spell, say
COLLOQ. shot, crack, stab, bash
4 ACT, appearance, routine, performance, performer
5 TREND, tendency, inclination, direction, bias, leaning, heading, drift
FORMAL propensity
6 *he did me a good turn*
kindness, act of kindness, service, favour, good deed, courtesy, benefit
7 *gave her quite a turn*
illness, nervousness, faintness, shock, fright, scare, surprise, start
■ **turn against**
dislike, disapprove of, distrust, make/become hostile to
F3 like, trust, support
■ **turn aside**
deviate, depart, diverge, deflect, ward off, fend off, parry, avert
■ **turn away**
reject, avert, deflect, refuse, deviate, depart, move away
COLLOQ. cold-shoulder
F3 accept, help, receive
■ **turn back**
1 GO BACK, return, retreat, retrace your steps
2 *turned back by the border guards*
drive back, force back, repel
■ **turn down**
1 *turn down an offer*
reject, decline, refuse, spurn, rebuff, repudiate, veto
2 LOWER, decrease, reduce, lessen, make quieter, quieten, soften, mute, muffle
F3 1 accept 2 turn up

■ **turn in**
1 GO TO BED, retire
COLLOQ. hit the hay, hit the sack; *N Am* sack out
2 HAND IN, give in, tender, submit, return, give back, hand over, give up, surrender, deliver
3 BETRAY, hand over, deliver, denounce, inform on, double-cross, turn traitor, be disloyal to, be unfaithful to, break faith with, go back on, renege on, let down
COLLOQ. tell on, rat on, sell (out), sell down the river, stab in the back, squeal on, blow the whistle on, walk out on, split on
SLANG shop, grass, rumble; *N Am* stool on
⊟ 1 get up **2** keep

■ **turn of events**
incident, happening, occurrence, result, affair, outcome, phenomenon

■ **turn of phrase**
expression, idiom, saying, style, diction, metaphor, phraseology, manner of speaking
FORMAL locution

■ **turn off**
1 BRANCH OFF, leave, depart from, deviate, divert, go along a different road
COLLOQ. quit
2 SWITCH OFF, turn out, stop, shut down, shut off, unplug, disconnect, pull off
3 REPEL, sicken, nauseate, disgust, offend, displease, disenchant, alienate, bore, discourage, put off, turn against
⊟ 1 join, meet **2** turn on, switch on, start up **3** *colloq.* turn on, excite, interest

■ **turn on**
1 SWITCH ON, put on, start (up), activate, plug (in), connect
2 AROUSE, stimulate, excite, thrill, please, attract
3 HINGE ON, depend on, rest on, hang on
FORMAL be contingent on
4 ATTACK, round on, fall on, set upon, lay into
⊟ 1 turn off, disconnect **2** *colloq.* turn off, bore

■ **turn out**
1 HAPPEN, come about, ensue, result, end up, become, develop, emerge
FORMAL transpire
COLLOQ. pan out
2 SWITCH OFF, turn off, unplug, disconnect
3 APPEAR, present, dress, clothe
4 ATTEND, turn up, come, go, arrive, appear, be present
COLLOQ. show up
5 PRODUCE, make, manufacture, fabricate, assemble
COLLOQ. churn out
6 EVICT, throw out, expel, deport, banish, dismiss, discharge, drum out
COLLOQ. chuck out, kick out, turf out, sack, fire
7 *turn out the attic*
empty, clear (out), clean out
⊟ 2 turn on, connect **6** admit, receive **7** fill

■ **turn over**
1 THINK OVER, think about, mull over, ponder, deliberate, reflect on, contemplate, consider, examine
FORMAL ruminate
2 HAND OVER, surrender, deliver, transfer, assign, consign
3 OVERTURN, upset, upend, turn turtle, invert, reverse, capsize, keel over

■ **turn up**
1 ATTEND, turn out, come, arrive, appear, be present
COLLOQ. show up
2 AMPLIFY, make louder, intensify, raise, increase
3 DISCOVER, find, uncover, unearth, dig up, expose, disclose, reveal, show, bring to light
⊟ 1 stay away **2** turn down

■ **to a turn**
perfectly, exactly, correctly, precisely, to perfection

PROVERBS
One good turn deserves another

SYNONYM NUANCES

verb sense 1
Spin suggests speedily going round: *he spun round when he heard a voice*, while **twirl** suggests a more graceful movement, and **whirl** a fast, but freer movement, as in a dance: *they whirled round the floor in a waltz*.
Spiral implies a closer, tighter motion either up or down: *snowflakes spiralling earthwards*, while **wind** suggests following a somewhat snaking route: *the path wound up the hillside*. The verb **reel** has connotations of staggering or loss of balance, while **twist** can be used to suggest an unnatural or forced turn: *he twisted round awkwardly in his chair*. **Gyrate**, meanwhile, returns to the idea of more regular, smoother movement going round in circles: *she gyrated her hips to the slow music*.
Pivot, **hinge**, **swivel** and **rotate** specifically describe remaining on a fixed point throughout making a turn: *he pivoted on one foot*. **Shift**, on the other hand, is more suggestive of a general, imprecise change of position: *he shifted round to face the other way*, while **invert** and **reverse** would refer more specifically to being moved in the opposite direction. **Veer** is suggestive of a more sudden change of course: *he veered to the left without warning*, while **swing** and **swerve** are again more appropriate for a fluid, swaying movement, although **swerve** has implications of last-minute avoidance: *she swerved when she noticed the oncoming car*.

turncoat *n*
traitor, defector, deserter, renegade, renegate, seceder, backslider, blackleg
FORMAL apostate, tergiversator
COLLOQ. fink, rat, scab

turning *n*
turn-off, junction, crossroads, fork, bend, curve, turn

turning-point *n*
crossroads, watershed, crux, crisis, critical/decisive moment, moment of truth

turnout *n*
1 ATTENDANCE, audience, gate, crowd, gathering, assembly, congregation, number
FORMAL assemblage
2 APPEARANCE, outfit, dress, clothes
FORMAL attire, array
COLLOQ. gear, clobber, togs, things, get-up

turnover *n*
income, profits, revenue, productivity, business, production, output, yield, volume, outturn, change, movement, flow, replacement

turpitude *n*
baseness, corruption, badness, corruptness, evil, criminality, immorality, vileness, wickedness, viciousness, depravity, degeneracy, foulness, sinfulness, villainy
FORMAL flagitiousness, nefariousness, iniquity
⊟ honour

tussle *v, n*
♦ *v*
struggle, battle, wrestle, compete, vie, fight, contend, grapple, scrap, brawl, scuffle, scramble, touse
OLD *Scot* tuilyie, tuilzie
♦ *n*
struggle, battle, conflict, contest, scramble, fight, brawl, bout, fracas, fray, mêlée, punch-up, scuffle, scrum, competition, contention, scrimmage
COLLOQ. dust-up, set-to, scrap

tutelage *n*
guidance, charge, custody, care, protection, guardianship, wardship, patronage, vigilance, eye, teaching, instruction, education, schooling, tuition, preparation
FORMAL aegis

tutor n, v
♦ n
teacher, instructor, coach, educator, lecturer, supervisor, guide, mentor, guru, guardian, governess
♦ v
teach, instruct, train, drill, coach, educate, school, lecture, supervise, direct, guide

tutorial n, adj
♦ n
class, lesson, seminar, teach-in
♦ adj
coaching, didactic, educative, educatory, guiding, instructional, teaching

TV n
television, receiver, set, small screen
COLLOQ. telly, the box, goggle-box, idiot box, the tube, tele; N Am boob tube

twaddle n
drivel, rubbish, nonsense, trash, garbage, gabble, waffle, gossip, tattle, balderdash, bunk, bunkum, claptrap, inanity, gobbledygook, poppycock, stuff; Scot blethers; dialect & N Am blathers
COLLOQ. hogwash, hot air, piffle, palaver, rot, tosh, baloney, blah, bosh, eyewash, rhubarb, guff, hooey, malarkey, moonshine
SLANG (vulgar) balls, bollocks, shit, bullshit
🖼 sense

tweak v, n
♦ v
1 TWIST, pinch, squeeze, nip, pull, tug, jerk, twitch
2 ADJUST, modify, change, adapt, fit, accommodate, suit, make adjustments
COLLOQ. fine-tune
♦ n
1 TWIST, pinch, squeeze, nip, pull, tug, jerk, twitch
2 ADJUSTMENT, modification, change, adaptation, alteration, conversion, remodelling, shaping, fitting, accommodation, amendment, revision, tuning, arranging, rearranging, rearrangement
COLLOQ. fine-tuning

twee adj
sweet, cute, pretty, dainty, quaint, sentimental, affected, precious

twiddle v
turn, twirl, swivel, twist, wiggle, adjust, fiddle, finger
■ twiddle your thumbs
have nothing to do, kick your heels, kill time, have time on your hands

twig¹ n
dried twigs
branch, sprig, spray, shoot, offshoot, stick, wattle, whip, withe, withy
FORMAL ramulus

twig² v
then I twigged
understand, see, realize, comprehend, grasp, fathom
COLLOQ. catch on, cotton on, get, tumble to, rumble

twilight n, adj
♦ n
dusk, half-light, dimness, sunset, evening, decline, ebb, evenfall, demi-jour
OLD gloaming, gloom, owl-light, cockshut
FORMAL crepuscule
Related adjective: crepuscular
♦ adj
darkening, dim, declining, evening, shadowy, final, last, ebbing, dying
FORMAL crepuscular

twin n, adj, v
♦ n
double, lookalike, likeness, duplicate, clone, match, counterpart, equivalent, complement, fellow, mate, couplet

OLD gemel
FORMAL corollary
COLLOQ. (dead) ringer
♦ adj
identical, matching, corresponding, symmetrical, parallel, matched, paired, double, dual, duplicate, twofold
TECHNICAL didymous
♦ v
match, pair, couple, link, join, combine, yoke

twine n, v
♦ n
string, cord, thread, yarn, whipping, twist, intorsion
♦ v
wind, coil, spiral, loop, curl, bend, twist, tangle, wreathe, wrap, surround, encircle, entwine, intertwine, plait, braid, knit, weave

twinge n
pain, pang, throb, spasm, ache, throe, stab, stitch, cramp, pinch, prick

twinkle v, n
♦ v
sparkle, glitter, shimmer, glisten, glimmer, flicker, wink, flash, glint, gleam, shine, scintillate, twink
FORMAL coruscate
♦ n
sparkle, scintillation, glitter, shimmer, glisten, glimmer, flicker, wink, flash, glint, shining, gleam, light
FORMAL coruscation

twinkling adj, n
♦ adj
bright, sparkling, glittering, shimmering, glistening, glimmering, flickering, gleaming, flashing, blinking, scintillating, shining, winking, polished
FORMAL coruscating, nitid
♦ n
moment, flash, short time, instant, minute, second
COLLOQ. sec, tick, jiff, jiffy, mo, trice, shake, wink, no time, two shakes of a lamb's tail

twirl v, n
♦ v
spin, whirl, pirouette, wheel, rotate, revolve, swivel, pivot, turn, curl, twist, gyrate, wind, coil, twiddle, twizzle, trill, trundle
♦ n
spin, whirl, pirouette, rotation, revolution, turn, curl, twist, gyration, convolution, spiral, coil, twiddle; Scot tirlie-wirlie

twirling adj
spinning, whirling, pirouetting, rotating, revolving, pivoting, pivotal, gyratory, swivelling
FORMAL gyral, rotatory

twist v, n
♦ v
1 TURN, screw, wring, spin, rotate, revolve, swivel, wind, zigzag, bend, coil, spiral, curl, wreathe, twirl, twine, entwine, intertwine, weave, braid, plait, entangle, wriggle, squirm, writhe, skew
2 twist your ankle
wrench, rick, sprain, strain
3 CHANGE, alter, garble, falsify, misquote, misrepresent, misreport, distort, contort, warp, bend, misshape, deform, pervert
♦ n
1 TURN, screw, spin, roll, bend, curve, arc, kink, curl, loop, zigzag, coil, spiral, convolution, squiggle, tangle
2 WRENCH, rick, sprain, strain
3 CHANGE, variation, angle, slant, break, turn, surprise, turnabout
4 PERVERSION, distortion, contortion, imperfection, defect, flaw
FORMAL aberration
5 QUIRK, oddity, peculiarity, idiosyncrasy, foible, freak, whim

■ **twist someone's arm**
persuade, force, intimidate, pressurize, bulldoze, bully, coerce, dragoon
COLLOQ. lean on, put the screws on

twisted *adj*
winding, wavy, squiggly, warped, perverted, deviant, unnatural, strange, peculiar, odd
FORMAL sinuous
E3 straight

twister *n*
1 SWINDLER, cheat, crook, fraud, rogue, deceiver, trickster, scoundrel, blackguard
COLLOQ. con man/woman, con artist, phoney
2 TORNADO, storm, cyclone, gale, hurricane, whirlwind, typhoon, monsoon, tempest, squall

twisty *adj*
winding, tortuous, meandering, curving, serpentine, zigzag, circuitous, roundabout, indirect
FORMAL sinuous
E3 straight

twit *n*
idiot, fool, imbecile, simpleton, clown
COLLOQ. ass, ninny, halfwit, dope, twerp, nitwit, clot, nincompoop, chump, blockhead, knuckle-head, proper Charlie, saphead
SLANG plonker, dork, geek, git, prat, goop, berk, nerk, nerd, airhead, dweeb, nig-nog; (*taboo*) dickhead

twitch *v, n*
♦ *v*
jerk, jump, start, blink, tremble, quiver, flutter, shake, pull, tug, tweak, snatch, pluck
♦ *n*
spasm, convulsion, tic, tremor, shiver, quiver, flutter, jerk, jump, start

twitchy *adj*
jumpy, nervous, anxious, agitated, apprehensive, uneasy, tense, panicky, fidgety, shaky, on edge
FORMAL restive
COLLOQ. edgy, nervy, het up, keyed up, wound up, jittery, uptight, with butterflies in your stomach, on pins and needles, shaking like a leaf/jelly, with your heart in your mouth, in a sweat, in a stew, in a tizzy

twitter *v, n*
♦ *v*
1 CHIRP, chirrup, tweet, cheep, sing, warble, whistle, chatter
2 PRATTLE, gabble, babble, jabber, chat, gossip, twaddle; *Scot* blether; *dialect & N Am* blather
COLLOQ. gab, witter
♦ *n*
chirping, chirruping, tweeting, song, cry, warble, chatter

two-faced *adj*
hypocritical, insincere, false, lying, deceitful, treacherous, double-dealing, devious, untrustworthy, Janus-faced
FORMAL perfidious, dissembling, duplicitous
E3 honest, candid, frank

twosome *n*
couple, pair, duo

tycoon *n*
industrialist, entrepreneur, captain of industry, magnate, mogul, baron, supremo, capitalist, financier
COLLOQ. fat cat, big noise, big cheese, moneybags, moneyspinner

type *n*
1 SORT, kind, form, set, style, variety, strain, species, breed, group, class, category, subdivision, classification, description, designation, stamp, mark, order, brand, model, make, standard
TECHNICAL genus
FORMAL genre
2 EMBODIMENT, prototype, original, model, pattern, specimen, example, epitome
FORMAL archetype, exemplar, quintessence
3 PRINT, printing, character(s), letter(s), number(s), symbol(s), lettering, typeface, face, fount, font

typhoon *n*
whirlwind, cyclone, tornado, hurricane, tempest, storm, squall
OLD typhon
COLLOQ. twister

typical *adj*
standard, normal, usual, average, ordinary, conventional, orthodox, classic, true, stereotype, stock, model, representative, illustrative, indicative, characteristic, distinctive
FORMAL archetypal, quintessential
COLLOQ. run-of-the-mill
E3 atypical, unusual

typically *adv*
usually, normally, ordinarily, characteristically, customarily, classically, routinely, habitually, as a rule
FORMAL quintessentially

typify *v*
embody, epitomize, encapsulate, personify, characterize, exemplify, symbolize, indicate, represent, illustrate, image, shadow, foreshadow

tyrannical *adj*
dictatorial, despotic, autocratic, absolute, totalitarian, arbitrary, authoritarian, domineering, overbearing, high-handed, imperious, magisterial, lordly, tyrannic, ruthless, harsh, severe, strict, cruel, oppressive, repressive, overpowering, unjust, unreasonable, Neronian, satrapal
FORMAL peremptory
E3 liberal, tolerant

tyrannize *v*
oppress, crush, intimidate, terrorize, coerce, repress, suppress, dictate, domineer, enslave, browbeat, bully, lord it over, tread on the neck of
FORMAL subjugate

tyranny *n*
dictatorship, despotism, autocracy, absolutism, authoritarianism, imperiousness, high-handedness, ruthlessness, harshness, severity, strictness, cruelty, oppression, injustice, domination
E3 democracy, freedom, liberty

> **QUOTATIONS**
> When laws end, tyranny begins
> WILLIAM PITT THE ELDER

tyrant *n*
dictator, despot, autocrat, absolutist, authoritarian, bully, oppressor, slave-driver, taskmaster, martinet
OLD tyranness

tyro
see **tiro, tyro.**

ubiquitous *adj*
ever-present, everywhere, universal, global, pervasive, common, frequent
FORMAL omnipresent
🞄 rare, scarce

ubiquity *n*
commonness, pervasiveness, universality, frequency, popularity, prevalence
FORMAL omnipresence
🞄 rarity

ugliness *n*
1 UNATTRACTIVENESS, unloveliness, plainness, unsightliness, hideousness, monstrosity, deformity; *N Am* homeliness
2 UNPLEASANTNESS, repulsiveness, offensiveness, frightfulness, enormity, horridness, horror, vileness
FORMAL heinousness
3 DANGER, evil, nastiness, menace
🞄 **1** beauty, charm, goodness **2** pleasantness, delightfulness

ugly *adj*
1 UNATTRACTIVE, unsightly, plain, unlovely, unprepossessing, hideous, revolting, repulsive, grotesque, monstrous, ogreish, misshapen, deformed, ill-favoured, evil-favoured, ill-faced, unfair, gorgon; *Scot* ill-faurd; *N Am* homely
OLD ouglie, oughly, loth; *(Shakesp)* foul; *(Spenser)* ill-faste
COLLOQ. ugly as sin; *N Am* plug-ugly
SLANG minging, butters; *N Am* butt-ugly
2 UNPLEASANT, disagreeable, nasty, horrid, hideous, objectionable, offensive, shocking, disgusting, loathsome, revolting, foul, repulsive, vile, frightful, obnoxious, terrible
COLLOQ. grotty
3 DANGEROUS, threatening, alarming, sinister, grave, nasty, hostile, evil
🞄 **1** attractive, good-looking, beautiful, handsome, pretty
2 pleasant, delightful

SYNONYM NUANCES

sense 1
Unattractive and **unlovely**, although they put the emphasis on a lack of redeeming features, are not particularly euphemistic and point to a visible ugliness: *one of the unlovely suburbs of this city.* Less emphatic synonyms to use are **unprepossessing**, and **plain**, which suggests a lack of any distinguishing features rather than ugliness: *she was what could be described as a plain child.* **Unsightly**, however, implies that something is particularly unpleasant to look at, and is rather more uncomplimentary: *unsightly warts.*
  Far more emotive are the terms **hideous, revolting** and **repulsive**, which suggest something frightful or abhorrent, **grotesque**, which suggests an unsettlingly bizarre element: *grotesque puppets,* and **monstrous**, which goes further by implying an abnormal deviation: *a monstrous toad-like face.* **Misshapen** and **deformed** specifically suggest disfigurement, while **ill-favoured** and **evil-favoured** are rather more poetic terms which also suggest being unkindly served by nature.

---

ulcer *n*
sore, open sore, fester, abscess, boil, canker, ulceration, noma, bedsore, issue, plague-sore
TECHNICAL rupia, aphtha, fistula, peptic ulcer, varicose ulcer, decubitus ulcer
OLD impostume, sycosis
Related adjective: helcoid

ulterior *adj*
secondary, hidden, concealed, undisclosed, unexpressed, unrevealed, underlying, covert, secret, private, personal, selfish
🞄 overt, declared

ultimate *adj, n*
  🞄 *adj*
1 FINAL, last, closing, concluding, eventual, terminal, furthest, end, remotest, extreme
2 RADICAL, basic, fundamental, primary
FORMAL elemental
3 BEST, utmost, greatest, topmost, highest, supreme, superlative, maximum, perfect, ideal
COLLOQ. the mostest
  🞄 *n*
best, greatest, peak, perfection, summit, culmination, greatest achievement, ideal, masterpiece, *chef d'oeuvre*, height, extreme
FORMAL consummation, epitome, *summum bonum*
COLLOQ. daddy of them all, last word

ultimately *adv*
1 FINALLY, eventually, at last, in the end, after all, sooner or later, in the last resort
COLLOQ. at the end of the day, when push comes to shove
2 BASICALLY, fundamentally, primarily

ultra- *prefix*
extremely, excessively, especially, exceptionally, unusually, extraordinarily, remarkably, extra

ululate *v*
howl, wail, screech, moan, lament, keen, mourn, cry, scream, weep, sob, holler, hoot

umbrage
■ **take umbrage**
take offence, resent, be angry, be annoyed, be exasperated, be hurt, be offended, be insulted, be upset, be/feel put out, take exception, take personally
COLLOQ. be miffed, get huffy, get your nose out of joint

umbrella *n*
1 *put up your umbrella*
parasol, sunshade, dumpy, en tout cas, chatta
COLLOQ. brolly, gamp; *N Am* bumbershoot
OLD COLLOQ. gingham
SLANG mushroom, mush
2 PROTECTION, cover, patronage, agency
FORMAL aegis, auspices

umpire *n, v*
  🞄 *n*
referee, linesman, judge, adjudicator, arbiter, arbitrator, mediator, moderator
COLLOQ. ref
  🞄 *v*
referee, judge, adjudicate, arbitrate, mediate, moderate, control

umpteen *adj*
numerous, very many, plenty, thousands, millions, gazillions, countless, innumerable
COLLOQ. a good many
‡ few

unabashed *adj*
unashamed, unembarrassed, brazen, blatant, bold, confident, undaunted, unconcerned, undismayed
‡ abashed, sheepish

unable *adj*
incapable, powerless, impotent, unequipped, unqualified, unfit, incompetent, inadequate
FORMAL ineffectual
‡ able, capable; *colloq.* up to

unabridged *adj*
complete, entire, full-length, full, whole, uncondensed, unshortened, uncut, unexpurgated
‡ abridged, shortened

unacceptable *adj*
intolerable, inadmissible, unsatisfactory, unsuitable, disappointing, undesirable, unwelcome, objectionable, disagreeable, offensive, unpleasant, obnoxious
COLLOQ. a bit off
‡ acceptable, satisfactory

unaccommodating *adj*
inflexible, uncompromising, unco-operative, unyielding, unbending, obstinate, stubborn, perverse, rigid, disobliging
FORMAL intransigent, uncomplaisant
‡ flexible, obliging

unaccompanied *adj*
alone, unescorted, unattended, by yourself, on your own, lone, solo, single, single-handed
‡ accompanied

unaccountable *adj*
1 INEXPLICABLE, unexplainable, unfathomable, impenetrable, insoluble, incomprehensible, baffling, puzzling, mysterious, astonishing, extraordinary, strange, odd, peculiar, singular, curious, bizarre, queer, unusual, uncommon, unheard-of
2 *unaccountable to the public*
not responsible, not answerable, free, immune
‡ 1 explicable, explainable 2 accountable, bound

unaccountably *adv*
inexplicably, incomprehensibly, unexplainably, incredibly, strangely, mysteriously, mystifyingly, bafflingly, puzzlingly, miraculously
‡ explicably

unaccustomed *adj*
1 *unaccustomed to such luxury*
unused, unacquainted, unfamiliar, unpractised, inexperienced
FORMAL unwonted
2 STRANGE, unusual, uncommon, different, new, unexpected, surprising, extraordinary, remarkable, unfamiliar, uncharacteristic, unprecedented
‡ 1 accustomed, familiar 2 customary

unacquainted *adj*
unfamiliar, unaccustomed, unused, inexperienced, strange, ignorant

unadorned *adj*
plain, simple, straightforward, undecorated, unornamented, unembellished, unvarnished, severe, stark, restrained
‡ decorated, embellished, ornate

unadulterated *adj*
1 *unadulterated gold*
pure, unalloyed, unmixed, undiluted, 100%, flawless, perfect, neat, straight, solid, simple, natural, real, authentic, genuine, true
2 *unadulterated bliss*
sheer, utter, pure, complete, total, thorough, absolute, perfect, unqualified, unmitigated, downright
‡ 1 impure, adulterated

unaffected *adj*
1 UNMOVED, unconcerned, indifferent, impervious, untouched, unchanged, unaltered, immune
2 GENUINE, natural, unsophisticated, artless, naive, ingenuous, guileless, unspoilt, plain, simple, straightforward, unpretentious, unassuming, candid, true, honest, sincere
‡ 1 moved, impressed, influenced 2 affected, pretentious, insincere

unafraid *adj*
fearless, confident, daring, undaunted, dauntless, brave, courageous, imperturbable, intrepid, unshak(e)able
‡ afraid, fearful, nervous

unalterable *adj*
unchangeable, invariable, unchanging, immutable, final, inflexible, unyielding, rigid, fixed, permanent
‡ alterable, flexible

unanimity *n*
consensus, unity, agreement, concurrence, like-mindedness, consistency, harmony, unison, concert
FORMAL accord, concord, congruence
‡ disagreement, disunity

unanimous *adj*
united, concerted, joint, common, as one, in agreement, like-minded, consistent, harmonious
FORMAL in accord, concordant
‡ disunited, divided

unanimously *adv*
unopposed, without opposition, without exception, as one, of one mind, with one voice, by common consent, in concert, *nem con*
FORMAL conjointly

unannounced *adj*
unexpected, unforeseen, unanticipated, unpredictable, unlooked-for, chance, accidental, sudden, abrupt, surprising, startling, amazing, astonishing, unusual
FORMAL fortuitous
‡ announced, expected, predictable

unanswerable *adj*
incontestable, incontrovertible, indisputable, unarguable, undeniable, absolute, final, conclusive, irrefutable
FORMAL irrefragable
‡ answerable, refutable

unanswered *adj*
undecided, unsettled, unresolved, open, in doubt, vexed
COLLOQ. up in the air
‡ decided, resolved, settled

unappetizing *adj*
unpleasant, tasteless, unpalatable, off-putting, distasteful, disagreeable, uninviting, unsavoury, insipid, unappealing, unattractive, unexciting, uninteresting
‡ appetizing

unapproachable *adj*
inaccessible, remote, distant, aloof, standoffish, withdrawn, reserved, unsociable, unfriendly, unresponsive, uncommunicative, forbidding, cold, cool
‡ approachable, friendly

unapt *adj*
unsuitable, unfit, unfitted, unsuited, inappropriate, inapplicable, untimely, unseasonable, inapt
FORMAL inapposite, malapropos
‡ apt

unarmed *adj*
defenceless, unprotected, exposed, open, vulnerable, weak, helpless
‡ armed, protected

unashamed *adj*
shameless, unabashed, impenitent, unrepentant, unconcealed, undisguised, direct, open, honest, blatant
‡ ashamed, abashed

unasked adj

uninvited, unbidden, unrequested, unsought, unsolicited, unwanted, voluntary, spontaneous, unannounced
F3 invited, wanted

unassailable adj

invulnerable, incontestable, impregnable, incontrovertible, indisputable, secure, sound, positive, proven, absolute, conclusive, invincible, inviolable, undeniable, irrefutable, well-armed, well-fortified
F3 assailable

unassertive adj

self-effacing, unassuming, backward, bashful, quiet, retiring, shy, timid, meek, diffident, timorous
COLLOQ. mous(e)y
F3 assertive, bold

unassuming adj

unassertive, self-effacing, retiring, modest, shy, demure, humble, meek, quiet, reticent, unobtrusive, unpretentious, simple, natural, restrained
F3 presumptuous, assertive, pretentious

unattached adj

unmarried, unengaged, uncommitted, single, on your own, by yourself, free, available, footloose, fancy-free, independent, unaffiliated, with no ties, loose
F3 engaged, committed

unattended adj

ignored, disregarded, abandoned, neglected, forgotten, forsaken, unguarded, unwatched, unsupervised, unaccompanied, unescorted, alone
F3 attended, escorted, looked after

unattractive adj

unappealing, disagreeable, unlovely, plain, unpleasant, unprepossessing, uninviting, unexciting, unsightly, ugly, objectionable, offensive, disgusting, distasteful, off-putting, undesirable, ill-favoured, uncomely, unwelcome, unpalatable, unsavoury, repellent, unappetizing; N Am homely
COLLOQ. N Am butt-ugly
SLANG skanky
See Synonym nuances panel at **ugly**.
F3 attractive

unauthorized adj

unofficial, unlicensed, unlawful, forbidden, prohibited, illegal, illicit, illegitimate, irregular, unapproved, unsanctioned, unwarranted
F3 authorized, legal; *formal* accredited

unavailing adj

unsuccessful, failed, abortive, vain, futile, useless, ineffective, fruitless, unproductive, unprofitable, sterile, luckless, unlucky, unfortunate, losing, beaten, defeated, frustrated, thwarted
F3 successful, effective

unavoidable adj

inevitable, inescapable, inexorable, certain, sure, fated, destined, predestined, obligatory, required, compulsory, necessary
FORMAL mandatory, ineluctable
F3 avoidable

unaware adj

oblivious, unconscious, ignorant, uninformed, unenlightened, in the dark, unknowing, unsuspecting, unmindful, heedless, blind, deaf, with no idea
OLD wareless, witless
FORMAL insentient, incognizant
F3 aware, conscious

unawares adv

off guard, by surprise, accidentally, inadvertently, mistakenly, suddenly, unexpectedly, aback, abruptly, unintentionally, unconsciously, unknowingly, unprepared, unthinkingly, unwittingly, insidiously, in the dark, *à l'improviste*

OLD unwares
COLLOQ. on the hop, red-handed, with your trousers down

unbalanced adj

1 INSANE, mad, lunatic, deranged, disturbed, demented, irrational, unsound, unstable, mentally ill
COLLOQ. crazy, nuts, barmy, crackers, round the bend/twist, needing your head examining
2 *an unbalanced report*
biased, prejudiced, one-sided, partisan, unfair, unjust, unequal, uneven, asymmetrical, lopsided, unsteady, unstable
FORMAL inequitable
F3 **1** sane, sound **2** unbiased, impartial

unbearable adj

intolerable, unacceptable, insupportable, insufferable, unendurable, excruciating
COLLOQ. too much, too bad, the limit, the last straw, the straw that broke the camel's back
F3 bearable, acceptable

unbeatable adj

invincible, unconquerable, unstoppable, unsurpassable, matchless, supreme, best, excellent
FORMAL indomitable

unbeaten adj

undefeated, unconquered, victorious, winning, supreme, triumphant, unsubdued, unsurpassed, unbowed
FORMAL unvanquished
F3 defeated; *formal* vanquished

unbecoming adj

unseemly, improper, unsuitable, inappropriate, unbefitting, indelicate, ungentlemanly, unladylike, unattractive, unsightly
OLD (Shakesp) ill-beseeming
FORMAL indecorous, unseemly
F3 suitable, attractive

unbeknown

■ **unbeknown to**
unbeknownst to, unknown, unrealized, unperceived, unheard of
F3 known

unbelief n

atheism, agnosticism, scepticism, doubt, incredulity, disbelief
F3 belief, faith

> **QUOTATIONS**
> Blind unbelief is sure to err, / And scan his work in vain; / God is his own interpreter, / And he will make it plain
> WILLIAM COWPER, *Olney Hymns*, 'Light Shining Out of Darkness'

unbelievable adj

incredible, inconceivable, unthinkable, unimaginable, amazing, astonishing, staggering, extraordinary, impossible, improbable, unlikely, implausible, unconvincing, far-fetched, preposterous, outlandish
F3 believable, credible

unbelievably adv

incredibly, amazingly, unimaginably, inconceivably, extraordinarily, outlandishly
F3 believably

unbeliever n

disbeliever, agnostic, atheist, doubter, doubting Thomas, sceptic, infidel
FORMAL nullifidian
F3 believer, supporter

unbelieving adj

sceptical, suspicious, disbelieving, distrustful, doubtful, doubting, dubious, unconvinced, unpersuaded, incredulous
FORMAL nullifidian
F3 credulous, trustful

unbend _v_
loosen up, relax, become less formal/strict, thaw, unfreeze, unbutton, uncoil, uncurl, straighten
E3 stiffen, withdraw

unbending _adj_
rigid, inflexible, strict, tough, uncompromising, unyielding, resolute, firm, formal, formidable, stubborn, severe, stiff, stern, hardline, forbidding, aloof, distant, reserved
FORMAL intransigent
E3 approachable, friendly, relaxed

unbiased _adj_
impartial, unprejudiced, objective, just, fair, fair-minded, open-minded, independent, equitable, balanced, even-handed, disinterested, dispassionate, neutral, uninfluenced, uncoloured, candid
E3 biased

unbidden _adj_
spontaneous, unforced, free, voluntary, unsolicited, unprompted, uninvited, willing, unasked, unwanted, unwelcome
E3 invited, solicited

unbind _v_
untie, unfasten, unloose, unloosen, unchain, undo, unshackle, free, liberate, loose, loosen, release, unyoke, unfetter
E3 bind, restrain

unblemished _adj_
untarnished, unspotted, unstained, unsullied, unimpeachable, unflawed, pure, clear, perfect, spotless, immaculate, irreproachable, flawless
E3 blemished, flawed, imperfect

unblinking _adj_
steady, unfaltering, unflinching, unshrinking, unwavering, imperturbable, emotionless, unemotional, fearless, unafraid, assured, calm, impassive, cool, composed
E3 fearful, cowed

unblushing _adj_
shameless, brazen, blatant, bold, immodest, unabashed, unashamed, unembarrassed, amoral, conscience-proof
E3 abashed, ashamed

unborn _adj_
embryonic, _in utero_, expected, awaited, coming, to-come, future, subsequent, succeeding

unbosom _v_
unburden, confess, admit, reveal, tell, lay bare, divulge, disclose, confide, uncover, let out, pour out, bare
COLLOQ. tell all
E3 hide, conceal, suppress

unbounded _adj_
boundless, limitless, unlimited, unrestricted, unrestrained, uncontrolled, unchecked, unbridled, infinite, endless, immeasurable, vast
E3 limited, restrained

unbreakable _adj_
indestructible, shatterproof, toughened, resistant, durable, strong, tough, rugged, solid
FORMAL infrangible
E3 breakable, fragile

unbridled _adj_
immoderate, excessive, rampant, riotous, wild, uncontrolled, unrestrained, unconstrained, ungoverned, uncurbed, unchecked, intemperate, licentious, profligate

unbroken _adj_
1 INTACT, whole, entire, complete, solid, undivided, single
OLD unbroke
2 UNINTERRUPTED, continuous, seamless, endless, non-stop, ceaseless, incessant, unceasing, constant, perpetual, progressive, successive, in a row
OLD unbroke; _(Shakesp)_ continuate
FORMAL unremitting

3 _an unbroken record_
unbeaten, unsurpassed, unrivalled, unequalled, unmatched
4 WILD, rough, untamed, undomesticated
OLD unbroke
E3 **1** broken, damaged **2** intermittent, fitful **4** broken, tamed, subdued

unburden _v_
confess, admit, reveal, tell, lay bare, divulge, offload, disclose, confide, uncover, let out, pour out, bare
COLLOQ. tell all
E3 hide, conceal, suppress

uncalled-for _adj_
unwarranted, gratuitous, unprovoked, unjustified, unasked, unsought, unsolicited, unprompted, undeserved, unwelcome, unnecessary, needless
E3 timely

uncannily _adv_
strangely, oddly, bizarrely, mysteriously, incredibly, remarkably, extraordinarily, unnaturally, supernaturally
COLLOQ. spookily

uncanny _adj_
weird, strange, queer, odd, bizarre, mysterious, unaccountable, incredible, remarkable, exceptional, extraordinary, fantastic, unnatural, unearthly, supernatural, eerie, creepy; _Scot_ eldritch
FORMAL preternatural
COLLOQ. spooky

uncared-for _adj_
1 UNAPPRECIATED, neglected, disregarded, abandoned, undervalued, deserted, stranded, forsaken
2 _uncared-for waste ground_
neglected, derelict, overgrown, uncultivated, unmaintained, untended, untilled, unweeded, unhusbanded, dilapidated
COLLOQ. run-down
E3 **1** cared-for, cherished, treasured **2** cared-for, tended

uncaring _adj_
unconcerned, unmoved, unsympathetic, inconsiderate, unfeeling, cold, callous, indifferent, apathetic, uninterested
E3 caring, concerned

unceasing _adj_
ceaseless, incessant, unending, endless, never-ending, non-stop, continuous, unbroken, constant, perpetual, continual, persistent, relentless, unrelenting, unremitting
E3 intermittent, spasmodic

unceremonious _adj_
1 INFORMAL, casual, easy-going, relaxed, unofficial
COLLOQ. laid-back
2 DIRECT, abrupt, sudden, impolite, rude, undignified, disrespectful, discourteous

uncertain _adj_
1 UNSURE, unconvinced, doubtful, dubious, undecided, unresolved, open, equivocating, ambivalent, hesitant, wavering, vacillating, conflicted
COLLOQ. in two minds
2 INCONSTANT, changeable, variable, erratic, irregular, shaky, fitful, unsteady, unreliable
3 UNPREDICTABLE, unforeseeable, undetermined, unsettled, unresolved, unconfirmed, unknown, unclear, speculative, indefinite, vague, insecure, risky
COLLOQ. iffy, up in the air, touch-and-go, (hanging) in the balance, in the lap of the gods
E3 **1** certain, sure **2** steady **3** predictable

uncertainly _adv_
hesitantly, reluctantly, unwillingly, half-heartedly, doubtfully, sceptically, dubiously, indecisively, irresolutely, vacillatingly, delayingly, waveringly, tentatively, warily, shyly, timidly, haltingly, stammeringly, stuttering
COLLOQ. in two minds
E3 confidently

uncertainty n
doubt, scepticism, irresolution, dilemma, ambiguity, ambivalence, hesitation, misgiving, qualm(s), uneasiness, confusion, vagueness, bewilderment, perplexity, puzzlement, unreliability, unpredictability, riskiness, insecurity
E3 certainty

unchallengeable adj
absolute, conclusive, incontestable, indisputable, incontrovertible, irrefutable, final, impregnable
FORMAL irrefragable, inappellable
E3 inconclusive

unchangeable adj
changeless, unchanging, invariable, irreversible, permanent, constant, fixed, stereotyped, final, eternal
FORMAL immutable, intransmutable
E3 changeable

unchanging adj
unvarying, changeless, same, invariable, steady, steadfast, constant, perpetual, lasting, enduring, abiding, eternal, permanent
E3 changing, changeable

uncharitable adj
unkind, cruel, hard-hearted, callous, hard, harsh, stern, severe, unfeeling, insensitive, unsympathetic, uncompassionate, unfriendly, mean, ungenerous, unforgiving
E3 kind, sensitive, charitable, generous

uncharted adj
unexplored, unsurveyed, undiscovered, unplumbed, foreign, alien, strange, unknown, unfamiliar, new, virgin
E3 familiar

unchaste adj
immoral, depraved, defiled, dissolute, dishonest, impure, immodest, promiscuous, fallen, loose, licentious, wanton, lewd
E3 chaste

unchecked adj
uncontrolled, unrestrained, unbridled, rampant, violent, wild, boisterous, riotous, unruly, uncurbed, undisciplined, unhindered
E3 controlled, restrained

uncivil adj
rude, impolite, discourteous, disrespectful, bad-mannered, ill-mannered, ill-bred, uncouth, unmannerly, ungracious, churlish, brusque, abrupt, gruff, curt, boorish, bearish, surly
E3 civil, polite

uncivilized adj
primitive, barbaric, barbarian, savage, wild, rough, boorish, brutish, untamed, uncultured, unrefined, unsophisticated, unenlightened, uneducated, illiterate, uncouth, antisocial
E3 civilized, cultured

unclassifiable adj
doubtful, indistinct, uncertain, undefinable, indescribable, unidentifiable, vague, elusive, ill-defined, indefinable, indefinite, indeterminate
E3 conformable, definable, identifiable

unclassified adj
1 *unclassified documents*
known, public, unrestricted, disclosed, published, revealed, official, on the record, for publication
2 *an unclassified country road*
general, basic, ungraded, minimum, minimal, lowest
E3 **1** secret, confidential **2** main

unclean adj
dirty, soiled, filthy, grimy, grubby, foul, polluted, contaminated, tainted, impure, unhygienic, unwholesome, corrupt, adulterated, defiled, sullied, profane, bad, evil, wicked

FORMAL ordurous
E3 clean, hygienic

unclear adj
indistinct, hazy, foggy, dim, obscure, vague, indefinite, ambiguous, inexplicit, equivocal, uncertain, undetermined, unsettled, unsure, doubtful, dubious
COLLOQ. iffy
E3 clear, evident

unclothed adj
naked, nude, stripped, undressed, disrobed, bare, stark-naked
FORMAL unclad
COLLOQ. in your birthday suit, in the altogether, in the buff, in the raw, starkers
E3 clothed, dressed

uncomfortable adj
1 CRAMPED, hard, cold, ill-fitting, irritating, painful, disagreeable
2 AWKWARD, embarrassed, self-conscious, nervous, uneasy, tense, on edge, troubled, worried, anxious, disturbed, distressed, disquieted, conscience-stricken
FORMAL discomfited
E3 **1** comfortable **2** relaxed

uncommitted adj
unattached, uninvolved, undecided, available, free, fancy-free, footloose, floating, non-aligned, non-partisan, neutral
E3 committed

uncommon adj
rare, scarce, infrequent, unusual, abnormal, atypical, unfamiliar, strange, odd, peculiar, queer, singular, curious, bizarre, extraordinary, remarkable, notable, outstanding, striking, exceptional, distinctive, special, out of the way
OLD seld
COLLOQ. thin on the ground, few and far between, like gold dust
E3 common, usual, normal

uncommonly adv
exceptionally, abnormally, peculiarly, remarkably, strangely, unusually, occasionally, singularly, rarely, seldom, infrequently, extremely, outstandingly, particularly, very
OLD seld
E3 commonly, frequently

uncommunicative adj
silent, taciturn, tight-lipped, close, secretive, unforthcoming, unresponsive, curt, brief, reticent, quiet, reserved, shy, retiring, diffident, withdrawn, aloof, unsociable
E3 communicative, forthcoming, talkative, conversational

uncomplicated adj
simple, easy, straightforward, direct, uninvolved, clear, undemanding
E3 complicated, complex, involved

uncompromising adj
unyielding, unbending, inflexible, unaccommodating, rigid, firm, stiff, strict, tough, hardline, hard-faced, immovable, inexorable, stubborn, obstinate, diehard
FORMAL obdurate, intransigent
E3 flexible, yielding

unconcealable adj
insuppressible, irrepressible, uncontrollable, obvious, manifest, plain, clear, insistent

unconcealed adj
open, obvious, patent, evident, manifest, conspicuous, overt, admitted, visible, blatant, frank, apparent, noticeable, unashamed, ill-concealed, self-confessed
E3 hidden, secret

unconcern n
aloofness, detachment, remoteness, apathy, nonchalance, indifference, disinterest, uninterestedness, negligence, callousness

FORMAL insouciance, pococurantism
≡ concern

unconcerned *adj*
indifferent, apathetic, uninterested, nonchalant, carefree, relaxed, casual, complacent, cool, composed, untroubled, unworried, unruffled, unmoved, uncaring, unsympathetic, callous, aloof, remote, distant, detached, dispassionate, disinterested, uninvolved, oblivious
FORMAL unperturbed, insouciant, pococurante
≡ concerned, worried, interested

unconditional *adj*
unqualified, unreserved, unrestricted, unlimited, absolute, utter, full, plenary, total, complete, entire, wholehearted, thoroughgoing, downright, outright, out-and-out, positive, definite, conclusive, categorical, unequivocal
≡ conditional, qualified, limited

unconditionally *adv*
unreservedly, without qualifications, absolutely, completely, fully, totally, entirely, wholeheartedly, categorically, unequivocally
COLLOQ. with no strings attached
≡ conditionally

unconfirmed *adj*
unproven, unproved, unratified, unverified, unauthenticated, unsubstantiated
FORMAL uncorroborated
≡ confirmed

unconformity *n*
discontinuity, irregularity, unconformability
FORMAL disconformity
≡ conformability

uncongenial *adj*
unfriendly, uninviting, unappealing, unattractive, unpleasant, displeasing, disagreeable, antagonistic, unsympathetic, incompatible, unsuited, unsavoury, discordant, distasteful
FORMAL antipathetic
≡ congenial

unconnected *adj*
1 IRRELEVANT, unrelated, beside/off the point, inappropriate, unattached, detached, separate, independent
COLLOQ. neither here nor there
2 DISCONNECTED, incoherent, irrational, illogical, confused, unco-ordinated, disjointed
≡ 1 connected, relevant **2** coherent, joined-up

unconquerable *adj*
irrepressible, enduring, ingrained, inveterate, undefeatable, unbeatable, invincible, unyielding, insuperable, insurmountable, irresistible, overpowering
FORMAL indomitable
≡ weak, yielding

unconscionable *adj*
unprincipled, amoral, outrageous, unethical, unjustifiable, unscrupulous, unreasonable, unwarrantable, unpardonable, preposterous, criminal, exorbitant, extreme, extravagant, excessive, immoderate, inordinate

unconscious *adj*
1 STUNNED, knocked out, dazed, out, passed out, fainted, collapsed, lifeless, drugged, in a coma, concussed, blacked out, senseless, asleep
TECHNICAL comatose
FORMAL insensible
COLLOQ. out cold, out for the count, put out, zonked, dead to the world
2 UNAWARE, oblivious, blind, deaf, heedless, unmindful, ignorant
OLD inconscious, inconscient
FORMAL insensible, incognizant
3 *an unconscious reaction*
involuntary, automatic, reflex, instinctive, impulsive, innate, subconscious, subliminal, repressed, suppressed, latent, unthinking, unwitting, inadvertent, accidental, unintentional

COLLOQ. knee-jerk
≡ 1 conscious **2** aware **3** intentional

unconsciously *adv*
1 OBLIVIOUSLY, heedlessly, unmindfully
FORMAL insensibly
2 INVOLUNTARILY, automatically, instinctively, impulsively, subliminally, unwittingly, unthinkingly, inadvertently, unintentionally, accidentally
≡ 1 mindfully **2** intentionally

unconsciousness *n*
blackout, coma, faint, torpor, numbness, stupefaction, trance, sleep, doze, snooze, daydream
OLD inconscience
FORMAL insensibility

unconstraint *n*
unreserve, unrestraint, openness, freedom, liberality, relaxation, abandon, laissez-faire

uncontrollable *adj*
ungovernable, unmanageable, unruly, out of control, disorderly, wild, mad, furious, violent, strong, irrepressible
FORMAL intractable
≡ controllable, manageable

uncontrolled *adj*
unrestrained, unbridled, unchecked, rampant, violent, wild, boisterous, riotous, unruly, uncurbed, undisciplined, unhindered
≡ controlled, restrained

unconventional *adj*
unorthodox, alternative, different, offbeat, eccentric, bohemian, idiosyncratic, individual, original, odd, unusual, uncommon, rare, uncustomary, irregular, abnormal, bizarre, weird, radical, experimental, avant-garde, long-haired, Gypsy
COLLOQ. fringe, out of the ordinary, left-field, freaky, freakish, wacky, oddball, zany
SLANG way-out, far-out; *N Am* spacy
≡ conventional, orthodox

SYNONYM NUANCES

While **unorthodox** is a straightforward synonym for diverging from the generally accepted way, both **alternative** and **different** imply that something is another option: *alternative medicine*. **Offbeat** and **eccentric**, however, are more suggestive of an endearing quirkiness, but **bohemian** has more to do with a rejection of the dominant social mores and lifestyle: *the bohemian atmosphere of the left bank is different from the rest of the city*. **Idiosyncratic** and **individual** suggest a singular approach to everything, and may be positive or negative depending on the context: *his highly idiosyncratic playing style can be irritating*.

The term **original**, on the other hand, can be used, usually in a positive way, to describe anything that is novel, unlike **odd**, which has less complimentary implications of strangeness. You can also use **uncustomary** to straightforwardly describe that something that is out of the ordinary: *uncustomary mealtimes*, whereas **irregular** implies something not conforming to accepted rules or norms in a way that is more disruptive: *this behaviour is most irregular*.

Abnormal, meanwhile, suggests total deviation from the norm and tends to suggest disapproval: *this is not just a bad, but an abnormal habit*, and both **bizarre** and **weird** return to the suggestion of unsettling peculiarity: *bizarre, disturbing artworks*. **Radical**, **experimental** and **avant-garde**, however, imply something daringly new, and are far more approving in tone.

---

unconvincing *adj*
implausible, unlikely, improbable, questionable, doubtful, dubious, suspect, weak, feeble, flimsy, lame
COLLOQ. fishy
≡ convincing, plausible

unco-operative *adj*
unhelpful, awkward, obstinate, stubborn, rude,
unpleasant, cubbish
COLLOQ. stroppy, bloody-minded
F3 co-operative, helpful, amenable, pleasant

unco-ordinated *adj*
clumsy, awkward, ungainly, ungraceful, bungling,
bumbling, clodhopping, inept, disjointed
FORMAL maladroit
F3 graceful

uncork *v*
open, crack, broach, break/burst/slide/push/force/prise
open, clear, expose, undo, uncover, unseal

uncouth *adj*
coarse, crude, vulgar, rude, bad-mannered, ill-mannered,
impolite, improper, clumsy, rustic, ungainly, awkward,
boorish, loutish, gauche, graceless, unrefined, uncultivated,
unsophisticated, uncultured, uncivilized, rough, rough-
hewn, rugged
OLD unrude
FORMAL unseemly
F3 polite, refined, urbane

uncover *v*
unveil, unmask, unwrap, strip, bare, lay bare, open, peel,
expose, reveal, bring to light, show, disclose, divulge,
make known, leak, unearth, dig up, exhume, discover,
detect, rake, unrake, dismask, unlid, unsheathe
OLD *(Spenser)* unhele
COLLOQ. take the lid off
F3 cover, conceal, suppress

uncritical *adj*
undiscerning, undiscriminating, unselective, unquestioning,
credulous, accepting, trusting, gullible, naive, non-
judgemental, unfussy, superficial
F3 discerning, discriminating, sceptical

unctuous *adj*
1 INSINCERE, fawning, ingratiating, smooth, suave,
sycophantic, gushing, slick, plausible, glib, sanctimonious,
servile, pietistic
FORMAL obsequious
COLLOQ. smarmy
2 GREASY, oily, creamy

uncultivated *adj*
fallow, wild, rough, natural
F3 cultivated

uncultured *adj*
unsophisticated, unrefined, uncultivated, uncivilized,
unintellectual, rough, uncouth, boorish, rustic, hick,
coarse, crude, ill-bred
F3 cultured, sophisticated

undaunted *adj*
undeterred, undiscouraged, undismayed, unbowed,
unflagging, resolute, steadfast, unafraid, brave, courageous,
fearless, bold, unalarmed, intrepid, dauntless, indomitable
F3 afraid, discouraged, timorous

undecided *adj*
uncertain, unsure, unknown, ambivalent, doubtful,
hesitant, dithering, equivocating, wavering, irresolute,
uncommitted, unestablished, indefinite, vague, dubious,
debatable, moot, unresolved, unsettled, open
COLLOQ. in two minds, the jury is still out, up in the air
F3 decided, certain, definite

undecorated *adj*
plain, simple, severe, stark, austere, unadorned,
unornamented, unembellished, functional, classical
FORMAL inornate
F3 decorated, ornate

undefeated *adj*
unbeaten, unconquered, victorious, winning, supreme,
triumphant, unsubdued, unsurpassed, unbowed
FORMAL unvanquished
F3 defeated; *formal* vanquished

undefended *adj*
defenceless, exposed, vulnerable, unprotected,
unguarded, open, unarmed, naked, pregnable
FORMAL unfortified
F3 armed, defended; *formal* fortified

undefiled *adj*
pure, spotless, unblemished, unsoiled, unspotted,
immaculate, flawless, sinless, chaste, clean, clear,
unstained, unsullied, intact, virginal
FORMAL inviolate

undefined *adj*
vague, hazy, ill-defined, indefinite, unclear, unexplained,
unspecified, indistinct, inexact, imprecise, woolly,
nebulous, formless, shadowy, tenuous
FORMAL indeterminate
F3 definite, precise

undemonstrative *adj*
aloof, distant, remote, withdrawn, reserved,
reticent, uncommunicative, unresponsive, stiff,
formal, cool, cold, unemotional, restrained, impassive,
phlegmatic
F3 demonstrative, communicative

undeniable *adj*
indisputable, incontrovertible, unquestionable, sure,
certain, undoubted, indubitable, beyond doubt, beyond
question, definite, positive, proven, clear, obvious,
manifest, patent, evident, unmistakable, irrefutable
F3 questionable

undeniably *adv*
incontrovertibly, indisputably, unquestionably, certainly,
positively, definitely, unmistakably, undoubtedly,
indubitably, beyond doubt, beyond question

undependable *adj*
unreliable, inconsistent, changeable, erratic, uncertain,
fickle, capricious, irresponsible, inconstant, unpredictable,
unstable, untrustworthy, variable, mercurial, treacherous,
fair-weather
F3 dependable, reliable

under *prep, adv*
♦ *prep*
1 BELOW, underneath, beneath, lower than, less than
2 INFERIOR TO, secondary to, junior to, subordinate to,
subservient to
F3 **1** over, above
♦ *adv*
below, underneath, beneath, down, downward, less,
lower

underclothes *n*
underwear, underclothing, undergarments, underlinen,
lingerie
COLLOQ. smalls, undies, unmentionables, frillies, scanties

undercover *adj*
secret, private, confidential, sly, intelligence, underground,
surreptitious, stealthy, furtive, covert, hidden, concealed
FORMAL clandestine
COLLOQ. hush-hush
F3 open, unconcealed

undercurrent *n*
1 *an undercurrent in the sea*
undertow, underflow
2 FEELING, undertone, overtone, hint, suggestion, tinge,
flavour, aura, atmosphere, sense, movement, tendency,
trend, drift, undertow

undercut *v*
1 UNDERPRICE, undersell, undercharge, charge less than,
underbid, undermine
2 EXCAVATE, hollow out, mine, gouge out, scoop out

underdog *n*
weaker party, outsider, loser, unfortunate, prey, victim,
outcast, the exploited

underestimate v
underrate, undervalue, misjudge, miscalculate, fail to appreciate, minimize, belittle, dismiss, look down on, sell short, trivialize
FORMAL disparage
COLLOQ. play down
➡ overestimate, exaggerate

undergo v
experience, suffer, sustain, submit to, go through, put up with, tolerate, bear, stand, endure, weather, withstand

underground adj, n, adv
♦ adj
1 *an underground passage*
subterranean, buried, sunken, covered, hidden, concealed
2 SECRET, covert, furtive, surreptitious, undercover, revolutionary, subversive, radical, experimental, avant-garde, alternative, unorthodox, unofficial, illegal
FORMAL clandestine
♦ n
underground railway, subway, metro
COLLOQ. tube
♦ adv
below the surface, below ground level, below ground, nether

undergrowth n
brush, brushwood, scrub, vegetation, shrubs, shrubbery, ground cover, bracken, thicket, bushes, brambles, briars

underhand adj
unscrupulous, unethical, immoral, improper, sly, crafty, sneaky, stealthy, secret, surreptitious, furtive, devious, dishonest, deceitful, deceptive, fraudulent, scheming
FORMAL clandestine
COLLOQ. crooked, shady
➡ honest, open; colloq. above board

underline v
mark, underscore, stress, emphasize, draw attention to, accentuate, italicize, highlight, foreground, point up
➡ play down; colloq. soft-pedal

underling n
minion, subordinate, inferior, lackey, menial, nonentity, flunkey, hireling, servant, slave, nobody
➡ boss, leader, master

underlying adj
basic, fundamental, essential, primary, elementary, root, intrinsic, inherent, latent, hidden, concealed, lurking, veiled
FORMAL basal

undermine v
1 WEAKEN, make less secure, destroy, erode, wear away, sap, damage, sabotage, subvert, injure, mar, impair, cripple, undercut
OLD underwork
FORMAL vitiate
COLLOQ. handbag
2 MINE, tunnel, dig, excavate
➡ **1** strengthen, fortify

undernourished adj
malnourished, underfed, starved, hungry, anorexic, anorectic

underprivileged adj
disadvantaged, deprived, poor, needy, in need, in distress, in want, impoverished, destitute, oppressed
FORMAL impecunious
➡ privileged, fortunate, affluent

underrate v
underestimate, undervalue, fail to appreciate, belittle, depreciate, dismiss, look down on, sell short
FORMAL disparage
➡ overrate, exaggerate

undersell v
undercharge, undercut, cut, mark down, reduce, slash, sell short, depreciate, play down, understate
FORMAL disparage

undersized adj
little, small, tiny, minute, miniature, pygmy, dwarf, stunted, underdeveloped, underweight, puny, runtish, atrophied; *Scot* wee
TECHNICAL achondroplastic
COLLOQ. pint-size(d), teeny, teensy
➡ oversized, big, overweight

understand v
1 *I don't understand*
grasp, take in, follow, fathom, comprehend, penetrate, make out, figure out, discern, perceive, construe, see, realize, recognize, appreciate, accept, take, conceive, make of, read, make sense of, catch, *dialect* gaum
OLD contrive
FORMAL apprehend
COLLOQ. get, get it, cotton on, click, twig, tumble to, latch onto, get the hang of, rumble, suss out, get the message, get the picture, get wise, get your head/mind round, know the ropes, the penny drops
SLANG grok, savvy
OLD SLANG dig
2 SYMPATHIZE, empathize, commiserate, comfort, feel sorry for, feel for, identify with, support, appreciate, enter into
3 BELIEVE, think, know, hear, learn, gather, assume, presume, suppose, conclude
➡ **1** misunderstand

> **QUOTATIONS**
> Adults never understand anything for themselves, and it is tiresome for children to be always and forever explaining things to them
> ANTOINE DE SAINT-EXUPÉRY, *Le Petit Prince*

understandable adj
1 *he reacted with understandable fury*
natural, unsurprising, reasonable, acceptable, admissible, expected, comprehensible
2 COMPREHENSIBLE, intelligible, penetrable, straightforward, clear, plain, direct, unambiguous, transparent, lucid, accessible
➡ **1** surprising, unreasonable **2** impenetrable, deep, complex, abstruse

understanding n, adj
♦ n
1 GRASP, knowledge, wisdom, intelligence, intellect, sense, comprehension, judgement, discernment, insight, appreciation, awareness, impression, feeling, perception, view, belief, idea, notion, opinion, interpretation, hindsight
OLD conceit
FORMAL apprehension, sagacity
2 AGREEMENT, arrangement, pact, bargain, harmony
FORMAL accord, compact, entente
3 SYMPATHY, empathy, compassion, comfort, support, consolation, commiseration, appreciation, trust
♦ adj
sympathetic, compassionate, kind, considerate, supportive, sensitive, thoughtful, tender, loving, patient, lenient, tolerant, forbearing, forgiving
➡ unsympathetic, insensitive, impatient, intolerant

understate v
underplay, play down, minimize, make light of, belittle, dismiss
COLLOQ. soft-pedal
➡ exaggerate, emphasize

understated adj
subtle, implied, indirect, low-key, faint, indistinct, indefinite, mild, toned-down
➡ exaggerated, overstated, emphasized

understatement n
minimization, restraint, underplaying, dismissal

TECHNICAL litotes, meiosis
F3 overstatement, exaggeration

understood *adj*
accepted, assumed, presumed, implied, implicit,
inferred, tacit, unstated, unspoken, unwritten

understudy *n*
stand-in, double, substitute, replacement, reserve, deputy,
relief, locum
COLLOQ. fill-in

undertake *v*
1 BEGIN, embark on, tackle, set about, try, attempt,
endeavour, take on, accept, assume, deal with, shoulder,
put/set your hand to, apply yourself to, turn your hand to,
get down to, get to grips with
OLD (*Spenser*) underfong
FORMAL commence
COLLOQ. grasp the nettle, get your teeth into, put your
shoulder to the wheel, set your hand to the plough, take
the bull by the horns
2 PLEDGE, promise, guarantee, agree, commit yourself,
contract, covenant

undertaker *n*
funeral director, funeral furnisher; *N Am* mortician
OLD upholder

undertaking *n*
1 ENTERPRISE, venture, business, affair, task, project,
operation, attempt, endeavour, effort, job, plan,
campaign, scheme
OLD emprise
2 PLEDGE, commitment, promise, vow, word, assurance,
guarantee, warrant

undertone *n*
hint, suggestion, whisper, murmur, intimation, trace,
tinge, touch, flavour, feeling, aura, atmosphere,
undercurrent
FORMAL connotation

undervalue *v*
underrate, underestimate, misjudge, minimize, depreciate,
dismiss, look down on, sell short
FORMAL disparage
F3 overrate, exaggerate

underwater *adj*
subaquatic, undersea, submarine, immersed, submerged,
sunken
TECHNICAL demersed
FORMAL subaqueous, demersal

underwear *n*
underclothes, undergarments, lingerie
COLLOQ. undies, smalls, frillies, scanties, unmentionables

underweight *adj*
thin, undersized, underfed, undernourished, half-starved
F3 overweight

underworld *n*
1 CRIMINAL WORLD, organized crime, gangland
SLANG the mob
2 NETHER WORLD, infernal regions, Hades, hell, inferno,
lower regions, abyss, fire, fire and brimstone, bottomless
pit, pit, Sheol, Acheron, Gehenna, Tophet, Abaddon,
Tartarus, Malebolge, Erebus
FORMAL perdition, abode of the devil
COLLOQ. below, down there, other place
Related adjectives: chthonian, chthonic

underwrite *v*
endorse, authorize, sanction, approve, confirm, back,
guarantee, insure, sponsor, support, fund, finance,
subsidize, subscribe, write, sign, initial, countersign

undesirable *adj*
unwanted, unwelcome, unacceptable, unwished-for,
disliked, unsuitable, unpleasant, disagreeable, distasteful,
offensive, objectionable, foul, nasty, obnoxious, repugnant
F3 desirable, pleasant

undeveloped *adj*
1 *undeveloped countries*
developing, underdeveloped, pre-industrialized, less
advanced, Third World
2 UNFORMED, embryonic, potential, latent, immature,
stunted, dwarfed
FORMAL inchoate, primordial
F3 **1** advanced, industrialized **2** developed, mature

undignified *adj*
inelegant, ungainly, clumsy, foolish, improper, unsuitable,
inappropriate, unbecoming
FORMAL unseemly, indecorous
F3 dignified, elegant

undiluted *adj*
1 *undiluted praise*
strong, pure, heady, unspoilt, unalloyed, sheer, utter,
unmitigated, unqualified
2 *an undiluted drink*
concentrated, neat, pure, straight, unmixed, unblended
F3 **1** qualified, weak **2** diluted, mixed

undisciplined *adj*
wild, unrestrained, unruly, uncontrolled, wayward,
disobedient, obstreperous, wilful, unpredictable,
unreliable, unschooled, unsteady, untrained, disorganized,
unsystematic
F3 disciplined, self-controlled

undisguised *adj*
unconcealed, open, overt, explicit, frank, genuine,
apparent, patent, obvious, evident, manifest, transparent,
blatant, naked, unadorned, stark, utter, outright,
thoroughgoing
F3 secret, concealed, hidden

undisguisedly *adv*
overtly, outright, openly, obviously, transparently, patently,
unreservedly, frankly, blatantly
F3 secretly

undisputed *adj*
uncontested, unchallenged, unquestioned, irrefutable,
undoubted, indisputable, incontrovertible, undeniable,
indubitable, accepted, acknowledged, recognized, sure,
certain, conclusive
OLD unargued
F3 debatable, uncertain

undistinguished *adj*
unexceptional, unremarkable, unimpressive, ordinary,
everyday, common, pedestrian, banal, indifferent,
mediocre, inferior
COLLOQ. run-of-the-mill, so-so, not up to much, not all
that it is cracked up to be, nothing to write home about,
no great shakes, not much cop
F3 distinguished, exceptional, remarkable

undisturbed *adj*
untouched, calm, composed, equable, collected, even,
quiet, placid, serene, tranquil, untroubled, motionless,
unconcerned, unaffected, uninterrupted, unruffled
FORMAL unperturbed
F3 disturbed, interrupted

undivided *adj*
solid, unbroken, intact, whole, total, entire, one, single,
individual, full, complete, combined, united, unanimous,
unqualified, unreserved, concentrated, exclusive,
wholehearted, serious, dedicated, sincere
TECHNICAL *pro indiviso*

undo *v*
1 UNFASTEN, untie, unbuckle, unbutton, unhook, unzip,
unlock, unwrap, unwind, open, free, release, loose,
loosen, separate, disentangle
2 ANNUL, invalidate, cancel, offset, neutralize, reverse,
overturn, repeal, revoke, set aside, upset, quash, defeat,
undermine, subvert, mar, spoil, ruin, wreck, crush, shatter,
destroy, obliterate
OLD defeat

FORMAL nullify
1 fasten, do up

undoing *n*
downfall, ruin, ruination, collapse, destruction, defeat, overthrow, reversal, weakness, shame, disgrace

undomesticated *adj*
wild, untamed, uncivilized, natural, savage
FORMAL feral
domesticated, tame

undone *adj*
1 UNACCOMPLISHED, unfulfilled, unfinished, uncompleted, incomplete, outstanding, left, omitted, neglected, ignored, forgotten, passed over
2 UNFASTENED, untied, unlaced, unbuttoned, unlocked, open, loose
3 RUINED, lost, destroyed, betrayed
1 done, accomplished, complete **2** fastened

undoubted *adj*
unchallenged, undisputed, acknowledged, uncontested, unquestionable, indisputable, incontrovertible, undesirable, sure, certain, definite, obvious, patent, indubitable, irrefutable

undoubtedly *adv*
certainly, definitely, doubtless, without doubt, without a shadow of a doubt, no doubt, beyond doubt, surely, of course, undeniably, unquestionably, unmistakably, assuredly, indubitably

undreamed-of *adj*
undreamt, inconceivable, unheard-of, unhoped-for, unimagined, unexpected, incredible, unforeseen, unsuspected, amazing, astonishing, miraculous

undress *v, n*
♦ *v*
strip, disrobe, divest, take off, remove, shed, unclothe
OLD make unready; (*Shakesp*) devest, discase, uncase; (*Spenser*) disattire
COLLOQ. peel off, streak, get your kit off
♦ *n*
nakedness, nudity, dishabille, *déshabillé*
OLD disarray

undressed *adj*
unclothed, disrobed, stripped, naked, stark-naked, nude, *en cueros*
COLLOQ. in the altogether, starkers, in your birthday suit, in the raw, in the buff, not a stitch on, naked as the day you were born
clothed

undue *adj*
unnecessary, needless, uncalled-for, unwarranted, undeserved, unjustified, unreasonable, disproportionate, excessive, immoderate, inordinate, extreme, superfluous, extravagant, exaggerated, obtrusive, improper, inappropriate
reasonable, moderate, proper

undulate *v*
rise and fall, swell, roll, surge, wave, ripple, billow, heave

undulating *adj*
rolling, wavy, rippling, billowing, sinuous
FORMAL flexuose, flexuous, undate, undulant
flat

unduly *adv*
too, over, excessively, immoderately, inordinately, disproportionately, out of all proportion, unreasonably, unjustifiably, unnecessarily, overmuch, exaggeratedly, obtrusively
COLLOQ. too ... by half
moderately, reasonably

undutiful *adj*
negligent, neglectful, careless, disloyal, remiss, slack, defaulting, delinquent
FORMAL unfilial
dutiful

undying *adj*
eternal, deathless, lasting, perpetual, everlasting, immortal, infinite, continuing, constant, perennial, permanent, unending, unfading, indestructible, inextinguishable, imperishable, undiminished
FORMAL abiding, sempiternal
impermanent, inconstant

unearth *v*
dig up, exhume, disinter, excavate, uncover, expose, reveal, bring to light, find, discover, detect
bury

unearthly *adj*
1 SUPERNATURAL, ghostly, phantom, eerie, uncanny, weird, strange, spine-chilling, otherworldly; *Scot* eldritch
FORMAL preternatural
COLLOQ. creepy
2 *at this unearthly hour*
unreasonable, preposterous, appalling, outrageous, ungodly, unheard-of
COLLOQ. horrendous
2 reasonable

unease *n*
uneasiness, anxiety, alarm, apprehension, apprehensiveness, worry, doubt, qualms, misgiving, nervousness, suspicion, disquiet, agitation
OLD dis-ease
FORMAL inquietude, perturbation
calm, composure

uneasiness *n*
anxiety, alarm, apprehension, apprehensiveness, worry, doubt, qualms, unease, discomfort, misgiving, nervousness, suspicion, disquiet, agitation
OLD dis-ease
FORMAL inquietude, perturbation
calm, composure

uneasy *adj*
1 UNCOMFORTABLE, anxious, worried, alarmed, apprehensive, tense, strained, nervous, agitated, shaky, on edge, upset, troubled, disturbed, unsettled, restless, impatient, unsure, insecure, disquieted
FORMAL perturbed
COLLOQ. trepidatious, edgy, nervy, twitchy, keyed up, wound up, jittery
2 WORRYING, troubling, disturbing, unsettling, unnerving, disconcerting, disquieting
FORMAL perturbing
1 calm, composed

uneconomic *adj*
unprofitable, uncommercial, loss-making, non-profit-making
economic, profitable, profit-making, remunerative

uneducated *adj*
unschooled, untaught, unread, ignorant, illiterate, uncultivated, uncultured, philistine, benighted
educated

unemotional *adj*
cool, cold, unfeeling, impassive, reserved, indifferent, apathetic, passionless, stoic, unresponsive, undemonstrative, unexcitable, phlegmatic, stolid, bland, bloodless, detached, objective, dispassionate
emotional, excitable

unemphatic *adj*
understated, unobtrusive, underplayed, played-down, unostentatious
COLLOQ. downbeat, soft-pedalled

unemployed *adj*
jobless, out of work, laid off, redundant, unwaged, idle, unoccupied, NEET
COLLOQ. on the dole
employed, occupied

unending *adj*
endless, never-ending, unceasing, ceaseless, incessant, interminable, continuous, uninterrupted, constant, continual, perpetual, everlasting, eternal, undying
FORMAL unremitting
ЕӠ transient, intermittent

unendurable *adj*
intolerable, unbearable, overwhelming, shattering, insufferable, insupportable
ЕӠ bearable, endurable

unenthusiastic *adj*
uninterested, unimpressed, cool, half-hearted, apathetic, bored, neutral, nonchalant, indifferent, unmoved, unresponsive, blasé, lukewarm, tepid, Laodicean
ЕӠ enthusiastic

unenviable *adj*
undesirable, unpleasant, disagreeable, uncongenial, uncomfortable, thankless, difficult, dangerous
ЕӠ enviable, desirable

unequal *adj*
1 DIFFERENT, varying, dissimilar, unlike, unfair, unjust, biased, inequitable, discriminatory
2 UNMATCHED, uneven, unbalanced, lopsided, disproportionate, asymmetrical, irregular
3 *unequal to a task*
incapable, unqualified, inadequate, unsuited, unfitted, incompetent
COLLOQ. not up to, not cut out for
ЕӠ **1, 2, 3** equal

unequalled *adj*
unmatched, unbeaten, unsurpassed, unrivalled, peerless, unique, paramount, matchless, incomparable, unparalleled, pre-eminent, surpassing, transcendent, supreme, exceptional, inimitable
FORMAL nonpareil

unequivocal *adj*
unambiguous, explicit, clear, plain, evident, distinct, unmistakable, express, direct, straight, straightforward, definite, positive, categorical, incontrovertible, absolute, outright, unqualified, unreserved
ЕӠ ambiguous, vague, qualified

unequivocally *adv*
unambiguously, unmistakably, clearly, directly, distinctly, explicitly, definitely, positively, firmly, unquestionably, incontrovertibly
ЕӠ ambiguously, vaguely

unerring *adj*
unfailing, perfect, impeccable, infallible, faultless, exact, certain, sure, accurate, uncanny
COLLOQ. dead
ЕӠ fallible

unerringly *adv*
unfailingly, infallibly, accurately
COLLOQ. bang, dead

unethical *adj*
unprofessional, immoral, improper, wrong, wicked, evil, unscrupulous, unprincipled, dishonourable, disreputable, illegal, illicit, dishonest, underhand
COLLOQ. shady
ЕӠ ethical

uneven *adj*
1 *uneven ground*
rough, bumpy, lumpy, stony, rugged, craggy, jagged, irregular, coarse, ruffled, rumpled, accidented
2 ODD, unequal, inequitable, unfair, unbalanced, one-sided, ill-matched, asymmetrical, lopsided, crooked
3 IRREGULAR, intermittent, spasmodic, fitful, jerky, unsteady, variable, changeable, fluctuating, erratic, inconsistent, patchy, streaky
OLD inequable
ЕӠ **1** even, flat, level **2** even, equal **3** regular, consistent

uneventful *adj*
uninteresting, unexciting, quiet, unvaried, boring, monotonous, tedious, dull, routine, humdrum, ordinary, everyday, commonplace, unremarkable, unexceptional, unmemorable
COLLOQ. run-of-the-mill
ЕӠ eventful, memorable, remarkable

unexampled *adj*
unprecedented, never before seen, incomparable, unequalled, unparalleled, unheard-of, unmatched, unique, novel

unexceptionable *adj*
inoffensive, harmless, innocuous, safe, innocent, unobjectionable, peaceable, mild, bland
ЕӠ exceptionable, offensive, objectionable

unexceptional *adj*
unremarkable, unmemorable, typical, average, normal, usual, ordinary, common, everyday, indifferent, mediocre, unimpressive, undistinguished
COLLOQ. run-of-the-mill, so-so, not up to much, not all that it is cracked up to be, nothing to write home about, no great shakes, not much cop
ЕӠ exceptional, impressive

unexcitable *adj*
self-possessed, cool, composed, relaxed, easy-going, serene, calm, contained, dispassionate, impassive, passionless, unimpassioned, phlegmatic
FORMAL imperturbable
COLLOQ. laid-back
ЕӠ excitable

unexpected *adj*
unforeseen, unanticipated, unpredictable, unlooked-for, chance, accidental, sudden, abrupt, surprising, startling, amazing, astonishing, unusual, emergent
OLD unhoped, inopinate, unware
FORMAL fortuitous
COLLOQ. snap, shock
ЕӠ expected, predictable

> **QUOTATIONS**
> If you do not expect the unexpected, you will not find it; for it is hard to be sought out, and difficult
> HERACLITUS

unexpectedly *adv*
suddenly, surprisingly, unpredictably, without warning, abruptly, by chance, fortuitously, unawares, accidentally, phenomenally, refreshingly, *ex improviso*, *à l'improviste*
OLD unware
COLLOQ. out of the blue, like a bolt from the blue

unexpressive *adj*
expressionless, emotionless, impassive, inexpressive, inscrutable, vacant, blank, deadpan, immobile
ЕӠ expressive, mobile

unfading *adj*
lasting, imperishable, durable, enduring, constant, undying, unfailing, fadeless, fast, evergreen
FORMAL abiding, immarcescible
ЕӠ changeable, transient

unfailing *adj*
constant, certain, dependable, reliable, sure, steady, true, steadfast, faithful, loyal, staunch, undying, unfading, inexhaustible, infallible, unerring
ЕӠ fickle, impermanent, transient

unfair *adj*
1 UNJUST, partial, biased, prejudiced, bigoted, discriminatory, unbalanced, weighted, one-sided, slanted, partisan, arbitrary, undeserved, unmerited, unwarranted, unreasonable, uncalled-for
FORMAL inequitable
COLLOQ. a bit off, thick
2 UNETHICAL, unscrupulous, unprincipled, wrongful, deceitful, dishonest, foul

COLLOQ. crooked, shady, bent, below the belt;
Aust & NZ crook
E3 1 fair, just, unbiased, deserved **2** honest, ethical

unfairly *adv*
unjustly, wrongly, improperly, unreasonably,
biasedly, partially, illegally, unlawfully, dishonestly
FORMAL inequitably
E3 fairly, justly

unfairness *n*
injustice, inequity, one-sidedness, partiality,
partisanship, prejudice, bigotry, bias, discrimination,
misusage
FORMAL inequitableness
E3 fairness, equity

unfaithful *adj*
disloyal, treacherous, false, untrue, insincere,
deceitful, dishonest, untrustworthy, unreliable, fickle,
inconstant, adulterous, double-dealing, faithless,
unbelieving, godless
FORMAL duplicitous, perfidious
COLLOQ. cheating, two-timing
E3 faithful, loyal, reliable

unfaltering *adj*
unfailing, unwavering, unyielding, unswerving, untiring,
tireless, unflagging, unflinching, constant, firm,
indefatigable, steady, steadfast, resolute, fixed
FORMAL pertinacious
E3 faltering, uncertain, wavering

unfamiliar *adj*
1 STRANGE, unusual, uncommon, curious, alien, foreign,
uncharted, unexplored, unknown, different, new, novel
2 UNACCUSTOMED, unacquainted, uninformed,
inexperienced, unpractised, unskilled, unversed,
unconversant
E3 1 familiar, customary **2** conversant, acquainted

unfashionable *adj*
outmoded, dated, out of date, out, passé, old-fashioned,
démodé, antiquated, obsolete, unpopular
COLLOQ. old hat, square
E3 fashionable

unfasten *v*
undo, untie, loosen, unwrap, unclasp, unlock, open,
uncouple, disconnect, separate, detach
E3 fasten, do up, bolt, lock

unfathomable *adj*
inexplicable, incomprehensible, impenetrable, baffling,
fathomless, immeasurable, unknowable, mysterious, deep,
profound, hidden, bottomless, unplumbed, unsounded,
inscrutable, indecipherable
FORMAL abstruse, esoteric
E3 comprehensible, explicable, penetrable

unfavourable *adj*
1 UNPROMISING, ominous, threatening, discouraging,
inopportune, untimely, unseasonable, ill-suited,
unfortunate, unlucky, in a bad light, disadvantageous, bad,
foul, poor, adverse, contrary, negative
FORMAL inauspicious
2 HOSTILE, critical, adverse, negative, bad, poor, unfriendly,
uncomplimentary, prejudiced
FORMAL inimical
E3 1 favourable, promising; *formal* auspicious **2** friendly,
complimentary, good

unfavourably *adv*
badly, poorly, adversely, negatively, disadvantageously,
unpromisingly, unfortunately
E3 favourably, positively, well

unfeeling *adj*
insensitive, cold, hard, stony, callous, heartless,
hard-hearted, numb, harsh, cruel, inhuman, pitiless,
uncaring, unsympathetic, iron-headed
E3 sensitive, sympathetic

unfeigned *adj*
genuine, natural, pure, real, sincere, unaffected, frank,
spontaneous, wholehearted, unforced, heartfelt
E3 insincere, pretended, feigned

unfettered *adj*
unconstrained, free, unhampered, unrestrained,
unhindered, unconfined, unchecked, unbridled,
uninhibited, unshackled, untrammelled
E3 constrained, fettered

unfinished *adj*
incomplete, uncompleted, half-done, sketchy, rough,
crude, imperfect, lacking, wanting, deficient, undone,
unaccomplished, unfulfilled
E3 finished, perfect

unfit *adj*
1 UNSUITABLE, inappropriate, unsuited, inapt, ill-equipped,
unqualified, disqualified, ineligible, untrained, unprepared,
unequal, incapable, unable, incompetent, inadequate,
ineffective, useless, condemned
2 UNHEALTHY, out of condition, out of shape, flabby,
feeble, weak, decrepit, disabled, incapacitated, debilitated
E3 1 fit, suitable, competent **2** healthy, fit

unflagging *adj*
unfaltering, unfailing, untiring, tireless, unswerving,
unceasing, undeviating, persevering, persistent, never-
failing, indefatigable, constant, steady, fixed, single-
minded, staunch
FORMAL unremitting
E3 faltering, inconstant

unflappable *adj*
calm, collected, composed, level-headed, unworried,
unexcitable, unruffled, equable, cool, impassive,
easy-going, self-possessed, phlegmatic
FORMAL imperturbable
COLLOQ. laid-back
E3 excitable, nervous, temperamental; *colloq.* panicky

unflattering *adj*
unbecoming, uncomplimentary, unattractive,
unfavourable, unprepossessing, critical, honest, blunt,
candid, outspoken
E3 complimentary, flattering

unflinching *adj*
steady, unfaltering, unwavering, unshaken,
unshrinking, unswerving, firm, fixed, determined, constant,
staunch, steadfast, sure, bold, resolute, stalwart,
unblinking
E3 unsteady, scared

unflinchingly *adv*
unfalteringly, unwaveringly, unshrinkingly, unswervingly,
steadily, firmly, staunchly, steadfastly, boldly, resolutely
E3 unsteadily, falteringly

unfold *v*
1 DEVELOP, evolve, grow, work out, come about, result,
emerge
2 REVEAL, disclose, show, display, present, tell, relate,
make known, describe, explain, clarify, expound,
elaborate, narrate, illustrate, interpret
OLD deploy
FORMAL explicate
3 *unfold a map*
open (out), spread (out), flatten, straighten (out),
stretch out, undo, unfurl, unroll, uncoil, unravel,
unwrap, uncover, extend, shake out, disenvelop,
disinvolve, undouble, untuck
OLD unclew
E3 2 withhold, suppress **3** fold, wrap

unforeseen *adj*
unpredicted, unpredictable, unexpected, unanticipated,
unlooked-for, surprising, amazing, astonishing, startling,
sudden, unavoidable, unusual
E3 expected, predictable

unforgettable adj
memorable, indelible, momentous, historic, noteworthy, notable, impressive, remarkable, significant, exceptional, extraordinary, striking, important, special, distinctive
E3 unmemorable, unexceptional

unforgivable adj
unpardonable, inexcusable, unjustifiable, indefensible, intolerable, shameful, outrageous, disgraceful, deplorable, contemptible
FORMAL reprehensible
E3 forgivable, venial

unforgiven adj
unredeemed, unabsolved, unregenerate, unrepentant
E3 absolved, forgiven

unfortunate adj
1 UNLUCKY, luckless, unsuccessful, poor, wretched, unhappy, doomed, ill, ill-fated, hopeless, calamitous, tragic, disastrous, ruinous, adverse, unpleasant, disadvantageous, untoward
OLD evil, disadventurous, misfortuned; (Shakesp) misadventured; (Spenser) disaventrous
FORMAL hapless
COLLOQ. tough
2 REGRETTABLE, lamentable, deplorable, adverse, unfavourable, unsuitable, inappropriate, inopportune, untimely, ill-timed, ill-advised
FORMAL injudicious
E3 **1** fortunate, happy **2** favourable, appropriate

unfortunately adv
regrettably, unhappily, unluckily, sadly, alas, sad to say, I am sorry to say, sad to relate
COLLOQ. worse luck
E3 fortunately

unfounded adj
baseless, groundless, unsupported, unsubstantiated, unproven, unjustified, idle, false, spurious, trumped-up, fabricated, without foundation
FORMAL uncorroborated, conjectural
E3 substantiated, justified

unfrequented adj
lonely, remote, secluded, uninhabited, unvisited, isolated, deserted, desolate, solitary, lone, god-forsaken
FORMAL sequestered
E3 busy, crowded, populous

unfriendly adj
unsociable, standoffish, aloof, distant, unapproachable, inhospitable, uncongenial, unneighbourly, unwelcoming, unkind, cold, chilly, chill, cool, frosty, frozen, wintry, hostile, strained, aggressive, quarrelsome, antagonistic, ill-disposed, unpleasant, disagreeable, surly, sour; Scot fremd
FORMAL inimical, inauspicious
E3 friendly, amiable, agreeable

SYNONYM NUANCES

The term **unsociable** could describe someone who does not enjoy company, but it tends to suggest disapproval: *although kind-hearted, he could be unsociable and stubborn*. **Standoffish**, however, is clearly suggestive of arrogance; similarly, **aloof** implies someone is behaving haughtily. **Distant**, on the other hand, is less judgemental and suggests reserve, but still has critical connotations, while **unapproachable** would imply that this reserve is discouraging or even frightening: *people feel banks are too unapproachable*.

 Inhospitable suggests an absence of comfort: *the inhospitable outback*, and **uncongenial** is similarly uninviting: *uncongenial surroundings*. **Unwelcoming** suggests a rather forbidding reception: *the unwelcoming look in his eyes*. **Unkind**, on the other hand, would suggest a degree of active cruelty: *she made an unkind comment the moment she met me*.

 Cold, **chilly**, **chill** and **cool** all share suggestions of remoteness, and the terms **frosty**, **frozen** and **wintry**

---

suggest an even more marked display of unfriendliness: *he met me with a frosty glare*. **Hostile**, **aggressive**, **quarrelsome** and **antagonistic** go further by implying an openly confrontational disposition, unlike **ill-disposed**, which describes an internal attitude: *he felt ill-disposed towards her but hid his emotions well*.

 Surly and **sour** can be used to suggest moroseness or peevishness behind unfriendliness: *sour criticism*, while **strained** would be reserved for a situation or relationship that causes uneasiness: *her words were met with a strained silence*.

---

unfrock v
dismiss, depose, degrade, demote, suspend
E3 restore, reinstate

unfruitful adj
unproductive, fruitless, barren, exhausted, impoverished, infertile, sterile, arid, unprofitable, unprolific, unrewarding
FORMAL infecund, infructuous
E3 fruitful, productive

unfurl v
1 *unfurl a flag*
unfold, open (out), spread (out), flatten, straighten (out), stretch out, extend, undo, unroll, uncoil, unravel, unwrap, uncover
2 DEVELOP, unfold, evolve, grow, work out, come about, result, emerge

ungainly adj
clumsy, awkward, gauche, inelegant, ungraceful, gawky, unco-ordinated, lumbering, gangling, unwieldy, uncouth, loutish
FORMAL maladroit
E3 graceful, elegant

ungodly adj
1 UNREASONABLE, outrageous, preposterous, intolerable, unearthly, unsocial
COLLOQ. horrendous
2 IMPIOUS, irreligious, godless, blasphemous, profane, immoral, corrupt, depraved, sinful, wicked
FORMAL iniquitous

ungovernable adj
uncontrollable, wild, disorderly, unmanageable, unrestrainable, unruly, ungoverned, rebellious, masterless
FORMAL refractory

ungracious adj
discourteous, uncivil, impolite, rude, disrespectful, graceless, bad-mannered, ill-bred, unmannerly, offhand, boorish, churlish
E3 gracious, polite

ungrateful adj
unthankful, unappreciative, rude, impolite, uncivil, ill-mannered, ungracious, selfish, thankless, heedless
E3 grateful, thankful

unguarded adj
1 *in an unguarded moment*
unwary, careless, inattentive, off guard, incautious, indiscreet, undiplomatic, thoughtless, unthinking, heedless, foolish, foolhardy, rash, ill-considered, imprudent
FORMAL impolitic, uncircumspect
2 UNDEFENDED, unprotected, exposed, vulnerable, defenceless, unpatrolled
E3 **1** guarded, cautious **2** defended, protected

unhappily adv
unfortunately, regrettably, unluckily, sadly, alas, sad to say, sad to relate
COLLOQ. worse luck
E3 fortunately

unhappy adj
1 SAD, sorrowful, miserable, melancholy, depressed, upset, dispirited, glum, despondent, dejected, downcast, discontent, crestfallen, long-faced, gloomy, mournful
FORMAL woebegone, disconsolate

COLLOQ. down, blue, fed up, low, down in the dumps
2 UNFORTUNATE, unlucky, ill-fated, ill-starred, luckless, unsuitable, inappropriate, inapt, ill-chosen, ill-advised, tactless, awkward, clumsy
FORMAL hapless, injudicious
F3 1 happy **2** fortunate, suitable

unharmed *adj*
undamaged, unhurt, uninjured, unscathed, untouched, whole, intact, safe, sound
F3 harmed, injured, hurt

unhealthy *adj*
1 UNWELL, sick, ill, poorly, ailing, sickly, infirm, invalid, weak, feeble, frail, debilitated, unsound, diseased, pasty
FORMAL indisposed
2 UNWHOLESOME, insanitary, unhygienic, harmful, injurious, detrimental, noxious, morbid, unnatural, unsanitary
FORMAL insalubrious, insalutary, epinosic
F3 1 healthy, fit **2** wholesome, hygienic, natural

unheard-of *adj*
1 UNTHINKABLE, inconceivable, unbelievable, unimaginable, undreamed-of, unprecedented, extraordinary, exceptional, unacceptable, offensive, shocking, outrageous, preposterous
2 UNKNOWN, unfamiliar, new, unusual, obscure, unsung, unheralded, undiscovered
F3 1 normal, acceptable **2** famous

unheeded *adj*
ignored, disregarded, disobeyed, unnoticed, unnoted, unobserved, unremarked, overlooked, neglected, forgotten
F3 noted, observed

unhelpful *adj*
awkward, obstructive, disobliging, troublesome, unaccommodating, unco-operative, obstinate, stubborn, irritable, touchy, prickly, oversensitive, rude, unpleasant, boorish, loutish, rustic, cubbish
COLLOQ. stroppy, bloody-minded
F3 helpful, accommodating, amenable, pleasant

unheralded *adj*
unsung, unrecognized, unproclaimed, unpublicized, unnoticed, surprise, unadvertised, unannounced, unexpected, unforeseen
F3 advertised, publicized, trumpeted, acclaimed

unhesitating *adj*
immediate, instant, instantaneous, prompt, ready, automatic, spontaneous, unquestioning, unwavering, unfaltering, wholehearted, confident, implicit
F3 hesitant, tentative

unhinge *v*
unbalance, unnerve, unsettle, upset, confuse, distract, disorder, drive mad, madden, craze, derange

unhinged *adj*
deranged, disordered, demented, crazy, mad, lunatic, insane, of unsound mind, *non compos mentis*, unbalanced, unsettled, disturbed, irrational, confused, frantic, delirious, distraught, berserk, out of your mind
COLLOQ. not all there, loopy, bonkers, barmy, potty, nuts, nutty, nutty as a fruitcake, round the bend, round the twist, out to lunch
SLANG loony, off your rocker, needing your head examined
F3 sane, calm

unholy *adj*
1 IMPIOUS, irreligious, godless, ungodly, blasphemous, sinful, immoral, corrupt, depraved, wicked, evil
FORMAL iniquitous
2 *an unholy mess*
unreasonable, shocking, outrageous, dreadful, terrible, ungodly, unearthly
COLLOQ. horrendous
F3 1 holy, pious, godly **2** reasonable

unhook *v*
undo, unfasten, untie, release, free, loose, loosen

unhoped-for *adj*
unexpected, unforeseen, unanticipated, unimaginable, unlooked-for, unbelievable, undreamed-of, incredible, surprising

unhurried *adj*
slow, leisurely, deliberate, easy, easy-going, relaxed, calm, sedate
COLLOQ. laid-back
F3 hurried, hasty, rushed

unhurt *adj*
unharmed, uninjured, unscathed, untouched, whole, intact, safe, sound
F3 hurt, injured

unhygienic *adj*
insanitary, unclean, impure, unhealthy, unsanitized, dirty, dirtied, contaminated, polluted, infected, disease-ridden, filthy, foul, infested
FORMAL unhealthful, noisome, noxious, insalubrious, feculent
F3 hygienic, sanitary, clean

unidentified *adj*
unknown, unrecognized, unmarked, unnamed, nameless, anonymous, incognito, unfamiliar, strange, mysterious, obscure, unclassified
F3 identified, known, named

unification *n*
union, uniting, merger, alliance, amalgamation, combination, federation, fusion, incorporation, coalescence, coalition, confederation
FORMAL enosis
F3 separation, split, division

uniform *n, adj*
♦ *n*
outfit, costume, livery, insignia, regalia, robes, dress, suit, habit, regimentals
COLLOQ. garb, rig
♦ *adj*
same, identical, like, alike, similar, homogeneous, consistent, regular, equal, smooth, level, even, flat, monotonous, of a piece, unvarying, unchanging, constant, unbroken, steady, stable, invariable, undeviating
F3 different, varied, changing

uniformity *n*
sameness, constancy, invariability, regularity, similarity, evenness, flatness, monotony, drabness, dullness, tedium
FORMAL homogeneity, homomorphism, similitude
F3 difference, dissimilarity, variation

unify *v*
unite, bring/come together, join, bind, combine, integrate, mix, blend, merge, amalgamate, consolidate, coalesce, fuse, weld
F3 separate, divide, split

unifying *adj*
uniting, reconciling, combinatory, consolidative
TECHNICAL esemplastic
FORMAL unific, henotic
F3 divisive

unimaginable *adj*
inconceivable, unbelievable, incredible, amazing, astonishing, staggering, extraordinary, preposterous, impossible, fantastic, undreamed-of, unthinkable, unheard-of, implausible, unlikely, unconvincing, far-fetched, outlandish
COLLOQ. mind-boggling

unimaginative *adj*
uninspired, unoriginal, predictable, hackneyed, banal, mundane, pedestrian, ordinary, dull, boring, routine, usual, dry, barren, lifeless, stale, unexciting, tame
COLLOQ. matter-of-fact, samey
F3 imaginative, creative, original

unimpeachable *adj*
blameless, perfect, unblemished, spotless,
faultless, immaculate, impeccable, irreproachable,
unchallengeable, unquestionable, unassailable, reliable,
dependable
F3 blameworthy, faulty

unimpeded *adj*
unrestrained, unconstrained, free, open, clear,
unhindered, unblocked, unchecked, unhampered,
uninhibited, untrammelled
COLLOQ. all-round
F3 hampered, impeded

unimportant *adj*
insignificant, irrelevant, immaterial, insubstantial, minor,
secondary, incidental, marginal, peripheral, trivial, trifling,
petty, slight, negligible, worthless, inconsiderable, light
FORMAL nugatory, inconsequential, of no consequence
COLLOQ. no great shakes, no big deal, not worth
mentioning
F3 important, significant, relevant, vital

unimpressive *adj*
unspectacular, undistinguished, unexciting,
unexceptional, unremarkable, uninteresting, dull,
ordinary, common, average, commonplace, indifferent,
mediocre
F3 impressive, memorable, notable, special

uninhabited *adj*
unoccupied, vacant, empty, deserted, abandoned,
desolate, unpeopled, unpopulated, unsettled

uninhibited *adj*
unconstrained, unreserved, unself-conscious, liberated,
free, unrestricted, uncontrolled, unrestrained, abandoned,
natural, spontaneous, frank, outspoken, candid, open,
relaxed, informal
F3 inhibited, repressed, constrained, restrained

uninspired *adj*
ordinary, boring, commonplace, dull, indifferent, stale,
trite, stock, unexciting, unimaginative, uninspiring,
uninteresting, arid, undistinguished, unexceptional,
unoriginal, pedestrian, prosaic, humdrum
COLLOQ. samey, dull as ditchwater
F3 original, inspired, exciting

uninspiring *adj*
boring, tedious, dull, monotonous, routine, repetitious,
uninteresting, unexciting, uneventful, dreary, humdrum,
tiring, tiresome, unvaried, commonplace, trite,
unimaginative, dry, stale, flat, insipid, prosaic,
long-winded
OLD stultifying, jejune
COLLOQ. samey, dull as ditchwater, soul-destroying,
with the novelty worn off, ho-hum
F3 inspiring, interesting, exciting, stimulating, original

unintelligent *adj*
stupid, foolish, silly, slow, half-witted, empty-headed,
fatuous, unreasoning, unthinking, dense, dull, obtuse,
brainless
COLLOQ. thick, dumb, gormless
F3 intelligent

unintelligible *adj*
incomprehensible, incoherent, inarticulate, garbled,
scrambled, jumbled, muddled, indecipherable,
unreadable, illegible, impenetrable, unfathomable,
puzzling, mysterious, obscure, complicated, complex,
involved
COLLOQ. double Dutch
F3 intelligible, comprehensible, clear

unintentional *adj*
unintended, accidental, inadvertent, unplanned,
unpremeditated, uncalculated, involuntary, unconscious,
unwitting, careless
FORMAL fortuitous
F3 intentional, deliberate

uninterested *adj*
indifferent, unconcerned, uninvolved, bored, listless,
apathetic, unenthusiastic, blasé, impassive, distant,
unresponsive, incurious, *pococurante*
COLLOQ. not giving a hoot, not giving two hoots
SLANG not giving a monkey's, not giving a damn, not
giving a toss, not giving a tinker's cuss
F3 interested, excited, enthusiastic, responsive, curious

> **!** **uninterested** or **disinterested**?
> *See panel at* **disinterested**.

uninteresting *adj*
boring, tedious, monotonous, humdrum, dull, drab,
dreary, dry, flat, tame, stale, prosaic, pedestrian,
uneventful, unexciting, uninspiring, unimpressive,
tiresome, wearisome
COLLOQ. samey, dull as ditchwater
F3 interesting, exciting, entertaining

uninterrupted *adj*
unbroken, continuous, non-stop, unending, unceasing,
ceaseless, endless, constant, continual, steady, sustained,
undisturbed, peaceful
FORMAL unremitting
F3 broken, intermittent

uninvited *adj*
unasked, unsought, unsolicited, unwanted,
unwelcome
F3 invited

uninviting *adj*
unappealing, unattractive, undesirable, unpleasant,
unwelcoming, repellent, repulsive, offensive,
off-putting, unsavoury, disagreeable, distasteful,
unappetizing
F3 inviting, welcome

uninvolved *adj*
unattached, uncommitted, unengaged, free, independent,
footloose, fancy-free, unhampered, unhindered,
untrammelled
F3 attached, committed

union *n*
1 FUSION, unification, unity, alliance, coalition, league,
association, confederation, amalgamation, merger,
combination, joining, juncture, consolidation, mixture,
synthesis, blend, coalescence, cementation
TECHNICAL coadunation, conglutination, consubstantiation
2 ASSOCIATION, trade union, alliance, coalition, league,
club, federation, confederacy, consortium
3 AGREEMENT, harmony, unity, unanimity
FORMAL accord, concurrence
4 MARRIAGE, wedding
OLD wedlock
FORMAL matrimony, nuptials, spousage, espousals
F3 1 separation, alienation; *formal* estrangement **4** divorce

unique *adj*
single, one-off, sole, only, one, one and only, one of a
kind, lone, alone, solitary, unmatched, matchless, peerless,
unequalled, unparalleled, unrivalled, incomparable,
unprecedented, inimitable, singular
FORMAL nonpareil, idiographic, *sui generis*
F3 common

uniquely *adv*
matchlessly, peerlessly, incomparably, inimitably, singly,
solely, only, specially, distinctively, markedly,
remarkably, peculiarly, idiosyncratically, singularly,
by itself, in its own way

unison *n*
agreement, co-operation, harmony, unanimity, unity
FORMAL concert, accord, concord
■ **in unison**
1 *sing in unison*
at the same time, simultaneously, at the same moment
2 *work in unison*
in agreement, in co-operation, in harmony

unit *n*
1 ITEM, part, element, constituent, piece, component, module, section, segment, portion, entity, whole, one, system, assembly
2 DETACHMENT, squad, force, corps, brigade, patrol, task force

unite *v*
join, connect, link, tie, couple, marry, wed, ally, co-operate, band, associate, federate, confederate, combine, join forces, pool, amalgamate, merge, blend, unify, consolidate, coalesce, weld, fuse, incorporate, make common cause, close, twist, knit, knot, lap, lock, splice, cement, consort, embody
TECHNICAL coadunate, conjugate, consubstantiate, synoecize
OLD concorporate, copulate, fay, ming
FORMAL accrete, cleave, conjoin, conglutinate
COLLOQ. pull together
Ｅ▆ separate, sever

united *adj*
allied, affiliated, corporate, unified, combined, amalgamated, pooled, incorporated, collective, concerted, one, unanimous, agreed, in agreement, like-minded, co-operative
OLD concorporated
FORMAL in accord, conjoined, conjoint
Ｅ▆ disunited

unity *n*
1 AGREEMENT, harmony, peace, consensus, unanimity, solidarity
FORMAL accord, concord, concert
COLLOQ. togetherness
2 UNION, integrity, oneness, wholeness, amalgamation, unification
Ｅ▆ 1 disunity, disagreement, discord, strife

universal *adj*
worldwide, global, cosmic, all, all-embracing, all-inclusive, general, comprehensive, common, across-the-board, total, whole, entire, all-round, unlimited
TECHNICAL ecumenic(al)
FORMAL ubiquitous, omnipresent, catholic
COLLOQ. varsal
OLD COLLOQ. versal

universality *n*
commonness, comprehensiveness, all-inclusiveness, entirety, totality, completeness, generalization, generality, predominance, prevalence
FORMAL ubiquity

universally *adv*
always, everywhere, uniformly, invariably
FORMAL ubiquitously

universe *n*
cosmos, world, nature, creation, firmament, heavens
FORMAL macrocosm

> **QUOTATIONS**
> Man cannot live without seeking to describe and explain the universe
> SIR ISAIAH BERLIN

university *n*
college, institute, varsity, academy
OLD polytechnic
FORMAL academia

unjust *adj*
unfair, wrong, partial, biased, prejudiced, one-sided, partisan, unreasonable, unjustified, undeserved
FORMAL inequitable
Ｅ▆ just, fair, reasonable

unjustifiable *adj*
indefensible, inexcusable, unforgivable, unpardonable, unreasonable, uncalled-for, unwarranted, immoderate, excessive, unacceptable, outrageous
Ｅ▆ justifiable, acceptable

unkempt *adj*
dishevelled, tousled, rumpled, uncombed, ungroomed, untidy, disordered, messy, sloppy, scruffy, shabby, shambolic, slovenly
COLLOQ. slobbish
Ｅ▆ well-groomed, tidy

unkind *adj*
cruel, harsh, inhuman, inhumane, callous, hard-hearted, cold-hearted, heartless, unfeeling, insensitive, thoughtless, inconsiderate, uncharitable, unkindly, pitiless, ruthless, nasty, malicious, malevolent, vicious, snide, spiteful, mean, unfriendly, uncaring, unsympathetic, disobliging
COLLOQ. shabby, bitchy
Ｅ▆ kind, kindly, considerate, generous, sympathetic

unkindness *n*
cruelty, harshness, uncharitableness, unfriendliness, inhumanity, callousness, hard-heartedness, insensitivity, maliciousness, meanness, spite
Ｅ▆ kindness, friendship

unknowable *adj*
unimaginable, unpredictable, untold, unascertainable, unfathomable, unforeseeable, incalculable, infinite
COLLOQ. in the lap of the gods

unknowing *adj*
unaware, unwitting, unsuspecting, unthinking, unconscious, involuntary, inadvertent, unplanned, accidental, chance, unintentional, unintended
Ｅ▆ knowing, conscious, deliberate

unknown *adj*
unfamiliar, unheard-of, strange, alien, foreign, mysterious, dark, obscure, hidden, concealed, undisclosed, secret, undivulged, untold, new, uncharted, unexplored, undiscovered, unrevealed, unidentified, unnamed, nameless, anonymous, incognito
Ｅ▆ known, familiar

unlawful *adj*
illegal, criminal, illicit, illegitimate, against the law, unconstitutional, outlawed, banned, prohibited, forbidden, unauthorized, unlicensed, unsanctioned
Ｅ▆ lawful, legal, allowed, permitted

unleash *v*
loose, let loose, (set) free, release, unloose, untie, untether
Ｅ▆ restrain

unlettered *adj*
illiterate, ignorant, uneducated, unlearned, unschooled, untaught, untutored, unlessoned
Ｅ▆ educated

unlike *adj, prep*
♦ *adj*
dissimilar, different, distinct, opposite, opposed, incompatible, contrasted, ill-matched, out of character, unrelated, unequal, divergent, diverse, various
OLD difform, unconform; (*Spenser*) unlich
FORMAL disparate, heterogeneous
Ｅ▆ similar, related
♦ *prep*
dissimilar to, different from, in contrast to, as opposed to, as against
Ｅ▆ like

unlikely *adj*
1 IMPROBABLE, implausible, far-fetched, unconvincing, unbelievable, incredible, inconceivable, fictional, unimaginable, unexpected, doubtful, dubious, questionable, suspect, suspicious, last
OLD (*Shakesp & Spenser*) unlike
COLLOQ. fishy

2 SLIGHT, faint, remote, distant, outside, slim, small, inconsiderable
E 1 likely, plausible

unlimited *adj*
limitless, unrestricted, unbounded, boundless, inexhaustible, illimitable, infinite, endless, countless, incalculable, immeasurable, measureless, untold, vast, immense, extensive, great, indefinite, absolute, total, unconditional, unqualified, all-encompassing, complete, full, unconstrained, unhampered, unimpeded, uncontrolled, unchecked
E limited

unload *v*
unpack, empty, discharge, dump, offload, unburden, remove, relieve
E load

unlock *v*
unbolt, unlatch, unfasten, undo, unbar, open, free, release
E lock, fasten

unlooked-for *adj*
unexpected, unforeseen, unanticipated, unpredicted, unhoped-for, unthought-of, undreamed-of, surprising, surprise, fortunate, chance, lucky
FORMAL fortuitous
E expected, predictable

unloved *adj*
unpopular, disliked, hated, detested, unwanted, rejected, spurned, forsaken, loveless, uncared-for, neglected
COLLOQ. dumped
E loved

unluckily *adv*
regrettably, unhappily, unfortunately, sadly, alas, sad to say, I am sorry to say, sad to relate
COLLOQ. worse luck
E luckily, fortunately

unlucky *adj*
1 UNFORTUNATE, luckless, unsuccessful, poor, wretched, unhappy, miserable, ill-fated, ill-starred, star-crossed, jinxed, doomed, cursed, ill-omened; *Aust* stiff
OLD infaust
FORMAL hapless
COLLOQ. down on your luck, tough
2 UNFAVOURABLE, adverse, unfortunate, unpleasant, unpromising, doomed, ill-fated, ominous, disadvantageous, untoward, calamitous, disastrous, catastrophic, black, left-handed, sinister; *Scot* donsie, unchancy, wanchancy
OLD (*Shakesp*) wicked; *Scot* mischancy
FORMAL inauspicious, unpropitious
E 1 fortunate, lucky 2 favourable, lucky

unmanageable *adj*
1 UNWIELDY, bulky, cumbersome, awkward, troublesome, inconvenient, unhandy
FORMAL incommodious
2 UNCONTROLLABLE, wild, unruly, disorderly, ungovernable, obstreperous, difficult
FORMAL recalcitrant, refractory
E 1 manageable 2 controllable

unmanly *adj*
effeminate, dishonourable, feeble, weak, weak-kneed, soft, weedy, cowardly, chicken-hearted, lily-livered, craven, namby-pamby
FORMAL effete
COLLOQ. cissy, wet, yellow, wimpish
SLANG wussy
E manly

unmannerly *adj*
impolite, rude, uncivil, uncouth, discourteous, ill-mannered, badly-behaved, bad-mannered, disrespectful, graceless, ungracious, ill-bred, boorish, low-bred
E polite

unmarried *adj*
single, unwed, divorced, separated, celibate, unattached, free, partnerless, available, lone, on your own
COLLOQ. footloose and fancy-free
E married

unmask *v*
unveil, uncloak, uncover, bare, expose, reveal, show, disclose, discover, detect
E mask, conceal

unmatched *adj*
unrivalled, unique, unparalleled, unequalled, unsurpassed, incomparable, beyond compare, matchless, supreme, peerless, paramount, unexampled
FORMAL consummate, nonpareil

unmentionable *adj*
unspeakable, unutterable, forbidden, taboo, immodest, indecent, embarrassing, unpleasant, shocking, scandalous, shameful, disgraceful, abominable

unmerciful *adj*
merciless, pitiless, ruthless, cruel, brutal, hard, callous, sadistic, heartless, implacable, relentless, remorseless, unrelenting, unsparing, uncaring, unfeeling
E merciful

unmethodical *adj*
unorganized, confused, muddled, disorderly, haphazard, illogical, irregular, unsystematic, unco-ordinated, random
FORMAL desultory
E methodical

unmindful *adj*
heedless, careless, negligent, remiss, unheeding, neglectful, lax, slack, indifferent, inattentive, unaware, unconscious, oblivious, forgetful, blind, deaf, regardless
E mindful, aware, heedful

unmistakable *adj*
clear, plain, distinct, pronounced, obvious, manifest, evident, patent, glaring, blatant, striking, explicit, conspicuous, clear-cut, well-defined, unambiguous, unequivocal, positive, definite, sure, certain, unquestionable, beyond question, indisputable, undeniable, indubitable
E unclear, ambiguous

unmistakably *adv*
clearly, plainly, manifestly, obviously, evidently, unquestionably, without question, without doubt, doubtlessly, definitely, surely, certainly, unambiguously, unequivocally, undeniably, indisputably, blatantly, conspicuously, indubitably
E unclearly, ambiguously

unmitigated *adj*
utter, absolute, complete, pure, rank, perfect, outright, downright, out-and-out, thorough, thoroughgoing, sheer, relentless, persistent, intense, unqualified, unalleviated, unrelieved, unbroken, unrelenting, unredeemed, unmodified, undiminished, harsh, grim
FORMAL arrant, consummate, unabated, unremitting

unmoved *adj*
unaffected, untouched, unshaken, unstirred, dry-eyed, unfeeling, cold, dispassionate, indifferent, impassive, unresponsive, unconcerned, unimpressed, firm, adamant, inflexible, unbending, undeviating, unwavering, steady, unchanged, resolute, resolved, determined
E moved, affected, shaken

unnatural *adj*
1 ABNORMAL, anomalous, freakish, irregular, against nature, unusual, strange, odd, peculiar, queer, bizarre, extraordinary, uncommon, uncanny, supernatural, inhuman, perverted, disnatured, monstrous
OLD absonant, cataphysical, unkindly; (*Shakesp*) kindless
2 AFFECTED, feigned, artificial, false, insincere, unspontaneous, contrived, laboured, stilted, forced,

strained, staged, self-conscious, stiff, wooden, constrained, far-fetched, formal, stiff-necked, pompous, fustian
F3 1 natural, normal **2** sincere, fluent

unnaturally *adv*
strangely, unusually, oddly, peculiarly, uncommonly, extraordinarily, irregularly, abnormally
F3 naturally, normally

unnecessarily *adv*
needlessly, excessively, immoderately, superfluously

unnecessary *adj*
unneeded, needless, uncalled-for, unrequired, wasted, unwanted, gratuitous, non-essential, inessential, excessive, dispensable, expendable, superfluous, redundant, tautological
F3 necessary, essential, indispensable

unnerve *v*
daunt, intimidate, frighten, scare, alarm, discourage, deject, demoralize, dishearten, dismay, disconcert, put out, disquiet, unsettle, upset, worry, shake, confound, fluster, unman
FORMAL perturb
COLLOQ. rattle
F3 nerve, brace, steel

unnoticed *adj*
unobserved, unremarked, unseen, unrecognized, undiscovered, overlooked, ignored, disregarded, neglected, unheeded
F3 noticed, noted

unobtrusive *adj*
inconspicuous, unnoticeable, unassertive, self-effacing, humble, modest, unassuming, unaggressive, unostentatious, unpretentious, restrained, low-key, subdued, quiet, retiring
F3 prominent, obtrusive, ostentatious

unobtrusively *adv*
inconspicuously, quietly, modestly, on the quiet, unostentatiously, surreptitiously, humbly, unpretentiously
F3 obtrusively, ostentatiously, showily, aggressively

unoccupied *adj*
1 UNINHABITED, unpopulated, vacant, empty, deserted, forsaken
2 JOBLESS, free, idle, inactive, workless, unemployed
F3 1 occupied **2** busy

unofficial *adj*
unauthorized, illegal, informal, off-the-record, personal, private, confidential, undeclared, unconfirmed, unauthenticated, unratified, alternative, fringe, black, kerb
F3 official, ratified; *formal* accredited, substantiated, corroborated

unoriginal *adj*
unimaginative, uninspired, hackneyed, stale, trite, copied, cliché-ridden, derivative, cribbed, second-hand, derived
F3 original, imaginative, creative, innovative, fresh

unorthodox *adj*
unconventional, nonconformist, heterodox, alternative, fringe, irregular, abnormal, unusual, eccentric, creative, cult, zany, innovative, new, novel, fresh
COLLOQ. left-field
SLANG way-out, off the wall
F3 orthodox, conventional

unpaid *adj*
1 *unpaid bills*
outstanding, overdue, unsettled, owing, due, payable, pending, uncollected, remaining
2 *unpaid work*
voluntary, honorary, unsalaried, unwaged, unremunerative, free
TECHNICAL pro bono(publico)
F3 1 paid

unpalatable *adj*
1 UNAPPETIZING, distasteful, insipid, bitter, uneatable, inedible, unsavoury, disgusting

2 UNPLEASANT, disagreeable, unattractive, distasteful, unsavoury, offensive, nasty, repellent, repugnant
F3 1 palatable **2** pleasant

unparalleled *adj*
unequalled, without equal, unmatched, matchless, peerless, beyond compare, incomparable, unrivalled, unsurpassed, supreme, superlative, rare, unique, exceptional, unprecedented

unpardonable *adj*
unforgivable, inexcusable, unjustifiable, indefensible, outrageous, deplorable, disgraceful, shocking, shameful, scandalous
FORMAL irremissible, reprehensible, unconscionable
F3 forgivable, understandable

unperturbed *adj*
calm, unexcited, unflustered, untroubled, unworried, undisturbed, unruffled, unflinching, self-possessed, composed, collected, tranquil, serene, placid, poised, cool, impassive
COLLOQ. unflappable
F3 anxious, perturbed

unpleasant *adj*
1 *an unpleasant smell*
disagreeable, nasty, objectionable, offensive, distasteful, unpalatable, unappetizing, unattractive, repulsive, repugnant, bad, foul, troublesome, disgusting, undesirable
FORMAL noisome
2 *an unpleasant person*
unfriendly, unkind, disagreeable, rude, impolite, discourteous, bad-tempered, ill-natured, nasty, objectionable, hostile, aggressive, quarrelsome, surly, sour, mean
F3 1, 2 pleasant, agreeable, nice

unpleasantness *n*
annoyance, nastiness, trouble, upset, bother, embarrassment, scandal, fuss, furore, ill-feeling, bad feeling/blood

unpolished *adj*
unfinished, unworked, rough and ready, sketchy, unrefined, unfashioned, unsophisticated, uncultivated, uncultured, uncivilized, coarse, crude, rough, home-bred, rude, uncouth, vulgar
F3 finished, polished, refined

unpopular *adj*
disliked, hated, detested, unloved, friendless, undesirable, unattractive, unsought-after, unfashionable, unwelcome, unwanted, rejected, shunned, avoided, ignored, neglected
F3 popular, fashionable

unprecedented *adj*
new, original, revolutionary, unknown, unheard-of, exceptional, remarkable, extraordinary, abnormal, unusual, uncommon, freakish, unparalleled, unrivalled, unequalled, unexampled
F3 usual

unpredictable *adj*
unforeseeable, unexpected, changeable, variable, inconstant, unreliable, fickle, unstable, volatile, erratic, random, chance
FORMAL mercurial, capricious
F3 predictable, foreseeable, constant, reliable

SYNONYM NUANCES

You can use **unforeseeable** of something, especially a problem, that could not have been anticipated, while **unexpected** can describe any event that comes as a surprise.

Changeable, **variable** and **inconstant**, on the other hand, are appropriate for something which is unpredictable because it is moving between different states: *his changeable moods*; *changeable weather*. The term **unreliable** has a similar meaning but is more critical, and implies a lack of dependability. **Fickle** is similar in implication, and would be used of a propensity for changing your mind or opinion: *the fickle world of fashion.*

Unstable is also rather negative in tone, and can suggest emotional fluctuations, while **volatile**, although similar, is perhaps suggestive of more sudden and dramatic, and therefore more problematic, variations: *his volatile temperament meant he could become violent; the shares market has proved volatile.*

The term **erratic**, meanwhile, may be used to suggest an unwelcome irregularity or inconsistency: *the child's erratic behaviour became difficult for his parents to handle,* whereas both **random** and **chance** can be used fairly generally of something haphazard: *random searches.*

unprejudiced *adj*
unbiased, fair, fair-minded, impartial, just, objective, non-partisan, open-minded, even-handed, balanced, detached, uncoloured, dispassionate, enlightened
E3 prejudiced, narrow-minded

unpremeditated *adj*
spontaneous, unintentional, unplanned, unprepared, unrehearsed, offhand, impulsive, impromptu, extempore
FORMAL fortuitous
COLLOQ. off-the-cuff, spur-of-the-moment
E3 premeditated

unprepared *adj*
unready, surprised, unsuspecting, ill-equipped, unwilling, unfinished, incomplete, half-baked, raw, crude, unplanned, unrehearsed, spontaneous, improvised, ad-lib, napping, on the wrong foot; *N Am* flat-footed
COLLOQ. off-the-cuff
E3 prepared, ready

unprepossessing *adj*
plain, ordinary, uninteresting, unexciting, unappealing, unexceptional, unremarkable, indifferent, undistinguished, unattractive, unlovely, ugly; *N Am* homely
E3 attractive, good-looking

unpretentious *adj*
unaffected, natural, plain, simple, ordinary, unobtrusive, honest, straightforward, humble, modest, unassuming, unostentatious
E3 pretentious, showy, ostentatious

unprincipled *adj*
unscrupulous, unprofessional, unethical, dishonest, dishonourable, immoral, underhand, deceitful, devious, corrupt, discreditable
COLLOQ. crooked
E3 ethical, principled

unproductive *adj*
infertile, sterile, barren, dry, arid, unfruitful, fruitless, futile, vain, idle, worthless, useless, ineffective, unprofitable, unremunerative, unrewarding
FORMAL inefficacious, otiose
E3 productive, fertile

unprofessional *adj*
amateurish, inexpert, unskilled, incompetent, inexperienced, untrained, inefficient, casual, sloppy, negligent, lax, unethical, unprincipled, unscrupulous, improper, unacceptable, inadmissible
FORMAL unseemly, indecorous
E3 professional, skilful

unpromising *adj*
unfavourable, adverse, discouraging, gloomy, depressing, doubtful, dispiriting, ominous
FORMAL inauspicious, unpropitious
E3 promising, favourable, auspicious

unprotected *adj*
defenceless, unguarded, unattended, undefended, unfortified, unarmed, unshielded, unsheltered, uncovered, exposed, open, naked, vulnerable, liable, helpless
E3 protected, safe, immune

unprovable *adj*
unverifiable, indemonstrable, undemonstrable, indeterminable, unascertainable
E3 verifiable

unqualified *adj*
1 UNTRAINED, inexperienced, amateur, ineligible, unlicensed, unfit, unsuitable, incompetent, incapable, inapt, unprepared, ill-equipped
2 ABSOLUTE, categorical, utter, total, complete, perfect, positive, thorough, round, plenary, downright, unmitigated, unreserved, wholehearted, outright, out-and-out, unconditional, unequivocal, unrestricted, unallayed
FORMAL consummate
E3 1 qualified, professional 2 conditional, tentative

unquestionable *adj*
unequivocal, beyond question, incontestable, faultless, flawless, indisputable, obvious, manifest, patent, clear, conclusive, definite, absolute, sure, certain, self-evident, unchallenged, undeniable, unmistakable, incontrovertible, indubitable, irrefutable
E3 dubious, questionable

unquestionably *adv*
unequivocally, unambiguously, unmistakably, clearly, manifestly, directly, distinctly, explicitly, definitely, positively, firmly, incontrovertibly, indubitably, irrefutably
E3 questionably, dubiously, vaguely

unquestioning *adj*
implicit, unhesitating, questionless, unconditional, unqualified, wholehearted
E3 doubtful

unravel *v*
unwind, undo, untangle, disentangle, free, extricate, separate, unknot, straighten out, resolve, sort out, clear up, solve, work out, figure out, puzzle out, penetrate, interpret, explain
E3 tangle, complicate

unreadable *adj*
unintelligible, too difficult to read, incomprehensible, incoherent, inarticulate, garbled, scrambled, jumbled, muddled, indecipherable, illegible, impenetrable, unfathomable, puzzling, mysterious, obscure, complicated, complex, involved
COLLOQ. double Dutch
E3 intelligible, comprehensible, clear

unreal *adj*
false, artificial, synthetic, mock, ersatz, fake, sham, faux, imaginary, visionary, fanciful, make-believe, fictitious, untrue, made-up, fairytale, legendary, mythical, fantastic, bizarre, illusory, illusive, immaterial, insubstantial, nebulous, hypothetical, non-existent, ungrounded, hollow, whimsical, notional, phantom, shadow, storybook, Alice-in-Wonderland, Disneyesque, moonshiny, aerial
FORMAL chimerical, phantasmagorical, aeriform
COLLOQ. pretend, phon(e)y
E3 real, genuine, authentic

unrealistic *adj*
impractical, idealistic, theoretical, romantic, quixotic, impracticable, unworkable, unreasonable, impossible, over-optimistic
E3 realistic, pragmatic

unreality *n*
irreality, artificiality, imaginariness, fancifulness, make-believe, bizarreness, insubstantiality, illusoriness, nebulousness, non-existence, hollowness
COLLOQ. phon(e)yness
E3 reality, genuineness, authenticity

unreasonable *adj*
1 UNFAIR, unjust, biased, unco-operative, unjustifiable, unjustified, unwarranted, unacceptable, undue, uncalled-for, unrealistic, exacting
COLLOQ. a bit much, unchristian
2 IRRATIONAL, illogical, inconsistent, arbitrary, absurd, nonsensical, ludicrous, far-fetched, outrageous,

preposterous, mad, senseless, silly, foolish, stupid,
headstrong, opinionated, perverse, froward
3 unreasonable prices
excessive, immoderate, extravagant, outrageous,
expensive, exorbitant, extortionate, undue, scandalous,
iniquitous, obscene
COLLOQ. steep, over the top, OTT
E3 1 reasonable, fair **2** rational, sensible **3** moderate

unreasoning adj
irrational, unreasonable, unsound, illogical,
inconsistent, invalid, groundless, implausible, arbitrary,
ridiculous, absurd, crazy, wild, foolish, silly, senseless,
beastlike, brute, brutish, nonsensical, unwise, beside
yourself, taken leave of your senses
E3 reasoning, rational, reasonable

unrecognizable adj
unidentifiable, disguised, incognito, changed,
altered, unknowable
FORMAL incognizable

unrecognized adj
unnoticed, unobserved, unremarked, unseen,
undiscovered, overlooked, ignored, disregarded,
neglected, unheeded
E3 recognized, noticed, noted

unrefined adj
raw, untreated, unprocessed, unpurified, unfinished,
unpolished, crude, coarse, vulgar, unsophisticated,
uncultivated, uncultured
E3 refined, finished

unregenerate adj
unconverted, hardened, impenitent, stubborn,
obstinate, unreformed, unrepentant, persistent,
abandoned, shameless, wicked, sinful
FORMAL intractable, obdurate, incorrigible, recalcitrant,
refractory
E3 reformed, repentant

unrelated adj
unconnected, unassociated, irrelevant, beside/off the point,
extraneous, different, dissimilar, unlike, distinct, foreign,
separate, independent
FORMAL disparate
COLLOQ. neither here nor there
E3 related, similar

unrelenting adj
relentless, uncompromising, inexorable, unceasing,
ceaseless, endless, unbroken, continuous, constant,
continual, perpetual, steady, remorseless, ruthless, cruel,
unmerciful, merciless, pitiless, unforgiving, unsparing,
implacable
FORMAL unremitting, incessant, unabated, intransigent
E3 spasmodic, intermittent

unreliable adj
unsound, fallible, deceptive, false, mistaken,
erroneous, inaccurate, doubtful, unconvincing,
questionable, implausible, uncertain,
undependable, untrustworthy, unstable, fickle,
irresponsible
COLLOQ. iffy, slippery, dodgy, in-and-out
E3 reliable, dependable, trustworthy, sound

unremitting adj
unrelenting, unceasing, ceaseless, relentless, remorseless,
tireless, constant, continual, continuous, perpetual,
unbroken
FORMAL incessant, unabated
E3 spasmodic, intermittent

unrepentant adj
impenitent, unapologetic, unabashed, unashamed,
shameless, confirmed, hardened, callous
FORMAL incorrigible, obdurate
E3 repentant, penitent, ashamed

unrequited adj
rejected, neglected, ignored, not returned, discarded,
unacknowledged, unrecognized, unreciprocated,
snubbed, spurned

unreserved adj
unqualified, unrestricted, unrestrained, unconditional,
unhesitating, uninhibited, unlimited, complete, full,
explicit, absolute, free, total, open, wholehearted, entire,
frank, forthright, direct, candid, heart-to-heart,
demonstrative, extrovert, outgoing, outspoken, talkative,
communicative
COLLOQ. whole-footed
E3 inhibited, tentative, hesitant

unreservedly adv
completely, entirely, utterly, fully, absolutely, totally,
wholeheartedly, outright, unhesitatingly, unconditionally

unresisting adj
submissive, docile, obedient, passive, meek
COLLOQ. like a lamb to the slaughter
E3 resisting, protesting

unresolved adj
undecided, unanswered, undetermined, unsettled,
unsolved, vexed, vague, indefinite, doubtful,
problematical, pending, moot
COLLOQ. up in the air
E3 definite, determined

unresponsive adj
unaffected, unmoved, unsympathetic, uninterested,
indifferent, aloof, apathetic, cool
E3 responsive, sympathetic

unrest n
protest, rebellion, turmoil, agitation, disorder,
restlessness, dissatisfaction, dissension, worry,
disquiet, discontent, unease, uneasiness, commotion
FORMAL disaffection, discord, perturbation
E3 peace, calm

unrestrained adj
unbridled, uncontrolled, unhindered, uninhibited,
unrepressed, unreserved, unchecked, unconstrained,
unbounded, irrepressible, inordinate, immoderate,
intemperate, free, natural, rampant, abandoned,
boisterous
E3 restrained, inhibited

unrestricted adj
unlimited, unbounded, unopposed, unhindered,
unimpeded, unobstructed, clear, free, open, public,
unconditional, absolute
COLLOQ. free-for-all
E3 restricted, limited

unripe adj
unripened, green, immature, undeveloped, unready
E3 ripe, mature

unrivalled adj
unequalled, unparalleled, unmatched, matchless,
peerless, incomparable, unsurpassed, without equal,
beyond compare, supreme, superlative
FORMAL inimitable, nonpareil

unruffled adj
undisturbed, untroubled, imperturbable, collected,
composed, cool, calm, tranquil, serene, peaceful, smooth,
level, even
FORMAL unperturbed
E3 troubled, anxious

unruly adj
uncontrollable, unmanageable, ungovernable, disorderly,
wild, rowdy, riotous, rebellious, mutinous, lawless,
insubordinate, disobedient, wayward, wilful, headstrong,
obstreperous
FORMAL recalcitrant, refractory, intractable
E3 manageable, orderly

SYNONYM NUANCES

Naturally, the synonyms tend to be marked by disapproval. You can use **uncontrollable** and **unmanageable** to suggest an unruliness that has gone beyond restraint, while **ungovernable** and **lawless**, although similar, are generally used with regard to a place or a people: *the country had become ungovernable.*

Disorderly and **rowdy**, however, suggest a more temporary state of disruption and noisiness: *a disorderly crowd gathered in the square,* whereas **wild** has stronger suggestions of being uncivilized and uncontrollable. **Riotous**, likewise, implies unrestrained, destructive behaviour, but **rebellious** and **mutinous** would be reserved for where there is a defiance of authority: *mutinous troops.* **Insubordinate** is similar, but does not convey the same sense of resulting turbulence.

You can use **wayward** of a person to suggest an element of unpredictability in their nature, while both **wilful** and **headstrong** have implications of stubbornness. **Obstreperous** returns to the idea of being noisy and unrestrained: *the barman threw him out because he was getting too obstreperous.*

unsafe *adj*
dangerous, perilous, risky, high-risk, hazardous, treacherous, chancy, unreliable, uncertain, unsound, unstable, precarious, insecure, vulnerable, exposed, defenceless
COLLOQ. dicey, hairy
E∃ safe, secure

unsaid *adj*
unspoken, unstated, unexpressed, unvoiced, unmentioned, undeclared, unuttered, unpronounced
E∃ spoken

unsatisfactory *adj*
unacceptable, imperfect, defective, faulty, inferior, poor, mediocre, weak, empty, lame, tame, wrong, off-colour, inadequate, insufficient, deficient, unsuitable, displeasing, dissatisfying, unsatisfying, frustrating, disappointing
COLLOQ. leaving a lot to be desired, rop(e)y, lousy, rocky
E∃ satisfactory, adequate, pleasing

unsavoury *adj*
distasteful, disagreeable, unpleasant, disgusting, nauseating, revolting, sickening, nasty, undesirable, repulsive, repugnant, objectionable, obnoxious, offensive, repellent, unattractive, sordid, squalid, unpalatable, unappetizing
E∃ palatable, pleasant

unscathed *adj*
unhurt, uninjured, unharmed, undamaged, untouched, whole, intact, safe, sound
E∃ hurt, injured, harmed

unscrupulous *adj*
unprincipled, ruthless, shameless, dishonourable, dishonest, corrupt, immoral, unethical, improper, unscrupled, unconscionable, villainous, Rottweiler
COLLOQ. crooked, stopping at nothing
E∃ scrupulous, ethical, proper

unseasonable *adj*
inappropriate, ill-timed, unsuitable, untimely, mistimed
FORMAL inopportune, intempestive, malapropos
E∃ seasonable, timely

unseasoned *adj*
unprepared, unprimed, unmatured, untreated, untempered
COLLOQ. green

unseat *v*
remove, depose, dethrone, dismount, displace, dismiss, discharge, oust, throw, overthrow, topple, unhorse, unsaddle, dishorse

unseemly *adj*
improper, indelicate, unbecoming, undignified, unrefined, disreputable, discreditable, undue, inappropriate, unsuitable, unbefitting
FORMAL indecorous
E∃ seemly, decorous

unseen *adj*
unnoticed, unobserved, undetected, unobtrusive, invisible, hidden, concealed, veiled, obscure, lurking
E∃ visible

QUOTATIONS
Greet the unseen with a cheer!
ROBERT BROWNING, *Asolando*

unselfish *adj*
selfless, altruistic, self-denying, self-sacrificing, self-forgetting, disinterested, noble, kind, generous, open-handed, liberal, charitable, philanthropic, public-spirited, humanitarian
FORMAL magnanimous
E∃ selfish

unsentimental *adj*
realistic, practical, pragmatic, hard-headed, hard-faced, tough, iron-headed, unemotional, unfeeling, unromantic, level-headed
E∃ sentimental, idealistic

unsettle *v*
disturb, upset, trouble, bother, discompose, ruffle, fluster, unbalance, destabilize, shake, agitate, disconcert, confuse
FORMAL perturb, discomfit
COLLOQ. rattle, throw

unsettled *adj*
1 DISTURBED, upset, troubled, restless, unstable, agitated, anxious, uneasy, tense, on edge, fidgety, flustered, shaken, unnerved, disoriented, confused, hesitant
OLD queasy
COLLOQ. edgy, fazed
2 UNRESOLVED, undetermined, indetermined, undecided, to be decided, open, uncertain, doubtful, in a state of flux
OLD undiscussed
COLLOQ. up in the air, in the balance
3 AIMLESS, directionless, pointless, purposeless, goalless, futile, unmotivated, irresolute, rambling, nomadic, drifting, undirected, unguided, wandering, roving, vagabond, with no fixed abode
4 *unsettled weather*
changeable, variable, unpredictable, inconstant, unstable, uncertain, insecure, unsteady, shaky
5 UNPAID, outstanding, owing, in arrears, payable, overdue
6 UNINHABITED, unoccupied, deserted, abandoned, desolate, unpeopled, unpopulated
E∃ **1** composed, calm **2** decided, certain **3** purposeful **4** settled **5** paid **6** settled, peopled

unshakable, unshakeable *adj*
firm, well-founded, fixed, stable, immovable, unassailable, unswerving, unwavering, constant, steadfast, staunch, sure, resolute, determined
E∃ insecure

unsightly *adj*
ugly, unattractive, unprepossessing, hideous, revolting, repulsive, repugnant, off-putting, unpleasant, disagreeable
E∃ attractive

unskilful *adj*
unskilled, amateurish, inexperienced, unprofessional, unqualified, untaught, untrained, uneducated, untalented, unpractised, incompetent, awkward, clumsy, fumbling, bungling, inept, inexpert, gauche
FORMAL maladroit
E∃ skilful, skilled

unskilled *adj*
untrained, unqualified, inexperienced, unpractised, inexpert, unprofessional, amateurish, incompetent
E3 skilled, professional

unsociable *adj*
unfriendly, aloof, distant, standoffish, withdrawn, introverted, uncompanionable, insociable, reclusive, solitary, retiring, reserved, taciturn, unforthcoming, uncommunicative, cold, chilly, cool, uncongenial, unneighbourly, inhospitable, hostile
E3 sociable, friendly, congenial

unsolicited *adj*
unrequested, unsought, uninvited, unasked, unwanted, unwelcome, uncalled-for, unasked-for, gratuitous, voluntary, spontaneous
E3 requested, invited

unsophisticated *adj*
1 *an unsophisticated person*
artless, guileless, innocent, ingenuous, naive, inexperienced, simple, unworldly, childlike, natural, unaffected, unpretentious
2 CRUDE, unrefined, plain, simple, basic, straightforward, rudimentary, undeveloped, uncomplicated, uninvolved
E3 1 sophisticated, worldly **2** complex, highly-developed

unsound *adj*
1 *unsound reasoning*
faulty, flawed, defective, ill-founded, unfounded, false, weak, erroneous, untenable, invalid, illogical, shaky
FORMAL fallacious
2 UNHEALTHY, unwell, ill, diseased, weak, ailing, delicate, frail, unbalanced, disordered, deranged, unhinged
3 UNSTABLE, unsteady, rickety, wobbly, shaky, insecure, broken, dangerous, unsafe, unreliable
E3 1 sound **2** well **3** stable

unsparing *adj*
1 GENEROUS, lavish, liberal, open-handed, ungrudging, unstinting, plenteous, abundant, bountiful, profuse
FORMAL munificent
2 HARSH, hard, merciless, unmerciful, ruthless, severe, stern, relentless, implacable, uncompromising, unforgiving
E3 forgiving, mean, sparing

unspeakable *adj*
unutterable, inexpressible, indescribable, unmentionable, awful, dreadful, frightful, terrible, horrible, shocking, appalling, monstrous, horrendous, inconceivable, unimaginable, unthinkable, unbelievable, nameless
FORMAL execrable, nefandous

unspeakably *adv*
indescribably, unutterably, inexpressibly, terribly, frightfully, awfully, appallingly, horrendously, inconceivably, unimaginably, unthinkably, unbelievably

unspecified *adj*
unknown, unnamed, uncertain, unidentified, undecided, indefinite, undefined, undetermined, obscure, mysterious, vague
E3 specified, known, certain

unspectacular *adj*
unremarkable, unimpressive, unexciting, uninteresting, dull, boring, ordinary, common, average, mediocre, plodding
E3 spectacular, impressive, memorable

unspoilt *adj*
preserved, unchanged, untouched, natural, unaffected, unsophisticated, unharmed, undamaged, unimpaired, unblemished, perfect
E3 spoilt, affected

unspoken *adj*
unstated, undeclared, unuttered, unexpressed, unsaid, voiceless, wordless, silent, tacit, implicit, implied, inferred, understood, assumed
E3 stated, explicit

unstable *adj*
1 CHANGEABLE, variable, fluctuating, vacillating, wavering, fitful, erratic, moody, inconsistent, volatile, inconstant, unpredictable, unreliable, untrustworthy, unsettled, brittle, flighty, light-minded, labile, unballasted, slippery; *dialect* wankle; *Scot* bruckle
OLD unstable
FORMAL capricious, mercurial
COLLOQ. dodgy
2 UNSTEADY, wobbly, shaky, rickety, insecure, unsafe, weak, infirm, risky, precarious, tottering, unbalanced, shifting
OLD instable, tickle
3 *emotionally/mentally unstable*
deranged, insane, mad, disturbed, unsound, unhinged, off balance
OLD instable
COLLOQ. crazy, nuts, nutty, nutty as a fruitcake, barmy, bonkers, batty, crackers, dippy, daffy, loopy, off your head, wrong in the head, off the wall, out to lunch, round the bend, round the twist, having bats in the belfry
SLANG bananas, loony, off your rocker, off your trolley, needing your head examined, having a screw/tile loose, having lost your marbles, meshuga, mental
E3 1 stable **2** steady **3** stable, sane

unsteady *adj*
unstable, wobbly, shaky, rickety, doddery, insecure, unsafe, treacherous, precarious, tottering, unreliable, inconstant, irregular, flickering
COLLOQ. *Aust* warby
E3 steady, firm, stable

unstinting *adj*
abounding, abundant, ample, bountiful, full, generous, large, lavish, liberal, plentiful, profuse, ungrudging, unsparing
FORMAL munificent, prodigal
E3 grudging, mean

unstoppable *adj*
unrelenting, unremitting, unending, unceasing, undying, without a let-up, inevitable, unavoidable

unsubstantiated *adj*
unconfirmed, debatable, dubious, questionable, disputable, unestablished, unproved, unproven, unsupported, unverified
FORMAL unattested, uncorroborated
E3 proved, proven

unsuccessful *adj*
failed, lost, abortive, vain, futile, useless, ineffective, unavailing, miscarried, fruitless, unproductive, unprofitable, sterile, luckless, unlucky, unfortunate, losing, beaten, defeated, frustrated, thwarted, fumbled, bungled
FORMAL ineffectual
COLLOQ. going down like a lead balloon
E3 successful, effective, fortunate, winning

unsuitable *adj*
inappropriate, inapt, unsuited, unfit, unacceptable, out of place, improper, incompatible
FORMAL unseemly, unbecoming, incongruous, inapposite, infelicitous, malapropos
E3 suitable, appropriate

unsullied *adj*
untainted, unspotted, spotless, unstained, stainless, untarnished, unblemished, uncorrupted, undefiled, unspoiled, unsoiled, untouched, perfect, clean, pure, immaculate, intact, unblackened
FORMAL pristine
E3 dirty, stained

unsung *adj*
unhonoured, unpraised, unacknowledged, uncelebrated, unhailed, unacclaimed, unknown, unrecognized, overlooked, disregarded, neglected, forgotten, anonymous, obscure
E3 honoured, famous, renowned

unsure *adj*
1 *unsure of yourself*
uncertain, hesitant, insecure, lacking self-confidence, tentative, doubtful, dubious, suspicious, sceptical, unconvinced, unpersuaded, undecided
2 *unsure about what to do*
undecided, uncertain, unknown, ambivalent, doubtful, hesitant, dithering, equivocating, wavering, irresolute, uncommitted, indefinite, vague
COLLOQ. in two minds
◪ **1** confident, sure, certain **2** sure, certain, decided

unsurpassed *adj*
surpassing, supreme, transcendent, unbeaten, unexcelled, unequalled, unparalleled, unrivalled, incomparable, unmatched, matchless, superlative, exceptional, second-to-none, state-of-the-art
◪ surpassed

unsurprising *adj*
expected, anticipated, promised, hoped-for, predicted, predictable, forecast, foreseen, forseeable, looked-for, wished-for
COLLOQ. just as you thought
◪ surprising, unexpected

unsuspecting *adj*
unwary, unaware, off guard, unconscious, trusting, trustful, unsuspicious, credulous, gullible, ingenuous, naive, innocent
◪ suspicious, knowing

unswerving *adj*
unflagging, unwavering, unfaltering, untiring, undeviating, staunch, steadfast, dedicated, devoted, steady, sure, true, firm, constant, fixed, immovable, resolute, single-minded, direct
◪ irresolute, tentative

unsympathetic *adj*
unpitying, unconcerned, uncaring, unmoved, unresponsive, indifferent, insensitive, unfeeling, cold, heartless, pitiless, soulless, hard-hearted, hard-faced, harsh, callous, cruel, inhuman, unkind, hard, stony, hostile, antagonistic
◪ sympathetic, compassionate

unsystematic *adj*
unmethodical, unco-ordinated, irregular, disorganized, unorganized, unstructured, unplanned, disorderly, untidy, haphazard, illogical, confused, muddled, jumbled, chaotic, indiscriminate, random, slapdash, sloppy, shambolic
◪ logical, systematic

untamed *adj*
wild, fierce, savage, undomesticated, unmellowed, untameable, barbarous
FORMAL feral
◪ domesticated, tame

untangle *v*
disentangle, extricate, unravel, undo, resolve, solve, work out, straighten out
◪ tangle, complicate

untarnished *adj*
unblemished, unstained, stainless, unspotted, spotless, unsullied, unsoiled, unspoilt, clean, immaculate, impeccable, intact, bright, pure, burnished, shining, glowing, polished, unimpeachable
FORMAL pristine
◪ tarnished, blemished

untenable *adj*
indefensible, unreasonable, unmaintainable, unsound, unjustifiable, inexcusable, insupportable, unsustainable, flawed, illogical, fallacious, rocky, shaky
OLD intenable
◪ tenable, sound

unthinkable *adj*
inconceivable, unimaginable, unheard-of, unbelievable, incredible, impossible, improbable, unlikely, implausible,

unreasonable, illogical, absurd, preposterous, outrageous, shocking, staggering

unthinking *adj*
thoughtless, inconsiderate, insensitive, tactless, indiscreet, undiplomatic, unkind, rude, impolite, heedless, careless, negligent, rash, impulsive, instinctive, involuntary, unconscious, automatic, mechanical
COLLOQ. knee-jerk
◪ considerate, conscious

unthinkingly *adv*
thoughtlessly, inconsiderately, insensitively, unfeelingly, tactlessly, undiplomatically, indiscreetly, impolitely, rudely, inattentively, foolishly, stupidly, carelessly, recklessly, rashly
◪ thoughtfully, considerately, carefully

untidily *adv*
messily, disorderly, scruffily, dirtily, chaotically, unsystematically, shambolically, sluttishly, topsy-turvily
COLLOQ. sloppily, like a dog's breakfast/dinner
◪ tidily, neatly

untidy *adj*
messy, cluttered, disorderly, muddled, jumbled, unsystematic, chaotic, haywire, disorganized, shambolic, topsy-turvy, dirty, scruffy, bedraggled, rumpled, dishevelled, foul, unkempt, slovenly, slipshod, tatty, slatternly, sluttish
COLLOQ. sloppy, higgledy-piggledy, ratty, raunchy
◪ tidy, neat

untie *v*
undo, unfasten, unhitch, unknot, unbind, unwrap, free, release, loose, loosen
◪ tie, fasten

until
♦ *prep, conj*
1 *work until six o'clock*
till, to, up till, up to, up to the time, as late as
2 *not until the spring*
before, prior to, before the coming of, earlier than

untimely *adj*
early, premature, unseasonable, ill-timed, inopportune, inconvenient, awkward, unsuitable, inappropriate, unfortunate
FORMAL inauspicious, infelicitous, malapropos
◪ timely, opportune

untiring *adj*
unflagging, unfaltering, tireless, indefatigable, dogged, persevering, persistent, tenacious, determined, resolute, devoted, dedicated, constant, incessant, unceasing, steady, staunch, unfailing
FORMAL unremitting
◪ inconstant, wavering

untold *adj*
1 *cause untold damage*
indescribable, unimaginable, inconceivable, inexpressible, unutterable
2 COUNTLESS, uncounted, unnumbered, unreckoned, incalculable, innumerable, uncountable, infinite, measureless, immeasurable, boundless, inexhaustible, undreamed-of, unimaginable

untouched *adj*
unharmed, undamaged, unimpaired, unhurt, uninjured, unscathed, safe, intact, unchanged, unaltered, unaffected, unimpressed, unstirred
◪ damaged, affected

untoward *adj*
unfortunate, troublesome, inconvenient, annoying, adverse, unfavourable, unexpected, unsuitable, unfitting, untimely, vexatious, irritating, worrying, awkward, amiss, disastrous, improper, contrary, unlucky, inappropriate, ominous, ill-timed

FORMAL inauspicious, indecorous, inopportune, unbecoming, unpropitious, unseemly
E∃ suitable, auspicious

untrained adj
unskilled, untaught, unschooled, uneducated, inexperienced, unpractised, unqualified, amateur, unprofessional, inexpert, incompetent
E∃ trained, expert

untried adj
untested, unproved, unestablished, experimental, exploratory, new, novel, innovative, innovatory
E∃ tried, tested, proven

untroubled adj
unworried, unconcerned, undisturbed, unexcited, unstirred, unflustered, unruffled, steady, calm, composed, peaceful, impassive, cool, placid, serene, tranquil
FORMAL unperturbed
COLLOQ. unflappable
E∃ anxious, troubled

untrue adj
1 FALSE, fallacious, deceptive, misleading, wrong, incorrect, inaccurate, inexact, mistaken, erroneous, fabricated, inauthentic, unofficial, legendary, mythical
COLLOQ. made-up, trumped-up
2 UNFAITHFUL, disloyal, untrustworthy, dishonest, deceitful, fraudulent, untruthful
FORMAL perfidious
COLLOQ. two-faced, two-timing
E∃ 1 true, correct **2** faithful, honest

untrustworthy adj
dishonest, deceitful, untruthful, disloyal, unfaithful, faithless, treacherous, false, untrue, dishonourable, capricious, fickle, fly-by-night, unreliable, untrusty
FORMAL duplicitous
COLLOQ. two-faced
E∃ trustworthy, reliable

untruth n
lie, story, tale, fiction, invention, fabrication, falsehood, lying, untruthfulness, deceit, perjury
COLLOQ. fib, whopper, porky, tall story, made-up story, cock-and-bull story
SLANG (vulgar) bullshit, crap
E∃ truth

untruthful adj
lying, deceitful, dishonest, hypocritical, insincere, false, untrue, fictional, fabricated, invented, erroneous, fallacious
FORMAL mendacious, unveracious
COLLOQ. crooked, two-faced
E∃ truthful, honest

untutored adj
untrained, unschooled, unpractised, uneducated, unlearned, unversed, inexperienced, inexpert, illiterate, ignorant, unrefined, unsophisticated, simple, artless, unlessoned
E∃ educated, trained

untwine v
unravel, uncoil, untwist, unwind, disentwine
E∃ twine, wind

untwist v
uncoil, unravel, untwine, unwind
E∃ twist

unused adj
1 LEFT OVER, remaining, surplus, extra, spare, available, new, fresh, blank, clean, untouched, unexploited, untapped, unemployed, idle
2 UNACCUSTOMED, unacquainted, unfamiliar, unpractised, inexperienced
FORMAL unwonted
E∃ 1, 2 used

unusual adj
uncommon, rare, unfamiliar, strange, odd, curious, peculiar, queer, bizarre, weird, unconventional,

unorthodox, irregular, abnormal, atypical, phenomenal, extraordinary, out of the ordinary, out of the way, remarkable, special, exceptional, different, anomalous, surprising, unexpected, unprecedented, eccentric, exotic; Scot unco
OLD (Spenser) unacquainted
FORMAL singular
COLLOQ. offbeat, freaky, freakish, kinky
See Synonym nuances panel at **strange**.
E∃ usual, normal, ordinary

unutterable adj
unspeakable, indescribable, unimaginable, extreme, overwhelming, ineffable
FORMAL egregious, nefandous

unvarnished adj
unembellished, unadorned, straightforward, undisguised, simple, sincere, plain, candid, frank, bare, naked, honest, pure, sheer, stark
E∃ disguised, embellished, exaggerated

unveil v
uncover, expose, lay open, bare, lay bare, unmask, betray, reveal, disclose, divulge, bring to light, bring out into the open, make known, discover
COLLOQ. take the lid off
E∃ cover, hide

unwanted adj
undesired, uninvited, unwelcome, outcast, rejected, discarded, unrequired, unneeded, unnecessary, surplus, extra, superfluous, redundant, useless
TECHNICAL otiose
FORMAL unsolicited
E∃ wanted, needed, necessary

unwarranted adj
unjustified, undeserved, unprovoked, uncalled-for, gratuitous, unnecessary, groundless, unreasonable, unjust, wrong, inexcusable, unjustifiable, indefensible
E∃ warranted, justifiable, deserved

unwary adj
unguarded, off guard, incautious, imprudent, careless, indiscreet, thoughtless, unthinking, heedless, reckless, rash, hasty
E∃ wary, cautious

unwashed adj
dirty, grubby, filthy, grimy, mucky, soiled, greasy, unclean, unhygienic, foul, messy, muddy, dusty, sooty, polluted, slimy, squalid, insanitary, miry, scruffy, shabby, sullied, stained, defiled, tarnished, clouded, cloudy, black, dark, dull, grungy; dialect clarty, grufted; Aust & NZ scungy
COLLOQ. grotty, yucky, flea-bitten, cruddy, manky; Aust & NZ chatty
E∃ clean

■ **the (great) unwashed**
the masses, the crowd(s), the herd, the mob, the lower/working class(es), the common people, the proletariat, the rabble, the hoi polloi, the rank and file, riff-raff
COLLOQ. plebs

unwavering adj
unswerving, unshak(e)able, unfaltering, undeviating, unshaken, untiring, unflagging, unquestioning, staunch, steadfast, steady, sturdy, dedicated, consistent, determined, resolute, single-minded, tenacious
E∃ wavering, fickle

unwelcome adj
1 UNWANTED, undesirable, unpopular, uninvited, excluded, rejected
2 *unwelcome news*
unpleasant, disagreeable, upsetting, worrying, distasteful, unpalatable, unacceptable
E∃ 1 welcome, desirable **2** pleasant

unwell adj
ill, sick, poorly, off-colour, ailing, sickly, unhealthy, unfit, rough, bad, queer
FORMAL indisposed

COLLOQ. in a bad way, dicky, out of sorts, under the weather, run down, groggy, like death warmed up; *Aust* warby
E∃ well, healthy

unwholesome *adj*
unhealthy, bad, harmful, demoralizing, evil, wicked, immoral, degrading, depraving, corrupting, perverting, sickly, tainted, unhygienic, poisonous, insanitary, innutritious, pasty, noxious, wan, pale, pallid, anaemic
FORMAL insalubrious, insalutary
COLLOQ. junk
E∃ wholesome; *formal* salubrious

unwieldy *adj*
unmanageable, inconvenient, awkward, clumsy, ungainly, bulky, massive, hefty, hulking, weighty, ponderous, cumbersome
FORMAL incommodious
E∃ handy, dainty

unwilling *adj*
reluctant, disinclined, indisposed, hesitant, resistant, opposed, averse, loath, slow, unenthusiastic, grudging, backward
OLD repugnant
FORMAL loathful
COLLOQ. not having any of
E∃ willing, enthusiastic

unwillingness *n*
reluctance, disinclination, indisposition, hesitancy, slowness, lack of enthusiasm, backwardness
FORMAL loathfulness, nolition
E∃ enthusiasm, willingness

unwind *v*
1 UNROLL, unreel, unwrap, undo, uncoil, untwist, unravel, disentangle
2 RELAX, wind down, calm down
COLLOQ. take it/things easy, let yourself go, make yourself at home, let your hair down, put your feet up, hang loose, cool it, chill (out), veg (out)
E∃ 1 wind, roll

unwise *adj*
ill-advised, inadvisable, inexpedient, short-sighted, improvident, ill-considered, ill-judged, foolish, stupid, silly, senseless, thoughtless, indiscreet, imprudent, foolhardy, irresponsible, rash, reckless
FORMAL impolitic, injudicious
E∃ wise, sensible, prudent

unwitting *adj*
1 UNAWARE, unknowing, unsuspecting, unthinking, unconscious, involuntary
2 INADVERTENT, accidental, chance, unintentional, unintended, unplanned
E∃ 1 knowing **2** conscious, deliberate

unwonted *adj*
unusual, uncommon, unfamiliar, unexpected, unheard-of, strange, rare, peculiar, infrequent, exceptional, extraordinary, unaccustomed, uncustomary, atypical
FORMAL singular
E∃ wonted, usual

unworldly *adj*
1 NAIVE, visionary, idealistic, impractical, unsophisticated, inexperienced, innocent, gullible, ingenuous
COLLOQ. green
2 SPIRITUAL, transcendental, metaphysical, otherworldly, extra-terrestrial
E∃ 1 sophisticated, worldly **2** worldly, materialistic

unworried *adj*
untroubled, relaxed, undismayed, unruffled, unabashed, composed, collected
FORMAL unperturbed
E∃ worried, anxious

unworthy *adj*
undeserving, inferior, ineligible, unsuitable, inappropriate, unfitting, improper, unprofessional, shameful, disgraceful, dishonourable, disreputable, discreditable, ignoble, base, contemptible, despicable
FORMAL unbecoming, unseemly, unbefitting, incongruous
E∃ worthy, commendable

unwritten *adj*
verbal, oral, word-of-mouth, unrecorded, unpenned, tacit, implicit, understood, accepted, recognized, traditional, customary, conventional
E∃ written, recorded

unyielding *adj*
unrelenting, uncompromising, relentless, unwavering, unbending, immovable, inflexible, hardline, adamant, steadfast, stubborn, obstinate, tough, firm, determined, resolute, staunch, rigid, solid
FORMAL implacable, inexorable, intractable, intransigent, obdurate
E∃ yielding, flexible

unzip *v*
undo, loosen, open, free, release, unhook, unwind, separate, detach

up-and-coming *adj*
promising, ambitious, eager, assertive, enterprising
COLLOQ. go-getting, pushing

upbeat *adj*
positive, buoyant, hopeful, optimistic, encouraging, favourable, promising, forward-looking, bright, cheerful, heartening, cheery, rosy
COLLOQ. bullish
E∃ downbeat, gloomy

upbraid *v*
reprimand, admonish, rebuke, reprove, reproach, scold, chide, criticize, censure
FORMAL castigate, berate
COLLOQ. *Aust & NZ* go crook on/at
E∃ praise, commend

upbringing *n*
bringing-up, raising, rearing, breeding, parenting, care, nurture, cultivation, tending, education, training, instruction, teaching

upcoming *adj*
imminent, impending, forthcoming, in the offing, (fast) approaching, coming, on the way, near, close, looming, in the air, at hand, about to happen, almost upon you, on the horizon
COLLOQ. round the corner
E∃ distant, remote, far-off

update *v*
modernize, revise, amend, correct, renew, renovate, revamp, upgrade

up-front *adj, adv*
♦ *adj*
1 FRANK, direct, open, honest, truthful, sincere, genuine, candid, blunt, free, plain, plain-spoken, forthright, straight, straightforward, downright, hard-hitting, outspoken, explicit, bluff
COLLOQ. straight from the shoulder
2 *an up-front payment*
advance, initial, first, introductory, primary
E∃ 1 insincere, evasive
♦ *adv*
in advance, initially, beforehand, early, earlier, sooner

upgrade *v*
improve, make better, better, modernize, enhance, promote, advance, elevate, raise
FORMAL ameliorate
E∃ downgrade, demote

upheaval n
disruption, disturbance, upset, chaos, confusion, disorder,
turmoil, revolution, overthrow
COLLOQ. shake-up

uphill adj
hard, difficult, arduous, tough, taxing, strenuous, laborious,
tiring, wearisome, exhausting, gruelling, punishing,
burdensome, onerous
E3 easy, downhill

uphold v
support, maintain, confirm, keep, hold to, stand by,
defend, champion, advocate, promote, back, endorse,
sustain, strengthen, justify, vindicate
FORMAL fortify
E3 abandon, reject

upkeep n
1 MAINTENANCE, preservation, conservation, care, running,
repair, support, sustenance, subsistence, keep
2 RUNNING COSTS, expenditure, outlay, overheads,
operating costs, oncosts, expenses
E3 **1** neglect

uplift v, n
♦ v
improve, better, boost, upgrade, advance, enlighten, exalt,
inspire, elate, lift, elevate, raise, hoist, heave, refine,
cultivate, edify, civilize
FORMAL ameliorate
♦ n
improvement, lift, enlightenment, enrichment,
advancement, enhancement, refinement, edification,
boost, cultivation
FORMAL betterment

up-market adj
expensive, high, good-quality, superior, prestige,
prestigious, respectful, reputable, excellent, first-class,
first-rate, high-class, exclusive, prime, quality, prize,
choice, select, fine, de luxe, admirable, distinguished,
exceptional, unrivalled, par excellence
COLLOQ. top-notch, top-flight
E3 down-market, inferior, average

upper adj
higher, loftier, superior, greater, senior, top, topmost,
uppermost, high, elevated, exalted, eminent, important
E3 lower, inferior, junior
■ **upper hand**
advantage, dominance, control, sway, supremacy,
superiority, mastery, domination, dominion
FORMAL ascendancy
COLLOQ. edge

upper-class adj
aristocratic, noble, well-bred, well-born, high-born,
high-class, patrician, blue-blooded, exclusive, élite
COLLOQ. swanky, top-drawer
E3 humble, working-class

uppermost adj
highest, loftiest, top, topmost, greatest, supreme, first,
primary, foremost, leading, principal, main, major, chief,
dominant, predominant, paramount, pre-eminent
E3 lowest

uppity adj
arrogant, self-important, conceited, presumptuous,
snobbish, supercilious, impertinent, affected, assuming,
overweening, bumptious, cocky
COLLOQ. bigheaded, hoity-toity, stuck-up, swanky, toffee-
nosed
E3 unassertive, diffident

upright adj
1 VERTICAL, perpendicular, erect, straight, at right angles,
sheer, steep
2 RIGHTEOUS, good, virtuous, upstanding, noble, worthy,
decent, respectable, reputable, honourable, moral, ethical,
principled, high-minded, incorruptible, honest, trustworthy
E3 **1** horizontal, flat **2** dishonest

uprising n
rebellion, revolt, mutiny, rising, overthrow, insurgence,
insurrection, revolution, coup d'état, putsch

uproar n
noise, din, racket, hubbub, hullabaloo, brouhaha,
pandemonium, ballyhoo, tumult, turmoil, turbulence,
commotion, confusion, disorder, mayhem, bedlam,
clamour, outcry, furore, riot, rumpus, fracas, ruction, hell,
rough music, flaw, randan, émeute; Scot collieshangie,
dirdum, rammy, reird; N Am katzenjammer
OLD garboil

uproarious adj
hilarious, riotous, rip-roaring, side-splitting, hysterical,
boisterous, noisy, loud, rollicking, rowdy, confused,
clamorous, deafening, wild, unrestrained
COLLOQ. killing, rib-tickling
E3 quiet

uproot v
pull up, rip up, root out, weed out, remove, displace,
eradicate, destroy, wipe out

upset v, n, adj
♦ v
1 DISTRESS, grieve, dismay, trouble, worry, agitate, disturb,
hurt, bother, fluster, ruffle, sadden, discompose, shake
(up), unnerve, aggrieve, disconcert, put out, confuse,
disorganize, mess about, disrupt, disquiet, break up, take
on, irritate, jangle, overset; Scot coup the cran
FORMAL perturb
COLLOQ. chew up, eat, play havoc with, ruffle someone's
feathers, throw a spanner in the works
SLANG piss off; N Am discombobulate
2 TIP, spill, overturn, capsize, topple, knock over, tumble
over, overthrow, destabilize, unsteady
OLD renverse
♦ n
1 TROUBLE, worry, agitation, distress, disturbance, bother,
disruption, upheaval, reverse, surprise, shock, purl; Scot
coup, upcast
FORMAL perturbation
COLLOQ. shake-up
2 *stomach upset*
disorder, complaint, illness, sickness, ailment
FORMAL malady
COLLOQ. bug
♦ adj
distressed, grieved, aggrieved, hurt, annoyed, dismayed,
troubled, worried, ailed, agitated, disturbed, unsettled,
discomposed, put out, flustered, bothered, shaken,
disconcerted, confused, jealous, in a bad way
FORMAL perturbed
COLLOQ. in a state, het up, uptight, worked up, choked,
gutted, shattered
SLANG pissed off

upsetting adj
distressing, worrying, alarming, disturbing, unsettling, off-
putting, disconcerting, frightening, startling
FORMAL perturbing
E3 comforting

upshot n
result, consequence, outcome, issue, end, conclusion,
finish, culmination, dénouement
COLLOQ. pay-off

upside down
♦ adj, adv
inverted, upturned, up-ended, wrong way up, wrong side
up, upset, overturned, disordered, in disarray, muddled,
jumbled, confused, topsy-turvy, chaotic
COLLOQ. messed up
■ **turn upside down**
disturb, upset, disorganize, make untidy, demolish,
overthrow, turn inside out
COLLOQ. mess up

upstage *v*
outshine, outclass, outstrip, outdo, overshadow, transcend, eclipse, surpass, beat, best, excel, dwarf, outrank, top, put in the shade, put to shame

upstanding *adj*
upright, honest, honourable, strong, true, trustworthy, ethical, moral, principled, incorruptible, erect, good, virtuous, firm, four-square
⊟ untrustworthy

upstart *n*
social climber, arriviste, parvenu, *nouveau riche*, nobody

upsurge *n*
increase, rise, growth, surge, upturn, gain, boost, addition, increment, advance, step-up, build-up, intensification, heightening, development, enlargement, extension, expansion, spread, proliferation, escalation, mushrooming, snowballing, rocketing, skyrocketing
FORMAL augmentation
COLLOQ. hike
⊟ decrease, reduction, decline

uptight *adj*
on edge, tense, uneasy, anxious, hung-up, irritated, prickly, nervy
COLLOQ. edgy
⊟ calm, cool, relaxed

upturn *n*
revival, recovery, upsurge, upswing, rise, increase, boost, improvement, betterment
FORMAL amelioration
⊟ downturn, drop

upward *adj*
ascending, rising, going/moving up, uphill
⊟ downward

■ **upwards of**
over, above, higher than, exceeding, more than, in excess of
⊟ less than

urban *adj*
town, city, inner-city, metropolitan, municipal, civic, built-up, megalopolitan
FORMAL oppidan
⊟ country, rural

> ⚠ **urban** or **urbane**?
> *Urban* means 'of a town': *urban development; urban life; urban violence*. *Urbane* means 'cultured, elegant, refined': *urbane wit*.

urbane *adj*
cultivated, suave, sophisticated, refined, polished, mannerly, civilized, courteous, cultured, debonair, well-bred, well-mannered, civil, elegant, smooth
⊟ gauche, uncouth, inurbane

urbanity *n*
refinement, cultivation, sophistication, suavity, mannerliness, polish, ease, smoothness, grace, elegance, culture, civility, courtesy, charm, worldliness
OLD eutrapelia
⊟ awkwardness, gaucheness

urchin *n*
brat, rascal, rogue, imp, guttersnipe, ragamuffin, waif, gamin, street Arab, kid; *Scot* hurcheon
OLD townskip
OLD SLANG mudlark

urge *v, n*
♦ *v*
1 PERSUADE, encourage, press, push, incite, drive, impel, prod, goad, spur, constrain, compel, force, hasten, induce, instigate, stimulate
COLLOQ. egg on
2 BEG, entreat, appeal, implore, plead
FORMAL beseech
3 ADVISE, counsel, recommend, advocate, encourage

FORMAL exhort
⊟ 1 discourage, dissuade, deter, hinder
♦ *n*
desire, wish, inclination, fancy, longing, yearning, impulse, compulsion, need, impetus, drive, eagerness
COLLOQ. itch, yen
⊟ disinclination

> ▣ **SYNONYM NUANCES**
>
> *verb sense 1*
> You can use **persuade** of bringing someone round to a particular way of thinking, and **encourage** of inspiring someone to do something, but **press** and **push**, **compel** and **force** imply the exertion of strong pressure: *he was pushed into the business by parental desire.*
>   **Drive** and **impel** are more suggestive of being firmly guided to a particular action: *driven by hunger, he went hunting*, while **prod** and **spur** imply arousal from inactivity: *he prodded me to start writing the show.* **Goad**, however, suggests that an irritant is acting as a stimulus: *the crowd goaded the players with their chants.* **Incite** also suggests rousing into action, but often a negative one: *emotive speakers incited people to riot.*
>   You can use **constrain** to suggest that restrictions have a bearing: *decisions constrained by financial difficulty*, unlike **hasten**, which is more suggestive of increased momentum: *ill health hastened his retirement.* **Induce**, on the other hand, returns to the idea of providing an incentive, albeit a less forceful one, while **instigate** is appropriate where something is acting as a catalyst for a particular action or event: *the rise in violent crime instigated tougher jail sentences.* **Stimulate** has more to do with increasing interest: *the lowering of prices stimulated consumer demand.*

urgency *n*
hurry, haste, pressure, stress, priority, importance, seriousness, extremity, gravity, imperativeness, need, necessity
OLD instance
FORMAL exigency, importunity

urgent *adj*
1 PRESSING, immediate, instant, top-priority, emergency, important, critical, necessary, vital, essential, crucial, acute, imperative, prior
OLD importune
FORMAL exigent, emergent
COLLOQ. crying out for ..., dire
2 COMPELLING, persuasive, earnest, serious, grave, eager, insistent, persistent, strident, strenuous
⊟ 1 unimportant

urinate *v*
pass water, make water, relieve yourself, answer the call of nature, be caught/taken short, wet, stale
OLD urine
FORMAL micturate
COLLOQ. leak, pee, piddle, spend a penny, tinkle, wee, tiddle, take a leak, widdle
OLD COLLOQ. ease yourself
SLANG (*vulgar*) piss, slash

usable *adj*
working, operational, serviceable, functional, fit to use, practical, exploitable, available, current, valid
⊟ unusable, useless

usage *n*
1 TREATMENT, handling, management, control, running, operation, employment, application, use
2 TRADITION, custom, practice, habit, convention, etiquette, rule, regulation, form, routine, procedure, way, method, law, formalism, institution, usance
TECHNICAL practic
FORMAL mode, consuetude

3 *contemporary English usage*
style, form, meaning, way of speaking/writing, phraseology, expression, idiom, parlance, terminology
≡ 1 abuse, mistreatment, maltreatment, misusage **3** abusage, misusage

use *v, n*
◆ *v*
1 UTILIZE, employ, make use of, exercise, service, practise, operate, work, apply, ply, wield, handle, deal with, treat, manoeuvre, enjoy, resort to, draw on, take advantage of, bring into play, put to use
2 EXPLOIT, manipulate, take advantage of, impose on, misuse, abuse, take liberties with
COLLOQ. cash in on, bleed, milk, wrap/twist someone round your little finger
3 CONSUME, exhaust, get through, go through, expend, spend, waste
◆ *n*
1 USAGE, application, employment, operation, exercise, utilization, manipulation, exploitation
2 USEFULNESS, value, worth, profit, service, advantage, benefit, good, avail, help, point, object, end, purpose
3 *have the use of the car*
right, permission, privilege, ability
4 EXPLOITATION, manipulation, imposition, mistreatment, misuse, abuse
5 NEED, cause, occasion, necessity, demand, call

■ use up
finish, exhaust, drain, sap, deplete, consume, devour, absorb, waste, squander, fritter

■ used to
accustomed to, adjusted to, in the habit of, familiar with, acclimatized to, given to, prone to, practised in
FORMAL habituated to, inured to, wont to
COLLOQ. at home with, no stranger to

used *adj*
second-hand, cast-off, hand-me-down, nearly-new, worn, dog-eared, soiled; *N Am* pre-owned
≡ unused, new, fresh

useful *adj*
1 CONVENIENT, handy, all-purpose, practical, effective, productive, fruitful, profitable, valuable, worthwhile, rewarding, advantageous, beneficial, helpful, functional, general-purpose
COLLOQ. nifty
2 SKILLED, proficient, practised, experienced, competent, expert, able, skilful, handy
≡ 1 useless, ineffective, worthless

usefulness *n*
utility, use, value, worth, profit, advantage, benefit, good, help, avail, service, convenience, practicality, functionality, efficiency, fitness, serviceableness
FORMAL efficacy

useless *adj*
1 FUTILE, fruitless, unproductive, vain, idle, unavailing, to no avail, hopeless, unhelpful, pointless, worthless, unusable, unprofitable, broken-down, unworkable, impractical
FORMAL ineffectual, inefficacious
COLLOQ. clapped-out, kaput; *Aust* bung
2 INCOMPETENT, ineffective, incapable, inefficient, bad, weak
COLLOQ. hopeless, awful, terrible, botched, lousy, pathetic, rop(e)y, a load of rubbish/garbage
SLANG half-arsed
≡ 1 useful, helpful, effective **2** good

uselessness *n*
futility, hopelessness, impracticality, incompetence, ineffectiveness, ineptitude, idleness
FORMAL ineffectuality, inutility
≡ effectiveness, usefulness

usher *n, v*
◆ *n*
usherette, doorkeeper, attendant, escort, guide
◆ *v*
escort, accompany, conduct, lead, direct, guide, show, pilot, steer

■ usher in
herald, inaugurate, initiate, introduce, launch, precede, announce, ring in, mark the start of, pave the way for

usual *adj*
normal, typical, stock, standard, regular, routine, habitual, customary, conventional, traditional, orthodox, accepted, recognized, accustomed, established, familiar, common, everyday, general, ordinary, average, unexceptional, expected, predictable
FORMAL wonted
≡ unusual, strange, rare

usually *adv*
normally, generally, as a rule, ordinarily, typically, traditionally, regularly, routinely, habitually, commonly, by and large, on the whole, mainly, chiefly, mostly, for the most part, on average, in the main
COLLOQ. nine times out of ten
≡ exceptionally

usurer *n*
extortionist, money-lender, Shylock; *Irish* gombeen-man; *N Am* note-shaver
COLLOQ. loan-shark
SLANG (*offensive Jew old slang*) gripe

usurp *v*
take over, assume, arrogate, seize, take, take possession of, annex, appropriate, commandeer, steal

usury *n*
money-lending, extortion, interest; *Irish* gombeen
OLD (*Shakesp*) excess

utensil *n*
tool, implement, instrument, device, contrivance, gadget, apparatus, appliance
See also panels at **cutlery**; **domestic appliances**; **kitchen utensils**.

utilitarian *adj*
functional, practical, convenient, serviceable, sensible, useful, unpretentious, effective, efficient, pragmatic, down-to-earth, lowly
≡ decorative, impractical

utility *n*
usefulness, use, value, worth, profit, advantage, benefit, good, help, avail, service, convenience, practicality, efficiency, fitness, serviceableness
FORMAL efficacy

utilize *v*
use, employ, make use of, put to use, resort to, take advantage of, turn to account, exploit, adapt

utmost *adj, n*
◆ *adj*
1 *with the utmost care*
extreme, maximum, most, greatest, highest, supreme, paramount
2 FARTHEST, furthest, furthermost, remotest, outermost, ultimate, final, last
◆ *n*
best, hardest, most, maximum, top, peak

Utopia *n*
paradise, Eden, Garden of Eden, bliss, Elysium, heaven, heaven on earth, Shangri-la
COLLOQ. seventh heaven
≡ cacotopia, dystopia

Utopian *adj*
ideal, idealistic, illusory, imaginary, perfect, visionary, wishful, fanciful, fantastic, airy, dream, romantic, unworkable, impractical, Elysian
FORMAL chimerical
≡ cacotopian, dystopian

utter[1] *v*
not utter a word

speak, say, voice, vocalize, verbalize, put into words, express, articulate, enunciate, sound, pronounce, deliver, state, declare, announce, proclaim, tell, reveal, divulge

> **QUOTATIONS**
> What I utter, I think, and spend my malice in my breath
> WILLIAM SHAKESPEARE, *Coriolanus*

utter[2] *adj*
to my utter amazement

absolute, complete, total, entire, thoroughgoing, thorough, out-and-out, downright, pure, sheer, stark, arrant, unmitigated, unqualified, positive, categorical, perfect, consummate

utterance *n*

statement, remark, comment, opinion, expression, word, articulation, delivery, speech, declaration, announcement, proclamation, pronouncement, enunciation

utterly *adv*

absolutely, completely, totally, fully, entirely, wholly, thoroughly, downright, perfectly, categorically, pure, stark, to the wide; *dialect* rank
OLD *N Am* plumb
COLLOQ. dead

U-turn *n*

about-turn, volte-face, reversal, backtrack

vacancy *n*
opportunity, opening, position, post, job, place, room, situation

vacant *adj*
1 EMPTY, unoccupied, unfilled, free, available, void, not in use, unused, deserted, abandoned, uninhabited
2 BLANK, expressionless, vacuous, inane, poker-faced, straight-faced, deadpan, impassive, inattentive, absent, absent-minded, unthinking, dreamy
1 occupied, engaged, in use, busy

vacate *v*
leave, depart, evacuate, abandon, withdraw
COLLOQ. quit

vacation *n*
holiday, trip, leave, leave of absence, time off, break, rest, recess, furlough

vaccinate *v*
inoculate, immunize, protect, syringe
COLLOQ. jab; *Scot* jag

vaccination *n*
injection, inoculation, immunization, dose
COLLOQ. jab, shot

vacillate *v*
waver, hesitate, fluctuate, sway, oscillate, keep changing your mind, haver, temporize, teeter, wobble, dither, halt, back and fill, go back and forth, whiffle
OLD wave
FORMAL tergiversate
COLLOQ. shilly-shally, blow hot and cold, waffle

vacillating *adj*
wavering, hesitant, irresolute, uncertain, unresolved, shuffling, oscillating
COLLOQ. shilly-shallying, blowing hot and cold, waffling
3 resolute, unhesitating

vacillation *n*
wavering, inconstancy, hesitancy, hesitation, fluctuation, irresolution, indecision, indecisiveness, unsteadiness, temporization, teetering, wobbling, dithering
FORMAL tergiversation
COLLOQ. shilly-shallying, blowing hot and cold

vacuity *n*
emptiness, space, nothingness, blankness, vacuousness, vacuum, void, apathy, inanity, incomprehension, incuriosity
FORMAL incognizance

vacuous *adj*
empty, blank, vacant, glassy, void, unfilled, inane, unintelligent, stupid, uncomprehending, incurious, apathetic, idle

vacuum *n*
emptiness, void, nothingness, hollowness, vacuity, space, chasm, gap
FORMAL lacuna
3 *technical* plenum

vagabond *n*
vagrant, tramp, wanderer, wayfarer, down-and-out, rascal, beggar, rover, runabout, itinerant, migrant, outcast,

nomad, piker, clochard, floater, straggle, stroller; *dialect* walker; *Scot* caird, gangrel, hallan-shaker, landloper, rinthereout,
(*derog*) tinkler; *N Am* hobo; *Aust* sundowner
OLD cursitor, rogue, scatterling, truant, vagrom
COLLOQ. loser, knight of the road, Weary Willie
SLANG bum, dosser, gook, toerag; *N Am* dingbat

vagary *n*
fancy, notion, prank, quirk, whim, whimsy, humour, crotchet; *Scot* megrim
FORMAL caprice

vagina *n*
TECHNICAL vulva, introitus
SLANG
(*taboo*) cunt, pussy, fanny, box, hole, muff, crack, beaver, punani

vagrancy *n*
wandering, travelling, shiftlessness, rootlessness, unsettledness, nomadism, itinerancy, homelessness

vagrant *n, adj*
♦ *n*
tramp, wanderer, drifter, itinerant, beggar, stroller, hobo, dosser, *Scot* gangrel
COLLOQ. rolling stone
SLANG bum
♦ *adj*
wandering, vagabond, travelling, shiftless, rootless, unsettled, roaming, roving, nomadic, itinerant, homeless

vague *adj*
1 ILL-DEFINED, blurred, unfocused, out of focus, indistinct, hazy, dim, faint, shadowy, foggy, misty, fuzzy, woozy, nebulous, obscure
FORMAL amorphous, transcendental
2 INDEFINITE, imprecise, unclear, unsure, uncertain, undefined, undetermined, unspecific, unspecified, rough, sketchy, incomplete, approximate, generalized, general, inexact, ambiguous, evasive, loose, lax, woolly, woolly-minded; *dialect* yonderly
FORMAL indeterminate
3 **1** clear **2** definite, precise, specific

vaguely *adv*
slightly, imprecisely, faintly, dimly, inexactly, obscurely, vacantly, absent-mindedly, distantly

vagueness *n*
unclearness, fuzziness, haziness, uncertainty, dimness, faintness, impression, notion, obscurity, imprecision, looseness, ambiguity, generality, inexactitude, woolliness
FORMAL amorphousness
3 clarity, precision

vain *adj*
1 *a vain attempt*
useless, worthless, futile, fruitless, pointless, unproductive, unprofitable, unavailing, hollow, groundless, empty, idle, trivial, insubstantial, unimportant, insignificant
FORMAL abortive, nugatory
2 CONCEITED, proud, haughty, self-satisfied, arrogant, self-important, self-conceited, self-glorious, egotistical, affected, pretentious, ostentatious, swaggering, narcissistic, peacockish

COLLOQ. bigheaded, swell-headed, swollen-headed, stuck-up, snooty, high and mighty
E3 1 fruitful, successful **2** modest, self-effacing

■ **in vain**
for nothing, to no avail, unsuccessfully, uselessly, fruitlessly, to no end, vainly
OLD (*Shakesp*) for vain
FORMAL ineffectually
COLLOQ. no go
E3 successfully

vainglorious *adj*
boastful, proud, conceited, vain, puffed up, bragging, crowing, cocky, swaggering, arrogant, self-flattering, egotistical
COLLOQ. bigheaded, swollen-headed, swanky
E3 modest, self-effacing, humble

vainly *adv*
for nothing, to no avail, unsuccessfully, uselessly, fruitlessly, to no end
OLD (*Shakesp*) for vain
FORMAL ineffectually
COLLOQ. no go
E3 successfully

valediction *n*
goodbye, farewell, leave-taking, adieu
COLLOQ. send-off
E3 welcome, greeting

valedictory *adj*
farewell, parting, departing, final, last

valet *n*
manservant, man, gentleman's gentleman, body servant, *valet de chambre*

valetudinarian *adj*
sickly, invalid, infirm, weakly, feeble, frail, delicate, hypochondriac, neurotic

valiant *adj*
brave, courageous, gallant, fearless, intrepid, bold, dauntless, determined, audacious, heroic, plucky, staunch, stout-hearted, lion-hearted
FORMAL indomitable, valorous
E3 cowardly, fearful, dismayed

valiantly *adv*
bravely, courageously, gallantly, fearlessly, intrepidly, boldly, dauntlessly, audaciously, heroically, pluckily, staunchly, stout-heartedly
FORMAL indomitably
E3 cowardly, fearfully

valid *adj*
1 LOGICAL, well-founded, well-grounded, reasonable, justifiable, sound, good, convincing, telling, conclusive, credible, reliable, substantial, forceful, weighty, powerful, just, meaningful
FORMAL cogent
2 OFFICIAL, legal, lawful, legitimate, authentic, effective, bona fide, genuine, binding, contractual, proper, acknowledged, licensed, accredited, formalized, consummated
TECHNICAL available; *Scot* approbated
E3 1 false, weak **2** unofficial, invalid, null and void

validate *v*
confirm, authenticate, endorse, legalize, authorize, substantiate, underwrite, ratify, certify, accredit, formalize, consummate
FORMAL attest, corroborate

validation *n*
confirmation, authentication, endorsement, authorization, ratification, accreditation, formalization
FORMAL attestation, corroboration

validity *n*
soundness, legality, lawfulness, legitimacy, foundation, grounds, justifiability, strength, power, force, weight, substance, logic, point, authority

FORMAL cogency
E3 invalidity

valley *n*
dale, vale, dell, glen, hollow, depression, slade, gulch, coomb, dean, dene, ria, dingle, gill; *dialect* griff, grike; *Scot* den, heuch, strath; *Welsh* cwm

valorous *adj*
brave, bold, heroic, courageous, fearless, plucky, lion-hearted, stout-hearted, valiant, intrepid, gallant, hardy, mettlesome, dauntless, doughty, stalwart
E3 cowardly, weak

valour *n*
boldness, courage, bravery, heroism, intrepidity, lion-heartedness, fearlessness, mettle, spirit, gallantry, hardiness, doughtiness
FORMAL fortitude
E3 cowardice, weakness

valuable *adj*
1 *a valuable necklace*
precious, prized, valued, costly, expensive, dear, high-priced, treasured, cherished, priceless, estimable
COLLOQ. worth a pretty penny, worth its weight in gold
2 *valuable suggestions*
helpful, worthwhile, useful, beneficial, invaluable, constructive, fruitful, profitable, advantageous, important, serviceable, worthy, handy
E3 1 worthless **2** useless

SYNONYM NUANCES

sense 1
You can use **precious** of something of great financial or emotional value, while **prized** further implies a degree of pride involved: *his prized trophies*. **Valued**, too, suggests that something is held in esteem, while the even more expressive **treasured** and **cherished** imply great love and care: *his treasured family photographs*. **Estimable** is more suggestive of being worthy of admiration rather than emotional attachment: *a surgeon of estimable skill*.
   Other synonyms, such as **costly**, **expensive**, **dear** and **high-priced** emphasize financial value. **Priceless** is rather more emotive in that it suggests being invaluable, and therefore irreplaceable.

---

valuation *n*
evaluation, value, assessment, estimate, computation, survey
FORMAL appraisement

value *n, v*
♦ *n*
1 COST, price, rate, worth
2 WORTH, use, usefulness, utility, merit, importance, desirability, benefit, advantage, significance, good, profit, gain, avail
3 *moral values*
morals, principles, moral principles, standards, ethics
♦ *v*
1 PRIZE, appreciate, treasure, hold dear, admire, respect, esteem, cherish, set great store by
2 EVALUATE, assess, estimate, price, put a price on, survey, rate
FORMAL appraise
E3 1 disregard, neglect **2** undervalue

valued *adj*
highly regarded, esteemed, cherished, treasured, prized, respected, dear, loved, beloved

valueless *adj*
worthless, useless, pointless, meaningless, futile, unavailing, unimportant, insignificant, trivial, unusable, cheap, poor, rubbishy, trashy, trifling, paltry
FORMAL ineffectual, nugatory
SLANG naff

vamp *n*
seductress, temptress, siren, *femme fatale*, Delilah, Lorelei, Circe, enchantress, flirt, coquette, charmer

van *n*
lorry, truck, wagon, trailer, carriage, pick-up, black Maria, prison van, box van, deliveryvan, mailvan, furniture van, pantechnicon, camper van, Dormobile®, caravan, mobile home; *N Am* motor home, recreational vehicle, RV, Winnebago®, guard's van, freight-car, railroad car
SLANG *N Am* meat wagon

vandal *n*
hooligan, ruffian, rowdy, hoodlum, mobster, thug, tough, rough, lout, delinquent, wrecker, annihilator, demolisher, desolater, despoiler, ransacker, ravager, locust
COLLOQ. mugger
SLANG bovver boy, yob

vandalize *v*
wreck, trash, destroy, ruin, demolish, devastate, shatter, smash, break, sink, torpedo, ravage, write off

vane *n*
fan, wing, blade, windsail, weathercock, plume, web
TECHNICAL dogvane
OLD fane

vanguard *n*
forefront, most advanced part, front, front line, firing line, spearhead, lead, fore, leading/foremost position

vanish *v*
disappear, fade, fade away/out, dissolve, evaporate, disperse, melt (away), die out, leave, depart, exit, fizzle out, peter out, ghost, end/go up in smoke
OLD evanish, faint
FORMAL evanesce, dematerialize
E3 appear, materialize

vanity *n*
1 CONCEIT, conceitedness, pride, arrogance, haughtiness, self-conceit, self-love, self-satisfaction, self-glorification, narcissism, egotism, pretension, ostentation, affectation, airs
COLLOQ. bigheadedness, swollen-headedness, snootiness
2 WORTHLESSNESS, uselessness, emptiness, futility, pointlessness, unreality, unproductiveness, unprofitableness, hollowness, fruitlessness, triviality, idleness, unimportance, insignificance
OLD (*Spenser*) vainesse
E3 **1** modesty, worth

vanquish *v*
defeat, conquer, beat, triumph over, overcome, overpower, overwhelm, subdue, humble, master, repress, quell, confound, crush, rout
FORMAL subjugate
COLLOQ. hammer, slaughter, clobber, thrash, lick, thump, trounce, drub, annihilate, smash, devastate, make mincemeat (out) of, run rings round, paste, wipe the floor with
SLANG take to the cleaners

vapid *adj*
vacuous, uninteresting, lifeless, dead, banal, bland, boring, dull, tedious, flat, insipid, limp, stale, tame, flavourless, tasteless, watery, wishy-washy, colourless, tiresome, trite, weak, uninspiring
OLD jejune
E3 interesting, vigorous

vaporous *adj*
1 STEAMY, misty, gaseous, fumy, fumous, foggy
2 FANCIFUL, flimsy, insubstantial, vain
FORMAL chimerical
E3 **2** substantial

vapour *n*
steam, mist, fog, smoke, breath, fumes, haze, damp, dampness, exhalation

variable *adj, n*
♦ *adj*
changeable, inconstant, varying, shifting, mutable, unpredictable, fluctuating, fitful, unstable, unsteady, uneven, wavering, vacillating, temperamental, fickle, flexible
FORMAL chameleonic, Protean
E3 fixed, invariable, stable
♦ *n*
factor, parameter

SYNONYM NUANCES

adjective
You can use **changeable** and **varying** fairly generally of anything continually altering: *changeable weather*, while **shifting** can also be used of a change of stance: *their shifting alliances*. **Mutable**, on the other hand, might be used of something that is subject to change: *truth is a mutable commodity*, whereas **inconstant** and **unpredictable** have negative overtones of a lack of dependability: *an inconstant friend*.
  While **fluctuating** suggests a strongly alternating movement: *the fluctuating tides*, **fitful** would describe something more intermittent and, often, unwelcome: *fitful sleep*.
  Wavering has connotations of a lack of resolve, and **vacillating**, while sharing this connotation, also echoes the image of moving back and forth: *the leaders vacillated between confrontation and compromise*. **Temperamental** could be used, with negative overtones, of someone displaying mood swings, while **fickle** is equally uncomplimentary when applied to someone constantly changing his or her opinion. **Flexible** is more suggestive of being accommodating, and therefore more positive in tone.

---

variance *n*
1 VARIATION, difference, discrepancy, divergence, inconsistency, disagreement
TECHNICAL covariance
2 DISAGREEMENT, disharmony, conflict, discord, division, dissent, dissension, quarrelling, opposition, strife, odds
E3 **1** agreement **2** agreement, harmony
■ **at variance**
at odds, disagreeing, in disagreement, in conflict, conflicting, differing, clashing, quarrelling, arguing, at loggerheads, out of step; *N Am* at outs

variant *n, adj*
♦ *n*
alternative, variation, modification, development, deviant, rogue
♦ *adj*
alternative, different, divergent, modified, derived, deviant, exceptional
E3 normal, standard, usual

variation *n*
diversity, variety, deviation, discrepancy, diversification, alteration, change, difference, vacillation, fluctuation, departure, modification, modulation, inflection, novelty, innovation
E3 monotony, uniformity

varied *adj*
assorted, diverse, miscellaneous, mixed, various, sundry, motley, different, wide-ranging
FORMAL heterogeneous, multifarious
E3 standardized, uniform

variegated *adj*
multicoloured, many-coloured, parti-coloured, varicoloured, speckled, mottled, dappled, pied, streaked, marbled, jaspe, motley
TECHNICAL poikilitic
E3 monochrome, plain

variety n
1 ASSORTMENT, miscellany, mixture, collection, medley, pot-pourri, range
2 DIVERSITY, difference, dissimilarity, discrepancy, variation
FORMAL multiplicity, multifariousness
3 SORT, kind, class, category, species, type, breed, brand, make, strain, classification
F3 **2** uniformity; *formal* similitude

> **PROVERBS**
> Variety is the spice of life

> **QUOTATIONS**
> Variety is the soul of pleasure
> APHRA BEHN, *The Rover*

various adj
different, differing, dissimilar, unlike, diverse, varied, varying, assorted, miscellaneous, distinct, diversified, mixed, many, several, motley
FORMAL heterogeneous, disparate, variegated

varnish n, v
♦ n
lacquer, lac, glaze, enamel, shellac, resin, polish, gloss, coating, veneer, japan
♦ v
lacquer, glaze, enamel, shellac, polish, gloss, coat, veneer, japan

vary v
1 CHANGE, alter, modify, qualify, modulate, diversify, re-order, transform, alternate, permutate, waver, spice
FORMAL metamorphose, variate
2 DIFFER, diverge, disagree, depart, fluctuate, oscillate, range, be dissimilar, clash, be in conflict, be at odds
TECHNICAL hunt

vase n
container, jar, jug, pitcher, urn, vessel, ewer, amphora, hydria, flask, cornucopia, lustre, potiche
OLD diota, Canopus

vassal n
serf, slave, subject, thrall, man, vassaless, bond(s)man, bondservant, retainer, villein, liege, liegeman, client

vassalage n
dependence, bondage, servitude, slavery, subjection, serfdom, thraldom, villeinage
FORMAL subjugation

vast adj
huge, immense, massive, gigantic, enormous, great, colossal, bulky, extensive, tremendous, sweeping, unlimited, fathomless, limitless, boundless, immeasurable, infinite, never-ending, teeming, monumental, monstrous, far-flung, gargantuan, cyclopean
OLD vasty
FORMAL prodigious

vastly adv
hugely, immensely, greatly, massively, enormously, extensively, boundlessly, limitlessly, without limits, immeasurably, infintely

vat n
barrel, tank, tub, container, kier, keeve, fat, back, stand, case, cuvée, tan-pit; *Scot* girnel
OLD pressfat

vault[1] v, n
♦ v
vault over the wall
leap, spring, bound, clear, jump, hurdle, leap-frog
♦ n
leap, spring, jump, bound, hurdle, clearance

vault[2] n
1 CELLAR, crypt, strongroom, repository, cavern, depository, wine-cellar, underground chamber, basement, catacomb, tomb, ossuary, mausoleum
2 ARCH, roof, span, concave

vaunt v
boast, brag, exult in, flaunt, parade, trumpet, crow
COLLOQ. show off, swank, blow your own trumpet; *N Am* blow your own horn
F3 belittle, minimize

veer v
swerve, swing, change, shift, diverge, deviate, wheel, turn, sheer, tack

vegetable

Vegetables include:

artichoke	chicory	onion
asparagus	courgette (or	parsnip
aubergine (or	N Am & Aust	pepper
N Am eggplant)	zucchini)	potato
baby corn	cucumber	pumpkin
beetroot	daikon	radish
bok choy (or pak	fennel	rocket
choi)	garlic	romanesco
broccoli	globe artichoke	shallot
Brussels sprout	Jerusalem	spinach
cabbage	artichoke	spring onion
calabrese	kale	*colloq.* spud
capsicum	leek	squash
carrot	lettuce	swede
cassava (or	lollo rosso	sweetcorn
manioc)	marrow	sweet potato
cauliflower	mibuna	turnip
cavolo nero (or	mizuna	water chestnut
black cabbage)	mooli	yam
celeriac	mushroom	
celery	okra	

See also **food**.

Legumes and pulses include:

BEANS:	French bean (or	winged bean
adzuki bean	green or kidney	**LENTILS:**
asparagus bean (or	or string bean)	brown lentil
yard-long bean)	haricot bean	continental lentil
asparagus pea (or	jicama	Egyptian lentil
Goa bean)	lablab	German lentil
bean sprout	lima bean (or	green lentil
black bean	sugar bean)	Puy lentil
black-eye(d) bean	mung bean	red lentil
(or cowpea)	navy bean (or	
borlotti bean	Yankee bean)	**PEAS:**
broad bean (or	pinto bean	chickpea (or
N Am fava bean)	red kidney bean	garbanzo)
butter bean	runner bean	d(h)al (or pigeon
cannellini bean (or	scarlet runner	pea)
fasolia)	bean	mangetout (or
carob bean (or	N Am snap bean	snow pea or
locust bean)	soy bean (or soya	sugar pea)
chilli bean	bean)	petit pois
edamame	tonka bean	split pea
flageolet	urd bean (or black	string pea
	gram)	sugar snap pea
	wax bean	

See also **bean**.

Salad leaves include:

arugula (or rocket)	cos lettuce	mizuna
borage	cress	radicchio
chard	endive	round lettuce
chicory	iceberg lettuce	salad burnet
corn-salad (or	lollo rosso	watercress
lamb's lettuce)	lovage	

vegetate v
stagnate, degenerate, deteriorate, rusticate, go to seed, idle, rust, languish, moulder, do nothing

vegetation n
plants, trees, flowers, flora, green plants, greenery
FORMAL herbage, verdure

vehemence n
passion, energy, enthusiasm, keenness, fervency, eagerness, earnestness, emphasis, strength, power, animation, intensity, zeal, verve, vigour, ardour, fervour, force, forcefulness, urgency, impetuosity, violence, warmth, heat, fire
E3 indifference

vehement adj
impassioned, passionate, ardent, fervent, intense, forceful, emphatic, heated, hot, warm, strong, zpowerful, spirited, vigorous, urgent, enthusiastic, animated, eager, keen, earnest, forcible, fierce, violent, zealous, thunderous
FORMAL fervid
E3 apathetic, indifferent

vehicle n
1 CONVEYANCE, transport
2 MEANS, agency, channel, medium, mechanism, instrument, organ

---

Vehicles include:

S Afr bakkie	hybrid electric	sledge
barouche	vehicle (HEV)	sleeper
bicycle	hybrid vehicle	sleigh
colloq. bike	*Aust* jinker	snowmobile
boat	juggernaut	stagecoach
bobsleigh	landau	steam-roller
colloq. bone-	litter	sulky
shaker	lorry	surrey
brougham	maglev	tandem
S Afr buck-wagon	minibus	tank
bus	minivan	taxi
cab	monorail	toboggan
camper	motorbike	tractor
S Afr Cape cart	motorcycle	trailer
car	omnibus	train
caravan	motorhome	tram
caravanette	pantechnicon	Transit®
charabanc	penny-farthing	trap
coach	phaeton	tricycle
cycle	plane	troika
dog-cart	post-chaise	trolleybus
double-decker	Pullman	truck
dray	*N Am* recreational	tube
fork-lift truck	vehicle (RV)	van
four-in-hand	scooter	Vespa®
gig	*S Afr* Scotch cart	wagon
golf cart	sedan-chair	wagon-lit
hackney-carriage	*NZ* service car	wetbike
hansom	ship	*N Am*
N Am Humvee®	sled	Winnebago®

See also **aircraft**; **bicycle**; **boat**; **car**.

---

veil v, n
♦ v
screen, cloak, cover (up), mask, mantle, blanket, shadow, shield, obscure, conceal, hide, shroud, disguise, shade, camouflage, mist, overveil, encurtain
E3 expose, uncover
♦ n
cover, covering, veiling, cloak, curtain, hood, mask, mantle, blanket, scarf, screen, disguise, film, blind, shade, canopy, shroud, purdah, chadar, yashmak, kalyptra, wimple, chrismal, lambrequin, mantilla, kiss-me, kiss-me-quick, weeper
OLD vail, caul, scene, volet; *(Spenser)* veale, vele

veiled adj
1 *veiled threats*
hidden, concealed, disguised, obscure, secret, masked, shrouded, cloaked, indirect, covert, surreptitious
2 COVERED, masked, shrouded, cloaked, disguised
E3 1 clear, open, obvious

vein n
1 STREAK, stripe, stratum, seam, lode, blood vessel
Related adjective: venous
2 MOOD, tendency, bent, strain, streak, temper, tenor, tone, frame of mind, humour, mode, style, disposition, temperament, attitude, inclination

veined adj
streaked, variegated, marbled, mottled, jaspe

velocity n
speed, rate, quickness, rapidity, pace, impetus, swiftness
OLD fleetness
FORMAL celerity

venal adj
corrupt, corruptible, bribable, mercenary, grafting, simoniacal
COLLOQ. bent, buyable
E3 incorruptible

vendetta n
feud, blood-feud, enmity, rivalry, quarrel, bad blood, bitterness

vendor n
seller, trader, salesperson, merchant, supplier, stockist
See panel at **seller**.

veneer n
1 FAÇADE, front, appearance, display, show, mask, gloss, camouflage, pretence, guise
2 LAYER, coating, surface, finish, gloss, covering, lamination

venerable adj
respected, esteemed, revered, honoured, venerated, dignified, grave, wise, august, aged, worshipped
FORMAL hallowed

venerate v
revere, respect, esteem, honour, worship, adore
FORMAL hallow
E3 despise, anathematize

veneration n
respect, esteem, reverence, deference, adoration, awe, worship, devotion

vengeance n
retribution, revenge, retaliation, reprisal, requital
OLD avengement, wrack; *(Spenser)* vengement
COLLOQ. tit for tat, an eye for an eye (and a tooth for a tooth)
E3 forgiveness
■ **with a vengeance**
1 FORCEFULLY, violently, vigorously, powerfully, energetically, furiously, vehemently
OLD with a (wild) wanion, with a witness
COLLOQ. flat out, like crazy
2 TO A GREAT DEGREE, greatly, to a great extent, fully, to the full, thoroughly, to the utmost
COLLOQ. with no holds barred

vengeful adj
spiteful, rancorous, unforgiving, vindictive, avenging, revengeful, retaliatory, relentless, retributive, punitive, implacable
E3 forgiving

venial adj
forgivable, excusable, pardonable, slight, minor, insignificant, trivial, trifling, negligible
E3 mortal, unforgivable, unpardonable

venom n
1 POISON, toxin, virus
OLD swelter

2 RANCOUR, ill-will, malice, malevolence, acrimony, vindictiveness, spite, bitterness, resentment, hate, enmity, hostility, animosity, virulence, virus

venomous *adj*
1 POISONOUS, toxic, lethal, deadly, fatal, virulent, harmful
FORMAL noxious
2 MALICIOUS, spiteful, vicious, rancorous, vindictive, bitter, resentful, baleful, hostile, virulent, malignant, malevolent, baneful
1 harmless

vent *n, v*
♦ *n*
opening, hole, aperture, outlet, gap, passage, orifice, duct, pipe, blowhole, breather, chimney, flue, vomitory
TECHNICAL mud volcano, solfatara, spiracle
♦ *v*
air, express, voice, utter, release, discharge, emit, let out, pour out, wreak, let off steam, take it out on, give vent to, give a loose to
OLD disclose

ventilate *v*
1 *ventilate a room*
air, aerate, freshen, cool
2 *ventilate your feelings*
express, air, broadcast, debate, discuss, bring out into the open

ventilation *n*
airing, cooling, freshening, aeration

venture *v, n*
♦ *v*
1 DARE, advance, go, embark, make bold, be so bold as to, put forward, presume, suggest, volunteer, pretend, adventure, take the liberty, make so free as to; *Scot* mint
OLD venter, ventre
FORMAL assay
2 RISK, hazard, chance, endanger, imperil, jeopardize, put in jeopardy, speculate, gamble, wager, stake, come in on, invest, sink
OLD venter, ventre
♦ *n*
risk, chance, hazard, speculation, gamble, undertaking, project, adventure, exploit, endeavour, enterprise, operation, fling, promotion, foray
OLD venter, portage; (*Shakesp*) jump
COLLOQ. throw

venturesome *adj*
adventurous, enterprising, courageous, bold, brave, daring, fearless, intrepid, spirited, plucky, audacious, dauntless, doughty
COLLOQ. daredevil
1 unenterprising, cowardly

veracious *adj*
truthful, true, trustworthy, genuine, frank, honest, reliable, credible, dependable, straightforward, exact, factual, faithful, accurate
1 untruthful

veracity *n*
truthfulness, truth, trustworthiness, integrity, honesty, frankness, precision, accuracy, candour, credibility, exactitude
FORMAL probity, rectitude
1 untruthfulness

veranda *n*
terrace, decking, gallery, lanai; *N Am* piazza, porch; *S Afr* stoep
OLD viranda, virando

verbal *adj*
spoken, oral, said, uttered, vocal, linguistic, verbatim, unwritten, word-of-mouth
1 written

verbalize *v*
put in/into words, articulate, utter, voice, give voice to, say, speak, state, communicate, put/get over, pronounce, word, tell, announce, report, assert, declare, put across, formulate, point out, convey
FORMAL enunciate

verbatim *adv*
word for word, exactly, literally, to the letter, precisely, closely

verbiage *n*
repetition, verbosity, waffle
FORMAL circumlocution, pleonasm, periphrasis, prolixity
1 succinctness, briefness

verbose *adj*
long-winded, wordy, windy, garrulous, diffuse, voluble
OLD wordish
FORMAL prolix, loquacious, circumlocutory, periphrastic, pleonastic
1 succinct, brief

verbosity *n*
verboseness, windiness, wordiness, long-windedness, garrulity, logorrhoea, verbiage
FORMAL loquaciousness, loquacity, multiloquy, prolixity
1 economy, succinctness

verdant *adj*
lush, green, grassy, fresh, leafy
FORMAL viridescent, virid, graminaceous, gramineous

verdict *n*
decision, judgement, conclusion, finding, adjudication, assessment, opinion, ruling, sentence, rough justice
TECHNICAL recovery
OLD verdit, vardy

verdure *n*
grass, greenery, greenness, herbage, foliage, leafage, pasture, meadows
FORMAL verdancy, viridity, viridescence

verge *n, v*
♦ *n*
border, edge, margin, limit, rim, brim, brink, boundary, wayside, threshold, extreme, extremity, edging
■ **verge on**
approach, border on, come close to, near, tend towards, incline to

verification *n*
confirmation, checking, proof, substantiation, validation, authentication, ascertaining
TECHNICAL audit
FORMAL attestation, corroboration

verify *v*
confirm, substantiate, authenticate, bear out, prove, support, endorse, validate, testify, ascertain, check
TECHNICAL audit
FORMAL corroborate, attest, accredit
1 invalidate, discredit

verisimilitude *n*
authenticity, credibility, resemblance, realism, likeliness, plausibility, semblance, colour
COLLOQ. ring of truth
1 implausibility

veritable *adj*
positive, absolute, utter, sheer, complete, rank, perfect, unmitigated, outright, out-and-out, thorough
FORMAL consummate

verity *n*
truth, truthfulness, validity, factuality, actuality, authenticity, soundness
FORMAL veracity
1 untruth

vernacular *adj, n*
♦ *adj*
indigenous, local, native, popular, vulgar, informal, colloquial, common

◆ *n*

language, speech, tongue, parlance, dialect, idiom, slang, cant, jargon
COLLOQ. lingo, patter

versatile *adj*

adaptable, flexible, all-round, all-purpose, multipurpose, multifaceted, adjustable, many-sided, general-purpose, functional, resourceful, handy, variable
⊟ inflexible

verse *n*

poetry, rhyme, stanza, strophe, metre, doggerel, jingle; *Welsh* pennill

Verse forms include:

ballad stanza	Petrarchan	Shakespearean
blank verse	(or Italian) sonnet	sonnet
cinquain	quatrain	sicilian octave
free verse	rubai	sonnet
Miltonic sonnet	sapphic	Spenserian stanza
ottava rima	sestina	tercet
		terza rima

See also **poem**; **prosody**.

versed *adj*

skilled, proficient, practised, experienced, familiar, acquainted, learned, read, knowledgeable, conversant, seasoned, qualified, competent, accomplished

versifier *n*

poet, poetess, poetaster, rhymer, rhymester, rhymist, verser, verse-maker, verse-monger, verse-smith, versificator, poeticule
OLD verse-man

version *n*

1 RENDERING, reading, interpretation, understanding, account, report, edition, translation, paraphrase, adaptation, portrayal
2 TYPE, kind, sort, variant, form, model, style, design, reproduction

versus *prep*

1 *Arsenal versus Manchester United*
against, v, playing, facing, opposing, in opposition to
2 *expense versus convenience*
as opposed to, rather than, instead of, in contrast to, as against

vertex *n*

peak, top, apex, summit, acme, apogee, zenith, height, highest point, pinnacle, culmination, crown, extremity
⊟ nadir

vertical *adj*

upright, perpendicular, straight up, upstanding, sheer, plumb, erect, on end
⊟ horizontal

vertigo *n*

dizziness, giddiness, light-headedness, sickness
COLLOQ. wooziness
Related adjective: dinic

verve *n*

vitality, vivacity, animation, energy, dash, élan, liveliness, sparkle, vigour, passion, fervour, enthusiasm, gusto, life, relish, spirit, force, brio
COLLOQ. pizzazz, zip
⊟ apathy, lethargy

very *adv, adj*

◆ *adv*

extremely, greatly, highly, deeply, truly, remarkably, excessively, exceedingly, most exceptionally, acutely, particularly, really, quite, absolutely, noticeably, unbelievably, incredibly, unusually, uncommonly; *Scot* unco; *N Am* mighty
COLLOQ. pretty, terribly, dreadfully, awfully, ever so, real

SLANG majorly, mega
⊟ slightly, scarcely

◆ *adj*

actual, real, same, selfsame, identical, true, genuine, simple, utter, sheer, pure, perfect, ideal, plain, mere, bare, exact, suitable, appropriate, fitting

---

SYNONYM NUANCES

adverb

You can use **extremely**, **greatly** and **highly** in many contexts to suggest a large extent: *highly critical*. **Deeply**, however, implies being emotionally affected: *deeply disturbing*, and **acutely** can also imply something is keenly felt: *acutely embarrassed*. **Truly** suggests something is irrefutable: *this is a truly momentous event*. **Remarkably**, however, might be used approvingly of something with a degree of distinction: *a remarkably clever novel*, and while **exceptionally** and **exceedingly** also convey this idea of standing out in a more neutral way, the word **excessively** implies it is too much: *an excessively clever novel that does not engage the emotions*.

The term **particularly** sets up a comparison against other examples: *of all novels, this one is particularly bad*, while **really** is more informal in tone and tends to suggest strong feeling on the part of the speaker: *it was a really good day*, and **absolutely** would convey even less reservation: *an absolutely brilliant day*. **Quite**, on the other hand, is rather more formal in tone, and suggests a degree of qualification or restraint: *I was quite beside myself with anger*.

The term **noticeably**, in its suggestion that something is simply apparent, does not give the same sense of intensity: *he was noticeably upset*, whereas both **unbelievably** and **incredibly**, in their suggestion of an unlikely degree, have far greater force: *you have been unbelievably stupid*.

---

vessel *n*

1 SHIP, boat, craft, barque
2 CONTAINER, bowl, receptacle, holder, jar, pot, pitcher, jug, cruse

vest *v*

give, endow, entrust, supply, grant, empower, authorize, sanction
FORMAL bestow, confer

vestibule *n*

foyer, hall, hallway, entrance, entrance hall, entranceway, lobby, porch, anteroom, portico

vestige *n*

trace, suspicion, touch, indication, sign, mark, track, impression, print, hint, evidence, inkling, glimmer, token, scrap, remains, remainder, remnant, residue, relics
COLLOQ. whiff

vestigial *adj*

remaining, surviving, rudimentary, undeveloped, imperfect, incomplete, reduced, functionless

vet *v*

investigate, examine, check (out), scrutinize, scan, inspect, survey, review, screen, audit
FORMAL appraise

veteran *n, adj*

◆ *n*

master, pastmaster, old hand, old stager, old-timer, warhorse
COLLOQ. pro
⊟ novice, recruit

◆ *adj*

experienced, practised, seasoned, long-serving, expert, adept, proficient, old, battle-scarred, case-hardened
⊟ inexperienced

veto v, n

♦ v

reject, turn down, forbid, ban, prohibit, rule out, block, negate, blackball
FORMAL disallow, proscribe, interdict
COLLOQ. give the thumbs-down to
SLANG nix
E3 approve, sanction

♦ n

rejection, ban, embargo, prohibition
FORMAL proscription
COLLOQ. thumbs-down
E3 approval, assent

vex v

irritate, annoy, provoke, pester, trouble, upset, worry, bother, harass, disturb, distress, agitate, enrage, exasperate, torment, fret, rile
FORMAL perturb
COLLOQ. put out, hassle, aggravate, needle, bug, brass off, cheese off, get someone's blood up, get someone's back up, wind up, rub up the wrong way, get on someone's nerves, get up someone's nose, get under someone's skin, get someone's goat, get on someone's wick, make someone's hackles rise; N Am tick/hack off
E3 calm, soothe

vexation n

annoyance, exasperation, displeasure, chagrin, anger, fury, pique, dissatisfaction, frustration, nuisance, misfortune, irritant, problem, trouble, upset, worry, bother, difficulty, bore
COLLOQ. headache, pain, bind, thorn in the flesh, aggravation
SLANG pain in the backside/arse; N Am pain in the ass/butt

vexatious adj

annoying, irritating, troublesome, upsetting, worrying, irksome, nagging, exasperating, infuriating, distressing, disappointing, bothersome, burdensome, disagreeable, unpleasant, trying, worrisome, provoking, teasing, tormenting, afflicting
FORMAL pestiferous
COLLOQ. aggravating, pesky
E3 pleasant, soothing

vexed adj

1 IRRITATED, annoyed, provoked, upset, troubled, worried, irate, incensed, infuriated, put out, exasperated, bothered, confused, perplexed, harassed, ruffled, riled, disturbed, flustered, distressed, displeased, agitated
COLLOQ. nettled, aggravated, hassled, peeved, miffed, narked
2 a vexed question
difficult, controversial, contested, disputed, in dispute, debated, awkward, tough, knotty, tricky, ticklish
FORMAL moot
COLLOQ. dicey, sticky

viability n

feasibility, practicability, achievability, workability, practicality, reasonableness, possibility, expedience

viable adj

feasible, practicable, possible, workable, usable, operable, achievable, sustainable, sound
E3 impossible, unworkable

vibes n

atmosphere, aura, ambience, feel, feelings, emotions, vibrations, reaction, response, emanation

vibrancy n

vitality, life, liveliness, animation, vigour, energy, vivacity, spirit, sparkle, exuberance, zest, strength, stamina
COLLOQ. go, get-up-and-go, oomph, pizzazz

vibrant adj

1 ANIMATED, vivacious, lively, energetic, vigorous, responsive, sparkling, spirited, sensitive, thrilling, dynamic, electrifying, electric

2 vibrant colours
vivid, bright, brilliant, colourful, striking

vibrate v

quiver, pulsate, shudder, shiver, resonate, reverberate, resound, throb, oscillate, tremble, undulate, sway, swing, shake, flutter, jar, quake, tingle, twinkle, warble, shimmy; dialect thirl; Scot dinnle, dirl, hotter
FORMAL pendulate

vibration n

quiver, pulsation, pulse, shudder, judder, juddering, resonance, reverberation, resounding, throb, throbbing, oscillation, trembling, tremor, shaking, flutter, jarring, quake, tingle, twinkle, frisson; Scot dirl, hotter

vicar n

minister, priest, chaplain, clergyman, clergywoman, parson, pastor, rector, curate, cleric, preacher
OLD arch-priest

vicarious adj

indirect, second-hand, substituted, surrogate, delegated, deputed, acting, commissioned
FORMAL empathetic

vice n

1 EVIL, evil-doing, wrongdoing, immorality, depravity, wickedness, sin, corruption, degeneracy
FORMAL iniquity, profligacy, transgression
2 FAULT, failing, defect, shortcoming, weakness, imperfection, foible, flaw, blemish, bad habit, besetting sin
E3 1 virtue, morality

vice versa adv

conversely, reciprocally, oppositely, contrariwise, the other way round, inversely

vicinity n

neighbourhood, surroundings, surrounding district/area, area, locality, district, precincts, environs, proximity
FORMAL propinquity

vicious adj

1 SAVAGE, wild, violent, fierce, barbarous, brutal, cruel, ferocious, dangerous, lethal
2 MALICIOUS, spiteful, vindictive, virulent, cruel, malevolent, mean, nasty, slanderous, venomous, caustic, defamatory, brutal, Rottweiler
COLLOQ. bitchy, catty
3 WICKED, bad, wrong, immoral, depraved, unprincipled, degenerate, diabolical, corrupt, debased, perverted, vile, heinous
FORMAL profligate
E3 1 gentle **2** kind **3** virtuous

viciously adv

brutally, savagely, wildly, violently, fiercely, cruelly, lethally
E3 gently, kindly

viciousness n

savagery, brutality, cruelty, ferocity, virulence, spite, spitefulness, venom, malice, wickedness, badness, rancour, immorality, corruption, sinfulness, depravity
FORMAL profligacy, vitiosity, viciosity
COLLOQ. bitchiness
E3 goodness, gentleness, virtue

vicissitude n

change, variation, alteration, alternation, shift, turn, revolution, deviation, divergence, fluctuation, twist
FORMAL mutation

victim n

sufferer, casualty, prey, quarry, scapegoat, fool, martyr, sacrifice, fatality, murderee, nebbich
OLD host
COLLOQ. dupe, sucker, fall guy, sitting target, sitting duck, muggee, angel, mark
SLANG N Am patsy
E3 offender, attacker

■ **fall victim to**
succumb to, be overcome by, be attacked by,
be stricken with, catch, contract, develop, fall prey to,
become a target of, be deceived by, be taken in by
COLLOQ. fall for
SLANG be taken for a ride by

victimize *v*
1 OPPRESS, persecute, discriminate against, pick on,
zprey on, bully, exploit, take (unfair) advantage of
COLLOQ. have it in for
2 CHEAT, deceive, trick, defraud, dupe, hoodwink, fleece,
fool
COLLOQ. swindle, frame, do, con, bamboozle, sting, rook,
stitch up, shaft, put one over on, pull the wool over
someone's eyes
SLANG rip off, take for a ride, take to the cleaners

victor *n*
winner, conqueror, champion, first, prize-winner
FORMAL subjugator, vanquisher, victor ludorum
COLLOQ. champ, top dog
E∃ loser; *formal* vanquished

victorious *adj*
conquering, champion, triumphant, winning,
unbeaten, successful, prize-winning, top, first
FORMAL vanquishing
E∃ defeated, unsuccessful

victory *n*
conquest, win, triumph, success, superiority,
mastery, subjugation, overcoming, landslide;
dialect gree
FORMAL vanquishment
TECHNICAL triple crown
COLLOQ. walk-away, walkover
E∃ defeat, loss, failure

victuals *n*
food, provisions, supplies, stores, edibles, bread,
rations, sustenance, comestibles
FORMAL aliment, viands
COLLOQ. eatables, eats, tuck, scran
SLANG grub, nosh, chow

vie *v*
strive, compete, contend, struggle, contest,
fight, rival

view *n, v*
♦ *n*
1 OPINION, attitude, belief, judgement, point of view,
viewpoint, angle, thought, conviction, estimation,
feeling, sentiment, impression, idea, notion
2 SIGHT, scene, vision, range of vision, vista, spectacle,
outlook, prospect, perspective, panorama, landscape,
composition
3 SURVEY, inspection, examination, observation, study,
contemplation, scrutiny, scan, assessment, review
4 DESCRIPTION, account, impression, picture, portrait,
portrayal, sketch
5 GLIMPSE, look, sight, perception
♦ *v*
1 OBSERVE, watch, see, look at, examine, inspect,
gaze at, scrutinize, scan, survey, witness, perceive
FORMAL descry, espy
2 CONSIDER, regard, contemplate, judge, reflect on,
think about, speculate
■ **in view of**
considering, bearing in mind, taking into account,
taking into consideration
■ **on view**
on show, showing, shown, on display, displayed,
made public, presented, exhibited

viewer *n*
spectator, watcher, observer, onlooker

viewpoint *n*
attitude, position, perspective, slant, standpoint, stance,
opinion, angle, feeling

vigil *n*
watch, wakefulness, wake, lookout, sleeplessness,
stake-out
FORMAL pernoctation

vigilance *n*
watchfulness, alertness, attentiveness, observation,
carefulness, caution, guardedness, wakefulness
FORMAL circumspection

vigilant *adj*
watchful, alert, attentive, observant,
on your guard, on the lookout, on the watch,
on the qui vive, cautious, jealous, aware, careful,
wide-awake, awake, wakeful, waking, sleepless,
unsleeping
FORMAL circumspect
E∃ careless

vigilante *n*
guard, neighbourhood watch, watch(man),
watchperson, security guard, armed guard, lookout,
sentinel; *N Am* Guardian Angel

vignette *n*
sketch, drawing, design, plan, diagram, outline,
skeleton, abstract, draft, representation, scene,
act, turn, cameo

vigorous *adj*
1 HEALTHY, energetic, active, lively, strong, strenuous,
tough, athletic, robust, lusty, sound, vital
2 DYNAMIC, forceful, forcible, powerful, stout,
spirited, full-blooded, effective, efficient, brisk,
enterprising, flourishing, lively, animated, punchy,
sparkling, intense
E∃ **1, 2** weak, feeble

vigorously *adv*
briskly, hard, forcefully, energetically,
eagerly, heartily, powerfully, strongly,
strenuously, lustily
E∃ feebly, weakly

vigour *n*
energy, vitality, liveliness, health, robustness,
stamina, strength, resilience, sturdiness, toughness,
soundness, spirit, verve, gusto, activity, animation,
power, potency, force, forcefulness, might, dash,
dynamism
FORMAL vivacity
COLLOQ. zip, oomph, pep, brio, pizzazz
E∃ weakness

SYNONYM NUANCES

Energy is a widely applicable synonym for the body's
capacity for physical and mental activity, while **vitality**
and **liveliness** have connotations of a zest for life, and
health, **robustness**, **soundness** and **strength**
emphasize physical wellbeing and fortitude. **Stamina**, on
the other hand, is more suggestive of the ability to last,
whereas **sturdiness** and **toughness** suggest
intractability, and **resilience** an ability to endure and
recover from misfortune: *he fought his illness with
characteristic resilience.*

    While **activity** is widely used to suggest any
movement, **animation** conveys the idea of spirit and
feeling: *we knew by his animation that he was thrilled at
the idea of a party.* **Spirit**, **verve** and **gusto** return to the
idea of vibrancy and enthusiasm: *the sheer verve of his
music makes you want to dance,* while **dash** also
suggests a degree of swaggering.

    Power, **potency** and **force** return to the idea of
effectiveness, and **dynamism** has very positive
implications of powerful drive: *I love the dynamism of
contemporary jazz.* **Forcefulness**, although similar, has
less positive overtones, and possible further implications
of imposition: *the forcefulness with which he projected
his views was disturbing,* while **might** suggests potential
supremacy: *military might.*

vile *adj*

1 *vile weather; a vile meal*
disgusting, foul, nasty, unpleasant, disagreeable, horrible, horrid, nauseating, sickening, repulsive, repugnant, revolting, obnoxious, offensive, distasteful, loathsome
OLD vild, vilde
FORMAL noxious
COLLOQ. beastly
2 EVIL, base, contemptible, debased, low, depraved, degenerate, bad, wicked, wretched, worthless, sinful, detestable, miserable, mean, impure, corrupt, earthly, despicable, disgraceful, degrading, vicious, appalling, infamous, villainous, scurvy
OLD vild, vilde, scabbed
FORMAL iniquitous
E3 **1** pleasant, lovely **2** pure, worthy

vileness *n*
foulness, nastiness, unpleasantness, dreadfulness, meanness, offensiveness, outrage, ugliness, wickedness, corruption, depravity, baseness, evil, profanity
FORMAL degeneracy, noxiousness

vilification *n*
criticism, defamation, abuse, denigration, scurrility
FORMAL aspersion, calumniation, calumny, contumely, disparagement, invective, revilement, vituperation
COLLOQ. mud-slinging

vilify *v*
criticize, snipe, slate, revile, denigrate, run down, denounce, slander, defame, stigmatize, abuse, smear, debase
FORMAL malign, disparage, asperse, berate, calumniate, decry, traduce, vilipend, vituperate
COLLOQ. badmouth, slam, knock, rubbish
SLANG slag (off)
E3 praise, compliment, adore, eulogize, glorify

village *n*
hamlet, community, settlement, town
COLLOQ. one-horse town

villain *n*
evildoer, wrongdoer, scoundrel, rogue, criminal, reprobate, knave, rascal, wretch, devil, heavy, thug, bravo
OLD scelerate
FORMAL miscreant, malefactor
COLLOQ. baddy
E3 hero, heroine; *colloq.* goody

villainous *adj*
wicked, bad, criminal, evil, sinful, vicious, notorious, cruel, inhuman, vile, depraved, debased, degenerate, disgraceful, terrible, fiendish
FORMAL heinous, nefarious, iniquitous, opprobrious
E3 good

villainy *n*
wickedness, viciousness, badness, crime, criminality, delinquency, atrocity, depravity, baseness, vice, sin, rascality, roguery, knavery
FORMAL iniquity, turpitude

vindicate *v*
1 CLEAR, acquit, excuse, absolve, rehabilitate
FORMAL exonerate, exculpate
2 JUSTIFY, right, uphold, support, back, maintain, sustain, champion, defend, establish, advocate, assert, verify, confirm, warrant
OLD darraign, salve
FORMAL corroborate

vindication *n*
justification, defence, plea, excuse, assertion, apology, support, maintenance, substantiation, verification, rehabilitation, extenuation
FORMAL exculpation, exoneration
E3 accusation, conviction

vindictive *adj*
spiteful, unforgiving, implacable, vengeful, relentless, unrelenting, revengeful, resentful, punitive, venomous, malicious, malevolent, rancorous
OLD (*Shakesp*) vindicative
E3 forgiving

vintage *n, adj*
♦ *n*
year, period, era, epoch, generation, time, origin, harvest, gathering, crop
♦ *adj*
1 CHOICE, best, fine, prime, quality, high-quality, select, superior, supreme, mature, ripe
2 *a vintage Beatles song*
classic, archetypal, ageless, timeless, enduring, old, veteran

violate *v*
1 CONTRAVENE, disobey, disregard, break, flout, offend, infringe, breach
OLD (*Shakesp*) fract
FORMAL transgress, infract
2 OUTRAGE, debauch, defile, abuse, rape, ravish, molest, dishonour, desecrate, profane, invade, disturb, interfere with, disrupt, wreck
OLD stuprate, vitiate
FORMAL despoil
E3 **1** observe

violation *n*
breach, contravention, offence, outrage, infringement, trespass, abuse, disruption, encroachment, profanation, sacrilege, defilement, rape, desecration
OLD stupration, vitiation
FORMAL infraction, spoliation, transgression
E3 obedience, observance

violence *n*
1 FORCE, strength, power, forcefulness, vehemence, intensity, passion, ferocity, fierceness, severity, tumult, turbulence, wildness
FORMAL might
2 BRUTALITY, aggression, roughness, destructiveness, cruelty, bloodshed, murderousness, savagery, passion, wildness, fighting, frenzy, fury, hostilities

violent *adj*
1 CRUEL, brutal, aggressive, fierce, ferocious, bloodthirsty, impetuous, hot-headed, headstrong, murderous, savage, wild, vicious, unrestrained, uncontrollable, ungovernable, passionate, furious, intemperate, maddened, outrageous, riotous, fiery, destructive
2 INTENSE, strong, severe, sharp, acute, extreme, great, dramatic, harmful, destructive, devastating, injurious, powerful, painful, agonizing, excruciating, forceful, forcible, harsh, ruinous, rough, vehement, passionate, tumultuous, turbulent
E3 **1** peaceful, gentle **2** calm, moderate

violently *adv*
1 CRUELLY, brutally, aggressively, wildly, savagely, viciously, fiercely, ferociously, impetuously, hot-headedly, uncontrollably
2 INTENSELY, strongly, severely, sharply, extremely, greatly, powerfully, dramatically
E3 **1** gently, peacefully **2** moderately

VIP *n*
celebrity, luminary, magnate, somebody, notable, personage, dignitary, star, headliner, lion
COLLOQ. bigwig, big name, big noise, big shot, big cheese, heavyweight, top dog
E3 nobody, nonentity

virago *n*
shrew, termagant, vixen, tartar, scold, harridan, dragon, fury, gorgon, Xanthippe
COLLOQ. battle-axe

virgin *n, adj*
- *n*

girl, maiden, celibate, vestal
OLD maid, pucelle
- *adj*

virginal, chaste, intact, immaculate, maiden, maidenly, pure, modest, new, fresh, spotless, stainless, undefiled, unblemished, untainted, untouched, unspoilt, unsullied

virginal *adj*

pure, spotless, virgin, untouched, undefiled, uncorrupted, undisturbed, stainless, white, snowy, vestal, immaculate, chaste, fresh, celibate, maidenly
FORMAL pristine

virginity *n*

purity, chastity, chasteness, maidenhood, virtue, honour, innocence

virile *adj*

man-like, masculine, male, manly, robust, muscular, strapping, vigorous, potent, lusty, red-blooded, forceful, strong, rugged
COLLOQ. macho
E3 effeminate, impotent

virility *n*

manhood, manliness, masculinity, ruggedness, vigour, huskiness, potency, machismo
E3 effeminacy, impotence, weakness

virtual *adj*

effective, in effect, essential, practical, for all practical purposes, in all but name, implied, implicit, potential, prospective

virtually *adv*

practically, effectively, in effect, almost, nearly, as good as, more or less, for all practical purposes, in all but name, in essence, conceivably, to all intents and purposes

virtue *n*

1 GOODNESS, morality, uprightness, worthiness, righteousness, integrity, honesty, honour, incorruptibility, justice, high-mindedness, excellence
FORMAL rectitude, probity
2 QUALITY, worth, merit, advantage, benefit, asset, credit, strength
COLLOQ. plus
E3 **1** vice
■ **by virtue of**
because of, on account of, by means of, owing to, with the help of, thanks to, by way of
FORMAL by dint of

> **QUOTATIONS**
> For that which all men then did virtue call, / Is now called vice, and that which vice was hight, / Is now hight virtue, and so used of all: / Right now is wrong, and wrong that was is right
> EDMUND SPENSER, *The Faerie Queen*

virtuosity *n*

skill, mastery, expertise, artistry, brilliance, polish, finesse, flair, panache, éclat, finish, wizardry, bravura

virtuoso *n, adj*
- *n*

expert, master, maestro, prodigy, genius
- *adj*

skilful, masterly, expert, brilliant, excellent, dazzling

virtuous *adj*

good, moral, righteous, upright, upstanding, worthy, honourable, honest, irreproachable, incorruptible, exemplary, unimpeachable, ethical, high-principled, blameless, respectable, decent, clean-living, temperate, moderate, continent, innocent, excellent, angelic, above/beyond suspicion, keeping to the straight and narrow
OLD graced, virtual
COLLOQ. squeaky-clean
E3 immoral, vicious

virulence *n*

1 POISON, venom, toxicity, deadliness
2 HOSTILITY, bitterness, resentment, hurtfulness, harmfulness, spite, vindictiveness, viciousness, acrimony, antagonism, malevolence, malice, malignancy, spleen, vitriol, hatred
FORMAL rancour

virulent *adj*

1 POISONOUS, toxic, venomous, deadly, fatal, lethal, malignant, injurious, pernicious, severe, intense, extreme
2 HOSTILE, resentful, spiteful, acrimonious, bitter, blistering, vicious, vindictive, malicious, malevolent, rancorous, vitriolic, waspish
E3 **1** harmless **2** amicable, kind

visa *n*

permit, pass, passport, licence, warrant, authorization, sanction, permission, safe-conduct, docket, carnet, green card, laissez-passer, *permis de séjour*

vis-à-vis *prep*

in comparison with, as regards, in relation to, over against, opposite, facing

viscera *n*

innards, insides, intestines, vitals, bowels, entrails, gralloch

viscous *adj*

sticky, adhesive, gluey, thick, clammy, mucous, tacky, syrupy, treacly, gummy, tenacious, viscid
FORMAL gelatinous, glutinous, mucilaginous
COLLOQ. gooey
E3 runny, thin, watery

visible *adj*

perceptible, discernible, detectable, apparent, noticeable, observable, perceivable, recognizable, distinguishable, discoverable, evident, in evidence, in sight, visual, unconcealed, undisguised, unmistakable, conspicuous, showing, clear, exposed, obvious, open, overt, palpable, plain, patent, manifest
OLD aspectable
E3 invisible, indiscernible, hidden

visibly *adv*

perceptibly, noticeably, evidently, clearly, obviously, manifestly, openly, overtly, plainly, conspicuously, patently
E3 invisibly, indiscernibly

vision *n*

1 SIGHT, seeing, eyesight, perception, discernment, far-sightedness, foresight, penetration
2 IDEA, ideal, conception, insight, perception, intuition, view, picture, image, mental image/picture, imagination, fantasy, dream, daydream; *Irish* aisling
3 APPARITION, hallucination, dream, illusion, optical illusion, delusion, mirage, phantom, ghost, chimera, spectre, wraith

> **QUOTATIONS**
> Where there is no vision, the people perish
> *Bible, Proverbs*

visionary *adj, n*
- *adj*

idealistic, impractical, romantic, dreamy, unrealistic, utopian, quixotic, unreal, fanciful, prophetic, perceptive, discerning, far-sighted, speculative, unworkable, illusory, imaginary
COLLOQ. moonshiny, ivory-tower
- *n*

idealist, romantic, dreamer, daydreamer, fantasist, prophet, mystic, seer, utopian, Don Quixote, rainbow-chaser, theorist
E3 pragmatist

visit v, n

♦ v

1 *visit her brother*
call on, call in, call round, go and see, go round/over to, stay with, stay at, look in, look up, see, spend time with, stop off at/over at/in at, take, frequent, haunt; *dialect* mump; *N Am* come by, stop by
FORMAL wait on/upon
COLLOQ. drop in on, drop by, swing by, pop in, blow in
2 INFLICT, punish, trouble, afflict, curse, plague
OLD smite

♦ n

call, stay, stop, excursion, pop-visit
OLD salutation
FORMAL sojourn

visitation n
1 VISIT, inspection, examination
2 INFLICTION, punishment, retribution, catastrophe, disaster, calamity, bane, blight, scourge, ordeal, trial, cataclysm
3 APPEARANCE, manifestation

visitor n
caller, guest, company, tourist, traveller, holidaymaker

vista n
view, prospect, panorama, perspective, outlook, scene, vision

visual adj
visible, observable, discernible, perceptible, optical
FORMAL ocular, optic, specular

visualize v
picture, envisage, imagine, see, conceive (of), contemplate

vital adj
1 CRITICAL, crucial, important, imperative, key, significant, basic, fundamental, essential, necessary, indispensable, urgent, life-and-death, decisive, forceful
FORMAL requisite
2 LIVELY, alive, living, life-giving, invigorating, spirited, vivacious, vibrant, vigorous, forceful, dynamic, animated, energetic
FORMAL quickening
1 inessential, peripheral **2** dead

vitality n
life, liveliness, animation, vigour, energy, vivacity, spirit, sparkle, exuberance, zest, strength, stamina, juice; *Scot* foison, fushion, fizzen
OLD vivency
COLLOQ. go, get-up-and-go, oomph, pizzazz, bounce, zap, zing

vitally adv
crucially, critically, significantly, importantly, fundamentally, essentially, urgently, decisively

vitamin

Vitamins include:

aneurin (or thiamine)	ergocalciferol	phylloquinone
ascorbic acid	folic acid	pteroic acid
bioflavonoid/citrin	linoleic acid	pyridoxine (or
biotin	linolenic acid	adermin)
calciferol	menadione	retinol
cholecalciferol	nicotinic acid (or	riboflavin
cyanocobalamin	niacin)	tocopherol
	pantothenic acid	

---

vitiate v
spoil, mar, weaken, undermine, deteriorate, harm, injure, blemish, ruin, sully, taint, corrupt, pervert, pollute, debase, contaminate, blight, defile, invalidate, nullify, devalue, deprave, impair

vitriolic adj
bitter, abusive, virulent, vicious, venomous, malicious, acrimonious, caustic, biting, sardonic, scathing, destructive
FORMAL acerbic, mordant, trenchant, vituperative

vituperate v
blame, revile, slate, run down, reproach, censure, denounce, abuse
FORMAL berate, castigate, upbraid, vilify
COLLOQ. slam, nag, knock, rubbish
SLANG slag (off)
praise, applaud, extol

vituperation n
censure, rebuke, reprimand, reproach, blame, abuse, fault-finding, scurrility
FORMAL castigation, invective, obloquy, revilement, contumely, diatribe, philippic, vilification, objurgation
COLLOQ. flak, stick, knocking, rubbishing
SLANG slagging(-off)
acclaim, praise

vituperative adj
censorious, harsh, insulting, abusive, scornful, derogatory, defamatory, scurrilous, withering, belittling, sardonic
FORMAL calumniatory, denunciatory, fulminatory, opprobrious
laudatory

vivacious adj
lively, animated, spirited, high-spirited, effervescent, cheerful, jolly, merry, sparkling, light-hearted
FORMAL ebullient
COLLOQ. bubbly, chirpy, bouncy

vivacity n
liveliness, spirit, animation, energy, quickness, vitality, dynamism, activity, élan, effervescence, light-heartedness, merriness
FORMAL ebullience
COLLOQ. brio, go, get-up-and-go, oomph, pizzazz, bounce, zap, zing

vivid adj
1 BRIGHT, colourful, intense, strong, rich, vibrant, brilliant, glowing, dazzling, glaring, lurid, vigorous, expressive, dramatic, flamboyant, animated, dynamic, lively, lifelike, spirited
2 MEMORABLE, powerful, graphic, clear, distinct, striking, dramatic, lively, sharp, realistic
1 colourless, dull **2** vague

vividly adv
1 *vividly coloured*
brightly, intensely, strongly, richly, vibrantly, brilliantly, dramatically, flamboyantly
2 *I remember her vividly*
clearly, distinctly, powerfully, memorably, graphically
1 dully **2** vaguely

vividness n
intensity, strength, glow, brilliancy, brightness, lucidity, radiance, realism, clarity, sharpness, immediacy, life, liveliness, distinctness
FORMAL refulgence, resplendence
dullness, lifelessness

viz adv
namely, that is, ie, specifically, that is to say, in other words
FORMAL to wit

vocabulary n
language, words, glossary, lexicon, dictionary, wordbook, thesaurus, idiom, cant, pidgin, slang
TECHNICAL lexis, idioticon
OLD nomenclature
COLLOQ. vocab
Related adjective: vocabularian

vocal adj
1 SPOKEN, said, oral, uttered, expressed, voiced
2 ARTICULATE, eloquent, expressive, noisy, clamorous, shrill, strident, outspoken, frank, blunt, forthright, plain-spoken, vociferous
1 unspoken **2** inarticulate

vocalize v
express, articulate, verbalize, put into words, utter, voice, give voice to, say, speak, state, communicate, put/get over, pronounce, word, tell, announce, report, assert, declare, put across, formulate, point out, intimate, convey, vent, ventilate, air
FORMAL enunciate

vocally adv
articulately, eloquently, expressively, stridently, forthrightly

vocation n
calling, pursuit, career, métier, mission, profession, occupation, trade, employment, work, craft, role, line, post, job, business, office

vociferous adj
noisy, vocal, clamorous, loud, obstreperous, strident, vehement, thundering, shouting, outspoken, frank, blunt, forthright
🗲 quiet

vociferously adv
loudly, noisily, vocally, stridently, vehemently, bluntly, frankly, outspokenly
🗲 quietly

vogue n
fashion, style, taste, craze, popularity, trend, prevalence, acceptance, custom
FORMAL mode
COLLOQ. fad, the latest, the rage, the thing
■ **in vogue**
fashionable, on-trend, modish, popular, stylish, trendy, up-to-the-minute, voguish, current, prevalent
COLLOQ. in, with it

voice n, v
♦ n
1 SPEECH, utterance, articulation, language, words, sound, tone, intonation, inflection, expression, mouthpiece, agency, vehicle, medium, instrument, organ
Related adjective: vocal
2 SAY, vote, opinion, view, decision, option, will, desire, wish, airing
♦ v
express, say, utter, air, articulate, speak of, talk of, mention, verbalize, assert, convey, disclose, divulge, declare, enunciate

void adj, n, v
♦ adj
1 EMPTY, emptied, free, unfilled, unoccupied, vacant, clear, bare, blank, drained, lacking, devoid
2 ANNULLED, inoperative, invalid, cancelled, nullified, ineffective, futile, useless, vain, worthless, nugatory
🗲 1 full 2 valid, binding
♦ n
emptiness, vacuity, vacuum, abyss, chasm, blank, blankness, space, lack, want, cavity, gap, hollow, opening
FORMAL lacuna
♦ v
1 NULLIFY, cancel, annul, invalidate, rescind
TECHNICAL avoid
FORMAL abnegate
2 DISCHARGE, eject, defecate, emit, empty, drain, evacuate
🗲 1 validate 2 fill

volatile adj
changeable, inconstant, unstable, variable, erratic, irregular, temperamental, unsteady, unsettled, fickle, whimsical, unpredictable, fitful, restless, giddy, flighty, lively, volcanic, explosive, skittish, light-winged, rattle-brained, rattle-headed, rattle-pated
FORMAL mercurial, capricious
COLLOQ. up and down
🗲 constant, steady

volatility n
instability, capriciousness, flightiness, fitfulness, fickleness, inconstancy, unsteadiness, shakiness, irresolution, uncertainty, changeableness, variability, fluctuation, unreliability, insecurity, precariousness
🗲 constancy, stability

volition n
will, free will, choice, choosing, determination, option, election, preference, discretion, purpose, resolution
■ **of your own volition**
of your own free will, voluntarily, willingly, freely, intentionally, consciously, deliberately, purposely, spontaneously, by choice, on your own initiative, of your own accord
🗲 involuntarily, unwillingly

volley n
barrage, salvo, bombardment, cannonade, fusillade, hail, shower, burst, blast, discharge, explosion

volte-face n
about-turn, about-face, (complete) reversal, turnabout
FORMAL enantiodromia
COLLOQ. U-turn

voluble adj
fluent, glib, articulate, talkative, forthcoming, garrulous
FORMAL loquacious
COLLOQ. chatty

volume n
1 BOOK, tome, publication
FORMAL omnibus
2 BULK, size, capacity, space, dimensions, amount, mass, quantity, aggregate, amplitude, body
3 LOUDNESS, sound, noise, amplification
TECHNICAL decibels

voluminous adj
roomy, big, ample, spacious, billowing, vast, full, bulky, huge, large
FORMAL capacious

voluntarily adv
willingly, freely, intentionally, consciously, deliberately, purposely, spontaneously, of your own free will, by choice, on your own initiative, of your own accord
🗲 involuntarily, unwillingly

voluntary adj
1 FREE, gratuitous, optional, spontaneous, unforced, willing, volunteer, unpaid, without pay, unsalaried, honorary
2 CONSCIOUS, deliberate, purposeful, intended, intentional, wilful, optional, of your own free will
FORMAL of your own volition
🗲 1 compulsory, obligatory 2 involuntary

volunteer v, n
♦ v
offer, propose, put forward, come forward, present, suggest, step forward, advance, tender
OLD voluntary
FORMAL proffer
♦ n
voluntary worker, community-service worker, doer, activist, participant, recruit, helping hand
COLLOQ. do-gooder

voluptuary n
hedonist, sensualist, epicurean, pleasure-seeker, libertine, sybarite, debauchee, bon vivant, bon viveur
FORMAL profligate
COLLOQ. playboy
🗲 ascetic

voluptuous adj
1 SENSUAL, licentious, luxurious, self-indulgent, hedonistic, sensuous, opulent
2 EROTIC, shapely, buxom, full-figured, curvaceous, seductive, provocative, enticing
COLLOQ. sexy, beddable

vomit v
be sick, bring up, heave, retch, regurgitate

COLLOQ. throw up, puke, spew, sick up, chuck up, fetch up
SLANG *N Am* barf, upchuck; *Aust* chunder

vomiting *n*
sickness, retching, regurgitation, emission, ejection, chundering
TECHNICAL emesis
OLD parbreak
COLLOQ. puking, spewing
SLANG *N Am* barfing

voracious *adj*
insatiable, greedy, hungry, gluttonous, acquisitive, avid, devouring, ravenous, ravening, uncontrolled, unquenchable
FORMAL edacious, omnivorous, prodigious, rapacious

voracity *n*
greed, hunger, ravenousness, eagerness, acquisitiveness, avidity
FORMAL edacity, rapacity

vortex *n*
whirlpool, maelstrom, eddy, whirlwind, whirl

votary *n*
believer, follower, disciple, devotee, addict, adherent

vote *n, v*
♦ *n*
1 *to cast your vote*
ballot, poll, election, franchise, referendum, plebiscite, yes, no
OLD yea, nay
2 *give everyone the vote*
franchise, suffrage, enfranchisement
⊟ disenfranchisement
♦ *v*
elect, ballot, go to the polls, re-elect, choose, opt for, go for, plump for, suggest, put in, declare, return
■ **vote in**
elect, vote for, choose, pick, opt for, select, decide on, prefer, adopt, designate, appoint, determine, co-opt, return
OLD voice
COLLOQ. plump for
■ **vote out**
remove, oust, overthrow, dismiss, unseat, topple, displace, demote, dethrone
COLLOQ. boot out, turf out

> **QUOTATIONS**
> Vote, n. The instrument and symbol of a freeman's power to make a fool of himself and a wreck of his country
>   AMBROSE BIERCE, *The Cynic's Word Book*

voter *n*
vote, constituent, member of the electorate, franchiser, balloter, floating voter, no, yes, citizen, free person, burgher, outvoter
OLD yea, nay, faggot, ten-pounder; *N Am* colonist

vouch
■ **vouch for**
guarantee, assure, warrant, support, back, endorse, confirm, answer for, certify, affirm, verify, assert, speak for, swear to, uphold
FORMAL attest to, asseverate

voucher *n*
coupon, token, ticket, document, paper, chit, note, warrant, gift token/voucher, book token, luncheon voucher

vouchsafe *v*
give, grant, impart, deign, yield, cede
FORMAL bestow, confer, accord

vow *v, n*
♦ *v*
promise, pledge, swear, give your word, undertake, dedicate, devote, profess, consecrate, affirm; *Scot* hight
OLD behight, bename; *(Shakesp)* protest
FORMAL nuncupate
♦ *n*
promise, oath, pledge
OLD avow, hest; *(Spenser)* heast, heaste
FORMAL nuncupation
Related adjectives: votive

voyage *n, v*
♦ *n*
journey, travel(s), trip, passage, expedition, crossing, cruise, sail, tour, safari, course, rough passage
OLD navigation, shipping, traffic, middle passage
FORMAL odyssey
♦ *v*
journey, travel, go, cruise, sail, tour, go/put to sea

vulgar *adj*
1 INDECENT, obscene, coarse, improper, dirty, filthy, crude, suggestive, risqué, rude, indelicate, distasteful, offensive, off-colour, ribald, lewd, bawdy
COLLOQ. near the bone
2 UNREFINED, uncouth, coarse, rude, rough, common, crude, ill-bred, impolite, boorish
FORMAL indecorous
3 TASTELESS, flashy, showy, ostentatious, kitsch, garish, loud, gaudy, tawdry
COLLOQ. cheap and nasty, tacky, glitzy
4 ORDINARY, general, popular, vernacular, common, low, unsophisticated, uncultured
⊟ **1** decent **2** correct **3** tasteful, refined **4** sophisticated

vulgarity *n*
1 CRUDENESS, indecency, crudity, dirtiness, rudeness, suggestiveness, ribaldry, coarseness
2 TASTELESSNESS, tawdriness, gaudiness, showiness, ostentation, garishness
⊟ **1** decency, politeness **2** tastefulness

vulnerable *adj*
unprotected, exposed, unguarded, insecure, defenceless, in danger, exposed to danger, susceptible, weak, powerless, helpless, sensitive, open, open to attack, wide open
⊟ protected, strong, safe

W

wacky *adj*
crazy, silly, wild, eccentric, offbeat, irrational, odd, unpredictable, zany, erratic, daft
COLLOQ. bonkers, goofy, loopy, nutty, screwy
SLANG loony
E3 sensible

wad *n*
chunk, plug, roll, bundle, ball, lump, hunk, mass, block
COLLOQ. wodge

wadding *n*
packing, padding, stuffing, filling, filler, lining, cotton wool

waddle *v*
toddle, totter, wobble, sway, rock, shuffle

wade *v*
cross, ford, wallow, roll, welter, lurch, flounder, splash
FORMAL traverse

■ **wade in**
pitch in, launch in, tear in, set to, get stuck in, wade through, trawl through, plough through

waffle *v, n*
♦ *v*
jabber, prattle, babble; *Scot* blether; *dialect & N Am* blather
COLLOQ. rabbit on, witter on
♦ *n*
prattle, wordiness, verbosity, padding, nonsense; *Scot* blethers; *dialect & N Am* blathers
COLLOQ. gobbledygook, hot air, guff, wittering

waft *v, n*
♦ *v*
drift, float, glide, blow, transport, carry, transmit
♦ *n*
breath, puff, draught, current, breeze, scent, whiff

wag *v, n*
♦ *v*
shake, waggle, wave, sway, swing, bob, nod, wiggle, oscillate, wobble, flutter, vibrate, quiver, rock
♦ *n*
wit, joker, humorist, jester, comic, comedian, clown, fool, droll, banterer, gagman

wage *n, v*
♦ *n*
pay, fee, earnings, salary, wage-packet, payment, stipend, remuneration, allowance, reward, hire, compensation, returns, recompense, pittance
OLD meed, pension, imprest, penny-fee
FORMAL emolument
SLANG screw
♦ *v*
carry on, conduct, engage in, undertake, execute, practise, pursue, levy, war

> **QUOTATIONS**
> I don't pay good wages because I have a lot of money; I have a lot of money because I pay good wages
> ROBERT BOSCH

wager *v, n*
♦ *v*
bet, gamble, chance, risk, speculate, venture, stake, pledge, lay odds, hazard, punt
♦ *n*
bet, gamble, speculation, stake, venture, hazard, pledge, punt, flutter

waggish *adj*
amusing, mischievous, playful, sportive, funny, humorous, comical, droll, facetious, witty, impish, roguish, jesting, frolicsome, puckish, merry, bantering
FORMAL risible, jocular, jocose
E3 grave, serious, staid

waggle *v*
wiggle, wobble, shake, jiggle, wave, oscillate, wag, bobble, flutter

wagon *n*
cart, dray, carriage, truck, van, train, float, buggy

waif *n*
orphan, stray, ragamuffin, urchin, foundling

wail *v, n*
♦ *v*
moan, cry, howl, lament, weep, sob, complain, groan, keen
FORMAL ululate
COLLOQ. yowl
♦ *n*
moan, cry, howl, lament, complaint, groan, weeping, sob
FORMAL ululation

wait *v, n*
♦ *v*
delay, linger, hold back, hesitate, pause, remain, rest, stand, stand by, sit out, stay, await
OLD watch, expect, bide tryst
FORMAL abide, tarry, bide, bide your time
COLLOQ. hang around, hang on, hang fire, lick your chops
E3 proceed, go ahead
♦ *n*
hold-up, hesitation, delay, interval, pause, halt

■ **wait on**
serve, attend to, minister to, look after, take care of, tend, work for, see, dance attendance on

> **PROVERBS**
> All things come to those who wait

waiter, waitress *n*
server, attendant, steward, stewardess, host, hostess, butler, *garçon, maître d'hôtel*, sommelier, commis; *N Am* waitron, busboy, busgirl
COLLOQ. pannier, maître d'

waive *v*
give up, do without, for(e)go, abandon, set aside, resign, surrender, yield, cede, postpone, defer
FORMAL renounce, relinquish
E3 enforce, claim, maintain

waiver *n*
disclaimer, postponement, resignation, surrender, abandonment
FORMAL abdication, deferral, relinquishment, remission, renunciation

wake[1] v, n

♦ v

1 RISE, get up, arise, waken, awake, awaken, rouse, stir, come to, bring round
2 STIMULATE, stir, activate, arouse, animate, excite, fire, galvanize, prod, goad, whet
COLLOQ. egg on
3 ALERT, notify, warn, signal, make/become aware of, make/become conscious of
E3 1 sleep

♦ n

funeral, death-watch, vigil, watch, lichwake; *Scot* lykewake

wake[2] n

in the wake of the ship
trail, track, path, aftermath, backwash, wash, rear, train, waves

wakeful adj

sleepless, restless, insomniac, unsleeping, watchful, vigilant, observant, heedful, attentive, alert, wary; *Scot* wakerife, waukrife
E3 inattentive, sleepy, unwary

wakefulness n

sleeplessness, restlessness, insomnia, watchfulness, vigilance, attentiveness

waken v

wake, rise, get up, awake, awaken, arouse, rouse, stimulate, stir, whet, quicken, animate, activate, enliven, kindle, fire, ignite, galvanize

walk v, n

♦ v

1 GO ON FOOT
FORMAL perambulate
COLLOQ. hoof it, go on shanks's pony/mare, stretch your legs
2 ACCOMPANY, escort, guide, lead, conduct, usher, shepherd

♦ n

1 *he has an odd walk*
carriage, gait, step, pace, stride
2 *go for a walk*
stroll, amble, ramble, saunter, march, hike, tramp, promenade, trek, traipse, trudge, trail
3 *a tree-lined walk*
footpath, path, way, walkway, avenue, pathway, promenade, alley, esplanade, lane, drive, track, pavement, sidewalk
4 BEAT, round, rounds, circuit, way, path, route, trail

■ **walk of life**
occupation, profession, trade, field, area, sphere, line, activity, arena, course, pursuit, career, vocation, calling, métier, background

■ **walk off/away with**
go off with, make off with, run off with, steal, pocket
COLLOQ. pinch, nick, lift, filch, snaffle, knock up, nobble, knock off, swipe, whip, bag, nip, liberate, relieve of, help yourself to, have your fingers in the till; *Aust & NZ* duckshove, souvenir

■ **walk out**
go on strike, strike, stop work, down tools, protest, mutiny, revolt, take industrial action

■ **walk out on**
abandon, desert
FORMAL forsake
COLLOQ. run out on, jilt, dump, leave in the lurch, leave high and dry

■ **walk over**
trample on, take advantage of, take liberties, misuse, abuse, profiteer, oppress, ill-treat, impose on, manipulate
COLLOQ. put something across someone, pull a fast one on, play off against
SLANG take for a ride

Ways of walking include:

amble	*formal*	stride
bestride	perambulate	stroll
clump	plod	strut
crawl	potter	stumble
creep	power walking	stump
dodder	promenade	swagger
expatiate	prowl	tiptoe
hike	ramble	*colloq.* toddle
Scot hirple	roam	totter
hobble	sashay	traipse
Scot lamp	saunter	tramp
limp	scuttle	trample
lope	shamble	tread
lurch	shuffle	trek
march	sleepwalk	trip
mince	slink	troop
colloq. mooch	sneak	trot
colloq. mosey	somnambulate	trudge
pace	stagger	trundle
pad	stalk	waddle
paddle	steal	wade
parade	step	*colloq.* waltz
patter	stomp	wander
	Scot stot	*colloq.* yomp

walker n

pedestrian, rambler, hiker

walk-out n

strike, stoppage, industrial action, protest, rebellion, revolt

walkover n

easy win/victory
COLLOQ. pushover, doddle, child's play, piece of cake, cakewalk, cinch

walkway n

path, pathway, passage, footpath, lane, pavement, promenade, esplanade; *N Am* sidewalk

wall

Related adjective: mural

■ **wall in**
enclose, surround, encircle, encompass, ring, circle, fence, hedge, hem in, bound, envelop, confine, frame, cage, hold, shut in, close in, wrap, pen, corral
OLD *(Shakesp)* circummure
FORMAL circumscribe

■ **go to the wall**
collapse, fail, founder, break down, fall through, finish, disintegrate, come to an end, come to nothing, slump
COLLOQ. go bust, fold, flop

Types of wall include:

abutment	dyke (or dike)	paling
bailey	embankment	palisade
barricade	enclosure wall	parapet
barrier	fence	partition
block	flying buttress	party wall
breeze-block wall	fortification	rampart
brick wall	garden wall	retaining wall
bulkhead	green wall (or	screen
bulwark	living wall)	sea-wall
buttress	hedge	shield wall
cavity wall	inner wall	stockade
climbing wall	load-bearing wall	stud partition
curtain wall	mural	wall of death
dam	obstacle	
divider	outer bailey	

wallet n

pouch, purse, folder, holder, case, notecase, pochette; *N Am* bill-fold

wallop *v, n*

♦ *v*

beat, hit, smack, punch, pummel, buffet, swat, swipe, bash, strike, thrash, thump, pound, clout, batter, defeat, crush, trounce, rout, drub, hammer
FORMAL vanquish
COLLOQ. belt, lick, paste, clobber, whack, thwack, wallop, clock, bonk, whop
SLANG *N Am* lam

♦ *n*

blow, kick, thump, clout, swat, swipe, smack, punch, bash
COLLOQ. whack, thwack, wallop, bonk

wallow *v*

1 *wallow in mud*
loll, lie, roll, wade, welter, lurch, flounder, splash
2 *wallow in nostalgia*
indulge, relish, revel, bask, enjoy, glory, delight
FORMAL luxuriate

wan *adj*

pale, washed out, ashen, white, weak, discoloured, faint, colourless, anaemic, ghastly, feeble, whey-faced, waxen, pallid, pasty, sickly, bleak, mournful, weary

wand *n*

rod, baton, staff, stick, sprig, mace, sceptre, twig

wander *v, n*

♦ *v*

1 ROAM, rove, ramble, meander, saunter, stroll, prowl, drift, range, traipse, stray, straggle, cruise, gad, swan off, moon about/around, roll, walk the streets, maraud, maunder, vagabondize, pilgrim; *dialect* stroam; *Scot* ratch about, stravaig, taver; *Irish* streel
OLD expatiate, extravagate, forwander, squander, stooge around, wend, wilder; (*Shakesp*) wheel; *Scot* vague
FORMAL peregrinate
COLLOQ. kick about/around, mooch
SLANG bat around
2 DIGRESS, diverge, deviate, depart, go astray, stray, turn away, swerve, veer, err, lose your way, aberrate; *dialect* moider
FORMAL divagate
3 RAMBLE, rave, babble, gibber, talk nonsense

♦ *n*

excursion, ramble, amble, stroll, saunter, meander, prowl, cruise

---

SYNONYM NUANCES

verb sense 1
You can use **roam** to suggest a lack of purpose in one's wanderings, and **rove** and **ramble** are similarly directionless, but are more suggestive of wandering for recreation or pleasure. **Meander**, meanwhile, implies a slow, circuitous route: *the river meandered through the town.* Similarly, **saunter** and **stroll** imply walking at a slow pace, with connotations of being carefree, whereas **prowl** has rather furtive or sinister implications: *journalists prowled, on the lookout for a story.* **Drift**, on the other hand, implies the absence of a plan: *he drifted through life,* while **range** suggests covering a wide area: *the troops ranged hundreds of miles into the country.*
   Other terms have negative connotations. **Traipse** is suggestive of weariness. **Stray** implies deviating from the intended route, and **straggle** suggests falling behind. You can use **cruise** more narrowly to imply wandering in search of something, and this term is often associated with looking for a sexual partner, while **gad** also most often suggests the pursuit of pleasure: *gadding off on expensive holidays.* **Swan off** also suggests nonchalance but has a rather critical tone, while **roll** implies swagger: *what kind of time is this to roll in at?* **Maraud** is reserved for wandering with the aim of raiding or plundering.

---

wanderer *n*

itinerant, traveller, voyager, drifter, rover, rambler, stroller, stray, straggler, ranger, wayfarer, nomad, Gypsy, vagrant, vagabond, prodigal
COLLOQ. rolling stone

wandering *adj, n*

♦ *adj*
itinerant, travelling, rambling, wayfaring, roving, strolling, voyaging, rootless, homeless, unsettled, drifting, migratory, nomadic, vagabond, vagrant
FORMAL peripatetic

♦ *n*
1 TRAVELS, drift(ing), journey(ing), meander(ing), walkabout
FORMAL odyssey, peregrination
2 DIGRESSION, divergence, deviation, departure
FORMAL evagation

wane *v, n*

♦ *v*
diminish, decrease, decline, weaken, subside, fade (away), dwindle, ebb, lessen, sink, drop, taper off, peter out, dim, droop, contract, shrink, fail, wither, vanish
OLD welk, welke
FORMAL abate
F∃ increase, wax

♦ *n*
fading, dwindling, decline, decrease, lessening, sinking, ebb, contraction, subsidence, weakening, decay, degeneration, failure, fall, drop, tapering off, atrophy
FORMAL abatement, diminution
F∃ increase

■ **on the wane**
deteriorating, declining, degenerating, weakening, withering, fading, subsiding, dwindling, lessening, ebbing, tapering off, dropping, on the decline, obsolescent
FORMAL moribund
COLLOQ. on its last legs, on the way out

wangle *v*

manipulate, arrange, contrive, engineer, fix, scheme, manoeuvre, work, pull off, manage
COLLOQ. fiddle, wheel and deal

want *v, n*

♦ *v*
1 DESIRE, wish, like, feel like, crave, covet, fancy, hope for, long for, pine for, yearn for, hunger for, thirst for
2 NEED, require, demand, lack, miss, be without, be deficient in, call for

♦ *n*
1 DESIRE, demand, longing, pining, yearning, craving, coveting, hunger, thirst, requirement, wish, need, lust, appetite
2 LACK, dearth, insufficiency, absence, deficiency, shortage, inadequacy, scarcity, scantiness
FORMAL paucity
3 POVERTY, destitution
FORMAL privation, indigence, penury

wanting *adj*

1 ABSENT, missing, lacking, short, insufficient
2 INADEQUATE, imperfect, faulty, defective, substandard, poor, deficient, unsatisfactory, unacceptable, disappointing
COLLOQ. not up to scratch
F∃ **1** sufficient **2** adequate

wanton *adj, n*

♦ *adj*
1 *a wanton action*
malicious, malevolent, arbitrary, unprovoked, unjustifiable, groundless, gratuitous, pointless, unrestrained, rash, reckless, wild, extravagant
2 *a wanton woman*
immoral, promiscuous, shameless, immodest, impure, abandoned, dissipated, dissolute, lewd, lecherous, lascivious, sportive; *Scot* cadgy
OLD cork-heeled, petulant, smicker, toyish, toysome; (*Shakesp*) nice, riggish

♦ *n*

slut, harlot, strumpet, trollop, prostitute, whore, voluptuary, debauchee, lecher, libertine, rake, roué, Don Juan, Casanova
SLANG tart

war *n, v*

♦ *n*

warfare, hostilities, fighting, fight, battle, combat, conflict, clash, skirmish, strife, struggle, bloodshed, contest, confrontation, campaign, contention, enmity, antagonism, ill-will
COLLOQ. *Aust & NZ* stoush
Related adjective: martial
⊟ peace, ceasefire

♦ *v*

wage war, fight, take up arms, cross swords, make war, battle, clash, combat, strive, skirmish, struggle, contest, contend

■ **war cry**

rallying-cry, battle-cry, war song, slogan, watchword

> **QUOTATIONS**
> And blood in torrents pour / In vain – always in vain, / For war breeds war again
>   JOHN DAVIDSON, 'War Song'
> There never was a good war or a bad peace
>   BENJAMIN FRANKLIN

Types of war include:

ambush	counter-attack	manoeuvres
armed conflict	cyberwarfare	nuclear war
assault	effects-based	private war
asymmetric(al)	warfare	resistance
warfare	engagement	skirmish
attack	germ warfare	state of siege
battle	guerrilla warfare	struggle
biological warfare	holy war	total war
blitz	hot war	trade war
blitzkrieg	intifada	trench warfare
bombardment	invasion	war of attrition
chemical warfare	jihad	war of nerves
civil war	jungle warfare	world war
cold war	limited war	

---

warble *v, n*

♦ *v*

sing, chirrup, chirp, twitter, quaver, yodel, trill

♦ *n*

song, cry, call, chirp, chirrup, quaver, trill, twitter

ward *n, v*

♦ *n*

1 ROOM, apartment, compartment, cubicle, unit
2 DIVISION, area, district, quarter, precinct, zone
3 CHARGE, dependant, protégé(e), pupil, minor

■ **ward off**

avert, fend off, deflect, parry, repel, drive back, stave off, thwart, beat off, forestall, evade, turn aside, turn away, block, avoid
COLLOQ. dodge

warden *n*

keeper, custodian, guardian, protector, warder, caretaker, curator, ranger, steward, watchman, superintendent, supervisor, overseer, administrator, janitor, concierge, housekeeper, constable
COLLOQ. meter maid/man

warder *n*

jailer, keeper, prison officer, guard, wardress, custodian, warden
SLANG screw

wardrobe *n*

1 CUPBOARD, closet, locker, cabinet
2 CLOTHES, outfit, garments
FORMAL attire, apparel

warehouse *n*

store, storehouse, depot, depository, repository, stockroom, entrepôt, shed, goods shed, freight shed, bodega, godown, hong
COLLOQ. lock-up

wares *n*

goods, merchandise, commodities, stock, products, produce, stuff

warfare *n*

war, fighting, hostilities, battle, arms, combat, strife, struggle, passage of arms, contest, confrontation, campaign, conflict, contention, discord, blows
⊟ peace

warily *adv*

cautiously, carefully, with care, guardedly, watchfully, vigilantly, hesitantly, apprehensively, gingerly, cagily, charily, suspiciously, uneasily, distrustfully
FORMAL circumspectly
⊟ heedlessly, recklessly, thoughtlessly, unwarily

wariness *n*

caution, carefulness, attention, mindfulness, alertness, care, prudence, heedfulness, watchfulness, vigilance, foresight, discretion, caginess, apprehension, hesitancy, suspicion, distrust, unease
FORMAL circumspection
⊟ heedlessness, recklessness, thoughtlessness

warlike *adj*

martial, belligerent, aggressive, combative, bloodthirsty, warmongering, militaristic, militant, hostile, antagonistic, hawkish, unfriendly
OLD (*Spenser*) battailous
FORMAL bellicose, pugnacious
⊟ friendly, peaceable

warlock *n*

witch, wizard, sorcerer, enchanter, conjurer, magician, demon
FORMAL necromancer

warm *adj, v*

♦ *adj*

1 HEATED, hot, tepid, lukewarm
2 ARDENT, passionate, fervent, vehement, intense, earnest, eager, enthusiastic, heartfelt, sincere, zealous
3 *warm colours*
rich, intense, mellow, cheerful, relaxing
4 FRIENDLY, amiable, cordial, affable, kind, kindly, genial, hearty, hospitable, caring, sympathetic, loving, affectionate, tender
5 FINE, sunny, balmy, temperate, close
⊟ 1 cold, cool **2** indifferent **3** cold, cool **4** unfriendly, hostile **5** cool, chilly

♦ *v*

1 HEAT (UP), make warm, reheat, melt, thaw
2 ANIMATE, interest, please, delight, stimulate, liven up, enliven, put some life into, stir, rouse, excite, cheer up
⊟ 1 cool

■ **warm to**

begin to like, become enthusiastic about, become friendly towards

■ **warm up**

limber up, loosen up, exercise, prepare

warm-blooded *adj*

passionate, enthusiastic, excitable, fervent, hot-blooded, emotional, ardent, earnest, lively, spirited, vivacious, impetuous, rash

warm-hearted *adj*

kind, kind-hearted, kindly, affectionate, loving, sympathetic, tender, tender-hearted, compassionate, generous, cordial, ardent, genial
⊟ cold, unsympathetic

warmonger n
hawk, militarist, aggressor, sabre-rattler

warmth n
1 WARMNESS, heat, hotness, fire
2 FRIENDLINESS, affection, cordiality, tenderness, kindness, kindliness, care, love, compassion, sympathy, hospitality
3 ARDOUR, enthusiasm, passion, fervour, zeal, vehemence, intensity, eagerness, sincerity
1 coldness **2** unfriendliness **3** indifference

warn v
1 INFORM, notify, tell, let know, advise, alert, give (advance) notice, put on your guard, sound the alarm; *Scot* shore
OLD (*Spenser*) awarn
FORMAL forewarn, portend, presage
COLLOQ. tip off
2 ADVISE, counsel, urge, caution, exhort
TECHNICAL *N Am* factorize
3 REBUKE, caution, reprimand, reprove
OLD premonish
FORMAL admonish

warning n, adj
♦ n
1 CAUTION, alert, advice, notification, information, notice, advance notice, counsel, hint, lesson, alarm, threat
FORMAL admonition
COLLOQ. heads-up, tip-off, shot across the bows, wake-up call
2 OMEN, threat, sign, premonition, signal
FORMAL augury, presage, portent
♦ adj
ominous, threatening, cautionary
FORMAL admonitory, premonitory, monitory

warp v, n
♦ v
twist, bend, contort, deform, distort, buckle, kink, misshape, pervert, corrupt, deviate
straighten
♦ n
twist, bend, contortion, deformation, distortion, bias, kink, irregularity, turn, bent, defect, deviation, quirk, perversion

warrant n, v
♦ n
authorization, authority, sanction, validation, permit, permission, consent, licence, guarantee, warranty, security, pledge, commission, voucher, assurance, pardon, death warrant, execution, search warrant, peace-warrant, bench-warrant; *Scot* fudgie-warrant
TECHNICAL detainer, diligence, precept, transire, fiat, mittimus, *lettre de cachet*
♦ v
1 GUARANTEE, pledge, swear, certify, assure, promise, declare, affirm, vouch for, answer for, underwrite, uphold, support, back, endorse, deserve, earn
OLD vouchsafe, sepad; (*Shakesp*) able, warn; (*Spenser*) behight, behote
FORMAL avouch
2 AUTHORIZE, entitle, empower, sanction, permit, allow, consent to, license, justify, excuse, approve, support, call for, commission, require, necessitate

warrantable adj
permissible, allowable, defensible, excusable, justifiable, right, reasonable, proper, legal, lawful, accountable, necessary
indefensible, unjustifiable, unwarrantable

warranty n
guarantee, contract, certificate, bond, authorization, assurance, pledge, justification
FORMAL covenant

warring adj
fighting, hostile, opposing, opposed, conflicting, contending, combatant, embattled, belligerent, at war, at daggers drawn

warrior n
fighter, soldier, fighting man, combatant, champion, warhorse, wardog

wart n
growth, lump, protuberance, verruca, anbury, angleberry
OLD wen
FORMAL excrescence, keratosis, papilloma

wary adj
cautious, prudent, guarded, careful, chary, on your guard, on the lookout, distrustful, suspicious, heedful, attentive, (on the) alert, watchful, vigilant, wide-awake, leery; *Scot* tentie
OLD aware, ware
FORMAL circumspect
COLLOQ. cagey
unwary, careless, heedless

wash v, n
♦ v
1 CLEAN, cleanse, launder, shampoo, scrub, mop, swab down, sponge, wipe, rinse, soak, swill
2 BATHE, bath, freshen up, get cleaned up, have a wash, have a bath, (have a) shower, douche, shampoo
3 FLOW, sweep, wave, swell, stream, beat, splash, dash
4 *that excuse won't wash*
be believable, be plausible, be accepted, be convincing, hold, hold water, stand up, bear examination, bear scrutiny, carry weight, pass muster
COLLOQ. stick
♦ n
1 CLEANING, cleansing, bath, bathe, laundry, laundering, scrub, shower, shampoo, washing, rinse
2 FLOW, roll, sweep, wave, swell, surge
3 LAYER, coat, coating, rinse, stain
■ **wash your hands of**
abandon, give up on, have nothing to do with, leave to your own devices, abdicate responsibility

washed-out adj
pale, pallid, blanched, bleached, faded, wan, colourless, ashen, drained, drawn, exhausted, tired-out, fatigued, worn-out, weary, spent, flat, lacklustre, haggard
COLLOQ. all in, dead on your feet, dog-tired, knackered

washout n
failure, disaster, disappointment, fiasco, debacle, mess
COLLOQ. flop, lead balloon
success, triumph

waspish adj
critical, irritable, bad-tempered, cross, ill-tempered, captious, irascible, peevish, petulant, prickly, snappish, testy, touchy
FORMAL cantankerous, vitriolic
COLLOQ. grumpy, bitchy, crabbed, crabby, crotchety, grouchy

wastage n
1 *wastage of scarce natural resources*
squandering, loss, exhausting, draining, frittering away, dissipation
2 DEGENERATION, atrophy, decay, emaciation
TECHNICAL marasmus

waste v, n, adj
♦ v
1 SQUANDER, misspend, misuse, fritter away, lavish, spend, throw away, get/go through
FORMAL dissipate
COLLOQ. blow, splurge
2 CONSUME, erode, exhaust, drain, destroy, spoil, devastate
3 WITHER, shrivel, shrink, become emaciated, atrophy
4 LAY WASTE, desolate, ravage, destroy, devastate, raze, ruin, sack, spoil, pillage, rape
FORMAL depredate, despoil
1 economize **2** preserve
♦ n
1 SQUANDERING, wastefulness, extravagance, loss
FORMAL dissipation, prodigality

2 MISAPPLICATION, misuse, abuse, neglect
3 RUBBISH, refuse, leftovers, debris, dregs, effluent, litter, scrap, e-waste, slops, offscouring(s), dross; *N Am* trash, garbage
E3 **1** thriftiness
♦ *adj*
1 USELESS, worthless, unwanted, unused, left-over, superfluous, extra
FORMAL supernumerary
2 BARREN, desolate, empty, uninhabited, bare, devastated, uncultivated, unprofitable, unproductive, wild, dismal, bleak, dreary

> **PROVERBS**
> Waste not, want not

> **SYNONYM NUANCES**
> *verb sense 1*
> Many of the synonyms are, naturally, disapproving in tone. You can use **squander** of the profligate disposal of a resource: *he squandered his talent*, while the more restrained **misspend** and **misuse** suggest an inappropriate application: *the problems resulting from a misspent youth.* **Fritter away** could be used of using something up, bit by bit, in a worthless way: *I frittered away the morning*, while the stronger **throw away**, again, implies lost opportunities: *he threw away his athletics career with his tendency for nights on the town.*
>   **Spend**, on the other hand, is widely applied to any expenditure, and the terms **get through** and **go through** can be used similarly without suggesting an opinion: *he got through his salary very quickly.* **Lavish**, however, implies prodigious extravagance: *he lavished too much on fine food and wine.*

wasted *adj*
1 UNNECESSARY, needless, useless, unrequired
2 EMACIATED, withered, weak, weakened, shrivelled, shrunken, gaunt, washed-out, spent, atrophied
E3 **1** necessary **2** robust

wasteful *adj*
extravagant, spendthrift, prodigal, uneconomical, thriftless, unthrifty, ruinous, lavish, improvident; *Scot* wasterife, wastrife
OLD wastfull
FORMAL profligate
E3 economical, thrifty

wasteland *n*
wilderness, desert, barrenness, waste, wild(s), void, emptiness

wasting *adj*
destroying, emaciating, enfeebling, devastating
TECHNICAL marasmic
E3 strengthening

wastrel *n*
good-for-nothing, idler, layabout, loafer, ne'er-do-well, malingerer, spendthrift
FORMAL profligate
COLLOQ. lounger, shirker, skiver, lazybones
SLANG *N Am* goof-off

watch *v, n*
♦ *v*
1 OBSERVE, see, look at, look on, regard, note, notice, mark, stare at, peer at, gape at, leer at, contemplate, scan, survey, gaze at, view
2 GUARD, look after, keep an eye on, mind, protect, superintend, inspect, take care of, keep
COLLOQ. keep tabs on, not take your eyes off
3 PAY ATTENTION, be careful, take care, take heed, look out
♦ *n*
1 TIMEPIECE, wristwatch, clock
FORMAL chronometer

2 VIGILANCE, watchfulness, vigil, guard, observation, surveillance, notice, lookout, attention, heed, alertness, inspection, supervision
■ **watch out**
notice, be vigilant, look out, keep a lookout, keep your eyes open, keep a weather eye out
COLLOQ. keep your eyes peeled/skinned
■ **watch over**
guard, protect, stand guard over, keep an eye on, look after, take care of, mind, shield, defend, shelter, preserve

---

Types of watch include:

analogue watch	hunter watch	ring watch
automatic watch	kinetic watch	skeleton watch
bracelet watch	lever-watch	*N Am* stemwinder
chronograph	nurse's watch	stopwatch
digital watch	pendant watch	Swatch®
dive watch	pocket watch	wristwatch
fob watch	quartz watch	
half-hunter watch	repeating watch	

---

watchdog *n*
1 GUARD DOG, house-dog
2 MONITOR, inspector, scrutineer, vigilante, ombudsman, regulator, guardian, custodian, protector

watcher *n*
spectator, observer, onlooker, looker-on, viewer, (member of the) audience, lookout, spy, witness, eyewitness

watchful *adj*
vigilant, attentive, heedful, observant, alert, guarded, on your guard, wide awake, keeping your eyes open/peeled/ skinned, on the lookout, on the qui vive, suspicious, wary, chary, cautious; *Scot* wakerife, waukrife
OLD adviceful; *(Spenser)* avizefull; *(Shakesp)* open-eyed
FORMAL circumspect
E3 unobservant, inattentive

watchfulness *n*
vigilance, alertness, attention, attentiveness, heedfulness, caution, cautiousness, circumspection, suspicion, suspiciousness, wariness
OLD observance
E3 inattention

watchman *n*
guard, security guard, caretaker, custodian

watchword *n*
catchphrase, slogan, catchword, maxim, password, principle, motto, rallying-cry, battle-cry, signal, byword, buzz word, magic word, shibboleth

water *n, v*
♦ *n*
rain, sea, ocean, lake, river, current, stream, moisture, flooding, torrent
Related adjective: aqueous
♦ *v*
wet, moisten, dampen, soak, spray, sprinkle, irrigate, saturate, drench, flood, hose, douse
E3 dry out, parch
■ **water down**
dilute, thin, water, weaken, adulterate, mix, tone down, play down, soften, moderate, qualify
FORMAL mitigate
COLLOQ. soft-pedal
■ **hold water**
stand up, remain valid, cohere, hold (up), stand (up), be believable, be plausible, be accepted, be convincing, bear examination, bear scrutiny, carry weight
COLLOQ. wash, stick

> **PROVERBS**
> Still waters run deep

watercourse *n*
river, stream, channel, ditch, canal, wadi, water-channel;
S Afr spruit

waterfall *n*
fall, falls, cascade, chute, cataract, torrent, rapid(s),
overfall, spout, force, foss, lasher, linn; *Can* sault, salt

waterproof *adj*
impervious, watertight, water-resistant, damp-proof,
rubberized, impermeable, water-repellent, coated, proofed
ꜰꜱ leaky

watertight *adj*
1 WATERPROOF, sound, sealed, hermetic
2 IMPREGNABLE, unassailable, airtight, flawless, foolproof,
firm, sound, incontrovertible, indisputable
ꜰꜱ **1** leaky

watery *adj*
1 LIQUID, fluid, moist, wet, damp
TECHNICAL hydrous
FORMAL aqueous
2 WEAK, watered-down, diluted, adulterated, insipid,
tasteless, thin, runny, soggy, squelchy, flavourless, washy
COLLOQ. wishy-washy
ꜰꜱ **1** dry

wave *v, n*
♦ *v*
1 BECKON, gesture, gesticulate, indicate, sign, signal, direct
2 BRANDISH, flourish, flap, flutter, stir, shake, sway, swing,
waft, quiver, ripple, surge, move from side to side
FORMAL undulate
♦ *n*
1 BREAKER, roller, billow, ripple, comber, foam, froth,
swell, surf, tidal wave, wavelet, undulation
COLLOQ. white horse
2 SURGE, sweep, swell, flow, upsurge, ground swell,
current, drift, movement, rush, tendency, trend, stream,
flood, outbreak, rash
■ **wave aside**
dismiss, brush aside, disregard, reject, set aside, shelve,
spurn
COLLOQ. pour cold water on
■ **wave down**
flag down, signal to stop, summon
■ **make waves**
stir up/cause trouble, disturb things, cause a disturbance,
challenge the status quo

waver *v*
1 VACILLATE, falter, hesitate, dither, fluctuate, vary, seesaw,
equivocate, be undecided, haver, teeter
OLD wave
COLLOQ. shilly-shally, hum and haw, waffle, wobble
2 TREMBLE, oscillate, shake, sway, wobble, stagger, give
way, reel, teeter, totter, rock
ꜰꜱ **1** decide

waverer *n*
ditherer, doubter, haverer, wobbler
COLLOQ. shilly-shallier

wavering *adj*
hesitant, doubting, doubtful, dithering, dithery, havering, in
two minds
COLLOQ. shilly-shallying
ꜰꜱ determined

wavy *adj*
undulating, rippled, curly, curling, curvy, curving, ridged,
sinuous, winding, zigzag

wax *v*
1 GROW, increase, get bigger, rise, swell, develop, enlarge,
expand, extend, spread, magnify, broaden, widen, mount,
fill out, become
2 *wax lyrical*
speak, talk, say, state, declare, express, utter, voice,
articulate, enunciate, pronounce, tell, communicate,
address, hold forth
FORMAL converse, declaim
ꜰꜱ **1** decrease, wane

waxen *adj*
pale, colourless, ashen, wan, white, whitish, pallid,
ghastly, anaemic, bloodless, livid
ꜰꜱ ruddy

waxy *adj*
soft, pallid, pasty, waxen, impressible, impressionable
FORMAL ceraceous, cereous

way *n*
1 METHOD, approach, manner, technique, process, plan,
course of action, strategy, procedure, means, instrument,
tool, system, style, fashion, lines
FORMAL mode, instrumentality
2 CUSTOM, practice, behaviour, manner, habit, usage,
characteristic, idiosyncrasy, peculiarity, mannerism,
personality, temper, temperament, disposition, trait, style,
conduct, nature
FORMAL wont
3 ROAD, direction, course, route, path, pathway, channel,
access, avenue, track, passage, highway, roadway, street,
thoroughfare, terrace, lane
■ **way of life**
lifestyle, life, living conditions, position, situation, world
■ **ways and means**
methods, procedure, way, resources, wherewithal,
capability, capacity, tools, cash, funds, reserves, capital
■ **by the way**
incidentally, in passing, secondarily, parenthetically, *en
passant*
■ **give way**
1 COLLAPSE, break, fall in, sink, disintegrate, subside, cave
in
2 GIVE IN, yield, surrender, capitulate, submit, concede
■ **under way**
in progress, moving, in motion, going, begun, started, in
operation, afoot

wayfarer *n*
traveller, walker, wanderer, journeyer, globetrotter, rover,
trekker, voyager, itinerant, nomad, Gypsy
ꜰꜱ resident, stay-at-home

wayfaring *adj*
journeying, walking, travelling, wandering, rambling,
roving, drifting, itinerant, voyaging, nomadic
FORMAL peripatetic
ꜰꜱ resident, stay-at-home

waylay *v*
lie in wait for, ambush, attack, accost, set upon, surprise,
catch, hold up, intercept, seize, buttonhole

way-out *adj*
weird, crazy, bizarre, outlandish, unusual, unorthodox,
unconventional, fantastic, eccentric, wild, experimental,
avant-garde, progressive
COLLOQ. far-out, freaky, off-beat, wacky, left-field
ꜰꜱ ordinary

wayward *adj*
wilful, perverse, contrary, changeable, fickle,
unpredictable, stubborn, self-willed, unmanageable,
ungovernable, headstrong, obstinate, disobedient,
rebellious, insubordinate, unruly, incorrigible
FORMAL intractable, obdurate, contumacious, refractory,
capricious
ꜰꜱ tractable, good-natured

waywardness *n*
unmanageableness, unruliness, stubbornness, obstinacy, wilfulness, perverseness, perversity, contrariness, disobedience, rebelliousness, insubordination
FORMAL obduracy, contumacy
F∃ tractableness

weak *adj*
1 FEEBLE, frail, infirm, shaky, unhealthy, sickly, puny, delicate, exhausted, worn out, fatigued, debilitated, fragile, flimsy
FORMAL enervated
COLLOQ. weedy
2 VULNERABLE, unprotected, unguarded, defenceless, exposed
3 POWERLESS, impotent, spineless, cowardly, indecisive, irresolute, poor, flimsy, feeble, lacking, lame, inadequate, faulty, imperfect, useless, defective, deficient, inconclusive, unconvincing, unsound, untenable
FORMAL ineffectual
4 FAINT, slight, dim, low, soft, muffled, stifled, dull, imperceptible, indistinct
5 INSIPID, tasteless, watery, thin, diluted, runny, adulterated
F∃ **1** strong, healthy **2** secure, protected **3** powerful, determined **4** strong, clear **5** strong

---

SYNONYM NUANCES

sense 1
You can use **feeble** to suggest something rather pitiful and ineffective: *their feeble efforts*, while **frail** and **infirm** are more appropriate to describe an ailing physical condition. **Puny**, likewise, can suggest a deficient physique: *his puny chest*, but may also imply insignificance: *a puny gesture of defiance*. In both instances, the tone is more contemptuous.
    A less critical and even slightly euphemistic synonym is **delicate**, which is more suggestive of something dainty or valuable. **Fragile** similarly suggests a lack of robustness, but has stronger connotations of a propensity for getting damaged: *a fragile unity*, whereas **flimsy** is rather more disapproving, and implies insubstantiality. **Shaky**, on the other hand, has connotations of a degree of uncertainty: *a shaky economy*.

---

weaken *v*
1 ENFEEBLE, tire, exhaust, sap, undermine, incapacitate, debilitate, disable, paralyse, cripple, impair, dilute, diminish, lower, lessen, reduce, moderate, mitigate, temper, soften (up), thin, water down, craze, effeminate, effeminize, kill, take the edge off, extenuate, taint, unnerve, disconcert
OLD disinvigorate, appal, pall, entender; *(Spenser)* deduct, delay
FORMAL enervate
2 TIRE, flag, fail, give way, droop, fade, ease up, dwindle
FORMAL abate
F∃ **1** strengthen

weakening *n*
fading, failing, flagging, reduction, diminishment, dwindling, easing, lessening, lowering, moderation, dilution, waning, undermining, impairment, extenuation, debilitation
FORMAL abatement, enervation
F∃ strengthening

weakling *n*
coward, underling, underdog, milksop, namby-pamby, mouse
OLD softling
COLLOQ. wimp, wet, wally, weed, drip, doormat, cissy
SLANG wuss; *Aust* tonk
F∃ hero, stalwart

weakly *adv*
1 *she sank weakly into the armchair*
feebly, frailly, faintly, slightly, powerlessly, helplessly, dispiritedly

2 *weakly argue a case*
ineffectively, indecisively, implausibly, tenuously, lamely
COLLOQ. pathetically
F∃ **1** strongly, powerfully **2** effectively, plausibly, convincingly

weak-minded *adj*
pliable, faint-hearted, irresolute, persuasible, submissive, compliant, weak-kneed, persuadable
FORMAL complaisant, pusillanimous
COLLOQ. spineless
F∃ strong-willed

weakness *n*
1 FEEBLENESS, infirmity, impotence, incapacity, debility, delicateness, frailty, powerlessness, vulnerability
FORMAL enervation
2 FAULT, failing, flaw, imperfection, shortcoming, blemish, defect, deficiency, foible, weak point, Achilles' heel
3 LIKING, inclination, fondness, passion
FORMAL penchant, predilection, proclivity, predisposition
COLLOQ. soft spot
4 *the weakness of the argument*
implausibility, improbability, uncertainty, flimsiness, ineffectiveness, tenuousness, unsoundness, doubt, doubtfulness, dubiousness, unlikelihood, unlikeliness, far-fetchedness
F∃ **1** strength **2** strength, virtue **3** dislike, distaste **4** effectiveness, plausibility

weal *n*
welt, stripe, streak, scar, ridge, mark, wound, contusion, cicatrice, cicatrix

wealth *n*
1 MONEY, cash, riches, assets, affluence, prosperity, funds, mammon, fortune, treasure, capital, finance, means, substance, resources, goods, possessions, property, estate
OLD lucre
FORMAL opulence
SLANG bling
2 ABUNDANCE, plenty, mass, bounty, fullness, store, treasury, copiousness, profusion
FORMAL cornucopia, plenitude
F∃ **1** poverty

wealthy *adj*
rich, prosperous, affluent, well-off, moneyed, comfortable, well-heeled, well-to-do, solid, substantial
FORMAL opulent
COLLOQ. flush, rolling in it, made of money, fat-cat, posh
OLD COLLOQ. oofy
SLANG loaded, filthy rich, stinking rich
F∃ poor, impoverished

weapon
See panel on next page

wear *v, n*
♦ *v*
1 DRESS IN, be dressed in, have on, put on, be clothed in, don, sport, carry, bear, have, display, show, exhibit, assume
2 DETERIORATE, erode, corrode, consume, fray, become thinner/weaker/threadbare, rub, abrade, waste, grind
♦ *n*
1 CLOTHES, clothing, dress, garments, outfit, costume
FORMAL attire
2 DETERIORATION, erosion, corrosion, damage, wear and tear, friction, abrasion
3 USE, service, employment, usefulness, utility, durability

■ **wear down**
reduce, rub away, corrode, abrade, erode, grind down, chip away at, consume, undermine, diminish, lessen, overcome
FORMAL macerate

Weapons include:

GUNS:
airgun
air rifle
anti-aircraft gun
anti-tank gun
automatic
bazooka
BB gun
blunderbuss
Bren gun
cannon
carbine
Colt®
elephant gun
field gun
gatling-gun
gun
howitzer
kalashnikov
Luger®
machine-gun
magnum
Mauser
mortar
musket
pistol

revolver
rifle
rocket-launcher
shotgun
six-gun
six-shooter
sten gun
stun gun
submachine-gun
Taser®
tommy-gun
turret-gun
Uzi
Winchester® rifle

BLADES:
arrow
battleaxe
bayonet
bowie knife
broadsword
caltrop
claymore
dagger
dirk
épée

flick-knife
foil
foot-claw
glaive
hand-claw
knife
lance
machete
panga
pike
poniard
quarterstaff
rapier
sabre
samurai sword
scimitar
spear
stiletto
sword
sword-stick (or
  sword-cane)
tomahawk
vouge

BOMBS:
atom bomb

binary weapon (or
  munition)
bomb
bomblet
colloq. bunker
  buster
cluster-bomb
daisy-cutter
depth-charge
H-bomb
incendiary bomb
landmine
Mills bomb
mine
nail bomb
napalm bomb
smart bomb
submunition
thermobaric bomb
time-bomb

MISSILES:
ballistic missile
bolas
boomerang
Cruise missile

Exocet®
hand grenade
rocket
colloq. Scud
shuriken
torpedo

PROJECTORS:
ballista
blowpipe
bow
catapult
crossbow
flame-thrower
harpoon
longbow
sling
trebuchet

STICKS:
billy
cosh
cudgel
halberd
partisan
poleaxe
shillelagh

taiaha
threshel
tomboc
truncheon

GASES:
Agent Orange
CS gas
N Am Mace®
mustard gas
nerve gas
tear-gas

OTHER:
bioweapon
knuckleduster
kubotan
kusari
kusari-gama
kyoketsu-shoge
maurikigusari
nunchaku

See also **bomb**; **gun**.

■ **wear off**
decrease, dwindle, diminish, subside, wane, weaken, fade, lessen, ebb, peter out, disappear
FORMAL abate
F∃ increase

■ **wear on**
go on, go by, pass, elapse

■ **wear out**
1 EXHAUST, consume, use up, fatigue, tire (out), strain, stress, drain, sap
FORMAL enervate
2 DETERIORATE, wear through, erode, impair, consume, fray

wearily *adv*
tiredly, lethargically, drowsily, sleepily, listlessly, unenthusiastically, unexcitedly
F∃ freshly, energetically

weariness *n*
fatigue, tiredness, exhaustion, lassitude, lethargy, ennui, drowsiness, sleepiness, listlessness, prostration
FORMAL enervation, languor
F∃ freshness, energy

wearing *adj*
exhausting, fatiguing, tiring, tiresome, wearisome, trying, taxing, oppressive, irksome, exasperating, erosive
F∃ refreshing

wearisome *adj*
tiresome, troublesome, wearing, fatiguing, exhausting, dreary, burdensome, bothersome, boring, monotonous, humdrum, tedious, annoying, trying, exasperating, irksome, vexatious, dull
F∃ refreshing

weary *adj, v*
♦ *adj*
1 TIRED, exhausted, fatigued, sleepy, worn out, drained, drowsy, jaded, overweary, toil-worn
OLD aweary, awearied; (*Shakesp*) dog-weary
COLLOQ. all in, done in, fagged out, knackered, bushed, dead beat, whacked, dog-tired, zonked, half-dead, wiped out; *N Am* pooped (out), tuckered out
2 *weary of trying to please him*
bored, unenthusiastic, tired, uninterested, unexcited

COLLOQ. sick and tired, bored to tears, browned off, brassed off, cheesed off
F∃ 1 refreshed, energetic **2** excited, interested
♦ *v*
tire (out), exhaust, debilitate, wear out, fatigue, bore, fail, jade, sap, sicken, drain, burden, fade, annoy, irritate, exasperate, irk, tax, cloy; *Scot* ramfeezle, trauchle
OLD betoil, think long; (*Spenser*) forweary
FORMAL enervate, ennui
COLLOQ. bug, fag

wearying *adj*
tiring, fatiguing, exhausting, wearisome, wearing, taxing, draining, trying
F∃ refreshing

weather *n, v*
♦ *n*
climate, conditions, temperature, humidity, dryness, windiness, sunniness, cloudiness, meteorological reports, atmospheric conditions, forecast, outlook
See panel on next page
♦ *v*
1 ENDURE, survive, live through, come through, get through, ride out, rise above, stick out, withstand, surmount, stand, brave, overcome, resist, pull through, suffer
2 EXPOSE, toughen, season, harden, dry
F∃ 1 succumb

■ **under the weather**
ill, sick, poorly, queer, ailing, off-colour, the worse for wear, groggy, below par, squeamish, nauseous, hung over, out of sorts
FORMAL indisposed
COLLOQ. grotty, lousy, rough, rop(e)y, seedy

QUOTATIONS
When two Englishmen meet, their first talk is of the weather
  SAMUEL JOHNSON

We welcome all enquiries about the UK climate – after all, we have more weather available in this country than anywhere else
  SIR SYDNEY SAMUELSON, *Check Book*

Types of weather include:

black ice	heatwave	snow
blizzard	hoar frost	snowfall
breeze	hurricane	snowstorm
chinook	ice	squall
cloud	lightning	storm
cyclone	mist	sunshine
deluge	mistral	tempest
dew	monsoon	thaw
downpour	rain	thunder
drizzle	rainbow	tornado
drought	rainfall	*colloq.* twister
fog	rainstorm	typhoon
frost	shower	whirlwind
gale	sleet	wind
hail	slush	
haze	smog	

See also **wind**[1].

weave *v*
1 INTERLACE, lace, plait, braid, intertwine, spin, knit, entwine, intercross, interweave, interwork, inweave, fuse, merge, unite, texture, tissue, twill, cane, damask
OLD plight; *(Spenser)* wind
2 CREATE, compose, construct, contrive, make up, put together, fabricate
3 WIND, twist, zigzag, criss-cross

web *n*
network, net, netting, lattice, latticework, lacework, mesh, mesh-work, complex, webbing, interlacing, weft, snare, knot, tangle, trap, mat, skein, tela
OLD texture

wed *v*
1 MARRY, get married, yoke
OLD take to wife
FORMAL espouse
COLLOQ. get hitched, splice, tie the knot, get spliced, take the plunge, lead to the altar, lead up the aisle, make an honest woman of
2 JOIN, unite, unify, coalesce, blend, ally, combine, link, interweave, fuse, merge
FORMAL commingle
E3 1 divorce **2** separate

wedded *adj*
married, marital, joined, husbandly, wifely
FORMAL conjugal, connubial, matrimonial, nuptial, spousal

wedding *n, adj*
♦ *n*
marriage, union, marriage service, marriage ceremony, celebration of marriage
OLD wedlock
FORMAL matrimony, nuptials, spousage, espousals
E3 divorce
♦ *adj*
bridal, marriage
FORMAL matrimonial, nuptial, hymeneal, hymenean, epithalamic

wedge *n, v*
♦ *n*
lump, block, piece, doorstop, chunk, wodge, chock, triangle, trig, feather, key, scotch, cleat, cotter
TECHNICAL gad, quoin, whipstock
Related adjectives: cuneiform, cuneal, cuneatic, sphenic, sphenoid
♦ *v*
jam, cram, pack, ram, squeeze, stuff, push, lodge, fit, block, thrust, crowd, force, quoin

wedlock *n*
marriage, union
FORMAL holy matrimony, matrimony

wee *adj*
small, little, tiny, miniature, minute, negligible, insignificant, diminutive, minuscule, microscopic, midget, Lilliputian
COLLOQ. itsy-bitsy, teeny, teensy, teeny-weeny, weeny
E3 big, large

weed
■ **weed out**
get rid of, remove, root out, isolate, eradicate, eliminate, purge
FORMAL extirpate
E3 add, fix, infiltrate

Weeds include:

annual nettle	deadnettle	oxalis
bindweed	dock	pearlwort
birdsfoot trefoil	duckweed	perennial nettle
bracken	fat hen	perennial oat-grass
broad-leaved dock	field wood rush	petty spurge
burnet saxifrage	greater (or rat-	pineapple weed
Canadian pond-	tailed) plantain	ragweed
weed	ground elder	ribwort
chickweed	ground ivy	rosebay
cinquefoil	groundsel	willowherb
coltsfoot	hairy bittercress	rough hawkbit
common burdock	horsetail	salad burnet
common chick-	Japanese knotgrass	self-heal
weed	knapweed	sheep's sorrel
common persi-	knotgrass	shepherd's-purse
caria	large bindweed	small bindweed
common plantain	lesser celandine	snakeweed
common reed	lesser yellow	sow thistle
couch grass	trefoil	speedwell
creeping buttercup	liverwort	spurge
creeping thistle	meadow grass	stemless thistle
creeping yellow	mind your own	sun spurge
cress	business	thale cress
curled dock	moss	vetch
daisy	mouse-ear chick-	white clover
dandelion	weed	yarrow

See also **wild flower**.

weedy *adj*
thin, skinny, puny, scrawny, undersized, gangling, weak, feeble, frail, weak-kneed, insipid
COLLOQ. wet, wimpish
SLANG wussy
E3 strong

weekly *adv, adj*
♦ *adv*
every week, by the week, once a week
FORMAL hebdomadally
♦ *adj*
FORMAL hebdomadal, hebdomadary

weep *v, n*
♦ *v*
cry, sob, be in/shed tears, moan, lament, wail, mourn, grieve, bawl, blubber, snivel, whine, whimper, outweep, pipe, pipe your eye, put a finger in the eye; *Scot* greet
OLD beweep
COLLOQ. blub, boo-hoo, turn on the waterworks
See Synonym nuances panel at **cry**.
E3 rejoice
♦ *n*
cry, sob, moan, snivel, blub, lament; *Scot* greet
COLLOQ. boo-hoo

> **QUOTATIONS**
> How much better it is to weep at joy than to joy at weeping!
> WILLIAM SHAKESPEARE, *Much Ado About Nothing*

weepy *adj, n*
* *adj*

crying, tearful, sobbing, blubbering, weeping, teary;
Scot greeting
FORMAL labile, lachrymose
* *n*

melodrama, sob-stuff, tear-jerker

weigh *v*
1 *it weighs one kilogram*
have a weight of, tip the scales at
2 *weigh the apples*
measure the weight of, see/measure how heavy
something is
3 BEAR DOWN, oppress, burden, depress, afflict,
trouble, worry
COLLOQ. get down
4 CONSIDER, contemplate, evaluate, meditate on,
mull over, ponder, think over, examine, reflect on,
deliberate
■ **weigh down**
oppress, overload, load, burden, bear down,
weigh upon, press down, depress, afflict,
trouble, worry
COLLOQ. get down
E∃ lighten, hearten
■ **weigh up**
assess, examine, size up, evaluate, balance, compare,
consider, contemplate, deliberate, mull over, ponder, think
over, discuss
COLLOQ. chew over

weight *n, v*
* *n*

1 HEAVINESS, gravity, burden, load, pressure, mass,
quantity, force, ballast, tonnage, poundage
FORMAL avoirdupois
2 IMPORTANCE, significance, substance, consequence,
impact, moment, influence, force, value, authority, power,
consideration
FORMAL preponderance
COLLOQ. clout
3 BURDEN, load, onus, responsibility, duty, worry, trouble,
strain, encumbrance
E∃ **1** lightness
* *v*

1 LOAD, weigh down, burden, oppress, handicap
2 BIAS, unbalance, slant, prejudice, angle, load, twist, sway

weightless *adj*
light, insubstantial, airy
FORMAL imponderous
E∃ heavy

weighty *adj*
1 HEAVY, substantial, massive, bulky, hefty
2 IMPORTANT, significant, consequential, crucial, critical,
momentous, vital, serious, influential, authoritative, grave,
solemn
3 DEMANDING, burdensome, onerous, difficult, exacting,
taxing
E∃ **1** light **2** unimportant, insignificant

weird *adj*
strange, uncanny, bizarre, eerie, creepy, supernatural,
unnatural, ghostly, fey, freakish, mysterious, queer,
grotesque, unearthly, witching; *Scot* eldritch
OLD weyard, weyward
FORMAL preternatural
COLLOQ. spooky, far-out, way-out, left-field, rum
E∃ normal, usual

weirdly *adv*
strangely, bizarrely, eerily, unnaturally, supernaturally,
mysteriously
COLLOQ. spookily
E∃ normally, usually

weirdo *n*
eccentric, freak, crank

COLLOQ. case, character, card, crackpot, oddball, nut,
nutter, nutcase, fruitcake, kook, queer fish, odd fish,
square peg in a round hole, fish out of water; N Am flake
SLANG cure, geek, loony, loon; N Am dingbat, cupcake,
wack; *Aust* dag

welcome *adj, n, v*
* *adj*

acceptable, desirable, popular, pleasing, pleasant,
agreeable, gratifying, appreciated, delightful, refreshing
E∃ unwelcome
* *n*

reception, greeting, acceptance, hospitality, acclamation;
N Am ticker-tape welcome, glad hand, salutary
TECHNICAL the right hand of fellowship
COLLOQ. salutation, red carpet
* *v*

greet, hail, receive, salute, meet, befriend, accept,
approve of, be pleased with, be satisfied with, embrace,
acclaim
OLD gratulate
COLLOQ. roll out the red carpet for, kill the fatted calf for
E∃ reject, snub

welcoming *adj*
1 *a welcoming person*
friendly, cordial, amicable, affable, affectionate, agreeable,
cheerful, genial, sociable, pleasant, heartfelt, warm, warm-
hearted, wholehearted, earnest, hearty, stimulating,
invigorating
2 *a welcoming room*
pleasant, comfortable, cosy, warm, friendly, relaxing,
homelike, *gemütlich*
E∃ **1** hostile, aloof, cool **2** cold, unfriendly

weld *v, n*
* *v*

fuse, unite, bond, join, solder, bind, connect, seal, link,
cement
E∃ separate
* *n*

joint, bond, seal, seam

welfare *n*
1 WELLBEING, health, prosperity, happiness, comfort,
soundness, security, benefit, good, fortune, advantage,
interest, profit, success
2 *live off welfare*
benefit, income, allowance, pension, sick pay, payment,
social security

well¹ *adv, adj*
* *adv*

1 *speak Czech well*
competently, skilfully, properly, ably, expertly, proficiently,
effectively, adeptly, excellently, rightly, correctly
2 *everything turned out well*
satisfactorily, adequately, suitably, fittingly, sufficiently
3 *treat someone well*
kindly, genially, generously, hospitably, agreeably, fairly,
decently, pleasantly, happily
4 *Did you know her well?*
thoroughly, properly, fully, deeply, profoundly, closely,
intimately, completely, greatly, considerably
5 THOROUGHLY, completely, intensively, comprehensively,
carefully, efficiently, rigorously, industriously
6 *live well*
successfully, prosperously, comfortably, splendidly, luckily,
fortunately
7 *think/speak well of someone*
highly, approvingly, favourably, glowingly, admiringly,
warmly
8 *well over a thousand people*
substantially, considerably, very much, to a great
extent, far
9 *you may well be right*
conceivably, quite possibly, very likely, probably, certainly
E∃ **1** badly, inadequately, incompetently, wrongly **2, 3**
badly **6** poorly **7** unfavourably

♦ *adj*
1 HEALTHY, in good health, fit, able-bodied, sound, robust, strong, thriving, flourishing, hale and hearty
2 SATISFACTORY, right, all right, good, pleasing, proper, agreeable, fine, lucky, fortunate
COLLOQ. OK
🔄 **1** ill **2** bad

■ **as well**
too, also, in addition, furthermore, besides, moreover
COLLOQ. into the bargain

■ **well done**
bravo, congratulations, hurrah, encore

■ **as well as**
in addition to, together with, along with, including, over and above, not to mention, to say nothing of

well² *n, v*
♦ *n*
dig a well
spring, wellspring, fountain, fount, source, reservoir, pool, wellhead, water hole, supply; *Aust* Mickery
♦ *v*
flow, spring, surge, gush, stream, brim over, jet, spout, spurt, swell, issue, rush, pour, flood, ooze, run, trickle, rise, seep

---

Types of well include:

artesian well	hot spring	stairwell
borehole	inkwell	thermal spring
draw-well	lift-shaft	waterhole
gas well	mineral spring	wishing well
geyser	oil well	
gusher	pump-well	

---

well-advised *adj*
wise, reasonable, sensible, sound, far-sighted, long-sighted, shrewd, prudent, politic
FORMAL judicious, sagacious, circumspect

well-balanced *adj*
1 RATIONAL, reasonable, level-headed, well-adjusted, stable, sensible, sane, sound, sober
COLLOQ. together
2 SYMMETRICAL, even, harmonious, balanced, well-proportioned, well-ordered
🔄 **1** unbalanced, maladjusted **2** asymmetrical, disordered

well-behaved *adj*
well-mannered, good, polite, respectful, under control, obedient, compliant, considerate, co-operative
COLLOQ. good as gold
🔄 disobedient, naughty

wellbeing *n*
welfare, good, happiness, comfort, (good) health

well-bred *adj*
well-mannered, polite, well-brought-up, mannerly, courteous, civil, refined, cultivated, cultured, genteel, gentlemanly, ladylike, aristocratic, blue-blooded, upper-crust, gallant, urbane
🔄 ill-bred

well-built *adj*
strong, muscular, brawny, strapping, sturdy, burly, beefy, stout

well-deserved *adj*
deserved, due, just, justified, merited, rightful, appropriate
OLD meet
FORMAL condign
🔄 undeserved

well-disposed *adj*
favourable, friendly, well-placed, sympathetic, agreeable, amicable, well-arranged, well-minded, well-aimed
🔄 ill-disposed

well-dressed *adj*
smart, well-groomed, elegant, fashionable, chic, stylish, neat, trim, dapper, spruce, tidy

COLLOQ. natty
🔄 badly-dressed, scruffy

well-founded *adj*
justifiable, reasonable, acceptable, warranted, sustainable, right, sensible, sound, proper, fit, valid, plausible

well-groomed *adj*
neat, tidy, smart, trim, spruce, dapper, well-turned-out, well-dressed

well-heeled *adj*
rich, wealthy, prosperous, affluent, well-off, moneyed, comfortable, well-to-do, solid, substantial
FORMAL opulent
COLLOQ. flush, rolling in it, made of money, fat-cat, posh
OLD COLLOQ. oofy
SLANG loaded, filthy rich, stinking rich

well-known *adj*
famous, renowned, celebrated, notorious, famed, eminent, notable, noted, illustrious, familiar, widely-known, usual, common
🔄 unknown

well-mannered *adj*
well-bred, polite, well-brought-up, mannerly, courteous, civil, refined, cultivated, cultured, genteel, gentlemanly, ladylike, aristocratic, blue-blooded, upper-crust, gallant, urbane
🔄 ill-mannered

well-nigh *adv*
almost, nearly, practically, virtually, all but, just about, to all intents and purposes

well-off *adj*
1 RICH, wealthy, affluent, prosperous, well-to-do, moneyed, thriving, successful, comfortable
COLLOQ. well-heeled, flush, rolling in it, made of money, in the money, with money to burn
SLANG loaded, filthy rich, stinking rich
2 FORTUNATE, lucky, prosperous, thriving, successful, comfortable
🔄 **1** poor, badly-off **2** unfortunate, unlucky

well-read *adj*
educated, literate, well-informed, knowledgeable, cultured, lettered

well-spoken *adj*
articulate, fluent, eloquent, clear, coherent, well-expressed

well-thought-of *adj*
respected, highly regarded, esteemed, venerated, admired, looked up to, honoured, revered
🔄 despised, looked down on

well-to-do *adj*
rich, wealthy, affluent, moneyed, prosperous, well-off, comfortable
COLLOQ. flush, rolling in it, made of money, fat-cat, posh
OLD COLLOQ. oofy
SLANG loaded, filthy rich, stinking rich
🔄 poor

well-versed *adj*
knowledgeable, familiar, acquainted, experienced, conversant, au fait, trained

well-wisher *n*
supporter, sympathizer, fan, well-willer

well-worn *adj*
1 *a well-worn phrase*
timeworn, stale, tired, trite, cliché(e)d, overused, unoriginal, hackneyed, commonplace, stock, stereotyped, threadbare
COLLOQ. corny
2 *well-worn clothing*
threadbare, worn, worn-out, frayed, ragged, scruffy, shabby
🔄 **1** original **2** new

welsh *v*
cheat, defraud, swindle
COLLOQ. diddle, do

welt *n*
weal, scar, mark, ridge, contusion, wound, streak, stripe, cicatrice, cicatrix

welter *v, n*
♦ *v*
roll, flounder, pitch, toss, wallow, splash, wade, lurch, heave
♦ *n*
mess, confusion, jumble, muddle, tangle, web, hotchpotch
COLLOQ. mish-mash

wend
■ **wend your way**
go, move, make your way, proceed, progress, travel, walk, hike, wander, trudge, plod, meander, amble
F⅃ stay

wet *adj, n, v*
♦ *adj*
1 DAMP, moist, soaked, soaking, sodden, saturated, soggy, sopping (wet), soppy, watery, waterlogged, drenched, dripping, dank, clammy, slippery, slippy, sloppy, sour, soused, spongy, squidgy, madid; *dialect* weet; *Scot* wat
2 RAINING, rainy, showery, teeming, pouring, drizzling, dank, damp, humid, clammy, muggy
3 WEAK, feeble, weedy, spineless, timorous, soft, namby-pamby, ineffective, irresolute
FORMAL ineffectual, effete
COLLOQ. pathetic, wimpish, cissy, drippy
F⅃ **1, 2** dry **3** strong
♦ *n*
1 WETNESS, moisture, moistness, damp, dampness, liquid, water, clamminess, condensation, humidity, rain, drizzle; *dialect* weet
OLD imbruement, madefaction
2 *don't be such a wet*
fool, idiot, softy, weakling, namby-pamby, milksop
COLLOQ. wimp, wally, drip, cissy, weed
SLANG jerk, nerd, wuss
F⅃ **1** dryness
♦ *v*
moisten, damp, dampen, wash, soak, saturate, drench, steep, flood, swamp, water, irrigate, spray, splash, sprinkle, imbue, douse, dip, sluice, sweat; *dialect* weet
OLD bedabble, bedrench, beweep, daggle, draggle, imbrue, madefy, moil; (*Shakesp*) bewet
F⅃ dry
■ **wet behind the ears**
new, untrained, inexperienced, immature, raw, innocent, naive, callow
COLLOQ. green
F⅃ experienced

SYNONYM NUANCES

adjective sense 1
You can use **damp** and **moist** of something showing traces of moisture, although **moist** in particular has positive connotations: *a moist sponge cake*. **Soggy** has more unwelcome connotations of something gone soft: *a disgusting breakfast of soggy corn flakes and warm milk*.
   More tactile sensations are emphasized with the terms **spongy**, which might be used of something porous or springy, or **squidgy**, which suggests being soft and pulpy to the touch. **Sloppy** suggests a more nauseating excess of wetness: *sloppy kisses*.
   Wet, humid atmospheres can be described using the terms **dank**, which suggests a somewhat unpleasant mustiness, and **clammy**, which suggests a disagreeable sticky warmth: *her heart raced and her skin felt clammy*.
   Soaked, **soaking**, **drenched**, **sopping** and **sodden** can all be used to suggest being completely imbued with liquid: *she peeled off her sodden clothes*, while **saturated** and **dripping** suggest an excess of water

running off: *her dripping hair and sodden dress*. The term **soused** would be used in the context of marinading or preserving food in liquid. **Waterlogged**, however, would be reserved for something rendered unusable by a surfeit of water: *a waterlogged pitch*.

wetness *n*
damp, dampness, moisture, wet, water, liquid, soddenness, sogginess, condensation, dankness, clamminess, humidity
F⅃ dryness

whack *v, n*
♦ *v*
hit, strike, smack, thrash, slap, beat, bang, clout, cuff, thump, box, buffet, rap
COLLOQ. bash, wallop, belt, clobber, biff, sock
♦ *n*
1 SMACK, slap, blow, hit, rap, stroke, thump, clout, cuff, box, bang
COLLOQ. bash, wallop
2 SHARE, portion, quota, allowance, allocation, lot, part, division, stint, proportion, percentage
COLLOQ. cut, rake-off, slice of the cake

whacking *adj*
enormous, huge, immense, vast, gigantic, massive, colossal, large-scale, gross, gargantuan, astronomic, monstrous, mammoth, considerable, tremendous, stupendous, prodigious, giant, Titanic
COLLOQ. jumbo, great big, whopping, walloping, whaling, plonking, ginormous, humongous, almighty, God-almighty
SLANG mega
F⅃ small, tiny

wharf *n*
dock, dockside, quay, quayside, jetty, landing-stage, dockyard, marina, pier; *dialect* staithe

what's-its-name *n*
thing
COLLOQ. thingummy, thingamy, thingy, thingummyjig, thingummybob, what-d'you-call-it, whatsit, doodah, doobrey, whatnot, gismo; *N Am* whatchamacallit, doodad, doofus, doohickey

wheedle *v*
cajole, coax, persuade, talk into, win over, charm, flatter, beguile, entice, induce, court, draw
FORMAL inveigle
COLLOQ. sweet-talk, butter up, soft-soap; *N Am* cozy up
F⅃ force

wheel *n, v*
♦ *n*
turn, revolution, circle, ring, hoop, rotation, gyration, pivot, roll, spin, twirl, whirl
♦ *v*
turn, rotate, circle, gyrate, orbit, spin, go round, pivot, twirl, whirl, swing, roll, revolve, swivel
■ **at the wheel**
1 DRIVING, steering, behind the wheel, in the driver's seat, turning
2 IN CHARGE, at the helm, in control, in command, responsible, directing
COLLOQ. heading up

Types of wheel include:

balance wheel	escape wheel	roulette wheel
big wheel	Ferris wheel	spinning jenny
buff-wheel	flywheel	spinning-wheel
cartwheel	gearwheel	sprocket
castor	idle wheel	spur gear
Catherine-wheel	mill wheel	steering wheel
charka	paddle wheel	wagon wheel
cogwheel	potter's wheel	water wheel
crown-wheel	prayer wheel	wheel of fortune
driving wheel	ratchet-wheel	worm wheel

wheeze v, n

♦ v
pant, gasp, cough, hiss, rasp, whistle
♦ n
1 RASP, gasp, cough, hiss, whistle
2 TRICK, joke, gag, crack, prank, ruse, practical joke, ploy, scheme, plan, stunt, idea, story, anecdote, catchphrase
COLLOQ. chestnut, one-liner, wrinkle

whereabouts n
location, position, place, situation, site, vicinity

wherewithal n
means, resources, supplies, money, cash, funds, capital, necessary
SLANG loot, readies, ready, megabucks, dough, dosh, bread, lolly, spondulicks, brass, gravy, greens, shekels, moolah, greenies, scratch, smash, stumpy

whet v
1 SHARPEN, hone, file, grind, edge
OLD stroke
2 STIMULATE, stir, rouse, arouse, excite, provoke, kindle, quicken, incite, awaken, titillate, increase
OLD appetize
☷ **1** blunt **2** dampen

whiff n
1 *a whiff of fresh air*
breath, puff, hint, trace, blast, gust, draught, odour, smell, aroma, sniff, scent, reek, stink, stench
2 *a whiff of scandal/danger*
trace, hint, suspicion, suggestion, soupçon, touch

while n, v
♦ n
time, period, spell, stretch, season, span, interval
■ **while away**
spend, pass, occupy, use (up), devote

whim n
fancy, caprice, notion, idea, quirk, freak, humour, conceit, fad, craze, passion, vagary, urge, impulse

whimper v, n
♦ v
cry, sob, weep, snivel, sniffle, whine, grizzle, mewl, moan, groan
COLLOQ. whinge
♦ n
sob, cry, snivel, whine, moan, groan

whimsical adj
fanciful, quirky, playful, mischievous, impulsive, unpredictable, eccentric, funny, droll, curious, whimsy, queer, unusual, weird, odd, peculiar, quaint
FORMAL capricious
COLLOQ. dotty

whimsy adj
playful, whimsical, fanciful, quirky, unpredictable, eccentric, funny, droll, curious, unusual, weird, odd, peculiar, quaint

whine v, n
♦ v
1 CRY, sob, whimper, grizzle, moan, wail
2 COMPLAIN, carp, grumble, moan, groan, grouse
COLLOQ. gripe, whinge, grouch, beef, bellyache
♦ n
1 CRY, sob, whimper, moan, wail
2 COMPLAINT, moan, grumble, groan, grouse
COLLOQ. gripe, grouch, beef, bellyache

whinge v, n
♦ v
complain, grumble, moan, carp; *Scot* greet, peenge
COLLOQ. gripe, grouse, beef, bellyache; *Scot* wheenge; *Aust* winge
♦ n
complaint, grumble, moan, groan, grouse
COLLOQ. gripe, beef, bellyache

whip v, n

♦ v
1 BEAT, flog, lash, scourge, birch, cane, strap, thrash, punish, discipline, rawhide, cowhide, kurbash
OLD feague; (*Shakesp*) firk
FORMAL flagellate, chastise, castigate
COLLOQ. tan, belt, whack, wallop, hide, larrup, whop, whap, give someone a good hiding
2 PULL, jerk, snatch, whisk, flash
OLD braid
COLLOQ. yank
3 DASH, dart, rush, tear, flit, fly
4 *whip the cream*
stir, mix, whisk, beat, beat up, switch
5 GOAD, drive, spur, prod, push, urge, stir, rouse, agitate, incite, provoke, prompt, instigate
♦ n
lash, scourge, switch, birch, cane, horsewhip, crop, riding-crop, cat-o'-nine-tails, flagellum, thong, black snake, bullwhip, bullwhack, cowhide, hunting-crop, hunting-whip, stock whip, lunge whip, longe whip, lunging whip, coachwhip, kurbash, ash-plant; *S Afr* sjambok
OLD knout, taw
■ **whip up**
stimulate, stir up, work up, agitate, excite, arouse, incite, inflame, kindle, instigate, provoke, foment
COLLOQ. psych up
☷ dampen, deter

whippersnapper n
scamp, scallywag, imp, rascal, nipper, upstart, pipsqueak, hobbledehoy

whipping n
beating, punishment, spanking, flogging, lashing, thrashing, birching, caning, hiding, scourging, knout; *Scot* laldie
FORMAL castigation, flagellation
COLLOQ. belting, tanning, walloping

whirl v, n
♦ v
spin, swirl, turn, twist, twirl, pivot, pirouette, swivel, wheel, rotate, revolve, turn round, eddy, reel, roll, gyrate, circle
♦ n
1 SPIN, twirl, twist, gyration, revolution, pirouette, swirl, turn, wheel, rotation, circle, reel, pivot, roll
2 BUSTLE, flurry, round, series, succession, merry-go-round, commotion, agitation, hubbub, hurly-burly, confusion, daze, muddle, jumble, giddiness, tumult, uproar
■ **give something a whirl**
try, attempt, strive, endeavour, venture
COLLOQ. have a go, have a bash/crack/shot/stab

whirlpool n
maelstrom, vortex, eddy, sea purse; *Scot* weel, weil, swelchie
OLD gulf, gurge
Related adjective: voraginous

whirlwind n, adj
♦ n
1 TORNADO, cyclone, vortex, typhoon, eddy, tourbillion, sand-devil, white squall
OLD typhon
2 BEDLAM, chaos, pandemonium, madhouse, commotion, confusion, furore, clamour, hubbub, hullabaloo, noise, tumult, turmoil, uproar, babel, anarchy
♦ adj
hasty, impulsive, quick, rapid, speedy, swift, lightning, headlong, impetuous, rash
☷ deliberate, slow

whisk v, n
♦ v
1 WHIP, beat, stir, mix
2 DART, dash, rush, hurry, speed, fly, tear, bolt, hasten, race, shoot, dive, whip
COLLOQ. belt, bomb, pelt, scoot, zip, go like the clappers
3 BRUSH, sweep, flick, wipe, twitch

♦ *n*
beater, brush, swizzle-stick

whisky *n*
whiskey, Scotch, bourbon, malt, rye, usquebaugh, moonshine
COLLOQ. *Scot & Irish* the cratur

whisper *v, n*
♦ *v*
1 MURMUR, mutter, mumble, say/speak quietly, breathe, hiss, rustle, sigh, burr, buzz, sough; *dialect* tittle; *Scot* whittie-whattie
OLD susurrate, round
2 HINT, intimate, insinuate, gossip, divulge
▣ **1** shout
♦ *n*
1 MURMUR, soft/quiet/low voice, undertone, sigh, hiss, rustle, breath, stage whisper, whisht, sough; *dialect* pig's whisper; *Scot* hark
OLD susurrus
2 HINT, suggestion, suspicion, breath, whiff, rumour, report, innuendo, insinuation, trace, tinge, soupçon, buzz

whistle *v, n*
♦ *v*
pipe, sing, call, cheep, chirp, warble
♦ *n*
song, call, cheep, warble, chirp, siren, hooter

whit *n*
atom, little, drop, bit, scrap, shred, piece, fragment, particle, crumb, pinch, speck, trace, iota, jot, spot, grain, mite, modicum, dash, hoot
▣ lot

white *adj*
1 PALE, light-skinned, pallid, wan, ashen, colourless, anaemic, pasty, waxen
2 LIGHT, snowy, milky, creamy, ivory, hoary, silver, grey
3 PURE, immaculate, spotless, stainless, undefiled, moral, virtuous, blameless
▣ **1** black, dark, ruddy **2** dark **3** defiled

white-collar *adj*
executive, office, professional, salaried, clerical, non-manual
▣ blue-collar, manual

whiten *v*
bleach, blanch, whitewash, pale, fade
OLD dealbate
FORMAL etiolate
▣ blacken, darken

whitewash *n, v*
♦ *n*
cover-up, concealment, deception, camouflage, -gate
▣ exposure
♦ *v*
1 COVER UP, conceal, hide, make light of, suppress, gloss over, camouflage
2 THRASH, beat, defeat utterly, crush, drub, best; *Scot* granny
COLLOQ. clobber, hammer, lick, paste, trounce
▣ **1** expose

whittle *v*
1 CARVE, cut, scrape, shave, trim, pare, hew, shape
2 ERODE, eat away, wear away, diminish, consume, use (up), reduce, undermine

whole *adj, n*
♦ *adj*
1 COMPLETE, entire, integral, full, total, unabridged, uncut, undivided, unedited
2 INTACT, unharmed, undamaged, unbroken, perfect, sound, in one piece, mint, uninjured, unhurt
FORMAL inviolate
3 WELL, healthy, fit, sound, strong
▣ **1** partial **2** damaged **3** ill

♦ *n*
total, aggregate, sum total, entirety, all, fullness, totality, ensemble, entity, unit, lot, piece, everything
COLLOQ. *Aust & NZ* the whole box and dice
▣ part
■ **on the whole**
generally, mostly, in general, generally speaking, in the main, as a rule, for the most part, all in all, all things considered, by and large, predominantly

> QUOTATIONS
> All are but parts of one stupendous whole, / Whose body, Nature is, and God the soul
> ALEXANDER POPE, *An Essay on Man*

wholehearted *adj*
enthusiastic, earnest, committed, dedicated, devoted, hearty, passionate, heartfelt, emphatic, warm, sincere, unfeigned, genuine, unreserved, unstinting, unqualified, complete, true, real, zealous
COLLOQ. *Aust & NZ* boots and all
▣ half-hearted

wholeheartedly *adv*
completely, enthusiastically, emphatically, warmly, heartily, passionately, sincerely, genuinely, unreservedly
▣ half-heartedly

wholesale *adj, adv*
♦ *adj*
comprehensive, far-reaching, extensive, sweeping, wide-ranging, mass, broad, all-inclusive, outright, total, massive, indiscriminate
▣ partial
♦ *adv*
indiscriminately, totally, extensively, comprehensively, massively, en bloc
▣ partially

wholesome *adj*
1 *wholesome food; a wholesome climate*
good, healthy, healthful, hygienic, sanitary, nutritious, nourishing, beneficial, salutary, refreshing, invigorating, bracing, sweet, healthsome; *Scot* healsome
FORMAL salubrious
2 *wholesome entertainment*
moral, decent, clean, proper, improving, edifying, uplifting, pure, virtuous, righteous, beneficial, helpful, ethical, honourable, respectable, sound
COLLOQ. squeaky-clean
▣ **1** unhealthy **2** unwholesome, immoral

wholly *adv*
completely, entirely, fully, purely, absolutely, totally, utterly, comprehensively, altogether, perfectly, thoroughly, all, exclusively, only, in every respect
COLLOQ. one hundred per cent
▣ partly

whoop *v, n*
shout, cry, yell, cheer, scream, shriek, roar, hoop, hoot, hurrah
COLLOQ. holler

whopper *n*
1 LIE, falsehood, fabrication, untruth, fable
COLLOQ. cracker, fairy story, tall story
2 GIANT, monster, mammoth, colossus, whale, hippopotamus, leviathan
OLD *N Am* scrouger
SLANG stonker, plumper, slapper
OLD SLANG swapper; *N Am* sockdologer

whopping *adj*
large, big, huge, massive, extraordinary, immense, vast, great, mammoth, tremendous, staggering, monumental, enormous, giant, gigantic
FORMAL prodigious
COLLOQ. jumbo, great big, walloping, whacking, whaling, plonking, ginormous, humongous, almighty, God-almighty

SLANG mega
⊟ tiny

whore *n*

prostitute, harlot, callgirl, rent-boy, woman of the streets, woman of the town, woman of ill repute, loose woman, fallen woman, scarlet woman, trollop, street-walker, cocotte, courtesan, bawd, *fille de joie, fille des rues,* drab, grande cocotte, lorette, lady of the night, geisha, hetaera, hierodule, loose fish, magdalen, night-walker, vizard-mask
OLD bulker, convertite, trull, moll, strumpet, cockatrice, public woman, wench, pug, punk, stew, stale; (*Shakesp*) quail, bona-roba, callet, polecat, road, venture
COLLOQ. hooker, hustler, pro, hostess, fancy woman; *N Am* working girl
SLANG *poule de luxe,* quiff, rough trade, tart, tom, tramp, brass, floozie; *N Am* broad
OLD SLANG dell, mutton, dolly-mop, plover; (*Shakesp*) laced mutton

whorehouse *n*

brothel, bordello, bawdy-house, house of ill fame, house of ill repute, bagnio, disorderly house; *Irish* kip; *N Am* sporting house
OLD bordel, flash-house, stew, vaulting-house, Corinth; (*Shakesp*) hothouse, leaping-house
COLLOQ. red light
SLANG knocking-shop, crib; *N Am* cathouse

whorl *n*

spiral, twist, turn, coil, loop, helix, vortex, corkscrew
FORMAL convolution

wicked *adj*

1 EVIL, sinful, immoral, bad, depraved, corrupt, vicious, unprincipled, debased, abominable, ungodly, devilish, unrighteous, unholy, shameful, black-hearted, villainous, guilty, ill, perverse, abandoned, miscreant
OLD facinorous, felon, felonious, flagitious, scelerate, unkind, wick; (*Shakesp*) high-viced, naughty
FORMAL iniquitous, heinous, dissolute, egregious, nefarious
2 BAD, unpleasant, harmful, offensive, scandalous, vile, worthless, difficult, terrible, dreadful, distressing, awful, atrocious, severe, intense, nasty, injurious, troublesome, foul, fierce
3 NAUGHTY, mischievous, roguish, impish, rascally
4 EXCELLENT, admirable
COLLOQ. terrific, amazing, fantastic, brilliant, neat, ace, brill, boffo, out of this world, second to none, divine, heavenly, fabulous, sensational, not half bad
SLANG mega, cool, mean, the business, stonking, radical, rad, crucial, way-out, shit-hot, the dog's bollocks, groovy, clinking, def, fab
⊟ 1 good, upright 2 harmless

wickedness *n*

evil, depravity, vileness, atrocity, abomination, corruption, corruptness, foulness, fiendishness, immorality, shamefulness, sin, sinfulness, impiety, unrighteousness, devilishness, enormity, amorality
FORMAL dissoluteness, heinousness, iniquity, reprobacy
⊟ uprightness

wickerwork *n*

wicker, basket-work, wattle, wattle-work

wide *adj, adv*

♦ *adj*
1 BROAD, roomy, spacious, extensive, vast, immense, ample
2 DILATED, expanded, full
3 EXTENSIVE, wide-ranging, comprehensive, great, broad, vast, immense, far-reaching, general
4 LOOSE, baggy, full, roomy
FORMAL capacious
5 OFF-TARGET, off-course, off the mark, distant, remote
⊟ 1 narrow 3 restricted 5 near
♦ *adv*
1 ASTRAY, off course, off target, off the mark
2 FULLY, completely, to the full extent, all the way
⊟ 1 on target

┃ **wide** or **broad**?
See panel at **broad**.

wide-awake *adj*

conscious, aware, fully awake, wakened, observant, watchful, vigilant, wary, sharp, alert, astute, roused, heedful, keen, quick-witted, on your toes, on the alert, on the qui vive
COLLOQ. on the ball
⊟ asleep

wide-eyed *adj*

1 INEXPERIENCED, innocent, artless, guileless, ingenuous, naive, fresh, natural, simple, open, frank, unsophisticated, unworldly, childlike, angelic, credulous, gullible, trusting, trustful, dewy-eyed, unsuspecting
2 ASTONISHED, surprised, startled, amazed, astounded, stunned, dazed, staggered, dumbfounded, taken aback, shocked, confounded, bewildered, open-eyed, open-mouthed
COLLOQ. lost for words, knocked for six, bowled over, flabbergasted, gobsmacked, thunderstruck

widely *adv*

broadly, extensively, generally, comprehensively

widen *v*

broaden, expand, extend, spread, increase, stretch, enlarge
FORMAL distend, dilate
⊟ narrow

wide-open *adj*

open, gaping, wide, outspread, outstretched, spread, unprotected, vulnerable, defenceless, exposed, susceptible
FORMAL unfortified
⊟ closed, narrow

wide-ranging *adj*

far-reaching, broad, extensive, widespread, comprehensive, thorough, thoroughgoing, important, significant, momentous, sweeping

widespread *adj*

extensive, prevalent, rife, general, sweeping, universal, global, wholesale, far-reaching, unlimited, broad, common, pervasive, far-flung
⊟ limited

widow *n*

feme sole, dowager, war widow, grass widow, hempen widow, suttee; *dialect* widdy
OLD relict
Related adjective: vidual

width *n*

breadth, broadness, diameter, wideness, compass, thickness, largeness, span, scope, range, measure, girth, beam, amplitude, extent, extensiveness, reach

wield *v*

1 *wield a weapon*
brandish, flourish, swing, wave, handle, ply, shake, play, manage, manipulate, apply
OLD weld, wild, sway, wind; (*Spenser*) sownd
2 *wield power*
have, hold, possess, employ, exert, exercise, use, utilize, control, maintain, command, manage, apply

wife *n*

partner, spouse, companion, mate, bride, woman, lady, married woman, *femmefrau,* consort, daughter-in-law, sister-in-law, stepmother, child-wife, concubine, first lady, helpmate, princess, queen
OLD helpmeet, dame; (*Shakesp*) kickie-wickie
COLLOQ. better half, other half, missus, old lady, rib
OLD COLLOQ. little woman
SLANG dutch, trouble and strife
Related adjective: uxorial

wig *n*

hairpiece, toupee, postiche, scratch-wig, spencer, bobwig, Brutus, buzz-wig, tie-wig; *Scot* gizz, jiz

OLD periwig, peruke, transformation, bagwig, caxon, major, Ramilie
OLD COLLOQ. jasey

wiggle *v, n*
jiggle, shake, jerk, wriggle, wag, waggle, twist, squirm, twitch, writhe

wild *adj*
1 UNTAMED, undomesticated, savage, barbarous, primitive, uncivilized, natural, unbroken, ferocious, fierce, brutish
FORMAL feral
2 UNCULTIVATED, natural, desolate, waste, barren, forsaken, unpopulated, uninhabited, unsettled, rugged, inhospitable
3 UNRESTRAINED, unruly, undisciplined, unmanageable, violent, turbulent, rowdy, lawless, out of control, uncontrollable, ungovernable, rampant, disorderly, riotous, boisterous
4 STORMY, tempestuous, raging, rough, furious, violent, blustery, choppy, turbulent
5 UNTIDY, unkempt, messy, dishevelled, tousled, uncombed
6 RECKLESS, rash, impulsive, foolish, foolhardy, impracticable, impractical, irrational, outrageous, preposterous, absurd, ridiculous, wayward, extravagant, fantastic, unwise, imprudent
7 MAD, frenzied, distraught, demented, berserk, frantic, beside yourself
COLLOQ. crazy, nuts, nutty, bonkers, bananas
8 ANGRY, furious, raging, enraged, infuriated, incensed, blazing, fuming
COLLOQ. crazy, mad, hopping mad, foaming at the mouth
9 ENTHUSIASTIC, keen, fervent, vehement, passionate, excited, fanatical
COLLOQ. crazy, mad, nuts, daft, potty
10 *a wild guess*
random, arbitrary, chance, casual, incidental, haphazard, irregular, accidental, aimless, purposeless, indiscriminate
FORMAL fortuitous, serendipitous
COLLOQ. hit-or-miss
Fa 1 tame, civilized **2** cultivated **3** restrained **4** calm **5** tidy **6** sensible **7** sane

wilderness *n*
desert, wasteland, waste, wilds, jungle

wild flower

Wild flowers include:

Aaron's rod	cuckoo flower	ragged robin
ale hoof	daisy	rock rose
bird's foot trefoil	edelweiss	rough-fruited
birth-wort	field cow-wheat	cinquefoil
bistort	foxglove	self-heal
black-eyed susan	goatsbeard	shepherd's club
bladder campion	goldcup	solomon's seal
bluebell	goldenrod	stiff-haired
broomrape	great mullein	sunflower
butter-and-eggs	harebell	stonecrop
buttercup	heartsease	teasel
campion	heather	toadflax
celandine	horsetail	violet
clary	lady's slipper	water lily
clover	lady's smock	white campion
clustered bell-	lungwort	wild chicory
flower	marguerite	wild endive
columbine	masterwort	wild gladiolus
comfrey	moneywort	wild iris
common	multiflora rose	wild orchid
evening-primrose	New England aster	wild pansy
common mallow	oxeye daisy	wood anemone
common toadflax	oxslip	yarrow
cowslip	pennyroyal	yellow rocket
crane's bill	poppy	
crowfoot	primrose	

See also **weed**.

---

wildlife *n*
animals, fauna

wildly *adv*
1 *behave wildly*
irresponsibly, rebelliously, anarchically, defiantly, recklessly, chaotically
2 *yell wildly*
unrestrainedly, uncontrollably, noisily, riotously, boisterously, angrily, furiously
3 *wildly impractical*
foolishly, outrageously, absurdly, preposterously, ridiculously, fantastically, extravagantly
4 *guess wildly*
arbitrarily, casually, haphazardly, aimlessly, indiscriminately, unmethodically, unsystematically
Fa 1 responsibly **2** calmly **3** sensibly

wilds *n*
outback, remote areas, wasteland, wilderness, desert
COLLOQ. the back of beyond, the sticks, the middle of nowhere; *N Am* the boondocks, the boonies

wiles *n*
tricks, stratagems, ruses, ploys, devices, contrivances, guile, manoeuvres, subterfuge, cunning, deceit, deception, cheating, trickery, fraud, craftiness, artfulness, chicanery
COLLOQ. dodges
Fa guilelessness

wilful *adj*
1 DELIBERATE, conscious, intentional, voluntary, willing, calculated, planned, premeditated
2 SELF-WILLED, headstrong, obstinate, stubborn, pig-headed, mulish, inflexible, unyielding, uncompromising, perverse, wayward, contrary, determined, dogged; *Scot* willyard
FORMAL obdurate, refractory, intransigent, intractable
Fa 1 unintentional, spontaneous **2** good-natured, easy-going

will *n, v*
♦ *n*
1 VOLITION, choice, option, prerogative, preference, decision, discretion
2 WISH, desire, inclination, feeling, fancy, disposition, mind, attitude
3 PURPOSE, resolve, resolution, determination, purposefulness, willpower, single-mindedness, aim, intention, command
♦ *v*
1 WANT, desire, wish, intend, choose, compel, direct, command, decree, order, ordain
2 BEQUEATH, leave, hand down, pass on, pass down, dispose of
FORMAL transfer, confer

> **PROVERBS**
> Where there's a will, there's a way

willing *adj*
disposed, inclined, agreeable, ready, prepared, consenting, content, amenable, biddable, compliant, co-operative, pleased, well-disposed, so-minded, favourable, happy, glad, eager, enthusiastic, keen
COLLOQ. game, up for it
Fa unwilling, disinclined, reluctant

willingly *adv*
readily, unhesitatingly, eagerly, freely, happily, cheerfully, by choice, voluntarily, gladly, nothing loath, lief
Fa unwillingly

willingness *n*
readiness, inclination, will, wish, consent, compliance, desire, favour, enthusiasm, agreeableness, agreement, disposition, volition
FORMAL complaisance
Fa unwillingness

willowy *adj*
slender, slim, tall, graceful, svelte, sylph-like, limber,
lissom, lithe, lithesome, supple
E3 buxom

willpower *n*
determination, resolution, resolve, single-mindedness,
commitment, will, strength of will, self-control, self-
discipline, self-mastery, self-command, persistence,
doggedness, drive
COLLOQ. grit

willy-nilly *adv*
1 WHETHER YOU LIKE IT OR NOT, necessarily, compulsorily,
of necessity
FORMAL perforce
2 HAPHAZARDLY, randomly, by chance, arbitrarily,
carelessly, indiscriminately, irregularly, unmethodically,
unsystematically

wilt *v*
droop, sag, wither, shrivel, flop, flag, dwindle, weaken,
faint, diminish, lessen, grow less, fail, fade, languish, taint,
ebb, sink, wane
E3 perk up

wily *adj*
shrewd, cunning, scheming, artful, sharp, crafty, foxy,
intriguing, tricky, underhand, shifty, deceitful, cheating,
deceptive, astute, sly, guileful, designing, crooked
COLLOQ. fly
E3 guileless

wimp *n*
fool, softy, clown, milksop, weed, namby-pamby
COLLOQ. clot, drip, wally, wet
SLANG jerk, nerd, wuss; *Aust* tonk

wimpish *adj*
weak, feeble, weedy, spineless, timorous, soft, namby-
pamby, ineffective, irresolute
FORMAL ineffectual, effete
COLLOQ. wet, pathetic, drippy, cissy
SLANG wussy

win *v, n*
♦ *v*
1 BE VICTORIOUS, triumph, succeed, achieve success,
prevail, overcome, conquer, come (in) first, carry off,
finish first
COLLOQ. win the day, win hands down,
come out on top, turn up trumps, strike gold, hit the
jackpot
2 GAIN, acquire, achieve, attain, accomplish, receive,
secure, obtain, get, earn, collect, catch, net
FORMAL procure
E3 1 fail, lose
♦ *n*
victory, triumph, conquest, success, mastery
E3 defeat
■ **win over**
persuade, convince, influence, convert, sway,
win/talk/bring round, charm, allure, attract
FORMAL prevail upon

> **QUOTATIONS**
> Winning isn't everything, but wanting to win is
>   VINCE LOMBARDI

wince *v, n*
♦ *v*
start, jump, draw back, recoil, flinch, jerk, shrink, pull a
face, cringe, blench, cower, quail
♦ *n*
start, cringe, flinch, jerk

wind[1] *n*
blowing in the wind
air, breeze, draught, gust, puff, breath, air-current, blast,
current, airstream, bluster, gale, hurricane, tornado
Related adjective: aeolian

■ **get wind of**
hear about, learn of, find out about, discover, become
aware of
COLLOQ. hear on the grapevine
■ **in the wind**
likely, probable, expected, about to happen
COLLOQ. on the cards
■ **put the wind up**
scare, frighten, discourage, alarm, unnerve, startle, panic,
agitate, daunt, sound the alarm
FORMAL perturb
COLLOQ. rattle, spook, boggle, scare someone out of their
wits, make someone's blood run cold, scare the living
daylights out of, make someone's hair stand on end, make
someone jump out of their skin, put the frighteners on
SLANG scare the shit out of

> **PROVERBS**
> It's an ill wind that blows nobody any good

Types of wind include:

anticyclone	harmattan	samiel
austral wind	helm wind	simoom
berg wind	khamsin	sirocco
bise	La Niña	snow eater
bora	levant	southerly
Aust buster	libeccio	southerly buster
Cape doctor	marin	trade wind
chinook	meltemi	tramontana
cyclone	mistral	westerly
doctor	monsoon	wet chinook
east wind	north wind	williwaw
El Niño	nor'wester	willy-willy
etesian	ostro	zephyr
Favonian wind	pampero	zonda
föhn	poniente	
gregale	prevailing wind	

wind[2] *v, n*
♦ *v*
1 CURVE, bend, loop, spiral, zigzag, twine, turn, twist and
turn, snake, deviate, meander, ramble
2 COIL, wrap, twist, turn, curl, twine, encircle, furl,
wreathe, roll, reel
♦ *n*
bend, curve, turn, twist, zigzag, meander
■ **wind down**
1 SLOW (DOWN), slacken off, lessen, reduce, subside,
diminish, dwindle, decline, stop, bring/come to
an end
2 RELAX, unwind, quieten down, ease up, calm down,
de-stress
COLLOQ. take it/things easy, let yourself go, make yourself
at home, let your hair down, put your feet up, hang loose,
cool it, chill (out), lighten up
E3 1 increase
■ **wind up**
1 CLOSE (DOWN), end, finalize, finish, stop, bring to a
close, bring to an end, liquidate
FORMAL conclude, terminate
2 END UP, finish up, find yourself, settle
3 ANNOY, irritate, disconcert, tease, fool, trick, make fun of
COLLOQ. kid, rib, pull someone's leg, rub someone up the
wrong way, take the mickey out of
SLANG take the piss out of; *N Am* goof
E3 1 begin

windbag *n*
boaster, gossip, bore, braggart, blether
COLLOQ. gasbag, bigmouth

winded *adj*
puffed out, breathless, out of breath, panting,
puffed, out of puff
E3 fresh

windfall n
stroke of luck, bonanza, godsend, jackpot, treasure-trove, find, manna, pennies from heaven

winding adj
curving, turning, twisting, twisting and turning, bending, crooked, tortuous, indirect, roundabout, spiral, twining, coiling, circuitous, meandering, serpentine
FORMAL sinuous, sinuate(d), flexuose, flexuous, anfractuous, convoluted
Ⅲ straight

window n
pane, light, opening

Types of window include:

astragal	French	rose window
bay	lancet	sash
bow	louvre window	secondary-glazed
bull's eye	lucarne	shop window
casement	mullioned win-	skylight
Catherine-wheel	dow	sliding window
compass	Norman	stained glass
decorated	oeil-de-boeuf	window
dormer	oriel	ticket window
double-glazed	patio door	Velux® window
double-glazing	perpendicular	windscreen
early English	porthole	
fanlight	quarterlight	

windpipe n
throat, pharynx, larynx, pipes, throttle, thropple; Scot thrapple
OLD weasand, weasand-pipe
TECHNICAL trachea
Related adjective: tracheal

windswept adj
1 a windswept mountainside
windy, blowy, exposed, unprotected, unsheltered, open, barren, desolate, bleak
2 windswept hair
dishevelled, disordered, ruffled, tousled, unkempt, untidy, messy, in a mess

windy adj
1 windy weather
breezy, blowy, blustery, squally, windswept, stormy, wild, tempestuous, gusty
2 windy speech
long-winded, wordy, verbose, garrulous, rambling, turgid, pompous, bombastic
FORMAL prolix
3 NERVOUS, uneasy, on edge, anxious, stressed, afraid, frightened, scared, timid
COLLOQ. chicken, nervy
Ⅲ 1 calm, windless 3 fearless

wine n
SLANG vino, plonk
Related adjective: vinous

Types of wine include:

alcohol-free	house white	sherry
amontillado	house wine	sparkling
blush wine	ice wine	straw wine
Aust colloq.	medium sherry	sweet
bombo	mulled wine	sweet sherry
brut	oloroso	table wine
demi-sec	plonk	tawny port
dry	port	tonic wine
dry sherry	red wine	vintage port
fino	rosé	vintage wine
fortified wine	ruby port	white port
house red	sec	

Varieties of wine include:

alicant	Frascati	Petite Sirah
Alsace	Gewürztraminer	Piesporter
Asti	Graves	Pinotage
Auslese	Grenache	Pinot Grigio
bacharach	(or Garnacha)	Pinot Noir
Bardolino	Hermitage	retsina
Barolo	hock	Rhine wine
Barsac	jerepigo	Riesling
Beaujolais	Johannisberg	Rioja
Beaujolais	Kabinett	Rüdesheimer
Nouveau	lachryma Christi	Sancerre
Beaune	Lambrusco	sangiovese
Bordeaux	Langue d'oc	Sauterne
bucellas	Liebfraumilch	Sauvignon Blanc
Burgundy	Mâcon	scuppernong
Cabernet	Madeira	Sekt
Sauvignon	Malaga	Sémillon
canary	Malbec	Shiraz (or Syrah)
Carménère	Marcobrunner	Soave
Cava	Marsala	Spätlese
Chablis	Médoc	Steinberger
Chambertin	Merlot	St Julien
champagne	Minervois	Sylvaner
Chardonnay	Montepulciano	Tarragona
Chenin Blanc	d'Abruzzo	Tavel
Chianti	Montilla	Tempranillo
claret	Moselle	Tokay
Constantia	muscat	Valpolicella
Côtes du Rhône	Muscadet	vinho verde
Crémant d'Alsace	muscatel	Viognier
Crémant de Loire	nebbiolo	Vouvray
Dão	Niersteiner	Zinfandel
Douro	Orvieto	

wine bottle sizes

Sizes of wine bottles include:

magnum	jeroboam	salmanazar
flagon	methuselah	balthazar
Marie-Jeanne	rehoboam	nebuchadnezzar

wine glass n
glass, goblet, flute, schooner

wing n, v
♦ n
1 SECTION, branch, arm, faction, group, grouping, flank, circle, coterie, set, segment, side
2 ANNEXE, adjunct, extension, attachment, part, side
♦ v
fly, glide, flit, hurry, move, travel, pass, speed, race, soar, zoom
FORMAL hasten
■ **wing it**
extemporize, ad-lib, compose/perform without preparation, vamp
COLLOQ. say whatever comes into your head/mind, speak off the cuff, speak off the top of your head, play by ear

wink v, n
♦ v
blink, flutter, glimmer, glint, glitter, twinkle, gleam, sparkle, flicker, flash
FORMAL nictate, nictitate
♦ n
1 BLINK, flutter, sparkle, twinkle, glimmering, gleam, glitter, glint, flash
FORMAL nictation, nictitation
2 INSTANT, moment, second, split second, flash
■ **wink at**
ignore, disregard, overlook, neglect, pass over, condone, take no notice of
COLLOQ. turn a blind eye to

winkle *v*
extract, extricate, draw out, worm, force, prise, flush

winner *n*
champion, victor, prizewinner, medallist, title-holder, world-beater, conqueror
FORMAL vanquisher
COLLOQ. champ
E∃ loser

winning *adj*
1 CONQUERING, triumphant, unbeaten, undefeated, victorious, successful
FORMAL vanquishing
2 WINSOME, charming, attractive, captivating, engaging, beguiling, bewitching, fetching, enchanting, endearing, delightful, amiable, alluring, lovely, pleasing, sweet
E∃ **1** losing **2** unappealing

winnings *n*
jackpot, gains, proceeds, profits, takings, prize(s), prize money, booty, spoils
E∃ losses

winnow *v*
sift, separate, screen, divide, cull, select, sort, part, comb, fan

winsome *adj*
charming, attractive, captivating, engaging, beguiling, bewitching, fetching, enchanting, endearing, appealing, cheerful, pleasant, delightful, amiable, alluring, lovely, pleasing, pretty, prepossessing, sweet
OLD comely
FORMAL delectable
E∃ unattractive

wintry *adj*
1 *wintry weather*
cold, chilly, bleak, cheerless, biting, piercing, raw, desolate, dismal, harsh, snowy, arctic, frosty, freezing, frozen, icy, glacial
FORMAL hibernal, hiemal
2 UNFRIENDLY, hostile, bleak, cheerless, desolate, dismal, cold, frosty, icy, cool, harsh

wipe *v, n*
♦ *v*
1 RUB, clean, cleanse, dry, dust, brush, sweep, mop, swab, sponge, clear, dab; *Scot* dicht, dight
TECHNICAL absterge
FORMAL deterge
2 REMOVE, erase, take away, take off, get rid of
OLD expunct, null
FORMAL expunge, purge
♦ *n*
rub, clean, dry, dust, brush, mop, sponge, swab, dab
■ **wipe out**
eradicate, obliterate, destroy, massacre, exterminate, annihilate, erase, expunge, raze, abolish, blot out, demolish
FORMAL efface, extirpate
COLLOQ. liquidate, rub out, decimate, polish off, waste, blow away, zap

wire-pulling *n*
scheming, plotting, influence, intrigue, conspiring, manipulation, pull, Machiavellianism
COLLOQ. clout

wiry *adj*
1 SINEWY, muscular, lean, tough, strong
2 *wiry hair*
coarse, wavy, rough
E∃ **1** puny, flabby **2** soft

wisdom *n*
discernment, penetration, reason, sense, astuteness, comprehension, enlightenment, judgement, insight, common sense, prudence, understanding, knowledge, learning, intelligence, foresight, experience
OLD sapience
FORMAL sagacity, judiciousness, erudition, circumspection

Related adjective: Palladian
E∃ folly, stupidity

QUOTATIONS
Wisdom comes not from reason but from love
ANDRÉ GIDE, *Les Nourritures terrestres*

wise *adj*
1 DISCERNING, perceptive, rational, informed, well-informed, understanding, enlightened, knowing, educated, knowledgeable, intelligent, clever, aware, experienced
OLD sapient
FORMAL sage, sagacious, erudite
2 WELL-ADVISED, reasonable, sensible, sound, far-sighted, long-sighted, shrewd, prudent, politic, common-sense
FORMAL judicious, sagacious, circumspect
E∃ **1** foolish, stupid **2** ill-advised, foolhardy
■ **put wise**
inform, notify, tip off, warn, tell, alert, fill in, intimate to, put in the picture, clue in
FORMAL apprise
COLLOQ. wise up

PROVERBS
It's easy to be wise after the event

wiseacre *n*
wise guy, wiseling
COLLOQ. smart alec, smartypants, clever dick

wisecrack *n*
quip, joke, jest, funny, witticism, gag, barb, gibe, pun, in-joke
COLLOQ. one-liner

wisely *adv*
sensibly, soundly, shrewdly, perceptively, rationally, knowingly, intelligently, clearly
FORMAL sagely, sagaciously
E∃ foolishly, stupidly

wish *v, n*
♦ *v*
1 DESIRE, want, yearn, long, hanker, pine, covet, crave, aspire, hope, fancy, hunger, thirst, prefer, need, lust
COLLOQ. yen
2 ASK, bid, require, order, instruct, direct, command
♦ *n*
1 DESIRE, want, hankering, aspiration, inclination, longing, craving, hunger, thirst, liking, fondness, preference, yearning, urge, whim, hope, fancy
COLLOQ. yen
2 REQUEST, desire, bidding, order, instruction, command, will

PROVERBS
The wish is father to the thought

wishy-washy *adj*
feeble, weak, insipid, thin, watered-down, watery, flat, bland, ineffective, vapid, tasteless
FORMAL ineffectual
COLLOQ. namby-pamby, vanilla
E∃ strong, firm

wisp *n*
shred, strand, thread, twist, piece, lock

wispy *adj*
thin, straggly, frail, fine, insubstantial, light, flimsy, fragile, delicate, ethereal, gossamer, faint
FORMAL attenuated
E∃ substantial

wistful *adj*
1 THOUGHTFUL, pensive, musing, reflective, wishful, contemplative, dreamy, dreaming, meditative
2 MELANCHOLY, sad, forlorn, longing, yearning, mournful, regretful
FORMAL disconsolate

wistfully *adv*
thoughtfully, pensively, sadly, forlornly, longingly, mournfully, plaintively

wit *n*
1 HUMOUR, funniness, wittiness, repartee, facetiousness, drollery, banter, badinage, jocularity, levity, waggishness, liveliness, *esprit*, salt, sparkle
OLD eutrapelia
2 INTELLIGENCE, cleverness, sense, reason, common sense, wisdom, understanding, judgement, insight, shrewdness, astuteness, faculties, intellect, concetto, mother wit
FORMAL sagacity
COLLOQ. brains, gumption, nous, marbles
3 HUMORIST, comedian, comic, satirist, joker, gagman, wag, *bel esprit, homme d'esprit*
OLD wagha
≠ 1 seriousness 2 stupidity

SYNONYM NUANCES

sense 1
You can use **humour** to suggest an inherent sense of delight in the ludicrous, while **funniness** implies the ability to cause laughter or smiles. **Wittiness**, on the other hand, is more redolent of sharp, intelligent humour which one admires, and **repartee** would be used likewise of sharp witty retorts. **Facetiousness**, however, is less approbatory, and implies an element of flippancy.
   Drollery suggests wry wit, unlike **banter**, which implies a degree of teasing, while **badinage** has implications of playfulness. You can use **jocularity** to suggest a propensity for joking, whereas **levity** has more to do with frivolity and being carefree. **Waggishness**, on the other hand, implies an element of mischievousness: *the waggishness of his cartoons satirizing politicians.*

---

witch *n*
sorceress, enchantress, occultist, magician, hex, hag, besom-rider, night-hag, pythoness, sibyl, weird, wise woman; *Scot* carline, gyre-carline
OLD *Scot* galdragon
FORMAL necromancer

witchcraft *n*
sorcery, magic, wizardry, Wicca, occultism, the occult, the black art, black magic, enchantment, voodoo, spell, incantation, divination
FORMAL necromancy, conjuration

witch doctor *n*
magician, medicine man/woman, shaman, angekok, mganga; *S Afr* sangoma

witch hunt *n*
hounding, hue and cry, McCarthyism

with *prep*
accompanied by, in the company of, in association with, by, using, among, including, together

withdraw *v*
1 REMOVE, take away, take out, pull back, draw back, draw out, pull out, extract
2 DEPART, go (away), absent yourself, retire, remove, leave, back out, draw back, fall back, recede, drop out, pull out, retreat, secede, scratch, opt out, contract out
3 RECANT, disclaim, take back, revoke, retract, cancel, annul, abolish, recall, take away
FORMAL rescind, abjure, nullify
4 RECOIL, shrink back, cower, draw back, pull back

withdrawal *n*
1 REMOVAL, taking away, pulling back, drawing back/out, extraction, disengagement
2 DEPARTURE, exit, exodus, falling back, retirement, retreat, evacuation, disengagement
3 REPUDIATION, recantation, disclaimer, revocation, recall, secession
FORMAL disavowal, abjuration

withdrawn *adj*
1 RESERVED, unsociable, shy, introvert, introverted, quiet, retiring, retired, aloof, detached, shrinking, private, uncommunicative, unforthcoming, taciturn, silent
2 REMOTE, isolated, distant, secluded, out-of-the-way, private, hidden, solitary
≠ 1 extrovert, outgoing, forthcoming

wither *v*
shrink, shrivel, dry (up), wilt, droop, weaken, decay, disintegrate, dwindle, wane, perish, atrophy, die (off), disappear, fade (away), languish, decline, waste, taint, scorch, welt; *Scot* gizzen
OLD arefy, blast, welk
COLLOQ. miff off
≠ flourish, thrive

withering *adj*
scornful, contemptuous, scathing, snubbing, humiliating, mortifying, wounding, destructive, deadly, death-dealing, devastating
≠ encouraging, supportive

withhold *v*
keep back, retain, hold back, suppress, restrain, repress, control, curb, check, keep in check, reserve, deduct, refuse, hide, conceal
FORMAL decline
≠ give, accord

within *prep*
inside, not over, in reach of, inside the limits/bounds of, enclosed by, surrounded by

with it *adj*
fashionable, vogue, modern, contemporary, progressive, up-to-date, up-to-the-minute, fashion-forward, modish
COLLOQ. cool, hip, in, trendy, groovy, all the rage, natty, glitzy, ritzy, snazzy, funky
≠ out-of-date

without *prep*
lacking, not having, in need of, needing, deprived of, free from

withstand *v*
resist, oppose, stand your ground, stand, stand up to, stand firm/fast, fight, confront, brave, face, cope with, take on, thwart, defy, hold your ground, hold out, last out, hold off, endure, bear, tolerate, put up with, survive, weather
≠ give in, yield

witless *adj*
stupid, mindless, foolish, silly, senseless, unintelligent, inane, crazy, imbecilic, idiotic, moronic, gormless, dull, empty-headed, half-witted, cretinous
COLLOQ. daft, loopy, barmy, potty, bonkers, nuts, nutty, nutty as a fruitcake, off the rails, cuckoo, mad as a hatter, raving, up the wall, wrong in the head
SLANG loony, off your chump, off your rocker, doolally, mental
≠ intelligent

witness *n, v*
♦ *n*
1 *witness in a court*
testifier, evidence, expert, signatory, vouchee; *Scot* man of skill
OLD compurgator
FORMAL attestant, deponent
2 ONLOOKER, eyewitness, looker-on, observer, spectator, viewer, watcher, bystander
3 TESTIMONY, evidence, authority
TECHNICAL teste
OLD *(Shakesp)* attest
♦ *v*
1 SEE, observe, notice, note, view, watch, look on, mark, perceive
2 TESTIFY, bear witness, give evidence, confirm, affirm, prove, verify, support, endorse, be evidence of, bear out, speak for

OLD obtest
FORMAL attest, depose, corroborate
3 ENDORSE, sign, countersign, validate
■ **bear witness**
record, testify, prove, confirm, corroborate, demonstrate, show, display, manifest, endorse, certify, affirm, assert, declare, vouch for, verify
FORMAL attest, adjure, aver, asseverate, evince, evidence

witter *v*
chat, chatter, gabble, babble, jabber, rattle, twitter, twaddle, twattle, patter, drivel, gossip; *Scot* blether; *dialect & N Am* blather

witticism *n*
quip, riposte, pun, play on words, joke, repartee, pleasantry, *bon mot*, wisecrack, epigram
COLLOQ. one-liner

wittingly *adv*
knowingly, intentionally, willingly, on purpose, purposely, consciously, studiedly, wilfully, deliberately, designedly, by design, calculatedly
E3 unwittingly

witty *adj*
humorous, amusing, comic, sharp-witted, droll, whimsical, original, brilliant, clever, ingenious, lively, light, sparkling, funny, facetious, waggish, fanciful, jocular
FORMAL coruscating, lambent
E3 dull, unamusing

wizard *n, adj*
♦ *n*
1 SORCERER, magician, warlock, enchanter, occultist, witch, conjurer, hex; *dialect* wise man
OLD wisard
FORMAL necromancer, thaumaturge
2 EXPERT, adept, virtuoso, ace, master, maestro, prodigy, genius
COLLOQ. star, whiz, hotshot
♦ *adj*
wonderful, great, good, marvellous, brilliant, enjoyable, tremendous, super, superb, sensational
COLLOQ. fantastic, terrific, smashing

wizened *adj*
shrivelled, shrunken, dried up, withered, wrinkled, gnarled, thin, worn, lined

wobble *v, n*
♦ *v*
shake, oscillate, tremble, quake, sway, stagger, teeter, totter, rock, seesaw, vibrate, waver, quiver, dodder, fluctuate, hesitate, dither, vacillate
COLLOQ. shilly-shally, wibble-wobble
♦ *n*
shake, unsteadiness, tremor, quaking, rock, tremble, vibration, oscillation

wobbly *adj*
unstable, shaky, rickety, unsteady, quavering, trembling, teetering, tottering, doddering, doddery, uneven, unbalanced, unsafe
COLLOQ. wonky
E3 stable, steady

woe *n*
misery, adversity, distress, sadness, sorrow, unhappiness, wretchedness, grief, melancholy, misfortune, suffering, hardship, trouble, pain, agony, anguish, gloom, curse, trial, depression, dejection, burden, disaster, calamity, heartache, heartbreak, tears
FORMAL affliction, tribulation
E3 joy

woebegone *adj*
miserable, wretched, sad, sorrowful, troubled, downcast, downhearted, gloomy, forlorn, grief-stricken, long-faced, dejected, crestfallen, mournful, doleful, dispirited, tearful, tear-stained
FORMAL disconsolate, lugubrious

COLLOQ. blue, down in the mouth
E3 joyful

woeful *adj*
1 SAD, miserable, wretched, mournful, sorry, unhappy, gloomy, grieving, grievous, heartbreaking, heart-rending
FORMAL disconsolate, doleful
2 DISTRESSING, disappointing, lamentable, pitiable, disgraceful, deplorable, shocking, sorrowful, tragic, cruel, hopeless, inadequate, mean, paltry, feeble, dreadful, appalling, awful, bad, terrible, poor, rotten, calamitous, catastrophic, disastrous
COLLOQ. lousy, pathetic
E3 1 joyful

woefully *adv*
1 SADLY, unhappily, miserably, mournfully, gloomily, wretchedly, forlornly
FORMAL disconsolately, dolefully
2 *woefully inadequate*
lamentably, pitiably, disgracefully, deplorably, shockingly, tragically, hopelessly, appallingly, dreadfully, awfully, terribly, disastrously
COLLOQ. lousily, pathetically
E3 1 joyfully

wolf *n, v*
♦ *n*
womanizer, seducer, ladies' man, lady-killer, lecher, philanderer, Casanova, Don Juan, Romeo
■ **wolf down**
gobble, gulp, devour, cram, bolt, stuff, gorge, scoff
COLLOQ. put away, pack away
E3 nibble

woman *n*
1 FEMALE, lady, girl, maiden, maid, lass, madam, au pair, tomboy, hussy, *fille*, shiksa, geisha, belle, cutie, dolly, dolly bird, baby, beauty queen, Cinderella, bag lady, flirt, moppet, princess, nymphet; *Scot* lassie, gillet, jillet, cummer, kimmer, cutty, randy; *N Am* bachelorette
OLD damsel, wench, peat, popsy, blowze, quean
COLLOQ. puss, plain Jane, bobby-dazzler; *Aust* sheila
OLD COLLOQ. filly
SLANG bird, chick, biddy, bint, peach, Judy, bit, number, mystery, bit of stuff, tart, tottie
Related adjective: female
2 PARTNER, wife, lover, girlfriend, girl, lass, sweetheart, fiancée, mistress
SLANG bird, chick

> **QUOTATIONS**
> The silliest woman can manage a clever man; but it needs a very clever woman to manage a fool
>   RUDYARD KIPLING, *Plain Tales from the Hills*, 'Three and – an Extra'

womanhood *n*
1 ADULTHOOD, maturity
FORMAL muliebrity
2 WOMANKIND, woman, womenkind, womenfolk(s)

womanizer *n*
philanderer, seducer, wolf, lady-killer, ladies' man, lecher, Casanova, Don Juan, Romeo

womanly *adj*
feminine, female, ladylike, womanish, motherly, kind, warm, tender, effeminate, well-formed, shapely

wonder *n, v*
♦ *n*
1 AWE, amazement, astonishment, admiration, wonderment, fascination, surprise, pleasure, bewilderment
2 MARVEL, phenomenon, miracle, prodigy, sight, spectacle, rarity, curiosity; *Scot* ferly
FORMAL nonpareil
♦ *v*
1 ASK YOURSELF, meditate, speculate, ponder, question, puzzle, inquire, query, doubt, think, reflect
FORMAL conjecture

2 MARVEL, gape, be amazed, be surprised, be astonished, be astounded, stand in awe, be dumbfounded, be lost for words; *Scot* ferly
OLD admire, muse

wonderful *adj*
1 MARVELLOUS, magnificent, outstanding, excellent, superb, admirable, delightful, phenomenal, sensational, stupendous, tremendous
OLD (*Shakesp*) mirable
COLLOQ. super, terrific, brilliant, great, fabulous, fantastic, smashing, ace, top-notch, stunning, neat, brill, boffo, out of this world, second to none, divine, heavenly, not half bad, boss, bully, classic, crack, dilly, famous, jammy, knockout; *Aust & NZ* trimmer; *N Am* hunky, jim-dandy
OLD COLLOQ. capital, champion, spiffing
SLANG mega, cool, mean, wicked, stonking, radical, rad, crucial, way-out, shit-hot, groovy, clinking, def, fab, peachy, elegant, stellar, triff, triffic; *N Am* copacetic, dicty, righteous, socko; *Aust* beaut, castor
OLD SLANG lummy, ripping, tipping, topping
2 AMAZING, astonishing, astounding, startling, surprising, extraordinary, incredible, remarkable, staggering, awesome, strange
Eⁿ **1** appalling, awful, dreadful **2** ordinary, unremarkable

wonderfully *adv*
fantastically, extremely, tremendously, terrifically, incredibly, unbelievably, amazingly, phenomenally

wonky *adj*
shaky, wobbly, weak, wrong, unsound, unsteady, crooked, askew, amiss
COLLOQ. skew-whiff
Eⁿ stable, straight, balanced

wont *adj, n*
♦ *adj*
inclined, used, accustomed, given
FORMAL habituated
♦ *n*
habit, custom, routine, practice, rule, use, way

wonted *adj*
usual, customary, familiar, normal, regular, common, daily, frequent, routine, accustomed, conventional
FORMAL habitual
Eⁿ unwonted

woo *v*
1 *woo a lover*
court, pay court to, chase, pursue, seek the hand of
OLD address, make love to; (*Spenser*) wow
2 *woo custom*
encourage, cultivate, attract, look for, seek, pursue

wood *n*
1 TIMBER, lumber, planks
Related adjective: ligneous
See panel on next page
2 FOREST, woods, woodland, trees, plantation, thicket, grove, coppice, copse, spinney
Related adjective: sylvan
■ **out of the wood(s)**
out of danger, safe, safe and sound, secure, in the clear, out of difficulty, home and dry

wooded *adj*
forested, timbered, woody, tree-covered
FORMAL sylvan
Eⁿ open

wooden *adj*
1 TIMBER, woody
2 EMOTIONLESS, expressionless, awkward, clumsy, stilted, stodgy, lifeless, spiritless, graceless, impassive, unemotional, unresponsive, stiff, rigid, leaden, deadpan, blank, empty, vacant, vacuous, slow
Eⁿ **2** lively

woodland *n*
wood(s), forest, trees, plantation, thicket, grove, coppice, copse, spinney
FORMAL boscage

woody *adj*
wooded, wooden, forested, tree-covered
FORMAL bosky, ligneous, sylvan, xyloid
Eⁿ open

wool *n*
fleece, down, hair, coat, floccus, yarn
Related adjective: lanate
See panel at **thread**.
■ **pull the wool over someone's eyes**
deceive, fool, trick, hoodwink, take in, bamboozle, delude, dupe
COLLOQ. con, lead up the garden path, pull a fast one on, put one over on

wool-gathering *n*
absent-mindedness, day-dreaming, forgetfulness, distraction, inattention, preoccupation

woolly *adj, n*
♦ *adj*
1 WOOLLEN, fleecy, woolly-haired, hairy, downy, fluffy, shaggy, fuzzy, frizzy
FORMAL flocculent
2 UNCLEAR, indistinct, ill-defined, hazy, fuzzy, blurred, foggy, cloudy, confused, muddled, vague, indefinite, nebulous
Eⁿ **2** clear, distinct
♦ *n*
jumper, sweater, jersey, pullover, cardigan

woozy *adj*
dazed, dizzy, nauseated, light-headed, fuddled, confused, blurred, wobbly, unsteady, rocky, befuddled, bemused, tipsy
Eⁿ alert

word *n, v*
♦ *n*
1 NAME, term, expression, designation, utterance
FORMAL vocable
Related adjectives: verbal, lexical
2 CONVERSATION, chat, talk, discussion, consultation, tête-à-tête
3 INFORMATION, news, report, communication, notice, message, bulletin, communiqué, intelligence, statement, utterance, dispatch, declaration, comment, assertion, account, remark, advice, warning
FORMAL tidings
COLLOQ. gen, info, low-down, dope
4 PROMISE, pledge, oath, assurance, honour, vow, guarantee, undertaking
5 COMMAND, instruction, signal, order, decree, will, commandment, mandate
COLLOQ. go-ahead, green light, thumbs-up
6 RUMOUR, hearsay, gossip, talk, speculation, scandal, whisper
7 *the words of a song*
lyrics, libretto, script, text, book
♦ *v*
phrase, express, couch, put, say, state, explain, write
■ **have words**
argue, dispute, quarrel, disagree, row, squabble, bicker
■ **in a word**
briefly, in short, in brief, to be brief, to put it briefly, concisely, succinctly, summarizing, to sum up
COLLOQ. in a nutshell, to cut a long story short
■ **word for word**
verbatim, literally, exactly, precisely, accurately, closely

PROVERBS
Fine words butter no parsnips

Types of wood include:

acacia	canary-wood	hazel	olive	sheesham	**GENERAL**
afara	candlewood	hemlock	opepe	sissoo	**CATEGORIES:**
African mahogany	cedar	hickory	orange-wood	sneezewood	bitterwood
afrormosia	cheesewood	hornbeam	paddle-wood	spruce	brushwood
alerce	cherry	iroko	palay	stinkwood	chipboard
Amboina-wood	chestnut	ironwood	palmyra wood	sycamore	cordwood
apple	chittagong wood	jacaranda	Paraná pine	tallow wood	driftwood
arrowwood	citron wood	jatoba (or Brazilian	partridge-wood	tamarack	firewood
ash	coachwood	cherry)	peach-wood	teak	fruitwood
balsa	coco-wood (or	kingwood (or	pine	thorn	green wood
bamboo	cocoa-wood)	violet-wood)	poon	tigerwood	hardboard
barwood	corkwood	kempass	poplar	toon	hardwood
basswood	coromandel wood	kokra	porcupine wood	torchwood	heartwood
beech	cottonwood	lana	purple heart (or	tulipwood	kindling
beefwood	deal	lancewood	purple wood)	wagenboom	*N Am* lumber
black walnut	deodar cedar	larch	quassia	wallaba	matchwood
blackwood	Douglas fir	lignum vitae	quebracho	walnut	nutwood
bloodwood	durmast	lima-wood	rata	wandoo	plywood
boxwood	eaglewood	lime	red sandalwood	white cedar	pulpwood
brazil (or	ebony	mahogany	redwood	willow	sapwood
brazil-wood or	elm	maple	rosewood	yacca	seasoned wood
sappanwood)	fiddlewood	meranti	rubberwood (or	yellowwood	softwood
cabreuva	fir	myall	hevea)	yew	timber
calamander	fustic	nutwood	sandalwood	zante (or zante-	whitewood
campeachy wood	hackberry	oak	sapele	wood)	wood veneer
camwood	hackmatack	obeche	satinwood	zebrawood	

See also **tree**.

wordiness *n*

verboseness, verbosity, verbiage, wordage, long-windedness, diffuseness, garrulity, garrulousness, loquacity, logorrhoea
FORMAL prolixity, perissology
COLLOQ. waffle, verbal diarrhoea

wording *n*

words, choice of words, language, phrasing, expression, phraseology, terminology, style, diction, wordage, verbiage

word-perfect *adj*

accurate, faithful, exact, spot-on, letter-perfect
Ea inaccurate

wordplay *n*

puns, punning, wit, witticisms, repartee
TECHNICAL paronomasia

wordy *adj*

verbose, long-winded, garrulous, rambling, diffuse, discursive, phrasy, windy
FORMAL loquacious, prolix
Ea concise

work *n, v*

♦ *n*
1 OCCUPATION, job, employment, profession, trade, business, career, calling, vocation, pursuit, field, line, line of business, métier, livelihood, craft, skill, art, workmanship
2 TASK, assignment, undertaking, job, chore, responsibility, duty, charge, mission, commission
3 TOIL, labour, drudgery, trouble, effort, exertion, industry

FORMAL travail
COLLOQ. slog, graft, elbow grease
4 CREATION, production, achievement, accomplishment, composition, piece, poem, painting, book, play, writing, oeuvre, opus
5 *steel works*
factory, plant, workshop, mill, foundry, shop
6 *good works*
actions, acts, doings, deed
7 *the works of a clock*
machinery, mechanism, workings, action, movement, parts, working parts, installations
COLLOQ. innards, guts
Ea 1 play, rest, hobby
♦ *v*
1 BE EMPLOYED, have a job, earn your living
2 LABOUR, toil, exert yourself, drudge, slave
COLLOQ. slog, graft, peg away, plug away, work your fingers to the bone, slog your guts out
3 FUNCTION, go, operate, perform, run, handle
4 OPERATE, run, handle, manage, use, drive, control
5 BRING ABOUT, accomplish, perform, execute, achieve, create, do, cause
FORMAL effect
COLLOQ. pull off
6 BE SUCCESSFUL, succeed, be effective, be satisfactory, have the desired effect, go well, prosper
7 MANIPULATE, manoeuvre, engineer, arrange, contrive
COLLOQ. fix, pull strings, fiddle, wangle
8 *work your way forward*
shift, guide, edge, move, make, penetrate, manoeuvre
9 CULTIVATE, farm, dig, till
10 MOULD, manipulate, knead, shape, form, ply, fashion, model, make, process, squeeze
Ea 1 be unemployed **2** play, rest **3** fail

■ **work out**
1 SOLVE, resolve, calculate, figure out, puzzle out, sort out, understand, clear up
COLLOQ. *N Am* dope (out)
2 DEVELOP, evolve, go well, succeed, be effective, prosper, turn out
COLLOQ. pan out

3 PLAN, devise, organize, arrange, contrive, invent, construct, formulate, develop, put together
4 ADD UP TO, amount to, total, come out, come to
5 EXERCISE, train, drill, practise, keep fit, warm up
■ **work up**
1 *work up a crowd*
excite, agitate, incite, arouse, stir up, move
2 *work something up*
incite, stir up, rouse, arouse, animate, move, stimulate, build up, inflame, spur, instigate, kindle, agitate, generate, whet
■ **the works**
everything, the lot, the whole lot, lock stock and barrel
COLLOQ. the whole caboodle, the whole kit and caboodle, the whole shooting-match, the whole shebang, the whole bag of tricks

---

PROVERBS
All work and no play makes Jack a dull boy

QUOTATIONS
When work is a pleasure, life is a joy! When work is a duty, life is slavery
MAXIM GORKY, *The Lower Depths*

Work expands so as to fill the time available for its completion
C NORTHCOTE PARKINSON, *Parkinson's Law: the Pursuit of Progress*

SYNONYM NUANCES

noun sense 3
The term **labour** could be used of any arduous work, but you might use **toil** of something that is even more exhausting to do. **Drudgery**, on the other hand, is a very negative term suggestive of work that is habitual and repetitive: *the constant drudgery of housework*. **Effort**, however, returns to the idea of struggle: *with some effort and application, he passed the exam*, while **exertion** tends to suggest more strenuous physical activity: *breathing heavily from their exertions*. To suggest work involving steady application, then the word **industry** is appropriate.

---

workable *adj*
practicable, feasible, possible, practical, realistic, viable, doable
⊟ unworkable

workaday *adj*
everyday, ordinary, routine, work-day, working, practical, mundane, average, humdrum, dull, common, commonplace, familiar, labouring, toiling
COLLOQ. run-of-the-mill
⊟ exciting

worker *n*
employee, labourer, working man/woman, member of staff, artisan, workman/workwoman, craftsman/craftswoman, tradesman/tradeswoman, hand, operative, wage-earner, breadwinner, proletarian
COLLOQ. workhorse, workaholic

QUOTATIONS
The workers have nothing to lose but their chains. They have a world to gain. Workers of the world, unite!
KARL MARX AND FRIEDRICH ENGELS, *The Communist Manifesto*

---

workforce *n*
workers, employees, personnel, labour force, staff, labour, human resources, manpower, workpeople, shop floor

working *n, adj*
♦ *n*
1 FUNCTIONING, operation, running, routine, manner, process, system, method, action
2 *mine workings*
mine, quarry, pit, shaft, diggings, excavations
3 *the workings of a clock*
works, machinery, mechanism, action, movement, parts, working parts, installations
COLLOQ. innards, guts
♦ *adj*
1 EMPLOYED, active, in work, in a job
2 FUNCTIONING, operational, running, operating, operative, going, in working order
COLLOQ. up and running
⊟ 1 unemployed, idle **2** inoperative, broken

workman, workwoman *n*
worker, employee, labourer, hand, artisan, craftsman/craftswoman, operative, manual worker, tradesperson, mechanic, journeyman, navvy, artificer

---

PROVERBS
A bad workman blames his tools

---

workmanlike *adj*
efficient, proficient, satisfactory, careful, adept, skilful, skilled, competent, thorough, painstaking, expert, professional, businesslike, masterly
⊟ amateurish

workmanship *n*
skill, craft, craftsmanship, expertise, art, artistry, handicraft, handiwork, technique, execution, manufacture, work, finish

workmate *n*
colleague, associate, co-worker, fellow-worker, work-fellow, yoke-fellow

workout *n*
exercise, training, drill, practice, warm-up, limbering up, aerobics, gymnastics, isometrics, eurhythmics, callisthenics

workshop *n*
1 WORKS, workroom, atelier, studio, garage, factory, plant, mill, shop, machine-shop, forge, smithery, cooperage, rigging-loft, plumbery
2 STUDY GROUP, seminar, symposium, discussion group, class

work-shy *adj*
lazy, idle, slothful, slack, inactive, inert, slow, slow-moving, good-for-nothing, lethargic, sluggish
OLD laesie, lither, lusk, luskish
FORMAL indolent, torpid, languid, languorous, tardy, fainéant
COLLOQ. bone-idle
⊟ busy, industrious, hard-working

world *n*
1 EARTH, globe, sphere, planet, star, heavenly body, universe, cosmos, creation, nature
2 EVERYBODY, everyone, people, population, human race, humankind, humanity, mankind, man
3 SPHERE, realm, field, area, domain, milieu, department, division, section, group, system, society, province, kingdom
4 TIMES, epoch, era, period, age, days, life
5 WAY OF LIFE, life, reality, existence, experience, situation
Related adjectives: terrestrial, global, mondial
■ **on top of the world**
overjoyed, delighted, elated, euphoric, ecstatic, in raptures, joyful, enraptured, rapturous, thrilled, jubilant, in transports of delight
COLLOQ. over the moon, tickled pink, on cloud nine, in seventh heaven, pleased as Punch, high as a kite
⊟ sad, disappointed

worldly

■ **out of this world**
wonderful, excellent, incredible, marvellous, remarkable, great, fantastic, superb, unbelievable, phenomenal, indescribable
COLLOQ. smashing, stunning, terrific, neat, ace, brill, second to none, divine, heavenly, fabulous, sensational
SLANG mega, cool, mean, wicked, stonking, radical, rad, crucial, way-out, shit-hot

> **QUOTATIONS**
> The world is so full of a number of things, / I'm sure we should all be as happy as kings
> ROBERT LOUIS STEVENSON, *A Child's Garden of Verses*, 'Happy Thought'

worldly *adj*
1 TEMPORAL, earthly, material, mundane, terrestrial, physical, secular, unspiritual, profane, carnal
FORMAL corporeal
2 WORLDLY-WISE, sophisticated, urbane, cosmopolitan, experienced, knowing
COLLOQ. streetwise
3 MATERIALISTIC, selfish, ambitious, grasping, greedy, covetous, avaricious
F3 1 spiritual, eternal 2 unsophisticated

worldly-wise *adj*
worldly, sophisticated, urbane, cosmopolitan, experienced, knowing, perceptive, shrewd, cultivated
COLLOQ. streetwise

worldwide *adj*
international, global, transglobal, general, universal, catholic
FORMAL mondial, ubiquitous
F3 local

worn *adj*
1 SHABBY, threadbare, worn-out, tatty, tattered, in tatters, frayed, ragged, dog-eared
2 EXHAUSTED, tired, weary, spent, fatigued, careworn, drawn, strained, haggard, jaded
COLLOQ. done in, all in, dog-tired, bushed, knackered
F3 1 new, unused 2 fresh, energetic

■ **worn out**
1 SHABBY, threadbare, useless, used, tatty, tattered, on its last legs, ragged, moth-eaten, dog-eared, frayed, decrepit
COLLOQ. tacky; *Aust* warby
2 TIRED OUT, exhausted, weary
COLLOQ. done in, all in, dog-tired, bushed, knackered, whacked, shattered, beat, dead-beat, zonked, clapped-out, rough, ready to drop, washed-out, hardly able to keep your eyes open; *N Am* pooped (out), tuckered out
SLANG (*taboo*) shagged out
3 HACKNEYED, stale, overworked, overused, tired, worn-out, time-worn, threadbare, wearing thin, unoriginal, cliché-ridden, cliché(e)d, stereotyped, stock, banal, trite, commonplace, common, pedestrian, uninspired, unimaginative
FORMAL platitudinous
COLLOQ. corny, run-of-the-mill, yawn-making
F3 1 new, unused 2 fresh, energetic 3 original, new, fresh

worried *adj*
anxious, troubled, uneasy, ill at ease, on edge, apprehensive, concerned, bothered, upset, fearful, afraid, frightened, overwrought, tense, strained, nervous, disturbed, distraught, distracted, disquieted, dismayed, fretful, distressed, agonized
FORMAL perturbed
COLLOQ. uptight, (all) hot and bothered, jittery, het up, beside yourself, in a stew, in a tizzy, having butterflies (in your stomach), tearing your hair out, with your knickers in a twist, a bundle of nerves
SLANG wired
F3 calm, unworried, unconcerned

worrisome *adj*
worrying, upsetting, troublesome, frightening, bothersome, agonizing, distressing, disturbing, insecure, vexing, irksome, disquieting
FORMAL perturbing
COLLOQ. nail-biting, hairy, scary
F3 calm, reassuring

worry *v, n*
♦ *v*
1 BE ANXIOUS, be troubled, be distressed, agonize, fret, stew; *dialect* worrit
COLLOQ. sweat, stress, climb the walls
2 IRRITATE, plague, pester, torment, upset, unsettle, agitate, annoy, bother, disturb, trouble, concern, vex, tease, nag, harass, harry, badger, dog, faze, niggle; *dialect* frab, worrit; *Scot* deave, pingle
FORMAL perturb
COLLOQ. aggravate, bug, hassle, eat (up)
3 ATTACK, go for, tear at, bite, savage, touse
F3 1 be unconcerned 2 comfort
♦ *n*
1 PROBLEM, trouble, responsibility, burden, concern, care, trial, annoyance, nuisance, pest, plague, irritation, vexation
COLLOQ. headache
2 ANXIETY, apprehension, trouble, distress, disquiet, concern, unease, misgiving, fear, fearfulness, tension, stress, strain, disturbance, agitation, torment, anguish, misery, perplexity; *dialect* worrit
OLD tew
FORMAL perturbation
COLLOQ. hang-up, tizzy, tiz, stew
F3 2 comfort, reassurance

worrying *adj*
anxious, troublesome, trying, unsettling, upsetting, niggling, disturbing, alarming, distressing, harassing, disquieting, worrisome, uneasy, agonizing
FORMAL perturbing
COLLOQ. nail-biting, hairy, scary
F3 calm, reassuring

worsen *v*
1 AGGRAVATE, exacerbate, intensify, increase, heighten
2 GET WORSE, weaken, deteriorate, degenerate, decline, slip, sink
COLLOQ. go from bad to worse, go down the tube(s), go to pot, go downhill
F3 2 improve

worsening *n*
deterioration, decline, degeneration, decay, retrogression
FORMAL exacerbation, pejoration
F3 improvement

worship *v, n*
♦ *v*
revere, reverence, adore, exalt, glorify, honour, praise, idolize, adulate, admire, love, be devoted to, extol, respect, pray to, deify
FORMAL venerate, laud
F3 despise, hate
♦ *n*
reverence, adoration, devotion(s), homage, honour, glory, glorification, exaltation, praise, prayer(s), respect, regard, love, adulation, deification, idolatry
FORMAL veneration, laudation

> **SYNONYM NUANCES**
> *verb*
> You can use **revere**, and the less common **reverence**, to suggest regarding with high esteem, while **adore** implies an element of passion. **Honour** and **praise**, on the other hand, suggest expression and paying tribute: *he honoured their achievements*. The stronger term **extol**, however, suggests lavish approbation: *court singers extolled the deeds of their princes*.
> **Exalt** could be used of according something with an elevated status: *his exalted heroes*, whereas **glorify** goes

even further and suggests raising to an even higher level. **Deify** is more strictly reserved for elevating to the status of a god.

   Idolize implies an excessive, and perhaps even unhealthy fixation: *he idolized and sought to imitate him*, and **adulate** also suggests a degree of fawning. However, the words **love**, **admire** and **respect** could be used where a more restrained term is required, as can **be devoted to**, although this has deeper implications of dedication.

Places of worship include:

abbey	fane	mosque
basilica	fire temple	pagoda
bethel	gurdwara	pathi
cathedral	jinja	shrine
chantry	kingdom hall	shul
chapel	kirk	synagogue
church	mandir	tabernacle
daoguan	masjid	temple
derasar	meeting-house	wat
dom	minster	

See also **religion**.

---

worshipful *adj*
reverential, respectful, admiring, deferential, humble, dutiful, devoted, awed, solemn, pious, devout, adoring, loving
OLD obeisant
E3 irreverent, disrespectful

worst *v*
beat, defeat, get the better of, overcome, overpower, overthrow, conquer, crush, master, subdue, drub, whitewash, best
FORMAL subjugate, vanquish
COLLOQ. thrash, lick, hammer, thump, trounce, clobber, annihilate, smash, devastate, slaughter, make mincemeat (out) of, run rings round, paste
SLANG take to the cleaners

worth *n*
worthiness, merit, value, benefit, profit, gain, advantage, importance, significance, eminence, use, usefulness, utility, service, quality, good, virtue, excellence, credit, desert(s), cost, rate, price, help, assistance, avail
E3 worthlessness

worthily *adv*
commendably, creditably, well, honourably, valuably, admirably, reliably
FORMAL laudably

worthless *adj*
1 VALUELESS, useless, pointless, meaningless, futile, unavailing, unimportant, insignificant, trivial, unusable, cheap, poor, rubbishy, trashy, trifling, measly, paltry
FORMAL ineffectual, nugatory
SLANG naff, cruddy
2 CONTEMPTIBLE, despicable, good-for-nothing, corrupt, vile, low, useless
E3 1 valuable **2** worthy

worthlessness *n*
lack of worth, uselessness, futility, meaninglessness, pointlessness, lack of importance/significance, unusability, cheapness
FORMAL ineffectualness
E3 valuableness, worth, importance, significance

worthwhile *adj*
profitable, useful, valuable, of value, rewarding, worthy, good, helpful, advantageous, beneficial, constructive, gainful, justifiable, productive
E3 worthless

worthy *adj, n*
♦ *adj*
praiseworthy, creditable, commendable, valuable, worthwhile, admirable, reliable, fit, deserving, appropriate, respectable, trustworthy, reputable, good, moral, honest, honourable, excellent, decent, upright, righteous, virtuous
FORMAL laudable, meritorious
E3 unworthy, disreputable
♦ *n*
dignitary, personage, somebody, VIP, name, luminary, notable
COLLOQ. bigwig, big cheese/noise/shot/gun, top brass, top dog

would-be *adj*
aspiring, budding, striving, endeavouring, ambitious, enterprising, keen, eager, hopeful, optimistic, wishful, longing
COLLOQ. wannabe

wound *n, v*
♦ *n*
1 INJURY, trauma, hurt, cut, gash, graze, scratch, lesion, laceration, scar
2 HURT, distress, trauma, torment, heartbreak, blow, insult, harm, damage, pain, ache, anguish, grief, shock
♦ *v*
1 DAMAGE, harm, hurt, injure, hit, cut, gash, tear, graze, scratch, lacerate, slash, stab, puncture, pierce
2 DISTRESS, hurt, offend, shock, insult, pain, traumatize, mortify, upset, slight, grieve

wraith *n*
ghost, spirit, phantom, apparition, spectre, revenant, shade
COLLOQ. spook

wrangle *n, v*
♦ *n*
argument, quarrel, dispute, controversy, squabble, tussle, tiff, bickering, disagreement, clash, contest
FORMAL altercation
COLLOQ. row, slanging match, set-to, barney, scrap, spat, dust-up, punch-up, argy-bargy
E3 agreement
♦ *v*
argue, quarrel, disagree, dispute, bicker, contend, have words, clash, row, squabble, fight, spar
FORMAL altercate
COLLOQ. be at each other's throats, be at loggerheads, fall out, hassle, have it out (with), cross swords, scrap, have a bone to pick
E3 agree

wrap *v, n*
♦ *v*
envelop, fold, enfold, enclose, cover, pack, shroud, wind, surround, package, parcel (up), gift-wrap, muffle, cocoon, encase, cloak, roll (up), bind, bundle up, swathe, immerse, lap, sheet, scarf, shawl, swaddle, enswathe, flannel, snug, wimple; *dialect* hap
OLD bemuffle, mail, wap; (*Spenser*) emboss
E3 unwrap
♦ *n*
shawl, stole, cape, robe, cloak, mantle, rug, shroud, amice; *dialect* hap; *N Am* throw
OLD night-rail
■ **wrap up**
1 *wrap up well on a winter morning*
dress warmly, wear warm clothes, wear something warm, muffle up
2 *wrap up a present*
wrap, gift-wrap, pack up, package, parcel (up)
3 CONCLUDE, finish off, end, bring to a close, terminate, wind up, close the book on, complete, round off
4 SHUT UP, be quiet
COLLOQ. dry up, belt up, pipe down, give it a rest, hold your tongue, put a sock in it, shut your mouth

wrapper *n*
wrapping, packaging, envelope, Jiffy bag®, cover, covering, jacket, dust jacket, sheath, casing, case, sleeve, paper

wrapping *n*
packaging, wrapper, envelope, Jiffy bag®, paper, case, carton, blister card, blister pack, bubble pack, Cellophane®, foil, tinfoil, silver paper

wrath *n*
anger, bitterness, rage, fury, exasperation, indignation, irritation, annoyance, temper, resentment, passion, displeasure, spleen, choler
FORMAL ire
E3 calm, pleasure

wrathful *adj*
angry, furious, incensed, enraged, infuriated, raging, indignant, bitter, displeased, irate, ireful
OLD wroth
FORMAL furibund
COLLOQ. aggravated, cross, ratty, uptight, mad, hopping mad, raving mad, seeing red, in a lather, disgruntled, up in arms, hot under the collar, stroppy, choked, fit to be tied, on the warpath, in a paddy; *N Am* ticked off; *Aust* spewy, ropable; *Aust & NZ* crooked
SLANG pissed off, hairless; *N Am* burned up
E3 calm, pleased

wreak *v*
inflict, exercise, create, cause, bring about, perpetrate, vent, unleash, express, execute, carry out
FORMAL bestow

wreath *n*
garland, coronet, chaplet, festoon, crown, band, loop, ring, circle, circlet

wreathe *v*
encircle, surround, enfold, entwine, twine, twist, wind, coil, wrap, envelop, crown, adorn, shroud, enwrap, festoon, intertwine, interweave

wreck *v, n*
♦ *v*
destroy, ruin, demolish, devastate, shatter, smash, break, sabotage, split, sink, spoil, mar, play havoc with, torpedo, ravage, write off, shipwreck, cast away, crab; *Scot* stramash
COLLOQ. trash, handbag
SLANG gum up
E3 conserve, repair
♦ *n*
1 RUIN, destruction, devastation, shattering, smashing, breaking, mess, demolition, ruination, write-off, disaster, loss, undoing, disruption, shipwreck, derelict, debris, remains, rubble, ruins, fragments, flotsam, pieces; *dialect* wrack; *Scot* stramash
2 *a nervous wreck*
neurotic, mouse, chicken
COLLOQ. bag/bundle of nerves
SLANG basket-case

wreckage *n*
debris, remains, rubble, ruin, fragments, flotsam, pieces, wrack
FORMAL detritus

wrench *v, n*
♦ *v*
yank, wrest, jerk, pull, tug, force, sprain, strain, rick, tear, twist, wring, rip, distort
♦ *n*
1 PULL, jerk, tear, twist, tug, sprain, pain, ache, pang
2 UPROOTING, upheaval, shock, sorrow, sadness, blow

wrest *v*
seize, force, extract, pull, take, win, wring, wrench, twist, strain

wrestle *v*
struggle, strive, fight, scuffle, grapple, tussle, combat, contend, contest, vie, battle

wretch *n*
scoundrel, rogue, villain, good-for-nothing, ruffian, rascal, vagabond, miscreant, outcast, devil, snake, miserable, pilgarlick
OLD cullion, rakeshame, recreant, scroyle; *(Shakesp)* vassal; *(Shakesp & Spenser)* miser
COLLOQ. rat, swine, worm, blighter, rapscallion, rascallion, insect

wretched *adj*
1 MISERABLE, sad, unhappy, sorry, melancholy, depressed, dejected, disconsolate, downcast, forlorn, anguished, gloomy, doleful, distressed, broken-hearted, crestfallen, woeful
OLD woe; *(Shakesp)* life-weary; *(Spenser)* wretch
2 PATHETIC, pitiable, pitiful, sad, unhappy, miserable, piteous, unfortunate, unlucky, sorry, hopeless, poor, woeful; *dialect* seely
OLD wretch
FORMAL hapless
3 CONTEMPTIBLE, despicable, vile, worthless, shameful, inferior, bad, low, base, mean, paltry, rascal
OLD wretch
4 ATROCIOUS, awful, miserable, deplorable, appalling, shocking, outrageous, dreadful, terrible, horrible, woeful, ratty
OLD wretch
5 *that wretched car*
damned, cursed, detestable, despicable, confounded, infernal, hateful, loathsome, odious, vile, fiendish, annoying, unpleasant
COLLOQ. blasted, blooming, flipping, darned, dashed, dratting, flaming, blinking
SLANG bloody, effing; *(taboo)* fucking, frigging
E3 **1** happy **2** enviable **3** worthy **4** excellent

wretchedly *adv*
1 SADLY, woefully, unhappily, miserably, mournfully, gloomily, forlornly
FORMAL disconsolately, dolefully
2 *wretchedly small*
lamentably, pitiably, woefully, disgracefully, deplorably, shockingly, tragically, hopelessly, appallingly, dreadfully, awfully, terribly, disastrously
COLLOQ. lousily, pathetically

wriggle *v, n*
♦ *v*
1 SQUIRM, writhe, wiggle, worm, twist, snake, slink, crawl, edge, sidle, manoeuvre, squiggle, dodge, extricate, zigzag, waggle, turn
2 *wriggle out of a responsibility*
evade, stay/keep away from, elude, sidestep, escape, run away from, get out of, get round, shun, abstain from, steer clear of
FORMAL eschew, circumvent, refrain from, forbear
COLLOQ. hedge, duck, dodge, shirk, worm your way out of, give a miss, give a wide berth to, body-swerve
♦ *n*
wiggle, twist, squirm, writhe, jiggle, jerk, turn, twitch

wring *v*
1 SQUEEZE, twist, wrench, wrest, extract, mangle, screw
2 EXACT, extort, coerce, force
3 DISTRESS, pain, hurt, rack, tear, rend, pierce, torture, wound, lacerate, stab

wrinkle *n, v*
♦ *n*
furrow, crease, corrugation, line, ridge, trench, fold, gather, pucker, crumple, wimple, crinkle, crankle, seam, ruck, ruckle, runkle, whelk; *Scot* lirk
OLD rumple, frounce
♦ *v*
crease, corrugate, furrow, line, fold, crinkle, crumple, shrivel, gather, pucker, ruck (up), ruckle, ruffle, unsmooth,

frown, plough, ridge, crimple, runkle, shrivel; *dialect* frumple, rivel; *Scot* lirk
OLD rumple, frounce

wrinkled *adj*
crumpled, wrinkly, crinkled, creased, furrowed, furrowy, ridged, puckered, puckery, rivelled, rumpled, crinkly, crimpy, corrugated, rucked, ruffled, crankled; *dialect* rivelled
OLD frounced; (*Spenser*) wrizled
FORMAL rugose, rugate, rugous
E3 smooth

writ *n*
court order, summons, decree, subpoena, warrant, brief, injunction, precept, extent, process, jury-process
TECHNICAL habeas corpus, replevin, ad inquievendum, audita querela, capias, certiorari, dedimus, devastavit, latitat, mandamus, mittimus, fiera facias, nisi prius, noverint, quare impedit, quo warranto, scire facias, supersedeas; *Scot* law-burrows
OLD inhibition, distringas, elegit, praemunire, supplicavit, tolt, venire facias; *Scot* letters of intercommuning

write *v*
pen, inscribe, record, register, jot down, note (down), set down, put down, take down, make a note of, transcribe, print, scribble, scrawl, correspond, communicate, draft, draw up, copy, compose, create
COLLOQ. dash off, put down in black and white
■ **write off**
1 DELETE, cancel, annul, cross out, wipe out, disregard, forget about
FORMAL nullify
2 WRECK, destroy, crash, demolish, smash (up), damage beyond repair

> QUOTATIONS
> There is an impression abroad that everyone has it in him to write one book; but if by this is implied a good book the impression is false
>   W SOMERSET MAUGHAM, *The Summing Up*

writer *n*
man/woman of letters

Writers include:

annalist	editor	penwoman
author	elegiast	playwright
autobiographer	essayist	poet
bard	fabler	poet laureate
biographer	fiction writer	reporter
blogger	ghost writer	rhymer
calligraphist	hack	satirist
chronicler	historian	scribbler
clerk	journalist	scribe
columnist	leader-writer	scriptwriter
composer	lexicographer	short-story writer
contributor	librettist	sonneteer
copyist	lyricist	speechwriter
copywriter	novelist	stenographer
correspondent	pen-friend	*colloq.* storyteller
court reporter	penman	technical writer
diarist	pen-pal	web author
dramatist	*colloq.* penpusher	

write-up *n*
review, assessment, criticism, critique, evaluation, appraisal, judgement, report, commentary, examination, scrutiny, analysis, study, survey, rating, summing-up
FORMAL recension

writhe *v*
squirm, wriggle, thresh, thrash, twist, wiggle, jerk, toss, coil, contort, struggle
COLLOQ. twist and turn

writing *n*
1 HANDWRITING, calligraphy, script, penmanship, scrawl, scribble, hand, text, words, print
2 DOCUMENT, composition, work, opus, volume, publication
Related adjective: literary

Types of writing include:

account	editorial	profile
advertising copy	epistle	propaganda
annals	essay	record
article	feature	report
autobiography	haiku	review
biography	history	satire
blog (or weblog)	journal	scientific writing
book	legal document	script
chronicle	letter	sketch
commentary	life story	sonnet
confessions	literature	speech
copywriting	lyric	statement
correspondence	memoir	story
criticism	monograph	study
critique	narrative	tale
curriculum vitae	news	thesis
diary	newspaper	travelogue
discourse	column	treatise
dissertation	paper	yearbook
documentary	parable	
drama	poem	

See also **book**; **literature**; **poem**; **sacred writings**; **story**.

Writing instruments include:

ballpoint	dip pen	propelling pencil
Biro®	eraser pen	quill
board marker	felt-tip pen	reed
brailler	fountain pen	Roman metal pen
calligraphy pen	highlighter	steel pen
cane pen	ink pencil	stylus
cartridge pen	laundry marker	typewriter
CD marker	lead-pencil	word-processor
chinagraph pencil	marker pen	writing brush
coloured pencil	pencil	
crayon	permanent marker	

written *adj*
set down, recorded, drawn up, transcribed, documented, documentary
FORMAL documental
E3 unwritten, verbal

wrong *adj, adv, n, v*
♦ *adj*
1 INACCURATE, incorrect, mistaken, erroneous, false, in error, imprecise
FORMAL fallacious
COLLOQ. wide of the mark, off beam, off target
2 INAPPROPRIATE, unsuitable, improper, unconventional, unfitting, inapt
FORMAL unseemly, indecorous, incongruous, infelicitous, inapposite, malapropos
COLLOQ. hardly the place/time
3 UNJUST, unethical, unfair, unlawful, immoral, illegal, illicit, dishonourable, unjustified, dishonest, criminal, blameworthy, guilty, to blame, bad, wicked, sinful, evil
FORMAL reprehensible, iniquitous, felonious
COLLOQ. crooked; *Aust & NZ* crook
4 DEFECTIVE, faulty, out of order, amiss, awry
COLLOQ. up the spout
5 REVERSE, opposite, inside, inverse, inverted, back, contrary
E3 **1** correct, right **2** suitable, right **3** good, moral **4** in order **5** right, front

♦ *adv*

amiss, astray, awry, inaccurately, incorrectly, inexactly, imprecisely, wrongly, mistakenly, faultily, badly, erroneously, improperly

🔁 right

♦ *n*

sin, misdeed, offence, crime, trespass, immorality, sinfulness, wickedness, unlawfulness, wrongdoing, grievance, abuse, injustice, iniquity, inequity, infringement, unfairness, error

FORMAL transgression, injury

🔁 right

■ **in the wrong**

at fault, guilty, in error, mistaken, to blame, blameworthy

🔁 in the right

♦ *v*

abuse, ill-treat, mistreat, maltreat, injure, ill-use, hurt, harm, discredit, dishonour, misrepresent, malign, oppress, cheat

■ **go wrong**

1 BREAK DOWN, stop working, fail

FORMAL malfunction

COLLOQ. pack up, conk out, go phut, go on the blink, seize up; *N Am* go on the fritz

2 FAIL, be unsuccessful, collapse, come to grief, come to nothing, stray, go astray

COLLOQ. not make it, crash and burn, come a cropper, come unstuck, come unglued

> **QUOTATIONS**
> To do wrong is the greatest of evils
> PLATO, *Gorgias*

wrongdoer *n*

offender, lawbreaker, criminal, delinquent, felon, miscreant, evildoer, sinner, trespasser, culprit

FORMAL transgressor, malefactor

wrongdoing *n*

crime, offence, lawbreaking, error, evil, misdeed, fault, felony, immorality, delinquency, sin, sinfulness, wickedness, mischief

FORMAL iniquity, maleficence, transgression

wrongful *adj*

immoral, improper, unfair, unethical, unjust, unlawful, illegal, illegitimate, illicit, dishonest, criminal, blameworthy, dishonourable, wrong, unjustified, unwarranted, reprehensible, wicked, evil

🔁 rightful

wrongfully *adv*

unjustly, unfairly, improperly, immorally, unethically, illegally, against the law, illicitly, illegitimately, dishonestly, criminally

🔁 justly, rightfully

wrongly *adv*

incorrectly, mistakenly, badly, by mistake, in error, inaccurately, erroneously

🔁 rightly

wrought *adj*

shaped, fashioned, hammered, beaten, made, manufactured, ornamental, ornate, decorative, ornamented

■ **wrought up**

agitated, worried, troubled, upset, disturbed, anxious, unsettled, flustered, ruffled, distraught, unnerved, disconcerted, nervous

COLLOQ. in a lather, in a tizzy

🔁 calm, composed

wry *adj*

1 *wry humour*

ironic, sardonic, dry, witty, sarcastic, mocking, scoffing, droll; *Scot* pawky, canny

2 TWISTED, distorted, deformed, contorted, warped, uneven, askew, crooked

🔁 **2** straight

X

xenophobia *n*
racism, ethnocentrism, racialism, xenophoby
 xenomania

xenophobic *adj*
racist, racialist, parochial, ethnocentrist

xerox *v*
photocopy, copy, duplicate, Photostat®, reproduce, print, run off

Xerox® *n*
photocopy, duplicate, facsimile, Photostat®

Xmas *n*
Christmas, Noel, Christmas-time, Christmas-tide, Nativity, Yule, Yuletide
COLLOQ. Chrissie, Crimbo

X-ray *n*
X-ray photograph, X-ray image, radiograph, radiogram, shadowgraph, angiogram, skiagram, skiagraph, röntgen ray
TECHNICAL encephalogram, encephalograph, mammogram, mammograph, pyelogram, sialogram

Y

yack *v, n*
- ♦ *v*

chatter, gossip, prattle, tattle, twattle, jabber, witter on, blather; *dialect & N Am* babble

COLLOQ. jaw, gab, yack-yack, yap
- ♦ *n*

chat, gossip, prattle, rant, harp on, twattle, jaw; *dialect & N Am* blather

COLLOQ. blah, chinwag, confab, hot air, yackety-yack

yank *v, n*
jerk, tug, pull, wrench, snatch, haul, heave

yap *v*
1 BARK, yelp
2 CHATTER, prattle, yatter, natter, witter on, jabber, babble

COLLOQ. jaw, gab

yard *n*
courtyard, court, garden, quadrangle

COLLOQ. quad

yardstick *n*
measure, gauge, criterion, standard, scale, guideline, benchmark, touchstone, comparison

yarn *n*
1 THREAD, fibre, strand, cotton
2 STORY, tale, anecdote, fable, fabrication

COLLOQ. tall story, cock-and-bull story

yawning *adj*
gaping, wide, wide-open, huge, vast, cavernous

year *n*
twelve-month period, calendar year
OLD twelvemonth
Related adjective: annual

■ **year in, year out**
regularly, repeatedly, again and again, time and (time) again, continually, endlessly, persistently, monotonously

---

Types of year include:

academic	financial	lunar
anomalistic	fiscal	Platonic (or great
astronomical (or	gap	or perfect)
equinoctial or	Galactic	sabbatical
natural or solar	Gaussian	seasonal
or tropical)	Gregorian	sidereal
Besselian	Hebrew	Sothic (or
calendar	heliacal	canicular)
draconic	Julian	tropical
ecclesiastical	leap	

---

yearly *adj, adv*
- ♦ *adj*

annual, per year, per annum, perennial
- ♦ *adv*

annually, every year, once a year, perennially

yearn *v*
long, pine, desire, want, wish, sigh, crave, covet, hunger, thirst, hanker, ache, fancy, languish, itch, pant
OLD earn, think long; *Scot* green
COLLOQ. yen

yearning *n*
longing, pining, desire, wish, craving, hunger, thirst, hankering, fancy, panting
COLLOQ. yen

yell *v, n*
- ♦ *v*

shout, scream, cry (out), bellow, roar, bawl, shriek, squeal, howl, yelp, screech, squall, yowl, whoop
COLLOQ. holler
EJ whisper
- ♦ *n*

shout, scream, cry, roar, bellow, shriek, howl, screech, squall, whoop
COLLOQ. holler
EJ whisper

yellow *adj*
1 *yellow butter*
lemon, gold, golden, buff, tawny, light-brown, canary, primrose, saffron, flaxen
TECHNICAL xanthous, xanthic, xanthochroic, vitellary, vitelline
FORMAL flavescent, fulvous, fulvid
2 COWARDLY, faint-hearted, craven, fearful, timid, coward, dastardly, timorous, scared, unheroic, unmanly, chicken-hearted, chicken-livered, white-livered, lily-livered, spiritless, spineless, weak, weak-spirited, weak-kneed, soft, jittery; *dialect* mangy, nesh
OLD faint, cowish, milk-livered, nithing; (*Shakesp*) meacock
FORMAL pusillanimous
COLLOQ. chicken, gutless, wimpish, yellow-bellied, showing the white feather
EJ 2 brave, courageous, bold

yelp *v, n*
- ♦ *v*

yap, bark, squeal, cry, yell, yowl, bay
- ♦ *n*

yap, bark, yip, squeal, cry, yell, yowl

yen *n*
longing, yearning, hunger, desire, craving, hankering, itch, passion, lust
COLLOQ. thing
EJ dislike

yes *adv, interj*
right, quite, absolutely, certainly, agreed, of course, affirmative, very well, sure, indeed, all right, OK, definitely, by all means, rather, yah, aye, *ja wohl*; *Scot* ou ay
OLD yea
COLLOQ. yeah, yep, and how
EJ no

yes-man *n*
sycophant, crawler, toady, lackey, minion, bootlicker
OLD toad-eater
SLANG
(*vulgar*) arse-licker

yet *adv, conj*
- ♦ *adv*

1 UP TILL NOW, until now, up to this time, up till then, by now, by then, now, already, as yet, so far, still

OLD hitherto, heretofore
FORMAL thus far
2 IN ADDITION, still, even, too, also, further, furthermore, besides, moreover
COLLOQ. into the bargain
♦ *conj*
but, however, nevertheless, nonetheless, anyway, even so, all/just the same, for all that
FORMAL notwithstanding

yield *v, n*
♦ *v*
1 SURRENDER, give up, for(e)go, abandon, abdicate, cede, part with, give over
FORMAL relinquish, renounce
2 GIVE WAY, capitulate, surrender, concede, submit, succumb, give in, admit defeat, bow, cave in, knuckle under, resign yourself, go along with, permit, allow, accede, agree, comply, consent
FORMAL acquiesce
COLLOQ. throw in the towel/sponge
3 PRODUCE, bear, supply, provide, give, generate, bring in, bring forth, furnish, return, earn, fetch, pay, net, gross
FORMAL fructify, fructuate
⊟ 1 hold **2** resist, withstand
♦ *n*
return, product, earnings, harvest, crop, produce, output, profit, revenue, takings, proceeds, income, haul

---

SYNONYM NUANCES

verb sense 2
Give way can be generally applied as a synonym of yield, while **surrender** suggests relinquishing any claims. **Capitulate**, however, has overtones of weakness: *he capitulated without any fight at all*, whereas **concede** makes the gentler suggestion of acknowledgement that you are defeated or wrong: *the ruling party conceded leadership to the democrats.* **Submit** also suggests admitting your opponent's superiority, although it implies that it has not been without a struggle, while **succumb** and **give in** would appropriately refer to being defeated in a struggle against difficulty: *she succumbed to weariness.*
  Bow, on the other hand, could be used of yielding to pressure: *they bowed to public opinion*, whereas **cave in** implies a rather sudden and ignominious collapse. The term **knuckle under** has more to do with acting in accordance with authority, but the tone suggests that this is not a desirable course of action. **Resign yourself** again implies acceptance, but **go along with** and **comply** have further implications of a lack of questioning.

---

yielding *adj*
1 FLEXIBLE, pliable, pliant, resilient, elastic, springy, soft, supple, spongy, quaggy
2 SUBMISSIVE, obedient, compliant, amenable, biddable, obliging, unresisting, accommodating, easy
FORMAL acquiescent, complaisant, tractable
⊟ 1 solid **2** obstinate

yob *n*
lout, oaf, boor, dolt, barbarian, yahoo, gawk, lubber, calf, bull-calf, hob, lob, hallion, lumpkin, chuckle-head; *dialect* loblolly, swad; *Scot* coof, cuif; *N Am* jake
COLLOQ. clod, clodhopper, hick, hobbledehoy, slob, yobbo, bumpkin, oik; *N Am* roughneck; *Aust* hoon

yobbish *adj*
loutish, uncouth, oafish, boorish, doltish, ill-mannered, ill-bred, gawky, rude, coarse, rough, crude, vulgar, churlish, unmannerly, unrefined, uncivilized, gruff, impolite, rustic, uneducated, ignorant, bungling
COLLOQ. clodhopping
⊟ polite, refined, cultured, genteel

yoke *n, v*
♦ *n*
1 HARNESS, bond, link, tie, coupling, halter
OLD
(*Shakesp*) bow
Related adjective: jugal
2 BURDEN, bondage, enslavement, slavery, tyranny, oppression, servility
FORMAL servitude, subjugation
♦ *v*
couple, link, join, tie, bond, harness, hitch, bracket, connect, unite, team, span; *S Afr* inspan

yokel *n*
country bumpkin, clodhopper, country cousin, hick, peasant, rustic, boor, bucolic
COLLOQ. hillbilly, hayseed
⊟ sophisticate, towny

young *adj, n*
♦ *adj*
1 YOUTHFUL, juvenile, childlike, baby, infant, junior, small, little, teenage, adolescent
COLLOQ. kid
2 IMMATURE, childish, early, new, recent, green, growing, fledgling, unfledged, inexperienced, undeveloped
⊟ 1 adult, old **2** mature, old
♦ *n*
offspring, babies, little ones, issue, litter, brood, children, family
FORMAL progeny

SYNONYM NUANCES

adjective sense 2
The word **immature** can be used straightforwardly of a state of not being fully developed, but in certain contexts it can have critical overtones: *an immature way to behave for a 30-year-old.* The term **childish** is also suggestive of behaving in a manner that belies your more advanced years: *his childish petulance.*
  Early, on the other hand, simply suggests being in the initial stages: *it's still early days.* Similarly, **fledgling** could be used a venture in its infancy: *this fledgling democracy*, while **unfledged** suggests something that has yet to take its first steps and is, as a result, untried. **Undeveloped** suggests that some input is required before full potential can be achieved: *undeveloped countries.*
  Inexperienced and **green** can be used of people to suggest that they are unpractised in life, and have connotations of innocence: *the green child in me slipped out of the older woman, and I made a silly remark.*

---

youngster *n*
child, boy, lad, girl, lass, toddler, stripling, young person, young adult, young man, youth, young woman, teenager, adolescent; *Scot* bairn, wean, tyke, knave-bairn, gyte, smout; *N Am* subteen
COLLOQ. kid, young 'un, shaver, nipper, tot, tiny tot, brat, sprog; *N Am* hellion
SLANG ankle-biter; *N Am* rug rat

youth *n*
1 ADOLESCENT, teenager, youngster, juvenile, boy, lad, young man, young adult
COLLOQ. kid, teen
OLD COLLOQ. teeny-bopper
2 YOUNG PEOPLE, the young, younger generation
3 ADOLESCENCE, teenage years, teens, childhood, immaturity, inexperience, boyhood, girlhood
⊟ 3 adulthood, maturity

QUOTATIONS
The Youth of a Nation are the trustees of Posterity
BENJAMIN DISRAELI, *Sybil*

youthful *adj*
young, boyish, girlish, childish, immature,
juvenile, inexperienced, fresh,
active, vigorous, lively, sprightly, spry, well-preserved

◼ aged

youthfulness *n*
liveliness, vigour, spryness, sprightliness, vivaciousness,
freshness, juvenileness, juvenility

FORMAL vivacity

◼ agedness, languor

yowl *v, n*
◆ *v*
wail, yell, yelp, cry, howl, screech, squall, bay, yawl,
caterwaul
FORMAL ululate
◆ *n*
wail, cry, howl, screech, yell, yelp, yawl

yucky *adj*
disgusting, revolting, horrible, unpleasant, messy, mucky,
filthy, dirty, foul, sickly
COLLOQ. grotty, gross
SLANG grungy
◼ nice

Z

zany *adj*
comical, funny, amusing, eccentric, odd, bizarre, absurd, ridiculous, droll, clownish
COLLOQ. crazy, daft, wacky; *N Am* kooky
serious

zap *v*
kill, destroy, hit, shoot, finish off
COLLOQ. do in, wipe out
SLANG bump off, rub out, zot

zeal *n*
enthusiasm, ardour, fervour, passion, warmth, fire, devotion, spirit, energy, vigour, keenness, zest, eagerness, earnestness, dedication, commitment, wholeheartedness, vehemence, intensity, gusto, verve, study, bigotry, fanaticism, propagandism
OLD zelotypia
apathy, indifference, coolness, half-heartedness

zealot *n*
fanatic, radical, extremist, bigot, militant, partisan
FORMAL zealant
COLLOQ. eager beaver

zealous *adj*
ardent, fervent, impassioned, passionate, devoted, wholehearted, burning, fiery, enthusiastic, intense, warm, fanatical, militant, keen, committed, dedicated, eager, earnest, spirited, staunch, strenuous, diehard, bigoted
OLD true-devoted
FORMAL fervid
SLANG gung-ho
apathetic, indifferent, cold, half-hearted

zealously *adv*
ardently, fervently, enthusiastically, keenly, eagerly, earnestly, passionately, staunchly, fanatically
apathetically, indifferently, half-heartedly

zenith *n*
summit, peak, height, pinnacle, apex, high point, highest point, top, optimum, climax, culmination, meridian, acme, vertex, apogee
nadir

zero *n, v*
♦ *n*
nothing, nought, naught, nil, null, nadir, bottom, cipher, duck, love, duck's egg; *N Am* goose-egg
TECHNICAL absolute zero
COLLOQ. zilch, diddly-squat
SLANG blob, zip, zippo
■ **zero in on**
aim for, concentrate on, converge on, home in on, direct at, level at, pinpoint, fix on, focus on, centre on, train on, head for

zest *n*
1 GUSTO, appetite, enthusiasm, enjoyment, relish, keenness, zeal, brio, eagerness, liveliness, vigour, exuberance, interest, joie de vivre
COLLOQ. zing

2 FLAVOUR, taste, relish, savour, spice, tang, piquancy
3 RIND, peel, skin, husk, crust, shell
OLD rine
FORMAL epicarp, integument
1 apathy

zigzag *v, adj*
♦ *v*
meander, snake, wind, twist, curve
♦ *adj*
meandering, crooked, serpentine, sinuous, twisting, winding
straight

zing *n*
liveliness, life, energy, vitality, vigour, spirit, enthusiasm, animation, zest, sparkle, élan, joie de vivre
COLLOQ. go, get-up-and-go, oomph, pizzazz, zip, pep, punch, dash, brio
listlessness

zip *n, v*
♦ *n*
energy, verve, vitality, life, liveliness, enthusiasm, drive, sparkle, spirit, vigour, zest, gusto, élan
COLLOQ. go, get-up-and-go, oomph, pizzazz, pep, punch, zing
listlessness
♦ *v*
fly, dash, tear, rush, race, hurry, speed, shoot, flash, whisk, zoom
COLLOQ. pelt, belt, vroom, scoot, whiz, whoosh

zodiac *n*
baldric
OLD (*Spenser*) baudricke

The signs of the zodiac (with their symbols) are:

Aries (*Ram*)	Virgo (*Virgin*)	Aquarius
Taurus (*Bull*)	Libra (*Balance*)	(*Water-bearer*)
Gemini (*Twins*)	Scorpio (*Scorpion*)	Pisces (*Fishes*)
Cancer (*Crab*)	Sagittarius (*Archer*)	
Leo (*Lion*)	Capricorn (*Goat*)	

zone *n*
region, area, district, territory, province, section, sector, belt, sphere, tract, stratum, zona

zoo *n*
zoological garden(s), zoological park, safari park, animal park, aquarium, aviary, menagerie

zoom *v*
race, rush, tear, dash, speed, fly, hurtle, streak, flash, shoot, whirl, dive, buzz, zip
COLLOQ. go all out, pelt, belt, vroom, whiz, zap